June 16–19, 2013
Seattle, Washington, USA

Association for
Computing Machinery

Advancing Computing as a Science & Profession

PLDI'13

Proceedings of the 2013 ACM SIGPLAN Conference on
Programming Language Design and Implementation

Sponsored by:

ACM SIGPLAN

Supported by:

Oracle, Microsoft Research, Google, Intel, LogicBlox, Facebook, HP Labs, IBM Research, Galois, NSF, and NEC Labs

Association for
Computing Machinery

Advancing Computing as a Science & Profession

The Association for Computing Machinery
2 Penn Plaza, Suite 701
New York, New York 10121-0701

ISBN: 978-1-4503-2014-6

Additional copies may be ordered prepaid from:

ACM Order Department
PO Box 30777
New York, NY 10087-0777, USA

Phone: 1-800-342-6626 (USA and Canada)
+1-212-626-0500 (Global)
Fax: +1-212-944-1318
E-mail: acmhelp@acm.org
Hours of Operation: 8:30 am – 4:30 pm ET

ACM Order Number: 548130

Printed in the USA

Welcome from the Chairs

It is our great pleasure to welcome you to PLDI 2013, the 34th ACM SIGPLAN Conference on Programming Language Design and Implementation. PLDI is the premier research conference on programming languages and their implementation. This year's program includes research papers, tutorials, keynotes, a Student Research Competition (SRC), a Fun and Interesting Thoughts (FIT) session, and several co-located conferences (SAS, ISMM, and LCTES) and workshops (PASTE, PLAS, SOAP, MSPC, X10, SASB, TAPAS, SSP, PSY, and PLOOC).

PLDI 2013 received a record 267 submissions, of which 46 were selected for presentation, an acceptance rate of 17%. Reviewing was "first read double-blind", meaning that author identities were withheld from reviewers until they submitted an initial review, to avoid potential bias. Together, the 31 members of the Program Committee (PC), the 66 members of the External Review Committee (ERC), and 40 additional outside reviewers wrote over 1000 reviews. Authors were given the opportunity to comment on these reviews during the January 15–18 rebuttal period. Over 1000 messages were contributed by the PC and ERC during the January 19–30 on-line discussion period. Subsequently, the program committee met for two days at the University of California, Santa Cruz, to select the final program. For submissions co-authored by a PC member, reviewing was done exclusively by the ERC and outside reviewers, and acceptance required a consensus among reviewers that the submission was in the top 80% of accepted PLDI papers from prior years.

Putting together PLDI 2013 was a team effort. First of all, we would like to thank the authors and workshop and tutorial organizers for providing the contents of the program. We are very grateful to the members of the PC and the ERC, and to the outside reviewers for evaluating many submissions on a tight schedule. In addition, we owe a debt of gratitude to the Student Research Competition Chair Isil Dillig, the Fun and Interesting Thoughts Session Chair Martin Rinard, the Publicity and Website Chair Matt Might, the Tutorials Chair Dan Grossman, and the Finance and Sponsorship Chair Iulian Neamtiu for their assistance with various aspects of organizing PLDI 2013. We gratefully acknowledge our sponsor ACM SIGPLAN, our corporate supporters (Microsoft Research, Oracle, Google, Intel, LogicBlox, Facebook, Galois, HP, IBM, and NEC) for their generous contributions and an equally generous student travel grant from the National Science Foundation. These enable subsidized student registration fees and travel grants, which make it much easier for students to attend the conference, allowing it to fulfill a critical part of its mission.

Finally, we want to thank all of the conference attendees for contributing to making the conference a success. We hope that you will find the PLDI 2013 program interesting and inspiring, and that the conference will give you valuable opportunities to share ideas with other members of our vibrant programming languages community.

Hans Boehm
PLDI'13 General Chair
HP Labs

Cormac Flanagan
PLDI'13 Program Chair
University of California, Santa Cruz

Table of Contents

PLDI 2013 Conference Organization ix

PLDI 2013 Sponsor and Supporters xiii

Session 1: Keynote Address
Session Chair: Yannis Smaragdakis *(University of Athens)*

- **Look Up! Your Future Is in the Cloud** 1
  James R. Larus *(Microsoft Research)*

Session 2A: Synthesis
Session Chair: Martin Vechev *(ETH Zurich)*

- **Optimizing Database-Backed Applications with Query Synthesis** 3
  Alvin Cheung, Armando Solar-Lezama, Samuel Madden *(Massachusetts Institute of Technology)*
- **Automated Feedback Generation for Introductory Programming Assignments** 15
  Rishabh Singh *(Massachusetts Institute of Technology)*, Sumit Gulwani *(Microsoft Research, Redmond)*,
  Armando Solar-Lezama *(Massachusetts Institute of Technology)*
- **Complete Completion Using Types and Weights** 27
  Tihomir Gvero, Viktor Kuncak, Ivan Kuraj *(École Polytechnique Fédérale de Lausanne)*,
  Ruzica Piskac *(Max Planck Institute for Software Systems)*

Session 2B: Low Level Issues
Session Chair: Tatiana Shpeisman *(Intel Labs)*

- **Fast Condensation of the Program Dependence Graph** 39
  Nick P. Johnson, Taewook Oh *(Princeton University)*, Ayal Zaks *(Intel Corporation)*,
  David I. August *(Princeton University)*
- **Scalable Variable and Data Type Detection in a Binary Rewriter** 51
  Khaled ElWazeer, Kapil Anand, Aparna Kotha, Matthew Smithson, Rajeev Barua
  (University of Maryland, College Park)
- **Fast RMWs for TSO: Semantics and Implementation** 61
  Bharghava Rajaram, Vijay Nagarajan *(University of Edinburgh)*, Susmit Sarkar *(University of St. Andrews)*,
  Marco Elver *(University of Edinburgh)*

Session 3A: Types
Session Chair: John Regehr *(University of Utah)*

- **Rely-Guarantee References for Refinement Types Over Aliased Mutable Data** 73
  Colin S. Gordon, Michael D. Ernst, Dan Grossman *(University of Washington)*
- **Harmonizing Classes, Functions, Tuples, and Type Parameters in Virgil III** 85
  Ben L. Titzer *(Google)*
- **It's Alive! Continuous Feedback in UI Programming** 95
  Sebastian Burckhardt, Manuel Fähndrich, Peli de Halleux, Sean McDirmid, Michal Moskal, Nikolai Tillmann
  (Microsoft Research), Jun Kato *(The University of Tokyo)*

Session 3B: High Performance Computing
Session Chair: Ben Zorn *(Microsoft Research, Redmond)*

- **Terra: A Multi-Stage Language for High-Performance Computing** 105
  Zachary DeVito, James Hegarty, Alex Aiken, Pat Hanrahan *(Stanford University)*, Jan Vitek *(Purdue University)*

- **SMAT: An Input Adaptive Auto-Tuner for Sparse Matrix-Vector Multiplication** 117
  Jiajia Li *(Chinese Academy of Sciences & University of Chinese Academy of Sciences)*,
  Guangming Tan, Mingyu Chen, Ninghui Sun *(Chinese Academy of Sciences)*
- **When Polyhedral Transformations Meet SIMD Code Generation** 127
  Martin Kong *(Ohio State University)*, Richard Veras *(Carnegie Mellon University)*,
  Kevin Stock *(Ohio State University)*, Franz Franchetti *(Carnegie Mellon University)*,
  Louis-Noël Pouchet *(University of California, Los Angeles)*, P. Sadayappan *(Ohio State University)*

Session 4: Keynote Address

Session Chair: Mike Hicks *(University of Maryland, College Park)*

- **Programming Languages in Security** 139
  Fred B. Schneider *(Cornell University)*

Session 5A: Dynamic Analysis

Session Chair: Satish Narayanasamy *(University of Michigan)*

- **CLAP: Recording Local Executions to Reproduce Concurrency Failures** 141
  Jeff Huang, Charles Zhang *(Hong Kong University of Science and Technology)*,
  Julian Dolby *(IBM T.J. Watson Research Center)*
- **CONCURRIT: A Domain Specific Language for Reproducing Concurrency Bugs** 153
  Tayfun Elmas, Jacob Burnim, George Necula, Koushik Sen *(University of California, Berkeley)*
- **Dynamic Determinacy Analysis** 165
  Max Schäfer *(Nanyang Technological University)*,
  Manu Sridharan, Julian Dolby *(IBM T.J. Watson Research Center)*, Frank Tip *(University of Waterloo)*

Session 5B: Compiler Validation

Session Chair: Mayur Naik *(Georgia Tech)*

- **Formal Verification of SSA-Based Optimizations for LLVM** 175
  Jianzhou Zhao *(University of Pennsylvania)*, Santosh Nagarakatte *(Rutgers University)*,
  Milo M. K. Martin, Steve Zdancewic *(University of Pennsylvania)*
- **Compiler Testing via a Theory of Sound Optimisations in the C11/C++11 Memory Model** 187
  Robin Morisset *(ENS & INRIA)*, Pankaj Pawan *(IIT Kanpur & INRIA)*, Francesco Zappa Nardelli *(INRIA)*
- **Taming Compiler Fuzzers** 197
  Yang Chen *(University of Utah)*,
  Alex Groce, Chaoqiang Zhang, Weng-Keen Wong, Xiaoli Fern *(Oregon State University)*,
  Eric Eide, John Regehr *(University of Utah)*

Session 6A: Verification 1

Session Chair: Swarat Chaudhuri *(Rice University)*

- **Almost-Correct Specifications: A Modular Semantic Framework for Assigning Confidence to Warnings** 209
  Sam Blackshear *(University of Colorado, Boulder)*, Shuvendu K. Lahiri *(Microsoft Research)*
- **Reasoning about Nondeterminism in Programs** 219
  Byron Cook *(Microsoft Research Cambridge & University College London)*,
  Eric Koskinen *(New York University)*
- **Natural Proofs for Structure, Data, and Separation** 231
  Xiaokang Qiu, Pranav Garg, Andrei Ştefănescu, Parthasarathy Madhusudan
  (University of Illinois at Urbana-Champaign)

Session 6B: Concurrency 1

Session Chair: Mira Mezini *(Technische Universitaet Darmstadt)*

- **General Data Structure Expansion for Multi-threading** 243
  Hongtao Yu, Hou-Jen Ko, Zhiyuan Li *(Purdue University)*

- **AutoSynch: An Automatic-Signal Monitor Based on Predicate Tagging** 253
  Wei-Lun Hung, Vijay K. Garg *(The University of Texas at Austin)*
- **Concurrent Libraries with Foresight** 263
  Guy Golan-Gueta *(Tel Aviv University)*, G. Ramalingam *(Microsoft Research)*, Mooly Sagiv *(Tel Aviv University)*, Eran Yahav *(Technion)*

Session 7A: Symbolic Execution

Session Chair: Koushik Sen *(University of California, Berkeley)*

- **Thresher: Precise Refutations for Heap Reachability** 275
  Sam Blackshear, Bor-Yuh Evan Chang *(University of Colorado, Boulder)*, Manu Sridharan *(IBM T.J. Watson Research Center)*
- **TRANSIT: Specifying Protocols with Concolic Snippets** 287
  Abhishek Udupa, Arun Raghavan, Jyotirmoy V. Deshmukh, Sela Mador-Haim, Milo M. K. Martin, Rajeev Alur *(University of Pennsylvania)*

Session 7B: Memory Management

Session Chair: Emery Berger *(University of Massachusetts, Amherst)*

- **Using Managed Runtime Systems to Tolerate Holes in Wearable Memories** 297
  Tiejun Gao *(Australian National University)*, Karin Strauss *(Microsoft Research)*, Stephen M. Blackburn *(Australian National University)*, Kathryn S. McKinley, Doug Burger, James Larus *(Microsoft Research)*
- **Limitations of Partial Compaction: Towards Practical Bounds** 309
  Nachshon Cohen, Erez Petrank *(Technion)*

Session 8A: Language Design

Session Chair: Umut A. Acar *(Carnegie Mellon University)*

- **P: Safe Asynchronous Event-Driven Programming** 321
  Ankush Desai, Vivek Gupta, Ethan Jackson, Shaz Qadeer, Sriram Rajamani *(Microsoft)*, Damien Zufferey *(IST Austria)*
- **Quipper: A Scalable Quantum Programming Language** 333
  Alexander S. Green *(Dalhousie University)*, Peter LeFanu Lumsdaine *(Institute of Advanced Studies)*, Neil J. Ross, Peter Selinger *(Dalhousie University)*, Benoît Valiron *(University of Pennsylvania)*
- **Reconciling Exhaustive Pattern Matching with Objects** 343
  Chinawat Isradisaikul, Andrew C. Myers *(Cornell University)*

Session 8B: Analysis

Session Chair: Ben Liblit *(University of Wisconsin–Madison)*

- **SPL^{LIFT} — Statically Analyzing Software Product Lines in Minutes Instead of Years** 355
  Eric Bodden *(Technische Universität Darmstadt)*, Társis Tolêdo *(Federal University of Pernambuco)*, Márcio Ribeiro *(Federal University of Pernambuco & Federal University of Alagoas)*, Claus Brabrand *(IT University of Copenhagen)*, Paulo Borba *(Federal University of Pernambuco)*, Mira Mezini *(Technische Universität Darmstadt)*
- **Finding Optimum Abstractions in Parametric Dataflow Analysis** 365
  Xin Zhang, Mayur Naik *(Georgia Institute of Technology)*, Hongseok Yang *(University of Oxford)*
- **How to Combine Widening and Narrowing for Non-monotonic Systems of Equations** 377
  Kalmer Apinis, Helmut Seidl, Vesal Vojdani *(Technische Universität München)*

Session 9A: Monads and FRP

Session Chair: Arjun Guha *(Cornell University)*

- **Verifying Higher-order Programs with the Dijkstra Monad** 387
  Nikhil Swamy *(Microsoft Research)*, Joel Weinberger *(University of California, Berkeley)*, Cole Schlesinger *(Princeton University)*, Juan Chen, Benjamin Livshits *(Microsoft Research)*

- **Monadic Abstract Interpreters** 399
  Ilya Sergey *(IMDEA Software Institute)*, Dominique Devriese *(KU Leuven)*, Matthew Might *(University of Utah)*,
  Jan Midtgaard *(Aarhus University)*, David Darais *(Harvard University)*,
  Dave Clarke, Frank Piessens *(KU Leuven)*
- **Asynchronous Functional Reactive Programming for GUIs** 411
  Evan Czaplicki, Stephen Chong *(Harvard University)*

Session 9B: Alias Analysis

Session Chair: Manu Sridharan *(IBM T.J. Watson Research Center)*

- **Hybrid Context-Sensitivity for Points-To Analysis** 423
  George Kastrinis, Yannis Smaragdakis *(University of Athens)*
- **Fast Algorithms for Dyck-CFL-Reachability with Applications to Alias Analysis** 435
  Qirun Zhang, Michael R. Lyu *(The Chinese University of Hong Kong)*, Hao Yuan *(BOPU Technologies)*,
  Zhendong Su *(University of California, Davis)*
- **Static Analysis for Probabilistic Programs: Inferring Whole Program Properties from Finitely Many Paths** 447
  Sriram Sankaranarayanan, Aleksandar Chakarov *(University of Colorado, Boulder)*,
  Sumit Gulwani *(Microsoft Research, Redmond)*

Session 10A: Verification 2

Session Chair: Steve Blackburn *(Australian National University)*

- **Modular Verification of Linearizability with Non-Fixed Linearization Points** 459
  Hongjin Liang, Xinyu Feng *(University of Science and Technology of China)*
- **Translation Validation for a Verified OS Kernel** 471
  Thomas Sewell *(NICTA & UNSW)*, Magnus Myreen *(Cambridge University)*, Gerwin Klein *(NICTA & UNSW)*
- **Machine-Verified Network Controllers** 483
  Arjun Guha, Mark Reitblatt, Nate Foster *(Cornell University)*

Session 10B: Concurrency 2

Session Chair: Sebastian Burckhardt *(Microsoft Research, Redmond)*

- **A General Constraint-centric Scheduling Framework for Spatial Architectures** 495
  Tony Nowatzki, Michael Sartin-Tarm, Lorenzo De Carli, Karthikeyan Sankaralingam
  (University of Wisconsin–Madison), Cristian Estan *(Broadcom)*,
  Behnam Robatmili *(Qualcomm Research Silicon Valley)*
- **Steal Tree: Low-Overhead Tracing of Work Stealing Schedulers** 507
  Jonathan Lifflander *(University of Illinois Urbana-Champaign)*,
  Sriram Krishnamoorthy *(Pacific Northwest National Lab)*,
  Laxmikant V. Kale *(University of Illinois Urbana-Champaign)*
- **Halide: A Language and Compiler for Optimizing Parallelism, Locality, and Recomputation in Image Processing Pipelines** 519
  Jonathan Ragan-Kelley *(Massachusetts Institute of Technology)*, Connelly Barnes *(Adobe)*,
  Andrew Adams *(Massachusetts Institute of Technology)*, Sylvain Paris *(Adobe)*,
  Frédo Durand, Saman Amarasinghe *(Massachusetts Institute of Technology)*

Author Index 531

PLDI 2013 Conference Organization

General Chair: Hans-J. Boehm, *HP Labs*

Program Chair: Cormac Flanagan, *University of California, Santa Cruz*

Tutorials Chair: Dan Grossman, *University of Washington*

Publicity Chair: Matt Might, *University of Utah*

Student Research Competition Chair: Isil Dillig, *College of William & Mary*

Finance and Sponsorship Chair: Iulian Neamtiu, *University of California, Riverside*

Fun and Interesting Thoughts Session Chair: Martin Rinard, *Massachusetts Institute of Technology*

Steering Committee Chair: Kathleen Fisher, *DARPA and Tufts University*

Steering Committee:
Hans-J. Boehm, *HP Labs*
Jack Davidson, *University of Virginia*
Cormac Flanagan, *University of California, Santa Cruz*
Jeremy Gibbons, *University of Oxford*
Mary Hall, *University of Utah*
Graham Hutton, *University of Nottingham*
David Padua, *University of Illinois at Urbana-Champaign*
Frank Tip, *University of Waterloo*
Jan Vitek, *Purdue University*
Philip Wadler, *University of Edinburgh*

Program Committee:
Umut A. Acar, *Carnegie Mellon University*
Vikram Adve, *University of Illinois at Urbana-Champaign*
David I. August, *Princeton University*
Emery Berger, *University of Massachusetts, Amherst*
Michael Bond, *The Ohio State University*
Swarat Chaudhuri, *Rice University*
Perry Cheng, *IBM Research*
Trishul Chilimbi, *Microsoft Research, Redmond*
Thomas Dillig, *College of William & Mary*
Matthew Flatt, *University of Utah*
Laurie Hendren, *McGill University*
Michael Hicks, *University of Maryland, College Park*
Martin Hirzel, *IBM T.J. Watson Research Center*
Suresh Jagannathan, *Purdue University*
Pramod Joisha, *HP Labs*
Sorin Lerner, *University of California, San Diego*
Shan Lu, *University of Wisconsin-Madison*

Program Committee (continued):

Mira Mezini, *Technische Universitaet Darmstadt*
Mayur Naik, *Georgia Tech*
Toshio Nakatani, *IBM Research - Tokyo*
Satish Narayanasamy, *University of Michigan*
Keshav Pingali, *University of Texas at Austin*
Lawrence Rauchwerger, *Texas A&M University*
Tatiana Shpeisman, *Intel Labs*
Jeremy Siek, *University of Colorado at Boulder*
Yannis Smaragdakis, *University of Athens*
Armando Solar-Lezama, *Massachusetts Institute of Technology*
Martin Vechev, *ETH Zurich*
Jan Vitek, *Purdue University*
Katherine Yelick, *University of California, Berkeley*

External Review Committee:

Amal Ahmed, *Northeastern University*
Alex Aiken, *Stanford University*
Jonathan Aldrich, *Carnegie Mellon University*
J. Nelson Amaral, *University of Alberta*
Steve Blackburn, *Australian National University*
Sebastian Burckhardt, *Microsoft Research, Redmond*
Adam Chlipala, *Massachusetts Institute of Technology*
Byron Cook, *Microsoft Research, Cambridge*
Sophia Drossopoulou, *Imperial College London*
Matthew Dwyer, *University of Nebraska*
Laura Effinger-Dean, *Carleton College*
Tayfun Elmas, *Google*
Erik Ernst, *Aarhus University*
Robby Findler, *Northwestern University*
Stephen Fink, *IBM T.J. Watson Research Center*
Kathleen Fisher, *Tufts University*
Jeffrey Foster, *University of Maryland, College Park*
Michael Franz, *University of California, Irvine*
Stephen Freund, *Williams College*
Andreas Gal, *Mozilla*
David Gregg, *Trinity College Dublin*
Robert Grimm, *New York University*
Dan Grossman, *University of Washington*
Arjun Guha, *Cornell University*
Sumit Gulwani, *Microsoft Research, Redmond*
Aarti Gupta, *NEC Labs America*
Rajiv Gupta, *University of California, Riverside*
Mary Hall, *University of Utah*
Tim Harris, *Oracle Labs, Cambridge*
Hiroshi Inoue, *IBM Research - Tokyo*

External Review Committee (continued):

Tomas Kalibera, *University of Kent*
Christoph Kessler, *Linkoping University*
Gary T. Leavens, *University of Central Florida*
Xavier Leroy, *INRIA*
Ondřej Lhoták, *University of Waterloo*
Ben Liblit, *University of Wisconsin–Madison*
Ben Livshits, *Microsoft Research, Redmond*
Rupak Majumdar, *Max Planck Institute for Software Systems*
Yitzhak Mandelbaum, *Google*
Todd Millstein, *University of California, Los Angeles*
Madanlal Musuvathi, *Microsoft Research, Redmond*
Anders Møller, *Aarhus University*
Aditya Nori, *Microsoft Research, India*
Klaus Ostermann, *Philipps-Universitaet Marburg*
David Pearce, *Victoria University of Wellington*
Erez Petrank, *Technion*
David Pichardie, *INRIA & Harvard University*
Filip Pizlo, *Apple Inc.*
Bill Pugh, *University of Maryland*
Sriram Rajamani, *Microsoft Research, India*
John Regehr, *University of Utah*
Susmit Sarkar, *University of Cambridge*
Max Schaefer, *IBM T.J. Watson Research Center*
Koushik Sen, *University of California, Berkeley*
Zhong Shao, *Yale University*
Manu Sridharan, *IBM T.J. Watson Research Center*
Emina Torlak, *University of California, Berkeley*
Viktor Vafeiadis, *Max Planck Institute for Software Systems*
Mandana Vaziri, *IBM T.J. Watson Research Center*
Christoph von Praun, *University of Applied Sciences Nuremberg*
Stephanie Weirich, *University of Pennsylvania*
Adam Welc, *Oracle Labs*
Eran Yahav, *Technion*
Greta Yorsh, *ARM*
Ben Zorn, *Microsoft Research, Redmond*

Student Research Competition Committee:

Isil Dillig (Chair), *College of William & Mary*
Mike Bond, *The Ohio State University*
Manuel Faehndrich, *Microsoft Research*
Ranjit Jhala, *University of California, San Diego*
Emina Torlak, *University of California, Berkeley*
Eran Yahav, *Technion*

Fun and Interesting Thoughts Committee:

Martin Rinard (Chair), *Massachusetts Institute of Technology*
Thomas Dillig, *College of William & Mary*
Mary Hall, *University of Utah*
Milind Kulkarni, *Purdue University*

Additional reviewers:

George Balatsouras
Michael Bauer
Aggelos Biboudis
Jens Brandt
Mark Chapman
Will Cook
James Demmel
Alastair Donaldson
Prodromos Gerakios
Patrice Godefroid
Philip Guo
Amber Hassaan
Matthew Hammer
David Helmbold
Chin Isradisaikul
George Kastrinis
Yit Phang Khoo
Doug Lea
Andrew Lenharth
Roman Manevich
Piotr Mardziel
Kris Micinski
Andrew Myers
Rupesh Nasre
Donald Nguyen
Peter Ohmann
Dimitris Prountzos
Rodric Rabbah
Tristan Ravitch
Noam Rinetzky
Andrey Rybalchenko
Kristoffer Rose
Amr Sabry
Marc Shapiro
Rahul Sharma
Stevie Strickland
Rei Thiessen
Sean Treichler
Andreas Voellmy
Herbert Wiklicky

PLDI 2013 Sponsor & Supporters

Sponsor:

acm SIGPLAN

Gold Supporters:

ORACLE

Microsoft Research

Silver Supporters:

Google

intel

LOGICBLOX

Bronze Supporters:

facebook

hp

IBM Research

galois

Other Supporters:

NSF

NEC

Look Up!

Your Future is in the Cloud

James R. Larus
Microsoft Research
larus@microsoft.com

Categories and Subject Descriptors H.0 [*Information Systems*]: General

General Terms Languages, Management, Performance, Reliability

Keywords Cloud computing; programming languages; distributed computing

1. Talk Abstract

The "Cloud" is a wonderfully expansive phrase used to denote computation and data storage centralized in a large datacenter and elastically accessed across a network. The concept is not new; web sites and business servers have run in datacenters for a long time. These, however, were specialized applications, outside of the mainstream of desktop programs. The past few years has seen enormous change as the mainstream shifts from a single computer to mobile devices and clusters of computers. Three factors are driving this change. 1) Mobile computing, where apps run on a size- and power-constrained device and would be far less interesting without backend systems to augment computation and storage capacity. 2) Big data, which uses clusters of computers to extract valuable information from vast amounts of unstructured data. 3) Inexpensive, elastic computing, pioneered by Amazon Web Services, which enables everyone to rapidly obtain and use many servers.

As a researcher from the language and compiler community, I firmly believe this sea change is at heart a programming problem.[1] Cloud computing is far different from the environment in which most of today's languages and tools were developed, and few programmers have mastered its complexity. New challenges include pervasive parallelism, partial failure, high and variable communication latency, and replication for reliability and throughput.

The Cloud is an intrinsically parallel and distributed world in which computation runs across many processors on many computers. The workload, fortunately, is inherently parallel, as a single server can be shared by hundreds or thousands of simultaneous and independent users. Moreover, the Cloud is built on inexpensive, commodity hardware that fails in perverse ways. Because of scale, failures are common and software must treat failure as normal. At the same time, services in the cloud face stringent requirements to handle large and unpredictable loads while providing consistent response latency and to maintain high availability and reliability. Redundancy and replication are the principal tools to achieve these ends. And, of course, all of these new demands are layered on the familiar challenges of constructing secure, reliable, scalable, elastic, and efficient software! If this is not a programming problem, what is it?

Language designers and implementers have a remarkable opportunity to contribute by providing first-class support and tools to address these new challenges. Languages such as Erlang, C#, Javascript, and Scala have started down this path by supporting asynchronous communication. But, much more can be done. Shared memory and message passing concurrency needs to be integrated into a single, easy-to-use model with an appropriate balance among performance, usability, consistency, and reliability. Richer data models that embrace replication, consistency, partitioning, and persistence would greatly aid software development. And life cycle issues, such as updating continuously running systems and monitoring and controlling large configurations, are appropriate as elements of a language's runtime system.

I will briefly describe Orleans, a software framework developed at Microsoft Research for building reliable, scalable, and elastic cloud applications. Its programming model encourages the use of simple concurrency patterns that are easy to understand and employ correctly. It is based on distributed actor-like components called grains, which are isolated units of state and computation that communicate through asynchronous messages. Within a grain, promises are the mechanism for managing both asynchronous messages and local task-based concurrency. Isolated state and a constrained execution model allow Orleans to persist, migrate, replicate, and reconcile grain state. In addition, Orleans provides lightweight transactions that support a consistent view of state and provide a foundation for automatic error handling and failure recovery. Orleans enables a developer to concentrate on application logic, while the Orleans runtime provides scalability, availability, and reliability. The system is in use by Microsoft, supporting production services.

[1] Yes, it also poses challenges for the networking, database, system management, . . . communities as well.

PLDI'13, June 16–19, 2013, Seattle, WA, USA.
ACM 978-1-4503-2014-6/13/06.

Optimizing Database-Backed Applications with Query Synthesis

Alvin Cheung Armando Solar-Lezama Samuel Madden *

MIT CSAIL

{akcheung, asolar, madden}@csail.mit.edu

Abstract

Object-relational mapping libraries are a popular way for applications to interact with databases because they provide transparent access to the database using the same language as the application. Unfortunately, using such frameworks often leads to poor performance, as modularity concerns encourage developers to implement relational operations in application code. Such application code does not take advantage of the optimized relational implementations that database systems provide, such as efficient implementations of joins or push down of selection predicates.

In this paper we present QBS, a system that automatically transforms fragments of application logic into SQL queries. QBS differs from traditional compiler optimizations as it relies on synthesis technology to generate invariants and postconditions for a code fragment. The postconditions and invariants are expressed using a new theory of ordered relations that allows us to reason precisely about both the contents and order of the records produced complex code fragments that compute joins and aggregates. The theory is close in expressiveness to SQL, so the synthesized postconditions can be readily translated to SQL queries. Using 75 code fragments automatically extracted from over 120k lines of open-source code written using the Java Hibernate ORM, we demonstrate that our approach can convert a variety of imperative constructs into relational specifications and significantly improve application performance asymptotically by orders of magnitude.

Categories and Subject Descriptors. D.3.2 [*Programming Languages*]: Processors—Compilers; I.2.2 [*Artificial Intelligence*]: Automatic Programming—Program Synthesis

Keywords. program optimization; program synthesis; performance

1. Introduction

In this paper, we develop QBS (Query By Synthesis), a new code analysis algorithm designed to make database-backed applications more efficient. Specifically, QBS identifies places where application logic can be pushed into the SQL queries issued by the application, and automatically transforms the code to do this. Moving application code into the database reduces the amount of data sent from the database to the application, and it also allows the database query optimizer to choose more efficient implementations of some operations—for instance, using indices to evaluate predicates or selecting efficient join algorithms.

One specific target of QBS is programs that interact with the database through object-relational mapping layers (ORMs) such as Hibernate for Java. Our optimizations are particularly important for such programs because ORM layers often lead programmers to write code that iterates over collections of database records, performing operations like filters and joins that could be better done inside of the database. Such ORM layers are becoming increasingly popular; for example, as of March, 2013, on the job board `dice.com` 15% of the 17,000 Java developer jobs are for programmers with Hibernate experience.

We are not the first researchers to address this problem; Wiedermann *et al.* [37, 38] identified this as the *query extraction problem*. However, our work is able analyze a significantly larger class of source programs and generate a more expressive set of SQL queries than this prior work. Specifically, to the best of our knowledge, our work is the first that is able to identify joins and aggregates in general purpose application logic and convert them to SQL queries. Our analysis ensures that the generated queries are *precise* in that both the contents and the order of records in the generated queries are the same as those produced by the original code.

At a more foundational level, our paper is the first to demonstrate the use of constraint-based synthesis technology to attack a challenging compiler optimization problem. Our approach builds on the observation by Iu *et al.* [20] that if we can express the postcondition for an imperative code block in relational algebra, then we can translate that code block into SQL. Our approach uses constraint-based synthesis to automatically derive loop invariants and postconditions, and then uses an SMT solver to check the resulting verification conditions. In order to make synthesis and verification tractable, we define a new *theory of ordered relations* (TOR) that is close in expressiveness to SQL, while being expressive enough to concisely describe the loop invariants necessary to verify the codes of interest. The postconditions expressed in TOR can be readily translated to SQL, allowing them to be optimized by the database query planner and leading in some cases to orders of magnitude performance improvements.

In summary, this paper makes the following contributions:

1. We demonstrate a new approach to compiler optimization based on constraint-based synthesis of loop invariants and apply it to the problem of transforming low-level loop nests into high-level SQL queries.
2. We define a theory of ordered relations that allows us to concisely represent loop invariants and postconditions for code fragments that implement SQL queries, and to efficiently translate those postconditions into SQL.
3. We define a program analysis algorithm that identifies candidate code blocks that can potentially be transformed by QBS.
4. We demonstrate our full implementation of QBS and the candidate identification analysis for Java programs by automatically identifying and transforming 75 code fragments in two large open source projects. These transformations result in order-of-magnitude performance improvements. Although those projects

* The authors are grateful for the support of Intel Corporation and NSF Grants 1065219 and 1139056.

PLDI'13, June 16–19, 2013, Seattle, WA, USA.

```
List<User> getRoleUser () {
  List<User> listUsers = new ArrayList<User>();
  List<User> users = this.userDao.getUsers();
  List<Role> roles = this.roleDao.getRoles();
  for (User u : users) {
    for (Roles r : roles) {
      if (u.roleId().equals(r.roleId())) {
        User userok = u;
        listUsers.add(userok);
  }}}
  return listUsers;
}
```

Figure 1: Sample code that implements join operation in application code, abridged from actual source for clarity

```
List listUsers := [ ]; int i, j = 0;
List users := Query(SELECT * FROM users);
List roles = Query(SELECT * FROM roles);
while (i < users.size()) {
  while (j < roles.size()) {
    if (users[i].roleId = roles[j].roleId)
      listUsers := append(listUsers, users[i]);
    ++j;
  }
  ++i;}
```

Figure 2: Sample code expressed in kernel language

Postcondition

$listUsers = \pi_{\ell}(\bowtie_{\varphi}(users, roles))$
where
$\varphi(e_{users}, e_{roles}) := e_{users}.roleId = e_{roles}.roleId$
ℓ contains all the fields from the *User* class

Translated code

```
List<User> getRoleUser () {
  List<User> listUsers = db.executeQuery(
       "SELECT u
        FROM users u, roles r
        WHERE u.roleId == r.roleId
        ORDER BY u.roleId, r.roleId");
  return listUsers; }
```

Figure 3: Postcondition as inferred from Fig. 1 and code after query transformation

use ORM libraries to retrieve persistent data, our analysis is not specific to ORM libraries and is applicable to programs with embedded SQL queries.

2. Overview

This section gives an overview of our compilation infrastructure and the QBS algorithm to translate imperative code fragments to SQL. We use as a running example a block of code extracted from an open source project management application [2] written using the Hibernate framework. The original code was distributed across several methods which our system automatically collapsed into a single continuous block of code as shown in Fig. 1. The code retrieves the list of users from the database and produces a list containing a subset of users with matching roles.

The example implements the desired functionality but performs poorly. Semantically, the code performs a relational join and projection. Unfortunately, due to the lack of global program information, the ORM library can only fetch all the users and roles from the database and perform the join in application code, without utilizing indices or efficient join algorithms the database system has access to. QBS fixes this problem by compiling the sample code to that

$$
\begin{array}{rcl}
c \in \text{constant} & ::= & \text{True} \mid \text{False} \mid \text{number literal} \mid \text{string literal} \\
e \in \text{expression} & ::= & c \mid [\,] \mid var \mid e.f \mid \{f_i = e_i\} \mid e_1 \; op \; e_2 \mid \neg\, e \\
 & \mid & \text{Query}(\ldots) \mid \text{size}(e) \mid \text{get}_{e_r}(e_s) \\
 & \mid & \text{append}(e_r, e_s) \mid \text{unique}(e) \\
c \in \text{command} & ::= & \text{skip} \mid var := e \mid \text{if}(e) \text{ then } c_1 \text{ else } c_2 \\
 & \mid & \text{while}(e) \text{ do } c \mid c_1 \,;\, c_2 \mid \text{assert } e
\end{array}
$$

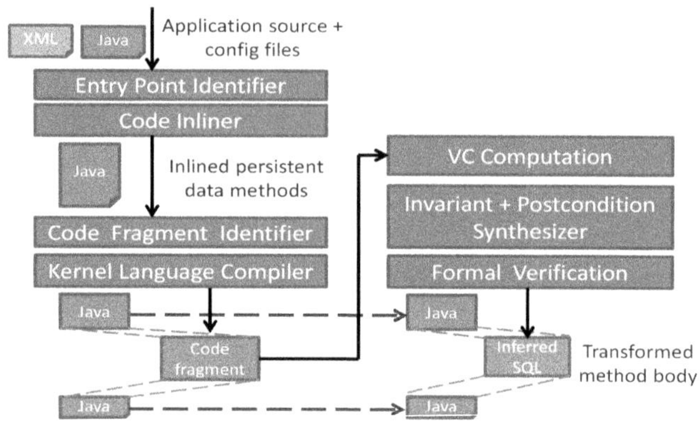

Figure 5: QBS architecture

shown at the bottom of Fig. 3. The nested loop is converted to an SQL query that implements the same functionality in the database where it can be executed more efficiently. Note that the query imposes an order on the retrieved records; this is because in general, nested loops can constraint the ordering of the output records in ways that need to be captured by the query.

In order to apply the QBS algorithm to perform the desired conversion, our system must be able to cope with the complexities of real-world Java code such as aliasing and method calls, which obscure opportunities for transformations. For example, it would not be possible to transform the code fragment in Fig. 1 without knowing that getUsers and getRoles execute specific queries on the database and return non-aliased lists of results, so the first step of the system is to identify promising code fragments and translate them into a simpler kernel language shown in Fig. 4.

The kernel language operates on three types of values: scalars, immutable records, and immutable lists. Lists represent the collections of records and are used to model the results that are returned from database retrieval operations. Lists store either scalar values or records constructed with scalars, and nested lists are assumed to be appropriately flattened. The language currently does not model the three-valued logic of null values in SQL, and does not model updates to the database. The semantics of the constructs in the kernel language are mostly standard, with a few new ones introduced for record retrievals. Query(...) retrieves records from the database and the results are returned as a list. The records of a list can be randomly accessed using get, and records can be appended to a list using append. Finally, unique takes in a list and creates a new list with all duplicate records removed. Fig. 2 shows the example translated to the kernel language.

2.1 QBS Architecture

We now discuss the architecture of QBS and describe the steps in inferring SQL queries from imperative code. The architecture of QBS is shown in Fig. 5.

Identify code fragments to transform. Given a web application written in Java, QBS first finds the persistent data methods in the application, which are those that fetch persistent data via ORM library calls. It also locates all entry points to the application such as servlet handlers. From each persistent data method that is reachable from the entry points, the system inlines a neighborhood of calls, *i.e.* a few of the parent methods that called the persistent data method and a few of the methods called by them. If there is ambiguity as to the target of a call, all potential targets are considered up to a budget. A series of analyses is then performed on each inlined method body to identify a continuous code fragment that can be potentially transformed to SQL; ruling out, for example, code fragments with side effects. For each candidate code fragment, our system automatically detects the program variable that will contain the results from the inferred query (in the case of the running example it is listUsers) — we refer this as the "result variable." At the end of the process, each code fragment is converted to our kernel language as discussed.

Compute verification conditions. As the next step, the system computes the verification conditions of the code fragment expressed in the kernel language. The verification conditions are written using the predicate language derived from the theory of ordered relations to be discussed in Sec. 3. The procedure used to compute verification conditions is a fairly standard one [12, 16]; the only twist is that the verification condition must be computed in terms of an unknown postcondition and loop invariants. The process of computing verification conditions is discussed in more detail in Sec. 4.1.

Synthesize loop invariants and postconditions. The definitions of the postcondition and invariants need to be filled in and validated before translation can proceed. QBS does this using a synthesis-based approach that is similar to [31], where a synthesizer is used to come up with a postcondition and invariants that satisfy the computed verification conditions. The synthesizer uses a symbolic representation of the space of candidate postconditions and invariants and efficiently identifies candidates within the space that are correct according to a bounded verification procedure. It then uses a theorem prover (Z3 [3], specifically) to check if those candidates can be proven correct. The space of candidate invariants and postconditions is described by a template generated automatically by the compiler. To prevent the synthesizer from generating trivial postconditions (such as True), the template limits the synthesizer to only generate postconditions that can be translated to SQL as defined by our theory of ordered relations, such as that shown at the top of Fig. 3.

We observe that it is not necessary to determine the strongest (in terms of logical implication) invariants or postconditions: we are only interested in finding postconditions that allow us transform the input code fragment into SQL. In the case of the running example, we are only interested in finding a postcondition of the form listUsers = *query*, where *query* is an expression translatable to SQL. Similarly, we only need to discover loop invariants that are strong enough to prove the postcondition of interest. From the example shown in Fig. 1, our system infers the postcondition shown at the top of Fig. 3, where π, σ, and $\bowtie$ are ordered versions of relational projection, selection, and join, respectively to be defined in Sec. 3. The process of automatic template generation from the input code fragment and synthesis of the postcondition from the template are discussed in Sec. 4.

Unfortunately, determining loop invariants is undecidable for arbitrary programs [6], so there will be programs for which the necessary invariants fall outside the space defined by the templates. However, our system is significantly more expressive than the state of the art as demonstrated by our experiments in Sec. 7.

Convert to SQL. After the theorem prover verifies that the computed invariants and postcondition are correct, the input code fragment is translated to SQL, as shown in the bottom of Fig. 3. The predicate language defines syntax-driven rules to translate any expressions in the language into valid SQL. The details of validation is discussed in Sec. 5 while the rules for SQL conversion are introduced in Sec. 3.2. The converted SQL queries are patched back into the original code fragments and compiled as Java code.

$$
\begin{array}{rcl}
c \in \text{constant} & ::= & \text{True} \mid \text{False} \mid \text{number literal} \mid \text{string literal} \\
e \in \text{expression} & ::= & c \mid [\,] \mid \text{program var} \mid \{f_i = e_i\} \mid e_1 \; op \; e_2 \mid \neg\, e \\
 & \mid & \text{Query}(...) \mid \text{size}(e) \mid \text{get}_{e_s}(e_r) \mid \text{top}_{e_s}(e_r) \\
 & \mid & \pi_{[f_{i_1},\ldots,f_{i_N}]}(e) \mid \sigma_{\varphi_\sigma}(e) \mid \bowtie_{\varphi_\bowtie}(e_1, e_2) \\
 & \mid & \text{sum}(e) \mid \text{max}(e) \mid \text{min}(e) \\
 & \mid & \text{append}(e_r, e_s) \mid \text{sort}_{[f_{i_1},\ldots,f_{i_N}]}(e) \mid \text{unique}(e) \\
op \in \text{binary op} & ::= & \wedge \mid \vee \mid > \mid = \\
\varphi_\sigma \in \text{select func} & ::= & p_{\sigma_1} \wedge \ldots \wedge p_{\sigma_N} \\
p_\sigma \in \text{select pred} & ::= & e.f_i \; op \; c \mid e.f_i \; op \; e.f_j \mid \text{contains}(e, e_r) \\
\varphi_\bowtie \in \text{join func} & ::= & p_{\bowtie_1} \wedge \ldots \wedge p_{\bowtie_N} \\
p_\bowtie \in \text{join pred} & ::= & e_1.f_i \; op \; e_2.f_j
\end{array}
$$

Figure 6: Abstract syntax for the predicate language based on the theory of ordered relations

3. Theory of Finite Ordered Relations

QBS uses a theory of finite ordered relations to describe postconditions and invariants. The theory is defined to satisfy four main requirements: precision, expressiveness, conciseness and ease of translation to SQL. For precision, we want to be able to reason about *both* the contents and order of records retrieved from the database. This is important because in the presence of joins, the order of the result list will not be arbitrary even when the original list was arbitrary, and we do not know what assumptions the rest of the program makes on the order of records. The theory must also be expressive enough not just to express queries but also to express invariants, which must often refer to partially constructed lists. For instance, the loop invariants for the sample code fragment in Fig. 1 must express the fact that listUsers is computed from the first i and j records of users and roles respectively. Conciseness, *e.g.*, the number of relational operators involved, is important because the complexity of synthesis grows with the size of the synthesized expressions, so if we can express invariants succinctly, we will be able to synthesize them more efficiently. Finally, the inferred postconditions must be translatable to standard SQL.

There are many ways to model relational operations (see Sec. 8), but we are not aware of any that fulfills all of the criteria above. For example, relational algebra is not expressive enough to describe sufficiently precise loop invariants. Defined in terms of sets, relational algebra cannot naturally express concepts such as "the first i elements of the list." First order logic (FOL), on the other hand, is very expressive, but it would be hard to translate arbitrary FOL expressions into SQL.

3.1 Basics

Our theory of finite ordered relations is essentially relational algebra defined in terms of lists instead of sets. The theory operates on three types of values: scalars, records, and ordered relations of finite length. Records are collections of named fields, and an ordered relation is a finite list of records. Each record in the relation is labeled with an integer index that can be used to fetch the record. Figure 6 presents the abstract syntax of the theory and shows how to combine operators to form expressions.

The semantics of the operators in the theory are defined recursively by a set of axioms; a sample of which are shown in Fig. 7. get and top take in an ordered relation e_r and return the record stored at index e_s or all the records from index 0 up to index e_s respec-

top

$$\frac{r = [\,]}{\mathsf{top}_r(i) = [\,]} \quad \frac{i = 0}{\mathsf{top}_r(i) = [\,]} \quad \frac{i > 0 \quad r = h : t}{\mathsf{top}_r(i) = h : \mathsf{top}_t(i-1)}$$

join ($\bowtie$)

$$\frac{r_1 = [\,]}{\bowtie_\varphi(r_1, r_2) = [\,]} \quad \frac{r_2 = [\,]}{\bowtie_\varphi(r_1, r_2) = [\,]} \quad \frac{r_1 = h : t}{\bowtie_\varphi(r_1, r_2) = \mathsf{cat}(\bowtie'_\varphi(h, r_2), \bowtie_\varphi(t, r_2))}$$

$$\frac{r_2 = h : t \quad \varphi(e, h) = \mathsf{True}}{\bowtie'_\varphi(e, r_2) = (e, h) : \bowtie'_\varphi(e, t)} \quad \frac{r_2 = h : t \quad \varphi(e, h) = \mathsf{False}}{\bowtie'_\varphi(e, r_2) = \bowtie'_\varphi(e, t)}$$

projection (π)

$$\frac{r = [\,]}{\pi_\ell(r) = [\,]} \quad \frac{r = h : t \quad f_i \in \ell \quad h.f_i = e_i}{\pi_\ell(r) = \{f_i = e_i\} : \pi_\ell(t)}$$

selection (σ)

$$\frac{r = [\,]}{\sigma_\varphi(r) = [\,]} \quad \frac{r = h : t \quad \varphi(h) = \mathsf{True}}{\sigma_\varphi(r) = h : \sigma_\varphi(t)} \quad \frac{r = h : t \quad \varphi(h) = \mathsf{False}}{\sigma_\varphi(r) = \sigma_\varphi(t)}$$

max

$$\frac{r = [\,]}{\mathsf{max}(r) = -\infty} \quad \frac{r = h : t \quad h > \mathsf{max}(t)}{\mathsf{max}(r) = h} \quad \frac{r = h : t \quad h \leq \mathsf{max}(t)}{\mathsf{max}(r) = \mathsf{max}(t)}$$

Figure 7: Some of the axioms that define the theory of ordered relations, Appendix C contains the full list of axioms

tively. The definitions for π, σ and $\bowtie$ are modeled after relational projection, selection, and join respectively, but they also define an order for the records in the output relation relative to those in the input relations. The projection operator π creates new copies of each record, except that for each record only those fields listed in $[f_{i_1}, \dots, f_{i_N}]$ are retained. Like projection in relational algebra, the same field can be replicated multiple times. The σ operator uses a selection function φ_σ to filter records from the input relation. φ_σ is defined as a conjunction of predicates, where each predicate can compare the value of a record field and a constant, the values of two record fields, or check if the record is contained in another relation e_r using contains. Records are added to the resulting relation if the function returns True. The $\bowtie$ operator iterates over each record from the first relation and pairs it with each record from the second relation. The two records are passed to the join function $\varphi_\bowtie$. Join functions are similar to selection functions, except that predicates in join functions compare the values of the fields from the input ordered relations. The axioms that define the aggregate operators max, min, and sum assume that the input relation contains only one numeric field, namely the field to aggregate upon.

The definitions of unique and sort are standard; in the case of sort, $[f_{i_1}, \dots, f_{i_N}]$ contains the list of fields to sort the relation by. QBS does not actually reason about these two operations in terms of their definitions; instead it treats them as uninterpreted functions with a few algebraic properties, such as

$$\bowtie_\varphi(\mathsf{sort}_{\ell_1}(r_1), \mathsf{sort}_{\ell_2}(r_2)) = \mathsf{sort}_{\mathsf{cat}(\ell_1, \ell_2)}(\bowtie_\varphi(r_1, r_2)).$$

Because of this, there are some formulas involving sort and unique that we cannot prove, but we have not found this to be significant in practice (see Sec. 7 for details).

3.2 Translating to SQL

The expressions defined in the predicate grammar can be converted into semantically equivalent SQL queries. In this section we prove that any expression that does not use append or unique can be compiled into an equivalent SQL query. We prove this in three steps; first, we define base and sorted expressions, which are formulated based on SQL expressions without and with ORDER BY clauses respectively. Next, we define *translatable expressions* and show that any expression that does not use append or unique can be converted into a translatable expression. Then we show how to produce SQL from translatable expressions.

Definition 1 (Translatable Expressions). *Any* transExp *as defined below can be translated into SQL:*

$$\begin{array}{rcl} b \in \mathsf{baseExp} & ::= & \mathsf{Query}(\dots) \mid \mathsf{top}_e(s) \mid \bowtie_{\mathsf{True}}(b_1, b_2) \mid \mathsf{agg}(t) \\ s \in \mathsf{sortedExp} & ::= & \pi_{\ell_\pi}(\mathsf{sort}_{\ell_s}(\sigma_\varphi(b))) \\ t \in \mathsf{transExp} & ::= & s \mid \mathsf{top}_e(s) \end{array}$$

where the term agg *in the grammar denotes any of the aggregation operators (*min, max, sum, size*).*

$$\begin{array}{rcl}
[\![\mathsf{Query}(string)]\!] & = & (\ string\ ) \\
[\![\mathsf{top}_e(s)]\!] & = & \mathsf{SELECT} * \mathsf{FROM}\ [\![s]\!]\ \mathsf{LIMIT}\ [\![e]\!] \\
[\![\bowtie_{\mathsf{True}}(t_1, t_2)]\!] & = & \mathsf{SELECT} * \mathsf{FROM}\ [\![t_1]\!], [\![t_2]\!] \\
[\![\mathsf{agg}(t)]\!] & = & \mathsf{SELECT}\ \mathsf{agg}(field)\ \mathsf{FROM}\ [\![t]\!] \\
[\![\pi_{\ell_1}(\mathsf{sort}_{\ell_2}(\sigma_{\varphi_\sigma}(t)))]\!] & = & \mathsf{SELECT}\ [\![\ell_1]\!]\ \mathsf{FROM}\ [\![t]\!]\ \mathsf{WHERE}\ [\![\varphi_\sigma]\!] \\
 & & \mathsf{ORDER\ BY}\ [\![\ell_2]\!], \mathsf{Order}(t) \\
[\![\mathsf{unique}(t)]\!] & = & \mathsf{SELECT\ DISTINCT} * \mathsf{FROM}\ [\![t]\!] \\
 & & \mathsf{ORDER\ BY\ Order}(t) \\
[\![\varphi_\sigma(e)]\!] & = & [\![e]\!].f_1\ op\ [\![e]\!]\ \mathsf{AND} \ \dots\ \mathsf{AND}\ [\![e]\!].f_N\ op\ [\![e]\!] \\
[\![\mathsf{contains}(e, t)]\!] & = & [\![e]\!]\ \mathsf{IN}\ [\![t]\!] \\
[\![[f_{i_1}, \dots, f_{i_N}]]\!] & = & f_{i_1}, \dots, f_{i_N}
\end{array}$$

Figure 8: Syntactic rules to convert translatable expressions to SQL

Theorem 1 (Completeness of Translation Rules). *All expressions in the predicate grammar in Fig. 6, except for those that contain* append *or* unique*, can be converted into translatable expressions.*

The theorem is proved by defining a function Trans that maps any expression to a translatable expression and showing that the mapping is semantics preserving. Definition of Trans is shown in Appendix B. Semantic equivalence between the original and the translated expression is proved using the expression equivalences listed in Thm. 2. Using those equivalences, for example, we can show that for $s \in \mathsf{sortedExp}$ and $b \in \mathsf{baseExp}$:

$$\begin{array}{rll}
\mathsf{Trans}(\sigma_{\varphi'_\sigma}(s)) & = \mathsf{Trans}(\sigma_{\varphi'}(\pi_{\ell_\pi}(\mathsf{sort}_{\ell_s}(\sigma_\varphi(b))))) & [\mathsf{sortedExp}\ \text{def.}] \\
& = \pi_{\ell_\pi}(\mathsf{sort}_{\ell_s}(\sigma_{\varphi_\sigma \wedge \varphi'_\sigma}(b))) & [\mathsf{Trans}\ \text{def.}] \\
& = \pi_{\ell_\pi}(\sigma_{\varphi'_\sigma}(\mathsf{sort}_{\ell_s}(\sigma_{\varphi_\sigma}(b)))) & [\text{expression equiv.}] \\
& = \sigma_{\varphi'_\sigma}(\pi_{\ell_\pi}(\mathsf{sort}_{\ell_s}(\sigma_{\varphi_\sigma}(b)))) & [\text{expression equiv.}] \\
& = \sigma_{\varphi'_\sigma}(s) & [\mathsf{sortedExp}\ \text{def.}]
\end{array}$$

Thus the semantics of the original TOR expression is preserved.

Translatable expressions to SQL. Following the syntax-directed rules in Fig. 8, any translatable expression can be converted into an equivalent SQL expression. Most rules in Fig. 8 are direct translations from the operators in the theory into their SQL equivalents.

One important aspect of the translation is the way that ordering of records is preserved. Ordering is problematic because although the operators in the theory define the order of the output in terms of the order of their inputs, SQL queries are not guaranteed to preserve the order of records from nested sub-queries; *e.g.*, the ordering imposed by an ORDER BY clause in a nested query is not guaranteed to be respected by an outer query that does not impose any ordering on the records.

To solve this problem, the translation rules introduce a function Order—defined in Fig. 9—which scans a translatable expression t and returns a list of fields that are used to order the subexpressions

$$\mathsf{Order}(\mathsf{Query}(\ldots)) = [\text{record order in DB}] \quad \mathsf{Order}(\mathsf{agg}(e)) = [\,]$$
$$\mathsf{Order}(\mathsf{top}_i(e)) = \mathsf{Order}(e) \quad \mathsf{Order}(\mathsf{unique}(e)) = \mathsf{Order}(e)$$
$$\mathsf{Order}(\pi_\ell(e)) = \mathsf{Order}(e) \quad \mathsf{Order}(\sigma_\varphi(e)) = \mathsf{Order}(e)$$
$$\mathsf{Order}(\bowtie_\varphi(e_1, e_2)) = \mathsf{cat}(\mathsf{Order}(e_1), \mathsf{Order}(e_2))$$
$$\mathsf{Order}(\mathsf{sort}_\ell(e)) = \mathsf{cat}(\ell, \mathsf{Order}(e))$$

Figure 9: Definition of Order

in t. The list is then used to impose an ordering on the outer SQL query with an ORDER BY clause. One detail of the algorithm not shown in the figure is that some projections in the inner queries need to be modified so they do not eliminate fields that will be needed by the outer ORDER BY clause, and that we assume Query(...) is ordered by the order in which the records are stored in the database (unless the query expression already includes an ORDER BY clause).

Append and Unique. The append operation is not included in translatable expressions because there is no simple means to combine two relations in SQL that preserves the ordering of records in the resulting relation [1]. We can still translate unique, however, using the SELECT DISTINCT construct at the outermost level, as Fig. 8 shows. Using unique in nested expressions, however, can change the semantics of the results in ways that are difficult to reason about (*e.g.*, $\mathsf{unique}(\mathsf{top}_e(r))$ is not equivalent to $\mathsf{top}_e(\mathsf{unique}(r))$). Thus, the only expressions with unique that we translate to SQL are those that use it at the outermost level. In our experiments, we found that omitting those two operators did not significantly limit the expressiveness of the theory.

With the theory in mind, we now turn to the process of computing verification conditions of the input code fragments.

4. Synthesis of Invariants and Postconditions

Given an input code fragment in the kernel language, the next step in QBS is to come up with an expression for the result variable of the form $\mathit{resultVar} = e$, where e is a translatable expression as defined in Sec. 3.2.

4.1 Computing Verification Conditions

In order to infer the postcondition, we compute *verification conditions* for the input code fragment using standard techniques from axiomatic semantics [19]. As in traditional Hoare style verification, computing the verification condition of the while statements involves a loop invariant. Unlike traditional computation of verification conditions, however, both the postcondition and the loop invariants are unknown when the conditions are generated. This does not pose problems for QBS as we simply treat invariants (and the postcondition) as unknown predicates over the program variables that are currently in scope when the loop is entered.

As an example, Fig. 11 shows the verification conditions that are generated for the running example. In this case, the verification conditions are split into two parts, with invariants defined for both loops.

The first two assertions describe the behavior of the outer loop on line 5, with the first one asserting that the outer loop invariant must be true on entry of the loop (after applying the rule for the assignments prior to loop entry), and the second one asserting that the postcondition for the loop is true when the loop terminates. The third assertion asserts that the inner loop invariant is true when it is first entered, given that the outer loop condition and loop invariant

Verification conditions for the outer loop (oInv = outerLoopInvariant, iInv = innerLoopInvariant, pcon = postCondition)	
initialization	$\mathsf{oInv}(0, \mathit{users}, \mathit{roles}, [\,])$
loop exit	$i \geq \mathsf{size}(\mathit{users}) \wedge \mathsf{oInv}(i, \mathit{users}, \mathit{roles}, \mathit{listUsers}) \rightarrow \mathsf{pcon}(\mathit{listUsers}, \mathit{users}, \mathit{roles})$
perservation	(same as inner loop initialization)
Verification conditions for the inner loop	
initialization	$i < \mathsf{size}(\mathit{users}) \wedge \mathsf{oInv}(i, \mathit{users}, \mathit{roles}, \mathit{listUsers}) \rightarrow \mathsf{iInv}(i, 0, \mathit{users}, \mathit{roles}, \mathit{listUsers})$
loop exit	$j \geq \mathsf{size}(\mathit{roles}) \wedge \mathsf{iInv}(i, j, \mathit{users}, \mathit{roles}, \mathit{listUsers}) \rightarrow \mathsf{oInv}(i+1, \mathit{users}, \mathit{roles}, \mathit{listUsers})$
preservation	$j < \mathsf{size}(\mathit{roles}) \wedge \mathsf{iInv}(i, j, \mathit{users}, \mathit{roles}, \mathit{listUsers}) \rightarrow (\mathsf{get}_i(\mathit{users}).\mathit{id} = \mathsf{get}_j(\mathit{roles}).\mathit{id} \wedge \mathsf{iInv}(i, j+1, \mathit{users}, \mathit{roles}, \mathsf{append}(\mathit{listUsers}, \mathsf{get}_i(\mathit{users})))) \vee (\mathsf{get}_i(\mathit{users}).\mathit{id} \neq \mathsf{get}_j(\mathit{roles}).\mathit{id} \wedge \mathsf{iInv}(i, j+1, \mathit{users}, \mathit{roles}, \mathit{listUsers}))$

Figure 11: Verification conditions for the running example

are true. The preservation assertion is the inductive argument that the inner loop invariant is preserved after executing one iteration of the loop body. The list *listUsers* is either appended with a record from $\mathsf{get}_i(\mathit{users})$, or remains unchanged, depending on whether the condition for the if statement, $\mathsf{get}_i(\mathit{users}).\mathit{id} = \mathsf{get}_j(\mathit{roles}).\mathit{id}$, is true or not. Finally, the loop exit assertion states that the outer loop invariant is valid when the inner loop terminates.

4.2 Constraint based synthesis

The goal of the synthesis step is to derive postcondition and loop invariants that satisfy the verification conditions generated in the previous step. We synthesize these predicates using the SKETCH constraint-based synthesis system [30]. In general, SKETCH takes as input a program with "holes" and uses a counterexample guided synthesis algorithm (CEGIS) to efficiently search the space of all possible completions to the holes for one that is correct according to a bounded model checking procedure. For QBS, the program is a simple procedure that asserts that the verification conditions hold for all possible values of the free variables within a certain bound. For each of the unknown predicates, the synthesizer is given a *sketch* (*i.e.*, a template) that defines a space of possible predicates which the synthesizer will search. The sketches are automatically generated by QBS from the kernel language representation.

4.3 Inferring the Space of Possible Invariants

Recall that each invariant is parameterized by the current program variables that are in scope. Our system assumes that each loop invariant is a conjunction of predicates, with each predicate having the form $\mathit{lv} = e$, where lv is a program variable that is modified within the loop, and e is an expression in TOR.

The space of expressions e is restricted to expressions of the same static type as lv involving the variables that are in scope. The system limits the size of expressions that the synthesizer can consider, and incrementally increases this limit if the synthesizer fails to find any candidate solutions (to be explained in Sec. 4.5).

Fig. 10 shows a stylized representation of the set of predicates that our system considers for the outer loop in the running example. The figure shows the potential expressions for the program variable i and *listUsers*. One advantage of using the theory of ordered relations is that invariants can be relatively concise. This has a big impact for synthesis, because the space of expressions grows exponentially with respect to the size of the candidate expressions.

4.4 Creating Templates for Postconditions

The mechanism used to generate possible expressions for the result variable is similar to that for invariants, but we have stronger

[1] One way to preserve record ordering in list append is to use case expressions in SQL, although some database systems such as SQL Server limit the number of nested case expressions.

$$
i \; op \left\{ \begin{array}{c} i \mid \mathsf{size}(\mathit{users}) \mid \mathsf{size}(\mathit{roles}) \mid \mathsf{size}(\mathit{listUsers}) \mid \\ \mathsf{sum}(\pi_\ell(\mathit{users}) \mid \mathsf{sum}(\pi_\ell(\mathit{roles}) \mid \mathsf{max}(\pi_\ell(\mathit{users}) \mid \\ \text{[other relational expressions that return a scalar value]} \end{array} \right\} \wedge \mathit{listUsers} = \left\{ \begin{array}{c} \mathit{listUsers} \mid \sigma_\varphi(\mathit{users}) \mid \\ \pi_\ell(\bowtie_\varphi(\mathsf{top}_{e_1}(\mathit{users}), \mathsf{top}_{e_2}(\mathit{roles}))) \mid \\ \pi_\ell(\bowtie_{\varphi_3}(\sigma_{\varphi_1}(\mathsf{top}_{e_1}(\mathit{users}), \sigma_{\varphi_2}(\mathsf{top}_{e_2}(\mathit{roles}))))) \mid \\ \text{[other relational expressions that return an ordered list]} \end{array} \right\}
$$

Figure 10: Space of possible invariants for the outer loop of the running example.

restrictions, since we know the postcondition must be of the form $\mathit{resultVar} = e$ in order to be translatable to SQL.

For the running example, QBS considers the following possible set of postconditions:

$$
\mathit{listUsers} = \left\{ \begin{array}{c} \mathit{users} \mid \sigma_\varphi(\mathit{users}) \mid \mathsf{top}_e(\mathit{users}) \mid \\ \pi_\ell(\bowtie_\varphi(\mathsf{top}_{e_1}(\mathit{users}), \mathsf{top}_{e_2}(\mathit{roles}))) \mid \\ \pi_\ell(\bowtie_{\varphi_3}(\sigma_{\varphi_1}(\mathsf{top}_{e_1}(\mathit{users}), \sigma_{\varphi_2}(\mathsf{top}_{e_2}(\mathit{roles}))))) \mid \\ \text{[other relational expressions that return an ordered list]} \end{array} \right\}
$$

4.5 Optimizations

The basic algorithm presented above for generating invariant and postcondition templates is sufficient but not efficient for synthesis. In this section we describe two optimizations that improve the synthesis efficiency.

Incremental solving. As an optimization, the generation of templates for invariants and postconditions is done in an iterative manner: QBS initially scans the input code fragment for specific patterns and creates simple templates using the production rules from the predicate grammar, such as considering expressions with only one relational operator, and functions that contains one boolean clause. If the synthesizer is able to generate a candidate that can be used to prove the validity of the verification conditions, then our job is done. Otherwise, the system repeats the template generation process, but increases the complexity of the template that is generated by considering expressions consisting of more relational operators, and more complicated boolean functions. Our evaluation using real-world examples shows that most code examples require only a few (< 3) iterations before finding a candidate solution. Additionally, the incremental solving process can be run in parallel.

Breaking symmetries. Symmetries have been shown to be one of sources of inefficiency in constraint solvers [11, 34]. Unfortunately, the template generation algorithm presented above can generate highly symmetrical expressions. For instance, it can generate the following potential candidates for the postcondition:

$$
\sigma_{\varphi_2}(\sigma_{\varphi_1}(\mathit{users})) \\
\sigma_{\varphi_1}(\sigma_{\varphi_2}(\mathit{users}))
$$

Notice that the two expressions are semantically equivalent to the expression $\sigma_{\varphi_1 \wedge \varphi_2}(\mathit{users})$. These are the kind of symmetries that are known to affect solution time dramatically. The template generation algorithm leverages known algebraic relationships between expressions to reduce the search space of possible expressions. For example, our algebraic relationships tell us that it is unnecessary to consider expressions with nested σ like the ones above. Also, when generating templates for postconditions, we only need to consider translatable expressions as defined in Sec. 3.2 as potential candidates. Our experiments have shown that applying these symmetric breaking optimizations can reduce the amount of solving time by half.

Even with these optimizations, the spaces of invariants considered are still astronomically large; on the order of 2^{300} possible combinations of invariants and postconditions for some problems. Thanks to these optimizations, however, the spaces can be searched very efficiently by the constraint based synthesis procedure.

Type	Expression inferred
outer loop invariant	$i \leq \mathsf{size}(\mathit{users}) \wedge$ $\mathit{listUsers} = \pi_\ell(\bowtie_\varphi(\mathsf{top}_i(\mathit{users}), \mathit{roles}))$
inner loop invariant	$i < \mathsf{size}(\mathit{users}) \wedge j \leq \mathsf{size}(\mathit{roles}) \wedge$ $\mathit{listUsers} = \mathsf{append}($ $\pi_\ell(\bowtie_\varphi(\mathsf{top}_i(\mathit{users}), \mathit{roles})),$ $\pi_\ell(\bowtie_\varphi(\mathsf{get}_i(\mathit{users}), \mathsf{top}_j(\mathit{roles})))$
postcondition	$\mathit{listUsers} = \pi_\ell(\bowtie_\varphi(\mathit{users}, \mathit{roles}))$

where $\varphi(e_{users}, e_{roles}) := e_{users}.\mathit{roleId} = e_{roles}.\mathit{roleId}$,
ℓ contains all the fields from the *User* class

Figure 12: Inferred expressions for the running example

5. Formal Validation and Source Transformation

After the synthesizer comes up with candidate invariants and postconditions, they need to be validated using a theorem prover, since the synthesizer used in our prototype is only able to perform bounded reasoning as discussed earlier. We have implemented the theory of ordered relations in the Z3 [3] prover for this purpose. Since the theory of lists is not decidable as it uses universal quantifiers, the theory of ordered relations is not decidable as well. However, for practical purposes we have not found that to be limiting in our experiments. In fact, given the appropriate invariants and postconditions, the prover is able to validate them within seconds by making use of the axioms that are provided.

If the prover can establish the validity of the invariants and postcondition candidates, the postcondition is then converted into SQL according to the rules discussed in Sec. 3.2. For instance, for the running example our algorithm found the invariants and postcondition as shown in Fig. 12, and the input code is transformed into the results in Fig. 3.

If the prover is unable to establish validity of the candidates (detected via a timeout), we ask the synthesizer to generate other candidate invariants and postconditions after increasing the space of possible solutions as described in Sec. 4.5. One reason that the prover may not be able to establish validity is because the maximum size of the relations set for the synthesizer was not large enough. For instance, if the code returns the first 100 elements from the relation but the synthesizer only considers relations up to size 10, then it will incorrectly generate candidates that claim that the code was performing a full selection of the entire relation. In such cases our algorithm will repeat the synthesis process after increasing the maximum relation size.

5.1 Incorporating inferred queries into original code

After verifying the transformation, the inferred queries are merged back into the code fragment. Before replacing the original fragment, we run a def-use analysis (which uses the points-to information to be described in Sec. 6.2) starting at the beginning of the code fragment until the end of the inlined method body. This is to ensure that none of the variables that are defined in the code fragment to be replaced is used in the rest of the inlined method after replacement.

6. Preprocessing of Input Programs

In order to handle real-world Java programs, QBS performs a number of initial passes to identify the code fragments to be transformed to kernel language representation before query inference. The code identification process makes use of several standard analysis techniques, and in this section we describe them in detail.

6.1 Generating initial code fragments

As discussed in Sec. 2, code identification first involves locating application entry point methods and data persistent methods. From each data persistent method, our system currently inlines a neighborhood of 5 callers and callees. We only inline callees that are defined in the application, and provide models for native Java API calls. For callers we only inline those that can be potentially invoked from an entry point method. The inlined method bodies are passed to the next step of the process. Inlining improves the precision of the points-to information for our analysis. While there are other algorithms that can be used to obtain such information [36, 40], we chose inlining for ease of implementation and is sufficient in processing the code fragments used in the experiments.

6.2 Identifying code fragments for query inference

Given a candidate inlined method for query inference, we would like to identify the code fragment to transform to our kernel language representation. While we can simply use the entire body of the inlined method for this purpose, we would like to limit the amount of code to be analyzed, since including code that does not manipulate persistent data will increase the difficulty in synthesizing invariants and postconditions with no actual benefit. We accomplish this goal using a series of analyses. First, we run a flow-sensitive pointer analysis [27] on the body of the inlined method. The results of this analysis is a set of points-to graphs that map each reference variable to one or more abstract memory locations at each program point. Using the points-to information, we perform two further analyses on the inlined method.

Location tainting. We run a dataflow analysis that conservatively marks values that are derived from persistent data retrieved via ORM library calls. This analysis is similar to taint analysis [35], and the obtained information allows the system to remove regions of code that do not manipulate persistent data and thus can be ignored for our purpose. For instance, all reference variables and list contents in Fig. 1 will be tainted as they are derived from persistent data.

Value escapement. After that, we perform another dataflow analysis to check if any abstract memory locations are reachable from references that are outside of the inlined method body. This analysis is needed because if an abstract memory location m is accessible from the external environment (*e.g.*, via a global variable) after program point p, then converting m might break the semantics of the original code, as there can be external references to m that rely on the contents of m before the conversion. This analysis is similar to classical escape analysis [36]. Specifically, we define an abstract memory location m as having escaped at program point p if any of the following is true:

- It is returned from the entry point method.
- It is assigned to a global variable that persists after the entry point method returns (in the web application context, these can be variables that maintain session state, for instance).
- It is assigned to a Runnable object, meaning that it can be accessed by other threads.
- It is passed in as a parameter into the entry point method.
- It can be transitively reached from an escaped location.

With that in mind, we define the beginning of the code fragment to pass to the QBS algorithm as the program point p in the inlined method where tainted data is first retrieved from the database, and the end as the program point p' where tainted data first escapes, where p' appears after p in terms of control flow. For instance, in Fig. 1 the return statement marks the end of the code fragment, with the result variable being the value returned.

App	# persistent data code fragments	translated	rejected	failed
Wilos	33	21	9	3
itracker	16	12	0	4
Total	**49**	**33**	**9**	**7**

Figure 13: Real-world code fragments experiment

6.3 Compilation to kernel language

Each code fragment that is identified by the previous analysis is compiled to our kernel language. Since the kernel language is based on value semantics and does not model heap updates for lists, during the compilation process we translate list references to the abstract memory locations that they point to, using the results from earlier analysis. In general, there are cases where the preprocessing step fails to identify a code fragment from an inlined method (*e.g.*, persistent data values escape to multiple result variables under different branches, code involves operations not supported by the kernel language, etc.), and our system will simply skip such cases. However, the number of such cases is relatively small as our experiments show.

7. Experiments

In this section we report our experimental results. The goal of the experiments is twofold: first, to quantify the ability of our algorithm to convert Java code into real-world applications and measure the performance of the converted code fragments, and second to explore the limitations of the current implementation.

We have implemented a prototype of QBS. The source code analysis and computation of verification conditions are implemented using the Polyglot compiler framework [25]. We use Sketch as the synthesizer for invariants and postconditions, and Z3 for validating the invariants and postconditions.

7.1 Real-World Evaluation

In the first set of experiments, we evaluated QBS using real-world examples from two large-scale open-source applications, Wilos and itracker, written in Java. Wilos (rev. 1196) [2] is a project management application with 62k LOC, and itracker (ver. 3.0.1) [1] is a software issue management system with 61k LOC. Both applications have multiple contributors with different coding styles, and use the Hibernate ORM library for data persistence operations. We passed in the entire source code of these applications to QBS to identify code fragments. The preprocessor initially found 120 unique code fragments that invoke ORM operations. Of those, it failed to convert 21 of them into the kernel language representation, as they use data structures that are not supported by our prototype (such as Java arrays), or access persistent objects that can escape from multiple control flow points and hence cannot be converted.

Meanwhile, upon manual inspection, we found that those 120 code fragments correspond to 49 distinct code fragments inlined in different contexts. For instance, if A and C both call method B, our system automatically inlines B into the bodies of A and C, and those become two different code fragments. But if all persistent data manipulation happens in B, then we only count one of the two as part of the 49 distinct code fragments. QBS successfully translated 33 out of the 49 distinct code fragments (and those 33 distinct code fragments correspond to 75 original code fragments). The results are summarized in Fig. 13, and the details can be found in Appendix A.

This experiment shows that QBS can infer relational specifications from a large fraction of candidate fragments and convert them into SQL equivalents. For the candidate fragments that are reported as translatable by QBS, our prototype was able to synthesize post-conditions and invariants, and also validate them using the prover. Furthermore, the maximum time that QBS takes to process any one code fragment is under 5 minutes (with an average of 2.1 minutes). In the following, we broadly describe the common types of relational operations that our QBS prototype inferred from the fragments, along with some limitations of the current implementation.

Projections and Selections. A number of identified fragments perform relational projections and selections in imperative code. Typical projections include selecting specific fields from the list of records that are fetched from the database, and selections include filtering a subset of objects using field values from each object (*e.g.*, user ID equals to some numerical constant), and a few use criteria that involve program variables that are passed into the method.

One special case is worth mentioning. In some cases only a single field is projected out and loaded into a set data structure, such as a set of integer values. One way to translate such cases is to generate SQL that fetches the field from all the records (including duplicates) into a list, and eliminate the duplicates and return the set to the user code. Our prototype, however, improves upon that scheme by detecting the type of the result variable and inferring a postcondition involving the unique operator, which is then translated to a SELECT DISTINCT query that avoids fetching duplicate records from the database.

Joins. Another set of code fragments involve join operations. We summarize the join operations in the application code into two categories. The first involves obtaining two lists of objects from two base queries and looping through each pair of objects in a nested for or while loop. The pairs are filtered and (typically) one of the objects from each pair is retained. The running example in Fig. 1 represents such a case. For these cases, QBS translates the code fragment into a relational join of the two base queries with the appropriate join predicate, projection list, and sort operations that preserve the ordering of records in the results.

Another type of join also involves obtaining two lists of objects from two base queries. Instead of a nested loop join, however, the code iterates through each object e from the first list, and searches if e (or one of e's fields) is contained in the second. If true, then e (or some of its fields) is appended to the resulting list. For these cases QBS converts the search operation into a contains expression in the predicate language, after which the expression is translated into a correlated subquery in the form of SELECT * FROM r1, r2 WHERE r1 IN r2, with r1 and r2 being the base queries.

QBS handles both join idioms mentioned above. However, the loop invariants and postconditions involved in such cases tend to be more complex as compared to selections and projections, as illustrated by the running example in Fig. 12. Thus, they require more iterations of synthesis and formal validation before finding a valid solution, with up to 5 minutes in the longest case. Here, the majority of the time is spent in synthesis and bounded verification. We are not aware of any prior techniques that can be used to infer join queries from imperative code, and we believe that more optimizations can be devised to speed up the synthesis process for such cases.

Aggregations. Aggregations are used in fragments in a number of ways. The most straightforward ones are those that return the length of the list that is returned from an ORM query, which are translated into COUNT queries. More sophisticated uses of aggregates include iterating through all records in a list to find the max or min values, or searching if a record exists in a list. Aggregates such as maximum and minimum are interesting as they introduce loop-carried dependencies [5], where the running value of the aggregate is updated conditionally based on the value of the current record as compared to previous ones. By using the top operator from the theory of ordered relations, QBS is able to generate a loop invariant of the form $v = agg(top_i(r))$ and then translate the postcondition into the appropriate SQL query.

As a special case, a number of fragments check for the existence of a particular record in a relation by iterating over all records and setting a result boolean variable to be true if it exists. In such cases, the generated invariants are similar to other aggregate invariants, and our prototype translates such code fragments into SELECT COUNT(*) > 0 FROM ... WHERE e, where e is the expression to check for existence in the relation. We rely on the database query optimizer to further rewrite this query into the more efficient form using EXISTS.

Limitations. We have verified that in all cases where the generated template is expressive enough for the invariants and postconditions, our prototype does indeed find the solution within a preset timeout of 10 minutes. However, there are a few examples from the two applications where our prototype either rejects the input code fragment or fails to find an equivalent SQL expression from the kernel language representation. Fragments are rejected because they involve relational update operations that are not handled by TOR. Another set of fragments include advanced use of types, such as storing polymorphic records in the database, and performing different operations based on the type of records retrieved. Incorporating type information in the theory of ordered relations is an interesting area for future work. There are also a few that QBS fails to translate into SQL, even though we believe that there is an equivalent SQL query without updates. For instance, some fragments involve sorting the input list by Collections.sort, followed by retrieving the last record from the sorted list, which is equivalent to max or min depending on the sort order. Including extra axioms in the theory would allow us to reason about such cases.

7.2 Performance Comparisons

Next, we quantify the amount of performance improvement as a result of query inference. To do so, we took a few representative code fragments for selection, joins, and aggregation, and populated databases with different number of persistent objects. We then compared the performance between the original code and our transformed versions of the code with queries inferred by QBS. Since Hibernate can either retrieve all nested references from the database (eager) when an object is fetched, or only retrieve the top level references (lazy), we measured the execution times for both modes (the original application is configured to use the lazy retrieval mode). The results shown in Fig. 14 compare the time taken to completely load the webpages containing the queries between the original and the QBS inferred versions of the code.

Selection Code Fragment. Fig. 14a and Fig. 14b show the results from running a code fragment that includes persistent data manipulations from fragment #40 in Appendix A. The fragment returns the list of unfinished projects. Fig. 14a shows the results where 10% of the projects stored are unfinished, and Fig. 14b shows the results with 50% unfinished projects. While the original version performs the selection in Java by first retrieving all projects from the database, QBS inferred a selection query in this case. As expected, the query inferred by QBS outperforms the original fragments in all cases as it only needs to retrieve a portion (specifically 10 and 50%) of all persistent objects.

Join Code Fragment. Fig. 14c shows the results from a code fragment with contents from fragment #46 in Appendix A (which is the same as the example from Fig. 1). The fragment returns the projection of User objects after a join of Roles and Users in the

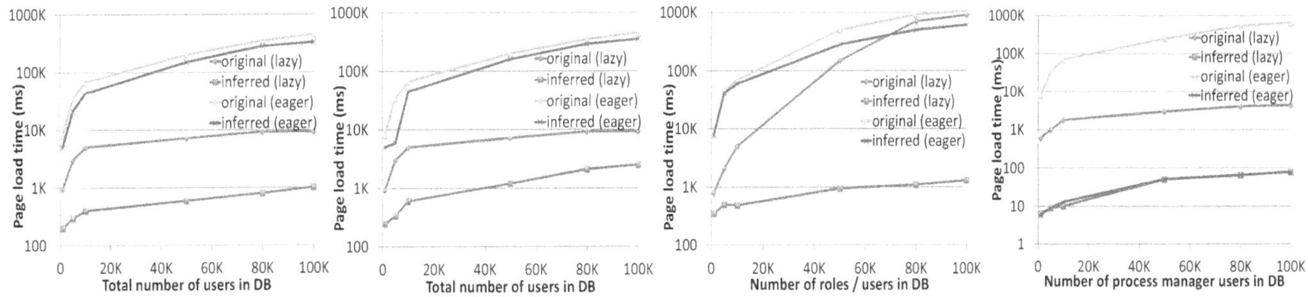

(a) Selection with 10% selectivity (b) Selection with 50% selectivity (c) Join code fragment (d) Aggregation code fragment

Figure 14: Webpage load times comparison of representative code fragments

database on the roleld field. The original version performs the join by retrieving all User and Role objects and joining them in a nested loop fashion as discussed in Sec. 2. The query inferred by QBS however, pushes the join and projection into the database. To isolate the effect of performance improvement due to query selectivity (as in the selection code fragment), we purposefully constructed the dataset so that the query returns all User objects in the database in all cases, and the results show that the query inferred by QBS version still has much better performance than the original query. This is due to two reasons. First, even though the number of User objects returned in both versions are the same, the QBS version does not need to retrieve any Role objects since the projection is pushed into the database, unlike the the original version. Secondly, thanks to the automatically created indices on the Role and User tables by Hibernate, the QBS version essentially transforms the join implementation from a nested loop join into a hash join, *i.e.*, from an $O(n^2)$ to an $O(n)$ implementation, thus improving performance asymptotically.

Aggregation Code Fragment. Finally, Fig. 14d shows the results from running code with contents from fragment #38, which returns the number of users who are process managers. In this case, the original version performs the counting by bringing in all users who are process managers from the database, and then returning the size of the resulting list. QBS, however, inferred a COUNT query on the selection results. This results in multiple orders of magnitude performance improvement, since the QBS version does not need to retrieve any objects from the database beyond the resulting count.

7.3 Advanced Idioms

In the final set of experiments, we used synthetic code fragments to demonstrate the ability of our prototype to translate more complex expressions into SQL. Although we did not find such examples in either of our two real-world applications, we believe that these can occur in real applications.

Hash Joins. Beyond the join operations that we encountered in the applications, we wrote two synthetic test cases for joins that join relations r and s using the predicate r.a = s.b, where a and b are integer fields. In the first case, the join is done via hashing, where we first iterate through records in r and build a hashtable, whose keys are the values of the a field, and where each key maps to a list of records from r that has that corresponding value of a. We then loop through each record in s to find the relevant records from r to join with, using the b field as the look up key. QBS currently models hashtables using lists, and with that our prototype is able recognize this process as a join operation and convert the fragment accordingly, similar to the join code fragments mentioned above.

Sort-Merge Joins. Our second synthetic test case joins two lists by first sorting r and s on fields a and b respectively, and then iterating through both lists simultaneously. We advance the scan of r as long as the current record from r is less than (in terms of fields a and b) the current record from s, and similarly advance the scan of s as long as the current s record is less than the current r record. Records that represent the join results are created when the current record from r equals to that from s on the respective fields. Unfortunately, our current prototype fails to translate the code fragment into SQL, as the invariants for the loop cannot be expressed using the current the predicate language, since that involves expressing the relationship between the current record from r and s with all the records that have been previously processed.

Iterating over Sorted Relations. We next tested our prototype with two usages of sorted lists. We created a relation with one unsigned integer field id as primary key, and sorted the list using the sort method from Java. We subsequently scanned through the sorted list as follows:

```
List records = Query("SELECT id FROM t");
List results = new ArrayList();
Collections.sort(records); // sort by id
for (int i = 0; i < 10; ++i)
{ results.add(records.get(i)); }
```

Our prototype correctly processes this code fragment by translating it into SELECT id FROM t ORDER BY id LIMIT 10. However, if the loop is instead written as follows:

```
List records = Query("SELECT id FROM t");
List results = new ArrayList();
Collections.sort(records); // sort by id
int i = 0;
while (records.get(i).id < 10)
{ results.add(records.get(i)); ++i;}
```

The two loops are equivalent since the id field is a primary key of the relation, and thus there can at most be 10 records retrieved. However, our prototype is not able to reason about the second code fragment, as that requires an understanding of the schema of the relation, and that iterating over id in this case is equivalent to iterating over i in the first code fragment. Both of which require additional axioms to be added to the theory before such cases can be converted.

8. Related Work

Inferring relational specifications from imperative code was studied in [37, 38]. The idea is to compute the set of data access paths that the imperative code traverses using abstract interpretation, and replace the imperative code with SQL queries. The analysis is applicable to recursive function calls, but does not handle code with loop-carried dependencies, or those with join or aggregation. It is unclear how modeling relational operations as access paths can be extended to handle such cases. Our implementation is able to infer both join and aggregation from imperative code. We currently do not handle recursive function calls, although we have not encountered such uses in the applications used in our experiments.

Modeling relational operations. Our ability to infer relational specifications from imperative code relies on using the TOR to connect the imperative and relational worlds. There are many prior work in modeling relational operations, for instance using bags [9], sets [22], and nested relational calculus [39]. There are also theoretical models that extend standard relational algebra with order, such as [4, 24]. Our work does not aim to provide a new theoretical model. Instead, one key insight of our work is that TOR is the right abstraction for the query inference, as they are similar to the interfaces provided by the ORM libraries in the imperative code, and allow us to design a sound and precise transformation into SQL.

To our knowledge, our work is the first to address the ordering of records in relational transformations. Record ordering would not be an issue if the source program only operated on orderless data structures such as sets or did not perform any joins. Unfortunately, most ORM libraries provide interfaces based on ordered data structures, and imperative implementations of join proves to be common at least in the benchmarks we studied.

Finding invariants to validate transformations. Our verification-based approach to finding a translatable postcondition is similar to earlier work [20, 21], although they acknowledge that finding invariants is difficult. Similar work has been done for general-purpose language compilers [33]. Scanning the source code to generate the synthesis template is inspired by the PINS algorithm [32], although QBS does not need user intervention. There has been earlier work on automatically inferring loop invariants, such as using predicate refinement [14] or dynamic detection [13, 18].

Constraint-based synthesis. Constraint-based program synthesis has been an active topic of research in recent years. For instance, there has been work on using synthesis to discover invariants [31]. Our work differs from previous approaches in that we only need to find invariants and postconditions that are *strong enough* to validate the transformation, and our predicate language greatly prunes the space of invariants to those needed for common relational operations. Synthesis has also been applied in other domains, such as generating data structures [29], processor instructions [15], and learning queries from examples [8].

Integrated query languages. Integrating application and database query languages into has been an active research area, with projects such as LINQ [23], Kleisli [39], Links [10], JReq [20], the functional language proposed in [9], Ferry [17], and DBPL [28]. These solutions embed database queries in imperative programs without ORM libraries. Unfortunately, many of them do not support all relational operations, and the syntax of such languages resemble SQL, thus developers still need to learn new programming paradigms and rewrite existing applications.

Improving performance of database programs by code transformation. There is also work in improving application performance by transforming loops to allow query batching [26], and pushing computations into the database [7]. Our work is orthogonal to this line of research. After converting portions of the source code into SQL queries, such code transformation can be applied to gain additional performance improvement.

9. Conclusions

In this paper, we presented QBS, a system for inferring relational specifications from imperative code that retrieves data using ORM libraries. Our system automatically infers loop invariants and postconditions associated with the source program, and converts the validated postcondition into SQL queries. Our approach is both sound and precise in preserving the ordering of records. We developed a theory of ordered relations that allows efficient encoding of relational operations into a predicate language, and we demonstrated the applicability using a set of real-world code examples.

References

[1] itracker Issue Management System. `http://itracker.sourceforge.net/index.html`.

[2] Wilos Orchestration Software. `http://www.ohloh.net/p/6390`.

[3] z3 Theorem Prover. `http://research.microsoft.com/en-us/um/redmond/projects/z3`.

[4] S. Abiteboul, R. Hull, and V. Vianu. *Foundations of Databases*. Addison-Wesley, 1995.

[5] J. R. Allen and K. Kennedy. Automatic loop interchange. In *Proc. CC*, pages 233–246, 1984.

[6] A. Blass and Y. Gurevich. Inadequacy of computable loop invariants. *ACM Trans. Comput. Log.*, 2(1):1–11, 2001.

[7] A. Cheung, O. Arden, S. Madden, and A. C. Myers. Automatic partitioning of database applications. *PVLDB*, 5, 2011.

[8] A. Cheung, A. Solar-Lezama, and S. Madden. Using program synthesis for social recommendations. In *Proc. CIKM*, pages 1732–1736, 2012.

[9] E. Cooper. The script-writer's dream: How to write great sql in your own language, and be sure it will succeed. In *Proc. DBPL Workshop*, pages 36–51, 2009.

[10] E. Cooper, S. Lindley, P. Wadler, and J. Yallop. Links: Web programming without tiers. In *Proc. Int.l Symp. on Formal Methods for Components and Objects*, pages 266–296, 2006.

[11] D. Déharbe, P. Fontaine, S. Merz, and B. W. Paleo. Exploiting symmetry in smt problems. In *Proc. Int.l Conf. on Automated Deduction*, pages 222–236, 2011.

[12] E. W. Dijkstra. Guarded commands, nondeterminacy and formal derivation of programs. *Commun. ACM*, 18(8):453–457, 1975.

[13] M. D. Ernst, J. Cockrell, W. G. Griswold, and D. Notkin. Dynamically discovering likely program invariants to support program evolution. In *Proc. ICSE*, pages 213–224, 1999.

[14] C. Flanagan and S. Qadeer. Predicate abstraction for software verification. In *Proc. POPL*, pages 191–202, 2002.

[15] P. Godefroid and A. Taly. Automated synthesis of symbolic instruction encodings from I/O samples. In *Proc. PLDI*, pages 441–452, 2012.

[16] D. Gries. *The Science of Programming*. Springer, 1987.

[17] T. Grust, M. Mayr, J. Rittinger, and T. Schreiber. FERRY: database-supported program execution. In *Proc. SIGMOD*, pages 1063–1066, 2009.

[18] A. Gupta and A. Rybalchenko. Invgen: An efficient invariant generator. In *Proc. CAV*, pages 634–640, 2009.

[19] C. A. R. Hoare. An axiomatic basis for computer programming. *Commun. ACM*, 12(10):576–580, 1969.

[20] M.-Y. Iu, E. Cecchet, and W. Zwaenepoel. Jreq: Database queries in imperative languages. In *Proc. CC*, pages 84–103, 2010.

[21] M.-Y. Iu and W. Zwaenepoel. HadoopToSQL: a mapreduce query optimizer. In *Proc. EuroSys*, pages 251–264, 2010.

[22] D. Jackson. Alloy: a lightweight object modelling notation. *ACM Trans. Softw. Eng. Methodol.*, 11(2):256–290, 2002.

[23] E. Meijer, B. Beckman, and G. Bierman. LINQ: Reconciling objects, relations and XML in the .NET framework. In *Proc. SIGMOD*, pages 706–706, 2006.

[24] W. Ng. An extension of the relational data model to incorporate ordered domains. *Trans. Database Syst.*, 26(3):344–383, Sept. 2001.

[25] N. Nystrom, M. R. Clarkson, and A. C. Myers. Polyglot: An extensible compiler framework for Java. In *Proc. CC*, pages 138–152, 2003.

[26] K. Ramachandra, R. Guravannavar, and S. Sudarshan. Program analysis and transformation for holistic optimization of database applications. In *Proc. SOAP Workshop*, pages 39–44, 2012.

[27] M. Sagiv, T. Reps, and R. Wilhelm. Parametric shape analysis via 3-valued logic. In *Proc. POPL*, pages 105–118, 1999.

[28] J. W. Schmidt and F. Matthes. The DBPL project: Advances in modular database programming. *Inf. Syst.*, 19(2):121–140, 1994.

[29] R. Singh and A. Solar-Lezama. Synthesizing data structure manipulations from storyboards. In *Proc. FSE*, pages 289–299, 2011.

[30] A. Solar-Lezama, L. Tancau, R. Bodík, S. Seshia, and V. Saraswat. Combinatorial sketching for finite programs. In *Proc. ASPLOS*, pages 404–415, 2006.
[31] S. Srivastava and S. Gulwani. Program verification using templates over predicate abstraction. In *Proc. PLDI*, pages 223–234, 2009.
[32] S. Srivastava, S. Gulwani, S. Chaudhuri, and J. S. Foster. Path-based inductive synthesis for program inversion. In *Proc. PLDI*, pages 492–503, 2011.
[33] Z. Tatlock and S. Lerner. Bringing extensibility to verified compilers. In *Proc. PLDI*, pages 111–121, 2010.
[34] E. Torlak and D. Jackson. Kodkod: a relational model finder. In *Proc. TACAS*, pages 632–647, 2007.
[35] O. Tripp, M. Pistoia, S. J. Fink, M. Sridharan, and O. Weisman. Taj: effective taint analysis of web applications. In *Proc. PLDI*, pages 87–97, 2009.
[36] J. Whaley and M. Rinard. Compositional pointer and escape analysis for java programs. In *Proc. OOPSLA*, pages 187–206, 1999.
[37] B. Wiedermann and W. R. Cook. Extracting queries by static analysis of transparent persistence. In *Proc. POPL*, pages 199–210, 2007.
[38] B. Wiedermann, A. Ibrahim, and W. R. Cook. Interprocedural query extraction for transparent persistence. In *Proc. OOPSLA*, pages 19–36, 2008.
[39] L. Wong. Kleisli, a functional query system. *J. Funct. Program.*, 10(1):19–56, 2000.
[40] Y. Xie and A. Aiken. Scalable error detection using boolean satisfiability. In *Proc. POPL*, pages 351–363, 2005.

A. Persistent Data Code Fragment Details

In this section we describe the code fragments from real-world examples that are used in our experiments. The table below shows the details of the 49 distinct code fragments as mentioned in Sec. 7.1. The times reported correspond to the time required to synthesize the invariants and postconditions. The time taken for the other initial analysis and SQL translation steps are negligible.

wilos code fragments

#	Java Class Name	Line	Oper.	Status	Time (s)
17	ActivityService	401	A	†	–
18	ActivityService	328	A	†	–
19	AffectedtoDao	13	B	✓	72
20	ConcreteActivityDao	139	C	*	–
21	ConcreteActivityService	133	D	†	–
22	ConcreteRoleAffectationService	55	E	✓	310
23	ConcreteRoleDescriptorService	181	F	✓	290
24	ConcreteWorkBreakdownElementService	55	G	†	–
25	ConcreteWorkProductDescriptorService	236	F	✓	284
26	GuidanceService	140	A	†	–
27	GuidanceService	154	A	†	–
28	IterationService	103	A	†	–
29	LoginService	103	H	✓	125
30	LoginService	83	H	✓	164
31	ParticipantBean	1079	B	✓	31
32	ParticipantBean	681	H	✓	121
33	ParticipantService	146	E	✓	281
34	ParticipantService	119	E	✓	301
35	ParticipantService	266	F	✓	260
36	PhaseService	98	A	†	–
37	ProcessBean	248	H	✓	82
38	ProcessManagerBean	243	B	✓	50
39	ProjectService	266	K	*	–
40	ProjectService	297	A	✓	19
41	ProjectService	338	G	†	–
42	ProjectService	394	A	✓	21
43	ProjectService	410	A	✓	39
44	ProjectService	248	H	✓	150
45	RoleDao	15	I	*	–
46	RoleService	15	E	✓	150
47	WilosUserBean	717	B	✓	23
48	WorkProductsExpTableBean	990	B	✓	52
49	WorkProductsExpTableBean	974	J	✓	50

itracker code fragments

#	Java Class Name	Line	Operation	Status	Time (s)
1	EditProjectFormActionUtil	219	F	✓	289
2	IssueServiceImpl	1437	D	✓	30
3	IssueServiceImpl	1456	L	*	–
4	IssueServiceImpl	1567	C	*	–
5	IssueServiceImpl	1583	M	✓	130
6	IssueServiceImpl	1592	M	✓	133
7	IssueServiceImpl	1601	M	✓	128
8	IssueServiceImpl	1422	D	✓	34
9	ListProjectsAction	77	N	*	–
10	MoveIssueFormAction	144	K	*	–
11	NotificationServiceImpl	568	O	✓	57
12	NotificationServiceImpl	848	A	✓	132
13	NotificationServiceImpl	941	H	✓	160
14	NotificationServiceImpl	244	O	✓	72
15	UserServiceImpl	155	M	✓	146
16	UserServiceImpl	412	A	✓	142

where:
A: selection of records
B: return literal based on result size
C: retrieve the max / min record by first sorting and then returning the last element
D: projection / selection of records and return results as a set
E: nested-loop join followed by projection
F: join using `contains`
G: type-based record selection
H: check for record existence in list
I: record selection and only return the one of the records if multiple ones fulfill the selection criteria
J: record selection followed by count
K: sort records using a custom comparator
L: projection of records and return results as an array
M: return result set size
N: record selection and in-place removal of records
O: retrieve the max / min record

✓ indicates those that are translated by. QBS
* indicates those that QBS failed to find invariants for.
† indicates those that are rejected by QBS due to TOR / preprocessing limitations.

B. TOR Expression Equivalences and Definition of Trans

Before defining Trans, we first list the set of TOR expression equivalences that are used in the definition.

Theorem 2 (Operator Equivalence). *The following equivalences hold, both in terms of the contents of the relations and also the ordering of the records in the relations:*

- $\sigma_\varphi(\pi_\ell(r)) = \pi_\ell(\sigma_\varphi(r))$
- $\sigma_{\varphi_2}(\sigma_{\varphi_1}(r)) = \sigma_{\varphi'}(r)$, *where* $\varphi' = \varphi_2 \wedge \varphi_1$
- $\mathsf{top}_e(\sigma_\varphi(r)) = \sigma_\varphi(\mathsf{top}_e(r))$
- $\pi_{\ell_2}(\pi_{\ell_1}(r)) = \pi_{\ell'}(r)$, *where* ℓ' *is the concatenation of all the fields in* ℓ_1 *and* ℓ_2.
- $\mathsf{top}_e(\pi_\ell(r)) = \pi_\ell(\mathsf{top}_e(r))$
- $\mathsf{top}_{e_2}(\mathsf{top}_{e_1}(r)) = \mathsf{top}_{\max(e_1,e_2)}(r)$
- $\bowtie_\varphi(r_1, r_2) = \sigma_{\varphi'}(\bowtie_{\mathsf{True}}(r_1, r_2))$, *i.e., joins can be converted into cross products with selections with proper renaming of fields.*
- $\bowtie_\varphi(\mathsf{sort}_{\ell_1}(r_1), \mathsf{sort}_{\ell_2}(r_2)) = \mathsf{sort}_{\ell_1:\ell_2}(\bowtie_\varphi(r_1, r_2))$
- $\bowtie_\varphi(\pi_{\ell_1}(r_1), \pi_{\ell_2}(r_2)) = \pi_{\ell'}(\bowtie_\varphi(r_1, r_2))$, *where* ℓ' *is the concatenation of all the fields in* ℓ_1 *and* ℓ_2.

Except for the equivalences involving sort, the other ones can be proven easily from the axiomatic definitions.

B.1 Definition of Trans

Let $s = \pi_{\ell_\pi}(\mathsf{sort}_{\ell_s}(\sigma_\varphi(b)))$. Trans is defined on expressions whose subexpressions (if any) are in translatable form, so we have to consider cases where the sub-expressions are either s or $\mathsf{top}_e(s)$. Each case is defined below.

$$\boxed{\mathsf{Query}(\ldots)}$$

$$\mathsf{Trans}(\mathsf{Query}(\ldots))) = \pi_\ell(\mathsf{sort}_{[\,]}(\sigma_{\mathsf{True}}(\mathsf{Query}(\ldots))))$$

where ℓ projects all the fields from the input relation.

$$\boxed{\pi_{\ell_2}(t)}$$

$$\begin{aligned}\mathsf{Trans}(\pi_{\ell_2}(s)) &= \pi_{\ell'}(\mathsf{sort}_{\ell_s}(\sigma_\varphi(b)))\\ \mathsf{Trans}(\pi_{\ell_2}(\mathsf{top}_e(s))) &= \mathsf{top}_e(\pi_{\ell'}(\mathsf{sort}_{\ell_s}(\sigma_\varphi(b))))\end{aligned}$$

where ℓ' is the composition of ℓ_π and ℓ_2.

$$\boxed{\sigma_{\varphi_2}(t)}$$

$$\begin{aligned}\mathsf{Trans}(\sigma_{\varphi_2}(s)) &= \pi_{\ell_\pi}(\mathsf{sort}_{\ell_s}(\sigma_{\varphi\wedge\varphi_2}(b)))\\ \mathsf{Trans}(\sigma_{\varphi_2}(\mathsf{top}_e(s))) &= \mathsf{top}_e(\pi_{\ell_\pi}(\mathsf{sort}_{\ell_s}(\sigma_{\varphi\wedge\varphi_2}(b))))\end{aligned}$$

$$\boxed{\bowtie_{\varphi_\bowtie}(t_1, t_2))}$$

$$\mathsf{Trans}(\bowtie_{\varphi_\bowtie}(s_1, s_2)) = \pi_{\ell'_\pi}(\mathsf{sort}_{\ell'_s}(\sigma_{\varphi'_\sigma}(\bowtie_{\mathsf{True}}(b_1, b_2))))$$

where $\varphi'_\sigma = \varphi_{\sigma_1} \wedge \varphi_{\sigma_2} \wedge \varphi_\bowtie$ with field names properly renamed, $\ell'_s = \mathsf{cat}(\ell_{s_1}, \ell_{s_2})$, and $\ell'_\pi = \mathsf{cat}(\ell_{\pi_1}, \ell_{\pi_2})$.

$$\begin{aligned}&\mathsf{Trans}(\bowtie_\varphi(\mathsf{top}_e(s_1), \mathsf{top}_e(s_2)))\\ &\quad = \pi_\ell(\mathsf{sort}_{[\,]}(\sigma_\varphi(\bowtie_{\mathsf{True}}(\mathsf{top}_e(s_1), \mathsf{top}_e(s_2)))))\end{aligned}$$

where ℓ contains all the fields from s_1 and s_2.

$$\boxed{\mathsf{top}_{e_2}(t)}$$

$$\begin{aligned}\mathsf{Trans}(\mathsf{top}_{e_2}(s)) &= \mathsf{top}_{e_2}(s)\\ \mathsf{Trans}(\mathsf{top}_{e_2}(\mathsf{top}_{e_1}(s))) &= \mathsf{top}_{e'}(s)\end{aligned}$$

where e' is the minimum value of e_1 and e_2.

$$\boxed{\mathsf{agg}(t)}$$

$$\begin{aligned}\mathsf{Trans}(\mathsf{agg}(s)) &= \pi_\ell(\mathsf{sort}_{[\,]}(\sigma_{\mathsf{True}}(\mathsf{agg}(s))))\\ \mathsf{Trans}(\mathsf{agg}(\mathsf{top}_e(s))) &= \pi_\ell(\mathsf{sort}_{[\,]}(\sigma_{\mathsf{True}}(\mathsf{agg}(s))))\end{aligned}$$

where ℓ contains all the fields from s.

$$\boxed{\mathsf{sort}_{\ell_{s_2}}(t)}$$

$$\begin{aligned}\mathsf{Trans}(\mathsf{sort}_{\ell_{s_2}}(s)) &= \pi_{\ell_\pi}(\mathsf{sort}_{\ell'_s}(\sigma_\varphi(b)))\\ \mathsf{Trans}(\mathsf{sort}_{\ell_{s_2}}(\mathsf{top}_e(s))) &= \mathsf{top}_e(\pi_{\ell_\pi}(\mathsf{sort}_{\ell'_s}(\sigma_\varphi(b))))\end{aligned}$$

where $\ell'_s = \mathsf{cat}(\ell_s, \ell_{s_2})$.

C. TOR Axioms

Below is a listing of all the axioms currently defined in the theory of ordered relations (TOR). $\mathsf{cat}(\ell_1, \ell_2)$ concatenates the contents of lists ℓ_1 and ℓ_2.

$$\boxed{\mathsf{size}}$$

$$\frac{r = [\,]}{\mathsf{size}(r) = 0} \qquad \frac{r = h : t}{\mathsf{size}(r) = 1 + \mathsf{size}(t)}$$

$$\boxed{\mathsf{get}}$$

$$\frac{i = 0 \quad r = h : t}{\mathsf{get}_i(r) = h} \qquad \frac{i > 0 \quad r = h : t}{\mathsf{get}_i(r) = \mathsf{get}_{i-1}(t)}$$

$$\boxed{\mathsf{append}}$$

$$\frac{r = [\,]}{\mathsf{append}(r, t) = [t]} \qquad \frac{r = h : t}{\mathsf{append}(r, t) = h : \mathsf{append}(t, r)}$$

$$\boxed{\mathsf{top}}$$

$$\frac{r = [\,]}{\mathsf{top}_r(i) = [\,]} \qquad \frac{i = 0}{\mathsf{top}_r(i) = [\,]} \qquad \frac{i > 0 \quad r = h : t}{\mathsf{top}_r(i) = h : \mathsf{top}_t(i-1)}$$

$$\boxed{\mathsf{join}\ (\bowtie)}$$

$$\frac{r_1 = [\,]}{\bowtie_\varphi(r_1, r_2) = [\,]} \qquad \frac{r_2 = [\,]}{\bowtie_\varphi(r_1, r_2) = [\,]}$$

$$\frac{r_1 = h : t}{\bowtie_\varphi(r_1, r_2) = \mathsf{cat}(\bowtie'_\varphi(h, r_2), \bowtie_\varphi(t, r_2))}$$

$$\frac{r_2 = h : t \quad \varphi(e, h) = \mathsf{True}}{\bowtie'_\varphi(e, r_2) = (e, h) : \bowtie'_\varphi(e, t)} \qquad \frac{r_2 = h : t \quad \varphi(e, h) = \mathsf{False}}{\bowtie'_\varphi(e, r_2) = \bowtie'_\varphi(e, t)}$$

$$\boxed{\mathsf{projection}\ (\pi)}$$

$$\frac{r = [\,]}{\pi_\ell(r) = [\,]} \qquad \frac{r = h : t \quad f_i \in \ell \quad h.f_i = e_i}{\pi_\ell(r) = \{f_i = e_i\} : \pi_\ell(t)}$$

$$\boxed{\mathsf{selection}\ (\sigma)}$$

$$\frac{r = [\,]}{\sigma_\varphi(r) = [\,]} \qquad \frac{r = h : t \quad \varphi(h) = \mathsf{True}}{\sigma_\varphi(r) = h : \sigma_\varphi(t)} \qquad \frac{r = h : t \quad \varphi(h) = \mathsf{False}}{\sigma_\varphi(r) = \sigma_\varphi(t)}$$

$$\boxed{\mathsf{sum}}$$

$$\frac{r = [\,]}{\mathsf{sum}(r) = 0} \qquad \frac{r = h : t}{\mathsf{sum}(r) = h + \mathsf{sum}(t)}$$

$$\boxed{\mathsf{max}}$$

$$\frac{r = [\,]}{\mathsf{max}(r) = -\infty} \qquad \frac{r = h : t \quad h > \mathsf{max}(t)}{\mathsf{max}(r) = h} \qquad \frac{r = h : t \quad h \le \mathsf{max}(t)}{\mathsf{max}(r) = \mathsf{max}(t)}$$

$$\boxed{\mathsf{min}}$$

$$\frac{r = [\,]}{\mathsf{min}(r) = \infty} \qquad \frac{r = h : t \quad h < \mathsf{min}(t)}{\mathsf{min}(r) = h} \qquad \frac{r = h : t \quad h \ge \mathsf{min}(t)}{\mathsf{min}(r) = \mathsf{min}(t)}$$

$$\boxed{\mathsf{contains}}$$

$$\frac{r = [\,]}{\mathsf{contains}(e, r) = \mathsf{False}}$$

$$\frac{e = h \quad r = h : t}{\mathsf{contains}(e, r) = \mathsf{True}} \qquad \frac{e \neq h \quad r = h : t}{\mathsf{contains}(e, r) = \mathsf{contains}(e, t)}$$

Automated Feedback Generation for Introductory Programming Assignments

Rishabh Singh
MIT CSAIL, Cambridge, MA
rishabh@csail.mit.edu

Sumit Gulwani
Microsoft Research, Redmond, WA
sumitg@microsoft.com

Armando Solar-Lezama
MIT CSAIL, Cambridge, MA
asolar@csail.mit.edu

Abstract

We present a new method for automatically providing feedback for introductory programming problems. In order to use this method, we need a reference implementation of the assignment, and an error model consisting of potential corrections to errors that students might make. Using this information, the system automatically derives minimal corrections to student's incorrect solutions, providing them with a measure of exactly how incorrect a given solution was, as well as feedback about what they did wrong.

We introduce a simple language for describing error models in terms of correction rules, and formally define a rule-directed translation strategy that reduces the problem of finding minimal corrections in an incorrect program to the problem of synthesizing a correct program from a sketch. We have evaluated our system on thousands of real student attempts obtained from the Introduction to Programming course at MIT (6.00) and MITx (6.00x). Our results show that relatively simple error models can correct on average 64% of all incorrect submissions in our benchmark set.

Categories and Subject Descriptors D.1.2 [*Programming Techniques*]: Automatic Programming; I.2.2 [*Artificial Intelligence*]: Program Synthesis

Keywords Automated Grading; Computer-Aided Education; Program Synthesis

1. Introduction

There has been a lot of interest recently in making quality education more accessible to students worldwide using information technology. Several education initiatives such as EdX, Coursera, and Udacity are racing to provide online courses on various college-level subjects ranging from computer science to psychology. These courses, also called massive open online courses (MOOC), are typically taken by thousands of students worldwide, and present many interesting scalability challenges. Specifically, this paper addresses the challenge of providing personalized feedback for programming assignments in introductory programming courses.

The two methods most commonly used by MOOCs to provide feedback on programming problems are: (i) test-case based feedback and (ii) *peer-feedback* [12]. In test-case based feedback, the student program is run on a set of test cases and the failing test cases are reported back to the student. This is also how the 6.00x course (Introduction to Computer Science and Programming) offered by MITx currently provides feedback for Python programming exercises. The feedback of failing test cases is however not ideal; especially for beginner programmers who find it difficult to map the failing test cases to errors in their code. This is reflected by the number of students who post their submissions on the discussion board to seek help from instructors and other students after struggling for hours to correct the mistakes themselves. In fact, for the classroom version of the Introduction to Programming course (6.00) taught at MIT, the teaching assistants are required to manually go through each student submission and provide qualitative feedback describing exactly what is wrong with the submission and how to correct it. This manual feedback by teaching assistants is simply prohibitive for the number of students in the online class setting.

The second approach of peer-feedback is being suggested as a potential solution to this problem [43]. For example in 6.00x, students routinely answer each other's questions on the discussion forums. This kind of peer-feedback is helpful, but it is not without problems. For example, we observed several instances where students had to wait for hours to get any feedback, and in some cases the feedback provided was too general or incomplete, and even wrong. Some courses have experimented with more sophisticated peer evaluation techniques [28] and there is an emerging research area that builds on recent results in crowd-powered systems [7, 30] to provide more structure and better incentives for improving the feedback quality. However, peer-feedback has some inherent limitations, such as the time it takes to receive quality feedback and the potential for inaccuracies in feedback, especially when a majority of the students are themselves struggling to learn the material.

In this paper, we present an automated technique to provide feedback for introductory programming assignments. The approach leverages program synthesis technology to automatically determine minimal fixes to the student's solution that will make it match the behavior of a reference solution written by the instructor. This technology makes it possible to provide students with precise feedback about what they did wrong and how to correct their mistakes. The problem of providing automatic feedback appears to be related to the problem of automated bug fixing, but it differs from it in following two significant respects:

- **The complete specification is known.** An important challenge in automatic debugging is that there is no way to know whether a fix is addressing the root cause of a problem, or simply masking it and potentially introducing new errors. Usually the best one can do is check a candidate fix against a test suite or a partial specification [14]. While providing feedback on the other hand, the solution to the problem is known, and it is safe to assume that the instructor already wrote a correct reference implementation for the problem.

PLDI'13, June 16–19, 2013, Seattle, WA, USA.

- **Errors are predictable.** In a homework assignment, everyone is solving the same problem after having attended the same lectures, so errors tend to follow predictable patterns. This makes it possible to use a *model-based* feedback approach, where the potential fixes are guided by a model of the kinds of errors students typically make for a given problem.

These simplifying assumptions, however, introduce their own set of challenges. For example, since the complete specification is known, the tool now needs to reason about the equivalence of the student solution with the reference implementation. Also, in order to take advantage of the predictability of errors, the tool needs to be parameterized with models that describe the classes of errors. And finally, these programs can be expected to have higher density of errors than production code, so techniques which attempts to correct bugs one path at a time [25] will not work for many of these problems that require coordinated fixes in multiple places.

Our feedback generation technique handles all of these challenges. The tool can reason about the semantic equivalence of student programs with reference implementations written in a fairly large subset of Python, so the instructor does not need to learn a new formalism to write specifications. The tool also provides an *error model* language that can be used to write an error model: a very high level description of potential corrections to errors that students might make in the solution. When the system encounters an incorrect solution by a student, it symbolically explores the space of all possible combinations of corrections allowed by the error model and finds a correct solution requiring a *minimal* set of corrections.

We have evaluated our approach on thousands of student solutions on programming problems obtained from the 6.00x submissions and discussion boards, and from the 6.00 class submissions. These problems constitute a major portion of first month of assignment problems. Our tool can successfully provide feedback on over 64% of the incorrect solutions.

This paper makes the following key contributions:

- We show that the problem of providing automated feedback for introductory programming assignments can be framed as a synthesis problem. Our reduction uses a constraint-based mechanism to model Python's dynamic typing and supports complex Python constructs such as closures, higher-order functions, and list comprehensions.
- We define a high-level error model language EML that can be used to provide correction rules to be used for providing feedback. We also show that a small set of such rules is sufficient to correct thousands of incorrect solutions written by students.
- We report the successful evaluation of our technique on thousands of real student attempts obtained from 6.00 and 6.00x classes, as well as from PEX4FUN website. Our tool can provide feedback on 64% of all submitted solutions that are incorrect in about 10 seconds on average.

2. Overview of the approach

In order to illustrate the key ideas behind our approach, consider the problem of computing the derivative of a polynomial whose coefficients are represented as a list of integers. This problem is taken from week 3 problem set of 6.00x (PS3: Derivatives). Given the input list `poly`, the problem asks students to write the function `computeDeriv` that computes a list `poly'` such that

$$\texttt{poly'} = \begin{cases} \{\texttt{i} \times \texttt{poly[i]} \mid 0 < \texttt{i} < \texttt{len(poly)}\} & \text{if } \texttt{len(poly)} > 1 \\ [0] & \text{if } \texttt{len(poly)} = 1 \end{cases}$$

For example, if the input list `poly` is $[2, -3, 1, 4]$ (denoting $f(x) = 4x^3 + x^2 - 3x + 2$), the `computeDeriv` function should return $[-3, 2, 12]$ (denoting the derivative $f'(x) = 12x^2 + 2x - 3$). The reference implementation for the `computeDeriv` function is shown in Figure 1. This problem teaches concepts of conditionals and iteration over lists. For this problem, students struggled with many low-level Python semantics issues such as the list indexing and iteration bounds. In addition, they also struggled with conceptual issues such as missing the corner case of handling lists consisting of single element (denoting constant function).

```
def computeDeriv_list_int(poly_list_int):
    result = []
    for i in range(len(poly_list_int)):
        result += [i * poly_list_int[i]]
    if len(poly_list_int) == 1:
        return result       # return [0]
    else:
        return result[1:]  # remove the leading 0
```

Figure 1. The reference implementation for `computeDeriv`.

One challenge in providing feedback for student submissions is that a given problem can be solved by using many different algorithms. Figure 2 shows three very different student submissions for the `computeDeriv` problem, together with the feedback generated by our tool for each submission. The student submission shown in Figure 2(a) is taken from the 6.00x discussion forum[1]. The student posted the code in the forum seeking help and received two responses. The first response asked the student to look for the first if-block return value, and the second response said that the code should return [0] instead of empty list for the first if statement. There are many different ways to modify the code to return [0] for the case `len(poly)=1`. The student chose to change the initialization of the `deriv` variable from [ ] to the list [0]. The problem with this modification is that the result will now have an additional 0 in front of the output list for all input lists (which is undesirable for lists of length greater than 1). The student then posted the query again on the forum on how to remove the leading 0 from result, but unfortunately this time did not get any more response.

Our tool generates the feedback shown in Figure 2(d) for the student program in about 40 seconds. During these 40 seconds, the tool searches over more than 10^7 candidate fixes and finds the fix that requires minimum number of corrections. There are three problems with the student code: first it should return [0] in line 5 as was suggested in the forum but wasn't specified how to make the change, second the if block should be removed in line 7, and third that the loop iteration should start from index 1 instead of 0 in line 6. The generated feedback consists of four pieces of information (shown in bold in the figure for emphasis):

- the location of the error denoted by the line number.
- the problematic expression in the line.
- the sub-expression which needs to be modified.
- the new modified value of the sub-expression.

The feedback generator is parameterized with a feedback-level parameter to generate feedback consisting of different combinations of the four kinds of information, depending on how much information the instructor is willing to provide to the student.

2.1 Workflow

In order to provide the level of feedback described above, the tool needs some information from the instructor. First, the tool needs to know what the problem is that the students are supposed to solve. The instructor provides this information by writing a reference im-

[1] https://www.edx.org/courses/MITx/6.00x/2012_Fall/discussion/forum/600x_ps3_q2/threads/5085f3a27d1d422500000040

Three different student submissions for `computeDeriv`

```
1 def computeDeriv(poly):
2     deriv = []
3     zero = 0
4     if (len(poly) == 1):
5         return deriv
6     for e in range(0,len(poly)):
7         if (poly[e] == 0):
8             zero += 1
9         else:
10            deriv.append(poly[e]*e)
11    return deriv
```

(a)

```
1 def computeDeriv(poly):
2     idx = 1
3     deriv = list([])
4     plen = len(poly)
5     while idx <= plen:
6         coeff = poly.pop(1)
7         deriv += [coeff * idx]
8         idx = idx + 1
9         if len(poly) < 2:
10            return deriv
```

(b)

```
1 def computeDeriv(poly):
2     length = int(len(poly)-1)
3     i = length
4     deriv = range(1,length)
5     if len(poly) == 1:
6         deriv = [0]
7     else:
8         while i >= 0:
9             new = poly[i] * i
10            i -= 1
11            deriv[i] = new
12    return deriv
```

(c)

Feedback generated by our Tool

The program requires **3** changes:

- In the return statement **return deriv** in **line 5**, replace **deriv** by **[0]**.
- In the comparison expression **(poly[e] == 0)** in **line 7**, change **(poly[e] == 0)** to **False**.
- In the expression **range(0, len(poly))** in **line 6**, increment **0** by **1**.

(d)

The program requires **1** change:

- In the function **computeDeriv**, add the base case at the top to return **[0]** for **len(poly)=1**.

(e)

The program requires **2** changes:

- In the expression **range(1, length)** in **line 4**, increment **length** by **1**.
- In the comparison expression **(i >= 0)** in **line 8**, change operator **>=** to **!=**.

(f)

Figure 2. Three very different student submissions ((a), (b), and (c)) for the `computeDeriv` problem and the corresponding feedback generated by our tool ((d), (e), and (f)) for each one of them using the same reference implementation.

plementation such as the one in Figure 1. Since Python is dynamically typed, the instructor also provides the types of function arguments and return value. In Figure 1, the instructor specifies the type of input argument to be list of integers (`poly_list_int`) by appending the type to the name.

In addition to the reference implementation, the tool needs a description of the kinds of errors students might make. We have designed an error model language EML, which can describe a set of correction rules that denote the potential corrections to errors that students might make. For example, in the student attempt in Figure 2(a), we observe that corrections often involve modifying the return value and the range iteration values. We can specify this information with the following three correction rules:

$$\begin{aligned} \texttt{return}\ a &\rightarrow \texttt{return}\ [0] \\ \texttt{range}(a_1, a_2) &\rightarrow \texttt{range}(a_1 + 1, a_2) \\ a_0 == a_1 &\rightarrow \texttt{False} \end{aligned}$$

The correction rule `return` $a \rightarrow$ `return` $[0]$ states that the expression of a `return` statement can be optionally replaced by $[0]$. The error model for this problem that we use for our experiments is shown in Figure 8, but we will use this simple error model for simplifying the presentation in this section. In later experiments, we also show how only a few tens of incorrect solutions can provide enough information to create an error model that can automatically provide feedback for thousands of incorrect solutions.

The rules define a space of candidate programs which the tool needs to search in order to find one that is equivalent to the reference implementation and that requires minimum number of corrections. We use constraint-based synthesis technology [16, 37, 40] to efficiently search over this large space of programs. Specifically, we use the SKETCH synthesizer that uses a SAT-based algorithm to complete program sketches (programs with holes) so that they meet a given specification. We extend the SKETCH synthesizer with support for *minimize* hole expressions whose values are computed efficiently by using incremental constraint solving. To simplify the presentation, we use a simpler language MPY (*miniPython*) in place of Py
sup
ord

2.2

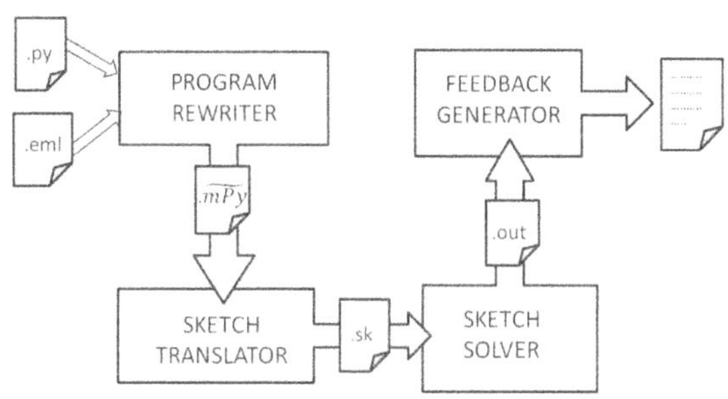

Figure 3. The architecture of our feedback generation tool.

The architecture of our tool is shown in Figure 3. The solution strategy to find minimal corrections to a student's solution is based on a two-phase translation to the Sketch synthesis language. In the first phase, the `Program Rewriter` uses the correction rules to translate the solution into a language we call $\widetilde{\text{MPY}}$; this language provides us with a concise notation to describe sets of MPY candidate programs, together with a cost model to reflect the number of corrections associated with each program in this set. In the second phase, this $\widetilde{\text{MPY}}$ program is translated into a sketch program by the `Sketch Translator`.

```
1  def computeDeriv(poly):
2      deriv = []
3      zero = 0
4      if ({ len(poly) == 1 , False}):
5          return { deriv ,[0]}
6      for e in range ({ 0 ,1}, len(poly)):
7          if ({ poly[e] == 0 ,False}):
8              zero += 1
9          else:
10             deriv.append(poly[e]*e)
11     return { deriv ,[0]}
```

Figure 4. The resulting $\widetilde{\text{MPY}}$ program after applying correction rules to program in Figure 2(a).

In the case of example in Figure 2(a), the `Program Rewriter` produces the $\widetilde{\text{MPY}}$ program shown in Figure 4 using the correction rules from Section 2.1. This program includes all the possible corrections induced by the correction rules in the model. The $\widetilde{\text{MPY}}$ language extends the imperative language MPY with expression choices, where the choices are denoted with squiggly brackets. Whenever there are multiple choices for an expression or a statement, the zero-cost choice, the one that will leave the expression unchanged, is boxed. For example, the expression choice $\{\boxed{a_0}, a_1, \cdots, a_n\}$ denotes a choice between expressions $a_0, \cdots, a_n$ where a_0 denotes the zero-cost default choice.

For this simple program, the three correction rules induce a space of 32 different candidate programs. This candidate space is fairly small, but the number of candidate programs grow exponentially with the number of correction places in the program and with the number of correction choices in the rules. The error model that we use in our experiments induces a space of more than 10^{12} candidate programs for some of the benchmark problems. In order to search this large space efficiently, the program is translated to a sketch by the `Sketch Translator`.

2.3 Synthesizing Corrections with Sketch

The SKETCH [37] synthesis system allows programmers to write programs while leaving fragments of it unspecified as *holes*; the contents of these holes are filled up automatically by the synthesizer such that the program conforms to a specification provided in terms of a reference implementation. The synthesizer uses the CEGIS algorithm [38] to efficiently compute the values for holes and uses bounded symbolic verification techniques for performing equivalence check of the two implementations.

There are two key aspects in the translation of an $\widetilde{\text{MPY}}$ program to a SKETCH program. The first aspect is specific to the Python language. SKETCH supports high-level features such as closures and higher-order functions which simplifies the translation, but it is statically typed whereas MPY programs (like Python) are dynamically typed. The translation models the dynamically typed variables and operations over them using struct types in SKETCH in a way similar to the union types. The second aspect of the translation is the modeling of set-expressions in $\widetilde{\text{MPY}}$ using ?? (holes) in SKETCH, which is language independent.

The dynamic variable types in the MPY language are modeled using the `MultiType` struct defined in Figure 5. The `MultiType` struct consists of a `flag` field that denotes the dynamic type of a variable and currently supports the following set of types: {`INTEGER`, `BOOL`, `TYPE`, `LIST`, `TUPLE`, `STRING`, `DICTIONARY`}. The `val` and `bval` fields store the value of an integer and a Boolean

```
struct MultiType{
  int val, flag;                    struct MTList{
  bit bval;                           int len;
  MTString str; MTTuple tup;          MultiType[len] lVals;
  MTDict dict;  MTList lst;         }
}
```

Figure 5. The `MultiType` struct for encoding Python types.

variable respectively, whereas the `str`, `tup`, `dict`, and `lst` fields store the value of string, tuple, dictionary, and list variables respectively. The `MTList` struct consists of a field `len` that denotes the length of the list and a field `lVals` of type array of `MultiType` that stores the list elements. For example, the integer value 5 is represented as the value `MultiType(val=5, flag=INTEGER)` and the list `[1,2]` is represented as the value `MultiType(lst=new MTList(len=2,lVals={new MultiType(val=1,flag=INTEGER), new MultiType(val=2,flag=INTEGER)}), flag=LIST)`.

The second key aspect of this translation is the translation of expression choices in $\widetilde{\text{MPY}}$. The SKETCH construct ?? denotes an unknown integer hole that can be assigned any constant integer value by the synthesizer. The expression choices in $\widetilde{\text{MPY}}$ are translated to functions in SKETCH that based on the unknown hole values return either the default expression or one of the other expression choices. Each such function is associated with a unique Boolean choice variable, which is set by the function whenever it returns a non-default expression choice. For example, the set-statement `return {`$\boxed{\texttt{deriv}}$`,[0]};` (line 5 in Figure 4) is translated to `return modRetVal0(deriv)`, where the `modRetVal0` function is defined as:

```
MultiType modRetVal0(MultiType a){
  if(??) return a; // default choice
  choiceRetVal0 = True; // non-default choice
  MTList list = new MTList(lVals={new
      MultiType(val=0, flag=INTEGER)}, len=1);
  return new MultiType(lst=list, type = LIST);
}
```

The translation phase also generates a SKETCH harness that compares the outputs of the translated student and reference implementations on all inputs of a bounded size. For example in case of the `computeDeriv` function, with bounds of $n = 4$ for both the number of integer bits and the maximum length of input list, the harness matches the output of the two implementations for more than 2^{16} different input values as opposed to 10 test-cases used in 6.00x. The harness also defines a variable `totalCost` as a function of choice variables that computes the total number of corrections performed in the original program, and asserts that the value of `totalCost` should be minimized. The synthesizer then solves this minimization problem efficiently using an incremental solving algorithm `CEGISMIN` described in Section 4.2.

After the synthesizer finds a solution, the `Feedback Generator` extracts the choices made by the synthesizer and uses them to generate the corresponding feedback in natural language. For this example, the tool generates the feedback shown in Figure 2(d) in less than 40 seconds.

3. EML: Error Model Language

In this section, we describe the syntax and semantics of the error model language EML. An EML error model consists of a set of rewrite rules that captures the potential corrections for mistakes that students might make in their solutions. We define the rewrite rules over a simple Python-like imperative language MPY. A rewrite rule transforms a program element in MPY to a set of weighted MPY program elements. This weighted set of MPY program elements is

$$
\begin{aligned}
[\![a]\!] &= \{(a, 0)\} \\
[\![\{\boxed{\tilde{a}_0}, \cdots, \tilde{a}_n\}]\!] &= [\![\tilde{a}_0]\!] \cup \{(a,\ c+1) \mid (a, c) \in [\![\tilde{a}_i]\!]_{0<i\leq n}\} \\
[\![\tilde{a}_0[\tilde{a}_1]]\!] &= \{(a_0[a_1],\ c_0 + c_1) \mid (a_i, c_i) \in [\![\tilde{a}_i]\!]_{i\in\{0,1\}}\} \\
[\![\texttt{while}\ \tilde{b} : \tilde{s}]\!] &= \{(\texttt{while}\ b :\ s,\ c_b + c_s) \mid \\
&\qquad (b, c_b) \in [\![\tilde{b}]\!], (s, c_s) \in [\![\tilde{s}]\!]\}
\end{aligned}
$$

Figure 7. The $[\![\ ]\!]$ function (shown partially) that translates an $\widetilde{\text{MPY}}$ program to a weighted set of MPY programs.

represented succinctly as an $\widetilde{\text{MPY}}$ program element, where $\widetilde{\text{MPY}}$ extends the MPY language with set-exprs (sets of expressions) and set-stmts (sets of statements). The weight associated with a program element in this set denotes the cost of performing the corresponding correction. An error model transforms an MPY program to an $\widetilde{\text{MPY}}$ program by recursively applying the rewrite rules. We show that this transformation is deterministic and is guaranteed to terminate on *well-formed* error models.

3.1 MPY and $\widetilde{\text{MPY}}$ languages

The syntax of MPY and $\widetilde{\text{MPY}}$ languages is shown in Figure 6(a) and Figure 6(b) respectively. The purpose of $\widetilde{\text{MPY}}$ language is to represent a large collection of MPY programs succinctly. The $\widetilde{\text{MPY}}$ language consists of set-expressions ($\tilde{a}$ and $\tilde{b}$) and set-statements ($\tilde{s}$) that represent a weighted set of corresponding MPY expressions and statements respectively. For example, the set expression $\{\boxed{n_0}, \cdots, n_k\}$ represents a weighted set of constant integers where n_0 denotes the default integer value associated with cost 0 and all other integer constants ($n_1, \cdots, n_k$) are associated with cost 1. The sets of composite expressions are represented succinctly in terms of sets of their constituent sub-expressions. For example, the composite expression $\{\boxed{a_0}, a_0 + 1\}\{\boxed{<}, \leq, >, \geq, ==, \neq\}\{\boxed{a_1}, a_1 + 1, a_1 - 1\}$ represents 36 MPY expressions.

Each MPY program in the set of programs represented by an $\widetilde{\text{MPY}}$ program is associated with a cost (weight) that denotes the number of modifications performed in the original program to obtain the transformed program. This cost allows the tool to search for corrections that require minimum number of modifications. The weighted set of MPY programs is defined using the $[\![\ ]\!]$ function shown partially in Figure 7, the complete function definition can be found in [36]. The $[\![\ ]\!]$ function on MPY expressions such as a returns a singleton set $\{(a, 0)\}$ consisting of the corresponding expression associated with cost 0. On set-expressions of the form $\{\boxed{\tilde{a}_0}, \cdots, \tilde{a}_n\}$, the function returns the union of the weighted set of MPY expressions corresponding to the default set-expression ($[\![\tilde{a}_0]\!]$) and the weighted set of expressions corresponding to other set-expressions ($\tilde{a}_1, \cdots, \tilde{a}_n$), where each expression in $[\![\tilde{a}_i)]\!]$ is associated with an additional cost of 1. On composite expressions, the function computes the weighted set recursively by taking the cross-product of weighted sets of its constituent sub-expressions and adding their corresponding costs. For example, the weighted set for composite expression $\tilde{x}[\tilde{y}]$ consists of an expression $x_i[y_j]$ associated with cost $c_{x_i} + c_{y_j}$ for each $(x_i, c_{x_i}) \in [\![\tilde{x}]\!]$ and $(y_j, c_{y_j}) \in [\![\tilde{y}]\!]$.

3.2 Syntax of EML

An EML error model consists of a set of correction rules that are used to transform an MPY program to an $\widetilde{\text{MPY}}$ program. A *correction rule* $\mathcal{C}$ is written as a rewrite rule $L \rightarrow R$, where L and R denote a *program element* in MPY and $\widetilde{\text{MPY}}$ respectively. A program element can either be a term, an expression, a statement, a method or the program itself. The left hand side (L) denotes an MPY program element that is pattern matched to be transformed to an $\widetilde{\text{MPY}}$ program element denoted by the right hand side (R). The left hand side of the rule can use free variables whereas the right hand side can only refer to the variables present in the left hand side. The language also supports a special $'$ (prime) operator that can be used to *tag* sub-expressions in R that are further transformed recursively using the error model. The rules use a shorthand notation $?a$ (in the right hand side) to denote the set of all variables that are of the same type as the type of expression a and are in scope at the corresponding program location. We assume each correction rule is associated with cost 1, but it can be easily extended to different costs to account for different severity of mistakes.

$$
\begin{aligned}
\textsc{IndR}:\ v[a] &\rightarrow v[\{a+1, a-1, ?a\}] \\
\textsc{InitR}:\ v = n &\rightarrow v = \{n+1, n-1, 0\} \\
\textsc{RanR}:\ \texttt{range}(a_0, a_1) &\rightarrow \texttt{range}(\{0, 1, a_0 - 1, a_0 + 1\}, \\
&\qquad\qquad \{a_1 + 1, a_1 - 1\}) \\
\textsc{CompR}:\ a_0\ op_c\ a_1 &\rightarrow \{\{a_0' - 1, ?a_0\}\ \widetilde{op}_c\ \{a_1' - 1, 0, 1, ?a_1\}, \\
&\quad \texttt{True}, \texttt{False}\} \\
&\quad \text{where } \widetilde{op}_c = \{<, >, \leq, \geq, ==, \neq\} \\
\textsc{RetR}:\ \texttt{return}\ a &\rightarrow \texttt{return}\{[0]\ \texttt{if len}(a) == 1\ \texttt{else}\ a, \\
&\qquad a[1:]\ \texttt{if}\ (\texttt{len}(a) > 1)\ \texttt{else}\ a\}
\end{aligned}
$$

Figure 8. The error model $\mathcal{E}$ for the `computeDeriv` problem.

Example 1. *The error model for the* `computeDeriv` *problem is shown in Figure 8. The* INDR *rewrite rule transforms the list access indices. The* INITR *rule transforms the right hand size of constant initializations. The* RANR *rule transforms the arguments for the range function; similar rules are defined in the model for other range functions that take one and three arguments. The* COMPR *rule transforms the operands and operator of the comparisons. The* RETR *rule adds the two common corner cases of returning* $[0]$ *when the length of input list is* 1*, and the case of deleting the first list element before returning the list. Note that these rewrite rules define the corrections that can be performed optionally; the zero cost (default) case of not correcting a program element is added automatically as described in Section 3.3.*

Definition 1. *Well-formed Rewrite Rule : A rewrite rule* $\mathcal{C} : L \rightarrow R$ *is defined to be well-formed if all tagged sub-terms* t' *in* R *have a smaller size syntax tree than that of* L.

The rewrite rule $\mathcal{C}_1 : v[a] \rightarrow \{(v[a])' + 1\}$ is not a well-formed rewrite rule as the size of the tagged sub-term ($v[a]$) of R is the same as that of the left hand side L. On the other hand, the rewrite rule $\mathcal{C}_2 : v[a] \rightarrow \{v'[a'] + 1\}$ is well-formed.

Definition 2. *Well-formed Error Model : An error model* $\mathcal{E}$ *is defined to be well-formed if all of its constituent rewrite rules* $\mathcal{C}_i \in \mathcal{E}$ *are well-formed.*

3.3 Transformation with EML

An error model $\mathcal{E}$ is syntactically translated to a function $\mathcal{T}_{\mathcal{E}}$ that transforms an MPY program to an $\widetilde{\text{MPY}}$ program. The $\mathcal{T}_{\mathcal{E}}$ function first traverses the program element w in the default way, i.e. no transformation happens at this level of the syntax tree, and the function is called recursively on all of its top-level sub-terms t to obtain the transformed element $w_0 \in \widetilde{\text{MPY}}$. For each correction rule $\mathcal{C}_i : L_i \rightarrow R_i$ in the error model $\mathcal{E}$, the function contains a

$$
\begin{array}{rcl}
\text{Arith Expr } a & := & n \mid [\,] \mid v \mid a[a] \mid a_0 \; op_a \; a_1 \\
& \mid & [a_1, \cdots, a_n] \mid f(a_0, \cdots, a_n) \\
& \mid & a_0 \; \texttt{if} \; b \; \texttt{else} \; a_1 \\
\text{Arith Op } op_a & := & + \mid - \mid \times \mid / \mid ** \\
\text{Bool Expr } b & := & \texttt{not} \; b \mid a_0 \; op_c \; a_1 \mid b_0 \; op_b \; b_1 \\
\text{Comp Op } op_c & := & == \mid < \mid > \mid \leq \mid \geq \\
\text{Bool Op } op_b & := & \texttt{and} \mid \texttt{or} \\
\text{Stmt Expr } s & := & v = a \mid s_0; s_1 \mid \texttt{while} \; b : \; s \\
& \mid & \texttt{if} \; b : \; s_0 \; \texttt{else:} \; s_1 \\
& \mid & \texttt{for} \; a_0 \; \texttt{in} \; a_1 : \; s \mid \texttt{return} \; a \\
\text{Func Def. } p & := & \texttt{def} \; f(a_1, \cdots, a_n) : \; s
\end{array}
$$

(a) MPY

$$
\begin{array}{rcl}
\text{Arith set-expr } \tilde{a} & := & a \mid \{\boxed{\tilde{a}_0}, \cdots, \tilde{a}_n\} \mid \tilde{a}[\tilde{a}] \mid \tilde{a}_0 \; \widetilde{op}_a \; \tilde{a}_1 \\
& \mid & [\tilde{a}_0, \cdots, \tilde{a}_n] \mid \tilde{f}(\tilde{a}_0, \cdots, \tilde{a}_n) \\
\text{set-op } \widetilde{op}_x & := & op_a \mid \{\boxed{\widetilde{op}_{x_0}}, \cdots, \widetilde{op}_{x_n}\} \\
\text{Bool set-expr } \tilde{b} & := & b \mid \{\boxed{\tilde{b}_0}, \cdots, \tilde{b}_n\} \mid \texttt{not} \; \tilde{b} \mid \tilde{a}_0 \; \widetilde{op}_c \; \tilde{a}_1 \mid \tilde{b}_0 \; \widetilde{op}_b \; \tilde{b}_1 \\
\text{Stmt set-expr } \tilde{s} & := & s \mid \{\boxed{\tilde{s}_0}, \cdots, \tilde{s}_n\} \mid \tilde{v} := \tilde{a} \mid \tilde{s}_0; \tilde{s}_1 \\
& \mid & \texttt{while} \; \tilde{b} : \; \tilde{s} \mid \texttt{for} \; \tilde{a}_0 \; \texttt{in} \; \tilde{a}_1 : \; \tilde{s} \\
& \mid & \texttt{if} \; \tilde{b} : \; \tilde{s}_0 \; \texttt{else} : \; \tilde{s}_1 \mid \texttt{return} \; \tilde{a} \\
\text{Func Def } \tilde{p} & := & \texttt{def} \; f(a_1, \cdots, a_n) \; \tilde{s}
\end{array}
$$

(b) $\widetilde{\text{MPY}}$

Figure 6. The syntax for (a) MPY and (b) $\widetilde{\text{MPY}}$ languages.

`Match` expression that matches the term w with the left hand side of the rule L_i (with appropriate unification of the free variables in L_i). If the match succeeds, it is transformed to a term $w_i \in \widetilde{\text{MPY}}$ as defined by the right hand side R_i of the rule after calling the $\mathcal{T}_\mathcal{E}$ function on each of its tagged sub-terms t'. Finally, the method returns the set of all transformed terms $\{\boxed{w_0}, \cdots, w_n\}$.

Example 2. *Consider an error model $\mathcal{E}_1$ consisting of the following three correction rules:*

$$
\begin{array}{rcl}
\mathcal{C}_1 : \; v[a] & \rightarrow & v[\{a-1, a+1\}] \\
\mathcal{C}_2 : \; a_0 \; op_c \; a_1 & \rightarrow & \{a_0' - 1, 0\} \; op_c \; \{a_1' - 1, 0\} \\
\mathcal{C}_3 : \; v[a] & \rightarrow & ?v[a]
\end{array}
$$

The transformation function $\mathcal{T}_{\mathcal{E}_1}$ for the error model $\mathcal{E}_1$ is shown in Figure 9.

$$
\begin{array}{l}
\mathcal{T}_{\mathcal{E}_1}(w : \text{MPY}) : \widetilde{\text{MPY}} \quad = \\
\textbf{let } w_0 = w[t \rightarrow \mathcal{T}_{\mathcal{E}_1}(t)] \textbf{ in } \; (*\; t : \text{a sub-term of } w \; *) \\
\textbf{let } w_1 = \textbf{Match } w \textbf{ with} \\
\qquad\qquad v[a] \rightarrow v[\{a+1, a-1\}] \textbf{ in} \\
\textbf{let } w_2 = \textbf{Match } w \textbf{ with} \\
\qquad\qquad a_0 \; op_c \; a_1 \rightarrow \{\mathcal{T}_{\mathcal{E}_1}(a_0) - 1, 0\} \; op_c \\
\qquad\qquad\qquad\qquad \{\mathcal{T}_{\mathcal{E}_1}(a_1) - 1, 0\} \textbf{ in} \\
\{\boxed{w_0}, w_1, w_2\}
\end{array}
$$

Figure 9. The $\mathcal{T}_{\mathcal{E}_1}$ method for error model $\mathcal{E}_1$.

The recursive steps of application of $\mathcal{T}_{\mathcal{E}_1}$ function on expression $(x[i] < y[j])$ are shown in Figure 10. This example illustrates two interesting features of the transformation function:

- **Nested Transformations :** Once a rewrite rule $L \rightarrow R$ is applied to transform a program element matching L to R, the instructor may want to apply another rewrite rule on only a few sub-terms of R. For example, she may want to avoid transforming the sub-terms which have already been transformed by some other correction rule. The EML language facilitates making such distinction between the sub-terms for performing nested corrections using the $'$ (prime) operator. Only the sub-terms in R that are tagged with the prime operator are visited for applying further transformations (using the $\mathcal{T}_\mathcal{E}$ function recursively on its tagged sub-terms t'), whereas the non-tagged sub-terms are not transformed any further. After applying the rewrite rule $\mathcal{C}_2$ in the example, the sub-terms $x[i]$ and $y[j]$ are further transformed by applying rewrite rules $\mathcal{C}_1$ and $\mathcal{C}_3$.
- **Ambiguous Transformations :** While transforming a program using an error model, it may happen that there are multiple rewrite rules that pattern match the program element w. After applying rewrite rule $\mathcal{C}_2$ in the example, there are two rewrite rules $\mathcal{C}_1$ and $\mathcal{C}_3$ that pattern match the terms $x[i]$ and $y[j]$. After applying one of these rules ($\mathcal{C}_1$ or $\mathcal{C}_3$) to an expression $v[a]$, we cannot apply the other rule to the transformed expression. In such ambiguous cases, the $\mathcal{T}_\mathcal{E}$ function creates a separate copy of the transformed program element (w_i) for each ambiguous choice and then performs the set union of all such elements to obtain the transformed program element. This semantics of handling ambiguity of rewrite rules also matches naturally with the intent of the instructor. If the instructor wanted to perform both transformations together on array accesses, she could have provided a combined rewrite rule such as $v[a] \rightarrow ?v[\{a+1, a-1\}]$.

Theorem 1. *Given a well-formed error model $\mathcal{E}$, the transformation function $\mathcal{T}_\mathcal{E}$ always terminates.*

Proof. From the definition of well-formed error model, each of its constituent rewrite rule is also well-formed. Hence, each application of a rewrite rule reduces the size of the syntax tree of terms that are required to be visited further for transformation by $\mathcal{T}_\mathcal{E}$. Therefore, the $\mathcal{T}_\mathcal{E}$ function terminates in a finite number of steps. □

4. Constraint-based Solving of $\widetilde{\text{MPY}}$ programs

In the previous section, we saw the transformation of an MPY program to an $\widetilde{\text{MPY}}$ program based on an error model. We now present the translation of an $\widetilde{\text{MPY}}$ program into a SKETCH program [37].

4.1 Translation of $\widetilde{\text{MPY}}$ programs to SKETCH

The $\widetilde{\text{MPY}}$ programs are translated to SKETCH programs for efficient constraint-based solving for minimal corrections to the student solutions. The two main aspects of the translation include : (i) the translation of Python-like constructs in $\widetilde{\text{MPY}}$ to SKETCH, and (ii) the translation of set-expr choices in $\widetilde{\text{MPY}}$ to SKETCH functions.

$$\mathcal{T}(x[i] < y[j]) \equiv \{ \boxed{\mathcal{T}(x[i]) < \mathcal{T}(y[j])}, \{\mathcal{T}(x[i]) - 1, 0\} < \{\mathcal{T}(y[j]) - 1, 0\}\}$$

$$\mathcal{T}(x[i]) \equiv \{ \boxed{\mathcal{T}(x)[\mathcal{T}(i)]}, x[\{i+1, i-1\}], y[i]\}$$

$$\mathcal{T}(y[j]) \equiv \{ \boxed{\mathcal{T}(y)[\mathcal{T}(j)]}, y[\{j+1, j-1\}], x[j]\}$$

$$\mathcal{T}(x) \equiv \{\boxed{x}\} \qquad \mathcal{T}(i) \equiv \{\boxed{i}\} \qquad \mathcal{T}(y) \equiv \{\boxed{y}\} \qquad \mathcal{T}(j) \equiv \{\boxed{j}\}$$

`Therefore, after substitution the result is:`

$$\mathcal{T}(x[i] < y[j]) \equiv \{ \boxed{\{ \boxed{\boxed{x}[\boxed{i}]}, x[\{i+1, i-1\}], y[i]\} < \{ \boxed{\boxed{y}[\boxed{j}]}, y[\{j+1, j-1\}], x[j]\}},$$

$$\{\{ \boxed{\boxed{x}[\boxed{i}]}, x[\{i+1, i-1\}], y[i]\} - 1, 0\} < \{\{ \boxed{\boxed{y}[\boxed{j}]}, y[\{j+1, j-1\}], x[j]\} - 1, 0\}\}$$

Figure 10. Application of $\mathcal{T}_{\mathcal{E}_1}$ (abbreviated $\mathcal{T}$) on expression $(x[i] < y[j])$.

Handling dynamic typing of $\widetilde{\text{MPY}}$ variables The dynamic typing in $\widetilde{\text{MPY}}$ is handled using a `MultiType` variable as described in Section 2.3. The $\widetilde{\text{MPY}}$ expressions and statements are transformed to SKETCH functions that perform the corresponding transformations over `MultiType`. For example, the Python statement `(a = b)` is translated to `assignMT(a, b)`, where the `assignMT` function assigns `MultiType` b to a. Similarly, the binary add expression `(a + b)` is translated to `binOpMT(a, b, ADD_OP)` that in turn calls the function `addMT(a,b)` to add a and b as shown in Figure 11.

```
MultiType addMT(MultiType a, MultiType b){
  assert a.flag == b.flag; // same types can be added
  if(a.flag == INTEGER)     // add for integers
   return new MultiType(val=a.val+b.val, flag =
        INTEGER);
  if(a.flag == LIST){       // add for lists
    int newLen = a.lst.len + b.lst.len;
    MultiType[newLen] newLVals = a.lst.lVals;
    for(int i=0; i<b.lst.len; i++)
      newLVals[i+a.lst.len] = b.lst.lVals[i];
  return new MultiType(lst = new
        MTList(lVals=newLVals, len=newLen),
        flag=LIST);}
  ... ...
}
```

Figure 11. The `addMT` function for adding two `MultiType` a and b.

Translation of $\widetilde{\text{MPY}}$ set-expressions The set-expressions in $\widetilde{\text{MPY}}$ are translated to functions in SKETCH. The function bodies obtained by the application of translation function (Φ) on some of the interesting $\widetilde{\text{MPY}}$ constructs are shown in Figure 12. The SKETCH construct ?? (called *hole*) is a placeholder for a constant value, which is filled up by the SKETCH synthesizer while solving the constraints to satisfy the given specification.

The singleton sets consisting of an MPY expression such as $\{a\}$ are translated simply to the corresponding expression itself. A set-expression of the form $\{\boxed{\tilde{a}_0}, \cdots, \tilde{a}_n\}$ is translated recursively to the `if` expression :`if` $(??)$ $\Phi(\tilde{a}_0)$ `else` $\Phi(\{\tilde{a}_1, \cdots, \tilde{a}_n\})$, which means that the synthesizer can optionally select the default set-expression $\Phi(\tilde{a}_0)$ (by choosing ?? to be `true`) or select one of the other choices $(\tilde{a}_1, \cdots, \tilde{a}_n)$. The set-expressions of the form $\{\tilde{a}_0, \cdots, \tilde{a}_n\}$ are similarly translated but with an additional statement for setting a fresh variable $\texttt{choice}_k$ if the synthesizer selects the non-default choice $\tilde{a}_0$.

$$\begin{aligned}
\Phi(\{a\}) &= a \\
\Phi(\{\boxed{\tilde{a}_0}, \cdots, \tilde{a}_n\}) &= \texttt{if } (??)\ \Phi(\tilde{a}_0) \texttt{ else } \Phi(\{\tilde{a}_1, \cdots, \tilde{a}_n\}) \\
\Phi(\{\tilde{a}_0, \cdots, \tilde{a}_n\}) &= \texttt{if } (??)\ \{\texttt{choice}_k = \texttt{True}; \Phi(\tilde{a}_0)\} \\
&\quad\ \texttt{else } \Phi(\{\tilde{a}_1, \cdots, \tilde{a}_n\}) \\
\Phi(\tilde{a}_0[\tilde{a}_1]) &= \Phi(\tilde{a}_0)[\Phi(\tilde{a}_1)] \\
\Phi(\tilde{a}_0 = \tilde{a}_1) &= \Phi(\tilde{a}_0) := \Phi(\tilde{a}_1)
\end{aligned}$$

Figure 12. The translation rules (shown partially) for converting $\widetilde{\text{MPY}}$ set-exprs to corresponding SKETCH function bodies.

The translation rules for the assignment statements $(\tilde{a}_0 := \tilde{a}_1)$ results in `if` expressions on both left and right sides of the assignment. The `if` expression choices occurring on the left hand side are desugared to individual assignments. For example, the left hand side expression `if` $(??)$ x `else` $y := 10$ is desugared to `if` $(??)$ $x := 10$ `else` $y := 10$. The infix operators in $\widetilde{\text{MPY}}$ are first translated to function calls and are then translated to sketch using the translation for set-function expressions. The remaining $\widetilde{\text{MPY}}$ expressions are similarly translated recursively and the translation can be found in more detail in [36].

Translating function calls The translation of function calls for recursive problems and for problems that require writing a function that uses other sub-functions is parmeterized by three options: 1) use the student's implementation of sub-functions, 2) use the teacher's implementation of sub-functions, and 3) treat the sub-functions as uninterpreted functions.

Generating the driver functions The SKETCH synthesizer supports the equivalence checking of functions whose input arguments and return values are over SKETCH primitive types such as `int`, `bit` and arrays. Therefore, after the translation of $\widetilde{\text{MPY}}$ programs to SKETCH programs, we need additional driver functions to integrate the functions over `MultiType` input arguments and return value to the corresponding functions over SKETCH primitive types. The driver functions first converts the input arguments over primitive types to corresponding `MultiType` variables using library functions such as `computeMTFromInt`, and then calls the translated $\widetilde{\text{MPY}}$ function with the `MultiType` variables. The returned `MultiType` value is translated back to primitive types using library functions such as `computeIntFromMT`. The driver function for student's programs also consists of additional statements of the form `if(choice_k) totalCost++;` and the statement `minimize(totalCost)`, which tells the synthesizer to compute a solution to the Boolean variables $\texttt{choice}_k$ that minimizes the `totalCost` variable.

4.2 CEGISMIN: Incremental Solving for the Minimize holes

Algorithm 1 CEGISMIN Algorithm for Minimize expression

```
σ0 ← σrandom,  i ← 0,  Φ0 ← Φ,  φp ← null
while (True)
    i ← i + 1
    Φi ← Synth(σi−1, Φi−1)                        ▷ Synthesis Phase
    if (Φi = UNSAT)                               ▷ Synthesis Fails
        if (Φprev = null) return UNSAT_SKETCH
        else return PE(P,φp)
    choose φ ∈ Φi
    σi ← Verify(φ)                                ▷ Verification Phase
    if (σi = null)                                ▷ Verification Succeeds
        (minHole, minHoleValue) ← getMinHoleValue(φ)
        φp ← φ
        Φi ← Φi ∪ {encode(minHole < minHoleVal)}
```

We extend the CEGIS algorithm in SKETCH [37] to obtain the CEGISMIN algorithm shown in Algorithm 1 for efficiently solving sketches that include a `minimize` hole expression. The input state of the sketch program is denoted by σ and the sketch constraint store is denoted by Φ. Initially, the input state σ_0 is assigned a random input state value and the constraint store Φ_0 is assigned the constraint set obtained from the sketch program. The variable ϕ_p stores the previous satisfiable hole values and is initialized to `null`. In each iteration of the loop, the synthesizer first performs the inductive synthesis phase where it shrinks the constraints set Φ_{i-1} to Φ_i by removing behaviors from Φ_{i-1} that do not conform to the input state σ_{i-1}. If the constraint set becomes unsatisfiable, it either returns the sketch completed with hole values from the previous solution if one exists, otherwise it returns `UNSAT`. On the other hand, if the constraint set is satisfiable, then it first chooses a conforming assignment to the hole values and goes into the verification phase where it tries to verify the completed sketch. If the verifier fails, it returns a counter-example input state σ_i and the synthesis-verification loop is repeated. If the verification phase succeeds, instead of returning the result as is done in the CEGIS algorithm, the CEGISMIN algorithm computes the value of `minHole` from the constraint set ϕ, stores the current satisfiable hole solution ϕ in ϕ_p, and adds an additional constraint `{minHole<minHoleVal}` to the constraint set Φ_i. The synthesis-verification loop is then repeated with this additional constraint to find a conforming value for the `minHole` variable that is smaller than the current value in ϕ.

4.3 Mapping SKETCH solution to generate feedback

Each correction rule in the error model is associated with a feedback message, e.g. the correction rule for variable initialization $v = n \rightarrow v = \{n + 1\}$ in the `computeDeriv` error model is associated with the message "Increment the right hand side of the initialization by 1". After the SKETCH synthesizer finds a solution to the constraints, the tool maps back the values of unknown integer holes to their corresponding expression choices. These expression choices are then mapped to natural language feedback using the messages associated with the corresponding correction rules, together with the line numbers. If the synthesizer returns `UNSAT`, the tool reports that the student solution can not be fixed.

5. Implementation and Experiments

We now briefly describe some of the implementation details of the tool, and then describe the experiments we performed to evaluate our tool over the benchmark problems.

5.1 Implementation

The tool's frontend is implemented in Python itself and uses the Python `ast` module to convert a Python program to a SKETCH program. The backend system that solves the sketch is implemented as a wrapper over the SKETCH system that is extended with the CEGISMIN algorithm. The feedback generator, implemented in Python, parses the output generated by the backend system and translates it to corresponding high level feedback in natural language. Error models in our tool are currently written in terms of rewrite rules over the Python AST. In addition to the Python tool, we also have a prototype for the C# language, which we built on top of the Microsoft Roslyn compiler framework. The C# prototype supports a smaller subset of the language relative to the Python tool but nevertheless it was useful in helping us evaluate the potential of our technique on a different language.

5.2 Benchmarks

We created our benchmark set with problems taken from the Introduction to Programming course at MIT (6.00) and the EdX version of the class (6.00x) offered in 2012. Our benchmark set includes most problems from the first four weeks of the course. We only excluded (i) a problem that required more detailed floating point reasoning than what we currently handle, (ii) a problem that required file i/o which we currently do not model, and (iii) a handful of trivial finger exercises. To evaluate the applicability to C#, we created a few programming exercises[2] on PEX4FUN that were based on loop-over-arrays and dynamic programming from an AP level exam[3]. A brief description of each benchmark problem follows:

- `prodBySum-6.00` : Compute the product of two numbers `m` and `n` using only the `sum` operator.
- `oddTuples-6.00` : Given a tuple `l`, return a tuple consisting of every other element of `l`.
- `compDeriv-6.00` : Compute the derivative of a polynomial `poly`, where the coefficients of `poly` are represented as a list.
- `evalPoly-6.00` : Compute the value of a polynomial (represented as a list) at a given value `x`.
- `compBal-stdin-6.00` : Print the values of monthly installment necessary to purchase a car in one year, where the inputs `car price` and `interest rate` (compounded monthly) are provided from `stdin`.
- `compDeriv-6.00x` : `compDeriv` problem from the EdX class.
- `evalPoly-6.00x` : `evalPoly` problem from the EdX class.
- `oddTuples-6.00x` : `oddTuples` problem from the EdX class.
- `iterPower-6.00x` : Compute the value $\texttt{m}^{\texttt{n}}$ using only the multiplication operator, where `m` and `n` are integers.
- `recurPower-6.00x` : Compute the value $\texttt{m}^{\texttt{n}}$ using recursion.
- `iterGCD-6.00x` : Compute the greatest common divisor (`gcd`) of two integers `m` and `n` using an iterative algorithm.
- `hangman1-str-6.00x` : Given a string `secretWord` and a list of guessed letters `lettersGuessed`, return `True` if all letters of `secretWord` are in `lettersGuessed`, and `False` otherwise.

[2] `http://pexforfun.com/learnbeginningprogramming`

[3] AP exams allow high school students in the US to earn college level credit.

- hangman2-str-6.00x : Given a string secretWord and a list of guessed letters lettersGuessed, return a string where all letters of secretWord that have not been guessed yet (i.e. not present in lettersGuessed) are replaced by the letter '_'.
- stock-market-I(C#) : Given a list of stock prices, check if the stock is stable, i.e. if the price of stock has changed by more than $10 in consecutive days on less than 3 occasions over the duration.
- stock-market-II(C#) : Given a list of stock prices and a start and end day, check if the maximum and minimum stock prices over the duration from start and end day is less than $20.
- restaurant rush (C#) : A variant of maximum contiguous subset sum problem.

5.3 Experiments

We now present various experiments we performed to evaluate our tool on the benchmark problems.

Performance Table 1 shows the number of student attempts corrected for each benchmark problem as well as the time taken by the tool to provide the feedback. The experiments were performed on a 2.4GHz Intel Xeon CPU with 16 cores and 16GB RAM. The experiments were performed with bounds of 4 bits for input integer values and maximum length 4 for input lists. For each benchmark problem, we first removed the student attempts with syntax errors to get the Test Set on which we ran our tool. We then separated the attempts which were correct to measure the effectiveness of the tool on the incorrect attempts. The tool was able to provide appropriate corrections as feedback for 64% of all incorrect student attempts in around 10 seconds on average. The remaining 36% of incorrect student attempts on which the tool could not provide feedback fall in one of the following categories:

- **Completely incorrect solutions:** We observed many student attempts that were empty or performing trivial computations such as printing strings and variables.
- **Big conceptual errors:** A common error we found in the case of eval-poly-6.00x was that a large fraction of incorrect attempts (260/541) were using the list function index to get the index of a value in the list (e.g. see Figure 13(a)), whereas the index function returns the index of first occurrence of the value in the list. Another example of this class of error for the hangman2-str problem in shown in Figure 13(b), where the solution replaces the guessed letters in the secretWord by '_' instead of replacing the letters that are not yet guessed. The correction of some other errors in this class involves introducing new program statements or moving statements from one program location to another. These errors can not be corrected with the application of a set of local correction rules.
- **Unimplemented features:** Our implementation currently lacks a few of the complex Python features such as pattern matching on list enumerate function and lambda functions.
- **Timeout:** In our experiments, we found less than 5% of the student attempts timed out (set as 4 minutes).

Number of Corrections The number of student submissions that require different number of corrections are shown in Figure 14(a) (on a logarithmic scale). We observe from the figure that a significant fraction of the problems require 3 and 4 coordinated corrections, and to provide feedback on such attempts, we need a technology like ours that can symbolically encode the outcome of different corrections on all input values.

Repetitive Mistakes In this experiment, we check our hypothesis that students make similar mistakes while solving a given problem. The graph in Figure 14(b) shows the number of student attempts corrected as more rules are added to the error models of the benchmark problems. As can be seen from the figure, adding a single rule to the error model can lead to correction of hundreds of attempts. This validates our hypothesis that different students indeed make similar mistakes when solving a given problem.

Generalization of Error Models In this experiment, we check the hypothesis that the correction rules generalize across problems of similar kind. The result of running the compute-deriv error model on other benchmark problems is shown in Figure 14(c). As expected, it does not perform as well as the problem-specific error models, but it still fixes a fraction of the incorrect attempts and can be useful as a good starting point to specialize the error model further by adding more problem-specific rules.

6. Capabilities and Limitations

Our tool supports a fairly large subset of Python types and language features, and can currently provide feedback on a large fraction (64%) of student submissions in our benchmark set. In comparison to the traditional test-cases based feedback techniques that test the programs over a few dozens of test-cases, our tool typically performs the equivalence check over more than 10^6 inputs. Programs that print the output to console (e.g. compBal-stdin) pose an interesting challenge for test-cases based feedback tools. Since beginner students typically print some extra text and values in addition to the desired outputs, the traditional tools need to employ various heuristics to discard some of the output text to match the desired output. Our tool lets instructors provide correction rules that can optionally drop some of the print expressions in the program, and then the tool finds the required print expressions to eliminate so that a student is not penalized much for printing additional values.

Now we briefly describe some of the limitations of our tool. One limitation of the tool is in providing feedback on student attempts that have big conceptual errors (see Section 5.3), which can not be fixed by application of a set of local rewrite rules. Correcting such programs typically requires a large global rewrite of the student solution, and providing feedback in such cases is an open question. Another limitation of our tool is that it does not take into account structural requirements in the problem statement since it focuses only on functional equivalence. For example, some of the assignments explicitly ask students to use bisection search or recursion, but our tool can not distinguish between two functionally equivalent solutions, e.g. it can not distinguish between a bubble sort and a merge sort implementation of the sorting problem.

For some problems, the feedback generated by the tool is too low-level. For example, a suggestion provided by the tool in Figure 2(d) is to replace the expression poly[e]==0 by False, whereas a higher level feedback would be a suggestion to remove the corresponding block inside the comparison. Deriving the high-level feedback from the low-level suggestions is mostly an engineering problem as it requires specializing the message based on the context of the correction.

The scalability of the technique also presents a limitation. For some problems that use large constant values, the tool currently replaces them with smaller teacher-provided constant values such that the correct program behavior is maintained. We also currently need to specify bounds for the input size, the number of loop unrollings and recursion depth as well as manually provide specialized error models for each problem. The problem of discovering these optimizations automatically by mining them from the large corpus of datasets is also an interesting research question. Our tool also currently does not support some of the Python language features, most notably classes and objects, which are required for providing feedback on problems from later weeks of the class.

```python
def evaluatePoly(poly, x):
    result = 0
    for i in list(poly):
        result += i*x**poly.index(i)
    return result
```

(a) an `evalPoly` solution

```python
def getGuessedWord(secretWord, lettersGuessed):
    for letter in lettersGuessed:
        secretWord = secretWord.replace(letter, '_')
    return secretWord
```

(b) a `hangman2-str` solution

Figure 13. An example of big conceptual error for a student's attempt for (a) `evalPoly` and (b) `hangman2-str` problems.

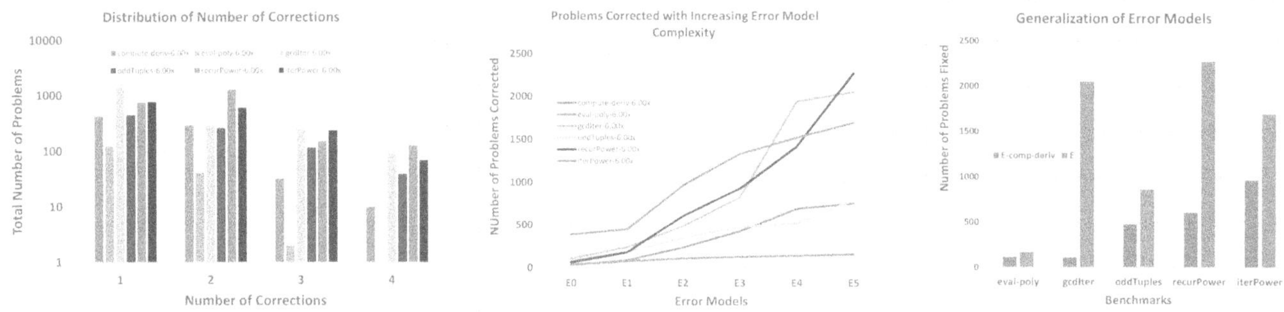

(a) (b) (c)

Figure 14. (a) The number of incorrect problem that require different number of corrections (in log scale), (b) the number of problems corrected with adding rules to the error models, and (c) the performance of compute-deriv error model on other problems.

Benchmark	Median (LOC)	Total Attempts	Syntax Errors	Test Set	Correct	Incorrect Attempts	Generated Feedback	Average Time(in s)	Median Time(in s)
`prodBySum-6.00`	5	1056	16	1040	772	268	218 (81.3%)	2.49s	2.53s
`oddTuples-6.00`	6	2386	1040	1346	1002	344	185 (53.8%)	2.65s	2.54s
`compDeriv-6.00`	12	144	20	124	21	103	88 (85.4%)	12.95s	4.9s
`evalPoly-6.00`	10	144	23	121	108	13	6 (46.1%)	3.35s	3.01s
`compBal-stdin-6.00`	18	170	32	138	86	52	17 (32.7%)	29.57s	14.30s
`compDeriv-6.00x`	13	4146	1134	3012	2094	918	753 (82.1%)	12.42s	6.32s
`evalPoly-6.00x`	15	4698	1004	3694	3153	541	167 (30.9%)	4.78s	4.19s
`oddTuples-6.00x`	10	10985	5047	5938	4182	1756	860 (48.9%)	4.14s	3.77s
`iterPower-6.00x`	11	8982	3792	5190	2315	2875	1693 (58.9%)	3.58s	3.46s
`recurPower-6.00x`	10	8879	3395	5484	2546	2938	2271 (77.3%)	10.59s	5.88s
`iterGCD-6.00x`	12	6934	3732	3202	214	2988	2052 (68.7%)	17.13s	9.52s
`hangman1-str-6.00x`	13	2148	942	1206	855	351	171 (48.7%)	9.08s	6.43s
`hangman2-str-6.00x`	14	1746	410	1336	1118	218	98 (44.9%)	22.09s	18.98s
`stock-market-I(C#)`	20	52	11	41	19	22	16 (72.3%)	7.54s	5.23s
`stock-market-II(C#)`	24	51	8	43	19	24	14 (58.3%)	11.16s	10.28s
`restaurant rush (C#)`	15	124	38	86	20	66	41 (62.1%)	8.78s	8.19s

Table 1. The percentage of student attempts corrected and the time taken for correction for the benchmark problems.

7. Related Work

In this section, we describe several related work to our technique from the areas of automated programming tutors, automated program repair, fault localization, automated debugging, automated grading, and program synthesis.

7.1 AI based programming tutors

There has been a lot of work done in the AI community for building automated tutors for helping novice programmers learn programming by providing feedback about semantic errors. These tutoring systems can be categorized into the following two major classes:

Code-based matching approaches: LAURA [1] converts teacher's and student's program into a graph based representation and compares them heuristically by applying program transformations while reporting mismatches as potential bugs. TALUS [31] matches a student's attempt with a collection of teacher's algorithms. It first tries to recognize the algorithm used and then tentatively replaces the top-level expressions in the student's attempt with the recognized algorithm for generating correction feedback. The problem with these approach is that the enumeration of all possible algorithms (with its variants) for covering all corrections is very large and tedious on part of the teacher.

Intention-based matching approaches: LISP tutor [13] creates a model of the student goals and updates it dynamically as the student makes edits. The drawback of this approach is that it forces students to write code in a certain pre-defined structure and limits their freedom. MENO-II [39] parses student programs into a deep syntax tree whose nodes are annotated with plan tags. This annotated tree is then matched with the plans obtained from teacher's solution. PROUST [24], on the other hand, uses a knowledge base of goals and their corresponding plans for implementing them for each programming problem. It first tries to find correspondence of these plans in the student's code and then performs matching to find discrepancies. CHIRON [32] is its improved version in which the goals and plans in the knowledge base are organized in a hierarchical manner based on their generality and uses machine learning techniques for plan identification in the student code. These approaches require teacher to provide all possible plans a student can use to solve the goals of a given problem and do not perform well if the student's attempt uses a plan not present in the knowledge base.

Our approach performs semantic equivalence of student's attempt and teacher's solution based on exhaustive bounded symbolic verification techniques and makes no assumptions on the algorithms or plans that students can use for solving the problem. Moreover, our approach is modular with respect to error models; the local correction rules are provided in a declarative manner and their complex interactions are handled by the solver itself.

7.2 Automated Program Repair

Könighofer et. al. [27] present an approach for automated error localization and correction of imperative programs. They use model-based diagnosis to localize components that need to be replaced and then use a template-based approach for providing corrections using SMT reasoning. Their fault model only considers the right hand side (RHS) of assignment statements as replaceable components. The approaches in [23, 41] frame the problem of program repair as a game between an environment that provides the inputs and a system that provides correct values for the buggy expressions such that the specification is satisfied. These approaches only support simple corrections (e.g. correcting RHS side of expressions) in the fault model as they aim to repair large programs with arbitrary errors. In our setting, we exploit the fact that we have access to the dataset of previous student mistakes that we can use to construct a *concise and precise* error model. This enables us to model more sophisticated transformations such as introducing new program statements, replacing LHS of assignments etc. in our error model. Our approach also supports minimal cost changes to student's programs where each error in the model is associated with a certain cost, unlike the earlier mentioned approaches.

Mutation-based program repair [10] performs mutations repeatedly to statements in a buggy program in order of their suspiciousness until the program becomes correct. The large state space of mutants (10^{12}) makes this approach infeasible. Our approach uses a symbolic search for exploring correct solutions over this large set. There are also some genetic programming approaches that exploit redundancy present in other parts of the code for fixing faults [5, 14]. These techniques are not applicable in our setting as such redundancy is not present in introductory programming problems.

7.3 Automated Debugging and Fault localization

Techniques like Delta Debugging [44] and QuickXplain [26] aim to simplify a failing test case to a minimal test case that still exhibits the same failure. Our approach can be complemented with these techniques to restrict the application of rewrite rules to certain failing parts of the program only. There are many algorithms for fault localization [6, 15] that use the difference between faulty and successful executions of the system to identify potential faulty locations. Jose et. al. [25] recently suggested an approach that uses a MAX-SAT solver to satisfy maximum number of clauses in a formula obtained from a failing test case to compute potential error locations. These approaches, however, only localize faults for a single failing test case and the suggested error location might not be the desired error location, since we are looking for common error locations that cause failure of multiple test cases. Moreover, these techniques provide only a limited set of suggestions (if any) for repairing these faults.

7.4 Computer-aided Education

We believe that formal methods technology can play a big role in revolutionizing education. Recently, it has been applied to multiple aspects of Education including problem generation [2, 4, 35] and solution generation [17]. In this paper, we push the frontier forward to cover another aspect namely automated grading. Recently [3] also applied automated grading to automata constructions and used syntactic edit distance like ours as one of the metrics. Our work differs from theirs in two regards: (a) our corrections for programs (which are much more sophisticated than automata) are teacher-defined, while [3] considers a small pre-defined set of corrections over graphs, and (b) we use the Sketch synthesizer to efficiently navigate the huge search space, while [3] uses brute-force search.

7.5 Automated Grading Approaches

The survey by Douce et al. [11] presents a nice overview of the systems developed for automated grading of programming assignments over the last forty years. Based on the age of these systems, they classify them into three generations. The first generation systems [21] graded programs by comparing the stored data with the data obtained from program execution, and kept track of running times and grade books. The second generation systems [22] also checked for programming styles such as modularity, complexity, and efficiency in addition to checking for correctness. The third generation tools such as RoboProf [9] combine web technology with more sophisticated testing approaches. All of these approaches are a form of test-cases based grading approach and can produce feedback in terms of failing test inputs, whereas our technique uses program synthesis for generating tailored feedback about the changes required in the student submission to make it correct.

7.6 Program Synthesis

Program synthesis has been used recently for many applications such as synthesis of efficient low-level code [29, 38], data structure manipulations [34], inference of efficient synchronization in concurrent programs [42], snippets of excel macros [18, 33], relational data representations [19, 20] and angelic programming [8]. The SKETCH tool [37, 38] takes a partial program and a reference implementation as input and uses constraint-based reasoning to synthesize a complete program that is equivalent to the reference implementation. In general cases, the template of the desired program as well as the reference specification is unknown and puts an additional burden on the users to provide them; in our case we use the student's solution as the template program and teacher's solution as the reference implementation. A recent work by Gulwani et al. [17] also uses program synthesis techniques for automatically synthesizing solutions to ruler/compass based geometry construction problems. Their focus is primarily on finding a solution to a given geometry problem whereas we aim to provide feedback on a given programming exercise solution.

8. Conclusions

In this paper, we presented a new technique of automatically providing feedback for introductory programming assignments that can complement manual and test-cases based techniques. The technique uses an error model describing the potential corrections and constraint-based synthesis to compute minimal corrections to student's incorrect solutions. We have evaluated our technique on a large set of benchmarks and it can correct 64% of incorrect solutions in our benchmark set. We believe this technique can provide a basis for providing automated feedback to hundreds of thousands of students learning from online introductory programming courses that are being taught by MITx, Coursera, and Udacity.

9. Acknowledgements

This work is supported in part by National Science Foundation grants Expeditions in Computer Augmented Program Engineering (ExCAPE NSF-1139056) and NSF-1139056, MIT EECS Super UROP program, Microsoft Research and a Microsoft Research PhD fellowship.

We thank Ned Batchelder, Sarina Canelake, Piotr Mitros, and Victor Shnayder from the EdX team for their support and for providing us the `6.00x` data. We thank the anonymous reviewers for their valuable feedback. We also thank the UROP students Tuan Andrew Nguyen, Xola Ntumy, and Eugene Oh for their contributions to this project. Finally, we thank Nikolai Tillmann and Jonathan de Halleux from the Pex4Fun team at Microsoft Research for providing us the C# data for the initial version of our tool.

References

[1] A. Adam and J.-P. H. Laurent. LAURA, A System to Debug Student Programs. *Artif. Intell.*, 15(1-2):75–122, 1980.

[2] U. Ahmed, S. Gulwani, and A. Karkare. Automatically generating problems and solutions for natural deduction. In *IJCAI*, 2013.

[3] R. Alur, L. D'Antoni, S. Gulwani, D. Kini, and M. Viswanathan. Automated grading of dfa constructions. In *IJCAI*, 2013.

[4] E. Andersen, S. Gulwani, and Z. Popovic. A trace-based framework for analyzing and synthesizing educational progressions. In *CHI*, 2013.

[5] A. Arcuri. On the automation of fixing software bugs. In *ICSE Companion*, 2008.

[6] T. Ball, M. Naik, and S. K. Rajamani. From symptom to cause: localizing errors in counterexample traces. In *POPL*, 2003.

[7] M. S. Bernstein, G. Little, R. C. Miller, B. Hartmann, M. S. Ackerman, D. R. Karger, D. Crowell, and K. Panovich. Soylent: a word processor with a crowd inside. In *UIST*, 2010.

[8] R. Bodík, S. Chandra, J. Galenson, D. Kimelman, N. Tung, S. Barman, and C. Rodarmor. Programming with angelic nondeterminism. In *POPL*, 2010.

[9] C. Daly. Roboprof and an introductory computer programming course. ITiCSE, 1999.

[10] V. Debroy and W. Wong. Using mutation to automatically suggest fixes for faulty programs. In *ICST*, 2010.

[11] C. Douce, D. Livingstone, and J. Orwell. Automatic test-based assessment of programming: A review. *J. Educ. Resour. Comput.*, 5(3), Sept. 2005.

[12] P. Ertmer, J. Richardson, B. Belland, D. Camin, P. Connolly, G. Coulthard, K. Lei, and C. Mong. Using peer feedback to enhance the quality of student online postings: An exploratory study. *Journal of Computer-Mediated Communication*, 12(2):412–433, 2007.

[13] R. G. Farrell, J. R. Anderson, and B. J. Reiser. An interactive computer-based tutor for lisp. In *AAAI*, 1984.

[14] S. Forrest, T. Nguyen, W. Weimer, and C. L. Goues. A genetic programming approach to automated software repair. In *GECCO*, 2009.

[15] A. Groce, S. Chaki, D. Kroening, and O. Strichman. Error explanation with distance metrics. *STTT*, 8(3):229–247, 2006.

[16] S. Gulwani, S. Srivastava, and R. Venkatesan. Program analysis as constraint solving. In *PLDI*, 2008.

[17] S. Gulwani, V. A. Korthikanti, and A. Tiwari. Synthesizing geometry constructions. In *PLDI*, 2011.

[18] S. Gulwani, W. R. Harris, and R. Singh. Spreadsheet data manipulation using examples. In *CACM*, 2012.

[19] P. Hawkins, A. Aiken, K. Fisher, M. C. Rinard, and M. Sagiv. Data representation synthesis. In *PLDI*, 2011.

[20] P. Hawkins, A. Aiken, K. Fisher, M. C. Rinard, and M. Sagiv. Concurrent data representation synthesis. In *PLDI*, 2012.

[21] J. B. Hext and J. W. Winings. An automatic grading scheme for simple programming exercises. *Commun. ACM*, 12(5), May 1969.

[22] D. Jackson and M. Usher. Grading student programs using assyst. SIGCSE, 1997.

[23] B. Jobstmann, A. Griesmayer, and R. Bloem. Program repair as a game. In *CAV*, pages 226–238, 2005.

[24] W. L. Johnson and E. Soloway. Proust: Knowledge-based program understanding. *IEEE Trans. Software Eng.*, 11(3):267–275, 1985.

[25] M. Jose and R. Majumdar. Cause clue clauses: error localization using maximum satisfiability. In *PLDI*, 2011.

[26] U. Junker. QUICKXPLAIN: preferred explanations and relaxations for over-constrained problems. In *AAAI*, 2004.

[27] R. Könighofer and R. P. Bloem. Automated error localization and correction for imperative programs. In *FMCAD*, 2011.

[28] C. Kulkarni and S. R. Klemmer. Learning design wisdom by augmenting physical studio critique with online self-assessment. Technical report, Stanford University, 2012.

[29] V. Kuncak, M. Mayer, R. Piskac, and P. Suter. Complete functional synthesis. PLDI, 2010.

[30] G. Little, L. B. Chilton, M. Goldman, and R. C. Miller. Turkit: human computation algorithms on mechanical turk. In *UIST*, 2010.

[31] W. R. Murray. Automatic program debugging for intelligent tutoring systems. *Computational Intelligence*, 3:1–16, 1987.

[32] W. Sack, E. Soloway, and P. Weingrad. From PROUST to CHIRON: Its design as iterative engineering: Intermediate results are important! In *In J.H. Larkin and R.W. Chabay (Eds.), Computer-Assisted Instruction and Intelligent Tutoring Systems: Shared Goals and Complementary Approaches.*, pages 239–274, 1992.

[33] R. Singh and S. Gulwani. Learning semantic string transformations from examples. *PVLDB*, 5, 2012.

[34] R. Singh and A. Solar-Lezama. Synthesizing data structure manipulations from storyboards. In *SIGSOFT FSE*, 2011.

[35] R. Singh, S. Gulwani, and S. K. Rajamani. Automatically generating algebra problems. In *AAAI*, 2012.

[36] R. Singh, S. Gulwani, and A. Solar-Lezama. Automated semantic grading of programs. *CoRR*, abs/1204.1751, 2012.

[37] A. Solar-Lezama. *Program Synthesis By Sketching*. PhD thesis, EECS Dept., UC Berkeley, 2008.

[38] A. Solar-Lezama, R. Rabbah, R. Bodik, and K. Ebcioglu. Programming by sketching for bit-streaming programs. In *PLDI*, 2005.

[39] E. Soloway, B. P. Woolf, E. Rubin, and P. Barth. Meno-II: An Intelligent Tutoring System for Novice Programmers. In *IJCAI*, 1981.

[40] S. Srivastava, S. Gulwani, and J. Foster. From program verification to program synthesis. *POPL*, 2010.

[41] S. S. Staber, B. Jobstmann, and R. P. Bloem. Finding and fixing faults. In *Correct Hardware Design and Verification Methods*, Lecture notes in computer science, pages 35 – 49, 2005.

[42] M. Vechev, E. Yahav, and G. Yorsh. Abstraction-guided synthesis of synchronization. In *POPL*, 2010.

[43] D. S. Weld, E. Adar, L. Chilton, R. Hoffmann, and E. Horvitz. Personalized online education - a crowdsourcing challenge. In *Workshops at the Twenty-Sixth AAAI Conference on Artificial Intelligence*, 2012.

[44] A. Zeller and R. Hildebrandt. Simplifying and isolating failure-inducing input. *IEEE Transactions on Software Engineering*, 28:183–200, 2002.

Complete Completion using Types and Weights

Tihomir Gvero Viktor Kuncak
Ivan Kuraj

École Polytechnique Fédérale de Lausanne (EPFL),
Switzerland

firstname.lastname@epfl.ch

Ruzica Piskac

Max Planck Institute for Software Systems (MPI-SWS),
Germany

piskac@mpi-sws.org

Abstract

Developing modern software typically involves composing functionality from existing libraries. This task is difficult because libraries may expose many methods to the developer. To help developers in such scenarios, we present a technique that synthesizes and suggests valid expressions of a given type at a given program point. As the basis of our technique we use type inhabitation for lambda calculus terms in long normal form. We introduce a succinct representation for type judgements that merges types into equivalence classes to reduce the search space, then reconstructs any desired number of solutions on demand. Furthermore, we introduce a method to rank solutions based on weights derived from a corpus of code. We implemented the algorithm and deployed it as a plugin for the Eclipse IDE for Scala. We show that the techniques we incorporated greatly increase the effectiveness of the approach. Our evaluation benchmarks are code examples from programming practice; we make them available for future comparisons.

Categories and Subject Descriptors I.2.2 [*Artificial Intelligence*]: Automatic Programming–Program synthesis; D.2.6 [*Software Engineering*]: Coding Tools and Techniques–Program Editors; D.2.13 [*Software Engineering*]: Reusable Software–Reuse Models

General Terms Languages, Algorithms

Keywords program synthesis, type inhabitation, code completion, type-driven synthesis, ranking

1. Introduction

Libraries are one of the biggest assets for today's software developers. Useful libraries often evolve into complex application programming interfaces (APIs) with a large number of classes and methods. It can be difficult for a developer to start using such APIs productively, even for simple tasks. Existing Integrated Development Environments (IDEs) help developers to use APIs by providing *code completion* functionality. For example, an IDE can offer a list of applicable members to a given receiver object, extracted by finding the declared type of the object. Eclipse [26] and IntelliJ [15] recommend methods applicable to an object, and allow the developer to fill in additional method arguments. Such completion typically considers one step of computation. IntelliJ can additionally compose simple method sequences to form a type-correct expression, but requires both the receiver object as well as assistance from the developer to fill in the arguments. These efforts suggest a general direction for improving modern IDEs: introduce the ability to synthesize entire type-correct code fragments and offer them as suggestions to the developer.

In this paper we describe a tool for automated synthesis of code snippets. The tool generates and suggests a list of expressions that have a desired type. One observation behind our work is that, in addition to the forward-directed completion in existing tools, developers can benefit from a backward-directed completion. Indeed, when identifying a computation step, the developer often has the type of a desired object in mind. We therefore do not require the developer to indicate a starting value (such as a receiver object) explicitly. Instead, we follow a more ambitious approach that considers all values in the current scope as the candidate leaf values of expressions to be synthesized. Our approach therefore requires fewer inputs than the pioneering work on the Prospector tool [18], or than the recent work of Perelman et al. [20]. A general idea of our approach and a first prototype implementation was demonstrated already in [10].

Finding a code snippet of the given type leads us directly to the type inhabitation problem: given a desired type T, and a type environment Γ (a map from identifiers to their types), find an expression e of this type T. Formally, find e such that $\Gamma \vdash e : T$. In our deployment, the tool computes Γ from the position of the cursor in the editor buffer. It similarly looks up T by examining the declared type appearing left of the cursor in the editor. The goal of the tool is to find an expression e, and insert it at the current program point, so that the overall program type checks. When there are multiple solutions, the tool prompts the developer to select one, much like in simpler code completion scenarios.

The type inhabitation in the simply typed lambda calculus corresponds to provability in propositional intuitionistic logic; it is decidable and PSPACE-complete [24, 28]. We developed a version of the algorithm that is complete in the lambda calculus sense (up to $\alpha\beta\eta$-conversion): it is guaranteed to synthesize a lambda expression of the given type, if such an expression exists. Moreover, if there are multiple solutions, it can enumerate all of them. If there are infinitely many solutions, then the algorithm can enumerate any desired finite prefix of the list of all solutions. Note also that each synthesized expression is a complete in that method calls have all of their arguments synthesized. Because of all these aspects of the algorithm we describe our technique as *complete completion*.

We present our algorithm using a calculus of *succinct types*, which we tailored for efficiently solving type inhabitation queries. The calculus computes equivalence classes of types that reduce the search space in goal-directed search, without losing completeness.

PLDI'13, June 16–19, 2013, Seattle, WA, USA.

```
import java.io._
object Main {
  def main(args:Array[String]) = {
    var body = "email.txt"
    var sig = "signature.txt"

    var inStream:SequenceInputStream = |
                                            new SequenceInputStream(new FileInputStream(sig), new FileInputStream(sig))
    var eof:Boolean = false                 new SequenceInputStream(new FileInputStream(sig), new FileInputStream(body))
    var byteCount:Int = 0                   new SequenceInputStream(new FileInputStream(body), new FileInputStream(sig))
    while (!eof) {                          new SequenceInputStream(new FileInputStream(body), new FileInputStream(body))
      var c:Int = inStream.read()           new SequenceInputStream(new FileInputStream(sig), System.in)
      if (c == -1)
```

Figure 1. InSynth suggesting five highest-ranked well-typed expressions synthesized from declarations visible at a given program point

Moreover, our algorithm generates a representation of *all* solutions, from which it can then extract any desired finite subset of solutions.

Given a possibility of an infinite number of type inhabitants, it is natural to consider the problem of finding the *best* one. To solve this problem, we introduce *weights* to guide the search and rank the presented solutions. Initially we assign the weight to each type declaration. Those weights play a crucial role in the algorithm, since they guide the search and rank the presented solutions. The weight is defined in a way that a smaller weight indicates a more desirable formula. To estimate the initial weights of declarations we leverage 1) the lexical nesting structure, with closer declarations having lower weight, and 2) implicit statistical information from a corpus of code, with more frequently occurring declarations having smaller weight, and thus being preferred. In addition, we used a corpus of open-source Java and Scala projects as well as the standard Scala library to collect the usage statistics for the initial weights of declarations.

We implemented our tool, InSynth, within the Scala Eclipse plugin. Our experience shows fast response times as well as a high quality of the offered suggestions, even in the presence of thousands of candidate API calls. We evaluated InSynth on a set of 50 benchmarks constructed from examples found on the Web, written to illustrate API usage, as well as examples from larger projects. To estimate the interactive nature of InSynth, we measured the time needed to synthesize the expected snippet. The running times of InSynth were always a fraction of a second. In the great majority of cases we found that the expected snippets were returned among the top dozen solutions.

Furthermore, we evaluated a number of techniques deployed in our final tool and found that all of them are important for obtaining good results. We also observed that, even for checking existence of terms InSynth outperforms recent propositional intuitionistic provers [9, 19] on our benchmarks. Our overall experience suggests that InSynth is effective in providing help to developers.

2. Motivating Examples

We illustrate the functionality of InSynth through three examples. The first example is taken from the online repository of Java API usage samples `http://www.java2s.com/`. The second example is a real-world fragment of the code base of the Scala IDE for Eclipse, `http://scala-ide.org/`, and requires invoking a higher-order function. For these two examples, the original code imports only declarations from a few specific classes; to make the problems more challenging and illustrate the task that a programmer faces, we import all declarations from packages where those classes reside. The third example illustrates that InSynth supports subtyping.

2.1 Sequence of Streams

In this example the goal is to create a SequenceInputStream object, which is a concatenation of two streams. Suppose that the developer has the code shown in the Eclipse editor in Figure 1. If she invokes InSynth at the program point indicated by the cursor, in a fraction of a second InSynth displays the ranked list of five expressions. Seeing the list, the developer can decide that e.g. the second expression in the list matches their intention, and select it to be inserted into the editor buffer.

This example illustrates that InSynth only needs the current program context, and does not require additional information from the developer. InSynth is able to use both imported values (such as the constructors in this example) and locally declared ones (such as body and sig). InSynth supports methods with multiple arguments and synthesizes expressions for each argument. In this example InSynth loads over 3000 declarations from the context, including local and imported values, and finds the expected solution in less than 250 milliseconds.

The effectiveness of InSynth is characterized by both scalability to many declarations and the quality of the returned suggestions. InSynth ranks the resulting expressions according to the weights and selects the ones with the lowest weight. The weights of expressions and types guide the final ranking and also make the search itself more goal-directed and effective. InSynth derives weights from a corpus of declarations, assigning lower weight to declarations appearing more frequently, and therefore favoring their appearance in the suggested fragments over more exotic declarations.

2.2 TreeFilter: Using Higher-Order Functions

We demonstrate the generation of expressions with higher-order functions on real code from the Scala IDE project. The example shows how a developer should properly check if a Scala AST tree satisfies a given property. In the code, the tree is an argument of the class TreeWrapper, whereas the property p is an input of the method filter.

```
import scala.tools.eclipse.javaelements._
import scala.collection.mutable._
trait TypeTreeTraverser {
  val global: tools.nsc.Global
  import global._
  class TreeWrapper(tree: Tree) {
    def filter(p: Tree => Boolean): List[Tree] = {
      val ft:FilterTypeTreeTraverser = |
      ft.traverse(tree)
      ft.hits.toList
    }
  }
}
```

The property p is a predicate function that takes the tree and returns **true** if the tree satisfies it. In order to properly use p inside filter, the developer first needs to create an object of the type FilterTypeTreeTraverser. If the developer calls InSynth at the place **I**, the tool offers several expressions, and the one ranked first turns out to be precisely the one found in the original code, namely

```
new FilterTypeTreeTraverser(var1 => p(var1))
```

The constructor FilterTypeTreeTraverser is a higher-order function that takes as input another function, in this case p. In this example, InSynth loads over 4000 initial declarations and finds the snippets in less than 300 milliseconds.

2.3 Drawing Layout: Using Subtyping

The next example illustrates a situation often encountered when using java.awt: implementing a getter method that returns a layout of an object Panel stored in a class Drawing. To implement such a method, we use code of the following form.

```
import java.awt._
class Drawing(panel:Panel) {
  def getLayout:LayoutManager = I
}
```

Note that handling this example requires support for subtyping, because the type declarations are given by the following code.

```
class Panel extends Container with Accessible { ... }
class Container extends Component {
  ...
  def getLayout():LayoutManager = { ... }
}
```

The Scala compiler has access to the information about all supertypes of all types in a given scope. InSynth supports subtyping and, in 426 milliseconds, returns a number of solutions among which the second one is the desired expression panel.getLayout(). While doing so, it examines 4965 declarations.

For more experience with InSynth, we encourage the reader to download it from:

`http://lara.epfl.ch/w/insynth`

The rest of the paper describes a formalization of the problem that InSynth solves as well as the algorithms we designed to solve it. We then describe the implementation and the evaluation, provide a survey of related efforts, and conclude.

3. Type Inhabitation Problem for Succinct Types

To answer whether there exists a code snippet of a given type, our starting point is the *type inhabitation problem*. In this section we establish a connection between type inhabitation and the synthesis of code snippets.

Let T be a set of types. A *type environment* Γ is a finite set $\{x_1 : \tau_1, \ldots, x_n : \tau_n\}$ of pairs of the form $x_i : \tau_i$, where x_i is a variable of a type $\tau_i \in T$. We call the pair $x_i : \tau_i$ a *type declaration*.

The type judgment, denoted by $\Gamma \vdash e : \tau$, states that from the environment Γ, we can derive the type declaration $e : \tau$ by applying rules of some calculus. The type inhabitation problem for a given calculus is defined as follows: given a type τ and a type environment Γ, does there exist an expression e such that $\Gamma \vdash e : \tau$?

In the sequel we first describe type rules for the standard lambda calculus restricted to normal-form terms. We denote the corresponding type judgment relation $\vdash_\lambda$. We then introduce a new *succinct* representation of types and terms, with the corresponding type judgment relation $\vdash_c$.

3.1 Simply Typed Lambda Calculus for Deriving Terms in Long Normal Form

As background we present relevant rules for the simply typed lambda calculus, focusing on terms in long normal form. Let B be a set of basic types. Types are formed according to the following syntax:

$$\tau ::= \tau \to \tau \mid v, \quad \text{where } v \in B$$

We denote the set of all types as $\tau_\lambda(B)$.

Let V be a set of typed variables. Typed expressions are constructed according to the following syntax:

$$e ::= x \mid \lambda x.e \mid e\, e, \quad \text{where } x \in V$$

Figure 2 shows the type derivation rules used to derive terms in long normal form. This calculus is slightly more restrictive than

$$\textsc{App}\ \frac{\begin{array}{c}(f : \tau_1 \to \ldots \to \tau_n \to \tau) \in \Gamma_o \\ \Gamma_o \vdash_\lambda e_i : \tau_i,\ i = 1..n \qquad \tau \in B\end{array}}{\Gamma_o \vdash_\lambda f e_1 \ldots e_n : \tau}$$

$$\textsc{Abs}\ \frac{\Gamma_o \cup \{x_1 : \tau_1, \ldots, x_m : \tau_n\} \vdash_\lambda e : \tau \qquad \tau \in B}{\Gamma_o \vdash_\lambda \lambda x_1 \ldots x_m.e : \tau_1 \to \ldots \to \tau_m \to \tau}$$

Figure 2. Rules for deriving lambda terms in long normal form

the standard lambda calculus: the APP rule requires that only those functions present in the original environment Γ_o can be applied on terms.

DEFINITION 3.1 (Long Normal Form). *A judgement $\Gamma_o \vdash_\lambda e : \tau_e$ is in long normal form if the following holds:*

- $e \equiv \lambda x_1 \ldots x_m.f e_1 ... e_n$, *where* $m, n \geq 0$
- $(f : \rho_1 \to \ldots \to \rho_n \to \tau) \in \Gamma_o$, *where* $\tau \in B$
- $\tau_e \equiv \tau_1 \to \ldots \to \tau_m \to \tau$
- $\Gamma'_o \vdash_\lambda e_i : \rho_i$ *are in long normal form, where* $\Gamma'_o = \Gamma_o \cup \{x_1 : \tau_1, \ldots, x_m : \tau_m\}$

Note that m can be zero. Then, $\tau_e \equiv \tau$ and Definition 3.1 reduces to the App rule. Otherwise, if $M \equiv f e_1 ... e_n$, then $M : \tau$ can be derived by App and $\lambda x_1 \ldots x_m.M : \tau_e$ by Abs rule.

In long normal form a variable f is followed by exactly the same number of sub-terms as the number of arguments indicated by the type of f. As an illustration, consider $f : \tau_1 \to \tau_2 \to \tau_3$ and $x : \tau_1$. There is no derivation resulting in a judgement $\Gamma_o \vdash_\lambda fx : \tau_2 \to \tau_3$ in long normal form, but $\lambda y.fxy : \tau_2 \to \tau_3$ has a long normal form derivation.

When solving the type inhabitation problem it suffices to derive only terms in long normal form, which restricts the search space. This does not affect the completeness of search, because each simply-typed term can be converted to its long normal form [6].

We define the depth $\mathcal{D}$ of a term from a long normal form judgement as follows:
$\mathcal{D}(\lambda x_1 \ldots x_m.a) = 1$
$\mathcal{D}(\lambda x_1 \ldots x_m.f e_1, \ldots, e_n) = \max(\mathcal{D}(e_1), \ldots, \mathcal{D}(e_n)) + 1$,
where a and f belong to V.

3.2 Succinct Types

To make the search more efficient we introduce *succinct types*, which are types modulo isomorphisms of products and currying, that is, according to the Curry-Howard correspondence, modulo commutativity, associativity, and idempotence of the intuitionistic conjunction.

DEFINITION 3.2 (Succinct Types). *Let B be a set containing basic types. Succinct types t_s are constructed according to the grammar:*

$$t_s ::= \{t_s, \ldots, t_s\} \rightarrow v, \quad \text{where } v \in B$$

We denote the set of all succinct types with $t_s(B)$, sometimes also only with t_s.

A type declaration $f : \{t_1, \ldots, t_n\} \rightarrow t$ is a type declaration for a function that takes arguments of n different types and returns a value of type t. The type $\emptyset \rightarrow t$ plays a special role: it is a type of a function that takes no arguments and returns a value of type t, i.e. we consider types t and $\emptyset \rightarrow t$ equivalent.

Every type $\tau \in \tau_\lambda(B)$ can be converted into a succinct type in $t_s(B)$. With $\sigma : \tau_\lambda(B) \rightarrow t_s(B)$ we denote this conversion function. Every basic type $v \in B$ becomes an element of the set of basic succinct types, and $\sigma(v) = \emptyset \rightarrow v$. We also denote $\emptyset \rightarrow v$ only with v. Let A (arguments) and R (return type) be two functions defined on $t_s(B)$ as follows:

$$\begin{array}{rcl} A(\{t_1, \ldots, t_n\} \rightarrow v) & = & \{t_1, \ldots, t_n\} \\ R(\{t_1, \ldots, t_n\} \rightarrow v) & = & v \end{array}$$

Using A and R we define the σ function as follows:

$$\sigma(\tau_1 \rightarrow \tau_2) = \{\sigma(\tau_1)\} \cup A(\sigma(\tau_2)) \rightarrow R(\sigma(\tau_2))$$

In particular, for $v \in B$, a type of the form

$$\tau_1 \rightarrow \ldots \rightarrow \tau_n \rightarrow v$$

which often occurs in practice, has the succinct representation

$$\{\sigma(\tau_1), \ldots, \sigma(\tau_n)\} \rightarrow v$$

Given a type environment $\Gamma_o = \{x_1 : \tau_1, \ldots, x_n : \tau_n\}$ where τ_i are types in the simply type lambda calculus, we define

$$\Gamma = \sigma(\Gamma_o) = \{\sigma(\tau_1), \ldots, \sigma(\tau_n)\}$$

It follows immediately that the conversion distributes over unions:

$$\sigma(\bigcup_{i \in I} \Gamma_o^i) = \bigcup_{i \in I} \sigma(\Gamma_o^i)$$

To demonstrate the power of the succinct representation, we provide the statistics from the example in Figure 1. In this example, the original type environment with 3356 declarations is reduced to the compact succinct environment with 1783 succinct types, after the σ transformation. This drastically reduces the search space later explored by our main algorithm.

3.3 Succinct Patterns

Succinct patterns have the following structure:

$$\Gamma @ \{t_1, \ldots, t_n\} : t$$

where $t_i \in t_s(B)$, $i = 1..n$, and $t \in B$.

A pattern $\Gamma @ \{t_1, \ldots, t_n\} : t$ indicates that types $t_1, \ldots, t_n$ are inhabited in Γ and an inhabitant of type t can be computed from them also in Γ. They abstractly represent an application term in lambda calculus.

Our algorithm for finding all type inhabitants works in two phases. In the first phase we derive all succinct patterns. They can be seen as a generalization of terms, because they describe all the ways in which a term can be computed. In the second phase we do a term reconstruction based on the original type declarations (Γ_o) and the set of succinct patterns.

3.4 Succinct Calculus

Figure 3 describes the calculus for succinct types. Note that the patterns are derived only in the APP rule. The rule ABS modifies Γ – it can either reduce Γ or enlarge it, depending on whether we are doing backward or forward reasoning.

$$\text{APP}\ \frac{\{t_1, \ldots, t_n\} \rightarrow t \in \Gamma \qquad \Gamma \vdash_c t_i,\ i = 1..n \qquad t \in B}{\Gamma \vdash_c \Gamma @ \{t_1, \ldots, t_n\} : t}$$

$$\text{ABS}\ \frac{\Gamma \cup S \vdash_c (\Gamma \cup S) @ \pi : t \qquad t \in B}{\Gamma \vdash_c S \rightarrow t}$$

Figure 3. Calculus rules for deriving succinct patterns

Consider the example given at the beginning of this section and its type environment $\Gamma_o = \{a : \text{Int}, f : \text{Int} \rightarrow \text{Int} \rightarrow \text{Int} \rightarrow \text{String}\}$. From the type environment Γ_o we compute $\Gamma = \{\emptyset \rightarrow \text{Int}, \{\emptyset \rightarrow \text{Int}\} \rightarrow \text{String}\} = \{\text{Int}, \{\text{Int}\} \rightarrow \text{String}\}$. By applying the APP rule on Int, we derive a succinct pattern $\Gamma @ \emptyset : \text{Int}$ that we add to a set of derived patterns. Having a pattern for Int we apply the ABS rule. By setting $S = \emptyset$, we derive $\Gamma \vdash_c \emptyset \rightarrow \text{Int}$. Finally, by applying again the APP rule, we directly derive a pattern $\Gamma @ \{\text{Int}\} : \text{String}$, for the String type and store it into the set of derived patterns.

3.5 Soundness and Completeness of Succinct Calculus

In this section we show that the calculus in Figure 3 is sound and complete with respect to synthesis of lambda terms in long normal form. We are interested in generating any desired number of expressions of a given type without missing any expressions equivalent up to β reduction. To formulate a completeness that captures this ability, we introduce two functions, CL and RCN, shown in Figure 4. These functions describe the terms in long normal form of a desired type, up to a given depth d. They refer directly to $\vdash_c$ and are therefore not meant as algorithms, but as a way of expressing the completeness of succinct representation and as specifications for the algorithms we outline in Section 5.

```
fun CL(Γ, S→t) = {(Γ ∪ S)@S₁ : t | (S₁→t) ∈ (Γ ∪ S),
                                     ∀t' ∈ S₁.Γ ∪ S ⊢c t'}
fun Select(Γo, t) := {v:τ | v:τ ∈ Γo and σ(τ) = t}
fun RCN(Γo, τ1→···→τn→v, d) :=
  if (d = 0) return ∅
  else
    S→v := σ(τ1→···→τn→v)
    Γ := σ(Γo)
    Γ'o := Γo ∪ {x1 : τ1, ..., xn : τn} //x1, ..., xn are fresh
    TERMS := ∅
    foreach ((Γ ∪ S)@{t1, ..., tm'} : v) ∈ CL(Γ, S→v)
      foreach (f : τ) ∈ Select(Γ'o, {t1, ..., tm'}→v)
        (ρ1→···→ρm→v) := τ
        if (m=0) TERMS := TERMS ∪ {λx1 ... xn.f}
        else
          foreach i ← [1..m]
            Ti := RCN(Γ'o, ρi, d−1)
          foreach (e1, ..., em) ← (T1 × ··· × Tm)
            TERMS := TERMS ∪ {λx1 ... xn.f e1 ... em}
  return TERMS
```

Figure 4. The function RCN constructs lambda terms in long normal form up to given depth d, invoking the auxiliary functions CL and Select.

The CL function in Figure 4 takes as arguments a succinct type environment Γ and a succinct type $S \rightarrow t$. It returns the set of all patterns $(\Gamma \cup S) @ S_1 : t$ that describe the derivation of t. The function RCN uses the initial environment and the desired type to reconstruct lambda terms. Additionally, RCN takes a non-negative integer d to limit the reconstruction to terms with depth smaller or equal to d. It uses type $\tau_1 \rightarrow \cdots \rightarrow \tau_n \rightarrow v$ to extend the environment and find all patterns that witness inhabitation of v. We extend the environment with fresh variables $x_1 : \tau_1, \ldots, x_n : \tau_n$, and use CL to find the patterns. Further, we find all declarations f with a return type v in the extended environment. If f has a function type $\rho_1 \rightarrow \cdots \rightarrow \rho_m \rightarrow v$, we recursively generate corresponding sub-terms with types $\rho_1, \ldots, \rho_m$. Finally, we use $x_1, \ldots, x_n$, f and sub-terms to construct terms in long normal form.

Given the functions CL and RCN we can formalize the completeness theorem: each judgement in long normal form derived in the standard lambda calculus can also be derived by reconstruction using derivations (patterns) of the succinct calculus.

THEOREM 3.3 (Soundness and Completeness). *Let Γ_o be an original environment, e an lambda expression, $\tau \in \tau_\lambda(B)$ and functions RCN and $\mathcal{D}$ defined as above, then:*

$$\Gamma_o \vdash_\lambda e : \tau \Leftrightarrow e \in \mathsf{RCN}(\Gamma_o, \tau, \mathcal{D}(e))$$

We provide the proof of Theorem 3.3 in [11].

4. Quantitative Type Inhabitation Problem

When answering the question of the type inhabitation problem, there might be many terms having the required type τ. A question that naturally arises is how to find the "best" term, for some adequate meaning of "best". For this purpose we assign a weight to every term. As in resolution-based theorem proving, a lower weight indicates a higher relevance of the term. Using weights we extend the type inhabitation problem to the *quantitative type inhabitation problem* – given a type environment Γ, a type τ and a weight function w, is τ inhabited and if it is, return a term that has the lowest weight.

Nature of Declaration or Literal	Weight
Lambda	1
Local	5
Coercion	10
Class	20
Package	25
Literal	200
Imported	$215 + \frac{785}{1+f(x)}$

Table 1. Weights for names appearing in declarations. We found these values to work well in practice, but the quality of results is not highly sensitive to the precise values of parameters.

Let w be a function that assigns a weight (a non-negative number) to each symbol primarily determined by:

1. the proximity to the point at which InSynth is invoked. We assume that the user prefers a code snippet composed from values and methods defined closer to the program point and assign the lower weight to the symbols which are declared closer. As shown in Table 1, we assign the lowest weight to local symbols declared in the same method. We assign a higher weight to symbols defined in the class where the query is initiated and the highest weight to symbols that are only in the same package.
2. the frequency with which the symbol appears in the training data corpus, as described in Section 7.3. For an imported symbol x, we determine its weight using the formula in Table 1. Here $f(x)$ is the number of occurrences of x in the corpus.

We also assign a low weight to a conversion function that witnesses the subtyping relation, as explained in Section 6. While we believe that our strategy is fairly reasonable, we arrived at the particular constants via trial and error, so further improvements are likely possible.

The function w also assigns a weight to a term such that the weight of the term $\lambda x_1 \ldots x_m.fe_1 \ldots e_n$ is the sum of the weights of all elements that occur in the expression:

$$w(\lambda x_1 \ldots x_m.fe_1 \ldots e_n) = \sum_{i=1}^{m} w(x_i) + w(f) + \sum_{i=1}^{n} w(e_i)$$

We use the weight of succinct types to guide the algorithm in Figure 5. Given Select in Figure 4, the weight of a succinct type t in Γ_o is defined as:

$$w(t, \Gamma_o) = min(\{w(f) \mid (f : \tau) \in \mathsf{Select}(\Gamma_o, t)\})$$

5. Synthesis of All Terms in Long Normal Form

In this section we first motivate and introduce the backward search as the core mechanism of the algorithm, then we illustrate the algorithm and optimizations we implement in InSynth.

5.1 Backward Search

If we were to apply the rules in Figure 3 in a forward manner we could have started from any environment in the premise(s). However, there are infinitely many such environments. Moreover, rule Abs states that we can split Γ' in $3^{|\Gamma'|}$ possible ways into two subsets S and Γ, such that $\Gamma' = \Gamma \cup S$. However, only some environments and splittings will lead to the final conclusion $\Gamma_{init} \vdash_c S_{init} \rightarrow t_{init}$, where Γ_{init} and $S_{init} \rightarrow t_{init}$ are the initial environment and the desired type, respectively. This means we would have many unnecessary guesses and computations, leading to the wrong conclusions.

In contrast, if we use a backward search, then we start from the conclusion $\Gamma_{init} \vdash_c S_{init} \rightarrow t_{init}$ in Abs rule, and use a premise to create a hypothesis that a pattern $(\Gamma_{init} \cup S_{init})@\pi : t_{init}$ is derivable. Further, we need to check that it is indeed derivable by applying App rule. Now, unlike in the forward manner, thanks to the conclusion in App, we know the exact environment and the type t of the first premise. Selecting only types in Γ that have return types t introduce constraints on the other premises as well. The entire process is applied recursively until the initial hypothesis is proven or disproved. However, the constraints allow us to narrow the search. This is the main advantage of the backward search. All this suggest that the backward search is more efficient, revealing only the search space reachable from the initial environment and the desired type, unlike the forward search.

To formalize the backward search we reformulate the earlier rules by splitting them into the five new rules shown in Figures 6 and 8. One should read and apply the new rules in the forward manner. In the following subsections we explain those rules in more detail.

5.2 Main Algorithm

In this section we present an algorithm based on the succinct ground calculus that we use for finding type inhabitants. This algorithm is further used as an interactive tool for synthesizing expression suggestions from which a developer can select a suitable expression. To be applicable, such an algorithm needs to 1) generate multiple solutions, and 2) rank these solutions to maximize the chances of returning relevant expressions to the developer.

The algorithm is illustrated in Figure 5. As input Synthesize takes a desired type τ_o, and an environment Γ_o and outputs at most N terms in long normal form with a type τ_o. We first transform Γ_o and τ_o by σ into a succinct environment and a type, respectively. Then we execute the algorithm in three phases. First, Explore takes the succinct type and the environment as input, and returns the discovered search space reachable from the desired type and the initial environment. Next, GenerateP takes the space as input and outputs a set of patterns. Finally, GenerateT takes patterns, Γ_o, τ_o and the integer N, and produces at most N ranked terms.

The Explore and GenerateP use succinct types to prune the search space in a light way. They leave only a portion where declaration argument-return types conform. This helps GenerateT to perform heavy reconstruct only when needed, returning compilable terms.

```
fun Synthesize(Γo, τo, N):= {
  space := Explore(σ(Γo), σ(τo))
  patterns := GenerateP(space)
  return GenerateT(patterns, Γo, τo, N)
}
```

Figure 5. The algorithm that generates all terms with a given type τ_o and an environment Γ_o

The algorithm Synthesize represents the imperative description of RCN, in Figure 4. It is the RCN version with a bound on the number of terms, N. Moreover, it uses weights to steer the search towards useful terms. We discuss this at the end of the section. The backward search and search driven by weights make the new algorithm effective, practical and interactive. Synthesize produces the same set of solutions as RCN, given the same input, if we remove bounds d and N or gradually increase them. Note that the set of solutions might be infinite.

5.3 Exploration phase

The goal of Explore is to start from the desired succinct type and environment and gradually explore the search space. We split the algorithm into three key steps:

1. **Type reachability.** Given a succinct type t and Γ we want to find all types reachable from t. We specify this request by $t \underset{\Gamma}{\leadsto} ?$. We use the request to trigger the Match rule in Figure 3. By the rule, types in set S are reachable from type t, $A(t) = \emptyset$, in Γ, if $(S \to t) \in \Gamma$ holds. We denote this with *reachability* term, $t \underset{\Gamma}{\leadsto} (S, \Pi)$ (later we explain what the set Π is).
2. **Request propagation.** Once we discover that types S are reachable from t, we want to discover what types are reachable from any type $t' \in S$. Thus, we generate a new request $t' \underset{\Gamma}{\leadsto} ?$. New requests are issued with the Prop rule. In other words, we use the Prop rule to propagate the search.
3. **Environment extension.** However, t can be a function type, i.e., $t \equiv S' \to t'$ and $S' \neq \emptyset$. Thus, we introduce the Strip rule that transforms a request $(S \to t) \underset{\Gamma}{\leadsto} ?$ to a request $t \underset{\Gamma \cup S}{\leadsto} ?$. Now, we can further use the request $t \underset{\Gamma \cup S}{\leadsto} ?$ in the Match rule.

$$\textsc{Match}\ \frac{t \underset{\Gamma}{\leadsto} ? \qquad (S \to t) \in \Gamma \qquad A(t) = \emptyset}{t \underset{\Gamma}{\leadsto} (S, \emptyset)}$$

$$\textsc{Prop}\ \frac{t \underset{\Gamma}{\leadsto} (S, \emptyset) \qquad t' \in S}{t' \underset{\Gamma}{\leadsto} ?} \qquad \textsc{Strip}\ \frac{(S \to t) \underset{\Gamma}{\leadsto} ?}{t \underset{\Gamma \cup S}{\leadsto} ?}$$

Figure 6. Type reachability rules.

A set of reachability terms keep the information about the explored search space. Thus our goal is to derive all such terms starting from the desired type and the environment. We next give the detailed description of the Explore algorithm.

```
fun Explore(Γ, S→t) := {
  queue := {S→t ~>Γ ?}
  visited := ∅
  space := ∅
  while(queue ≠ ∅) {
    curr := queue.dequeue
    visited := visited ∪ {curr}
    t' ~>Γ' ? := Strip(curr)
    found := {Match(t' ~>Γ' ?, S'→t') | S'→t' ∈ Γ'}
    space := space ∪ found
    newr := {Prop(tf ~>Γf (Sf, ∅), t') | tf ~>Γf (Sf, ∅) ∈ found
                                           and t' ∈ Sf}
    queue := queue ∪ (newr \ visited)
  }
  return space
}
```

Figure 7. The algorithm that explores the search space.

To initiate the Explore algorithm in Figure 7 we create the request $(S \to t) \underset{\Gamma}{\leadsto} ?$, where $S \to t$ is the desired type, and Γ is the initial type environment. We put the request into a working queue. In the loop we process one request at the time, until queue is empty. First, we use Strip to obtain a new request $t' \underset{\Gamma'}{\leadsto} ?$ with an extended environment Γ'. Here, Strip is the function that implements the corresponding rule, Strip in Figure 3. It takes request $(S \to t) \underset{\Gamma}{\leadsto} ?$ and returns new request $t \underset{\Gamma \cup S}{\leadsto} ?$. In the same fashion, we implement the other two functions, Match that returns a reachability term, and Prop that returns a request. Next, by applying Match to $t' \underset{\Gamma'}{\leadsto} ?$ and every type in Γ' we find a set of reachability terms, found. We store the terms in the set space. The space set represents the entire search space discovered from the desired type and the initial environment. Finally, we propagate the search by issuing newr requests using the Prop function onto found. We update queue with these requests. We additionally keep the set of all visited requests, to avoid cycles in the exploration.

5.4 Pattern generation phase

In this phase we use the space explored by the Explore algorithm to create patterns. We start from the reachability terms with inhabited types, and use them to produce patterns and new inhabited types. We repeat the process until no new types can be inhabited.

$$\textsc{Prod}\ \frac{t \underset{\Gamma}{\leadsto} (\emptyset, \Pi)}{\Gamma @ \Pi : t}$$

$$\textsc{Transfer}\ \frac{t \underset{\Gamma}{\leadsto} (S \cup \{S' \to t'\}, \Pi) \qquad t' \underset{\Gamma \cup S'}{\leadsto} (\emptyset, \Pi')}{t \underset{\Gamma}{\leadsto} (S, \Pi \cup \{S' \to t'\})}$$

Figure 8. Pattern synthesis rules.

Initially, we divide the search space, space, into two groups: 1) leaves that contains reachability terms in the form $t \underset{\Gamma}{\leadsto} (\emptyset, \Pi)$, i.e., reachability terms with inhabited types, and 2) others that contains the remaining terms. The set Π collects succinct types that have an inhabitant. It is initialized by Match to an empty set. The Transfer rule, in Figure 8, turns $t \underset{\Gamma}{\leadsto} (S \cup \{S' \to t'\}, \Pi)$ into

```
fun GenerateP(space) := {
  patterns := ∅
  visited := ∅
  leaves := {x | x = t ~>_Γ (∅, ∅) and x ∈ space}
  others := space \ leaves
  while (leaves ≠ ∅) {
    t ~>_Γ (∅, Π) := leaves.dequeue
    visited := visited ∪ {t ~>_Γ (∅, Π)}
    patterns := patterns ∪ {Prod(t ~>_Γ (∅, Π))}
    compatible := {x | x = t' ~>_Γ' (S ∪ {S' → t}, Π')
                   and Γ = Γ' ∪ S' and x ∈ others}
    newt := {Transfer(x, t ~>_Γ (∅, Π)) | x ∈ compatible}
    newLeaves := {x | x = t' ~>_Γ' (∅, Π') and x ∈ newt}
    others := (others \ compatible) ∪ (newt \ newLeaves)
    leaves := leaves ∪ (newLeaves \ visited)
  }
  return patterns
}
```

Figure 9. The algorithm that generates patterns.

$t \underset{\Gamma}{\leadsto} (S, \Pi \cup \{S' \to t'\})$ if $\{S' \to t'\}$ is inhabited. We use Π to produce a pattern by the Prod rule.

In the loop we remove one term $t \underset{\Gamma}{\leadsto} (\emptyset, \Pi)$ from leaves to generate: 1) a pattern $\Gamma @ \Pi : t$ by the Prod function, and 2) the newt reachability terms by the Transfer function. To perform the latter we first calculate the set of compatible terms. Those are the reachability terms in form $t \underset{\Gamma}{\leadsto} (S \cup \{S' \to t'\}, \Pi)$, such that $\Gamma = \Gamma' \cup S'$ holds. Every term in compatible can be resolved with $t \underset{\Gamma}{\leadsto} (\emptyset, \Pi)$ by the Transfer rule. The result is the set of newt terms. These reachability terms can be split into two groups. The first group contains terms of the form $t' \underset{\Gamma'}{\leadsto} (\emptyset, \Pi')$, that we add to leaves. The second group contains the remaining terms and we add them to others. We also keep the set of visited leaves in order to avoid cycles in generation.

5.5 Term generation phase

In Figure 10 we illustrate the algorithm that finds at most N lambda expressions with the smallest weight. First, we introduce the notion of holes to define the partial expressions, and later we describe the algorithm GenerateT.

A typed hole $[\ ]_h : \tau$ is a constant $[\ ]$ with a name h and a type τ. Let V be a set of typed variables, and H a set of typed holes. Partial typed expressions are constructed according to the following syntax:

$$e ::= x \mid [\ ]_h : \tau \mid \lambda x{:}\tau.e \mid e\,e, \quad \text{where } x \in V \text{ and } [\ ]_h : \tau \in H$$

To derive the partial expressions in *long normal form* one can use the same APP and ABS rules in Figure 2, where $e_i, i = [1..m]$ and e are partial types expressions. Moreover, one can substitute all holes in a partial expression and get a new partial or complete expression, without holes. A hole $[\ ]_h : \tau$, in a judgment $\Gamma_o \vdash [\ ]_h : \tau$, can be substituted only with a partial expression $e : \tau$, where $\Gamma_o \vdash e : \tau$.

We next describe the GenerateT algorithm. We start from the desired type and original environment, follow patterns and gradually create and unfold partial expressions. During the process we keep partial expressions in the queue. Once a partial expression becomes complete, we store it in the set of snippets.

We use a priority queue to process partial expressions. The expressions are sorted by the weight in ascending order. We initiate the queue with $[\ ]_x : \tau_{init}$, where τ_{init} is the desired type. In the loop we process one partial expression at a time. The loop terminates either when the queue is empty or we find N expression. First, we remove the highest ranked partial expression, expr_p, from the priority queue. Then, we call the function findFirstHole, that for a given judgment $\Gamma_{init} \vdash \mathsf{expr}_p$ finds (if it exists) a hole $[\ ]_h : \tau_1 \to \cdots \to \tau_n \to v$ and its corresponding environment Γ_o. If expr_p has no holes, it is a complete lambda expression, i.e., a snippet that we will output to a user. Hence, we append it to snippets. If there is a hole in expr_p we build all partial expressions that can substitute the hole. We extend the environment and use patterns with the return type v to find declarations f. If the declaration has function type, we build the expression filling all arguments with fresh holes. (Note that the new holes might be substituted in a later iteration.) For each expression expr_{newp}, we build a substitution that maps a name of the hole to the expressions. We apply the substitution to substitute the hole with the new expression. We use the function w to calculate expression weights and store them in the priority queue. The weight of a hole is equal to zero. We find

```
fun GenerateT(patterns, Γ_init, τ_init, N) := {
  snippets := NIL
  pq := PriorityQueue.empty
  pq.put(0, [ ]_x : τ_init)
  while(pq.size > 0 and |snippets| < N){
    expr_p = pq.dequeue
    findFirstHole(Γ_init,expr_p) match {
      case None ⇒
        snippets.append(expr_p) //appends to the end
      case Some((Γ_o, [ ]_h : τ1→···→τn→v)) ⇒
        S→v := σ(τ1→···→τn→v)
        Γ := σ(Γ_o)
        //x1,...,xn are fresh
        Γ'_o := Γ_o ∪ {x1 : τ1,...,xn : τn}
        foreach ((Γ ∪ S)@S' : v) ∈ patterns //S' is binder
         foreach (f : ρ1→···→ρm→v) ∈ Select(Γ'_o, S'→v)
          expr_newp :=
           sub(expr_p, h ↣ (λx1...xn.f[ ]_r1 : ρ1...[ ]_rm : ρm))
          //r1,...,rm are fresh names
          pq.put(w(expr_newp), expr_newp)
    }
  }
  return snippets
}

fun findFirstHole(Γ_o, exp):= exp match {
   case [ ]_x : τ ⇒ Some((Γ_o, [ ]_x : τ))
   case λx1...xn.fe1...em ⇒
    Γ'_o := Γ_o ∪ {x1 : τ1,...,xn : τn} //x1,...,xn are fresh
    for(i ∈ [1..m])
      findFirstHole(Γ'_o, e_i) match {
        case Some(hole) ⇒ return Some(hole)
        case Node ⇒
      }
    None
 }

 fun sub(expr1, y ↣ expr2):= expr1 match {
  case [ ]_x : τ ⇒ if (x = y) expr2 else expr1
  case λx1...xn.fe1...em ⇒
     λx1...xn.f sub(e1, y ↣ exp2) ... sub(em, y ↣ exp2)
 }
```

Figure 10. A function that constructs the best N lambda terms in long normal form.

the partial expressions that replace the hole using patterns. First we calculate a succinct type $S \to v$ and environment Γ. We expand the environment to $\Gamma \cup S$ and use it with type v to find all patterns with form $(\Gamma \cup S)@S' : v$ in the pattern set. When we find all such sets S' we use them to select all type variables in Γ'_o whose type maps to a succinct type $S' \rightarrow v$. Once we have such a variable we use it to create the most general partial expression $\lambda x_1 \ldots x_n.f[\ ]_{r_1} : \rho_1 \ldots [\ ]_{r_m} : \rho_m$. Such an expression has holes at the places of f's arguments. In this way we gradually unfold a partial expression until it becomes complete.

5.6 Responsiveness

We use first two phases to synthesize patterns starting from the desired type and the initial environment. We referred to those phases as a *prover*. To be interactive we allow a user to specify a time limit for the prover. Due to time bound, we decide to interleave the two phases, such that whenever Explore discovers a new leaf, it immediately triggers GenerateP. Every time GenerateP is called it uses all discovered reachability terms to generate as many new patterns as possible. Moreover, to generate the best solutions, within a given time, we use a priority queue in Explore instead of the regular queue. Requests in the priority queue are sorted by weights. A weight of a request $t \underset{\Gamma}{\leadsto} ?$ is equal to a weight of type t in the initial environment. Additionally, we allow a user to specify a time limit for GenerateT.

5.7 Optimizations

To efficiently find the compatible set in GenerateP, we create a backward map that maps a term to its predecessor terms. Last reachability term_f that initiated creation of term, through propagation, is the predecessor of term. We build the map in Explore, that records all predecessors of a given term, by storing an entry (term, predecessors). By using the map, compatible becomes the predecessors set of $t \underset{\Gamma}{\leadsto} (\emptyset, \Pi)$. This way we do not preform expensive calculation of compatible. However, whenever a new term x is generate by Transfer(y, z) in GenerateP, we need to update the map by substituting every occurrence of y with x in the map. To speed up this process, for every term in the map we keep the list of entries where the term occurs.

6. Subtyping using Coercion Functions

We use a simple method of coercion functions [2, 17, 21] to extend our approach to deal with subtyping. We found that this method works well in practice. On the given set of basic types, we model each subtyping relation $v_1 <: v_2$ by introducing into the environment a fresh coercion expression $c_{12} : \{v_1\} \rightarrow v_2$. If there is an expression $e : \tau$, and e was generated using the coercion functions, then while translating e into simply typed lambda terms, the coercion is removed. Up to η-conversion, this approach generates all terms of the desired type in a system with subtyping on primitive types with the usual subtyping rules on function types.

In the standard lambda calculus there are three additional rules to handle subtyping: transitivity ($\tau_1 <: \tau_2$ and $\tau_2 <: \tau_3$ imply $\tau_1 <: \tau_3$), subsumption (if $e : \tau_1$ and $\tau_1 <: \tau_2$ then $e : \tau_2$), and the cvariant rule ($\tau_1 <: \rho_1$ and $\rho_2 <: \tau_2$ imply $\rho_1 \rightarrow \rho_2 <: \tau_1 \rightarrow \tau_2$). We proved that even with those new rules the complexity of the problem does not change and the type inhabitation remains a PSPACE-complete problem. If subtyping constraints are present, then the coercion functions are used in the construction of succinct patterns. However, in the RCN function the coercion functions are omitted when deriving new lambda terms.

7. Evaluation of the Effectiveness of InSynth

This section discusses our implementation, a set of benchmarks we used to evaluate InSynth, and the experimental results.

7.1 Implementation in Eclipse

We implemented InSynth as an Eclipse plugin that extends the code completion feature. It enables developers to accomplish a complex action with only a few keystrokes: declare a type of a term, invoke InSynth, and select one of the suggested expressions.

InSynth provides its functionality in Eclipse as a contribution to the standard Eclipse content assist framework and contributes its results to the list of content assist proposals. These proposals can be returned by invoking the content assist feature when Scala source files are edited (usually with Ctrl + Space). If the code completion is invoked at any valid program point in the source code, InSynth attempts to synthesize and return code snippets of the desired type. Only the top specified number of snippets are displayed as proposals in the content assist proposal list, in the order corresponding to the weighted ranking. InSynth supports invocation at any location immediately following declaration of a typed value, variable or a method, i.e. in the place of its definition and also at the place of method parameters, if condition expressions, and similar (where the type can be inferred). InSynth uses the Scala presentation compiler to extract program declarations and imported API functions visible at a given point. InSynth can be easily configured though standard Eclipse preference pages, and the user can set maximum execution time of the synthesis process, desired number of synthesized solutions and code style of Scala snippets.

7.2 Creating Benchmarks

There is no standardized set of benchmarks for the problem that we examine, so we constructed our own benchmark suite. We collected examples primarily from `http://www.java2s.com/`. These examples illustrate correct usage of Java API functions and classes in various scenarios. We manually translated the examples from Java into equivalent Scala code. Since only single class imports are used in the original examples, we generalized the import statements for the benchmarks to include more declarations and thereby made the synthesis problem more difficult by increasing the size of the search space.

One idea of measuring the effectiveness of a synthesis tool is to estimate its ability to reconstruct certain expressions from existing code. We arbitrarily chose some expressions from the collected examples, removed them and marked them as goal expressions that needed to be synthesized (we replaced them with a fresh value definition if the place of the expression was not valid for InSynth invocation). The resulting benchmark is a partial program, similar to a program sketch [23]. We measure whether InSynth can reconstruct an expression equal to the one removed, modulo literal constants (of integer, string, or boolean type). Our benchmark suite is available for download from the InSynth web site.

7.3 Corpus for Computing Symbol Usage Frequencies

Our algorithm searches for typed terms that can be derived from the initial environment and that minimize the weight function. To compute initial declaration weights we follow the steps presented in Section 4. The key step is to derive declarations frequencies. Hence, we collected a code corpus which dictates those initial weights. The corpus contains code statistics from 18 Java and Scala open-source projects. Table 3 lists those projects together with their description.

One of the analyzed projects is the Scala compiler, which is mainly written in the Scala language itself. In addition to the projects listed in Table 3, we analyzed the Scala standard library, which mainly consists of wrappers around Java API calls. We extracted the relevant information only about Java and Scala APIs, and ignored information specific to the projects themselves. Overall, we extracted 7516 declarations and identified a total of 90422 uses of these declarations. 98% of declarations have less than 100

	Benchmarks	Size	#Initial	No weights		No corpus		All				Provers	
				Rank	Total	Rank	Total	Rank	Prove	Recon	Total	Imogen	fCube
1	AWTPermissionStringname	2/2	5615	>10	5157	1	101	**1**	8	125	133	127	20123
2	BufferedInputStreamFileInputStream	3/2	3364	>10	2235	1	45	**1**	7	46	53	44	5827
3	BufferedOutputStream	3/2	3367	>10	2009	1	18	**1**	7	11	19	44	5781
4	BufferedReaderFileReaderfileReader	4/2	3364	>10	2276	2	69	**1**	7	43	50	44	0176
5	BufferedReaderInputStreamReader	4/2	3364	>10	2481	2	66	**1**	7	42	49	44	0175
6	BufferedReaderReaderin	5/4	4094	>10	5185	>10	4760	**6**	7	237	244	61	0228
7	ByteArrayInputStreambytebuf	4/4	3366	>10	5146	**3**	94	>10	4	18	22	44	5836
8	ByteArrayOutputStreamintsize	2/2	3363	>10	2583	2	51	**2**	8	63	70	44	5204
9	DatagramSocket	1/1	3246	>10	5024	1	74	**1**	7	80	88	38	5555
10	DataInputStreamFileInput	3/2	3364	>10	2643	1	20	**1**	6	46	52	44	5791
11	DataOutputStreamFileOutput	3/2	3364	>10	5189	1	29	**1**	7	38	45	44	5839
12	DefaultBoundedRangeModel	1/1	6673	>10	3353	1	220	**1**	10	257	266	193	36337
13	DisplayModeintwidthintheightintbit	2/2	4999	>10	6116	1	136	**1**	6	147	154	99	10525
14	FileInputStreamFileDescriptorfdObj	2/2	3366	>10	3882	3	24	**2**	6	17	23	44	3929
15	FileInputStreamStringname	2/2	3363	>10	2870	1	125	**1**	9	100	109	44	4425
16	FileOutputStreamFilefile	2/2	3364	>10	4878	1	86	**1**	8	51	60	44	4415
17	FileReaderFilefile	2/2	3365	>10	3484	2	37	**2**	7	13	20	44	4495
18	FileStringname	2/2	3363	>10	3697	1	169	**1**	7	155	163	44	5859
19	FileWriterFilefile	2/2	3366	>10	4255	1	40	**1**	8	28	36	45	4515
20	FileWriterLPT1	2/2	3363	6	3884	1	139	**1**	7	89	96	44	4461
21	GridBagConstraints	1/1	8402	>10	3419	1	3241	**1**	19	323	342	290	0121
22	GridBagLayout	1/1	8401	>10	2	1	1	**1**	0	1	1	290	56553
23	GroupLayoutContainerhost	4/2	6436	>10	4055	1	24	**1**	10	26	36	190	29794
24	ImageIconStringfilename	2/2	8277	>10	3625	2	495	**1**	13	154	167	300	50576
25	InputStreamReaderInputStreamin	3/3	3363	>10	3558	8	90	**4**	7	177	184	44	4507
26	JButtonStringtext	2/2	6434	>10	3289	2	117	**1**	9	85	95	184	27828
27	JCheckBoxStringtext	2/2	8401	>10	3738	3	134	**2**	18	50	68	188	4946
28	JformattedTextFieldAbstractFormatter	3/2	10700	>10	3087	**2**	2048	4	21	101	122	520	99238
29	JFormattedTextFieldFormatterformatter	2/2	9783	>10	3404	2	67	**2**	15	85	100	419	74713
30	JTableObjectnameObjectdata	3/3	8280	>10	3676	2	109	**2**	13	129	142	300	46738
31	JTextAreaStringtext	2/2	6433	>10	2012	**2**	232	>10	9	293	302	183	29601
32	JToggleButtonStringtext	2/2	8277	>10	3171	2	177	**2**	12	123	135	299	5231
33	JTree	1/1	8278	2	3534	1	3162	**1**	16	2022	2039	298	52417
34	JViewport	1/1	8282	8	5017	**1**	20	8	12	7	19	298	22946
35	JWindow	1/1	6434	3	4274	1	296	**1**	10	425	434	194	2862
36	LineNumberReaderReaderin	5/4	3363	>10	2315	>10	3770	**9**	6	233	239	44	5876
37	ObjectInputStreamInputStreamin	3/2	3367	>10	3093	1	20	**1**	6	29	35	44	5849
38	ObjectOutputStreamOutputStreamout	3/2	3364	>10	4883	1	31	**1**	7	47	54	44	5438
39	PipedReaderPipedWritersrc	2/2	3364	>10	2762	2	54	**2**	8	60	68	44	262
40	PipedWriter	1/1	3359	>10	4801	1	107	**1**	6	133	139	44	5432
41	Pointintxinty	3/1	4997	>10	2068	5	133	**2**	6	96	103	101	8573
42	PrintStreamOutputStreamout	3/2	3365	>10	2100	6	16	**1**	7	20	27	44	5841
43	PrintWriterBufferedWriter	4/3	3365	>10	2521	4	135	**4**	8	36	44	44	448
44	SequenceInputStreamInputStreams	5/3	3365	>10	4777	2	35	**2**	8	20	28	44	5862
45	ServerSocketintport	2/2	4094	>10	2285	2	28	**1**	6	57	63	61	11123
46	StreamTokenizerFileReaderfileReader	3/2	3365	>10	2012	1	34	**1**	8	57	65	44	5782
47	StringReaderStrings	2/2	3363	>10	2006	1	35	**1**	6	37	43	45	5746
48	TimerintvalueActionListeneract	3/3	6665	>10	2051	1	123	**1**	10	189	199	186	34841
49	TransferHandlerStringproperty	2/2	8648	>10	3911	1	27	**1**	14	17	31	319	67997
50	URLStringspecthrows	3/3	4093	>10	3302	6	124	**1**	8	175	183	60	11197

Table 2. Results of measuring overall effectiveness. The first 4 columns denote the ordinal and name of a benchmark, size of the desired snippet (in terms of number of declarations: with coercion function accounted/only visible) and the initial number of declarations seen at the invocation point. The subsequent columns denote the rank at which the desired snippet was found and (averaged) execution times in milliseconds for the algorithm with no weights, with weight but without use of input statistics, and with weights and input statistics (with the distribution of execution time between the engine and reconstruction parts). The last two columns show execution time for checking provability using the Imogen and fCube provers.

uses in the entire corpus, whereas the maximal number of occurrences of a single declaration is 5162 (for the symbol `&&`).

7.4 Platform for Experiments

We ran all experiments on a machine with a 3Ghz clock speed processor and 8MB of cache. We imposed a 2GB limit for allowed memory usage. Software configuration consisted of Ubuntu 12.04.1 LTS (64b) with Scala 2.9.3 (a nightly version), and Java(TM) Virtual Machine 1.6.0_24. The reconstruction part of InSynth is implemented sequentially and does not make use of multiple CPU cores.

7.5 Measuring Overall Effectiveness

In each benchmark, we invoked InSynth at the place where the goal expression was missing. We parametrized InSynth with N=10 and used a time limit of 0.5s seconds for *prover* (Section 5.6) and 7s for the reconstruction. By using a time limit, our goal was to evaluate the usability of InSynth in an interactive environment (which IDEs usually are).

We ran InSynth on the set of 50 benchmarks. Results are shown in Table 2. The Size column represents the size of the goal expression in terms of number of declarations in its structure. It is illustrated in the form `c/nc` where `c` is the size with coercion functions and `nc` is the size without. Note that when `c>nc` holds, InSynth needs to deal with subtyping to synthesize the goal expression. The #Initial column represents the size of the initial environment, i.e. the number of initial type declarations that InSynth extracts at a given program point. The following columns are partitioned into three groups, one for each variant of the synthesis algorithm: 1) the

Project	Description
Akka	Transactional actors
CCSTM	Software transactional memory
GooChaSca	Google Charts API for Scala
Kestrel	Tiny queue system based on starling
LiftWeb	Web framework
LiftTicket	Issue ticket system
O/R Broker	JDBC framework with support for externalized SQL
scala0.orm	O/R mapping tool
ScalaCheck	Unit test automation
Scala compiler	Compiles Scala source to Java bytecode
Scala Migrations	Database migrations
ScalaNLP	Natural language processing
ScalaQuery	Typesafe database query API
Scalaz	"Scala on steroidz" - scala extensions
simpledb-scala-binding	Bindings for Amazon's SimpleDB
smr	Map Reduce implementation
Specs	Behaviour Driven Development framework
Talking Puffin	Twitter client

Table 3. Scala open-source projects used for the corpus extraction.

algorithm without weights (the No weights column), 2) the algorithm with weights derived without the corpus (the No corpus column) and 3) finally, the full algorithm, with weights derived using the corpus (the All column).

In all groups, Rank represents the rank of the goal expression in the resulting list, and Total represents the total execution time of synthesis. The distribution of the execution time between *prover* and the reconstruction is shown in columns Prove and Recon, respectively. The last column group gives execution times of two state-of-the-art intuitionistic theorem provers (`Imogen` [19] and `fCube` [9]) employed for checking provability of inhabitation problems for the benchmarks.

Table 2 shows the differences in both effectiveness and execution time between the variants of the algorithm.

First, the table shows that the algorithm without weights does not perform well and finds the goal expressions in only 4 out of 50 cases and executes by more than an order of magnitude slower than the other variants. This is due to the fact that without the utilization of the weight function to guide the search, InSynth is driven into a wrong direction toward less important solutions, whose ranks are as low as the actual solutions.

Second, we can see that adding weights to terms helps the search drastically and the algorithm without corpus fails to find the goal expression in only 2 cases. Also, the running times are decreased substantially. In 33 cases, this variant finds the solution with the same rank as the variant which incorporates corpus, while on 4 of them it finds the solution of a higher rank. This suggests that in some cases, synthesis does not benefit from the derived corpus – initial weights defined by it are not biased favorably and do not direct the search toward the goal expression.

Third, we show the times for `Imogen` and `fCube` provers on the same set of benchmarks. We can see that our *prover* is up to 2 orders of magnitude faster than `Imogen` and up to 4 orders than `fCube`. Note that reconstruction of terms in `Imogen` was limited to 10 seconds and `Imogen` failed to reconstruct a proof within that time limit in all cases.

In the case of the full algorithm, the results show that the desired expressions appear in the top 10 suggested snippets in 48 benchmarks (96%). They appear as the top snippet (with rank 1) in 32 benchmarks (64%). Note that our corpus (Section 7.3) is derived from a source code base that is disjoint (and somewhat different in nature) from the one used for benchmarks. This suggests that even a knowledge corpus derived from unrelated code increases the effectiveness of the synthesis process; a specialized corpus would probably further increase the quality of results.

In summary, the expected snippets were found among the top 10 solutions in many benchmarks. Weights play an important role in finding and ranking those snippets high in a short period of time (on average around just 145ms). Finally, our *prover* outperforms two state of the art provers `Imogen` and `fCube`. These results suggest that InSynth is effective in quickly finding (i.e. synthesizing) desired expressions at various places in source code.

8. Related Work

Several tools including Prospector [18], XSnippet [22], Strathcona [13], PARSEWeb [27] and SNIFF [4] that generate or search for relevant code examples have been proposed. In contrast to all these tools we support expressions with higher order functions. Additionally, we synthesize snippets using all visible methods in a context, whereas the other existing tools build or present them only if they exist in a corpus. Prospector, Strathcona and PARSEWeb do not incorporate the extracted examples into the current program context; this requires additional effort on the part of the programmer. Moreover, Prospector does not solve queries with multiple argument methods unless the user initiates multiple queries. In contrast, we generate full expressions using just a single query. We could not effectively compare InSynth with those tools, since unfortunately, the authors did not report exact running times.

We next provide more detailed descriptions for some of the tools, and we compare their functionality to InSynth. InSynth is similar in operation to Eclipse content assist proposals [26] and it implements the same behaviour. More advanced solutions appeared recently, such as [3], that proposes declarations, and the Eclipse code recommenders [8], that suggests declarations and code templates. Both systems use API declaration call statistics from the existing code examples in order to offer suggestions to the developer with appropriate statistical confidence value. InSynth is fundamentally different from these approaches (it even subsumes them) and can synthesize even code fragments that never previously occurred in code.

Prospector [18] uses a type graph and searches for the shortest path from a receiver type, $type_{in}$, to the desire type, $type_{out}$. The nodes of the graph are monomorphic types, and the edges are the names of the methods. The nodes are connected based on the method signature. Prospector also encodes subtypes and downcasts into the graph. The query is formulated through $type_{in}$ and $type_{out}$. The solution is a chain of method calls that starts at $type_{in}$ and ends at $type_{out}$. Prospector ranks solutions by the length, preferring shorter solutions. In contrast, we find solutions that have minimal weights. This potentially enables us to get solutions that have better quality, since the shortest solution may not be the most relevant. Furthermore, in order to fill in the method parameters, a user needs to initiate multiple queries in Prospector. In InSynth this is done automatically. Prospector uses a corpus for down-casting, whereas we use it to guide the search and rank the solutions. Moreover, Prospector has no knowledge of what methods are used most frequently. Unfortunately, we could not compare our implementation with Prospector, because it was not publicly available. XSnippet [22] offers a range of queries from generalized to specialized. The tool uses them to extract Java code from the sample repository. XSnippet ranks solutions based on their length, frequency, and context-sensitive as well as context-independent heuristics. In order to narrow the search the tool uses the parental structure of the class where the query is initiated to compare it with the parents of the classes in the corpus. The returned examples are not adjusted automatically into a context—the user needs to do this manually. Similar to Prospector the user needs to initiate additional queries to fill in the method parameters. In Strathcona [13], a query based on the structure of the code under development is automatically extracted. One cannot explicitly specify the desired type. Thus, the returned set of examples is often irrelevant. Moreover, in contrast to InSynth, those examples can not be fitted into the code without additional interventions. PARSEWeb [27] uses the Google code search engine to get relevant code examples. The solutions are ranked by length and frequency. In InSynth the length of a returned snippet also plays an important role in ranking the snippets but InSynth also has an additional component by taking into account also the proximity of derived snippets and the point where InSynth was invoked. The main idea behind the SNIFF [4] tool is to use natural language to search for code examples. The authors collected the corpus of examples and annotated them with keywords, and attached them to corresponding method calls in the examples. The keywords are collected from the available API documentation. InSynth is based on a logical formalism, so it can overcome the gap between programming languages and natural language.

The synthesized code in our approach is extracted from the proof derivation. Similar ideas have been exploited in the context of sophisticated dependently typed languages and proof assistants [1]. Our goal is to apply it to simpler scenarios, where propositions are only partial specifications of the code, as in the current programming practice. Agda is a dependently typed programming language and proof assistant. Using Agda's Emacs interface, programs can be developed incrementally, leaving parts of the program unfinished. By type checking the unfinished program, the programmer can get useful information on how to fill in the missing parts. The Emacs interface also provides syntax highlighting and code navigation facilities. However, because it is a new language and lacks large examples, it is difficult to evaluate this functionality on larger numbers of declarations.

There are several tools for the Haskell API search. The Hoogle [14] search engine searches for a single function that has either a given type or a given name in Haskell, but it does not return a composed expression of the given type. The Hayoo [12] search engine does not use types for searching functions: its search is based on function names. The main difference between Djinn [25] and our system is that Djinn generates a Haskell expression of a given type, but unlike our system it does not use weights to guide the algorithm and rank solutions. Recently we have witnessed a renewed interest in semi-automated code completion [20]. The tool [20] generates partial expressions to help a programmer write code more easily. While their tool helps to guess the method name based on the given arguments, or it suggests arguments based on the method name, we generate complete expressions based only on the type constraints. In addition, our approach also supports higher order functions, and the returned code snippets can be arbitrarily nested and complex: there is no bound on the number and depth of arguments. This allows us to automatically synthesize larger pieces of code in practice, as our evaluation shows. In that sense, our result is a step further from simple completion to synthesis.

The use of type constraints was explored in interactive theorem provers, as well as in synthesis of code fragments. SearchIsos [5] uses type constraints to search for lemmas in Coq, but it does not use weights to guide the algorithm and rank the solutions. Having the type constraints, a natural step towards the construction of proofs is the use of the Curry-Howard isomorphism. The drawback of this approach is the lack of a mechanism that would automatically enumerate all the proofs. By representing proofs using graphs, the problem of their enumeration was shown to be theoretically solvable [29], but there is a large gap between a theoretical result and an effective tool. Furthermore, InSynth can not only enumerate terms but also rank them and return a desired number of best-ranked ones.

Having a witness term that a type is inhabited is a vital ingredient of our tool, so one could think of InSynth as a prover for propositional intuitionistic logic (with substantial additional functionality). Among recent modern provers are Imogen [19] and fCube [9]. These tools can reason about more expressive fragments of logic: they support not only implication but also intuitionistic counterparts for other propositional operators such as $\vee$, $\Rightarrow$, $\Leftrightarrow$, and Imogen also supports first-order and not only propositional fragment. Our results on fairly large benchmarks suggests that InSynth is faster for our purpose. This is not entirely surprising because these tools are not necessarily optimized for the task that we aim to solve (looking for shallow proofs from many assumptions), and often do not have efficient representation of large initial environments. The main purpose of our comparison is to show that our technique is no worse than the existing ones for our purpose, even when used to merely check the existence of proofs. What is more important than performance is that InSynth produces not only one proof, but a representation of *all* proofs, along with their ranking. This additional functionality of our algorithm is essential for the intended application: using type inhabitation as a generalization of code completion.

For a given type InSynth produces a finite representation of all the type inhabitants. In general, if an expression is an inhabitant of the given type, there is a derivation that proves that fact. Using Curry-Howard isomorphism for each proof derivation there is a lambda term representing it. The problem of enumerating all the proofs for a given formula is an important research topic, since it can be also used to answer other problems like provability or definability. We keep the system of patterns to represent all the type inhabitants, achieving this way finite representation of a possibly infinite set of the proofs. In [7] the authors used a semi-grammatically description of all proof-terms for minimal predicate logic and a positive sequent calculus. The use of grammars is an alternative to our use of graphs as the representation for all solutions; we therefore expect that grammars could similarly be used as the starting point for a practical system such as ours.

9. Conclusions

We have presented the design and implementation of a code completion inspired by complete implementation of type inhabitation for the simply typed lambda calculus. Our algorithm uses succinct types, an efficient representation for types, terms, and environments that takes into account that the order of assumptions is unimportant. Our approach generates a representation of all solutions (a set of pattens), from which it can extract any desired number of solutions.

To further increase the usefulness of generated results, we introduce the ability to assign weights to terms and types. The resulting algorithm performs search for expressions of a given type in a type environment while minimizing the weight, and preserves the completeness. The presence of weights increases the quality of the generated results. To compute weights we use the proximity to the declaration point as well as weights mined from a corpus. We have deployed the algorithm in an IDE for Scala. Our evaluation on synthesis problems constructed from API usage indicate that the technique is practical and that several technical ingredients had to come together to make it powerful enough to work in practice. Our tool and additional evaluation details are publicly available.

Our experience suggests that the idea of computing type inhabitats using succinct types and weights is useful by itself. Moreover, our subsequent exploration suggests that these techniques can also serve as the initial phase of semantic-based synthesis [16]. The idea is to generate a stream of type-correct solutions and then filter it to contain only expressions that meet given specifications, such as postconditions (or, in the special case, input/output examples).

Note that the approach based on the techniques we presented can also generate programs with various control patterns, because conditionals, loops, and recursion schemas can themselves be viewed as higher-order functions. Although we believe the current results to be a good starting point for such tasks, further techniques may be needed to control larger search spaces for more complex code correctness criteria and larger expected code sizes.

Acknowledgments

We thank the anonymous reviewers of PLDI 2013 for useful feedback. We are grateful to Iulian Dragos and the Scala IDE team for the collaboration on integrating InSynth into Scala IDE. We thank Martin Odersky, Aleksandar Prokopec, and Sean McLaughlin for useful discussions. Tihomir Gvero is supported by the European Research Council (ERC) Project "Implicit Programming", `http://lara.epfl.ch/w/impro`. Ivan Kuraj was supported by a Google Summer of Code project.

References

[1] A. Bove, P. Dybjer, and U. Norell. A brief overview of Agda - a functional language with dependent types. In *TPHOLs*, 2009.

[2] V. Breazu-Tannen, T. Coquand, C. A. Gunter, and A. Scedrov. Inheritance as implicit coercion. *Inf. Comput.*, 93:172–221, July 1991. ISSN 0890-5401. doi: 10.1016/0890-5401(91)90055-7.

[3] M. Bruch, M. Monperrus, and M. Mezini. Learning from examples to improve code completion systems. In *ESEC/SIGSOFT FSE*, pages 213–222, 2009.

[4] S. Chatterjee, S. Juvekar, and K. Sen. SNIFF: A search engine for java using free-form queries. FASE '09, pages 385–400, 2009.

[5] D. Delahaye. Information retrieval in a Coq proof library using type isomorphisms. In *TYPES*, pages 131–147, 1999.

[6] G. Dowek. Higher-order unification and matching. *Handbook of automated reasoning*, II:1009–1062, 2001.

[7] G. Dowek and Y. Jiang. Enumerating proofs of positive formulae. *Comput. J.*, 52(7):799–807, Oct. 2009. ISSN 0010-4620.

[8] Eclipse Code Recommenders. `http://www.eclipse.org/recommenders/`.

[9] M. Ferrari, C. Fiorentini, and G. Fiorino. fCube: An efficient prover for intuitionistic propositional logic. In *LPAR (Yogyakarta)*, 2010.

[10] T. Gvero, V. Kuncak, and R. Piskac. Interactive synthesis of code snippets (tool demonstration). In *23rd Int. Conf. Computer Aided Verification, July 14-20*, 2011.

[11] T. Gvero, V. Kuncak, I. Kuraj, and R. Piskac. On complete completion using types and weights. Technical report, EPFL, December 2012.

[12] Hayoo! API Search. `http://holumbus.fh-wedel.de/hayoo/hayoo.html`.

[13] R. Holmes and G. C. Murphy. Using structural context to recommend source code examples. ICSE '05, pages 117–125, 2005.

[14] Hoogle API Search. `http://www.haskell.org/hoogle/`.

[15] IntelliJ IDEA website, 2011. URL `http://www.jetbrains.com/idea/`.

[16] I. Kuraj. Interactive code generation. Master's thesis, EPFL, February 2013.

[17] Z. Luo. Coercions in a polymorphic type system. *Mathematical Structures in Computer Science*, 18(4):729–751, 2008.

[18] D. Mandelin, L. Xu, R. Bodík, and D. Kimelman. Jungloid mining: helping to navigate the api jungle. In *PLDI*, 2005.

[19] S. McLaughlin and F. Pfenning. Efficient intuitionistic theorem proving with the polarized inverse method. In *CADE*, 2009.

[20] D. Perelman, S. Gulwani, T. Ball, and D. Grossman. Type-directed completion of partial expressions. In *PLDI*, pages 275–286, 2012.

[21] J. C. Reynolds. Using category theory to design implicit conversions and generic operators. In *Semantics-Directed Compiler Generation*, pages 211–258, 1980.

[22] N. Sahavechaphan and K. Claypool. Xsnippet: mining for sample code. In *OOPSLA*, 2006. ISBN 1-59593-348-4.

[23] A. Solar-Lezama, G. Arnold, L. Tancau, R. Bodík, V. A. Saraswat, and S. A. Seshia. Sketching stencils. In *PLDI*, 2007.

[24] R. Statman. Intuitionistic propositional logic is polynomial-space complete. *Theoretical Computer Science*, 9(1):67 – 72, 1979.

[25] The Djinn Theorem Prover. `http://www.augustsson.net/Darcs/Djinn/`.

[26] The Eclipse Foundation. `http://www.eclipse.org/`.

[27] S. Thummalapenta and T. Xie. PARSEWeb: a programmer assistant for reusing open source code on the web. In *ASE*, 2007.

[28] P. Urzyczyn. Inhabitation in typed lambda-calculi (a syntactic approach). In *TLCA*, 1997.

[29] J. B. Wells and B. Yakobowski. Graph-based proof counting and enumeration with applications for program fragment synthesis. In *LOPSTR*, pages 262–277, 2004.

Fast Condensation of the Program Dependence Graph

Nick P. Johnson Taewook Oh Ayal Zaks† David I. August

Princeton University, Princeton, NJ
{npjohnso, twoh, august}@princeton.edu

†Intel Corporation, Haifa, Israel
ayal.zaks@intel.com

Abstract

Aggressive compiler optimizations are formulated around the Program Dependence Graph (PDG). Many techniques, including loop fission and parallelization are concerned primarily with dependence cycles in the PDG. The Directed Acyclic Graph of Strongly Connected Components (DAG_{SCC}) represents these cycles directly. The naïve method to construct the DAG_{SCC} first computes the full PDG. This approach limits adoption of aggressive optimizations because the number of analysis queries grows quadratically with program size, making DAG_{SCC} construction expensive. Consequently, compilers optimize small scopes with weaker but faster analyses.

We observe that many PDG edges do not affect the DAG_{SCC} and that ignoring them cannot affect clients of the DAG_{SCC}. Exploiting this insight, we present an algorithm to omit those analysis queries to compute the DAG_{SCC} efficiently. Across 366 hot loops from 20 SPEC2006 benchmarks, this method computes the DAG_{SCC} in half of the time using half as many queries.

Categories and Subject Descriptors D.3.4 [*Programming Languages*]: Processors—Compilers

Keywords Demand-driven analysis; Dependence analysis; Program Dependence Graph; Strongly connected components.

1. Introduction

Users expect compilers to be fast; one study [34] indicates that programmer productivity drops when compilation takes more than a few seconds. If the benefit of aggressive optimizations does not outweigh the cost of long compile times, users will avoid them. Making matters worse, analysis precision drastically affects optimization quality [3, 8, 28, 29, 36], and precise analyses tend to be more expensive than their less-precise counterparts [7, 15] and scale poorly [16, 26]. Despite the performance potential of state-of-the-art transformations, common compilers optimize small, intra-procedural scopes, instead favoring short compilation times.

To extend the benefits of precise analysis to the wider community, we must first address compiler scalability. We envision a future where common compilers feature aggressive optimizations such as automatic parallelization [4, 24, 28–30, 35, 36] by default. The critical path to this end is the precise analysis of large program scopes.

Many compiler techniques are formulated around the Program Dependence Graph (PDG) [6]. Many of those techniques (*clients* of the PDG) focus primarily on dependence cycles, identified as the Strongly Connected Components (SCCs) of the PDG (Figure 1(b)).

The Directed Acyclic Graph of the SCCs (*DAG_{SCC}*) or *condensation* of the PDG is a representation that makes dependence cycles explicit (Figure 1(c)). The DAG_{SCC} contains enough information to support a broad class of compiler techniques. For instance, automatic parallelization [4, 24, 28–30, 35, 36] asks: *can two operations execute concurrently without races, or is synchronization needed?* Determine whether their respective components are ordered in the DAG_{SCC}. Program slicing [17, 37, 39] asks: *Which earlier operations may affect an operation?* All operations in the same component and operations in components ordered before it in the DAG_{SCC}. Loop fission [2, 20] asks: *Can a loop be split?* Ensure that no operations in the second half belong to the same component as, or any component ordered before components from the first half.

The DAG_{SCC} holds less information than the PDG and should be cheaper to compute. Yet, standard practice wastefully builds the full PDG before condensing it to a DAG_{SCC}. The number of potential PDG edges grows quadratically with the scope size (in vertices). Each potential edge adds a quantum of analysis effort (a *query*) to determine whether that edge exists. The running times of these queries sum to make DAG_{SCC} construction prohibitively expensive, especially since precise analyses are costly [7, 15, 16, 26].

Compiler authors should not sacrifice analysis precision for cost since imprecision limits optimization [3, 8, 28, 29, 36]. Instead, they should use the most precise analyses and reduce compilation time by exploiting the reduced information of the DAG_{SCC}.

This paper presents a technique that computes the DAG_{SCC} more efficiently than by finding SCCs of the full PDG. Using partial dependence information, the algorithm identifies dependence edges which cannot affect the clients of the DAG_{SCC}. Next, the algorithm uses a Demand-Driven Analysis framework [13, 32, 40] to elide those analysis queries and thus expend effort only on important analysis queries rather than the whole program. This improvement is orthogonal to speeding up each query; it reduces DAG_{SCC} construction time yet maintains high analysis quality since no analysis algorithms change. With these savings, compiler authors may pursue more aggressive and costlier analyses while providing the same quality of service to compiler end-users. This work contributes:

- a fast client-agnostic DAG_{SCC} algorithm (Section 3.2);
- an extension of that algorithm for PS-DSWP [28] (Section 3.3);
- a proof of correctness (Section 4); and,
- evaluation of the performance benefit (Section 5).

Averaged across 366 hot loops from 20 SPEC2006 benchmarks, the proposed method computes the DAG_{SCC} with 49.0% fewer queries, reducing construction time by 53.1% (Section 5.2). These savings dramatically affect compiler scalability. The proposed method analyzes half of the hot loops (weighted by coverage) in 456.6s on average, saving 111.5s over the baseline (Section 5.3). These savings broaden the class of transformations that fit the user's time constraints without reducing analysis precision.

PLDI'13, June 16–19, 2013, Seattle, WA, USA.

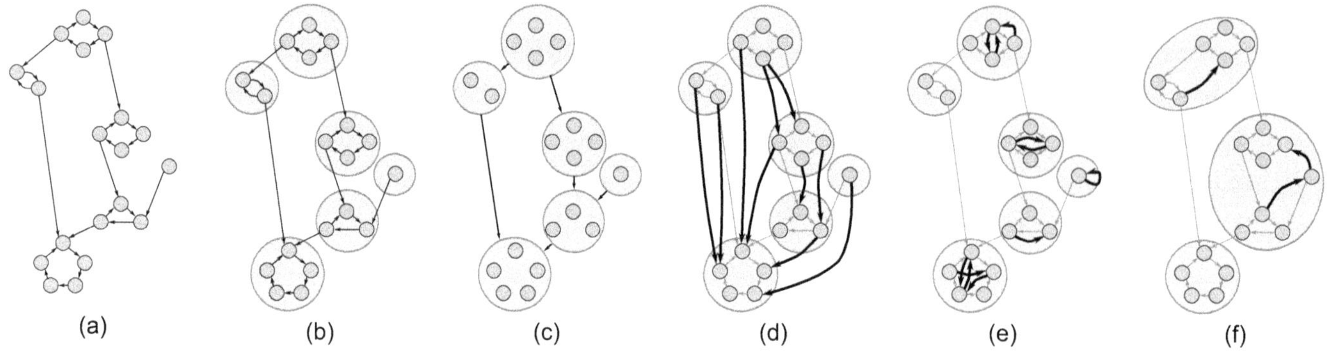

Figure 1: (a) Example PDG; (b) Strongly Connected Components; (c) Condensation of the example; (d) Additional edges which redundantly order components do not change the condensation, thus have no marginal value; (e) Additional edges within a component do not change the condensation, thus have no marginal value; (f) Additional edges which violate ordering are valuable since they may change condensation.

2. Insight

To construct the DAG_{SCC} of a loop, a naïve compiler considers the presence or absence of a dependence edge between every pair of vertices (operations), and condenses that into a DAG_{SCC}. However, not all dependences in the PDG contribute equally to the structure of the DAG_{SCC}. Once a PDG is partially computed, some edges have no marginal value since they do not affect the structure of the DAG_{SCC} and thus cannot affect the answer to optimization questions. By eliminating these redundant dependence edges, a compiler computes the DAG_{SCC} with fewer dependence queries in less time. Compiler authors may spend these savings on costlier analyses in pursuit of aggressive optimization.

An ideal algorithm would perform queries only for those edges found in a transitive reduction of the PDG (to *join* components), as well as queries to ensure the absence of back edges (to *separate* components). This, however, leads to a problem: the compiler does not know the PDG *a priori*, and so it cannot distinguish redundant edges from important ones. Instead, this paper proposes an approximation of that ideal.

Figure 1(d) demonstrates one class of redundant dependences: edges that order two vertices whose components are already ordered. This is a large class of dependences, which grows quadratically in the number of components and quadratically in component size. Across SPEC2006, empirical study indicates that two-thirds of all loops have 5–968 SCCs and two-thirds of all components have 8.4–1118.0 vertices.

Another class of redundant dependences are demonstrated by Figure 1(e): edges within a component other than a minimum cycle that spans the component. This class grows quadratically in component size and linearly in the number of components.

The only dependences which contribute to finding the condensation graph are the class which join separate components, demonstrated in Figure 1(f). These grow quadratically in the size of components and quadratically in the number of components. Although this is a large class, any one dependence between a pair of components will constrain the entire component. Conversely, the absence of these dependences also has value, since only after analysis returns *negative* results can the algorithm confidently report that the separate components are separate.

By periodically interrupting PDG construction to recompute strongly connected components, the proposed algorithm eliminates queries for dependences which are definitely in classes (d) and (e) while focusing on those dependence queries which seem to be within class (f). This approach is informed by the following heuristic: if the compiler can build large components quickly, it can safely exclude more edges. Further, this technique performs more computation to actively search for opportunities to elide queries. This strategy will not be faster in the worst case since the overhead of recomputing components may overwhelm the benefits for loops with a very low average component size. However, the common case is more amenable to this strategy; experiments show that the proposed method is faster for all but 14 of 366 loops.

3. Efficient DAG_{SCC} Construction Algorithm

In a Program Dependence Graph (PDG), each instruction in the loop is represented as a vertex. Edges are drawn to represent control and data dependences. Figure 2(a) shows an example of a PDG.

Control dependences represent cases where one instruction may prevent another instruction from executing; for instance, an `if`-statement controls its `then`- and `else`-clauses. Data dependences represent the flow of data between instructions. We distinguish *register* data dependences from *memory* data dependences. Register and control dependences are computed quickly in practice.

Memory dependences represent data *flow* through a memory location, or additional constraints such as *anti-* and *output*-dependences. Exactly determining memory dependences is undecidable. To mitigate this, standard practice allows analyses to fail: given a pair of operations which access memory, report *no-* or *must*-depend, or fall-back to *may*-depend when an answer cannot be decided. Clients interpret may-depend conservatively.

We use `Query`(v_1.inst, v_2.inst, type) to denote a demand-driven analysis query that determines whether there is a memory dependence from the instruction associated with vertex v_1 to the instruction associated with vertex v_2; type is either *Loop-Carried* or *Intra-Iteration*. Any analysis—no matter its internal structure or operation—can be packaged to provide this query interface.

In the algorithms below, `TarjanSCC` refers to Tarjan's Algorithm for Strongly Connected Components [33]. Tarjan's algorithm reports SCC structure as well as a topological sort of those components and runs in time linear in the number of vertices and edges.

3.1 Baseline Algorithm

The baseline algorithm (Algorithm 1) builds a full PDG, including all register, control and memory dependences. To find memory dependences, it queries every pair of vertices (corresponding to instructions in the IR) which access memory to determine if there is a loop-carried or intra-iteration memory dependence. It then computes the strongly connected components of that PDG.

Algorithm 1: Baseline computeDagScc(V)

```
let E := computeRegisterDeps(V) ∪ computeControlDeps(V);
foreach vertex v_src ∈ V which accesses memory do
    foreach vertex v_dst ∈ V which accesses memory do
        if Query(v_src.inst, v_dst.inst, Loop-Carried) then
            let E := E ∪ {⟨v_src, v_dst, Loop-Carried⟩};
        end
        if Query(v_src.inst, v_dst.inst, Intra-Iteration) then
            let E := E ∪ {⟨v_src, v_dst, Intra-Iteration⟩};
        end
    end
end
return TarjanSCC(V, E);
```

3.2 Client-Agnostic Algorithm

We first present a client-agnostic version of the proposed algorithm, listed in Algorithm 2. This algorithm is written without destructive updates to simplify the proofs in Section 4, though a real implementation may save space by overwriting old values. We label points "X" and "Y" to clarify those proofs.

Similar to the baseline algorithm, the client-agnostic method starts by computing register and control dependences. This yields a PDG at Point X which is only partially computed since it lacks memory dependences. Next, it performs queries only between the vertices of select components in `withTheGrain` and `againstTheGrain`. These components are selected so that they will quickly cause components to merge into larger components. This leads to a savings in the number of memory dependence queries since dependences between vertices in a common component cannot further constrain the DAG_{SCC}.

For simplicity of implementation, we chose to recompute the SCCs by invoking `TarjanSCC` multiple times rather than using an incremental component maintenance algorithm. This reduces the amount of code to write and allows us to use simpler data structures internally. The cost of computing SCCs does not have a significant impact on overall performance.

Algorithm 2: Client-Agnostic computeDagScc(V)

```
let E := computeRegisterDeps(V) ∪ computeControlDeps(V) ;
let TopSort_0 := TarjanSCC(V, E) ;
• (Point X)
let E_0 := E ∪ withTheGrain(E, TopSort_0) ;
for i = 1 to ∞ do
    • (Point Y)
    let E' := againstTheGrain(TopSort_{i-1}) ;
    if E' = ∅ then
        return TopSort_{i-1} ;
    end
    let E'_i := E_{i-1} ∪ E' ;
    let TopSort_i := TarjanSCC(V, E'_i) ;
    let E_i := E'_i ∪ withTheGrain(E'_i, TopSort_i) ;
end
```

The routine `withTheGrain` (Algorithm 3) considers pairs of components c_{early} and c_{late} where c_{early} appears *before* c_{late} in the topological sorting of components. We exploit the feature that Tarjan's algorithm provides a topological sorting of the components with no additional computation. Figure 2(a) shows a topological sort. `withTheGrain` only performs queries that flow along topological order (i.e. from c_{early} to c_{late}), and only between components that are not already immediately ordered.[1] Such queries neither cause separate components to merge, nor invalidate the topological sorting of components, as illustrated in Figure 2(b).

[1] This test should exclude components that are *ordered*. We use *immediate ordering* as a fast approximation to avoid transitive closure. Consequently, `withTheGrain` may conservatively add some edges from class 1(d).

Algorithm 3: withTheGrain(E_0, TopSort)

```
let E' := ∅;
let N := size(TopSort);
for i = N-1 down to 0 do
    let c_late := TopSort(i);
    for j = i-1 down to 0 do
        let c_early := TopSort(j);
        if ¬hasEdge(c_early, c_late, E_0) then
            let E' := E' ∪ findOneEdge(c_early, c_late);
        end
    end
end
return E' ;
```

The routine `againstTheGrain` (Algorithm 4) searches for dependences between pairs of components. Unlike `withTheGrain`, `againstTheGrain` only performs queries which may add edges that violate topological sort order, i.e. those from a vertex in a component c_{late} to a vertex in a topologically-earlier c_{early}. The rationale is that such queries quickly form larger components (Figure 2(c)). Large components have a compounding effect, further reducing the number of queries performed later. This routine performs enough queries to test every absence of an edge if none exists, allowing the algorithm to report that two components are separate.

It may surprise some readers that `againstTheGrain` has a `break` statement in its inner loop. This `break` stops searching for edges *from* a given component after it finds one, allowing the algorithm to recompute SCCs before resuming the search. This `break` is not necessary for correctness, however, it benefits performance. By recomputing SCCs, this formulation of `againstTheGrain` merges SCCs early, actively searching for opportunities to skip more queries. Later invocations of `againstTheGrain` perform fewer queries because there are fewer, larger components.

Algorithm 4: againstTheGrain(TopSort)

```
let E := ∅;
let N := size(TopSort);
for i = N-1 down to 0 do
    let c_late := TopSort(i);
    for j = i-1 down to 0 do
        let c_early := TopSort(j);
        let E' := findOneEdge(c_late, c_early);
        let E := E ∪ E';
        if E' ≠ ∅ then
            break;
        end
    end
end
return E;
```

The routine `findOneEdge` (Algorithm 5) performs queries from a source component to destination component. It stops after it finds the first edge between them since additional edges would order those two components redundantly.

3.3 Client-Aware DAG_{SCC} Constructions

The DAG_{SCC} guides clients such as DSWP [29] or loop fission [2, 20]. Some clients want more information than the DAG_{SCC} offers. The proposed algorithm may be extended to needs of particular clients. Despite these additional requirements, one can implement these extensions while achieving comparable performance improvements over the baseline. Two dimensions characterize client-specific extensions of the algorithm: additional requirements of dependence information and opportunities to abort early.

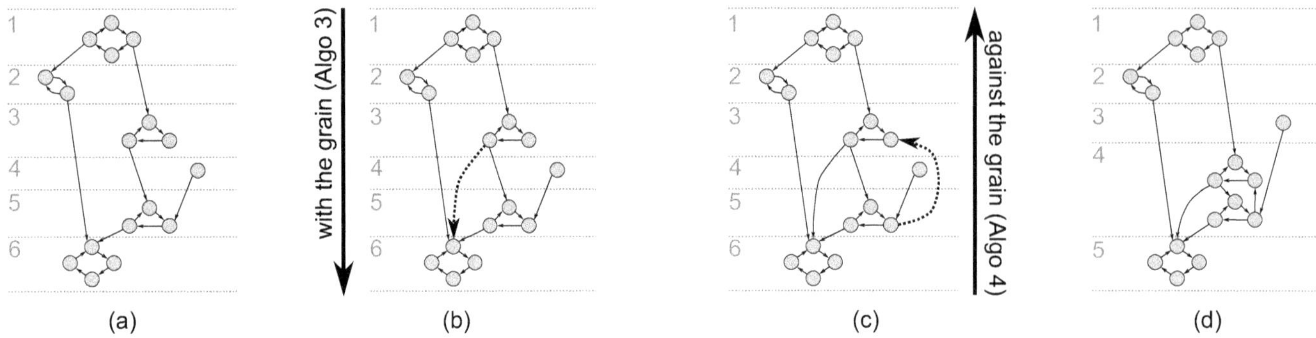

Figure 2: A partially computed PDG. (a) Topological sort (grey lines) imposes a total order on the partially ordered components. (b) `withTheGrain` (Algorithm 3) performs queries to discover edges between components with increasing position. Such edges neither cause SCCs to merge nor invalidate the topological sort. Here, a new edge is discovered from component three to six. (c) `againstTheGrain` (Algorithm 4) performs queries to discover edges between components with decreasing position. Here, a new edge is discovered from component five to three. (d) When `againstTheGrain` discovers new edges the topological sort is invalidated and components may merge.

Algorithm 5: findOneEdge(c_{src}, c_{dst})

```
foreach vertex v_src ∈ c_src which accesses memory do
    foreach vertex v_dst ∈ c_dst which accesses memory do
        if Query(v_src.inst, v_dst.inst, Loop-Carried) then
            return {⟨v_src, v_dst, Loop-Carried⟩};
        end
    end
end
foreach vertex v_src ∈ c_src which accesses memory do
    foreach vertex v_dst ∈ c_dst which accesses memory do
        if Query(v_src.inst, v_dst.inst, Intra-Iteration) then
            return {⟨v_src, v_dst, Intra-Iteration⟩};
        end
    end
end
return ∅;
```

Parallel Stage Decoupled Software Pipelining (PS-DSWP) is an illustrative example of such a client. PS-DSWP is an automatic thread-extraction technique with great performance potential [28, 36]. PS-DSWP partitions the $\mathrm{DAG_{SCC}}$ into pipeline stages such that all communication and synchronization flow forward in pipeline order (i.e. forbidding cyclic communication among worker threads). PS-DSWP delivers scalable speedups when a large *parallel stage* is available; conversely, PS-DSWP does not transform the code when no significant parallel stage is present.

PS-DSWP requires slightly more dependence information than is present in the $\mathrm{DAG_{SCC}}$, thus creating a meaningful evaluation scenario. Beyond the $\mathrm{DAG_{SCC}}$, PS-DSWP classifies each SCC as either *DOALL* or *Sequential* according to the absence or presence of loop-carried dependences. Parallel stages are assembled from the DOALL SCCs such that no loop-carried dependence exists among the operations in the parallel stage. Algorithm 2 does not guarantee that such queries will be performed. To support PS-DSWP, the algorithm must perform additional queries to classify each SCC as DOALL or Sequential. These additional queries are still fewer than the full PDG and $\mathrm{DAG_{SCC}}$ guides the compiler to search for such queries. Furthermore, $\mathrm{DAG_{SCC}}$ construction may abort as soon as no significant parallel stage is possible.

We extend Algorithm 2 for the needs of PS-DSWP in Algorithm 6. The routine `checkReflexiveLC` checks for loop-carried dependences from any operation in a DOALL SCC to itself, stopping after it finds one. `checkWithinSccLC` checks for loop-carried dependences from any operation located in a DOALL SCC to any other operation in the same SCC. The latter contains the former, but experience suggests that prioritizing reflexive queries tends to exclude many components from the parallel stage after only a linear number of queries, whereas querying in `checkWithinSccLC` is quadratic. At the end, the algorithm invokes `checkWithinSccLC` again since components have grown, potentially including more loop-carried dependences. These checks are cheaper than full PDG construction since they only query among DOALL SCCs.

Algorithm 6: PS-DSWP-Aware computeDagScc(V)

```
let E := computeRegisterDeps(V) ∪ computeControlDeps(V);
let TopSort := TarjanSCC(V, E);
abortIfPsInsubstantial(V,E,TopSort);
let E := E ∪ checkReflexiveLC(V);
abortIfPsInsubstantial(V,E,TopSort);
let E := E ∪ checkWithinSccLC(TopSort) ;
abortIfPsInsubstantial(V,E,TopSort);
let E := E ∪ withTheGrain(E, TopSort);
while true do
    let E' := againstTheGrain(TopSort);
    if E' = ∅ then
        break;
    end
    let E := E ∪ E';
    let TopSort := TarjanSCC(V, E);
    abortIfPsInsubstantial(V,E,TopSort);
    let E := E ∪ withTheGrain(E, TopSort) ;
end
let E := E ∪ checkBetweenDoallSccs(TopSort) ;
abortIfPsInsubstantial(V,E,TopSort);
let E := E ∪ checkWithinSccLC(TopSort) ;
return TopSort ;
```

Loop-carried dependences between DOALL SCCs prevent the simultaneous assignment of those components to the parallel stage. The routine `checkBetweenDoallSccs` performs queries to find such dependences. These checks are cheaper than full PDG construction, since they only consider pairs of DOALL SCCs. `abortIfPsInsubstantial` cancels construction if no substantial parallel stage is present whenever the upper bound on the parallel stage may change. For evaluation, we say a stage is "substantial" if it contains memory accesses or calls.

4. Proof of Correctness

We present a proof that our proposed method (Algorithm 2) produces a $\mathrm{DAG_{SCC}}$ that is equivalent to the one produced by the baseline method (Algorithm 1), both in terms of partitioning the set of vertices V into the same SCCs, and in terms of drawing the same edges between SCCs.

Both algorithms partition the same set of vertices V. Let C_B, C_P represent the components returned by the baseline and proposed algorithms, respectively. Each algorithm computes its own set of edges E_B and E_P, respectively, between pairs of vertices in V. Two components in the DAG_{SCC} are connected with an edge if there exists an edge between members of those components: for any components $c_1, c_2 \in C_B$, we write $c_1 \rightarrow_B c_2$ iff there is an edge $\langle v_1, v_2 \rangle \in E_B$ such that $v_1 \in c_1$ and $v_2 \in c_2$. Similarly, for any components $c_1, c_2 \in C_P$, we write $c_1 \rightarrow_P c_2$ iff there is an edge $\langle v_1, v_2 \rangle \in E_P$ such that $v_1 \in c_1$ and $v_2 \in c_2$.

Let $B(v) \in C_B$ denote the strongly connected component which contains vertex v as reported by the baseline algorithm. Let $P(v) \in C_P$ denote the strongly connected component which contains v as reported by the proposed algorithm.

We state our equivalence in Theorems 1 and 2.

Theorem 1 (C_B and C_P induce the same partition of V). *For every $t, u \in V$, $B(t) = B(u)$ iff $P(t) = P(u)$.*

Proof. Follows immediately from Lemmas 3 and 5. □

Theorem 2 ($\langle C_B, \rightarrow_B \rangle$ is isomorphic to $\langle C_P, \rightarrow_P \rangle$). *For every $t, u \in V$, $B(t) \rightarrow_B B(u)$ iff $P(t) \rightarrow_P P(u)$.*

Proof. We construct a correspondence $\Psi = B(v) \mapsto P(v)$.

Lemmas 3 and 5 show that Ψ is a bijective function.

Lemmas 4 and 6 show that $t \rightarrow_B u$ iff $\Psi(t) \rightarrow_P \Psi(u)$. □

We prove both Theorems using the following lemmas.

Lemma 1 (Forward Preservation of Edges, Simplified). *Ignoring the* `break` *in Algorithm 4, if $\langle t, u \rangle \in E_B$ then $P(t) \rightarrow_P P(u)$.*

Proof. During an invocation of the proposed method (Algorithm 2), execution will necessarily reach Point Y.

Components evolve during the execution of the proposed algorithm; to avoid confusion we refer to specific versions of the components. Let $P_i(v)$ denote the strongly connected component which contains vertex v at Point Y in the i-th iteration of the loop. In other words, $P_i(v)$ finds the component that contains v within the variable TopSort_{i-1}. Note that $P(v)$ is the value of $P_i(v)$ during the final iteration.

We consider three cases based on the relative positions of $P_i(t)$ and $P_i(u)$ in the topological sort of components reported by `TarjanSCC`, observed at Point Y.

Case 1: During any iteration i, $P_i(u)$ appears before $P_i(t)$ in the topological sort.

During that iteration, the invocation of `againstTheGrain` (Algorithm 4) necessarily reaches an iteration during which $c_{\text{late}} = P_i(t)$. It visits every earlier component c_{early}, invoking `findOneEdge` on each until an edge is discovered. Ignoring the `break` statement in Algorithm 4, we will reach an iteration in which $c_{\text{early}} = P_i(u)$.

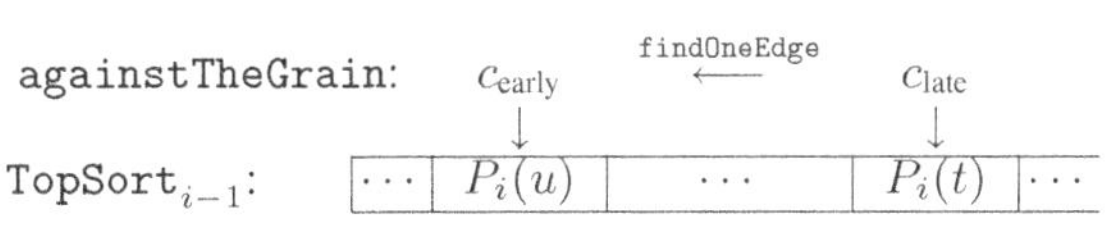

`findOneEdge` (Algorithm 5) will perform queries between the elements of $P_i(t)$ and $P_i(u)$ until an edge is found.

During the execution of the baseline algorithm, the call to Query(t.inst, u.inst, f) returns `true` given that $\langle t, u \rangle \in E_B$. Note that `Query` depends only on its arguments, so it behaves the same during the execution of the proposed algorithm.

If `findOneEdge` reaches the iteration where $(v_{\text{src}}, v_{\text{dst}}) = (t, u)$, then Query($t$.inst, u.inst, f) will again return `true`, thus adding the edge $\langle t, u \rangle$. The only case it may not reach that iteration is when `findOneEdge` finds some other edge between those components. Thus, $P_i(t) \rightarrow_P P_i(u)$.

Case 2: During any iteration i, $P_i(t)$ appears at the same position as $P_i(u)$ in the topological sort. That is, $P_i(t) = P_i(u)$.

By reflexivity, $P_i(t) \rightarrow_P P_i(u)$.

Case 3: $P_i(u)$ never appears before or at the same position as $P_i(t)$ in the topological sort during any iteration.

$P_1(t)$ appears before $P_1(u)$ in the topological sort of components during the first iteration of the loop. The topological sort is not updated between Point X and Point Y in the first iteration, so $P_1(t)$ appears before $P_1(u)$ in the topological ordering before the invocation of `withTheGrain` (Point X in Algorithm 2).

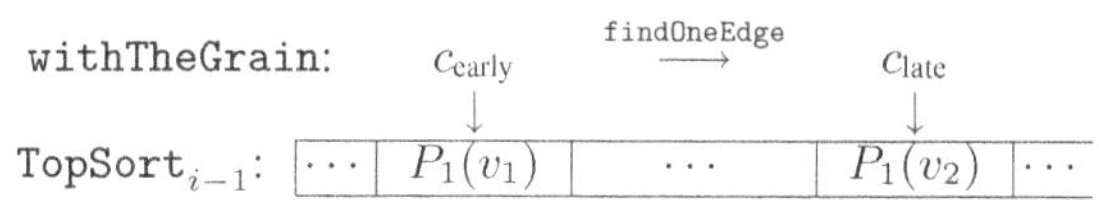

The algorithm `withTheGrain` necessarily reaches an iteration during which $c_{\text{early}} = P_1(t)$ and $c_{\text{late}} = P_1(u)$. If there is not already an immediate ordering relationship $P_1(t) \rightarrow_P P_1(u)$, `withTheGrain` passes those components to `findOneEdge`. Since $\langle t, u \rangle \in E_B$, we know that Query($t$.inst, u.inst, f) returned `true`. Thus, `findOneEdge` must find an edge (either $\langle t, u \rangle$ or an earlier one) between these components: $P_1(t) \rightarrow_P P_1(u)$.

In all cases, we have $P_i(t) \rightarrow_P P_i(u)$ for some i.

Observe that the proposed algorithm may add edges to the graph, but never removes edges from the graph. Adding edges may cause two separate components to merge into one, but never splits a component. Thus, for any vertex v and iteration i: $P_{i-1}(v) \subseteq P_i(v)$. Since $P(v)$ is the value of $P_j(v)$ in the final iteration j, it follows that $P(t) \rightarrow_P P(u)$. □

Lemma 2. *Considering the* `break` *in Algorithm 4, if $\langle t, u \rangle \in E_B$ then $P(t) \rightarrow_P P(u)$.*

Proof. The only difference between the simplified and proposed algorithms occurs in Lemma 1, Case 1: during iteration i, $P_i(u)$ appears before $P_i(t)$ in the topological sort.

The invocation of `againstTheGrain` (Algorithm 4) necessarily reaches an iteration during which $c_{\text{late}} = P_i(t)$. It visits every earlier component c_{early} invoking `findOneEdge` until an edge is discovered.

Suppose there is an intervening component $P_i(x) \neq P_i(u)$ such that `findOneEdge` discovers an edge $\langle w, x \rangle$ from $w \in P_i(t)$ to $x \in P_i(x)$. This edge causes the loop to break before visiting $c_{\text{early}} = P_i(u)$.

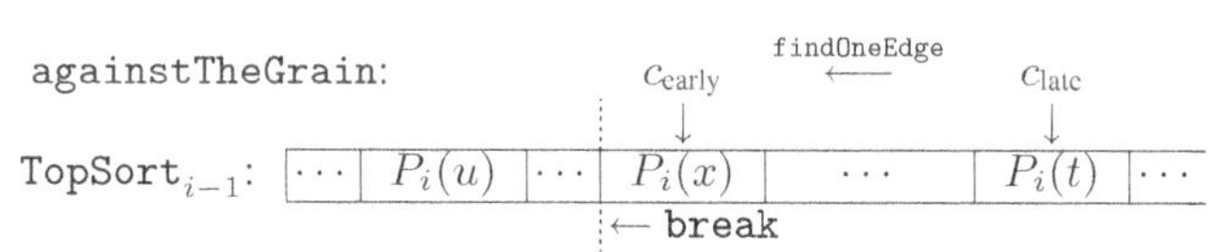

After the new edge is found, the algorithm recomputes components and may change their relative positions. Either $P_{i+1}(u)$ precedes $P_{i+1}(t)$ in the topological sort TopSort_{i+1}, or they merge, or $P_{i+1}(t)$ precedes $P_{i+1}(u)$. In the latter case, the subsequent invocation of `withTheGrain` immediately detects an edge from a vertex in $P_{i+1}(t)$ to a vertex in $P_{i+1}(u)$. Thus we need only consider the case in which they maintain their relative topological order.

We argue inductively that such an iteration of Algorithm 2 will be followed by another iteration that falls into Case 1, yet has one fewer intervening component. Assume that $P_{i+1}(u)$ precedes

$P_{i+1}(t)$. Observe that the component $P_{i+1}(x)$ cannot appear before $P_{i+1}(t)$ because of the newly discovered edge $\langle w, x\rangle$. Consequently, there is one fewer intervening component that could cause an later invocations of `againstTheGrain` to break. As a new edge $\langle w, x\rangle$ was found, the loop in Algorithm 2 will perform at least one more iteration. Thus, in the next iteration `againstTheGrain` will be one `break` closer to Lemma 1. After sufficient iterations, all intervening components have been eliminated and Lemma 1 Case 1 applies.

□

Lemmas 1 and 2 demonstrate that edges in E_B will order components in C_P. We next strengthen this statement to show that edges between components in C_B will order components in C_P in Lemma 4, but first we prove the following.

Lemma 3 (Wholeness of Components, Forward). *For any vertices $t, u \in V$, if $B(t) = B(u)$ then $P(t) = P(u)$.*

Proof. Vertices t and u belong to the same strongly connected component of C_B, so there is a path from t to u:

$$\langle t, t_1\rangle, \langle t_1, t_2\rangle, \ldots, \langle t_{j-1}, t_j\rangle, \langle t_j, u\rangle \in E_B$$

and a path from u to t:

$$\langle u, u_1\rangle, \langle u_1, u_2\rangle \ldots, \langle u_{k-1}, u_k\rangle, \langle u_k, t\rangle \in E_B.$$

By Lemma 2 this implies that there is a cycle across the corresponding components of C_P: $P(t) \rightarrow_P P(t_1) \rightarrow_P \ldots \rightarrow_P P(t_j) \rightarrow_P P(u) \rightarrow_P P(u_1) \rightarrow_P \ldots \rightarrow_P P(u_k) \rightarrow_P P(t)$.

This, in turn, implies that $P(t) = P(t_1) = \ldots = P(t_j) = P(u) = P(u_1) = \ldots = P(u_k)$. □

Lemma 4 (Preservation of Structure, Forward). *For any vertices $t, u \in V$, if $B(t) \rightarrow_B B(u)$ then $P(t) \rightarrow_P P(u)$.*

Proof. By definition of $\rightarrow_B$, there is an edge $\langle x, y\rangle \in E_B$ such that $x \in B(t)$ and $y \in B(u)$. By Lemma 2 we know $P(x) \rightarrow_P P(y)$.

Since components are a partition of all vertices, $x \in B(t)$ implies $B(t) = B(x)$. Similarly, $B(u) = B(y)$.

By Lemma 3, $P(t) = P(x)$ and $P(u) = P(y)$.

Thus, $P(t) \rightarrow_P P(u)$. □

Lemma 5 (Wholeness of Components, Reverse). *For any two vertices $t, u \in V$, if $P(t) = P(u)$ then $B(t) = B(u)$.*

Proof. Vertices t and u belong to the same strongly connected component of C_P, so there is a path from t to u:

$$\langle t, t_1\rangle, \langle t_1, t_2\rangle, \ldots, \langle t_{j-1}, t_j\rangle, \langle t_j, u\rangle \in E_P$$

and a path from u to t:

$$\langle u, u_1\rangle, \langle u_1, u_2\rangle \ldots, \langle u_{k-1}, u_k\rangle, \langle u_k, t\rangle \in E_P.$$

Since the baseline performs *all* queries, $E_P \subseteq E_B$, and the same a cycle connects the corresponding components of C_B: $B(t) \rightarrow_P B(t_1) \rightarrow_P \ldots \rightarrow_P B(t_j) \rightarrow_P B(u) \rightarrow_P B(u_1) \rightarrow_P \ldots \rightarrow_P B(u_k) \rightarrow_P B(t)$.

This, in turn, implies that $B(t) = B(t_1) = \ldots = B(t_j) = B(u) = B(u_1) = \ldots = B(u_k)$. □

Lemma 6 (Preservation of Structure, Reverse). *For any vertices $t, u \in V$, if $P(t) \rightarrow_P P(u)$ then $B(t) \rightarrow_B B(u)$.*

Proof. By definition of $\rightarrow_P$, there is an edge $e = \langle x, y\rangle \in E_P$ such that $x \in P(t)$ and $y \in P(u)$. Since components are a partition of vertices, $P(x) = P(t)$ and $P(y) = P(u)$. By Lemma 5, it follows that $B(x) = B(t)$ and $B(y) = B(u)$. Since $E_P \subseteq E_B$, $e \in E_B$ and therefore $B(x) \rightarrow_B B(y)$. By substitution we obtain that $B(t) \rightarrow_B B(u)$ as desired. □

5. Empirical Validation

To evaluate this technique, we implement the baseline (Section 3.1), client-agnostic (Section 3.2), and PS-DSWP-aware (Section 3.3) algorithms in the LLVM infrastructure [21] revision 164307. Each algorithm is augmented with a 30 minute timeout.

Each algorithm uses the same data structures to represent the program dependence graph and strongly connected components. The PDG data structure is a sorted adjacency-list representation, which performs well since PDGs tend to be sparse graphs. The data structure is capable of representing partial knowledge of memory dependences: between any pair of vertices, a memory dependence is *present*, *absent*, or *unknown*. Thus, none of the algorithms will ever perform the same query more than once. The cost of manipulating the data structure had negligible effect on most experiments.

We evaluated these techniques on 20 SPEC 2006 benchmarks [31]. The experiments exclude eight FORTRAN benchmarks because the front-end supports only C and C++. Each benchmark was compiled under two optimization regimens. The less-optimized regimen uses `clang -O1`. The more-optimized regimen is designed to create larger scopes that are harder to analyze. Specifically, we apply internalization,[2] devirtualization of indirect calls, and `-O3`.

We profile each benchmark to identify 366 hot loops. Hot loops are those loops whose running time consumes at least 5% of application running time, and which perform at least five iterations per invocation, on average. The hot loops found among the benchmarks are summarized in Table 1. It is not always possible to correlate hot loops between the less- and more-optimized regimens; optimization may break a hot loop into several, or reduce the execution time of a loop below the threshold.

Experiments run on an eight core 1.6GHz Xeon E5310. The machine has 8GB RAM and runs 64-bit Linux 2.6.32. All benchmarks are compiled to 64-bit, little-endian code. In this section, we use *instruction* to refer to an LLVM virtual instruction. All measurements experienced negligible variance.

5.1 Evaluation Analysis Framework

The overall performance benefit of the proposed algorithms depends greatly upon the performance characteristics of the underlying analysis framework. Many algorithms implement dependence analysis [9, 10, 13, 18, 22, 23, 32, 38, 40], yet these algorithms are not easily compared. Each occupies a distinct niche in the precision-efficiency trade-off [14].

We fix a single dependence analysis framework across all experiments. This framework combines separate analyses under a common, demand-driven interface. The interface accepts *queries* about the intra-/inter-iteration dependence relationship between two memory operations with respect to a loop of interest. As each query enters the analysis framework, it passes through each analysis in turn to find the most optimistic answer; thus, the combination features the strengths of each member.

The evaluation analysis includes nineteen separate analyses developed internally at Princeton. These analyses are designed to support automatic thread-extraction in general purpose codes such as SPEC INT [31]. Thus, our analyses emphasize precision in codes with linked-data structures and are sensitive to loops. The suite of analyses includes control- and data-flow sensitive analyses, calling-context sensitive analyses, induction-variable analyses, analyses specializing in external functions from the C and C++ standard libraries, a rudimentary shape analysis, and analyses which reason about call sites. These analyses are either purely demand-driven or

[2] Internalization asserts that the input program is the *whole* program, i.e. that no external libraries reference any of the program's exported symbols. It is similar to marking all global symbols with C's `static` keyword.

Benchmark	Less-Optimized Regimen					More-Optimized Regimen				
	Hot Loops	Coverage		Size		Hot Loops	Coverage		Size	
		Hottest	Coldest	Largest	Smallest		Hottest	Coldest	Largest	Smallest
400.perlbench	4	25.6%	5.5%	163 (#1)	9 (#4)	3	25.8%	11.1%	266 (#2)	66 (#3)
401.bzip2	9	73.5%	8.5%	597 (#7)	7 (#9)	9	71.5%	5.6%	2236 (#9)	7 (#8)
403.gcc	16	79.2%	5.0%	5800 (#1)	7 (#12)	11	79.8%	5.4%	11326 (#1)	40 (#2)
429.mcf	7	99.9%	6.3%	81 (#4)	26 (#1)	8	99.7%	8.6%	1352 (#1)	47 (#8)
433.milc	9	52.5%	7.5%	159 (#1)	12 (#9)	15	32.5%	5.4%	298 (#1)	19 (#7)
435.gromacs	5	99.9%	18.6%	671 (#1)	23 (#5)	8	99.4%	6.2%	10191 (#1)	72 (#7)
444.namd	16	99.9%	5.2%	1266 (#10)	9 (#2)	21	100.0%	6.1%	1271 (#14)	66 (#10)
445.gobmk	20	100.0%	5.0%	3868 (#7)	12 (#11)	20	99.9%	5.3%	3099 (#7)	39 (#13)
447.dealII	20	100.0%	5.5%	140 (#17)	10 (#10)	16	100.0%	5.6%	788 (#4)	6 (#6)
450.soplex	6	50.7%	6.4%	118 (#5)	15 (#6)	9	69.4%	5.5%	1034 (#4)	15 (#7)
453.povray	6	99.9%	28.8%	90 (#5)	23 (#6)	7	99.9%	5.6%	258 (#1)	13 (#7)
456.hmmer	6	100.0%	6.4%	277 (#2)	11 (#4)	6	100.0%	7.2%	240 (#1)	13 (#5)
458.sjeng	7	100.0%	9.5%	779 (#4)	147 (#1)	9	99.9%	5.4%	3359 (#7)	13 (#8)
462.libquantum	15	74.2%	4.9%	49 (#4)	5 (#6)	12	94.6%	5.7%	97 (#1)	9 (#11)
464.h264ref	8	100.0%	6.7%	680 (#8)	159 (#3)	8	100.0%	11.1%	1483 (#8)	128 (#3)
470.lbm	2	99.8%	99.1%	475 (#2)	23 (#1)	2	99.6%	99.0%	1175 (#1)	475 (#2)
471.omnetpp	2	100.0%	13.2%	23 (#1)	23 (#1)	2	100.0%	19.0%	37 (#2)	22 (#1)
473.astar	9	65.4%	5.8%	61 (#3)	9 (#9)	12	56.6%	6.7%	238 (#1)	17 (#6)
482.sphinx3	10	95.0%	6.6%	429 (#2)	12 (#10)	8	94.5%	5.0%	2170 (#2)	12 (#1)
483.xalancbmk	2	98.0%	7.2%	28 (#2)	12 (#1)	1	97.6%	97.6%	36 (#1)	36 (#1)

Table 1: Hot loops from SPEC2006. "Coverage" is the percent of running time spent in the loop. "Size" is the number of LLVM IR instructions contained in the loop. "Largest" and "smallest" also contain the loop id, where #1 is the hottest loop, and #n is the coldest.

are largely demand-driven, i.e., a significant portion of analysis effort is performed in response to a query, not ahead of time.

Analysis services most queries quickly: half of all queries take less than 287.6μs (460K cycles); two thirds take less than 601.3μs (962K cycles); 90% take less than 1.0ms (2M cycles). Differences in query running time are due to differences in query complexity: for instance, analyzing a call site is generally more expensive than analyzing a `load` instruction. Across multiple runs, the running time of any one query exhibits negligible variance, suggesting that noise has minimal impact on timing results.

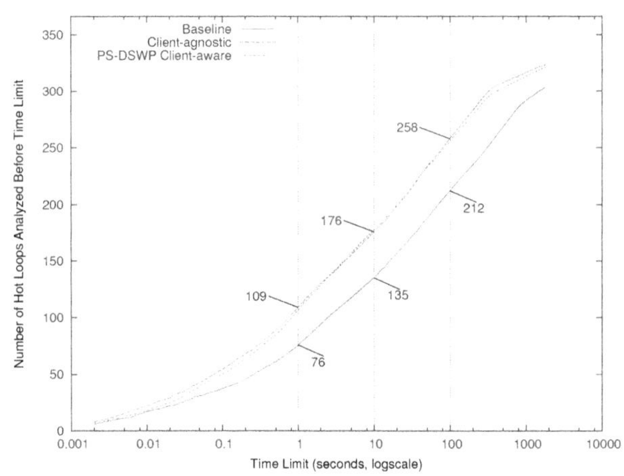

Figure 3: Largest sequence of hot loops analyzed before timeout.

5.2 Performance Improvement

The most direct impact of the proposed algorithm is a reduction in DAG_{SCC} construction latency.

Figure 4(a) shows the time required to construct a DAG_{SCC} for both the client-agnostic and PS-DSWP-aware algorithms. Each point represents a loop from the less- or more-optimized regimen, normalized to the running time of the baseline algorithm (smaller is better). The client-agnostic method is faster for all but 14 of 366 loops.

Performance improvements are due primarily to a reduction in the number of dependence analysis queries. Empirical results concur with the claim that the client-agnostic algorithm normalized running time is linear in the normalized number of queries. The Pearson's Correlation between the normalized construction time and normalized number of queries is 0.63.

Figures 4(b)–(d) show factors which contribute to the reduction in queries. The fraction of queries performed by the client-agnostic method is related to both the average size of SCCs as well as the number of SCCs, yet is only mildly affected by the size of the region. This is because the algorithm elides queries for a class of redundant edges that grows with both average SCC size and number of SCCs (illustrated in Figure 1(d)–(e)). Empirical results concur with the claim that the client-agnostic method elides a greater fraction of queries in loops with fewer or larger components. The Spearman's Rank[3] between the average SCC size and normalized number of queries is -0.52. The Spearman's Rank between the number of SCCs and the normalized number of queries is 0.24.

One extreme outlier experiences more than 2× slowdown: the fourth-hottest loop from `458.sjeng`, located in function `std_eval`. In that loop, the proposed methods decrease the number of queries and the time spent on analysis queries. The cost of computing SCCs several times is less than the savings from fewer queries. However, the overhead of manipulating the sparse graph data structure is exceptionally high for this loop, canceling the savings. Further engineering work could reduce this overhead.

[3] Spearman's Rank is a measure of statistical dependence [19]. We use Spearman's Rank to support the claim of a *monotone* relationship, which is strictly weaker than a *linear* relationship indicated by Pearson's Correlation.

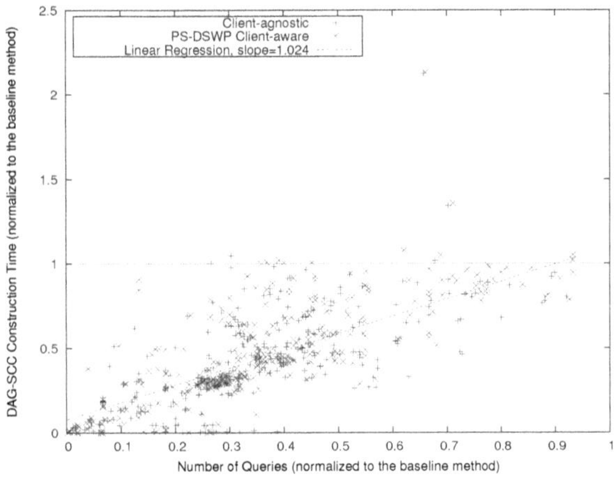

(a) Improvement in Time vs Improvement in Queries

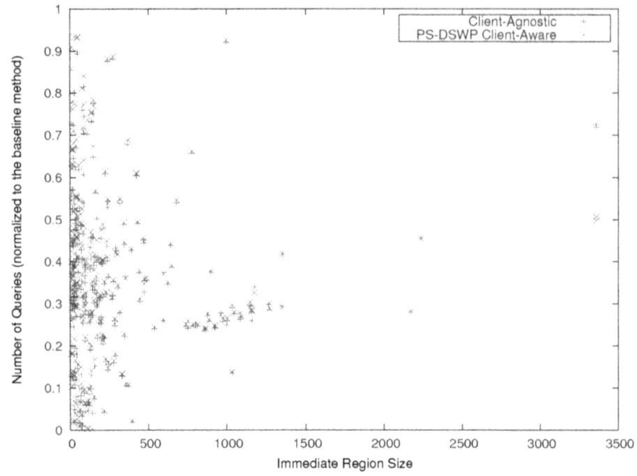

(b) Improvement in Queries vs Size of Region

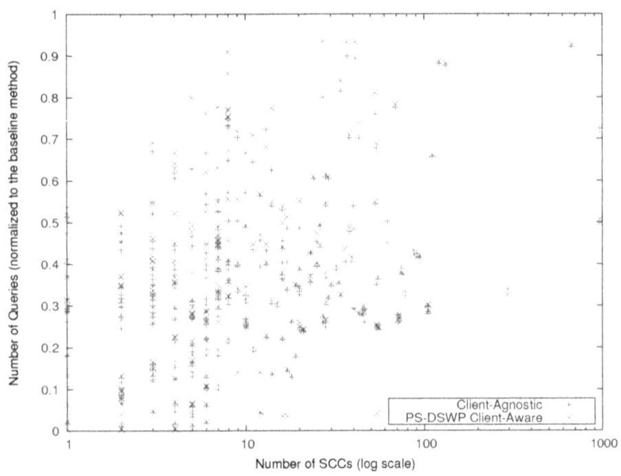

(c) Improvement in Queries vs Number of SCCs (log scale)

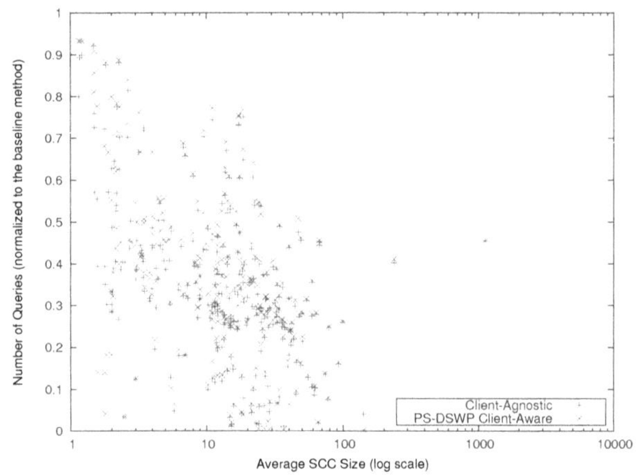

(d) Improvement in Queries vs Average SCC Size (log scale)

Figure 4: Improvement in running time and in number of queries, normalized to the baseline method.

5.3 Effect on Compiler Scalability

Analysis of whole benchmarks matters more than analysis of single loops. Compilers consider hot loops to plan an optimization strategy. We consider the question: *what is the largest sequence of loops which can be analyzed?* both in terms of the total number of loops, and in terms of the sum of execution coverage.

Figure 3 considers the largest sequences of loops that can be analyzed before varying limits on analysis time (log scale). To simulate a very large application, this experiment allows the compiler to select any of the loops from the entire benchmark suite. The client-agnostic method analyzes more loops than the baseline under the same time constraints. The PS-DSWP client-aware extensions cause a slight performance degradation from client-agnostic yet are still more efficient than the baseline.

Not all loops are equally valuable. Amdahl's law encourages compilers to ration their time budget towards hot loops. Figure 5 explores how many hot loops (weighted by coverage) each method analyzes by a certain time. The compiler considers each loop from hottest to least-hot. On average, the client-agnostic method analyzes 50% of the hot loops 111.5s before the baseline, and the client-aware method achieves that 106.1s before the baseline. The proposed methods allow an optimizing compiler to analyze the code which most contributes to running time in shorter use cycles.

6. Related Work

Harrold et al. [12] present an algorithm to efficiently compute control dependences for a PDG. This technique does not address memory dependence analysis. In our setup, control analysis is cheap; memory analysis dominates construction time. There is theoretical evidence that precise analysis *must* be expensive [16, 26].

Scalability of memory analysis is an area of ongoing research. Approaches can be classified along levels of abstraction: low-level approaches improve the efficiency of the analysis, without considering the client; mid-level approaches assume some properties of the client to improve efficiency; high-level approaches modify the client so it more judiciously employs analysis or restructure the code so analysis will perform better.

Low-Level Many analyses are implemented as Maximum Fixed Points (MFP) of a set of data-flow equations. Several works optimize how programs are reduced to data-flow equations. Johnson et al. observe that formulating these equations with respect to the control flow graph is wasteful, proposing instead to formulate them along the Data-Flow Graph thereby reducing the number of identity relationships [18]. Similarly, Duesterwald et al. attempt to optimize the set of equations by identifying congruent equations through idempotency and common sub-expression elimination prior to computing the MFP [5]. Both techniques eliminate

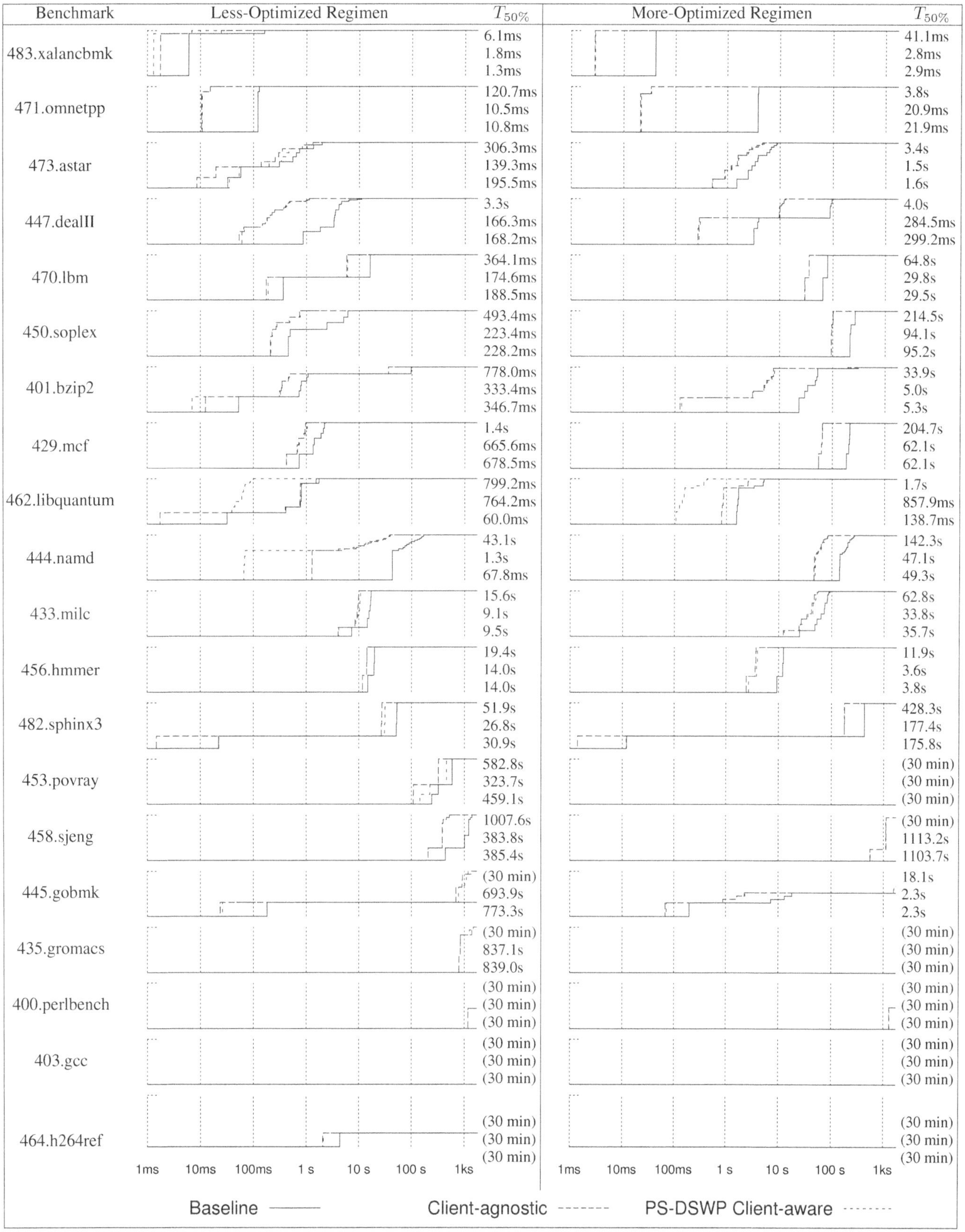

Figure 5: The client-agnostic, client-aware and baseline methods analyzing each benchmark. The horizontal axis measures time (seconds) from 1ms to 30 minutes on a log scale. The vertical axis is the fraction of loops analyzed before a that time, weighted by loop coverage. The compiler analyzes loops from hottest to coldest. $T_{50\%}$ shows the times when the Baseline, Client-agnostic, and PS-DSWP Client-aware methods reach 50% or *(30 min)* if they time out first. The client-agnostic method reaches 50% on average 111.5s earlier than baseline.

unnecessary relationships among program points, reducing MFP convergence time.

Calling-context sensitivity is a challenge for scalability: procedures exhibit drastically different memory access behavior depending on actual parameters and global state. One response has been the use of "procedure summaries," i.e. functions which compute a points-to set for a procedure as a function of its parameters and globally accessible state [9, 22]. In such solutions, there are still exponentially many calling contexts, yet summaries allow large numbers of contexts to be evaluated quickly. A complementary approach employs Datalog solvers which scale to the huge number of calling contexts using Binary Decision Diagrams [38]. This approach is restricted to analyses expressible in Datalog.

Mid-Level Demand-driven analyses employ an orthogonal approach [13, 32, 40]. Under the observation that many clients need only a fraction of all analysis queries, a demand-driven approach shifts effort from preprocessing into each query. This scales better as it only expends effort on queries which affect the client.

However, these approaches do not inform compiler authors of how to (re-)structure analysis clients as to perform the minimum number of analysis queries. The algorithms proposed in this paper have a synergistic relationship with demand-driven analyses since the proposed algorithms actively attempts to perform only select queries while still supporting advanced clients.

The Pruning-Refinement method [23] considers a spectrum of Datalog dependence analyses ranging from cheap-yet-imprecise to expensive-yet-precise. It first applies cheaper analyses to queries and, if successful, returns that answer to the client. Otherwise, it runs the slower, more precise analyses, using a byproduct of cheap analyses to prune extraneous inputs and reduce running times. This method has dramatic benefits on memory usage, but its running time improvements are less pronounced. This method is only applicable to analyses which can be formulated in Datalog.

High-Level The structure of input code, in particular the division into procedures, has an effect on analysis and optimization. Program restructuring techniques can improve analyzability. Procedure inlining and partial inlining not only reduce the overhead of a procedure call, but also improve memory analysis by disambiguating the relationship of call sites and callees [1, 25]. Region formation chooses scopes independently of procedure boundaries to make interprocedural analysis and optimization scale [11].

Ohata et al. [27] propose merging program statements before building a PDG to reduce memory consumption and analysis time. They modify analysis to treat groups of statements as one, leading to faster convergence, similar to Duesterwald et al. [5]. However, this approach is imprecise and falsely reports that some statements belong to a slice because they are merged with a statement truly in the slice. This technique can only merge non-call statements which are adjacent in the program source code and control equivalent, and requires tight integration with analysis. Our technique calls for no modifications to analysis.

Client-driven approaches [10] use cheap analyses first and retroactively apply precise analyses when imprecision limits the client. This approach requires analysis to track imprecision due to *polluting assignments*, and clients to request greater precision in important cases. This approach improves performance only when those important cases are less common than polluting assignments. In terms of the DAG_{SCC}, an augmented client must identify those conservative edges whose removal would split a component into several. In contrast, our method always uses the most precise analysis available and only queries edges that may merge components.

When used to improve analysis quality, the high-level approaches share a common failing: they conflate the separate concerns of analysis and transformation and break abstractions that are useful for the development of compilers.

7. Conclusion

The DAG_{SCC} provides strong insight into dependence structure over a large program scope and is sufficient to drive a large class of compiler optimizations. This paper demonstrates that the DAG_{SCC} can be computed much more efficiently than the naïve method of computing the strongly connected components of the full PDG. The savings from this technique allow a compiler to analyze larger scopes while still providing short turnaround times to the compiler's user. This makes aggressive optimization of large scopes palatable to a wider audience, and contributes to the universal deployment of aggressive whole-program optimization.

Acknowledgments

We thank the entire Liberty Research Group for their support and feedback during this work. We also thank the anonymous reviewers for their insightful comments. Additionally, we thank CJ Bell, Sid Sen, Sushant Sachdeva, and Chris Monsanto for commenting on early drafts. This material is based on work supported by National Science Foundation Grants 0964328 and 1047879. All opinions, findings, conclusions, and recommendations expressed throughout this work are those of the authors and do not necessarily reflect the views of the aforementioned funding agencies.

References

[1] R. Allen and S. Johnson. Compiling C for vectorization, parallelization, and inline expansion. In *Proceedings of the ACM SIGPLAN 1988 Conference on Programming Language Design and Implementation (PLDI)*, pages 241–249, June 1988.

[2] U. Banerjee. *Loop Transformations for Restructuring Compilers: The Foundations*. Kluwer Academic Publishers, Norwell, MA, 1993.

[3] T. Chen, J. Lin, W. Hsu, and P. Yew. An empirical study on the granularity of pointer analysis in C programs. *Languages and Compilers for Parallel Computing (LCPC)*, pages 157–171, 2005.

[4] R. Cytron. DOACROSS: Beyond vectorization for multiprocessors. In *Proceedings of the 1986 International Conference on Parallel Processing (ICPP)*, pages 836–884, 1986.

[5] E. Duesterwald, R. Gupta, and M. L. Soffa. Reducing the cost of data flow analysis by congruence partitioning. In *In International Conference on Compiler Construction*, pages 357–373. Springer-Verlag, 1994.

[6] J. Ferrante, K. J. Ottenstein, and J. D. Warren. The program dependence graph and its use in optimization. *ACM Transactions on Programming Languages and Systems*, 9:319–349, July 1987.

[7] J. S. Foster, M. Fähndrich, and A. Aiken. Polymorphic versus monomorphic flow-insensitive points-to analysis for C. In *Proceedings of the 7th International Symposium on Static Analysis (SAS)*, pages 175–198, London, UK, UK, 2000. Springer-Verlag.

[8] R. Ghiya, D. Lavery, and D. Sehr. On the importance of points-to analysis and other memory disambiguation methods for C programs. In *Proceedings of the ACM SIGPLAN 2001 Conference on Programming Language Design and Implementation (PLDI)*, pages 47–58. ACM Press, 2001.

[9] B. Guo, M. J. Bridges, S. Triantafyllis, G. Ottoni, E. Raman, and D. I. August. Practical and accurate low-level pointer analysis. In *Proceedings of the 3rd International Symposium on Code Generation and Optimization (CGO)*, March 2005.

[10] S. Z. Guyer and C. Lin. Client-driven pointer analysis. In *In International Static Analysis Symposium*, pages 214–236. Springer-Verlag, 2003.

[11] R. E. Hank, W. W. Hwu, and B. R. Rau. Region-based compilation: An introduction and motivation. In *Proceedings of the 28th Annual International Symposium on Microarchitecture*, pages 158–168, December 1995.

[12] M. J. Harrold, B. Malloy, and G. Rothermel. Efficient construction of Program Dependence Graphs. In *Proceedings of the 1993 ACM*

SIGSOFT international symposium on Software testing and analysis (ISSTA), pages 160–170, New York, NY, 1993.

[13] N. Heintze and O. Tardieu. Demand-driven pointer analysis. In *Proceedings of the ACM SIGPLAN 2001 conference on Programming language design and implementation (PLDI)*, pages 24–34, New York, NY, 2001.

[14] M. Hind. Pointer analysis: Haven't we solved this problem yet? In *2001 ACM SIGPLAN-SIGSOFT Workshop on Program Analysis for Software Tools and Engineering (PASTE)*, 2001.

[15] M. Hind and A. Pioli. Evaluating the effectiveness of pointer alias analyses. In *Science of Computer Programming*, pages 31–55, 1999.

[16] S. Horwitz. Precise flow-insensitive may-alias analysis is NP-hard. *ACM Transactions on Programming Languages and Systems*, 19(1), January 1997.

[17] S. Horwitz and T. Reps. The use of program dependence graphs in software engineering. In *In proceedings of the Fourteenth International Conference on Software Engineering (CSE)*, pages 392–411, 1992.

[18] R. Johnson and K. Pingali. Dependence-based program analysis. In *In Proceedings of the SIGPLAN '93 Conference on Programming Language Design and Implementation (PLDI)*, pages 78–89, 1993.

[19] M. G. Kendall. *Rank Correlation Methods*. Charles Griffin and Company, Limited, London, 1948.

[20] K. Kennedy and J. R. Allen. *Optimizing compilers for modern architectures: a dependence-based approach*. Morgan Kaufmann Publishers Inc., San Francisco, CA, USA, 2002.

[21] C. Lattner and V. Adve. LLVM: A compilation framework for lifelong program analysis & transformation. In *Proceedings of the Annual International Symposium on Code Generation and Optimization (CGO)*, pages 75–86, 2004.

[22] C. Lattner, A. Lenharth, and V. Adve. Making Context-Sensitive Points-to Analysis with Heap Cloning Practical For The Real World. In *Proceedings of the 2007 ACM SIGPLAN Conference on Programming Language Design and Implementation (PLDI)*, San Diego, California, June 2007.

[23] P. Liang and M. Naik. Scaling abstraction refinement via pruning. In *Proceedings of the 2011 ACM SIGPLAN Conference on Programming Language Design and Implementation (PLDI)*.

[24] W. Liu, J. Tuck, L. Ceze, W. Ahn, K. Strauss, J. Renau, and J. Torrellas. POSH: a TLS compiler that exploits program structure. In *PPoPP '06: Proceedings of the 11th ACM SIGPLAN Symposium on Principles and Practice of Parallel Programming*, pages 158–167, 2006.

[25] R. Muth and S. Debray. Partial inlining. Technical report, Department of Computer Science, University of Arizona, 1997.

[26] R. Muth and S. Debray. On the complexity of flow-sensitive dataflow analyses. In *In Proc. ACM Symp. on Principles of Programming Languages*, pages 67–80. ACM Press, 2000.

[27] F. Ohata, A. Nishimatsu, and K. Inoue. Analyzing dependence locality for efficient construction of program dependence graph. *Information and Software Technology*, 42(13):935 – 946, 2000.

[28] E. Raman, G. Ottoni, A. Raman, M. Bridges, and D. I. August. Parallel-stage decoupled software pipelining. In *Proceedings of the Annual International Symposium on Code Generation and Optimization (CGO)*, 2008.

[29] R. Rangan, N. Vachharajani, M. Vachharajani, and D. I. August. Decoupled software pipelining with the synchronization array. In *Proceedings of the 13th International Conference on Parallel Architectures and Compilation Techniques (PACT)*, pages 177–188, September 2004.

[30] L. Rauchwerger and D. A. Padua. The LRPD test: Speculative runtime parallelization of loops with privatization and reduction parallelization. *IEEE Transactions on Parallel Distributed Systems*, 10:160–180, February 1999.

[31] Standard Performance Evaluation Corporation. http://www.spec.org.

[32] M. Sridharan, D. Gopan, L. Shan, and R. Bodík. Demand-driven points-to analysis for java. In *Proceedings of the 20th annual ACM SIGPLAN conference on Object-oriented programming, systems, languages, and applications (OOPSLA)*, pages 59–76, New York, NY, 2005.

[33] R. E. Tarjan. Depth-first search and linear graph algorithms. *SIAM Journal on Computing*, 1(2):146–160, 1972.

[34] A. J. Thadhani. Factors affecting programmer productivity during application development. *IBM Systems Journal*, 23(1):19 -35, 1984.

[35] C. Tian, M. Feng, V. Nagarajan, and R. Gupta. Copy or discard execution model for speculative parallelization on multicores. In *Proceedings of the 41st Annual IEEE/ACM International Symposium on Microarchitecture (MICRO)*, pages 330–341, Washington, DC, 2008. IEEE Computer Society.

[36] H. Vandierendonck, S. Rul, and K. De Bosschere. The Paralax infrastructure: Automatic parallelization with a helping hand. In *Proceedings of the 19th International Conference on Parallel Architecture and Compilation Techniques (PACT)*, pages 389–400, 2010.

[37] M. Weiser. Program slicing. In *Proceedings of the 5th international conference on Software engineering*, (ICSE), pages 439–449, Piscataway, NJ, 1981.

[38] J. Whaley and M. S. Lam. Cloning-based context-sensitive pointer alias analysis using binary decision diagrams. In *Proceedings of the ACM SIGPLAN 2004 conference on Programming language design and implementation*, (PLDI), pages 131–144, New York, NY, 2004.

[39] *The Wisconsin Program-Slicing Tool, Version 1.1*, 2000. http://research.cs.wisc.edu/wpis/slicing_tool/.

[40] X. Zheng and R. Rugina. Demand-driven alias analysis for C. In *Proceedings of the 35th Annual ACM SIGPLAN-SIGACT Symposium on Principles of Programming Languages (POPL)*, pages 197–208, New York, NY, 2008.

Scalable Variable and Data Type Detection in a Binary Rewriter

Khaled ElWazeer   Kapil Anand   Aparna Kotha   Matthew Smithson   Rajeev Barua

Electrical and Computer Engineering Department, University of Maryland College Park, MD, 20742, USA

{wazeer,kapil,akotha,msmithso,barua}@umd.edu

Abstract

We present scalable static analyses to recover variables, data types, and function prototypes from stripped x86 executables (without symbol or debug information) and obtain a functional intermediate representation (IR) for analysis and rewriting purposes. Our techniques on average run 352X faster than current techniques and still have the same precision. This enables analyzing executables as large as millions of instructions in minutes which is not possible using existing techniques. Our techniques can recover variables allocated to the floating point stack unlike current techniques. We have integrated our techniques to obtain a compiler level IR that works correctly if recompiled and produces the same output as the input executable. We demonstrate scalability, precision and correctness of our proposed techniques by evaluating them on the complete SPEC2006 benchmarks suite.

Categories and Subject Descriptors D.2.7: Software Engineering [*Distribution, Maintenance, and Enhancement*]: Restructuring, reverse engineering, and reengineering

Keywords reverse engineering; binary rewriting; variable recovery; type recovery;

1. Introduction

Reverse engineering binary executable code is commonplace today, especially for untrusted code and malware. Agencies as diverse as anti-virus companies, security consultants, code forensics consultants, law-enforcement agencies and national security agencies routinely try to understand binary code. Existing tools such as the IDAPro disassembler and the Hex-Rays decompiler [1] help, with the latter producing (non-executable) C-like pseudocode text.

However, existing reverse engineering tools do not exhibit several desired characteristics. First, previous tools do not aim to recover a *fully-functional high-level code* (similar to source code) from executables. These tools neglect variables allocated on the floating point stack and generate intermediate representation (IR) containing incomplete interprocedural interfaces. The recovered IR is suitable for human understanding but does not capture the complete functionality of the input executable. Second, they are either imprecise [1] or recover precise information at the cost of *scalability*. For example, DIVINE [5], the most precise variable identification tool proposed in the literature, spends two hours while analyzing programs of the order of 55,000 assembly instructions.

Recovering a functional IR in a scalable and accurate manner would be invaluable to security professionals. It would enable them to write compiler passes to extract properties of interest. The recovered IR can be updated with insertion, deletion, or modification. Running the updated rewritten program enables dynamic source-level debugging techniques such as judiciously placed print statements, and many more.

Recovering functional IR is also valuable for legacy binaries for which the source code has been lost. It enables users to fix bugs in such binaries, modify the functionality, optimize such binaries, or even port them to new hardware systems.

In this work, we present static analyses that can recover source level variable and type information from x86 binaries as large as millions of instructions in a few minutes. The produced information is as accurate as the current state of the art x86 binary analysis systems. The recovered information is represented in a high level compiler IR that is completely functional and produces a correct rewritten executable when recompiled. Our static techniques combine functionality, precision and scalability; features that collectively do not exist in today's binary analysis tools.

Our methods also improve the scope of variable analysis and type recovery in two ways. First, unlike current binary analysis techniques, our recovery mechanisms are able to recognize variables allocated on the floating point stack. Recognizing such variables is a hard problem in the presence of unknown indirect and external calls. Recognizing floating-point stack variables is imperative for obtaining a functional IR from executables.

Another way our methods improve the scope of analysis is by accurately identifying all register allocated variables used as arguments and returns from functions. Most x86 binary analyses will only identify memory allocated arguments [4], but do not identify register allocated ones. This is acceptable when recovering pseudocode, but unacceptable when recovering functional code. Some methods perform either brute force techniques [22] that are imprecise, or use dynamic analysis to detect arguments and returns [7] which is precise but produces incomplete information.

This work presents a step towards a system that rewrites executables into a functional high-level program representation and incorporates as much source level information as possible in a scalable manner. We envision the need for such a system in various security and binary analysis applications. This work has the following contributions:

* It produces a correct and running IR that can be recompiled to obtain a rewritten executable that works exactly the same way as the input executable.

PLDI'13, June 16–19, 2013, Seattle, WA, USA.

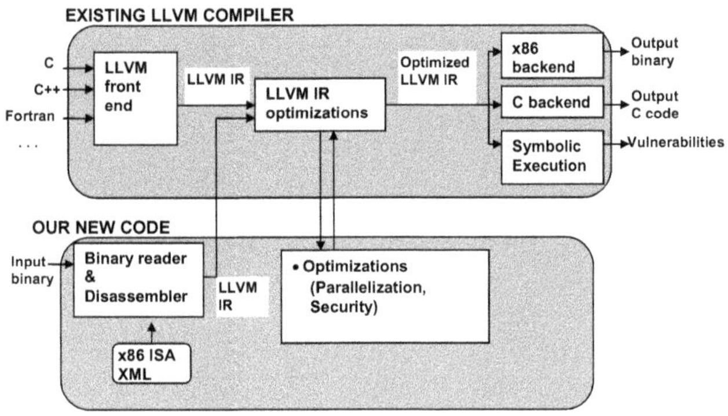

Figure 1. SecondWrite Flow

* It presents algorithms for solving problems missed while analyzing executables like resolving floating point stack accesses and accurately identifying interprocedural interfaces.
* It presents a highly scalable mechanism for identifying variables and types which is orders of magnitude faster than current analysis techniques. Our techniques do not rely on symbol or debug information to be present in binaries.
* It utilizes a compiler's intermediate representation (LLVM) in its internals which opens the domain of running existing source-level analysis and optimization passes built up over decades by hundreds of developers.
* It is evaluated and shown to recover accurate and precise information from C, C++, and Fortran binaries obtained from the SPEC2006 benchmarks suite; compiled using two different compilers in a reasonable amount of time.

2. Analysis and Rewriting Framework

Figure 1 presents an overview of SecondWrite [6], [3]; our executables analysis and rewriting framework. SecondWrite translates the input x86 binary code to the intermediate format of the LLVM compiler [2]. The disassembler along with the binary reader translates every x86 instruction to an equivalent LLVM instruction.

A key challenge in binary frameworks is discovering which portions of the code section in an input executable are definitely code. Smithson et. al. [20] proposed *speculative disassembly*, coupled with *binary characterization*, to efficiently address this problem. SecondWrite speculatively disassembles the unknown portions of the code segments as if they were code. However, it also retains the unchanged code segments in the IR to guarantee the correctness of data references in case the disassembled region was actually data.

SecondWrite employs *binary characterization* to limit such unknown portions of code. It leverages the restriction that an indirect control transfer instruction (CTI) requires an absolute address operand, and that these address operands must appear within the code and/or data segments. The binary segments are scanned for values that lie within the range of the code segment. The resulting values are guaranteed to contain, at a minimum, all of the indirect CTI targets. More information on how we form functions and function boundaries using binary characterization is found in [11].

Memory stack analysis is done for every procedure to detect its corresponding memory arguments as explained in [3]. The techniques presented in [3] along with [4] are used to split the physical stack into individual abstract stack frames. Global and stack regions appear as arrays of bytes in the IR.

3. Decoding the floating point variables

In this section, we describe our technique to decode all the floating point stack operations and represent them in higher level code using floating point variables, function arguments and function returns, instead of the low level stack layout used in the assembly.

We begin by introducing the x86 floating point stack. The floating point hardware stack has a maximum height of 8 which means there are only 8 physical floating point registers that can be used at any time. The names of those registers, as used by the hardware instructions, are dynamic and are relative to the current top of the floating point stack. If we assume the fixed physical register names are: PST_0 - PST_7, then the assembly instructions will refer to another set of names ST_0 - ST_7, where ST_0 always refers to the register at the top of the stack. For example, if the height of the stack is one, then ST_0 refers to PST_0. If the stack is full, then ST_0 refers to PST_7. In general, ST_x is mapped to PST_y where $y = TOP(\text{I}) - 1 - \text{x}$ where *TOP*(I) is the stack height at instruction I and $0 \leq y < TOP(\text{I})$. Whenever a function returns a floating point value in a register, it pushes the value on the floating point stack. Whenever a function takes floating point values as arguments in registers, the caller pushes the values on the floating point stack. It is assumed that *TOP*(I) cannot be negative at any instruction I.

Decoding the floating point stack means mapping every assembly operand among ST_0 - ST_7 into a corresponding IR register among PST_0 - PST_7. To do so in the IR, we declare the registers PST_0 - PST_7 as local variables inside each procedure. It turns out from the previous equations that we only need to identify for every instruction I, what is the corresponding *TOP*(I) in order to decode the floating point operands successfully. This task is not trivial because of the existence of indirect and external calls.

If there is no indirect or unknown external call in the program, the problem is trivial because we can traverse the control flow of the program, tracking the floating point stack height at every point, and set the value of *TOP*(I) at every instruction I depending on the floating point operations observed. This analysis will not work in the presence of indirect and external calls because when we hit such a call, we will not know what function is being called and how the height of the stack will be affected by this call.

We use a symbolic analysis scheme to solve this problem by maintaining a symbolic value X_i for every indirect and external call i representing the difference of the floating point stack height before and after the call. Sometimes we refer to that difference as *StackDiff* in the paper. After doing the symbolic analysis, each *TOP*(I) will become a symbolic expression in terms of the X_is. We build symbolic linear equations to solve for X_is. Once the X_is are calculated, *TOP*(I) will be known for every instruction.

It is statically indeterminable to be able to decode the floating point operations correctly in all cases in the presence of indirect and external calls. In this work, we show that if we lay out some assumptions, we can actually guarantee a correct and functional representation of the floating point stack operations in all cases that adhere to those assumptions. Our assumptions are:

1. At control-flow join points, the floating point stack height must be the same for every predecessor basic block.
2. At indirect and external calls, the floating point stack height must be zero before the call.
3. Every indirect or external call can return at most a single floating point value on the floating point stack.

The above assumptions are correct in compiled code in every case in every compiler we are aware of. They are also true in most hand written assembly code, but may not be always true in theory. The justifications for the assumptions are as follows. (1) If the stack height is not balanced at join points, any subsequent floating point stack access will be indeterminable as it might access different values depending on the path taken at run time. (2) For indirect and external calls, the behavior of their targets is usually unknown to the compiler, and hence the compiler must assume they might use all the floating point stack registers, hence it has to clean the stack before such calls. We can state this assumption by saying we assume floating point registers are scratch registers. Theoretically, a compiler might know in some cases the behavior of the functions being called and may not clean the floating point stack, but practically we are not aware of such a compiler. (3) The last assumption above is coming from the fact that we are not aware of any calling convention that allows the return of more than one floating point stack register from indirect calls and externals.

We translate the above assumptions into the symbolic analysis propagation rules present in figure 2, explained as follows. For internal function calls, we use helper variables $Y(F)$ to represent the symbolic expression representing *StackDiff* of every function F. The executable is traversed in a depth first search manner starting from the entry point function for the binary, and from functions that are never called directly in the code. Then we analyze the remaining strongly connected components in the call graph. The assumptions (1) through (3) above represent the symbolic equations in lines (1) through (3) in figure 2. The actual values of X_is can only be zero or one because before the call, the stack height is zero according to assumption (2), and the call can return at most one value according to assumption (3). The height of the stack cannot go negative and hence the actual value of the X_is cannot be negative.

The symbolic equations represented by equations (1) through (3) in figure 2 along with the symbolic unknowns X_is are transformed into a linear system of equations. To solve those equations, we employ our custom linear solver that categorize the equations into disjoint groups based on the variables used in every equation, and then solve every group only if the number of equations is equal to the number of unknowns. We keep propagating calculated values to other groups until no more calculated values are present. Most of the X_is are usually solved using equation (3) in figure 2.

The remaining unknowns are assumed to take a value of $X_i = 1$ conservatively. This will be always correct because from our second assumption above, the stack height is zero before every indirect and external call. In this case, if we declare by mistake that a particular call modifies the stack height by adding one element; this element will never be accessed. In this case, even if there are subsequent floating point stack operations, they have to push values on the stack before reading them.

The floating point register arguments and returns are declared in the IR as follows: a) Whenever a function has $TOP(\mathrm{I}) > 0$ at its entry point instruction I, the function is declared in the IR to take as many floating point values as the value of $TOP(\mathrm{I})$. They will be passed as arguments and copied to the correct local variables according to the mapping we described earlier. b) Whenever X_i or $Y(F)$ are greater than zero at a call site, this call site will be returning one or more floats in the IR and they will be copied to the corresponding local variables in the callers according to the $TOP(\mathrm{I})$ value at the call site.

Unknown Symbolic Values :

X_i, where X_i = *StackDiff* of indirect/external callsite i

Helper Variables :

$Y(F)$ = *StackDiff* of function F, where F is an internal function
$TOP(\mathrm{I})$ = top of the stack after executing instruction I
I' = the previous instruction to I. At a basic block (*BB*) entry, it is the first instruction of *BB*.

Initial Conditions :

Root functions "not called directly anywhere" as well as the entry point function have entry $TOP(\mathrm{I}) = 0$ where I is a NOP instruction inserted at the entry point of each of those functions.

Data flow rules :

At every basic block (BB) entry:

$TOP(\mathrm{I}) = TOP(\mathrm{I_n})$, where I_n are the terminators of the predecessors of BB ———————(1)

For every instruction I:

I = push ... $\Rightarrow TOP(\mathrm{I}) = TOP(\mathrm{I'}) + 1$

I = pop ... $\Rightarrow$

if $(TOP(\mathrm{I'}) = \mathrm{X_i})\ X_i = 1$ ———————(3)

$TOP(\mathrm{I}) = TOP(\mathrm{I'}) - 1$

I = call $F \Rightarrow$

if (F is an external or indirect)

$TOP(\mathrm{I'}) = \text{zero}$ ——————— (2)

$TOP(\mathrm{I}) = \mathrm{X_i}$

else

$TOP(\mathrm{A}) = TOP(\mathrm{I'})$ where A is the first NOP instruction in F

Analyze F to get $Y(F) = func(X_1, ..., X_n)$

$TOP(\mathrm{I}) = TOP(\mathrm{I'}) + \mathrm{Y(F)}$

I = return from $F \Rightarrow$

$Y(F) = TOP(\mathrm{I'}) - TOP(\mathrm{A})$, A is the first NOP instruction in F

$\forall Z$ = return from $F \Rightarrow TOP(\mathrm{Z}) = TOP(\mathrm{I'})$

Figure 2. Data flow rules used to decode the floating point stack

4. Function Prototypes Recovery

Detecting the complete and accurate set of function arguments and returns is essential in producing a high quality code that can run correctly if recompiled. If some arguments are missing, the code will not work correctly in all cases. If more unnecessary arguments are identified, the code will run correctly, but will be less understandable by users.

We show how to accurately identify the register arguments and returns. Existing techniques show how to identify the exact set of memory arguments. SecondWrite already uses a variant of the algorithm used by Balakrishnan et. al. [4] to identify memory arguments [3]. Surprisingly, we did not find any related work that recognizes correctly and accurately register arguments and returns. Not recognizing register arguments and returns is acceptable if the goal is to help human understanding of binaries (as for existing methods), but unacceptable if the goal is to generate correct rewritten code (as for our method.) Typical x86 codes have less register arguments than memory arguments, but they still have large numbers of register arguments especially for optimized executables.

A brute force algorithm for identifying register arguments and returns is to define the set of registers read without being initialized inside a procedure as arguments, and the registers modified inside a procedure and then later used at some of the call sites as returns. This technique will result in many spurious arguments since all registers which are saved and then restored back in a function (such as callee saves) will be declared as arguments and returns for this function, which is not true. Further, this algorithm might miss some arguments if not carefully implemented. For example, a procedure not accessing any register at all might be declared as taking no register arguments, which may not be true since it might be calling a function which is taking a register argument.

We propose below an algorithm which identifies accurately all register arguments and returns. Our algorithm is conservative since it will not miss any arguments. It is also accurate since it prunes out unnecessary extra arguments in many cases.

The main challenge in being accurate and yet conservative is that the stack locations used to save registers need to be tracked to make sure they are only used for this purpose, thus allowing those registers to be pruned from the arguments or returns. The stores of the register values at the beginning of the function should dominate the loads used to restore them back. There should not be any write to those stack locations in between. If those stack locations are read in the middle of a function, the corresponding registers must be declared as arguments.

Our register arguments and returns detection algorithm is composed of five steps. 1) We assume all registers are arguments to every function and there are no register returns. 2) We declare all registers written to inside a function or any of its callees as potential return registers. 3) We run our algorithm for detecting saved locations by detecting the set of stores to the memory stack which are never loaded back except before the return from the function. We call those store instructions *DeadStores* since they will be eventually removed from the code. For each of the detected dead stores, we determine the corresponding saved register and remove it from the potential returns set. 4) We run our algorithm to propagate the register arguments correctly and prune unused ones. 5) We prune the unused return registers out. Next, we describe each of those steps in details. Step 1 is trivial. We proceed from step two.

The second step in our algorithm is to detect the initial set of potential return registers. The simple idea is that any register which is being written to inside a function is a potential return register from this function. For example, if a function `foo` is calling function `bar`, and `bar` is modifying `eax`, then `foo` and `bar` will be declared as potentially returning `eax` despite the fact that there is no write to `eax` inside of `foo`. We do a post-order depth-first search traversal of the call graph (which visits child nodes before their parents) and propagate the set of potential return registers upwards in the call graph by looking for the written-to registers. Whenever we find a call to a function, we add its potential returns to the caller function potential returns. We handle recursion using a work list mechanism such that whenever we detect a call to a function which has not been analyzed yet, we add the caller function back to the work list.

After detecting the potential returns, we add them to the IR in every return statement inside every function. If more than one register is returned, we return a structure containing all combined potential return registers.

The third step in our algorithm is to detect the callee saves registers and exclude them from the list of potential returns. Since callee-saves values are saved to the memory stack, we need a memory analysis technique to track the memory stack locations where they are saved. Tracking memory in executables is not a trivial task. Our saved registers detection does not need a sophisticated memory tracking algorithm because it only needs to track stack memory. Neither heap nor global memory need to be tracked.

We modify the Value Set Analysis (VSA) algorithm proposed by Balakrishnan et. al. [4] by removing global and heap memory tracking, keeping only stack memory tracking. We also remove the context sensitivity from the algorithm since it is not needed in this application. The resulting algorithm is less powerful for general memory tracking but is sufficient for this purpose.

As a quick summary of the VSA algorithm, it derives a conservative estimate of the set of addresses and integer values every memory location and register can contain at any program point. Every set of values is represented as a strided interval with a lower and upper bounds; and a stride. In our modified implementation of VSA, we only keep track of the lower and upper bounds.

Before we run the saved registers detection algorithm, we convert the registers inside of each function into the SSA form. This is straight forward; indeed in our implementation LLVM already does that. Our algorithm works on a temporary copy of the IR.

Algorithm 1 detects the dead stores used to save registers and prunes those saved registers from the potential return register set. Lines 6 through 12 in the algorithm collect the addresses on the stack that are used to store register values. For each of those addresses, a simple memory liveness analysis is being conducted using standard memory-to-register promotion and dead code elimi-

Algorithm 1: The callee-saves detection algorithm

```
Input: A copy of the LLVM IR for a binary
Input: PotArgs : maps functions to their potential register arguments
Input: PotRets : maps functions to their potential return registers
Output: DeadStores : maps functions to the dead register stores
Output: PotRets : The input map after pruning saved registers
1  foreach reg ∈ PotArgs do
2  |   Create a dummy register dummy ; DummyRegs(reg) = dummy
3  end
4  ADDRS = ϕ
5  foreach Function F do
6  |   foreach Instruction I in F do
7  |   |   if I = store reg, Ptr AND reg ∈ PotArgs then
8  |   |   |   if ValueSet(Ptr) = {address} (Singleton) then
9  |   |   |   |   ADDRS = ADDRS ∪ {(reg,address,I)}
10 |   |   |   end
11 |   |   end
12 |   end
13 |   foreach (reg,address, I) ∈ ADDRS do
14 |   |   allocate a dummy pointer DummyPtr((reg, address)) at the
   |   |   beginning of F
15 |   |   store DummyRegs(reg) to DummyPtr((reg, address))
16 |   end
17 |   foreach Instruction I in F do
18 |   |   if I is UnsafeInstruction(address) where (reg,address,X) ∈
   |   |   ADDRS then
19 |   |   |   insert a volatile load from DummyPtr((reg, address))
20 |   |   end
21 |   |   if I = store value, Ptr AND ValueSet(Ptr) ⊇ {address}
   |   |   AND (reg,address,X) ∈ ADDRS then
22 |   |   |   insert a store value to DummyPtr((reg, address))
23 |   |   end
24 |   |   if I = load Ptr AND ValueSet(Ptr) ⊇ {address} AND
   |   |   (reg,address,X) ∈ ADDRS then
25 |   |   |   insert I' = load DummyPtr((reg, address))
26 |   |   |   for every use of I insert a cloned use of I'
27 |   |   end
28 |   end
29 |   Run LLVM Memory to Register Promotion on All DummyPtr
30 |   Run LLVM Dead Code Elimination on F
31 |   foreach (reg,address, I) ∈ ADDRS do
32 |   |   if DummyPtr(reg, address) is deleted AND
   |   |   DummyRegs(reg) has no uses OR only used in return
   |   |   instructions then
33 |   |   |   DeadStores(F) = DeadStores(F) ∪ {I}
34 |   |   end
35 |   |   if DummyRegs(reg) has no uses OR DummyRegs(reg) is
   |   |   used in all return instructions of F then
36 |   |   |   PotRets(F) = PotRets(F) - {reg}
37 |   |   end
38 |   end
39 end
```

nation compiler passes (both these passes are already available in LLVM). Lines 13 through 16 create a dummy memory location in the IR for each pair of address and register identified. We initially store a dummy value we create to each one of those memory locations. Lines 17 through 28 examine the uses of every address using VSA. At every possible read of an address, we insert a load from the dummy memory location we create. At every possible write to that address, we insert a store to that dummy memory location of the stored value. After that, we run the memory-to-register promotion compiler pass again on those memory locations. Finally, lines 31 through 38 determine the final set of dead stores. If the dummy memory location is promoted successfully to registers, and the only use of the dummy value is at the return then it is saved and can safely be removed from the potential return. The corresponding initial register stores are declared to be dead in this case. If the same previous conditions occur and also there are other uses of the dummy value, then the register is removed from the potential returns, but the initial store is not dead and is considered a real use of the register; i.e. the register becomes an argument.

The *UnsafeInstruction(address)* functions appearing in line 18 in the algorithm is responsible of deciding whether the instruction may have side effects which can potentially access that *address*. External calls where any stack address appears in the value sets of one of the arguments are considered unsafe as they may do arithmetic on those addresses and potentially read from or write to our *address*. An example of this behavior is `memcpy`, `strcpy` and other string manipulating functions from the standard C library. Some external functions are pre-identified safe and known not to do arithmetic on pointer arguments. For example, we parse format strings of `printf`, `scanf` and similar functions and in some cases we can prove those functions are safe.

After detecting the dead stores used to save registers and pruning the callee-saves from the potential returns, we proceed to step four which identifies the actual register arguments. We traverse the call graph of the executable in post-order depth-first search traversal, which ensures child nodes are visited before their parents. For each potential register argument inside a function, we declare it as an argument if and only if we see a "real" use of this register in the function. If a register is used in a store instruction among the dead stores identified by algorithm 1, the store is not considered a real use. Uses in calls are only considered "real" if the callee takes the register as an actual identified argument. A work list mechanism is maintained to handle the dependencies between functions. PHI nodes that link multiple SSA versions of the same register are not considered uses and are tracked. Returns are not considered real uses because if the return is the only use of a register, there is no need to pass it as an argument. Propagating the actual return registers (step 5 in our algorithm) is done in a similar way to the one above except that it works on functions in the forward call graph order and looks for uses of return values at call sites.

The correctness of our register arguments and returns algorithm is guaranteed for internal functions. The reason is that we start our algorithm initially by having all registers as arguments, and then remove those which are not really used. For returns, we start the algorithm by adding all registers that are written to inside of a function or one of its callees, we then remove the ones which are unused at call sites. The correctness in the presence of indirect calls, external calls and call backs is described below.

Our algorithm runs the same way on indirect calls and is correct. At every indirect call, SecondWrite inserts a call translator function that checks the value of the function pointer and calls the corresponding IR function accordingly. In this case, this call translator is treated the same way as any normal function in this algorithm under the assumption that the call translator will call all possible target functions.

Regarding external calls, they are treated correctly by our algorithm in all compiler generated code where the external function has a standard compiler calling convention; ex; *cdecl*, *fastcall*, *thiscall*, *stdcall* and others. Some external functions like standard C and C++ libraries are known to SecondWrite; hence our algorithm will know from the prototypes what registers are needed passing. For the unknown prototypes, we pass all registers that form the union of all the possible known calling conventions, and return all possible returns from the same union. This is not efficient, but will produce correct code under the above assumption. We insert assembly instructions before the external call to make sure we pass the correct register values from the IR to the corresponding physical register in hardware, and copy the physical returns into the correct IR registers after the call. Only if the external call has a non-standard compiler calling convention is when we might not be able to handle it correctly. We never experienced any such external call in all our tested programs.

5. Variable and Type Recovery

In this section, we present our techniques to recover source-level variable information from executables, and then present them with meaningful data types in the IR. Our techniques focus only on memory allocated variables. Register-allocated variables can be handled after detecting register arguments and returns using any compiler liveness analysis that detects a variable for every live range of a register in the executable.

Variable and type recovery from executables is a hard problem because symbol tables are absent. Every memory-allocated variable access in the source code is represented by a memory store or load in the executable. Those memory accesses are either direct accesses to locations represented by constant addresses, or indirect memory accesses to locations represented by some register value. Direct memory accesses can be used to infer variable information by examining the constant memory address being accessed, but indirect memory accesses are unknown accesses and need more advanced memory analysis to reveal the underlying memory locations. That is why pointer analysis is important while recovering variables and data types from executables since it reveals what are the possible memory locations an indirect memory reference can possibly access.

Researchers in this field know this and the best known variable identification technique from executables (DIVINE [5]) uses an advanced memory analysis technique called value set analysis [4], which is a generalized form of alias analysis. DIVINE presents accurate variable identification that detects 88% of the memory-allocated variables in executables. The problem with DIVINE is that it is not scalable and requires a very long time to analyze even small programs. Our aim is to present techniques with the same accuracy as DIVINE, but run orders of magnitudes faster.

Our key insight that enables scalability is that efficient variable detection and type recovery do not require a sound pointer analysis. Unsound pointer analysis usually means incomplete points-to sets. As an example, if variable `x` points to `y` and `z`, an unsound pointer analysis might report `x` points to `y` only. Usually unsound pointer analysis is unacceptable, but variable detection from executables is a best-effort analysis and no method claims to detect 100% of the variables. If we are going to miss some variables anyways because of the nature of the problem we are solving, then we can sacrifice the soundness of the analysis at the expense of losing some variable information – as losing variable `z` in the given example above, but with the gains of having a practical analysis that scales well for large executables.

The correctness of the recovered IR, while missing some variables due to the unsound pointer analysis, comes from the fact that the relative ordering between variables in the memory layout is

store y, x (store value y to location x of size S)	$\forall z \in$ ALocs(PtSet(x)) : PtSet(z) $\cup =$ PtSet(y) **Variables:** UpdateALocs (PtSet(x), S)
y = load x (load location x of size S to y)	$\forall$ z $\in$ ALocs(PtSet(x)) : PtSet(y) $\cup =$ PtSet(z) **Variables:** UpdateScalar (PtSet(x), S)
$y = x$	PtSet(y) = PtSet(x)
$y = x + z$, PtSet(x) is not empty	**if** z is a constant **then** PtSet(y) = PtSet(x) $>> z$ **Variables:** **if** z is a constant **then** UpdateStructure (PtSet(x), z) **else if** z has SCEV bounds and stride **then** UpdateArray (PtSet(y), stride, bounds)

Table 1. Points-to sets propagation and variable detection rules

A = call $foo\,(arg_1, ..., arg_n)$ foo has the known prototype: $retType\ foo\,(type_1, ..., type_n)$	$\forall$ x $\in$ [1,n] setType(arg_x, $type_x$) setType(A, $retType$)
$A = B$ op C $op \in \{+, -, *, /, \%, >>, <<\}$ op has type: $opType$ A, B, C has empty points-to sets	setType($\{A, B, C\}$, $opType$)
A = load B store A, B	unifyType(A, ALocs(PtSet(B)))
$op_1 = \phi\,(op_2, ..., op_n)$ op_1 = typecast op_2 to $type$	unifyType($\{op_1,$ ..., $op_n\}$)

Table 2. Typing rules

maintained in the recovered IR. For example, if we detect two integer local variables at offsets 0 and 20 on a stack frame of size 24 bytes, we will lay out those variables in a structure which has the following three members: a) An integer in the range [0-3]. b) A generic array of bytes in the range [4-19]. c) An integer in the range [20-23]. Preserving the layout of the variables in such a structure maintains the correctness of any indirect memory access to this region. The arrays inserted fill the unknown gaps between variables and maintain the memory layout. This representation helps understanding what variables are detected along with their types, and at the same time maintains the functionality of the rewritten program.

We introduce the concept of a best-effort pointer analysis; where the identified points-to set of each pointer may not be complete, but we terminate the analysis in a certain amount of time nevertheless to prevent it from taking too long even before it converges. This analysis is not correct given the usual criteria for correctness, but suffices in the way we use it to identify as many discrete variables as possible. Our best-effort pointer analysis is a flow and context insensitive data flow analysis that has the following properties:

* It limits the cardinality of the points-to sets to a fixed number.
* It does not track interprocedural information via indirect calls.
* The number of analysis iterations is set to a fixed number.

Having the above relaxations makes our analysis much faster at an extremely small loss in precision. The intuition behind this is as follows: a) A flow and context sensitive pointer analysis is not needed since the variables usually have the same size and type in all flows and contexts of a program. Some exceptions to this might happen which is not common in the programs. b) Limiting the cardinality of points-to sets does not affect the precision that much since only few variables will have large points-to sets. c) Propagating interprocedural information through indirect calls will only affect functions which are only called indirectly. Those functions are still analyzed, but their arguments will have unknown points-to sets. Given that there are relatively few such functions in executables, skipping their arguments propagation is not a big loss. d) Limiting the total number of iterations will only affect longer chains of pointers. For example, the first iteration will always reveal some pointers. The second will reveal two-level (double) pointers. Subsequent iterations reveal more pointer levels. Usually most variables do not have more than four level pointers, which means subsequent iterations will only reveal very little information.

5.1 Best Effort Static Variable Recovery

We show in this section how a simple best-effort pointer analysis can be used for identifying variables. This pointer analysis should be suitable to run on executables where no variables yet identified. We could have modified current memory analysis schemes on executables like [4] to fit our needs, but we show a simpler analysis with similar precision and much better scalability.

Before we begin the analysis, we identify all base memory regions in the executable. An executable has three base memory regions. 1) The global memory region where global variables are located. 2) The stack memory region where local variables inside functions are located. Stack regions are allocated at the beginning of a function and deallocated at the end of the function. SecondWrite already represents those as large arrays in every function. 3) The heap memory region where dynamically allocated variables are usually located. Those are identified by detecting calls to functions like `malloc` and `new` in the executable.

Every detected memory-allocated variable is represented by an abstraction called *ALoc* which stands for Abstract Location. The name is similar to the name used by DIVINE [5]. An *ALoc* contains an offset inside a base memory region and a size representing the variable size. Variables allocated to registers are represented by IR symbols which represent the SSA form of those registers.

Our pointer analysis conservatively assumes that every detected variable can be a pointer. We assign points-to sets to every IR symbol and detected ALoc. When the analysis is done, the actual pointers are identified by tracking if the corresponding points-to sets are not empty.

We implement the points-to sets using the efficient LLVM sparse bit vector data structure. For every base memory region, we assign it a series of unique bits where the number of bits equals the size of the region in bytes. If the size of the base memory region is not known (usually in heap allocated arrays), we assume an arbitrary size. This allows us to detect variables with offsets up to that size. Whenever an access is detected beyond that arbitrary size, we do not track it. This is an important part of our best-effort analysis that allows us to recover a subset of the variables on unsized base memory regions instead of totally giving up on them as the case in DIVINE [5]. Whenever a symbol or an ALoc points to some variable in a certain memory region, the bit corresponding to the starting address of the variable will be set to one. The number of bits set to one equals the number of variables pointed to by a symbol or an ALoc.

Table 1 shows our detailed propagation rules for the best-effort pointer analysis as well as for detecting the variables. We introduce the following definitions to ease the understanding. 1) PtSet(x): takes an ALoc or an IR symbol x and retrieves its points-to set 'bit-vector'. 2) ALocs(x): takes a bit-vector x and retrieves the set of ALocs starting at the addresses that correspond to the set-bits in the bit vector x. 3) UpdateALocs(x,y): takes a bit-vector x and a size y and creates ALocs starting at the addresses corresponding to the set-bits in the bit-vector x with the given size y. If existing ALocs overlap the new ALocs, the new and old ALocs will be split into smaller ALocs to avoid the overlap. 4) UpdateStructure(x,y):

takes a bit-vector x and a number y. It defines a set of structures starting at the addresses corresponding to the set-bits in the bit-vector x. Each structure has its last member at offset y. If a structure already starts at one of the starting addresses, its last member offset will be updated with the maximum of the existing offset and the new one (y). 5) UpdateArray(x,y,z): takes a bit-vector x, a number y representing a stride, and another number z representing the upper bound of the array. It defines arrays starting at the addresses corresponding to the set-bits in the bit-vector x. Each array has a maximum size z. The arrays will be declared to have an element size y. Existing arrays will be merged with the new declared ones and the element size will be set to one if overlapping arrays have conflicting element sizes.

Here we describe briefly the propagation rules in table 1. For a store instruction, the points-to sets of the ALocs pointed to by the pointer operand will be unioned with the points-to set of the value stored. This is called a weak update in the domain of pointer analysis. A load will set the loaded value points-to set to whatever is pointed to by the pointer operand. Stores and loads will create ALocs as they are resolved using the UpdateALocs function described earlier. For pointer arithmetic, the points-to sets will be shifted right according to the positive constant added. If the constant is negative, the shift will become to the left. Adding a constant to a pointer is a hint about the existence of a structure where the pointer address is the start address, and the constant represents one field offset inside the structure. We use this hint and declare a structure identified by the starting address and the last member offset. The structure's last member offset might be updated in subsequent pointer arithmetic operations that start from the same base. The structure's last member offset will eventually be the maximum observed constant that was added to the pointer in the program. Adding a non-constant value is an indication that an array exists. An array will be declared in this case. We use the Scalar EVolution (SCEV) analysis by LLVM to deduce the bounds and the stride of the arithmetic and use this information to describe the array. If such information is not present, we do not declare an array.

The more pointer analysis rounds done, the more ALocs, structures and arrays are identified in all base memory regions. More pointer analysis rounds help identifying multi-level pointers since the first round will always reveal single level pointers. The second round will propagate the points-to sets for those ALocs and identify their points-to sets leading to the identification of two level pointers. More rounds will reveal more levels.

After all iterations are done, collected information about arrays gets resolved. For every base memory region, we fill in the gaps between ALocs using arrays. The bounds and stride information are available from our earlier propagation. If no bounds are available, previously defined ALocs are used as bounds. If no stride information is available, a stride of one is used which means the array is an array of bytes. Overlapping arrays are combined into one bigger array as described earlier.

At the end of this process, a structure hierarchy is created based on the structure information calculated for every base memory region. Using the starting and ending offsets previously calculated for every structure, we construct nested hierarchy structures. We define inner and outer structures such that any outer structure must have its starting address less than any starting address of any nested inner structure, and its ending address larger than any ending address of any nested inner structure. A straight forward algorithm is employed to produce this hierarchy.

5.2 Data Type Recovery

Data type recovery aims at representing every symbol in the IR with a meaningful type. It declares a map between every symbol in the IR and the corresponding detected data type. It uses this map to rewrite the complete IR such that the instructions use the detected types instead of the generic types that are used by SecondWrite.

Without integrating type recovery with some pointer analysis, detected types will be less accurate because of two reasons: 1) Instructions like memory loads and stores will usually be untyped since there is no memory tracking possible. 2) Multi-level pointer types will not be detected because there is no way to track them without having some sort of pointer analysis.

To achieve the goal of typing memory accesses and IR symbols; and detecting multi-level pointer types, we integrate our best-effort pointer analysis and variable recovery techniques described above with our type recovery system. Any other pointer analysis like [4] can be theoretically used, but will be orders of magnitude slower which makes it less practical in large executables. That is the disadvantage of TIE [14] which is the state of the art binary type recovery technique.

Integrating our variable identification system with type recovery makes the type recovery simpler because it will need only recover scalar types like integers, floats and doubles. Structures and arrays are detected as part of the variable identification. A pointer is detected if the points-to set of the corresponding ALoc or IR symbol is not empty. In this case, we get the ALocs pointed to by that pointer and type them according to our rules. We keep doing this for longer pointer chains as needed.

Table 5.1 shows the most important typing rules we have. There are two main type sources. a) Known external function calls like standard C/C++ library calls. For those, we set the types of actual arguments passed to be the same as the known argument types from the prototypes and we do the same thing for the return value. b) Arithmetic operations with non-pointers: in this case the type is deduced from the semantics of the operation itself – whether it is an integer or a floating point operation –. We use the function *setType* to update the type of the symbol or the ALoc in the type map we declare. For pointer types, we type the ALocs represented by the points-to sets of the corresponding variables.

For the other operations in the table, we propagate the types using the function *unifyType*. This function attempts to set the data type of all the given symbols and ALocs to be the same. At least one of the symbols or the ALocs given to that function should be typed. Whenever this function finds conflicting types, it gives up and does not update any types. It is used for copy operations like type casts and phi nodes. It is also used to propagate types through memory as shown in the rules for stores and loads. Interprocedural information is propagated by unifying the formal and actual arguments types at a call instruction. The return value data type at the call site is unified with all the data types of all return values appearing in the return statements inside the called function body.

IR Correctness. We are able to produce a correct and functional IR even if we do not detect some variables and data types. To be able to do that, we rewrite the IR using the following restrictions:

1. We use generic types for the symbols we could not detect types for. The generic types will be wide enough to handle the largest possible variable size that can be allocated to a physical register in the hardware. Type casts are used as needed to convert the generic type to actual types used in different operations.
2. We never assign a type to an IR symbol that conflicts with its use. For example, if we see a 4 byte load, we will never type the pointer as a pointer to short (2 bytes) even if our analysis detects it this way. Otherwise, the load will be wrong.
3. All variables identified for a certain memory allocation will be surrounded by a structure data type. The order of the variables inside that structure is the same as the order they appear in the original executable. The memory regions with no variables declared will be declared as arrays of bytes and will be placed at

Application	Lang	# Inst	# Proc	Time(s)
mcf	C	3,357	36	0.15
lbm	C	7,740	30	0.11
astar	C++	12,677	111	0.39
libquantum	C	13,800	73	0.41
bwaves	F	19,002	22	0.87
bzip2	C	21,408	51	1.14
sjeng	C	32,238	121	2.86
milc	C	34,183	172	2.38
sphinx	C	41,669	210	6.68
leslie3d	F	43,432	32	2.78
hmmer	C	85,981	242	5.29
namd	C++	103,365	193	11.71
soplex	C++	116,743	1523	20.09
zeusmp	F	118,429	68	5.44
omnetpp	C++	148,453	3980	59.58
h264	C	170,684	462	19.78
gobmk	C	196,230	4188	35.34
cactus	C	218,896	962	25.57
povray	C++	288,957	3678	72.49
perlbench	C	313,036	2183	67.89
gromacs	C/F	396,450	674	38.14
calculix	C/F	506,725	771	54.79
dealII	C++	766,555	15619	815.05
gcc	C	934,292	6426	354.68
tonto	F	1,303,359	2878	342.99

Figure 3. Benchmarks Table

the correct offsets inside those structures. This guarantees that every unresolved pointer arithmetic will still point to the correct variable in the rewritten executable.

6. Results

In this section, we present the results showing the effectiveness of our schemes to identify variables and data types. We first show results on the overall variable and data type detection process and then we show specific in-depth results for floating point variables and function prototypes. We evaluate our techniques on the SPEC2006 benchmark suite which represents C, C++ and Fortran executables using different optimization levels and compiled using two different compilers (GCC 4.3 for Linux, and Visual Studio 2010 for Windows). We use a machine with an Intel Core i7 3.33GHz processor with 24 GB of RAM.

All the recovered code in all the experiments was recompiled using LLVM 3.0, linked using GCC (Linux) and MinGW (Windows), and then tested on the ref and test inputs provided by the SPEC2006 test suite. All rewritten executables worked successfully and produced the correct answer as provided in the test suite. In the following sections, we show our detailed analysis results.

6.1 Variable and data types detection

In this section, we show the accuracy, scalability and quality of the recovered variables and types and compare them to the state of the art. We compile C benchmarks from SPEC2006 with all debugging information present and only use them for comparison. We currently do not support reading complete debugging information for C++ and Fortran, yet we collected results on those benchmarks without comparing with source code.

The first experiment shows the quality of the recovered variables using the same metrics DIVINE [5] used for comparison purposes. DIVINE [5] compares recovered variables in the binary to corresponding variables in the source code of those binaries to determine how well it did. It defines four variable categories as a result: 1) a matched variable is a recovered variable whose exact size and position matches the variable from the source code. 2) An over refined variable is when the source code variable is divided into more recovered variables; for example, an integer identified as four characters. 3) Under refined variables which are recovered as part of a larger source code variable ; for example, an un-identified structure member. 4) An unknown variable is a variable which is not one of those mentioned categories.

As shown from figure 4, an average of 86% of the variables are matched to the debugging information. We run this experiment on programs ranging from 2,149 instructions (mcf) to 934,292 instructions (gcc). DIVINE [5] reports an average of 88% matched variables on programs ranging between 252 to 5,371 instructions. This shows that our schemes has comparable precision to DIVINE [5] but on much bigger benchmarks. The largest benchmark they report variables results on is *deltablue* with 5,371 instructions.

The scalability of the variables and type detection is shown in figure 7. Our analysis scales linearly with program size for larger binaries. The detailed benchmarks sizes and analysis time are shown in table 3. The analysis takes around 6 minutes to analyze *tonto* which is a Fortran benchmark whose size is 1.3 million instructions. The average analysis speed is 1.7 seconds per 10000 instructions compared to 10 minutes per 10000 instructions in DIVINE. Thus our method is 352X faster than DIVINE on average. As mentioned before, the underlying reason for our much-faster analysis is using an underlying best-effort pointer analysis that is not guaranteed to have complete points-to sets. We consider that while recovering the IR to maintain correctness as we discussed earlier in section 5. dealII is the only program (out of 25) that did not scale well. dealII has very large number of procedures as shown in table 3. The interprocedural data flow propagation took most of the time in dealII. Still, it is finishing in around 13 minutes given that it has 766,555 instructions.

In order to evaluate our type analysis techniques, we calculate the same metrics that TIE [14] uses. TIE defines a type range for every variable recovered from the executable. An ordering between basic types is specified by a type lattice shown in their paper. The first metric they define is the *distance* which is the difference between the lattice heights of the upper and lower bounding types for each type range. The smaller the *distance*, the more accurate the identified types are. The maximum distance is 4. They also define their detected type range to be *conservative* if the actual source code type falls inside the detected range.

In order to compare with TIE [14], we define a range of types for every variable we detect where the lower bound is the single detected type by our analysis and the upper bound is the generic `reg32_t` type they define in their lattice. Based on that range, we calculate our distances and conservativeness rates.

In addition to the distance and conservativeness, we define our own metric that measures the precision of multi-level pointers detection. TIE metrics do not show how multi-level pointers are precisely typed since all pointer types have the same height on their lattice [14]. Our precision metric is defined as the ratio between the correctly recovered pointer levels to the source level pointer levels. For example, if a variable has a double pointer to integer type (`int**`) in the source code and we identified it as a single pointer to an integer (`int*`), then we identified one level only out of the three levels in source, which are *pointer* to *pointer* to *integer*. Our precision in this example will be 33%.

Figure 5 shows the conservativeness as well as the precision of our detected types. The conservativeness rate is 96% on average which is slightly higher than 90% that TIE reports. Our precision metric shows that we detect 73% of the pointer levels on average. The average distance detected for our type recovery system is 1.7 which is slightly better than the distance of 2 that TIE [14] reports.

Some of the larger binaries have lower type precision than other smaller ones. This is expected since larger programs tend to have more higher level pointers than smaller ones and those are usually

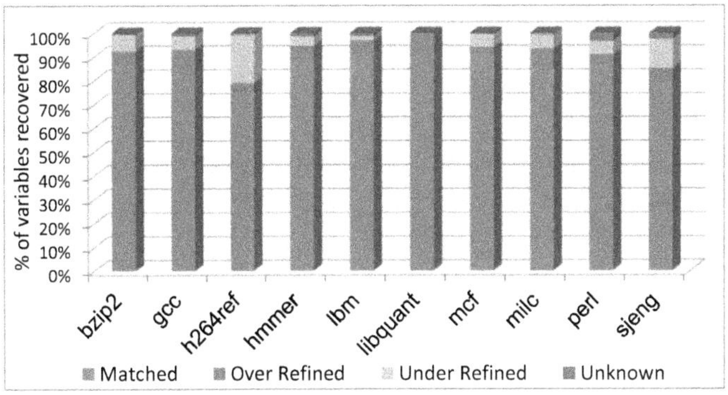

Figure 4. Accuracy of variable detection

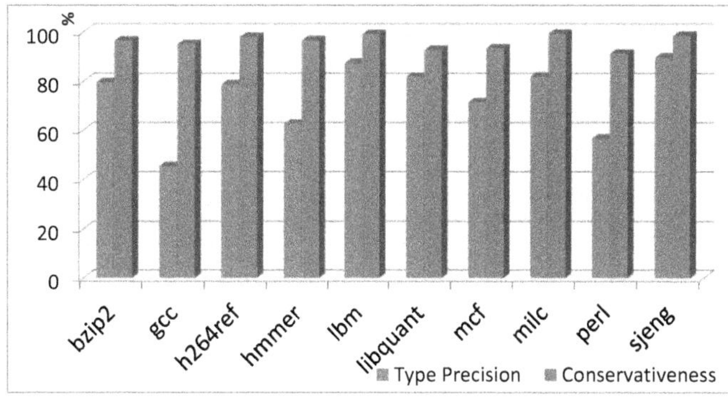

Figure 5. Accuracy of type detection

hard to detect since they rely on the effectiveness of the underlying pointer analysis. The conservativeness and distance measures used by TIE do not capture this fact as it is clear from figure 5.

It is worth mentioning that our variable and type recovery are integrated together in our system. The scalability shown in figure 7 as well as the detailed analysis time results shown in table 3 are capturing both the variable recovery and the type analysis.

6.2 Decoding the floating point stack

In this section, we show the effectiveness of our techniques in identifying floating point stack variables. We show the percentage of the symbolic values that were not solved using our linear solver and required the conservative assumption of $X_i = 1$. As mentioned in section 3, the main challenge while decoding the floating point stack is to identify whether an indirect or an external call is modifying the floating point stack height. According to our assumptions, whenever we are not sure about an indirect or an external call site, we decide conservatively that it is modifying the floating point stack by pushing a single value. We show how often we took that conservative decision in different binaries.

All register allocated floating point stack variables were recovered correctly and all the rewritten benchmarks ran correctly and produced correct answers. The conservative decision taken does not affect correctness as we explained in section 3. It only adds extra return values to some indirect and external calls and this might reflect adding more return values to internal functions as well. The next results section quantifies this effect.

On average, we took the conservative decision 28% of the time for non-optimized executables and 25% of the time for optimized ones. This means we are able to identify the exact floating point arguments and returns for more than 72% of the indirect and external calls on average. We are not aware of any work that identifies such information. Optimized binaries often have less variables than non-optimized binaries which translates to less floating point stack usage and less number of times when the conservative decision is taken. The conservative decision is usually taken more often in C++ binaries because they have more indirect calls with more straight line code and smaller functions than C and Fortran binaries, which translates into smaller number of equations.

6.3 Register Arguments and Returns

In this section we show the accuracy of the detected register arguments and returns. We run our algorithm only for the C and C++ benchmarks shown in table 3 and present the average number of added register arguments and returns (false positives). We never had any false negatives in any of the binaries we tested. We could not compare Fortran binaries since currently, we do not support reading Fortran prototypes from debugging information.

As shown from the figure 6, the average number of false positive arguments is 0.2 per function. The average number of false positive returns is 0.44 registers per function. These results include the conservative floating point returns we declare in our analysis, which explains why the average number of returns is higher. C++ executables tend to have more indirect calls than C executables which explains why they have more false positives.

In contrast to the work in [7], our method has three advantages: (i) it is guaranteed to discover all arguments; (ii) it has been demonstrated on a much larger programs; and (iii) it is orders of magnitude faster. First, their method cannot guarantee full coverage of arguments and returns because of being a dynamic analysis. Any unused argument or return during an execution trace can be missed. Missing arguments or returns is acceptable for human understanding of binaries, but unacceptable for rewriting binaries. Second, although our method produces slightly more false positives then their method (0.2 vs. 0.15 false positive arguments per function), it has been evaluated on far more functions (48,854 functions for our method, vs. just 13 functions for theirs.) Third, our analysis is much faster: for example, it takes only 30 seconds to analyze a program like *soplex* which has 116,743 instructions containing 1,523 procedures and produces prototypes for all of them. In their case, they need the same 30 seconds to only extract `MD5_Final` which is a single function of 67 instructions. This shows that our analysis is two to three orders of magnitude faster than their method, at the expense of a small loss in precision.

7. Related Work

Throughout the paper, we compared our work with the most recent work done in the areas of variable and type recovery [5, 14] and function prototypes identification [7]. In this section, we discuss other work that is relevant to our techniques.

Binary rewriting has been considered by a number of researchers. There are two main categories when talking about binary rewriters, dynamic binary rewriters and static binary rewriters. Dynamic binary rewriters rewrite the binary during its execution. Examples are PIN [16], BIRD [18] and others. None of the dynamic binary rewriters found produce high-level compiler IR. Examples of existing static binary rewriters include ATOM [13], PLTO [19] and UQBT [8]. None of those binary rewriters employ a compiler level intermediate format, like LLVM IR or similar; rather they define their own low-level custom intermediate format. They do not detect high level features such as floating point stack variables, register arguments to functions and data types.

Boomerang [12] is an open source decompiler. It has very limited capabilities and cannot handle large binaries. Register arguments has to be specified manually. It does not detect any floating point stack operations. Zhang et al. present a technique to re-

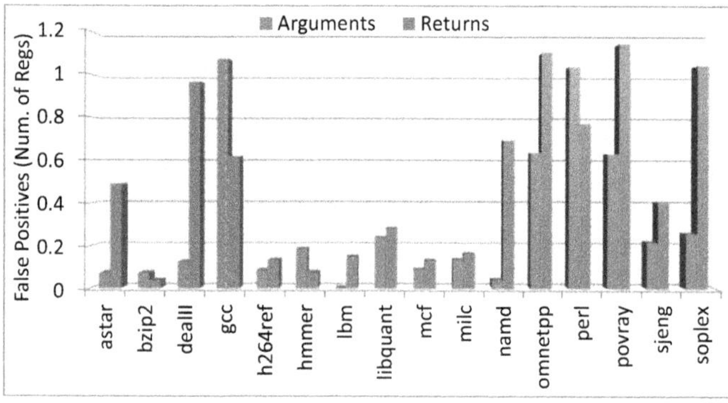

Figure 6. Accuracy of register arguments and returns

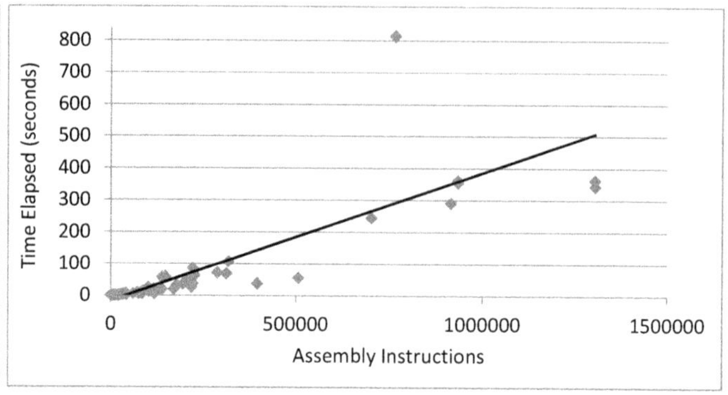

Figure 7. Scalability of variable and type detection

cover function arguments and returns from executable [22]. Their technique is similar the brute force technique described in section 4 which leads to imprecise results. Another technique recovering function prototypes is presented in [9]. It defines a language that can be used to specify machine independent calling conventions. It depends on ABI standards to recover the calling conventions.

REWARDS [15] presents a dynamic type recovery technique; TIE [14] shows better precision than REWARDS. We already compared to TIE [14] in our results. A technique to automatically reconstruct data types from binaries is presented in [10]. It is used in a tool that aims to produce C code from binaries; however no actual C code generation is demonstrated. One main disadvantage in their work is they do not track memory. As we have shown, tracking memory is very important in identifying accurate types. The analysis they produce is intraprocedural which limits its accuracy. Their algorithm is used by Torshina et. al. [21] in another attempt to reverse engineer data types in a tool named TyDec for program decompilation. An early work on type construction from binaries is by Mycroft [17]. It tries to construct C code from binaries with correct type information. However, it does not actually show results producing C code. The algorithm does not track memory locations and it is not clear if it can produce valid IR or C output code.

We are not aware of any work done to recover floating point stack variables except Hex-Rays [1]. Hex-Rays produces inline assembly in case it cannot resolve the variables which is not acceptable for our goal. As far as we know, their work is not published.

8. Conclusion

This paper shows how an executable can be represented by a compiler IR with source code level variables, data types and function prototypes. The analysis we present in this paper is scalable to large executables which makes it more practical than current techniques. The obtained high level IR is guaranteed to work correctly for compiled executables. The schemes are shown to work on executables containing up to million instructions.

References

[1] Idapro, Hexrays. `http://www.hex-rays.com/idapro/`.

[2] The LLVM Compiler Infrastructure. URL `http://www.llvm.org`.

[3] K. Anand, M. Smithson, K. ElWazeer, A. Kotha, J. Gruen, N. Giles, and R. Barua. A compiler-level intermediate representation based binary analysis and rewriting system. In *EuroSys*, 2013.

[4] G. Balakrishnan and T. Reps. Analyzing memory accesses in x86 executables. In *CC*, 2004.

[5] G. Balakrishnan and T. Reps. DIVINE: Discovering variables in executables. In *VMCAI*, 2007.

[6] R. Barua and M. Smithson. Binary rewriting without relocation information, May 24 2010. US Patent App. 12/785,923.

[7] J. Caballero, N. M. Johnson, S. McCamant, and D. Song. Binary code extraction and interface identification for security applications. In *NDSS*, 2010.

[8] C. Cifuentes and M. V. Emmerik. UQBT: Adaptable Binary Translation at Low Cost. *Computer*, 33(3):60–66, Mar. 2000.

[9] C. Cifuentes and D. Simon. Procedure abstraction recovery from binary code. In *Software Maintenance and Reengineering*, 2000.

[10] E. Dolgova et al. Automatic reconstruction of data types in the decompilation problem. *Programming and Computer Software*, 35: 105–119, 2009.

[11] K. Elwazeer, K. Anand, M. Smithson, A. Kotha, and R. Barua. Recovering function boundaries from executables. Technical report, 2013. URL `http://www.ece.umd.edu/~barua/function-boundaries.pdf`.

[12] M. Emmerik and T. Waddington. Using a decompiler for real-world source recovery. In *Working Conference on Reverse Engineering*, 2004.

[13] A. Eustace and A. Srivastava. ATOM: a flexible interface for building high performance program analysis tools. In *Proceedings of the USENIX 1995 Technical Conference Proceedings*, TCON'95, 1995.

[14] J. Lee, T. Avgerinos, and D. Brumley. TIE: Principled reverse engineering of types in binary programs. In *NDSS*, 2011.

[15] Z. Lin, X. Zhang, and D. Xu. Automatic reverse engineering of data structures from binary execution. In *NDSS*, 2010.

[16] C.-K. Luk, R. Cohn, R. Muth, H. Patil, A. Klauser, G. Lowney, S. Wallace, V. J. Reddi, and K. Hazelwood. Pin: building customized program analysis tools with dynamic instrumentation. *SIGPLAN Not.*, 40:190–200, June 2005.

[17] A. Mycroft. Type-based decompilation. In *Proceedings of the 8th European Symposium on Programming*, 1999.

[18] S. Nanda, W. Li, L.-C. Lam, and T.-c. Chiueh. BIRD: Binary Interpretation using Runtime Disassembly. In *CGO*, 2006.

[19] B. Schwarz et al. PLTO: A Link-Time Optimizer for the Intel IA-32 Architecture. In *In Proc. 2001 Workshop on Binary Translation*, 2001.

[20] M. Smithson, K. Anand, A. Kotha, K. Elwazeer, N. Giles, and R. Barua. Binary rewriting without relocation information. Technical report, 2010. URL `http://www.ece.umd.edu/~barua/without-relocation-technical-report10.pdf`.

[21] K. Troshina, Y. Derevenets, and A. Chernov. Reconstruction of composite types for decompilation. In *Source Code Analysis and Manipulation (SCAM)*, 2010.

[22] J. Zhang, R. Zhao, and J. Pang. Parameter and return-value analysis of binary executables. In *COMPSAC*, 2007.

Fast RMWs for TSO: Semantics and Implementation

Bharghava Rajaram
University of Edinburgh
r.bharghava@ed.ac.uk

Vijay Nagarajan
University of Edinburgh
vijay.nagarajan@ed.ac.uk

Susmit Sarkar
University of St Andrews
ss265@st-andrews.ac.uk

Marco Elver
University of Edinburgh
marco.elver@ed.ac.uk

Abstract

Read-Modify-Write (RMW) instructions are widely used as the building blocks of a variety of higher level synchronization constructs, including locks, barriers, and lock-free data structures. Unfortunately, they are expensive in architectures such as x86 and SPARC which enforce (variants of) Total-Store-Order (TSO). A key reason is that RMWs in these architectures are ordered like a memory barrier, incurring the cost of a write-buffer drain in the critical path. Such strong ordering semantics are dictated by the requirements of the strict atomicity definition (type-1) that existing TSO RMWs use. Programmers often do not need such strong semantics. Besides, weakening the atomicity definition of TSO RMWs, would also weaken their ordering – thereby leading to more efficient hardware implementations.

In this paper we argue for TSO RMWs to use weaker atomicity definitions – we consider two weaker definitions: type-2 and type-3, with different relaxed ordering differences. We formally specify how such weaker RMWs would be ordered, and show that type-2 RMWs, in particular, can seamlessly replace existing type-1 RMWs in common synchronization idioms – except in situations where a type-1 RMW is used as a memory barrier. Recent work has shown that the new C/C++11 concurrency model can be realized by generating conventional (type-1) RMWs for C/C++11 SC-atomic-writes and/or SC-atomic-reads. We formally prove that this is equally valid using the proposed type-2 RMWs; type-3 RMWs, on the other hand, could be used for SC-atomic-reads (and optionally SC-atomic-writes). We further propose efficient microarchitectural implementations for type-2 (type-3) RMWs – simulation results show that our implementation reduces the cost of an RMW by up to 58.9% (64.3%), which translates into an overall performance improvement of up to 9.0% (9.2%) on a set of parallel programs, including those from the SPLASH-2, PARSEC, and STAMP benchmarks.

Categories and Subject Descriptors C.1.2 [*Processor Architectures*]: Multiple Data Stream Architectures (Multiprocessors)–Parallel processors; D.1.3 [*Concurrent Programming*]: Parallel programming

General Terms Design, Performance, Experimentation

Keywords Read-Modify-Write (RMW), Total-Store-Order (TSO), Atomics

1. Introduction

Read-Modify-Write (RMW) instructions are primitive synchronization operations used to solve a variety of concurrency problems. Herlihy [15] showed that the ability to read and write to an address atomically is critical to solve the *consensus* problem, which abstracts important synchronization problems. Most modern processor architectures have support for such RMW instructions – examples include test-and-set (TAS), fetch-and-add (FAA), compare-and-swap (CAS), and load-linked/store conditional (LL/SC).

In this paper, we concentrate on *Total-Store-Order* (TSO) architectures, variants of which are implemented on mainstream processors like x86 and SPARC, and on the use of RMWs to implement synchronization constructs in TSO. The most pertinent study of such techniques [6, 27] deals with the new C/C++11 concurrency model [7, 10], a model which introduces synchronization reads and writes of various flavors; these reads and writes are referred to as atomics. Batty et al. [6] have shown that this model is correctly implementable on TSO by replacing C/C++11 SC-atomic-writes and/or SC-atomic-reads by RMWs, leaving other language constructs (reads, writes, fences) to be implemented by plain TSO reads, writes and barriers.

Unfortunately, RMWs are costly in current TSO architectures, where they are ordered similarly to a memory barrier [16, 26], incurring the cost of a write-buffer drain in the critical path. When an RMW is issued, the write-buffer is first drained; then the read and the write (of the RMW) are performed atomically – typically by locking the cache-line locally and denying coherence requests to the locked cache-line until the write completes. Thus, instructions following the RMW are allowed to complete only after the write (of the RMW) and the pending writes prior to it complete [24]. As a quick illustration, we measured an average latency of 67 cycles for an RMW on an 8-core *Intel Sandybridge* processor, using the Splash-2 benchmark suite. The latency does not significantly change if we insert a memory barrier (`mfence` instruction) after each RMW, strengthening the hypothesis of a forced write-buffer drain. Since efficient synchronization is important to effectively harness the power of multicores, it is highly desirable that RMWs are efficient. Nevertheless, the optimization of RMWs has historically received little attention [3].

T0	T1	T0	T1	T0	T1	T0	T1	T0	T1
x=1	y=1	W(x)	W(y)	W(x)	W(y)	W(x)	W(y)	RMW(x)	RMW(y)
if(y==0)	if(x==0)	R(y)	R(x)	RMW(z_1)	RMW(z_2)	RMW(y)	RMW(x)	R(y)	R(x)
// critical	// critical			R(y)	R(x)				
(a)		(b)		(c)		(d)		(e)	

Figure 1. Dekker's Algorithm: (a) code snippet. (b) reads and writes involved: $W(x)$ denotes a write to address x, $R(x)$ denotes a read from address x. (c) using RMWs as memory barriers. (d) replacing reads with RMWs. (e) replacing writes with RMWs. In all subfigures, initially, x=y=0.

Semantically speaking, why are TSO RMWs ordered like a memory barrier? We observe that the ordering of RMWs with other memory accesses in TSO depends on the precise semantics of how *atomic* they have to be with respect to those other accesses. TSO can be defined in terms of a global memory order, a relation over memory accesses in the program. Existing TSO RMWs are defined to prevent *writes to any address* from appearing between the read and the write in this global memory order [16, 26]. We call this strict definition *type-1* atomicity. We show that this strict atomicity definition, combined with the other TSO ordering rules, results in type-1 RMWs being strongly ordered with respect to memory operations before and after it, just like a memory barrier.

This strong ordering is exploited by programmers in various synchronization primitives. Fig. 1(a) shows the key steps involved in the implementation of Dekker's algorithm for achieving mutual exclusion and Fig. 1(b) shows the same code in terms of reads and writes. For correctness, at least one of the reads should return a value of 1; otherwise both of the threads can enter the critical section simultaneously. One way to ensure this is by inserting memory barriers between the writes and the reads. In fact, since type-1 RMWs behave like memory barriers, they can be used instead of memory barriers as shown in Fig. 1(c). Alternatively, as shown in Fig. 1d (Fig. 1e), correctness can also be ensured by replacing reads (and/or writes) with RMWs, since type-1 RMWs are strongly ordered with respect to memory operations before and after it in program order. For the same reason, the C/C++11 concurrency model can be implemented on TSO by replacing SC-atomic-reads (and/or SC-atomic-writes) with RMWs [6].

The goal of this paper is to examine whether the ordering of TSO RMWs can be weakened in ways that enable a more efficient implementation, while remaining strong enough for it to replace existing RMWs in synchronization idioms. In other words, can we design fast yet portable RMWs for TSO?

Our approach here is guided by the requirements of general programs, in particular by just what properties are needed for the C/C++11 implementation. Thus, this is hardware design exploiting the freedom provided by language-level concurrency models, and sufficing for those requirements.

Since the ordering semantics of an RMW depends on its atomicity semantics, our approach to weakening the ordering semantics is through weakening the atomicity semantics. In contrast to the strict *type-1* atomicity which disallows writes of *any* address between the read and the write, we consider two weaker atomicity definitions: the *type-2* atomicity which disallows only reads and writes of the same address as the RMW; and the even weaker *type-3* atomicity, which disallows only writes to the same address as the RMW.

Our key contribution is to derive the ordering semantics of the proposed weaker RMWs, and examine if the ordering is strong enough to replace existing RMWs in synchronization idioms (§2.4, §2.5). Unlike a type-1 RMW, a type-2 RMW is not explicitly ordered with respect to memory operations before and after it. Thus, a type-2 RMW cannot be used as a memory barrier like in Fig. 1(c). However, we show that a type-2 RMW appears strongly ordered with respect to any memory operation that synchronizes with the RMW i.e. any memory operation from another thread that is to the same address as the RMW. Indeed, like before, Dekker's algorithm can be ported to TSO by replacing reads (and/or writes) with type-2 RMWs. It is worth noting that in the scenario shown in Fig. 1c (Fig. 1d), each of the RMWs appear to be strongly ordered with respect to the writes (reads) from the other thread which synchronize with the RMW; this strong ordering is again able to guarantee correctness. For similar reasons, C/C++11 can be ported to TSO by replacing SC-atomic-writes (and/or SC-atomic-reads) with type-2 RMWs. Thus, type-2 RMWs are able to replace existing type-1 RMWs in all synchronization idioms, except when used as a memory barrier.

A type-3 RMW is also not explicitly ordered with respect to memory operations before and after it, and hence cannot be used a memory barrier (like a type-2 RMW). However, unlike a type-2 RMW, it appears strongly ordered only with respect to a write/RMW (but not a read) that synchronizes with the RMW. Therefore, Dekker's algorithm can be ported to TSO by replacing reads (but not writes) with type-3 RMWs. Similarly, C/C++11 can be ported to TSO by replacing SC-atomic-reads (but not SC-atomic-writes) with type-3 RMWs. Table 1 summarizes the use of type-1, type-2 and type-3 RMWs in various synchronization idioms.

In our final contribution, we propose efficient microarchitectural implementations of the weaker RMWs, which, in contrast to existing implementations, do not incur the cost of a write-buffer drain (§3). Our implementation of a type-2 RMW allows instructions following it to retire as soon as the read obtains exclusive ownership of the cache-line and locks it locally. The write simply retires into the tail of the write-buffer – thus the write-buffer drain is moved out of the critical path. To guarantee atomicity, coherence requests to the locked cache-line are denied until the write (of the RMW) and the pending writes prior to it complete. However, to prevent a potential deadlock we need to ensure that the above pending writes will eventually complete, and not be blocked by an RMW from another processor. We ensure this by tracking the list of unique RMW addresses in per-processor bloom filters. When a pending write (before the RMW) is found to conflict with the list of maintained RMW addresses, we revert to draining the write-buffer, thus avoiding the possibility of a deadlock (§3.2).

The type-3 RMW implementation is almost identical, with one difference. Since type-3 atomicity permits reads to the same ad-

Table 1. Conventional RMW (type-1) vs proposed RMWs (type-2, type-3)

Atomicity Definition	Dekker's with reads replaced by RMWs?	Dekker's with writes replaced by RMWs?	Dekker's with RMWs as barriers?	C/C++11 by replacing SC-atomic-reads with RMWs?	C/C++11 by replacing SC-atomic-writes with RMWs?
type-1	✓	✓	✓	✓	✓
type-2	✓	✓	✗	✓	✓
type-3	✓	✗	✗	✓	✗

dress as the RMW between the read and the write, the read need not obtain exclusive ownership of the cache-line – leading to a potentially more efficient implementation (§3.3). Our experimental results (§4) from benchmarks chosen from Splash-2, PARSEC, STAMP, and lock-free data structures show that in comparison with the existing type-1 RMW, our proposed type-2 RMW (type-3 RMW) is up to 58.9% (64.3%) cheaper, which translates into an overall performance improvement of upto 9.0%(9.2%)

We are not the first to propose weaker atomicity semantics for RMWs in general. In fact, Gharachorloo et al. [12] have already observed that it is sufficient for RMWs to use a type-3 definition for atomicity. However, in order for their TSO specification to be compliant with the original TSO specification, additional program order edges are added to RMWs, making the RMWs strongly ordered. In other words, by explicitly adding additional program order edges, the RMWs in their specification are effectively made equivalent to type-1 RMWs. In this paper, we consider the case in which the atomicity definitions are weakened, but additional program order edges are not added to the RMW. Besides, our proposed type-2 atomicity definition, to the best of our knowledge has not been considered before. More on related work in §5.

2. Semantics of TSO RMWs

In this section we will propose definitions of atomicity weaker than the standard strong definition for RMWs in TSO, and derive the ordering properties that apply. We will then use those ordering properties to demonstrate the use of weakened RMWs in synchronization – in particular, we will demonstrate when they are sufficient to implement the C/C++11 concurrency model.

We begin with recalling the base TSO model (without RMWs), and then add our new formulations of atomicity. The base TSO model follows Alglave [2], where our atomicity definitions fit most naturally. We present here only a brief introduction to Alglave's formulation published previously. Readers, particularly those familiar with alternative TSO formulations, should refer to Alglave's thesis for more details. The thesis has a proof of equivalence with the SPARC definition of TSO [25] is given, which is separately shown by Owens et al [22] to resemble the x86 multiprocessor model.

2.1 Base TSO

As usual in axiomatic memory models, we first derive a set of candidate executions from a program. Each candidate execution contains a set of events and relations over them, and represents a conceivable execution path (with control-flow unfolded, and values for each read in the program). In the next step, the memory model will carve out (via conditions on those relations) which of these candidate executions are allowed by the model.

The events (memory reads, writes, and barriers) are annotated with their thread, type, and for memory accesses the associated address and value. From the program we derive the program order (po) relation, a local (per-thread) total order over events from the same thread as they appear in the program. We also consider two relations which are existentially quantified over: a reads-from map (rf) and write-serialization (ws), both relations over events. The relation rf maps, for each read, the write that the read takes its value from to the read. The relation ws is a linear order per location relating all (and only) the writes to the same location, and represents the coherence order of the system (in prior work, this relation is also called coherence co).

For ease of stating the memory model, we derive various additional relations from the above. The from-reads relation (fr) relates a read to all writes to the same location that come after (in ws) the write it reads from (given by rf). The external-reads-from relation (rfe) is the subrelation of rf which is restricted to reads which read from a different-thread write. The communication relation com is the union of ws, rfe, and fr.

A preserved-program-order relation (ppo) relates all memory operations from the same thread in program order, according to TSO ordering rules. Thus it relates all memory operations, except writes to program order-subsequent reads: In other words, $W \xrightarrow{\text{po}} W$, $R \xrightarrow{\text{po}} W$, $R \xrightarrow{\text{po}} R$ all belong to ppo also.

A barrier-separated relation (bar) relates memory operations (on the same thread) separated in program order by a memory barrier.

The behavior of a program is the set of corresponding execution witnesses which are valid. A valid execution witness is one where the union of com, ppo, and bar is acyclic, and satisfies the uniproc condition. The uniproc condition states that the relation com is consistent with the per-thread order of memory operations to the same location. The first condition says that a happens-before-like relation is acyclic. In this case we call a linear extension of of com, ppo, and bar the global-happens-before relation (ghb). Informally, it is the global memory order (also known as execution order) in which memory operations appear to perform.

2.2 Adding RMWs to the model

We now consider events coming from RMWs. These correspond to one read and one write to the same location – we denote the read part of the RMW as R_a and the write part of the RMW as W_a. In an RMW, the read part comes before the write in program order – consequently, the read R_a reads an earlier value and not the value written by W_a. In addition to this, R_a and W_a need to be performed atomically, where atomicity is one of the following three definitions:

- **Type-1 Atomicity.** This is a strict definition of atomicity, used by existing TSO RMWs [16, 26], that prevents *writes of any address* from appearing between the read and the write in the global memory order. More formally, with type-1 RMWs added to the TSO model, valid execution witnesses are ones which further impose that there is no event in ghb between R_a and W_a.
- **Type-2 Atomicity.** This is a weakening which only prevents *reads and writes of the same address as the RMW* from appearing between R_a and W_a in the global memory order. More formally: $\{\forall M(x) : M(x) \xrightarrow{ghb} R_a(x) \vee W_a(x) \xrightarrow{ghb} M(x)\}$.
- **Type-3 Atomicity.** This is a further weakening which merely prevents *writes of the same address as the RMW* from appearing between R_a and W_a in the global memory order. More formally: $\{\forall W(x) : W(x) \xrightarrow{ghb} R_a(x) \vee W_a(x) \xrightarrow{ghb} W(x)\}$.

It is important to note that even type-3 atomicity, the weakest of the atomicity definitions, satisfies the notion of atomicity required for solving the *consensus* problem [15] – consensus being the abstract problem that models synchronization idioms. Nonetheless, this does not imply that the three types of RMWs can be used interchangeably. In fact, we shall see that each of the three atomicities gives rise to RMWs that are ordered differently.

Atomicity-induced orderings. Each atomicity definition, by disallowing a specific set of memory operations between R_a and W_a in the global memory order – effectively requires both R_a and W_a of the RMW to be ordered identically with such disallowed memory operations. For example, if just R_a (and not W_a) is originally ordered before a disallowed memory operation M in the ghb ($R_a \xrightarrow{ghb} M$), then atomicity requires W_a to also be ordered before M ($W_a \xrightarrow{ghb} M$) – otherwise M could end up between R_a and W_a in the ghb. In other words, the atomicity constraint induces additional memory orderings – the atomicity relation ato is used to refer to such atomicity-induced orderings. In the above example, the ordering $W_a \xrightarrow{ato} M$ would be an atomicity-induced ordering. Accounting for such atomicity-induced orderings, the global memory order (ghb) is the linear extension of the union of com, ppo, bar, and ato. A valid execution witness, like before, is one which has an acyclic union of the above relations (including ato), and satisfies the uniproc condition. Next, we will derive the atomicity-induced memory ordering constraints for each of the atomicity definitions.

2.3 Type-1 RMWs

The strict type-1 definition of atomicity combined with TSO's preserved program order ensures that a type-1 RMW is strongly ordered with respect to memory operations before and after it.

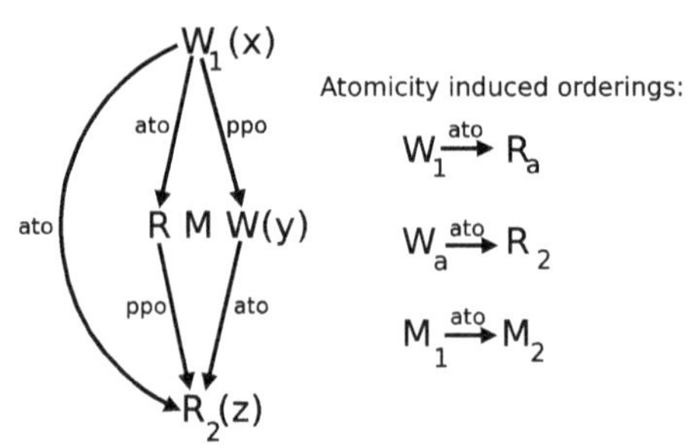

Figure 2. Additional memory orderings induced by type-1 RMW

Lemma 1. *An RMW placed between a write W_1 and a read R_2, results in the enforcement of $W_1 \xrightarrow{ato} R_a$, $W_a \xrightarrow{ato} R_2$ and consequently, $W_1 \xrightarrow{ato} R_2$.*

Proof. Type-1 atomicity mandates that either $W_a \xrightarrow{ghb} W_1$ or $W_1 \xrightarrow{ghb} R_a$. As shown in Fig. 2, $W_1 \xrightarrow{ppo} W_a$. This implies $W_1 \xrightarrow{ato} R_a$. Next, we prove the second part: $W_a \xrightarrow{ato} R_2$. As shown in Fig. 2, $R_a \xrightarrow{ppo} R_2$. This implies that either R_2 occurs after W_a in the ghb or R_2 is between R_a and W_a. Meanwhile, type-1 atomicity mandates that there cannot be any writes between R_a and W_a in the ghb; in particular there cannot be any writes to location z. This implies that even if R_2 were to occur between R_a and W_a, it can be safely be moved after W_a. This in turn implies $W_a \xrightarrow{ato} R_2$. Finally, $W_1 \xrightarrow{ato} R_2$, because of transitivity ($W_1 \xrightarrow{ato} R_a$ and $R_a \xrightarrow{ppo} R_2$). □

Such strongly ordered type-1 RMWs result in costly implementations that involve a write-buffer drain; however, they can be used to port synchronization idioms to TSO without requiring additional memory barriers. Below, we demonstrate how type-1 RMWs are used in various synchronization idioms:

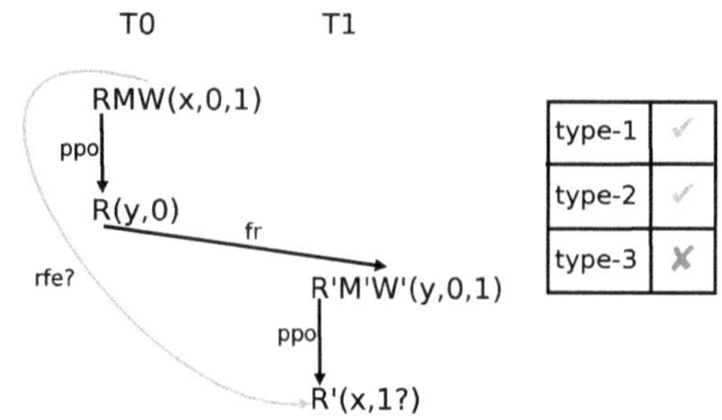

Figure 3. Dekker's with writes replaced by RMWs. In this and other examples that follow, $RMW(x, 0, 1)$ means that the RMW reads a value of 0 from location x and updates it to 1

Dekker's: write-replacement. One way to ensure that Dekker's algorithm works on TSO architectures is to replace the writes with type-1 RMWs as shown in Fig. 3 [16, 26] In the above example, we assume that the read $R(y)$ from thread 0 reads the initial value of 0. For Dekker's algorithm to work the read $R'(x)$ should read a value of 1. The following sequence of orderings ensure this: $W_a(x) \xrightarrow{ato} R(y) \xrightarrow{fr} W'_a(y) \xrightarrow{ato} R'(x)$ – where ato denotes the additional orderings induced by atomicity.

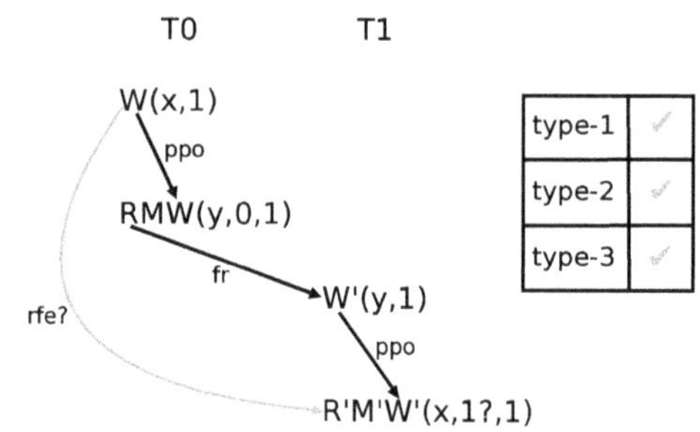

Figure 4. Dekker's with reads replaced by RMWs.

Dekker's: read-replacement. Using similar reasoning, it is easy to see that replacing reads with type-1 RMWs will also ensure that Dekker's algorithm works on TSO (Fig. 4).

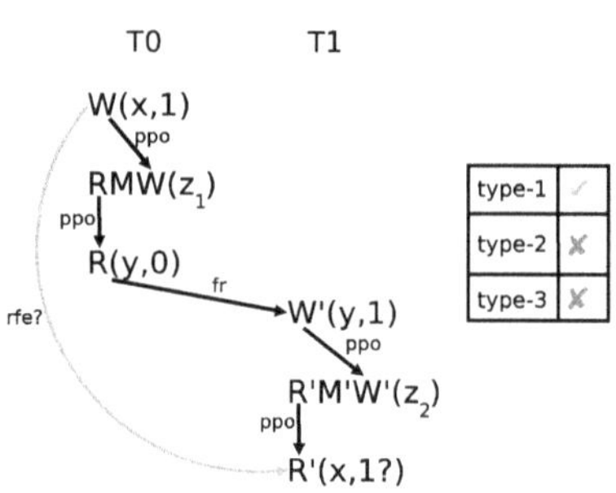

Figure 5. Dekker's with RMWs used as memory barriers. The two RMWs access different addresses z_1 and z_2.

Dekker's: RMWs as barriers. One simple way to make Dekker's algorithm work on TSO is to insert memory barriers between the writes and the reads, as the $W \rightarrow R$ ordering enforced by the memory barriers would ensure correctness. Since type-1 RMWs order memory operations before and after it, they can very well be used instead of the barriers. As shown in Fig. 5, the following sequence of ordering ensures correctness: $W(x) \xrightarrow{ato} R(y) \xrightarrow{fr} W'(y) \xrightarrow{ato} R'(x)$.

Implementing C/C++11 using type-1 RMWs. The C/C++11 concurrency model [7, 10] is an adaptation of *data-race-free-0* [1] which guarantees SC for data race free programs. It introduces a variety of atomic memory operations parameterized by different *memory order* parameters. Correct compilation depends (among other things) on mapping these atomic memory operations to hardware primitives. Batty et al. [6] recently proved that C/C++11 can be implemented on X86-TSO by mapping C/C++11 SC-atomic-reads and SC-atomic-writes to type-1 RMWs supported by x86 architectures (non-SC atomic reads and writes and non-atomic accesses can simply be mapped to ordinary TSO reads and writes). In fact, it is easy to adapt this proof and show that it is sufficient to map at least one of the SC-atomic-writes or the SC atomic reads to type-1 RMWs (see appendix). Informally, since TSO already preserves all program orders except the $W \rightarrow R$ order, we only need to ensure SC-atomic-writes are ordered with subsequent SC-atomic-reads; similarly to Dekker's algorithm, this can be accomplished by replacing either the reads or writes with type-1 RMWs.

2.4 Type-2 RMWs

We show that, unlike a type-1 RMW, a type-2 RMW placed between a write W_1 and a read R_2 does not explicitly enforce any of $W_1 \xrightarrow{ghb} R_a$, $W_a \xrightarrow{ghb} R_2$, or $W_1 \xrightarrow{ghb} R_2$. However, it disallows $R_a \xrightarrow{ghb} W_1$ and $R_2 \xrightarrow{ghb} W_a$ from being enforced [1] – in effect, a type-2 RMW is *implicitly ordered with respect to memory operations before and after it.*

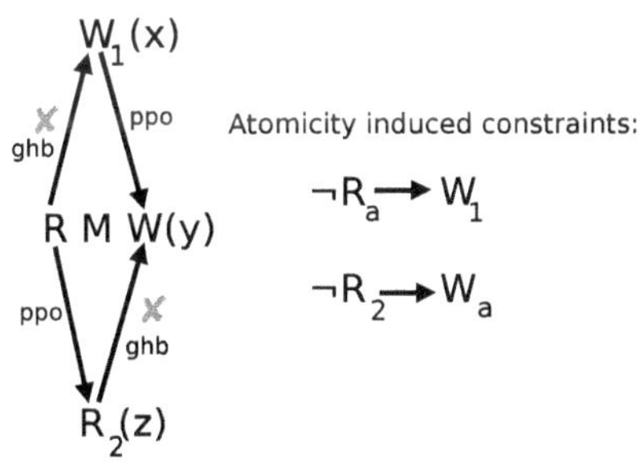

Figure 6. Memory ordering disallowed by a type-2 RMW

Lemma 2. *A type-2 RMW placed between two memory operations W_1 and R_2, disallows the enforcement of the following two orderings: $R_a \xrightarrow{ghb} W_1$ and $R_2 \xrightarrow{ghb} W_a$.*

Proof. Let us attempt to prove by contradiction by assuming the ordering $R_a \xrightarrow{ghb} W_1$ is enforced. Since there is no ppo edge directly connecting R_a and W_1, $R_a \xrightarrow{ghb} W_1$ we will need to be enforced via a sequence of edges as shown in Fig. 7. More specifically, there has to be a write $W'(y)$ which conflicts with $R_a(y)$ such that: $R_a(y) \xrightarrow{fr} W'(y) \xrightarrow{ghb} W_1(x)$. But, $R_a(y) \xrightarrow{fr} W'(y)$ implies $W_a(y) \xrightarrow{ato} W'(y)$, due to type-2 atomicity. This leads to a cycle: $W_a(y) \xrightarrow{ato} W'(y) \xrightarrow{ghb} W_1(x) \xrightarrow{ppo} W_a(y)$.

Similarly for the other part let us assume $R_2 \xrightarrow{ghb} W_a$. As shown in Fig. 7, this implies that there has to be a read $R''(y)$

[1] Disallowing an ordering $M_1 \xrightarrow{ghb} M_2$ (say) is not the same as enforcing $M_2 \xrightarrow{ghb} M_1$. The latter implies that M_2 will occur before M_1 in every valid global memory order, while the former implies that it is not necessary for M_1 to occur before M_2 in every valid global memory order

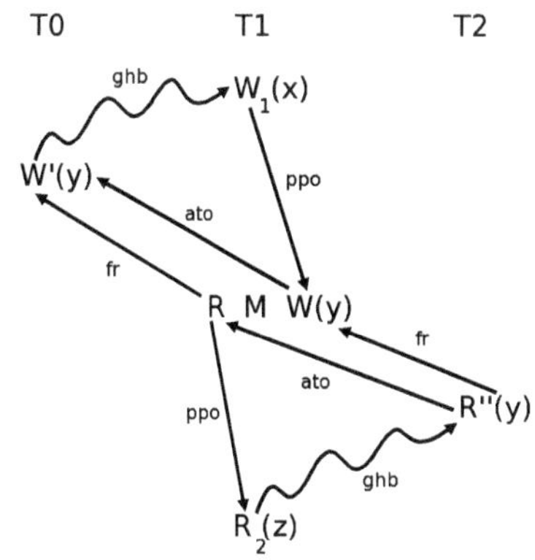

Figure 7. Scenario for proof of lemma 2.

which conflicts with $W_a(y)$ such that: $R_2(z) \xrightarrow{ghb} R''(y) \xrightarrow{fr} W_a(y)$. But, $R''(y) \xrightarrow{fr} W_a(y)$ implies $R''(y) \xrightarrow{ato} R_a(y)$, due to type-2 atomicity. This leads to a cycle: $R_a(y) \xrightarrow{ppo} R_2(z) \xrightarrow{ghb} R''(y) \xrightarrow{ato} R_a(y)$. □

Effect of implicitly ordered type-2 RMWs. Since a type-2 RMW neither enforces $W_1 \rightarrow R_a$ nor $W_a \rightarrow R_2$, it also does not transitively enforce $W_1 \rightarrow R_2$. Consequently, a type-2 RMW is not ordered like a memory barrier; in the next section we will propose an efficient implementation that does not incur the cost of a write-buffer drain. At the same time, a type-2 RMW appears to be strongly ordered with respect to any memory operation that synchronizes with the RMW i.e any memory operation from another thread that is to the same address as the RMW. As shown in Fig. 7, with respect to $W'(y)$ which synchronizes with R_a, W_1 appears to be ordered before the RMW. This is because, type-2 atomicity induces the ordering $W_a(y) \xrightarrow{ato} W'(y)$, which results in the sequence of orderings: $W_1(x) \xrightarrow{ppo} W_a(y) \xrightarrow{ato} W'(y)$, thereby ensuring $W_1(x) \rightarrow W'(y)$. Likewise, with respect to $R''(y)$ which synchronizes with W_a, $R_2(z)$ appears to perform after the RMW – the sequence of orderings $R_{\prime\prime}(y) \xrightarrow{ato} R_a(y) \xrightarrow{ppo} R_2(z)$ ensures this. Consequently, type-2 RMWs can seamlessly replace existing RMWs in synchronization idioms, as we will demonstrate next.

Dekker's: write-replacement. Similarly to type-1 RMWs, Dekker's algorithm will continue to work with writes replaced by type-2 RMWs as shown in in Fig. 3. Since $R(y) \xrightarrow{fr} W'_a(y)$, $R(y) \xrightarrow{ato} R'_a(y)$ (due to type-2 atomicity). Now, the sequence of orderings $R_a(x) \xrightarrow{ppo} R(y) \xrightarrow{ato} R'_a(y) \xrightarrow{ppo} R'(x)$ ensures that $R_a(x) \xrightarrow{ghb} R'(x)$. This in turn implies that $W_a(x) \xrightarrow{ato} R'(x)$, again due to type-2 atomicity.

Dekker's: read-replacement. Using a similar reasoning, replacing reads with type-2 RMWs will also ensure that Dekker's algorithm works on TSO (Fig. 4). Since $R_a(y) \xrightarrow{fr} W'(y)$, $W_a(y) \xrightarrow{ato} W'(y)$ (due to type-2 atomicity). Now, the sequence of orderings $W(x) \xrightarrow{ppo} W_a(y) \xrightarrow{ato} W'(y) \xrightarrow{ppo} W'_a(x)$ ensures that $W(x) \xrightarrow{ghb} W'_a(x)$. This in turn implies that $W(x) \xrightarrow{ato} R'_a(x)$, again due to type-2 atomicity.

Dekker's: RMWs as barriers (different addresses). A type-2 RMW cannot be used as a memory barrier in Dekker's algorithm if the RMWs used to replace the barriers access different addresses, since they would not appear strongly ordered with one another. As shown in Fig. 5, it can potentially allow the following sequence of operations – $R_a(z_1), R(y), R'_a(z_2), R'(x), W(x),$

$W_a(z_1), W'(x), W'_a(z_1)$ – which would lead to $R'(x)$ to read a value of 0.

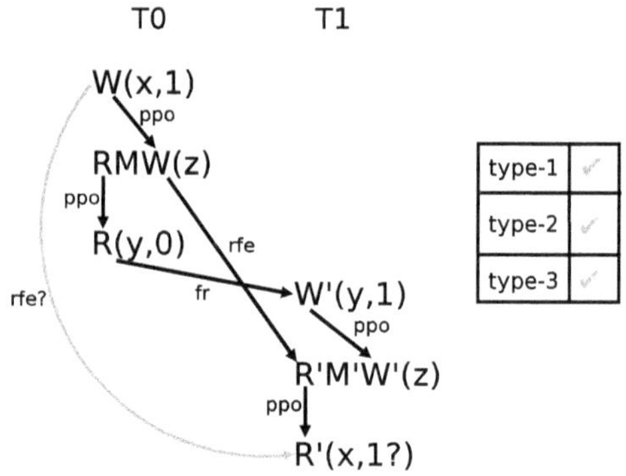

Figure 8. Dekker's with RMWs used as a memory barrier. The two RMWs access the same addresses z.

Dekker's: RMWs as barriers (same address). A type-2 RMW, however, can be used as a memory barrier in Dekker's algorithm if the inserted RMWs access the same address, since this ensures that the RMWs appear strongly ordered to one another. As shown in Fig. 8, type-2 RMWs used in the above fashion ensure that $R'(x)$ will read the correct value of 1. To see why, first recall that based on our assumption $R(y) \xrightarrow{fr} W'(y)$. This implies that $W_a(z) \xrightarrow{rfe} R'_a(z)$ (as the other possibility $W'_a(z) \xrightarrow{rfe} R_a(z)$ would result in the following cycle: $W'_a(z) \xrightarrow{rfe} R_a(z) \xrightarrow{ppo} R(y) \xrightarrow{fr} W'(y \xrightarrow{ppo} W'_a(z))$. This in turn leads to the sequence $W(x) \xrightarrow{ppo} W_a(z) \xrightarrow{rfe} R'_a(z) \xrightarrow{ppo} R'(x)$, ensuring that $R'(x)$ reads the correct value.

Implementing C/C++11 using type-2 RMWs. We formally show that, similarly to type-1 RMWs, C/C++11 can be implemented by mapping at least one of SC-atomic-writes or SC-atomic-reads to type-2 RMWs. Recall that, since TSO already preserves all program orders except the $W \rightarrow R$ order, we only need to ensure SC-atomic-writes are ordered with subsequent SC-atomic-reads. Intuitively, since type-2 RMWs appear strongly ordered when used in synchronization idioms, this can be accomplished by replacing either the SC-atomic-reads or SC-atomic-writes with RMWs. See appendix for the formal proof.

2.5 Type-3 RMWs

We show that, similarly to a type-2 RMW, a type-3 RMW placed between W_1 and R_2 does not explicitly enforce any of $W_1 \xrightarrow{ghb} R_a$, $W_a \xrightarrow{R}_2\ ghb$, or $W_1 \xrightarrow{ghb} R_2$. However, unlike a type-2 RMW it disallows only $R_a \rightarrow W_1$ (but could allow $R_2 \rightarrow W_a$) – in effect, a type-3 RMW is implicitly ordered with respect to memory operations before it, but not with those after it.

Lemma 3. *A type-3 RMW placed between two memory operations W_1 and R_2, disallows $R_a \xrightarrow{ghb} W_1$ (but could allow $R_2 \xrightarrow{ghb} W_a$ to be enforced).*

Proof. Proof of $\neg R_a \xrightarrow{ghb} W_1$ is identical to the first part of the proof of lemma 2. To understand why $R_2 \xrightarrow{ghb} W_a$ is not disallowed, let us consider the second part of the proof of lemma 2, where we assumed $R_2 \xrightarrow{ghb} W_a$. As shown in Fig. 7, this implies that there has to be a read $R''(y)$ which conflicts with $W_a(y)$ such that: $R_2(z) \xrightarrow{ghb} R''(y) \xrightarrow{fr} W_a(y)$. Recall that type-2 atomicity induced the ordering: $R''(y) \xrightarrow{ato} R_a(y)$, which led to a cycle. However, such an ordering is not induced by type-3 atomicity, which allows for reads to happen between the $R_a(y)$ and $W_a(y)$, and so there is no cycle. □

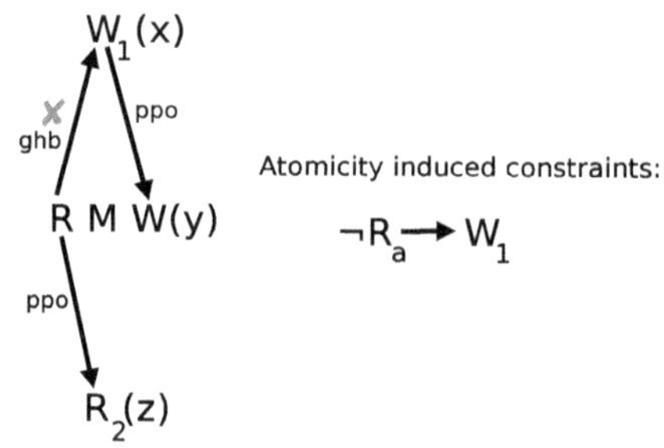

Figure 9. Memory ordering disallowed by a type-3 RMW

Effect of implicitly ordered type-3 RMWs. Since a type-3 RMW enforces neither $W_1 \rightarrow R_a$ nor $W_a \rightarrow R_2$, it also does not transitively enforce $W_1 \rightarrow R_2$. Consequently, a type-3 RMW is not ordered like a memory barrier. At the same time, a type-3 RMW appears to be strongly ordered with respect to any write/RMW that synchronizes with the RMW. As shown in Fig. 7, with respect to $W'(y)$ which synchronizes with R_a, W_1 appears to be ordered before the RMW. This is because type-3 atomicity induces $W_a(y) \xrightarrow{ato} W'(y)$, which in turn results in the sequence of orderings: $W_1(x) \xrightarrow{ppo} W_a(y) \xrightarrow{ato} W'(y)$ which ensures this. On the other hand, with respect to the read $R''(y)$ which synchronizes with W_a, $R_2(z)$ does not appear to be ordered after the RMW, since type-3 atomicity allows $R''(y)$ to occur between $R_a(y)$ and $W_a(y)$. Consequently, type-3 RMWs cannot seamlessly replace existing RMWs in synchronization idioms, as we will demonstrate next.

Dekker's: write-replacement. Unlike type-1 or type-2 RMWs, replacing writes with type-3 RMWs cannot guarantee correctness (Fig. 3). This is because type-3 atomicity is not able to induce $R(y) \xrightarrow{ato} R'_a(y)$. Hence, the following sequence is allowed: $R_a(x), R(y), R'_a(y), R'(x), W_a(x), W'_a(y)$ – which would lead to $R'(x)$ to read 0.

Other Dekker's scenarios. For the other Dekker's algorithm scenarios (Fig. 4, Fig. 5, and Fig. 8) a type-3 RMW behaves identically to a type-2 RMW.

Implementing C/C++11 using type-3 RMWs. We formally show that C/C++11 can be implemented by mapping SC-atomic-reads (and optionally SC-atomic-writes) to type-3 RMWs. However, it is not sufficient (unlike type-1 and type-2 RMWs) for only the SC-atomic-writes to be so mapped. Intuitively, since type-3 RMWs appear strongly ordered only when synchronizing with writes or RMWs, but not reads, all SC-atomic-reads need to replaced with RMWs. See appendix for the formal proof.

2.6 Summary

We show that type-2 RMWs can seamlessly replace type-1 RMWs in various synchronization idioms, except when a type-1 RMW is used purely as a memory barrier. Given that all modern TSO(-like) architectures have a dedicated memory barrier instruction, there is no need to use an RMW as a barrier. Furthermore, type-2 RMWs can still be used as a memory barrier provided such RMWs are forced to synchronize with each other (by forcing them to access the same address). Similarly to type-2 RMWs, type-3 RMWs also do not behave like memory barriers. However, unlike type-2 RMWs, type-3 RMWs only appear ordered with respect to writes/RMWs (but not reads) that synchronize with the RMW; thus type-3 RMWs cannot seamlessly replace type-1 RMWs. Nevertheless, we show that by replacing synchronization reads with type-3 RMWs, the above synchronization idioms can still be implemented using type-3 RMWs.

3. TSO RMWs: Implementation

In this section we first discuss how existing type-1 RMWs are implemented. We then describe our proposed type-2 and type-3 RMW implementations. For the following discussion we assume a chip multiprocessor with local L1 caches and a shared L2 cache; the local caches are kept coherent at the L2 cache using a distributed directory based coherence protocol.

3.1 Type-1 RMW

Recall that a type-1 RMW is strongly ordered with respect to memory operations before and after it: a type-1 RMW placed between write W_1 and read R_2 results in the enforcement of $W_1 \rightarrow R_a$ and $W_a \rightarrow R_2$, where R_a/W_a are the read/write of the RMW respectively. To enforce $W_1 \rightarrow R_a$, pending writes in the write-buffer (if any) must complete before R_a can retire.

Furthermore, type-1 atomicity mandates that there should not be any conflicting reads or writes (to the same address as the RMW) between R_a and W_a. To ensure this, existing RMW implementations use a cache-line locking mechanism [16, 20, 26]. The R_a obtains read/write permissions for the cache-line, and locks it before it retires, thereby denying coherence requests to the cache-line. Once W_a completes, the cache-line is unlocked.

To ensure that $W_a \rightarrow R_2$ is enforced, R_2 is allowed to retire only after W_a completes. In other words, reads that follow the RMW have to wait until: (a) all writes prior to the RMW are performed (the write-buffer is drained) and (b) R_a and W_a are performed. Thus, the type-1 RMW incurs the cost of a write-buffer drain and the cost of performing R_a and W_a.

Gharachorloo et al. [13] proposed two techniques to provide efficient memory ordering. Both these techniques can be used to improve the performance of type-1 RMWs. The first one involves issuing the read-exclusive request for all pending writes in parallel, to efficiently enforce the write-buffer drain. The actual writes, however, are completed in-order, keeping with TSO. Parallel issue of the read-exclusives will be serialized at the local L1 cache and at the directory, but will make full use of the interconnect and overlap invalidation and acknowledgement messages for all the pending writes. The second technique is to hide part of the write-buffer drain latency through in-window speculation. Here, the instructions following the RMW are speculatively executed, but are allowed to complete only after the RMW and all the pending writes before it complete.

3.2 Type-2 RMW

Recall that a type-2 RMW is not explicitly ordered with respect to memory operations before and after it in the program order. Since a type-2 RMW that is placed between memory operations W_1 and R_2, does not enforce $W_1 \rightarrow R_a$, R_a need not wait for the write-buffer to be drained. However, type-2 atomicity still disallows conflicting reads or writes from appearing between R_a and W_a in the global memory order. Similarly to a type-1 RMW, this is ensured using the cache-line locking mechanism. Like before, R_a obtains read/write permissions for the cache-line, locks the cache-line, and then retires. After this, W_a simply retires into the tail of the write-buffer. At this point the RMW effectively retires, and allows memory operations following it (e.g. R_2) to retire (since $W_a \rightarrow R_2$ is not enforced). Finally, when W_a reaches the head of the write-buffer and completes, the cache-line is unlocked.

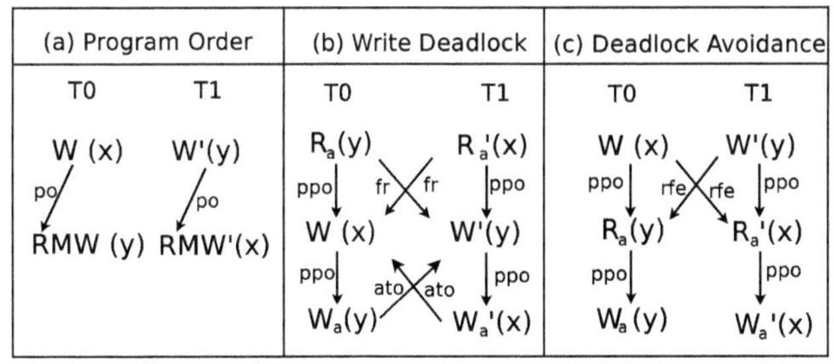

Figure 10. (a) shows a code segment that can cause a write-deadlock. (b) shows an execution order with a cyclic dependency of non-occurring events resulting in a write-deadlock. fr ordering

Write-deadlocks. The above implementation, while simple, can potentially result in a deadlock. To guarantee type-2 atomicity, coherence requests to the cache-line locked by an RMW are denied until W_a and the pending writes prior to it complete. If such a pending write W_1 is to a cache-line which has already been locked by another RMW$'$ from a different processor, then W_1 (and hence W_a) will have to wait until W'_a completes. If W'_a itself is stalled because of a similar write in its write-buffer, a deadlock manifests.

This is illustrated in the code segment shown in Fig. 10(a), where $W(x)$ occurs before RMW(y), and $W'(y)$ occurs before RMW$'(x)$ in program order. As shown in Fig. 10(b), let us assume that $R_a(y)$ and $R'_a(x)$ have retired after locking their respective cache-lines, while the writes ($W(x)$ and $W'(y)$) have retired into the write-buffer and are yet to complete. Cache-line locking ensures that $W(x)$ cannot complete until $W'_a(x)$ has completed, and $W'(y)$ cannot complete until $W_a(y)$ has completed. However, since writes are ordered in TSO, $W_a(y)$ cannot complete until $W(x)$ completes, and $W'_a(x)$ cannot complete until $W'(y)$ completes. This leads to a write-deadlock.

More formally, our assumptions can be represented by the two fr orderings: $R'_a(x) \xrightarrow{fr} W(x)$ and $R_a(y) \xrightarrow{fr} W'(y)$. Now, type-2 atomicity induces the two orderings: $W'_a(x) \xrightarrow{ato} W(x)$ and $W_a(y) \xrightarrow{ato} W'(y)$. This in turn results in a cycle: $W(x) \xrightarrow{ppo} W_a(y) \xrightarrow{ato} W'(y) \xrightarrow{ppo} W'_a(x) \xrightarrow{ato} W(x)$. Since each of the memory operations which are part of the cycle have not yet performed, a deadlock ensues.

Deadlock avoidance. In order to ensure that the deadlock scenario discussed above never occurs, we should guarantee that none of the pending writes before an RMW, are to cache-lines locked by other RMWs – the deadlock safety property. To ensure this, we propose a mechanism to dynamically maintain the set of unique RMW addresses accessed by RMWs from all processors – the *addr-list*. Furthermore, we make this addr-list available locally to each of the processors.

Now, when an RMW is performed, if none of the pending writes in the write-buffer conflict with the addr-list, we can safely say that these writes are not to locked cache-lines. On the other hand, if any of the pending writes conflicts with the addr-list, the deadlock safety property is not guaranteed. In such a case, we revert to type-1 implementation by draining the write-buffer before performing the RMW – thereby avoiding a deadlock.

There are two challenges to efficiently implementing this mechanism in hardware: (a) keeping track of the RMW addresses in the addr-list efficiently; (b) keeping the addr-list coherent across all processors. We implement the addr-list using a bloom filter [8], which is a well understood mechanism for maintaining sets and supporting membership queries. In order to keep the addr-list coherent we simply broadcast the address whenever a new RMW address is encountered by a processor. Our design exploits the fact that the number of unique RMW addresses is relatively small – our experiments show that typically around 1% of the number of dynamic RMWs are to unique addresses. This in turn means that the addresses of the RMWs can be stored efficiently in a relatively small-sized bloom filter, with a low probability of false positives. More importantly, the number of broadcasts required to keep the addr-list coherent is minimal.

We now explain the working of our mechanism in more detail. When an RMW is ready to perform, we first query the bloom filter for the RMW address. If the address is not found in the filter, we insert the RMW address into the local bloom filter. In addition to this, since the addr-list has changed, we broadcast the new address to all processors. Each of the other processors, upon receiving the address, inserts the address into its respective bloom filter and sends back an acknowledgement. Once all acknowledgements have been received (or if the RMW's address is found in the addr-list in the first place), we query the bloom filter with the pending writes' addresses. If any of these write addresses are found in the addr-list, this flags a potential deadlock. Consequently, the write-buffer is drained before performing the RMW like a type-1 RMW. On the other hand, if none of the pending writes' addresses are found, the RMW does not wait for the write-buffer to drain. It locks the cache-line and simply retires, while the write of the RMW is retired into the write-buffer.

To see why our scheme is correct note that an RMW can lock the cache-line and retire (with pending writes in the write-buffer) only when:

- c1: the RMW's address is made visible to all processors
- c2: none of the pending writes conflict with the addr-list.

Now, c1 implies that any write (W') that could be potentially involved in a deadlock with the original RMW will conflict with the local addr-list. c2 implies that an RMW with W' in its write-buffer will revert to type-1, thereby avoiding a deadlock. Consider the deadlock scenario shown in Fig. 10(c). Recall that in the deadlock scenario, $R_a(y)$ and $R'_a(x)$ have retired, but their respective pending writes $W(x)$ and $W'(y)$ are unable to complete (inducing the two fr orderings: $R'_a(x) \xrightarrow{fr} W(x)$ and $R_a(y) \xrightarrow{fr} W'(y)$). The fact that $R_a(y)$ and $R'_a(x)$ have retired implies that both x and y must be present in the bloom filter (from c1). In addition to this, $W(x)$ and $W'(y)$ should have checked the filter for conflicts (from c2). The assumed fr orderings imply that neither of the writes conflicted with the bloom filter. This in turn implies that neither x nor y are in the bloom filter leading to a contradiction.

False Positives. Bloom filters suffer from false positives. The correctness of our scheme, however, is not compromised. The false positive may result from either an RMW or a pending write checking the bloom filter. When an RMW, whose address has not been encountered before, queries the bloom filter and the bloom filter returns a false positive, the RMW address ends up not being broadcast. This is safe, however, because any write which conflicts with this address will also similarly return a false positive. It is worth noting that false positives in this case may reduce the number of RMW broadcasts. Likewise, When a pending write queries the bloom filter and the filter returns a false positive, the write-buffer is unnecessarily drained. The correctness of the mechanism, however, is not affected.

Finally, in our design, the bloom filter keeps track of RMW addresses of all contexts. In other words, each bloom filter is independent of the thread context. While this may increase the probability of false positives, it again does not present any correctness issues.

It is worth noting that, the probability of false positives in the filter increases with the number of elements inserted into it, leading to a performance degradation over time. To handle this, we reset the bloom filters of all processors when the number of RMW addresses inserted into the filter exceeds a certain threshold, which is a function of the bloom filter configuration. To ensure correctness, when a processor receives a reset request, it waits until all in-flight RMWs have completed, and responds subsequently.

3.3 Type-3 RMW

Recall that a type-3 RMW, like a type-2 RMW, is not explicitly ordered with respect to memory operations before and after it. R_a need not wait for the write-buffer to be drained – it can retire even if there are pending entries in the write-buffer. However, type-3 atomicity still disallows conflicting writes and other RMWs from appearing between R_a and W_a in the global memory order. Since reads to the same memory address can appear between R_a and W_a, it is sufficient for R_a to get read permissions for the cache-line, unlike type-1/type-2 RMW which require read/write permission.

If the RMW is to a cache-line owned by the local cache, then it is locked in the cache itself before retiring R_a, similar to type-1/type-2 RMWs. If the RMW is to cache-line in *shared* state, however, locking the cache-line locally cannot prevent an RMW from another processor, which also has the cache-line in its local cache, from performing. To resolve this, we propose a *directory locking* protocol, wherein R_a to a cache-line in shared state is locked in the directory by transitioning the cache-line to a *locked* state. When W_a is issued from the write-buffer, the cache-line is transitioned out of the locked state allowing subsequent coherence requests to the cache-line to be serviced. This optimization removes any invalidation delay, incurred by the RMW, from the critical execution path.

Once R_a obtains a lock and retires, W_a simply retires into the tail of the write-buffer. At this point the RMW effectively retires, and allows memory operations following it to retire. Thus reads that follow a type-3 RMW will only have to wait until R_a obtains read permission for the cache-line and locks it. Finally, when W_a reaches the head of the write-buffer and completes, the lock on the cache-line is released. Similarly to type-2 RMWs, the implementation of type-3 RMWs also makes use of the bloom filter mechanism to avoid deadlocks.

4. Experimental Evaluation

The primary goal of our experiments was to compare the cost of type-1, type-2, and type-3 RMWs. Furthermore, we evaluated the impact of the different types of RMWs on the overall execution time of the benchmark programs. Since RMWs are also used to implement C/C++11 SC-atomic-reads and/or SC-atomic-writes, we also investigated the performance of supporting C/C++11 concurrency model with type-1, type-2 and type-3 RMWs. We briefly describe our implementation before discussing the results.

4.1 Implementation

Table 2. Architectural Parameters

Processor	32 core CMP, inorder
Write Buffer	32-entry deep
L1 Cache	private, 32 KB 4-way 2-cycle latency
L2 Cache	shared, 1 MB per-core, 16-way 6-cycle latency
Memory	300 cycle latency
Coherence	MOESI distributed directory
Interconnect	2D Mesh, 1-cycle link, 4-cycle router latency

Simulator. We use the GEM5 simulator to implement our baseline system, which is an x86-based CMP composed of inorder processors, with local L1 caches and a shared-distributed L2 cache.

Table 3. Benchmark Characteristics

Code	Suite	Problem Size	Ratio of RMWs per 1000 memops	% Unique RMWs	% write-buffer drains for type-2/type-3 RMW	RMW broadcasts per 100 RMW ops
radiosity	SPLASH-2	room	15.56	0.28	0.06	0.26
raytrace	SPLASH-2	car	13.83	0.02	0.12	0.02
fluidanimate	PARSEC	simmedium	17.43	0.46	0.09	0.46
dedup	PARSEC	simmedium	8.10	3.31	0.20	3.12
bayes	STAMP	bayes+	34.15	0.91	0.01	0.80
genome	STAMP	genome+	6.19	0.64	0.10	0.52
wsq-mst	Lockfree	10000 nodes	23.41	3.80	0.07	3.71

Cache latencies were obtained from CACTI [21]. The baseline uses type-1 RMWs. The local caches are kept coherent using a distributed directory based on the MOESI coherence protocol. We chose inorder cores for our simulation as the GEM5's out-of-order processor model is unstable for full system simulation of the x86 processor architecture. The choice of inorder cores, however, is a valid design point owing to the fact that several present and future many-core processors, like the Intel Xeon Phi, Sun Niagara T2, and NVIDIA GPUs, make use of inorder cores as opposed to out-of-order cores to achieve better performance to power ratios. As mentioned in the previous section, we implemented a parallel write-buffer drain mechanism. This improves the baseline significantly over the serial write-buffer drain. We did not implement in-window speculation as it is not applicable to inorder processors. The architectural parameters for our implementation are presented in Table 2.

We modified the simulator to implement type-2 and type-3 RMWs with deadlock avoidance. In our implementation, we used a 128B bloom filter with 3 hash functions. It is worth noting that the only hardware overhead for type-2/type-3 RMWs is the 128B bloom filter and a RMW threshold counter per processor. Also, we did not make use of the threshold counter in our simulations as we ran only a single context which did not require a bloom filter reset for good performance.

Benchmarks. We evaluate our technique using benchmarks in Table 3, which includes both lock-based and a lock-free program. *radiosity* and *raytrace* are benchmarks from the Splash-2 suite which primarily use RMWs in lock/unlock primitives. Similarly, *fluidanimate* and *dedup* (from PARSEC) are also lock-based benchmarks. It is worth noting here that we chose only the top two benchmarks from each suite, in terms of the ratio of RMW instructions to other memory operations. We do this as traditional lock-based algorithms are highly scalable and do not communicate (or synchronize) very much and thus do not benefit from reducing the cost of RMWs. On the other hand, lock-free programs use more RMWs taking advantage of low-latency communication on multicores. *wsq-mst* is a lock-free parallel spanning tree algorithm [4] using Chase-Lev work stealing queue. *bayes* and *genome*, from the STAMP (using TL2 [11]), use RMWs for locking writes in transactions and to commit transactions. We ran the benchmarks in their regions of interest, with the input sizes mentioned in Table 3.

C/C++11 concurrency. Because of the recency of the C/C++11 concurrency model, there is no corpus of C/C++11 code to test our ideas on. We therefore modified the *wsq-mst* program to make use of atomic reads/writes as prescribed by the C/C++11 model. *wsq-mst* uses Dekker-like synchronization to update the task queue pointers while removing tasks from the queue; thus the read and write of this synchronization primitive corresponds to an SC-atomic-read and SC-atomic-write respectively. As mentioned earlier, the C/C++11 concurrency model can be realized by replacing SC-atomic-writes and/or SC-atomic-reads with RMWs. We compare the performance of the different types of RMWs by replacing either the SC-atomic-reads (*wsq-mst_rr*) or SC-atomic-writes (wsq-mst_wr) with RMWs. We do not consider type-3 RMWs for write replacement here as that cannot guarantee correctness (as described in §2.5).

4.2 Cost of RMWs

We split the cost of an RMW in two parts: the cost of performing the read and write (R_a/W_a); and the cost of handling the writes in the write-buffer. The average cost of an RMW across the chosen benchmarks for type-1, type-2, and type-3 RMWs is presented in Fig. 11(a). As we can see, RMWs are expensive – the average cost of type-1 RMWs is as high as 69 cycles. We also observe that the write-buffer drain significantly contributes to the overall cost of an RMW (58.0% on average). We can infer from this that a significant number of RMWs have at least one write in the write-buffer which needs to send out invalidation requests. Also, a significant number of RMWs are to shared cache-lines which explains the cost contributed by R_a/W_a.

Using type-2 RMWs, the cost of an RMW reduces by 38.6%-58.9% when compared to type-1 RMWs across the benchmarks. As seen from Fig. 11(a), a significant portion of the performance improvement is by avoiding the write-buffer drain in the general case. Recall that we revert to a write-buffer drain, when a write hits in the bloom filter. As seen from Table 3, the average number of hits of pending writes in the bloom filter is negligible for each benchmark, and is sometimes zero. This explains the low write-buffer drain cost for type-2 and type-3 RMWs. It is worth noting that the cost of R_a/W_a itself slightly increases when compared with type-1 RMWs as a portion of the RMWs require broadcasts in addition to the invalidation request. The number of such RMW broadcasts depends on the accuracy of the bloom filter. As shown in the table, the percentage of RMWs that require a broadcast is less than 1.0% for most lock-based benchmarks except for *dedup* (3.1%), which has a higher ratio of unique RMWs to begin with. We have not presented the increase in network traffic due to RMW broadcasts, as this number is negligible across all chosen benchmarks (<0.5%).

Type-3 RMWs reduce the cost of the RMW even further. The average cost of a type-3 RMWs is lower than type-1 RMWs by up to 64.3%. Type-3 RMWs reduce the cost of R_a/W_a but incur a similar write-buffer drain delay as type-2 RMWs.

C/C++11 concurrency. Similarly to lock-based benchmarks, we observe that using type-2 RMWs reduces the average cost of RMWs by 44.6% (write-replacement), and 43.2% (write-replacement) respectively, over type-1 RMWs. As mentioned earlier, type-3 RMWs cannot be used for write-replacement. For read-replacement, type-3 RMWs provide an additional 11.6% improvement over type-1 RMWs.

It is worth noting that the cost of RMWs in read-replacement (*wsq-mst_rr*) is higher than in write-replacement (*wsq-mst_wr*) for all types of RMWs; with read replacement, there are more entries

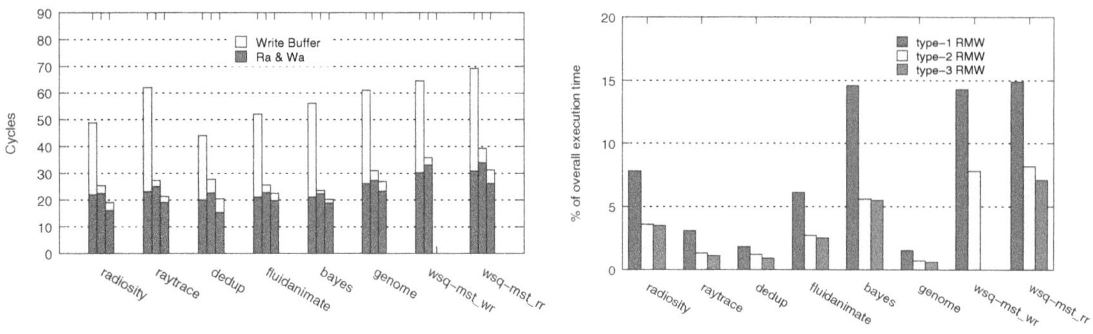

(a) Cost of type-1(left), type-2(center), and type-3(right) RMWs

(b) Execution time overhead of RMWs

Figure 11. Experimental Results

in the write-buffer per-RMW, which increases draining cost. The cost of R_a/W_a, however, is oblivious to whether SC-atomic-read or SC-atomic-write were replaced. In case of type-2 RMWs, we observe that the number of writes conflicting with the bloom filter increases, thereby increasing the cost of an RMW. Also note that this lock-free program, unlike traditional benchmarks, have more RMW broadcasts (3.7%) owing to a relatively larger number of unique RMWs. This affects the performance of type-2 and type-3 RMWs. However, the write-buffer drain cost eclipses the broadcast overhead.

4.3 Execution time overhead

Although we achieve a significant reduction in the cost of an RMW in all chosen benchmarks, its impact on the overall execution time depends on the ratio of RMW operations to other memory operations. We call this the *density* of RMWs. Thus, benchmarks with a larger RMW density benefit more from cheaper RMWs. Table 3 shows the ratio of the number of RMWs to the number of other memory operations in each of the benchmarks. From Fig. 11(b) shows the impact of RMWs on the overall execution time for all the chosen benchmarks. As expected, lock-free algorithms suffer more from expensive RMWs than lock-based algorithms. Similarly, *bayes* and *wsq-mst* also spend a lot of time performing RMWs. Although *genome* is a lock-free benchmark, the impact of RMWs on the overall execution time is less owing to a lower RMW density. This is because genome performs a lot more operations per transaction. As for lock-based benchmarks, *radiosity* and *fluidanimate* spend more than 5.0% of their execution time on RMWs. This, however, is not the case with *raytrace* and *dedup*. This is a result of the effort put into optimizing traditional lock-based benchmarks. We can extrapolate that other benchmarks from Splash-2 and Parsec will show an even lesser impact of RMWs.

With type-2 RMWs, we get up to 9.0% reduction for *bayes*, where the write-buffer drain almost but eliminated, as seen from Table 3. We also observe a significant reduction in the contribution of RMWs to the overall execution time in all other lock-free benchmarks as well. Even *radiosity* and *fluidanimate* show a reduction in overall execution time albeit lesser than 4%. Type-3 RMWs further improve the overall performance over type-2 RMWs, but only by a minimal amount (<0.5%).

C/C++11 concurrency. As for the C/C++11 concurrency model, replacing read atomics with RMWs results in a slightly higher overhead of RMWs as can be seen from the figure. The best performance can be obtained by replacing read atomics with type-3 RMWs (7.7% improvement over type-1 RMWs).

In summary, type-2 and type-3 RMWs are significantly cheaper than type-1 RMWs across all chosen benchmarks. This translates to a significant reduction in the overall execution time for the lock-free work stealing queue program which exhibits a higher RMW density. Traditional lock-based programs also show an improvement in performance. This improvement, however, is only visible in programs with a high RMW density. Other benchmarks show a negligible improvement in performance.

5. Related Work

Memory ordering. Over the years, researchers have proposed a number of techniques for achieving memory ordering efficiently [9, 14, 17, 18, 23]. While any of the above techniques can be used to efficiently implement the barrier-like ordering of a type-1 RMW, the goal of our work, however, is orthogonal. Instead of striving to implement the barrier-like ordering, we ask the question as to why a TSO RMW should be ordered like a memory barrier in the first place. Indeed, as we have shown through our weaker type-2/type-3 RMWs, implementing a barrier-like ordering is not necessary.

Weaker atomicity RMWs. Gharachorloo et al. [12] were the first to observe that it is sufficient for RMWs to use type-3 atomicity in the context of various memory consistency models. However, in order for their TSO specification to be compliant with the original TSO specification, they then added additional program order edges to RMWs, making the RMWs strongly ordered – hence equivalent to type-1 RMWs.

The load-reserve/store-conditional instruction is a classic example of an RMW in weaker models such as Power [19] which uses type-3 atomicity semantics. None of the mainstream TSO architectures, however, provide such an RMW. However, even if a TSO architecture were to support such an RMW, it would be ordered like a type-1 RMW. Because of its speculative nature, memory operations following such an RMW can only be retired after the store-conditional succeeds, and thus, such memory operations will have to wait for pending writes in the write-buffer, making the store-conditional act as a full barrier.

Hardware locking mechanisms. There have been several proposals (e.g. [28]) which address issues related to hardware based locking mechanisms. It is worth noting that these locks refer to the synchronization primitive as a whole and not the RMW instructions used in these primitives. These proposals primarily deal with lock contention and fairness. Our proposal is orthogonal to such work as we deal with the overhead added by the RMW to the local thread.

6. Conclusion

We observed that the atomicity semantics of an RMW is the key factor which affects the RMW's ordering semantics, its programmability, and its implementation cost. Existing TSO RMWs use a strict definition of atomicity (type-1) which results in the RMW being strongly ordered like a memory barrier. Whereas type-1 RMWs are costly to implement, they can be easily used in synchronization idioms on TSO without requiring additional memory barriers. In this paper, we proposed two weaker atomicity definitions: type-2 and type-3 atomicity; we formally derived how type-2 and type-3 RMWs would be ordered, and demonstrated that the resultant ordering is strong enough to implement various synchronization idioms using the weaker RMWs. We then proposed efficient architectural implementations of the weaker RMWs – experimental results show that our proposed type-2 RMW (type-3 RMW) is 58.9% (64.3%) cheaper than an existing type-1 RMW on average.

Based on our analysis and experimental evidence, type-2 RMWs, while performing almost as well as type-3 RMWs, are also able to seamlessly replace existing type-1 RMWs in common synchronization idioms – except in situations where an RMW is used as a memory barrier. Thus, they appear to be a promising alternative to existing type-1 RMWs. We also show how the proposed type-2 and type-3 RMWs can be used to implement C/C++11 atomics – thus making it possible for the compiler to transparently utilize the proposed RMWs to realize C/C++11 more efficiently.

A. C/C++11 implementation proofs

Recall that the C/C++11 concurrency model [7, 10] has marked memory accesses of various kinds (only SC is important on TSO, the properties of the others are automatically satisfied by normal reads and writes on TSO). We work with the formal description in Batty et al [6]. For a particular execution of a program, various relations among the actions corresponding to these operations are defined, including a happens-before relation; modification order mo, a total order per atomic location on writes to that location; and SC order sc, a total order on all SC atomic actions in the execution. There are several consistency conditions which these relations must satisfy for the execution to be consistent (briefly, both mo and sc must be consistent with happens-before; the ithb part of happens-before must be acyclic; certain shapes contradicting coherence must not occur within happens-before; and reads must read from a happens-before consistent write). Furthermore, if any consistent execution in the sense above has a data race, then the program as a whole has no defined semantics.

Correct compilation to TSO depends (among other things) on mapping the atomic accesses to TSO hardware primitives. Batty et al [6] prove correctness for a few variant mappings on X86-TSO; specifically, the *read-write-mapping* of Table 4(a) (from a prototype by Terekhov [27]), which maps SC-atomic-reads and SC-atomic-writes to X86-TSO RMWs. It is easy to adapt their proof and weaken the mapping, making only the SC-atomic-reads RMW's as in Table 4(b): *read-mapping*, or only the SC-atomic-writes RMW's as in Table 4(c): *write-mapping*. We now show that each mapping above would suffice for correctly implementing C/C++11 using type-2 RMWs (and reprove for type-1), while for type-3 RMWs, the read-write mapping and the read-mapping work. The write-mapping would not work for type-3 RMWs, by Dekker's counterexample in the paper (Fig. 3).

A.1 A generic outline of the proof strategy

The proof is fairly standard, following the proofs in [5, 6]. In particular, the way of constructing SC orders is derived from the earlier paper.

Mapping read-from maps, and mo First, the events occurring in the hardware models are related to the C/C++ actions from the corresponding program. For everything except the C/C++11 SC atomics, this is straightforward, as ordinary reads and writes correspond to C/C++11 reads and writes. For the SC actions, we assume that there is a unique mapping that can be derived. Then the hardware rf relation corresponds to the reads-from map of C/C++11, and the hardware ws relation (restricted to *atomic* locations) corresponds to mo of C/C++11.

ghb contains the C/C++11 ithb Here we notice that under any mapping (and any kind of RMW), each of the components of C/C++11 inter-thread-happens-before are part of ghb, by the construction via release sequences. Thus the ghb is a greater relation than the C/C++11 ithb.

Constructing the C/C++11 SC order. This part of the proof crucially depends on the mapping, so we will have to parametrize the proof by the mapping. We consider, as in the proof of SC actions on Power [5], an arbitrary linearization of the union of po_{SC}, program-order on SC actions; ws_{SC}, ws restricted to SC actions; fr_{SC}, which relates SC reads to all SC writes to the same location coherence-after the write the read reads from; and erf_{SC}, which relates a SC read and the last SC write in coherence before the write, or that write if a SC write, that the read reads-from.

We will then show that these relations are included in the ghb relation, and thus their union is consistent with ghb. As a corollary, by the acyclicity of ghb, we get that the union is acyclic and thus can be extended to a linear SC order.

C/C++11 concurrency. Assuming we can construct the SC order as above, we are now in a position to verify the consistency in C/C++11 of all behaviors permitted by TSO (with the variant RMWs) for race-free C/C++11 programs:

- Acyclicity of ithb: First, the ithb is contained within ghb, which is acyclic.
- Consistency of happens-before and mo: Second, mo should be consistent with C/C++ happens-before (which we get by ws being included in ghb, and the uniproc condition).
- Coherence diagrams: Third, the coherence diagrams [6] CoRR, CoRW, CoWR, and CoWW, must not be contradicted by the happens-before, which we get by the construction of ghb.
- Consistency of SC order: Fourth, sc should be consistent with happens-before and mo, which we get by our construction of sc.
- Reads read from a consistent write: Fifth, SC reads must read-from a write not happens-after the sc-last SC write, which we get by construction of sc. Other reads must read from a happens-before consistent write, where we note that all reads read from the last write to the same location in ghb. It is possible, however, that there is no C/C++11 happens-before relating the read and write (hb is smaller than ghb). Then, we find a race in the original C/C++ program, contradicting the race-free assumption.
- Constructing a race: Suppose we have found a read and a write that it reads-from that are not C/C++11 happens-before related. We find the minimal such pair in ghb (we know ghb is acyclic, so this is well-founded). Cut off the program without this read, and anything program-order after that write. Now we add back the read, but read from a C/C++11 allowed write; and it races with the original write. We complete the program execution in any consistent way, to get a racy consistent execution. Note that without speculative execution as in Power, this proof is much simpler than the corresponding proof for Power [5].

A.2 Instantiating the generic proof

Now we fill in the pieces above for each atomicity definition and each mapping. The remaining obligation is finding events in the TSO execution corresponding to the C/C++11 SC atomics, and proving that po_{SC}, ws_{SC}, fr_{SC}, and erf_{SC} are contained within ghb.

Read-write-mapping and read-mapping. For these mappings, we consider the write W_a of the RMW for the SC read, and the write

Table 4. Mapping from C/C++11 to X86

(a) read-write-mapping

Operation	x86 Impl.
non-SC read	mov
SC read	lock xadd(0)
non-SC write	mov
SC write	lock xchg

(b) read-mapping

Operation	x86 Impl.
non-SC read	mov
SC read	lock xadd(0)
non-SC write	mov
SC write	mov

(c) write-mapping

Operation	x86 Impl.
non-SC read	mov
SC read	mov
non-SC write	mov
SC write	lock xchg

(either by itself in the read-mapping, or from the RMW for the read-write-mapping) for the SC write. Then $\mathsf{po}_{SC}$is a part of ghb (they are same-thread writes). $\mathsf{ws}_{SC}$is a part of ghb by definition of write-serialization. Every fr_{SC}edge must be consistent with ghb, since the subsequent write cannot be in ghb between R_a and W_a of the RMW, using any atomicity definition. Every erf_{SC}edge must be consistent with ghb, since the write read-from must be coherence-before the W_a of the SC read, and cannot come between R_a and W_a in any atomicity definition.

Write-mapping Here SC reads are mapped to plain reads, and thus there is no write to use as above. Instead, we use the read as is for SC reads, and the read R_a of the RMW for the SC write. Using this mapping, $\mathsf{po}_{SC}$is a part of ghb (they are same-thread reads). For write-serialization, $\mathsf{ws}_{SC}$is a part of the ghb, since R_a of each write must be before that write in fr. Likewise, $\mathsf{erf}_{SC}$is a part of ghb, but the proof has two cases. For same threads, R_a of the write is ghb-before the read (same-thread reads). For different threads, R_a from the write is ghb before W_a in fr, and W_a is before the SC read in rfe. The last piece required is fr_{SC}. The SC read is certainly before in fr W_a of the RMW, but we are now considering R_a as representing the SC action. For Type-1 and Type-2 RMWs, it is consistent to impose that the SC read is before R_a, since they are to the same location, and no same-location actions can be in ghb between R_a and W_a. Then we get the required result.

For Type-3 RMWs, since a *read* can be in between R_a and W_a of a RMW, this strategy will not work. This is the point where the proof fails for Type-3 RMWs.

Acknowledgements

We would like to thank Peter Sewell and the anonymous reviewers for their helpful comments and advice for improving this paper. This work is supported by the Centre for Numerical Algorithms and Intelligent Software, funded by EPSRC grant EP/G036136/1 and the Scottish Funding Council to the University of Edinburgh. Susmit Sarkar was supported by EPSRC grant EP/H027351.

References

[1] S. V. Adve. *Designing memory consistency models for shared-memory multiprocessors*. PhD thesis, Madison, WI, USA, 1993. UMI Order No. GAX94-07354.

[2] J. Alglave. *A Shared Memory Poetics*. PhD thesis, 2010.

[3] H. Attiya, R. Guerraoui, D. Hendler, P. Kuznetsov, M. M. Michael, and M. T. Vechev. Laws of order: expensive synchronization in concurrent algorithms cannot be eliminated. In *POPL*, pages 487–498, 2011.

[4] D. A. Bader and G. Cong. A fast, parallel spanning tree algorithm for symmetric multiprocessors (smps). *J. Parallel Distrib. Comput.*, 65(9):994–1006, 2005.

[5] M. Batty, K. Memarian, S. Owens, S. Sarkar, and P. Sewell. Clarifying and compiling C/C++ concurrency: from C++11 to POWER. In *Proc. POPL*, 2012.

[6] M. Batty, S. Owens, S. Sarkar, P. Sewell, and T. Weber. Mathematizing C++ concurrency. In *POPL*, pages 55–66, 2011.

[7] P. Becker, editor. *Programming Languages — C++*. 2011. ISO/IEC 14882:2011. A non-final recent version is available at `http://www.open-std.org/jtc1/sc22/wg21/docs/papers/2011/n3242.pdf`.

[8] B. H. Bloom. Space/time trade-offs in hash coding with allowable errors. *Commun. ACM*, 13(7):422–426, 1970.

[9] C. Blundell, M. M. K. Martin, and T. F. Wenisch. Invisifence: performance-transparent memory ordering in conventional multiprocessors. In *ISCA*, 2009.

[10] *Programming Languages — C*. 2011. ISO/IEC 9899:2011. A non-final recent version is available at `http://www.open-std.org/jtc1/sc22/wg14/docs/n1539.pdf`.

[11] D. Dice, O. Shalev, and N. Shavit. Transactional locking ii. In *DISC*, pages 194–208, 2006.

[12] K. Gharachorloo, S. Adve, A. Gupta, J. Hennessy, and M. Hill. *Specifying system requirements for memory consistency models*. Computer Systems Laboratory, Stanford University, 1993.

[13] K. Gharachorloo, A. Gupta, and J. L. Hennessy. Two techniques to enhance the performance of memory consistency models. In *ICPP (1)*, pages 355–364, 1991.

[14] C. Gniady, B. Falsafi, and T. N. Vijaykumar. Is sc + ilp=rc? In *ISCA*, pages 162–171, 1999.

[15] M. Herlihy. Wait-free synchronization. *ACM Trans. Program. Lang. Syst.*, 13:124–149, January 1991.

[16] Intel Corporation. *Intel® 64 and IA-32 Architectures Software Developer's Manual*. Number 253669-033US. December 2009.

[17] E. Ladan-Mozes, I.-T. A. Lee, and D. Vyukov. Location-based memory fences. In *SPAA*, pages 75–84, 2011.

[18] C. Lin, V. Nagarajan, R. Gupta, and B. Rajaram. Efficient sequential consistency via conflict ordering. In *ASPLOS*, pages 273–286, 2012.

[19] I. B. Machine and A. C. I. Staff. *PowerPC Microprocessor Common Hardware Reference Platform: A System Architecture*. Morgan Kaufmann Publishers Inc., San Francisco, CA, USA, 1995.

[20] M. Michael and M. Scott. Implementation of atomic primitives on distributed shared memory multiprocessors. In *Proc. HPCA*, 1995.

[21] N. Muralimanohar and R. Balasubramonian. Cacti 6.0: A tool to understand large caches.

[22] S. Owens, S. Sarkar, and P. Sewell. A better x86 memory model: x86-TSO. In *Proc. TPHOLs*, 2009.

[23] A. Singh, S. Narayanasamy, D. Marino, T. D. Millstein, and M. Musuvathi. End-to-end sequential consistency. In *ISCA*, pages 524–535, 2012.

[24] D. J. Sorin, M. D. Hill, and D. A. Wood. *A Primer on Memory Consistency and Cache Coherence*. Morgan and ClayPool Publishers, 2011.

[25] C. SPARC International, Inc. *The SPARC architecture manual (version 8)*. Prentice-Hall, Inc., Upper Saddle River, NJ, USA, 1992.

[26] C. SPARC International, Inc. *The SPARC architecture manual (version 9)*. Prentice-Hall, Inc., Upper Saddle River, NJ, USA, 1994.

[27] A. Terekhov. Brief tentative example x86 implementation for C/C++ memory model. cpp-threads mailing list, `http://www.decadent.org.uk/pipermail/cpp-threads/2008-December/001933.html`, Dec. 2008.

[28] E. Vallejo, R. Beivide, A. Cristal, T. Harris, F. Vallejo, O. Unsal, and M. Valero. Architectural support for fair reader-writer locking. In *Proc. MICRO*, 2010.

Rely-Guarantee References for Refinement Types Over Aliased Mutable Data

Colin S. Gordon, Michael D. Ernst, and Dan Grossman
University of Washington
{csgordon,mernst,djg}@cs.washington.edu

Abstract

Reasoning about side effects and aliasing is the heart of verifying imperative programs. Unrestricted side effects through one reference can invalidate assumptions about an alias. We present a new type system approach to reasoning about safe assumptions in the presence of aliasing and side effects, unifying ideas from reference immutability type systems and rely-guarantee program logics. Our approach, *rely-guarantee references*, treats multiple references to shared objects similarly to multiple threads in rely-guarantee program logics. We propose statically associating rely and guarantee conditions with individual references to shared objects. Multiple aliases to a given object may coexist only if the guarantee condition of each alias implies the rely condition for all other aliases. We demonstrate that existing reference immutability type systems are special cases of rely-guarantee references.

In addition to allowing precise control over state modification, rely-guarantee references allow types to depend on mutable data while still permitting flexible aliasing. Dependent types whose denotation is stable over the actions of the rely and guarantee conditions for a reference and its data will not be invalidated by any action through any alias. We demonstrate this with refinement (subset) types that may depend on mutable data. As a special case, we derive the first reference immutability type system with dependent types over immutable data.

We show soundness for our approach and describe experience using rely-guarantee references in a dependently-typed monadic DSL in Coq.

Categories and Subject Descriptors D.2.4 [*Software/Program Verification*]: Correctness Proofs; F.3.2 [*Semantics of Programming Languages*]: Program Analysis

Keywords reference immutability, rely-guarantee, refinement types

1. Introduction

A common way to reason about side effects in imperative languages is to restrict (disable) mutating some state in some code sections. This is seen most clearly in reference immutability [22, 44, 49, 50], but also in ownership [14] and region-based type systems [6]. The common approach is to attach permission/ownership/region information to references, where certain operations (mainly writes to the heap) through references with certain permissions are prohibited.

The program logic literature includes work ensuring that actions by one section of code do not interfere destructively with the assumptions of another section of code. This appears most often in the form of concurrent program logics, where the goal is to prevent destructive interference between threads. This reaches at least as far back as Owicki and Gries's technique [37], which checks thread non-interference by ensuring that no action would invalidate any intermediate assumption of another thread. Jones abstracted cross-thread interactions to a *rely* relation bounding interference by other threads, and a *guarantee* relation bounding actions of the current thread [27]. Each thread's local proof then requires all local actions to fall within its guarantee, and that all of its intermediate assertions are stable with respect to (that is, not invalidated by) any possible action permitted by the rely. Parallel composition of threads is then safe if each thread's guarantee implies each other thread's rely.

Our central idea is to treat aliases to objects similarly to threads of control in rely-guarantee program logics. Each reference's type carries a rely and a guarantee, bounding actions on an object through other references (rely) and bounding actions through the reference itself (guarantee). We call these augmented reference types *rely-guarantee references*. The type system maintains the invariant that the guarantee of any reference implies the rely of any alias. The type system checks these constraints when a program duplicates an alias. This raises the issue that some references cannot soundly coexist: no two references to the same object can each guarantee nothing (the reference permits arbitrary actions) and rely on restricted behavior through aliases. This presents us with a logical account of aliasing: some references may not be aliased without weakening the rely or guarantee of the source, and a reference with an empty rely necessarily has no aliases.

Rely-guarantee references generalize *reference immutability* [22, 44, 49, 50] to finer-grained control over interference through aliases. The traditional reference immutability qualifiers correspond to simple rely and guarantee conditions. For ref τ[R,G] as a reference to data of type τ with rely R and guarantee G:

- readable $\tau \equiv$ ref τ[any interference, no writes]
- writable $\tau \equiv$ ref τ[any interference, any writes]
- immutable $\tau \equiv$ ref τ[no interference, no writes]

Rely-guarantee references let us reason about some refinements of referents. Let a *stable* predicate over a reference be one that is preserved by its rely. Then a stable predicate cannot be invalidated by actions through an alias, and any new predicate that is stable and ensured by a guarantee-permitted action (on an object satisfying the old predicate) is true after the action, providing a form of strong update on arbitrarily aliased mutable data. (An action allowed by the guarantee that preserves the current predicate is a special case.)

PLDI'13, June 16–19, 2013, Seattle, WA, USA.

1.1 Contributions

Refinement Types Over Mutable Data Rely-guarantee references permit refinement types [21] that depend on mutable data, without requiring any aliasing restrictions to support strong updates. We leverage the notion of a *stable assertion* from rely-guarantee program logics, allowing any refinements that are not invalidated by actions performed through other references. We prove that our type system is sound.

Generalizing Reference Immutability We generalize reference immutability by combining it with rely-guarantee techniques. This is of independent interest, but also outlines an effort/precision spectrum from unrestricted references to reference immutability to rely-guarantee references.

A Prototype Implementation We prototype an implementation as a shallow monadic embedding in COQ. We have used it to verify the examples in the paper, including implementing reference immutability as a special case. We briefly discuss our experience implementing a language as a COQ DSL and the manual proof burden for our technique versus purely functional versions. The implementation is available at
`https://github.com/csgordon/rgref/`.

We believe rely-guarantee references make a compelling argument that rely-guarantee reasoning is a promising way to statically reason about aliasing. Further, any technique traditionally used to reason about thread interference can be adapted to modularly reason about effects in the presence of aliasing (we present rely-guarantee references as a type system, but our ideas could be implemented in other ways, such as a program logic). Ultimately we believe the proper way to support unknown aliases in program verification is by treating aliases as different threads of control.

2. Rely-Guarantee References

A rely-guarantee reference is a reference to a heap structure of a given type, as in ML's ref τ, with three additional type components:

- A refinement predicate P over the τ and a heap h that can enforce local properties and/or data-structure well-formedness.
- A guarantee relation G over pairs of τs and heaps, restricting the effects to the referent (and state heap-reachable from that referent) that may be performed through this reference or those produced by dereferencing it.
- A rely relation R specifying the actions permitted by (the guarantees of) other aliases to the referent.

We use the form $\mathsf{ref}\{\tau \mid P\}[R,G]$ for a rely-guarantee reference. Predicates and relations are defined not only over the τ a reference refers to, but also over heaps, to refine data reachable from the immediate referent. For a rely-guarantee reference type to be well-formed, the predicate P must be *stable* with respect to the rely R: for all values and heaps for which the predicate holds, if the rely R allows another value and heap to be produced by actions on another alias, then the predicate holds for the new value and heap as well: $P\ v\ h \wedge R\ v\ v'\ h\ h' \implies P\ v'\ h'$. This ensures that actions through aliases do not invalidate the refinement, and that all actions that may invalidate the refinement are local, so reasoning about such changes allows strong updates to the refinement. These issues are formally treated in Section 4.

A simple example of rely-guarantee references is a monotonically increasing counter, which we can represent as a value of type

$$\mathsf{ref}\{\mathtt{nat} \mid \mathsf{any}\}[\mathsf{increasing},\mathsf{increasing}]$$

where any is the trivial (always true) refinement, and increasing (Section 3.1) is a relation on natural numbers and heaps that requires the second `nat` to be greater than or equal to the first. Given a variable x with the type above, $x \leftarrow\ !x+1$ type-checks (! is ML's dereference operator). By contrast, incorrect code that decrements the counter cannot satisfy the guarantee relation increasing.

A read-only alias to an increasing counter can be expressed as:

$$\mathsf{ref}\{\mathtt{nat} \mid \mathsf{any}\}[\mathsf{increasing},\approx]$$

where $\approx$ is a relation permitting no change.

We might wish to know more about a counter value, for example that it is greater than 0 so it is safe as a divisor to compute an average. Any write to the counter via any reference will increase its value, and may therefore conclude the result is greater than 0.[1] Furthermore, it is safe to continue assuming the value is greater than 0 because the reference's rely ensures no alias can decrease the value. We say $\lambda x : \mathtt{nat}.\,\lambda h : \mathsf{heap}.\, x > 0$ is *stable* with respect to the rely increasing. When a write establishes a new stable predicate over the data, strong updates to the reference's predicate (changing the predicate in the type) are sound. (Similarly, when a write invalidates a reference's predicate, a strong update is required, to a new predicate stable over the rely.)

Many verification techniques for imperative programs struggle to verify examples of this kind. Reference immutability and fractional permissions [7, 28] can only allow or outright prevent mutation, not control it. Separation logic cannot concisely specify the counter's intended semantics, only code's behavior. Rely-guarantee and related systems can express the semantics among threads [18, 27, 45], but only coarsely [46] among different program sections. Most program logics can constrain the actions of a function on an argument, but the specification must deal with aliasing, either by giving linear semantics to knowledge of the counter (as in separation logic), or by explicitly treating aliasing (as in more traditional Hoare logics [24]).

With rely-guarantee references, functions are written without concern for aliasing among their arguments. A function cannot be called with unsafe aliasing among arguments: since each alias's guarantee must imply each other's rely, each function explicitly accounts for its possible actions. If two arguments of the same type have conflicting rely/guarantee conditions, they cannot be aliased.

2.1 Subtleties of Rely-Guarantee References

While the intuition behind rely-guarantee references is straightforward, this section overviews some more subtle features of our system that avoid problems.

Non-duplicable References A reference may be freely duplicated if its guarantee implies its own rely, as with the monotonically increasing counter. But consider a reference

$$y : \mathsf{ref}\{\mathtt{nat} \mid \mathsf{any}\}[\mathsf{decreasing},\mathsf{increasing}]$$

Making an alias to y where the the alias has the same type as y violates soundness, because the guarantee of the duplicate does not imply the rely of y! Instead, aliasing y requires splitting it into two aliases with weaker rely/guarantee conditions. We support such splitting via a novel substructural resource semantics (Section 4).

Reference to References We need a reference's guarantee to restrict all actions performed using that reference, which must include actions performed via references acquired by dereferencing the first reference. Otherwise, reading a reference out of the heap and writing through it could violate the original reference's guarantee, violating the "capability to perform effects in the guarantee" intuition, and potentially invalidating a predicate. So reading from the heap must somehow transform the type of the referent to restrict resulting references. Reference immutability systems can give a simple binary function on permissions [22], to capture the transitive meaning of

[1] Because the type nat of natural numbers contains no negative numbers.

qualifiers. For example, dereferencing a `readable` reference to a `writable` reference returns a `readable` reference (assuming a *deep* interpretation of reference immutability, where permissions apply transitively). By contrast, our type system combines *arbitrary* relations (Section 3.2). Furthermore, if one reference points to another, how should the rely of the "inner" reference be related to the outer one? It is unsound if it permits more interference than the outer rely, so our type system prevents this.[2]

Footprint How much of the heap may a rely-guarantee reference's predicate or conditions mention? It is not productive or sound to let a reference constrain unrelated heap data: letting a reference arbitrarily constrain the heap could lead to allocating a new heap cell whose rely is not implied by existing references. The type system restricts the expressiveness of these predicates to ensure sound and tractable reasoning: predicates and relations may depend only on the heap reachable from the reference.

Cycles Many useful data structures contain cycles, so we wish to reason effectively about them. The solution turns out to be simple (propositions describing cycles require finite proofs, and recursion based on heap structure is not permitted in predicates), but was not immediately obvious to us.

3. Examples

We present examples using rely-guarantee references to verify programs. The examples are small, but highlight distinct capabilities of rely-guarantee references. Rather than writing examples in our core language RGREF (Section 4), we present them using a slight simplification of our shallow embedding in COQ [12]. The embedding is largely in the style of YNOT [11, 34], using axioms for heap interactions.

Reading* COQ *Source COQ's language for defining functions and types is based strongly on ML, though many keywords are different: `Definition` and `Fixpoint` for non- and recursive definitions, `Inductive` for defining inductive variant datatypes by specifying constructors. `Parameter` declares assumptions, external functions, or abstract elements in a module signature. Functions and parameterized type definitions can put some arguments in braces rather than parentheses; these arguments are implicit, and inferred when possible from later arguments. Another notable syntactic change from ML is that = is an operator for *propositional* equality, not a boolean decision procedure for structural equality. Therefore, := is often used where ML would use = in definitions. The set of types is much richer than ML, not only due to dependent types but because there are universes (types of types): Prop is the type of propositional types (erasable during extraction, such as proof terms with conjunction, implications, etc.), and Set is the type of normal (computationally relevant) data types. COQ also includes a notation feature that allows users to extend the grammar with additional parsing rules, allowing programs to use syntax closer to mathematical definitions (such as $\mathsf{ref}\{T \mid P\}[R,G]$). Our notation uses ML's dereference operator (`!`) and uses $r \leftarrow e$ for writing e to the location referenced by r. We introduce further notations as they arise.

The PROGRAM extension [42] (used via definitions prefixed with `Program`) allows the omission of explicit proof terms in programs. Omitted terms are either solved automatically via a (customizable) proof search tactic, or set aside for subsequent manual interactive solving, improving readability.

[2] This is actually a design decision that simplifies checking stability. An alternative design could check a predicate for stability over any change permitted by any reference reachable from the predicate's target referent.

3.1 Monotonic Counter

Consider again our running example of a monotonically increasing counter. Generally, rely and guarantee conditions must be defined over pre- and post-heaps as well as values, to describe the interference they tolerate on reachable substructures. For a simple counter, there is no other reachable data, so the pre- and post-heaps may be ignored. Thus the relation for increasing over time is defined as:

```
Definition increasing (n n':nat) (h h':heap) : Prop :=
  n' ≥ n.
```

Code to allocate a counter is straightforward:

```
Program Definition mkCounter (_:unit)
  : ref{nat|any}[increasing,increasing] :=
    alloc 0.
```

The allocation function `mkCounter` generates well-formedness proof obligations for the resulting type:

- that any is stable with respect to increasing
- that any and increasing are precise: they access only the (empty) heap segment reachable from the natural number they apply to
- that any is true of 0

In our prototype implementation (Section 5), most of these obligations are proven automatically by lightly-guided automatic proof search. Type errors for actions that fall outside the guarantee (or ill-formed rely/guarantee relations, or predicates that are not precise, etc.) manifest as unsolvable proof obligations.

Using a monotonic counter is also straightforward:

```
Program Definition example (_:unit) :=
let x = mkCounter () in x ← !x + 1;
```

An assignment typechecks only if the change implied by the write is permitted by the reference's guarantee relation, for any pre-heap and pre-value satisfying the reference's refinement. In this case, the assignment generates a proof obligation of the form

$$\forall x, h.\, \mathtt{any}\ (!x)\ h \implies \mathtt{increasing}\ (!x)\ (!x+1)\ h\ h[x \mapsto h[x]+1].$$

which is easily solved, with little effort beyond what is required to verify a pure-functional increment function (see Section 5.3). Each read also generates a proof obligation that the guarantee `increasing` is "reflexive": it allows a reference to be used without modifying the heap ($\forall n, h.\, \mathsf{increasing}\ n\ n\ h\ h$). By contrast, an empty guarantee relation would disallow using a reference.

The monotonically increasing counter was proposed by Pilkiewicz and Pottier [40] as a challenging goal for program verification. Unlike their solution and another in fictional separation logic [26], we can state the monotonicity property plainly and require no abstraction to prevent unchecked interference. On the other hand, their solutions verify that the increment occurs, while ours ensures that increment is the only permitted action.

3.2 Monotonic List

We can define a monotonically growing (prepend-only) list, either using a mutable reference to a pure-functional list, or using mutable nodes. The former approach is similar to the monotonic counter, so to show the power of rely-guarantee references for recursive data structures, Figure 1 shows the latter.[3]

We first define `hpred` and `hrel`, type-level functions that allow shorter type declarations. We use them throughout this paper. Next we define a linked list structure, with restricted references to the

[3] The most natural design uses mutual inductive types where one indexes the other, which we assume here. COQ does not support this, so we use an encoding, discussed further in Section 5 and our technical report [23].

```
Definition hpred (A:Set) := A -> heap -> Prop.
Definition hrel (A:Set) := A -> A -> heap -> heap -> Prop.
Inductive list : Set :=
  | nil : list
  | cons : forall (n:nat),
                ref{list|any}[list_imm,list_imm] -> list
with (* list tails are immutable (_imm) *)
  list_imm : list -> list -> heap -> heap -> Prop :=
  | imm_nil : forall h h', list_imm nil nil h h'
  | imm_cons: forall n tl h h',
      list_imm h[tl] h'[tl] h h' ->
        list_imm (cons n tl) (cons n tl) h h'.
(* Convenient allocation functions *)
Program Definition Nil {P:hpred list}
  : ref{list|P}[list_imm,list_imm] := alloc nil.
Program Definition Cons {P P':hpred list}
    (n:nat)(tl:ref{list|P}[list_imm,list_imm])
  : ref{list|P'∩(λ l h=>l=cons n tl)}[list_imm,list_imm]
  := alloc (cons n tl).
(* A prepend-only list container *)
Record list_container (P:hpred list) :=
  mkList { head : ref{list|P}[list_imm,list_imm] }.
Inductive prepend : hrel (list_container P) :=
  | prepended : forall c c' h h' n,
      h'[head c']=cons n (head c) -> prepend c c' h h'
  | prepend_nop : forall c h h', prepend c c h h'.
Program Definition newList (P:hpred list)
  : ref{list_container|any}[prepend,prepend] :=
    let x = Nil in alloc (mkList P x).
Program Definition doPrepend {P:hpred list}(n:nat)
  (l:ref{list_container|any}[prepend,prepend]) : unit :=
    let x = Cons n (head l) in
      l ← mkList P x.
```

Figure 1. RGREF code for a prepend-only linked list.

tail. list_imm constrains the tail to be immutable. For the reader unfamiliar with COQ, list_imm is a GADT [48] constructing a proposition on different constructions of lists. The first constructor declares that an empty list must remain empty, regardless of heaps. The second constructor accepts a nat, a tail, two heaps, and a proof that list_imm holds over the tail of the list in those heaps, returning a declaration that a cons cell must remain constant. The immutability requirement is not essential to this example (we could, for example, permit the numbers to change but require the length to increase), but is included for completeness. We then define convenient helper functions for heap-allocating nil or cons cells.

We enforce the prepend-only behavior through reference to a list_container structure, which holds a reference to a list parameterized by some predicate. The prepend relation on list_containers allows prepending and no-ops (required for reading the reference). Finally we have helper functions to allocate a new list and to prepend the list with a new cell. prepend is essentially the specification of what doPrepend is permitted to do with the list.

Note the predicate conjunction (⋂) in the return type of Cons. This, along with the predicate conversion rule, is how flow-sensitive assumptions can be handled (notice that the equality is stable with respect to list_imm). This is important in doPrepend, where information from the result of one write (inside Cons) must be carried into another (the assignment through l), because it is otherwise unavailable in the expression stored.

Not shown in Figure 1 are implicit obligations such as $\forall h. P\ \mathtt{nil}\ h$ in Nil. Other such obligations include:

- $\forall tl, h. P\ tl\ h \implies P'\ (\mathrm{cons}\ n\ tl)\ h$ in Cons
- That prepend permits the write in doPrepend (under the trivial assumption that any holds of the initial list container and heap). This obligation requires a richer type for the allocation result, because mkList must know x is a cons cell whose tail is the old list. This information is not available locally (within the write statement itself). Other systems propagate hypotheses separately, but we only need to track variables: the required equality is present in x's predicate because of Cons's return type.
- The stability and precision properties that must hold for various predicates and list_imm.
- Propagations of these obligations to indirect polymorphic callers, such as newList and prepend.

Also omitted in Figure 1 are obligations related to *folding* and *containment*. Folding is the restriction of read result types to ensure that for any reference r with guarantee G, references produced via reads of r do not allow actions exceeding those permitted by G on r's referent. This ensures actions via a reference read from inside a data structure cannot invalidate predicates over the whole structure. Containment is a check that the rely R for a reference r captures all interference allowed by the interference summaries of references reachable from r. This ensures that any predicate preserved by R is also preserved by actions on aliases to internal structures.

Both operations require projecting a given relation component-wise onto a datatype's members. For our prepend-only list, projecting prepend is trivial (it does not constrain the list cells' values), and the result of projecting list_imm is logically equivalent to list_imm itself.

3.3 Reference Immutability as a Special Case

Reference immutability [22, 44, 49, 50] adds permissions (type qualifiers) to references to permit or disallow side effects through a particular reference. Multiple aliases at different permissions may coexist if compatible: for example, there may be write-permitting and read-only aliases to an object. We can define the permissions of reference immutability like this:

```
Definition havoc {A:Set} : hrel A :=
   fun x => fun x' => fun h => fun h' => True.
Definition readable (T:Set) := ref{T|any}[havoc,≈].
Definition writable (T:Set) := ref{T|any}[havoc,havoc].
Definition immutable (T:Set) := ref{T|any}[≈,≈].
```

Our definitions encode the standard semantics for reference immutability qualifiers: only immutable assumes limited interference via other aliases, and readable and immutable disallow mutation through a reference. Restrictions on aliasing among reference immutability permissions are reflected in the rely and guarantee relations: no heap cell may have writable and immutable aliases simultaneously, as the guarantee of the writable reference (havoc) is not a subrelation of the immutable rely (≈). The "containment" requirement (Section 3.2) for rely conditions on nested datatypes is satisfied by the rely for readable and writable, and for immutable the rely prevents it from (transitively) referencing mutable data.

Reading through one of these references requires considering how the rely and guarantee affect the read's result. In reference immutability, result types are adapted using a simple binary function on permissions (Figure 2). Our rely-guarantee reference type system must combine arbitrary relations (folding), using the type of the referent. Intuitively, folding is projection of the reference's guarantee onto the referent type. Any projection of havoc and ≈ correspond with the simplified version in Figure 2. Projecting havoc is equivalent to reading through a writable reference, which simply produces the inner type. Projecting ≈ is equivalent to the weakening that occurs when reading through readable or immutable references.

We can also give a reference immutability system with limited dependent types by a small extension:

_	$\triangleright$	immutable	=	immutable
immutable	$\triangleright$	_	=	immutable
readable	$\triangleright$	_	=	readable
writable	$\triangleright$	q	=	q

Figure 2. Combining reference immutability permissions, from [22]. Using a p reference to read a $q\ T$ field produces a $(p \triangleright q)\ T$.

```
Definition refined (T:Set) (P:hpred T) := ref{T|P}[≈,≈].
```

At first glance this is weaker than proposed systems that let mutable data's type depend on arbitrary immutable data, because we require any reference predicate to access only heap state reachable from its referent. At the cost of some space the referent could maintain its own extra reference to relevant immutable data. Careful code extraction work can improve the space overhead in executables.

Another benefit of implementing reference immutability via rely-guarantee references is interoperability between reference immutability and richer rely-guarantee references. For example, a function accepting a `readable` reference to a natural number can be passed a read-only monotonically-increasing counter from Section 3.1. This offers a natural path for gradually adding stronger verification guarantees to code using reference immutability (which itself is a gradual refinement of unrestricted references [22]).

3.4 RCC/Java with Reference Immutability

The core of RCC/Java [20] is also implementable as a small library using our COQ DSL, and we present a translation of an early version [19]. The key idea in these type systems and related systems is to parameterize the type of a reference by the identity of a particular lock. The type system tracks the set of held locks and permits reads and writes through a reference only when the reference's lock parameter is statically known to be held.

A COQ module wraps standard acquire and release primitives and exposes a new reference type that quantifies over a lock. The RCC reference type can be abstracted with a module signature, but can be concretely represented by a RGREF `ref` type:

```
(* Signature *)
Parameter rccref : forall (A:Set),
   hpred A -> hrel A -> hrel A -> lock -> Set.
...
(* Implementation *)
Definition rccref A P R G (l:lock) := ref A P R G.
```

The module then exposes its own read and write primitives, and external ways of proving goals like guarantee satisfaction that do not expose the internal `rccref` representation. This mostly consists of re-exporting existing axioms using new names. Then an explicit lock witness (since the type system is not specialized to track lock witnesses) can be abstracted using:

```
Parameter lockwitness : lock -> Set.
Parameter locked : forall {l:lock}, hpred (lockwitness l).
Parameter unlocked : forall {l:lock}, hpred (lockwitness l).
```

The acquire and release operations must respectively produce and consume a witness that a lock is held, that permits release. Using a binary operator `-->` on predicates that produces a relation allowing changes from states where the first predicate holds to states where the second holds (a limited encoding of protocols), a witness may have type ref{lockwitness | locked}[empty, locked-->unlocked]. Using an empty rely implies uniqueness, and requiring such a witness to release the lock prevents splitting the witness, which would requiring weakening the rely of both resulting references. The read and write for `rccref`s would need to also require some witness that the lock was held:

Expressions	e	::=	x	Variable
		|	$e\ e$	Application
		|	$!e$	Dereference
		|	$e[e]$	Heap Select
		|	$\mathsf{alloc}\ e$	Allocation
		|	$(\lambda x:\tau.\ e)$	Pure Function
		|	$(\lambda_{\mathcal{M}}(x:\tau).\ e)$	Procedure
		|	τ	Types
		|	$x \leftarrow e$	Store
		|	$\mathsf{swap}(x,e)$	Atomic swap
Types	τ	::=	$=$	Propositional equality
		|	Prop	Propositions
		|	$\mathsf{ref}\{\tau \mid e\}[e,e]$	Reference
		|	Type	Type of Prop
		|	$\Pi x:\tau \rightarrow \tau'$	Dep. Product (pure)
		|	$\tau \overset{\mathcal{M}}{\rightarrow} \tau'$	Impure Function
		|	heap	Heaps
		|	e	Expressions

Figure 3. Syntax, omitting booleans (b : `bool`), unary natural numbers (n : `nat`), unit, pairs, propositional True and False, and standard recursors. The expression/type division is presentational; the language is a single syntactic category of PTS-style [2] pseudoterms.

```
Program Definition rcc_read ...{l:lock}
    (w:ref{lockwitness l | locked}[empty,locked-->unlocked])
    (r:rccref A P R G l)... := (!r,w).(* return the witness *)
```

This encoding of RCC/Java using dependent types is not novel, but note the rely, guarantee, and predicate of the underlying reference are exposed, yielding the first combination of race-free lock acquisition and reference immutability we are aware of, in addition to exposing the full power of rely-guarantee references over lock-guarded data.

4. A Type System for Rely-Guarantee References

Figure 3 gives the syntax for a core language RGREF with rely-guarantee references. The expressions combine features from the ML-family (e.g., references) and dependently typed languages (e.g., dependent product), specifically from the Calculus of Constructions [2, 13]. We include a few basic datatypes (natural numbers, booleans, pairs, unit), a type for propositional equality, and their standard recursors [25]. We also distinguish effectful functions through the term former $\lambda_{\mathcal{M}}$ and the effectful non-dependent function type former $\tau \overset{\mathcal{M}}{\rightarrow} \tau'$ ($\mathcal{M}$ for mutation).

The language supports reasoning about heaps: not only is there a standard form of dereference, but there is a term for dereferencing a reference in a particular heap, used to specify predicates and rely/guarantee relations using the propositions-as-types principle. The language is designed to use propositions-as-types to specify predicates and relations, and to use the pure sublanguage as a computational language amenable to rich reasoning, but to use external means for discharging obligations like a write satisfying a guarantee. The presence of current-heap-dereference makes the pure term language itself unsound as a logic, internally offering assurances similar to Cayenne [1]. In general, the language for predicates and relations can be distinct from the term language, and the term language does not require advanced types; our design is motivated by our implementation as a COQ DSL (Section 5).

Figure 4 presents the primary typing rules for the core language. There are two key judgments: $\Gamma \vdash e : \tau$ for pure terms (useful for proofs), and $\Gamma \vdash e : \tau \Rightarrow \Gamma'$ for impure and substructural computation. Those pure rules omitted here (recursors for the assumed inductive types, typing the primitive types in Prop, etc.) are standard for a pure type system.

The imperative typing judgment $\Gamma \vdash e : \tau \Rightarrow \Gamma'$ is flow-sensitive to allow reasoning about when references are duplicated. Crucially, it allows reasoning about when a reference must not be duplicated because its guarantee does not imply its own rely. For this reason, we have two impure variable rules: one consumes the variable (V-$\emptyset$), and the other uses an auxiliary relation $\Gamma \vdash \tau \prec \tau \circledast \tau$ to split a type (V-$\circledast$). Primitive types (`nat`, `bool`, `unit`) freely split into two copies of themselves. We require that any variable captured by a closure has a self-splitting type (Π-I and FUN), and thus functions may be duplicated freely. We require that only values of self-splitting types are captured by dependent type constructors (Π-F and the not-shown propositional equality rule), so types are also self-splitting. Variables read in pure computation must also be self-splitting (V).

References (and structures that may contain them, like pairs) are the only types with non-trivial splitting. Reference types split into reference types that may coexist (each guarantee implies the other rely, both relies are no stronger than the original rely, stable predicates, etc.), and pairs split into pairs of the component-wise split results. For example, the problematic reference from Section 2.1 has non-trivial splitting behavior, mediated by REF-$\circledast$:

$$y : \mathsf{ref}\{\mathtt{nat} \mid \mathsf{any}\}[\mathsf{decreasing}, \mathsf{increasing}]$$

Splitting this reference requires consuming the original and producing two "weaker" references: each guarantee may permit at most what the original guarantee allowed, and each rely must assume at least as much interference as the original. For example,

$$\begin{aligned}\varepsilon \vdash\ & \mathsf{ref}\{\mathtt{nat} \mid \mathsf{any}\}[\mathsf{decreasing}, \mathsf{increasing}]\\ \prec\ & \mathsf{ref}\{\mathtt{nat} \mid \mathsf{any}\}[\mathsf{havoc}, \mathsf{increasing}]\\ \circledast\ & \mathsf{ref}\{\mathtt{nat} \mid \mathsf{any}\}[\mathsf{havoc}, \mathsf{increasing}]\end{aligned}$$

The natural use of simply duplicating a reference whose guarantee implies its own rely (as in the monotonic counter) is a degenerate case of the very general rule REF-$\circledast$.

The conversion relation $\Gamma \vdash \tau \rightsquigarrow \tau$ is a directed call-by-value β-conversion (so for example β-reduction is not used with arguments containing dereferences) plus reducing abstractions whose bound variable is free in the result, and what amounts to subtyping by converting predicates and relations to weaker versions: P-$\Rightarrow$ weakens the predicate; R-$\subset$ assumes more interference may occur; and G-$\subset$ sacrifices some permissions; P and R changes may affect stability.

Mutation The most interesting rules are those for mutation, particularly for writing to the heap (WRITE). This rule requires (beyond basic type safety) that the effects fall within the guarantee, assuming the reference's predicate holds in the current heap.[4] It also allows the option of a strong update to the reference's predicate, if the change establishes some new stable predicate. For example,

$$\begin{aligned}&x : \mathsf{ref}\{\mathtt{nat} \mid \lambda x.\lambda h.x = 3\}[\mathsf{empty}, \mathsf{havoc}] \vdash\\ &\quad x \leftarrow 4 : \mathtt{unit}\\ &\quad \Rightarrow x : \mathsf{ref}\{\mathtt{nat} \mid \lambda x.\lambda h.x = 4\}[\mathsf{empty}, \mathsf{havoc}]\end{aligned}$$

Thus RGREF naturally supports strong updates on unique references as a degenerate case. The atomic swap operation (which permits modifying substructural fields) leverages the heap-write rule's premises. Allocation simply requires a well-formed type as a result and establishing the predicate over the value in any heap. The imperative part of the language also includes non-dependent function types, application, and the use of pure expressions.

Dereference uses the *relation folding* function $[R,G] \gg \tau$ (Figure 5) to reason about the rely and guarantee in result types. It has no effect for non-reference types. For types containing references, the result type is rewritten by intersecting the projection of the guarantee onto each component with the stated guarantee for the component itself. This can cause some precision loss. The effect of folding on the rely has no impact: because the rely for any well-formed reference type has to contain / admit the effects allowed by the rely of any reachable reference type, the intersection on the rely component would produce a relation semantically equivalent to the syntactically present rely on the inner reference (the same type of relation projection is used to check rely containment as is used in folding the guarantee). In general, relation folding and checking containment are straightforward for types whose members are always reflected in a type index (e.g., pairs, references). Folding for richer types, such as full inductive types [39] is left to future work. The Deref rule also checks that the source type is self-splitting. This ensures that the (possibly weaker) guarantee of the result implies the original location's rely, and the original value's guarantee(s) will imply the (unaltered) rely relations of the result.

The rule for typing reference types themselves (WF-REF) imposes several additional requirements on predicates and relations. First, the predicate P must be stable with respect to R. Second, the relations and predicates must be *precise*: all depend only on heap state reachable from the referent. This prevents code from rendering the system unsound by allocating a new cell whose rely condition requires the heap to be invariant: that rely would be undesirable if enforced as it prevents all mutation and allocation, but unsound if ignored because all predicates are stable over such a rely. Finally, the rely must be *closed* (contained): any changes permitted by relies of references reachable from the referent are also permitted by the checked rely. This ensures that checking $\mathsf{stable}\ P\ R$ is sufficient to ensure P is not violated (otherwise P could depend on other references reachable from the referent, whose rely relations might permit P to be invalidated). Figure 5 defines these notions precisely. WF-REF also requires as a side condition that P, R, and G are free of dereference expressions ($!e$), since implicitly heap-dependent predicates are not sensible.

We foresee no technical difficulty in building the system directly atop stronger calculi such as the Calculus of Inductive Constructions [4] (CIC) beyond richer treatment of folding for the full spectrum of inductive types (Section 5.2). There are a few essential qualities required for soundness. First, effectful terms and abstractions are encapsulated in a separate judgment (which corresponds to a monadic treatment of effects in translation to a pure system). Any term in the pure fragment must be reflexively splittable, to avoid introducing resource semantics into the pure sublanguage. Captured variables have reflexively splittable types ($\Gamma \vdash \tau \prec \tau \circledast \tau$). In principle this could be weakened, but we prefer the simplicity of allowing function terms to be arbitrarily duplicated. We build upon CC for simpler presentation.

4.1 Soundness Sketch

Soundness follows a preservation-like structure. Evaluation must preserve a couple invariants beyond standard heap soundness:

- For each reference $r : \mathsf{ref}\{T \mid P\}[R,G]$ in the stack, heap, or expression under reduction, there exists a proof of $P\ (h[r])\ h$ for the current heap h.
- For each pair of references $p : \mathsf{ref}\{T \mid P\}[R,G]$ and $q : \mathsf{ref}\{T \mid P'\}[R',G']$ in the stack, heap, or expression under reduction, if p and q alias (point to the same heap cell) then $\emptyset \subset G' \subseteq R$ and $\emptyset \subset G \subseteq R'$.

Initially there are no references, so these hold trivially. On allocation, the predicate for the new object is true in all heaps by inversion on the allocation typing, so the result is immediate. On any action through a reference, the type system ensures the action falls within the guarantee. The action either preserves the predicate or produces a new (stable) one, and the proof for that reference's new refinement is easy to construct from the typing derivation results. For aliases, the used reference's guarantee must imply the rely of any alias, and the alias's predicate is stable over its rely, and therefore preserved by the

[4] The reflexivity goals DEREF generates could also assume the predicate (i.e., reflexive on states satisfying the predicate), but we haven't needed this.

$$\boxed{\Gamma \vdash \tau \prec \tau \divideontimes \tau} \qquad \frac{\tau \in \{\mathtt{nat}, \mathtt{bool}, \mathtt{unit}, \mathsf{Prop}, \mathsf{Type}, \mathsf{heap}, \_ = \_, \Pi x : \tau \to \tau', \tau \stackrel{\mathcal{M}}{\to} \tau'\}}{\Gamma \vdash \tau \prec \tau \divideontimes \tau} \qquad \frac{\Gamma \vdash \tau \prec \tau_a \divideontimes \tau_b \qquad \Gamma \vdash \sigma \prec \sigma_a \divideontimes \sigma_b}{\Gamma \vdash (\tau, \sigma) \prec (\tau_a, \sigma_a) \divideontimes (\tau_b, \sigma_b)}$$

$$\textsc{Ref-}\divideontimes\ \frac{\Gamma \vdash \mathsf{ref}\{b \mid \phi'\}[R', G'] \qquad \Gamma \vdash \mathsf{ref}\{b \mid \phi''\}[R'', G''] \qquad \emptyset \subset [\![G']\!] \subseteq [\![R'']\!] \qquad \emptyset \subset [\![G'']\!] \subseteq [\![R]\!]' \qquad [\![G']\!] \cup [\![G'']\!] \subseteq [\![G]\!] \qquad [\![R]\!] \subseteq [\![R']\!] \qquad [\![R]\!] \subseteq [\![R'']\!]}{\Gamma \vdash \mathsf{ref}\{b \mid \phi\}[R, G] \prec \mathsf{ref}\{b \mid \phi'\}[R', G'] \divideontimes \mathsf{ref}\{b \mid \phi''\}[R'', G'']}$$

$$\boxed{\Gamma \vdash e : \tau} \qquad \frac{}{\Gamma \vdash n : \mathtt{nat}} \qquad \frac{}{\Gamma \vdash b : \mathtt{bool}} \qquad \frac{}{\Gamma \vdash \mathsf{tt} : \mathtt{unit}} \qquad \textsc{Axiom}\ \frac{}{\Gamma \vdash \mathsf{Prop} : \mathsf{Type}} \qquad \textsc{V}\ \frac{\Gamma \vdash \tau \prec \tau \divideontimes \tau}{\Gamma, x : \tau \vdash x : \tau}$$

$$\Pi\text{-I}\ \frac{\Gamma \vdash \tau \prec \tau \divideontimes \tau \qquad \forall \tau \in \Gamma. \vdash \tau \prec \tau \divideontimes \tau \qquad \Gamma \vdash (\Pi x : \tau \to \tau') : \sigma \qquad \sigma \in \{\mathsf{Type}, \mathsf{Prop}\} \qquad \Gamma, x : \tau \vdash e : \tau'}{\Gamma \vdash (\lambda x : \tau. e) : \Pi x : \tau \to \tau'} \qquad \Pi\text{-E}\ \frac{\Gamma \vdash e_1 : \Pi x : \tau \to \tau' \qquad \Gamma \vdash e_2 : \tau}{\Gamma \vdash e_1\ e_2 : \tau'[x/e_2]}$$

$$\frac{\varepsilon \vdash \tau \qquad \varepsilon \vdash \tau' \qquad x : \tau \vdash e : \tau' \Rightarrow \Gamma'}{\Gamma \vdash (\lambda_{\mathcal{M}} x : \tau. e) : \tau \stackrel{\mathcal{M}}{\to} \tau'} \qquad \textsc{Deref}\ \frac{\Gamma \vdash e : \mathsf{ref}\{\tau \mid P\}[R, G] \qquad \tau' = [R, G] \gg \tau \qquad \Gamma \vdash \tau \prec \tau \divideontimes \tau \qquad G\ \mathsf{reflexive}}{\Gamma \vdash !e : \tau'}$$

$$\Pi\text{-F}\ \frac{\Gamma \vdash \tau : \gamma \qquad \Gamma \vdash \tau \prec \tau \divideontimes \tau \qquad \Gamma, x : \tau \vdash \tau' : \sigma \qquad \gamma, \sigma \in \{\mathsf{Type}, \mathsf{Prop}\}}{\Gamma \vdash \Pi x : \tau \to \tau' : \sigma} \qquad \textsc{Conv}\ \frac{\Gamma \vdash e : \tau \qquad \Gamma \vdash \tau \leadsto \tau'}{\Gamma \vdash e : \tau'}$$

$$\boxed{\Gamma \vdash \tau \leadsto \tau} \qquad \text{P-}\Rightarrow\ \frac{\forall v, h. P\ v\ h \to P'\ v\ h \qquad \mathsf{stable}\ P'\ R}{\Gamma \vdash \mathsf{ref}\{\tau \mid P\}[R, G] \leadsto \mathsf{ref}\{\tau \mid P'\}[R, G]} \qquad \text{R-}\subset\ \frac{[\![R]\!] \subseteq [\![R']\!] \qquad \mathsf{stable}\ P\ R'}{\Gamma \vdash \mathsf{ref}\{\tau \mid P\}[R, G] \leadsto \mathsf{ref}\{\tau \mid P\}[R', G]} \qquad \text{G-}\subset\ \frac{[\![G']\!] \subseteq [\![G]\!]}{\Gamma \vdash \mathsf{ref}\{\tau \mid P\}[R, G] \leadsto \mathsf{ref}\{\tau \mid P\}[R, G']}$$

$$\boxed{\Gamma \vdash e : \tau \Rightarrow \Gamma} \qquad \text{V-}\emptyset\ \frac{}{\Gamma, x : \tau \vdash x : \tau \Rightarrow \Gamma} \qquad \text{V-}\divideontimes\ \frac{\Gamma \vdash \tau \prec \tau' \divideontimes \tau''}{\Gamma, x : \tau \vdash x : \tau' \Rightarrow \Gamma, x : \tau''} \qquad \mathcal{M}\text{-I}\ \frac{\forall \tau \in \Gamma. \vdash \tau \prec \tau \divideontimes \tau \qquad \Gamma, x : \tau \vdash e : \tau' \Rightarrow \Gamma'}{\Gamma \vdash (\lambda_{\mathcal{M}}(x : \tau). e) : \tau \stackrel{\mathcal{M}}{\to} \tau' \Rightarrow \Gamma} \qquad \mathcal{M}\text{-E}\ \frac{\Gamma \vdash e_1 : \tau \stackrel{\mathcal{M}}{\to} \tau' \Rightarrow \Gamma_1 \qquad \Gamma_1 \vdash e_2 : \tau \Rightarrow \Gamma_2}{\Gamma \vdash e_1\ e_2 : \tau' \Rightarrow \Gamma_2}$$

$$\textsc{Write}\ \frac{\Gamma \vdash e : \tau \Rightarrow \Gamma', x : \mathsf{ref}\{\tau \mid P\}[R, G] \qquad \forall h, h' : heap. h' = [\![e]\!](h) \to P\ (!x)\ h' \to P'\ [\![e]\!]\ h'[x \mapsto [\![e]\!]] \qquad \mathsf{stable}\ P'\ R \qquad \forall h, h' : heap. h' = [\![e]\!](h) \to P\ (!x)\ h' \to G\ (!x)\ e\ h'\ h'[x \mapsto [\![e]\!]]}{\Gamma \vdash x \leftarrow e : \mathsf{unit} \Rightarrow \Gamma', x : \mathsf{ref}\{\tau \mid P'\}[R, G]}$$

$$\textsc{IDeref}\ \frac{\Gamma \vdash e : \mathsf{ref}\{\tau \mid P\}[R, G] \qquad \tau' = [R, G] \gg \tau \qquad \Gamma \vdash \tau \prec \tau \divideontimes \tau \qquad G\ \mathsf{reflexive}}{\Gamma \vdash !e : \tau' \Rightarrow \Gamma'}$$

$$\textsc{Alloc}\ \frac{\Gamma \vdash e : \tau \Rightarrow \Gamma' \qquad \emptyset \subset G \qquad \mathsf{stable}\ P\ R \qquad \forall h : heap. P\ e\ h}{\Gamma \vdash \mathsf{alloc}\ e : \mathsf{ref}\{\tau \mid P\}[R, G] \Rightarrow \Gamma'} \qquad \textsc{Swap}\ \frac{\Gamma \vdash x \leftarrow e : \mathsf{unit} \Rightarrow \Gamma', x : \mathsf{ref}\{\tau \mid P'\}[R, G]}{\Gamma \vdash \mathsf{swap}(x, e) : \tau \Rightarrow \Gamma', x : \mathsf{ref}\{\tau \mid P'\}[R, G]} \qquad \textsc{Pure}\ \frac{\varepsilon \vdash e : \tau \qquad \varepsilon \vdash \tau : \mathsf{Prop}}{\Gamma \vdash e : \tau \Rightarrow \Gamma}$$

$$\text{I}\Pi\text{-E}\ \frac{\Gamma \vdash e_1 : \Pi x : \tau \to \tau' \Rightarrow \Gamma' \qquad \Gamma' \vdash e_2 : \tau \Rightarrow \Gamma'' \qquad x \notin FV(\tau')}{\Gamma \vdash e_1\ e_2 : \tau' \Rightarrow \Gamma''} \qquad \boxed{\Gamma \vdash \tau : \sigma} \qquad \textsc{wf-Ref}\ \frac{\varepsilon \vdash R : hrel(\tau) \qquad \varepsilon \vdash G : hrel(\tau) \qquad \varepsilon \vdash P : hprop(\tau) \qquad \mathsf{closed}\ R \qquad \mathsf{precise}\ R \qquad \mathsf{precise}\ G \qquad \mathsf{precise}\ P \qquad \mathsf{stable}\ P\ R \qquad \varepsilon \vdash \tau : \mathsf{Prop}}{\Gamma \vdash \mathsf{ref}\{\tau \mid P\}[R, G] : \mathsf{Prop}}$$

with metafunctions $hrel(\tau) \stackrel{\text{def}}{=} \tau \to \tau \to \mathsf{heap} \to \mathsf{heap} \to \mathsf{Prop}$ and $hprop(\tau) \stackrel{\text{def}}{=} \tau \to \mathsf{heap} \to \mathsf{Prop}$

Figure 4. Typing. Not shown: standard recursors for naturals, booleans, pairs, identity types [25]. Also not shown: standard well-formed contexts, most of (pure) expression/type conversion ($\Gamma \vdash \tau \leadsto \tau$) (see our technical report [23]).

action within the used reference's guarantee. For other references, the action will fall within its rely (by containment) and thus a similar use of a stability proof suffices, or the changed cell is not reachable from the reference in question, in which case the predicate is preserved by precision.

This proof is simplified by slightly nonstandard operational semantics. First, we execute an elaborated language where conversions, strong updates, and substructural reads of variables are explicit (translation from a typed source program is straightforward). To prove soundness of substructural manipulation, impure code manipulates a mutable stack, and references are "fat pointers" of the underlying pointer, rely, guarantee, and predicate. Variable capture in imperative closures occurs via a rule that inlines all free variables when reducing to a value. Folding has a runtime representation, since folded types sometimes occur as part of runtime values. Finally, the semantics sometimes reduce multiple dereferences at once inside pure expressions, when type equivalence requires the dereference expressions to be definitionally equal. This avoids trouble where the naïve reduction might reduce definitionally equal dereferences in different heaps (with different values). We have yet to conceive of desirable computational code that observes this behavior. Our technical report provides more details [23].

5. Implementation

To understand RGREF's effect on data structure design and the effort required for verification, we have implemented RGREF as a shallow embedding in COQ, and used it to implement Section 3's examples. This includes implementing reference immutability, meaning our RGREF implementation can be used to write programs using reference immutability, and to gradually refine parts of those programs to use more fine-grained rely and guarantee conditions and predicates. Overall, we found that RGREF required careful choice of type refinements, but did not affect algorithm design and had reasonable proof burden (commensurate with the complexity of the code verified).

The implementation is done largely in the style of YNOT [11, 34], with axioms for heap interaction, and using COQ's notation facilities to elaborate source terms to COQ terms with proof holes, which are then elaborated and semi-automatically solved by Sozeau's PROGRAM extension [42]. Each structure typically requires its own slightly customized PROGRAM tactic for effectively solving most goals, but we find that following the tactic development style Chlipala recommends [10] tends to work well, as each module typically handles its own family of predicates and relations. Proofs involving heaps are carried out using a small set of axioms reflecting invariants maintained by the semantics. The most useful axiom is $\mathsf{heap\_lookup} : \forall h, A, P, R, G. \forall r : \mathsf{ref}\{A \mid P\}[R, G]. P\ (h[r])\ h$ which means that in any heap, the type system ensures there is a proof of the refinement for every valid reference. The implementation also relaxes some restrictions present in the formal language, such as allowing values to be projected into predicates (as in Section 3.2); predicates, rely and guarantee relations must simply abstain from dereference.

$$\mathsf{stable}_\tau\ (P : hprop(\tau))\ (R : hrel(\tau)) \stackrel{\text{def}}{=} \forall x : \tau. \forall h, h' : \mathsf{heap}. P\ x\ h \rightarrow R\ x\ h\ h' \rightarrow P\ x\ h'$$

$$\mathsf{precise}_\tau\ (P : hpred(\tau)) \stackrel{\text{def}}{=} \forall x, h, h'. (\forall l, \mathsf{ReachFromIn}\ l\ x\ h \rightarrow h[l] = h'[l]) \rightarrow P\ x\ h \rightarrow P\ x\ h'$$

$$\mathsf{precise}_\tau\ (R : hrel(\tau)) \stackrel{\text{def}}{=} \forall x, x', h, h', \overline{h}, \overline{h'}. (\forall l, \mathsf{ReachFromIn}\ l\ x\ h \rightarrow h[l] = h'[l]) \rightarrow (\forall l, \mathsf{ReachFromIn}\ l\ x'\ \overline{h} \rightarrow \overline{h}[l] = \overline{h'}[l]) \rightarrow R\ x\ x'\ h\ \overline{h} \rightarrow R\ x\ x'\ h'\ \overline{h'}$$

$$\mathsf{closed}_\tau\ (R : hrel(\tau)) \stackrel{\text{def}}{=} \begin{cases} \mathsf{True} & \text{if } \tau \in \{\mathtt{nat}, \mathtt{bool}, \mathsf{unit}, \Pi x : \tau' \rightarrow \tau'', \tau \stackrel{\mathcal{M}}{\rightarrow} \tau', \mathsf{True}, \mathsf{False}, \mathsf{heap}, \_ = \_\} \\ \mathsf{closed}\ R.1 \wedge \mathsf{closed}\ R.2 & \text{if } \tau = (\sigma * \sigma') \\ \mathsf{closed}\ R' \wedge \forall l, h, h'. R'\ h[l]\ h'[l]\ h\ h' \rightarrow R\ l\ l\ h\ h' & \text{if } \tau = \mathsf{ref}\{\tau' \mid P'\}[R', G'] \end{cases}$$

$$[R, G] \gg \tau \stackrel{\text{def}}{=} \begin{cases} \tau & \text{if } \tau \in \{\mathtt{nat}, \mathtt{bool}, \mathsf{unit}, \Pi x : \tau' \rightarrow \tau'', \tau \stackrel{\mathcal{M}}{\rightarrow} \tau', \mathsf{True}, \mathsf{False}, \mathsf{heap}, \_ = \_\} \\ ([R.1, G.1] \gg \sigma * [R.2, G.2] \gg \gamma) & \text{if } \tau = (\sigma * \gamma) \\ \mathsf{ref}\{\sigma \mid P\}[R', \begin{array}{l}(\lambda a, a', h, h'. G'\ a\ a'\ h\ h' \wedge \\ \quad (\forall l, h[l] = a \rightarrow h'[l] = a' \rightarrow G\ l\ l\ h\ h'))\end{array}] & \text{if } \tau = \mathsf{ref}\{\sigma \mid P\}[R', G'] \end{cases}$$

where for $R : hrel(\sigma * \sigma')$: $R.1 \stackrel{\text{def}}{=} \lambda x, x' : \sigma. \lambda h, h' : \mathsf{heap}. \forall y : \sigma'. R\ (x, y)\ (x', y)\ h\ h'$ and $R.2 \stackrel{\text{def}}{=} \lambda y, y' : \sigma. \lambda h, h' : \mathsf{heap}. \forall x : \sigma'. R\ (x, y)\ (x, y')\ h\ h'$

Figure 5. Selected auxiliary judgments and predicates

We made compromises to fit into COQ. Notably, COQ lacks support for mutual inductive types where one indexes the other (e.g., a datatype simultaneously defined with an inductive predicate on that type). Our implementation adapts a standard encoding [8] of induction-recursion [17] outlined in our technical report [23] to support examples like the list in Section 3.2. Any use of this encoding somewhat complicates generated proof obligations and data structure designs. Thus our current implementation is best-suited to "functional-first" designs that make only light use of references, as is common in OCaml, Scala, and F# code. We stress that this is a limitation of our implementation by embedding in COQ, not a fundamental limitation of rely-guarantee references.

To use COQ's rich support for inductive types, we require trusted user-provided definitions of relation folding, immediate reachability (without heap access) of references from a pure datatype, and relation containment. These are provided as typeclass instances. The definitions are fairly mechanical, and can be synthesized automatically for simple types if we extend COQ's support for inductive datatypes.

We also move some proof obligations such as stability, precision, and containment from type formation to allocation. This allows the definition of functions over ill-formed types, but such functions are unusable: only well-formed types may actually be constructed. This avoids some redundant proof obligations.

Our implementation is publicly available at `https://github.com/csgordon/rgref/`.

5.1 Proving Obligations with Dependent Types

RGREF contains as a sublanguage the full Calculus of Constructions (CC). Specifically, it contains a full Pure Type System (PTS) with sorts $\mathcal{S} = \{\mathsf{Prop}, \mathsf{Type}\}$, axioms $\mathcal{A} = \{\mathsf{Prop} : \mathsf{Type}\}$, and product formation rules $\mathcal{R} = \{(s_1, s_2) \mid s_1, s_2 \in \mathcal{S}\}$ as formulated by Barendregt [2]. This sublanguage is part of the pure $(\Gamma \vdash e : \tau)$ subset of RGREF. Thus the language is amenable to embedding directly into CC with a few extensions (natural numbers, etc.) and RGREF-specific axioms. Our technical report details the translation [23].

This provides us with an approach to proving predicate and guarantee obligations in a way well-integrated with the source language, justifying the use of proof terms in RGREF's implementation. This also allows straightforward translation of proof goals from our typing derivations into COQ, where we can use tactic-based theorem proving to solve proof obligations.

The only subtleties arise from the fact that our embedding treats dereference as an uninterpreted function, allowing two potential inconsistencies. First, we permit recursion through the store, so applying a function read (via dereference) from the heap could result in an infinite loop; by treating dereference as an uninterpreted function in the embedding, this potential recursion is lost. The prototype may accept proofs about non-terminating terms. Second, there is a potential to equate dereference expressions that will be evaluated in different heaps (e.g., when a returned pure closure dereferences some reference). Our implementation only uses full equational reasoning for cases where all dereferences occur in the same heap, and otherwise abstracts terms with only their type.

5.2 Data Structure Design

We were able to use natural data structures for the examples in Section 3, but the types require careful consideration for propagating information through data flow. For example, the return type of `Cons` in Figure 1 must carry the additional refinement that the reference points to a cons cell whose tail is the `tl` argument, or the obligation to prove that the write prepends a cell in `doPrepend` is unprovable.

From Simple Types to Inductive Types For the types whose splitting, folding, and containment we have examined formally (first-order data types, pairs, and references), the structure of the types is simple enough to provide a straightforward structural projection for each type. Much imperative code (e.g. in C, Java, etc.) heap-allocates similarly-simple structures. We have not worked out the theory for full inductive types. For types whose constructor arguments are not reflected as type indices, splitting and the like depend on the values passed to constructors, complicating the definitions for splitting because they then depend not only on type indices, but the actual value being potentially-split. This is an issue even though we expect to only require support for small inductive types. For self-referential datatypes, such as the list, we have only used guarantees for which folding is idempotent. In general, folding a restricted guarantee when dereferencing an datatype defined with concrete relations on "recursive" references is not expressible in the current system; if the guarantee on the recursive member changes, the result may not match a constructor of the type! Supporting this would require some sort of datatype-generic support, or a hybrid dereference-and-pattern-match to avoid directly representing not-quite-typed read results. We leave full support for inductive types to future work.

5.3 Proof Burden

RGREF imposes proof obligations for precision, folding, containment, and guarantee satisfaction. For verifying the examples in Sections 3.1, 3.2, and 3.3, the proof burden is not substantially different from verifying the analogous pure-functional version. This section will call out which parts were particularly straightforward, as well as the few challenging aspects.

Precision obligations are typically easy to prove when they are true, as are the reflexive relation goals generated when references are used for reading: most are discharged by a simple induction, use of constructors for the relevant relation, and/or first order reasoning (e.g., COQ's `firstorder` tactic). When the goals are not true (e.g., a relation or predicate is not precise), the goal is simply not provable, and it is up to the developer to recognize this. In this respect, RGREF is similar to verifying a functional program in COQ: a developer can waste time on unsolvable (false) proof goals.

In cases where relation folding is a no-op (e.g., $[R,G] \gg \tau = \tau$ as in the monotonic counter) folding goals are a simple matter of reduction and basic equality. In cases where relation folding is not a no-op (e.g., for references to references where the outer reference's guarantee bounds effects on other reachable objects), the folding obligations' complexity depends on the relations involved.

The most difficult proof obligations generated are those checking that heap writes satisfy the guarantee.[5] This is partly because these goals sometimes require reasoning about reads from an updated heap, in particular proving non-aliasing between references to different base types. Some goals are also complicated by non-identity folding results in types. In the formal system, we abstract away the mechanism for checking guarantee satisfaction through a denotational semantics for writes. Our implementation uses COQ's notation facilities for a sort of "punning," to duplicate expressions into two contexts with different semantics for dereference.

The normal program's use of the dereference expression chooses the appropriate relation folding type class instance, while the duplicated version used to check guarantee satisfaction is placed inside a context where a no-op fold instance overrides all others. This way the guarantee and predicates, which are specified as predicates over a type A, can be applied directly to $!x$ at type A in the proofs instead of at a weakened type. The disadvantage of this approach is that the expression duplication also duplicates proof goals. Many of the smaller goals are automatically discharged when using COQ's PROGRAM extension, but because the generated goals are formed in slightly different contexts, the solved lemmas' proof terms have different arities, and are therefore not interchangeable in equalities. We encountered this twice, and solved it by using the proof irrelevance axiom on applications of the equivalent lemmas.

Because stability, reflexivity, and satisfaction results tend to be reused within a module and by clients, it should be considered proper practice for modules exporting a given API to also export most goals proven internally about properties of rely and guarantee relations, and predicates, as lemmas registered in a module-specific hint database. This is best practice for verifying purely functional programs in COQ as well; in general most of the useful habits in verifying functional programs can be reused in our implementation.

6. Future Work: Extensions and Adaptations

The type system we present in this paper has a few limitations (these are orthogonal to the implementation-specific limitations described in Section 5). We briefly mention a couple here, and discuss them in more detail in our technical report [23].

One weakness is that every individual write must fall within a guarantee relation. This means that a series of writes that individually violate a guarantee but in aggregate satisfy it are disallowed. This is a common challenge for verification techniques [3, 5, 41], and we expect related work to inspire sufficient solutions.

Also, as execution progresses, the actions permitted on an object through all references strictly decreases, by weakening and splitting guarantees. We have no way to strengthen guarantees based on additional information, as in the *recovery* technique [22] used to combine reference immutability with uniqueness, allowing uniqueness to be temporarily lost and then recovered. A resource-based approach to splitting, as in deny-guarantee program logics [16], suggests one promising approach to preserving possible actions.

Finally, it would be useful to separate out a logically-consistent fragment of the pure sublanguage (possibly using techniques like F*'s kind system [43]).

7. Related Work

The most closely related work falls into three categories: restricting mutation on a per-reference basis, techniques for reasoning about interference among threads (which can be adapted to interference among aliases), and dependent types for imperative languages.

Alias-based Mutation Control Many techniques exist to control side effects by restricting actions through particular references. Notable examples include reference immutability [22, 44, 49, 50], and the owner-as-modifier interpretation of ownership and universe types [14]. Rely-guarantee references generalize reference immutability permissions (Section 3.3), allowing precise control over what modification is permitted through a given alias, not simply a choice between arbitrary mutation and local immutability. The fact that reference immutability is a special case of rely-guarantee references suggests a natural transition path from reference immutability to stronger verification guarantees. Developers could employ a "pay-as-you-go" model for verification, where a code base first transitions to using reference immutability (which need not be onerous [22]), and then gradually enrich the types for some parts of the system where more assurance is desired.

Typestate approaches typically use reference immutability like access permissions to control sharing of objects in a certain typestate, which is a weak form of refinement [5, 29, 31, 35]. Nistor and Aldrich describe a program-logic style type system [35] using abstract predicates [38] and connectives inspired by separation logic to specify *object propositions*, essentially an enriched typestate much closer to a full predicate logic; we believe object propositions and RGREF have similar expressivity in terms of what predicates they can verify. They pair access permissions with refinements to let aliases share coinciding views of an object's properties, and handle non-atomic updates. However, propositions on aliased objects cannot change over time and all aliases must have identical capabilities (simply preserving the proposition if the object is aliased), while RGREF allows asymmetric permissions and some strong updates to refinements even with aliasing.

Militão and Aldrich present a system that splits objects into substates that each carry their own typestate, and ways to merge particular substates into a typestate of the parent object [29]. Aliases to an object may exist and allow modification provided each reference is to a different substate, rather than to the full substate.

Concurrently with our work, they have proposed a rely-guarantee typestate [30], where the rely is a typestate each alias assumes an object may be in, and the guarantee is a typestate each alias is required to produce when unpacked. The properties they can verify are limited to those expressible as typestate (finite state partitioning) and the system requires the programmer to add many dynamic typestate checks to aid verification, but using their system is easier than the theorem-proving RGREF requires. RGREF can express stronger properties and forces no extra dynamic checks.

Reasoning About Thread Interference Generally, any technique that can reason about interference among threads can be adapted to reason about interference among references. The most closely related system for reasoning about thread interference is rely-guarantee reasoning [27] described in Section 1.

The original rely-guarantee approach focused on global relations and assertions, hampering modularity. Several adaptations exist to treat interference over disjoint state separately. Vafeiadis and Parkinson integrated rely-guarantee reasoning with separation logic [45], allowing separation of state with linear resource semantics from shared state with interference. Feng later generalized this

[5] Not all are difficult; Section 3.1's guarantee obligation is discharged by automatic proof search with arithmetic hints: `auto with arith`.

to add separating conjunction of rely and guarantee conditions [18]. The conditions split into separate relations over separated pieces of shared state. Rely-guarantee references are heavily inspired by these approaches. However, RGREF allows substantial overlap among heap segments.

Dodds et al. adapted standard (non-separating) rely-guarantee reasoning to give resource semantics to rely and guarantee relations as assumptions in a context [16]. This allows the interference on shared state to change over time as permission to modify disjoint parts in particular ways is split, rejoined, and split again differently. This style of strong changes to the rely and guarantee over time could be adapted in a rely-guarantee reference system to allow the natural rely-guarantee reference generalization of the *recovery* technique of Gordon et al. [22], which allows recovering unique (or immutable) references from writable (or readable) references in a flow-sensitive type system given some constraints on the input context to a block of code.

Wickerson et al. [46] apply a modularized rely-guarantee logic to treat (non-)interference in the degenerate case of sequential access to the UNIXv7 memory manager. Related systems [15, 18, 45] could be applied similarly, but to our knowledge haven't. Most have only first-order treatment of interference. Only Concurrent Abstract Predicates [15] can (with some effort) store capabilities into the heap, while RGREF naturally supports this since mutation capabilities are tied to data. Our design closely follows a technique already shown successful in large-scale uses (reference-immutability [22]).

Dependent Types for Imperative Code Many others have worked on integrating dependent types into imperative programming languages. Most take the approach of using refinement types [21, 43] that restrict modification to mutable data, but the refinements themselves may depend only on immutable data. Examples include DML [47], ATS [9], and X10's constrained types [36]. The refinement language is often also restricted to some theory that can be effectively decided by an SMT solver, as in Liquid Types [41]. RGREF allows refinements to depend on mutable heap data, and does not artificially restrict the properties that can be verified (at the cost of requiring manual guidance for proofs).

A notable approach to dependent types in imperative code is Hoare Type Theory (HTT) [32, 33] and its implementation YNOT [11, 34]. HTT uses a monadic Hoare Triple to encode effectful computation. It allows using effectful code in specifications: it decides equality of effectful specification terms by using canonical forms where traditional dependent type systems use β-conversion. This approach could be adapted for rely-guarantee references as well. YNOT implements the core ideas of HTT as a domain specific language embedded in COQ. It supports traditional Hoare logic specifications and, by embedding, separation logic specifications as well. A later version [11] builds a family of targeted proof search tactics that can automatically discharge most separation logic proof goals generated while typechecking YNOT programs. We modeled our implementation after YNOT, and are currently building a library of combinators and transformers in hopes of supporting similarly robust automatic proof discharge.

HTT (and separation logic in general) support proving functional correctness rather than the somewhat weaker safety properties verified by rely-guarantee references (and most other stable-assertion-based approaches [18, 27, 45]). But this comes at the cost of specifications explicitly specifying aliasing constraints through choice of standard or separating conjunction. Separation logic specifies the behavior of code, not the restrictions on data transformation. Rely-guarantee reference types specify the possible evolution of data in the description of data itself. This means that assumptions and permission to modify state follow data-flow, rather than the control-flow-centric passing of assertions in most program logics.

8. Conclusion

We have introduced *rely-guarantee references*, an adaptation of rely-guarantee program logics to reasoning about interference among aliases to shared objects. The technique generalizes reference immutability, connecting two previously-separate lines of research and addressing a fundamental problem in verifying imperative programs. We have shown the technique's usefulness by verifying correctness for several small examples (which are difficult to specify or verify with other approaches) in a prototype implementation. Our experience suggests that at least for small examples, the proof burden is reasonable. Rely-guarantee references demonstrate that aliasing in program verification can be addressed by adapting ideas from reasoning about thread interference.

Acknowledgments

This work was supported by NSF grants CNS-0855252 and CCF-1016701; and by DARPA contracts FA8750-12-C-0174 and FA8750-12-2-0107. We thank the anonymous referees for their comments, which helped improve the paper.

References

[1] L. Augustsson. Cayenne — A Language with Dependent Types. In *ICFP*, 1998.

[2] H. Barendregt. *Lambda Calculi with Types*. 1991.

[3] M. Barnett, M. Fähndrich, K. R. M. Leino, P. Müller, W. Schulte, and H. Venter. Specification and Verification: The Spec# Experience. *Commun. ACM*, 54(6):81–91, June 2011.

[4] Y. Bertot and P. Castéran. *Interactive Theorem Proving and Program Development; Coq'Art: The Calculus of Inductive Constructions*. Springer Verlag, 2004.

[5] K. Bierhoff and J. Aldrich. Modular Typestate Checking of Aliased Objects. In *OOPSLA*, 2007.

[6] R. L. Bocchino, Jr., V. S. Adve, D. Dig, S. V. Adve, S. Heumann, R. Komuravelli, J. Overbey, P. Simmons, H. Sung, and M. Vakilian. A Type and Effect System for Deterministic Parallel Java. In *OOPSLA*, 2009.

[7] R. Bornat, C. Calcagno, P. O'Hearn, and M. Parkinson. Permission Accounting in Separation Logic. In *POPL*, 2005.

[8] V. Capretta. A Polymorphic Representation of Induction-Recursion. Retrieved 9/12/12. URL: `http://www.cs.ru.nl/~venanzio/publications/induction_recursion.pdf`, March 2004.

[9] C. Chen and H. Xi. Combining Programming with Theorem Proving. In *ICFP*, 2005.

[10] A. Chlipala. *Certified Programming with Dependent Types*. `http://adam.chlipala.net/cpdt/`.

[11] A. Chlipala, G. Malecha, G. Morrisett, A. Shinnar, and R. Wisnesky. Effective Interactive Proofs for Higher-order Imperative Programs. In *ICFP*, 2009.

[12] Coq Development Team. The COQ Proof Assistant Reference Manual: Version 8.4, 2012.

[13] T. Coquand and G. Huet. The Calculus of Constructions. *Information and Computation*, 76, 1988.

[14] W. Dietl, S. Drossopoulou, and P. Müller. Generic Universe Types. In *ECOOP*, 2007.

[15] T. Dinsdale-Young, M. Dodds, P. Gardner, M. Parkinson, and V. Vafeiadis. Concurrent Abstract Predicates. In *ECOOP*, 2010.

[16] M. Dodds, X. Feng, M. Parkinson, and V. Vafeiadis. Deny-Guarantee Reasoning. In *ESOP*. 2009.

[17] P. Dybjer. Inductive Families. *Formal Aspects of Computing*, 6:440–465, 1994.

[18] X. Feng. Local Rely-Guarantee Reasoning. In *POPL*, 2009.

[19] C. Flanagan and M. Abadi. Types for Safe Locking. In *ESOP*, 1999.

[20] C. Flanagan and S. N. Freund. Type-Based Race Detection for Java. In *PLDI*, 2000.

[21] T. Freeman and F. Pfenning. Refinement types for ml. In *PLDI*, 1991.

[22] C. S. Gordon, M. J. Parkinson, J. Parsons, A. Bromfield, and J. Duffy. Uniqueness and Reference Immutability for Safe Parallelism. In *OOPSLA*, 2012.

[23] C. S. Gordon, M. D. Ernst, and D. Grossman. Rely-Guarantee References for Refinement Types Over Aliased Mutable Data (Extended Version). Technical Report UW-CSE-13-03-02, University of Washington, March 2013.

[24] C. A. R. Hoare. An Axiomatic Basis for Computer Programming. *Commun. ACM*, 12(10):576–580, Oct. 1969.

[25] M. Hofmann. *Syntax and Semantics of Dependent Types, in Semantics and Logics of Computation*, chapter 3. 1997.

[26] J. B. Jensen and L. Birkedal. Fictional Separation Logic. In *ESOP*, 2012.

[27] C. B. Jones. Tentative Steps Toward a Development Method for Interfering Programs. *ACM TOPLAS*, 5(4):596–619, Oct. 1983.

[28] K. R. Leino and P. Müller. A Basis for Verifying Multi-threaded Programs. In *ESOP*, 2009.

[29] F. Militão, J. Aldrich, and L. Caires. Aliasing Control with View-based Typestate. In *FTfJP*, 2010.

[30] F. Militão, J. Aldrich, and L. Caires. Rely-Guarantee View Typestate. Retrieved 8/24/12, July 2012. URL `http://www.cs.cmu.edu/~foliveir/papers/rgviews.pdf`.

[31] K. Naden, R. Bocchino, J. Aldrich, and K. Bierhoff. A Type System for Borrowing Permissions. In *POPL*, 2012.

[32] A. Nanevski, G. Morrisett, and L. Birkedal. Polymorphism and Separation in Hoare Type Theory. In *ICFP*, 2006.

[33] A. Nanevski, A. Ahmed, G. Morrisett, and L. Birkedal. Abstract Predicates and Mutable ADTs in Hoare Type Theory. In *ESOP*. 2007.

[34] A. Nanevski, G. Morrisett, A. Shinnar, P. Govereau, and L. Birkedal. Ynot: Dependent Types for Imperative Programs. In *ICFP*, 2008.

[35] L. Nistor and J. Aldrich. Verifying Object-Oriented Code Using Object Propositions. In *IWACO*, 2011.

[36] N. Nystrom, V. Saraswat, J. Palsberg, and C. Grothoff. Constrained Types for Object-Oriented Languages. In *OOPSLA*, 2008.

[37] S. Owicki and D. Gries. An Axiomatic Proof Technique for Parallel Programs I. *Acta Informatica*, pages 319–340, 1976.

[38] M. Parkinson and G. Bierman. Separation Logic and Abstraction. In *POPL*, 2005.

[39] C. Paulin-Mohring. Inductive Definitions in the System Coq: Rules and Properties. In *Typed Lambda Calculi and Applications*, 1993.

[40] A. Pilkiewicz and F. Pottier. The Essence of Monotonic State. In *TLDI*, 2011.

[41] P. M. Rondon, M. Kawaguchi, and R. Jhala. Low-Level Liquid Types. In *POPL*, 2010.

[42] M. Sozeau. Program-ing Finger Trees in Coq. In *ICFP*, 2007.

[43] N. Swamy, J. Chen, C. Fournet, P.-Y. Strub, K. Bhargavan, and J. Yang. Secure Distributed Programming with Value-dependent Types. In *ICFP*, 2011.

[44] M. S. Tschantz and M. D. Ernst. Javari: Adding Reference Immutability to Java. In *OOPSLA*, 2005.

[45] V. Vafeiadis and M. Parkinson. A Marriage of Rely/Guarantee and Separation Logic. In *CONCUR*. 2007.

[46] J. Wickerson, M. Dodds, and M. Parkinson. Explicit Stabilisation for Modular Rely-Guarantee Reasoning. In *ESOP*, 2010.

[47] H. Xi and F. Pfenning. Dependent Types in Practical Programming. In *POPL*, 1999.

[48] H. Xi, C. Chen, and G. Chen. Guarded Recursive Datatype Constructors. In *POPL*, 2003.

[49] Y. Zibin, A. Potanin, M. Ali, S. Artzi, A. Kiezun, and M. D. Ernst. Object and Reference Immutability Using Java Generics. In *ESEC-FSE*, 2007.

[50] Y. Zibin, A. Potanin, P. Li, M. Ali, and M. D. Ernst. Ownership and Immutability in Generic Java. In *OOPSLA*, 2010.

Harmonizing Classes, Functions, Tuples, and Type Parameters in Virgil III

Ben L. Titzer
Google
titzer@google.com

Abstract

Languages are becoming increasingly multi-paradigm. Subtype polymorphism in statically-typed object-oriented languages is being supplemented with parametric polymorphism in the form of generics. Features like first-class functions and lambdas are appearing everywhere. Yet existing languages like Java, C#, C++, D, and Scala seem to accrete ever more complexity when they reach beyond their original paradigm into another; inevitably older features have some rough edges that lead to nonuniformity and pitfalls. Given a fresh start, a new language designer is faced with a daunting array of potential features. Where to start? What is important to get right first, and what can be added later? What features must work together, and what features are orthogonal? We report on our experience with Virgil III, a practical language with a careful balance of classes, functions, tuples and type parameters. Virgil intentionally lacks many advanced features, yet we find its core feature set enables new species of design patterns that bridge multiple paradigms and emulate features not directly supported such as interfaces, abstract data types, ad hoc polymorphism, and variant types. Surprisingly, we find variance for function types and tuple types often replaces the need for other kinds of type variance when libraries are designed in a more functional style.

Categories and Subject Descriptors D.3.3 [*Programming Languages*]: Language Constructs and Features

Keywords Multi-paradigm languages; parametric types; object-oriented programming; functional programming; monomorphization; variance; closures; tuples; flattening; unboxing; static compilation

1. Introduction

Mainstream languages are becoming increasingly multi-paradigm and increasingly complex. Statically-typed object-oriented languages have now ventured beyond the subtype polymorphism of class and object inheritance and begun adding parametric polymorphism in various forms; erased generics in Java 5.0, reified generics in C# 2.0, C++ templates, and even more complex generics in Scala.

Functional programming constructs are now appearing in nearly all active languages, further adding to language complexity. Languages like Java first offered object-oriented emulation of functions in the form of single-method interfaces like `Runnable` and `Comparator`. Generics gave rise to even more complex emulations of functions such as `java.util.concurrent`'s `Callable` and Guava's `Function` [13] and `Predicate`. Now Java has proposals for syntax for function types and closures in JSR 335 [17]. Similar developments occurred in both C++ and C#, with libraries first evolving functional patterns before languages added syntactic support. C# first allowed *delegates*, which are closures bound to a method of an object, and then full lambdas. Scala set out to blend object-oriented and functional styles while still primarily targeting the JVM. Not to be outdone, C++11 has added support for lambdas and a host of other new features. Of course the relationship between functions and objects goes back even further in dynamically-typed languages. Smalltalk had blocks [12], popular dynamic languages such as JavaScript, Python and Ruby have first class functions, and newcomers such as Newspeak, Groovy and Dart also incorporate some kind of functional features.

A designer of a new programming language faces a daunting lineup of features from which to choose. What features work best? How does this feature enhance or hinder another feature? What feature should be implemented first? Should objects be primary, or functions be primary? What tools should programmers have to express polymorphism and reuse, model side-effects or state, and how can the constructs be implemented efficiently?

Of course, these are the tough design questions to which the whole of language research is directed. This paper explores just *one* potential combination of four language features and the implications of that combination. In seeking to find a smaller, more cohesive language core made from existing parts, and seeking to implement a practical language in which efficient systems can be written, we've found a number of surprising patterns arising from just a small set of features.

This paper finds that integrating four particular features in a statically-typed language achieves a surprising cohesiveness and simplicity. **Classes** provide data abstraction, encapsulation, and information hiding; first-class **functions** allow fine-grained reuse; **tuples** allow for the uniform treatment of multi-argument and multi-return function types and simplify composing values, and **type parameters** allow type abstraction and representation independence for more reuse of functions and data structures represented by objects. None of these features are novel, and all of them exhibit implementations in mainstream languages, but their seamless integration is key in Virgil's design. This integration yields surprising power; enough to build new design patterns that emulate other language features not in the language, including interfaces, abstract data types, ad hoc polymorphism, and variants. An interesting aside is Virgil's approach to type variance; a key design difficulty in recent statically typed languages with both subtyping and parametric polymorphism. Surprisingly, we find type variance for class types

PLDI'13, June 16–19, 2013, Seattle, WA, USA.

to be far less important when libraries are designed in a more functional style because built-in variance for tuple and function type constructors is often sufficient.

2. Four Pieces of the Puzzle

Virgil I was originally designed [31] for programming severely resource-constrained devices with only a few hundred bytes of RAM. A staged computation model allows applications to execute initialization code during compilation, building a heap of objects that is compiled into a binary that executes directly on the hardware. Virgil I supported objects and functions but had no dynamic memory allocation, no type parameters, and no tuples, making it unsuitable for general-purpose programming. Virgil III is a clean redesign for a more general-purpose setting. It retains the staged compilation model of Virgil I but improves classes and functions, adds tuples, type parameters, dynamic memory allocation, and garbage collection.

Virgil includes primitive types such as `int`, `byte`, `bool`, and `void`[1]. All types support four basic operators: equality `==`, inequality `!=`, type cast `!`, and type query `?`. Control structures, basic statements and expression syntax are similar to most C language descendants, but declarations and classes look more like Scala.

2.1 Classes

Virgil provides classes that allow encapsulation, data abstraction and polymorphism through inheritance. Classes resemble those in Java and C# in that only single inheritance is allowed between classes and all methods are virtual except those declared private. All objects are created by instantiating classes and are always passed by reference, never by value. Unlike most object-oriented languages, Virgil has no universal superclass akin to `Object` from which all classes ultimately inherit. A class declared without a parent class begins a new hierarchy which is unrelated to other class hierarchies. This means that there is no unifying supertype for all objects, and there are no default methods available on all objects. Classes are further limited in that there is no concept of an *interface* which a class can implement. The example below illustrates the basics of Virgil classes.

```
(a1)  class A {
(a2)    var f: int;                    // mutable field
(a3)    def g: int;                    // immutable field
(a4)    new(f, g) { ... }              // constructor
(a5)    def m(a: byte) -> int { ... }  // method
(a6)    def n(a: X, b: T) { ... }
(a7)  }
(a8)  class B extends A {              // subclass
(a9)    def m(a: byte) -> int { ... }  // override
(a10) }
```

Pure object-oriented philosophy views all values as objects with some universal type and a default set of methods. The lack of a universal supertype in Virgil or any kind of interface mechanism at first seems crippling, but as we will see in this section, the other features of the language more than make up for the loss of expressiveness. Virgil does not hold the everything-is-an-object philosophy for several reasons. First, domains such as system software [9] [20] and scientific computing [21] demand efficient primitive types; modeling these primitives as objects can be cumbersome, performance can be unpredictable, and mapping certain object types onto hardware primitives requires significant extra-lingual and compiler support. Second, a universal type in object-oriented languages of the past was most often used to implement reuseable datastructures and provide default methods; these roles are better served with proper design of type parameters and use of first class functions, as we will see in the next section. Third, the possibility of subsumption to a universal type weakens confinement [34] properties and may reduce the precision of other static analyses [6][25][31].

[1] `void` has one value, `()`, which is always equal to itself.

2.2 First-class Functions

Virgil provides support for statically-typed first-class functions. Function types take the form T_p `->` T_r, where T_p is the parameter type and T_r is the return type. The type `void` becomes the parameter type of methods with no parameters and the return type of methods without a declared return type. Function types are unrelated to object types, forming a separate universe of values. Function types are co-variant in their return type and contra-variant in their parameter type. A function type can legally appear anywhere any other type can appear, such as the type of a class field, method parameter, local variable, or return type of a method. Unlike most traditional functional languages, tuples are used to model multi-argument functions instead of currying.

To bridge the object-oriented and functional worlds, any method of any object can be used as an *object method*, a function which is bound to the object as its closure. Similarly, *class methods* are not bound to an object but are functions that accept the receiver object as their first parameter followed by the method parameters. All of the basic primitive operators can be used as first-class functions as well, and all three kinds of functions can be used interchangeably.

Examples (b1-7) illustrate the basics, with the types of each expression given in comments. Continuing with the class `A` from (a1-6), we can (b1) create an object of that class and (b2) create a closure bound to the `m` method of that object. In (b3) we use the method `m` of class `A` as a first-class function that is not bound to an object, but accepts the receiver object as the first parameter. In (b4) we invoke `m` directly on the object, in (b5) apply the function `m1` to arguments, and in (b6) apply the function `m2`, supplying the object as the first argument. Notice that we can also use the `new` operator for a class `A` as a function as well (b7).

```
(b1) var a = A.new(0, 1); // A
(b2) var m1 = a.m;        // byte -> int
(b3) var m2 = A.m;        // (A, byte) -> int
(b4) var x = a.m('5');    // int
(b5) var y = m1('4');     // int
(b6) var z = m2(a, '6');  // int
(b7) var w = A.new;       // (int, int) -> A
```

The four basic operators `==` `!=` `!` `?` of every type T are available as first class functions. Though normally written with infix notation, comparisons (b8-9) can be used as functions by referring to them as members of a type, as can primitive and integer arithmetic operators (b10-11).

```
(b8)  var z = byte.==; // (byte, byte) -> bool
(b9)  var w = A.!=;    // (A, A) -> bool
(b10) var p = int.+;   // (int, int) -> int
(b11) var m = int.-;   // (int, int) -> int
```

Type casts (b12) express all type conversions, including downcasts of objects and conversions between primitive values. Type queries (b13) evaluate to `true` if the value is of type T, `false` otherwise. Type casts and type queries of class types check the dynamic type of their input objects. Both operators each have a type parameter that abstracts the type of the input value. Parameterization allows dynamic casts and dynamic type queries between any two types, even polymorphic types. This is a blatant violation of the *parametricity* property of type parameters, but is an intentional tradeoff that allows dynamic casts to emulate other language features, as we will see later. In practice, the compiler rejects casts and queries between unrelated types wherever possible, such as between a function type and a primitive type or between unrelated classes. Like the other operators, casts and queries can be used as functions (b14-15).

```
(b12) var x = A.!(...);    // A
(b13) var y = A.?(...);    // bool
(b14) var z = A.!<B>;      // B -> A
(b15) var w = A.?<B>;      // B -> bool
```

2.3 Tuples

Tuples are a lightweight mechanism to group multiple values into a single value. The resulting tuple value is not an object and has no identity; tuples with equivalent elements are always equal, no matter when or where in the program they are computed. No restrictions are placed on what types may appear as element types of a tuple; if `A` and `B` are valid types, then `(A, B)` is a valid tuple type. Inductively, this means that tuples can be inside of tuples, but not recursively, since tuple types have no names. Elements are ordered and accessed as if they were fields named as integer literals beginning at `0`. Tuples are not arrays; they cannot be indexed by expressions.

```
(c1) var x: (int, int) = (0, 1);
(c2) var y: (byte, bool) = ('a', true);
(c3) var z: ((int, int), (byte, bool)) = (x, y);
(c4) var w: (int) = x.0;
(c5) var u: byte = (z.1.0);
(c6) var v: () = ();
```

Tuple types with any number of element types are possible, with two degenerate cases: (c6) a tuple type $T =$ `()` with no elements is exactly the same as the `void` type, and (c4) a tuple type $T =$ `(A)` with just one element is exactly the same as the type `A`. Similarly, tuple values with any number of element values can be created, with (c6) a tuple value $V =$ `()` with no elements equivalent to the one `void` value, and (c5) a tuple $V =$ `(e)` is equivalent to `e`.

Immutability admits straightforward covariant type rules for tuples. $T = (T_0...T_m)$ is a subtype of $S = (S_0...S_n)$ if and only if $m = n$ and all elements T_i of T are subtypes of the corresponding S_i.[2]

Like all types in Virgil, every tuple type T has the four basic operators `== != ! ?`. Equality and inequality operators operate recursively on the elements of a tuple: two tuple values are equivalent if the positionally-correspondent elements are equivalent. Casts and queries are also defined recursively: a cast of a tuple value to a tuple type succeeds if a cast of each element to the positionally-corresponding element type succeeds, and a type query of a tuple value against a tuple type is `true` if all type queries of elements against the positionally-corresponding element type are `true`.

Syntactic choices for tuples give rise to familiar looking calls. For example, a typical method invocation such as `a.m(foo, bar)` parses as an application of the expression `a.m` to the tuple expression `(foo, bar)`. The expression `a.m` itself is an object method expression, but could be any expression that evaluates to a function of the appropriate type. Nested calls like `f(g(x))` compose nicely, even if the inner call has a tuple or `void` return type. This represents semantics similar to tuples in Haskell and ML, but with syntax that resembles Java and C#.

Tuple type syntax leads to familiar syntax for function types. `(A, B) -> C` denotes a function type with two parameters and `A -> (B, C)` denotes a function that returns two values. The degenerate rules for tuple types imply intuitive equivalences, such as `() -> ()` = `void -> void` and `(A) -> (B)` = `A -> B`. This also allows the tuple type constructor `()` to be used as a grouping mechanism, either to emphasize the right-associative nature of `->` by writing `A -> (B -> C)`, or override it with `(A -> B) -> C`. For type rules, covariance of tuple types means that variance rules for function types operate exactly as one would expect when applied to functions that accept or return tuples.

2.4 Type Parameters

Classes, functions and tuples all coexist in Virgil, but an important abstraction mechanism is missing. Without abstraction over types, the nonoverlapping universe of primitive types, the separate class hierarchies of user classes, the system of tuple types, and the system of function types would be independent of each other forever. *Type parameters* provide this capability, allowing classes and methods to be parameterized over the types of values they manipulate, greatly increasing the expressive power of the language.

A type parameter T introduces a new name for a unknown type within the scope of its declaration. The unknown type is *universally quantified* in the sense that it could be instantiated to *any* type at a usage site. Within the scope of declaration, the new unknown type T is unrelated to all other types except itself. The compiler typechecks the body of the class or method without any information about T except that it supports the same four basic operators that all types support, namely `== != ! ?`. *Separate typechecking* means that the bodies of parameterized declarations are checked independently of any instantiation and type errors in the declaration do not generate type errors at the usage sites[3].

```
(d1) class List<T> {
(d2)   var head: T;
(d3)   var tail: List<T>;
(d4)   new(head, tail) { }
(d5) }
(d6) def apply<A>(list: List<A>, f: A -> void) {
(d7)   for (l = list; l != null; l = l.tail) f(l.head);
(d8) }
```

In (d1-8) we implement a cons list using a generic class. Objects of the class (d1) store a value (d2) of the generic type and a reference to the next link (d3) in the list. A generic convenience method (d6) provides a handy way of iterating over the elements of a list and applying a function to each element.

```
(d9)   def print(i: int) { ... }
(d10)  var a = List<int>.new(0, null);
(d11)  var b = List<(int, int)>.new((3, 4), null);
(d12)  apply<int>(a, print);
(d10') var c = List.new(0, null);
(d11') var d = List.new((3, 4), null);
(d12') apply(c, print);
(d13)  var e = List<bool>.?(a);
(d14)  var f = List<void>.?(a);
```

At every usage site of a parameterized class or method, *type arguments* are supplied for the type parameters, either explicitly by the programmer or inferred by the compiler. Explicit type arguments to a parameterized class or method can always be supplied with a `<...>` suffix (d10-12) immediately following the identifier, but the compiler can usually infer them (d10'-12'). Virgil uses a best-effort type inference algorithm[4] for type arguments to both classes and methods. Virgil does not perform type erasure; instead, enough information is always retained to recover the type argu-

[2] Subtyping rules for tuples could also allow a longer tuple to be a subtype of a shorter tuple, but too much static checking would be lost: basic errors such as passing more arguments to a function than it expects would go unnoticed.

[3] C++ templates are typechecked at instantiation time, leading to famously huge and inscrutable error messages where type arguments are already substituted for type parameters.

ments of any parameterized usage. That means, among other things, that polymorphic types can be distinguished at runtime (d13-14).

Any type can appear as a type argument. That means we can use our list class to create and manipulate homogeneous lists of any type, including primitives, objects, tuples, functions, and even `void`. Allowing unrestricted type arguments has subtle but important benefits. First, since there are no exceptions or special cases to remember, the language is actually simpler and more intuitive; any type can be a type argument, no exceptions. Secondly, reuse of data structures and functions is greatly enhanced by *composability*; we can easily create lists of functions, or lists of tuples of functions, or functions of arrays of lists of functions. Third, it promotes a programming style based on representation independence where no information about the representation of a type is necessary for the class or function to perform its role.

```
(e1) def time<A, B>(func: A -> B, a: A) -> (B, int) {
(e2)   var start = clock.ticks();
(e3)   return (func(a), clock.ticks() - start);
(e4) }
(e5) print(time(sqrt, 37).1);
```

In (e1-5) we make use of three language features to implement a method that times the execution of a function applied to some given arguments. First, our utility accepts a function as the routine to be timed. Second, it has type parameters that abstract the parameter and return type of that function, allowing it to be used with *any* function and arguments, including tuples or even `void`. Third, it uses a tuple to return both the time elapsed and function's result, even if the function returned `void` or another tuple.

2.5 Type Constructor Summary

Virgil's type system employs five kinds of type constructors. Four language-provided type constructors represent primitive types, arrays, tuples, and functions. The fifth kind of type constructor represents the types of class objects; a new class type constructor is created for each user-defined class. The table below summarizes the type constructors, their type parameters, and their syntax. In this table, the symbol $\ominus$ means *contravariant*, and $\oplus$ means *covariant*.

<table>
<tr><th>Typecon</th><th>Type Parameters</th><th>Syntax</th></tr>
<tr><td>Primitive</td><td></td><td>void|int|byte|bool</td></tr>
<tr><td>Array</td><td>T</td><td>Array<T></td></tr>
<tr><td>Tuple</td><td>$\oplus T_0 \cdots \oplus T_n$</td><td>([$T$(,$T$)*])</td></tr>
<tr><td>Function</td><td>$\ominus T_p \oplus T_r$</td><td>T -> T</td></tr>
<tr><td>class X</td><td>$T_0 \cdots T_n$</td><td>X[<T(,T)*>]</td></tr>
</table>

3. Patterns

Language designers face an unending series of tradeoffs when choosing which features to add, tradeoffs which become more complex and difficult as the language grows. Abstract data types, interfaces, ad hoc polymorphism, and variant types are useful, but how should they be prioritized relative to other features? Our experience with the design of Virgil suggests that these features can at least be postponed. Instead we found that the four principal language features were often powerful enough to *emulate* these other features with multi-paradigm design patterns made possible by the close collaboration of several features at once.

3.1 Interface Adapters

While other OO languages offer complex patterns of inheritance such as interfaces and traits, Virgil offers only single inheritance between classes. More complex patterns of inheritance and interface specification can be emulated with first class functions.

The most straightforward technique for emulating interfaces in Virgil is to define a class whose fields store first-class functions representing the methods of the interface, each with a name and a type. This class is essentially a dictionary of named interface methods. What would be somewhat awkward and verbose to define in other languages is actually quite easy in Virgil thanks to a compact syntax for declaring immutable public fields that are initialized in the constructor. In (f1-5) we see an example where the `DatastoreInterface` defines a dictionary with `create`, `load`, and `store` operations, each of which is a field which stores a function.

```
(f1) class DatastoreInterface(
(f2)   create: () -> Record,
(f3)   load: Key -> Record,
(f4)   store: Record -> ()) {
(f5) }
```

Virgil's ability to bridge the object and functional paradigms with class and object methods makes it easy for another unrelated class to simply construct an instance of the interface using its own methods. In (g6-7), the `DatastoreImpl` class *adapts* itself to the `DatastoreInterface` by instantiating an instance of the class, passing *object methods* bound to itself (i.e. the `this` object); invocations of those functions through the interface will receive the bound `this` as the receiver object.

```
(g1) class DatastoreImpl {
(g2)   def create() -> Record { ... }
(g3)   def load(k: Key) -> Record { ... }
(g4)   def store(r: Record) { ... }
(g5)   def adapt() -> DatastoreInterface {
(g6)     return DatastoreInterface.new(
(g7)       create, load, store);
(g8)   }
(g9) }
```

Tradeoffs. One advantage to this pattern is that an adapter object can be constructed from any set of functions, regardless of their names. A class can implement multiple interfaces, and the names of the methods it uses to implement the interface are immaterial, as long as the methods have the correct signature, which avoids name clashes. In fact, there is no requirement that an interface be constructed from class methods at all. An interface adapter object could as well be constructed from top-level functions, built-in operators, or any other functions at hand. Notice that in (g2-4), the methods could as well have had any names, since they are simply used as functions when constructing the interface adapter object (g6-7). Unfortunately, because Virgil has no implicit type conversions, object types do not subsume to the interface types they implement. Thus the primary disadvantage of this pattern is that to use an object as an instance of the interface always requires an extra step, usually the construction of another object. Another drawback is that the programmer must manually specify the mapping between existing functions to the interface by supplying them to the constructor of the interface object, as done in the `adapt` method in (g5).

3.2 Emulating Abstract Data Types

Abstract data types (ADTs) are useful when modeling a type that has unknown representation but has a set of associated operations with names and signatures. One way to model an ADT in Virgil is to parameterize an interface (h1-7). In this example we model a number that has an unknown representation but a known set of associated operations and some named values. The availability of the basic operators like `int.+` as first class functions makes it easy to adapt the basic primitive type `int` to the ADT interface (h8-9).

[4] Type inference with both subtyping and type parameters is tricky business; see for example [23]. Our compiler uses a bi-directional typechecking approach, but the details are beyond the scope of this paper.

In this pattern the interface is not bound to a particular value or object instance; instead, the values are external so that they can be manipulated by the client.

```
(h1) class NumberInterface<T>(
(h2)    add: (T, T) -> T,
(h3)    sub: (T, T) -> T,
(h4)    compare: (T, T) -> bool,
(h5)    one: T,
(h6)    zero: T) {
(h7) }
(h8) var IntInterface = NumberInterface.new(
(h9)    int.+, int.-, int.==, 1, 0);
```

A class interface is not always necessary, especially if the number of operations associated with the type is very small. In (i1-8) we see one way to design a hash table using the abstract data type pattern, but without the need to supply an interface object.

```
(i1) class HashMap<K, V> {
(i2)    def hash: K -> int;          // hash function
(i3)    def equals: (K, K) -> bool; // equality function
(i4)    new(hash, equals) { }
(i5)    def get(key: K) -> V { ... }
(i6)    def set(key: K, val: V) { ... }
(i7)    def apply(f: (K, V) -> void) { ... }
(i8) }
```

`HashMap` abstracts over the key and value types using type parameters and accepts the `hash` and `equals` functions as parameters to the constructor (i4). This allows this one `HashMap` implementation to be used with *any* key or value type. This is in contrast to the typical object-oriented approach, where every key type would necessarily be a class type and implement `hash` and `equals` methods with appropriate signatures. With unrestricted type parameters, even primitives (i15) and tuples (i18) can serve as the key, as long as they have the associated methods. Moreover, different `hash` and `equals` methods can be used on a per-instance basis (i13-14) with the help of *class methods* and first-class operators like == that bridge the gap between the object-oriented and functional worlds.

```
(i9)  class X {
(i10)   def deepEquals(x: X) -> bool { ... }
(i11)   def hash() -> int { ... }
(i12) }
(i13) HashMap<X, int>.new(X.hash, X.deepEquals);
(i14) HashMap<X, int>.new(X.hash, X.==);
(i15) HashMap<int, X>.new(int.!, int.==);
(i16) var h2: (int, int) -> int;
(i17) var e2: ((int, int), (int, int)) -> bool;
(i18) HashMap<(int, int), X>.new(h2, e2);
```

Tradeoffs. The primary disadvantage to using type parameters and functions to model abstract data types, rather than a module system, is that type parameters require the client code to be parameterized over the abstract data type. There must be a scope where the client code has declared a type parameter, whereas with a module system the type can be made available in the namespace of the client code. In the `HashMap` example, the client code instantiates the `HashMap` code with the types of the keys and values, but in another example, such as the `NumberInterface`, the code that provides the abstract data type must instantiate not only the number interface, but the code manipulating the numbers.

3.3 Emulating Ad-hoc Polymorphism

Virgil provides no direct support for ad-hoc polymorphism such as method overloading. While other languages make use of arguments' types at call sites to perform overload resolution, Virgil allows methods to be used in a first-class way where enough context may not be available. For example, suppose a method `m` has several overloaded variants but is used simply as `o.m`, lacking any arguments for overload resolution. The inherent ambiguity would require a manual resolution mechanism. Virgil chooses to disallow overloading altogether, requiring every method in the same class to have a unique name. It views overloaded methods as parameterized methods, with the type parameters being instantiated with the various overloadings at call sites. This approach admits an emulation of method overloading and still allows methods to be used in a first-class way without ambiguity.

Consider a use case like `print`. Remembering to call `printInt` versus `printBool` versus `printString` can become cumbersome. A somewhat cleaner solution is to use a design pattern that admits a small number of overloads, making use of type parameters and casts:

```
(j1) def print1<T>(fmt: string, a: T) {
(j2)    if (int.?(a)) printInt(fmt, int.!(a));
(j3)    if (bool.?(a)) printBool(fmt, bool.!(a));
(j4)    if (string.?(a)) printString(fmt, string.!(a));
(j5)    if (byte.?(a)) printByte(fmt, byte.!(a));
(j6) }
(j7) print1("Result: %1\n", 0);
(j8) print1("Boolean: %1\n", false);
(j9) print1("Hello %1!", name);
```

A parameterized method (j1) is the starting point of this pattern. The parameterized method dispatches to the appropriate `print*` method through a chain of dynamic type queries and type casts. The user of the library calls the parameterized method (j7-9), with the compiler inferring the type arguments. The chain of dynamic casts in (j2-5) will be optimized by the compiler. First, the compiler will specialize the parameterized method for each unique type argument, then optimize each version independently. The type queries and casts in each version can be decided statically, the chain of `if` statements will be folded away, and only a call to the corresponding version remains, which the compiler may then inline, resulting in code just as efficient as if the caller had called the appropriate `print*` method directly.

Tradeoffs. One clear disadvantage of this approach is that some static checking is lost since the parameterized method must necessarily accept any type for its type argument. Unless all possible types are covered by some case, the programmer will have to resort to producing a runtime error or defining some default behavior [5]. The benefit, aside from not needing to remember to call the appropriate unique method, is that there is no longer any ambiguity in first-class functions, and the parameterized method can be used in a first-class way like other methods, supplying explicit type arguments if necessary. Multi-argument overloads are possible with tuples, but type matching can become painfully ugly, so in practice one tends to write `print1`, `print2`, etc. For complex cases this is admittedly an unsatisfyingly clunky solution, but it works and is very efficient. It does not require boxing arguments in any situation, it optimizes away dynamic type tests, and does not require a *varargs* mechanism.

3.4 A Polymorphic Matcher

Subtyping provides a language with a form of information hiding where the exact type of an expression is intentionally forgotten when it is used in a context requiring only the supertype. This ability of subtyping can also hide information about type parameters. For example, declaring a base class `Any` and a subclass `Box<T> extends Any` allows any value to be boxed and used

[5] Our implementation of `print` accepts the standard primitive types and also functions of type `StringBuffer -> void`; we equip those classes that need to be printed with methods that render the object into a `StringBuffer`; we can then simply pass `o.render` to the `print` method.

wherever the type Any is accepted. Instead of language-provided classes for each primitive type such as java.lang.Integer, java.lang.Double, etc, a single pair of user-defined classes suffices.

```
(k1)  class Matcher {
(k2)    var matches: List<Any>;
(k3)    def add<T>(f: T -> void) {
(k4)      matches = List.new(Box.new(f), matches);
(k5)    }
(k6)    def dispatch<T>(v: T) {
(k7)      for (l = matches; l != null; l = l.tail) {
(k8)        var f = l.head;
(k9)        if (Box<T -> void>.?(f))
(k10)         return Box<T -> void>.!(f).unbox()(v);
(k11)     }
(k12)   }
(k13) }
```

Hiding information about type parameters using class subtyping allows us to improve upon our previous emulation of method overloading. In (k2-5), the matcher wraps each function in a Box and intentionally forgets its type, treating it as Any, in order to put it in a list. To dispatch on a polymorphic value, since Virgil does not erase type parameters but can in fact distinguish a Box<int -> void> from a Box<bool -> void>, the matcher can search the list for a Box that contains a function of the right type that can handle the polymorphic value. In (m1-8) we see examples of how we could use the Matcher to accomplish polymorphic dispatching for printing without having to write a series of type queries and casts. The Matcher class need only be written once, and it can be reused in whatever context is necessary. [6]

```
(m1) var m = Matcher.new();
(m2) m.add(printInt);
(m3) m.add(printBool);
(m4) m.add(printString);
(m5) ...
(m6) m.dispatch("Result: %1", 1);        // printInt
(m7) m.dispatch("Boolean: %1", true);  // printBool
(m8) m.dispatch("Hello %1", name);      // printString
```

Tradeoffs. The polymorphic matcher pattern improves upon the manual type dispatching approach but still lacks static checking. Since the matcher's dispatch method can be instantiated with any type argument, it may fail at runtime if an appropriate method is not found in the list.

3.5 Emulating Variant types

The ability of subtyping to hide information can emulate a variety of ad-hoc polymorphism patterns, including the ability to have a number of variant types, each with the same operation.

```
(n1)  class Instr {
(n2)    def emit(buf: Buffer);
(n3)  }
(n4)  class InstrOf<T> extends Instr {
(n5)    var emitFunc: (Buffer, T) -> void;
(n6)    var val: T;
(n7)    new(emitFunc, val) { }
(n8)    def emit(buf: Buffer) {
(n9)      emitFunc(buf, val);
(n10)   }
(n11) }
(n12) var i = InstrOf.new(asm.add, (rax, rbx));
(n13) var j = InstrOf.new(asm.addi, (rax, -11));
(n14) var k = InstrOf.new(asm.neg, rax);
```

[6] Notice also that (m2-8) uses functions with multiple parameters, which works seamlessly due to the clean integration between functions and tuples.

The example above shows one approach to representing machine instructions in the backend of a compiler. Instead of manually defining classes that represent instructions with one operand, two operands, an operand and immediate, etc, the four main features of Virgil can be used to model all variants of instructions with just two class definitions. We first declare a base class for instructions (n1) with an abstract method (n2) that emits the instruction to some buffer. Then a parameterized subclass (n4) can be instantiated to each of the different variants, with the function that assembles the instruction and the operands themselves stored as fields (n5-6). The implementation of emit then simply calls the supplied function with the operands and the buffer (n9). Without writing any more classes, we can reuse methods from the assembler itself (n12-14) with various kinds of operands to create instruction variants. The Instr class in this case is like a super-closure: it not only closes over the unknown (variant) parts of the instruction, but can have more than one operation, such as iterating over the register operands of the instruction for register allocation.

If pattern matching is required on instructions, we can use a cascade of dynamic type casts and type queries (n15-20), or use a polymorphic matcher from (k1-13).

```
(n15) if (InstrOf<Reg>.?(i))
(n16)   printReg(InstrOf<Reg>.!(i));
(n17) if (InstrOf<(Reg, Reg)>.?(i))
(n18)   printRegReg(InstrOf<(Reg, Reg)>.!(i));
(n19) if (InstrOf<(Reg, int)>.?(i))
(n20)   printRegInt(InstrOf<Reg>.!(i));
```

This pattern requires all four features to work. Without classes and inheritance, we couldn't hide the actual representation type by having an unparameterized superclass, but would instead need some other form of existential quantification, a universal supertype, support for algebraic data types, etc. Without first-class functions, some other form of polymorphism would be required to supply the logic for assembling each instruction, e.g. subclassing the Instr class with a lot of redundant classes or using a switch or enumeration, all of which mean writing calls to assembler methods instead of just passing them around. Without tuples, any variant that consisted of more than one parameter would require an aggregate datastructure of some kind, such as another class. And finally, without type parameters, some universal representation would have been required to store all the different variants in some polymorphic location.

Tradeoffs. Emulating variants suffers from two main problems. The first problem is similar to emulating ad hoc polymorphism with dynamic casts: a loss of static checking in pattern matches (n15-20), where the programmer can too easily miss a case. The second problem is both an advantage and a disadvantage. This pattern allows an unbounded number of new variants to be created simply by instantiating the InstrOf class with new values and methods, which is an advantage for extensibility but is a disadvantage if the programmer wants to intentionally bound the set of variants that can be created.

3.6 Type Variance

Languages that contain both subtyping and type parameters face type variance problems. Java, C#, and Scala have various solutions that range from use-site annotations to declaration site annotations, wildcards, raw types, unsafe casts, or all of the above. Virgil only offers variance for tuples and function types; but surprisingly these two features reduce the need for other kinds of variance.

Returning to the cons list example (p1-p10), assume for the moment that the fields of this class are immutable, written only once in the constructor. Suppose we have types Animal and Bat with Bat extends Animal. We might intuitively consider List to be covariant, i.e. List<Bat> <: List<Animal>. In the example below (o2), we have a function `f` that performs an operation on every element in a list, and (o5) we have `b` of type `List<Bat>`. Virgil classes are invariant in their type parameters, so applying `f` to `b` is not well-typed (o6).

```
(o1) def g(a: Animal) { ... }
(o2) def f(list: List<Animal>) {
(o3)    for (l = list; l != null; l = l.tail) g(l.head);
(o4) }
(o5) var b: List<Bat>;
(o6) f(b);          // ERROR
(o7) apply(b, g); // OK
```

However, we can invert the control flow; instead we pass a function `g` of type `Animal -> void` which performs the operation for just one `Animal` to our utility function `apply` from (d6). Due to contra-variant function parameter types, `Animal -> void` <: `Bat -> void`, and (o7) is well-typed.

As another example, consider again the `HashMap` class (h1-h8). If Virgil supported declaration-site variance annotations, the designer of this class might want to add a contra-variance annotation to `K` so that `HashMap<A, V>` <: `HashMap<B, V>` for `B` <: `A`. In another situation, a client might accept a `HashMap<K, V>` but only use the `get` method. In this case, it would be tempting to add variance at the use site, since the map could be considered co-variant in `V` and contra-variant in `K` at that use site. But notice that this is exactly the variance of the `get` method itself, and since function types *do* have variance, it would be better if the client simply accepted a function of type `K -> V`, and users could pass the `get` method of their `HashMap`, or some other function of their choosing. The client is thus more general, no longer dependent at all on the type of the object (if any) bound to the closure.

The prolific reuse of methods from objects radically simplifies libraries. For example, with help from tuples, functions, and variance, the call `a.apply(b.add)` copies the contents of `HashMap a` into `HashMap b`, without even writing a loop or burdening the library with another convenience method such as `addAll`. A more terse functional style transfers well to other kinds of datastructures, including arrays, sequences, maps, matrices, etc. All manner of familiar operators from functional libraries such as `map`, `fold`, `zip`, and `unzip` are easily defined, and surprisingly they don't require variance annotations.

Tradeoffs. The lack of variance for class types and the lack of either declaration or use site constraints on type parameters forces a different kind of programming style. This can make it hard to port code from existing languages that makes use of these features, necessitating both local refactorings and some redesign to rely more on a functional style. C# 2.0 debuted without variance annotations for generics, but they were later added. We believe this design choice was made because first-class functions were only timidly employed in their first inception as invariant, named delegate types. It may be that evolution of existing programs to a more functional style was deemed too radical at the time.

4. Implementation Issues

Language goals such as supporting system and low-level programming bring important efficiency considerations, posing challenges for implementing advanced features. This has driven Virgil's design throughout its earliest embodiment for microcontroller programming until today. The pressure to implement all of Virgil's constructs without undue reliance on implicitly allocating memory on the heap has been a substantial motivator for keeping its feature set conservative. Key in meeting these efficiency considerations is proper implementation of tuples and type parameters. This section describes the unique problems posed by tuples in Virgil and presents a solution based on a flattening strategy that guarantees that no implicit boxing or unboxing operations need to be inserted. In fact, Virgil's native implementation *never* allocates memory on the heap except when done explicitly by the programmer but still retains all the language flexibility described in previous sections.

4.1 Tuple Ambiguity

The uniform treatment of functions that accept multiple parameters as functions that accept a single tuple parameter is unfortunately not so uniform in implementation. The interaction between tuples and the other features of Virgil can give rise to implementation ambiguity in several different ways. In (p1-5) `f` and `g` are both of type `(int, int) -> void`, and the variable `x` could refer to either at runtime (p3). Two potential problems arise. The caller could legally pass either two integers (p4) or a tuple of two integers (p5). What calling convention would the compiler use at these call sites? What about within the body of `f` which expects two integers and `g` which expects a tuple? In this case, using tuple types to model multiple arguments creates a potential ambiguity because functions can be first-class.

```
(p1) def f(a: int, b: int) { ... }
(p2) def g(a: (int, int)) { ... }
(p3) var x = z ? f : g, t = (0, 1);
(p4) x(0, 1);    // ambiguous invocation
(p5) x(t);       // ambiguous invocation
(p6) def r<A>(a: A) { ... }
(p7) var y = z ? r<(int, int)> : f;
(p8) y(0, 2);    // ambiguous invocation
```

A parameterized function like the one defined in (p6) can also give rise to ambiguity. The method `r<(int, int)>` (p7) could be used anywhere a function of type `(int, int) -> void` is expected (p8). Ambiguity can also arise with simple method overriding. A class may declare a method (p11) with individual parameters that is overridden in a subclass (p14) with an implementation that has a single tuple parameter, leading to ambiguity at virtual method invocation sites (p17).

```
(p10) class A {
(p11)    def m(a: int, b: int) { ... }
(p12) }
(p13) class B extends A {
(p14)    def m(a: (int, int)) { ... }
(p15) }
(p16) var a = z ? A.new() : B.new();
(p17) a.m(1, 2); // ambiguous invocation
```

One solution is to place dynamic checks at invocation sites to determine whether the function to be invoked requires a tuple (i.e. boxed) or multiple scalars (i.e. unboxed) representation for its arguments. The Virgil interpreter uses this approach, but the checks are expensive. A small improvement can be made when compiling to a target machine by eliminating the dynamic checks at call sites where receiver methods can be statically determined. This is still suboptimal since too many such sites would give poor performance and might require allocating memory on the heap for tuples. Instead our compiler *normalizes* the program, rewriting all uses of tuples to eliminate such overhead. This ensures that all method calls pass scalar arguments regardless of whether the parameters were originally tuples or scalars, arrays and fields store dense scalar values, and operations on tuples never allocate on the heap, on both the JVM target and the native x86 targets.

4.2 Normalization

Tuples are ideal values: they are immutable, have no identity, and are not extensible. A program cannot discern implementation details such as whether a tuple is represented by a record or by individual scalars. *Normalization* is the process by which the Virgil compiler converts all uses of tuples into uses of scalars, regardless of where they occur, including parameters, return values, local variables, array elements, fields, and elements inside other tuples. Variants of normalization (also known as scalar replacement of aggregates or flattening) have been employed in numerous functional language implementations, e.g. [3] and [36]. Reducing tuples to individual scalar values simplifies the program to a *normal form* where tuples no longer appear and exposes the individual values to classical compiler optimizations. It also eliminates the ambiguities demonstrated in the previous section; all normalized functions accept zero or more scalars and return zero or more scalars.

The compiler performs normalization on an internal representation of the program, but we can illustrate the basics of the algorithm with source-to-source translations. First, we see how the compiler treats local variables (q1) and parameters (q2) that are tuples, replacing them with multiple local variables (q1') or parameters (q2'). A use of a variable which was formerly a tuple (q3) is expanded to the normalized (q3') variables. An access of a tuple element (q4) is replaced with a reference to the corresponding normalized variable (q4'). Parameters (q6) and variables (q7) of type `void` are replaced with nothing (q6'-7') [7].

```
(q1) var b = ("hello", 15);
(q2) def m(a: (string, int)) { ... }
(q3) m(b);
(q4) m("goodbye", b.1);
(q5) m("cheers", (11, 22).0);
(q6) def f(v: void) { ... }
(q7) var t: void;
(q8) f(t);

  =>

(q1') var b0 = "hello", b1 = 15;
(q2') def m(a0: string, a1: int) { ... }
(q3') m(b0, b1);
(q4') m("goodbye", b1);
(q5') m("cheers", 11);
(q6') def f() { ... }
(q7')
(q8') f();
```

Normalization can potentially rewrite every expression in the program, whether it be a field access, array element access, array creation, method call, comparison, etc. Care is taken to avoid duplicating or reordering side-effects in expressions; this is facilitated by the compiler's internal SSA representation of the code. Fields are normalized by replacing with them with zero or more normalized fields; field accesses are normalized into multiple reads or writes as appropriate. Array element accesses require similar normalization. Depending on the compilation target, an array of tuples may be normalized to an array whose elements store tuple elements next to each other in memory, or to be multiple arrays, each of which stores one element of the tuple. Returns of a tuple become a return of multiple values, utilizing multiple return registers on native targets.

There are several corner cases that are not immediately obvious. Accesses to fields of type `void` are simply removed and replaced with null checks; this ensures that a null dereference always throws an exception, regardless of the field's type. Similarly, arrays of `void` require no storage for their elements, but accesses are dutifully bounds checked. The JVM does not support arrays of `void` so such arrays are represented with a `java.lang.Integer` object which distinguishes between `null` and an array with a length. On native targets a two-word array object that only stores the array length is sufficient. The JVM also does not support returning multiple values from a method call. In this case the Virgil compiler inserts a tuple creation at the return site and deconstructs the tuple return value after call sites.

[7] Normally programmers do not explicitly use variables of type `void`, but they often appear when expanding polymorphic code.

Normalization is modular; normalizing a method's body does not require knowledge of the call sites, nor do call sites require knowledge of the methods which they call. However, normalization relies on knowing the types of all expressions and methods; this is only possible if type arguments have been substituted for type parameters, which is the subject of the next section.

Tradeoffs. Normalization removes all boxing related to tuples, achieving Virgil's implementation goal of avoiding implicit memory allocations. For small tuples, normalization has much better performance than boxing, but large tuples might actually perform better if allocated on the heap, depending on how the program uses them; in a program that uses large tuples, reading and writing pointers to objects on the heap may be cheaper than reading and writing the many tuple elements individually.

4.3 Monomorphization

In Virgil, runtime information about type arguments is needed in some operations, such as allocating or accessing an array of polymorphic type, performing a dynamic type cast or type query involving polymorphic types, or accessing a field of a polymorphic type. We saw dynamic type casts and queries were key in allowing several patterns such as the polymorphic matcher. In the Virgil interpreter, type arguments are passed as invisible arguments to polymorphic function calls and stored as type information within objects, arrays and closures. Even with lazy evaluation of the type expressions that represent type arguments, this exacts a considerable runtime cost.

The Virgil compiler instead employs *monomorphization*, where a specialized version of each polymorphic class or method is generated for each distinct assignment of type arguments to type parameters. Thus an object of type `List<(int, int)>` has a different representation than `List<byte>`, and similarly the method `id<int>` has a distinct representation from `id<byte>`. Once the representation of all classes and methods is obtained through specialization, no type parameters appear in the program. The resulting code is therefore monomorphic and can use the most efficient, dense representations. Monomorphization affords the opportunity for whole-program normalization which eliminates all tuples from the program, and therefore guarantees that programs can be compiled to a form where implicit memory allocations on the heap are not required. This is key for some systems programming problems where some code must be able to run without interruption from the garbage collector, and thus may not allocate memory [8].

Tradeoffs. The implementation of parametric polymorphism is full of tradeoffs and has been the subject of much research which we cannot fully summarize in the space alotted. The main drawback to monomorphization is that polymorphic code can be duplicated repeatedly, perhaps exponentially, even infinitely if the language allows polymorphic recursion, which Virgil disallows [9]. The result can be code explosion where polymorphic methods are duplicated repeatedly. In our experience, this has not been an issue in real programs. Other language implementations use monomorphization as well, including MLton [35] which employs whole-program monomorphization quite sucessfully for ML, and C++ does complete template expansion, which is similar to monomorphization. Some programming guidelines can reduce code explo-

[8] This has been a constant source of problems in system code written in Java like Jikes RVM and Maxine VM, especially when writing the garbage collectors themselves in Java. We wrote our GC in Virgil without encountering these problems.

sion [33]. Another drawback is that monomorphization also requires the whole program to be available, or it must fall back on a universal representation when instantiations are not known across compilation unit boundaries.

One alternative to monomorphization is to remove type parameters from the program by simply *erasing* them [22]. This is only possible if all values have a universal representation (e.g. Scala), the compiler forces a universal representation through boxing (most functional language implementations), or by disallowing some types as type arguments (e.g. Java). With erasure, some polymorphic operations can only be implemented by passing a representation of the type arguments at runtime [15]. Both Scala and Java perform type erasure, but *do not* pass a runtime representation of type parameters, meaning that some polymorphic operations, such as allocating an array of a polymorphic type or casting a polymorphic type, are simply not allowed. Simply put, type erasure cannot work for Virgil. Also note that both Scala and Java target the JVM, which does not support type parameters; dynamic type casts must be inserted to satisfy the JVM's bytecode verifier. In contrast, monomorphization requires no casts to be inserted.

To be fair, Scala recently attempted to address the problem of missing type information with *manifests*, which are indeed a representation of type parameters, but at first they were manual and not fully integrated with the rest of the language. Scala 2.10 uses type tags which can be passed as implicit parameters, subsuming the role of manifests. However, they require the programmer to request a type tag be passed to a class or method in order to perform some polymorphic operations. Scala also recently experimented with annotations to allow programmers to manually instruct the compiler to perform specialization [7].

In Java, a programmer can explicitly pass instances of `java.lang.Class` along with type parameters to act as the missing type information, but only one level deep: class objects do not contain information about type arguments to parameterized classes.

C# coined the term *reified generics*; the semantics are closest to Virgil's type parameters. C# mainly targets the CLR which provides support for type parameters in bytecode, and the virtual machine performs specialization on demand [18], sharing identical machine code for some specializations. When one can assume a VM with a dynamic compiler, late specialization has strong advantages: it avoids the need for the whole program at compile time and reduces code explosion. However it is not an option for compiling Virgil statically. Other differences are that C# has no tuples, does not allow `void` as a type argument, and does not allow casts between, e.g., a type parameter and a concrete type.

Most functional language implementations use a mix of specialization and boxing, where the overhead of boxing is removed wherever the compiler has full knowledge of the representation of values [35], even for tuples [36]. There are more complicated schemes for implementing parametric polymorphism, such as intensional type analysis [15] which relies on representation passing. In some sense, this is the implementation adopted by the Virgil interpreter as discussed before.

5. Experience

The balance of features in Virgil has proven to be quite practical in writing small to medium-scale programs. Our experience in writing over 100,000 lines of Virgil code has motivated continual refinement of the language. A self-hosted, fully-bootstrapped compiler written in Virgil is the primary implementation. It features compilation to both the JVM and native x86 targets, includes a standard suite of intraprocedural compiler optimizations, array bounds check elimination, sophisticated instruction selection, a linear-scan register allocator, whole-program optimizations such as monomorphization, as well as sophisticated dead code and dead data elimination [31]. On native targets Virgil provides a precise semi-space garbage collector (also written in Virgil), a runtime system (written in Virgil) and direct access to kernel system calls. The compiler also offers ancillary tools such as a full interpreter, a profiler, and a code coverage tool. Despite its small size (just 25,000 lines of code), the Virgil compiler generates decent quality machine code and compiles very fast. Virgil III is open source and freely available at `http://code.google.com/p/virgil`.

We also wrote a small number of applications, ported several benchmarks, and created a vast battery of test programs. We found, like many Scala programmers, that the free intermixing of functions with objects brings a new kind of expressiveness beyond pure object-oriented and pure functional styles. Objects work well for encapsulating state and related methods, while functions excel at small-scale reuse, such as that found in operations like `map`, `fold`, and `sort`. Our experience has been that unrestricted type arguments and cheap access to tuples have markedly increased expressiveness beyond simply throwing objects and functions together into the same language. For example, the ability to quickly define a list of tuples and then sort them by, say, the first element, has been very convenient for rapid prototyping.

Every pattern described in this paper has made it into practical use. The emulation of abstract data types has direct applicability in the design of reusable data structures like maps; the emulation of ad hoc polymorphism has been useful in printing and logging; and the emulation of variant types is used the Virgil compiler backend to represent and manipulate machine instructions without requiring a complete duplication of the x86 assembler's interface, nor the definition of many small variant classes.

6. Conclusion

Virgil brings a new kind of harmony between classes, functions, tuples, and type parameters in a statically-typed setting. The whole is more than the sum of its parts; these features complement each other in subtle and powerful ways that reduce the need for more language features, including complex patterns of inheritance, type variance annotations, and a universal super type. Perhaps most interestingly, multi-paradigm design patterns can be built that allow emulation of features not directly supported in the language, including abstract data types, ad-hoc polymorphism, and variant types. Each emulation presents some tradeoffs, and balancing the inclusion of new features versus those tradeoffs is ongoing challenge in the art of language design; a challenge which we by no means claim to have conquered. Moreover, we do not argue that any of the emulated features should necessarily be excluded from this or any other language; rather that the use of patterns can give designers more time to prioritize new language features and ensure they compose well.

6.1 Future Work

Virgil lacks many advanced features and there are still rough edges. For example, we find our own emulation of `printf`-like cases still somewhat cumbersome; a well-developed pattern matching system coupled with a kind of *varargs* mechanism could greatly increase expressive power without upsetting the existing design. Our experience programming in the language suggests that enumerated types are of high priority, and certainly other languages offer excellent examples of potential design.

Virgil lacks a module system, which can offer representation independence and separate compilation units for modularity on a larger scale. Higher-rank polymorphism (i.e. polymorphism over type constructors) allows more forms of generic programming [24]. We believe both extensions to be important in the future, and like

[9] Virgil disallows polymorphic recursion but it is not currently enforced.

the other features mentioned, Virgil's core design has done nothing to preclude them.

We mentioned issues with full monomorphization in section 4.3. We continually track the amount of code expansion due to specialization for the compiler and applications we have already built. We consider it an important goal to avoid code explosion, and a hybrid approach to monomorphization is the subject of current research. See for example [29].

Acknowledgments

Thanks to Alex Warth, Jan-Willem Maessen, Marek Gilbert, and Jens Palsberg for comments on early drafts of this paper.

References

[1] E. Allen and R. Cartwright. The case for run-time types in generic Java. *In Proceedings of the 1st Conference on the Principles and Practice of Programming in Java (PPPJ '02).* Dublin, Ireland. Jun 2002.

[2] C. Baker-Finch, K. Glynn, and S. P. Jones. Constructed product result analysis for Haskell. *In Journal of Functional Programming (JFP)*, Volume 14, Issue 2. Mar 2004.

[3] L. Bergstrom and J. Reppy. Arity raising in Manticore. *In Proceedings of the 21st International Conference on Implementation and Application of Functional Languages (IFL '09).* South Orange, NJ. Sep 2009.

[4] N. H. Cohen. Type-extension type tests can be performed in constant time. *In ACM Transactions on Programming Languages and Systems (TOPLAS)*, Volume 13, Issue 4. Oct 1991.

[5] J. Dean, D. Grove and C. Chambers. Optimization of object-oriented programs using static class hierarchy analysis. In *Proceedings of the 9th European Conference on Object-Oriented Programming (ECOOP '95).* Aarhus, Denmark. Aug 1995.

[6] A. Diwan, K. McKinley, and J. E. B. Moss. Using types to analyze and optimize object-oriented programs. *In ACM Transactions on Programming Languages and Systems (TOPLAS)*, Volume 23, Issue 1. Jan 2001.

[7] I. Dragos and M. Odersky. Compiling generics through user-directed type specialization. *In Proceedings of the 4th workshop on the Implementation, Compilation, Optimization of Object-Oriented Languages and Programming Systems (ICOOOLPS '09).* Genova, Italy. Jul 2009.

[8] B. Emir, A. Kennedy, C. Russo, and D. Yu. Variance and generalized constraints for C# generics. *In Proceedings of the 20th Annual European Conference on Object-Oriented Programming (ECOOP '06).* Nantes, France. Jul 2006.

[9] D. Frampton, S. M. Blackburn, P. Cheng , R. J. Garner, D. Grove, J. E. B. Moss, and S. I. Salishev. Demystifying magic: high-level low-level programming. *In Proceedings of the International Conference on Virtual Execution Environments (VEE '09).* Washington, DC. Mar 2009.

[10] K. Faxén. Representation analysis for coercion placement. *In Proceedings of the 9th International Symposium on Static Analysis (SAS '02).* Madrid, Spain. Sep 2002.

[11] E. Gamma, R. Helm, R. Johnson and J. Vlissides. Design patterns: elements of reusable object-oriented software. Addison-Wesley Longman Publishing Co., Inc. Boston, MA. 1995.

[12] A. Goldberg and D. Robson. Smalltalk-80: the language and its implementation. Addison-Wesley Longman Publishing Co., Inc. Boston, MA. 1983.

[13] Guava: Google Core Libraries for Java 1.5+ http://code.google.com/p/guava-libraries/

[14] J. J. Hallett, V. Luchangco, S. Ryu and G. L. Steele Jr. Integrating coercion with subtyping and multiple dispatch. *In Science of Computer Programming*, Volume 75, Issue 9. 2010.

[15] R. Harper and G. Morrisett. Compiling polymorphism with intensional type analysis. *In Proceedings of the 22nd Symposium on Principles of Programming Languages (POPL '95).* San Francisco, CA. Jan 1995.

[16] A. Igarashi and M. Viroli. On variance-based subtyping for parametric types. *In Proceedings of the 16th Annual European Conference on Object-Oriented Programming (ECOOP '02).* Malaga, Spain. June 2002.

[17] JSR 335: Lambda expressions for the Java(TM) programming language. http://jcp.org/en/jsr/detail?id=335

[18] A. J. Kennedy and D. Syme. Design and implementation of generics for the .NET Common Language Runtime. *In Proceedings of the 23rd Conference on Programming Language Design and Implementation (PLDI 2001).* Snowbird, UT. Jun 2001.

[19] A. J. Kennedy and D. Syme. Combining generics, pre-compilation and sharing between software-based processes. Jan 2004.

[20] The Maxine Virtual Machine. http://labs.oracle.com/projects/maxine/

[21] J. E. Moreira, S. P. Midkiff, M. Gupta, P. V. Artigas, M. Snir, and R. D. Lawrence. Java programming for high performance numerical computing. *In IBM Systems Journal*, Volume 39, Issue 1. Jan 2000.

[22] M. Odersky and P. Wadler. Pizza into Java: translating theory into practice. *In Proceedings of the 24th Symposium on Principles of Programming Languages (POPL '97).* Paris, France. Jan 1997.

[23] M. Odersky, M. Sulzmann and M. Wehr. Type inference with constrained types. *In Proceedigns of the 4th International Workshop on Foundations of Object-Oriented Programming (FOOL '97).* Paris, France. Jan 1997.

[24] B. Oliveira and J. Gibbons. Scala for generic programmers. *In Proceedings of the Workshop on Generic Programming (WGP '08).* Victoria, BC. Sep 2008.

[25] J. Palsberg. Type-based analysis and applications. *In Proceedings of the Workshop on Program Analysis for Software Tools (PASTE 01).* Snowbird, UT. Jun 2001.

[26] B. C. Pierce. Advanced topics in types and programming languages. MIT Press. 2004.

[27] B. C. Pierce and D. N. Turner. Local type inference. *In Proceedings of the 25th Symposium on Principles of Programming Languages (POPL '98).* San Diego, California. Jan 1998.

[28] C. van Reeuwijk and H. J. Sips. Adding tuples to Java: a study in lightweight data structures. *In Proceedings of the Joint Java Grande/ISCOPE Conference (JGI '02).* Seattle, Washington. Nov 2002.

[29] O. Sallenave and R. Ducournau. Lightweight generics in embedded systems through static analysis. *In Languages, Compilers, Tools and Theory for Embedded Systems (LCTES '12).* Beijing, China. Jun 2012.

[30] D. Smith and R. Cartwright. Java type inference is broken: can we fix it? *In Proceedings of the 23rd Annual Conference on Object-Oriented Programming Systems, Languages, and Applications (OOPSLA '08).* Nashville, Tennesee. Oct 2008.

[31] B. L. Titzer. Virgil: Objects on the head of a pin. *In Proceedings of the 21st Annual Conference on Object-Oriented Programming Systems, Languages, and Applications (OOPSLA '06).* Portland, Oregon. Oct 2006.

[32] B. L. Titzer and J. Palsberg. Vertical object layout and compression for fixed heaps. *In Proceedings of the International Conference on Compilers, Architecture, and Synthesis for Embedded Systems (CASES '07).* Salzburg, Austria. Oct 2007.

[33] D. Tsafrir, R. W. Wisniewski, D. F. Bacon, and B. Stroustrup. Minimizing dependencies within generic classes for faster and smaller programs. *In Proceedings of the 24th Annual Conference on Object-Oriented Programming, Systems, Languages, and Applications (OOPSLA '09).* Orlando, FL. Oct 2009.

[34] J. Vitek and B. Bokowski. Confined types. *In Proceedings of the 14th Annual Conference on Object-Oriented Programming, Systems, Languages, and Applications (OOPSLA '99).* Denver, CO. Oct 1999.

[35] S. Weeks. Whole-program compilation in MLton. *In Proceedings of the 2006 workshop on ML.* Portland, OR. Sep 2006. Slides available: http://mlton.org/pages/References/attachments/060916-mlton.pdf

[36] L. Ziarek, S. Weeks and S. Jagannathan. Flattening tuples in an SSA intermediate representation. *In Journal of Higher-Order and Symbolic Computation*, Volume 21, Issue 3. Sept 2008.

It's Alive! Continuous Feedback in UI Programming

Sebastian Burckhardt Manuel Fähndrich
Peli de Halleux Sean McDirmid
Michal Moskal Nikolai Tillmann
Microsoft Research
{sburckha,maf,jhalleux,smcdirm,micmo,nikolait}@microsoft.com

Jun Kato
The University of Tokyo
i@junkato.jp

Abstract

Live programming allows programmers to edit the code of a running program and immediately see the effect of the code changes. This tightening of the traditional edit-compile-run cycle reduces the cognitive gap between program code and execution, improving the learning experience of beginning programmers while boosting the productivity of seasoned ones. Unfortunately, live programming is difficult to realize in practice as imperative languages lack well-defined abstraction boundaries that make live programming responsive or its feedback comprehensible.

This paper enables live programming for user interface programming by cleanly separating the rendering and non-rendering aspects of a UI program, allowing the display to be refreshed on a code change without restarting the program. A type and effect system formalizes this separation and provides an evaluation model that incorporates the code update step. By putting live programming on a more formal footing, we hope to enable critical and technical discussion of live programming systems.

Categories and Subject Descriptors D.3.3 [*Language Constructs and Features*]; D.2.2 [*Design Tools and Techniques*]: User Interfaces; D.2.6 [*Programming Environments*]

General Terms Languages, Human Factors

Keywords Live Programming, Graphical User Interface

1. Introduction

One major difficulty in writing programs is that a programmer must effectively simulate parts of the execution of the program in his mind during development [14, 19]. If we can narrow the gap between the program text and seeing how the program behaves, productivity during code editing and debugging could be improved substantially. This gap takes two forms: 1) the time gap between making an edit and seeing the effect of the change is dominated by rebuilding the program, executing the program and guiding it (possibly with manual input) to the place where the edit can be observed. Speeding up this "edit-compile-run" cycle can narrow the time gap, but the re-execution part remains critical and cannot be narrowed by improvements in development tools. 2) the perception gap is the cognitive distance between looking at the code and understanding what the code will do when it is run. Addressing this perception gap requires an environment where code can be edited continuously with uninterrupted "live" feedback, showing the consequences of those edits. This so-called *live programming* [11] enables more fluid problem solving compared to today's common "edit-compile-debug" style of programming.

Most people are familiar with live programming in the context of spreadsheets, where data and formulae can be edited and the effect of those edits be seen immediately. Besides spreadsheets, languages based on mostly declarative programming models, including many visual languages like Pure Data [20], already provide a live programming experience, but these languages are not expressive enough for more complex general purpose programs [6].

Grafting live programming features onto existing mainstream imperative programming languages such as Java or C# is daunting. Currently, such languages support fix-and-continue features that allow a restricted set of code changes to a live program and then continue execution. However, fix-and-continue alone does not provide a live programming experience. Live programming requires at a minimum some state snapshot, some re-execution of changed code, and some re-displaying of results. Exactly what data to save, what code to re-execute, and which parts of the UI to maintain is difficult to answer in a general purpose language. A natural starting point is re-execution of a trace of the entire program to the current point. However, apart from the cost of trace capturing and re-execution, traces are problematic since code changes can cause the re-execution to diverge from the previous trace. In light of this observation, it seems difficult to establish a precise technical definition of live programming to start with.

This paper tackles the question of live programming in the domain of user interface (UI) programming by proposing a formal model, where a program consists of both code and persistent data. The program is event based and viewed as continually executing. A code change is simply one possible transition of the program in our model. The benefit of formalizing such a language and execution model is that it unambiguously answers questions about what state is saved, what state is rebuilt, and what code is re-executed as a result of a code change. Our language is imperative and has an explicit imperative way of building up user-interface state in the form of nested *boxes*, akin to TeX and HTML, on a stack of pages. We separate both the UI state from ordinary state, and the render code that builds UI state from ordinary code. As a result, upon code changes, we throw away the UI state, and then rebuild the UI state for the currently displayed page using the separated render code for that page.

Beyond achieving live feedback, our model also reduces the perceptive gap between code and the UI components rendered on a page by the use of a boxed construct that builds a UI element as a side effect. Using syntactic nesting and arbitrary code such

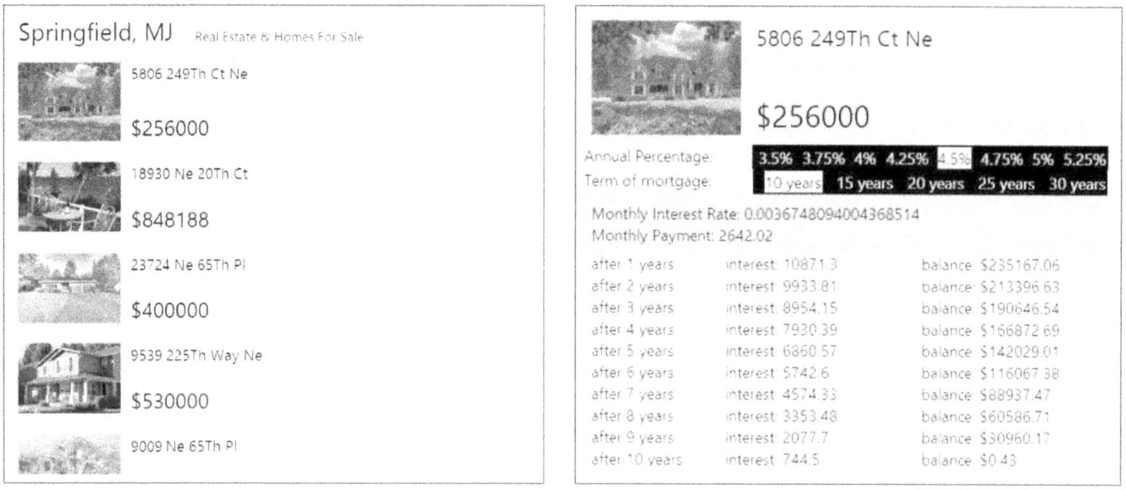

Figure 1. The two pages of the mortgage calculator example: a start page is on the left; a detail page is on the right.

as loops, conditionals, and procedure abstraction, UI construction is very expressive and not limited to a specialized declarative sub-language. We make the following contributions:

- We propose a programming model where UI state is built using procedural code, but maintained separate from the normal state of the program. UI's are organized as page stacks with operations to push a new page or pop the current page.
- We put live programming on a formal footing by providing an execution model in which one can argue what parts of the code are re-executed upon a program change.
- Although live programming has recently been demonstrated [10, 27] to much fanfare, designing and building these systems is so far a black art. We report on our experience implementing and using our programming model in TouchDevelop [1, 25], a device independent browser-based programming language and development environment.

Section 2 further motivates live programming while Section 3 introduces how our language and environment supports it. Section 4 describes and formalizes our implementation, providing insights on how to design and build future systems. Section 5 presents our experience with our implementation and a discussion of the trade-offs made in its construction. Section 6 presents related work while Section 7 concludes.

2. Motivation

We now explain the motivation for live programming with a discussion of how it improves on existing programming practice. For this discussion, we use as a running example a simple program to browse local listings of houses for sale, and calculate mortgage payments and an amortization schedule. On startup, the application issues a web request to obtain listings that are displayed on the program's start page (Figure 1, left). When the user taps an entry, the program navigates to a detail page that displays the monthly mortgage payment and an amortization schedule (Figure 1, right). The user can modify the term of the mortgage and the annual percentage rate by tapping the corresponding box.

Suppose that the programmer is not satisfied with the UI and wishes to make the following fixes and improvements: (I1) adjust various margins to improve the visual appearance; (I2) print the monthly balance in properly formatted dollars and cents; and (I3) highlight every fifth line of the amortization schedule with a different color. If the code were written in a conventional language and programming environment, a programmer implementing the three improvements (I1-I3) would have to iterate the following steps:

1. Stop the program execution.
2. Discover and navigate to the code location that needs to be fixed.
3. Edit the code to change the behavior.
4. Compile the code, and restart the program.
5. Navigate to the appropriate UI context by waiting for the list to download, and clicking on an entry.
6. Inspect the display to verify the fix.
7. If not satisfied, continue with step 1.

This cycle is time-consuming and tiring since temporal delays drain programmer concentration; e.g., consider the waiting for code compilation or the list to download, navigating to the correct UI screen, and, while debugging, remembering procedure names and the call graph to retrieve relevant code. Hancock [11] compares this way of programming to the activity of an archer: "you aim, shoot, string another arrow, carefully correct the aim, shoot again, and so on." This productivity drain is particularly harmful when dealing with design properties that require many iterations in practice, such as margins, font sizes, or colors.

Conventional programming can currently be made more fluid in a couple of ways. First, a programmer could use a read-eval-print loop (REPL) to quickly experiment with code statements, such as monthly interest rate printing, on a command line. However, using a REPL precludes debugging the UI directly, and each feature must be developed as a command-line computation. Second, many IDEs for languages such as LISP [23], Smalltalk [9], Java, and C# support a "fix-and-continue" feature where the programmer can modify their code without restarting the debugging process. Unfortunately, fix-and-continue often does not result in responsive feedback: for the common "retained" UI where a program builds and modifies a tree of widget objects to be rendered, changing the code that initially builds this widget tree is meaningless as that code has already executed and will not execute again!

If editing and debugging a program were to occur simultaneously, the programmer could make an adjustment to interest rate printing, observe immediately what this change produces, and then

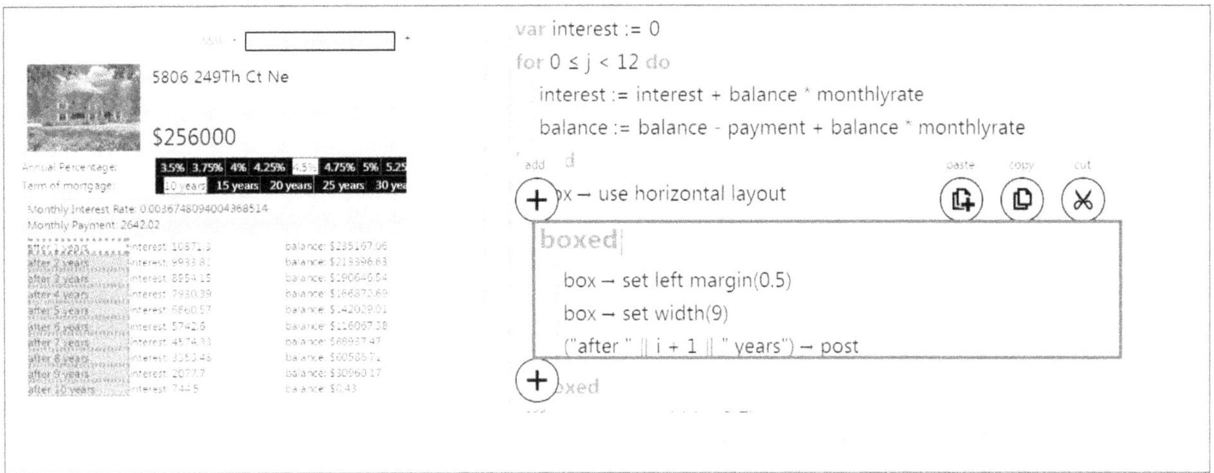

Figure 2. Code edited in the right *code view* is continuously type-checked, compiled, and executed, where its behavior is instantly visible in the left *live view*. Selecting a box in the left live view (highlighted red outline) causes the corresponding *boxed* statement to be selected in the right code view, and vice versa.

quickly make another edit to adjust the formatting based on that observation. Although parts of the program must be re-executed, the application and UI state of the program must be maintained so that the programmer can focus on editing and observing. Hancock [11] compares *live programming* to using a water hose in contrast to archery: "as we adjust which way the hose is pointed, the stream of water from us toward the target reflects back as an uninterrupted stream of information about the consequences of our aim."

Live programming has long been supported by many visual programming languages; e.g., a program in PureData [20] is expressed as a data flow graph that is continuously executing while the user is adding nodes and edges in this graph. Such visual languages realize live programming with inexpressive declarative programming models of simplified control flow constructs and heavily encapsulated state. For example, editing a PureData program simply causes re-execution of its data flow graph where any state encapsulated in a node is easily preserved.

Unfortunately, a large class of programs, including our running example, cannot easily be rewritten using existing declarative live visual languages given their inexpressive programming models. On the other hand, building an IDE that can support live programming for a more expressive language like C# is technically daunting given their support for complex control flow and imperative state. Many programming environments for conventional languages do offer a limited live experience by separating declarative style declarations from the imperative code that generates content; e.g., HTML and cascading style sheets (CSS) allow designers to change box structure and stylistic properties of web pages and inspect the result immediately while ignoring embedded Javascript code. This live experience can handle aesthetic tweaks like the I1 improvement in the list above, but unfortunately cannot support a wide variety of program alterations, such as the I2 and I3 improvements.

As observed in [17], updating a UI based on changes in the code is really not that different from updating the UI based on model changes. The important question is how to ensure that the view is up-to-date with respect to the model in the first place. The widely used model-view-controller (MVC) pattern (pioneered in [21]) requires the programmer to write code that reacts to model changes and performs the corresponding updates to the view. If the view is a complex function of the state, writing such code can be challenging (in database systems, this is known as the view-update problem), and it is questionable whether the programmer should be bothered to perform such dangerous mental acrobatics. We adopt a more straightforward solution: the programmer writes code that directly specifies how the view is constructed from the model, and just rerun this code whenever the model changes. We thus construct a fresh view instead of updating the existing one, known as the *immediate* vs. *retained* approach to GUI programming [18]. The immediate approach naturally enables live programming, because in response to a code change we can simply re-render the UI with the new code applied to the program's old state. The next section describes how we leverage this technique to enable live programming in our language.

3. Live Programming in TouchDevelop

We modify the TouchDevelop language [25] with programming model changes that enable live UI programming in an enhanced programming environment. The traditional edit-compile-run cycle is tightened and enhanced via the following three features:

Live Editing. The program keeps running while the programmer edits their code. Our editor provides a split screen that shows program execution on the left in the *live view*, and program code being edited on the right in the *code view* (Figure 2). All changes to UI-rendering code are immediately visible in the live view because the program is continuously being type-checked, compiled, and executed as the programmer edits.

UI-Code Navigation. The environment maintains navigable bi-directional connections between rendered elements in the live view and code that created these elements in the code view. If the user taps a UI element, which we call a *box*, in the live view, the editor on the right selects the boxed statement in the code view that created the UI element (Figure 2). Likewise, if the user selects a boxed statement in the code view, the corresponding box (or boxes) is selected in the live view. Note that a selected boxed statement appearing inside a loop corresponds to multiple boxes in the display, which are collectively selected in the live view (Figure 2).

Direct Manipulation. Combining both live editing and UI-code navigation, the programmer can directly change the attributes of a box in the live view, where the code view is updated automatically to reflect these changes (known as direct manipulation in [24]). For example, to insert a command to change the size of a margin, the programmer can first select the corresponding box in the live view and then choose the margin property from a button menu, which inserts (if not present) a command in the code and positions the code cursor on the margin number. The programmer can then edit this number while observing the result in the live view.

Although one may imagine an implementation that provides some or all of these features without any changes to the programming language, such as by using deterministic replay or program analysis, we focus here on the programming language design rather than heroic tool construction. Thus, our main contribution is to demonstrate how to enable a simple and transparent implementation of a live experience by *specializing the programming model.*

We take concepts from UI programming—event-based programming, model-view separation, box-based layout, and page-stack navigation—and bake them directly into the execution model, language, and type system. We first present an example-based description of this model; an in depth description of the programming model appears in Section 4.

As usual, programmers can define global procedures and variables in TouchDevelop. In addition, programmers can now define *pages* that take arguments like procedures (an idea we borrowed from the Mobl programming language [13]). The TouchDevelop code for the start page of our example program in Section 2 is shown in Figure 3. Unlike procedures, pages have two bodies rather than one:

- The *initialization body* is executed before the page is rendered for the first time. It can update global variables, but it cannot create any UI elements (boxes). The initialization body for the **startup** page is the init code at the top in Figure 3. It downloads the list of properties for sale and stores it in the variable **listings**.
- The *render body* is called to build or refresh the display with interactive UI elements known as *boxes*; the render body in Figure 3 defines two top-level vertically-stacked boxes[1]. The first top-level box is the header. It contains two boxes of text laid out horizontally. The second top-level box contains all listings, where a box for each entry is created by iterating over each listing stored in the **listings** variable. Note that, while render code can read global variables, such as **listings**, it cannot write global variables. The only effects of render code are the construction of UI elements through boxed constructs.

In model-view terminology, the *view* of the program is thus defined by the render body of a page, while the *model* is expressed as the program's global variables. The render body is re-executed in response to changes to the model or to code called during rendering. The latter guarantees that the live view is always consistent with the current code. Since render code cannot modify global variables, re-execution of a render body preserves the model (values of global variables). Initialization of the model must occur in the initialization body, which is not automatically re-executed and therefore cannot undergo live programming.

Boxes, which are TouchDevelop's UI elements, are defined in a page as nested boxed statements in much the same way that DOM elements are defined in HTML. We refer to them collectively as a page's *box tree*. Unlike widgets in conventional UI libraries, boxes are not first-class values in TouchDevelop, meaning code does not manipulate the box tree structure directly. Instead, the box tree is created as a "side effect" of the execution weaving in and out of boxed statements. This execution is free to use loops, arbitrary conditionals, and procedure calls. For example, the last boxed statement in the code of Figure 3 is embedded in a for-loop,

[1] Vertical stacking is the default.

```
page startpage ()
init
  □ listings := ▷ getlistings()
  □ term := 20
  □ apr := 0.045
render
  boxed
    boxed
      box → use horizontal layout
      boxed
        box → set left margin(0.5)
        box → set font size(2.3)
        "Springfield, MJ" → post
      boxed
        box → set font size(1.3)
        box → set top margin(1.08)
        "Real Estate & Homes For Sale" → post
    boxed
      for 0 ≤ i < □ listings → count do
        boxed
          ▷ display listentry(□ listings → at(i))
          on box → tapped do
            push ▷ detailpage(□ listings → at(i))
```

Figure 3. The source code for the start page of our mortgage calculator example, whose rendering was shown on the left of Figure 1 in Section 2. **Note on syntax:** attributes and methods are accessed via → rather than the typical `.`; global functions calls are preceded by ▷; and global variable references are preceded by a square symbol.

producing a number of boxes equal to the number of items in the **listings** variable. Additionally, it creates nested boxes by calling the **display listentry** procedure. Boxes have attributes that include layout parameters (margins, size, layout direction, font sizes), and event handlers.

Event handlers can be registered on boxes using the on statement to respond to interactions such as tapping or editing by the user. To respond to an event, event handlers can modify global variables as model state, or perform page nagivation such as popping the current page or pushing a new page. Handlers are not part of render code and are never executed as part of rendering. The last two lines in Figure 3 define a **tapped** event handler for each listing entry. When activated, it pushes the "detail" page for that entry, whose code is defined in Figure 4.

To maintain a clean separation between the model (global variables) and the view (boxes and render code) and to guarantee that the view is a well-defined function of the model, we enforce the following rules:

- The view is stateless: the display content (the box tree, including attributes and handlers) cannot be read by the code, and is discarded as soon as it becomes stale. Boxes are second class values and so cannot be referenced (aka aliased) outside rendering code. Attributes of a box can only be modified by statements inside the dynamic scope of the corresponding boxed statement.
- Render code can only read, but not modify global variables (model state).
- Non-render code, such as initialization bodies and event handlers, can modify global variables, but cannot produce boxes.

We show in Section 4 how we enforce these rules at compile time using a type and effect system.

```
page detailpage (
  listing : ⊞listing)
init
  do nothing
render
  boxed
    ▷ display listentry(listing)
  ▷ display apr menu
  ▷ display term menu
  var principal := listing → price → get
  var monthlyrate := math → exp(math → loge(1 + ◫apr) / 12) - 1
  var rr := math → pow(1 + monthlyrate, ◫term * 12)
  var payment := math → round with precision(principal * ((monthlyrate
  * rr) / (rr - 1)), 2)
  ▷ display results(monthlyrate, payment)
  boxed
    box → set font size(1)
    ▷ display amortization(principal, monthlyrate, payment)
```

Figure 4. The source code of the detail page.

This separation between model and view is sufficient for achieving the live editing feature of TouchDevelop's live programming experience. Code-execution reification and direct manipulation in turn are supported by TouchDevelop's simple box model, which allows the environment to easily keep track of code/box mappings. Our enhanced programming model also helps to keep UI code concise and readable. Although the code in Figure 3 *looks* a bit like declarative code, it executes just like any other procedural code: it is free to use loops to create multiple boxes, procedural abstraction to keep the code organized, and conditional statements to customize the display based on arbitrary conditions.

3.1 Example Improvements

We now discuss how the three improvements (I1–I3) described at the beginning of Section 2 are applied by the programmer in the live programming enhanced version of TouchDevelop. The programmer starts the program and begins editing our example program's **startpage**, whose code is shown in Figure 3. The first improvement made is to tweak the margins of the page (I1), which is done through direct manipulation: one simply selects the box to modify in the output display which brings up a menu on the code side to change it.

When the programmer taps an entry on the start page, its detail page opens (Figure 2) and the code view shows the code in Figure 4. The monthly amortization table of this page is generated by calling the **display amortization** function defined in Figure 5. Selecting one of the "balance" cells in the detail page selects the corresponding boxed statement in the code view (last boxed in Figure 5. Changing this statement to:

```
boxed
  var dollars := math → floor(balance)
  var cents := math → round((balance - dollars) * 100) || ""
  if cents → count < 2 then
    cents := "0" || cents
  ("balance: $" || dollars || "." || cents) → post
```

will cause the balance to print correctly in dollars and cents, implementing our I2 improvement; balance printing is updated for all amortization table rows as soon as we complete the last line of this modification.

The last improvement, high-lighting every fifth year of the amortization in another color (I3), involves selecting an amortization row in in the live view, which causes the first top-level box

```
private action display amortization (
  balance : Number,
  monthlyrate : Number,
  payment : Number)
do
  for 0 ≤ i < ◫term do
    var interest := 0
    for 0 ≤ j < 12 do
      interest := interest + balance * monthlyrate
      balance := balance - payment + balance * monthlyrate
    boxed
      box → use horizontal layout
      boxed
        box → set left margin(0.5)
        box → set width(9)
        ("after " || i + 1 || " years") → post
      boxed
        box → set width(13.7)
        ("interest: " || math → round with precision(interest, 2)) → post
      boxed
        box → set width(13)
        ("balance: $" || math → round with precision(balance, 2))
        → post
```

Figure 5. The procedure to display the amortization schedule.

of Figure 5 to be selected in the code view. The programmer can add the code

```
if math → mod(i, 5) == 4 then
  box → set background(colors → light blue)
```

to set the background of every fifth row to a light blue color. This improvement demonstrates how our live programming improves on UI editors that operate over purely declarative languages. E.g., HTML/CSS has special support for even-odd coloring, but cannot go beyond that without the loss of live feedback.

4. Formal Model

In this section, we develop a formal operational model. This model removes any ambiguities that are often a source of confusion in reactive systems, where user actions (back button, box tapping, code updates) are interleaved with program execution (event handling, rendering). It also clarifies how we avoid some typical problems, such as (1) the programmer unintentionally violating the view-model separation, or (2) strange failures due to inconsistencies between various versions of the code. We start with the syntax for writing code (Section 4.1). Then, we present an operational model that defines how the system state (which includes the code) evolves when handling user events, receiving code updates, or performing execution steps (Section 4.2). Finally, we present and discuss our type and effect system (Section 4.3). We do not formalize the visual layout of box trees.

4.1 Expression Syntax

We show the expression syntax in Fig. 6. It is based on the simply typed lambda calculus with the following additions:

- We use tuples to simplify the passing of multiple values to functions and page code. Also, empty tuples serve as the unit value, which we use heavily (since many of our operations are imperative in nature).
- We use global variables (representing the model state) and global function definitions (representing the current code). This

Identifiers:

g	$::=$	$\ldots$	global variables
f	$::=$	$\ldots$	global functions
p	$::=$	start | ...	page names
a	$::=$	ontap | margin | ...	box attributes
μ	$::=$	p | r | s	pure, render, state effect

Types:

τ	$::=$	number	(number)
	|	string	(string)
	|	$(\tau_1, \ldots, \tau_n)$	(tuple), $(n \geq 0)$
	|	$\tau \xrightarrow{\mu} \tau$	(function)

Environment:

Γ	$::=$	ϵ	
	|	$\Gamma, x : \tau$	(variable type)
	|	$\Gamma, a : \tau$	(attribute type)

Values:

v	$::=$	n	(number literal)
	|	s	(string literal)
	|	x	(variable)
	|	$(v_1, \ldots, v_n)$	(tuple)
	|	$\lambda(x : \tau).e$	(lambda)

Expressions:

e	$::=$	v	(value)
	|	$e_1 e_2$	(application)
	|	f	(function)
	|	$(e_1, \ldots, e_n)$	(tuple), $(n \geq 0)$
	|	$e.n$	(projection), $(n \geq 1)$
	|	g	(read global)
	|	$g := e$	(write global)
	|	push p e	(push new page)
	|	pop	(pop page)
	|	boxed e	(create box)
	|	post e	(post content)
	|	box.a := e	(set box attribute)

Evaluation Contexts:

E	$::=$	$[] \mid E\,e \mid v\,E$
	|	$(v_1, \ldots, v_i, E, e_j, \ldots, e_n) \mid E.n \mid g := E$
	|	push p E | post E | box.a := E

Figure 6. The syntax of types, values, expressions, and evaluation contexts.

separation is important during code updates, when we need to fix up the model state and purge stale code.

- We use page names to identify pages, and we support operations for pushing a new page (passing a parameter) and popping the current page.
- We support boxed statements to create a box, post e to add content to the current box, and box.a := e to modify an attribute of the current box.

Our calculus is intentionally kept concise even though our examples use a higher level syntax. Loops are expressible in our calculus via recursion through global functions, conditionals via lambda abstractions and thunks. Handlers on boxes are simply attributes that can be set to lambda expressions. These differences are purely syntactic and no expressivity is lost.

System State:

$\sigma \quad ::= \quad (C, D, S, P, Q)$

System Components:

C	$::=$	$\epsilon \mid C\,d$	(program code)
D	$::=$	$\bot \mid B$	(display)
S	$::=$	$\epsilon \mid S[g \mapsto v]$	(store)
P	$::=$	$\epsilon \mid P\,(p, v)$	(page stack)
Q	$::=$	$\epsilon \mid Q\,q$	(event queue)

Program Definitions:

d	$::=$	global $g : \tau = v$	(global)
	|	fun $f : \tau$ is e	(function)
	|	page $p(\tau)$ init e_1 render e_2	(page)

Box Content:

B	$::=$	ϵ	(empty)
	|	$B\,v$	(leaf content)
	|	$B\,[a = v]$	(box attribute)
	|	$B\,\langle B \rangle$	(nested box)

Events:

q	$::=$	[exec v]	(execute thunk)
	|	[push p v]	(push new page)
	|	[pop]	(pop page)

Figure 7. Definitions for system states, programs, box content, and events.

4.2 System Model

Our operational model is defined by a set of system states and a set of system transitions. A system state is a tuple (C, D, S, P, Q) as defined in Fig. 7. Note that for simplicity, we represent our data structures as sequences (with ϵ being the empty sequence), though an actual implementation would use specialized data structures such as maps, sets, queues, and so on. The meaning of the components is as follows:

- C represents the code (i.e. the program). It contains (1) global variable definitions that specify a name, a type, and an initial value, (2) function definitions that specify a name, a function type, and a lambda expression, and (3) page definitions that specify a page name, the type of the argument passed to the page on construction, and two functions to respectively be called on initialization and rendering. To save space, we write $C(p) = (f_i, f_r)$ as a shorter form for (page $p(\tau)$ init f_i render f_r) $\in C$.
- D represents what is currently displayed to the user. It contains either box content B (recursively defined as a sequence of layout attributes, values, and nested boxes), or the special value $\bot$ to indicate that the display is stale and needs to be refreshed.
- S represents the store (i.e. the values of global variables). We represent S as a sequence of key-value pairs $[g \mapsto v]$; the rightmost occurrence of a key g defines its current value, denoted $S(g)$.
- P represents the page stack. It is a sequence of pairs (p, v) where p is a page identifier and v is the argument value that was supplied when the page was created. We add and remove entries at the end of the sequence.
- Q represents the event queue. It contains three kinds of events: [exec v], [push p x], [pop]. We enqueue by adding elements

Pure execution steps:

$$\text{(EP-FUN)}\ \frac{(\mathsf{fun}\ f : \tau\ \mathsf{is}\ e) \in C}{(C, S, E[f]) \rightarrow_{\mathsf{p}} (C, S, E[e])}$$

$$\text{(EP-APP)}\ \frac{}{(C, S, E[\lambda(x : \tau).e)\ v]) \rightarrow_{\mathsf{p}} (C, S, E[e[v/x]])}$$

$$\text{(EP-TUPLE)}\ \frac{}{((C, S, E[(v_1, ..., v_m).n]) \rightarrow_{\mathsf{p}} (C, S, E[v_n])}$$

$$\text{(EP-GLOBAL-1)}\ \frac{S(g) = v}{((C, S, E[g]) \rightarrow_{\mathsf{p}} (C, S, E[v])}$$

$$\text{(EP-GLOBAL-2)}\ \frac{g \notin dom\ S \qquad \mathsf{global}\ g : \tau = v \in C}{((C, S, E[g]) \rightarrow_{\mathsf{p}} (C, S, E[v])}$$

Execution steps for standard mode:

$$\text{(ES-PURE)}\ \frac{(C, S, e) \rightarrow_{\mathsf{p}} (C, S, e')}{(C, S, Q, e) \rightarrow_{\mathsf{s}} (C, S, Q, e')}$$

$$\text{(ES-ASSIGN)}\ \frac{}{(C, S, Q, E[g := v]) \rightarrow_{\mathsf{s}} (C, S[g \mapsto v], Q, E[()])}$$

$$\text{(ES-PUSH)}\ \frac{}{(C, S, Q, E[\mathsf{push}\ p\ v]) \rightarrow_{\mathsf{s}} (C, S, [\mathsf{push}\ p\ v]\ Q, E[()])}$$

$$\text{(ES-POP)}\ \frac{}{(C, S, Q, E[\mathsf{pop}]) \rightarrow_{\mathsf{s}} (C, S, [\mathsf{pop}]\ Q, E[()])}$$

Execution steps for render mode:

$$\text{(ER-PURE)}\ \frac{(C, S, e) \rightarrow_{\mathsf{p}} (C, S, e')}{(C, S, B, e) \rightarrow_{\mathsf{r}} (C, S, B, e')}$$

$$\text{(ER-POST)}\ \frac{}{((C, S, B, E[\mathsf{post}\ v]) \rightarrow_{\mathsf{r}} (C, S, B\ v, E[()])}$$

$$\text{(ER-ATTR)}\ \frac{}{((C, S, B, E[\mathsf{box}.a := v]) \rightarrow_{\mathsf{r}} (C, S, B\ [a = v], E[()])}$$

$$\text{(ER-BOXED)}\ \frac{(C, S, \epsilon, e) \rightarrow_{\mathsf{r}}^{*} (C, S, B', v)}{(C, S, B, E[\mathsf{boxed}\ e]) \rightarrow_{\mathsf{r}} (C, S, B\ \langle B' \rangle, E[v])}$$

Figure 8. Expression evaluation steps are defined by $\rightarrow_{\mathsf{p}}$, $\rightarrow_{\mathsf{s}}$ and $\rightarrow_{\mathsf{r}}$ for pure mode, standard mode, and render mode, respectively. $\rightarrow_{\mu}^{*}$ is the reflexive transitive closure of $\rightarrow_{\mu}$.

to the left of the sequence, and dequeue by removing elements from the right end of the sequence.

At the heart of our operational semantics are the small expression evaluation steps, defined in Fig. 8. We distinguish three different steps based on their effects. Pure steps are side-effect free, but may depend on the code C and the current global state S, thus they are of the form $(C, S, e) \rightarrow_{\mathsf{p}} (C, S, e')$. Standard execution steps are of the form $(C, S, Q, e) \rightarrow_{\mathsf{s}} (C, S', Q', e')$; they may modify the state S or add elements to the event queue Q. Render steps are of the form $(C, S, B, e) \rightarrow_{\mathsf{r}} (C, S, B', e')$; they may be pure, or can append an element to the current box content B.

Our evaluation rules enforce that render functions have no side effects other than updating the display, and that the display cannot be accessed by any other user code. This is important, because it is otherwise much too easy for programmers to (intentionally or unintentionally) break the principles of our model-view separation, with highly confusing consequences.

At the system level, We define the *system step relation* $\rightarrow_{\mathrm{g}}$ as a binary relation on system states in Fig. 9. We call a system state *stable* if the event queue is empty, and the page stack is non-empty. In stable states, the system is waiting for user actions such as (TAP)

Three rules that enqueue events:

$$\text{(STARTUP)}\ \frac{}{(C, D, S, \epsilon, \epsilon) \rightarrow_{\mathrm{g}} (C, \bot, S, \epsilon, [\mathsf{push\ start}\ ()])}$$

$$\text{(TAP)}\ \frac{[\mathsf{ontap} = v] \in B}{(C, B, S, P, Q) \rightarrow_{\mathrm{g}} (C, \bot, S, P, [\mathsf{exec}\ v]\ Q)}$$

$$\text{(BACK)}\ \frac{}{(C, D, S, P, Q) \rightarrow_{\mathrm{g}} (C, \bot, S, P, [\mathsf{pop}]\ Q)}$$

Three rules that handle events:

$$\text{(THUNK)}\ \frac{(C, S, Q, v\ ()) \rightarrow_{\mathsf{s}}^{*} (C, S', Q', ())}{(C, D, S, P, Q\ [\mathsf{exec}\ v]) \rightarrow_{\mathrm{g}} (C, \bot, S', P, Q')}$$

$$\text{(PUSH)}\ \frac{C(p) = (f_i, f_r) \qquad (C, S, Q, (f_i\ v)) \rightarrow_{\mathsf{s}}^{*} (C, S', Q', ())}{(C, D, S, P, Q\ [\mathsf{push}\ p\ v]) \rightarrow_{\mathrm{g}} (C, \bot, S', P\ (p, v), Q')}$$

$$\text{(POP)}\ \frac{P = P'(p, v) \quad \text{or} \quad P = P' = \epsilon}{(C, D, S, P, Q\ [\mathsf{pop}]) \rightarrow_{\mathrm{g}} (C, \bot, S, P', Q)}$$

One rule to refresh the display:

$$\text{(RENDER)}\ \frac{C(p) = (f_i, f_r) \qquad (C, S, \epsilon, (f_r\ v)) \rightarrow_{\mathsf{r}}^{*} (C, S, B, ())}{(C, \bot, S, P\ (p, v), \epsilon) \rightarrow_{\mathrm{g}} (C, B, S, P\ (p, v), \epsilon)}$$

One rule to change the program code:

$$\text{(UPDATE)}\ \frac{C'' \vdash C' \qquad C' : S \triangleright S' \qquad C' : P \triangleright P'}{(C, D, S, P, \epsilon) \rightarrow_{\mathrm{g}} (C', \bot, S', P', \epsilon)}$$

Figure 9. System steps are defined by $\rightarrow_{\mathrm{g}}$.

for tapping a box in the display, (BACK) for hitting the back button, and (UPDATE) for code updates.

We define the initial system state to be $(C, \bot, \epsilon, \epsilon, \epsilon)$, which is unstable. While the system state is unstable, one of the following transitions is always enabled:

- If the page stack is empty, we can perform the transition (STARTUP) which enqueues an event [push start ()] causing the system to create the start page.
- If the event queue is not empty, we can dequeue the next element with one of the following transitions:
  - (THUNK) dequeues [exec v] and executes the thunk v (which is a lambda function that takes a unit value and returns a unit value). It executes v in standard execution mode, taking as many small steps as necessary to reduce the expression v () to a value.
  - (PUSH) dequeues [push p v], pushes a new page (p, v) onto the page stack, and executes the page initialization code (passing v as the argument), in standard execution mode. It takes as many small steps as necessary to reduce to a value.
  - (POP) dequeues [pop], and either pops the top page, or does nothing (if the page stack is already empty).

Some of these transitions can enqueue more events onto the queue (for example, executing a push or pop expression in user code enqueues a push or pop event). This can lead to an infinite loop of pushing new pages. Also, the execution of user code may of course diverge. Apart from those nonterminating cases, however, we eventually reach a stable state (we never get stuck, as discussed in Section 4.3). Thus the system is always live, either in an active state (executing some user code), or in a stable state (ready to handle user events or code updates).

All global transitions, except for (RENDER), also invalidate the display (set it to $\bot$). The display remains invalid until we do the (RENDER) transition. This transition executes the render code for the page that is currently at the top of the stack, in render mode, taking as many small steps as necessary. This mechanism guarantees that the display is never stale, but either invalid or current with respect to the model state and the code. In particular, it is not possible to activate tap handlers on a stale display: the prerequisite of the rule (TAP) can only be satisfied if the display is valid, which also implies that Q is empty.

In a stable state, the transition (UPDATE) allows the user to update the code (swap new code C' for old code C). Its first prerequisite (to be formally defined in Section 4.3) is $C' \vdash C'$, which means that C' must be well-typed and satisfy a number of sanity conditions. Note that there is no requirement that C' is related in any way to C. Instead, our transition performs a fix-up of the global state (defined by the relations $C' : S \triangleright S'$ and $C' : P \triangleright P'$ which we discuss in Section 4.3). Supporting arbitrary code changes is important in practice: limiting the changes a user can make is both complex to implement and explain, and unpleasant for the user.

Another important guarantee we make is that after a code update, the system contains no stale code (such as closures taken in earlier versions). The reason is that after applying rule (UPDATE), the display and the event queue are empty. Since neither global variables nor the page stack contain function values (we enforce this using the type system), the state contains no code.

4.3 Typing of Expressions and States

Fig. 10 shows how we type expressions. Our judgments have the form $C; \Gamma \vdash_\mu e : \tau$, meaning that we can type e as τ given the code C, context Γ, and effect μ (which is one of p, s, r for pure, state, or render). We define an attribute environment Γ_a that contains types for box attributes, such as ontap : $() \xrightarrow{s} ()$ and margin : number. Note that our model has an implicit top-level box, so render code can set attributes even outside a boxed statement.

The rules in Fig. 10 are mostly standard [15]. Rules indexed by effect variable μ can be instantiated to all three effect modes p, s, r. The types relate to the operational semantics in that an expression e typable under effect μ reduces to a value under $\rightarrow_\mu^*$, thereby guaranteeing that render code can be reduced by $\rightarrow_r$ rules, and that stateful code can be reduced by $\rightarrow_s$ rules.

Fig. 11 shows how we type system states. Not surprisingly, it involves separate typing judgements for almost all system components. The top rule (T-SYS) ensures that there is a definition for the start page (otherwise we would be stuck before execution even starts). The typing judgments $C \vdash D$, $C \vdash S$, $C \vdash P$, and $C \vdash Q$ are straightforward typings for the display, global variables, page stack, and event queue. The typing judgments $C \vdash C$ enforce that no name is defined twice, and that definitions use correct typings. In particular, global variables must have function-free types (notated as $\rightarrow$-free), functions must be typable with the type they declare, and the render and init functions must be typeable under the corresponding effect.

Preservation. All small evaluation steps preserve the type of the evaluated expression (i.e. if $e \rightarrow_\mu e'$, we can type e' with the same type and effect as e), and leave the store and the queue well typed. This is a simple consequence of our type and effect system (we are using a widely known standard construction). System steps also preserve the typeability of the system state. This is mostly a simple consequence of manipulating the state correctly, and of the preservation guarantee for small evaluation steps. However, the (UPDATE) rule is interesting since it completely replaces the code. In this case, to ensure typeability of the state, we need to fix up the global state and page stack. The algorithm for this fix-up is shown in Fig. 12. Essentially, it just deletes whatever does not type.

$$\text{(S-EMPTY)}\ \frac{}{C : \epsilon \triangleright \epsilon} \qquad \text{(S-SKIP)}\ \frac{C : S \triangleright S' \quad g \notin C \vee (C; \epsilon \not\vdash_s v : \tau)}{C : S\,[g \mapsto v] \triangleright S'}$$

$$\text{(S-OKAY)}\ \frac{C : S \triangleright S' \quad \text{global } g : \tau = \in C \quad C; \epsilon \vdash_s v : \tau}{C : S\,[g \mapsto v] \triangleright S'\,[g \mapsto v]}$$

$$\text{(P-EMPTY)}\ \frac{}{C : \epsilon \triangleright \epsilon} \qquad \text{(P-SKIP)}\ \frac{C : P \triangleright P' \quad p \notin C \vee (C; \epsilon \not\vdash_s v : \tau)}{C : P\,(p, v) \triangleright P'}$$

$$\text{(P-OKAY)}\ \frac{C : P \triangleright P' \quad C; \epsilon \vdash_s v : \tau \quad \text{page } p(\tau) \text{ init } e_1 \text{ render } e_2 \in C}{C : P\,(p, v) \triangleright P'\,(p, v)}$$

Figure 12. Rules for fixing up the globals and the page stack.

Progress. Any expression e that is not a value and that types as $C; \Gamma \vdash_\mu e : \tau$, with $\mu = p$ or $\mu = s$, can take a step $e \rightarrow_\mu e'$. However, if $\mu = r$, progress may be only indirect: if $e = E[\text{boxed } e']$ and e' has a diverging computation, then it is only e' that makes progress, but not e. At the system level, progress is also guaranteed with some restrictions. In a stable system state, the system makes no progress unless there are user-initiated actions. In unstable states, the system can always make progress except if there is a diverging expression evaluation (again, progress in that case is indirect: the expression evaluation makes progress, but the system as a whole does not).

5. Experience

We now present our experiences in designing, building, and using an enhanced version of TouchDevelop, along with a discussion of the various tradeoffs we had to make to achieve a reasonable live programming experience. TouchDevelop is public, free to use, and runs in most browsers on any device; we encourage the reader to check it out [1]. We have also produced an 8-minute video that demonstrates the live programming feature.[2]

Much of our work was focused on improving the user experience for the programmer. Our key finding here was to place the live and code view side by side while making elements in each view navigable to elements in the other view. The live view is automatically scaled down to fit on a smaller portion of the screen, but we support interactive zooming to allow programmers to inspect the effect of detail adjustments (such as margins and font sizes). Also, because nested boxes often cover their containers completely, we support a nested selection mode where the user can tap the same box multiple times to select enclosing boxes.

One limitation of our system is the representation of a UI program's model as a collection of global variables, where the view itself cannot retain any state. For example, the value of a slider widget must be defined as a global variable, which is then passed into render code to be read and manipulated. Our strict separation of model and view thus conflicts with the encapsulation principle. How to support encapsulation of state in view elements, and how to deal with tricky initialization semantics, remain to be addressed by future work.

Live programming can be an alternative to step-wise debuggers, given the easy navigability between code and rendered UI artifacts.

[2] `http://bit.ly/itsalive13` or directly `http://youtu.be/XnWgX6cORJM`. Please use HD quality setting.

$$\text{(T-INT)}\ \frac{}{C;\Gamma \vdash_\mu n : \mathsf{number}}$$

$$\text{(T-STRING)}\ \frac{}{C;\Gamma \vdash_\mu s : \mathsf{string}}$$

$$\text{(T-VAR)}\ \frac{}{C;\Gamma, x : \tau \vdash_\mu x : \tau}$$

$$\text{(T-TUPLE)}\ \frac{C;\Gamma \vdash_\mu e_i : \tau_i}{C;\Gamma \vdash_\mu (e_1..e_n) : (\tau_1..\tau_n)}$$

$$\text{(T-LAM)}\ \frac{C;\Gamma, x : \tau_1 \vdash_{\mu_1} e : \tau_2}{C;\Gamma \vdash_{\mu_2} \lambda(x : \tau).e : \tau_1 \xrightarrow{\mu_1} \tau_2}$$

$$\text{(T-SUB)}\ \frac{C;\Gamma \vdash_\mu e : \tau_1 \xrightarrow{\mathsf{p}} \tau_2}{C;\Gamma \vdash_\mu e : \tau_1 \xrightarrow{\mu_2} \tau_2}$$

$$\text{(T-APP)}\ \frac{C;\Gamma \vdash_\mu e_1 : \tau_1 \xrightarrow{\mu} \tau_2 \qquad C;\Gamma \vdash_\mu e_2 : \tau_1}{C;\Gamma \vdash_\mu e_1 e_2 : \tau_2}$$

$$\text{(T-FUN)}\ \frac{\mathsf{fun}\ f : \tau_1 \xrightarrow{\mu_2} \tau_2\ \mathsf{is}\ e_2 \in C}{C;\Gamma \vdash_\mu f : \tau_1 \xrightarrow{\mu_2} \tau_2}$$

$$\text{(T-BOXED)}\ \frac{C;\Gamma \vdash_{\mathsf{r}} e : \tau}{C;\Gamma \vdash_{\mathsf{r}} \mathsf{boxed}\ e : \tau}$$

$$\text{(T-POST)}\ \frac{C;\Gamma \vdash_{\mathsf{r}} e : \tau}{C;\Gamma \vdash_{\mathsf{r}} \mathsf{post}\ e : ()}$$

$$\text{(T-ATTR)}\ \frac{\Gamma_{\mathsf{a}}(a) = \tau \qquad C;\Gamma \vdash_{\mathsf{r}} e : \tau}{C;\Gamma \vdash_{\mathsf{r}} \mathsf{box}.a := e : ()}$$

$$\text{(T-GLOBAL)}\ \frac{\mathsf{global}\ g : \tau = v \in C}{C;\Gamma \vdash_\mu g : \tau}$$

$$\text{(T-ASSIGN)}\ \frac{\mathsf{global}\ g : \tau = \in C \qquad C;\Gamma \vdash_{\mathsf{s}} e : \tau}{C;\Gamma \vdash_{\mathsf{s}} g := e : ()}$$

$$\text{(T-PUSH)}\ \frac{C(p) = (e_1, e_2) \qquad C;\Gamma \vdash_{\mathsf{s}} e : \tau}{C;\Gamma \vdash_{\mathsf{s}} \mathsf{push}\ p\ e : ()}$$

$$\text{(T-POP)}\ \frac{}{C;\Gamma \vdash_{\mathsf{s}} \mathsf{pop} : ()}$$

$$\text{(T-PROJ)}\ \frac{C;\Gamma \vdash_\mu e : (\tau_1..\tau_n)}{C;\Gamma \vdash_\mu e.i : \tau_i}$$

Figure 10. Expression type rules.

$$\text{(T-SYS)}\ \frac{C \vdash C \qquad C \vdash D \qquad C \vdash S \qquad C \vdash P \qquad C \vdash Q \qquad \mathsf{page\ start}()..\in C}{\vdash (C, D, S, P, Q)}$$

$$\text{(T-EMPTY)}\ \frac{}{C \vdash \epsilon}$$

$$\text{(T-D-INV)}\ \frac{}{C \vdash \bot}$$

$$\text{(T-B-VAL)}\ \frac{C \vdash B}{C \vdash B\ v}$$

$$\text{(T-B-ATTR)}\ \frac{C \vdash B \qquad \Gamma_{\mathsf{a}}(a) = \tau \qquad C;\epsilon \vdash_{\mathsf{p}} v : \tau}{C \vdash B\ [a = v]}$$

$$\text{(T-B-NEST)}\ \frac{C \vdash B_i}{C \vdash B_1\ \langle B_2 \rangle}$$

$$\text{(T-C-GLOBAL)}\ \frac{C \vdash C' \qquad g \notin \mathit{Defs}(C') \qquad \tau \text{ is } \rightarrow\text{-free} \qquad C;\epsilon \vdash_{\mathsf{p}} v : \tau}{C \vdash C'\ \mathsf{global}\ g : \tau = v}$$

$$\text{(T-C-FUN)}\ \frac{C \vdash C' \qquad f \notin \mathit{Defs}(C') \qquad C;\epsilon \vdash_{\mathsf{p}} e : \tau_1 \xrightarrow{\mu} \tau_2}{C \vdash C'\ \mathsf{fun}\ f : \tau_1 \xrightarrow{\mu} \tau_2\ \mathsf{is}\ e}$$

$$\text{(T-C-PAGE)}\ \frac{C \vdash C' \qquad p \notin \mathit{Defs}(C') \qquad \tau \text{ is } \rightarrow\text{-free} \qquad C;\epsilon \vdash_{\mathsf{s}} e_1 : \tau \xrightarrow{\mathsf{s}} () \qquad C;\epsilon \vdash_{\mathsf{s}} e_2 : \tau \xrightarrow{\mathsf{r}} ()}{C \vdash C'\ \mathsf{page}\ p(\tau)\ \mathsf{init}\ e_1\ \mathsf{render}\ e_2}$$

$$\text{(T-S-ENTRY)}\ \frac{C \vdash S \qquad C;\epsilon \vdash_{\mathsf{p}} v : \tau}{C \vdash S\ [g \mapsto v]}$$

$$\text{(T-R-ENTRY)}\ \frac{C \vdash P \qquad C;\epsilon \vdash_{\mathsf{p}} v : \tau \qquad \mathsf{page}\ p(\tau)\ \mathsf{init}\ e_1\ \mathsf{render}\ e_2 \in C}{C \vdash P\ (p, v)}$$

$$\text{(T-Q-EXEC)}\ \frac{C \vdash Q \qquad C;\epsilon \vdash_{\mathsf{p}} v : () \xrightarrow{\mathsf{s}} ()}{C \vdash Q\ [\mathsf{exec}\ v]}$$

$$\text{(T-Q-PUSH)}\ \frac{C \vdash Q \qquad C;\epsilon \vdash_{\mathsf{p}} v : \tau \qquad \mathsf{page}\ p(\tau)\ \mathsf{init}\ e_1\ \mathsf{render}\ e_2 \in C}{C \vdash Q\ [\mathsf{push}\ p\ v]}$$

$$\text{(T-Q-POP)}\ \frac{C \vdash Q}{C \vdash Q\ [\mathsf{pop}]}$$

Figure 11. System state type rules.

However, not all aspects of program execution may be sufficently visible in the view. Also, the code in event handlers and initialization bodies is not debuggable via live programming. Thus, a step-wise debugger is still useful and future work may look at how live programming and step-wise debugging can work together. Alternatively, we may explore enhancing the programming model so that even state-changing code can be debugged through live programming, as in the Subtext language [7]. One avenue to explore is the use of boxed statements to produce debugging output in batch computations.

Our model re-executes the render code of the current page being viewed, whenever this render code or the program's model changes. Recreating the entire box tree on a redraw can become slow if there are many boxes on the screen. We are currently working on a simple optimization where we can reuse box tree elements that have not changed. An intriguing avenue for future work is the application of research on self-adjusting computation [2], which would allow redundant parts of the render computation to be elided automatically.

6. Related Work

As mentioned previously, visual programming languages have long supported live programming. Burnett *et al.* [5] survey these languages and detail how they can support live programming efficiently. In contrast, we describe how live programming can be supported in the context of a fully expressive textual, imperative language with standard control flow constructs.

Superglue [17] is a textual language that adopts a model inspired by dataflow visual languages; live programming is indeed achieved, but many programs are hard to express with dataflow alone.

Flogo II [11] is another textual live language that supports *live text*, where the state of an executing program is presented as graphical annotations in the code. Rather than annotating code with execution details, our work focuses on making the connection navigable between code and the program's execution (as the rendered UI).

Live programming depends on a "model" that persists between program edits, which originates from Smalltalk's support for image-based persistence [9]. Although Smalltalk supports "fix-and-continue," it does not provide live programming as code edits and execution are independent. Self [26] with its Morphic [16] UI library gets around this limitation by supporting the direct manipulation [24] of object run-time structures, although such edits only persist and do not affect the object's code. In contrast, our work is able to support liveness through a deep connection between code and program execution as well as direct manipulation whose effects are enshrined in code.

Going beyond live programming, Subtext [7] explores how code and program execution can be represented using the same encoding; code in Subtext is not so much executed as it is copied. Our goal is less ambitious: we view live programming as a promising next step in bridging the gap between code and program execution.

Mobl [13] is a programming language for mobile devices. It provides page stack navigation and view-model separation (using data binding), but no live programming. HyperCard [4] provides an overall experience that is quite similar to ours (page stack navigation, persistent state, event handling, and quick switching between editing the code and interacting with the program). However, programming is not live, as code does not automatically reexecute, nor is there any support for writing specialized code to express the relationship between view and state.

Live programming is also related to the hot swapping of code, introduced by Fabry [8], an important capability of the Erlang language [3], both of which allow the code of an executing program to be updated without losing its state and context. However, live programming is concerned with program development while code hot swapping is concerned with updating programs already deployed. The former focuses more on navigable connections between code and execution, while the latter focuses more on uptime and robustness.

Hicks et al. [12] propose live software updating via state snapshots, state transformations, and re-starting of the changed program. The reconstruction of the call-stack and application of data transformation is the responsibility of the programmer, rather than an automated system. This provides maximum flexibility, while making it unsuitable for live programming.

7. Conclusion

Live programming is an idea whose time has come: emerging interactive programming systems [10, 22, 27] capture the imagination of today's programmers and promise to narrow the temporal and perceptive gap between program development and code execution. This paper has shown how live programming can be conceptualized and realized in an expressive procedural language, by tightly integrating UI construction techniques (model-view separation and page-stack navigation) with programming language techniques (syntactically nested boxes and a type and effect system). By providing a formal model, we have established a foundation for critical discussions at a technical level. Future work on live programming may explore improvements in expressiveness, such as support for state encapsulation in the view, or improvements in performance, such as optimizations that help to scale to larger and more complex user interfaces.

References

[1] TouchDevelop website and web application (Microsoft Research). `http://www.touchdevelop.com`.

[2] U. A. Acar. Self-adjusting computation: (an overview). In *Proc. of Partial Evaluation and Program Manipulation (PEPM)*, pages 1–6, 2009.

[3] J. L. Armstrong and S. R. Virding. Erlang - an experimental telephony programming language. In *Proc. of International Switching Symposium*, pages 2–7, 1990.

[4] B. Atkinson. Hypercard. Apple Computer, 1987.

[5] M. M. Burnett, J. W. Atwood Jr, and Z. T. Welch. Implementing level 4 liveness in declarative visual programming languages. In *Proc. of the IEEE Symposium on Visual Languages*, pages 126–134, 1998.

[6] M. M. Burnett, M. J. Baker, C. Bohus, P. Carlson, P. J. V. Zee, and S. Yang. The scaling-up problem for visual programming languages. Technical report, Oregon State University, 1994.

[7] J. Edwards. Subtext: uncovering the simplicity of programming. In *Proc. of OOPSLA Onward!*, pages 505–518, 2005.

[8] R. S. Fabry. How to design a system in which modules can be changed on the fly. In *Proc. of ICSE*, pages 470–476, 1976.

[9] A. Goldberg and D. Robson. *Smalltalk-80: the language and its implementation*. Addison-Wesley Longman Publishing Co., Inc., 1983.

[10] C. Granger. Light Table - a reactive work surface for programming. `http://www.kickstarter.com/projects/ibdknox/-light-table`, 2012.

[11] C. M. Hancock. *Real-time programming and the big ideas of computational literacy*. PhD thesis, Massachusetts Institute of Technology, 2003. AAI0805688.

[12] C. M. Hayden, E. K. Smith, M. Denchev, M. Hicks, and J. S. Foster. Kitsune: efficient, general-purpose dynamic software updating for C. In *Proc. of OOPSLA*, Oct. 2012.

[13] Z. Hemel and E. Visser. Declaratively programming the mobile web with mobl. In *Object oriented programming systems languages and applications (OOPSLA)*, pages 695–712. ACM, 2011.

[14] H. Lieberman and C. Fry. Bridging the gulf between code and behavior in programming. In *Proc. of CHI*, pages 480–486, 1995.

[15] J. M. Lucassen and D. K. Gifford. Polymorphic effect systems. In *In Principles of Programming Languages (POPL*, pages 47–57. ACM Press, 1988.

[16] J. H. Maloney and R. B. Smith. Directness and liveness in the Morphic user interface construction environment. In *Proc. of UIST*, pages 21–28, nov 1995.

[17] S. McDirmid. Living it up with a live programming language. In *Proc. of OOPSLA Onward!*, pages 623–638, October 2007.

[18] C. Muratori. Immediate-mode graphical user interfaces. `www.molly-rocket.com/861`, 2005.

[19] D. A. Norman and S. W. Draper. *User Centered System Design; New Perspectives on Human-Computer Interaction*. L. Erlbaum Associates Inc., 1986.

[20] M. Puckette. Pure Data: another integrated computer music environment. In *Proc. of International Computer Music Conference*, pages 37–41, 1996.

[21] T. Reenskaug. Thing-model-view-editor an example from a planningsystem. `http://heim.ifi.uio.no/~trygver/1979`. Technical report, Xerox PARC, 1979.

[22] J. Resig. Khan Academy - computer science. `http://www.khan-academy.org/cs`.

[23] E. Sandewall. Programming in an interactive environment: the "LISP" experience. *ACM Computing Surveys*, 10(1):35–71, Mar. 1978.

[24] B. Shneiderman. Direct manipulation. a step beyond programming languages. *IEEE Transactions on Computers*, 16(8):57–69, August 1983.

[25] N. Tillmann, M. Moskal, J. de Halleux, and M. Fahndrich. TouchDevelop - programming cloud-connected mobile devices via touchscreen. In *Proc. of SPLASH Onward!*, 2011.

[26] D. Ungar and R. B. Smith. Self: the power of simplicity. In *Proc. of OOPSLA*, pages 227–242, December 1987.

[27] B. Victor. Inventing on principle. Invited talk at the Canadian University Software Engineering Conference (CUSEC), Jan. 2012.

Terra: A Multi-Stage Language for High-Performance Computing

Zachary DeVito James Hegarty Alex Aiken Pat Hanrahan Jan Vitek
Stanford University Purdue University
(zdevito|jhegarty|aiken|hanrahan)@cs.stanford.edu jv@cs.purdue.edu

Abstract

High-performance computing applications, such as auto-tuners and domain-specific languages, rely on generative programming techniques to achieve high performance and portability. However, these systems are often implemented in multiple disparate languages and perform code generation in a separate process from program execution, making certain optimizations difficult to engineer. We leverage a popular scripting language, Lua, to stage the execution of a novel low-level language, Terra. Users can implement optimizations in the high-level language, and use built-in constructs to generate and execute high-performance Terra code. To simplify metaprogramming, Lua and Terra share the same lexical environment, but, to ensure performance, Terra code can execute independently of Lua's runtime. We evaluate our design by reimplementing existing multi-language systems entirely in Terra. Our Terra-based auto-tuner for BLAS routines performs within 20% of ATLAS, and our DSL for stencil computations runs 2.3x faster than hand-written C.

Categories and Subject Descriptors D.3.4 [*Programming Languages*]: Processors – Code Generation, Compilers

General Terms Design, Performance

Keywords Lua, Staged computation, DSL

1. Introduction

There is an increasing demand for high-performance power-efficient applications on devices ranging from phones to supercomputers. Programming these applications is challenging. For optimum performance, applications need to be tailored to the features of the target architecture, e.g., multi-core, vector instructions, and throughput-oriented processors such as GPUs. Applications have turned to generative programming to adapt to complex hardware. Auto-tuners like SPIRAL [23], ATLAS [33], or FFTW [12] can express a range of implementations for specific applications such as FFTs, and choose the best optimizations for a given architecture. In areas such as machine learning [4], or physical simulation [9], domain-specific languages (DSLs) can achieve the same goal for a range of similar applications through domain-specific optimizations.

PLDI'13, June 16–19, 2013, Seattle, WA, USA.

However, high-performance applications that rely on code generation are often implemented as ad hoc source-to-source translators. For instance, consider FFTW which implements its `genfft` compiler in OCaml and emits C code [12], or Liszt, a DSL which uses Scala for its transformations and generates code that links against a runtime written in C [9].

While these designs produce high-performance code, they are hard to engineer. A DSL or auto-tuner typically has three components: an optimizer that performs domain-specific transformations to generate a plan of execution, a compiler that generates high-performance code based on the plan, and a runtime that supports the generated code and provides feedback to the optimizer. If, as in FFTW and Liszt, the optimizer and compiler are separate from the runtime, it is difficult to feed runtime statistics back to the compiler to perform problem-specific optimizations. Transformations also require careful engineering to separate compile-time and runtime optimizations, making it difficult to prototype new optimizations.

Ideally, it should be easy for domain experts to experiment with domain and problem-specific transformations, generate high-performance code dynamically, and provide runtime feedback to improve performance. Furthermore, all parts of the toolchain, compiler, generated code, and runtimes, should inter-operate amongst themselves and with legacy high-performance libraries. Achieving these goals in a single system is complicated by the fact that each component has different design constraints. It is easier to prototype compiler transformations in an expressive high-level language, but achieving high performance in the generated code and runtime requires fine-grained control over execution and memory resources, which is easier in a low-level language.

To address these problems, we use multi-stage programming [30] to couple an existing high-level language, Lua, with a new low-level language, Terra. Lua is a high-level dynamically-typed language with automatic memory management and first-class functions [14]. Terra, on the other hand, is a statically-typed language similar to C with manual memory management. Terra code is embedded in Lua. Using multi-stage programming, programmers can generate and execute Terra code dynamically from Lua.

This two-language design allows domain experts to experiment with high-level transformations using Lua, while still generating high-performance code using Terra. To simplify code generation, the evaluation of Lua and the *generation* of Terra code share the same lexical environment and variable references are hygienic across the two languages. To ensure fine-grained control of execution, Terra executes in a *separate* environment: Terra code runs independently of the Lua runtime. It can run in a different thread, or (in the future) on accelerators like GPUs. This separation ensures that the high-level features of Lua do not creep into the execution of Terra. Furthermore, Terra exposes the low-level features of modern hardware such as vector instructions. Finally, we leverage the fact that Lua was specifically designed to be embedded in low-level languages such as C [15]. Lua's stack-based C API makes it easy to interface with legacy code, while a built-in foreign-function interface [1] makes it possible to pass values between Lua and Terra.

Furthermore, we provide support for type reflection on Terra types that enables the creation of new types via meta-programming. This design keeps the Terra language simple while still allowing the creation of libraries to implement higher-level components such as class systems that can be used in high-performance runtimes.

This paper makes the following contributions:

- We present the design of Terra which uniquely combines the staging of a low-level language using a high-level one, shared lexical scoping, separate evaluation, and type reflection.[1]
- We provide a formal semantics of core Terra to elucidate the interaction between Terra and Lua, focusing on how staging operates in the presence of side effects in Lua.
- We show that we can reimplement a number of existing multi-language systems entirely in Terra, but still achieve similar performance. In particular, we show an auto-tuner for matrix multiply that performs within 20% of ATLAS, but uses fewer than 200 lines of Terra code, and we present a stencil computation language that performs 2.3x faster than hand-written C. Finally, we implement a class system and container with parameterizable data layout as JIT-compilable Terra libraries, which would be difficult to engineer in existing languages.

2. Writing Multi-stage Code in Terra

We use an example image-processing algorithm to introduce Terra. At the top-level, a program executes as Lua, augmented with constructs to create Terra functions, types, variables, and expressions. The terra keyword introduces a new Terra function (Lua functions are introduced with function):

```
terra min(a: int, b: int) : int
  if a < b then return a
  else return b end
end
```

Terra functions are lexically-scoped and statically-typed, with parameters and return types explicitly annotated. In contrast, Lua has no type annotations. Terra is also backwards-compatible with C:

```
std = terralib.includec("stdlib.h")
```

The Lua function includec imports the C functions from stdlib.h. It creates a Lua *table*, an associative map. It then fills the table with Terra functions that invoke the corresponding C functions found in stdlib.h. In Lua, the expression table.key is syntax sugar for table["key"]. So, for example, std.malloc is C's malloc.

Terra entities (functions, types, variables and expressions) are first-class Lua values. For example, the follow statement constructs a Terra type that holds a square greyscale image:

```
struct GreyscaleImage {
  data : &float;
  N : int;
}
```

GreyscaleImage is a Lua variable whose value is a Terra type. Terra's types are similar to C's. They include standard base types, arrays, pointers, and nominally-typed structs. Here data is a pointer to floats, while GreyscaleImage is a type that was created by the struct constructor.

We might want to parameterize the image type based on the type stored at each pixel (e.g., an RGB triplet, or a greyscale value).

We can define a Lua function Image that creates the desired Terra type at runtime. This is conceptually similar to a C++ template:

```
   function Image(PixelType)
     struct ImageImpl {
       data : &PixelType,
       N : int
5    }
     -- method definitions for the image:
     terra ImageImpl:init(N: int): {} --returns nothing
       self.data =
         [&PixelType](std.malloc(N*N*sizeof(PixelType)))
10     self.N = N
     end
     terra ImageImpl:get(x: int, y: int) : PixelType
       return self.data[x*self.N + y]
     end
15   --omitted methods for: set, save, load, free
     return ImageImpl
   end
```

In addition to its layout declared on lines 2–5, each struct can have a set of methods (lines 6–15). Methods are normal Terra functions stored in a Lua table associated with each type (e.g., ImageImpl.methods). The method declaration syntax is sugar for:

```
ImageImpl.methods.init =
  terra(self : &ImageImpl, N : int) : {}
    ...
  end
```

Method invocations (myimage:init(128)) are also just syntactic sugar (ImageImpl.methods.init(myimage,128)). In the init function, we call std.malloc to allocate memory for our image. Since std is a Lua table, Terra will evaluate the table select operator (std.malloc) during compilation and resolve it to the malloc function. We also define a get function to retrieve each pixel, as well as some utility functions which we omit for brevity.

Outside of the Image function, we call Image(float) to define GreyscaleImage. We use it to define a laplace function and a driver function runlaplace that will run it on an image loaded from disk to calculate the Laplacian of the image:

```
GreyscaleImage = Image(float)
terra laplace(img: &GreyscaleImage,
              out: &GreyscaleImage) : {}
  --shrink result, do not calculate boundaries
  var newN = img.N - 2
  out:init(newN)
  for i = 0,newN do
    for j = 0,newN do
      var v = img:get(i+0,j+1) + img:get(i+2,j+1)
            + img:get(i+1,j+2) + img:get(i+1,j+0)
            - 4 * img:get(i+1,j+1)
      out:set(i,j,v)
    end
  end
end
terra runlaplace(input: rawstring,
                 output: rawstring) : {}
  var i = GreyscaleImage {}
  var o = GreyscaleImage {}
  i:load(input)
  laplace(&i,&o)
  o:save(output)
  i:free(); o:free()
end
```

To actually execute this Terra function, we can call it from Lua:

```
runlaplace("myinput.bmp","myoutput.bmp")
```

Invoking the function from Lua will cause the runlaplace function to be JIT compiled. A foreign function interface converts the Lua string type into a raw character array rawstring used in Terra code.

[1] Our implementation and additional examples are available at github.com/zdevito/terra

Alternatively, we can save the Terra function to a `.o` file which can be linked to a normal C executable:

```
terralib.saveobj("runlaplace.o",
                 {runlaplace = runlaplace})
```

We may want to optimize the `laplace` function by blocking the loop nests to make the memory accesses more friendly to cache. We could write this optimization manually, but the sizes and numbers of levels of cache can vary across machines, so maintaining a multi-level blocked loop can be tedious. Instead, we can create a Lua function, `blockedloop`, to *generate* the Terra code for the loop nests with a parameterizable number of block sizes. In `laplace`, we can replace the loop nests (lines 7–12) with a call to `blockedloop` that generates Terra code for a 2-level blocking scheme with outer blocks of size 128 and inner blocks of size 64:

```
[blockedloop(newN,{128,64,1}, function(i,j)
  return quote
    var v = img:get(i+0,j+1) + img:get(i+2,j+1)
          + img:get(i+1,j+2) + img:get(i+1,j+0)
          - 4 * img:get(i+1,j+1)
    out:set(i,j,v)
  end
end)]
```

The brackets (`[]`) around the expression are the Terra equivalent of the *escape* operator from multi-stage programming, allowing a value evaluated in Lua (the code for the loop nest generated by `blockedloop`) to be spliced into the Terra expression. The third argument to `blockedloop` is a Lua function that is called to create the inner body of the loop. Its arguments (`i,j`) are the loop indices. The `quote` expression creates a *quotation*, a block of Terra code that can be spliced into another Terra expression. Here, we use it to create the loop body using the loop indices.

The implementation of `blockedloop` walks through the list of `blocksizes`. It uses a quote to create a level of loop nests for each entry and recursively creates the next level using an escape. At the inner-most level, it calls `bodyfn` to generate the loop body:

```
function blockedloop(N,blocksizes,bodyfn)
  local function generatelevel(n,ii,jj,bb)
    if n > #blocksizes then
      return bodyfn(ii,jj)
    end
    local blocksize = blocksizes[n]
    return quote
      for i = ii,min(ii+bb,N),blocksize do
        for j = jj,min(jj+bb,N),blocksize do
          [ generatelevel(n+1,i,j,blocksize) ]
        end
      end
    end
  end
  return generatelevel(1,0,0,N)
end
```

A more general version of this function is used to implement multi-level blocking for our matrix multiply example.

This example highlights some important features of Terra. We provide syntax sugar for common patterns in runtime code such as namespaces (`std.malloc`) or method invocation (`out:init(newN)`). Furthermore, during the generation of Terra functions, both Lua and Terra share the same lexical environment. For example, the loop nests refer to `blocksize`, a Lua number, while the Lua code that calls `generatelevel` refers to `i` and `j`, Terra variables. Values from Lua such as `blocksize` will be specialized in the staged code as constants, while Terra variables that appear in Lua code such as `i` will behave as variable references once placed in a Terra quotation.

3. Terra Core

To make the interaction between Lua and Terra precise, we formalize the essence of both languages focusing on how Terra functions are created, compiled, and called during the evaluation of a Lua program and in the presence of side-effects. We will use this formalism in Section 4.1 to illustrate key design decisions in Terra.

The calculus, called Terra Core, is equipped with a big step operational semantics. Evaluation starts in Lua ($\xrightarrow{L}$). When a Terra term is encountered it is specialized ($\xrightarrow{S}$), a process analogous to macro expansion in LISP that evaluates any escapes in the term to produce concrete Terra terms. Specialized Terra functions can then be executed ($\xrightarrow{T}$). We distinguish between Lua expressions e, Terra expressions $\dot{\mathsf{e}}$, and specialized Terra expressions $\underline{\dot{\mathsf{e}}}$ (we use a dot to distinguish Terra terms from Lua terms, and a bar to indicate a Terra term is specialized). For simplicity we model Lua as an imperative language with first-class functions and Terra as a purely functional language. A namespace Γ maps variables (x) to addresses a, and a store S maps addresses to Lua values v. The namespace Γ serves as the *value* environment of Lua (resolving variables to values, v), and the *syntactic* environment of Terra specialization (resolving variables to specialized Terra terms $\underline{\dot{\mathsf{e}}}$, which are a subset of Lua values). In contrast, Terra is executed in a separate environment ($\dot{\Gamma}$).

The Lua (Core) syntax is given in the following table:

$$
\begin{array}{lcl}
\mathsf{e} & ::= & \mathsf{b} \mid \dot{\mathsf{T}} \mid \mathsf{x} \mid \mathtt{let}\,\mathsf{x} = \mathsf{e}\;\mathtt{in}\;\mathsf{e} \mid \mathsf{x} := \mathsf{e} \mid \; \mid \mathsf{e}(\mathsf{e}) \mid \\
 & & \mathtt{fun}(\mathsf{x})\{\mathsf{e}\} \mid \mathtt{tdecl} \mid \mathtt{ter}\;\mathsf{e}(\mathsf{x} : \mathsf{e}) : \mathsf{e}\,\{\,\dot{\mathsf{e}}\,\} \mid \grave{}\dot{\mathsf{e}} \\
\mathsf{v} & ::= & \mathsf{b} \mid l \mid \dot{\mathsf{T}} \mid \langle \Gamma, \mathsf{x}, \mathsf{e} \rangle \mid \underline{\dot{\mathsf{e}}} \\
\dot{\mathsf{T}} & ::= & \dot{\mathsf{B}} \mid \dot{\mathsf{T}} \rightarrow \dot{\mathsf{T}}
\end{array}
$$

A Lua expression can be a base value (b), a Terra type expression ($\dot{\mathsf{T}}$), a variable (x), a scoped variable definition (`let x = e in e`), an assignment (`x := e`), a function call `e(e)`, a Lua function (`fun(x){e}`), or a quoted Terra expression ($\grave{}\dot{\mathsf{e}}$). We separate declaration and definition of Terra functions to allow for recursive functions. A Terra function declaration (`tdecl`) creates a new address for a Terra function, while a Terra definition ($\mathtt{ter}\;\mathsf{e}_1(\mathsf{x} : \mathsf{e}_2) : \mathsf{e}_3\;\{\,\dot{\mathsf{e}}\,\}$) fills in the declaration at address e_1. For example, the following declares and defines a Terra function, storing it in x:

$$\mathtt{let}\;\mathsf{x} = \mathtt{ter}\;\mathtt{tdecl}(\mathsf{x}_2 : \mathtt{int}) : \mathtt{int}\;\{\,\mathsf{x}_2\,\}\;\mathtt{in}\;\mathsf{x}$$

Alternatively, `tdecl` creates just a declaration that can be defined later:

$$\mathtt{let}\;\mathsf{x} = \mathtt{tdecl}\;\mathtt{in}\;\mathtt{ter}\;\mathsf{x}(\mathsf{x}_2 : \mathtt{int}) : \mathtt{int}\;\{\,\mathsf{x}_2\,\}$$

In real Terra code, a Terra definition will create a declaration if it does not already exist. Lua values range over base types (b), addresses of Terra functions (l), Terra types ($\dot{\mathsf{T}}$), Lua closures ($\langle \Gamma, \mathsf{x}, \mathsf{e} \rangle$) and specialized Terra expressions ($\underline{\dot{\mathsf{e}}}$). The syntax of Terra terms is defined as follows:

$$\dot{\mathsf{e}} \;::=\; \mathsf{b} \mid \mathsf{x} \mid \dot{\mathsf{e}}(\dot{\mathsf{e}}) \mid \mathtt{tlet}\;\mathsf{x} : \mathsf{e} = \dot{\mathsf{e}}\;\mathtt{in}\;\dot{\mathsf{e}} \mid [\mathsf{e}]$$

A Terra expression is either a base type, a variable, a function application, a let statement, or a Lua escape (written [e]). The syntax of specialized terms is given next:

$$\underline{\dot{\mathsf{e}}} \;::=\; \mathsf{b} \mid \underline{\dot{\mathsf{x}}} \mid \underline{\dot{\mathsf{e}}}(\underline{\dot{\mathsf{e}}}) \mid \mathtt{tlet}\;\underline{\dot{\mathsf{x}}} : \dot{\mathsf{T}} = \underline{\dot{\mathsf{e}}}\;\mathtt{in}\;\underline{\dot{\mathsf{e}}} \mid l$$

In contrast to an unspecialized term, a specialized Terra term does not contain escape expressions, but can contain Terra function addresses (l). The let statement must assign Terra types to the bound variable and variables are replaced with specialized Terra variables $\underline{\dot{\mathsf{x}}}$.

The judgment $\mathsf{e}\;\Sigma_1 \xrightarrow{L} \mathsf{v}\;\Sigma_2$ describes the evaluation of a Lua expression. It operates over an environment Σ consisting of Γ, S, and a Terra function store F which maps addresses (l)

$$\mathsf{v}\ \Sigma \xrightarrow{L} \mathsf{v}\ \Sigma \ \text{(LVAL)} \qquad \frac{\Sigma = \Gamma, S, F}{\mathsf{x}\ \Sigma \xrightarrow{L} S(\Gamma(\mathsf{x}))\ \Sigma}\ \text{(LVAR)}$$

$$\frac{\mathsf{e}_1\ \Sigma_1 \xrightarrow{L} \mathsf{v}_1\ \Sigma_2 \qquad \Sigma_2 = \Gamma, S, F \qquad \mathsf{e}_2\ \Sigma_2[\mathsf{x} \leftarrow \mathsf{v}_1] \xrightarrow{L} \mathsf{v}_2\ \Sigma_3}{\mathtt{let}\ \mathsf{x} = \mathsf{e}_1\ \mathtt{in}\ \mathsf{e}_2\ \Sigma \xrightarrow{L} \mathsf{v}_2\ (\Sigma_3 \leftarrow \Gamma)}\ \text{(LLET)}$$

$$\frac{\mathsf{e}\ \Sigma \xrightarrow{L} \mathsf{v}\ \Gamma, S, F \qquad \Gamma(\mathsf{x}) = a}{\mathsf{x} := \mathsf{e}\ \Sigma \xrightarrow{L} \mathsf{v}\ \Gamma, S[a \leftarrow \mathsf{v}], F}\ \text{(LASN)}$$

$$\frac{\Sigma = \Gamma, S, F}{\mathtt{fun(x)\{e\}}\ \Sigma \xrightarrow{L} \langle \Gamma, \mathsf{x}, \mathsf{e} \rangle\ \Sigma}\ \text{(LFUN)}$$

$$\frac{\begin{array}{c}\mathsf{e}_1\ \Sigma_1 \xrightarrow{L} \langle \Gamma_1, \mathsf{x}, \mathsf{e}_3 \rangle\ \Sigma_2 \qquad \mathsf{e}_2\ \Sigma_2 \xrightarrow{L} \mathsf{v}_1\ \Gamma_2, S, F \\ a\ \mathsf{fresh} \qquad \mathsf{e}_3\ \Gamma_1[\mathsf{x} \leftarrow a], S[a \leftarrow \mathsf{v}_1], F \xrightarrow{L} \mathsf{v}_2\ \Sigma_3\end{array}}{\mathsf{e}_1(\mathsf{e}_2)\ \Sigma_1 \xrightarrow{L} \mathsf{v}_2\ (\Sigma_3 \leftarrow \Gamma_2)}\ \text{(LAPP)}$$

$$\frac{l\ \mathsf{fresh} \qquad \Sigma = \Gamma, S, F}{\mathtt{tdecl}\ \Sigma \xrightarrow{L} l\ \Gamma, S, F[l \leftarrow \bullet]}\ \text{(LTDECL)}$$

$$\frac{\begin{array}{c}\mathsf{e}_1\ \Sigma_1 \xrightarrow{L} l\ \Sigma_2 \qquad \mathsf{e}_2\ \Sigma_2 \xrightarrow{L} \dot{\mathsf{T}}_1\ \Sigma_3 \qquad \mathsf{e}_3\ \Sigma_3 \xrightarrow{L} \dot{\mathsf{T}}_2\ \Sigma_4 \\ \Sigma_4 = \Gamma_1, S_1, F_1 \qquad \underline{\dot{\mathsf{x}}}\ \mathsf{fresh} \\ \dot{\mathsf{e}}\ \Sigma_4[\mathsf{x} \leftarrow \underline{\dot{\mathsf{x}}}] \xrightarrow{S} \underline{\dot{\mathsf{e}}}\ \Gamma_2, S_2, F_2 \qquad F_2(l) = \bullet\end{array}}{\mathtt{ter}\ \mathsf{e}_1(\mathsf{x} : \mathsf{e}_2) : \mathsf{e}_3\ \{\ \dot{\mathsf{e}}\ \}\ \Sigma_1 \xrightarrow{L} l\ \Gamma_1, S_2, F_2[l \leftarrow \langle \underline{\dot{\mathsf{x}}}, \dot{\mathsf{T}}_1, \dot{\mathsf{T}}_2, \underline{\dot{\mathsf{e}}} \rangle]}\ \text{(LTDEFN)}$$

$$\frac{\dot{\mathsf{e}}\ \Sigma_1 \xrightarrow{S} \underline{\dot{\mathsf{e}}}\ \Sigma_2}{\text{`}\dot{\mathsf{e}}\ \Sigma_1 \xrightarrow{L} \underline{\dot{\mathsf{e}}}\ \Sigma_2}\ \text{(LTQUOTE)}$$

$$\frac{\begin{array}{c}\mathsf{e}_1\ \Sigma_1 \xrightarrow{L} l\ \Sigma_2 \qquad \mathsf{e}_2\ \Sigma_2 \xrightarrow{L} \mathsf{b}_1\ \Sigma_3 \\ \Sigma_3 = \Gamma, S, F \qquad F(l) = \langle \underline{\dot{\mathsf{x}}}, \dot{\mathsf{T}}_1, \dot{\mathsf{T}}_2, \underline{\dot{\mathsf{e}}} \rangle \qquad \mathsf{b}_1 \in \dot{\mathsf{T}}_1 \\ [\underline{\dot{\mathsf{x}}} : \dot{\mathsf{T}}_1], [l : \dot{\mathsf{T}}_1 \rightarrow \dot{\mathsf{T}}_2], F_2 \vdash \underline{\dot{\mathsf{e}}} : \dot{\mathsf{T}}_2 \qquad \underline{\dot{\mathsf{e}}}\ [\underline{\dot{\mathsf{x}}} \leftarrow \mathsf{b}], F \xrightarrow{T} \mathsf{b}_2\end{array}}{\mathsf{e}_1(\mathsf{e}_2)\ \Sigma_1 \xrightarrow{L} \mathsf{b}_2\ \Sigma_3}\ \text{(LTAPP)}$$

Figure 1. The rules $\xrightarrow{L}$ for evaluating Lua expressions.

to Terra functions. Terra functions can be defined ($\langle \underline{\dot{\mathsf{x}}}, \dot{\mathsf{T}}, \dot{\mathsf{T}}, \underline{\dot{\mathsf{e}}} \rangle$), or undefined ($\bullet$). Figure 1 defines the Lua evaluation rules. We use two notational shortcuts:

$$\Sigma_1[\mathsf{x} \leftarrow \mathsf{v}] = \Gamma_2, S_2, F \quad \text{when } \Sigma_1 = \Gamma_1, S_1, F \wedge \Gamma_2 = \Gamma_1[\mathsf{x} \leftarrow a] \wedge S_2 = S_1[a \leftarrow \mathsf{v}] \wedge a \text{ fresh}$$

$$\Sigma \leftarrow \Gamma_1 = \Gamma_1, S, F \quad \text{when } \Sigma = \Gamma_2, S, F$$

Rule LTDECL creates a new Terra function at address l and initializes it as undefined ($\bullet$). Rule LTDEFN takes an undefined Terra function (e_1) and initializes it. First, e_2 and e_3 are evaluated as Lua expressions to produce the type of the function, $\dot{\mathsf{T}}_1 \rightarrow \dot{\mathsf{T}}_2$. The body, $\dot{\mathsf{e}}$, is specialized. During specialization, Terra variables (x) are renamed to new symbols ($\underline{\dot{\mathsf{x}}}$) to ensure hygiene. Renaming has been previously applied in staged-programming [30] and hygienic macro expansion [2]. In the case of LTDEFN, we generate a fresh name $\underline{\dot{\mathsf{x}}}$ for the formal parameter x, and place it in the environment. Variable x will be bound to the value $\underline{\dot{\mathsf{x}}}$ in the scope of any Lua code evaluated during specialization of the function. During specialization, Rule SVAR will replace uses of x in Terra code with the value of x in the environment.

$$\mathsf{b}\ \Sigma \xrightarrow{S} \mathsf{b}\ \Sigma \ \text{(SBAS)}$$

$$\frac{\dot{\mathsf{e}}_1\ \Sigma_1 \xrightarrow{S} \underline{\dot{\mathsf{e}}}_1\ \Sigma_2 \qquad \dot{\mathsf{e}}_2\ \Sigma_2 \xrightarrow{S} \underline{\dot{\mathsf{e}}}_2\ \Sigma_3}{\dot{\mathsf{e}}_1(\dot{\mathsf{e}}_2)\ \Sigma_1 \xrightarrow{S} \underline{\dot{\mathsf{e}}}_1(\underline{\dot{\mathsf{e}}}_2)\ \Sigma_3}\ \text{(SAPP)}$$

$$\frac{\begin{array}{c}\mathsf{e}\ \Sigma_1 \xrightarrow{L} \dot{\mathsf{T}}\ \Sigma_2 \qquad \dot{\mathsf{e}}_1\ \Sigma_2 \xrightarrow{S} \underline{\dot{\mathsf{e}}}_1\ \Sigma_3 \qquad \underline{\dot{\mathsf{x}}}\ \text{fresh} \\ \Sigma_3 = \Gamma, S, F \qquad \dot{\mathsf{e}}_2\ \Sigma_3[\mathsf{x} \leftarrow \underline{\dot{\mathsf{x}}}] \xrightarrow{S} \underline{\dot{\mathsf{e}}}_2\ \Sigma_4\end{array}}{\mathtt{tlet}\ \mathsf{x} : \mathsf{e} = \dot{\mathsf{e}}_1\ \mathtt{in}\ \dot{\mathsf{e}}_2\ \Sigma_1 \xrightarrow{S} \mathtt{tlet}\ \underline{\dot{\mathsf{x}}} : \dot{\mathsf{T}} = \underline{\dot{\mathsf{e}}}_1\ \mathtt{in}\ \underline{\dot{\mathsf{e}}}_2\ (\Sigma_4 \leftarrow \Gamma)}\ \text{(SLET)}$$

$$\frac{\mathsf{e}\ \Sigma_1 \xrightarrow{L} \underline{\dot{\mathsf{e}}}\ \Sigma_2}{[\mathsf{e}]\ \Sigma_1 \xrightarrow{S} \underline{\dot{\mathsf{e}}}\ \Sigma_2}\ \text{(SESC)} \qquad \frac{[\mathsf{x}]\ \Sigma_1 \xrightarrow{S} \underline{\dot{\mathsf{e}}}\ \Sigma_2}{\mathsf{x}\ \Sigma_1 \xrightarrow{S} \underline{\dot{\mathsf{e}}}\ \Sigma_2}\ \text{(SVAR)}$$

Figure 2. The rules $\xrightarrow{S}$ for specializing Terra expressions.

$$\mathsf{b}\ \dot{\Gamma}, F \xrightarrow{T} \mathsf{b}\ \text{(TBAS)} \qquad l\ \dot{\Gamma}, F \xrightarrow{T} l\ \text{(TFUN)}$$

$$\underline{\dot{\mathsf{x}}}\ \dot{\Gamma}, F \xrightarrow{T} \dot{\Gamma}(\underline{\dot{\mathsf{x}}}) \ \text{(TVAR)}$$

$$\frac{\underline{\dot{\mathsf{e}}}_1\ \dot{\Gamma}, F \xrightarrow{T} \mathsf{v}_1 \qquad \underline{\dot{\mathsf{e}}}_2\ \dot{\Gamma}[\underline{\dot{\mathsf{x}}} \leftarrow \mathsf{v}_1], F \xrightarrow{T} \mathsf{v}_2}{\mathtt{tlet}\ \underline{\dot{\mathsf{x}}} : \dot{\mathsf{T}} = \underline{\dot{\mathsf{e}}}_1\ \mathtt{in}\ \underline{\dot{\mathsf{e}}}_2\ \dot{\Gamma}, F \xrightarrow{T} \mathsf{v}_2}\ \text{(TLET)}$$

$$\frac{\begin{array}{c}\underline{\dot{\mathsf{e}}}_1\ \dot{\Gamma}, F \xrightarrow{T} l \qquad \underline{\dot{\mathsf{e}}}_2\ \dot{\Gamma}, F \xrightarrow{T} \mathsf{v}_1 \\ F(l) = \langle \underline{\dot{\mathsf{x}}}, \dot{\mathsf{T}}_1, \dot{\mathsf{T}}_2, \underline{\dot{\mathsf{e}}}_3 \rangle \qquad \underline{\dot{\mathsf{e}}}_3\ \dot{\Gamma}[\underline{\dot{\mathsf{x}}} \leftarrow \mathsf{v}_1], F \xrightarrow{T} \mathsf{v}_2\end{array}}{\underline{\dot{\mathsf{e}}}_1(\underline{\dot{\mathsf{e}}}_2)\ \dot{\Gamma}, F \xrightarrow{T} \mathsf{v}_2}\ \text{(TAPP)}$$

Figure 3. The rules $\xrightarrow{T}$ for evaluating Terra expressions.

$$\frac{\hat{F}(l) = \dot{\mathsf{T}}}{\dot{\Gamma}, \hat{F}, F \vdash l : \dot{\mathsf{T}}}\ \text{(TYFUN1)}$$

$$\frac{l \notin \hat{F} \qquad F(l) = \langle \mathsf{x}, \dot{\mathsf{T}}_1, \dot{\mathsf{T}}_2, \underline{\dot{\mathsf{e}}} \rangle \qquad [\mathsf{x} : \dot{\mathsf{T}}_1], \hat{F}[l : \dot{\mathsf{T}}_1 \rightarrow \dot{\mathsf{T}}_2], F \vdash \underline{\dot{\mathsf{e}}} : \dot{\mathsf{T}}_2}{\dot{\Gamma}, \hat{F}, F \vdash l : \dot{\mathsf{T}}_1 \rightarrow \dot{\mathsf{T}}_2}\ \text{(TYFUN2)}$$

Figure 4. Typing rules for references to Terra functions.

Rule LTAPP describes how to call a Terra function from Lua. The actual parameter e_2 is evaluated. The Terra function is then typechecked. Semantically, typechecking occurs every time a function is run. In practice, we cache the result of typechecking. For simplicity, Terra Core only allows values b of base types to be passed and returned from Terra functions (full Terra is less restricted).

Figure 2 defines judgment $\dot{\mathsf{e}}\ \Sigma_1 \xrightarrow{S} \underline{\dot{\mathsf{e}}}\ \Sigma_2$ for specializing Terra code, which evaluates all embedded Lua expressions in type annotations and escape expressions. Similar to LTDEFN, rule SLET generates a unique name $\underline{\dot{\mathsf{x}}}$ to ensure hygiene. Rule SESC evaluates escaped Lua code: it splices the result into the Terra expression if the resulting value is in the subset of values that are Terra terms $\underline{\dot{\mathsf{e}}}$ (e.g., a variable $\underline{\dot{\mathsf{x}}}$ or base value b). Variables in Terra can refer to variables defined in Lua and in Terra; they behave as if they are escaped, as defined by Rule SVAR. If x is a variable defined in Terra code and renamed $\underline{\dot{\mathsf{x}}}$ during specialization, then rule SVAR will just produce $\underline{\dot{\mathsf{x}}}$ (assuming no interleaving mutation of x).

Figure 3 presents the judgment $\underline{\dot{\mathsf{e}}}\ \dot{\Gamma}, F \xrightarrow{T} \mathsf{v}$ for evaluating specialized Terra expressions. These expressions can be evaluated independently from the Lua store S, and do not modify F, but are otherwise straightforward. A Terra function is typechecked right before it is run (LTAPP) with the judgment $\dot{\Gamma}, \hat{F}, F \vdash \underline{\dot{\mathsf{e}}} : \dot{\mathsf{T}}$, where $\hat{\Gamma}$ is the typing environment for variables and $\hat{F}$ is the typing environment for Terra function references (F is the Terra function store from before). The rules (omitted for brevity) are standard, except for the handling of Terra function references l. If a Terra function l_1 refers to another Terra function l_2, then l_2 must be typechecked when typechecking l_1. The rules for handling these references in the presence of mutually recursive functions are shown in Figure 4. They ensure all functions that are in the connected component of a function are typechecked before the function is run.

4. Key Design Decisions

We want to make it easier to prototype domain- and problem-specific transformations, dynamically compile the results of the transformations into high-performance code, and support this code with high-performance runtime libraries. We highlight some important design decisions in the semantics of Terra Core that make these goals possible. We then present engineering decisions that also address these issues.

4.1 Language Design

Hygienic staged programming with a shared lexical environment. The combination of staged programming, shared lexical environment, and hygiene provides several benefits. The staged programming of Terra from Lua provides interoperability between compiler, generated code, and runtime of a DSL. DSL compilers written in Lua can generate arbitrary code using a combination of quotations, escapes, and `terra` definitions. The shared lexical environment makes it possible to organize Terra functions in the Lua environment, and refer to them directly from Terra code without explicit escape expressions. To further reduce the need for escape expressions, we also treat lookups into nested Lua tables of the form $\mathtt{x.id_1.id_2 \ldots id_n}$ (where $\mathtt{id_1 \ldots id_n}$ are valid entries in nested Lua tables) as if they were escaped. This syntactic sugar allows Terra code to refer to functions organized into Lua tables (e.g., `std.malloc`), removing the need for an explicit namespace mechanism in Terra. Finally, maintaining hygiene during staging ensures that it is always possible to determine the relationship between variables and their declarations (across both Lua and Terra) using only the local lexical scope.

Terra Core illustrates how we provide a shared lexical environment and hygiene. The evaluation of Lua code and the specialization of Terra code share the same lexical environment Γ and store S. This environment and store always map variables x to Lua values v. Terra *syntax* $\dot{\underline{e}}$ is one type of Lua *value*. This example illustrates the shared environment:

```
let x1 = 0 in
let x2 = `(tlet y1 : int = 1 in x1) in
let x3 = ter tdecl(y2 : int) : int { x2 } in x3
```

The specialization of the quoted `tlet` expression occurs in the surrounding Lua environment, so Rule SVAR will evaluate x_1 to 0. This results in the specialized expression:

$$\mathtt{tlet}\ \dot{\underline{\mathsf{y}}}_1 : \mathtt{int} = 1\ \mathtt{in}\ 0$$

This Terra expression will be stored as a Lua value in x_2. Since the Terra function refers to x_2, specialization will result in the following Terra function:

$$\langle \dot{\underline{\mathsf{y}}}_2, \mathtt{int}, \mathtt{int}, \mathtt{tlet}\ \dot{\underline{\mathsf{y}}}_1 : \mathtt{int} = 1\ \mathtt{in}\ 0 \rangle$$

Furthermore, during specialization variables introduced by Terra functions and Terra `let` expressions are bound in the shared lexical environment. Consider this example:

```
let x1 = fun(x2){`tlet y : int = 0 in [x2]} in
let x3 = ter tdecl(y : int) : int { [x1(y)] } in x3
```

The variable y on line 2 is introduced by the Terra function definition. It is referenced by the Lua expression inside the escape ($[\mathsf{x}_1(\mathsf{y})]$). The variable y is then passed as an argument to Lua function x_1, where it is spliced into a `tlet` expression.

When Terra variables are introduced into the environment, they are given fresh names to ensure hygiene. For example, without renaming, x_3 would specialize to the following, causing the `tlet` expression to unintentionally capture y:

$$\langle \mathsf{y}, \mathtt{int}, \mathtt{int}, \mathtt{tlet}\ \mathsf{y} : \mathtt{int} = 1\ \mathtt{in}\ \mathsf{y} \rangle$$

To avoid this, rules LTDEFN and SLET generate fresh names for variables declared in Terra expressions. In this case, the LTDEFN will generate a fresh name $\dot{\underline{\mathsf{y}}}_1$ for the argument y binding it into the shared environment ($\Sigma[\mathsf{y} \leftarrow \dot{\underline{\mathsf{y}}}_1]$), and SLET will similarly generate the fresh name $\dot{\underline{\mathsf{y}}}_2$ for the `tlet` expression. Since y on line 2 has the *value* $\dot{\underline{\mathsf{y}}}_1$ during specialization, the variable x_2 will get the value $\dot{\underline{\mathsf{y}}}_1$, and x_3 will specialize to the following, avoiding the unintentional capture:

$$\langle \dot{\underline{\mathsf{y}}}_1, \mathtt{int}, \mathtt{int}, \mathtt{tlet}\ \dot{\underline{\mathsf{y}}}_2 : \mathtt{int} = 1\ \mathtt{in}\ \dot{\underline{\mathsf{y}}}_1 \rangle$$

Eager specialization with lazy typechecking Statically-typed languages such as Terra are normally compiled ahead-of-time, resolving symbols, typechecking, and linking in a separate process from execution. However, since Lua is dynamically-typed and can generate arbitrary Terra code, it is not possible to typecheck a combined Lua-Terra program statically. Instead, the normal phases of Terra compilation become part of the evaluation of the Lua program, and we must decide when those phases run in relation to the Lua program. To better understand how Terra code is compiled in relation to Lua, consider where Terra can "go wrong." While *specializing* Terra code, we might encounter an undefined variable, resolve a Lua expression used in an escape to a value v that is not also a Terra term $\dot{\underline{e}}$, or resolve a Lua expression used as a Terra type to a value v that is not a Terra type $\dot{\mathsf{T}}$. While *typechecking* Terra code, we might encounter a type error. And, while *linking* Terra code, we might find that a Terra function refers to a declared but undefined function. In Terra (and reflected in Terra Core), we perform specialization *eagerly* (as soon as a Terra function or quotation is defined), while we perform typechecking and linking *lazily* (only when a function is called, or is referred to by another function being called).

Eager specialization prevents mutations in Lua code from changing the meaning of a Terra function between when it is compiled and when it is used. For instance, consider the following example (we use the syntax `e:e` as sugar for `let _ = e in e`):

```
let x1 = 0 in
let y = ter tdecl(x2 : int) : int { x1 } in
x1 := 1;
y(0)
```

Since specialization is performed eagerly, the statement y(0) will evaluate to 0. In contrast, if specialization were performed *once* lazily, then it would capture the value of x_1 the first time y is called and keep that value for the rest of the program, which would lead to surprising results (e.g., if y were used before $\mathsf{x}_1 := 1$ then it would always return 0, otherwise it would always return 1). Alternatively, we could re-specialize (and hence re-compile) the function when a Lua value changes, but this behavior could lead to large compiler overheads that would be difficult to track down.

Eager specialization requires all symbols used in a function to be defined before it is used, which can be problematic for mutually recursive functions. In order to support recursive functions with eager specialization, we separate the declaration and definition of Terra functions:

```
let x2 = tdecl in
let x1 = ter tdecl(y : int) : int { x2(y) } in
ter x2(y : int) : int { x1(y) };
x1(0)
```

Alternatively, we could have provided a form of Terra definition that allows the definition of multiple mutually-recursive functions at one time. However, this approach does not inter-operate well with generative programs such as a DSL compiler that may need to create an arbitrarily sized connected-component based on dynamic information.

In contrast to specialization, typechecking is performed lazily. In Terra Core, it would be possible to perform typechecking eagerly if declarations also had types. For instance, in our previous example we could typecheck x_1 when it is defined if x_2 was given a type during declaration. However, even though x_1 would typecheck, we would still receive a *linking* error if $x_1(0)$ occurred before the definition of x_2. So performing typechecking eagerly would not reduce the number of places an error might occur for function x_1. Furthermore, unlike specialization where the result can change arbitrarily depending on the Lua state, the result of typechecking and linking x can only change monotonically from a type-error to success as the functions it references are defined (it can also stay as a type-error if the function is actually ill-typed). This property follows from the fact that Terra functions can be defined, but not re-defined by Rule LTDEFN.

In the full Terra language, performing typechecking lazily also provides several advantages. Forward declarations of functions do not have to have type annotations making them easier to maintain, and user-defined `struct` types do not need all their members or methods specified before being used in a Terra function. In the default case, we can keep type-checking monotonic by ensuring that members and methods can only be added to user-defined types and not removed. In actuality, the mechanisms for type-reflection described later in this section allow user-defined libraries to override the default behavior of a type (e.g., by adding inheritance). In this case, to maintain monotonic typechecking, implementors must ensure that the functionality of a type only grows over the execution of the program.

Separate evaluation of Terra code. After Terra code is compiled, it can run independently from Lua. This behavior is captured in Terra Core by the fact that Terra expressions are evaluated independently from the environment Γ and the store S, as illustrated by this example:

$$\begin{array}{l}\texttt{let } x_1 = 1 \texttt{ in}\\ \texttt{let } y = \texttt{ter tdecl}(x_2 : \texttt{int}) : \texttt{int} \{ x_1 \} \texttt{ in}\\ x_1 := 2; y(0)\end{array}$$

The Terra function will specialize to $\langle \dot{x}, \texttt{int}, \texttt{int}, 1 \rangle$, so the function call will evaluate to the value 1, despite x_1 being re-assigned to 2. An alternative design would allow Terra evaluation to directly refer to x_1. For instance, in MetaOCaml [29], `ref` cells share the same store across different stages, allowing mutations in staged code to be seen outside of the staged code. This alternative makes sharing state easier, but it would couple Terra and Lua's runtimes. The reliance on the Lua runtime, which includes high-level features such as garbage collection, would make it more difficult to reason about the performance of Terra code. Furthermore, the required runtime support would make it difficult to port Terra to new architectures such as GPUs, run code in multiple threads, or link code into existing C programs without including the Lua runtime.

Mechanisms for type reflection. Terra is a low-level monomorphic language. Its simplicity makes it easier to implement, but can make programming libraries such as DSL runtimes tedious. For instance, a DSL writer may want to experiment with different data layouts such as array-of-structs or struct-of-arrays. Instead of adding this functionality to Terra, we provide a type reflection API for creating and examining Terra types so this higher-level functionality can be implemented as libraries. The basis of the API lies in the fact that Terra types are Lua values, as illustrated in Terra Core:

$$\begin{array}{l}\texttt{let } x_3 = \texttt{fun}(x_1)\{\texttt{ter tdecl}(x_2 : x_1) : x_1 \{ x_2 \}\} \texttt{ in}\\ x_3(\texttt{int})(1)\end{array}$$

The Lua function x_3 will generate a Terra identity function for any given type. Here we call it with `int`, which will result in the specialized Terra function $\langle \dot{x}, \texttt{int}, \texttt{int}, \dot{x} \rangle$.

In the full language we supplement this behavior with an API to introspect and create types in Lua. Terra types include methods for introspection (e.g., `t:ispointer()`, or `t:isstruct()`) that can be called from Lua. Furthermore, structs can be created programmatically. In addition to the `methods` table presented in Section 2, structs also contain an `entries` table that describes their in-memory layout. Here we layout complex number type using its `entries` table directly:

```
struct Complex {}
Complex.entries:insert { field = "real", type = float }
Complex.entries:insert { field = "imag", type = float }
```

A struct also contains a `metamethods` table that can override certain compile-time behaviors. For instance, we might want to allow the promotion of a `float` to a complex number. A user-defined implicit conversion can be created using a Lua function `__cast` in the struct's `metamethod` table. During typechecking, when Terra needs to convert one type to another and no default conversions apply, it will call the `__cast` metamethod of either type to see if it could implement the conversion (if both are successful, we favor the metamethod of the starting type). The following example defines a conversion from a `float` to a complex number, `Complex`:

```
Complex.metamethods.__cast = function(fromtype,totype,exp)
  if fromtype == float then
    --valid, construct a complex number from the float exp
    return `Complex { exp, 0.f }
  end
  error("invalid conversion")
end
```

If there is a valid conversion, the method returns a quotation that implements the conversion (the back-tick is a shorthand for creating single-expression quotations). Using a Lua function to determine the behavior of conversions provides expressibility without the need for a more complicated mechanism.

To organize functions related to a particular type, we also provide a method invocation syntax `obj:my_method(arg)` that is desugared during typechecking to `[T.methods.my_method] (obj,arg)`, where `T` is the static type of `obj`. The combination of these features allows many components such as polymorphic class systems to be implemented as libraries (shown later in section 6.3).

4.2 Engineering Design

A high-level language for prototyping. Lua provides automatic memory management, first-class functions, and built-in tables that make it easy to manage structures like ASTs and graphs, which are frequently used in DSL transformations. Its dynamic typing makes it easier to prototype different data structures and to construct arbitrary functions of Terra types and expressions.

A low-level language for performance. High-level programming languages can make it difficult to control when and what optimizations will take place. Auto-tuners and DSLs already capture the knowledge of how to generate high-performance code, so it is important to give them as much control as reasonable to express optimizations. We designed Terra to be a thin abstraction layer on modern processors. Terra provides much the same functionality as C including manual memory management, pointer arithmetic, and monomorphic functions. Global state, though not present in Terra Core, is possible in the full language using global variables created with the `global` function. Additionally, Terra includes fixed-length vectors of basic types (e.g., `vector(float,4)`) to reflect the presence of SIMD units on modern processors. Since the design of Terra is close to the hardware, users can more precisely express the execution behavior that they desire, and get predictable performance.

Cross-language interoperability using a foreign-function interface. In Terra Core, Lua can only pass base values to Terra functions and receive them as results. In the full language, when a Lua environment *is* available, we use LuaJIT's foreign function interface(FFI) [1] to translate values between Lua and Terra both along function call boundaries and during specialization. The similarity of Terra's type system to C's enables us to adapt the FFI to work with Terra. In addition to base types, it supports conversion of higher-level objects. For instance, Lua tables can be converted into structs when they contain the required fields. Lua functions can also be converted into Terra functions by generating wrapper code to dynamically convert the types on entry and exit. Since conversions are defined for Lua functions, calling a Lua function from Terra code is just a special case of converting a Lua value into a Terra value during specialization.

Backwards compatible with C. We believe that the lack of interoperability with existing code is a key factor limiting the adoption of DSLs. Terra can call C functions, making it possible to use existing high-performance libraries in the implementation of runtimes, and produce code that is binary compatible with C programs. Since Lua is easily embedded in C programs, it is easy to incorporate a mixed Lua-Terra program into existing C code. Since most languages have interfaces for calling C functions, this design makes it possible to use Terra in existing systems.

5. Implementation

Terra expressions are an extension of the Lua language. We use LuaJIT [1], an implementation of Lua that includes a trace-based JIT compiler. Lua itself is implemented as a library in C, with calls to initialize the runtime, load Lua programs, and evaluate them. We add additional functions to this library to load combined Lua-Terra programs. This process is implemented as a preprocessor that parses the combined Lua-Terra text. This design allows us to implement Terra without having to modify the LuaJIT implementation. The preprocessor parses the text, building an AST for each Terra function. It then replaces the Terra function text with a call to specialize the Terra function in the local environment. This constructor takes as arguments the parsed AST, as well as a Lua closure that captures the local lexical environment. When this code is executed, it will call into an internal library that actually constructs and returns the specialized Terra function. The preprocessed code is then passed to the Lua interpreter to load.

Terra code is compiled when a Terra function is typechecked the first time it is run. We use LLVM [17] to compile Terra code since it can JIT-compile its intermediate representation directly to machine code. To implement backwards compatibility with C, we use Clang, a C front-end that is part of LLVM. Clang is used to compile the C code into LLVM and generate Terra function wrappers that will invoke the C code when called.

6. Evaluation

To evaluate Terra, we use it to reimplement a number of multi-language applications and compare our implementations with existing approaches. We present evidence that the design decisions of Terra make the implementations simpler to engineer compared to existing implementations while achieving high performance. First, we evaluate an auto-tuner for BLAS and a DSL for stencil computations. Next, we show a high-performance class system and container with programmable data layout that can be JIT compiled. Each would be difficult to implement in a single existing language.

6.1 Tuning DGEMM

BLAS routines like double-precision matrix multiply (DGEMM) are used in a wide range of applications and form a basis for many of the algorithms used in high-performance scientific computing. However, their performance is dependent on characteristics of the machine such as cache sizes, vector length, or number of floating-point machine registers. In our tests, a naïve DGEMM can run over 65 times slower than the best-tuned algorithm.

```
function genkernel(NB, RM, RN, V,alpha)
  local vector_type = vector(double,V)
  local vector_pointer = &vector_type
  local A,B,C = symbol("A"),symbol("B"),symbol("C")
  local mm,nn = symbol("mn"),symbol("nn")
  local lda,ldb,ldc = symbol("lda"),symbol("ldb"),symbol("ldc")
  local a,b = symmat("a",RM), symmat("b",RN)
  local c,caddr = symmat("c",RM,RN), symmat("caddr",RM,RN)
  local k = symbol("k")
  local loadc,storec = terralib.newlist(),terralib.newlist()
  for m = 0, RM-1 do for n = 0, RN-1 do
    loadc:insert(quote
      var [caddr[m][n]] = C + m*ldc + n*V
      var [c[m][n]] =
        alpha * @vector_pointer([caddr[m][n]])
    end)
    storec:insert(quote
      @vector_pointer([caddr[m][n]]) = [c[m][n]]
    end)
  end end
  local calcc = terralib.newlist()
  for n = 0, RN-1 do
    calcc:insert(quote
      var [b[n]] = @vector_pointer(&B[n*V])
    end)
  end
  for m = 0, RM-1 do
    calcc:insert(quote
      var [a[m]] = vector_type(A[m*lda])
    end)
  end
  for m = 0, RM-1 do for n = 0, RN-1 do
    calcc:insert(quote
      [c[m][n]] = [c[m][n]] + [a[m]] * [b[n]]
    end)
  end end
  return terra([A] : &double, [B] : &double, [C] : &double,
               [lda] : int64,[ldb] : int64,[ldc] : int64)
    for [mm] = 0, NB, RM do
      for [nn] = 0, NB, RN*V do
        [loadc];
        for [k] = 0, NB do
          prefetch(B + 4*ldb,0,3,1);
          [calcc];
          B,A = B + ldb,A + 1
        end
        [storec];
        A,B,C = A - NB,B - ldb*NB + RN*V,C + RN*V
      end
      A,B,C = A + lda*RM, B - NB, C + RM * ldb - NB
end end end
```

Figure 5. Parameterized Terra code that generates a matrix-multiply kernel optimized to fit in L1.

The ATLAS project [33] was created to maintain high performance BLAS routines via auto-tuning. To demonstrate Terra's usefulness in auto-tuning high-performance code, we implemented a version of matrix multiply, the building block of level-3 BLAS routines. We restrict ourselves to the case $C = AB$, with both A and B stored non-transposed, and base our optimizations on those of ATLAS [33]. ATLAS breaks down a matrix multiply into smaller operations where the matrices fit into L1 cache. An optimized kernel for L1-sized multiplies is used for each operation. Tuning DGEMM involves choosing good block sizes, and generating optimized code for the L1-sized kernel. We found that a simple two-level blocking scheme worked well. To generate the L1-sized kernel, we use staging to implement several optimizations. We implement register-blocking of the inner-most loops, where a block of the output ma-

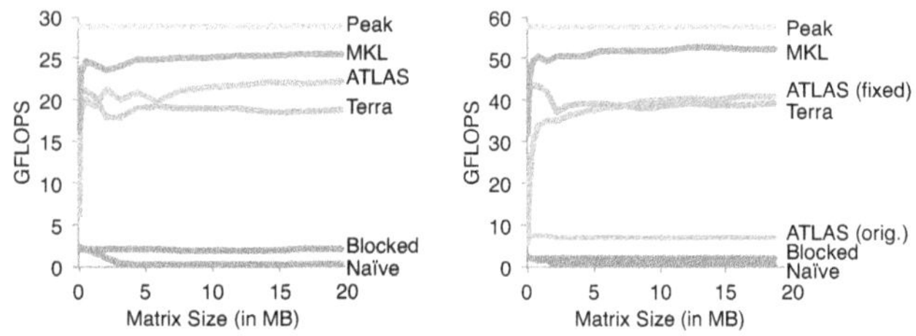

(a) DGEMM Performance (b) SGEMM Performance

Figure 6. Performance of matrix multiply using different libraries as a function of matrix size. Size reported is the total footprint for both input and output matrices. All matrices are square.

trix is stored in machine registers; we vectorize this inner-most loop using vector types; and we use prefetch intrinsics to optimize non-contiguous reads from memory.

The code that implements our L1-sized kernel is shown in Figure 5. It is parameterized by the blocksize (`NB`), the amount of the register blocking in 2 dimensions (`RM` and `RN`), the vector size (`V`), and a constant (`alpha`) which parameterizes the multiply operation, `C = alpha*C + A*B`. When generating code with a parameterizable number of variables (e.g., for register blocking) it is sometimes useful to selectively violate hygiene. Terra provides the function `symbol`, equivalent to LISP's `gensym`, which generates a globally unique identifier that can be used to define and refer to a variable that will not be renamed. We use it on lines 4–9 to generate the intermediate variables for our computation (`symmat` generates a matrix of symbols). On lines 10–20, we generate the code to load the values of `C` into registers (`loadc`), and the code to store them back to memory (`storec`). Lines 21–31 load the `A` and `B` matrices, and lines 32–36 generate the unrolled code to perform the outer product(`calcc`). We compose these pieces into the L1-sized matrix multiply function (lines 37–51). The full matrix-multiply routine (not shown) calls the L1-sized kernel for each block of the multiply.

In Lua, we wrote an auto-tuner that searches over reasonable values for the parameters (`NB`, `V`, `RA`, `RB`), JIT-compiles the code, runs it on a user-provided test case, and choses the best-performing configuration. Our implementation is around 200 lines of code.

We evaluate the performance by comparing to ATLAS and Intel's MKL on a single core of an Intel Core i7-3720QM. ATLAS 3.10 was compiled with GCC 4.8. Figure 6 shows the results for both double- and single- precision. For DGEMM, the naïve algorithm performs poorly. While blocking the algorithm does improve its performance for large matrices, it runs at less than 7% of theoretical peak GFLOPs for this processor. In contrast, Terra performs within 20% of the ATLAS routine, over 60% of peak GFLOPs of the core, and over 65 times faster than the naïve unblocked code. The difference between Terra and ATLAS is likely caused by a register spill in Terra's generated code that is avoided in ATLAS's generated assembly. Terra is also competitive with Intel's MKL, which is considered state-of-the-art. For SGEMM, Terra outperforms the unmodified ATLAS code by a factor of 5 because ATLAS incurs a transition penalty from mixing SSE and AVX instructions. Once this performance bug is fixed, ATLAS performs similarly to Terra.

ATLAS is built using Makefiles, C, and assembly programs generated with a custom preprocessor. The Makefiles orchestrate the creation and compilation of the code with different parameters. Code generation is accomplished through a combination of preprocessors and cross-compilation written in C. Auto-tuning is performed using a C harness for timing. Different stages communicate through the file system.

The design of Terra allows all of these tasks to be accomplished in one system and as a single process. Terra provides low-level features like vectors and prefetch instructions needed for high-

```
void diffuse(int N, int b, float* x, float* x0, float* tmp,
             float diff, float dt ){
  int i, j, k; float a=dt*diff*N*N;
  for (k = 0; k<= iter; k++){
    for (j = 1; j <= N; j++)
      for (i = 1; i <= N; i++)
        tmp[IX(i,j)] = (x0[IX(i,j)] + a*(x[IX(i-1,j)]+
          x[IX(i+1,j)]+x[IX(i,j-1)]+x[IX(i,j+1)]))/(1+4*a);
    SWAP(x,tmp);
  }
}
```

```
function diffuse ( x, x0, diff, dt )
  local a=dt*diff*N*N
  for k=0,iter do
    x = (x0+a*(x(-1,0)+x(1,0)+x(0,-1)+x(0,1)))/(1+4*a)
  end
  return x,x0
end
```

Figure 7. A kernel from a real-time fluid solver written in C (top) compared to Orion (bottom).

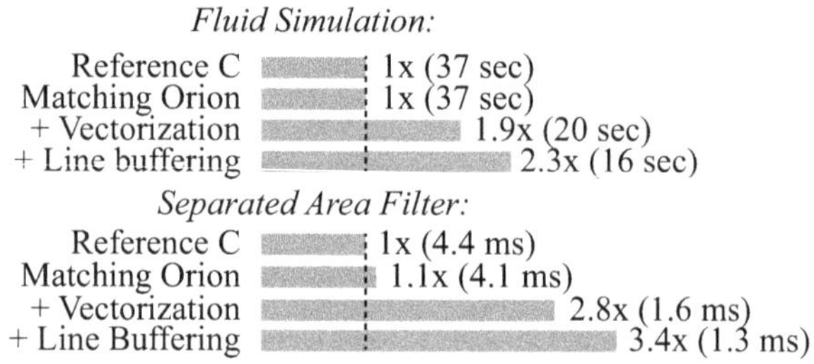

Figure 8. Speedup from choosing different Orion schedules. All results on Intel Core i7-3720QM, 1024x1024 floating point pixels.

performance. In contrast, ATLAS needed to target x86 directly, which resulted in a performance bug in SGEMM. Staging annotations made it easy to write parameterized optimizations like register unrolling without requiring a separate preprocessor. Interoperability through the FFI made it possible to generate and evaluate the kernels in the same framework. Finally, since Terra code can run without Lua, the resulting multiply routine can be written out as a library and used in other programs; or, for portable performance, it can be shipped with the Lua runtime and auto-tuning can be performed dynamically, something that is not possible with ATLAS.

6.2 Orion: A Stencil DSL for Images

To test Terra's suitability for DSL development, we created Orion, a DSL for 2D stencil computations on images. Stencil computations are grid-based kernels in which each value in the grid is dependent on a small local neighborhood. They are used in image processing and simulation. They present a number of opportunities for optimization, but implemented like the C code in Figure 7, it is difficult to exploit the performance opportunities. For example, fusing two iterations of the outer loop in `diffuse` may reduce memory traffic, but testing this hypothesis can require significant code changes. Figure 7 shows the same `diffuse` operation written in Orion. Rather than specify loop nests directly, Orion programs are written using image-wide operators. For instance, `f(-1,0) + f(0,1)` adds the image `f` translated by -1 in x to `f` translated by 1 in y. The offsets must be constants, which guarantees the function is a stencil.

We base our design on Halide [24], a language for the related domain of image processing. The user guides optimization by specifying a *schedule*. An Orion expression can be *materialized*, *inlined*, or *line buffered*. Materialized expressions are computed once and stored to main memory. Inlined expressions are recomputed once for each output pixel. Line buffering is a compromise in which computations are interleaved and the necessary intermediates are stored in a scratchpad. Additionally, Orion can vectorize any schedule using Terra's vector instructions. Being able to easily change the schedule is a powerful abstraction. To demonstrate this, we implemented a pipeline of four simple memory-bound point-wise image processing kernels (blacklevel offset, brightness, clamp, and invert). In a traditional image processing library, these functions would likely be written separately so they could be composed in an arbitrary order. In Orion, the schedule can be changed independently of the algorithm. For example, we can choose to inline the four functions, reducing the accesses to main memory by a factor of 4 and resulting in a 3.8x speedup.

To implement Orion, we use operator overloading on Lua tables to build Orion expressions. These operators build an intermediate representation (IR) suitable for optimization. The user calls `orion.compile` to compile the IR into a Terra function. We then use Terra's staging annotations to generate the code for the inner loop.

To test that the code generated by Terra performs well, we implemented an area filter and a fluid simulation. We compare each to equivalents hand-written in C. The area filter is a common image processing operation that averages the pixels in a 5x5 window. Area filtering is separable, so it is normally implemented as a 1-D area filter first in Y then in X. We compare against a hand-written C implementation with results in Figure 8. Given a schedule that matches the C code, Orion performs similarly, running 10% faster. Enabling vectorization in Orion yields a 2.8x speedup over C, and then line buffering between the passes in Y and X yields a 3.4x speedup. Explicit vectors are not part of standard C, and writing line-buffering code is tedious and breaks composability, so these optimizations are not normally done when writing code by hand.

We also implemented a simple real-time 2D fluid simulation based on an existing C implementation [26]. We made small modifications to the reference code to make it suitable to a stencil language. We converted the solver from Gauss-Seidel to Gauss-Jacobi so that images are not modified in place and use a zero boundary condition since our implementation does not yet support more complicated boundaries. We also corrected a performance bug in the code caused by looping over images in row-major order that were stored in column-major order. We compare against the corrected version. With a matching schedule, Orion performs the same as reference C. Enabling 4-wide vectorization results in a 1.9x speedup over the matching code, making each materialized operation memory bound. Finally, line buffering pairs of the iterations of the diffuse and project kernels yielded a 1.25x speedup on the vectorized code, or a 2.3x total speedup over the reference C code.

A number of features of Terra facilitated the implementation of Orion. High-level features of Lua made it easy to express transformations on the Orion IR. Terra's built-in support of vector types made it easy to vectorize the compiler by simply changing scalar types into vectors. Backwards compatibility with C allowed us to link to an existing library for loading images. The FFI made it possible to use Lua to implement non-performance-critical code such as the kernel scheduler, saving development time. Furthermore, the fluid simulation that we ported included a semi-Lagrangian advection step, which is not a stencil computation. In this case, we were able to allow the user to pass a Terra function to do the necessary computation, and easily integrate this code with generated Terra code. This interoperability would have been more difficult to accomplish with a stand-alone compiler.

In contrast to Orion, Halide, a related image processing language, requires three different languages to provide the same functionality as Orion. It uses C++ for the front-end, ML for manipulating the IR, and LLVM for code generation [24]. From our experience implementing Orion, using Lua to stage Terra code accomplishes the same tasks, but results in a simpler architecture.

6.3 Building reuseable components via type reflection

Type reflection makes it possible to define the behavior and layout of types at a low-level. First, we show the flexibility of Terra's type reflection by using it to implement a class system with subtyping. Then we show how it can be applied specifically to building runtimes for high-performance computing by implementing a type constructor that can automatically generate a data table with either array-of-structs or struct-of-arrays layout.

6.3.1 Class Systems

Using type-reflection, we can implement a single-inheritance class system with multiple subtyping of interfaces similar to Java's. We specify classes using an interface implemented in Lua:

```
J = terralib.require("lib/javalike")
Drawable = J.interface { draw = {} -> {} }
struct Square { length : int; }
J.extends(Square,Shape)
J.implements(Square,Drawable)
terra Square:draw() : {} ... end
```

The function `interface` creates a new interface given a table of method names and types. The functions `J.extends` and `J.implements` install metamethods on the `Square` type that will implement the behavior of the class system.

Our implementation, based on vtables, uses the subset of Stroustrup's multiple inheritance [27] that is needed to implement single inheritance with multiple interfaces. For each class, we define a `__finalizelayout` metamethod. This metamethod is called by the Terra typechecker right before a type is examined, allowing it to compute the layout of the type at the latest possible time. For our class system, this metamethod is responsible for calculating the concrete layout of the class, creating the class's vtable, and creating vtables for any interface that the class implements. If the user specified a parent class using `J.extends`, then the class and its vtables are organized such that the beginning of each object has the same layout as an object of the parent, making it safe to cast a pointer to the class to a pointer to the parent. If the user specified an interface using `J.implements` then we create a vtable that implements the interface, and insert a pointer to the vtable in the layout of the class. Finally, for each method defined on `class`, we create a stub method to invoke the real method through the class's vtable:

```
for methodname,fn in pairs(concretemethods) do
  local fntype = fn:gettype()
  local params = fntype.parameters:map(symbol)
  local self = params[1]
  class.methods[methodname] =
    terra([params]) : fntyp.returns
      return self.__vtable.[methodname]([params])
    end
end
```

At this point, child classes can access the methods and members of a parent class, but the Terra compiler will not allow the conversion from a child to its parent or to an interface. To enable conversions, we create a user-defined conversion that reflects the subtyping relations of our class system (e.g., `&Square <: &Shape`). We implement the conversion generically by defining a `__cast` metamethod:

```
class.metamethods.__cast = function(from,to,exp)
  if from:ispointer() and to:ispointer() then
    if issubclass(from.type,to.type) then
      return `[to](exp) --cast expression to 'to' type
    elseif implementsinterface(from.type,to.type) then
      local imd = interfacemetadata[to.type]
      return `&exp.[imd.name] --extract subobject
  end end
  error("not a subtype")
end
```

Since the beginning of a child class has the same layout as its parent, we can convert a child into a parent by simply casting the object's pointer to the parent's type (`[to](exp)`). Converting an object to one of its interfaces requires selecting the subobject that holds the pointer to the interface's vtable (`&exp.[imd.name]`). The stubs generated for the interface restore the object's pointer to the original object before invoking the concrete method implementation.

We measured the overhead of function invocation in our implementation using a micro-benchmark, and found it performed within 1% of analogous C++ code. The implementation requires only 250 lines of Terra code to provide much of the functionality of Java's class system. Users are not limited to using any particular class system or implementation. For instance, we have also implemented a system that implements interfaces using fat pointers that store both the object pointer and vtable together.

6.3.2 Data Layout

Terra's type reflection should help programmers build reusable components in high-performance runtimes. One common problem in high-performance computing is choosing between storing records as an array of structs (AoS, all fields of a record stored contiguously), or as a struct of arrays (SoA, individual fields stored contiguously). We implement a solution to this problem, and contrast it with existing languages.

Changing the layout can substantially improve performance. We implemented two micro-benchmarks based on mesh processing. Each vertex of the mesh stores its position, and the vector normal to the surface at that position. The first benchmark calculates the vector normal as the average normal of the faces incident to the vertex. The second simply performs a translation on the position of every vertex. Figure 9 shows the performance using both AoS and SoA form. Calculating vertex normals is 55% faster using AoS form. For each triangle in the mesh, positions of its vertices are gathered, and the normals are updated. Since this access is sparse, there is little temporal locality in vertex access. AoS form performs better in this case since it exploits spatial locality of the vertex data — all elements of the vertex are accessed together. In contrast, translating vertex positions is 43% faster using SoA form. In this case, the vertices are accessed sequentially, but the normals are not needed. In AoS form these normals share the same cache-lines as the positions, and memory bandwidth is wasted loading them.

To facilitate the process of choosing a data layout in Terra, we implemented a function that can generate either version, but presents the same interface. A Lua function `DataTable` takes a Lua table specifying the fields of the record and how to store them (AoS or SoA), returning a new Terra type. For example, a fluid simulation might store several fields in a cell:

```
FluidData = DataTable({ vx = float, vy = float,
            pressure = float, density = float },"AoS")
```

The `FluidData` type provides methods to access a row (e.g., `fd:row(i)`). Each row can access its fields (e.g., `r:setx(1.f)`, `r:x()`). The interface abstracts the layout of the data, so it can be changed just by replacing `"AoS"` with `"SoA"`.

This behavior can be emulated ahead-of-time in low-level languages, for example using X-Macros [19] in C, or template meta-programming in C++, but unlike Terra cannot be generated dynamically based on runtime feedback. Dynamic languages such as Javascript support this ad hoc creation of data types dynamically but do not provide the same low-level of control.

Benchmark	Array-of-Structs	Struct-of-Arrays
Calc. vertex normals	3.42 GB/s	2.20 GB/s
Translate positions	9.90 GB/s	14.2 GB/s

Figure 9. Performance of mesh transformations using different data layouts.

7. Related Work

Much work on multi-stage programming has focused on homogeneous meta-programming [22, 29, 30]. MetaML [30] and MetaOCaml [29] add staging annotations to ML. Staged code is lexically scoped, and a type system ensures that the annotations can only produce well-typed programs. MetaHaskell is an extension of Haskell for heterogeneous meta-programming that supports embedding new object languages while ensuring that the staging is type-safe [18]. Unlike Terra, the object languages implemented in MetaHaskell do not share Haskell's lexical environment and are currently unhygienic. Eckhardt et al. propose implicit heterogeneous programming in OCaml with a translation into C [10] but the type language is limited to basic types and arrays. In contrast to statically-typed approaches, Terra supports the creation of user-defined types using arbitrary code but precludes static typing of the full Lua-Terra program.

Heterogeneous multi-stage languages with shared lexical scope and different execution environments have occurred organically in the past [10, 32]. Separating compile-time and runtime-time environments has also been used to make macro expansion composable [11]. To our knowledge, we are the first to argue for these design choices as a way to generate portable high-performance code, retaining interoperability through an optional FFI.

Multi-stage programming has been used to generate high-performance programs [12, 23, 33]. Carette investigates staging of Gaussian elimination in MetaOCaml [5], while Cohen et al. investigate applying MetaOCaml to problems in high-performance computing like loop unrolling/tiling and pipelining [8]. This work has focused on using staging to improve the performance of specific problems. More generally, Chafi et al. use lightweight modular staging [25]—a type-directed staging approach that can be implemented as a library—to stage a subset of the Scala language. The staged code is used to implement DSLs in the Delite framework that can be translated to run on GPUs [4, 7]. Additionally, Intel's ArBB enables runtime generation of vector-style code using a combination of operator overloading and macros in C++ [21]. In contrast to Terra, ArBB and Delite do not have explicit staging annotations, instead relying on types to distinguish object-language expressions from meta-language ones. In practice we have found that this type-directed staging makes it difficult to know when code will execute.

The macro systems of Lisp and Scheme have also been used to build DSLs. In particular, Racket [31] provides an interface to the static semantics of the language using macros. Using this interface they implement a typed variant of Racket, as well as other DSLs. The macro system is used to translate typed Racket to standard Racket with a few extensions to support unchecked access to fields. Terra, by contrast, is implemented as a separate language from Lua, which allows for different design decisions in each (e.g., automatic memory management in Lua, manual management in Terra).

Previous work examined the combination of staging and type reflection for statically-typed languages. Template meta-programming in C++ is widely used and allows generation and introspection on types. Garcia and Lumsdaine describe a core calculus for compile-time meta-programming based on template meta-programming in C++ [13]. Similar to Terra, their semantics support code generation and type reflection, but like C++ they focus only on ahead-of-time code generation. F# allows type-providers which can specify types and methods based on external data like a SQL schema [28]. Metaphor is a multi-stage language with support for type reflection on a built-in class system [20]. In contrast, Terra's type reflection allows the creation of class-systems as libraries.

Dynamic languages have added extensions to produce low-level code. Cython is an extension to the Python language that allows the creation of C extensions while writing in Python's syntax [3]. Copperhead supplements Python with a vector-style language that can run on GPUs [6]. In both cases, the low-level code depends on the Python runtime to execute.

Other languages have been proposed as a portable target for low-level code [16, 17]. Terra is also usable directly as a low-level programming language, making it possible to write runtime code in Terra.

8. Discussion and Future Work

We have presented Terra, a staged language embedded in Lua and designed for high-performance computing. By comparing to existing multi-language systems, we have shown that the combination of high- and low-level languages, shared lexical environment, separate execution, and type reflection make designing autotuners, DSLs, and runtime components simpler, while retaining high-performance.

We plan to extend Terra in several ways. Accelerators like GPUs or Intel's MIC architecture provide more performance for data-parallel problems. We plan to extend our implementation so that Terra can generate code that runs on these architectures. Currently Terra does not provide a seamless way to mix Terra code compiled ahead-of-time with dynamically compiled code, which can be problematic for DSLs with a large runtime. We plan to address this with a module system that will allow some code to be generated ahead-of-time, while still allowing JIT compilation of code at runtime.

Terra addresses the problem of generating high-performance code and interoperating with existing applications. We want to generalize the way Terra is embedded and staged to make it easy to embed custom DSLs in Lua in the same way that Terra is embedded. In particular, we think that having DSLs share the same lexical environment during compilation will open up more opportunities for interoperability between different languages. In the future, we envision a programming ecosystem where the right language can be used for a particular task without loss of performance, or significant effort to integrate the language with existing systems.

Acknowledgments This work has been supported by the DOE Office of Science ASCR in the ExMatEx and ExaCT Exascale Co-Design Centers, program manager Karen Pao; DARPA Contract No. HR0011-11-C-0007; and the Stanford Pervasive Parallelism Lab (supported by Oracle, AMD, Intel, and NVIDIA). Any opinions, findings and conclusion or recommendations expressed in this material are those of the authors and do not necessarily reflect the views of DARPA. We thank our reviewers for suggesting improvements to specialization.

References

[1] The LuaJIT project. `http://http://luajit.org/`.

[2] A. Bawden and J. Rees. Syntactic closures. In *LFP*, 1988.

[3] S. Behnel, R. Bradshaw, C. Citro, L. Dalcin, D. S. Seljebotn, and K. Smith. Cython: The best of both worlds. *Computing in Science and Engineering*, 13.2:31–39, 2011.

[4] K. J. Brown, A. K. Sujeeth, H. J. Lee, T. Rompf, H. Chafi, M. Odersky, and K. Olukotun. A heterogeneous parallel framework for domain-specific languages. In *PACT*, 2011.

[5] J. Carette. Gaussian elimination: A case study in efficient genericity with MetaOCaml. *Sci. Comput. Program.*, 62(1):3–24, Sept. 2006.

[6] B. Catanzaro, M. Garland, and K. Keutzer. Copperhead: Compiling an embedded data parallel language. In *PPoPP*, 2011.

[7] H. Chafi, A. K. Sujeeth, K. J. Brown, H. Lee, A. R. Atreya, and K. Olukotun. A domain-specific approach to heterogeneous parallelism. In *PPoPP*, 2011.

[8] A. Cohen, S. Donadio, M. Garzaran, C. Herrmann, and D. Padua. In search of a program generator to implement generic transformations for high-performance computing. In *MetaOCaml Workshop*, 2004.

[9] Z. DeVito, N. Joubert, F. Palacios, S. Oakley, M. Medina, M. Barrientos, E. Elsen, F. Ham, A. Aiken, K. Duraisamy, E. Darve, J. Alonso, and P. Hanrahan. Liszt: A domain specific language for building portable mesh-based PDE solvers. In *SC*, 2011.

[10] J. Eckhardt, R. Kaiabachev, E. Pasalic, K. Swadi, and W. Taha. Implicitly heterogeneous multi-stage programming. *New Gen. Comput.*, 25(3):305–336, Jan. 2007.

[11] M. Flatt. Composable and compilable macros: You want it when? In *ICFP*, 2002.

[12] M. Frigo and S. Johnson. The design and implementation of FFTW3. *Proc. of the IEEE*, 93(2):216 –231, 2005.

[13] R. Garcia and A. Lumsdaine. Toward foundations for type-reflective metaprogramming. In *GPCE*, 2009.

[14] R. Ierusalimschy, L. H. de Figueiredo, and W. C. Filho. Lua - an extensible extension language. *Software: Practice and Experience*, 26 (6), 1996.

[15] R. Ierusalimschy, L. H. De Figueiredo, and W. Celes. Passing a language through the eye of a needle. *CACM*, 54(7):38–43, 2011.

[16] S. Jones, T. Nordin, and D. Oliva. C--: A portable assembly language. In *Workshop on Implementing Functional Languages*, 1997.

[17] C. Lattner and V. Adve. LLVM: A Compilation Framework for Lifelong Program Analysis & Transformation. In *CGO*, 2004.

[18] G. Mainland. Explicitly heterogeneous metaprogramming with metahaskell. In *ICFP*, 2012.

[19] R. Meyers. X macros. *C/C++ Users J.*, 19(5):52–56, May 2001.

[20] G. Neverov and P. Roe. Metaphor: A multi-staged, object-oriented programming language. In *GPCE*, 2004.

[21] C. Newburn, B. So, Z. Liu, M. McCool, A. Ghuloum, S. Toit, Z. G. Wang, Z. H. Du, Y. Chen, G. Wu, P. Guo, Z. Liu, and D. Zhang. Intel's Array Building Blocks: A retargetable, dynamic compiler and embedded language. In *CGO*, 2011.

[22] M. Poletto, W. C. Hsieh, D. R. Engler, and M. F. Kaashoek. C and tcc: A language and compiler for dynamic code generation. *TOPLAS*, 21 (2):1999.

[23] M. Püschel, J. M. F. Moura, B. Singer, J. Xiong, J. Johnson, D. Padua, M. Veloso, and R. W. Johnson. Spiral: A generator for platform-adapted libraries of signal processing algorithms. *Int. J. High Perform. Comput. Appl.*, 18(1):2004.

[24] J. Ragan-Kelley, A. Adams, S. Paris, M. Levoy, S. Amarasinghe, and F. Durand. Decoupling algorithms from schedules for easy optimization of image processing pipelines. In *SIGGRAPH*, 2012.

[25] T. Rompf and M. Odersky. Lightweight modular staging: A pragmatic approach to runtime code generation and compiled DSLs. In *GPCE*, 2010.

[26] J. Stam. Real-time fluid dynamics for games. In *GDC*, 2003.

[27] B. Stroustrup. Multiple inheritance for C++. In *European Unix Systems Users's Group Conference*, 1987.

[28] D. Syme, K. Battocchi, K. Takeda, D. Malayeri, J. Fisher, J. Hu, T. Liu, B. McNamara, D. Quirk, M. Taveggia, W. Chae, U. Matsveyeu, and T. Petricek. F#3.0 – Strongly-typed language support for internet-scale information sources. Technical report, 2012.

[29] W. Taha. A gentle introduction to multi-stage programming. In *Domain-Specific Program Generation*, 2004.

[30] W. Taha and T. Sheard. MetaML and multi-stage programming with explicit annotations. In *Theoretical Computer Science*, 1999.

[31] S. Tobin-Hochstadt, V. St-Amour, R. Culpepper, M. Flatt, and M. Felleisen. Languages as libraries. In *PLDI*, 2011.

[32] Z. Wan, W. Taha, and P. Hudak. Real-time FRP. In *ICFP*, 2001.

[33] R. C. Whaley and A. Petitet. Minimizing development and maintenance costs in supporting persistently optimized BLAS. *Softw. Pract. Exper.*, 35(2):101–121, 2005.

SMAT: An Input Adaptive Auto-Tuner for Sparse Matrix-Vector Multiplication

Jiajia Li[1,2], Guangming Tan[1], Mingyu Chen[1], Ninghui Sun[1]

[1]State Key Laboratory of Computer Architecture, Institute of Computing Technology, Chinese Academy of Sciences

[2]University of Chinese Academy of Sciences

{lijiajia, tgm, cmy, snh}@ict.ac.cn

Abstract

Sparse Matrix Vector multiplication (SpMV) is an important kernel in both traditional high performance computing and emerging data-intensive applications. By far, SpMV libraries are optimized by either application-specific or architecture-specific approaches, making the libraries become too complicated to be used extensively in real applications. In this work we develop a Sparse Matrix-vector multiplication Auto-Tuning system (SMAT) to bridge the gap between specific optimizations and general-purpose usage. SMAT provides users with a unified programming interface in compressed sparse row (CSR) format and automatically determines the optimal format and implementation for any input sparse matrix at runtime. For this purpose, SMAT leverages a learning model, which is generated in an off-line stage by a machine learning method with a training set of more than 2000 matrices from the UF sparse matrix collection, to quickly predict the best combination of the matrix feature parameters. Our experiments show that SMAT achieves impressive performance of up to 51GFLOPS in single-precision and 37GFLOPS in double-precision on mainstream x86 multi-core processors, which are both more than 3 times faster than the Intel MKL library. We also demonstrate its adaptability in an algebraic multigrid solver from Hypre library with above 20% performance improvement reported.

Categories and Subject Descriptors F.2.1 [*Numerical Algorithms and Problems*]: Computations on matrices; C.1.2 [*Multiple Data Stream Architectures (Multiprocessors)*]: Parallel processors

General Terms Algorithms, Performance

Keywords sparse matrix-vector multiplication, SpMV, auto-tuning, data mining, algebraic multi-grid

1. Introduction

Nowadays, high performance computing technologies are driven simultaneously by both Exascale FLOPs (ExaFlops) and data-intensive applications. Although the grand challenges of these applications are diverse, an interesting observation is that they share an intersection in terms of sparse linear system solvers. For example, the well-known ExaFlops applications, laser fusion in international thermonuclear experimental reactor (ITER) [3] and global cloud system resolving climate modeling [20], spend most of the execution time on solving large-scale sparse linear systems. Similarly, lots of large-scale graph analysis applications like PageRank [9] and HITS [26] involve sparse matrix solvers in identifying relationships. All of these algorithms rely on a core Sparse Matrix Vector multiplication (SpMV) kernel consuming a large percentage of their overall execution time. For example, the algebraic multigrid (AMG) solver [13], an iterative algorithm widely used in both laser fusion and climate modeling, reports above 90% SpMV operation of its overall iterations.

Since 1970s, plenty of researches have been dedicated to optimizing SpMV performance for its fundamental importance, which are generally separated into two paths, one for developing new application-specific storage formats [7, 21, 29–32, 36], and the other for tuning on emerging processor architectures [10, 11, 16, 22, 27, 28, 34, 35]. This separation leads to low performance and low productivity in SpMV solvers and applications:

- *Low Performance: sparse solvers are not aware of the diversity of input sparse matrices.*
  It is well-known that for a specific sparse matrix SpMV performance is sensitive to storage formats. More than ten formats have been developed during the last four decades. However, most of them show good performance only for a few specific applications, and are rarely adopted in widely used numeric solvers such as Hypre [14], PETSc [6], Trilinos [18] etc. In fact, these solvers mainly support one popular storage format CSR (compressed sparse row, explained in Section 2.1). Thus, they usually perform poorly in some applications whose sparse matrices are not appropriate for the supported CSR format. Besides, even considering only one application, patterns of sparse matrices may change at runtime. Take AMG as an example again, it generates a series of different sparse matrices by the coarsen algorithm on successive grid levels. Figure 1 illustrates an example of the need for dynamic storage formats in Hypre AMG solver. At the first few levels, SpMVs desire DIA or COO format (see Section 2.1) for the optimal performance. While at the coarser-level grids, other formats like CSR may be more desirable due to high zero-filling ratio in DIA format. Therefore, a numerical solver should be adaptive to different sparse matrix formats for achieving better performance.
- *Low Productivity: sparse libraries provide multiple interfaces to users*
  An alternative solution to the above low performance issue is to rewrite these solvers for every storage format. Unfortunately, such changes are too time-consuming for legacy software. An easier option may be to provide an SpMV library, which can automatically adapt to various sparse matrix formats for

PLDI'13, June 16–19, 2013, Seattle, WA, USA.

numerical solvers and real applications. However, none of the available sparse libraries accommodate us with a consistent programming interface to replace the original SpMV kernels. All these libraries including Intel MKL [1] and OSKI [31] provide different interfaces for every format supported, which leaves the burden of determining and integrating the optimal format to application programmers. As a consequence, although these libraries are highly optimized by either hand-tuning or auto-tuning techniques [4, 5, 7, 8, 10, 11, 17, 21, 29, 31, 35, 36] with processor architectures evolving, it is still difficult to integrate them into high level solvers or applications. This fact results in an embarrassing situation: on one hand, there are several high performance sparse libraries available; on the other hand, solver or application developers seldom use them in practice.

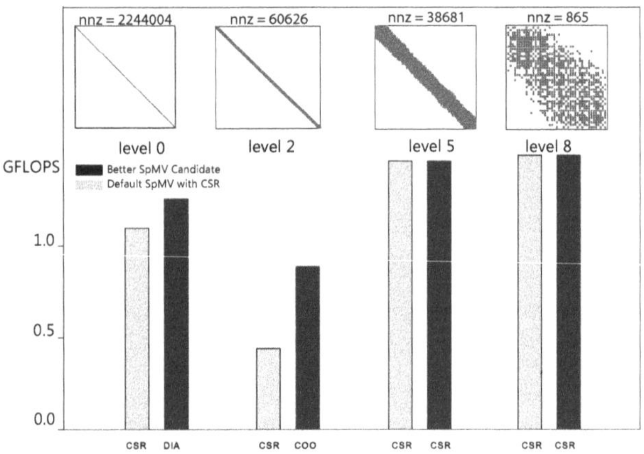

Figure 1. An example of dynamic sparse matrix structures in AMG solver and their SpMV performance using different formats. The *nnz* represents the number of nonzero elements in matrices.

In this paper we propose a novel Sparse Matrix-vector multiplication Auto-Tuner (SMAT) to provide both application- and architecture-aware SpMV kernels. A distinct feature of SMAT is the unified programming interface for different storage formats. Based on a comprehensive investigation (in Section 2) that shows CSR performs the best for most sparse matrices, we define the unified interface as CSR format. In this way users only need to prepare their sparse matrices in CSR format as the input, and SMAT automatically determines the optimal storage format and implementation on a given architecture. Our auto-tuning approach takes advantage of a black-box machine learning model to train representative performance parameters extracted from the sparse matrix pattern and architectural configuration. Once the model is trained on the target architecture, SMAT evaluates candidate storage formats and determines the optimal format and implementation by leveraging either existing auto-tuning work [11, 17, 21, 29, 31, 35, 36] or available hand-tuned codes.

Apart from the conventional auto-tuning techniques considering architectural parameters, the novelty of SMAT system is *cooperatively auto-tuning between algorithms and architectures.* In other words, SMAT searches for the optimal storage format based on sparse matrix structures at the algorithm level while generating the optimal implementation based on the processor architecture. Though auto-tuning techniques for optimizing libraries and applications have been explored for a long time, the originality of our work lies in an input adaptive mechanism that identifies characteristics of both applications and architectures. Besides, the main contributions of this paper are:

- We enable reusable training by adopting more than 2000 sparse matrices from real applications and systematically sampling the parameter space, including sparse structure characteristics and architecture configuration.
- We propose a unified interface on top of SpMV kernels to avoid the tedious work of manually choosing among sparse storage formats. SMAT facilitates users to adopt the tuned library for improving performance with little extra programming effort.
- We develop a flexible and extension-free framework, with which users can add not only new formats and novel implementations in terms of their needs, but also more features and larger datasets.

We implement SMAT and train it using sparse matrix collection from the university of Florida [12] on two x86 multi-core processors, Intel Xeon X5680 and AMD Opteron 6168. With sparse matrices selected from various application areas, SpMV kernels generated by SMAT achieve impressive performance of up to 51GFLOPS in single-precision (SP) and 37GFLOPS in double-precision (DP). The improvement of SMAT over Intel MKL is more than 3.2 times on average. We also evaluate the adaptability of SMAT in AMG algorithm of sparse solver Hypre [14], and the results show above 20% performance improvement.

The rest of the paper is organized as follows. Section 2 presents several storage formats of sparse matrices and our motivation. In Section 3 we propose an overview of SMAT system. Then the three important contributions are described in the following sections. Section 4 shows the parameter extraction process to build the feature database. After that, we illustrate the machine learning and kernel searching process in Section 5, and the runtime procedure in Section 6. We give the performance results on representative sparse matrices and a real application in Section 7, as well as analyze the accuracy and overhead of SMAT. Related work is presented in Section 8, and conclusion in Section 9.

2. Background

2.1 Sparse Matrix Storage Format

In order to reduce the complexity of both space and computation, a compressed data structure is commonly used to only store nonzero elements of a sparse matrix. Since sparse structure is closely related to compression effectiveness and SpMV behavior on specific processor architectures (i.e.,vector machine, cache, etc.), more than ten compressed data structures (i.e. formats) have been developed since 1970s. However, most of them were customized only for certain special cases. By far four basic storage formats CSR, DIA, ELL, COO are extensively used in mainstream applications, from which most other formats can be derived. For example, when there exist many dense sub-blocks in a sparse matrix, the corresponding blocking variants (i.e. BCSR, BDIA, etc.) may perform better if an appropriate blocking factor is selected. Here, COO is specially noted because it usually performs better in large scale graph analysis applications [36]. In this proof-of-concept work, we start from the four basic formats and make it possible to extend for supporting other formats in our auto-tuning system.

Figure 2 illustrates a sparse matrix example represented in the four basic formats respectively. CSR (Compressed Sparse Row) format contains three arrays: "data" stores nonzero elements of the sparse matrix, "indices" stores their corresponding column indices, and the beginning positions of each row are stored in "ptr". COO (COOrdinate) format explicitly stores the row indices. The "rows", "cols" and "data" arrays store the row indices, the column indices, and the values of all nonzero elements respectively. DIA (Diagonal) format stores non-zeros by the order of diagonals. "data" array stores the dense diagonals, and "offsets" records the offsets of each diagonal to the principal one. The idea of the ELL (ELLPACK) format is to pack all non-zeros towards left, and store the packed dense matrix. "data" array stores this dense matrix, and "indices" stores the corresponding column indices. Please refer to [25] for more detailed illustration. The corresponding basic implementations of the four formats are also presented in Figure 2.

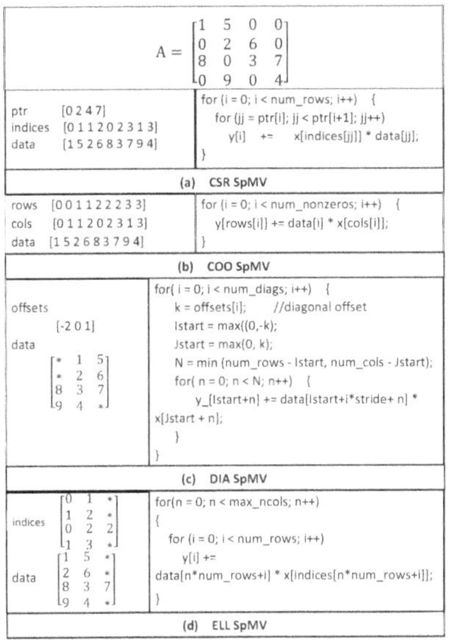

Figure 2. Data structures and basic SpMV implementations

2.2 Motivation

Although it is a common sense to store sparse matrices in a proper format, it is non-trivial to figure out how to automatically select the combination of appropriate storage format and its optimal implementation on a specific architecture. A distinct difference is that previous auto-tuning techniques [11, 17, 21, 29, 31, 35, 36] only take architectural impact into account while the storage format is predefined by users. Actually, it is really a challenging job because sufficient performance characteristics must be extracted from diverse sparse matrices and then used to quickly determine the optimal format and implementation.

For extracting characteristics and showing potential benefits from tuning storage format based on sparse structures, we conduct comprehensive experiments on the UF collection [12], which consists of more than 2000 sparse matrices from real applications covering extensive application areas. For simplicity without loss of accuracy, we exclude the matrices with complex values and too small size, and eventually studied 2386 sparse matrices in total in this work. Table 1 lists their application areas spread in more than 20 domains.

Table 1 also summarizes the distribution of the optimal storage formats for all 2386 sparse matrices. Column 2 – 5 represent the number of sparse matrices that have affinity with CSR, COO, DIA, and ELL formats, respectively. The last row calculates the proportion of the matrices have affinity with each format to the whole matrix set respectively. Apparently, CSR is favored by most sparse matrices. Furthermore, for highlighting performance variance and plotting legible graphs, we select 16 representatives from the 2386 matrices and compare the performance in GFLOPS among the four storage formats without meticulous implementations. As shown in Figure 3 the largest performance gap is about 6 times. The reasons for the variance will be explained in Section 4. Obviously it is not reasonable to apply only one storage format in sparse numeric solvers.

Given a specific format, there are already well-studied auto-tuning tools or libraries [11, 17, 21, 29, 31, 35, 36], which can be leveraged to generate the optimal SpMV implementation on a specific platform. If the matrix structure stays the same during the whole lifetime of an application, even a brute-force search algorithm might be reasonable to generate the best candidate. As noted in Section 1, certain applications like AMG dynamically change sparse matrix structures (see Figure 1). Therefore, two key issues will be addressed in this paper: (i). *determine the optimal storage format for any input sparse matrix*; (ii). *generate the optimal combination of format and implementation at runtime with low overhead.*

Table 1. Application and distribution of affinity to each format

Application Domains	CSR	COO	DIA	ELL	Total
graph	187	114	6	27	334
linear programming	267	52	3	5	327
structural	224	14	35	4	277
combinatorial	122	50	10	84	266
circuit simulation	110	149	0	1	260
computational fluid dynamics	110	8	47	3	168
optimization	113	15	8	2	138
2D_3D	64	21	19	17	121
economic	67	4	0	0	71
chemical process simulation	47	14	2	1	64
power network	45	15	0	1	61
model reduction	29	34	6	1	60
theoretical quantum chemistry	21	0	26	0	47
electromagnetics	17	1	12	3	33
semiconductor device	28	1	3	1	33
thermal	19	3	3	4	29
materials	12	3	11	0	26
least squares	10	2	0	9	21
computer graphics vision	8	1	1	2	12
statistical mathematical	2	1	3	4	10
counter-example	3	4	1	0	8
acoustics	5	0	2	0	7
robotics	3	0	0	0	3
Percentage	63%	21%	9%	7%	2386

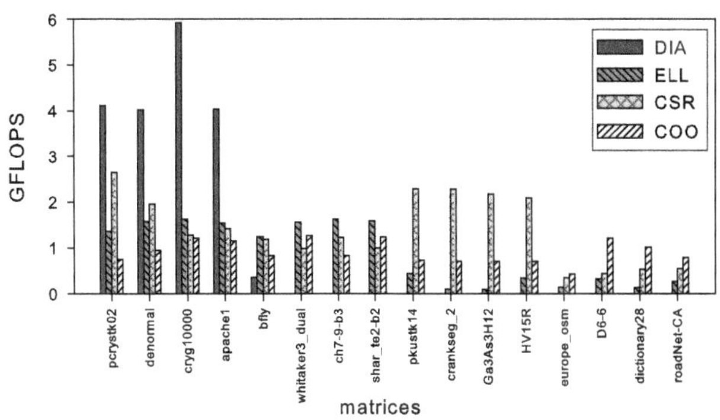

Figure 3. Performance variance among different storage formats for 16 representative matrices.

3. SMAT Overview

We develop SpMV Auto-Tuner (SMAT) to choose the optimal storage format and implementation of SpMV, whose framework is shown in Figure 4. We consider both architecture parameters (such as TLB size, cache and register size, prefetch, threading policy, etc., details in [35]) and application parameters (such as matrix dimension, diagonal situation, nonzero distribution, etc., to be described in Section 4) to optimize an SpMV kernel and evaluate its performance on sparse matrices from different applications. The large parameter space makes it difficult to find the most suitable sparse matrix format and optimization method on a specific architecture. For this reason, we generate a learning model using data mining to find the optimal result.

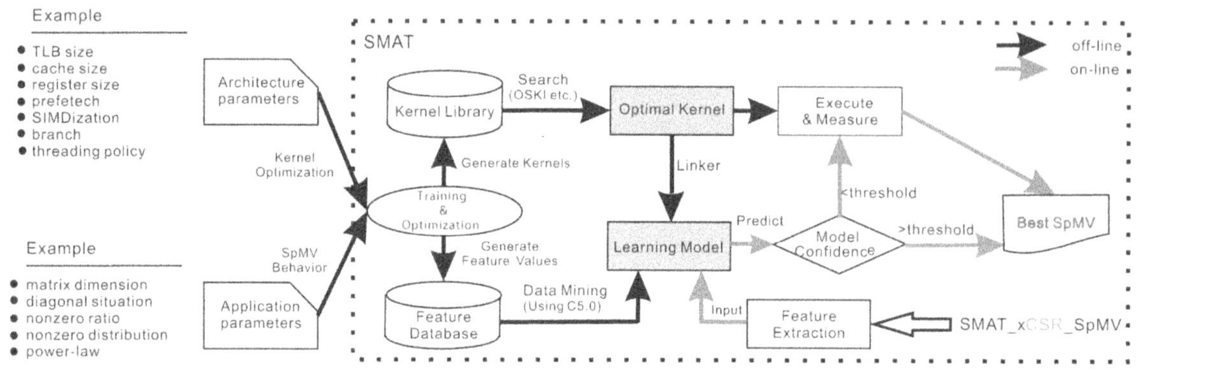

Figure 4. SMAT architecture

Since each sparse matrix has different SpMV behaviors, we train the corresponding parameter values using UF collection to generate a feature record for each matrix. Data mining is used to generate a learning model from the feature database. Besides, since a variety of kernel optimization methods consider architecture parameters (like cache blocking, register blocking, parallelization, etc.), a large kernel library is built. The optimal kernel implementation is searched based on particular architecture characteristics. Thus, a learning model, which combines application features and architecture characteristics together, is built to generate high performance kernels quickly.

Given a sparse matrix in the most popular CSR format, SMAT extracts its sparse features first. The feature values are used to predict the optimal format and implementation of SpMV. However, there are still some cases that the learning model may fail to make the right prediction. A confidence factor is added to rule the model. When the confidence factor is larger than the threshold, we determine the optimal SpMV format with the optimal implementation through the model. Otherwise, an execution-measure process is triggered to benchmark available candidates and outputs the one with the highest performance. In this way, users do not need to think about which format and implementation should be chosen. All they need to do is to input the sparse matrix in CSR format and then SMAT will give the optimal answer. Figure 5 compares application programming interfaces between Intel MKL [1] and SMAT. MKL implements six storage formats and provides the same number of function calls to users, while SMAT exposes only one function in CSR format, as most sparse matrices favor CSR according to statistical results (see Table 1).

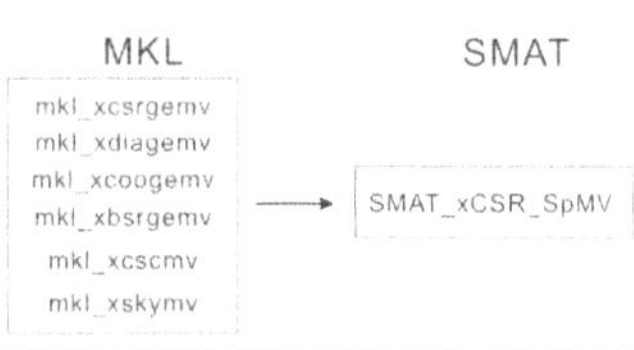

Figure 5. Application programming interface. The character "*x*" denotes numerical precision (single- or double-precision).

In addition to the benefit of the unified programming interface, there are two more advantages of SMAT – reusability and portability: First, on a specific architecture, SMAT generates the learning model once in off-line stage, and use this model repeatedly for different input matrices; Second, SMAT extends well to different architectures as the architecture features have been considered already. Besides, SMAT performs beyond existing auto-tuners by employing the performance of SpMV implementations to quantize architecture features, instead of using architecture features directly. This innovation brings two advantages: First, it makes SMAT smoothly compatible to new architectures, which is the most important thing to auto-tuners and the biggest difference from other ones; Second, it is more accurate to conduct learning using performance values instead of a band of architecture features, to narrow down the parameter space while considering both application and architecture features.

Another main advantage of SMAT is extensibility. With the nature of data mining methods, SMAT is really easy for users to add new algorithms and/or more meticulous implementation. Besides, it is also open to add new matrices and corresponding records into the database to improve the prediction accuracy. Third, if there is a need to balance accuracy and training time, it is also convenient to add or remove parameters from the learning model with SMAT.

In the following sections, three compositions of SMAT will be discussed, which are respectively parameter extraction, learning model generation, and runtime process.

4. Parameter Extraction

SMAT is an application and architecture aware auto-tuner, and it can apparently leverage the well-studied architecture-aware auto-tuners [17, 21, 31, 36] to extract architecture parameters. In this section, we present how to extract sparse structure feature parameters. To build an application-aware auto-tuner, we extract feature parameters from more than 2000 sparse matrices of UF collection [12]. Table 2 summaries a complete list of sparse structure parameters used in SMAT system.

Firstly, four parameters are used to represent the basic structure of a sparse matrix applicable to all four formats (marked by $\surd$): `M` (the number of rows), `N` (the number of columns), `NNZ` (the number of non-zeros), and `aver_RD` (the average number of non-zeros per row). Besides, a couple of advanced parameters are added to describe SpMV behavior for non-default formats in SMAT such as DIA, ELL and COO. Note: the up(down) arrows indicate that the corresponding SpMV performance gets higher once the parameter becomes larger(smaller), .

The advantages of DIA and ELL formats come from regular data access behavior to the matrix, especially the X-vector. Since DIA and ELL store matrices in a diagonal and column major layout respectively, DIA reads continuous elements of X-vector, while ELL has a large possibility to reuse X-elements. However, these two formats also suffer from the following drawbacks: First, when there are only a few elements distributed in a diagonal(row), DIA(ELL) will fill up these diagonals(rows) with zero-padding and has to do useless computation on zero elements, which will dramatically hurt the overall performance. Second, the diagonal(column)-order loop requires Y-elements to be written once per diagonal(column), which will produce frequent cache evict and memory write back operation for large sparse matrices. In order to address these issues, four parameters ({`Ndiags, max_RD, ER_DIA, ER_ELL`} in Table 2) are extracted to represent the DIA and ELL kernels' behavior.

Table 2. Feature parameters of a sparse matrix and the relationship with the formats

Parameter		Meaning	Formula	DIA	ELL	CSR	COO
Matrix Dimension	M	the number of rows	-	√	√	√	√
	N	the number of columns	-	√	√	√	√
Diagonal Situation	Ndiags	the number of diagonals	-	↓			
	NTdiags_ratio	the ratio of "true" diagonals to total diagonals	$NTdiags\_ratio = \frac{number\ of\ \text{"}true\ diagonals\text{"}}{Ndiags}$	↑			
Nonzero Distribution	NNZ	the number of nonzeros	-	√	√	√	√
	aver_RD	the number of nonzeros per row	$aver\_RD = \frac{NNZ}{M}$	√	√	√	√
	max_RD	the maximum number of nonzeros per row	$max\_RD = \max_1^M\{number\ of\ nonzeros\ per\ row\}$		↓		
	var_RD	the variation of the number of nonzeros per row	$var\_RD = \frac{\Sigma_1^M \lvert row\_degree - aver\_RD \rvert^2}{M}$			↓	
Nonzero Ratio	ER_DIA	the ratio of nonzeros in DIA data structure	$ER\_DIA = \frac{NNZ}{Ndiags \times M}$	↑			
	ER_ELL	the ratio of nonzeros in ELL data structure	$ER\_ELL = \frac{NNZ}{max\_RD \times M}$		↑		
Power-Law	R	a factor of power-law distribution	$P(k) \sim k^{-R}$				[1, 4]

Our methodology is to perform a statistical analysis based on experiments on UF sparse matrix collection, by plotting the distribution of beneficial matrices to reflect the parameter influence and then defining their ranks accordingly. In Figure 6(a) X-axis gives the intervals of `Ndiags` and `max_RD`, and the distribution of DIA and ELL matrices among the intervals is presented on Y-axis in percentage. When `Ndiags or max_RD` becomes larger, less number of matrices gain performance benefits from DIA or ELL format, which means small `Ndiags` and `max_RD` indicate good performance for DIA and ELL. Similarly, Figure 6(b) shows the beneficial matrix distribution among nonzero ratio intervals, from which we can conclude that large nonzero ratio is good for DIA (less obvious) and ELL formats.

However, we also observe exceptions from these two figures above. For `ER_DIA` parameter there are still nearly half of matrices benefiting from DIA format even when the nonzero ratio is no more than 50%. To improve the combinational accuracy of the rules, we introduce two more parameters – `NTdiags_ratio` and `var_RD`. We firstly define a new type of diagonal – "true diagonal", to represent one occupied mostly with non-zeros. A "true diagonal" features continuous X access pattern, minor part of zero-padding, and writing Y-vector only once, which will show competitive SpMV performance. We use the ratio of "true diagonals" out of all diagonals (`NTdiags_ratio`) as another parameter. The beneficial DIA matrix distribution is shown in Figure 6(c), which indicates DIA also gains higher performance with larger `NTdiags_ratio` just as `ER_DIA` parameter. However, `NTdiags_ratio` shows more obvious rules than `ER_DIA` so that it captures application features more accurately. Similarly, we add `var_RD` parameter for ELL format. As we know, if a sparse matrix has a significantly variable number of non-zeros per row, its SpMV performance degrades due to a lot of zero-padding operations. So we introduce `var_RD` to represent the variation of the number of non-zeros per row. Figure 6(d) indicates that small `var_RD` value is good for ELL SpMV performance. Finally, we learn from [36] that COO format gains good performance on small-world network. Thus, we choose power-law distribution $P(k) \sim k^{-R}$ as its criterion. Figure 6(e) depicts the distribution on `R`, of which the interval $[1, 4]$ is preferred by COO matrices.

So far, we extract 11 feature parameters to abstract sparse matrix structure and draw several rules to achieve higher SpMV performance with a certain format. However, it is still far from predicting the optimal format and implementation only based on rules with the thresholds generated from the simple observations in Table 2. First, for each format there are multiple parameters which are not completely orthogonal to each other. That makes it hard to set accurate threshold values for decision making. Second, from Figure 6, there are quite a few exceptions to the simple rules, which may bring too many wrong predictions. Last, a careful balance is needed for determining the threshold values. Since a rule has both advantages and disadvantages, although it can predict accurately for its favored format, it might hurt the prediction accuracy of other formats. For example, if we conclude a rule of $var\_RD < 0.5$ from Figure 6(d), even when the matrix satisfies this rule SpMV performance with ELL format still may be lower than CSR format. In this case, it is necessary to balance the overall accuracy of four formats rather than only one. Therefore, we introduce a data mining method based on the parameters in Table 2 to build a learning model, with which SMAT can generate practical and reliable prediction.

5. Machine Learning Model

In this section, we discuss details of the data mining method used to the generate learning model and search for optimal implementation from the kernel library.

5.1 Model Generation

We define an attribute collection {`M, N, Ndiags, NTdiags_ratio, NNZ, max_RD, var_RD, ER_DIA, ER_ELL, R, Best_Format`} for each matrix, where "Best_Format" is the target attribute. Through training with 2055 UF matrices, we get accurate parameter values of all training matrices. For example, matrix t2d_q9 (in training set) has a record of parameter values as {9801, 9801, 9, 1.0, 87025, 9, 0.35, 0.99, 0.99, inf, DIA}, where "inf" means the power-law distribution cannot calculate the R value from this matrix since it has no attribute of scale-free network. All of these records together constitute the matrix feature database.

As the target attribute, "Best_Format" is used to classify possible candidates (DIA, ELL, CSR, COO) for a particular sparse matrix. Thus, a mapping from the parameters set to the "Best_Format" needs to be built. This falls into a classification problem that can be solved by data mining tools. The formulation of mapping is described in Equation 1, where $\vec{x_i}(i = 1, \ldots, n)$ represents the set of parameters of a sparse matrix in the training set, and $\vec{TH}$ stands for the set of thresholds for each attribute. $C_n(DIA, ELL, CSR, COO)$ represents one of the four categories. With the help of data mining method, $\vec{TH}$ is generated along with the decision tree.

$$f(\vec{x_1}, \vec{x_2}, \ldots, \vec{x_n}, \vec{TH}) \rightarrow C_n(DIA, ELL, CSR, COO) \quad (1)$$

SMAT system uses C5.0 [2] data mining tool to generate the decision tree from the training matrix set. With its user-friendly design, little knowledge besides the feature database is needed to generate the model. The tool extracts informative patterns from the input data and outputs the learning model.

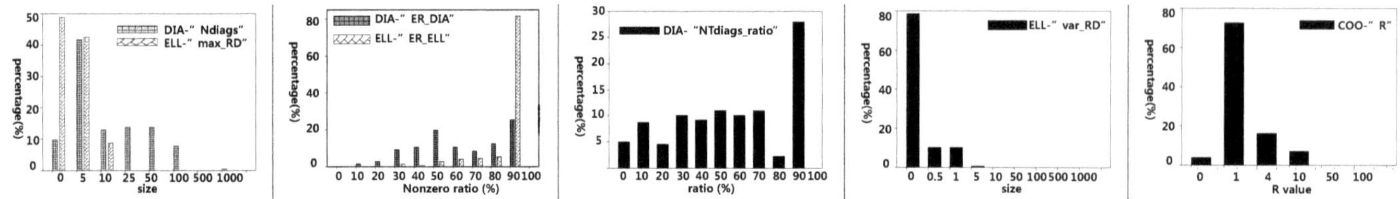

(a) Ndiags and max_RD (b) ER_DIA and ER_ELL (c) NTdiags_ratio (d) var_RD (e) R

Figure 6. The distribution of the beneficial matrices (gain SpMV performance benefit using the corresponding formats) with different parameter values, where Y-axis shows the percentage of matrices falling into each parameter value interval.

As we know, C5.0 can generate either decision tree or ruleset pattern. Though the two patterns represent similar information, we eventually chose ruleset for two reasons. First, ruleset classifiers are most likely more accurate than decision tree. Although this higher accuracy increases the execution time of the data mining method, it only impacts the off-line stage of SMAT and is reusable after one time decision. Second, it is convenient to convert the rules to IF-THEN sentences, so ruleset is more straightforward to integrate with our system. In order to reduce model inaccuracy, we guide C5.0 to generate a confidence factor along with each rule. The confidence factor is the ratio of the number of correctly classified matrices to the number of matrices falling in this rule, the range of which is between 0 and 1. The larger the confidence factor is, the more reliable the rule is. We will show the role of this confidence factor in Section 6.

Using a matrix feature database, SMAT generates a learning model in ruleset pattern with a confidence factor. The usage of the ruleset model will also be discussed in Section 6.

5.2 Kernel Searching

Previous literature [10, 11, 22, 31, 35] discussed architectural optimization strategies (such as blocking methods, software prefetching, SSE intrinsic usage, multi-thread, etc.) for specific architectures. In SMAT a collection of strategies are grouped together as a large kernel library in Figure 4. It is important to narrow down the optimization implementations of the library to find potential optimal kernels on a given architecture. SMAT can leverage existing auto-tuning tools to facilitate search in off-line stage.

Kernel searching is conducted with a performance record table and scoreboard algorithm. We run all possible implementations (up to 24 in current SMAT system) and record corresponding performance in a table. The implementations are arranged in a specific order in this table, and each performance number in a record can be indexed by all of the optimization strategies it used. Based on the performance table, a scoreboard is created to find the most efficient strategy according to SpMV behavior on the target architecture. Beginning from the implementation with a single optimization method, if it shows performance gain compared with basic implementation, the corresponding optimization method is marked as 1 on the scoreboard, otherwise it is marked by -1. When performance gap between two implementations is less than 0.01, we consider this optimization strategy showing no effect on this architecture and neglect it by default. In this way, an implementation with multiple optimization strategies should compare its performance with those that have just one less optimization strategy. Thus, we eventually obtain the score of each optimization strategy, and then the score of each implementation can be calculated by summing the scores of strategies used in it. Through these two algorithms, the implementation with the highest score is considered to be the optimal one for the corresponding format on the architecture. The optimal kernels will be invoked when the data mining method builds the learning model and the execute-measure module runs.

6. Runtime Process

In this section, we discuss runtime components (labeled by red arrows in Figure 4) of SMAT. This procedure depends on a black-box machine learning model with details depicted in Figure 7. We also discuss several optimization methods to reduce runtime overhead.

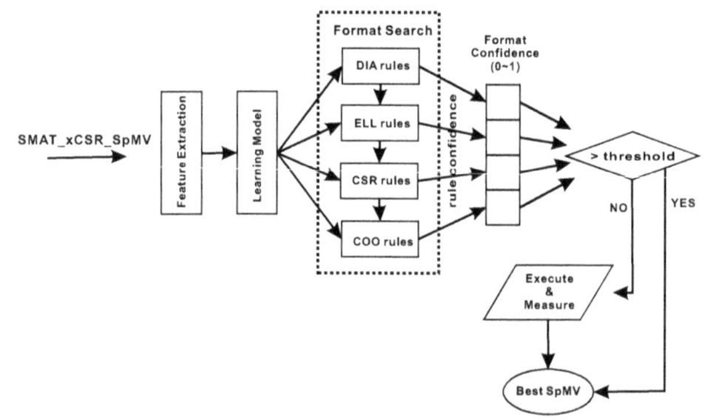

Figure 7. Runtime procedure of SMAT

Feature Extraction In this component the parameters listed in Table 2 are calculated without actually running SpMV in two separated steps: First, we extract diagonal information for DIA format. For reducing the number of times we traverse the whole matrix, we count the diagonals and nonzero distribution together. Thus, we extract the parameter values of DIA, ELL, and CSR formats in this step. Second, we need to evaluate parameter R for COO format, which will spends non-trivial time due to the heavy computation of power-law distribution. From the feature extraction process, we learn that the two separated steps are independent, which will be useful to accelerate the runtime process as described in the next paragraph.

Rule Tailoring and Grouping C5.0 generates tens of rules in the learning model. As many of these rules are suitable for only a small group of matrices and inaccuracy, we re-order them according to corresponding estimated contribution (a concept from C5.0) to the overall training set. That is, rules reducing error rate the most appear first, and rules contributing the least appear last. Then we tailor rules top-down until the subset of rules achieve predictive accuracy close to whole ruleset (1% accuracy gap is acceptable). From our experiments, we choose rules No.1-15 on Intel platform, which decrease the error rate to 9.6%, which is very close to the result 9.0% achieved by the whole ruleset of 40 rules.

After finishing the rule tailoring step, we assign the rules to different format groups. According to the rule confidence factor generated with learning model, we pick the largest one within the same format group as format confidence factor. The format confidence factor reflects the reliability when a corresponding format is chosen by the model, and we compare it with the threshold to decide the reliability of the prediction.

Since it is quite time-consuming when executing all steps in order, we employ an optimistic strategy to accelerate this process. The basic idea is that we can make the decision and do not need to go through all rules if the prediction has sufficiently high confidence. For example, after the feature parameters are calculated in the first step, the learning model will check DIA rule group and get DIA confidence. If DIA confidence is larger than the threshold, DIA format and its optimal implementation will be output as the result. With this strategy, the format group order should be carefully set. As we know, DIA achieves the highest performance (Figure 3) once a matrix satisfies specific conditions, so we arrange DIA rule group in the first place for high performance. ELL takes the second place for its regular and easy-to-predict behavior, which is followed by CSR as the parameters needed have been calculated already (with DIA and ELL), and COO takes the last place. With this order, the prediction procedure reduces quite a lot of time while retaining prediction accuracy.

No.	Graph	Name	Dimensions	Nonzeros (NNZ / M)	Application area
1	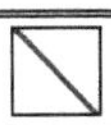	pcrystk02	14K×14K	491K (35)	duplicate materials problem
2	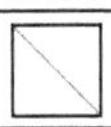	denormal	89K×89K	623K (7)	counter-example
3	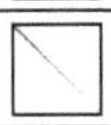	cryg10000	10K×10K	50K (5)	materials problem
4	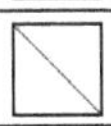	apache1	81K×81K	311K (4)	structural problem
5		bfly	49K×49K	98K (2)	undirected graph sequence
6	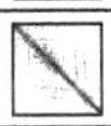	whitaker3_dual	19K×19K	29K (1)	2D/3D problem
7		ch7-9-b3	106K×18K	423K (4)	combinatorial problem
8		shar_te2-b2	200K×17K	601K (3)	combinatorial problem
9	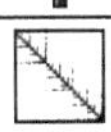	pkustk14	152K×152K	15M (98)	structural problem
10		crankseg_2	64K×64K	14M (222)	structural problem
11	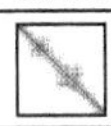	Ga3As3H12	61K×61K	6M (97)	theoretical/quantum chemistry
12		HV15R	2M×2M	283M (140)	computational fluid dynamics
13		europe_osm	51M×51M	108M (2)	undirected graph
14		D6-6	121K×24K	147K (1)	combinatorial problem
15		dictionary28	53K×53K	178K (3)	undirected graph
16	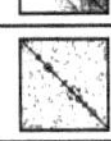	roadNet-CA	2M×2M	6M (3)	undirected graph

Figure 8. Representative matrices

7. Experiments and Analysis

In this section, we evaluate the performance of SMAT by running benchmark matrices and a real application, followed by accuracy and overhead analysis.

7.1 Experimental Setup

Platform The experiments are conducted on two x86 multicore processors: One is a Intel Xeon X5680 with 12 3.3GHz cores, 12MB shared last-level cache, and 31GB/s memory bandwidth; and the other one is AMD Opteron 6168 with 12 1.9GHz cores, 12MB shared last-level cache, and 42GB/s memory bandwidth. All executions are configured to run with 12 threads.

Benchmark The off-line data mining component processes a training set of 2055 sparse matrices randomly chosen from UF sparse matrix collection. Excluding the training matrices, we use the rest 331 matrices for performance evaluation, and 16 matrices (described in Figure 8) of them for plotting visualized graphs of their contents.

Application To demonstrate the usability of SMAT, we integrate it with Hypre [14], a scalable linear solver library from LLNL. Wherein, Algebraic Multigrid (AMG) is used as a preconditioner such as conjugate gradients to solve large-scale scientific simulation problems on unstructured grids. As noted in Section 1, the sparse matrices show dynamic patterns to some extent among different levels. We anticipate it will benefit from SMAT's co-tuning approach.

7.2 Performance

We measure SpMV performance in GFLOPS, which is a ratio of the number of floating-point operations to execution time. Figure 9 plots GFLOPS of both single- and double-precision on the two platforms. X-axis represents the matrix number as listed in Figure 8 and Y-axis gives the performance of SpMV generated by SMAT. The highest SMAT performance on Intel platform is 51GFLOPS with an efficiency of 32% in single-precision and 37GFLOPS (23%) in double-precision. On AMD platform, SMAT achieves 38GFLOPS (42%) in single-precision and 22GFLOPS (24%) in double-precision. This peak performance is even higher than the reported maximum performance of 18 GFLOPs on GPU [7].

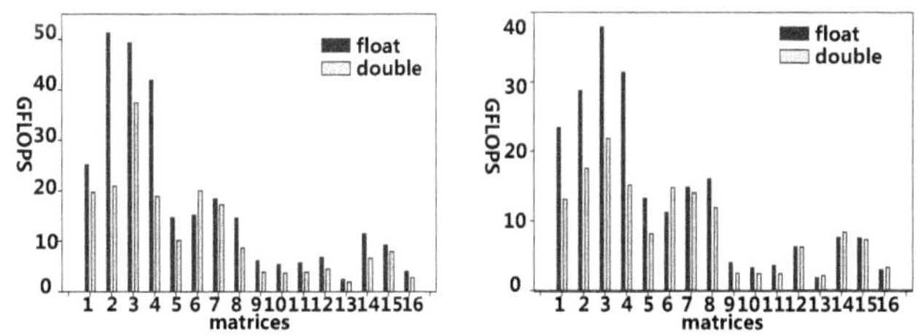

(a) Intel (b) AMD

Figure 9. SMAT performance in single- and double-precision on the two platforms

Figure 9 shows up to 5 times performance variation among the matrices, which proves it is worth adopting SMAT in different applications owing to its adaptability to diverse sparse matrices. For matrices that have affinity to DIA, ELL or COO format (No.1-8 and No.13-16), the corresponding SpMVs achieve higher performance than those in CSR format (No.9-12). The performance gap indicates that it is meaningful to implement a high performance SpMV library being aware of sparse structures (applications).

Moreover, we give performance comparison between SMAT and Intel MKL multi-threaded library in Figure 10 in single- and double-precision on Intel platform. MKL performance shown in this figure is the maximum performance number of DIA, CSR, and COO SpMV functions in this library. Compared with MKL, SMAT obtains the maximum speedup of 6.1 times in single-precision and 4.7 times in double-precision. Although this figure only shows 16 representative matrices, we do collect experimental data for all 331 matrices and the average speedup over MKL is **3.2** times in single-precision and **3.8** times in double-precision. SMAT shows big advantages in performance due to the following reasons. First, we take advantage of optimized SpMV implementations us-

Table 3. Analysis of SMAT

Matrix Number	Matrix Name	Model Prediction Format	Execution	SMAT Prediction Format	Actual Best Format	Model Accuracy	SMAT Overhead (times of CSR-SpMV)
1	pcrystk02	DIA	-	DIA	DIA	R	2.28
2	denormal	DIA	-	DIA	DIA	R	2.09
3	cryg10000	DIA	-	DIA	DIA	R	2.11
4	apache1	DIA	-	DIA	DIA	R	1.94
5	bfly	ELL	-	ELL	ELL	R	1.18
6	whitaker3_dual	ELL	-	ELL	ELL	R	4.89
7	ch7-9-b3	ELL	-	ELL	ELL	R	2.25
8	shar_te2-b2	ELL	-	ELL	ELL	R	2.24
9	pkustk14	$confidence < TH$	CSR+COO	CSR	CSR	W	16.39
10	crankseg_2	$confidence < TH$	CSR+COO	CSR	CSR	W	16.28
11	Ga3As3H12	$confidence < TH$	CSR+COO	CSR	CSR	W	16.2
12	HV15R	$confidence < TH$	CSR+COO	CSR	CSR	W	15.43
13	europe_osm	COO	-	COO	COO	R	2.3
14	D6-6	COO	-	COO	COO	R	5.79
15	dictionary28	COO	-	COO	COO	R	2.05
16	roadNet-CA	COO	-	COO	COO	R	2.38

"R" and "W" represent Right and Wrong prediction respectively.

ing SIMDization, branch optimization, data prefetch, and task parallelism policy. Second, as SMAT can determine the optimal format and implementation, the highest SpMV performance achieved by these optimization methods is eventually revealed. We also observe one matrix (No.8) shows lower performance than MKL due to inaccuracy of SMAT. We will analyze accuracy and prediction overhead of SMAT in the next section.

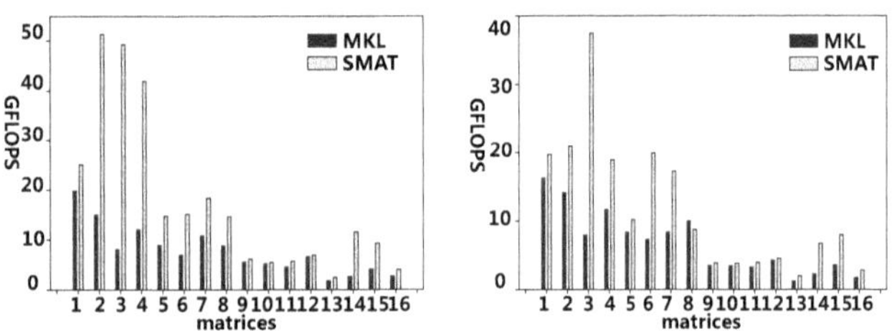

(a) float (b) double

Figure 10. The performance of SMAT V.S. MKL

7.3 Analysis

Accuracy Table 3 shows the details of on-line decision making process and its accuracy. When a sparse matrix is input to SMAT system, the learning model performs prediction on-line and outputs the predicted format (noted by "Model Prediction Format"). However, there are some exceptions that the learning model cannot predict their formats confidently. SMAT actually executes SpMV kernels for once and measures the performance for part of formats, which is noted as "Execution" in this table. For example, the execution process runs CSR- and COO- based SpMVs to determine the final format for matrix No.9-12. In this table "Best Format" represents the best result of exhaustive search. Though the learning model cannot predict correctly in some cases due to relatively intricate features of CSR as the most general format, SMAT still can obtain good results on the 16 matrices. For all 331 matrices, the accuracy is 92% (SP) and 82% (DP) on Intel platform, and 85% (SP) and 82% (DP) on AMD platform respectively.

Prediction Overhead Table 3 also shows the "SMAT Overhead" in the last column, which is represented by ratio of the overall execution time to the basic CSR-SpMV execution time. In most cases, the overhead is no more than 5 times, which is very competitive comparing to existing auto-tuning tools [11, 17, 17, 21, 29, 31, 35, 36] and practical for real applications. But when the learning model fails to get a confident prediction, SMAT overhead increases to about 15 times. This is acceptable when an application executes an SpMV kernel hundreds of times. In fact, compared with the overhead of existing auto-tuners – OSKI (40 times), clSpMV (1-20 times), the overhead of SMAT appears acceptable.

As a straightforward way to search for the optimal result, one option is to run SpMV kernels for all formats one by one. Despite plenty of implementation variants of one format, the simplest search across basic implementations of the four formats takes more time than SMAT. The overhead of this search method comes from format conversion and SpMV execution. For example, the conversion from CSR to ELL consumes 39.6 times of CSR-SpMV for the No.11 matrix. The overhead of simple search reaches up to 45 times even if only four implementations are explored, which is much higher than the case (16.2) in Table 3. Remember that SMAT is only a proof of concept system, and its adoption of reusable machine learning model makes it feasible to extend for more formats and implementations.

7.4 SMAT-based AMG

Considering a problem of solving equation $Au = f$ with certain precision criterion, where A is a large sparse matrix, u and f are dense vectors, Hypre AMG solves this by building N levels of virtual grids with a series of grid operators $(A_0, ...A_{N-1})$ and grid transfer operators $(P_0, ...P_{N-2})$ in a setup process. Figure 11 illustrates a typical V-cycle in AMG. Apparently, P-operators perform SpMV between adjacent grids, and A-operators are used to do relaxations like Jacobi and Gauss-Seidel methods with SpMV kernel, too. Without a doubt, SpMV consumes most of the V-cycle's execution time. We observe an interesting phenomenon that the two series of sparse matrices dynamically show different sparse features from the original input matrix A. Thus, SMAT is useful on determining the optimal format and implementation for the operators at each level, and improving the overall performance.

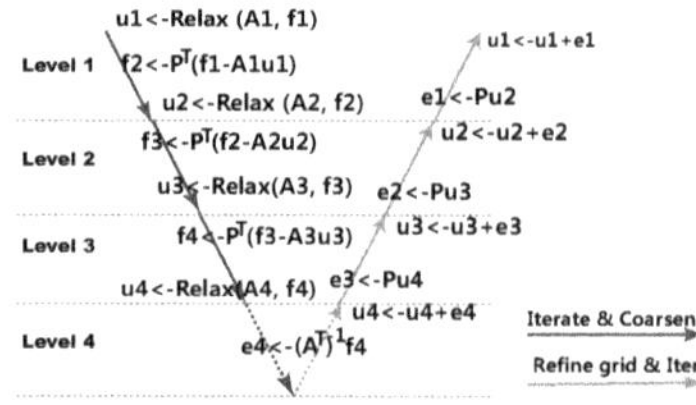

Figure 11. V-cycle involved with SpMV kernels in AMG solver.

We perform experiments on *cljp* and *rugeL* coarsen methods in the setup process to generate A-operators with different structures. The input matrices are generated by 7-point and 9-point Laplacian methods, respectively. Instead of using CSR format all the time, SMAT chooses DIA format for A-operators at the first few levels, and ELL format for most P-operators. To do this, we simply replace the SpMV kernel codes with SMAT interfaces with no changes to the original CSR data structure in Hypre. As shown in Table 4, the solving part of SMAT AMG achieves more than 20% performance gain than Hypre AMG.

Table 4. SMAT-based AMG execution time (millisecond)

Coarsen	Rows	Hypre AMG	SMAT AMG	Speedup
cljp_7pt_50	125K	3034	2487	1.22
rugeL_9pt_500	250K	388	300	1.29

8. Related Work

There has been a flurry of work related to optimizing sparse matrix vector multiplication performance. While we could not hope to provide a comprehensive set, we attempt to contrast our work with several key representatives.

Storage Format Basically, SMAT discovers optimal storage formats for sparse matrices. This idea is reflected in previous work. By far, more than ten storage formats [7, 21, 25, 28, 29, 31] have been proposed, most of which are either application-specific or architecture-specific so that their applicable domains are limited. Recently, several hybrid storage formats have been developed. Bor-Yiing Su et al. [29] proposed a Cocktail format that splits a matrix and represents these sub-matrices in different formats according to relative advantages of different sparse matrix formats. Similarly, on NVIDIA GPU CuSparse [23] stores one sparse matrix with a hybrid format HYB, which is a combination of two basic formats. These new hybrid storage formats show much better performance than conventional formats for certain sparse matrices. The major difference from SMAT is that the hybrid formats are determined statically and not applicable to dynamic sparse structures as shown at different levels of AMG solver. In the other aspect, researchers are developing relatively flexible formats. Richard Vuduc et al. [31] improved BCSR format to VBR to explore dense blocks with different sizes. Kourtis et al. [21] proposed CSX to exploit dense structures not limited to dense blocks, but also 1-dimension bars and dense diagonals by compressing metadata. However, the process of searching sub-blocks costs too much to be conducted on-line. In contrast, in terms of storage format optimization, SMAT selects the optimal format from the existing formats, instead of designing a new one. The machine learning model makes an on-line decision feasible. It is possible to add new formats by extracting novel parameters and integrating its implementations in kernel library in SMAT.

Auto-tuning Approach For developing a domain-specific performance-critical library, auto-tuning approach is promising to resolve both performance and portability problems. There are several successful auto-tuning libraries, such as ATLAS [33], FFTW [15], SPIRAL [24], and OSKI [31], widely used in scientific computing area. Specifically for SpMV, auto-tuning techniques are actively investigated. Eun-jin Im et al. [19] created BCSR format to better develop the performance of dense blocks in a sparse matrix. Richard Vuduc et al. [31] built OSKI to tune the block size for a matrix in BCSR or VBR formats. Williams et al. [35] deployed a hierarchical strategy to choose the optimal architectural parameter combinations. Choi et al. [11] implemented Blocked Compress Sparse Row (BCSR) and Sliced Blocked ELLPACK (SBELL) formats on Nvidia GPUs, and tuned the block sizes of them. X.Yang et al. [36] proposed a mixed format and automatically chose the partition size for each format with the help of a model. A common feature of these auto-tuning designs is to focus on implementation tuning on diverse processing architectures only for a single pre-defined storage format. In addition to architectural auto-tuning, SMAT extends to cooperatively tune storage formats by extracting key performance parameters from input sparse matrices. In fact, algorithm and architecture co-tuning was advocated in PetaBricks compiler [4]. Our work further proves the value of auto-tuning techniques.

Prediction Model A core component of SMAT is the machine-learning based prediction model for determining the optimal format and implementation. It is a common strategy to apply prediction model in auto-tuning approach. ATLAS [33] performed an empirical search to determine optimal parameter values bounded by architecture features. But an actual run of generated code is needed to measure and record its performance to choose the best implementation. This empirical search has been proven efficient to generate high quality BLAS codes, although the search process takes a lot of time. Recently, many arising auto-tuners adopt model-driven method such as [11, 21, 29, 31, 36] without the need of actually running the code. Though the model-driven method decreases the prediction time, the generated code performance is considered lower than empirical search in most cases. Kamen Yotov et. al. [37] did experiments on ATLAS and got this conclusion on ten platforms. Our SMAT system combines learning model and empirical search invoked rarely that ensures the code performance and reduces prediction time at the same time. Although clSpMV [29] also used a prediction model to tune its Cocktail format, there are certain crucial differences from SMAT. First and foremost, in on-line decision making stage, clSpMV uses the maximum GFLOPS measured in offline stage. Unfortunately, as our experiments on UF collection shows (see Table 1 and Figure 3) the maximum performance of one format is not representative enough to reflect the SpMV performance of all the matrices suitable in this format. It is more accurate to use the features of each input matrix to determine its own best format rather than using a single maximum performance for each format. Second, we extract more features from real matrices in UF collection, which can feed more training data to data mining tools so as to generate more reliable rules for the learning model. W. Armstrong et al. [5] uses reinforcement learning to choose the best format, but users should decide the factor values which influence the accuracy of the learning model. SMAT system is more convenient to automatically generate the model and still achieve similar prediction accuracy.

9. Conclusion

In this paper, we propose SMAT, an input adaptive SpMV auto-tuner, which encompasses several statistical and machine learning techniques to enable both application- and architecture-dependent, incremental model training and black-box performance prediction. In particular, we provide a unified interface to eliminate tedious work on determining optimal formats and implementations for diverse sparse matrices. Due to cooperatively auto-tuning with both algorithms and architectures, SMAT achieves impressive performance of up to 51 (38) GFLOPS in single-precision and 37 (22) GFLOPS in double-precision on Intel (AMD) multi-core processor. The average speedup is above 3 times over Intel MKL sparse library. SMAT is also used to improve the performance of algebraic multi-grid algorithm from Hypre sparse linear system solver by about 20%. Our work suggests that algorithm and architecture co-tuning is a promising approach for developing domain-specific auto-tuning libraries or tools.

Acknowledgments

We would like to express our gratitude to Yin Li from Intel China and Dr. Trishul Chilimbi for helping us polishing this paper. This work is supported by National Natural Science Foundation of China (61272134, 61033009, 61003062, 60925009), the National Basic Research Program of China (973 Program) (2011CB302502, 2012CB316502), and the joint lab of Institute of Computing Technology and Intel.

References

[1] *Intel Math Kernel Library*. URL http://software.intel.com/en-us/intel-mkl.

[2] *Data Mining Tools See5 and C5.0*. URL http://www.rulequest.com/see5-info.html.

[3] M. D. Adam Hill. The international thermonuclear experimental reactor. Technical report, 2005.

[4] J. Ansel, C. Chan, Y. L. Wong, M. Olszewski, Q. Zhao, A. Edelman, and S. Amarasinghe. Petabricks: a language and compiler for algorithmic choice. In *Proceedings of the 2009 ACM SIGPLAN conference on Programming language design and implementation*, PLDI '09, pages 38–49. ACM, 2009. ISBN 978-1-60558-392-1.

[5] W. Armstrong and A. Rendell. Reinforcement learning for automated performance tuning: Initial evaluation for sparse matrix format selection. In *Cluster Computing, 2008 IEEE International Conference on*, pages 411 –420, 2008.

[6] S. Balay, J. Brown, , K. Buschelman, V. Eijkhout, W. D. Gropp, D. Kaushik, M. G. Knepley, L. C. McInnes, B. F. Smith, and H. Zhang. PETSc users manual. Technical Report ANL-95/11 - Revision 3.3, Argonne National Laboratory, 2012.

[7] N. Bell and M. Garland. Efficient sparse matrix-vector multiplication on CUDA. NVIDIA Technical Report NVR-2008-004, NVIDIA Corporation, Dec. 2008.

[8] G. Belter, E. R. Jessup, I. Karlin, and J. G. Siek. Automating the generation of composed linear algebra kernels. In *Proceedings of the Conference on High Performance Computing Networking, Storage and Analysis*, SC '09, pages 59:1–59:12, New York, NY, USA, 2009. ACM. ISBN 978-1-60558-744-8.

[9] S. Brin and L. Page. The anatomy of a large-scale hypertextual web search engine. In *Proceedings of the seventh international conference on World Wide Web 7*, WWW7, pages 107–117. Elsevier Science Publishers B. V., 1998.

[10] A. Buluc, S. Williams, L. Oliker, and J. Demmel. Reduced-bandwidth multithreaded algorithms for sparse matrix-vector multiplication. In *Proceedings of the 2011 IEEE International Parallel & Distributed Processing Symposium*, IPDPS '11, pages 721–733. IEEE Computer Society, 2011.

[11] J. W. Choi, A. Singh, and R. W. Vuduc. Model-driven autotuning of sparse matrix-vector multiply on gpus. In *Proceedings of the 15th ACM SIGPLAN Symposium on Principles and Practice of Parallel Programming*, PPoPP '10, pages 115–126. ACM, 2010.

[12] T. A. Davis. The university of florida sparse matrix collection. *NA DIGEST*, 92, 1994.

[13] R. Falgout. An introduction to algebraic multigrid computing. *Computing in Science Engineering*, 8(6):24 –33, nov.-dec. 2006. ISSN 1521-9615.

[14] R. D. Falgout and U. M. Yang. hypre: a library of high performance preconditioners. In *Preconditioners, Lecture Notes in Computer Science*, pages 632–641, 2002.

[15] M. Frigo and S. G. Johnson. The design and implementation of FFTW3. *Proceedings of the IEEE*, 93(2):216–231, 2005. Special issue on "Program Generation, Optimization, and Platform Adaptation".

[16] D. Grewe and A. Lokhmotov. Automatically generating and tuning gpu code for sparse matrix-vector multiplication from a high-level representation. In *Proceedings of the Fourth Workshop on General Purpose Processing on Graphics Processing Units*, GPGPU-4, pages 12:1–12:8. ACM, 2011.

[17] J. Harris. poski: An extensible autotuning framework to perform optimized spmvs on multicore architectures. 2009.

[18] M. A. Heroux, R. A. Bartlett, V. E. Howle, R. J. Hoekstra, J. J. Hu, T. G. Kolda, R. B. Lehoucq, K. R. Long, R. P. Pawlowski, E. T. Phipps, A. G. Salinger, H. K. Thornquist, R. S. Tuminaro, J. M. Willenbring, A. Williams, and K. S. Stanley. An overview of the trilinos project. *ACM Trans. Math. Softw.*, 31(3):397–423, Sept. 2005. ISSN 0098-3500.

[19] E. jin Im, K. Yelick, and R. Vuduc. Sparsity: Optimization framework for sparse matrix kernels. *International Journal of High Performance Computing Applications*, 18:2004, 2004.

[20] M. F. Khairoutdinov and D. A. Randall. A cloud resolving model as a cloud parameterization in the near community climate system model: Preliminary results. *Geophys. Res. Lett.*, 28(18):3617C3620, 2001.

[21] K. Kourtis, V. Karakasis, G. Goumas, and N. Koziris. Csx: an extended compression format for spmv on shared memory systems. In *Proceedings of the 16th ACM symposium on Principles and practice of parallel programming*, PPoPP '11, pages 247–256. ACM, 2011.

[22] K. Nagar and J. Bakos. A sparse matrix personality for the convey hc-1. In *Field-Programmable Custom Computing Machines (FCCM), 2011 IEEE 19th Annual International Symposium on*, pages 1 –8, may 2011.

[23] *CUDA CUSPARSE Library*. NVIDIA, 2010.

[24] M. Püschel, J. M. F. Moura, J. Johnson, D. Padua, M. Veloso, B. Singer, J. Xiong, F. Franchetti, A. Gacic, Y. Voronenko, K. Chen, R. W. Johnson, and N. Rizzolo. SPIRAL: Code generation for DSP transforms. *Proceedings of the IEEE, special issue on "Program Generation, Optimization, and Adaptation"*, 93(2):232– 275, 2005.

[25] Y. Saad. Sparskit : a basic tool kit for sparse matrix computations. *Technical Report*, 1994.

[26] N. Spirin and J. Han. Survey on web spam detection: principles and algorithms. *SIGKDD Explor. Newsl.*, 13(2):50–64, May 2012. ISSN 1931-0145.

[27] A. Srinivasa and M. Sosonkina. Nonuniform memory affinity strategy in multithreaded sparse matrix computations. In *Proceedings of the 2012 Symposium on High Performance Computing*, HPC '12, pages 9:1–9:8, 2012.

[28] J. P. Stevenson, A. Firoozshahian, A. Solomatnikov, M. Horowitz, and D. Cheriton. Sparse matrix-vector multiply on the hicamp architecture. In *Proceedings of the 26th ACM international conference on Supercomputing*, ICS '12, pages 195–204, New York, NY, USA, 2012. ACM. ISBN 978-1-4503-1316-2.

[29] B.-Y. Su and K. Keutzer. clspmv: A cross-platform opencl spmv framework on gpus. In *Proceedings of the 26th ACM international conference on Supercomputing*, ICS '12, pages 353–364. ACM, 2012.

[30] X. Sun, Y. Zhang, T. Wang, G. Long, X. Zhang, and Y. Li. Crsd: application specific auto-tuning of spmv for diagonal sparse matrices. In *Proceedings of the 17th international conference on Parallel processing - Volume Part II*, Euro-Par'11, pages 316–327, 2011.

[31] R. Vuduc, J. W. Demmel, and K. A. Yelick. OSKI: A library of automatically tuned sparse matrix kernels. In *Proc. SciDAC, J. Physics: Conf. Ser.*, volume 16, pages 521–530, 2005.

[32] R. W. Vuduc and H.-J. Moon. Fast sparse matrix-vector multiplication by exploiting variable block structure. In *Proceedings of the First international conference on High Performance Computing and Communications*, HPCC'05, pages 807–816. Springer-Verlag, 2005.

[33] R. C. Whaley and J. J. Dongarra. Automatically tuned linear algebra software. In *Proceedings of the 1998 ACM/IEEE conference on Supercomputing (CDROM)*, Supercomputing '98, pages 1–27, Washington, DC, USA, 1998. IEEE Computer Society. ISBN 0-89791-984-X.

[34] S. Williams, L. Oliker, R. Vuduc, J. Shalf, K. Yelick, and J. Demmel. Optimization of sparse matrix-vector multiplication on emerging multicore platforms. In *Proceedings of the 2007 ACM/IEEE conference on Supercomputing*, SC '07, pages 38:1–38:12. ACM, 2007.

[35] S. Williams, L. Oliker, R. Vuduc, J. Shalf, K. Yelick, and J. Demmel. Optimization of sparse matrix-vector multiplication on emerging multicore platforms. *Parallel Comput.*, 35(3):178–194, Mar. 2009.

[36] X. Yang, S. Parthasarathy, and P. Sadayappan. Fast sparse matrix-vector multiplication on gpus: implications for graph mining. *Proc. VLDB Endow.*, 4(4):231–242, Jan. 2011.

[37] K. Yotov, X. Li, G. Ren, M. Garzaran, D. Padua, K. Pingali, and P. Stodghill. Is search really necessary to generate high-performance blas?, 2005.

When Polyhedral Transformations Meet SIMD Code Generation

Martin Kong
Ohio State University
kongm@cse.ohio-state.edu

Richard Veras
Carnegie Mellon University
rveras@cmu.edu

Kevin Stock
Ohio State University
stockk@cse.ohio-state.edu

Franz Franchetti
Carnegie Mellon University
franzf@ece.cmu.edu

Louis-Noël Pouchet
University of California Los Angeles
pouchet@cs.ucla.edu

P. Sadayappan
Ohio State University
saday@cse.ohio-state.edu

Abstract

Data locality and parallelism are critical optimization objectives for performance on modern multi-core machines. Both coarse-grain parallelism (e.g., multi-core) and fine-grain parallelism (e.g., vector SIMD) must be effectively exploited, but despite decades of progress at both ends, current compiler optimization schemes that attempt to address data locality and both kinds of parallelism often fail at one of the three objectives.

We address this problem by proposing a 3-step framework, which aims for integrated data locality, multi-core parallelism and SIMD execution of programs. We define the concept of *vectorizable codelets*, with properties tailored to achieve effective SIMD code generation for the codelets. We leverage the power of a modern high-level transformation framework to restructure a program to expose good ISA-independent vectorizable codelets, exploiting multi-dimensional data reuse. Then, we generate ISA-specific customized code for the codelets, using a collection of lower-level SIMD-focused optimizations.

We demonstrate our approach on a collection of numerical kernels that we automatically tile, parallelize and vectorize, exhibiting significant performance improvements over existing compilers.

Categories and Subject Descriptors D 3.4 [*Programming languages*]: Processor — Compilers; Optimization

General Terms Algorithms; Performance

Keywords Compiler Optimization; Loop Transformations; Affine Scheduling; Program synthesis; Autotuning

1. Introduction

The increasing width of vector-SIMD instruction sets (e.g., 128 bits in SSE, to 256 bits in AVX, to 512 bits in LRBni) accentuates the importance of effective SIMD vectorization. However, despite the significant advances in compiler algorithms [15, 26, 28, 30, 31, 43] over the last decade, the performance of code vectorized by current compilers is often far below a processor's peak.

A combination of factors must be addressed to achieve very high performance with multi-core vector-SIMD architectures: (1) effective reuse of data from cache — the aggregate bandwidth to main memory on multi-core processors in words/second is far lower than the cumulative peak flop/second; (2) exploitation of SIMD parallelism on contiguously located data; and (3) minimization of load, store and shuffle operations per vector arithmetic operation.

PLDI'13, June 16–19, 2013, Seattle, WA, USA.

While hand tuned library kernels such as GotoBLAS address all the above factors to achieve over 95% of machine peak for specific computations, no vectorizing compiler today comes anywhere close. Recent advances in polyhedral compiler optimization [5, 11] have resulted in effective approaches to tiling for cache locality, even for imperfectly nested loops. However, while significant performance improvement over untiled code has been demonstrated, the absolute achieved performance is still very far from machine peak. A significant challenge arises from the fact that polyhedral compiler transformations to produce tiled code generally require auxiliary transformations like loop skewing, causing much more complex array indexing and loop bound expressions than the original code. The resulting complex code structure often leads to ineffective vectorization by even sophisticated vectorizing compilers such as Intel ICC. Further, locality enhancing transformations, e.g. loop fusion, can result in dependences in the innermost loops, inhibiting vectorization.

In this paper, we present a novel multi-stage approach to overcome the above challenges to effective vectorization of imperfectly nested loops. First, data locality at the cache level is addressed by generating tiled code that operates on data footprints smaller than L1 cache. Code within L1-resident tiles is then analyzed to find affine transformations that maximize stride-0 and stride-1 references in parallel loops as well as minimization of unaligned loads and stores. This results in the decomposition of a L1-resident tile into *codelets*. Finally, a specialized back-end codelet optimizer addresses optimization of register load/store/shuffle operations, maximization of aligned versus unaligned load/stores, as well as register level reuse. Target-specific intrinsics code is generated for the codelet by the back-end optimizer.

This paper makes the following contributions. (1) It presents a novel formalization for an affine loop transformation algorithm that is driven by the characteristics of codelets.(2) Unlike most previous approaches that focus on a single loop of a loop-nest for vectorization, it develops an approach that performs integrated analysis over a multi-dimensional iteration space for optimizing the vector-SIMD code. (3) It represents the first demonstration of how high-level polyhedral transformation technology can be effectively integrated with back-end codelet optimization technology through a model-driven approach, with significant performance improvement over production and research compilers.

This paper is organized as follows. Sec. 2 gives a high-level overview of our approach, and Sec. 3 defines the concept of vectorizable codelets, the interface between a high-level loop transformation engine and a low-level ISA-specific SIMD code generator. Sec. 4 details our new framework for automatically extracting maximal codelets. Sec. 5 details the framework for ISA-specific SIMD code generation. Experimental results are presented in Sec. 6, and related work is discussed in Sec. 7.

2. Overview

The key to our approach to vectorization is a separation of tasks between a high-level program restructuring stage and an ISA-specific SIMD code generation stage. High-level program transformation frameworks such as the polyhedral/affine framework excel at finding loop transformation sequences to achieve high-level, cost-model-based objectives. Examples such as maximizing data locality [7], maximizing parallelism (fine-grain or coarse-grain [11, 16, 29]) and possibly balancing the two [33, 34] illustrate the ability of the polyhedral framework to aggressively restructure programs. On the other hand, SIMD-specific concerns such as ISA-specific vector instruction selection, scheduling, and register promotion have been implemented using frameworks that depart significantly from classical loop transformation engines [15, 28, 30].

In this work we formalize the interface between these two optimization stages — the vectorizable codelet: a tile of code with specific, SIMD-friendly properties. We develop a novel and complete system to generate and optimize vectorizable codelets.

High-level overview of algorithm The data locality optimization algorithm in a system like Pluto [11] is geared towards exposing parallelism and tilability for the outer-most loops first, through aggressive loop fusion. This is critical for achieving good L1 cache data locality through tiling, as well as coarse-grained multi-core parallelization. However, for L1-resident code, those objectives are often detrimental: for effective exploitation of vector-SIMD ISA's, we need inner-most parallel loops, and the addressing of stride and alignment constraints. Other work has looked at the impact of unroll-and-jam for SIMD vectorization [12], but they do not consider the problem of restructuring programs to maximize the applicability of unroll-and-jam, nor any access stride constraint.

In this work, we develop an integrated system aimed at reconciling the different considerations in optimizing for coarse-grain parallelism and cache data locality versus effective SIMD vectorization. Our end-to-end strategy is as follows.

1. Transform the program for cache data locality (see Sec. 4.2), using: (1) a model-driven loop transformation algorithm for maximizing data locality and tilability [11]; (2) a parametric tiling method to tile all tilable loops found [5]; and (3) an algorithm to separate partial tiles and full tiles [1].
2. For each full tile, transform it to expose maximal vectorizable codelets (see Sec. 4), using: (1) a new polyhedral loop transformation algorithm for codelet extraction; (2) unroll-and-jam along permutable loops to increase data reuse potential in the codelet(s); and (3) an algorithm for abstract SIMD vectorization, addressing hardware alignment issues.
3. For each vectorizable codelet, generate high-performance ISA-specific SIMD code (see Sec. 5), using a special *codelet compiler* akin to FFTW's `genfft` or the SPIRAL system. Further, use instruction statistics or runtime measurements to autotune the codelets if alternative implementations exist.

3. Vectorizable Codelets

the original program, which satisfy some specific properties that enable effective SIMD code to be synthesized for it using an ISA-specific back-end code generator. In order to illustrate the properties, we proceed backwards by first describing the process of abstract SIMD vectorization on a code satisfying those properties.

3.1 Abstract SIMD Vectorization

We use the term abstract SIMD vectorization for the generation of ISA-independent instructions for a vectorizable innermost loop. The properties to be satisfied by this inner-most loop are summarized in the following definition:

DEFINITION 1 (Line codelet). *A line codelet is an affine inner-most loop with constant trip count such that:*
1. *there is no loop-carried dependence,*
2. *all array references are stride-1 (fastest varying array dimension increments by one w.r.t. the innermost loop) or stride-0 (innermost loop absent from array index expressions),*
3. *unaligned load/stores are avoided whenever possible.*

To illustrate the process of abstract SIMD vectorization, Fig. 1 shows a code example which satisfies the above requirements. It is the transformed output of a sample full tile by our codelet exposure algorithm, to be discussed later. Fig. 3 shows its abstract vector variant, after performing a basic unroll-and-jam as shown in Fig. 2. The abstract vector code generation involves peeling the vectorizable loop with scalar prologue code so the first store (and all subsequent ones) will be aligned modulo V, the vector length. Similarly, an epilogue with scalar code is peeled off. All arithmetic operators are replaced by equivalent vector operations, stride-0 references are replicated in a vector by "splatting", stride-1 references are replaced by vload/vstore calls, and the vectorized loop has its stride set to the vector length V. The arrays in this example, and the remainder of this paper, are assumed to be padded to make each row a multiple of the vector length V.

```
for (i = lbi; i < ubi; ++i)
  for (j = lbj; j < ubj; ++j) {
R:  A[i-1][j] = B[i-1][j];
S:  B[i][j] = C[i]*A[i-1][j];
  }
```

Figure 1. After transfo. for codelet exposure

```
for (i = lbi; i < ubi; i += 2)
  for (j = lbj; j < ubj; ++j) {
R:  A[i-1][j] = B[i-1][j];
S:  B[i][j] = C[i]*A[i-1][j];
R:  A[i][j] = B[i][j];
S:  B[i+1][j] = C[i+1]*A[i][j];
  }
```

Figure 2. After unroll-and-jam 2×1

```
for (i = lbi; i < ubi; i += 2)
  // Prolog: peel for alignment.
  lbj2 = &(A[i-1][j]) % V
  for (j = lbj; j < lbj + lbj2; ++j) {
     A[i-1][j] = B[i-1][j];
     B[i][j] = C[i]*A[i-1][j];
  }
  // Body: codelet (abstract vectorization)
  ubj2 = (lbj2 - ubj) % V
  for (j = lbj2; j < ubj - ubj2; j += V) {
     vstore(A[i-1][j], vload(B[i-1][j]));
     vstore(B[i][j], vmul(vsplat(C[i]),
                          vload(A[i-1][j]));
     vstore(A[i][j], vload(B[i][j]));
     vstore(B[i+1][j], vmul(vsplat(C[i+1]),
                          vload(A[i][j]));
  }
  // Epilog: peel for multiple of V.
  for (j = ubj - ubj2; j < ubj; ++j) {
     A[i-1][j] = B[i-1][j];
     B[i][j] = C[i]*A[i-1][j];
  }
```

Figure 3. After abstract SIMD vect.

Our objective in this work is to automatically transform full tiles into code fragments satisfying Definition 1 (i.e., Fig. 1), possibly interleaved with other code fragments not matching those requirements. Each vectorizable inner-loop is a *vectorizable codelet*. We show in Sec. 4 how to leverage the restructuring power of the polyhedral transformation framework to automatically reshape the loop nests to satisfy the requirements when possible.

3.2 Vectorizable Codelet Extraction

Efficient vector code generation requires to exploit data reuse potential. Specifically, given a program segment that is L1-resident, we should maximize the potential for register reuse while increasing the number of vector computations in the codelet. To do so we use register tiling, or unroll-and-jam, which amounts to unrolling outer loops and fusing the unrolled statements together.

Our framework is well suited to perform this optimization: the polyhedral framework can restructure a loop nest to maximize the number of *permutable loops*, along which unroll-and-jam can be applied. Arbitrarily complex sequences of fusion/distribution/skewing/shifting may be required to make unroll-and-jam possible, and we show in Sec. 4 how to automatically generate effective sequences for a given program to maximizes the applicability of unroll-and-jam. As a result of our framework, the innermost vectorizable loops (the line codelets) will contain an increased number of vector operations and operands for the ISA-specific synthesizer to optimize. Definition 2 lists the various optimization objectives that drive the high-level transformation engine to ensure the creation of good (i.e. large) candidate vector codelets.

DEFINITION 2 (Maximal Codelet Extraction). *Given a program P, maximal codelets are obtained by applying polyhedral loop transformations on P to obtain a program P′ such that:*

1. *the number of innermost loop(s) iterations which are parallel is maximized;*
2. *the number of references in P′ which are not stride-0 or stride-1 is minimized;*
3. *the number of permutable dimensions is maximized.*
4. *the number of unaligned stores is minimized;*
5. *the number of unaligned loads is minimized;*

In this work, we apply maximal codelet extraction on each full tile in the program. We then apply unroll-and-jam on all permutable loops, apply abstract SIMD vectorization on all candidate codelets, before synthesizing ISA-specific SIMD code for each of them.

4. Framework for Codelet Extraction

We now present our high-level framework to automatically transform the program to extract candidate vectorizable codelets.

4.1 Polyhedral Framework

To meet our goal of effectively transforming a program (region) to expose maximal codelets, we use a powerful and expressive mathematical framework for program representation: the polyhedral model. In the present work, we leverage recent developments on expressing various optimization constraints (e.g. loop permutability, data reuse, parallelism, etc.) into a single optimization problem that can then be optimally solved using Integer Linear Programming [34, 39]. We first review the basis of program representation and optimization in the polyhedral model, using the same notation as in [34].

Background and program representation The polyhedral framework is a flexible and expressive representation for imperfectly nested loops with statically predictable control flow. Loop nests amenable to this algebraic representation are called *static control parts* (SCoP) [16, 19], roughly defined as a set of consecutive statements such that all loop bounds and conditional expressions are affine functions of the enclosing loop iterators and variables that are constant during the SCoP execution (whose values are unknown at compile-time). Numerous scientific kernels exhibit those properties; they are found frequently in image processing filters (such as medical imaging algorithms) and dense linear algebra operations.

Unlike the abstract syntax trees used as internal representation in traditional compilers, polyhedral compiler frameworks internally represent imperfectly nested loops and their data dependence information as a collection of parametric polyhedra. Programs in the polyhedral model are represented using four mathematical structures: each statement has an *iteration domain*, each memory reference is described by an affine *access function*, data dependences are represented using *dependence polyhedra* and finally the program transformation to be applied is represented using a *scheduling function*.

Iteration domains For all textual statements in the program (e.g. R and S in Fig. 1) the set of its dynamic instances is described by a set of affine inequalities. When the statement is enclosed by one or more loops, all iterations of the loops are captured in the iteration domain of the statement. Each executed instance of the statement corresponds to a point in the iteration domain; the coordinate of this point is defined by the value of the surrounding loop iterators when the statement instance is executed. Parametric polyhedra are used to capture loop bounds whose values are invariant through loop execution but unknown at compilation time. These polyhedra use *parameters* in the inequalities defining their faces, and are a natural extension to standard polyhedra. For instance, in Fig. 1, the iteration domain of R is:

$$\mathcal{D}_R = \{(i,j) \in \mathbb{Z}^2 \mid \texttt{lbi} \le i < \text{ubi} \wedge \texttt{lbj} \le j < \text{ubj}\}.$$

We denote by $\vec{x}_R$ the vector of the surrounding loop iterators; for R it is (i,j) and takes values in $\mathcal{D}_R$.

Access functions They represent the location of the data accessed by the statement, in the form of an affine function of the iteration vector. For each point in $\mathcal{D}_R$, the access function $F_A^R(\vec{x}_R)$ returns the coordinate of the cell of A accessed by this instance of the memory reference. We restrict ourselves to subscripts of the form of affine expressions which may depend on surrounding loop counters and global parameters. For instance, the subscript function for the read reference `A[i-1][j]` of statement R is $F_R^A(i,j) = (i-1, j)$.

Data dependences The sets of statement instances between which there is a producer-consumer relationship are modeled as equalities and inequalities in a *dependence polyhedron*. Dependences are defined at the reference granularity of an array element. If two instances $\vec{x}_R$ and $\vec{x}_S$ refer to the same array cell and one of these references is a write, a data dependence exists between them. To respect program semantics, the producer instance must be executed before the consumer instance. Given two statements R and S, a dependence polyhedron, written $\mathcal{D}_{R,S}$, contains all pairs of dependent instances $\langle \vec{x}_R, \vec{x}_S \rangle$. Multiple dependence polyhedra may be required to capture all dependent instances, at least one for each pair of array references accessing an array (scalars being a particular case of array). It is possible to have several dependence polyhedra per pair of textual statements, as they may contain multiple array references.

Program transformation Program transformations in the polyhedral model are represented by a scheduling function. This function is used to reorder the points in the iteration domain, and the corresponding source code can be generated using polyhedral code generation [6]. A scheduling function captures, in a single step, what may typically correspond to a sequence of several tens of basic loop transformations [19]. It takes the form of a scheduling matrix Θ^R, whose coefficients drive the program restructuring to be performed.

DEFINITION 3 (Affine multi-dimensional schedule). *Given a statement R, an affine schedule Θ^R of dimension m is an affine form of the d loop iterators (denoted $\vec{x}_R$) and the p global parameters (denoted $\vec{n}$). $\Theta^R \in \mathbb{Z}^{m \times (d+p+1)}$ can be written as:*

$$\Theta^S(\vec{x}_R) = \begin{pmatrix} \theta_{1,1} & \cdots & \theta_{1,d+p+1} \\ \vdots & & \vdots \\ \theta_{m,1} & \cdots & \theta_{m,d+p+1} \end{pmatrix} \cdot \begin{pmatrix} \vec{x}_R \\ \vec{n} \\ 1 \end{pmatrix}$$

The scheduling function Θ^R maps each point in $\mathcal{D}_R$ to a multidimensional time-stamp (a vector) of dimension m. In the transformed code, the instances of R defined in $\mathcal{D}_R$ will be executed in lexicographic order of their associated time-stamp. Multidimensional timestamps can be seen as logical clocks: the first dimension similar to days (most significant), the next one to hours (less significant), etc.

The optimization of a full program requires a collection of affine schedules, one for each syntactic program statement. Even seemingly non-linear transformations like loop tiling (also known as blocking) and unrolling can be modeled [19].

4.2 Program Transformation for L1-resident Blocking

Tiling for locality involves grouping points in an iteration space into smaller blocks (tiles) [43], enabling reuse in multiple directions when the block fits in a faster level of the memory hierarchy (registers, L1, or L2 cache). Tiling for coarse-grained parallelism partitions the iteration space into tiles that may be executed concurrently on different processors with a reduced frequency and volume of inter-processor communication. A tile is atomically executed on a processor, with communication required only before and after execution. The tiling hyperplane method [11] is an effective approach for tiling of imperfectly nested affine loops. However, it can only generate tiled code for tile sizes that are fixed at compile-time. Alternatively, *parametric tiling* [5, 22], used in the present work, enables run-time selection of tile sizes. It has the advantage that tile sizes can be adapted to the problem size and machine used without recompiling the code.

The first stage of our optimization flow is as follows. Given an input program, we first apply a model-driven optimization geared towards maximizing the applicability of tiling [11]. Then parallel parametric tiling is applied, followed by full-tile separation. The process of separating full tiles leads to rectangular blocks of code whose loop bounds are functions of the tile sizes (which are run-time parameters). Each full tile is a potential candidate for effective SIMD execution using the codelet extraction and synthesis approach detailed below. We note that the codelet extraction and synthesis techniques are not limited to tilable programs. However, in our experiments in Sec. 6 we use benchmarks which can be processed by parallel parametric tiling.

The downside of parametric tiling is the generation of very complex loop bounds for the loops iterating on the various blocks (inter-tile loops), typically involving complex compositions of *ceil*(), *floor*() and *round*() expressions. Current production compilers often fail to successfully analyze the dependences in such loops, and therefore are unable to automatically generate the best SIMD code for the full tiles. This leads to significant performance loss in the generated program. However, using the information extracted by the polyhedral compilation framework, full tiles can be manipulated, transformed and vectorized using our proposed approach.

4.3 Convex Set of Semantics-Preserving Transformations

A key reason for the power and effectiveness of the polyhedral transformation framework is the ability to formulate, with a single set of (affine) constraints, a set of *semantics-preserving (affine) program transformations* [34, 39]. An optimization problem whose solutions are subject to these constraints will necessarily lead to a semantics-preserving program transformation.

To build such a set of constraints, the reasoning is as follows. First, we observe that for all pairs of dependent instances $\langle \vec{x}_R, \vec{x}_S \rangle$, the dependence is strongly satisfied if $\Theta(\vec{x}_R) < \Theta(\vec{x}_S)$, that is if the producer is scheduled before the consumer. As Θ is in practice a multi-dimensional function, we can more precisely state that the dependence is strongly satisfied if $\Theta(\vec{x}_R) \prec \Theta(\vec{x}_S)$, where $\prec$ is the lexicographic precedence operator. This can be rewritten as $\Theta(\vec{x}_S) - \Theta(\vec{x}_R) \succ \vec{0}$. Alternatively, given Θ_p, row p of Θ, we have $\forall p,\ \Theta_p(\vec{x}_S) - \Theta(\vec{x}_R) \geq \delta_p$ with $\delta_p \in \{0,1\}$. We note that once a dependence has been strongly satisfied at a dimension d, then it does not contribute to the semantics constraint and so we have instead $\forall p > d,\ \Theta_p(\vec{x}_S) - \Theta_p(\vec{x}_R) \geq -\infty$ (that is, a "void" constraint with no impact on the solution space).

The constraints for semantics preservation are summarized in Def. 4, and are the starting basis for our new optimization algorithm. For each row p of the scheduling matrix Θ and each dependence polyhedron $\mathcal{D}_{R,S}$, we associate a Boolean decision variable $\delta_p^{\mathcal{D}_{R,S}}$; these decision variables are used to encode semantics-preserving properties of a schedule so that for each pair of instances in dependence the source instance will be scheduled necessarily before the target instance. We bound the coefficients of Θ to be in some arbitrary range, so that we can find some arbitrarily large $K \in \mathbb{Z}$ such that the form $(K.\vec{n}+K)$ is an upper bound of the schedule latency [34], therefore $\Theta_p(\vec{x}_S) - \Theta_p(\vec{x}_R) \geq -(K.\vec{n}+K)$ is equivalent to $\Theta_p(\vec{x}_S) - \Theta_p(\vec{x}_R) \geq -\infty$.

DEFINITION 4 (Semantics-preserving affine schedules). *Given a set of affine schedules $\Theta^R, \Theta^S \ldots$ of dimension m, the program semantics is preserved if the three following conditions hold:*

$$(i) \quad \forall \mathcal{D}_{R,S},\ \forall p,\ \delta_p^{\mathcal{D}_{R,S}} \in \{0,1\}$$

$$(ii) \quad \forall \mathcal{D}_{R,S},\ \sum_{p=1}^{m} \delta_p^{\mathcal{D}_{R,S}} = 1 \tag{1}$$

$$(iii) \quad \forall \mathcal{D}_{R,S},\ \forall p \in \{1,\ldots,m\},\ \forall \langle \vec{x}_R, \vec{x}_S \rangle \in \mathcal{D}_{R,S}, \tag{2}$$

$$\Theta_p^S(\vec{x}_S) - \Theta_p^R(\vec{x}_R) \geq -\sum_{k=1}^{p-1} \delta_k^{\mathcal{D}_{R,S}}.(K.\vec{n}+K) + \delta_p^{\mathcal{D}_{R,S}}$$

As Feautrier proposed, the affine form of the Farkas lemma is used to build the set of all non-negative functions over a polyhedron [16], a straightforward process as Eq. 2 represents a non-negative function and $\mathcal{D}_{R,S}$ is a polyhedron. As a result, a convex set of constraints linking the various $\theta_{i,j}$ coefficients and the δ variables is obtained, such that each point in this space is a semantics-preserving schedule [34].

4.4 Codelet-Specific Cost Functions

We now present the set of additional constraints we use to formulate our scheduling optimization problem. The complete scheduling algorithm works in two steps: first we find a schedule for the program that maximizes parallelism, the number of stride-0/1 references, and permutability. Then we apply a second algorithm for minimizing the number of unaligned load/stores on the transformed program.

4.4.1 Additional Properties on the Schedule

In the present work, we impose specific properties on Θ: $\theta_{i,j} \in \mathbb{N}$. Enforcing non-negative coefficients greatly simplifies the process of finding good schedules. Large coefficients for Θ can lead to complex code being generated, containing modulo operations [6], and small values for the coefficients are usually preferred [32]. Our ILP formulation attempts to minimize the value of coefficients, therefore making them as close to 0 as possible when $\theta_{i,j} \geq 0$.

In addition, we use the so-called 2d+1 schedule form [19], which forces the scheduling function to be an interleaving of linear and constant dimensions. The number of rows of Θ^S is set to $2d+1$ if S is surrounded by d loops in the original sub-program, and every odd row of Θ^S is made constant (that is, $\theta_{i,j} = 0$ for all j except $j = d+n+1$). For instance, in this 2d+1 form, the original schedule of Fig 1 is $\Theta^R : (0,i,0,j,0)$ and $\Theta^S : (0,i,0,j,1)$. Those are computed simply by building the AST of the sub-program with loops and statements as nodes, and edges between a parent and its children in the AST. Edges are labeled by the syntactic order of appearance of the children, and to compute the original schedule one simply takes the path from the root to the statement, collecting the node labels and the edge labels along this path.

While not technically required for this work, the 2d+1 form provides a standardized notation for the schedules, ensures that at least one schedule exists in the considered search space (the identity schedule, as shown above), and tends to simplify the generated loop bounds when implementing full distribution through the scalar dimensions.

4.4.2 Minimizing Dependence Distance

The first objective we encode is designed to find solutions with good data locality. It also helps with other objectives. The minimization finds a function that bounds the dependence distance [11], for each non-constant scheduling level (the even rows). This function is a form of the program parameters $\vec{n}$, and requires additional constraints on Θ: all coefficients associated with the parameters $\vec{n}$ are set to 0. This only removes parametric shifts, and is therefore not a limiting factor unless there are dependences of parametric distances in the program, a rare case. This bounding function is defined as follows, for each row k of the schedule:

$$\mathbf{u}_k.\vec{n} + w_k \geq \Theta^S(\vec{x}_S) - \Theta^R(\vec{x}_R) \qquad \langle \vec{x}_R, \vec{x}_S \rangle \in \mathcal{D}_{R,S} \qquad (3)$$
$$\mathbf{u}_k \in \mathbb{N}^p, w_k \in \mathbb{N}$$

Intuitively, the value of $\mathbf{u}_k.\vec{n} + w_k$ is an indicator of an upper bound on the distance between dependent iterations. To minimize the distance between dependent iterations, we minimize the value of $\mathbf{u}_k$ and w_k. If, after minimization, $\mathbf{u}_k.\vec{n} + w_k = 0$, then the dependent iterations are scheduled at exactly the same time for this loop level, i.e., the loop is parallel.

4.4.3 Maximizing Fine-grain Parallelism

Maximizing fine-grain parallelism requires that no dependences in the generated code are carried by the innermost loop(s). Feautrier addressed the problem of maximizing fine-grain parallelism through an aggressive strategy of strongly satisfying all dependences as early as possible [16]. We propose a different form: minimization of the number of dependences to be solved by the schedule dimension $2d$ (e.g., the one corresponding to the inner-most loop), together with the objective of minimizing the dependence distance at that level. We use the following optimization objective:

$$\min \sum_{\mathcal{D}_{R,S}} \delta_{2d}^{\mathcal{D}_{R,S}} \qquad (4)$$

Indeed, if this sum is equal to 0, and if $\mathbf{u}_{2d}.\vec{n} + w_{2d}$ (from the minimization of the dependence distance at that level) is also equal to 0, then the inner-most loop is parallel as no dependence is carried by this loop. Minimizing both objectives at the same time ensures that we discover inner-most parallel loops whenever possible.

4.4.4 Maximizing Stride-0/1 References

We propose a framework to embed directly, as constraints on the coefficients of Θ, the maximization of the number of stride-0/1 references. It is a complex task to model such a constraint as a convex optimization problem, so that we can use standard solvers to find coefficients of Θ. The reader is referred to a technical report [27] for detailed examples.

Access functions after scheduling In a nutshell, we aim for sufficient conditions for an array reference to be stride-0/1, when the innermost loop is parallel. These conditions come from properties of the polyhedral code generation process which builds the expressions connecting the input iterator symbols (e.g., `i`, `j`) with the new loop iterators created (e.g., `t2`, `t4`). For instance, $\Theta^R = (0, i+j, 0, j, 0)$ is a valid schedule for R in Fig. 1. Two loops are created after code generation, and their schedule is given by the even dimensions of Θ: $t2 = i + j$, $t4 = j$. In the access `A[i-1][j]`, after loop transformation, `i` and `j` are replaced by expressions in the form of the new loop iterators `t2`, `t4`. This process is done by constructing a system of equalities between the `tX` variables and the original iterators, based on the schedule, and performing Gaussian elimination. Equalities with one original iterator on the left hand side are then obtained. With the above example, we would get `A[t2-t4-1][t4]`, which is not a stride-1 reference along `t4`, the inner loop.

Our approach to model sufficient conditions for the stride of a reference to be 0 or 1 is to reason about the system of equalities built to create the new references after loop transformations. Specifically, we want to ensure that the innermost loop iterator (to be vectorized) appears only in the right-most index function (the Fastest Varying Dimension, FVD) of an array reference, or does not appear at all in the reference. Otherwise, the reference is not stride-0/1.

As an illustration of a sufficient condition for stride-1: assuming the innermost non-constant schedule dimension p represents a parallel loop, then for a reference to be stride-1 it is enough to have (1) the schedule coefficients for rows less than p corresponding to the iterators present in non-FVD functions are non-zero at least once; (2) for at least one of the iterators present in the FVD function, the schedule coefficients for rows less than p corresponding to this iterator are all zero.

Convex encoding of access stride properties To encode this kind of property, we resort to two complementary structures in the ILP. First, a new set of Boolean variables $\gamma_{i,j}$ is introduced, to help us model when a schedule coefficient $\theta_{i,j}$ is 0 or not. There are as many $\gamma_{i,j}$ variables as there are $\theta_{i,j}$ variables, and for each of them we set $\gamma_{i,j} \leq \theta_{i,j}$. Intuitively, we sum these γ variables to count how many schedule coefficients are non-zero. For $\gamma_{i,j}$ to accurately capture when a schedule coefficient is non-zero, we maximize $\sum \gamma_{i,j}^R$ so that $\gamma_{i,j}^R$ is set to 1 as soon as $\theta_{i,j}^R$ is greater or equal to 1.[1]

Second, we use an auxiliary representation of the access functions, using a normalized matrix G^F for an access function F. Intuitively, it is used to represent which iterators appear in the non-FVD index functions, and which appear in the FVD with a coefficient of 1. G^F has two rows: all iterators appearing in the non-FVD are represented in the first row, and in the second row iterators appearing in the FVD with a coefficient of 1 are represented. Precisely, for the access function matrix F of dimension $l \times d + n + 1$, G^F is constructed as follows. (1) G^F has 2 rows and d columns. (2) $\forall i \in \{1..l-1\}$, $\forall j \in \{1..d\}$, if $F_{i,j} \neq 0$ then $G^F_{1,j} = 1$, $G^F_{1,j} = 0$ otherwise; (3) $\forall j \in \{1..d\}$, if $F_{l,j} = 1$ then $G^F_{2,j} = 1$, $G^F_{2,j} = 0$ otherwise.

This leads to the following definition [27], wherein besides the γ variables we also define new Boolean variables μ_F^j and ν_F^j (one pair per loop surrounding the reference F), and σ_1^F and σ_2^F to model this seemingly non-convex problem in a convex fashion.

DEFINITION 5 (Constraint for Stride-0/1). *Given a statement R surrounded by d loops; a legal schedule Θ^R where all loop-carried dependences have been strongly satisfied before level $2d$; a memory reference F_R^A for an array A of dimension l with stride-0/1 potential; μ_F^j, ν_F^j, σ_1^F and σ_2^F, a collection of Boolean decision variables; and G^F the normalized matrix for F. When given semantics-preserving Θ^R with parallel inner-dimension, the following constraints*

$$\left(\sum_{k=1}^{d-1} g_{1,j}.\gamma_{2k,j} \geq g_{1,j}.\mu_F^j\right) \wedge \left(\sum_{k=1}^{d-1} g_{2,j}.\gamma_{2k,j} \leq (d-1).g_{2,j}.\nu_F^j\right) \quad \forall j \in \{1..d\}$$
$$\left(\sum_{j=1}^{d} g_{1,j}.\mu_F^j \geq \sum_{j=1}^{d} g_{1,j}.\sigma_1^F\right) \wedge \left(\sum_{j=1}^{d} g_{2,j}.\nu_F^j \leq \sum_{j=1}^{d} g_{2,j} - \sigma_2^F\right)$$

are verified if $\sigma_1^F = 1$ and $\sigma_2^F = 1$ (stride-1), or if $\sigma_1^F = 1$ and $\sigma_2^F = 0$ (stride-0). Otherwise it is not stride-1/0.

The optimization objective is formulated as follows.

[1] As we perform lexicographic optimization, we can place this maximization as the very last optimization objective to not disrupt the actual performance-driven optimization objectives.

DEFINITION 6 (Maximization of Stride-0/1 References). *The number of non-stride-0/1 references is minimized by encoding, for each memory reference F in the program, the constraints of Def. 5, and optimizing the following objectives:*

$$\max \sum_F \sigma_1^F, \ \max \sum_F \sigma_2^F$$

Example To illustrate the above definitions, Fig. 4 shows how they are applied on a simple program with a single reference. The stride optimization objectives yield the optimum value of $\sigma_1 = 1$ and $\sigma_2 = 1$. $\sigma_1 = 1$ implies that $\mu^2 = 1$, which in turn makes $\gamma_{2,2} = 1$. Thus, in the final schedule $\theta_{2,2} \geq 1$. $\sigma_2 = 1$ forces $\nu^1 = 0$, which propagates and sets $\gamma_{2,1} = 0$. In the final schedule, $\theta_{2,1} = 0$ and $\theta_{2,2} \geq 1$. This corresponds to making the loop j the outer loop.

`for (i = 0; i < M; ++i)`
`  for (j = 0; j < N; ++j)`
`    A[j][i] = 0;`
	$G = \begin{bmatrix} 0 & 1 \\ 1 & 0 \end{bmatrix}$

$0 \cdot \mu^1 + 1 \cdot \mu^2 \geq (0+1) \cdot \sigma_1$	$1 \cdot \nu^1 + 0 \cdot \nu^2 \leq 1 - \sigma_2$
$0 \cdot \gamma_{2,1} \geq 0 \cdot \mu^1$ $1 \cdot \gamma_{2,2} \geq 1 \cdot \mu^2$	$1 \cdot \gamma_{2,1} \leq 1 \cdot \nu^1$ $0 \cdot \gamma_{2,2} \leq 0 \cdot \nu^2$

Figure 4. Example of stride-0/1 constraints

4.4.5 Maximizing Permutability

Our approach to maximize permutability is to add constraints to capture level-wide permutability [11], and maximizing the number of such dimensions. We first recall the definition of permutable dimensions.

DEFINITION 7 (Permutability condition). *Given two statements R, S. Given the conditions for semantics-preservation as stated by Def. 4. Their schedule dimensions are permutable up to dimension k if in addition:*

$$\forall \mathcal{D}_{R,S},\ \forall p \in \{1,\dots,k\},\ \forall \langle \vec{x}_R, \vec{x}_S \rangle \in \mathcal{D}_{R,S},$$
$$\Theta_p^S(\vec{x}_S) - \Theta_p^R(\vec{x}_R) \geq \delta_p^{\mathcal{D}_{R,S}} \quad (5)$$

Enforcing this constraint on all schedule dimensions may lead to an empty solution set, if not all dimensions are permutable. So, we need to relax this criterion in order to capture *when* it is true, while not removing schedules from the solution set. We start by introducing Boolean decision variables, $\rho_p^{\mathcal{D}_{R,S}}$, i.e., one ρ variable per δ variable, and set $\delta_p^{\mathcal{D}_{R,S}} \geq \rho_p^{\mathcal{D}_{R,S}}$. These variables, when set to 1, will make Eq. (2) equal to Eq. (5), and will not impact the solution set when set to 0. This is achieved by replacing Eq. (2) by:

$$\Theta_p^S(\vec{x}_S) - \Theta_p^R(\vec{x}_R) \geq -\sum_{k=1}^{p-1} (\delta_k^{\mathcal{D}_{R,S}} - \rho_k^{\mathcal{D}_{R,S}}).(K.\vec{n} + K) + \delta_p^{\mathcal{D}_{R,S}}$$

When a dependence has been previously satisfied ($\delta_p^{\mathcal{D}_{R,S}} = 1$ for some p), instead of nullifying the legality constraint at subsequent levels, we will attempt to maximize the number of cases where Eq. (5) holds, with the following optimization objective for a given dimension p:

$$\max \sum_{\mathcal{D}_{R,S}} \rho_p^{\mathcal{D}_{R,S}}$$

We note that as δ and ρ variables are connected by an inequality, maximizing ρ variables implicitly forces the strong satisfaction of dependences as early as possible.

4.5 Putting It All Together

The above constraints are all embedded into a single optimization problem, containing numerous Boolean decision variables, as well as the schedule coefficients for all statements. We combine all our optimization objectives into a single optimization problem that is solved by Integer Linear Programming, by finding the lexicographically smallest point in the space. The order of the optimization objectives determines which objective will be maximally/minimally solved first, with succeeding objectives being optimally solved given the max/min solution of the previous objectives. Our combined problem P is:

$$P: \left\{ \min \sum_{\mathcal{D}_{R,S}} \delta_{2d}^{\mathcal{D}_{R,S}},\ \min \mathbf{u}_{2d}.\vec{n} + w_{2d},\ \max \sum_F \sigma_1^F,\ \max \sum_F \sigma_2^F, \right.$$
$$\left. \forall k\ \max \sum_{\mathcal{D}_{R,S}} \rho_k^{\mathcal{D}_{R,S}},\ \forall k \neq 2d\ \min \mathbf{u}_k.\vec{n} + w_k,\ \max \sum_{i,j} \gamma_{i,j} \right\}$$

There may still be multiple solutions to this optimization problem, each satisfying the criteria for extraction of maximal codelets as per Def. 2. While technically enumerating all optimal solutions should be performed for best performance, in practice we limit ourselves to the lexicographically smallest solution of the above problem. The resulting schedule is then applied to the program, polyhedral code generation is performed, and candidate codelets are detected on the generated code (all parallel innermost loops with only stride-0/1 references are candidate codelets). Those candidate codelets are the input to the second stage of our optimization framework, which performs retiming+skewing of statements to minimize the number of unaligned load/stores. In addition, permutable loops are detected through dependence analysis on the generated code, and are marked as candidate loops for unroll-and-jam.

4.6 Minimizing Unaligned Stores and Loads

The final stage of our method to extract valid candidate codelets for ISA-specific SIMD synthesis is to minimize the number of unaligned stores and loads in each candidate codelet found by the previous loop transformation step. Despite the fact that hardware alignment constraints are usually dealt with at a lower compilation level [15], this task should more naturally belong to the high-level transformation engine, where multidimensional loop transformations as well as precise array dataflow analysis can be performed.

To achieve this objective, we perform a combination of *statement retiming* at the codelet level, and additional loop skewing for the unroll-and-jammed loops. Intuitively, we 'shift' statements in the codelet such that (when possible) all array elements which are referenced by the vectorizable loop become aligned if the first element being referenced by the loop is aligned. Previous work by Henretty et al. [23] develops a complete framework for statement retiming so as to minimize stream alignment conflict on innermost vectorizable loops. Our candidate codelets fit their definition of vectorizable loops, and to find the relevant retiming factor for our optimization purpose, we use a slightly adapted version of that algorithm. The main difference is that we add an additional scalar quantity to the shifts found by their algorithm so that stores to different arrays need the same iteration peeling quantity to ensure alignment with the technique shown in Sec. 3.1. This is not strictly necessary, but simplifies the code generation and can reduce the number of peeled iterations in the scalar prologue/epilogue codes.

Finally, we need to take care of alignment properties in case of unroll-and-jam of the loops. For this purpose, we resort to skewing the unroll-and-jammable loops by a positive factor, so that the array index expression along the FVD is a multiple of the vector length. Such transformation is always legal, as a positive skew cannot change the dependence direction. As an illustration, for a Jacobi-2D example the access function after parametric tiling and full tile extraction, but before retiming is of the form `A[-2t+i][-2t+j]`. Assuming $V = 4$, we apply an additional skew by 2 to unroll-and-jam along t, to get `A[-4t+i][-4t+j]`. In this manner, when unrolling by any factor along t and jamming in j, references will still be vector-aligned in j.

In summary, to minimize store/load alignment even in the presence of unroll-and-jam, for each candidate codelet we compute an ad-hoc polyhedral transformation made only of shifts and skews, and apply this transformation using a polyhedral code generator. The resulting codelet is then transformed to abstract vector code using the technique depicted in Sec. 3.1, creating valid inputs to the next optimization stage: ISA-specific SIMD synthesis of vectorizable codelets, as detailed in Sec. 5.

5. ISA-specific SIMD Generation

In this section we discuss the back-end compilation step that translates pre-vectorized code into machine-specific high-performance code. The final high-performance code is structurally similar to the popular auto-tuning package FFTW [18], the auto-tuning BLAS package ATLAS [42], and general-size auto-tuning libraries generated by SPIRAL [35, 41]: the main work is performed in small, highly optimized code blocks called codelets, which are automatically generated. A higher-level approach (the polyhedral framework to parallelization) breaks down the bigger computation into a skeleton that performs all the book-keeping and calls the codelets appropriately. The first important question is how to restructure the computation to enable the utilization of efficient codelets, which we discuss in Sec. 4. The remaining problem to solve is how to compile codelet specifications into highly efficient code, a problem similar to the role of `genfft` [17] in FFTW.

5.1 Overview

Our line codelet generator takes as input a specification of the tile code in a LISP-like intermediate representation (a one-to-one translation is systematically possible from our abstract SIMD form to this LISP-like form) that captures the necessary amount of information needed to generate highly efficient SIMD code. The representation is designed to convey everything that is known by construction (alignments, loop trip count properties, aliasing, etc.) without over-specifying the problem. Our codelet generator then performs various platform independent transformations such as common subexpression elimination (CSE), array scalarization and strength reduction. Furthermore more advances optimizations such as converting unaligned loads into aligned loads or ISA-specific strength reduction and pattern transformation are performed. Loops are unrolled in a reuse-conscious way that depends on the problem type. The output of the codelet generator is highly optimized sequential C code augmented by ISA-specific intrinsics. The code contains well-shaped simple loops, large basic blocks in single static assignment (SSA) form, easily analyzable array index expressions, and explicit SIMD vector instructions. This code is finally compiled with the target vendor compiler.

5.2 Line Codelet Specification

The input to our codelet generator is a program in a LISP-like code representation. The representation enables SIMD architecture-independent meta programs that construct architecture specific instances when instantiated. Only the information needed for performing the operation is captured in the abstraction, details regarding the hardware and the exact calling convention for the SIMD intrinsics are abstracted away using vector primitives that have a type and a length. During the code generation and optimization process the codelet generator will translate the polymorphic vector operations to their exact implementation according to the targeted platform and compiler.

The input language expresses the following operations in an ISA-independent way: 1) loads and stores that are guaranteed to be naturally aligned (e.g, in 128-bit SSE a 128-bit vector load for which the start address is 16-byte aligned), 2) vector splats and compile-time constants, 3) unaligned loads and stores and their displacement loop-carried or constant displacement modulo vector length, 4) in-register transposes across 2, 4,..., V registers (including pack/unpack and interleave/deinterleave), and 5) in-register partial and full reductions (e.g., horizontal adds or a dot-product instruction).

We show an illustrative example that is generated by the pre-vectorization stage below. The SIMD tile meta-program is represented as a tree data structure, using standard C-like commands (`decl` for variable declarations, `loop` for `for` loops, `assign` for assignments, etc.). Multi-dimensional array access is directly supported (`sv_nth2D_addr`), and the meta-program aspect can be seen in expressions like `isa.vload` and `isa.vloadu` (aligned and unaligned load instruction in the current SIMD ISA passed into the meta-program through `isa`). SSA code is supported by constructing "fresh" variables. The input language including meta-programming capabilities is extensible and new primitives needed by new types of kernels or new vector ISAs can be added easily. Our example show an editorially simplified input to the codelet generator specifying a 2D Jacobi SIMD vector line codelet. The full example contains more annotations attached to the variables.

```
Jacobi2D_tile := isa ->
  let(range0 := var.fresh_t(TInt), ...,
    vreg0 := var.fresh_t(isa.vtype),...,
    func(TInt, "jacobi2d_tile",[loop_bound_aligned_1,
      loop_bound_aligned_2, c4, c6, shift_0, shift_1, local_c8, B, A],
      decl([range0,k0,c8,vreg0,vreg1,vreg2,vreg3,...],
        chain(
          ...
          assign(vreg1,isa.vload(sv_nth2D_addr(A,add(mul(V(-2),
            c4),c6),sub(add(mul(V(-2),c4),c8),1),n,1))),
          assign(vreg2,isa.vloadu(sv_nth2D_addr(A,add(mul(V(-2),
            c4),c6),sub(sub(add(mul(V(-2),c4),c8),1),1),n,1))),
          ...
          assign(vreg0,mul(0.200000,add(add(add(add(vreg1,
            vreg2),vreg3),vreg4),vreg5))),
          ...
          assign(deref(tcast(TPtr(datatype),sv_nth2D_addr(A,add(
            add(mul(V(-2),c4),c6),sub(0,1)),add(add(mul(V(-2),c4),
            add(c8,sub(shift_0,shift_1))),sub(0,1)),n,1))),vreg6)
      ))
));
```

5.3 Code Generation and Optimization

Our codelet generator is a full-fledged highly aggressive basic block compiler with very limited support for loops. It instantiates the generic tile specification for a particular SIMD ISA and then optimizes the resulting code, and outputs a C function with compiler and architecture specific SIMD intrinsics.

Loop unrolling We aggressively unroll loops to produce large basic blocks. Modern superscalar out-of-order processors have huge instruction caches, reorder windows, store-to-load forwarding, multiple outstanding loads, and many other architectural features that are fully exercised in steady state only by basic blocks with hundreds of instructions. We convert the massive basic blocks into single static assignment (SSA) form to enable better register allocation through the compiler. In addition, unrolling a time loop by a factor of two allows transparently moving between an input vector and a temporary space, avoiding extra copy operations.

Loop pipelining and blocking The best loop unrolling strategy depends on the type of code that is underlying the tile codelet. Our codelet generator at present supports three patterns:

First, stencil and filter-type data flow graphs require software pipelining and register rotation. This is either supported in hardware (as on Itanium) or must be done in software through unrolling and multi-versioning of variables. Proper loop pipelining achieves the optimal steady state load/store to computation ratio (e.g., one load, one store and 3 flops per loop iteration for 1D Jacobi). Jacobi or wavelet filters are examples of this pattern.

Second, dense linear algebra-type data flow graphs have high arithmetic intensity. This enables register-level double buffering: on half of the register file a register tile computation is performed while on the other half of the register file in parallel the results from the previous register tile are stored and the data for the new register tile is loaded. The L1 tile of BLAS3 DGEMM is an example of this pattern [42].

Third, $O(N \log N)$-type data flow graphs require depth first source code scheduling [17]. This utilizes the available registers most efficiently and the slow-growing reuse help tolerating a limited amount of register spilling. FFTW's codelets, and SPIRAL-generated fixed-size FFT and DCT kernels as well as, sorting networks are examples of this pattern.

Unaligned vector array scalarization Unaligned load operations following aligned store operations are common in stencil-like codes and introduce two performance penalties. Firstly, unaligned loads are substantially more expensive than aligned loads, even on the latest Intel processors (SandyBridge and Nehalem). Secondly, the read-after-write dependency introduced by an aligned store followed by an unaligned load that touch an overlapping memory area is costly as it introduces hard barriers for the compiler to reorder instructions to hide memory latencies. They also can introduce problems in write buffers and store-to-load forwarding hardware and reduce the number of registers that can be used.

Our codelet generator performs an important optimization to eliminate unaligned load operations. It first unrolls the outer (time) loop of a stencil to collect the store and load operations from neighboring iterations of the outer loop in the same basic block. Next, it replaces unaligned loads with aligned loads and in-register permutations (vector shifts). Then, it replaces the ensuing matching aligned store/load pairs by automatic (register) vector variables, in effect scalarizing the SIMD vector array. Finally, it performs ISA-specific strength reduction and common subexpression elimination on the introduced permutation instructions to minimize their cost. Often, more than one instruction sequence can be used to implement the vector shift and carefully choosing the sequences allows to reuse partial results across multiple iterations of the innermost loop. The result is a large basic block free of unaligned memory accesses and thus free of unaligned read-after-write dependencies that would stall the pipeline. The basic block further can take better advantage of large register files and fully benefits from super-scalar out-of-order cores.

Alignment versioning On many SIMD ISAs the instructions required to shift data within SIMD registers to resolve miss-alignment take the shift value as immediate and thus require it to be a compile-time constant. On other ISAs different instruction sequences are required for different shift values. The miss-alignment may be introduced through a loop variable or may vary across codelet invocations. Finally, there may be multiple arrays that are independently misaligned.

When necessary our codelet generator performs code specialization with respect to unknown array miss-alignment. The largest scope within the codelet for which the miss-alignment is constant (usually either the whole codelet or the outermost loop body) becomes a `switch` statement that contains one `case` for each combination of miss-alignments. Each `case` contains specialized code that inlines the miss-alignment values and the resulting specific vector shift instruction sequences. The potentially large code size blowup is usually no problem given the big instruction cache size and can be compensated through slightly less aggressive unrolling.

Generic optimizations Finally, the codelet generator applies standard basic block optimizations used by program generators such as FFTW's `genfft`, SPIRAL and ATLAS. This includes copy propagation, constant folding, common subexpression elimination, array scalarization, and source code scheduling. The codelet generator also performs simplification of array indexing expression and expresses them using patterns supported by the ISA, and can generate array-based and pointer-based code.

5.3.1 Quality of the Generated Codelets

Below we show the code generated for an 1D Jacobi tile for Intel SSSE3. The instruction set operates on 4-way 32-bit float vectors and supports the `palignr` instruction. For readability we extract the kernel as inline function. In the actual generated code the function would be inlined. The example code is a partial tile codelet that does not have a time loop inside and thus unaligned store-to-load forwarding through unaligned vector array scalarization is not applied. Nevertheless, all unaligned loads have been replaced by aligned loads and the `palignr` instruction. The codelet generator implements a software pipeline that for every loop iteration of the unrolled loop loads one SIMD vector, computes one SIMD vector result with two vector adds, one vector multiply and two vector alignment operations, and stores the result.

```
__m128 __forceinline kernel(__m128 in0, __m128 in1, __m128 in2) {
  return _mm_mul_ps(_mm_set1_ps(0.333333333),
    _mm_add_ps(_mm_castsi128_ps(_mm_alignr_epi8(_mm_castps_si128(in0),
      _mm_castps_si128(in1), 4)),
    _mm_add_ps(in1,_mm_castsi128_ps(_mm_alignr_epi8(_mm_castps_si128(in1),
      _mm_castps_si128(in2), 12)))));
}

void jacobild_tile(__m128 *in, __m128*out, int n) {
  __m128 t0, t1, t2, t3, t4, t5, t6, t7,..., t17, t18, t19;
    t0 = in[0]; t1 = in[1];
        for (i=1; i<n-1; i+=20) {
      t2 = in[i+1]; out[i+0] = kernel(t0, t1, t2);
      t3 = in[i+2]; out[i+1] = kernel(t1, t2, t3);
      t4 = in[i+3]; out[i+2] = kernel(t2, t3, t4);
      ...
      t18 = in[i+17]; out[i+16] = kernel(t16, t17, t18);
      t19 = in[i+18]; out[i+17] = kernel(t17, t18, t19);
      t0 = in[i+19]; out[i+18] = kernel(t18, t19, t0);
      t1 = in[i+20]; out[i+19] = kernel(t19, t0, t1);
  }
}
```

Below we show the assembly generated for this function by the Intel C++ compiler 11.1 in 64-bit mode (EM64T), targeting a SandyBridge processor supporting the VEX encoding and 3-operand instructions. We see the compact addressing encoding and that on this processor the code looks almost perfect.

```
jacobild_tile   PROC
; parameter 1(in): rcx
; parameter 2(out): rdx
; parameter 3(n): r8d
        vmovaps   xmm1, XMMWORD PTR [rcx]
        vmovaps   xmm3, XMMWORD PTR [16+rcx]
        mov       r8d, 1
        mov       eax, 16
        vmovaps   xmm0, XMMWORD PTR [_2il0floatpacket.287]
.B2.2:: vmovaps   xmm4, XMMWORD PTR [16+rax+rcx]
        vpalignr  xmm1, xmm1, xmm3, 4
        add       r8, 20
        vpalignr  xmm5, xmm3, xmm4, 12
        vaddps    xmm2, xmm3, xmm5
        vaddps    xmm5, xmm1, xmm2
        vmulps    xmm1, xmm0, xmm5
        vmovaps   XMMWORD PTR [rax+rdx], xmm1
        ... ; about 300 lines of assembly repeating the last 5 lines
        ... ; cycling through the 16 XMM registrer
        vmovaps   xmm3, XMMWORD PTR [320+rax+rcx]
        vpalignr  xmm2, xmm1, xmm3, 12
        vaddps    xmm2, xmm1, xmm2
        vaddps    xmm5, xmm4, xmm2
        vmulps    xmm2, xmm0, xmm5
        vmovaps   XMMWORD PTR [304+rax+rdx], xmm2
        add       rax, 320
        cmp       r8, 401
        jl        .B2.2
        ret

_2il0floatpacket.287    DD      03eaaaaabH,03eaaaaabH,03eaaaaabH,03eaaaaabH
```

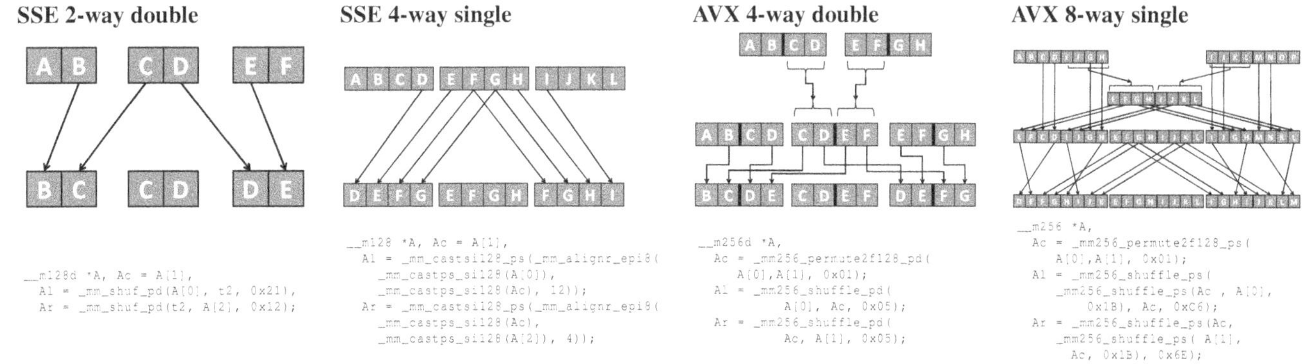

Figure 5. Extraction of left-shifted (denoted by `Al`), centered (`Ac`) and right-shifted (`Ar`) SIMD vectors from three aligned vectors `A[0]`, `A[1]`, and `A[2]` through permutation instructions. We display the data flow and instruction sequence for shifting on SSE 2-way double and 4-way single, and AVX 4-way double and 8-way single, as supported on Intel's SandyBridge processors.

One concern is the large size SSE instructions and decoder limitations, however, post-decoder micro-op caches can alleviate this problem on high performance processors. In Sec. 6 we will analyze the tile performance for a collection of kernels, machines and vector lengths.

5.4 Cost Model

Our codelet generator provides a simple cost model for the generated codelets to aid codelet (pre-)selection without the need for profiling the code. The line codelets are in steady state run cache resident (in hot L1 cache). Thus a weighted instruction count is a good first order metric to predict the relative performance of codelets. The metric captures the fact that generated codelets run close to the machine peak and this places a cost on every instruction, even if executed in parallel. The metric in particular allows to measure the vectorization overhead (number of arithmetic operations versus number of all operations). By counting source-level SIMD operations like `_mm_add_ps`, `_mm_sub_ps`, and `_mm_unpacklo_ps` instead of assembly instructions like `movaps`, `lea` and `mov` the metric is more resilient to effects on aggressive superscalar out-of-order processors like the Intel Core i7. We pick the coefficients for various operations to provide a relative ordering that favors cheaper operations over more expensive operations and models the relative cost of operations in the target micro-architecture. While the metric cannot predict actual execution times it is sufficient to prune the search space and find good candidates and aids auto-tuning in the high-level framework.

6. Experimental Results

6.1 Experimental Protocol

We evaluate our framework on a collection of benchmarks where the core computational part is a SCoP. Specifically, we experiment with 5 stencil computations that arise in typical image processing and physical simulation applications, and 3 linear algebra benchmarks. Problem sizes are selected to be larger than the last level cache (LLC) size of 8 MB. Each benchmark is evaluated using single-precision (`float`) and double-precision (`double`). Experiments are performed on an Intel SandyBridge i7-2600K (3.4GHz, 4 cores, 32KB L1, 256KB L2, 8MB L3), using either the SSE or AVX vector instruction set. The testbed runs a native 64-bit Linux distribution. We use Intel ICC 13.0 with `-fast -parallel -openmp`, except for the sequential baseline where we use `-fast`. For AVX experiments, the flag `-xAVX` is used.

For each benchmark, we apply the following flow: (1) loop transformations for parallel parametric tiling with full-tile separation, and coarse-grain shared-memory parallel execution; (2) for each full-tile, perform loop transformation to expose maximal codelets, and perform abstract SIMD vectorization; (3) for each codelet found, perform ISA-specific SIMD synthesis. This framework is implemented using PolyOpt/C, a polyhedral compiler based on the LLNL ROSE infrastructure [2]. The SIMD codelet generator is implemented in the SPIRAL system's back-end infrastructure. A web page and codelet generation web service with makefile tie-in can be found at [3]. On average, our end-to-end framework (not considering auto-tuning time) takes about 25 seconds to generate a program version for benchmarks like Jacobi-2d, laplacian-2d, or correlation; and about 3 minutes for benchmarks like Jacobi-3D, laplacian-3D, or doitgen.

6.2 Codelet Extraction Statistics

Table 1 reports statistics on the ILP scheduling problem developed in this paper. We report for some representative benchmarks the number of dependence polyhedra for array references, the total number of schedule coefficient variables $\theta_{i,j}$, the total number of additional variables inserted to model our problem, the total number of constraints in the system to be solved (this includes the semantics preserving constraints from dependence polyhedra), and the time to optimally solve the ILP using PIPLib. More details can be found in a technical report [27].

Benchmark	# deps	# refs	# $\theta_{i,j}$	# others	# cst.	Time (s)
jacobi-2d	20	8	140	486	3559	3.0711
laplacian-2d	20	10	140	502	3591	3.1982
poisson-2d	32	12	140	674	5277	5.8132
correlation	5	9	70	177	640	0.0428
covariance	3	4	70	176	593	0.0415
doitgen	3	4	117	269	911	0.1383

Table 1. ILP statistics

6.3 Tile Codelet Performance

Table 2 summarizes the operation count in steady state for the Jacobi kernels. This establishes the performance of the tile codelets in a stand-alone fashion. Here each codelet is made L1-resident, and is the result of unroll-and-jamming multiple loops in the codelet, leading to multi-loop vectorization in practice. We list the theoretical maximum floating-point operations per cycle and the actually measured floating-point operations per cycle for SSE and AVX on the processor described above, and also for a 2.66 GHZ Intel Nehalem processor. The SandyBridge processor supports SSE 4.2 and

Problem					SandyBridge 3.4 GHz								Nehalem 3.3 GHz			
					SSE 2-way		SSE 4-way		AVX 4-way		AVX 8-way		SSE 2-way		SSE 4-way	
Name	+	×	mem	shft	peak	meas	peak	meas	peak	meas	peak	meas	peak	meas	peak	meas
Jacobi 1D 3pt	2	1	2	1-5	3	2.5	6	5.5	4	2.7	8	8.2	3	1.4	6	2.9
Jacobi 2D 5pt	4	1	2	1-5	2.5	2.5	5	4.8	5	4.3	10	7.5	2.5	2.4	5	2.4
Jacobi 3D 7pt	6	1	2	1-5	2.3	1.2	4.6	4.5	4.6	3.8	9.3	8.9	2.3	1.1	4.6	4

Table 2. Cost analysis of the tile codelet specifications and performance (flop/cycle) on two different machines (Intel SandyBridge Core i7 2600K and Intel Nehalem X5680). We provide operation counts in steady state for adds/subtracts, multiply, vector shifts, loads and stores.

AVX and provides the three-operand VEX encoding for SSE instructions, which results in very compact code.

A three-point 1D Jacobi stencil in steady state requires one load, one store, two additions, one multiplication and two shift operations. The SandyBridge processor can transfer 48 bytes/cycle between the L1 cache and the register file, execute one vector (SSE or AVX) addition and vector multiplication each cycle and can perform one shift/permute operation per cycle. The decoder can decode 4 to 5 x86 instructions per cycle and caches decoded micro-ops. The hard limiting factor is the two additions needed per stencil result and thus the maximum performance is 6 flops/cycle for 4-way single-precision SSE (one addition every cycle and a multiplication every other cycle). We achieve 5.5 flops/cycle steady-state L1 performance. In the 2D case the maximum is 5 flop/cycle, which we achieve. This is a testament to the power of the latest generation of Intel processors and shows that our tile codelets are very efficient. The table summarizes further results across kernels and ISAs.

6.4 Full Program Performance

One of the key aspects of our framework is the ability to perform extensive auto-tuning on a collection of parameters with significant impact on performance. The two categories of parameters we empirically tune are (1) the tile sizes, so as to partition the computation in L1-resident blocks; and (2) the unroll-and-jam factor, that affects the number of operations in a codelet. While technically the parameter space is extremely large, it can be greatly pruned based on a number of observations. (1) We test tile sizes whose footprint is L1-cache resident. (2) We set the tile size of the vector dimension to be some multiple of the unrolling factor of this loop by the vector length, so as to minimize the peeling required for alignment. (3) We keep only tile sizes where the percentage of total computation performed by the full tiles is above a given threshold, so as to avoid tile shapes where a significant fraction of the computation is done by partial tiles. For 2D benchmarks we use a threshold of 80%, and a threshold of 60% for 3D benchmarks. (4) We unroll-and-jam all permutable dimensions, using unrolling factors of 1, 2, 4 and 8.

The auto-tuning is broken into two phases. In the first phase, approximately 100 tile sizes are tested and the 10 with the most iteration points in full tiles are selected. This process takes 2-3 minutes. The second phase tests 6-8 codelet optimizations for each of the 10 tile sizes, taking about 10-15 minutes.

Time breakdown over full/partial tiles and tile codelets To gain insights into the effectiveness and potential limitations of our framework, we first present a breakdown of time expended within tile codelets, within full tiles, and in partial tiles. Table 3 shows the performance comparison using 3 metrics: ATC, the time spent in all tile codelets; AFT, the time spent in all full tiles; FP, and the total time of the full program. We make the following observations: Peeling is the main reason for loss of performance when moving from ATC to AFT, and slowdowns can vary between 1.1× and 2×. The fraction of performance loss depends on the vector length and unrolling factors used in the FVD. Thus, these two parameters must be tightly coupled with the FVD tile size while remaining tile sizes must be relatively small for minimizing the peeling overhead. Also, partial tiles have a considerable impact on the FP performance. In general partial tiles can cause between 1.3× to 3× slowdown over AFT, and they are particularly detrimental for higher dimensional iteration spaces (e.g. Jacobi-3D and doitgen). In general, bigger tile sizes improve performance but only up to a certain point, as they also gradually push more iterations from full tiles into partial tiles, even reducing the number of tiles that can be executed concurrently. Finally, the accumulated effect of peeling and partial tiles execution can yield between 1.4× and 6× slowdown from ATC to FP.

Benchmark	SIMD ISA	ATC (sec)	AFT (sec)	FP (sec)
jacobi-2d	SSE	0.040	0.046	0.068
jacobi-3d	SSE	0.458	0.514	1.113
jacobi-2d	AVX	0.036	0.054	0.077
jacobi-3d	AVX	0.188	0.354	1.062
laplacian-2d	SSE	0.046	0.056	0.071
laplacian-3d	SSE	0.482	0.538	1.131
laplacian-2d	AVX	0.031	0.042	0.061
laplacian-3d	AVX	0.197	0.373	0.993
poisson-2d	SSE	0.051	0.064	0.090
poisson-2d	AVX	0.029	0.049	0.075
correlation	SSE	0.840	0.915	1.179
correlation	AVX	0.752	0.917	1.139
covariance	SSE	0.846	0.922	1.159
covariance	AVX	0.733	0.883	1.121
doitgen	SSE	0.191	0.353	0.865
doitgen	AVX	0.158	0.308	0.834

Table 3. Time breakdown for kernels: All Tile Codelets (ATC), All Full Tiles (AFT=ATC+Peeling) and Full Program (FP=AFT+Partial Tiles)

Overall performance Finally, we report in Table 4 the full-application performance for the benchmarks. For each benchmark × vector ISA × data type, we compare our performance in GF/s to that attained by ICC on the input program (both sequentially and with automatic parallelization flags) and PTile, the performance of PTile [5], a state-of-the-art Parallel Parametric Tiling software (tile sizes have been auto-tuned). The performance achieved using only the front-end of our framework (transformation for codelet extraction) is reported in the Prevect columns, i.e., we restructure the program to expose codelets but simply emit standard C code for the codelet body and use the C compiler's vectorizer. SIMD reports the performance achieved by using our ISA-specific SIMD synthesizer on each codelet after codelet extraction.

We observe very significant performance improvements over ICC and PTile, our two reference compilers. Up to 50× improvement is achieved using AVX for the covariance benchmark, for instance. We systematically outperform ICC (both with and without auto-parallelization enabled) with our complete framework using AVX (the SIMD/AVX column) since ICC fails to effectively vectorize most of the benchmarks. However, we note that due to the polyhedral model's limitation of not allowing explicit pointer management, the stencil codes have an explicit copy-back loop nest instead of a pointer flip. We note that the stencil benchmarks are

Benchmark	PB Size	single							double						
		ICC		PTile	Prevect		SIMD		ICC		PTile	Prevect		SIMD	
		seq	par		SSE	AVX	SSE	AVX	seq	par		SSE	AVX	SSE	AVX
jacobi-2d	20×2000^2	2.96	3.71	6.24	17.15	13.22	25.39	20.96	1.79	1.86	6.25	13.35	11.80	17.86	15.72
laplacian-2d	20×2000^2	4.30	4.44	6.29	18.7	17.85	24.86	26.57	2.15	2.23	6.30	13.19	13.13	16.01	18.53
poisson-2d	20×2000^2	4.23	6.68	17.47	19.56	14.75	31.77	42.23	3.08	3.36	16.86	15.19	11.31	20.67	29.77
jacobi-3d	20×256^3	4.21	4.70	3.82	5.38	5.04	3.84	5.53	2.22	2.06	4.01	2.70	2.87	2.67	3.41
laplacian-3d	20×256^3	4.80	5.44	4.39	6.13	5.67	6.99	6.26	2.55	2.38	4.58	3.34	3.17	4.15	3.98
correlation	2000^3	0.94	0.81	26.21	18.78	19.89	33.35	52.43	0.64	0.63	14.38	9.56	9.66	21.28	26.29
covariance	2000^3	0.97	0.99	26.53	18.70	20.08	34.85	55.92	0.65	2.16	13.52	9.66	9.70	21.88	27.23
doitgen	256^4	8.63	8.56	14.72	31.35	30.76	41.63	52.66	4.85	4.68	9.14	16.85	16.80	26.45	25.96

Table 4. Performance data in GFLOP/s.

severely memory-bandwidth bounded. Although ICC is able to automatically parallelize and vectorize the benchmarks, it is unable to perform time-tiling on the benchmarks and therefore the memory bandwidth limits the speedup achieved from parallelism. We also outperform, usually very significantly, the PTile research compiler in all but two cases (Jacobi-3D and Laplacian-3D, DP). These anomalies are due to our criteria of "good tile sizes" during the auto-tuning phase: tile sizes are selected based on the percentage of points that will be executed in full tiles vs. partial tiles. Therefore, a good configuration for our line codelet is not necessarily the overall best tile configuration. As explained before, increasing tile sizes shift iterations from full to partial tiles (which are slower) and reduce the number of concurrent tiles down to possibly a single one.

We also remark that the Prevect performance does not necessarily follow the vector length (and hence the arithmetic throughput), nor does it necessarily outperform ICC or PTile. One of the main reason is the complexity, in terms of number of basic blocks, of the codelets which are generated. By exploiting large tile sizes and unroll-and-jam, codelets with hundreds of blocks are generated and ICC simply cannot process the loop nest without splitting it, therefore negating the potential benefit of our approach. In general, we have observed that despite being in a form that satisfies the vectorizability criteria, the C code generated by our high-level framework does not lead to effectively exploited SIMD parallelism by the compiler, emphasizing the impact from an explicit coupling with a SIMD synthesizer. In some cases, ICC degrades performance with automatic parallelization, possibly due to inaccurate profitability models. PTile can also be slower than ICC parallel, due to complicated loop bound expressions as seen for single precision Jacobi and Laplacian 3D. The 3D stencils require a careful balance between maximization of the size of full tiles for high performance of the codelets, and keeping the size small enough to ensure that a high percentage of operations are in full tiles. Other tile shapes such as diamond tiling [4] may be needed for better performance.

7. Related Work

Automatic SIMD vectorization has been the subject of intense research in the past decades, i.e. [15, 26, 28, 30, 43]. These work are usually focusing on the back-end part, that is the actual SIMD code generation from a parallel loop [15, 28, 30], or on the high-level loop transformation angle only [12, 26, 38, 40]. To the best of our knowledge, our work is the first to address simultaneously both problems by setting a well-defined interface between a powerful polyhedral high-level transformation engine and a specialized SIMD code generator. Vasilache et al. also integrated SIMD and contiguity constraints in a polyhedral framework, in the R-Stream compiler [40], with similar objectives as ours. However, to the best of our knowledge, they are not considering the coupling of this framework with a powerful back-end SIMD code generator as we do. Other previous work considered inner- and outer-loop vectorization [31], our proposed work makes also a step forward by doing (tiled) *loop nest* vectorization, as codelets embed in their body up to all iterations of the surrounding loops.

Program generation (also called generative programming) has gained considerable interest in recent years [8, 9, 13, 21, 36]. The basic goal is to reduce the development, maintenance, and analysis of software. Among the key tools for achieving these goals, domain-specific languages provide a compact representation that raises the level of abstraction for specific problems and hence enables the manipulation of programs [10, 20, 24, 37]. Our codelet generator is an example of such a program generation system.

Automating the optimization of performance libraries is the goal in recent research efforts on automatic performance tuning, program generation, and adaptive library frameworks that can offer high performance with greatly reduced development time. Examples include ATLAS [42], Bebop/Sparsity [14, 25], and FFTW [18] for FFTs. SPIRAL [35] automatically generates highly efficient fixed-size and general-size libraries for signal processing algorithms across a wide range of platforms. SPIRAL and FFTW provide automatic SIMD vector codelet generation while ATLAS utilizes contributed hand-written SIMD vector kernels. While our transformation+synthesis approach bears some resemblance with those work, we address a much more general problem which requires to combine highly complex program transformations – that can be modeled effectively only by means of the polyhedral framework – with ISA-specific code generation.

8. Conclusion

Automatic short-vector SIMD vectorization is ubiquitous in modern production and research compilers. Nevertheless, the task of automatically generating effective programs — addressing the data locality, coarse-grain and SIMD parallelism challenges — remains only partly solved in the vast majority of cases.

We have made a statement about a viable scheme to achieve this goal, for a class of programs that arises frequently in compute-intensive programs. We have isolated and formalized program optimizations that can be effectively performed by a high-level loop transformation engine, from those optimizations that can be effectively implemented by SIMD code generation. We have used the power and expressiveness of the polyhedral compilation framework to formalize a series of scheduling constraints so as to form maximal *vectorizable codelets*, targeting parallelization, data reuse, alignment, and the stride of memory references in a single combined problem. As a result, we have unleashed the power of a custom ISA-specific SIMD code synthesizer, which translates those codelets into very effective (up to near-peak) SIMD execution. We have demonstrated the power of our approach on a collection of benchmarks, providing very significant performance improvement over an auto-parallelizing production compiler as well as a state-of-the-art research compiler.

Acknowledgments

The authors acknowledge support by DOE through awards DE-SC0005033 and DE-SC0008844, NSF through awards 0926688, 1116802 and 0926127, by the U.S. Army through contract W911NF-10-1-0004, and by Intel ECG.

References

[1] PoCC, the polyhedral compiler collection. http://pocc.sourceforge.net.

[2] PolyOpt/C. http://hpcrl.cse.ohio-state.edu/wiki/index.php/polyopt/c.

[3] www.spiral.net/software/stencilgen.html.

[4] V. Bandishti, I. Pananilath, , and U. Bondhugula. Tiling stencil computations to maximize parallelism. In *ACM/IEEE Conf. on Supercomputing (SC'12)*, 2012.

[5] M. Baskaran, A. Hartono, S. Tavarageri, T. Henretty, J. Ramanujam, and P. Sadayappan. Parameterized tiling revisited. In *CGO*, April 2010.

[6] C. Bastoul. Code generation in the polyhedral model is easier than you think. In *IEEE Intl. Conf. on Parallel Architectures and Compilation Techniques (PACT'04)*, pages 7–16, Juan-les-Pins, France, Sept. 2004.

[7] C. Bastoul and P. Feautrier. More legal transformations for locality. In *Euro-Par'10 Intl. Euro-Par conference, LNCS 3149*, pages 272–283, Pisa, august 2004.

[8] D. Batory, C. Johnson, B. MacDonald, and D. von Heeder. Achieving extensibility through product-lines and domain-specific languages: A case study. *ACM Transactions on Software Engineering and Methodology (TOSEM)*, 11(2):191–214, 2002.

[9] D. Batory, R. Lopez-Herrejon, and J.-P. Martin. Generating product-lines of product-families. In *Proc. Automated Software Engineering Conference (ASE)*, 2002.

[10] J. Bentley. Programming pearls: little languages. *Communications of the ACM*, 29(8):711–721, 1986.

[11] U. Bondhugula, A. Hartono, J. Ramanujam, and P. Sadayappan. A practical automatic polyhedral program optimization system. In *PLDI*, June 2008.

[12] C. Chen, J. Chame, and M. Hall. Chill: A framework for composing high-level loop transformations. Technical Report 08-897, USC Computer Science Technical Report, 2008.

[13] K. Czarnecki and U. Eisenecker. *Generative Programming: Methods, Tools, and Applications*. Addison-Wesley, 2000.

[14] J. Demmel, J. Dongarra, V. Eijkhout, E. Fuentes, A. Petitet, R. Vuduc, C. Whaley, and K. Yelick. Self adapting linear algebra algorithms and software. *Proc. of the IEEE*, 93(2):293–312, 2005.

[15] A. Eichenberger, P. Wu, and K. O'Brien. Vectorization for simd architectures with alignment constraints. In *PLDI*, 2004.

[16] P. Feautrier. Some efficient solutions to the affine scheduling problem, part II: multidimensional time. *Intl. J. of Parallel Programming*, 21(6):389–420, Dec. 1992.

[17] M. Frigo. A fast Fourier transform compiler. In *PLDI*, pages 169–180, 1999.

[18] M. Frigo and S. G. Johnson. The design and implementation of FFTW3. *Proc. of the IEEE*, 93(2):216–231, 2005.

[19] S. Girbal, N. Vasilache, C. Bastoul, A. Cohen, D. Parello, M. Sigler, and O. Temam. Semi-automatic composition of loop transformations. *International Journal of Parallel Programming*, 34(3):261–317, June 2006.

[20] K. J. Gough. Little language processing, an alternative to courses on compiler construction. *SIGCSE Bulletin*, 13(3):31–34, 1981.

[21] GPCE. ACM conference on generative programming and component engineering.

[22] A. Hartono, M. Baskaran, C. Bastoul, A. Cohen, S. Krishnamoorthy, B. Norris, J. Ramanujam, and P. Sadayappan. Parametric multi-level tiling of imperfectly nested loops. In *ICS*, 2009.

[23] T. Henretty, K. Stock, L.-N. Pouchet, F. Franchetti, J. Ramanujam, and P. Sadayappan. Data layout transformation for stencil computations on short simd architectures. In *ETAPS International Conference on Compiler Construction (CC'11)*, pages 225–245, Saarbrcken, Germany, Mar. 2011. Springer Verlag.

[24] P. Hudak. Domain specific languages. Available from author on request, 1997.

[25] E.-J. Im, K. Yelick, and R. Vuduc. Sparsity: Optimization framework for sparse matrix kernels. *Int'l J. High Performance Computing Applications*, 18(1), 2004.

[26] K. Kennedy and J. Allen. *Optimizing compilers for modern architectures: A dependence-based approach*. Morgan Kaufmann, 2002.

[27] M. Kong, L.-N. Pouchet, and P. Sadayappan. Abstract vector SIMD code generation using the polyhedral model. Technical Report Technical Report 4/13-TR08, Ohio State University, Apr. 2013.

[28] S. Larsen and S. P. Amarasinghe. Exploiting superword level parallelism with multimedia instruction sets. In *PLDI*, 2000.

[29] A. W. Lim and M. S. Lam. Maximizing parallelism and minimizing synchronization with affine transforms. In *POPL*, pages 201–214, 1997.

[30] D. Nuzman, I. Rosen, and A. Zaks. Auto-vectorization of interleaved data for simd. In *PLDI*, 2006.

[31] D. Nuzman and A. Zaks. Outer-loop vectorization: revisited for short simd architectures. In *PACT*, 2008.

[32] L.-N. Pouchet, C. Bastoul, A. Cohen, and J. Cavazos. Iterative optimization in the polyhedral model: Part II, multidimensional time. In *PLDI*, pages 90–100. ACM Press, 2008.

[33] L.-N. Pouchet, U. Bondhugula, C. Bastoul, A. Cohen, J. Ramanujam, and P. Sadayappan. Combined iterative and model-driven optimization in an automatic parallelization framework. In *ACM Supercomputing Conf. (SC'10)*, New Orleans, Lousiana, Nov. 2010.

[34] L.-N. Pouchet, U. Bondhugula, C. Bastoul, A. Cohen, J. Ramanujam, P. Sadayappan, and N. Vasilache. Loop transformations: Convexity, pruning and optimization. In *POPL*, pages 549–562, Austin, TX, Jan. 2011.

[35] M. Püschel, J. M. F. Moura, J. Johnson, D. Padua, M. Veloso, B. Singer, J. Xiong, F. Franchetti, A. Gacic, Y. Voronenko, K. Chen, R. W. Johnson, and N. Rizzolo. SPIRAL: Code generation for DSP transforms. *Proc. of the IEEE*, 93(2):232– 275, 2005.

[36] D. R. Smith. Mechanizing the development of software. In M. Broy, editor, *Calculational System Design, Proc. of the International Summer School Marktoberdorf.* NATO ASI Series, IOS Press, 1999. Kestrel Institute Technical Report KES.U.99.1.

[37] W. Taha. Domain-specific languages. In *Proc. Intl Conf. Computer Engineering and Systems (ICCES)*, 2008.

[38] K. Trifunovic, D. Nuzman, A. Cohen, A. Zaks, and I. Rosen. Polyhedral-model guided loop-nest auto-vectorization. In *PACT*, Sept. 2009.

[39] N. Vasilache. *Scalable Program Optimization Techniques in the Polyhedra Model*. PhD thesis, University of Paris-Sud 11, 2007.

[40] N. Vasilache, B. Meister, M. Baskaran, and R. Lethin. Joint scheduling and layout optimization to enable multi-level vectorization. In *Proc. of IMPACT'12*, Jan. 2012.

[41] Y. Voronenko and M. Püschel. Algebraic signal processing theory: Cooley-tukey type algorithms for real dfts. *IEEE Transactions on Signal Processing*, 57(1), 2009.

[42] R. C. Whaley and J. Dongarra. Automatically Tuned Linear Algebra Software (ATLAS). In *Proc. Supercomputing*, 1998. `math-atlas.sourceforge.net`.

[43] M. J. Wolfe. *High Performance Compilers For Parallel Computing*. Addison-Wesley, 1996.

Programming Languages in Security

Keynote

Fred B. Schneider

Samuel B. Eckert Professor of Computer Science
Department of Computer Science
Cornell University
Ithaca, New York 14853
U. S. A.
fbs@cs.cornell.edu

Categories and Subject Descriptors D.4.6 [*Security and Protection*]: Access controls, Information flow controls, Verification; F.3.1 [*Specifying and Verifying and Reasoning about Programs*]: Specification techniques

General Terms Security

Keywords Science of Security

Extended Abstract

Are programming languages part of the problem or are they part of the solution for building secure systems? We explore this question, starting with the roles that programming languages currently do play in building secure systems and roles that they could play. But to focus on language details misses some key opportunities.

Progress in programming languages is an exemplar for a discipline's transition from an art to a craft to a science that informs engineering. Moreover, evidence mounts that the same science base developed within the programming languages community is also useful for building a science of security. We will explore the similarities and discuss how a science of security is likely to be different.

We characterize properties that one might expect for a science of security, and we discuss the utility and limitations of existing language-based techniques in supporting that agenda. To illustrate, we explore some foundational problems in cyber-security:

- What does security mean for a system? This is clearly a specification question, but it has different scope than specifications for ordinary programs. Fundamental models studied in the formal methods community need to be revisited.
- How can we characterize classes of defense mechanisms and impose useful structure on that space? Is it in terms of attacks that will be resisted, policies that will be enforced, or orthogonality and limits to compositionality?
- How do we reconcile the two primary metaphors for authorization: access control versus information-flow control. Are they linked by notions of universality or by interesting reduction relations?

Acknowledgments Schneider is supported in part by AFOSR grants F9550-06-0019 and FA9550-11-1-0137, National Science Foundation grants 0430161, 0964409, and CCF-0424422 (TRUST), ONR grants N00014-01-1-0968 and N00014-09-1-0652, and grants from Microsoft.

PLDI'13, June 16–19, 2013, Seattle, WA, USA.
ACM 978-1-4503-2014-6/13/06.

CLAP: Recording Local Executions to Reproduce Concurrency Failures

Jeff Huang
Hong Kong University of Science and Technology
smhuang@cse.ust.hk

Charles Zhang
Hong Kong University of Science and Technology
charlesz@cse.ust.hk

Julian Dolby
IBM Thomas J. Watson Research Center
dolby@us.ibm.com

Abstract

We present CLAP, a new technique to reproduce concurrency bugs. CLAP has two key steps. First, it logs thread local execution paths at runtime. Second, offline, it computes memory dependencies that accord with the logged execution and are able to reproduce the observed bug. The second step works by combining constraints from the thread paths and constraints based on a memory model, and computing an execution with a constraint solver.

CLAP has four major advantages. First, logging purely local execution of each thread is substantially cheaper than logging memory interactions, which enables CLAP to be efficient compared to previous approaches. Second, our logging does not require any synchronization and hence with no added memory barriers or fences; this minimizes perturbation and missed bugs due to extra synchronizations foreclosing certain racy behaviors. Third, since it uses no synchronization, we extend CLAP to work on a range of relaxed memory models, such as TSO and PSO, in addition to sequential consistency. Fourth, CLAP can compute a much simpler execution than the original one, that reveals the bug with minimal thread context switches. To mitigate the scalability issues, we also present an approach to parallelize constraint solving, which theoretically scales our technique to programs with arbitrary execution length.

Experimental results on a variety of multithreaded benchmarks and real world concurrent applications validate these advantages by showing that our technique is effective in reproducing concurrency bugs even under relaxed memory models; furthermore, it is significantly more efficient than a state-of-the-art technique that records shared memory dependencies, reducing execution time overhead by 45% and log size by 88% on average.

Categories and Subject Descriptors D.2.5 [*Software Engineering*]: Testing and Debugging—Diagnostics; Tracing; Symbolic execution; Debugging aids

General Terms Algorithms, Design, Performance, Theory

Keywords Concurrency, Bug Reproduction, Local Execution, Constraint Solving

PLDI'13, June 16–19, 2013, Seattle, WA, USA.

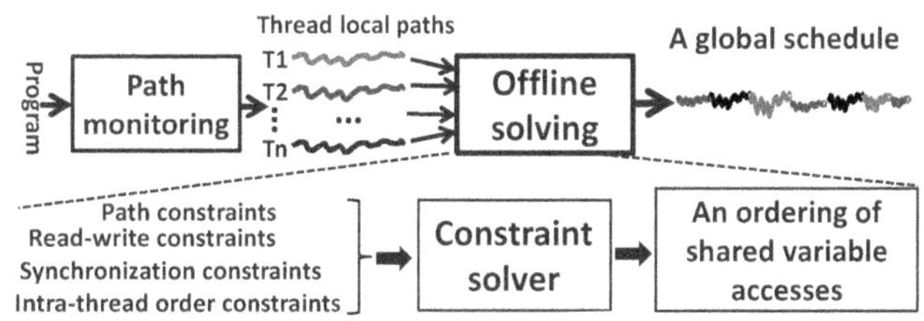

Figure 1. CLAP technical overview

1. Introduction

When diagnosing the root cause of a concurrency bug, to be able to reproduce the bug is crucial but notoriously difficult due to the nondeterministic memory races. Researchers have proposed a wide spectrum of techniques to address the bug reproduction problem. At one end, the deterministic record-replay techniques [12, 14, 21, 22, 26, 32] faithfully capture shared memory dependencies online. At the other end, execution synthesis techniques [36, 40] completely rely on offline analysis to search for shared memory dependencies without any runtime monitoring. Standing in between are several hybrid techniques [1, 23, 24, 29, 41] that explore the right balance between online recording and offline search.

Considering the production-like environments where we should minimize the diagnostic perturbation to the program execution, there are several critical drawbacks of the aforementioned bug reproduction techniques. First, the techniques that introduce locks [14, 21, 22, 41] to track race orders often make the program run much slower (LEAP[14]>6x and Chimera[21]>2.4x for programs with heavy shared memory dependencies). What is worse is that they can also exert the so-called Heisenberg effect by eliminating the concurrency bugs while trying to capture them. The locks they insert act as memory barriers and can prevent the instruction reordering common to most modern commodity multiprocessors. Second, recording values traces [23, 24, 41] to match the shared loads and stores usually incurs a considerable program slowdown and a large disk space to store the logs (Lee *et al.* [23, 24] and Zhou *et al.* [41] reported average trace sizes from 2MB/s to 200MB/s). Third, the complete offline analysis has limited bug reproduction capabilities due to the explosion of both the number of program paths and choices of thread schedules.

In this work, we propose a new technique, CLAP, that reproduces concurrency bugs without recording any shared memory dependency nor any value or order information, and without introducing any extra synchronization. Our key insight is to reduce this problem into two well-known problems: monitoring thread local execution paths and solving symbolic constraints. Since these two problems have been studied for decades, many highly optimized solutions can be directly leveraged. For example, for path collection, efficient solutions are widely available on both software and hardware levels, such as the classical Ball-Larus path profiling algorithm [4, 20] (around 30% overhead) and the hardware monitoring techniques based on branch predictors [17] and path descriptors [31] (as low as 0.6% overhead); for constraint solving, the SMT solvers such as Yices [8] and Z3 [7] are becoming increasingly powerful with the advances of theorem provers and decision procedures.

As illustrated in Figure 1, CLAP has two key phases:

1. Monitoring an instrumented execution of the program. Unlike most dynamic techniques that collect a global trace, this phase records only the local control-flow choices of each thread. In threads that exhibit bugs, these local traces lead to the occurrence of the bug.

2. Assembling a global execution that exhibits the bug. This phase in turns has several key steps:

- Find all the possible shared data access points (called SAP - a read, write, or synchronization) on the thread local paths that may cause non-determinism, via a static escape analysis.
- Compute the path conditions for each thread with symbolic execution. Given the program input, the path conditions are all symbolic formulae with the unknown values read by the SAPs.
- Encode all the other necessary execution constraints – *i.e.*, the bug manifestation, the synchronization order, the memory order, and the read-write constraints – into a set of formulae in terms of the symbolic value variables and the order variables.
- Use a SMT solver to solve the constraints, which computes a schedule represented by an ordering of all the SAPs, and this schedule is then used by an application-level thread scheduler to deterministically reproduce the bug.

With thread local path monitoring and constraint solving, CLAP achieves several important advances over previous approaches:

1. CLAP obviates logging of shared memory dependencies and program states, and completely avoids adding extra synchronizations. This not only substantially reduces the logging overhead compared to the shared memory recorders [14, 21, 41], but also minimizes the perturbation that extra synchronizations foreclose certain racy behaviors.

2. CLAP not only works for sequential consistent executions, but also for a range of relaxed memory models such as TSO and PSO [2]. We show that the memory order constraints between SAPs can be correctly modeled to respect the memory model relaxation. This is of tremendous importance, because it makes CLAP applicable for real production setting on commodity multiprocessors that allows the reordering of instructions.

3. CLAP can produce simpler bug-reproducing schedules than the original one. We are able to encode preemption-bounding constraints over the order of shared data accesses to always produce a schedule with the minimal number of thread context switches. With this property, it becomes much easier to understand how the bug occurs due to the prolonged sequential reasoning [15, 16]. Moreover, through preemption-bounding, the complexity of constraint solving is dramatically reduced from exponential to polynomial with respect to the execution length.

4. The constraint solving in CLAP is much easier to scale. The solver does not need to directly solve the complex path constraints (such as non-linear arithmetic or string constraints), but only to find a solution for the order variables that satisfies the path constraints. Thus, the solving task can be divided into two parts – generating candidate schedules (that respect the memory order) and validating them (using the other constraints). Since the first part which is searching possible executions does not have complex constraints, and the second which does have complex constraints is focused on a single execution, our approach is easier than traditional model checking. Moreover, observing that generating and validating multiple candidate schedules can be done in parallel, we have also developed a parallel constraint solving algorithm, which theoretically scales CLAP to programs with arbitrary execution length when there are sufficient computation cores.

We have implemented CLAP for C/C++ programs and evaluated it on a range of multithreaded benchmarks as well as several real world applications with intensive shared memory dependencies. Our experimental results show that CLAP is highly effective in reproducing concurrency bugs. CLAP was able to compute correct schedules that deterministically reproduce all of the evaluated bugs, and incurred only 9.3%-269% runtime overhead based on an extension of the Ball-Larus algorithm [4, 20] for collecting the thread paths. The constraint solving took 0.5s to 2280s for the sequential solver, while on an eight-core machine with our parallel solving algorithm, it typically took much less time (0.2s-63s). The computed schedules by CLAP typically contain less than three preemptive thread context switches, which is much easier to reason about for diagnosing the bug. Moreover, compared to a state of art record-replay technique LEAP [14], CLAP achieved significantly smaller overhead in both runtime (with 10%-93.9% reduction) and space (with 72%-97.7% reduction).

We highlight our contributions as follows:

- We present the design and implementation of CLAP, a new concurrency bug reproduction technique that computes shared memory dependencies through thread local path collection and constraint solving.
- We present a sound modeling of the execution constraints with respect to both the sequential consistent and TSO/PSO models. Any schedule that satisfies the constraints is guaranteed to reproduce the bug.
- We formulate the thread context switches into the constraints, which enables CLAP to produce the bug-reproducing schedule with minimal thread context switches and also bound the search space of the solver to be polynomial to the execution length.
- We present a parallel constraint solving algorithm that scales CLAP to programs with arbitrary execution length in theory.
- We evaluate CLAP on a set of real world concurrent applications. The result demonstrates the efficiency and the effectiveness of our technique.

2. Overview

We first provide an example to illustrate the key challenges in reproducing concurrency bugs. We then show how CLAP works for the example and outline the core constraint modeling.

2.1 Example

Figure 2 shows an example with two threads accessing two shared variables (`x` and `y`). Consider the two assertions `assert①` and `assert②` at line 9 and line 18, respectively. On the sequential consistent (SC) model, `assert①` will be violated if the two threads execute following the annotated interleaving `1-10-2-11-3-12-13-4-5-14-9`. However, this assertion violation is difficult to reproduce because the program contains more than `10000` different interleavings [25, 27] and a slightly different one may make the bug disappear. Worse, `assert②` will never be violated under the SC model, but can be violated under the PSO model that allows the reordering of writes to different memory addresses. For example, suppose line 4 and line 5 are reordered, `assert②` will be violated following the schedule `1-10-2-11-3-12-5-13-14-4-18`.

For the state of the art bug reproduction solutions [14, 21, 32, 41], having a small runtime perturbation is challenging, even for

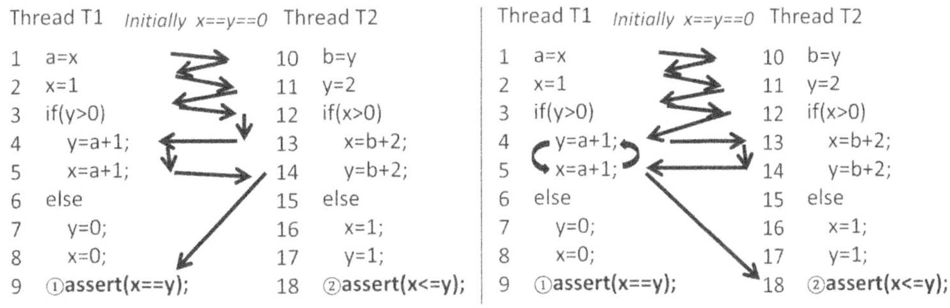

Figure 2. Example: concurrency errors on sequential consistent (left) and partial store order (right) memory models.

Thread T1 *Initially x==y==0;* Thread T2

path	***constraints***	***path***	***constraints***
1 a=x	a=R^1x	**10** b=y	b=R^{10}y
2 x=1	W^2x=1	**11** y=2	W^{11}y=2
3 if(y>0)	**R^3y>0**	**12** if(x>0)	**R^{12}x>0**
4 x=a+1;	W^4x=a+1	**13** x=b+2;	W^{13}x=b+1
5 y=a+1;	W^5y=a+1	**14** y=b+2;	W^{14}y=b+1
9 ① **assert(x==y);**	***R^9x!=R^9y***	**18** ② **assert(x<=y);**	***R^{18}x>R^{18}y***

(a)

read-write constraints

(R^1x=0 & O^1x<O^{13}x) | (R^1x=W^{13}x & O^1x>O^{13}x)
(R^3y=0 & O^3y<O^{11}y) | (R^3y=W^{11}y&O^{11}y<O^3y<O^{14}y)
| (R^3y=W^{14}y&O^3y>O^{14}y)
(R^9x=W^4x & (O^9x<O^{13}x | O^4x>O^{13}x))
| (R^9x=W^{13}x & O^4x<O^{13}x<O^9x)
(R^9y=W^5y & (O^9y<O^{14}y | O^5y>O^{14}y))
| (R^9y=W^{11}y&O^5y<O^{11}y<O^9y<O^{14}y)
| (R^9y=W^{14}y&O^5y<O^{14}y<O^9y)
...

(b)

SC order constraints

O^1x<O^2x<O^3y<O^4x<O^5y<O^9x<O^9y
O^{10}y<O^{11}y<O^{12}x<O^{13}x<O^{14}y<O^{18}x<O^{18}y

PSO order constraints

O^1x<O^2x<O^4x<O^9x & O^3y<O^5y<O^9y
O^{12}x<O^{13}x<O^{18}x & O^{10}y<O^{11}y<O^{14}y<O^{18}y

(c)

Figure 3. CLAP constraint modeling of the example program in Figure 2.

this simple example of less than 20 lines. For instance, to replay either of the assertions, there are at least 12 race pairs that need to be tracked. A more subtle but critical point is that the PSO bug might never be captured if one is not careful enough in adding locks in tracking the race orders. The memory fencing effect of locks can prevent the reordering in Figure 2 (right) to happen in test runs. And, if the runtime monitoring is disabled in production runs, the bug will surface to bite.

Both of these two assertion violations can be reproduced by the value-based approaches [23, 24, 36, 40], however, at the price of expensive logging of the value trace. Because both of the two buggy executions contain 12 reads and writes, there are 12 corresponding value cells (one per each read/write) needed to be recorded and stored into the value logs at runtime. Yet, the search space of the shared memory dependencies based on the value trace is still enormous, and the search problem has been shown to be still NP-complete in theory [11].

We next show how CLAP reproduces these two bugs without recording any race order or program state and without using any extra synchronization.

2.2 CLAP

In CLAP, we formulate the problem of reproducing concurrency bugs as a constraint solving problem, the goal of which is to compute a schedule (*i.e.*, an ordering) of the shared data accesses in the execution such that the bug can be reproduced. For simplicity, we shall refer to such access to shared data as shared access point (SAP), the read-SAP as Read, and the write-SAP as Write. At runtime, CLAP logs only the execution path of each individual thread. Then, offline, CLAP performs symbolic execution along the thread paths to collect and encode all the necessary execution constraints over the order of the SAPs. During the symbolic execution, since the value returned by each Read is unknown, we first mark it by a fresh symbolic value and later match it with a Write using the constraints.

Figure 3 shows our constraint modeling of the example program for both SC and PSO. There are two type of unknown variables: R^i_v – the value of read access to v (here v is x or y) at line i, and O^i_v – the order of the corresponding access to v in the to-be-computed schedule. For the value of each Write, given the program input, it could be either a concrete value or a value computed from the symbolic values of the Reads. To aid the presentation, we also use a symbolic variable W^i_v to denote the value of Write to v at line i in the example.

Figure 3(a) shows the path constraints. For instance, the constraints for the violation of `assert②` are written as $R^3_y > 0 \wedge R^{12}_x > 0 \wedge R^{18}_x > R^{18}_y$, meaning that, for this assertion to be violated, both the value returned by the read of y at line 3, R^3_y, and that by the read of x at line 12, R^{12}_x, should be larger than 0, and, of course, the value returned by the read of x at line 18, R^{18}_x, should be larger than that of the read of y at line 18, R^{18}_y.

Figure 3(b) shows the read-write constraints. The idea is to match each Read with a corresponding Write, following the rule that a read always returns the value by the most recent write (on the same data). For example, consider the read of x at line 1 (R^1_x), it may return either the initial value 0, or the value written by the write access at line 13 (W^{13}_x). If R^1_x returns 0, it should be executed before W^{13}_x, and we shall have the order constraint $O^1_x < O^{13}_x$. Otherwise, if R^1_x returns the value by W^{13}_x (which is b+1), it should be executed after W^{13}_x, and we shall have the order constraint $O^1_x > O^{13}_x$. Therefore, as shown in the first row, the read-write constraint for R^1_x is written as (R^1_x=0 $\wedge$ $O^1_x < O^{13}_x$) $\vee$ (R^1_x=W^{13}_x $\wedge$ $O^1_x > O^{13}_x$).

Figure 3(c) shows the memory order constraints, determined by the memory model. The memory order constraint for SC is the same as the program order among all the per-thread SAPs. For instance, we have $O^1_x < O^2_x < O^3_y$ in the SC order constraints, meaning that the statement at line 1 should be executed before line 2, and line 2 before line 3. For PSO, the memory order constraint is more relaxed compared to that of SC. Because reads and writes on different memory addresses are allowed to be re-ordered, the strict program order constraint is only applied to the SAPs on the same shared variable. For instance, we only have $O^1_x < O^2_x$, but not $O^2_x < O^3_y$, as line 2 and line 3 are accessing different data.

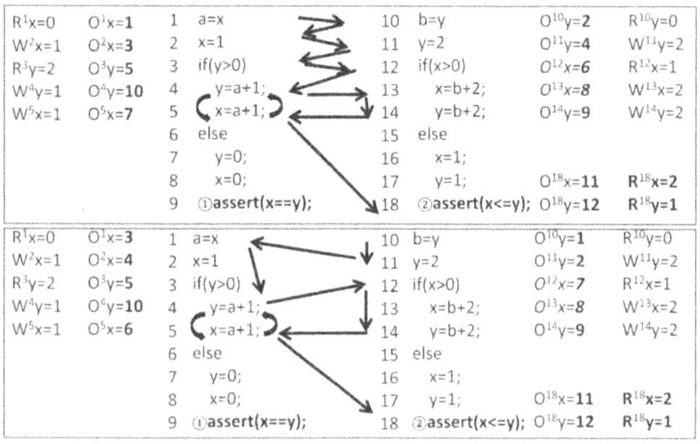

Figure 4. Two possible solutions returned by the solver for the PSO case. The first solution (top) is identical to the original schedule. The second (bottom) has the minimal thread context switches.

Taking all these constraints, CLAP invokes a SMT solver to solve them. Figure 4 shows two possible solutions returned by the solver for the PSO case (the result for SC is similar but simpler so we omit it). In the first solution (top), the computed schedule is identical to the original one. Following this schedule, at line `18`, the values of `x` and `y` are 2 and 1, respectively, and the violation of `assert②` can be reproduced. Better, in the second solution (bottom), the computed schedule has only four context switches, much fewer than that of the original schedule, but is still sufficient to reproduce the assertion violation. The power of our approach is that we can easily add additional constraints to always produce a solution like the second one, which has the minimal number of thread context switches. We will present more details on this property in Section 4.2.

The above example illustrates how CLAP works in a nutshell. We next answer the following two important questions:

- How to correctly model all the execution constraints? For example, for presentation easiness, we do not have any synchronization in the example program. How to model them? (§3)
- How difficult it is to solve the constraints? How to scale the constraint solving task in our approach? (§4)

3. CLAP Execution Constraint Modeling

From a high level view, we encode all the necessary execution constraints into a formula Φ containing two type of unknown variables: V - the symbolic value variables denoting the value returned by Reads, and O - the order variables denoting the order of SAPs in the schedule. Φ is constructed by a conjunction of five sub-formulae:

$$\Phi = \Phi_{path} \wedge \Phi_{bug} \wedge \Phi_{so} \wedge \Phi_{rw} \wedge \Phi_{mo}$$

where Φ_{path} denotes the path constraints, Φ_{bug} the bug predicate, Φ_{so} the inter-thread order constraints determined by synchronizations, Φ_{rw} read-write constraints over Reads and Writes, and Φ_{mo} the memory order constraints determined by the memory model. These constraints are complete because the intra-thread data and control dependencies are captured by Φ_{path} and Φ_{bug}, and the inter-thread dependencies are captured by Φ_{rw}, Φ_{so} and Φ_{mo}. We next present each of the constraints in detail.

3.1 Intra-Thread Constraints

The intra-thread constraints serve two purposes: they force every thread in the computed execution to follow the same control flow as the corresponding threads in the original execution, and they force the same bug to happen, *i.e.*, the same assertion to fail. Forcing the same control flow eliminates the search over all possible branches that common to the static techniques, thus simplifying the problem.

Path Constraints **(**Φ_{path}**)** The path constraints consist of the conjunction of the path conditions for all threads. The thread path conditions are collected by a symbolic execution of the program following the recorded thread path profiles. On each branch instruction, a new constraint that specifies the condition of the branch taken by the thread, is generated and added to the path constraint.

Bug Manifestation Constraint **(**Φ_{bug}**)** In our modeling, the bug is not limited to a crash or a segfault, but general to all properties over the program state. Φ_{bug} is modeled as a predicate over the final program state. For example, a null pointer dereference $x.f()$ can be defined as $V_x = NULL$, and a buffer overflow error can be defined as $V_{len} > V_{size}$. In practice, the predicate could be extracted from the core dump when the program crashed, or from the program assertion when the assertion is violated at runtime, or from any other properties checked at runtime.

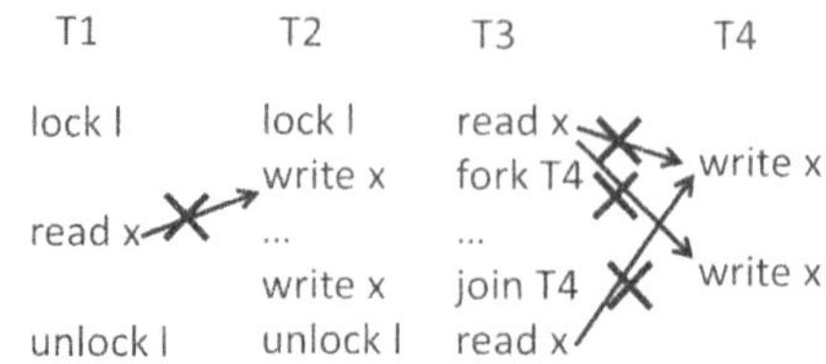

Figure 5. An illustration of the synchronization constraints

3.2 Inter-Thread Constraints

Inter-thread constraints are of two kinds: the synchronization constraints that govern the control flow between multiple threads, and memory constraints that govern the data flow between threads. We cover the synchronization constraints and then the memory constraints. For the memory order constraints Φ_{mo}, we also prove that our approach is applicable to both SC and a range of relaxed memory models such as TSO and PSO.

Synchronization Order Constraints (Φ_{so}**)**

We model the synchronization order constraints according to the locking and the partial order semantics. The locking semantics determines that two sequences of Reads/Writes protected by the same lock should not be interleaved, while the partial order semantics determines that one SAP should always happen before the other. For example, consider the program in Figure 5. The read of `T1` cannot be mapped to the first write of `T2`, because it cannot be executed between the two writes due to the lock. The first read of `T3` cannot be mapped to any of the two writes of `T4`, because it must happen before them due to the *fork* operation; similarly, the second read of `T3` cannot be mapped to the first write of `T4`, because the second write of `T4` always executes between them due to the *join* operation.

Φ_{so} is encoded as the conjunction of the locking constraints and the partial order constraints. We extract the synchronization operations for each thread and group them by the lock, signal, or thread they operate on. We use the memory address in the symbolic execution to identify locks and signals. For thread objects, because each thread creates its children threads in a deterministic order (i.e., following the program order), we create a consistent identification for all threads based on the parent-children order relationship. For example, suppose a thread t_i forks its jth child thread, this child thread is identified as $t_{i:j}$, and when the thread $t_{i:j}$ forks its kth child thread, the new thread is then identified as $t_{i:j:k}$. Readers can find more details in our previous work [13].

Locking constraints The locking semantics is concerned with the *lock* and *unlock* operations only. For each lock object, we first extract the set of *lock/unlock* pairs that operate on it, following the program order locking semantics, *i.e.*, an unlock operation is paired with the most recent lock operation on the same lock by the same thread. For each *lock/unlock* pair, we then enumerate all the other pairs in the set and add their corresponding order constraints with the chosen pair. Specifically, let S denote the set of *lock/unlock* pairs on a certain lock and consider a pair a_l/a_u. The constraint is written as follows:

$$\bigwedge_{\forall a'_l/a'_u \in S} O_{a_u} < O_{a'_l} \quad \vee$$

$$\bigvee_{\forall a'_l/a'_u \in S} (O_{a_l} > O_{a'_u} \wedge \bigwedge_{\forall a''_l/a''_u \in S} O_{a''_l} > O_{a_u} \vee O_{a''_u} < O_{a'_l})$$

The constraint above states that the *lock* operation a_l acquires either the initial lock, or the lock released by another *unlock* operation a'_u. In the first case, the order of the *unlock* operation a_u should be smaller than that of all the other *unlock* operations. In the second case, the order of a_l should be larger than that of a'_u, and for any other *lock/unlock* pair a''_l/a''_u, either the order of a''_l is larger than that of a_u, or the order of a''_u is smaller than that of a'_l. The total size of the locking constraints for each lock object is $2|S|^2 + 2|S|$.

Partial order constraints The partial order semantics is related to the thread *fork/join* and *wait/signal* operations. For *fork* and *join*, their order constraint is simple to model, because they can only be mapped to one unique operation. For *fork*, it is the corresponding *start* operation of the newly forked thread, and for *join*, it is the *exit* operation of the joined thread. Therefore, we can simply add the constraints that the order of a *fork* operation is smaller than that of its corresponding *start* operation. Similarly, the order of a *join* operation is larger than that of its corresponding *exit* operation. For *wait* and *signal* operations, the constraint is slightly more complex. Because a *wait* operation could have multiple candidate *signal* operations that it could be mapped to, we have to enumerate all the candidates. Also, because a *signal* operation can only signal at most one *wait* operation, we need to constrain the number of operations a *signal* can be mapped to.

To model this constraint, we introduce a set of binary variables for each *signal* operation. Each binary variable denotes whether the *signal* operation is mapped to a *wait* operation or not. We then constrain the sum of these binary variables to be less than or equal to one. Consider a *wait* operation a_{wt}, and let SG denote the set of *signal* operations that operate on the same *signal* variable as that of a_{wt} and by a thread different from that of a_{wt}. We model the constraint as follows:

$$(\bigvee_{\forall a_{sg} \in SG} O_{a_{sg}} < O_{a_{wt}} \wedge b_{a_{wt}}^{a_{sg}} = 1) \bigwedge \sum_{x \in WT} b_x^{a_{sg}} \leq 1$$

In the constraint above, WT denotes the set of wait operations the signal operation a_{sg} can be mapped to, and $b_x^{a_{sg}}$ the binary variable that indicates whether a_{sg} is mapped to a wait operation, x, or not. The total size of the constraints is $2|SG||WT| + |SG|$.

Memory Model Constraints

A crucial factor of the constraint modeling is the memory model under which the buggy execution occurred, as it determines what values each Read could return. The memory model is a parameter to our system in the sense that we take a declarative specification of the memory model, and combine it with the concrete program actions from the trace to produce a set of constraints that determine which reads can see values from which writes in the program. Conceptually, this approach is taken from previous work like MemSAT [3]; indeed, we could employ specifications in that style directly, since our thread path constraints and SAPs correspond to the elements of that model.

However, in this work, we are focusing on memory models for bus-based shared memory machines in which there is a global order among memory operations as they appear to the main memory. This allows us to simplify and use O as a total order; however, this is not an inherent limit and we could employ other kinds of models directly. Specifically, in CLAP, we currently implement Sequential Consistency (SC), Total Store Order (TSO), and Partial Store Order (PSO). We next discuss how Reads and Writes are constrained with respect to the memory order O, and then how O is constrained to model SC, TSO and PSO.

Read-Write Constraints (Φ_{rw}) For a Read, it may be mapped to a Write by the same or a different thread, depending on the order relation between the Writes. Consider a Read r on a shared variable s, and let W denote the set of Writes on s. We use O_r to denote the order of r, V_r the value returned by r, and O_{w_i} the order of the Write w_i in W. Φ_{rw} is written as:

$$\bigvee_{\forall w_i \in W} (V_r = w_i \wedge O_{w_i} < O_r \bigwedge_{\forall w_j \neq w_i} O_{w_j} < O_{w_i} \vee O_{w_j} > O_r)$$

The constraint above states that, if a Read is mapped to a Write, for this Write, its order is smaller than that of the Read, and there is no other Write that is between them. In our constraint construction, we first group all the Reads/Writes by the accessed memory address, and then encode the read-write constraint for each Read. Let N_r and N_w denote the number of Reads and Writes on a certain shared address, the size of the read-write constraints is $4N_rN_w^2$, which is polynomial to the size of SAPs. Note that this constraint is identical to the corresponding constraints in [3], with the change of O to be a single global order.

Memory order constraints (Φ_{mo}) For the sequential consistent memory model, the memory order for SAPs is the same as the program order. Consider two consecutive SAPs a and b by a thread t in the program order, their order constraint is written as $O_a < O_b$. We encode this constraint for each pair of successive accesses by each thread, following the recorded path profile. The size of the constraints is linear to the total number of SAPs in the execution.

For TSO, it does not require the program order and allows reordering Read and Write on different addresses. The hard constraint is that the original program order among all the Writes and among all the Reads is preserved. Hence, for all Writes and for all Reads by the same thread, we model the same order relation as the program order. In addition, for Reads, we need to make sure each Read returns the value written by the most recent Write on the same data. Therefore, for each Read, we first find the two Writes that 1) access the same address as that by the Read, and 2) are immediately before and after the Read, respectively, in the program order. We then model the order between the Read and the two Writes to be the same as that in the program order. Compared to TSO, PSO further relaxes the order relation between Writes and between Reads on different addresses. Our constraint model for PSO is hence similar to TSO, except that the order relation between Writes and between Reads on different addresses are removed.

Soundness With respect to different models, although the execution order of the SAPs by each thread may or may not be the same as the program order, we prove that our approach of computing a schedule among the SAPs is sound to SC/TSO/PSO memory models. More formally, we have the following theorem:

Theorem 1. *For SC/TSO/PSO, there always exists a schedule of the SAPs in which each load return the value by the most recent store to the same address, and following which the same program state can be achieved as that of the original buggy execution.*

Proof For all these models, once a store is visible to a second processor, it is instantly visible to all processors. It is impossible for two processors to observe different orders for any pair of stores. Hence, there always exists a total ordering of all the stores under these models. For loads, their order in the schedule can be determined by placing them after the stores whose value they accessed in the original execution and before the subsequent store, such that a load always return the value by the most recent store.

4. Constraint Complexity and Scalable Solving

Our constraint solving task is much easier than conventional ones involving complex constraints such as strings and non-linear mathematics. In CLAP, the solver only needs to compute a solution for the order variables that essentially maps each Read to a certain Write in a discrete finite domain (*i.e.*, the set of Writes on the same data as that of the Read), subject to the order constraints. To further scale CLAP, we have also developed two core techniques to improve the performance of constraint solving: preemption bounding and parallel solving. We next conduct a brief analysis of the constraint complexity, followed by the detailed discussion of the two techniques.

4.1 Constraint Complexity

Let N_{br} denote the number of conditional branching instructions in the execution. Let N_{sync} denote the number of synchronizations. And let N_{sap}, N_r, and N_w denote the number of SAPs, read-SAPs, and write-SAPs, respectively. Among the synchronizations, let N_l the number of *lock/unlock* pairs, and N_{wt}/N_{sg} the number of *wait/signal* operations.

Recall Section 3 that our constraint formulae consist of the path constraints Φ_{path}, the bug manifestation constraint Φ_{bug}, the synchronization constraints Φ_{so}, the read-write constraints Φ_{rw}, and the memory order constraints Φ_{mo}. The size of Φ_{path} is equal to N_{br} because each branching instruction generates a new conjunction clause over the symbolic value variables. Recall Section 3.2, the size of Φ_{so} is $2N_l^2$+$2N_l$+$2N_{sg}N_{wt}$+N_{sg}; assuming all SAPs are accessing a single shared variable, the worst case size of Φ_{rw} is $4N_rN_w^2$, and the worst case size of Φ_{mo} is equal to N_{sap}+N_{sync} (for all the three memory models). Because N_{sap}=N_r+N_w+N_{sync} and normally $N_{sap} \gg N_{sync}$, the size of Φ_{rw} is far larger than Φ_{mo} and Φ_{so}. Therefore, the total size of the constraints can be approximated as N_{br}+N_{sap}^3.

In sum, the worst case complexity of our constraints is linear to the number of conditional branches and cubic to the number of shared data accesses in the execution.

4.2 Thread Context Switch Constraint

Researchers have observed that most real world concurrency bugs can be manifested by a small number of thread context switches [28]. In CLAP, this observation can be directly encoded as additional constraints to bound the search space of the solver.

Recall that each SAP is assigned with an order variable, representing its position in the computed schedule. Our basic idea is to use the order difference between consecutive SAPs within the same thread to determine whether a context switch occurs between them. If the execution of two consecutive SAPs is not interleaved by other threads, their order difference will be equal to one; otherwise, the difference will be larger. To obviate modeling the non-preemptive context switches (as they always occur) and to create a uniform constraint for different memory models, we group a sequence of SAPs into segments, and use the number of interleaved segments to approximate the size of real context switches. This is a good approximation in practice because the context switch number is often small.

We first extract all the synchronization operations that cause non-preemptive context switches, including *wait*, *join*, *yield*, and *exit*. For brevity, we call them *must-interleave* operations. We use these operations to divide the SAPs into segments for each thread. Each segment contains only one must-interleave operation which leads or ends the segment. Note that the must-interleave operations are not allowed to be reordered (because they are synchronizations). In the final schedule, the leading (ending) operation in each segment will always have the smallest (largest) order among all the SAPs in the same segment. For each segment, we then use the difference between the orders of the ending and the leading operations to determine whether a context switch occurs or not in the segment. Let S_t denote the set of segments by thread t, a_l and a_e the leading and ending SAP in a segment s, and N_{cs} the specified context switch bound. The constraint is written as:

$$\Sigma_{t \in T} \Sigma_{s \in S_t} \begin{cases} 1 & \text{if } O_{a_e} - O_{a_l} > |s| - 1 \\ 0 & \text{otherwise.} \end{cases} \leq N_{cs}$$

The above formula states that the total number of interleaved segments for all threads is bounded by N_{cs}.

Minimal thread context switches The method above not only bounds the search space, but can also be used to produce the schedules with minimal number of context switches. Specifically, we can start from the constraint with zero thread context switch, and increment the context switch number when the solver fails to return a solution. We repeat this process until a solution is found. In this way, we can always produce a schedule with the fewest thread context switches among all the bug-reproducing schedules.

4.3 Parallel Constraint Solving Algorithm

Our core idea to parallelize the constraint solving is to treat the memory order constraints Φ_{mo} separately from the other constraints. We first generate candidate schedules that satisfy Φ_{mo}, and then employ the solver to validate each candidate schedule, *i.e.*, checking if it satisfies all the other constraints. This method has two salient features. First, we can generate different schedules and validate them in parallel. Each single schedule generation and validation is independent and fast (requiring only a linear scan of the SAPs and the constraints). The whole constraint solving task can then be divided into many independent subtasks that each works on a candidate schedule. Second, we can generate the schedules with the increasing number of context switches, allowing us to bound the search space similar to that of the bounded dynamic schedule exploration approaches [27, 28].

A key challenge in this approach is how to avoid generating duplicated schedules. To address this problem, we represent the context switches in a schedule by a set of *context switching points* (CSP). A CSP is a location in the schedule where a context switch occurs. It can be uniquely identified in an ordered way by a triple ($t1$,k,$t2$), denoting that a thread $t1$ is interleaved by another thread $t2$ immediately before the kth SAP of $t1$. Different CSPs are then combined together into a CSP set, and the set is used to guide the schedule generation procedure.

Preemption-bounded schedule generation Given a context switch number c (= 0,1,2,. . .), we first generate all the CSP sets of size c. For each CSP set (including the empty set), we fork a separate process that generates the corresponding schedules. Each generated schedule is then validated by the solver to determine its correctness. Our algorithms for generating schedules for SC and for TSO/PSO are mostly the same with only slight difference. The complexity of our algorithm is linear to the total number of SAPs. The size of the schedules is bounded by $\binom{c}{N}(N + c)!$, where c is the number of context switches and N is the total number of SAPs.

SC We associate each thread with a stack that contains the SAPs of the thread in the program order. Starting from the main thread, each schedule-generation process attempts to pop up one SAP from the thread's stack, subject to a condition: the input set S contains no CSP ($t1$,k,$t2$) that matches the current thread (t) and the current SAP (i). If the condition is not met ($t = t1$ and $i = k$), it means that a context switch should happen at this point, so we jump to the stack of the interleaving thread ($t2$). This process is repeated until all SAPs are popped up.

Note that each process usually generates more than one schedule. This is because, when the stack of the current thread becomes empty, we have multiple remaining threads to jump to and each choice will generate a different schedule. In that case, we remove the current thread and fork multiple children processes to continue the schedule generation. Each child process jumps to the stack of a different thread in the remaining thread set and repeat the process.

TSO/PSO As Reads/Writes are allowed to be reordered in TSO and PSO models, we can no longer use a stack to represent the memory order constraints. Instead, we use a tree structure (called SAP-tree) to represent the order relation between SAPs for each thread. Each node in the SAP-tree represents a SAP and the parent-child relation between nodes represents a store-load data dependence or a memory-model determined order relation. In TSO, the parent-child relation is applied on all Writes in the program order, while in PSO it is applied on the Writes for each memory address.

Similar to that of SC, the schedule generation process for TSO/PSO repeatedly removes an ancestor node (which has no parent) from a SAP-tree, until the SAP-trees for all threads become empty. Whenever there are multiple ancestor nodes in the tree (because an ancestor node with multiple children nodes may be removed in the previous step), we fork the same number of sub-processes each of which continues the schedule generation starting with one of the ancestor nodes.

5. Implementation

We have implemented CLAP on top of LLVM and KLEE-2.9 [5] with the STP solver [10]. To adapt KLEE to CLAP, we made four key modifications. First, KLEE works only with sequential programs, thus we extended it to support multiple threads. Specifically, we modified KLEE to spawn a new instance for each new thread and added the necessary extension to uniquely identify threads (see Section 3). Second, we changed KLEE to only follow the recorded path profile for each thread, and to only collect the path constraints without solving them. At the end of the run, we unify the constraints collected from each thread as the path constraints. Third, we adapted KLEE to return a new symbolic value for the load instructions that access shared memory addresses. Fourth, we modified the constraint solving utility, Kleaver, to incorporate the path constraints with the other execution constraints. We wrote our own constraint generation engine based on the SAPs collected from the thread local paths during the symbolic analysis phase.

Thread Local Path Collection Path monitoring is a pluggable component in our approach. Ideally, we can use hardware monitoring techniques such as the work of Vaswani *et al.* [31] which has negligible (around 0.6%) overhead. Our current implementation is an extension of the classical Ball-Larus algorithm [4, 20] based on a LLVM function pass. It works for multithreaded C/C++ programs that use PThreads and incurs 9.3%-269% runtime overhead in our experiment. From a high level view, we break the whole path into a sequence of segments, each of which is a Ball-Larus (BL) profile. A new segment starts when a new function is called, or an intra-procedural path is re-entered. We analyze the control flow graph of each function and insert instrumentations at the following points: the entrance/exit of each function, the beginning of basic blocks that have a back edge, and the branching points analyzed by the Ball-Larus algorithm. Each function is uniquely labeled (represented by a number), and each BL path inside the same function is also uniquely labeled (computed as the sum of the encoded edge weights at runtime). During the execution, we collect the whole path profile for each thread by recording the sequence of the labels for the function calls and for the BL paths. To distinguish between the BL paths that have the same label but are in different functions, we also log the exit of each function to demarcate the sequence of BL paths. The recorded labels are then decoded to produce the whole path profile, and to guide our symbolic analysis.

Shared Memory Access Identification Identifying shared data accesses is orthogonal to our approach but important for reducing the size of the constraints. Naively, we would mark all loads and stores as shared data accesses. This would produce a huge amount of unnecessary constraints, since the constraints with only the thread local data accesses are essentially redundant. A better way is to detect shared data accesses at runtime, where the accessed address is available for every memory operation. To overcome the virtual address recycling issue, we also need to record malloc/free operations to identify truly shared memory locations. However, this method does not fit our design as it inevitably causes additional program slowdown. In CLAP, we perform a static thread sharing analysis based on the Locksmith [30] race detector to identify shared variable accesses, including also the treatment of shared pointers and heap locations. Though being conservative, it is very effective to determine thread-local locations and, more importantly, does not introduce any runtime cost.

Deterministic Bug Reproduction Our application level thread scheduler is implemented based on Tinertia [16]. We add instrumentations before each SAP in the program and employ the dynamic thread interpolation to intercept PThread library calls. Through the inserted instrumentations, we are able to enforce the thread execution order of the SAPs to strictly follow that of the computed bug-reproducing schedule. Whenever a thread is going to execute a SAP, we first check the schedule to decide whether it is the correct turn for the thread to continue execution. If not, we put the thread in a postponed thread queue and make it wait until all the SAPs before it have been executed.

Challenges and Treatments

External Function Calls A known challenge in symbolic execution is the existence of external function calls that make the path constraints incomplete. Although KLEE tried its best to simulate the external environments (i.e., file systems and system libraries), it still suffers from this problem when facing unresolved external calls. However, this problem is not fundamental to CLAP because, for bug reproduction, we can record the runtime input/return values of all the external calls, and use the value pairs to construct the constraints of the external interfaces. A negative side of this method is that it would over-approximate the behavior of the external functions, which reduces the scheduling space explored by CLAP. In practice, to avoid limiting the capability of CLAP too much, we choose to first resolve the external functions as much as possible. In addition, we try to avoid flagging as symbolic the variables that have value flows to unresolved external calls. In our experiments, the external functions are seldom related to symbolic variables, and we did not face much difficulty in this problem.

Symbolic Address Resolution Another known issue in symbolic execution is the resolution of symbolic memory addresses. As KLEE does not perform any pointer tracking, when facing reads or writes to symbolic addresses, it would exhaustively search all allocated objects and forks execution for each possible base object. This usually takes a long time and also produces quite a number of unnecessary memory states. In CLAP, since the symbolic analysis phase follows the recorded thread execution path, we only need to explore one memory state for each thread. To avoid the state explosion, we choose to delay the object resolution for symbolic addresses to the constraint solving phase. Specifically, during symbolic execution, we keep track of the base object for each memory operation. For each base object, we maintain an ordered list of writes to symbolic addresses performed so far. Each write is remembered as a pair consisting of the location that was updated, and the expression that was written to that location. For any subsequent read, the loaded value is resolved from the ordered list with a set of constraints. As an example, suppose the ordered list of writes to an array is $\langle a[0] = 0, a[1] = 0, \ldots, a[n] = 0, a[i1] = x, a[i2] = y \rangle$. For a read $b = a[j]$, we create the constraint $(j = i2 \wedge b = y) \vee (j \neq i2 \wedge j = i1 \wedge b = x) \vee (j \neq i2 \wedge j \neq i1 \wedge b = 0)$, and add it to the path constraints.

Input Non-determinism Currently, CLAP assumes that the program input is deterministic. CLAP does not record the program input as we mainly address the problem of scheduling non-determinism in this work (which is more significant and difficult). If the program input is non-deterministic, CLAP might not be able to reproduce the bug. Nevertheless, similar to the treatment of external functions, this problem can be addressed by recording and enforcing the same input value during the bug reproduction execution.

6. Experiments

We have evaluated CLAP on a variety of real world multithreaded C/C++ applications with known or seeded bugs collected from [16, 39], including *pbzip2-0.9.4*, a parallel implementation of bzip; *aget-0.4.1*, a parallel FTP/HTTP downloading utility; *ctrace*, a multithreaded tracing library; *pfscan*, a parallel file scanner; *swarm*, a parallel sort implementation; *bbuf*, a shared bounded buffer implementation; and the *apache-2.2.9* web server. To assess the limit of CLAP, we also examined with *simp_race*, a simple racey program [16], and *racey*, a benchmark for deterministic replay systems [38]. To evaluate CLAP for reproducing bugs on relaxed memory models, we also examined with the implementations of three classical mutual exclusion algorithms - *dekker*, *bakery* and *peterson*.

Setup CLAP works in three phases: 1) online path collection; 2) offline constraint generation and solving; 3) bug replay execution. In phase 1, the thread paths are dumped to disk when the bug occurs. Due to the rare erroneous thread interleaving, most concurrency bugs are difficult to manifest. To trigger the bug in our experiment, we typically inserted timing delays at key places in the program and ran it many times until the bug occurred, and we added the corresponding assertion to denote the bug manifestation. In phase 2, the constructed constraints were first saved to a file which is then provided to the solver to compute a schedule. In phase 3, CLAP enforced the replay to follow the computed schedule to reproduce the bug. All our experiments were conducted on an eight-core 3GHz machine with 16GB memory and Linux 2.6.22.

6.1 CLAP Bug Reproduction Effectiveness

Table 1 summarizes our experimental results. Overall, CLAP is highly effective in reproducing concurrency bugs. For all the eleven evaluated bugs and injected violations including three relaxed memory model related failures, CLAP is able to reproduce all of them by producing a schedule with a small number of thread context switches. Most of the computed schedules contain less than three preemptive context switches, except for the *racey* benchmark, in which at least 276 context switches are needed to reproduce the injected violation. The size of the constraints range from 341 to more than 400M clauses with 26 to 2M unknown variables, and the total time for constructing and solving these constraints ranges from 2s to around 50 mins. We next discuss the results for several interesting applications in detail.

pbzip2-0.9.4 contains a known order violation bug frequently studied in concurrency defect analysis techniques [16, 18, 19, 35, 39]. The main thread communicates with a set of consumer threads through a FIFO queue with a mutex protecting the data accesses. The bug occurs intermittently when the main thread nullifies the mutex before some consumer threads are still using it, causing program crashes. The buggy execution contains four threads compressing a 80K file. There are 18 variables identified as shared (including all the global variables and the variables associated with the FIFO queue) by the static escape analysis [30] and are marked as symbolic. Upon crash, it executed a total number of 4K instructions with 65 SAPs and 473 conditional branches (excluding calls to external libraries). It took CLAP 4s to construct the symbolic constraints, containing 102 unknown variables and 5K clauses. The STP solver took around 5s to compute a bug-reproducing schedule with two preemptive thread context switches.

apache-2.2.9 bug #45605 is a multi-variable atomicity violation between a set of listener threads and worker threads on accessing a shared queue data structure, causing an assertion violation that finally crashes the server. We started four clients to simultaneously send a number of requests until the assertion was violated. The collected path profiles contain 28 threads executing a total number of 6.8M instructions with 962K branches. We identified a total number of 22 variables as shared symbolic variables in the buggy run. To bound the search space, we constrained the size of preemptive thread context switches to be less than three. It took CLAP around 13 minutes to collect and encode the execution constraints, which contain 81K unknown variables and 10M clauses. CLAP solved the constraints in 344s and produced a bug-reproducing schedule with three preemptive thread context switches.

racey is a specially designed benchmark [38] with numerous intentional races that make it very likely to produce a different output if a different race occurs. We assessed the bug reproduction capability of CLAP by applying it to reproduce the same output in racey. There are three shared variables: a 64-union array upon which the core computation between threads is operated, and two volatile variables for coordinating the start of the threads. To avoid out of memory error, we set the loop iterations (*MAX_LOOP*) to 500000. The test execution contained 3 threads, 7.1M branches, 93M instructions, and 1.36M SAPs. It took CLAP around 15 minutes to collect the constraints containing 513M clauses and 2M unknown variables. CLAP took 38 minutes to solve the constraints and successfully computed a schedule with 276 context switches. Since racey is a benchmark specifically designed to have many races, it is an outlier in our data. It does not follow the observation that most bugs require few thread switches to reproduce, and hence it causes worst-case behavior in our system. Note that real programs have much better results.

Relaxed memory model bugs

Dekker's and Peterson's algorithms, and Lamport's Bakery algorithm all work well for the SC model, but not for TSO and PSO models. We evaluated with them to demonstrate the capability of CLAP for reproducing concurrency bugs on relaxed memory models. To trigger the bugs, we simulated the memory model effects by actively controlling the value returned by shared data loads in a similar style to [9]. For TSO, we simulated a FIFO store buffer for each thread, and for PSO, we simulated multiple FIFO store buffers, with one per shared variable.

Bakery We forked four worker threads, each of which increments a shared integer variable by one in the critical section. Due to the

Program	LOC	#Threads	#SV	#Inst	#Br	#SAPs	#Constraints	#Variables	Time (secs) symbolic	Time (secs) solve	#cs	success?
sim_race	75	5	2	103	18	23	341	26	0.8	0.5	0	**Y**
pbzip2	1.8K	4	18	4203	473	65	5324	102	4	5	2	**Y**
aget	1.2K	4	30	39401	4017	1951	1366923	2485	125	89	1	**Y**
bbuf	381	5	11	2643	189	64	2784	75	3	5	1	**Y**
swarm	2.2K	3	13	840193	73728	1265	1226098	1776	27	64	2	**Y**
pfscan	925	3	13	2261926	287713	2864	7255156	3101	332	160	3	**Y**
apache	643K	28	22	6806939	961779	81237	10153562	15534	770	344	3	**Y**
racey	200	3	3	93035842	7133586	1361588	513086300	2010082	857	2280	276	**Y**
bakery	73	5	3	1181	182	218	16355	331	1	8	1	**Y**
dekker	48	3	3	223	28	39	699	52	1	2	1	**Y**
peterson	44	3	3	215	28	35	696	48	1	2	1	**Y**

Table 1. Overall results - Columns 3-6 report the number of threads (*#Threads*), the number of shared variables (*#SV*), the number of executed instructions (*#Inst*) and branches (*#Br*) in the original buggy execution. Columns 7 reports the number of shared data accesses (*#SAPs*) in the schedule. Columns 8-9 report the size of the constraints (*#Constraints*) and the number of unknown variables in it (*#Variables*). Columns 10-11 report the symbolic analysis time (*Time-symbolic*) for collecting the constraints, and the constraint solving time (*Time-solve*) using the STP solver on a single core. For all the evaluated programs, CLAP was able to compute a bug-reproducing schedule, and most of the computed schedules contain less than 3 context switches. The total time for collecting and solving the constraints ranges from 2s to 50mins.

bug, the mutual exclusion for executing the critical section does not hold, and threads accessing the shared variable can race with each other, which may produce a wrong final result of the shared integer. The recorded path profiles of the buggy execution contain 5 threads with a total of 1181 instructions and 182 branches. It took CLAP less than 1s to collect the constraints that contain 331 unknown variables and 16K clauses for both TSO and PSO. CLAP solved the constraints in 8s and produced a bug-reproducing schedule with one preemptive thread context switch.

Dekker/Perterson We forked two threads each of which loops twice in the critical section for incrementing a shared integer. Due to the bug, the final result of the shared integer could be wrong. The recorded path profiles of *dekker* contain 3 threads with a total of 223 instructions and 28 branches. It took CLAP less than 1s to collect the constraints that contain 52 unknown variables and 699 clauses for both TSO and PSO. CLAP solved the constraints in 2s and produced a bug-reproducing schedule with one preemptive thread context switch. The result for *peterson* is similar, as Peterson's algorithm is a slightly simplified version over Dekker's algorithm.

6.2 CLAP Runtime Performance

We compared the runtime performance of CLAP with an implementation of LEAP [14], which is one of the state of art record-replay techniques that track shared memory dependencies. Because none of the concurrency bug reproduction tools [1, 21, 29, 32, 40, 41] is available, we choose LEAP for the reason that it incurs minimum implementation bias and it puts the quantifications of various runtime characteristics of CLAP into perspective. We ran each benchmark under three different settings – natively (without instrumentation and logging), with LEAP, and with CLAP, and we measured the corresponding execution time and log size.

Table 2 reports the results. All data were average over five runs. As expected, since LEAP requires synchronizations to record the shared variable access orders, its overhead is large when there are intensive shared memory dependencies in the execution. Because most of these benchmarks have frequent shared data accesses (especially *racey*, in which the majority of memory operations are on shared data), both the runtime overhead for recording the shared data accesses and the space needed for storing the log are significant for LEAP. The runtime overhead of LEAP ranges from 21.4% in *pbzip2* to as large as 4289% in *racey*, and the corresponding space cost ranges from 19.5K-68.2M. Compared to LEAP, CLAP incurred much less runtime overhead and space cost, because it only records the thread local paths and does not use any synchronization. The runtime overhead of CLAP ranges from 9.3%-269%, which achieves 10% to 93.9% reduction compared to LEAP. For the space cost (1.1K-3.81M), the improvement by CLAP is also significant, with 72% to 97.7% reduction compared to LEAP.

Program	Schedules #worst	Schedules #gen(#cs)	Schedules #good	Time par	Time seq
sim_race	$> 10^{6}$	128(0)	3	0.3s	0.5s
pbzip2	$> 10^{15}$	140(2)	8	0.3s	5s
aget	$> 10^{40}$	13725(1)	16	16s	89s
bbuf	$> 10^{20}$	324(1)	36	0.6s	5s
swarm	$> 10^{30}$	30855(2)	27	19s	64s
pfscan	$> 10^{50}$	118714(3)	12	63s	160s
apache	$> 10^{100}$	5634627(3)	15	195s	344s
racey	$> 10^{10000}$	2528316(2)	**0**	**2h**	2280s
bakery	$> 10^{25}$	1071(1)	22	1.5s	8s
dekker	$> 10^{6}$	31(1)	12	0.2s	2s
peterson	$> 10^{6}$	28(1)	11	0.2s	2s

Table 3. The performance of parallel constraint solving

6.3 CLAP Parallel Constraint Solving Performance

We have evaluated the performance of our parallel constraint solving algorithm on an eight-core machine. We repeated the schedule generation process with a larger context switch number (recall Section 4.3) until we found at least one correct schedule that satisfies the constraints. Each task of generating and validating one schedule is handled by a separate thread. Because normally there exist a set of correct schedules and multiple threads may work on them simultaneously, we typically have found multiple correct schedules before the whole process is terminated.

Table 3 reports the results. Columns 2-4 report the worst number of possible schedules (computed according to the theoretical results in [25, 27]), the number of generated schedules before we stopped (#cs–the largest number of context switches among these schedules), and the number of correct schedules among the generated ones. Column 5 reports the total amount of time it took for finding these correct schedules. As the table shows, although the worst number of different schedules is exponential, CLAP successfully generated correct schedules for most of the benchmarks within 200s.

For comparison, Column 6 shows the constraint solving time of the sequential version (as also reported in Table 1). For most benchmarks, using our parallel algorithm is much faster than the

Program	Native	Time			Space		
		LEAP (Overhead%)	CLAP (Overhead%)	Reduction%	LEAP	CLAP	Reduction%
sim_race	2ms	4ms (-)	4ms (-)	-	448B	126B	↓**72%**
bbuf	2ms	6ms (-)	4ms (-)	↓**33%**	12.2K	1.1K	↓**91%**
swarm	68ms	0.770s (**1032%**)	0.101s (**48.5%**)	↓**87%**	9.20M	215.6K	↓**97.7%**
pbzip2	0.140s	0.170ms (**21.4%**)	0.153ms (**9.3%**)	↓**10%**	19.5K	1.8K	↓**91%**
aget	0.231s	0.490s (**112%**)	0.270s (**17%**)	↓**45%**	683.8K	24.3K	↓**96.4%**
pfscan	0.135s	1.537s (**1172%**)	0.260s (**92.6%**)	↓**83.1%**	1.61M	330.5K	↓**79.5%**
apache	0.185s	0.248s (**34%**)	0.220 (**19%**)	↓**11.3%**	15.4M	2.30M	↓**85%**
racey	0.262s	11.5s (**4289%**)	0.705 (**269%**)	↓**93.9%**	68.2M	3.81M	↓**94.4%**

Table 2. Runtime and space overhead comparison between CLAP and LEAP

sequential solution. For example, for the constraint of *apache*, it took the sequential solver 344s to return a correct schedule, while with the parallel algorithm, CLAP generated 27 correct schedules in 195 seconds. The only exception is *racey*, which we use as a stress test for worst case behavior. Using the parallel algorithm, we did not find a correct schedule within two hours. The reason is that a correct schedule for *racey* should contain at least 276 thread context switches, but in two hours we did not even finish enumerating the schedules with only two context switches, due to the large number of shared data accesses in the execution.

6.4 Discussion

Long running traces Our evaluation results demonstrate that CLAP has good scalability with fairly substantial traces in real-world executions. For very long runs, reproducing the failure is more challenging that the solver may not be able to find a solution within a reasonable time budget. In such cases, we need to break up the execution so that each execution segment has tractable size of constraints. Checkpointing is a common technique used in such contexts. We plan to integrate CLAP with checkpointing in future.

Recording synchronizations Previous work [32, 42, 43] has shown that recording synchronization operations is lightweight for many applications. Recording the synchronization order can also reduce the size of generated constraints, and it is easy for CLAP to do so. We do not record synchronizations in our current version of CLAP, because it would need extra synchronization operations, which could limit our ability to capture non-sequential bugs. Also, it could still be costly for a certain range of programs containing intensive high-level races on synchronizations.

7. Related Work

Lee *et al.* [23, 24] pioneered the use of offline symbolic analysis for deterministic replay on SC and TSO models at the hardware level. While being much inspired by their work, their solution does not meet our goal of designing a lightweight and software-only solution. Without the hardware support, their reliance on collecting load values for the SMT solvers to search for shared memory dependencies will create a significant space overhead and a considerable program slowdown. In contrast, we do not collect any values but only the paths taken by the threads, which has much lower recording overhead. Taking a leap from their symbolic analysis, we perform symbolic execution along the program paths to replace "value matching" with "path constraint satisfaction". This not only allows us to exploring more and possibly simpler schedules (*i.e.*, with minimal number of thread context switches), but more importantly, it enables us to encode the preemption bound into the constraint model, converting the NP-complete problem [11] to a polynomial search.

ODR [1] presents a high-level framework that is similar with CLAP: using constraint solving to figure out a schedule that satisfies the recorded information. However, ODR did not provide a concrete constraint solving algorithm and implementation that considers real-world memory consistency and synchronization. Its constraint solving approximates many issues that CLAP provides concrete and accurate solution to.

Wang *et al.* [33, 34] develop a verification framework for predictive concurrency trace analysis. Our modeling of the read-write constraints is similar to their symbolic model, but has several specializations treatments tailored to bug reproduction. For instance, we do not use any synchronization nor log any program state online, and we do not require a sequential consistent execution which is needed in their work to obtain a global trace.

ESD [40] performs symbolic execution to synthesize program failures without any runtime logging. A key difference between CLAP and ESD is that we explore only a single path (*i.e.*, the original path) that is guaranteed to exhibit the same failure, while ESD essentially has to search all program paths and thread interleavings to find the bug, which faces particular challenges in addressing programs with loops and recursive calls. To improve scalability, ESD relies on heuristics to synthesize races and deadlocks (which is unsound and could miss real bugs), while CLAP is built upon a sound modeling of the execution constraints.

Weeratunge *et al.* [36] present a technique that reproduces concurrency bugs by analyzing the failure core dump. Powered by execution indexing [37], their technique actively searches for a failure inducing schedule by comparing the core dump differences between the failing run and the passing run. Compared to [36], CLAP does not require the core dump information and hence is able to reproduce a wider range of concurrency errors.

CHESS [28] detects and reproduces concurrency bugs through dynamic exploration of thread interleaving. To mitigate the schedule explosion, CHESS employs a context-bounded algorithm [27] to explore schedules up to a certain small number of context switches. Our mechanism for encoding the number of thread interleavings shares the same spirit as CHESS. Differently, our technique is parallelizable because of the static nature, while CHESS is difficult to parallelize due to the dynamic exploration strategy.

PRES [29] proposes probabilistic replay that intelligently explores the thread interleavings through a feedback-based replayer. By continuously rectifying the schedule in the previous failing replay, the technique successfully trades multiple replay attempts for efficient online recording.

The idea of doing lightweight recording at runtime and making up for it with a solver has also been successfully applied by Cheung *et al.* [6] for replaying long-running single-threaded programs. The technique achieves low recording overhead by logging only the branch choices at runtime and using symbolic analysis to reconstruct the inputs and memory states.

8. Conclusion

Reproducing concurrency bugs is notoriously challenging due to non-determinism. We have presented a new technique, CLAP, that achieves significant advances over previous approaches. CLAP does not log any runtime shared memory dependency or program state, works for sequential consistent as well as a range of relaxed memory models, and produces the bug-reproducing schedule in parallel with minimal thread context switches. With all these properties, we believe CLAP is promising for production settings.

Acknowledgements

We thank the anonymous reviewers for their insightful feedback which has substantially improved the content and presentation of this paper. We are also grateful to Thomas Ball for his invaluable comments on CLAP. The work of the first two authors is supported by Hong Kong RGC GRF grants 622208 and 622909.

References

[1] Gautam Altekar and Ion Stoica. ODR: output deterministic replay for multicore debugging. In *SOSP*, 2009.

[2] The SPARC Architecture Manual V9. *SPARC International, Inc.* 1994.

[3] Emina Torlakand, Mandana Vaziri, and Julian Dolby. MemSAT: checking axiomatic specifications of memory models. In *PLDI*, 2010.

[4] Thomas Ball and James Larus. Efficient path profiling. In *MICRO*, 1996.

[5] Cristian Cadar, Daniel Dunbar, and Dawson Engler. Klee: unassisted and automatic generation of high-coverage tests for complex systems programs. In *OSDI*, 2008.

[6] Alvin Cheung, Armando Solar-Lezama, and Samuel Madden. Partial replay of long-running applications. In *ESEC/FSE*, 2011.

[7] Leonardo De Moura and Nikolaj Bjørner. Z3: an efficient SMT solver. In *TACAS*, 2008.

[8] Bruno Dutertre and Leonardo De Moura. The Yices SMT solver. Technical report, 2006.

[9] Cormac Flanagan and Stephen Freund. Adversarial memory for detecting destructive races. In *PLDI*, 2010.

[10] Vijay Ganesh and David Dill. A decision procedure for bit-vectors and arrays. In *CAV*, 2007.

[11] Phillip Gibbons and Ephraim Korach. Testing shared memories. 1997.

[12] Derek Hower and Mark Hill. Rerun: Exploiting episodes for lightweight memory race recording. In *ISCA*, 2008.

[13] Jeff Huang, and Charles Zhang. LEAN: Simplifying concurrency bug reproduction via Replay-supported Execution Reduction. In *OOPSLA*, 2012.

[14] Jeff Huang, Peng Liu, and Charles Zhang. LEAP: Lightweight deterministic multi-processor replay of concurrent Java programs. In *FSE*, 2010.

[15] Jeff Huang and Charles Zhang. An efficient static trace simplification technique for debugging concurrent programs. In *SAS*, 2011.

[16] Nicholas Jalbert and Koushik Sen. A trace simplification technique for effective debugging of concurrent programs. In *FSE*, 2010.

[17] Daniel Jiménez. Fast path-based neural branch prediction. In *MICRO*, 2003.

[18] Guoliang Jin, Linhai Song, Wei Zhang, Shan Lu, and Ben Liblit. Automated atomicity-violation fixing. In *PLDI*, 2011.

[19] Guoliang Jin, Aditya Thakur, Ben Liblit, and Shan Lu. Instrumentation and sampling strategies for cooperative concurrency bug isolation. In *OOPSLA*, 2010.

[20] James R. Larus. Whole program paths. In *PLDI*, 1999.

[21] Dongyoon Lee, Peter M. Chen, Jason Flinn, and Satish Narayanasamy. Chimera: hybrid program analysis for determinism. In *PLDI*, 2012.

[22] Michael D. Bond and Milind Kulkarni. Respec: efficient online multiprocessor replay via speculation and external determinism. *Technical report, Ohio State University*, 2012.

[23] Dongyoon Lee, Mahmoud Said, Satish Narayanasamy, and Zijiang Yang. Offline symbolic analysis to infer total store order. In *HPCA*, 2011.

[24] Dongyoon Lee, Mahmoud Said, Satish Narayanasamy, Zijiang Yang, and Cristiano Pereira. Offline symbolic analysis for multi-processor execution replay. In *MICRO*, 2009.

[25] Shan Lu, Weihang Jiang, and Yuanyuan Zhou. A study of interleaving coverage criteria. In *ESEC-FSE*, 2007.

[26] Pablo Montesinos, Luis Ceze, and Josep Torrellas. Delorean: Recording and deterministically replaying shared-memory multi-processor execution efficiently. In *ISCA*, 2008.

[27] Madanlal Musuvathi and Shaz Qadeer. Iterative context bounding for systematic testing of multithreaded programs. In *PLDI*, 2007.

[28] Madanlal Musuvathi, Shaz Qadeer, Thomas Ball, Gérard Basler, Piramanayagam A. Nainar, and Iulian Neamtiu. Finding and reproducing heisenbugs in concurrent programs. In *OSDI*, 2008.

[29] Soyeon Park, Yuanyuan Zhou, Weiwei Xiong, Zuoning Yin, Rini Kaushik, Kyu H. Lee, and Shan Lu. PRES: probabilistic replay with execution sketching on multi-processors. In *SOSP*, 2009.

[30] Polyvios Pratikakis, Jeffrey Foster, and Michael Hicks. Locksmith: context-sensitive correlation analysis for race detection. In *PLDI*, 2006.

[31] Kapil Vaswani, Matthew J. Thazhuthaveetil, and Y. N. Srikant. A programmable hardware path profiler. In *CGO*, 2005.

[32] Kaushik Veeraraghavan, Dongyoon Lee, Benjamin Wester, Jessica Ouyang, Peter M. Chen, Jason Flinn, and Satish Narayanasamy. Doubleplay: parallelizing sequential logging and replay. In *ASPLOS*, 2011.

[33] Chao Wang, Sudipta Kundu, Malay K. Ganai, and Aarti Gupta. Symbolic predictive analysis for concurrent programs. In *FM*, 2009.

[34] Chao Wang, Rhishikesh Limaye, Malay Ganai, and Aarti Gupta. Trace based symbolic analysis for atomicity violations. In *TACAS*, 2010.

[35] Dasarath Weeratunge, Xiangyu Zhang, and Suresh Jaganathan. Accentuating the positive: Atomicity inference and enforcement using correct executions. In *OOPSLA*, 2011.

[36] Dasarath Weeratunge, Xiangyu Zhang, and Suresh Jagannathan. Analyzing multicore dumps to facilitate concurrency bug reproduction. In *ASPLOS*, 2010.

[37] Bin Xin, William Sumner, and Xiangyu Zhang. Efficient program execution indexing. In *PLDI*, 2008.

[38] Min Xu, Rastislav Bodik, and Mark Hill. A "flight data recorder" for full-system multiprocessor deterministic replay. In *ISCA*, 2003.

[39] Jie Yu and Satish Narayanasamy. A case for an interleaving constrained shared-memory multi-processor. In *ISCA*, 2009.

[40] Cristian Zamfir and George Candea. Execution synthesis: a technique for automated software debugging. In *EuroSys*, 2010.

[41] Jinguo Zhou, Xiao Xiao, and Charles Zhang. Stride: Search-based deterministic replay in polynomial time via bounded linkage. In *ICSE*, 2012.

[42] Dongyoon Lee, Benjamin Wester, Kaushik Veeraraghavan, Satish Narayanasamy, Peter M. Chen, and Jason Flinn. Respec: efficient online multiprocessor replayvia speculation and external determinism. In *ASPLOS*, 2010.

[43] A. Georges, M. Christiaens, M. Ronsse, and K. De Bosschere. JaRec: a portable record/replay environment for multi-threaded Java applications. In *SPE*, 2004.

CONCURRIT: A Domain Specific Language for Reproducing Concurrency Bugs

Tayfun Elmas [†] Jacob Burnim [‡] George Necula Koushik Sen

Department of Electrical Engineering and Computer Sciences, University of California, Berkeley

{elmas,jburnim,necula,ksen}@cs.berkeley.edu

Abstract

We present CONCURRIT, a domain-specific language (DSL) for reproducing concurrency bugs. Given some partial information about the nature of a bug in an application, a programmer can write a CONCURRIT script to formally and concisely specify a set of thread schedules to explore in order to find a schedule exhibiting the bug. Further, the programmer can specify how these thread schedules should be searched to find a schedule that reproduces the bug. We implemented CONCURRIT as an embedded DSL in C++, which uses manual or automatic source instrumentation to partially control the scheduling of the software under test. Using CONCURRIT, we were able to write concise tests to reproduce concurrency bugs in a variety of benchmarks, including the Mozilla's SpiderMonkey JavaScript engine, Memcached, Apache's HTTP server, and MySQL.

Categories and Subject Descriptors D.2.5 [*Software Engineering*]: Testing and Debugging; F.3.1 [*Logics and Meanings of Programs*]: Specifying and Verifying and Reasoning about Programs

Keywords Concurrency Errors; Domain-Specific Languages; Software Testing

1. Introduction

To diagnose and fix a software bug, a programmer often needs to first reproduce the bug. That is, given some partial information about the nature of the bug — e.g., from a bug report or from directly observing erroneous program behavior — the programmer constructs a test scenario in which they execute some piece of their software so that it reliably exhibits the bugs. Reproducing such bugs can require controlling a number of sources of nondeterminism in a program's execution, including program inputs, library dependencies, and interactions with the underlying operating system. This task is especially challenging for concurrent programs, where a bug may occur only under very specific interleavings of a program's threads.

To reproduce concurrent bugs in practice, programmers often do *stress testing*. In stress testing, a programmer imposes *no control* over the scheduling of threads. Rather, to increase the chance of examining different and interesting schedules, the programmer creates a long-running test scenario with a large number of threads. In addition, the programmer adds perturbations to the timings of the threads by exploiting her (partial) knowledge about the bug. For example, if the programmer has intuition about potentially problematic locations in the code, she inserts *sleep* statements at these locations to perturb the thread schedule in a certain way. Such tests can be long-running and the resulting buggy executions can be very difficult to understand and debug due to the large number of threads and complex test setups. Manually controlling the schedule, e.g., by inserting sleeps, can be ad hoc and unreliable and may require nontrivial modifications in the program text.

In this paper, we propose CONCURRIT, a domain-specific language (DSL) for reproducing concurrency bugs. When using CONCURRIT to reproduce a bug, as with the existing approaches described above, a programmer begins with partial knowledge about the bug, for example, a number of threads and some intuition about how to schedule these threads to exhibit the bug. Then, the programmer also writes a *test script* in the CONCURRIT language. This CONCURRIT test script expresses the programmer's knowledge about the bug formally and concisely. In particular, the test script describes a set of potentially-problematic thread schedules among which the programmer intends to search for the target, buggy interleaving. For this, the test script dictates partial constraints on the thread schedule, for example, which threads are allowed to be interleaved at which point of the execution, or at which code location or under what conditions a context switch will happen. At runtime, the script guides the interleaving of threads, within the constraints given in the script, to generate these thread schedules.

CONCURRIT also gives the programmer the ability to implement various techniques to search for the target schedules. For example, combined with automatic or manual instrumentation of the program under test, the programmer can impose any level of control from none at all, as in random search, to full control of the thread schedule, as in model checking (e.g., [19]). For this, the programmer uses DSL constructs to explicitly indicate nondeterministic choices in the interleaving (e.g., a set of threads one of which will be scheduled next). At each execution of the test, these choices are resolved in a controlled manner, in order to search for distinct thread schedules with respect to these choices. While the choice points for the schedule are explicitly indicated in the CONCURRIT test, the underlying mechanics of the search are transparent to the programmer. For example, the search can be implemented independently from the test by employing one of a number of search strategies we provide, such as depth- and breadth-first searches. This approach also enables rapid prototyping and evaluation of a custom search strategy by writing and exploring a CONCURRIT test.

[†] The author is currently affiliated with Google, Inc., and can be reached at tayfunelmas@gmail.com.

[‡] The author is currently affiliated with Sift Science, Inc., and can be reached at jburnim@gmail.com.

PLDI'13, June 16–19, 2013, Seattle, WA, USA.

CONCURRIT allows a programmer to simply specify and explore a set of thread schedules with various degrees of flexibility. For example, the programmer may start with little intuition about a bug and write a fully nondeterministic CONCURRIT test (i.e., any thread may be scheduled any time), which results in a high number of thread schedules. As she gains more insight about the bug based on the results of the CONCURRIT test, she can refine the test to incorporate new insights, search fewer schedules, and reproduce the target bug more quickly. For example, if the programmer thinks that the bug resides in a small number of critical functions, she can modify the test to express her interest in different interleavings of threads only when the program is in one of these functions, leaving a reasonable number of interleavings to explore. Furthermore, one can write a fully deterministic test, which specifies an exact schedule triggering the bug. A CONCURRIT test specifying one or few schedules can be used to formally document the bug and for regression testing after the bug is fixed.

Searching for thread schedules in our work carries similarities to model checking techniques that enumerate thread schedules, e.g., [6, 14, 19, 21]. However, our approach diverges from the traditional model checking in two significant aspects. First, in the CONCURRIT approach, the programmer can guide the exploration of the schedules by imposing, within the test script, constraints on individual schedules. This allows the programmer to restrict and localize the search, and to focus on small number of interesting program states and interleavings, and have the search terminate earlier. Second, the traditional notion of model checking assumes that (1) the thread schedule is a primary source of nondeterminism, and (2) the entire thread schedule can be controlled. These assumptions are fundamental for the soundness guarantees of such model checking. Nevertheless, these assumptions only hold for relatively small programs, not for large, complex software, such as web browsers and servers. Controlling the entire schedule is challenging for large programs, because precisely repeating an entire execution prefix is very difficult due to sources of nondeterminism (e.g., timing of computations and network events) other than the thread schedule. Therefore, we accept that totally avoiding uncontrolled nondeterminism is not realistic in practice, and we develop our testing approach to embrace the possibility of uncontrollable nondeterminism. A CONCURRIT test can describe the controlled nondeterminism for part of the thread schedule and leave the rest of the schedule unspecified. As a result, for example, a search for distinct thread schedules with respect to the controlled nondeterministic choices in the CONCURRIT test can be performed in the presence of partially uncontrolled interleavings of threads. In fact, we do not have to control the entire thread schedule, because concurrency bugs in general can be triggered by controlling only a small (but critical) part of the schedule. From this point of view, our approach inherits the imperfect but lightweight and tolerant notion of control from sleep-based approaches, and formal notion of search from model checking.

Contributions and outline. In Section 2, we present a case study showing how to use CONCURRIT to reproduce a real bug in Mozilla's SpiderMonkey JavaScript engine. We formally present the CONCURRIT DSL, discuss how to write CONCURRIT search strategies, and present several high-level CONCURRIT constructs and patterns for writing effective and concise CONCURRIT test scripts, in Sections 3, 4, and 5, respectively. In Section 6, we present our implementation of CONCURRIT as an embedded DSL in C++. Our framework supports the use of CONCURRIT for both unit testing within a single process and system testing involving multiple processes. In Section 7, we describe our experimental evaluation of CONCURRIT, on a number of of multithreaded programs from well-known Inspect [26], PARSEC [3], and RADBench [12] benchmark suites. Our benchmarks include large software such as the Mozilla's SpiderMonkey JavaScript engine, Memcached, the Apache HTTP server, and MySQL. We demonstrate the expressiveness and usefulness of CONCURRIT by writing tests to reproduce concurrency bugs in these benchmarks. Our implementation is available at `http://code.google.com/p/concurrit/`.

2. Overview: Writing tests in CONCURRIT

We present a case study of using CONCURRIT from the perspective of a programmer who wants to write a test to reproduce a concurrency bug. We consider a real concurrency bug in the Mozilla SpiderMonkey JavaScript Engine (version 1.8RC1), a large software system with 121K lines of code. (In Section 7 this bug is named *spidermonkey2*.) The related bug report can be found at: `https://bugzilla.mozilla.org/show_bug.cgi?id=478336`. The bug manifests itself as an assertion violation and can be triggered using the multithreaded program given in Figure 1 (supplied with the bug report). We refer to this program as the *software-under-test (SUT)*.

The bug report shows a progressive understanding of the buggy interleaving. The report starts from the stress testing of the code in Figure 1 with 100 threads to reproduce the bug. Then, the programmers collect information from the stack traces of buggy executions to identify problematic code locations and schedules. Finally, they figure out a scenario, given in Figure 2, describing of a suspicious interleaving of three threads A, B, and C executing `testfunc` in Figure 1.

Notice that, this scenario is still partial: It explains the key scheduling decisions to bring the execution to a problematic program state, say **S**, after which it will be highly likely that the bug will manifest. But, the description leaves unspecified the rest of the schedule, from **S** to the assertion violation. By writing a CONCURRIT test, we can specify 1) the known scheduling decisions until **S** and 2) a search for the missing part of the buggy schedule after **S**.

In this section, we demonstrate how to write tests in CONCURRIT to incrementally capture the different stages of understanding of the bug in the bug report. We will start with simple CONCURRIT tests that assume little knowledge about the bug—i.e., having three threads running the code in Figure 1, but not knowing how to interleave them. To begin, we found it useful to first check whether the bug is due to concurrency (Section 2.1), then continue with tests with many possible thread schedules, but that do trigger the bug. These tests will require searching among a large number of thread schedules for a buggy one. We will subsequently incorporate more and more intuition from the bug report to make our test more precise and efficient, by searching among fewer schedules. In this way: (1) we show that a CONCURRIT script can formally and concisely express the intuition of the programmer at various levels of detail,

```
static JSRuntime *rt;
static void* testfunc(void* ignored) {
  JSContext *cx = JS_NewContext(rt, 0x1000);
  if (cx) {
     JS_BeginRequest(cx);
     JS_DestroyContext(cx);
  }
  return NULL;
}
int main(void) {
  rt = JS_NewRuntime(0x100000);
  if (rt == NULL) return 1;
  ... // create threads to run testfunc (and join all)
  return 0;
}
```

Figure 1. Test code manifesting a bug in SpiderMonkey (taken from the related bug report).

Now suppose there are 3 threads, A, B, C running `testfunc`.
Threads A and B call js_DestroyContext and thread˜C calls js_NewContext.
First thread˜A removes its context from the runtime list. That context is not
the last one so thread does not touch rt−>state and eventually calls js_GC.
The latter skips the above check and tries to to take the GC lock.
Before this moment the thread˜B takes the lock, removes its context from the
runtime list, discovers that it is the last, sets rt−>state to LANDING, runs
the-last-context-cleanup, runs the GC and then sets rt−>state to DOWN.
At this stage the thread˜A gets the GC lock, setup itself as the thread that
runs the GC and releases the GC lock to proceed with the GC
when rt−>state is DOWN.
Now the thread˜C enters the picture. It discovers under the GC lock in
js_NewContext that the newly allocated context is the first one. Since
rt−>state is DOWN, it releases the GC lock and starts the first context
initialization procedure. That procedure includes the allocation of the initial
atoms and it will happen when the thread˜A runs the GC.
This may lead precisely to the first stack trace from the comment 4.

Figure 2. Bug scenario, taken from Comment #5 of the bug report, describing an interleaving of threads for the program in Figure 1.

and (2) we highlight the common usage patterns of our DSL that we follow in our experiments. (In Section 5.1 we revisit the general form of these patterns.)

While we demonstrate only a few steps of refining CONCURRIT tests, in reality, we do not always expect to have a quick transition between tests, and there may be more steps before obtaining a practical test. We expect the error information (such as stack traces) from the failing executions in earlier steps will play the role of bug reports to refine tests for the later steps. Although the earlier tests find the bug, our goal is not only to trigger the bug, but to have concise, informative, and targeted (towards the bug) tests.

2.1 First test: Run threads sequentially until completion

To begin, suppose that our intuition about our target interleaving is limited: We know that three distinct threads, A, B, and C, are sufficient to reproduce the bug, but we do not know how to schedule these threads to trigger the error. Indeed, we do not even know whether the bug is sequential or concurrent. Thus, before interleaving the threads, we want to check if the bug is really related to concurrency. For this, we want to run every thread sequentially, i.e., without being interleaved with another thread until its completion. Our first CONCURRIT test is as follows:

```
SearchSeqTest :
1 Tid tA, tB, tC = WaitForDistinctThreads(3, ThreadStarts);
2 while(!HasEnded(tA) || !HasEnded(tB) || !HasEnded(tC)) {
3    Tid t = ChooseThread(tA, tB, tC);
4    RunThreadUntil(t, ThreadEnds);
5 }
```

A CONCURRIT test is run concurrently with the SUT (in Figure 1) and controls the scheduling of the threads in the SUT. Test **SearchSeqTest** demonstrates two kinds of control CONCURRIT can impose on the schedule: (1) It describes how the threads A, B, and C in each execution should be scheduled; in our case, each thread runs sequentially (without interleaving with another thread) until completion. (2) It describes a set of schedules satisfying the constraint in (1) and differ in the scheduling order of threads. In order to realize this control, the SUT is instrumented to interact with the CONCURRIT script. The CONCURRIT script hides the mechanism for this interaction from the programmer and allows her to specify the thread schedule without thinking about the low-level details of how the SUT is controlled.

The diagram in Figure 3 illustrates the interaction between three threads in the SUT and the test **SearchSeqTest**. Function **WaitForDistinctThreads** at Line 1 waits for three distinct threads in the SUT to run and reach a point satisfying its second argument (**ThreadStarts**), then binds variables **tA**, **tB**, and **tC** to the identifiers of those threads. The predicate **ThreadStart** indicates that this binding occurs when the threads start executing. On binding, each thread is blocked until re-enabled by the test.

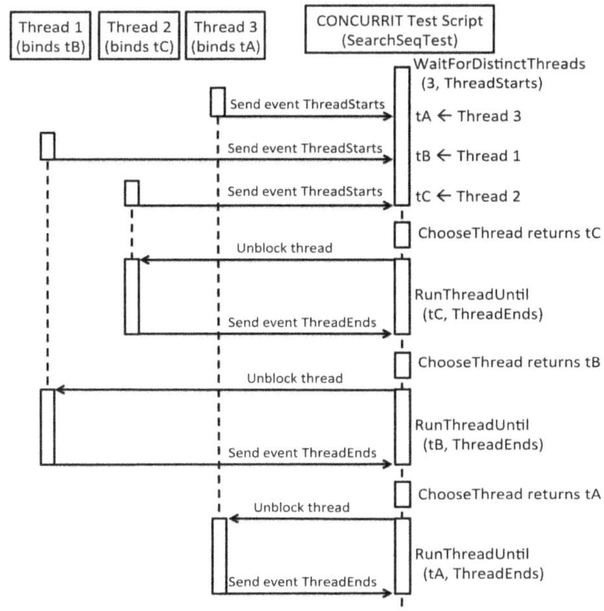

Figure 3. Interaction between the SUT threads and test script.

At lines 2-5, the test controls the execution of threads **tA**, **tB**, and **tC** in a loop, which iterates until all the threads terminate (line 2). At each iteration, **ChooseThread** nondeterministically chooses one of the variables **tA**, **tB**, and **tC** (line 3) and assigns it to variable **t**. Then, **RunThreadUntil** enables the chosen thread referred to by **t** to execute (line 4). The second argument of **RunThreadUntil** indicates until when the thread will be allowed to execute. The predicate **ThreadEnds** indicates that thread **t** should keep running until it terminates. While **t** is executing, the other two threads remain blocked. In addition, since the test binds only three threads, all other threads in the SUT remain blocked until the loop ends, after which the control on the SUT imposed by the test is removed.

Controlled nondeterminism. The command **ChooseThread** specifies a nondeterministic choice of given arguments. This nondeterminism is controlled by our test and resolved to implement a search for thread schedules. For example, one can implement random testing by using a random number generator to choose the thread.

In our work, we provide a search strategy that restarts the SUT multiple times and explores a distinct combination of these choices until all distinct combinations are enumerated. This provides the mechanism to search for all possible thread schedules specified by the CONCURRIT test. During this search, for example, if **ChooseThread** chooses an already-terminated thread, **RunThreadUntil** timeouts and restarts the SUT to explore a different schedule. While the choice points for the schedule are indicated explicitly using **ChooseThread**, the underlying search strategy is transparent to the programmer. Thus, as explained in Section 4, one can customize the search independently of the test, for example to follow a depth-first or breath-first order.

When guided by the test **SearchSeqTest**, our search generates 6 thread schedules in which threads **tA**, **tB**, **tC** are run in different orders (but sequentially). However, these schedules do not trigger the assertion violation. This confirms our intuition that the bug is due to concurrency. Thus, we need to allow threads to interleave with each other to trigger the bug.

2.2 Second test: Interleave threads at finest granularity

In our second test we want to interleave the threads. But, suppose we still do not have any knowledge about what interleavings will trigger the bug. Our next step is to allow threads to interleave arbitrarily, and search for the buggy interleaving among these fine-grained interleavings. We can slightly change `SearchSeqTest` to permit such interleaving of threads `tA`, `tB`, and `tC` as follows:

```
SearchAllTest :
1 Tid tA, tB, tC = WaitForDistinctThreads(3, ThreadStarts);
2 while(!HasEnded(tA) || !HasEnded(tB) || !HasEnded(tC)) {
3    Tid t = ChooseThread(tA, tB, tC);
4    RunThreadUntil(t, ReadsMem || WritesMem || CallsFunc|| ThreadEnds);
5 }
```

We modify line 4 to replace the predicate `ThreadEnds` with `ReadsMem || WritesMem || CallsFunc|| ThreadEnds`. The new predicate indicates that thread `t` (chosen at line 3) should run until it attempts to access the memory (read from or write to an address), calls a function, or terminates. When thread `t` attempts to perform one of these operations, the command `RunThreadUntil` ends and leaves thread `t` blocked before that operation. When `RunThreadUntil` is called again with `t` bound to the same thread, it first unblocks the thread to let it complete the operation, and then runs the thread until next operation satisfying the predicate.

As it allows threads to interleave at fine granularity, our second test `SearchAllTest` can generate the buggy thread schedule violating the assertion. However, the buggy schedule is generated after exploring *millions* of schedules of the test. This means, whenever we want to reproduce the bug using this test, we have to wait for *days* to see the assertion violation. Although the test allows us to examine all schedules, there are a huge number of them. Moreover, the bug is triggered by a small number of tricky interleavings; thus, most of the schedules do not create the buggy situation. Thus, it will not be practical to use `SearchAllTest` for the purpose of reproducing the bug. (It is for this reason that traditional model checking is often impractical to use for large software.)

2.3 Third test: Localize search to suspicious states

The real power of CONCURRIT can be seen when we need to restrict the search space of interleavings. Note that, `SearchAllTest` runs the search for the entire lifetime of the threads. After examining the executions with assertion violations generated by `SearchAllTest`, we next localize the search for interleavings to a shorter period of the execution in order to enumerate fewer interleavings and to more quickly reach the intended state at which the assertion is violated. We refine our test as follows:

```
SearchInBuggyTest :
1 Tid tA, tB, tC = WaitForDistinctThreads(3, EntersFunc(JS_NewContext));
2 RunThreadsUntil(tA, tB, EntersFunc(JS_DestroyContext));
3 RunThreadUntil(tA, InFunc(js_GC) && ReadsMem(&rt-> state));
4 RunThreadUntil(tB, ThreadEnds); // thread B does not involve after this point
5 RunThreadUntil(tA, InFunc(js_GC) && WritesMem(&rt-> gcThread));
6 while(InFunc(tA, JS_DestroyContext) || InFunc(tC, JS_NewContext)) {
7    Tid t = ChooseThread(tA, tC);
8    RunThreadUntil(t, ReadsMem || WritesMem || CallsFunc|| ThreadEnds);
9 }
```

We first notice that the problematic portion of the interleaving is after threads A and B call `JS_DestroyContext` and thread C calls `JS_NewContext`. Thus, we want to only examine interleavings starting not from the beginning of the execution, but after the threads enter these functions. We incorporate this new insight to our CONCURRIT test as follows. First, we replace the condition `ThreadStart` at line 1 with `EntersFunc(JS_NewContext)`. The new version of `WaitForDistinctThreads` waits until the threads all start executing `JS_NewContext`—and then get blocked. Then, the command `RunThreadsUntil` at line 2 runs threads `tA` and `tB` (permitting them to interleave) until both threads start running `JS_DestroyContext`, at which point they are blocked.

Furthermore, at lines 3-5 we explicitly schedule the threads to lead the execution towards a problematic state (discussed below). The search for distinct interleavings starts after this point and is performed at lines 6-9. The body of the loop to interleave threads differs from that of `SearchAllTest` in two ways. First, as thread B terminates (at line 4) before the search starts, we remove references to `tB` from the loop. Second, the loop condition indicates that we are only interested in distinct interleavings of threads while running `JS_NewContext` and `JS_DestroyContext`.

Compared to `SearchAllTest`, our test `SearchInBuggyTest` is more effective in reproducing the bug: it generates the buggy interleaving after exploring less than 10 schedules of the test.

Capturing the programmer's knowledge in the bug report. Test `SearchInBuggyTest` indeed concisely and formally expresses the interleaving scenario in Figure 2. Our test also includes a search for the final portion of the interleaving to address the (missing) rest of the scenario. While the test scenario in Figure 2 explains our intuition about why the assertion is violated, the test formally documents and implements this intuition to reproduce the bug.

In detail, we realize that the assertion is violated because in a buggy execution there exists a problematic state **S** at which thread A starts a garbage collection routine `js_GC` to deallocate some shared data structures of the JavaScript engine, and thread C starts initializing these data structures. The scenario describes an interleaving to lead the execution towards state **S** and the commands between lines 1-5 of `SearchInBuggyTest` guides the threads to follow this interleaving. During this interleaving thread B terminates (at line 4), and the rest of the execution after **S** involves only threads A and C executing functions `JS_DestroyContext` and `JS_NewContext`, respectively. Interleaving of A and C after **S** results in a data race between A and C on a shared data structure, leading to an assertion violation about the data structure. Note that, our knowledge about the buggy interleaving is still partial, because we do not know how A and C should interleave after **S** to trigger the assertion violation. Thus, at lines 6-9, we search for interleavings A and C during this final part of the execution.

Uncontrolled nondeterminism. In addition to the controlled nondeterminism in command `ChooseThread`, `SearchInBuggyTest` also allows uncontrolled nondeterminism. Except when specifically blocked and sequentialized by the CONCURRIT script, the threads in the SUT are allowed to run in parallel following a nondeterministic schedule. For example, at Lines 1 and 2, the threads run in parallel until they start executing functions from `JS_NewContext` and `JS_DestroyContext`. The test does not control the nondeterminism in the thread schedule until they start executing these functions. Thus, a search guided by `SearchInBuggyTest` may generate another execution in which the threads follow a different interleaving before they enter these functions; such interleavings are not distinguished from each other. Moreover, after Line 1, any threads other than `tA`, `tB`, and `tC` run in parallel without any interruption by the CONCURRIT test. By embracing uncontrolled nondeterminism in this way, a CONCURRIT test can tolerate changes in the execution context across different executions of the SUT and can still explore different schedules. In addition, our tests highlight that the CONCURRIT script can express a very complicated schedule in a compact form, as it specifies only the key scheduling decisions and choices. Therefore, a programmer can conveniently use CONCURRIT to test her partial knowledge about the thread schedules without needing to specify uninteresting and irrelevant parts of the schedule.

2.4 Final test: Generate exact buggy interleaving

In `SearchInBuggyTest` we have localized the search (lines 6-9) for the latter, short part of the schedule. As a result, each interleaving explored by the loop in `SearchInBuggyTest` contains few context switches of threads `tA` and `tC`. Moreover, since we have also increased the likelihood of hitting the bug in `SearchInBuggyTest`, we will have many buggy interleavings to compare and find the common scheduling decisions in the latter part of the schedule. Thus, it becomes manageable to analyze the latter part of the interleavings and extract a test without search that will trigger the bug at every execution.

To develop the final, exact schedule, we select buggy executions with the least number of context switches and (manually) alternated two refinement steps: *Strengthen:* Using the execution trace, translate an exact, buggy schedule to a CONCURRIT test, i.e., express a sequence of operations by the same threads to a `RunThreadUntil` command. *Weaken:* Try to remove some `RunThreadUntil` commands and check if the bug is still triggered. After several refinement steps, we figure out an exact interleaving after the problematic state S to reach the assertion violation, and replace the loop in `SearchInBuggyTest` with a sequence of `RunUntilThread` commands to guide the execution of the SUT along the buggy interleaving. Our final test `ExactScheduleTest` is as follows:

```
ExactScheduleTest :
Tid tA, tB, tC = WaitForDistinctThreads(3, EntersFunc(JS_NewContext));
RunThreadsUntil(tA, tB, EntersFunc(JS_DestroyContext));
RunThreadUntil(tA, InFunc(js_GC) && ReadsMem(&rt-> state));
RunThreadUntil(tB, ThreadEnds);
RunThreadUntil(tA, InFunc(js_GC) && WritesMem(&rt-> gcNumber));
RunThreadUntil(tC, EntersFunc(js_AddRoot));
RunThreadUntil(tA, ReturnsFunc(js_GC)); // violates assertion!
```

Our final test concisely describes few key scheduling decisions causing the bug and leaves other parts of the thread schedule unspecified. The control imposed by the CONCURRIT script is enough to guide the SUT to the assertion violation at every execution. Thus, we can use this test to file a bug report and to check if any fix for the bug prevents the problem; after the fix, we can add the test to our regression suite.

In summary, we demonstrated an iterative process for one to refine a CONCURRIT test by incorporating new insights about the target schedules. At each step, we fixed a longer, former portion of the target interleaving and localized the search for unknown portion of the interleaving around a smaller region of the interleaving space. Finally, we were able to simplify our test to describe an exact, buggy schedule in a concise and formal form.

3. DSL for controlling thread schedules

In this section, we provide a low-level, imperative language to describe and control intended thread schedules of the SUT.

3.1 Software-under-test (SUT)

We do not assume any specific syntax and semantics for the Software-under-Test (SUT)—we leave abstract (1) the structure of SUT-states and (2) transitions between such states. Let $SUTState$ refer to the set of all SUT-states, S range over $SUTState$, and $S_0 \in SUTState$ be the unique initial state of SUT.

We assume that each SUT-state consists of a set of threads, each of which is referred to via a unique thread identifier. Let Tid be the set of all thread identifiers and t range over Tid. In case the SUT consists of multiple processes, the set Tid contains all the threads contained in these processes.

To present the operation of a CONCURRIT test, we assume a standard interleaving semantics for the execution of threads in the SUT: At any time only one thread is allowed to execute, modifying its own local variables, and possibly, some global variables. We also abstract away the memory model issues by assuming a sequentially consistent memory model. We use the notation $S \xrightarrow{t} S'$ to indicate that a thread $t \in Tid$ in the SUT can execute from state S and leads to SUT-state S'.

In addition, the SUT code is instrumented, so that when a thread t visits an instrumentation point, it generates an event carrying information about the operation to be performed next by t and blocks. (See Section 6 for details of this instrumentation). For this, we extend the notation for SUT-transitions as follows. We write $S \xrightarrow{t} S'/e$ to indicate that thread t also generates an event e as a result of the state transition.

Event. We represent each *event* as a record from fields to values describing an operation performed by a thread, such as accessing a memory location, entering or exiting a function, and terminating. Let $Event$ be the set of events, and e range over $Event$.

Given an event e, we write $e.f$ to refer to field f of the event. Each event contains at least two fields, $kind$ and tid, to indicate the type of the operation for which the event is generated and the generating thread's identifier, respectively. Other fields are used to store more information about the operation, for example, *addr* field for the memory address read or written, $func$ field for the function being called, and *pc* field for the related source location.

CONCURRIT scripts use a special form of boolean expression, called *event predicates*, to represent sets of events. Let `EPred` contain all event predicates and `p` range over `EPred`. Following is the list of event predicates we commonly use in our tests:

```
WritesMem      ≡ λe. e.kind == MemWrite
WritesMem(a)   ≡ λe. e.kind == MemWrite && e.addr == a
EntersFunc(f)  ≡ λe. e.kind == FuncEnter && e.func == f
CallsFunc      ≡ λe. e.kind == FuncCall
ThreadEnds     ≡ λe. e.kind == ThreadEnd
AtControl(x)   ≡ λe. e.kind == Control && e.pc == x
```

Predicate `AtControl` is used to refer to events generated at particular source locations (control point) in the SUT code.

The events generated by SUT threads are communicated to the CONCURRIT script, and they provide the mechanism to interact with and control the execution of the SUT. In particular, generating an event causes the originating thread to block until the CONCURRIT script observes the event and explicitly enables the generating thread to continue.

3.2 CONCURRIT: Syntax

Figure 4 shows the core syntax of CONCURRIT. We will extend this syntax in Section 4 to support exploring multiple test executions.

A statement in our DSL is denoted by `C`. Our DSL extends an imperative language with two special commands: `select` and `release`. (Command `endrun` represents an instruction that marks the end of the execution.) These special commands can be implemented as a library of procedures on top of an imperative language, in our case, C/C++. Thus, we follow the C language syntax for standard imperative constructs and expressions in CONCURRIT.

Symbols `b`, `t`, and `e` refer to CONCURRIT variable names storing Boolean values, thread identifiers, and events, respectively. The variables have types `bool`, `Tid`, and `Event`, respectively. We also use `x` to refer to a variable of an arbitrary type.

$$\frac{t \in Tid \quad E(t) = \bot \quad S \xrightarrow{t} S'}{(S, D, E, \mathtt{C}) \dashrightarrow (S', D, E, \mathtt{C})}\ \textsc{SUT-Step-Without-Event}$$

$$\frac{t \in Tid \quad E(t) = \bot \quad S \xrightarrow{t} S'/e}{(S, D, E, \mathtt{C}) \dashrightarrow (S', D, E[t \mapsto e], \mathtt{C})}\ \textsc{SUT-Step-With-Event}$$

$$\frac{t \in D \Downarrow \mathtt{T} \quad E(t) = e \quad D' = D[\mathtt{e} \mapsto e]}{(S, D, E, \mathtt{e} = \mathtt{select(T)}; \mathtt{C}) \dashrightarrow (S, D', E, \mathtt{C})}\ \textsc{Select}$$

$$\frac{\forall t \in D \Downarrow \mathtt{T}.\ E(t) = \bot \quad (\textit{Time limit for } \mathtt{select} \textit{ expires})}{(S, D, E, \mathtt{e} = \mathtt{select(T)}; \mathtt{C}) \dashrightarrow (S, D, E, \mathtt{endrun})}\ \textsc{Select-Timeout}$$

$$\frac{\forall t \in D \Downarrow \mathtt{T}.\ (E(t) \neq \bot \wedge E'(t) = \bot) \quad \forall t \notin D \Downarrow \mathtt{T}.\ E'(t) = E(t)}{(S, D, E, \mathtt{release(T)}; \mathtt{C}) \dashrightarrow (S, D, E', \mathtt{C})}\ \textsc{Release}$$

$$\frac{\mathtt{C}' = (D(\mathtt{b}) = \textit{true})\ ?\ (\mathtt{C_1}; \mathtt{C})\ :\ (\mathtt{C_2}; \mathtt{C})}{(S, D, E, \mathtt{if(b)}\ \{\mathtt{C_1}\}\ \mathtt{else}\ \{\mathtt{C_2}\}; \mathtt{C}) \dashrightarrow (S, D, E, \mathtt{C}')}\ \textsc{If}$$

$$\frac{\mathtt{C}' = (D(\mathtt{b}) = \textit{true})\ ?\ (\mathtt{C_1}; \mathtt{while(b)}\ \{\mathtt{C_1}\}; \mathtt{C})\ :\ \mathtt{C}}{(S, D, E, \mathtt{while(b)}\ \{\mathtt{C_1}\}; \mathtt{C}) \dashrightarrow (S', D, E, \mathtt{C}')}\ \textsc{While}$$

Figure 5. The operational semantics of CONCURRIT.

b, t, e, x ∈ *Var*		
T ::=	AnyThread | t | T+t | T−t	*Thread expressions*
C ::=	e = select(T)	*Wait for event from thread(s)*
|	release(T)	*Unblock thread(s)*
|	endrun	*End of execution*
|	if(b) C else C	*Conditional*
|	while(b) C | break	*Loop*
|	C; C	*Sequential composition*
|	...	*Other imperative constructs*

Figure 4. Syntax of CONCURRIT.

3.3 CONCURRIT: Semantics

We next give an operational semantics to CONCURRIT. For this, we think of the software-under-test (SUT) and the test written in CONCURRIT running together as a single system, in which the SUT and the DSL script run concurrently and in interaction with each other (events provide the mechanism for their interaction). Thus, we define a *test state* as the composed state of the SUT and the DSL script in CONCURRIT.

3.3.1 Test state

A test state is described by a tuple $(S, D, E, \mathtt{C})$:

- $S \in SUTState$ is a state of SUT as described in Section 3.1. Note that we abstract out the details of SUT states.
- $D \in DSLState$ is the state of the DSL script written in CONCURRIT. Let Var be a set of variable names. State D is a map from Var to $Value$. Let $dom(D)$ denote the set of variables defined at state D. We write $D(\mathtt{x})$ to denote the value of a variable $\mathtt{x} \in dom(D)$ in state D. We write $D[\mathtt{x} \mapsto v]$ to denote the DSL state that agrees with D for all variables except that x is mapped to value v.
- E is a map from Tid to $Event$. For a thread $t \in Tid$, $E(t) = \bot$ indicates that t has no event associated with it, and $E(t) \in Event$ indicates that t is blocked at an event and waiting for the CONCURRIT script to unblock it. We write $E = [\lambda t \in Tid.\ \bot]$ to indicate that no thread in E is mapped to an event. We use similar notation to D to update the map E (e.g., $E[t \mapsto e]$).
- C is the rest of the DSL program (a statement from Figure 4) to evaluate next.

3.3.2 Test executions

Figure 5 gives an operational semantics for an execution of the SUT composed by the test in CONCURRIT. Such an execution is expressed as a sequence of test-state transitions governed by the rules in Figure 5:

$$(S_0, D_0, [\lambda t \in Tid.\ \bot], \mathtt{C_0}; \mathtt{endrun}) \dashrightarrow^* (S_n, D_n, E_n, \mathtt{endrun})$$

In the initial test-state, S_0 and D_0 denote the unique initial states of the SUT and the DSL, and $\mathtt{C_0}$ denotes the CONCURRIT script written by the programmer. Notice that, we sequentially compose the DSL statement $\mathtt{C_0}$ with special command **endrun**. During the execution, the statement $\mathtt{C_0}$; **endrun** is modified by the operational semantics rules to indicate the next DSL statement to be evaluated, and the execution terminates when the DSL statement is fully evaluated to **endrun**.

Without loss of generality, we use an interleaved semantics for the execution, where at any time either an SUT thread or the DSL script may take a transition.

SUT-transitions. As stated by rules SUT-STEP-WITHOUT-EVENT and SUT-STEP-WITH-EVENT, a thread t in the SUT may execute and lead the SUT from state S to a new state S' (expressed by $S \xrightarrow{t} S'$). The transitions by an SUT thread t is enabled only when $E(t) = \bot$ holds, i.e., there is no event associated with t in the current test state. If thread t generates an event e as a result of this transition, it is associated with that event using the map E (see SUT-STEP-WITH-EVENT). This causes thread t to be blocked until the DSL script executes a **release** command on thread t to remove this mapping (see rule RELEASE).

DSL-transitions. Each DSL transition evaluates the current script C to result in a new script $\mathtt{C}'$, and possibly modifies the internal DSL state D and the mapping E. These transitions are governed by the semantics rules other than SUT-STEP-WITHOUT-EVENT and SUT-STEP-WITH-EVENT. Transitions by the DSL do not affect the SUT-state S. The DSL script can only control the execution of the SUT by modifying the map E, which affects the further transitions of the SUT by, for example, unblocking a thread waiting on an event.

3.3.3 Controlling thread schedule with select and release

Thread expressions. The DSL commands **select** and **release** operate on a set of thread identifiers. We use thread expressions (T of type **TExpr**) to identify a set of thread identifiers. Syntax for thread expressions is given in Figure 4. First, the special DSL constant **AnyThread** represents the set of all thread identifiers, i.e., Tid. Second, each thread variable **t** (storing the identifier of a thread) is also treated a thread expression representing the set $\{D(\mathtt{t})\}$. Finally, we overload the $+$ and $-$ operators to include or exclude a thread identifier to/from the set.

We write $D \Downarrow \mathtt{T}$ to refer to the set of thread identifiers (subset of Tid) represented by the expression T in D. This set is defined recursively as follows:

$$D \Downarrow \mathtt{AnyThread} = Tid \qquad D \Downarrow (\mathtt{T} + \mathtt{t}) = D \Downarrow \mathtt{T} \cup \{D(\mathtt{t})\}$$
$$D \Downarrow \mathtt{t} = \{D(\mathtt{t})\} \qquad D \Downarrow (\mathtt{T} - \mathtt{t}) = D \Downarrow \mathtt{T} \setminus \{D(\mathtt{t})\}$$

We say that a thread with identifier t *satisfies* T (or T is satisfied by thread t) at a state D if $t \in D \Downarrow \mathtt{T}$.

Waiting for an event. The command `e = select(T)` takes a thread expression and waits for a thread whose identifier is in the set $D \Downarrow \mathtt{T}$ to generate an event. The command then binds variable `e` to the generated event. For example, `e = select(AnyThread)` waits for any thread, `e = select(t)` waits for thread `t`, and `e = select(AnyThread − t)` waits for any thread except `t` to generate an event.

Semantics rule SELECT governs this operation of `select`. Note that an event generated by a thread t is recorded at $E.t$, so the rule simply queries E to retrieve this event.

Timeout. Due to an incorrect test script or uncontrolled nondeterminism in the SUT (as explained in Section 2), no thread in $D \Downarrow \mathtt{T}$ may generate an event from the current test state. In order to detect such situations, we allow the implementation of a timeout mechanisms. For this, we include the rule SELECT-TIMEOUT, which allows `select` to end the execution by evaluating the current DSL statement to **endrun**, when no thread in $D \Downarrow \mathtt{T}$ is associated with an event.

Nondeterminism in `select`**.** Notice that rules SELECT and SELECT-TIMEOUT bring some nondeterminism to the semantics. For example, consider a command `e = select(T)`. First, the command can choose an arbitrary thread from the set $D \Downarrow \mathtt{T}$, or, before taking effect it can even wait for a state in which more threads generate events and satisfy T. Second, if no thread in $D \Downarrow \mathtt{T}$ has generated an event, the command may evaluate to **endrun** before waiting a thread to generate an event. For the former case, our high-level constructs in Section 5 give examples to controlling this nondeterminism. For the latter case, the programmer can set, in the CONCURRIT test, a time limit for each invocation of a `select` command.

Unblocking threads. The command `release(T)` takes a thread expression and unblocks all threads whose identifiers are in the set $D \Downarrow \mathtt{T}$. This is governed by the rule RELEASE. The rule requires that all threads that are specified by T are associated with an event. Thus, `release` should be called for threads that have already generated and associated with an event at the current test state. A common way to ensure this condition, which we consistently followed in our case studies, is to match each `release` on a thread t to a previous `select` on the same thread t.

4. Searching for thread schedules

Having introduced the CONCURRIT constructs to control the scheduling of threads, we next extend our DSL to express a set of schedules and present mechanisms to search for these schedules in the presence of uncontrolled nondeterminism.

To accommodate the notion of search in CONCURRIT, we first add to the syntax of CONCURRIT a new command: (Let k refer to a constant value.)

$$\begin{array}{lll} \mathtt{C} & ::= & \cdots & \textit{Constructs from Figure 4} \\ & | & \mathtt{x} = \mathtt{choose}(\mathtt{k_1}, ..., \mathtt{k_n}) & \textit{Ask oracle to choose a value} \end{array}$$

The new construct `choose` is used to guide the execution (in addition to `select` and `release`) to support the search for schedules. To explain the semantics of `choose`, we include in our formalism an *oracle* denoted, $\mathcal{O}$, which resolves controlled nondeterminism in the test. We extend the test state (defined in Section 3.3.1) to include an oracle, and add to the operational semantics two new rules shown in Figure 6. The original rules in Figure 4 remain the same, except that they preserve $\mathcal{O}$ as is during the transition. The oracle $\mathcal{O}$ may change only by the new rules in Figure 6.

CHOOSE

$$\frac{\mathcal{O}.\mathit{choose}(\mathtt{k_1}, ..., \mathtt{k_n}) = (k, \mathcal{O}') \qquad k \in \{\mathtt{k_1}, ..., \mathtt{k_n}\} \qquad D' = D[\mathtt{x} \mapsto k]}{(S, D, E, \mathtt{x} = \mathtt{choose}(\mathtt{k_1}, ..., \mathtt{k_n}); \mathtt{C}, \mathcal{O}) \dashrightarrow (S, D', E, \mathtt{C}, \mathcal{O}')}$$

RESTART

$$\frac{\mathcal{O}.\mathit{restart}() = \mathit{Some}(\mathcal{O}')}{(S, D, E, \mathbf{endrun}, \mathcal{O}) \dashrightarrow (S_0, D_0, [\lambda t \in \mathit{Tid}.\ \bot], \mathtt{C_0}; \mathbf{endrun}, \mathcal{O}')}$$

Figure 6. The extended operational semantics of CONCURRIT for search. We keep the original rules in Figure 5 except that we include an oracle $\mathcal{O}$ to the test state and preserve $\mathcal{O}$ during the transition.

Choose. Rule CHOOSE governs the operation of the command $\mathtt{x} = \mathtt{choose}(\mathtt{k_1}, ..., \mathtt{k_n})$. The command is used to request an *input* from the oracle $\mathcal{O}$ to be used to guide the current execution. Operation $\mathcal{O}.\mathit{choose}(k_1, ..., k_n)$ returns a pair $(k, \mathcal{O}')$, where k is the value chosen by the oracle from $k_1, ..., k_n$, and $\mathcal{O}'$ is the new state of the oracle. The oracle can choose nondeterministically or it can track choices across multiple executions to implement a search.

Restart. Rule RESTART allows the oracle $\mathcal{O}$ to start a new execution of the SUT when the current one terminates (when the CONCURRIT script evaluates to **endrun**). For this, we define the $\mathcal{O}.\mathit{restart}()$ operation to return either $\mathit{Some}(\mathcal{O}')$ or None. If the oracle decides to start a new execution, it returns $\mathit{Some}(\mathcal{O}')$, where $\mathcal{O}'$ is the oracle to guide the SUT during the new execution. In this case, the SUT and the CONCURRIT script are restarted from their initial states. Recall that, in the initial test-state, the CONCURRIT script $\mathtt{C_0}$ is sequentially composed with **endrun**. If the oracle decides that there are no more executions to explore, it terminates the overall test by returning None.

Modularity of Test Scripts and Oracles. The interface of the oracle cleanly separates (1) the description of a set of thread schedules in CONCURRIT and (2) the exploration of these schedules. The oracle guides the exploration in (2) by defining a search strategy and related heuristics transparently to the CONCURRIT script. To explain this separation, consider the following test:

```
InterleaveTwoThreads :
1 Event e1 = select(AnyThread); Tid t1 = e1.tid;
2 Event e2 = select(AnyThread − t1).tid; Tid t2 = e2.tid;
3 while(!HasEnded(t1) || !HasEnded(t2)) {
4   Tid t = choose(t1, t2);    // Oracle chooses one of the threads.
5   do {                       // Loop until thread t accesses the memory.
6     release(t);              // Enable thread t to execute.
7     Event e = select(t);     // Wait until thread t blocks at another event.
8   } while(!ReadsMem(e) && !WritesMem(e));
9 }
```

The test binds variables `t1` and `t2` to two distinct threads at Line 1 and 2, respectively. At each outer loop iteration, one of the threads `t1` or `t2` is chosen by the `choose(t1, t2)` construct at Line 4. Then, the chosen thread `t` is enabled to execute using `release` at Line 6, until the thread is blocked at another event. When the chosen thread is blocked at an event before an access (read or write) to the memory, the test repeats the outer loop and choses a new thread. Irrespective of the choice made by the oracle $\mathcal{O}$ at Line 4, the test describes a set of interleavings, say **I**, of two distinct threads where a new scheduling decision is made (at Line 4) after every memory access event. The described interleaving ends when both threads terminate (`HasEnded(t)` at Line 3 returns true iff thread `t` has terminated). Different oracles, however, will differ in the order in which the interleavings are explored.

Implementing oracles. With our oracle interface—`choose` and `restart`—it is straightforward to implement various search strate-

```
O.choose(k1, ..., kn):
  if O.index > |O.τ| then
    // EXTEND PREFIX: Record chosen value in the prefix
    let K = {k1, ..., kn}
    k = nondeterministically choose from set K
    O.τ.append((k, K \ {k}))
  else
    // REPLAY PREFIX: Use previously chosen value in the prefix
    let (k, K) = O.prefix[O.index]
  endif
  O.index = O.index + 1
  return (k, O)

O.restart():
  R = {i | 1 ≤ i ≤ |O.τ| ∧ O.τ[i] = (k, K) ∧ K ≠ ∅}
  if R ≠ ∅ then
    m = max(R)
    let (k, K) = O.τ[m] and k' ∈ K
    O.τ.pruneAfter(m − 1)
    O.τ.append((k', K\{k'}))
    O.index = 1
    return Some(O)
  else
    return None
  endif
```

Figure 7. Oracle implementing depth-first search.

gies, such as breadth-first and depth-first search. In the following, we give an abstract, declarative description of an oracle implementing search. To make our point concrete, we explain how to instantiate this oracle for depth-first search; other search techniques and heuristics (e.g., [17]) can be integrated to our framework following a similar methodology.

4.1 Implementing oracles for search

Our oracle $\mathcal{O}$ tracks a *trace* of each execution, denoted τ. The trace consists of the inputs and outputs interchanged between the oracle and the CONCURRIT test—in particular the sequence of choices taken by the oracle in response to `choose` commands. The oracle also keeps a set $\mathcal{T}$ of traces for the complete executions it observes.

Initially, set $\mathcal{T}$ is empty, and the oracle starts with an empty trace τ. During the execution, calls to operation $\mathcal{O}.choose()$ extend trace τ. Note that, when the execution terminates, the semantic rule RESTART invokes $\mathcal{O}.restart()$ to decide whether to start a new execution or to terminate the search. Operation $\mathcal{O}.restart()$ first adds τ to set $\mathcal{T}$, and then computes from $\mathcal{T}$ a new trace τ' satisfying the following: *(i) Trace τ' is non-empty, (ii) it is not a prefix of another trace in $\mathcal{T}$, and (iii) the longest prefix τ'' of τ' such that $\tau'' \neq \tau'$ is a prefix of some trace in $\mathcal{T}$.* Thus, trace τ' may be used to generate an execution (particularly, a thread schedule) distinct from the previously explored ones. If no such τ' exists, $\mathcal{O}.restart()$ returns $None$, which terminates the exploration. Otherwise, during the next execution, the oracle first replays τ'—i.e., it uses the records in τ' to respond to calls to $\mathcal{O}.choose()$. When all records in τ' are used, the oracle extends τ' to a complete trace in the rest of the execution.

4.1.1 Oracle for depth-first search

In our framework, we implement search by following a depth-first search (DFS) strategy. Figure 7 gives an implementation of the oracle $\mathcal{O}$ following a depth-first search strategy. We implement the trace τ as a sequence of pairs (k, K). Each pair records in the first element k a choice taken by the oracle in response to a `choose` command. The second element K is the set of values that has not been chosen yet. The oracle also keeps an index $index$, which points to an element of τ to be considered next while replaying the trace.

```
1  Tid WaitForThread
       (TExpr T, EPred p) {
2    while(true) {
3      Event e = select(T);
4      if(p(e)) return e.tid;
5      release(e.tid);
6    }
7  }

8  TidList WaitForDistinctThreads
       (int n, EPred p) {
9    TExpr T = AnyThread;
10   TidList ts;
11   while(0 < n--) {
12     Tid t = WaitForThread(T, p);
13     ts.add(t);
14     T = T − t;
15   }
16   return ts;
17 }

18 void RunThreadsUntil
       (Tid t1, ..., tn, EPred p) {
19   TExpr T = t1 + ··· + tn;
20   release(T);
21   int c = n;
22   while(0 < c--) {
23     Tid t = WaitForThread(T, p);
24     T = T − t;
25   }
26 }

27 Tid ChooseThread
       (Tid t1, ..., tn) {
28   int k = choose(1, ..., n);
29   switch(k) {
30     case 1 : return t1;
31     ...
32     case n : return tn;
33   }
34 }
```

Figure 8. Our test library with high-level functions

For the entire search, the oracle modifies the trace τ as a DFS stack, which eliminates the need for additional traces. Thus, during the $\mathcal{O}.restart()$ operation, the set $\mathcal{T}$ only contains the last explored trace τ. The oracle computes the new trace τ' (to replay in the next execution) from τ by backtracking to the last record (k, K) of a `choose` command in the trace such that K contains at least one unchosen element, say k', and updating that record to $(k', K\backslash\{k'\})$. This ensures that during the replay of τ' the oracle responds to the corresponding invocation of `choose` by returning k'.

5. A high-level library for writing concise tests

While the core CONCURRIT DSL introduced in Sections 3 and 4 is useful to formally explain the control obtained by a CONCURRIT test, the low-level primitives in the DSL may not be appropriate for programmers to write concise tests. In this section, we show how these low-level primitives can be combined to implement higher-level constructs, as a library of functions. Our library is shown in Figure 8. We found this library sufficient and convenient to write tests for our benchmarks (Section 7). In fact, we conclude this section by describing common usage patterns of the library that we have learned from our experiments.

Waiting for a thread. We define two functions to wait for threads. Function `WaitForThread` takes a thread expression `T` and an event predicate `p`, and repeatedly runs the threads satisfying `T` until one thread in `T` generates an event satisfying `p`. A common use of `WaitForThread` is with `T = AnyThread`, to enable all threads in the SUT until the expected event is generated.

Function `WaitForDistinctThreads` waits for a fixed number of threads each to generate an event satisfying `p`. Once a thread generates such an event, we ensure at Line 14 that the thread is no longer run by removing its identifier from the thread expression `T`.

Running threads. The library functions `WaitForThread` and `WaitForDistinctThreads` return one or a set of blocked thread identifiers, respectively. Function `RunThreadsUntil` takes a list of already-blocked threads and reenables them (via `release`). Then, the function runs each reenabled thread until the thread generates an event satisfying predicate `p`. For readability, when using only a single thread identifier `t`, we call the function `RunThreadUntil(t, epred)`.

Selecting a thread variable. We define function `ChooseThread` for selecting from a given set of thread variables, using the primitive `choose` explained in Section 4. Thus, we use this function when we want to introduce a scheduling point for which all possible choices must be explored.

5.1 Test patterns using high-level constructs

In this section, we present common test patterns. Most of our patterns are based on the following generic pattern:

```
GenericPattern(int n, EPred p_start, p_schedule, BExpr loop_cond) :
1 Tid t1, ..., tn = WaitForDistinctThreads(n, p_start);
2 ...... // Run threads t1, ..., tn to follow a fixed interleaving
3 while(loop_cond) {
4    Tid t = ChooseThread(t1, ..., tn);
5    RunThreadUntil(t, p_schedule);
6 }
```

The pattern has four parameters: the number (`n`) of threads to be controlled during the test, the event predicates, `p_start` and `p_schedule`, and a boolean expression `loop_cond`. We first wait for `n` threads until each of the `n` threads generates an event satisfying `p_start` (line 1). Then, we use functions of our library in Figure 8 to guide the threads to follow a particular schedule (line 2). Finally, we schedule threads in a loop–at each iteration running one of the threads until it generates an event satisfying `p_schedule`. Then, the SUT is restarted to explore a new thread interleaving.

SearchAll: Traditional model checking. In order to apply model checking to the SUT in the traditional way, we instrument the entire code for the SUT. In particular, the instrumentation ensures that (i) every memory access (read and write) and (ii) every operation that may cause the executing thread to block (e.g., synchronization operations such as acquiring a mutex) generate an event. We over-approximate (ii) by inserting instrumentation before every function call. Under the assumption that the only source of non-determinism in the program is the thread schedule, rescheduling threads at (1) and (2) is sufficient to enumerate all possible thread schedules of the SUT. The pattern `SearchAll` instantiates our generic pattern `GenericPattern` as follows: (1) `p_start` = `ThreadStart`. (2) Line 2 is omitted. (3) `p_schedule` = (`ReadsMem` ‖ `WritesMem` ‖ `CallsFunc` ‖`ThreadEnds`). (4) `loop_cond` =!`HasEnded(t1)` || ··· || !`HasEnded(tn)`.

SearchInFunc: Restricting search to particular functions. The pattern `SearchInFunc` restricts the search for the interleaving of threads within a set of functions, say **F**. In this pattern, we modify `GenericPattern` as follows: (1) We only instrument the code so that a thread generates events only when executing a function in **F**. (2) `p_start` = `EntersFunc(f1)` ‖ ··· ‖ `EntersFunc(fm)`, where **F** = `f1`, ..., `fm`. (3) Similarly to `SearchAll`, Line 2 is omitted. (4) `loop_cond` = `InFunc(f1)` || ··· || `InFunc(fm)`, which holds if at least one of `t1`, ..., `tn` is running a function from **F**.

SearchInFuncLS: Interleaving threads at large steps. For some benchmarks, we found it useful to limit the scheduling points to a few special locations in the SUT code. For this, we manually instrument these locations in the SUT code to generate user-defined events of the form `AtControl(pc)`. In particular, we associate each of these locations with a user-defined program counter (`pc`), an integer value. Then, we extend the pattern `SearchInFunc` by setting `p_schedule` to (`AtControl` ‖ `ThreadEnds`).

SearchInBuggy: Starting search from a suspicious state. Similarly to the pattern `SearchInFunc`, `SearchInBuggy` searches for interleavings within a set **F** of functions. However, instead of starting the search from the beginning of the functions, this pattern includes a fixed schedule before starting the search (at line 2 of `GenericPattern`). This fixed schedule is benchmark-specific and is described by few lines each running `RunThread(s)Until`.

ExactSchedule. This pattern describes the exact thread schedule intended by the programmer to generate, for example, to document a buggy interleaving in a reliable way. In this case, the schedule only consists of line 1 of `GenericPattern` and a sequence of `RunThread(s)Until`, omitting the search loop at lines 3-8.

SearchInFuncCB: Context-bounded search of interleavings. There are many reduction techniques for software model checking, including partial-order reduction [5, 7], preemption bounding [19], and fair stateless model checking [20]. These optimizations are orthogonal to our technique. One can implement these optimizations within the test script instead of modifying the underlying search algorithm (i.e., the interface for oracle $\mathcal{O}$). In our experiments, we found context bounding quite useful to reduce the interleavings searched when using `SearchInFunc`. The following is an implementation of the context-bounded version of `GenericSearch`.

```
GenericPatternCB(int n, EPred p_start, p_schedule,
                 BExpr loop_cond, int context_bound) :
Tid t1, ..., tn = WaitForDistinctThreads(n, p_start);
...... // Run threads t1, ..., tn to follow a fixed schedule
for(int i = 1; i ⩽ context_bound && loop_cond; ++i){
   Tid t = ChooseThread(t1, ..., tn);
   do { // Run next context by thread t
      RunThreadUntil(t, p_schedule);
   } while(loop_cond && choose(true, false));
}
...... // Interleave each thread sequentially until completion
```

6. Implementation

We have implemented CONCURRIT as an embedded DSL for C/C++. Our implementation is available at http://code.google.com/p/concurrit/. A test in CONCURRIT is simply a C++ program. Our implementation supports the use of CONCURRIT tests in both unit testing and system testing.

6.1 Unit testing with CONCURRIT

For unit testing, the programmer provides the SUT as a shared library with an entry function named `test_main`. The executable CONCURRIT test loads this shared library and calls `test_main` multiple times to explore different executions of the SUT.

To instrument the SUT we provide a library with a collection of functions. We give example instrumentation functions below.

```
void concurritThreadStart();
void concurritThreadEnd();
void concurritFuncEnter(void* function, long arg0, long arg1);
void concurritFuncReturn(void* function, long return_value);
void concurritFuncCall(void* caller, void* callee, long arg0);
void concurritMemRead(void* address, int size, long value);
void concurritMemWrite(void* address, int size, long value);
void concurritControlPoint(int pc);
```

CONCURRIT can operate with different event granularities. At one extreme the programmer can insert these functions manually, or one can use our Pin tool [18] for automatically instrumenting (the binary of) the SUT at runtime, capturing all memory operations and function calls/returns. While the the cost can be 10-100x in the former case, the overhead is very small in the latter case. In our experiments with larger programs we needed to insert (manually) very few instrumentation points with negligible cost, which made our approach lightweight.

6.2 System testing with CONCURRIT

We applied CONCURRIT in system testing of three large servers: Memcached, Apache httpd, and MySQL. System tests for these servers carry unique challenges. First, the SUT is composed of many components with nondeterministic behaviors, such as arbitrary network-packet delays and arbitrary assignment of worker threads to connections. Second, the SUT consists of multiple processes interacting with each other using various mechanisms.

To test such servers, first, we run the CONCURRIT test in a separate process and perform the event communication between the SUT processes and the CONCURRIT process using named (FIFO) pipes. Except when specifically blocked and sequentialized by the CONCURRIT test, all the threads in these SUT processes run in parallel. Except for the threads controlled by the CONCURRIT test, all the threads in the distributed processes run in parallel with each other. Second, we define two special events: `TestStart` and `TestEnd` to signal the beginning and the end of an SUT execution. For example, in `memcached`, these events are generated when the requestor process starts and terminates, respectively. The CONCURRIT test only controls the events generated (by the `memcached` server) between `TestStart` and `TestEnd`.

7. Evaluation

In our evaluation of our proposal, we used our implementation of CONCURRIT described in Section 6 and conducted a case study on a collection of multithreaded programs. These programs are from well-known benchmark suits: Inspect [26], PARSEC [3], and RADBench [12]. Each of our benchmarks contains a concurrency bug, either real or manually inserted by existing work [11].

For each benchmark, we followed the testing process that we demonstrated in Section 2 for one of the benchmarks. During this process, we wrote one or more tests in the high-level DSL described in Section 5, aiming at reproducing the bug in the benchmark. We started by writing less exact tests (which are not `SearchAll`) for each bug using partial information about the bug. Based on the information obtained from these test executions we made the tests more precise so that they could reproduce the bug by describing only a small number of key scheduling decisions. We found that we can write concise tests for all of our benchmarks by applying the usage patterns we described in Section 5.1. For small benchmarks we also wrote tests that will search all thread schedules (`SearchAll`) in order to see if model checking could find these bugs efficiently. Moreover, for some benchmarks we managed to write tests that are exact schedules (`ExactSchedule`). The CONCURRIT code for these tests are available at `http://code.google.com/p/concurrit/`. We give sample tests from our benchmarks in Appendix A.

Table 1 shows the results of our study. For each benchmark, the table shows the various tests we wrote to reproduce a bug in the benchmark. Our CONCURRIT tests detected the regarding bugs in all the cases. For each test, we give the number of functions involved in the test, how many extra instrumentation calls were manually inserted in addition to the automated Pin instrumentation, the number of CONCURRIT DSL lines, number of threads involved in the test, and the (average) number of schedules explored before hitting the bug. Note that, in the sixth column we only give the number of threads explicitly controlled by the test; the execution may contain other threads, which are either blocked or executed in an uncontrolled manner. For benchmarks *streamcluster*, *memcached*, *apache-httpd*, and *mysql-server* we did not use Pin and inserted all the instrumentation manually (as reported in the forth column). In this way, our tests become portable as they require no heavy-weight automated instrumentation.

Full model checking. In our study, we were able to apply traditional notion of model checking on small benchmarks, namely bbuf, bzip2, ctrace, pbzip2. The test type "SearchAll" refers to tests of this kind, which was explained in Section 5.1. In these tests, we control the scheduling decision after every memory access (read or write) and function call. We had to instrument all operations that may introduce nondeterminism and change the thread schedule. However, we did not control synchronization operations for locks and condition variables; instead, we inserted scheduling choices before every function call. This gives two benefits. First, it ensures that all model checking tests were able to hit the bug, since instrumenting every function call over-approximates the effect of synchronization-related functions on the thread schedule. Second, it makes our approach *portable*; we do not have to control and implement the semantics of different synchronization operations. Finally, as expected, we should note that full model checking works only for small programs, such a data structures. In our experiments, we bounded the number of executions to $10K$, but even for some small programs `SearchAll` generated more than $10K$ executions.

Customizing the search using information about the bug. While full model checking is impractical, we found that if we use information about a bug to restrict the number of explored schedules in a CONCURRIT test, we can efficiently and reliably reproduce the bugs. As discussed in Section 5.1, we restricted the traditional notion of model checking to customize the search in three aspects: (1) In tests "SearchInFunc", we instrumented only the body of several functions, say **F**, that we found related to the bug. The third column of Table 1 gives the size of **F**. Then, we started to search for thread schedules only when threads were executing functions in **F**. The size of **F** highlights a common characteristics of concurrency bugs: they occur due to incorrect synchronization of few functions and can be detected by focusing the search on these functions. (2) In tests "SearchInFuncCB2" and "SearchInFuncCB3", we applied context-bounded model checking techniques [19] with bounds 2 and 3, respectively. (3) In tests "SearchInFuncLS", we scheduled threads at coarse granularity, only after reaching a manually inserted control point. We obtained information about these control points either from the bug report (if the bug report has these details) or from insight obtained from triggering the bug with less exact CONCURRIT tests. For example, to check for atomicity violations using SearchInFuncLS, we inserted these control points around the accesses to the shared variables that we think will involve in the violation, and for ordering violations, we inserted the control points to mark the beginning and end of the code blocks whose different orderings may create an error. We found that, when used in conjunction with restricting the search to functions in **F**, context bounding and interleaving threads at coarse granularity are quite effective to reproduce the bugs in a small number of executions.

Generating exact buggy schedule. For 8 of our benchmarks, we were able to refine the test to "ExactSchedule", after observing a buggy execution and generalizing its thread schedule in a CONCURRIT test, which guides the execution towards the buggy states. Notice that, compared to tests for search, the size of ExactSchedule tests are not longer. This highlights the fact that in many concurrency bugs only few scheduling decisions involve; by enforcing these decisions, the bug can still happen in spite of the larger, uncontrolled part of the schedule. While sleep-based approaches exploit this fact to effectively reproduce simple concurrency bugs, our technique goes further by making such approches more formal and reliable for reproducing even more complex bugs.

8. Related work

We observe a spectrum of approaches to specifying and controlling the thread schedule in testing of concurrent programs. At one end of the spectrum, there are manual approaches, in which the programmer implements synchronization mechanisms to restrict the possible schedules of threads towards a particular scenario. However, such mechanisms are either ad hoc and unreliable (e.g., in the case of sleep statements) or may require nontrivial and unportable modifications in the program text. Techniques have been proposed to guide the execution to intended thread schedules in more portable and reliable ways, where the intended schedules are specified by the

Benchmark	Test pattern	Funcs involved	Manual instr.	Test LOC	Threads controlled	Schedules explored
bbuf	SearchAll	all	0	4	4	20
	SearchInFunc1	2	0	5	4	12
	SearchInFunc2	2	0	4	2	3
bzip2	SearchAll	all	0	4	3	>10K
	SearchInFunc	2	0	5	3	510
	SearchInFuncLS	2	3	5	3	8
	ExactSchedule	2	3	6	3	1
ctrace	SearchAll	all	0	4	2	>10K
	SearchLargeSteps	4	2	5	2	15
	ExactSchedule	2	2	6	2	1
pbzip2	SearchAll	all	0	4	4	>10K
	SearchLargeSteps	3	1	4	4	71
	ExactSchedule	2	1	4	4	1
pfscan	SearchInFunc	1	0	4	2	67
	SearchInFuncLS	1	1	4	2	51
	ExactSchedule	1	1	4	2	1
dedup	SearchInFunc	1	0	4	2	8
	SearchInFuncLS	1	1	4	2	3
	ExactSchedule	1	1	5	2	1

Benchmark	Test pattern	Funcs involved	Manual instr.	Test LOC	Threads controlled	Schedules explored
streamcluster	SearchInFuncLS	all	9	11	4	>10K
	ExactSchedule	3	9	11	4	1
mozilla-nspr1	SearchInFunc	1	0	4	2	1020
	SearchInFuncCB2	1	0	6	2	4
mozilla-nspr2	SearchInFuncCB2	2	0	6	2	6
	ExactSchedule	2	1	5	2	1
mozilla-nsp3	SearchSeqFuncs	1	0	5	2	38
spidermonkey1	SearchAll	all	0	4	2	>10K
	SearchInFunc	2	0	5	2	>10K
	SearchInFuncCB3	2	0	10	2	451
	SearchInFuncCB2	2	0	7	2	226
spidermonkey2	SearchAll	all	0	4	3	>10K
	SearchInFunc	4	0	5	3	>10K
	SearchInBuggy	4	0	8	3	8
	ExactSchedule	4	0	7	3	1
memcached	SearchInFuncLS	2	12	4	2	10
	ExactSchedule	2	12	4	2	1
apache-httpd	SearchInFuncLS	2	14	4	3	7
mysql-server	SearchInFuncLS	2	9	5	3	30

Table 1. Experimental results. Our CONCURRIT tests detect the bugs in all the cases.

programmer relative to a global timer (ConAn [16], MultithreadedTC [23]) or a sequence of user-defined events expressed in linear temporal logic (IMUnit [9]). While these techniques give the programmer the ability to impose constraints on the interleaving of threads, they do not support exploration of all executions satisfying these constraints.

At the other end of the spectrum, there are fully automated approaches. To alleviate the nondeterminism in the execution, software model checking techniques have been combined with testing to control the thread scheduler so that distinct interleavings of the threads in the test are systematically enumerated and checked against the test criteria [6, 14, 19, 21]. However, these techniques require controlling all sources of nondeterminism in the program, which is impractical for large programs, such as web servers.

Many model checking exploration techniques have been developed that seek to achieve high coverage of executions in a scalable way [13]—such as partial-order reduction [5, 7], symmetry reduction [8], preemption bounding [19], fair stateless model checking [20], and commutativity guided scheduling [25]. These techniques do not directly help to efficiently examine interesting and potentially-problematic interleaving scenarios. Our proposal allows the tester to customize the model checking to target such scenarios. Meanwhile, the tester can still implement these reduction techniques within the CONCURRIT test.

Recent studies proposed techniques to control the scheduling of a model checker to target suspicious executions more quickly than traditional state-space exploration. Among them, active testing [24], probabilistic scheduling [4], and change-aware preemption prioritization [10] are fully automated and rely on heuristics. However, we believe that programmers' help to guide the exploration of executions is also valuable, and testing tools should be designed to allow the programmer to interact with the test runtime to express her intents and insights about the test scenario. In fact, work on preemption sealing [2] proposed to disable preemptions that the programmer thinks are not interesting or can cause false warnings. In our work, we would like to give more control and flexibility to the programmer in this direction.

Note that our approach enables rapid prototyping and evaluation of a custom search strategy by writing and exploring a CONCURRIT test. The work in [15] is in the same spirit of ours, but it focuses on Boolean programs and allows the user to describe the model checking algorithm as a compact and high-level fixed-point formulation that can be fed to a general-purpose fixed-point solver.

Recent work in record/replay systems propose recording the thread schedule partially and reproducing the missing parts of the schedule during the replay [1, 22]. These systems do search in order to reproduce a single, feasible schedule, while in our work we do search to enumerate a space of specified schedules.

Acknowledgments

This research supported in part by Microsoft (Award #024263) and Intel (Award #024894) funding and by matching funding by U.C. Discovery (Award #DIG07-10227), by NSF Grants CCF-101781, CCF-0747390, CCF-1018729, and CCF-1018730, and by a DoD NDSEG Graduate Fellowship. The last author is supported in part by a Sloan Foundation Fellowship. Additional support comes from Oracle (formerly Sun Microsystems), from a gift from Intel, and from Par Lab afliates National Instruments, NEC, Nokia, NVIDIA, and Samsung.

References

[1] G. Altekar and I. Stoica. ODR: Output-deterministic replay for multicore debugging. In *SOSP*, 2009.

[2] T. Ball, S. Burckhardt, K. Coons, M. Musuvathi, , and S. Qadeer. Preemption sealing for efficient concurrency testing. *Technical Report MSR-TR-2009-143*, 2009.

[3] C. Bienia, S. Kumar, J. P. Singh, and K. Li. The PARSEC Benchmark Suite: Characterization and Architectural Implications. In *PACT*, 2008.

[4] S. Burckhardt, P. Kothari, M. Musuvathi, and S. Nagarakatte. A randomized scheduler with probabilistic guarantees of finding bugs. In *ASPLOS*, 2010.

[5] P. Godefroid. *Partial-order methods for the verification of concurrent systems: an approach to the state-explosion problem.* Springer-Verlag Inc., 1996. URL `citeseer.ist.psu.edu/godefroid95partialorder.html`.

[6] P. Godefroid. Software model checking: The verisoft approach. *In Form. Methods Syst. Des.*, 2005.

[7] G. Gueta, C. Flanagan, E. Yahav, and M. Sagiv. Cartesian partial-order reduction. In *SPIN*, 2007.

[8] R. Iosif. Symmetry reduction criteria for software model checking. In *SPIN*, 2002.

[9] V. Jagannath, M. Gligoric, D. Jin, Q. Luo, G. Rosu, and D. Marinov. Improved multithreaded unit testing. In *ESEC/FSE*, 2011.

[10] V. Jagannath, Q. Luo, and D. Marinov. Change-aware preemption prioritization. In *ISSTA*, 2011.

[11] N. Jalbert and K. Sen. A trace simplification technique for effective debugging of concurrent programs. In *FSE*, 2010.

[12] N. Jalbert, C. Pereira, G. Pokam, and K. Sen. RADBench: A concurrency bug benchmark suite. In *HOTPAR*, 2011.

[13] R. Jhala and R. Majumdar. Software model checking. *In ACM Comput. Surv.*, 2009.

[14] M. Kim, Y. Kim, and H. Kim. A comparative study of software model checkers as unit testing tools: An industrial case study. *In IEEE Trans. Softw. Eng.*, 2011.

[15] S. La Torre, M. Parthasarathy, and G. Parlato. Analyzing recursive programs using a fixed-point calculus. In *PLDI*, 2009.

[16] B. Long, D. Hoffman, and P. Strooper. Tool support for testing concurrent Java components. *In IEEE Trans. Softw. Eng.*, 2003.

[17] S. Lu, J. Tucek, F. Qin, and Y. Zhou. AVIO: Detecting atomicity violations via access interleaving invariants. In *ASPLOS*, 2006.

[18] C.-K. Luk, R. Cohn, R. Muth, H. Patil, A. Klauser, G. Lowney, S. Wallace, V. J. Reddi, and K. Hazelwood. Pin: Building customized program analysis tools with dynamic instrumentation. In *PLDI*, 2005.

[19] M. Musuvathi and S. Qadeer. Iterative context bounding for systematic testing of multithreaded programs. In *PLDI*, 2007.

[20] M. Musuvathi and S. Qadeer. Fair stateless model checking. In *PLDI*, 2008.

[21] V. Mutilin. Concurrent testing of Java components using Java PathFinder. In *ISoLA*, 2006.

[22] S. Park, Y. Zhou, W. Xiong, Z. Yin, R. Kaushik, K. H. Lee, and S. Lu. PRES: Probabilistic replay with execution sketching on multiprocessors. In *SOSP*, 2009.

[23] W. Pugh and N. Ayewah. Unit testing concurrent software. In *ASE*, 2007.

[24] K. Sen. Race directed random testing of concurrent programs. In *PLDI*, 2008.

[25] O. Shacham, N. Bronson, A. Aiken, M. Sagiv, M. Vechev, and E. Yahav. Testing atomicity of composed concurrent operations. In *OOPSLA*, 2011.

[26] Y. Yang, X. Chen, and G. Gopalakrishnan. Inspect: A runtime model checker for multithreaded C programs. *Technical Report UUCS-08-004*, 2008.

A. Sample CONCURRIT tests

Parallel tracing library (ctrace)

```
ExactSchedule :
Tid t1, t2 = WaitForDistinctThreads(2, EntersFunc(HASH_READ_ENTER));
RunThreadUntil(t1, AtControl(43) && InFunc(HAS_READ_EXIT));
RunThreadUntil(t2, ReturnsFunc(HASH_READ_ENTER));
RunThreadUntil(t1, ReadsMem &&InFunc(HASH_READ_ENTER));
RunThreadUntil(t2, ReturnsFunc(HASH_READ_EXIT));
RunThreadUntil(t1, ThreadEnds);
```

Online clustering kernel (streamcluster)

```
ExactSchedule :
// Control locations and other events (FuncEnter, FuncReturn) are all manually inserted in functions
// localSearch, localSearchSub, and pkmedian
Tid tmain = WaitForThread(AnyThread, EntersFunc(pkmedian));
RunThreadUntil(tmain, AtControl(42));
Tid t1, t2, t3 = WaitForThread(AnyThread − tmain, AtControl(42));
RunThreadsUntil(t1, t2, EntersFunc(barrier) ‖ ReturnsFunc(pkmedian));
while(InFunc(t1, pkmedian)) {
      RunThreadUntil(t3, EntersFunc(barrier) ‖ ReturnsFunc(pkmedian));
      RunThreadsUntil(t1, t2, t3, ExitsFunc(barrier) ‖ ReturnsFunc(pkmedian));
      RunThreadsUntil(t1, t2, EntersFunc(barrier) ‖ ReturnsFunc(pkmedian));
}
RunThreadsUntil(t1, t2, ThreadEnds);
RunThreadUntil(tm, ThreadEnd);
RunThreadsUntil(t1, t2, ThreadEnds);
```

RADBench Bug 4 (Mozilla NSPR Library – mozilla-nspr1)

```
SearchInFuncCB2 :
Tid t1, t2 = WaitForDistinctThreads(2, EntersFunc(MT_safe_localtime));
Tid t = ChooseThread(t1, t2);
while(choose(true, false)) {
      RunThreadUntil(t, ReadsMem ‖ WritesMem ‖ CallsFunc ‖ ThreadEnds);
}
t = (t == t1) ? t2 : t1;
RunThreadUntil(t, ReturnsFunc(MT_safe_localtime)); // assertion violation!
```

RADBench Bug 5 (Mozilla NSPR Library – mozilla-nspr2)

```
ExactSchedule :
// Control location 42 is in function PR_WaitCondVar
Tid t1 = WaitForThread(AnyThread, EntersFunc(PR_WaitCondVar));
RunThreadUntil(t1, AtControl(42));
Tid t2 = WaitForThread(AnyThread − t1, EntersFunc(PR_Interrupt));
RunThreadUntil(t2, ReturnsFunc(PR_Interrupt));
RunThreadUntil(t1, ReturnsFunc(PR_WaitCondVar));
```

RADBench Bug 6 (Mozilla NSPR Library – mozilla-nspr3)

```
SearchSeqFuncs :
Tid t1 = WaitForThread(AnyThread, EntersFunc(reader_main));
Tid t2 = WaitForThread(AnyThread − t1, EntersFunc(writer_main));
while(InFunc(t1, reader_main) ‖ InFunc(t2, writer_main) {
   Tid t = ChooseThread(t1, t2);
   RunThreadUntil(t, ReturnsFunc(PR_RWLock_Wlock) ‖ ReturnsFunc(PR_RWLock_Rlock)
      ‖ ReturnsFunc(PR_RWLock_Unlock) ‖ ThreadEnds);
}
```

RADBench Bug 2 (Mozilla SpiderMonkey JS – spidermonkey1)

```
SearchInFuncCB3 :
Tid t1 = WaitForThread(AnyThread, EntersFunc(js_GC));
Tid t2 = WaitForThread(AnyThread − t1, EntersFunc(JS_ClearContextThread));
Tid t = ChooseThread(t1, t2);
while(choose(true, false)) {
      RunThreadUntil(t, ReadsMem ‖ WritesMem ‖ CallsFunc ‖ ThreadEnds);
}
t = (t == t1) ? t2 : t1;
while(choose(true, false)) {
      RunThreadUntil(t, ReadsMem ‖ WritesMem ‖ CallsFunc ‖ ThreadEnds);
}
t = (t == t1) ? t2 : t1;
RunThreadUntil(t, ThreadEnds); // segmentation fault!
```

RADBench Bug 8 (Memcached server – memcached)

```
ExactSchedule :
// Control locations (including 42) and other events (FuncEnter, FuncReturn) are all manually
// inserted in functions complete_incr_bin and process_arithmetic_command
Tid t1, t2 = WaitForDistinctThreads(2, EntersFunc(complete_incr_bin)
    ‖ EntersFunc(process_arithmetic_command));
RunThreadUntil(t1, AtControl(42));
RunThreadUntil(t2, ReturnsFunc);
RunThreadUntil(t1, ReturnsFunc);
```

RADBench Bug 15 (MySQL Server – mysql-server)

```
SearchInFuncLS :
// Control locations and other events (FuncEnter, FuncReturn) are all manually inserted in functions
// mysql_insert and MYSQL_LOG::new_file
Tid t1, t2 = WaitForDistinctThreads(2, EntersFunc(MYSQL_LOG::new_file);
Tid t3 = WaitForThread(AnyThread − t1 − t2, EntersFunc(mysql_insert);
while(InFunc(t1, MYSQL_LOG::new_file)
    ‖ InFunc(t2, MYSQL_LOG::new_file) ‖ InFunc(t3, mysql_insert) {
   Tid t = ChooseThread(t1, t2, t3);
   RunThreadUntil(t, AtControl ‖ ThreadEnds);
}
```

Dynamic Determinacy Analysis

Max Schäfer *
Nanyang Technological University
schaefer@ntu.edu.sg

Manu Sridharan   Julian Dolby
IBM T.J. Watson Research Center
{msridhar, dolby}@us.ibm.com

Frank Tip
University of Waterloo
ftip@uwaterloo.ca

Abstract

We present an analysis for identifying *determinate* variables and expressions that always have the same value at a given program point. This information can be exploited by client analyses and tools to, e.g., identify dead code or specialize uses of dynamic language constructs such as `eval`, replacing them with equivalent static constructs. Our analysis is completely dynamic and only needs to observe a single execution of the program, yet the determinacy facts it infers hold for any execution. We present a formal soundness proof of the analysis for a simple imperative language, and a prototype implementation that handles full JavaScript. Finally, we report on two case studies that explored how static analysis for JavaScript could leverage the information gathered by dynamic determinacy analysis. We found that in some cases scalability of static pointer analysis was improved dramatically, and that many uses of runtime code generation could be eliminated.

Categories and Subject Descriptors F.3.2 [*Logics and Meanings of Programs*]: Semantics of Programming Languages—Program analysis

Keywords static analysis; dynamic analysis; JavaScript

1. Introduction

Most modern programming languages offer support for reflective programming. For instance, Java programs can inspect an object's class at runtime to discover or access its fields and methods, and they can dynamically load classes by name, or even create new classes from scratch. Modern dynamic languages such as Ruby or JavaScript are even more liberal and permit almost arbitrary reflective changes to a running program's state. JavaScript, for example, provides `for-in` loops to discover an object's properties, and dynamic property accesses to read, write or even delete properties referenced by a computed name. Finally, the notorious `eval` function can execute arbitrary text as code, which can access or even declare local variables of the enclosing scope.

While cherished by many programmers for their conciseness and expressiveness, these features make any form of sound program analysis very hard. As an extreme example, a program could evaluate arbitrary user input as program code, thus defeating any attempts to obtain useful analysis results. In practice, however, programmers tend to use reflective features in a more disciplined fashion. For instance, Bodden et al. [5] found that Java programs using reflective class loading tend to always load the same classes, so by observing the classes loaded on some test runs, an analysis can gain a fairly complete picture of the program's reflective behavior. Similarly, Furr et al. [13] report that while dynamic features in Ruby are used pervasively, most uses are "highly constrained" and can be replaced with static alternatives, and Jensen et al. [17] show similar results for uses of `eval` in JavaScript.

This paper proposes a general approach for soundly identifying such constrained uses of dynamic language features. The basic concept behind our approach is *determinacy*.[1] Roughly speaking, a variable `x` is *determinate* at a program point p if `x` must have the same value, say v, whenever program execution reaches p. In that case, we will also say that x *determinately has value* v at p. We allow the program point p to be qualified by a calling context c to account for cases where `x` is only guaranteed to have value v if p is reached while executing inside calling context c. By extension, an expression is determinate at at program point p if its value is computed only from variables that are determinate at p.

Determinacy information can be used by a client to reason about reflective code. For instance, if for some use of `eval` the argument is known to determinately have some string value s, then a static analysis can analyze the code represented by s and maintain soundness. Type checkers, program transformation tools, and static optimizers could also benefit from this kind of specialization.

Determinacy information is not only useful for dealing with dynamic features. For example, in JavaScript it is not uncommon for highly polymorphic functions to behave very differently depending on the type and number of arguments they are passed. Figure 1 shows a short, highly simplified excerpt from the popular jQuery library,[2] which defines a utility function `$` that performs different

* This paper was written while the author was with IBM Research.

[1] Determinacy should not be confused with the notion of determinism in concurrent programming.

[2] See `http://www.jquery.com`

```
function $(selector) {
  if(typeof selector === "string") {
    if(isHTML(selector))
      // parse as HTML and return DOM tree
    else
      // interpret as CSS query
  } else if(typeof selector === "function") {
    // install as event handler for document ready
  } else {
    return [selector];
  }
}
```

Figure 1. Example of polymorphic function in JavaScript

PLDI'13, June 16–19, 2013, Seattle, WA, USA.

tasks depending on its argument. If the argument is a string (line 2), it is either parsed as HTML and the corresponding DOM fragment is returned (line 3), or it is interpreted as a CSS selector and all matching elements are returned (line 5). If the argument is a function (line 7), it is installed as an event handler to be executed once the HTML document has finished loading. Otherwise (line 9), the argument is wrapped in a single-element array and returned.

Individual call sites of `$` tend to be monomorphic, i.e., they only exercise one particular functionality of the function, so the conditions of the `if` statements become determinate for that site. For instance, under a call `$(function() { ... })`, the conditional expression on line 2 must be false, whereas line 7 must evaluate to `true`. A flow-insensitive static analysis can use this information to identify code that is unreachable for this particular invocation of `$`, thereby gaining a degree of flow sensitivity. Similarly, a partial evaluator could use determinacy information to complement binding time analysis for specializing a program with respect to determinate input, and an optimizer could use it to detect dead code.

Statically computing determinacy information, however, is very challenging, especially for dynamic languages like JavaScript, where even a call graph is hard to construct without an effective approach to dealing with dynamic language features [30], the very problem determinacy analysis is supposed to help with.

In this paper, we propose a *dynamic determinacy analysis* that analyzes one or more concrete executions to infer determinacy facts that are guaranteed to hold in *any* execution. Our analysis is similar in spirit to dynamic information flow analysis [32], in the sense that we consider indeterminate program inputs to be "tainted" and track the flow of this taint. Any value that is not tainted must then be determinate. As in dynamic information flow, our analysis must consider how indeterminate inputs can influence other values both directly (by participating in computations) and indirectly (e.g., by being used as an `if` condition).

Since our determinacy analysis is dynamic, it can only observe one execution at a time and has to carefully account for the possible effects of code that was not exercised in this execution, but may be exercised in another. Determinacy information itself can help here: if the conditional expression of an `if` statement is determinate, for instance, the dynamic analysis only has to explore one branch, since the other branch is definitely not run in any execution. To handle indeterminate conditionals, we introduce the technique of *counterfactual execution*, where we explore both the branch that would ordinarily be executed, *and* the other branch that would not normally be run. In this way, we can more precisely account for the behavior of other executions and infer more determinacy facts.

We have formalized our analysis for a simple imperative language with records and higher-order functions and proved its correctness: variables marked as determinate by the analysis at a certain program point will in fact have the predicted value any time an execution reaches that point. We have implemented a prototype determinacy analysis that handles all of JavaScript, and obtained promising results on two case studies where we combined the determinacy analysis with a static analysis: first, we extended the static points-to analysis for JavaScript implemented in WALA [30] to make use of determinacy facts, dramatically increasing precision and scalability in some cases; second, we further extended the static analysis to use determinacy facts for eliminating uses of `eval`.

In summary, this paper makes the following main contributions:

- We introduce a **dynamic determinacy analysis**, which analyzes one or more concrete executions to identify variables and expressions that have the same value at a given program point in any execution. (Section 2).
- We give a **formalization** and a **correctness proof** of our determinacy analysis for a simple imperative language. (Section 3).

```
1  (function() {
2    function checkf(p) {
3      // ⟦p.f<32⟧16→4 = true; ⟦p.f<32⟧25→4 = ?
4      if(p.f < 32)
5        setg(p, 42);
6    }
7
8    function setg(r, v) {
9      r.g = v;
10   } // ⟦r.g⟧18→5→10 = 42
11
12   var x = { f : 23 },
13       y = { f : Math.random()*100 };
14   // ⟦x.f⟧14 = 23, ⟦y.f⟧14 = ?
15
16   checkf(x);
17   // ⟦x.f⟧17 = 23, ⟦x.g⟧17 = 42
18   checkf(y);
19   // ⟦y.g⟧19 = ?
20
21   (y.f > 50 ? checkf : setg)(x, 72);
22   // ⟦x.g⟧22 = ?
23
24   var z = { f: x.g - 16, h: true };
25   checkf(z);
26 })();
```

Figure 2. Example program for illustrating dynamic determinacy analysis. Some key determinacy facts are given in comments.

- We present a **prototype implementation** of the analysis for JavaScript. (Section 4).
- We report on **two case studies**, demonstrating that the information gathered by our dynamic determinacy analysis can significantly improve the precision of static pointer analysis and identify many uses of `eval` that can be eliminated. (Section 5).

Finally, Section 6 surveys related work, and Section 7 concludes.

2. Overview

This section provides a high-level overview of determinacy and its applications. First, we introduce some terminology and informally explain how determinacy facts can be computed using dynamic analysis, using a small JavaScript example that was carefully contrived to demonstrate the key issues involved. Then, we illustrate the usefulness of determinacy analysis by showing how determinacy facts can be used to improve static pointer analysis for JavaScript and eliminate common uses of the `eval` function.

2.1 Determinacy

To illustrate key challenges for determinacy analysis, consider the example program in Figure 2. It consists of two functions `checkf` (lines 2–6) and `setg` (lines 8–10), and a sequence of statements (lines 12–25). These functions and statements are wrapped into an anonymous function call to provide lexical scope.

Running the example program. Program execution starts with the call on line 26, which invokes the anonymous function defined on lines 1–26. Executing its body, we first encounter the function definitions for `checkf` and `setg`. Then, when line 12 is reached, variables `x` and `y` are initialized to object literals, both containing a single property `f`. While property `x.f` is set to the constant value 23, property `y.f` is initialized to `Math.random()*100`, a random floating point number between `0` and `100`; let us assume that it evaluates to `31.4` in our concrete execution.

Execution then proceeds by calling `checkf` twice, on lines 16 and 18, passing `x` and `y` as the argument, respectively. If the condition on line 4 evaluates to true, `checkf` calls `setg`, which assigns the value `42` to the `g` property of the argument. In our example execution, the condition evaluates to true for both calls, so `x.g` and `y.g` both hold the value `42` after line 18. Then, line 21 invokes a function whose name is determined by the conditional expression `(y.f > 50 ? checkf : setg)`. Since `y.f` holds the value `31.4` at this point, `setg` is called, with arguments `x` and `72`, causing the value `72` to be assigned into `x.g`. Next, on line 24, a third local variable `z` is initialized to an object literal with properties `f` and `h` containing values `56` and `true`, respectively. Finally, when `checkf` is called with `z` as an argument on line 25, the condition on line 4 evaluates to false so that `setg` is not called.

Determinacy facts. The goal of determinacy analysis is to identify situations where a variable or expression must hold the same value at a given location in *any* execution of the program.

For example, `x.f` is determinate on line 14: it must always have the value 23 here because its initialization does not depend in any way on program input, or on values in the environment. On the other hand, `y.f` is *indeterminate* on line 14, because the value returned by `Math.random` may vary in different executions. We express these observations using the following *determinacy facts*:

$$[\![\texttt{x.f}]\!]_{14} = 23$$
$$[\![\texttt{y.f}]\!]_{14} = ?$$

Likewise, variables `x` and `y` are both determinate at line 14.[3]

Sometimes, determinacy facts only hold under a given calling context. For instance, for the call to `checkf` on line 16, the condition `p.f < 32` on line 4 will evaluate to true in any program execution, but this is not the case for the calls to `checkf` on lines 18 and 25. We express this as a *qualified determinacy fact*

$$[\![\texttt{p.f < 32}]\!]_{16\to 4} = \texttt{true}$$

stating that the condition `p.f < 32` is determinately true on line 4 if this line is reached from the call at line 16. Determinacy facts inferred by our dynamic analysis are always qualified with a complete call stack reaching all the way back to the program's entrypoint.

Dynamic determinacy analysis. To infer determinacy facts, we instrument the program to compute not only the values of variables, properties and other expressions, but also whether they are determinate at the current program point. This is done using techniques reminiscent of dynamic information flow analysis, where instead of high and low security levels we track indeterminacy.

Program inputs (including, for JavaScript, the DOM) are considered indeterminate, as are the results of certain functions like `Math.random`. Constants, on the other hand, are determinate, so the analysis marks `x` and `x.f` as determinate on line 12.

Starting from these sources, indeterminacy (like high-security annotations in information flow) propagates both directly and indirectly: a variable becomes indeterminate when it is assigned an expression involving other indeterminate variables, but also when it is modified in code that is control dependent on an indeterminate condition and hence not necessarily run in every execution.

Direct propagation of indeterminacy is easy to track by computing a compound expression's determinacy from its constituent expressions: e.g., `Math.random()*100` is indeterminate, so `y.f` is indeterminate at line 13. To track indirect flow of indeterminacy, the dynamic analysis has to carefully reason about conditionals.

Conditionals and counterfactual execution. Conditionals where the condition is itself determinate are easy to handle, since any other execution will take the same branch as the one we are observing. This case arises in the call to `checkf` on line 16, where the condition `p.f < 32` is determinately true, so by simply continuing execution we can infer the fact $[\![\texttt{x.g}]\!]_{17} = \texttt{42}$.

Indeterminate conditions require a more careful treatment. For the second call to `checkf` (line 18), the condition `p.f < 32` on line 4 is indeterminate, but happens to be true. In another execution it may well be false, causing the branch not to be executed. To account for this possibility, we execute the branch as usual, but record any variable or property write. After the branch has finished executing, we mark all written variables and properties (in this case only `y.g`) as indeterminate, giving $[\![\texttt{y.g}]\!]_{19} = ?$.

By marking variables indeterminate only *after* the branch has finished executing, we can infer more determinacy facts inside it. Note that both arguments to `setg` are determinate at line 5 when `checkf` is invoked from line 18. So, we infer $[\![\texttt{r.g}]\!]_{18\to 5\to 10} = \texttt{42}$, even though `y.g` is later marked indeterminate. Of course, `x.f` and `x.g` stay determinate, as they are not written to in the branch.

The third, and most difficult, case arises with conditions that are indeterminate and happen to be false, as is the case for `p.f < 32` in the third call to `checkf` on line 25. Here, we have to account for the fact that the condition may evaluate to true in another execution, causing the branch to be taken.

A simple approach would be to statically examine the code to determine which local variables it could write to (none in this case) and mark them indeterminate. However, this does not account for possible heap writes by functions called within the branch. Since a dynamic analysis does not have access to a static call graph, a conservative approach is to "flush" the heap, marking every property of every object as indeterminate.

This is clearly very imprecise, so our analysis takes another approach, which we refer to as *counterfactual execution*. Even though the condition is false, we still (counterfactually) execute the branch, recording any determinacy facts that may arise. After it has finished executing, we (i) undo the effect of any writes to variables or properties (since the branch was not originally meant to execute), and (ii) mark any written variables and properties as indeterminate (since other executions may not perform these writes). In our case, this leads to `z.g` being marked indeterminate after the conditional, while, for instance, `z.h` is still determinate.

Indeterminate calls. Since JavaScript functions are first-class, the target of a function call must itself be computed as a value, which may be indeterminate. An example is the call on line 21, where the callee is computed by the indeterminate expression `y.f > 50 ? checkf : setg`. In the concrete execution we are considering, it evaluates to `setg`, which is then invoked to set `x.g` to `72`. However, the value of the callee expression is indeterminate since `y.f` is indeterminate at line 21, so another execution may well invoke `checkf` instead, which would result in `x.g` being `42`.

To account for this, we conservatively flush the heap, marking all properties as indeterminate after every indeterminate call. In our example, this means that `x.f`, `x.g`, `y.f` and `y.g` are indeterminate at line 22. While this is overly conservative (`x.f` is, in fact, still determinate), it is the best thing we can do, since we do not track alternative values for indeterminate expressions. Note that `x` and `y` need not be made indeterminate, since they are local variables and cannot possibly be written by any called function.

2.2 Improving pointer analysis

We now show how determinacy facts can be used to improve static pointer analysis for JavaScript. Static analysis of JavaScript is very challenging [18, 27, 30], due to pervasive use of reflective constructs in JavaScript programs and the absence of of static types. Determinacy facts can be used to rewrite uses of reflection into more verbose code that is easier to analyze, as we illustrate below.

[3] While `y.f` is indeterminate, `y` itself must hold the object literal assigned to it at line 13.

```
1 function Rectangle(w, h) {
2   this.width = w;
3   this.height = h;
4 }
5
6 Rectangle.prototype.toString = function() {
7   return "["+this.width+"x"+this.height+"]";
8 };
9
10 String.prototype.cap = function() {
11   return this[0].toUpperCase()+this.substr(1);
12 };
13
14 function defAccessors(prop) {
15   Rectangle.prototype["get" + prop.cap()] =
16     function() { return this[prop]; };
17
18   Rectangle.prototype["set" + prop.cap()] =
19     function(v) { this[prop] = v; };
20 }
21
22 var props = ["width", "height"];
23 for (var i=0; i < props.length; i++)
24   defAccessors(props[i]);
25
26 var r = new Rectangle(20, 30);
27 r.setWidth(r.getWidth()+20);
28 alert(r.toString());  // [40x30]
```

Figure 3. Example program illustrating the use of determinacy facts for improving a static pointer analysis

Example. Consider the example program in Figure 3, which is loosely modeled after code seen in jQuery and other commonly-used JavaScript frameworks. The program defines a `Rectangle` constructor function on lines 1–4, which initializes properties `width` and `height` to the values passed in parameters `w` and `h`, respectively. A `toString()` method is defined on the `Rectangle.prototype` object (lines 6–8), thereby making it available on all objects created by `Rectangle`. Similarly, a utility method `cap` for performing string capitalization is defined on `String.prototype` (line 10), which means that it can be invoked on any string object.

We now use a standard trick employing dynamic property accesses to concisely define getter and setter methods for the `width` and `height` properties. We iterate over the array `["width", "height"]` using the for loop on lines 23–24, invoking the `defAccessors` function twice, first with `prop` set to `"width"`, then to `"height"`. Function `defAccessors` (lines 14–20) defines a getter function (line 15–16) and a setter function (line 18–19), and stores them into `Rectangle.prototype`. The names of these accessor methods are computed dynamically, capitalizing the property name using `cap` and prepending `"get"` and `"set"`, respectively. Thus, the getter methods end up in properties `getWidth` and `getHeight`, and similar for the setters. Lines 26–28 illustrate how these getter and setter methods can be used: Executing these lines will bring up an alert box that reads `[40x30]`.

Applying static pointer analysis. Now let us consider how a standard static pointer analysis algorithm such as 0-CFA [29] would analyze this program. Since such algorithms typically do not track string values, they would conservatively treat the writes on lines 15 and 18 as possibly writing to *any* property of `Rectangle.prototype`. From this, they would conclude that the call to `getWidth` on line 27 could invoke *either* of these functions, and that the call to `toString` on line 28 could invoke the getter, the setter, or the actual `toString` method, which is very imprecise. Even a recent, more advanced analysis that reasons about correlated dynamic property accesses [30] is unable to determine the result of applying `cap` to the property name, yielding the same result.

Static string analyses [8] can reason abstractly about string operations, but are expensive and rely on a call graph. If, as in this example, such reasoning is required to construct a precise call graph to begin with, an iterative scheme interleaving call graph construction and string analysis would have to be devised. By contrast, a context-sensitive static analysis can be adapted to leverage determinacy facts in a fairly straightforward manner, as we now show.

Using determinacy facts. Our determinacy analysis produces facts that can help the static pointer analysis handle complex string operations. For example:

- The analysis shows that the `prop` argument to `defAccessors` is determinate in the first iteration of the loop at lines 23–24:

  $$[\![\texttt{prop}]\!]_{24^0 \rightarrow 15} = \texttt{"width"}$$

  Here, 24^0 denotes the first time execution reaches line 24.
- Within the `defAccessors` call, the result of the `prop.cap()` call is also determinate:

  $$[\![\texttt{this[0].toUpperCase()+...}]\!]_{24^0 \rightarrow 15 \rightarrow 11} = \texttt{"Width"}$$

  which makes the result of the string concatenation determinate:

  $$[\![\texttt{"get" + prop.cap()}]\!]_{24^0 \rightarrow 15} = \texttt{"getWidth"}$$

Similar facts hold for the second loop iteration, and since `props.length` is determinate at line 23, the determinacy analysis can also show that the loop executes at most two times. Given these determinacy facts, the pointer analysis can use loop unrolling and context sensitivity to precisely handle the property writes at lines 15 and 18. First, the analysis unrolls the loop at lines 23–24 twice, using the iteration bound given by the determinacy analysis. Then, via context sensitivity, each call site of `defAccessors` in the unrolled loop is treated as invoking a function specialized by the corresponding determinacy facts. For example, the first call site, corresponding to the loop iteration with `props[i] == "width"`, invokes the following specialized function:

```
function defAccessors(prop) {
  Rectangle.prototype.getWidth =
    function() { return this.width; };
  Rectangle.prototype.setWidth =
    function(v) { this.width = v; };
}
```

For this specialized code, the pointer analysis can easily prove that only the getter function is written into property `getWidth`, and that only the setter function is written into property `setWidth`, thus enabling precise resolution of the function call at line 27.

Besides replacing dynamic property accesses with static ones, determinacy facts can also be used to eliminate conditionals where the condition is determinate, helping to analyze cases like that shown in Figure 1. In Section 5.1, we shall show how our implementation of these techniques achieved large speedups when analyzing certain versions of jQuery.

2.3 Eliminating `eval`

JavaScript's `eval` function transforms text into executable code at run time. Although strongly discouraged by leading practitioners [11], it is pervasively used in practice [26], leaving static analyses with a stark choice: if `eval` is not handled, soundness is compromised; if it is handled conservatively, analysis results will become extremely imprecise, and thus useless for most applications.

Recent research suggests that many uses of `eval` could, in fact, be replaced by equivalent `eval`-free code [17, 23]. For example,

```
1 ivymap = window.ivymap || {};
2 function showIvyViaJs(locationId) {
3   var _f = undefined;
4   var _fconv = "ivymap[\'"+locationId+"\']";
5   try {
6     _f = eval(_fconv);
7     if (_f!=undefined) {
8       _f();
9     }
10  } catch(e) {
11  }
12 }
13
14 showIvyViaJs('pc.sy.banner.tcck.');
15 showIvyViaJs('pc.sy.banner.duilian.');
```

Figure 4. Program (taken from [17]) for which determinacy analysis can show that all calls to `eval` have a determinate argument.

consider the code in Figure 4, taken from Jensen et al. [17], who extracted it from a real-world website.

Clearly, the strings passed to `eval` are determinate in both invocations of `showIvyViaJS`:

$$[\![\texttt{\_fconv}]\!]_{14\to 6} = \texttt{"ivymap['pc.sy.banner.tcck.']"}$$

$$[\![\texttt{\_fconv}]\!]_{15\to 6} = \texttt{"ivymap['pc.sy.banner.duilian.']"}$$

Using the same approach as in the previous subsection, a static analysis can specialize each call to `showIvyViaJS`, replacing calls to `eval` with the code obtained by (statically) parsing the string values found by the determinacy analysis, thus eliminating the calls to `eval` altogether. Section 5.2 presents encouraging results from an initial experiment using this approach, which showed that `eval` elimination via determinacy facts can complement existing purely-static approaches like that of TAJS [17].

3. Formalization

In this section, we formalize the dynamic determinacy analysis from Section 2 on a simple imperative language μJS with records, dynamic property accesses and first-order functions. μJS contains most of the features that make determinacy analysis for JavaScript challenging. We exclude prototypes, constructors and other features usually modeled in JavaScript-based core calculi [15], since they are orthogonal to determinacy analysis. For simplicity, we also exclude unstructured control flow.

We start out by formalizing the syntax and (concrete) semantics of μJS. Then, the analysis is formalized as an instrumented semantics over values with determinacy annotations $\cdot^!$ and $\cdot^?$. Finally, we show soundness of the analysis: if a variable has a value $v^!$ at some program point p in *some* instrumented execution, it has value v at the same point in *every* concrete execution.

3.1 Syntax and semantics of μJS

Figure 5 presents the syntax of μJS, which is mostly a subset of that of JavaScript, except that we abbreviate the keyword **function** as **fun**. Instead of the complex statement and expression syntax of JavaScript, μJS only allows simple statements reminiscent of three address code. In particular, conditionals have only a single branch and their conditional expression must be a variable.

Values in μJS are either primitive values, closures, or heap-allocated records. Primitive values are taken from an unspecified set PrimVal containing a special value **undefined**. We assume that all primitive values are silently coerced to strings or Boolean values where necessary. When viewed as a Boolean value, addresses and records evaluate to `true`. We also assume a set PrimOp of binary operators on primitive values. Closures are represented as

$l \in$ Literal	$::=$	pv	primitive value
	$\mid$	$\textbf{fun}(x)$ { **var** $\overline{y}$; $\overline{s}$; **return** z; }	function value
	$\mid$	{}	empty record
$s \in$ Stmt	$::=$	$x = l$	literal load
	$\mid$	$x = y$	variable copy
	$\mid$	$x = y[z]$	property load
	$\mid$	$x[y] = z$	property store
	$\mid$	$x = y \diamond z$	primitive operator
	$\mid$	$x = f(y)$	function call
	$\mid$	$\textbf{if}(x)\{\overline{s}\}$	conditional
	$\mid$	$\textbf{while}(x)\{\overline{s}\}$	loop

$x, y, z, f \in$ Name; $\diamond \in$ PrimOp; $pv \in$ PrimVal; $a \in$ Address

$v \in$ Value	$::=$	$pv \mid a \mid (\textbf{fun}(x)\ \{b\}, \rho)$
$r \in$ Rec	$::=$	$\{\overline{x : v}\}$
$\rho \in$ Env	$:=$	Name $\rightharpoonup$ Value
$h \in$ Heap	$:=$	Address $\rightharpoonup$ Rec

Figure 5. Syntax and semantic domains of μJS; b abbreviates function bodies

$e \in$ Event	$::=$	$x = v$	variable write
	$\mid$	$a[x] = v$	heap write
	$\mid$	$\textbf{if}(v)\{t\}$	conditional
	$\mid$	$\textbf{fun}(v)\{t\}_\rho$	function call
$t \in$ Trace	$:=$	$\overline{e}$	

Figure 6. Concrete execution traces

a function value plus an environment, as usual. Record literals are always empty, but property load and store statements can be used to add more properties; we do not model property deletion. Note that the name of the property accessed by these statements is itself a variable, and hence can be computed at runtime, just as in JavaScript. There is no designated prototype property, since μJS does not model JavaScript's prototype system. For convenience, we treat records r as total functions from names to values: if $r = \{\overline{x : v}\}$, then $r(x_i) = v_i$, and $r(y) =$ **undefined** for $y \notin \overline{x}$.

Our semantics for μJS is big-step. While a small-step semantics would allow more direct reasoning about individual program points, it makes it hard to match up control flow forks and joins, which play a crucial role in computing determinacy information. To be able to speak about intermediate states, we use a trace-based semantics [22] with an evaluation judgement of the form $(h, \rho, s) \downarrow (h', \rho', t)$: h and ρ are the initial heap and environment, s is the statement to evaluate; h' and ρ' are the resulting heap and environment, and t is a *trace* recording all assignments, conditionals and function calls executed during evaluation of s.

Figure 6 gives the grammar of trace events and traces; the environment ρ in a function call event denotes the closure environment of the called function. Figure 8 lists the evaluation rules, which are mostly standard, except that they each add an event to the trace. We assume that the semantics of built-in primitive operators $\diamond$ is given by a partial function $[\![\diamond]\!]$. If this function is undefined on the provided arguments, execution gets stuck, as is the case when accessing undefined local variables or trying to invoke a non-function. In full JavaScript, these situations give rise to elaborate implicit conversions or exceptions, which we do not model.

Local variables have to be declared before use (hence the precondition $x \in \text{dom}(\rho)$ in most rules), and we do not model globals.

$$
\begin{array}{lcl}
d \in D & := & \{!, ?\} \\
\hat{v} \in \widehat{\text{Value}} & ::= & pv^d \mid a^d \mid (\mathbf{fun}(x)\ \{b\}, \hat{\rho})^d \\
\hat{r} \in \widehat{\text{Rec}} & ::= & \{\overline{x : \hat{v}}\} \mid \{\overline{x : \hat{v}}, \ldots\} \\
\hat{h} \in \widehat{\text{Heap}} & := & \text{Address} \rightharpoonup \widehat{\text{Rec}} \\
\hat{\rho} \in \widehat{\text{Env}} & := & \text{Name} \rightharpoonup \widehat{\text{Value}} \\
\hat{e} \in \widehat{\text{Event}} & ::= & x = \hat{v} \mid a^d[x^{d'}] = \hat{v} \mid \mathbf{if}(\hat{v})\{\hat{t}\} \\
 & \mid & (\mathbf{fun}(\hat{v})\{\hat{t}\})^d_{\hat{\rho}} \\
\hat{t} \in \widehat{\text{Trace}} & := & \overline{\hat{e}}
\end{array}
$$

Figure 7. Instrumented semantic domains and traces

While local variables can be modified, their semantics is quite idiosyncratic: updates are only visible inside the updating function, so updating a closure variable will not have the desired effect. A more standard semantics can be achieved by modeling local variables that are accessed in a nested functions as immutable references to records with a single property, and accessing that property instead.

Given a trace t, we can reconstruct what effects the execution that produced it had on the heap and the environment. Its *variable domain* $\mathrm{vd}(t)$ is the set of all variables written during the execution; it consists of all variables x such that t or one of its sub-traces (excluding sub-traces inside function calls[4]) contains an event $x = v$. The *property domain* $\mathrm{pd}(t)$ contains all address-property name pairs $\langle a, p\rangle$ such that property p of the record at a was modified during the execution, which is the case iff t or one of its sub-traces (*including* sub-traces inside function calls) contains an event $a[p] = v$. We also define the variable domain of a sequence of statements, $\mathrm{vd}(\overline{s})$, to contain all variables x such that one of the statements in $\overline{s}$ (without nested functions) is an assignment to x.

Clearly, if $\langle h, \rho, s\rangle \downarrow \langle h', \rho', t\rangle$, then $\forall x \notin \mathrm{vd}(t).\rho(x) = \rho'(x)$, and similarly $\forall (a, p) \notin \mathrm{pd}(t).h(a)(p) = h'(a)(p)$.[5]

3.2 Instrumented semantics

We formalize determinacy analysis via an instrumented semantics of μJS where variables and properties are bound to annotated values of the form $v^!$ and $v^?$, representing determinate and indeterminate values, respectively.

Instrumented values, records, heaps, environments and traces are defined in Figure 7. An instrumented value of the form $v^!$ represents the single concrete value v, whereas $v^?$ represents any concrete value. For records, a *closed record* of the form $\{\overline{x : \hat{v}}\}$ represents all records that have precisely the properties $\overline{x}$ with values represented by the corresponding instrumented values $\overline{\hat{v}}$; an *open record* of the form $\{\overline{x : \hat{v}}, \ldots\}$, on the other hand, represents all records that have *at least* the properties $\overline{x}$ (again with the same restrictions on their values), but may have more.

Like their concrete counterparts, we also interpret instrumented records as functions; looking up a non-existent property on a closed record yields $\mathbf{undefined}^!$, and on an open record $\mathbf{undefined}^?$.

For an instrumented value $\hat{v}$, we define $\hat{v}^?$ as $\hat{v}$ with all $\cdot^!$ annotations replaced by $\cdot^?$. For records $\hat{r}$, $\hat{r}^?$ additionally turns $\hat{r}$ into an open record. For heaps, we let $\hat{h}^?$ be the heap resulting from $\hat{h}$ by replacing every record $\hat{r}$ with $\hat{r}^?$, which corresponds to a heap flush. We also define $\hat{v}^! := \hat{v}$, $\hat{r}^! := \hat{r}$, $\hat{h}^! := \hat{h}$ i.e., the extant determinacy annotations are retained.

[4] Function calls need not be considered, since callees cannot update their caller's local variables.

[5] These equalities should be considered to hold if either both sides are undefined, or both are defined and equal.

$$
(\textsc{LdLit})\ \frac{x \in \mathrm{dom}(\rho)}{\langle h, \rho, x = pv\rangle \downarrow \langle h, \rho[x \mapsto pv], x = pv\rangle}
$$

$$
(\textsc{LdClos})\ \frac{F \equiv \mathbf{fun}(y)\ \{\ \mathbf{var}\ \overline{y};\ \overline{s};\ \mathbf{return}\ z;\ \} \quad x \in \mathrm{dom}(\rho)}{\langle h, \rho, x = F\rangle \downarrow \langle h, \rho[x \mapsto (F, \rho)], x = (F, \rho)\rangle}
$$

$$
(\textsc{LdRec})\ \frac{x \in \mathrm{dom}(\rho) \quad a \notin \mathrm{dom}(\rho)}{\langle h, \rho, x = \{\}\rangle \downarrow \langle h[a \mapsto \{\}], \rho[x \mapsto a], x = a\rangle}
$$

$$
(\textsc{Assign})\ \frac{x \in \mathrm{dom}(\rho) \quad \rho(y) = v}{\langle h, \rho, x = y\rangle \downarrow \langle h, \rho[x \mapsto v], x = v\rangle}
$$

$$
(\textsc{Ld})\ \frac{x \in \mathrm{dom}(\rho) \quad \rho(y) = a \quad \rho(z) = z' \quad h(a) = r \quad r(z') = v}{\langle h, \rho, x = y[z]\rangle \downarrow \langle h, \rho[x \mapsto v], x = v\rangle}
$$

$$
(\textsc{Sto})\ \frac{\rho(x) = a \quad \rho(y) = y' \quad h(a) = r \quad \rho(z) = v}{\langle h, \rho, x[y] = z\rangle \downarrow \langle h[a \mapsto r[y' \mapsto v]], \rho, a[y'] = v\rangle}
$$

$$
(\textsc{PrimOp})\ \frac{x \in \mathrm{dom}(\rho)\ \rho(y) = pv_1\ \rho(z) = pv_2\ pv_1 [\![\diamond]\!] pv_2 = pv_3}{\langle h, \rho, x = y \diamond z\rangle \downarrow \langle h, \rho[x \mapsto pv_3], x = pv_3\rangle}
$$

$$
(\textsc{Inv})\ \frac{\begin{array}{c} x \in \mathrm{dom}(\rho) \quad \rho(f) = (\mathbf{fun}(z)\ \{\mathbf{var}\ \overline{x'}; \overline{s};\ \mathbf{return}\ y';\}, \rho') \quad \rho(y) = v \\ \langle h, \rho'[z \mapsto v, \overline{x' \mapsto \mathbf{undefined}}], \overline{s}\rangle \overline{\downarrow} \langle h', \rho'', t\rangle \quad \rho''(y') = v' \end{array}}{\langle h, \rho, x = f(y)\rangle \downarrow \langle h', \rho[x \mapsto v'], (\mathbf{fun}(v)\{t\}_{\rho'}; x = v')\rangle}
$$

$$
(\textsc{If}_1)\ \frac{\rho(x) = v \quad v = \mathbf{true} \quad \langle h, \rho, \overline{s}\rangle \overline{\downarrow} \langle h', \rho', t\rangle}{\langle h, \rho, \mathbf{if}(x)\{\overline{s}\}\rangle \downarrow \langle h', \rho', \mathbf{if}(v)\{t\}\rangle}
$$

$$
(\textsc{If}_2)\ \frac{\rho(x) = v \quad v = \mathbf{false}}{\langle h, \rho, \mathbf{if}(x)\{\overline{s}\}\rangle \downarrow \langle h, \rho, \mathbf{if}(v)\{\}\rangle}
$$

$$
(\textsc{While})\ \frac{\langle h, \rho, \mathbf{if}(x)\{\overline{s};\ \mathbf{while}(x)\{\overline{s}\}\}\rangle \downarrow \langle h', \rho', t\rangle}{\langle h, \rho, \mathbf{while}(x)\{\overline{s}\}\rangle \downarrow \langle h', \rho', t\rangle}
$$

$$
(\textsc{Seq})\ \frac{\langle h_i, \rho_i, s_i\rangle \downarrow \langle h_{i+1}, \rho_{i+1}, e_i\rangle}{\langle h_0, \rho_0, \overline{s}\rangle \overline{\downarrow} \langle h_n, \rho_n, \overline{e}\rangle}
$$

Figure 8. Concrete semantics of μJS

An instrumented trace looks like a concrete trace, except that it contains instrumented values instead of concrete ones. For a function call event $(\mathbf{fun}(\hat{v})\{\hat{t}\})^d_{\hat{\rho}}$, for instance, $\hat{v}$ is the argument value, $\hat{\rho}$ is the closure environment of the callee, and $\hat{t}$ is the trace resulting from the call. The annotation d indicates whether the callee is determinate or not. The variable and property domains $\mathrm{vd}(\hat{t})$ and $\mathrm{pd}(\hat{t})$ are defined exactly as for concrete traces, simply disregarding determinacy annotations.

As described in Section 2, after executing a branch guarded by an indeterminate but true condition, the analysis marks every variable written in the branch as indeterminate. Similarly, after counterfactually executing a branch, every written variable is reset to its previous value *and* marked indeterminate.

To model this in our semantics, we use the notation $\hat{\rho}'[V := \hat{\rho}^d]$, where $\hat{\rho}, \hat{\rho}'$ are instrumented environments, V is a set of variable names, and d is a determinacy flag. Roughly, this means that $\hat{\rho}'$ is updated so that every variable $x \in V$ is reset to the value it had in $\hat{\rho}$, and marked as indeterminate if $d = ?$. More precisely, we define

$$
\hat{\rho}'[V := \hat{\rho}^d](x) := \begin{cases} \hat{\rho}(x)^d & \text{if } x \in \mathrm{dom}(\hat{\rho}) \cap V \\ \hat{\rho}'(x) & \text{otherwise} \end{cases}
$$

Thus, for a trace $\hat{t}$, $\hat{\rho}'[\mathrm{vd}(\hat{t}) := \hat{\rho}'^?]$ marks every variable x written by $\hat{h}$ as indeterminate, and $\hat{\rho}'[\mathrm{vd}(\hat{t}) := \hat{\rho}^?]$ additionally resets its value to $\hat{\rho}(x)$.

For records $\hat{r}, \hat{r}'$, we define $\hat{r}'[V := \hat{r}^d]$ as for environments. For heaps $\hat{h}, \hat{h}'$, a set $A \subseteq \mathrm{Address} \times \mathrm{Name}$ of address-property name pairs and a determinacy flag d, we define

$$\hat{h}'[A := \hat{h}^d](a) := \begin{cases} \hat{h}'(a)[A_a := \hat{h}(a)^d] & \text{if } a \in \mathrm{dom}(\hat{h}') \cap \mathrm{dom}(\hat{h}) \\ \hat{h}'(a) & \text{otherwise} \end{cases}$$

where $A_a := \{p \mid (a, p) \in A\}$.

Given these technical preliminaries, we can now define the evaluation judgement $\langle \hat{h}, \hat{\rho}, s\rangle \hat{\downarrow}^n \langle \hat{h}', \hat{\rho}', \hat{t}\rangle$ of the instrumented semantics as shown in Figure 9. The index n is used to bound the nesting depth of counter-factual executions, to be discussed shortly.

We omit ($\widehat{\text{LdClos}}$), ($\widehat{\text{LdRec}}$), ($\widehat{\text{Assign}}$), ($\widehat{\text{While}}$) and ($\widehat{\text{Seq}}$), which are straightforward adaptations of their concrete counterparts. In ($\widehat{\text{PrimOp}}$), the determinacy flags d_1 and d_2 of both operands are applied to the result, so it will be indeterminate if at least one of the operands is. Similarly in ($\widehat{\text{Ld}}$), the result of a property load is only determinate if both the address and the property name are. Rule ($\widehat{\text{Sto}}$) applies the determinacy flag d of the address to be accessed to the whole heap: if $d = ?$, the heap is flushed. Similarly, the flag d' of the property name is applied to the record being accessed: if $d' = ?$, all properties are made indeterminate and it becomes an open record, since any of the existing properties may be written, or a new one added.

The most interesting rules are the ones concerning conditionals. ($\widehat{\text{If}_1}$) handles the case where the condition is (determinate or indeterminate) true by simply executing the branch, and afterwards marking all written properties and variables as indeterminate if the condition is indeterminate. ($\widehat{\text{If}_2\text{-Det}}$) applies when the condition is determinate false; in this case, the conditional is a no-op.

($\widehat{\text{Cntr}}$) initiates counterfactual execution if the condition is indeterminate false, executing the branch while increasing the counterfactuality level to $n+1$. After the branch has finished executing, ($\widehat{\text{Cntr}}$) reverts to the heap and environment before the counterfactual (i.e., assignments performed by the counterfactually executed branch are not visible), and marks any variable or property possibly written by counterfactual code as indeterminate.

In general, counterfactually executing branches may lead to non-termination, so we introduce a cut-off: when the number of nested counterfactual executions is about to exceed some fixed number k, the pre-condition $n < k$ prevents the ($\widehat{\text{Cntr}}$) from applying; instead, rule ($\widehat{\text{CntrAbort}}$) shortcuts evaluation and conservatively flushes the heap and marks any variable that may possible be assigned anywhere in the branch indeterminate.

$$(\widehat{\text{LdLit}})\ \frac{x \in \mathrm{dom}(\hat{\rho})}{\langle \hat{h}, \hat{\rho}, x = pv\rangle \hat{\downarrow}^n \langle \hat{h}, \hat{\rho}[x \mapsto pv^!], x = pv^!\rangle}$$

$$(\widehat{\text{Ld}})\ \frac{x \in \mathrm{dom}(\hat{\rho}) \quad \hat{\rho}(y) = a^d \quad \hat{\rho}(z) = z'^{d'} \quad \hat{h}(a) = \hat{r} \quad \hat{r}(z') = \hat{v}}{\langle \hat{h}, \hat{\rho}, x = y[z]\rangle \hat{\downarrow}^n \langle \hat{h}, \hat{\rho}[x \mapsto (\hat{v}^d)^{d'}], x = (\hat{v}^d)^{d'}\rangle}$$

$$(\widehat{\text{Sto}})\ \frac{\hat{\rho}(x) = a^d \quad \hat{\rho}(y) = y'^{d'} \quad \hat{h}(a) = \hat{r} \quad \hat{\rho}(z) = \hat{v}}{\langle \hat{h}, \hat{\rho}, x[y] = z\rangle \hat{\downarrow}^n \langle (\hat{h}[a \mapsto (\hat{r}[y' \mapsto \hat{v}])^{d'}])^d, \hat{\rho}, a^d[y'^{d'}] = \hat{v}\rangle}$$

$$(\widehat{\text{PrimOp}})\ \frac{x \in \mathrm{dom}(\hat{\rho}) \quad \hat{\rho}(y) = pv_1^{d_1} \quad \hat{\rho}(z) = pv_2^{d_2} \quad pv_1 [\![\diamond]\!] pv_2 = pv_3}{\langle \hat{h}, \hat{\rho}, x = y \diamond z\rangle \downarrow \langle \hat{h}, \hat{\rho}[x \mapsto (pv_3^{d_1})^{d_2}], x = (pv_3^{d_1})^{d_2}\rangle}$$

$$(\widehat{\text{Inv}})\ \frac{\begin{array}{c} x \in \mathrm{dom}(\hat{\rho}) \quad \hat{\rho}(f) = (\mathbf{fun}(z)\,\{\mathbf{var}\ \overline{x'};\ \overline{s};\ \mathbf{return}\ z';\}, \hat{\rho}')^d \quad \hat{\rho}(y) = \hat{v} \\ \langle \hat{h}, \hat{\rho}'[z \mapsto \hat{v}, \overline{x' \mapsto \mathbf{undefined}^!}], \overline{s}\rangle \overline{\hat{\downarrow}^n} \langle \hat{h}', \hat{\rho}'', \hat{t}\rangle \quad \hat{\rho}''(z') = \hat{v}' \end{array}}{\langle \hat{h}, \hat{\rho}, x = f(y)\rangle \hat{\downarrow}^n \langle \hat{h}'^d, \hat{\rho}[x \mapsto \hat{v}'^d], (\mathbf{fun}(\hat{v})\ \{\hat{t}\}^d_{\hat{\rho}'}; x = \hat{v}'^d)\rangle}$$

$$(\widehat{\text{If}_1})\ \frac{\hat{\rho}(x) = v^d \quad v = \mathbf{true} \quad \langle \hat{h}, \hat{\rho}, \overline{s}\rangle \overline{\hat{\downarrow}^n} \langle \hat{h}', \hat{\rho}', \hat{t}\rangle}{\langle \hat{h}, \hat{\rho}, \mathbf{if}(x)\{\overline{s}\}\rangle \hat{\downarrow}^n \langle \hat{h}'[\mathrm{pd}(\hat{t}) := \hat{h}'^d], \hat{\rho}'[\mathrm{vd}(\hat{t}) := \hat{\rho}'^d], \mathbf{if}(v^d)\{\hat{t}\}\rangle}$$

$$(\widehat{\text{If}_2\text{-Det}})\ \frac{\hat{\rho}(x) = v^! \quad v = \mathbf{false}}{\langle \hat{h}, \hat{\rho}, \mathbf{if}(x)\{\overline{s}\}\rangle \downarrow \langle \hat{h}, \hat{\rho}, \mathbf{if}(v^!)\{\}\rangle}$$

$$(\widehat{\text{Cntr}})\ \frac{\hat{\rho}(x) = v^? \quad v = \mathbf{false} \quad n < k \quad \langle \hat{h}, \hat{\rho}, \overline{s}\rangle \overline{\hat{\downarrow}^{n+1}} \langle \hat{h}', \hat{\rho}', \hat{t}\rangle}{\langle \hat{h}, \hat{\rho}, \mathbf{if}(x)\{\overline{s}\}\rangle \hat{\downarrow}^n \langle \hat{h}'[\mathrm{pd}(\hat{t}) := \hat{h}^?], \hat{\rho}'[\mathrm{vd}(\hat{t}) := \hat{\rho}^?], \mathbf{if}(v^?)\{\hat{t}\}\rangle}$$

$$(\widehat{\text{CntrAbort}})\ \frac{\hat{\rho}(x) = v^? \quad v = \mathbf{false} \quad n \geq k}{\langle \hat{h}, \hat{\rho}, \mathbf{if}(x)\{\overline{s}\}\rangle \hat{\downarrow}^n \langle \hat{h}^?, \hat{\rho}[\mathrm{vd}(\overline{s}) := \hat{\rho}^?], \mathbf{if}(v^?)\{\}\rangle}$$

Figure 9. Instrumented semantics for determinacy analysis.

$$v^? \models_\mu v' \qquad pv^! \models_\mu pv \qquad \mu(a)^! \models_\mu a \qquad \frac{F \equiv \mathbf{fun}(y)\ \{b\} \quad \hat{\rho} \models_\mu \rho}{(F, \hat{\rho})^! \models_\mu (F, \rho)}$$

$$\frac{\forall x \in \mathrm{dom}(\rho).\hat{\rho}(x) \models_\mu \rho(x)}{\hat{\rho} \models_\mu \rho} \qquad \frac{\forall a \in \mathrm{dom}(h).\hat{h}(\mu(a)) \models_\mu h(a)}{\hat{h} \models_\mu h}$$

$$\frac{\forall x.\hat{r}(x) \models_\mu r(x)}{\hat{r} \models_\mu r} \qquad \frac{\hat{v} \models_\mu v}{x = \hat{v} \models_\mu x = v} \qquad \frac{a^d \models_\mu a' \quad p^{d'} \models_\mu p' \quad \hat{v} \models_\mu v}{a^d[p^{d'}] = \hat{v} \models_\mu a'[p'] = v}$$

$$\frac{\hat{v} \models_\mu v \quad \hat{t} \models_\mu t}{\mathbf{if}(\hat{v})\{\hat{t}\} \models_\mu \mathbf{if}(v)\{t\}} \qquad \frac{v' = \mathbf{false}}{\mathbf{if}(v^?)\{\hat{t}\} \models_\mu \mathbf{if}(v')\{\}}$$

$$\frac{\hat{v} \models_\mu v}{(\mathbf{fun}(\hat{v})\{\hat{t}\})^?_{\hat{\rho}} \models_\mu \mathbf{fun}(v)\{t\}_\rho} \qquad \frac{\hat{t} \models_\mu t \quad \hat{v} \models_\mu v \quad \hat{\rho} \models_\mu \rho}{(\mathbf{fun}(\hat{v})\{\hat{t}\})^!_{\hat{\rho}} \models_\mu \mathbf{fun}(v)\{t\}}$$

Figure 10. Modeling relations between instrumented values, environments, records, heaps, traces and their concrete counterparts

3.3 Soundness

To show soundness, we will now prove that the instrumented trace generated by an execution under the instrumented semantics correctly predicts any concrete trace produced by an execution under the normal semantics: where the instrumented trace has $v^!$, a concrete trace must have v; where the instrumented trace has $v^?$, we cannot predict the corresponding value in the concrete trace.

Obviously, however, this can only hold if instrumented and concrete execution start in compatible states. To formalize this notion, we inductively define a modeling relation $\cdot \models_\mu \cdot$ relating instrumented values, environments, records, heaps and traces to their concrete counterparts (Figure 10). The mapping μ: Address $\rightarrow$ Address maps addresses of the concrete execution to corresponding addresses of the instrumented execution, since the choice of a in (LdRec) is not constrained enough to require both executions to choose precisely the same addresses.

The rules for values, environments, records and heaps are fairly straightforward. For traces, note that the instrumented and concrete traces of the branches of a conditional need not match if the condition variable is indeterminate false. Similarly, for a function call event we do not require the traces of the called function to correspond if the called function is not determinate.

We can now state the soundness of the instrumented semantics:

Theorem 1. *If* $\langle \hat{h}, \hat{\rho}, s\rangle \hat{\downarrow}^n \langle \hat{h}', \hat{\rho}', \hat{t}\rangle$ *and* $\langle h, \rho, s\rangle \downarrow \langle h', \rho', t\rangle$ *where* $\hat{h} \models_\mu h$ *and* $\hat{\rho} \models_\mu \rho$ *for some* μ *that is injective on* $\mathrm{dom}(h)$, *then* $\hat{h}' \models_{\mu'} h'$, $\hat{\rho}' \models_{\mu'} \rho'$, *and* $\hat{t} \models_{\mu'} t$ *for some* μ' *that is injective on* $\mathrm{dom}(h')$, *and agrees with* μ *and* $\mathrm{dom}(h)$.

A proof of this theorem and its mechanization in Coq are available online at `http://github.com/xiemaisi/determinacy`.

To relate this result to our intuitive description of a determinacy analysis, note that every event in a (concrete or instrumented) trace corresponds to a statement in the program being executed under a certain call stack. The soundness result essentially shows that the instrumented heap and environment at some position p in an instrumented trace correctly model all concrete heaps and environments that may be encountered by a concrete execution at p, provided its initial heap and environment are correctly modeled by the initial instrumented heap and environment.

4. Implementation

We have implemented a prototype dynamic determinacy analysis for JavaScript, which instruments a program to track determinacy flags as in the instrumented semantics of the previous section. Instrumented programs can run in a browser or atop Node.js, using ZombieJS for DOM emulation.[6]

For instrumentation, the program is first translated into a form similar to μJS with a small number of additional statement forms. Almost all of the ECMAScript 5.1 standard is handled, except implicit conversions using `toString` and `valueOf`; getters and setters are partially supported. To handle unstructured control flow, the instrumented program adjusts determinacy information at every control flow merge point, not just after `if`s.

To implement heap flushes, we keep a global *epoch counter*. Every property has a recency annotation, and is only considered determinate if this annotation equals the current epoch. Thus, incrementing the epoch counter flushes the heap.

Native functions from the standard library cannot be instrumented. For some of them, we provide hand-written models that conservatively approximate their effects on determinacy information; e.g., most string handling functions do not affect the determinacy of heap objects. Calling a native function without a model, however, yields an indeterminate result and causes a heap flush.

For DOM functions, we assume that they can only modify DOM data structures, so calling them does not affect the determinacy of other heap locations. Return values of DOM functions, however, are always considered indeterminate, as is any value that is read from a DOM data structure. This is very conservative, and could be improved by providing a more detailed model of the DOM. Since DOM events can fire in any order, we perform a heap flush immediately upon entering an event handler. In practice, this means that few useful determinacy facts can be derived for them.

If counterfactual execution encounters a call to a native function that is not known to be side effect-free, we immediately abort the counterfactual execution and flush the heap. Exceptions during counterfactual execution are handled similarly.

Finally, note that `eval` is easy to handle in a dynamic analysis: calls to `eval` are instrumented to recursively instrument any code loaded at runtime, flushing the heap if the code is not determinate.

Currently, our instrumentation is not optimized, so instrumented code is expected to run slower. In typical applications, however, the main focus of the analysis is on the program's initialization phase, which for most JavaScript programs tends to be fairly short.

[6] See `http://nodejs.org` and `http://zombie.labnotes.org`.

jQuery Version	Baseline	Spec		Spec+DetDOM	
1.0	✗	✓	(82)	✓	(2)
1.1	✗	✗	(107)	✓	(4)
1.2	✓	✓	(>1000)	✓	(0)
1.3	✗	✗	(>1000)	✗	(>1000)

Table 1. Comparison of pointer analysis scalability on several jQuery versions; the number of heap flushes is given in parentheses.

5. Case Studies

This section reports on two case studies combining determinacy analysis with static analysis to improve pointer analysis scalability and to eliminate calls to `eval` as suggested in Section 2.

5.1 Improving pointer analysis

We enhanced the points-to analysis of WALA [30] to exploit determinacy facts computed by our dynamic analysis. This is done by creating clones of functions based on the full call stacks present in determinacy facts to enable specialization, extending the baseline context sensitivity policy used in [30], as discussed in Section 2. We perform three kinds of specializations: (i) removing branches guarded by determinately false conditions; (ii) making dynamic property accesses with determinate property names static; (iii) unrolling loops with a determinate maximum number of iterations if this enables other specializations.

We compared our specializing analysis (**Spec**) to the analysis of [30] (**Baseline**) on several versions of jQuery, as shown in Table 1. For each version, we analyzed an HTML file that includes the jQuery library itself with no additional client code; this is not trivial due to jQuery's complex initialization code [30]. In all cases, the static analysis either completed in less than 5 seconds, indicated by ✓ in the table,[7] or it did not complete within a 10-minute timeout, indicated by ✗. We also give the number of heap flushes performed by the dynamic analysis in parentheses; note that we stop the dynamic analysis after 1000 heap flushes, since at this point it is unlikely to detect new determinacy facts.

Since the DOM model used by the dynamic analysis is very limited, we also ran the dynamic analysis with the additional (unsound) assumption that all properties of DOM objects are determinate, and that operations on the DOM return determinate values (column **Spec+DetDOM**). This avoids many heap flushes and yields more determinacy facts, effectively specializing the code to one particular browser and one HTML document. While unsound in general, this configuration is an indicator of possible improvements to be gained from a richer DOM model.

The results show that determinacy facts can dramatically enhance the scalability of a static pointer analysis: while **Baseline** fails to analyze jQuery 1.0 in 10 minutes, **Spec** analyzes it in a matter of seconds. All specializations listed above were necessary to make this version analyzable; in particular, one loop had to be unrolled 21 times to enable specialization of two critical property writes (similar in style to Figure 3) to make the pointer analysis terminate. The additional context sensitivity needed to make use of determinacy facts is moderate: up to four levels of calling context are required, but only for call sites where a determinacy fact is available; this additional effort pays for itself, since the specialized functions are much easier to analyze than their unspecialized counterparts.

For jQuery 1.1, the determinacy facts were insufficient to make our specializing analysis terminate. Further investigation suggested

[7] As measured on a Lenovo ThinkPad W520 with a 2.20 GHz Intel Core i7-2720QM processor and 8GB RAM running Linux 3.2.0-32, using the OpenJDK 64-Bit Server VM, version 1.7.0_09, with a 5GB maximum heap.

that our imprecise DOM model was to blame, and indeed assuming a determinate DOM makes this version analyzable as well. Again, adding determinacy facts required no more than four levels of context sensitivity and made the analysis dramatically faster.

Interestingly, jQuery 1.2 is easy to analyze for all analysis configurations, even the baseline. This is due to a change that made complex initialization code execute lazily; without client code, this code is dead and need not be analyzed.

jQuery 1.3 (and later versions) are not yet analyzable, even using a determinate DOM. We suspect this is due to more complex event handlers being installed during initialization. Some handlers are not exercised by the dynamic analysis, but even for the ones that are we need to perform a heap flush on entry (see Section 4). Nonetheless, it is clear from our experiments that determinacy analysis has the potential for significantly improving the scalability of pointer analysis of complex JavaScript frameworks such as jQuery.

5.2 Eliminating calls to `eval`

We further enhanced our analysis to also specialize calls to `eval` where `eval` is the only call target and its argument string is determinate. We ran this analysis on the benchmark suite used by Jensen et al. [17]. As they note, there are some difficulties in eliminating uses of `eval` even with constant arguments. Many of these issues do not arise in our case, since we perform specialization on an intermediate representation with fully resolved name bindings.

Jensen et al. report that their *unevalizer* tool could eliminate all uses of `eval` in 19 of 28 benchmarks. Our dynamic analysis needs to be able to run the program, so we had to disregard 3 benchmarks that are missing required code, and one that cannot be run in ZombieJS. On 14 out of the remaining 24 programs, our analysis could specialize all uses of `eval`. Interestingly, this includes six programs that *unevalizer* cannot handle, including the code shown in Figure 4. In this program, the code to be evaluated results from a string concatenation, but their analysis requires the concatenation to be a syntactic part of the `eval` argument expression, which is not the case here. Other cases involve `for-in` loops: if the set of properties to iterate over is determinate, our analysis assumes that the iteration order is also determinate. This is true for all major JavaScript implementations, but *unevalizer* does not assume this.

In the remaining 10 programs, our analysis fails to specialize away at least one use of `eval`. This is either because the evaluated string is genuinely indeterminate (1 case); the dynamic analysis does not cover a use that WALA considers reachable (4 cases); or incomplete DOM modeling causes heap flushes, making the callee of a use of `eval` indeterminate (1 case). In the remaining 4 cases, `eval` occurs inside a loop for which the dynamic analysis cannot derive a determinate upper bound, and which hence cannot be specialized. In only one of these cases is the loop bound truly indeterminate; in the other cases, the imprecision is again caused by heap flushes due to missing DOM modeling.

We also ran our analysis with the potentially unsound determinate DOM assumption described in Section 5.1. This enabled better inference of determinate loop bounds and detection of unreachable code, allowing it to handle 20 benchmarks.

In conclusion, we found that determinacy analysis can be an effective tool for eliminating calls to `eval`.

5.3 Discussion

The case studies above show that determinacy facts can be useful for client analyses like flow-insensitive static analyses. In principle, the additional context sensitivity needed to take advantage of the facts could be very expensive, but it seems that, in practice, scalability problems are often due to a *lack* of determinacy facts.

A more sophisticated DOM model could help finding more determinacy facts, as could a more precise treatment of event handlers. However, soundly reasoning about all possible interleavings of event handlers is a challenging task that we leave to future work.

6. Related Work

Constant Propagation Like determinacy analysis, constant propagation aims to discover expressions that have the same value in every execution. Unlike in determinacy analysis, this value is usually required to be independent of calling context (though context-qualified constants have also been considered [24]) and primitive (i.e., not an object or array). Constant propagation typically relies on a sound static call graph, which is hard to obtain in dynamic languages like JavaScript. Our approach does not require a static call graph, but can only produce fully qualified determinacy facts.

Partial Evaluation Partial evaluation [19] seeks to identify and evaluate program parts that only depend on designated *static inputs*, yielding a *residual program* that can be run on the remaining inputs. *Online* partial evaluation generates the residual program in one pass, whereas *offline* evaluation relies on static analysis to specialize the program. Usually, it first computes a call graph, and then performs a *binding time analysis* to determine expressions whose value only depends on static inputs. A *monovariant* binding time analysis assigns a single classification to every expression, whereas a *polyvariant* analysis [10] takes contexts into account.

Our determinacy analysis can be viewed as a polyvariant binding time analysis where static program inputs are considered determinate. Typical binding time analyses are completely static and hence do not need to know the concrete values of any inputs. Online partial evaluators, on the other hand, operate on given concrete values for the static inputs. By contrast, our analysis is completely dynamic, and hence requires concrete values for *all* inputs.

The main advantage of our approach for JavaScript is that it does not rely on a static analysis. Unlike an online partial evaluator, we do not need heuristics for ensuring termination: our analysis can be run as long as desired and aborted at any point without endangering the soundness of the results.

Symbolic Execution Our counterfactual execution can be viewed as a very limited form of symbolic execution [20]. Unlike symbolic execution, our analysis performs a merge at control-flow join points, rather than maintaining two "forked" executions. This trades precision for performance, since we cannot reason about all possible values of indeterminate expressions.

Information Flow Analysis Our determinacy analysis is similar to a dynamic information flow analysis [3, 32] with indeterminate inputs corresponding to high-security inputs. Since we want to infer determinacy facts even under indeterminate conditionals, we do not mark constants under such conditionals as indeterminate immediately (as an information flow analysis would), but only after the branch has finished executing. Counterfactual execution is similar to faceted execution [4], but rather than creating faceted values at control-flow merge points, we mark the values as indeterminate.

Self-Adjusting Computation The goal of *self-adjusting computation* [1] (a generalization of incremental computation [25]) is to incrementally update the result of a computation given changes to some of its inputs. This is achieved using a dynamic dependence graph tracking computations that depend on changeable inputs. Earlier systems for self-adjusting computation require programs to follow a particular programming style, whereas our analysis works on arbitrary programs. More recent systems [6, 7] automatically transform appropriately annotated programs into the required form, using an inference algorithm based on static information flow. Such a system could be used for static determinacy analysis of typed languages. Conversely, our analysis (which is similar to *dynamic* information flow) may itself be useful for self-adjusting computation.

Trace-Based Abstract Interpretation The instrumented traces in our formalization are similar to abstract derivation trees used in trace-based abstract interpretation [28] in that they describe a class of concrete executions. However, our traces are obtained by dynamic analysis, not static abstract interpretation. Our semantics does not yet cover infinite derivations and infinite traces.

Combinations of Static and Dynamic Analysis Several researchers have proposed using information gathered by a dynamic analysis to specialize uses of dynamic language constructs. Furr et al. [13] present a type inferencer for Ruby that uses information obtained during a profile run to replace dynamic features with statically analyzable alternatives. While their approach is technically similar to ours, their dynamic analysis is not sound, so a client has to account for cases where later runs do not match the profile. Bodden et al. [5] use a similar approach to specialize reflective Java programs, also without soundness guarantees.

Kneuss et al. [21] describe an (unsound) analysis for finding type errors in PHP that uses a flow-sensitive static analysis starting from a program state recorded by a dynamic analysis.

Dufour et al. [12] perform static analysis for Java based on a dynamic call graph, thus essentially analyzing only a single execution; this suffices for their application area of performance analysis. Wei et al. [31] apply the same approach to JavaScript, additionally using dynamic information to eliminate uses of `eval`. They argue that this approach, while unsound, can be useful for applications such as taint analysis where soundness is not always required.

Combining static and dynamic analysis the other way around, an unsound static analysis can be supplemented with additional runtime checks to catch cases not covered by the analysis. This technique has been used to enforce information flow policies [9, 14], and to infer type information for JIT compilation [16].

7. Conclusions

We have presented a purely dynamic analysis for identifying determinate expressions which always have the same value at a given program point. While the analysis only observes one program execution at a time, the facts it derives hold for *all* executions. We have proved the analysis correct for a simple imperative language, implemented it for full JavaScript, and shown how its results can be used by a static analysis to deal with reflective language features.

While our results are promising, more work is needed for the combined static-dynamic analysis to realize its full potential. To generate *more* determinacy facts, we plan to explore automated test generation [2] to improve coverage of the dynamic analysis. Running the determinacy analysis on different inputs yields more facts, which are all sound and hence can be used together. To generate *better* determinacy facts, we will work on inferring determinacy facts with shallower calling contexts. We will investigate whether these improvements are enough to make WALA scale to realistic web applications, or whether more work is needed. Finally, we also plan to apply determinacy analysis to other problems such as partial evaluation and dead code detection, and explore potential uses for counterfactual execution outside the setting of determinacy analysis, for instance in dynamic taint analysis.

References

1. Umut A. Acar. *Self-Adjusting Computation*. Ph.D. thesis, CMU, 2005.
2. Shay Artzi, Julian Dolby, Simon Holm Jensen, Anders Møller, and Frank Tip. A Framework for Automated Testing of JavaScript Web Applications. In *ICSE*, 2011.
3. Thomas H. Austin and Cormac Flanagan. Efficient Purely-Dynamic Information Flow Analysis. In *PLAS*, 2009.
4. Thomas H. Austin and Cormac Flanagan. Multiple Facets for Dynamic Information Flow. In *POPL*, 2012.
5. Eric Bodden, Andreas Sewe, Jan Sinschek, Hela Oueslati, and Mira Mezini. Taming Reflection: Aiding Static Analysis in the Presence of Reflection and Custom Class Loaders. In *ICSE*, 2011.
6. Yan Chen, Joshua Dunfield, and Umut A. Acar. Type-Directed Automatic Incrementalization. In *PLDI*, 2012.
7. Yan Chen, Joshua Dunfield, Matthew Hammer, and Umut Acar. Implicit Self-Adjusting Computation for Purely Functional Programs. In *ICFP*, 2011.
8. Aske Simon Christensen, Anders Møller, and Michael I. Schwartzbach. Precise Analysis of String Expressions. In *SAS*, 2003.
9. Ravi Chugh, Jeffrey A. Meister, Ranjit Jhala, and Sorin Lerner. Staged Information Flow for JavaScript. In *PLDI*, 2009.
10. Charles Consel. Polyvariant Binding-Time Analysis For Applicative Languages. In *PEPM*, 1993.
11. Douglas Crockford. *JavaScript: The Good Parts*. O'Reilly, 2008.
12. Bruno Dufour, Barbara G. Ryder, and Gary Sevitsky. Blended Analysis for Performance Understanding of Framework-based Applications. In *ISSTA*, 2007.
13. Michael Furr, Jong-hoon An, and Jeffrey S. Foster. Profile-guided Static Typing for Dynamic Scripting Languages. In *OOPSLA*, 2009.
14. Salvatore Guarnieri and V. Benjamin Livshits. GATEKEEPER: Mostly Static Enforcement of Security and Reliability Policies for JavaScript Code. In *USENIX Security Symposium*, 2009.
15. Arjun Guha, Claudiu Saftoiu, and Shriram Krishnamurthi. The Essence of JavaScript. In *ECOOP*, 2010.
16. Brian Hackett and Shu-yu Guo. Fast and Precise Hybrid Type Inference for JavaScript. In *PLDI*, 2012.
17. Simon Holm Jensen, Peter A. Jonsson, and Anders Møller. Remedying the Eval That Men Do. In *ISSTA*, 2012.
18. Simon Holm Jensen, Anders Møller, and Peter Thiemann. Type Analysis for JavaScript. In *SAS*, 2009.
19. Neil D. Jones, Carsten K. Gomard, and Peter Sestoft. *Partial evaluation and automatic program generation*. Prentice-Hall, Inc., 1993.
20. James C. King. Symbolic Execution and Program Testing. *Communications of the ACM*, 19(7), July 1976.
21. Etienne Kneuss, Philippe Suter, and Viktor Kuncak. Runtime Instrumentation for Precise Flow-Sensitive Type Analysis. In *RV*, 2010.
22. Xavier Leroy and Hervé Grall. Coinductive Big-Step Operational Semantics. *Inf. Comput.*, 207(2):284–304, 2009.
23. Fadi Meawad, Gregor Richards, Floréal Morandat, and Jan Vitek. Eval Begone! Semi-Automated Removal of Eval from JavaScript Programs. In *OOPSLA*, 2012.
24. Thomas W. Reps, Stefan Schwoon, Somesh Jha, and David Melski. Weighted Pushdown Systems and Their Application to Interprocedural Dataflow Analysis. *Sci. Comput. Program.*, 58(1-2):206–263, 2005.
25. Thomas W. Reps and Tim Teitelbaum. The Synthesizer Generator. In *SDE*, 1984.
26. Gregor Richards, Christian Hammer, Brian Burg, and Jan Vitek. The Eval That Men Do—A Large-Scale Study of the Use of Eval in JavaScript Applications. In *ECOOP*, 2011.
27. Gregor Richards, Sylvain Lebresne, Brian Burg, and Jan Vitek. An Analysis of the Dynamic Behavior of JavaScript Programs. In *PLDI*, 2010.
28. David A. Schmidt. Trace-Based Abstract Interpretation of Operational Semantics. *Lisp and Symbolic Computation*, 10(3):237–271, 1998.
29. O. Shivers. Control Flow Analysis in Scheme. In *PLDI*, 1988.
30. Manu Sridharan, Julian Dolby, Satish Chandra, Max Schäfer, and Frank Tip. Correlation Tracking for Points-To Analysis of JavaScript. In *ECOOP*, 2012.
31. Shiyi Wei and Barbara G. Ryder. A Practical Blended Analysis for Dynamic Features in JavaScript. TR 12-18, Virginia Tech, 2012.
32. Steve Zdancewic. *Programming Languages for Information Security*. PhD thesis, Cornell University, 2002.

Formal Verification of SSA-Based Optimizations for LLVM

Jianzhou Zhao Santosh Nagarakatte[†] Milo M. K. Martin Steve Zdancewic

Computer and Information Science Department, University of Pennsylvania [†]Rutgers University

jianzhou@cis.upenn.edu santosh.nagarakatte@cs.rutgers.edu milom@cis.upenn.edu stevez@cis.upenn.edu

Abstract

Modern compilers, such as LLVM and GCC, use a *static single assignment* (SSA) intermediate representation (IR) to simplify and enable many advanced optimizations. However, formally verifying the correctness of SSA-based optimizations is challenging because SSA properties depend on a function's entire control-flow graph.

This paper addresses this challenge by developing a proof technique for proving SSA-based program invariants and compiler optimizations. We use this technique in the Coq proof assistant to create mechanized correctness proofs of several "micro" transformations that form the building blocks for larger SSA optimizations. To demonstrate the utility of this approach, we formally verify a variant of LLVM's `mem2reg` transformation in Vellvm, a Coq-based formal semantics of the LLVM IR. The extracted implementation generates code with performance comparable to that of LLVM's unverified implementation.

Categories and Subject Descriptors D.2.4 [*Software Engineering*]: Software/Program Verification - Correctness Proofs; F.3.1 [*Logics and Meanings of Programs*]: Specifying and Verifying and Reasoning about Programs - Mechanical verification; F.3.2 [*Logics and Meanings of Programs*]: Semantics of Programming Languages - Operational semantics

General Terms Languages, Verification, Reliability

Keywords LLVM, Coq, single static assignment

1. Introduction

Compiler bugs can manifest as crashes during compilation, or, much worse, result in the silent generation of incorrect programs. Such mis-compilations can introduce subtle errors that are difficult to diagnose and generally puzzling to software developers. A recent study by Yang *et al.* [20] used random test-case generation to expose serious bugs in mainstream compilers including GCC, LLVM, and commercial compilers. Whereas few bugs were found in the front end of the compiler, various optimization phases of the compiler that aim to make generated programs faster were a prominent source of bugs.

Projects like CompCert [9, 16–18] are tackling the problem of compiler bugs by *mechanically verifying* the correctness of compilers. Indeed, although the aforementioned study uncovered many bugs in other compilers, the only bugs found in CompCert were in those parts of the compiler not (yet) formally verified. Yang *et al.* write [20]: *"The apparent unbreakability of CompCert supports a strong argument that developing compiler optimizations within a proof framework, where safety checks are explicit and machine-checked, has tangible benefits for compiler users."*

Despite CompCert's groundbreaking compiler-verification efforts, there still remain many challenges in applying its technology to industrial-strength compilers. In particular, the original CompCert development, and the bulk of the subsequent work—with the notable exception of CompCertSSA [4]—did not use a *static single assignment (SSA)* [7] intermediate representation (IR) [9].

In SSA intermediate representations, each variable of a function is assigned statically only once, and each variable definition must dominate all of its uses in the control-flow graph. These SSA properties simplify or enable many compiler optimizations [14], including: constant folding, sparse conditional constant propagation, aggressive dead code elimination, global value numbering, global code motion, partial redundancy elimination, and inductive variable analysis. Consequently, open-source and commercial compilers such as GCC, LLVM, and Intel CC all use SSA-based intermediate representations when performing such optimizations.

Despite their importance, there are few mechanized formalizations of the correctness properties of SSA transformations. This paper tackles this problem by developing proof techniques suitable for mechanically verifying the correctness of SSA-based optimizations. We do so in the context of our Vellvm framework [21, 22], which formalizes the operational semantics of programs expressed in LLVM's SSA-based IR [10] and provides Coq [6] infrastructure to facilitate mechanized proofs of properties about transformations on the LLVM IR.

The key idea is to generalize the "SSA scoping" predicate, which is an invariant of the operational semantics, to more complex safety predicates. The main proof obligation then becomes a preservation argument, but one that takes the dominance relation of the SSA form into account. Instances of this idea are found in the literature (see, for example, Menon, *et al.* [13]), and related proof techniques have been recently used in CompCertSSA [4], which uses translation validation to check SSA optimizations (see Section 8). This work is the first to verify SSA algorithms in the context of an industrial-strength compiler like the LLVM.

To demonstrate the utility of these techniques, we use them to establish the correctness of a variant of `mem2reg`, a crucial LLVM pass that is responsible for promoting un-aliased local variables and stack-based temporary values into registers. We build our `vmem2reg` pass by "pipelining" several simpler transformations, such as load-after-store elimination, which are common building blocks of many SSA-based optimizations. To improve compilation time, we also investigate how to fuse such multiple such passes into one. To summarize our contributions, this paper:

- introduces general-purpose proof techniques for verifying SSA optimizations,
- shows that the proposed SSA proof techniques are viable for use in mechanized proofs, and verifies several simple transformations,

PLDI'13, June 16–19, 2013, Seattle, WA, USA.

- describes and proves correct vmem2reg, an easier-to-verify variant of LLVM's mem2reg optimization, which is a key SSA-based transformation used by LLVM, and
- demonstrates that the extracted implementation of the fully verified vmem2reg is effective: The vmem2reg fully-verified pass yields an average speedup over a LLVM -O0 of 77% versus a speedup of 81% speedup obtained by LLVM's implementation of mem2reg.

To streamline the explanation (Section 3), we describe the proof techniques in the context of Vminus, a simplified subset the full Vellvm framework [22], but one that still captures the essence of SSA. We mechanically verified *all* the claims of the paper both for Vminus and full Vellvm in Coq.[1]

2. Background

2.1 Program refinement

In this paper, we use program refinement to reason about the correctness of compilation. Following the CompCert project [9], we define program refinement in terms of programs' external behaviors (which include program traces of input-output events, whether a program terminates, and the returned value if a program terminates): a transformed program *refines* the original if the behaviors of the original program include all the behaviors of the transformed program. We define the operational semantics using traces of a labeled transition system.

Events	e	$::=$	$v = fid(\overline{v_j}^{\,j})$
Finite traces	t	$::=$	$\epsilon \mid e, t$
Finite or infinite traces	T	$::=$	$\epsilon \mid e, T$ (coinductive)

We denote one small-step of evaluation as $config \vdash S \xrightarrow{t} S'$: in program environment $config$, program state S transitions to the state S', recording events e of the transition in the trace t. An event e describes the inputs v_j and output v of an external function call named fid. $config \vdash S \xrightarrow{t}{}^{*} S'$ denotes the reflexive, transitive closure of the small-step evaluation with a finite trace t. $config \vdash S \xrightarrow{T} \infty$ denotes a diverging evaluation starting from S with a finite or infinite trace T. Program refinement is given by the following definition.

DEFINITION 1 (Program refinement).

1. $\textbf{init}\,(prog, fid, \overline{v_j}^{\,j}, S)$ *means* S *is the initial program state of the program* $prog$ *with the main entry* fid *and inputs* v_j.
2. $\textbf{final}\,(S, v)$ *means* S *is the final state with the return value* v.
3. $\Downarrow(prog, fid, \overline{v_j}^{\,j}, t, v)$ *means* $\exists S\, S'.\ \textbf{init}\,(prog, fid, \overline{v_j}^{\,j}, S)$, $config \vdash S \xrightarrow{t}{}^{*} S'$ *and* $\textbf{final}\,(S', v)$.
4. $\Uparrow(prog, fid, \overline{v_j}^{\,j}, T)$ *means* $\exists S.\ \textbf{init}\,(prog, fid, \overline{v_j}^{\,j}, S)$ *and* $config \vdash S \xrightarrow{T} \infty$.
5. $\not\Downarrow(prog, fid, \overline{v_j}^{\,j}, t)$ *means* $\exists S\, S'.\ \textbf{init}\,(prog, fid, \overline{v_j}^{\,j}, S)$, $config \vdash S \xrightarrow{t}{}^{*} S'$ *and* S' *is stuck.*
6. $\textbf{defined}\,(prog, fid, \overline{v_j}^{\,j})$ *means* $\forall\, t, \neg \not\Downarrow(prog, fid, \overline{v_j}^{\,j}, t)$
7. $prog_2$ ***refines*** *program* $prog_1$, *written* $prog_1 \supseteq prog_2$, *if*
   - (a) $\textbf{defined}\,(prog_1, fid, \overline{v_j}^{\,j})$
   - (b) $\Downarrow(prog_2, fid, \overline{v_j}^{\,j}, t, v) \Rightarrow \Downarrow(prog_1, fid, \overline{v_j}^{\,j}, t, v)$
   - (c) $\Uparrow(prog_2, fid, \overline{v_j}^{\,j}, T) \Rightarrow \Uparrow(prog_1, fid, \overline{v_j}^{\,j}, T)$
   - (d) $\not\Downarrow(prog_2, fid, \overline{v_j}^{\,j}, t) \Rightarrow \not\Downarrow(prog_1, fid, \overline{v_j}^{\,j}, t)$

Note that refinement requires only that a transformed program preserves the semantics of a well-defined original program, but does not constrain the transformation of undefined programs.

[1] Annotated Coq source available at http://cis.upenn.edu/~stevez/vellvm/release.tgz.

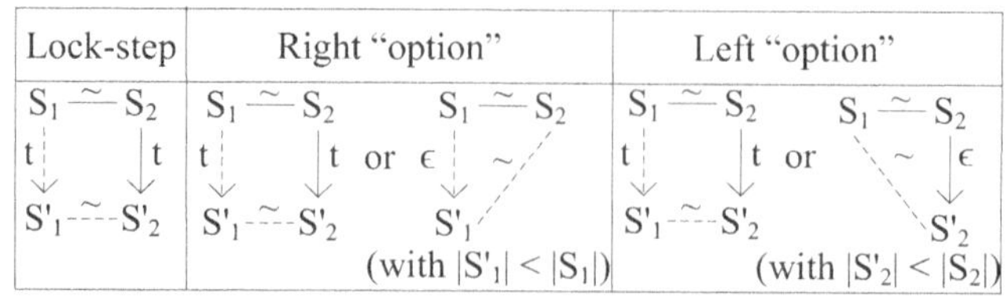

Figure 1. Backward simulation diagrams that imply program refinement. In each diagram, the program states of original and compiled programs are on the left and right respectively. A line denotes a relation $\sim$ between program states. Solid lines or arrows denote hypotheses; dashed lines or arrows denote conclusions.

We use the backward simulation diagrams in Figure 1 to prove that a program transformation satisfies the refinement property. The CompCert project uses similar diagrams for forward simulation [9]. At a high-level, we first need to find a relation $\sim$ between program states and their transformed counterparts. The relation must hold initially, imply equivalent returned values finally, and imply that stuck states are related. Then, depending on the transformation, we prove that a specific diagram holds: lock-step simulation is for variable substitution, right "option" simulation is for instruction removal, and left "option" simulation is for instruction insertion. Because the existence of a diagram implies that the source and target programs share traces, we can prove the equivalence of program traces by decomposing program transitions into matched diagrams. To ensure co-termination, the "option" simulations are parameterized by a measure of program states $|S|$ that must decrease to prevent "infinite stuttering" problems.

2.2 SSA

Static Single Assignment (SSA) form [7] is an intermediate representation distinguished by its treatment of temporary variables—each such variable may be defined only once, statically, and each use of the variable must be dominated by its definition with respect to the control-flow graph of the containing function.[2] Intuitively, the variable definition dominates a use if all possible execution paths to the use go through the definition first.

To maintain these invariants in the presence of branches and loops, SSA form uses ϕ-instructions, which act like control-flow dependent move operations. Such ϕ-instructions appear only at the start of a basic block and, crucially, they are handled specially in the dominance relation to "cut" apparently cyclic data dependencies.

The left part of Figure 2 shows an example program in SSA form, written using the stripped-down notation of Vminus (defined more formally in Section 3). The temporary r_3 at the beginning of the block labeled l_2 is defined by a ϕ-instruction: if control enters the block l_2 by jumping from basic block l_1, r_3 will get the value 0; if control enters from block l_2 (via the back edge of the branch at the end of the block), then r_3 will get the value of r_5.

The SSA form is good for implementing optimizations because it identifies variable names with the program points at which they are defined. Maintaining the SSA invariants thus makes definition and use information of each variable more explicit. Also, because each variable is defined only once, there is less mutable state to be considered (for purposes of aliasing, *etc.*) in SSA form, which makes certain code transformations easier to implement.

Program transformations like the one in Figure 2 are correct if the transformed program refines the original program (in the sense described above) and the result is well-formed SSA. Proving that

[2] In the literature, there are different variants of SSA forms [1]. We use LLVM' version: memory locations are not in SSA form; LLVM does not maintain any connection between a variable name in the IR and its original name in the source; the live ranges of variables can overlap.

Original	Transformed
$l_1 : \cdots$	$l_1 : \cdots$
$\cdots$	$r_4 := r_1 * r_2$
$\mathbf{br}\ r_0\ l_2\ l_3$	$\mathbf{br}\ r_0\ l_2\ l_3$
$l_2 : r_3 = \mathbf{phi}\,\mathbf{int}[0, l_1][r_5, l_2]$	$l_2 : r_3 = \mathbf{phi}\,\mathbf{int}[0, l_1][r_5, l_2]$
$r_4 := r_1 * r_2$	
$r_5 := r_3 + r_4$	$r_5 := r_3 + r_4$
$r_6 := r_5 \geq 100$	$r_6 := r_5 \geq 100$
$\mathbf{br}\ r_6\ l_2\ l_3$	$\mathbf{br}\ r_6\ l_2\ l_3$
$l_3 : r_7 = \mathbf{phi}\,\mathbf{int}[0, l_1][r_5, l_2]$	$l_3 : r_7 = \mathbf{phi}\,\mathbf{int}[0, l_1][r_5, l_2]$
$r_8 := r_1 * r_2$	
$r_9 := r_8 + r_7$	$r_9 := r_4 + r_7$

Figure 2. An SSA-based optimization. In the original program with entry l_1, $r_1 * r_2$ is a partial common expression for the definitions of r_4 and r_8, because there is no domination relation between r_4 and r_8. Therefore, eliminating the common expression directly is not correct: we cannot simply replace $r_8 := r_1 * r_2$ by $r_8 := r_4$ since r_4 is not available at the definition of r_8 if l_2 does not execute before l_3 runs. To transform this program, we might first move the instruction $r_4 := r_1 * r_2$ from the block l_2 to the block l_1, because the definitions of r_1 and r_2 must dominate the end of l_1, and l_1 dominates l_2. Then we can safely replace all the uses of r_8 by r_4, because the definition of r_4 in l_1 dominates l_3 and therefore dominates all the uses of r_8. Finally, r_8 is removed, because there are no uses of r_8.

such code transformations are correct is nontrivial because they involve non-local reasoning about the program.

3. Proof Techniques for SSA

This section describes the proof techniques we have developed for formalizing properties of SSA-style intermediate representations. To most clearly articulate the approach, we present the results using a language called Vminus, which is a minimalist SSA language containing only those features salient to the proof technique. Vminus is a subset of the LLVM IR formalized in Vellvm [22].

The key idea of the technique is to generalize the invariant used for Vminus's preservation lemma for proving safety to other predicates that are also shown to be invariants of the operational semantics. Crucially, these predicates all share the same form, which only constrains variable definitions that *strictly dominate* the current program counter.

The remainder of this section first presents the syntax and operational semantics of Vminus, then it gives the static semantics and proves safety (which in this context simply amounts to showing that all variables are well-scoped). With these properties established, we then show how to generalize the safety invariant to a form that is useful for proving program transformations correct and demonstrate its applicability to a number of standard optimizations. Because Vminus is such a stripped-down language, the relevant lemmas are relatively straightforward to establish; Section 4 shows how to scale the proof technique to the full Vellvm model of LLVM to verify the `mem2reg` pass.

3.1 The simple SSA language—Vminus

Syntax Figure 3 gives the syntax of Vminus. Every Vminus expression is of type integer. Operations in Vminus compute with values val, which are either temporaries r or constants $cnst$ that must be integer values. We use R to range over sets of identifiers.

All code in Vminus resides in a top-level function, whose body is composed of blocks b. Here, $\overline{b}$ denotes a list of blocks; we also use similar notation for other lists. As is standard, a basic block consists of a labeled entry point l, a series of ϕ nodes, a list of commands cs, and a terminator instruction tmn. In the following, we also use the label l of a block to denote the block itself.

Types	typ	$::=$	$\mathbf{int}$
Constants	$cnst$	$::=$	Int
Values	val	$::=$	$r \mid cnst$
Binops	bop	$::=$	$+ \mid * \mid \&\& \mid = \mid \geq \mid \leq \mid \cdots$
Right-hand-sides	rhs	$::=$	$val_1\ bop\ val_2$
Commands	c	$::=$	$r := rhs$
Terminators	tmn	$::=$	$\mathbf{br}\ val\ l_1\ l_2 \mid \mathbf{ret}\ typ\ val$
Phi Nodes	ϕ	$::=$	$r = \mathbf{phi}\ typ\ \overline{[val_j, l_j]}^j$
Instructions	$insn$	$::=$	$\phi \mid c \mid tmn$
Non-ϕs	ψ	$::=$	$c \mid tmn$
Blocks	b	$::=$	$l\ \overline{\phi}\ \overline{c}\ tmn$
Functions	f	$::=$	$\mathbf{fun}\ \{\overline{b}\}$

Values v	$::=$	Int	Locals	δ	$::=$	$r \mapsto v$
Frames σ	$::=$	(pc, δ)	Prog Counters	pc	$::=$	$l.i \mid l.\mathbf{t}$

$$\frac{[\![val]\!]_\delta = \lfloor v \rfloor \quad l_3 = (v?l_1 : l_2) \qquad f[l_3] = \lfloor (l_3\ \overline{\phi}_3\ \overline{c}_3\ tmn_3) \rfloor \quad [\![\overline{\phi}_3]\!]^l_\delta = \lfloor \delta' \rfloor}{f \vdash (l, [], \mathbf{br}\ val\ l_1\ l_2, \delta) \longrightarrow (l_3, \overline{c}_3, tmn_3, \delta')}\ \text{E\_BR}$$

$$\frac{[\![val_1]\!]_\delta = \lfloor v_1 \rfloor \quad [\![val_2]\!]_\delta = \lfloor v_2 \rfloor \qquad c = r := val_1\ bop\ val_2 \quad \mathbf{eval}\,(bop, v_1, v_2) = v_3}{f \vdash (l, (c, \overline{c}), tmn, \delta) \longrightarrow (l, \overline{c}, tmn, \delta\{v_3/r\})}\ \text{E\_BOP}$$

Figure 3. Syntax and Operational Semantics of Vminus

The set of blocks making up the top-level function constitutes a control-flow graph with a well-defined entry point that cannot be reached from other blocks. We write $f[l] = \lfloor b \rfloor$ if there is a block b with label l in function f. Here, the $\lfloor\ \rfloor$ (pronounced "some") indicates that the function is partial (might return "none" instead).

As usual in SSA, the ϕ nodes join together values from a list of predecessor blocks of the control-flow graph—each ϕ node takes a list of (value, label) pairs that indicates the value chosen when control transfers from a predecessor block with the associated label. The commands c include the usual suite of binary arithmetic or comparison operations. We denote the right-hand-sides of commands by rhs. Block terminators (**br** and **ret**) branch to another block or return a value from the function. We also use metavariable $insn$ to range over ϕ-nodes, commands and terminators, and non-phinodes ψ to represent commands and terminators.

Dynamic Semantics The operational semantics rules in Figure 3 are parameterized by the top-level function f, and relate evaluation frames σ before and after an evaluation step. An evaluation frame keeps track of the integer values v bound to local temporaries r in δ and current program counter. We also use $\sigma.pc$ and $\sigma.\delta$ to denote the program counter and locals of σ respectively. Because Vminus has no function calls, the rules ignore program traces. This simplification does not affect the essence of the proof techniques. Section 5 shows the full Vellvm semantics with traces.

Instruction positions are denoted by program counters pc: $l.i$ indicates the i-th command in the block l; $l.\mathbf{t}$ indicates the terminator of the block l. We write $f[pc] = \lfloor insn \rfloor$ if some $insn$ is at the program counter pc of function f. We also use $l.(i+1)$ to denote the next program counter of $l.i$. When $l.i$ is the last command of block l, $l.(i+1) = l.\mathbf{t}$. To simplify presentation of the operational semantics, we use $l, \overline{c}, tmn$ to "unpack" the instructions at a program counter in function f. Here, l is the current block, $\overline{c}$ and tmn are the instructions of l that are not executed yet. It is easy to see how the "block & offset" specification is equivalent to the "continuation commands" representation so we omit the details of the correspondence here.

$$\frac{\forall r.(\psi\ \mathbf{uses}\ r \Rightarrow r \in \mathbf{sdom}_f(pc))}{f \Vdash_{\succ} \psi\ @\ pc}\ \textsc{NonPhi} \qquad \frac{f \rightsquigarrow l \Rightarrow (\overline{f, l \Vdash_{\succ} \phi_j}^{\,j} \wedge \overline{f \vdash c_i\ @\ l.i}^{\,i} \wedge f \vdash tmn\ @\ (l.\mathbf{t}))}{f \vdash l\,\overline{\phi_j}^{\,j}\,\overline{c_i}^{\,i}\,tmn}\ \textsc{WF\_B}$$

$$\frac{\mathbf{uniq}\,(\overline{l_j}^{\,j}) \quad \overline{l_j}^{\,j} = \mathbf{preds}\,(f, l) \quad \overline{\forall r_j.(val_j\ \mathbf{uses}\ r_j \Rightarrow r_j \in \mathbf{sdom}_f(l_j.\mathbf{t}))}^{\,j} \quad \mathbf{len}\,(\overline{[val_j, l_j]}^{\,j}) > 0 \quad \overline{f \vdash val_j : typ}^{\,j}}{f, l \Vdash_{\succ} r = \mathbf{phi}\ typ\ \overline{[val_j, l_j]}^{\,j}}\ \textsc{Phi}$$

$$\frac{f \vdash val_1 : \mathbf{int} \quad f \vdash val_2 : \mathbf{int}}{f \vdash r := val_1\ bop\ val_2}\ \textsc{WF\_BOP} \qquad \frac{f \vdash val : \mathbf{int} \quad f[l_1] = \lfloor b_1 \rfloor \quad f[l_2] = \lfloor b_2 \rfloor}{f \vdash \mathbf{br}\ val\ l_1\ l_2}\ \textsc{WF\_BR}$$

$$\frac{f \Vdash_{\succ} \psi\ @\ pc \quad f \vdash \psi}{f \vdash \psi\ @\ pc}\ \textsc{WF\_NonPhi} \qquad \frac{\mathbf{uniq}\,(\mathbf{defs}\,(f)) \quad \mathbf{uniq}\,(\mathbf{labels}\,(f)) \quad f = \mathbf{fun}\,\{\overline{b_j}^{\,j}\} \quad \overline{f \vdash b_j}^{\,j} \quad \mathbf{wf\_entry}\,f}{\vdash f}\ \textsc{WF\_F}$$

Figure 4. Static Semantics of Vminus (excerpt)

Most of the Vminus commands have straight-forward interpretation. The arithmetic and logic instructions are all unsurprising—the $[\![val]\!]_\delta$ function computes a value from the local state δ and val, looking up the meanings of variables in the local state as needed; **eval** implements arithmetic and logic operations. We use $[\![rhs]\!]_\delta$ to denote evaluating the right-hand-side rhs in the state δ.

There is one wrinkle in specifying the operational semantics when compared to a standard environment-passing call-by-value language. All of the ϕ instructions for a block must be executed atomically and with respect to the "old" local value mapping due to the possibility of self loops and dependencies among the ϕ nodes. For example the well-formed code fragment bellow has a circular dependency between r_1 and r_2

$$\begin{array}{ll} l_0: & \cdots \\ l_1: & r_1 = \mathbf{phi}\ \mathbf{int}[r_2, l_1][0, l_0] \\ & r_2 = \mathbf{phi}\ \mathbf{int}[r_1, l_1][1, l_0] \\ & r_3 := r_1 = r_2 \\ & \mathbf{br}\ r_3\ l_2\ l_1 \\ l_2: & \cdots \end{array}$$

If control enters this block from l_0, r_1 will map to 0 and r_2 to 1, which causes the conditional branch to fail, jumping back to the label l_1. The new values of r_1 and r_2 should be 1 and 0, and not 1 and 1 as might be computed if they were handled sequentially. This atomic update of the local state, similar to "parallel assignment," is handled by the $[\![\overline{\phi}_3]\!]^l_\delta$ function as shown in rule E_BR.

Static semantics Vminus requires that a program satisfy certain invariants to be considered well formed: every variable in the top-level function must dominate all its uses, and be assigned exactly, once statically. At a minimum, any reasonable Vminus transformation must preserve these invariants; together they imply that the program is in SSA form [7].

Figure 4 shows the judgments to check the SSA invariants with respect to the control-flow graph and program points of the function f. To explain the judgments we need the following definitions.

DEFINITION 2 (Domination).

1. *val **uses** $r \triangleq val = r$.*
2. *$insn$ **uses** $r \triangleq \exists val.\ val$ **uses** $r \wedge val$ is an operand of $insn$.*
3. *A variable r is defined at a program counter pc of function f, written f **defines** $r\ @\ pc$ if and only if $f[pc] = \lfloor insn \rfloor$ and r is the left-hand side of $insn$. We write **defs** (f) to denote the set of all variables defined in f.*
4. *In function f, block l_1 **dominates** block l_2, written $f \vdash l_1 \succeq l_2$, if every path from the entry block of f to l_2 must go through l_1; l_1 **strictly dominates** l_2, written $f \vdash l_1 \succ l_2$, if every path from the entry block of f to l_2 must go through l_1 and $l_1 \neq l_2$.*
5. *In function f, pc_1 **strictly dominates** pc_2, written $f \vdash pc_1 \succ pc_2$, if pc_1 and pc_2 are at distinct blocks l_1 and l_2 respectively and $f \vdash l_1 \succ l_2$; if pc_1 and pc_2 are in the same block, then pc_1 appears earlier than pc_2.*
6. *$\mathbf{sdom}_f(pc)$ is the set of variables strictly dominating pc:*

$$\mathbf{sdom}_f(pc) = \{r \mid f\ \mathbf{defines}\ r\ @\ pc' \text{ and } f \vdash pc' \succ pc\}$$

Rule WF_F of Figure 4 ensures that variables **defs** (f) defined in the top-level function are unique, which enforces the single-assignment part of the SSA property. Additionally, all block labels **labels** (f) in the function must be unique for a well-formed control-flow graph, and the entry block should have no predecessors (**wf_entry** f).

The rule WF_B checks that all instructions in reachable blocks (written $f \rightsquigarrow l$) satisfy the SSA domination invariant. Because unreachable blocks have no effects at runtime, the rule does not check them. Rule NONPHI ensures that a ψ at pc is strictly dominated by the definitions of all variables used by ψ. The rule PHI ensures that the number of incoming values is not zero, that all incoming labels are unique, and that the current block's predecessors is the same as the set of incoming labels. If an incoming value val_j from a predecessor block l_j uses a variable r_j at pc_j, then pc_j must strictly dominate the terminator of l_j. Importantly, this rule allows "cyclic" uses of SSA variables of the kind shown in the example above.

Dominance analysis Dominance analysis plays an important role in the type system, so we must first prove the following lemmas about the domination relations. They are needed to establish the SSA-based program properties in the following sections. Details about these lemmas can be found our prior work [21].

LEMMA 1 (Domination is transitive).

LEMMA 2 (Strict domination is acyclic).

By Lemma 1, $\mathbf{sdom}_f(pc)$ has the following properties:

LEMMA 3 (sdom step).

1. *If $l.i$ and $l.(i+1)$ are valid program counters of f, then $\mathbf{sdom}_f(l.(i{+}1)) = \mathbf{sdom}_f(l.i) \cup \{r\}$ where f **defines** $r\ @\ l.i$.*
2. *If $l.\mathbf{t}$ and $l'.0$ are valid program counters of f, and l' is a successor of l, then $\mathbf{sdom}_f(l'.0) - \mathbf{defs}\,(\overline{\phi}) \subseteq \mathbf{sdom}_f(l.\mathbf{t})$ where $\overline{\phi}$ are from the block l' and $\mathbf{defs}\,(\overline{\phi})$ denotes all variables defined by $\overline{\phi}$.*

3.2 Safety of Vminus

There are two ways that a Vminus program might get stuck. First, it might try to jump to an undefined label, but this property is ruled out statically by WF_BR. Second, it might try to access a variable whose value is not defined in δ. We can prove that this second case never happens by establishing the following safety theorem:

THEOREM 4 (Safety). *If $\vdash f$ and $f \vdash (entry.0, \emptyset) \longrightarrow^* \sigma$, then σ is not stuck.*

The proof takes the standard form using preservation and progress lemmas with the invariant for frames shown bellow:

$$\frac{pc \in f \quad \forall r.(r \in \mathbf{sdom}_f(pc) \Rightarrow \exists v.\delta[r] = \lfloor v \rfloor)}{f \vdash (pc, \delta)} \text{ WF\_FR}$$

This rule is similar to the predicate used in prior work for verifying the type safety of an SSA-based language [13]. The invariant WF_FR shows that a frame (pc, δ) is well-formed if every definition that strictly dominates pc is defined in δ. The initial program state satisfies this invariant trivially:

LEMMA 5 (Initial State). *If* $\vdash f$ *then* $f \vdash (entry.0, \emptyset)$.

The preservation and progress lemmas are straightforward—but note that they crucially rely on the interplay between the invariant on δ "projected" onto $\mathbf{sdom}_f(pc)$ (Lemma 3), and the PHI and NONPHI rules of the static semantics.

LEMMA 6 (Preservation). *If* $\vdash f$, $f \vdash \sigma$ *and* $f \vdash \sigma \longrightarrow \sigma'$, *then* $f \vdash \sigma'$.

LEMMA 7 (Progress). *If* $\vdash f$, $f \vdash \sigma$, *then* σ *is not stuck.*

3.3 Generalizing Safety to other SSA Invariants

The main feature of the preservation proof, Lemma 6, is that the constraint on $\mathbf{sdom}_f(pc)$ is an invariant of the operational semantics. But—*and this is a key observation*—we can parameterize rule WF_FR by a predicate P, which is an arbitrary proposition about functions and frames:

$$\frac{\sigma.pc \in f \qquad P\ f\ (\sigma|_f)}{f, P \vdash \sigma} \text{ GWF\_FR}$$

Here, $\sigma|_f$ is $(\sigma.pc, (\sigma.\delta)|_{(\mathbf{sdom}_f(\sigma.pc))})$ and we write $(\delta|_R)[r] = \lfloor v \rfloor$ iff $r \in R$ and $\delta[r] = \lfloor v \rfloor$ and observe that $\mathbf{dom}(\delta|_R) = R$. These restrictions say that we don't need to consider *all* variables: Intuitively, because SSA invariants are based on dominance properties, when reasoning about a program state we need only consider the variable definitions that strictly dominate the program counter in a given state.

For proving Theorem 4, we instantiated P to be:

$$P_{\text{safety}} \triangleq \lambda f.\, \lambda\sigma.\, \forall r. r \in \mathbf{dom}(\sigma.\delta) \Rightarrow \exists v.(\sigma.\delta)[r] = \lfloor v \rfloor$$

For safety, it is enough to show that each variable in the domination set is well defined at its use. To prove program transformations correct, we instantiate P with a different predicate, P_{sem}, that relates the syntactic definition of a variable with the semantic value:

$$\lambda f.\, \lambda\sigma.\, \forall r. f[r] = \lfloor rhs \rfloor \Rightarrow (\sigma.\delta)[r] \neq \cdot \Rightarrow (\sigma.\delta)[r] = [\![rhs]\!]_{(\sigma.\delta)}$$

Just as we proved preservation for P_{safety}, we can also prove preservation for P_{sem} (using Lemma 2):

THEOREM 8. *If* $\vdash f$ *and* $f, P_{\text{sem}} \vdash \sigma$ *and* $f \vdash \sigma \longrightarrow \sigma'$, *then* $f, P_{\text{sem}} \vdash \sigma'$.

As we show next, Theorem 8 can be used to justify the correctness of many SSA-based transformations. Instantiating P with other predicates can also be useful—Section 5 shows how.

3.4 The correctness of SSA-based transformations

Consider again the example code transformation from Figure 2. It, and many other SSA-based optimizations, can be defined by using a combination of simpler transformations: deleting an unused definition, substituting a constant expression for a variable, substituting one variable by another, or moving variable definitions. Each such transformation is subject to the SSA constraints—for example, we can't move a definition later than one of its uses—and each transformation preserves the SSA invariants. By pipelining these basic transformations, we can define more sophisticated SSA-based program transformations whose correctness is established by the composition of the proofs for the basic transformations.

In general, an SSA-based transformation from f to f' is *correct* if it preserves both well-formedness and program behavior.

1. Preserving well-formedness: if $\vdash f$, then $\vdash f'$.
2. Program refinement: if $\vdash f$, then $f \supseteq f'$ (see Section 2.1).

Each of the basic transformations mentioned above can be proved correct by using Theorem 8. For the sake of space, here we present only the correctness of variable substitution (though we proved correct all the mentioned transformations in our Coq development). Section 4 shows how to extend the transformations to implement memory-aware optimizations in the full Vellvm.

Variable substitution Consider the step of the program transformation from Figure 2 in which the use of r_8 on the last line is replaced by r_4 (this is valid only after hoisting the definition of r_4 so that it is in scope). This transformation is correct because both r_4 and r_8 denote the same value, and the definition of r_4 (after hoisting) strictly dominates the definition of r_8. In Figure 2, it is enough to do *redundant variable elimination*—this optimization lets us replace one variable by another when their definitions are syntactically equal; other optimizations, such as *global value numbering*, allow a coarser, more semantic, equality to be used. Proving them correct follows the same basic pattern as the proof shown below.

DEFINITION 3 (Redundant Variable). *In a function* f, *a variable* r_2 *is* ***redundant*** *with variable* r_1 *if:*

1. f **defines** r_1 @ pc_1, f **defines** r_2 @ pc_2 *and* $f \vdash pc_1 \succ pc_2$
2. $f[pc_1] = \lfloor c_1 \rfloor$, $f[pc_1] = \lfloor c_2 \rfloor$ *and* c_1 *and* c_2 *have syntactically equal right-hand-sides.*

We would like to prove that eliminating a redundant variable is correct, and therefore must relate a program f with $f\{r_1/r_2\}$. Since substitution does not change the control-flow graph, it preserves the domination relations.

LEMMA 9.

1. $f \vdash l_1 \succcurlyeq l_2 \iff f\{r_2/r_1\} \vdash l_1 \succcurlyeq l_2$
2. $f \vdash pc_1 \succ pc_2 \iff f\{r_2/r_1\} \vdash pc_1 \succ pc_2$

Applying Lemma 1 and Lemma 9, we have:

LEMMA 10. *Suppose that in* f, r_1 *is redundant with* r_2. *If* $\vdash f$, *then* $\vdash f\{r_2/r_1\}$.

Let two program states simulate each other if they have the same local state δ and program counter. We assume that the original program and its transformation have the same initial state.

LEMMA 11. *If* $\vdash f$, r_2 *is redundant with* r_1 *in* f, *and* (pc, δ) *is a reachable state, then*

1. *If* val *is an operand of a non-phinode at program counter* pc, *then* $\exists v. [\![val]\!]_\delta = \lfloor v \rfloor \wedge [\![val\{r_1/r_2\}]\!]_\delta = \lfloor v \rfloor$.
2. *If* pc *is* $l_i.\mathbf{t}$, *and* l_i *is a previous block of a block with* ϕ*-nodes* $\overline{\phi_j}^j$, *then* $\exists\delta'. [\![\overline{\phi_j}^j]\!]_\delta^{l_i} = \lfloor \delta' \rfloor \wedge [\![\overline{\phi_j\{r_1/r_2\}}^j]\!]_\delta^{l_i} = \lfloor \delta' \rfloor$.

Proof (sketch): The proof makes crucial use of Theorem 8. For example, to show part 1 for a source instruction $r := rhs$ (with transformed instruction $r := rhs\{r_1/r_2\}$) located at program counter pc, we reason like this: if r_2 is an operand used by rhs, then $r_2 \in \mathbf{sdom}_f(pc)$ and by Theorem 8, property P_{sem}, implies that $\delta[r_2] = [\![rhs_2]\!]_\delta$ for some rhs_2 defining r_2. Since r_1 is used as an operand in $rhs\{r_1/r_2\}$, similar reasoning shows that $\delta[r_1] =$

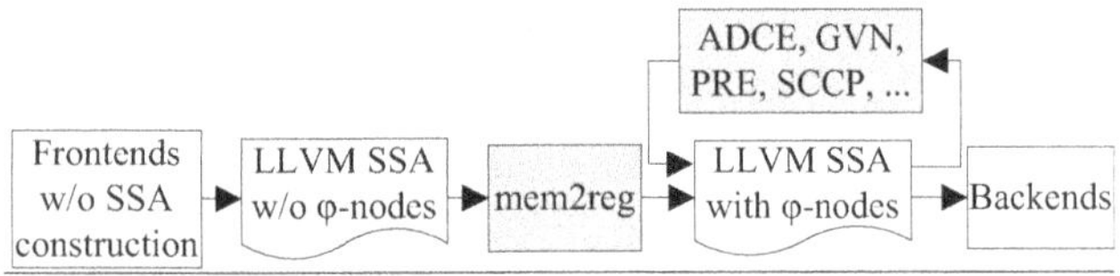

Figure 5. The tool chain of the LLVM compiler

$[\![rhs_1]\!]_\delta$, but since r_2 is redundant with r_1, we have $rhs_2 = rhs_1$, and the result follows immediately. □

Using Lemma 11, we can easily show the lock-step simulation lemma, which completes the correctness proof:

LEMMA 12. *If* $\vdash f$, r_2 *is redundant with* r_1 *in* f, $f\{r_1/r_2\} \vdash \sigma_1 \longrightarrow \sigma_2$, *then* $f \vdash \sigma_1 \longrightarrow \sigma_2$.

4. LLVM and mem2reg

From Vminus to Vellvm Vminus provides a convenient minimal setting in which to study SSA-based optimizations, but it omits many features necessary in a real intermediate representation. To demonstrate that our proof techniques can be used for practical compiler optimizations, we next show how to apply them to the LLVM IR used in Vellvm [22].

LLVM [10] (*Low-Level Virtual Machine*) is a robust, industrial-strength, and open-source compilation framework that competes with GCC in terms of compilation speed and performance of the generated code. LLVM uses a platform-independent SSA-based intermediate representation [10], and provides a large suite of optimization passes, including aggressive dead code elimination, global value numbering, partial redundancy elimination, and sparse conditional constant propagation, among others. Each transformation pass consumes and produces code in this SSA form, and they typically have the flavor of the code transformations described above in Section 3. Figure 5 depicts LLVM's tool chain.

The Vellvm infrastructure provides a Coq implementation of the full LLVM 3.0 intermediate language and defines (several) operational semantics along with some useful metatheory about the memory model. Figure 6 shows the additional Vellvm features needed to explain the following proofs; more details about the operational semantics can be found in our earlier Vellvm work [22].

A program $prog$ includes a list of products $prod$ that are either global constants or function definitions. The address of a global constant with type typ is a constant $typ * gid$ of type $typ*$. Vellvm also has memory operations that include stack allocation, loads, and stores. At runtime, a pointer in is represented by a block name blk and an offset ofs within the block. All globals are allocated before the start of a program and stored in a mapping g. A program state S is composed of a memory state M and a list of stack states $\overline{\sigma}$. We denote small-step evaluation by $config \vdash S \xrightarrow{t} S'$ where a program configuration $config$ includes a program $prog$ and globals. Judgment $\vdash prog$ denotes a well-formed program—it checks that all definitions of globals and functions are unique, each function is well-formed, *etc.*

4.1 The mem2reg Optimization Pass

A critical piece of LLVM's compilation strategy is the `mem2reg` pass, which takes code that is "trivially" in SSA form and converts it into a *minimal, pruned* SSA program [15]. This strategy simplifies LLVM's many front ends by moving work in to `mem2reg`. An SSA form is "minimal" if each ϕ is placed only at the dominance frontier of the definitions of the ϕ node's incoming variables [7]. A minimal SSA form is "pruned" if it contains only live ϕ nodes [15]. This pass enables many subsequent optimizations (and, in particular, backend optimizations such as register allocation) to work effectively.

Programs	$prog$	$::=$	$\overline{prod}$
Products	$prod$	$::=$	$gid = \textbf{global}\ typ\ const \mid f$
Functions	f	$::=$	$\textbf{define}\ typ\ fid(\overline{arg})\ \{\overline{b}\}$
Types	typ	$::=$	$\cdots \mid typ*$
Constants	$cnst$	$::=$	$\cdots \mid typ * gid$
Commands	c	$::=$	$\cdots$
		$\mid$	$r := \textbf{alloca}\ typ$
		$\mid$	$r := \textbf{load}\ (typ*)\ r_1$
		$\mid$	$\textbf{store}\ typ\ val_1\ r_2$
		$\mid$	$option\ r = \textbf{call}\ typ\ fid\ \overline{param}$
Values	v	$::=$	$\cdots \mid blk.ofs$
Globals	g	$::=$	$r \mapsto v$
Configurations	$config$	$::=$	$prog, g$
Allocas	α	$::=$	$\emptyset \mid blk, \alpha$
Frames	σ	$::=$	(f, pc, δ, α)
Call stacks	$\overline{\sigma}$	$::=$	$\emptyset \mid \sigma, \overline{\sigma}$
Program states	S	$::=$	$M, \overline{\sigma}$

Figure 6. The syntax and program states of Vellvm (excerpt)

Figure 7 demonstrates the importance of the `mem2reg` pass for LLVM's generated code performance. In our experiments, running *only* the `mem2reg` pass yields a 81% speedup (on average) compared to LLVM without any optimizations; doing the full suite of `-O1` level optimizations (which includes `mem2reg`) yields a speedup of 102%, which means that `mem2reg` alone captures all but %12 of the benefit of the `-O1` level optimizations. Comparison with `-O3` optimizations yields similar results. These observations make `mem2reg` an obvious target for our verification efforts.

The "trivial" SSA form is generated directly by compiler front ends, and it uses the **alloca** instruction to allocate stack space for *every* source-program local variable and temporary needed. In this form, an LLVM SSA variable is used either only locally to access those stack slots, in which case the variable is never live across two basic blocks, or it is a reference to the stack slot, whose lifetime corresponds to the source-level variable's scope. These constraints mean that no ϕ instructions are needed—it is extremely straightforward for a front end to generate code in this form.

As an example, consider this C program:

```
int i = 0; while (i<=100) i++; return i;
```

The "trivial" SSA form that might be produced by the frontend of a compiler is shown in the left-most column of Figure 8. The $r_0 := \textbf{alloca int}$ instruction on the first line allocates space for the source variable `i`, and r_0 is a reference from which local **load** and **store** instructions access `i`'s contents.

The `mem2reg` pass converts *promotable* uses of stack-allocated variables to SSA temporaries. An **alloca**'ed variable like r_0 is considered to be promotable, written $\textbf{promotable}\,(f, r_0)$, if it is created in the entry block of function f and it doesn't escape—*i.e.*, its value is never written to memory or passed as an argument to a function call. The `mem2reg` pass identifies promotable stack allocations and then replaces them by temporary variables in SSA form. It does this by placing ϕ nodes, substituting each variable defined by a **load** with the previous value stored into the stack slot, and then eliminating the memory operations (which are now dead). The right-most column of Figure 8 shows the resulting pruned SSA program for this example.

Proving that `mem2reg` is correct is nontrivial because it makes significant, non-local changes to the use of memory locations and temporary variables. Furthermore, the specific `mem2reg` algorithm used by LLVM is not directly amenable to the proof techniques developed in Section 3—it was not designed with verification in mind, so it produces intermediate stages that break the SSA invariants or do not preserve semantics. This section therefore describes an alternate algorithm that is more suitable to formalization.

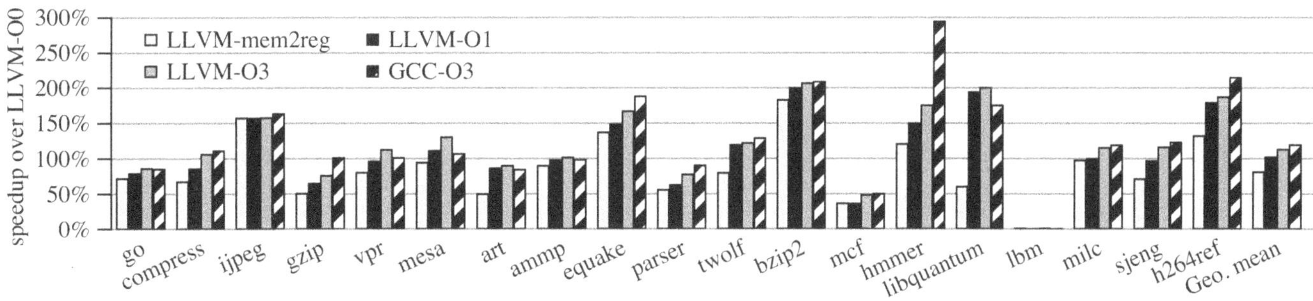

Figure 7. Normalized execution time improvement of the LLVM's mem2reg, LLVM's O1, and LLVM's O3 optimizations over the LLVM baseline with optimizations disabled. For comparison, GCC-O3's speedup over the same baseline is also shown.

"trivial" SSA	Maximal ϕ nodes placement	After LAS/LAA/SAS	After DSE/DAE	After ϕ nodes elimination
$l_1: r_0 :=$ **alloca int**	$l_1: r_0 :=$ **alloca int**	$l_1: r_0 :=$ **alloca int**	$l_1:$	$l_1:$
store int $0\ r_0$	**store int** $0\ r_0$	**store int** $0\ r_0$		
	$r_7 :=$ **load** (**int** $*$) r_0			
br l_2	**br** l_2	**br** l_2	**br** l_2	**br** l_2
$l_2:$	$l_2: r_6 =$ **phi** $[r_7, l_1][r_9, l_3]$	$l_2: r_6 =$ **phi** $[0, l_1][r_9, l_3]$	$l_2: r_6 =$ **phi** $[0, l_1][r_4, l_3]$	$l_2: r_6 =$ **phi** $[0, l_1][r_4, l_3]$
	store int $r_6\ r_0$	**store int** $r_6\ r_0$		
$r_1 :=$ **load** (**int** $*$) r_0	$r_1 :=$ **load** (**int** $*$) r_0			
$r_2 := r_1 \leq 100$	$r_2 := r_1 \leq 100$	$r_2 := r_6 \leq 100$	$r_2 := r_6 \leq 100$	$r_2 := r_6 \leq 100$
	$r_8 :=$ **load** (**int** $*$) r_0			
br $r_2\ l_3\ l_4$	**br** $r_2\ l_3\ l_4$	**br** $r_2\ l_3\ l_4$	**br** $r_2\ l_3\ l_4$	**br** $r_2\ l_3\ l_4$
$l_3:$	$l_3: r_{10} =$ **phi** $[r_8, l_2]$	$l_3: r_{10} =$ **phi** $[r_6, l_2]$	$l_3: r_{10} =$ **phi** $[r_6, l_2]$	$l_3:$
	store int $r_{10}\ r_0$			
$r_3 :=$ **load** (**int** $*$) r_0	$r_3 :=$ **load** (**int** $*$) r_0			
$r_4 := r_3 + 1$	$r_4 := r_3 + 1$	$r_4 := r_{10} + 1$	$r_4 := r_{10} + 1$	$r_4 := r_6 + 1$
store int $r_4\ r_0$	**store int** $r_4\ r_0$	**store int** $r_4\ r_0$		
	$r_9 :=$ **load** (**int** $*$) r_0			
br l_2	**br** l_2	**br** l_2	**br** l_2	**br** l_2
$l_4:$	$l_4: r_{11} =$ **phi** $[r_8, l_2]$	$l_4: r_{11} =$ **phi** $[r_6, l_2]$	$l_4: r_{11} =$ **phi** $[r_6, l_2]$	$l_4:$
	store int $r_{11}\ r_0$	**store int** $r_{11}\ r_0$		
$r_5 :=$ **load** (**int** $*$) r_0	$r_5 :=$ **load** (**int** $*$) r_0			
ret int r_5	**ret int** r_5	**ret int** r_{11}	**ret int** r_{11}	**ret int** r_6

Figure 8. The SSA construction by the `vmem2reg` pass

4.2 The `vmem2reg` Algorithm

The `vmem2reg` algorithm is structured to lead to a clean formalism and yet still produce programs with effectiveness similar to the LLVM `mem2reg` pass. To demostrate the main ideas of `vmem2reg`, this section describes an algorithm that uses straightforward micro-pass pipelining. Section 6 presents a smarter way to "fuse" the micro passes, thereby reducing compilation time. Proving pipeline fusion correct is (by design) independent of the proofs for the `vmem2reg` algorithm shown in the section.

At a high level, `vmem2reg` (whose code is shown in Figure 10) traverses all functions of the program, applying the transformation `vmem2reg_fn` to each. Figure 9 depicts the main loop, which is an extension of Aycock and Horspool's SSA construction algorithm [3]. `vmem2reg_fn` first iteratively promotes each promotable **alloca** by adding ϕ nodes at the beginning of every block. After processing all promotable **alloca**s, `vmem2reg_fn` removes redundant ϕ nodes, and eventually will produce a program almost in pruned SSA form,[3] in a manner similar to previous algorithms [15].

[3] Technically, fully pruned SSA requires a more aggressive dead-ϕ-elimination pass that we omit for the sake of simplicity. Section 7 shows that this omission is negligible.

The transformation that `vmem2reg_fn` applies to each function is a composition of a series of micro transformations (LAS, LAA, SAS, DSE, and DAE, shown in Figure 9). Each of these transformations preserves the well-formedness and semantics of its input program; moreover, these transformations are relatively small and local, and can therefore be reasoned about more easily.

At each iteration of **alloca** promotion, `vmem2reg_fn` finds a promotable allocation r. Then ϕ-`nodes_placement` (code shown in Figure 10) adds ϕ nodes for r at the beginning of every block. To preserve both well-formedness and the original program's semantics, ϕ-`nodes_placement` also adds additional **load**s and **store**s around each inserted ϕ node. At the end of every block that has successors, ϕ-`nodes_placement` introduces a **load** from r, and stores the result in a fresh temporary; at the beginning of every block that has a predecessor, ϕ-`nodes_placement` first inserts a fresh ϕ node whose incoming value from a predecessor l is the value of the corresponding **load** added at the end of l, then inserts a **store** to r with the value of the new ϕ node.

The second column in Figure 8 shows the result of running the ϕ-node placement pass starting from the example program in its trivial SSA form. It is not difficult to check that this code is in SSA form. Moreover, the output program also preserves the meaning of the original program. For example, at the end of block l_1, the pro-

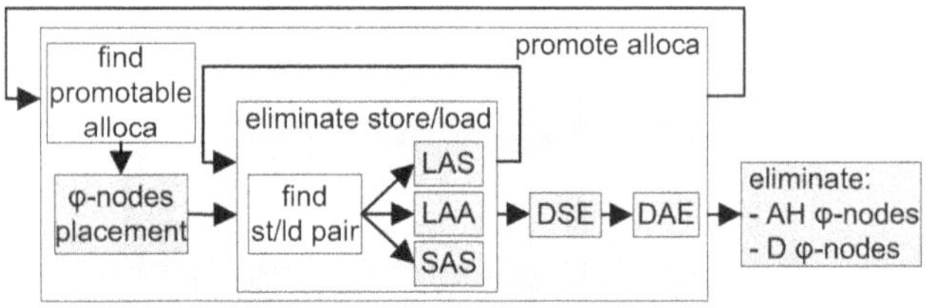

Figure 9. Basic structure of vmem2reg_fn

```
let vmem2reg prog =
  map (function f → vmem2reg_fn f
                | prod → prod) prog
let φ-nodes_placement f r =
  let define typ fid(arg‾) {b‾} = f in
  let (ldnms, phinms) = gen_fresh_names b‾ in
  define typ fid(arg‾) { (map
    (function l φ‾ c‾ tmn →
      let r := alloca typ ∈ f in
      let (φ‾', c‾1) =
        match predecessors_of f l with
        | [] → (φ‾, c‾)
        | l‾j^j → let r‾j^j = map (find ldnms) l‾j^j in
                  let r' = find phinms l in
                  (r' = phi typ [r_j, l_j]‾^j ::φ‾, store typ r' r ::c‾)
        end in
      let c‾' = match successors_of f l with
                | [] → c‾1
                | _ → let r' = find ldnms l in
                      c‾1 ++ [r' := load (typ*) r]
                end in
      l φ‾' c‾' tmn) b‾)}
let rec eliminate_stld f r =
  match find_stld_pair f r with
  | LAS (pc2, val2, r1) →
      eliminate_stld (f{val2/r1} − r1) r
  | LAA r1 → eliminate_stld (f{0/r1} − r1) r
  | SAS (pc1, pc2) → eliminate_stld (f − pc1) r
  | NONE → f
  end
```

Figure 10. The algorithm of vmem2reg

gram loads the value stored at r_0 into r_7. After jumping to block l_2, the value of r_7 is stored into the location r_0, which should contain the same values as r_7. Therefore, the additional store does not change the status of memory. Although the output program contains more temporaries than the original program, these temporaries are used only to connect inserted **load**s and **store**s, and so they do not interfere with the original temporaries.

To remove the additional **loads** and **stores** introduced by the ϕ-node placement pass and eventually promote **allocas** to registers, vmem2reg_fn next applies a series of micro program transformations until no more optimizations can be applied.

First, vmem2reg_fn iteratively does the following transformations (implemented by eliminate_stld shown in Figure 10):

1. LAS (r_1, pc_2, val_2) "Load After Store": r_1 is **load**ed from r after a store of val_2 to r at program counter pc_2, and there are no other **stores** of r in any path (on the control-flow graph) from pc_2 to r_1. In this case, all uses of r_2 can be replaced by val_2, and the **load** can be removed.
2. LAA r_1 "Load After Alloca": As above, but the load is from an uninitialized memory location at r. r_1 can be replaced by LLVM's default memory value, and the **load** can be removed.
3. SAS (pc_1, pc_2): The **store** at program counter pc_2 is a store after the store at program counter pc_1. If both of them access r, and there is no **load** of r in any path (on the control-flow graph) from pc_1 to pc_2, then the **store** at pc_1 can be removed.

At each iteration step of eliminate_stld, the algorithm uses the function find_stld_pair to identify each of the above cases. Because the ϕ-node placement pass only adds a **store** and a **load** as the first and the last commands at each block respectively, find_stld_pair only needs to search for the above cases within blocks. This simplifies both the implementation and proofs. Moreover, eliminate_stld must terminate because each of its transformations removes one command. The third column in Figure 8 shows the code after eliminate_stld.

Next, the algorithm uses DSE (Dead Store Elimination) and DAE (Dead Alloca Elimination) to remove the remaining unnecessary **stores** and **allocas**. The fourth column in Figure 8 shows the code after DSE and DAE.

Finally, vmem2reg_fn eliminates unnecessary and dead ϕ nodes. A ϕ-node is unnecessary [3] if ϕ is of the form $r = \textbf{phi}\ typ\ \overline{[val_j, l_j]}^j$ where all the val_j's are either equal to r or to val. In this case, uses of r can be replaced by val, and the ϕ node can be removed. Aycock and Horspool [3] proved that when there is no such ϕ node in a reducible program, the program is of the minimal SSA form. The right-most column in Figure 8 shows the final output of the algorithm.

5. Correctness of vmem2reg

We prove the correctness of vmem2reg using the techniques developed in Section 3. At a high level, the correctness of vmem2reg is the composition of the correctness of each micro transformation of vmem2reg shown in Figure 10. Given a well-formed input program, each shaded box must produce a well-formed program that preserves the semantics of the input program. Moreover, the micro transformations except DAE and ϕ-nodes elimination must preserve the **promotable** predicate, because the correctness of subsequent transformations relies on fact that promotable allocations aren't aliased.

Formally, let $prog\{f'/f\}$ be the substitution of f by f' in $prog$, and let $(\!|f|\!)$ be a micro transformation of f applied by vmem2reg. $(\!|\_|\!)$ must satisfy:

1. Preserving **promotable**: when $(\!|\_|\!)$ is not DAE or ϕ-nodes elimination, if **promotable** (f, r), then **promotable** $((\!|f|\!), r)$.
2. Preserving well-formedness: if **promotable** (f, r) when $(\!|\_|\!)$ is ϕ-nodes placement, and $\vdash prog$, then $\vdash prog\{(\!|f|\!)/f\}$.
3. Program refinement: if **promotable** (f, r) when $(\!|\_|\!)$ is not ϕ-nodes elimination, and $\vdash prog$, then $prog \supseteq prog\{(\!|f|\!)/f\}$.

5.1 Preserving promotability

At the beginning of each iteration for promoting **allocas**, the algorithm indeed finds promotable allocations.

LEMMA 13. *If* $prog \vdash f$, *and* vmem2reg_fn *finds a promotable allocation* r *in* f, *then* **promotable** (f, r).

We next show that ϕ-nodes placement preserves **promotable**:

LEMMA 14. *If* **promotable** (f, r), *then* **promotable** (ϕ-nodes_placement $f\ r, r$).

Each of the other micro transformations is composed of one or two more basic transformations: variable substitution, denoted by $f\{val/r\}$, and instruction removal, denoted by **filter check** f where **filter** removes an instruction $insn$ from f if **check** $insn$ =

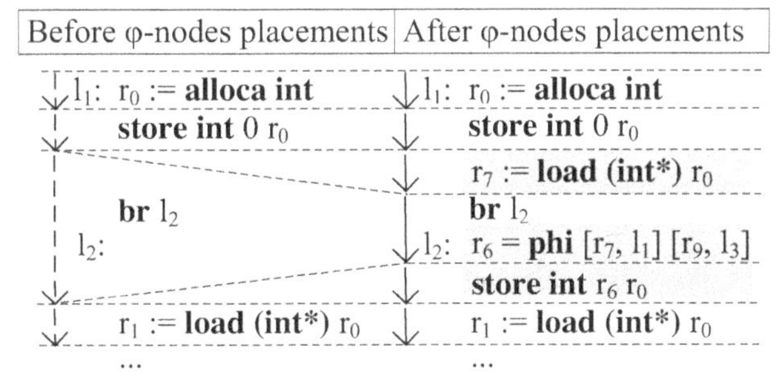

Figure 11. The simulation relation for ϕ-node placement

false. For example, $f\{val_2/r_1\} - r_1$ (LAS) is a substitution followed by a removal in which **check** $insn$ = **false** iff $insn$ defines r_1; DSE of a promotable **alloca** r is a removal in which **check** $insn$ = **false** iff $insn$ is a store to r. We first establish that substitution and removal preserve **promotable**.

LEMMA 15. *Suppose* **promotable** (f, r),

1. *If* $\neg(val_1$ **uses** $r)$, *then* **promotable** $(f\{val_1/r_1\}, r)$.
2. *If* **check** $insn$ = **false** $\Rightarrow$ *insn does not define r, then* **promotable** (**filter check** f, r).

We can show that the other micro transformations preserve **promotable** by checking the preconditions of Lemma 15.

LEMMA 16. *Suppose* **promotable** (f, r), *r is still* **promotable** *after LAS, LAA, SAS or DSE.*

The substituted value of LAS is written to memory by a **store** in f, which cannot use r because r is promotable in f. The substituted value of LAA is a constant that cannot use r trivially. Moreover, LAS, LAA, SAS and DSE remove only **load**s or **store**s.

5.2 Preserving well-formedness

It is sufficient to check the following conditions to show that a function-level transformation preserves well-formedness:

LEMMA 17. *Suppose*

1. $(\!|f|\!)$ *and* f *have the same signature.*
2. *if* $prog \vdash f$, *then* $prog\{(\!|f|\!)/f\} \vdash (\!|f|\!)$.

If $\vdash prog$, *then* $\vdash prog\{(\!|f|\!)/f\}$.

It is easy to see that all transformations vmem2reg applies satisfy the first condition. We first prove that ϕ-nodes placement preserves the second condition:

LEMMA 18. *If* **promotable** (f, r), $prog \vdash f$ *and let* f' *be* ϕ*-nodes_placement* $f\ r$, *then* $prog\{f'/f\} \vdash f'$.

Similarly, to reason about other transformations, we first establish that substitution and removal preserve well-formedness.

LEMMA 19. *Suppose* $prog \vdash f$,

1. *If* $f \vdash val_1 \succ r_2$, $f' = f\{val_1/r_2\}$, *then* $prog\{f'/f\} \vdash f'$.
2. *If* **check** $insn$ = **false** $\Rightarrow$ *f does not use insn, and let* f' *be* **filter check** f, *then* $prog\{f'/f\} \vdash f'$.

Here, $f \vdash val_1 \succ r_2$ if $f \vdash r_1 \succ r_2$ when val_1 **uses** r_1. Note that the first part of Lemma 19 is an extension of Lemma 10 that only allows substitution on commands. In vmem2reg, LAS and ϕ-nodes elimination may transform ϕ-nodes.

LAS, LAA and ϕ-nodes elimination remove instructions after substitution. The following auxiliary lemma shows that the substituted definition is removable after substitution (by Lemma 2):

LEMMA 20. *If* $f \vdash val_1 \succ r_2$, *then* $f\{val_1/r_2\}$ *does not use* r_2.

By Lemma 19, Lemma 20 and the proofs [3], we have:

LEMMA 21. *LAS, LAA, SAS, DSE, DAE and* ϕ*-nodes elimination preserve well-formedness.*

5.3 Program refinement

The proofs of program refinement use the simulation diagrams in Section 2 and different instantiations of the GWF_FR rule we developed in Section 3, where instead of just a function f and frame σ, we now have a configuration *config* that also includes the program memory.

Promotability As we discussed above, the micro transformations (except ϕ-nodes elimination) rely on the **promotable** property. We start by establishing the invariants related to promotability, namely that promotable allocations aren't aliased. This proof is itself an application of GWF_FR.

The **promotable** property ensures that a promotable **alloca** of a function does not escape—the function can access the data stored at the allocation, but cannot pass the address of the allocation to other contexts. Therefore, in the program, the promotable **alloca** and all other pointers (in memory, local temporaries and temporaries on the stack) must not alias. Formally, given a promotable allocation r with type $typ*$ in f, we define $P_{\text{noalias}}(f, r, typ)$:

$$
\begin{array}{l}
\lambda config.\ \lambda S.\\
\quad \forall \overline{\sigma}_1 +\!\!+\ \sigma :: \overline{\sigma}_2 = S.\overline{\sigma}.\ f = \sigma.f \wedge [\![r]\!]_{\sigma.\delta} = \lfloor blk \rfloor \Longrightarrow\\
\qquad\quad \exists v.\mathbf{load}\,(S.M, typ, blk) = \lfloor v \rfloor\\
\qquad \wedge \quad \forall blk'.\forall typ'.\neg\mathbf{load}\,(S.M, typ', blk') = \lfloor blk \rfloor\\
\qquad \wedge \quad \forall r' \neq r \Longrightarrow \neg [\![r']\!]_{\sigma.\delta} = \lfloor blk \rfloor\\
\qquad \wedge \quad \forall \sigma' \in \overline{\sigma}_1.\forall r'.\neg [\![r']\!]_{\sigma'.\delta} = \lfloor blk \rfloor
\end{array}
$$

The last clause ensures that the **alloca** and the variables in the callees reachable from f do no alias. In CompCert, the translation from C#minor to Cminor uses properties (in non-SSA form) similar to $P_{\text{noalias}}(f, r, typ)$ to allocate local variables on stack.

LEMMA 22 (A promotable alloca is not aliased). *At any reachable program state S, config,* $P_{\text{noalias}}(f, r, typ) \vdash S$ *holds.*

The invariant holds initially. At all reachable states, the invariant holds because a promotable allocation cannot be copied to other temporaries, stored to memory, passed into a function, or returned. Therefore, in a well-defined program no external code can get its location by accessing other temporaries and memory locations. Importantly, the memory model ensures that from a consistent initial memory state, all memory blocks in temporaries and memory are allocated—it is impossible to forge a fresh pointer from an integer.

ϕ-node placement Figure 11 pictorially shows an example (which is the code fragment from Figure 8) of the simulation relation $\sim$ for proving that the ϕ-node placement preserves semantics. It follows left "option" simulation, because ϕ-node placement only inserts instructions. We use the number of unexecuted instructions in the current block as the measure function.

The dashed lines indicate where the two program counters must be synchronized. Although the pass defines new variables and **store**s (shaded in Figure 11), the variables are only passed to the new ϕ nodes, or stored into the promotable allocation; additional **store**s only update the promotable allocation with the same value. Therefore, by Lemma 22, $\sim$ requires that two programs have the same memory states and the original temporaries match.

LEMMA 23.
If $f' = \phi$*-nodes_placement* $f\ r$, *and* **promotable** (f, r), *and* $\vdash prog$, *then* $prog \supseteq prog\{f'/f\}$.

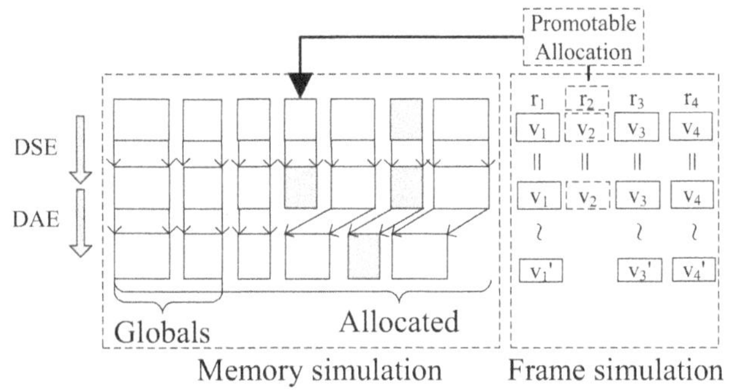

Figure 12. The simulation relation for DSE and DAE

The interesting case is to show that $\sim$ implies a correspondence between stuck states. Lemma 22 ensures that the promotable allocation cannot be dereferenced by operations on other pointers. Therefore, the inserted memory accesses are always safe.

LAS/LAA We present the proofs for the correctness of LAS. The proofs for the correctness of LAA is similar. In the code after ϕ-node placement of Figure 8, r_7 := **load** (**int** ∗) r_0 is an LAS of **store int** 0 r_0. We observe that at any program counter pc between the **store** and **load**, the value stored at r_0 must be 0 because **alive** (pc_1, pc_2) holds—the **store** defined at pc_1 is not overwritten by other writes until pc.

To formalize the observation, consider a promotable r with type $typ*$ in f. Suppose `find_stld_pair f r = LAS (`pc_2`,` val_2`,` r_1`)`. Consider the invariant $P_{\text{las}}(f, r, typ, pc_2, val_2)$:

$$\lambda config.\, \lambda S.\, \forall \sigma \in S.\overline{\sigma}.$$
$$(f = \sigma.f \wedge [\![val_2]\!]_{\sigma.\delta} = \lfloor v_2 \rfloor \wedge [\![r]\!]_{\sigma.\delta} = \lfloor blk \rfloor \wedge$$
$$\textbf{alive}\,(pc_2, \sigma.pc)) \Longrightarrow \textbf{load}\,(S.M, typ, blk) = \lfloor v_2 \rfloor$$

Using Lemma 22, we have that:

LEMMA 24. *If* **promotable** (f, r), *then* **alive** (pc_2, r_1) *and at any reachable state* S, $config, P_{\text{las}}(f, r, typ, pc_2, val_2) \vdash S$ *holds.*

Let two programs relate to each other if they have the same program states. Lemma 24 establishes that the substitution in LAS is correct. The following lemma shows that removal of unused instructions preserves semantics in general.

LEMMA 25. *If* **check** $insn$ = **false** ⇒ f *does not use* $insn$, *and* $\vdash prog$, *then* $prog \supseteq prog\{$**filter check** $f/f\}$.

Lemma 20 shows that the precondition of Lemma 25 holds after the substitution in LAS. Finally, we have that:

LEMMA 26. *LAS preserves semantics.*

SAS/DSE/DAE Here we discuss only the simulation relations used by the proofs. SAS removes a **store** to a promotable allocation overwritten by a following memory write. We consider a memory simulation that is the identity when the program counter is outside the SAS pair, but ignores the promotable **alloca** when the program counter is between the pair. Due to Lemma 22 and the fact that there is no **load** between a SAS pair, no temporaries or other memory locations can observe the value stored at the promotable **alloca** between the pair.

Figure 12 pictorially shows the simulation relations between the program states before and after DSE or DAE. Shaded memory blocks contain uninitialized values. The program states on the top are before DSE, where r_2 is a temporary that holds the promotable stack allocation and is not used by any loads. After DSE, the memory values for the promotable allocation may not match the original program's corresponding block. However, values in temporaries and all other memory locations must be unchanged (by Lemma 22). Note that unmatched memory states only occur after the promotable allocation; before the allocation, the two memory states should be the same.

The bottom part of Figure 12 illustrates the relations between programs before and after DAE. After DAE, the correspondence between memory blocks of the two programs is not bijective, due to the removal of the promotable **alloca**. However, there must exist a mapping $\sim$ from the output program's memory blocks to the original program's memory blocks. The simulation requires that all values stored in memory and temporaries (except the promotable allocation) are equal modulo the mapping $\sim$.

ϕ-nodes elimination Consider r = **phi** $typ\ \overline{[val_j, l_j]}^{\,j}$ (an AH ϕ-node) where all the val_j's are either equal to r or some val'. Lemma 21 showed that $f \vdash val' \succ r$. Intuitively, at any pc that both val' and r strictly dominate, the values of val' and r must be the same. Consider the invariant $P_{\text{ah}}(f, r, val')$:

$$\lambda config.\, \lambda S.\, \forall \sigma \in S.\overline{\sigma}.$$
$$f = \sigma.f \wedge [\![r]\!]_{\sigma.\delta} = \lfloor v_1 \rfloor \wedge [\![val']\!]_{\sigma.\delta} = \lfloor v_2 \rfloor \Longrightarrow v_1 = v_2$$

LEMMA 27. $config, P_{\text{ah}}(f, r, val') \vdash S$ *holds for any reachable program state* S.

Lemma 27 establishes that the substitution in ϕ-nodes elimination is correct by using the identity relation. Lemma 20 and Lemma 25 show that removing dead ϕ-nodes is correct.

5.4 The correctness of `vmem2reg`

Our main result, fully verified in Coq, is the composition of the correctness proofs for all the micro program transformations:

THEOREM 28 (vmem2reg is correct). *If* f' = *vmem2reg* f *and* $\vdash prog$, *then* $\vdash prog\{f'/f\}$ *and* $prog \supseteq prog\{f'/f\}$.

6. Pipeline Fusion

In vmem2reg (show in Figure 9), there are two loops of micro pass-pipelinings: `eliminate_stld` and the redundant ϕ-node elimination. This section gives a smarter pipelining vmem2reg-O that "fuses" the micro passes, reducing compilation time. For the sake of space, we present the fused version of `eliminate_stld`; the fused ϕ-node elimination follows similarly (see our Coq development). The design and correctness proofs described here should be applicable to other optimizations besides vmem2reg.

At a high level, Figure 13 gives `eliminate_stld_O`, the fused `eliminate_stld`, which first takes a pass to find all initial eliminations, fuses them, and then takes another pass that eliminates **load**'s and **store**'s in terms of fused eliminations.

We use actions ac to denote micro eliminations:

$$\text{Actions } ac \quad ::= \quad r \mapsto val \mid pc \mapsto \#$$

Here, $r \mapsto val$ denotes LAS (r, pc, val) or LAA r with the default memory value val and $pc \mapsto \#$ denotes SAS (pc, pc'). We use AC to denote a list of actions, and $AC(f)$ to denote a single pass of f that, for each $r \mapsto val$, replaces all uses of r by val, then removes the definition of r and, for each $pc \mapsto \#$, removes the **store** at pc.

To find all initial actions, `eliminate_stld_O` traverses the blocks of a function, uses `find_stld_pairs_block` to find actions for each block, and then concatenates them. At each block, `find_stld_pairs_block` traverses each command (by `find_stld_pairs_cmd`), and uses `stld_state` to keep track of the search state: `ST_INIT` is the initial state; `ST_AL` typ records the element type of the promotable allocation; `ST_ST` pc val records the value stored by the latest **store** at pc to the promotable allocation.

```
let find_stld_pair_cmd r acc c =
  let (st, AC) = acc in
  match c with
  | r0 := alloca typ →
      if r = r0 then (ST_AL typ, AC) else acc
  | pc0 : store typ val1 r2 →
      let st' = ST_ST pc0 val1 in
      if r = r2 then
         match st with
         | ST_ST pc _ → (st', (pc ↦ #, AC))
         | _ →  (st', AC)
         end
      else acc
  | r0 := load (typ *) r1 →
      if r = r1 then
         match st with
         | ST_ST _ val → (st, (r0 ↦ val, AC))
         | ST_AL typ → (st, (r0 ↦ undef typ, AC))
         | _ → acc
         end
      else acc
  | _ → acc
  end
let find_stld_pairs_block r b =
  let (_ _ c̄ _) = b in
  fold_left (find_stld_pair_cmd r) c̄ (ST_INIT, ∅)
let rec fuse_actions AC =
  match AC with
  | ∅ → ∅
  | r ↦ val, AC' →
      let AC'' = fuse_actions AC' in
      let val' = find_parent AC'' val in
      r ↦ val', AC''{val'/r}
  | pc ↦ #, AC' → pc ↦ #, fuse_actions AC'
  end
let eliminate_stld_O r f =
  let fheader{b̄} = f in
  let AC = flat_map (rev (snd
    (find_stld_pairs_block r))) b̄ in
  (fuse_actions AC)(f)
```

Figure 13. **eliminate_stld** of `vmem2reg-O`

`eliminate_stld_O` must fuse the initial actions before transforming f. Let values be vertices, and elements in actions be edges. A list of actions found from a well-formed function forms a forest because SSA ensures acyclicity of def/use chains. `fuse_actions` fuses the forest to be a forest with depth one: each non-root node in a tree of the original forest maps to the root of the tree. In `fuse_actions`, `find_parent` AC val returns the parent of val in the forest formed by AC if val has a parent; otherwise returns val; $AC\{val/r\}$ substitutes r in the codomain of AC by val. Suppose that `eliminate_stld_O` finds a list of actions: $r_4 \mapsto r_3, r_5 \mapsto r_4, r_2 \mapsto r_1, r_3 \mapsto r_2, r_6 \mapsto r_3, []$. `fuse_actions` returns $r_4 \mapsto r_1, r_5 \mapsto r_1, r_2 \mapsto r_1, r_3 \mapsto r_1, r_6 \mapsto r_1, []$.

The interesting part for the correctness of `vmem2reg-O` is showing that the fused pass produces the same output as the pipelined transformations:

LEMMA 29 (`eliminate_stld_O` is correct). *If prog* $\vdash f$*, then* `eliminate_stld` $r\ f$ = `eliminate_stld_O` $r\ f$.

By Lemma 29 and Theorem 30, we have that

THEOREM 30 (`vmem2reg-O` is correct). *If* f' = `vmem2reg-O` f *and* $\vdash$ *prog, then* $\vdash prog\{f'/f\}$ *and* $prog \supseteq prog\{f'/f\}$.

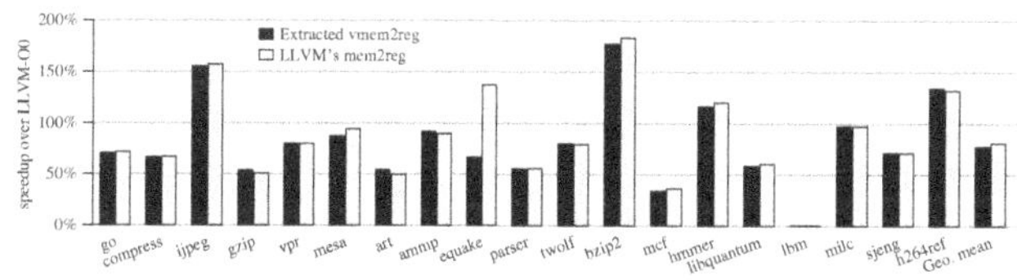

Figure 14. Execution speedup over LLVM `-O0` for both the extracted `vmem2reg` and LLVM's original `mem2reg` pass.

7. Discussion and Evaluation

Coq Development Our Coq development for SSA optimizations consists of approximately 838 lines of algorithm implementations and 50k lines of (not particularly automated) correctness proof scripts and supporting infrastructure. We expect that much of these proofs can be reused for other SSA-based optimizations—that is the reason why we chose the pipeline of micro transformations structure. The development relies on about a dozen axioms, almost all of which define either the initial state of the machine (*i.e.*, where in memory functions and globals are stored) or the behavior of external function calls. One axiom asserts that memory alignment is a power of two, which is not necessary for LLVM programs in general, but is true of almost all real-world platforms.

Extracted* `vmem2reg` *and experimental methodology We used the Coq extraction mechanism to obtain a certified implementation of the `vmem2reg` optimization directly from the Coq sources. `mem2reg` is the first optimization pass applied by LLVM[4], so we tested the efficacy of the extracted implementation on LLVM IR bitcode generated directly from C source code using the clang compiler. At this stage, the LLVM bitcode is unoptimized and in "trivial" SSA form. To prevent the impact of this optimization pass from being masked by subsequent optimizations, we apply either LLVM's `mem2reg` or the extracted `vmem2reg` to the unoptimized LLVM bitcode and then immediately invoke the back-end code generator. We evaluate the performance of the resultant code on a 2.66 GHz Intel Core 2 processor running benchmarks selected from the SPEC CPU benchmark suite that consist of over 336k lines of C source code in total.

Figure 14 reports the execution time speedups (larger is better) over a LLVM's-O0 compilation baseline for various benchmarks. The left bar of each group shows the speedup of the extracted `vmem2reg`, which provides an average speedup of 77% over the baseline. The right bar of each group is the benefit provided by LLVM's `mem2reg`, which provides 81% on average; `vmem2reg` captures much of the benefit of the LLVM's `mem2reg`.

***Comparing* `vmem2reg` *and* `mem2reg`** The `vmem2reg` pass differs from LLVM's `mem2reg` in a few ways. First, `mem2reg` promotes **alloca**s used by LLVM's intrinsics, while `vmem2reg` conservatively considers such **alloca**s to potentially escape, and so does not promote them. We determined that such intrinsics (used by LLVM to annotate the liveness of variable definitions) lead to almost all the difference in performance in the *equake* benchmark. Second, although `vmem2reg` deletes most unused ϕ-nodes, it does not aggressively remove them and, therefore, does not generate fully pruned SSA as `mem2reg` does. However, our results show that this does not impose a significant difference in performance.

Compilation time The focus of this work is *compiler correctness*, not *compilation time*. Although the code generated by `vmem2reg` is comparable to that of `mem2reg`, their compilation times differ, for two reasons. First, the extracted OCaml programs use purely functional data structures that impose $O(\log n)$ overhead compared to the efficient imperative hash tables available in C++. Second, the

[4] All results reported are for LLVM version 3.0.

pessimistic ϕ-node placement algorithm introduces unnecessary ϕ nodes. In our future work, we plan to use the minimal ϕ-node placement algorithm in vmem2reg, whose correctness is (by design) independent of the proofs presented in this paper. Moreover, unlike "all or nothing" translations, vmem2reg maintains the SSA invariants at each pass and can thus be applied incrementally to boost performance. In practice, should compilation time be an issue, it is always possible to use mem2reg for development and vmem2reg to ensure correctness for a final release.

8. Related Work and Conclusions

Verifying the correctness of compiler transformations is an active research area with a sizable amount of literature. We focus here on the work relevant to SSA-based optimizations.

CompCertSSA CompCertSSA [4] improves the CompCert compiler with a verified SSA-based middle-end and a GVN optimization pass. CompCertSSA verified a *translation validator* for an SSA construction algorithm that takes imperative variables to variables in a pruned SSA form. In contrast, our work fully verifies the SSA construction pass vmem2reg for LLVM directly. A bug in the CompCertSSA compiler will cause the validator to abort the compilation, whereas verifying the compiler rules out such a possibility. More pragmatically, translation validation is harder to apply in the context of LLVM, because the compiler infrastructure was not created with verification in mind. For example, the CompCertSSA translations maintain a close mapping between source and target variable names so that simulation can be checked by simple erasure; this is not feasible in the LLVM framework. The CompCertSSA project reports performance measurements of only small benchmarks totaling about 6k lines, whereas we have tested our pass on 336k lines, including larger programs.

Unsurprisingly, the CompCertSSA and Vellvm proofs share some similarities. For example, CompCertSSA's GVN proof uses an invariant similar to the one in our Theorem 8 and Lemma 12. However, the LLVM's strategy of promoting **alloca**s means that our proofs need a combination of both SSA and aliasing properties to prove correctness. Moreover, our proof technique of pipelining "micro" transformations is novel, and should be broadly applicable.

Other related work In less closely related work, Mansky *et al.* designed an Isabelle/HOL framework that uses control-flow graph rewrites to transform programs and uses temporal logic and model-checking to specify and prove the correctness of program transformations [11]. They verified an SSA construction algorithm in the framework. Other researchers have formalized specific SSA-based optimizations by using SSA forms with different styles of semantics: an informal semantics that describes the intuitive idea of the SSA form [7]; an operational semantics based on a matrix representation of ϕ nodes [19]; a data-flow semantics based term graphs using the Isabelle/HOL proof assistant [5]. Matsuno *et al.* defined a type system equivalent to the SSA form and proved that dead code elimination and common subexpression elimination preserve types [12]. There are also conversions between the programs in SSA form and functional programs [2, 8].

Conclusion We have presented a proof technique for formally verifying SSA-based compiler optimizations. Using the Coq proof assistant, we fully mechanized the proof technique and the correctness of several micro optimizations. For the full LLVM IR semantics in Vellvm, we have formalized and implemented an extractable SSA optimization pass vmem2reg that is an easier-to-prove variant of LLVM's mem2reg pass but that delivers most of its benefits.

Acknowledgments We would like to thank Delphine Demange, Vivien Durey, and Dmitri Garbuzov for their comments and suggestions about this work.

References

[1] Static Single Assignment Book, 2012. Working draft available at http://ssabook.gforge.inria.fr/latest/book.pdf.

[2] A. W. Appel. SSA is functional programming. *SIGPLAN Not.*, 33(4): 17–20, April 1998. ISSN 0362-1340.

[3] J. Aycock and N. Horspool. Simple generation of static single assignment form. In *CC*, 2000.

[4] G. Barthe, D. Demange, and D. Pichardie. A formally verified SSA-based middle-end - Static Single Assignment meets CompCert. In *ESOP*, 2012.

[5] J. O. Blech, S. Glesner, J. Leitner, and S. Mülling. Optimizing code generation from SSA form: A comparison between two formal correctness proofs in Isabelle/HOL. *Electron. Notes Theor. Comput. Sci.*, 141(2):33–51, 2005.

[6] *The Coq Proof Assistant Reference Manual (Version 8.3pl1)*. The Coq Development Team, 2011.

[7] R. Cytron, J. Ferrante, B. K. Rosen, M. N. Wegman, and F. K. Zadeck. Efficiently computing static single assignment form and the control dependence graph. *TOPLAS*, 13:451–490, 1991.

[8] R. A. Kelsey. A correspondence between continuation passing style and static single assignment form. In *IR*, number 3, 1995.

[9] X. Leroy. A formally verified compiler back-end. *Journal of Automated Reasoning*, 43(4):363–446, December 2009. ISSN 0168-7433.

[10] *The LLVM Reference Manual (Version 3.0)*. The LLVM Development Team, 2011. http://llvm.org/releases/3.0/docs/LangRef.html.

[11] W. Mansky and E. L. Gunter. A framework for formal verification of compiler optimizations. In *ITP*, 2010.

[12] Y. Matsuno and A. Ohori. A type system equivalent to static single assignment. In *PPDP*, 2006.

[13] V. S. Menon, N. Glew, B. R. Murphy, A. McCreight, T. Shpeisman, A. Adl-Tabatabai, and L. Petersen. A verifiable SSA program representation for aggressive compiler optimization. In *POPL*, 2006.

[14] S. S. Muchnick. *Advanced compiler design and implementation*. Morgan Kaufmann Publishers Inc., San Francisco, CA, USA, 1997. ISBN 1-55860-320-4.

[15] V. C. Sreedhar and G. R. Gao. A linear time algorithm for placing ϕ-nodes. In *POPL*, 1995.

[16] J.-B. Tristan and X. Leroy. Formal verification of translation validators: a case study on instruction scheduling optimizations. In *POPL*, 2008.

[17] J.-B. Tristan and X. Leroy. Verified validation of lazy code motion. In *PLDI*, 2009.

[18] J. B. Tristan and X. Leroy. A simple, verified validator for software pipelining. In *POPL*, 2010.

[19] B. Yakobowski. Étude sémantique d'un langage intermédiaire de type Static Single Assignment. Rapport de dea (Master's thesis), ENS Cachan and INRIA Rocquencourt, Sept. 2004.

[20] X. Yang, Y. Chen, E. Eide, and J. Regehr. Finding and understanding bugs in C compilers. In *PLDI*, 2011.

[21] J. Zhao and S. Zdancewic. Mechanized verification of computing dominators for formalizing compilers. In *CPP*, 2012.

[22] J. Zhao, S. Nagarakatte, M. M. K. Martin, and S. Zdancewic. Formalizing the LLVM intermediate representation for verified program transformations. In *POPL*, 2012.

This research was funded in part by the U.S. Government. The views and conclusions contained in this document are those of the authors and should not be interpreted as representing the official policies, either expressed or implied, of the U.S. Government. This research was funded in part by DARPA contract HR0011-10-9-0008 and ONR award N000141110596. This material is based upon work supported by the National Science Foundation under Grant No. CNS-1116682, CCF-1065166, and CCF-0810947. Any opinions, findings, and conclusions or recommendations expressed in this material are those of the author(s) and do not necessarily reflect the views of the National Science Foundation.

Compiler Testing via a Theory of Sound Optimisations in the C11/C++11 Memory Model

Robin Morisset
ENS & INRIA

Pankaj Pawan
IIT Kanpur & INRIA

Francesco Zappa Nardelli
INRIA

Abstract

Compilers sometimes generate correct sequential code but break the concurrency memory model of the programming language: these subtle compiler bugs are observable only when the miscompiled functions interact with concurrent contexts, making them particularly hard to detect. In this work we design a strategy to reduce the hard problem of hunting concurrency compiler bugs to differential testing of sequential code and build a tool that puts this strategy to work. Our first contribution is a theory of sound optimisations in the C11/C++11 memory model, covering most of the optimisations we have observed in real compilers and validating the claim that common compiler optimisations are sound in the C11/C++11 memory model. Our second contribution is to show how, building on this theory, concurrency compiler bugs can be identified by comparing the memory trace of compiled code against a reference memory trace for the source code. Our tool identified several mistaken write introductions and other unexpected behaviours in the latest release of the gcc compiler.

Categories and Subject Descriptors D3.4 [*Programming Languages*]: Processors – compilers; D2.4 [*Software Engineering*]: Software/Program Verification; F.3.1 [*Specifying and Verifying and Reasoning about Programs*]

Keywords C11/C++11 memory model; compiler testing

1. Random testing for concurrency compiler bugs

The C and C++ languages were originally designed without concurrency support: threads were available via external libraries, yielding unexpected behaviours and misunderstandings between programmers and compiler writers.[1] The recent revision of the C and C++ standards [6] does provide a precise semantics for threads (formalised in [4]): well-synchronised programs must exhibit only sequentially consistent behaviours, racy programs can have any behaviour, and an escape mechanism with a complex semantics, called *low-level atomics*, enables programmers to write high-performance but portable concurrent code. The resulting model is intricate and the interactions with compiler optimisations are not entirely understood. Today's C and C++ compilers, whose optimisers were initially developed in absence of any well-defined memory model, are being extended to support the new concurrency standard. This is a hard task. Past research showed that all production-quality C compilers used to generate incorrect code for accessing volatile variables [10]: the memory model defined by the volatile modifier is trivial compared to the new C11/C++11 model. Correctly supporting the new memory model in today's compilers will be an error-prone enterprise, requiring significant development effort. It is thus vital to investigate techniques to build assurance in widely used implementations of C and C++.

```
#include <stdio.h>
#include <pthread.h>

int g1 = 1; int g2 = 0;

void *th_1(void *p) {
  for (int l = 0; (l != 4); l++) {
    if (g1) return NULL;
    for (g2 = 0; (g2 >= 26); ++g2)
      ;
  }
}

void *th_2(void *p) {
  g2 = 42;
  printf("%d\n",g2);
}

int main() {
  pthread_t th1, th2;
  pthread_create(&th1, NULL, th_1, NULL);
  pthread_create(&th2, NULL, th_2, NULL);
  (void)pthread_join (th1, NULL);
  (void)pthread_join (th2, NULL);
}
```

Figure 1: `foo.c`, a concurrent program miscompiled by `gcc` 4.7.0.

Consider for instance the C program in Figure 1. Can we guess its output? This program spawns two threads executing the functions `th_1` and `th_2` and waits for them to terminate. The two threads share two global memory locations, `g1` and `g2`, but a careful reading of the code reveals that the inner loop of `th_1` is never executed and `g2` is only accessed by the second thread, while `g1` is only accessed by the first thread. According to the C11/C++11 standards this program should always print `42` on the standard output: the two threads do not access the same variable in conflicting

[1] as an example, this recent discussion illustrates the mismatch and tensions between what Linux kernel developers expect from compilers and what `gcc` does: `http://gcc.gnu.org/ml/gcc/2012-02/msg00005.html`.

PLDI'13, June 16–19, 2013, Seattle, Washington, USA.

ways, so the program is *data-race free*, and its semantics is defined as the interleavings of the actions of the two threads.

If we compile the above code with the version 4.7.0 of `gcc` on an x86_64 machine running Linux, and we enable some optimisations with the `-O2` flag (as in `g++ -std=c++11 -lpthread -O2 -S foo.c`) then, sometimes, the compiled code prints `0` to the standard output. This unexpected outcome is caused by a subtle bug in `gcc`'s implementation of the loop invariant code motion (LIM) optimisation. If we inspect the generated assembly we discover that `gcc` saves and restores the content of `g2`, causing `g2` to be overwritten with `0`:

```
th_1:
    movl  g1(%rip), %edx     # load g1 (1) into edx
    movl  g2(%rip), %eax     # load g2 (0) into eax
    testl %edx, %edx         # if g1 != 0
    jne   .L2                #   jump to .L2
    movl  $0, g2(%rip)
    ret
.L2:
    movl  %eax, g2(%rip)     # store eax (0) into g2
    xorl  %eax, %eax         # return 0 (NULL)
    ret
```

This optimisation is sound in a sequential world because the extra store always rewrites the initial value of `g2` and the final state is unchanged. However, as we have seen, this optimisation is unsound in the concurrent context provided by `th_2`, and the C11/C++11 standards forbid it.

How to search for concurrency compiler bugs? We have a *compiler bug* whenever the code generated by a compiler exhibits a behaviour not allowed by the semantics of the source program. Differential random testing has proved successful at hunting compiler bugs. The idea is simple: a test harness generates random, *well-defined*, source programs, compiles them using several compilers, runs the executables, and compares the outputs. The state of the art is represented by the Csmith tool by Yang, Chen, Eide and Regehr [24], which over the last four years has discovered several hundred bugs in widely used compilers, including `gcc` and `clang`. However this work cannot find *concurrency compiler bugs* like the one we described above: despite being miscompiled, the code of `th_1` still has correct behaviour in a sequential setting.

A naive approach to extend differential random testing to concurrency bugs would be to generate *concurrent* random programs, compile them with different compilers, record *all* the possible outcomes of each program, and compare these sets. This works well in some settings, such as the generation and comparison of litmus tests to test hardware memory models; see for instance the work by Alglave et al. [3]. However this approach is unlikely to scale to the complexity of hunting C11/C++11 compiler bugs. Concurrent programs are inherently *non-deterministic* and optimisers can compile away non-determism. In an extreme case, two executables might have disjoint sets of observable behaviours, and yet both be correct with respect to a source C11 or C++11 program. To establish correctness, comparing the final checksum of the different binaries is not enough: we must ensure that all the behaviours of a compiled executable are allowed by the semantics of the source program. The Csmith experience suggests that large program sizes (~80KB) are needed to maximise the chance of hitting corner cases of the optimisers; at the same time they must exhibit subtle interaction patterns (often unexpected, as in the example above) while being well-defined (in particular data-race free). Capturing the set of all the behaviours of such large concurrent programs is tricky as it can depend on rare interactions between threads; computing all the behaviours allowed by the C11/C++11 semantics is even harder.

Despite this, we show that differential random testing can be used successfully for hunting concurrency compiler bugs. First, C and C++ compilers must support separate compilation and the concurrency model allows any function to be spawned as an independent thread. As a consequence compilers must always assume that the *sequential* code they are optimising can be run in an *arbitrary concurrent context*, subject only to the constraint that the whole program is well-defined (race-free on non-atomic accesses, etc.), and can only apply optimisations that are sound with respect to the concurrency model. Second, it is possible to characterise which optimisations are correct in a concurrent setting by observing how they eliminate, reorder, or introduce, memory accesses in the traces of the sequential code with respect to a reference trace. Combined, these two remarks imply that testing the correctness of compilation of concurrent code can be reduced to validating the traces generated by running optimised sequential code against a reference (unoptimised) trace for the same code.

We illustrate this idea with program `foo.c` from Figure 1. Traces only report accesses to global (potentially shared) memory locations: optimisations affecting only the thread-local state cannot induce concurrency compiler bugs. On the left below, the reference trace for `th_1` initialises `g1` and `g2` and loads the value `1` from `g1`:

```
                         Init  g1 1
Init  g1 1               Init  g2 0
Init  g2 0               Load  g1 1
Load  g1 1               Load  g2 0
                         Store g2 0
```

On the right above, the trace of the `gcc -O2` generated code performs an extra load and store to `g2` and, since arbitrary store introduction is provably incorrect in the C11/C++11 concurrency model we can detect that a miscompilation happened. Figure 2 shows another example, of a randomly generated C function together with its reference trace and an optimised trace. In this case it is possible to match the reference trace (on the left) against the optimised trace (on the right) by a series of sound eliminations and reordering of actions.

Contributions This approach to compiler testing crucially relies on a theory of sound optimisations over executions of C11/C++11 programs. Building on the work by Ševčík [17, 19] for an idealised DRF model, our **first contribution** is the study and correctness proof of several criteria for sound optimisations in the C11/C++11 model, covering all the optimisations we observed in testing real compilers (with the exception of irrelevant read introductions and merging of accesses), presented in Section 3. The **second contribution** of this work is a strategy to perform differential testing of compilers against a memory model, reducing the hard problem of hunting concurrency compiler bugs to matching memory traces realised by sequential code. The `cmmtest` tool, which we designed and developed, puts the testing strategy to work building on our theory of C11/C++11 optimisations. These are presented in Section 4. Our **third contribution**, in Section 5, is a report on some concurrency compiler bugs and other unexpected behaviours caught by preliminary testing of `gcc`. The `gcc` developers promptly fixed all the reported bugs and are integrating our soundness criteria with the `gcc` optimiser. We begin in Section 2 by introducing our theory of semantic optimisations and recalling the C11/C++11 memory model and conclude with a discussion of related work. Complete proofs and an evaluation release of `cmmtest` are on the web [1].

2. Program Transformations and the C11/C++11 Memory Model

Compiler optimisations are usually described as program transformations over an intermediate representation of the source code; a typical compiler performs literally hundreds of optimisation passes. Although it is possible to prove the correctness of individual transformations, this presentation does not lend itself to a thorough characterisation of what program transformations are valid.

```
const unsigned int g3 = 0UL;
long long g4 = 0x1;
int g6 = 6L;
unsigned int g5 = 1UL;

void f(){
  int *l8 = &g6;
  int l36 = 0x5E9D070FL;
  unsigned int l107 = 0xAA37C3ACL;
  g4 &= g3;
  g5++;
  int *l102 = &l36;
  for (g6 = 4; g6 < (-3); g6 += 1);
  l102 = &g6;
  *l102 = ((*l8) && (l107 << 7)*(*l102));
}
```

This randomly generated function generates the following traces if compiled with gcc -O0 and gcc -O2.

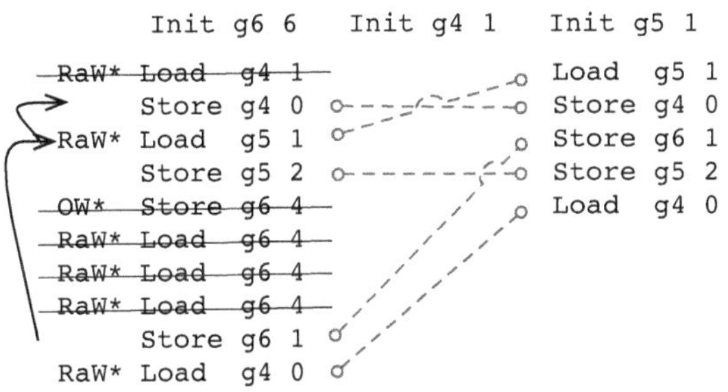

All the events in the optimised trace can be matched with events in the reference trace by performing valid eliminations and reorderings of events. Eliminated events are ~~struck-off~~ while the reorderings are represented by the arrows.

Figure 2: successful matching of reference and optimised traces

In a source program each thread consists of a sequence of *instructions*. During the execution of a program, any given static instruction may be iterated multiple times (for example due to looping) and display many behaviours. For example reads may read from different writes and conditional branches may be taken or not. We refer to each such instance of the dynamic execution of an instruction as an *instruction instance*. More precisely, each instruction instance performs zero, one, or more shared memory accesses, which we call *actions*. We account for all the differing ways a given program can execute by identifying a source program with the set of sets of all the actions (annotated with additional information as described below) it can perform when it executes in an arbitrary context. We call the set of the actions of a particular execution an *opsem* and the set of all the opsems of a program an *opsemset*. For instance, the snippet of code below:

```
x = 1; y = 1; if (x == y){x = 42;}
```

has, among others, the two opsems below:

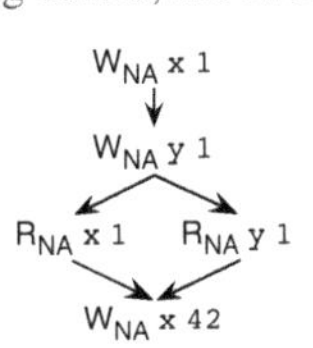

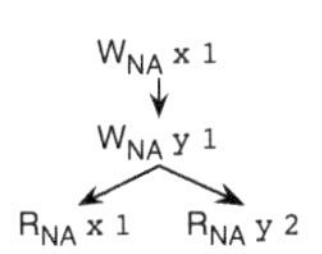

The opsem on the left corresponds to an execution where the reads read the last values written by the thread itself; the opsem on the right accounts for an arbitrary context that concurrently updated the value of y to 2. Nodes represent actions and black arrows show

```
for (i=0; i<2; i++) {              t = y; x = t;
  z = z + y + i;          ⇒       for (i=0; i<2; i++) {
  x = y;                             z = z + t + i;
}                                  }
```

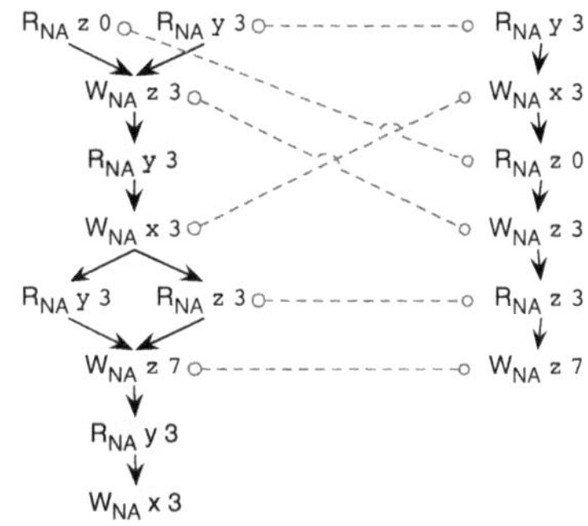

Figure 3: effect of loop invariant code motion (LIM) on an opsem

the *sequenced-before relation*, which orders actions (by the same thread) according to their program order. The sequenced-before relation is not total because the order of evaluation of the arguments of functions, or of the operands of most operators, is underspecified in C and C++. The memory accesses are non-atomic, as denoted by the NA label.

We can then characterise the effect of arbitrary optimisations of source code directly on opsemsets. On a given opsem, the effect of any transformation of the source code is to eliminate, reorder, or introduce actions. If the optimiser performs constant propagation, the previous code is rewritten as:

```
x = 1; y = 1; if (1 == 1){x = 42;}
```

and its unique opsem is depicted here on the right. This opsem can be obtained from the one above on the left by eliminating the two read actions. A more complex example is shown in Figure 3, where the loop on the left is optimised by LIM. The figure shows opsems for the initial state z=0, y=3 assuming that the code is not run in parallel with an interfering context. Here the effect of the LIM optimisation is not only to remove some actions (shaded) but also to reorder the write to x.

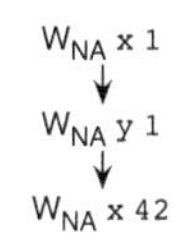

An opsem captures a possible execution of the program, so by applying a transformation to an opsem we are actually optimising one particular execution. Lifting pointwise this definition of *semantic transformations* to opsemsets enables optimising all the execution paths of a program, one at a time, thus abstracting from actual source program transformation.

In the rest of this section we give a high-level overview of the C11/C++11 memory model as formalised by Batty et al. [4], defining opsems, opsemsets and executions, while in the next section we formalise program transformations and prove their correctness.

2.1 Background: overview of the C11/C++11 memory model

Let l range over locations (which are partitioned into non-atomic and atomic), v over values and $tid \in \{1..n\}$ over thread identifiers. We consider the following actions:

$$\mathsf{mem\_ord}, \mu \ ::= \ \mathsf{NA} \mid \mathsf{SC} \mid \mathsf{ACQ} \mid \mathsf{REL} \mid \mathsf{R/A} \mid \mathsf{RLX}$$

$$\phi \ ::= \ \mathsf{R}_\mu\, l\, v \mid \mathsf{W}_\mu\, l\, v \mid \mathsf{Lock}\, l \mid \mathsf{Unlock}\, l \mid \mathsf{Fence}_\mu \mid \mathsf{RMW}_\mu\, l\, v_1\, v_2$$

$$\mathsf{actions} \ ::= \ aid, tid{:}\phi$$

The possible actions are loads from and stores to memory, lock and unlock of a mutex, fences, and read-modify-writes of memory locations. Each action is identified by an action identifier aid (ranged over by $r, w, \ldots$) and specifies its thread identifier tid, the location l it affects, the value read or written v (when applicable), and the memory-order μ (when applicable).[2] In the drawings we omit the action and thread identifiers.

The thread-local semantics identifies a program with a set of *opsems* (ranged over by O): triples $(A, \mathsf{sb}, \mathsf{asw})$ where $A \in \mathcal{P}(\mathsf{actions})$ and $\mathsf{sb}, \mathsf{asw} \subseteq A \times A$ are the *sequenced-before* and *additional-synchronised-with* relations. Sequenced-before (denoted sb) was introduced above; it is transitive and irreflexive and only relates actions by the same thread; *additional-synchronised-with* (denoted asw) contains additional edges from thread creation and thread join, and in particular orders initial writes to memory locations before all other actions in the execution.

The thread-local semantics assumes that all threads run in an arbitrary concurrent context which can update the shared memory at will. This is modelled by reads taking unconstrained values. We say that a set of opsems S is *receptive* if, for every opsem O, for every read action $r, t{:}\mathsf{R}_\mu\, l\, v$ in the opsem O, for all values v' there is an opsem O' in S which only differs from O because the read r returns v' rather than v, and for the actions that are sequenced-after r. Intuitively a set of opsems is receptive if it defines a behaviour for each possible value returned by each read.

We call the set of all the opsems of a program an *opsemset*, ranged over by P. The thread local semantics ensures that opsemsets are receptive. Opsems and opsemsets are subject to several well-formedness conditions, e.g. atomic accesses must access only atomic locations, which we omit here and can be found in [4]. We additionally require opsemsets to be sb-prefix closed, assuming that a program can halt at any time. Formally, we say that an opsem O' is an sb-prefix of an opsem O if there is an injection of the actions of O' into the actions of O that behaves as the identity on actions, preserves sb and asw, and, for each action $x \in O'$, whenever $x \in O$ and $y <_{\mathsf{sb}} x$, it holds that $y \in O'$.

Executions The denotation of each thread in an opsem is agnostic to the behaviour of the other threads of the program: the thread-local semantics takes into account only the structure of every thread's statements, not the semantics of memory operations. In particular, the values of reads are chosen arbitrarily, without regard for writes that have taken place. The memory model filters inconsistent opsems by constructing additional relations and checking the resulting candidate executions against the axioms of the model. For this an *execution witness* (denoted by W) for an opsem specifies an interrelationship between memory actions of different threads via three relations: *reads-from* (rf) relates a write to all the reads that read from it; the *sequential consistent order* (sc) is a total order over all SC actions; and *modification order* (mo) – or *coherence* – is the union of a per-location total order over writes to each atomic location. From these, the model infers the relations *synchronises-with* (denoted sw), which defines synchronisation and is described in detail below, and *happens-before* (denoted hb), showing the precedence of actions in the execution. Key constraints on executions depend on the happens-before relation, in particular a *non-atomic read* must not read any write related to it in hb other than its immediate predecessor. This property is called *consistent non-atomic read values*, and for writes w_1 and w_2 and a read r accessing the same non-atomic location, the following shapes are forbidden:

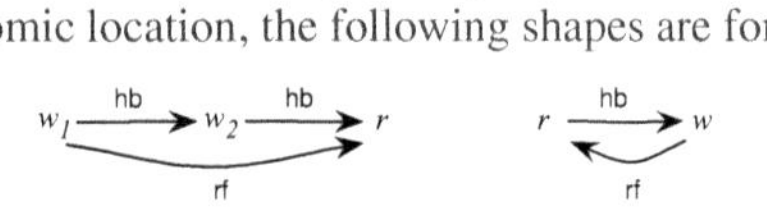

[2] we omit *consume* atomics: their semantics is intricate (e.g. happens-before is not transitive in the full model) and at the time of writing no major compiler profits from the their weaker semantics, treating consume as acquire. By general theorems [5], our results remain valid in the full model.

For atomic accesses the situation is more complex, and atomic reads can read from hb-unrelated writes.

Happens-before is a partial relation defined as the transitive closure of sb, asw and sw: $\mathsf{hb} = (\mathsf{sb} \cup \mathsf{asw} \cup \mathsf{sw})^+$.

We refer to a pair of an opsem and witness (O, W) as a *candidate execution*. A pair (O, W) that satisfies a list of *consistency predicates* on these relations (including consistent non-atomic read values) is called a *pre-execution*. The model finally checks if none of the pre-executions contain an *undefined behaviour*. Undefined behaviours arise from *unsequenced races* (two conflicting accesses performed by the same thread not related by sb), *indeterminate reads* (an access that does not read a written value), or *data races* (two conflicting accesses not related by hb), where two accesses are *conflicting* if they are to the same address and at least one is a non-atomic write. Programs that exhibit an undefined behaviour (e.g. a data-race) in one of their pre-executions are undefined; programs that do not exhibit any undefined behaviour are called *well-defined*, and their semantics is given by the set of their pre-executions.

Synchronisation Synchronisation between threads is captured by the sw relation. The language provides two mechanisms for establishing synchronisation between threads and enabling race-free concurrent programming: *mutex locks* and *low-level atomics*. The semantics of mutexes is intuitive: the sc relation, part of the witness, imposes a total order over all lock and unlock accesses, and a synchronised-with (sw) edge is added between every unlock action, and every lock of the same mutex that follows it in sc-order. Low-level atomics are specific to C/C++ and designed as an escape hatch to implement high-performance racy algorithms. Atomic operations do not race with each other, by definition, and their semantics is specified by a memory-order attribute. *Sequentially consistent* atomics have the strongest semantics: all SC reads and writes are part of the total order sc (acyclic with hb). An SC read can only read from the closest sc-preceding write to the same location. A subtlety of the model is that, although sc and hb must be compatible, sc is not included in hb. Sequentially consistent atomics, as well as release-acquire atomics, generate synchronisation edges, which are included in hb. This is best explained for a classic message-passing idiom. Imagine that one thread writes some (perhaps multi-word) data x and then an atomic flag a, while another waits to see that flag write before reading the data:

```
                    x=0; atomic a=0
x = 1;              || while (0 == a.load(acq)) {};
a.store(1, rel);    || int r = x;
```

The synchronisation between the release and acquire ensures that the sender's write of x will be seen by the receiver. Below we depict a typical opsem for this program; we represent the asw relation with the double horizontal line: the init actions are asw-before all other events. The witness has an rf arrow between the write-release and read-acquire on a to justify that the read returns 1. A read between a write-release and a read-acquire generates an sw edge. Since hb includes sb and sw, the write of 1 to x is the last write in the hb order before the read of the second thread, which is then forced to return 1. *Relaxed atomics* instead do not generate synchronisation edges sw; they are only forbidden to read from the future, i.e. from writes later in hb.

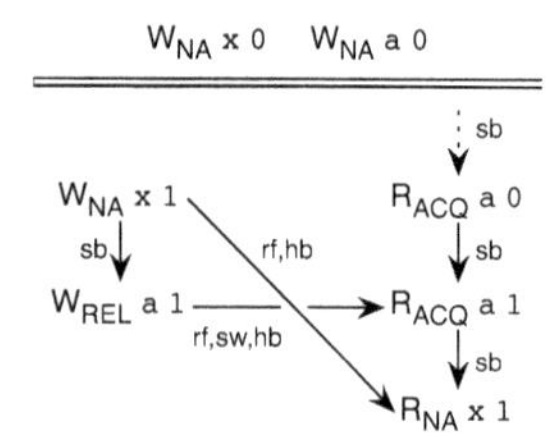

Observable behaviour The C11/C++11 memory model does not explicitly define the *observable behaviour* of an execution. We extend the model with a special atomic location called `world`, and model the observable side-effects of the program (e.g., writes on `stdout`) by relaxed writes to that location. The relaxed attribute guarantees that these accesses are totally ordered with each other, as captured by the mo relation. As a result, the *observable behaviour* of a pre-execution is the restriction of the mo relation to the distinguished `world` location. If none of its pre-executions exhibit an undefined behaviour, then the observable behaviour of a program is the set of all observable behaviours of its executions.

3. Sound Optimisations in the C Memory Model

C and C++ are shared-memory-concurrency languages with explicit thread creation and implicit sharing: any location might be read or written by any thread for which it is reachable from variables in scope. It is the programmer's responsibility to ensure that such accesses are race-free. This implies that compilers can perform optimisations that are not sound for racy programs and common thread-local optimisations can still be done without the compiler needing to determine which accesses might be shared.

Ševčík showed that a large class of elimination and reordering transformations are correct (that is, do not introduce any new behaviour when the optimised code is put in an arbitrary data-race free context) in an idealised DRF model [17, 19]. In this section we adapt and extend his results to optimise non-atomic accesses in the C11/C++11 memory model. As we have discussed, we classify program transformations as *eliminations*, *reorderings*, and *introductions* over opsemsets.

3.1 Eliminations of actions

The semantic elimination transformation is general enough to cover optimisations that eliminate memory accesses based on data-flow analysis, such as common subexpression elimination, induction variable elimination, and global value numbering, including the cases when these are combined with loop unrolling.

We define semantic elimination and discuss informally its soundness criterion; we then state the soundness theorems and briefly describe the proof structure.

Definition 3.1. An action is a *release* if it is an unlock action, an atomic write with memory-order REL or SC, a fence or read-modify-write with memory-order REL, R/A or SC.

Semantically, release actions can be seen as potential sources of sw edges. The intuition is that they "release" permissions to access shared memory to other threads.

Definition 3.2. An action is an *acquire* if it is a lock action, or an atomic read with memory-order ACQ or SC, or a fence or read-modify-write with memory order ACQ, R/A or SC.

Acquire actions can be seen as potential targets of sw edges; the intuition is that they "acquire" permissions to access shared memory from other threads.

To simplify the presentation we omit dynamic thread creation. This is easily taken into account by stating that spawning a thread has release semantics, while the first accesses in sb-order of the spawned function have acquire semantics. Reciprocally, the last actions of a thread have release semantics and a thread-join has acquire semantics.

A key concept is that of a *same-thread release-acquire pair*:

Definition 3.3. A *same-thread release-acquire pair* (shortened *st-release-acquire pair*) is a pair of actions (r, a) such that r is a release, a is an acquire, and $r <_{\mathsf{sb}} a$.

Note that these may be to different locations and never synchronise together. To understand the role they play in optimisation soundness, consider the code on the left, running in the concurrent context on the right:

```
x=0; atomic a1,a2=0
x = 1;                         || while(0==a1.load(acq)) {};
a1.store(1,rel);               || printf("%i",x);
while(0==a2.load(acq)) {};     || a2.store(1,rel);
x = 2;                         ||
```

All executions have similar opsems and witnesses, depicted below (we omitted rf arrows from initialisation writes). No consistent execution has a race and the only observable behaviour is printing `1`.

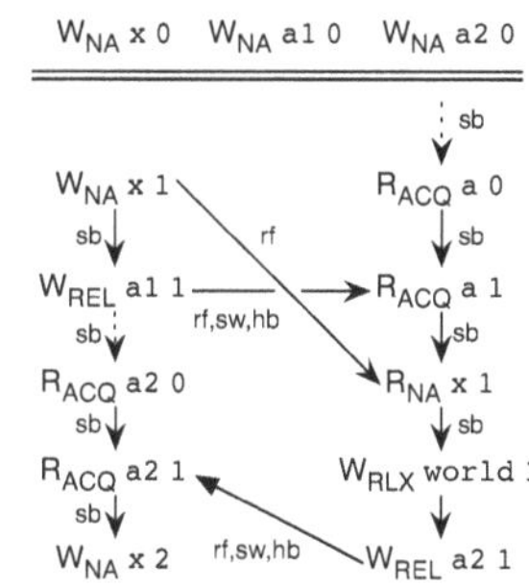

Eliminating the first store to `x` (which might appear redundant as `x` is later overwritten by the same thread) would preserve DRF but would introduce a new behaviour where `0` is printed. However, if either the release or the acquire were not in between the two stores, then this context would be racy (respectively between the load performed by the print and the first store, or between the load and the second store) and it would be correct to optimise away the first write. More generally, the proof of the Theorem 3.1 below clearly shows that the presence of an intervening same-thread release-acquire is a necessary condition to allow a discriminating context to interact with a thread without introducing data races.

Definition 3.4. A read action $a, t{:}\mathsf{R}_{\mathsf{NA}}\, l\, v$ is *eliminable* in an opsem O of the opsemset P if one of the following applies:

Read after Read (RaR): there exists another action $r, t{:}\mathsf{R}_{\mathsf{NA}}\, l\, v$ such that $r <_{\mathsf{sb}} a$, and there does not exist a memory access to location l or a st-release-acquire pair sb-between r and a;

Read after Write (RaW): there exists an action $w, t{:}\mathsf{W}_{\mathsf{NA}}\, l\, v$ such that $w <_{\mathsf{sb}} a$, and there does not exist a memory access to location l or a st-release-acquire pair sb-between w and a;

Irrelevant Read (IR): for all values v' there exists an opsem $O' \in P$ and a bijection f between actions in O and actions in O', such that $f(a) = a', t{:}\mathsf{R}_{\mathsf{NA}}\, l\, v'$, for all actions $u \in O$ different from a, $f(u) = u$, and f preserves sb and asw.

A write action $a, t{:}\mathsf{W}_{\mathsf{NA}}\, l\, v$ is *eliminable* in an opsem O of the opsemset P if one of the following applies:

Write after Read (WaR): there exists an action $r, t{:}\mathsf{R}_l\, v$ such that $r <_{\mathsf{sb}} a$, and there does not exist a memory access to location l or a st-release-acquire pair sb-between r and a;

Overwritten Write (OW): there exists another action $w, t{:}\mathsf{W}_{\mathsf{NA}}\, l\, v'$ such that $a <_{\mathsf{sb}} w$, and there does not exist a memory access to location l or a st-release-acquire pair sb-between a and w;

Write after Write (WaW): there exists another action $w, t{:}\mathsf{W}_{\mathsf{NA}}\, l\, v$ such that $w <_{\mathsf{sb}} a$, and there does not exist a memory access to location l or a st-release-acquire pair sb-between w and a.

Note that the OW rule is the only rule where the value can differ between the action eliminated and the action that justifies the elimination. The IR rule can be rephrased as "a read in an execution is irrelevant if the program admits other executions (one for each value) that only differ for the value returned by the irrelevant read".

Definition 3.5. An opsem O' is an *elimination* of an opsem O if there exists a injection $f : O' \to O$ that preserves actions, sb, and asw, and such that the set $O \backslash f(O')$ contains exactly one eliminable action. The function f is called an *unelimination*.

To simplify the proof of Theorem 3.1 the definition above allows only one elimination at a time (this avoids a critical pair between the rules OW and WaW whenever we have two writes of the same value to the same location), but, as the theorem shows, this definition can be iterated to eliminate several actions from one opsem while retaining soundness. The definition of eliminations lifts pointwise to opsemsets:

Definition 3.6. An opsemset P' is an *elimination* of an opsemset P if for all opsem $O' \in P'$ there exists an opsem $O \in P$ such that O' is an elimination of O.

In the previous section we did not describe all the intricacies of the C11/C++11 model but our theory takes all of them into account. For example, a release fence followed by an atomic write behaves as if the write had the REL attribute, except that the sw edge starts from the fence action. Another example is given by *release sequences*: if an atomic write with attribute `release` is followed immediately in mo-order by one or more `relaxed` writes in the same thread (to the same location), and an atomic load with attribute `acquire` reads-from one of these relaxed stores, an sw edge is created between the write release and the load acquire, analogously to the case where the acquire reads directly from the first write. These subtleties must be taken into account in the elimination correctness proof but do not invalidate the intervening same-thread release-acquire pair criterion. This follows from a property of the C11/C++11 design that makes every sw edge relate a release action to an acquire action. For instance, in the program below it is safe to remove the first write to `x` as OW, because all discriminating contexts will be necessarily racy:

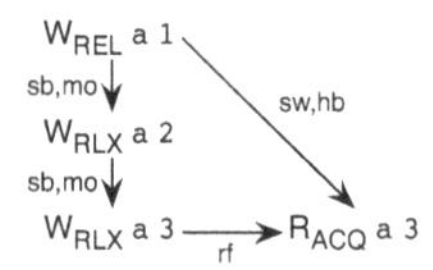


```
a1.store(1,rel);
x = 1;
a1.store(2,rlx);
while(0==a2.load(acq)) {};
x = 2;
```

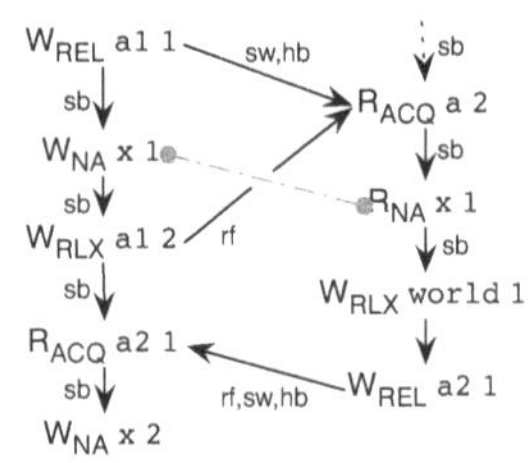

We establish that our semantic transformations have the following properties: any execution of the transformed opsemset has the same observable behaviour of some execution of the original opsemset, and the transformation preserves data-race freedom. As C11 and C++11 do not provide any guarantee for racy programs we cannot prove any result about out-of-thin-air value introduction.

Theorem 3.1. *Let the opsemset P' be an elimination of the opsemset P. If P is well-defined, then so is P', and any execution of P' has the same observable behaviour of some execution of P.*

We sketch the structure of the proof; details can be found online [ ]. Let the opsemset P' be an elimination of the opsemset P, and let (O', W') be an execution of P' (that is, a pair of an opsem and a witness). Since P' is an elimination of P, there is at least one opsem $O \in P$ such that O' is an elimination of O, and an unelimination function f that injects the events of the optimised opsem into the events of the unoptimised opsem. We build the mo and sc relations of the witness of O by lifting the mo$'$ and sc$'$ relations of the witness W': this is always possible because our program transformations do not alter any atomic access. Analogously it is possible to build the rf relation on atomic accesses by lifting the rf$'$ one. To complete the construction of the witness we lift the rf$'$ relation on non-atomic events as well, and complete the rf relation following the case analysis below on the eliminated events in O:

- RaR: if i is a read action eliminated with the RaR rule because of a preceding read action r, and $w <_{\mathsf{rf}} r$, then add $w <_{\mathsf{rf}} i$;
- RaW: if i is a read action eliminated with the RaW rule because of a preceding write action w, then add $w <_{\mathsf{rf}} i$;
- IR: if i is an irrelevant read, and there is a write event to the same location that happens before it, then let w be a write event to the same location maximal with respect to hb and add $w <_{\mathsf{rf}} i$;
- OW: rf is unchanged;
- WaW: if i is a write event eliminated by the WaW rule because of the preceding write event w, then for all actions r such that $w <_{\mathsf{rf}'} r$ and $i <_{\mathsf{hb}} r$, replace $w <_{\mathsf{rf}} r$ by $i <_{\mathsf{rf}} r$;
- WaR: if i is a read event eliminated by the WaR rule, then every read of the same value at the same location, that happens-after i and that either read from a write $w <_{\mathsf{hb}} i$ or does not read from any write, now reads from i.

This completes the construction of the witness W and in turn of the candidate execution (O, W) of P. We must now prove that (O, W) is consistent, in particular that it satisfies *consistent non-atomic read values*, for which the construction has been tailored. This proceeds by a long case disjunction that relies on the following constructions:

- the absence of a release-acquire pair between two accesses a and b in the same thread guarantees the absence of an access c in another thread with $a <_{\mathsf{hb}} c <_{\mathsf{hb}} b$.
- in some cases the candidate execution (O, W) turns out to have conflicting accesses a and b that are not ordered by hb. We use the fact that opsemsets are receptive and closed under sb-prefix to build another candidate pre-execution of P where a and b are still hb-unordered, but for which we can prove it is a pre-execution (not necessarily with the same observable behaviour). From this we deduce that P is not data-race free and ignore these cases.

By construction the pre-execution (O, W) has the same observable behaviour as (O', W'); we conclude by showing that (O', W') can not have undefined behaviours that (O, W) does not have.

3.2 Reorderings of actions

Most compiler optimisations do not limit themselves to eliminating memory accesses, but also reorder some of them. In this category fall all the code motion optimisations. Of course not all accesses are reorderable without introducing new behaviours. In this section we state and prove the correctness of the class of reorderings we have observed being performed by `gcc` and `clang`, ignoring more complex reordering schemes. In particular we omit reorderings across synchronisation actions: neither `gcc` or `clang` perform them and a more complex statement taking into account partial reorderings on prefix-closures of an opsemset would be needed.

Definition 3.7. Two actions a and b are *reorderable* if they access different memory locations and neither is a synchronisation action (that is a lock, unlock, atomic access, rmw, or fence action).

Definition 3.8. An opsem O' is a *reordering* of an opsem O if: (i) the set of actions in O and O' are equal; (ii) O and O' define the same asw; (iii) for all actions $a, b \in O$, if $a <_{\mathsf{sb}} b$ then either $a <_{\mathsf{sb}'} b$ or $b <_{\mathsf{sb}'} a$ and a is reorderable with b.

Like for eliminations, the definition of reorderings lifts pointwise to opsemsets:

Definition 3.9. An opsemset P' is a *reordering* of an opsemset P if for all opsems $O' \in P'$ there exists an opsem $O \in P$ such that O' is a reordering of O.

The soundness theorem for reorderings can be stated analogously to the one for eliminations and, although the details are different, the proofs follow the same structure. In particular the proof shows that, given a witness for an execution of a reordered opsem, it is possible to build the happens-before relation for the witness for the corresponding source opsem by lifting the synchronise-with relation, which is unchanged by the reorderings and relates the same release/acquire events in the two witnesses.

Theorem 3.2. *Let the opsemset P' be a reordering of the opsemset P. If P is well-defined, then so is P', and any execution of P' has the same observable behaviour of some execution of P.*

As the sb relation is partial, reordering instructions in the source code can occasionally introduce sb arrows between reordered actions. For instance, the optimised trace of Figure 3 not only reorders the $\mathsf{W}_{\mathsf{NA}}\,\mathtt{x}\,3$ with the $\mathsf{R}_{\mathsf{NA}}\,\mathtt{z}\,0$ and $\mathsf{W}_{\mathsf{NA}}\,\mathtt{z}\,3$ actions but also introduces an sb arrow between the first two events $\mathsf{R}_{\mathsf{NA}}\,\mathtt{y}\,3$ and $\mathsf{R}_{\mathsf{NA}}\,\mathtt{z}\,0$. Unsurprisingly, adding sb arrows to an opsem reduces the non-determinism of the candidate executions and does not introduce new behaviours on well-defined programs.

Definition 3.10. We say that an opsem O' is a *linearisation* of an opsem O if they contain the same actions and asw relation, and whenever $x <_{\mathsf{sb}} y \in O'$ it holds that $x <_{\mathsf{sb}} y \in O$. This definition lifts pointwise to opsemsets.

Theorem 3.3. *Let the opsemset P' be a linearisation of the opsemset P. If P is well-defined then so is P', and any execution of P' has the same observable behaviour of some execution of P.*

3.3 Introductions of actions

Even if it seems counterintuitive, compilers tend to introduce loads when optimising code (introducing writes is incorrect in DRF models most of the time [7], and always dubious — see the final example in Section 5). Usually the introduced loads are irrelevant, that is their value is never used. This program transformation sounds harmless but it can introduce data races and does not lend itself to a theorem analogous to those for eliminations and reorderings. Worse than that, if combined with DRF-friendly optimisations it can introduce unexpected behaviours [19]. We conjecture that a soundness property can be stated relating the source semantics to the actual hardware behaviour, along the lines of: if an opsem O' is obtained from an opsem O by introducing irrelevant reads, and it is then compiled naively following the standard compilation schemes for a given architecture [15, 23], then all the behaviours observable on the architecture are allowed by the original opsem. In some cases the introduced loads are not irrelevant, but are RaR-eliminable or RaW-eliminable. We proved that RaR-eliminable and RaW-eliminable introductions preserve DRF and do not introduce new behaviours under the hypothesis that there is no *release* action in sb order between the introduced read and the action that justifies it. Details are available online [1].

4. Compiler Testing

Building on the theory of the previous section, we designed and implemented a bug-hunting tool called `cmmtest`. The tool performs random testing of C and C++ compilers, implementing a variant of Eide and Regehr's *access summary testing* [10]. A test case is any well-defined, sequential C program; for each test case, `cmmtest`:

1. compiles the program using the compiler and compiler optimisations that are being tested;
2. runs the compiled program in an instrumented execution environment that logs all memory accesses to global variables and synchronisations;
3. compares the recorded trace with a reference trace for the same program, checking if the recorded trace can be obtained from the reference trace by valid eliminations, reorderings and introductions.

Test-case generation We rely on a small extension of Csmith [24] to generate random programs that cover a large subset of C while avoiding undefined and unspecified behaviours. We added mutex variables (as defined in `pthread.h`) and system calls to `pthread_mutex_lock` and `pthread_mutex_unlock`. Enforcing balancing of calls to lock and unlock along all possible execution paths of the generated test-cases is difficult, so mutex variables are declared with the attribute `PTHREAD_MUTEX_RECURSIVE`. We also added atomic variables and atomic accesses to atomic variables, labelled with a memory order attribute. For atomic variables we support both the C and the C++ syntax, the former not yet being widely supported by today's compilers. Due to limitations of our tracing infrastructure, for now we instruct Csmith to not generate programs with unions or consts.

Compilation Compilation is straightforward provided that the compiler does not attempt to perform whole-program optimisations. With whole-program optimisation, the compiler can deduce that some functions will never run in a concurrent context and perform more aggressive optimisations, such as eliminating all memory accesses after the last I/O or synchronisation. It is very hard to determine precise conditions under which these aggressive whole-program optimisations remain sound; for instance Ševčík's criteria are overly conservative and result in false positives when testing Intel's `icc -O3`. Neither `gcc` nor `clang` perform whole-program optimisations at the typical optimisation levels `-O2` or `-O3`.

Test case execution and tracing The goal of this phase is to record an execution trace for the compiled object file, that is the linearly-ordered sets of actions it performs. For the x86_64 architecture we implemented a tracing framework by binary instrumentation using the Pin tool [13]. Our Pin application intercepts all memory reads and writes performed by the program and for each records the address accessed, the value read or written, and the size. In addition it also traces calls to `pthread_mutex_lock` and `pthread_mutex_unlock`, recording the address of the mutex. With the exception of access size information, entries in the execution trace correspond to the actions of Section 2. Access size information is needed to analyse optimisations that merge adjacent accesses, discussed below.

The "raw" trace depends on the actual addresses where the global variables have been allocated, which is impractical for our purposes. The trace is thus processed with additional informations obtained from the ELF object file (directly via `objdump` or by parsing the debugging informations). The addresses of the accesses are mapped to variable names and similarly for values that refer to addresses of variables; in doing so we also recover array and struct access information. For example, if the global variable `int g[10]` is allocated at `0x1000`, the raw action `Store 0x1008 0x1004 4` is mapped to the action `Store g[2] &g[1] 4`. After this analysis execution traces are independent of the actual allocation addresses of the global variables. Finally, information about the initialisation of the global variables is added to the trace with the `Init` tag.

Irrelevant reads The Pin application also computes some data-flow information about the execution, recording all the store actions which *depend* on each read. This is done by tracking the flow of each read value across registers and thread-local memory. A dependency is reported if either the value read is used to compute the value written or used to determine the control that leads to a later write or synchronisation. With this information we reconstruct an approximation of the set of *irrelevant reads* of the execution: all reads whose returned value is never used to perform a write (or synchronisation) are labelled as irrelevant.

In addition, we use a second algorithm to identify irrelevant reads following their characterisation on the opsems: the program is replayed and its trace recorded again but binary instrumentation injects a different value for the read action being tested. The read is irrelevant if, despite the different value read, the rest of the trace is unchanged. This approach is slower but accurately identifies irrelevant reads inserted by the optimiser (for instance when reorganising chains of conditions on global variables).

Reference trace In the absence of a reference interpreter for C11, we reuse our tracing infrastructure to generate a trace of the program compiled at `-O0` and use this as the reference trace. By doing so our tool might miss potential front-end concurrency bugs but there is no obvious alternative.

Trace matching Trace matching is performed in two phases. Initially, eliminable actions in the reference trace are identified and labelled as such. The labelling algorithm linearly scans the trace, recording the last action performed at any location and whether release/acquire actions have been encountered since; using this information each action is analysed and labelled following the definition of eliminable actions of Section 3.1. Irrelevant reads reported by the tracing infrastructure are labelled as such. To get an intuition for the occurrences of eliminable actions in program traces, out of 200 functions generated by Csmith with `-expr_complexity 3`, the average trace has 384 actions (max 15511) of which 280 (max 14096) are eliminable, distributed as follows:

IR	RaW	RaR	OW	WaR	WaW
8 (94)	94 (1965)	95 (10340)	75 (1232)	5 (305)	1 (310)

Additional complexity in labelling eliminable actions is due to the fact that a compiler performs many passes over the program and some actions may become eliminable only once other actions have been eliminated. Consider for instance this sequence of optimisations from the example in Figure 2:

```
Store g6 4
Load  g6 4        RaW    Store g6 4     OW
Load  g6 4       ---->   Store g6 1    ---->   Store g6 1
Load  g6 4
Store g6 1
```

In the original trace, the first store cannot be labelled as OW due to the intervening loads. However, if the optimiser first removes these loads (which is correct since they are RaW), it can subsequently remove the first store (which becomes an OW). Our analysis thus keeps track of the critical pairs between eliminations and can label actions eliminable under the assumption that other actions are themselves eliminated. Irrelevant and eliminable reads are also labelled in the optimised trace, to account for potential introductions.

Before describing the matching algorithm, we must account for one extra optimisation family we omitted in the previous section: *merging of adjacent accesses*. Consider the following loop updating the global array `char g[10]`:

```
for (int l=0; l<10; l++) g[l] = 1;
```

The reference trace performs ten writes of one byte to the array `g`. The object code generated by `gcc -O3` performs only two memory accesses: `Store g 101010101010101 8` and `Store g[8] 101 2`. This optimisation is sound under hypothesis similar to those of eliminations: there must not be intervined accesses or release/acquire pairs between the merged accesses; additionally the size of the merged access must be a power of two and the merged store must be aligned. Since the C11/C++11 memory model, as formalised by Batty et al., is agnostic to the size of accesses, we could not formally prove the soundness of this optimisation.

The matching algorithm takes two annotated traces and scans them linearly, comparing one annotated action of the reference trace and one of the optimised trace at a time. It performs a depth-first search exploring at each step the following options:

- if the reference and optimised actions are equal, then consider them as matched and move to the next actions in the traces;
- if the reference action is eliminable, delete it from the reference trace and match the next reference action; similarly if the optimised action is eliminable;
- if the reference action merges with later reference actions to match the the optimised action, then consider the merged actions as matched and move to the next actions in the traces; and
- if the optimised action can be matched by reordering actions in the reference trace, reorder the reference trace and match again.

The algorithm succeeds if it reaches a state where all the actions in the two input traces are either deleted or matched.

Some of these options are very expensive to explore (for instance when combinations of reordering, merging and eliminations must be considered), and we guide the depth-first search with a critical heuristic to decide the order in which the tree must be explored. The heuristic is dependent on the compiler being tested. The current implementation can match in a few minutes `gcc` traces of up to a few hundreds of actions on commodity hardware; these traces are well beyond manual analysis.

Outcome During tracing, `cmmtest` records one "execution" of a C or C++ program; using the terminology of the previous section, it should observe a witness for an opsem of the program. Since `cmmtest` traces sequential deterministic code in an empty concurrent environment, all reads of the opsem always return the last (in sb order) value written by the same thread to the same location. The witness is thus trivial: reads-from derives from sb while mo and sc are both included in sb. Note that the tool traces an execution of the generated assembler and as such it records a linearisation of the opsem's sb. Theorem 3.3 guarantees that this cannot introduce false positives due to extra sb arrows added between non-atomic accesses. Overestimating the sb relation between atomic accesses might induce false positives because `cmmtest` cannot reconstruct the original sb relation and considers all atomic accesses as unreorderable. To prevent this our version of Csmith never generates programs with atomic accesses not related by sb.

The `cmmtest` tool compares two opsems and returns true if the optimised opsem can be obtained from the reference opsem by a sequence of sound eliminations/reorderings/introductions, and false otherwise. If `cmmtest` returns *true* then we deduce that this opsem (that is, this execution path of the program) has been compiled correctly, even if we cannot conclude that the whole program has been compiled correctly (which would require exploring all the opsems of the opsemset, or, equivalently, all the execution paths of the program). More interestingly, whenever `cmmtest` returns *false*, then either the code has been miscompiled, or an exotic optimisation has been applied (since our theory of sound optimisations is not complete). In this case we perform test-case reduction using CReduce [16], and manually inspect the assembler. Reduced test-cases have short traces (typically less than 20 events) and it is immediate to build discriminating contexts and produce bug-reports. Currently the tool reports no false positives for `gcc` on any of the many thousands of test-cases we have tried without structs and atomics; we are getting closer to a similar result for arbitrary programs (with the restriction of a single atomic access per expression).

Stability against the HW memory model Compiled programs are executed on shared-memory multiprocessors which may expose behaviours that arise from hardware optimisations. Reference mappings of atomics instructions to x86 and ARM/POWER architectures have been proved correct [4, 5]: these mappings insert all the necessary assembly synchronisation instructions to prevent hardware optimisations from breaking the C11/C++11 semantics. On x86_64, `cmmtest` additionally traces memory fences and locked instructions, and under the hypothesis that the reference trace is obtained by applying a correct mapping (e.g., by putting fence instructions after all SCatomic writes), then `cmmtest` additionally ensures that the optimiser does not make hardware behaviours observable (for instance by moving a write after a fence).

5. Impact on compiler development

Concurrency compiler bugs While developing `cmmtest` and tuning the matching heuristic, we tested the latest svn version of the 4.7 and 4.8 branches of the `gcc` compiler. During these months we reported several concurrency bugs (including bugs no. 52558, 54149, 54900, and 54906 in the `gcc` bugzilla), which have all been promptly fixed by the `gcc` developers. In one case the bug report highlights an obscure corner case of the `gcc` optimiser, as shown by a discussion on the `gcc-patches` mailing list;[3] even though the reported test-case has been fixed, the bug has been left open until a general solution is found. In all cases the bugs were wrongly introduced writes, speculated by the LIM or IFCVT (if-conversion) phases, similar to the example in Figure 1. These bugs do not only break the C11/C++11 memory model, but also the Posix DRF-guarantee which is assumed by most concurrent software written in C and C++. The corresponding patches are activated via the `---param allow-store-data-races=0` flag, which will eventually become default standard for `-std=c11` or `-std=c++11` flags. All these are *silent wrong-code bugs* for which the compiler issues no warning.

Unexpected behaviours Each compiler has its own set of internal invariants. If we tune the matching algorithm of `cmmtest` to check for compiler invariants rather than for the most permissive sound optimisations, it is possible to catch unexpected compiler behaviours. For instance, in the current phase of development, `gcc` forbids all reorderings of a memory access with an atomic one. We baked this invariant into `cmmtest` and in less than two hours of testing on an 8-core machine we found the following testcase:

```
atomic_uint a; int32_t g1, g2;
int main (int, char *[]) {
  a.load () & a.load ();
  g2 = g1 != 0;
}
```

whose traces for the function `main` compiled with `gcc 4.8.0 20120627 (experimental)` at optimisation levels `-O0` and `-O2` (or `-O3`) are:

```
ALoad  a  0 4  o-.          .-o  Load   g1 0 4
ALoad  a  0 4  o-.\        /.-o  ALoad  a  0 4
Load   g1 0 4  o-' \------/ '-o  ALoad  a  0 4
Store  g2 0 4  o--------------o  Store  g2 0 4
```

As we can observe, the optimiser moved the load of `g1` before the two atomic SC loads. Even though we conjecture that this reordering is not observable by a non-racy context, this unexpected compiler behaviour was fixed nevertheless (`rr190941`).

Interestingly, `cmmtest` found one unexpected compiler behaviour whose legitimacy is arguable. Consider the program below:

```
atomic_int a; uint16_t g;
void func_1 () {
  for (; a.load () <= 0; a.store (a.load () + 1))
    for (; g; g--);
}
```

Traces for the `func_1` function, compiled with `gcc 4.8.0 20120911 (experimental)` at optimisation levels `-O0` and `-O2` (or `-O3`), are:

```
ALoad  a 0 4   o-------?-------o   ALoad  a 0 4
Load   g 0 2   )---------------(   Store  g 0 2
ALoad  a 0 4   o---------------o   ALoad  a 0 4
AStore a 0 4   o---------------o   AStore a 0 4
ALoad  a 1 4   o---------------o   ALoad  a 1 4
```

[3] http://gcc.gnu.org/ml/gcc-patches/2012-10/msg01411.html

The optimiser here replaced the inner loop with a single write:

```
for (; g; g--);        ⟶       g = 0;
```

thus substituting a read access with a write access in the execution path where `g` already contains `0`. The introduced store is *idempotent*, as it rewrites the value that is already stored in memory. Since in the unoptimised trace there is already a load at the same location, this extra write cannot be observed by a non-racy context. Strictly speaking, this is not a compiler bug. However, whether this should be allowed or not is subject to debate. Although we believe no architecture can detect this introduced write, in a world with hardware or software race detection it might fire a false positive. Also, possibly a bigger issue, the introduced write can introduce cache contention where there should not be any, potentially resulting in an unexpected performance loss.

6. Related work

Randomised techniques for testing compilers have been popular since the 60's and have been applied to a variety of languages, ranging from Cobol [22] and Fortran [9] to C [12, 14, 21] and C++ [25]. A survey (up to 1997) can be found in Boujarwah and Saleh [8], while today the state of art is represented by Yang et al.'s work on Csmith [24]. None of these works addresses concurrency compiler bugs and the techniques presented are unable to detect any of our bug reports.

The notable exception is Eide and Regehr's work [10] on hunting miscompilation of the `volatile` qualifier in production-quality C compilers. Eide and Regehr generate random well-defined *deterministic, sequential* programs with volatile memory accesses: miscompilations are detected by counting how many accesses to volatile variables are performed during the execution of an unoptimised and an optimised binary of the program. The semantics of the volatile attribute requires that accesses to volatile variables are never optimised away, so comparing the number of runtime accesses is enough to detect bugs in the optimiser. We were inspired by Eide and Regehr's approach to reduce hunting concurrency compilation bugs to analysis to differential testing of sequential code, but the complexity of the C11/C+11 memory model requires us to build a theory of sound optimisations and makes the analysis phase far more complicated.

As we discussed in Section 3, soundness of optimisations in an idealised DRF model was studied by Ševčík [17, 19]. We reuse Ševčík's classification of optimisations as eliminations, reorderings and introductions, but moving from an idealised DRF model to the full C11/C++11 memory model brings new challenges:

- we cannot identify a program with the set of linear orders of actions it can realise because in C and C++ the sequenced-before order is not total; although reasoning about opsems seems unintuitive, partial orders turn out be be easier to work with than the explicit manipulation of trace indices that Ševčík performs;
- the semantics of low-level atomic accesses and fences must be taken into account when computing synchronisations; in particular the weaker consistency and coherency conditions of the release/acquire/relaxed attributes made the soundness proof much more complex.

There are other minor differences, for instance Ševčík assumes that every variable has a default value, while C/C++ forbids accessing an uninitialised variable. Initially Ševčík gave a more restrictive condition for soundness of eliminations [17], namely eliminations are forbidden if there is an intervening release *or* acquire operation rather than a release/acquire pair. This simpler condition appears to be too strong as we have observed compilers eliminate accesses across a release or acquire access. All our analysis was driven by what optimisations we could actually observe: this led to identifying WaW eliminations and RaR/RaW introductions, and motivated us to omit roach-motel reorderings.

More generally, reasoning about the C11/C++11 memory model is in its infancy. We follow the formalisation of the C11/C++11 memory model given in [4]; the original presentation of the model design [7] mentions (Sec. 2.1) that the soundness of reorderings under some conditions follows from previous work [2], with no mention of eliminations or introductions. Although the C11/C++11 model is based on the DRF design, we do believe that its complexity deserves careful proofs taking into account its whole design.

There is a long tradition of research on compiler optimisations that preserve sequential consistency dating back to Shasha and Snir [20], mostly focusing on whole program analyses. While these works show that a restricted class of optimisations can maintain the illusion of sequential consistency for all programs, we show that common compiler transformations maintain the illusion of sequential consistency for correctly synchronised programs.

7. Conclusion

This paper validates the belief that common compiler optimisations are sound in C11/C++11 memory model, contrary to the situation for the Java Memory Model [18]. With the exception of optimisations that change the size of memory accesses (which cannot be expressed in the current formalisation of the memory model) and irrelevant read introduction (which does not preserve DRF), we proved correct all the classes of optimisations performed by widely used optimising compilers (under the hypothesis that a program can halt at any time). We presented a general strategy to perform differential testing of real compilers against memory models, and designed and implemented a bug-hunting tool, `cmmtest`, building on our theory of optimisations in the C11/C++11 memory model. Subtle concurrency bugs and unexpected behaviours of the latest `gcc` optimiser have been discovered using `cmmtest`. None of these could have been found using the existing compiler testing methods.

Future work Bug-hunting via random testing is a slow process: each reported bug must be fixed before continuing testing, otherwise with high probability the tool keeps on rediscovering the same bug. Our priority now is to complete the tracing infrastructure to support all the features of the C language, most notably bit-fields, and to put `cmmtest` to work conducting extensive testing of `gcc` and `clang`. Since our testing strategy considers the compiler as a black box, it is easy to extend the tool to test other compilers. A preliminary trial run with `clang` suggests that only minor changes to the matching heuristic are required; contrary to `gcc`, `clang` systematically reorders accesses around relaxed atomic accesses and performs simultaneous merge and reorder of memory actions. Although this article focuses on the x86_64 architecture and x86_64 compiler backends, only the tracer module (and IR data-flow analysis) of the tool are dependent on the binary architecture. Building on Fox's ARM emulator [11], we are implementing a tracing infrastructure for ARMv7 binaries that will allow testing the ARM backends of compilers. By instrumenting an executable semantics for the LLVM IR (e.g., [26]), it would even be possible to run our analysis internally within the LLVM optimisers, comparing the traces before and after each optimisation pass.

Last but not least, the `gcc` developers expressed a keen interest in adopting our `cmmtest` tool as part of their testing infrastructure.

Acknowledgments We are grateful to Jaroslav Ševčík, Kayvan Memarian, and Peter Sewell for enlightening discussions, to John Regehr and Xuejun Yang for help with Csmith, to Aldy Hernandez, Andrew MacLeod and Torvald Riegel for promptly addressing our bug-reports. This work was partially supported by IRILL and ANR grant WMC (ANR-11-JS02-011).

References

[1] The `cmmtest` tool. http://www.di.ens.fr/~zappa/projects/cmmtest/.

[2] S. V. Adve and M. D. Hill. Weak ordering - a new definition. In *ISCA*, 1990.

[3] J. Alglave, L. Maranget, S. Sarkar, and P. Sewell. Litmus: Running tests against hardware. In *TACAS*, 2011.

[4] M. Batty, S. Owens, S. Sarkar, P. Sewell, and T. Weber. Mathematizing C++ concurrency. In *POPL*, 2011.

[5] M. Batty, K. Memarian, S. Owens, S. Sarkar, and P. Sewell. Clarifying and compiling C/C++ concurrency: from C++11 to POWER. In *POPL*, 2012.

[6] P. Becker. *Standard for Programming Language C++ - ISO/IEC 14882*, 2011.

[7] H.-J. Boehm and S. V. Adve. Foundations of the C++ concurrency memory model. In *PLDI*, 2008.

[8] A. S. Boujarwah and K. Saleh. Compiler test case generation methods: a survey and assessment. *Information & Software Technology*, 39(9): 617–625, 1997.

[9] C. J. Burgess and M. Saidi. The automatic generation of test cases for optimizing fortran compilers. *Information & Software Technology*, 38 (2):111–119, 1996.

[10] E. Eide and J. Regehr. Volatiles are miscompiled and what to do about it. *EMSOFT*, 2008.

[11] A. C. J. Fox and M. O. Myreen. A trustworthy monadic formalization of the ARMv7 instruction set architecture. In *ITP*, 2010.

[12] C. Lindig. Random testing of C calling conventions. In *AADEBUG*, 2005.

[13] C.-K. Luk, R. Cohn, R. Muth, H. Patil, A. Klauser, G. Lowney, S. Wallace, V. J. Reddi, and K. Hazelwood. Pin: building customized program analysis tools with dynamic instrumentation. In *PLDI*, 2005.

[14] W. M. McKeeman. Differential testing for software. *Digital Technical Journal*, 10(1):100–107, 1998.

[15] P. E. McKenney and R. Silvera, 2011. http://www.rdrop.com/users/paulmck/scalability/!paper/N2745r.2011.03.04a.html.

[16] J. Regehr, Y. Chen, P. Cuoq, E. Eide, C. Ellison, and X. Yang. Test-case reduction for C compiler bugs. In *PLDI*, 2012.

[17] J. Ševčík. *Program Transformations in Weak Memory Models*. PhD thesis, University of Edinburgh, 2008.

[18] J. Ševčík. The Sun Hotspot JVM does not conform with the Java memory model. Technical Report EDI-INF-RR-1252, School of Informatics, University of Edinburgh, 2008.

[19] J. Ševčík. Safe optimisations for shared-memory concurrent programs. In *PLDI*, 2011.

[20] D. Shasha and M. Snir. Efficient and correct execution of parallel programs that share memory. *ACM Transactions on Programming Languages and Systems*, 10(2), 1988.

[21] F. Sheridan. Practical testing of a C99 compiler using output comparison. *Software: Practice and Experience*, 37(14):1475–1488, 2007.

[22] R. L. Solder. A general test data generator for COBOL. In *AFIPS Joint Computer Conferences*, 1962.

[23] A. Terekhov. Brief tentative example x86 implementation for C/C++ memory model, 2008. http://www.decadent.org.uk/pipermail/~cpp-threads/2008-December/001933.html.

[24] X. Yang, Y. Chen, E. Eide, and J. Regehr. Finding and understanding bugs in C compilers. In *PLDI*, 2011.

[25] C. Zhao, Y. Xue, Q. Tao, L. Guo, and Z. Wang. Automated test program generation for an industrial optimizing compiler. In *AST*, 2009.

[26] J. Zhao, S. Nagarakatte, M. M. K. Martin, and S. Zdancewic. Formalizing the LLVM intermediate representation for verified program transformations. In *POPL*, 2012.

Taming Compiler Fuzzers

Yang Chen Alex Groce† Chaoqiang Zhang† Weng-Keen Wong†
Xiaoli Fern† Eric Eide John Regehr

University of Utah
Salt Lake City, UT

†Oregon State University
Corvallis, OR

chenyang@cs.utah.edu agroce@gmail.com zhangch@onid.orst.edu wong@eecs.oregonstate.edu
xfern@eecs.oregonstate.edu eeide@cs.utah.edu regehr@cs.utah.edu

Abstract

Aggressive random testing tools ("fuzzers") are impressively effective at finding compiler bugs. For example, a single test-case generator has resulted in more than 1,700 bugs reported for a single JavaScript engine. However, fuzzers can be frustrating to use: they indiscriminately and repeatedly find bugs that may not be severe enough to fix right away. Currently, users filter out undesirable test cases using ad hoc methods such as disallowing problematic features in tests and grepping test results. This paper formulates and addresses the *fuzzer taming problem*: given a potentially large number of random test cases that trigger failures, order them such that diverse, interesting test cases are highly ranked. Our evaluation shows our ability to solve the fuzzer taming problem for 3,799 test cases triggering 46 bugs in a C compiler and 2,603 test cases triggering 28 bugs in a JavaScript engine.

Categories and Subject Descriptors D.2.5 [*Software Engineering*]: Testing and Debugging—testing tools; D.3.4 [*Programming Languages*]: Processors—compilers; H.3.3 [*Information Storage and Retrieval*]: Information Search and Retrieval—selection process

Keywords compiler testing; compiler defect; automated testing; fuzz testing; random testing; bug reporting; test-case reduction

1. Introduction

Modern optimizing compilers and programming language runtimes are complex artifacts, and their developers can be under significant pressure to add features and improve performance. When difficult algorithms and data structures are tuned for speed, internal modularity suffers and invariants become extremely complex. These and other factors make it hard to avoid bugs. At the same time, compilers and runtimes end up as part of the trusted computing base for many systems. A code-generation error in a compiler for a critical embedded system, or an exploitable vulnerability in a widely deployed scripting language runtime, is a serious matter.

Random testing, or fuzzing, has emerged as an important tool for finding bugs in compilers and runtimes. For example, a single fuzzing tool, `jsfunfuzz` [31], is responsible for identifying more than 1,700 previously unknown bugs in SpiderMonkey, the JavaScript engine used in Firefox [32]. LangFuzz [14], a newer randomized testing tool, has led to the discovery of more than 500 previously unknown bugs in the same JavaScript engine. Google's proprietary ClusterFuzz effort "hammers away at it [Chrome, including its V8 JavaScript engine] to the tune of around fifty-million test cases a day," with apparent success [2]: "ClusterFuzz has detected 95 unique vulnerabilities since we brought it fully online at the end of last year [a four-month period]." For C compilers, Csmith [44] has identified more than 450 previously unknown bugs.

While fuzzers are powerful bug-finding tools, their use suffers from several drawbacks. The first problem is that failures due to random test cases can be difficult to debug. This has been largely solved by Delta Debugging [45], an automated greedy search for small failure-inducing test cases. In fact, there is some evidence that debugging based on short random test cases is easier than debugging based on human-created test cases [3]. A second problem is the sheer volume of output: an overnight run of a fuzzer may result in hundreds or thousands of failure-inducing test cases. Moreover, some bugs tend to be triggered much more often than others, creating needle-in-a-haystack problems. Figure 1 shows that some of the bugs studied in this paper were triggered thousands of times more frequently than others. Compiler engineers are an expensive and limited resource, and it can be hard for them to find time to sift through a large collection of highly redundant bug-triggering test cases. A third problem is that fuzzers are indiscriminate: they tend to keep finding more and more test cases that trigger noncritical bugs that may also already be known. Although it would be desirable to fix these bugs, the realities of software development—where resources are limited and deadlines may be inflexible—often cause low-priority bugs to linger unfixed for months or years. For example, in November 2012 we found 2,403 open bugs in GCC's bug database, considering priorities P1, P2, and P3, and considering only bugs of "normal" or higher severity. The median-aged bug in this list was well over two years old. If a fuzzer manages to trigger any appreciable fraction of these old, known bugs, its raw output will be very hard to use.

A typical workflow for using a random tester is to (1) start running the random tester against the latest version of the compiler; (2) go to bed; and (3) in the morning, sift through the new failure-inducing test cases, creating a bug report for each that is novel and important. Step 3 can be time-consuming and unrewarding. We know of several industrial compiler developers who stopped using Csmith not because it stopped finding bugs, but because step 3 became uneconomical. This paper represents our attempt to provide fuzzer users with a better value proposition.

Thus far, little research has addressed the problem of making fuzzer output more useful to developers. In a blog entry, Ruderman,

PLDI'13, June 16–19, 2013, Seattle, WA, USA.

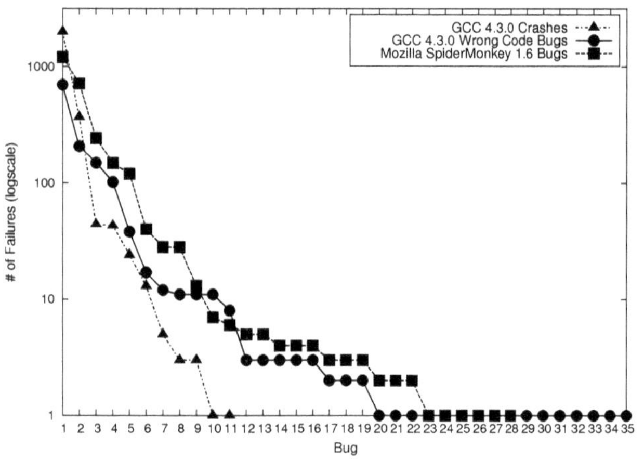

Figure 1. A fuzzer tends to hit some bugs thousands of times more frequently than others

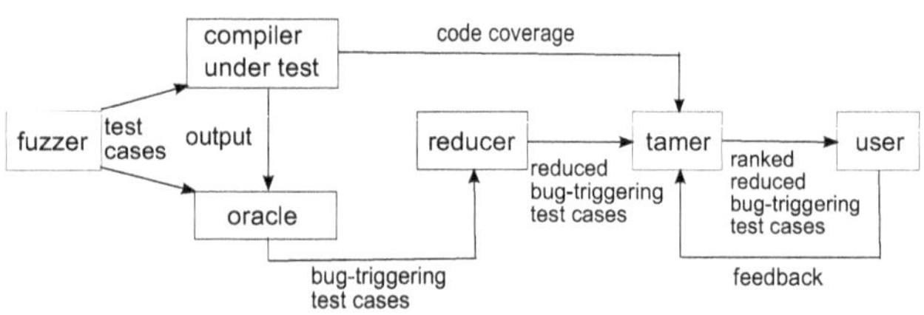

Figure 2. Workflow for a fuzzer tamer

the original author of the `jsfunfuzz` tool, reports using a variety of heuristics to avoid looking at test cases that trigger known bugs, such as turning off features in the test-case generator and using tools like `grep` to filter out test cases triggering bugs that have predictable symptoms [33]. During testing of mission file systems at NASA [12], Groce et al. used hand-tuned rules to avoid repeatedly finding the same bugs during random testing—e.g., "ignore any test case with a reset within five operations of a rename."

We claim that much more sophisticated automation is feasible and useful. In this paper we describe and evaluate a system that does this for two fuzzers: one for JavaScript engines, the other for C compilers. We characterize the *fuzzer taming problem*:

> Given a potentially large collection of test cases, each of which triggers a bug, rank them in such a way that test cases triggering distinct bugs are early in the list.
>
> **Sub-problem:** If there are test cases that trigger bugs previously flagged as undesirable, place them late in the list.

Ideally, for a collection of test cases that triggers N distinct bugs (none of which have been flagged as undesirable), each of the first N test cases in the list would trigger a different bug. In practice, perfection is unattainable because the problem is hard and also because there is some subjectivity in what constitutes "distinct bugs." Thus, our goal is simply to improve as much as possible upon the default situation where test cases are presented to users in effectively random order.

Figure 2 shows the workflow for a fuzzer tamer. The "oracle" in the figure detects buggy executions, for example by watching for crashes and by running the compiler's output against a reference compiler's output. Our rank-ordering approach was suggested by the prevalence of ranking approaches for presenting alarms produced by static analyses to users [18, 19].

Our contributions are as follows. First, we frame the fuzzer taming problem, which has not yet been addressed by the research community, as far as we are aware. Second, we make and exploit the observation that automatic triaging of test cases is strongly synergistic with automated test-case reduction. Third, based on the insight that bugs are highly diverse, we exploit diverse sources of information about bug-triggering test cases, including features of the test case itself, features from execution of the compiler on the test case, and features from the compiler's output. Fourth, we show that diverse test cases can be ranked highly by first placing test cases in a metric space and then using the *furthest point first* (FPF) technique from machine learning [10]. The more obvious approach to fuzzer taming is to use a clustering algorithm [27] to place tests into homogeneous groups, and then choose a representative test from each cluster. We show that FPF is both faster and more effective than clustering for all of our case studies. Finally, we show that our techniques can effectively solve the fuzzer taming problem for 2,603 test cases triggering 28 bugs in a JavaScript engine and 3,799 test cases triggering 46 bugs in a C compiler. Using our methods over this test suite, a developer who inspects the JavaScript engine's test cases in ranked order will more quickly find cases that trigger the 28 bugs found during the fuzzing run. In comparison to a developer who examines cases in a random order, the developer who inspects in ranked order will be 4.6× faster. For wrong-code bugs and crash bugs in the C compiler, the improvements are 2.6× and 32×, respectively. Even more importantly, users can find many more distinct bugs than would be found with a random ordering by examining only a few tens of test cases.

Taming a fuzzer differs from previous efforts in duplicate bug detection [37, 38, 42] because user-supplied metadata is not available: we must rely solely on information from failure-inducing test cases. Compared to previous work on dealing with software containing multiple bugs [15, 22, 28], our work differs in the methods used (ranking bugs as opposed to clustering), in the kinds of inputs to the machine learning algorithms (diverse, as opposed to just predicates or coverage information), and in its overall goal of taming a fuzzer.

2. Approach

This section describes our approach to taming compiler fuzzers and gives an overview of the tools implementing it.

2.1 Definitions

A *fault* or *bug* in a compiler is a flaw in its implementation. When the execution of a compiler is influenced by a fault—e.g., by wrong or missing code—the result may be an *error* that leads to a *failure* detected by a test oracle. In this paper, we are primarily concerned with two kinds of failures: (1) compilation or interpretation that fails to follow the semantics of the input source code, and (2) compiler crashes. The goal of a compiler fuzzer is to discover source programs—test cases—that lead to these failures. The goal of a *fuzzer tamer* is to rank failure-inducing test cases such that any prefix of the ranked list triggers as many different faults as possible. Faults are not directly observable, but a fuzzer tamer can estimate which test cases are related by a common fault by making an assumption: the more "similar" two test cases, or two executions of the compiler on those test cases, the more likely they are to stem from the same fault [23].

A *distance function* maps any pair of test cases to a real number that serves as a measure of similarity. This is useful because our goal is to present fuzzer users with a collection of highly dissimilar test cases. Because there are many ways in which two test cases can be similar to each other—e.g., they can be textually similar, cause similar failure output, or lead to similar executions of the compiler—our work is based on several distance functions.

2.2 Ranking Test Cases

Our approach to solving the fuzzer taming problem is based on the following idea.

> **Hypothesis 1:** If we (1) define a distance function between test cases that appropriately captures their static and dynamic characteristics and then (2) sort the list of test cases in *furthest point first* (FPF) order, then the resulting list will constitute a usefully approximate solution to the fuzzer taming problem.

If this hypothesis holds, the fuzzer taming problem is reduced to defining an appropriate distance function. The FPF ordering is one where each point in the list is the one that maximizes the distance to the nearest of all previously listed elements; it can be computed using a greedy algorithm [10]. We use FPF to ensure that diverse test cases appear early in the list. Conversely, collections of highly similar test cases will be found towards the end of the list.

Our approach to ignoring known bugs is based on the premise that fuzzer users will have labeled some test cases as exemplifying these bugs; this corresponds to the "feedback" edge in Figure 2.

> **Hypothesis 2:** We can lower the rank of test cases corresponding to bugs that are known to be uninteresting by "seeding" the FPF computation with the set of test cases that are labeled as uninteresting.

Thus, the most highly ranked test case will be the one maximizing its minimum distance from any labeled test case.

2.3 Distance Functions for Test Cases

The fundamental problem in defining a distance function that will produce good fuzzer taming results is that we do not know what the trigger for a generic compiler bug looks like. For example, one C compiler bug might be triggered by a struct with a certain sequence of bitfields; another bug might be triggered by a large number of local variables, which causes the register allocator to spill. Our solution to this fundamental ambiguity has been to define a variety of distance functions, each of which we believe will usefully capture some kinds of bug triggers. This section describes these distance functions.

Levenshtein Distance Also known as edit distance, the Levenshtein distance [20] between two strings is the smallest number of character additions, deletions, and replacements that suffices to turn one string into the other. For every pair of test cases we compute the Levenshtein distance between the following, all of which can be treated as plain text strings:

- the test cases themselves;
- the output of the compiler as it crashes (if any); and
- the output of Valgrind [25] on a failing execution (if any).

Computing Levenshtein distance requires time proportional to the product of the string lengths, but the constant factor is small (a few tens of instructions), so it is reasonably efficient in practice.

Euclidean Distance Many aspects of failure-inducing test cases, and of executions of compilers on these test cases, lend themselves to summarization in the form of *feature vectors*. For example, consider this reduced JavaScript test case, which triggers a bug in SpiderMonkey 1.6:

```
__proto__=__parent__
new Error(this)
```

Lexing this code gives eight tokens, and a feature vector based on these tokens contains eight nonzero elements. The overall vector contains one element for every token that occurs in at least one test case, but which does not occur in every test case, out of a batch of test cases that is being processed by the fuzzer tamer. The elements in the vector are based on the number of appearances of each token in the test case. We construct lexical feature vectors for both C and JavaScript.

Given two n-element vectors v_1 and v_2, the Euclidean distance between them is:

$$\sqrt{\sum_{i=1..n} (v_1[i] - v_2[i])^2}$$

For C code, our intuition was that lexical analysis in some sense produced shallower results than it did for JavaScript. To compensate, we wrote a Clang-based detector for 45 additional features that we guessed might be associated with compiler bugs. These features include:

- common types, statement classes, and operator kinds;
- features specific to aggregate data types such as structs with bitfields and packed structs;
- obvious divide-by-zero operations; and
- some kinds of infinite loops that can be detected statically.

In addition to constructing vectors from test cases, we also constructed feature vectors from compiler executions. For example, the *function coverage* of a compiler is a list of the functions that it executes while compiling a test case. The overall feature vector for function coverage contains an element for every function executed while compiling at least one test case, but that is not executed while compiling all test cases. As with token-based vectors, the vector elements are based on how many times each function executed. We created vectors of:

- functions covered;
- lines covered;
- tokens in the compiler's output as it crashes (if any); and
- tokens in output from Valgrind (if any).

In the latter two cases, we use the same tokenization as with test cases (treating output from the execution as a text document), except that in the case of Valgrind we abstract some non-null memory addresses to a generic ADDRESS token. The overall hypothesis is that most bugs will exhibit some kind of dynamic signature that will reveal itself in one or more kinds of feature vector.

Normalization Information retrieval tasks can often benefit from *normalization*, which serves to decrease the importance of terms that occur very commonly, and hence convey little information. Before computing distances over feature vectors, we normalized the value of each vector element using *tf-idf* [34]; this is a common practice in text clustering and classification. Given a count of a feature (token) in a test case or its execution (the "document"), the tf-idf is the product of the term-frequency (tf) and the inverse-document-frequency (idf) for the token. Term-frequency is the ratio of the count of the token in the document to the total number of tokens in the document. (For coverage we use number of times the entity is executed.) Inverse-document-frequency is the logarithm of the ratio of the total number of documents and the total number of documents containing the token: this results in a uniformly zero value for tokens appearing in all documents, which are therefore not included in the vector. We normalize Levenshtein distances by the length of the larger of the two strings, which helps handle varying sizes for test cases or outputs.

3. A Foundation for Experiments

To evaluate our work, we need a large collection of reduced versions of randomly generated test cases that trigger compiler bugs. Moreover, we require access to ground truth: the actual bug triggered by each test case. This section describes our approach to meeting these prerequisites.

3.1 Compilers Tested

We chose to test GCC 4.3.0 and SpiderMonkey 1.6, both running on Linux on x86-64. SpiderMonkey, best known as the JavaScript engine embedded in Firefox, is a descendant of the original JavaScript implementation; it contains an interpreter and several JIT compilers. Our selection of these particular versions was based on several considerations. First, the version that we fuzzed had to be buggy enough that we could generate useful statistics. Second, it was important that most of the bugs revealed by our fuzzer had been fixed by developers. This would not be the case for very recent compiler versions. Also, it turned out not to be the case for GCC 4.0.0, which we initially started using and had to abandon, since maintenance of its release branch—the 4.0.x series—terminated in 2007 with too many unfixed bugs.

3.2 Test Cases for C

We used the default configuration of Csmith [44] version 2.1.0, which over a period of a few days generated 2,501 test cases that crash GCC and 1,298 that trigger wrong-code bugs. The default configuration of Csmith uses swarm testing [13], which varies test features to improve fault detection and code coverage. Each program emitted by Csmith was compiled at `-O0`, `-O1`, `-O2`, `-Os`, and `-O3`.

To detect crash bugs, we inspected the return code of the main compiler process; any nonzero value was considered to indicate a crash. To detect wrong-code bugs, we employed *differential testing*: we waited for the compiler's output to produce a result different from the result of executing the output of a reference compiler. Since no perfect reference compiler exists, we approximated one by running GCC 4.6.0 and Clang 3.1 at their lowest optimization levels and ensuring that both compilers produced executables that, when run, had the same output. (We observed no mismatches during our tests.)

Csmith's outputs tend to be large, often exceeding 100 KB. We reduced each failure-inducing test case using C-Reduce [29], a tool that uses a generalized version of Delta debugging to heuristically reduce C programs. After reduction, some previously different tests became textually equivalent; this happens because C-Reduce tries quite hard to reduce identifiers, constants, data types, and other constructs to canonical values. For crash bugs, reduction produced 1,797 duplicates, leaving only 704 different test cases. Reduction was less effective at canonicalizing wrong-code test cases, with only 23 duplicate tests removed, leaving 1,275 tests to examine. In both cases, the typical test case was reduced in size by two to three orders of magnitude, to an average size of 128 bytes for crash bugs and 243 bytes for wrong-code bugs.

3.3 Test Cases for JavaScript

We started with the last public release of `jsfunfuzz` [31], a tool that, over its lifetime, has led to the discovery of more than 1,700 faults in SpiderMonkey. We modified `jsfunfuzz` to support swarm testing and then ran it for several days, accumulating 2,603 failing test cases. Differential testing of JavaScript compilers is problematic due to their diverging implementations of many of the most bug-prone features of JavaScript. However, `jsfunfuzz` comes with a set of built-in test oracles, including semantic checks (e.g., ensuring that compiling then decompiling code is an identity function) and watchdog timers to ensure that infinite loops can only result from faults. For an ahead-of-time compiler like GCC, it is natural to divide bugs into those that manifest at compile time (crashes) and those that manifest at run time (wrong-code bugs). This distinction makes less sense for a just-in-time compiler such as SpiderMonkey; we did not attempt to make it, but rather lumped all bugs into a single category. Test cases produced by `jsfunfuzz` were also large, over 100 KB on average. We reduced test cases using a custom reducer similar in spirit to C-Reduce, tuned for JavaScript. Reduction resulted in 854 duplicate test cases that we removed, leaving 1,749 test cases for input to the fuzzer taming tools. The typical failure-inducing test case for SpiderMonkey was reduced in size by more than three orders of magnitude, to an average size of 68 bytes.

3.4 Establishing Ground Truth

Perhaps the most onerous part of our work involved determining ground truth: the actual bug triggered by each test case. Doing this the hard way—examining the execution of the compiler for each of thousands of failure-inducing test cases—is obviously infeasible.

Instead, our goal was to create, for each of the 74 total bugs that our fuzzing efforts revealed, a patched compiler fixing only that bug. At that point, ground-truth determination can be automated: for each failure-inducing test case, run it through every patched version of the compiler and see which one changes its behavior. We only partially accomplished our goal. For a collection of arbitrary bugs in a large application that is being actively developed, it turns out to be very hard to find a patch fixing each bug, and only that bug.

For each bug, we started by performing an automated forward search to find the patch that fixed the bug. In some cases this patch (1) was small; (2) clearly fixed the bug triggered by the test case, as opposed to masking it by suppressing execution of the buggy code; and (3) could be back-ported to the version of the compiler that we tested. In other cases, some or all of these conditions failed to hold. For example, some compiler patches were extraordinarily complex, changing tens of thousands of lines of code. Moreover, these patches were written for compiler versions that had evolved considerably since the GCC 4.3.0 and SpiderMonkey 1.6 versions that are the basis for our experiments.

Although we spent significant effort trying to create a minimal patch fixing each compiler bug triggered by our fuzzing effort, this was not always feasible. Our backup strategy for assessing ground truth was first to approximately classify each test case based on the revision of the compiler that fixed the bug that it triggered, and second to manually inspect each test case in order to determine a final classification for which bug it triggered, based on our understanding of the set of compiler bugs.

3.5 Bug Slippage

When the original and reduced versions of a test case trigger different bugs, we say that *bug slippage* has occurred. Slippage is not hard to avoid for bugs that have an unambiguous symptom (e.g., "assertion violation at line 512") but it can be difficult to avoid for silent bugs such as those that cause a compiler to emit incorrect code. Although slippage is normally difficult to recognize or quantify, these tasks are easy when ground truth is available, as it is here.

Of our 2,501 unreduced test cases that caused GCC 4.3.0 to crash, almost all triggered the same (single) bug that was triggered by the test case's reduced version. Thirteen of the unreduced test cases triggered two different bugs, and in all of these cases the reduced version triggered one of the two. Finally, we saw a single instance of actual slippage where the original test case triggered one bug in GCC leading to a segmentation fault and the reduced version triggered a different bug, also leading to a segmentation fault. For the 1,298 test cases triggering wrong-code bugs in GCC, slippage during reduction occurred fifteen times.

For JavaScript, bug slippage was a more serious problem: 23% of reduced JavaScript test cases triggered a different bug than the original test case. This problem was not mitigated (as we had originally hoped) by re-reducing test cases using the slower "debug" version of SpiderMonkey.

In short, bug slippage was a problem for SpiderMonkey 1.6 but not for GCC 4.3.0. Although the dynamics of test-case reduction are complex, we have a hypothesis about why this might have been the case. Test-case reduction is a heuristic search that explores one particular path through the space of all possible programs. This path stays in the subset of programs that trigger a bug and also follows a gradient leading towards smaller test cases. Sometimes, the trajectory will pass through the space of programs triggering some completely different bug, causing the reduction to be "hijacked" by the second bug. We would expect this to happen more often for a compiler that is buggier. Our observation is that GCC 4.3.0 is basically a solid and mature implementation whereas SpiderMonkey 1.6 is not—it contains many bugs in fairly basic language features.

4. Results and Discussion

For 1,979 reduced test cases triggering 46 bugs in GCC 4.3.0 and 1,749 reduced test cases triggering 28 bugs in SpiderMonkey 1.6, our goal is to rank them for presentation to developers such that diverse faults are triggered by test cases early in the list.

4.1 Evaluating Effectiveness using Bug Discovery Curves

Figures 3–8 present the primary results of our work using *bug discovery curves*. A discovery curve shows how quickly a ranking of items allows a human examining the items one by one to view at least one representative of each different category of items [26, 40]. Thus, a curve that climbs rapidly is better than a curve that climbs more slowly. Here, the items are test cases and categories are the underlying compiler faults. The top of each graph represents the point at which all faults have been presented. As shown by the y-axes of the figures, there are 28 SpiderMonkey bugs, 11 GCC crash bugs, and 35 GCC wrong-code bugs in our study.

Each of Figures 3–8 includes a baseline: the expected bug discovery curve without any fuzzer taming. We computed it by looking at test cases in random order, averaged over 10,000 orders. We also show the theoretical best curve where for N faults each of the first N tests reveals a new fault.

In each graph, we show in solid black the first method to find all bugs (which, in all of our examples, is also the method with the best area under the full curve). For GCC crash bugs and SpiderMonkey, this method also has the best climb for the first 50 tests, and for GCC wrong-code bugs, it is almost the best for the first 50 tests (and, in fact, discovers one more bug than the curve with the best area). For this best curve, we also show points sized by the log of the frequency of the fault; our methods do not always find the most commonly triggered faults first. Finally, each graph additionally shows the best result that we could obtain by ranking test cases using clustering instead of FPF, using X-means to generate clusterings by various features, sorting all clusterings by isolation and compactness, and using the centermost test for each cluster. (See Section 4.6 for details.)

4.2 Are These Results Any Good?

Our efforts to tame fuzzers would have clearly failed had we been unable to significantly improve on the baseline. On the other hand, there is plenty of room for improvement: our bug discovery curves do not track the "theoretical best" lines in Figures 3 and 7 for very long. For GCC crash bugs, however, our results are almost perfect.

Perhaps the best way to interpret our results is in terms of the value proposition they create for compiler developers. For example, if a SpiderMonkey team member examines 15 randomly chosen reduced test cases, he or she can expect them to trigger five different bugs. In contrast, if the developer examines the first 15 of our ranked tests, he or she will see 11 distinct bugs: a noticeable improvement.

4.3 Selecting a Distance Function

In Section 2 we described a number of ways to compute distances between test cases. Since we did not know which of these would work, we tried all of them individually and together, with Figures 3–8 showing our best results. Since we did not consider enough case studies to be able to reach a strong conclusion such as "fuzzer taming should always use Levenshtein distance on test case text and compiler output," this section analyzes the detailed results from our different distance functions, in hopes of reaching some tentative conclusions about which functions are and are not useful.

SpiderMonkey and GCC Crash Bugs For these faults, the best distance function to use as the basis for FPF, based on our case studies, is the normalized Levenshtein distance between test cases plus normalized Levenshtein distance between failure outputs. Our tentative recommendation for bugs that (1) reduce very well and (2) have compiler-failure outputs is: use normalized Levenshtein distance over test-case text plus compiler-output text, and do not bother with Valgrind output or coverage information.

Given that using Levenshtein distance on the test-case text plus compiler output worked so well for both of these bug sets, where all faults had meaningful failure symptoms, we might expect using output or test-case text alone to also perform acceptably. In fact, Levenshtein distance based on test-case text alone (not normalized) performed moderately well for SpiderMonkey, but otherwise the results for these distance functions were uniformly mediocre at best. For GCC, using compiler output plus C features (Section 2.3) performed nearly as well as the best distance function, suggesting that the essential requirement is compiler output combined with a good representation of the test case, which may not be satisfied by a simple vectorization: vectorizing test case plus output performed badly for both GCC and SpiderMonkey.

Coverage-based methods worked fairly well for SpiderMonkey, appearing in six of the top ten functions and only two of the worst ten. Interestingly, these best coverage methods for SpiderMonkey all included both line and function coverage. Both coverage-based functions were uniformly mediocre for GCC crashes (coverage did not appear in any of the best ten or worst ten methods). For GCC, Valgrind was of little value, as most failures did not produce any Valgrind output. Memory-safety errors were more common in SpiderMonkey, so most test cases did produce Valgrind output; however, for the most part, adding the information to a distance function still made the function perform worse in the long run. Valgrind output alone performed extremely poorly in the long run for both GCC crashes and SpiderMonkey bugs.

GCC Crash Bugs For these bugs, every distance function increased the area under the curve for examining less than 50 tests by a factor or four or better, compared to the baseline. Clearly there is a significant amount of redundancy in the information provided by different functions. All but five of the 63 distance functions we used were able to discover all bugs within at most 90 tests: a dramatic improvement over the baseline's 491 tests. Only Valgrind output alone performed worse than the baseline. The other four poorly performing methods all involved using vectorization of the test case, with no additional information beyond Valgrind output and/or test-case output.

GCC crash bugs were, however, our easiest target: there are only 11 crash outputs and 11 faults. Even so, the problem is not trivial, as the faults and outputs do not correspond perfectly—two faults have two different outputs, and there are two outputs that are each produced by two different faults. Failure output alone provides a great deal of information about a majority of the faults, and test-case distance completes the story.

SpiderMonkey Bugs The story was less simple for SpiderMonkey bugs, where many methods performed poorly and seven methods per-

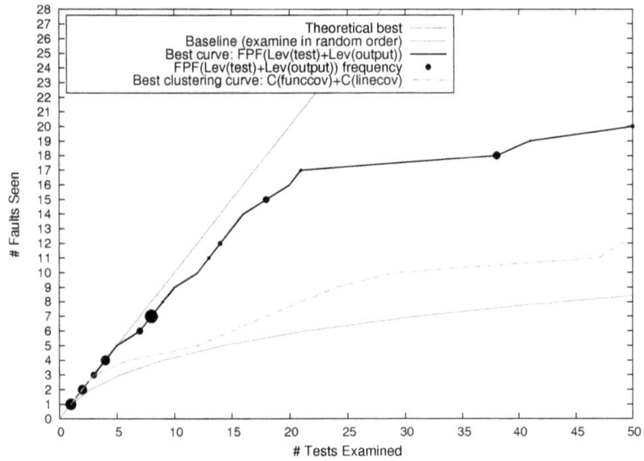

Figure 3. SpiderMonkey 1.6 bug discovery curves, first 50 tests

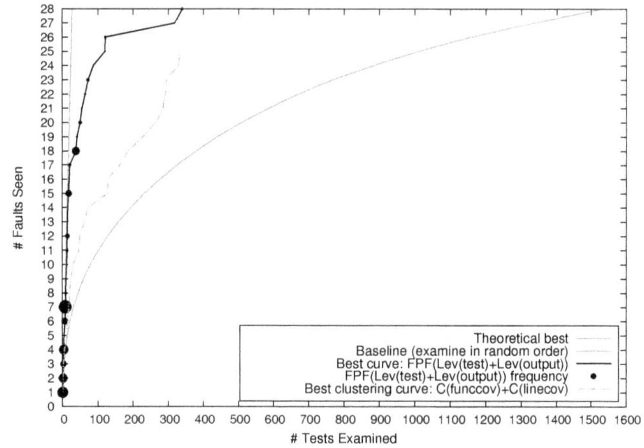

Figure 4. SpiderMonkey 1.6 bug discovery curves, all tests

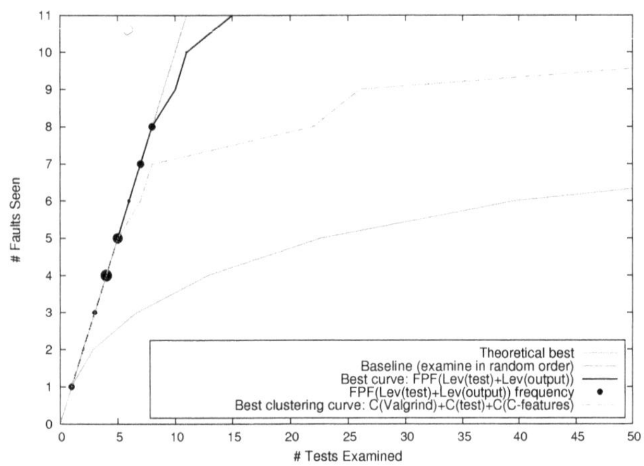

Figure 5. GCC 4.3.0 crash bug discovery curves, first 50 tests

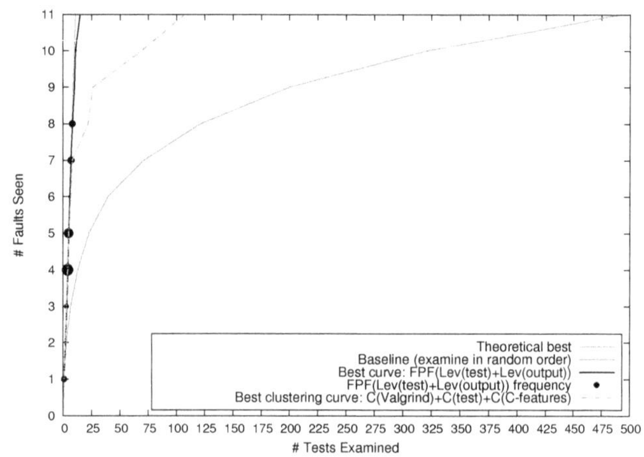

Figure 6. GCC 4.3.0 crash bug discovery curves, all tests

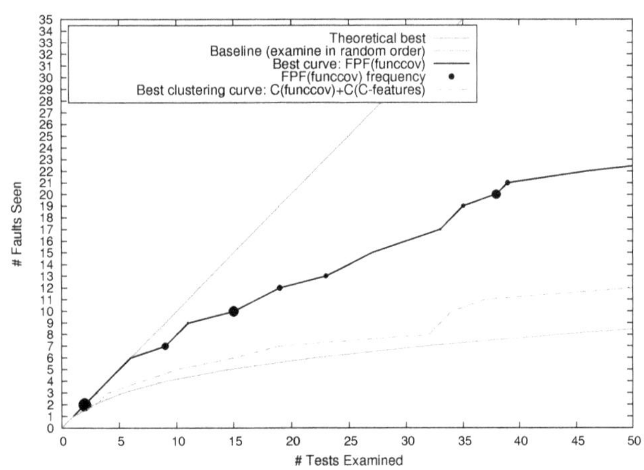

Figure 7. GCC 4.3.0 wrong-code bug discovery curves, first 50 tests

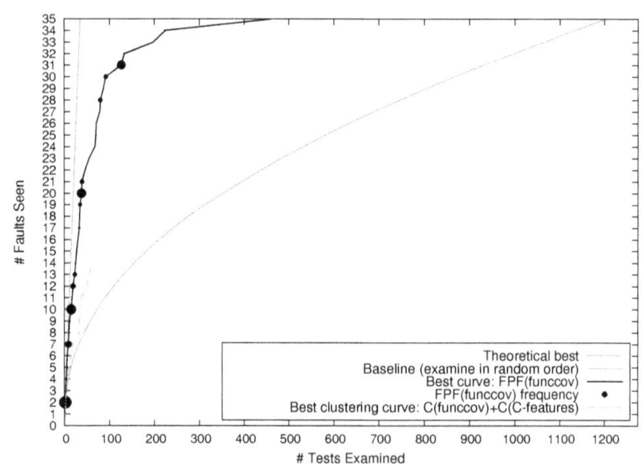

Figure 8. GCC 4.3.0 wrong-code bug discovery curves, all tests

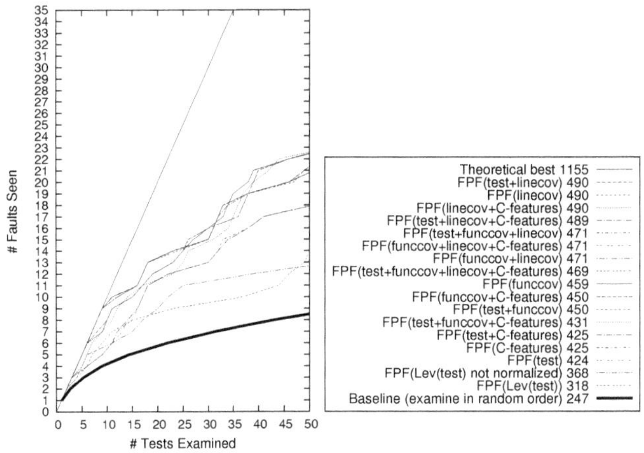

Figure 9. All bug discovery curves for GCC 4.3.0 wrong-code bugs, sorted by increasing area under the curve if examining only the 50 top-ranked test cases

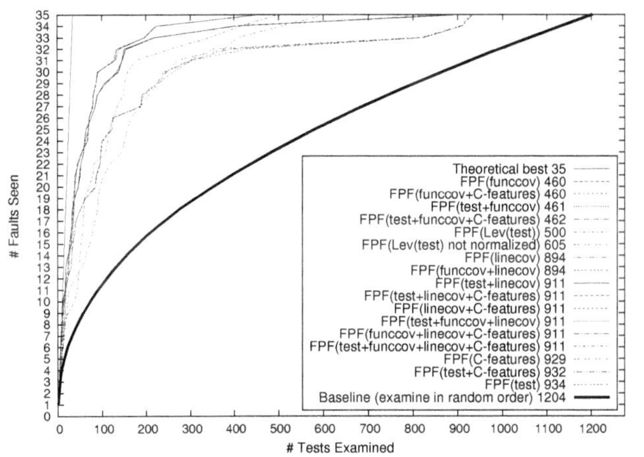

Figure 10. All bug discovery curves for GCC 4.3.0 wrong-code bugs, sorted by increasing number of test cases that must be examined to discover all faults

formed worse than the baseline. In this case, compiler output alone did not provide as much direct guidance: there were 300 different failure outputs, and only four of 28 faults had a unique identifying output. As a result, while compiler output alone performed very well over the first 50 tests (where it was one of the best five functions), it proved one of the worst functions for finding all faults, detecting no new faults between the 50th and 100th tests ranked. Test-case text by itself performed well for SpiderMonkey with Levenshtein distance, or when combined with line coverage, but performed badly as a vectorization without line coverage, appearing in six of the worst ten functions. As with GCC crashes, Valgrind output alone performed very badly, requiring a user to examine 1,506 tests to discover all bugs. Levenshtein-based approaches (whether over test case, compiler output, Valgrind output, or a combination thereof) performed very well over the first 50 tests examined.

GCC Wrong-Code Bugs Wrong-code bugs in GCC were the trickiest bugs that we faced: their execution does not provide failure output and, in the expected case where the bug is in a "middle end" optimizer, the distance between execution of the fault and actual emission of code (and thus exposure of failure) can be quite long.

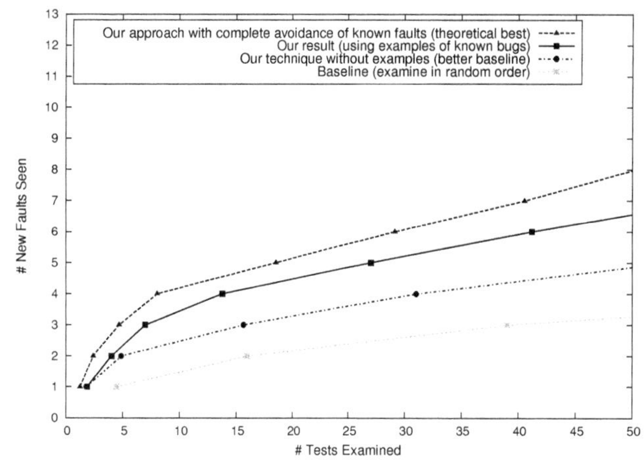

Figure 11. Avoiding known bugs in SpiderMonkey 1.6

For these bugs, the best method to use for fuzzer taming was less clear. Figures 9 and 10 show the performance of all methods that we tried, including a table of results sorted by area under the curve up to 50 tests (Figure 9) and number of test cases to discover all faults (Figure 10). It is clear that code coverage (line or function) is much more valuable here than with crash bugs, though Levenshtein distance based on test case alone performs well in the long run (but badly initially). Line coverage is useful for early climb, but eventually function coverage is most useful for discovering all bugs. Perhaps most importantly, given the difficulty of handling GCC wrong-code bugs, all of our methods perform better than the baseline in terms of ability to find all bugs, and provide a clear advantage over the first 50 test cases. We do not wish to overgeneralize from a few case studies, but these results provide hope that for difficult bugs, if good reduction is possible, the exact choice of distance function used in FPF may not be critical.

We were disappointed to see that Figures 9 and 10 show no evidence that our domain-specific feature detector for C programs is useful for wrong-code bugs; in the tables it appears as "C-Feature."

4.4 Avoiding Known Faults

In Section 2.2 we hypothesized that FPF could be used to avoid reports about a set of known bugs; this is accomplished by lowering the rankings of test cases that appear to be caused by those bugs. Figure 11 shows, for our SpiderMonkey test cases, an averaged bug discovery curve for the case where half of the bugs were assumed to be already known, and five test cases (or fewer, if five were not available) triggering each of those bugs were used to seed FPF. This experiment models the situation where, in the days or weeks preceding the current fuzzing run, the user has flagged these test cases and does not want to see more test cases triggering the same bugs. The curve is the average of 100 discovery curves, each corresponding to a different randomly chosen set of known bugs.

The topmost bug discovery curve in Figure 11 represents an idealized best case where all test cases corresponding to known bugs are removed from the set of test cases to be ranked. The second curve from the top is our result. The third curve from the top is also the average of 100 discovery curves; each corresponds to the case where the five (or fewer) test cases for each known bug are discarded instead of being used to seed the FPF algorithm, and then the FPF algorithm proceeds normally. This serves as a baseline: our result would have to be considered poor if it could not improve on this. Finally, the bottom curve is the "basic baseline" where the labeled test cases are again discarded, but then the remaining test cases are examined in random order.

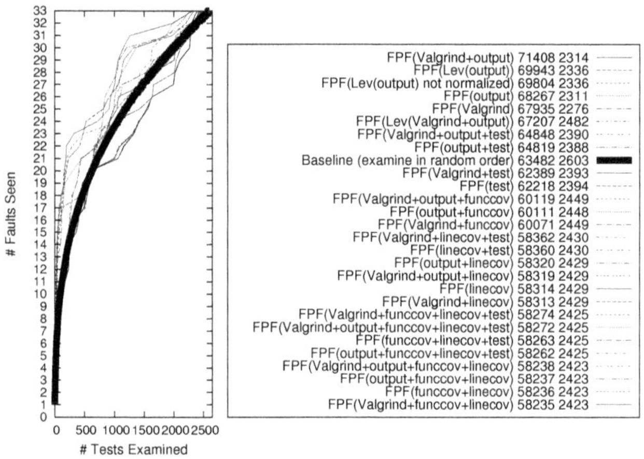

Figure 12. All bug discovery curves for SpiderMonkey 1.6 using unreduced test cases. It is difficult to significantly improve on the baseline without test case reduction.

As can be seen, our current performance for SpiderMonkey is reasonably good. Analogous results for GCC bugs (not included for reasons of space) were similar, but not quite as good for wrong-code bugs. We speculate that classification, rather than clustering or ranking, might be a better machine-learning approach for this problem if better results are required.

4.5 The Importance of Test-Case Reduction

Randomly generated test cases are more effective at finding bugs when they are large [1]. There are several reasons for this. First, large tests are more likely to bump into implementation limits and software aging effects in the system under test. Second, large tests amortize start-up costs. Third, undesirable feature interactions in the system under test are more likely to occur when a test case triggers more behaviors.

The obvious drawback of large random test cases is that they contain much content that is probably unrelated to the bug. They consequently induce long executions that are difficult to debug. Several random testers that have been used in practice, including McKeeman's C compiler fuzzer [24] and QuickCheck [6], have included built-in support for greedily reducing the size of failure-inducing inputs. Zeller and Hildebrandt [45] generalized and formalized this kind of test-case reduction as Delta Debugging.

While previous work has assumed that the consumer for reduced test cases is a human, our observation is that machine-learning-based methods can greatly benefit from reduced test cases. First, machine-learning algorithms can be overwhelmed by noisy inputs: reduced test cases have a vastly improved "signal to noise ratio." Second, a suitably designed test-case reducer has a canonicalizing effect.

Figure 12 shows the discovery curves for the FPF ordering on unreduced JavaScript test cases, accompanied by a table sorted by area under the discovery curve for all 2,603 unreduced tests (first column after distance function name) and also the number of tests required to discover all faults (second column). Note that this is a different baseline than in previous graphs, as there are no duplicates among the unreduced test cases. While all methods improve (slightly) on the baseline for finding all faults, it is difficult to consider these approaches acceptable: many methods produce an overall discovery curve that is worse than the baseline. Without test-case reduction, it is essentially impossible to efficiently find the more obscure SpiderMonkey bugs.

Based on these poor results, and on the fact that ranking unreduced test cases (which have much longer feature vectors) is expensive, our view is that attempting to tame a fuzzer without the aid of a solid test-case reducer is inadvisable. The most informative sources of information about root causes are rendered useless by overwhelming noise. Although we did not create results for unreduced GCC test cases that are analogous to those shown in Figure 12 (the line coverage vectors were gigantic and caused problems by filling up disks), we have no reason to believe the results would have been any better than they were for JavaScript.

4.6 Clustering as an Alternative to Furthest Point First

The problem of ranking test cases is not, essentially, a clustering problem. On the other hand, if our goal were simply to find a single test case triggering each fault, an obvious approach would be to cluster the test cases and then select a single test from each cluster, as in previous approaches to the problem [9, 28]. The FPF algorithm we use is itself based on the idea of approximating optimal clusters [10]; we simply ignore the clustering aspect and use only the ranking information.

Our initial approach to taming compiler fuzzers was to start with the feature vectors described in Section 2.3 and then, instead of ranking test cases using FPF, use X-means [27] to cluster test cases. A set of clusters does not itself provide a user with a set of representative test cases, however, nor a ranking (since not all clusters are considered equally likely to represent true categories). Our approach therefore followed clustering by selecting the member of each cluster closest to its center as that cluster's representative test. We ranked each test by the quality of its cluster, as measured by compactness (whether the distance between tests in the cluster is small) and isolation (whether the distance to tests outside the cluster is large) [40]. This approach appeared to be promising as it improved considerably on the baseline bug discovery curves (Figures 3–8).

We next investigated the possibility of independently clustering different feature vectors, then merging the representatives from these clusterings [36], and ranking highest those representatives appearing in clusterings based on multiple feature sets. This produced better results than our single-vector method, and it was also more efficient, as it did not require the use of large vectors combining multiple features. This approach is essentially a completely unsupervised variation (with the addition of some recent advances in clustering) of earlier approaches to clustering test cases that trigger the same bug [9]. Our approach is unsupervised because we exploit test-case reduction as a way to select relevant features, rather than relying on the previous approaches' assumption that features useful in predicting failure or success would also distinguish failures from each other.

However, in comparison to FPF for all three of our case studies, clustering was (1) significantly more complex to use, (2) more computationally expensive, and (3) most importantly, less effective. The additional complexity of clustering should be clear from our description of the algorithm, which omits details such as how we compute normalized isolation and compactness, the algorithm for merging multiple views, and (especially) the wide range of parameters that can be supplied to the underlying X-means algorithm.

Table 1 compares runtimes, with the time for FPF including the full end-to-end effort of producing a ranking and the clustering column only showing the time for computing clusters using X-means, with settings that are a compromise between speed and effectiveness. (Increased computation time to produce "more accurate" clusters in our experience had diminishing returns after this point, which allowed up to 40 splits and a maximum of 300 clusters.) Computing isolation and compactness of clusters and merging clusters to produce a ranking based on multiple feature vectors adds additional significant overhead to the X-means time shown, if multiple clusterings are combined, but we have not measured this time because our implementation is highly unoptimized Python (while X-means

Program / Feature	Time (s) FPF	Clustering	Figures
SpiderMonkey / Valgrind	8.27	23.68	–
SpiderMonkey / output	8.38	46.71	–
SpiderMonkey / test	8.12	94.26	–
SpiderMonkey / funccov	9.56	227.78	3, 4
SpiderMonkey / linecov	48.29	1,594.04	3, 4
SpiderMonkey / Lev. test+output	998.21	N/A	3, 4
GCC crash bugs / output	0.08	0.71	–
GCC crash bugs / Valgrind	0.09	0.75	5, 6
GCC crash bugs / C-Feature	0.10	1.95	5, 6
GCC crash bugs / test	0.14	15.12	5, 6
GCC crash bugs / funccov	1.37	162.22	–
GCC crash bugs / linecov	18.70	2,021.08	–
GCC crash bugs / Lev. test+output	75.07	N/A	5, 6
GCC wrong-code bugs / C-Feature	0.49	4.26	7, 8
GCC wrong-code bugs / test	0.72	67.72	–
GCC wrong-code bugs / funccov	4.12	1,046.07	7, 8
GCC wrong-code bugs / linecov	60.60	7,127.42	–
GCC wrong-code bugs / Lev. test	667.21	N/A	–

Table 1. Runtimes for FPF versus clustering

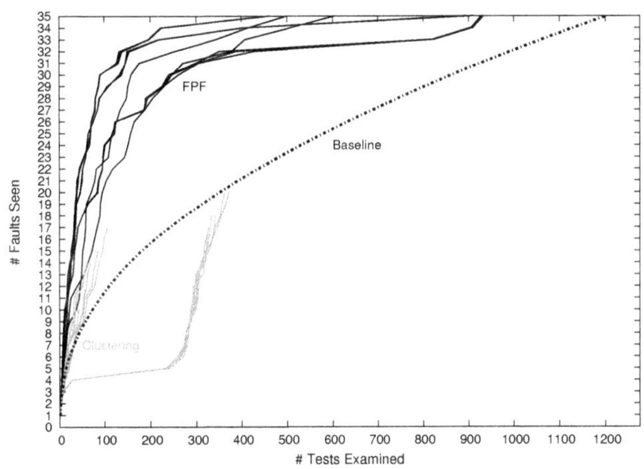

Figure 13. GCC 4.3.0 wrong-code bug clustering comparison

is a widely used tool written in C). Because the isolation and compactness computations require many pairwise distance results, an efficient implementation should be approximately equal in time to running FPF. The final column of the table lists the figures in this paper that show a curve based on the indicated results. If a curve relies on multiple clusterings, its generation time is (at least) the sum of the clustering times for each component. Note that because X-means expects inputs in vector form, we were unable to apply our direct Levenshtein-distance approach with clustering, but we include some runtimes for FPF Levenshtein to provide a comparison.

That clustering is more expensive and complex than FPF is not surprising; clustering has to perform the additional work of computing clusters, rather than simply ranking items by distance. That FPF produces considerably better discovery curves, as shown in Figures 3–8, *is* surprising. The comparative ineffectiveness of clustering is twofold: the discovery curves do not climb as quickly as with FPF, and (perhaps even more critically) clustering does not ever find all the faults in many cases. In general, for almost all feature sets, clustering over those same features was worse than applying FPF to those features. The bad performance of clustering was particularly clear for GCC wrong-code bugs: Figure 13 shows all discovery curves for GCC wrong-code, with clustering results shown in gray. Clustering at its "best" missed 15 or more bugs, and in many cases performed much worse than the baseline, generating a small number of clusters that were not represented by distinct faults. In fact, the few clustering results that manage to discover 20 faults also did so more slowly than the baseline curve. While GCC wrong-code clustering was particularly bad, clustering also always missed at least three bugs for SpiderMonkey. Our hypothesis as to why FPF performs so much better than clustering is that the nature of fuzzing results, with a long tail of outliers, is a mismatch for clustering algorithm assumptions. FPF is not forced to use any assumptions about the size of clusters, and so is not "confused" by the many single-instance clusters. A minor point supporting our hypothesis is that the rank ordering of clustering effectiveness matched that of the size of the tail for each set of faults: GCC crash results were good but not optimal, SpiderMonkey results were poor, and GCC wrong-code results were extremely bad.

5. Related Work

A great deal of research related to fuzzer taming exists, and some related areas such as fault localization are too large for us to do more than summarize the high points.

Relating Test Cases to Faults Previous work focusing on the core problem of "taming" sets of redundant test cases differs from ours in a few key ways. The differences relate to our choice of primary algorithm, our reliance on unsupervised methods, and our focus on randomly generated test cases.

First, the primary method used was typically clustering, as in the work of Francis et al. [9] and Podgurski et al. [28], which at first appears to reflect the core problem of grouping test cases into equivalence classes by underlying fault. However, in practice the user of a fuzzer does not usually care about the tests in a cluster, but only about finding at least one example from each set with no particular desire that it is a perfectly "representative" example. The core problem we address is therefore better considered as one of *multiple output identification* [8] or rare category detection [8, 40], given that many faults will be found by a single test case out of thousands. This insight guides our decision to provide the first evaluation in terms of discovery curves (the most direct measure of fuzzer taming capability we know of) for this problem. Our results suggest that this difference in focus is also algorithmically useful, as clustering was less effective than our (novel, to our knowledge) choice of FPF.

One caveat is that, as in the work of Jones et al. on debugging in parallel [15], clusters may not be directly useful to users, but might assist fault localization algorithms. Jones et al. provide an evaluation in terms of a model of debugging effort, which combines clustering effectiveness with fault-localization effectiveness. This provides an interesting contrast to our discovery curves: it relies on more assumptions about users' workflow and debugging process and provides less direct information about the effectiveness of taming itself. In our experience, sufficiently reduced test cases make localization easy enough for many compiler bugs that discovery is the more important problem. Unfortunately, it is hard to compare results: cost-model results are only reported for SPACE, a program with only around 6,200 LOC, and their tests included not only random tests from a simple generator but 3,585 human-generated tests. In the event that clusters are needed, FPF results for any k can be transformed into k clusters with certain optimality bounds for the chosen distance function [10].

Second, our approach is completely unsupervised. There is no expectation that users will examine clusters, add rules, or intervene in the process. We therefore use test-case reduction for feature selection, rather than basing it on classifying test cases as successful or failing [9, 28]. Because fuzzing results follow a power law, many faults will be represented by far too few tests for a good classifier to include their key features; this is a classic and extreme case of class imbalance in machine learning. While bug slippage is a problem, reduction remains highly effective for feature selection, in that the features selected are correct for the reduced test cases, essentially by the definition of test-case reduction.

Finally, our expected use case and experimental results are based on a large set of failures produced by large-scale random testing for complex programming languages implemented in large, complex, modern compilers. Most previous results in failure clustering used human-reported failures or human-created regression tests (e.g., GCC regression tests [9, 28]), which are essentially different in character from the failures produced by large-scale fuzzing, and/or concerned much smaller programs with much simpler input domains [15, 23], i.e., examples from the Siemens suite. Liblit et al. [22] in contrast directly addressed scalability by using 32,000 random inputs (though not from a pre-existing industrial-strength fuzzer for a complex language) and larger programs (up to 56 KLOC), and noted that they saw highly varying rates of failure for different bugs. Their work addresses a somewhat different problem than ours—that of isolating bugs via sampled predicate values, rather than straightforward ranking of test cases for user examination—and did not include any systems as large as GCC or SpiderMonkey.

Distance Functions for Executions and Programs Liu and Han's work [23], like ours, focuses less on a particular clustering method and proposes that the core problem in taming large test suites is that of embedding test cases in a metric space that has good correlation with underlying fault causes. They propose to compute distance by first applying fault localization methods to executions, then using distance over localization results rather than over the traces themselves. We propose that the reduction of random test cases essentially "localizes" the test cases themselves, allowing us to directly compute proximity over test cases while exhibiting the good correlation with underlying cause that Liu and Han seek to achieve by applying a fault-localization technique. Reduction has advantages over localization in that reduction methods are more commonly employed and do not require storing—or even capturing or sampling—information about coverage, predicates, or other metrics for passing test cases. Liu and Han show that distance based on localization algorithms better captures fault cause than distance over raw traces, but they do not provide discovery curves or a detailed clustering evaluation. They provide correlation results only over the Siemens suite's small subjects and test case sets.

More generally, the problems of distance functions over executions and test cases [5, 11, 23, 30, 39] and programs themselves [4, 35, 41] have typically been seen as essentially different problems. While this is true for many investigations—generalized program understanding and fault localization on the one hand, and plagiarism detection, merging of program edits, code clone, or malware detection on the other—the difference collapses when we consider that every program compiled is an input to some other program. A program is therefore both a program and a test input, which induces an execution of another program. Distance between (compiled) programs, therefore, is a distance between executions. We are the first, to our knowledge, to essentially erase the distinction between a metric space for programs and a metric space for executions, mixing the two concepts as needed. Moreover, we believe that our work addresses some of the concerns noted in fault-localization efforts based on execution distances (e.g., poor results compared to other methods [16]), in that distance functions should perform much better on executions of reduced programs, due to the power of feature selection, and distances over programs (highly structured and potentially very informative inputs) can complement execution-based distance functions.

Fault Localization Our work shares a common ultimate goal with fault localization work in general [5, 7, 11, 16, 17, 21, 22, 30] and specifically for compilers [43]: reducing the cost of manual debugging. We differ substantially in that we focus our methods and evaluation on the narrow problem of helping the users of fuzzers deal with the overwhelming amount of data that a modern fuzzer can produce when applied to a compiler. As suggested by Liu and Han [23], Jones et al. [15], and others, localization may support fuzzer taming and fuzzer taming may support localization. As part of our future work, we propose to make use of vectors based on localization information to determine if, even after reduction, localization can improve bug discovery. A central question is whether the payoff from keeping summaries of successful executions (a requirement for many fault localizations) provides sufficient improvement to pay for its overhead in reduced fuzzing throughput.

6. Conclusion

Random testing, or fuzzing, has emerged as an important way to test compilers and language runtimes. Despite their advantages, however, fuzzers create a unique set of challenges when compared to other testing methods. First, they indiscriminately and repeatedly find test cases triggering bugs that have already been found and that may not be economical to fix in the short term. Second, fuzzers tend to trigger some bugs far more often than others, creating needle-in-the-haystack problems for engineers who are triaging failure-inducing outputs generated by fuzzers.

Our contribution is to *tame* a fuzzer by adding a tool to the back end of the random-testing workflow; it uses techniques from machine learning to rank test cases in such a way that interesting tests are likely to be highly ranked. By analogy to the way people use ranked outputs from static analyses, we expect fuzzer users to inspect a small fraction of highly ranked outputs, trusting that lower-ranked test cases are not as interesting. If our rankings are good, fuzzer users will get most of the benefit of inspecting every failure-inducing test case discovered by the fuzzer for a fraction of the effort. For example, a user inspecting test cases for SpiderMonkey 1.6 in our ranked order will see all 28 bugs found during our fuzzing run 4.6× faster than will a user inspecting test cases in random order. A user inspecting test cases that cause GCC 4.3.0 to emit incorrect object code will see all 35 bugs 2.6× faster than one inspecting tests in random order. The improvement for test cases that cause GCC 4.3.0 to crash is even higher: 32×, with all 11 bugs exposed by only 15 test cases.

Acknowledgments

We thank Michael Hicks, Robby Findler, and the anonymous PLDI '13 reviewers for their comments on drafts of this paper; Suresh Venkatasubramanian for nudging us towards the furthest point first technique; James A. Jones for providing useful early feedback; and Google for a research award supporting Yang Chen. A portion of this work was funded by NSF grants CCF-1217824 and CCF-1054786.

References

[1] James H. Andrews, Alex Groce, Melissa Weston, and Ru-Gang Xu. Random test run length and effectiveness. In *Proc. ASE*, pages 19–28, September 2008.

[2] Abhishek Arya and Cris Neckar. Fuzzing for security, April 2012. `http://blog.chromium.org/2012/04/fuzzing-for-security.html`.

[3] Mariano Ceccato, Alessandro Marchetto, Leonardo Mariani, Cu D. Nguyen, and Paolo Tonella. An empirical study about the effectiveness of debugging when random test cases are used. In *Proc. ICSE*, pages 452–462, June 2012.

[4] Silvio Cesare and Yang Xiang. Malware variant detection using similarity search over sets of control flow graphs. In *Proc. TRUSTCOM*, pages 181–189, November 2011.

[5] Sagar Chaki, Alex Groce, and Ofer Strichman. Explaining abstract counterexamples. In *Proc. FSE*, pages 73–82, 2004.

[6] Koen Claessen and John Hughes. QuickCheck: a lightweight tool for random testing of Haskell programs. In *Proc. ICFP*, pages 268–279, 2000.

[7] Holger Cleve and Andreas Zeller. Locating causes of program failures. In *Proc. ICSE*, pages 342–351, May 2005.

[8] Shai Fine and Yishay Mansour. Active sampling for multiple output identification. *Machine Learning*, 69(2–3):213–228, 2007.

[9] Patrick Francis, David Leon, Melinda Minch, and Andy Podgurski. Tree-based methods for classifying software failures. In *Proc. ISSRE*, pages 451–462, November 2004.

[10] Teofilo F. Gonzalez. Clustering to minimize the maximum intercluster distance. *Theoretical Computer Science*, 38:293–306, 1985.

[11] Alex Groce. Error explanation with distance metrics. In *Proc. TACAS*, pages 108–122, March 2004.

[12] Alex Groce, Gerard Holzmann, and Rajeev Joshi. Randomized differential testing as a prelude to formal verification. In *Proc. ICSE*, pages 621–631, May 2007.

[13] Alex Groce, Chaoqiang Zhang, Eric Eide, Yang Chen, and John Regehr. Swarm testing. In *Proc. ISSTA*, pages 78–88, July 2012.

[14] Christian Holler, Kim Herzig, and Andreas Zeller. Fuzzing with code fragments. In *Proc. USENIX Security*, pages 445–458, August 2012.

[15] James A. Jones, James F. Bowring, and Mary Jean Harrold. Debugging in parallel. In *Proc. ISSTA*, pages 16–26, July 2007.

[16] James A. Jones and Mary Jean Harrold. Empirical evaluation of the Tarantula automatic fault-localization technique. In *Proc. ASE*, pages 273–282, November 2005.

[17] James A. Jones, Mary Jean Harrold, and John Stasko. Visualization of test information to assist fault localization. In *Proc. ICSE*, pages 467–477, May 2002.

[18] Yungbum Jung, Jaehwang Kim, Jaeho Shin, and Kwangkeun Yi. Taming false alarms from a domain-unaware C analyzer by a Bayesian statistical post analysis. In *Proc. SAS*, pages 203–217, September 2005.

[19] Ted Kremenek and Dawson Engler. Z-ranking: using statistical analysis to counter the impact of static analysis approximations. In *Proc. SAS*, pages 295–315, June 2003.

[20] Vladimir I. Levenshtein. Binary codes capable of correcting deletions, insertions, and reversals. *Soviet Physics Doklady*, 10:707–710, 1966.

[21] Ben Liblit, Alex Aiken, Alice X. Zheng, and Michael I. Jordan. Bug isolation via remote program sampling. In *Proc. PLDI*, pages 141–154, June 2003.

[22] Ben Liblit, Mayur Naik, Alice X. Zheng, Alex Aiken, and Michael I. Jordan. Scalable statistical bug isolation. In *Proc. PLDI*, pages 15–26, June 2005.

[23] Chao Liu and Jiawei Han. Failure proximity: a fault localization-based approach. In *Proc. FSE*, pages 46–56, November 2006.

[24] William M. McKeeman. Differential testing for software. *Digital Technical Journal*, 10(1):100–107, December 1998.

[25] Nicholas Nethercote and Julian Seward. Valgrind: a framework for heavyweight dynamic binary instrumentation. In *Proc. PLDI*, pages 89–100, June 2007.

[26] Dan Pelleg and Andrew Moore. Active learning for anomaly and rare-category detection. In *Advances in Neural Information Processing Systems 18*, December 2004.

[27] Dan Pelleg and Andrew W. Moore. X-means: Extending K-means with efficient estimation of the number of clusters. In *Proc. ICML*, pages 727–734, June/July 2000.

[28] Andy Podgurski, David Leon, Patrick Francis, Wes Masri, Melinda Minch, Jiayang Sun, and Bin Wang. Automated support for classifying software failure reports. In *Proc. ICSE*, pages 465–475, May 2003.

[29] John Regehr, Yang Chen, Pascal Cuoq, Eric Eide, Chucky Ellison, and Xuejun Yang. Test-case reduction for C compiler bugs. In *Proc. PLDI*, pages 335–346, June 2012.

[30] Manos Renieris and Steven Reiss. Fault localization with nearest neighbor queries. In *Proc. ASE*, pages 30–39, October 2003.

[31] Jesse Ruderman. Introducing jsfunfuzz. `http://www.squarefree.com/2007/08/02/introducing-jsfunfuzz/`.

[32] Jesse Ruderman. Mozilla bug 349611. `https://bugzilla.mozilla.org/show_bug.cgi?id=349611` (A meta-bug containing all bugs found using jsfunfuzz.).

[33] Jesse Ruderman. How my DOM fuzzer ignores known bugs, 2010. `http://www.squarefree.com/2010/11/21/how-my-dom-fuzzer-ignores-known-bugs/`.

[34] G. Salton, A. Wong, and C. S. Yang. A vector space model for automatic indexing. *CACM*, 18(11):613–620, November 1975.

[35] Saul Schleimer, Daniel S. Wilkerson, and Alex Aiken. Winnowing: local algorithms for document fingerprinting. In *Proc. SIGMOD*, pages 76–85, June 2003.

[36] Alexander Strehl and Joydeep Ghosh. Cluster ensembles—a knowledge reuse framework for combining multiple partitions. *The Journal of Machine Learning Research*, 3:583–617, 2003.

[37] Chengnian Sun, David Lo, Siau-Cheng Khoo, and Jing Jiang. Towards more accurate retrieval of duplicate bug reports. In *Proc. ASE*, pages 253–262, November 2011.

[38] Chengnian Sun, David Lo, Xiaoyin Wang, Jing Jiang, and Siau-Cheng Khoo. A discriminative model approach for accurate duplicate bug report retrieval. In *Proc. ICSE*, pages 45–54, May 2010.

[39] Vipindeep Vangala, Jacek Czerwonka, and Phani Talluri. Test case comparison and clustering using program profiles and static execution. In *Proc. ESEC/FSE*, pages 293–294, August 2009.

[40] Pavan Vatturi and Weng-Keen Wong. Category detection using hierarchical mean shift. In *Proc. KDD*, pages 847–856, June/July 2009.

[41] Andrew Walenstein, Mohammad El-Ramly, James R. Cordy, William S. Evans, Kiarash Mahdavi, Markus Pizka, Ganesan Ramalingam, and Jürgen Wolff von Gudenberg. Similarity in programs. In *Duplication, Redundancy, and Similarity in Software*, Dagstuhl Seminar Proceedings, July 2006.

[42] Xiaoyin Wang, Lu Zhang, Tao Xie, John Anvik, and Jiasu Sun. An approach to detecting duplicate bug reports using natural language and execution information. In *Proc. ICSE*, pages 461–470, May 2008.

[43] David B. Whalley. Automatic isolation of compiler errors. *TOPLAS*, 16(5):1648–1659, September 1994.

[44] Xuejun Yang, Yang Chen, Eric Eide, and John Regehr. Finding and understanding bugs in C compilers. In *Proc. PLDI*, pages 283–294, June 2011.

[45] Andreas Zeller and Ralf Hildebrandt. Simplifying and isolating failure-inducing input. *IEEE TSE*, 28(2):183–200, February 2002.

Almost-Correct Specifications

A Modular Semantic Framework for Assigning Confidence to Warnings

Sam Blackshear
University of Colorado, Boulder
samuel.blackshear@colorado.edu

Shuvendu K. Lahiri
Microsoft Research, Redmond
shuvendu@microsoft.com

Abstract

Modular assertion checkers are plagued with false alarms due to the need for precise environment specifications (preconditions and callee postconditions). Even the fully precise checkers report assertion failures under the most demonic environments allowed by unconstrained or partial specifications. The inability to preclude overly adversarial environments makes such checkers less attractive to developers and severely limits the adoption of such tools in the development cycle.

In this work, we propose a parameterized framework for prioritizing the assertion failures reported by a modular verifier, with the goal of suppressing warnings from overly demonic environments. We formalize *almost-correct specifications* as the minimal weakening of an angelic specification (over a set of predicates) that precludes any dead code intraprocedurally. Our work is inspired by and generalizes some aspects of semantic inconsistency detection. Our formulation allows us to lift this idea to a general class of warnings. We have developed a prototype ACSPEC, which we use to explore a few instantiations of the framework and report preliminary findings on a diverse set of C benchmarks.

Categories and Subject Descriptors D.2.4 [*Software Engineering*]: Software/Program Verification

Keywords Program verifiers, false alarms, predicate abstraction

1. Introduction

> *Talking about false positive rate is simplistic since false positives are not all equal. The initial reports matter inordinately; ... Furthermore, you never want an embarrassing false positive. A stupid false positive implies the tool is stupid. ("It's not even smart enough to figure* that *out?").* [2]

Automatic program verifiers are doomed to report false alarms. False alarms can be the result of analysis imprecision or the result of underspecified environment assumptions. The problem is relevant not only to modular checkers that analyze each procedure in isolation [12] (and therefore need specification of inputs and callees), but also to the more general setting when interprocedural specification inference (e.g., based on abstract interpretation [4]) converges with the best invariants expressible in the domain. Finally, this problem is inevitable when analyzing any open program that has under-constrained inputs and external procedures without source code.

This is unfortunate because excessive false alarms (especially stupid ones) act as a deterrent to the initial adoption of verification tools by average developers. Current best practices (often undocumented) in designing usable static analysis tools mitigate this issue by using several less-than-ideal techniques for reducing false positives. For example, a tool may bake unsound decisions into the analysis, which precludes the tool from finding a class of bugs. A tool may require user annotations, which often hurts initial adoption by average developers. Finally, a tool may suppress alarms using domain-specific and often ad-hoc heuristics, which makes the tool brittle and unpredictable. In spite of the severity of the problem, the subject of prioritizing warnings from program verifiers systematically is relatively under-studied.

In this work, we focus on a post-processing framework for prioritizing alarms in an intraprocedural setting. We assume that the interprocedural specification inference [4] has converged with a set of invariants expressible in the underlying analysis. This assumption allows us to decouple the analysis and the framework for displaying warnings, which is important because our goal is not to define a new static analysis technique. We seek to solve a problem similar to one addressed by statistical methods for ranking alarms [17] or user-guided classification of alarms [10]. Our method is based on deep semantic reasoning of a program (unlike [17]), and can complement the work in [10] by identifying the initial set of warnings to display to the user for further classification.

In this work, we propose a framework for reporting a high-confidence subset of the assertion failures reported by a modular verifier. Our framework is parameterized by a set of predicates Q. We use the following heuristic: if a warning can be suppressed by a *simple environment specification* over Q, it is likely to be a "stupid" false alarm. On the other hand, if a warning can only be suppressed by a complicated environment specification, it is more more likely to be a true alarm. In this work, we limit ourselves to three metrics for characterizing simple specifications: (i) the specification should not preclude the set of angelic environments, (ii) the specification should at least be permissive enough to allow all program locations in a procedure to be reachable (unless they are unreachable even in an unconstrained environment), and (iii) the representation of the specification should satisfy some quality measures such as (but not limited to) the number of disjunctions in a clausal representation.

This paper describes a framework for inferring these *almost-correct specifications*. We refer to the high-confidence warnings that these specifications reveal as *abstract inconsistency bugs*. When the set of predicates Q contains all the atomic predicates in the representation of the weakest precondition for a procedure, our framework reports a set of warnings corresponding to *semantic*

```
void Foo(int *c, char *buf, CMD cmd) {
1:  if (*) {
2:    free(c);//A1:assert(!Freed[c]);Freed[c] := true;
3:    free(buf);//A2:assert(!Freed[buf]);Freed[buf] := true;
4:    return;
5:  }
6:  if (cmd == READ) {
7:   if (*) {
8:     free(c);//A3:assert(!Freed[c]);Freed[c] := true;
9:     free(buf);//A4:assert(!Freed[buf]);Freed[buf] := true;
10:    /* ERROR: missing return */
11:  }
12: }
13: free(c);//A5:assert(!Freed[c]);Freed[c] := true;
14: free(buf);//A6:assert(!Freed[buf]);Freed[buf] := true;
15: return;
}
```

Figure 1. An example of a C double `free` bug.

inconsistency bugs [9, 11, 21], a class of high-confidence bugs that can be identified in a modular fashion. On the other hand, when the set of predicates Q is empty, our framework reports all of the warnings from the underlying modular verifier. Our framework can be instantiated with other predicate sets between these extremes in order to construct various schemes for filtering warnings.

1.1 Overview

We begin by providing an informal overview of our work with the help of two illustrative examples.

1.1.1 Semantic inconsistency detection

Consider the C program in Figure 1, which is a simplified version of a real program [11]. Initially, we will ignore the "//"-commented text. The program frees the pointers `c` and `buf` by invoking the `free` procedure. The "*" denotes a non-deterministic choice. The procedure `free` has a precondition that the argument should not already be freed; the effect of the procedure is to free the pointer. The procedure has a double-free bug when the sequence of locations `1,6,7,8,9,10,11,13,14,15` is executed; the pointers `c` and `buf` would be freed twice. The error in the program is the missing return in line `10`.

The comments in "//" encode the program statements into a simple intermediate language (described in detail in § 2.1). The program makes the type-state for *freed* explicit by maintaining an array `Freed` that is indexed by an integer address. The `free` procedure is replaced by its precondition and the update to the `Freed` array.

Demonic environments. Given this program, let us consider what a sound and precise modular program verifier (such as BOOGIE [1]) would do: (1) It would report a violation of the assertion at `A1` by pretending that `Freed[c]` could be true at entry to `Foo`. Looking at the code, it seems likely that the programmer does not expect this scenario. (2) It would next report a violation of the assertion at `A2` by pretending that `Freed[buf]` holds on input, or that the `c` and `buf` pointers could be aliased (assuming we don't trust the static types of C). Looking at the code, there is no indication that the programmer expects any such aliasing (probably because he/she trusts the static types). (3) It would next complain about locations `A3` and `A4` for similar reasons. (4) Finally, it would complain about `A5` and `A6` by assuming that `c` and `buf` are not freed on entry and that they are not aliased, which corresponds to the real bug.

The exercise illustrates the most severe limitation of modular checking: the absence of precise environment assumptions yields a flood of stupid false alarms that obscure interesting alarms. For this example, the environment consists of inputs `c`, `buf`, `cmd` and the global `Freed`. Sound modular checkers assume the most demonic environments not precluded by the existing procedure contracts (preconditions and callee postconditions).

Angelic environments. Now consider the other extreme. The *weakest (liberal) precondition* WP(`Foo`) is the largest set of input states for `Foo` that do not fail any assertion; in other words, the weakest *angelic* environment specification. WP(`Foo`) can be represented as:

```
(cmd != READ  &&  !Freed[c] && !Freed[buf] && c != buf)
```

However, the weakest precondition for this example is too strong. It makes code unreachable (namely `A3`, `A4`), which prevents the bug from being reported. This intuition has been exploited by prior work on semantic inconsistency detection [9, 11, 21], and has inspired our work.

Our insight is that if the weakest precondition is too strong according to some metric (such as the absence of intraprocedurally dead code), then we can progressively weaken it until it satisfies the metric (makes all code reachable). The weakening process will reveal assertion failures that were previously suppressed by the weakest precondition. We formalize the notion of *almost-correct specifications* as the set of specifications that can be obtained by *minimally* weakening the representation of weakest precondition as a conjunction of *maximal clauses* (§3.3). For the current example, our method infers a single almost-correct specification:

```
(!Freed[c] && !Freed[buf] && c != buf)
```

which fails only `A5`, the assertion failure corresponding to the true bug.[1]

```
void Bar(..) {
    twoints * data = NULL; /* Initialize data */
L1: data = (twoints *)calloc(100, sizeof(twoints));
L2: if(static_returns_t()) {
        /* FLAW: should check if memory allocation failed */
A1:     data[0].a = 1; ...
    } else {
        if (data != NULL) {
A2:         data[0].a = 1; ...
L3:     } else { }
    }
}
```

Figure 2. Example for abstract semantic inconsistency bug.

1.1.2 Abstract semantic inconsistency bug

Consider the following C example in Figure 2 from the SAMATE suite of benchmarks [20]. Let us assume that there is an assertion `data != 0` before the access to `data` in lines `A1` and `A2`. The environment for this example consists of the variables modified or returned by the two procedure calls `calloc` and `static_returns_t`. In the absence of any specification about the two procedures, a demonic environment would suggest that the assertion at line `A1` can fail. However, the code alone does not give us enough information to determine if this the environment is too demonic. On the angelic end, the weakest precondition conjures up a correlation between the two procedures and makes it a precondition to the procedure under analysis:

$$\theta_{L1}.\texttt{static\_returns\_t.return} \implies \theta_{L2}.\texttt{calloc.return} != 0$$

[1] In our semantics, assertion failures terminate execution and therefore two assertion failures cannot happen for the same input. Since every input that fails `A6` also fails `A5` under this environment, `A6` is unreachable and never reported as a failure.

Here θ_L.pr.return is a fresh constant that denotes the return value of the call to a procedure pr at some location L. The angelic weakest precondition tries to create correlations between various values in the program (parameters, returns, globals) in order to avoid an assertion failure.

Unlike the previous example, the metric of creating unreachable code cannot be used to counter the angelic specification. There is little evidence to suggest that either the angelic or demonic specification is (or isn't) the intended one.

Our insight is that we can report this warning (albeit with lesser confidence) by lifting semantic inconsistency detection to a more abstract setting. The idea is to take away some of the angelic power of the weakest precondition by restricting the vocabulary over which it can be expressed (i.e., the set of predicates Q). One natural abstraction that we describe in this paper is treating conditionals in a program as non-deterministic for the purpose of collecting the set of predicates in Q. This abstraction prevents the correlation between the return values of calloc and static_returns_t that the (concrete) weakest precondition inferred for this example. Instead, the most angelic specification possible under this abstraction of Q is θ_{L2}.calloc.return != 0, which creates dead code by making location L3 unreachable. The almost-correct specification (over Q) for this example is **true**, which reveals the bug in location A1. We call such bugs *abstract semantic inconsistency bugs*, as they are parameterized by the set of predicates Q.

The example shows that we are able to lift the idea of semantic inconsistency detection from the concrete domain to an abstraction, which allows us to classify more failures using the same underlying principle. This greatly increases the applicability of semantic inconsistency detection.

1.2 Contributions

In this work, we propose a parameterized post-processing framework for prioritizing the assertion failures reported by a modular verifier. Specifically, we make the following contributions: (1) We generalize the notion of semantic inconsistency bugs ([9, 11, 21]) by parameterizing it with a set of *predicates*. This allows us to apply the idea of semantic inconsistency to larger classes of warnings. (2) We formalize the concept of *almost-correct specifications* as the minimal weakening of the angelic specifications over a set of predicates. These specifications can be used to report high-confidence warnings to the user. (3) We provide a set of generic predicate choices that can be automatically constructed and instantiate our framework with them. (4) We have implemented our techniques in a tool called ACSPEC. Our tool is based on BOOGIE program verifier, but can be used with any off-the-shelf program verifier. (5) We have applied our tool on a diverse set of C programs measuring over 1.5 million LOC from open source and Windows software, and report our preliminary findings.

2. Background

In this section, we describe a simple programming language that we use to formalize the ideas in the paper.

2.1 Programs

Figure 3 defines the syntax of a simple loop-free and call-free programming language. A program consists of a set of procedures. Each program consists of a set of integer valued variables denoted by *Vars*. Variables are partitioned into globals, procedure parameters, returns, and locals. Integer expressions (denoted by *Expr*) can be constructed from variables, or by applying a function symbol f to a (possibly empty) list of expressions. Boolean expressions (denoted by *Formula*) can be constructed from Boolean constants, or by applying a predicate symbol p to a (possibly empty) list of expressions. The expressions are closed under Boolean connectives $\{\wedge, \neg\}$. Array expressions are modeled with the use of special function symbols *read* (to read a location in an array) and *write* (to return a new array updated at a location) that are constrained by the theory of arrays [6].

x, y	$\in$	*Vars*		
e	$\in$	*Expr*	::	x | $f(e,\ldots,e)$
ϕ, ψ	$\in$	*Formula*	::	**true** | **false** | $p(e,\ldots,e)$ | $\phi \wedge \phi$ | $\neg\phi$
s, t	$\in$	*Stmt*	::	skip | assert ϕ | assume ϕ | x := e | havoc x | $s; s$ | if (ϕ) then s else s

Figure 3. A simple programming language.

A (simple) statement can be either a skip (skip), an assertion (assert ϕ), an assumption (assume ϕ), or an assignment to a variable. In addition to the usual assignment x := e, the statement havoc x assigns a non-deterministic value to the variable x — this is used to model a non-deterministic value "*" in an expression. A (compound) statement can be either a sequential composition of two statements or a conditional statement if (ϕ) then s else t that executes the statement s if ϕ is true, or t otherwise.

Procedure calls are not part of the programming language. Instead, a procedure call is replaced by its specification. Consider a procedure pr(x) : ret that takes a parameter x, returns ret, and modifies a global gl $\in$ *Vars*. Further, it has a precondition ψ_1 (a formula over parameters and globals) and a postcondition ψ_2 (a formula over parameters, globals, and returns). A call to a procedure r := call $pr(e)$ at a control location l is expressed as:

assert $\psi_1[e/\mathtt{x}]$; r, gl := $\theta_l.pr.$r, $\theta_l.pr.$gl ; assume $\psi_2[\mathtt{r}/\mathtt{ret}]$;

where $\theta_l.pr.$r, $\theta_l.pr.$gl are fresh constants unique to the location l.

The constructs in the programming language are fairly standard, and we refer the reader to earlier work for an operational semantics of the language [7]. The expressive power of the simple language suffices to precisely provide semantics to many imperative languages such as C, C#, and Java. Fields and objects can be modeled by a map indexed by object identifiers. Object allocation and deallocation can be simulated using extra ghost variables. We refer the reader to previous work on modeling Java [12] and C [3].

2.2 Program to logic

DEFINITION 1 (*WP(pr)*). *For a procedure pr, the weakest precondition WP(pr) is the largest set of input states from which no execution fails an assertion.*

A procedure satisfies its contracts if $WP(pr)$ is the set $\lambda x.\mathbf{true}$. For a loop-free and call-free procedure, the check for partial correctness can be reduced to checking satisfiability (modulo the background theories) of a logical formula by variants of Dijkstra's *weakest (liberal) precondition* predicate transformer [8]. The predicate transformer $wp(s, \psi)$ takes as inputs a statement $s \in Stmt$ and a formula $\psi \in Formula$, and constructs a formula. It is defined recursively over the structure of statements as follows:

$$
\begin{array}{lcl}
wp(\mathtt{skip}, \psi) & = & \psi \\
wp(\mathtt{assume}\ \phi, \psi) & = & \neg\phi \vee \psi \\
wp(\mathtt{assert}\ \phi, \psi) & = & \phi \wedge \psi \\
wp(\mathtt{x} := e, \psi) & = & \psi[e/\mathtt{x}] \\
wp(\mathtt{havoc}\ \mathtt{x}, \psi) & = & \forall x.\psi[x/\mathtt{x}] \\
wp(s; t, \psi) & = & wp(s, wp(t, \psi)) \\
wp(\mathtt{if}\ (c)\ \mathtt{then}\ s\ \mathtt{else}\ t, \psi) & = & (\neg c \vee wp(s, \psi)) \wedge (c \vee wp(t, \psi))
\end{array}
$$

To verify that $pr(\ldots)\{body\}$ does not fail any assertions, we check that the formula $\neg wp(body, \mathbf{true})$ is unsatisfiable. Since computing $wp(body, \mathbf{true})$ can incur an exponential blowup, program verifiers compute an equisatisfiable formula by first passifying the program [13]. We often overload the expression $wp(pr, \mathbf{true})$ to mean $wp(body, \mathbf{true})$, where *body* is the body of pr. The satisfiability of the resultant formula can be checked by suitable decision procedures such as modern Satisfiability Modulo Theories (SMT) solvers [6]. We will refer to the process of converting a program to a formula as verification condition (VC) generation.

2.3 Dead and fail set

For a procedure pr, let $Locs$ denote the set of locations inside pr, and $Asserts$ denote the set of assertions inside pr. For rest of the discussion, the procedure pr, the set of assertions $Asserts$ and the set of locations $Locs$ are implicit in every context, unless otherwise noted.

For a formula $\phi \in Formula$ representing a set of input states, we define the following concepts:

1. The set of *dead* locations $Dead(\phi) \doteq \{l \in Locs \mid l$ is not reachable for any state in $\phi\}$.
2. The set of *failed* assertions $Fail(\phi) \doteq \{a \in Asserts \mid a$ can fail on at least one execution from an input in $\phi\}$.

Note that for non-deterministic programs, both $Dead(\phi)$ and $Fail(\phi)$ account for all possible executions starting from a given input state.

We assume that $Dead(\mathbf{true}) = \{\}$; that is, that there are no dead locations from the local perspective of pr. In practice, we can ensure that this assumption holds by removing $Dead(\mathbf{true})$ from $Locs$ before starting our analysis. To determine the set of dead locations, it suffices to restrict ourselves to only a subset of locations — namely the locations that appear immediately inside "then", and "else" branches as well as the locations that appear after each `assume` statement. The former ensures that each branch can be taken both ways, and the latter ensures that `assume` statements do not block subsequent statements.

Although we choose to define $Dead(\phi)$ in terms of branch coverage in this paper, the definition of $Dead(\phi)$ can be a parameter of our analysis. We can easily replace our definition with any computable metric for expressing when a specification is too strong. For example, we could have defined $Dead(\phi)$ as the set of paths that are infeasible under ϕ (i.e., in terms of path coverage rather than in terms of branch coverage), or as the set of observed runtime values at some locations that are precluded by ϕ.

2.4 Clauses

A *predicate* p is an atomic formula over some theory (say arithmetic) without any Boolean connectives $(\neg, \wedge, \vee)$ at the outermost scope. A *literal* l is either a predicate or its negation. A *clause* $c \doteq l_1 \vee l_2 \ldots l_k$ is a disjunction over literals. Dually, a *cube* $d \doteq l_1 \wedge l_2 \ldots l_k$ is a conjunction over literals. For a set of clauses C, we denote $\Pi(C)$ to be the formula $\left(\mathbf{true} \wedge \bigwedge_{c \in C} c\right)$.

LEMMA 1. *For any two sets of input clauses* $C_1 \subseteq C_2$,

- $Dead(\Pi(C_1)) \subseteq Dead(\Pi(C_2))$, *and*
- $Fail(\Pi(C_2)) \subseteq Fail(\Pi(C_1))$.

3. Semantic inconsistency and almost-correct specifications

In this section, we formalize the notion of abstract semantic inconsistency bugs (*SIB*). First, we capture the essential intuition behind semantic inconsistency [11] in the context of modular assertion checking (§ 3.1). We then lift the idea of inconsistency to a more general setting by parameterizing it with a set of predicates (abstract *SIB*). In § 3.3, we describe almost-correct specifications as a witness for abstract *SIB*s.

3.1 Semantic inconsistency bugs

Let us start by formalizing semantic inconsistency bugs in the context of modular assertion checking and explaining their relationship with weakest precondition.

DEFINITION 2 (*SIB*). *A procedure pr has a semantic inconsistency bug (SIB) if the largest set of input states ϕ that satisfies all assertions (i.e. $Fail(\phi) = \{\}$) creates dead code (i.e. $Dead(\phi) \neq \{\}$).*

We can establish a connection between inconsistency bugs and weakest precondition for a procedure:

PROPOSITION 1. *A procedure pr containing at least one assertion has a SIB if and only if $Dead(WP(pr)) \neq \{\}$.*

Note that the above formulation is purely semantic and only relies on the assertions present in the code. For the double `free()` example in § 1.1.1, the weakest precondition can be expressed as:

```
(cmd != READ && !Freed[c] && !Freed[buf] && c != buf)
```

However, this causes `A3` and `A4` to become unreachable, and thus the procedure has a *SIB*.

The case where $WP(pr)$ is equivalent to $\{\}$ (that is, when every input fails at least one assertion) is a special case of *SIB* bugs where $Dead(WP(pr))$ contains every statement in the procedure.

3.2 Abstract semantic inconsistency bugs

Although *SIB*s are interesting and useful to detect, they represent only a small fraction of all possible bugs. As the example in § 1.1.2 shows, the concrete $WP(pr)$ is the most angelic specification on the environment, and therefore examining the dead locations it creates will not reveal any errors except *SIB*s. Our goal in this section is to lift the connection between $WP(pr)$ and *SIB*s to a more general setting. Our intuition is simple: by restricting the abstraction (or vocabulary) over which we can describe the environment specifications, some warnings can be categorized as *SIB* bugs *with respect to that abstraction*, even though there may be no *SIB* bugs by the concrete definition defined earlier in Proposition 1.

We lift the notion of *SIB* to *abstract* semantic inconsistency bugs by parameterizing the definition of inconsistency with respect to a *predicate abstraction* [4, 14]. Given a set of atomic formulas Q, the abstraction function $\alpha_Q : Formula \rightarrow Formula$ maps a formula ϕ to the strongest approximation of ϕ expressible as Boolean combinations of Q. For example, if $Q = \{x = 0, y = 0\}$ and $\phi \doteq (x = 0 \wedge y = 0) \vee (x = 1 \wedge y = 1)$, then $\alpha_Q(\phi) \doteq (x = 0 \wedge y = 0) \vee (x \neq 0 \wedge y \neq 0)$. For a given formula $\phi \in Formula$, we denote β_Q as the weakest underapproximation of ϕ with respect to a given set of predicates Q. It is represented as $\neg\alpha_Q(\neg\phi)$. We can establish a partial order on the set of all predicate abstractions by a subset relation $\subseteq$ on the set of predicates. It is not hard to see that given a formula ϕ and two sets of predicates $Q \subseteq P$, $\phi \implies \alpha_P(\phi) \implies \alpha_Q(\phi)$ and $\beta_Q(\phi) \implies \beta_P(\phi) \implies \phi$. In other words, a larger set of predicates provides a more precise approximation (both over and under) of ϕ.

DEFINITION 3 (Abstract *SIB*). *A procedure pr has an abstract semantic inconsistency bug (abstract SIB) with respect to a set of predicates Q if $Dead(\beta_Q(wp(pr, \mathbf{true}))) \neq \{\}$.*

The intuition behind this definition is quite simple: the set of environments $\beta_Q(wp(pr, \mathbf{true}))$ is the weakest set of angelic environments expressible using Q that do not fail any assertion in the procedure. If this set of states gives rise to dead code, then the procedure has an abstract *SIB*. Henceforth, we will implicitly assume Q as the set of predicates under consideration unless otherwise noted.

Note that when Q contains all the atomic predicates from $wp(pr, \mathbf{true})$, then abstract *SIB*s (with respect to Q) and *SIB*s coincide. Unlike concrete *SIB*s, abstract *SIB*s are not guaranteed to correspond to either true bugs or dead code. However, the example in § 1.1.2 illustrates that some true bugs can be categorized as abstract *SIB*s, but not as concrete *SIB*s. At the other extreme when $Q \doteq \{\}$, any assertion failure will manifest itself as an abstract *SIB* since the only specifications allowed over $Q = \{\}$ are **true** and **false**. We can establish the following relationship between two sets of predicates:

PROPOSITION 2. *For two sets of predicates $Q \subseteq P$, if pr has an abstract SIB under P, then pr has an abstract SIB under Q.*

3.3 Almost-correct specifications

So far, we have only shown how to determine whether a procedure has an abstract *SIB* or not. In this section, we explain how to find the assertions that might fail in a procedure with a *SIB* (abstract or concrete). We provide a witness for each potential assertion failure by providing an *almost-correct* specification under which that assertion might fail. For this section, we assume that the procedure pr is fixed and therefore implicit in the definitions.

Let $Formula_Q \subseteq Formula$ be the set of all formulas that can be constructed by a Boolean combination over the predicates in Q.

DEFINITION 4 ($AlmostCorrectSpecs(Q)$). *For a set of predicates Q and an integer $k \geq 0$, $AlmostCorrectSpecsK(Q, k) \subseteq Formula_Q$ is defined as set of formulas ϕ where*

1. $\beta_Q(wp(pr, \mathbf{true})) \implies \phi$, *and*
2. $Dead(\phi) = \{\}$, *and*
3. $|Fail(\phi)| = k$, *and*
4. *for any* $\psi \in Formula_Q$ *such that* $\beta_Q(wp(pr, \mathbf{true})) \implies \psi \implies \phi$, *either* $\phi \implies \psi$ *or* $Dead(\psi) \neq \{\}$.

$AlmostCorrectSpecs(Q)$ *is* $AlmostCorrectSpecsK(Q, k)$ *for the smallest* $k \geq 0$ *such that* $AlmostCorrectSpecsK(Q, k) \neq \{\}$.

$AlmostCorrectSpecsK(Q, k)$ contains precisely those formulas ϕ that are at least as weak as the $\beta_Q(wp(pr, \mathbf{true}))$, do not create any dead code, induce k assertion failures, and cannot be strengthened over the vocabulary Q without creating dead code. $AlmostCorrectSpecs(Q)$ contains the set of specifications that induce the minimum number of failures. When a procedure has no abstract *SIB*s, then $AlmostCorrectSpecs(Q)$ is precisely the set of formulas representing $\beta_Q(wp(pr, \mathbf{true}))$, which (by definition) induce $k = 0$ failures.

Algorithm 1 $FindAbstractSIBs(pr, Q)$

Require: A procedure pr with a set of assertions $Asserts$
Require: A set of predicates Q
1: $\phi \leftarrow \beta_Q(wp(pr, \mathbf{true}))$
2: **if** $Dead(\phi) \neq \{\}$ **then**
3: $s \leftarrow$ *SIB* /* abstract */
4: **else**
5: $s \leftarrow$ *MAYBUG* /* low confidence warnings */
6: **end if**
7: $\Psi \leftarrow FindAlmostCorrectSpecs(pr, Q)$
8: $E \leftarrow \bigcup_{\psi \in \Psi} Fail(\psi)$
9: return (s, E)

Algorithm 1 shows how to find abstract *SIB*s. Line 7 invokes a method for generating a set of almost-correct specifications over Q; we describe this method in the next section. Finally, line 8 collects the set of assertion failures that are possible under the almost-correct specifications.

4. Computing almost-correct specifications

In this section, we describe one method to compute the set of almost-correct specifications formulated in Definition 4. The steps consist of obtaining a *canonical* representation of $\beta_Q(wp(pr, \mathbf{true}))$ in a conjunctive normal form (§ 4.1), and then performing a greedy search (with pruning) to find the almost-correct specifications (§ 4.2). We discuss Boolean simplification of the resultant specifications and further weakening the specifications based on some syntactic clause quality measures (§ 4.3). Finally, we provide different methods for constructing the set of predicates Q starting with the precise set of predicates for representing $wp(pr, \mathbf{true})$.

4.1 Predicate cover $PredicateCover_Q(pr)$

For a procedure pr, let $VC(pr) \in Formula$ be the verification condition (VC) that is equisatisfiable with $\neg wp(pr, \mathbf{true})$ — the size of $VC(pr)$ is usually almost linear in the size of pr [1] when pr is converted to static single assignment (SSA) form. Given a set of predicates Q, the predicate cover $\beta_Q(wp(pr, \mathbf{true}))$ is computed by enumerating all the assignments (ALL-SAT) over Q that satisfy $VC(pr)$ and then obtaining a set of clauses by negating these assignments. The clauses obtained this way are *maximal* — i.e., each predicate in Q either appears in a positive or negative polarity in each clause. Let us denote this operation as $PredicateCover_Q(pr)$. Such a conjunctive normal form over maximal clauses provides a canonical representation of $\beta_Q(wp(pr, \mathbf{true}))$. The canonical representation is important for computing the almost-correct specifications, as we will describe in the next section. The algorithm is fairly standard in predicate abstraction and we refer readers to earlier work [19].

4.2 Weakening predicate cover

The algorithm $FindAlmostCorrectSpecs(pr, Q)$ finds the set of almost-correct specifications. It first computes the set of maximal clauses C using the predicate cover operation described earlier. It performs a greedy search over the space of clauses by selecting a clause to drop and then inspecting the $Dead()$ and $Fail()$ counts of the resulting clause sets. The algorithm starts with the set of clauses C satisfying $Fail(\Pi(C)) = \{\}$ and computes the minimum number of failures that can result from dropping clauses from C to make all the code reachable. The procedure returns a set of formulas, each representing an almost-correct specification.

For the purpose of this section, we will treat the operations $Normalize$ and $PruneClauses$ as identity functions that simply return the input set of clauses — we will consider more interesting uses in § 4.3. The algorithm maintains a frontier set S of sets of clauses that have a non-empty dead set and iterates (via the outer while loop) until S is empty. It also maintains the minimum failure count ($MinFail$) for any clause set with an empty dead set. This count is initialized to the size of $Asserts$. At each step, the algorithm extracts a clause set $C_1 \in S$, and enumerates each subset of clauses C_2 (the inner for loop) by dropping a clause c from C_1. Each sub-clause C_2 is either added to S (if $Dead(C_2) \neq \{\}$ and $|Fail(C_2)| \leq MinFail$, or $Dead(C_2) = \{\}$ and $|Fail(C_2)| = 0$) or pruned (if $Dead(C_2) \neq \{\}$ and $|Fail(C_2)| > MinFail$). If $|Dead(C_2)| = 0$ and $|Fail(C_2)| \leq MinFail$, then we add C_2 to the output set U. When $|Fail(C_2)| < MinFail$, then the output set is flushed and the $MinFail$ is reduced to $|Fail(C_2)|$.

THEOREM 1. *The following statements are true:*

1. $FindAlmostCorrectSpecs(pr, Q) \subseteq AlmostCorrectSpecs(Q)$.
2. *For each* $\phi \in AlmostCorrectSpecs(Q)$, *there exists a* $\psi \in FindAlmostCorrectSpecs(pr, Q)$ *such that* $\phi \Leftrightarrow \psi$.

The set $AlmostCorrectSpecs(Q)$ may contain different syntactic representations of the same specification and therefore may con-

Algorithm 2 *FindAlmostCorrectSpecs*(pr, Q)

Require: A procedure pr with a set of assertions $Asserts$
Require: A set of predicates Q
Ensure: Set of formulas representing $AlmostCorrectSpecs(C)$
$C \leftarrow PredicateCover_Q(pr)$
if $Dead(\Pi(C)) = \{\}$ **then**
  return $\{\Pi(PruneClauses(Normalize(C)))\}$
end if
$S \leftarrow \{C\}$ /*Frontier set */
$T \leftarrow \{\}$ /* Visited set */
$U \leftarrow \{\}$ /* Output set */
$MinFail \leftarrow |Asserts|$ /* Smallest set of failures*/
while $S \neq \{\}$ /* Frontier is non-empty */ **do**
  $C_1 \leftarrow Choose(S)$
  for each clause $c \in C_1$ **do**
    $C_2 \leftarrow C_1 \setminus \{c\}$ /* Weaken by one clause */
    if $C_2 \in T$ **then**
      continue /* Visited already */
    end if
    $T \leftarrow T \cup \{C_2\}$ /* Add to Visited */
    if $|Fail(C_2)| > MinFail$ **then**
      continue /* $MinFail$ can only decrease */
    end if
    if $|Dead(C_2)| \neq 0$ **then**
      $S \leftarrow S \cup \{C_2\}$ /* Add to the frontier set */
    else if $|Fail(C_2)| = 0$ **then**
      $S \leftarrow S \cup \{C_2\}$ /* Add to the frontier set */
    else if $|Fail(C_2)| = MinFail$ **then**
      $U \leftarrow U \cup \{C_2\}$ /* Add it to U */
    else
      /* $|Fail(C_2)| < MinFail$ */
      $MinFail \leftarrow |Fail(C_2)|$ /* Decrease $MinFail$ */
      $U \leftarrow \{C_2\}$ /* Clear U and add C_2 */
    end if
  end for
end while
return $\bigcup_{C_1 \in U} \Pi(PruneClauses(Normalize(C_1)))$

tain more formulas than $FindAlmostCorrectSpecs(pr, Q)$. The proof follows from the observations that (a) the set of maximal cubes (negation of maximal clause) over Q partitions the set of all states, and (b) dropping a maximal clause from the set of maximal clauses representing a formula weakens the formula by exactly one maximal cube.

4.3 Clause simplification and pruning

We can additionally parameterize the almost-correct specifications by providing a syntactic quality measure for the set of clauses. For instance, the number of literals in a clause can be a measure of goodness of a specification. Under the hypothesis that good specifications are usually simple and do not contain many disjunctions, we can prune clauses that contain a large number of literals. Alternately, we might try to avoid clauses that correlate the return values of multiple procedure calls.

However, such quality measures cannot be applied directly on the maximal clauses. Consider the maximal clauses $(a \vee b) \wedge (a \vee \neg b)$ over $Q = \{a, b\}$. These clauses have two literals per clause and may be undesirable, whereas an equivalent clause (a) has only one literal. We address this problem by first performing Boolean simplification of the maximal clauses.

The operation $Normalize(C)$ takes a set of clauses C and performs Boolean clause simplification on the set of clauses. It applies the following three rules to a set of clauses (starting with C) until a fix-point is reached: (1) *Resolution:* If there are two clauses $(c \vee l), (d \vee \neg l) \in C$, then add $(c \vee d)$ to C. (2) *Subsumption:* If there are two clauses $c, (c \vee l) \in C$, then remove $(c \vee l)$ from C. (3) *Tautologies:* If there is a clause $(c \vee l \vee \neg l) \in C$, then remove it from C.

The function $PruneClauses$ takes a set of clauses and returns a subset of clauses that satisfy the quality measure. Note that the pruning makes the almost-correct specifications weaker and can reveal more warnings — it is not just a syntactic transformation. For the example in § 1.1.2, both schemes (limiting the number of literals per clause to one, or removing clauses containing returns from multiple procedures) will reveal the warning by pruning the clause θ_{L1}`.static_returns_t.return` $\Longrightarrow$ θ_{L2}`.calloc.return != 0`.

4.4 Mining predicates

We now describe a few choices for constructing the set of predicates in Q automatically for any given procedure pr. We start with a method for collecting all the atomic predicates that appear in the expression representing the weakest precondition (§ 4.4.1), followed by two methods that generate smaller sets of predicates (§ 4.4.2 and § 4.4.3).

4.4.1 Predicates in $wp(pr, \mathbf{true})$

Recall that if Q contains all the atomic predicates that constitute $wp(pr, \mathbf{true})$, then $\beta_Q(wp(pr, \mathbf{true}))$ is equivalent to $wp(pr, \mathbf{true})$, and abstract *SIB*s and *SIB*s coincide. For a procedure pr with body $body$, the set of predicates collected is $Preds(body, \{\})$, where $Preds(,)$ is defined recursively as follows:

$$
\begin{array}{lcl}
Preds(\texttt{skip}, Q) & = & Q \\
Preds(\texttt{assume}\ \phi, Q) & = & Atoms(\phi) \cup Q \\
Preds(\texttt{assert}\ \phi, Q) & = & Atoms(\phi) \cup Q \\
Preds(\texttt{x} := e, Q) & = & Atoms(Q[e/\texttt{x}]) \\
Preds(\texttt{havoc x}, Q) & = & Drop(Q, \texttt{x}) \\
Preds(s; t, Q) & = & Preds(s, Preds(t, Q)) \\
Preds(\texttt{if}\ (c)\ \texttt{then}\ s\ \texttt{else}\ t, Q) & = & Atoms(c) \cup Preds(s, Q) \\
 & & \cup\ Preds(t, Q)
\end{array}
$$

Here $Atoms(\phi)$ collects the set of atomic predicates (those do not contain any Boolean connectives), and $Drop(Q, \texttt{x})$ removes any atomic predicate in Q that contains the variable `x`. Note the similarity with the $wp(s, \phi)$ transformer from § 2.2, as the goal of the predicate collection above is to collect the atomic predicates that may appear in the $wp(pr, \mathbf{true})$. We describe a few important details about the predicates in $Preds(body, \{\})$.

First, recall that a variable `x` that is modified by a call to a procedure pr_l at line l is assigned a special constant $\theta_l.pr_l.\texttt{x}$ (§ 2.1). These constants appear in the set of predicates Q and in the specifications (see the example in § 1.1.2).

Second, consider the problem of generating atomic predicates in the presence of arrays or maps. For example,

$$wp(\texttt{x} := write(\texttt{x}, e_1, e_2), p(read(\texttt{x}, e_3), e_4))$$

results in the formula $p(read(write(\texttt{x}, e_1, e_2), e_3), e_4)$ that contains $write$ symbol. We apply rewrite rules (omitted for brevity) to eliminate the $write$ symbols in the predicates in order to make input specifications more readable and intuitive. After eliminating $write$, the above expression corresponds to $e_1 = e_3\ ?\ p(e_2, e_4) : p(read(\texttt{x}, e_3), e_4)$. The set of atomic predicates in this expression are $\{e_1 = e_3,\ p(e_2, e_4),\ p(read(\texttt{x}, e_3), e_4)\}$. This explains the presence of the predicate `c` $=$ `buf` in the weakest precondition for the example of double-free (§ 1.1.1).

4.4.2 Ignoring conditionals

Consider the following example:

Alias	Havoc returns	Ignore conditionals
Conc	F	F
A_0	T	F
A_1	F	T
A_2	T	T

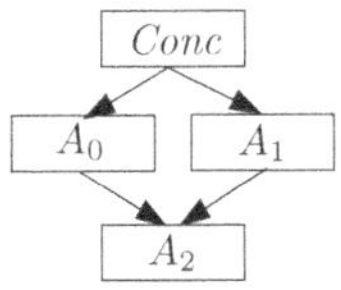

Figure 4. The four abstract configurations defined by combining our two abstractions, along with their aliases. Arrows flow from higher precision to lower precision.

```
void Foo(bool c1, bool c2, int *x) {
    if (c1) {...; if (x) {*x = 1;} ... }
    if (c2) {... ; *x = 2; ...}
}
```

The weakest precondition avoids non-null errors by conjuring $\mathtt{c2} \implies \mathtt{x} \neq 0$ as a possible precondition. This precondition does not create any concrete *SIB*s. One way to take away this angelic power (and reveal warnings as abstract *SIB*s) is to avoid considering the predicates that guard conditionals. We can obtain this by treating a conditional **if** (c) **then** s **else** t as $\{$**havoc** x; **if** (x) **then** s **else** $t;\}$ during predicate collection (where x is a fresh program variable). The set of predicates collected for this examples is $Q = \{\mathtt{x} \neq 0\}$.

4.4.3 Havoc returns

Another way to restrict the set of predicates is to avoid predicates about callee modifications. Instead of assigning fresh constants (e.g. $\theta_l.pr_1$.x) to modified variables (as done by default in § 2.1), we can **havoc** these variables. However, this can also lead to undesired imprecision in cases such as:

```
void Bar(...) {
    havoc x;    // x = getValidPointer(..);
    M[x] := 1; // *x = 1;
}
```

For this example, $wp(\mathtt{Bar}, \mathbf{true})$ will be **false** because the predicate set is empty.

We henceforth refer to the first abstraction described as "ignore conditionals" (§ 4.4.2) and the second as "havoc returns" (§ 4.4.3). The product of the these two abstractions naturally yields $2^2 = 4$ abstract configurations which we name and describe in Figure 4. The configuration *Conc* refers to concrete *SIB*s (§ 4.4.1). The rest of the configurations A_0, A_1, A_2 correspond to abstract *SIB*s resulting from combining the schemes in the previous two sections (§ 4.4.2 and § 4.4.3).

5. Implementation and evaluation

Implementation. We have constructed a prototype tool ACSPEC (Almost-Correct SPECifications) that implements the ideas presented in the paper. The tool consists of around 2000 lines of C# code. It accepts a source file in the BOOGIE language [7] and a list of abstractions as input. It outputs whether the procedure has a *SIB* under the abstractions, searches for the set of almost-correct specifications in the predicate vocabulary allowed by the abstractions, and prints the set of errors induced by the specifications. We leverage BOOGIE's optimized verification condition generation along with the Z3 SMT solver [6] for checking the satisfiability of the verification conditions. The current prototype does not yet use the incremental interface to the Z3 prover and regenerates VC for every call to Z3 — this is a major source of inefficiency in the current implementation.

The main modules implemented in the tool are (a) computing the $Fail()$ and $Dead()$ sets, (b) generating the set of predicates under the different options from Figure 4, (c) computing the predicate cover and checking for *SIB*s, (d) searching for almost-correct specifications over a set of clauses, and (e) normalizing clauses and performing clause pruning. We only mention the computation of $Dead()$ briefly here. For each location $l \in Locs$ (one for each block that has an **assume** statement), we introduce an assertion **assert** b_l. To compute $Dead(\phi)$, we ask for all assertion failures (over the location asserts) under ϕ — the set of assertions that *do not fail* constitute $Dead(\phi)$. For computing $Dead()$, we rely on the completeness of the theorem prover. For the logics we use (equalities, arithmetic, arrays), Z3 ensures completeness.

Bench	LOC (C)	LOC (BPL)	Procs	Asserts
CWE476	24582	267510	561	228
CWE690	85855	941045	1865	1009
ansicon	2972	38145	289	325
space	9566	185878	263	2144
cancel	827	7411	9	9
event	872	6430	7	4
firefly	622	8669	9	22
moufilter	631	7073	7	25
vserial	1396	21617	23	102
Drv1	97615	1401949	799	14402
Drv2	77180	1536078	1218	13843
Drv3	31011	77760	67	692
Drv4	82720	542049	401	3582
Drv5	151516	981682	661	11250
Drv6	18577	562477	490	7381
Drv7	1171514	21845268	21626	227573
Lib1	96158	1121121	1158	10051
Total	1853614	29552162	29453	292642

Figure 5. Benchmark statistics. For each benchmark, we give the lines of code in both C and BOOGIE, the number of procedures, and number of assertions.

Benchmarks. We chose a set of 17 C benchmarks drawn from open source programs and the Windows codebase (Figure 5). The CWE benchmarks are from the NIST SAMATE test suite for static analysis[2], space is a flight control software[3], ansicon is a console text processor, and the rest of the small benchmarks are sample drivers from Windows Driver Kit[4]. The set of larger Windows benchmarks has been anonymized. Each Drv* is a set of multiple drivers in Windows and Lib1 is a core component of the Windows kernel. All benchmarks were compiled from C to the BOOGIE programming language using the HAVOC tool [3]. Although our technique works for arbitrary assertions, the only assertions contained in these programs are assertions of the form `x != null` automatically inserted by HAVOC before each pointer dereference `*x`. For each procedure, we unroll the loops twice. This allows us to focus on the (still substantial) subset of warnings from program verifiers that do not arise from analysis imprecision in handling loops.

Experiments. We performed experiments with the goal of evaluating both the reduction in warnings (Section 5.1.1) and the precision/completeness trade offs (Section 5.1.2) induced by the abstractions and clause pruning. Finally, we evaluated the usability of ACSPEC on larger programs by running the tool on over 1M lines of Windows code (Section 5.1.3). We triaged the highest priority warnings and compiled statistics on the performance of the tool.

Experimental setup. For each benchmark we checked for *SIB*s with the *Conc* configuration and abstract *SIB*s with the A_0, A_1, and A_2 configurations. *Cons* refers to the conservative verifier we

[2] http://samate.nist.gov/SRD/testsuite.php

[3] http://sir.unl.edu/portal/index.html

[4] http://www.microsoft.com/whdc/devtools/ddk/default.mspx

Bench	Proc	Asrt	*Conc*	k=3	k=2	k=1	A_1	k=3	k=2	k=1	A_2	k=3	k=2	k=1	*Cons*	TO
CWE476	561	228	32	32	32	34	32	32	32	34	36	36	36	36	126	0
CWE690	1865	1009	36	36	36	60	54	54	54	60	105	105	105	105	348	0
ansicon	289	325	1	4	5	5	2	17	18	20	5	26	26	28	60	9
space	263	2144	2	94	131	150	6	27	18	243	9	22	28	30	313	39
cancel	9	9	0	0	0	0	0	0	0	2	0	0	0	2	2	1
event	7	4	0	0	0	1	0	0	0	0	0	0	0	0	1	0
firefly	9	22	0	2	4	5	0	0	2	2	4	4	4	4	7	0
moufilter	7	25	0	0	0	0	0	0	0	0	5	5	5	5	8	0
vserial	23	102	0	10	2	11	0	0	10	11	8	10	12	12	24	1
Total	3033	3868	71	178	210	266	94	130	134	372	172	208	216	222	889	50

Figure 6. Comparison of abstract configurations and clause pruning on small benchmarks. For each abstract configuration (*Conc*, A_1, A_2), we show results with no clause pruning ($k = \infty$) and with pruning from $k = 3$ to 1."TO" denotes the number of timeouts.

use (BOOGIE). We omit results for A_0 because it performed the same as A_2 on all benchmarks we tried. Timeout was set to 10 seconds; we omit procedures that timed out in any configuration. Experiments were run on a Windows 7 desktop machine with a 2.66 GHz processor and 6 GB of RAM and a Windows 7 laptop with a 1.3 GHz processor and 4 GB of RAM.

5.1 Evaluation

5.1.1 Warning reduction

In our first experiment, we compared the the number of warnings reported by *Conc*, A_1, and A_2 abstract configurations both without clause pruning and with k-clause pruning for $k = 1$ to 3 (Figure 6). In k-clause pruning, we prune clauses with $> k$ literals out of specifications (§ 4.3). We observe that:

- Without clause pruning, all abstract configurations report many fewer warnings than *Cons*. Even the coarsest abstract configuration (A_2) reported at least 2X fewer alarms than the conservative verifier on almost all benchmarks.
- Clause pruning steadily increases the number of alarms reported as k decreases. This effect is relatively stable across abstract configurations, but is much more dramatic for *Conc* and A_1. Even with clause pruning, all configurations still report less than half as many alarms as *Cons* on most benchmarks.

Interestingly, combining aggressive clause pruning with a coarser abstraction can sometimes result in a *lower* number of errors than a finer abstraction at the same level of clause pruning (for example, the firefly benchmark under 1-clause pruning in the *Conc* and A_1 configurations). This is because abstractions remove predicates and consequently force the generation of simpler (and less disjunctive) specs. An example illustrates how this can occur:

```
L1: grid_ptr = malloc();
L2: if (grid_ptr == NULL) return;
L3: x = *key;
```

The weakest specification for *Conc* (θ_{L1}`.malloc.return == 0 || key != 0`) has a disjunction. However, A_1's predicate vocabulary does not allow predicates from conditionals, so the angelic specification is the simpler `key != 0`. Though both specs prove the program correct without creating dead code, the former contains one disjunction, so it is pruned to **true** by 1-clause pruning and reports a warning.

5.1.2 Precision and completeness trade offs

Our next experiment investigated whether the additional alarms revealed by adding abstractions and/or clause pruning to the *Conc* configuration were real bugs or false positives. We performed a complete classification of the error reports for *Cons*, *Conc*, and

		Conc			A_1			A_2			*Cons*		
Bnch	Asrt	C	FP	FN	C	FP	FN	C	FP	FN	C	FP	FN
CWE476	228	179	0	49	179	0	49	179	2	47	183	45	0
CWE490	1009	775	0	234	793	0	216	844	0	165	931	78	0
Total	1237	954	0	283	972	0	265	1023	2	212	1114	123	0

Figure 7. Full classification of alarms for the SAMATE benchmark suite across abstract configurations with no clause pruning. We give the number of assertions classified correctly (C), number of false positives (FP), and number of false negatives (FN).

the abstract configurations for two benchmarks: CWE476 and CWE690. We chose these because they are from a NIST test suite for static analysis tools in which dereferences are labeled as safe or buggy (with 36% and 27% assertions buggy for CWE476 and CWE690 respectively). We omit the results for clause pruning because they were nearly identical to the results shown. Figure 7 shows the results. We can observe the following:

- Adding abstractions (such as A_1 and A_2) to *Conc* allows us to report more real bugs than the concrete domain while barely increasing the number of false positives. The few false positives our abstract domains report are due to the "havoc return values" abstraction as shown in § 4.4.2 and § 4.4.3.
- Even the coarsest abstraction fails to report lots of real bugs. This is expected — our stated goal is to report a small number of high confidence bugs with a low false positive rate. Many false negatives occur because there is no (abstract) inconsistency when the procedures bodies are simple, but buggy (e.g. `void Foo(x) { *x = 1;}`). To catch such bugs, we plan to extend our current method to assert the weakest precondition of simple procedures at call sites.

5.1.3 Larger benchmarks

In this section, we evaluate ACSPEC on the set of core Windows benchmarks, measuring over a million lines. The results are shown[5] in Figure 8.

Bench	Proc	Asrt	*Conc*	A_1	A_2	*Cons*	TO
Drv1	799	14402	2	5	44	399	401
Drv2	1218	13843	0	0	61	766	370
Drv3	67	692	0	0	1	63	18
Drv4	401	3582	0	0	12	262	61
Drv5	661	11250	0	0	31	353	294
Drv6	490	7381	0	0	84	287	114
Drv7	16753	172973	1	11	876	12596	1369
Lib1	1158	10051	1	3	171	552	317
Total	21547	234174	4	19	1280	15278	2944

Figure 8. Comparison of abstract configurations on large benchmarks. "TO" denotes the number of timeouts.

We briefly comment on trends in the data:

- As on the smaller benchmarks, the abstract configurations provide a "knob" through which gradually more errors can be viewed by adding abstractions to *Conc*.
- With the possible exception of A_2, the abstract configurations show a number of warnings small enough that a willing user could feasibly examine them. As expected, the conservative verifier reports more warnings than most users would reasonably want to examine.

[5] Our tool did not analyze around 5000 procedures in Drv7 due to an out-of-memory error. The results do not include these procedures or their assertions.

We investigated most of the warnings reported by the *Conc* and A_1 configurations. All of the reports we examined were false positives, which is perhaps not entirely surprising since the property we are testing for is very shallow and these benchmarks are old and well-tested Windows code.

Many false positives were due to expansion of macros (a problem also encountered by [11] [21]). One extensively used macro pattern defensively checks for `NULL` before dereferencing a field:

```
#define CheckFieldF(x, a) (x != NULL && x->f == a)
```

The short-circuiting semantics of "&&" causes us to view this as a conditional expression, which means that a code snippet such as `y = *x; if(CheckFieldF(x, a)) ...` is expanded to `y = *x; if (x != NULL) {...} else {L1: ...}`. *Conc* flags this as a *SIB* since the location `L1` is unreachable for the specification `x != NULL`. We manually validated that `x` can never be never be `NULL` in each of these cases, which means that this check is too defensive, but not buggy. Another cause for the *Conc* warnings is the presence of macros that encode an assertion in terms of **assert false** as follows:

```
#define SL_ASSERT(e)  if (!e) assert(false)
```

Our tool insists that the "then" branch of such code be reachable, although the user expects it to be reachable only when the assertion fails. Macro expansion corresponds to a form of inlining callees, and the heuristic of absence of dead code can sometimes be too strong interprocedurally [9] (due to defensive coding in the callees).

Most of the A_1 warnings happen either due to one of the reasons above, or due to the removal of correlations that appear to be true preconditions. A common pattern that we observe (names anonymized) is the following:

```
void Process(size_t mBufferLength, char *mBuffer, ..){ ...
1:  if (mBufferLength >= 0) { ...
2:      for (size_t i = 0; i < mBufferLength; ++i) { ...
3:          assert(mBuffer != null); mBuffer[i] = ..;
        }
      ....
    }
5:  if (mBuffer != null) { .... }
```

where the tool avoids the error in Line 3 during *Conc* analysis by inferring the correct precondition: `mBufferLength >= 0` $\Longrightarrow$ `mBuffer != 0`, which does not create any dead code. However, A_1 results in a stronger specification `mBuffer != 0`, which creates dead code for the "else" branch for Line 5 and reveals a *SIB*.

A vast majority of the A_2 warnings are due to an overly conservative modeling of calls in HAVOC, where all fields (modeled as maps) are present in the set of modified globals for a call. Any nested dereference of a field `x->f->g` (modeled as `g[f[x]]`) after a call to (say) `bar` results in a warning since A_2 can't capture that `x->f != 0` (expressed as `f[x] != 0`) after the call to `bar`. On the other hand, both *Conc* and A_1 can add a specification θ`.bar.f[x] != 0` since the modified values have associated symbolic constants.

5.1.4 Performance

Figure 9 describes the performance of our tool on the large benchmark set. We do not report any statistics for procedures that the conservative verifier labels as correct. We note that: (1) As expected, A_1 and A_2 collect fewer predicates than *Conc*. (2) Interestingly, the number of clauses in the predicate cover is relatively stable across all three configurations even though *Conc* runs noticeably slower than the other two domains.

	Conc			A_1			A_2		
Bench	P	C	T	P	C	T	P	C	T
Drv1	3.5	1.1	2.7	2.0	1.0	2.2	1.8	0.9	2.1
Drv2	4.5	1.1	2.0	2.4	1.1	1.3	2.2	1.0	1.2
Drv3	3.6	1.3	2.3	2.8	1.3	1.6	2.6	1.3	1.6
Drv4	4.1	1.6	2.7	2.6	1.5	1.9	2.5	1.5	1.9
Drv5	3.6	1.0	2.3	1.7	0.9	1.4	1.4	0.8	1.4
Drv6	5.3	1.6	2.8	2.8	1.5	1.7	2.8	1.3	1.9
Drv7	3.3	1.3	1.1	2.5	1.2	0.8	2.4	1.1	0.8
Lib1	6.1	1.5	2.3	3.1	1.2	1.3	2.0	1.0	1.2

Figure 9. Performance on large benchmarks expressed as per-procedure averages. P is av. predicates/procedure, C is av. clauses in the predicate cover/procedure, and T is av. time/procedure in seconds.

Finally, as we can see from Figure 8, we time out on 14% of the procedures that the conservative verifier does not label as correct[6]. We found that the sources of timeouts are mixed. Some of the larger procedures take more than 10 seconds to compute $Fail()$ and $Dead()$; others time out during the predicate cover generation, and a smaller number time out during the search for almost-correct specifications. In the latter case, we can at least answer the question about the existence of a *SIB* in the procedure. We believe that using the incremental Z3 interface will significantly reduce timeouts by preventing redundant VC generation.

6. Related work

Engler *et al.* introduced inconsistency detection [11] as a practical approach for finding bugs in real programs. They identify a set of templates for inconsistent programmer beliefs such as "`*`<p> ... `if (`<p>` != null)`" that can be matched to patterns in real code in order to find likely bugs. They rank occurrences of these patterns using statistical analysis and use this simple but powerful combination to discover hundreds of new bugs in open source software. They build on this work with techniques for suppressing false alarms stemming from "polluted" analysis results [17] and a combination of this approach with factor-based statistical techniques to automatically infer rich function specifications, such as which functions allocate and de-allocate memory [18].

Dillig *et al.* provide the first semantic formulation of inconsistency errors [9]. In their framework, an inconsistency is a discrepancy between two related "checks" (i.e., a dereference): an inconsistency exists when there are two checks on the same predicate such that one check always succeeds, but the other may fail. They formally distinguish inconsistency errors from *source-sink* errors which require directly tracking the flow of a bad value across the program. Finally, they provide a scheme for interprocedural inconsistency detection based on inlining failure summaries for procedures at their call sites.

The recent work of Tomb and Flanagan [21] is the closest to identifying a connection between weakest precondition and (concrete) inconsistency checking in terms of assertions. Their inconsistency detection works by splitting a procedure pr with c conditionals into $2c$ *wedge programs*, where each wedge blocks one of the two branches of a conditional statement. An inconsistency is reported if any wedge program fails on all inputs. Both of these works [9, 21] validate that numerous bugs can be found using semantic inconsistency checking.

Our approach is inspired by both of these formulations of inconsistency checking, although our goal is not limited to finding inconsistency bugs. There are several differences between our work and

[6] We ignore the 5000 procedures that were not analyzed due to the memory problem.

theirs. First, our formulation of inconsistency checking can be parameterized with an abstraction, which allows us to apply the idea to a more general class of errors. Second, we compute the almost-correct specifications for a procedure, which allows us to witness inconsistency bugs as the failures induced by these specifications.

Finally, there are subtle discrepancies in the definition of inconsistency due to differences in formalism. For example, [21] would not report an inconsistency error for the procedure `Foo` in § 4.4.2, whereas [9] would [21]. Our formulation agrees with [21] in that we would characterize this program as an abstract *SIB* rather than a concrete *SIB*. On the other hand, we would report a concrete *SIB* for the program `if` $(*)$ **`then`** `assert` e **`else`** `assert` $\neg e$, since there are no inputs that satisfy both assertions. [21] would not flag this program since neither of the two wedge programs is guaranteed to fail. We believe that [9] would not report this as an error since neither assertion is guarded by a check that guarantees its success. Similar reasoning (due to the presence of non-determinism) shows that [21] will miss reporting a *SIB* for the example in Figure 1.

In addition to prior work on semantic inconsistency, there are other generic approaches to reducing false alarms in static analysis. *Necessary preconditions* [5] are conditions that are shared by all non-faulting execution traces. Even without abstraction, the preconditions inferred by our approach are (in general) incomparable to necessary preconditions. For the program `if (x) { assert x; } assert x`, the necessary precondition is `x`, but the almost-correct specification is `true`, and thus the necessary precondition is stronger. For the program `if (*) assert x`, the necessary precondition is `true`, and the almost-correct specification is `x`, and so the almost-correct specification is stronger. The work on *doomed program points* [15] reduces false alarms by looking for assertions that will fail for all possible inputs. Such assertions are a special case of our *SIB*s. Recent work by Dillig *et al.* [10] use *abductive inference* with user feedback to classify alarms. We believe that the two approaches are largely complementary. The framework in [10] mainly addresses the problem of false alarms resulting from analysis imprecision instead of imprecision from the environment. Our framework can aid this work by identifying the initial set of warnings to display to the user for further classification. On the other hand, the use of quantifier elimination for abduction can provide an alternate way to discover almost-correct specifications. The work on *interleaved bugs* [16] addresses the underspecified precondition problem for the specific case of checking concurrency bugs by using the "simpler" sequential executions as a filter. Our approach applies in the sequential setting and does not use any simpler behaviors as oracles.

7. Conclusions and future work

In this paper, we make the case for using semantic methods to make program verifiers less demonic in the face of uncertainty. We introduce the concepts of *abstract* semantic inconsistency bugs and almost-correct specifications, which allow program verifiers to avoid reporting a class of stupid false alarms without being overly angelic. We show that our framework can be instantiated to find the demonstrably useful class of semantic inconsistency bugs. Our preliminary results demonstrate that the technique can be useful in suppressing many obviously demonic environments and improving the quality of warnings.

There are several directions for extending this work: We would like to discover more interesting abstractions, possibly by using user feedback for guidance. Extending our current work to perform limited interprocedural analysis [9] by asserting failure preconditions at call sites will increase the scope of analysis and increase the set of abstract *SIB*s. Finally, we plan to conduct a user study to understand the quality of the alarms we report initially.

References

[1] M. Barnett, K. R. M. Leino, and W. Schulte. The Spec# programming system: An overview. In *Construction and Analysis of Safe, Secure and Interoperable Smart Devices*, LNCS, 2005.

[2] A. Bessey, K. Block, B. Chelf, A. Chou, B. Fulton, S. Hallem, C. Henri-Gros, A. Kamsky, S. McPeak, and D. Engler. A few billion lines of code later: using static analysis to find bugs in the real world. *Commun. ACM*, 53(2):66–75, Feb. 2010.

[3] J. Condit, B. Hackett, S. K. Lahiri, and S. Qadeer. Unifying type checking and property checking for low-level code. In *Principles of Programming Languages (POPL '09)*, pages 302–314, 2009.

[4] P. Cousot and R. Cousot. Abstract interpretation : A Unified Lattice Model for the Static Analysis of Programs by Construction or Approximation of Fixpoints. In *Symposium on Principles of Programming Languages (POPL '77)*. ACM Press, 1977.

[5] P. Cousot, R. Cousot, M. Fähndrich, and F. Logozzo. Automatic inference of necessary preconditions. In *VMCAI*, pages 128–148, 2013.

[6] L. de Moura and N. Bjørner. Z3: An efficient SMT solver. In *International Conference on Tools and Algorithms for the Construction and Analysis of Systems (TACAS '08)*, 2008.

[7] R. DeLine and K. R. M. Leino. BoogiePL: A typed procedural language for checking object-oriented programs. Technical Report MSR-TR-2005-70, Microsoft Research, 2005.

[8] E. W. Dijkstra. Guarded commands, nondeterminacy and formal derivation of programs. *Communications of the ACM*, 1975.

[9] I. Dillig, T. Dillig, and A. Aiken. Static error detection using semantic inconsistency inference. In *Programming Language Design and Implementation (PLDI '07)*, pages 435–445, 2007.

[10] I. Dillig, T. Dillig, and A. Aiken. Automated error diagnosis using abductive inference. In *Proceedings of the 33rd ACM SIGPLAN conference on Programming Language Design and Implementation*, PLDI '12, pages 181–192, New York, NY, USA, 2012. ACM.

[11] D. R. Engler, D. Y. Chen, and A. Chou. Bugs as inconsistent behavior: A general approach to inferring errors in systems code. In *Symposium on Operating Systems Principles (SOSP '01)*, pages 57–72, 2001.

[12] C. Flanagan, K. R. M. Leino, M. Lillibridge, G. Nelson, J. B. Saxe, and R. Stata. Extended static checking for Java. In *Programming Language Design and Implementation (PLDI'02)*, 2002.

[13] C. Flanagan and J. B. Saxe. Avoiding exponential explosion: generating compact verification conditions. In *Symposium on Principles of Programming Languages (POPL '01)*, pages 193–205. ACM, 2001.

[14] S. Graf and H. Saïdi. Construction of abstract state graphs with PVS. In *Computer-Aided Verification (CAV '97)*.

[15] J. Hoenicke, K. R. M. Leino, A. Podelski, M. Schäf, and T. Wies. Doomed program points. *Formal Methods in System Design*, 37(2-3):171–199, 2010.

[16] S. Joshi, S. K. Lahiri, and A. Lal. Underspecified harnesses and interleaved bugs. In *Principles of Programming Languages (POPL '12)*, pages 19–30. ACM, 2012.

[17] T. Kremenek and D. R. Engler. Z-ranking: Using statistical analysis to counter the impact of static analysis approximations. In *Static Analysis Symposium (SAS '03)*, LNCS 2694, pages 295–315, 2003.

[18] T. Kremenek, P. Twohey, G. Back, A. Y. Ng, and D. R. Engler. From uncertainty to belief: Inferring the specification within. In *OSDI*, 2006.

[19] S. K. Lahiri, R. Nieuwenhuis, and A. Oliveras. Smt techniques for fast predicate abstraction. In *Computer Aided Verification (CAV '06)*, Lecture Notes in Computer Science, 2006.

[20] NIST SAMATE Benchmarks. `http://samate.nist.gov/SRD/testsuite.php`.

[21] A. Tomb and C. Flanagan. Detecting inconsistencies via universal reachability analysis. In *International Symposium on Software Testing and Analysis (ISSTA '12)*, 2012.

Reasoning about Nondeterminism in Programs

Byron Cook
Microsoft Research Cambridge
& University College London

Eric Koskinen *
New York University

Abstract

Branching-time temporal logics (*e.g.* CTL, CTL*, modal μ-calculus) allow us to ask sophisticated questions about the nondeterminism that appears in systems. Applications of this type of reasoning include planning, games, security analysis, disproving, precondition synthesis, environment synthesis, etc. Unfortunately, existing automatic branching-time verification tools have limitations that have traditionally restricted their applicability (*e.g.* push-down systems only, universal path quantifiers only, etc).

In this paper we introduce an automation strategy that lifts many of these previous restrictions. Our method works reliably for properties with non-trivial mixtures of universal and existential modal operators. Furthermore, our approach is designed to support (possibly infinite-state) programs.

The basis of our approach is the observation that existential reasoning can be reduced to universal reasoning if the system's state-space is appropriately restricted. This restriction on the state-space must meet a constraint derived from recent work on proving non-termination. The observation leads to a new route for implementation based on existing tools. To demonstrate the practical viability of our approach, we report on the results applying our preliminary implementation to a set of benchmarks drawn from the Windows operating system, the PostgreSQL database server, Soft-Updates patching system, as well as other hand-crafted examples.

Categories and Subject Descriptors D.2.4 [*Software Engineering*]: Software/Program Verification—Model checking; Correctness proofs; Reliability; D.4.5 [*Operating Systems*]: Reliability—Verification; F.3.1 [*Logics and Meanings of Programs*]: Specifying and Verifying and Reasoning about Programs; F.3.2 [*Logics and Meanings of Programs*]: Semantics of Programming Languages—Program analysis

General Terms Verification, Theory, Reliability

Keywords CTL, temporal logic, formal verification, termination, program analysis, model checking

1. Introduction

Branching-time temporal logics facilitate reasoning about the nondeterminism that exists within the transition relations of systems. For example we might wish to prove that a program P could (but is not forced to) terminate from every reachable state, and furthermore if and when termination does occur, p will hold. In the branching-time logic CTL, we can express this as[1]

$$P \models \mathsf{A}[\mathsf{EF}p \;\mathsf{W}\; p]$$

Here we are using two temporal operators:

- $\mathsf{A}[a \;\mathsf{W}\; b]$ specifies that a and b are temporally sequenced in all executions through the system: either a might happen forever, or b must happen if a ever ceases to hold. $\mathsf{A}[a \;\mathsf{W}\; b]$ is a *universal* temporal operator: it must hold over *all* executions of the system, no matter which nondeterministic choices are made.
- $\mathsf{EF}a$ specifies that there exist nondeterministic choices that can be made such that a will eventually hold.

Applications of this type of reasoning include planning, games, security analysis, disproving, precondition synthesis, environment synthesis, and many others. In the area of planning, for example, nondeterministic choices in a system often represent choices that can be manipulated by a plan. With a proof that $P \models \mathsf{A}[\mathsf{EF}p \;\mathsf{W}\; p]$, we could devise a plan that would cause the system P to terminate in state p whenever desired [32]. As another example, consider environment synthesis: Imagine that we would like to find a condition that—if maintained—would guarantee whenever p holds, q will eventually hold: $\mathsf{AG}(p \Rightarrow \mathsf{AF}\; q)$. Towards this goal we can prove $\mathsf{EG}(p \Rightarrow \mathsf{AF}\; q)$, which states that it's *possible* but not guaranteed that whenever p then eventually q. With a proof in hand we can then work out the conditions required to guarantee such a desired condition, thus giving us a restriction on the state-space such that $\mathsf{AG}(p \Rightarrow \mathsf{AF}\; q)$ would be true.

At first glance the above applications of CTL reasoning look appealing. Unfortunately, there is a problem: The question of how to reliably automate proofs in CTL and similar branching-time logics (*e.g.* CTL*, modal μ-calculus) for infinite-state programs remains an open problem.

In this paper we report on the first known robust automatic proof method to support both universal and existential branching-time modal operators for programs. Our approach is based on the observation that existential reasoning can be reduced to universal reasoning when an appropriate restriction is placed on the the state-space of the system. For soundness we require that the restriction used meets a condition adapted from recent approaches to non-termination proving [22]. For example, to prove that there *exists* a path in a program P such that p holds (*i.e.* $P \models \mathsf{EF}p$), we search for a restriction $\mathcal{C}$ on P's state-space such that in the program restricted to $\mathcal{C}$-states, *for all* paths p eventually holds (*i.e.* $P|_{\mathcal{C}} \models \mathsf{AF}p$). To ensure that there still exists at least one path to p in $P|_{\mathcal{C}}$ we must check a condition that the restriction $\mathcal{C}$ be a *recurrent* set [22].

The advantage of our approach is that there are known solutions to the problem of universal branching-time, as well proving non-termination. Thus, to construct a full-fledged CTL prover for infinite-state programs, we need only develop a method that synthesizes appropriate restrictions $\mathcal{C}$. Towards this goal we give a procedure that refines candidate restrictions on demand using failed proof attempts with insufficient restrictions.

To demonstrate the practical viability of our approach we have built a preliminary unoptimized prover and applied it to toy bench-

* Supported in part by the CMACS NSF Expeditions in Computing award 0926166.

[1] We abuse notation slightly; we mean that $s \models \mathsf{A}[\mathsf{EF}p \;\mathsf{W}\; p]$ for every initial state s in program P.

marks with a variety of combinations of temporal operators, as well as examples drawn the PostgreSQL database server, the SoftUpdates patch system, the Windows OS kernel.

Limitations. The formal treatment given in this paper is defined over general transitions systems. Thus, we make no assumption about the structure of programs (recursive, higher-order, etc). In practice, however, our implementation uses constraint-based methods as well as safety and termination proving techniques that limit the applicability of the tool to non-recursive programs with variables that range over arithmetic domains. Heap-based programs can be handled by first constructing a numerical abstraction (*e.g.* [26], [29]).

For the purpose of brevity we have limited ourselves here to the logic CTL, as CTL is a simple logic that supports mixtures of existential and universal reasoning. Applying these techniques to more expressive logics (*e.g.* CTL* or modal μ-calculus) is left as future work.

While the CTL proof rules we develop are sound and complete, our practical implementation is not complete for several reasons:

- The underlying technique for proving the universal subset of CTL is not complete.
- Our heuristics for synthesizing restrictions on the state-space is not complete.
- The refinement procedure for state-space restrictions may make incorrect choices early during the iterative proof search that limit the choices available later in the search. In these circumstances we a form of backtracking could potentially be used to consider alternative decisions.

2. Example

In this section we informally discuss a simple example. In the following sections we develop the approach more rigorously.

```
1  x = 0;
2  while (true) {
3    ρ^1 = *;
4    y = ρ^1;
5    x = 1;
6    ρ^2 = *;
7    n = ρ^2;
8    while (n>0) {
9      n = n - y;
10   }
11   x = 0;
12 }
```

Here we have made all of the nondeterminism explicit through the use of variables ρ^1 and ρ^2. The symbol $*$ represents nondeterministic choice. Imagine that we would like to prove that it is *possible* to maintain the invariant that, whenever $\mathtt{x} = 1$, then eventually $\mathtt{x} = 0$. In CTL we would express this property as:

$$\mathsf{EG}(\mathtt{x} = 1 \Rightarrow \mathsf{AF}(\mathtt{x} = 0))$$

Here $\mathsf{EG}p$ specifies that there exist nondeterministic choices such that p holds forever. $\mathsf{AF}p$ says that in all nondeterministic choices p eventually becomes true.

Our method is based on the search for a restriction on the nondeterministic choices made (*i.e.* the ρ-variables) such that we can use tools that support only universal reasoning to do the hard work. In this case, if we restrict the nondeterministic choice $\rho^1 = *$ at line 3 to be positive then the *universal* variation of original property, $\mathsf{AG}(\mathtt{x} = 1 \Rightarrow \mathsf{AF}(\mathtt{x} = 0))$, holds of a similar program:

```
1  x = 0;
2  while (true) {
3    ρ^1 = *; assume(ρ^1 ≥ 1);
4    y = ρ^1;
5    x = 1;
6    ρ^2 = *;
7    n = ρ^2;
8    while (n>0) {
9      n = n - y;
10   }
11   x = 0;
12 }
```

Here we have used a restriction on the state space:

$$\mathcal{C} \equiv (\text{program is at line 3} \Rightarrow \rho^1 \geq 1)$$

which we have implemented using an `assume` instruction [31].

$$\rho^1 = *;\ \underline{\mathtt{assume}(\rho^1 \geq 1);}$$

We have to be careful when choosing restrictions, as we have done above. For example, the restriction

$$\mathcal{C} \equiv (\text{ program is at line 3} \Rightarrow \mathsf{false})$$

would cause the universal reasoning to succeed. However, the `assume(false)` command that would appear on Line 3 would cause there to be no executions of this restricted program. Consequently, EG does not hold. In this paper we will describe a requirement on our choice of chute so that we guarantee non-emptiness.

Finding restrictions. To automate the discovery of restrictions we begin with $\mathcal{C} \equiv \mathsf{true}$. We then use failed proof attempts in the universal subset of CTL to guide where further restrictions need to be added. In our example we would try proving $\mathsf{AG}(\mathtt{x} = 1 \Rightarrow \mathsf{AF}(\mathtt{x} = 0))$ using $\mathcal{C} \equiv \mathsf{true}$, which fails. As a result we will get the following counterexample:

A path to $(\mathtt{x} = 1)$:

```
x = 0;
ρ^1 = *;
y = ρ^1;
x = 1;
ρ^2 = *;
n = ρ^2;
```

A cyclic path where $(\mathtt{x} = 0)$ *never occurs*:

```
assume(n>0);
n = n - y;
```

Because the cyclic path is executed forever we can infer that $\mathtt{y} \leq 0$ is invariant in the cyclic path. That is, we can strengthen the cyclic path to:

```
assume(y<=0);
assume(n>0);
n = n - y;
```

As is standard in tools based on counterexample-guided abstraction refinement (*e.g.* [30], [2]) we can represent this command sequence as a logical formula expressed using static single assignment variables:

$$\bigwedge \left\{ \begin{array}{c} \mathtt{x}_1 = 0 \\ \mathtt{y}_1 = \rho^1_1 \\ \mathtt{x}_2 = 1 \\ \mathtt{n}_1 = \rho^2_1 \\ \mathtt{y}_1 \leq 0 \\ \mathtt{n}_1 > 0 \\ \mathtt{n}_2 = \mathtt{n}_1 - \mathtt{y}_1 \end{array} \right\}$$

We would like to compute a condition using one of the ρ variables that would make this path spurious. Take ρ^1_1 as our candidate. We can compute a condition by performing quantifier elimination on the variables ($\mathtt{x}_1, \mathtt{y}_1, \mathtt{x}_2, \mathtt{n}_1, \mathtt{n}_2, \rho_1^2$) that are not in scope just after the command $\rho^1 := *$. The elimination is thus:

$$\exists \mathtt{y}_1, \mathtt{x}_1, \mathtt{x}_2, \mathtt{n}_1, \mathtt{n}_2, \rho_1^2, \rho_1^0. \bigwedge \left\{ \begin{array}{l} \mathtt{x}_1 = 0 \\ \mathtt{y}_1 = \rho_1^1 \\ \mathtt{x}_2 = 1 \\ \mathtt{n}_1 = \rho_1^2 \\ \mathtt{y}_1 \le 0 \\ \mathtt{n}_1 > 0 \\ \mathtt{n}_2 = \mathtt{n}_1 - \mathtt{y}_1 \end{array} \right\} \equiv \rho_1^1 \le 0$$

Finally, we can restrict the original program such that this path is not possible. To this end, we instrument the negation of this condition $\neg(\rho^1 \le 0)$, after the assignment $\rho^1 := *$. Hence, we strengthen $\mathcal{C}$ with

$$\mathcal{C} := \mathcal{C} \wedge (\text{ program is at line 3 } \Rightarrow \rho^1 > 0)$$

In more complex cases with nested temporal existential operators we must find families of restrictions, maintaining a set of $\mathcal{C}$ restrictions, indexed by their use in a CTL proof search. In the next section we describe our procedure more formally and discuss this complexity in some detail.

3. Treating the Existential Fragment of CTL

We now turn to a formal description of our technique. We begin with new proof rules for CTL. These generalize our previous rules for ∀CTL [10, 11]. Our rules are given in terms of sets of states, allowing us to partition the state space rather than enumerate the state space.

In this paper we introduce a new proof rule for existential operators that characterizes the existence of traces as a subset of the transition relation called a *chute*. This allows us to apply *universal* reasoning to the subset, in order to prove *existential* properties. We characterize the side condition of non-emptiness with *recurrent sets*. In later sections, we will describe how proof derivations (including discovery of chutes) can be obtained automatically.

3.1 Preliminaries

Transition systems. A transition system $M = (S, R, I)$ is a set of states S, a transition relation $R \subseteq S \times S$, and a set of initial states $I \subseteq S$. We use the notation $r|_1$ to mean the first projection of relation r. A *trace* π of a transition system is an infinite sequence of states $(s_0, s_1, ...)$ such that $s_0 \in I$, $\forall i \ge 0.\ s_i \in S$ and $\forall i \ge 0.\ (s_i, s_{i+1}) \in R$. We denote by $\Pi(S, R, I)$ the set of all such traces. For convenience, we do not allow finite traces. The transition relation must be such that every state has at least one successor state: $\forall s \in S.\ \exists s'.\ (s, s') \in R$. This is without a loss of generality, as final states can be encoded as states that loop back to themselves. The notation π^i indicates a *suffix* of a trace starting at the ith state in the sequence. We use π_0 to denote the first element in π. The superscript binds tighter than the subscript, i.e. $\pi_0^i = (\pi^i)_0$. We will use similar notation for a *finite* path ϖ. Additionally, we will say that ϖ^{end} denotes the final element of ϖ.

Ranking functions. For a state space S, a ranking function f is a total map from S to a well-ordered set with ordering relation $\prec$. A relation $R \subseteq S \times S$ is *well-founded* if and only if there exists a ranking function f such that $\forall (s, s') \in R.\ f(s') \prec f(s)$. We denote a finite set of ranking functions (or *measures*) as $\mathcal{M}$. Note that the existence of a finite set of ranking functions for a relation R is equivalent to containment of R^+ within a finite union of well-founded relations [34]. That is to say that a set of ranking functions $\{f_1, ..., f_n\}$ can denote the disjunctively well-founded relation $\{(s, s') \mid f_1(s') \prec f_1(s) \vee ... \vee f_n(s') \prec f_n(s)\}$.

Temporal logic. The syntax of a CTL formula is

$$\Phi ::= p \mid \Phi \vee \Phi \mid \Phi \wedge \Phi \mid \mathsf{AF}\Phi \mid \mathsf{EF}\Phi \mid \mathsf{A}[\Phi \mathsf{W} \Phi] \mid \mathsf{E}[\Phi \mathsf{W} \Phi]$$

Note that $\mathsf{AG}p$ can be defined as $\mathsf{A}[p\ \mathsf{W}\ \mathsf{false}]$, and $\mathsf{EG}p$ can be defined as $\mathsf{E}[p\ \mathsf{W}\ \mathsf{false}]$. The standard semantics of CTL is given in Figure 1. p is an atomic proposition. There are two classes of temporal constructors: constructors that quantify universally over paths (AF, AW) and constructors that quantify existentially over paths (EF, EW). The AF and EF constructors specify that a state in which Φ holds must be reached. The $[\Phi_1 \mathsf{W} \Phi_2]$ operator specifies that Φ_1 holds in every state where Φ_2 does not yet hold.

We use F and W as our base temporal operators (as opposed to the more standard U and R), as each corresponds to a distinct form of proof: F to termination, and W to safety. We omit the next state operator X as it is not particularly useful in an imperative programming language: the next step simply is a transition across a command and can be supported via F. We assume that formulae are written in negation normal form, in which negation only occurs next to atomic propositions, and assume that the domain of atomic propositions is closed under negation. A formula that is not in negation normal form can be easily normalized.

Definition 3.1 (CTL machine entailment)**.** *For every* $M = (S, R, I)$ *and CTL property* Φ, $M \models \Phi \;\equiv\; \forall s \in I.\ R, s \models \Phi$.

Our rules are composed structurally over a CTL formula. In order to track components of a proof we need to uniquely identify subformulae. To this end, our definition of subformulae maintains a context path: $\kappa \;\equiv\; \epsilon \mid \mathsf{L}\,\kappa \mid \mathsf{R}\,\kappa$ that indicates the path from the root ϵ (the outermost property Φ), to the particular subproperty of interest, at each step taking either the left or right subformula ($\mathsf{L}\kappa$ or $\mathsf{R}\kappa$). For a CTL property Φ, the set of subformulae is a set of (κ, Φ) pairs as follows:

$$\begin{aligned}
\mathsf{sub}(\Phi) &\equiv \mathsf{sub}(\epsilon, \Phi) \\
\mathsf{sub}(\kappa, p) &\equiv \{(\kappa, p)\} \\
\mathsf{sub}(\kappa, \Phi \vee \Phi') &\equiv \{(\kappa, \Phi \vee \Phi')\} \cup \mathsf{sub}(\mathsf{L}\kappa, \Phi) \cup \mathsf{sub}(\mathsf{R}\kappa, \Phi') \\
\mathsf{sub}(\kappa, \Phi \wedge \Phi') &\equiv \{(\kappa, \Phi \wedge \Phi')\} \cup \mathsf{sub}(\mathsf{L}\kappa, \Phi) \cup \mathsf{sub}(\mathsf{R}\kappa, \Phi') \\
\mathsf{sub}(\kappa, \mathsf{AF}\Phi) &\equiv \{(\kappa, \mathsf{AF}\Phi)\} \cup \mathsf{sub}(\mathsf{L}\kappa, \Phi) \\
\mathsf{sub}(\kappa, \mathsf{EF}\Phi) &\equiv \{(\kappa, \mathsf{EF}\Phi)\} \cup \mathsf{sub}(\mathsf{L}\kappa, \Phi) \\
\mathsf{sub}(\kappa, \mathsf{A}[\Phi \mathsf{W} \Phi']) &\equiv \{(\kappa, \mathsf{A}[\Phi \mathsf{W} \Phi'])\} \cup \mathsf{sub}(\mathsf{L}\kappa, \Phi) \cup \mathsf{sub}(\mathsf{R}\kappa, \Phi') \\
\mathsf{sub}(\kappa, \mathsf{E}[\Phi \mathsf{W} \Phi']) &\equiv \{(\kappa, \mathsf{E}[\Phi \mathsf{W} \Phi'])\} \cup \mathsf{sub}(\mathsf{L}\kappa, \Phi) \cup \mathsf{sub}(\mathsf{R}\kappa, \Phi')
\end{aligned}$$

3.2 A Proof System for CTL

Our proof system given in Figure 2 is a relation between a set of states X and a CTL context/formula κ, Φ. Atomic proposition RAP and conjunction RAND are as expected (note that $[\![p]\!]$ means the set of states such that p holds). Disjunction ROR partitions the set of states into two sets X_1 and X_2 where Φ_1 holds of X_1 and Φ_2 holds of X_2.

Quantification operators. In this paper, we generalize the proof system to encompass the universal and existential temporal operators. To this end, we decompose the temporal operators based on quantification, so we have:

$$\begin{aligned}
\gamma &::= \mathsf{F}\Phi \mid [\Phi\ \mathsf{W}\ \Phi] \\
\Phi &::= p \mid \Phi \vee \Phi \mid \Phi \wedge \Phi \mid \mathsf{A}\gamma \mid \mathsf{E}\gamma
\end{aligned}$$

This decomposition allows us to treat universal and existential temporal operators similarly. When an $\mathsf{A}\gamma$ or $\mathsf{E}\gamma$ quantification operator is reached, a corresponding rule (RA or RE) is used to identify three key sets of states that will be relevant to γ:

1. The initial states X
2. The *chute* states $\mathcal{C}$
3. The *frontier* [10, 11] states $\mathcal{F}$

$$
\begin{array}{rcl}
R, s \models p & \iff & s \in [\![p]\!] \\
R, s \models \Phi_1 \wedge \Phi_2 & \iff & R, s \models \Phi_1 \text{ and } R, s \models \Phi_2 \\
R, s \models \Phi_1 \vee \Phi_2 & \iff & R, s \models \Phi_1 \text{ or } R, s \models \Phi_2 \\
R, s \models \mathsf{AF}\Phi & \iff & \forall (s_0, s_1, \ldots) \in \Pi(S, R, \{s\}).\ \exists i \geq 0.\ R, s_i \models \Phi \\
R, s \models \mathsf{EF}\Phi & \iff & \exists (s_0, s_1, \ldots) \in \Pi(S, R, \{s\}).\ \exists i \geq 0.\ R, s_i \models \Phi \\
R, s \models \mathsf{A}[\Phi_1 \mathsf{W} \Phi_2] & \iff & \forall (s_0, s_1, \ldots) \in \Pi(S, R, \{s\}).\ (\forall i \geq 0.\ R, s_i \models \Phi_1) \vee (\exists j \geq 0.\ R, s_j \models \Phi_2 \wedge \forall i \in [0, j).\ R, s_i \models \Phi_1) \\
R, s \models \mathsf{E}[\Phi_1 \mathsf{W} \Phi_2] & \iff & \exists (s_0, s_1, \ldots) \in \Pi(S, R, \{s\}).\ (\forall i \geq 0.\ R, s_i \models \Phi_1) \vee (\exists j \geq 0.\ R, s_j \models \Phi_2 \wedge \forall i \in [0, j).\ R, s_i \models \Phi_1)
\end{array}
$$

Figure 1: Standard CTL semantics, a relation from a state to a formula.

$$
\frac{X \subseteq [\![p]\!]}{X \vdash \kappa, p}\ \textsc{Rap} \qquad
\frac{X \vdash \mathsf{L}\kappa, \Phi_1 \quad X \vdash \mathsf{R}\kappa, \Phi_2}{X \vdash \kappa, \Phi_1 \wedge \Phi_2}\ \textsc{Rand}
$$

$$
\frac{X = X_1 \cup X_2 \quad X_1 \vdash \mathsf{L}\kappa, \Phi_1 \quad X_2 \vdash \mathsf{R}\kappa, \Phi_2}{X \vdash \kappa, \Phi_1 \vee \Phi_2}\ \textsc{Ror}
$$

$$
\frac{X, S, \mathcal{F}^\kappa \Vdash \kappa, \gamma}{X \vdash \kappa, \mathsf{A}\gamma}\ \textsc{Ra} \qquad
\frac{(X, \mathcal{C}^\kappa, \mathcal{F}^\kappa) \text{ is rcr} \quad X, \mathcal{C}^\kappa, \mathcal{F}^\kappa \Vdash \kappa, \gamma}{X \vdash \kappa, \mathsf{E}\gamma}\ \textsc{Re}
$$

$$
\frac{\mathcal{R}^{\mathcal{F}^\kappa}_{\underset{X}{\mathcal{C}^\kappa}} \text{ is w.f.} \quad \mathcal{F}^\kappa \vdash \mathsf{L}\kappa, \Phi}{X, \mathcal{C}^\kappa, \mathcal{F}^\kappa \Vdash \kappa, \mathsf{F}\Phi}\ \textsc{Rf} \qquad
\frac{\mathcal{R}^{\mathcal{F}^\kappa}_{\underset{X}{\mathcal{C}^\kappa}}|_1 \vdash \mathsf{L}\kappa, \Phi_1 \quad \mathcal{F}^\kappa \vdash \mathsf{R}\kappa, \Phi_2}{X, \mathcal{C}^\kappa, \mathcal{F}^\kappa \Vdash \kappa, [\Phi_1 \mathsf{W} \Phi_2]}\ \textsc{Rw}
$$

$$
\frac{(s,t) \in R \quad s \in X \quad s \notin \mathcal{F} \quad s, t \in \mathcal{C}}{\mathcal{R}^{\mathcal{F}}_{\underset{X}{\mathcal{C}}}\ (s,t)}
\qquad
\frac{\mathcal{R}^{\mathcal{F}}_{\underset{X}{\mathcal{C}}}\ (s,t) \quad (t,u) \in R \quad t \notin \mathcal{F} \quad u \in \mathcal{C}}{\mathcal{R}^{\mathcal{F}}_{\underset{X}{\mathcal{C}}}\ (t,u)}
$$

Figure 2: On the left is a proof system for CTL that unifies the temporal treatment of universal A and existential E. There is a side condition on the existential rule that the relevant states form a recurrent set. The definition of $\mathcal{R}$ is given on the right.

We can think about these as: the start states X, the relevant region of the transition relation $\mathcal{C}$ through which execution is allowed to pass, and a stopping point at the frontier $\mathcal{F}$. Visually:

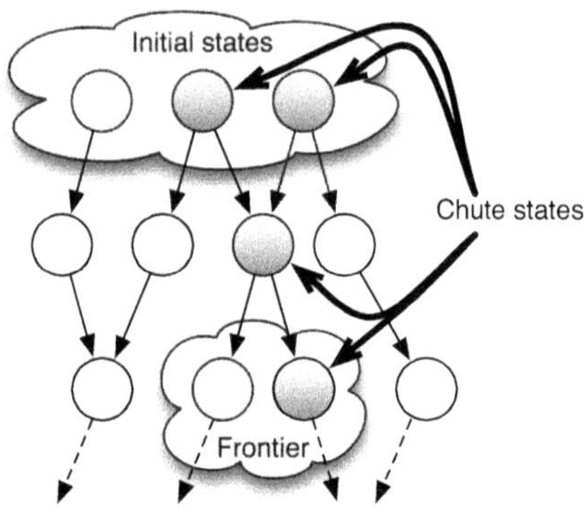

The chute $\mathcal{C}$ effectively carves out the portion of the state space that will be relevant to the subproperty. This generalization with chutes provides a means of treating each quantification fragment of CTL:

1. For a given subformula, *existential* properties can be treated by restricting the state space to a chute and applying universal reasoning on that chute (RE). The non-emptiness side condition is that this chute must be recurrent, discussed below.
2. For a given subformula, *universal* properties can be treated by letting the chute be the entire state space (RA).

The quantification proof rules (Figure 2) each involve a proof obligation for the temporal operator γ, in terms of this triple: $X, \mathcal{C}, \mathcal{F} \Vdash \kappa, \gamma$. In the case of RA, we use the entire state space S as the chute. In the case of RE, we must identify a chute $\mathcal{C}$ and ensure a special side condition that the triple $(X, \mathcal{C}, \mathcal{F})$ be a recurrent set, defined as follows:

Definition 3.2 (Recurrent set)**.** *For sets of states $X, \mathcal{C}, \mathcal{F}$ and transition relation R, we say that $\mathcal{C}$ is a* recurrent set *w.r.t. X and $\mathcal{F}$ (denoted $(X, \mathcal{C}, \mathcal{F})$ is rcr) provided that $X \cap \mathcal{C} \neq \varnothing$ and:*

1. $X \cap \mathcal{C} \subseteq \mathcal{F}$, or
2. *For every $x \in \mathcal{C}$, there exists x' such that $(x, x') \in R$ and $x' \in \mathcal{F} \vee x' \in \mathcal{C}$.*

Intuitively, a recurrent set $\mathcal{C}$ is such that either: (i) there is a path from X that either immediately intersects with $\mathcal{F}$, (ii) there is a path that reaches $\mathcal{F}$ by following $\mathcal{C}$ at each transition or (iii) there is a path that remains in $\mathcal{C}$ forever, never reaching $\mathcal{F}$. Note that this is a generalization of a previously described notion of a recurrent set [22]. For proving non-termination, the simpler notion of recurrent set is sufficient because there is no frontier. With nested temporal operators, we must account for a set being recurrent modulo a frontier, wherein the subproperty is satisfied.

Temporal operators. The quantification operators discussed above are designed to be compatible with either temporal operator. First we identify the region (*i.e.* subset) of the transition relation that is relevant to a given triple $X, \mathcal{C}, \mathcal{F}$ via the relation $\mathcal{R}^{\mathcal{F}}_{\underset{X}{\mathcal{C}}}$, given on the right-hand side of Figure 2. Notice that $\mathcal{R}^{\mathcal{F}}_{\underset{X}{\mathcal{C}}} \subseteq R$. In the base case, a transition (s,t) is in $\mathcal{R}^{\mathcal{F}}_{\underset{X}{\mathcal{C}}}$ if $s \in X, s \in \mathcal{C}$, and $s \notin \mathcal{F}$. In the inductive case, a transition (t,u) is included in $\mathcal{R}^{\mathcal{F}}_{\underset{X}{\mathcal{C}}}$ whenever some $(s,t) \in \mathcal{R}^{\mathcal{F}}_{\underset{X}{\mathcal{C}}}$, $t \notin \mathcal{F}$ and $u \in \mathcal{C}$. Intuitively, these are all of the double-line edges in the following diagram:

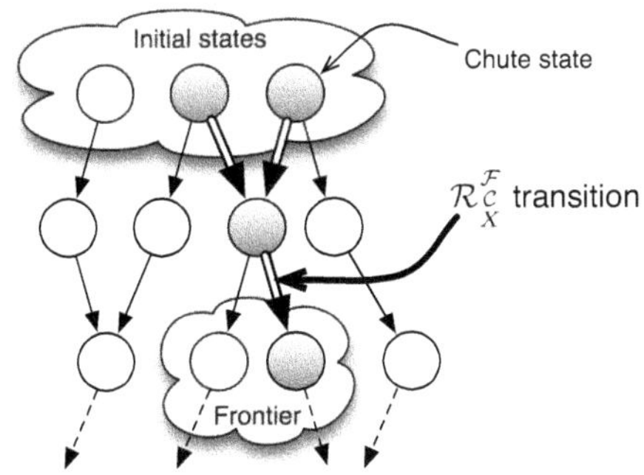

The proof that $X, \mathcal{C}, \mathcal{F} \Vdash \mathsf{F}\Phi$ involves showing that $\mathcal{R}^{\mathcal{F}}_{\substack{\mathcal{C}\\X}}$ is well-founded. This well-foundedness condition ensures that all traces through $X, \mathcal{C}, \mathcal{F}$ reach the frontier $\mathcal{F}$ after finitely many steps. Moreover, the RF rule requires that $\mathcal{F} \vdash \Phi$. The proof rule RW requires that along every path from X through the chute $\mathcal{C}$, Φ_1 holds (by requiring that the first projection of $\mathcal{R}^{\mathcal{F}}_{\substack{\mathcal{C}\\X}}$ satisfies Φ_1) unless the frontier $\mathcal{F}$ has been reached at which point Φ_2 holds.

Remark: CTL*. Note that our decomposition of quantification and temporal operators bares some resemblance to CTL* [16]. CTL* is a generalization of CTL (and of LTL) that includes state propositions (E, A) as well as path propositions (F,W). The difference is that a path proposition F or W is already fixed on a particular path. By contrast, our treatment relates F or W to the triple $(X, \mathcal{C}, \mathcal{F})$, giving us more structure to work with in the temporal operators. For example, using chutes and frontiers allows us to characterize eventuality as the well-foundedness of a subset of the transition relation $\mathcal{R}^{\mathcal{F}}_{\substack{\mathcal{C}\\X}}$.

Example 1. *Consider the following program for which we would like to prove that the nested property $\Phi = \mathsf{EF}(\mathsf{EG}(p > 0))$ holds.*

```
   assume(p == 0 ∧ x > 0); // Initial state
1  while(x>0) {
2    ρ¹ = *;
3    if (ρ¹ > 0) {
4       x = x + 1;
5    } else {
6       x = x - 1;
7    }
8  }
9  while(1) {
10   ρ² = *;
11   if (ρ² > 0)
12     p = 1;
13   else
14     p = 0;
15 }
```

Intuitively, the property holds because there is an execution that exits the first loop, enters the second loop, sets `p = 1` and then forever iterates the second loop, each time avoiding `p = 0`. If we restrict the nondeterministic choices, then we can treat EFEGp like AFAGp. This can be accomplished by constraints on the ρ variables.

A derivation for this example is given in Figure 3 where $I = [\![p = 0 \wedge x > 0]\!]$. On the left-hand side is the proof tree, built syntactically from Φ. Note that we are using EGp which is a special case: EGp = E[p W false]. On the right-hand side are values for the chutes and frontiers. (Note that pc is a special variable containing the value of the program counter, i.e., *line number.) Chute $\mathcal{C}^{\epsilon}$ ensures that in the first loop, executions always take the second branch, and decrement* `x`. *Chute $\mathcal{C}^{\epsilon}$ also ensures that once an execution exits the first loop and enters the second loop, it immediately takes the* `p=1` *branch, satisfying that $p > 0$. This is also the point at which frontier $\mathcal{F}^{\epsilon}$ is reached.*

From this state, we can ensure that $\mathsf{EG}(p > 0)$ holds using chute $\mathcal{C}^{L_\epsilon}$, which specifies that executions of the second loop only take the `p=1` *branch. This must hold in every subsequently reachable state (i.e. the semantics of EG), so we choose $\mathcal{F}^{L_\epsilon}$ = false. What remains are the proof obligations:*

1. *$(I, \mathcal{C}^{\epsilon}, \mathcal{F}^{\epsilon})$ is rcr. This triple is recurrent because there is at least one state in I (in fact, we can choose any initial state), and whenever we are at the first loop there is at least* some *successor in the chute (iterating* `x=x-1` *or proceeding along the path* `8,9,10,11,12`*) until the frontier $\mathcal{C}^{\epsilon}$ is reached at location* `12`*.*
2. *$\mathcal{R}^{\mathcal{F}^{\epsilon}}_{\substack{\mathcal{C}^{\epsilon}\\I}}$ is well-founded. This holds because, when executions are restricted to the second branch in the first loop, they are well-founded:* `x` *is decremented and bounded from below by 0.*
3. *$(\mathcal{F}^{\epsilon}, \mathcal{C}^{L_\epsilon}, \mathcal{F}^{L_\epsilon})$ is rcr. This set is recurrent because there is always a successor state in $\mathcal{C}^{L_\epsilon}$: taking the first branch of the second loop ad infinitum.*

This program appears in the EFEGp benchmark in Figure 6.

Equivalence to CTL semantics. The following theorem shows that our treatment in Figure 2 is equivalent to CTL. The proof involves representing traces as infinite sequences (*i.e* streams), and numerous support lemmas based on coinduction. We also incorporate recurrent sets and several corresponding lemmas.

Theorem 3.1 (Equivalence to CTL). *For all Φ, $M = (S, R, I)$,*

$$I \vdash \epsilon, \Phi \quad \Longleftrightarrow \quad \forall s \in I.\ R, s \vDash \Phi.$$

Proof. (sketch) We first expand our proof rules for $X \vdash \kappa, \mathsf{A}\gamma$ and $X \vdash \kappa, \mathsf{E}\gamma$ for each γ case, obtaining four direct $\vdash$ rules: $X \vdash \kappa, \mathsf{AF}\Phi$, $X \vdash \kappa, \mathsf{EF}\Phi$, $X \vdash \kappa, \mathsf{A}[\Phi_1 \ \mathsf{W}\ \Phi_2]$, and $X \vdash \kappa, \mathsf{E}[\Phi_1 \ \mathsf{W}\ \Phi_2]$ (and no $\Vdash$ rules). The proof then proceeds by induction on the (negation normal form) CTL property Φ. □

4. Automation

In this section we present an algorithm for automatically discovering the chutes necessary for proving a CTL property. Our method assumes an underlying proof technique for applying *universal* reasoning to CTL verification, such as the one we previously described [10, 11]. We extend this underlying prover slightly, by adding cases for the *existential* subformulae that are identical to their universal counterparts, except that the transition relation is constrained by the per-subformula chute. Our algorithm begins by assuming that no chute restriction is necessary for proving existential subformulae. This typically leads to counterexamples from the underlying prover. From counterexamples, we synthesize chutes by attempting to eliminate the behaviors witnessed by the counterexamples.

We begin with a symbolic treatment of chutes. Chutes, as seen in Section 3, are (potentially infinite) sets of states. In our refinement procedure we will work with predicates instead, written in first-order logic:

Definition 4.1 (Chute predicate *cp*). *A chute predicate cp is a first-order logic formula over the states of a transition system.*

For a given CTL property Φ, we use the notation $\vec{\mathcal{C}}$ to mean an indexed set of chutes, consisting of a conjunctive chute predicate $\mathcal{C}^{\kappa}$ for every $(\kappa, \_) \in \mathsf{sub}(\Phi)$. We will abuse notation and sometimes use $\mathcal{C}^{\kappa}$ to refer to a chute predicate. When this is then used in the

$$\dfrac{(I,\mathcal{C}^{\epsilon},\mathcal{F}^{\epsilon})\text{ is rcr} \qquad \dfrac{\mathcal{R}^{\mathcal{F}^{\epsilon}}_{\mathcal{C}^{\epsilon},I}\text{ is w.f.} \qquad \dfrac{(\mathcal{F}^{\epsilon},\mathcal{C}^{\mathsf{L}\epsilon},\mathcal{F}^{\mathsf{L}\epsilon})\text{ is rcr} \qquad \dfrac{\dfrac{\mathcal{R}^{\mathcal{F}^{\mathsf{L}\epsilon}}_{\mathcal{C}^{\mathsf{L}\epsilon},\mathcal{F}^{\epsilon}}|_1 \subseteq [\![p > 0]\!]}{\mathcal{R}^{\mathcal{F}^{\mathsf{L}\epsilon}}_{\mathcal{C}^{\mathsf{L}\epsilon},\mathcal{F}^{\epsilon}}|_1 \vdash \mathsf{LL}\epsilon, p}}{\mathcal{F}^{\epsilon},\mathcal{C}^{\mathsf{L}\epsilon},\mathcal{F}^{\mathsf{L}\epsilon} \Vdash \mathsf{L}\epsilon, \mathsf{G}p}}{\mathcal{F}^{\epsilon} \vdash \mathsf{L}\epsilon, \mathsf{EG}p}}{I,\mathcal{C}^{\epsilon},\mathcal{F}^{\epsilon} \Vdash \epsilon, \mathsf{FEG}p}}{I \vdash \epsilon, \mathsf{EFEG}p}$$

$$\begin{aligned}
\mathcal{C}^{\epsilon} &\equiv \mathsf{pc} = 2 \Rightarrow \rho^1 \leq 0 \wedge \mathsf{pc} = 10 \Rightarrow \rho^2 > 0\\
\mathcal{F}^{\epsilon} &\equiv \mathsf{pc} = 12\\
\mathcal{C}^{\mathsf{L}\epsilon} &\equiv \mathsf{pc} = 10 \Rightarrow \rho^2 > 0\\
\mathcal{F}^{\mathsf{L}\epsilon} &\equiv \mathsf{false}
\end{aligned}$$

Figure 3: Derivation for CTL property $\mathsf{EF}(\mathsf{EG}(p > 0))$. On the left is the proof tree and on the right are the values for the chutes and frontiers. Note that we use EG which is a simple case of EW where the second subproperty is simply false.

context of a set of states, we mean the set of all states such that $\mathcal{C}^{\kappa}$ holds: $[\![\mathcal{C}^{\kappa}]\!]$.

Algorithm. Given a CTL property Φ and a program P, our refinement algorithm discovers a proof that $P \models \Phi$ by iteratively refining an indexed set of chute predicates $\bar{\mathcal{C}}$. Our algorithm is given in Figure 4. It begins by initializing each $\mathcal{C}^{\kappa}$ to true. We then use an underlying method for attempting to prove that Φ holds, given the set $\bar{\mathcal{C}}$:

$$\mathsf{attempt}\ M \vdash \epsilon, \Phi\ \mathsf{using}\ \bar{\mathcal{C}}$$

We discuss our implementation of attempt in Section 5. When attempt succeeds, a candidate proof is returned. This candidate includes an indexed set of frontiers $\bar{\mathcal{F}}$. Together, $\bar{\mathcal{C}}$ and $\bar{\mathcal{F}}$ specify the chutes and frontiers in a $\vdash$ proof tree. Moreover, attempt returns an indexed set of rank functions $\bar{\mathcal{M}}$, which are the proofs of each well-foundedness obligation in F subformulae. What remains are the recurrent set proof obligations for $\mathsf{E}\gamma$ subformulae, accomplished in RCRCHECK (Section 5.3).

When attempt fails, it has discovered a counterexample to Φ in the form of a path ϖ : list $(S \times \mathsf{sub}(\Phi))$.[2] The path ϖ is part of a counterexample to Φ and traverses the $S \times \mathsf{sub}(\Phi)$ state space. (A discussion of counterexamples is given in [9].) Although attempt has failed, Φ may still hold of P. Choices may have been made in $\mathsf{E}\gamma$ subformulae which exercised a region of the state space where γ does not hold. For example, consider the property $\mathsf{EG}(\mathtt{x} = 1)$ and the program:

```
1 x = 1; ρ = *; // init
2 if(ρ > 0)
3   while(1) { x = 0 }
4 else
5   while(1) { x = 1 }
```

Here, attempt may return the path

$$(\mathsf{pc} = 1, \mathsf{x} = 1, \rho = 1),\ (\mathsf{pc} = 3, \mathsf{x} = 0, \rho = 1),\ (\mathsf{pc} = 3, \mathsf{x} = 0, \rho = 1), \ldots$$

While this path proves that $\mathsf{AG}(\mathtt{x} = 1)$ does not hold, it is still the case that $\mathsf{EG}(\mathtt{x} = 1)$ does hold. If we restrict the transition relation's state space to exclude such paths, alternative decisions may be possible, leading to an alternative proof that Φ holds of P. In the case above, if we exclude all of the states where $\mathsf{pc} = 3$ (by ensuring that ρ is never more than zero) then we are left with a transition system for which $\mathsf{AG}(\mathtt{x} = 1)$ holds.

Synthesizing chute predicates. The procedure $\textsc{Synth}_{cp}$ is used to automatically discover predicates such as $(\rho \leq 0)$, which are

[2] In our implementation (see Section 5) this path is represented as a sequence of program commands rather than concrete states.

```
let SYNTH_cp(ϖ) ≡
  { (cp, κ)     ∃(κ, Eγ) ∈ sub(Φ). ∃i.
                  1. ϖ_0^i ∈ ⟦C^κ⟧ × {(κ, Eγ)}
                  2. ϖ_0^{i+1} ∈ ⟦C^κ⟧ × {(κ, Eγ)}
                  3. ϖ_0^{i+1} ∉ ⟦C^κ ∧ cp⟧ × {(κ, Eγ)}
  { Not_found   otherwise

let prove(M, Φ) =
  C̄ := {κ ↦ true | (κ, Eγ) ∈ sub(Φ)};
  loop
    match (attempt M ⊢ ε, Φ using C̄) with
    | Counterexample(ϖ, F̄) ⟶
        let (cp, κ) = SYNTH_cp(ϖ) in
          C^κ := C^κ ∧ cp
        with Not_found ⟶ return Fail(F̄, C̄)

    | MaybeProof(F̄, M̄) ⟶
        if (∀κ, Eγ ∈ sub(Φ).  RCRCHECK(F̄, C^κ, F^κ))
          return Succeed
  done
```

Figure 4: Chute-refinement procedure. Counterexamples from failed proofs using $\forall$CTL techniques with chutes $\bar{\mathcal{C}}$ are used to help refine $\bar{\mathcal{C}}$.

necessary to restrict the transition relation to the states in which the existential subproperty holds. The path ϖ returned from attempt is part of a counterexample to Φ and traverses the $S \times \mathsf{sub}(\Phi)$ state space. $\textsc{Synth}_{cp}$ must discover a predicate cp such that path ϖ is not possible. To this end, it examines ϖ to find regions of ϖ that are existential temporal operators. Let $(\kappa, \mathsf{E}\gamma)$ be such a region. $\textsc{Synth}_{cp}$ must then look for nondeterministic choices that were made in that scope within ϖ where some other alternative choice was possible. In our implementation we can easily find such cases because we have automatically lifted all nondeterministic choice into assignments to special variables denoted ρ_i.

Theorem 4.1 (Soundness of refinement algorithm). *For every transition system M and CTL property Φ,*

$$\mathit{prove}(M, \Phi) \quad \Rightarrow \quad M \models \Phi$$

Proof. (Sketch) We first argue that $\mathsf{prove}(M, \Phi) \Rightarrow M \vdash \epsilon, \Phi$ and then use Theorem 3.1. Our algorithm iteratively prunes nondeterministic choices by restricting the transition relation, within a particular subformula, via chute predicates. When proving that a set of

```
E(P, M̄, C̄, Φ) ≡ ∪_{(κ,ψ)∈sub(Φ)} {enc^κ_ψ : s → 𝔹}   where
bool enc^κ_{ψ∧ψ'}(state s) {
  if (*) return enc^{Lκ}_ψ(s);
  else return enc^{Rκ}_{ψ'}(s);
}
bool enc^κ_{ψ∨ψ'}(state s) {
  if (enc^{Lκ}_ψ(s)) return true;
  else return enc^{Rκ}_{ψ'}(s);
}
bool enc^κ_p(state s) { return p(s); }

bool enc^κ_{A[ψ W ψ']}(state s) {
  P[ c / [ if (*) return true;
           if (¬ enc^{Lκ}_ψ(s)) return enc^{Rκ}_{ψ'}(s); ] ; c]
}

bool enc^κ_{E[ψ W ψ']}(state s) {
  P[ c / [ if (*) return true;
           assume(C^κ);
           if (¬ enc^{Lκ}_ψ(s)) return enc^{Rκ}_{ψ'}(s); ] ; c]
}

bool enc^κ_{AFψ}(state s) {
 bool dup = false; state 's;
  P[ c / [ if (*) return true;
           if (enc^{Lκ}_ψ(s)) return true;
           if (dup && ¬(∃f ∈ M. f(s) < f('s)))
           return false;
           if (¬ dup && *) { dup:=true;'s:=s;} ] ; c]
}

bool enc^κ_{EFψ}(C^κ)(state s) {
 bool dup = false; state 's;
  P[ c / [ if (*) return true;
           assume(C^κ);
           if (enc^{Lκ}_ψ(s)) return true;
           if (dup && ¬(∃f ∈ M. f(s) < f('s)))
           return false;
           if (¬ dup && *) { dup:=true; 's:=s; } ] ; c]
}
```

Figure 5: Encoding CTL verification as a finite set of procedures. Universal rules discussed in [10, 11]. The two new existential rules, which account for (κ,ψ)-subformula indexed sets of chute predicates are highlighted with shadow-boxes.

states $X \vdash \kappa, \mathsf{E}\gamma$, it is always sound to remove behaviors and apply universal reasoning (in attempt), provided that before we conclude that $\mathsf{E}\gamma$ holds, we ensure that there is at least *one* behavior (accomplished in RCRCHECK). □

In some cases, our refinement algorithm will give an answer that is not the expected one due to an incorrect refinement choice. In cases where an incorrect chute is synthesized we can easily backtrack.

5. Implementation

In this section we describe some implementation-level details that proved important when developing our prototype tool.

5.1 CTL Proof Attempts

Assume for now that we have a set of chute predicates $\bar{\mathcal{C}}$. In Section 4 we assumed the following method:

$$\text{attempt } (M \vdash \epsilon, \Phi) \text{ using } \bar{\mathcal{C}}$$

When this procedure fails to prove the property, it returns a path ϖ : $(S \times \mathsf{sub}(\Phi))$ list that is part of a counterexample that demonstrates how Φ can be violated given the current state-space restriction to chutes $\bar{\mathcal{C}}$.

In our implementation we developed this attempt procedure as an extension to our previous method [10, 11], which handles the universal subset of CTL. In our previous work, we introduced a reduction which, when given a transition system P and an $\forall$CTL temporal logic property Φ, generates a procedural program $\mathcal{E}$ that encodes the search for the proof that Φ holds of P [10, 11]. Existing program analysis tools can then be used to reason about the validity of the property.

Our encoding $\mathcal{E}$ is given in Figure 5 and has been extended with the two new rules in large shadowed boxes so that we can now handle full CTL properties. The notation $P[c/c']$ indicates that the program P is modified such that each command c is replaced with a new command c'. When given a program P and a CTL property Φ, the new program $\mathcal{E}$ encodes the search for the proof that Φ holds of P. The arguments $(\langle s,\psi\rangle, \mathcal{M}, R)$ passed to $\mathcal{E}$ are a pair consisting of the state s and a Φ-subformula ψ of interest, a finite set of ranking functions $\mathcal{M}$, an indexed set of chute predicates $\bar{\mathcal{C}}$ and the program source P. Executions of the procedure $\mathcal{E}$ explore the $S \times \mathsf{sub}(\Phi)$ state space from an initial state $s_0 \in I$ in a depth-first manner. At each recursive call, $\mathcal{E}$ is attempting to determine whether ψ holds of s. Rather than explicitly tracking this information, however, $\mathcal{E}$ returns false (recursively) whenever ψ does not hold of s. Consequently, if $\mathcal{E}$ can be proved to never return false, it must be the case that the overall property Φ holds of the initial state s. When a program analysis is applied to $\mathcal{E}$ it is implementing what is needed to prove branching-time behaviors of the original transition system (*e.g.* backtracking, eventuality checking, tree counterexamples, abstraction, abstraction-refinement, etc). Formally the relationship between $\mathcal{E}$ and $\vdash$ is: for a program P (with initial states I) and CTL property Φ,

$$\exists\bar{\mathcal{C}}.\ \exists\bar{\mathcal{M}}.\ \forall s \in I.\ \mathcal{E}(s,\Phi,\bar{\mathcal{M}},\bar{\mathcal{C}},R) \text{ cannot return false}$$
$$\Rightarrow$$
$$\forall s \in I.\ R, s \models \Phi$$

What remains is to understand how $\mathcal{E}$ determines whether a subformula ψ holds of a state s. By passing the state on the stack, we can consider multiple branching scenarios. When a particular ψ is a $\wedge$ or AW/EW subformula, then $\mathcal{E}$ ensures that all possibilities are considered by establishing feasible paths to all of them. When a particular ψ is a $\vee$ or AF/EF subformula, $\mathcal{E}$ enables executions to consider all of the possible cases that might cause ψ to hold of s. As soon as one is found, true is returned. Otherwise, false will be returned if none are found.

New existential cases. The encoding has two new cases, in large shadowed boxes, for the existential operators: the new subformula encoding $\mathtt{enc}^{\kappa}_{\mathsf{EF}\psi}$ which is similar to $\mathtt{enc}^{\kappa}_{\mathsf{AF}\psi}$, as well as encoding $\mathtt{enc}^{\kappa}_{\mathsf{E}[\psi_1\ \mathsf{W}\ \psi_2]}$ which is similar to $\mathtt{enc}^{\kappa}_{\mathsf{A}[\psi_1\ \mathsf{W}\ \psi_2]}$. They are designed such that we can again apply the universal reasoning and try to prove that $\mathtt{enc}^{\kappa}_{\mathsf{EF}\psi}$ (or $\mathtt{enc}^{\kappa}_{\mathsf{E}[\psi_1\ \mathsf{W}\ \psi_2]}$) cannot return false. What is new is that $\mathtt{enc}^{\kappa}_{\mathsf{EF}\psi}$ and $\mathtt{enc}^{\kappa}_{\mathsf{E}[\psi\mathsf{W}\psi']}$ must take care to restrict possible proofs/counterexamples as specified by the chute predicates we have discovered. This is where the indexed vector of chute predicates $\bar{\mathcal{C}}$ is used. The encodings for $\mathtt{enc}^{\kappa}_{\mathsf{EF}\psi}$ and $\mathtt{enc}^{\kappa}_{\mathsf{E}[\psi\mathsf{W}\psi']}$ include wavy underlined assume($\mathcal{C}^{\kappa}$) statements in Figure 5. These statements restrict the behavior of the transition system to chute $\mathcal{C}^{\kappa}$.

5.2 Synthesizing Chute Predicates

Our refinement algorithm, given in Figure 4, then assumes a method for synthesizing new chute predicates, given counterexamples to proof attempts. In our implementation, when the proof attempt fails a path $\varpi : (c, \kappa, \psi)$ list is returned, which is a sequence of commands in the original program P, annotated with the relevant subformula. Our implementation of $\textsc{Synth}_{cp}$ must return a chute predicate cp and subformula index κ that meets the interface given in Figure 4. When our implementation of attempt generates the encoding $\mathcal{E}$, it introduces a variable ρ_i at each nondeterministic choice. For example, we would transform nondeterministic assignments as follows:

$$\texttt{x := read();} \quad \rightsquigarrow \quad \rho_x \texttt{ := *; x :=} \rho_x\texttt{;}$$

We similarly transform nondeterministic branching:

$$\texttt{if (read()) then } C_1 \texttt{ else } C_2$$
$$\rightsquigarrow \quad \rho_i \texttt{ := *; if (}\rho_i\texttt{>0) then } C_1 \texttt{ else } C_2$$

These transformations simplify chute predicate synthesis by standardizing the sources of nondeterminism as values of ρ-variables. When we are given a path ϖ, we look for a ρ-variable:

$$\ldots, (c_{i-1}, \kappa_{i-1}, \psi_{i-1}), (\underset{\sim}{\rho_i}\texttt{:=*}, \kappa_i, \mathsf{E}\gamma_i), (c_{i+1}, \kappa_{i+1}, \psi_{i+1}), \ldots$$

Given such a path, we restrict our attention to the commands that are annotated with $(\kappa_i, \mathsf{E}\gamma_i)$, as the other commands are only relevant to other subformulae. We then build a formula T that is the conjunction of inequalities in static single-assignment form that represents the remaining commands. Assume that V is the variables *not* in the $(\kappa_i, \mathsf{E}\gamma_i)$ scope. Using quantifier elimination we compute $T' = \exists V.T$. Our procedure then ensures that T' is in CNF form: $T' = \bigwedge_i T'_i$ where each T'_i is an inequality . We prune T' ensuring that each conjunct mentions the variable ρ:

$$T_\rho = \neg \bigwedge \{T'_i \mid \rho \in \textsc{FreeVars}(T'_i)\}$$

The new candidate for chute refinement is thus $\mathsf{pc} = \ell \Rightarrow T_\rho$ where ℓ is assumed to be the location of the command $\rho := *$.

Example. Imagine that we have the following path:

```
(...;                              , (Rε, Eγ ∨ AFp))
(x:=a; y:=b; v:=c; y:=k;           , (LRε, Eγ))
(rho := *;                         , (LRε, Eγ))
(assume(rho>3);                    , (LRε, Eγ))
(x := w;                           , (LRε, Eγ))
(y := y-1;                         , (LRε, Eγ))
(assume(x<z);                      , (LRε, Eγ))
(rho := *;                         , (LRε, Eγ))
(assume(rho>x);                    , (LRε, Eγ))
(x := x - 1;                       , (LRε, Eγ))
(v := y;                           , (LRε, Eγ))
(rho := *;                         , (LRε, Eγ))
(assume(rho>3);                    , (LRε, Eγ))
```

The SSA formula representing this would be:

$$\begin{array}{rcl} \texttt{x}_1 & = & a_0 \\ \texttt{y}_1 & = & b_0 \\ \texttt{v}_1 & = & c_0 \\ \texttt{y}_1 & = & \texttt{k}_0 \\ \texttt{rho}_1 & > & 3 \\ \texttt{x}_2 & = & \texttt{w}_0 \\ \texttt{y}_2 & = & \texttt{y}_1 - 1 \\ \texttt{x}_2 & < & z_0 \end{array} \qquad \begin{array}{rcl} \texttt{rho}_2 & > & \texttt{x}_2 \\ \texttt{x}_3 & = & \texttt{x}_2 - 1 \\ \texttt{v}_2 & = & \texttt{y}_1 \\ \texttt{rho}_3 & > & 3 \\ a_1 & = & \texttt{x}_3 \\ b_1 & = & \texttt{y}_2 \\ c_1 & = & \texttt{v}_2 \end{array}$$

Imagine that we'd like to find a condition from the second $\texttt{rho} := *$. In this case we quantify out all variables except $\texttt{x}_2$, $\texttt{y}_2$, $\texttt{v}_1$, $\texttt{k}_0$, $\texttt{z}_0$, and $\texttt{rho}_2$. That leaves us with the condition: $\texttt{rho}_2 > x_2$

Thus we might use $\neg(\texttt{rho}_2 > x_2)$ as the refinement for $\mathcal{C}^{\mathsf{LR}\epsilon}$. There are usually many choices available, some of which may lead to failed proofs due to a violation in $\textsc{RCRcheck}$. To filter out potentially bad chute predicates, our implementation performs a simple non-termination check of the scope in question. If multiple candidates still exist we choose the one that appears as the last assignment in the inner most scope. We have found that these heuristics for choosing chute predicates was effective at proving a wide variety of CTL properties, as seen in our experimental results (Section 6).

5.3 Checking Recurrent Sets

Finally, when a proof attempt succeeds, recall that we must check that our chutes have not restricted the state space to empty traces. To this end, we must check that chutes for existential subformulae are *recurrent*. This does not necessarily mean that we must check all subformula. For example, the property $(\mathsf{EG}p) \vee (\mathsf{EG}q)$ holds if $\mathsf{EG}p$ holds. In this case, we only need to ensure that the chute $\mathcal{C}^{\mathsf{LL}\epsilon}$ for the left operator is recurrent. A proof that $M \vdash \epsilon, \Phi$ involves indexed sets $\bar{\mathcal{C}}$ and $\bar{\mathcal{F}}$. For each recurrent set obligation, we can use a simple reduction to satisfiability.

Inside our implementation of attempt, for every subformula $(\kappa, \mathsf{E}\gamma)$, there is an encoding of the relevant subset of the transition relation, restricted by chute predicate $\mathcal{C}^\kappa$. Our implementation uses known non-termination proving techniques to prove, in the case of EG, that there is at least one non-terminating execution and, in the case of EF that there at least one execution to a place where the subproperty may hold.

6. Evaluation

Using our prototype implementation we performed two sets of experiments. First, we ran the tool on a series of small benchmarks crafted to explore the various combinations of temporal operators. We then used the tool on a set of examples drawn from industrial code bases. In both cases, we generated the encoding and ran our algorithm on an Intel x64-based 2.8 GHz single-core processor. The sources of our experiments are available—please contact the authors. As discussed in Section 1, our tool is the first to handle mixtures of universal and existential quantifiers. Thus at this time there are no competing tools to compare against. Note that, as our tool is not especially optimized, the purpose of these experiments is only to demonstrate the promise of the approach.

For our small benchmarks, we wrote example programs in C. For each example, we wrote down corresponding CTL properties. The results of these experiments are given in Figure 6. Some of the CTL properties are meant to hold (denoted $\checkmark$) and others are meant not to hold (denoted χ). We report the time it took to prove or discover a counterexample in the **Time** column. In each case, we constructed another benchmark for the corresponding negated property (using the same program). For example, in the benchmark 22 where $\mathsf{EGAG}p$ holds, we ensure that $\mathsf{AFEF}\neg p$ does not hold of benchmark 49. The $\mathsf{EFEG}p$ benchmark is displayed in Example 1.

In all but two cases we were able to prove that the property held or discover a counterexample in less than a minute, often in seconds or less. Benchmark #20 ran out of memory during abstraction refinement in the underlying safety proof. In benchmark #24 of Figure 6, our tool failed to report the correct answer for the property $\mathsf{EG}(q \Rightarrow \mathsf{EF}p)$. This is because our tool made the wrong choice about synthesizing chute, but restricting execution to a particular set of paths (via a predicate on ρ). However, a more mature version of our tool can simply backtrack and make other choices. Understanding these tradeoffs is an important direction for future work.

SMALL BENCHMARKS

#	Property	Result Exp.	Result Act.	Time (s)
1.	$\mathsf{AF}p$	✓	✓	1.2
2.	$\mathsf{AF}p$	χ	χ	0.8
3.	$\mathsf{AG}p$	✓	✓	0.3
4.	$\mathsf{AG}p$	χ	χ	0.5
5.	$\mathsf{EF}p$	✓	✓	
6.	$\mathsf{EF}p$	χ	χ	1.7
7.	$\mathsf{EG}p$	✓	✓	0.9
8.	$\mathsf{EG}p$	χ	χ	0.9
9.	$\mathsf{AGAF}p$	✓	✓	10.8
10.	$\mathsf{AGAF}p$	χ	χ	1.9
11.	$\mathsf{AGEF}p$	✓	✓	29.0
12.	$\mathsf{AGEG}p$	✓	✓	1.2
13.	$\mathsf{AFEG}p$	✓	✓	55.8
14.	$\mathsf{AFEF}p$	✓	✓	3.7s
15.	$\mathsf{AFAG}p$	✓	✓	1.3
16.	$\mathsf{AFAG}p$	χ	χ	11.0
17.	$\mathsf{EFEG}p$	✓	✓	44.3
18.	$\mathsf{EFEG}p$	χ	χ	54.7
19.	$\mathsf{EFAG}p$	✓	✓	0.6
20.	$\mathsf{EFAF}p$	✓	?	*mem*
21.	$\mathsf{EGEF}p$	χ	χ	10.4
22.	$\mathsf{EGAG}p$	✓	✓	0.8
23.	$\mathsf{EGAF}p$	✓	✓	12.5
24.	$\mathsf{EG}(q \Rightarrow \mathsf{EF}p)$	✓	χ	33.9
25.	$\mathsf{EG}(q \Rightarrow \mathsf{AF}p)$	χ	χ	150.2
26.	$\mathsf{AG}(q \Rightarrow \mathsf{EG}p)$	✓	✓	2.2
27.	$\mathsf{AG}(q \Rightarrow \mathsf{EF}p)$	✓	✓	29.5
28.	$\mathsf{EG}\ \neg p$	χ	χ	0.8
29.	$\mathsf{EG}\ \neg p$	✓	✓	0.9
30.	$\mathsf{EF}\ \neg p$	χ	χ	0.5
31.	$\mathsf{EF}\ \neg p$	✓	✓	0.6
32.	$\mathsf{AG}\ \neg p$	χ	χ	0.8
33.	$\mathsf{AG}\ \neg p$	✓	✓	2.0
34.	$\mathsf{AF}\ \neg p$	χ	χ	0.5
35.	$\mathsf{AF}\ \neg p$	✓	✓	0.4
36.	$\mathsf{EFEG}\neg p$	χ	χ	1.9
37.	$\mathsf{EFEG}\neg p$	✓	✓	3.6
38.	$\mathsf{EFAG}\neg p$	χ	χ	3.9
39.	$\mathsf{EFAF}\neg p$	χ	χ	6.3
40.	$\mathsf{EGAF}\neg p$	χ	χ	10.9
41.	$\mathsf{EGAG}\neg p$	χ	χ	37.7
42.	$\mathsf{EGEF}\neg p$	χ	χ	2.7
43.	$\mathsf{EGEF}\neg p$	✓	✓	5.8
44.	$\mathsf{AGAF}\neg p$	χ	χ	3.6
45.	$\mathsf{AGAF}\neg p$	✓	✓	10.2
46.	$\mathsf{AGEF}\neg p$	χ	χ	23.8
47.	$\mathsf{AGEG}\neg p$	χ	χ	7.5
48.	$\mathsf{AFAG}\neg p$	✓	✓	40.3
49.	$\mathsf{AFEF}\neg p$	χ	χ	0.9
50.	$\mathsf{AFEG}\neg p$	χ	χ	13.8
51.	$\mathsf{AF}(q \wedge \mathsf{AG}\neg p)$	χ	χ	2.0
52.	$\mathsf{AF}(q \wedge \mathsf{EG}\neg p)$	χ	χ	13.8
53.	$\mathsf{EF}(q \wedge \mathsf{AF}\neg p)$	χ	χ	6.3
54.	$\mathsf{EF}(q \wedge \mathsf{AG}\neg p)$	χ	χ	3.9

Figure 6: The performance of our tool when applied to small benchmarks. We report the property proved/disproved, the expected/actual result, and the time. For each property (1–27) we have also attempted to prove/disprove the negated property (28–54). Benchmarks 28–54 are the same as 1–27 but with the property negated.

INDUSTRIAL EXAMPLES

#	Example	LOC	Property shape	Result Exp.	Result Act.	Time (s)
1	OS frag. 1	29	$\mathsf{AG}(p \Rightarrow \mathsf{AF}q)$	✓	✓	4.6
2	OS frag. 1	29	$\mathsf{AG}(p \Rightarrow \mathsf{AF}q)$	χ	χ	9.1
3	OS frag. 1	29	$\mathsf{AG}(p \Rightarrow \mathsf{EF}q)$	✓	✓	9.5
4	OS frag. 1	29	$\mathsf{AG}(p \Rightarrow \mathsf{EF}q)$	χ	χ	1.5
5	OS frag. 2 [8]	58	$\mathsf{AG}(p \Rightarrow \mathsf{AF}q)$	✓	✓	2.1
6	OS frag. 2 [8]	58	$\mathsf{AG}(p \Rightarrow \mathsf{AF}q)$	χ	χ	1.8
7	OS frag. 2 [8]	58	$\mathsf{AG}(p \Rightarrow \mathsf{EF}q)$	✓	✓	3.7
8	OS frag. 2 [8]	58	$\mathsf{AG}(p \Rightarrow \mathsf{EF}q)$	χ	χ	1.5
9	OS frag. 3	370	$\mathsf{AG}(p \Rightarrow \mathsf{AF}q)$	✓	✓	38.9
10	OS frag. 3	370	$\mathsf{AG}(p \Rightarrow \mathsf{AF}q)$	χ	χ	18.0
11	OS frag. 3	370	$\mathsf{AG}(p \Rightarrow \mathsf{EF}q)$	✓	✓	90.0
12	OS frag. 3	370	$\mathsf{AG}(p \Rightarrow \mathsf{EF}q)$	χ	χ	107.8
13	OS frag. 4	370	$\mathsf{AF}q \vee \mathsf{AF}p$	✓	✓	34.3
14	OS frag. 4	370	$\mathsf{AF}q \vee \mathsf{AF}p$	χ	χ	18.8
15	OS frag. 4	370	$\mathsf{EF}q \wedge \mathsf{EF}p$	✓	✓	1261
16	OS frag. 4	370	$\mathsf{EF}q \wedge \mathsf{EF}p$	χ	?	*mem*
17	OS frag. 5	43	$\mathsf{AGAF}p$	✓	✓	569.7
18	OS frag. 5	43	$\mathsf{AGAF}p$	χ	χ	65.1
19	OS frag. 5	43	$\mathsf{AGEF}p$	✓	?	*time*
20	OS frag. 5	43	$\mathsf{AGEF}p$	χ	?	*mem*
21	PgSQL arch	90	$\mathsf{AGAF}p$	✓	?	*mem*
22	PgSQL arch	90	$\mathsf{AGAF}p$	χ	χ	38.1
23	PgSQL arch	90	$\mathsf{AGEF}p$	✓	?	*mem*
24	PgSQL arch	90	$\mathsf{AGEF}p$	χ	χ	42.7
25	S/W Updates	36	$p \Rightarrow \mathsf{AF}q$	✓	✓	70.2
26	S/W Updates	36	$p \Rightarrow \mathsf{AF}q$	χ	χ	32.4
27	S/W Updates	36	$p \Rightarrow \mathsf{EF}q$	✓	✓	18.5
28	S/W Updates	36	$p \Rightarrow \mathsf{EF}q$	χ	χ	1.3
29	OS frag. 1	29	$\mathsf{EF}(p \wedge \mathsf{EG}\neg q)$	χ	χ	12.5
30	OS frag. 1	29	$\mathsf{EF}(p \wedge \mathsf{EG}\neg q)$	✓	✓	3.5
31	OS frag. 1	29	$\mathsf{EF}(p \wedge \mathsf{AG}\neg q)$	χ	χ	18.1
32	OS frag. 1	29	$\mathsf{EF}(p \wedge \mathsf{AG}\neg q)$	✓	✓	105.7
33	OS frag. 2 [8]	58	$\mathsf{EF}(p \wedge \mathsf{EG}\neg q)$	χ	χ	6.5
34	OS frag. 2 [8]	58	$\mathsf{EF}(p \wedge \mathsf{EG}\neg q)$	✓	✓	1.2
35	OS frag. 2 [8]	58	$\mathsf{EF}(p \wedge \mathsf{AG}\neg q)$	χ	χ	8.7
36	OS frag. 2 [8]	58	$\mathsf{EF}(p \wedge \mathsf{AG}\neg q)$	✓	✓	5.6
37	OS frag. 3	370	$\mathsf{EF}(p \wedge \mathsf{EG}\neg q)$	χ	χ	1930.9
38	OS frag. 3	370	$\mathsf{EF}(p \wedge \mathsf{EG}\neg q)$	✓	✓	1680.7
39	OS frag. 3	370	$\mathsf{EF}(p \wedge \mathsf{AG}\neg q)$	χ	?	*mem*
40	OS frag. 3	370	$\mathsf{EF}(p \wedge \mathsf{AG}\neg q)$	✓	?	*mem*
41	OS frag. 4	370	$\mathsf{EG}\neg p \wedge \mathsf{EG}\neg q$	χ	χ	61.3
42	OS frag. 4	370	$\mathsf{EG}\neg p \wedge \mathsf{EG}\neg q$	✓	✓	7.6
43	OS frag. 4	370	$\mathsf{AF}\neg q \vee \mathsf{AF}\neg p$	χ	χ	0.9
44	OS frag. 4	370	$\mathsf{AF}\neg q \vee \mathsf{AF}\neg p$	✓	✓	0.6
45	OS frag. 5	43	$\mathsf{EFEG}\neg p$	χ	χ	1471.7
46	OS frag. 5	43	$\mathsf{EFEG}\neg p$	✓	✓	351.1
47	OS frag. 5	43	$\mathsf{EFAG}\neg p$	χ	χ	85.5
48	OS frag. 5	43	$\mathsf{EFAG}\neg p$	✓	✓	255.8
49	PgSQL arch	90	$\mathsf{EFEG}\neg p$	χ	χ	45.3
50	PgSQL arch	90	$\mathsf{EFEG}\neg p$	✓	✓	35.2
51	PgSQL arch	90	$\mathsf{EFAG}\neg p$	χ	?	*mem*
52	PgSQL arch	90	$\mathsf{EFAG}\neg p$	✓	✓	30.2
53	S/W Updates	36	$p \wedge \mathsf{EG}\neg q$	χ	χ	0.4
54	S/W Updates	36	$p \wedge \mathsf{EG}\neg q$	✓	✓	4.5
55	S/W Updates	36	$p \wedge \mathsf{AG}\neg q$	χ	χ	0.5
56	S/W Updates	36	$p \wedge \mathsf{AG}\neg q$	✓	✓	0.3

Figure 7: The results of applying our refinement algorithm on a variety of examples from industrial code. In each case, we report the shape of the property, the expected/actual result returned by our tool, and the time it took to prove the property or discover a counterexample. Benchmarks 29–56 are the same as 1–28 but with the property negated.

In Figure 7 we report the results of applying our tool to CTL challenge problems drawn from industrial code bases. The examples were taken from code models of the I/O subsystem of the Windows kernel, the back-end infrastructure of the PostgreSQL database server, and the SoftUpdates patch system [25]. Line counts are given in the third column. In many of these cases, heap-commands from the original sources have been abstracted away using the approach due to Magill *et al.* [29]. This abstraction introduces new arithmetic variables that track the sizes of recursive predicate found as a byproduct of a successful memory safety analysis using an abstract domain based on separation logic. Note that this abstraction often allows us to reason about nondeterminism related to data-structures (e.g. a subroutine that increases the length of a list by some nondeterministic amount).

For each benchmark, we considered a meaningful property. Many are standard acquire/release or malloc/free-style properties ($\mathsf{AG}[p \Rightarrow \mathsf{AF}q]$) and, for example, the OS frag. 4 property (Figure 7, #13) says that either an I/O completion occurs successfully or else a failure code is returned. Figure 7 reports the shape of these properties (eliding the details of the atomic propositions p, q, etc.).

The final columns of Figure 7 report the expected/actual result returned by our tool, and the time it took to prove the property or discover a counterexample. In the vast majority of the cases, we were able to prove/disprove the property, often very quickly. In some cases, our implementation ran out of memory (*mem*) while performing SYNTH_{cp}. We believe that these examples could be proved if we applied program slicing on the encoding $\mathcal{E}$. In one case our implementation timed out (*time*) after 24 hours.

In summary, we can prove CTL properties of C functions that have hundreds of lines of code. For example, OS frag. 3 is 370 LOC. The majority of the examples (both the small benchmarks in Figure 6 and industrial code in Figure 7) were examples that previously could not be proved. The exceptions are the single-temporal-operator small benchmarks (which reduce to simple safety/liveness) and the strictly-universal industrial examples such as #21, which can be treated by previous work [11].

It is reasonable to ask about a comparison between our tool on the property AFfalse (which encodes termination) and a termination prover, or EGtrue and a non-termination prover. In fact, in our system the encoding of AFfalse is isomorphic to the reduction used in tools such as TERMINATOR [12], similarly EGtrue in our system reduces immediately to the identical techniques used in current non-termination provers. Thus, the experimental results are essentially identical, with the variability in the performance only due to the level of optimizations implemented in the underlying tools.

7. Related Work

Temporal property verification (and related problems such as finding winning strategies in games) have been extensively studied for finite-state systems (*e.g.* [1, 4, 6, 7, 28, 37]). Temporal property verification for some limited types of infinite-state systems have also been studied (*e.g.* pushdown systems [36, 39, 40], parameterized systems [17], etc). In limited cases we can abstract programs to finite-state systems and apply these known methods, but existing abstraction methods usually do not allow us to reliably prove properties that mix universal and existential modal operators in non-trivial ways. Methods for proving *linear-time* properties of infinite-state programs have been studied in recent work (*e.g.* [8, 9, 13, 33]). These techniques do not, however, facilitate reasoning about the nondeterminism in systems (see [9] for a discussion on this).

Methods of proving branching-time properties with only universal path quantifiers are known (*e.g.* [5, 10, 11, 13]). Techniques are also known for proving AF false (*a.k.a.* termination [3, 12, 18]) as well as EG true (*a.k.a.* non-termination [22]). In this work we build on these known techniques.

Previous tools based on fixed *a priori* abstractions are known for CTL. The abstraction used by YASM [23] is aimed primarily at the unnested existential subset of CTL. The work of Song and Touili [36] abstracts the program to pushdown systems. The difference here is that we reduce the problem of CTL (in a way that information is not lost) to different problems, which allows abstractions to be computed by refinement later using known techniques.

Although we solve a problem more general than termination, our iterative algorithm for finding restrictions on the state-space shares some similarity with the idea of alternation used in Harris *et al.* [24]. Related approaches are also seen in Godefroid *et al.* [19] and Gulavani *et al.* [20] for proving safety properties.

Our work characterizes CTL verification in a way that is complete upto a certain parameter (*chutes*) and gives a method and implementation for discovering these parameters automatically. In this sense it may be applicable to discovering focus sets [14] or the necessary ingredients in a games-based abstraction framework [15]. Our paper also might contribute towards novel approaches to the known problem of supporting mixtures of may/must [19]. Specifically we contribute a reduction that facilitates existing successful universal techniques (*e.g.* predicate abstraction, interpolation, etc) and gives a more general underapproximation for existential properties than previously known approaches to may/must abstraction.

Kesten and Pnueli [27] describe a proof system for CTL*. Due to our desire for full automation, ours differs in significant ways. For example, while a proof of eventuality ($\mathsf{AF}q$ or $\mathsf{EF}q$) in our case involves reasoning along paths until q, we do not decompose into path assertions in the proof system. Instead, we identify the appropriate fragment of the transition relation (*i.e.* $\mathcal{R}^{\mathcal{F}}_{\mathcal{C}\,X}$) and a general property that must hold of this transition relation (well-foundedness). In this way, we leave the details of eventuality proving to underlying abstraction techniques such as interpolation or abstraction refinement. This simplifies the proof system and lends itself many different forms of reasoning over $\mathcal{R}^{\mathcal{F}}_{\mathcal{C}\,X}$.

There are a few other connections to existing work. Pruning paths (as we do in chute refinement) appears in many static analysis techniques [21, 41]. Second, in our work we synthesize program variables that correspond to properties of the transition system (or of the desired system). The success of similar techniques in other contexts [35] reinforces the practical potential and experimental results of our paper. Finally, Vardhan and Viswanathan [38] describe tool called Lever which uses language inference to discover fixed points. These fixed points could potentially be used in conjunction with our method once we have discovered the appropriate state restrictions.

8. Concluding Remarks

Until now, the question of how to reliably automate proofs in branching-time logics (such as CTL, CTL* and the modal μ-calculus) for infinite-state programs remained an open problem. In this paper we have reported on the first known robust automatic proof method to support both universal and existential branching-time temporal operators (in CTL) for programs. In our approach existential reasoning is reduced to universal reasoning together with the search for a restrictions on the program's state-space. The advantage of the approach is that there are known solutions for universal reasoning. To demonstrate the practical viability of our approach we discussed the outcome of an experimental evaluation with a prototype implementation using examples drawn the PostgreSQL database server, the SoftUpdates patch system, the Windows OS kernel.

There are a few open problems left as future work. It would be helpful to have a more extensive evaluation considering, for example, performance of properties that have high levels of nesting in the temporal operators. Further, one might bring these techniques to the interprocedural level, investigating the use of temporal lemmas to optimize the performance of the proof search. Finally, these techniques could be extended to more expressive logics such as CTL* and the modal μ-calculus.

Acknowledgments

We thank Carsten Fuhs, Peter O'Hearn, John Wickerson, and the anonymous reviewers for their valuable feedback.

References

[1] BERNHOLTZ, O., VARDI, M. Y., AND WOLPER, P. An automata-theoretic approach to branching-time model checking (extended abstract). In *CAV'94* (1994), D. L. Dill, Ed., vol. 818, Springer, pp. 142–155.

[2] BEYER, D., HENZINGER, T. A., JHALA, R., AND MAJUMDAR, R. The software model checker blast. *STTT 9*, 5-6 (2007), 505–525.

[3] BRADLEY, A., MANNA, Z., AND SIPMA, H. The polyranking principle. *Automata, Languages and Programming* (2005), 1349–1361.

[4] BURCH, J., CLARKE, E., ET AL. Symbolic model checking: 10^{20} states and beyond. *Information and computation 98*, 2 (1992), 142–170.

[5] CHAKI, S., CLARKE, E. M., GRUMBERG, O., OUAKNINE, J., SHARYGINA, N., TOUILI, T., AND VEITH, H. State/event software verification for branching-time specifications. In *IFM'05* (2005), J. Romijn, G. Smith, and J. van de Pol, Eds., vol. 3771, pp. 53–69.

[6] CLARKE, E., JHA, S., LU, Y., AND VEITH, H. Tree-like counterexamples in model checking. In *LICS* (2002), pp. 19–29.

[7] CLARKE, E. M., EMERSON, E. A., AND SISTLA, A. P. Automatic verification of finite-state concurrent systems using temporal logic specifications. *TOPLAS 8* (April 1986), 244–263.

[8] COOK, B., GOTSMAN, A., PODELSKI, A., RYBALCHENKO, A., AND VARDI, M. Y. Proving that programs eventually do something good. In *POPL'07* (2007), pp. 265–276.

[9] COOK, B., AND KOSKINEN, E. Making prophecies with decision predicates. In *POPL'11* (2011), T. Ball and M. Sagiv, Eds., ACM, pp. 399–410.

[10] COOK, B., KOSKINEN, E., AND VARDI, M. Temporal verification as a program analysis task [extended version]. *FMSD* (2012).

[11] COOK, B., KOSKINEN, E., AND VARDI, M. Y. Temporal property verification as a program analysis task. In *CAV'11* (2011), G. Gopalakrishnan and S. Qadeer, Eds., vol. 6806, Springer, pp. 333–348.

[12] COOK, B., PODELSKI, A., AND RYBALCHENKO, A. Termination proofs for systems code. In *PLDI'06* (2006), M. I. Schwartzbach and T. Ball, Eds., pp. 415–426.

[13] COUSOT, P., AND COUSOT, R. An abstract interpretation framework for termination. In *POPL'12* (2012), ACM, pp. 245–258.

[14] DAMS, D., AND NAMJOSHI, K. S. The existence of finite abstractions for branching time model checking. In *LICS* (2004), pp. 335–344.

[15] DE ALFARO, L., GODEFROID, P., AND JAGADEESAN, R. Three-valued abstractions of games: Uncertainty, but with precision. In *LICS* (2004), pp. 170–179.

[16] EMERSON, E. A., AND HALPERN, J. Y. "sometimes" and "not never" revisited: on branching versus linear time temporal logic. *J. ACM 33*, 1 (1986), 151–178.

[17] EMERSON, E. A., AND NAMJOSHI, K. S. Automatic verification of parameterized synchronous systems (extended abstract). In *CAV'96* (1996), vol. 1102, pp. 87–98.

[18] GIESL, J., SCHNEIDER-KAMP, P., AND THIEMANN, R. Aprove 1.2: Automatic termination proofs in the dependency pair framework. *Automated Reasoning* (2006), 281–286.

[19] GODEFROID, P., NORI, A. V., RAJAMANI, S. K., AND TETALI, S. Compositional may-must program analysis: unleashing the power of alternation. In *POPL'10* (2010), ACM, pp. 43–56.

[20] GULAVANI, B. S., HENZINGER, T. A., KANNAN, Y., NORI, A. V., AND RAJAMANI, S. K. SYNERGY: a new algorithm for property checking. In *FSE'06* (2006), ACM, pp. 117–127.

[21] GULWANI, S., JAIN, S., AND KOSKINEN, E. Control-flow refinement and progress invariants for bound analysis. In *PLDI'09* (2009), pp. 375–385.

[22] GUPTA, A., HENZINGER, T. A., MAJUMDAR, R., RYBALCHENKO, A., AND XU, R.-G. Proving non-termination. *SIGPLAN Not. 43* (January 2008), 147–158.

[23] GURFINKEL, A., WEI, O., AND CHECHIK, M. Yasm: A software model-checker for verification and refutation. In *CAV'06* (2006), vol. 4144, pp. 170–174.

[24] HARRIS, W. R., LAL, A., NORI, A. V., AND RAJAMANI, S. K. Alternation for termination. In *SAS* (2010).

[25] HAYDEN, C. M., MAGILL, S., HICKS, M., FOSTER, N., AND FOSTER, J. S. Specifying and verifying the correctness of dynamic software updates. In *VSTTE'12* (2012), vol. 7152, pp. 278–293.

[26] IOSIF, R., BOZGA, M., BOUAJJANI, A., HABERMEHL, P., MORO, P., , AND VOJNAR, T. Programs with lists are counter automata. In *CAV* (2006).

[27] KESTEN, Y., AND PNUELI, A. A compositional approach to ctl* verification. *Theor. Comput. Sci. 331*, 2-3 (2005), 397–428.

[28] KUPFERMAN, O., VARDI, M., AND WOLPER, P. An automata-theoretic approach to branching-time model checking. *Journal of the ACM 47*, 2 (2000), 312–360.

[29] MAGILL, S., TSAI, M.-H., LEE, P., AND TSAY, Y.-K. Automatic numeric abstractions for heap-manipulating programs. In *POPL'10* (2010), ACM, pp. 211–222.

[30] MCMILLAN, K. L. Lazy abstraction with interpolants. In *CAV'06* (2006), T. Ball and R. B. Jones, Eds., vol. 4144, pp. 123–136.

[31] NELSON, G. A generalization of Dijkstra's calculus. *TOPLAS 11*, 4 (1989), 517–561.

[32] PISTORE, M., AND TRAVERSO, P. Planning as model checking for extended goals in non-deterministic domains. In *IJCAI'01* (2001), Springer.

[33] PNUELI, A., AND ZAKS, A. Psl model checking and run-time verification via testers. In *FM* (2006), pp. 573–586.

[34] PODELSKI, A., AND RYBALCHENKO, A. Transition invariants. In *LICS* (2004), pp. 32–41.

[35] SOLAR-LEZAMA, A., TANCAU, L., BODÍK, R., SESHIA, S. A., AND SARASWAT, V. A. Combinatorial sketching for finite programs. In *PLDI* (2006), ACM, pp. 404–415.

[36] SONG, F., AND TOUILI, T. Pushdown model checking for malware detection. In *TACAS* (2012).

[37] STIRLING, C. Games and modal mu-calculus. In *TACAS* (1996), vol. 1055, pp. 298–312.

[38] VARDHAN, A., AND VISWANATHAN, M. Learning to verify branching time properties. *FMSD 31*, 1 (2007), 35–61.

[39] WALUKIEWICZ, I. Pushdown processes: Games and model checking. In *CAV* (1996), vol. 1102, pp. 62–74.

[40] WALUKIEWICZ, I. Model checking ctl properties of pushdown systems. In *FSTTCS* (2000), S. Kapoor and S. Prasad, Eds., vol. 1974, pp. 127–138.

[41] YANG, Z., AL-RAWI, B., SAKALLAH, K. A., HUANG, X., SMOLKA, S. A., AND GROSU, R. Dynamic path reduction for software model checking. In *IFM* (2009), vol. 5423, pp. 322–336.

Natural Proofs for Structure, Data, and Separation

Xiaokang Qiu Pranav Garg Andrei Ştefănescu P. Madhusudan

University of Illinois at Urbana-Champaign, USA

{qiu2, garg11, stefane1, madhu}@illinois.edu

Abstract

We propose *natural proofs* for reasoning with programs that manipulate data-structures against specifications that describe the structure of the heap, the data stored within it, and separation and framing of sub-structures. Natural proofs are a subclass of proofs that are amenable to completely automated reasoning, that provide sound but incomplete procedures, and that capture common reasoning tactics in program verification. We develop a dialect of separation logic over heaps, called DRYAD, with recursive definitions that avoids explicit quantification. We develop ways to reason with heaplets using classical logic over the theory of sets, and develop natural proofs for reasoning using proof tactics involving disciplined unfoldings and formula abstractions. Natural proofs are encoded into decidable theories of first-order logic so as to be discharged using SMT solvers.

We also implement the technique and show that a large class of more than 100 correct programs that manipulate data-structures are amenable to full functional correctness using the proposed natural proof method. These programs are drawn from a variety of sources including standard data-structures, the Schorr-Waite algorithm for garbage collection, a large number of low-level C routines from the Glib library and OpenBSD library, the Linux kernel, and routines from a secure verified OS-browser project. Our work is the first that we know of that can handle such a wide range of full functional verification properties of heaps automatically, given pre/post and loop invariant annotations. We believe that this work paves the way for deductive verification technology to be used by programmers who do not (and need not) understand the internals of the underlying logic solvers, significantly increasing their applicability in building reliable systems.

Categories and Subject Descriptors F.3.1 [*Logics and Meanings of Programs*]: Specifying and Verifying and Reasoning about Programs: Mechanical verification; D.2.4 [*Software Engineering*]: Software/Program Verification: Assertion checkers

Keywords heap analysis; data structures; natural proofs; separation logic; SMT solvers

1. Introduction

In recent years, the *automated deductive verification paradigm* for software verification that combines user written modular contracts and loop invariants with automated theorem proving of the resulting verification conditions has become very powerful. The latter process is often executed by automated logical decision procedures supported by SMT solvers, which have emerged as robust and powerful engines to automatically find proofs. Several techniques and tools have been developed [2, 16, 20] and there have been several success stories of large software verification projects using this approach (the Verve OS project [42], the Microsoft hypervisor verification project using VCC [16], and a recent verified-for-security OS+browser for mobile applications [29], to name a few).

Verification conditions do not, however, always fall into decidable theories. In particular, the verification of properties of the *dynamically modified heap* is a big challenge for logical methods. The dynamically manipulated heap poses several challenges, as typical correctness properties of heaps require complex combinations of structure (e.g., *p* points to a tree structure, or to a doubly-linked list, or to an almost balanced tree, with respect to certain pointer-fields), data (the integers stored in data-fields of the tree respect the binary search tree property, or the data stored in a tree is a max-heap), and separation (the procedure modifies one list and not the other and leaves the two lists disjoint at exit, etc.).

The fact that the dynamic heap contains an unbounded number of locations means that expressing the above properties requires *quantification* in some form, which immediately precludes the use of most SMT decidable theories (there are only a few of them known that can handle quantification; e.g., the array property fragment [12] and the STRAND logic [25, 26]). Consequently, *expressing* such properties naturally and succinctly in a logical formalism has been challenging, and reasoning with them automatically even more so.

For instance, in the Boogie line of tools (including VCC) of writing specifications using first-order logic and employing SMT solvers to validate verification conditions, the specification of invariants of even simple methods like *singly-linked-list insert* is tedious. In such code[1], second-order properties (reachability, acyclicity, separation, etc.) are smuggled in using carefully chosen *ghost variables*; for example, acyclicity of a list is encoded by assigning a ghost number (idx) to each node in the list, with the property that the numbers associated with adjacent nodes strictly increase going down the list. These ghost variables require careful manipulation when the structures are updated; for example, inserting a node may require updating the ghost numbers for other nodes in the list, in order to maintain the acyclicity property. Once such a ghost-encoding of the specification is formulated, the validation of verification conditions, which typically have quantifiers, are dealt with using sound heuristics (a wide variety of them including e-matching, model-based quantifier instantiation, etc. are available), but are still often not enough and have to be augmented by *instantiation triggers* from the verification engineer to help the proof go through.

PLDI'13, June 16–19, 2013, Seattle, WA, USA.

[1] http://vcc.codeplex.com/SourceControl/changeset/view/dcaa4d0ee8c2#vcc/Docs/Tutorial/c/7.2.list.c

In recent years, *separation logic*, especially in combination with recursive definitions, has emerged as a much more succinct and natural logic to express properties about structure and separation [32, 36]. However, the validation of verification conditions resulting from separation logic invariants are also complex, and has eluded automatic reasoning and exploitation of SMT solvers (even more so than tools such as Boogie that use classical logic). Again, help from the user in proving the verification conditions are currently necessary— the tools VERIFAST [20] and BEDROCK [15], for instance, admit separation logic specifications but require the user to write low-level lemmas and proof tactics to guide the verification. For example, in verifying an in-place reversal of a linked list[2], BEDROCK would require several lemmas and a hint package be supplied at the level of the code in order for the proof to go through.

The work in this paper is motivated by the opinion that entirely decidable logics are too restrictive, in general, to support the verification of complex specifications of functional correctness for heap manipulating programs, and the other extreme of user-supplied proof tactics and lemmas is too tedious, requiring of the user too much knowledge of the underlying proof systems/decision procedures. Our aim is to build completely automatic, sound, but incomplete proof techniques that can solve a large class of properties involving complex data-structures.

The natural proof methodology:
Our proof methodology of natural proofs was first proposed in a paper by Madhusudan et al on natural proofs for tree data-structures last year at POPL [27]. Natural proofs exploit a *fixed* set of proof tactics, keeping the expressiveness of powerful logics, retaining the automated nature of proving validity, but giving up on completeness (i.e., giving up decidability, retaining soundness). The idea of natural proofs [27] is to identify a subclass of proofs $\mathcal{N}$ such that (a) a large class of valid verification conditions of real-world programs have a proof in $\mathcal{N}$, and (b) searching for a proof in $\mathcal{N}$ is *decidable*. In fact, we would even like the search for a proof in $\mathcal{N}$ to be efficiently decidable, possibly utilizing the automatic logic solvers (SMT solvers) that exist today. Natural proofs are hence a fixed set of proof tactics whose application is itself expressible in a decidable logic. The natural proofs developed in [27] were too restrictive, however, handling only *single* trees, with no scope for handling multiple or more complex data-structures and their separation (see section on Related Work for more details).

The aim of this paper is to provide natural proofs for general properties of structure, data, and separation. Our contributions are: (a) we propose DRYAD, a dialect of separation logic for heaps, with no explicit (classical) quantification but with recursive definitions, to express second-order properties; (b) show that DRYAD is both powerful in terms of expressiveness, and that the strongest-post of DRYAD specifications with respect to bounded code segments can be formulated in DRYAD, (c) show how DRYAD has been designed so that it can be systematically converted to *classical* logic using the theory of sets, allowing us to connect the more natural and succinct specifications to more verbose but classical logic, and (d) develop a natural proof mechanism for classical logics with recursion and sets that implement sound but incomplete reductions to decidable theories that can be handled by an SMT solver.

DRYAD*: A separation logic with determined heaplets*
The primary design principle behind separation logic is the decision to express *strict specifications*— logical formulas must naturally refer to *heaplets* (subparts of the heap), and, by default, the smallest heaplets over which the formula needs to refer to. This is in contrast to classical logics (such as FOL) which implicitly refer to the entire heap globally. Strict specifications permit elegant ways to capture how a particular sub-part of the heap changes due to a procedure, implicitly leaving the rest of the heap and its properties unchanged across a call to this procedure. Separation logic is a particular framework for strict specifications, where formulas are implicitly defined on strictly defined heaplets, and where heaplets can be combined using a *spatial conjunction operator* denoted by $*$. The frame rule in separation logic captures the main advantage of strict specifications: if the Hoare-triple $\{P\}C\{Q\}$ holds for some program C, then $\{P * R\}C\{Q * R\}$ also holds (with side-conditions that the modified variables in C are disjoint from the free variables in R).

Consider, for example, expressing that the location x is the root of a tree. This is a *second-order* property and formulations of it in classical logic using set or path quantification are quite complex and not easily amenable to automated verification. We prefer *inductive* definitions of structural properties without any explicit quantification. The separation logic syntax with recursive definitions and heaplet semantics allows simple quantifier-free formulas to express structural restrictions; for example. tree-ness can be expressed simply as:

$$tree(x) :: (x = \texttt{nil} \wedge \texttt{emp}) \vee (x \longmapsto (l, r) * tree(l) * tree(r))$$

We first define a new logic, DRYAD, that permits no explicit quantification, but permits powerful recursive definitions to define integers, sets/multisets of integers, and sets of locations, using least fixed-points. The logic DRYAD furthermore has a heaplet semantics and allows the spatial conjunction operator $*$. However, a key design feature of DRYAD is that the heaplet for recursive formulas is essentially *determined* by the syntax as opposed to the semantics. In classical separation logic, a formula of the form $\alpha * \beta$ says that the heaplet can be partitioned into *any* two disjoint heaplets, one satisfying α and the other β. In DRYAD, the heaplet for a (complex) formula is *determined* and hence if there is a way to partition the heaplet, there is precisely *one* way to do so. We have found that most uses of separation logic to express properties can be written quite succinctly and easily using DRYAD (in fact, it is *easier* to write such deterministic-heap specifications). The key advantage is that this eliminates implicit existential quantification the separation operator provides. In a verification condition that combines the precondition in the negative and the post-condition in the positive, the classical semantics for separation logic invariably introduces universal quantification in the satisfiability query for the negation of the verification condition, which in turn is extremely hard to handle.

In DRYAD, the semantics of a recursive definition $r(x)$ (such as *tree* above), requires that the heaplet be determined and defined as the set of all locations reachable from the node x through a set of pointer-fields $f_1, \ldots, f_k$ without passing through a set of locations (given by a set of location terms $t_1, \ldots t_n$). While our logical mechanisms can be extended beyond this notion (in deterministic ways), we have found that this captures most common properties required in proving data-structure manipulating programs correct.

Translating* DRYAD *to classical logic with recursion:
The second key step in our paradigm is a technique to bridge the gap from separation logic to classical logic in order to utilize efficient decision procedures supported by SMT solvers. We show that heaplet semantics and separation logic constructs of DRYAD can be effectively translated to classical logic where heaplets are modeled as *sets of locations*. We show that DRYAD formulas can be translated into classical logic with free set variables that capture the heaplets corresponding to the strict semantics. This translation does not, of course, yield a decidable theory yet, as recursive definitions are still present (the recursion-free formulas are in a decidable theory). The carefully designed DRYAD logic with determined heaplet semantics ensures that there is no quantification in the resulting formula in classical logic. The heaplets of recursively defined prop-

[2] http://plv.csail.mit.edu/bedrock/Tutorial.html

erties, which are defined using the set of all *reachable* nodes, are translated to recursively defined sets of locations.

Natural proofs for* DRYAD*:
Finally, we develop a natural proof methodology for DRYAD by showing a natural proof mechanism for the equivalent formulas in classical logic. The basic proof tactic that we follow is not just dependent on the formula embodying the verification condition, but also on the precise footprint touched by the program segment being verified. We unfold recursive definitions precisely across footprints, translating them to the frontier of the footprint, and then use a form of *formula abstraction* that treats recursive formulas on frontier nodes as uninterpreted functions. The resulting formula falls in a logic over sets and integers, which is then decided using the theory of uninterpreted functions and arrays using SMT solvers. The key feature is that heaplets and separation logic constructs, which get translated to recursively defined sets of locations, are unfolded along with other user-defined recursive definitions and formula-abstracted using this uniform natural proof strategy,

While our proof strategy is roughly as above, there are many technical details that are complex. For example, the heaplets defined by pre/post conditions intrinsically specify the modified locations of the heap, which have to be considered when processing procedure calls in order to ensure which recursively defined metrics on locations continue to hold after a procedure call. Also, the final decidable theories that we compile our conditions down to does require a bit of quantification, but it turns out to be in the *array property fragment* which admits automatic decision procedures.

Implementation and Evaluation:
Our proof mechanisms are essentially a class of decidable proof tactics that result in sound but incomplete validation procedures. To show that this class of natural proofs is effective in practice, we provide a prototype implementation of our technique, which handles a low-level programming language with pre-conditions and post-conditions written in DRYAD. We show, using a large class of correct programs manipulating lists, trees, cyclic lists, and doubly linked lists as well as *multiple* data-structures of these kinds, that the natural proof mechanism succeeds in proving the verifications conditions automatically. These programs are drawn from a range of sources, from textbook data-structure routines (binary search trees, red-black trees, etc.) to routines from Glib low-level C-routines used in GTK+/Gnome to implement file-systems, from the Schorr-Waite garbage collection algorithm, to several programs from a recent secure framework developed for mobile applications [29]. Our work is by far the only one that we know of that can handle such a large class of programs, completely automatically. Our experience has been that the user-provided contracts and invariants are easily expressible in DRYAD, and the automatic natural proof mechanisms work extremely fast. In fact, contrary to our own expectations, we also found that the tool is useful in *debugging*: in several cases, when the annotations supplied were incorrect, the model provided by the SMT solver for the natural proof was useful in detecting errors and correcting the invariants/program.

2. Related Work

The natural proof methodology was introduced in [27] (see also [39]), but was exclusively built for tree data-structures. In particular, this work could only handle *recursive* programs, i.e., no while-loops, and even for tree data-structures, imposed a large number of restrictions on pre/post conditions for methods— the input to a procedure had to be only a single tree, the method can only return a single tree, and even then must havoc the input tree given to it. The lack of handling of multiple structures means that even simple programs like mergesort (that merges two lists), cannot be handled, and simple programs that manipulate two lists or two trees cannot be reasoned with. Also, structures such as doubly-linked lists, trees with parent pointers, etc. are out of scope of this work. Technically, in our present work, we can handle user-defined structures expressible in separation logic, multiple structures and their separation, programs with while-loops, etc., because of our *logical* treatment of separation logic using classical logic.

There is a rich literature on analysis of heaps in software. We omit discussing literature on general interactive theorem provers (like ISABELLE [31]) that require considerable manual guidance. We also omit a lot of work on analyzing shape properties of the heap [6, 13, 18, 28, 41], as they do not handle complex functional properties.

There are several proof systems and assistants for separation logic [32, 36] that incorporate proof heuristics and are incomplete. However, [3] gives a small decidable fragment of separation logic on lists which has been further extended in [11] to include a restricted form of arithmetic. Symbolic execution with separation logic has been used in [4, 5, 8] to prove structural specifications for various list and tree programs. These tools come hardwired with a collection of axioms and their symbolic execution engines check the entailment between two formulas modulo these axioms. VERIFAST [20], on the other hand, chooses flexibility of writing richer specifications over complete automation, but requires the user to provide inductive lemmas and proof tactics to aid verification. Similarly, BEDROCK [15] is a Coq library that aims at mostly automated (but not completely automated) procedures that requires some proof tactics to be given by the user to prove verification conditions. The idea of using regions (sets of locations) for describing heaps in our work also extends to describing frames for function calls, and the use for the latter is similar to implicit dynamic frames [38] in the literature. The crucial difference in our framework is that the implicit dynamic frames are syntactically determined, and amenable to quantifier-free reasoning. A work that comes very close to ours is a paper by Chin et al. [14], where the authors allow user-defined recursive predicates (similar to ours) and build a terminating procedure that reduces the verification condition to standard logical theories. However, their procedure does not search for a proof in a well-defined simple and decidable class, unlike our natural proof mechanism; in fact, the resulting formulas are quantified and incompatible with decidable logics handled by SMT solvers.

In all of the above cited work and other manual and semi-automatic approaches to verification of heap-manipulating programs like [37], inductive definitions of algebraic data-types is extremely common for capturing second-order data-structure properties. Most of these approaches use proof tactics which unroll inductive definitions and do extensive unification to try to match terms to find simple proofs. Our notion of natural proofs is very much inspired by such kinds of semi-automatic and manual heap reasoning that we have seen in the literature.

There is also a variety of verification tools based on classical logics and SMT solvers. DAFNY [23] and VCC [16] compile to BOOGIE [2] and generate VCs that are passed to SMT solvers. This approach requires significant ghost annotations, and annotations that explicitly express and manipulate frames. The JAHOB system [43, 44] is one of the first attempts at full functional verification of linked data structures, which integrates a variety of theorem provers, including SMT solvers, and makes the process mostly automated. However, complex specifications combining structure, data and separation usually require more complex provers such as MONA [21], or even interactive theorem provers such as ISABELLE [31] in the worst case. The success of the proof search also relies on users' manual guidance.

```
void heapify(loc x) {
  if (x.left = nil)
    s := x.right;
  else if (x.right = nil)
    s := x.left;
  else {
    lx := x.left
    rx := x.right;
    if (lx.key < rx.key)
      s := x.right;
    else
      s := x.left;
  }
  if (s =/= nil)
    if (s.key > x.key) {
      t := s.key;
      s.key := x.key;
      x.key := t;
      heapify(s);
    }
}
```

$$\varphi_{pre} \equiv \Big(x \overset{key,left,right}{\longmapsto} (k,\ l,\ r) * mheap^{\Delta}_{\vec{pf}}(l) * mheap^{\Delta}_{\vec{pf}}(r)\Big) \wedge keys^{\Delta}_{\vec{pf}}(x) = K$$

$$\varphi_{post} \equiv mheap^{\Delta}_{\vec{pf}}(x) \wedge keys^{\Delta}_{\vec{pf}}(x) = K$$

assume $x.left_0 \neq nil$
assume $x.right_0 \neq nil$
$lx := x.left_0$
$rx := x.right_0$
assume $lx.key_0 < rx.key_0$
$s := x.right_0$
assume $s \neq nil$
assume $s.key_0 > x.key_0$
$t := s.key_0$
$s.key_1 := x.key_0$
$x.key_2 := t$
heapify(s)

$$\boldsymbol{mheap}^{\Delta}_{\vec{pf}}(x) \overset{def}{=} \Big(x = \mathtt{nil} \wedge \mathtt{emp} \vee \big(x \overset{key,left,right}{\longmapsto} (k,\ l,\ r) * (mheap^{\Delta}_{\vec{pf}}(l) \wedge \{k\} \geq keys^{\Delta}_{\vec{pf}}(l)) * (mheap^{\Delta}_{\vec{pf}}(r) \wedge \{k\} \geq keys^{\Delta}_{\vec{pf}}(r))\big)\Big)$$

$$\boldsymbol{keys}^{\Delta}_{\vec{pf}}(x) \overset{def}{=} \Big(x = \mathtt{nil} \wedge \mathtt{emp} : \emptyset\ ;\ x \overset{key,left,right}{\longmapsto} (k,\ l,\ r) * \mathtt{true} : keys^{\Delta}_{\vec{pf}}(l) \cup \{k\} \cup keys^{\Delta}_{\vec{pf}}(r)\ ;\ \text{default} : \emptyset\Big)$$

Figure 1. Motivating example: Heapify

The idea of unfolding recursive definitions and formula abstraction also features in the work by Suter et al. [39, 40], where a procedure for algebraic data-types is presented. However, this work focuses on soundness and completeness, and is not terminating for several complex data structures like red-black trees. Moreover, the work limits itself to functional program correctness; in our opinion, functional programs are very similar to algebraic inductive specifications, leading to much simpler proof procedures.

There is also a rich literature on completely automatic decision procedures for restricted heap logics, some of which combine structure-logic and arbitrary data-logic. These logics are usually FOLs with restricted quantifiers, and usually are decided using SMT solvers. The logics LISBQ [22] and CSL [9, 10] offer such reasoning with restricted reachability predicates and quantification; see also the logics in [1, 7, 30, 33–35]. STRAND is a relatively expressive logic that can handle some data-structure properties (like BSTs) and admits decidable fragments [25, 26], but is again not expressive enough for more complex properties of inductive data-structures. None of these logics can express the class of VCs for full functional verification explored in this paper.

3. Motivating Example

In this section we give intuition into our verification approach through a motivating example. Recall that a max-heap is a binary tree such that for each node n the key stored at n is greater than or equal to the keys stored at each of its children. Heaps are often used to implement priority queues. In Figure 1, in the lower right corner, we express the property that a location x points to a max-heap using recursive definitions $keys^{\Delta}_{\vec{pf}}(x)$ and $mheap^{\Delta}_{\vec{pf}}(x)$, with $\vec{pf} \equiv \{left, right\}$. These recursive definitions are written in DRYAD, which is formally introduced in Section 4. Intuitively, DRYAD extends quantifier free separation logic [32, 36] with recursive predicates and functions. These recursive definitions allow us to express structural and data properties on the heap, like those of max-heap, without explicit quantification.

For a location x, the recursive definition $keys^{\Delta}_{\vec{pf}}(x)$ returns the set of keys at the nodes of the tree rooted at x: if x is `nil` and the heaplet is empty, then the empty-set; otherwise, the union of the key stored at x and the keys stored in the left and right subtrees of x. Similarly, the recursive definition $mheap^{\Delta}_{\vec{pf}}(x)$ states that x points to a max-heap if: x is `nil` and the heaplet is empty; or x and the heaplets of the left and right subtrees of x are mutually disjoint (x points to a tree) and the key at x is greater than or equal to the keys of the left and right subtrees of x.

The method `heapify` in Figure 1 is at the heart of the procedure for deleting the root from a max-heap (removing the node with the maximum priority). If the max-heap property is violated at a node x while satisfied by its descendants, then `heapify` restores the max-heap property at x. It does so by recursively descending into the tree, swapping the key of the root with the key at its left or right child, whichever is greater. The precondition φ_{pre} binds the free variable K to the set of keys of x. The postcondition states that after the procedure call, x satisfies the max-heap property and the set of keys of x is unchanged (same as K).

One of the main aspects of our approach is to reduce reasoning about heaplet semantics and separation logic constructs to reasoning about sets of locations. We use set operations like union, intersection and membership to describe separation constraints on a heaplet satisfying a formula. This translation from DRYAD formulas, like those in Figure 1, to formulas in classical logic with recursive predicates and functions is formally presented in Section 5. Intuitively, we associate a set of locations to each (spatial) atomic formula, which is the domain of the heaplet satisfying that formula. DRYAD requires that this heaplet is *syntactically* determined for each formula. For example, the heaplet associated to the formula $x \mapsto \ldots$ is the singleton $\{x\}$; for recursive definitions like $mheap^{\Delta}_{\vec{pf}}(x)$ and $keys^{\Delta}_{\vec{pf}}(x)$, the domain of the heaplet is $reach_{\{left,right\}}(x)$, which intuitively is the set of locations reachable from x using the pointer fields *left* and *right*, and can be defined recursively.

As shown in Figure 1, φ_{pre} is a conjunction of two formulas. If G_{pre} is the domain of the heaplet associated to φ_{pre}, then the first conjunct requires G_{pre} to be the disjoint union of the sets $\{x\}$, $reach_{\{left,right\}}(left(x))$ and $reach_{\{left,right\}}(right(x))$. The second conjunct requires $G_{pre} = reach_{\{left,right\}}(x)$. From these heaplet constraints, we can translate φ_{pre} to the following formula in classical logic *over the global heap*:

$$\begin{aligned}
& G_{pre} = \{x\} \cup reach_{\{left,right\}}(left(x)) \cup reach_{\{left,right\}}(right(x)) \\
\wedge\ & x \notin reach_{\{left,right\}}(left(x)) \wedge x \notin reach_{\{left,right\}}(right(x)) \\
\wedge\ & reach_{\{left,right\}}(left(x)) \cap reach_{\{left,right\}}(right(x)) = \emptyset \wedge x \neq nil \\
\wedge\ & mheap(left(x)) \wedge mheap(right(x)) \\
\wedge\ & G_{pre} = reach_{\{left,right\}}(x) \wedge keys(x) = K
\end{aligned}$$

Similarly, we translate φ_{post} to

$$G_{post} = reach_{\{left,right\}}(x) \wedge mheap(x) \wedge keys(x) = K$$

Note that the recursive definitions *mheap* and *keys* without the "Δ" superscript are in the classical logic (without the heaplet constraint). Hence the recursive predicate *mheap* satisfies

$$\begin{aligned}
mheap(x) \leftrightarrow\ & x = nil \wedge reach_{\{left,right\}}(x) = \emptyset) \\
\vee\ & \big(x \neq nil \wedge x \notin reach_{\{left,right\}}(left(x)) \wedge x \notin reach_{\{left,right\}}(right(x)) \\
& \wedge reach_{\{left,right\}}(left(x)) \cap reach_{\{left,right\}}(right(x)) = \emptyset \\
& \wedge (reach_{\{left,right\}}(x) = \{x\} \cup reach_{\{left,right\}}(left(x)) \\
& \quad \cup reach_{\{left,right\}}(right(x))) \\
& \wedge mheap(left(x)) \wedge \{key(x)\} \geq keys(left(x)) \\
& \wedge mheap(right(x)) \wedge \{key(x)\} \geq keys(right(x))\big)
\end{aligned}$$

The right side of Figure 1 presents a basic path from method `heapify`, corresponding to the case when both children of x are not *nil* and the key of the right child is greater than the keys of the left child and the root. The subscript of a pointer/data field denotes the timestamp. A key insight is that any basic path touches a finite number of locations and may call some recursive procedures. We refer to the touched locations as the *footprint*, and to the adjacent locations which are not part of the footprint as the *frontier*. For this example, the footprint is $\{ x, lx, rx \}$ (s is known to be equal with rx) and the frontier is $\{ left_0(lx), right_0(lx), left_0(rx), right_0(rx) \}$. We capture the effect of the path until the call to `heapify` by

$$\begin{aligned} & left_0(x) \neq nil \wedge right_0(x) \neq nil \wedge lx = left_0(x) \wedge rx = right_0(x) \\ \wedge\ & key_0(lx) < key_0(rx) \wedge\ s = right_0(x) \wedge s \neq nil \\ \wedge\ & key_0(s) > key_0(x) \wedge t = key_0(s) \\ \wedge\ & key_1 = key_0\{s \leftarrow key_0(x)\} \wedge key_2 = key_1\{x \leftarrow t\} \end{aligned}$$

Once we have expressed the verification condition in classical logic with recursive definitions over the global heap, we prove it using the *natural proof* methodology. We unfold the recursive definitions $mheap(x)$, $keys(x)$ and $reach_{\{left,right\}}(x)$ for x, lx and rx (the footprint), thus evaluating them in terms of their values on the frontier. The call to `heapify` preserves the recursive definitions on locations reachable from lx, and modifies those on rx according to the pre/post condition. Finally, we abstract the recursive definitions on the frontier with uninterpreted functions. We decide the resulted formula (which is in a decidable logic) using an SMT solver. Section 6 describes this process in detail.

4. The Logic Dryad

In this section we present our logic Dryad_{sep}; this redefines the logic Dryad [27] on arbitrary data-structures (not just trees), using heaplet semantics and separation logic primitives; the logic hence is a quantifier-free heaplet logic augmented with recursively defined predicates/functions. However, for brevity, we will refer to the new logic we propose as Dryad, and refer to the logic in [27] as Dryad_{tree}.

4.1 Syntax

Let us fix a finite set of *pointer-fields* PF and a finite set of *data-fields* DF. A record consists of a set of pointer-fields from PF and a set of data-fields from DF. Our logic also presumes that locations refer to entire records rather than particular fields, and that address arithmetic is precluded. We will use the term *locations* hence to refer to these records. We assume that every field is defined at every location, i.e., all memory records have the same layout (to simplify the presentation); our logic can easily be extended with record types.

Let $Bool = \{\texttt{true}, \texttt{false}\}$ stand for the set of Boolean values, Int stand for the set of integers and Loc stand for the universe of locations. For any set A, let $\mathcal{S}(A)$ denote the set of all finite subsets of A, and let $\mathcal{MS}(A)$ denote the set of all finite multisets with elements in A.

The Dryad logic allows expressing quantifier-free first-order properties over heaps/heaplets augmented with recursively defined notions for a location to express second-order properties, denoted as a function $r : Loc \rightarrow D$. The codomain D can be Int_L, $\mathcal{S}(Loc)$, $\mathcal{S}(Int)$, $\mathcal{MS}(Int)_L$ or $Bool$, where Int_L and $\mathcal{MS}(Int)_L$ extend Int and $\mathcal{MS}(Int)$ to lattice domains, respectively, in order to give least fixed-point semantics (explained later in this section). Typical examples of these recursive definitions include the definitions of the height of a tree or the height of black-nodes in the tree rooted at a node (recursively defined integers), the set of nodes reachable from a location following certain pointer fields (recursively defined sets of locations), the set/multiset of keys stored at a particular data-field under nodes reachable from a location (recursively defined set/multiset of integers), and the property that the tree rooted at a node is a binary search tree or a balanced tree or just a tree (recursively defined predicates).

A Dryad formula φ is quantifier-free, but parameterized by a set of recursive definitions Def^{Δ}. The syntax of Dryad logic is given in Figure 2, where the syntax of formulas is followed by the syntax for recursive definitions. Most symbols in Dryad are common and self-explanatory. Note that the inequality ($<$ or $\leq$) between integer sets/multisets indicates that any integer in the left-hand side is less-than/not-greater-than any integer in the right-hand side. It is also noteworthy that the separating conjunction ($*$) from separation logic is also allowed, but only if it is not above any negation ($\neg$). We require that every recursive function/predicate used in the formula φ has a unique definition in Def^{Δ}. Each recursive function is parameterized by a set of pointer fields $\overrightarrow{pf}$ and a set of program variables $\vec{v}$, denoted as $f^{\Delta}_{\overrightarrow{pf},\vec{v}}$. The subscripts are used in defining the semantics of recursive functions in Section 4.2. We usually simply use f^{Δ} when the subscripts are not relevant in the context. Similarly, recursive predicates are denoted as $p^{\Delta}_{\overrightarrow{pf},\vec{v}}$ or simply p^{Δ}. The recursive functions are defined using the syntax:

$$(\varphi^f_1(x, \vec{v}, \vec{s}) : t^f_1(x, \vec{s})\ ;\ \ldots\ ;\ \varphi^f_k(x, \vec{v}, \vec{s}) : t^f_k(x, \vec{s})\ ;\ \text{default} : t^f_{k+1}(x, \vec{s}))$$

where $\varphi^f_u(x, \vec{v}, \vec{s})/t^f_u(x, \vec{s})$ is a formula/term in our logic with $\vec{s}$ implicitly existentially quantified. The recursively defined predicates are defined using the syntax: $\varphi^p(x, \vec{v}, \vec{s})$, which is a formula in our logic with $\vec{s}$ implicitly existentially quantified. The recursive function syntax above expresses a case-split, with the function evaluating to the first term whose guard evaluates to true. The restrictions on the recursive definitions are:

- Subtraction, set-difference, and negation are disallowed;
- Every variable in $\vec{s}$ should appear in the right hand side of a points-to relation binding it to x *exactly once*.

For examples of recursive functions and predicates, see the definitions $keys^{\Delta}_{\overrightarrow{pf}}(x)$ and $mheap^{\Delta}_{\overrightarrow{pf}}(x)$ in Figure 1, respectively. The set of program variables $\vec{v}$ parameterizing the definitions is empty in both these definitions and the set of implicitly existentially-quantified variables $\vec{s}$ is $\{k, l, r\}$.

4.2 Semantics

Our logic is interpreted on models that are *program states*:

Definition 4.1. *A program state is a tuple $C = (R, s, h)$ where*

- *$R \subseteq Loc \setminus \{nil\}$ is a finite set of locations;*
- *$s : Vars \rightarrow Int \cup Loc$ is a store mapping program variables to locations or integers (of appropriate type);*
- *$h : R \times (PF \cup DF) \rightarrow Int \cup Loc$ is a heaplet mapping non-nil locations and each pointer-field/data-field to values of the appropriate type.* □

Note that the set of locations is, in general, larger than the state R and hence R defines a subset of heap locations. The store maps variables to locations (not necessarily in R), but the heaplet h gives interpretations for pointer and data-fields only for elements in R.

Given a heaplet h, for every pointer field pf, we denote the projection of h on $R \times (PF \setminus \{pf\} \cup DF)$ as $h \nmid pf$; similarly, for every data-field df, we denote the projection of h on $R \times (PF \cup DF \setminus \{df\})$ as $h \nmid df$. Also, for every subset $S \subseteq R$, we denote the projection of h on $S \times (PF \cup DF)$ as $h \mid S$.

A term/formula with free variables F is interpreted by interpreting the free variables in F using the map s from variables to values. The semantics of Dryad is similar to that of classical Separation Logic (SL). In particular, a term/formula without recursive definitions is interpreted exactly in the same way in Dryad and SL. Hence we first give the semantics of the non-recursive part, followed by the semantics of recursive definitions.

$$
\begin{array}{lllll}
i^{\Delta} : Loc \to Int_L & sl^{\Delta} : Loc \to \mathcal{S}(Loc) & si^{\Delta} : Loc \to \mathcal{S}(Int) & msi^{\Delta} : Loc \to \mathcal{MS}(Int)_L & p^{\Delta} : Loc \to Bool \\
j \in Int_L \text{ Variables} & L \in \mathcal{S}(Loc) \text{ Variables} & S \in \mathcal{S}(Int) \text{ Variables} & MS \in \mathcal{MS}(Int)_L \text{ Variables} & q \in Bool \text{ Variables} \\
x \in Loc \text{ Variables} & c : Int_L \text{ Constant} & pf \in PF & df \in DF &
\end{array}
$$

$$
\begin{array}{rrcl}
Loc \text{ Term:} & lt & ::= & x \mid \texttt{nil} \\
Int_L \text{ Term:} & it & ::= & c \mid j \mid i^{\Delta}_{\vec{pf},\vec{v}}(lt) \mid it + it \mid it - it \\
\mathcal{S}(Loc) \text{ Term:} & slt & ::= & \emptyset_l \mid L \mid \{lt\} \mid sl^{\Delta}_{\vec{pf},\vec{v}}(lt) \mid slt \cup slt \mid slt \cap slt \mid slt \setminus slt \\
\mathcal{S}(Int) \text{ Term:} & sit & ::= & \emptyset_s \mid S \mid \{it\} \mid si^{\Delta}_{\vec{pf},\vec{v}}(lt) \mid sit \cup sit \mid sit \cap sit \mid sit \setminus sit \\
\mathcal{MS}(Int)_L \text{ Term:} & msit & ::= & \emptyset_m \mid MS \mid \{it\}_m \mid msi^{\Delta}_{\vec{pf},\vec{v}}(lt) \mid msit \cup msit \mid msit \cap msit \mid msit \setminus msit
\end{array}
$$

$$
\begin{array}{rcl}
\text{Positive Formula: } \varphi & ::= & \texttt{true} \mid \texttt{false} \mid q \mid p^{\Delta}_{\vec{pf},\vec{v}}(lt) \mid \texttt{emp} \mid lt \overset{\vec{pf},\vec{df}}{\longmapsto} (\vec{lt},\vec{it}) \mid lt = lt \mid lt \neq lt \mid it \leq it \mid it < it \mid sit \leq sit \mid sit < sit \mid msit \leq msit \mid msit < msit \\
& & \mid slt \subseteq slt \mid slt \nsubseteq slt \mid sit \subseteq sit \mid sit \nsubseteq sit \mid msit \sqsubseteq msit \mid msit \not\sqsubseteq msit \mid lt \in slt \mid lt \notin slt \mid it \in sit \mid it \notin sit \mid it \in msit \mid it \notin msit \\
& & \mid \varphi \wedge \varphi \mid \varphi \vee \varphi \mid \varphi * \varphi \\
\text{Formula: } \psi & ::= & \varphi \mid \psi \wedge \psi \mid \psi \vee \psi \mid \neg \psi
\end{array}
$$

$$
\begin{array}{rcl}
\text{Recursive function : } f^{\Delta}_{\vec{pf},\vec{v}}(x) & \overset{def}{=} & (\varphi^f_1(x,\vec{v},\vec{s}) : t^f_1(x,\vec{s})\ ;\ \ldots\ ;\ \varphi^f_k(x,\vec{v},\vec{s}) : t^f_k(x,\vec{s})\ ;\ \text{default} : t^f_{k+1}(x,\vec{s})) \\
\text{Recursive predicate : } p^{\Delta}_{\vec{pf},\vec{v}}(x) & \overset{def}{=} & \varphi^p(x,\vec{v},\vec{s})
\end{array}
$$

Figure 2. Syntax of DRYAD

Before defining the semantics of formulas, we define the *pure* property for terms/formulas. Intuitively, a term/formula is pure if it is independent of the heap. Syntactically, a term/formula is pure if it does not contain emp, $\longmapsto$ or any recursive definition. Note that in *SL* all terms are pure, but in DRYAD, a term can be impure if it contains a recursive function f^{Δ}.

Semantics of terms

Each $\mathcal{T}$-term evaluates to either a normal value of type $\mathcal{T}$, or to `undef`, which is only used in interpreting recursive functions (will be explained later). As a special value, `undef` will be propagated throughout the formula: if a formula φ contains a sub-term that evaluates to `undef`, then φ will evaluate to `false` if it appears positively, and will evaluate to `true` otherwise. Intuitively, `undef` cannot help in making the formula true over a model.

The *Loc* terms are evaluated as follows:

$$
\begin{array}{rcl}
[\![x]\!]_C & = & s(x) \\
[\![\texttt{nil}]\!]_C & = & nil
\end{array}
$$

For any binary operator op, t op t' is evaluated as follows:

$$
[\![t \text{ op } t']\!]_C = \begin{cases}
[\![t]\!]_C \text{ op } [\![t']\!]_C & \text{if } t \text{ or } t' \text{ is pure} \\
[\![t]\!]_{C|R_1} \text{ op } [\![t']\!]_{C|R_2} & \text{else if there exist } R_1, R_2 \text{ such that} \\
& \quad R = R_1 \cup R_2, [\![t]\!]_{C|R_1} \neq \texttt{undef} \\
& \text{and } [\![t']\!]_{C|R_2} \neq \texttt{undef} \\
\texttt{undef} & \text{otherwise}
\end{cases}
$$

where op is interpreted in the natural way.

For singletons, $\{it\}$ will evaluate to $\emptyset$ if it evaluates to $-\infty$ or ∞:

$$
[\![\{it\}]\!]_C = \begin{cases}
\texttt{undef} & \text{if } [\![it]\!]_C = \texttt{undef} \\
\emptyset & \text{if } [\![it]\!]_C = -\infty \text{ or } \infty \\
\{[\![it]\!]_C\} & \text{otherwise}
\end{cases}
$$

$\{it\}_m$ and $\{lt\}$ evaluate similarly.

Semantics of formulas

The formula `true` is always interpreted to be *true*:

$$(R, s, h) \models \texttt{true}$$

The formula emp asserts that the heap is empty:

$$(R, s, h) \models \texttt{emp} \quad \text{iff} \quad R = \emptyset$$

The formula $lt \overset{\vec{pf},\vec{df}}{\longmapsto} (\vec{lt},\vec{it})$ asserts that the heap contains exactly one record consisting of fields $\vec{pf}$ and $\vec{df}$, at address lt, with values $\vec{lt}$ and $\vec{it}$, respectively. Formally, the semantics of this formula is given as:

$$
\begin{array}{ll}
(R, s, h) \models lt \overset{\vec{pf},\vec{df}}{\longmapsto} (\vec{lt},\vec{it}) \quad \text{iff} \quad R = \{[\![lt]\!]_{R,s,h}\} \text{ and} & \\
\qquad h([\![lt]\!]_{R,s,h}, pf_i) = [\![lt_i]\!]_{R,s,h} & \text{for corresponding } pf_i \text{ and } lt_i, \\
\qquad h([\![lt]\!]_{R,s,h}, df_i) = [\![it_i]\!]_{R,s,h} & \text{for corresponding } df_i \text{ and } it_i.
\end{array}
$$

Note that, as in separation logic, the above has a *strict semantics*—the heaplet must be a singleton set and cannot be a larger set.

For binary relations $t \sim t'$ between integers, sets, and multisets, including equality, the pure property plays an important role. Remember that in *SL* all terms are pure. To be consistent with *SL*, if both t and t' are pure, it is interpreted in the normal way. Otherwise, $t \sim t'$ is only defined on the minimum heaplet required by t and t', more concretely the union of the heaplet associated with t and t'.

$$
\begin{array}{lll}
(R, s, h) \models t \sim t' & \text{iff} & t \text{ or } t' \text{ is pure and } [\![t]\!]_C \sim [\![t']\!]_C \\
& \text{or} & t \text{ and } t' \text{ are impure and there exist } R_1, R_2 \text{ s.t. } R = R_1 \cup R_2 \\
& & \text{and } [\![t]\!]_{C|R_1} \neq \texttt{undef}, [\![t']\!]_{C|R_2} \neq \texttt{undef} \text{ and } [\![t]\!]_{C|R_1} \sim [\![t']\!]_{C|R_2}
\end{array}
$$

where $\sim$ is interpreted in the natural way.

The semantics of the disjoint conjunction operator $*$ is defined as follows. The formula $\varphi_0 * \varphi_1$ asserts that the heap can be split into two disjoint parts in which φ_0 and φ_1 hold respectively:

$$
\begin{array}{lll}
(R, s, h) \models \varphi_0 * \varphi_1 & \text{iff} & \text{there exist } R_0, R_1 \text{ s.t. } R_0 \cap R_1 = \emptyset \text{ and} \\
& & R_0 \cup R_1 = R \text{ and } (R_0, s, h \mid R_0) \models \varphi_0 \text{ and } (R_1, s, h \mid R_1) \models \varphi_1
\end{array}
$$

Boolean combinations are defined in the standard way:

$$
\begin{array}{rll}
(R, s, h) \models \varphi_0 \wedge \varphi_1 & \text{iff} & (R, s, h) \models \varphi_0 \text{ and } (R, s, h) \models \varphi_1 \\
(R, s, h) \models \varphi_0 \vee \varphi_1 & \text{iff} & (R, s, h) \models \varphi_0 \text{ or } (R, s, h) \models \varphi_1 \\
(R, s, h) \models \neg\varphi & \text{iff} & (R, s, h) \not\models \varphi
\end{array}
$$

Semantics of recursive definitions

The main semantical difference between DRYAD and *SL* is on recursive definitions. We would like to *deterministically delineate* the heap domain for any recursive definition, so that the heap domain required by any DRYAD formula can be *syntactically determined.* Given a recursive definition $rec^{\Delta}_{\vec{pf},\vec{v}}$, the subscripts $\vec{pf}$ and $\vec{v}$ play a role in delineating the heap domain. Intuitively, the heap domain for $rec^{\Delta}_{\vec{pf},\vec{v}}(l)$ is the set of locations reachable from l using pointer-fields in $\vec{pf}$, but *without* going through the locations $\vec{v}$. In other words, we want to take the set of locations that lie *in between* l and $\vec{v}$. Precisely, this set is determined by a location l and a program state (R, s, h).

We denote it as $\text{reachset}_{\vec{pf},\vec{v}}(l,(R,s,h))$. Formally it is the smallest set of locations L satisfying the following two conditions:

1. l is in the set L if l is not in $\vec{v}$ and $l \neq nil$;
2. for each c in L, with $c \in R$, and for each pointer pf, if $h(c, pf)$ is not in $\vec{v}$ and is not nil, then $h(c, pf)$ is also in L.

Note that even though the reach set is defined with respect to the edges in the heaplet, we can determine whether R includes all nodes reachable from l without going through $\vec{v}$ in the *global heap* by checking whether $R = \text{reachset}_{\vec{pf},\vec{v}}(l,(R,s,h))$.

For each recursive definition $rec^{\Delta}_{\vec{pf},\vec{v}}$, we usually simply denote $\text{reachset}_{\vec{pf},\vec{v}}$ as reachset^{rec}, as the subscripts are implicitly known.

Now, given a program state $C = (R,s,h)$ and a recursive function/predicate rec^{Δ}, the semantics on a location l depends on whether the heap domain R is exactly the required reach set $\text{reachset}^{rec}(l,(R,s,h))$. If this is not true, we simply interpret it as `undef` or `false`.

If the heap domain matches the reach set (i.e., $R = \text{reachset}_{\vec{pf},\vec{v}}(l,(R,s,h))$), the semantics is defined in the natural way (using least fixed-points). The colon operator in the syntax of recursive function $f^{\Delta}_{\vec{pf},\vec{v}}$ translates into a nested if-then-else (ITE) operator. Formally,

$$[\![f^{\Delta}_{\vec{pf},\vec{v}}(l)]\!]_C = \text{ITE}(\varphi^f_1, [\![t^f_1]\!]_{C|R_1}, \text{ITE}(\varphi^f_2, [\![t^f_2]\!]_{C|R_2}, \ldots [\![t^f_{k+1}]\!]_{C|R_{k+1}} \cdots))$$

where $R_1 \ldots R_{k+1} \subseteq R$ such that $[\![t^f_i]\!]_{C|R_i} \neq \texttt{undef}$. In order to give least fixed-point semantics for recursive definitions in the logic, we extend the primitive data-types to lattice domains. *Bool* with the order $\texttt{false} \sqsubseteq \texttt{true}$ forms a complete lattice, and $\mathcal{S}(Loc)$ and $\mathcal{S}(Int)$ ordered by inclusion, with join as union and meet as intersection, form complete lattices. Integers and multisets are extended to lattices. Let $(Int_L, \leq)$ denote the complete lattice, where $Int_L = Int \cup \{-\infty, \infty\}$, and where the ordering is $\leq$, join is *max*, meet is *min*. Also, $\mathcal{MS}(Int)_L, \sqsubseteq$ denote the complete lattice constructed from $\mathcal{MS}(Int)$, where $\mathcal{MS}(Int)_L = \mathcal{MS}(Int) \cup \{\top\}$, and $\sqsubseteq$ extends the inclusion relation with $S \sqsubseteq \top$ for any $M \in \mathcal{MS}(Int)$. It is easy to see that $(Int_L, \sqsubseteq)$ and $(\mathcal{MS}(Int)_L, \sqsubseteq)$ are complete lattices.

Formally, let *Def* consists of definitions of integer functions *I*, set-of-locations functions *SL*, set-of-integers functions *SI*, multiset-of-integers functions *MSI* and predicates *P*. Since these definitions could rely on each other, we evaluate them altogether as a function vector

$$r^{\Delta} = (\vec{i^{\Delta}}, \vec{sl^{\Delta}}, \vec{si^{\Delta}}, \vec{msi^{\Delta}}, \vec{p^{\Delta}})$$

We take the cartesian product lattice of the individual lattices and take the least fixed-point of r^{Δ} to obtain the semantics for each definition. Let $\text{select}_{rec}(lfp(r^{\Delta}))$, for each recursive definition rec^{Δ}, denote the selection of the coordinate for rec^{Δ} in $lfp(r^{\Delta})$.

Now we can formally define the semantics of recursive definitions. For any configuration C, the semantics of a recursive function f^{Δ} is defined as:

$$[\![f^{\Delta}(lt)]\!]_C = \begin{cases} \text{select}_f(lfp(r^{\Delta}))([\![lt]\!]_C) & \text{if } R = \text{reachset}^f([\![lt]\!]_C, C) \\ \texttt{undef} & \text{otherwise} \end{cases}$$

and the semantics of a recursive predicate p^{Δ} is defined as

$$[\![p^{\Delta}(lt)]\!]_C = \begin{cases} \text{select}_p(lfp(r^{\Delta}))([\![lt]\!]_C) & \text{if } R = \text{reachset}^p([\![lt]\!]_C, C) \\ \texttt{false} & \text{otherwise} \end{cases}$$

Remark: Note that we disallow negative operations (subtraction, set-difference and negation) in defining recursive definitions. This syntactical restriction guarantees that each iteration of r^{Δ} is monotonic. By Knaster-Tarski theorem, r^{Δ} admits a least fixed-point.

Examples

The DRYAD logic was already used in Section 3 to define max-heaps. Note that the definition of a max-heap is precisely defined on the heaplet that includes the underlying tree nodes of the max-heap only, as the heaplet for a recursive definition is the set of all reachable nodes according to the two pointers.

To clarify the difference between DRYAD and *SL*, consider now this recursive definition:

$$p^{\Delta}_{\{l,r\}}(x) \stackrel{def}{=} (x = \texttt{nil} \wedge \texttt{emp}) \vee \left[(x \stackrel{l,r}{\longmapsto} y, z) * \left(p^{\Delta}_{\{l,r\}}(y) \vee p^{\Delta}_{\{l,r\}}(z)\right)\right]$$

Now consider a global heap that has a tree rooted at x with pointer fields l and r. The above recursive formula, in separation logic, will be true on any heaplet that contains the nodes of a path in this tree from x to *nil*. However, in Dryad, we require that the heaplet must satisfy the heap constraints of the formula and also be the precise set of locations reachable from x using the pointer fields l and r. Consequently, if the tree pointed to by x has more than one path, the Dryad formula will be *false for any heaplet*.

The above example shows the advantage of Dryad; when heaplets are determined, we can avoid quantification. We have not found natural examples where an undetermined heaplet semantics helps in specifying properties of heaps.

DRYAD can express structures beyond trees. The main restriction we do impose is that we allow only *unary* recursive definitions, as this allows us to find simpler natural proofs since there is only one way to unfold the definition across a footprint. However, DRYAD can express structures like cyclic lists and doubly-linked lists.

A cyclic-list is captured as $(v \mapsto y) * lseg^{\Delta}_{next,v}(y)$. Here, v is a program variable which denotes the head of the cyclic-list and $lseg^{\Delta}_{next,v}(y)$ captures the list segment from y back to the head v, where the subscripts *next* and v indicate that the heaplet of the list segment is the locations that can be reached using the field *next*, but without going through v:

$$lseg^{\Delta}_{next,v}(y) \stackrel{def}{=} (y = v \wedge \texttt{emp}) \vee ((y \stackrel{next}{\mapsto} z) * lseg^{\Delta}_{next,v}(z))$$

Another interesting example is a doubly-linked list. We define a doubly-linked list as the following unary predicate:

$$\begin{aligned} dll^{\Delta}_{next}(x) \quad = \quad & (x = \texttt{nil} \wedge \texttt{emp}) \vee (x \stackrel{next}{\mapsto} \texttt{nil}) \vee \\ & (x \stackrel{next}{\mapsto} y * ((y \stackrel{prev}{\mapsto} x * \texttt{true}) \wedge dll^{\Delta}_{next}(y))) \end{aligned}$$

The first two disjuncts in the definition cover the base case when x is *nil* or the location next to x is *nil*; otherwise, let y be the location next to x, then the *prev* pointer at y points to x and location y is recursively defined as a doubly-linked list.

5. Translation to a Logic over the Global Heap

We now show one of the main contributions of this paper— a translation from DRYAD logic to classical logic with recursive predicates and functions, but over the global heap. The formulation of separation logic primitives in the global heap allows us to express complex structural properties, like disjointness of heaplets and treeness, using recursive definitions over *sets of locations*, which are defined locally, and are amenable to unfolding across the footprint and hence amenable to natural proofs.

For example, consider the formula $mheap^{\Delta}(x) * mheap^{\Delta}(y)$, where $mheap^{\Delta}$ is defined in Section 3. Since the heaplets for $mheap^{\Delta}(x)$ and $mheap^{\Delta}(y)$ are precise, it can get translated to an equivalent formula with a *free* set variable G that denotes the global heap over which the formula is evaluated:

$$\begin{aligned} & mheap(x) \wedge mheap(y) \wedge (reach^{mheap}(x) \cap reach^{mheap}(y) = \emptyset) \\ & \qquad \wedge (reach^{mheap}(x) \cup reach^{mheap}(y) = G) \end{aligned}$$

where *mheap* and $reach^{mheap}$ are corresponding recursive definitions in classical logic, which will be defined later in this section. Note that we use italics and remove the $^{\Delta}$ superscript to show the difference from their counterpart in DRYAD.

We assume the DRYAD formula to be translated is in *disjunctive normal form*, i.e., $\vee$ operators should be above all $*$ and $\wedge$ operators.

Construct	Domain-exact	Scope
$var/const$	false	$\emptyset$
$\{t\}/\{t\}_m$	dom-ext(t)	scope(t)
t op t'	dom-ext(t) $\vee$ dom-ext(t')	scope(t) $\cup$ scope(t')
$f^{\Delta}(lt)$	true	reachset$^f(lt)$
true/false	false	$\emptyset$
emp	true	$\emptyset$
$lt \overset{\vec{pf},\vec{df}}{\longmapsto} (\vec{lt}, \vec{it})$	true	$\{lt\}$
$p^{\Delta}(lt)$	true	reachset$^p(lt)$
$t \sim t'$	dom-ext(t) $\vee$ dom-ext(t')	scope(t) $\cup$ scope(t')
$\varphi \wedge \varphi'$	dom-ext(φ) $\vee$ dom-ext(φ')	scope(φ) $\cup$ scope(φ')
$\varphi * \varphi'$	dom-ext(φ) $\wedge$ dom-ext(φ')	scope(φ) $\cup$ scope(φ')

Figure 3. Domain-exact property and Scope function. Both are defined only for terms and formulas without disjunction and negation. A formula is assumed in its disjunctive normal form.

This is not a real restriction as one can always push the disjunction out. This normal form ensures that for all occurrences of the separation operator in a formula, there exists a unique way of splitting the heap so as to satisfy the $*$ separated sub-formulas. Also, it ensures that this unique heap-split can be determined syntactically from the structure of those sub-formulas.

In our translation, we model the heaplets associated with a formula or a term as a set of locations and all operations on these heaplets are modeled as set operations like set union, set intersections, etc. over set-of-location variables. For example the separating conjunction $P{*}Q$ is translated to the following set constraint: the intersection of the sets associated with the heaplets in the formulas P and Q is empty. Given a formula φ in Dryad and its associated heap domain modeled by a set variable G, we define an inductive translation T into a classical logic formula $T(\varphi,\ G)$ in the quantifier-free theory of finite sets, integers and uninterpreted functions. The translated formula is not interpreted on a heaplet, but interpreted on a global heap (i.e., with the heap domain *Loc*).

The translation uses an auxiliary *domain-exact* property and an auxiliary *scope* function. The domain-exact property indicates whether a term evaluates to a well-defined value or a positive formula evaluates to true on a fixed heap domain or not. This is different from the property *pure*; a pure formula or term is not domain-exact but the reverse implication is not true, in general. For example, the formula $(lt \longmapsto it) * true$ is not domain-exact but is also not pure. The scope function maps a term to the minimum heap domain required to evaluate it to a normal value, and maps a positive formula to the minimum heap domain required to evaluate it to *true*. The domain-exact property and the scope function are defined inductively in Figure 3.

We describe the logic translation in detail in Figure 4. The ITE expression used in the translation is short for "if-then-else". It is just a conditional expression defined as follows: ITE(ϕ, t_1, t_2) evaluates to t_1 if ϕ is true, otherwise evaluates to t_2.

In general, our translation restricts an impure term/formula to be evaluated only on the syntactically determined heap domain according to the semantics of Dryad. In particular, when evaluating a recursive formula or predicate p^{Δ}, we ensure that the heaplet is precisely the reach set $reach^p(lt)$. For a formula $\varphi * \varphi'$, translation to classical logic depends on whether the sub-formulas φ and φ' are domain-exact or not. If a sub-formula is domain-exact then it is evaluated on its scope. If it is not domain-exact, then it is evaluated on the rest of the heaplet.

Recursive definitions in Dryad are also translated to recursive definitions in classical logic. Translating a recursive definition rec^{Δ} uses the corresponding definitions rec and $reach^{rec}$, both of which are defined recursively in classical logic. The set $reach^{rec}$ represents the domain of the required heaplet for evaluating rec^{Δ}, and the Δ-eliminated definition rec captures the value of rec^{Δ} when the heaplet is restricted to $reach^{rec}$. Formally, suppose rec^{Δ} is a recursive definition w.r.t. pointer fields $\vec{pf}$ and stopping locations $\vec{v}$, then $reach^{rec}$ is recursively defined as the least fixed-point of

$$reach^{rec}(x) \overset{def}{=} \text{ITE}\Big(x = \texttt{nil} \vee x \in \vec{v},\ \emptyset,\ \{x\} \cup \bigcup_{pf \in \vec{pf}} (reach^{rec}(pf(x)))\Big)$$

$$
\begin{aligned}
T(var\ /\ const,\ G) &\equiv var\ /\ const \\
T(\{t\}\ /\ \{t\}_m,\ G) &\equiv \{t\}\ /\ \{t\}_m \\
T(t\ \text{op}\ t',\ G) &\equiv T(t,G)\ \text{op}\ T(t',G) \\
T(f^{\Delta}(lt),\ G) &\equiv \text{ITE}\,(reach^f(lt) = G,\ f(lt),\ \texttt{undef}) \\
T(\texttt{true}\ /\ \texttt{false},\ G) &\equiv \texttt{true}\ /\ \texttt{false} \\
T(\texttt{emp},\ G) &\equiv G = \emptyset \\
T(lt \overset{\vec{pf},\vec{df}}{\longmapsto} (\vec{lt}, \vec{it}),\ G) &\equiv G = \{lt\} \wedge \textstyle\bigwedge_{pf_i} pf_i(T(lt,G)) = T(lt_i, G) \\
&\qquad \wedge \textstyle\bigwedge_{df_i} df_i(T(lt,G)) = T(it_i, G) \\
T(p^{\Delta}(lt),\ G) &\equiv p(lt) \wedge G = reach^p(lt) \\
T(t \sim t',\ G) &\equiv \begin{cases} t \sim t' & \text{if } t \sim t' \text{ is not domain-exact} \\ t \sim t' \wedge G = \text{scope}(t \sim t') & \text{otherwise} \end{cases} \\
T(\varphi \wedge \varphi',\ G) &\equiv T(\varphi, G) \wedge T(\varphi', G) \\
T(\varphi \vee \varphi',\ G) &\equiv T(\varphi, G) \vee T(\varphi', G) \\
T(\neg\varphi,\ G) &\equiv \neg T(\varphi, G)
\end{aligned}
$$

$$
T(\varphi * \varphi',\ G) \equiv \begin{cases}
T(\varphi,\ \text{scope}(\varphi)) \wedge T(\varphi',\ \text{scope}(\varphi')) \\
\quad \wedge\ \text{scope}(\varphi) \cup \text{scope}(\varphi') = G \\
\quad \wedge\ \text{scope}(\varphi) \cap \text{scope}(\varphi') = \emptyset \\
\qquad\qquad \text{if both } \varphi \text{ and } \varphi' \text{ are domain-exact} \\
T(\varphi,\ \text{scope}(\varphi)) \wedge T(\varphi',\ G \setminus \text{scope}(\varphi)) \\
\quad \wedge\ \text{scope}(\varphi) \subseteq G \qquad \text{if only } \varphi \text{ is domain-exact} \\
T(\varphi',\ \text{scope}(\varphi')) \wedge T(\varphi,\ G \setminus \text{scope}(\varphi')) \\
\quad \wedge\ \text{scope}(\varphi') \subseteq G \qquad \text{if only } \varphi' \text{ is domain-exact} \\
T(\varphi,\ \text{scope}(\varphi)) \wedge T(\varphi',\ \text{scope}(\varphi')) \\
\quad \wedge\ \text{scope}(\varphi) \cup \text{scope}(\varphi') \subseteq G \\
\quad \wedge\ \text{scope}(\varphi) \cap \text{scope}(\varphi') = \emptyset \\
\qquad\qquad \text{if neither } \varphi \text{ nor } \varphi' \text{ is domain-exact}
\end{cases}
$$

Figure 4. Translating Dryad terms/formulas to classical logic

For each recursive predicate p^{Δ} defined as $p^{\Delta}(x) \overset{def}{=} \varphi^p(x, \vec{v}, \vec{s})$, we define

$$p(x) \overset{def}{=} T(\ \varphi^p(x,\ \vec{v}, \vec{s}),\ reach^p(x)\ )$$

Similarly, for each recursive function f^{Δ} defined as

$$f^{\Delta}(x) \overset{def}{=} (\varphi_1^f(x, \vec{v}, \vec{s}) : t_1^f(x, \vec{s})\ ;\ \ldots\ \varphi_k^f(x, \vec{v}, \vec{s}) : t_k^f(x, \vec{s})\ ;\ \text{default} : t_{k+1}^f(x, \vec{s}))$$

we define

$$
\begin{aligned}
f(x) \overset{def}{=} \text{ITE}\Big(&T(\varphi_1^f(x, \vec{v}, \vec{s}), reach^f(x)),\ t_1^{f-\Delta}(x, \vec{s}) \\
&\text{ITE}\Big(T(\varphi_2^f(x, \vec{v}, \vec{s}), reach^f(x)),\ t_2^{f-\Delta}(x, \vec{s}) \\
&\qquad \ldots, t_{k+1}^{f-\Delta}(x, \vec{s})\ \ldots\Big)\Big)
\end{aligned}
$$

where $t_i^{f-\Delta}(x, \vec{s})$ is just the classical logic counterpart of $t_i^f(x, \vec{s})$, when interpreted in a heap domain within $reach^f(x)$. Formally it is short for

$$\text{ITE}\big(\text{scope}(t_i^f(x, \vec{s})) \subseteq reach^f(x),\ T(t_i^f(x, \vec{s}),\ \text{scope}(t_i^f(x, \vec{s}))),\ \texttt{undef}\big)$$

Now for each set of recursive definitions Def^{Δ} in Dryad, we can translate it to a set of recursive definitions *Def* in classical logic.

Theorem 5.1. *Let φ be a* Dryad *formula w.r.t. a set of recursive definitions Def^{Δ}. For every program state C with heap domain Loc, and for every interpretation of variables I including a valuation for set-variable G, $(C,\ I) \models T(\varphi,\ G)$ w.r.t. Def if and only if $(C\ |_G,\ I \setminus \{G\}) \models \varphi$ w.r.t. Def^{Δ}.* □

$$
\begin{array}{lll}
P & :- & P\,;P \mid stmt \\
stmt & :- & u := v \mid u := \texttt{nil} \mid u := v.pf \mid u.pf := v \\
 & & \mid j := u.df \mid u.df := j \mid j := aexpr \\
 & & \mid u := \texttt{new} \mid \texttt{free}\ u \mid \texttt{assume}\ bexpr \\
 & & \mid u := f(\vec{v},\vec{z}) \mid j := g(\vec{v},\vec{z}) \\
aexpr & :- & int \mid j \mid aexpr + aexpr \mid aexpr - aexpr \\
bexpr & :- & u = v \mid u = \texttt{nil} \mid aexpr \leq aexpr \\
 & & \mid \neg bexpr \mid bexpr \vee bexpr
\end{array}
$$

Figure 5. Syntax of programs

6. Natural Proofs for DRYAD

In this section we show how DRYAD can be used in reasoning about the correctness of imperative heap-manipulating programs, in terms of verifying Hoare-triples where the pre- and post-conditions are expressed in DRYAD. We first introduce a simple programming language and the corresponding Hoare-triples, generate a classical logic formula as the verification condition, utilizing in part the translation defined in Section 5. Then we present the natural proof framework which consists of two steps. In the first step, we utilize the idea of unfolding across the footprint to strengthen the verification condition. In the second step, we prove the validity of the VC soundly using the technique of formula abstraction.

6.1 Programs and Hoare-triples

We consider straight-line program segments that do destructive pointer-updates, data-updates and procedure calls. Parameterized by a set of pointer fields PF and a set of data-fields DF, the syntax of the programs is defined in Figure 5, where $pf \in PF$, $f \in DF$, u and v are program variables of type location, j and z are program variables of type integer, *int* is an integer constant. To simplify the presentation, we assume all program variables are local and are either pre-assigned or assigned once in the program.

We allow two kinds of recursive procedures, one returning a location $f(\vec{v},\vec{z})$ and one returning an integer $g(\vec{v},\vec{z})$. Each procedure/program is annotated with its pre- and post-conditions in DRYAD. The pre-condition is denoted as a formula $\psi_{pre}(\vec{v},\vec{z},\vec{c})$, where $\vec{v}$ and $\vec{z}$ are variables as the formal parameters/program variables, $\vec{c}$ is a set of implicitly existentially quantified complimentary variables (e.g., variable K in the pre-condition φ_{pre} in Figure 1). The post-condition is denoted as a formula $\psi_{post}(ret,\vec{v},\vec{z},\vec{c})$, where *ret* is the variable representing the returned value, of corresponding type, $\vec{v}$ and $\vec{z}$ are program variables, $\vec{c}$ is a set of complimentary variables that have appeared in the pre-condition ψ_{pre}.

Given a straight-line program with its pre- and post-conditions $\{\psi_{pre}\}\ P\ \{\psi_{post}\}$, we define its partial correctness without considering memory errors[3]: P is partially correct iff for every normal execution (memory-error free) of P, which transits state C to state C', if $C \models \psi_{pre}$, then $C' \models \psi_{post}$.

Given a Hoare-triple $\{\psi_{pre}\}\ P\ \{\psi_{post}\}$ as defined above, a set of recursive definitions and a set of annotated procedure declarations are presented here. Assume that P consists of n statements, then consider a normal execution $\mathcal{E}$, which can be represented as a sequence of program states $(C_0,\ldots,C_n)$, where each $C_i = (R_i, s_i, h_i)$ represents the program state after executing the first i statements. The verification condition is just a formula interpreted on a state sequence $(C_0,\ldots,C_n)$. Let $pf_i : Loc \to Loc$ be the function mapping every location l to its pf pointer, i.e., $pf_i(l) = h_i(l, pf)$ for every location l. Similarly, $df_i : Loc \to Int$ is defined such that $df_i(l) = h_i(l, df)$ for every l. Recall that every program variable is either pre-assigned or assigned once in the program, each s_i is an expantion of the previous one, and s_n is the store with all program variables defined.

[3] We exclude memory errors in order to simplify the presentation. Memory errors can be handled using a similar VC generation for assertions that negate the conditions for memory errors to occur.

Hence we simply use v to denote $s_n(v)$. Moreover, every recursive predicate/function is also indexed by i. For example, p_i is the recursive predicate such that $p_i(l)$ is true iff $C_i \models T(p^{\Delta}(l), \mathrm{reachset}^{p}(l))$. Now for every formula φ and every index i, we can give the index i to all the pointer fields, data fields and recursive definitions. We denote the indexed formula as $\varphi[i]$.

We algorithmically derive the verification condition ψ_{VC} corresponding to it in classical logic with recursive definitions on the global heap (the algorithm is quite involved, and is presented in Appendix A in the supplemental material).

Theorem 6.1. *Given a Hoare-triple $\{\psi_{pre}\}\ P\ \{\psi_{post}\}$, assume that each procedure call in P satisfies its associated pre- and post-conditions. Then the triple is valid if the formula ψ_{VC} derived above is valid. Moreover, when P contains no procedure calls, the triple is valid iff ψ_{VC} is valid.*

Proof. Presented in Appendix B in the supplemental material. □

6.2 Unfolding Across the Footprint

The verification condition obtained above is a quantifier-free formula involving recursive definitions and the reachable sets of the form $reach^{p}(x)$, which are also defined recursively. While these recursive definitions can be unfolded *ad infinitum*, we exploit a proof tactic called *unfolding across the footprint*. Intuitively, the footprint is the set of locations explored by the program *explicitly* (not including procedure calls). More precisely, a location is in the footprint if it is dereferenced explicitly in the program. The idea is to unfold the recursive definitions over the footprint of the program, so that recursive definitions on the footprint nodes are related, as precisely as possible, to the recursive definitions on frontier nodes. This will enable effective use of the formula abstraction mechanism, as when recursive definitions on frontier nodes are made uninterpreted, the unfolding formulas ensure tight conditions that the frontier nodes have to satisfy.

Furthermore, to enable effective frame reasoning, it is also necessary to strengthen the verification condition with a set of instances of the frame rule. More concretely, we need to capture the fact that a recursive definition (or a field) on a location is unchanged during a segment or procedure call of the program, if the reachable locations (or only the location itself) are not affected by the segment or procedure call.

We incorporate the above facts formally into the verification condition. Let us introduce a macro function *fp* that identifies the location variables that are in (or aliased to something in) the footprint. The footprint of P, FP, is the set of dereferenced variables in P (we call a location variable dereferenced if it appears on the left-hand side of a dereferencing operator "." in P). Then $fp(u) \equiv \bigvee_{v \in FP}(u = v)$.

Now we state the unfoldings and framings using a formula UNFOLDANDFRAME. Assume there are m procedure calls in P, then P can be divided into $m+1$ basic segments (subprograms without procedure calls): $S_0\ ;\ g_1\ ;\ S_1\ ;\ \ldots\ ;\ g_m\ ;\ S_m$ where S_d is the $(d+1)$-th basic segment and g_d is the d-th procedure call. Then

$$
\textsc{UnfoldAndFrame} \equiv \bigwedge_{rec} \bigwedge_{0 \leq d \leq m} \bigwedge_{u \in LVars \cup \{nil\}} \Big[\Big(\big(fp(u) \vee u = nil\big) \Rightarrow \big(\textsc{Unfold}^{rec}_{d}(u) \wedge \textsc{FieldUnchanged}_{d}(u)\big) \Big) \wedge \Big(\big(\neg fp(u) \vee u = nil\big) \Rightarrow \textsc{RecUnchanged}^{rec}_{d}(u) \Big) \Big]
$$

The formula enumerates every recursive definition *rec* and every index d, and for each location u that is either pointed to by a location variable or is *nil*, the formula checks if u is in the footprint, and then unfolds it or frames it accordingly. If u is in the footprint, then we unfold *rec* for the timestamps before and after S_d (represented by the formula $\textsc{Unfold}^{rec}_{d}(u)$); moreover, all fields of

u are unchanged if it is not affected during calling g_d (represented by the formula $\textsc{FieldUnchanged}_d(u)$). If u is not in the footprint, i.e., in the frontier, then *rec* and its corresponding reach set $reach^{rec}$ are unchanged after executing S_d, if S_d does not modify any location in $reach^{rec}$; they are also unchanged if $reach^{rec}$ is not affected by calling g_d. These frame assertions are represented by the formula $\textsc{RecUnchanged}_d^{rec}(u)$. All the sub-formulas mentioned above are formulated in Appendix C in the supplemental material.

Now we can strengthen the verification condition by incorporating the derived formula above:

$$\psi'_{\text{VC}} \equiv \psi_{\text{VC}} \wedge \textsc{UnfoldAndFrame}$$

Since the incorporated formula is implied by the verification condition, we can reduce the validity of ψ_{VC} to the validity of ψ'_{VC}.

Theorem 6.2. *Given a Hoare-triple* $\{\psi_{pre}\}\ P\ \{\psi_{post}\}$, *its verification condition* ψ_{VC} *is valid if and only if* ψ'_{VC} *is valid.* □

6.3 Formula Abstraction

While checking the validity of the strengthened verification condition ψ'_{VC} is still undecidable, as we argued before, it is often sufficient to prove it by assuming that the recursive definitions are arbitrary, or uninterpreted. Moreover, the uninterpreted formula falls in the array property fragment [12], whose satisfiability is decidable and is supported by modern SMT solvers such as Z3 [17]. This tactic roughly corresponds to applying *unification* in proof systems.

To prove ψ'_{VC}, we first replace each recursive predicate rec_d with an uninterpreted predicate $\widehat{rec}_d$, and replacing the corresponding reach-set function $reach_d^{rec}$ with an uninterpreted function $\widehat{reach}_d^{rec}$. Let the result formula be $\psi_{\text{VC}}^{\text{abs}}$. This conversion, called *formula abstraction*, is sound: if $\psi_{\text{VC}}^{\text{abs}}$ is valid, so is ψ'_{VC}. When a proof for $\psi_{\text{VC}}^{\text{abs}}$ is found, we call it a natural proof for ψ'_{VC} (and also for ψ_{VC}).

The formula abstraction step is the only step that introduces incompleteness in our framework, but helps us transform the verification condition to a decidable theory. Formula abstraction (combined with unfolding recursive definitions across the footprint) discovers *recursive proofs* where the recursion is structural recursion on the definitions of the data-structures. The use of these tactics comes from the observation that such programs often have such recursive proofs (see [39] also for use of formula abstractions).

Our goal now is to check the satisfiability of $\neg\psi_{\text{VC}}^{\text{abs}}$ in a decidable theory. The resulting formula can be expressed using the theory of maps (to model sets) and corresponding map operations to model set operations. Formulas of the kind $S_1 \leq S_2$, where S_1 and S_2 are sets/multi-sets of integers, are the only ones that introduce quantification, but they can be translated to formulas in the array property fragment, which is decidable [12]. We hence obtain a formula ψ^{APF} in the array property fragment combined with the theory of uninterpreted functions, maps, and arithmetic (details are in Appendix D in the supplementary material).

Theorem 6.3. *Given a Hoare-triple* $\{\psi_{pre}\}\ P\ \{\psi_{post}\}$, *if the derived array formula* ψ^{APF} *is satisfiable, then the Hoare-triple is valid.* □

User-provided axioms:

While natural proofs are often effective in finding recursive proofs that unfold recursive definitions and do unification, they are not geared towards finding *relationships* between various recursive definitions themselves. We hence require the user to provide certain obvious relationships between the different recursive definitions as axioms. For example, $lseg(x, y) * list(y) \Rightarrow list(x)$ is such an axiom saying that a list segment concatenated with a list yields a list. Note that these axioms are *not* program-dependent, and hence are not program-specific tactics that the user provides. These axioms are necessary typically to relate partial data-structure properties (like list segments) to complete ones (like lists), especially in iterative programs (as opposed to recursive ones), and we can fix them for each class of data-structures. We also allow the use of the separating implication, $-*$, from separation logic while specifying these axioms. User-defined axioms are instantiated, using the natural proof philosophy, on precisely the footprint nodes uniformly, and get translated to quantifier-free formulas.

Data-structure	Routine	Time (s) / Routine
Singly-Linked List	`find_rec, insert_front, insert_back_rec, delete_all_rec, copy_rec, append_rec, reverse_iter`	< 1s
Sorted List	`find_rec, insert_rec, merge_rec, delete_all_rec, insert_sort_rec, reverse_iter, find_last_iter`	< 1s
	`insert_iter`	1.4
	`quick_sort_iter`	64.8
Doubly-Linked List	`insert_front, insert_back_rec, delete_all_rec, append_rec, mid_insert, mid_delete, meld`	< 1s
Cyclic List	`insert_front, insert_back_rec, delete_front, delete_back_rec`	< 1s
Max-Heap	`heapify_rec`	8.8
BST	`find_rec, find_iter, insert_rec, delete_rec, remove_root_rec`	< 1s
	`insert_iter`	72.4
	`find_leftmost_iter`	4.7
	`remove_root_iter`	65.6
	`delete_iter`	225.2
Treap	`find_rec, delete_rec`	< 1s
	`insert_rec`	12.7
	`remove_root_rec`	9.5
AVL-Tree	`balance, leftmost_rec`	< 1s
	`insert_rec`	4.1
	`delete_rec`	13.9
RB-Tree	`insert_rec`	73.9
	`insert_left_fix_rec`	8.1
	`insert_right_fix_rec`	5.1
	`delete_rec`	12.1
	`delete_left_fix_rec`	7.6
	`delete_right_fix_rec`	5.5
	`leftmost_rec`	< 1s
Binomial Heap	`find_min_rec`	1.1
	`merge_rec`	152.7
Schorr-Waite (for trees)	`marking_iter`	< 1s
Tree Traversals	`inorder_tree_to_list_rec`	2.4
	`inorder_tree_to_list_iter`	42.7
	`preorder_rec, postorder_rec`	< 1s
	`inorder_rec`	3.76

Figure 6. Results of verifying data-structure algorithms. (more details at `http://www.cs.uiuc.edu/~madhu/dryad/sl/`)

7. Experimental Evaluation

We have implemented a prototype of the natural proof methodology for Dryad presented in this paper. The prototype verifier takes as input a set of user-defined recursive definitions, a set of procedure declarations with contracts, and a set of straight-line programs (or *basic blocks*) annotated with a pre-condition and a post-condition specifying a set of partial correctness properties including structural, data and separation requirements. Both the contracts and pre-/post-conditions are written in Dryad. For each basic block, the verifier automatically generates the abstracted formula ψ^{APF} as described in Section 6, and passes ψ^{APF} to Z3 [17], a state-of-the-art SMT solver, to check the satisfiability in the decidable theory of array property fragment. The front-end of our verifier is based on

ANTLR and our tool is around 4000 lines of C# code. Using the verifier, we successfully proved the partial correctness of 59 routines over a large class of programs involving heap data structures like sorted lists, doubly-linked lists, cyclic lists and trees. Additionally, we pit our natural proofs methodology against real-world programs and successfully verified, in total, 47 routines from different projects including the list and queue implementations in the Glib open source library, the OpenBSD library, the Linux kernel and the memory regions and the page cache implementations from two different operating systems. Experimental details are available at `http://www.cs.uiuc.edu/~madhu/dryad/sl/` .

We conducted the experiments on a machine with a dual-core, 2.4GHz CPU and 6GB RAM. The first part of our experimental results is tabulated in Figure 6. In general, for every routine, we checked the properties formalizing the complete verification of the routines— capturing the precise structure of the resulting heap-structure, the precise change to the data stored in the nodes and the precise heaplet modified by the respective routines.

For every routine, the suffix `rec` or `iter` indicates if the routine was implemented recursively or iteratively using while loops. The names for most of the routines are self-descriptive. Routines like `find`, `insert`, `delete`, `append`, etc. are the natural implementations of the corresponding data structure operations. The routine `delete_all` for singly-linked lists, sorted lists and doubly-linked lists recursively deletes all occurrences of a particular key in the input list. The max-heap routine `heapify` accepts an almost max-heap in which the heap property is violated only at the root, both of whose children are max-heaps, and recursively descends the tree to restore the max-heap property. The routine `remove_root` for binary search trees and treaps is an auxiliary routine which is called in `delete`. Similarly, the routines `leftmost` for AVL-trees and RB-trees and `delete_fix` and `insert_fix` for RB-trees are also auxiliary routines.

Schorr-Waite is a well-known graph marking algorithm which marks all the reachable nodes of the graph using very little additional space. The algorithm achieves this by manipulating the pointers in the graph such that the stack of nodes along the path from the root is encoded in the graph itself. The Schorr-Waite algorithm is used in garbage collectors and it is traditionally considered as a challenging problem for verification [19]. The routine `marking` is an implementation of Schorr-Waite for trees [24] and we check the property that the resulting output tree is well-marked.

The routines `inorder_tree_to_list` construct a list consisting of the keys of the input tree, which is traversed inorder. The iterative version of this algorithm achieves this by maintaining a worklist/stack of sub-trees which remain to be processed at any given time. The routines `inorder`, `preorder` and `postorder` number the nodes of an input tree according to the inorder, preorder and postorder traversal algorithm, respectively.

Figure 7 shows the results of applying natural proofs to the verification of various other real world programs and libraries. Glib is the low-level C library that forms the basis of the GTK+ toolkit and the GNOME desktop environment, apart from other open source projects. Using our prototype verifier, we efficiently verified Glib implementation of various routines for manipulating singly-linked and doubly-linked lists. We also verified the queue library which forms part of the OpenBSD operating system.

ExpressOS is an operating-system/browser implementation which provides security guarantees to the user via formal verification [29]. The module `cachePage` maintains a cache of the recently used disc pages. The cache is implemented as a priority queue based on a sorted list. We prove that the methods `add_cachepage` and `lookup_prev` (both called whenever a disc page is accessed) maintain the sortedness property of the cache page.

Example	Routine	Time (s) / Routine
glib/gslist.c Singly Linked-List LOC: 1.1K	`free, prepend, concat, insert_before, remove_all, remove_link, delete_link, copy, reverse, nth, nth_data, find, position, index, last, length`	< 1s
	`append`	4.9
	`insert_at_pos`	11.4
	`remove`	3.1
	`insert_sorted_list`	16.6
	`merge_sorted_lists`	6.1
	`merge_sort`	3.0
glib/glist.c Doubly Linked-List LOC: 0.3K	`free, prepend, reverse, nth, nth_data, position, find, index, last, length`	< 1s
OpenBSD/queue.h Queue LOC: 0.1K	`simpleq_init, simpleq_remove_after`	< 1s
	`simpleq_insert_head`	1.6
	`simpleq_insert_tail`	3.6
	`simpleq_insert_after`	18.3
	`simpleq_remove_head`	2.1
ExpressOS/cachePage.c LOC: 0.1K	`lookup_prev`	2.4
	`add_cachepage`	6.4
ExpressOS/ memoryRegion.c LOC: 0.1K	`memory_region_init`	< 1s
	`create_user_space_region`	3.6
	`split_memory_region`	5.8
linux/mmap.c LOC: 0.1K	`find_vma, remove_vma, remove_vma_list`	< 1s
	`insert_vm_struct`	11.6

Figure 7. Results of verifying open-source libraries. (more details at `http://www.cs.uiuc.edu/~madhu/dryad/sl/`)

In an OS kernel, a process address space consists of a set of intervals of linear addresses represented as a *memory region*. In the ExpressOS implementation, a memory region is implemented as a sorted doubly-linked list where each node of the list with a *start* and an *end* address represents an interval included in the address space. We also verified some key components of the Linux implementation of a memory region, present in the file *mmap.c*. In Linux, a memory region is represented as a red-black tree where each node, again, represents an address interval. We proved methods which find, remove and insert a *vma_struct* (*vma* is short for virtual memory address) into a memory region.

It also worth mentioning that in the process of experiments, we did make some unintentional mistakes, in writing both the basic blocks and the annotations. For example, forgetting to free the deleted node, or using $\wedge$ instead of $*$ in the specification between two disjoint heaplets, were common mistakes. In these cases, Z3 provided counter-examples to the verification condition that captured the essence of the bugs, and turned out to be very helpful for us to debug the specification. These debugging hints are usually not available in other incomplete proof systems.

Our experiments show that the natural proof methodology set forth in this paper is successful in efficiently proving full-functional correctness of a large variety of algorithms. Most of the VCs generated for the above examples were discharged by Z3 in a few seconds. To the best of our knowledge, this is the first automatic mechanism that can prove such a wide variety of algorithms correct, handling such complex properties of structure, data and separation.

Acknowledgments

This work is partially funded by NSF CAREER award #0747041, NSF CCF #1018182, and NSA contract H98230-10-C-0294.

References

[1] I. Balaban, A. Pnueli, and L. D. Zuck. Shape analysis of single-parent heaps. In *VMCAI'07*, volume 4349 of *LNCS*, pages 91–105. Springer, 2007.

[2] M. Barnett, B.-Y. E. Chang, R. DeLine, B. Jacobs, and K. R. M. Leino. Boogie: A modular reusable verifier for object-oriented programs. In *FMCO'05*, volume 4111 of *LNCS*, pages 364–387. Springer, 2005.

[3] J. Berdine, C. Calcagno, and P. W. O'Hearn. A decidable fragment of separation logic. In *FSTTCS'04*, volume 3328 of *LNCS*, pages 97–109. Springer, 2004.

[4] J. Berdine, C. Calcagno, and P. W. O'Hearn. Symbolic execution with separation logic. In *APLAS'05*, volume 3780 of *LNCS*, pages 52–68. Springer, 2005.

[5] J. Berdine, C. Calcagno, and P. W. O'Hearn. Smallfoot: Modular automatic assertion checking with separation logic. In *FMCO'05*, volume 4111 of *LNCS*, pages 115–137. Springer, 2005.

[6] J. Berdine, C. Calcagno, B. Cook, D. Distefano, P. W. O'Hearn, T. Wies, and H. Yang. Shape analysis for composite data structures. In *CAV'07*, volume 4590 of *LNCS*, pages 178–192. Springer, 2007.

[7] N. Bjørner and J. Hendrix. Linear functional fixed-points. In *CAV'09*, volume 5643 of *LNCS*, pages 124–139. Springer, 2009.

[8] M. Botinčan, M. Parkinson, and W. Schulte. Separation logic verification of C programs with an SMT solver. *ENTCS*, 254:5 – 23, 2009.

[9] A. Bouajjani, C. Drăgoi, C. Enea, and M. Sighireanu. A logic-based framework for reasoning about composite data structures. In *CONCUR'09*, volume 5710 of *LNCS*, pages 178–195. Springer, 2009.

[10] A. Bouajjani, C. Drăgoi, C. Enea, and M. Sighireanu. On inter-procedural analysis of programs with lists and data. In *PLDI'11*, pages 578–589. ACM, 2011.

[11] M. Bozga, R. Iosif, and S. Perarnau. Quantitative separation logic and programs with lists. In *IJCAR'08*, volume 5195 of *LNCS*, pages 34–49. Springer, 2008.

[12] A. R. Bradley, Z. Manna, and H. B. Sipma. What's decidable about arrays? In *VMCAI'06*, volume 3855 of *LNCS*, pages 427–442. Springer, 2006.

[13] B.-Y. E. Chang and X. Rival. Relational inductive shape analysis. In *POPL'08*, pages 247–260. ACM, 2008.

[14] W.-N. Chin, C. David, H. H. Nguyen, and S. Qin. Automated verification of shape, size and bag properties via user-defined predicates in separation logic. *Science of Computer Programming*, 77(9):1006 – 1036, 2012.

[15] A. Chlipala. Mostly-automated verification of low-level programs in computational separation logic. In *PLDI'11*, pages 234–245. ACM, 2011.

[16] E. Cohen, M. Dahlweid, M. A. Hillebrand, D. Leinenbach, M. Moskal, T. Santen, W. Schulte, and S. Tobies. VCC: A practical system for verifying concurrent C. In *TPHOLs'09*, volume 5674 of *LNCS*, pages 23–42. Springer, 2009.

[17] L. M. de Moura and N. Bjørner. Z3: An efficient SMT solver. In *TACAS'08*, volume 4963 of *LNCS*, pages 337–340. Springer, 2008.

[18] D. Distefano, P. W. O'Hearn, and H. Yang. A local shape analysis based on separation logic. In *TACAS'06*, volume 3920 of *LNCS*, pages 287–302. Springer, 2006.

[19] T. Hubert and C. Marché. A case study of C source code verification: the Schorr-Waite algorithm. In *SEFM'05*, pages 190–199. IEEE-CS, 2005.

[20] B. Jacobs, J. Smans, P. Philippaerts, F. Vogels, W. Penninckx, and F. Piessens. Verifast: A powerful, sound, predictable, fast verifier for C and Java. In *NFM'11*, volume 6617 of *LNCS*, pages 41–55. Springer, 2011.

[21] N. Klarlund and A. Møller. *MONA*. BRICS, Department of Computer Science, Aarhus University, January 2001. Available from `http://www.brics.dk/mona/`.

[22] S. Lahiri and S. Qadeer. Back to the future: revisiting precise program verification using SMT solvers. In *POPL'08*, pages 171–182. ACM, 2008.

[23] K. R. M. Leino. Dafny: An automatic program verifier for functional correctness. In *LPAR-16*, volume 6355 of *LNCS*, pages 348–370. Springer, 2010.

[24] A. Loginov, T. W. Reps, and M. Sagiv. Automated verification of the Deutsch-Schorr-Waite tree-traversal algorithm. In *SAS'06*, volume 4134 of *LNCS*, pages 261–279. Springer, 2006.

[25] P. Madhusudan and X. Qiu. Efficient decision procedures for heaps using STRAND. In *SAS'11*, volume 6887 of *LNCS*, pages 43–59. Springer, 2011.

[26] P. Madhusudan, G. Parlato, and X. Qiu. Decidable logics combining heap structures and data. In *POPL'11*, pages 611–622. ACM, 2011.

[27] P. Madhusudan, X. Qiu, and A. Stefanescu. Recursive proofs for inductive tree data-structures. In *POPL'12*, pages 123–136. ACM, 2012.

[28] S. Magill, M.-H. Tsai, P. Lee, and Y.-K. Tsay. THOR: A tool for reasoning about shape and arithmetic. In *CAV'08*, volume 5123 of *LNCS*, pages 428–432. Springer, 2008.

[29] H. Mai, E. Pek, H. Xue, S. T. King, and P. Madhusudan. Verifying security invariants in ExpressOS. In *ASPLOS'13*, pages 293–304. ACM, 2013.

[30] G. Nelson. Verifying reachability invariants of linked structures. In *POPL'83*, pages 38–47. ACM, 1983.

[31] T. Nipkow, L. C. Paulson, and M. Wenzel. *Isabelle/HOL - A Proof Assistant for Higher-Order Logic*, volume 2283 of *Lecture Notes in Computer Science*. Springer, 2002.

[32] P. W. O'Hearn, J. C. Reynolds, and H. Yang. Local reasoning about programs that alter data structures. In *CSL'01*, volume 2142 of *LNCS*, pages 1–19. Springer, 2001.

[33] Z. Rakamarić, J. D. Bingham, and A. J. Hu. An inference-rule-based decision procedure for verification of heap-manipulating programs with mutable data and cyclic data structures. In *VMCAI'07*, volume 4349 of *LNCS*, pages 106–121. Springer, 2007.

[34] Z. Rakamarić, R. Bruttomesso, A. J. Hu, and A. Cimatti. Verifying heap-manipulating programs in an SMT framework. In *ATVA'07*, volume 4762 of *LNCS*, pages 237–252. Springer, 2007.

[35] S. Ranise and C. Zarba. A theory of singly-linked lists and its extensible decision procedure. In *SEFM'06*, pages 206–215. IEEE-CS, 2006.

[36] J. Reynolds. Separation logic: a logic for shared mutable data structures. In *LICS'02*, pages 55–74. IEEE-CS, 2002.

[37] G. Rosu, C. Ellison, and W. Schulte. Matching logic: An alternative to Hoare/Floyd logic. In *AMAST'10*, volume 6486 of *LNCS*, pages 142–162. Springer, 2010.

[38] J. Smans, B. Jacobs, and F. Piessens. Implicit dynamic frames. *ACM Trans. Program. Lang. Syst.*, 34(1):2:1–2:58, 2012.

[39] P. Suter, M. Dotta, and V. Kuncak. Decision procedures for algebraic data types with abstractions. In *POPL'10*, pages 199–210. ACM, 2010.

[40] P. Suter, A. S. Köksal, and V. Kuncak. Satisfiability modulo recursive programs. In *SAS'11*, volume 6887 of *LNCS*, pages 298–315. Springer, 2011.

[41] H. Yang, O. Lee, J. Berdine, C. Calcagno, B. Cook, D. Distefano, and P. W. O'Hearn. Scalable shape analysis for systems code. In *CAV'08*, volume 5123 of *LNCS*, pages 385–398. Springer, 2008.

[42] J. Yang and C. Hawblitzel. Safe to the last instruction: automated verification of a type-safe operating system. In *PLDI'10*, pages 99–110. ACM, 2010.

[43] K. Zee, V. Kuncak, and M. C. Rinard. Full functional verification of linked data structures. In *PLDI'08*, pages 349–361. ACM, 2008.

[44] K. Zee, V. Kuncak, and M. C. Rinard. An integrated proof language for imperative programs. In *PLDI'09*, pages 338–351. ACM, 2009.

General Data Structure Expansion for Multi-threading

Hongtao Yu Hou-Jen Ko Zhiyuan Li

Department of Computer Science
Purdue University
West Lafayette, IN 47907
{htyu, ko16, zhiyuanli}@purdue.edu

Abstract

Among techniques for parallelizing sequential codes, privatization is a common and significant transformation performed by both compilers and runtime parallelizing systems. Without privatization, repetitive updates to the same data structures often introduce spurious data dependencies that hide the inherent parallelism. Unfortunately, it remains a significant challenge to compilers to automatically privatize dynamic and recursive data structures which appear frequently in real applications written in languages such as C/C++. This is because such languages lack a naming mechanism to define the address range of a pointer-based data structure, in contrast to arrays with explicitly declared bounds. In this paper we present a novel solution to this difficult problem by expanding general data structures such that memory accesses issued from different threads to contentious data structures are directed to different data fields. Based on compile-time type checking and a data dependence graph, this aggressive extension to the traditional scalar and array expansion isolates the address ranges among different threads, without struggling with privatization based on thread-private stacks, such that the targeted loop can be effectively parallelized. With this method fully implemented in GCC, experiments are conducted on a set of programs from well-known benchmark suites such as Mibench, MediaBench II and SPECint. Results show that the new approach can lead to a high speedup when executing the transformed code on multiple cores.

Categories and Subject Descriptors D.3.4 [*Programming Languages*]: Processors—Compilers, run-time environments; F.3.2 [*Logics And Meanings Of Programs*]: Semantics of Programming Languages—Program Analysis

General Terms Algorithms, Languages, Performance

Keywords Parallelization, privatization, multithreading

1. Introduction

Data privatization is an important technique that has been used by both compilers and runtime parallelizing systems to enable loop parallelization. This technique duplicates data structures for each thread, in order to remove spurious data dependencies due to the reuse of such data structures for storing intermediate results. Mature data privatization techniques, such as scalar expansion [4, 5] and array privatization [15, 16, 18, 22, 23, 36], are widely adopted by parallelizing compilers.

Unfortunately, existing compile-time privatization techniques primarily target statically allocated variables. They lack the capability of privatizing dynamic and recursive data structures which are extensively used in non-numerical programs. This is because dynamic data structures are allocated at run time through allocation routines (e.g. `malloc`, `calloc` and `realloc`). A program often makes many of such calls under various program contexts to create a dynamic data structure (such as linked lists, trees and graphs) that are nonconsecutive in the memory. Therefore, the program does not have a single address "range" to precisely contain such data structures, which makes it difficult to apply traditional privatization methods. This difficulty is certainly compounded by the ambiguity of pointer-induced aliases.

Several proposals have emerged recently to offer language constructs to aid the privatization of dynamic data structures. For example, in Paralax [37], the allocation site of a heap-allocated object expressed with a base pointer variable is annotated as a constructor. If one wishes to privatize that object, one can call its constructor. This method, however, is not effective for programs that have complicated pointer aliases and scattered allocation sites. Alternatively, Feng *et al.* [12] attempted to solve the problem by devising new language support to guide run time copying of data structures to thread-local spaces for private use. Conceptually, such a method can be universal and it is not restricted by insufficient static analysis. Their system, *SpiceC*, monitors every memory access at run time in order to forward them to private copies when necessary. In spite of their efforts to make runtime monitoring less costly, the overhead seems still too high in practice, as we shall show in subsequent sections.

In this paper, we propose a novel compiler technique to expand dynamic data structures such that dependences due to contentious data updates from different threads can be removed. This method in essence keeps N copies of the same data structures in a program by expanding the original data types in the thread-shared address space, each copy for one thread. The original copy serves as both the shared copy (for all N threads) and the private copy for the first thread. Given a data dependence graph, the method also partitions all memory accesses in a program into two classes, namely, the *shared* accesses and the *thread-private* accesses. A shared memory access should access the shared copy of the data structure while a private memory access should only access its own thread-private copy. Memory accesses are redirected to their designated copies by adjusting the code at compile time. As the result, thread-private memory accesses from different threads have no cross-thread data dependencies and can be performed in parallel. This new approach to removing data contention for arbitrary data structures does not need to know the shape of the data structure, where it is allocated

PLDI'13, June 16–19, 2013, Seattle, WA, USA.

or where it is referenced. In this sense, it is a universal framework. Our experiments show that the average running overhead is below 5% of the original execution time, making the method practical.

The rest of this paper is organized as follows. We discuss the technical background of this work in Section 2. We then present our new technique, i.e., the compile-time general data structure expansion, in Section 3. Experimental results are given in Section 4. We discuss related work in Section 5 and conclude in Section 6.

2. A Dependence-based Approach

A variable is said to be privatizable if it is written before each read in every loop iteration. By allocating private copies for privatizable variables in each thread participating in the loop execution, memory accesses to these variables in iterations executed by different threads do not interfere with each other, thus exposing parallelism in loops that otherwise appear to be sequential. For Fortran-like numerical programs, privatization can often be performed well by parallelizing compilers, which are sometimes guided by the "private" clause in OpenMP [6]. At run time, each thread will have a private copy of each privatized variable stored in the local stack maintained for that thread.

Unfortunately, the privatization process becomes more complicated for non-numerical programs which manipulate dynamic data structures. Take the benchmark *Dijkstra* in *Mibench* suite [17] for example. This program has a loop that finds the shortest path between a distinct pair of nodes in each iteration. An internal priority queue, which is essentially a linked list, is manipulated such that new nodes are created and old nodes removed from iteration to iteration, with no guarantee of contiguous allocation in the memory. Furthermore the graph may be annotated during the search. Conceptually, it is possible to run 10 iterations in parallel to find 10 shortest paths between 10 pairs of nodes, but the priority queue must first be privatized. As discussed in the introduction, no simple way exists to privatize these internal data structures, unfortunately.

Our new approach is to perform general data structure expansion in the shared address space based on a loop-level data dependence graph. Such a graph can be obtained either from the programmer, the compiler, or tools that perform data dependence profiling [21, 38–40] with programmer verification. It can also be obtained at runtime when candidate loops are running speculatively [27, 28]. The rest of the paper assumes the availability of such a loop-level dependence graph at compile time.

3. Data Structure Expansion

We first use a sample program in Figure 1(a) to illustrate the idea of general data structure expansion. For this example we aim to parallelize the `while` loop, which cannot be handled by traditional array privatization. To create thread private copies, we extend the memory allocation in line 1 by enlarging the allocation size by a factor of N, where N is the number of threads to run the program, which may be determined as late as runtime. After that, we direct memory accesses to appropriate data copies to satisfy all flow dependencies according to the data dependence graph for the loop. Note that in Figure 1(b) the memory accesses in shaded lines are directed to thread-private copies. To simplify the illustration, we do not show data expansion for every scalar variable that must be privatized or expanded in this program.

In the rest of this section, we will first present our method to create the thread-private copies and then discuss the redirection of memory accesses. After that, we discuss methods to lower the redirection overhead.

3.1 Creating Private Data Copies

Thread-private data copies can be logically formed by expanding types for each data structure. Table 1 shows the expanding rules. Column "Declaration" lists several general cases of C variable instantiation, including a heap allocation. We show the rules for the `int` primitive type only, but the rules concerning other primitive types, such as `char, float, double` and all pointer types, have obvious counterparts. Column "Expansion", shows the corresponding instantiations after type expansion. The type expansion simply enlarges the size of a data structure by a factor equal to the thread count (denoted by N) at run time. Note that the expansion for a stack variable can be implemented by using a variable-length array. However, statically expanding global variables of a variable length is impossible because the global data section must have a fixed size in the final binary file. To deal with global variables we first substitute each of them with a dynamically allocated heap object and then convert each access to the global variable to referencing the heap object. After that, the converted global variables can be treated as normal heap objects.

Table 1: Type Expansion rules.

Rule	Declaration	Expansion
Local scalar	int a	int a[N]
Local record	struct S a	struct S a[N]
Local array	int a[n]	int a[N][n]
Global scalar	int a	int *pa = malloc(sizeof(int) * N)
Global record	struct S a	S *pa = malloc(sizeof(S) * N)
Global array	int a[n]	int *pa=malloc(sizeof(int)*n*N)
Heap object	malloc(size)	malloc(size*N)

Note that when expanding an aggregate data structure, such as an array variable or a structure variable, we lay out multiple copies of the variable adjacently in their entireties. We call this layout mode the *bonded mode*, in which a data structure is replicated entirely with copies for different threads being adjacent in memory, as shown in Figure 2(a). Alternatively, there is the *interleaved mode*, in which each primitive member of a structure is replicated such that its copies are allocated consecutively in memory, but different primitive members of the same structure are interleaved in memory, as shown in Figure 2(b). We prefer the bonded mode for a number of reasons. For one thing, the interleaved mode fails to work in some cases in which a data structure is recast between different-sized types. For example, the `zptr` array in 256.bzip2 of the SPEC2000 benchmark suite is frequently recast between the types of 2-byte short integer and 4-type integer. Without knowing the exact size of the array elements, it is unclear to the compiler how to place the duplicates of each array element in the interleaved mode. Another benefit of the bonded mode is the potentially lower cache misses in coarse-grain parallel threads because data items used by a single thread are placed as near as possible, rendering a better data locality than in the interleaved mode.

3.2 Partitioning Memory Accesses

After creating private data copies for threads, we revise memory accesses to make sure that they refer to the correct data. We partition memory accesses in a program into two mutually exclusive classes, namely the shared accesses and the private accesses. As mentioned previously, shared accesses should be directed to the first thread's data copy while private accesses should reference the corresponding thread-private copies. The partition is based on the given loop-level data dependence graph as defined below.

Definition 1. *(Loop-level Data dependence graph) A loop-level data dependence graph G of a loop is represented by $< V, E >$*

```
1  int *zptr = malloc ( sizeof(int) * m);
2  while (1) {
3      ...
4      initialize (zptr);
5      ...
6      for (k = 0; k < m; k++)
7          b += zptr [k];
8      ...
9  }
```

(a) A sample program.

```
1  int *zptr = malloc ( sizeof(int) * m * N );
2  while (1) {
3      ...
4      initialize (zptr);
5      ...
6      for (k = 0; k < m; k++)
7          b += zptr [k + tid * m];
8      ...
9  }
```

(b) The sample program after expanding.

Figure 1: Data structure expansion. The sample program is extracted from SPEC CPU2000/Bzip2. In every iteration of the `while` loop, the memory chunk that the variable `zptr` points to is initialized in line 4 and then referenced throughout the loop body. The corresponding code after data structure expansion is shown in (b).

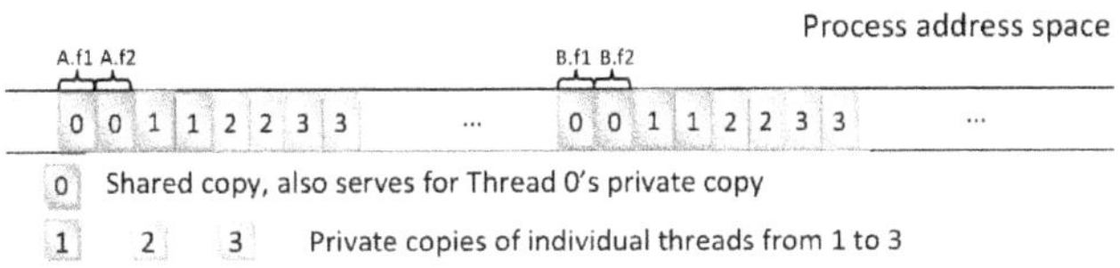

(a) Bonded mode

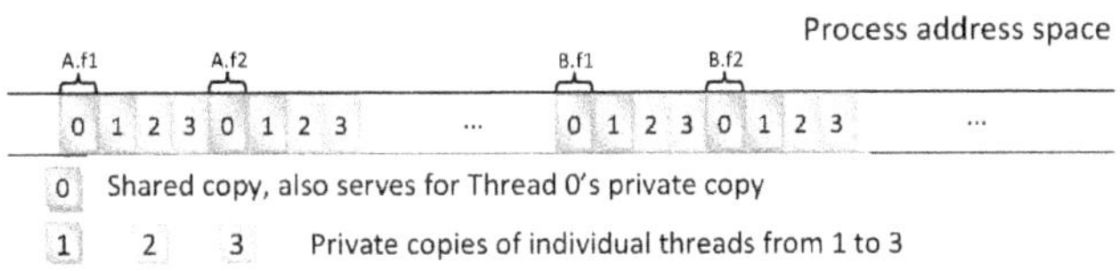

(b) Interleaved mode

Figure 2: Expansion of struct {int f1, f2;} A, B; under four threads.

where the vertex set V consists of all memory accesses potentially executed in the loop and E is a set of directed edges each of which denotes a possible data dependence from the source memory access to the sink memory access.

A data dependence between its source memory access a and its sink memory access b may occur in different ways:

- A loop-independent flow dependence occurs when b reads from an address to which a writes prior to b in the same iteration.
- A loop-carried flow dependence occurs when b reads from an address to which a writes in a previous iteration, and b is not covered by previous writes to the same address in the same loop iteration.
- A loop-independent or loop-carried anti-dependence occurs when b writes to an address from which a reads prior to b in the same iteration (loop-independent) or a previous iteration (loop-carried).
- A loop-independent or loop-carried output dependence occurs when b writes to an address to which a also writes prior to b in the same iteration (loop-independent) or in a previous iteration (loop-carried).

Note that we have extended the definition of loop-carried flow dependence to account for privatizable variables. In addition to a loop-level data dependence graph we introduce an additional property for each memory load or store, respectively.

Definition 2. *(Upwards-exposed load) A memory load is said to be upwards-exposed in a loop if and only if the value which it reads comes from outside the loop.*

Definition 3. *(Downwards-exposed store) A memory store is said to be downwards-exposed in a loop if and only if the value which it writes is used after the loop.*

It is straightforward to define private memory accesses at the instruction instance level. A load instance is said to be thread-private if it reads a value defined by previous instructions of the the same thread. Similarly, a store instance is said to be thread-private if the value it writes will be used only in the same thread. However, extending such definitions to the program statement level is not as simple. A static write memory access may induce multiple store instances at run time, some of which may be thread-private while others may not. For instance, suppose the following code snippet is embedded in a loop body. Further assume that the write to $*p$ in line L3 is thread-private if and only if condition c holds. Even though the load $*p$ in line L4 is always thread-private, we cannot decide at compile time the iterations in which the store $*p$ in line L3 must write to the private copy instead of the shared copy.

```
L1:   if (c) p = &a;
L2:   else   p = &b;
L3:   *p = 0;
L4:   if (c) a[i] = *p;
```

The main problem encountered here is that privatizing only one of the two `*p` will violate the potential loop-independent dependence between them. To avoid the semantic violation, we regard a loop-independent dependence as an equivalence relationship between its source and sink memory accesses. Noting that an equivalence relationship has the transitive property, we place all equivalent memory accesses into a single access class.

Definition 4. *(Access class) We consider a loop-independent dependence between its source memory access a and its sink memory access b as an equivalence relation $a \sim b$, which is reflexive, symmetric and transitive. The access class of a memory access a is the equivalence class of a defined as the set $[a] = \{b \in MEMOPS \mid a \sim b\}$ of all memory accesses that are related to a by $\sim$. MEMOPS represents all the memory accesses in the loop.*

Based on the definition of access classes, we define thread-private memory accesses.

Definition 5. *(Thread-private access class) Suppose a loop is to have its iterations executed by multiple threads. An access class is said to be private to a thread if and only if all the following conditions are satisfied:*

1. *No memory access in the class is an upwards-exposed load or a downwards-exposed store;*
2. *No memory access in the class is involved in any loop-carried flow dependence; and*
3. *At least one memory access in the class is involved in a loop-carried anti- or output dependence.*

A memory access is said to be *private* if and only if its access class is thread-private. Non-private memory accesses are called *shared* memory accesses. One could relax the conditions in Definition 5 to create more privatization opportunities. Note that even if a memory access of a class is involved in a loop-carried flow dependence, privatization is still possible for the class as long as the dependence does not occur across threads. We do not explore these relaxations in this paper.

3.3 Redirecting Memory Accesses

The memory access redirection can be accomplished by applying rules listed in Table 2 to each memory access which has been identified as either a shared access or a private access. The variable *tid*, which represents the index of the current thread, is used to index thread-private copies. Thread-private copies for a whole data structure are organized consecutively in memory, from the first thread to the last thread, as shown in Figure 2(a). The first thread copy (when the value of *tid* is zero) also serves as the shared copy. Note that in some cases we need to know the original size of the data structure expanded (denoted by the symbol *span*) in order to index into thread private copies. This is because, in C/C++, it is difficult to infer the size of a data structure based on the base pointer alone.

Table 2: Redirection rules.

Rule	Original	Shared	Private
Local scalar	a	a[0]	a[tid]
Local field	a.field	a[0].field	a[tid].field
Local array	a[i]	a[0][i]	a[tid][i]
Global scalar	a	pa[0]	pa[tid]
Global field	a.field	pa[0].field	pa[tid].field
Global array	a[i]	pa[i]	pa[i+tid*span/sizeof(*pa)]
Pointer deref	*p	*p	*(p+tid*span/sizeof(*p))

We use an example shown in Figure 3(a) to explain the necessity of the symbol *span*. The example is extracted from SPEC CPU2006/456.hmmer. In this example, suppose the variable declarations are local to a function and the program segment is embedded in a loop (in that function) targeted for parallelization. The variables `m1`, `m2` and `k` are of integer types. In line 6, whether pointer `mx` points to the `m1`-sized memory chunk allocated in line 3 or the `m2`-sized memory chunk allocated in line 5 can only be determined at run time. After the thread copy creation, the intermediate representation will be in the form shown in the right-hand side. Because we use the bonded mode, without knowing at compile time the exact size of the data structure that `mx` points to, we have no idea where to redirect `mx[k]` in line 6. The symbol *span* has the meaning of a shadow variable allocated for each pointer, in order to record the original size of the data structure pointed to by the pointer. We also insert additional statements in the right place to compute the symbol *span*. The creation and computation of the symbol *span* is prior to the data structure expansion.

3.3.1 Creating Span

The symbol *span* can be implemented by attaching a field to each pointer variable. We promote a pointer variable to a structure variable whose first field is the pointer variable itself and the second field is the *span*, which is an integer. For the example in Figure 3(a), the promoted version is shown in Figure 4(a). The transformed program has the same semantics as the original program. Note that we do not create thread private copies at this stage. After the promotion, we insert additional statements to compute the symbol *span*. This will be addressed in Section 3.3.2.

We proceed by promoting pointer declarations first. If the original type of a variable declaration is a pointer type, we promote its pointee type first and then promote the pointer type to a structure type. If the original type is an array type, we promote the element

```
1  int *mx;
2  if (...)
3    mx=malloc(m1);
4  else
5    mx=malloc(m2);
6  mx[k] = 0;
```

(a) Original program

```
int *mx;
if (...)
  mx=malloc(m1*N);
else
  mx=malloc(m2*N);
mx[k+tid*?] = 0;
```

(b) After expansion

Figure 3: Thread space creation

```
struct {
  int *pointer,
  int span,
} mx;
if (...)
  mx.pointer=malloc(m1);

else
  mx.pointer=malloc(m2);

mx.pointer[k]=0;
```

(a) Creating span

```
struct {
  int *pointer,
  int span,
} mx;
if (...) {
  mx.pointer=malloc(m1);
  mx.span=m1; }
else {
  mx.pointer=malloc(m2);
  mx.span=m2; }
mx.pointer[k+tid*
 mx.span/sizeof(int)]=0;
```

(b) Computing span

Figure 4: Computing span before thread space creation

type correspondingly. Similarly, if the original type is a structure type we promote each of its field types. The whole promotion process proceeds recursively because there may exist various combinations of aggregate types and pointer types.

Figure 5 lists the promotion rules. We apply promotion to all variable instantiations in a program, including global variable declarations, local variable declarations, formal parameter declarations and heap variable allocations. Figure 6 lists the *promotion* function used in Figure 5. Note that the *promotion* function uses *int* type as the example for all primitive types. After promoting all declarations, we adjust each reference site to ensure that after promotion each reference refers to the same data as in the original program. As shown in those *Ref* and *Deref* rules, this is done by replacing each original reference with a new reference to the *pointer* field if its type is promoted. We do not list rules for all kinds of references here. Instead we use *store* assignments to illustrate the idea. *Load* sites and call-site argument passing are processed similarly. Assignments to structure variables are treated as a series of scalar assignments.

3.3.2 Computing Span

For each pointer variable to which a *span* field is attached, we insert an assignment statement to compute the *span* field immediately after each assignment to that pointer. Table 3 lists the rules for computing a *span* field. The third column shows the statement being inserted after the original assignment shown in the second column. Note that for the rule Address taken 2, we fetch the size of the whole structure rather than the size of its corresponding field. For the rule Pointer arithmetic 2, an integer variable i is used to keep the difference between two pointers. In the subsequent program code, the integer variable can be used to recover any of the two pointers, e.g., by performing $p - i$ or $q + i$. We promote the type of integer variables that are used to keep pointer differences to a structure similar to the one for pointer promotion, whose first field is the integer variable itself and the second field represents the *span*. The *span* field for such integer variables are used in the two rules for pointer arithmetic. For the sample program in Figure 3(a), Figure 4(b) lists the corresponding program after creating and inserting statements for computing the *span* field.

[Decl Pointer]

$$\frac{\Gamma \vdash v : T*}{\Gamma' \vdash v : \text{promote}(T*)}$$

[Decl Array]

$$\frac{\Gamma \vdash v : T[n]}{\Gamma' \vdash v : \text{promote}(T)[n]}$$

[Decl Struct]

$$\frac{\Gamma \vdash v : \textbf{struct}(f_1 : T_1, ..., f_m : T_m)}{\Gamma' \vdash v : \textbf{struct}(f_1 : \text{promote}(T_1), ..., f_m : \text{promote}(T_m))}$$

[Decl Heap]

$$\frac{\Gamma \vdash v = malloc(sizeof(T))}{\Gamma' \vdash v = malloc(sizeof(\text{promote}(T)))}$$

[Decl Function]

$$\frac{\Gamma \vdash f_m : T_m\ func(f_1 : T_1, ..., f_{m-1} : T_{m-1})}{\Gamma' \vdash f_m : \text{promote}(T_m)\ func(f_1 : \text{promote}(T_1), ..., f_{m-1} : \text{promote}(T_{m-1}))}$$

[Ref Pointer]

$$\frac{\Gamma \vdash v : T* \quad \Gamma \vdash v = val}{\Gamma' \vdash v.pointer = val}$$

[Ref Array]

$$\frac{\Gamma \vdash v : T*[n] \quad \Gamma \vdash v[i] = val}{\Gamma' \vdash v[i].pointer = val}$$

[Ref Field]

$$\frac{\Gamma \vdash v : \textbf{struct}(f_1 : T_1, ..., f_i : T*, ...f_m : T_m) \quad \Gamma \vdash v.f_i = val}{\Gamma' \vdash v.f_i.pointer = val}$$

[Deref Pointer]

$$\frac{\Gamma \vdash v : T** \quad \Gamma \vdash *v = val}{\Gamma' \vdash (*(v.pointer)).pointer = val}$$

Figure 5: Pointer promotion rules.

```
promote(t):
  case t of
   [int] :
    return int
   [int*] :
    return struct(int* pointer, int span)
   [T*] :
    return struct(promote(T)* pointer, int span)
```

Figure 6: Auxiliary function in promotion rules.

Table 3: Span computing rules.

Rule	Original	Insert after
Address taken 1	p = &a	p.span = sizeof(a)
Address taken 2	p = &s.a	p.span = sizeof(s)
Memory allocation	p = malloc(n)	p.span = n
Pointer assignment	p = q	p.span = q.span
Pointer arithmetic 1	p = q ± 1	p.span = q.span
Pointer arithmetic 2	i = p - q	i.span = p.span - q.span
Pointer arithmetic 3	p = p ± i	p.span = p.span ± i.span

3.4 Reducing Time and Memory Overhead

Obviously, the memory access redirection will incur overhead. For example, in Table 2, the private memory operation `*(p + tid*span/sizeof(*p))` costs more than in the original program because of the complicated memory accessing expression. Operations to compute the *span* field (c.f. Table 3) also take extra time. Fortunately, several compiler optimizations can be applied to lower the overhead. First of all, the pointer assignment `p=p+1` does not cause the *span* field of pointer `p` to be changed. Hence, it is unnecessary to place a `p.span=p.span` after `p=p+1`. By applying dead store elimination, `p.span=p.span` can be removed. Secondly, by constant propagation and copy propagation, `p` and `q` may be found to always point to the same-sized data structure. In this case, `p.span=q.span` can be eliminated. Furthermore, if the object that a pointer points to is not involved in privatization, we do not promote the pointer at all.

To avoid memory overhead due to unnecessary expansion, we perform alias analysis in the compiler to find out whether a data structure gets referenced by private memory accesses (as defined in Definition 5) in the targeted loop, no matter whether the data structure is local, global or heap-allocated. If not, the data structure will not be expanded.

4. Evaluation

4.1 Experimentation Setup

We have implemented the techniques presented above in the GCC compiler, version 4.7. Our experiment was conducted on a multicore machine with two 2.00GHz Quad-Core AMD Opteron 8350 processors and 32GB RAM, with Linux 3.4.10 installed. In order to assess how these techniques enable loop parallelization to speed up sequential programs, our experiment was performed on a set of programs from well-known benchmark suites such as Mibench [17], MediaBench II [14] and SPEC CPU [1]. Table 4 shows the characteristics of these benchmarks. Note that H263-encoder has two promising loops which take most of the computation. We select these benchmarks because of their inherent parallelism which justifies the use of privatization or data structure expansion, although our techniques are not limited to particular data structures. The benchmarks not selected lack sufficient parallelism to justify the synchronization overhead, regardless of the privatization techniques used. To our best knowledge, among previous automatic multi-threading methods, only the dynamic privatization technique can handle the DOALL and DOACROSS loops in these benchmarks. The dynamic privatization technique, however, incurs a much higher runtime overhead than general data structure expansion, as indicated in our results below. Previous work has exploited pipeline parallelism for MediaBench [12, 31], but the speedup is not as good as ours.

The workflow of our tool is shown in Figure 7. Our experiment consists of two stages, namely, estimating the overhead of our techniques and evaluating the impact of our techniques on parallelization. In our experiment, we obtained the data dependence graph for each loop candidate first by data dependence profiling [38, 39]. We then inspect the program to verify the general validity of the graph. The reason for using profiler-generated graphs is because, for all benchmark programs in our experiment, current compile-time data dependence analysis algorithms are still too conservative and they report false positives that prevent loop parallelization. Figure 8 shows the breakdown of dynamic memory accesses of each loop candidate. These accesses are measured at runtime by collecting only load/store instructions. In this chart, the bars marked as "Free of loop-carried dep" refer to the memory accesses that are free of any loop-carried data dependence. The "Expandable" bars refer to the thread-private memory accesses according to Definition 5. Consequently, "With loop-carried dep" refers to all the remaining memory accesses involved in at least one loop-carried dependence. Although we cannot infer any real speedup from this chart, it is quite obvious that, for some of these benchmarks, if we do not

Table 4: From left to right: benchmark name, benchmark suite, code size counted by lines, function containing the parallelized loop, loop nesting level (1 meaning the outermost loop), type of parallelism, loop execution time as percentage of the whole program.

Benchmark	Suite	#LOC	Function	Level	Parallelism	%Time
dijkstra	MiBench	375	main	1	DOACROSS	99.9%
md5	MiBench	420	main	1	DOALL	99.8%
mpeg2-encoder	MediaBench II	7605	motion_estimation	3	DOALL	70.6%
mpeg2-decoder	MediaBench II	9832	picture_data	2	DOALL	97.8%
h263-encoder	MediaBench II	8105	NextTwoPB	2	DOALL	43.2%
			MotionEstimatePicture	2	DOALL	37.1%
256.bzip2	SPEC CPU2000	4649	compressStream	2	DOACROSS	99.8%
456.hmmer	SPEC CPU2006	35992	main_loop_serial	2	DOACROSS	99.9%
470.lbm	SPEC CPU2006	1155	LBM_performStreamCollide	2	DOALL	99.1%

have an effective way to remove the data dependences due to contentious data structures, we will have to resort to synchronization across threads in order to execute the target loop in parallel, with high overhead.

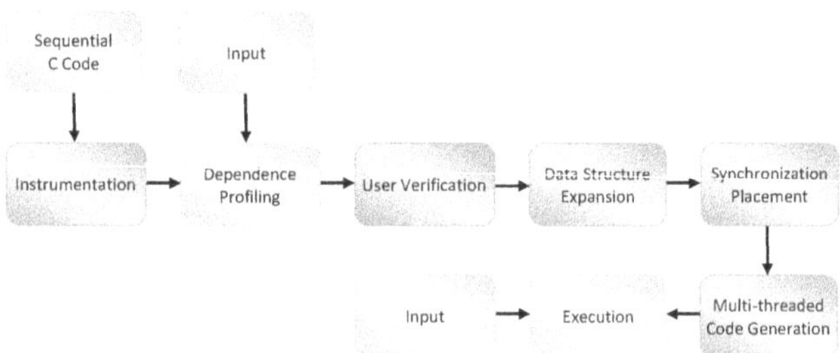

Figure 7: Our parallelization framework.

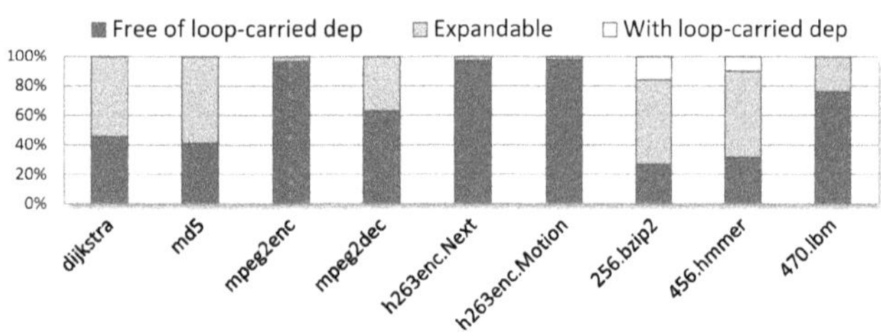

Figure 8: Breakdown of memory accesses of promising loops.

4.2 Evaluating the Overhead

Table 5 lists the number of dynamic data structures privatized for each benchmark. Note that none of these loops can be parallelized by production compilers, such as Intel ICC [3]. We evaluate the overhead due to our techniques at two levels, namely, with and without optimizations. Figure 9a shows the slowdown caused by our data structure expansion without any optimizations mentioned in Section 3.4, with native running time normalized to 1. The numbers are collected when the measured programs are executed sequentially on a single core. For most of the benchmarks, the overhead is high before optimizations for the kind of challenging loops we target. The last two bars show the harmonic average overhead for all benchmarks, which brings an 1.8x slowdown. On the contrary, Figure 9b shows the slowdown caused by data structure expansion with optimizations mentioned in Section 3.4. We can see from the chart that the overhead is kept below 5% of the original program execution time on average, which makes our techniques quite practical as the result.

To further assess the time efficiency of our techniques, we compare with an alternative method, i.e., an implementation of the runtime privatization. The memory overhead is also measured when a benchmark is executed in parallel. We show the results below.

Table 5: The number of dynamic data structures privatized for each benchmark.

Benchmark	#Privatized
dijkstra	2
md5	1
mpeg2-encoder	7
mpeg2-decoder	3
h263-encoder	6
256.bzip2	4
456.hmmer	8
470.lbm	2

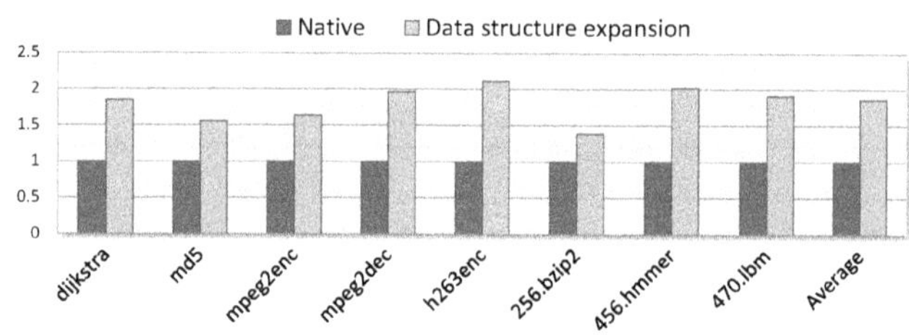

(a) Without optimizations.

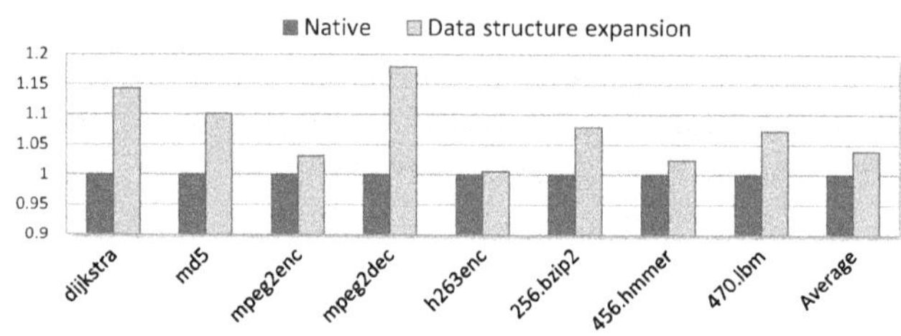

(b) With optimizations.

Figure 9: Overhead of data structure expansion with/without optimizations.

4.2.1 Runtime Privatization

Runtime privatization aims at privatizing data structures at run time, by transferring data between the shared space and thread-private spaces. This scheme for handling various kinds of data structures has been adopted by several recent parallel programming models [12] as well as thread-level speculation (TLS) systems [19, 33]. While there is no available runtime privatization techniques ready for a given data dependence graph, we borrow and adapt the idea from SpiceC [12].

In SpiceC, all memory accesses are monitored by a runtime access control system which assures that the data being accessed by one thread are copied from the shared space to the corresponding thread-private space properly. Besides the copying-in operations, the access control system is also responsible for committing thread-local changes to the shared space. For the purpose of evaluating its performance for privatization, we identify private memory accesses in the way described in Section 3.2 and insert a function call before each private access. These function calls invoke the functions implemented in a user-level runtime library and they are in charge of dynamically locating thread-local storage. According to the presentation in [12], the access control of global or stack variables can be performed statically by allocating thread-local copies at compile time and adjusting private memory accesses accordingly. The access control for heap-allocated objects, however, must be performed at runtime by invoking those functions in the runtime library for each private pointer dereference because of the compiler's inability to resolve alias relations. We also implement their *Heap prefix* technique for fast locating thread-local storage. Simply speaking, a heap prefix is the meta-data of a data structure which contains the location information of the data structure in each private space, and it is located adjacent to the data structure in the shared space. Given a pointer pointing to the beginning of a data structure, a fast way to redirect it to the corresponding thread-local copies is by accessing the heap prefix. However, as the authors of SpiceC [12] suggest, there is no known method yet to decide whether this fast scheme is safe. Hence, we extend the scheme in a safe way such that it adapts to the situation in which a given pointer may point to any part of a data structure rather than just the start of that data structure.

Figure 10 compares our static data structure expansion with dynamic privatization as we implemented. For most of the benchmarks, the result shows that runtime privatization incurs much higher time overhead than ours. However, there also exist a few programs that issue just a small number of private memory accesses, for which the monitoring overhead is low for runtime privatization. On the other hand, such memory accesses are involved in ambiguous alias relations involving many program statements, causing our technique to promote types in a large program scope.

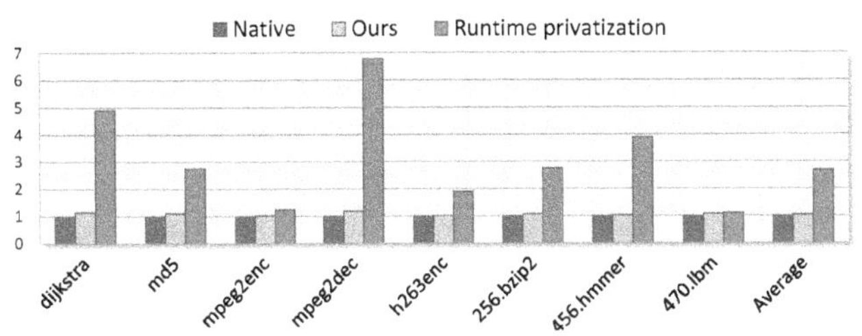

Figure 10: Slowdowns of runtime privatization with optimizations.

4.3 Evaluating the Effect

Our parallelized loops invoke the Gomp library [2]. For DOALL loops, we use static chunk scheduling. For DOACROSS loops, we use dynamic scheduling with the chunk size of one. Besides data structure expansion, we also place necessary inter-thread synchronization for the safety of DOACROSS parallelization. Figures 11a and 11b plot the parallel speedups (Y-axis) of the target loops and the whole program, respectively, over the original program. The X-axis marks the number of cores used. The slowdown in the single-core case reflects the overhead due to privatization, synchronization and the calls to the Gomp library. Speedups are good with `md5`, `mpeg2-encoder` and `h263-encoder`. On the other hand, for `dijkstra`, `mpeg2-decoder`, `256.bzip2`, `456.hmmer` and `470.lbm`, the speedups have plateaued as the number of cores exceeds 4.

To explain the cause for the observed plateau, we list the instruction counts breakdown of an 8-core run for each benchmark in Figure 12. For `256.bzip2` and `456.hmmer`, of which the parallelized loops are DOACROSS, inter-thread synchronization takes the majority of the running time. This means that our synchronization placement algorithm still has room for improvement. Recent literature has reported several techniques that are effective for enhancing the performance of some of these benchmark programs, but we have not incorporated them in our experiments. Loop parallelism can be enhanced by exploiting I/O parallelism in `256.bzip2` [13] and by recognizing commutative code regions in `456.hmmer` [26]. As for `470.lbm` and `mpeg2-decoder`, there is room for load balance improvement, since Figure 12 shows that a large portion of time was spent on calling `do_wait` and `cpu_relax` in Gomp. Memory access efficiency is also an area for improvement. The performance profiling tool Perf [8] reports that the parallel performance of `470.lbm` suffers from the memory bandwidth constraint when the number of cores exceeds 4. Programs `dijkstra` and `mpeg2-decoder`, on the other hand, suffer from increased cache misses as the number of cores increases.

Figure 13 shows the speedup attained by applying runtime privatization instead of our expansion technique. For most of the benchmarks, there is nearly no speedup due to the large runtime overhead. We have also measured the performance of the parallelized code without privatization for each benchmark. Unfortunately, this would require excessive synchronization due to the spurious loop-carried dependences, causing a slowdown instead of speedup for the loops.

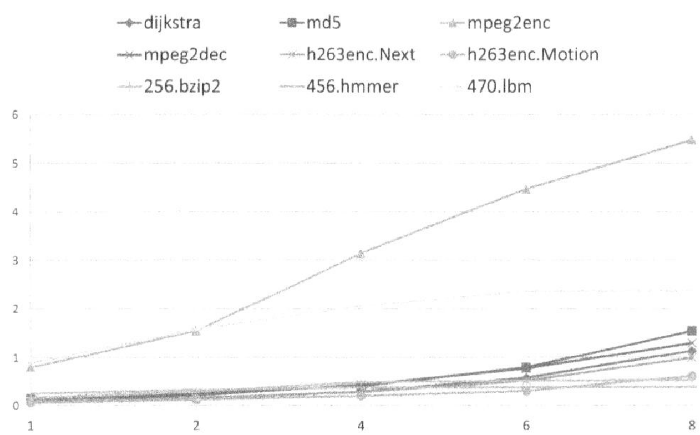

Figure 13: Loop speedup by runtime privatization.

Obviously, data expansion method and runtime privatization will both increase the memory use. Figure 14 shows the memory use after applying these two methods respectively, measured as a multiple of the usage by the original sequential program. The runtime privatization, as we implement it, never privatizes any memory location that is not recognized as thread-private. Hence, one can regard their memory usage to be necessary for achieving the loop speedup that has been shown. In comparison, the figure also shows that our data expansion method adds quite little to that memory overhead except for the program `h263.encoder` executed on eight cores, in which case our method has increased the memory use by 50%. Note that we have not yet implemented the memory reduction technique in Section 3.4. Nonetheless, the virtual memory management in Linux system that we used in the experiment is quite efficient in physical memory use – a virtual block does not

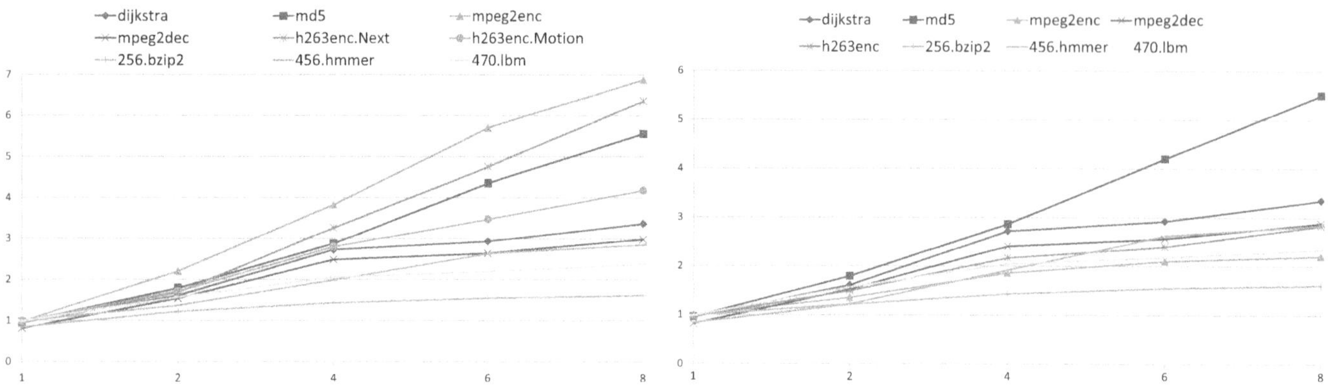

(a) Loop speedup. (b) Total speedup.

Figure 11: Speedup obtained by data structure expansion.

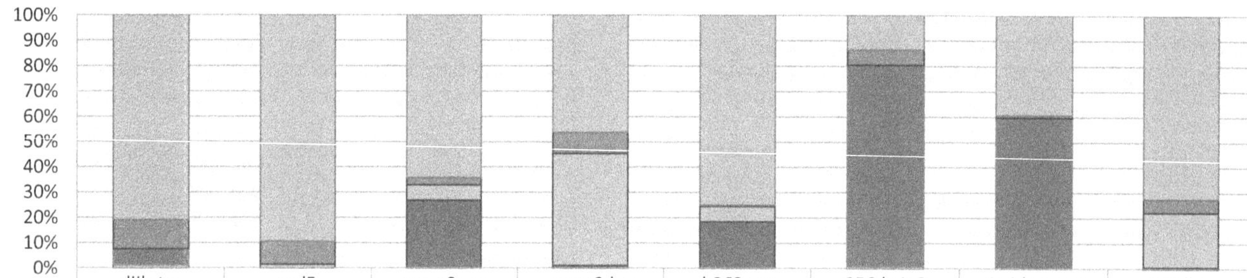

	dijkstra	md5	mpeg2enc	mpeg2dec	h263enc	256.bzip2	456.hmmer	470.lbm
target loop	81.01%	89.59%	64.34%	46.36%	75.07%	13.52%	39.36%	72.65%
expansion	11.56%	9.08%	2.80%	8.51%	0.47%	6.26%	0.94%	5.29%
post/wait	6.23%	0.00%	0.00%	0.00%	0.00%	79.46%	59.57%	0.00%
libgomp	1.14%	1.15%	6.13%	44.08%	6.11%	0.74%	0.10%	21.41%
others	0.07%	0.18%	26.73%	1.05%	18.35%	0.03%	0.02%	0.65%

Figure 12: Breakdown of instruction counts on 8 cores. From top to bottom: native instructions executed by parallelized loops, extra instructions introduced by data structure expansion, inter-thread synchronization, underlying multi-threading facility provided by Gomp library, and the remaining serial native code.

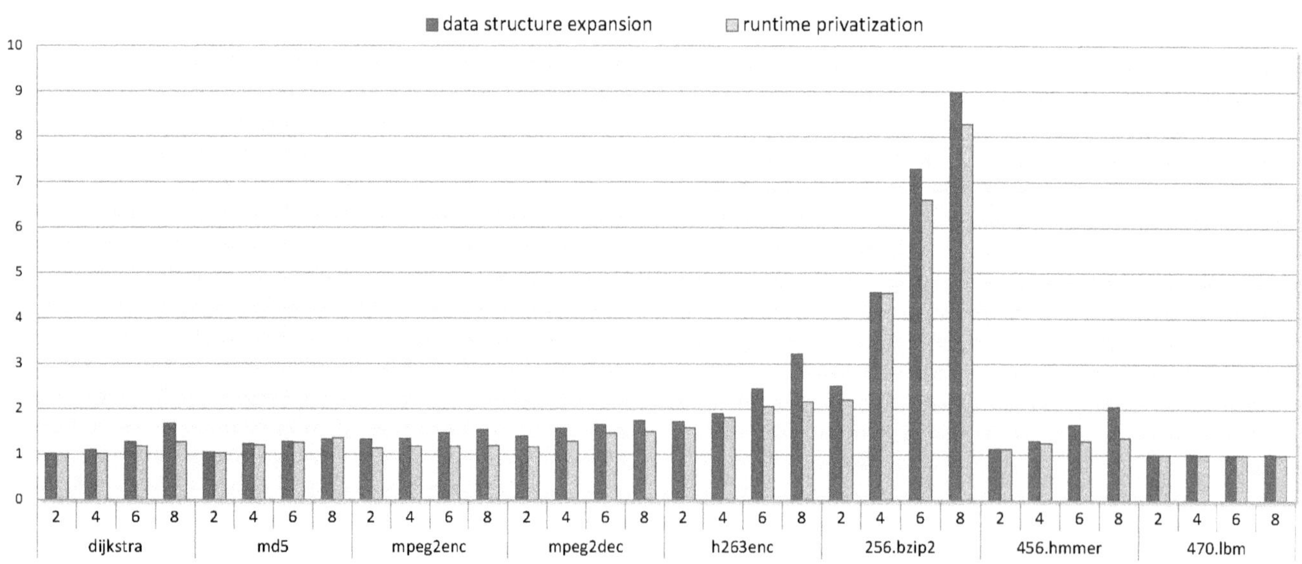

Figure 14: Memory use increase.

get a physical allocation until the block is actually referenced in the program.

5. Related Work

Parallelizing compilers have traditionally used scalar expansion [4, 5, 25] to eliminate the loop-carried anti- and output data dependences associated with scalar variables. Some research studies have also found that applying this technique to arrays can help expose parallelism in loops which would otherwise be sequential [10]. Array expansion or privatization techniques [11, 15, 16, 18, 22, 23, 36], which are based on array dataflow analysis and works well for Fortran-like programs, are now essential facilities in parallelizing compilers.

Going beyond static privatization method, researches have also resorted to dynamically constructing individual data structures for simultaneous multiple threads. The PD Test [28] inspects variable privatizability and performs parallelization at runtime immediately before a candidate loop is executed in parallel, in an inspector/executor way. The LRPD Test [29] and R-LRPD Test [7] improves the PD Test for speculatively parallelization. Furthermore, to accelerate dynamic privatization, Hybrid Analysis [30] utilizes compiler-generated predicates to aid runtime memory reference analysis. These techniques are still limited to handling Fortran-like array-based programs.

To extend the generality for handling dynamic data structures, the recent software-based thread level speculation (TLS) system CorD [32–34] moves shared data structures copies that may be modified by speculative threads into thread-local memory space for private use. Another dynamic privatization technique, called Privateer [19], also supports speculative execution, but it is based on processes. With processes, privatization overhead is reduced because different simultaneous processes maintain separate address spaces. The process-based Privateer, however, does not parallelize DOACROSS and pipelined loops. Behavior-oriented parallelization (BOP) [9, 20] also performs speculative privatization based on multi-processes. In BOP, OS-assisted techniques for copying data between spaces are heavily used and page-level access tracking is employed to detect misspeculations.

Software Transactional Memory (STM) systems for thread level speculation also provide facilities to privatize data structures at run time during a transaction. For example, STMlite [24] manipulates transactional store operations on a thread-local write set. Every time when a transactional load is about to be executed, the system first checks the transaction's write signature to see if this transaction has previously written to the same address as the load. If so, the load is redirected to read data from the thread-local write set; otherwise the load reads directly from the memory location that saves the value computed by other threads previously. Hash tables are employed for conflict checking, which incurs considerable computational overhead.

Several parallel programming models provide privatization directives to be inserted in sequential codes for parallelization. For example, OpenMP allows user-specified privatization for scalar or array variables. Paralax [37] makes an improvement to OpenMP by providing KILL(var) annotations to indicate that a data structure is privatizable. The KILL annotation applies to the scalar, array or structure that var points to. Unfortunately, it does not apply recursively to deeper data structures that can be referenced by chasing pointers starting from var. SpiceC [12] supports data privatization involving dynamic data structures implicitly after parallel regions are identified by the programmer. We have analyzed the run-time cost for the copy-in and copy-out operations used in SpiceC in the previous section.

Tournavitis *et al.* [35] propose a profile-driven parallelizing compiler which successfully parallelizes many numeric benchmark programs. Unfortunately, their privatization technique is based on named memory locations such as scalar and array variables. Hence, it can not handle dynamic data structures. Thies *et al.* [31] presents a profile-based approach to exploiting coarse-grained pipeline parallelism in C programs. They privatize necessary data by simply forking the original program into multiple processes. The memory spaces of the processes are isolated from one another, yet the processes share exactly the same data layout such that no pointers or instructions need to be adjusted either at compile time or run time. A standard inter-process communication mechanism (such as pipes) is used to send shared data from one process to another. At the end of a parallel loop's execution, all of the processes commit their modified data into a single process that continues after the loop. While such a multi-processes approach works well for streaming applications which utilize simple data structures (mainly consecutive linear buffers), it has difficulties in privatizing highly dynamic discrete data structures. For example, a process enlarging/shrinking a data structure (by using `malloc`, `realloc` or `free`) will cause other processes to see different data layouts, making the synchronization and commit difficult to manage.

6. Conclusion

Variable privatization is a crucial step in parallelization of many nonnumerical programs. We have proposed a compile-time technique to expand arbitrary data structures, thus overcoming the difficulties faced by other techniques when trying to privatize dynamic and irregular data structures. Experiments with eight benchmark programs show the harmonic mean of 1.93 for the total program speedup with four cores and 2.24 with eight cores. Future work to improve our work can be conducted in several areas. Most importantly, the state of the art compilers are not yet powerful enough to obtain the data dependence graph required for applying our technique to the benchmarks used in our experiments. As such, we have used off-line data dependence profiling to obtain such a graph, with manually performed verification afterwards. In addition to pursuing advanced compiler analysis for building such a graph, we will explore effective ways for the programmer to interact with the compiler in the verification of the data dependence graph. We have used fat pointers to facilitate type promotion, which will face interoperability issues when the program calls library routines with no source code for compiler analysis. Binary analysis on such routines can be a useful tool in such situations. Lastly, the bonded mode and the interleaved mode for data structure allocation have their respective strengths and weaknesses, as discussed in the paper, which naturally raises the prospect of devising an adaptive scheme to switch between these two modes.

Acknowledgments

The authors thank Xinmin Tian for his advice concerning the use of Intel's ICC compiler. This work is sponsored in part by the National Science Foundation through grants CNS-0915414, CCF-0811587, and CCF-0702245, and by an Intel research grant and an Intel gift.

References

[1] `http://http://www.spec.org/cpu/`.

[2] `http://gcc.gnu.org/projects/gomp/`.

[3] `http://software.intel.com/en-us/intel-compilers/`.

[4] M. G. Burke, R. Cytron, J. Ferrante, and W. C. Hsieh. Automatic generation of nested, fork-join parallelism. *The Journal of Supercomputing*, pages 71–88, 1989.

[5] R. Cytron and J. Ferrante. What's in a name? -or- the value of renaming for parallelism detection and storage allocation. In *ICPP'87*, pages 19–27, 1987.

[6] L. Dagum and R. Menon. OpenMP: An industry-standard API for shared-memory programming. *IEEE Comput. Sci. Eng.*, 5(1):46–55, Jan. 1998.

[7] F. Dang, H. Yu, and L. Rauchwerger. The R-LRPD test: Speculative parallelization of partially parallel loops. In *Proceedings of the 16th International Symposium on Parallel and Distributed Processing*, IPDPS '02, pages 20–, 2002.

[8] A. de Melo. The new linuxperftools. In *Slides from Linux Kongress*, 2010.

[9] C. Ding, X. Shen, K. Kelsey, C. Tice, R. Huang, and C. Zhang. Software behavior oriented parallelization. In *Proceedings of the 2007 ACM SIGPLAN Conference on Programming Language Design and Implementation*, PLDI '07, pages 223–234, 2007.

[10] R. Eigenmann, J. Hoeflinger, Z. Li, and D. A. Padua. Experience in the automatic parallelization of four perfect-benchmark programs. In *Proceedings of the 4th International Workshop on Languages and Compilers for Parallel Computing*, LCPC '92, pages 65–83, 1992.

[11] P. Feautrier. Array expansion. In *Proceedings of the 2nd International Conference on Supercomputing*, ICS '88, pages 429–441, 1988.

[12] M. Feng, R. Gupta, and Y. Hu. SpiceC: scalable parallelism via implicit copying and explicit commit. In *Proceedings of the 16th ACM Symposium on Principles and Practice of Parallel Programming*, PPoPP '11, pages 69–80, 2011.

[13] M. Feng, R. Gupta, and I. Neamtiu. Effective parallelization of loops in the presence of I/O operations. In *Proceedings of the 33rd ACM SIGPLAN Conference on Programming Language Design and Implementation*, PLDI '12, pages 487–498, 2012.

[14] J. E. Fritts, F. W. Steiling, J. A. Tucek, and W. Wolf. Mediabench II video: Expediting the next generation of video systems research. *Microprocess. Microsyst.*, 33(4):301–318, June 2009.

[15] J. Gu, Z. Li, and G. Lee. Experience with efficient array data flow analysis for array privatization. In *Proceedings of the 6th ACM SIGPLAN Symposium on Principles and Practice of Parallel Programming*, P-POPP '97, pages 157–167, 1997.

[16] M. Gupta. On privatization of variables for data-parallel execution. In *Proceedings of the 11th International Symposium on Parallel Processing*, IPPS '97, pages 533–541, 1997.

[17] M. R. Guthaus, J. S. Ringenberg, D. Ernst, T. M. Austin, T. Mudge, and R. B. Brown. Mibench: A free, commercially representative embedded benchmark suite. In *Proceedings of the Workload Characterization, 2001. WWC-4. 2001 IEEE International Workshop*, WWC '01, pages 3–14, 2001.

[18] M. H. Hall, S. P. Amarasinghe, B. R. Murphy, S.-W. Liao, and M. S. Lam. Detecting coarse-grain parallelism using an interprocedural parallelizing compiler. In *Proceedings of the 1995 ACM/IEEE Conference on Supercomputing (CDROM)*, Supercomputing '95, 1995.

[19] N. P. Johnson, H. Kim, P. Prabhu, A. Zaks, and D. I. August. Speculative separation for privatization and reductions. In *Proceedings of the 33rd ACM SIGPLAN Conference on Programming Language Design and Implementation*, PLDI '12, pages 359–370, 2012.

[20] K. Kelsey, T. Bai, C. Ding, and C. Zhang. Fast track: A software system for speculative program optimization. In *Proceedings of the 7th Annual IEEE/ACM International Symposium on Code Generation and Optimization*, CGO '09, pages 157–168, 2009.

[21] M. Kim, H. Kim, and C.-K. Luk. SD3: A scalable approach to dynamic data-dependence profiling. In *Proceedings of the 43rd Annual IEEE/ACM International Symposium on Microarchitecture*, MICRO '43, pages 535–546, 2010.

[22] Z. Li. Array privatization for parallel execution of loops. In *Proceedings of the 6th International Conference on Supercomputing*, ICS '92, pages 313–322, 1992.

[23] D. E. Maydan, S. P. Amarasinghe, and M. S. Lam. Array-data flow analysis and its use in array privatization. In *Proceedings of the 20th ACM SIGPLAN-SIGACT Symposium on Principles of Programming Languages*, POPL '93, pages 2–15, 1993.

[24] M. Mehrara, J. Hao, P.-C. Hsu, and S. Mahlke. Parallelizing sequential applications on commodity hardware using a low-cost software transactional memory. In *Proceedings of the 2009 ACM SIGPLAN Conference on Programming Language Design and Implementation*, PLDI '09, pages 166–176, 2009.

[25] D. A. Padua and M. J. Wolfe. Advanced compiler optimizations for supercomputers. *Commun. ACM*, 29(12):1184–1201, Dec. 1986.

[26] P. Prabhu, S. Ghosh, Y. Zhang, N. P. Johnson, and D. I. August. Commutative set: a language extension for implicit parallel programming. In *Proceedings of the 32nd ACM SIGPLAN Conference on Programming Language Design and Implementation*, PLDI '11, pages 1–11, 2011.

[27] L. Rauchwerger, N. M. Amato, and D. A. Padua. A scalable method for run-time loop parallelization. *Int. J. Parallel Program.*, 23(6):537–576, Dec. 1995.

[28] L. Rauchwerger and D. Padua. The privatizing DOALL test: a runtime technique for DOALL loop identification and array privatization. In *Proceedings of the 8th International Conference on Supercomputing*, ICS '94, pages 33–43, 1994.

[29] L. Rauchwerger and D. Padua. The LRPD test: speculative run-time parallelization of loops with privatization and reduction parallelization. In *Proceedings of the 1995 ACM SIGPLAN Conference on Programming Language Design and Implementation*, PLDI '95, pages 218–232, 1995.

[30] S. Rus, L. Rauchwerger, and J. Hoeflinger. Hybrid analysis: static & dynamic memory reference analysis. In *Proceedings of the 16th International Conference on Supercomputing*, ICS '02, pages 274–284, 2002.

[31] W. Thies, V. Chandrasekhar, and S. Amarasinghe. A practical approach to exploiting coarse-grained pipeline parallelism in C programs. In *Proceedings of the 40th Annual IEEE/ACM International Symposium on Microarchitecture*, MICRO '40, pages 356–369, 2007.

[32] C. Tian, M. Feng, and R. Gupta. Speculative parallelization using state separation and multiple value prediction. In *Proceedings of the 2010 International Symposium on Memory Management*, ISMM '10, pages 63–72, 2010.

[33] C. Tian, M. Feng, and R. Gupta. Supporting speculative parallelization in the presence of dynamic data structures. In *Proceedings of the 2010 ACM SIGPLAN Conference on Programming Language Design and Implementation*, PLDI '10, pages 62–73, 2010.

[34] C. Tian, M. Feng, V. Nagarajan, and R. Gupta. Copy or discard execution model for speculative parallelization on multicores. In *Proceedings of the 41st Annual IEEE/ACM International Symposium on Microarchitecture*, MICRO '41, pages 330–341, 2008.

[35] G. Tournavitis, Z. Wang, B. Franke, and M. F. O'Boyle. Towards a holistic approach to auto-parallelization: integrating profile-driven parallelism detection and machine-learning based mapping. In *Proceedings of the 2009 ACM SIGPLAN Conference on Programming Language Design and Implementation*, PLDI '09, pages 177–187, 2009.

[36] P. Tu and D. A. Padua. Automatic array privatization. In *Proceedings of the 6th International Workshop on Languages and Compilers for Parallel Computing*, LCPC '94, pages 500–521, 1994.

[37] H. Vandierendonck, S. Rul, and K. De Bosschere. The Paralax infrastructure: automatic parallelization with a helping hand. In *Proceedings of the 19th International Conference on Parallel Architectures and Compilation Techniques*, PACT '10, pages 389–400, 2010.

[38] H. Yu and Z. Li. Fast loop-level data dependence profiling. In *Proceedings of the 26th ACM International Conference on Supercomputing*, ICS '12, pages 37–46, 2012.

[39] H. Yu and Z. Li. Multi-slicing: a compiler-supported parallel approach to data dependence profiling. In *Proceedings of the 2012 International Symposium on Software Testing and Analysis*, ISSTA '12, pages 23–33, 2012.

[40] X. Zhang, A. Navabi, and S. Jagannathan. Alchemist: A transparent dependence distance profiling infrastructure. In *Proceedings of the 7th Annual IEEE/ACM International Symposium on Code Generation and Optimization*, CGO '09, pages 47–58, 2009.

AutoSynch: An Automatic-Signal Monitor Based on Predicate Tagging

Wei-Lun Hung   Vijay K. Garg

Department of Electrical and Computer Engineering
The University of Texas at Austin
wlhung@utexas.edu, garg@ece.utexas.edu

Abstract

Most programming languages use monitors with *explicit signals* for synchronization in shared-memory programs. Requiring programmers to signal threads explicitly results in many concurrency bugs due to missed notifications, or notifications on wrong condition variables. In this paper, we describe an implementation of an automatic signaling monitor in Java called *AutoSynch* that eliminates such concurrency bugs by removing the burden of signaling from the programmer. We show that the belief that automatic signaling monitors are prohibitively expensive is wrong. For most problems, programs based on *AutoSynch* are almost as fast as those based on explicit signaling. For some, *AutoSynch* is even faster than explicit signaling because it never uses *signalAll*, whereas the programmers end up using *signalAll* with the explicit signal mechanism.

AutoSynch achieves efficiency in synchronization based on three novel ideas. We introduce an operation called *closure* that enables the predicate evaluation in every thread, thereby reducing context switches during the execution of the program. Secondly, *AutoSynch* avoids *signalAll* by using a property called *relay invariance* that guarantees that whenever possible there is always at least one thread whose condition is true which has been signaled. Finally, *AutoSynch* uses a technique called *predicate tagging* to efficiently determine a thread that should be signaled. To evaluate the efficiency of *AutoSynch*, we have implemented many different well-known synchronization problems such as the producers/consumers problem, the readers/writers problems, and the dining philosophers problem. The results show that *AutoSynch* is almost as efficient as the explicit-signal monitor and even more efficient for some cases.

Categories and Subject Descriptors D.1.3 [*Concurrent Programming*]: Parallel programming; D.3.3 [*Language Constructs and Features*]: Concurrent programming structures; classes and objects; control structures

General Terms Algorithms, Languages, Performance

Keywords automatic signal, explicit signal, implicit signal, monitor, concurrency, parallel

1. Introduction

Multicore hardware is now ubiquitous. Programming these multicore processors is still a challenging task due to bugs resulting from concurrency and synchronization. Although there is widespread acknowledgement of difficulties in programming these systems, it is surprising that by and large the most prevalent methods of dealing with synchronization are based on ideas that were developed in early 70's [2, 9, 14]. For example, the most widely used threads package in C++ [19], pthreads [6], and the most widely used threads package in Java [11], java.util.concurrent [18], are based on the notion of monitors [2, 14](or semaphores [8, 9]). In this paper, we propose a new approach, *AutoSynch*, based on automatic signaling monitor that allows gains in productivity of the programmer as well as gain in performance of the system.

Both pthreads and Java require programmers to explicitly signal threads that may be waiting on certain condition. The programmer has to explicitly declare condition variables and then signal one or all of the threads when the associated condition becomes true. Using the wrong waiting notification (*signal* versus *signalAll* or notify versus notifyAll) is a frequent source of bugs in Java multithreaded programs. In our proposed approach, *AutoSynch*, there is no notion of explicit condition variables and it is the responsibility of the system to signal appropriate threads. This feature significantly reduces the program size and complexity. In addition, it allows us to completely eliminate signaling more than one thread resulting in reduced context switches and better performance. The idea of automatic signaling was initially explored by Hoare in [14], but rejected in favor of condition variables due to efficiency considerations. The belief that automatic signaling is extremely inefficient compared to explicit signaling is widely held since then and all the prevalent concurrent languages based on monitors use explicit signaling. For example, Buhr, Fortier, and Coffin claim that automatic monitors are 10 to 50 times slower than explicit signals [4]. We show in this paper that the widely held belief is wrong. The reason for this drastic slowdown in previous implementations of automatic monitor is that they evaluate all possible conditions on which threads are waiting whenever the monitor becomes available. With careful analysis of the conditions on which the threads are waiting and evaluating as few conditions as possible, automatic signaling can be as efficient as explicit signaling. In *AutoSynch*, the programmer simply specifies the predicate P on which the thread is waiting by using the construct *waituntil(P)* statement. When a thread executes the *waituntil* statement, it checks whether P is true. If it is true, the thread can continue; otherwise, the thread must wait for the system to signal it. The *AutoSynch* system has a condition manager that is responsible for determining which thread to signal by analyzing the predicates and the state of the shared object.

Fig. 1 shows the difference between the Java and the *AutoSynch* implementation for the parameterized bounded-buffer problem, a variant bounded-buffer problem (also known as the producer-consumer problem) [8, 10]. In this problem, producers put items into a shared buffer, while consumers take items out of the buffer. The *put* function has a parameter *items*; the *take* function has a parameter, *num*, indicating the number of items taken. There are two requirements for synchronization. First, every operation on a shared variable, such as *buff*, should be done under mutual exclusion. Second, we need *conditional synchronization*; a producer must wait when the buffer does not have sufficient space, and a consumer must wait when the buffer has no sufficient items. The explicit-signal bounded-buffer is written in Java. Programmers need to explicitly associate conditional predicates with condition variables and call *signal* (*signalAll*) or *await* statement manually. Note that, the *unlock* statement should be done in a *finally* block, *try* and *catch* blocks are also need for the *InterruptedException* that may be thrown by *await*. However, for simplicity, we avoid the exception handling in Fig. 1. The automatic-signal bounded-buffer is written using *AutoSynch* framework. We use *AutoSynch* modifier to indicate that the class is a monitor as in line 1. An *AutoSynch* class provides mutually exclusive access to its member functions. For conditional synchronization, we use *waituntil* as in line 9. There are no *signal* or *signalAll* calls in the *AutoSynch* program. Note that, the *waituntil* statement can take any boolean condition just like the *if* and *while* statements. Clearly, the automatic-signal monitor is much simpler than the explicit-signal monitor.

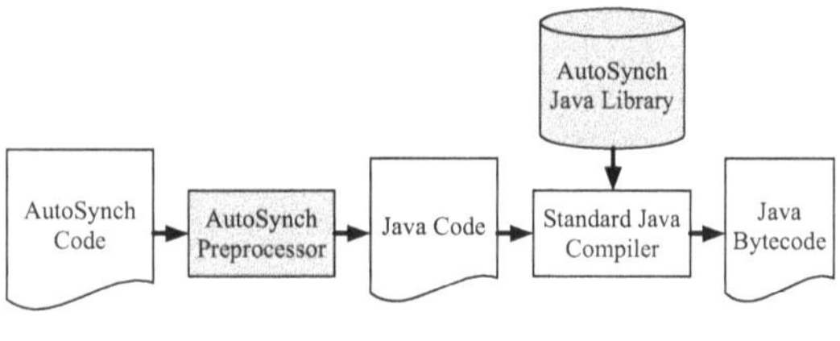

Figure 2: The framework of *AutoSynch*

The framework for the implementation is shown if Fig. 2. It is composed of a preprocessor and a Java condition manager library. The preprocessor translates *AutoSynch* code into traditional Java code. Our automatic-signal mechanism and developed techniques were implemented in the Java condition manager library, which is responsible for monitoring the state of the monitor object and signaling an appropriate thread.

In this paper, we argue that automatic signaling is generally as fast as explicit signaling (and even faster for some examples). The explicit signaling has to resort to *signalAll* in some examples; however, our automatic signaling never uses *signalAll*. Thus *AutoSynch* is considerably faster for synchronization problems that requires *signalAll*. The design principle underlying *AutoSynch* is to reduce the number of context switches and predicate evaluations.

Context switch: A context switch requires a certain amount of time to save and load registers and update various tables and lists. Reducing unnecessary context switches boosts the performance of the system. A *signalAll* call introduces unnecessary context switches; therefore, *signalAll* calls are never used in *AutoSynch*.

Predicate evaluation: In the automatic-signal mechanism, signaling a thread is the responsibility of the system. The number of predicate evaluations is crucial for efficiency in deciding which thread should be signaled. By analyzing the structure of the predicate, our system reduces the number of predicate evaluations.

There are three important novel concepts in *AutoSynch* that enable efficient automatic signaling — *closure of predicates, relay invariance*, and *predicate tagging*.

The technique of *closure* of a predicate P is used to reduce the number of context switches for its evaluation. In the current systems, only the thread that is waiting for the predicate P can evaluate it. When the thread is signaled, it wakes up, acquires the lock to the monitor and then evaluates the predicate P. If the predicate P is false, it goes back to wait resulting in an additional context switch. In *AutoSynch* system, the thread that is in the monitor evaluates the condition for the waiting thread and wakes it only if the condition is true. Since the predicate P may use variables local to the thread waiting on it, *AutoSynch* system derives a closure predicate P' of the predicate P, such that other threads can evaluate P'. The details of closure are in Section 3.1.

The idea of *relay invariance* is used to avoid *signalAll* calls in *AutoSynch*. The relay invariance ensures that if there is any thread whose waiting condition is true, then there exists at least one thread whose waiting condition is true and is signaled by the system. With this invariance, the *signalAll* call is unnecessary in our automatic-signal mechanism. This mechanism reduces the number of context switches by avoiding *signalAll* calls. The details of this approach are in Section 3.2.

The idea of *predicate tagging* is used to accelerate the process of deciding which thread to signal. All the waiting conditions are analyzed and tags are assigned to every predicate according to its semantics. To decide which thread should be signaled, we identify tags that are most likely to be true after examining the current state of the monitor. Then we only evaluate the predicates with those tags. The details of predicate tagging are in Section 3.3.

Our experimental results indicate that *AutoSynch* can significantly improve performance compared to other automatic-signal mechanisms [5]. In [4, 5] the automatic-signal mechanism is 10-50 times slower than the explicit-signal mechanism; however, *AutoSynch* is only 2.6 times slower than the explicit-signal mechanism even in the worst case of our experiment results. Furthermore, *AutoSynch* is 26.9 times faster than the explicit-signal mechanism in the parameterized bounded-buffer problem that relies on *signalAll* calls. Besides, the experimental results also show that *AutoSynch* is scalable; the performance of *AutoSynch* scales well even if the number of threads increases for many problems studied in the paper.

Although the experiment results show that *AutoSynch* is 2.6 times slower than the explicit-signal mechanism in the worst case, it is still desirable to have automatic signaling. First, automatic signaling simplifies the task of concurrent programming. In explicit-signal monitor, it is the responsibility of programmers to explicitly invoke a *signal* call on some condition variable for conditional synchronization. Using the wrong notification, and signaling a wrong condition variable are frequent sources of bugs. The idea is analogous to automatic garbage collection. Although garbage collection leads to decreased performance because of the overhead in deciding which memory to free, programmers avoid manual memory deallocation. As a consequence, memory leaks and certain bugs, such as dangling pointers and double free bugs, are reduced. Similarly, automatic-signal mechanism consumes computing resources in deciding which thread to be signaled; programmers avoid explicitly invoking *signal* calls. As a result, some bugs, such as using wrong notification and signaling a wrong condition variable, are eliminated. Secondly, in explicit-signal monitor, the principle of separation of concerns is violated. Any method that changes the state of the monitor must be aware of all the conditions, which other threads could be waiting for, in other methods of the monitor. The intricate relation between threads for conditional synchronization breaks the modularity and encapsulation of programming. Finally,

Explicit-Signal

```
1 class BoundedBuffer {
2   Object[] buff;
3   int putPtr, takePtr, count;
4   Lock mutex = new ReentrantLock();
5   Condition insufficientSpace = mutex.newCondition();
6   Condition insufficientItem = mutex.newCondition();
7   public BoundedBuffer(int n) {
8     buff = new Object[n];
9     putPtr = takePtr = count = 0;
10  }
11  public void put(Object[] items) {
12    mutex.lock();
13    while (items.length + count > buff.length) {
14      insufficientSpace.await();
15    }
16    for (int i = 0; i < items.length; i++) {
17      buff[putPtr++] = items[i];
18      putPtr %= buff.length;
19    }
20    count += items.length;
21    insufficientItem.signalAll();
22    mutex.unlock();
23  }
24  public Object[] take(int num) {
25    mutex.lock();
26    while (count < num) {
27      insufficientItem.await();
28    }
29    Object[] ret = new Object[num];
30    for (int i = 0; i < num; i++) {
31      ret[i] = buff[takePtr++];
32      takePtr %= buff.length;
33    }
34    count -= num;
35    insufficientSpace.signalAll();
36    mutex.unlock();
37    return ret;
38  }
39 }
```

Automatic-Signal

```
1 AutoSynch class BoundedBuffer {
2   Object[] buff;
3   int putPtr, takePtr, count;
4   public BoundedBuffer(int n) {
5     buff = new Object[n];
6     putPtr = takePtr = count = 0;
7   }
8   public void put(Object[] items) {
9     waituntil(count + items.length <= buff.length);
10    for (int i = 0; i < items.length; i++) {
11      buff[putPtr++] = items[i];
12      putPtr %= buff.length;
13    }
14    count += items.length;
15  }
16  public Object[] take(int num) {
17    waituntil(count >= num);
18    Object[] ret = new Object[num];
19    for (int i = 0; i < num; i++) {
20      ret[i] = buff[takePtr++];
21      takePtr %= buff.length;
22    }
23    count -= num;
24    return ret;
25  }
26 }
```

Figure 1: The parameterized bounded-buffer example

AutoSynch can provide rapid prototyping in developing programs and accelerating product time to market.

Although this paper focuses on Java, our techniques are also applicable to other programming languages and models, such as pthread and C# [13].

This paper is organized as follows. Section 2 gives the background of the monitor and explains why *signalAll* is required for explicit-signal monitor but not automatic-signal monitor. The concepts of *AutoSynch* are presented in Section 3 and the practical implementation details are discussed in Section 4. The proposed methods are then evaluated with experiments in Section 5. Section 6 gives the concluding remarks.

2. Background: monitor

According to Buhr and Harji [5], monitors can be divided into two categories according to the different implementations of conditional synchronization.

Explicit-signal monitor In this type of monitor, condition variables, *signal* and *await* statements are used for synchronization. Programmers need to associate assertions with condition variables manually. A thread waits on some condition variable if its predicate is not true. When another thread detects that the state has changed and the predicate is true, it explicitly signals the appropriate condition variable.

Automatic-signal (implicit-signal) monitor This kind of monitor uses *waituntil* statements, such as line 9 in automatic-signal program in Fig. 1, instead of condition variables for synchronization. Programmers do not need to associate assertions with variables, but use *waituntil* statements directly. In monitor, a thread will wait as long as the condition of a *waituntil* statement is false, and execute the remaining tasks only after the condition becomes true. The responsibility of signaling a waiting thread is that of the system rather than of the programmers.

We note that the *signalAll* call is essential in explicit-signal mechanism when programmers do not know which thread should be signaled. In Fig. 1, a producer must wait if there is no space to put *num* items, while a consumer has to wait when the buffer has insufficient items. Since producers and consumers can put and take different numbers of items every time, they may wait on different conditions to be met. Programmers do not know which producer or consumer should be signaled at runtime. Therefore, the *signalAll* call is used instead of *signal* calls in line 21 and 35. Although programmers can avoid using *signalAll* calls by writing complicated code that associates different conditions to different condition variables; the complicated code makes the maintenance of the program hard.

The *signalAll* call is expensive; it generally decreases the performance because it introduces redundant context switches, requiring computing time to save and load registers and update various tables and lists. Furthermore, *signalAll* calls cannot increase parallelism because threads are forbidden to access a monitor simultaneously. Although multiple threads are signaled at a time, only one thread is able to acquire the monitor. Other threads may need to go back to waiting state since another thread may change the status of the monitor.

3. *AutoSynch* concepts

3.1 Predicate evaluation

In *AutoSynch*, it is the responsibility of the system to signal appropriate threads automatically. The predicate evaluation is crucial in deciding which thread should be signaled. We discuss how to preform predicate evaluations of *waituntil* statements.

A predicate $P(\vec{x}) : X \rightarrow \mathbb{B}$ is a Boolean condition, where X is the space spanned by the variables $\vec{x} = (x_1, \ldots, x_n)$. A variable of a monitor object is a shared variable if it is accessible by every thread that is accessing the monitor. The set of shared variables is denoted by S. The set of local variables, denoted by L, is accessible only by a thread calling a function in which the variables are declared.

Predicates can be used to describe the properties of conditions. In our approach, every condition of *waituntil* statement is represented by a predicate. We say a condition has been met if its representing predicate is true; otherwise, the predicate is false. Furthermore, we assume that every predicate, $P = \vee_{i=1}^{n} c_i$, is in disjunctive normal form (DNF), where c_i is defined as the conjunction of a set of atomic Boolean expressions. For example, a predicate $(x = 1) \wedge (y = 6) \vee (z \neq 8)$ is in DNF, where $c_1 = (x = 1) \wedge (y = 6)$ and $c_2 = (z \neq 8)$. Note that, every Boolean formula can be converted into DNF using De Morgan's laws and distributive law.

Predicates can be divided into two categories based on the type of their variables [5].

Definition 1 (Shared and complex predicate). *Consider a predicate $P(\vec{x}) : X \rightarrow \mathbb{B}$. If $X \subseteq S$, P is a shared predicate. Otherwise, it is a complex predicate.*

The automatic-signal monitor has an efficient implementation [16] by limiting the predicate of a *waituntil* to a shared predicate; however, we do not limit the predicate of a *waituntil* statement to a shared predicate. The reason is that this limitation will lead *AutoSynch* to be less attractive and practical since conditions including local variables cannot be represented in *AutoSynch*.

Evaluating a complex predicate in all the threads is unattainable because the accessibility of the local variables in the predicate is limited to the thread declaring them. To evaluate a complex predicate in all the threads, we treat local variables as constant values at runtime and define closure as follows.

Definition 2 (Closure). *Given a complex predicate $P(\vec{x}, \vec{a}) : X \times A \rightarrow \mathbb{B}$, where $X \subseteq S$ and $A \subseteq L$. The closure of P at runtime **t** is the new shared predicate*

$$G_t(\vec{x}) = P(\vec{x}, \vec{a_t}),$$

*where $\vec{a_t}$ is the values of $\vec{a}$ at runtime **t**.*

The closure can be applied to any complex predicate; a shared predicate can be derived from the closure. For example, in Fig. 1, the consumer C wants to take 48 items at some instant of time. Applying the closure to the complex predicate $(count \geq num)$ in line 19, we derive the shared predicate $(count \geq 48)$.

The following proposition shows that the complex predicate evaluation of *waituntil* statement in all threads can be achieved through the closure.

Proposition 1. *Consider a complex predicate $P(\vec{x}, \vec{a})$ in a **waituntil** statement. $P(\vec{x}, \vec{a})$ and its closure $P(\vec{x}, \vec{a_t})$ are semantically equivalent during the **waituntil** period, where t is the time instant immediately before invoking the **waituntil** statement.*

Proof. Only the thread invoking the *waituntil* statement can access the local variables of the predicate; all other threads are unable to change the values of those local variables. Therefore, the value of $\vec{a}$ cannot be changed during the *waituntil* period. Since $\vec{a_t}$ is the value of $\vec{a}$ immediately before invoking the *waituntil* statement, $P(\vec{x}, \vec{a})$ and $P(\vec{x}, \vec{a_t})$ are semantic equivalent during the *waituntil* period. ■

Proposition 1 enables the complex predicate evaluation of *waituntil* statement in all threads. Given a complex predicate in a *waituntil* statement, in the sequel we substitute all the local variables with their values immediately before invoking the statement. The predicate can now be evaluated in all other threads during the *waituntil* period.

3.2 Relay invariance

As mentioned in Section 2, *signalAll* calls are sometimes unavoidable in the explicit-signal mechanism. In *AutoSynch*, *signalAll* calls are avoided by providing the *relay invariance*.

Definition 3 (Active and inactive thread). *Consider a thread that tries to access a monitor. If it is not waiting in a* waituntil *statement or has been signaled, then it is an* active *thread for the monitor. Otherwise, it is an* inactive *thread.*

Definition 4 (Relay invariance). *If there is a thread waiting for a predicate that is true, then there is at least one active thread; i.e., suppose W_T is the set of waiting threads whose conditions have become true, A_T is the set of active threads, then*

$$W_T \neq \phi \Rightarrow A_T \neq \phi$$

holds at all time.

AutoSynch uses the following mechanism for signaling.

Relay signaling rule: When a thread exits a monitor or goes into waiting state, it checks whether there is some thread waiting on a condition that has become true. If at least one such waiting thread exists, it signals that thread.

Proposition 2. *The relay signaling rule guarantees relay invariance.*

Proof. Suppose a thread T is waiting on the predicate P that is true. Since T is waiting on P, P must be false before T went to waiting state. There must exist another active thread R after T such that R changed the state of the monitor and made P true. According to the rule, R must signal T or another thread waiting for a condition that is true before leaving the monitor or going into waiting state. The thread signaled by R then becomes active. Therefore, the relay invariance holds. ■

Our framework guarantees progress by providing *relay invariance*. The concept behind relay invariance is that, the privilege to enter the monitor is transmitted from one thread to another thread whose condition has become true. For example, in Fig. 1, the consumer C tries to take 32 items; however, only 24 items are in the buffer at this moment. Then, C waits for the predicate $P : (count \geq 32)$ to be true. A producer, D, becomes active after C; D puts 16 items into the buffer and then leaves the monitor. Before leaving, D finds that P is true and then signals C; therefore, C becomes active again and takes 32 items of the buffer. Proposition 2 shows that the relay invariance holds in our automatic-signaling mechanism. Thus, *signalAll* calls are avoidable in *AutoSynch*. Note that, although at most one thread is signaled at any time; the signaled thread is not guaranteed to get the lock. Some other thread trying to acquire the lock could also get the lock. The signaled thread may need to go back as a waiting thread, since the state of the monitor may be changed. However, this situation is very rare in comparison with the *signalAll* call. The problem is now reduced to finding a thread waiting for a condition that is true.

3.3 Predicate tag

In order to efficiently find an appropriate thread waiting for a predicate that is true, we analyze every waiting condition and assign different tags to every predicate according to its semantics. These tags help us prune predicates that are not true by examining the state of the monitor. The idea behind the predicate tag is that, local variables cannot be changed during the *waituntil* period; thus the values of local variables are used as keys when we evaluate predicates. First, we define two types of predicates according to their semantics.

Definition 5 (Local and shared expression). *Consider an expression $E(\vec{x}) : X \rightarrow \mathbb{D}$, where $\mathbb{D}$ represents one of the primitive data types in Java. If $X \subseteq L$, then E is a local expression. Otherwise, if $X \subseteq S$, E is a shared expression.*

We use SE to denote a shared expression, and LE to denote a local expression.

Definition 6 (Equivalence predicate). *A predicate $P : (SE = LE)$ is an equivalence predicate.*

Definition 7 (Threshold predicate). *A predicate $P : (SE$ **op** $LE)$ is a threshold predicate, where* **op** $\in \{<, \leq, >, \geq\}$.

Note that, many predicates that are not equivalence or threshold predicates can be transformed into them. Consider the predicate $(x - a = y + b)$, where $x, y \in S$ and $a, b \in L$. This predicate is equivalent to $(x - y = a + b)$ which is an equivalence predicate. Thus, these two types of predicates can represent a wide range of conditions in synchronization problems.

Given an *Equivalence* or a *Threshold* predicate, we can apply the *closure* operation to derive a constant value on the right hand side of the predicate. In *AutoSynch*, there are three types of tags, $Equivalence$, $Threshold$, and *None*. Every $Equivalence$ or $Threshold$ tag represents an equivalence predicate or a threshold predicate, respectively. If the predicate is neither equivalence nor threshold, it acquires the *None* tag. For example, consider the $Threshold$ predicate $x + b > 2y + a$ where a and b are local variables with values 11 and 2. We first use the closure to convert it to $(x - 2y > 9)$, which is represented by the tag $(Threshold,\ x - 2y,\ 9,\ >)$. The formal definition of tag is as follows.

Definition 8. *A tag is a four-tuple $(M,\ expr,\ key,\ op)$, where*

- $M \in \{Equivalence,\ Threshold,\ None\}$;
- *$expr$ is a shared expression if $M \in \{Equivalence,\ Threshold\}$; otherwise, $expr = \perp$;*
- *key is the value of a local expression after applying closure if $M \in \{Equivalence,\ Threshold\}$; otherwise, $key = \perp$;*
- *$op \in \{<, \leq, >, \geq\}$ if $M = Threshold$; otherwise, $op = \perp$.*

We say that a tag is true (false) if the predicate representing the tag is true (false).

3.3.1 Predicate tagging

Tags are given to every predicate by the algorithm shown in Fig. 3. A tag is assigned to every conjunction. The tags of conjunctions of a predicate constitute the set of tags of the predicate. When assigning a tag to a conjunction, the equivalence tag has the highest priority because the set of values that make an equivalence predicate true is smaller than the set of values that make a threshold predicate true. For example, the equivalence predicate $x = 8$ is true only when the value of x is 8, whereas the threshold predicate $x > 3$ is true for a much larger set of values. Therefore, the $Equivalence$ tags can help us prune predicates that are false more efficiently than other kinds of tags. If a conjunction does not include any equivalence predicate, then we check whether it includes any threshold predicate. If yes, then a $Threshold$ tag is assigned to the conjunction; otherwise, the conjunction has a *None* tag.

```
tags = empty
foreach conjunction c
  if c contains an equivalence predicate se=le
    tag t = (Equivalence, se, closure(le), null)
  else if c contains a threshold predicate se op le
    tag t = (Threshold, se, closure(le), op)
  else
    tag t = (None, null, null, null)
  add t to tags
return tags
```

Figure 3: Predicate Tagging

Creating all tags for a conjunction is unnecessary. If a conjunction includes multiple equivalence predicates or threshold predicates, only one arbitrary $Equivalence$ tag or $Threshold$ tag is assigned to the conjunction. If there are a large number of tags, then the performance may decrease because of the cost of maintaining tags. Assigning multiple tags to a conjunction cannot accelerate the searching process. For example, consider a conjunction $(x = 8) \wedge (y = 9)$. If only a tag $(Equivalence,\ x,\ 8,\ null)$ is assigned to the conjunction, we check the predicate when the tag is true. Adding another tag $(Equivalence,\ y,\ 9,\ null)$ cannot accelerate the searching process since we need to check both the tags. Note that multiple predicates with a shared conjunct may share a tag. For example, the predicates $(x = 5) \wedge (z \leq 4)$ and $(x = 5) \wedge (y \geq 4)$ would have a shared equivalence tag of $(x = 5)$.

As another example, consider the predicate $p = ((x < 5) \wedge (y = 3)) \vee ((x > 5) \wedge (foo2())) \vee foo1()$, where x and y are shared variables, and, $foo1()$ and $foo2()$ are boolean functions. The predicate p has three tags, $(Equivalence,\ y,\ 3,\ null)$ for the clause $(x < 5) \wedge (y = 3)$, $(Threshold,\ x, 5, >)$ for the clause $(x > 5) \wedge (foo2())$, and *None* tag for $foo1()$.

3.3.2 Tag signaling

Signaling mechanism is based on tags in *AutoSynch*. Since the equivalence tag is more efficient in pruning the search space than the threshold tag, the predicates with equivalence are checked prior to the predicates with other tags. If no true predicate is found after checking *Equivalence* tags and *Threshold* tags, our algorithm does the exhaustive search for the predicates with a *None* tag.

Equivalence tag signaling: Observe that, an equivalence predicate becomes true only when its shared expression equals the specific value of its local expression after applying *closure*. For distinct equivalence tags related to the same shared expression, at most one tag can be true at a time because the value of its local expression is deterministic and unique at any time. By observing the value of its local expression, the appropriate tag can be identified. For example, suppose there are three *Equivalence* tags for predicates $x = 3$, $x = 6$, and $x = 8$. We examine x and find that its value is 8. Then we know that only the third predicate $x = 8$ is true. Based on this observation, for each unique shared expression of an equivalence tag, we create a hash table, where the value of the local expression is used as the key. By using this hash table and evaluating the shared expression at runtime, we can find a tag that is true in $O(1)$ time if there is any. Then we check the predicates having the tag.

Threshold tag signaling: Threshold tag signaling exploits monotonicity of the predicate to reduce the complexity of evaluating predicates. For example, suppose there are two predicates, $x > 5$ and $x > 3$. We know that if $x > 3$ is false, then $x > 5$ cannot be true. Hence, we only need to check the predicate with the smallest local expression value for $>$ and $\geq$ operations. Similarly, the predicate $x > 3$ cannot be true when $x \geq 3$ is false; i.e., we only need to check the predicate $x \geq 3$. We use a min-heap data structure for storing the threshold tags related to a same shared expression with ***op*** $\in \{>, \geq\}$. If two predicates have the same local expression value but different operations, then the predicate with $\geq$ is considered to have a smaller value than the predicate with $>$ in the min-heap. Dually, the max-heap is used for threshold tags with ***op*** $\in \{<, \leq\}$.

The signaling mechanism for $Threshold$ tag is shown if Fig. 4. In general, the tag in the root of a heap is checked. If the tag is false, all the descendant nodes are also false. Otherwise, all predicates having the tag need to be checked for finding a true predicate. To maintain the correctness, if no predicate is true, the tag is removed from the heap temporarily. Then the tag in the position of the new heap root is checked again until a true predicate is found or a false tag is found. Those tags removed temporarily are reinserted in the heap. The reason to remove the tags is that the descendants of the tags may also be true since the tags are true. So we also need to check the descendant tags. For example, consider the predicates $P_1 : (x \geq 5) \wedge (y \neq 1)$ and $P_2 : (x > 7)$. P_1 has the tag $Q_1 : (Threshold,\ x,\ 5,\ \geq)$ and P_2 has the tag $Q_2 : (Threshold,\ x,\ 7,\ >)$. Q_1 is the root and Q_2 is its descendant. Suppose at some time instant $x = 3$, then Q_1 is false; thus, there is no need to check Q_2. Now, suppose $x = 9$ and $y = 1$, then Q_1 is true. We check all predicates that have tag Q_1. Since P_1 is false, no predicate having tag Q_1 is true. Then Q_1 is removed form the heap temporarily. We find the new root Q_2 is true and P_2 that has tag Q_2 is also true. We signal a thread waiting for P_2 and then add Q_1 back to the heap.

```
list backup = empty;
tag t = heap.peek(); //retrieve but not remove the root
while t is true
  foreach predicate p with t
    if p is true
      signal a thread waiting on p
      foreach b in backup
        heap.add(b)
      return
  backup.insert(heap.poll()) //retrieve and remove the root
  t = heap.peek()
foreach b in backup
  heap.add(b)
```

Figure 4: Threshold tag signaling

Suppose there are n $Threshold$ tags for a shared expression with different keys, and these tags are assigned to m predicates. The time complexity for maintaining the heap is $O(n \log(n))$ However, the performance is generally much better because we only need to check the predicates of the tags in the root position in the most cases. The time complexity for finding the root is $O(1)$. In the worst case, we need to check all predicates; thus, the time complexity is $O(n \log(n) + m)$. However, this situation is rare. Furthermore, this algorithm is optimized for evaluating threshold predicates by sacrificing performance in tag management.

4. *AutoSynch* implementation

The *AutoSynch* implementation involves two parts, the preprocessor and the Java library of condition manager. The preprocessor, built using JavaCC [17], translates *AutoSynch* code to Java code. Our signal-mechanism is implemented in the condition manager library that creates condition variables, and maintains the association between predicates and condition variables. Furthermore, predicate tags are also maintained by the condition manager. It is the responsibility of the condition manager to decide which thread should be signaled.

4.1 Preprocessor

The *AutoSynch* class provides both mutual exclusion and conditional synchronization. To maintain these two properties, our preprocessor adds some additional variables for any *AutoSynch* class. Fig. 5 summarizes the definitions of additional variables in the constructor of an *AutoSynch* class. The lock variable, $mutex$, is declared for mutual exclusion, which is acquired at the beginning of every member function and released before the return statement. In addition, a condition manager, $condMgr$, is declared for synchronization. The details of the condition manager are discussed in the next section.

```
Lock mutex
ConditionManager condMgr
foreach shared predicate P
  tags = AnalyzePredicate(toDNF(P))
  condMgr.registerSharedPredicate(P, tags)
foreach shared expression E
  condMgr.registerSharedExpression(E)
```

Figure 5: The additional variables for an *AutoSynch* class

All predicates are transformed to DNF in the preprocessing process by De Morgan's laws and distributive law. Then predicates are analyzed to derive tags by our preprocessor. The shared predicates and shared expressions are identified in the preprocessing stage and registered to the condition manager in the constructor of the class for predicate evaluation at runtime as in Fig. 5. Shared predicates and shared expressions (but not complex predicates) are registered in the construct because their semantics is static and never changes. A complex predicate is registered dynamically because its closure may change according to the value of its local variables at runtime. In Java, the predicates and shared expressions are created as inner classes that can access the shared variables appearing in them with $isTrue()$ or $getValue()$ functions for the condition manager to evaluate. The function $isTrue()$ returns the evaluation of a predicate and the function $getValue()$ returns the value of a shared expression.

For every member function of an *AutoSynch* class, the *mutex.lock()* and *mutex.unlock()* are inserted at the beginning of the function and immediately before the *return* statement, respectively.

In the *waituntil* statement, the predicate is checked initially at runtime. If it is true, then the thread can continue. Otherwise, the type of predicate is checked. If the predicate is complex, then $closure$ is applied to it for deriving a new shared predicate. Then the condition manager is queried to determine whether the derived predicate has been registered earlier. If not, the condition manager registers the predicate with its tags. The corresponding condition variable can be obtained by calling *getCondition()* function of the condition manager. The *relaySignal()* function is called to maintain relay invariance and signal an appropriate thread. Then, the thread goes into the waiting state until its predicate becomes true and some other thread signals it. After exiting the waiting state, if the predicate is complex and the corresponding condition has no other waiting thread, the predicate is deactivated by the condition manager.

```
if P is false
  if P is a complex predicate
    P := Closure(toDNF(P))
    if P is not in condMgr
      tags = AnalyzePredicate(P)
      condMgr.registerComplexPredicate(P, tags)
  C = condMgr.getCondition(P)
  do
    condMgr.relaySignal()
    wait C
  while P is false
  if P is complex predicate and C has no waiting thread
    condMgr.deactivate(P)
```

Figure 6: Preprocessing for a *waituntil(P)* statement

4.2 *AutoSynch* Java library: condition manager

The condition manager maintains the predicates and condition variables, and provides the signaling mechanism. To avoid creating redundant predicates and condition variables, predicates that have the same meaning should be mapped to the same condition variable. Two predicates are syntax equivalent if they are identical after applying closure. A predicate table, which is implemented by using a hash table, records predicates and their associated condition variables.

When a predicate is added to the condition manager, its tags are stored in an appropriate data structure depending upon the type of its tag. Fig. 7 shows an example. The symbol • indicates a condition variable. The gray blank indicates that the predicate is deactivated, that is, no thread waits on it. A hash table is used for storing equivalence tags with the shared expression x. In addition, a min-heap and a max-heap are used for storing threshold tags.

For finding a predicate that is true in Fig. 7, the value of the shared expression x is evaluated. The hash table of the equivalence tag is checked (with $O(1)$ time complexity) using the value of the shared expression as the key. If a tag is found, then the predicates that have the tag are evaluated. If there exists a predicate that is true, then its corresponding condition variable is signaled. Otherwise, the max-heap and the min-heap of the threshold tag are checked. If both tags of their roots are false, the predicates with the *None* tag are searched exhaustively. If one of these predicates is true, its corresponding condition variable is signaled. As can be expected, the equivalence and threshold tags are helpful for searching predicates that are true.

A predicate must be removed from the predicate table once it has become deactivated to avoid unnecessary predicate evaluation. A threshold tag also needs to be removed once all of its predicates have become deactivated.

Predicates may be reused. Instead of removing deactivated predicates, those predicates are moved to a deactivated list. If they are used later, then we remove them from the deactivated list and add them back to the predicate table and its tags. Otherwise, when the length of the deactivated list exceeds some predefined threshold, we remove the oldest predicates from the list. Note that, the shared predicates are never removed since they are static and are added only at the constructor level.

5. Evaluation

We present the experimental setup and its results to evaluate the performance of *AutoSynch* in this section. We compare the performance of different signaling mechanisms in three sets of classical conditional synchronization problems. The first set of problems relies on only shared predicates for synchronization. Next, we explore the performance for problems using complex predicates. Finally, we evaluate the problems in which *signalAll* calls are required in the explicit-signal mechanism.

5.1 Experimental environment

All of the experiments were conducted on a machine with 16 Intel(R) Xeon(R) X5560 Quad Core CPUs (2.80 GHz) and 64 GBs memory running Linux 2.6.18.

We conducted two types of experiments. The first is a *saturation* test [5], in which only monitor accessing functions performed. That is, no extra work is performed in the monitor or out of the monitor. The other set of experiments simulate different workloads of the monitors [4]. For each monitor operation, there is a fixed time to perform other operations out of the monitor. For every experiment, we ran the program 25 times, and removed the best and the worst results. Then we compared the average runtime for different signaling mechanisms.

We do not report memory usage due to space limitations. Although some additional data structures are created in our framework, the additional memory consumption is insignificant. The reason is that, whenever a predicate has no waiting thread, it is put in an inactive list for reuse. If the size of the inactive list exceeds a predefined threshold, e.g. $2n$ (n is the number of threads), then we remove the oldest predicate and the conditional variable from the list and the table. Moreover, the size of active predicates is always less than n.

5.2 Signaling mechanisms

Four implementations using different signaling mechanisms have been compared.

Explicit-signal Using the original Java explicit-signal mechanism.

Baseline Using the automatic-signal mechanism relying on only one condition variable. It calls *signalAll* to wake every waiting thread. Then each thread that wakes up re-evaluates its own predicate after re-acquiring the monitor.

AutoSynch-T Using the approach described in this paper but excluding predicate tagging.

AutoSynch Using the approach described in this paper.

5.3 Test problems

Seven conditional synchronization problems are implemented for evaluating our approach.

5.3.1 Shared predicate synchronization problems

Bounded-buffer [8, 10] This is the traditional bounded-buffer problem. Every producer waits if the buffer is full, while every consumer waits if the buffer is empty.

H_2O **problem [1]** This is the simulation of water generation. Every H atom waits if there is no O atom or another H atom. Every O atom waits if the number of H atoms is less than 2.

5.3.2 Complex predicate synchronization problems

Round-Robin Access Pattern Every test thread accesses the monitor in round-robin order.

Readers/Writers [7] We use the approach given in [5], where a ticket is used to maintain the accessing order of readers and

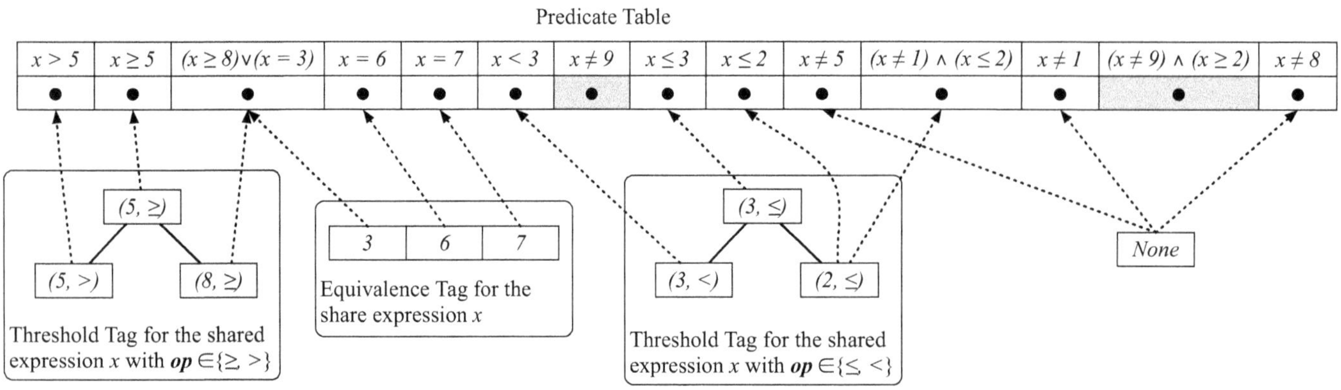

Figure 7: A example of the condition manager in *AutoSynch*

writers. Every reader and writer gets a ticket number indicating its arrival order. Readers and writers wait on the monitor for their turn.

Dining philosophers [10] This problem requires coordination among philosophers sitting around a table and is described in [10].

5.3.3 Synchronization problems requiring *signalAll* in explicit

Parameterized bounded-buffer [8, 10] The parameterized bounded-buffer problem shown in Fig. 1.

5.4 Experimental results

Fig. 8 and 9 plot the results for the bounded-buffer and the H_2O problem. The y-axis shows the runtime in seconds. The x-axis represents the number of simulating threads. Note that, in the H_2O problem, only one thread simulates an O atom. The x-axis represents the number of threads simulating H atoms. As expected, the baseline is much slower than other three signaling mechanisms, which have similar performance in the both problems. This phenomenon can be explained as follows. There is only a constant number of shared predicates in *waituntil* statements for automatic-signal mechanisms. For example, in the bounded-buffer problem, there are two *waituntil* statements with global predicates, $count > 0$ (not empty condition) and $count < buff.length$ (not full condition). Therefore, the complexity for signaling a thread in *AutoSynch* and *AutoSynch-T* is also constant. Hence, both *AutoSynch* and *AutoSynch-T* are as efficient as the explicit-signal mechanism. These experiments illustrate that the automatic-signal mechanisms are as efficient as the explicit-signal mechanisms for synchronization problems relying on only shared predicates.

Fig. 10, 11 12 present the experimental results for the round-robin access pattern, the readers/writers problem, and the dining philosophers problem. The result of the baseline is not plotted in these figures since its performance is extremely inefficient in comparison with other mechanisms. In this set of experiments, the explicit-signal mechanism has an advantage since it can explicitly signal the next thread to enter the monitor. For example, in the round-robin access pattern, an array of condition variables is used for associating the id of each thread and its condition variable. Each thread waits on its condition variable until its turn. When a thread leaves the monitor, it signals the condition variable of the next thread. As can be seen, the performance of explicit-signal mechanism is steady as the number of threads increases in the round-robin access pattern and the reader/writers problem. In *AutoSynch-T*, its runtime increases significantly as the number of threads increase. For *AutoSynch*, the performance is between 1.2 to 2.6 times slower

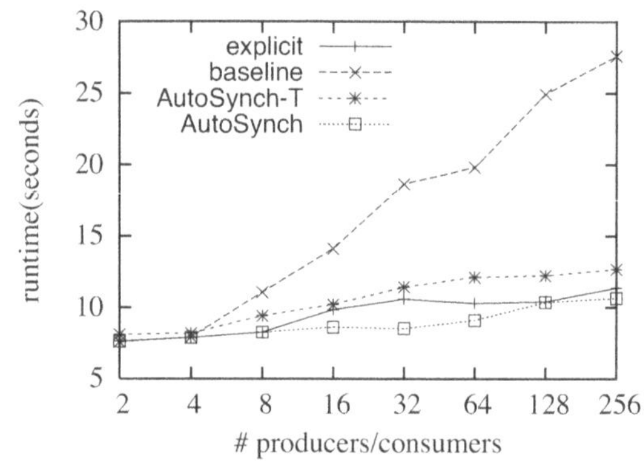

Figure 8: The results of bounded-buffer problem

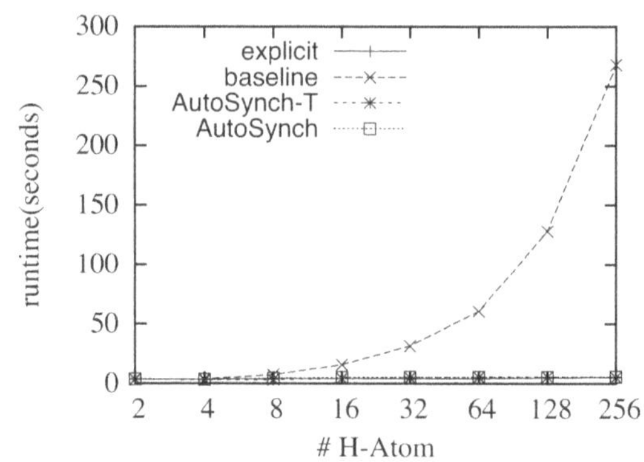

Figure 9: The results of H_2O problem

than the explicit-signal mechanism for the round-robin access pattern. However, the performance of *AutoSynch* does not decrease as the number of threads increases. Note that, in the readers/writers problem, the *AutoSynch-T* is more efficient than *AutoSynch* when the number of threads is small. The reason is that *AutoSynch* sacrifices performance for maintaining predicate tags. The benefit of predicate tagging increases as the number of threads increases. Another interesting point is that the performance of the explicit signal mechanism does not outperform implicit signal mechanisms much in the dining philosophers problem. The reason is that a philosopher only competes with two other philosophers sitting near him even when the number of philosophers increases.

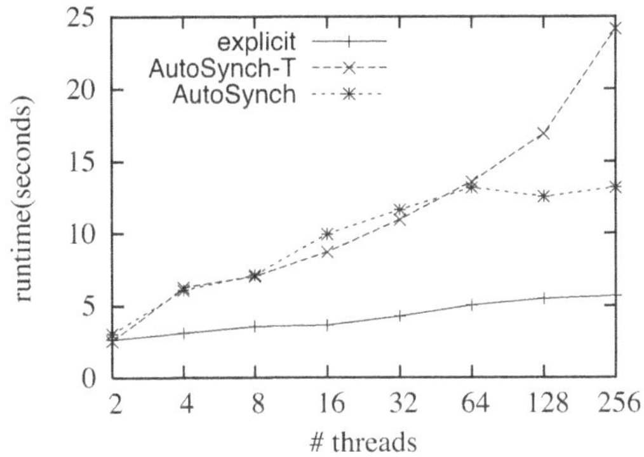

Figure 10: The results of round-robin access pattern

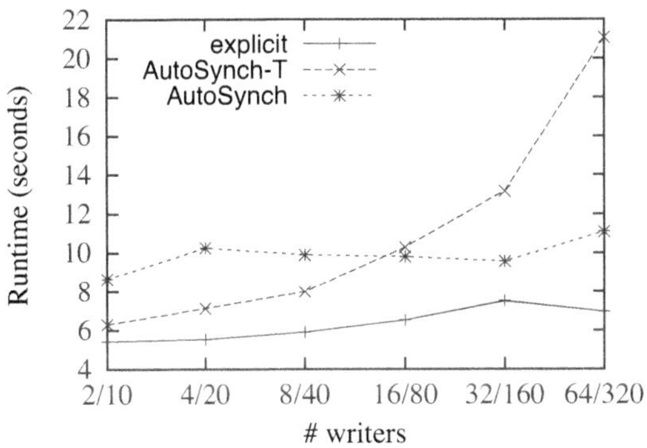

Figure 11: The results of readers/writers problem

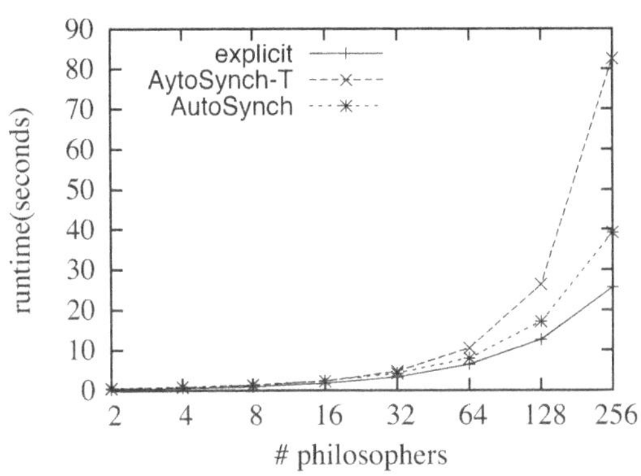

Figure 12: The results of dining philosophers problem

Table 1 presents the CPU usage (profiled by YourKit [20]) for the round-robin access pattern with 128 threads. The *relaySignal* is the process of deciding which thread should be signaled in both *AutoSynch* and *AutoSynch-T*. *Tag Mger* is the computation for maintaining predicate tags in *AutoSynch*. As can be seen, the predicate tagging significantly improves the process for finding a predicate that is true. The CPU time of *relaySingal* process is reduced 95% with a slightly increased cost in tag management.

In Fig. 13, we compare the results of the parameterized bounded-buffer in which *signalAll* calls are required in the explicit-signal mechanism. In this experiment, there is one producer, which randomly puts 1 to 128 items every time. The y-axis indicates the number of consumers. Every consumer randomly takes 1 to 128 items every time. As can be seen, the performance of the explicit-signal mechanism decreases as the number of consumers increases. *AutoSynch* outperforms the explicit-signal mechanism by 26.9 times when the number of threads is 256. This can be explained by Fig. 14 that depicts the number of contexts switches. The number of context switches increases in the explicit-signal mechanism in which the number of context switches is around 2.7 million when the number of threads is 256. However, the numbers of context switches are stable in *AutoSynch* even when the number of threads increase. It has around 5440 context switches when the number of threads is 256. This experiment demonstrates that the number of context switches can be dramatically reduced and the performance can be increased in *AutoSynch* for the problems requiring *signalAll* calls in the explicit-signal mechanism.

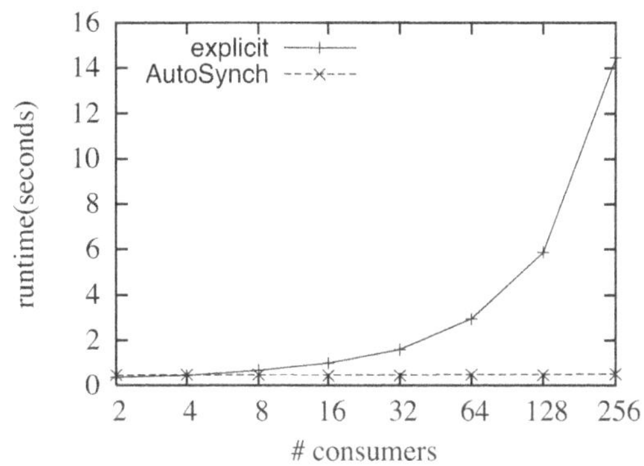

Figure 13: The results of the parameterized bounded-buffer problem

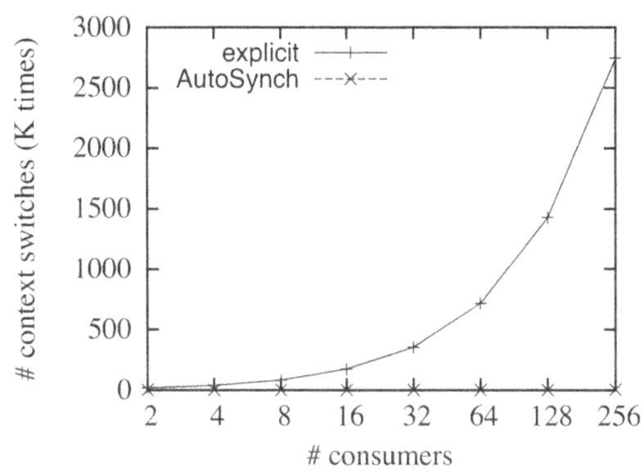

Figure 14: The number of context switches of the parametrized bounded-buffer problem

Fig. 15 and 16 present the run time ratio of our approaches and the *explicit* approach for the round-robin access pattern with 256 threads and the readers/writers problem with 64 writers and 320 readers. The y-axis indicates the runtime ratio and the x-axis shows the delay time, the amount of time in which the threads perform operations out of the monitor between every two monitor operations, in microseconds. As expected, the performance difference decreases as the duration of delay time increases. *AutoSynch* is two times slower than the explicit approach with no delay time (saturation test) for round-robin access pattern. However, when the duration of delay time is 5000 microseconds, *AutoSynch* is only 7.7%

	await		lock		relaySignal		Tag Mger		others		total
	T	%	T	%	T	%	T	%	T	%	T
explicit	21365	99.7%	28	0.15%	NA	NA	NA	NA	28	0.15%	21433
AutoSynch-T	410377	98.5%	3140	0.7%	2108	0.5%	NA	NA	1033	0.2%	416658
AutoSynch	96754	98.8%	812	0.8%	112	0.1%	124	0.1%	148	0.02%	97950

Table 1: The CPU usage for the round robin access pattern

slower than the explicit approach. Note that, even *AutoSynch-T* performs well when the duration of delay time increases. The similar observation can be seen for the readers/writers problem in Fig. 16. The results suggest that our approach could be more useful for practical problems that perform more monitor unrelated operations.

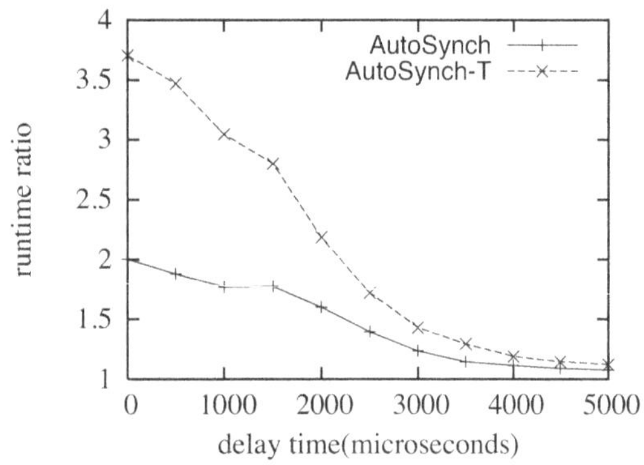

Figure 15: The runtime ratio of round-robin

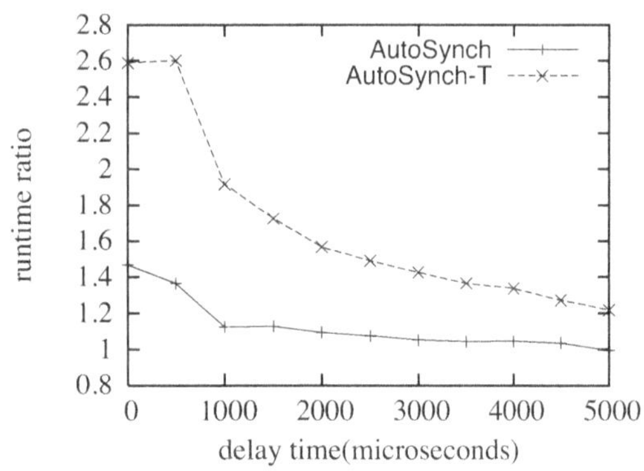

Figure 16: The runtime ratio of ticket readers/writers

6. Future Work

Fairness is not guaranteed in our system. Our approach favors signaling a thread waiting on a predicate that is likely to be true. We focus on the efficiency of our automatic-signal monitor at this point. Fairness may be an important issue for some concurrent applications and we plan to address it in future. Buhr and Harji simulated implicit-signal monitors with explicit monitors [5]. Their approach provides fairness and deals with staleness/freshness issues. However, their approach does not focus on the efficiency.

In the future, we plan to optimize our framework through using the architecture information. For example, we can get the number of cores of a machine, and then limit the number of executing threads to avoid unnecessary contention. Our current implementation of *AutoSynch* is built upon constructs provided by Java. Thus, there is possibility of further performance improvement if the approach was to be implemented within the JVM.

Acknowledgement

The authors thank Himanshu Chauhan, Yen-Jung Chang, John Bridgman, and Craig Chase for the helpful discussions and comments to improve the paper. This work was supported in part by the NSF Grants CNS-1115808, CNS-0718990, and Cullen Trust for Higher Education Endowed Professorship.

References

[1] G. R. Andrews. *Multithreaded, Parallel, and Distributed Programming*. Addison-Wesley, MA, 2000.

[2] P. Brinch Hansen, *The Programming language concurrent Pascal*. IEEE Trans. Software Engineering, 1(2), 199–207, June, 1975.

[3] P. Brinch Hansen, *Structured multiprogramming*. Commun. ACM 15(7), 574–578, July 1972.

[4] P. A. Buhr, M. Fortier, and M. H. Coffin, *Monitor Classification*. ACM Computing Surveys, ACM, 27(1), 63–107, Mar. 1995.

[5] P. A. Buhr and A. S. Harji, *Implicit-signal monitors*. ACM Transactions on Programming Languages and Systems ACM, 27(6):1270–1343, Nov. 2005.

[6] D. R. Butenhof, *Programming With Posix Threads*. Addison-Wesley, MA, 1997.

[7] P. J. Courtois, F. Heymans, D. L. Parnars, *Concurrent control with "readers" and "writers"*. Commun. ACM, 14(10), 667–668, Oct. 1971.

[8] E. W. Dijkstra, *Cooperating Sequential Processes*. Technical Report EWD-123, 1965.

[9] E. W. Dijkstra, *The structure of the "THE"-multiprogramming system*. Commun. ACM, 11(5), 341 – 346, May 1968.

[10] E. W. Dijkstra, *Hierarchical Ordering of Sequential Processes*. Acta Informatica, 1, 115 – 138, 1971.

[11] J. Gosling, B. Joy, and G. Steele, *The Java Language Specification*. 2nd ed. Addison-Wesley, MA, 2000.

[12] V. K. Garg and N. Mittal, *A Critique of Java for Concurrent Programming*, IEEE Distributed Systems online 6(9), 2005.

[13] A. Hejisberg, S. Wiltamuth, and P. Golde, *C# Language Specification*. Addison-Wesley, MA, 2003.

[14] C. A. R. Hoare, *Monitors: an operating system structuring concept*. Commun. ACM, 17(10), 549–557, Oct. 1974.

[15] Y.-J. Joung, *Asynchronous group mutual exclusion*. ACM Symposium on Principles of Distributed Computing, 51–60, Aug. 1998.

[16] J. L. W. Kessels. *An alternative to event queues for synchronization in monitors*. Commun. ACM, 20(7), 500–503, July 1977.

[17] V. Kodaganallur, *Incorporating language processing into Java applications: a JavaCC tutorial*. IEEE Software, 21(4), 70–77, July–Aug. 2004.

[18] D. Lea, *The java.util.concurrent synchronizer framework*. Science of Computer Programming, 58(3), 293 – 309, Dec. 2005.

[19] B. Stroustrup, *The C++ Programming Language*. 3rd ed. Addison-Wesley, MA, 1997.

[20] Yourkit LLC, *Yourkit profiler*. http://www.yourkir.com

Concurrent Libraries with Foresight

Guy Golan-Gueta
Tel Aviv University
ggolan@tau.ac.il

G. Ramalingam
Microsoft Research
grama@microsoft.com

Mooly Sagiv
Tel Aviv University
msagiv@tau.ac.il

Eran Yahav
Technion
yahave@cs.technion.ac.il

Abstract

Linearizable libraries provide operations that appear to execute atomically. Clients, however, may need to execute a sequence of operations (a *composite operation*) atomically. We consider the problem of extending a linearizable library to support arbitrary atomic composite operations by clients. We introduce a novel approach in which the concurrent library ensures atomicity of composite operations by exploiting information (*foresight*) provided by its clients. We use a correctness condition, based on a notion of dynamic right-movers, that guarantees that composite operations execute atomically without deadlocks, and without using rollbacks.

We present a static analysis to infer the foresight information required by our approach, allowing a compiler to automatically insert the foresight information into the client. This relieves the client programmer of this burden and simplifies writing client code.

We present a generic technique for extending the library implementation to realize foresight-based synchronization. This technique is used to implement a general-purpose Java library for Map data structures — the library permits composite operations to simultaneously work with multiple instances of Map data structures.

We use the Maps library and the static analysis to enforce atomicity of a wide selection of real-life Java composite operations. Our experiments indicate that our approach enables realizing efficient and scalable synchronization for real-life composite operations.

Categories and Subject Descriptors D.1.3 [*Programming Techniques*]: Concurrent Programming; D.3.1 [*Programming Languages*]: Formal Definitions and Theory; D.3.3 [*Programming Languages*]: Language Constructs and Features—Abstract data types, Concurrent programming structures, Data types and structures

Keywords Concurrency, Composition, Transactions, Data Structures, Automatic Synchronization

PLDI'13, June 16–19, 2013, Seattle, WA, USA.

1. Introduction

Writing concurrent software is hard and error prone. To ease the programmer's burden, programming languages such as Java, Scala, and C# provide libraries of efficient concurrent data structures. These libraries provide operations that are guaranteed to be *atomic*, while hiding the complexity of the implementation from clients. Unfortunately, clients often need to perform a *sequence of library operations that appears to execute atomically*, referred to hereafter as an *atomic composite operation*.

The problem of realizing atomic composite operations is an important and widespread one [9]. Atomic composite operations are a restricted form of *software transactions* [15]. However, general-purpose software transaction implementations have not gained acceptance [10] due to their high overhead as well as difficulties in using libraries that are incompatible with software transactions. Programmers typically realize such composite operations using ad-hoc synchronization leading to many concurrency bugs in practice [27].

Concurrency Control with Foresight In this paper, we address the problem of extending a linearizable library [19] to allow clients to execute an arbitrary composite operation atomically. Our basic methodology requires the client code to demarcate the sequence of operations for which atomicity is desired and provide declarative information to the library (*foresight*) about the library operations that the composite operation may invoke (as illustrated later). It is the library's responsibility to ensure the desired atomicity, exploiting the foresight information for effective synchronization.

Our first contribution is a formalization of this approach. We formalize the desired goals and present a sufficient correctness condition. As long as the clients and the library extension satisfy the correctness condition, all composite operations are guaranteed atomicity without deadlocks. Furthermore, our condition does not require the use of rollbacks. Our sufficiency condition is broad and permits a range of implementation options and fine-grained synchronization. It is based on a notion of *dynamic right-movers*, which generalizes traditional notions of static right-movers and commutativity [21, 23].

Our formulation decouples the implementation of the library from the client. Thus, the correctness of the client does not depend on the way the foresight information is used by library implementation. The client only needs to ensure the correctness of the foresight information.

Automatic Foresight for Clients We then present a simple static analysis to infer calls (in the client code) to the API used to pass the foresight information. Given a description of a library's API, our algorithm conservatively infers the required calls. This relieves the client programmer of this burden and simplifies writing atomic composite operations.

Library Extension Realization Our approach permits the use of customized, hand-crafted, implementations of the library extension. However, we also present a generic technique for extending a linearizable library with foresight. The technique is based on a variant of the tree locking protocol in which the tree is designed according to semantic properties of the library's operations.

We used our technique to implement a general-purpose Java library for Map data structures. Our library permits composite operations to simultaneously work with multiple instances of Map data structures.

Experimental Evaluation We use the Maps library and the static analysis to enforce atomicity of a wide selection of real-life Java composite operations, including composite operations that manipulate multiple instances of Map data structures. Our experiments indicate that our approach enables realizing efficient and scalable synchronization for real-life composite operations.

Main Contributions We develop the concept of *concurrent libraries with foresight* along several dimensions, providing the theoretical foundations, an implementation methodology, and an empirical evaluation. Our main contributions are:

- We introduce the concept of concurrent libraries with foresight, in which the concurrent library ensures atomicity of composite operations by exploiting information (foresight) provided by its clients. The main idea is to shift the responsibility of synchronizing composite operations of the clients to the hands of the library, and have the client provide useful foresight information to make efficient library-side synchronization possible.
- We define a sufficient correctness condition for clients and the library extension. Satisfying this condition guarantees atomicity and deadlock-freedom of composite operations (Sec. 4).
- We show how to realize both the client-side (Sec. 5) and the library-side (Sec. 6) for leveraging foresight. Specifically, we present a static analysis algorithm that provides foresight information to the library (Sec. 5), and show a generic technique for implementing a family of libraries with foresight (Sec. 6).
- We realized our approach and evaluated it on a number of real-world composite operations. We show that our approach provides efficient synchronization (Sec. 7).

2. Overview

We now present an informal overview of our approach, for extending a linearizable library into a library with foresight-based synchronization, using a toy example. Fig. 1 presents the specification of a single Counter (library). The counter can be incremented (via the `Inc()` operation), decremented (via the `Dec()` operation), or read (via the `Get()` operation). The counter's value is always nonnegative: the execution of `Dec()` has an effect only when the counter's value is positive. All the counter's procedures are atomic.

Fig. 2 shows an example of two threads each executing a *composite operation*: a code fragment consisting of multiple counter operations. (The **mayUse** annotations will be explained later.) Our goal is to execute these composite operations atomically: a *serializable* execution of these two threads is one that is equivalent to either thread T_1 executing completely before T_2 executes or vice versa. Assume that the counter value is initially zero. If T_2 executes first, then neither decrement operation will change the counter value, and the subsequent execution of T_1 will produce a counter value of 2. If T_1 executes first and then T_2 executes, the final value of the counter will be 0. Fig. 3 shows a slightly more complex example.

```
int value = I;
void Inc() { atomic { value=value+1; } }
void Dec() { atomic { if (value > 0) then value=value-1; } }
int Get() { atomic { return value; } }
```

Figure 1. Specification of the Counter library. *I* denotes the initial value of the counter.

```
/* Thread T1 */
/* @atomic */ {
  @mayUseInc()
  Inc();
  Inc();
  @mayUseNone()
}
```

```
/* Thread T2 */
/* @atomic */ {
  @mayUseDec()
  Dec();
  Dec();
  @mayUseNone()
}
```

Figure 2. Simple compositions of counter operations.

```
/* Thread T1 */
/* @atomic */ {
  @mayUseAll()
  c = Get();
  @mayUseInc()
  while (c > 0) {
    c = c-1;
    Inc();
  }
  @mayUseNone()
}
```

```
/* Thread T2 */
/* @atomic */ {
  @mayUseDec()
  Dec();
  Dec();
  @mayUseNone()
}
```

Figure 3. Compositions of counter dependent operations.

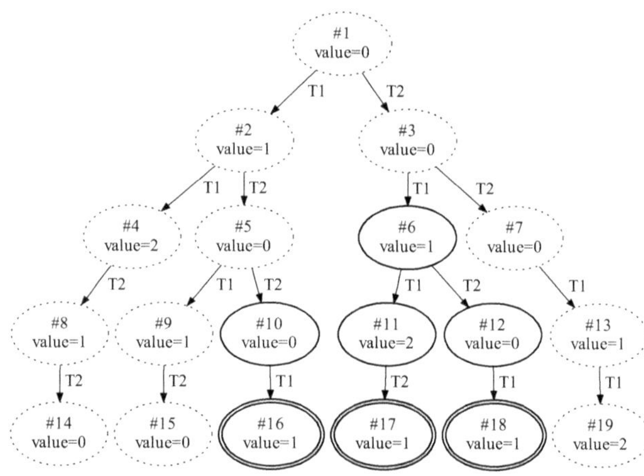

Figure 4. Execution prefixes of the code shown in Fig. 2, for a counter with $I = 0$. Each node represents a prefix of an execution; a leaf node represents a complete execution.

2.1 Serializable and Serializably-Completable Executions

Fig. 4 shows prefixes of various interleaved executions of the code shown in Fig. 2 for an initial counter value of 0. Nodes are annotated with the values of the counter. Bold double circles depict *non-serializable* nodes: these nodes denote execution prefixes that are not serializable. E.g., node #18 is a non-serializable node since it represents the non-serializable execution $T_2.Dec(); T_1.Inc(); T_2.Dec(); T_1.Inc()$ (which produces a final counter value of 1).

Bold single circles depict *doomed* nodes: once we reach a doomed node, there is no way to order the remaining operations in a way that achieves serializability. E.g., node #6 is a doomed node since it only leads to non-serializable complete executions (represented by nodes #17 and #18). Finally, dashed circles depict *safe* nodes, which represent *serializably-completable* executions. We formalize this notion later, but safe nodes guarantee that the execution can make progress, while ensuring serializability.

Our goal is to ensure that execution stays within safe nodes. Even in this simple example, the set of safe nodes and, hence, the potential for parallelism depends on the initial value I of the counter. For $I \geq 1$ all nodes are safe and thus no further synchronization is necessary. Using our approach enables realizing all available parallelism in this example (for every $I \geq 0$), while avoiding the need for any backtracking (i.e., rollbacks).

2.2 Serializably-Completable Execution: A Characterization

We now present a characterization of serializably-completable executions based on a generalization of the notion of *static right movers* [23]. We restrict ourselves to executions of two threads here, but our later formalization considers the general case.

We define an operation o by a thread T to be a *dynamic right-mover with respect to thread T' after an execution p*, iff for any sequence of operations s executed by T', if $p; T.o; s$ is feasible, then $p; s; T.o$ is feasible and equivalent to the first execution. Given an execution ξ, we define a relation $\sqsubset$ on the threads as follows: $T \sqsubset T'$ if ξ contains a prefix $p; T.o$ such that o is not a dynamic right-mover with respect to T' after p. As shown later, if $\sqsubset$ is acyclic, then ξ is a serializably-completable execution (as long as every sequential execution of the threads terminates).

In Fig. 4, node #2 represents the execution prefix $T_1.Inc()$ for which $T_1 \sqsubset T_2$.This is because $T_2.Dec()$ is a possible suffix executed by T_2, and $T_1.Inc(); T_2.Dec()$ is not equivalent to $T_2.Dec(); T_1.Inc()$. On the other hand, node #5 represents the execution prefix $T_1.Inc(); T_2.Dec()$ for which $T_2 \not\sqsubset T_1$.This execution has one possible suffix executed by T_1 (i.e., $T_1.Inc()$), and the execution $T_1.Inc(); T_2.Dec(); T_1.Inc()$ is equivalent to the execution $T_1.Inc(); T_1.Inc(); T_2.Dec()$.

Observe that the relation $\sqsubset$ corresponding to any non-serializable or doomed node has a cycle, while it is acyclic for all safe nodes.

Note that the use of a *dynamic* (i.e., *state-dependent*) right-mover relation is critical to a precise characterization above. E.g., Inc and Dec are not static right-movers with respect to each other.

2.3 Synchronization Using Foresight

We now show how we exploit the above characterization to ensure that an interleaved execution stays within safe nodes.

Foresight. A key aspect of our approach is to exploit knowledge about the possible future behavior of composite operations for more effective concurrency control. We enrich the interface of the library with operations that allow the composite operations to assert temporal properties of their future behavior. In the Counter example, assume that we add the following operations:

- **mayUseAll()**: indicates transaction may execute arbitrary operations in the future.
- **mayUseNone()**: indicates transaction will execute no more operation.
- **mayUseDec()**: indicates transaction will invoke only `Dec` operations in the future.
- **mayUseInc()**: indicates transaction will invoke only `Inc` operations in the future.

The code in Fig. 2 is annotated with calls to these operations in a straightforward manner. The code shown in Fig. 3, is conservatively annotated with a call to mayUseAll() since the interface does not provide a way to indicate that the transaction will only invoke `Get` and `Inc` operations.

Utilizing Foresight. We utilize a suitably modified definition of the dynamic right mover relation, where we check for the right mover condition only with respect to the set of all sequences of operations the other threads are allowed to invoke (as per their foresight assertions). To utilize foresight information, a library implementation maintains a conservative over-approximation $\sqsubset'$ of the $\sqsubset$ relation. The implementation permits an operation to proceed iff it will not cause the relation $\sqsubset'$ to become cyclic (and blocks the operation otherwise until it is safe to execute it). This is sufficient to guarantee that the composite operations appear to execute atomically, without any deadlocks.

We have created an implementation of the counter that (implicitly) maintains a conservative over-approximation $\sqsubset'$ (see [14]). Our implementation permits all serializably-completable execution prefixes for the example shown in Fig. 2 (for every $I \geq 0$). Our implementation also provides high degree of parallelism for the example shown in Fig. 3 — for this example the loop of T_1 can be executed in parallel to the execution of T_2.

Fine-grained Foresight. We define a library operation to be a tuple that identifies a procedure as well as the values of the procedure's arguments. For example, `removeKey(1)` and `removeKey(2)` are two **different** operations of a library with the procedure `removeKey(int k)`. In order to distinguish between different operations which are invoked using the same procedure, a *mayUse* procedure (which is used to pass the foresight information) can have parameters. For example, a library that represents a single Map data structure can have a *mayUse* procedure `mayUseKey(int k)`, where `mayUseKey(1)` is defined to refer to all operations on key 1 (including, for example, `removeKey(1)`), and `mayUseKey(2)` is defined to refer to all operations on key 2 (including, for example, `removeKey(2)`).

Special Cases. Our approach generalizes several ideas that have been proposed before. One example, from databases, is locking that is based on operations-commutativity (e.g., see [8, chapter 3.8]). Such locking provides several lock modes where each mode corresponds to a set of operations; two threads are allowed to execute in parallel as long as they do not hold lock modes that correspond to non-commutative operations. A simple common instance is a read-write lock [12], in which threads are allowed to simultaneously hold locks in a read-mode (which corresponds with read-only operations that are commutative with each other). Interestingly, the common `lock-acquire` and `lock-release` operations used for locking, can be seen as special cases of the procedures used to pass the foresight information.

2.4 Realizing Foresight Based Synchronization

What we have described so far is a methodology and formalism for foresight-based concurrency control. This prescribes the conditions that must be satisfied by the clients and library implementations to ensure atomicity for composite operations.

Automating Foresight For Clients. One can argue that adding calls to *mayUse* operations is an error prone process. Therefore, in Section 5 we show a simple static analysis algorithm which conservatively infers calls to *mayUse* operations (given a description of the *mayUse* operations supported by the library). Our experience indicates that our simple algorithm can handle real-life programs.

Library Implementation. We permit creating customized, handcrafted, implementations of the library extension (a simple example is demonstrated in [14]). However, in order to simplify creating such libraries, we present a generic technique for implementing a family of libraries with foresight (Section 6). The technique is based on a variant of the tree locking protocol in which the tree is designed according to semantic properties of the library's operations. We have utilized the technique to implement a general purpose Java library for Map data structures. Our library permits a composite operation to simultaneously work with multiple maps.

3. Preliminaries

3.1 Libraries

A library $\mathcal{A}$ exposes a set of procedures $\text{PROCS}_{\mathcal{A}}$. We define a library *operation* to be a tuple $(p, v_1, \cdots, v_k)$ consisting of a procedure name p and a sequence of values (representing actual values of the procedure arguments). The set of operations of a library $\mathcal{A}$ is denoted by $\text{OP}_{\mathcal{A}}$. Library operations are invoked by client threads (defined later). Let $\mathcal{T}$ denote the set of all thread identifiers. An *event* is a tuple (t, m, r), where t is a thread identifier, m is a library operation, and r is a return value. An event captures both an operation invocation as well as its return value.

A *history* is defined to be a finite sequence of events. The semantics of a library $\mathcal{A}$ is captured by a set of histories $H_{\mathcal{A}}$. If $h \in H_{\mathcal{A}}$, then we say that h is *feasible* for $\mathcal{A}$. Histories capture the interaction between a library and its client (a set of threads). Though multiple threads may concurrently invoke operations, this simple formalism suffices in our setting, since we assume the library to be linearizable. An *empty history* is an empty sequence of events.

Let $h \circ h'$ denote the concatenation of history h' to the end of history h. Note that the set $H_{\mathcal{A}}$ captures multiple aspects of the library's specification. If h is feasible, but $h \circ (t, m, r)$ is not, this could mean one of three different things: r may not be a valid return value in this context, or t is not allowed to invoke m is this context, or t is allowed to invoke m in this context, but the library will block and not return until some other event has happened.

A library $\mathcal{A}$ is said to be *total* if for any thread t, operation $m \in \text{OP}_{\mathcal{A}}$ and $h \in H_{\mathcal{A}}$, there exists r such that $h \circ (t, m, r) \in H_{\mathcal{A}}$.

3.2 Clients

We now briefly describe clients and their semantics. (A more complete definition appears in [14].) A client $t_1 \mid\mid t_2 \mid\mid \cdots \mid\mid t_n$ consists of the parallel composition of a set of client programs t_i (also referred to as threads). Each t_i is a sequential program built out of two types of statements: statements that change only the thread's local-state, and statements that invoke a library operation. Threads have no shared state except the (internal) state of the library, which is accessed or modified only via library operations.

The semantics $[\![t_i]\!]$ of a single thread t_i is defined to be a labelled transition system $(\Sigma_i, \Rightarrow_i)$ over a set of thread-local states Σ_i, with some states designated as initial and final states. The execution of any instruction other than a library operation invocation is represented by a (thread-local) transition $\sigma \overset{\epsilon}{\Rightarrow}_i \sigma'$. The execution of a library operation invocation is represented by a transition of the form $\sigma \overset{e}{\Rightarrow}_i \sigma'$, where event e captures both the invocation as well as the return value. This semantics captures the semantics of the "open" program t_i. When t_i is "closed" by combining it with a library $\mathcal{A}$, the semantics of the resulting closed program is obtained by combining $[\![t_i]\!]$ with the semantics of $\mathcal{A}$, as illustrated later.

A t_i-execution is defined to be a sequence of t_i-transitions $s_0 \overset{a_1}{\Rightarrow}_i s_1, s_1 \overset{a_2}{\Rightarrow}_i s_2, \cdots, s_{k-1} \overset{a_k}{\Rightarrow}_i s_k$ such that s_0 is an initial state of t_i and every a_j is either ϵ or an event. Such an execution is said to be *complete* if s_k is a final state of t_i.

The semantics of a client $\mathcal{C} = t_1 \mid\mid \cdots \mid\mid t_n$ is obtained by composing the semantics of the individual threads, permitting any arbitrary interleaving of the executions of the threads. We define the set of transitions of $\mathcal{C}$ to be the disjoint union of the set of transitions of the individual threads. A $\mathcal{C}$-execution is defined to be a sequence ξ of $\mathcal{C}$-transitions such that each $\xi \mid t_i$ is a t_i-execution, where $\xi \mid t_i$ is the subsequence of ξ consisting of all t_i-transitions.

We now define the semantics of the composition of a client $\mathcal{C}$ with a library $\mathcal{A}$. Given a $\mathcal{C}$-execution ξ, we define $\phi(\xi)$ to be the sequence of event labels in ξ. The set of $(\mathcal{C}, \mathcal{A})$-executions is defined to be the set of all $\mathcal{C}$-executions ξ such that $\phi(\xi) \in H_{\mathcal{A}}$. We abbreviate "$(\mathcal{C}, \mathcal{A})$-execution" to *execution* if no confusion is likely.

Threads as Transactions Our goal is to enable threads to execute code fragments containing multiple library operations as atomic transactions (i.e., in *isolation*). For notational simplicity, we assume that we wish to execute each thread as a single transaction. (Our results can be generalized to the case where each thread may wish to perform a sequence of transactions.) In the sequel, we may think of threads and transactions interchangeably. This motivates the following definitions.

Non-Interleaved and Sequential Executions An execution ξ is said to be a *non-interleaved execution* if for every thread t all t-transitions in ξ appear contiguously. Thus, a non-interleaved execution ξ is of the form $\xi_1, \cdots, \xi_k$, where each ξ_i represents a different thread's (possibly incomplete) execution. Such a non-interleaved execution is said to be a *sequential execution* if for each $1 \leq i < k$, ξ_i represents a complete thread execution.

Serializability Two executions ξ and ξ' are said to be *equivalent* iff for every thread t, $\xi \mid t = \xi' \mid t$. An execution ξ is said to be *serializable* iff it is equivalent to some non-interleaved execution.

Serializably Completable Executions For any execution ξ, let $W(\xi)$ denote the set of all threads that have at least one transition in ξ. An execution ξ is said to be a *complete execution* iff $\xi \mid t$ is complete for every thread $t \in W(\xi)$. A client execution ξ is *completable* if ξ is a prefix of a complete execution ξ_c such that $W(\xi) = W(\xi_c)$. An execution ξ is said to be *serializably completable* iff ξ is a prefix of a complete serializable execution ξ_c such that $W(\xi) = W(\xi_c)$. Otherwise, we say that ξ is a *doomed* execution.

An execution may be incompletable due to problems in a client thread (e.g., a non-terminating loop) or due to problems in the library (e.g., *blocking* by a library procedure leading to deadlocks).

4. Foresight-Based Synchronization

We now formalize our goal of extending a base library $\mathcal{B}$ into a foresight-based library $\mathcal{E}$ that permits clients to execute arbitrary composite operations atomically.

4.1 The Problem

Let $\mathcal{B}$ be a given total library. (Note that $\mathcal{B}$ can also be considered to be a specification.) We say that a library $\mathcal{E}$ is a *restrictive extension* of $\mathcal{B}$ if (i) $\text{PROCS}_{\mathcal{E}} \supset \text{PROCS}_{\mathcal{B}}$, (ii) $\{h \downarrow \mathcal{B} \mid h \in H_{\mathcal{E}}\} \subseteq H_{\mathcal{B}}$, where $h \downarrow \mathcal{B}$ is the subsequence of events in h that represent calls of operations in $\text{OP}_{\mathcal{B}}$, and (iii) $\text{PROCS}_{\mathcal{E}} \setminus \text{PROCS}_{\mathcal{B}}$ do not have a return value. We are interested in extensions where the extension procedures ($\text{PROCS}_{\mathcal{E}} \setminus \text{PROCS}_{\mathcal{B}}$) are used for synchronization to ensure that each thread appears to execute in isolation.

Given a client $\mathcal{C}$ of the extended library $\mathcal{E}$, let $\mathcal{C} \downarrow \mathcal{B}$ denote the program obtained by replacing every extension procedure invocation in $\mathcal{C}$ by the skip statement. Similarly, for any execution ξ of $(\mathcal{C}, \mathcal{E})$, we define $\xi \downarrow \mathcal{B}$ to be the sequence obtained from ξ by omitting transitions representing extension procedures. We say that an execution ξ of $(\mathcal{C}, \mathcal{E})$ is $\mathcal{B}$-serializable if $\xi \downarrow \mathcal{B}$ is a serializable execution of $(\mathcal{C} \downarrow \mathcal{B}, \mathcal{B})$. We say that ξ is $\mathcal{B}$-serializably-completable if $\xi \downarrow \mathcal{B}$ is a serializably completable execution of $(\mathcal{C} \downarrow \mathcal{B}, \mathcal{B})$. We say that $\mathcal{E}$ is a *transactional extension* of $\mathcal{B}$ if for any (correct) client $\mathcal{C}$ of $\mathcal{E}$, every $(\mathcal{C}, \mathcal{E})$-execution is $\mathcal{B}$-serializably-completable. Our goal is to build transactional extensions of a given library.

4.2 The Client Protocol

In our approach, the extension procedures are used by transactions (threads) to provide information to the library about the future operations they may perform. We refer to procedures in $\text{PROCS}_{\mathcal{E}} \setminus \text{PROCS}_{\mathcal{B}}$ as *mayUse* procedures, and to operations in $MU_{\mathcal{E}} = \text{OP}_{\mathcal{E}} \setminus \text{OP}_{\mathcal{B}}$ as *mayUse* operations. We now formalize the *client protocol*, which captures the preconditions the client must satisfy, namely that the foresight information provided via the *mayUse* operations must be correct.

The semantics of *mayUse* operations is specified by a function $may_{\mathcal{E}} : MU_{\mathcal{E}} \mapsto \mathcal{P}(\text{OP}_{\mathcal{B}})$ that maps every *mayUse* operation to a set of base library operations[1]. In Section 5 we show simple procedure annotations that can be used to define the set $MU_{\mathcal{E}}$ and the function $may_{\mathcal{E}}$.

The *mayUse* operations define an *intention-function* $I_{\mathcal{E}} : H_{\mathcal{E}} \times \mathcal{T} \mapsto \mathcal{P}(\text{OP}_{\mathcal{B}})$ where $I_{\mathcal{E}}(h,t)$ represents the set of (base library) operations thread t is allowed to invoke after the execution of h. For every thread $t \in \mathcal{T}$ and a history $h \in H_{\mathcal{E}}$, the value of $I_{\mathcal{E}}(h,t)$ is defined as follows. Let M denote the set of all *mayUse* operations invoked by t in h. (I) IF M IS NON-EMPTY, THEN $I_{\mathcal{E}}(h,t) = \bigcap_{m \in M} may_{\mathcal{E}}(m)$. (II) IF M IS EMPTY, THEN $I_{\mathcal{E}}(h,t) = \{\}$. We extend the notation and define $I_{\mathcal{E}}(h,T)$, for any set of threads T, to be $\bigcup_{t \in T} I_{\mathcal{E}}(h,t)$.

Once a thread executes its first *mayUse* operation, the intention set $I_{\mathcal{E}}(h,t)$ can only shrink as the execution proceeds. Subsequent *mayUse* operations cannot be used to increase the intention set.

DEFINITION 1 (Client Protocol). *Let h be a history of library $\mathcal{E}$. We say that h follows the client protocol if for any prefix $h' \circ (t,m,r)$ of h, we have $m \in I_{\mathcal{E}}(h',t) \cup MU_{\mathcal{E}}$.*

We say that an execution ξ follows the client protocol, if $\phi(\xi)$ follows the client protocol.

4.3 Dynamic Right Movers

We now consider how the library extension can exploit the foresight information provided by the client to ensure that the interleaved execution of multiple threads is restricted to safe nodes (as described in Section 2). First, we formalize the notion of a *dynamic right mover*.

Given a history h of a library $\mathcal{A}$, we define the set $E_{\mathcal{A}}[h]$ to be $\{h' \mid h \circ h' \in H_{\mathcal{A}}\}$. (Note that if h is not feasible for $\mathcal{A}$, then $E_{\mathcal{A}}[h] = \emptyset$.) Note that if $E_{\mathcal{A}}[h_1] = E_{\mathcal{A}}[h_2]$, then the concrete library states produced by h_1 and h_2 cannot be distinguished by any client (using any sequence of operations). Dually, if the concrete states produced by histories h_1 and h_2 are equal, then $E_{\mathcal{A}}[h_1] = E_{\mathcal{A}}[h_2]$.

DEFINITION 2 (Dynamic Right Movers). *Given a library $\mathcal{A}$, a history h_1 is said to be a dynamic right mover with respect to a history h_2 in the context of a history h, denoted $h : h_1 \triangleright_{\mathcal{A}} h_2$, iff*

$$E_{\mathcal{A}}[h \circ h_1 \circ h_2] \subseteq E_{\mathcal{A}}[h \circ h_2 \circ h_1].$$

An operation m is said to be a dynamic right mover with respect to a set of operations M_s in the context of a history h, denoted $h : m \triangleright_{\mathcal{A}} M_s$, iff for any event (t,m,r) and any history h_s consisting of operations in M_s, we have $h : (t,m,r) \triangleright_{\mathcal{A}} h_s$.

The following example shows that an operation m can be a dynamic right mover with respect to a set M after some histories but not after some other histories.

[1] Our approach can be extended to use a more precise semantic function $may_{\mathcal{E}} : MU_{\mathcal{E}} \mapsto \mathcal{P}(\text{OP}^*_{\mathcal{B}})$ that maps each *mayUse* operation to a set of sequence of operations, enabling client transactions to more precisely describe their future behavior.

EXAMPLE 4.1. *Consider the Counter described in Section 2. Let h_p be a history that ends with a counter value of $p > 0$. The operation `Dec` is a dynamic right mover with respect to the set $\{$`Inc`$\}$ in the context of h_p since for every n the histories $h_p \circ (t, Dec, r) \circ (t_1, Inc, r_1), \ldots, (t_n, Inc, r_n)$ and $h_p \circ (t_1, Inc, r_1), \ldots, (t_n, Inc, r_n) \circ (t, Dec, r)$ have the same set of suffixes (since the counter value is $p - 1 + n$ after both histories).*

Let h_0 be a history that ends with a counter value of 0. The operation `Dec` is not *a dynamic right mover with respect to the set $\{$`Inc`$\}$ in the context of h_0 since after a history $h_0 \circ (t, Dec, r) \circ (t', Inc, r')$ the counter's value is 1, and after $h_0 \circ (t', Inc, r') \circ (t, Dec, r)$ the counter's value is 0. Thus, $(t, Get, 1)$ is a feasible suffix after the first history but not the second.*

The following example shows that the dynamic right mover is not a symmetric property.

EXAMPLE 4.2. *Let h_i be a history that ends with a counter value of $i > 0$. The operation `Inc` is* not *a dynamic right mover with respect to the set $\{$`Dec`$\}$ in the context of h_i since after a history $h_i \circ (t, Inc, r) \circ (t_1, Dec, r_1), \ldots, (t_{i+1}, Dec, r_{i+1})$ the Counter's value is 0, and after $h_i \circ (t_1, Dec, r_1), \ldots, (t_{i+1}, Dec, r_{i+1}) \circ (t, Inc, r)$ the Counter's value is 1.*

One important aspect of the definition of dynamic right movers is the following: it is possible to have $h : m \triangleright_{\mathcal{A}} \{m_1\}$ and $h : m \triangleright_{\mathcal{A}} \{m_2\}$ but not $h : m \triangleright_{\mathcal{A}} \{m_1, m_2\}$.

Static Movers. We say that an operation m is a *static right mover* with respect to operation m', if every feasible history h satisfies $h : m \triangleright_{\mathcal{A}} \{m'\}$. We say that m and m' are *statically-commutative*, if m is a *static right mover* with respect to m' and vice versa.

4.4 Serializability

It follows from the preceding discussion that an incomplete history h may already reflect some execution-order constraints among the threads that must be satisfied by any other history that is equivalent to h. These execution-order constraints can be captured as a partial-ordering on thread-ids.

DEFINITION 3 (Safe Ordering). *Given a history h of $\mathcal{E}$, a partial ordering $\sqsubseteq \subseteq \mathcal{T} \times \mathcal{T}$, is said to be safe for h iff for any prefix $h' \circ (t,m,r)$ of h, where $m \in OP_{\mathcal{B}}$, we have $h' \downarrow \mathcal{B} : m \triangleright_{\mathcal{B}} I(h',T)$, where $T = \{t' \in \mathcal{T} \mid t \not\sqsubseteq t'\}$.*

A safe ordering represents a conservative over-approximation of the execution-order constraints among thread-ids (required for serializability). Note that in the above definition, the right-mover property is checked only with respect to the *base library* $\mathcal{B}$.

EXAMPLE 4.3. *Assume that the Counter is initialized with a value $I > 0$. Consider the history (return values omitted for brevity):*

$$h = (t, mayUseDec), (t', mayUseInc), (t, Dec), (t', Inc).$$

If $\sqsubseteq$ is a safe partial order for h, then $t' \sqsubseteq t$ because after the third event `Inc` is not *a dynamic right mover with respect to the operations allowed for t (i.e., $\{$`Dec`$\}$). Dually, the total order defined by $t' \sqsubseteq' t$ is safe for h since after the second event, the operation `Dec` is a dynamic right mover with respect to the operations allowed for t' (i.e., $\{$`Inc`$\}$) because the Counter's value is larger than 0.*

DEFINITION 4 (Safe Extension). *We say that library $\mathcal{E}$ is safe extension of $\mathcal{B}$, if for every $h \in H_{\mathcal{E}}$ that follows the client protocol there exists a partial ordering $\sqsubseteq_h$ on threads that is safe for h.*

The above definition prescribes the synchronization (specifically, *blocking*) that a safe extension must enforce. In particular, assume that h is feasible history allowed by the library. If the history $h \circ (t, m, r)$ has no safe partial ordering, then the library must block the call to m by t rather than return the value r.

THEOREM 4.1 (Serializability). *Let $\mathcal{E}$ be a safe extension of a library $\mathcal{B}$. Let $\mathcal{C}$ be a client of $\mathcal{E}$. Any execution ξ of $(\mathcal{C}, \mathcal{E})$ that follows the client protocol is $\mathcal{B}$-serializable.*

The proofs appear in [14].

4.5 $\mathcal{B}$-Serializable-Completability

We saw in Section 2 and Fig. 4 that some serializable (incomplete) executions may be doomed: i.e., there may be no way of *completing* the execution in a serializable way. Safe extensions, however, ensure that all executions avoid doomed nodes and are serializably completable. However, we cannot guarantee completability if a client thread contains a non-terminating loop or violates the client protocol. This leads us to the following conditional theorem.

THEOREM 4.2 ($\mathcal{B}$-Serializable-Completability). *Let $\mathcal{E}$ be a safe extension of a total library $\mathcal{B}$. Let $\mathcal{C}$ be a client of $\mathcal{E}$. If every sequential execution of $(\mathcal{C}, \mathcal{E})$ follows the client protocol and is completable, then every execution of $(\mathcal{C}, \mathcal{E})$ is $\mathcal{B}$-serializably-completable.*

The precondition in the above theorem is worth noting. We require client threads to follow the client protocol and terminate. However, it is sufficient to check that clients satisfy these requirements in *sequential executions*. This simplifies reasoning about the clients.

4.6 $\mathcal{E}$-Completability

The preceding theorem about $\mathcal{B}$-Serializable-Completability has a subtle point: it indicates that *it is possible* to complete any execution of $(\mathcal{C}, \mathcal{E})$ in a serializable fashion *in* $\mathcal{B}$. The extended library $\mathcal{E}$, however, could choose to *block* operations unnecessarily and prevent progress. This is undesirable. We now formulate a desirable progress condition that the extended library must satisfy.

In the sequel we assume that every thread (transaction) always executes a *mayUse* operation m such that $may_{\mathcal{E}}(m) = \{\}$ before it terminates. (Essentially, this is an *end-transaction* operation.) Given a history h and a thread t, we say that t is *incomplete* after h iff $I_{\mathcal{E}}(h, t) \neq \emptyset$. We say that history h is *incomplete* if there exists some incomplete thread after h.

We say that a thread t is *enabled* after history h, if for all events (t, m, r) such that $h \circ (t, m, r)$ satisfies the client protocol and $h \circ (t, m, r) \downarrow \mathcal{B} \in H_{\mathcal{B}}$, we have $h \circ (t, m, r) \in H_{\mathcal{E}}$. Note that this essentially means that $\mathcal{E}$ will not block t from performing any legal operation.

DEFINITION 5 (Progress Condition). *We say that a library $\mathcal{E}$ satisfies the* progress condition *iff for every history $h \in H_{\mathcal{E}}$ that follows the client protocol the following holds:*

- *If h is incomplete, then at least one of the incomplete threads t is enabled after h.*
- *If h is complete, then every thread t that does not appear in h is enabled after h.*

THEOREM 4.3 ($\mathcal{E}$-Completability). *Let $\mathcal{E}$ be a safe extension of a total library $\mathcal{B}$ that satisfies the progress condition. Let $\mathcal{C}$ be a client of $\mathcal{E}$. If every sequential execution of $(\mathcal{C}, \mathcal{E})$ follows the client protocol and is completable, then every execution of $(\mathcal{C}, \mathcal{E})$ is completable and $\mathcal{B}$-serializable.*

4.7 Special Cases

In this subsection we describe two special cases of safe extension.

```
int createNewMap();
int put(int mapId,int k,int v);
int get(int mapId,int k);
int remove(int mapId,int k);
bool isEmpty(int mapId);
int size(int mapId);
```

Figure 5. Base procedures of the example Maps library.

Eager-Ordering Library Our notion of safe-ordering permits $\sqsubseteq$ to be a partial order. In effect, this allows the system to determine the execution-ordering between transactions lazily, only when forced to do so (e.g., when one of the transactions executes a non-right-mover operation). One special case of this approach is to use a total order on threads, eagerly ordering threads in the order in which they execute their first operations. The idea of shared-ordered locking [7] in databases is similar to this. Using such approach guarantees *strict-serializability* [25] which preserves the runtime order of the threads.

DEFINITION 6. *Given a history h we define an order $\leq_h$ of the threads in h such that: $t \leq_h t'$ iff $t = t'$ or the first event of t precedes the the first event of t' (in h).*

DEFINITION 7 (Eager-Ordering Library). *We say that library $\mathcal{E}$ is eager-ordering if for every $h \in H_{\mathcal{E}}$ that follows the client protocol, $\leq_h$ is safe for h.*

Commutative-Blocking Library A special case of eager-ordering library is *commutative-blocking library*. (This special case is common in the database literature, e.g., see [8, chapter 3.8]). The idea here is to ensure that two threads are allowed to execute concurrently only if any operations they can invoke commute with each other. This is achieved by treating each *mayUse* operation as a lock acquisition (on the set of operations it denotes). A *mayUse* operation m by any thread t, after a history h, will be blocked if there exists a thread $t' \neq t$ such that some operation in $may_{\mathcal{E}}(m)$ does not statically commute with some operation in $I_{\mathcal{E}}(h, t')$.

DEFINITION 8 (Commutative-Blocking Library). *We say that library $\mathcal{E}$ is commutative-blocking, if for every $h \in H_{\mathcal{E}}$ that follows the client protocol:*
if $t \neq t'$, $m \in I_{\mathcal{E}}(h, t)$ and $m' \in I_{\mathcal{E}}(h, t')$, then m and m' are statically-commutative.

Note that, for the examples shown in Section 2 such library will not allow the threads to run concurrently. This is because the operations `Inc` and `Dec` are not statically-commutative.

5. Automatic Foresight for Clients

In this section, we present our static analysis to infer calls (in the client code) to the API used to pass the foresight information. The static analysis works for the general case covered by our formalism, and does not depend on the specific implementation of the extended library.

We assume that we are given the interface of a library $\mathcal{E}$ that extends a base library $\mathcal{B}$, along with a specification of the semantic function $may_{\mathcal{E}}$ using a simple annotation language. We use a static algorithm for analyzing a client $\mathcal{C}$ of $\mathcal{B}$ and instrumenting it by inserting calls to *mayUse* operations that guarantee that (all sequential executions of) $\mathcal{C}$ correctly follows the client protocol.

Example Library. In this section, we use a library of Maps as an example. The base procedures of the library are shown in Fig. 5 (their semantics will be described later). The *mayUse* procedures are shown in Fig. 6 — their semantic function is specified using the annotations that are shown in this figure.

```
void mayUseAll();@{(createNewMap),(put,*,*,*),(get,*,*),
(remove,*,*),(isEmpty,*),(size,*)}
void mayUseMap(int m);@{(put,m,*,*),(get,m,*),(remove,m,*),
(isEmpty,m),(size,m)}
void mayUseKey(int m,int k);@{(put,m,k,*),(get,m,k),
(remove,m,k)}
void mayUseNone();@{}
```

Figure 6. Annotated *mayUse* procedures of the example library.

```
mayUseMap(m);
if (get(m,x) == get(m,y)) {
  mayUseKey(m,x); remove(m,x); mayUseNone();
} else {
  remove(m,x); mayUseKey(m,y); remove(m,y); mayUseNone(); }
```

Figure 7. Code section with inferred calls to *mayUse* procedures.

Fig. 7 shows an example of a code section with calls to the base library procedures. The calls to *mayUse* procedures shown in bold are inferred by our algorithm.

5.1 Annotation Language

The semantic function is specified using annotations. These annotations are described by *symbolic operations* and *symbolic sets*.

Let *PVar* be a set of variables, and $*$ be a symbol such that $* \notin PVar$. A *symbolic operation* (over *PVar*) is a tuple of the form $(p, a_1, \cdots, a_n)$, where p is a base library procedure name, and each $a_i \in PVar \cup \{*\}$. A *symbolic set* is a set of symbolic operations.

EXAMPLE 5.1. *Here are four symbolic sets for the example library (we assume that $m, k \in PVar$):*

$$SY_1 = \{(createNewMap), (put, *, *, *), (get, *, *), (remove, *, *), (isEmpty, *), (size, *)\}$$
$$SY_2 = \{(put, m, *, *), (get, m, *), (remove, m, *), (isEmpty, m), (size, m)\}$$
$$SY_3 = \{(put, m, k, *), (get, m, k), (remove, m, k)\}.$$
$$SY_4 = \{\}$$

Let *Value* be the set of possible values (of parameters of base library procedures). Given a function $asn : PVar \mapsto Value$ and a symbolic set SY, we define the set of operations $\mathrm{SY}(asn)$ to be

$$\bigcup_{(p,a_1,\ldots,a_n)\in \mathrm{SY}} \{(p, v_1, \ldots, v_n) \mid \forall i.(a_i \neq *) \Rightarrow (v_i = asn(a_i))\}.$$

EXAMPLE 5.2. *Consider the symbolic sets from Example 5.1. The set $SY_3(asn)$ contains all operations with the procedures* `put`, `get`, *and* `remove` *in which the first parameter is equal to $asn(m)$ and the second parameter is equal to $asn(k)$. The sets $SY_1(asn)$ and $SY_4(asn)$ are not dependent on asn. The set $SY_1(asn)$ contains all operations with the procedures* `createNewMap`, `put`, `get`, `remove`, `isEmpty` *and* `size`. *The set $SY_4(asn)$ is empty.*

The Annotations Every *mayUse* procedure p is annotated with a symbolic set over the the set of formal parameters of p.

In Fig. 6, the procedure *mayUseAll* is annotated with SY_1, *mayUseMap* is annotated with SY_2, *mayUseKey* is annotated with SY_3, and *mayUseNone* is annotated with SY_4.

Let p be a *mayUse* procedure with parameters $x_1, \ldots, x_n$ which is annotated with SY_p. An invocation of p with the values $v_1, \ldots, v_n$ is a *mayUse* operation that refers to the set defined by SY_p and a function that maps x_i to v_i (for every $1 \leq i \leq n$).

EXAMPLE 5.3. *In Fig. 6, the procedure* `mayUseAll()` *is annotated with SY_1, hence its invocation is a* mayUse *operation that refers to all the base library operations . The procedure* `mayUseKey(int m, int k)` *is annotated with SY_3, hence* `mayUseKey(0, 7)` *refers to all operations with the procedures* `put`, `get`, *and* `remove` *in which the first parameter is 0 and the the second parameter is 7.*

5.2 Inferring Calls to *mayUse* Procedures

We use a simple abstract interpretation algorithm to infer calls to *mayUse* procedures. Given a client $\mathcal{C}$ of $\mathcal{B}$ and annotated *mayUse* procedures, our algorithm conservatively infers calls to the *mayUse* procedures such that the client protocol is satisfied in all sequential executions of $\mathcal{C}$. We have implemented the algorithm for Java programs in which the relevant code sections are annotated as *atomic*. More details are described in [14].

Assumptions. The algorithm assumes that there exists a *mayUse* procedure (with no parameters) that refers to the set of all base library operations (the client protocol can always be enforced by adding a call to this procedure at the beginning of each code section). It also assumes that there exists a *mayUse* procedure (with no parameters) that refers to an empty set, the algorithm adds a call to this procedure at the end of each code section.

Limitations. Our implementation may fail to enforce atomicity of the code sections because: (i) Java code can access shared-memory which is not part of the extended library (e.g., by accessing a global variable); (ii) our simple implementation does not analyze the procedures which are invoked by the annotated code sections. The implementation reports (warnings) about suspected accesses (to shared-memory) and about invocations of procedures that do not belong to the extended library. These reports should be handled by a programmer or by a static algorithm (e.g., purity analysis [28]) that verifies that they will not be used for inter-thread communication (in our formal model, they can be seen as thread-local operations).

6. Implementing Libraries with Foresight

In this section we present a generic technique for realizing an eager-ordering safe extension (see Definition 7) of a given base library $\mathcal{B}$. Our approach exploits a variant of the tree locking protocol over a tree that is designed according to semantic properties of the library's operations.

In Section 6.1 we describe the basic idea of our technique which is based on locking and static commutativity. In Section 6.2 we show how to utilize dynamic properties like dynamic right-movers. In Section 6.3 we show an optimistic synchronization that enables mitigating *lock contention* that may be caused by the locking in our approach. Further extensions of our technique are described in [14].

6.1 The Basic Approach

Example Library. Here, we use the example from Section 5. The procedures of the base library are shown in Fig. 5. The procedure `createNewMap` creates a new Map and returns a unique identifier corresponding to this Map. The other procedures have the standard meaning (e.g., as in *java.util.Map*), and identify the Map to be operated on using the unique `mapId` identifier. In all procedures, `k` is a key, `v` is a value.

We now describe the *mayUse* procedures we use to extend the library interface (formally defined in Fig. 6): (1) `mayUseAll()`: indicates that the transaction may invoke any library operations. (2) `mayUseMap(int mapId)`: indicates that the transaction will invoke operations only on Map `mapId`; (3) `mayUseKey(int mapId, int k)` : indicates that the transaction will invoke operations only on Map `mapId` and key `k`; (4) `mayUseNone()`: indicates the end of transaction (it will invoke no more operations).

In the following, we write $may_{\mathcal{E}}(m)$ to denote the the set of operations associated with the *mayUse* operation m.

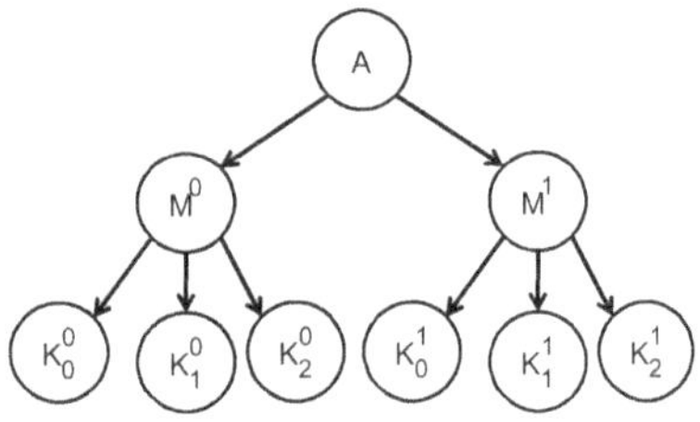

Figure 8. A *locking-tree* used in the example.

Implementation Parameters Our technique is parameterized and permits the creation of different instantiations offering tradeoffs between concurrency granularity and overheads. The parameters to our extension are a *locking-tree* and a *lock-mapping*.

A *locking-tree* is a directed static tree where each node n represents a (potentially unbounded) set of library operations O_n, and satisfies the following requirements: (i) the root of the locking-tree represents all operations of the base library; (ii) if n' is a child of n, then $O_{n'} \subseteq O_n$; (iii) if n and n' are roots of disjoint sub-trees, then every $m \in O_n$ and $m' \in O_{n'}$ are statically-commutative.

EXAMPLE 6.1. *Fig. 8 shows a possible locking-tree for the Map library. The root A represents all (library) operations. Each M^i ($i = 0, 1$) represents all operations with argument* `mapId` *that satisfies*[2] *: $i = mapId \,\%\, 2$. Each K^i_j ($i = 0,1$ and $j = 0, 1, 2$) represents all operations with arguments* `mapId` *and k that satisfy: $i = mapId \,\%\, 2 \wedge j = k\%\, 3$.*

The *lock-mapping* is a function P from *mayUse* operations to tree nodes and a special value $\perp$. For a *mayUse* operation m, $P(m)$ is the node which is associated with m. For each *mayUse* operation m, P should satisfy: if $may_{\mathcal{E}}(m) \neq \emptyset$, then $may_{\mathcal{E}}(m) \subseteq O_{P(m)}$, otherwise $P(m) = \perp$.

EXAMPLE 6.2. *Here is a possible lock-mapping for our example.* `mayUseAll()` *is mapped to the root A.* `mayUseMap(mapId)` *is mapped to M^i where $i = mapId \,\%\, 2$.* `mayUseKey(mapId, k)` *is mapped to K^i_j where $i = mapId \,\%\, 2 \wedge j = k\%\, 3$.* `mayUseNone()` *is mapped to $\perp$.*

Implementation We associate a lock with each node of the locking-tree. The *mayUse* operations are implemented as follows:

- The first invocation of a *mayUse* operation m by a thread or transaction (that has not previously invoked any *mayUse* operation) acquires the lock on $P(m)$ as follows. The thread follows the path in the tree from the root to $P(m)$, locking each node n in the path before accessing n's child. Once $P(m)$ has been locked, the locks on all nodes except $P(m)$ are released.[3]
- An invocation of a *mayUse* operation m' by a thread that holds the lock on $P(m)$, locks all nodes in the path from $P(m)$ to $P(m')$ (in the same tree order), and then releases all locks except $P(m')$. If $P(m') = P(m)$ or $P(m')$ is not reachable from $P(m)$,[4] then the execution of m' has no impact.
- If a *mayUse* operation m is invoked by t and $P(m) = \perp$, then t releases all its owned locks .

Furthermore, our extension adds a wrapper around every base library procedure, which works as follows. When a *non-mayUse* operation m is invoked, the current thread t must hold a lock on some node n (otherwise, the client protocol is violated). Conceptually, this operation performs the following steps: (1) wait until all the nodes reachable from n are unlocked; (2) invoke m of the base library and return its return value. Here is a possible pseudo-code for `isEmpty`:

```
bool isEmpty(int mapId) {
  n := the node locked by the current thread
  if(n is not defined) error // optional
  wait until all nodes reachable from n are unlocked
  return baseLibrary.isEmpty(mapId);
}
```

Correctness The implementation satisfies the **progress condition** because: if there exist threads that hold locks, then at least one of them will never wait for other threads (because of the tree structure, and because the base library is total).

We say that t is smaller than t', if the lock held by t is reachable from the lock held by t'. The following property is guaranteed: if $t \leq_h t'$ (see Definition 6) then either t is smaller than t' or all operations allowed for t and t' are statically-commutative. In an implementation, a *non-mayUse* operation waits until all smaller threads are completed, hence the extended library is a **safe extension**.

Further Extensions In [14] we show extensions of the basic approach. We show how to associate several nodes with the same *mayUse* operation — this enables, for example, *mayUse* operation that is associated with operations on several different keys. We also show how to utilize read-write locks — this enables situations in which several threads hold the same lock (node).

6.2 Using Dynamic Information

The dynamic information utilized by the basic approach is limited. In this section we show two ways that enable (in some cases) to avoid blocking by utilizing dynamic information.

6.2.1 Utilizing the State of the Locks

In the basic approach, a *non-mayUse* operation, invoked by thread t, waits until all the reachable nodes (i.e., reachable from the node which is locked by t) are unlocked — this ensures that the operation is a right-mover with respect to the preceding threads. In some cases this is too conservative; for example:

EXAMPLE 6.3. *Consider the example from Section 6.1, and a case in which thread t holds a lock on M^0 (assume t is allowed to use all operations of a single Map). If t invokes* `remove(0, 6)` *it will wait until K^0_0, K^0_1 and K^0_2 are unlocked. But, waiting for K^0_1 and K^0_2 is not needed, because threads that hold locks on these nodes are only allowed to invoke operations that are commutative with* `remove(0, 6)`*. In this case it is sufficient to wait until K^0_0 is unlocked.*

So, if a *non-mayUse* operation m is invoked, then it is sufficient to wait until all reachable nodes in the following set are unlocked:

$$\{n \mid \exists m' \in O_n : m \text{ is not static-right-mover with } m'\}$$

6.2.2 Utilizing the State of the Base Library

In some cases, the state of the base library can be used to avoid waiting. For example:

EXAMPLE 6.4. *Consider the example from Section 6.1, and a case in which thread t holds a lock on M^0 (assume t is allowed to use all operations of a single Map), and other threads hold locks on K^0_0, K^0_1 and K^0_2. If t invokes* `isEmpty`*, it will have to wait until all the other threads unlock K^0_0, K^0_1 and K^0_2. This is not always needed, for example, if the Map manipulated by t has 4 elements, then the other threads will never be able to make the Map empty (because,*

[2] We write % to denote the *modulus* operator. Note that we can use a hash function (before applying the modulus operator).

[3] This is simplified version. Other variants, such as hand-over-hand locking, will work as well.

[4] This may happen, for example, when $O_{P(m')} \supset O_{P(m)}$.

according to the Map semantics, they can only affect 3 keys, so they cannot remove more than 3 elements). Hence, the execution of `isEmpty` *by t is a dynamic-right-mover.*

A library designer can add code that observes the library's state and checks that the operation is a dynamic-right-mover; in such a case, it executes the operation of the base library (without waiting). For example, the following code lines can be added to the beginning of `isEmpty(int mapId)`:

```
bool c1 = M^0 or M^1 are held by the current thread ;
bool c2 = baseLibrary.size(mapId) > 3 ;
if(c1 and c2) return baseLibrary.isEmpty(mapId);
... // the remaining code of isEmpty
```

This code verifies that the actual Map cannot become empty by the preceding threads; in such a case we know that the operation is a dynamic-right-mover. Note that writing code that dynamically verifies right-moverness may be challenging, because it may observe inconsistent state of the library (i.e., the library may be concurrently changed by the other threads).

6.3 Optimistic Locking

In the approach, the threads are required to lock the root of the locking-tree. This may create *contention* (because of several threads trying to lock the root at the same time) and potentially degrade performance [18].

To avoid contention, we use the following technique. For each lock we add a counter — the counter is incremented whenever the lock is acquired. When a *mayUse* operation m is invoked (by a thread that has not invoked a *mayUse* operation) it performs the following steps: **(1)** go over all nodes from the root to $P(m)$ and read the counter values; **(2)** lock $P(m)$; **(3)** go over all nodes from the root to $P(m)$ (again), if one node is locked or its counter has been modified then unlock $P(m)$ and restart (i.e., go to step 1).

The idea is to simulate hand-over-hand locking by avoid writing to shared memory. This is done by only locking the node $P(m)$ (and only read the state of the other nodes). When we do not restart in step **3**, we know that the execution is equivalent to one in which the thread performs hand-over-hand locking from the root to $P(m)$.

7. Experimental Evaluation

In this section we present an experimental evaluation of our approach. The goals of the evaluation are: (i) to measure the precision and applicability of our simple static analysis algorithm (ii) to compare the performance of our approach to a synchronization implemented by experts, and (iii) to determine if our approach can be used to perform synchronization in realistic software with reasonable performance.

Towards these goals, we implemented a general purpose Java library for Map data structures using the technique presented in Section 6 (we used the extensions from Sections 6.2 and 6.3). Implementation details can be found in [14]. In all cases, in which our library is used, the calls to the *mayUse* operations have been automatically inferred by our static algorithm.

Evaluation Methodology For all performance benchmarks (except the *GossipRouter*), we followed the evaluation methodology of [17]. We used a Sun SPARC enterprise T5140 server machine running Solaris 10 — this is a 2-chip Niagara system in which each chip has 8 cores (the machine's hyperthreading was disabled). More details about the evaluation methodology can be found in [14].

7.1 Applicability and Precision Of The Static Analysis

We applied our static analysis to 58 Java code sections (composite operations) from [27] that manipulate Maps (taken from open-source projects). We have found that for all composite operations,

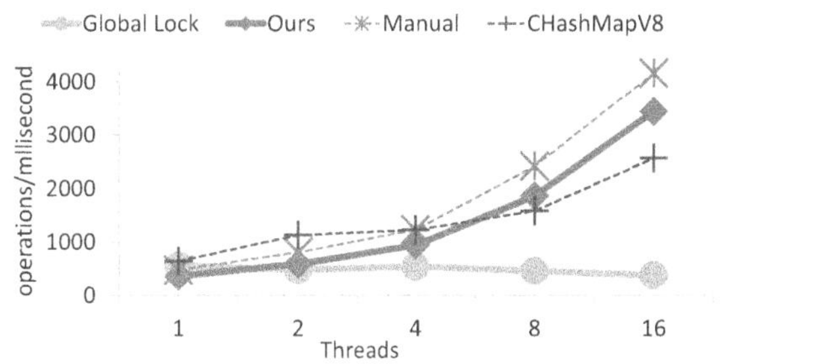

Figure 9. Throughput of *ComputeIfAbsent*.

our simple algorithm infers calls to *mayUse* operations which cannot be further improved manually. For 18 composite operations, our implementation reported (warnings) about procedure invocations that did not belong to the library — we manually verified that these invocations are *pure*[5] (so they can be seen as thread-local operations). These results are summarized in [14].

7.2 Comparison To Hand-Crafted Implementations

We selected several composite operations over a single Map: the *computeIfAbsent* pattern [1], and a few other common composite Map operations (that are supported by [2]). For these composite operations, we compare the performance of our approach to a synchronization implemented by experts in the field. The results of the *computeIfAbsent* pattern are reported here, and the rest of the results are reported in [14].

ComputeIfAbsent The *ComputeIfAbsent* pattern appears in many Java applications. Many bugs in Java programs are caused by non-atomic realizations of this simple pattern (see [27]). It can be described with the following pseudo-code:

```
if(!map.containsKey(key)) {
  value = ... // pure computation
  map.put(key, value);
}
```

The idea is to compute a value and store it in a Map, if and only if, the given key is not already present in the Map. We chose this benchmark because there exists a new version of Java Map, called *ConcurrentHashMapV8*, with a procedure that gets the computation as a parameter (i.e., a function is passed as a parameter), and atomically executes the pattern's code [1].

We compare four implementations of this pattern: (i) an implementation which is based on a global lock; (ii) an implementation which is based on our approach; (iii) an implementation which is based on *ConcurrentHashMapV8*; (iv) an implementation which is based on hand-crafted fine-grained locking (we used *lock stripping*, similar to [16], with 32 locks; this is an attempt to estimate the benefits of manual hand-crafted synchronization w/o changing the underlying library). The computation was emulated by allocating a relatively-large Java object ($\sim$ 128 bytes).

The results are shown in Fig. 9. We are encouraged by the fact that our approach provides better performance than *ConcurrentHashMapV8* for at least 8 threads. Also, it is (at most) 25% slower than the hand-crafted fine-grained locking.

7.3 Evaluating The Approach On Realistic Software

We applied our approach to three benchmarks with multiple Maps — in these benchmarks, several Maps are simultaneously manipulated by the composite operations. We used the *Graph* benchmark [16], Tomcat's *Cache* [3], and a multi-threaded application

[5] We have found that the purity of the invoked procedures is obvious, and can be verified by existing static algorithms such as [28].

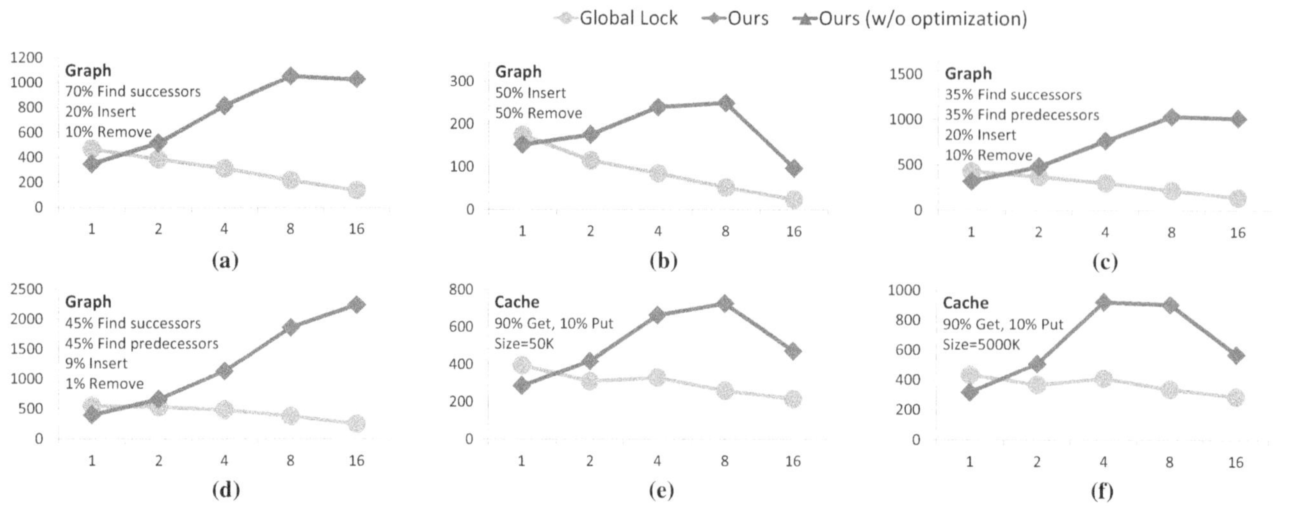

Figure 10. Throughput (operations/millisecond) as a function of the number of threads (1-16).

GossipRouter [6]. In these benchmarks, we compare the performance to coarse grained locking.

Graph This benchmark is based on a Java implementation of the Graph that has been used for the evaluation of [16]. The Graph consists of four composite operations: *find successors*, *find predecessors*, *insert edge*, and *remove edge*. Its implementation uses two Map data structures in which several different values can be associated with the same key (such type of Maps is supported by our library; also [5] contains an example for such type of Maps).

We compare a synchronization which is based on a global lock, and a synchronization which is based on our approach. We use the workloads from [16]. The results are shown in Fig. 10(a)–(d).

For some of the workloads, we see that there is a drop of performance between 8 and 16 threads. This can be explained by the fact that each chip of the machine has 8 cores, so using 16 threads requires using both chips (this creates more overhead).

Tomcat's Cache This benchmark is based on a Java implementation of Tomcat's cache [3]. This cache uses two types of Maps which are supported by our library: a standard Map, and a *weak Map* (see [4]). The cache consists of two composite operations `Put` and `Get` which manipulate the internal Maps. In this cache, the `Get` is not a read-only operation (in some cases, it copies an element from one Map to another). The cache gets a parameter (*size*) which is used by its algorithm. Fig. 10(e) and Fig. 10(f) show results for two workloads.

GossipRouter The *GossipRouter* is a Java multi-threaded routing service from [6]. Its main state is a *routing table* which consists of several Map data structures. (The exact number of Maps is dynamically determined).

We use a version of the router (*"3.1.0.Alpha3"*) with several bugs that are caused by an inadequate synchronization in the code that access the *routing table*. We have manually identified all code sections that access the *routing table* as atomic sections; and verified (manually) that: whenever these code sections are executed atomically, the known bugs are not occurred.

We compare two ways to enforce atomicity of the code sections: a synchronization which is based on a global lock, and a synchronization which is based on our approach. We used a performance tester from [6] (called *MPerf*) to simulate 16 clients where each client sends 5000 messages. In this experiment the number of threads cannot be controlled from the outside (because the threads are autonomously managed by the router). Therefore, instead of changing the number of threads, we changed the number of active cores. The results are shown in Fig. 11.

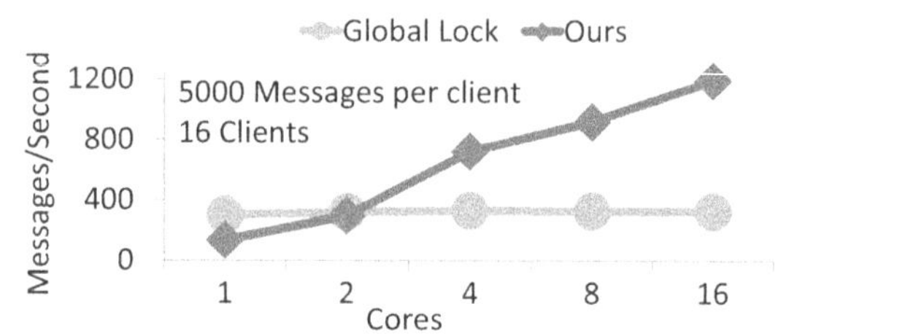

Figure 11. Throughput of *GossipRouter*.

For the router's code, our static analysis has reported (warnings) about invocations of procedures that do not belong to the Maps library. Interestingly, these procedures perform I/O and do not violate atomicity of the code sections. Specifically, they perform two types of I/O operations: logging operation (used to print debug messages), and operations that send network messages (to the router's clients). They do not violate the atomicity of the atomic sections, because they are not used to communicate between the threads (from the perspective of our formal model, they can be seen as thread-local operations).

8. Related Work

8.1 Concurrent Data Structures

Many sophisticated concurrent data structures (e.g., [2, 18, 24]) were developed and integrated into modern software libraries. These data structures ensure atomicity of their basic operations, while hiding the complexity of synchronization inside their libraries. Unfortunately as shown in [27] employing concurrent data structures in client code is error prone. The problem stems from the inability of concurrent data structures to ensure atomicity of client operations composed from several data structure operations.

In this paper we focus on enabling efficient atomicity of client operations composed from several data structure operations. The foresight information enables the library to provide concurrency without violating atomicity of composite client operations. This prevents the errors reported in [27] without the need for the library to directly support composite operations as suggested in [1].

8.2 Synchronization by Utilizing Semantics Properties

Many synchronization approaches aim to utilize semantics properties of concurrent operations for the sake of concurrency and efficiency. (e.g., by utilizing commutativity of read-only operations.) These approaches are developed for databases (e.g.,[26, 29]) and for general programming models (e.g.,[21, 22]).

Rollbacks A notable property of most approaches (e.g., all the approaches discussed in [21, 22, 26, 29]) is that they require a rollback mechanism (otherwise atomicity and deadlock-freedom are not guaranteed). In contrast, in this paper we show an approach that ensures atomicity and deadlock-freedom without using a rollback mechanism. This may be an advantage in some cases (e.g., when a rollback mechanism has a high runtime and memory overhead [10], or when I/O operations are involved).

Using foresight may also be beneficial for approaches with a rollback mechanism. Though, in this work we focus on synchronization that does not require rollback mechanisms.

Commutativity and Movers We base our approach on right-movers whereas most approaches are based on commutativity. Indeed, [21] shows that many synchronization schemes can be based on either right-movers or left-movers. In [21], they use a variant of a "static" right-mover which is a special case of our definition for dynamic-right-mover.

Locking Mechanisms Locking mechanisms are widely used for synchronization, some of them utilize semantics properties of shared operations (e.g., [12, 20]). Usually these mechanisms do not allow several threads to hold locks which correspond to non-commutative operations. An interesting locking mechanism is shared-ordered locking [7] which allow several threads to hold locks which correspond to non-commutative operations. Such locking mechanisms can be seen as special cases of libraries with foresight-based synchronization.

8.3 Synchronization via Locking

Locking is a widely used approach for software synchronization. Writing software with locking that permits concurrency, such as fine-grain locking, is considered hard and error prone.

In order to mitigate this problem several algorithms for automatically inferring locks using static analysis were recently suggested (e.g. [11, 13]). Our algorithm for inferring *mayUse* operations is similar to these algorithms; still with the following differences: (i) we deal *mayUse* operations which can be seen as generalizations of *lock-acquire* and *lock-release* operations — this enables our approach to utilize non-trivial semantic properties of shared operations; (ii) lock inference algorithms usually need to consider the structure of a dynamically manipulated state, we avoid this by considering a single shared library that can be statistically identified.

Acknowledgments

We thank Yehuda Afek, Adam Morrison, Noam Rinetzky, Omer Tripp and the anonymous referees for their insightful feedbacks. This work was partially supported by Microsoft Research through its PhD Scholarship Programme, and by The Israeli Science Foundation (grant no. 965/10).

References

[1] gee.cs.oswego.edu/dl/jsr166/dist/jsr166edocs/jsr166e/ConcurrentHashMapV8.html.

[2] docs.oracle.com/javase/6/docs/api/java/util/concurrent/ConcurrentHashMap.html.

[3] www.devdaily.com/java/jwarehouse/apache-tomcat-6.0.16/java/org/apache/el/util/ConcurrentCache.java.shtml.

[4] docs.oracle.com/javase/6/docs/api/java/util/WeakHashMap.html.

[5] guava-libraries. code.google.com/p/guava-libraries/.

[6] Jgroups toolkit. www.jgroups.org/index.html.

[7] AGRAWAL, D., AND EL ABBADI, A. Constrained shared locks for increasing concurrency in databases. In *Selected papers of the ACM SIGMOD symposium on Principles of database systems* (1995).

[8] BERNSTEIN, P. A., HADZILACOS, V., AND GOODMAN, N. *Concurrency Control and Recovery in Database Systems*. Addison-Wesley, 1987.

[9] BRONSON, N. *Composable Operations on High-Performance Concurrent Collections*. PhD thesis, Stanford University, Dec. 2011.

[10] CASCAVAL, C., BLUNDELL, C., MICHAEL, M., CAIN, H. W., WU, P., CHIRAS, S., AND CHATTERJEE, S. Software transactional memory: Why is it only a research toy? *Queue 6*, 5 (Sept. 2008), 46–58.

[11] CHEREM, S., CHILIMBI, T., AND GULWANI, S. Inferring locks for atomic sections. In *PLDI* (2008).

[12] COURTOIS, P. J., HEYMANS, F., AND PARNAS, D. L. Concurrent control with *readers* and *writers*. *Commun. ACM 14*, 10 (Oct. 1971).

[13] GOLAN-GUETA, G., BRONSON, N., AIKEN, A., RAMALINGAM, G., SAGIV, M., AND YAHAV, E. Automatic fine-grain locking using shape properties. In *OOPSLA* (2011).

[14] GOLAN-GUETA, G., RAMALINGAM, G., SAGIV, M., AND YAHAV, E. Concurrent libraries with foresight. Tech. Rep. TR-2012-89, Tel Aviv University, 2012.

[15] HARRIS, T., LARUS, J., AND RAJWAR, R. Transactional memory, 2nd edition. *Synthesis Lectures on Computer Architecture 5*, 1 (2010).

[16] HAWKINS, P., AIKEN, A., FISHER, K., RINARD, M., AND SAGIV, M. Concurrent data representation synthesis. In *PLDI* (2012).

[17] HERLIHY, M., LEV, Y., LUCHANGCO, V., AND SHAVIT, N. A provably correct scalable concurrent skip list. In *OPODIS* (2006).

[18] HERLIHY, M., AND SHAVIT, N. *The Art of Multiprocessor Programming*. Morgan Kauffman, Feb. 2008.

[19] HERLIHY, M. P., AND WING, J. M. Linearizability: a correctness condition for concurrent objects. *ACM Trans. Program. Lang. Syst. 12* (July 1990).

[20] KORTH, H. F. Locking primitives in a database system. *J. ACM 30* (January 1983), 55–79.

[21] KOSKINEN, E., PARKINSON, M., AND HERLIHY, M. Coarse-grained transactions. In *POPL* (2010), pp. 19–30.

[22] KULKARNI, M., PINGALI, K., WALTER, B., RAMANARAYANAN, G., BALA, K., AND CHEW, L. P. Optimistic parallelism requires abstractions. In *PLDI* (2007).

[23] LIPTON, R. J. Reduction: a method of proving properties of parallel programs. *Commun. ACM 18*, 12 (Dec. 1975), 717–721.

[24] MICHAEL, M. M., AND SCOTT, M. L. Simple, fast, and practical non-blocking and blocking concurrent queue algorithms. In *PODC* (1996), pp. 267–275.

[25] PAPADIMITRIOU, C. H. The serializability of concurrent database updates. *J. ACM 26*, 4 (1979), 631–653.

[26] SCHWARZ, P. M., AND SPECTOR, A. Z. Synchronizing shared abstract types. *ACM Trans. Comput. Syst. 2*, 3 (Aug. 1984), 223–250.

[27] SHACHAM, O., BRONSON, N., AIKEN, A., SAGIV, M., VECHEV, M., AND YAHAV, E. Testing atomicity of composed concurrent operations. In *OOPSLA* (2011).

[28] SĂLCIANU, A., AND RINARD, M. Purity and side effect analysis for Java programs. In *VMCAI* (2005), pp. 199–215.

[29] WEIHL, W. E. Commutativity-based concurrency control for abstract data types. *IEEE Trans. Comput. 37* (December 1988), 1488–1505.

Thresher: Precise Refutations for Heap Reachability

Sam Blackshear
University of Colorado Boulder
samuel.blackshear@colorado.edu

Bor-Yuh Evan Chang
University of Colorado Boulder
evan.chang@colorado.edu

Manu Sridharan
IBM T.J. Watson Research Center
msridhar@us.ibm.com

Abstract

We present a precise, path-sensitive static analysis for reasoning about *heap reachability*; that is, whether an object can be reached from another variable or object via pointer dereferences. Precise reachability information is useful for a number of clients, including static detection of a class of Android memory leaks. For this client, we found that the heap reachability information computed by a state-of-the-art points-to analysis was too imprecise, leading to numerous false-positive leak reports. Our analysis combines a symbolic execution capable of path-sensitivity and strong updates with abstract heap information computed by an initial flow-insensitive points-to analysis. This novel *mixed* representation allows us to achieve both precision and scalability by leveraging the pre-computed points-to facts to guide execution and prune infeasible paths. We have evaluated our techniques in the THRESHER tool, which we used to find several developer-confirmed leaks in Android applications.

Categories and Subject Descriptors D.2.4 [*Software Engineering*]: Software/Program Verification

Keywords heap reachability; path-sensitive analysis; symbolic execution

1. Introduction

Static reasoning about nearly any non-trivial property of modern programs requires effective analysis of heap properties. In particular, a heap analysis can be used to reason about *heap reachability*—whether one heap object is reachable from another via pointer dereferences at some program point. Precise heap reachability information improves heap-intensive static analyses, such as escape analysis, taint analysis, and cast checking. A heap reachability checker would also enable a developer to write statically checkable assertions about, for example, object lifetimes, encapsulation of fields, or immutability of objects.

Our interest in heap-reachability analysis arose while developing a tool for detecting an important class of memory leaks in Android applications. Briefly, such a leak occurs when an object of type Activity remains reachable from a static variable after the end of its life cycle and thus cannot be freed by the garbage collector (explained further in Sections 2 and 4). For this client, we found that highly precise reasoning about heap reachability, including flow-, context-, *and* path-sensitivity *with* materialization [43], was required to avoid emitting too many spurious warnings. We are unaware of an existing analysis that can provide such precision for heap-reachability queries while scaling to our target applications (40K SLOC with up to 1.1M SLOC of libraries). While approaches based on predicate abstraction or symbolic execution [2, 4, 11, 31] could provide the necessary precision in principle, to our best knowledge such approaches have not been shown to handle heap-reachability queries for real-world object-oriented programs (further discussion in Section 5).

We present an analysis for precise reasoning about heap reachability via on-demand refinement of a flow-insensitive points-to analysis. When the points-to analysis cannot refute a heap-reachability query Q, our technique performs a backwards search for a path program [7] witnessing Q; a failed search means Q is refuted. Our analysis is flow-, context-, and path-sensitive with location materialization, yielding the precision required by clients like the Android memory leak detector in an on-demand fashion.

In contrast to previous approaches to refinement-based or staged heap analysis [25, 26, 28, 36, 44], our approach refines points-to facts directly and is capable of path-sensitive reasoning. Also, unlike some prior approaches [28, 36, 44], our analysis does *not* attempt to refine the heap abstraction of the initial points-to analysis. Instead, we focus on the orthogonal problem of on-demand flow- and path-sensitive reasoning given a points-to analysis with a sufficiently precise heap abstraction.

Our analysis achieves increased scalability through two novel uses of the initial points-to analysis result. First, we introduce a *mixed symbolic-explicit* representation of heap reachability queries and transfer functions that simultaneously enables strong updates during symbolic execution, exploits the initial points-to analysis result, and mitigates the case split explosion seen with a fully explicit representation. Crucially, our representation allows the analysis to avoid case-splitting over entire points-to sets when handling heap writes, key to scaling beyond small programs. We also maintain *instance constraints* for memory locations during analysis, based on points-to facts, and use these constraints during query simplification to obtain contradictions earlier, improving performance.

Second, our analysis utilizes points-to facts to handle loops effectively, a well-known source of problems for symbolic analyses. Traditionally, such analyses either require loop invariant annotations or only analyze loops to some fixed bound. We give a sound algorithm for *inferring loop invariants over points-to constraints on path programs* during backwards symbolic execution. Our algorithm takes advantage of the heap abstraction computed by the up-front points-to analysis to effectively over-approximate the effects of the loop during the backwards refinement analysis (Section 3.3). Our technique maintains constraints from path conditions separately from the heap reachability constraints, enabling heuristic "dropping" of path constraints at loops to avoid divergence without significant precision loss in most cases.

PLDI'13, June 16–19, 2013, Seattle, WA, USA.

Contributions. This paper makes the following contributions:

- We describe a technique for refining a points-to analysis with strong updates, path sensitivity, and context sensitivity to improve precision for heap-reachability queries. Our technique centers on enriching a backwards symbolic execution with the over-approximate information from the up-front points-to analysis to guide the execution and prune infeasible paths.
- We introduce a *mixed symbolic-explicit* representation of heap reachability queries and corresponding transfer functions that enable strong updates and precise disaliasing information during symbolic execution while reducing case splitting compared to a fully explicit approach. This representation is important both for finding contradictions early and for collapsing paths effectively.
- We present a method for *inferring loop invariants for heap-reachability queries* during symbolic execution based on over-approximating the heap effects of loops and dropping path constraints that may lead to divergence.
- We demonstrate the usefulness of our analysis by applying it to the problem of finding memory leaks in Android applications. Our tool refuted many of the false alarms that a flow-insensitive analysis reported for real-world Android applications and finished in less than twenty minutes on most programs we tried. We used our tool to successfully identify real (and developer-confirmed) memory leaks in several applications.

2. Overview

Here we present a detailed example to motivate our precise heap-reachability analysis and illustrate our technique. The example is based on real code from Android applications and libraries, and verifying the desired heap-reachability property requires strong updates, context sensitivity, *and* path sensitivity, which our technique provides in an on-demand fashion.

Our techniques were motivated by the need to detect leaks of Activity objects in Android applications. Every Android application has least one associated Activity object to control the user interface. Android development guidelines state that application code should not maintain long-lived pointers to Activity objects, as such pointers prevent the objects from being garbage collected at the end of their lifetimes, causing significant memory leaks (we discuss this issue further in Section 4). To detect such leaks in practice, it is sufficient to verify that Activity objects are *never* reachable from a static field via object pointers.

Figure 1 is a simple application that illustrates the difficulties of precisely checking this heap reachability property (ignore the boxed assertions for now). The `Main` class initializes and starts the application's Activity, the `Act` class. The `Vec` class captures the essence of a list data structure, as implemented in Android. This example is free of the leak described above, as the `Act` object allocated on line 1 is never made reachable from a static field.

For this example program, flow-insensitive points-to analysis techniques cannot prove the desired heap (un)reachability property due to the manner in which the `Vec` class is implemented. In the inset, we show a heap graph obtained by applying Andersen's analysis [1] with one level of object sensitivity [40] to the example. Graph nodes represent classes or abstract locations (whose names are shown at the corresponding allocation site in Figure 1), and edges represent possible values of field pointers. Object-sensitive abstract locations are named appropriately, for example, $\text{vec}_0\text{.arr}_1$ for arr_1 instances allocated when `Vec.push(−)` is invoked on instances of vec_0. Each edge indicates a may points-to relationship, written as $a_1 \cdot f \mapsto a_2$, meaning there may be an execution where field f of abstract location a_1 contains the address of location a_2. The graph imprecisely shows that

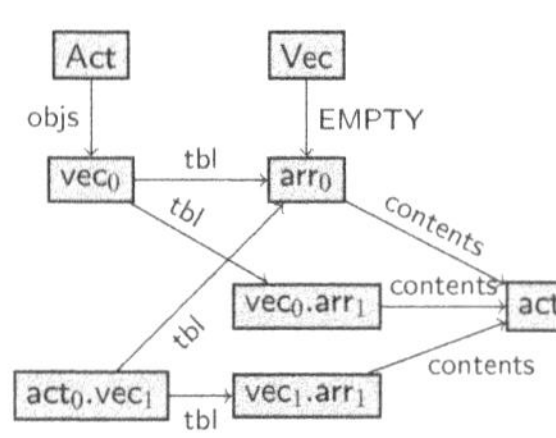

Figure 2.

```
   public class Main {
     public static void main(String[] args) {
1      Act a = new_{act_0} Act(); a.onCreate();
2    }
   }
   public class Act extends Activity {
     private static final Vec objs = new_{vec_0} Vec();
     public void onCreate() {
3      Vec acts = new_{vec_1} Vec();
4        [ $\widehat{v}^{int}_{sz} < \widehat{v}^{int}_{cap}$, $\widehat{acts}\cdot sz \mapsto \widehat{v}^{int}_{sz}$, $\widehat{acts}\cdot cap \mapsto \widehat{v}^{int}_{cap}$;
           $this \mapsto \widehat{this}$, $acts \mapsto \widehat{acts}$, $\widehat{acts}\cdot tbl \mapsto arr_0$, $\widehat{this} \mapsto act_0$ ]
       acts.push(this
5        [ $\widehat{v}^{int}_{sz} < \widehat{v}^{int}_{cap}$, $\widehat{this}\cdot sz \mapsto \widehat{v}^{int}_{sz}$, $\widehat{this}\cdot cap \mapsto \widehat{v}^{int}_{cap}$;
           $this \mapsto vec_1$, $vec_1\cdot tbl \mapsto arr_0$, $\underline{val \mapsto act_0}$ ]   ——
       );
6      ...
7      objs.push("hello"
8        [ $\widehat{v}^{int}_{sz} < \widehat{v}^{int}_{cap}$, $\widehat{this}\cdot sz \mapsto \widehat{v}^{int}_{sz}$, $\widehat{this}\cdot cap \mapsto \widehat{v}^{int}_{cap}$;
           $this \mapsto vec_0$, $vec_0\cdot tbl \mapsto arr_0$, $\underline{val \mapsto act_0}$ ] †  ——
       );
9    }
   }
   public class Vec {
     private static final Object[] EMPTY = new_{arr_0} Object[1];
     private int sz; private int cap; private Object[] tbl;

     public Vec() {
10     this.sz = 0; this.cap = -1; this.tbl = EMPTY;
11       [ $\widehat{v}^{int}_{sz} < \widehat{v}^{int}_{cap}$, $\widehat{this}\cdot sz \mapsto \widehat{v}^{int}_{sz}$, $\widehat{this}\cdot cap \mapsto \widehat{v}^{int}_{cap}$;
           $this \mapsto \widehat{this}$, $\widehat{this}\cdot tbl \mapsto arr_0$ ] †
     }

     public void push(Object val) {
12     Object[] oldtbl = this.tbl;
13       [ $\widehat{v}^{int}_{sz} < \widehat{v}^{int}_{cap}$, $\widehat{this}\cdot sz \mapsto \widehat{v}^{int}_{sz}$, $\widehat{this}\cdot cap \mapsto \widehat{v}^{int}_{cap}$;
           $this \mapsto \widehat{this}$, $\widehat{this}\cdot tbl \mapsto arr_0$, $val \mapsto act_0$ ]   ——
       if (this.sz >= this.cap) {
14       this.cap = this.tbl.length * 2;
15       this.tbl = new_{arr_1} Object[this.cap];
16         [ $this \mapsto \widehat{this}$, $\widehat{this}\cdot tbl \mapsto arr_0$, $val \mapsto act_0$ ] †  ——
         for (int i = 0; i < this.sz; i++) {
17         this.tbl[i] = oldtbl[i]; // copy from oldtbl
18       }
19     }
20       [ $this \mapsto \widehat{this}$, $\widehat{this}\cdot tbl \mapsto arr_0$, $val \mapsto act_0$ ]
       this.tbl[this.sz] = val;
21       [ $\underline{arr_0\cdot contents \mapsto act_0}$ ]
       this.sz = this.sz + 1;
22   }
   }
```

Figure 1. Refuting a false alarm with context-sensitive, path-sensitive witness search. We show witness queries in the boxes. The † indicate refuted branches of the witness search.

Activity object act_0 is reachable from both static fields Act·objs and Vec·EMPTY, hence falsely indicating that a leak is possible.

The root cause of the imprecision in Figure 2 is the edge $\mathsf{arr}_0 \cdot \mathsf{contents} \mapsto \mathsf{act}_0$, which indicates that the array assigned to Vec·EMPTY may contain the Activity object. `Vec` is implemented using the *null object pattern* [45]: rather than allocating a separate internal array for each empty `Vec`, all `Vec` objects initially use Vec·EMPTY as their internal array. The code in `Vec` is carefully written to avoid ever adding objects to Vec·EMPTY while also avoiding additional branches to check for the empty case. But, a flow-insensitive points-to analysis is incapable of reasoning precisely about this code, and hence it models the statement `this.tbl[this.sz] = val` on line 20 as possibly writing to Vec·EMPTY, polluting the points-to graph. Real Android collections are implemented in this way.[1] Note that a more precise heap abstraction would not help in this case—because the (concrete) null object is shared among *all* instances the `Vec` class, *no refinement on the heap abstraction* alone would be sufficient to rule out this false alarm.

More precise analysis of this example requires reasoning about the relationship between the `sz` and `cap` fields of each `Vec`. This relationship is established in the `Vec`'s constructor and must be preserved until its `push` method is called. Though there is a large body of work focused on the important problem of refining heap abstractions (e.g., [36, 44]), this example shows that doing so alone is sometimes not sufficient for precise results. An analysis that lacks path sensitivity and strong updates will be unable to prove that `Vec`'s never write into the shared array and must therefore conflate the contents of all `Vec` objects. The *witness-refutation* technique that we detail in this paper enables after-the-fact, on-demand refinement to address this class of *control-precision* issues.

Refinement by Witness Refutation. We refine the results of the flow-insensitive points-to analysis by attempting to refute all executions that could possibly witness an edge involved in a leak alarm. The term "witness" is highly overloaded in the program analysis literature, so we begin by carefully defining its use in our context. We first define a *path* as a sequence of program transitions. A *path witness* for a *query Q* is a path that ends in a state that satisfies Q. Such a path witness may be concrete/under-approximate/must in that it describes a sequence of program transitions according to a concrete semantics that results in a state where Q holds (e.g., a test case execution). Analogously, an abstract/over-approximate/may path witness is such a sequence over an abstract semantics (e.g., a trace in an abstract interpreter). Building on the definition of a path program [7], we define a *path program witness* for a query Q as a path program that ends in a state satisfying Q. A *path program* is a program projected onto the transitions of a given execution trace (essentially, paths augmented with loops). Note that a path program witness may be under- or over-approximate in its handling of loops. In this paper, we use the term "witness" to refer to over-approximate path program witnesses unless otherwise stated, as our focus is on sound refutation of queries.

Our analysis performs a goal-directed, backwards search for a path program witness ending in a state that satisfies a query Q. We *witness* a query by giving a witness that produces it, or we *refute* a query by proving that no such witness can exist. Our technique proceeds in three phases.

Obtain a Conservative Analysis Result. First, we perform a standard points-to analysis to compute an over-approximation of the set of reachable heaps, such as the points-to graph in Figure 2.

[1] In fact, we discovered buggy logic in the actual Android libraries that allowed writing to a null object, thereby polluting all empty containers! The bug was acknowledged and fixed by Google (`https://code.google.com/p/android/issues/detail?id=48055`).

Formulate Queries. Second, we formulate queries to refute alarms generated using the points-to analysis result. For the Activity leak detection client, an alarm is a points-to path between a **static** field and an Activity object. For example, the following points-to path from the graph in Figure 2 is a (false) leak alarm:

$$\mathsf{Act}\cdot\mathsf{objs} \mapsto \mathsf{vec}_0, \mathsf{vec}_0\cdot\mathsf{tbl} \mapsto \mathsf{arr}_0, \mathsf{arr}_0\cdot\mathsf{contents} \mapsto \mathsf{act}_0$$

To refute an alarm, we attempt to refute each individual edge in the corresponding points-to path. If we witness all edges in the path, we report a leak alarm. If we refute some edge e in the path, we delete e from the points-to graph and attempt to find another path between the source node and the sink node. If we find such a path, we restart the process with the new path. If we refute enough edges to disconnect the source and sink in the points-to graph, we have shown that the alarm raised by the flow-insensitive points-to analysis is false.

For our client, we wish to show the flow-insensitive property that a particular points-to constraint cannot hold at any program point. Thus, for each points-to edge e to witness, we consider a query for e at every program statement that could produce e. This information can be obtained by simple post-processing or instrumentation of the up-front points-to analysis [8].

Search for Witnesses. Finally, given a query Q at a particular program point, we search for path program witnesses on demand. In Figure 1, we illustrate a witness search that produces a refutation for the points-to constraint $\mathsf{arr}_0\cdot\mathsf{contents} \mapsto \mathsf{act}_0$ holding at program point 21. That is, we prove that the points-to constraint is unrealizable at that program point. By starting a witness search from each statement that potentially produces the edge, we will see that $\mathsf{arr}_0\cdot\mathsf{contents} \mapsto \mathsf{act}_0$ is in fact unrealizable at any program point.

Notationally, we use a single arrow $\mapsto$ to denote an *exact points-to constraint*, whose source and sink are symbolic values typically denoting addresses of memory cells, and a double arrow $\Mapsto$ to denote a may points-to edge between abstract locations (cf., Section 3.1). For example, the exact points-to constraint $\mathsf{arr}_0\cdot\mathsf{contents} \mapsto \mathsf{act}_0$ describes a single memory cell whose address is some instance in the concretization of arr_0 and contents is some instance in the concretization of act_0. This distinction is critical for enabling strong updates in a backwards analysis.

2.1 Mixed Symbolic-Explicit Queries

We illustrate the witness search by showing the sub-queries (boxed) that arise as the search progresses. Moving backwards from our starting point at line 21, the sub-query at program point 20 says that we need the following heap state at that point:

$$\mathsf{this} \mapsto \widehat{this}, \widehat{this}\cdot\mathsf{tbl} \mapsto \mathsf{arr}_0, \mathsf{val} \mapsto \mathsf{act}_0 \qquad (\dagger)$$

where $\widehat{this}$ is a *symbolic variable* that represents the receiver of the method. A symbolic variable (written as a hatted letter $\hat{v}$) is an existential standing for an arbitrary instance drawn from some definite set of abstract locations. Here, $\widehat{this}$ represents some instance drawn from the points-to set of local variable this, which is $\{\mathsf{vec}_0, \mathsf{vec}_1\}$. We represent this fact with an *instance constraint*:

$$\widehat{this} \text{ from } \{\mathsf{vec}_0, \mathsf{vec}_1\} \qquad (\ddagger)$$

that we track as part of the query at program point 20. For the moment, we elide such 'from' constraints and discuss them further in Section 2.2 and Section 3. This sub-query conjoining the heap state from (†) and the instance constraint from (‡) is an example of a *mixed* symbolic-explicit state because we introduce a fresh symbolic variable for the contents of **this**, but also have named abstract locations arr_0 and act_0. We say that a query is fully *explicit* if all of its points-to constraints are between named abstract locations from the points-to abstraction. A named abstract location can be seen as a symbolic variable that is constrained to be from a singleton abstract location set. This connection to the points-to abstraction in an explicit query enables our witness search to prune paths that are inconsistent with the up-front points-to analysis result, as we demonstrate in Section 2.2.

Backwards Path-By-Path Analysis. Returning to the example, the path splits into two prior to program point 20, one path entering the **if** control-flow branch at point 19, the other bypassing the branch to point 13. We consider both possibilities and indicate the fork in Figure 2 by indenting from the right margin. For the path into the branch, the loop between program points 16 and 19 has no effect on the query in question from point 20, so it simply continues backward to program point 16. Observe that because we are only interested in answering a specific query, this irrelevant loop poses no difficulty. At program point 16, we encounter a refutation for this path: the preceding assignment statement writes an instance of arr_1 to the *this*·tbl field, which contradicts the requirement that *this*·tbl hold an instance of arr_0 (underlined). Thus, we have discovered that no concrete program execution can assign a newly allocated array to **this**.`tbl` at line 15, that is, an instance of arr_1 and then place an Activity object in the `EMPTY` array at line 20 because **this**.`tbl` will point to that newly allocated array by then.

Resuming the path that bypasses the **if** branch, the analysis at program point 13 determines that entering the **if** branch changed the query and thus adds a *control-path constraint* to the abstract state indicating that the value of the **this**.`sz` field (i.e., $\widehat{v}^{\mathsf{int}}_{\mathsf{sz}}$) must be less than the value of the **this**.`cap` field (i.e., $\widehat{v}^{\mathsf{int}}_{\mathsf{cap}}$). As we will see, tracking the path constraint above is critical to obtaining a refutation for the example. From here, this path reaches the method boundary, leading the analysis to process the possible call sites at program points 8 and 5. The path at program point 8 can be refuted at this point, as the query requires that the val parameter be bound to an instance of act_0 (underlined), but the actual argument is the string `"hello"`. Thus, we have identified that this call to `push` cannot be the reason that an Activity object is placed into the `EMPTY` array because it is pushing a string, not an Activity.

The other path from the `acts.push` call site (i.e., program point 5) can continue. The query at program point 4 before the call simply changes the program variables of the callee to those of the caller. Continuing this path, we enter the constructor of `Vec` at program point 11. Here, we discover that the values of the `sz` and `cap` fields as initialized in the constructor contradict the control constraint $\widehat{v}^{\mathsf{int}}_{\mathsf{sz}} < \widehat{v}^{\mathsf{int}}_{\mathsf{cap}}$. Intuitively, the witness search has observed the invariant that a `Vec`'s `tbl` field cannot point to the `EMPTY` array after a call to its `push` method. We have refuted the last path standing, and so we have shown that the statement at line 21 cannot produced the edge $\mathsf{arr}_0{\cdot}\mathsf{contents} \mapsto \mathsf{act}_0$.

In the above, we have been rather informal in describing why certain points-to facts can be propagated back unaffected and why producing certain facts can be done with a strong update-style transfer function. Furthermore, in the example program from Figure 1, there is one (and only one) more statement that could produce the constraint $\mathsf{arr}_0{\cdot}\mathsf{contents} \mapsto \mathsf{act}_0$, which is the assignment at line 17 inside the copy loop. A witness search for this query starting at line 17 leads to a refutation similar to the one described above, but to discover it we must first infer a non-trivial loop invariant. Because we are interested in an over-approximate path program witness-refutation search, we have to obtain loop invariants. We consider these issues further in Section 3.

2.2 Taming Path Explosion From Aliasing

In the previous subsection, we focused on how refutations can occur. For example, backwards paths were pruned at line 15 and at program point 8 because we reach an allocation site that conflicts with our instance constraints in the query (e.g., we need an arr_0 not an arr_1 at line 15). In this section, we present a simple example to explain how our mixed symbolic-explicit representation enables our analysis to derive such contradictions earlier and thus mitigates the *aliasing path explosion problem*.

1 $\mathsf{x} \mapsto \widehat{y}, \mathsf{y} \mapsto \widehat{y}, \mathsf{p} \mapsto \widehat{z} \wedge \widehat{z}$ from $\mathsf{pt}_{\mathring{G}}(\mathsf{p}) \cap \mathsf{pt}_{\mathring{G}}(\mathsf{y.f}) \cap \mathring{r}, \widehat{y}$ from $\mathsf{pt}_{\mathring{G}}(\mathsf{x}) \cap \mathsf{pt}_{\mathring{G}}(\mathsf{y})$ —

$\mathsf{x} \mapsto \widehat{x}, \mathsf{y} \mapsto \widehat{y}, \widehat{y}{\cdot}\mathsf{f} \mapsto \widehat{z} \wedge \widehat{z}$ from $\mathsf{pt}_{\mathring{G}}(\mathsf{y.f}) \cap \mathring{r}, \widehat{y}$ from $\mathsf{pt}_{\mathring{G}}(\mathsf{y}) \wedge \widehat{x} \neq \widehat{y}$ —

```
x.f = p;
```

2 $\mathsf{y} \mapsto \widehat{y}, \widehat{y}{\cdot}\mathsf{f} \mapsto \widehat{z} \wedge \widehat{z}$ from $\mathsf{pt}_{\mathring{G}}(\mathsf{y.f}) \cap \mathring{r}, \widehat{y}$ from $\mathsf{pt}_{\mathring{G}}(\mathsf{y})$

```
z = y.f;
```

3 $\mathsf{z} \mapsto \widehat{z} \wedge \widehat{z}$ from $\mathring{r}$

Figure 3. An example illustrating how 'from' constraints help tame path explosion from aliasing. Note that the set of abstract locations to which symbolic variable $\widehat{z}$ might belong is restricted each time we observe $\widehat{z}$ flow through a variable or field.

An over-approximate backwards symbolic executor that lacks information about aliasing will be forced to fork a number of cases to account for aliasing at every field write, quickly causing a case explosion that is worst-case exponential in the number of field writes. This case explosion is independent of (but compounded by) the well-known scalability problems caused by conditional branching in a path-sensitive analysis.

To address this aliasing path explosion problem, the key observation that we make is that contradictions from instance constraints can be derived *before* the allocation site by exploiting information from the up-front points-to analysis. In particular, the set of possible allocation sites for any instance can be restricted as we reason about how they flow into and out of program variables and heap locations. This observation motivates our mixed symbolic-explicit representation, which we demonstrate with a simple example shown in Figure 3. Our initial query at point 3 asks if program variable `z` can point to an instance $\widehat{z}$ from some set of abstract locations $\mathring{r}$—we call this a *points-to region*. Moving backwards across the statement `z = y.f`, we derive a pre-query at point 2 that says our original query can be witnessed if `y` points to some instance $\widehat{y}$ and that instance points to $\widehat{z}$ through its f field (i.e., $\mathsf{y} \mapsto \widehat{y}, \widehat{y}{\cdot}\mathsf{f} \mapsto \widehat{z}$). Additionally, we now know that the instance $\widehat{z}$ must be drawn from the *intersection* of $\mathring{r}$ and the abstract locations in the points-to set of y.f, which we write as $\mathsf{pt}_{\mathring{G}}(\mathsf{y.f})$. If we can use the points-to graph $\mathring{G}$ to determine that no such abstract location exists (e.g., if we had $\mathring{r} = \{a_0, a_2\}$ and $\mathsf{pt}_{\mathring{G}}(\widehat{y}.\mathsf{f}) = \{a_1\}$), then we have refuted this query and can prune this path immediately.

Assuming $\mathring{r}$ and $\mathsf{pt}_{\mathring{G}}(\mathsf{y.f})$ are not disjoint (i.e., $\mathring{r} \cap \mathsf{pt}_{\mathring{G}}(\mathsf{y.f}) \neq \emptyset$), we proceed with our backwards analysis to the field write `x.f = p`. We must consider two cases at program point 1: one where `x` and `y` are aliased (the top query) and one where they are not (the bottom query). In the aliased case, we can further constrain the instance $\widehat{u}$ to be from $\mathsf{pt}_{\mathring{G}}(\mathsf{x}) \cap \mathsf{pt}_{\mathring{G}}(\mathsf{y})$. Some previous tools have used an up-front, over-approximate points-to analysis as an aliasing oracle to rule out aliased cases like this one (e.g., PSE [39])—if `x` and `y` cannot possibly point to the same abstract location (i.e., $\mathsf{pt}_{\mathring{G}}(\mathsf{x}) \cap \mathsf{pt}_{\mathring{G}}(\mathsf{y}) = \emptyset$), this aliased case is ruled out. Our approach generalizes this kind of aliasing check by explicitly introducing 'from' constraints that are incrementally restricted. For example, we also constrain $\widehat{z}$ to be from $\mathsf{pt}_{\mathring{G}}(\mathsf{p}) \cap \mathsf{pt}_{\mathring{G}}(\mathsf{y.f}) \cap \mathring{r}$, where the additional restriction is $\mathsf{pt}_{\mathring{G}}(\mathsf{p})$. This constraint says that the field write `x.f = p` produced the query in question only if the instance $\widehat{z}$ is drawn from some abstract location shared by these three sets.

Finally, we consider the case where `x` and `y` are not aliased (i.e., $\widehat{x} \neq \widehat{y}$). Here, the only change to the query is the addition of the constraints $\mathsf{x} \mapsto \widehat{x}$ and $\widehat{x} \neq \widehat{y}$. This disequality further constrains the query so that if we later discover that `x` and `y` are in fact aliased, we can refute this query. Accumulation of this kind of disaliasing constraint is common (e.g., [11]), but expensive (cf., Section 3.3).

We remark that the instance 'from' constraints can be viewed as a generalization of a fully explicit representation. To represent 'from' constraints explicitly, instead of a symbolic points-to constraint $\mathsf{x} \mapsto \widehat{x}$, we disjunctively consider all cases where we replace the symbolic variable $\widehat{x}$ with an abstract location from $\mathrm{pt}_{\mathring{G}}(\mathsf{x})$ (the points-to set of x) For example, suppose $\mathrm{pt}_{\mathring{G}}(\mathsf{x}) = \{a_1, a_2\}$; then we case split and consider two heap states: (1) $\mathsf{x} \mapsto a_1$ and (2) $\mathsf{x} \mapsto a_2$. This representation corresponds roughly to a backwards extension of *lazy initialization* [33] over abstract locations instead of types. Note that while PSE-style path pruning only applies to ruling out the aliased case in field writes, the explicit representation of 'from' constraints permits the same kind of flow-based restriction shown in Figure 3. However, the cost is case splitting a separate query for each possible abstract location from which each symbolic variable is drawn (e.g., $|\mathrm{pt}_{\mathring{G}}(\mathsf{y.f}) \cap \mathring{r}| \cdot |\mathrm{pt}_{\mathring{G}}(\mathsf{y})|$ queries at program point 2).

3. Refuting Path Program Witnesses

We formalize our witness-refutation analysis and argue that our technique is *refutation sound*—that we only declare an edge refuted when no concrete path producing that query can exist. The language providing the basis for our formalization is defined as follows: This language is a standard imperative programming language with object fields and dynamic memory allocation.

statements	$s ::= c \mid \texttt{skip} \mid s_1 \,;\, s_2 \mid s_1 [] s_2 \mid \texttt{loop}\, s$
commands	$c ::= x \texttt{ := } y \mid x \texttt{ := } y.f \mid x.f \texttt{ := } y \mid x \texttt{ := } \texttt{new}_a\, \tau\texttt{()} \mid \texttt{assume}\, e$
expressions	$e ::= x \mid \cdots$
types	$\tau ::= \{f_1, \ldots, f_n\} \mid \cdots$

program variables x, y object fields f abstract locations a

Atomic commands c include assignment, field read, field write, object allocation, and a guard. For the purposes of our discussion, it is sufficient if an object type is just a list of field names. We leave unspecified a sub-language of pure expressions, except that it allows reading of program variables. The label a on allocation names the allocation site so that we can tie it to the points-to analysis. Compound statements include a do-nothing statement, sequencing, non-deterministic branching, and looping. Standard `if` and `while` statements can be defined in the usual way (i.e., $\texttt{if}\,(e)\, s_1\, \texttt{else}\, s_2 \stackrel{\text{def}}{=} (\texttt{assume}\, e \,;\, s_1) [] (\texttt{assume}\, !e \,;\, s_2)$ and $\texttt{while}\,(e)\, s \stackrel{\text{def}}{=} \texttt{loop}\,(\texttt{assume}\, e \,;\, s) \,;\, \texttt{assume}\, !e$).

For ease of presentation, our formal language is intraprocedural. However, our implementation is fully interprocedural. We handle procedure calls by modeling parameter binding using assignment and keeping an explicit abstraction of the call stack. The call stack is initially empty representing an arbitrary calling context but grows as we encounter call instructions during symbolic execution. If we reach the entry block of a function with an empty call stack, we propagate symbolic state backwards to all possible callers of the current function. We determine the set of possible callers using the call graph constructed alongside the points-to analysis.

3.1 Formulating a Witness Query over Heap Locations

Given a program, we first do a standard points-to analysis to obtain a points-to graph $\mathring{G}\colon \langle \mathring{V}, \mathring{E} \rangle$ consisting of a set of vertices $\mathring{V}$ and a set of edges $\mathring{E}$ (e.g., Figure 2). A vertex represents a set of memory addresses, which include program variables $x \in \mathbf{Var}$ and abstract locations $a \in \mathbf{AbsLoc}$ (i.e., $\mathring{V} \supseteq \mathbf{Var} \cup \mathbf{AbsLoc}$). An abstract location a abstracts non–program-variable locations (e.g., from dynamic memory allocation). We do not fix the heap abstraction, such as the level of context sensitivity, but we do assume that we are given the abstract location to which any `new` allocation belongs (via the subscript annotation). A points-to edge from $\mathring{E}$ is either of the form $x \mapsto\!\!\!\Rightarrow a$ or $a_0 \cdot f \mapsto\!\!\!\Rightarrow a_1$. The form $x \mapsto\!\!\!\Rightarrow a$ means a concrete memory address represented by the program variable x may contain a value represented by abstract location a. We write $a_0 \cdot f \mapsto\!\!\!\Rightarrow a_1$ to denote that f is the label for the edge between nodes a_0 and a_1. This edge form means that $a_0 \cdot f$ is a field of an object in the concretization of a_0 that may contain a value represented by abstract location a_1. A **static** field in Java can be modeled as a global program variable.

Our analysis permits formulating a query Q over a finite number of heap locations along with constraints over data fields:

queries	$Q ::= M \wedge P \mid \mathsf{false}$
memories	$M ::= \mathsf{any} \mid x \mapsto \widehat{v} \mid \widehat{v} \cdot f \mapsto \widehat{u} \mid M_1 * M_2$
pure formulæ	$P ::= \mathsf{true} \mid P_1 \wedge P_2 \mid \widehat{v}\; \mathsf{from}\; \mathring{r} \mid \cdots$
points-to regions	$\mathring{r}, \mathring{s} ::= a \mid \mathsf{data} \mid \mathring{r}_1 \uplus \mathring{r}_2$
instances	$\widehat{v}, \widehat{u}$
refutation states	$R ::= Q \mid R_1 \vee R_2 \mid \exists \widehat{v}. R$

We give a heap location via an *exact points-to edge constraint* having one of two forms: $x \mapsto \widehat{v}$ or $\widehat{v} \cdot f \mapsto \widehat{u}$. Recall that in contrast to points-to edges that summarize a *set* of concrete memory cells, an exact points-to constraint expresses a single memory cell. The first form $x \mapsto \widehat{v}$ means a memory address represented by the program variable x contains a value represented by a symbolic variable $\widehat{v}$ (and similarly for the second form for a field). Since we are mostly concerned with memory addresses for concrete object instances, we often refer to symbolic variables as *instances*. The memory any stands for an arbitrary memory.

We introduce one non-standard pure constraint form: the *instance constraint* $\widehat{v}\; \mathsf{from}\; \mathring{r}$ says the symbolic variable $\widehat{v}$ is an instance of a points-to region $\mathring{r}$ (i.e., is in the set of values described by region $\mathring{r}$). A *points-to region* is a set of abstract locations a or the special region data. For uniformity, the region data is used to represent the set of values that are not memory addresses, such as integer values. As we have seen in Section 2.2, instance constraints enable us to use information from the up-front points-to analysis in our witness-refutation analysis. As an example, the informal query $\mathsf{arr}_0 \cdot \mathsf{contents} \mapsto \mathsf{act}_0$ from Section 2 is expressed as follows:

$$\widehat{v}_1 \cdot \mathsf{contents}_{[\widehat{v}_3]} \mapsto \widehat{v}_2 \wedge \widehat{v}_1\; \mathsf{from}\; \{\mathsf{arr}_0\} \wedge \widehat{v}_2\; \mathsf{from}\; \{\mathsf{act}_0\} \wedge \widehat{v}_3\; \mathsf{from}\; \mathsf{data}$$

where $\widehat{v}_3$ stands for the index of the array. This query considers existentially an instance of each abstract location arr_0 and act_0.

When writing down queries, we assume the usual commutativity, associativity, and unit laws from separation logic [41]. Since we are interested in witnessing or refuting a subset of edges corresponding to part of the memory, we interpret any memory M as $M * \mathsf{any}$ (or intuitionistically instead of classically [32, 41]).

3.2 Witness-Refutation Search with Instance Constraints

As described in Section 2, we perform a path-program–by–path-program, backwards symbolic analysis to find a witness for a given query Q. A refutation state R is simply a disjunction of queries, which we often view as a set of candidate witnesses. We include an existential binding of instances $\exists \widehat{v}. R$ to make explicit when we introduce fresh instances, but we implicitly view instances as renamed so that they are all bound at the top-level (i.e., all formulæ are in prenex normal form). Informally, a path program witness is a query Q_{wit} bundled with a sub-program examined so far s_{wit} and a sub-program left to be explored s_{pre}.

Definition 1 (Path Program Witness). A *path program witness* for an input statement-query pair $\langle s, Q \rangle$ is a triple $\langle s_{\mathrm{pre}}, Q_{\mathrm{wit}}, s_{\mathrm{wit}} \rangle$ where (1) $s \equiv s_{\mathrm{pre}} \,;\, s_{\mathrm{post}}$, and (2) s_{wit} is a sub-statement of s_{post} such that (a) if an execution of s_{post} leads to a store σ_{post} satisfying the input query Q, then it must be from a store σ_{wit} satisfying Q_{wit} and (b) executing s_{wit} from σ_{wit} also leads to σ_{post}.

$$\boxed{\vdash \{R\}\, s\, \{Q\} \qquad \vdash \{R'\}\, s\, \{R\}}$$

$$\textsc{WitRefuted}\ \frac{}{\vdash \{\mathsf{false}\}\, s\, \{\mathsf{false}\}} \qquad \textsc{WitCases}\ \frac{\vdash \{R'_1\}\, s\, \{R_1\} \qquad \vdash \{R'_2\}\, s\, \{R_2\}}{\vdash \{R'_1 \vee R'_2\}\, s\, \{R_1 \vee R_2\}}$$

$$\textsc{WitSkip}\ \frac{}{\vdash \{\mathsf{any} \wedge \mathsf{true}\}\, s\, \{\mathsf{any} \wedge \mathsf{true}\}} \qquad \textsc{WitFrame}\ \frac{\vdash \{\bigvee_i M'_i \wedge P'_i\}\, s\, \{M \wedge P\} \quad s \text{ must not modify } M_{\mathrm{fr}}}{\vdash \{\bigvee_i (M_{\mathrm{fr}} \ast M'_i) \wedge P'_i\}\, s\, \{(M_{\mathrm{fr}} \ast M) \wedge P\}}$$

$$\boxed{\vdash \{R\}\, c\, \{Q\}}$$

$$\textsc{WitNew}\ \frac{}{\vdash \{\mathsf{any} \wedge \ \boxed{\widehat{v}\ \mathsf{from}\ a \cap \mathring{r}}\ \wedge P\}\ x := \mathtt{new}_a\, \tau()\ \{x \mapsto \widehat{v} \wedge \widehat{v}\ \mathsf{from}\ \mathring{r} \wedge P\}}$$

$$\textsc{WitAssign}\ \frac{}{\vdash \{y \mapsto \widehat{v} \wedge \ \boxed{\widehat{v}\ \mathsf{from}\ \mathrm{pt}_{\mathring{G}}(y) \cap \mathring{r}}\ \wedge P\}\ x := y\ \{x \mapsto \widehat{v} \wedge \widehat{v}\ \mathsf{from}\ \mathring{r} \wedge P\}}$$

$$\textsc{WitRead}\ \frac{P' = \widehat{u}\ \mathsf{from}\ \mathrm{pt}_{\mathring{G}}(y) \wedge \ \boxed{\widehat{v}\ \mathsf{from}\ \mathrm{pt}_{\mathring{G}}(y.f) \cap \mathring{r}}\ \wedge P}{\vdash \{\exists \widehat{u}.\, y \mapsto \widehat{u} \ast \widehat{u}\cdot f \mapsto \widehat{v} \wedge P'\}\ x := y.f\ \{x \mapsto \widehat{v} \wedge \widehat{v}\ \mathsf{from}\ \mathring{r} \wedge P\}}$$

$$\textsc{WitWrite}\ \frac{\begin{array}{c} M_i = x \mapsto \widehat{v}_i \ast y \mapsto \widehat{u}_i \ast (\bigast_{j \neq i} \widehat{v}_j \cdot f \mapsto \widehat{u}_j \wedge \widehat{v}_j\ \mathsf{from}\ \mathring{r}_j \wedge \widehat{u}_j\ \mathsf{from}\ \mathring{s}_j) \\ Q_i = M_i \wedge \ \boxed{\widehat{v}_i\ \mathsf{from}\ \mathrm{pt}_{\mathring{G}}(x) \cap \mathring{r}_i}\ \wedge \ \boxed{\widehat{u}_i\ \mathsf{from}\ \mathrm{pt}_{\mathring{G}}(y) \cap \mathring{s}_i}\ \wedge (\bigwedge_{j \neq i} \widehat{v}_j \neq \widehat{v}_i) \wedge P \\ Q = \exists \widehat{x}.\, x \mapsto \widehat{x} \ast (\bigast_i \widehat{v}_i \cdot f \mapsto \widehat{u}_i \wedge \widehat{v}_i\ \mathsf{from}\ \mathring{r}_i \wedge \widehat{u}_i\ \mathsf{from}\ \mathring{s}_i \wedge \widehat{v}_i \neq \widehat{x}) \wedge \widehat{x}\ \mathsf{from}\ \mathrm{pt}_{\mathring{G}}(x) \wedge P \end{array}}{\vdash \{Q \vee \bigvee_i Q_i\}\ x.f := y\ \{(\bigast_i \widehat{v}_i \cdot f \mapsto \widehat{u}_i \wedge \widehat{v}_i\ \mathsf{from}\ \mathring{r}_i \wedge \widehat{u}_i\ \mathsf{from}\ \mathring{s}_i) \wedge P\}}$$

Figure 4. Witness-refutation search is a path-program–by–path-program backwards analysis. Boxed terms emphasize opportunities for refuting paths using instance constraints.

Any intermediate state in our backwards analysis is such a path program witness. Intuitively, the statement s_{wit} captures the path sub-program identified by the backwards analysis that is relevant to producing the input query Q (so far). A refutation occurs when Q_{wit} is false, that is, we have discovered that it is not possible to end up in a state satisfying Q. A "full" witness is when Q_{wit} is any; that is, we can no longer find a refutation. A "partial" witness is a witness where Q_{wit} is a query other than any or false.

We formalize a backwards path program enumeration transforming queries into sub-queries to eventually produce an any or a false refutation state. To describe the analysis, we define the judgment form $\vdash \{R'\}\ s\ \{R\}$ in Figure 4. This judgment form is a standard Hoare triple, but because our analysis is backwards, we read this judgment form from right-to-left. It says, "Given a post-formula R, we find a pre-formula R' such that executing statement s from a state satisfying R' yields a state satisfying R (up to termination)." Conceptually, the post-formula R is a (disjunctive) set of queries, and the pre-formula R' is the set of sub-queries. The path program s_{wit} can be obtained by a simple instrumentation of the rules similar to our prior work [8].

Deriving Refutations. At any point, we can extend the witness-refutation search for some disjunct. Here, we express this step with WitCases, which says a disjunctive refutation state $R_1 \vee R_2$ can be derived by finding a witness for R_1 and R_2. We make this system algorithmic for an implementation by representing cases as a disjunctive set of pending queries $\cdots \vee Q_i \vee \cdots$ that we extend individually. Rule WitRefuted simply says if we have derived false in the post-state for a statement, then we have false in the pre-state as well. To scale beyond the tiniest of programs, we need to be able to refute queries quickly so that the number of queries to consider, that is, the number of symbolic execution paths to explore, remains small. We have three tools for refuting queries: (1) separation (i.e., a query where a single memory cell would need to point to two locations simultaneously), (2) instance constraints (i.e., a query where an instance cannot be in any points-to region), and (3) other pure constraints (i.e., a query with pure constraints that are unsatisfiable, such as, from detecting an infeasible control-flow path). In our inference rules, we assume a refutation state R is always normalized to false if the formula is unsatisfiable. Since we are interested in sound refutations and over-approximate witnesses, for scaling, we can also weaken queries at the cost of potentially losing precision. We revisit this notion in Section 3.3.

Instance constraints are pure constraints that tie the exact points-to constraints in the query to the accumulated information from the up-front points-to analysis and the flow of the symbolic variables as discussed in Section 2.2. They can axiomatized as follows:

$$\widehat{v}\ \mathsf{from}\ \emptyset \iff \mathsf{false} \tag{1}$$

$$\widehat{v}\ \mathsf{from}\ \mathring{r}_1 \wedge \widehat{v}\ \mathsf{from}\ \mathring{r}_2 \iff \widehat{v}\ \mathsf{from}\ \mathring{r}_1 \cap \mathring{r}_2 \tag{2}$$

$$\mathsf{true} \iff \widehat{v}\ \mathsf{from}\ \mathbf{AbsLoc} \cup \{\mathsf{data}\} \tag{3}$$

In particular, we derive a contradiction when we discover an instance that can be drawn from any abstract location (axiom 1). Though our formalism groups instance constraints and other pure constraints together, our implementation keeps them separate for simplicity in checking. Instance constraints are checked using basic set operations and other pure constraints are checked with an off-the-shelf SMT solver, though it should be possible to encode instance constraints into the solver using this axiomatization.

We include a frame rule on M, WitFrame, to simplify our presentation, which together with WitSkip allow us to isolate the parts of the query that a block of code may affect and to ignore irrelevant statements. In other words, any statements that cannot affect the memory state in the query can be skipped. We can thus focus our discussion on an auxiliary judgment form $\vdash \{R\}\ c\ \{Q\}$ that describes how the assignment commands affect a query and its point-to and instance constraints. Informally, it says, "We can witness a query Q after assignment command c by executing c if we can also witness one of the sub-queries R before c." From an algorithmic perspective, we can view $\vdash \{R\}\ c\ \{Q\}$ as generating sub-queries that when combined with a frame may yield additional contradictions. We assume this judgment implicitly has access to the points-to graph $\mathring{G}\colon \langle \mathring{V}, \mathring{E} \rangle$ computed by the up-front analysis. We use the $\mathrm{pt}_{\mathring{G}}(\cdot)$ function to get the points-to set of a program variable via $\mathrm{pt}_{\mathring{G}}(x) \stackrel{\text{def}}{=} \{a \mid (x \mapsto a) \in \mathring{E}\}$ or a field of a program variable via $\mathrm{pt}_{\mathring{G}}(y.f) \stackrel{\text{def}}{=} \{a_j \mid a_i \in \mathrm{pt}_{\mathring{G}}(y) \text{ and } (a_i \cdot \mathsf{f} \mapsto a_j) \in \mathring{E}\}$.

Backwards Transfer Functions and Instance Constraints. Rule WitNew says that the exact points-to constraint $x \mapsto \widehat{v}$ can be witnessed, or *produced*, by the allocation command $x := \mathtt{new}_a\, \tau()$ if instance $\widehat{v}$ may have been created at allocation site a. Following our axiomatization, the instance constraint $\widehat{v}\ \mathsf{from}\ a \cap \mathring{r}$ may immediately reduce to false if $a \notin \mathring{r}$. Or, we can drop it (without loss of precision) because this instance cannot exist before its allocation at this statement. Such a contradiction is precisely the reason for refuting the path at the new arr_1 allocation (program point 16) in our motivating example (Figure 1).

Now, consider rule WitAssign: it says that the exact points-to constraint $x \mapsto \widehat{v}$ can be produced by the assignment command $x := y$ if $y \mapsto \widehat{v}$ can be witnessed before this assignment *and* the instance $\widehat{v}$ can come from a region common to the points-to set of y and the region $\mathring{r}$. If the points-to set of y and the region $\mathring{r}$ are disjoint, we can derive a contradiction because the instance $\widehat{v}$ cannot come from any allocation site. Observe that WitAssign leverages the 'from' constraint and the up-front points-to analysis result to eagerly discover that *no* allocation site satisfies the conditions required for a witness (rather than observing that a *particular* allocation site does not satisfy the conditions required for a witness, as in WITNEW). To get a sense for why these eager refutations are critical for scaling, consider the path refutation due to the binding of val to `"hello"` at the `objs.push` call site (program point 8). In our example, this refutation is via WITNEW because `"hello"` is a `String` allocation, but we can easily imagine a variant where `objs.push` is called with a program variable y that can conservatively point-to a large set of non-Activity objects. For such a program, WITASSIGN would allow us to discover a path refutation at the assignment corresponding to the binding rather than requiring us to continue exploration across the potentially exponential number of paths to the allocation sites that flow to y.

The WITREAD rule is quite similar to WITASSIGN except that we existentially quantify over the instance to which y points (i.e., $\widehat{u}$). We set up an initial points-to region constraint for the fresh symbolic variable $\widehat{u}$ based on the points-to set of y and narrow the points-to region of $\widehat{v}$ using the points-to set of $y.f$. As in WITASSIGN, we can derive a contradiction based on this narrowing if the region $\mathring{r}$ and the points-to set of $y.f$ are disjoint. Here, we have taken some liberty with notation placing, for example, 'from' constraints under the iterated separating conjunctions; we recall that $*$ collapses to $\wedge$ for pure constraints.

In the WITWRITE rule, the post-formula consists of two cases for each edge $\widehat{v}_i{\cdot}f \mapsto \widehat{u}_i$ in the pre-formula: (1) the field write $x.f$ `:=` y did not produce the edge $\widehat{v}_i{\cdot}f \mapsto \widehat{u}_i$ (the first disjunct Q), or (2) the field write did produce the edge (the second set of disjuncts over all Q_i). If the write $x.f$ `:=` y did produce the points-to edge $\widehat{v}_i{\cdot}f \mapsto \widehat{u}_i$, then the points-to regions of $\widehat{v}_i$ and $\widehat{u}_i$ are restricted based on the points-to sets of x and y, respectively. The "not produced" case represents the possibility that this write updates an instance other than a $\widehat{v}_i$ (as reflected by the $x \mapsto \widehat{x}$ and $\widehat{v}_i \neq \widehat{x}$ conditions).

While WITWRITE can theoretically generate a huge case split, we have observed that the combination of instance constraints and separation typically allow us to find refutations quickly in practice (see Section 4). In particular, the "not written" case can often be immediately refuted by separation. For example, we end up with a contradictory query where a local variable x has to point to two different instances simultaneously (i.e., $\mathsf{x} \mapsto \widehat{v} * \mathsf{x} \mapsto \widehat{u} \wedge \widehat{v} \neq \widehat{u}$).

Guards and Control Flow. Except for loops (see Section 3.3), the remaining rules mostly relate to control flow and are quite standard (shown inset). To discover a contradiction on pure constraints, we state that the guard condition of an `assume` must hold in the pre-query. We write $e[M]$ for interpreting the program expression e in the memory state M.

WITASSUME

$$\frac{}{\vdash \{ M \wedge P \wedge e[M] \}\ \texttt{assume}\, e\ \{ M \wedge P \}}$$

WITSEQ

$$\frac{\vdash \{ R'' \}\ s_1\ \{ R' \} \qquad \vdash \{ R' \}\ s_2\ \{ R \}}{\vdash \{ R'' \}\ s_1\ ;\ s_2\ \{ R \}}$$

WITCHOICE

$$\frac{\vdash \{ R_1 \}\ s_1\ \{ R \} \qquad \vdash \{ R_2 \}\ s_2\ \{ R \}}{\vdash \{ R_1 \vee R_2 \}\ s_1 \,[\,]\, s_2\ \{ R \}}$$

The WITCHOICE rule analyzes each branch independently. Our implementation avoids path explosion due to irrelevant path sensitivity by adding pure constraints from `if`-guards only when the queries on each side of the branch are different (as in previous work [18, 39]), though our rules do not express this.

3.3 Loop Invariant Inference and Query Simplification

In this section, we finish our description of witness-refutation search by discussing our loop invariant inference scheme.

Roughly speaking, we infer loop invariants by repeatedly performing backwards symbolic execution over the loop body until we reach a fixed point over the domain of points-to constraints. To ensure termination, we drop all pure constraints affected by the loop body and fix a static bound on the number of instances of each abstract location to materialize. In our experiments, a static bound of one has been sufficient for precise results. The WITLOOP rule (shown inset) simply states that if the loop body has no effect on the query, the loop has no effect on it.

WITLOOP

$$\frac{\vdash \{ R \}\ s\ \{ R \}}{\vdash \{ R \}\ \texttt{loop}\, s\ \{ R \}}$$

WITABSTRACTION

$$\frac{R_2' \models R_1' \quad \vdash \{ R_2' \}\ s\ \{ R_2 \} \quad R_1 \models R_2}{\vdash \{ R_1' \}\ s\ \{ R_1 \}}$$

By itself, this rule only handles the degenerate case where a loop can be treated as `skip` with respect to the query. For this case, the disjunctive set of queries R is trivially a loop invariant. For more interesting cases, we use WITCASES to consider each query in the refutation state individually so that we can infer an over-approximate loop invariant for each one. Thus, we infer a loop invariant on-the-fly for each *path program* rather than joining all queries at the loop exit and then inferring an invariant for all backwards paths into the loop (similar to [35] but with heap constraints).

To preserve refutation soundness, we want to ensure that a contradiction false is only derived when there does not exist a concrete path witnessing the given query and thus must over-approximate loops. A sound, backwards over-approximation can be obtained by weakening the post-loop query Q_i. Since an individual query is purely conjunctive, we can weaken it quite easily by "dropping" constraints (i.e., removing conjuncts). Intuitively, dropping constraints is refutation-sound because it can only make it more difficult to derive a contradiction. This over-approximation is captured by the WITABSTRACTION rule. The rule says that at any program point, we can drop constraints, and doing so preserves refutation soundness (Theorem 1).

We write $R_1 \models R_2$ for the semantic entailment and correspondingly rely on a sound decision procedure in our implementation (used in WITABSTRACTION). Entailment between a finite separating conjunction exact points-to constraints can be resolved in a standard way by subtraction [5]. Without inductive predicates, the procedure is a straightforward matching. Entailment between the 'from' instance constraints can be defined as follows:

$$(\widehat{v}_1 \text{ from } \mathring{r}_1) \models (\widehat{v}_2 \text{ from } \mathring{r}_2) \quad \text{iff} \quad \widehat{v}_1 = \widehat{v}_2 \text{ and } \mathring{r}_1 \subseteq \mathring{r}_2 \qquad (\S)$$

As previously mentioned, 'from' constraints are represented as sets associated with a symbolic variable and solved with ordinary set operations. We discharge other pure constraints using an off-the-shelf SMT solver, so precision of reasoning about those constraints is with respect to the capabilities of the solver.

With these tools, our loop invariant inference is a rather straightforward fixed-point computation. For a loop statement $\texttt{loop}\,s$ and a post-loop query Q, we iteratively apply the backwards predicate transformer for the loop body s to saturate a set of sub-queries at the loop head. Let R_0 be some refutation state such that $\vdash \{ R_0 \}\ s\ \{ Q \}$, and let $R_{i+1} = R_i \vee R'$ where $\vdash \{ R' \}\ s\ \{ R_i \}$. We ensure that the chain of $R_0 \models R_1 \models \cdots$ converges by bounding the number of instances or materializations from the abstract locations. Since there are a finite number of abstract locations, the number of points-to constraints in any particular query is bounded by the number of edges in the points-to graph (i.e., $|\mathring{E}|$). For the base domain of pure constraints, widening [14] can be used to ensure convergence. Our implementation uses a trivial widening that drops pure constraints that may be modified by the loop.

Query Simplification with Disaliasing. The WITABSTRACTION rule captures backwards over-approximation by saying that at any point, we can weaken a refutation state without losing refutation soundness. Conceptually, we can weaken by replacing any symbolic join $\vee$ with an over-approximate join $\sqcup$. We perform one such join by replacing the refutation state $Q_1 \vee Q_2$ with Q_2 if $Q_1 \models Q_2$. Note that this join does not lose precision. Intuitively, for a refutation state R, we are interested in witnessing *any* query in R or refuting *all* queries in R. Here, a refutation of query Q_2 implies a refutation of Q_1, so we only need to consider Q_2.

To enable this join to apply often, we enforce a normal form for our queries by dropping certain kinds of constraints. As formalized in Figure 4, the backwards transfer functions for assignment commands c are as precise as possible, including the generation of disequality constraints in WITWRITE. These disequality constraints are needed locally to check for refutations due to separation, as detailed in Section 3.2. However, if this check passes, we drop them before proceeding and instead keep only the disaliasing information implied by separation and the instance from constraints. While this weakening could lose precision (e.g., if the backwards analysis would later encounter an `if`-guard for the aliasing condition), we hypothesize that this situation is rare and that the most useful disaliasing information is captured by separation and instance constraints.

In our implementation, we are much closer to a path-by-path analysis than our formalization would indicate. Refutation states are represented as a worklist of pending (non-disjunctive) queries to explore. To apply the simplification described above, we must keep a history of queries seen at a given program point: if we have previously seen a weaker query at this program point, then we can drop the current query. We keep a query history only at procedure boundaries and loop heads. This simplification has been especially critical for procedures.

Soundness. We define a concrete store σ be a finite mapping from variables or address-field pairs to concrete values (i.e., $\sigma : \mathbf{Var} \uplus (\mathbf{Addr} \times \mathbf{Field}) \rightharpoonup_{\text{fin}} \mathbf{Val}$) and give a standard big-step operational semantics to our basic imperative language The judgment form $\sigma \vdash s \downarrow \sigma'$ says, "In store σ, statement s evaluates to store σ'." Furthermore, we write $\sigma \models R$ to say that the store σ is in the concretization of the refutation state R. The definition of $\sigma \models R$ is as would be expected in comparison to separation logic. We need to utilize two other concrete semantic domains: a valuation η that maps instances to values (i.e., $\eta : \mathbf{Instance} \to \mathbf{Val}$) and a *regionalization* ρ that maps abstract locations to sets of concrete addresses (i.e., $\rho : \mathbf{AbsLoc} \to \wp(\mathbf{Addr})$). The regionalization gives meaning to the 'from' instance constraint. With these definitions, we precisely state the soundness theorem.

Theorem 1 (Refutation Soundness). *If* $\vdash \{R_{\text{pre}}\}\ s\ \{R_{\text{post}}\}$ *and* $\sigma_{\text{pre}} \vdash s \downarrow \sigma_{\text{post}}$ *such that* $\sigma_{\text{post}} \models R_{\text{post}}$, *then* $\sigma_{\text{pre}} \models R_{\text{pre}}$. *As a corollary, refutations (i.e., when* R_{pre} *is* false*) are sound.*

Interestingly, the standard consequence rule from Hoare logic states the opposite in comparison to WITABSTRACTION by permitting the strengthening of queries. Doing so would instead preserve witness precision; that is, any path program witness exhibits some witness path (up to termination).

4. Case Study: Activity Leaks in Android

We evaluated our witness-refutation analysis by using it to find Activity leaks, a common class of memory leaks in open-source Android applications. We explain this client in more detail below. Our experiments were designed to test two hypotheses. The first and most important concerns the *precision* of our approach: we hypothesized that witness-refutation analysis reports many fewer false alarms than a flow-insensitive points-to analysis. We tried using a flow-insensitive analysis to find leaks, but found that the number of alarms reported was too large to examine manually. To be useful, our technique needs to prune this number enough for a user to effectively triage the results and identify real leaks. Our second hypothesis concerns the *utility* of our techniques: we posited that (1) our mixed symbolic-explicit is an improvement over both a fully explicit and a fully symbolic representation, (2) our query simplification significantly speeds up analysis, and (3) our on-the-fly loop invariant inference is needed to preserve precision in the presence of loops.

Client. Activity leaks occur when a pointer to an Activity object can outlive the Activity. The operating system frequently destroys Activity's when configuration changes occur (e.g., rotating the phone). Once an Activity is destroyed, it can never be displayed to the user again and thus represents unused memory that should be reclaimed by the garbage collector. However, if an application developer maintains a pointer to an Activity after it is destroyed, the garbage collector will be unable to reclaim it. In our experiments, we check if *any* Activity instance is ever reachable from a static field, a flow-insensitive property. Though a developer could safely keep a reference to an Activity object via a static field that is cleared each time the Activity is destroyed, this is recognized as bad practice.

Activity leaking is a serious problem. It is well-documented that keeping persistent references to Activity's is bad practice; we refer the reader to an article[2] in the Android Developers Blog as evidence. The true problem is that it is quite easy for developers to inadvertently keep persistent references to an Activity. Sub-components of Activity's (such as Adapter's, Cursor's, and View's) typically keep pointers to their parent Activity, meaning that any persistent reference to an element in the Activity's hierarchy can potentially create a leak.

Precision of Our Techniques: Threshing Alarms. We implemented our witness-refutation analysis in the THRESHER tool, which is publicly available.[3] Additional details on our implementation are included at the end of this section. All of our experiments were performed on a machine running Ubuntu 12.04.2 with a 2.93 GHz Intel Xeon processor and 32GB of memory. Though our analysis is quite amenable to parallelization in theory, our current implementation is purely sequential.

To evaluate the precision of our approach, we computed a flow-insensitive points-to graph for each application and the Android library (version 2.3.3) using WALA's 0-1-Container-CFA pointer analysis (a variation of Andersen's analysis with unlimited context sensitivity for container classes). For each heap path from a static field f to an Activity instance A in the points-to graph, we asked THRESHER to witness or refute each edge in the path from source to sink. If we refuted an edge in the heap path, we searched for a new path. We repeated this until THRESHER either witnessed each edge in the heap path (i.e., confirmed the flow-insensitive alarm) or refuted enough edges to prove that no heap path from f to A can exist (i.e., filtered out the leak report). We allowed an exploration budget of 10,000 path programs for each edge; if the tool exceeded the budget, we declared a timeout for that edge and considered it to be not refuted. On paths with call stacks of depth greater than three, we soundly skipped callees by dropping constraints that executing the call might produce (according to a mod/ref analysis computed alongside the points-to analysis). We limited the size of the path constraint set to at most two. Allowing larger path constraint sets slowed down the symbolic executor without increasing precision. We ran in two configurations: one with the Android library as-is (**Ann?**=N), and one where we added a single annotation to the HashMap class to indicate that the shared `EMPTY_TABLE` field can never point to anything (**Ann?**=Y). We did this because we observed that the use of the null object pattern in the HashMap class was a major source of imprecision for the flow-insensitive analysis (cf. Figure 1), but we wanted to make sure that it was not the only one our tool was able to handle.

[2] `http://developer.android.com/resources/articles/avoiding-memory-leaks.html`

[3] `https://github.com/cuplv/thresher`

	Benchmark *Size*			*Filtering* Effectiveness						Computational *Effort*			
Benchmark	**SLOC**	**CGB**	**Ann?**	**Alrms**	**RefA(%)**	**TruA(%)**	**FalA(%)**	**Flds**	**RefFlds**	**RefEdg**	**WitEdg**	**TO**	**T (s)**
PulsePoint♠	no src	198K	N	24	16 (67)	8 (33)	0 (0)	3	2	47	40	1	750
			Y	16	8 (50)	8 (50)	0 (0)	2	1	40	31	0	95
StandupTimer♣	2K	240K	N	25	15 (60)	0 (0)	10 (40)	5	3	18	26	0	1199
			Y	25	15 (60)	0 (0)	10 (40)	5	3	18	26	0	1068
DroidLife♠	3K	132K	N	3	0 (0)	3 (100)	0 (0)	1	0	0	4	0	1
			Y	3	0 (0)	3 (100)	0 (0)	1	0	0	4	0	1
OpenSudoku	6K	229K	N	7	1 (14)	0 (0)	6 (86)	1	0	2	21	1	1596
			Y	0	0 (0)	0 (0)	0 (0)	0	0	0	0	0	0
SMSPopUp♠	7K	232K	N	5	1 (20)	4 (80)	0 (0)	1	0	10	24	0	49
			Y	5	1 (20)	4 (80)	0 (0)	1	0	10	24	0	46
aMetro♠	20K	326K	N	144	18 (12)	36 (25)	90 (63)	8	1	62	66	3	4226
			Y	54	18 (33)	36 (67)	0 (0)	3	1	55	24	0	18
K9Mail♠	40K	394K	N	364	78 (21)	64 (18)	222 (61)	14	3	141	106	1	1130
			Y	208	130 (63)	64 (49)	14 (7)	8	5	124	80	0	374
Total	78K	1751K	N	572	129 (22)	115 (20)	332 (58)	33	9	280	287	6	8991
			Y	311	172 (55)	115 (37)	24 (8)	20	10	247	189	0	1602

Table 1. This table characterizes the size of our benchmarks, highlights our success in distinguishing false alarms from real leaks, and quantifies the effort required to find refutations. ♠'s indicate a benchmark in which we found an observable leak, and ♣ indicates a latent leak. The *Size* column grouping gives the number of source lines of code **SLOC** and the number of bytecodes in the call graph **CGB** for each app as well as the annotation configuration **Ann?**=Y/N. The *Filtering* column grouping characterizes the effectiveness of our approach for filtering false alarms. The first four columns list the number of (static field, Activity) alarm pairs reported by the points-to analysis **Alarms**, number of alarms refuted by our approach **RefA**, number of true alarms **TruA**, and the number of false alarms **FalA**. The final two columns of this group give the number of leaky fields reported by the points-to analysis **Fields** and the number of these fields **RefFlds** that we can refute (i.e., prove that the field in question cannot point to *any* Activity). The *Effort* columns describe the amount of work required by our filtering approach. We list the number of edges refuted **RefEdg**, edges witnessed **WitEdg**, edge timeouts **TO**, and the time **T (s)** taken by the symbolic execution phase in seconds. This number does not include points-to analysis time, which ranged from 8–46 seconds on all benchmarks.

Table 1 shows the results of this experiment. We first comment on the most interesting part of the experiment: the *filtering effectiveness* of our analysis. As we hoped, our analysis is able to refute many of the false alarms produced by the flow-insensitive points-to analysis. Overall, we refute 129/457 = 28% of these false alarms in the un-annotated configuration and 172/196 = 87% of these false alarms in the annotated configuration. Contrary to our expectations, we found many *more* refutations in the **Ann?**=Y configuration, confirming that our technique can indeed remedy imprecision other than the pollution caused by HashMaps.

Unfortunately, this also means that our analysis is not always able to remedy the imprecision caused by HashMaps. The major problem is that the **Ann?**=N configuration fails to refute many of the HashMap-related edges due to timeouts. In fact, most of the false alarms that are not common to both configurations stem from (soundly) not considering timed-out edges to be refuted. We observed that a timeout commonly corresponds to a refutation that the analysis was unable to find within the path program budget. This is not surprising; finding a witness for an edge only requires finding a single path program that produces the edge (which we can usually do quickly), but to find a refutation we must refute *all* path programs that might produce an edge (which is slow and sometimes times out, potentially causing precision loss).

For example, the single timeout in the **Ann?**=N run of K9Mail occurs on a HashMap-related edge that is refutable, but quite challenging to refute. As it turns out, refuting this edge is extremely important for precision—upon further investigation, we discovered that the analysis would have reduced the number of false alarms reported by over 100 if it had been able to refute it! In the **Ann?**=Y configuration, this edge disappears from the flow-insensitive points-to graph. We can see that this increases the number of alarms we are able refute from 78 to 130 even though the number of alarms reported by the flow-insensitive points-to analysis falls from 364 to 208.

```
public class EmailAddressAdapter extends ResourceCursorAdapter {
  private static EmailAddressAdapter sInstance;
  public static EmailAddressAdapter getInstance(Context context) {
    if (sInstance == null)
      sInstance = new_adr0 EmailAddressAdapter(context);
    return sInstance;
  }
  private EmailAddressAdapter(Context context) { super(context); }
}
```

Figure 5. A confirmed Activity leak discovered in K9Mail.

We now comment on the *computational effort* required to refute/witness edges. We first observe that the number of edges refuted is almost always greater then the number of alarms refuted, indicating that it is frequently necessary to refute several edges in order to refute a single (source, sink) alarm pair. For example, in the un-annotated run of aMetro, we refute 62 edges in order to refute 18 alarms. This demonstrates that the flow-insensitive points-to analysis is imprecise enough to find many different ways to produce the same false alarm.

We note that the running times are quite reasonable for an analysis at this level of precision, especially in the annotated configuration. No benchmark other than aMetro takes more than a half hour. Our tool would be fast enough to be used in a heavyweight cloud service or as part of an overnight build process.

Real **Activity** ***Leaks.*** As hypothesized, our tool's precision enabled us to ignore most false alarms and focus on likely leaks. We found genuine leaks in PulsePoint, DroidLife, SMSPopUp, aMetro, and K9Mail. Many of the leaks we found would only manifest under specialized and complex circumstances, but a few of the nastiest leaks we found would almost always manifest and are due to the same simple problem: an inappropriate use of the singleton pattern. We briefly explain one such leak from the K9Mail app.

In the code in Figure 5, the developer uses the singleton pattern to ensure that only one instance of EmailAddressAdapter is ever created. The leak arises when `getInstance()` is called with an Activity instance passed as the `context` parameter (which happens in several places in K9Mail). The Activity instance is passed backwards through the constructors of two superclasses via the `context` parameter until it is finally stored in the `mContext` instance field of the CursorAdapter superclass. For *every* Activity act_0 that calls `getInstance()`, the flow-insensitive points-to analysis reports a heap path $\mathsf{EmailAddressAdapter{\cdot}sInstance} \mapsto \mathsf{adr}_0, \mathsf{adr}_0{\cdot}\mathsf{mContext} \mapsto \mathsf{act}_0$. When the Activity instance is destroyed, the garbage collector will never be able to reclaim it because none of the pointers involved in the leak are ever cleared.

We found this leak in a version of K9Mail that was downloaded in September 2011 (all versions of the benchmarks we used are available in project's GitHub repository). We looked at the current version and noticed that the EmailAddressAdapter class had been refactored to remove the singleton pattern. We found the commit that performed this refactoring and asked the developers of K9Mail if the purpose of this commit was to address a leak issue; they confirmed that it was.[4]

We also discovered a very simple latent leak in StandupTimer that was also due to a bad use of the singleton pattern. We noticed that several of the path programs THRESHER produced for a field in this app would be a full witness for a leak if a single boolean flag `cacheDAOInstances` were enabled. Our tool correctly recognizes that this flag cannot ever be set and refutes the alarm report, but a modification to the program that enabled this flag would result in a leak. The path program witnesses our tool produces are always helpful in triaging reported leak alarms, but in this case even the *refuted* path program witness provided useful information that allowed us to identify an almost-leak. With a less constructive refutation technique, we might have missed this detail.

Utility of Our Techniques. To test our second set of hypotheses, we ran THRESHER on the benchmarks from Table 1 without using each of three key features of our analysis: mixed symbolic-explicit query representation, query simplification, and loop invariant inference. We hypothesized that: (1) using an alternative query representation would negatively affect scalability and/or performance, (2) not simplifying queries would negatively affect scalability and/or performance, and (3) the absence of loop invariant inference would negatively affect precision.

To test hypothesis (1), we implemented a fully symbolic query representation. In a fully symbolic representation, we do not track the set of allocation sites that a variable might belong to. We have up-front points-to information, but use it only to confirm that two symbolic variables are *not* equal (i.e., to prevent aliasing case splits in the style of [39]) and to confirm that a symbolic variable was allocated at a given site (as in WITNEW). This precludes both pruning paths based on the boxed 'from' constraints in Figure 4 and performing the entailment check between symbolic variables defined in Equation § in Section 3.3.

Using this fully symbolic representation, our analysis ran slower and timed out more often, but did not refute any fewer alarms

Benchmark	Ann?	T (slowdown)	TO (Δ)
PulsePoint	N	1237 (1.6X)	7 (+6)
	Y	220 (1.9X)	3 (+3)
StandupTimer	N	4946 (4.1X)	4 (+4)
	Y	4104 (3.8X)	4 (+4)
OpenSudoku	N	2984 (1.9X)	4 (+3)
	Y	-	-
SMSPopUp	N	95 (1.9X)	0 (+0)
	Y	76 (1.7X)	0 (+0)
aMetro	N	6863 (1.6X)	5 (+2)
	Y	18 (1X)	0 (+0)
K9Mail	N	990 (0.9X)	2 (+1)
	Y	454 (1.2X)	0 (+0)

Table 2. Performance of the fully symbolic representation as compared to the mixed symbolic-explicit representation.

than the run with the mixed representation. We observed several cases where a timeout caused the fully symbolic representation to miss refuting an edge that the mixed representation was able to refute, but in each case the edge turned out not to be important for precision (that is, it was one of many edges that needed to be refuted in order to refute an alarm, but both representations failed to refute all of these edges).

The results of this experiment are shown in Table 2. We omit the results for DroidLife since they were unaffected by the choice of representation. For every other benchmark, we give the time taken with a fully symbolic representation, the number of times slower than the mixed representation this was (**T (slowdown)**), the number of edges that timed out, and how many timeouts were added over the mixed representation (**TO (Δ)**).

We can see that in both the annotated and un-annotated configurations, most benchmarks run at least 1.6X slower and time out on at least one more edge than they did with the mixed representation. The anomalous behavior of K9Mail in the un-annotated configuration occurs because the mixed representation is able to refute an edge that the fully symbolic representation times out on. Ultimately, this leads the mixed representation to make more progress towards (but ultimately fail in) refuting a particular alarm. The fully symbolic representation declares this particular alarm witnessed after the edge in question times out, which allows it to skip this effort and finish faster. Thus, hypothesis (1) seems to hold: using a fully symbolic representation negatively affected both performance and scalability as predicted, but choosing a fully symbolic representation did not ultimately affect the precision of the analysis in terms of alarms filtered.

To test hypothesis (2), we re-ran THRESHER on our benchmarks using the annotated Android library without performing any query simplification at all. This significantly hurt the performance of THRESHER on PulsePoint (102.4X slower), K9Mail (3.2X slower), and SMSPopUp (4.3X slower), but did not change the number of alarms refuted or witnessed for these benchmarks. On StandupTimer, not performing simplification caused the tool to run out of memory before completing the analysis, thus affecting both precision and performance. The performance of the tool on other apps was not significantly affected. Thus, hypothesis (2) seems to hold for the benchmarks that require significant computational effort.

Finally, to test hypothesis (3), we implemented a simple loop invariant inference that simply drops all possibly-affected constraints at any loop. With only this simple inference, the analysis was unable to refute some critical HashMap-related edges (using the un-annotated library). This meant that the analysis could never distinguish the contents of different HashMap objects. This imprecision

[4] `https://groups.google.com/forum/?fromgroups=#!topic/k-9-mail/JhoXL2c4UfU`

prevented the analysis from refuting leak reports involving multiple HashMap's even on small, hand-written test cases. Our full loop invariant inference (Section 3.3) handled the hand-written cases precisely, but due to unrelated analysis limitations, it did not achieve any fewer overall refutations on our real benchmarks. Nevertheless, our testing confirmed hypothesis (3): our loop invariant inference was clearly necessary to properly handle Android HashMap's and similar data structures.

Implementation. THRESHER is built on top of the on the WALA program analysis framework for Java and uses the Z3 [19] SMT solver with JVM support via ScalaZ3 [34] to determine when path constraints are unsatisfiable. Like most static analysis tools that handle real-world programs, our tool has a few known sources of unsoundness. We do not reason about reflection or handle concurrency. We have source code for most (but not all) non-native Java library methods. In particular, the Android library custom implementations of core Java library classes (including collections) that we analyze. To focus our reasoning on Android library and application code, we exclude classes from Apache libraries, `java/nio/Charset`, and `java/util/concurrent` from the call graph. Though we track control flow due to thrown exceptions, we do not handle the **catch**() construct; instead, we assume that thrown exceptions are never caught.

Android apps are event-driven and (in general) Android event handlers can be called any number of times and in (almost) any order. We use a top-level harness that invokes every event handler defined for an application. Our harness allows event handlers to be invoked in any order, but insists that each handler is called only once in order to prevent termination issues. In our experiments, we did not observe any unsound refutations due to these limitations.

We do not do any modeling for special Android components such as Intent's and BroadcastReceiver's. Since most special components are used for communication between applications that run in separate memory spaces, we would not expect THRESHER to miss any memory leaks due to this modeling issue.

5. Related Work

Dillig et al. present precise heap analyses for programs manipulating arrays and containers [21, 22], with path and context sensitivity [20]. Our analysis introduces path and context sensitivity via on-demand refinement, in contrast to their exhaustive, summary-based approach. Our symbolic variables are similar to their index variables [21, 22] in that both symbolically represent concrete locations and enable lazy case splits. Unlike index variables, our symbolic variables do not distinguish specific array indices or loop iterations, since this was not required for our memory leak client. Also, our analysis does not require container specifications [22]; instead, we analyze container implementations directly. Hackett and Aiken [29] present a points-to analysis with intra-procedural path sensitivity, which is insufficient for our needs.

Several previous systems focused on performing effective backward symbolic analysis. The pioneering ESC/Java system [27] performed intra-procedural backward analysis, generating a polynomially-sized verification condition and checking its validity with a theorem prover. Snugglebug [11] performed inter-procedural backward symbolic analysis, employing directed call graph construction and custom simplifiers to improve scalability. Cousot et al. [17] present backward symbolic analysis as one of a suite of techniques for transforming intermittent assertions in a method into executable pre-condition checks. PSE [39] used backward symbolic analysis to help explain program failures, but for greater scalability, it did not represent full path conditions. Our work is distinguished from these previous systems by the integration of points-to analysis information, which enables key optimizations like mixed symbolic-explicit states and abstraction for loop handling.

Our analysis can be seen as refining the initial flow-insensitive abstraction of the points-to analysis based on a "counterexample" reachability query deemed feasible by that analysis. However, instead of gradually refining this abstraction as in, for example, counterexample-based abstraction refinement (CEGAR) [13] and related techniques [16] , our technique immediately employs concrete reasoning about the program, and then re-introduces abstraction as needed (e.g., to handle loops). In general, the above predicate-abstraction-based approaches have not been shown to work well for proving properties of object-oriented programs, which present additional challenges due to intensive heap usage, frequent virtual dispatch, etc. Architecturally, our system is more similar to recent staged analyses for typestate verification [25, 26], but our system employs greater path sensitivity and more deeply integrates points-to facts from the initial analysis stage. A path program [7] was originally defined in the context of improving CEGAR by pruning multiple counterexample traces through a loop at once. SMPP [30] performs SMT-based verification by exhaustively enumerating path programs in a forward-chaining manner (in contrast to our goal-directed search). The recent DASH system [4] refines its abstraction based on information from dynamic runs and employs dynamic information to reduce explosion due to aliasing.

Our witness-refutation search uses the "bounded" fragment of separation logic [41] and thus has a peripheral connection to recent separation-logic–based shape analyzers [6, 12]. In contrast to such analyzers, we do not use inductive summaries and instead use materializations from a static points-to analysis abstraction. Shape analysis using bi-abductive inference [10] enables a compositional analysis by deriving pre- and post-conditions for methods in a bottom-up manner and making a best effort to reach top-level entry points. The derivation of heap pre-conditions is somewhat similar to our witness-refutation search over points-to constraints, but our backwards analysis is applied on demand from a flow-insensitive query and is refined by incorporating information from an up-front, whole program points-to analysis. Recent work [24] has applied bi-abduction to detect real Java memory leaks in the sense of an object that is allocated but never used again. In contrast, our client is a flow-insensitive heap reachability property that over-approximates a leak that is not explicit in the code, but is realized in the Android run-time.

Similar to our path program witnesses, other techniques have aimed to either produce a concrete path witness for some program error or help the user to discover one. Bourdoncle [9] presents a system for "abstract debugging" of program assertions, in which the compiler aims to discover inputs leading to violations statically. Rival [42] presents a system based on combined forward and backward analysis for elucidating and validating error reports from the Astrée system [15]. Work by Ball et al. [3] observes that for showing the *existence* of program errors (as opposed to verifying their absence), a non-standard notion of abstraction suffices in which one only requires the existence of a concrete state satisfying any particular property of the corresponding abstract state (as opposed to all corresponding concrete states satisfying the property). We observe an analogous difference between refutation and witness discovery in Section 3. Similar notions underlie the "proof obligation queries" and "failure witness queries" in recent work on error diagnosis [23].

Previous points-to analyses have included refinement to improve precision. Guyer and Lin's client-driven pointer analysis [28] introduced context and flow sensitivity at possibly-polluting program points based on client needs. Sridharan and Bodik [44] presented an approach for adding field and context sensitivity to a Java points-to analysis via refinement. Recently, Liang et al. [36–38] have shown that highly-targeted refinements of a heap abstraction can yield sufficient precision for certain clients. Unlike our work, none of the aforementioned techniques can introduce path sensitivity via refinement. A recent study on Andersen's analysis [8] used dependency rules akin to a fully-explicit analog of our mixed symbolic-explicit transfer functions in a flow-insensitive context.

6. Conclusion

We have presented THRESHER, a precise static analysis for reasoning about heap reachability with flow-, context-, and path-sensitivity and location materialization. THRESHER introduces such precision in an on-demand manner after running a flow-insensitive points-to analysis. By integrating flow-insensitive points-to facts directly into a mixed symbolic-explicit representation of the program state and computing sufficiently strong loop invariants automatically, our techniques scale well while maintaining good precision. In our evaluation, we applied THRESHER to the problem of detecting an important class of Android memory leaks and discovered real leaks while significantly improving precision over points-to analysis alone.

Acknowledgments. We thank Sriram Sankaranarayanan and the CUPLV group for insightful discussions, as well as the anonymous reviewers for their helpful comments. This research was supported in part by NSF under grant CCF-1055066.

References

[1] L. O. Andersen. *Program Analysis and Specialization for the C Programming Language*. PhD thesis, University of Copenhagen, DIKU, 1994.

[2] T. Ball and S. K. Rajamani. Automatically validating temporal safety properties of interfaces. In *SPIN*, 2001.

[3] T. Ball, O. Kupferman, and G. Yorsh. Abstraction for falsification. In *CAV*, 2005.

[4] N. Beckman, A. V. Nori, S. K. Rajamani, and R. J. Simmons. Proofs from tests. In *ISSTA*, 2008.

[5] J. Berdine, C. Calcagno, and P. W. O'Hearn. Symbolic execution with separation logic. In *APLAS*, 2005.

[6] J. Berdine, C. Calcagno, B. Cook, D. Distefano, P. W. O'Hearn, T. Wies, and H. Yang. Shape analysis for composite data structures. In *CAV*, 2007.

[7] D. Beyer, T. A. Henzinger, R. Majumdar, and A. Rybalchenko. Path invariants. In *PLDI*, 2007.

[8] S. Blackshear, B.-Y. E. Chang, S. Sankaranarayanan, and M. Sridharan. The flow-insensitive precision of andersen's analysis in practice. In *SAS*, 2011.

[9] F. Bourdoncle. Abstract debugging of higher-order imperative languages. In *PLDI*, 1993.

[10] C. Calcagno, D. Distefano, P. W. O'Hearn, and H. Yang. Compositional shape analysis by means of bi-abduction. In *POPL*, 2009.

[11] S. Chandra, S. J. Fink, and M. Sridharan. Snugglebug: a powerful approach to weakest preconditions. In *PLDI*, 2009.

[12] B.-Y. E. Chang and X. Rival. Relational inductive shape analysis. In *POPL*, 2008.

[13] E. M. Clarke, O. Grumberg, S. Jha, Y. Lu, and H. Veith. Counterexample-guided abstraction refinement for symbolic model checking. *J. ACM*, 50(5), 2003.

[14] P. Cousot and R. Cousot. Abstract interpretation: A unified lattice model for static analysis of programs by construction or approximation of fixpoints. In *POPL*, 1977.

[15] P. Cousot, R. Cousot, J. Feret, L. Mauborgne, A. Miné, D. Monniaux, and X. Rival. The ASTREÉ analyzer. In *ESOP*, 2005.

[16] P. Cousot, P. Ganty, and J.-F. Raskin. Fixpoint-guided abstraction refinements. In *SAS*, 2007.

[17] P. Cousot, R. Cousot, and F. Logozzo. Precondition inference from intermittent assertions and application to contracts on collections. In *VMCAI*, 2011.

[18] M. Das, S. Lerner, and M. Seigle. ESP: Path-sensitive program verification in polynomial time. In *PLDI*, 2002.

[19] L. M. de Moura and N. Bjørner. Z3: An efficient SMT solver. In *TACAS*, 2008.

[20] I. Dillig, T. Dillig, and A. Aiken. Sound, complete and scalable path-sensitive analysis. In *PLDI*, 2008.

[21] I. Dillig, T. Dillig, and A. Aiken. Fluid updates: Beyond strong vs. weak updates. In *ESOP*, 2010.

[22] I. Dillig, T. Dillig, and A. Aiken. Precise reasoning for programs using containers. In *POPL*, 2011.

[23] I. Dillig, T. Dillig, and A. Aiken. Automated error diagnosis using abductive inference. In *PLDI*, 2012.

[24] D. Distefano and I. Filipović. Memory leaks detection in Java by bi-abductive inference. In *FASE*, 2010.

[25] N. Dor, S. Adams, M. Das, and Z. Yang. Software validation via scalable path-sensitive value flow analysis. In *ISSTA*, 2004.

[26] S. J. Fink, E. Yahav, N. Dor, G. Ramalingam, and E. Geay. Effective typestate verification in the presence of aliasing. *ACM Trans. Softw. Eng. Methodol.*, 17(2), 2008.

[27] C. Flanagan, K. R. M. Leino, M. Lillibridge, G. Nelson, J. B. Saxe, and R. Stata. Extended static checking for Java. In *PLDI*, 2002.

[28] S. Z. Guyer and C. Lin. Error checking with client-driven pointer analysis. *Sci. Comput. Program.*, 58(1-2), 2005.

[29] B. Hackett and A. Aiken. How is aliasing used in systems software? In *FSE*, 2006.

[30] W. R. Harris, S. Sankaranarayanan, F. Ivancic, and A. Gupta. Program analysis via satisfiability modulo path programs. In *POPL*, 2010.

[31] T. A. Henzinger, R. Jhala, R. Majumdar, and G. Sutre. Lazy abstraction. In *POPL*, 2002.

[32] S. S. Ishtiaq and P. W. O'Hearn. BI as an assertion language for mutable data structures. In *POPL*, 2001.

[33] S. Khurshid, C. S. Pasareanu, and W. Visser. Generalized symbolic execution for model checking and testing. In *TACAS*, 2003.

[34] A. S. Kksal, P. Suter, and V. Kuncak. Scala to the Power of Z3: Integrating SMT and Programming. In *CADE*, 2011.

[35] K. R. M. Leino and F. Logozzo. Loop invariants on demand. In *APLAS*, 2005.

[36] P. Liang and M. Naik. Scaling abstraction refinement via pruning. In *PLDI*, 2011.

[37] P. Liang, O. Tripp, M. Naik, and M. Sagiv. A dynamic evaluation of the precision of static heap abstractions. In *OOPSLA*, 2010.

[38] P. Liang, O. Tripp, and M. Naik. Learning minimal abstractions. In *POPL*, 2011.

[39] R. Manevich, M. Sridharan, S. Adams, M. Das, and Z. Yang. PSE: explaining program failures via postmortem static analysis. In *FSE*, 2004.

[40] A. Milanova, A. Rountev, and B. G. Ryder. Parameterized object sensitivity for points-to analysis for Java. *ACM Trans. Softw. Eng. Methodol.*, 14(1), 2005.

[41] J. C. Reynolds. Separation logic: A logic for shared mutable data structures. In *LICS*, 2002.

[42] X. Rival. Understanding the origin of alarms in Astrée. In *SAS*, 2005.

[43] M. Sagiv, T. Reps, and R. Wilhelm. Solving shape-analysis problems in languages with destructive updating. *ACM Trans. Program. Lang. Syst.*, 20(1), 1998.

[44] M. Sridharan and R. Bodík. Refinement-based context-sensitive points-to analysis for Java. In *PLDI*, 2006.

[45] B. Woolf. Null object. In *Pattern languages of program design 3*. Addison-Wesley Longman Publishing Co., Inc., 1997.

TRANSIT: Specifying Protocols with Concolic Snippets *

Abhishek Udupa, Arun Raghavan, Jyotirmoy V. Deshmukh†
Sela Mador-Haim, Milo M. K. Martin, Rajeev Alur
University of Pennsylvania
{audupa, arraghav, djy, selama, milom, alur}@cis.upenn.edu

Abstract

With the maturing of technology for model checking and constraint solving, there is an emerging opportunity to develop programming tools that can transform the way systems are specified. In this paper, we propose a new way to program distributed protocols using *concolic* snippets. Concolic snippets are sample execution fragments that contain both concrete and symbolic values. The proposed approach allows the programmer to describe the desired system partially using the traditional model of communicating extended finite-state-machines (EFSM), along with high-level invariants and concrete execution fragments. Our synthesis engine completes an EFSM skeleton by inferring guards and updates from the given fragments which is then automatically analyzed using a model checker with respect to the desired invariants. The counterexamples produced by the model checker can then be used by the programmer to add new concrete execution fragments that describe the correct behavior in the specific scenario corresponding to the counterexample.

We describe TRANSIT, a language and prototype implementation of the proposed specification methodology for distributed protocols. Experimental evaluations of TRANSIT to specify cache coherence protocols show that (1) the algorithm for expression inference from concolic snippets can synthesize expressions of size 15 involving typical operators over commonly occurring types, (2) for a classical directory-based protocol, TRANSIT automatically generates, in a few seconds, a complete implementation from a specification consisting of the EFSM structure and a few concrete examples for every transition, and (3) a published partial description of the SGI Origin cache coherence protocol maps directly to symbolic examples and leads to a complete implementation in a few iterations, with the programmer correcting counterexamples resulting from underspecified transitions by adding concrete examples in each iteration.

Categories and Subject Descriptors D.1 [*Programming Techniques*]: Automatic Programming; D.2.2 [*Design Tools and Techniques*]: Computer-aided Software Engineering; D.2.4 [*Software Verification*]: Model Checking

Keywords Program Synthesis; Distributed Protocol Synthesis; Cache Coherence Protocols; Programming by Example.

* This research was partially supported by NSF award CCF 0905464 and NSF Expeditions in Computing grant CCF 1138996.

† Jyotirmoy V. Deshmukh is currently a researcher at Toyota Technical Center, Gardena, CA.

PLDI'13, June 16–19, 2013, Seattle, WA, USA.

1. Introduction

Over the last few decades, technology for program analysis, model checking, and software verification has matured, and has witnessed growing adoption in industry. However, verification tools have largely been confined to discovering bugs in systems that have already been designed. This raises the question: how can we leverage the advances in analysis tools to assist programmers, during the program development phase, in an interactive manner? In this paper, we propose a methodology for programming distributed protocols, in which a programmer can express the intended design using multiple formats, which a synthesis tool then integrates into an executable implementation. Our approach is inspired by recent work on *sketching* and on *programming by examples*. In *sketching*, a programmer writes a partial program with incomplete details, and a synthesizer then fills in the missing details based on user-specified assertions [23, 24] (see also [15, 26]). With this approach, the programmer can continue to use the familiar imperative style of programming, but can use the synthesis tool to find intricate details necessary for fine-tuning code by supplying a few high-level invariants. In *programming by examples*, the programmer expresses the desired behavior using a set of example input/output traces, and the synthesis tool constructs an executable implementation consistent with these examples. This has been shown to be an intuitive and effective style for programming finite-state reactive controllers [9–11], Excel macros performing string manipulations [7], and pointer-manipulations for updating data structures [22].

This paper focuses on programming reactive systems such as distributed protocols. For such protocols, although the core algorithms are published with accompanying correctness proofs and performance analyses, these descriptions typically do not specify every detail, and translating them into a correct working implementation is challenging due to corner cases arising from asynchrony and concurrency [2]. A distributed protocol is typically described by listing the set of processes participating in the protocol, the set of channels connecting the processes, the types of messages each channel can carry, and the descriptions of individual processes given as *extended finite-state-machines* (EFSMs). An EFSM description consists of a list of internal state variables, a set of control states, and a set of transitions connecting control states. Each transition is specified by a guard condition and update code that refer to the internal state variables and fields of incoming and outgoing messages. This style of specifying distributed protocols is common in standardized descriptions of network protocols as RFCs, rigorous textbook descriptions of distributed algorithms [17], modeling languages supported by formal verification tools such as SPIN [12] and Murφ [5], and domain-specific languages such as SLICC [18]. The traditional programming style requires the programmer to fill in every detail of every transition, and our goal is to offer programmer assistance with this tedious and error-prone task.

Using the proposed language, TRANSIT, a programmer describes the communication architecture of a distributed protocol

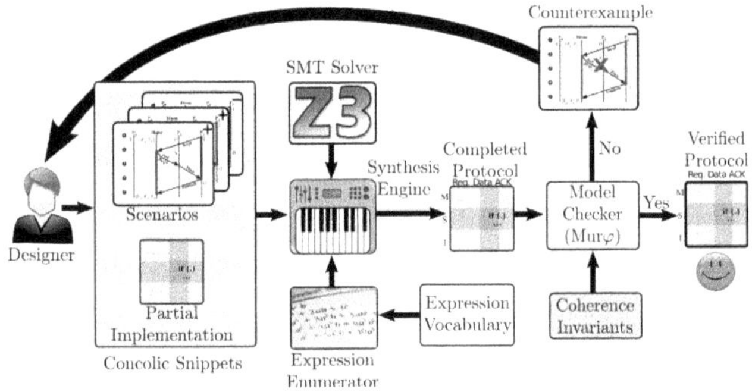

Figure 1. Design methodology using concolic snippets

by listing the set of processes, the set of channels connecting them, the types of messages each channel can carry, and the EFSM skeleton for each process by listing control states and internal state variables. TRANSIT also allows behavioral specification of each process using *concolic* snippets, which are fragments of desired execution that contain conditional updates to variables using both concrete and symbolic values (the term "concolic" was coined in the context of testing programs using both concrete and symbolic inputs [20]). This approach offers the programmer the flexibility to either describe each EFSM transition in the traditional way using symbolic expressions for guards and updates, or to specify only representative examples of such transitions. The TRANSIT synthesis tool then generates a complete protocol by inferring guards and update actions that are *consistent* with the specified snippets. The programmer also specifies high-level temporal invariants which the protocol needs to satisfy. A finite instance of the synthesized protocol is then checked against these invariants using a model checker. The programmer debugs any reported counterexamples with a visualizer and adds more snippets to rule out erroneous behaviors. Figure 1 illustrates the proposed methodology.

The main computational problem in our approach is to infer an expression to be used in a guard or an update appearing in an EFSM transition that is (1) built in a type-consistent manner using the specified vocabulary of function symbols and variables, and (2) is consistent with the given set of concrete and symbolic examples. Our solution is a variant of the *counterexample-guided inductive synthesis* (CEGIS) approach [8, 13, 23], and involves an interplay between pruning based on concrete examples and concretization of symbolic examples using an SMT solver. Specifically, our implementation enumerates expressions of increasing sizes, where the space of expressions is pruned significantly by considering two expressions equivalent if they evaluate to the same values for the given concrete examples. This results in an expression that is consistent with all the concrete examples. This expression is then checked for consistency with respect to the symbolic examples using an SMT solver. If the consistency check succeeds, then the expression is the desired answer. If it fails, the evidence for inconsistency returned by the solver contributes to a concrete example, which is considered in subsequent iterations.

The TRANSIT prototype implementation invokes the SMT solver Z3 [19] and the model checker Murφ [5]. To evaluate the algorithm for inferring an expression from concolic examples, we consider a vocabulary of the common operations on Booleans, integers, and bounded sets. The algorithm can infer expressions with a size of 15 symbols within a few minutes.

To evaluate the feasibility of the proposed methodology, we focus on cache coherence protocols, a class representative of distributed protocols. We performed two case studies where students with no experience with coherence protocols used the TRANSIT prototype to program two canonical cache coherence protocols from textbook descriptions using concolic examples [25]. Both case studies resulted in generating protocols that were successfully checked by the model checker. We found that: (1) the final, correctly generated protocol typically required one or two concrete snippets per transition, (2) synthesizing the protocol from snippets took only a few seconds, and (3) the entire iterative protocol development required a few hours of manual effort for either case study.

In our final case study, we used TRANSIT to specify the industrial-strength SGI Origin protocol. The published description [16] was directly mapped to symbolic snippets corresponding to typical transitions. However, as the published prose is not a complete specification, it results in an implementation that violates coherence invariants during the model-checking phase. Because the counterexamples produced by the model checker correspond to concrete executions, our methodology allowed the programmer to augment the original description with concrete fixes to these violating traces, culminating in a correct implementation of the protocol.

2. Illustrative Examples of Our Approach

We illustrate the use of TRANSIT using cache coherence protocols as an example application. Such protocols maintain a coherent view of shared memory among threads running in multi-core and multi-socket systems. Although programmers view memory as a single data store, most systems incorporate private per-core caches to reduce access latency. Coherence protocols prevent threads from reading stale data from caches by ensuring that reads to memory locations (addresses) receive the last value written to that location by *any* thread. Coherence is conventionally enforced using mutually exclusive read/write permissions: either multiple processors may simultaneously cache an address with read permissions (*i.e.*, *shared* readers) or a single processor may cache that address with read/write permissions (*i.e.*, *exclusive* writer). Although several different hardware and software approaches exist, this paper focuses on *invalidation-based directory* hardware implementations. In such a system, processors issue requests to a central directory which tracks the current permissions of each cache. On receiving a request for write permission, the directory issues *invalidation* messages to all caches that hold a valid copy (read or write permissions) and gathers acknowledgments from these caches before granting write permissions to the requester. Similarly, the directory redirects read requests to the last writer to that address (tracked as the "owner" in the directory) to ensure that valid data is transferred to the requesting processor.

As with existing approaches for modeling protocols using state machines, TRANSIT views the protocol in terms of a well defined structure (referred to as the *protocol skeleton*) and its behavioral description.

Protocol skeleton. A protocol description usually includes the high-level structural description of the desired protocol. For example, from Chapter 8 of the coherence primer [25], the specification would include: (1) Processes: a distinguished EFSM called the *Directory* and one EFSM per cache controller. (2) Communication architecture: three networks that the EFSMs use to send/receive messages, including any ordering guarantees. (3) Message types: such as `Get` and `Data` that may be carried on specific networks (for instance, the `Response` network can only carry `Data` and `Inv-Ack` message types). (4) Control states of each EFSM: such as M, S and I for the directory EFSM. (5) Internal variables for each EFSM: such as `Sharers` in directory, which is used to track the list of cache processes with a valid copy of data. The above *protocol skeleton* is usually expressed as type declarations and variable definitions in existing approaches. The programmer specifies the protocol skeleton similarly in the proposed approach as well.

Traditional behavioral description. Having set up the above structure, a protocol implementation next requires the behavioral specification of the EFSMs. Protocol designers typically describe behavior in terms of example flows [27] or interaction of processes when they exchange messages, triggering events and consequent actions. These descriptions are commonly expressed and communicated informally (using visual aids like example state diagrams and message sequence charts, or listing case-by-case actions textually) both in industrial protocols as well as in academic literature [16, 25]. Such informal descriptions can completely specify relatively straightforward protocols like the textbook MSI example [25]. In these cases, the programming task is largely to infer and symbolically codify the semantics implied by the examples. For more complex protocols, the informal descriptions convey salient features, like common-case behavior and perhaps some of the more interesting scenarios that might arise (usually in terms of rules). Implementing such protocols involves the additional step of filling in any unspecified details. However, it has been shown that this approach to implementing complete protocols symbolically as a program can be error-prone even for experts, with bugs manifesting even in released processors [1, 2].

Specifying behavior with snippets. We observe that the complexity in protocols does not usually stem from the code for individual transitions — these tend to be straight line code. The complexity is due to corner cases and race conditions arising from concurrency and asynchrony when protocols are considered in their entirety [2]. Using a concolic approach allows the programmer to mix symbolic snippets (transition code) describing well-defined behavior (like rules or state machine transitions) with concrete snippets describing specific example scenarios.

The TRANSIT tool composes the given concrete and symbolic snippets to generate an implementation which allows *at least* all the behaviors described in the input snippets. This implementation is then model checked for coherence invariants. Any underspecification or error in the specification of the EFSM behavior will result in a counterexample during model checking, which the programmer can then fix using concrete snippets to prevent subsequent occurrences of at least that specific violation.

Example using concolic snippets. We illustrate this mixed (or concolic) use of TRANSIT with an anecdote from our case study in implementing the SGI Origin protocol from published informal textual rules [16] (Section 6 contains more details on this case study, and using TRANSIT with concolic snippets to implement protocols which are completely specified). The protocol skeleton states that the directory EFSM has variables `Sharers` and `Owner` to maintain its internal state. One of the rules in the paper describes the behavior of a directory upon a read request from a cache as: *"If directory state is Exclusive with another owner, transitions to Busy-shared with requester as owner and send out an intervention shared request to the previous owner and a speculative reply to the requester. Go to 5b"*. Note that this description does not specify how the `Sharers` process variable in the directory EFSM needs to be updated. The programmer indicated that if the sender of the message was not the previous `Owner`, the value of the `Sharers` variable needs to contain *at least* the sender of the received message in addition to the old value of the `Sharers` variable. Based on this specification, TRANSIT generated the code:

`Sharers := Sharers` $\cup$ `{Msg.Sender}`

However, an attempt to verify the generated implementation using Murφ resulted in a coherence violation. TRANSIT provided a visual trace of the counterexample to the programmer, a simplified version of which is shown in Figure 2. Observe that the transition on the directory shown in Figure 2 is a concrete instance of the scenario described earlier, where `Msg.Sender` is `Cache2` and the `Owner` variable is initially set to `Cache1`. Upon inspecting the trace, the programmer recognized that in this particular scenario, with `Sharers` needed to include the previous value of the `Owner` as well. After a concrete snippet specifying this specific conditional update was added, TRANSIT then generated a new implementation including the correct update to `Sharers` as:

`Sharers := Sharers` $\cup$ `{Msg.Sender, Owner}`

This example illustrates how a programmer can benefit from using the concolic nature of TRANSIT. TRANSIT allows the programmer to combine the familiar symbolic programming style for specifying the protocol skeleton and well-understood behavior. TRANSIT also makes it convenient to fix bugs with concrete execution fragments that describe the desired outcome in the particular scenario where the bug manifests.

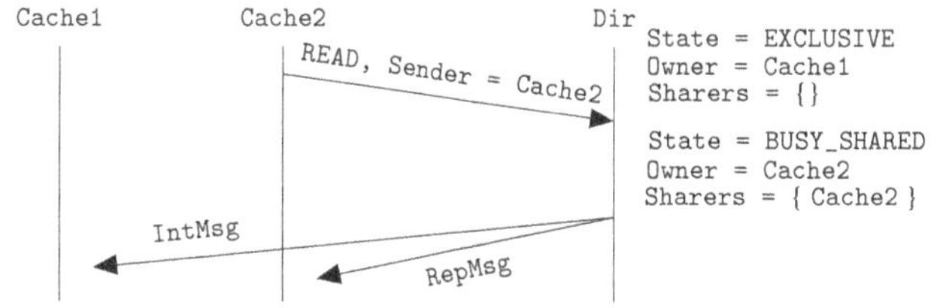

Figure 2. The counterexample trace

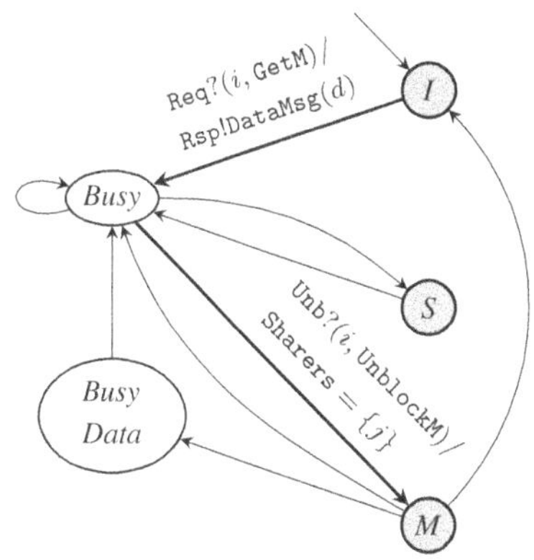

Figure 3. EFSM representing a directory process. The M (modified) state indicates read/write permissions. The S (shared) state indicates read-only permissions and the I (invalid) state indicates no permissions. The rest of the states are transient states.

3. Protocol Specification using Concolic Snippets

A protocol implementation results in transition code for communicating EFSMs. Figure 3 shows the EFSM for a directory process in a cache coherence protocol. TRANSIT borrows from traditional software [18] and hardware [4] protocol description languages to specify the protocol skeleton (*i.e.*, types and variable definitions) and transitions (using a guarded command language). However, TRANSIT offers the additional ability to mix concrete and symbolic transitions as snippets, and to under-specify elements of transitions for the tool to infer. We now describe how to specify a protocol using TRANSIT.

3.1 High-level Building Blocks of TRANSIT

Coherence protocols typically assume an *asynchronous, message-passing* based model of communication. Each process description includes a list of input channels to receive messages, and output channels on which messages are sent. A channel can be modeled as a multiset or a queue depending on the desired ordering guarantees.

```
Transition(CurrentState, InputEvent)
  [optional guard] => (NextState, OutMsg1, ...)
      Pre1 ==>
          Post11;
          Post12;
          ...
      Pre2 ==>
          ...
```

Figure 4. A concolic snippet. *CurrentState* and *NextState* are the start and end control states. The snippet specifies zero or more outbound messages. It also specifies a *guard-action* block for each *guard* containing a set of conditional updates. The expression Pre_i specifies the condition (on process variables and the fields of the received message) under which the boolean constraints Post_{ij} hold. Each Post_{ij} constrains the updated value of exactly one process variable or output message field in terms of the old values of the process variables and the fields of the received message.

The syntactic elements of TRANSIT, shown in Figure 4, are as follows:

Control states define the logical state of the directory and cache machines. These can be thought of as the *program counter* for these machines.

Process variables internal to each machine, such as `Sharers` in the directory. These may be Booleans, integers or bounded sets.

Input events correspond to receiving messages or external triggers (to issue requests). An input event is specified as a single message variable and the network on which it is received.

Guards are Boolean expressions over process variables and fields of received messages.

Output events correspond to sending messages to other processes. They are represented as a list of message variables and the name of network on which each message is sent.

Action statements update process variables to new values and specify values for the fields of outbound messages.

We defer a discussion on *Pre* and *Post* to Section 3.2. A complete specification of the behavior of an EFSM is thus a set of actions A that are to be executed, a set of output events O that are to be generated, the next control state s' to transition to, all predicated on a guard g, for each combination of input event and control state $\langle e, s\rangle$. The semantics of such a specification are that the EFSM executes actions A, generates events O, and finally transitions to control state s' in response to an input event e when the EFSM is in control state s, provided g evaluates to `true`. In the asynchronous model of computation, the order in which processes execute is nondeterministic. However, once a process has been chosen for execution, its actions are assumed to be deterministic.

3.2 Programming with TRANSIT

Figure 4 shows the composition of a single transition snippet in TRANSIT. Using existing approaches such as SLICC [18] or hardware description languages, the programmer would completely specify the guards and actions in the transition. However, TRANSIT allows for guards to be left empty and for actions to be specified as constraints governed by pre- and post-conditions as shown in Figure 4. In such cases, the tool computes expressions for the empty guards and update statements satisfying the given constraints.

The programmer has a choice of specifying completely symbolic, completely concrete, or mixed concolic snippets. In each case, TRANSIT generates a symbolic implementation. The pre- and post-conditions are Boolean predicates over process variables and message fields. Primed variables denote updated values of process variables. We assume a parallel assignment model, which precludes primed variables from appearing in pre-conditions and allows at most one primed variable per post-condition. Note that although guards and pre-conditions are both Boolean predicates ranging over the same variables, they have markedly different uses: guards appear in the *complete* protocol implementation of the EFSM in a guarded-command language, whereas pre-conditions are inputs to the inference engine which allow users to capture particular scenarios and are not part of the generated protocol implementation.

Symbolic snippets. By specifying the guard and actions symbolically, we obtain a symbolic snippet which completely specifies a transition. A non-empty guard is assumed to be symbolic (*i.e.*, completely specified and not generated by TRANSIT). Symbolic actions are specified by making the post-condition an equality constraint.

Concolic snippets. If the guard is left empty, or the actions are specified using pre- and post-condition constraints (instead of equality), the snippet is concolic in nature. The TRANSIT tool generates symbolic code for update statements and/or the guard to be consistent with the given constraints. The following concolic snippet specifies the transition for the directory process mentioned in the SGI-Origin anecdote in Section 2.

```
Transition(EXCLUSIVE, ReqNet Msg) {
  [] => (BUSY_SHARED, RepNet RMsg, IntNet IMsg) {
     (Msg.MType = READ & Msg.Sender != Owner) ==> {
        SubsetOf(SetUnion(Sharers, {Msg.Sender}),
                 Sharers');
        ...
}}}
```

This snippet is applicable only when the current state is `EXCLUSIVE` and a message is received on the network `ReqNet`. To be consistent with the snippet, TRANSIT must generate code to update the new value of `Sharers` to be a superset of the old value and the sender of the incoming message.

Concrete snippets. Concolic snippets may contain symbolic pre- and post-conditions over variables, but concrete snippets specify concrete values for any variables in these constraints. They may leave the guard empty as well. For example, the concrete snippet below shows the bug-fix described in Section 2:

```
Transition(EXCLUSIVE, ReqNet Msg) {
  [] => (BUSY_SHARED, RepNet RMsg, IntNet IMsg) {
     (Msg.MType = READ & Owner = C1 &
      Msg.Sender = C2) ==> {
        Sharers' = {C1, C2};
        ...
}}}
```

In summary, symbolic and concrete snippets can be thought of as instances of concolic snippets in which guards and actions are either completely specified (symbolic), or specified with concrete values for all variables (concrete). The task of the TRANSIT tool is to generate expressions for guards and update expressions for variables such that they are consistent with the given snippets. We formalize this problem in Section 5 after first describing our expression inference algorithm in the next section.

4. Inferring Expressions

We first define the problem of inferring an expression from concrete or concolic examples in Section 4.1, which our synthesis procedure uses as a subroutine. Section 4.2 presents a solution for a restricted version of this problem in which the examples involve only concrete values, whereas Section 4.3 presents a solution for the general case where the examples have concolic values.

The expression inference problem corresponds to the following computational problem: given a quantifier-free formula $\mathcal{C}$ over (typed) variables $\mathcal{V}$ and a distinguished (output) variable o, find an expression e such that the formula $\mathcal{C}[o := e]$ is valid, where $\mathcal{C}[o := e]$ is the usual notation for the formula obtained by syntactically substituting e for every occurrence of o in $\mathcal{C}$. Conceptu-

Function	Description
add (Int, Int) → Int	Integer Addition
sub (Int, Int) → Int	Integer Subtraction
inc (Int) → Int	Add one to an Integer
dec (Int) → Int	Subtract one from an Integer
setadd (Set, PID) → Set	Add an entry into a Set
setsize (Set) → Int	Cardinality of a Set
setunion (Set, Set) → Set	Set Union
setinter (Set, Set) → Set	Set Intersection
setminus (Set, Set) → Set	Set Difference
setof (PID) → Set	Create a singleton Set
or (Bool, Bool) → Bool	Boolean Disjunction
and (Bool, Bool) → Bool	Boolean Conjunction
not (Bool) → Bool	Boolean Negation
setcontains (Set, PID) → Bool	Membership test on a Set
iszero (Int) → Bool	Test if an integer is Zero
$\forall t \in \mathcal{T}$ equals (t, t) → Bool	Equality Test
ge (Int, Int) → Bool	Greater than or equal to
gt (Int, Int) → Bool	Greater than
$\forall t \in \mathcal{T}$, ite (Bool, t, t) → t	Conditional Expression
numcaches () → Int	# of Caches (constant)

Table 1. Expression Vocabulary used in Coherence Protocols

ally, this problem is similar to solving $\exists\forall$-formulas, and we use the *counterexample-guided inductive synthesis* (CEGIS) strategy that has previously been used to solve such problems [8, 23].

The algorithm enumerates expressions, with suitable pruning strategies, to find a candidate expression e that is consistent with the concrete examples that contribute to $\mathcal{C}$. It then checks if $\neg\mathcal{C}[o := e]$ is satisfiable. If $\neg\mathcal{C}[o := e]$ is unsatisfiable, then e is the desired expression. Otherwise, the satisfying model contributes a concrete example that is added to the set of concrete examples and the entire process is repeated. Thus, the algorithm handles "exists an expression" using enumerative techniques and "is valid for all variable values" using symbolic constraint solving.

4.1 Problem Definition

We define an *expression vocabulary* G as a tuple $(\mathcal{T}, \mathcal{F})$, where $\mathcal{T}$ is a set of *types*, and $\mathcal{F}$ is a set of typed function symbols, where for each $f \in \mathcal{F}$, $\mathsf{arity}(f) \in \mathbb{N}$ denotes the arity of f, $\mathsf{type}(f) \in \mathcal{T}$ denotes the type of the range of f, and $\mathsf{argtype}(f, i) \in \mathcal{T}, i \in [1, \mathsf{arity}(f)]$ denotes the type of the domain of the ith argument to f. Function symbols of arity zero are constants. $\mathcal{F}$ is finite, so we have a fixed number of constant symbols. However, constant expressions such as 2 are allowed as an abbreviation for $\mathsf{add}(1, 1)$.

Let $\mathcal{V}$ denote a set of typed variable symbols and let $\mathsf{type}(v) \in \mathcal{T}$ denote the type of a variable v in $\mathcal{V}$. Given an expression vocabulary $G = (\mathcal{T}, \mathcal{F})$ and a set of typed variables $\mathcal{V}$, we denote the set of expressions of type t as $\mathsf{Exp}(\mathcal{F}, \mathcal{V}, t)$. This set is defined inductively as follows: (1) If $v \in \mathcal{V}$ then $v \in \mathsf{Exp}(\mathcal{F}, \mathcal{V}, \mathsf{type}(v))$, and (2) If $f \in \mathcal{F}$, and $\forall i \in [1, k] : e_i \in \mathsf{Exp}(\mathcal{F}, \mathcal{V}, \mathsf{argtype}(f, i))$, then $f(e_1, e_2, \ldots, e_k) \in \mathsf{Exp}(\mathcal{F}, \mathcal{V}, \mathsf{type}(f))$, where $k = \mathsf{arity}(f)$.

If $e \in \mathsf{Exp}(\mathcal{F}, \mathcal{V}, t)$, then we write $\mathsf{type}(e) = t$. We assume that the Boolean type (denoted `Bool`) is always present in any instantiation of $\mathcal{T}$ and that the basic Boolean operators (conjunction, disjunction and negation) are part of $\mathcal{F}$.

For specifying cache coherence protocols, we use an expression vocabulary where the set of types is $\mathcal{T} = \{\texttt{Bool}, \texttt{Int}, \texttt{PID}, \texttt{Set}\} \cup \texttt{Enums}$. Here, `Int` denotes the integer type, `PID` is a special type for process identifiers, `Set` is a type denoting a set of values of type `PID`, and `Enums` is a set of user defined enumerated types. The set of functions $\mathcal{F}$ in the vocabulary is shown in Table 1.

The *size* of an expression e, $\mathsf{size}(e)$, is defined as the number of function symbols and variable symbols appearing in e. Further, we denote by $\mathsf{Exp}_k(\mathcal{F}, \mathcal{V}, t)$ the set $\{e : e \in \mathsf{Exp}(\mathcal{F}, \mathcal{V}, t) \wedge \mathsf{size}(e) = k\}$, *i.e.*, the subset of expressions of type t with size k.

Given a set of typed variables $\mathcal{V}$ and a distinguished typed variable $o \notin \mathcal{V}$ (henceforth known as the output variable), an *example* C is a Boolean formula of the form $\mathsf{pre} \Rightarrow \mathsf{post}$ where $\mathsf{pre} \in \mathsf{Exp}(\mathcal{F}, \mathcal{V}, \texttt{Bool})$ and $\mathsf{post} \in \mathsf{Exp}(\mathcal{F}, \mathcal{V} \cup \{o\}, \texttt{Bool})$. In other words, if the variables in $\mathcal{V}$ satisfy the pre-condition pre, then the output variable o should be assigned an expression over these variables such that the post-condition post holds. An *example set* over the output variable o, denoted $\mathcal{C}(o)$, is defined as the set of examples $\{C_1, \ldots, C_n\}$ such that the conjunction $\bigwedge_n(\mathsf{pre}_i \Rightarrow \mathsf{post}_i)$ is satisfiable. An expression e is *consistent* with the example set $\mathcal{C}(o)$ iff for all $C \in \mathcal{C}(o)$, $C[o := e]$ is a formula that is valid.

Example. Let $\mathcal{V} = \{x, y\}$, where $\mathsf{type}(x)$ and $\mathsf{type}(y)$ are both `Int`. Consider the example set $\{C_1\}$, where C_1 is $((x = 0) \wedge (y = 1)) \Rightarrow (o = 1)$. The expressions y and $x + y$ are all consistent with $\mathcal{C}(o)$, while the expression x is inconsistent, as $C_1[o := x]$ is the invalid formula $(x = 0) \wedge (y = 1) \Rightarrow (x = 1)$.

Now, consider the example set $\{C_1, C_2\}$, where C_2 is the example $(x = 1) \wedge (y = 1) \Rightarrow (o = 2)$. The expression y is not consistent with the new example set, as $C_2[o := y]$ is the invalid formula $(x = 1) \wedge (y = 1) \Rightarrow (y = 2)$; however, the expression $x + y$ is still consistent.

The expression inference problem can now be stated as: given an expression vocabulary $G = (\mathcal{T}, \mathcal{F})$ with a set of variables $\mathcal{V}$ and an example set $\mathcal{C}(o)$ over the typed output variable o, find an expression e in $\mathsf{Exp}(\mathcal{F}, \mathcal{V}, \mathsf{type}(o))$ which is consistent with $\mathcal{C}(o)$.

4.2 Inferring Expressions from Concrete Examples

We say that an example is *concrete* if it has the form: $(\bigwedge_{v \in \mathcal{V}}(v = k_v)) \Rightarrow (o = k_o)$, where for all $v \in \mathcal{V}$, k_v and k_o are concrete expressions[1] of types $\mathsf{type}(v)$ and $\mathsf{type}(o)$, respectively. An example set containing only concrete examples is called a concrete example set. An alternative representation for a concrete example is the tuple (S, k_o), where S is a valuation function mapping variables in $\mathcal{V}$ to values and k_o is the concrete value for the output variable o. We use the notation $S(e)$ to denote the evaluation of an expression e for the valuation S for its constituent variables. Checking if an expression e is consistent with a concrete example C is straightforward: we check if $S(e) = k_o$. Given a concrete example set $\mathsf{ConcreteExs} = \{C_1, \ldots, C_n\}$, e is consistent with ConcreteExs iff e is consistent with each C_i.

The algorithm enumerates expressions inductively until it finds an expression e that is consistent with ConcreteExs. In the first step, only expressions of size one are considered, *i.e.*, variable symbols or constants. In the nth step, expressions of size n are obtained by composing expressions obtained in previous steps using functions in $\mathcal{F}$. As each expression e is enumerated, it is checked for consistency with ConcreteExs.

To enhance scalability, the algorithm uses the examples to guide the search as well, rather than just to check for consistency. Intuitively, if two expressions e and e' evaluate to the same values for each example $C \in \mathsf{ConcreteExs}$, then only one of e or e' needs to be carried forward to the next iteration, as the information encoded in ConcreteExs is insufficient to distinguish e and e'. The algorithm exploits this property to prune the search space of expressions.

Let $\mathsf{ConcreteExs} = \{C_1, \ldots, C_n\}$ be a concrete example set. Suppose each C_i is represented as (S_i, k_i). Then the *signature* $\mathsf{Sig}(e, \mathsf{ConcreteExs})$ of an expression e with respect to ConcreteExs is a vector of values $\langle k_1, k_2, \ldots k_n \rangle$, where each $k_i = S_i(e)$. In other words, the signature of an expression e is the

[1] These are constant-valued expressions that do not contain variables. For example, if the only integer-valued constants in $\mathcal{F}$ are 0 and 1, then k_v is allowed to be the term 2 as an abbreviation for `add(1, 1)`.

Algorithm 1: SolveConcrete

Input : A concrete example set ConcreteExs on a typed variable o, an expression vocabulary $(\mathcal{T}, \mathcal{F})$ and a set of typed variables $\mathcal{V}$.
Output: An expression e, which is consistent with ConcreteExs.
Data : The sets $\mathsf{ExpSet}(t, i), t \in \mathcal{T}, i \in \mathbb{N}$, denoting sets of expressions of type t and size i, initialized to empty sets. A set SigSet which stores the signatures of all enumerated expressions e over ConcreteExs, initially empty.

Goal $\leftarrow \langle k_1, k_2, \ldots, k_n \rangle$, **for each** $C_i = (S_i, k_i) \in$ ConcreteExs
SizeOneExps $\leftarrow \perp$
foreach $v \in \mathcal{V}$ **do**
  SizeOneExps $\leftarrow$ SizeOneExps $\cup \{v\}$
foreach $(c \in \mathcal{F}) \wedge (\mathsf{arity}(c) = 0)$ **do**
  SizeOneExps $\leftarrow$ SizeOneExps $\cup \{c\}$
foreach $e \in$ SizeOneExps **do**
  if Sig(e, ConcreteExs) $\notin$ SigSet **then**
    SigSet $\leftarrow$ SigSet $\cup$ {Sig(e, ConcreteExs)}
    if Sig(e, ConcreteExs) $=$ Goal **then**
      return e
    ExpSet(type(e), 1) $\leftarrow$ ExpSet(type(e), 1) $\cup \{e\}$
$i \leftarrow 2$
while *true* **do**
  foreach $f \in \mathcal{F}$ **do**
    $m \leftarrow \mathsf{arity}(f)$
    foreach partition p of $i - 1$ into m-partitions **do**
      foreach $(e_1, e_2, \ldots, e_m) \in \prod_{j=1}^{m} \mathsf{ExpSet}(\mathsf{argtype}(f, j), p_j)$ **do**
        $e \leftarrow f(e_1, e_2, \ldots, e_m)$
        if Sig(e, ConcreteExs) $\notin$ SigSet **then**
          SigSet $\leftarrow$ SigSet $\cup$ {Sig(e, ConcreteExs)}
          if Sig(e, ConcreteExs) $=$ Goal **then**
            return e
          Add e to ExpSet(type(e), size(e))
  $i \leftarrow i + 1$

vector of values obtained by evaluating e over the concrete examples. Two expressions e and e' are said to be *indistinguishable* w.r.t a concrete example set ConcreteExs iff Sig(e, ConcreteExs) $=$ Sig(e', ConcreteExs).

Example. Consider the expression vocabulary shown in Table 1. Suppose that we wish to describe the expression to compute the maximum of two integers a and b. Consider concrete example $C_1 = (S_1, k_1)$, where S_1 is the map $\langle a : 5, b : 3, c : 4 \rangle$. Also consider the concrete example $C_2 = (\langle a : 3, b : 1, c : 2 \rangle, k_2)$. Let ConcreteExs $= \{C_1, C_2\}$. For expressions $e_1 = a + b$, $e_2 = b + a$, $e_3 = c + c$, the signatures Sig(e_1, ConcreteExs) $= \langle 8, 4 \rangle$, Sig(e_2, ConcreteExs) $= \langle 8, 4 \rangle$, and Sig(e_3, ConcreteExs) $= \langle 8, 4 \rangle$ are equal. Thus e_1, e_2, and e_3 are indistinguishable with respect to ConcreteExs. Note that this implies that larger expressions such as $a + (a + b)$ and $a + (c + c)$ are also indistinguishable w.r.t. ConcreteExs. □

Algorithm 1, referred to as SolveConcrete, implements the enumeration based strategy, with the pruning of the search space based on the notion of indistinguishability, to find an expression that is consistent with respect to a given set of concrete examples.

4.3 Inferring Expressions from Concolic Examples

We now describe an algorithm for the general problem defined in Section 4.1, *i.e.*, we relax the restriction that the examples be concrete. Each example $C \in$ ConcolicExs — where ConcolicExs

Algorithm 2: SolveConcolic

Input : A set of concolic examples ConcolicExs over a typed output variable o, an expression vocabulary $\mathcal{F}$ and a set of typed variables $\mathcal{V}$.
Output: An expression e, which is consistent with ConcolicExs.
Data : ConcreteExs, a set of concrete examples inferred from ConcolicExs.

ConcreteExs $\leftarrow \{\}$
while *true* **do**
  $e \leftarrow$ SolveConcrete (ConcreteExs, $\mathcal{F}$, $\mathcal{V}$)
  if *e is consistent with* ConcolicExs **then**
    return e
  else
    foreach $C \in$ ConcolicExs *such that* $\neg C[o := e]$ *is satisfiable* **do**
      $S \leftarrow$ a valuation of variables $v \in \mathcal{V}$ which satisfies the formula $\neg C[o := e]$
      $k_o \leftarrow$ a value that satisfies the formula $(\bigwedge_{v \in \mathcal{V}} v = S(v)) \wedge \mathsf{post}(C[o := k_o])$
      ConcreteExs $\leftarrow$ ConcreteExs $\cup$ (S, k_o)

is a set of *concolic* examples — has the form pre $\Rightarrow$ post, where the structure of pre and post are unrestricted.

Evaluating a candidate expression e is sufficient to check if e is consistent with respect to a given set of concrete examples. However, checking consistency of an expression w.r.t. a concolic example set requires a validity query involving terms from the expression vocabulary. For our expression vocabulary we can use a satisfiability modulo theories (SMT) solver to check consistency.

We now discuss how we can adapt Algorithm SolveConcrete to infer expressions consistent with respect to a set of concolic examples. The notion of indistinguishability has been defined only with respect to a set of concrete examples. It has no simple analogue with respect to concolic examples. But using indistinguishability to prune the search space contributes significantly to the scalability of our enumerative approach, as our experiments show in Section 4.4. Thus, it would be desirable to retain the benefits of using indistinguishability to prune the search space in the solution for the general problem of inferring an expression consistent w.r.t. a set of concolic examples. To this end, the algorithm which we now propose uses a set of *concretizations* of the concolic examples to serve as concrete examples w.r.t. which the search space is pruned.

Consider a concolic example set ConcolicExs over an output variable o and an expression e found to be inconsistent with some concolic example C of the form pre $\Rightarrow$ post. Then there must exist a valuation S over the variables $v \in \mathcal{V}$ which satisfies the formula $\neg C[o := e]$. Now, pre must necessarily be satisfiable under the valuation S. Let k_o be a value which satisfies the formula $(\bigwedge_{v \in V} v = S(v)) \wedge \mathsf{post}(C[o := k_o])$. The tuple (S, k_o) is now a *concretization* of the concolic example C. The proposed algorithm thus maintains a concrete example set ConcreteExs containing concretizations of concolic examples $C \in$ ConcolicExs. By ensuring that any expression e' enumerated henceforth is consistent with ConcreteExs before checking for consistency over ConcolicExs, the number of expensive SMT queries needed can be reduced. Whenever an expression e' that is consistent with ConcreteExs, but is inconsistent with ConcolicExs is found, additional concretizations of the concolic examples are added to ConcreteExs. This technique helps in two ways: (1) the number of queries to an SMT solver is reduced, and (2) the search space can be pruned on the basis of indistinguishability.

Algorithm 2, referred to as SolveConcolic, makes use of these pruning strategies. Note that it uses Algorithm SolveConcrete as a subroutine. It maintains a set of concrete examples, ConcreteExs

Expression	Counterexample	Inferred Example
—	—	$\langle a:0, b:-1, o:0\rangle$
a	$\langle a:0, b:1, o:0\rangle$	$\langle a:0, b:1, o:1\rangle$
$\mathsf{ite}(\mathsf{iszero}(\mathsf{dec}(b)), b, a)$	$\langle a:0, b:2, o:0\rangle$	$\langle a:0, b:2, o:2\rangle$
$\mathsf{ite}(\mathsf{gt}(b, a), b, a)$	—	—

Table 2. Illustration of the working of SolveConcrete

— which are concretizations of examples in ConcolicExs — and invokes the SolveConcrete algorithm on it. If SolveConcrete finds an expression e which is consistent w.r.t. ConcreteExs, the algorithm checks if e is consistent w.r.t. ConcolicExs with a query to an SMT solver. If e is inconsistent with ConcolicExs, then the algorithm augments ConcreteExs with new concrete examples as described earlier and repeats the entire process.

Example. To illustrate the working of the algorithm, consider finding an expression for $\mathsf{max}(a, b)$, with the expression vocabulary in Table 1. We can specify $\mathsf{max}(a, b)$ with the concolic example:

$$\texttt{true} \Rightarrow (o \geq a) \wedge (o \geq b) \wedge ((o = a) \vee (o = b))$$

Table 2 shows the expressions that were checked for consistency, the witness for the inconsistency of the expression obtained, and the concrete example inferred from the witness. The first row of the table seeds the set of concrete examples. The subsequent rows indicate the expression queried for symbolic validity and the concrete example inferred. We observe that the expression corresponding to $\mathsf{max}(a, b)$ was discovered after making only four calls to the SMT solver, although the algorithm enumerated approximately five hundred expressions. □

4.4 Evaluation of the Expression Inference Algorithm

To evaluate the utility of the expression inference algorithm, we focus on the *size* of the expressions which the algorithm is able to compute successfully as a key metric. To benchmark the performance of the algorithm `SolveConcrete`, a large number of random expressions of varying sizes were generated. For each expression, a set of ten concrete examples that were consistent with the expression was generated. For each such concrete example set, the Algorithm SolveConcrete was used to compute an expression that is consistent. Figure 5 shows that the "Pruned" variant — which prunes the search space using the notion of indistinguishability — often explores two to three orders of magnitude fewer expressions than the "Exhaustive" variant — which does not perform any pruning — for expression sizes larger than ten (note the logarithmic scale on the Y-axis in Figure 5).

To evaluate the algorithm SolveConcolic, we used the benchmarks shown in Table 3. The algorithm computes expressions of up to size 15 within a reasonable amount of time as shown in Table 3. The algorithm exceeds our 30 minute time-out on only one benchmark, whose solution has an expression size greater than 20. The right-most column in Table 3 shows that the algorithm reaches the desired solution within a few iterations of the CEGIS outer loop.

5. The TRANSIT Synthesis Tool

We now describe the implementation of TRANSIT, which uses the algorithms described in Section 4 to generate an implementation of the protocol from concolic snippets. To this end, TRANSIT needs to: (1) compute process-variable update expressions, and (2) compute guards for transitions.

5.1 Computing Update Expressions

TRANSIT employs a parallel assignment model, allowing the update for each primed variable to be computed independently. For each primed variable v', the TRANSIT snippets specify a set of concolic examples, each of the form Pre $\Rightarrow$ Post. This is precisely the form in which the Algorithm SolveConcolic expects a concolic example and can thus be solved directly by the algorithm. We instantiate o in Algorithm SolveConcolic with v', $\mathcal{V}$ with the set of all process variables and incoming message fields *i.e.*, all the variables which can be *read* in the current scope and ConcolicExs with the set of concolic examples provided in the TRANSIT snippets.

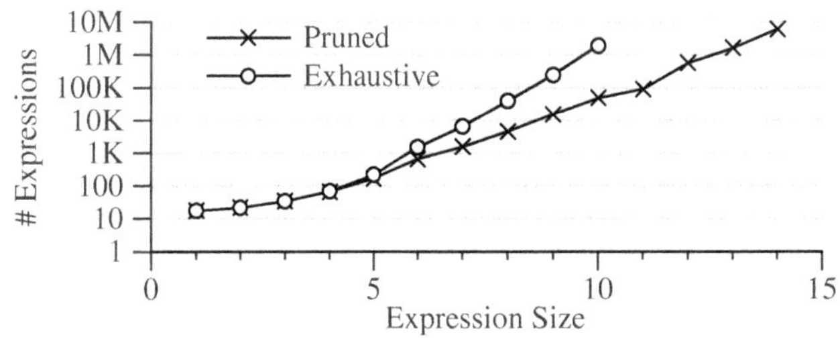

Figure 5. Average number of expressions explored for various expression sizes by the Pruned and Exhaustive variants of Algorithm SolveConcrete. We omit data for the Exhaustive variant for sizes greater than 10 where it exceeds the memory limit of 3.5 GB.

5.2 Computing Guard Expressions

A guard can be viewed as a Boolean-valued expression. The key difference between computing guards and computing update expressions is that for a given control state and input event, guards cannot be computed independently of each other. To ensure that the behavior of the EFSM implementations generated by TRANSIT are deterministic, the computed guards for each control state and input event pair are required to be pairwise mutually exclusive. To compute guards on transitions from a given state, TRANSIT groups the concolic snippets with the same starting state, input event and next state into one guard-action as shown in Figure 4. Therefore, given a starting state and input event, each possible next state has a corresponding guard-action associated with it.

Given a set of guard-actions $B_1, \ldots, B_n$, the jth guard-action block is a set of examples conditioned by $\mathsf{Pre}_{j1}, \ldots, \mathsf{Pre}_{jk_j}$. The algorithm for computing guards sequentially computes the guards for each of the blocks, starting with B_1. Thus, before synthesizing the jth guard, it has the guards $\varphi_1, \ldots, \varphi_{j-1}$ corresponding to the guard-action blocks $B_1, \ldots, B_{j-1}$ available to it. To compute a guard φ_j for the guard-action block B_j, we observe that φ_j must evaluate to false whenever the guard φ_i evaluates to true, for any $i < j$. This property is expressed with the concolic examples:

$$\mathsf{ConcolicExs}_1 = \{\varphi_i \Rightarrow \neg\varphi_j \mid i < j\}$$

Next, φ_j must evaluate to true whenever any of the preconditions $\mathsf{Pre}_{jl}, l \in [1, k_j]$ evaluate to true. This property can be expressed with the following concolic example:

$$\mathsf{ConcolicExs}_2 = \left\{ \left(\bigvee_{l=1}^{k_j} \mathsf{Pre}_{jl} \right) \Rightarrow \varphi_j \right\}$$

Also, corresponding to each block B_i for which a guard has not yet been synthesized (*i.e.*, $i > j$), φ_j must evaluate to false whenever any of preconditions in B_i evaluate to true. This property is expressed with the following symbolic examples

$$\mathsf{ConcolicExs}_3 = \left\{ \left(\bigvee_{l=1}^{k_i} \mathsf{Pre}_{il} \right) \implies \neg\varphi_j \middle| i > j \right\}$$

Finally the concolic example set required for inferring φ_j is the union of $\mathsf{ConcolicExs}_1$, $\mathsf{ConcolicExs}_2$ and $\mathsf{ConcolicExs}_3$. Again, $\mathcal{V}$ is instantiated to be the set of all process variables and the incoming

#	Description	Expected Expression	Exp. Size	Constraints	Time (s)	# Iters
1	Max. of a, b	$\mathsf{ite}(\mathsf{gt}(a, b), a, b)$	6	**(a)** $(a > b) \Rightarrow (o = a); (b > a) \Rightarrow (o = b)$	< 1	1
				(b) $\texttt{true} \Rightarrow (o \geq a \wedge o \geq b \wedge (o = a \vee o = b))$	< 1	2
2	Max. of a, b, c	Similar to 1	15	Similar to 1**(a)**	536	7
				Similar to 1**(b)**	762	16
3	Sym. Diff. of s_1, s_2	$\mathsf{setunion}($ $\mathsf{setminus}(s_1, s_2),$ $\mathsf{setminus}(s_2, s_1))$	7	$\texttt{true} \Rightarrow (o \subseteq (s_1 \cup s_2);$ $\texttt{true} \Rightarrow (o \cap (s_1 \cap s_2)) = \{\};$ $\texttt{true} \Rightarrow (o \cup (s_1 \cup s_2)) = (s_1 \cup s_2)$	< 1	2
4	Sym. Diff. of 3 sets	Similar to 3	11	Similar to 3	< 1	6
5	Sym. Diff. of 4 sets	Similar to 3	15	Similar to 3	132	14
6	Conditional Update	$\mathsf{ite}(\mathsf{equals}(e, c_1), a, b)$	6	$(e = c_1) \Rightarrow (o = a);$ $(e \neq c_1) \Rightarrow (o = b)$	< 1	4
7	Largest of 2 sets	$\mathsf{ite}(\mathsf{gt}(\mathsf{setsize}(s_1),$ $\mathsf{setsize}(s_2)), s_1, s_2)$	8	**(a)** $(\lvert s_1\rvert > \lvert s_2\rvert) \Rightarrow (o = s_1);$ $(\lvert s_2\rvert > \lvert s_2\rvert) \Rightarrow (o = s_2)$	< 1	1
				(b) $\texttt{true} \Rightarrow (\lvert o\rvert \geq \lvert s_1\rvert \wedge \lvert o\rvert \geq \lvert s_2\rvert$ $\wedge (o = s_1 \vee o = s_2))$	< 1	2
8	Largest of 3 sets	Similar to 7	> 20	Similar to 7**(b)**	TO	–

Table 3. Description of the benchmarks used to evaluate the algorithms and experimental results

Prot-ocol	# Sce-narios	Synthesis: Updates Num. synth.	Updates Exps tried	Updates Time (secs)	Guards Num. synth.	Guards Exps tried	Guards Time (secs)	State-Space
VI	19	49	449	< 1	17	525	< 1	140K
MSI	77	157	3330	< 1	45	3710	< 1	854K

Table 4. Performance of snippet-based design

message fields. o is instantiated to be φ_j. Algorithm SolveConcolic can now be used to infer the required guard expression φ_j.

6. Evaluating TRANSIT

To evaluate the proposed approach for specifying protocols with concolic snippets, we describe our experiences in using TRANSIT to specify some representative cache coherence protocols. As the proposed aims to be easy to use, a direct scientific comparison with existing approaches is challenging for two reasons: (1) a large user study, besides logistical difficulty, presents the problem of defining and extracting meaningful comparative metrics, and (2) a programmer attempting the same problem with two different approaches is subject to a familiarity bias. We instead document the experiences of three different programmers — each a co-author of this paper — in specifying three coherence protocols of varying complexity (two textbook examples and one industrial strength protocol) with TRANSIT. We summarize the perceived advantages as well as limitations of our approach based on these experiences. All experiments were performed using the expression vocabulary shown in Table 1.

We first validated the feasibility of using our expression enumeration approach by transcribing fully specified protocols from the GEMS simulation toolkit [18] into fully symbolic TRANSIT snippets. With four cache processes and one directory, the entire synthesis process took less than a second for each protocol. The key results are summarized in Table 4.

6.1 Case Study A: Non-blocking MSI Protocol.

We specified the non-blocking "MSI protocol" described in the synthesis lectures [25] using concolic snippets in TRANSIT. A non-blocking directory allows a greater number of concurrent requests to be in flight, requiring the programmer to consider a larger number of corner cases due to increased concurrency.

The scenarios described in the text resulted in a sparse initial set of snippets, as most of the tricky corner cases were either indirectly specified in the textual description or were left unspecified. Hence, the programmer added 67 more snippets over 13 debugging iterations before converging to a correct protocol. In each such iteration, the programmer either added symbolic snippets, when the behavior of the protocol in some corner case was completely unspecified, or concrete snippets, when a specification existed but was incomplete. Table 5 summarizes the effort and complexity in this experiment.

6.2 Case Study B: From MSI to MESI

The goal of our second case study was to augment the blocking MSI protocol with an "*E*" state to arrive at the MESI protocol. The *E* state (shorthand for *exclusive*) is an optimization that grants read-write permissions to the first reader of an unshared address (*i.e.*, not present in any cache) — as opposed to just read permission in MSI — thereby eliminating coherence traffic on a subsequent write to the same address. The synthesis lectures [25] describe this protocol in terms of new scenarios and modifications to scenarios in the MSI protocol. Our approach was to add the corresponding snippets to the existing set of snippets used to specify the MSI protocol. Because the examples describe a MESI protocol with a non-blocking directory, we modified our baseline MSI protocol correspondingly.

The extended protocol contained five new states (four for the cache, one for the directory), and seven new message types. In the first iteration, we added 19 snippets to specify transitions involving the *E* state and the non-blocking behavior of the directory. These snippets described the behavior of the protocol in under-specified corner cases and scenarios involving transient states and were added in response to the errors reported by the model checker. The programmer was able to obtain a fully verified protocol by adding twelve additional snippets over eight iterations. Additional metrics gathered during this case study are presented in Table 5.

6.3 Case Study C: The SGI Origin Protocol

For our final case study, we chose the coherence protocol used in the SGI-Origin 2000 servers [16], which is highly cited in the cache coherence literature. The Origin protocol is a directory-based, MESI protocol, and it supports multiple concurrent requests to the same address. Processes communicate through messages that may be arbitrarily re-ordered in the network. The consequent race conditions made it an interesting candidate for this case study.

Laudon and Lenoski [16] describe the common case protocol behavior using request flows. In this experiment, ignoring the "poisoned" directory state (used for page-migration), we transcribed each of the read, read exclusive, upgrade, and write-back flows using symbolic snippets in TRANSIT. Except for obvious cases, we left most of the guards empty and specified all conditional attributes on message fields and process variables with pre-conditions.

The protocol skeleton comprised of the cache process and directory processes, four request types, twelve response types, the request and response networks, and an intervention network used to buffer intervention requests. We initially specified 56 transitions in the cache machine and 18 transitions in the directory machine. We also specified the guards in instances where the incoming message type was found to be inconsequential; doing so prevented the tool from exploring artificially large expressions involving the disjunction of these enumerated types. The resulting protocol resulted in an error discovered by the model checker due to the cache process receiving an unexpected message. We fixed this case by adding a concrete snippet describing the desired behavior of the cache. Once again we left the guards unspecified, but the pre-conditions and update constraints were predicated by identical values for the input message fields and internal process variables, as seen in the violating trace.

Continuing similarly, we added concrete snippets to fix error traces. In some cases, the tool identified inconsistencies between the added trace and a pre-existing constraint. We found it straightforward to reconcile these differences before converging to a protocol that model checked. The final synthesis step took a little over 30 minutes, exploring over four million states during model checking. The generated TRANSIT specification had a total of 50 transitions.

6.4 Discussion and Limitations

We found the primary convenience of using TRANSIT to be the manner in which the initial specification phase and the iterative debugging phases could be expressed differently. Although it was natural to transcribe the bulk of the protocol symbolically from the algorithmic description of flows, corner cases invariably resulted. Most errors occurred due to unintended interactions between flows. The unexpected message condition cited above resulted from a cache process that was participating in a read-write-back race scenario. TRANSIT generalized the concrete fixes provided by the programmer in a manner that was guaranteed not to contradict the constituent flows. Fixing this bug symbolically would have required reasoning about the impact on both these flows. Similarly, another coherence violation was the result of the sharer set in the directory being updated incorrectly when a previous owner was downgraded. Again, the fix involved adding a snippet that concretely specified the next contents of the sharer set with the pre-condition specifying only the erroneous case.

Similar to other synthesis approaches, one limitation of TRANSIT is the readability of the produced code. Although expression size might sometimes approximate desirable metrics (like gate count in hardware descriptions), it can result in less intuitive code. For instance, consider the following code generated by TRANSIT in one of our case studies:

```
SetSize(SetAdd(Sharers, InMsg.Sender)) - 1
```

Although this code is more is compact than the equivalent, but more verbose:

```
if-then-else(SetContains(Sharers, (InMsg.Sender)),
             SetSize(Sharers) - 1,
             SetSize(Sharers))
```

the latter is more intuitive. Similarly, aggressive combining of guard-action blocks sometimes resulted in guard expressions that contained conjunctions of several different message types, making the generated code more difficult to read (although not less efficient than what a programmer would write).

	Case Study A	Case Study B
Snippets in the first/last version	19/86	96/108
Writing first set of snippets	2 hrs	6 hrs
Total manual effort	6 hrs	13 hrs
Number of iterations	13	8
Number of traces inspected	5	6
Number of updates/guards inferred	175/80	260/74
States in verified protocol	1.48M	1.5M

Table 5. Effectiveness Metrics for Protocol Design

7. Related Work

Broadly speaking, the topic of this paper can be classified as *program synthesis*, an active area of research with numerous approaches. We limit the comparison of our work to those that we feel are most closely related.

Methodologically, our approach is inspired by *program sketching* [23] and template-guided program synthesis [26]. In such approaches, a programmer specifies the scaffold of a program by listing the high-level structure, the variables, the functional specification as a pre and post condition, and the form of desired assignments inside the specified structure. The desired expressions are then formalized as terms with unknown parameters, whose values are computed using constraint solving techniques analogous to the ones used for automatic derivation of program invariants.

The problem of inferring an expression that matches a given set of concrete examples is addressed by the work by Gulwani on a variety of domains including end-user spreadsheet programming [7]. Although they do not use symbolic examples, their strategy for concrete examples, based on *version space algebra*, is different from the approach we adopt: the algorithm computes a representation of the set of all expressions that are consistent with each example, achieves compactness of the representation by a judicious use of data structures and pruning based on domain knowledge, and constructs the product of all such representations to choose an expression that is consistent with all the examples.

The problem of inferring expressions consistent with concrete and symbolic snippets can be viewed as an instance of the *counterexample-guided inductive synthesis* (CEGIS) strategy [8, 13, 23]. As mentioned earlier, the problem is analogous to solving an $\exists\forall$ formula. The solutions described in prior work [8, 13] explicitly encoded the problem into an SMT constraint, which was then solved using an SMT solver. The approach described in this work uses an enumerative technique to handle the existential quantifier and uses an SMT solver to check for universality.

Distributed protocols, such as cache coherence protocols, have been the canonical application for model checking [3]. In *reactive synthesis*, a finite-state controller is derived from correctness requirements in temporal logic, but this problem becomes undecidable when synthesizing a distributed protocol (see [28] for a survey and [6, 21] for recent approaches aimed at coping with the high computational complexity of the synthesis problem). An interesting recent approach to distributed protocol design relies on genetic programming [14]: given an initial protocol and correctness requirements, if the model checker finds that the protocol does not satisfy the requirements, the tool tries multiple mutations of the guards and updates used in the protocol, ranks the resulting versions by estimating how close they are to satisfying the requirements using state-space analysis, and iterates by probabilistically selecting a variant with weights proportional to ranks. Note that we require the programmer to specify the skeleton of the protocol (such as control states and state variables), and thus we focus not on deriving protocol logic from high-level requirements, but on providing assistance to complete the intended design correctly.

8. Conclusions

In this paper, we have proposed an approach for specifying distributed protocols by adopting verification tools that interact with the programmer. The approach relies on the observation that parts of the protocol behavior, as well as fixes during the debugging phase, can be naturally expressed in terms of example snippets. We described the concept of *concolic* snippets to allow a programmer to specify the protocol behavior as a mix of concrete examples and symbolic partial transitions. For the computational problem of inferring an expression that is consistent with the given set of concolic examples, we presented an algorithm that significantly prunes the space of expressions that need to be considered, and also limits the number of calls to an SMT solver needed to check consistency with respect to symbolic constraints. To demonstrate the feasibility of our methodology, we developed a prototype tool based on the algorithm for expression inference that generates complete protocol specifications from concolic snippets, which are then verified using a model checker.

Our preliminary case studies using this tool allowed inexperienced programmers to correctly synthesize representative cache coherence protocols of modest complexity with several hours of human effort. We were also able to translate an incomplete flow-based description of an industrial-strength protocol into a working implementation by effectively exploiting the flexibility afforded by concolic specifications. Encouraged by the initial experimental results, our next steps are to explore techniques to automatically analyze counterexamples returned by the model checker and alternate strategies for expression inference, and synthesizing EFSM descriptions from distributed scenarios such as message sequence charts.

References

[1] Intel Core2 Extreme Processor X6800 and Intel Core2 Duo Desktop Processor E6000 and E4000 Sequence — Specification Update, 2003. URL `http://www.intel.com/design/processor/specupdt/313279.htm`.

[2] D. Abts, D. J. Lilja, and S. Scott. So Many States, So Little Time: Verifying Memory Coherence in the Cray X1. In *Proceedings of the International Parallel and Distributed Processing Symposium*, IPDPS '03, pages 1–11, 2003.

[3] E. Clarke, O. Grumberg, H. Hiraishi, S. Jha, D. .Long, K. McMillan, and L. Ness. Verification of the Futurebus+ Cache Coherence Protocol. *Formal Methods in System Design*, 6:217–232, 1995.

[4] N. Dave, M. C. Ng, and Arvind. Automatic Synthesis of Cache-Coherence Protocol Processors Using Bluespec. In *Formal Methods and Models for Codesign*, MEMOCODE '05, pages 25–34, 2005.

[5] D. Dill, A. Drexler, A. Hu, and C. Yang. Protocol Verification as a Hardware Design Aid. In *Proceedings of the International Conference on Computer Design*, ICCD '92, pages 522–525, 1992.

[6] B. Finkbeiner and S. Jacobs. Lazy Synthesis. In *13th International Conference on Verification, Model Checking, and Abstract Interpretation*, VMCAI '12, LNCS 7148, pages 219–234, 2012.

[7] S. Gulwani. Automating String Processing in Spreadsheets using Input-output Examples. In *Proceedings of The 38th ACM SIGPLAN/SIGACT Symposium on Principles of Programming Languages*, POPL '11, pages 317–330, 2011.

[8] S. Gulwani, S. Jha, A. Tiwari, and R. Venkatesan. Synthesis of Loop-free Programs. In *Proceedings of the 32nd ACM SIGPLAN conference on Programming Language Design and Implementation*, PLDI '11, pages 62–73, 2011.

[9] D. Harel. Can Programming Be Liberated, Period? *IEEE Computer*, 41(1):28–37, Jan. 2008.

[10] D. Harel and R. Marelly. *Come, Let's Play: Scenario-Based Programming Using LSCs and the Play-Engine*. Springer-Verlag New York, 2003.

[11] D. Harel, A. Marron, and G. Weiss. Behavioral Programming. *Communications of the ACM*, 55(7):90–100, Jul. 2012.

[12] G. J. Holzmann. *The Spin Model Checker: Primer and Reference Manual*. Addison-Wesley, 2003.

[13] S. Jha, S. Gulwani, S. A. Seshia, and A. Tiwari. Oracle-guided Component-based Program Synthesis. In *Proceedings of the 32nd ACM/IEEE International Conference on Software Engineering - Volume 1*, ICSE '10, pages 215–224, 2010.

[14] G. Katz and D. Peled. MCGP: A Software Synthesis Tool Based on Model Checking and Genetic Programming. In *8th Internation Symposium on Automated Technology for Verification and Analysis*, ATVA '10, LNCS 6252, pages 359–364, 2010.

[15] V. Kuncak, M. Mayer, R. Piskac, and P. Suter. Software Synthesis Procedures. *Communications of the ACM*, 55(2):103–111, Feb. 2012.

[16] J. Laudon and D. Lenoski. The SGI Origin: A ccNUMA Highly Scalable Server. In *Proceedings of the 24th Annual International Symposium on Computer Architecture*, ISCA '97, pages 241–251, 1997.

[17] N. A. Lynch. *Distributed algorithms*. Morgan Kaufmann Publishers Inc., 1996.

[18] M. M. K. Martin, D. J. Sorin, B. M. Beckmann, M. R. Marty, M. Xu, A. R. Alameldeen, K. E. Moore, M. D. Hill, and D. A. Wood. Multifacet's General Execution-driven Multiprocessor Simulator (GEMS) Toolset. *SIGARCH Computer Architecture News*, 33(4):92–99, Nov. 2005.

[19] L. D. Moura and N. Bjørner. Z3: An Efficient SMT Solver. In *Proceedings of the 14th International Conference on Tools and Algorithms for the Construction and Analysis of Systems*, TACAS '08, pages 337–340, 2008.

[20] K. Sen, D. Marinov, and G. Agha. CUTE: A Concolic Unit Testing Engine for C. In *Proceedings of the 13th ACM SIGSOFT International Symposium on Foundations of Software Engineering*, FSE '05, pages 263–272, 2005.

[21] S. A. Seshia. Sciduction: Combining Induction, Deduction, and Structure for Verification and Synthesis. In *Proceedings of the 49th Annual Design Automation Conference*, DAC '12, pages 356–365, 2012.

[22] R. Singh and A. Solar-Lezama. Synthesizing Data Structure Manipulations from Storyboards. In *Proceedings of the 19th ACM Symposium on Foundations of Software Engineering*, FSE '11, pages 289–299, 2011.

[23] A. Solar-Lezama, R. Rabbah, R. Bodik, and K. Ebcioglu. Programming by Sketching for Bitstreaming Programs. In *Proceedings of the SIGPLAN 2005 Conference on Programming Language Design and Implementation*, PLDI '05, pages 281–294, 2005.

[24] A. Solar-Lezama, C. G. Jones, and R. Bodik. Sketching Concurrent Data Structures. In *Proceedings of the SIGPLAN 2008 Conference on Programming Language Design and Implementation*, PLDI '08, pages 136–148, 2008.

[25] D. J. Sorin, M. D. Hill, and D. A. Wood. *A Primer on Memory Consistency and Cache Coherence*. Morgan Claypool, 2011.

[26] S. Srivastava, S. Gulwani, and J. S. Foster. From Program Verification to Program Synthesis. In *Proceedings of the 37th annual ACM Symposium on Principles of Programming Languages*, POPL '10, pages 313–326, 2010.

[27] M. Talupur and M. R. Tuttle. Going with the Flow: Parameterized Verification using Flows: An Industrial Experience. In *Proceedings of the 2008 Internation Conference on Formal Methods in Computer-Aided Design*, FMCAD '08, pages 1–8, 2008.

[28] W. Thomas. Facets of Synthesis: Revisiting Church's Problem. In *Foundations of Software Science and Computational Structures, 12th International Conference*, FOSSACS '09, LNCS 5504, pages 1–14, 2009.

Using Managed Runtime Systems to Tolerate Holes in Wearable Memories

Tiejun Gao† Karin Strauss‡ Stephen M. Blackburn† Kathryn S. McKinley‡ Doug Burger‡ James Larus‡

†Australian National University
{tiejun.gao,steve.blackburn}@anu.edu.au

‡Microsoft Research
{kstrauss,mckinley,dburger,larus}@microsoft.com

Abstract

New memory technologies, such as phase-change memory (PCM), promise denser and cheaper main memory, and are expected to displace DRAM. However, many of them experience permanent failures far more quickly than DRAM. DRAM mechanisms that handle permanent failures rely on very low failure rates and, if directly applied to PCM, are extremely inefficient: Discarding a page when the first line fails wastes 98% of the memory.

This paper proposes low complexity cooperative software and hardware that handle failure rates as high as 50%. Our approach makes error handling transparent to the application by using the memory abstraction offered by managed languages. Once hardware error correction for a memory line is exhausted, rather than discarding the entire page, the hardware communicates the failed line to a failure-aware OS and runtime. The runtime ensures memory allocations never use failed lines and moves data when lines fail during program execution. This paper describes minimal extensions to an Immix mark-region garbage collector, which correctly utilizes pages with failed physical lines by skipping over failures. This paper also proposes hardware support that clusters failed lines at one end of a memory region to reduce fragmentation and improve performance under failures. Contrary to accepted hardware wisdom that advocates for wear-leveling, we show that with software support non-uniform failures delay the impact of memory failure. Together, these mechanisms incur no performance overhead when there are no failures and at failure levels of 10% to 50% suffer only an average overhead of 4% and 12%, respectively. These results indicate that hardware and software cooperation can greatly extend the life of wearable memories.

Categories and Subject Descriptors D. Software [*D.3 Programming Languages*]: D.3.4 Processors, Memory management (garbage collection); B. Hardware [*B.8 Performance and Reliability*]: B.8.1 Reliability, Testing, and Fault-Tolerance

General Terms Reliability

Keywords Failure tolerance, memory management, phase-change memory

1. Introduction

The semiconductor industry continues to exploit Moore's Law by scaling down lithographic feature sizes to improve chip density. However, due to increased process variation and smaller features, scaling charge-based memories such as DRAM is becoming increasingly difficult [12]. Errors increase as smaller features represent a bit with less charge. Process variation makes scaling even more challenging because different memory cells operate with a wider range of charges.

Memory manufacturers are delivering alternatives to charge-based memories, such as resistive and magneto-resistive memories. Among these, memristors are under advanced development and phase-change memory (PCM) is in production [15]. PCM's storage principle is based on physical atomic arrangements of the materials that constitute it, rather than charges it holds, resulting in more stable storage at smaller feature sizes. The result is better scaling for main memory storage, which will keep improving memory density and cost in smaller feature sizes. Moreover, PCM is non-volatile, which presents opportunities for new software designs [7] and lower power operation.

However, PCM comes with its own idiosyncrasies. Stable memory cells require more energy to write and fail much quicker compared to DRAM, as writes change the material's physical configuration and cause it to wear out. We call memories vulnerable to this issue *wearable memories*. This paper frames our solution as targeting PCM, but it is applicable to any main memory technology that suffers failures.

Current DRAM approaches assume failures occur extremely rarely. When one line in DRAM fails, software remaps its virtual page to another working physical page and discards the entire failed physical page [9]. Even recent work on error correction hardware tailored to wearable memories [16, 22, 23, 25] assumes that once the finite error correction resources are exhausted, the entire page, if not the entire memory, fails. Assuming only pages fail, 4 KB pages and 64 B lines, this solution wastes 98% of working memory. In other words, only 2% of lines need fail and the entire wearable memory becomes unusable.

This paper proposes a software/hardware cooperative mechanism to extend the life of wearable memories. We propose software mechanisms that handle failures at a fine granularity, e.g., a cache line, in which the OS and managed runtime extend the lifetime of wearable memory, with graceful performance degradation as the number of failures (*holes*) increases.

The first line of defense for failures is of course the hardware error correction of the memory system. When the number of failed bits exceeds the capacity of the error correction hardware, the memory communicates this failure to the OS. The OS keeps track of failures at the level of individual lines in a page. The OS reports failed lines when the runtime requests memory, and it may also communicate failures that occur during program execution.

The failure-aware memory manager never allocates live objects on failed lines and evacuates live objects from lines when they fail. We show how to minimize wasted space and performance degradation for garbage-collected managed languages, such as C#, Java, JavaScript, and PHP, using the hierarchical, *logical* line and block heap organization in the Immix mark-region garbage collector [3].

PLDI'13 June 16–19, 2013, Seattle, WA, USA.

This heap organization reflects hardware cache lines and pages and simplifies failure tolerance because it manages memory in sizes similar to the failure granularity.

This basic software design delivers a correct, simple failure-aware approach for heap data and dynamically generated code with modest performance degradation for low failure rates. Even though hardware-unassisted software results in correct behavior, we show that memory fragmentation causes significant overheads when the number of failures rises above 10%. Fragmentation makes it too time consuming to locate free memory for medium and large object allocations. Novel, low complexity *failure clustering* hardware comes to the rescue by redirecting failures within a region (one or more pages) to a cluster at one end, greatly reducing virtual memory fragmentation. This modest hardware support solves the fragmentation problem for software, increasing the number of failures that are performance-transparent.

We implement this approach in a Java virtual machine, but it generalizes to any managed language. Since PCM is not yet available as a DRAM replacement, we add fault injection between the OS and VM memory allocators and execute on current processors with DRAM. Experiments with DaCapo benchmarks [5] show that failure-aware software adds no overhead in the absence of failures, and with 10% and 50% failure ranges on average adds only 4% and 12%, respectively. We explore the sensitivity of our approach to different clustering granularities and software line granularities. These results show that hardware failure clustering brings additional benefits because it creates larger contiguous pieces of working memory, even entire working pages, with little performance degradation. These results contradict accepted hardware wisdom on wear leveling [17, 18, 26]. Wear leveling delays any one failure, but once memory begins to fail, uniformly distributed failures cause fragmentation, whereas concentrated failures fragment memory less and are more transparent to software.

The capability of a managed runtime to relocate objects increases the ability of the system to tolerate uncorrected hardware failures, independent of the underlying hardware error correction mechanism. By allocating around holes in non-homogeneous memory pages, our system increases the useful lifetime of PCM memory, making it more practical to use as main memory.

2. PCM Background and System Design

This section explains why DRAM technology is struggling to scale to smaller technologies. It then briefly describes PCM technologies, approaches to extending PCM lifetimes, and how future systems may incorporate PCM. We use the following failure terminology. (1) *Static* failures occur prior to an application executing. The runtime may never allocate into pre-existing failed memory. (2) *Dynamic* failures occur during an application's execution.

2.1 Scaling Problems for DRAM

DRAM technology manufacturers are running into difficulties scaling DRAM cells to smaller features (thus denser memory chips) because DRAM uses a capacitive storage principle. Each cell is a capacitor, which stores electrons. The charge held by the cell is later sensed to determine the state stored in the cell. As cells get smaller, the charge held in each cell drops, which increases the probability that charge escaping from the cell will cause a bit flip. Emerging technologies such as PCM are much more stable than DRAM, so they became interesting potential replacement technologies.

2.2 PCM Hardware

The basic storage principle of PCM is changing the state of a chalcogenide material [19]. Electrical current heats up cells and then the material cools down into an amorphous or a crystalline state that have different resistances, which encode logical zeroes and ones. Due to the physical nature of state changes on writes, cells tend to wear out. The average lifetime is currently about 10^8 writes per cell versus 10^{15} in DRAM. These changes are isolated and localized to individual cells, so failures have no spatial correlation. The peripheral circuitry responsible for performing the write detects failures by reading the value once the write completes.

Previous work advocates for hardware and software wear leveling [17, 18, 26] that uniformly distributes failures across memory with the purpose of wearing it equally and delaying failures. Hardware-only error correction replaces bits or entire lines on permanent failures [16, 22, 23, 25]. These papers assume that once the finite error correction resources are exhausted, the entire page, if not the entire memory, fails. This was inspired by how DRAM systems handle failures today, but it is not adequate for PCM because failures are not as rare as in DRAM. This paper shows that, with modest hardware and software support, only the failing line needs to be disabled and removed from the visible memory space. Furthermore, software tolerates failures better when they are clustered, rather than uniformly distributed throughout memory.

Our software/hardware cooperative approach extends system endurance to go beyond what is possible with hardware-only error correction because it successfully uses other lines in the same page. Effectively, the system gradually shifts from error correction to error tolerance. An additional benefit is that error correction resources previously used to correct the failed line can be repurposed to correct lines that are still in use when they experience additional bit failures, extending the system lifetime even further.

2.3 System Design

Even though the bulk of a system's main memory may eventually be composed of PCM, we assume in this paper that the system will have some DRAM protected by regular ECC for operations that must not fail. For example, DRAM should store essential OS and runtime data structures. The lower the software's dependency on DRAM and perfect PCM, the more failure-tolerant it will be. One may wonder what incentive application writers have to use PCM when DRAM is also available. The right balance between PCM and DRAM sizes will depend on costs and goals of the system, but if PCM reaches the scale required to service the main memory market, it will have to be significantly cheaper than DRAM. As such, main memories are likely to use a small DRAM module and a much larger PCM module, making DRAM scarce. A process storing data in DRAM would have a higher probability of having its pages swapped out into disk, which will likely degrade performance. If the process stores data in PCM, performance improves because this module is large and its contents are less likely to be swapped out, if at all.

3. Cooperatively Avoiding Faults

This section describes our proposed hardware, OS, and runtime support for handling PCM failures.

3.1 Hardware Support

We propose two simple hardware mechanisms. The first informs the software of failures, and is the foundation for cooperative failure tolerance. The other clusters failures to reduce fragmentation.

3.1.1 Hardware: Failure Tolerance

The hardware cooperates with software by (a) informing software when a write fails, and (b) transparently maintaining the data from a failed write while the software adapts to the failure.

When a PCM write fails, the PCM memory module: (1) copies the data and the corresponding physical address to a failure buffer,

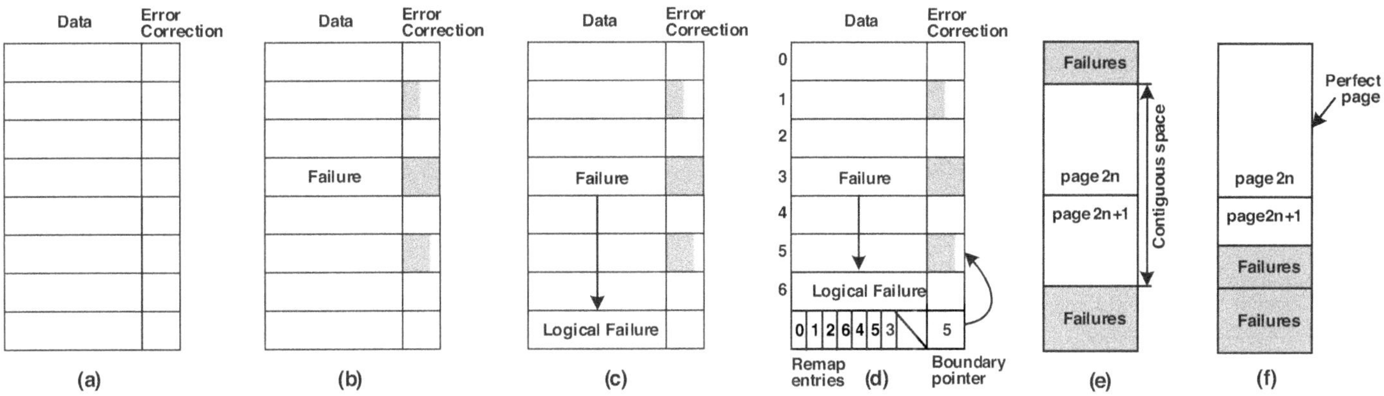

Figure 1. Hardware Failure Clustering

and (2) interrupts the processor. The failure buffer consists of a small quantity of SRAM or DRAM that is part of the PCM module itself, its peripheral DIMM circuit, or the memory controller. Every memory read request checks the buffer for the latest value written to a memory location. This search is performed in parallel with the actual access, so it does not affect read latency. If the memory module finds an entry in the buffer, it returns the corresponding data instead of the data read from the PCM array. The OS invalidates entries in this buffer once it finishes handling them. If other failures happen before a first failure is processed, information about these failures is stored in the failure buffer in FIFO order. The size of the buffer bounds the number of simultaneous failures that can be tolerated. The physics of PCM results in failures that are not naturally clustered in practice and do not happen frequently, so this buffer can be small (no larger than the processors' load/store queues, which have similar forwarding capabilities). An earlier entry with the same address is invalidated. When the failure buffer is about to fill up (enough entries are reserved to drain all outstanding writes to PCM), another type of interrupt is sent to the processor, and the PCM memory stops accepting any further write requests until the OS handles and clears at least one buffer entry. The hardware and OS thus prevent deadlocks and data loss.

3.1.2 Hardware: Minimizing Fragmentation

As failures accumulate, they increase memory fragmentation, making it more difficult to allocate data across multiple contiguous lines. We propose a hardware mechanism called *failure clustering* to mitigate this problem. Failure clustering logically pushes failures to one end of a region, consisting of one or more pages. Section 6.4 quantifies fragmentation due to failures and shows that reducing fragmentation greatly reduces software overhead.

Failure clustering logically remaps failed lines to edges of regions, as illustrated in Figure 1. Figure 1(a) shows a region with no failures. Figure 1(b) shows that, as the region wears out, lines run out of error correction resources and fail. Figure 1(c) shows that ideally these lines map to the edges of regions, maximizing the amount of contiguous space available for object allocation. To create contiguous space, we propose a simple line redirecting strategy. Figure 1(d) shows that every time a line fails, the hardware redirects it to the top or bottom of the region. Once the first line fails, the hardware installs a redirection map in the first line (or another pre-defined line) of the region and a pointer to the boundary between lines that work and lines that do not.

The redirection map has as many entries as lines in a region (128 by default in our experiments) and each entry requires as many bits as the logarithm of this number. Each entry is indexed by the physical address offset in the region and produces the actual line offset to which that line was redirected. On each failure, the hardware maps the failed address to the boundary pointer line, advances the boundary, and updates the redirection map, exchanging the offsets of the two lines being swapped. It increments or decrements the boundary, depending on which side of the region the failures cluster. If regions are page-sized, to further maximize the amount of contiguous memory, failures cluster to the top of even regions and to the bottom of odd regions, as shown in Figure 1 (e). Figure 1(f) illustrates regions larger than one page, in which case failures of both pages cluster in only one of them (as long as the number of unavailable lines corresponds to less than one page). Multiple-page clustering creates logically perfect PCM pages. Assuming a 4 KB page, 64 B lines, and a 2-page region size, the redirection map requires 889 bits, or two lines, for its metadata: 126 7-bit fields for redirection entries, and one 7-bit field for the boundary pointer. It uses the remaining bits for error correction.

When the first failure happens in a page, the hardware sets up a redirection map. The memory module first places a 'fake' failure at the location in which it intends to install the redirection map in its failure buffer, before inserting the entry corresponding to the first failure. Once the OS clears both entries from the list, the memory module installs the redirection map. The hardware handles failures in the redirection map with error correcting codes.

On memory operations, the memory module must identify which lines to redirect. The hardware uses a single bit in the original error correction metadata to indicate if the line is redirected. The memory module inserts the failure maps at fixed locations to ease lookup — the top of even regions and bottom of odd regions.

The implementation complexity of clustering hardware is modest. Upon an application reference to a region with failures, the memory module accesses the redirection map using the physical address offset it received from the cache hierarchy as the index. It retrieves a new offset and then accesses the corresponding line. In practice, this functionality requires very simple logic. However, it requires three memory accesses: (1) The first access finds the line is redirected, and (2) the second access goes to the redirection table, and (3) the third access reads or writes the redirected line. Three accesses could significantly increase latency. A simple solution is to cache recently used redirection maps. Note that in the common case of no failure, references require only one memory access irrespective of whether or not caching is in use.

3.2 Operating System Support

When the system is new, most, if not all, pages will be perfect (no failures). As PCM pages wear, their cells start to fail, and, at some point, hardware error correction is exhausted. Certain lines in a page become unusable, although other lines are still functional.

When a line fails, the operating system receives the interrupt notification of the failure. The memory access may have executed in a user process or the operating system itself. This paper focuses on the first case. The OS accesses PCM, as discussed below, and must handle situations in which its writes fail, but this paper does not consider storing OS data structures or code in PCM.

Operating systems can handle the failure in two fundamentally different ways. They can hide line failures from executing processes by replacing failed pages with perfect pages, changing the process's page tables and continuing the process without interruption. This approach masks the failure, preserving the illusion of perfect memory, at the cost of depleting the increasingly scarce resource of perfect pages.

The other approach is to notify the process of a line failure, to allow the runtime to reorganize data structures and avoid using memory locations in the failed line. The process continues using the page until its defect density renders it unusable. The focus of this paper is the design of failure-aware managed runtimes that may relocate data transparently to applications.

3.2.1 OS: Data Structures and System Calls

The OS manages DRAM, perfect PCM, and imperfect PCM pages in separate pools. Initially, all PCM pages start in the perfect pool. When a page first becomes imperfect, the OS moves the page to the imperfect page pool. The OS also tracks the failed lines in these pages. A system with 64 B lines and 4 KB pages requires a 64-bit bitmap per page. The OS stores these bitmaps in a table in DRAM with an entry corresponding to each physical PCM page in the system. Uncompressed, this table is approximately 1.6% of the size of the PCM page pool. Run-length encoding or other simple encoding techniques may provide high compression rates and reduce this overhead, especially when the system is new and the number of failures is low. When the system is shut down, the OS may save the failed line map to persistent storage and restore it on system initialization. Alternatively, the OS may rebuild the table by eagerly scanning memory or by lazily rediscovering failures at first write. Rediscovery is necessary after abnormal shutdowns and incurs a cost proportional to the size of PCM or the number of failures not recorded in persistent storage before the shutdown.

Failure-unaware processes may continue allocating perfect memory via normal mechanisms such as *mmap*. A failure-aware process can utilize both perfect and imperfect memory pages. Perfect memory grows scarcer as a system ages. Although imperfect pages require extra management and overhead, they are more abundant. A failure-aware runtime uses a special variation of *mmap* to acquire imperfect pages. This call returns the number of pages requested, however not all of the allocated memory may be usable. The runtime uses a *map-failures* call to get a failure map of the allocated memory region. If the runtime requires more space than the OS returned, it requests additional memory.

3.2.2 OS: Handling Dynamic Failures

When the memory module detects a failure, it raises an interrupt. This failure occurs asynchronously with respect to the write operation because a line is only written to PCM when it is evicted from the cache subsystem. When the interrupt is raised, the OS interrupt handler reads the failure information from the failure buffer. Before removing any entries from the failure buffer, the OS must prevent accesses to the failing addresses because, once it removes them, the memory module no longer forwards data to read operations on these addresses. The OS finds the corresponding virtual pages via reverse address translation, removes read and write permissions from them, and updates its own failure map. Reverse address translation is relatively expensive, but dynamic failures are very rare and either require copying a page or a garbage collection. The cost of reverse address translation is small compared to both.

The OS handler needs to resolve every failure. For failure-unaware processes, the only option is to copy the entire affected page to a perfect page. It must do the same for memory regions allocated when failure-aware processes request perfect memory. For imperfect memory requests, it may use the same approach or rely on the runtime to handle the failure.

A failure-aware runtime must register a handler with the OS before it uses imperfect memory. When a failure occurs, the OS performs an up-call on the handler, passing the addresses and data of all pending failures. The runtime must relocate affected data, updating whatever runtime structures are necessary to ensure correctness and transparency before returning from the handler.

As a convenience to the runtime, the OS may optionally reconstruct the affected page using a DRAM page for the duration of the runtime handler performing its work. Otherwise, the runtime uses the partially-failed PCM page and the information passed to the handler to reconstruct the affected data, and must avoid accessing the failed lines while it handles the failure.

3.2.3 OS: Paging and Other Issues

The OS may occasionally copy data from one imperfect page to another, for example, when an imperfect page is swapped out and then brought back into memory. If the failures on the destination page are a subset of the failure locations on the source page, copying is straightforward. However, keeping track of page compatibility is expensive, and prior work shows similar matching processes have limited efficacy in practice [11]. As we show below, failure clustering helps solve this problem.

When moving data from a previous imperfect page (possibly on disk) to another memory page, the OS has three options: (1) The OS may swap data into a perfect page. (2) The OS may swap data into an imperfect page with different failures compared to the previous physical page. The OS must inform the runtime of the new failure map by delivering an up-call on the runtime's handler. If the runtime cannot safely move data in the failed lines, the OS can try another imperfect page or fall back to a perfect page. (3) Failure clustering enables a third and simpler approach. Since clustering accumulates failures at one end of the page, the OS simply maps the page it is swapping in onto any available page with the same number or fewer failures.

3.3 Runtime and Application Software Support

We turn now to failure-aware runtimes. We start with the limitations inherent to native (unmanaged) applications. We then overview failure-aware runtime support for managed applications. Section 4 describes the basic Immix garbage collection algorithm and how we implement failure-tolerance in Immix.

3.3.1 Failure-Aware Applications and Runtimes

In principle, any application can be made failure-aware. In practice, forcing developers to manage failures without runtime support is impractical because it requires significant and pervasive changes to ensure live data never occupies failed memory.

Static failures to memory allocated to the *stack* for both native and managed languages could be addressed by the compiler and runtime stepping around failed lines as they allocate new stack frames. But given the frame allocation/deallocation frequency, the overhead of such a scheme is likely to be unreasonable. Handling dynamic failures to the stack is even more challenging.

Static failures to memory allocated to the *code and data segments* will be hard to handle because of hard-coded assumptions about offsets to code and data in these segments. In principle, this problem could be addressed via binary rewriting. However, because native programs may hold untyped and undiscoverable references to elements in the code and data segments, handling dynamic failures to these regions appears to be intractable.

The runtime memory manager may handle static failures in *heap* memory. Native runtimes use free list allocators, which could use imperfect memory, and mark as unavailable those units of allocation that coincide with failed memory. Such an implementation would increase the complexity of managing the free list. However, for large objects and large numbers of failures, native runtimes have a stronger requirement for perfect pages than managed runtimes. For example, managed languages can split large arrays [21] (see Section 4), whereas native languages require contiguous allocation.

Adding failure tolerance to the free-list used by native runtimes will incur additional complexity, fragmentation, or both. Most of the complexity arises due to (1) mismatches between failure granularity and the free-list heap layout, and (2) the need to differentiate between failed and in-use memory both to reduce fragmentation and for correctness with conservative collection. Granularity mismatches arise because native memory managers use segregated size free-list allocators [2, 6, 8, 14], carving up large fixed-sized regions (e.g., one or more pages) into same-sized objects on demand. To add failure tolerance, we have three choices: (a) to use only perfect small page size regions, which incurs fragmentation for medium size objects, and never uses pages with failures, or (b) incur fragmentation in each fixed-size large region, or (c) add complexity to allocate and recycle variable-sized regions. Note that these same issues arise for managed languages that use free-lists. None of these options are appealing.

To summarize, native applications could be made tolerant to static failures in the heap with non-trivial changes to a free-list allocator, but the OS must still handle all dynamic failures.

3.3.2 Failure-Aware Managed Runtimes

We design and implement a solution for failure-aware memory in a *managed* runtime that dynamically allocates code and data memory space. A large and growing set of applications are written in managed languages, such as C#, Java, JavaScript, Python, and PHP. These languages use safe pointer disciplines and execute in virtual machines (VMs) that include dynamic compilers and automatic memory management (garbage collection). Because these languages are memory safe, the garbage collector (GC) allocates and is free to move objects in memory (including code objects in some VMs). Moving objects is both safe and transparent to applications. We leverage this functionality to tolerate failures in PCM without putting a burden on developers. A failure-aware garbage collector never allocates objects in failed memory and relocates affected data when new failures happen.

In VMs that dynamically allocate code and data, our solution transparently handles both, but we focus on data here. A VM solution reduces the need for perfect memory to the VM itself, heap metadata, and large objects. A self-hosting VM may reduce the need even further. The next section provides an overview of how to make garbage collection failure-aware.

3.3.3 Garbage Collection

Two high-level modifications are necessary for a garbage collector to tolerate failures: (1) exposing information about failures to the garbage collector (GC), and (2) modifying the allocator to avoid allocating live objects in memory that contains failures.

The OS communicates a failure map to the GC. The GC adds the failure map to the heap metadata that records which memory contains live objects and which memory is free for allocation. The hardware determines the finest possible granularity of the failure map. This paper uses the cache line size as the finest failure granularity, which is also typically the same granularity of hardware write operations to PCM. The failure map may use coarser granularities that trade-off less storage overhead for less available memory as failures accrue. We evaluate this trade-off in Section 6.3. For simplicity, we assume here that the failure map and other heap metadata are stored in perfect memory and do not themselves fail.

In a failure-aware VM, (a) the GC must never allocate live objects in a failed region of memory, and (b) when a region of memory fails during execution, the collector must evacuate all objects in the failed region and allocate them elsewhere.

Static failures The GC already maintains the invariant that it only allocates objects into free memory. The GC treats all allocations the same regardless of whether an object allocation is the result the application's call to `new()`, or if the GC itself is allocating an object to evacuate (move) it during a collection. A failure-aware GC maintains the same invariant. It only allocates into free memory. It treats failed memory the same as memory with live objects on it (neither are free). With a static failure map in hand, the collector simply allocates into free memory.

At a minimum, all memory managers separately manage (i) small or medium objects and (ii) large objects. Given sufficient failures and a large enough object, imperfect memory will not accommodate a large object. As with any allocation, when the failure-aware memory manager first attempts to allocate an object and there is insufficient memory, it triggers a collection to reclaim free memory and then attempts to allocate again. If the GC still cannot accommodate the object in imperfect memory, the allocator requests perfect memory. We greatly reduce the probability of this situation with hardware clustering at the granularity of two or more pages to create logically perfect pages (see "Large Objects" below).

Dynamic failures If a failure occurs during program execution, the OS may notify the GC and provide it with the values the program intended to write into the affected region. The OS can specify dynamic failures at the granularity of lines or pages. Regardless, the collector must move any affected objects, allocating them elsewhere in the heap. This requires that all pointers to the affected object(s) be identified and retargeted to the moved object(s). In a typical generational collector, a failure to memory in the nursery will only require a nursery collection, but any other failure will require a full heap collection. If no live objects reside in the affected region, which is unlikely because writes cause the failures, the collector marks the memory as failed in the failure map and returns.

Pinning support is required in some languages, such as C#. If a live object in the failed region is pinned by the application, the VM cannot move it and must notify the OS that it cannot vacate the region. An alternative solution is to allocate pinned objects to memory that does not fail, but some systems require in-place pinning after allocation, so this solution will not always work. Since pinning is rare, the probability of a line failing that contains a pinned object is low and some expensive action, such as the OS remapping the affected page to another perfect or failure-compatible physical page would be appropriate.

While the collector recovers from a failure, other failures could happen. As explained earlier, the hardware and OS handle these failures until the collector is ready to deal with them.

Heap Layout To implement failure tolerance, the garbage collector must relate the PCM failure granularity to the data structures it uses to manage live objects and free memory. Modern garbage collectors use one of contiguous allocation, a free-list, or the Immix mark-region line and block hierarchy [3, 4]. The next section describes how to use the Immix heap, and Section 3.3.2 described why modifying a free list is possible, but complex. Modifying a contiguous heap layout is not even possible, because it simply has no way to skip over or manage small regions of memory without fundamental changes to the algorithm.

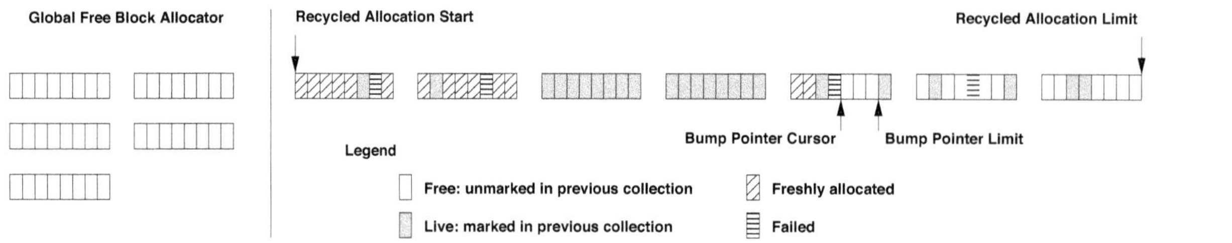

Figure 2. Immix Heap Organization and Amenability to Failure Tolerance

Large Objects Both memory managers and garbage collectors explicitly handle large objects separately [2, 4, 14, 21]. The exact large object size is a function of the granularity of the memory manager's block size, i.e., the granularity at which it manages the small and medium size objects. Typical block sizes range from 16 to 64 KB. Immix uses 32 KB by default. Most large objects in managed languages are arrays and, for DaCapo Java programs, they consume on average half the heap [21].

Without hardware clustering, if many failures are uniformly distributed in memory, large objects will not fit. A purely software solution is to use discontiguous arrays, which divide up arrays into a spine that points to smaller fixed-size *arraylets* and modify the array access code [1, 21]. Discontinuous arrays were invented to bound pause times for real-time systems. Sartor et al. showed how to make them relatively efficient, with average overheads below 13%, even with arraylets as small as 256 bytes.

With hardware clustering at a two-page granularity or higher, the hardware creates the logically perfect pages that large objects require. For example, with two-page clustering and failures in roughly 50% or less of the memory, at least 50% of memory will consist of perfect pages that the allocator may use for large objects.

4. Implementing a Failure-Aware Runtime

This section describes the modest changes required to make the Immix mark-region garbage collector failure-aware. The key attributes of Immix are well suited to the PCM failure mode, in which fixed-size lines fail. (a) Immix already tracks memory at a line granularity categorizing lines as: free, live, or live pinned. (b) Immix already maintains two invariants: (*i*) it only allocates into free lines, and (*ii*) it only ever moves unpinned objects. To make Immix failure-aware, we simply add a fourth line category to Immix, failed lines, and continue to enforce the same two invariants.

4.1 Basic Immix

The Immix design was motivated by the tension between three desirable performance objectives: space efficiency, collection time, and mutator (program) locality [3, 4]. Immix achieves all three performance objectives by combining bump-pointer allocation, efficient tracing, and occasional copying of live objects, as well as a memory-efficient two-level line and block heap organization. A key to this design is a bump-pointer allocator that can very efficiently skip over unavailable lines. This organization makes Immix an excellent match for our requirement that the allocator skip over failed PCM lines. Prior work established that Immix outperforms prior algorithms and heap organizations, and it is now the default collector in Jikes RVM [3].

Lines and Blocks Immix manages heap memory at coarse and fine granularity by dividing memory into blocks and blocks into lines, as depicted in Figure 2. Lines approximate cache lines and blocks approximate pages. Objects may span lines within a block, but cannot span blocks. Objects that fit within one line are regarded as *small*. Immix has a threshold that designates objects as *large* and delegates them to a separate page-grained large object space (LOS). This threshold is never larger than a block. Initially all blocks are free and Immix allocates objects contiguously into blocks until it fills the heap, which triggers a collection.

Collection Immix collection marks live objects by performing a transitive closure over the live object graph starting at the roots (global and stack variables) and then tracing references. When it encounters an object for the first time, it marks the object and its line as live. Immix does not copy objects by default; it deals with fragmentation by copying objects on occasion. Some managed languages, such as C# and JavaScript, require object pinning, in which applications can specify that an object may not be moved. This is typically supported for performant interoperability with native C. Immix respects pinned objects and never copies them.

After marking, Immix scans line mark tables, recycles partially filled blocks, and returns completely empty blocks to a global pool of pages for use by the whole runtime.

Allocation In steady state, Immix allocates objects into available recycled blocks first, as depicted in Figure 2. The allocator is parallel, with one thread-local allocator for each application thread. The allocator initializes a bump pointer to the first free line in a block and sets the limit to the end of the last free line in this contiguous set of free lines. When the bump pointer finds that an allocation request cannot be satisfied within the limit, it skips over any unavailable lines to identify the next set of free lines. When it exhausts a recycled block, it requests another from a shared pool of recycled blocks. Once all recycled blocks have been exhausted, the allocator requests completely free blocks from the global block pool. Once the global pool is exhausted the allocator triggers a collection. Other allocators, such as the large object space (LOS) compete for blocks from the global pool.

To make efficient use of recycled blocks, and avoid skipping otherwise usable smaller spaces, Immix heuristically allocates medium objects (those larger than a line) on a special overflow block if the object cannot immediately fit in the contiguous space available to the bump pointer. Overflow blocks are sourced from the global pool of completely free blocks, so have maximal contiguous space. Our failure-aware collector handles requests for completely free blocks by the LOS and overflow allocator by using perfect memory for such requests (see Section 3.3.3).

Sticky Immix The Sticky Immix algorithm adds high-performance generational behavior to the Immix collector. It combines sticky mark bits collection [8] with the Immix algorithm. Sticky mark bits collectors identify young objects by a bit in their header, rather than by allocating them into a distinct space. By default, it *opportunistically* copies nursery survivors into any available empty or partially filled blocks. If there is no available memory, it leaves them in place. This collector retains all of the attributes of Immix which make it amenable to failure tolerance and to the need to skip over failures, whilst gaining the performance of compacting and collecting younger objects first.

Performance Figure 3 shows a sample result that motivates Immix as a performant baseline for a failure-aware runtime. It shows the geometric mean of total execution time of the DaCapo benchmarks configured with full-heap mark-sweep (MS), Immix (IX), and the Sticky generational variants (S-MS and S-IX). We extend Immix to handle failures because of its high performance and its line-block organization simplifies the algorithmic design.

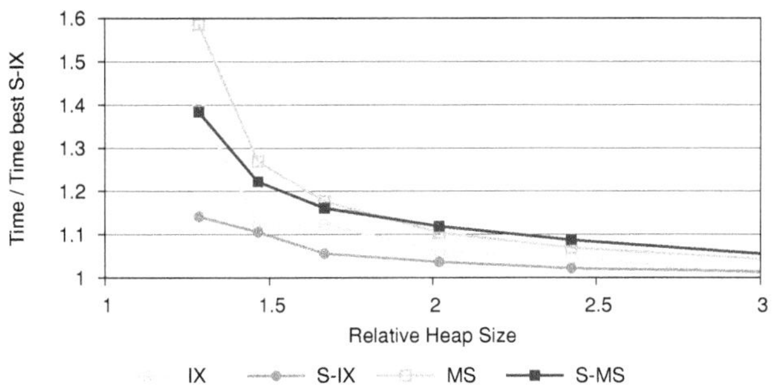

Figure 3. Performance of DaCapo benchmarks running with various memory management algorithms at multiple heap sizes.

4.2 Failure-Aware Immix

This section describes how we modify Sticky Immix to be failure-aware.

Static Failures When the OS gives Immix a region of memory and a failure bit map, failure-aware Immix marks corresponding lines as failed in its line-mark metadata. Because line marks are bytes and only some of the 256 available states are used, we add an additional state that denotes a failed line without space overhead. One subtlety is that the Immix line size is not necessarily the same as the PCM line size. For example, the best performing line size for Immix is 256 B without failures, whereas PCM line sizes are typically 64 B. When the Immix line size is greater than the PCM line size, we must mark the entire Immix line failed, even though only part of it failed. Section 6.3 explores this trade-off.

The previous section described how Immix uses free blocks for overflow allocation to accommodate medium sized objects that do not immediately fit in the space available at the bump pointer. With failure-aware Immix, the overflow block is not guaranteed to be perfect and the object may not fit. Thus we change the algorithm to search the remainder of the overflow block for suitably sized available space. If this search fails, the allocator resorts to requesting a free perfect block. Hardware failure clustering greatly reduces the likelihood of multiple overflow allocation failures.

Dynamic Failures To address dynamic failures, we use the same mechanism that Immix uses to defragment the heap. Immix opportunistically copies objects that reside on sparsely populated pages to free or partially free blocks during a defragmenting collection. For dynamic failures, we straightforwardly reuse this mechanism to move objects affected by dynamic PCM failures. We mark the affected object(s), the lines that contain it, and its block for evacuation, and then invoke a copying collection. Although a full heap collection is relatively expensive, dynamic failures are rare.

The full heap collection time is an estimate of the time needed by the runtime to handle a failure. For the DaCapo benchmarks on Intel Core i7 hardware, it takes 7 msec on average. The worst case is 44 msec (hsqldb). The next two are 22 and 12 msec (fop and xalan), with all others under 10 msec. To put this time in context, the average number of garbage collections is 14.7 and the average total execution time for these benchmarks is 1817 msec. We believe that for most applications, this simple strategy is sufficient for dealing with the rare occurrence of a dynamic failure.

5. Experimental Methodology

This section justifies our use of execution time results and then describes the hardware, benchmarks, collector configurations, and methodology for running experiments.

At the time of writing, direct evaluation on systems with PCM main memory is unfortunately not possible, as the only commercially available PCM parts today are NOR flash replacements, with very low capacities and incompatible physical interfaces. Simulation is slow, making whole benchmark execution prohibitively long. Instead, we evaluate our approach running natively on DRAM, and instrument the managed runtime with a fault injection module between the OS memory allocator and the VM memory allocation module. When the latter allocates memory, part of this memory is made 'defective' by the fault injection module.

Machine, benchmarks, and collector configurations All experiments execute on an Intel Core i7 2600 machine with 4 GB of DRAM main memory, running on Ubuntu 10.04.1 LTS. We use an implementation of Immix in Jikes RVM, a Java virtual machine. We execute the superset of all benchmarks in the DaCapo 9.12-bach and DaCapo-2006-10 suites that can run on Jikes RVM. We use lusearch-fix, which is the lusearch benchmark patched to fix a bug in the underlying lucene library that introduces pathological allocation behavior [24] by needlessly allocating a large data structure in a hot loop. This bug results in an allocation rate a factor of three higher than any other benchmark. Aside from reporting it in Figure 4 for completeness, we exclude the buggy version of lusearch from all of our analysis.

We compare to the Sticky Immix (S-IX) implementation in MMTk from Jikes RVM 3.1.2 described above with a block size of 32 KB and a line size of 256 B. Failures and garbage collection expose application performance to a space-time trade-off that we explore explicitly across a range of heap sizes. We use a modest default heap size that is 2× the minimum for each benchmark.

Failure map generation and memory accounting We model PCM failures via a failure map. The failure map has one bit for each 64 B PCM line, which indicates whether that line is working or has failed. The failure map generator distributes failures uniformly from a command line argument and produces clustered failure map distributions from uniform distributions.

Because the time-space trade-off is central to garbage collected systems, we explicitly control for heap size in all of our experiments. This introduces two important and distinct methodological considerations in the context of memory that may fail. First, we compensate the fixed heap sizes according to the failure rate to ensure that the *usable* memory is held constant. Section 6.2 discusses heap compensation in detail. Second, and quite separately, application memory requests now fall into two categories: those from *relaxed* allocators that are robust to failure because they can utilize fragmented pages, and those from *fussy* allocators that require perfect PCM or DRAM pages (because their allocations are page-grained). The balance between fussy and relaxed allocation varies greatly as a function of time and among benchmarks.

Because our modeling of PCM failure is not guaranteed to return a perfect page and a real implementation would have a limited supply of DRAM for such requests, we use a debit-credit based cost model to account for the cost of using a DRAM page when no perfect PCM page is available. Penalizing the use of DRAM is appropriate both because it would be scarce in practice and because, without a penalty, DRAM is highly attractive since it is never fragmented, which may lead to the counter-intuitive situation where higher failure rates offer better performance.

When a fussy allocator requests a perfect page and the allocator has sufficient memory, but no perfect page is available, we model giving it a perfect page (DRAM or PCM) with a one page space

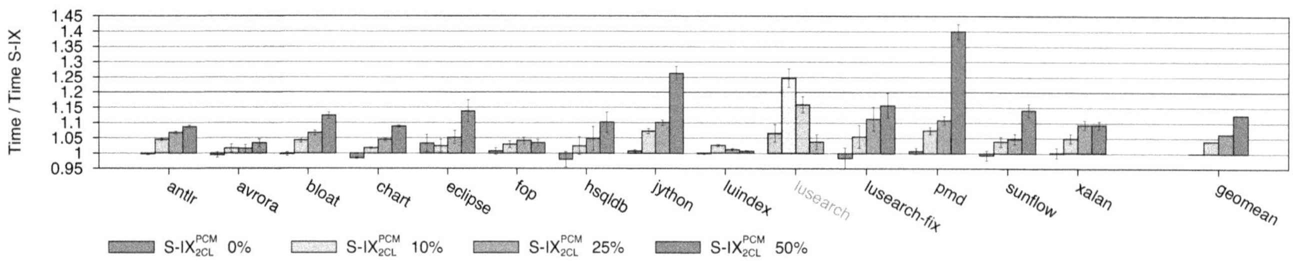

Figure 4. Performance of DaCapo benchmarks running with a failure-aware Immix implementation at multiple failure levels, normalized to the unmodified version of the algorithm.

penalty. Because garbage collection exists as a time-space trade-off, this space penalty ultimately translates to a time penalty. The relaxed allocator may 'repay' the debt of the fussy allocator. On subsequent allocations, which may follow a collection or not, each time the relaxed allocator is given a perfect page, it only takes the page if there is no outstanding debt. If there is a debt, we reduce the debt by one page and fetch another PCM page for the relaxed allocator.

Nondeterminism and experimental error To eliminate the effects of nondeterminism due to timer-driven adaptive recompilation, we used the current version of Jikes RVM's replay compilation mechanism [10, 13]. Compiler replay is driven by optimization profiles gathered ahead of time for each benchmark and then used for all experiments. Each profile identifies a good optimization plan, stating the optimization level (if any) for each method, and includes edge counts and a call graph which would normally be gathered dynamically. The replay mechanism first runs each benchmark for one iteration without any optimization (this forces all classes to be loaded). The system then compiles all methods according to the optimization plan, before commencing a second iteration of the benchmark. Our experiments evaluate this second, optimized, iteration. This methodology eliminates the chaotic nature of timer-based adaptive optimization while delivering performance slightly better than steady-state performance for an adaptively optimized system.

We perform 20 invocations of each benchmark, each using the replay methodology, and take the mean of these results, reporting 95% confidence intervals. The 95% confidence interval error is generally very low, around 1-2%. We aggregate results across benchmarks using geometric means. Some configurations cannot execute some of the benchmarks in very small heaps. When reporting aggregated results, we discard results at a given heap size when some of the benchmarks do not complete, which manifests in the graphs as lines that terminate before reaching the y-axis.

6. Evaluation

This section starts with an evaluation of PCM-aware Sticky Immix implementation with failure clustering hardware. It shows how together they dramatically mitigate the effect of PCM failures. The remainder of the section explores trade-offs in the design space and illustrates the effects of failure-induced memory fragmentation.

6.1 Performance and Memory Overheads

Figure 4 shows the performance overheads of failure-aware Sticky Immix with two-page failure clustering (S-IX$^{PCM}_{2CL}$) at multiple PCM failure rates (0, 10%, 25% and 50%). The figure normalizes time to the unmodified Sticky Immix (S-IX) collector (not shown). All of the Immix collectors use a logical line size of 256 B and block size of 32 KB, and receive the same amount of *usable* memory (the equivalent of two times the minimum heap required by each benchmark to run). Note that S-IX$^{PCM}_{2CL}$ incurs zero overhead when there are no PCM failures (the geometric mean of the green bars is 1.0, the same as unmodified Sticky Immix). The lack of any measurable overhead corroborates that, as described in Section 4.2, no additional metadata is required for failure-aware Sticky Immix (or we would see slowdowns at this constrained heap size).

As the number of failures increases, the performance overheads slowly increase. At failure levels of 10%, the overhead is 3.9% on average and never exceeds 7.4% (peach bars). Low overheads are a result of the positive effects of failure clustering, which are more thoroughly explained in Section 6.4. The overhead grows modestly with failure rate, increasing when the failure rate is 50% to an average of 12.4% with a maximum of 40% for pmd.

Some workloads, such as pmd and jython, experience high overheads. The reason is that they allocate many medium sized objects, which makes it more challenging to find free memory to fit these objects. Benchmarks such as xalan, which predominantly allocate very large objects, are quite resilient to failures because they utilize the entirely free pages delivered by two-page failure clustering. Virtual address translation transparently removes any problem of page-level fragmentation. As anticipated in Section 5, the buggy lusearch benchmark (which we gray-out here and exclude from all further analysis) gives a counter-intuitive result, with overhead *reducing* as failure rate rises. This result is due both to lusearch's pathological behavior, and an unobvious interplay between the two-page failure clustering and the way we use heap space compensation in our analysis (see Section 6.2 and Figure 5).

The remainder of this section explores the fragmentation problems and the inherent trade-offs due to failures in more detail.

6.2 Memory Reduction vs. Fragmentation

Three main factors impact performance as memory degrades. (1) As failures accumulate, the functional memory a VM receives when it requests a certain region of memory from the OS is reduced. This problem is addressed by compensation: the VM simply requests more memory until it gets as much working memory as originally intended. (2) Failures cause heap fragmentation, which reduces the usability of the available memory. (3) A more subtle effect is *false* failures, which occur when the PCM failure granularity is less than the granularity of allocation (similar to false sharing in caches). For example, if the Immix line size is greater than the failed cache line size specified by the PCM memory or the OS. With an allocation granularity of 256 B lines in Immix, an entire line becomes unusable when a single 64 B PCM line fails and false failures overstate the real failure by 192 B. This phenomenon is not specific to Immix, and will manifest whenever a request is made for contiguous memory greater than the PCM line granularity (regardless of the software algorithm).

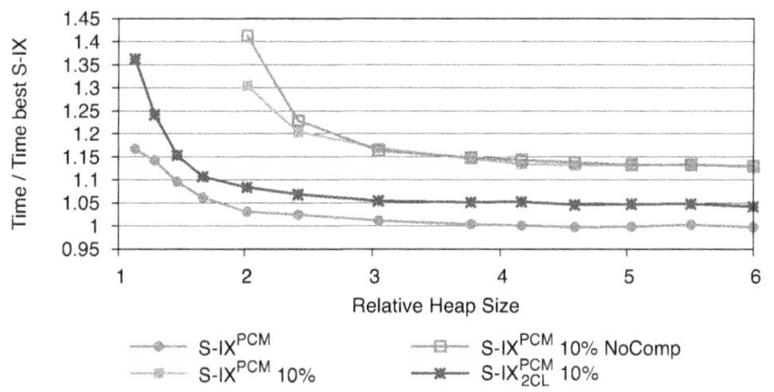

Figure 5. Compensation for memory failures is most noticeable at smaller heap sizes. This graph compares the baseline S-IX^{PCM} with no failures (green) to 10% PCM line failure rate and no clustering, with (red) and without (orange) memory compensation, and to S-IX^{PCM} with clustering and compensation (maroon), the best failure-tolerant configuration.

To break down these three effects, Figure 5 summarizes the behavior of different configurations by presenting normalized execution time geometric means (y-axis) over all workloads as a function of heap size (x-axis). It compares the baseline (green) with no failures (S-IX^{PCM}) to PCM-aware Sticky Immix with compensation (orange) and without (red), both *without* failure clustering hardware at a 10% failure rate (S-IX^{PCM} 10%). Space compensation provides the same amount of working memory if there were no failures. For example, given a heap size h used in the absence of failure, when the failure rate is f, we compensate with a heap size of $h/(1-f)$. Compensation ensures that the number of bytes of non-faulty memory available to the system is held constant.

Consider S-IX^{PCM} under no failures (S-IX^{PCM}, green), at 10% failure rates (S-IX^{PCM} 10% NoComp, red), and with working-memory space-compensation at 10% failure levels (S-IX^{PCM} 10%, orange). The gap between S-IX^{PCM} 10% NoComp and S-IX^{PCM} 10% (red and orange) in Figure 5 shows the effect of failures reducing available memory. In small to moderate heap sizes, this effect is pronounced until the heap grows to 3 times minimum, when the lines converge. The gap between the S-IX^{PCM} 10% (orange) and no failures (green) on the bottom shows the remaining two effects. Fragmentation and false failures, when spread uniformly over memory, significantly degrade performance, over 25% in small to moderate heaps and over 10% even in large heaps.

The large effects of fragmentation with or without heap compensation motivate hardware clustering. Comparing no clustering (the top two lines) to S-IX$^{PCM}_{2CL}$ 10% (two-page clustering, maroon) shows that the latter significantly improves performance by reducing the amount of fragmentation exposed to the software. Reducing fragmentation wins twice. First, the amount of usable memory is increased, which reduces memory management load, shifting the curve left. Second, application locality is improved, shifting the curve down. The next section examines in more detail the effect of line size on false failures.

Heap compensation can have an unexpected interplay with two-page failure clustering and our means of accounting for requests for perfect memory, as in lusearch in Figure 4. When allocation is dominated by page-grain requests, the number of failures on a page is unimportant; what matters is whether the page is completely free or not. Consequently, the impact of failure rate on such benchmarks is essentially constant for non-zero failure rates. On the other hand, heap compensation makes more memory available as failure rates grow. Thus although in practice the cost in terms of usable pages for failure rates of 10%, 25% and 50% remains similar for a benchmark like lusearch, compensation increases, which leads to the counter-intuitive improvement in performance as failure rates grow that we see in the lusearch result in Figure 4. However, this pathological behavior is rare, as Figure 4 shows.

In the remainder of the evaluation, we use compensated runs by default.

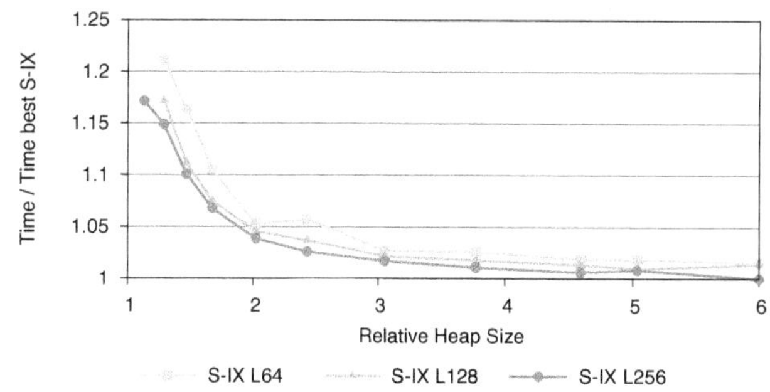

(a) The effect of line size on baseline S-IX.

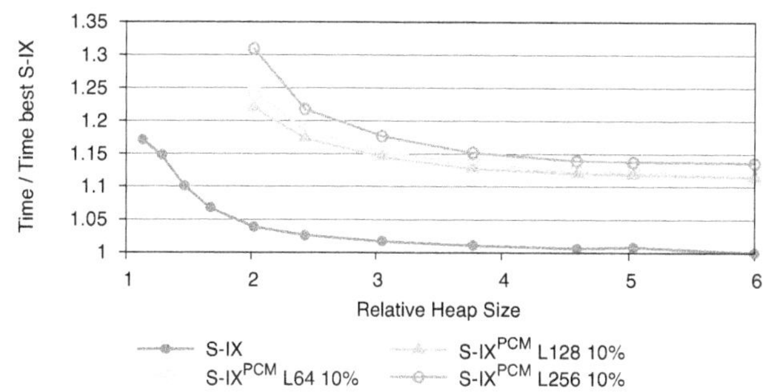

(b) The effect of line size on S-IX^{PCM} with 10% of lines failed.

Figure 6. The presence of failures without hardware clustering alters the performance behavior as Immix line size grows: While S-IX uniformly benefits from larger lines, in the presence of failures, S-IX^{PCM} L256 suffers.

6.3 The Effect of Line Size

Figure 6 shows the effect of Immix line size on performance, assuming a constant PCM line size of 64 bytes and no hardware failure clustering. Figure 6(a) corresponds to the baseline S-IX at three Immix line sizes: 64 bytes (S-IX L64), 128 bytes (S-IX L128), and 256 bytes (S-IX L256), all running without PCM failure. The interesting trend to note is that larger lines perform better on S-IX, and that this advantage increases as the heap becomes smaller. The primary reason is that in a tight heap, larger lines mean fewer slow-path operations and better locality. Smaller lines increase metadata overhead, which is felt most acutely in constrained heaps.

The presence of failures changes the Immix line size dynamics significantly. Figure 6(b) shows the same three Immix line sizes (S-IX^{PCM} L64, S-IX^{PCM} L128, and S-IX^{PCM} L256) at 10% failure levels, as well as S-IX. False failures make larger Immix line sizes less desirable when we constrain the heap without clustering. As the Immix line size increases, it takes only one PCM line failure to make an entire 128-byte or 256-byte line unusable. These false failures generate more severe loss of usable memory space, which affects performance negatively. Once again, the issue is alleviated, but not eliminated, at larger heap sizes.

Figure 7 further illustrates the relationship between performance, Immix line size and failures, this time holding heap size constant at 2× the minimum and varying failures between 0 and 50% of all lines. To more fully expose fragmentation behavior, these configurations do not use hardware failure clustering. In this

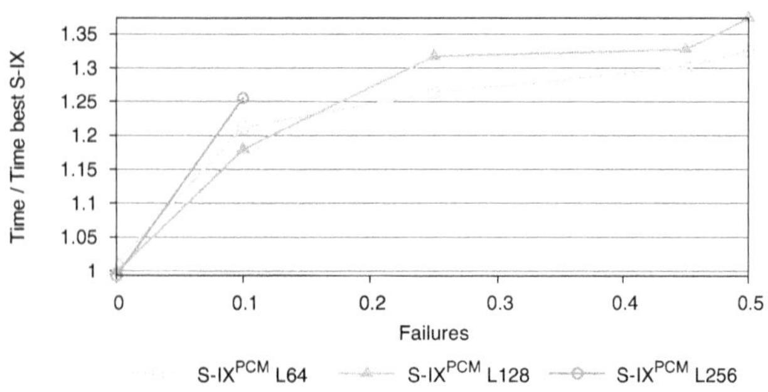

Figure 7. The effect of PCM failures on three different Immix line sizes at a fixed 2× heap size. With a 256 B Immix line, failures dramatically reduce useful memory causing benchmarks to fail without hardware clustering.

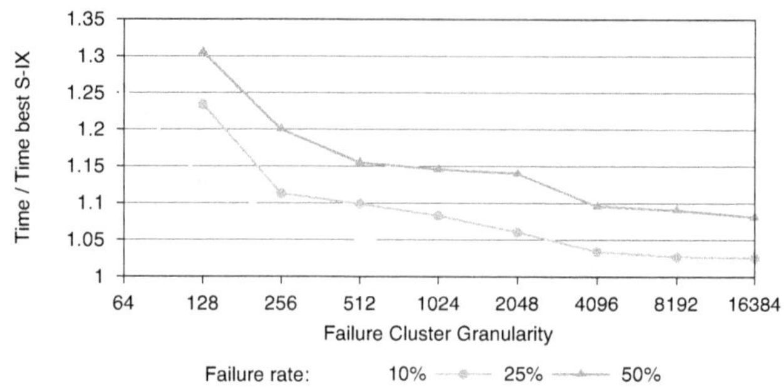

Figure 8. S-IX^{PCM} performance with default 256 B lines as failures are clustered at a variety of power-of-two granularities (x-axis) with 10%, 25% and 50% of lines failed. Clustering of failures dramatically mitigates performance penalties of failures.

case, the larger the line size, the earlier it starts causing excessive false failures and thus wasting memory, so the worse the performance. When the failure rate is zero, larger lines perform better, but as the failure rate increases, the effect of false failures dominates. With L256 this happens almost immediately, and with L128 the crossover is at about 15% failure rate.

Figures 6 and 7 illustrate the two opposing forces that influence the choice of Immix line size without clustering: lower memory management overhead versus higher usable memory waste.

6.4 Failure Clustering

The results in Section 6.3 assume that PCM failures occur with a uniform random distribution at the granularity of 64 B lines. When uniformly distributed, these failures cause significant fragmentation, and will lead to as much as 3× space overhead due to false failures with a 256 B Immix line. This section quantitatively explores the effect of clustering failures at granularities greater than 64 B. The number of failed lines remains 10%, 25%, and 50%, but we systematically distribute failures in clusters of 2^N failed lines, for sizes 64 B and greater to reveal the effects of fragmentation and how well clustering counterbalances them.

Failure Clustering Limit Study To conduct these experiments, we use the S-IX^{PCM} collector, but generate the PCM failure map slightly differently. Instead of failing individual 64 B lines with probability p, we step through aligned regions of size 2^N and fail the entire region with probability p. The effect is that the gaps between failures are guaranteed to be at least 2^N, but the probability of any given line having failed remains p. This analysis motivates hardware support for failure clustering.

Figure 8 shows performance when S-IX^{PCM} is exposed to 10%, 25%, and 50% failures with failures clustered at powers of two from 64 B to 16 KB. The x-axis is logarithmic. Performance is normalized to unmodified S-IX running on regular memory.

Performance dramatically improves with failure clustering. Clustering mitigates fragmentation by reducing or eliminating false failures and leaving larger chunks of usable memory for the memory manager to use. The greater the number of failures, the more dramatic the effect of failure clustering. The problem is so severe that starting at 25% failures, and at 64-byte failure cluster granularity, the VM cannot execute many workloads to completion even at a 2× heap, thus the 25% and 50% curves start at 128 bytes. Yet, using clustering at 256 bytes, the performance overhead is reduced to just 20% when 50% of lines fail.

Proposed Failure Clustering Hardware Figure 9 compares our failure-aware collector with and without clustering hardware support at one- and two-page granularity, for 64 B, 128 B, and 256 B Immix lines, and with 0, 10%, 25%, and 50% of PCM lines failed.

These experiments use a failure map with uniformly distributed 64-byte line failures, and then move those failures according to our one- and two-page clustering algorithm, alternatively moving all failures to the start or end of each clustering region.

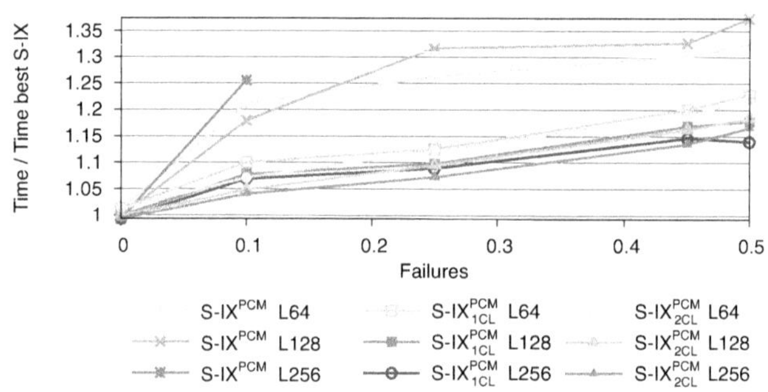

(a) Hardware failure clustering greatly improves performance.

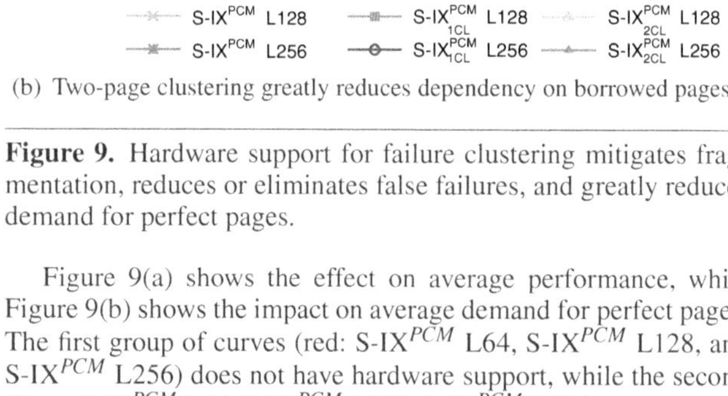

(b) Two-page clustering greatly reduces dependency on borrowed pages.

Figure 9. Hardware support for failure clustering mitigates fragmentation, reduces or eliminates false failures, and greatly reduces demand for perfect pages.

Figure 9(a) shows the effect on average performance, while Figure 9(b) shows the impact on average demand for perfect pages. The first group of curves (red: S-IX^{PCM} L64, S-IX^{PCM} L128, and S-IX^{PCM} L256) does not have hardware support, while the second (blue: S-IX$^{PCM}_{1CL}$ L64, S-IX$^{PCM}_{1CL}$ L128, S-IX$^{PCM}_{1CL}$ L256) has one-page clustering and the third (green: S-IX$^{PCM}_{2CL}$ L64, S-IX$^{PCM}_{2CL}$ L128, S-IX$^{PCM}_{2CL}$ L256) has two-page clustering.

Figure 9(a) shows that hardware failure clustering greatly reduces the performance overhead due to PCM failures. The first group of lines (red, top) consistently perform worse because frag-

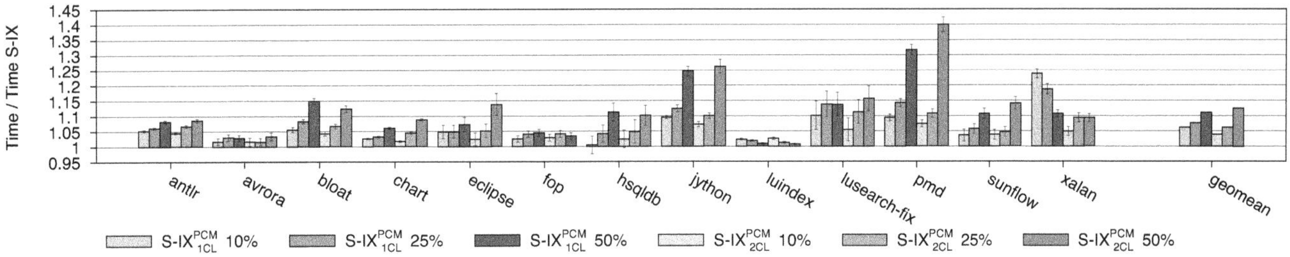

Figure 10. Performance of failure clustering at one- and two-page granularities for each of the DaCapo benchmarks.

mentation and false failures dominate performance, especially when lines are large and many lines fail. The 256 B line size fares worst, and the effect of false failures is so great that many benchmarks cannot run at 25% failure (hence no data for that point in the graph). Performance is much better and less variable with hardware support for failure clustering because clustering eliminates most false failures and greatly reduces fragmentation visible to software.

Two-page clustering (green) has the further advantage of creating completely failure-free pages. Note that for both one-page and two-page clustering, 256 B Immix lines result in the best performance. The reason is that clustering mitigates the negative effects of fragmentation, leaving only the positive effects of coarser Immix line granularity (lower memory management overheads).

Figure 10 shows the individual benchmark results for one- and two-page failure clustering at various failure rates. Consistent with Figure 9(a), two-page clustering reduces overheads considerably unless failure rates are very high. Figure 9(b) shows that the main reason is that hardware failure clustering greatly reduces demand for perfect pages. This reflects the fact that clustering has a defragmenting effect, which greatly increases the probability of a medium sized object being able to fit on a page suffering failed lines. Perfect pages are used when objects cannot be placed on a regular page, so the 3× reduction in demand for perfect pages by the two-page clustering algorithm reflects the strong defragmenting effect of failure clustering. The xalan benchmark makes very heavy use of perfect pages and consequently sees a huge advantage in two-page push at 10% failure rate. The counter-intuitive lowering of overhead with rising failure rate in xalan with one-page push is due to the effect of heap compensation, as it was with lusearch (Section 6.1).

Figure 9(b) also shows an interesting property of the two page clustering. The demand for clean pages is very robust to failure rates even as high as 50%. As long as a two-page region has a failure rate less than 50%, the clustering will yield at least one perfect page out of every two. Once the failure rate in a two-page region exceeds 50%, clustering will only yield a free region that is smaller than a page, greatly reducing the stock of failure-free pages. Figure 10 shows that two benchmarks, pmd and jython, are very sensitive to this threshold, but the others degrade gradually.

7. Discussion

This section discusses implications of our work.

7.1 Managed Language Incentives

Managed languages offer a layer of memory abstraction, which this paper exploits to attain fault tolerance transparently and which native languages lack. Our work thus creates an incentive to use managed languages for future memory technologies. Native applications will need to rely on the operating system to shield them from dynamic failures, losing an entire PCM page when the first line on the page has failed. Modifying a free-list allocator to handle static failures is possible. However, it is more complex than the solution offered by Immix. Without clustering, it would be even more complex. An additional consideration for native runtimes is that because C applications are unsafe they may generate illegal reads and writes to failed memory, which the OS will need to handle. Without support for pages with failures in a native runtime, native applications will have access to fewer and fewer pages as memory fails, making managed applications more attractive for PCM memory.

7.2 Wear Leveling Considered Harmful

Wear leveling strives to uniformly spread writes and wear all memory equally. However, the result is that failures end up being evenly spread out through memory, causing memory fragmentation. Our results show that clustering mitigates fragmentation, but only to a certain extent. We argue that evenly wearing memory is not the best wear management strategy because of the fragmentation it causes. Concentrating writes into certain regions of memory may reduce total system fragmentation and the effect of failures. We intend to investigate smarter wear management strategies in future work.

7.3 Balanced Hardware Clustering

Our results show that managed runtimes experience performance improvements with multiple-page regions because this keeps entire working pages available longer, making allocating medium and large objects less challenging. Native applications need entire working pages, so we expect them to benefit from this as well.

It may seem beneficial to use larger regions. Although initially a higher number of pages are logically intact (e.g., three in four-page region), these cases quickly degenerate to the two-page case. When failures reach roughly 25%, two of the four pages will be necessary to remap all failures in the region. Moreover, large regions may create additional complexity such as failure map cache pressure.

7.4 Possible Mitigation of Memory Fabrication Issues

As DRAM cells get smaller and closer to the atomic scale, precise manufacturing of these memory cells gets more challenging and fabrication variation causes cells to have wide ranges of sizes and electron-storage capacities. Manufacturing issues may cause certain cells to be 'born dead', i.e., not capable of holding any charge after fabrication. Similar issues may afflict other memory technologies. DRAM manufacturers today have on-chip provisions to replace a small number of failed cells before memory parts are shipped, but scaling this solution to a higher number of failures while keeping overheads low may be very challenging. This issue may cause low yields, i.e., only being able to ship the small portion of fabricated chips that have low number of failures, which increases costs and disrupts the memory industry business model. Our solution makes memory chips with arbitrary numbers of failures useful, without incurring high area or cost overhead. Instead of throwing the chips with high failures rates away, manufacturers can 'bin' them into classes. For example, the higher the number of failures, the cheaper the memory. This process is akin what processor manufacturers do today with chip frequency and power dissipation, which is also caused by process variation.

8. Conclusions

This paper explores an example of Rattner's "self-aware systems" [20], in which hardware and software cooperate to accomplish a shared system goal, in this case, system endurance. As hardware resources are gradually used up and exhausted, the OS and runtime come to the rescue to tolerate visible failures.

This work proposes a cooperative hardware/software system with low hardware and software complexity to mitigate failures in wearable memories. The OS and runtime coordinate to recover data from failed lines and migrate objects affected by failures. We use the memory abstraction provided by a managed runtime to handle failures transparently, and exploit the Immix garbage collector's capacity to efficiently skip over unusable holes. Even without hardware clustering, the runtime correctly handles failures, but overhead is 17% with 10% failed memory and 33% with 50% failed memory. When the hardware assists by clustering failures, software overhead reduces quite significantly to 3.9% with 10% failed memory and 12.4% with 50% failed memory. This paper is the first to observe that hardware and software cooperation has the potential to achieve substantially better failure tolerance with increasing numbers of hardware failures.

9. Acknowledgments

We thank Burton Smith for initial failure map implementation ideas, and our anonymous reviewers for their valuable feedback.

References

[1] D. Bacon, P. Cheng, and V. T. Rajan. Controlling fragmentation and space consumption in the Metronome, a real-time garbage collector for Java. In *Proceedings of the 2003 ACM SIGPLAN Conference on Languages, Compiler, and Tool Support for Embedded Systems*, pages 81–92, 2003.

[2] E. D. Berger, K. S. McKinley, R. D. Blumofe, and P. R. Wilson. Hoard: A scalable memory allocator for multithreaded applications. In *Proceedings of the 9th International Conference on Architectural Support for Programming Languages and Operating Systems*, pages 117–128, 2000.

[3] S. M. Blackburn and K. S. McKinley. Immix: A mark-region garbage collector with space efficiency, fast collection, and mutator performance. In *Proceedings of the 2008 ACM SIGPLAN Conference on Programming Languages Design and Implementation*, pages 22–32, 2008.

[4] S. M. Blackburn, P. Cheng, and K. S. McKinley. Myths and realities: The performance impact of garbage collection. In *Proceedings of the 2004 ACM SIGMETRICS Conference on Measurement & Modeling Computer Systems*, pages 25–36, 2004.

[5] S. M. Blackburn, R. Garner, C. Hoffman, A. M. Khan, K. S. McKinley, R. Bentzur, A. Diwan, D. Feinberg, D. Frampton, S. Z. Guyer, M. Hirzel, A. Hosking, M. Jump, H. Lee, J. E. B. Moss, A. Phansalkar, D. Stefanović, T. VanDrunen, D. von Dincklage, and B. Wiedermann. The DaCapo benchmarks: Java benchmarking development and analysis. In *Proceedings of the 21st Annual ACM SIGPLAN Conference on Object-Oriented Programming Systems, Languages, and Applications*, pages 169–190, 2006.

[6] H.-J. Boehm. Conservative GC algorithmic overview. http://www.hpl.hp.com/personal/Hans_Boehm/gc/gcdescr.html.

[7] J. Condit, E. B. Nightingale, C. Frost, E. Ipek, D. Burger, B. C. Lee, and D. Coetzee. Better I/O through byte-addressable, persistent memory. In *Proceedings of the 22nd ACM Sumposium on Operating Systems Principles*, pages 133–146, 2009.

[8] A. Demmers, M. Weiser, B. Hayes, H. Boehm, D. Bobrow, and S. Shenker. Combining generational and conservative garbage collection: Framework and implementations. In *Proceedings of the 17th ACM SIGPLAN-SIGACT Symposium on Principles of Programming Languages*, pages 261–269, 1990.

[9] *Avoiding server downtime from hardware errors in system memory with HP Memory Quarantine.* Hewlett-Packard Corporation.

[10] X. Huang, S. M. Blackburn, K. S. McKinley, J. E. B. Moss, Z. Wang, and P. Cheng. The garbage collection advantage: Improving program locality. In *Proceedings of the 19th Annual ACM SIGPLAN Conference on Object-Oriented Programming Systems, Languages, and Applications*, pages 69–80, 2004.

[11] E. Ipek, J. Condit, E. B. Nightingale, D. Burger, and T. Moscibroda. Dynamically replicated memory: Building reliable systems from nanoscale resistive memories. In *Proceedings of the 15th International Conference on Architectural Support for Programming Languages and Operating Systems*, pages 3–14, 2010.

[12] ITRS Working Group. ITRS report. Technical report, International Technology Roadmap for Semiconductors, 2011.

[13] Jikes RVM. *Compiler Replay*, Dec. 2011. http://jikesrvm.org/Experimental+Guidelines.

[14] D. Lea. A memory allocator. http://g.oswego.edu/dl/html/malloc.html.

[15] Micron Technology Inc. PCM-based MCP. http://www.micron.com/products/multichip-packages/pcm-based-mcp?source=mb.

[16] M. K. Qureshi. Pay-as-you-go: Low-overhead hard-error correction for phase change memories. In *Proceedings of the 44th Annual IEEE/ACM International Symposium on Microarchitecture*, pages 318–328, 2011.

[17] M. K. Qureshi, J. Karidis, M. Franceschini, V. Srinivasan, L. Lastras, and B. Abali. Enhancing lifetime and security of PCM-based main memory with start-gap wear leveling. In *Proceedings of the 42nd Annual IEEE/ACM International Symposium on Microarchitecture*, pages 14–23, 2009.

[18] M. K. Qureshi, V. Srinivasan, and J. Rivers. Scalable high performance main memory system using phase-change memory technology. In *Proceedings of the 36th Annual International Symposium on Computer Architecture*, pages 24–33, 2009.

[19] S. Raoux, G. Burr, M. Breitwisch, C. Rettner, Y. Chen, R. Shelby, M. Salinga, D. Krebs, S.-H. Chen, H. L. Lung, and C. Lam. Phase-change random access memory: A scalable technology. *IBM Journal of Research and Development*, 52(4.5):465–479, 2008.

[20] J. Rattner. Extreme scale computing. Keynote Speech at the 39th International Symposium on Computer Architecture, 2012.

[21] J. B. Sartor, S. M. Blackburn, D. Frampton, M. Hirzel, and K. S. McKinley. Z-rays: Divide arrays and conquer speed and flexibility. In *Proceedings of the 2010 ACM SIGPLAN Conference on Programming Languages Design and Implementation*, pages 471–482, 2010.

[22] S. Schechter, G. Loh, K. Strauss, and D. Burger. Use ECP, not ECC, for hard failures in resistive memories. In *Proceedings of the 37th Annual International Symposium on Computer Architecture*, pages 141–152, 2010.

[23] N. H. Seong, D. H. Woo, V. Srinivasan, J. A. Rivers, and H.-H. S. Lee. SAFER: Stuck-at-fault error recovery for memories. In *Proceedings of the 43rd Annual IEEE/ACM International Symposium on Microarchitecture*, pages 115–124, 2010.

[24] X. Yang, S. M. Blackburn, D. Frampton, J. B. Sartor, and K. S. McKinley. Why nothing matters: The impact of zeroing. In *Proceedings of the 26th Annual ACM SIGPLAN Conference on Object-Oriented Programming Systems, Languages, and Applications*, pages 307–324, 2011.

[25] D. H. Yoon, N. Muralimanohar, J. Chang, P. Ranganathan, N. P. Jouppi, and M. Erez. FREE-p: Protecting non-volatile memory against both hard and soft errors. In *Proceedings of the 17th International Symposium on High Performance Computer Architecture*, pages 466–477, 2011.

[26] P. Zhou, B. Zhao, J. Yang, and Y. Zhang. A durable and energy efficient main memory using phase change memory technology. In *Proceedings of the 36th Annual International Symposium on Computer Architecture*, pages 14–23, 2009.

Limitations of Partial Compaction: Towards Practical Bounds *

Nachshon Cohen
Technion
nachshonc@gmail.com

Erez Petrank
Technion
erez@cs.technion.ac.il

Abstract

Compaction of a managed heap is considered a costly operation, and is avoided as much as possible in commercial runtimes. Instead, partial compaction is often used to defragment parts of the heap and avoid space blow up. Previous study of compaction limitation provided some initial asymptotic bounds but no implications for practical systems. In this work, we extend the theory to obtain better bounds and make them strong enough to become meaningful for modern systems.

Categories and Subject Descriptors D.3.3 [*Language Constructs and Features*]: Dynamic Storage Management; D.3.4 [*Processors*]: Memory management (garbage collection); D.4.2 [*Storage Management*]: Allocation/deallocation strategies; D.1.5 [*Programming Technique*]: Object Oriented Programming

General Terms Algorithms, Theory, Languages.

Keywords Memory management, compaction, fragmentation, theory, lower bounds.

1. Introduction

The study of the theoretical foundations for memory management is mostly lacking. Little is known about the limitations of various memory management functionalities, and in particular on the space consumption of various memory management methods. Previous work consists of Robson's classical results on fragmentation when no compaction is employed [14, 15], a result on the hardness of achieving cache consciousness [11], and work on the effectiveness of conservative garbage collection and lazy reference counting [5, 6]. A recent new work by Bendersky et al. [4] attempted to bound the overhead mitigation that can be achieved by partial compaction.

Memory managers typically suffer from fragmentation. Allocation and de-allocation of objects in the heap create "holes" between objects that may be too small for future allocation and thus create a waste of available heap space. Compaction can eliminate this problem, but compaction algorithms are notoriously costly and are thus not frequently used [1, 9, 10]. Instead, memory managers today either use compaction seldom, or employ partial compaction, where only a (small) fraction of the heap objects are compacted to make space for further allocation [2, 3, 7, 8, 12].

The work in [4] studies limitations of partial compaction. But in spite of [4] being novel and opening a new direction for bounding the effectiveness of partial compaction, their results are only significant for huge heaps and objects. When used with realistic setting of system parameters today, their lower bounds become meaningless. For example, suppose a program uses a live heap space of 256MB and allocates objects of size at most 1MB. For such a program, even if the memory manager is limited and can only compact 1% of the allocated objects, the results in [4] would only imply that the heap must be of size at least $256MB$, which is obvious and not very useful.

In this work we extend the lower bounds on partial compaction to make them meaningful for practical systems. To this end, we propose a new "bad" program, that makes memory managers fail in preserving low space overheads. We then improve the mathematical analysis of the interaction between the bad program and the memory manager to obtain much better bounds. For example, using the parameters mentioned in the previous paragraph, our lower bound implies that a heap of size $896MB$ must be used, i.e., a space overhead of $3.5x$.

In general, the more objects we let the memory manager move, the lower the space overhead that it may suffer. To put a bound on the amount of compaction work that is undertaken by the memory manager, we use the model set in [4] and bound the fraction of allocated space that may be compacted by a constant fraction $1/c$. This means that at any point in the execution, if a space of s words has been allocated so far, then the amount of total compaction that is allowed up to this point in the execution is s/c words, where c is the compaction bound.

The results we obtain involve some non-trivial mathematical arguments and the obtained lower bound is presented in a complex formula that is not easy to digest. The general lower bound is stated in Theorem 1 (on Page 3). But in order to grasp the improvement over the previously known results, we have depicted in Figure 1 (on Page 3) the space overhead factor for the parameters mentioned above (which we consider realistic). Namely, for a program that uses live space of $M = 256MB$ and whose largest allocated object is of size at most $n = 1MB$, we drew for different values of c the required heap size as a factor of the $256MB$ live space. Note that if we were willing to execute a full compaction after each de-allocation, then the overhead factor would have been 1. We could have used a heap size of $256MB$ and serve all allocation and de-allocation requests. But with limited (partial) compaction, our results show that this is not possible. In Figure 1 we drew our lower bound as well as the lower bound obtained from [4] for these parameters. In fact, throughout the range of $c = 10, \ldots, 100$, the lower bound from [4] gives nothing but the trivial lower bound overhead factor of 1, meaning that $256MB$ are required to serve the program. In contrast, our new techniques show that the space overhead must be at least $2x$, i.e., $512MB$ when 10% of the allocated space can be

* This work was supported by the Israeli Science Foundation grant No. 283/10

compacted. And when the compaction is limited to 1% of the allocated space, then an overhead of $3.5x$ is required for guaranteeing memory management services for all programs.

In general, the result described in this work is theoretical, and does not provide a new system or algorithm. Instead, it describes a limitation that memory managers can never achieve. As such, it does serve a practical need, by letting practitioners know what they cannot aspire to, and should not spend efforts in trying to achieve. The lower bounds we provide are for a worst-case scenario and they do not rule out achieving a better behavior on a suite of benchmarks. But providing a better guaranteed bound on fragmentation (as required for critical systems such as real-time systems) is not possible. Note that this bound holds for manual memory managers as well as automatic one, even when applying sophisticated methods like copying collection, mark-compact, Lang-Dupont, MC^2, etc. [9].

Finally, we also make a slight improvement over the state-of-the-art related upper bound. The upper bound is shown by presenting a memory manager that keeps fragmentation low against all possible programs. The new upper bound slightly improves over the result of [4], and it does so by providing a better memory manager and a better analysis for its worst space overhead. This slight improvement is depicted in Figure 3 (on Page 4), where we depict the new upper bound and compare it to the previous upper bound of [4]. The upper bound theorem is stated rigorously as Theorem 2 (on Page 3). Note that the proposed memory manager is not meant to be a practical efficient memory manager that can be used in real systems, but it demonstrates the ability to deal with worst-case fragmentation.

To achieve the bounds presented in this paper, we stand on the shoulders of prior work, and in particular our techniques build on and extend the techniques proposed in [15] and [4].

Organization. In Section 2 we provide some preliminaries, explain the execution of a memory manager, and state our results. In Section 3 we provide an overview over the lower bound and its proof. In Section 4 we provide the actual proof of the the lower bound, and we conclude in Section 5. A full version of this work is available [13], and contains the complete proof of the lower bound and the upper bound.

2. Problem Description and Statement of Results

2.1 Framework

We think of an interaction between a program and a memory manager that serves its allocation and de-allocation requests as a series of sub-interactions of the form:

1. De-Allocation: The program declares objects as free
2. Compaction: The memory manager moves objects in the heap.
3. Allocation: The program requests to allocate objects by specifying their sizes to the memory manager and receiving in response the addresses in which the objects got allocated.

In this work, we question the ability of a memory manager to handle programs within a given heap size. But if a program allocates continuously and never de-allocates any memory, then the heap size required is trivially unbounded. So to let the question make sense, we assume a bound on the space that the program may use simultaneously. This bound is denoted by M.

A second important parameter of the execution of a program (from a memory management point of view) is the variance of sizes for the objects that it allocates. If all objects are of fixed size, say 1, a heap space of M is always sufficient. Although holes can be created by de-allocating objects, these holes can always be filled by newly allocated objects. If we denote the least size of an object by 1, the parameter n will denote the maximum size of an object. It can be thought of as the ratio between the largest and smallest allowable objects. We denote by $\mathscr{P}(M,n)$ the (infinite) set of all programs that never allocate more than M words simultaneously, and allocate objects of size at most n. We denote by $\mathscr{P}_2(M,n)$ the set of programs whose allocated objects sizes are always a power of two.

As explained in the introduction, if the heap is compacted after every de-allocation, fragmentation never occurs. However, frequent compaction is costly and so memory managers either perform a full compaction infrequently, or just move a small fraction of the objects occasionally. In this paper we adopt the definition of [4], and consider memory managers that limit their compaction efforts with a predetermined fraction of the allocated space. For a constant $c > 1$, a memory manager is c-partial memory manager if it compacts at most $\frac{1}{c}$ of the total space allocated by the program. We denote the set of c-partial memory manager by $\mathscr{A}(c)$.

Given a program P and a memory manager A, the execution of P where A serve as its memory manager is well defined. The total heap size that A uses in this case is denoted by $HS(A,P)$

In order to present a lower bound on the space overhead required by any memory manager, it is enough to present one bad program whose allocation and de-allocation demands would make all memory managers need a large heap space. For an upper bound, we need to provide a memory manager that would maintain a limited heap space for all possible programs.

Our model is phrased above as one that lets the program know the address of each allocated object. This knowledge helps the program create the fragmented memory. We remark that it is enough to let the program know the allocator's algorithm and when GC is invoked (namely, when de-allocation actually happens) in order to obtain this information and create the large fragmentation.

2.2 Previous work

For programs that allocate only objects with size that is a power of 2, and $M|n$, and for all memory managers that do not use compaction, Robson [14, 15] proved lower and upper bounds that match. For his lower bound, he presented a "bad" program $P_o \in \mathscr{P}_2(M,n)$ that makes any memory manager (that does not use compaction) need a large heap. Specifically, [1]

$$\min_{A \in \mathscr{A}(\infty)} HS(A,P_o) \geq M \cdot \left(\frac{1}{2}\log(n)+1\right) - n + 1$$

For an upper bound, Robson presented an allocator A_o that satisfies the allocation requests of any program in $\mathscr{P}_2(M,n)$ using a heap size of

$$\max_{P \in \mathscr{P}_2(M,n)} HS(A_o,P) \leq M \cdot \left(\frac{1}{2}\log(n)+1\right) - n + 1.$$

For programs that may allocate objects of arbitrary size (and not only powers of 2), one may round each allocation to the closest higher power of two. This rounding may (at the most) double the size of each object, which means that if the program is allowed to allocate $2M$ words simultaneously, then we obtain a doubled upper bound of $2(M(1/2 \cdot \log(n)+1)-n+1)$.

When some compaction is allowed (but not an unlimited compaction effort), much less is known. For the upper bound, Bendersky and Petrank [4] have shown a simple compacting collector $A_c \in \mathscr{A}(c)$, that uses a heap space of at most

$$\max_{P \in \mathscr{P}(M,n)} HS(A_c,P) \leq (c+1) \cdot M$$

words, when run with any program in $\mathscr{P}(M,n)$.

[1] Here, and throughout the paper, all logarithms are of base 2.

They have also shown a "bad" program P_W that makes all memory managers with a c-partial compaction bound use a large heap. In particular:
$\min_{A\in\mathscr{A}(c)} HS(A,P_W(c)) \geq$

$$\begin{cases} \frac{1}{10}M \cdot \min\left(c, \frac{\log n}{\log c+1} - \frac{5n}{M}\right) & \text{for} \quad c \leq 4\log n \\ \frac{1}{6}M \cdot \frac{\log n}{\log\log n+2} - \frac{n}{2} & \text{for} \quad c > 4\log n \end{cases}$$

2.3 This work

Our main contribution is a new lower bound on the ability of a memory manager to keep the heap de-fragmented. While the lower bound of [4] is important for modeling the problem, providing some tools for solving it, and an asymptotical lower bound, their bound is meaningful only for huge objects and heaps. In particular, it provides a lower bound that is higher than the obvious M only for $M > n \geq 16TB$. In this work we extend the theory enough to obtain meaningful results for practical values of M and n.

Theorem 1. *For any c-partial memory manager A, and for any* $M > n > 1$ *there exists a program* $P_F \in \mathscr{P}_2(M,n)$ *such that for any* $\gamma \leq \log(\frac{3}{4}c) : \gamma \in \mathbb{N}$

$$\min_{A\in\mathscr{A}(c)} HS(A,P_F) \geq M \cdot h \qquad (1)$$

where h is set to:

$$h = \frac{\frac{\gamma+2}{2} - \frac{2^\gamma}{c}\left(\gamma+1-\frac{1}{2}\sum_{i=1}^{\gamma}\frac{i}{2^i-1}\right) + \left(\frac{3}{4}-\frac{2^\gamma}{c}\right)\frac{\log(n)-2\gamma-1}{\gamma+1} - \frac{2n}{M}}{1+2^{-\gamma}(\frac{3}{4}-\frac{2^\gamma}{c})\frac{\log(n)-2\gamma-1}{\gamma+1}}$$

We remark that the theorem makes use of an integral parameter γ. The theorem holds for any $\gamma \leq \log(\frac{3}{4}c) : \gamma \in \mathbb{N}$, but obviously there is one γ that makes h the largest and optimizes the bound. Determining this γ mathematically is possible (if we do not require integral values) but the formula for that is complicated. In practice, there are very few (integral) γ values that are relevant for any given setting of the parameters, and so it can be easily computed in practice.

Since h is given in a complicated formula, the implications of $HS(A,P_F) \geq M \cdot h$ are not very intuitive. Therefore, we chose some realistic parameters to check how this bound behaves in practice. We chose M, the size of the allocated live space to be $256MB$, and n, the size of the largest allocatable object to be $1MB$. With these parameters fixed and with the parameter γ set to the value that maximizes the bound, we drew a graph of h as a function of the compaction quota bound c. This graph appears in Figure 1. The x-axis has c varying between 10 to 100. Setting $c = 10$ means that we have enough budget to move 10% of the allocated space, whereas setting $c = 100$ means that we have enough budget to move 1% of the allocated space. For these c's, the y-axis represents the obtained lower bound as a multiplier of M. For example, when compaction of 2% of all allocated space is allowed ($c = 50$), any memory manager will need to use a heap size of at least $3.15 \cdot M$. Even with 10% of the allocated space being compacted, a heap size of $2 \cdot M = 512MB$ is unavoidable. For these practical parameters, previous results in [4, 14] do not provide any bound, except for the obvious one, that the heap must be at least of size M.

We also depicted the lower bound as a function of a varying maximum object size n. We fixed the compaction budget to $c = 100$, and the total size of live objects to $M = 256n$. The rational for the last parameter setting is that it is uncommon for a single object to create a significant part of the heap (larger than half a percent). Setting M to a larger value does not change the bound. We let the size of the largest object n vary between $1KB$ and $1GB$, and for these n values, the y-axis represents the obtained lower bound as a multiplier of M. The graph is depicted in Figure 2.

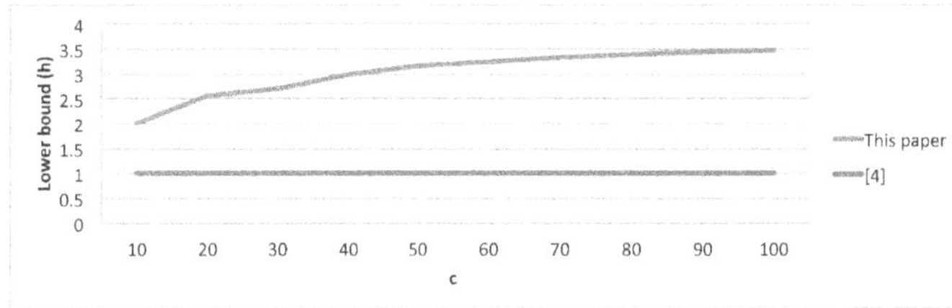

Figure 1. Lower bound on the waste factor h for realistic parameters ($M = 256MB$ and $n = 1MB$) as a function of c

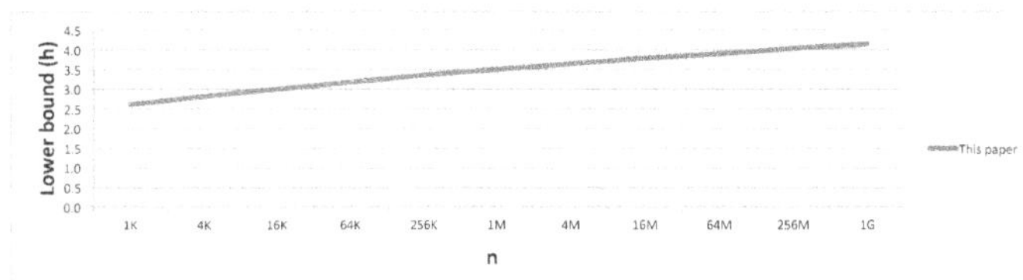

Figure 2. Lower bound on the waste factor h as a function of n (c=100, M=256n)

We could also depict the lower bound as a function of M, where n and c remain fixed. However, in a practical setting, the size of the largest object is much smaller than the total live space (i.e., n/M is small). Hence the lower bound as a function of M is very close to a constant function and it does not provide an additional interesting information.

We also consider the upper bound on the size of heap required. In [4] an upper bound of the form $(c+1)M$ was presented. However, this upper bound may become non-interesting when Robson's upper bound is stronger, meaning that the same heap size may be obtained without moving objects at all. This happens when $c > \log n + 1$. As partial compactors often use a large c to limit the fraction $1/c$ of moved objects, such a scenario seems plausible. We provide some improvement to Robson's algorithm when little compaction is allowed and obtain better upper bound as follows.

Theorem 2. *For any* $c > \frac{1}{2}\log n$*, there exists a c-partial memory manager* $A \in \mathscr{A}(c)$*, which satisfies allocation requests of any program* $P \in \mathscr{P}$ *with heap size at most*

$$\max_{P\in\mathscr{P}(M,n)} HS(A_C,P) \leq 2M \cdot \sum_{i=0}^{\log n} \max\left(a_i, \frac{1}{4-2/c}\right) + 2n\log n$$

Where $a_0 = 1$*, and the values of* a_i*,* $i = 1,\ldots,\log(n)$*, satisfy the following recursive formula:*

$$a_i = 1 - \sum_{j=0}^{i-1} \max\left(\frac{1}{c}, 2^{j-i}\right) \cdot a_j$$

As the formulas in this theorem are also not easy to grasp, we also drew a graph comparing previously known bounds with the new result. It can be seen in Figure 3 that for c's between 20 and 100 we get improvement with the largest improvement being 15% at $c = 20$. We consider this result minor and the lower bound the major result in this paper. The proof of the upper bound appears in the full paper [13].

3. Overview and Intuitions

In this section we review the proof of the lower bound. The main tool in this proof is the presentation of a "bad" program that cause large fragmentation. Our bad program will always allocate objects

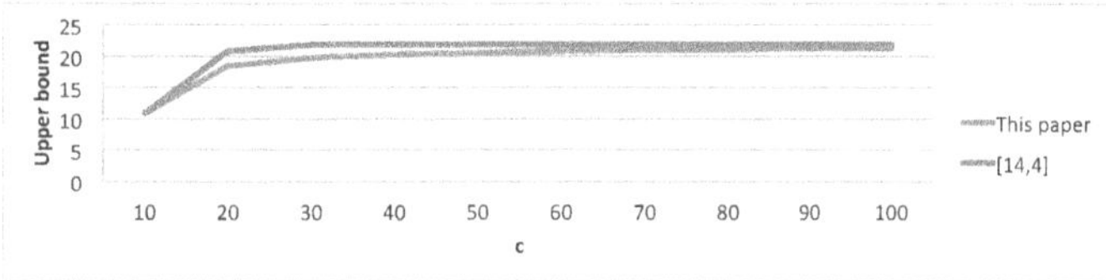

Figure 3. Upper bound on the waste factor for realistic parameters ($M = 256MB$ and $n = 1MB$) as a function of c

of size which is an exponent of 2, and to simplify the discussion (in this overview), we assume that the memory manager is restricted to using only aligned allocation. This means that an object of size 2^i is placed in an address that is dividable by 2^i.

The bad program will work in steps, where in each step of the execution, the bad program will allocate only objects of size 2^i, for some i that it will determine. Consider such a step and consider a memory region that starts at an address dividable by 2^i and spans 2^i words. Denote such a memory region a chunk. If a chunk is fully populated by objects, there is no fragmentation in this chunk. On the other extreme, if a chunk is empty, a new object of size 2^i can be placed in this "hole", creating a fully populated chunk. Fragmentation actually occurs (w.r.t. a chunk) when a chunk is sparsely populated. In this case, the utilization of this chunk is low, yet it can not be used for placing a new object. In the case that no compaction is allowed, a "bad" program should attempt to leave a small object in each such chunk, by de-allocating as many objects as possible, leaving one object in each chunk.

The bad program always tries to deallocate as much space as possible, while keeping chunks occupied by objects that hinder their reuse by the allocator. Recall that the program is restricted in allocating at most M words at any time. Therefore, the larger the de-allocated space, the larger the space that can be allocated in the next step, and the larger the heap that the allocator must use. This is the main design goal of the bad program: never allow chunk reuse, and allocate as much as possible at each step (by de-allocating as much as possible in the previous step).

In case compaction is allowed, avoiding reuse is more difficult. In particular, a sparsely populated chunk can be evacuated and reused by the memory manager. If the populated space on a chunk is of size $2^i/c$ or smaller, then the memory manager can move the allocated objects away, losing a compaction budget of at most $2^i/c$, but then allocating an object of size 2^i on the cleared chunk and gaining a compaction budget of $2^i/c$. So reuse of sparsely allocated chunks becomes beneficial for the memory manager.

In order to create fragmentation in the presence of compaction, the bad program attempts to maintain dense-enough chunks. If the allocated space for a chunk is, say, $2 \cdot 2^i/c$, then either the memory manager does not reuse this chunk, or it does reuse the chunk, but then it must pay at least $2 \cdot 2^i/c$ of its compaction budget. Allocation of a new object re-charge compaction budget by $2^i/c$, thus the memory manager remains with a minus of $2^i/c$ words. This allows bounding the overall reuse by bounding the overall compaction budget.

Finally, let us discuss how we deal with objects that are not aligned, and therefore, reside on the border of two chunks. If objects are aligned, then an object is allocated exactly on one full single chunk. In order to allocate an object, the chunk it is put on must be entirely free of objects. When an object's allocation is not aligned, it may reside on two chunks. We start by looking at smaller chunks, whose size is a quarter of the allocated object. This means that a non-aligned allocated object must entirely fill three chunks (and partially sit on two more chunks). These three chunks must be completely free of allocated objects before the allocation can take place. If one of these three chunks is about to be reused, then the memory manager must move away every object that resides (even partially) on the reused chunk, and lose some compaction budget. Note that we have to make sure that if two adjacent chunks are reused, then we do not double count budget loss due to the move of a non-aligned object that resides on both.

3.1 Improvements over prior work [4]

In this subsection we review the main improvements of this work over [4]. These improvements enabled the achievement of a better lower bound, which is meaningful with realistic parameter settings. We mention the three major improvements in this overview.

The first improvement follows from noting that in the first steps, the size of allocated objects are large compared to the chunk sizes (which are small in the first steps). Therefor, in these first steps, it is useful to run a program that is very similar to Robson's bad program [14]. Robson's program is designed for memory managers that do not compact objects, but when objects are large compared to the chunks, it is not beneficial to the memory manager to do any compaction, and a reduction theorem is developed to show that this program (or actually a similar program) creates fragmentation even where compaction is allowed. Furthermore, these first steps nicely integrate with the general algorithm that runs in the rest of the steps.

The second improvement consists of a small twist in the algorithm that creates a more regimented behavior during the execution, which then allows analyzing the execution and obtaining the improved bound. Recall that the bad program attempts to de-allocate as much space as possible in each step so that it can allocate as many objects as possible in the next step. It turns out that this behavior can create scenarios that are hard to analyze. This happens when we allocate a lot of objects in one step, and then very few in the following steps. The second improvement that helps us obtain higher fragmentation is in bounding the amount of memory that is allocated per step. This, perhaps, does not use all the space that can be used in one step, but it guarantees a sufficient amount of allocation in all steps. Allocating a fixed amount of memory at each step allows a stronger analysis of the program behavior and results in a better bound. Indeed the stronger analysis of the more regimented execution is another improvement of this new work.

Finally, the third improvement that we mention concerns non-aligned object allocation. When an object is not aligned, it consists of two parts that lie on two different chunks. The reuse of one of these chunks for allocation requires the moving of this object, but such a move may also allow use of the other neighboring chunk. The analysis of these scenarios is not simple. We gain more control over the analysis by virtually assigning the non-aligned object to one of its underlying chunks. Of-course, in order to reuse a chunk, this object must still be moved, but the virtual assignment of an object to one of its underlying chunk allows making easier algorithm decisions and also computing tighter bounds on the amount of reuse that the memory manager can achieve.

4. Lower bound: creating fragmentation

In this section we prove a lower bound on the ability of a memory manager to keep the heap defragmented when its compaction resources are bounded. In particular, we introduce a program P_F that forces any c-partial memory manager to use a large heap size to satisfy all of P_F's allocation requests.

Let us start by explaining the ideas behind the construction of P_F. The program P_F works in two stages. The second stage is probably the major contributor to the fragmentation achieved, but the first stage is also necessary to obtain our results. The first stage is an adaptation of Robson's malicious program [14] that attempts to fragment the memory as much as possible, when working against

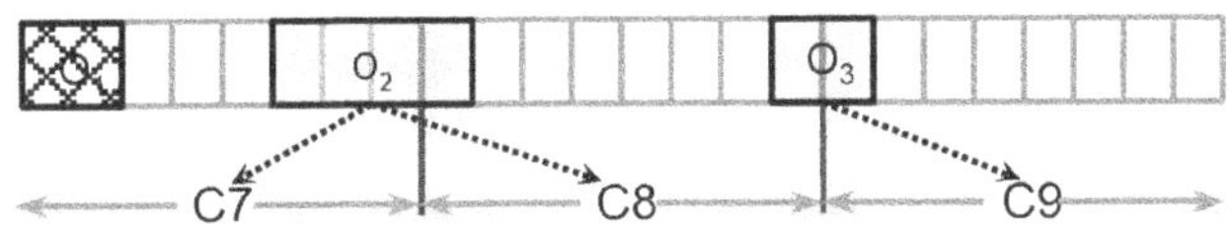

Figure 4. association of objects and half objects with chunks

a memory manager that cannot move objects. We will discuss in Section 4.2 how this algorithm behaves against a memory manager that can move objects and show that it buys some fragmentation in this case as well. After running for 2γ steps, a second stage starts, which behaves differently. The second stage works in steps $i = 2\gamma, \ldots, \log(n) - 2$ and in each step it only requests allocations of objects of size 2^{i+2} words. At each such step of the execution, we consider a partition of the heap space into aligned chunks of size 2^i words. This means, for example, that each allocated object either consumes four full consecutive chunks if its allocation is aligned, or it consumes at least three full consecutive chunks.

Our goal is to show that the memory manager must use many chunks. If at any point in the execution $x+1$ chunks of size 2^j are used, even if only one word of each chunk is used, then the heap must contain at least x chunks. (The last chunk may not be entirely contained in the heap.) This means that the memory manager must be using a heap size of at least $x \cdot 2^j$ words.

Since we do not assume aligned allocation, objects may spread over more than one chunk. Nevertheless, each chunk that has a word allocated on it (at any point of the execution) must be part of the heap. Given an execution of the program P_F with some given memory manager, we associate with each chunk a set of objects that were allocated on it at some point in the execution. This enables tighter analysis. An object is associated with one of the chunks it resides on. This means that at least one word of the object resides on the associated chunk at the time the object is allocated. We then aim to show that $x+1$ chunks have objects associated with them, and obtain the bound as above.

The association of objects with chunks is chosen carefully to establish the bound. Note that chunk sizes dynamically change as we move from step to step. On a step change, each pair of adjacent chunks become a single joint chunk. So, association of chunks with objects changes between steps. The association is also updated during the execution, as objects get allocated and de-allocated. The program actively maintains the set of objects associated with each chunk, and also uses this set in the second stage to determine which objects to de-allocate. Association of an object with a chunk is only removed when P_F de-allocates the object. It is not removed when an object is compacted. The fact that we do not "move" association during compaction and attempt to claim that an additional chunk must be used for the move follows from a analysis strategy: when an object is moved, usually it is possible to put it in used chunks, that are not fully occupied. Since the analysis can gain nothing from checking the object's new location, the bad program will just de-allocate any object that's being moved immediately, again, not attempting to consider the location to which it was moved into, but instead, de-allocating it and using its space for future allocation. Note that the chunk that it did occupy will remain part of the heap forever, so associating it with the old chunk makes sense.

We denote by $O_D(t)$ the set of objects that P_F associates with the chunk D at time t, and we sometimes omit the t, when its value is clear from the context. In fact, when an object lies on the border of two chunks, we sometimes choose to associate it with both chunks. In this case, we associate exactly half of it with each of the chunks (ignoring the actual way the object is split between the chunks). This even split in association is used to preserve the property that objects sizes are a power of two. This refinement of association implies that a chunk may be associated with half an object, and a single object may be associated with two chunks.

From the memory manager point of view, a chunk that contains a small number of allocated words is a good candidate for compaction and reuse. Compaction allows reuse of a chunk's space for more allocations. As the program P_F controls which objects get de-allocated, P_F will attempt to make sure that each chunk has enough associated objects to make it non-beneficial for the memory manager to clear a chunk. The *density* of a chunk is the total size of objects that are associated with it, divided by the chunk size. We define a *density parameter* $2^{-\gamma}$ so that P_F attempts to keep the density of a chunk at least $2^{-\gamma}$. This means that the program P_F will never choose to de-allocate an object if the de-allocation makes a chunk too sparse, in the sense that its density goes below $2^{-\gamma}$. This density will be chosen to be larger than $1/c$ to make the compaction of objects from such a chunk not beneficial.

Loosely speaking, according to the compaction budget rules, the memory manager gains an extra compaction budget of $\frac{1}{c}|o|$ when it allocates o. However, if it needs to move $2^{-\gamma} \cdot |o|$ words to make space for this allocation, then its overall compaction budget decreases. (Recall that $2^{-\gamma} > \frac{1}{c}$). An example of density threshold and association set is depicted in Figure 4. Let the density threshold $2^{-\gamma}$ be $1/4$, which consists of 2 words per chunk of size 8. Half of O_2 is associated with Chunk $C7$, the other half is associated with Chunk $C8$, and the object O_3 is associated with Chunk $C9$ only. These objects suffice to make the density of each chunk at least $1/4$. The program can free the object O_1 since a density of $1/4$ is preserved even without it.

The whole issue of maintaining a high enough density is not relevant for the first steps in the computation. In these steps chunks are small enough so that when even one word is allocated on the chunk, a density of $2^{-\gamma}$ is achieved. Therefore, we can simply adopt Robson's "bad" program [14] with a technical variation so that it can deal with the memory manager's compaction activity. Robson's program works well to blow the heap up for memory managers that do not compact the heap. In our scenario, where the chunks are small and so the density is always high, compaction is not very useful, and so Robson's original program can work for us too. However, while compaction is not beneficial to the memory manager, compaction may still occur and our bad program must deal with it. We build a program P_F that will be "similar" to Robson's program in the sense that it will keep a similar heap shape, it will make very similar decisions on which objects to de-allocate and it will allocate the same amount of space in each step. We will then show a reduction saying that if there exists a memory manager M that can maintain low fragmentation while serving P_F, then it is possible to create another memory manager M', that does not move objects, and maintains low fragmentation against Robson's program. Since no memory manager can keep low fragmentation against Robson's program, we get the lower bound we need.

In order to make P_F work similarly to Robson's program, we need to handle compaction. When objects are moved, several differences are created that might influence the execution. First, space gets occupied where an object is moved, so new objects can no longer be allocated there. Second, vacancy is created in the old space from which an object was moved, so objects might be allocated there. And finally, the different shape of allocated objects may change the de-allocation decisions of the bad program. To handle the first difference, P_F simply de-allocates each moved object immediately after it gets moved. This makes sure that new objects can be allocated as before. To handle the other two problems we introduce *ghost objects*, which are not really in the heap, but are used by P_F to remember where objects existed so that Robson's program behavior can still be imitated.

The program P_F maintains a list of ghost objects. These are objects that have been relocated by the memory manager along with their original location. For all of its de-allocation considerations, P_F treats ghost objects as if they still reside at their original location. In fact, each ghost object continue to exist until the de-allocation procedure (of Robson's) determines that it should be de-allocated. Of-course, these objects have been de-allocated when they became ghosts, so no actual de-allocation is required by the memory manager, but at that point, they are removed from the list of ghost objects and are not considered further by the de-allocation procedure.

Note that memory space on which ghost objects reside may receive allocations of new objects by the memory manager, who is not aware of the ghost objects. This is fine. The de-allocation procedure can view both objects as residing on the same location while making its decisions. This seeming collision is later resolved in the reduction theorem, by noting a property of the de-allocation procedure. The de-allocation procedure only cares about location of objects moduli 2^i. Therefore, one can think of the ghost objects as existing in a separate (far away) space at the same address moduli 2^i. This additional space will not be counted as part of the heap size, but it will allow the program P_F and a real memory manager to work consistently together. Details follow.

Definition 4.1. [A ghost object] *We call an object that was compacted by the memory manager during the execution and immediately de-allocated by the program P_F a* ghost *object. In the first stage of the algorithm, such objects are considered by P_F as still residing as ghosts in the original location where they were allocated. They do not impact the behavior of the memory manager, which can allocate objects on a space consumed by ghosts. When ghost objects are de-allocated by the program, they disappear and are no longer considered by P_F in subsequent steps.*

At each step i of the first stage, $i = 0, 1, \ldots, \gamma$, we start by considering a partition $\mathscr{D}(i)$ of the heap into all aligned chunks of size 2^i. (Aligned here means that they start on an address that is divisible by 2^i.) The main decision that is taken at each step is which objects should be de-allocated (by the malicious program). To this end, Robson picks an offset f_i and examines the word at offset f_i (from the beginning of the chunk) for all chunks. De-allocation then is executed for all objects that do not intersect the f_i word of a chunk. Note that all objects that will be allocated thereafter are all of size at least 2^i, and therefore, two adjacent chunks that have their f_i offset word occupied, will never be able to hold a new object between them.

Definition 4.2. [an f-occupying object with respect to step i] *An object is f-occupying with respect to step i if it occupies a word at address $k \cdot 2^i + f$ for some $k \in \mathbb{N}$.*

As a new step kicks in, the chunks sizes get doubled to 2^{i+1}, where each chunk contains two adjacent chunks of the previous step i. We would like to pick a new offset f_{i+1} for the larger chunks of size 2^{i+1}. The new offset will be either the old offset on the left 2^i-sized sub-chunk or the old offset on the right 2^i-sized sub-chunk. Robson chooses the new offset to be the one that maximizes the wasted space. In a way, Robson attempts to keep the smallest objects that will still occupy words at the f_{i+1} offset. So if one of these two offsets allows capturing more space with smaller objects, this becomes the new offset f_{i+1}. To formalize this, Robson chooses f_{i+1} to be either f_i or $f_i + 2^i$, according to which maximizes

$$\sum_{\text{o is } f_{i+1}\text{-occupying}} 2^{i+1} - |o|.$$

It is not necessary to understand the details of Robson's analysis, as we adopt it without repeating it for the first stage of our program. However, to be able to link Robson's program to P_F's first stage, we also work with ghost objects. In the summation above, Robson naturally considers all objects in the heap that have been allocated but not de-allocated yet, i.e., the set of live objects. In our modified algorithm, we also consider ghost objects. Namely, we sum over all live objects and also over all objects that were compacted from their original location and thereafter de-allocated by the program. The ghost objects are considered to reside at the location they were allocated (and are not considered at the location to which they were compacted into, as they were already deleted from the heap.)

After running Robson's program, P_F runs extra $\gamma - 1$ null steps in which it does not allocate anything. This is done just for making all objects in the heap be of size at most $2^{-\gamma}$ of a chunk size. As will be shown in the analysis, this helps ensuring that a lot of space can be de-allocated by P_F even while maintaining a density of $2^{-\gamma}$. With much space de-allocated, P_F gains ammunition for allocations in the steps of the second stage. Recall that P_F is limited and cannot allocate more than M words simultaneously, so it must de-allocate enough space before it can allocate again.

The bad program P_F is presented in Algorithm 1 (on Page 7). It starts by running some steps that are similar to Robson's algorithm and proceeds with newly designed algorithm to deal with compaction, and maintain some density in each chunk. When the memory manager moves objects using its compaction quota, the program will not try to take advantage of the moved objects in their new location. There are not enough of those to justify the trouble. Instead, it will simply immediately delete these objects, and use the reclaimed space for future allocation.

Recall that we denote the density that the program attempts to maintain in each chunk by $2^{-\gamma}$. Other inputs to P_F include M, n, which is the size of the largest allocatable object; and c, the compaction budget factor.

4.1 Analysis of Program P_F

Let us now analyze the behavior of the program P_F when executing against a c-partial memory manager A. We distinguish the behavior of the program in the two stages. Denote the set of objects that P_F allocates during the first stage by S_1 and during the second stage by S_2. Also, denote the total size of the objects in S_1 by s_1 and the total size of the objects in S_2 by s_2. Finally, denote the set of objects that the memory manager chooses to compact during the first stage by Q_1 and their total size by q_1. Similarly, the corresponding set of compacted objects in the second stage is Q_2 whose accumulated size is q_2.

The execution of P_F proceeds in in steps $i = 0, 1, \ldots, 2\gamma - 1, 2\gamma, \ldots, \log(n) - 2$. The steps $0, 1, \ldots, 2\gamma - 1$ define the first stage (yet, nothing is done in steps $\gamma + 1, \ldots, 2\gamma - 1$). The rest of the steps happen in the second stage. At each first stage step, we use a partition of the heap into chunks of size 2^i, in an aligned manner, i.e., each chunks starts at an address that is divisible by 2^i. Denote by $\mathscr{D}(i)$ the set of all aligned chunks of size 2^i.

Our analysis is simplified by using a potential function $u(t)$, which we define next. It will turn out that this function provides a lower bound on the heap usage during the execution, and our goal will be to show that it becomes large by the end of the execution. The function $u(t)$ will be written as a sum of chunk functions $u_D(t)$, one for each chunk in $\mathscr{D}(i)$. The function $u_D(t)$ will be zero for all chunks that are not used to allocate objects. On the other hand, $u_D(t)$ will always be at most 2^i (i.e., the size of the chunk D) for chunks that have been used until time t.

During the analysis of the second stage, we will need to give special treatment to some of the chunks. The set of special chunks

ALGORITHM 1: Program P_F

Input: M,n,c,γ

Initially: Compute $x = \frac{1-2^{\gamma}\cdot h}{\gamma+1}$

During the execution: If the memory manager compacts an object, ask the memory manager to de-allocate this object immediately (before any other action is taken), but add this object to the set of ghost objects, with the same address it held when it was allocated.

// **Stage I:**

$f_0 := 0$

Allocate as many objects of size 1 as is possible (i.e., M such objects.)

for $i = 1$ to γ **do**

  Pick f_i to be either f_{i-1} or $f_{i-1} + 2^{i-1}$, according to which of the two maximizes

$$\sum_{o \text{ is live or ghost and } o \text{ is } f_i\text{-occupying}} 2^i - |o|$$

  Free every live or ghost object that is non f_i-occupying

  Allocate $\left\lfloor \left(M - \sum_{o \text{ is live or ghost}} |o|\right) / 2^i \right\rfloor$ objects of size 2^i

end for

Associate objects with chunks: consider the chunk partition $\mathscr{D}(2\gamma-1)$ to chunks of size $2^{2\gamma-1}$. Each f_γ-occupying object is associated with the chunk that contains its f_γ-occupying word.

// **Stage II:**

for $i = 2\gamma$ to $\log(n) - 2$ **do**

  Consider the chunk partition $\mathscr{D}(i)$ of chunks of size 2^i. Each chunk D is composed of chunks D_1, D_2 of the previous step, we set the association: $O_D = O_{D_1} \cup O_{D_2}$

  For each 2^i chunk, Free as many objects from O_D as possible such that $\sum_{o \in O_D} |o| \geq 2^{i-\gamma}$.
  When a half object is freed, associate it with the chunk that contains the other half, and re-evaluate that chunk.

  Allocate $\lfloor x \cdot M \cdot 2^{-i-2} \rfloor$ objects of size 2^{i+2} if the total size of allocated memory will not exceed M.
  Each allocated object o fully cover 3 chunks D_1, D_2, D_3, if it cover four, pick the first three.
  Set $O_{D_1} := \{o'\}, O_{D_2} := \emptyset, O_{D_3} := \{o''\}$.

end for

will be denoted by $\mathscr{E}$ and defined later in Definition 4.12. For the analysis of the first stage, one can simply think of $\mathscr{E}$ as the empty set. Let us now set the terminology and then define the potential function.

Definition 4.3. [The chunk function $u_D(t)$] *Let A be a c-partial memory manager, and let t be any time during the execution of P_F against A which happen at step i. Let D be a chunk of size 2^i. The function $u_D(t)$ is defined as follows.*

$$u_D(t) = \begin{cases} 2^i & D \in \mathscr{E}(t) \\ \min(2^{i-\gamma} \cdot \sum_{o \in O_D(t)} |o|, 2^i) & \text{otherwise} \end{cases}$$

The above definition depends on the association of objects to the chunk D, as determined by the association function $O_D(t)$. This association is computed explicitly by the program P_F and it dynamically changes during the course of execution. Let us now define the potential function $u(t)$.

Definition 4.4. [The potential function $u(t)$] *Let A be a c-partial memory manager, and let t be any time during the execution of P_F against A. Let i be the step in which t occurs. The function $u(t)$ is defined as follows.*

$$u(t) = \left(\sum_{D \in \mathscr{D}(i)} u_D(t) \right) - \frac{n}{4}.$$

The function $u(t)$ is used to prove the lower bound as follows. It will later be shown that $u_D(t)$ is non-zero only if there exists an object o which intersected with D at some point during execution. We consider the heap to be the smallest consecutive space that the memory manager may use to satisfy all allocation requests. Now, if $x+1$ chunks of size 2^i are used during the execution, then at least x of them (all but the last chunk) must fully reside in the heap. Thus, the heap size must be at least $x \cdot 2^i$. As $u(t)$ sums over all used chunks, and as it accumulate at most 2^i for each of those, we get that $u(t)$ is a lower bound on the heap size. A caveat to that is that $u(t)$ may accumulate 2^i also for the last chunk that is not fully used in the heap. It is for this reason that $u(t)$ is defined as the sum of all $u_D(t)$ minus a single $n/4$ which is the largest 2^i possible. With this additional term, $u(t)$ is guaranteed to be a lower bound on the size of the heap used. Next, we analyze the increase of $u(t)$ during the execution.

When P_F allocates an object, either the memory manager places it on completely new chunks, which (as will be shown) increases in the value of $u(t)$, or, it places the new object in a chunk already occupied by other objects, that have been compacted away. As compaction is bounded, the latter will not happen too much, and furthermore, it will be shown that such a combination of compaction and allocation does not decrease $u(t)$. It will also be shown that a step change, which influences $u(t)$ do not decrease it. Finally, new objects may be placed on top of objects that have been de-allocated earlier by P_F. But the program P_F will manage its de-allocations to not allow reuse of a chunk unless some objects are compacted away from it. Thus, we get that the function grows sufficiently to provide a good lower bound on the heap usage.

The guaranteed growth of $u(t)$ and the implied lower bound are shown in two lemmas 4.5 and 4.6. The first lemma, Lemma 4.5, asserts the increase of $u(t)$ during the first stage. It also bounds from above the amount of space allocated during the first stage. This bound will be used to analyze the first stage.

Lemma 4.5. *Let A be a c-partial memory manager, and let t_{first} be the time that P_F finishes the execution of its first stage when executing with A as its memory manager. Then*

$$u(t_{first}) \geq M \cdot \frac{\gamma+2}{2} - 2^{\gamma} \cdot q_1 - \frac{n}{4}$$

Also, the total size of allocated memory during the execution of the first stage s_1 is bounded by

$$s_1 \leq M \left(\gamma + 1 - \frac{1}{2} \sum_{i=1}^{\gamma} \frac{i}{2^i - 1} \right)$$

The analysis of the second stage is summarized in Lemma 4.6. This lemma again asserts that $u(t)$ increases. However, the increase depends on the total space allocated in the second stage and also on the compaction budget in the second stage, which depends on the space allocated (in both stages). To show that the increase in the potential function $u(t)$ is high, this lemma also bounds from below the amount of allocated space s_2 in the second stage. This second bound uses an additional parameter h, which depends on γ, c, n, and M and is set to the following complicated expression in order to achieve the strongest possible bound.

$$h = \frac{\frac{\gamma+2}{2} - \frac{2^\gamma}{c}\left(\gamma + 1 - \frac{1}{2}\sum_{i=1}^{\gamma} \frac{i}{2^i-1}\right) + \left(\frac{3}{4} - \frac{2^\gamma}{c}\right)\frac{\log(n)-2\gamma-1}{\gamma+1} - \frac{2n}{M}}{1 + 2^{-\gamma}\left(\frac{3}{4} - \frac{2^\gamma}{c}\right)\frac{\log(n)-2\gamma-1}{\gamma+1}}$$

Intuitively, h is the wasted space factor. Namely, If M is a bound on the live space allocated simultaneously by P_F, then $h \cdot M$ is the lower bound we show on the size of the heap that the memory manager must use to satisfy the allocation requests of P_F. The analysis will show that either the memory manager uses more than $M \cdot h$ space, and we are done with the proof of Theorem 1, or the program allocates a lot of space, as in the second part of the lemma, which will then be used to show that the heap space used in both stages is larger than $M \cdot h$, satisfying the assertion of Theorem 1.

Lemma 4.6. *Let A be a c-partial memory manager, and let* t_{finish} *be the time that* P_F *finishes its execution with A as its memory manager. Then,*

$$u(t_{finish}) - u(t_{first}) \geq \frac{3}{4}s_2 - 2^{\gamma} \cdot q2$$

Additionally, either the memory manager uses more than $M \cdot h$ *space, or the amount of allocation* s_2 *in the second stage satisfies*

$$s_2 \geq M\left(\frac{\log(n) - 2\gamma - 1}{\gamma + 1}\right)(1 - 2^{-\gamma} \cdot h) - 2n$$

We now show how to obtain the lower bound stated in Theorem 1 using Lemma 4.5 and 4.6. Using the fact that the memory manager compacts at most $\frac{1}{c}$ of the total allocation, we know that $(q_1 + q_2) \leq \frac{1}{c}(s_1 + s_2)$. Thus,

$$\begin{aligned} HS(A, P_F) &\geq u(t_{finish}) = u(t_{first}) + (u(t_{finish} - u(t_{first})) \\ &\geq M \cdot \frac{\gamma+2}{2} + \frac{3}{4}s_2 - 2^{\gamma} \cdot (q_1 + q_2) - \frac{n}{4} \\ &\geq M \cdot \frac{\gamma+2}{2} + \frac{3}{4}s_2 - \frac{2^{\gamma}}{c}(s_1 + s_2) - \frac{n}{4} \\ &\geq M \cdot \frac{\gamma+2}{2} - \frac{2^{\gamma}}{c}s_1 + \left(\frac{3}{4} - \frac{2^{\gamma}}{c}\right)s_2 - \frac{n}{4} \end{aligned}$$

Now, if $HS(A, P_F) \geq M \cdot h$, then we are done. Otherwise, Lemma 4.6 gives us the lower bound on s_2:

$$s_2 \geq M\left(\frac{\log(n) - 2\gamma - 1}{\gamma + 1}\right)(1 - 2^{-\gamma} \cdot h) - 2n$$

In addition, Lemma 4.5 implies

$$s_1 \leq M\left(\gamma + 1 - \frac{1}{2}\sum_{i=1}^{\gamma}\frac{i}{2^i - 1}\right)$$

and using simple algebra we get that

$$HS(A, P_F) \geq M \cdot h$$

which completes the proof of Theorem 1. □

4.2 Analysis of the first stage

We now focus our attention on the first stage and prove Lemma 4.5. We consider an execution of the malicious program P_F with any memory manager A and look at the first γ steps. In Step i, the size of the chunks is 2^i words, and therefore the size of any chunk throughout the first stage is not larger than 2^{γ} words. If any object is associated with a chunk, and since any object is of size at least one word, then the fraction (or density) of live space associated with that chunk must be at least $2^{-\gamma}$. When the density is guaranteed to be that high, and compaction is limited by the $\frac{1}{c} < 2^{-\gamma}$ fraction, compaction is very limited and not very beneficial to the memory manager. Therefore, for these initial steps (of the first stage) we chose to use a program that is very similar to a program presented by Robson. Robson used his program for the case where no compaction is allowed. We will analyze the slightly modified program to show that it is still useful when limited compaction is used by the memory manager.

For completeness, let us recall Robson's program in Algorithm 2. In the algorithm we use the term *f-occupying objects* that was defined in Definition 4.2. Also, an object is *live* if it is in the heap, i.e., has not been de-allocated. A simple example to the behavior of Algorithm 2 is depicted in Figure 5. In this example, the object O_3 will be freed in Line 5, since it is not f_i occupying.

ALGORITHM 2: Robson's "bad" program P_R

1: **Initially:** $f_0 := 0$
2: Allocate M objects of size 1.
3: **for** $i = 1$ to γ **do**
4: Pick $f_i \in \{f_{i-1}, f_{i-1} + 2^{i-1}\}$ that maximizes $\sum_{o \text{ is live and } f_i\text{-occupying}} 2^i - |o|$.
5: Free all non-f_i-occupying objects
6: Allocate as many objects of size 2^i as possible (within the M live space bound.)
7: **end for**

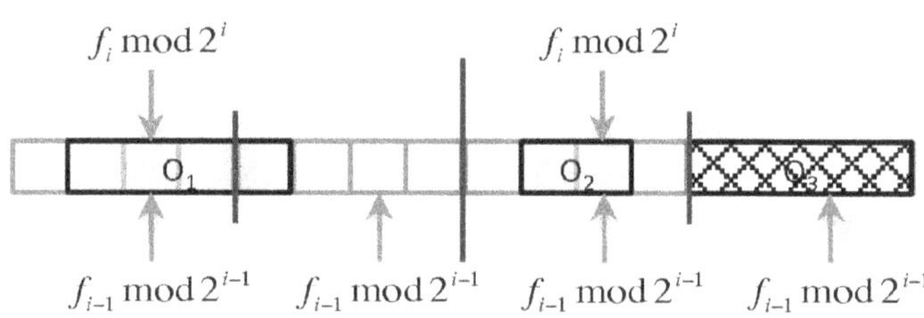

Figure 5. Lower bound on the waste factor h for realistic parameters ($M = 256MB$ and $n = 1MB$) as a function of c

The original program was designed to maximize fragmentation when no compaction is allowed. In our adaptation, appearing as the first stage of Program P_F, we also handle the case that the memory manager employs compaction. When a compaction occurs, P_F immediately de-allocates the moved objects. But we would still like to adopt the original analysis of Robson without redoing the entire analysis for the slightly modified version that was used in the first stage of P_F. To this end, we use a mind experiment in which we let Robson's malicious program P_R run against an imaginary memory manager A' that does not move objects. Clearly, Robson's analysis holds for the execution (P_R, A'), as it holds for all memory managers that do not move objects. From this analysis we will be able to also deduce a lower bound on the heap size that A uses while satisfying P_F's allocation and de-allocation sequence. To make a connection between the first stage of P_F and P_R we note that their only difference is that P_F must deal with compacted objects. (Such objects are de-allocated by P_F, but still count for the decisions on future de-allocation of all objects.) Otherwise, it behaves exactly like the original P_R.

In the discussion in this subsection we only care about the execution of the first stage of P_F. In what follows, when we mention P_F, we only look at the first stage of P_F.

The imaginary memory manager A' is constructed only for this proof and has no use otherwise. We therefore do not care much about its efficiency or generality. A' will be looking at the run of P_F against A in order to make its allocation decisions. Actually, it will make sure that the program P_R makes the same allocation requests as P_F makes when running against A. But A' will satisfy them with no compaction. Since P_R will make the same allocation sequence, A' knows exactly which allocations to expect during the execution against P_R.

The memory manager A' will require more heap space than the original memory manager, but it will make sure that the number of f_i-occupying objects in each step i is similar throughout the execution. This is done by maintaining a one to one mapping between objects in the execution of (P_F, A) and objects in the execution of (P_R, A'), such that mapped objects are always of the same size, and are either both f_i-occupying or are both not f_i-occupying. Since the allocation sequence of P_R and P_F is determined by the space consumed by f_i-occupying objects, we get that these sequences remains the same for both programs. Interestingly, the set of f_γ-occupying objects at the end of executing the first stage can be used to bound the value of the potential function $u(t_{first})$ (from below) at the end of P_F's first stage. This will be the final connection and the thing that will provide the desired bound.

It still remains to show how we handle the case that an object is compacted, and why this does not break the maintained mapping between objects. This is exactly the reason why ghost objects were defined and used. Objects that have been moved by the memory manager and de-allocated by the program P_F are considered by P_F as remaining in their original location (where they were allocated) as ghosts. This means that the memory manager can allocate space at this original location and it simply ignores these ghost objects. But the malicious program P_F does consider their sizes when it needs to decide on which objects to delete, and how many objects to allocate. If ghost objects are f-occupying, then they are counted in the summation there.

Let us now specify the imaginary memory manager A' (which depends on the execution (P_F, A)) such that the execution (P_F, A) is made similar to the execution (P_R, A').

Definition 4.7. [Memory manager $A'(A, P_F)$] *The memory manager $A'(A, P_F)$ works as follows. The k-th object that P' allocates is placed in a location in the memory whose address is equal modulo 2^γ to where A placed the k-th object that P_F allocated. There are infinitely many such locations and A' chooses one of them that does not contain any other object previously allocated in an arbitrary manner.*

Indeed the arbitrary location that A' uses to place the objects may seem too much, as it may use a huge heap for that. But all we care about in the end is the accumulated size of objects that are f_γ-occupying, and this set will be the same for both executions of (P_F, A) and (P_R, A'). Robson's analysis will guarantee that this set will be large, and we will deduce the bound we need.

We now prove that the mapping between objects in the execution of (P_F, A) and objects in the execution of (P_R, A') indeed exists and satisfies some nice properties.

Claim 4.8. *Consider the execution of P_F against a memory manager A, and the execution of P_R against $A'(A, P_F)$, and suppose that both finished their Step i. There is one to one mapping between objects in A and objects in A' with the following property.*

1. *A live or a (non-deleted) ghost object in the execution (P_F, A) is mapped to a live object in the execution (P_R, A') and vise verse (a live object in (P_R, A') is mapped to either live or ghost object in (P_F, A)).*
2. *The sizes of two mapped objects are equal.*
3. *The addresses of two mapped objects are equal modulo 2^γ.*

Moreover, the total number of objects allocated during Step i is equal in both execution.

Proof: The one to one mapping we chose maps the k-th object that P_F allocated to the k-th object that P_R allocated. By the definition of A' their address is equal modulo 2^γ and we are done with the third property. The other two properties are more involved. The full proof appears in [13].

We now quote an implicit lemma from Robson's analysis, that will help us in bounding the value of the potential function at the end of the first stage of P_F.

Claim 4.9 ([14], inequality 1). *After the execution of step i, there are at least $M\frac{i+1+1}{2^{i+1}} = M\frac{i+2}{2\cdot 2^i}$ objects that are f_i-occupying.*

By the end of the first stage execution, in P_F Line 9, an object o is associated with the chunk that contains its f_γ-occupying word. We now want to use Robson's guarantee for many f_γ-occupying objects in order to say that there are many associated objects, and prove the first part of Lemma 4.5.

Claim 4.10. *Let A be a memory manager, and let t_{first} be the time P_F finished the execution of its first stage against A. Then*

$$u(t_{first}) \geq M(\gamma/2+1) - 2^\gamma \cdot q_1 - \frac{n}{4}$$

Proof sketch: By Claim 4.9 there are lots of f_i-occupying objects and by Claim 4.8 this also holds for the execution of P_F. The proof follows from these two and the definition of $u_D(t)$. □

Next we bound from above the amount of memory allocated by Robson's algorithm. It is used to bound the amount of compaction allowed for a c-partial memory manager.

Claim 4.11. *Let A be a memory manager, and consider the execution of P_F's first stage against A. The total size of memory that P_F allocated is at most*

$$s_1 \leq M\left(\gamma + 1 - \frac{1}{2}\sum_{i=1}^{\gamma}\frac{i}{2^i - 1}\right)$$

Proof: Omitted for lack of space. □

The proof of Lemma 4.5 directly follows from Claim 4.10 and claim 4.11.

4.3 Analysis of the second stage

In this section we prove Lemma 4.6, which asserts a substantial growth in the potential function during the second stage. We let t_{first} represent the time where the first stage completes, and t_{finish} represent the time the second stage (and the entire algorithm) completes. Let us recall the statement of the lemma.

Lemma 4.6. *Let A be a c-partial memory manager, and let t_{finish} be the time that P_F finishes its execution with A as its memory manager. Then,*

$$u(t_{finish}) - u(t_{first}) \geq \frac{3}{4}s_2 - 2^\gamma \cdot q2.$$

Additionally, either the memory manager uses more than $M \cdot h$ space, or the allocated space s_2 in the second stage satisfies

$$s_2 \geq M\left(\frac{\log(n) - 2\gamma - 1}{\gamma + 1}\right)(1 - 2^{-\gamma} \cdot h) - 2n$$

To show that this lemma holds, we look at changes that might occur during the execution. This includes allocation of new objects (initiated by P_F), compaction of objects (by the memory manager), de-allocation of objects (by P_F), and a change of steps that changes the chunk sizes, and therefore the summation over the chunks and each chunks $u_D(t)$ function. We will show that we get substantial growth during allocations, and also that all other events do not decrease the potential function.

Recall that the potential function is defined as $u(t) = \sum_{D \in \mathcal{D}(i)} u_D(t) - \frac{n}{4}$ and we need to show that the value of the potential function grows by at least $\frac{3}{4}s_2 - 2^\gamma \cdot q_2$ during the second stage of the execution.

We start by looking at allocations and show that whenever P_F allocates an object, either the potential function gets larger, or some compaction occur (and the potential function does not decrease). We then use the fact that compaction is limited to get the potential function growth we need. Suppose an object o is allocated during Step i of the execution of P_F with A. The size of o is $4 \cdot 2^i$ (by the definition of P_F) and so when the memory manager places o in the heap, it consumes at least three full consecutive chunks (of size 2^i)

and maybe some additional space from the chunk preceding and the chunk that comes after these three consecutive chunks. Denote by D_1, D_2 and D_3 the three chunks that are fully covered by o and are selected at Step 14 of Algorithm 1. All three must be empty when o is placed. We claim that this transition from empty chunks to full chunks makes the potential function grow. We will show that the value of $u_{D_1}(t)+u_{D_2}(t)+u_{D_3}(t)$ grows, which implies that the value of $u(t)$ grows. Note that $u_D(t)$ for any other chunk D (other than D_1, D_2 or D_3) is not affected by this allocation, because the set of associated objects as well as membership in $\mathscr{E}$ (which we define in the next paragraph) only changes for D_1, D_2, and D_3.

During allocation step of P_F (Line 14), when an object o is allocated, P_F associates D_1 with the first half of object o and D_3 with the second half of Object o. But since an object is associated with at most two chunks (each half can be associated with a chunk), it follows that D_2 is left with no object associated with it, in spite of it being completely covered by the allocated object o. The goal of the set $\mathscr{E}$ is to deal with these middle chunks. This set will contain all such middle chunks and make $u_{D_2}(t)$ of Definition 4.3 be set to 2^i. We note that this "anomaly", of a chunk being covered by an object but with no associated object, is temporary and it disappears at the next step change since the middle chunk is joined with either its left or right chunk, and they become a single chunk with which o (or o's half) can be associated. Let us now define $\mathscr{E}$.

Definition 4.12. [The set $\mathscr{E}(t)$] *Let A be a memory manager, and consider any time t during the execution of P_F's second stage with A as its memory manager. Let i be the step where t happens. The* set of middle chunks $\mathscr{E}(t) \subset \mathscr{D}(i)$ *is the set of chunks that both their left adjacent chunk and their right adjacent chunk were fully covered by an object o allocated at step i (thus, the chunk itself is also covered by o), but half of o was not associated with it. A chunk remains in $\mathscr{E}(t)$ until either an new step kicks in, or an object is associated with this chunk. The later may happen if o was compacted during step i, and another object is allocated there.*

Let us now claim a simple property about chunks in $\mathscr{E}$. We'd like to say if a chunk is in $\mathscr{E}$, then the two chunks adjacent to it are associated with a "big", or "recently allocated" object.

Claim 4.13. *Let t be a time during the execution of P_F against a memory manager A, and let i be the step in which t occurs. Let D_1 and D_2 be two consecutive chunks such that $D_1 \in \mathscr{E}(t)$. Then there exists an object o that is allocated during Step i, such that at time t half of o is associated with D_2. The same holds for D_1 when $D_2 \in \mathscr{E}(t)$.*

Proof sketch: When a chunk joins $\mathscr{E}$ both chunks to its left and right are associated with half objects allocated in Step i. □

The chunks D_1, D_2 and D_3 were empty before the allocation. For each of these chunks, we distinguish between the case where an object was associated with it before the allocation, or that no object was so associated. In the latter case, the value of the function $u_D(t)$ for that chunk grows since an object gets associated with it. In the first case, it must be that the memory manager compacted away all objects that were allocated on the chunk and made it fully available for allocation. Note that the definition of P_F rules out a third possibility that these chunks were emptied due to de-allocation of the objects that previously resided on them. Object de-allocation is initiated by the program P_F only (and not by the memory manager). By the definition of P_F, it only de-allocates an object when there are enough other objects left on the chunk to make the remaining space size at least $2^{i-\gamma}$.

When the second case occurs, i.e., that the memory manager compacts away objects from a chunk before placing o, we are not able to show that the value of the potential function grows. However, we get that some compaction occurred, and we use that to bound the number of such events. To this end, we associate some compaction value with the newly allocated object. Recall that the objects that were compacted away from a chunk and then de-allocated immediately by P_F are still considered associated with the chunk until a new object is placed on the chunk. Therefore, to determine how much compaction occurred to free space for the allocation, we can just check the objects that were associated with these chunks right before the allocation. The formal definition follows.

Definition 4.14. [Compaction space associated with an object] *Let o be an object allocated during the execution of P_F's second stage against a memory manager A. Let $t+1$ be the allocation time (and t be the time just before the allocation), and let D_1, D_2, and D_3 be the chunks picked by P_F at Step 14 of P_F, after allocating o. Then we define* the compacted space associated with the object *o to be*

$$q(o) = \sum_{o' \in O_{D_1}(t)} |o'| + \sum_{o' \in O_{D_2}(t)} |o'| + \sum_{o' \in O_{D_3}(t)} |o'|$$

Next, we establish some properties of the set of objects associated with every chunk.

Claim 4.15. *Consider a time t during the execution of P_F's second stage against a memory manager A, and let i be the step where t happens. Then the following three properties hold:*

1. *The sets $\{O_D : D \in \mathscr{D}(i)\}$ are disjoint.*
2. *Every live object o is either associated with a single chunk or its two halves are associated with two chunks.*
3. *If a live object o is associated with a chunk D, then o intersects D.*

Proof sketch: The proof follows from the definition of the program P_F and its way of associating objects with chunks. The full proof is omitted for lack of space. □

We now show that the potential function $u(t)$ indeed increases substantially. We will show that no event causes a decrease in it, while allocations cause sufficient increase. We will compute the potential function $u(t)$ increase for each allocation, and then sum over all allocations to obtain the total increase in $u(t)$ during P_F's second stage.

Claim 4.16. *Let A be a memory manager, let $u(t)$ be the potential function as defined in Definition 4.4, and $q(o)$ be the compaction associated with an object as defined in Definition 4.14. Then during execution of P_F against A, the following properties of $u(t)$ holds*

1. *No event in the execution causes $u(t)$ to decrease.*
2. *During an allocation of an object o, $u(t)$ increase by at least $\frac{3}{4}|o| - 2^{\gamma} \cdot q(o)$.*

Proof. The potential function only changes when the set of chunks changes during step transition or when the set of associated objects of a chunk changes. There are three types of events that may cause such a change. Note that compaction of an object by A is not an event that influences the potential function, since the object association remains unchanged.

A step transition causes P_F to consider a new partition of the heap. Consider the time t when we consider a new partition of the heap (when a new step i kicks in). Let D be a chunk of Step i (of size 2^i). D is composed of two chunks D_1 and D_2 of Step $i-1$ (and of size 2^{i-1}). It suffices to show that $u_D(t) \geq u_{D_1}(t) + u_{D_2}(t)$.

If either $D_1, D_2 \in \mathscr{E}(t-1)$, then by Claim 4.13 there exists an object o that was allocated in Step $i-1$, and half of o is associated with either D_1 or D_2. Since half of o is associate with D, and the size of half of o is 2^i, it holds that $\sum_{o' \in O_D} |o'| = 2^i$. Thus (recall definition 4.3 of $u_D(t)$)

$$u_D(t) = \min(2^\gamma \cdot 2^i, 2^i) = 2^i \geq u_{D_1}(t-1) + u_{D_2}(t-1).$$

Otherwise, both chunks are not in $\mathscr{E}$ and we know that the objects that are associated with them are disjoint. Therefore, according to Step 12 in P_F,

$$\sum_{o \in O_D} |o| = \sum_{o \in O_{D_1}} |o| + \sum_{o \in O_{D_2}} |o|,$$

and the statement follows by definition of $u_D(t)$.

P_F de-allocates an object. By definition, P_F does not free an object if this decrease $\sum_{o \in O_D} |o|$ below $2^{i-\gamma}$, so $u_D(t)$ does not decrease.

P_F allocates an object o. Let t be the time P_F allocates an object o, and let D_1, D_2, D_3 be the three chunks that P_F picked. Only the sets $O_{D_1}, O_{D_2}, O_{D_3}$ are changed during allocation. After the allocation, size of each half an object is $2 \cdot 2^i$, so $u_{D_1}(t) = u_{D_3}(t) = \min(2^\gamma \cdot 2 \cdot 2^i, 2^i) = 2^i$, and $D_2 \in \mathscr{E}(t)$. Thus

$$u_{D_1}(t) + u_{D_2}(t) + u_{D_3}(t) = 3 \cdot 2^i = \frac{3}{4}|o|$$

Before the allocation, if either chunks was contained in $\mathscr{E}$, then by Claim 4.13 there exists an object o allocated at step i, and half of o is associated with D_1, D_2, or D_3. In this case $2^\gamma \cdot q(o) \geq 2^\gamma \cdot 2^{i+1} \geq 3 \cdot 2^i$. The last inequality follows since $\gamma \geq 1$. Otherwise, $u_{D_i}(t-1) \leq 2^\gamma \cdot \sum_{o' \in O_{D_i}(t-1)} |o'|$ for $i = 1,2,3$. In both case we have $2^\gamma \cdot q(o) \geq u_{D_1}(t-1) + u_{D_2}(t-1) + u_{D_3}(t-1)$. Subtracting the values before and after the allocation of o provides the bound in this case and we are done □

We now turn to bound the amount of memory that P_F allocates during the execution of its second stage. By its definition, In Step 14, P_F attempts to allocate a $\lfloor x \cdot M \cdot 2^{-i-2} \rfloor$ objects of size 2^{i+2} if the total size of allocated memory does not exceed M. In order to show that it allocates a lot, we need to show that the bound of not exceeding M simultaneously allocated words does not limit this allocation too much. To this end, we need to bound the space occupied by live objects in the heap from above, which implies a lower bound on the amount of memory available for allocation.

The next proposition asserts that any chunk D in the heap is either empty, or it contains a single large object, or the total space of its associated objects O_D is bounded exactly by $2^i/2^\gamma$, which is the density that P_F attempts to preserve in each chunk. This lemma will later be used to bound the total size of live objects in the heap.

Proposition 4.17. *Consider the execution of P_F's second stage against a memory manager A. Let t be a time when P_F allocates an object, and let i be the step in which t happens. Then for every chunk $D \in \mathscr{D}(i)$ either $|O_D(t)| \leq 1$, or $\sum_{o \in O_D(t)} |o| \leq 2^{i-\gamma}$.*

Proof sketch: The proof of this proposition follows from the behavior of P_F as defined in Line 13. □

Next, we bound the space P_F allocates during its second stage.

Claim 4.18. *Consider the execution of P_F against a memory manager A. Then either A uses more than $M \cdot h$ heap space, or the number of words that that P_F allocates during its second stage satisfies*

$$s_2 \geq (\log n - 2\gamma - 1)\frac{1 - h \cdot 2^{-\gamma}}{\gamma + 1} - 2n.$$

Proof sketch: Recall that x is set at the beginning of Algorithm 1 to: $\frac{1-h \cdot 2^{-\gamma}}{\gamma+1}$. We show that in each step P_F's allocation of $M \cdot x$ words does not exceed the M bound, and then show that the accumulated size of allocation is large enough. □

Recall that in Claim 4.16 we bounded the increase in $u(t)$ when an object o is allocated by $\frac{3}{4}|o| - 2^\gamma \cdot q(o)$. Summing $\frac{3}{4}|o|$ over all objects allocated during stage two of P_F gives $\frac{3}{4}s_2$, which we also computed. We now bound the total sum of $q(o)$ over all objects allocated during stage two of P_F. The precise value of $q(o)$ was given in Definition 4.14.

Proposition 4.19. *Consider the execution of P_F against a memory manager A. S_2 is the set of objects allocated at P_F second stage, and q_2 is the total size of objects that were compacted during the second stage. Then $q_2 \geq \sum_{o \in S_2} q(o)$.*

Proof. Omitted for lack of space. □

Now we are ready to bound to total increase in the unavailable space at P_t's second stage

Claim 4.20. *Consider the execution of P_F against a memory manager A, and let t_{finish} be the time when P_F finished it execution, and t_{first} be the time when P_F finished execution of first stage. Then*

$$u(t_{finish}) \geq u(t_{first}) + \frac{3}{4}s_2 - 2^\gamma \cdot q2$$

Proof: Omitted for lack of space. □

The proof of Lemma 4.6 directly follows from Claim 4.18 and Claim 4.20.

5. Conclusion

This work contributes to building a solid theoretical foundation for memory management. In particular, it extends previous work by providing new lower and upper bounds on the effectiveness of partial compaction. Our lower bound is the first bound in the literature that carries implications for practical systems existing today, by showing that some desirable (realistic) compaction goals cannot be achieved.

References

[1] D. Abuaiadh, Y. Ossia, E. Petrank, and U. Silbershtein. An efficient parallel heap compaction algorithm. In *OOPSLA 2004*.

[2] D. F. Bacon, P. Cheng, and V. Rajan. A real-time garbage collector with low overhead and consistent utilization. In *POPL 2003*.

[3] O. Ben-Yitzhak, I. Goft, E. Kolodner, K. Kuiper, and V. Leikehman. An algorithm for parallel incremental compaction. In ISMM 2002.

[4] A. Bendersky and E. Petrank. Space overhead bounds for dynamic memory management with partial compaction. *POPL 2011*.

[5] H.-J. Boehm. Bounding space usage of conservative garbage collectors. In *POPL 2002*.

[6] H.-J. Boehm. The space cost of lazy reference counting. *POPL 2004*.

[7] C. Click, G. Tene, and M. Wolf. The Pauseless GC algorithm. VEE 2005.

[8] D. Detlefs, C. Flood, S. Heller, and T. Printezis. Garbage-first garbage collection. In *ISMM 2004*.

[9] R. Jones, A. Hosking, and E. Moss. *The Garbage Collection Handbook: The Art of Automatic Memory Management*. Chapman & Hall, Aug. 2011.

[10] H. Kermany and E. Petrank. The Compressor: Concurrent, incremental and parallel compaction. In *PLDI 2006*.

[11] E. Petrank and D. Rawitz. The hardness of cache conscious data placement. In *POPL 2002*.

[12] F. Pizlo, E. Petrank, and B. Steensgaard. A study of concurrent real-time garbage collectors. In *PLDI 2008*.

[13] N. Cohen and E. Petrank. Limitations of Partial Compaction: Towards Practical Bounds. http://www.cs.technion.ac.il/%7eerez/%50apers/compaction-full.pdf.

[14] J. Robson. Bounds for some functions concerning dynamic storage allocation. *Journal of the ACM*, 21(3):491–499, 1974.

[15] J. Robson. An estimate of the store size necessary for dynamic storage allocation. *Journal of the ACM*, 18(3):416–423, 1971.

P: Safe Asynchronous Event-Driven Programming

Ankush Desai Vivek Gupta
Ethan Jackson Shaz Qadeer
Sriram Rajamani
Microsoft

Damien Zufferey
IST Austria

Abstract

We describe the design and implementation of P, a domain-specific language to write asynchronous event driven code. P allows the programmer to specify the system as a collection of interacting state machines, which communicate with each other using events. P unifies modeling and programming into one activity for the programmer. Not only can a P program be compiled into executable code, but it can also be tested using model checking techniques. P allows the programmer to specify the environment, used to "close" the system during testing, as nondeterministic ghost machines. Ghost machines are *erased* during compilation to executable code; a type system ensures that the erasure is semantics preserving.

The P language is designed so that a P program can be checked for responsiveness—the ability to handle every event in a timely manner. By default, a machine needs to handle every event that arrives in every state. But handling every event in every state is impractical. The language provides a notion of deferred events where the programmer can annotate when she wants to delay processing an event. The default safety checker looks for presence of unhandled events. The language also provides default liveness checks that an event cannot be potentially deferred forever.

P was used to implement and verify the core of the USB device driver stack that ships with Microsoft Windows 8. The resulting driver is more reliable and performs better than its prior incarnation (which did not use P); we have more confidence in the robustness of its design due to the language abstractions and verification provided by P.

Categories and Subject Descriptors D.2.4 [*Software Engineering*]: Software/Program Verification– Model checking; D.2.5 [*Software Engineering*]: Testing and Debugging; D.3.2 [*Programming Languages*]: Language Classifications– Specialized application languages, Concurrent, distributed, and parallel languages; D.3.3 [*Programming Languages*]: Language Constructs and Features– Concurrent programming structures, Control structures

Keywords domain-specific language; device driver; event-driven programming; state machine; verification; systematic testing

PLDI'13, June 16–19, 2013, Seattle, WA, USA.

1. Introduction

Asynchronous systems code that is both performant and correct is hard to write. Engineers typically design asynchronous code using state machine notations, use modeling and verification tools to make sure that they have covered corner cases, and then implement the design in a language like C. They use a variety of performance tricks, as a result of which the structure of the state machines is lost in myriad of details. Clean state machine diagrams that were initially written down become out-of-date with the actual code as it evolves, and the resulting system becomes hard to understand and maintain. During the development of Windows 8, the USB team took a bold step and decided to unify modeling and programming. Various components of the USB driver stack are now specified as state machines and asynchronous driver code is generated from these state machines. We are able to use state exploration techniques directly on the state machines to find and fix design bugs. Since the executable code was generated from the source, we could make changes at the level of state machines and perform both verification and compilation from one description. This methodology is used to design, validate and generate code for the USB stack that ships with Windows 8. The resulting driver stack is not only more reliable, but also more performant.

In this paper, we formalize and present the salient aspects of this methodology as a domain-specific language P. Though P has a visual programming interface, we represent P as a textual language with a simple core calculus, so that we can give a formal treatment of the language, compiler and verification algorithms. A P program is a collection of state machines communicating via events. Each state machine has a collection of states, local variables, and actions. The states and actions are annotated with code statements to read and update local variables, send events to other state machines, raise events locally, or call external C functions. The external C functions are used to write parts of the code that have do with data transfer. A machine responds to received events by executing transitions and actions which in turn causes the aforementioned code fragments to execute. For programming convenience, call transitions are used to factor out common code that needs to be reused (similar to nested modes in state charts [11]).

Components in an operating system are required to be responsive. Consequently P programs are required to handle every message that can possibly arrive in every state. Our notion of responsiveness is weaker than synchronous languages like Esterel [4] (which require input events to be handled synchronously during every clock tick, and are hence too strong to be implemented in asynchronous software), but stronger than purely asynchronous languages like Rhapsody [12] (where asynchronous events can be queued arbitrarily long before being handled). Thus, our notion of responsiveness lies in an interesting design point between synchrony and asynchrony. In practice, handling every event at every state would lead to combinatorial explosion in the number of control states, and is hence impractical. The language provides a notion of deferred events to handle such situations and allow a programmer to explicitly specify that it is acceptable to delay processing of certain events in certain states.

Reactive systems, such as device drivers, typically interact with their environment, both synchonously via function calls and asynchronously via events. The reliability of the system depends critically on the correct handling of all interactions via stateful protocols. To allow reasoning about such interactions, we allow programmers to model the environment of a P program using *ghost* machines and variables. These ghost elements are used only during modeling and verification and elided during compilation. The type system of P ensures that the ghost machines can be *erased* during compilation without changing the semantics of the program. It is worth noting that both the real and ghost parts of a P program are based on the computational model of communicating state machines. This aspect of the P language effectively blurs the distinction between modeling and programming and makes the specification capabilities in the language more accessible to programmers.

A P program is validated via *systematic testing* [9, 17] of its inherent nondeterminism. Systematic testing is accomplished by interpreting the operational semantics of a P program (closed using ghost machines) in the explicit-state model checker Zing [2]. All aspects of the operational semantics of the program are interpreted including the code statements labeling the states and actions of a P machine. The model checker takes care of systematically enumerating all implicit scheduling and explicit modeling choices in the program. The number of states and executions of a P program is unbounded in general (in fact, reachability analysis of P programs is undecidable). Therefore, in practice, the enumeration is controlled by bounding techniques.

The simplest approach to bounding the exploration of nondeterministic transition systems is depth-bounding [19]. We have implemented this approach and found it useful for discovering errors witnessed by short executions. However, the complexity of depth-bounded search increases exponentially with execution depth, and consequently does not scale for systematic testing of large P programs, in which errors may be lurking in long executions. We use delay-bounded scheduling [6] to overcome this problem. A delaying scheduler is a deterministic scheduler with a "delay" operation, whose invocation causes the scheduler to change its default scheduling strategy. Given a delay budget d, a delaying scheduler naturally defines a set of schedules obtained by nondeterministically invoking the "delay" operation at most d times; the number of generated schedules (under the assumption that scheduling is the only source of nondeterminism) is independent of execution length and exponential in d; thus arbitrarily long executions can be generated even with a delay bound of 0. We expect most bugs that occur in practice to be found using low values of the delay bound. We have developed a new delaying scheduler for P programs; our scheduler prioritizes schedules that follow the causal sequence of events in the program. We provide empirical evidence to demonstrate that our scheduler indeed finds common errors with a small delay bound.

In summary, our contributions are the following:

- We design a DSL P to program asynchronous interacting state machines at a higher level of abstraction than detailed event handlers that lose the state machine structure.
- We present formal operational semantics and a compiler and runtime that enables P programs to run as KMDF (Kernel Mode Driver Framework) device drivers.
- We show how to validate P programs using delay-bounded scheduling and provide a novel delaying scheduler that, by default, attempts to schedule events according to their causal order.
- We report on the use of P in a production environment; our case study is the USB stack in Windows 8.

2. Overview

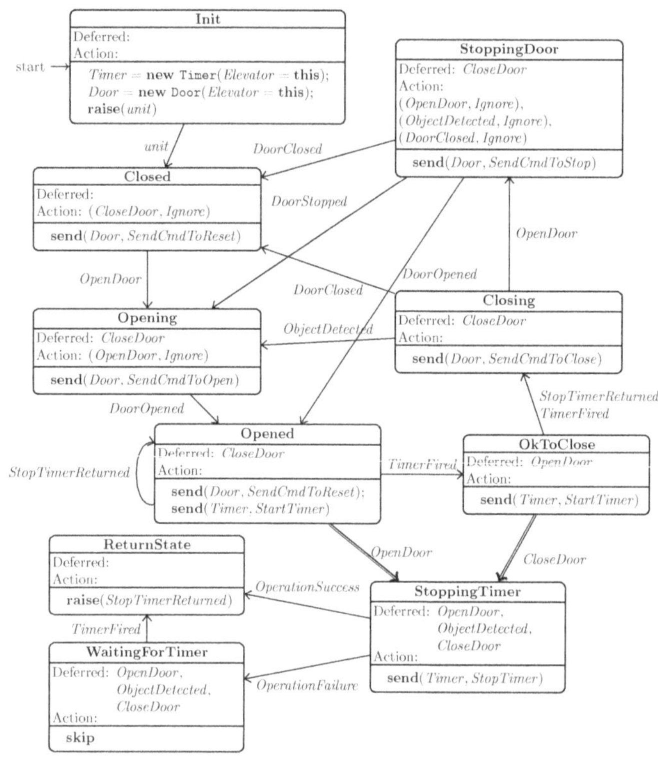

Figure 1: Elevator example

P is a domain-specific language for writing asynchronous event-driven programs. Protocols governing the interaction among concurrently executing components are essential for safe execution of such programs. The P language is designed to clearly explicate these control protocols; to process data and perform other functions irrelevant to control flow, P machines have the capability to call external functions written in C. We call those functions *foreign functions*.

A P program is a collection of *machines*. Machines communicate with each other asynchronously through *events*. Events are queued, but machines are required to handle them in a responsive manner (defined precisely later)—failure to handle events is detected by automatic verification.

We illustrate the features of P using the example of an elevator, together with a model of its environment. The elevator machine is shown in Figure 1 and the environment machines in Figure 2. The environment is composed of *ghost machines* which are used only during verification, and elided during compilation and actual execution. Machines that are not ghost are called *real machines*. We use the term *machine* in situations where it is not necessary to distinguish between real and ghost machines.

Machines communicate with each other using events. An event can be sent from one machine to another and or raised within a machine. Each machine is composed of control states, transitions, actions, and variables. The elevator machine has events *unit* and *StopTimerReturned* (which are used for communication locally inside the elevator machine), an action called *Ignore*, and two *ghost*

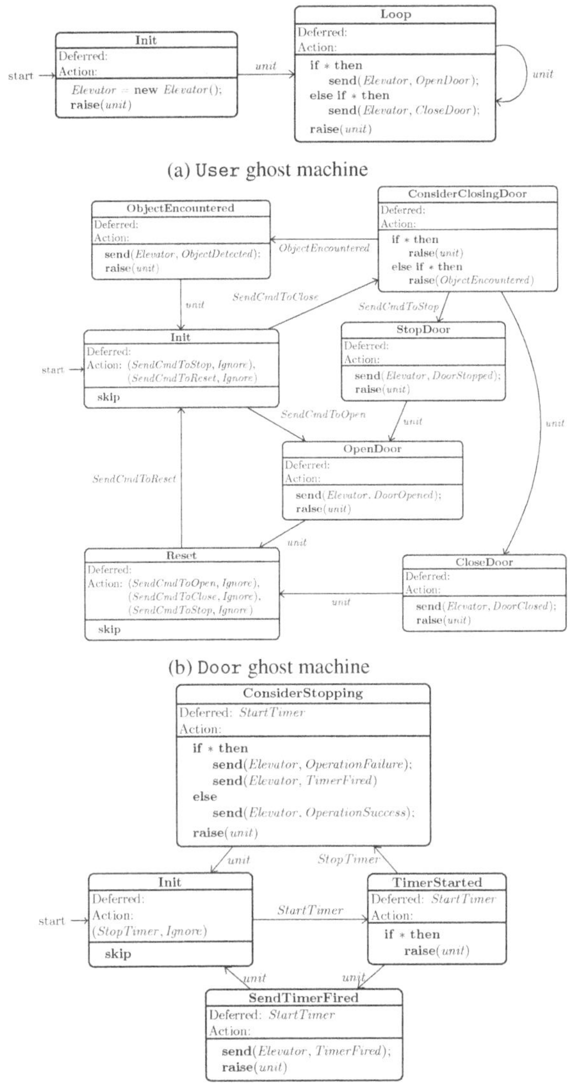

(a) User ghost machine

(b) Door ghost machine

(c) Timer ghost machine

Figure 2: Environment for elevator

variables `Timer` and `Door`. Ghost variables are used only during verification and are used to hold references to ghost machines.

Each state description consists of a 4-tuple (n, d, a, s), where (1) n is a state name, (2) d is a set of events (called *deferred set*), (3) a is a set of (event, action) pairs (called *action handlers*), and (4) s is a statement (called *entry statement*), which gets executed when the state is entered. For instance, the **Init** state in Figure 1 has an empty deferred set, no action handlers, and an entry statement that creates an instance of the `Timer` and `Door` machines and raises the event *unit*. As another example, the **Opening** state has $\{CloseDoor\}$ as the deferred set, a single action handler (*OpenDoor*, *Ignore*), and $\textbf{send}(Door, SendCmdToOpen)$ as the entry statement. If the state machine enters the **Opening** state, the following things happen: on entry to the state, the statement $\textbf{send}(Door, SendCmdToOpen)$ is executed, which results in the event *SendCmdToOpen* being sent to the *Door* machine. On finishing the execution of the entry statement, the machine waits for events on the input buffer. The initial state of the `Elevator` machine is **Init**. Whenever an instance of the `Elevator` machine is created (using the **new** statement), the state of this machine instance is initialized to **Init**.

Deferred events and action handlers. Events sent to a machine are stored in a FIFO queue. However, it is possible to influence the order in which the events are delivered. In a given state, some events can be deferred. When trying to receive an event a machine scans its event queue, starting from the front dequeuing the first event that is not in the deferred set. A dequeued event is either processed by executing an action handler or executing an outgoing transition. An action is simply a named piece of code. The *Elevator* machine has a single action called *Ignore* that does nothing. For instance, in the **Opening** state, the event *CloseDoor* is deferred and therefore never dequeued. If the event *OpenDoor* is dequeued, the *Ignore* action is executed (which just drops the event on the floor) and control stays in **Opening**. If the event *DoorOpened* is dequeued, the outgoing transition labeled by *DoorOpened* is taken and control moves to state **Opened**.

Step and call transitions. The edges in Figure 1 specify how the state of the `Elevator` machine transitions on events. There are two types of transitions: (1) *step* transitions, and (2) *call* transitions. Both these transition types have the form (n_1, e, n_2), where n_1 is the source state of the transition, e is an event name, and n_2 is the target state of the transition. Step transitions are shown by simple edges and call transitions by double edges. For instance, when the machine is in the **Init** state, if an *unit* event arrives the machine transitions to the **Closed** state. On the other hand, call transitions have the semantics of pushing the new state on the top of the call stack. Call transitions are used to provide a subroutine-like abstraction for machines. For instance, there is a call transition to the **StoppingTimer** state from the **Opened** state on the *OpenDoor* event, and a similar call transition to the **StoppingTimer** state from the **OkToClose** state on the *CloseDoor* event. One can think about the **StoppingTimer** state as the starting point of a subroutine that needs to be executed in both these contexts. This subroutine has 3 states: **StoppingTimer**, **WaitingForTimer** and **ReturnState**. The "return" from the call happens when **ReturnState** raises the *StopTimerReturned* event. This event gets handled by the callers of the subroutine **Opened** and **OkToClose** respectively.

Unhandled events. The P language has been designed to aid the implementation of responsive systems. Responsiveness is understood as follows. If an event e arrives in a state n, and there is no transition defined for e, then the verifier flags an "unhandled event" violation. There are certain circumstances under which the programmer may choose to delay handling of specific events or ignore the events by dropping them. These need to be specified explicitly by marking such events in the associated deferred set, so that they are not flagged by the verifier as unhandled. The verifier also implements a liveness check that prevents deferring events indefinitely. This check avoids trivial ways to silence the verifier by making every event deferred in every state.

Environment modeling. Figure 2 shows the environment machines (which are ghost machines) and initialization statement for the elevator. There are 3 ghost machines: `User`, `Door` and `Timer`. These machines are used to model the environment during verification, but no code is generated for these machines. For the purpose of modeling, the entry statements in the states of these machines are allowed to include nondeterminism. For example, the entry statement of the **TimerStarted** state is specified as "$\textbf{if} * \textbf{then raise}(unit)$". The $*$ expression evaluates nondeterministically to true or false. Thus, when the `Timer` machine enters this state, it can nondeterministically raise the *unit* event. The verifier considers both possibilities and ensures absence of errors in both circumstances. In the real world, the choice between these

program	::=	evdecl machine$^+$ m(init*)
machine	::=	optghost **machine** m
		vrdecl* actdecl* stdecl*
		spdecl* cldecl* acdecl*
optghost	::=	ϵ | **ghost**
evdecl	::=	**event** edecl$^+$
vrdecl	::=	optghost **var** vdecl$^+$
actdecl	::=	**action** $(a, \text{stmt})^+$
stdecl	::=	**state** $(n, \{e_1, e_2, \ldots, e_k\}, \text{stmt}, \text{stmt})^+$
spdecl	::=	**step** $(n, e, n)^+$
cldecl	::=	**call** $(n, e, n)^+$
acdecl	::=	**act** $(n, e, a)^+$
edecl	::=	e(type)
vdecl	::=	x : type
type	::=	**void** | **bool** | **int** | **event** | **id**
stmt	::=	**skip**
	|	$x :=$ expr
	|	$x :=$ **new** m(init*)
	|	**delete**
	|	**send**(expr, e, expr)
	|	**raise** (e, expr)
	|	**leave**
	|	**return**
	|	**assert**(expr)
	|	stmt; stmt
	|	**if** expr **then** stmt **else** stmt
	|	**while** expr stmt
init	::=	x = expr
expr	::=	**this** | **msg** | **arg** | b | c | $\perp$ | x | $*$
		| uop expr | expr bop expr
$c \in$ **int**		$b \in$ **bool**
$\neg, - \in$ uop		$+, -, \wedge, \vee \in$ bop
$r \in$ expr		$a, e, m, x \in$ name

Figure 3: Syntax

possibilities depends on environmental factors (such as timing), which we choose to ignore during modeling.

In this example, the initial machine is the `User` machine, and this is the starting point for a model checker to perform verification. Note that the initial state of the `User` machine creates an instance of `Elevator`, and the `Elevator` instance in turn creates instances of `Timer` and `Door` (in Figure 1). During execution, the external code is responsible for creating an instance of the `Elevator` machine.

3. P Syntax and Semantics

Figure 3 shows the syntax of the core of P. Some of the features presented in the examples of Section 2 can be compiled using a preprocessor into this core language. In particular, state descriptions in the core language are triples of the from (n, d, s_1, s_2), where n is a state name, d is a set of deferred events, s_1 is an entry statement, and s_2 is an exit statement.

A program in the core language consists of declaration of events, a nonempty list of machines, and one machine creation statement. Each event declaration also specifies a list of types, which are types of data arguments that are sent along with the event (can be thought of as "payload" of the event).

A machine declaration consists of (1) a machine name, (2) a list of events, (3) a list of variables, (4) a list of actions, (5) a list of states, (6) a list of transitions, and (7) a list of action bindings. Each variable has a declared type, which can be int, byte, bool, event or machine identifier type (denoted **id**). Actions associate an action name with a statement. Transitions are one of two types: steps or calls, and action bindings associate state-event pairs with actions.

A machine can optionally be declared as *ghost* by prefixing its declaration by the keyword **ghost**. Variables can be also declared as **ghost**. Events sent to ghost machines are (implicitly) ghost events. Ghost machines, events and ghost variables are used only during verification, and are elided during compilation and execution of the P program.

As mentioned in Section 2, a state declaration consists of a name n, a set of events (called deferred set), and two statements: (1) an entry statement and (2) an exit statement. Each state declaration must have a distinct name. Thus, we can use the name n to denote the state. The entry statement associated with a state n is executed whenever control enters n, and the exit statement associated with state n is executed whenever control leaves n. Given a machine name m and a state n in m, let $Deferred(m, n)$ denote the associated set of deferred events and let $Action(m, n, e)$ be an that action a is associated with event e in state n, if such a binding exists or $\perp$ otherwise. Let $Entry(m, n)$ denote the associated entry statement, and let $Exit(m, n)$ denote the associated exit statement. The initial state of the machine m is the first state in the state list and is denoted by $Init(m)$.

Each action declaration consists of an action name and a statement. Let $Stmt(m, a)$ denote the statement associated with action a in machine m.

Transition declarations describe how a state responds to events. The list of transitions is partitioned into step transitions, and call transitions. A step transition from state n to another state n_1 involves executing the exit statement of n and the entry statement of n_1. A call transition is similar to function calls in programming languages and is implemented using a stack (more details below). The set of transitions of m must be deterministic, that is, if (n, e, n_1) and (n, e, n_2) are two transitions then $n_1 = n_2$.

An action binding does not change the state, but merely executes the statement associated with the action.

A statement (be it an entry statement or exit statement associated with a state, or associated with an action) is obtained by composing primitive statements using standard control flow constructs such as sequential composition, conditionals, and loops. Primitive statements are described below. The **skip** statement does nothing. The assignment $x := r$ evaluates an expression r and writes the result into x. The statement $x :=$ **new** m(init*) creates a new machine and stores the identifier of the created machine into x. The initializers give the initial values of the variables in the created machine. The **delete** statement terminates the current machine (which is executing the statement) and release its resources. The statement **send**(r_1, e, r_2) sends event e to the target machine identified by evaluating the expression r_1, together with arguments obtained by evaluating r_2. When e does not have any argument `null` is expected. In the examples, we use **send**(r_1, e) as syntactic sugar for **send**$(r_1, e,$ `null`$)$. The statement **raise**(e, r) terminates the evaluation of the statement raising an event e with arguments obtained by evaluating r. The event e must be a local event. The **leave** statement jumps control to end of the entry function to wait for an event to be dequeued. The **return** statement terminates the evaluation of the statement and returns to the caller (see below for more details). The statement **assert**(r) moves the machine to an error state of the expression r evaluates to false, and behaves like **skip** otherwise.

Expressions and evaluation. The expressions in the language, in addition to the declared variables, can also refer to three special variables—**this**, **msg** and **arg**. While **this** is a constant containing the identifier of the executing machine, **msg** contains the event that is last received from the input buffer of the machine, and **arg** contains the payload from the last event. Expressions also include constants c, the special constant $\bot$, variables, and compound expressions constructed from unary and binary operations on primitive expressions. Binary and unary operators evaluate to $\bot$ if any of the operand expressions evaluate to $\bot$. The value $\bot$ arises either as a constant, or if an expression reads a variable whose value is uninitialized, and propagate through operators in an expression. The expression $*$ represents nondeterministic choice of a Boolean value. Nondeterministic expressions are allowed only in ghost machines to conveniently model the environment.

Memory management. P programs manage memory manually by using the **new** and **delete** commands. The **new** command allocates a new instance of a machine and returns its reference, and the **delete** command terminates the machine which executes the command and frees its resources. It is the responsibility of the P programmer to perform cleanup and ensure absence of dangling references, or pending message exchanges before calling **delete**. Manually managing the memory add some complexity in order to retain a precise control over the footprint of the program.

3.1 Operational semantics

The role played by the environment is different during execution and verification of a P program. During execution, the environment is responsible for creating initial machines in the P program, sending some initial messages to it, and responding to events sent by the P machines. During verification, the environment is specified using ghost machines, and the program starts execution with a single machine instance of the machine specified by the initialization statement at the end of the program, and this machine begins execution in its initial state with an empty input queue. However, once the initial configuration is specified (which is different during execution and verification), the transition rules are the same for execution as well as verification. We formally specify the transition semantics using a single set of transition rules below.

Since our language allows dynamic creation of machines, a global configuration would contain, in general, a collection of machines. A machine identifier id represents a reference to a dynamically-created machine; we denote by $Name(id)$ the name of the machine with identifier id. A global configuration M is a map from a machine identifier to a tuple representing the machine configuration. A machine configuration corresponding to identifier id is of the form (γ, σ, s, q) with components defined as follows:

- γ is a sequence of pairs (n, α), where n is a state name, and α is map from events to $A \cup \{\top, \bot\}$, where A is the set of all actions declared in machine $Name(id)$. This sequence functions as a call stack, to implement call and return, and the α values are used to inherit deferred events and actions from caller to callee. For an event e, $\alpha(e)$ can be an action a, or the value $\top$ indicating that the event is deferred, or the value $\bot$ which indicates that the event does not have an associated action and it is not deferred.
- σ is a map from variables declared in machine $Name(id)$ to their values; this map contains an entry for the local variables **this**, **msg** and **arg**.
- s is the statement remaining to be executed in machine id.
- q is a sequence of pairs of a event-argument pairs representing the input buffer of machine id.

Our type checker verifies that for any event e and state n, there is at most one outgoing transition labeled with e out of n and at most one action bound to e in s. We define $Step(m, n, e)$ to be equal to n' if there is a step transition labeled e between n and n' in machine m and $\bot$ otherwise. Similarly, we define $Call(m, n, e)$ to be equal to n' if there is a call transition labeled e between n and n' in machine m and $\bot$ otherwise. We define $Trans(m, n, e)$ to be the union

$$\frac{M[id] = (\gamma, \sigma, S[x := r], q) \qquad \sigma(r) \downarrow v}{M \longrightarrow M[id := (\gamma, \sigma[x := v], S[\mathbf{skip}], q)]} \ (\text{ASSIGN})$$

$$\frac{\begin{array}{c} M[id] = (\gamma, \sigma, S[x := \mathbf{new}\ m'(x_1 = r_1, x_2 = r_2, \ldots, x_n = r_n)], q) \\ id' = fresh(m') \qquad n' = Init(m') \\ \alpha_o = \lambda e.\ \bot \qquad \sigma(r_1) \downarrow v_1 \qquad \sigma(r_2) \downarrow v_2 \qquad \cdots \qquad \sigma(r_n) \downarrow v_n \\ \sigma' = \lambda x.\ \bot\ [\mathbf{this} := id'][x_1 := v_1][x_2 := v_2] \cdots [x_n := v_n] \end{array}}{\begin{array}{c} M \longrightarrow M[id := (\gamma, \sigma[x := id'], S[\mathbf{skip}], q)] \\ [id' := ((n', \alpha_o), \sigma', Entry(m', n'), \epsilon)] \end{array}} \ (\text{NEW})$$

$$\frac{M[id] = (\gamma, \sigma, S[\mathbf{delete}], q)}{M \longrightarrow M[id := \bot]} \ (\text{DELETE})$$

$$\frac{M[id] = (\gamma, \sigma, S[\mathbf{assert}(r)], q) \qquad \sigma(r) \downarrow \mathbf{true}}{M \longrightarrow M[id := (\gamma, \sigma, S[\mathbf{skip}], q)]} \ (\text{ASSERT-PASS})$$

$$\frac{M[id] = (\gamma, \sigma, S[\mathbf{skip}; s], q)}{M \longrightarrow M[id := (\gamma, \sigma, S[s], q)]} \ (\text{SEQ})$$

$$\frac{M[id] = (\gamma, \sigma, S[\mathbf{if}\ r\ \mathbf{then}\ s_1\ \mathbf{else}\ s_2], q) \qquad \sigma(r) \downarrow \mathbf{true}}{M \longrightarrow M[id := (\gamma, \sigma, S[s_1], q)]} \ (\text{IF-THEN})$$

$$\frac{M[id] = (\gamma, \sigma, S[\mathbf{if}\ r\ \mathbf{then}\ s_1\ \mathbf{else}\ s_2], q) \qquad \sigma(r) \downarrow \mathbf{false}}{M \longrightarrow M[id := (\gamma, \sigma, S[s_2], q)]} \ (\text{IF-ELSE})$$

$$\frac{M[id] = (\gamma, \sigma, S[\mathbf{while}\ r\ s], q) \qquad \sigma(r) \downarrow \mathbf{true}}{M \longrightarrow M[id := (\gamma, \sigma, S[s; \mathbf{while}\ r\ s], q)]} \ (\text{WHILE-ITERATE})$$

$$\frac{M[id] = (\gamma, \sigma, S[\mathbf{while}\ r\ s], q) \qquad \sigma(r) \downarrow \mathbf{false}}{M \longrightarrow M[id := (\gamma, \sigma, S[\mathbf{skip}], q)]} \ (\text{WHILE-DONE})$$

$$\frac{\begin{array}{c} M[id] = (\gamma, \sigma, S[\mathbf{send}(r_1, e, r_2)], q) \\ \sigma(r_1) \downarrow id' \qquad \sigma(r_2) \downarrow v \qquad M[id'] = (\gamma', \sigma', C', q') \end{array}}{M \longrightarrow M[id := (\gamma, \sigma, S[\mathbf{skip}], q)][id' := (\gamma', \sigma', C', q' \odot (e, v))]} \ (\text{SEND})$$

Figure 4: Operational semantics: statement execution

of $Step(m, n, e)$ and $Call(m, n, e)$. Note that $Trans(m, n, e)$ is the static transition in state s on event e, $Action(m, n, e)$ is the static action bound with state n and event e, and $Deferred(m, n)$ is the static set of events deferred in state n. During execution, both deferred events and actions associated with a state can be inherited from callers, and these are modeled in the second component of the call stack, which is a sequence of pairs (n, α).

Let S be constructed according to the following grammar:

$$S ::= \square \mid S; \mathsf{stmt}$$

The leftmost position in S is a *hole* denoted by $\square$; there is exactly one $\square$ in any derivation for S. We denote by $S[s]$ the substitution of statement $s \in \mathsf{stmt}$ for the unique hole in S. Finally, we have $|q| = \bigcup_{(e,v) \in q} \{e\}$.

The rules in Figures 4, 5, and 6 give the operational semantics of our programming language. The program starts execution in a configuration M defined at a single id_0 such that $Name(id_0) = m$, where m is the machine name specified in the program's initialization statement (at the end of the program). and $M[id_0] = ((Init(m), \lambda e.\ \bot), \lambda x.\ \bot, Entry(m, Init(m)), \epsilon)$. The semantics is defined as a collection of rules for determining transitions of the form $M \longrightarrow M'$. All existing state machines are running concurrently retrieving events from their input queue, performing local computation, and possibly sending events to other machines. Each rule picks an existing machine with identifier id and executes it for a step. To simplify the rule we use small steps ($\longrightarrow$) for statements and big steps ($\downarrow$) for the expression. The rules for expressions are as expected and therefore omitted.

Figure 4 gives the rules for executing code statements inside a state. These rules execute small steps performed during the computation of the entry function of a state. During this computation,

$$\frac{\begin{array}{c} M[id] = ((n, \alpha) \cdot \gamma, \sigma, S[\mathbf{raise}\,(e, r)], q) \\ \sigma(r) \downarrow v \qquad \sigma' = \sigma[\mathbf{msg} := e][\mathbf{arg} := v] \qquad m = \mathit{Name}(id) \\ s = \begin{array}{l} \mathbf{if}\ \mathit{Pop}(m, n, \alpha, e) \vee \mathit{Step}(m, n, e) \neq \bot \\ \mathbf{then}\ \mathit{Exit}(m, n) \\ \mathbf{else\ skip} \end{array} \end{array}}{M \longrightarrow M[id := ((n, \alpha) \cdot \gamma, \sigma', s; \overline{\mathbf{raise}}\,(e, v), q)]} \ (\text{RAISE})$$

$$\frac{M[id] = (\gamma, \sigma, S[\mathbf{leave}], q)}{M \longrightarrow M[id := (\gamma, \sigma, \mathbf{skip}, q)]} \ (\text{LEAVE})$$

$$\frac{M[id] = (\gamma, \sigma, S[\mathbf{return}], q)}{M \longrightarrow M[id := (\gamma, \sigma, \mathit{Exit}(m, n); \overline{\mathbf{return}}, q)]} \ (\text{RETURN})$$

$$\frac{\begin{array}{c} M[id] = ((n, \alpha) \cdot \gamma, \sigma, \mathbf{skip}, q_1 \cdot (e, v) \cdot q_2) \qquad m = \mathit{Name}(id) \\ t = \{e \mid \mathit{Trans}(m, n, e) \neq \bot \vee \mathit{Action}(m, n, e) \neq \bot\} \\ d = \{e \mid \alpha(e) = \top\} \qquad d' = (d \cup \mathit{Deferred}(m, n)) - t \\ |q_1| \subseteq d' \qquad e \notin d' \qquad \sigma' = \sigma[\mathbf{msg} := e][\mathbf{arg} := v] \\ s = \begin{array}{l} \mathbf{if}\ \mathit{Pop}(m, n, \alpha, e) \vee \mathit{Step}(m, n, e) \neq \bot \\ \mathbf{then}\ \mathit{Exit}(m, n) \\ \mathbf{else\ skip} \end{array} \end{array}}{M \longrightarrow M[id := ((n, \alpha) \cdot \gamma, \sigma', s; \overline{\mathbf{raise}}\,(e, v), q_1 \cdot q_2)]} \ (\text{DEQUEUE})$$

$$\frac{\begin{array}{c} M[id] = ((n, \alpha) \cdot \gamma, \sigma, \overline{\mathbf{raise}}\,(e, v), q) \\ m = \mathit{Name}(id) \qquad \mathit{Step}(m, n, e) = n' \end{array}}{M \longrightarrow M[id := ((n', \alpha) \cdot \gamma, \sigma, \mathit{Entry}(m, n'), q)]} \ (\text{STEP})$$

$$\frac{\begin{array}{c} M[id] = ((n, \alpha) \cdot \gamma, \sigma, \overline{\mathbf{raise}}\,(e, v), q) \\ m = \mathit{Name}(id) \qquad \mathit{Trans}(m, n, e) = \bot \\ (\alpha(e) = a \wedge \mathit{Action}(m, n, e) = \bot) \vee \mathit{Action}(m, n, e) = a \\ a \notin \{\bot, \top\} \end{array}}{M \longrightarrow M[id := ((n, \alpha) \cdot \gamma, \sigma, \mathit{Stmt}(m, a), q)]} \ (\text{ACTION})$$

$$\frac{\begin{array}{c} M[id] = ((n, \alpha) \cdot \gamma, \sigma, \overline{\mathbf{raise}}\,(e, v), q) \\ m = \mathit{Name}(id) \qquad \mathit{Call}(m, n, e) = n' \\ \alpha' = \lambda e. \begin{array}{l} \mathbf{if}\ (\mathit{Trans}(m, n, e) \neq \bot)\ \mathbf{then}\ \bot \\ \mathbf{else\ if}\ (\mathit{Action}(m, n, e) \neq \bot)\ \mathbf{then}\ \mathit{Action}(m, n, e) \\ \mathbf{else\ if}\ (e \in \mathit{Deferred}(m, n))\ \mathbf{then}\ \top \\ \mathbf{else}\ \alpha(e) \end{array} \end{array}}{M \longrightarrow M[id := ((n', \alpha') \cdot (n, \alpha) \cdot \gamma, \sigma, \mathit{Entry}(m, n'), q)]} \ (\text{CALL})$$

$$\frac{\begin{array}{c} M[id] = ((n, \alpha) \cdot \gamma, \sigma, \overline{\mathbf{raise}}\,(e, v), q) \\ m = \mathit{Name}(id) \qquad \mathit{Pop}(m, n, \alpha, e) \end{array}}{M \longrightarrow M[id := (\gamma, \sigma, \mathbf{raise}\,(e, v), q)]} \ (\text{POP1})$$

$$\frac{M[id] = ((n, \alpha) \cdot \gamma, \sigma, \overline{\mathbf{return}}, q) \qquad m = \mathit{Name}(id)}{M \longrightarrow M[id := (\gamma, \sigma, \mathbf{skip}, q)]} \ (\text{POP2})$$

Figure 5: Operational semantics: event handling

$$\frac{M[id] = (\gamma, \sigma, S[\mathbf{assert}(r)], q) \qquad \sigma(r) \downarrow \mathbf{false}}{M \longrightarrow \mathit{error}} \ (\text{ASSERT-FAIL})$$

$$\frac{M[id] = (\gamma, \sigma, S[\mathbf{send}(r_1, e, r_2)], q) \qquad \sigma(r_1) \downarrow \bot}{M \longrightarrow \mathit{error}} \ (\text{SEND-FAIL1})$$

$$\frac{\begin{array}{c} M[id] = (\gamma, \sigma, S[\mathbf{send}(r_1, e, r_2)], q) \\ \sigma(r_1) \downarrow id' \qquad M[id'] = \bot \end{array}}{M \longrightarrow \mathit{error}} \ (\text{SEND-FAIL2})$$

$$\frac{M[id] = (\epsilon, \sigma, s, q)}{M \longrightarrow \mathit{error}} \ (\text{POP-FAIL})$$

Figure 6: Operational semantics: error transitions

local variables could be modified and events could be sent to other state machines.

The rule SEND shows the semantics of the statement $\mathbf{send}(r_1, e, r_2)$. First, the target of the send $id' = \sigma(r_1)$, and the payload of the event $v = \sigma(r_2)$ are evaluated and the event (e, v) is appended to the queue of the target machine identified by id' using the special append operator $\odot$. The operator $\odot$ is defined as follows. If $(e, v) \notin q$, then $q \odot (e, v) = q \cdot (e, v)$. Otherwise, $q \odot (e, v) = q$. Thus, event-value pairs in event queues are unique, and if the same event-value pair is sent more than once to a machine, only one instance of it is added to the queue, avoiding flooding of the queue due to events generated by hardware, for instance. In some cases, the programmer may want multiple events to be queued, and they can enable this by differentiating the instances of these events using a counter value in the payload.

Figure 5 gives the rules for how events are generated and processed. These rules use $\overline{\mathbf{raise}}$ and $\overline{\mathbf{return}}$, which are dynamic instances of **raise** and **return** statements respectively. The computation terminates either normally via completion of all statements in the entry statement, execution of **leave** to jump control to the end of the entry function, execution of a **return** statement (which results in popping from the call stack), or by raising an event e. In the first two cases, the machine attempts to remove an event from the input queue via the rule DEQUEUE prior to raising the retrieved event.

Each state in a state machine can opt to defer a set of events received from the outside world. The logic for dequeuing an event from the input buffer is cognizant of the current set of deferred events and skips over all deferred events from the front of the queue. The deferred set of a stack of states is the union of the deferred set at the top of the call stack with the value resulting from evaluating the deferred set expression declared with that state. In case an event e is both in the deferred set and has a defined transition from a state, the defined transition overrides, and the event e is not deferred (see rule DEQUEUE).

Once an event is raised, using either dequeuing or a raise statement, it is handled using one of the three transition rules STEP, ACTION or CALL. The STEP transition results in leaving the current state n and entering a target state n'. The ACTION transition picks an appropriate action a either from $\mathit{Action}(m, n, e)$ or from the partial map α on the call stack, with the caveat that an action bound on the current state using $\mathit{Action}(m, n, e)$ overrides the action inherited in the call stack using α. Once a suitable action α is picked, the statement $\mathit{Stmt}(m, a)$ is executed. Also, if $\mathit{Step}(m, n, e)$ or $\mathit{Call}(m, n, e)$ is defined, it takes higher priority over actions. The CALL transition computes new values for the map α' in terms of the existing value of the map α on the top of the stack and the set of transitions and actions defined on the current state n. The map $\alpha'(e)$ is defined as follows: if a transition is defined for e then it is bound to $\bot$, otherwise if the event e is bound to an action in n then that binding is used, otherwise if event e is deferred in n then it is mapped to $\top$, and all the other events are mapped to the old value $\alpha(e)$. As a result of the transition, the machine enters the target state n' by pushing the pair (n', α') on the stack.

If these transition rules are not applicable due to the unavailability of a suitable transition, then the top most state on the machine stack is popped via the rules POP1 and POP2 to allow the next state to continue processing. These rules use the predicate $\mathit{Pop}(m, n, \alpha, e)$ to represent the condition under which a state is popped.

$$\begin{array}{rl} \mathit{Pop}(m, n, \alpha, e) = & \mathit{Step}(m, n, e) = \bot \wedge \\ & \mathit{Call}(m, n, e) = \bot \wedge \\ & \mathit{Action}(m, n, e) = \bot \wedge \\ & \alpha(e) \in \{\bot, \top\} \end{array}$$

If rule POP1 executes, the next state must process the unhandled event; if rule POP2 executes, the next state dequeues a new event from the input queue.

The exit function $Exit(m, n)$ of a state n in machine m is executed either when a step transition out of s is taken or s is popped. When an event e is raised or dequeued, the available transitions in s are examined to determined whether $Exit(m, n)$ needs to be executed, and if so, the code statement $Exit(m, n)$ is inserted into the state. $Exit(m, n)$ is always executed if the entry function terminates with a **return**. The rules in Figure 5 assume that $Exit(m, n)$ itself does not contain any explicit raise or return; however, our implementation allows that.

Figure 6 specifies error transitions. The error configuration, denoted by *error*, can be reached in one of 4 ways: (1) by failing an assertion (rule ASSERT-FAIL), (2) by executing a statement $\mathbf{send}(r_1, e, r_2)$ with r_1 evaluating to $\perp$ (rule SEND-FAIL1), (3) by executing a statement $\mathbf{send}(r_1, e, r_2)$ with r_1 evaluating to some id', but with $M[id'] = \perp$, thereby attempting to send to an uninitialized or deleted machine (rule SEND-FAIL1), and (4) The stack becomes empty after a pop (rule POP-FAIL). In Section 5, we show how to detect all these 4 types of errors using systematic testing.

Other features. We conclude the description of the core language and semantics with two additional features: (1) foreign functions, and (2) call statements. Both these features are very important to write real-world asynchronous code, but their semantics is standard. Consequently, we describe them informally below.

To interact with external code, a P program has the ability to call functions written in the C language. These functions needs to be introduced in the scope of a machine by a declaration that give the function's name and type signature. The runtime semantics of a function call to a foreign functions is similar to a standard C method call. For verification purposes we allow the user to give a P body to a foreign function. The body has to be erasable, i.e. uses only ghost variables and expressions.

The P language also has a call statement of the form **call** n', where n' is a state. This can be used to transition to the target state n' by pushing n' on the call stack, much like a call transition. Unlike a call transition, the call statement requires saving a continuation associated with the caller on the stack, so that execution can resume and complete the remaining statements when the callee state is popped.

3.2 Responsiveness

Beyond providing constructs for building safe programs, the design of the P language also contains constructs to build responsive programs. Explicitly deferring messages instead of doing so implicitly is such a design choice. However, it is still possible to excessively defer events, thus not processing them. Therefore, we propose two liveness properties that must be satisfied by a P program. We describe these two properties below in terms of a precise description of those infinite executions which *violate* these properties; we use linear temporal logic [18] for our specifications. Our specifications use the following predicates over events that occur during an execution:

1. $en(m)$ holds iff machine m is enabled, i.e., m can take a step.
2. $sched(m)$ holds iff machine m is enabled and takes a step.
3. $enq(m, e, m')$ holds iff machine m enqueues an event e into machine m'.
4. $deq(m', e)$ holds iff machine m' dequeues an event e.

The first property specifies that a machine cannot execute indefinitely without getting disabled. In particular, a machine should not get into a cycle of private operations, causing it to loop forever. The set of erroneous executions is given by

$$\exists m.\ \Diamond\Box(sched(m)).$$

The second property specifies that events are not deferred excessively; the goal is to prevent events from being always deferred, thus never processed. We first define the notion of *fairly scheduling* a machine m.

$$fair(m) \triangleq \Box\Diamond(en(m) \Rightarrow sched(m))$$

An erroneous execution is one in which every machine is fairly scheduled and an event is enqueued which is never subsequently dequeued. The set of all erroneous executions is given by

$$\forall m.\ fair(m) \wedge \exists m, e, m'.\ \Diamond(enq(m, e, m') \wedge \Box\neg deq(m', e)).$$

Our experience with real drivers suggests that in some cases, this property may be too strong. For instance, in a system with prioritized events, enough high priority events from the environment may postpone forever the processing of lower priority events. We allow programmers to indicate this expectation in a state s by annotating s with a list of postponed events. Our refinement of the second liveness specification uses the predicate $ppn(m, e)$ that holds whenever m is in a state whose list of postponed events contains e. The smaller set of erroneous executions is given by

$$\forall m.\ fair(m) \wedge \exists m, e, m'.\ \Diamond(enq(m, e, m') \wedge \Box\neg deq(m', e)) \wedge \Diamond\Box\neg ppn(m', e).$$

3.3 Type system and erasure

The type system of P is, on purpose, kept very simple. It mostly does simple checks to make sure the machines, transitions, and statements are well-formed. In particular, the following checks are performed: (1) identifiers for machines, state names, events, and variables are unique, (2) statements inside real machines are deterministic, and (3) ghost machines, ghost variables, and ghost events can be *erased* during compilation and execution.

The only non-trivial part of our type system is the rules that deal with the erasure property of ghost variables, and ghost machines. We identify "ghost terms" in statements of real machines, and check that they do not affect the runs of real machines (except for assertions). The separation is needed since ghost terms are kept only for verification purposes and are erased during the compilation. Therefore, only a limited flow of information is allowed between real and ghost terms. For machine identifiers we enforce complete separation, because we need to unambiguously identify the **send** operation that targets ghost machine, so that it can be preserved during verification and erased during compilation.

The error transitions specified in Figure 6 cannot be detected by our type checker. Instead, we use state-space exploration techniques (described in Section 5) to check for these errors statically.

4. Execution

This section explains how we generate code from a P program, so that the generated code can run as a Windows device driver. Execution requires a host driver framework; our current implementation uses Windows Kernel Mode Driver Framework (KMDF). The complete driver, which runs inside Windows, has four components:

1. The *generated code* is a C file which is produced by the P compiler from a state machine description.
2. The *runtime* is a library that interacts with the generated code and provides utilities for synchronization and management of state, execution, and memory.
3. The *interface code* is a skeletal KMDF driver which mediates between the OS and the generated code by creating instances

of P machines and getting the execution started, and translating OS callbacks into P state machine events that are queued into the queues of the respective machines.

4. The *foreign functions* are provided as C source files or libraries. The function calls occurring in the machines are linked to those files.

Generated code. The code generated from a P program comprises a collection of indexed and statically-allocated data structures that are examined by the runtime when it executes the operational semantics of the program. The set of names of events is compiled to a C enumeration, thus giving a globally-known unique index to each event. Similarly, names of machine types and names of local variables and states in each machine are also compiled to C enumerations. At the top level, there is a driver structure that contains pointers to an array of events and an array of machine types; these arrays are indexed by the corresponding enumerations for events and machine types respectively. Each entry in the machine array contains pointers to an array of variables and an array of states, each indexed by the corresponding enumeration. Each entry in the state array contains a table of outgoing transitions, a table of deferred events, a table of installed actions, and pointers for entry and exit functions. In addition to these data structures, the compiler also generates C code for the bodies of entry and exit functions of all states and all actions declared in the program.

When P is compiled to C, the state of a machine is wrapped into an object of type `StateMachineContext`. This object contains data structures to represent the state of the machine, as described in the formal operational semantics in Section 3. In addition, it also contains a `void*` pointer to external memory used only by the foreign functions and interface code.

To make the P compiler work for another driver framework or another operating system, the runtime and foreign code needs to be reimplemented appropriately but the generated code does not need to change.

Runtime. The runtime of P provides functionality for all operations required for executing the operational semantics of a P program, such as creating a machine, enqueueing an event into a machine, running a state machine, maintaining the call stack and available event handlers of each machine, etc. This functionality is mostly private to the runtime with a few exceptions for the benefit of interface code, which can interact with the P runtime using three APIs: create a new state machine using `SMCreateMachine`, queue an event into a machine using `SMAddEvent`, or request a pointer to the external memory associated with a machine using `SMGetContext`.

Windows drivers are parsimonious with threads. Worker threads are rarely created and drivers typically use calling threads to do all the work. Thus, when the OS calls the driver, either due to an application request or due to a hardware interrupt or deferred procedure call, the driver uses the calling thread to process the event and run to completion. Multiple such threads could be executing inside the runtime at any time; each dynamic instance of a state machine is protected by its own lock for safe synchronization.

Interface code. The interface code is used to mediate between the OS and the P code. It is written as a skeletal KMDF driver, which handles callbacks from the Windows OS and translates them into events it adds to the queue of the P machine, using the runtime API. In KMDF, the `EvtAddDevice` callback is used to create the state machine using the `SMCreateMachine` API. All events such as Plug and Play or Power management or other events are handled by the foreign code by queuing a corresponding event using the `SMAddEvent` API. The `EvtRemoveDevice` callback results in a special event `Delete` added to the P driver. Every P state machine is required to handle this event by cleaning up and executing the `delete` statement. Note that the P machine may have to do internal bookkeeping and keep track of other machines it has created, and the state of the interactions it has with other machines, cleanup the state of the interactions, and only then execute the `delete` statement. In our experience, the interface code is generic enough so that it can be automatically generated for a particular class of drivers.

Foreign functions. The foreign functions are provided by the programmer to complement the P machines. The foreign functions must have one additional argument on top of the ones declared in P. This argument, of type `void *`, points to external memory that can be used by the programmer to persist some information as part of the state of calling machine. The foreign functions are assumed to terminate and to limit any side effect to the provided memory. Unlike the interface code which is generic, foreign functions are typically driver-specific and consequently need to be specified by the programmer.

4.1 Efficiency of generated code and runtime

In order to evaluate the efficiency of the code generated by P and the runtime, we performed the following experiment. We developed two drivers for a simple switch-and-led device, one using P, and one directly using KMDF. Both drivers use the same level of asynchrony. The P code is about 150 lines with one driver machine and four ghost machines. The driver machine has 15 states and 23 transitions, and each ghost machines has approximately four states and transitions. The foreign code is 1720 lines, written directly in C, interfacing between KMDF and the P code. In contrast, the full KMDF driver (written without using P) is about 6000 lines of C code.

We tested both drivers in an environment which sends 100 events per second, and both drivers are able to process each event with an average processing time of 4ms, demonstrating that the P compiler and runtime do not introduce additional overhead. We present a more substantial case study in Section 6.

5. Systematic testing

P is designed to enable systematic testing of programs written in it. There are two kinds of nondeterminism in the semantics of P programs—explicit nondeterministic choice in the ghost machines and implicit nondeterministic choice of which machine to schedule next. Systematic testing of a P program is accomplished by interpreting its operational semantics (closed using ghost machines) in the explicit-state model checker Zing [2]. All aspects of the operational semantics of the program are interpreted including the code statements labeling the states and actions of a P machine. The model checker takes care of systematically enumerating all implicit scheduling and explicit modeling choices in the program and checks for the possible errors (see Figure 6) namely, (1) assertion failures, (2) executing send commands with uninitialized target identifiers, (3) sending events to machine that has been already freed, and (4) unhandled events. We leave verification of the liveness checks in P programs for future work.

Machines in P programs communicate via message-passing; there are only three operations at which a communication between two machines occurs—creating a machine, sending an event, and receiving an event. It suffices to introduce context-switches after only these operations; since a private operation in a machine commutes with operations of other machines, a context switch after is redundant. In other words, if an error occur in an execution with a more fine-grained context-switching, it can be shown to occur in another equivalent execution in which context-switches happen only at the points mentioned above. This optimization is an example of atomicity reduction [7]. Furthermore, it can be shown that a receive operation is a right mover [15]; therefore, a context switch after a receive operation can also be eliminated and it suffices to introduce context switches only after a machine is created or an event is sent.

Delay-bounded scheduling. Unfortunately, even the coarse-grained context-switching described above is not sufficient to prevent the state space explosion problem. If there are k machines enabled at each interleaving point, the number of possible schedules for runs with n context switches is k^n. Therefore, systematic exploration of long schedules becomes prohibitively expensive. Consequently, we have designed a delaying scheduler to scale our exploration to large P programs with long executions.

Intuitively, our delaying scheduler explores schedules that follow the causal sequence of events. Diverging from that sequence is done by delaying some machine. Given a bound d, the scheduler may introduce at most d delays. Suppose machine m_1 sends an event e to machine m_2. Then, at a later point m_2 removes e from its input buffer, and processes this message, thereby resulting in an event e' sent to machine m_3. The delay bounded scheduler follows the causal sequence of steps which consists of machine m_1 sending the event e to m_2, machine m_2 processing the event e and sending the event e' to m_3, and machine m_3 handling the event e'. A delay that the scheduler may choose to introduce is, for instance, at the second context-switch delaying m_3 and executing m_2.

More formally, our delaying scheduler maintains a stack S of P machine identifiers, and an integer delay score. Initially, the stack S contains a single machine identifier corresponding to the instance created by the initialization statement of the P program, and the delay score is set to 0. For example, in the `Elevator` example from Section 2, the stack initially contains the id of the `User` ghost machine.

The scheduler always chooses to schedule the machine whose identifier is at the top of S. The scheduled machine executes until it reaches a scheduling point (which is a send or the creation of a machine) at which point the scheduler again provides the next machine to be scheduled. The stack S and the delay score is updated in response to events happening in the execution as follows:

- If m is scheduled and m sends an event to machine m' and $m' \notin S$, m' is pushed on S.
- If m is scheduled and m creates a new machine m', then m' is pushed on S.
- If m is delayed, m is moved from top of S to the bottom of S, and the delay score is incremented by 1.

Given a delay bound d, a delay bounded scheduler explores only those schedules which have a delay score lesser than or equal to d.

We can show that for $d = 0$, the real part of schedules explored by the delay bounded scheduler are exactly the same as the one executed by the P runtime in Section 4, assuming no multithreading (that is, at most one thread calls into the P runtime from the kernel). Differences between the runtime and the delay bounded scheduler occur only in the interaction with the ghost machines/environment. Increasing the delay bound d let the scheduler explores more schedules and captures more interactions with the environment. We can also show that as d approaches infinity, in the limit, the delay bounded scheduler explores all possible schedules of a P program, and in particular includes all cases where the P runtime is invoked by an arbitrary number of parallel threads from the kernel. However, even for low values of d, the delay bounded scheduler is very useful in error detection, as shown below.

Empirical results. In order to evaluate the efficacy of delay bounding, we conducted the following experiments. For three benchmark

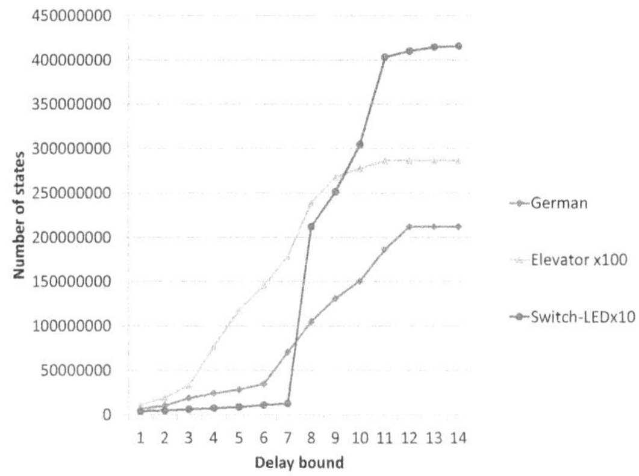

Figure 7: States explored with increasing delay bound.

P programs (elevator example from Section 2, driver for Switch-and-LED device, and for a software implementation of German's cache coherence protocol), we studied the behavior of delay bounding for varying values of the delay bound parameter d. Figure 7 shows how the number of explored states varies as we increase the value of the delay bound parameter. We scaled the number of states in the Switch-LED by a factor of 10 and Elevator by a factor of 100 to make the graphs legible. We also experimented with buggy versions of these designs and determined that bugs are found within a delay bound of 2. The data can be summarized as follows: bugs are found for low values of delay bound (note the low value of number of states explored for delay bound of 2 in Figure 7 within which bugs were found), and as we increase the delay bound we eventually explore all states within a delay bound of around 12.

6. Case Study

USB Hub Driver: Context and challenges. The state machine methodology described in this paper, together with code generation as well as verification, was used in the development of core components of the USB 3.0 stack that was released as part of Microsoft Windows 8. In particular, the USB hub driver ("USBHUB3.sys") was developed using our methodology. The USB hub driver is responsible for managing USB hubs, the ports in these hubs, enumerating the devices and other hubs connected to their downstream ports. It receives a large number of un-coordinated events sent from different sources such as OS, hardware and other drivers, in tricky situations when the system is suspending or powering down. It can receive unexpected events from disabled or stopped devices, non-compliant hardware and buggy drivers. The hub driver can fail requests from incorrect hardware or buggy function drivers. However, it is important that the USB hub itself handles all events and does not crash or hang itself.

State machine	P states	P transitions	Explored states (millions)	Time (hh:mm)	Memory MB
HSM	196	361	5.9	2:30	1712
PSM 3.0	295	752	1.5	3:30	1341
PSM 2.0	457	1386	2.2	5:30	872
DSM	1919	4238	1.2	5:30	1127

Figure 8: State machine sizes and exploration time

Experience using P in USB Hub. We designed the USB Hub in P as a collection of state machines. The hub, each of the ports, and each of the devices are designed as P machines. Using P helped us serialize the large number of uncoordinated events coming in from hardware, operating system, function drivers and other driver components. In order to make hub scalable, the processing in the hub should be as asynchronous as possible. We captured all the complexity of asynchronous processing using P state machines, and fine-grained and explicit states for each step in the processing. We used sub-state machines to factor common event handling code, and control the explosion in the number of states in the P code, and deferred events to delay processing of low-priority events. We made sure that any code in the driver that lives outside the P state machine (as foreign functions) is relatively simple and primarily does only data processing, and no control logic. This helped us ensure that the most complex pieces of our driver are verified using the state exploration tools of P.

We had to carefully constrain the environment machines in several cases to help direct the verification tools. Even with such constraints, the actual state spaces explored by the verifier were on the order of several millions, and the verifier runs took several hours to finish (even after using multicores to scale the state exploration), once our designs became mature and the shallow bugs were found and fixed. Figure 8 shows the size and scale of state spaces for the various state machines. The second and third columns show the number of states and transitions at the level of P. The fourth column shows the number of states explored by the explored (taking into account values of variables, state of queues, and state of ghost machines modeling the environment). The fifth and sixth column give the time and space needed to complete the exploration.

The systematic verification effort enabled by P helped us greatly flesh out corner cases in our design, forced us to handle every event (or explicitly defer it) in every state, and greatly contributed to the robustness of the shipped product. Overall, state exploration tools helped us identify and fix over 300 bugs, and justified their continued use throughout the development cycle. A majority of the bugs were due to unhandled events that we did not anticipate arriving. Other bugs were due to unexpected interactions between machines, or with the environment, which manifested in either unhandled messages or assertion violations.

Comparison with existing USB stack. The old USB driver in Windows has existed for several years and predates P. We compare the old USB driver and new driver in terms of functionality, performance, and reliability.

1. Functionality. The new USB hub driver has to deal with new USB 3.0 hardware in addition to all the requirements for the old driver. Therefore the new USB hub driver implements functionality that is a super set of the functionality of the old hub driver.
2. Reliability. The old USB hub driver had significantly more synchronization issues in PnP, power and error recovery paths even till date. The number of such issues has dropped dramatically in the new USB hub driver. The number of crashes in the new USB hub driver due to invalid memory accesses and race conditions is insignificant.
3. Performance. The new USB hub driver performs much better than the old USB hub driver —average enumeration time for a USB device is 30% faster. We have not seen any instances of worker item starvation that we used to see with the old hub driver.

This gain in performance is mainly due to the highly asynchronous nature of the new hub driver. In comparison, the old hub driver blocks processing of worker items in several situations, leading to performance degradation. It is theoretically possible to develop a driver that is not based on explicit state machines such as in P, but is equally (or more) performant. However, in practice, when we have tried to build such asynchronous drivers directly, we have run into myriad of synchronization issues and unacceptable degradation in reliability. The support for asynchrony in P in terms of explicitly documented states and transitions, and the verification tools in P that systematically identified corner cases due to asynchrony were the key reasons why we were able to design the new USB hub driver with both high performance and high reliability.

We note that the new USB hub driver has only been released to the public for about a month at the time of this writing. Once we get more empirical data from usage of USB by Windows 8 users, we can make a more thorough comparison on actual number of crashes and hangs with the old driver.

7. Related work

Synchronous languages. Synchronous languages such as Esterel [4], Lustre [10] and Signal [3] have been used to model, and generate code for real-time and embedded systems for several decades. All these languages follow the synchrony hypothesis, where time advances in steps, and concurrency is deterministic —that is, given a state and an input at the current time step, there is a unique possible state at the next time step. Lustre and Signal follow a declarative dataflow model. Every variable or expression in Lustre represents a *flow* which is a sequence of values. For a flow x, Lustre uses $pre(x)$ do denote a flow with values postponed by one time step. A Lustre program [10] is a set of definitions of flows, where each flow is defined using some constant flows or other flows. Even though flows can be recursively defined, each recursive cycle should be broken using the pre operator. In contrast, Esterel is an imperative language [4] where a program consists of a collection of nested concurrently running threads, and each step is triggered by an external event, and threads are scheduled until all internally generated events are consumed. The Esterel compiler ensures a property called *constructive causality*, which guarantees absence of cyclical dependencies in propagating events, and ensures that each step terminates. Harel's StateCharts [11] is a visual language, with hierarchical states, broadcast communication of events and a synchronous fixpoint semantics which involves executing a series of micro-steps within each time step until all internally generated events are consumed.

The synchronous model has the advantage that every event sent to machine is handled in the next clock tick, and is widely used in hardware and embedded systems. However, in an OS or a distributed system, it is impossible to have all the components of the system clocked using a global clock, and hence asynchronous models are used for these systems. In such models events are queued, and hence can be delayed arbitrarily before being handled. However, arbitrary delays are unacceptable in OS components such as device drivers, which require responsiveness in event handling. The main focus of our work is an asynchronous model where responsiveness is enforced using verification, with the ability do code generation.

Asynchronous languages. Asynchronous languages are used to model and program software systems. The adaptation of StateCharts in the Rhapsody tool has produced a variant, which is suitable for modeling asynchronous software systems. This variant (see [12]) allows steps that take non-zero time and resembles a collection of communicating and interacting state machines, where each machine has a named input queue, and each transition of a machine consumes a message from its input queue and possibly sends messages to the output queues of one or more machines. Other asynchronous models include the actor model [13] and process calculi, such as CSP [14] and CCS [16], and Join Calculus [8], which have asynchronous processes communicating with each other via messages. While these models are useful in modeling and reasoning about asynchronous systems, our goal is to unify modeling and verification with programming, and generate code that can run in an OS kernel.

Domain-specific languages. The Teapot [5] programming language shares similar goals to our work in that they attempt to unify modeling, programming and verification, although in a different application domain —cache coherence protocols. Teapot's continuation passing design is related to the design of P's call transitions. The notion of deferred sets, ghost machines and erasure property, default safety and liveness checks, delay bounding, and the ability of the P compiler and runtime to generate code that runs in an OS kernel are all unique to P.

Automatic stack management. There have been attempts to provide automatic stack management for event-driven programming to allow the possibility of blocking constructs inside procedure calls (e.g., [1]). In P, entry functions of states are written in non-blocking style and call transitions are provided to conveniently factor common event handling code. Thus, stack management is particularly simple in our current design.

8. Conclusion

We presented P, a domain specific language for writing asynchronous event-driven programs. We have given a full formal treatment of various aspects of P, including operational semantics, type system, and verifier. We also presented experience using P to program the USB stack that ships with Windows 8. The main technical contribution of our work is an asynchronous model which forces each event in the queue to be handled as soon as the machine associated with the queue is scheduled, and has a chance to dequeue the event. Our verifier systematically explores the state space of machines and ensures that there are no unhandled events. In certain circumstances, such as processing a high priority event, or processing a sequence of event exchanges during a transaction, some other lower priority events may have to be queued temporarily. P has features such as deferred events for a programmer to explicitly specify such deferrals. Thus, our main contribution is the design of an asynchronous language, which promotes a discipline of programming where deferrals need to be declared explicitly, and consequently leads to responsive systems.

Acknowledgments

We would like to acknowledge the contribution of Randy Aull, architect of the USB device driver stack in Windows 8, to the design of P. We would also like to thank him for his enthusiastic adoption of the P programming model. Damien Zufferey would like to acknowledge the support of the Austrian Science Fund NFN RiSE (Rigorous Systems Engineering) and the ERC Advanced Grant QUAREM (Quantitative Reactive Modeling).

References

[1] A. Adya, J. Howell, M. Theimer, W. J. Bolosky, and J. R. Douceur. Cooperative task management without manual stack management. In *USENIX Annual Technical Conference, General Track*, pages 289–302, 2002.

[2] T. Andrews, S. Qadeer, S. K. Rajamani, J. Rehof, and Y. Xie. Zing: A model checker for concurrent software. In *CAV: International Conference on Computer Aided Verification*, pages 484–487, 2004.

[3] A. Benveniste, P. L. Guernic, and C. Jacquemot. Synchronous programming with events and relations: the Signal language and its semantics. *Sci. Comput. Program.*, 16(2):103–149, 1991.

[4] G. Berry and G. Gonthier. The Esterel synchronous programming language: design, semantics, implementation. *Sci. Comput. Program.*, 19(2):87–152, Nov. 1992.

[5] S. Chandra, B. Richards, and J. R. Larus. Teapot: A domain-specific language for writing cache coherence protocols. *IEEE Trans. Software Eng.*, 25(3):317–333, 1999.

[6] M. Emmi, S. Qadeer, and Z. Rakamaric. Delay-bounded scheduling. In *POPL: ACM SIGPLAN-SIGACT Symposium on Principles of Programming Languages*, pages 411–422, 2011.

[7] C. Flanagan and S. Qadeer. A type and effect system for atomicity. In *PLDI: ACM SIGPLAN Conference on Programming Language Design and Implementation*, pages 338–349, 2003.

[8] C. Fournet and G. Gonthier. The reflexive CHAM and the join-calculus. In H.-J. Boehm and G. L. S. Jr., editors, *POPL*, pages 372–385. ACM Press, 1996.

[9] P. Godefroid. Model checking for programming languages using Verisoft. In *POPL: 24th ACM SIGPLAN-SIGACT Symposium on Principles of Programming Languages*, pages 174–186, 1997.

[10] N. Halbwachs, P. Caspi, P. Raymond, and D. Pilaud. The synchronous dataflow programming language Lustre. *Proceedings of the IEEE*, 79(9):1305–1320, September 1991.

[11] D. Harel. Statecharts: A visual formalism for complex systems. *Sci. Comput. Program.*, 8(3):231–274, 1987.

[12] D. Harel and H. Kugler. The Rhapsody semantics of Statecharts (or, on the executable core of the UML) - preliminary version. In H. Ehrig, W. Damm, J. Desel, M. Große-Rhode, W. Reif, E. Schnieder, and E. Westkämper, editors, *SoftSpez Final Report*, volume 3147 of *Lecture Notes in Computer Science*, pages 325–354. Springer, 2004.

[13] C. Hewitt, P. Bishop, and R. Steiger. A universal modular actor formalism for artificial intelligence. In *Proceedings of the 3rd international joint conference on Artificial intelligence*, IJCAI'73, pages 235–245, San Francisco, CA, USA, 1973. Morgan Kaufmann Publishers Inc.

[14] C. A. R. Hoare. Communicating sequential processes. *Commun. ACM*, 21(8):666–677, 1978.

[15] R. J. Lipton. Reduction: a new method of proving properties of systems of processes. In *POPL: ACM SIGPLAN-SIGACT Symposium on Principles of Programming Languages*, pages 78–86, 1975.

[16] R. Milner. *A Calculus of Communicating Systems*, volume 92 of *Lecture Notes in Computer Science*. Springer, 1980.

[17] M. Musuvathi, S. Qadeer, T. Ball, G. Basler, P. A. Nainar, and I. Neamtiu. Finding and reproducing Heisenbugs in concurrent programs. In *OSDI : USENIX Symposium on Operating Systems Design and Implementation*, pages 267–280, 2008.

[18] A. Pnueli. The temporal logic of programs. In *FOCS: IEEE Symposium on Foundations of Computer Science*, pages 46–67, 1977.

[19] S. Russell and P. Norvig. *Artificial Intelligence: A Modern Approach (3rd edition)*. Prentice Hall, 2009.

Quipper: A Scalable Quantum Programming Language

Alexander S. Green
Dalhousie University
agreen@mathstat.dal.ca

Peter LeFanu Lumsdaine
Institute of Advanced Studies
p.l.lumsdaine@gmail.com

Neil J. Ross
Dalhousie University
Neil.JR.Ross@Dal.Ca

Peter Selinger
Dalhousie University
selinger@mathstat.dal.ca

Benoît Valiron
University of Pennsylvania
benoit.valiron@monoidal.net

Abstract

The field of quantum algorithms is vibrant. Still, there is currently a lack of programming languages for describing quantum computation on a practical scale, i.e., not just at the level of toy problems. We address this issue by introducing Quipper, a scalable, expressive, functional, higher-order quantum programming language. Quipper has been used to program a diverse set of non-trivial quantum algorithms, and can generate quantum gate representations using trillions of gates. It is geared towards a model of computation that uses a classical computer to control a quantum device, but is not dependent on any particular model of quantum hardware. Quipper has proven effective and easy to use, and opens the door towards using formal methods to analyze quantum algorithms.

Keywords Quipper; Quantum Programming Languages

Categories and Subject Descriptors D.3.1 [*Programming Languages*]: Formal Definitions and Theory

1. Introduction

The earliest computers, such as the ENIAC and EDVAC, were both rare and difficult to program. The difficulty stemmed in part from the need to express algorithms in a vocabulary suited to the particular hardware, ranging from function tables for the ENIAC to more conventional arithmetic and movement operations for later machines. The introduction of symbolic programming languages such as FORTRAN (for "FORmula TRANslator") solved a major difficulty for the next generation of computing devices, by enabling the specification of algorithms in a form more suitable for human understanding, and then translating this specification into a form executable by the machine. Thus, programming languages assumed the important role of bridging a semantic gap between the human and the computing device. This was achieved, among other things, by two important principles: high-level abstractions and automated bookkeeping.

Quantum computation, which was envisioned in the later part of the 20th century, is a computational paradigm based on the laws of quantum physics. It has been amply demonstrated in the literature that quantum computing can, in theory, outperform classical computing for certain classes of computational problems. The design of new quantum algorithms is a vibrant area, as witnessed by the quantum algorithm "zoo" of S. Jordan [11], which references 45 algorithms and 160 papers, with no less than 14 written in 2011 and 2012.

PLDI'13, June 16–19, 2013, Seattle, WA, USA.

Although quantum computing is not yet ready to move from theory to practice, it is nevertheless possible to make informed guesses of what form an eventual quantum computer may take, or more importantly for programming language design, of the *interface* by which one may interact with such a quantum computer. It seems wise, then, to apply the lessons learned from programming classical computing to the emerging quantum computing capabilities.

This paper is a stepping stone towards meeting this challenge. We approach quantum computation from a programmer's perspective: how should one design a programming language that can implement real-world quantum algorithms in an efficient, legible and maintainable way? We introduce Quipper, a declarative language with a monadic operational semantics that is succinct, expressive, and scalable, with a sound theoretical foundation.

When we speak of Quipper being "scalable", we mean that it goes well beyond toy algorithms and mere proofs of concept. Many actual quantum algorithms in the literature are orders of magnitude more complex than what could be realistically implemented in previously existing quantum programming languages. We put Quipper to the test by implementing seven non-trivial quantum algorithms from the literature:

- Binary Welded Tree (BWT). To find a labeled node in a graph [4].
- Boolean Formula (BF). To evaluate a NAND formula [2]. The version of this algorithm implemented in Quipper computes a winning strategy for the game of Hex.
- Class Number (CL). To approximate the class group of a real quadratic number field [8].
- Ground State Estimation (GSE). To compute the ground state energy level of a particular molecule [23].
- Quantum Linear Systems (QLS). To solve a linear system of equations [9].
- Unique Shortest Vector (USV). To choose the shortest vector among a given set [17].
- Triangle Finding (TF). To exhibit a triangle inside a dense graph [13].

These algorithms were chosen by IARPA, in the context of its QCS program [10], to provide a reasonably representative cross-section of current algorithms. They make use of a wide variety of quantum primitives, such as amplitude amplification, quantum walks, the quantum Fourier transform, and quantum simulation. Several of the algorithms also require the implementation of complex classical oracles. The starting point for each of our algorithm implementations was a detailed description of the algorithm provided by IARPA.

Related work. Many formalisms for programming quantum computers have been developed in the last few decades. Some of them, such as the quantum Turing machine [6] or the quantum lambda calculus of van Tonder [22], are mainly theoretical tools for exploring particular aspects of quantum computation, and are not designed with practical quantum programming in mind.

There are many recent proposals for quantum programming languages [7]. Of these, we pinpoint three languages that represent important milestones and can be regarded as predecessors of Quipper.

In the realm of imperative programming languages, arguably the oldest "concrete" quantum programming language is Ömer's QCL [16]. Defined as a C-style language, QCL comes with many interesting features, collectively dubbed *structured quantum programming*. This provides a relatively natural way of writing simple quantum algorithms. One of QCL's innovations was the separation of functions into separate syntactic classes, based on their operational behavior; thus, QCL distinguishes classical procedures, which are unconstrained; "quantum functions", which are restricted to define unitary operations; and "pseudo-classical" operators, which are intended to implement oracles, featuring "quantum tests" and automatic uncomputation of ancillas. QCL lacks high-level quantum data types, and does not have a well-defined semantics, complicating the analysis of programs. Finally, since the language was designed with simulation in mind, many of its useful programming features incur a strong computational overhead. In spite of these drawbacks, QCL is a milestone in the development of quantum programming languages. We include a very brief comparison between circuits generated by Quipper and QCL in Section 6.

More recently, there have been two proposals for functional quantum programming languages that can be regarded as precursors of Quipper. Selinger and Valiron's quantum lambda calculus is an ML-style language with strong static type checking [18, 19]. It is designed to run on Knill's QRAM model [12], but lacks high-level facilities for circuit construction and manipulation. The quantum IO Monad of Green and Altenkirch [1] is, like Quipper, embedded in Haskell, provides extensible quantum data types, and comes with a consistent operational semantics. However, it uses a much simpler circuit model and lacks many of Quipper's advanced programming features.

Outline of the paper. In Section 2, we briefly present quantum computation, focusing particularly on the interface by which software would interact with a quantum device. Section 3 covers some of the main techniques that are used to describe quantum algorithms and hopefully makes the case for a quantum programming language. In Section 4, we introduce Quipper. Section 5 discusses our implementation of the Triangle Finding algorithm, and Section 6 contains a very brief comparison between Quipper and QCL. We summarize our conclusions at the end.

2. Quantum computation

We very briefly summarize some basic notions from quantum computation, primarily to provide hints on how a quantum programming language might interact with a quantum computer. One cannot really do this subject justice in such a limited space. For a much more thorough introduction to quantum computing, see e.g. [15].

In quantum computation, the storage and manipulation of data is governed by the law of quantum physics. We will here be concerned with *idealized* quantum computation, i.e., we ignore the effects of physical imprecisions, decoherence, etc. We will describe an idealized quantum device in terms of its *state* and *operations*.

The state of a quantum system is given by a normalized vector in a Hilbert space. The smallest unit of information in quantum computing is the *quantum bit* or *qubit*; the state of one qubit is a complex linear combination of two basis vectors $|0\rangle$ and $|1\rangle$. Similarly, the state of two qubits is given as a linear combination of four basis vectors $\{|00\rangle, |01\rangle, |10\rangle, |11\rangle\}$, and more generally, the state of n qubits is a linear combination of 2^n basis vectors. The available operations are *unitary transformations*, which allow the state to be transformed along a user-specified unitary map; and *measurements*, which are the only way to extract classical information from a quantum state. We usually assume that each quantum device has some built-in set of elementary unitary transformations, called *gates*. Measurement has a probabilistic behavior: for example, when measuring a qubit in state $\alpha|0\rangle + \beta|1\rangle$, the result will be 0 with probability $|\alpha|^2$ and 1 with probability $|\beta|^2$, and subsequently the state of the qubit will have been changed to $|0\rangle$ or $|1\rangle$, respectively. There is an analogous rule for measuring, say, one of several qubits in a multi-qubit state.

2.1 Interacting with a quantum device

We can now describe the operation of an idealized quantum device known as Knill's QRAM model for quantum computation [12]. In this model, we think of a quantum computer as a specialized device that is attached to and controlled by a classical computer, much in the way of a co-processor. The device holds n individually addressable qubits, for some fixed n. The operation of the quantum device is controlled by only two kinds of instructions, which can be interleaved. Instructions of the first kind are unitary operations. They take the form "apply the built-in unitary gate U to qubit k", "apply the gate V to qubits j and k", and so on. The quantum device responds with an acknowledgement that the operation has been performed, but there is no further information returned. Instructions of the second kind are measurements. They take the form "measure qubit k". The quantum device responds with a measurement result, which is either 0 or 1. One can also add a third kind of instruction called *initialization*: "reset qubit k to 0". However, this is derivable from the instructions already mentioned: namely, by first measuring qubit k, and then negating it if and only if the measurement outcome was 1.

2.2 Basic properties

In the above model of quantum computation, the control flow of an algorithm is purely classical: tests, loops, etc., are performed on the classical computer that controls the quantum co-processor. Both classical and quantum data are first class objects.

Because quantum measurement is a probabilistic operation, classical probabilistic computation is automatically included as a subset of quantum computation.

The laws of quantum mechanics imply that quantum information cannot be duplicated. This is the so-called *no-cloning* property of quantum mechanics. It would not be physically meaningful, for example, to apply a 2-qubit quantum gate to qubits k and k. Quantum programming languages should ensure that such non-physical operations cannot occur. This kind of property can either be checked at compile time or at run time.

2.3 Hardware independence

We do not claim that the idealized QRAM model is what an actual quantum computer will look like. An actual quantum computer might be far more difficult to control. Because of the relatively short life span of quantum states in experimental settings, many layers of quantum error correction and control will likely be required to enable meaningful quantum computation. Also, realistic quantum hardware may be highly sensitive to timing constraints, such as the exact timing of control pulses. So rather than performing one gate or measurement at a time, as suggested in the QRAM model, it may be more realistic to assume that a large number of gates will be pre-computed, then executed in a single batch operation on the quantum device, possibly measuring all qubits at the end. A sequence of pre-computed gates is called a *quantum circuit*, and this model of quantum computation is known as the *circuit model*.

One operation that is available in the QRAM model, but not in the circuit model, is the ability to change the sequence of quantum gates in response to the results of previous measurements. This restriction can be overcome by augmenting the circuit model with the ability to preserve some of the unmeasured qubits in some kind of long-term storage between successive circuit executions.

From the point of view of programming language design, the particular choice of physical quantum architecture should not be of much consequence. The purpose of a high-level programming language is precisely to abstract from such hardware specific details, and to present the user with the illusion of a uniform idealized computational model.

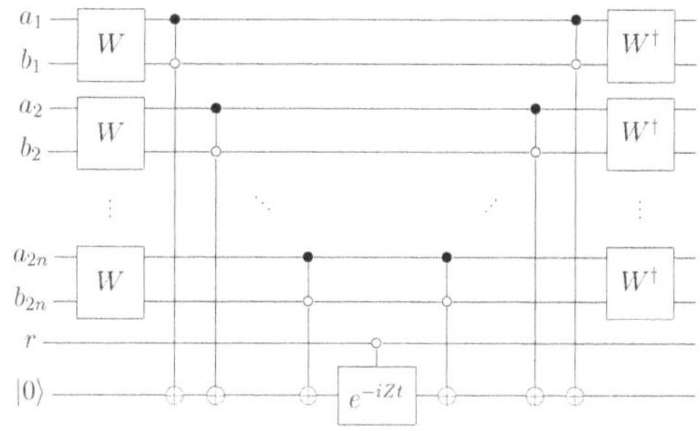

Figure 1. Example of a quantum circuit. Circuits are read left to right, with horizontal lines representing wires, boxes representing quantum gates, and vertical wires representing controls on a gate.

3. Techniques used in quantum algorithms

While every quantum algorithm can be ultimately specified as a sequence of gates and measurements, this is rarely how quantum algorithms are actually described in the literature. Rather, they are often described at a high level, for example in the style of: "Take the following function, which can obviously be implemented by a boolean circuit of polynomial size. Translate this to a reversible quantum circuit in the standard way. Apply m steps of amplitude amplification, then copy the result to a scratch register and uncompute". We believe that a good quantum programming language should be flexible enough to allow quantum algorithms to be expressed at a level of abstraction, high or low, that is as close as possible to the intent of the algorithm's human designer, while filling in enough details to be unambiguous. For this reason, prior to introducing Quipper's high-level programming features in the next section, let us briefly review some of the techniques that are commonly used in the design of quantum algorithms.

3.1 Quantum primitives

Most quantum algorithms make use of one or more of a few well-known primitive building blocks. The *quantum Fourier transform* is a unitary change of basis analogous to the classical Fourier transform, and is used in many quantum algorithms, for example to find the period of a periodic function. *Amplitude amplification* (also known as *Grover's search*) is used to increase the amplitude of certain basis states in a superposition, while decreasing others. *Quantum walks* can be described as the quantum counterpart to random walks. Due to quantum interference, some paths in the walk may cancel out (or at least, appear with decreased probability). In some situations, it is possible to outperform the success probability of a similar strategy that would have used a classical random walk. *Phase estimation* is a technique for estimating eigenvalues of a unitary operator. *State distillation* is a method by which one starts with a large noisy set of quantum states, and gradually narrows them down to a smaller cleaner set of states with desirable properties.

The above primitives are often at the heart of what makes a quantum algorithm potentially outperform its classical counterpart. But they are more than just off-the-shelf functions that can be directly used on a classical data structure, and they are typically combined in non-trivial ways.

3.2 Oracles

Another important part of many quantum algorithms is the description of an *oracle*. An oracle is usually given by a classical function $f : \texttt{Bool}^n \to \texttt{Bool}^m$, describing some aspect of the input to the algorithm, such as the edges of a graph, the winning positions of a game, arithmetic or number-theoretic functions, and so forth. To be useable in a quantum computation, the oracle must be made reversible. This can be done by lifting the function, such that $\hat{f} : \texttt{Bool}^{n+m} \to \texttt{Bool}^{n+m}$ is defined as $\hat{f}(x, y) = (x, y \oplus f(x))$. The reversible boolean function $\hat{f}$ can then be lifted into a unitary map working on quantum bits. Often, in the literature, the description of oracles is both low-level and high-level. It is low-level in the sense that, despite the fact that the oracle manipulates non-trivial data types (e.g., integers, real numbers, edges of a graph, etc.), the algorithm goes into detail about how to implement these in terms of quantum registers. But it is also high-level, in the sense that the details of how the oracle performs its operations are often only sketched.

3.3 Circuit families

At a low level, quantum algorithms take the form of a (potentially very long) sequence of unitary gates with occasional measurements. Such a sequence of operators is called a *quantum circuit* and is customarily described in diagrammatic form. An example of such a diagram, showing a diffusion step from the Binary Welded Tree algorithm [4], is shown in Figure 1. However, such diagrams are not in and by themselves good descriptions of quantum algorithms. The reason is that most quantum algorithms also depend on *parameters*, such as the number n in Figure 1, and thus a quantum algorithm really describes a *family* of circuits, which cannot be captured in a single diagram. Quipper permits a formal and precise description of such parameterized circuit families.

3.4 Circuit manipulation

Although ultimately, a quantum algorithm comes down to a sequence of elementary gates and measurements, many quantum algorithms are more naturally described in terms of manipulations at the level of entire sub-circuits, rather than individual gates. Examples of such operations are:

- reversing;
- iteration (e.g., Trotterization; amplitude amplification);
- automatic synthesis of classical circuits (e.g., oracles) and ancilla management (i.e., initialization and recollection of auxiliary quantum bits);
- circuit transformations (e.g., replacing one elementary gate set by another);
- whole-circuit optimizations.

3.5 Classical processing

To be useful, a complete quantum program must ultimately produce a classical answer to a classical question. In particular, any parameters to the algorithm are classical, as are the final outputs. Therefore, most quantum algorithms use some amount of classical pre- and post-processing. Typically, the algorithm consists of the description of a parameterized quantum circuit, followed by a final measurement.

In some algorithms, such as the Triangle Finding algorithm, the probabilistic measurement result can then be classically checked to see if a useful answer has been found, and if not, the whole procedure is repeated, possibly for a different set of parameters. In some algorithms, such as the Binary Welded Tree algorithm, the validity of a potential solution cannot be efficiently verified, and a statistical argument is used to determine how many times the algorithm should be repeated until the correct answer is found with the desired probability. A third class of algorithms, such as the Unique Shortest Vector algorithm, requires a more subtle interleaving of quantum and classical operations, whereby only a subset of the qubits are measured, and the quantum memory cannot be reset between each quantum circuit invocation. In the paradigm of quantum circuits, this amounts to saying that the circuit is constructed on-the-fly, where later pieces depend on the value of former intermediate measurements. This is typically the case for algorithms that incorporate state distillation.

We learn from this that a usable quantum programming language should also incorporate a general-purpose classical programming language, in which classical pre-, post-, and intermediate computations can be specified. It is desirable that the integration between the classical and quantum parts of the language is as seamless as possible, but that a clear distinction still exists.

4. Our proposal: Quipper

We introduce Quipper, an embedded functional programming language for quantum computation. Quipper is intended to offer a unified general-purpose programming framework for quantum computation. It provides, among other things, a notation for quantum circuits, a notation for quantum algorithms, and a notation for circuit transformations.

Quipper was designed with correctness, scalability and usability in mind. It was originally developed in the context of IARPA's Quantum Computer Science program [10]. We have demonstrated Quipper's viability by implementing seven non-trivial quantum algorithms from the literature [2, 4, 8, 9, 13, 17, 23], as selected by IARPA [10]. In this section, we describe some of the basic features of Quipper's design.

4.1 Quipper is an embedded language

We implemented Quipper as an embedded language, with Haskell as the host language. Therefore, Quipper can be seen as a collection of data types, combinators, and a library of functions within Haskell, together with an *idiom*, i.e., a preferred style of writing embedded programs. See [5, Sec. 1.3] for a general discussion of the advantages and disadvantages of embedded languages in programming language design.

We chose Haskell as the host language because Quipper contains many higher-order and overloaded operators, whose implementation makes heavy use of advanced features of Haskell's type system, including several GHC extensions. Both Haskell and Quipper are strongly-typed functional programming languages, and therefore they are a relatively good fit for each other. Of course, there are some trade-offs. In particular, Haskell lacks two features that would be useful for Quipper: *linear types* and *dependent types*. Therefore, certain properties of quantum programs that could be checked at compile time by a linear or dependent type system must currently be checked at run-time. For this reason, a future implementation of Quipper may be equipped with a stand-alone compiler, or at least a custom type-checker.

4.2 Quipper's extended circuit model

The quantum circuit model, as usually presented (see e.g. [15, Sec. 4]), is only concerned with unitary gates and circuits. While this is theoretically sufficient, we found it to be a cumbersome restriction in practice. Quipper natively supports a larger class of circuits that also includes:

- Explicit qubit initialization and termination. This is useful, among other things, for accurately representing the scope of ancillas.
- Measurements, classical bits, classical gates, and classically-controlled quantum gates.

4.2.1 Ancillas and scope

Many quantum algorithms require ancillas, i.e., "scratch space" qubits whose state is (say) $|0\rangle$ outside of certain well-defined regions where the ancilla is being "used". In settings where all gates must be unitary, ancillas are usually treated as additional global inputs and outputs to the algorithm, which are assumed to be in state $|0\rangle$ at the start of the algorithm, and which the algorithm is expected to reset to $|0\rangle$ after each "use". The following image shows a circuit with two ancillas, and the regions where the ancilla is in state $|0\rangle$ are highlighted:

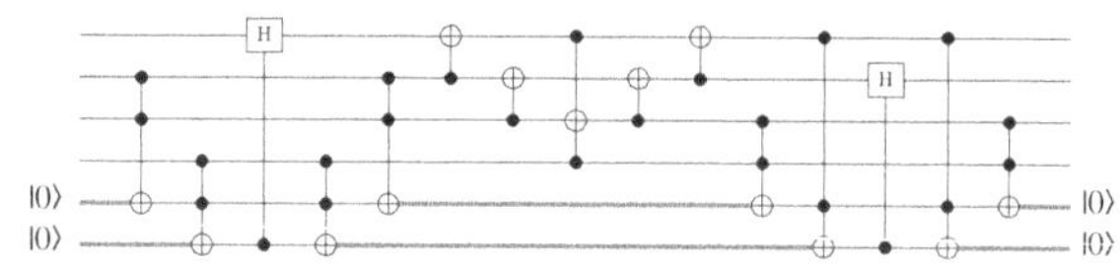

We refer to the regions where an ancilla may potentially be used as the *scope* of the ancilla. For a compiler of quantum programming languages, there are many potential benefits to tracking the scope of ancillas explicitly. For example, it would be wasteful for error correction to be applied to an ancilla while it is known to be unused (and therefore disentangled from the rest of the computation). Moreover, if an algorithm temporarily requires two ancillas at some point in time, and then again two ancillas at some later time, it does not actually matter whether the two later ancillas are "equal" to the earlier ancillas, whether they are swapped, or whether they are different ancillas altogether. For example, the following circuit is equivalent to the one above:

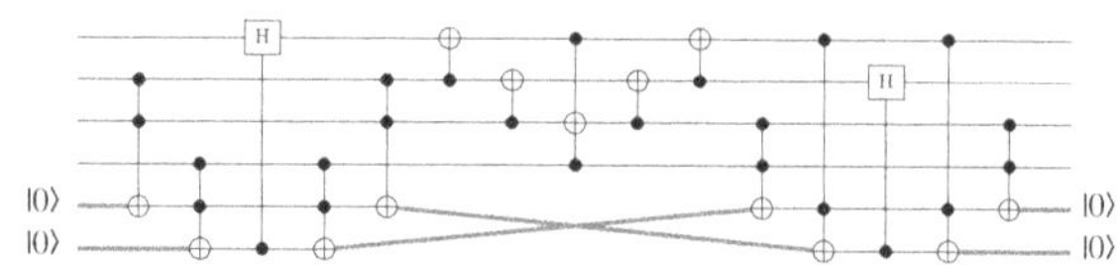

The problem of which particular ancillas to use from a "pool" of ancillas is analogous to the classical problem of register allocation, and is best left to a late compiler phase that is aware of the layout of physical qubits.

In Quipper's circuit model, we use the notation "0 ⊢" to denote the allocation of a new qubit initialized to state $|0\rangle$. Dually, we use the notation "⊣ 0" to denote the deallocation of a qubit that is *asserted* to be in stated $|0\rangle$. Here is the same circuit as above, represented with explicitly scoped ancillas:

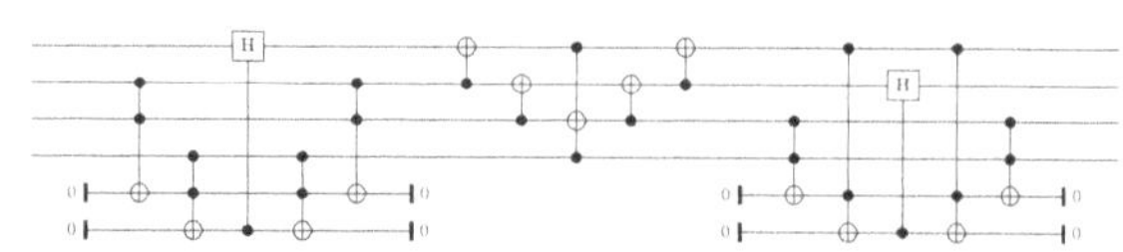

Keeping track of ancilla scopes also has an additional possible advantage. In certain physical machine models, such as photonics, it is generally better to work with "fresh" photons than with photons that have been in a holding loop. This is because photons have a relatively high dissipation rate. Scoped ancillas were used extensively in our seven algorithm implementations.

4.2.2 Assertive termination

As explained above, the gate $\dashv 0$ terminates (or deallocates) a qubit while asserting that it is in state $|0\rangle$. We call this an *assertive termination*, to distinguish it from the ordinary termination, denoted $\dashv$, which simply drops the qubit (therefore resulting in a possibly mixed state).

The concept of assertive qubit termination warrants some further thoughts. The first thing to note is that it is the *programmer*, and not the compiler, who is asserting that the qubit is in state $|0\rangle$ before being terminated. In general, the correctness of such an assertion depends on intricacies of the particular algorithm, and is not something that the compiler can verify automatically. It is therefore the programmer's responsibility to ensure that only correct assertions are made. The compiler is free to rely on these assertions, for example by applying optimizations that are only correct if the assertions are valid.

The second thing to note is that circuits containing qubit initializations and assertive terminations can never result in a mixed state, and are, in a suitable sense, unitary and reversible. More precisely, where assertive qubit terminations are used in a circuit, they determine a certain *subspace* of its domain: namely, the subspace of those states for which the assertions are true. Dually, the use of qubit initializations determines a certain subspace of the codomain: namely, the subspace of states that are reachable (or equivalently, in the *image* of the circuit). The circuit then defines a unitary bijection between these two subspaces. In particular, it follows that a circuit using n input qubits and n output qubits, and using any number of local ancillas, is unitary (provided, of course, that all termination assertions are correct, i.e., all ancillas are uncomputed correctly). For this reason, Quipper will, without complaint, reverse circuits containing qubit initializations and assertive terminations.

4.2.3 Mixed classical/quantum circuits

In the circuit model used by Quipper, classical and quantum data can co-exist. Classical wires (whose state is a classical bit), classical gates, and classically-controlled quantum gates can be freely combined with pure quantum gates. Measurement is a gate that turns a qubit into a classical bit. One reason for including these features is the construction of oracles, which we will discuss in more detail in Section 4.6.

4.3 The two run-times

4.3.1 Circuit generation and circuit execution

Because Quipper is (among other things) a circuit description language, Quipper programs have three distinct phases of execution: compile time, circuit generation time, and circuit execution time. We refer to circuit generation time and circuit execution times as the "two run-times". The phenomenon of having three distinct phases of execution is well-known and also occurs, for example, in hardware description languages (see e.g. [5]).

1. Compile time. Since Quipper is an embedded language, its compile time is the same as the Haskell compile time. It takes place on a classical computer in an off-line development environment (i.e., before specific algorithm parameters are known). The input to this phase is source code and *compile time parameters*. The output is executable object code.
2. Circuit generation time. This takes place on a classical computer in an on-line environment (i.e., when specific algorithm parameters are known). The input to this phase is executable object code and *circuit parameters* (for example, the size of registers, problem sizes, the size of time steps, error thresholds, etc.). The output is a representation of a quantum circuit.
3. Circuit execution time. This takes place on a physical quantum computer in an on-line real-time environment. The input to this phase is a quantum circuit, and possibly some *circuit inputs* (for example, qubits fetched from long-term storage to initialize circuit inputs, if supported by the physical device; classical bits to be used as classical circuit inputs). The output consists of circuit outputs (for example, classical bits that are measurement results; qubits to be moved to long-term storage, if supported).

Many quantum algorithms require an alternation between the second and third phases (circuit generation time and circuit execution time). In this model of execution, the classical controller generates a circuit, sends it to the physical device for execution, awaits measurement results, then generates another circuit, and so on. We note that this is the same as the usual quantum circuit model of computation. If, moreover, the physical quantum device has the ability to preserve qubits in long-term storage between real-time circuit invocations, then one can support a more general model of computation known in Quipper as *dynamic lifting*: this allows circuit outputs (for example, the results of measurements) to be re-used as circuit parameters (to control the generation of the next part of the circuit). An example of such a model of computation is Knill's QRAM model [12]. We believe that Quipper's abstract computational paradigm is general enough to support a variety of such concrete computational models.

4.3.2 The parameter/input distinction

We use the word "parameter" to refer to a value that is known at circuit generation time, and we use the word "input" or "state" to refer to a value that is only known at circuit execution time, i.e., the state of a bit or qubit on the physical quantum device, thought of as a "wire" in a circuit. The distinction between inputs and parameters must be taken seriously and requires special programming language support. For example, because inputs are not known at circuit generation time, if one would like to do an if-then-else operation conditioned on a boolean *input*, then one must generate the circuit for the then-part *and* the else-part. On the other hand, if the if-then-else operation is conditioned on a boolean *parameter*, then one only needs to generate the circuit for the then-part *or* the else-part, resulting in a smaller circuit.

Because of this distinction between generation-time parameters and execution-time inputs, the Quipper language has three basic types for bits and qubits, instead of the usual two:

- `Bool`: a boolean parameter, known at circuit generation time;
- `Bit`: a boolean input, i.e., a boolean wire in a circuit;
- `Qubit`: a qubit input, i.e., a quantum wire in a circuit.

A `Bool` is a parameter and can be easily converted to a `Bit`. The outcomes of quantum measurements are only known at circuit execution time, and are therefore Bits, not Bools. As mentioned above, the converse operation, converting a `Bit` to a `Bool`, is known as *dynamic lifting* in Quipper, and is usually an expensive operation, requiring circuit execution to be suspended while the next part of the circuit is generated.

The input/parameter distinction also applies to classical data types other than booleans; for example, there are integer parameters and integer inputs.

Moreover, some data is partly input and partly parameter. For example, if a quantum function inputs a list of qubits, then the *length* of the list is a parameter (affecting, for example, circuit size), whereas the actual qubits in the list are inputs. In Quipper terminology, when a piece of data has both input and parameter components, the parameter component is called the *shape* of the data.

4.4 Circuit description language

One can readily imagine a quantum programming language that operates by sending gate-by-gate instructions in real time to some physical quantum device. Indeed, this was the approach taken in [18, 19]. However, we found that this approach is not very practical when it comes to implementing larger-scale quantum algorithms. Quantum algorithms in the literature are often represented at a relatively high conceptual level, and many tasks in algorithm construction require manipulations at the level of entire circuits, rather than individual gates. Examples of such operations include inversion; iteration; ancilla management; circuit transformations (e.g., replacing one set of basic gates by another); and whole-circuit optimization. Another important use of whole-circuit manipulation is the automatic generation of reversible circuits from classical code. In our experience, it is perhaps fair to say that 99 percent of the quantum programmer's task is constructing and manipulating circuits, and only 1 percent is actually running them.

We therefore designed Quipper with the goal of supporting both gate-level operations and circuit-level operations in a natural way. Quipper combines a basic procedural paradigm for writing quantum functions "one gate at a time" with a powerful higher-order paradigm for whole-circuit manipulations.

4.4.1 Procedural paradigm

The basic philosophy of Quipper's procedural paradigm is that qubits are held in variables and gates are applied to them one at a time. Subroutines can be used to group gate-level operations together where the programmer finds it useful. When writing such procedural code, the programmer may safely pretend — although this is not actually true — that the variables hold actual physical qubits, and that the specified gates are applied to them in real time.

Thus, the basic abstraction offered by Quipper is that a quantum operation is a *function* that inputs some quantum data, performs state changes on it, and then outputs the changed quantum data. This is encapsulated in a Haskell monad called `Circ`. For example, the following is a simple quantum function that inputs a pair of quantum bits, performs some unitary operations (two Hadamard gates and a controlled not-gate), and outputs the modified pair of quantum bits. The code is shown on the left, and the generated circuit is shown on the right.

```
mycirc :: Qubit -> Qubit -> Circ (Qubit, Qubit)
mycirc a b = do
  a <- hadamard a
  b <- hadamard b
  (a,b) <- controlled_not a b
  return (a,b)
```

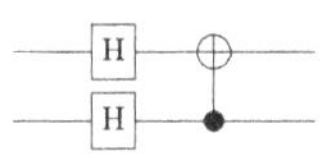

Gates can also be written in "imperative style", i.e., the return value of a gate can be ignored if it consists of the same physical qubits as the gate's input. For now, this is just a notational convention, but it could be formalized through the use of a *linear type system* in a future version of Quipper.

4.4.2 Block structure

Quipper provides operators for introducing block structure into circuits. For example, the operator

```
with_controls :: Qubit -> Circ a -> Circ a
```

can be used to let an entire block of gates be controlled by a qubit. The example also illustrates how subroutines (in this case, `mycirc` defined above) can be used to build up complex circuits from simpler ones.

```
mycirc2 :: Qubit -> Qubit -> Qubit
  -> Circ (Qubit, Qubit, Qubit)
mycirc2 a b c = do
  mycirc a b
  with_controls c $ do
    mycirc a b
    mycirc b a
  mycirc a c
  return (a,b,c)
```

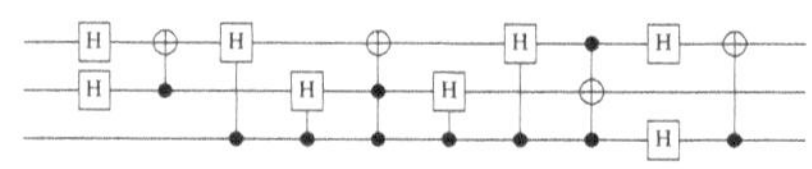

Another block structure operator provided by Quipper is

```
with_ancilla :: (Qubit -> Circ a) -> Circ a.
```

This operator can be used to provide an ancilla qubit (temporary scratch space) to a block of gates. The ancilla is initially in state $|0\rangle$, and the code is expected to return it to state $|0\rangle$ at the end of the block. The following example also illustrates the use of the `controlled` operator, which is an infix version of `with_controls`. The controls are specified to the right of the operator, and can be a tuple of qubits.

```
mycirc3 :: Qubit -> Qubit -> Qubit
  -> Circ (Qubit, Qubit, Qubit)
mycirc3 a b c = do
  with_ancilla $ \x -> do
    qnot x `controlled` (a,b)
    hadamard c `controlled` x
    qnot x `controlled` (a,b)
  return (a,b,c)
```

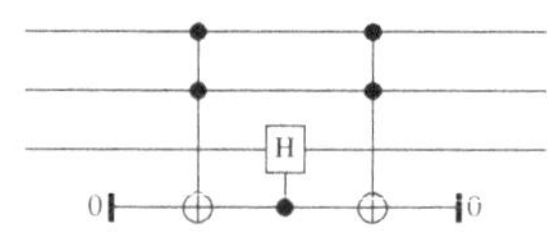

4.4.3 Circuit operators

In addition to the gate-by-gate circuit construction paradigm, Quipper also provides powerful higher-order operators that operate on entire quantum functions. The block-structuring commands of the previous subsection are examples of simple higher-order operators. Other high-level operators provided by Quipper include operators for reversing, iterating, and transforming quantum procedures, as well as a general mechanism for turning classical boolean procedures into quantum oracles.

The `reverse_simple` operator takes a quantum function and returns its inverse:

```
timestep :: Qubit -> Qubit -> Qubit
  -> Circ (Qubit, Qubit, Qubit)
timestep a b c = do
    mycirc a b
    qnot c `controlled` (a,b)
    reverse_simple mycirc (a,b)
    return (a,b,c)
```

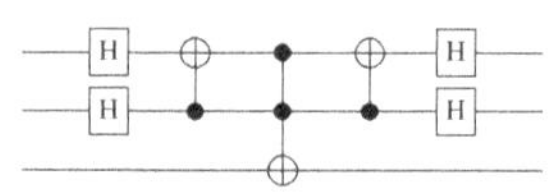

It is important to realize that reversing a circuit is not necessarily an operation to be performed just on the output of a program (say, by a separate tool). Many quantum algorithms require a circuit to be reversed in the middle of a computation, perhaps within a nested subroutine.

The operator `decompose_generic` decomposes a quantum circuit into a specified set of elementary gates. The inputs and outputs of the circuit are unchanged, so the resulting quantum circuit has the same type as the original circuit. The decomposition is achieved by first decomposing multiply-controlled gates into Toffoli gates, and then decomposing the Toffoli gates into binary gates [15, Sec. 4.3]. For example, the following decomposes the circuit from the previous example into binary gates:

```
timestep2 :: Qubit -> Qubit -> Qubit
  -> Circ (Qubit, Qubit, Qubit)
timestep2 = decompose_generic Binary timestep
```

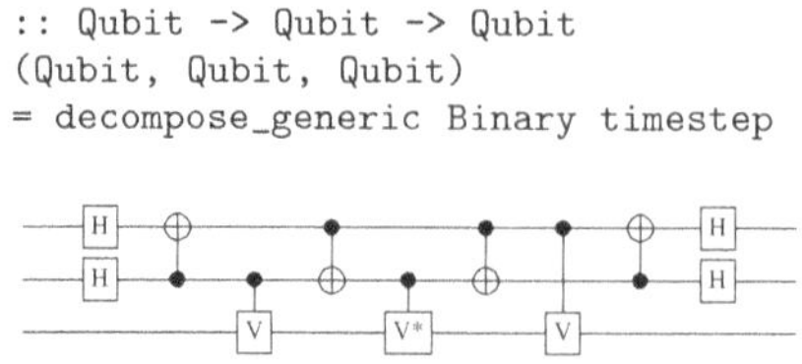

4.4.4 Boxed subcircuits

Quipper circuits can be very large; for example, in Section 5, we use Quipper to describe a circuit of over 30 trillion gates. In order to be able to store and manipulate such large circuits efficiently, Quipper provides a feature called *hierarchical circuits* or *boxed subcircuits*. The idea is simple: if a certain subcircuit is used multiple times throughout a larger circuit, the programmer has the option to "box" it. In this case, the subcircuit will be replaced by a single named gate, with a separate definition on the side. Boxed subcircuits can be nested, leading to a hierarchy of circuits. The Quipper operator for introducing a boxed subcircuit is called `box`. It takes a name and a circuit-generating function as its arguments. See Section 5 for examples.

4.4.5 Run functions

As we have already seen, in Quipper, the *description* of circuits is separated from *what to do* with them. Thus, the same subroutine can be used, for example, to run a circuit on a quantum device, or to construct and manipulate it in memory. We believe that this separation provides a useful abstraction to programmers.

What to do with a circuit is determined by different *run functions* for the `Circ` monad. For example, the function `print_generic` can be used to print a circuit in a number of available output formats (such as text, PostScript, and PDF). Quipper also provides a function `run_generic` to simulate a circuit (this is necessarily inefficient on a classical computer). The more specialized functions `run_classical_generic` and `run_clifford_generic` can be used to simulate certain classes of circuits efficiently; this is especially useful in testing oracles.

4.5 Quipper's extensible quantum data types

Following the strategy first presented in Altenkirch and Green's work on the Quantum IO monad [1], Quipper uses Haskell's type classes to provide an abstract view of the notion of quantum data. A type class can be thought of as a property that a type may satisfy; the property comes with a set of functions. The strength of type classes is that they can be defined by induction on the structure of types.

In Quipper, the notion of quantum data is represented by the type class `QCData`. The most basic members of this type class are `Qubit` and `Bit`, representing a quantum bit and a classical bit in a circuit, respectively. Expanding on this, tuples of quantum data are quantum data, lists of quantum data are quantum data, and so forth:

```
instance (QCData a, QCData b) => QCData (a,b) where ...
instance (QCData a)           => QCData [a]   where ...
```

Quipper also comes with a number of libraries defining additional kinds of quantum data. For example, there is an arithmetic library that defines `QDInt`, a type of fixed-size signed quantum integers, and a real number library defining a type `FPReal` of fixed-size, fixed-point real numbers.

Certain generic quantum operations can be defined at any `QCData` instance, rather than just qubits. For example, the built-in Quipper function `controlled_not`, which applies a controlled not operation to each corresponding pair of qubits from two quantum data structures, has type:

```
controlled_not :: (QCData q) => q -> q -> Circ (q, q).
```

Quipper also provides a type class `QShape`, which takes 3 arguments and represents the relationship between the quantum input, classical input, and classical parameter versions of a type, as described in Section 4.3.2. For example, we have

```
instance QShape Bool Qubit Bit
instance (QShape b q c, QShape b' q' c')
  => QShape (b,b') (q,q') (c,c')
instance QShape IntM QDInt CInt
```

Most of Quipper's built-in circuit generating functions natively use these representations. For example, the functions for initialization and measurement of quantum data have the type

```
qinit :: QShape b q c => b -> Circ q
measure :: QShape b q c => q -> Circ c
```

For example, we can use `qinit` to create a pair of quantum bits:

```
example = do
  (p,q) <- qinit (False,False)
  ...
```

4.6 Oracles in Quipper

Although appending gates to quantum circuits is an important part of many quantum algorithms, the most challenging part for the quantum programmer — and the biggest, in terms of number of gates produced — is often the implementation of classical oracles. Such oracles are boolean functions represented as reversible quantum circuits. They are problem specific and can be quite complicated. For example, Shor's factoring algorithm [21] relies on an oracle for computing the modular exponentiation $f(x) = a^x \pmod N$, where N is the integer to be factored. In the Triangle Finding algorithm, described in more detail in Section 5 below, an oracle is used to define the edges of the graph that is the input to the algorithm.

Quipper provides powerful facilities for programming oracles in a natural way.

4.6.1 Automatic generation of quantum oracles

The implementation of a quantum oracle "by hand" usually requires four separate steps. The first step is to express the oracle as a classical program acting on classical data types. The second step is to translate this program to a classical circuit for the given input size. The third step is to change the classical circuit to a quantum circuit, possibly introducing many ancillas to hold intermediate or "scratch space" values. The fourth step is to make this quantum circuit reversible, using the standard trick of replacing the function $x \mapsto f(x)$ by a reversible function $(x, y) \mapsto (x, y \oplus f(x))$, while also uncomputing any scratch space used by the function f.

In Quipper, all of these steps but the first one can be automated. Consider, for example, a very simple oracle that inputs a list of booleans and outputs their parity (even or odd). This can be naturally expressed as a functional program:

```
build_circuit
f :: [Bool] -> Bool
f as = case as of
  [] -> False
  [h] -> h
  h:t -> h `bool_xor` f t
```

The keyword `build_circuit` is built into Quipper (incidentally, it has been implemented in a very interesting way, using a custom pre-processor and Template Haskell [20]). Its purpose is to perform an operation that we call *circuit lifting*, automating steps 2 and 3 above. Specifically, the effect of the `build_circuit` keyword is to produce, at compile time, a circuit-generating function `template_f` in addition to the function `f`. The type of the function `template_f` is obscure, but can be made useful by passing it through Quipper's `unpack` operation:

```
unpack template_f :: [Qubit] -> Circ Qubit
```

The function `template_f` automatically produces a circuit computing the same operation as `f`. For example, when applied to a list of 4 qubits, it produces:

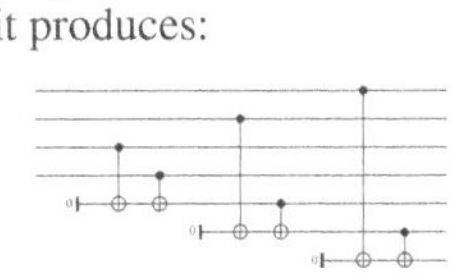

Note how the top four qubits are the inputs, the bottom qubit is the output, and the remaining two qubits are scratch space. Finally, the fourth step, to make the circuit reversible and uncompute the scratch space, is taken care of by the Quipper operator `classical_to_reversible`:

```
classical_to_reversible :: (Datable a, QCData b) =>
                 (a -> Circ b) -> (a,b) -> Circ (a,b)
```

For example, here is the circuit produced by

```
classical_to_reversible (unpack template_f):
```

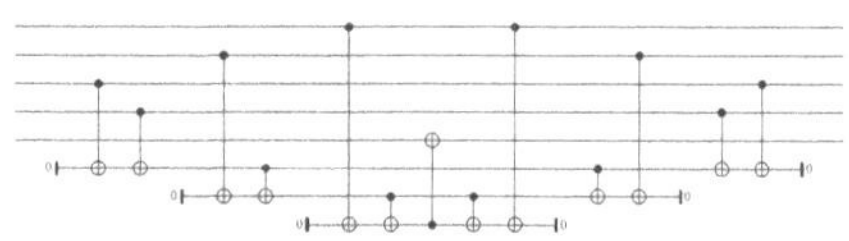

Note that in this circuit, the top four qubits are inputs, the fifth qubit is the output, and all intermediate ancillas have been uncomputed.

Quipper's circuit lifting operation is extremely versatile. We have used it to implement oracles containing millions of gates. For example, our implementation of the Boolean Formula algorithm uses an oracle that determines the winner for a given final position in the game of Hex. It uses a flood-fill algorithm, which we implemented as a functional program and converted to a circuit using the circuit lifting operation. The resulting oracle consists of 2.8 million gates. Similarly, our implementation of the Linear Systems algorithm makes liberal use of arithmetic and analytic functions, such as $\sin(x)$ and $\cos(x)$, which were implemented using the circuit lifting feature. The circuit created for $\sin(x)$, over a 32+32 qubit fixed-point argument, uses 3273010 gates.

5. The Triangle Finding algorithm in Quipper

We give some details of our implementation of the Triangle Finding algorithm in Quipper.

5.1 Background

An instance of the *Triangle Finding problem* [3, 14] is given by an undirected simple graph G containing exactly one triangle Δ. The graph is given by an oracle function f, such that, for any two nodes v, w of G, $f(v, w) = 1$ if (v, w) is an edge of G and $f(v, w) = 0$ otherwise. To solve an instance of the Triangle Finding problem is to find the set of vertices $\{e_1, e_2, e_3\}$ forming Δ by querying f.

The *Triangle Finding algorithm*, as described in [14] and [3], works by performing a Grover-based quantum walk on a larger graph H, called the *Hamming graph* associated to G. It is designed to find Δ with high probability. The algorithm is parametric on an oracle defining the graph G. In our implementation, the oracle is a changeable part, but we have implemented a particular pre-defined oracle specified by the QCS program. This oracle injects G into the space $\{0, 1, \ldots, 2^l - 1\}$ of l-bit integers, and each oracle call requires the extensive use of modular arithmetic.

The overall algorithm is parameterized on integers l, n and r specifying respectively the length l of the integers used by the oracle, the number 2^n of nodes of G and the size 2^r of Hamming graph tuples.

5.2 Top-level structure

The Quipper implementation of the Triangle Finding algorithm is broken down into six modules:

- `Definitions`: global definitions used throughout the algorithm.
- `QWTFP`: the quantum walk algorithm and its subroutines.
- `Oracle`: the oracle and its subroutines.
- `Main`: a command line interface.

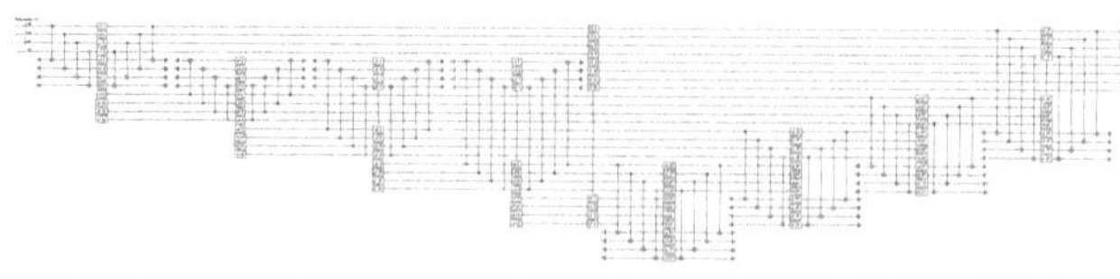

Figure 2. The circuit for `o4_POW17`

- `Simulate`: a test suite for the oracle.
- `Alternatives`: alternatives and/or generalization of certain algorithms.

These can be compiled into an executable program `tf`. Its command line interface allows the user, for example, to plug in different oracles, show different parts of the circuit, select a gate base, select different output formats, and select parameter values for l, n and r. Some usage examples are provided throughout the remainder of this section as we discuss our implementation.

5.3 Code samples

The quantum walk part of the algorithm is broken into about 20 subroutines, and the oracle consists of 8 subroutines. For brevity, we only present the code for one of each: `o4_POW17` and `a6_QWSH`. Although relatively simple, these subroutines are good illustrations of some of Quipper's key features.

5.3.1 The subroutine `o4_POW17`

The subroutine `o4_POW17` is an arithmetic function used by the oracle. It computes the seventeenth power of a quantum integer and stores the result in a fresh integer register. It proceeds by first raising its input x to the 16th power by repeated use of a squaring subroutine, and then multiplies x and x^{16} to get the desired result. In the following Quipper code, `QIntTF` denotes the type of quantum integers used by the oracle, which happen to be l-bit integers with arithmetic taken modulo $2^l - 1$ (not 2^l):

```
o4_POW17 :: QIntTF -> Circ (QIntTF,QIntTF)
o4_POW17 = box "o4" $ \x -> do
 comment_with_label "ENTER: o4_POW17" x "x"

 (x, x17) <- with_computed_fun x
  (\x -> do
   (x,x2) <- square x
   (x2,x4) <- square x2
   (x4,x8) <- square x4
   (x8,x16) <- square x8
   return (x,x2,x4,x8,x16))

  (\(x,x2,x4,x8,x16) -> do
   (x,x16,x17) <- o8_MUL x x16
   return ((x,x2,x4,x8,x16),x17))

 comment_with_label "EXIT: o4_POW17" (x,x17) ("x","x17")
 return (x, x17)
```

We note the use of the pre-defined Quipper operators `box`, `comment_with_label` and `with_computed_fun`. The operator `box` introduces a boxed subcircuit. The operator `comment_with_label` inserts a comment and some qubit labels in the generated circuits. Such comments have proven to be quite useful in reading large circuits. The operator `with_computed_fun` automates the reversing of intermediary computations: the first block of code (in this case, applications of `square` producing x^2, x^4, x^8 and x^{16}) is reversed once the second block of code (here `o8_MUL`) has been applied. Because the uncomputation of intermediate results is such a common operation in quantum computing, the use of operators like `with_computed_fun` helps to avoid unnecessary and error-prone code repetitions. All three of these Quipper features can be seen in

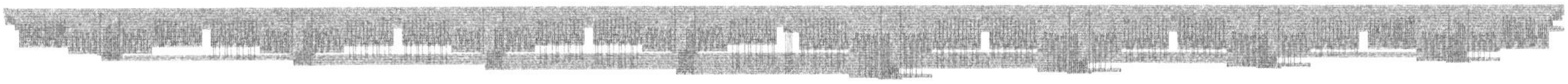

Figure 3. The circuit for o8_MUL

the circuit for o4_POW17 with parameter values $l = 4, n = 3$ and $r = 2$ shown in Figure 2. This circuit is produced by the command line `./tf -s pow17 -l 4 -n 3 -r 2`.

We note that some of the circuits shown here have too many gates to be legible in a printed version of this paper; however, in the PDF version, it is possible to zoom in to see individual gates.

In the circuit in Figure 2, the vertical strings of squares marked o8 represent invocations of a boxed subcircuit. Each of them denotes an invocation of the subroutine o8_MUL for multiplication, or its inverse. The full definition of o8_MUL is shown in Figure 3.

It is possible to inline the boxed subcircuits within o4_POW17, but the resulting circuit would be too large to be usefully included here. However, we can use Quipper's gate counting feature to provide some statistics about this circuit. The is done via the command line option **-f gatecount**. It will compute a gate count for each boxed subcircuit called by o4_POW17, together with an aggregated gate count for the circuit with all boxed subcircuits inlined. For $l = 4, n = 3, r = 2$, the aggregated gate count for o4_POW17 is:

```
Aggregated gate count:
 1636: "Init0"
 3484: "Not", controls 1
  288: "Not" controls 1+1
 2592: "Not", controls 2
 1632: "Term0"
Total gates: 9632
Inputs: 4
Outputs: 8
Qubits in circuit: 71
```

In words, this circuit has 4 inputs, 8 outputs, and uses a total of 71 qubits (including ancillas) and 9632 elementary gates. Of these gates, about one third are qubit initializations and terminations, and the remainder are controlled-not gates with 1 or 2 controls. In gate counts provided by Quipper a distinction is made between positive and negative controls. If a gate G has a positive controls ("filled dots") and b negative controls ("empty dots"), the gate count will read: **"G", controls a+b**. Moreover, a+0 is written a.

5.3.2 The subroutine a6_QWSH

The subroutine **a6_QWSH** implements a walk step on the Hamming graph. By definition, the nodes of the Hamming graph associated to G are tuples of nodes of G, such that two such tuples are adjacent if they differ in exactly one coordinate. **a6_QWSH** proceeds in two steps. In the first step, it arbitrarily chooses an index i and a node v of G. In the second step, it replaces a Hamming tuple T by an adjacent one T' by swapping the i-th component of T with v, and updates the register containing the edge information concerning nodes in T'. The corresponding Quipper code is the following:

```
a6_QWSH :: QWTFP_spec -> (IntMap QNode) -> QDInt
 -> QNode -> (IntMap (IntMap Qubit))
  -> Circ (IntMap QNode, QDInt, QNode,
           IntMap (IntMap Qubit))
a6_QWSH oracle@(n,r,edgeOracle,qram) =
  box "a6" $ \tt i v ee -> do
  comment_with_label "ENTER: a6_QWSH"
    (tt, i, v, ee) ("tt", "i", "v", "ee")
  with_ancilla_init (replicate n False) $ \ttd -> do
    with_ancilla_init (intMap_replicate (2^r) False) $
     \eed -> do
      (i,v) <- a7_DIFFUSE (i,v)
      ((tt,i,v,ee,ttd,eed),_) <-
       with_computed_fun (tt,i,v,ee,ttd,eed)
        (\(tt,i,v,ee,ttd,eed) -> do
          (i,tt,ttd) <- qram_fetch qram i tt ttd
          (i,ee,eed) <- a12_FetchStoreE i ee eed
          (tt,ttd,eed) <- a13_UPDATE oracle tt ttd eed
          (i,tt,ttd) <- qram_store qram i tt ttd
          return (tt,i,v,ee,ttd,eed))

        (\(tt,i,v,ee,ttd,eed) -> do
          (ttd,v) <- a14_SWAP ttd v
          return ((tt,i,v,ee,ttd,eed),()))

      comment_with_label "EXIT: a6_QWSH"
       (tt, i, v, ee) ("tt", "i", "v", "ee")
      return (tt,i,v,ee)
```

Here, the Quipper operator **with_ancilla_init** creates a list of n ancillas, whose scope is restricted to a local block of code. The circuit for **a6_QWSH** with parameter values $l = 4, n = 3$ and $r = 2$ is:

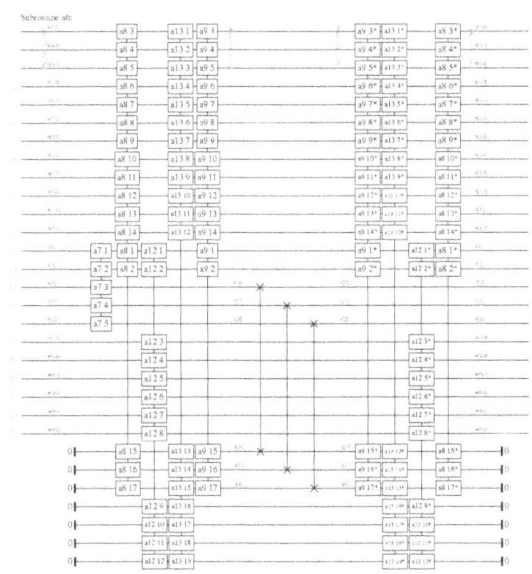

In this circuit, the first boxed subcircuit corresponds to the diffusion of the index i and node v. The remaining boxed subcircuits denote the qRam operations before and after the node swap.

5.4 Aggregate gate counts

The command line

```
./tf -f gatecount -O -o orthodox -l 31 -n 15 -r 9
```

computes the gate count for just the oracle, with parameter values $n = 15, l = 31$ and $r = 9$. It counts 2051926 total gates and 1462 qubits. The command line

```
./tf -f gatecount -o orthodox -l 31 -n 15 -r 6
```

produces the gate counts for the complete algorithm, including repeated quantum walk steps with inlined oracle invocations. On a standard laptop, this runs to completion in under two minutes and produces a count of 30189977982990 (over 30 trillion) total gates and 4676 qubits.

6. Comparing Quipper and QCL

To enable a direct comparison between Quipper and QCL, we implemented identical versions of the Binary Welded Tree algorithm [4] in both programming languages, using a hand-coded oracle. For further comparison, we also gave a second implementation of an equivalent oracle, using Quipper's `build_circuit` mechanism to automatically generate the (non-optimized) oracle from classical functional code as explained in Section 3.2. We generated the main circuit for the BWT algorithm for each of the three different implementations, using the same parameters in each case. The results are summarized in the following table.

	QCL "direct"	Quipper "orthodox"	Quipper "template"
Init	58	313	777
Not	746	8	0
$CNot_1$	9012	472	344
$CNot_2$	7548	768	1760
e^{-itZ}	4	4	4
W	48	48	48
Term	0	307	771
Meas	0	6	6
Total	17358	1300	2156
Qubits	58	26	108

Here "Init", "Term", and "Meas" refer to Quipper's qubit initialization, termination, and measurement gates. These are not directly comparable between QCL and Quipper, because Quipper explicitly tracks the scope of ancillas whereas QCL does not. "Total" refers to the total number of logical gates excluding initialization, termination, and measurement. "Qubits" refers to the total number of qubits used in each circuit, i.e., the height of the circuit.

It is apparent that the QCL code produces far more gates than its Quipper counterpart, even when the hand-coded oracle in QCL is compared to the automatically generated oracle in Quipper. Moreover, the QCL circuit uses twice as many qubits as the Quipper version with the same oracle. On the other hand, the Quipper implementation with automatically generated oracle uses more ancillas than QCL, but does so with fewer gates.

7. Conclusion

We have presented Quipper, a scalable functional quantum programming language. We demonstrated its usability by implementing seven non-trivial quantum algorithms, chosen to represent a broad range of quantum computing capabilities. The algorithms were implemented by a team of 11 geographically distributed Quipper programmers. Programming the seven algorithms required approximately 55 man months and resulted in a representation usable for resource estimation using realistic problem sizes. On this basis we conclude that Quipper is both usable and useful.

One of the issues left for future work in Quipper is the improvement of compile-time type checking. Thanks to its Haskell implementation, Quipper already catches many ordinary type errors at compile time. However, in the absence of a linear type system, certain properties, such as non-duplication of quantum data, must be checked at runtime. Developing a fully-featured type system is the next step in Quipper's development, and is a work in progress.

8. Acknowledgements

Thanks to Jonathan M. Smith for his helpful comments.

Supported by the Intelligence Advanced Research Projects Activity (IARPA) via Department of Interior National Business Center contract number D11PC20168. The U.S. Government is authorized to reproduce and distribute reprints for Governmental purposes notwithstanding any copyright annotation thereon. Disclaimer: The views and conclusions contained herein are those of the authors and should not be interpreted as necessarily representing the official policies or endorsements, either expressed or implied, of IARPA, DoI/NBC, or the U.S. Government. Supported by NSERC.

References

[1] T. Altenkirch and A. S. Green. The Quantum IO Monad. In S. Gay and I. Mackie, editors, *Semantic Techniques in Quantum Computation*, pages 173–205. Cambridge University Press, 2009.

[2] A. Ambainis, A. M. Childs, B. Reichardt, R. Špalek, and S. Zhang. Any AND-OR formula of size n can be evaluated in time $n^{\frac{1}{2}+o(1)}$ on a quantum computer. *SIAM J. Comput.*, 39:2513–2530, 2010.

[3] A. Childs and R. Kothari. Quantum query complexity of minor-closed graph properties. In *Proceedings of the 28th Symposium on Theoretical Aspects of Computer Science*, pages 661–672, 2011.

[4] A. M. Childs, R. Cleve, E. Deotto, E. Farhi, S. Gutmann, and D. A. Spielman. Exponential algorithmic speedup by a quantum walk. In *Proceedings of the Thirty-Fifth Annual ACM Symposium on Theory of Computing*, pages 59–68, 2003.

[5] K. Claessen. *Embedded Languages for Describing and Verifying Hardware*. PhD thesis, Chalmers University of Technology and Göteborg University, 2001.

[6] D. Deutsch. Quantum theory, the Church-Turing principle and the universal quantum computer. *Proceedings of the Royal Society of London, Series A*, 400(1818):97–117, 1985.

[7] S. J. Gay. Quantum programming languages: Survey and bibliography. *Mathematical Structures in Computer Science*, 16(04):581–600, 2006.

[8] S. Hallgren. Polynomial-time quantum algorithms for Pell's equation and the principal ideal problem. *J. ACM*, 54(1):4:1–4:19, Mar. 2007.

[9] A. W. Harrow, A. Hassidim, and S. Lloyd. Quantum algorithm for linear systems of equations. *Phys. Rev. Lett.*, 103(15):150502, 2009.

[10] IARPA Quantum Computer Science Program. Broad Agency Announcement IARPA-BAA-10-02. Available from https://www.fbo.gov/notices/637e87ac1274d030ce2ab69339ccf93c, April 2010.

[11] S. Jordan. `http://math.nist.gov/quantum/zoo/`. Electronic resource.

[12] E. H. Knill. Conventions for quantum pseudocode. LANL report LAUR-96-2724, 1996.

[13] F. Magniez, M. Santha, and M. Szegedy. Quantum algorithms for the triangle problem. quant-ph/0310134, 2003.

[14] F. Magniez, M. Santha, and M. Szegedy. Quantum algorithms for the triangle problem. In *Proceedings of the 16th annual ACM-SIAM symposium on Discrete algorithms*, pages 1109–1117, 2005.

[15] M. A. Nielsen and I. L. Chuang. *Quantum Computation and Quantum Information*. Cambridge University Press, 2002.

[16] B. Ömer. Quantum programming in QCL. Master's thesis, Institute of Information Systems, Technical University of Vienna, 2000.

[17] O. Regev. Quantum computation and lattice problems. *SIAM J. Comput.*, 33(3):738–760, 2004.

[18] P. Selinger and B. Valiron. A lambda calculus for quantum computation with classical control. *Mathematical Structures in Computer Science*, 16(3):527–552, 2006.

[19] P. Selinger and B. Valiron. Quantum lambda calculus. In S. Gay and I. Mackie, editors, *Semantic Techniques in Quantum Computation*, pages 135–172. Cambridge University Press, 2009.

[20] T. Sheard and S. Peyton Jones. Template metaprogramming for Haskell. In *Proc. Haskell Workshop*, 2002.

[21] P. Shor. Algorithms for quantum computation: discrete logarithms and factoring. In *Proceedings, 35th Annual Symposium on Foundations of Computer Science*. CA: IEEE Press, 1994.

[22] A. van Tonder. A lambda calculus for quantum computation. *SIAM Journal of Computing*, 33(5):1109–1135, 2004.

[23] J. D. Whitfield, J. Biamonte, and A. Aspuru-Guzik. Simulation of electronic structure Hamiltonians using quantum computers. *Molecular Physics*, 109(5):735–750, 2011.

Reconciling Exhaustive Pattern Matching with Objects

Chinawat Isradisaikul   Andrew C. Myers

Department of Computer Science
Cornell University
Ithaca, New York, United States
chinawat@cs.cornell.edu   andru@cs.cornell.edu

Abstract

Pattern matching, an important feature of functional languages, is in conflict with data abstraction and extensibility, which are central to object-oriented languages. Modal abstraction offers an integration of deep pattern matching and convenient iteration abstractions into an object-oriented setting; however, because of data abstraction, it is challenging for a compiler to statically verify properties such as exhaustiveness. In this work, we extend modal abstraction in the JMatch language to support static, modular reasoning about exhaustiveness and redundancy. New matching specifications allow these properties to be checked using an SMT solver. We also introduce expressive pattern-matching constructs. Our evaluation shows that these new features enable more concise code and that the performance of checking exhaustiveness and redundancy is acceptable.

Categories and Subject Descriptors D.3.3 [*Programming Languages*]: Language Constructs and Features—Patterns, Polymorphism; D.1.5 [*Programming Techniques*]: Object-oriented Programming; F.3.1 [*Logics and Meanings of Programs*]: Specifying and Verifying and Reasoning about Programs—Pre- and post-conditions, Mechanical verification

General Terms Design, Verification, Languages

Keywords JMatch; pattern matching; named constructor; equality constructor; matching specification; exhaustiveness; redundancy; modal abstraction; Java; data abstraction; subtyping

1. Introduction

Despite being an important feature of modern functional programming languages, pattern matching has not been adopted by most object-oriented languages. Data abstraction and extensibility, both primary goals of object-oriented languages, conflict with pattern matching. This work explores a language design for integrating pattern matching with object-oriented programming.

The following is a simple implementation of natural numbers in OCaml. The algebraic data type `nat`, with two constructors `Zero` and `Succ`, represents a natural number; the recursive `plus` function adds two naturals by matching them with one of three patterns.

```
type nat = Zero | Succ of nat
```

```
let rec plus m n =
  match (m, n) with
    (Zero, x)
  | (x, Zero) -> x
  | (Succ m', _) -> plus m' (Succ n)
```

This example illustrates two benefits of pattern matching in ML and other functional programming languages such as Haskell.

The first benefit is that patterns serve a dual role that enables algebraic reasoning and results in concise, intuitive code. A constructor such as `Succ` is also a pattern that matches the values produced by that constructor. Patterns can be nested to match complex values in a natural way, so a pattern like `Succ(Succ(n))` matches exactly the values constructed by expressions using the same syntax.

The second benefit is that pattern matching helps catch common programming errors. Patterns in a `match` expression can be checked to ensure that they are *exhaustive* and not *redundant*: that all possible values are matched by some pattern, and that every pattern can match some value. Without such checks, if the programmer forgot the first of the three cases above, the program could crash with an exception. With such checks, the compiler would warn that no cases match values of the form `(Zero, Succ _)`.

Relying on access to the concrete representation of data, however, makes the ML-style pattern matching inimical to data abstraction [30]. A value produced by one module can only be matched by patterns in another module if the second module knows the underlying representation of the value. Agreement on the concrete representation tightly couples the two modules in a way usually considered undesirable for large software systems. For example, we might initially implement natural numbers as above, then later want to change the representation to be an `int`. This change is not possible in ML without breaking client code.

To make pattern matching compatible with data abstraction, prior work has developed pattern-matching constructs that can be implemented by arbitrary code. Examples of this approach include views [30], extractors [5], and active patterns [29]. These mechanisms permit matching on deep patterns over abstract data, but sacrifice other benefits of algebraic pattern matching. There is no check that patterns are consistent with their corresponding constructors, so algebraic reasoning is weakened. Further, data abstraction interferes with checking exhaustiveness and redundancy.

The JMatch language [19] introduced another way to harmoniously integrate pattern matching into object-oriented languages, through *modal abstractions* that support multiple directions of computation. Modal abstractions allow a constructor and its pattern to be implemented by the same invertible computation, ensuring that they are inverses. Determining whether patterns are exhaustive or redundant, however, remained impossible under the data abstraction provided by JMatch. Furthermore, the added expressive power of patterns implemented by complex computations

```
1  class Nat {
2    private int value;
3    private Nat(int n) returns(n)
4      ( value = n )
5    public static Nat zero() returns()
6      ( result = Nat(0) )
7    public static Nat succ(Nat n) returns(n)
8      ( result = Nat(n.value + 1) )
9  }
10 ...
11 static Nat plus(Nat m, Nat n) {
12   switch (m, n) {
13     case (zero(), Nat x):
14     case (x, zero()):
15       return x;
16     case (succ(Nat k), _):
17       return plus(k, Nat.succ(n));
18   }
19 }
```

Figure 1. Natural numbers with data abstraction in JMatch.

means that programmers can accidentally omit patterns more easily than with algebraic data types.

The challenge for analysis of exhaustiveness and redundancy is to reason statically without violating data abstraction. The main contribution of this paper is, therefore, a way to extend modal abstractions with concise specifications that enable static reasoning about exhaustiveness and redundancy of pattern matching and, more generally, about the totality of computations.

Object-oriented programming involves more than just data abstraction; subtyping and inheritance are key ingredients supporting extensibility. For extensibility, different implementations of (subtypes of) the same interface should support the same patterns without clients knowing which implementation has been used. We therefore introduce *named constructors* that can be used as patterns in this way. We also introduce two first-class *or-patterns* that generalize both data-type constructors and or-patterns in ML.

We proceed as follows. Section 2 reviews modal abstraction in JMatch. Section 3 introduces mechanisms that improve the expressive power of pattern matching and its integration with objects. Section 4 describes new static annotations that support reasoning about exhaustiveness and redundancy. The verification procedure is explained in Section 5. Section 6 describes our implementation of an extended version of JMatch. Using various code examples, we evaluate its expressiveness, analytic power, and efficiency in Section 7. Section 8 discusses related work, and Section 9 concludes.

2. Background

Some background will be helpful on JMatch [17, 19], an extension to Java 1.4 that supports pattern matching and iteration through modal abstraction.

2.1 Modal abstraction

Section 1 observed that in OCaml, natural numbers cannot support pattern matching while being represented internally with an `int`. Figure 1 shows how this can be done in JMatch. The key idea is that JMatch methods may declare multiple *modes* that correspond to different "directions" of evaluation, analogously to predicate mode declarations in the logic programming language Mercury [26]. In addition to the ordinary *forward mode*, which acts like a Java method, a JMatch method may also provide *backward modes* which, given a desired result, compute corresponding argument values. Backward modes support pattern matching. For example, the method `succ` may be used in the forward mode to compute the successor of a number. As indicated by the clause `returns(n)` on line 7, it also has a backward mode that computes the number `n` for which the value given in `result` is the successor.

This implementation of `Nat` *is* more complex than in OCaml because the abstract view that supports pattern matching must be related to its concrete representation as an `int`. The methods of `Nat` demonstrates that JMatch programs can define patterns that both preserve data abstraction, because the field `value` is private, and are also usable outside the module that defines them. Lines 11–19 show how the backward modes of these methods can be used to implement the method `plus` similarly to the earlier OCaml code.

In general, a JMatch method implements a relation over its arguments and its result. Each of its modes is a different way of exploring the relation. For example, the `succ` operation is a binary relation on `Nat`: a subset of `Nat` × `Nat`. In each mode, some of the arguments or the return value are *knowns* supplied by the caller, and the others are *unknowns* to be solved for.

Individual method modes may be implemented by imperative, Java-like code, but one single declarative-style implementation of multiple modes is often more concise. As in each of `Nat`'s methods in Figure 1, a declarative method implementation is a boolean formula placed inside parentheses, directly expressing the implemented relation. For example, the equation `result = Nat(n.value + 1)` at line 8 exactly captures the `succ` relation.[1] For each mode of a method, the compiler generates an imperative algorithm that, given values for knowns, finds values of all unknowns that satisfy the formula. Thus, the backward mode often comes nearly for free, unlike with related approaches such as extractors [5].

Not only user-defined abstractions but also built-in types such as primitive types support modal abstractions. For example, integer operations such as + and - can solve for either of their arguments, given a result to match against.

2.2 Iterative modes

Modes need not be functions; viewed as relations, they may be one-to-many or many-to-many. A mode is *iterative* when there may be more than one solution to the unknowns for given knowns; the keyword `iterates` is used in place of `returns` to indicate such a mode. For example, the `contains` method of the `Collection` class has the signature

```
boolean contains(Object x) iterates(x)
```

meaning that its backward mode can be used to iterate over all contained objects. Using iterative modes, the Java collections framework could be made 35% more concise by implementing its operations, including iterators, as modes of relatively few methods [17].

2.3 Semantics and solving

The semantics of JMatch is defined as a syntax-directed, type-preserving translation to $\text{Java}_{\texttt{yield}}$ [18], which extends Java with *coroutine methods* in which control is yielded to the caller via the `yield` statement, much as in languages like C#, Ruby, and, originally, CLU [16].

JMatch supports imperative Java code, the translation of which is relatively straightforward. The interesting parts of the translation involve the solving of boolean formulas and pattern expressions. JMatch considers a formula or pattern *solvable* when the compiler can generate an algorithm that either finds satisfying assignments to unknowns or determines that there are none. In the latter case, the formula or pattern is not *satisfiable* but is still solvable. A formula or pattern may also be satisfiable but not solvable if the

[1] Note that the operator = is an equality test, which unambiguously *subsumes* its usual Java role as imperative assignment.

```
interface Nat {
  constructor zero() returns();
  constructor succ(Nat n) returns(n);
  ...
}
```

Figure 2. Natural number interface with named constructors.

```
1  class ZNat implements Nat {
2    int val;
3    private ZNat(int n) returns(n)
4      ( val = n && n >= 0 )
5    constructor zero() returns()
6      ( val = 0 )
7    constructor succ(Nat n) returns(n)
8      ( val >= 1 && ZNat(val - 1) = n )
9    ...
10 }
11
12 class PZero implements Nat {
13   constructor zero() returns() ( true )
14   constructor succ(Nat n) returns(n) ( false )
15   ...
16 }
17 class PSucc implements Nat {
18   Nat pred;
19   constructor zero() returns() ( false )
20   constructor succ(Nat n) returns(n) ( pred = n )
21   ...
22 }
```

Figure 3. Three implementations of Nat.

compiler does not know how to generate an appropriate algorithm for determining satisfying assignments.

As an extension to Java, JMatch allows side effects, although its new features encourage a declarative programming style. With side effects, programmers need to reason about the order in which computations occur. The JMatch solver therefore solves formulas in a well-defined order that is left-to-right as much as possible.

3. Pattern-matching extensions

We extend JMatch, adding new pattern-matching constructs to better support object-oriented programming and data abstraction and to increase expressive power in other ways.

3.1 Named constructors

In JMatch, pattern matching using procedures is successful only if the value being matched is either their result or one of their arguments. Therefore, a JMatch procedure can successfully match on its own receiver object (`this`) only if the procedure is a constructor or happens to return its receiver object as the result. Since a constructor belongs to a particular class, code using a constructor pattern is tightly coupled to that particular implementation. This tight coupling interferes with extensibility and code reuse.

To support implementation-oblivious pattern matching, we extend JMatch with *named constructors* that can pattern-match an object whose run-time class is unknown. Named constructors have an explicit name different from that of their class, and they can be declared in interfaces.

For example, Figure 2 shows a `Nat` interface exposing two named constructors, `zero` and `succ`. Figure 3 shows two partial implementations of `Nat`. The first (`ZNat`) corresponds to the implementation of Figure 1. The second is analogous to the OCaml version and consists of two classes: `PZero`, representing zero, and `PSucc`, representing the successor of its field `pred` at line 18.

```
1  class ZNat { ...
2    constructor equals(Nat n)
3      ( zero() && n.zero() |
4        succ(Nat y) && n.succ(y) )
5  }
6
7  class PZero { ...
8    constructor equals(Nat n)
9      ( n.zero() )
10 }
11 class PSucc { ...
12   constructor equals(Nat n)
13     ( n.succ(pred) )
14 }
```

Figure 4. Equality constructors.

Unlike ordinary constructors, a named constructor like `zero` can be applied to an object `x` of type `Nat` or of any subtype of `Nat`. It acts as a boolean predicate in this style of invocation. For example, `ZNat(0).zero()` evaluates to `true` because its implementation tests the equation `val = 0`. A named constructor for type T may be invoked without an explicit receiver object when it is used to pattern-match a value of type T. In this case, the receiver object is the value being matched. Finally, named constructors can be invoked to construct new objects of their class, as in the expression `ZNat.zero()`. In the forward mode, the fields of `this` are in scope as unknowns to be solved for either directly in the formula or via another constructor. For example, `val` in the equation `val = 0` at line 6 is solved directly by assigning zero to it.

3.2 Equality constructors

As written, the implementations of `Nat` in Figure 3 are incomplete. The problem is that the forward mode of `succ` in `ZNat` promises to construct a `ZNat` from an arbitrary `Nat` predecessor `n`. If `n` is not a `ZNat`, the equality test at line 8 between `ZNat(val - 1)` and `n` will fail. We fix this by adding an operation to `Nat` that allows solving for equality between objects of different classes:

```
constructor equals(Nat n);
```

Because `equals` is used to pattern-match on the receiver object, it becomes a special named constructor—an *equality constructor*—rather than an ordinary boolean method as in Java. If defined, `equals` is used for solving equality in addition to JMatch's default strategy of direct assignment. The code of `equals` for the classes implementing `Nat` is given in Figure 4.

Using `equals`, the equality `ZNat(val - 1) = n` is solved for non-`ZNat` objects `n` by invoking `ZNat.equals`, defined at lines 2–4. This method tests whether `n` is zero or the successor of some number. If the former, it returns `ZNat.zero`; if the latter, it invokes `ZNat.succ` recursively to retrieve the predecessor of `n`, which is bound to `y` by the constructor invocation `n.succ(y)`. Operationally, `ZNat`'s `equals` and `succ` interoperate to find successive predecessors until either zero or a `ZNat` representation (as in `PSucc.succ(ZNat(3))`, which is legal!) is encountered. Once `equals` converts `n` to a `ZNat` object, `succ` matches the internal representation of this `ZNat` object with `val - 1`, solving for `val`, which internally represents the desired successor.

3.3 Other extensions

A complete overview of the existing patterns in JMatch can be found in Section 2.2 of the JMatch technical report [18]. We extend the language with additional operators and a new pattern that increase expressive power:

```
1  public Expr CPS(Expr e) returns(e) (
2    Var k = freshVar("k", e) &&
3    (e, result) =
4      (Var(_),
5         Lambda(k, Apply(k, e)))
6    | (Lambda(Var vl, Expr body),
7         Lambda(k,
8           Apply(k, Lambda(vl,
9             Lambda(k, Apply(CPS(body), k))))))
10   | (Apply(Expr fn, Expr arg),
11        Lambda(k, Apply(CPS(fn),
12          Lambda(f, Apply(CPS(arg),
13            Lambda(Var("v") as Var va,
14              Apply(Apply(f, va), k))))))
15          where Var f = freshVar("f", arg))
16 )
```

Figure 5. Invertible CPS conversion.

- JMatch already has a pattern conjunction operator called `as`, which generalizes ML's pattern operator of the same name by requiring two arbitrary patterns to match the same value. We add a pattern *disjunction* operator, `#`, that combines two patterns into a single pattern that matches either or both of the two, and solves for the same unknowns. For example, the formula `int x = y-1 # y+1` (which should be read as `int x = (y-1 # y+1)`) generates the two solutions `x = y-1` and `x = y+1` when solving for `x`, and `y = x+1` and `y = x-1` when solving for `y`. Unlike Icon's alternation expression [9], a match is attempted against all alternatives even if one of them fails.
- We also add a *disjoint* disjunction operator, `|`, that behaves like `#` except that the patterns must be disjoint. A pattern constructed with this operator produces at most one solution when a value is matched against it, unlike `#`. The number of solutions is important because the pattern-matching statements require that there be only a single solution. The compiler verifies that patterns combined via `|` are disjoint. The formula `x = 1 | 2` would therefore be legal but `x = y-1 | y+1` would not if used to solve for `y`.
- A *tuple pattern*, written (p_1, ..., p_n), may be used to match multiple values at once. Tuples are not first-class values; uses of tuple patterns are equivalent to, but often more concise than, a set of equations expressed over the tuple components.

These new constructs add expressiveness. For example, the JMatch 1.1.6 release [18] includes an example of invertible conversion to continuation-passing style (CPS). The same two computations, CPS conversion and its inverse, are both expressed even more concisely in Figure 5 using the new pattern operators. In this code, the use of tuples enables the translation rules to be expressed essentially as inference rules. The pattern (p `where` f) on line 15 refines pattern p to succeed only when formula f is also satisfiable. The use of `|` ensures that CPS is one-to-one, though not total in its backward mode. Without `|`, the JMatch compiler would be unable to conclude that the three cases are disjoint and would raise the error that CPS is not one-to-one.

4. Static annotations for exhaustiveness reasoning

Several pattern-matching forms in JMatch can benefit from verification of exhaustiveness. As we saw in Figure 1, `switch` statements are one such form. Whether `switch` (e) {$\overrightarrow{\texttt{case}\ p_i : s_i}$} is exhaustive corresponds to (roughly) whether

$$\bigvee_{i=1}^{n} e = p_i \tag{1}$$

```
Nat n;
...
switch (n) {
  case succ(Nat p): ...
  case succ(succ(Nat pp)):  ...
  case zero(): ...
}
```

Figure 6. Redundant switch statement.

is a tautology. A second such form is the JMatch statement `cond` {$\overrightarrow{(f_i)\ \{s_i\}}$}, which executes the first statement s_i such that its corresponding formula f_i is true. For exhaustiveness, at least one such formula must be true. A third pattern-matching form is `let` f, which is equivalent to `cond {(`f`) {}}` except that variable bindings made in f are in scope for the remainder of the statement's block. The declaration `int x = 2` is in fact syntactic sugar for `let int x = 2`. Therefore, the formula f in a `let` statement should always be satisfiable.

In principle, exhaustiveness checking seems simple. Reasoning about exhaustiveness while preserving data abstraction, however, is challenging because the client code performing pattern matching is oblivious to the concrete representation (e.g., private fields) of objects. For example, given the code in Figure 6, the compiler does not know the implementation of `succ` and `zero` with which `n` will be matched. Even if it did know, using this knowledge would violate modularity, coupling correctness of this code to implementation choices internal to `Nat`. Moreover, given a value of type `Nat`, the compiler may not assume that `succ` and `zero` are the only ways to construct the value; there could be another constructor defined in `Nat` that could produce the same value. As a result, the compiler does not have enough information about the patterns to show that disjunction (1) is a tautology.

To enable the compiler to reason modularly about exhaustiveness, we must expose enough information to the client about the relation implemented by a method without exposing implementation details. Supplied with this information for the code in Figure 6, the compiler should be able to determine that all values of type `Nat` will be matched by some case. If that were not true (e.g., if the first case were omitted), the compiler should issue a warning. Also, in the code as written, the second case is redundant because anything matching `succ(succ(Nat pp))` must have matched `succ(Nat p)`. Redundant code often indicates errors in programmer's reasoning; the compiler ought to report this too. At the same time, the exposed information should let the compiler know that `zero` and `succ` are indeed disjoint and conclude that the third case and the first two are not redundant. Without such information, the compiler could generate a false redundancy warning.

To support static verification of exhaustiveness and other properties, three new kinds of concise and intuitive specifications provide the missing information: *class invariants*, *matches clauses*, and *ensures clauses*. As an orthogonal benefit, all of these specifications can exploit the new pattern operator `|` to prove patterns disjoint. We now explore these new features in more detail.

4.1 Class and interface invariants

One way to provide the information needed to determine exhaustiveness is as a *class* or *interface invariant*. For example, we can express that all instances of `Nat` match either `zero()` or `succ()` by adding the following invariant to the `Nat` interface, using `|` to assert that the two patterns are disjoint:

```
class ZNat implements Nat {
  int val;
  private invariant(val >= 0);
  private ZNat(int n) matches(n >= 0) returns(n)
    ( val = n && n >= 0 )
  ...
}
```

Figure 7. Private invariant and `matches` clause.

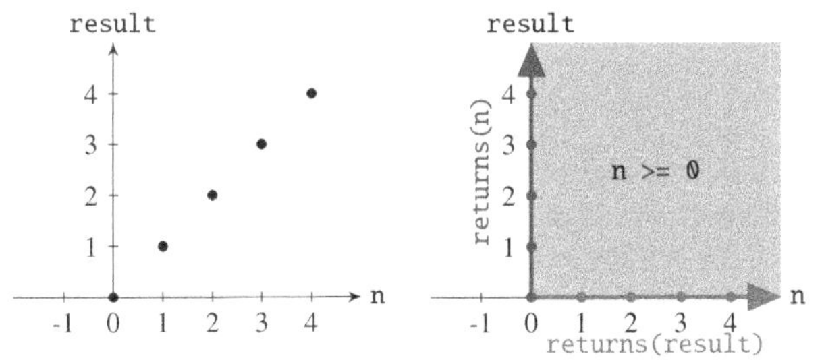

(a) actual relation (b) matching preconditions

Figure 8. The `ZNat` relation.

```
interface Nat {
  invariant(this = zero() | succ(_));
  ...
}
```

This example invariant shows how to obtain the exhaustiveness analysis provided by algebraic data types, while preserving data abstraction and allowing extensibility. New implementations of the `Nat` interface do not alter this invariant.

Class and interface invariants can be thought of as a kind of boolean-valued method whose value is always asserted to be true and whose implementation is visible to callers. Invariants may be given visibility modifiers (`public`, `protected`, or `private`). To maintain modularity, an invariant may only mention methods and fields that are at least as visible as the invariant itself.

Invariants not publicly visible may be useful for verifying the implementation of a class, such as the totality of the implementation of its methods. For instance, in the `ZNat` code of Figure 3, the field `val` cannot be negative. We can add a private invariant asserting this constraint, as in Figure 7. This invariant supports successful verification of the backward mode of the implementation of the constructor `ZNat()`, which should be total among all `ZNat` values. The invariant plus the first conjunct imply the second conjunct, `n >= 0`. The private invariant also helps verify both modes of `succ()`.

4.2 Matches clauses

One impediment to checking exhaustiveness is that a method mode may implement partial functions: on some inputs, its body might be unsatisfiable, in which case the method will fail rather than returning values for its unknowns. We extend the JMatch language with a way to specify when a method will successfully produce a result. This "matching precondition" is analogous to a precondition, but rather than specifying when a method call is legal, it specifies when pattern matching is guaranteed to succeed. The specification is conservative in that matching could succeed even when the condition does not hold.

For example, consider the constructor `ZNat()` in Figure 3. Any `ZNat` object must have a representation as a nonnegative integer. The corresponding matching precondition for the forward mode is `n >= 0`, meaning that for any nonnegative `n`, there exists a `ZNat` object matching that `n`. This matching precondition implies the constructor body, allowing successful verification of the forward mode. The backward mode of `ZNat()`, on the other hand, is total, corresponding to the matching precondition `true`.

Asking the programmer to specify matching preconditions for each mode would be verbose and repetitive, since different modes may share knowns (i.e., inputs). Our insight is that the programmer can write a single condition that captures when matching will succeed for the entire relation implemented by a method. We call this condition the *matches clause* for the method. Methods having no `matches` clause defaults to `matches(false)`, meaning that matching is not guaranteed to succeed for any input. The JMatch 2.0 compiler must extract the matching precondition for each mode from the consolidated `matches` clause. The extraction is described formally in Section 4.3; the rest of this section illustrates how extraction works for `ZNat()`.

The `matches` clause for `ZNat()` is shown in Figure 7. Figure 8(a) shows the actual relation implemented by `ZNat`; Figure 8(b) shows the `matches` clause, describing the relation consisting of integral points in the shaded region. This relation can be viewed as an approximation to the true `ZNat` relation. Informally, the extraction obtains the matching precondition by projecting this relation onto the axis corresponding to an appropriate mode, obtaining matching preconditions shown as thick arrows. For the forward mode (`returns(result)`), the relation is protected onto the `n` axis, obtaining `n >= 0`. For the backward mode (`returns(n)`), it is projected onto the `result` axis, obtaining `true`.

4.3 Extracting matching precondition from matches clause

In general, the body of a method implements some relation B and the `matches` clause specifies another relation M. Suppose that the method is a relation over a set of variables $\{\vec{x}\}$. For each mode $\mathcal{M}$ of the method, this set is partitioned into disjoint sets of knowns (inputs) $\{\vec{k}\}$ and unknowns (outputs) $\{\vec{u}\}$. We can then view the relations M and B as predicates over knowns and unknowns, $M(\vec{k},\vec{u})$ and $B(\vec{k},\vec{u})$, respectively. Given $\vec{k}$, the precise condition in which the body guarantees success is therefore $\exists\vec{u}.\ B(\vec{k},\vec{u})$. We call this formula the *precise matching precondition*.

For brevity, we define a function $\pi_{\mathcal{M}}$ that constructs the precise matching precondition for mode $\mathcal{M}$ by projecting an arbitary predicate B onto the knowns:

$$(\pi_{\mathcal{M}} B)(\vec{k}) \overset{\triangle}{\iff} \exists\vec{u}.\ B(\vec{k},\vec{u})$$

Given $\mathcal{M}$ and B, $\pi_{\mathcal{M}} B$ is a predicate on $\vec{k}$ that holds when $\vec{k}$ provides some way to satisfy B in mode $\mathcal{M}$ and hence to successfully pattern-match.

To preserve abstraction, reasoning about exhaustiveness must be done using the `matches` clause M, not B. Intuitively, if $M \Rightarrow B$, the body will be satisfiable whenever the `matches` clause holds; however, to require this implication would be unnecessarily restrictive. In the case of `ZNat` relation, for example, `n >= 0` does *not* imply the actual relation, and the only `matches` clause that does so while preserving abstraction is `false`. A more useful correctness condition is $M \Rightarrow \bigwedge_{\mathcal{M}'} \pi_{\mathcal{M}'} B$, where $\mathcal{M}'$ is ranges over declared modes. In other words, satisfiability of the `matches` clause only needs to imply satisfiability of the body in all the modes actually available. This can be visualized as expanding B (in the case of `ZNat`, the dots in Figure 8(a)) along all the dimensions corresponding to the supported modes (obtaining, in this case, the shaded area in Figure 8(b)).

It is easy to show that the formula $M \Rightarrow \bigwedge_{\mathcal{M}'} \pi_{\mathcal{M}'} B$ is equivalent to $\pi_{\mathcal{M}} M \Rightarrow \pi_{\mathcal{M}} B$ for each declared mode $\mathcal{M}$. This suggests that given the mode $\mathcal{M} = (\{\vec{k}\}, \{\vec{u}\})$ and the inputs $\vec{k}$, we should verify exhaustiveness by using $(\pi_{\mathcal{M}} M)(\vec{k})$ as the matching precondition. Unfortunately, the existential quantifiers in this formula make it ill-suited to automated reasoning. Instead, we construct a weakening of $\pi_{\mathcal{M}} M$ that does not mention existential quantifiers. Let us denote this weakened predicate on $\vec{k}$ as $\mathit{Extract}_{\mathcal{M}} M$.

The construction of $\mathit{Extract}_{\mathcal{M}} M$ proceeds as follows. We first convert the `matches` clause into negation normal form (NNF) so that the formula uses only positive logical operators over atomic formulas. We then use a variant of the usual JMatch algorithm for generating solutions to a formula. The first step is to reorder the atoms so that as many unknowns as possible can be solved from left to right. After this reordering, atoms that do not mention unknowns are left unchanged, as are atoms in which all unknowns are solvable in the left-to-right order. Atoms mentioning any unsolvable unknowns are dropped; that is, they are replaced with `true`. Any remaining occurrences of unknowns can be thought of as existentially quantified, but because each remaining unknown is solvable, it represents a solution expressed entirely in terms of knowns.

For instance, in the `ZNat` example, the atomic formula `n >= 0` is dropped in the backward mode because `n` is unsolvable, leaving only `true`. As another example, consider extracting a matching precondition for `x > 0 && y >= 0 && x+1 = y`, where `x` is unknown and `y` known. The formula is first reordered to allow solving for `x`, yielding `y >= 0 && x+1 = y && x > 0`. The first atom is left unchanged because it only mentions `y`. The second is also kept because it solves fore `x`, allowing the third atom to be retained as well. Because `x` is solved by the value `y-1`, the extracted precondition is `y >= 0 && (y-1)+1 = y && (y-1) > 0`, which is equivalent to `y > 1`. In general, `x` might be solved by a user-defined method. Section 5 explains how atoms containing such unknowns are handled.

Dropping unsolvable atoms is a heuristic, but it seems effective because such atoms are typically satisfiable for all possible values of the knowns. In general, however, dropped atoms might not be satisfiable, in which case $\mathit{Extract}_{\mathcal{M}} M$ may not be conservative. For example, if the `matches` clause were instead `y >= 0 && x < y && x > 0`, dropping the atoms `x < y` and `x > 0` would result in the extracted precondition `y >= 0`. The precise matching precondition $(\pi_{\mathcal{M}} M)(y)$ is rather `y >= 2`, since there is no satisfying assignment for `x` when $y < 2$.

$\mathit{Extract}_{\mathcal{M}} M$ can be used not only for analyzing exhaustiveness, but also for verifying that the method body implements its extracted precondition in mode $\mathcal{M}$. That is, when the method body is implemented as a formula, the compiler verifies in each mode $\mathcal{M}$ that for all inputs $\vec{k}$, $(\mathit{Extract}_{\mathcal{M}} M)(\vec{k}) \Rightarrow (\pi_{\mathcal{M}} B)(\vec{k})$. This ensures soundness for exhaustiveness analysis done using $\mathit{Extract}_{\mathcal{M}} M$. Verification is done using an SMT solver, as described in Section 6. For imperative method implementations, this verification is left to the programmer, though existing program logics might be used to obtain a verifiable logical interpretation in many cases.

4.4 Opaquely refining matches

In general, we may want to support modes in which precondition extraction fails because the `matches` clause does not or cannot capture the relationship among the arguments. For example, consider adding to `ZNat()` a *predicate mode* `returns()`, in which there are no unknowns. In this mode, the `matches` clause `n >= 0` does not correctly capture the matching precondition, yet the existing implementation is correct. To support such modes, `matches` clauses may be refined using the special opaque predicate `notall`. During precondition extraction, an atom $\texttt{notall}(\vec{x_i})$ is treated as unsolvable if any of the variables x_i is unknown, and is therefore dropped; if all of the variables are known or already solved, however, the predicate is treated as `false`.

Thus, to support a predicate mode for `ZNat()`, the predicate `notall(result, n)` is conjoined with `n >= 0` to indicate that pattern matching is not guaranteed to succeed when both `result` and `n` are known. This `notall` predicate corresponds to the refinement that converts the gray area in Figure 8(b) into just the black dots in Figure 8(a). The opaque `notall` is needed because this refinement cannot be characterized abstractly.

4.5 Ensures clauses

Matches clauses are a kind of multimodal precondition. To improve the precision of verification and exhaustiveness reasoning in JMatch, we add the *ensures clause*, a multimodal postcondition whose syntax resembles previous, unimodal postcondition specifications (e.g., [25, 27]). The `ensures` clause for a method is an abstraction of the relation implemented by the method, expressed in terms that client code can understand; that is, it only mentions names a legal caller could name, similar to the specifications proposed by Leavens and Müller [14].

Unlike the `matches` clause, the `ensures` clause must define an overapproximation (a superset) of the implemented relation. Thus, in any context where a method call is known to have succeeded, the `ensures` clause can be assumed to hold with respect to the values supplied as knowns and the values returned as unknowns.

Because the clauses for both `matches` and `ensures` are often identical, the syntax `matches ensures(`f`)` may be used as a shorthand for `matches(`f`) ensures(`f`)`.

5. Checking exhaustiveness and totality

JMatch 2.0 must show the exhaustiveness of various pattern-matching statements (`switch`, `cond`, and `let`). Similar verification is required for methods with a `matches` or `ensures` clause, since they promise to succeed in each mode when the extracted matching precondition is true, and since the postcondition must hold if the methods succeed. In addition, both arms of `|` must be verified as disjoint. In each case, the analysis constructs quantifier-free formulas that can be satisfied only if some cases are not handled by the appropriate patterns or formulas.

Section 4 described verification informally while pretending that formulas can be verified directly, e.g., by an SMT solver. This is not true in general, because formulas may contain user-defined predicates that must be treated abstractly.

To aid in constructing formulas to be verified the SMT solver, we introduce an intermediate representation language $\mathbb{F}$ that is similar to the language of quantifier-free logical formulas. Each formula is transformed to an $\mathbb{F}$ formula using function $\mathcal{V}_{\mathcal{F}}$ defined inductively on the syntax of formulas. $\mathcal{V}_{\mathcal{F}}$ takes a formula f to be transformed, along with the set U of unknowns to be solved in f, and an additional $\mathbb{F}$ formula F that represents the rest of the constraint. $\mathcal{V}_{\mathcal{F}}[\![f]\!]\ U\ F$ holds if (1) f is satisfiable and (2) F also holds under any solution to the unknowns in U satisfying f.

Because space is limited, the definitions of the translation are elided here; they are available in the technical report [11].

The Z3 theorem prover [3] is used to find a model satisfying these $\mathbb{F}$ formulas. This model can be used to construct a counterexample to explain the failure of exhaustiveness or totality to the user. The verification done by Z3 does not affect the dynamic semantics of JMatch 2.0; it only affects warnings given to the programmer.

In the remainder of this section, let μf be the set of variables declared in f.

5.1 Verifying exhaustiveness

Every `switch` and `if` statement can be written as a `cond` statement. Thus, verification of `switch` and `if` reduces to that of `cond`.

To verify a cond statement cond { $\overrightarrow{(f_i)\ \{s_i\}}$ else s }, we begin by asserting the invariants of all the known variables in the context. We then proceed case by case. The algorithm first checks whether f_i yields a solution to its unknowns. If not, the compiler issues a warning that this arm is redundant. In either case, the assertion is updated to rule out patterns matched up to the current arm. The else arm, if present, is equivalent to true.

Finally, the cond statement is exhaustive if the final assertion is unsatisfiable. If not, a counterexample is generated from a satisfying assignment, and a nonexhaustive warning is reported.

A cond statement can be used to refine patterns in the same way as a where pattern. Since both switch and if are syntactic sugar for cond, so can they. Let I be the invariant prior to the verification of a conditional case (f) {s}. We verify s with the stronger invariant $I' \triangleq I \wedge (\mathcal{V}_{\mathcal{F}}[\![f]\!]\ \mu f\ \texttt{true})$.

To verify let f, we check whether the negation of f is satisfiable. If so, a warning that the let statement may not always be total is reported to the programmer.

5.2 Verifying matching specifications

As described in Section 4.3, the bodies of methods are checked against the matches clause of the method to ensure that the body succeeds whenever the matches clause is true. Recall that this entails verifying the proposition $Extract_{\mathcal{M}} M \Rightarrow \pi_{\mathcal{M}} B$.

One complication is that the matches clause M of a method may refer to other methods. These method references may solve for unknown variables in M. In turn, these unknowns may be further referenced by other atoms in M, imposing additional matching preconditions.

The matches and ensures clauses of the referenced methods are used to resolve this complication. The matches clause imposes additional matching precondition to M, and the ensures clause constrains the values of unknowns that may be referenced later in M.

In the following example, the matches clause of method bar refers to foo:

```
int foo(int x)
  matches(x > 2) ensures(result >= x);
int bar(int y)
  matches(y > 0 && result = foo(y) && result < 4);
```

Now, suppose we want to extract bar's matching precondition for the forward mode, i.e., when y is known. The reordering and atom-dropping procedure does not alter the matches clause. This means bar(y) succeeds if y > 0, foo(y) returns a result, and foo(y) < 4. The invocation of foo in bar's matches clause succeeds if y > 2, and foo's ensures clause says result $\geq$ y. Therefore, bar(y) is guaranteed to succeed if y $> 0 \wedge$ y $> 2 \wedge$ result $\geq$ y $\wedge$ result < 4, which is equivalent to y $= 3$.

We now give the formal translation for $Extract_{\mathcal{M}} M$, where $\mathcal{M} = (\{\vec{k}\}, \{\vec{u}\})$. If $\hat{M}$ is the result of reordering and dropping atoms in M, and $\{\vec{\hat{u}}\} \subseteq \{\vec{u}\}$ is the set of unknowns remaining in $\hat{M}$, then we have

$$Extract_{\mathcal{M}} M \triangleq \mathcal{V}_{\mathcal{F}}[\![\hat{M}]\!]\ \left(\{\vec{\hat{u}}\} \cup \mu \hat{M}\right)\ \texttt{true}$$

Similarly, the precise matching precondition is defined as

$$\pi_{\mathcal{M}} B \triangleq \mathcal{V}_{\mathcal{F}}[\![B]\!]\ (\{\vec{u}\} \cup \mu B)\ \texttt{true}$$

With the above definitions, we are ready to formally define the verification conditions for JMatch methods. To verify a method

T_r foo($\overrightarrow{T_i\ x_i}$) **matches**($M$) **ensures**($E$)

in mode $\mathcal{M}$ with body B, we prove these two assertions:

$$Extract_{\mathcal{M}} M \Rightarrow \pi_{\mathcal{M}} B \qquad (2)$$

$$\pi_{\mathcal{M}} B \Rightarrow \mathcal{V}_{\mathcal{F}}[\![E]\!]\ \mu E\ \texttt{true} \qquad (3)$$

Assertion (2) says that if the extracted matching precondition for $\mathcal{M}$ holds, then B succeeds in generating a solution to all of its unknowns, which can be part of the arguments or declared in B itself. Assertion (3) says that if B succeeds in generating a solution, then the postcondition of the method holds.

For a method declared in an interface or declared abstract, and for each mode $\mathcal{M}$ declared in that method, the assertion

$$Extract_{\mathcal{M}} M \Rightarrow Extract_{\mathcal{M}} E$$

is proven instead. Since the matches clause must specify an underapproximation of the (unimplemented) relation and the ensures clause an overapproximation, this assertion says that by transitivity, if the matching precondition holds, then the postcondition should hold as well.

Failure to prove these assertions means that the method does not respect its contract. As a result, a warning for the violation is issued to the programmer.

5.3 Verifying disjoint patterns

JMatch 2.0 verifies multiplicity of formulas and patterns, ensuring that they generate at most one solution in non-iterative modes. Disjoint pattern disjunctions allow disjunctions to be expressed without generating multiple solutions, but this property must be verified. We also overload the | symbol as a logical operator; the formula f_1 | f_2 is a disjunction that may be used only if at most one of f_1 or f_2 is satisfiable. Let U be the set of unsolved unknowns in p_1 | p_2, and let p'_1 be the result of substituting each unsolved unknown in p_1 with a fresh variable, and similarly for p'_2. Patterns p_1 and p_2 are disjoint if $(\mathcal{V}_{\mathcal{F}}[\![x = p'_1]\!]\ U\ \texttt{true}) \wedge (\mathcal{V}_{\mathcal{F}}[\![x = p'_2]\!]\ U\ \texttt{true})$, where x is a fresh variable, is unsatisfiable. Similiarly, when | is used as a logical operator, formulas f_1 and f_2 are disjoint if $(\mathcal{V}_{\mathcal{F}}[\![f'_1]\!]\ U\ \texttt{true}) \wedge (\mathcal{V}_{\mathcal{F}}[\![f'_2]\!]\ U\ \texttt{true})$ is unsatisfiable.

Consider the examples in Section 3.3. The pattern 1 | 2 is disjoint because $x = 1 \wedge x = 2$ is unsatisfiable. The disjunction y-1 | y+1 is disjoint when y is known. When y is unknown, the verification procedure renames y in each arm to a fresh variable, yielding $x = y_1 - 1 \wedge x = y_2 + 1$, which is satisfiable, so the compiler generates a warning.

5.4 Soundness

As in most functional programming languages, we consider failures of exhaustiveness not as errors but rather as a reason to warn the programmer. Our goal is to help programmers be *effective*. Therefore, some unsoundness or incompleteness may be tolerable or even desirable if it rarely limits or annoys the programmer. Our verification procedures establish two main sources of unsoundness, possibly leading to erroneous warnings or lack of warnings. An obvious source is that JMatch is an imperative language, yet the reasoning procedures described here do not take side effects into account. We do not consider this a serious problem because JMatch encourages a programming style in which side effects are used sparingly and are encapsulated inside data abstractions. A second source of unsoundness arises from recursively defined methods, which are discussed in Section 6.2. In some cases, the compiler may report that it cannot prove exhaustiveness or lack of redundancy. This does not seem to be a problem in practice.

6. Implementation

We have built a prototype implementation of JMatch 2.0 by extending the JMatch 1.1.6 compiler [18] to add the new pattern matching

```
interface Nat {
  boolean zero() returns();
  boolean succ(Nat n) returns(n);
  ...
}
class PSucc implements Nat {
  Nat pred;
  boolean zero() returns() ( false )
  static PSucc create$zero() ( false )
  boolean succ(Nat n) returns(n)
    ( pred = n )
  static PSucc create$succ(Nat n)
    ( result = PSucc() && result.pred = n )
  ...
}
```

Figure 9. Translation of named constructors.

features in Section 3 and the static annotations in Section 4, and to use the Z3 theorem prover [3] to verify exhaustiveness, totality, and multiplicity.

6.1 Translating new features

Each named constructor `foo(...)` defined in class `C` is translated into two JMatch methods having the same visibility as that of `foo`. The first method is `boolean foo(...)` and contains all the modes where `result` is known. The other method is `static C create$foo(...)` and contains the remaining modes, whose body requires creating a fresh object. For named constructors defined in an interface, the latter translation is omitted. An invocation of a named constructor is also transformed to use one of the translated methods accordingly, with the exception of invocations appearing in invariants and `matches` and `ensures` clauses. These invocations are retained as a type object of the class and will be used directly during verifications. An example translation of `Nat` and `PSucc` is shown in Figure 9.

In the JMatch implementation, when a variable w of type T_w is matched against a value x of type T_x, only an `instanceof` check is introduced if T_w is not a supertype of T_x. To use the equality constructor, JMatch 2.0 further checks whether an equality constructor accepting one argument of type T_x exists in the implementation of T_w and invokes it on x if the `instanceof` check fails.

6.2 Handling recursion

The verification functions defined in Section 5 unwind all method invocations appearing in a formula being translated into assertions expressed in terms of the `matches` and `ensures` clauses of the methods. In general, these translations may not be well-founded when the `matches` and `ensures` clauses of methods are mutually dependent, or in invariants of mutually recursive types. Nevertheless, the verification may be successful without fully unrolling all facts about method calls and types. We use Z3's external theory plugin to implement lazy assertions by introducing interpreted theory predicates and functions. Our external theory for Z3 expands facts about type invariants and about matching preconditions and postconditions only when instances of the theory predicates are assigned a truth value. For example, if an instance of the predicate on procedure invocation is assigned false, the negation of the `matches` clause of the associated procedure is asserted on the procedure inputs. If the instance is assigned true, the `ensures` clause is asserted. An interpreted theory function is used to enforce the uniqueness of procedure outputs when the procedure is a (partial) function.

Because Z3 treats each asserted axiom as global, every instantiated axiom is asserted as an implication whose premise is the assigned predicate. Z3 also keeps track of every asserted theory predicate in its logical context, which allows proving exhaustiveness using class invariants without unrolling them entirely. To prevent unbounded unrolling, iterative deepening [12] is used to unroll as deeply as possible within a time budget. Since the theory will not further expand facts beyond the maximum depth, Z3 concludes that no satisfying assignment exists. If this happens when checking exhaustiveness, the compiler warns that it did not find a counterexample to exhaustiveness, but that there might be one.

7. Evaluation

Our evaluation of JMatch 2.0 aims to answer three kinds of questions:

- Is the extended language expressive? In particular, does it permit concise implementations? What annotation burden is incurred by programmers using the new verification procedures?
- Is the verification performed by our implementation effective on different kinds of code?
- What is the compile-time overhead of verification?

7.1 Code examples

We have evaluated our prototype JMatch 2.0 implementation on a variety of different coding problems. For each of these code examples, we have shown that the compiler correctly performs the three verification tasks described above, and we have measured the time taken by verification and compared it to total compilation time. To evaluate expressiveness, we have also implemented each example as concisely as we could using Java.

Natural numbers The implementations of natural numbers shown earlier in the paper are also used for our evaluation.

Lists A JMatch 2.0 interface `List` for immutable lists is shown in Figure 10. We implement this interface in four very different ways: the empty list (`EmptyList`), regular cons lists (`ConsList`), snoc lists (`SnocList`) in which elements are appended to the end, and lists with an array representation (`ArrList`), in which the underlying array is imperatively updated by `cons` but is shared as much as possible across multiple lists that record indices into it. To give the flavor of these implementations, the figure shows how the multimodal named constructor `snoc` is defined for `ConsList`. As the remaining code in the figure shows, these four list implementations interoperate smoothly, and list operations, even including `reverse`, can be used as patterns.

CPS We implement CPS conversion of a simple abstract syntax tree (AST) for lambda calculus; though Figure 5 shows only the key code, the implementation also includes AST classes.

Type inference We implement unification-based type inference over the same ASTs, augmented with type declarations. The code for type inference is placed within the AST node classes.

Trees A JMatch 2.0 interface `Tree` for binary trees is shown in Figure 11. We implement the AVL tree based on this interface. The `rebalance` method, also shown in the figure, returns the balanced version of the input subtree having `v` as the value at the root and `l` and `r` as its children. The invariant of `Tree` and the `ensures` clause of `branch` are crucial for the JMatch 2.0 compiler to verify that the formula in `rebalance` covers all the possible input subtrees. Checking the disjoint disjunctions also ensures that there is only one way to match each tree.

Collections We convert the prior JMatch reimplementation of the key collection classes from the Java collections framework [17] into JMatch 2.0. This code base includes implementations of various data structures: hash tables, red-black trees, and resizable arrays.

```
interface List {
  invariant(this = nil() | cons(_, _));
  constructor nil() matches(notall(result));
  constructor cons(Object hd, List tl)
    matches(notall(result)) returns(hd, tl);
  constructor snoc(List hd, Object tl)
    matches ensures(cons(_, _)) returns(hd, tl);
  constructor equals(List l);
  constructor reverse(List l) matches(true) returns(l);
  boolean contains(Object elem) iterates(elem);
  int size();
}
constructor snoc(List h, Object t) // in ConsList
  matches ensures(cons(_, _)) returns(h, t) (
    h = EmptyList.nil() && cons(t, h)
  | h = cons(Object hh, List ht) && cons(hh, snoc(ht, t))
)
static int length(List l) {
  switch (l) {
    case nil(): return 0;
    case snoc(List t, _): return length(t) + 1;
    case cons(_, List t): return length(t) + 1;
      // detected as redundant
  }
}
List l = EmptyList.nil();  // l = []
l = SnocList.cons(0, l);   // l = [[], 0]
l = ConsList.snoc(l, 1);   // l = [0, [1, []]]
l =  ArrList.snoc(l, 2);   // l = [0, 1, 2]
l = ConsList.cons(3, l);   // l = [3, [0, 1, 2]]
let l = reverse(List r1);  //r1 = [2, [1, [0, [3, []]]]]
l =  ArrList.cons(4, l);   // l = [4, 3, 0, 1, 2]
let l = reverse(List r2);  //r2 = [2, 1, 0, 3, 4]
```

Figure 10. List interface and sample usage.

Implementation	JMatch	Java	w/o verif	w/ verif
Nat	41 (21)	29	0.100	0.104
PZero	85	189	0.258	0.331
PSucc	98	226	0.280	0.435
ZNat	161	319	0.377	0.459
List	114 (72)	91	0.129	0.123
EmptyList	164	455	0.416	0.510
ConsList	309	1007	0.807	2.47
SnocList	311	1006	1.05	3.36
ArrList	473	1208	0.864	1.90
Expr	96 (57)	80	0.710	0.846
Variable	192	434	0.689	0.852
Lambda	239	500	1.20	1.52
TypedLambda	86	92	1.38	1.57
Apply	232	506	1.15	2.31
CPS	325	1279	7.88	8.37
Type	154	187	0.218	0.307
BaseType	73	163	0.350	0.443
ArrowType	82	189	0.357	0.444
UnknownType	154	245	0.372	0.490
Environment	211	310	0.695	0.862
Tree	114 (44)	69	0.165	0.170
Leaf	124	351	0.420	0.510
Branch	202	553	0.529	0.682
AVLTree	439	720	2.84	9.01
ArrayList	773	1098*	1.67	1.81
LinkedList	886	1232*	2.00	2.20
HashMap	1082	1874*	3.41	3.66
TreeMap	3606	3955*	5.90	6.43

Table 1. The number of tokens for implementations in JMatch 2.0 versus Java. Interface token counts are reported both with and without (in parentheses) `matches` and `ensures` clauses. Verification overhead is given in seconds as the average of 24 runs, with a standard deviation of at most 15%. Some comparisons (*) are versus a PolyJ [21] implementation that is more concise than the Java one. For example, the PolyJ `TreeMap` is 20% shorter than the Java equivalent [17].

7.2 Expressiveness

We can assess the expressiveness of JMatch 2.0 by comparing the number of language tokens needed to implement each of the examples. The resulting token counts shown in Table 1 indicate that JMatch 2.0 code is considerably more concise than in Java: 42.9% shorter on average. This conciseness is largely due to the JMatch support for modal abstraction and for equality constructors.

7.3 Effectiveness

There are three new verification tasks. First, `switch` and related constructs (`let`, `cond`, etc.) should be exhaustive. Second, method implementations must be correct with respect to both their declared `matches` clause and their `ensures` clause. Third, disjoint disjunctions must indeed be disjoint, to verify multiplicity.

All of the examples shown in the table, and all prior examples shown in the paper, are successfully verified for exhaustiveness, (non-)redundancy, and multiplicity. The compiler caught several subtle exhaustiveness bugs during development of this code, such as incorrect order of arguments to methods and invocation to an unexpected implementation of overloaded or overridden methods. In case of `TreeMap`, the absence of red-black tree invariants results in a nonexhaustive warning in the `balance` method.

7.4 Efficiency

Table 1 shows that verification time is reasonable for all of the code examples, even with our unoptimized prototype implementation. The reported numbers include compilation time of dependencies but exclude the overhead of initializing the compiler (689 ms) and the Z3 solver (680 ms). On average, the verification overhead on the evaluated code is 37.5% compared to the regular compilation time.

The speed of verification is not surprising, because verification is performed one method at a time. Verification is simple and tractable because the abstraction mechanisms we introduced to JMatch allow both programmers and the SMT solver to reason locally about code.

Because JMatch 2.0 does not significantly change the dynamic semantics of JMatch, the translation to Java is essentially unchanged. The performance of the compiled programs is therefore similar to one in the previous evaluation [17].

8. Related work

Integrating pattern matching with objects and data abstraction has been the subject of quite a few research efforts.

Case classes in the Scala programming language [22], as in Pizza [23], provide pattern matching by allowing case-class constructors in case arms. Scala uses *sealed classes* to limit the number of case classes that can inherit them. This makes exhaustiveness easy to verify, but sacrifices extensibility because only one implementation is allowed per declaration of a sealed class. Our `invariant` declaration achieves the same level of exhaustiveness checking but allows programmers to extend classes freely. Closely related approaches include extensible algebraic data types [32] and polymorphic variants [8], which support some extensibility and

```
interface Tree {
  invariant(this = leaf() | branch(_,_,_));
  constructor leaf() matches(height() = 0) ensures(height() = 0);
  constructor branch(Tree l, int v, Tree r) matches(height() > 0) ensures(height() > 0 &&
      (height() = l.height() + 1 && height() > r.height() || height() > l.height() && height() = r.height() + 1))
    returns(l, v, r);
  int height() ensures(result >= 0);
}

static Tree rebalance(Tree l, int v, Tree r) matches(true) (                                 // in AVLTree
  result = Branch(Branch(Tree a, int x, Tree b), int y, Branch(Tree c, int z, Tree d))
    && ( l.height() - r.height() > 1 && d = r && z = v                                        // rotation from left
        && ( l = branch(Tree ll, y, c) && ll = branch(a, x, b) && ll.height() >= c.height()   // case 1: single rot.
           | l = branch(a, x, Tree lr) && lr = branch(b, y, c) && a.height() < lr.height())  // case 2: double rot.
      | r.height() - l.height() > 1 && a = l && x = v                                         // rotation from right
        && ( r = branch(Tree rl, z, d) && rl = branch(b, y, c) && rl.height() > d.height()   // case 3: double rot.
           | r = branch(b, y, Tree rr) && rr = branch(c, z, d) && b.height() <= rr.height())) // case 4: single rot.
  | abs(l.height() - r.height()) <= 1 && result = Branch(l, v, r)
)
```

Figure 11. Tree interface and the AVL tree `rebalance` method, which uses the interface to check for totality.

deep pattern matching, but tie pattern matching to the data representation more than is ideal.

Wadler's views [30] were an early, influential generalization of pattern matching. Views require an explicitly defined bijection between the abstract view and the representation. Unlike in our language, views do not reconcile pattern matching with subtyping and do not allow matching without knowing the identity of the implementation.

Extractors are introduced in [5] as an alternative to case classes that is compatible with data abstraction. Each extractor contains `apply` and `unapply` methods, called implicitly during construction and pattern matching. There is no check that these methods are inverses, however. Modal abstractions in JMatch are less verbose and reduce the chance of such errors. No exhaustiveness checking was proposed for extractors. Dotta et al. [4] verify extractors by relying on sealed classes, and support user-defined constructor patterns. Their work does check for pattern disjointness; abstraction prevents us from making this guarantee.

Active patterns in F# [29] are similar to extractors, but support exhaustiveness checking by allowing the declaration that a set of patterns is complete. Because they offer only a backward mode, they do not support algebraic reasoning in the same way as modal abstractions. They also do not support object-oriented extensibility.

The RINV language of Wang et al. [31] also uses invertible computation to implement pattern matching that is compatible with data abstraction. Rather than extracting computations from a logical characterization of the computation, RINV instead uses a restricted language for abstraction functions that guarantees invertibility. These functions are bidirectional rather than fully multimodal and do not support iterative modes. RINV analyzes exhaustiveness via specifications of complete sets of constructors, but does not verify these specifications. RINV supports neither subtyping nor extensibility.

Suter et al. [27] also use abstraction functions to reduce algebraic data types to abstract values such as multisets, and use known theories of these abstract values to reason about data types. Methods may be annotated with a postcondition in terms of abstraction functions. Leon [28] extends this reasoning to recursive programs. Used in conjunction with sealed classes, these decision procedures assist in a more precise analysis of pattern exhaustiveness by taking type refinement into account. These decision procedures do not support modal abstraction.

An orthogonal approach to integrating pattern matching into object-oriented languages is predicate dispatch [6, 20], which extends multimethods with the ability to choose an implementation based on general predicates over the arguments. Predicate dispatch appears to be largely orthogonal and complementary to the pattern matching mechanisms described here. The predicates in prior work on predicate dispatch are, however, less expressive than those we have explored here. OOMatch [24] uses pattern matching in predicate dispatch. Its deconstructors are similar to the backward mode of JMatch constructors. OOMatch's pattern matching differs in that it can appear only in method headers as part of predicate dispatch, and no separation of specification and implementation is provided. HydroJ [15] uses predicate dispatch to express extensible communication patterns in distributed systems; however, pattern matching is done over concrete data structures, tagged trees.

Matchete [10] extends Java with pattern matching operators similar to extractors, but matches on regular expressions and other specialized expressions. It does not analyze exhaustiveness.

The Thorn language integrates patterns to make code more concise and robust [1]. Its rich set of patterns includes boolean combinations of patterns, general list patterns, regular expressions, and first-class patterns. First-class patterns in Thorn provide pattern abstraction that supports evolution of the data structure used in pattern matching, but Thorn does not support multiple implementations. As a dynamic language, Thorn does not check exhaustiveness.

Harmony and the Boomerang language [2, 7] support bidirectional computations over trees and strings through domain-specific lens combinators. The types in these languages support reasoning about the totality of transformations in these domains, but data abstraction is not a feature of these languages.

One focus of research on pattern matching has been on how to generate efficient code that shares computation across different patterns (e.g., [13]). Such optimizations are orthogonal to this work.

9. Conclusions

A clean integration of pattern matching into the object-oriented setting could simplify many programming tasks. Prior work has not managed to provide expressive pattern matching with strong data abstraction and subtyping, along with statically checked exhaustiveness. This is the first work that manages to combine these important features. We improved the integration of pattern matching with object-oriented programming, yet showed that even with this more powerful pattern matching, it is possible to reason statically about exhaustiveness, redundancy, totality, and multiplicity.

The most important insight was that programmers need to be able to specify the precondition for successful pattern matching in an abstract way. We showed that it is possible to do this while keeping the annotation burden low, by automatically extracting matching preconditions. The specification techniques introduced may be helpful for other models of multidirectional computation.

Acknowledgments

Soam Vasani and Denis Bueno got the JMatch exhaustiveness project off to a good start. Leo de Moura helped with using Z3. Ross Tate, Owen Arden, Aslan Askarov, Jed Liu, Harry Terkelsen, Mark Reitblatt, Robert Soulé, Mike George, and Danfeng Zhang offered many helpful suggestions for the presentation.

This research was supported in part by Office of Naval Research Grants N00014-09-1-0652 and N00014-13-1-0089, and by a grant administered by the Air Force Research Laboratory.

References

[1] Bard Bloom and Martin J. Hirzel. Robust scripting via patterns. In *Proc. 8th symposium on Dynamic languages (DLS)*, pp. 29–40, 2012.

[2] Aaron Bohannon, J. Nathan Foster, Benjamin C. Pierce, Alexandre Pilkiewicz, and Alan Schmitt. Boomerang: Resourceful lenses for string data. In *Proc. 35th ACM Symposium on Principles of Programming Languages (POPL)*, pp. 407–419, January 2008.

[3] Leonardo de Moura and Nikolaj Bjørner. Z3: an efficient SMT solver. In *Proceedings of the Theory and Practice of Software, 14th Int'l Conf. on Tools and Algorithms for the Construction and Analysis of Systems*, pp. 337–340, 2008.

[4] Mirco Dotta, Philippe Suter, and Viktor Kuncak. On static analysis for expressive pattern matching. Technical report, École Polytechnique Fédérale de Lausanne, February 2008.

[5] Burak Emir, Martin Odersky, and John Williams. Matching objects with patterns. In Erik Ernst, editor, *Proc. 21st European Conf. on Object-Oriented Programming*, volume 4609 of *Lecture Notes in Computer Science*, pp. 273–298. Springer Berlin Heidelberg, 2007.

[6] Michael Ernst, Craig Kaplan, and Craig Chambers. Predicate dispatching: A unified theory of dispatch. In *Proc. 12th European Conf. on Object-Oriented Programming*, pp. 186–211, 1998.

[7] J. Nathan Foster, Michael B. Greenwald, Jonathan T. Moore, Benjamin C. Pierce, and Alan Schmitt. Combinators for bidirectional tree transformations: A linguistic approach to the view-update problem. *ACM Trans. Program. Lang. Syst.*, 29(3), May 2007.

[8] Jacques Garrigue. Typing deep pattern-matching in presence of polymorphic variants. In *JSSST Workshop on Programming and Programming Languages*, 2004.

[9] Ralph E. Griswold, David R. Hanson, and John T. Korb. Generators in Icon. *ACM Transaction on Programming Languages and Systems*, 3(2):144–161, April 1981.

[10] Martin Hirzel, Nathaniel Nystrom, Bard Bloom, and Jan Vitek. Matchete: Paths through the pattern matching jungle. In *Proc. 10th Int'l Conf. on Practical Aspects of Declarative Languages*, pp. 150–166, 2008.

[11] Chinawat Isradisaikul and Andrew C. Myers. Reconciling exhaustive pattern matching with objects. Technical report, Computing and Information Science, Cornell University, March 2013. `http://hdl.handle.net/1813/33123`.

[12] Richard E. Korf. Depth-first iterative-deepening: an optimal admissible tree search. *Artificial Intelligence*, 27(1):97–109, September 1985.

[13] Fabrice Le Fessant and Luc Maranget. Optimizing pattern matching. In *Proc. 6th ACM SIGPLAN Int'l Conf. on Functional Programming*, pp. 26–37, 2001.

[14] Gary T. Leavens and Peter Müller. Information hiding and visibility in interface specifications. In *Proc. 33rd Int'l Conf. on Software Engineering (ICSE)*, pp. 385–395, 2007.

[15] Keunwoo Lee, Anthony LaMarca, and Craig Chambers. HydroJ: object-oriented pattern matching for evolvable distributed systems. In *Proc. 18th ACM SIGPLAN Conf. on Object-Oriented Programming, Systems, Languages and Applications*, pp. 205–223, 2003.

[16] Barbara Liskov, Russell Atkinson, Toby Bloom, J. Eliot Moss, J. Craig Schaffert, Robert Scheifler, and Alan Snyder. *CLU Reference Manual*. Springer-Verlag, 1984. Also published as Lecture Notes in Computer Science 114, G. Goos and J. Hartmanis, Eds., Springer-Verlag, 1981.

[17] Jed Liu, Aaron Kimball, and Andrew C. Myers. Interruptible iterators. In *Proc. 33rd ACM Symposium on Principles of Programming Languages (POPL)*, pp. 283–294, January 2006.

[18] Jed Liu and Andrew C. Myers. JMatch: Java plus pattern matching. Technical Report TR2002-1878, Computer Science Department, Cornell University, October 2002. Software release at `http://www.cs.cornell.edu/projects/jmatch`.

[19] Jed Liu and Andrew C. Myers. JMatch: Iterable abstract pattern matching for Java. In *Proc. 5th International Symposium on Practical Aspects of Declarative Languages*, pp. 110–127, January 2003.

[20] Todd Millstein. Practical predicate dispatch. In *Proc. 19th ACM SIGPLAN Conf. on Object-Oriented Programming, Systems, Languages and Applications*, pp. 345–364, 2004.

[21] Andrew C. Myers, Barbara Liskov, and Nicholas Mathewson. PolyJ: Parameterized types for Java. Software release, at `http://www.cs.cornell.edu/polyj`, July 1998.

[22] Martin Odersky, Lex Spoon, and Bill Venners. *Programming in Scala: A Comprehensive Step-by-step Guide*. Artima Incorporation, USA, 1st edition, 2008.

[23] Martin Odersky and Philip Wadler. Pizza into Java: translating theory into practice. In *Proc. 24th ACM Symposium on Principles of Programming Languages (POPL)*, pp. 146–159, 1997.

[24] Adam Richard and Ondřej Lhoták. OOMatch: pattern matching as dispatch in Java. In *Companion 22nd ACM SIGPLAN Conf. on Object-Oriented Programming, Systems, Languages and Applications*, pp. 771–772, 2007.

[25] Clyde Ruby and Gary T. Leavens. Safely creating correct subclasses without seeing superclass code. In *Proc. 15th ACM SIGPLAN Conf. on Object-Oriented Programming, Systems, Languages and Applications*, pp. 208–228, 2000.

[26] Zoltan Somogyi, Fergus Henderson, and Thomas Conway. The execution algorithm of Mercury, an efficient purely declarative logic programming language. *The Journal of Logic Programming*, 29(1–3):17–64, October–December 1996.

[27] Philippe Suter, Mirco Dotta, and Viktor Kuncak. Decision procedures for algebraic data types with abstractions. In *Proc. 37th ACM Symposium on Principles of Programming Languages (POPL)*, pp. 199–210, 2010.

[28] Philippe Suter, Ali Sinan Köksal, and Viktor Kuncak. Satisfiability modulo recursive programs. In *Proc. 18th Int'l Conf. on Static Analysis*, pp. 298–315, 2011.

[29] Don Syme, Gregory Neverov, and James Margetson. Extensible pattern matching via a lightweight language extension. In *Proc. 12th ACM SIGPLAN Int'l Conf. on Functional Programming*, pp. 29–40, 2007.

[30] Philip Wadler. Views: a way for pattern matching to cohabit with data abstraction. In *Proc. 14th ACM Symposium on Principles of Programming Languages (POPL)*, pp. 307–313, 1987.

[31] Meng Wang, Jeremy Gibbons, Kazutaka Matsuda, and Zhenjiang Hu. Refactoring pattern matching. *Science of Computer Programming*, in press. Available online 24 August 2012.

[32] Matthias Zenger and Martin Odersky. Extensible algebraic datatypes with defaults. In *Proc. 6th ACM SIGPLAN Int'l Conf. on Functional Programming*, pp. 241–252, September 2001.

SPL^{LIFT} — Statically Analyzing Software Product Lines in Minutes Instead of Years

Eric Bodden[1] Társis Tolêdo[3] Márcio Ribeiro[3,4] Claus Brabrand[2] Paulo Borba[3] Mira Mezini[1]

[1] EC SPRIDE, Technische Universität Darmstadt, Darmstadt, Germany
[2] IT University of Copenhagen, Copenhagen, Denmark
[3] Federal University of Pernambuco, Recife, Brazil
[4] Federal University of Alagoas, Maceió, Brazil

bodden@acm.org, {twt, phmb}@cin.ufpe.br, marcio@ic.ufal.br, brabrand@itu.dk, mira.mezini@cased.de

Abstract

A software product line (SPL) encodes a potentially large variety of software products as variants of some common code base. Up until now, re-using traditional static analyses for SPLs was virtually intractable, as it required programmers to generate and analyze all products individually. In this work, however, we show how an important class of existing inter-procedural static analyses can be transparently lifted to SPLs. Without requiring programmers to change a single line of code, our approach SPL^{LIFT} automatically converts any analysis formulated for traditional programs within the popular IFDS framework for inter-procedural, finite, distributive, subset problems to an SPL-aware analysis formulated in the IDE framework, a well-known extension to IFDS. Using a full implementation based on Heros, Soot, CIDE and JavaBDD, we show that with SPL^{LIFT} one can reuse IFDS-based analyses without changing a single line of code. Through experiments using three static analyses applied to four Java-based product lines, we were able to show that our approach produces correct results and outperforms the traditional approach by several orders of magnitude.

Categories and Subject Descriptors F.3.2 [*Logics and Meanings of Programs*]: Semantics of Programming Languages—Program analysis

General Terms Design, Languages, Performance

Keywords Software product lines, inter-procedural static analysis, context sensitive, flow sensitive


```
void main() {
  int x = secret();
  int y = 0;
  #ifdef F
    x = 0;
  #endif
  #ifdef G
    y = foo(x);
  #endif
  print(y);
}

int foo(int p) {
  #ifdef H
    p = 0;
  #endif
  return p;
}
```

(a) Example SPL

```
void main() {
  int x = secret();
  int y = 0;
  y = foo(x);
  print(y);
}

int foo(int p) {
  return p;
}
```

(b) Product for $\neg F \wedge G \wedge \neg H$

Figure 1: Example product line: secret is printed if `F` and `H` are disabled but `G` is enabled

1. Introduction

A Software Product Line (SPL) describes a set of software products as variations of a common code base. Variations, so-called features, are typically expressed through compiler directives such as the well-known **#ifdef** from the C pre-processor or other means of conditional compilation. Figure 1a shows a minimal example product line that assigns values through different methods. Figure 1b shows the product obtained by applying to the product line a pre-processor with the configuration $\neg F \wedge G \wedge \neg H$, i.e., a product with feature G enabled and features F and H disabled. Software product lines have become quite popular in certain application domains, for instance for the development of games and other applications for mobile devices. This is due to the tight resource restrictions of those devices: depending on the hardware capabilities of a certain mobile device, it may be advisable or not to include certain features in a software product for that device, or to include a variant of a given feature.

Static program analyses are a powerful tool to find bugs in program code [1–3] or to conduct static optimizations [4], and it is therefore highly desirable to apply static analyses also to software product lines. With existing approaches, though, it is often prohibitively expensive to reuse existing static analyses. The problem is that traditional static analyses cannot be directly applied to software product lines. Instead they have to be applied to pre-processed programs such as the one from Figure 1b. But for an SPL with n optional, independent features, there are 2^n possible products, which therefore demands thousands of analysis runs even for small product lines. This exponential blowup is particularly annoying because many of those analysis runs will have large overlaps for different feature combinations. It therefore seems quite beneficial to share analysis information wherever possible.

In this work we introduce SPL^{LIFT}, a simple but very effective approach to re-using existing static program analyses without an exponential blowup. SPL^{LIFT} allows programmers to transparently lift an important class of existing static analyses to software product lines. Our approach is fully inter-procedural. It works for any analysis formulated for traditional programs within Reps, Horwitz

PLDI'13, June 16–19, 2013, Seattle, WA, USA.

and Sagiv's popular IFDS [5] framework for inter-procedural, finite, distributive, subset problems. In the past, IFDS has been used to express a variety of analysis problems such as secure information flow [1], typestate [2, 3, 6], alias sets [7], specification inference [8], and shape analysis [9, 10]. SPL^{LIFT} automatically converts any such analysis to a feature-sensitive analysis that operates on the entire product line in one single pass. The converted analysis is formulated in the IDE framework [11] for inter-procedural distributed environment problems, an extension to IFDS. In cases in which the original analysis reports that a data-flow fact d may hold at a given statement s, the resulting converted analysis reports a feature constraint under which d may hold at s. As an example, consider again Figure 1. Imagine that we are conducting a taint analysis [1], determining whether information can flow from `secret` to `print`. In the traditional approach we would generate and analyze all $2^3 = 8$ possible products individually, eventually discovering that the product from Figure 1b may indeed leak the secret. SPL^{LIFT} instead analyzes the product line from Figure 1a in a single pass, informing us that `secret` may leak for the configuration $\neg F \wedge G \wedge \neg H$ (cf. Fig. 1b).

But a reduced analysis time is not the only advantage of a feature-sensitive static analysis. In the area of software product lines, conditional-compilation constructs may add much complexity to the code, and can yield subtle and unusual programming mistakes [12, 13]. As an example, a plain Java program will not compile if it uses a potentially undefined local variable. In a Java-based software product line, any pre-processor would accept such a program; the programming problem would only manifest later, when the pre-processed program is compiled. When the mistake is discovered, it is laborsome to map the resulting plain-Java error message back to the original product line. Analyzing the product line directly, as in SPL^{LIFT}, circumvents this problem.

To obtain meaningful results, SPL^{LIFT} further takes feature models into account. A feature model defines a Boolean constraint that describes the set of all feature combinations that a user intends to generate, the SPL's *valid* configurations (or *valid* products). For instance, if we were to evaluate the SPL from Figure 1a under the constraint $F \leftrightarrow G$ (stating that the user intends to generate only products for which both F and G are either enabled or disabled), SPL^{LIFT} would detect that the secret information cannot leak after all, as it holds that: $(\neg F \wedge G \wedge \neg H) \;\wedge\; (F \leftrightarrow G) \;=\; \textbf{false}$. Considering a feature model complicates the analysis, which may cause one to expect an increase in analysis cost. Fortunately, our experimental results show that this, in fact, is not usually the case. SPL^{LIFT} can gain speed by exploiting the model, terminating the analysis for constraint-violating program paths early. This balances out the expected slowdown in many cases.

We have fully implemented SPL^{LIFT} within Heros [14], a self-written IDE solver integrating with the program-analysis framework Soot [15], extending this solver to product lines and connecting Soot to CIDE, the Colored IDE [16], an Eclipse [17] extension for writing and maintaining Java-based software product lines. Using our solution, existing IFDS-based analyses are automatically converted to feature-sensitive versions without changing a single line of code.

We used SPL^{LIFT} to lift three standard inter-procedural static program analyses, and then applied them to four existing CIDE-based product lines, on which, due to the exponential blowup, the traditional analysis approach takes hours if not years to compute. Our experiments show that SPL^{LIFT} produces correct results, and outperforms the traditional approach by several orders of magnitude.

At http://bodden.de/spllift/ we make available our full implementation as open source, along with all data and scripts to reproduce our empirical results. To summarize, this paper presents the following original contributions:

- a mechanism for automatically and transparently converting any IFDS-based static program analysis to an IDE-based analysis over software product lines,
- a full open-source implementation for Java, and
- a set of experiments showing that our approach yields correct results and outperforms the traditional approach by several orders of magnitude.

The remainder of this paper is structured as follows. In Section 2, we introduce the IFDS and IDE frameworks, along with their strengths and limitations. Section 3 contains the core of this paper; here we explain the automated lifting of IFDS-based analyses to software product lines. Section 4 explains how we take into account the product line's feature model. In Section 5 we discuss our implementation, while we present our experimental setup and results in Section 6. The work presented in this paper bases itself on previous work presented at the 2012 ACM SIGPLAN Workshop on Programming Languages and Analysis for Security [18]. In Section 7 we explain the differences to this paper along with the differences to other related work.

2. The IFDS framework

Our approach builds on top of the so-called *IFDS framework* by Reps, Horwitz and Sagiv [5]. This framework defines a general solution strategy for the inter-procedural, flow-sensitive, and fully context-sensitive analysis of finite distributive subset problems. In this section we present the general concepts behind this framework and illustrate them by an example.

2.1 Overview of the IFDS Framework

The major idea of the IFDS framework is to reduce any program-analysis problem formulated in this framework to a pure graph-reachability problem. Based on the program's inter-procedural control-flow graph, the IFDS algorithm builds a so-called "exploded super graph", in which a node (s, d) is reachable from a selected start node $(s_0, \mathbf{0})$ if and only if the data-flow fact d holds at statement s. In this setting a "fact" may mean any logical statement that a static analysis can decide, such as "variable `x` may carry a secret value" or "variables `x` and `y` may alias." To achieve this goal, the framework encodes data-flow functions as nodes and edges.

Figure 2 shows how to represent compositions of typical *gen* and *kill* functions as they are often used in static analysis. The nodes at the top represent facts before the given statement s, the nodes at the bottom represent facts after s. The identity function **id** maps each data-flow fact before a statement onto itself. In IFDS, the unique special value **0**, represents a tautology, i.e., a fact that always holds. It is therefore an invariant that two nodes representing **0** at different statements will always be connected. This **0** value is used to generate data-flow facts unconditionally. The flow function α generates the data-flow fact a, and at the same time kills the data-flow fact b (as there is no edge from b to b). Function β, on the other hand kills a, generates b and leaves all other values (such as c) untouched.

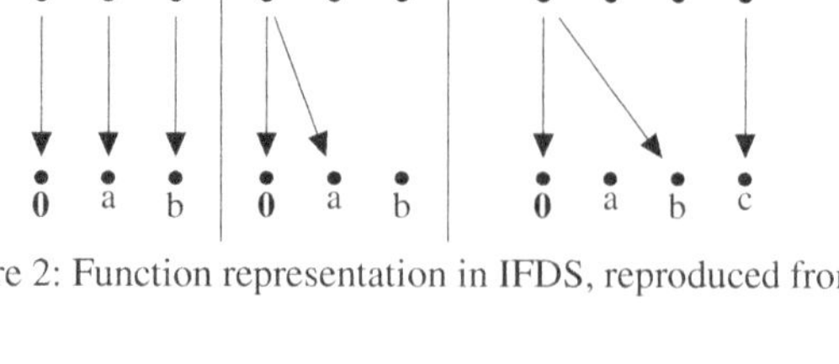

Figure 2: Function representation in IFDS, reproduced from [5]

The unconditional *kill*-and-*gen* functions above can be used to model analysis problems that are *locally separable*, i.e., in which a data-flow fact does not depend on the previous values of other facts. Such problems include the computation of reaching definitions or live variables. Many interesting analysis problems are not locally separable, however, for instance the taint analysis from our example in the introduction. For instance, the function representation to the right could be chosen to model an assignment `p=x`. Here, `x` has the same value as before the assignment, modeled by the arrow from x to x, and `p` obtains `x`'s value, modeled by the arrow from x to p. If `p` previously held a secret value, then it will only continue doing so if `x` holds a secret value, too. This is modeled by a missing arrow from p to p.

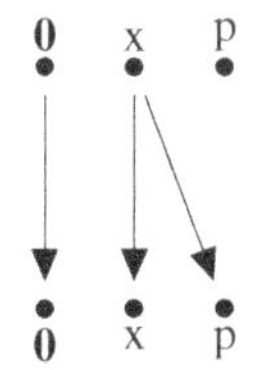

non-locally-separable flow function

It is important to note that data-flow facts are by no means limited to simple values such as the local variables in our example. Much more sophisticated abstractions exist, in which facts can, for instance, model aliasing through sets of access paths [1] or even the abstract typestate of combinations of multiple objects [3]. The IFDS framework itself, however, is oblivious to the concrete abstraction being used; the abstraction is a free parameter to the framework.

2.2 Different classes of flow functions

Users implement IFDS-based analyses by providing four classes of flow functions that can be denoted as:

- **normal**: modeling flow through a statement that is neither a call nor a return (incl. non-branching, unconditionally branching and conditionally branching statements),
- **call**: modeling flow from a call site to a possible callee,
- **return**: modeling flow from a possible callee back to a return site, i.e., a control-flow successor of the original method-call site, and
- **call-to-return**: modeling intra-procedural flow from just before a call site directly to a given return site.

Normal flow functions track simple intra-procedural flows. Call-to-return functions track intra-procedural flows at call sites; they are useful to propagate, for instance, information about local variables that are *not* passed to a method call, as the call cannot possibly change the value of those variables. Call functions map values from the caller's context to appropriate values in the callee's context. Return functions model the opposite flow, usually from return values to variables that receive those values. Due to this setup, the analysis of each method usually only processes information that is in scope within that method.

2.3 Example: Taint analysis in IFDS

To encode the assignment of a secret value to a variable `x` we generate a fact x. This fact would be killed to denote that `x` is assigned a definitely non-secret value.

To illustrate this encoding, Figure 3 shows the exploded super graph for our example client of the IFDS framework, the taint analysis applied to the product from the running example (Figure 1b). The analysis starts at the top-left node, which resembles the starting node $(s_0, \mathbf{0})$, s_0 being the starting statement. According to the encoding outlined above, the analysis "taints" the return value at the call to `secret()` by generating the data-flow fact for the variable `x` that holds this value. The analysis then tracks simple assignments to local variables and method parameters as stated above. (For now, let us ignore possible assignments through fields and arrays. We will comment on those in Section 5.) At the single call site in the example, the call-to-return function keeps `x` alive, stating that it is still tainted after the call if it was tainted earlier. At the same time, it kills `y` because the call statement is assigning `y` a new value. (Note that at this point `y` is already dead, due to the preceding assignment.) The call function encodes the transfer of actual to formal parameters. Since the only variable in scope within `foo` is `p`, the graph for method `foo` has nodes for `p` but not for `x` nor `y`. In the example, a taint violation is detected by observing the data flow marked with the red/thick arrow: the node for `y` just before the `print` statement is reachable in the graph, which means that a secret value, referred to by `y`, may be printed.

2.4 The IDE Framework

Sagiv, Reps and Horwitz also developed a more general, more expressive framework than IFDS, called *inter-procedural distributive environment transformers* (IDE) [11]. As in IFDS, the IDE framework models data flow through edges in an exploded super graph. In addition to IFDS, however, IDE allows for the computation of distributive functions along those edges: the label d of each node in the exploded super graph maps to a value v from a second, independent analysis domain, the so-called *value domain* V. The flow functions thus transform environments $\{d \mapsto v\}$ to other environments $\{d' \mapsto v'\}$. Every IFDS problem can be encoded as a special instance of the IDE framework using a binary domain $\{\top, \bot\}$ where $d \mapsto \bot$ states that data-flow fact d holds at the current statement, and $d \mapsto \top$ states that it does not hold [11]. But this binary domain is the least expressive instance of a large set of possible value domains. This we can exploit.

3. Using IDE to lift IFDS-based analyses to Software Product Lines

The main idea of SPL^LIFT is to leverage the gap in expressiveness between IFDS and IDE. To lift IFDS-based data-flow analyses to a feature-sensitive version for software product lines, we replace the binary domain for encoding any IFDS problem as a special instance of the IDE framework by a value domain that consists of feature constraints. The lifting is based on the following principle:

> Assume a statement s that is annotated with a feature constraint F (i.e., **#ifdef** `(F)` s **#endif**). Then s should have its usual data-flow effect if F holds, and should have no effect if F does not hold.

This principle effectively talks about two different flow functions: one function f^F for the *enabled* case F, and one function $f^{\neg F}$ for the *disabled* case $\neg F$. The idea of SPL^LIFT is to combine both flow functions into one, $f^{\text{LIFT}} := f^F \vee f^{\neg F}$, while using constraints to track traversals of edges labeled with F and $\neg F$ respectively. (The labeling effectively occurs within IDE's value domain V.) The above definition depends on the two notions of a what a statement's "usual effect" should be and what it means to have "no effect". The general principle of disjoining two labeled flow functions f^F and $f^{\neg F}$ into one applies to all flow functions in SPL^LIFT. The two component flow functions f^F and $f^{\neg F}$ differ, however, for the different classes of flow functions that we described in Section 2.2.

3.1 Intra-procedural flow functions

First we consider intra-procedural "normal" flow functions, which exist for non-branching, unconditionally branching and conditionally branching statements. Let us first discuss the most simple case of a non-branching statement s. For the *enabled* case F, assume that the statement's original flow function is $f(s)$. In Figure 4a we show on the left the function f^F, which we define as $f(s)^F$, i.e., a copy of $f(s)$ in which all edges are labeled with F, the feature annotation of s. In the figure, we show the edges as dashed because they are conditionalized by this feature annotation. A label F effectively

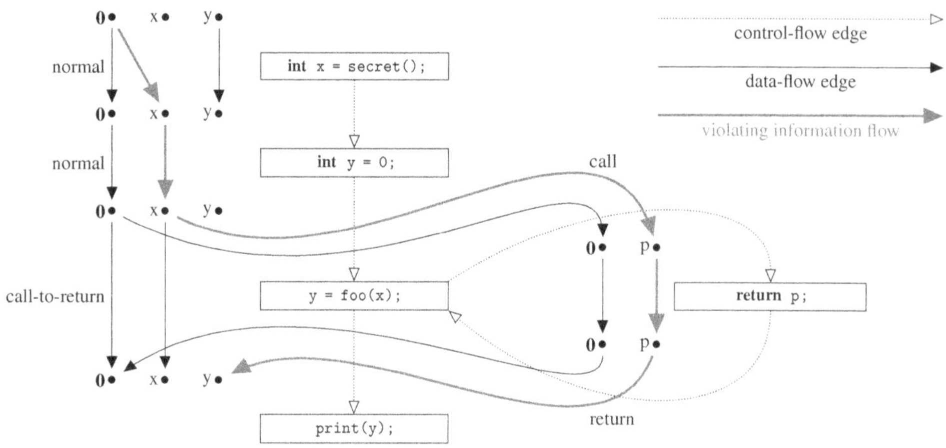

Figure 3: Exploded super graph for the *single* example product from Figure 1b; main method shown on left-hand side, `foo` shown to the right

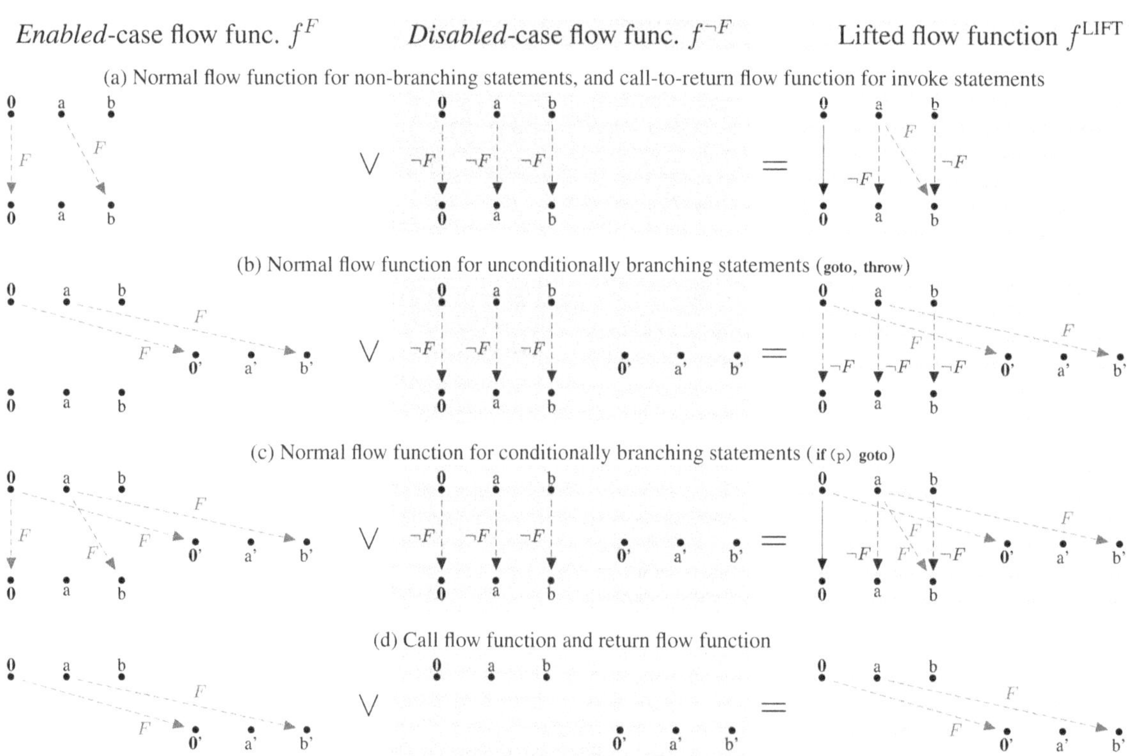

Figure 4: Lifting of different flow functions in SPL^{LIFT}

denotes the function $\lambda c.\ c \wedge F$ that will conjoin the incoming constraint c with F when the edge is traversed. In the *disabled* case $\neg F$, statement s is disabled because its feature annotation F contradicts the current product's feature selection. This means that the statement simply does not change the intra-procedural data-flow information at all (cf. the identity function in Figure 2). We hence define $f^{\neg F}$ as shown in the middle column: the identity function labeled with $\neg F$. Once both functions have been labeled, we can combine them into a single flow function as shown in the rightmost column. This function f^{LIFT} effectively represents both previous functions at the same time, as a disjunction $f^F \vee f^{\neg F}$. Edges such as the one from **0** to **0**, which are annotated with F in the one function and with $\neg F$ in the other, are implicitly annotated with **true**. In the following we show such edges as (unconditional) solid black edges. The intra-procedural call-to-return functions are treated exactly the same way.

But how about intra-procedural flows through branching statements? We conduct our analysis on the Jimple intermediate representation, a three-address code, for which we need to distinguish unconditional branches like **throw** `e` and **goto** `l`, from conditional branches of the form **if** `(p)` **goto** `l`.

Figure 4b shows how we lift flow functions for unconditional branches labeled with a feature annotation F. If the **throw** or **goto** statement is enabled, data flow only exists towards the nodes of the branch target (the primed nodes in Figure 4b). Both edges within this figure are assumed to be labeled with F. If the statement is disabled, data flows only along the fall-through branch, as the branch does not actually execute. Again we use the identity function in this case. Just as before, the lifted flow function f^{LIFT} is obtained through a disjunction of both functions.

For conditional branches of the form **if** `(p)` **goto** `1`, the lifted flow function is basically a combination of the cases for the unconditional branch and the "normal data flow", which models the case in which the branch falls through. We show the respective case in Figure 4c. The *disabled* case $\neg F$ is handled just as for unconditional branches; if a branch is disabled, it just falls through, no matter whether it is conditional or not.

3.2 Inter-procedural flow functions

The *call* and *return* flow functions model inter-procedural control flows caused by call and return statements. The general idea behind modeling those functions is the same as in the intra-procedural case, however this time we need to consider a different flow function for the *disabled* case, i.e., when $\neg F$ holds. Remember that a call flow function leads from a call site to its callee, and a return flow function from a return statement to just after the call site. Using the identity function to model such situations would be incorrect: If we were to use the identity function then this would propagate information from the call site to the callee (respectively vice versa) although under $\neg F$ the call (or return) never occurs. We must hence use the kill-all function to model this situation, as shown in Figure 4d (middle column). This function kills all data-flow facts, modeling that no flow between call site and callee occurs if the invoke statement is disabled.

3.3 Computing reachability as a useful side effect

It is an interesting question to ask whether we should conditionalize edges between **0** nodes. As explained earlier, in plain IFDS/IDE, **0** nodes are always connected, unconditionally. We decided for the design shown in Figure 4 where edges between **0** nodes are in fact conditionalized by feature annotations just as any other edges. This has the advantage that, as a side effect, our analysis computes reachability information: a constraint c that SPL^{LIFT} computes for a node $(s, \mathbf{0})$, i.e., an environment $(s, \{\mathbf{0} \mapsto c\})$, tells the programmer that s is reachable only in product configurations satisfying c. This design also prevents our implementation to propagate **0**-facts through code that is unreachable according to the feature model.

3.4 Combining flow functions and initializing flows

As the analysis explores a path in the exploded super graph, we combine all constraint annotations along the path using conjunction. After all, *all* constraints on that path must hold for the flow to be possible. At control-flow merge points we combine constraints using disjunction, as we could have reached the program point along different paths. We initialize the analysis with the constraint **true** at the program's start node $(s_0, \mathbf{0})$, and with **false** at all other nodes.

3.5 Application to running example

In Figure 5, we show how our generic flow-function conversion rules are applied to our specific running example of our inter-procedural taint analysis, operating on our example product line from Figure 1a. In the figure, the violating information flow leads to the following constraint:

$$(\mathbf{true} \wedge \neg F \wedge G \wedge \neg H \wedge G) \vee (\mathbf{false} \wedge \neg G) = \neg F \wedge G \wedge \neg H$$

Note that this is exactly the constraint that our introduction promised our analysis would compute.

4. Considering the SPL's feature model

In the introduction we already hinted at the fact that it is generally necessary to consider a product line's feature model during analysis. Without considering the feature model both the lifted and the traditional feature-oblivious analysis may simply produce useless information as the analysis would be unable to distinguish results for valid configurations from those for invalid ones (cf. Section 1).

4.1 Computing the feature-model constraint from the feature model

Feature models are usually given in the form of a graphical tree representation with additional propositional constraints. As proposed by Batory [19], we translate the model into a single propositional constraint by creating a conjunction of: (i) a bi-implication between every mandatory feature and its parent, (ii) an implication from every optional feature to its parent, (iii) a bi-implication from the parent of every OR group to the disjunction of the components of said group; and (iv) a bi-implication from the parent of every exclusive-OR group, E, to the conjunction of: the pair-wise mutual exclusion of the components E and the disjunction of the components of E.

4.2 Taking advantage of the feature-model constraint

SPL^{LIFT} uses the feature model as follows: for an edge label f and a Boolean feature-model constraint m SPL^{LIFT} implicitly assumes that the edge is instead labeled with $f \wedge m$. Our tool automatically reduces contradictory constraints to **false**, which causes the IDE algorithm to automatically terminate computations for paths that result in such a contradictory constraint.

Due to the fact that the constraint m complicates the overall constraint computation during the buildup of the exploded super graph, one may expect slowdowns over a version of SPL^{LIFT} that ignores the feature model. However, our particular style of implementation allows for an early termination of the IDE algorithm. As our experiments show, this often counterbalances the slowdown effect. Consider again the example of Figure 5, and in this figure the top-most node labeled with p. During our analysis, when we reach this node, we will have computed the path constraint $\neg F \wedge G$. In combination with the feature model $F \leftrightarrow G$, already at this point we obtain: $\neg F \wedge G \ \wedge \ F \leftrightarrow G \ = \ \mathbf{false}$. But this means that any further data flow along this path of the graph is actually infeasible. We can hence terminate further analysis along this path early.

Note that first we tried an even simpler solution: just replace the start value **true** at the program's start node by the feature-model constraint m [18]. While this yields the same analysis results eventually, we found that it wastes performance. The problem is that the IDE algorithm spends most time constructing the graph and internal summary functions, and spends only very little time actually propagating values through the graph. Exchanging the start value only leads to early termination in the propagation phase but not in the costly construction phase. By conjoining the edge constraints with m we terminate early in the construction phase already, saving the algorithm from computing summary functions that, according to the model, would carry contradictory Boolean constraints.

5. Implementation with Soot and CIDE

We have implemented SPL^{LIFT} based on Heros [14], our IDE solver which integrates with the Soot program analysis and transformation framework [15], the Colored Integrated Development Environment (CIDE) [16] and the JavaBDD[1] library. We have implemented an IDE solver [11] in Soot that works directly on Soot's intermediate representation "Jimple". Jimple is a three-address code representation of Java programs that is particularly simple to analyze. Jimple

[1] JavaBDD website: `http://javabdd.sourceforge.net/`

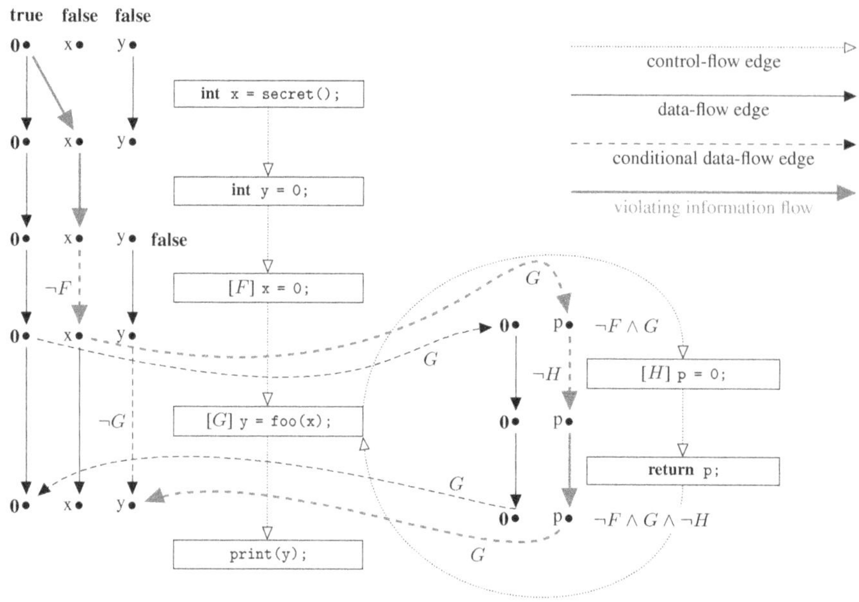

Figure 5: SPL^{LIFT} as it is applied to the entire example product line of Figure 1a; an edge labeled with feature constraint C represents the function $\lambda x.\ x \wedge C$. Constraints at nodes represent initial values (at the top) or intermediate results of the constraint computation.

statements are never nested, and all control-flow constructs are reduced to simple conditional and unconditional branches. Soot can produce Jimple code from Java source code or bytecode, and compile Jimple back into bytecode or into other intermediate representations.

To be able to actually parse software product lines, we used CIDE, an extension of the Eclipse IDE [17]. In CIDE, software produce lines are expressed as plain Java programs. This makes them comparatively easy to parse: there are no explicit compiler directives such as **#ifdef** that a parser would need to handle. Instead, code variations are expressed by marking code fragments with different colors. Each color is associated with a feature name. In result, every CIDE SPL is also a valid Java program. CIDE forbids so-called "undisciplined" annotations, i.e., enforces that users mark code regions that span entire statements, members or classes. Previous research has shown that undisciplined annotations do exist in real-world projects but that they can often be eliminated by code expansion [20].

One performance critical aspect of our implementation is what data structures we use to implement the feature constraints that SPL^{LIFT} tracks. After some initial experiments with a hand-written data structure representing constraints in Disjunctive Normal Form, we switched to an implementation based on Binary Decision Diagrams (BDDs) [21], using JavaBDD. Reduced BDDs have the advantage that they are compact and normalized, which allows us to easily detect and exploit contradictions. The size of a BDD can heavily depend on its variable ordering. In our case, because we did not perceive the BDD operations to be a bottleneck, we just pick one ordering and leave the search for an optimal ordering to future work.

Current Limitations

```
#ifdef F
x = new ArrayList();
#else
x = new LinkedList();
#endif
x.add(o);
```

Our current implementation is not as sensitive to feature annotations as it could be. This is mostly due to the fact that IFDS/IDE requires the presence of a call graph, and currently we compute this call graph without taking feature annotations into account. While we follow call-graph edges in a feature sensitive fashion (as defined by our call flow function), the feature-insensitive call graph is also used to compute points-to sets. This precludes us from precisely handling situations such as the one shown above. Here, we would conservatively resolve the `add`-call to both `ArrayList.add` and `LinkedList.add`, irrespective of whether F is enabled. In other words, we would propagate the constraint **true** along the respective call edges. This is sound but not maximally precise. Ideally, our points-to analysis should be feature sensitive as well, propagating F to `ArrayList.add` and $\neg F$ to `LinkedList.add`. One could solve this problem by ignoring the pre-computed points-to analysis and handling pointers as part of the IFDS abstraction, e.g., as done by Guarnieri et al. [1].

Due to our tool chain, our implementation is currently limited to software product lines expressed with CIDE. Having said that, there is nothing that precludes our approach from being applied to product lines described in different ways. We are, in fact, currently considering how SPL^{LIFT} could be applied to C, using the TypeChef parser [22]. The C pre-processor features **#ifdef** constructs that are more expressive than the ones in CIDE, and the C language includes more constructs for unstructured control flow than Java. Our current implementation ignores reflective calls, but those could be treated with approaches such as TamiFlex [23].

Last but not least, SPL^{LIFT} is limited to analyses expressed in the IFDS framework, which requires that the analyses must have flow functions that are distributive over the merge operator (set union). This is the case for many but not all analysis problems. In the future we plan to investigate to what extent the same ideas are transferable to more expressive static analysis frameworks, for instance weighted pushdown systems [24].

6. Experiments

We used a set of extensive experiments to answer the following research questions about our implementation:

- **RQ1: Correctness** Does SPL^{LIFT} compute a sound result?

- **RQ2: Efficiency** How much efficiency do we gain over the traditional feature-oblivious approach?
- **RQ3: Feature Model** What is the cost of using the feature model?

6.1 RQ1: Correctness

To validate the correctness of our SPL^{LIFT} implementation, we need an oracle that can tell apart correct from incorrect results. As an oracle, we implemented a second, simplistic analysis that is also feature aware but not constraint based. This analysis essentially corresponds to an inter-procedural version of the analysis *A2* from our earlier publication [25], and we therefore call the analysis *A2* in the remainder of this paper. *A2* operates on the feature-annotated control-flow graph just as SPL^{LIFT}, however unlike SPL^{LIFT} *A2* is configuration-specific, i.e., evaluates the product line only with respect to one concrete configuration $c = \{F_1, \ldots, F_n\}$ at a time. If a statement s is labeled with a feature constraint F then *A2* first checks whether c satisfies F to determine whether s is enabled. If it is, then *A2* propagates flow to s's standard successors using the standard IFDS flow function defined for s. If c does not satisfy F then *A2* uses the identity function to propagate intra-procedural flows to fall-through successor nodes only. The implementation of *A2* is so simple that we consider it as foolproof. We hence assume this *A2* implementation as correct, and can therefore use it as an oracle to cross-check the results of SPL^{LIFT}. Whenever *A2* computes a fact r for some configuration c, we fetch SPL^{LIFT}'s computed feature constraint C for r (at the same statement), and check that C allows for c. This ensures that SPL^{LIFT} is not overly restrictive. The other way around, we traverse all of SPL^{LIFT}'s results (r, c) for the given fixed c, and check that the instance of *A2* for c computed each such r as well (at the same statement). This ensures that SPL^{LIFT} is as precise as *A2*, i.e., does not report any false positives. Our cross-checks initially helped us to find bugs in the implementation of SPL^{LIFT}, but we quickly converged to an implementation that does not violate any cross-checks any more.

6.2 RQ2: Efficiency

To evaluate the performance of our approach, we chose four different product lines used in earlier work [25]. We apply to each benchmark subject three different static analyses both emulating the traditional approach (details below) and using SPL^{LIFT}. Table 1 summarizes some core data about these subjects. BerkeleyDB is a feature-enriched database library. GPL is a small product line for desktop applications, while Lampiro and MM08 are product lines for J2ME applications. Because whole-program analyses require entry points to start with, we programmed driver classes for three of the benchmarks. For the J2ME SPLs, those methods call life-cycle methods usually called by the J2ME framework. For BerkeleyDB, our main class calls the main methods of all driver classes that BerkeleyDB includes. The driver classes are available for download along with all other data and tools to reproduce the experiments.

The third column in Table 1 gives the total number of features as mentioned in the feature model. The fourth column states the number of features mentioned in feature annotations that are actually reachable from our main classes. For Lampiro this number is surprisingly low. Kästner reports that the current version of Lampiro is unusual in the sense that it contains many dead features and other anomalies, which may be the explanation of this effect [16, pages 131–132]. Column five states the number of configurations over those features, i.e., $2^{\text{Features-reachable}}$. The last column states the number of such configurations that are valid w.r.t. the feature model. For instance, for Lampiro the feature model ended up not constraining the 4 combinations of the 2 reachable features. For BerkeleyDB, we do not know the number of valid configurations. This is because we compute this number as a side-effect of running the traditional approach: for each possible configuration we first check whether it is valid and, if it is, next apply the traditional analysis approach to this configuration. But for BerkeleyDB, due to the $55 \cdot 10^{10}$ possible configurations, this process would take years to complete. For each benchmark/analysis combination we define a cutoff time of ten hours, which is why we cannot report the number of valid configurations for BerkeleyDB.

As analysis clients we used three different generic IFDS-based inter-procedural client analyses. *Possible Types* computes the possible types for a value reference in the program. Such information can, for instance, be used for virtual-method-call resolution [4]. We track typing information through method boundaries. Field and array assignments are treated with weak updates in a field-sensitive manner, abstracting from receiver objects through their context-insensitive points-to sets. *Reaching Definitions* is a reaching-definitions analysis that computes variable definitions for their uses. To obtain inter-procedural flows, we implement a variant that tracks definitions through parameter and return-value assignments. *Uninitialized Variables* finds potentially uninitialized variables. Assume a call `foo(x)`, where `x` is potentially uninitialized. Our analysis will determine that all uses of the formal parameter of `foo` may also access an uninitialized value. We provide the source code for all three clients (only approx. 550LOC) in our download package. We include the Java 1.7 runtime libraries in our analysis.

To evaluate the efficiency of SPL^{LIFT} against the actual traditional approach, we would ideally want to use a pre-processor to generate all possible products, and then apply the traditional analysis approach to each resulting product, an approach which in our earlier work [25] we called *A1*. However, we quickly found that this approach is so intractable that it would even preclude us from finishing our experiments in due time. This is because the traditional approach would need to generate, parse and analyze every single product. A prerequisite for each analysis is a call graph, whose computation can easily take minutes on its own. Given the large number of possible configurations, it would have taken us years to complete the experiments. (Brabrand et al. [25] did not have this problem because their intra-procedural analyses need no call graph and must only consider up to 2^k combinations where k is the maximal number of features within a single method. For our four benchmark subjects k is always ≤ 9.)

We hence decided to compare SPL^{LIFT} not to *A1* but instead to our implementation of *A2*, which only requires a single parsing step and call-graph computation. *A2* is thus naturally faster than *A1*, and therefore any performance gain we can show with respect to *A2* would be even higher with respect to *A1*. We found that even with using *A2*, some experiments would still take years to complete, though, which is why we nevertheless use a cutoff-time of ten hours.

For our performance measurements we used a Linux machine with kernel version 2.6.26-1 running on a Quad-Core AMD Opteron Processor 8356 at 2.3GHz and with 40GB RAM. As Java Virtual Machine we used the Hotspot server VM in version 1.7.0_05, configured to run with 32GB maximal heap space. To make our results easier to reproduce, we configured Eclipse to run all analyses without requiring a user interface. Our implementation is single-threaded. JavaBDD was configured to use the BuDDy[2] BDD package, which implements BDD operations in native code.

Table 2 shows our performance comparison between SPL^{LIFT} and *A2*, based on a single measured run each. In those experiments, both approaches make use of the feature model. For convenience, the second column shows again the number of valid configurations. The *A2* analysis needs to be executed that many times, once for each configuration. The third column shows the time it takes Soot to

[2]BuDDy website: `http://buddy.sf.net/`

Benchmark	Configurations valid	Soot/CG	Possible Types SPL^LIFT	Possible Types *A2*	Reaching Definitions SPL^LIFT	Reaching Definitions *A2*	Uninitialized Variables SPL^LIFT	Uninitialized Variables *A2*
BerkeleyDB	unknown	7m33s	24s	*years*	12m04s	*years*	10m18s	*years*
GPL	1,872	4m35s	42s	9h03m39s	8m48s	*days*	7m09s	*days*
Lampiro	4	1m52s	4s	13s	42s	3m30s	1m25s	3m09s
MM08	26	2m57s	3s	2m06s	59s	24m29s	2m13s	27m39s

Table 2: Performance comparison of SPL^{LIFT} over *A2*; values in gray show coarse estimates

Benchmark	KLOC	Features total	Features reachable	Configurations reachable	Configurations valid
BerkeleyDB	84.0	56	39	$55 \cdot 10^{10}$	unknown
GPL	1.4	29	19	524,288	1,872
Lampiro	45.0	20	2	4	4
MM08	5.7	34	9	512	26

Table 1: Key information about benchmarks used

construct a call graph and points-to sets for the respective benchmark. This time is the same for SPL^{LIFT} and *A2*, as both require a call graph as prerequisite.

As the table shows, SPL^{LIFT} outperforms *A2* clearly. While SPL^{LIFT} never takes more than about 12 minutes to terminate, *A2* always takes significantly longer. In five cases (shown in gray), *A2* even took longer than our cut-off time of ten hours. When this was the case we estimated the rough time it would take *A2* to terminate if we had run it to completion. We computed this estimate by taking the average of a run of *A2* with all features enabled and with no features enabled and then multiplying by the number of valid configurations. (For BerkeleyDB we estimated the number of valid configurations by extrapolating the results obtained within 10 hours.) As this estimation has a relatively low confidence, we only report a very coarse prognosis of days or years.

Notice that, while the absolute performance gain certainly differs depending on the client analysis and chosen product line, the gain is always substantial, and in particular the exponential blowup that *A2* suffers from cannot be observed with SPL^{LIFT}.

Qualitative performance analysis During our experiments, we found a relatively high variance in the analysis times. As we found, this is caused due to non-determinism in the order in which the IDE solution is computed. As a fixed-point algorithm, IDE computes the same result independently of iteration order, but some orders may compute the result faster (computing fewer flow functions) than others. The non-determinism is hard to avoid; it is caused by hash-based data structures within Soot and our solver. We did find, however, that the analysis time taken strongly correlates with the number of flow functions constructed in the exploded super-graph (the correlation coefficient was above 0.99 in all cases). Moreover, in all our benchmark setups, the *A2* analysis for the "full configuration", in which all features are enabled, constructed almost as many edges as SPL^{LIFT} did on its unique run. While SPL^{LIFT} deals with a much more complex analysis domain, i.e., performs more work per edge, our experimental results show that this additional cost is rather low.

6.3 RQ3: Feature Model

Regarding a product line's feature model is crucial to any analysis approach for software product lines, as otherwise the analysis would be unable to distinguish results for valid configurations from those for invalid ones, yielding analysis information that would be of little use to clients.

Nevertheless it is an interesting question to ask how high is the cost of regarding the feature model. Table 3 compares the running

Benchmark	Feature Model	P. Types	R. Def.	U. Var.
BerkeleyDB	regarded	24s	12m04s	10m18s
	ignored	23s	11m35s	10m47s
	average A2	*21s*	*9m35s*	*7m12s*
GPL	regarded	42s	8m48s	7m09s
	ignored	18s	8m21s	7m29s
	average A2	*17s*	*7m31s*	*6m42s*
Lampiro	regarded	4s	42s	1m25s
	ignored	4s	48s	1m13s
	average A2	*3s*	*42s*	*49s*
MM08	regarded	3s	59s	2m13s
	ignored	2s	45s	1m49s
	average A2	*2s*	*31s*	*1m37s*

Table 3: Performance impact of feature model on SPL^{LIFT}. Values in gray show the average time of the *A2* analysis. This number can be seen as lower bound for any feature-sensitive analysis.

time of SPL^{LIFT} with the running time of an instance of SPL^{LIFT} where the feature model was explicitly ignored. As our results show, there is usually no significant difference in analysis cost. Exceptions are GPL with *Possible Types* and, to a lesser extent, MM08 with all three analyses. In both cases, the cost of regarding the feature model is clearly observable, albeit far from prohibitive. Apel et al. [26] previously observed as well that regarding the feature model does usually not add much cost during analysis.

Interestingly, those results are quite different from the ones we obtained in our previous approach on intra-procedural analysis for software product lines [25]. There we found that regarding the feature model actually *saved* time. Our explanation for this difference in results is that the intra-procedural analyses from our earlier work use a different, bitset-based constraint representation. This representation is likely less efficient than the BDD-based one in SPL^{LIFT}, which causes the baseline to be much higher. With a higher baseline, the inclusion of the feature model can save more time, as the feature model can help to keep analysis configurations small. With SPL^{LIFT} the baseline is quite low already. To illustrate this, we included in Table 3 the average duration of all executed *A2* analyses for the respective setup. Since *A2* is so simple, it is hard to imagine a feature-sensitive analysis (which by its nature considers all configurations, not just one as *A2*) that would complete in less time. As the comparison with those values shows, the analysis time of SPL^{LIFT} is often actually quite close to this gold standard.

7. Related Work

The work presented in this paper extends an initial effort on applying the IFDS and IDE analysis frameworks to SPLs [18]. In the earlier work, we only considered "normal" flow functions. Here we significantly refine the technique and implementation. In particular, to achieve soundness and improve performance, we now consider feature model constraints. In our earlier work, we were still speculating about what could be an efficient representation for Boolean constraints. In this work we present a solution based on BDDs that is highly efficient. In our eyes, BDDs are crucial to the performance of SPL^{LIFT}; we found that others do not scale nearly as well for the Boolean operations we require. Finally, for the first time we present empirical evidence of the benefits of our approach.

Our work can also be seen as an extension to an approach by Brabrand et al., who present a number of mechanisms to lift intra-procedural data-flow analyses to SPLs by extending the analysis abstraction with feature constraints [25]. Our approach, on the other hand, lifts information and data-flow analyses to SPLs in an *inter*-procedural fashion, using a different analysis framework, and in particular requiring no extension of the analysis abstraction. In SPL^{LIFT}, the implementation of the IFDS flow functions can remain unchanged. To the best of our knowledge SPL^{LIFT} is the first work that supports such transparent reuse of analyses. Another crucial difference is our efficient encoding of the distributive Boolean operations through BDDs in the IDE framework.

TypeChef [22, 27] is a parser and analysis engine for product lines written in C. It can parse the entire Linux kernel, including macros and **#ifdef** constructs (including undisciplined uses), and performs data-flow analysis. Opposed to SPL^{LIFT}, all analyses are intra-procedural, though, and use a customized analysis domain, thus not providing no support for reusing standard analyses in the way we do. We plan to integrate SPL^{LIFT} with TypeChef.

Thüm et al. survey analysis strategies for SPLs [28], focusing on parsing [22], type checking [26, 29], model checking [30, 31], and verification [32–34]. The surveyed work does not include SPL data-flow analysis approaches, but shares with our work the general goal of checking properties of a SPL with reduced redundancy and efficiency. Similar to SPL^{LIFT}, a number of approaches covered by the survey adopt a *family-based* analysis strategy, manipulating only family artifacts such as code assets and feature model. Contrasting, *product-based* strategies, such as the generate-and-analyze approach we use as baseline, manipulate products and therefore might be too expensive for product lines having a large number of products. Product-based strategies, however, might be appealing because they can simply reuse existing analyses, but this is also the case of the specific family-based strategy proposed here.

In the testing context, Kim et al. use conventional inter-procedural data-flow analysis to identify features that are reachable from a given test case [35]. The test case is then only executed with the SPL products that have these features, reducing the number of combinations to test. They are able to use an off-the-shelf analysis because they express part of the variability using conditional statements, not conditional compilation or other feature tagging mechanisms. This is similar to the technique of configuration lifting [32], which converts compile time variability into runtime variability. In this paper we propose a feature-sensitive analysis to obtain more precision. By applying our family-based analysis followed by their product-based testing one could maybe further reduce the effort to test an SPL. Similar benefits might apply for other testing approaches based on conventional analyses [36] or even feature-sensitive model level analyses [37].

The idea of making dataflow analysis sensitive to statements that may or may not be executed is related to path-sensitive dataflow analysis. Such analyses compute different analysis information along different execution paths aiming to improve precision by disregarding spurious information from infeasible paths [38] or to optimize frequently executed paths [39]. Earlier, disabling infeasible dead statements has been exploited to improve the precision of constant propagation [40] by essentially running a dead-code analysis capable of tagging statements as executable or non-executable during constant propagation analysis.

Predicated dataflow analysis [41] introduced the idea of using propositional logic predicates over runtime values to derive so-called optimistic dataflow values guarded by predicates. Such analyses are capable of producing multiple analysis versions and keeping them distinct during analysis. However, their predicates are over dynamic state rather than SPL feature constraints for which everything is statically decidable.

SPL^{LIFT} can be applied to a number of contexts, but much motivation comes from the concept of emergent interfaces [42]. These interfaces emerge on demand to give support for specific SPL maintenance tasks and thus help developers understand and manage dependencies between features. Such dependencies are generated by feature-sensitive analyses such as the ones discussed here. In particular, the performance improvements we obtain are very important to make emergent interfaces useful in practice.

8. Conclusion

We have presented SPL^{LIFT}, an approach and framework for transparently lifting IFDS-based static analysis to software product lines using the more expressive framework IDE. Using a set of experiments we were able to show that it can outperform the traditional feature-oblivious generate-and-analyze approach by several orders of magnitude. In practice, SPL^{LIFT} successfully avoids the exponential blowup usually associated with SPL analysis.

We believe this to be primarily the case because, due to its fine-grained representation of analysis facts, SPL^{LIFT} performs splits and joins of configurations as sparsely as possible. Moreover, SPL^{LIFT} piggybacks onto the user-defined IFDS-based analysis a layer of Boolean feature constraints. The functions generating those Boolean constraints are distributive and hence find a very efficient encoding in the IDE framework. Moreover, we encode all Boolean constraints using minimized binary decision diagrams (BDDs). The Boolean operations we require are conjunction, disjunction, negation and "is false". The two latter operations are constant-time on minimized BDDs. Conjunction and disjunction are, on average, efficient on BDDs, too. The JavaBDD engine we use further memoizes the result of all BDD operations, which speeds up repetitive operations to constant time.

In the future we plan to apply SPL^{LIFT} to C. Further, we will investigate the performance impact of BDD variable orderings, and to what extent a similar lifting approach can be applied also to static-analysis frameworks that are more expressive than IFDS.

Acknowledgements Thanks to Ondřej Lhoták for providing useful hints on optimizing BDDs! We also wish to thank the developers of CIDE, JavaBDD and Soot for making their tools available to us and for their continuing support. Thanks to Phil Pratt-Szeliga and Marc-André Laverdière-Papineau, who provided help with analyzing J2ME MIDlets. Thanks also to Sven Apel who provided helpful feedback on an earlier version of this paper. This work was supported by the BMBF within EC SPRIDE, by the Hessian LOEWE excellence initiative within CASED, by the DFG within the project RUNSECURE, and the Brazilian National Institute of Science and Technology for Software Engineering (INES). Finally, we would like to acknowledge the financial support from CNPq, FACEPE and a CAPES PROBRAL project.

References

[1] S. Guarnieri, M. Pistoia, O. Tripp, J. Dolby, S. Teilhet, and R. Berg, "Saving the world wide web from vulnerable JavaScript," in *Proc. 2011 int. symp. on Software Testing and Analysis*, ser. ISSTA '11, 2011, pp. 177–187.

[2] S. J. Fink, E. Yahav, N. Dor, G. Ramalingam, and E. Geay, "Effective typestate verification in the presence of aliasing," *ACM Trans. Softw. Eng. Methodol.*, vol. 17, no. 2, pp. 9:1–9:34, May 2008.

[3] N. A. Naeem and O. Lhotak, "Typestate-like analysis of multiple interacting objects," in *OOPSLA*, 2008, pp. 347–366.

[4] V. Sundaresan, L. Hendren, C. Razafimahefa, R. Vallée-Rai, P. Lam, E. Gagnon, and C. Godin, "Practical virtual method call resolution for Java," in *OOPSLA*, 2000, pp. 264–280.

[5] T. Reps, S. Horwitz, and M. Sagiv, "Precise interprocedural dataflow analysis via graph reachability," in *Proc. 22nd ACM SIGPLAN-SIGACT symp. on Principles of programming languages*, ser. POPL '95, 1995, pp. 49–61.

[6] E. Bodden, "Efficient hybrid typestate analysis by determining continuation-equivalent states," in *ICSE 2010*, May 2010, pp. 5–14.

[7] N. A. Naeem and O. Lhoták, "Efficient alias set analysis using SSA form," in *Proc. 2009 int. symp. on Memory Management*, ser. ISMM '09, 2009, pp. 79–88.

[8] S. Shoham, E. Yahav, S. Fink, and M. Pistoia, "Static specification mining using automata-based abstractions," *IEEE TSE*, vol. 34, no. 5, pp. 651–666, 2008.

[9] N. Rinetzky, M. Sagiv, and E. Yahav, "Interprocedural shape analysis for cutpoint-free programs," in *Static Analysis*, ser. Lecture Notes in Computer Science, C. Hankin and I. Siveroni, Eds. Springer Berlin / Heidelberg, 2005, vol. 3672, pp. 284–302.

[10] H. Yang, O. Lee, J. Berdine, C. Calcagno, B. Cook, D. Distefano, and P. O'Hearn, "Scalable shape analysis for systems code," in *CAV*, 2008, pp. 385–398.

[11] M. Sagiv, T. Reps, and S. Horwitz, "Precise interprocedural dataflow analysis with applications to constant propagation," in *TAPSOFT '95*, 1996, pp. 131–170.

[12] C. Kästner and S. Apel, "Virtual separation of concerns - a second chance for preprocessors," *Journal of Object Technology*, vol. 8, no. 6, pp. 59–78, 2009.

[13] C. Kästner, S. Apel, and M. Kuhlemann, "Granularity in Software Product Lines," in *Proc. 30th int. conf. on Software Engineering (ICSE'08)*, 2008, pp. 311–320.

[14] E. Bodden, "Inter-procedural data-flow analysis with ifds/ide and soot," in *SOAP 2012*, Jul. 2012, pp. 3–8, heros website: http://sable.github.com/heros/.

[15] R. Vallée-Rai, L. Hendren, V. Sundaresan, P. Lam, E. Gagnon, and P. Co, "Soot - a Java optimization framework," in *Proceedings of CASCON 1999*, 1999, pp. 125–135. [Online]. Available: www.sable.mcgill.ca/publications

[16] C. Kästner, "Virtual separation of concerns," Ph.D. dissertation, Universität Magdeburg, 2010.

[17] "The Eclipse IDE," http://eclipse.org/.

[18] E. Bodden, "Position Paper: Static flow-sensitive & context-sensitive information-flow analysis for software product lines," in *PLAS 2012*, Jun. 2012, pp. 6:1–6:6.

[19] D. Batory, "Feature models, grammars, and propositional formulas," in *Software Product Lines (SPLC) 2005*, ser. LNCS, vol. 3714, 2005, pp. 7–20.

[20] J. Liebig, C. Kästner, and S. Apel, "Analyzing the discipline of preprocessor annotations in 30 million lines of c code," in *Proc. 10th int. conf. on Aspect-oriented software development*, ser. AOSD '11, 2011, pp. 191–202.

[21] R. Drechsler and B. Becker, *Binary decision diagrams: theory and implementation*. Springer, 1998.

[22] C. Kästner, P. G. Giarrusso, T. Rendel, S. Erdweg, K. Ostermann, and T. Berger, "Variability-aware parsing in the presence of lexical macros and conditional compilation," in *Proc. 2011 ACM int. conf. on Object oriented programming systems languages and applications*, ser. OOPSLA '11, 2011, pp. 805–824.

[23] E. Bodden, A. Sewe, J. Sinschek, H. Oueslati, and M. Mezini, "Taming reflection: Aiding static analysis in the presence of reflection and custom class loaders," in *ICSE 2011*, May 2011, pp. 241–250.

[24] T. Reps, S. Schwoon, and S. Jha, "Weighted pushdown systems and their application to interprocedural dataflow analysis," in *Static Analysis*, ser. Lecture Notes in Computer Science, R. Cousot, Ed. Springer Berlin / Heidelberg, 2003, vol. 2694, pp. 1075–1075.

[25] C. Brabrand, M. Ribeiro, T. Tolêdo, and P. Borba, "Intraprocedural dataflow analysis for software product lines," in *Proc. 11th annual int. conf. on Aspect-oriented Software Development*, ser. AOSD '12, 2012, pp. 13–24.

[26] S. Apel, C. Kästner, A. Grösslinger, and C. Lengauer, "Type safety for feature-oriented product lines," *Automated Software Eng.*, vol. 17, no. 3, pp. 251–300, Sep. 2010.

[27] "Typechef analysis engine," http://ckaestne.github.com/TypeChef/.

[28] T. Thüm, S. Apel, C. Kästner, M. Kuhlemann, I. Schaefer, and G. Saake, "Analysis strategies for software product lines," School of Computer Science, University of Magdeburg, Tech. Rep. FIN-004-2012, Apr. 2012.

[29] C. Kästner and S. Apel, "Type-checking software product lines - a formal approach," in *Proc. 2008 23rd IEEE/ACM int. conf. on Automated Software Engineering*, ser. ASE '08, 2008, pp. 258–267.

[30] A. Classen, P. Heymans, P.-Y. Schobbens, A. Legay, and J.-F. Raskin, "Model checking lots of systems: efficient verification of temporal properties in software product lines," in *Proc. 32nd ACM/IEEE int. conf. on Software Engineering - Volume 1*, ser. ICSE '10, 2010, pp. 335–344.

[31] A. Classen, P. Heymans, P.-Y. Schobbens, and A. Legay, "Symbolic model checking of software product lines," in *Proc. 33rd int. conf. on Software Engineering*, ser. ICSE '11, 2011, pp. 321–330.

[32] H. Post and C. Sinz, "Configuration lifting: Verification meets software configuration," in *Proc. 2008 23rd IEEE/ACM int. conf. on Automated Software Engineering*, ser. ASE '08, 2008, pp. 347–350.

[33] C. H. P. Kim, E. Bodden, D. Batory, and S. Khurshid, "Reducing configurations to monitor in a software product line," in *Proc. First int. conf. on Runtime verification*, ser. RV'10, 2010, pp. 285–299.

[34] S. Apel, H. Speidel, P. Wendler, A. von Rhein, and D. Beyer, "Detection of feature interactions using feature-aware verification," in *Proc. 2011 26th IEEE/ACM int. conf. on Automated Software Engineering*, ser. ASE '11, 2011, pp. 372–375.

[35] C. Hwan, P. Kim, D. Batory, and S. Khurshid, "Reducing combinatorics in testing product lines," in *Proc. 10th int. conf. on Aspect-oriented Software Development (AOSD'11)*, 2011, pp. 57–68.

[36] J. Shi, M. Cohen, and M. Dwyer, "Integration testing of software product lines using compositional symbolic execution," in *Fundamental Approaches to Software Engineering*, ser. Lecture Notes in Computer Science, J. de Lara and A. Zisman, Eds. Springer Berlin / Heidelberg, 2012, vol. 7212, pp. 270–284.

[37] V. Stricker, A. Metzger, and K. Pohl, "Avoiding redundant testing in application engineering," in *Software Product Lines: Going Beyond*, ser. Lecture Notes in Computer Science, J. Bosch and J. Lee, Eds. Springer Berlin / Heidelberg, 2010, vol. 6287, pp. 226–240.

[38] T. Ball and S. K. Rajamani, "Bebop: a path-sensitive interprocedural dataflow engine," in *Proc. 2001 ACM SIGPLAN-SIGSOFT workshop on Program analysis for software tools and engineering*, ser. PASTE '01, 2001, pp. 97–103.

[39] G. Ammons and J. R. Larus, "Improving data-flow analysis with path profiles," *SIGPLAN Not.*, vol. 39, no. 4, pp. 568–582, Apr. 2004.

[40] M. N. Wegman and F. K. Zadeck, "Constant propagation with conditional branches," *ACM Trans. Program. Lang. Syst.*, vol. 13, no. 2, pp. 181–210, Apr. 1991.

[41] S. Moon, M. W. Hall, and B. R. Murphy, "Predicated array dataflow analysis for run-time parallelization," in *Proc. 12th int. conf. on Supercomputing*, ser. ICS '98, 1998, pp. 204–211.

[42] M. Ribeiro, H. Pacheco, L. Teixeira, and P. Borba, "Emergent feature modularization," in *Proc. ACM int. conf. companion on Object oriented programming systems languages and applications companion*, ser. SPLASH '10, 2010, pp. 11–18.

Finding Optimum Abstractions in Parametric Dataflow Analysis

Xin Zhang
Georgia Institute of Technology, USA
xin.zhang@gatech.edu

Mayur Naik
Georgia Institute of Technology, USA
naik@cc.gatech.edu

Hongseok Yang
University of Oxford, UK
hongseok.yang@cs.ox.ac.uk

Abstract

We propose a technique to efficiently search a large family of abstractions in order to prove a query using a parametric dataflow analysis. Our technique either finds the cheapest such abstraction or shows that none exists. It is based on counterexample-guided abstraction refinement but applies a novel meta-analysis on abstract counterexample traces to efficiently find abstractions that are incapable of proving the query. We formalize the technique in a generic framework and apply it to two analyses: a type-state analysis and a thread-escape analysis. We demonstrate the effectiveness of the technique on a suite of Java benchmark programs.

Categories and Subject Descriptors D.2.4 [*SOFTWARE ENGINEERING*]: Software/Program Verification; F.3.2 [*LOGICS AND MEANINGS OF PROGRAMS*]: Semantics of Programming Languages—Program analysis

General Terms Languages, Verification

Keywords Dataflow analysis, CEGAR, abstraction refinement, optimum abstraction, impossibility, under-approximation

1. Introduction

A central problem in static analysis concerns how to balance its precision and cost. A *query-driven analysis* seeks to address this problem by searching for an abstraction that discards program details that are unnecessary for proving an individual query.

We consider query-driven dataflow analyses that are parametric in the abstraction. The abstraction is chosen from a large family that allow abstracting different parts of a program with varying precision. A large number of fine-grained abstractions enables an analysis to specialize to a query but poses a hard search problem in practice. First, the number of abstractions is infinite or intractably large to search naïvely, with most abstractions in the family being too imprecise or too costly to prove a particular query. Second, proving queries in different parts of the same program requires different abstractions. Finally, a query might be unprovable by all abstractions in the family, either because the query is not true or due to limitations of the analysis at hand.

We propose an efficient technique to solve the above search problem. It either finds the cheapest abstraction in the family that proves a query or shows that no abstraction in the family can prove the query. We call this the *optimum abstraction problem*. Our technique is based on counterexample-guided abstraction refinement (CEGAR) but differs radically in how it analyzes an abstract counterexample trace: it computes a sufficient condition for the failure of the analysis to prove the query along the trace. The condition represents a set of abstractions such that the analysis instantiated using any abstraction in this set is guaranteed to fail to prove the query. Our technique finds such unviable abstractions by doing a backward analysis on the trace. This backward analysis is a *meta-analysis* that must be proven sound with respect to the abstract semantics of the forward analysis. Scalability of backward analyses is typically hindered by exploring program states that are unreachable from the initial state. Our backward analysis avoids this problem as it is guided by the trace from the forward analysis. This trace also enables our backward analysis to do under-approximation while guaranteeing to find a non-empty set of unviable abstractions.

Like the forward analysis, the backward meta-analysis is a static analysis, and the performance of our technique depends on how this meta-analysis balances its own precision and cost. If it does under-approximation aggressively, it analyzes the trace efficiently but finds only the current abstraction unviable and needs more iterations to converge. On the other hand, if it does under-approximation passively, it analyzes the trace inefficiently but finds many abstractions unviable and needs fewer iterations. We present a generic framework to develop an efficient meta-analysis, which involves choosing an abstract domain, devising (backward) transfer functions, and proving these functions sound with respect to the forward analysis. Our framework uses a generic DNF representation of formulas in the domain and provides generic optimizations to scale the meta-analysis. We show the applicability of the framework to two analyses: a type-state analysis and a thread-escape analysis.

We evaluate our technique using these two client analyses on seven Java benchmark programs of 400K–600K bytecodes each. Both analyses are fully flow- and context-sensitive with 2^N possible abstractions, where N is the number of pointer variables for type-state analysis, and the number of object allocation sites for thread-escape analysis. The technique finds the cheapest abstraction or shows that none exists for 92.5% of queries posed on average per client analysis per benchmark program.

We summarize the main contributions of this paper:

- We formulate the optimum abstraction problem for parametric dataflow analysis. The formulation seeks a cheapest abstraction that proves the query or an impossibility result that none exists.
- We present a new refinement-based technique to solve the problem. The key idea is a meta-analysis that analyzes counterexamples to find abstractions that are incapable of proving the query.
- We present a generic framework to design the meta-analysis along with an efficient representation and optimizations to scale it. We apply the framework to two analyses in the literature.
- We demonstrate the efficacy of our technique in practice on the two analyses, a type-state analysis and a thread-escape analysis, for several real-world Java benchmark programs.

PLDI'13, June 16–19, 2013, Seattle, WA, USA.

The rest of the paper is organized as follows. Section 2 illustrates our technique on an example. Section 3 formalizes parametric dataflow analysis and the optimum abstraction problem. We first define a generic framework and then apply it to our two example analyses. Section 4 presents our meta-analysis, first in a generic setting and then for a domain that suffices for our two analyses. Section 5 gives our overall algorithm and Section 6 presents empirical results. Section 7 discusses related work and Section 8 concludes.

2. Example

We illustrate our technique using the program in Figure 1(a). The program operates on a File object which can be in either state *opened* or *closed* at any instant. It begins in state *closed* upon creation, transitions to state *opened* after the call to open(), and back to state *closed* after the call to close(). Suppose that it is an error to call open() in the *opened* state, or to call close() in the *closed* state. Statements $check_1$ and $check_2$ at the end of the program are queries which ask whether the state of the File object is *closed* or *opened*, respectively, at the end of every program run.

A static type-state analysis can be used to conservatively answer such queries. Such an analysis must track aliasing relationships between pointer variables in order to track the state of objects correctly and precisely. For instance, in our example program, the analysis must infer that variables x and y point to the same File object in order to prove query $check_1$. Analyses that track more program facts are typically more precise but also more costly. A query-based analysis enables striking a balance between precision and cost by not tracking program facts that are unnecessary for proving an individual query.

Making our type-state analysis query-based enables it to track only variables that matter for answering a particular query (such as $check_1$). We therefore parameterize this analysis by an *abstraction* π which specifies the set of variables that the analysis must track. An abstraction π_1 is cheaper than an abstraction π_2 if π_1 tracks fewer variables than π_2 (i.e., $|\pi_1| < |\pi_2|$). For a program with N variables there are 2^N possible abstractions. Figure 1(b) shows which abstractions in this family are suitable for each of our two queries. Any abstraction containing variables x and y is precise enough to let our analysis prove query $check_1$. The cheapest of these abstractions is $\{x, y\}$. On the other hand, our analysis cannot prove query $check_2$ using any abstraction in the family. This is because query $check_2$ is not true concretely, but the analysis may fail to prove even true queries due to its conservative nature.

We propose an efficient technique for finding the cheapest abstraction in the family that proves a query or showing that no abstraction in the family can prove the query. We illustrate our technique on our parametric type-state analysis. This analysis is fully flow- and context-sensitive, and tracks for each allocation site in the program a pair $\langle ts, vs\rangle$ or $\top$, where ts over-approximates the set of possible type-states of an object created at that site, and vs is a must-alias set—a set of variables that definitely point to that object. Only variables in the abstraction π used to instantiate the analysis are allowed to appear in any must-alias set. $\top$ denotes that the analysis has detected a type-state error.

Our technique starts by running the analysis with the cheapest abstraction. For our type-state analysis this corresponds to not tracking any variable at all. The resulting analysis fails to prove query $check_1$. Our technique is CEGAR-based and requires the analysis to produce an abstract counterexample trace as a failure witness. Such a trace showing the failure to prove query $check_1$ under the cheapest abstraction is shown in Figure 1(c). The trace is annotated with abstract states computed by the analysis, denoted $\downarrow$, that track information about the lone allocation site in the program. Note that state $\langle\{\textit{closed}\}, \{\}\rangle$ incoming into call x.open() results in outgoing state $\langle\{\textit{opened}, \textit{closed}\}, \{\}\rangle$ even though the File object cannot be in the *closed* state after the call. This is because the analysis does a weak update as x is not in the must-alias set of the incoming abstract state.

At this point our technique has eliminated abstraction $\pi = \{\}$ as incapable of proving query $check_1$ and must determine which abstraction to try next. Since the number of abstractions is large, however, it first analyzes the trace to eliminate abstractions that are guaranteed to suffer a failure similar to the current one. It does so by performing a backward meta-analysis that inspects the trace backwards and analyzes the result of the (forward) type-state analysis. This meta-analysis is itself a static analysis and the abstract states it computes are denoted by $\uparrow$ in Figure 1(c). Each abstract state of the meta-analysis represents a set of pairs (d, π) consisting of an abstract state d of the forward analysis and an abstraction π. An abstract state of the meta-analysis is a boolean formula over primitives of the form: (1) *err* representing the set of pairs where the d component is $\top$; (2) $\textit{closed} \in ts$ representing the set of pairs where the d component is $\langle ts, vs\rangle$ and ts contains *closed*; (3) $x \in vs$ which is analogous to (2) except that vs contains x; and (4) $x \in \pi$ meaning the π component contains x.

The meta-analysis starts with the weakest formula under which $check_1$ fails, which is $\textit{err} \vee (\textit{opened} \in ts)$, and propagates its weakest precondition at each step of the trace to obtain formula $(\textit{closed} \in ts) \wedge (\textit{opened} \notin ts) \wedge (x \notin \pi)$ at the start of the trace. This formula implies that any abstraction not containing variable x cannot prove query $check_1$. Our meta-analysis has two notable aspects. First, it does not require the family of abstractions to be finite: it can show that all abstractions in even an infinite family cannot prove a query. Second, it avoids the blowup inherent in backward analyses by performing under-approximation. It achieves this for the above domain of boolean formulae by dropping disjuncts in the DNF representation of the formulae. A crucial condition ensured by our meta-analysis during under-approximation is that the abstract state computed by the forward analysis is contained in the resulting simpler formula. Otherwise, it is not possible to guarantee that the eliminated abstractions cannot prove the query. Section 4 explains how our technique picks the best k disjuncts for a $k \geq 1$ specified by the analysis designer. Smaller k enables the meta-analysis to run efficiently on each trace but can require more iterations by eliminating only the current abstraction in each iteration in the extreme case. We use $k = 1$ for this example and highlight in bold the chosen (retained) disjunct in each formula with multiple disjuncts in Figure 1. For instance, we drop the second disjunct in formula $\textit{err} \vee (\textit{opened} \in ts)$ at the end point of the trace in Figure 1(c), since abstract state $\top$ computed by the forward analysis at that point is not in the set of states represented by $(\textit{opened} \in ts)$. The weakest precondition of the chosen disjunct *err* with respect to the call y.close() is $\textit{err} \vee (\textit{closed} \in ts)$, but this time we drop disjunct *err* as the abstract state $\langle\{\textit{closed}, \textit{opened}\}, \{\}\rangle$ computed by the forward analysis is not in the set of states represented by *err*.

Having eliminated all abstractions that do not contain variable x, our technique next runs the type-state analysis with abstraction $\pi = \{x\}$, but again fails to prove query $check_1$, and produces the trace showed in Figure 1(d). Our meta-analysis performed on this trace infers that any abstraction containing variable x but not containing variable y cannot prove the query. Hence, our technique next runs the type-state analysis with abstraction $\pi = \{x, y\}$, and this time succeeds in proving the query. Our technique is effective at slicing away program details that are irrelevant to proving a query. For instance, even if either of the traces in Figure 1 (c) or (d) contained the statement "if (*) z = x", variable z would not be included in any abstraction that our technique tries; indeed, tracking variable z is not necessary for proving query $check_1$.

Finally, consider the query $check_2$. Our technique starts with the cheapest abstraction $\pi = \{\}$, and obtains a trace identical

```
x = new File;
y = x;
if (*) z = x;
x.open();
y.close();
if (*)
    check₁(x, closed);
else
    check₂(x, opened);
```

(a) Example program.

query	abstraction
$check_1$	any $\pi \supseteq \{x, y\}$
$check_2$	none

(b) Feasible solutions.

$\uparrow$ *closed* $\in ts \wedge$ *opened* $\notin ts \wedge x \notin \pi$
x = new File;
$\downarrow \langle\{closed\}, \{\}\rangle$
$\uparrow$ *closed* $\in ts \wedge$ *opened* $\notin ts \wedge x \notin vs$
y = x;
$\downarrow \langle\{closed\}, \{\}\rangle$
$\uparrow$ *closed* $\in ts \wedge$ *opened* $\notin ts \wedge x \notin vs$
x.open();
$\downarrow \langle\{closed, opened\}, \{\}\rangle$
$\uparrow$ *err* $\vee$ ***closed*** $\in \boldsymbol{ts}$
y.close();
$\downarrow \top$
$\uparrow$ ***err*** $\vee$ *opened* $\in ts$
$check_1$(x, *closed*);

(c) Iteration 1 for query $check_1$ using $\pi = \{\}$.

$\uparrow$ *closed* $\in ts \wedge$ *opened* $\notin ts \wedge y \notin \pi \wedge x \in \pi$
x = new File;
$\downarrow \langle\{closed\}, \{x\}\rangle$
$\uparrow$ *closed* $\in ts \wedge$ *opened* $\notin ts \wedge y \notin \pi \wedge x \in vs$
y = x;
$\downarrow \langle\{closed\}, \{x\}\rangle$
$\uparrow$ *closed* $\in ts \wedge$ *opened* $\notin ts \wedge y \notin vs \wedge x \in vs$
x.open();
$\downarrow \langle\{opened\}, \{x\}\rangle$
$\uparrow$ *opened* $\in ts \wedge$ *closed* $\notin ts \wedge y \notin vs$
y.close();
$\downarrow \langle\{closed, opened\}, \{x\}\rangle$
$\uparrow$ *err* $\vee$ ***opened*** $\in \boldsymbol{ts}$
$check_1$(x, *closed*);

(d) Iteration 2 for query $check_1$ using $\pi = \{x\}$.

$\uparrow$ *closed* $\in ts \wedge$ *opened* $\notin ts \wedge x \in \pi$
x = new File;
$\downarrow \langle\{closed\}, \{x\}\rangle$
$\uparrow$ *closed* $\in ts \wedge$ *opened* $\notin ts \wedge x \in vs$
y = x;
$\downarrow \langle\{closed\}, \{x\}\rangle$
$\uparrow$ *closed* $\in ts \wedge$ *opened* $\notin ts \wedge x \in vs$
x.open();
$\downarrow \langle\{opened\}, \{x\}\rangle$
$\uparrow$ *opened* $\in ts \wedge$ *closed* $\notin ts$
y.close();
$\downarrow \langle\{closed, opened\}, \{x\}\rangle$
$\uparrow$ *err* $\vee$ ***closed*** $\in \boldsymbol{ts}$
$check_2$(x, *opened*);

(e) Iteration 2 for query $check_2$ using $\pi = \{x\}$.

Figure 1. Example illustrating our technique for a parametric type-state analysis.

to that in Figure 1(b) for query $check_1$, except that the meta-analysis starts by propagating formula $err \vee (closed \in ts)$ instead of $err \vee (opened \in ts)$. The same disjunct *err* in this formula is retained and the rest of the meta-analysis result is identical. Thus, in the next iteration, our technique runs the type-state analysis with abstraction $\pi = \{x\}$, and obtains the trace shown in Figure 1(e). This time, the meta-analysis retains disjunct $(closed \in ts)$, and concludes any abstraction containing variable x cannot prove the query. Since in the first iteration all abstractions without variable x were eliminated, our technique concludes that the analysis cannot prove query $check_2$ using any abstraction.

3. Formalism

This section describes a formal setting used throughout the paper.

3.1 Programming Language

We present our results using a simple imperative language:

$$\begin{aligned}(\text{atomic command})\ & a ::= \ldots \\ (\text{program})\ & s ::= a \mid s\,;\,s' \mid s + s' \mid s^*\end{aligned}$$

The language includes a (unspecified) set of atomic commands. Examples are assignments $v = w.f$ and statements $\mathsf{assume}(e)$ which filter out executions where e evaluates to false. The language also has the standard compound constructs: sequential composition, non-deterministic choice, and iteration. A ***trace*** τ is a finite sequence of atomic commands $a_1 a_2 \ldots a_n$. It records the steps taken during one execution of a program. Function $\mathsf{trace}(s)$ in Figure 2 shows a standard way to generate all traces of a program s.

3.2 Parametric Dataflow Analysis

We consider dataflow analyses whose transfer functions for atomic commands are parametric in the abstraction. We specify such a parametric analysis by the following data:

1. A set $(\mathbb{P}, \preceq)$ with a preorder $\preceq$ (i.e., $\preceq$ is reflexive and transitive). Elements $\pi \in \mathbb{P}$ are parameter values. We call them *abstractions* as they determine the degree of approximation performed by the analysis. The preorder $\preceq$ on π's dictates the cost of the analysis: using a smaller π yields a cheaper analysis. We require that every nonempty subset $P \subseteq \mathbb{P}$ has a *minimum* element $\pi \in P$ (i.e., $\pi \preceq \pi'$ for every $\pi' \in P$).

$$\begin{aligned}\mathsf{trace}(a) &= \{a\} \\ \mathsf{trace}(s + s') &= \mathsf{trace}(s) \cup \mathsf{trace}(s') \\ \mathsf{trace}(s\,;\,s') &= \{\tau\,\tau' \mid \tau \in \mathsf{trace}(s) \wedge \tau' \in \mathsf{trace}(s')\} \\ \mathsf{trace}(s^*) &= \mathsf{leastFix}\,\lambda T.\,\{\epsilon\} \cup \{\tau;\tau' \mid \tau \in T \wedge \tau' \in \mathsf{trace}(s)\}\end{aligned}$$

Figure 2. Traces of a program s. Symbol ϵ denotes an empty trace.

2. A finite set $\mathbb{D}$ of abstract states. Our analysis uses a set of abstract states to approximate reachable concrete states at each program point. Formally, this means the analysis is disjunctive.
3. A transfer function $[\![a]\!]_\pi : \mathbb{D} \to \mathbb{D}$ for each atomic command a. The function is parameterized by $\pi \in \mathbb{P}$.

A parametric analysis analyzes a program in a standard way except that it requires an abstraction to be provided before the analysis starts. The abstract semantics in Figure 3 describes the behavior of the analysis formally. In the figure, a program s denotes a transformer $F_\pi[s]$ on sets of abstract states, which is parameterized by $\pi \in \mathbb{P}$. Note that the abstraction π is used when atomic commands are interpreted. Hence, π controls the analysis by changing the transfer functions for atomic commands. Besides this parameterization all the defining clauses are standard.

Our parametric analyses satisfy a fact of disjunctive analyses:

LEMMA 1. *For all programs s, abstractions π, and abstract states d, we have $F_\pi[s](\{d\}) = \{F_\pi[\tau](d) \mid \tau \in \mathsf{trace}(s)\}$, where $F_\pi[\tau]$ is the result of analyzing trace τ as shown in Figure 3.*

The lemma ensures that for all final abstract states $d' \in F_\pi[s](\{d\})$, we can construct a trace τ transforming d to d'. This trace does not have loops and is much simpler than the original program s. We show later how our technique exploits this simplicity (Section 4). We now formalize two example parametric analyses.

Type-State Analysis. Our first example is a variant of the type-state analysis from [7]. The original analysis maintains various kinds of aliasing facts in order to track the type-state of objects correctly and precisely. Our variant only tracks must-alias facts.

We assume we are given a set $\mathbb{T}$ of type-states containing *init*, which represents the initial type-state of objects, and a function $[\![m]\!] : \mathbb{T} \to \mathbb{T} \cup \{\top\}$ for every method m, which describes how a call $x.m()$ changes the type-state of object x and when it leads to

$$
\begin{aligned}
F_\pi[s] &: 2^{\mathbb{D}} \to 2^{\mathbb{D}} \\
F_\pi[a](D) &= \{[\![a]\!]_\pi(d) \mid d \in D\} \\
F_\pi[s\,;\,s'](D) &= (F_\pi[s'] \circ F_\pi[s])(D) \\
F_\pi[s + s'](D) &= F_\pi[s](D) \cup F_\pi[s'](D) \\
F_\pi[s^*](D) &= \mathsf{leastFix}\ \lambda D_0.\, D \cup F_\pi[s](D_0)
\end{aligned}
$$

$$
\begin{aligned}
F_\pi[\tau] &: \mathbb{D} \to \mathbb{D} \\
F_\pi[\epsilon](d) &= d \\
F_\pi[a](d) &= [\![a]\!]_\pi(d) \\
F_\pi[\tau\,;\,\tau'](d) &= F_\pi[\tau'](F_\pi[\tau](d))
\end{aligned}
$$

Figure 3. Abstract semantics. In the case of loop, we take the least fixpoint with respect to the subset order in the powerset domain $2^{\mathbb{D}}$.

$$
\begin{array}{rl}
\text{(type-states)} & \sigma \in \mathbb{T} \text{ (we assume } init \in \mathbb{T}) \\
\text{(variables)} & x, y \in \mathbb{V} \\
\text{(analysis parameter)} & \pi \in \mathbb{P} = 2^{\mathbb{V}} \\
\text{(abstract state)} & d \in \mathbb{D} = (2^{\mathbb{T}} \times 2^{\mathbb{V}}) \cup \{\top\} \\
\text{(order on parameters)} & \pi \preceq \pi' \Leftrightarrow |\pi| \leq |\pi'|
\end{array}
$$

$$
\text{(transfer function)} \quad [\![a]\!]_\pi : \mathbb{D} \to \mathbb{D}
$$

$$
\begin{aligned}
[\![a]\!]_\pi(\top) &= \top \\
[\![x = y]\!]_\pi(ts, vs) &= \begin{cases} (ts, vs \cup \{x\}) \text{ if } y \in vs \wedge x \in \pi \\ (ts, vs \setminus \{x\}) \text{ otherwise} \end{cases} \\
[\![x = \mathtt{null}]\!]_\pi(ts, vs) &= (ts, vs \setminus \{x\}) \\
[\![x.m()]\!]_\pi(ts, vs) &= \begin{cases} \top & \text{if } \exists \sigma \in ts.\, [\![m]\!](\sigma) = \top \\ (\{[\![m]\!](\sigma) \mid \sigma \in ts\}, vs) & \text{else if } x \in vs \\ (ts \cup \{[\![m]\!](\sigma) \mid \sigma \in ts\}, vs) & \text{otherwise} \end{cases}
\end{aligned}
$$

Figure 4. Data for the type-state analysis.

an error, denoted $\top$. Using these data, we specify the domains and transfer functions of the analysis in Figure 4.

The abstraction π for the analysis is a set of variables that determines what can appear in the must-alias set of an abstract state during the analysis. An abstract state d has form (ts, vs) or $\top$, where vs should be a subset of π, and it tracks information about a single object. In the former case, ts represents all the possible type-states of the tracked object and vs, the must-alias set of this object. The latter means that the object can be in any type-state including the error state $\top$. For brevity, we show transfer functions only for simple assignments and method calls. Those for assignments $x = y$ and $x = \mathtt{null}$ update the must-alias set according to their concrete semantics and abstraction π. The transfer function for a method call $x.m()$ updates the ts component of the input abstract state using $[\![m]\!]$. In the case where the must-alias set is imprecise, this update includes both the old and new type-states.

According to our order $\preceq$, an abstraction π is smaller than π' when its cardinality is smaller than π'. Hence, running this analysis with a smaller π implies that the analysis would be less precise about must-alias sets, which normally correlates the faster convergence of the fixpoint iteration of the analysis.

Thread-Escape Analysis. Our second example is a variant of the thread-escape analysis from [17]. A heap object in a multithreaded shared-memory program is thread-local when it is reachable only from at most a single thread. A thread-escape analysis conservatively answers queries about thread locality.

Let $\mathbb{H}$ be the set of allocation sites, $\mathbb{L}$ that of local variables, and $\mathbb{F}$ that of object fields in a program. Using these data, we specify the domains and transfer functions of the analysis in Figure 5. There $\mathtt{N}$ means the null value, and $\mathtt{L}$ and $\mathtt{E}$ are abstract locations, representing disjoint sets of heap objects, except that both $\mathtt{L}$ and $\mathtt{E}$ include the null value. Abstract location $\mathtt{E}$ summaries null, all the thread-escaping objects, and possibly some thread-local ones. On the other hand, $\mathtt{L}$ denotes all the other heap objects and null; hence it means only thread-local objects, although it might miss some such objects. The analysis maintains an invariant that $\mathtt{E}$-summarized objects are closed under pointer reachability: if a heap object is summarized by $\mathtt{E}$, following any of its fields always gives null or $\mathtt{E}$-summarized objects, but not $\mathtt{L}$-summarized ones.

An abstraction π determines for each site $h \in \mathbb{H}$ whether $\mathtt{L}$ or $\mathtt{E}$ should be used to summarize objects allocated at h. An abstract element d is a function from local variables or fields of $\mathtt{L}$-summarized objects to abstract locations or $\mathtt{N}$. It records the values of local variables and those of the fields of $\mathtt{L}$-summarized heap objects. For instance, abstract state $[v \mapsto \mathtt{L}, f_1 \mapsto \mathtt{E}, f_2 \mapsto \mathtt{E}]$ means that local variable v points to some heap object summarized by $\mathtt{L}$, and fields f_1, f_2 of every $\mathtt{L}$ object point to those summarized by $\mathtt{E}$. Since all thread-escaping objects are summarized by $\mathtt{E}$, this abstract state implies that v points to a thread-local heap object.

We order abstractions $\pi \preceq \pi'$ based on how many sites are mapped to $\mathtt{L}$ by π and π'. This is because the number of $\mathtt{L}$-mapped sites usually correlates the performance of the analysis.

The thread-escape analysis includes transfer functions of the following heap-manipulating commands:

$$
\begin{aligned}
a ::= {} & v = \mathsf{new}\, h \mid g = v \mid v = g \mid v = \mathtt{null} \mid v = v' \mid \\
& v = v'.f \mid v.f = v'
\end{aligned}
$$

Here g and v are global and local variables, respectively, and $h \in \mathbb{H}$ is an allocation site. Transfer functions of these commands simulate their usual meanings but on abstract instead of concrete states.

Function $[\![v = \mathsf{new}\, h]\!]_\pi(d)$ makes variable v point to abstract location $\pi(h)$, simulating the allocation of a $\pi(h)$-summarized object and the binding of this object with v. The transfer function for $g = v$ models that if v points to a thread-local object, this assignment makes the object escape, because it exposes the object to other threads via the global variable g. When v points to $\mathtt{L}$, the transfer function calls $\mathsf{esc}(d)$, which sets all local variables to $\mathtt{E}$ (unless they have value $\mathtt{N}$) and resets all fields to $\mathtt{N}$. This means that after calling $\mathsf{esc}(d)$, the analysis loses most of the information about thread locality, and concludes that all variables point to potentially escaping objects. This dramatic information loss is inevitable because if v points to $\mathtt{L}$ beforehand, the assignment $g = v$ can cause any object summarized by $\mathtt{L}$ to escape. The transfer functions of the remaining commands in the figure can be understood similarly by referring to the concrete semantics and approximating it over abstract states.

Figure 6 shows the abstract state (denoted by $\downarrow$) computed by our thread-escape analysis at each point of an example program. The results of the analysis in parts (a) and (b1) of the figure are obtained using the same abstraction $[\mathtt{h1} \mapsto \mathtt{E}, \mathtt{h2} \mapsto \mathtt{E}]$ and are thus identical; the results in part (b2) are obtained using a different abstraction $[\mathtt{h1} \mapsto \mathtt{L}, \mathtt{h2} \mapsto \mathtt{E}]$.

3.3 Optimum Abstraction Problem

Parametric dataflow analyses are used in the context of query-driven verification where we are given not just a program to analyze but also a query to prove. In this usage scenario, the most important matter to resolve before running the analysis is to choose a right abstraction π. Ideally, we would like to pick π that causes the analysis to keep enough information to prove a given query for a given program, but to discard information unnecessary for this proof, so that the analysis achieves high efficiency.

The optimum abstraction problem provides a guideline on resolving the issue of abstraction selection. It sets a specific target on abstractions to aim at. Assume that we are interested in queries expressed as subsets of $\mathbb{D}$. The problem is defined as follows:

```
  ↓ [u ↦ N, v ↦ N]
  ↑ h1→E ∨ (h2→E ∧ h1→L)
u = new h1;
  ↓ [u ↦ E, v ↦ N]
  ↑ u→E ∨ (h2→E ∧ u→L) ∨ (h2→L ∧ f→E ∧ u→L)
v = new h2;
  ↓ [u ↦ E, v ↦ E]
  ↑ u→E ∨ (v→E ∧ u→L) ∨ (v→L ∧ f→E ∧ u→L)
v.f = u;
  ↓ [u ↦ E, v ↦ E]
  ↑ u→E
pc: local(u)?
```

(a) $\pi = [\mathtt{h1} \mapsto \mathtt{E}, \mathtt{h2} \mapsto \mathtt{E}]$

```
  ↓ [u ↦ N, v ↦ N]
  ↑ h1→E
u = new h1;
  ↓ [u ↦ E, v ↦ N]
  ↑ u→E
v = new h2;
  ↓ [u ↦ E, v ↦ E]
  ↑ u→E
v.f = u;
  ↓ [u ↦ E, v ↦ E]
  ↑ u→E
pc: local(u)?
```

(b1) $\pi = [\mathtt{h1} \mapsto \mathtt{E}, \mathtt{h2} \mapsto \mathtt{E}]$

```
  ↓ [u ↦ N, v ↦ N]
  ↑ h1→L ∧ h2→E
u = new h1;
  ↓ [u ↦ L, v ↦ N]
  ↑ u→L ∧ h2→E
v = new h2;
  ↓ [u ↦ L, v ↦ E]
  ↑ u→L ∧ v→E
v.f = u;
  ↓ [u ↦ E, v ↦ E]
  ↑ u→E
pc: local(u)?
```

(b2) $\pi = [\mathtt{h1} \mapsto \mathtt{L}, \mathtt{h2} \mapsto \mathtt{E}]$

Figure 6. Example showing our technique for thread-escape analysis with under-approximation (parts (b1) and (b2)) and without (part (a)).

(allocation sites)	$h \in \mathbb{H}$
(local variables)	$v \in \mathbb{V}$
(object fields)	$f \in \mathbb{F}$
(analysis parameter)	$\pi \in \mathbb{P} = \mathbb{H} \to \{\mathtt{L}, \mathtt{E}\}$
(abstract state)	$d \in \mathbb{D} = (\mathbb{L} \cup \mathbb{F}) \to \{\mathtt{L}, \mathtt{E}, \mathtt{N}\}$

(order on parameters) $\pi \preceq \pi' \Leftrightarrow |\{h \in \mathbb{H} \mid \pi(h) = \mathtt{L}\}| \leq |\{h \in \mathbb{H} \mid \pi'(h) = \mathtt{L}\}|$

$$\mathsf{esc} \;:\; \mathbb{D} \to \mathbb{D}$$
$$\mathsf{esc}(d) \;=\; \lambda u.\,\text{if } (d(u) = \mathtt{N} \vee u \in \mathbb{F}) \text{ then } \mathtt{N} \text{ else } \mathtt{E}$$

(transfer function) $[\![a]\!]_\pi \;:\; \mathbb{D} \to \mathbb{D}$

$$\begin{aligned}
[\![v = \mathsf{new}\, h]\!]_\pi(d) &= d[v \mapsto \pi(h)] \\
[\![g = v]\!]_\pi(d) &= \text{if } (d(v) = \mathtt{L}) \text{ then } \mathsf{esc}(d) \text{ else } d \\
[\![v = g]\!]_\pi(d) &= d[v \mapsto \mathtt{E}] \\
[\![v = \mathtt{null}]\!]_\pi(d) &= d[v \mapsto \mathtt{N}] \\
[\![v = v']\!]_\pi(d) &= d[v \mapsto d(v')] \\
[\![v = v'.f]\!]_\pi(d) &= \begin{cases} d[v \mapsto d(f)] & \text{if } (d(v') = \mathtt{L}) \\ d[v \mapsto \mathtt{E}] & \text{otherwise} \end{cases} \\
[\![v.f = v']\!]_\pi(d) &=
\end{aligned}$$
$$\begin{cases}
\mathsf{esc}(d) & \text{if } d(v) = \mathtt{E} \wedge d(v') = \mathtt{L} \\
d & \text{if } (d(v) = \mathtt{E} \wedge d(v') \neq \mathtt{L}) \vee d(v) = \mathtt{N} \\
\mathsf{esc}(d) & \text{if } d(v) = \mathtt{L} \wedge \{d(f), d(v')\} = \{\mathtt{L}, \mathtt{E}\} \\
d[f \mapsto \mathtt{L}] & \text{if } d(v) = \mathtt{L} \wedge \{d(f), d(v')\} = \{\mathtt{N}, \mathtt{L}\} \\
d[f \mapsto \mathtt{E}] & \text{if } d(v) = \mathtt{L} \wedge \{d(f), d(v')\} = \{\mathtt{N}, \mathtt{E}\} \\
d & \text{if } d(v) = \mathtt{L} \wedge d(f) = d(v')
\end{cases}$$

Figure 5. Data for the thread-escape analysis.

DEFINITION 2 (Optimal Abstraction Problem). *Given a program s, an initial abstract state d_I, and a query $q \subseteq \mathbb{D}$, find a minimum abstraction*[1] *π such that*

$$F_\pi[s]\{d_I\} \subseteq q, \tag{1}$$

or show that $F_\pi[s]\{d_I\} \subseteq q$ does not hold for any π.

The problem asks for not a minimal π but a minimum hence cheapest one. This requirement encourages any solution to exploit cheap abstractions (determined by $\preceq$) as much as possible. Note that the requirement is aligned with the intended meaning of $\preceq$, which compares abstractions in terms of the analysis cost. A different way of comparing abstractions in terms of precision rather than cost is taken in Liang et al. [15]. In their case, a minimum abstraction for proving a query often does not exist or it is expensive to compute, so they ask for a minimal abstraction instead.

Our approach to solve the problem is based on using a form of a backward meta-analysis that reasons about the behavior of a parametric dataflow analysis under different abstractions simultaneously. We explain this backward meta-analysis next.

[1] The condition that π be minimum means: if $F_{\pi'}[s]d_I \subseteq q$, then $\pi \preceq \pi'$. In contrast, the minimality of π means the absence of π' that satisfies (1) and is strictly smaller than π according to $\preceq$.

4. Backward Meta-Analysis

In this section, we fix a parametric dataflow analysis $(\mathbb{P}, \preceq, \mathbb{D}, [\![-]\!])$ and describe corresponding backward meta-analyses. To avoid the confusion between these two analyses, we often call the parametric analysis as ***forward analysis***.

A backward meta-analysis is a core component of our algorithm for the optimum abstraction problem. It is invoked when the forward analysis fails to prove a query. The meta-analysis attempts to determine why a run of the forward analysis with a specific abstraction π fails to prove a query, and to generalize this reason. Concretely, the inputs to the meta-analysis are a trace τ, an abstraction π, and an initial abstract state d_I, such that the π instance of the forward analysis fails to prove that a given query holds at the end of τ. Given such inputs, the meta-analysis analyzes τ backward, and collects abstractions that lead to a similar verification failure of the forward analysis. The collected abstractions are used subsequently when our top-level algorithm computes a necessary condition on abstractions for proving the given query and chooses a next abstraction to try based on this condition.

Formally, the meta-analysis is specified by the following data:

- A set $\mathbb{M}$ and a function

  $$\gamma : \mathbb{M} \to 2^{\mathbb{P} \times \mathbb{D}}.$$

  Elements in $\mathbb{M}$ are the main data structures used by the meta-analysis, and γ determines their meanings. We suggest to read elements in $\mathbb{M}$ as predicates over $\mathbb{P} \times \mathbb{D}$. The meta-analysis uses such a predicate $\phi \in \mathbb{M}$ to express a sufficient condition for verification failure: for every $(\pi, d) \in \gamma(\phi)$, if we instantiate the forward analysis with π and run this instance from the abstract state d (over the part of a trace analyzed so far), we will fail to prove a given query.
- A function

  $$[\![a]\!]^b : \mathbb{M} \to \mathbb{M}$$

  for each atomic command a. The input $\phi_1 \in \mathbb{M}$ represents a postcondition on $\mathbb{P} \times \mathbb{D}$. Given such ϕ_1, the function computes the weakest precondition ϕ such that running $[\![a]\!]$ from any abstract state in $\gamma(\phi)$ has an outcome in $\gamma(\phi_1)$. This intuition

$$B[\tau] : \mathbb{P} \times \mathbb{D} \times \mathbb{M} \to \mathbb{M}$$
$$B[\epsilon](\pi, d, \phi) = \phi$$
$$B[a](\pi, d, \phi) = \mathsf{approx}(\pi, d, [\![a]\!]^b(\phi))$$
$$B[\tau\,;\tau'](\pi, d, \phi) = B[\tau](\pi, d, B[\tau'](\pi, F_\pi[\tau](d), \phi))$$

Figure 7. Backward meta-analysis.

$\mathsf{toDNF}(\phi)$ transforms ϕ to the DNF form and sorts disjuncts by size

$$\mathsf{simplify}(\bigvee\{\phi_i \mid i \in \{1,\ldots,n\}\}) = \bigvee\{\phi_i \mid i \in \{1,\ldots,n\} \wedge \neg(\exists j < i.\phi_j \sqsubseteq \phi_i)\}$$

$$\mathsf{drop}_k(\pi, d, \bigvee\{\phi_i \mid i \in \{1,\ldots,n\}\}) = (\bigvee\{\phi_i \mid i \in \{1,\ldots,\min(k-1,n)\}\}) \vee \phi_j$$
(where $(\pi, d) \in \gamma(\phi_j)$ and j is the smallest such index)

Figure 8. Functions for manipulating ϕ's.

is formalized by the following requirement on $[\![a]\!]^b$:

$$\forall \phi_1 \in \mathbb{M}.\ \gamma([\![a]\!]^b(\phi_1)) = \{(\pi, d) \mid (\pi, [\![a]\!]_\pi(d)) \in \gamma(\phi_1)\}. \quad (2)$$

- A function
$$\mathsf{approx} : \mathbb{P} \times \mathbb{D} \times \mathbb{M} \to \mathbb{M}.$$
The function is required to meet the following two conditions:
  1. $\forall \pi, d, \phi.\ \gamma(\mathsf{approx}(\pi, d, \phi)) \subseteq \gamma(\phi)$; and
  2. $\forall \pi, d, \phi.\ (\pi, d) \in \gamma(\phi) \Rightarrow (\pi, d) \in \gamma(\mathsf{approx}(\pi, d, \phi))$.

  The first ensures that $\mathsf{approx}(\pi, d, \phi)$ under-approximates the input ϕ, and the second says that this under-approximation should keep at least (π, d), if it is already in $\gamma(\phi)$. The main purpose of approx is to simplify ϕ. For instance, when ϕ is a logical formula, approx converts ϕ to a syntactically simpler one. The operator is invoked frequently by our meta-analysis to keep the complexity of the $\mathbb{M}$ value (the analysis's main data structure) under control.

Using the given data, our backward meta-analysis analyzes a trace τ backward as described in Figure 7. For each atomic command a in τ, it transforms an input ϕ using $[\![a]\!]^b$ first. Then, it simplifies the resulting ϕ' using the approx operator.

Our meta-analysis correctly tracks a sufficient condition that the forward analysis fails to prove a query. This condition is not trivial (i.e., it is a satisfiable formula), and includes enough information about the current failed verification attempt on τ by the forward analysis. Our theorem below formalizes these guarantees. Proofs of all theorems are provided in the supplementary material.

THEOREM 3 (Soundness). *For all τ, π, d and $\phi \in \mathbb{M}$,*

1. $(\pi, F_\pi[\tau](d)) \in \gamma(\phi) \Rightarrow (\pi, d) \in \gamma(B[\tau](\pi, d, \phi))$; and
2. $\forall (\pi_0, d_0) \in \gamma(B[\tau](\pi, d, \phi)).\ (\pi_0, F_{\pi_0}[\tau](d_0)) \in \gamma(\phi)$.

4.1 Disjunctive Meta-Analysis and Underapproximation

Designing a good under-approximation operator approx is important for the performance of a backward meta-analysis, and it often requires new insights. In this subsection, we identify a special subclass of meta-analyses, called *disjunctive meta-analyses*, and define a generic under-approximation operator for these meta-analyses. Both our example analyses have disjunctive meta-analyses and use the generic under-approximation operator.

A meta-analysis is ***disjunctive*** if the following conditions hold:

- The set $\mathbb{M}$ consists of formulas ϕ:
$$\phi ::= p \mid \mathsf{true} \mid \mathsf{false} \mid \neg\phi \mid \phi \wedge \phi' \mid \phi \vee \phi' \quad (p \in \mathsf{PForm})$$

(primitive formula) $p \in \mathsf{PForm}$

$$p ::= \mathsf{err} \mid \mathsf{param}(x) \mid \mathsf{var}(x) \mid \mathsf{type}(\sigma)$$

$$\gamma(\mathsf{err}) = \{(\pi, \top)\}$$
$$\gamma(\mathsf{param}(x)) = \{(\pi, d) \mid x \in \pi\}$$
$$\gamma(\mathsf{var}(x)) = \{(\pi, (ts, vs)) \mid x \in vs\}$$
$$\gamma(\mathsf{type}(\sigma)) = \{(\pi, (ts, vs)) \mid \sigma \in ts\}$$

$p \sqsubseteq p' \Leftrightarrow p = p'$

$\phi \sqsubseteq \phi' \Leftrightarrow \phi = \phi'$, or both ϕ and ϕ' are conjunction of primitive formulas and for every conjunct p' of ϕ', there exists a conjunct p of ϕ such that $p \sqsubseteq p'$

Figure 9. Data for backward meta-analysis for type-state analysis.

where PForm is a set of primitive formulas, and the boolean operators have the standard meanings:

$$\gamma(\mathsf{true}) = \mathbb{P} \times \mathbb{D} \quad \gamma(\mathsf{false}) = \emptyset \quad \gamma(\neg\phi) = (\mathbb{P} \times \mathbb{D}) \setminus \gamma(\phi)$$
$$\gamma(\phi \wedge \phi') = \gamma(\phi) \cap \gamma(\phi') \qquad \gamma(\phi \vee \phi') = \gamma(\phi) \cup \gamma(\phi')$$

- The set $\mathbb{M}$ comes with a binary relation $\sqsubseteq$ such that
$$\forall \phi, \phi' \in \mathbb{M}.\ \phi \sqsubseteq \phi' \Rightarrow \gamma(\phi) \subseteq \gamma(\phi').$$

The domain $\mathbb{M}$ of a disjunctive meta-analysis in a sense contains all boolean formulas which are constructed from primitive ones in PForm. We define a generic under-approximation operator for disjunctive meta-analyses as follows:

$$\mathsf{approx} : \mathbb{P} \times \mathbb{D} \times \mathbb{M} \to \mathbb{M}$$
$$\mathsf{approx}(\pi, d, \phi) = \text{let } \phi' = (\mathsf{simplify} \circ \mathsf{toDNF})(\phi) \text{ in}$$
$$\text{if (number of disjuncts in } \phi' \le k) \text{ then } \phi'$$
$$\text{else } \mathsf{drop}_k(\pi, d, \phi')$$

Subroutines toDNF, simplify, and drop are defined in Figure 8. The approx operator first transforms ϕ to disjunctive normal form and removes redundant disjuncts in the DNF formula that are subsumed by other shorter disjuncts in the same formula. If the resulting formula ϕ' is simple enough in that it has no more than k disjuncts (where k is pre-determined by an analysis designer), then ϕ' is returned as the result. Otherwise, some disjuncts of ϕ' are pruned: the first $k-1$ disjuncts according to their syntactic size survive, together with the shortest disjunct ϕ_j that includes the input (π, d) (i.e., $(\pi, d) \in \gamma(\phi_j)$). Our pruning is an instance of beam search in Artificial Intelligence which keeps only the most promising k options during exploration of a search space.

Meta-Analysis for Type-State. We define a disjunctive meta-analysis for our type-state analysis using the above recipe. Doing so means defining three entities shown in Figures 9 and 10: the set of primitive formulas, the order $\sqsubseteq$ on formulas, and a function $[\![-]\!]^b$.

The meta-analysis uses three primitive formulas. The first is err which says the d component of a pair (π, d) is $\top$. The remaining three formulas describe elements that should be included in some component of (π, d). For instance, $\mathsf{var}(x)$ says that the d component is a non-$\top$ value (ts, vs) such that the vs part contains x.

We order formulas $\phi \sqsubseteq \phi'$ in $\mathbb{M}$ when ϕ and ϕ' are the same, or both ϕ and ϕ' are conjunction of primitive formulas and every primitive formula p' in ϕ' corresponds to some primitive formula p in ϕ that implies p'.

Finally, for each atomic command a, the meta-analysis uses transfer function $[\![a]\!]^b$, which we show in [23] satisfies requirement (2) of our framework. This requirement means that $[\![a]\!]^b$ collects all the abstractions π and abstract pre-states d such that the run of the π-instantiated analysis with d generates a result satisfying ϕ. That is, $[\![a]\!]^b(\phi)$ computes the weakest precondition of $[\![a]\!]_\pi$ with respect to the postcondition ϕ.

$$
\llbracket g = v \rrbracket^b(\delta{\to}o) \quad = \quad \begin{cases}
\mathsf{false} & \text{if } \delta \equiv v \wedge o = \mathtt{L} \\
v{\to}\mathtt{L} \vee v{\to}\mathtt{E} & \text{if } \delta \equiv v \wedge o = \mathtt{E} \\
v{\to}\mathtt{N} & \text{if } \delta \equiv v \wedge o = \mathtt{N} \\
(v{\to}\mathtt{E} \vee v{\to}\mathtt{N}) \wedge \delta{\to}\mathtt{L} & \text{if } \delta \in (\mathbb{L} \setminus \{v\}) \wedge o = \mathtt{L} \\
(v{\to}\mathtt{L} \wedge \delta{\to}\mathtt{L}) \vee \delta{\to}\mathtt{E} & \text{if } \delta \in (\mathbb{L} \setminus \{v\}) \wedge o = \mathtt{E} \\
\delta{\to}\mathtt{N} & \text{if } \delta \in (\mathbb{L} \setminus \{v\}) \wedge o = \mathtt{N} \\
(v{\to}\mathtt{E} \vee v{\to}\mathtt{N}) \wedge \delta{\to}o & \text{if } \delta \in \mathbb{F} \wedge o \in \{\mathtt{L}, \mathtt{E}\} \\
v{\to}\mathtt{L} \vee ((v{\to}\mathtt{E} \vee v{\to}\mathtt{N}) \wedge \delta{\to}\mathtt{N}) & \text{if } \delta \in \mathbb{F} \wedge o = \mathtt{N} \\
\delta{\to}o & \text{otherwise}
\end{cases}
$$

$$
\begin{aligned}
\llbracket v = g \rrbracket^b(\delta{\to}o) \quad &= \quad \text{if } (\delta \equiv v \wedge o = \mathtt{E}) \text{ then } (\mathsf{true}) \text{ else } (\text{if } (\delta \equiv v \wedge o \neq \mathtt{E}) \text{ then } (\mathsf{false}) \text{ else } (\delta{\to}o)) \\
\llbracket v = \mathsf{new}\, h \rrbracket^b(\delta{\to}o) \quad &= \quad \text{if } (\delta \equiv v) \text{ then } (h{\to}o) \text{ else } (\delta{\to}o) \\
\llbracket v = \mathtt{null} \rrbracket^b(\delta{\to}o) \quad &= \quad \text{if } (\delta \equiv v \wedge o = \mathtt{N}) \text{ then } (\mathsf{true}) \text{ else } (\text{if } (\delta \equiv v \wedge o \neq \mathtt{N}) \text{ then } (\mathsf{false}) \text{ else } (\delta{\to}o)) \\
\llbracket v = v' \rrbracket^b(\delta{\to}o) \quad &= \quad \text{if } (\delta \equiv v) \text{ then } (v'{\to}o) \text{ else } (\delta{\to}o)
\end{aligned}
$$

$$
\llbracket v = v'.f \rrbracket^b(\delta{\to}o) \quad = \quad \begin{cases}
(v'{\to}\mathtt{L} \wedge f{\to}\mathtt{E}) \vee v'{\to}\mathtt{E} \vee v'{\to}\mathtt{N} & \text{if } \delta \equiv v \wedge o = \mathtt{E} \\
v'{\to}\mathtt{L} \wedge f{\to}o & \text{if } \delta \equiv v \wedge o \neq \mathtt{E} \\
\delta{\to}o & \text{if } \delta \not\equiv v
\end{cases}
$$

$$
\llbracket v.f = v' \rrbracket^b(\delta{\to}o) \quad = \quad \begin{cases}
\delta{\to}o & \text{if } \delta \notin (\mathbb{L} \cup \mathbb{F}) \\
\begin{aligned}&\delta{\to}\mathtt{E} \vee (\delta{\to}\mathtt{L} \wedge v{\to}\mathtt{E} \wedge v'{\to}\mathtt{L}) \\ &\quad \vee (\delta{\to}\mathtt{L} \wedge v{\to}\mathtt{L} \wedge f{\to}\mathtt{L} \wedge v'{\to}\mathtt{E}) \\ &\quad \vee (\delta{\to}\mathtt{L} \wedge v{\to}\mathtt{L} \wedge f{\to}\mathtt{E} \wedge v'{\to}\mathtt{L})\end{aligned} & \text{if } \delta \in \mathbb{L} \wedge o = \mathtt{E} \\
\delta{\to}o & \text{if } \delta \in \mathbb{L} \wedge o = \mathtt{N} \\
\begin{aligned}&\delta{\to}o \wedge (v{\to}\mathtt{N} \vee (v{\to}\mathtt{E} \wedge (v'{\to}\mathtt{E} \vee v'{\to}\mathtt{N})) \\ &\qquad \vee (v{\to}\mathtt{L} \wedge (v'{\to}\mathtt{N} \vee f{\to}\mathtt{N} \\ &\qquad\qquad \vee (v'{\to}\mathtt{L} \wedge f{\to}\mathtt{L}) \\ &\qquad\qquad \vee (v'{\to}\mathtt{E} \wedge f{\to}\mathtt{E}))))\end{aligned} & \begin{aligned}&\text{if } (\delta \in \mathbb{L} \wedge o = \mathtt{L}) \\ &\quad \vee (\delta \in \mathbb{F} \wedge o = \mathtt{E} \wedge \delta \not\equiv f) \\ &\quad \vee (\delta \in \mathbb{F} \wedge o = \mathtt{L} \wedge \delta \not\equiv f)\end{aligned} \\
\begin{aligned}&\delta{\to}\mathtt{N} \vee (v{\to}\mathtt{E} \wedge v'{\to}\mathtt{L}) \\ &\quad \vee (v{\to}\mathtt{L} \wedge f{\to}\mathtt{L} \wedge v'{\to}\mathtt{E}) \\ &\quad \vee (v{\to}\mathtt{L} \wedge f{\to}\mathtt{E} \wedge v'{\to}\mathtt{L})\end{aligned} & \text{if } \delta \in \mathbb{F} \wedge o = \mathtt{N} \wedge \delta \not\equiv f \\
\begin{aligned}&(\delta{\to}\mathtt{N} \wedge (v{\to}\mathtt{E} \vee v{\to}\mathtt{N} \vee (v{\to}\mathtt{L} \wedge v'{\to}\mathtt{N}))) \\ &\quad \vee (v{\to}\mathtt{E} \wedge v'{\to}\mathtt{L}) \\ &\quad \vee (\delta{\to}\mathtt{L} \wedge v{\to}\mathtt{L} \wedge v'{\to}\mathtt{E}) \\ &\quad \vee (\delta{\to}\mathtt{E} \wedge v{\to}\mathtt{L} \wedge v'{\to}\mathtt{L})\end{aligned} & \text{if } \delta \in \mathbb{F} \wedge o = \mathtt{N} \wedge \delta \equiv f \\
\begin{aligned}&(\delta{\to}\mathtt{N} \wedge v{\to}\mathtt{L} \wedge v'{\to}\mathtt{L}) \\ &\quad \vee (\delta{\to}\mathtt{L} \wedge v{\to}\mathtt{N}) \\ &\quad \vee (\delta{\to}\mathtt{L} \wedge v{\to}\mathtt{E} \wedge (v'{\to}\mathtt{E} \vee v'{\to}\mathtt{N})) \\ &\quad \vee (\delta{\to}\mathtt{L} \wedge v{\to}\mathtt{L} \wedge (v'{\to}\mathtt{N} \vee v'{\to}\mathtt{L}))\end{aligned} & \text{if } \delta \in \mathbb{F} \wedge o = \mathtt{L} \wedge \delta \equiv f \\
\begin{aligned}&(\delta{\to}\mathtt{N} \wedge v{\to}\mathtt{L} \wedge v'{\to}\mathtt{E}) \\ &\quad \vee (\delta{\to}\mathtt{E} \wedge v{\to}\mathtt{N}) \\ &\quad \vee (\delta{\to}\mathtt{E} \wedge (v{\to}\mathtt{E} \vee v{\to}\mathtt{L}) \wedge (v'{\to}\mathtt{E} \vee v'{\to}\mathtt{N}))\end{aligned} & \text{if } \delta \in \mathbb{F} \wedge o = \mathtt{E} \wedge \delta \equiv f
\end{cases}
$$

Figure 11. Backward transfer function for thread-escape analysis. We use δ to range over h, v, f, and we use o to range over $\mathtt{L}, \mathtt{E}, \mathtt{N}$.

Meta-Analysis for Thread-Escape. The backward meta-analysis for the thread-escape analysis is also disjunctive. Its domain $\mathbb{M}$ is constructed from the following primitive formulas p:

$$p ::= h{\to}o \mid v{\to}o \mid f{\to}o$$

where o is an abstract value in $\{\mathtt{L}, \mathtt{E}, \mathtt{N}\}$, and h, v, f are an allocation site, a local variable, and a field, respectively. These formulas describe properties about pairs (π, d) of abstraction and abstract state. Formula $h{\to}o$ says that an abstraction π should map h to o. Formula $v{\to}o$ means that an abstract state d should bind v to o; formula $f{\to}o$ expresses a similar fact on the field f. We formalize these meanings via function $\gamma : \mathbb{M} \to 2^{\mathbb{P} \times \mathbb{D}}$ below:

$$\gamma(h{\to}o) = \{(\pi, d) \mid \pi(h) = o\} \quad \gamma(v{\to}o) = \{(\pi, d) \mid d(v) = o\}$$
$$\gamma(f{\to}o) = \{(\pi, d) \mid d(f) = o\}$$

We order formulas $\phi \sqsubseteq \phi'$ in $\mathbb{M}$ when our simple entailment checker concludes that ϕ' subsumes ϕ. This conclusion is reached when ϕ and ϕ' are the same, or both ϕ and ϕ' are conjunction of primitive formulas and all the primitive formulas in ϕ' appear in ϕ. This proof strategy is fast yet highly incomplete. However, we found it sufficient in practice for our application, where the order is used to detect redundant disjuncts in formulas in the DNF form.

Figure 11 shows transfer function $\llbracket a \rrbracket^b$ of the meta-analysis for each atomic command a. We show in [23] that it satisfies requirement (2) of our framework which determines the semantics of the function using weakest preconditions.

Figure 6 shows the backward meta-analysis for thread-escape analysis without and with under-approximation on an example program. The trace in part (a) is generated by the forward analysis using initial abstraction $[\mathtt{h1} \mapsto \mathtt{E}, \mathtt{h2} \mapsto \mathtt{E}]$. The abstract states computed by the meta-analysis at each point of this trace without under-approximation are denoted by $\uparrow$. It correctly computes the sufficient condition for failure at the start of the trace as $\mathtt{h1}{\to}\mathtt{E} \vee (\mathtt{h2}{\to}\mathtt{E} \wedge \mathtt{h1}{\to}\mathtt{L})$, thus yielding the cheapest abstraction that proves the query as $[\mathtt{h1} \mapsto \mathtt{L}, \mathtt{h2} \mapsto \mathtt{L}]$. Despite taking a single iteration, however, the lack of under-approximation causes a blow-up in the size of the formula tracked by the meta-analysis.

$$
\begin{aligned}
[\![x = y]\!]^b(\mathsf{err}) &= \mathsf{err} \\
[\![x = \mathtt{null}]\!]^b(\mathsf{err}) &= \mathsf{err} \\
[\![x.m()]\!]^b(\mathsf{err}) &= \mathsf{err} \vee \bigvee\{\mathsf{type}(\sigma) \mid [\![m]\!](\sigma) = \top\} \\
[\![x = y]\!]^b(\mathsf{param}(z)) &= \mathsf{param}(z) \\
[\![x = \mathtt{null}]\!]^b(\mathsf{param}(z)) &= \mathsf{param}(z) \\
[\![x.m()]\!]^b(\mathsf{param}(z)) &= \mathsf{param}(z) \\
[\![x = y]\!]^b(\mathsf{var}(z)) &= \begin{cases} \mathsf{param}(x) \wedge \mathsf{var}(y) & \text{if } x \equiv z \\ \mathsf{var}(z) & \text{otherwise} \end{cases} \\
[\![x = \mathtt{null}]\!]^b(\mathsf{var}(z)) &= \begin{cases} \mathsf{false} & \text{if } x \equiv z \\ \mathsf{var}(z) & \text{otherwise} \end{cases} \\
[\![x.m()]\!]^b(\mathsf{var}(z)) &= \mathsf{var}(z) \wedge \bigwedge\{\neg\mathsf{type}(\sigma) \mid [\![m]\!](\sigma) = \top\} \\
[\![x = y]\!]^b(\mathsf{type}(\sigma)) &= \mathsf{type}(\sigma) \\
[\![x = \mathtt{null}]\!]^b(\mathsf{type}(\sigma)) &= \mathsf{type}(\sigma) \\
[\![x.m()]\!]^b(\mathsf{type}(\sigma)) &= \neg\mathsf{err} \\
&\quad \wedge (\bigwedge\{\neg\mathsf{type}(\sigma') \mid [\![m]\!](\sigma') = \top\}) \\
&\quad \wedge ((\neg\mathsf{var}(x) \wedge \mathsf{type}(\sigma)) \\
&\qquad \vee \bigvee\{\mathsf{type}(\sigma') \mid [\![m]\!](\sigma') = \sigma\})
\end{aligned}
$$

Figure 10. Backward transfer function for type-state analysis.

Part (b) shows the result with under-approximation, using $k = 1$ in the beam search via function drop_k. This time, the first iteration, shown in part (b1), yields a stronger sufficient condition for failure, h1→E, causing our technique to next run the forward analysis using abstraction $[\mathtt{h1} \mapsto \mathtt{L}, \mathtt{h2} \mapsto \mathtt{E}]$. But the analysis again fails to prove the query, and the second iteration, shown in part (b2), computes the sufficient condition for failure as ($\mathtt{h1}\to\mathtt{L} \wedge \mathtt{h2}\to\mathtt{E}$). By combining these conditions from the two iterations, our technique finds the same cheapest abstraction as that without under-approximation in part (a). Despite needing an extra iteration, the formulas tracked in part (b) are much more compact than those in part (a).

5. Iterative Forward-Backward Analysis

This section presents our top-level algorithm, called TRACER, which brings a parametric analysis and a corresponding backward meta-analysis together, and solves the parametric static analysis problem. Throughout the section, we fix a parametric analysis and a backward meta-analysis, and denote them by $(\mathbb{P}, \preceq, \mathbb{D}, [\![-]\!])$ and $(\mathbb{M}, \gamma, [\![-]\!]^b, \mathsf{approx})$, respectively.

Our TRACER algorithm assumes that queries are expressed by elements ϕ in $\mathbb{M}$ satisfying the following condition:

$$\exists D_0 \subseteq \mathbb{D}.\, \gamma(\phi) = \mathbb{P} \times D_0 \wedge (\exists \phi' \in \mathbb{M}.\, \gamma(\phi') = \mathbb{P} \times (\mathbb{D} \setminus D_0)).$$

The first conjunct means that ϕ is independent of abstractions, and the second, that the negation of ϕ is expressible in $\mathbb{M}$. A ϕ satisfying these two conditions is called a ***query*** and is denoted by symbol q. The negation of a query q is also a query and is denoted $\mathsf{not}(q)$.

TRACER takes as inputs initial abstract state d_I, a program s, and a query $q \in \mathbb{M}$. Given such inputs, TRACER repeatedly invokes the forward analysis with different abstractions, until it proves the query or finds that the forward analysis cannot prove the query no matter what abstraction is used. The key part of TRACER is to choose a new abstraction π' to try after the forward analysis fails to prove the query using some π. TRACER does this abstraction selection using the backward meta-analysis which goes over an abstract counterexample trace of the forward analysis and computes a condition on abstractions that are necessary for proving the query. TRACER chooses a minimum-cost abstraction π' among such abstractions.

The TRACER algorithm is shown in Algorithm 1. It uses variable Π_{viable} to track abstractions that can potentially prove the query. Whenever TRACER calls the forward analysis, it picks a minimum π from Π_{viable}, and instantiates the forward analysis with π before running the analysis (lines 8-9). Also, whenever TRACER learns a necessary condition from the backward meta-analysis for proving a query (i.e., $\mathbb{P} \setminus \Pi$ in line 14), it conjoins the condition with Π_{viable} (line 15). In the description of the algorithm, we do not specify how to choose an abstract counterexample trace τ from a failed run of the forward analysis. Such traces can be chosen by well-known techniques from software model checking [1, 20]. We show the correctness of our algorithm in [23].

Algorithm 1 TRACER(d_I, s, q): *iterative forward-backward analysis*

1: **INPUTS:** Initial abstract state d_I, program s, and query q
2: **OUTPUTS:** Minimum π according to $\preceq$ such that $F_\pi[s](\{d_I\}) \subseteq \{d \mid (\pi, d) \in \gamma(q)\}$. Or impossibility meaning that $\nexists \pi : F_\pi[s](\{d_I\}) \subseteq \{d \mid (\pi, d) \in \gamma(q)\}$.
3: **var** $\Pi_{viable} := \mathbb{P}$
4: **while** true **do**
5:   **if** $\Pi_{viable} = \emptyset$ **then**
6:     **return** impossible
7:   **end if**
8:   choose a minimum $\pi \in \Pi_{viable}$ according to $\preceq$
9:   **let** $D = (F_\pi[s](\{d_I\}) \cap \{d \mid (\pi, d) \in \gamma(\mathsf{not}(q))\})$ **in**
10:     **if** $D = \emptyset$ **then**
11:       **return** π
12:     **end if**
13:     choose any $\tau \in \mathsf{trace}(s) : F_\pi[\tau](d_I) \in D$
14:     **let** $\Pi = \{\pi' \mid (\pi', d_I) \in \gamma(B[\tau](\pi, d_I, \mathsf{not}(q)))\}$ **in**
15:       $\Pi_{viable} := \Pi_{viable} \cap (\mathbb{P} \setminus \Pi)$
16:     **end let**
17:   **end let**
18: **end while**

6. Experiments

We implemented our parametric dataflow analysis technique in Chord [16], an extensible program analysis framework for Java bytecode. The forward analysis is expressed as an instance of the RHS tabulation framework [19] while the backward meta-analysis is expressed as an instance of a trace analysis framework that implements our proposed optimizations.

We implemented our type-state and thread-escape analyses in our framework, and we evaluated our technique on both of them using a suite of seven real-world concurrent Java benchmark programs. Table 1 shows characteristics of these programs. All experiments were done using JDK 1.6 on Linux machines with 3.0 GHz processors and a maximum of 8GB memory per JVM process.

The last two columns of Table 1 show the size of the family of abstractions searched by each analysis for each benchmark. For the type-state analysis, it is 2^N where N is the number of pointer-typed variables in reachable methods, since an abstraction determines which variables the analysis can track in must-alias sets. For thread-escape analysis, it is 2^N where N is the number of object allocation sites in reachable methods, since the abstraction determines whether to map each such site to L or E.

We presented our technique for a single query but in practice a client may pose multiple queries in the same program. Our framework has the same effect as running our technique separately for each query but it uses a more efficient implementation: at any instant, it maintains a set of groups $\{G_1, ..., G_n\}$ of unresolved queries (i.e., queries that are neither proven nor shown impossible to prove). Two queries belong to the same group if the sets of unviable abstractions computed so far for those queries are the same. All queries start in the same group with an empty set of unviable abstractions but split into separate groups when different sets of unviable abstractions are computed for them.

	description	# classes		# methods		bytecode (KB)		KLOC		$\log_2$(# abstractions)	
		app	total	app	total	app	total	app	total	type-state	thread-esc.
tsp	Traveling Salesman implementation	4	997	21	6,423	2.6	391	0.7	269	569	6,175
elevator	discrete event simulator	5	998	24	6,424	2.3	390	0.6	269	352	6,180
hedc	web crawler from ETH	44	1,066	234	6,881	16	442	6	283	1,400	7,326
weblech	website download/mirror tool	57	1,263	312	8,201	20	504	13	326	2,993	7,663
antlr	A parser/translator generator	118	1,134	1,180	7,786	131	532	29	303	16,563	7,748
avrora	microcontroller simulator/analyzer	1,160	2,192	4,253	10,985	224	634	64	340	37,797	10,151
lusearch	text indexing and search tool	229	1,236	1,508	8,171	101	511	42	314	14,508	7,395

Table 1. Benchmark statistics computed using a 0-CFA call graph analysis. The "total" and "app" columns report numbers with and without counting JDK library code, respectively. The last two columns determine the (log of the) number of abstractions for our two client analyses.

To avoid skewing our results by using a real type-state property to evaluate our type-state analysis, we used a fictitious one that tracks the state of every object allocated in the application code of the program (as opposed to, say, only file objects). The type-state automaton for this property has two states, $init$ and $error$. The type-state analysis tracks a separate abstract object for each allocation site h in application code that starts in the $init$ state, and transitions to $error$ upon any method call $v.m()$ in application code if the following two conditions hold: (i) v may point to an object created at site h according to a 0-CFA may-alias analysis that is used by the type-state analysis, and (ii) v is not in the current must-alias set tracked by the type-state analysis. If neither of these conditions holds, then the abstract object remains in the $init$ state, which corresponds to precise type-state tracking by the analysis.

To enable a comprehensive evaluation of our technique, we generated queries pervasively and uniformly from the application code of each benchmark. For the type-state analysis, we generated a query at each method call site, and for the thread-escape analysis, we generated a query at each instance field access and each array element access. Specific clients of these analyses may pose queries more selectively but our technique only stands to benefit in such cases by virtue of being query-driven. To avoid reporting duplicate results across different programs, we did not generate any queries in the JDK standard library, but our analyses analyze all reachable bytecode including that in the JDK.

Our type-state analysis answers each query (pc, h) such that the statement at program point pc is a method call $v.m()$ in application code and variable v may point to an object allocated at a site h that also occurs in application code. The query is proven if every object allocated at site h that variable v may refer to at the point of this call is in state $init$ (i.e., not $error$). These queries stress-test our type-state analysis since they fail to be proven if the underlying may-alias or must-alias analysis loses precision along any program path from the point at which any object is created in application code to the point at which any application method is called on it.

Our thread-escape analysis answers each query (pc, v) such that the statement at program point pc in application code accesses (reads or writes) an instance field or an array element of the object denoted by variable v. Such queries may be posed by a client such as static datarace detection.

We chose type-state and thread-escape analyses as they are challenging to scale: both are fully flow- and context-sensitive analyses that use radically different heap abstractions. The thread-escape analysis is especially hard to scale: simply mapping all allocation sites to L in the abstraction causes the analysis to run out of memory even on our smallest benchmark. Moreover, these analyses are useful in their own right: type-state analysis is an important general analysis for object state verification while thread-escape analysis is beneficial to a variety of concurrency analyses.

We next summarize our evaluation results, including precision, scalability, and useful statistics of proven queries.

Precision. Figure 12 shows the precision of our technique. The absolute number of queries for each benchmark appears at the top. The queries are classified into three categories: those proven using a cheapest abstraction, those shown impossible to prove using any abstraction, and those that could not be resolved by our technique in 1,000 minutes (we elaborate on these queries below).

All queries are resolved in the type-state analysis. Of these queries, 25% are proven on average per benchmark. Queries impossible to prove are notably more than proven queries for the type-state analysis primarily due to the stress-test nature of the type-state property that the analysis checks. In contrast, for the thread-escape analysis, our technique proves 38% queries and it shows 47% queries impossible to prove, for a total of 85% resolved queries on average per benchmark. We manually inspected several queries that were unresolved, and found that all of them were true but impossible to prove using our thread-escape analysis, due to its limit of two abstract locations (L and E). There are two possible ways to address such queries depending on the desired goal: alter the backward meta-analysis to show impossibility more efficiently or alter the forward analysis to make the queries provable.

In summary, we found our technique useful at quantifying the limitations of a parametric dataflow analysis, and inspecting the queries deemed impossible to prove suggests what aspects of the analysis to change to overcome those limitations.

Scalability. It is challenging to scale backward static analyses. We found that underapproximation is crucial to the scalability of our backward meta-analysis: disabling it caused our technique to timeout for *all* queries even on our smallest benchmark. Recall that for disjunctive meta-analysis (Section 4.1) the degree of underapproximation can be controlled by specifying the maximum number of disjuncts k retained in the boolean formulae that are propagated backward by the meta-analysis. We found it optimal to set $k = 5$ for our two client analyses on all our benchmarks. We arrived at this setting by experimenting with different values of k. Figure 13 illustrates the effect of setting k to 1, 5, and 10 on the running time of our thread-escape analysis. We show these results only for our smallest four benchmarks as the analysis ran out of memory on the larger three benchmarks for $k = 1$ and $k = 10$. Intuitively, the reason is that doing underapproximation aggressively ($k = 1$) reduces the running time of the backward analysis in each iteration but it increases the number of iterations to resolve a query, whereas doing underapproximation passively ($k = 10$) reduces the number of iterations but increases the running time of the backward analysis in each iteration. Compared to these two extremes, setting $k = 5$ results in much fewer timeouts and better scalability overall.

Table 2 shows statistics about the number of iterations of our technique for resolved queries using $k = 5$. Minimum, maximum, and average number of iterations are shown separately for proven queries and for queries found impossible to prove. The table highlights the scalability of our technique as queries for most benchmarks are resolved in under ten iterations on average. The only exception is the type-state analysis on avrora which takes 48 iterations on average for proven queries. The reason is that, compared to the remaining benchmarks, for avrora our type-state analysis requires many more variables in the cheapest abstraction for most

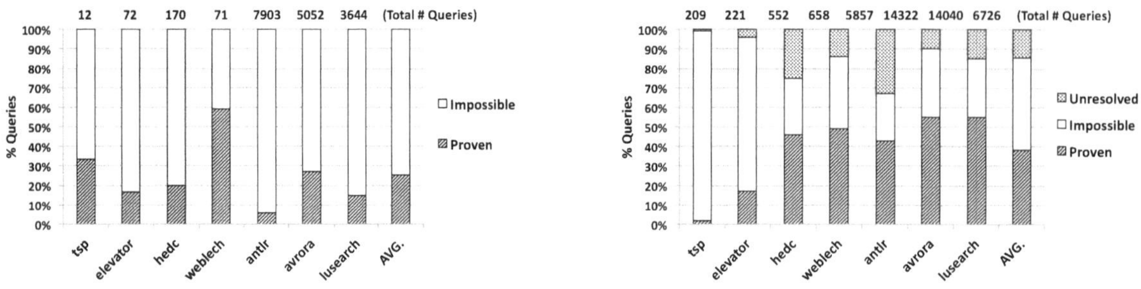

(a) Type-state analysis. (b) Thread-escape analysis.

Figure 12. Precision measurements.

	number of iterations												running time of thread-escape analysis (s = seconds, m = minutes, h = hours)					
	type-state analysis						thread-escape analysis											
	proven			impossible			proven			impossible			proven			impossible		
	min	max	avg	min	max	avg	min	max	avg	min	max	avg	min	max	avg	min	max	avg
tsp	2	2	2	1	2	1.5	2	2	2	1	1	1	14s	29s	21s	6s	8s	7s
elevator	2	3	2.1	1	9	3.8	2	3	2	1	5	1.3	12s	107s	34s	6s	144s	15s
hedc	2	3	2.3	1	2	1	2	6	2.4	1	4	1.8	17s	6m	89s	10s	5m	51s
weblech	2	3	2.1	1	3	1.4	2	17	6.9	1	3	1.2	20s	16m	5m	11s	150s	28s
antlr	2	18	8.9	1	47	7.8	2	88	3	1	18	1.4	18s	77m	98s	6s	21m	64s
avrora	2	82	47.7	1	30	3.5	2	97	3	1	38	1.4	16s	28m	67s	5s	3h	41s
lusearch	2	32	2.1	1	23	2	2	19	2.7	1	20	2.3	14s	13m	112s	6s	45m	131s

Table 2. Scalability measurements.

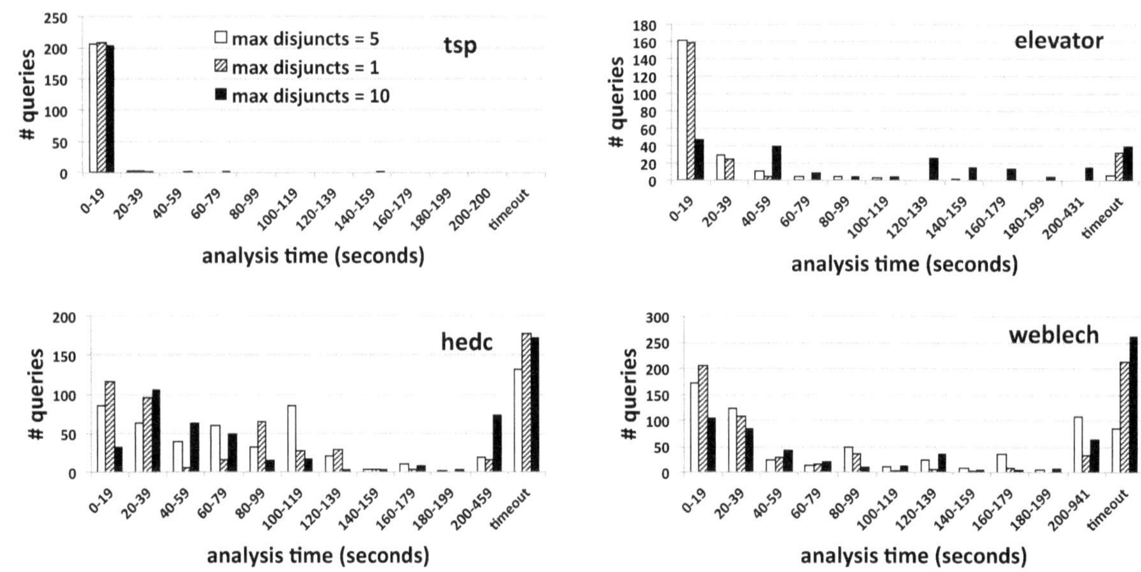

Figure 13. Running time of thread-escape analysis per query for different degrees of underapproximation $k = 1, 5, 10$ in its meta-analysis on our smallest four benchmarks. The timeout columns denote queries that could not be resolved in 1,000 minutes. Setting k to 1 or 10 resolves fewer queries than $k = 5$ for the shown benchmarks and also caused the analysis to run out of memory for the largest three benchmarks.

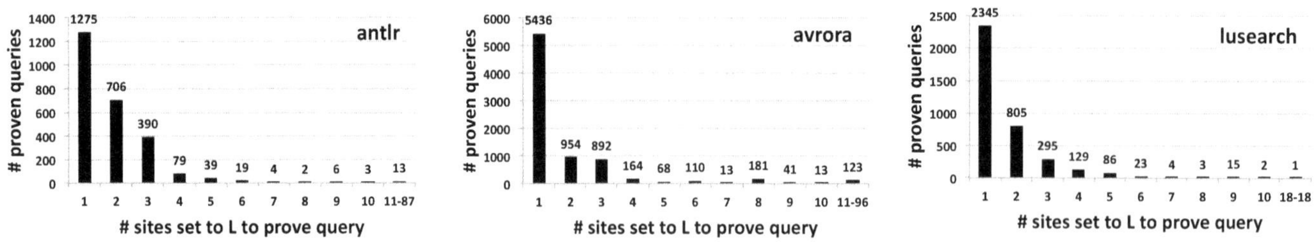

Figure 14. Sizes of the cheapest abstractions computed for proven queries of the thread-escape analysis on our largest three benchmarks.

	type-state analysis			thread-escape analysis		
	min	max	avg	min	max	avg
tsp	2	3	2.3	1	1	1
elevator	2	4	2.8	1	2	1.1
hedc	2	5	2.9	1	5	1.4
weblech	2	4	3.3	1	16	6.1
antlr	2	20	10.9	1	87	1.9
avrora	2	84	50.2	1	96	2.1
lusearch	2	34	16.5	1	18	1.7

Table 3. Statistics of cheapest abstraction size for proven queries.

	type-state analysis				thread-escape analysis			
	# groups	min	max	avg	# groups	min	max	avg
tsp	4	1	1	1	3	1	3	2
elevator	8	1	5	1.5	10	1	13	3.8
hedc	26	1	4	1.3	34	1	50	7.6
weblech	18	1	17	2.3	51	1	88	6.4
antlr	101	1	106	4.6	237	1	374	10.7
avrora	158	1	368	8.6	890	1	262	9
lusearch	151	1	139	3.6	270	1	256	13.7

Table 4. Statistics of cheapest abstraction reuse for proven queries.

of the proven queries (this is confirmed below by statistics on the sizes of the cheapest abstractions). The numbers of iterations also show that our technique is effective at finding queries that are impossible to prove since for most benchmarks it finds such queries in under four iterations on average. We also show the running time for thread-escape analysis in the table as it is relatively harder to scale than type-state analysis. For each benchmark, our technique takes one to two minutes on average for resolved queries.

Statistics of Proven Queries. We now present some useful statistics about proven queries. Table 3 shows the minimum, maximum, and average sizes of the cheapest abstraction computed by our technique for these queries. For type-state analysis, the size of the cheapest abstraction correlates the benchmark size and is greatly affected by the depth of method calls. The average number of variables that must be tracked in must-alias sets ranges from 2 to 50 from our smallest benchmark to our largest. On the other hand, thread-escape analysis only needs 1 to 2 sites mapped to L on average for most benchmarks, though there are queries that need upto 96 such sites (this means that no abstraction with fewer than those many sites can prove those queries). The graphs in Figure 14 show the distribution of the cheapest abstraction sizes for thread-escape analysis on our largest three benchmarks. We see that most queries are indeed proven using 1 or 2 allocation sites mapped to L.

Finally, it is worth finding how different the cheapest abstractions computed by our technique are for these proven queries. Table 4 answers this question by showing the numbers of queries grouped together sharing the same cheapest abstraction. The table shows that around ten or less queries on average share the same cheapest abstraction for both analyses, indicating that the cheapest abstraction tends to be different for different queries, though there are also a few large groups containing up to 368 queries for type-state analysis and 374 queries for thread-escape analysis.

These statistics underscore both the promise and the challenge of parametric static analysis: on one hand, most queries can be proven by instantiating the analysis using very inexpensive abstractions, but on the other hand, these abstractions tend to be very different for queries from different parts of the same program.

7. Related Work

Our work is related to iterative refinement analyses but differs in the goal and the technique. They aim to find a cheap enough abstraction to prove a query while we aim to find a cheapest abstraction or show that none exists. We next contrast the techniques.

CEGAR-based model checkers such as SLAM [2] and BLAST [13] compute a predicate abstraction of the given program to prove an assertion (query) in the program. Yogi [3, 8] combines CEGAR-based model checking and directed input generation to simultaneously search for proofs and violations of assertions. All these approaches can be viewed as parametric in which program predicates to use in the predicate abstraction. They differ from our approach primarily in the manner in which they analyze an abstract counterexample trace that is produced as a witness to the failure to prove a query using the currently chosen abstraction. In particular, these approaches compute an interpolant, which can be viewed as a minimal sufficient condition for the model checker to *succeed* in proving the query on the trace, whereas our meta-analysis computes a sufficient condition for the *failure* of the given analysis to prove the query on the trace. Intuitively, our meta-analysis attempts to find as many other abstractions destined to a similar proof failure as the currently chosen abstraction; the next abstraction our approach attempts is simply a cheapest one not discarded by the meta-analysis. One advantage of the above approaches over our approach is that they can produce *concrete* counterexamples for false queries, whereas our approach can at best declare such queries impossible to prove using the given analysis. Conversely, our approach can declare when true queries are impossible to prove using the given analysis, whereas the above approaches can diverge for such queries.

Refinement-based pointer analyses compute cause-effect dependencies for finding aspects of the abstraction that might be responsible for the failure to prove a query and then refine these aspects in the hope of proving it. These aspects include field reads and writes to be matched [21, 22], methods or object allocation sites to be cloned [14, 18], or memory locations to be treated flow-sensitively [12]. A drawback of these analyses is that they can refine much more than necessary and thereby sacrifice scalability.

Combining forward and backward analysis has been proposed (e.g., [4]) but our approach differs in three key aspects. First, existing backward analyses are proven sound with respect to the program's concrete semantics, whereas ours is a *meta-analysis* that is proven sound with respect to the abstract semantics of the forward analysis. Second, existing backward analyses only track abstract states (to prune the over-approximation computed by the forward analysis), whereas ours also tracks parameter values. Finally, existing backward analyses may not scale due to tracking of program states that are unreachable from the initial state, whereas ours is guided by the abstract counterexample trace provided by the forward analysis, which also enables underapproximation.

Parametric analysis is a search problem that may be tackled using various algorithms with different pros and cons. Liang et al. [15] propose iterative coarsening-based algorithms that start with the most precise abstraction (instead of the least precise one in the case of iterative refinement-based algorithms). Besides being impractical, these algorithms solve a different problem and cannot be adapted to ours: they find a *minimal* abstraction in terms of precision as opposed to a *minimum* or *cheapest* abstraction. Naik et al. [17] use dynamic analysis to infer a necessary condition on the abstraction to prove a query. They instantiate the parametric analysis using a cheapest abstraction that satisfies this condition. However, there is no guarantee that it will prove the query, and the approach does not do refinement in case the analysis fails.

Finally, constraint-based and automated theorem proving techniques have been proposed that use search procedures similar in spirit to our approach: they too combine over- and under-approximations, and compute strongest necessary and weakest sufficient conditions for proving queries (e.g, [5, 6, 10, 11]). A key difference is that none of these approaches address finding minimum-cost abstractions or proving impossibility results.

8. Conclusion

We presented a new approach to parametric dataflow analysis with the goal of finding a cheapest abstraction that proves a given query or showing that no such abstraction exists. Our approach is CEGAR-based and applies a novel meta-analysis on abstract counterexample traces to efficiently eliminate unsuitable abstractions. We showed the generality of our approach by applying it to two example analyses in the literature. We also showed its practicality by applying it to several real-world Java benchmark programs.

Our approach opens intriguing new problems. First, our approach requires the abstract domain of the parametric analysis to be disjunctive in order to be able to provide a counterexample trace to the meta-analysis. Our meta-analysis relies on the existence of such a trace for scalability: the trace guides the meta-analysis in deciding which parts of the formulae it tracks represent infeasible states that can be pruned. One possibility is to generalize our meta-analysis to operate on DAG counterexamples that have been proposed for non-disjunctive analyses [9]. Second, the meta-analysis is a static analysis, and designing its abstract domain is an art. We proposed a DNF representation along with optimizations that were very effective in compacting the formulas tracked by the meta-analysis for our type-state analysis and our thread-escape analysis. It would be useful to devise a generic semantics-preserving simplification process to assist in compacting such formulas. Finally, manually defining the transfer functions of the meta-analysis can be tedious and error-prone. One plausible solution is to devise a general recipe for synthesizing these functions automatically from a given abstract domain and parametric analysis.

Acknowledgments

We thank Ravi Mangal for discussions and help with the implementation. We also thank the anonymous reviewers for many insightful comments. This research was supported in part by DARPA contract #FA8750-12-2-0020, NSF award #1253867, awards from Google and Microsoft, and EPSRC.

References

[1] T. Ball and S. Rajamani. Bebop: a path-sensitive interprocedural dataflow engine. In *Proceedings of the ACM Workshop on Program Analysis For Software Tools and Engineering (PASTE'01)*, 2001.

[2] T. Ball and S. Rajamani. The SLAM project: Debugging system software via static analysis. In *Proceedings of the 29th ACM Symposium on Principles of Programming Languages (POPL'02)*, 2002.

[3] N. Beckman, A. Nori, S. Rajamani, R. Simmons, S. Tetali, and A. Thakur. Proofs from tests. *IEEE Trans. Software Eng.*, 36(4):495–508, 2010.

[4] P. Cousot and R. Cousot. Refining model checking by abstract interpretation. *Autom. Softw. Eng.*, 6(1):69–95, 1999.

[5] I. Dillig, T. Dillig, and A. Aiken. Sound, complete and scalable path-sensitive analysis. In *Proceedings of the 29th ACM Conference on Programming Language Design and Implementation (PLDI'08)*, 2008.

[6] I. Dillig, T. Dillig, and A. Aiken. Fluid updates: beyond strong vs. weak updates. In *Proceedings of the 19th European Symposium on Programming (ESOP'10)*, 2010.

[7] S. Fink, E. Yahav, N. Dor, G. Ramalingam, and E. Geay. Effective typestate verification in the presence of aliasing. *ACM Trans. Softw. Eng. Methodol.*, 17(2), 2008.

[8] B. Gulavani, T. Henzinger, Y. Kannan, A. Nori, and S. Rajamani. Synergy: a new algorithm for property checking. In *Proceedings of the 14th ACM SIGSOFT International Symposium on Foundations of Software Engineering (FSE'06)*, 2006.

[9] B. Gulavani, S. Chakraborty, A. Nori, and S. Rajamani. Automatically refining abstract interpretations. In *Proceedings of the 14th International Conference on Tools and Algorithms for the Construction and Analysis of Systems (TACAS'08)*, 2008.

[10] S. Gulwani and A. Tiwari. Assertion checking unified. In *Proceedings of the 8th International Conference on Verification, Model Checking, and Abstract Interpretation (VMCAI'07)*, 2007.

[11] S. Gulwani, B. McCloskey, and A. Tiwari. Lifting abstract interpreters to quantified logical domains. In *Proceedings of the 35th ACM Symposium on Principles of Programming Language (POPL'08)*, 2008.

[12] S. Guyer and C. Lin. Client-driven pointer analysis. In *Proceedings of the 10th International Symposium on Static Analysis (SAS'03)*, 2003.

[13] T. Henzinger, R. Jhala, R. Majumdar, and K. McMillan. Abstractions from proofs. In *Proceedings of the 31st ACM Symposium on Principles of Programming Languages (POPL'04)*, 2004.

[14] P. Liang and M. Naik. Scaling abstraction refinement via pruning. In *Proceedings of the 32nd ACM Conference on Programming Language Design and Implementation (PLDI'11)*, 2011.

[15] P. Liang, O. Tripp, and M. Naik. Learning minimal abstractions. In *Proceedings of the 38th ACM Symposium on Principles of Programming Languages (POPL'11)*, 2011.

[16] M. Naik. Chord: A static and dynamic program analysis platform for Java. `http://code.google.com/p/jchord/`.

[17] M. Naik, H. Yang, G. Castelnuovo, and M. Sagiv. Abstractions from tests. In *Proceedings of the 39th ACM Symposium on Principles of Programming Languages (POPL'12)*, 2012.

[18] J. Plevyak and A. Chien. Precise concrete type inference for object-oriented languages. In *Proceedings of the 9th ACM Conference on Object-Oriented Programming Systems, Languages, and Applications (OOPSLA'94)*, 1994.

[19] T. Reps, S. Horwitz, and M. Sagiv. Precise interprocedural dataflow analysis via graph reachability. In *Proceedings of the 22nd ACM Symposium on Principles of Programming Languages (POPL'95)*, 1995.

[20] T. Reps, S. Schwoon, S. Jha, and D. Melski. Weighted pushdown systems and their application to interprocedural dataflow analysis. *Sci. Comput. Program.*, 58(1-2):206–263, 2005.

[21] M. Sridharan and R. Bodík. Refinement-based context-sensitive points-to analysis for Java. In *Proceedings of the 27th ACM Conference on Programming Language Design and Implementation (PLDI'06)*, 2006.

[22] M. Sridharan, D. Gopan, L. Shan, and R. Bodík. Demand-driven points-to analysis for Java. In *Proceedings of the 20th ACM Conference on Object-Oriented Programming, Systems, Languages, and Applications (OOPSLA'05)*, 2005.

[23] X. Zhang, M. Naik, and H. Yang. Finding optimum abstractions in parametric dataflow analysis. Technical report, Georgia Institute of Technology, 2013. Available at `http://pag.gatech.edu/pubs/pldi13.pdf`.

How to Combine Widening and Narrowing for Non-monotonic Systems of Equations

Kalmer Apinis   Helmut Seidl   Vesal Vojdani

Technische Universität München

{apinis,seidl,vojdanig}@in.tum.de

Abstract

Non-trivial analysis problems require complete lattices with infinite ascending and descending chains. In order to compute reasonably precise post-fixpoints of the resulting systems of equations, Cousot and Cousot have suggested accelerated fixpoint iteration by means of widening and narrowing [6, 7].

The strict separation into phases, however, may unnecessarily give up precision that cannot be recovered later. While widening is also applicable if equations are non-monotonic, this is no longer the case for narrowing. A narrowing iteration to improve a given post-fixpoint, additionally, must assume that all right-hand sides are monotonic. The latter assumption, though, is not met in presence of widening. It is also not met by equation systems corresponding to context-sensitive interprocedural analysis, possibly combining context-sensitive analysis of local information with flow-insensitive analysis of globals [1].

As a remedy, we present a novel operator $\boxminus$ that combines a given widening operator $\sqcup\!\!\!\!\!\;\,\!\lrcorner$ with a given narrowing operator $\sqcap\!\!\!\!\!\;\,\urcorner$. We present adapted versions of round-robin as well as of worklist iteration, local, and side-effecting solving algorithms for the combined operator $\boxminus$ and prove that the resulting solvers always return sound results and are guaranteed to terminate for monotonic systems whenever only finitely many unknowns (constraint variables) are encountered.

Categories and Subject Descriptors D.2.4 [*Software Engineering*]: Software/Program Verification; F.3.2 [*Logics and Meanings of Programs*]: Semantics of Programming Languages—Program analysis; F.2.2 [*Analysis of Algorithms and Problem Complexity*]: Nonnumerical Algorithms and Problems—Computations on discrete structures

Keywords Static Program Analysis, Fixpoint Iteration, Constraint Solving

1. Introduction

From an algorithmic point of view, static analysis typically boils down to solving systems of equations over a suitable domain of values. The unknowns of the system correspond to the invariants to be computed, e.g., for each program point or for each program point in a given calling context or instances of a class. For abstract interpretation, often complete lattices are chosen as domains of (abstract) values [7]. Then variants of Kleene iteration can be applied to determine solutions. Right from the beginning of abstract interpretation, it has been observed that many interesting invariants are best expressed by means of lattices that have *infinite* strictly ascending chains. Possibly infinite strictly ascending chains, though, imply that naive Kleene iteration may not terminate. For that reason, Cousot and Cousot proposed a *widening* iteration, followed by a *narrowing* iteration in order to determine reasonably precise invariants or, technically speaking, reasonably small *post* solutions [6]. The widening phase can be considered as a Kleene iteration that is accelerated by means of a widening operator which enforces that only finitely many increases of values occur for an unknown. While enforcing termination, it may result in a crude over-approximation of the invariants of the program. In order to compensate for that, the subsequent narrowing iteration tries to improve a given post solution by means of a downward fixpoint iteration, which again may be accelerated by means of a *narrowing* operator.

Trying to recover precision once it has been thrown away, though, in general is not possible (see, e.g., [18] for a recent discussion). Some attempts try to improve precision by reducing the number of points where widening applied [4, 10], others rely on refined widening or narrowing operators (see, e.g., [5, 27]). Recent work has focused methods to guide or stratify the exploration of the state space [13–15, 19, 23], including techniques for automatic transformation of irregular loops [16, 26].

Our approach here is complementary to such techniques and can, possibly, be combined with these. Our idea is not to postpone narrowing to a second phase where all losses of information have already occurred and been propagated. Instead, an attempt is made to systematically improve the current information by narrowing immediately. In particular, this means that widening and narrowing are applied in an *interleaved* manner. A similar idea has been proposed for the static analyzer ASTRÉE [2].

Narrowing and the narrowing operator are only guaranteed to return meaningful results, i.e., a post solution of the given system of equations, if the right-hand sides of equations are *monotonic*. This assumption, however, is violated in presence of widening. This requirement is also not met by the equation systems for context-sensitive interprocedural analysis [1, 12]. Moreover, for more complicated abstract domains, these systems may be infinite and thus can be handled by *local* solvers only. Local solvers query the value of an interesting unknown and explore the space of unknowns only insofar as required for answering the query. For this type of algorithm, the set of evaluated unknowns is not known beforehand. In particular the values of new unknowns may be queried in the narrowing phase that have not yet been considered before. As a consequence, the strict separation into a widening and a narrowing phase can no longer be maintained. Although, narrowing iteration

PLDI'13, June 16–19, 2013, Seattle, WA, USA.

in case of non-monotonicity has been considered before [9], such approaches are not directly applicable for local solving.

In order to remedy these obstacles, we introduce an operator $\boxminus$ which is a generic combination of a given widening $\underline{\sqcup}$ with a given narrowing operator $\overline{\sqcap}$ and show that this new operator can be plugged into a generic solver of equation systems, be they monotonic or non-monotonic. As a result, solvers are obtained that return reasonably precise post solutions in one go—given that they terminate.

Termination, though, is indeed an issue. We present two simple example systems of monotonic equations where standard fixpoint algorithms such as round robin or work-list iteration, when enhanced with the new operator, fail to terminate. Therefore, we develop a variant of round robin as well as a variant of work-list iteration which in absence of widening and narrowing are not or at least not much worse than their standard counter parts—but which additionally are guaranteed to terminate for monotonic systems when the $\boxminus$-operator is used.

The idea of plugging the new operator $\boxminus$ into a generic *local* solver in principle, i.e., modulo termination, works as well. A local solver such as [21], however, is not generic in the sense of the present paper—meaning that a naive enhancement with the operator $\boxminus$ is no longer guaranteed to return sound results. As our main contribution, we therefore present a variation of this algorithm which always returns a (partial) post solution and, moreover, is guaranteed to terminate—at least for monotonic equation systems and if only finitely many unknowns are encountered. This algorithm is then extended to a solver for *side-effecting* constraint systems. Such systems allow to conveniently specify analyses that combine context-sensitive analysis of local information with flow-insensitive analysis of globals [1] as provided, e.g., by the program analyzer GOBLINT [29]. Since the different contributions to a global unknown are generated during the evaluation of a subset of right-hand sides, which is not known before-hand and may vary during fixpoint iteration, further non-trivial changes are required to handle this situation.

The remaining paper is organized as follows. In section 2, we present the concept of generic solvers. In section 3, we show that any such solver, when instantiated with $\boxminus$, returns a post solution of an arbitrary equation system (be it monotonic or not) whenever the solver terminates. In order to enforce termination at least for finite systems of monotonic equations, we provide in section 4 new generic variants of round-robin iteration as well as of work-list based fixpoint computation. Section 5 introduces the new generic local $\boxminus$-solver **SLR**, which then is generalized to equation systems with side effects in section 6. In section 7, we report about preliminary experiments with the novel $\boxminus$-solver within the analyzer framework GOBLINT and conclude in section 8.

2. Chaotic fixpoint iteration

Consider a system S of equations $x = f_x$, for a set of unknowns $x \in X$, and over a set D of values where the right-hand sides f_x are mappings $(X \to D) \to D$. Furthermore, let $\Box : D \to D \to D$ be a binary operator to combine old values with the new contributions of the right-hand sides.

A $\Box$-solution of S is a assignment $\rho : X \to D$ such that for all unknowns $x \in X$, $\rho[x] = \rho[x] \Box f_x\, \rho$ holds. In the case that $\Box$ is defined as $a \Box b = b$, a $\Box$-solution is an ordinary solution of the system, i.e., a mapping ρ with $\rho[x] = f_x\, \rho$ for all unknowns x. In case D is a lattice, and the $\Box$-operator equals the least upper bound operator $\sqcup$, a $\Box$-solution is a *post* solution of the system, i.e., a mapping ρ with $\rho[x] \sqsupseteq f_x\, \rho$ for all unknowns x. Likewise in case $\Box$ equals the greatest lower bound operator $\sqcap$, a $\Box$-solution is a *pre* solution of the system, i.e., a mapping ρ with $\rho[x] \sqsubseteq f_x\, \rho$ for all unknowns x.

The operator $\Box$ can also be instantiated with widening and narrowing operators. According to [6, 7, 11], a widening operator $\underline{\sqcup}$ for a lattice D must satisfy that $a \sqcup b \sqsubseteq a \,\underline{\sqcup}\, b$ for all $a, b \in D$. This implies that a $\Box$-solution then again provides a post solution of the original system S. The situation is slightly more complicated for narrowing operators. For a narrowing operator $\overline{\sqcap}$, $a \sqsupseteq b$ implies that $a \sqsupseteq (a \,\overline{\sqcap}\, b) \sqsupseteq b$. This means that narrowing can only be applied if the right-hand side of equations are guaranteed to return values that are less or equal than the values of the current left-hand sides. Thus a mapping ρ can only be a $\overline{\sqcap}$-solution, if it is a post solution of the system.

A (chaotic) solver for systems of equations is an algorithm that maintains a mapping $\rho : X \to D$ and performs a sequence of *update steps*, starting from an initial mapping ρ_0. Each update step selects an unknown x, evaluates the right-hand side f_x of x w.r.t. the current mapping ρ_i and updates the value for x, i.e.,

$$\rho_{i+1}[y] = \begin{cases} \rho_i[x] \Box f_x\, \rho_i, & \text{if } x = y \\ \rho_i[y], & \text{otherwise.} \end{cases}$$

Then the algorithm is a $\Box$-solver if upon termination the final mapping (after completing n steps) ρ_n is a $\Box$-solution of S. The algorithm is a generic solver, if it works for any binary update operator $\Box$. In this sense, the round-robin iteration of Fig. 1 is a generic solver. Note that, in most cases, we omit update step indices and, additionally, use imperative assignment syntax of the form $\rho[x] \leftarrow w$ to change the value of the unknown x to w in the mapping ρ.

In order to prove that a given algorithm is a generic solver, i.e., upon termination returns a $\Box$-solution, one typically verifies the invariant that for every terminating run of the algorithm producing the sequence $\rho_0, \rho_1, \ldots, \rho_n$ of mappings, and every unknown x, $\rho_i[x] \neq \rho_i(x) \Box f_x\, \rho_i$ implies that for some $j \geq i$, an update $\rho_{j+1}[x] \leftarrow \rho_j[x] \Box f_x\, \rho_j$ occurs.

Not every solver algorithm, though, may consider right-hand sides of equations as black boxes, as the round-robin algorithm does. The worklist algorithm from Fig. 2 can only be used as generic solver—given that all dependences are provided beforehand. This means that for each right-hand side f_x a (super-)set dep_x of unknowns is given such that for all mappings ρ, ρ', $f_x\, \rho = f_x\, \rho'$ whenever ρ and ρ' agree on all unknowns in dep_x. From these sets, we define the sets infl_y of unknowns possibly influenced by (a change of the value of) unknown y, i.e.,

$$\mathsf{infl}_y = \{x \in X \mid y \in \mathsf{dep}_x\} \cup \{y\}\,.$$

In the case that the value of some unknown y changes, all right-hand sides of unknowns in the set infl_y must be re-computed. Note that whenever an update to a unknown y provides a new value, we re-schedule y for evaluation as well. This is a precaution for the case that the operator $\Box$ is *not* (right) idempotent. Here, an operator $\Box$ is called *idempotent* if the following equality:

$$(a \Box b) \Box b = a \Box b$$

holds for all a, b. In this sense, the operators $\sqcup$ and $\sqcap$ are idempotent and often also $\underline{\sqcup}$ and $\overline{\sqcap}$. An operator such as $\frac{a+b}{2}$, however, for $a, b \in \mathbb{R}$ is not idempotent.

3. Enhancing Narrowing

First, we observe:

FACT 1. *Assume that all right-hand sides of the system S of equations over a lattice D are monotonic and that ρ_0 is a post solution of S, and $\Box$ is a narrowing operator $\overline{\sqcap}$. Then the sequence $\rho_0, \rho_1, \ldots$ of mappings produced by a generic $\Box$-solver, is defined and decreasing.* ∎

```
do {
    dirty ← false;
    forall (x ∈ X) {
        new ← ρ[x] □ f_x ρ;
        if (ρ[x] ≠ new) {
            ρ[x] ← new;
            dirty ← true;
        }
    }
} while (dirty);
```

Figure 1. The solver **RR**.

```
W ← X;
while (W ≠ ∅){
    x ← extract(W);
    new ← ρ[x] □ f_x ρ;
    if (ρ[x] ≠ new) {
        ρ[x] ← new;
        W ← W ∪ infl_x;
    }
}
```

Figure 2. The Solver **W**.

Thus, any generic solver can be applied to improve a post solution by means of a narrowing iteration—given that all right-hand sides of equations are monotonic.

Equation systems for context-sensitive interprocedural analysis, though, are not necessarily monotonic. In the following we show how to lift the the technical restrictions to the applicability of narrowing. Given a widening operator $\sqcup\!\!\!\!\!-$ and a narrowing operator $\sqcap\!\!\!\!\!-$, we define a new binary operator $\boxminus$ by:

$$a \boxminus b = \begin{cases} a \sqcap\!\!\!\!\!- b, & \text{if } b \sqsubseteq a \\ a \sqcup\!\!\!\!\!- b, & \text{otherwise.} \end{cases}$$

Note that the operator $\boxminus$ is not necessarily idempotent, but whenever narrowing is idempotent the following holds:

$$(a \boxminus b) \boxminus b = (a \boxminus b) \sqcap\!\!\!\!\!- b$$

and therefore also

$$((a \boxminus b) \boxminus b) \boxminus b = (a \boxminus b) \boxminus b\,.$$

A fixpoint algorithm equipped with the operator $\boxminus$ applies widening as long as values grow. Once the evaluation of the right-hand side of a unknown results in a smaller or equal value, narrowing is applied and values may shrink. For the operator $\boxminus$, we observe:

LEMMA 1. *Consider a finite system S of equations over a lattice D. Then every $\boxminus$-solution ρ of S is a post solution, i.e., for all unknowns x, $\rho[x] \sqsupseteq f_x\,\rho$.*

Proof. Consider a mapping ρ that is a $\boxminus$-solution of S and an arbitrary unknown x. For a contradiction assume that $\rho[x] \not\sqsupseteq f_x\,\rho$. But then we have:

$$\rho[x] \;=\; \rho[x] \boxminus f_x\,\rho \;=\; \rho[x] \sqcup\!\!\!\!\!- f_x\,\rho \;\sqsupseteq\; f_x\,\rho$$

in contradiction to our assumption! Accordingly, ρ must be a post solution of the system of equations S. ∎

Thus, every generic solver for lattices D can be turned into a solver computing post solutions by using the combined widening and narrowing operator. The intertwined application of widening and narrowing, which naturally occurs when solving the system of equations by means of $\boxminus$, has the additional advantage that values may also *shrink* in-between. Improving possibly too large values, thus, may take place immediately resulting in overall smaller, i.e., better post solutions. Moreover, no restriction is imposed any longer concerning monotonicity of right-hand sides.

4. Enforcing termination

For the new operator $\boxminus$, termination cannot generally be guaranteed for all solvers. In this section, we therefore present a modification of worklist iteration which is guaranteed to terminate—given that all right-hand sides of equations are monotonic.

EXAMPLE 1. *Consider the system:*

$$\begin{array}{rcl} x_1 & = & x_2 \\ x_2 & = & x_3 + 1 \\ x_3 & = & x_1 \end{array}$$

with $D = \mathbb{N} \cup \{\infty\}$, the lattice of non-negative integers, equipped with the natural ordering $\sqsubseteq$ given by $\leq$ and extended with ∞. Consider a widening $\sqcup\!\!\!\!\!-$ where $a \sqcup\!\!\!\!\!- b = a$ if $a = b$ and $a \sqcup\!\!\!\!\!- b = \infty$ otherwise, together with a narrowing $\sqcap\!\!\!\!\!-$ where for $a \geq b$, and $a \sqcap\!\!\!\!\!- b = b$ if $a = \infty$, and $a \sqcap\!\!\!\!\!- b = a$ otherwise. Round-robin iteration with the operator $\boxminus$ for this system starting from the mapping $\rho_0 = \{x_1 \mapsto 0, x_2 \mapsto 0, x_3 \mapsto 0\}$, will produce the following sequence of mappings:

	0	1	2	3	4	5	
x_1	0	0	∞	1	∞	2	...
x_2	0	∞	1	∞	2	∞	...
x_3	0	0	∞	1	∞	2	...

thus does no not terminate—although right-hand sides are monotonic. ∎

A similar example shows that ordinary worklist iteration, enhanced with $\boxminus$, also may not terminate, even if all equations are monotonic.

EXAMPLE 2. *Consider the two equations:*

$$x_1 = (x_1 + 1) \sqcap (x_2 + 1)$$
$$x_2 = (x_2 + 1) \sqcap (x_1 + 1)$$

using the same lattice as in example 1 where $\sqcap$ denotes minimum, i.e., the greatest lower bound. Assume that the work-set is maintained with a lifo discipline. For $W = [x_1, x_2]$, worklist iteration, starting with the initial mapping $\rho_0 = \{x_1 \mapsto 0, x_2 \mapsto 0\}$, results in the following iteration sequence:

W	$[x_1, x_2]$	$[x_1, x_2]$	$[x_1, x_2]$	$[x_2]$	$[x_2, x_1]$	$[x_2, x_1]$	$[x_1]$	$[x_1, x_2]$	
x_1	0	∞	1	1	1	1	1	∞	...
x_2	0	0	0	0	∞	2	2	2	...

which does not terminate. ∎

We present modified versions of the round-robin solver as well as of the worklist solver for which termination can be guaranteed. The worst case complexity for the new round-robin solver turns out to be even by a factor of 2 faster than ordinary round-robin iteration. For the new worklist solver, the theoretical complexity is at least not far away from the classical iterator.

For both algorithms, we assume that we are given a fixed *linear ordering* on the set of unknowns so that $X = \{x_1, \ldots, x_n\}$. The ordering will affect the iteration strategy, and therefore, as shown by Bourdoncle [3], has a significant impact on performance. Hence, the linear ordering should be chosen in a way that innermost loops would be evaluated before iteration on outer loops. For unknowns

x_i and the system of equations given by $x_i = f_i$, for $i = 1, \ldots, n$, the new round-robin algorithm is shown in Fig. 3.

Let us call the new algorithm **SRR** (*structured* round-robin). For a given initial mapping ρ_0, structured round-robin is started by calling solve n. The idea of the algorithm is, when called for a number i, to iterate on the unknown x_i until stabilization. Before every update of the unknown x_i, however, all unknowns $x_j, j < i$ are recursively solved. Clearly, the resulting algorithm is a generic $\Box$-solver.

Recall that a lattice $\mathbb{D}$ has height h if h is the maximal length of a strictly increasing chain $\bot \sqsubset d_1 \sqsubset \ldots \sqsubset d_h$. We find:

THEOREM 1. *Consider the algorithm* **SRR** *for a system of n equations over a complete lattice where all right-hand sides are monotonic and $\Box = \boxminus$. Then the following holds:*

1. *Assume that the lattice has bounded height h and $\underline{\sqcup} = \sqcup$. Then* **SRR** *when started with the initial mapping $\rho_0 = \{x_i \mapsto \bot \mid i = 1, \ldots, n\}$, terminates after at most $n + \frac{h}{2}n(n+1)$ evaluations of right-hand sides f_i.*
2. *Also in presence of unbounded ascending chains, the algorithm* **SRR** *will terminate for* every *initial mapping.*

Proof. Recall that ordinary round robin iteration performs at most $h \cdot n$ rounds due to increases of values of unknowns plus one extra round to detect termination, giving in total

$$n + h \cdot n^2$$

evaluations of right-hand sides. In contrast for structured round robin iteration, termination for unknown x_i requires one evaluation when solve i is called for the first time and then one further evaluation for every update of one of the unknowns $x_n, \ldots, x_{i+1}$. This sums up to $h \cdot (n - i) + 1$ evaluations throughout the whole iteration. This gives overhead

$$n + h \cdot \sum_{i=1}^{n} (n - i) = n + \frac{h}{2} \cdot n \cdot (n - 1)$$

Additionally, there are $h \cdot n$ evaluations that increase values. In total, the number of evaluations, therefore, is

$$n + \frac{h}{2} \cdot n \cdot (n - 1) + h \cdot n = n + \frac{h}{2} n(n + 1)$$

giving us statement 1. For the second statement, we proceed by induction on i. The case $i = 0$ is vacuously true. For the induction step assume $i > 0$. For a contradiction assume that solve i for the current mapping does not terminate. First assume that $f_i\ \rho$ returns a value smaller than $\rho[x_i]$ while for all $j < i$, $\rho[x_j] = \rho[x_j] \boxminus f_j\ \rho$ implying that $\rho[x_j] \sqsupseteq f_j\ \rho$ for all $j < i$. Then due to monotonicity, the subsequent iteration of solve i will produce a decreasing sequence of mappings implying that the operator $\boxminus$ during all occurring updates behaves like $\overline{\sqcap}$. Since all decreasing chains produced by narrowing are ultimately stable, the call solve i will terminate—in contradiction to our assumption.

Therefore during the whole run of solve i the mapping ρ' when evaluating f_i, must always return a value that is not subsumed by $\rho[x_i]$. Since all calls solve $(i - 1)$ inbetween terminate by induction hypothesis, a strictly increasing sequence of values for x_i is obtained that is produced by repeatedly applying the widening operator. Due to the properties of widening operators, any such sequence is eventually stable—in contradiction to our assumption. We conclude that solve i is eventually terminating. ■

EXAMPLE 3. *Recall the equation system, for which round-robin iteration did not terminate. With structured round-robin iteration, however, we obtain the following sequence of updates:*

```
void solve i {
    if (i = 0) return;
    solve (i − 1);
    new ← ρ[x_i] □ f_i ρ;
    if (ρ[x_i] ≠ new) {
        ρ[x_i] ← new;
        solve i;
    }
}
```

Figure 3. The new solver **SRR**.

```
Q ← ∅;
for (i ← 1; i ≤ n; i++) add Q x_i;
while (Q ≠ ∅) {
    x_i ← extract_min (Q);
    new ← ρ[x_i] □ f_i ρ;
    if (ρ[x_i] ≠ new) {
        ρ[x_i] ← new;
        add Q x_i;
        forall (x_j ∈ infl_i) add Q x_j;
    }
}
```

Figure 4. The new solver **SW**.

i		2	1	2	1	3	2	1
x_1	0	0	∞	∞	1	1	1	∞
x_2	0	∞	∞	1	1	1	∞	∞
x_3	0	0	0	0	0	∞	∞	∞

where the evaluations of unknowns not resulting in an update, have been omitted. Thus, structured fix-point solving quickly stabilizes for this example. ■

The idea of structured iteration can also be lifted to worklist iteration. Consider again a system $x_i = f_i$, for $i = 1, \ldots, n$, of equations. As for the ordinary worklist algorithm, we assume that we are given for each right-hand side f_i a (super-)set dep_i of unknowns is given such that for all mappings ρ, ρ', $f_i\,\rho = f_i\,\rho'$ whenever ρ and ρ' agree on all unknowns in dep_i. As before for each unknown x_j, let infl_j denote the the set consisting of the unknown x_j together with all unknowns influenced by x_j. Instead of a plain worklist, the modified algorithm maintains the set of unknowns to be reevaluated, within a *priority queue* Q. In every round, not an arbitrary element is extracted from Q — but the unknown with the least index. The resulting algorithm is presented in Fig. 4.

Here, the function add inserts an element into the priority queue or leaves the queue unchanged if the element is already present. Moreover, the function extract_min removes the unknown with the smallest index from the queue and returns it as result.

Let us call the resulting algorithm **SW** (structured worklist iteration). Clearly, the resulting algorithm is a generic solver.

EXAMPLE 4. *Consider again the system from example 2. Structured worklist iteration using $\boxminus$ for this system results in the following iteration:*

Q	$[x_1, x_2]$	$[x_1, x_2]$	$[x_1, x_2]$	$[x_2]$	$[x_1, x_2]$	$[x_1, x_2]$	$[x_2]$	$[]$
x_1	0	∞	1	1	1	∞	∞	∞
x_2	0	0	0	0	∞	∞	∞	∞

and thus terminates. ■

In general, we have:

THEOREM 2. *Assume the algorithm* **SW** *is applied to a system of equations over a complete lattice $\mathbb{D}$ and that each right-hand side is monotonic.*

1. *Assume that the maximal length of a strictly ascending chain is bounded by h. When instantiated with $\square = \sqcup$, and started with an initial mapping ρ mapping each unknown to $\bot$, the algorithm terminates after at most $h \cdot N$ evaluations of right-hand sides where $N = \sum_{i=1}^{n}(2 + |\mathsf{dep}_i|)$.*
2. *When instantiated with $\square = \boxminus$ and started on any mapping, the algorithm is guaranteed to terminate and, thus, always to return a post solution.*

The first statement of the theorem indicates that **SW** behaves complexity-wise like ordinary worklist iteration: the only overhead to be paid for is an extra logarithmic factor for maintaining the priority queue. The second statement, perhaps, is more surprising: it provides us with a termination guarantee for the operator $\boxminus$.

Proof. We proceed by induction on the number n of unknowns. The case $n = 1$ is true by definition of widening and narrowing. For the induction step assume that the assertion holds for systems of equations of $n - 1$ unknowns. Now consider a system of equations for a set X of cardinality n, and assume that x_n is the unknown which is larger than all other unknowns in X.

For a contradiction assume that **SW** does not terminate for the system of equations for X. First assume that the unknown x_n is extracted from the queue Q only finitely many times, say k times where d is the last value computed for x_n. This means that after the last extraction, an infinite iteration occurs on the subsystem on the unknowns $X' = X \setminus \{n\}$ where for $x_r \in X'$, the right-hand side is given by $f'_r\,\rho = f_r\,(\rho \oplus \{x_n \mapsto d\})$. By inductive hypothesis, however, the algorithm **SW** for this system terminates — in contradiction to our assumption.

Therefore, we may assume that the unknown x_n is extracted infinitely often from Q. Let $\rho_i, i \in \mathbb{N}$, denote the sequence of mappings at these extractions. Since Q is maintained as a priority queue, we know that for all unknowns x_r with $r < n$, the inequalities $\rho_i[x_r] \sqsupseteq f_r\,\rho_i$ hold. Let $d_i = \rho_i[x_n]$. If for any i, $f_n\,\rho_i \sqsubseteq d_i$, the next value d_{i+1} for x_n then is obtained by $d_{i+1} = d_i \sqcap\!\!\!\!\sqcap f_n\,\rho_i$ which is less or equal to ρ_i. By monotonicity, this implies that in the subsequent iteration, the values for all unknowns $x_r, r \leq n$, may only decrease. The remaining iteration therefore is a pure narrowing iteration and therefore terminates. In order to obtain an infinite sequence of updates for z, we conclude that for no i, $f_n\,\rho_i \sqsubseteq d_i$. Hence for every i, $d_{i+1} = d_i \sqcup\!\!\!\!\sqcup f_n\,\rho_i$ where $d_i \sqsubseteq d_{i+1}$. This, however, is impossible due to the properties of the widening operator. In summary, we conclude that x_n is extracted only finitely often from Q. Hence the fixpoint iteration terminates. ■

Since the algorithm **SW** is a generic solver, it can also be applied to non-monotonic systems. There, however, termination can no longer be guaranteed. One generic idea, though, to enforce termination for *all* $\boxminus$-solvers and in all cases, is to equip each unknown with a separate counter that counts how often the solver has switched from narrowing back to widening. That number then may be taken into account by the $\boxminus$-operator, e.g., by choosing successively less aggressive narrowing operators $\sqcap\!\!\!\!\sqcap_0, \sqcap\!\!\!\!\sqcap_1, \ldots$, and, ultimately, to give up improving the obtained values. The latter is achieved by defining $a \sqcap\!\!\!\!\sqcap_k b = a$ for a certain threshold k.

5. Local generic solvers

Similar to generic solvers, we define generic *local* solvers. Use of local solvers can be considered if systems of equations are infeasibly large or even infinite. Such systems are, e.g., encountered for context-sensitive analysis of procedural languages [1, 8]. Local solvers query the system of equations for the value of a given unknown of interest and try to evaluate only the right-hand sides of those unknowns that are needed for answering the query [12, 22, 28]. For that, it seems convenient that the *dynamic* dependences between unknowns are approximated. For a mapping ρ, a set $X' \subseteq X$ subsumes all dynamic dependences of a function $f : (X \to \mathbb{D}) \to \mathbb{D}$ (w.r.t. ρ) in the case that $f\,\rho = f\,\rho'$ whenever $\rho'|_{X'} = \rho|_{X'}$. Such sets can be constructed on the fly whenever the function f is *pure* in the sense of [20].

Essentially, purity for a right-hand side f means that evaluating $f\,\rho$ for a mapping ρ operationally consists of a finite sequence value lookups in ρ where the next unknown whose value to be looked up may only depend on the values that have already been queried. Once the sequence of lookups has been completed, the final value is determined depending on the sequence of values and finally returned.

A *partial* $\square$-solution of an (infinite) system of pure equations S is a set $\mathsf{dom} \subseteq X$ and a mapping $\rho : \mathsf{dom} \to D$ with the following two properties:

1. $\rho[x] = \rho[x] \,\square\, f_x\,\rho$ for all $x \in \mathsf{dom}$; and
2. $\mathsf{dep}_x \subseteq \mathsf{dom}$ for all $x \in \mathsf{dom}$

In essence, this means that a partial $\square$-solution is a $\square$-solution of the subsystem of S restricted to unknowns in dom.

EXAMPLE 5. *The following equation system (for $n \in \mathbb{N} = D$)*

$$y_{2n} = \max(y_{y_{2n}}, n)$$
$$y_{2n+1} = y_{6n+4}$$

is infinite as it uses infinitely many unknowns, but has at least one finite partial $\max$*-solution—the set* $\mathsf{dom} = \{y_1, y_2, y_4\}$ *together with the mapping* $\rho = \{y_1 \mapsto 2, y_2 \mapsto 2, y_4 \mapsto 2\}$. ■

A *local* generic solver instantiated with an operator $\square$, then, is an algorithm that, when given a system of pure equations S, and an initial mapping ρ_0 for all unknowns, and an unknown x_0, performs a sequence of update operations that, upon termination, results in a partial $\square$-solution (dom, ρ), such that $x_0 \in \mathsf{dom}$.

At first sight, it may seem surprising that such local generic solvers may exist. In fact, one such instance can be derived from the round-robin algorithm. For that, the evaluation of right-hand sides is instrumented in such a way that it keeps track of the set of accessed unknowns. Each round then operates on a growing set of unknowns. In the first round, just x_0 alone is considered. In any subsequent round all unknowns are added whose values have been newly accessed during the last iteration.

One more elaborate algorithm for local solving is formalized by Hofmann et al. [21], namely the solver **RLD** as shown in Figure 5. This algorithm has the benefit of visiting nodes in a more efficient order, first stabilizing innermost loops before iterating on outer loops. However, when enhanced with an operator $\square$, this algorithm is *not* a generic solver in our sense, since it is not guaranteed to execute as a sequence of *atomic* updates. Due to the recursive call to procedure solve at the beginning of eval, one evaluation of a right-hand side may occur nested into the evaluation of another right-hand side. Therefore, conceptually, it may happen that an evaluation of a right-hand side uses the values of unknowns from several different mappings ρ_i from the sequence $\rho_0, \rho_1, \ldots, \rho_n$, instead of the latest mapping ρ_n. Accordingly, the solver **RLD** is not guaranteed to return a $\square$-solution—even if it terminates. Here, we therefore, provide a variant of **RLD** where right-hand sides (conceptually) are executed atomically.

Clearly, a local generic solver does not terminate if infinitely many unknowns are encountered. Therefore, a reasonable local

```
let rec solve x =
  if x ∉ stable then
    stable ← stable ∪ {x};
    tmp ← σ[x] ⊔ f_x(eval x);
    if tmp ≠ σ[x] then
      W ← infl[x];
      σ[x] ← tmp;
      infl[x] ← [];
      stable ← stable \ W;
      foreach x ∈ W do solve x
    end
  end

and eval x y =
  solve y ;
  infl[y] ← infl[y] ∪ {x};
  σ[y]

in
  stable ← ∅; infl ← ∅; σ ← ∅;
  solve x_0; σ
```

Figure 5. The solver **RLD** from [21].

solver will try to consider as few unknowns as possible. Our solver, thus, explores the values of unknowns by recursively descending into solving unknowns *newly* detected while evaluating a right-hand side. Certain equation systems, though, introduce infinite chains of dependences for the unknowns of interest. Those systems then cannot be solved by any local solver. Here, we show that the new solver is guaranteed to terminate for the operator ⊟ at least for equation systems which are monotonic and either finite, or infinite but where only finitely many unknowns are encountered.

Let us call the new solver, on Fig. 6, **SLR** (*structured local recursive* solver). The new algorithm maintains an explicit set dom $\subseteq X$ of unknowns that have already been encountered. Beyond **RLD**, it additionally maintains a counter count which counts the number of elements in dom, and a mapping key : dom $\to \mathbb{Z}$ that equips each unknown with its priority. Moreover, a global assignment infl : dom $\to 2^X$ records for each unknown in $y \in$ dom, the unknown y itself together with the set of unknowns $x \in$ dom with the following two properties:

- the last evaluation of f_x has accessed the unknown y;
- since then, the value of the unknown y has not changed.

Unknowns whose equations may possibly be no longer valid, will be scheduled for reevaluation. This means that they are inserted into the global priority queue Q. Finally, there is a global mapping ρ : dom $\to \mathbb{D}$ that records the current values for the encountered unknowns.

As in the algorithm **RLD**, right-hand sides f_x are not directly evaluated for the current mapping ρ, but instead for a helper function eval which in the end, returns values for unknowns. Before that, however, the helper function eval provides extra book keeping of the encountered dependence between unknowns. Also, if the encountered unknown is new, then it tries not just to return the value $\bot$, but to compute the best possible value for the new unknown before-hand. In order to be able to track dependences between unknowns, the helper function eval receives as a first argument the unknown x whose right-hand side is under evaluation. The function eval first checks whether the unknown y is already contained in the domain dom of ρ. If this is not the case, y is first initialized by calling the procedure init. Subsequently, the best possible value for y is computed by calling the procedure solve for y. Then eval

```
let rec solve x =
  if x ∉ stable then
    stable ← stable ∪ {x}
    tmp ← ρ[x] □ f_x(eval x);
    if tmp ≠ ρ[x] then
      W ← infl[x];
      foreach y ∈ W do add Q y;
      ρ[x] ← tmp;
      infl[x] ← {x};
      stable ← stable \ W;
      while (Q≠∅)∧(min_key Q ≤ key[x]) do
        solve (extract_min Q);
    end
  end

and init y =
  dom ← dom ∪ {y};
  key[y] ← −count; count++;
  infl[y] ← {y}; ρ[y] ← ρ_0[y]

and eval x y =
  if y ∉ dom then
    init y; solve y
  end;
  infl[y] ← infl[y] ∪ {x};
  ρ[y]

in
  stable ← ∅; infl ← ∅; ρ ← ∅;
  dom ← ∅;
  Q ← empty_queue(); count ← 0;
  init x_0; solve x_0; ρ
```

Figure 6. The new solver **SLR**.

records the fact that x depends on y, by adding x to the set infl$[y]$. Only then is the corresponding value $\rho[y]$ returned.

Initialization of a fresh unknown y means that y is inserted into dom where it receives a key less than the keys of all other unknowns in dom. For that, the variable count is used. Moreover, infl$[y]$ and $\rho[y]$ are initialized with $\{y\}$ and $\rho_0[y]$, respectively. Thus, the given function eval differs from the corresponding function in **RLD** in that solve is recursively called only for *fresh* unknowns, and also that every unknown y always depends on itself.

The main fixpoint iteration is implemented by the procedure solve. When solve is called for an unknown x, we assume that there is currently no unknown $x' \in$ dom with key$[x'] <$ key$[x]$ that violates its equation, i.e., for which $\rho[x'] \neq \rho[x'] \,\square\, f_{x'}\,\rho$ holds. In the procedure solve for x, the call min_key Q returns the minimal key of an element in Q, and extract_min Q returns the unknown in Q with minimal key and additionally removes it from Q. Besides the global priority queue Q, the procedure solve also requires a set stable of all unknowns introduced so far such that for all unknowns x' in stable one of the following properties hold at each call of procedure solve:

- a call to the procedure solve x' has been started and the update of $\rho[x']$ has not yet occurred; or
- the equality $\rho[x'] = \rho[x'] \,\square\, f_{x'}\,\rho$ holds.

The new function solve essentially behaves like the corresponding function in **RLD** with the notable exception that not necessarily all unknowns that have been found unstable after the update of the value for x in ρ, are recursively solved right-away. Instead, all these unknowns are inserted into the global priority queue Q and then solve is only called for those unknowns x' in Q whose keys are less or equal than key$[x]$. Since x_0 has received the largest key, the initial call solve x_0 will result, upon termination, in an empty priority queue Q.

EXAMPLE 6. *Consider again the infinite equation system from example 5. The solver* **SLR**, *when solving for* y_1, *will return the partial* max*-solution* $\{y_0 \mapsto 0, y_1 \mapsto 2, y_2 \mapsto 2, y_4 \mapsto 2\}$. ■

The modifications of the algorithm **RLD** to obtain algorithm **SLR** allow us not only to prove that it is a generic local solver, but also a strong result concerning termination. Our main theorem is:

THEOREM 3. *1. When applied to any system of pure equations and interesting unknown* x_0, *the algorithm* **SLR** *returns a partial* $\square$*-solution—whenever it terminates.*

2. Assume that **SLR** *is applied to a system of pure equations over a complete lattice* $\mathbb{D}$ *where each right-hand side is monotonic. If the operator* $\square$ *is instantiated with* $\boxminus$, *then for any initial mapping* ρ_0 *and interesting unknown* x_0, **SLR** *is guaranteed to terminate and thus always to return a partial post solution—whenever only finitely many unknowns are encountered.*

Proof. We first convince ourselves that, upon termination, each right-hand side can be considered as being evaluated atomically. For that, we notice that a call solve y will never modify the value $\rho[x]$ of an unknown x with key$[x]$ > key$[y]$. A recursive call to solve may only occur for an unknown y that has not been considered before, i.e., is fresh. Therefore, it will not affect any unknown that has been encountered earlier. From that, we conclude that reevaluating a right-hand side f_x for ρ immediately after a call f_x (eval x), will return the same value — but by a computation that does not change ρ and thus is atomic.

In order to prove that **SLR** is a local generic solver, it therefore remains to verify that upon termination, ρ is a partial $\square$-solution with $x_0 \in$ dom. Since x_0 is initialized before solve x_0 is called, x_0 must be contained in dom. Upon termination, evaluation of no unknown is still in process and the priority queue is empty. All unknowns in dom $\setminus$ stable are either fresh and therefore solved right-away, or non-fresh and then inserted into the priority queue. Therefore, we conclude that the equation $\rho[x] = \rho[x] \;\square\; f_x\,\rho$ holds for all $x \in$ dom. Furthermore, the invariant for the map infl implies that upon termination, $x \in$ infl$[y]$ whenever $x = y$ or $y \in \text{dep}_x\,\rho$. In particular, infl is defined for y implying that $y \in$ dom.

In summary, correctness of the algorithm **SLR** follows from the stated invariants. The invariants themselves follow by induction on the number of function calls. Therefore, statement 1 holds.

For a proof of statement 2, assume that all equations are monotonic and only finitely many unknowns are encountered during the call solve x_0. Let dom denote this set of unknowns. We proceed by induction on key values of unknowns in dom. First consider the unknown $x \in$ dom with minimal key value. Then for all mappings ρ and infl, the call solve x will perform a sequence of updates to $\rho[x]$. In an initial segment of this sequence, the operator $\boxminus$ behaves like $\sqcup\!\!\!\!\sqcup$. As soon as the same value $\rho[x]$ or a smaller value is obtained, the operator $\boxminus$ behaves like the operator $\sqcap\!\!\!\!\sqcap$. Due to monotonicity, the remaining sequence may only consist of narrowing steps. By the properties of widening and narrowing operators, the sequence therefore must be finite.

Now consider a call solve x for an unknown $x \in$ dom where by inductive hypothesis, solve y terminates for all unknowns y with smaller keys and all mappings ρ, infl, sets stable and priority queue Q satisfying the invariants of the algorithm. In particular, this means that every recursive call to a fresh unknown terminates.

Assume for a contradiction that the assertion were wrong and the call to solve x would not terminate. Then this means that the unknown x must be destabilized after every evaluation of f_x (eval x). Upon every successive call to solve x all unknowns with keys smaller than key$[x]$, are no longer contained in Q and therefore are stable. Again we may deduce that the successive updates for $\rho[x]$ are computed by $\sqcup\!\!\!\!\sqcup$ applied to the former value of $\rho[x]$ and a new value provided by the right-hand side for x, until a narrowing phase starts. Then, however, again due to monotonicity a decreasing sequence of values for $\rho[x]$ is encountered where each new value now is combined with the former value by means of $\sqcap\!\!\!\!\sqcap$. Due to the properties of $\sqcup\!\!\!\!\sqcup$ and $\sqcap\!\!\!\!\sqcap$, we conclude that the iteration must terminate. ■

6. Side-effecting systems of equations

Generic solving, as we have discussed in the preceding sections cannot generally be extended to right-hand sides f_x that not only return a value for the left-hand side x of the equation $x = f_x$, but additionally may produce *side effects* to other unknowns. This extension, which recasts *assert*-statements of PROLOG or DATALOG programs, has been advocated in [1] for an elegant treatment of interprocedural analysis using partial contexts and flow-insensitive unknowns and thus also of multi-threaded programs [25].

EXAMPLE 7. *Consider the following program.*

```
int g = 0;
void f(int b) {
    if (b) g = b + 1;
    else g = -b - 1;
}
int main() {
    f(1);
    f(2);
    return 0;
}
```

The goal is to determine a tight interval for the global program variable g. A flow-insensitive analysis of globals aims at computing a single interval which should comprise all values possibly assigned to g. Besides the initialization with 0, this program has two asignments, one inside the call $f(1)$, *the other inside the call* $f(2)$. *A context-sensitive analysis of the control-flow should therefore collect the three values* $0, 2, 3$ *and combine them into the interval* $[0, 3]$ *for g. This requires to record for which contexts the function f is called. This task can nicely be accomplished by means of a local solver. That solver, however, has to be extended to deal with the contributions to global unknowns.* ■

In general, several side effects may occur to the same unknown z. Over an arbitrary domain of values, though, it remains unclear how the multiple contributions to z should be combined. Therefore in this section, we assume that the values of unknowns are taken from a *lattice* $\mathbb{D}$ and also that right-hand sides are *pure*. For side-effecting constraint systems this means that evaluating a right-hand side f_x applied to functions get : $X \to \mathbb{D}$ and side : $X \to \mathbb{D} \to$ **unit**, consists of a sequence of value lookups for unknowns by means of calls to the first argument function get and side effects to unknowns by means of calls to the second argument function side which is terminated by returning a contribution in $\mathbb{D}$ for the corresponding left-hand side.

Subsequently, we assume that each right-hand side f_x produces no side effect to x itself and also to each unknown $z \neq x$ at most one side effect. Technically, the right-hand side f_x of x with side effects can be considered as a succinct representation of a function $\bar{f}_x$ that takes a mapping ρ and does not return just a single value, but again another mapping ρ' where $\rho'[x]$ equals the return value computed by f_x for get $= \rho$, and for $z \neq x$, $\rho'[z] = d$ if during evaluation of f_x get side, side is called for z and d. Otherwise, i.e., if no side effect occurs to z, $\rho'[z] = \bot$. A post solution of a system $x = f_x, x \in X$, of equations with side effects then is a mapping $\rho : X \to \mathbb{D}$ such that for every $x \in X$, $\rho \sqsupseteq \bar{f}_x\, \rho$. A *partial* post solution with domain $\mathsf{dom} \subseteq X$ is a mapping $\rho : \mathsf{dom} \to \mathbb{D}$ such that for every $x \in \mathsf{dom}$, evaluation of f_x for ρ accesses only unknowns in dom and also produces side effects only to unknowns in dom; moreover, $\bar{\rho} \sqsupseteq \bar{f}_x\, \bar{\rho}$ where $\bar{\rho}$ is the total variable assignment obtained from ρ by setting $\bar{\rho}[y] \leftarrow \bot$ for all $y \notin \mathsf{dom}$.

In the following, we present a side-effecting variant $\mathbf{SLR}^+$ of the algorithm **SLR** from section 5 that for such systems returns a partial $\boxminus$-solution—whenever it terminates. Moreover, the enhanced solver $\mathbf{SLR}^+$ is guaranteed to terminate whenever all right-hand sides f_x are *monotonic*, i.e., the functions $\bar{f}_x$ all are monotonic.

EXAMPLE 8. *Consider again the analysis of example 7. The contributions to the global program variable g by different contexts may well be combined individually by widening to the current value of the global. When it comes to narrowing, though, an individual combination may no longer be sound. Therefore, the extension of the local solver* **SLR** *should collect all occurring contributions into* a set, *and use the* joint value *of all these to possibly improve the value of* g. ■

Conceptually, the algorithm $\mathbf{SLR}^+$ therefore creates for each side effect to unknown z inside the right-hand side of x, a fresh unknown $\langle x, z\rangle$ which receives that single value during evaluation of the right-hand side f_x. Furthermore, the algorithm maintains for every unknown z an auxiliary set $\mathsf{set}[z]$ which consists of all unknowns x whose right-hand sides may possibly contribute to the value of z by means of side effects. Accordingly, the original system of side-effecting equations is (implicitly) transformed in the following way:

1. Inside a right-hand side f_x, the side effect $\mathsf{side}\; z\; d$ is implicitly replaced with
$$\mathsf{side}\; \langle x, z\rangle\; d$$
while additionally, x is added to the set $\mathsf{set}[z]$.
2. The new right-hand side for an unknown x is extended with a least upper bound of all $\langle z, x\rangle$, $z \in \mathsf{set}[x]$.

The $\boxminus$-operator is applied whenever the return value of the new right-hand side for x is combined with the previous value of x. Let us now list the required modifications of the algorithm **SLR**.

First, the function $\mathsf{init}\; y$ is extended with an extra initialization of the set $\mathsf{set}[y]$ with $\emptyset$. The function eval remains unchanged. Additionally, a function side is required for realizing the side-effects during an evaluation of a right-hand side. As the function eval, also function side receives the left-hand side of the equation under consideration as its first argument. We define:

```
side x y d = if ⟨x,y⟩ ∉ dom then
                 ρ[⟨x,y⟩] ← ⊥;
             if d ≠ ρ[⟨x,y⟩] then
                 ρ[⟨x,y⟩] ← d;
               if y ∈ dom then
                 set[y] ← set[y] ∪ {x};
                 stable ← stable \ {y};
                 add Q y
               else
                 init y;
                 set[y] ← {x};
                 solve y
               end
             end
```

When called with x, y, d, the function side first initializes the unknown $\langle x, y\rangle$ if it is not yet contained in dom. If the new value is different from the old value of ρ for $\langle x, y\rangle$, $\rho[\langle x, y\rangle]$ is updated. Subsequently, the set $\mathsf{set}[y]$ receives the unknown x, and the unknown y is triggered for reevaluation. If y has not yet been encountered, y is initialized, $\mathsf{set}[y]$ is set to $\{x\}$, and $\mathsf{solve}\; y$ is called. Otherwise, x is only added to $\mathsf{set}[y]$, and y is scheduled for reevaluation by destabilizing y first and then inserting y into the priority queue Q.

The third modification concerns the procedure solve. There, the call of the right-hand side f_x now receives $\mathsf{side}\; x$ as a second argument and additionally evaluates all unknowns collected in $\mathsf{set}[x]$. The corresponding new line reads:

$$\mathsf{tmp} \leftarrow \rho(x) \boxminus (f_x\; (\mathsf{eval}\; x)\; (\mathsf{side}\; x) \sqcup \bigsqcup\{\rho\, \langle z, x\rangle \mid z \in \mathsf{set}\; x\});$$

EXAMPLE 9. *Consider again interval analysis for the program from example 7. Concerning the global program variable g, the initialization $g = 0$ is detected first, resulting in the value $\rho[g] = [0, 0]$. Then g is scheduled for reevaluation. This occurs immediately, resulting in no further change. Then the calls $f(1)$, $f(2)$ are analyzed, the side effects of 2 and 3 are recorded and g is rescheduled for evaluation. When that happens, the value $\rho[g]$ is increased to*

$$[0, 0] \boxminus [0, 3] = [0, 0] \sqcup\!\!\!\!\sqcup [0, 3] = [0, \infty]$$

if the standard widening for intervals is applied. Since $\rho[g]$ has changed, z again is scheduled for evaluation resulting in the value

$$[0, \infty] \boxminus [0, 3] = [0, \infty] \sqcap\!\!\!\!\sqcap [0, 3] = [0, 3]$$

Further evaluation of g will not change this result any more. ■

Analogously to theorem 3 from the last section, we obtain:

THEOREM 4. *1. When applied to any system of pure equations with side effects and interesting unknown x_0, the algorithm $\mathbf{SLR}^+$ returns a partial post solution—whenever it terminates.*
2. Assume that $\mathbf{SLR}^+$ is applied to a system of pure equations over a complete lattice $\mathbb{D}$ where each right-hand side is monotonic. Then for any initial mapping ρ_0 and interesting unknown x_0, $\mathbf{SLR}^+$ is guaranteed to terminate and thus always to return a partial post solution—whenever only finitely many unknowns are encountered.

7. Experimental evaluation

We have implemented the generic local solver $\mathbf{SLR}^+$ and included into the analyzer GOBLINT for multi-threaded C programs. Goblint uses CIL as C front-end [24] and is written in OCAML. The tests were performed on 2.7GHz Intel Core i7 laptop, with 8GB DDR3 RAM, running OS X 10.8.2.

In order to compare the precision attained by two-phase solving according to [6] using widening and narrowing, and $\boxminus$-solving, we used the benchmark suite[1] from the Märdalen WCET research group [17] which collects a series of interesting small examples for WCET analysis, varying in size from about 40 lines to 4000 lines of code. On top of standard analyses of pointers, we performed an interval analysis where local variables are analyzed context-insensitively while global variables are treated flow-insensitively. Within this setting, we determined the precision achieved by the $\boxminus$-solver compared to a corresponding solver which realizes a distinct widening phase, followed by a distinct narrowing phase. The results of this comparison is displayed in fig. 7. Since the absolute run-times are negligible (about 14 seconds for all programs together), we only display the relative precision. For that, we list, sorted

[1] available at www.mrtc.mdh.se/projects/wcet/benchmarks.html

	$\sqcup$ without context		$\boxminus$ without context		$\sqcup$ with context		$\boxminus$ with context	
Program	Time(s)	Unknowns	Time(s)	Unknowns	Time(s)	Unknowns	Time(s)	Unknowns
401.bzip2	3.3	6 565	3.3	6 578	3.3	7 033	3.3	7 028
429.mcf	0.4	1 245	0.4	1 245	0.5	1 673	0.5	1 673
433.milc	9.3	8 206	9.3	8 206	13.5	36 720	13.4	36 711
456.hmmer	11.2	11 446	11.2	11 446	12.6	80 938	13.3	81 038
458.sjeng	49.1	13 306	52.1	13 306	121.0	97 785	131.0	108 371
470.lbm	0.3	784	0.3	784	0.4	1 577	0.2	899
482.sphinx	14.0	11 963	13.9	11 963	6.3	21 610	6.3	21 610

Table 1. Results for programs from the SpecCpu2006 benchmark suite.

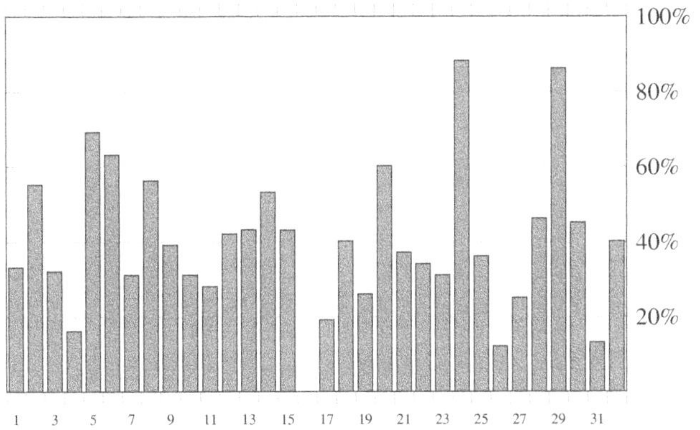

Figure 7. The percentage of program points with improvement.

by program size, the percentage of program points where the $\boxminus$-solver returns better results. With the notable exception of the benchmark `qsort-exam.c` without improvement (number 16 in the list), all other benchmarks show significant improvements, with an weighted average improvement of 39%.

In a second experiment, we explored the efficiency of our implementation of a generic local $\boxminus$-solver. Our collection of benchmarks consists of all C projects of the SpecCpu2006 benchmark suite that can be handled by CIL. The programs `400.perlbench` and `445.gobmk` could not be analyzed in this setting, as there was (to our best understanding) insufficient memory to do so. For the other programs, we performed interval analysis in two variants. The first variant (reported in the table 1 to the left) performs a context-insensitive analysis, while the second variant (reported to the right) analyzes local variables depending on a calling context which includes all non-interval values of locals. While the first variant of analysis can be realized by means of clearly separated phases of widening and narrowing, the second variant cannot, since right-hand sides are not monotonic and the sets of contexts and thus also the sets of unknowns encountered during the widening and narrowing phases may vary. In order to explore the extra costs incurred by the operator $\boxminus$ for each variant, we then compared the run-times if just widening is applied or $\boxminus$. While in size, the programs range from 1 to 33 kloc, the effective run-times essentially depend on the number of unknowns to be handled by the solvers.

Not surprisingly, the run-times for context-*insensitive* analysis, (as reported to the left) are faster than those if context is taken into account, with the exception of `482.sphinx`. As we can see here, sometimes the dependency-breaking property of context-sensitive analysis succeeds in performing the analysis faster—even when the context-sensitive case needs substantially more unknowns.

In absence of context, the $\boxminus$-solver is only marginally slower than the corresponding $\sqcup$-solver. The efficiency picture for context-*sensitive* analysis, however, is less clear. Here, it seems that the efficiency crucially depends on the number of needed unknowns.

For some programs the numbers of encountered unknowns do not depend greatly on the chosen solver, since the sets of occurring contexts are largely independent of the computed intervals. In these cases, the solvers essentially perform equally well. For the remaining benchmarks, the number of contexts may increase (456 and 458) or decrease (470) with $\boxminus$, implying that the run-time of the $\boxminus$-solver may increase or decrease compared to the $\sqcup$-solver.

In summary, the $\boxminus$-solver $\mathbf{SLR}^+$ turns out to be a robust algorithm with decent run-times. The new solver allows to significantly improve precision over the two-phase widening/narrowing approach and also is successfully applicable in more general analysis scenarios, where the two-phase approach was not applicable.

8. Conclusion

We have presented a generic combination of widening and narrowing into a single operator $\boxminus$ and systematically explored solver algorithms which, when instantiated with $\boxminus$ will solve general systems of equations. Perhaps surprisingly, standard versions of fixpoint algorithms, when enhanced with $\boxminus$, may fail to terminate even for finite systems of monotonic equations. Therefore, we presented variants of round-robin iteration, of ordinary worklist iteration as well as of recursive local solving with and without side effects where for monotonic equations and finitely many unknowns, termination can be guaranteed whenever only finitely many unknowns are encountered.

Furthermore, we provided preliminary practical evidence that fixpoint iteration based on the combined operator $\boxminus$ may increase precision significantly, and that it also behaves well for interprocedural analysis where right-hand sides of equations can no longer be considered as monotonic. Our experiments were performed independent of other methods of increasing the precision of the widening/narrowing approach. It remains for future work to explore how well different methods to increase precision may cooperate for computing precise analysis results at a decent cost.

Acknowledgments

The research leading to these results has received funding from the ARTEMIS Joint Undertaking under grant agreement n° 269335 and from the German Science Foundation (DFG). The last author is partially supported by the Estonian Science Foundation (EstSF) under grant n° 8421.

References

1. K. Apinis, H. Seidl, and V. Vojdani. Side-Effecting Constraint Systems: A Swiss Army Knife for Program Analysis. In *APLAS*, pages 157–172. LNCS 7705, Springer, 2012.
2. Bruno Blanchet, Patrick Cousot, Radhia Cousot, Jérome Feret, Laurent Mauborgne, Antoine Miné, David Monniaux, and Xavier Rival. A static analyzer for large safety-critical software. In *ACM SIGPLAN Notices*, volume 38, pages 196–207. ACM, 2003.
3. François Bourdoncle. Interprocedural abstract interpretation of block structured languages with nested procedures, aliasing and recursivity. In *Programming Language Implementation and Logic Programming, 2nd International Workshop PLILP'90*, volume 456 of *Lecture Notes in Computer Science*, pages 307–323. Springer-Verlag, 1990.
4. François Bourdoncle. Efficient chaotic iteration strategies with widenings. In *In Proceedings of the International Conference on Formal Methods in Programming and their Applications*, pages 128–141. Springer-Verlag, 1993.
5. Agostino Cortesi and Matteo Zanioli. Widening and narrowing operators for abstract interpretation. *Computer Languages, Systems & Structures*, 37(1):24–42, 2011.
6. P. Cousot and R. Cousot. Static determination of dynamic properties of programs. In B. Robinet, editor, *Second International Symposium on Programming, Paris, France*, page 106—130. Dunod, Paris, 1976.
7. P. Cousot and R. Cousot. Abstract Interpretation: A unified lattice model for static analysis of programs by construction or approximation of fixpoints. In *4th ACM Symp. on Principles of Programming Languages (POPL'77)*, pages 238–252. ACM Press, 1977.
8. P. Cousot and R. Cousot. Static Determination of Dynamic Properties of Recursive Procedures. In *IFIP Conf. on Formal Description of Programming Concepts*, pages 237–277. North-Holland, 1977.
9. P. Cousot, R. Cousot, J. Feret, L. Mauborgne, A. Miné, D. Monniaux, and X. Rival. Combination of abstractions in the ASTRÉE static analyzer. In M. Okada and I. Satoh, editors, *Eleventh Annual Asian Computing Science Conference (ASIAN'06)*, pages 272–300, Tokyo, Japan, LNCS 4435, 2007. Springer, Berlin.
10. Patrick Cousot. Semantic foundations of program analysis. In S.S. Muchnick and N.D. Jones, editors, *Program Flow Analysis: Theory and Applications*, chapter 10, page 303—342. Prentice-Hall, Inc., Englewood Cliffs, New Jersey, U.S.A., 1981.
11. Patrick Cousot and Radhia Cousot. Comparing the galois connection and widening/narrowing approaches to abstract interpretation. In Maurice Bruynooghe and Martin Wirsing, editors, *PLILP*, volume 631 of *LNCS*, pages 269–295. Springer, 1992.
12. Christian Fecht and Helmut Seidl. A Faster Solver for General Systems of Equations. *Science of Computer Programming*, 35(2):137–161, 1999.
13. Denis Gopan and Thomas Reps. Lookahead widening. In Thomas Ball and Robert Jones, editors, *Computer Aided Verification*, volume 4144 of *LNCS*, pages 452–466. Springer, 2006.
14. Denis Gopan and Thomas Reps. Guided static analysis. In Hanne Nielson and Gilberto Filé, editors, *Proc. of the 14th International Static Analysis Symposium (SAS)*, volume 4634 of *LNCS*, pages 349–365. Springer, 2007.
15. Bhargav Gulavani, Supratik Chakraborty, Aditya Nori, and Sriram Rajamani. Automatically refining abstract interpretations. In C. Ramakrishnan and Jakob Rehof, editors, *Tools and Algorithms for the Construction and Analysis of Systems (TACAS'08)*, volume 4963 of *LNCS*, pages 443–458. Springer, 2008.
16. Sumit Gulwani, Sagar Jain, and Eric Koskinen. Control-flow refinement and progress invariants for bound analysis. In *Proceedings of the 2009 ACM SIGPLAN conference on Programming language design and implementation (PLDI'09)*, page 375–385, June 2009.
17. Jan Gustafsson, Adam Betts, Andreas Ermedahl, and Björn Lisper. The Mälardalen WCET benchmarks – past, present and future. In Björn Lisper, editor, *WCET2010*, pages 137–147, Brussels, Belgium, July 2010. OCG.
18. Nicolas Halbwachs and Julien Henry. When the decreasing sequence fails. In Antoine Miné and David Schmidt, editors, *SAS*, volume 7460 of *LNCS*, pages 198–213. Springer, 2012. ISBN 978-3-642-33124-4.
19. Julien Henry, David Monniaux, and Matthieu Moy. Succinct representations for abstract interpretation. In Antoine Miné and David Schmidt, editors, *Static Analysis Symposium (SAS'12)*, volume 7460 of *LNCS*, pages 283–299. Springer Berlin / Heidelberg, 2012.
20. Martin Hofmann, Aleksandr Karbyshev, and Helmut Seidl. What is a pure functional? In *ICALP (2)*, pages 199–210. LNCS 6199, Springer, 2010.
21. Martin Hofmann, Aleksandr Karbyshev, and Helmut Seidl. Verifying a local generic solver in Coq. In *SAS'10*, pages 340–355. LNCS 6337, Springer, 2010.
22. B. Le Charlier and P. Van Hentenryck. A Universal Top-Down Fixpoint Algorithm. Technical Report 92–22, Institute of Computer Science, University of Namur, Belgium, 1992.
23. David Monniaux and Julien Le Guen. Stratified static analysis based on variable dependencies. In *The Third International Workshop on Numerical and Symbolic Abstract Domains*, 2011.
24. George C. Necula, Scott McPeak, S. P. Rahul, and Westley Weimer. CIL: Intermediate Language and Tools for Analysis and Transformation of C Programs. In *CC'02*, volume 2304 of *LNCS*, pages 213–228. Springer, 2002.
25. Helmut Seidl, Varmo Vene, and Markus Müller-Olm. Global invariants for analyzing multithreaded applications. *Proc. of the Estonian Academy of Sciences: Phys., Math.*, 52(4):413–436, 2003.
26. Rahul Sharma, Isil Dillig, Thomas Dillig, and Alex Aiken. Simplifying loop invariant generation using splitter predicates. In Ganesh Gopalakrishnan and Shaz Qadeer, editors, *Computer Aided Verification (CAV'11)*, volume 6806 of *LNCS*, pages 703–719. Springer, 2011.
27. Axel Simon and Andy King. Widening polyhedra with landmarks. In Naoki Kobayashi, editor, *APLAS*, volume 4279 of *LNCS*, pages 166–182. Springer, 2006. ISBN 3-540-48937-1.
28. B. Vergauwen, J. Wauman, and J. Lewi. Efficient fixpoint computation. In *SAS'94*, volume 864 of *LNCS*, pages 314–328. Springer, 1994.
29. Vesal Vojdani and Varmo Vene. Goblint: Path-sensitive data race analysis. *Annales Univ. Sci. Budapest., Sect. Comp.*, 30:141–155, 2009.

Verifying Higher-order Programs with the Dijkstra Monad

Nikhil Swamy[1] Joel Weinberger[2] Cole Schlesinger[3] Juan Chen[1] Benjamin Livshits[1]

Microsoft Research[1] UC Berkeley[2] Princeton University[3]

{nswamy, juanchen, livshits}@microsoft.com jww@cs.berkeley.edu cschlesi@princeton.edu

Abstract

Modern programming languages, ranging from Haskell and ML, to JavaScript, C# and Java, all make extensive use of higher-order state. This paper advocates a new verification methodology for higher-order stateful programs, based on a new monad of predicate transformers called the *Dijkstra monad*.

Using the Dijkstra monad has a number of benefits. First, the monad naturally yields a weakest pre-condition calculus. Second, the computed specifications are structurally simpler in several ways, e.g., single-state post-conditions are sufficient (rather than the more complex two-state post-conditions). Finally, the monad can easily be varied to handle features like exceptions and heap invariants, while retaining the same type inference algorithm.

We implement the Dijkstra monad and its type inference algorithm for the F* programming language. Our most extensive case study evaluates the Dijkstra monad and its F* implementation by using it to verify JavaScript programs.

Specifically, we describe a tool chain that translates programs in a subset of JavaScript decorated with assertions and loop invariants to F*. Once in F*, our type inference algorithm computes verification conditions and automatically discharges their proofs using an SMT solver. We use our tools to prove that a core model of the JavaScript runtime in F* respects various invariants and that a suite of JavaScript source programs are free of runtime errors.

Categories and Subject Descriptors D.2.4 [*Software/ Program Verification*]: Validation

General Terms Verification

Keywords Predicate transformer, Hoare monad, refinement types, dynamic languages

1. Introduction

Once the preserve of languages like Haskell and ML, programming with a mixture of higher-order functions and state is now common in the mainstream. C# and Java provide first-class closures, which interact with imperative objects in subtle ways, and in languages like JavaScript, higher-order state is pervasive. When used properly, programming with these features can promote code re-use, modularity, and programmer productivity. However, the complexity of higher-order state poses serious difficulties for program verification tools. Consider the JavaScript program below.

```
function incf(x) {x.f = x.f + 1; return x;};
assert (incf({f:0}).f == 1); incf=0;
```

To understand this program, we turn to Guha et al. (2010), who desugar JavaScript to λJS, an untyped lambda calculus with references and key/value dictionaries. We show the desugared JavaScript program below, with some superficial modifications—notably, rather than use an untyped lambda calculus, we present the desugared program in ML, where the typing is made explicit using a standard ML variant type *dynamic* (Henglein 1994).

```
1 let incf this args = let x = select args "0" in
2                 update x "f" (plus (select x "f") (Int 1)); x in
3 update global "incf" (Fun incf);
4 let args = let x = update (allocObject()) "f" (Int 0) in
5           update (allocObject()) "0" x in
6 let res = apply (select global "incf") global args in
7 assert(select res "f" = Int 1);
8 update global "incf" (Int 0)
```

The JavaScript function `incf` is translated to the **let**-bound λ-term incf, with two arguments: this, corresponding to JavaScript's implicit `this` parameter, and args, an object containing all the (variable number of) arguments that a JavaScript function may receive. An object is a dictionary indexed by string keys, rather than containing statically known field names. In the body of incf, the `x` argument is the value stored at the key `"0"` in the args object.

At line 3, the function incf is stored in the global object (an implicit object in JavaScript) at the key `"incf"`. At line 6 we see that a function call proceeds by reading a value out of the global object (using the library function select), calling the apply library function, which checks that its first argument is a Fun f, and then applies f to its next two arguments—here, the global object, the receiver object for the call; and the args object containing a single argument.

Now, suppose that one wished to prove that the assertion at line 7 succeeds. One needs to reason that line 6 was indeed a call to incf. But, even proving this is non-trivial, since the call occurs via a lookup into a higher-order store, in this case, the global object. Making matters harder, the store is subject to arbitrary updates, e.g., at line 8, the incf field is modified to be Int 0 instead. Thus, in a language like JavaScript, even to reason about simple function calls one needs to reason precisely about higher-order state.

1.1 SMT-based verification of higher-order stateful programs

Our main technical contribution is a new way of structuring specifications for higher-order, stateful programs, and of inferring and automatically solving verification conditions (VCs) for these programs using an SMT solver.

Specifically, we present the *Dijkstra monad*, a new variant of the Hoare state monad of Nanevski et al. (2008a). The Dijkstra monad equips a state monad with a predicate transformer (Dijkstra 1975) that can be used to compute a pre-condition for a computation, for any context in which that computation may be used. We show how to encode the Dijkstra monad in F*, a dependently typed dialect of ML (Swamy et al. 2011a), and present several examples of F* pro-

PLDI'13, June 16–19, 2013, Seattle, Washington, USA.

grams verified using this monad, ranging from higher-order combinators and data structures, to implementations of cryptographic protocols with stateful invariants (§2).

Verification is facilitated by a new type inference algorithm that allows stateful programs written in "direct style" to be interpreted in the Dijkstra state monad, yielding a VC for the program. We prove our inference algorithm sound, which (informally) means that if the VC computed for an F* program is provable, then the program contains no failing assertions. Despite our liberal use of predicate transformers and other higher-order logic constructs, we prove that the VCs computed by our algorithm can be represented in a first-order theory, and hence can often be discharged effectively by SMT solvers like Z3 (de Moura and Bjørner 2008) (§2.3).

To illustrate the expressiveness of our approach, we show how to program and verify implementations of abstract datatypes involving a mixture of higher-order functions and local state. Our verification technique employs a mixture of existentially quantified abstract predicates and a lightweight specification style reminiscent of separation logic, all encoded using F*'s higher-order logic. Nevertheless, we are still able to discharge verification conditions automatically using an SMT solver (§3).

1.2 An extended case study: JavaScript verification

Our most extensive case study to date involves applying the Dijkstra monad to verify JavaScript programs, a problem of growing practical importance. Our verification tool chain first translates JavaScript programs to JS* (a subset of F*), then uses our type inference algorithm to compute VCs, and, finally, solves the VCs automatically using Z3. The diagram below depicts this workflow.

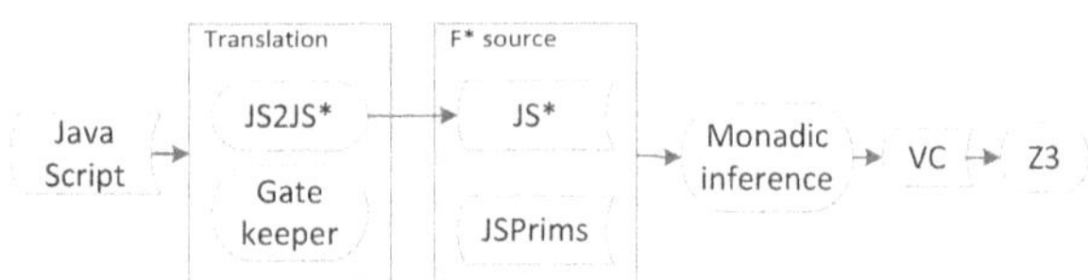

Our translation, JS2JS*, adapts λJS, retargeting it to a typed language. We show how to make use of Gatekeeper (Guarnieri and Livshits 2009), an unsound but efficient pointer analysis for JavaScript, to convey verification hints in the translation, thereby improving verification times while still maintaining soundness.

Besides higher-order state, a program verifier for JavaScript programs also has to deal with dynamic typing. We show how to smoothly integrate the Dijkstra monad within a variant type dyn, a new refinement of type dynamic (Cartwright and Fagan 1991; Henglein 1994). Using this type, we program a library of runtime support for JavaScript (called JSPrims). The full version of JSPrims (available online[1]) contains approximately 1,200 lines of carefully hand-written, mechanically verified F* code, making heavy use of the Dijkstra monad and type dyn to prove that several key invariants related to the JavaScript heap are respected. Additionally, our verification guarantees that well-typed clients of JSPrims do not raise any JavaScript runtime errors. We present a simplified version of JSPrims in §4.

We report on our experience using our tools to verify a collection of JavaScript web-browser extensions for the absence of JavaScript runtime errors. We provide a verification harness that includes a partial specification of a sequential fragment of the Document Object Model (DOM)—this specification makes heavy use of the Dijkstra monad, illustrating its versatility. In each case, apart from the annotation of loop invariants, verification was automatic. The soundness of our verification results rides conveniently on the mechanized metatheory and certified implementation of F*—no JavaScript-specific extensions to the type system are required (§5).

As such, using F* as an intermediate verification language, we bring a methodology proven effective for first-order programs (using tools like Boogie (Leino and Rümmer 2010) or Why (Filliâtre and Marché 2007)), to higher-order, stateful programs.

2. The Dijkstra Monad

Monads have traditionally been used to structure effectful computations in functional programs. For example, the state monad, ST a, is the type of a computation that when evaluated in an initial heap, produces a result of type a and a final heap. In a purely functional language like Coq, ST a can be represented by the type heap $\rightarrow$(a $*$ heap). In a language that provides primitive support for state, e.g., ML, the type ST a can just be an abstract alias for a. As a monad, the abstract type ST comes with two operations: returnST : $\forall$a. a $\rightarrow$ST a and bindST: $\forall$a,b. ST a $\rightarrow$(a $\rightarrow$ST b) $\rightarrow$ST b, and these are expected to satisfy certain laws.

To verify stateful programs, Nanevski et al. (2008b) propose Hoare Type Theory (HTT), where the main typing construct is a state monad augmented with pre- and post-conditions. The resulting monad, the *Hoare monad*, written HST pre a post, can be understood as the type h:heap{pre h} $\rightarrow$(x:a $*$ h':heap{post x h'})[2] That is, HST pre a post is the type of a computation which when run in an input heap h satisfying the predicate pre h, produces a result x:a and an output heap h' satisfying post x h'. The HST monad comes with two operations, returnHST: $\forall$a, p. a $\rightarrow$HST (p x) a p, which allows a pure value to be treated as a computation; and bindHST: $\forall$p a q b r. HST p a q $\rightarrow$(x:a $\rightarrow$HST (q x) b r) $\rightarrow$HST p b r, which allows two computations to be composed, so long as the post-condition of the first matches the pre-condition of the second.

While the Hoare monad has proven effective in verifying stateful code in a functional language, it has some shortcomings:

–Usually, with the Hoare monad one writes specifications in the form of valid triples. This style does not lead directly to a VC generation algorithm. In order to extract a VC generation algorithm from specifications in this style, Nanevski et al. have adopted a variety of strategies in several papers. The original presentation of HTT (Nanevski et al. 2008b) employs a custom-built bidirectional typing algorithm to exploit the specific structure of HST to infer VCs. Subsequent works (Nanevski et al. 2008a) show how to embed HTT in Coq, where using a slightly different style of specification, Coq's type inference algorithm can be used to compute VCs for programs in the HST monad. However, the VCs thus computed involve a proliferation of existential quantifiers to state properties of intermediate program states. Reasoning with these quantifiers, particularly using automated SMT solvers, can be problematic.

–Additionally, writing precise specifications with the Hoare monad requires post-conditions that circumscribe the write effects of a computation, e.g., to say that the input and output heaps are the same on some domain. To achieve this, one usually requires two-state (a.k.a binary) post-conditions, or designs patterns like separation logic, adding complexity to the system.

Our key observation is that writing specifications for programs using a monad of predicate transformers (Dijkstra 1975) can alleviate the above difficulties. We call the monad the *Dijkstra monad*,

[1] Supplementary material associated with this paper is available from `http://research.microsoft.com/fstar`, and includes a compiler download, several example programs, and a technical report including proofs of all the theorems in this paper.

[2] Notation: we write x:t $\rightarrow$t' for a dependent function whose formal parameter x of type t is named and is in scope in the return type t'; and (x:t $*$ t') for a dependent pair where x names the t-typed first component and is bound in the second component t'; and x:t{ϕ} for a refinement of the type t to those elements x that satisfy the proposition ϕ.

and write it DST a wp. This is the type of a stateful computation producing a result x:a, and whose behavior is described by the weakest pre-condition predicate transformer, wp. In a purely functional language, one may view DST a wp as an abbreviation for the type ∀p. h:heap{wp p h} → (x:a ∗ h':heap{p x h'}). That is, in order for the output heap h' to satisfy p x h', for any predicate p, one needs to prove wp p h of the input heap h. DST provides two operations, return and bind, with the signatures shown below:

```
return: ∀a. x:a → DST a (Λp. p x)

bind: ∀a wp1 b wp2. DST a wp1
        → (x:a → DST b (wp2 x))
        → DST b (Λp. wp1 (λx. wp2 x p))
```

To inject a value x:a into the monad, one uses return, where the weakest pre-condition is simply to prove the post-condition p for x on the input heap. To compose computations, one can use bind, where the weakest pre-condition of the result is simply computed by composing the weakest pre-conditions of each component.

2.1 Simple examples

For a flavor of the Dijkstra monad, we show a selection of small ML programs and their specifications. These examples illustrate (1) the expressive power of the DST monad, in particular, the way we describe precise effects using unary, parametric post-conditions, and, how, using parametricity over the predicate transformers themselves, one can write precise specifications for higher-order programs; (2) the way in which the DST monad provides a VC generation algorithm by construction; and, (3), how the general construction can be varied to accommodate features like heap invariants for monotonic state, as well as language features like exceptions.

Primitive operations on references. We start with types for the primitives that manipulate references, where, as usual, the type heap is viewed in the logic as a partial map from references of type **ref** t to values of type t. We model the map using McCarthy's select/update theory of functional maps (McCarthy 1962), with the usual interpretation. To reduce clutter in the notation, we assume all function types are prenex quantified with their free type variables.

```
ref : x:a → DST (ref a) (Λp.λh. ∀l. l ∉ dom h ⟹ p l (update h l x))
(!) : x:ref a → DST a (Λp.λh. p (select h x) h)
(:=): x:ref a → v:a → DST unit (Λp.λh. p () (update h x v))
```

We use the function **ref** to allocate a reference cell of type **ref** a, initializing its contents to x:a. The weakest pre-condition of **ref** states that for any post-condition p, the proposition to prove on the input heap h is ∀l. l ∉ dom h ⟹ p l (update h l x), i.e., **ref** x returns a new heap location l not in the input heap h, and updates h at location l with the argument x. We type the dereference !(x:**ref** a) at the type a, as usual, and give it the weakest pre-condition Λp.λh. p (select h x) h, i.e., dereference returns the contents of the input heap h at location x, and leaves the heap unchanged. The type of x := v is analogous, except we return ():unit, and the weakest pre-condition states that the input heap h is updated just at x.

Note that in each case we were able to precisely state the relation between the input and output heaps by relying on a parametric unary post-condition, instead of binary post-conditions. In general, given a Hoare triple with a binary post-condition, i.e., the type h:heap{pre h} → (x:a ∗ h':heap{post2 x h h'}), one can always represent it using unary post-conditions and the Dijkstra monad as DST a (Λp.λh. pre h ∧ ∀x h'. post2 x h h' ⟹ p x h').

Swapping references. Take the following ML program:

```
let swap x y = let tmp = !x in let _ = x := !y in y := tmp
```

To compute a weakest pre-condition for swap, one simply computes the weakest pre-condition for each of the three commands, which are then composed using two monadic binds. The resulting type is:

```
swap: x:ref a → y:ref b → DST unit
      (Λp.λh. p () (update (update h x (select h y)) y (select h x)))
```

In contrast, using bidirectional VC generation for HST, one begins with a user-provided post-condition which is then "pushed" back through the computation. This is usually interleaved with a forward phase that computes types for **let**-bound variables. At each **let**-binding, one must close over the bound variable with an existential quantifier. The additional quantifiers make proof obligations more cumbersome to manipulate. These difficulties are avoided with predicate transformers.

Higher-order functions. Predicate parametricity is also essential for writing specifications for higher-order programs. Take the following combinator: **let** app f x = f x. Its type is

```
app: (y:a → DST b (wp y)) → x:a → DST b (wp x)
```

By being parametric in wp, app is able to abstract over the specification of its function-typed argument. Similarly, the type of **let** twice f x = f (f x), abstracts over the wp of the argument.

```
twice: (z:a → DST a (wp z)) → x:a → DST a (Λp. wp x (λy. wp y p))
```

If we were to instead abstract over the pre- and post-condition of the function argument f (rather than its wp) we would be forced to reason about twice f using invariants only, e.g., it would be impossible to prove that twice (λx. x:=!x+1) x added 2 to x. Of course, for programs with loops, we must resort to invariants. For example, here is the type of the while-combinator.

```
while: guard:(unit → DST bool wpg)
    → body:(unit → DST unit wpb)
    → DST unit (Λp.λh0. inv h0
        ∧ ∀h1. inv h1 ⟹ wpg (λb h2. b=true ⟹ wpb (λ_. inv) h2
                                    ∧ b=false ⟹ inv h2) h1
        ∧ ∀h1. inv h1 ⟹ p () h1)
```

The type above is parametric in wpg, the specification of the guard; in wpb, the specification of the loop body; and in inv, the loop invariant. The three clauses of the wp of while require the invariant to hold on the initial heap (inv h0); for the weakest pre-condition of the body (with respect to the invariant once again) to hold if the guard returns true, and otherwise for the invariant to hold immediately; and finally, for the invariant to imply the post-condition, i.e., the DST monad makes it easy to embed the standard weakest pre-condition rule for a while-loop inside the types.

Monotonic state with two-state invariants. Some applications demand variations on the basic DST monad. For instance, our supplementary material contains an example of an authentication protocol based on digital signatures, verified using the Dijkstra monad. A feature in our model of this protocol is the use of monotonic state. In particular, we make use of a stateful log of protocol events, log : **ref** (list event). For our model to be sound, at each state update, we need to verify that no event has been removed from the log. Rather than insert an explicit assertion at every command (which would be impractically tedious), we would like a variant of the DST monad that yields VCs with the necessary checks.

Our approach makes this easy to do. We provide the monad iDST, a variant of DST with a bind that checks the invariant, as shown in the signature below.

```
bind: iDST a wp1 → (x:a → iDST b (wp2 x))
      → iDST b (Λp.λh0. wp1 (λx h1. δ h0 h1 ∧ wp2 x post h1) h0).
```

This type ensures that as the heap evolves, every pair of adjacent heaps h0, h1 are related by the predicate δ h0 h1. The particular instantiation of δ depends on the application. For our authorization protocol, we instantiate δ to λh0 h1. ∀x. In x (select h0 log) ⟹ In x (select h1 log), (where In is for list membership), to ensure that the list grows monotonically.

As we will see, our type inference algorithm is generic enough to support arbitrary bind signatures, thereby allowing VC generation to be customized for the application at hand. In contrast, most program verifiers, e.g., the tools based on the Boogie framework, bake in a specific verification condition generation strategy into the tool. For example, without explicitly sprinkling assertions between every pair of commands, it is impossible to make Dafny (Leino 2010) check a two-state heap evolution invariant.

While the signature of bind requires us to prove that successive heaps are related by δ, dually, we would like to benefit from the invariant as well. When δ is reflexive and transitive, we show that a heap and any of its descendants that may result during a program execution are related by δ. Reflecting this property, we can provide two axiomatic functions, witness, which takes a snapshot of the current heap, and recall, which guarantees that the current heap is related to any prior snapshot by δ:

```
witness: unit →iDST heap (Λp. λh. p h h)
recall: h0:heap →iDST unit (Λp. λh. δ h0 h ⟹ p () h)
```

The validity of these axioms is justified by our metatheory. Intuitively, since heap is abstract, the only heap values that are available to a program are those produced by witness. Thus, in recall, we know that h0 is a heap snapshot, and by reflexivity and transitivity, it must be related to the current heap by δ.

Combining monads. Handling language features like exceptions within the Dijkstra monad is straightforward. For example, given a monad for exceptions, we can combine it with the Dijkstra monad to yield a monad for state and exceptions, with VC generation provided by construction. We first define a type result a to capture the two kinds of results a computation may produce. Normal results are tagged with the constructor V : a →result a, and exceptional results are represented using E: exn →result a, for some type of exceptions exn. Now, combining the result type with the DST monad, we write eDST a wp, which can be understood as the type ∀p. h:heap{wp p h} →(x:result a ∗ h':heap{p x h'}).

```
val return: x:a →eDST a (Λp.p (V x))
val bind: eDST a wp1 →(x:a →eDST b (wp2 x)) →eDST b wpBindE
  where wpBindE = (Λp. wp1 (λr h1. (∀ x. r=V x ⟹ wp2 x p h1)
                                    ∧ r=E _ ⟹ p r h1))
val raise: e:exn →eDST a (Λp.p (E e))
val tryWith: (unit →eDST a wp1) →(e:exn →eDST a (wp2 e))
         →eDST a (Λp. wp1 (λr h. (∀ v. r=V v ⟹ p r h)
                                  ∧(∀ e. r=E e ⟹ wp2 e p h)))
```

2.2 Monadic F*

To develop a type inference algorithm and metatheory for the Dijkstra monad, we introduce monadic F*, a programming language with a runtime semantics similar to ML (i.e., a call-by-value, higher-order programming language, with primitive support for general recursion, state, and exceptions), but with a type system that extends ML's with dependent refinements and the Dijkstra monad for functional correctness verification using an SMT solver.

Figure 1 shows the syntax of monadic F*. Values include variables, n-ary data constructors, abstractions, and ascriptions. Expressions additionally include applications, let bindings, and operations on references. We exclude a fix-point form, since these can be encoded using recursive data types. The full version of the paper also includes support for raising and handling exceptions.

Types include type variables a, formulas ϕ, constants for the heap, unit and references, user-defined inductive types T, type application, refinement types, and polymorphic types. We have two kinds of dependent function types: x:t →t' is the type of a pure function, and is typically used to type data constructors only. The type of effectful functions is more generally described using x:t →M t' ϕ, a dependent function with a monadic co-domain. The choice of monad M is left as a parameter in the system, except that it must be indexed by both a result type t' and a predicate transformer ϕ. By restricting monadic types to the co-domain of functions only, we borrow an insight from Swamy et al. (2011b), who use a similar restriction to develop a type inference algorithm for monadic ML. We generalize their work to the setting of a dependently typed language. However, unlike that work which supports typing a program with respect to multiple monads, in monadic F* there is only a single monad. Note, polymorphic types have non-monadic co-domains corresponding to a value restriction.

$$
\begin{array}{lcll}
v & ::= & x \mid D\,\bar{t}\,\bar{v} \mid \lambda x{:}t.e \mid \Lambda a{::}\kappa.v \mid v{:}t & \text{value}\\
e & ::= & v \mid v\,v \mid v\,t \mid \textbf{let}\ x = e\ \textbf{in}\ e \mid !v \mid v := v \mid \textbf{ref}\ v & \text{expression}\\
 & \mid & \textbf{match}\ v\ \textbf{with}\ D\,\bar{a}\,\bar{x} \rightarrow\ e\ \textbf{else}\ e & \\
t & ::= & a \mid \phi \mid \mathsf{heap} \mid \mathsf{unit} \mid \textbf{ref}\ t \mid T \mid t\,t & \text{type}\\
 & \mid & x{:}t\{\phi\} \mid \forall a{::}\kappa.t \mid x{:}t \rightarrow t \mid x{:}t \rightarrow \mathsf{M}\ t\ \phi & \\
\phi & ::= & a \mid T \mid \mathsf{true} \mid \mathsf{false} \mid u = u \mid u \in u \mid \phi \wedge \phi & \text{formula}\\
 & \mid & \phi \vee \phi \mid \neg\phi \mid \phi \implies \phi \mid \forall x{:}t.\phi \mid \exists x{:}t.\phi & \\
 & \mid & \forall a{::}\kappa.\phi \mid \exists a{::}\kappa.\phi \mid \lambda x{:}t.\phi \mid \phi\ u \mid \Lambda a{::}\kappa.\phi \mid \phi\ t & \\
u & ::= & v \mid t \mid \mathsf{select}\ u\ u \mid \mathsf{update}\ u\ u\ u \mid \mathsf{dom}\ u \mid \mathsf{op}\ \bar{u} & \text{logic term}\\
\kappa & ::= & \star \mid E \mid x{:}t \Rightarrow \kappa \mid \alpha{::}\kappa \Rightarrow \kappa & \text{kind}\\
\Gamma & = & \cdot \mid \Gamma, x{:}t \mid \Gamma, a{::}\kappa & \text{typ. env.}\\
\Sigma & = & \mathsf{M}{::}\kappa, \mathsf{ret} = \phi, \mathsf{bind} = \phi' \mid \Sigma, T{::}\kappa\{\overline{D{:}t}\} & \text{signature}
\end{array}
$$

Figure 1. Syntax of monadic F* (partial)

Formulas ϕ describe a standard, higher-order predicate logic over a term language u that includes the values v and types t, interpreted functions from the select/update theory, other theories like arithmetic, and uninterpreted functions of the user's choosing. The logic includes variables a, uninterpreted predicates T, constants, equality, set membership, and all the usual connectives. We also include abstraction over terms and types (the two lambda forms) and the corresponding application forms.

Types are organized into kinds, κ, with two base kinds: $\star$ is the kind of types given to computationally relevant values; and kind E is for purely specificational types. In general, formulas ϕ are types with kind E. We have dependent function kinds, both on values $x{:}t \Rightarrow \kappa$ and on types $a{::}\kappa \Rightarrow \kappa$.

Type environments Γ bind variables to types and type variables to kinds. A signature Σ defines the set of inductive types $T{::}\kappa$ and their data constructors, the kind of the monad M, and the weakest pre-condition specifications of its return and bind operators.

We generally omit explicit type applications and kind annotations on type variables. These can usually be inferred.

2.3 Typing monadic F*

Figure 2 presents the two central judgments in the type system of monadic F*. The first judgment, $\Gamma \vdash e : t$, infers a value-type t for a term e in a context Γ. For effectful expressions, we have $\Gamma \vdash e : \mathsf{M}\ t\ \phi$, which infers a type t and a weakest pre-condition ϕ for an expression e from a context Γ. In both cases, the judgments are implicitly parameterized by the signature Σ (when omitted).

Monadic signature. We define K(a) as KPost(a) ⇒ heap ⇒ E for the kind of a predicate transformer from post-conditions on a-computations to pre-conditions. The type system is parametric in the choice of KPost(a)—one may pick KPost(a) to be a ⇒ heap ⇒ E for the DST monad, or result a ⇒ heap ⇒ E for the eDST monad, etc. We expect M to have kind a::⋆⇒ K(a) ⇒ ⋆; Σ.ret : a::⋆⇒ a ⇒ K(a); and Σ.bind : a::⋆⇒ b::⋆⇒ K(a) ⇒ (a ⇒ K(b)) ⇒ K(b). Observe how the signatures of Σ.ret and Σ.bind evoke a monad "one level up", i.e., they are monadic in the *kind* K(a). We expect the following three monad laws to hold, where equality is to be interpreted

$$\frac{\Gamma\ \mathsf{ok}}{\Gamma \vdash x : \Gamma(x)} \qquad \frac{\Gamma\ \mathsf{ok} \quad \Sigma(D) = \forall \overline{a{::}\kappa}.\overline{x{:}t'} \to t'' \quad \forall i.\Gamma \vdash t_i :: \kappa_i[\overline{t/a}] \quad \forall i.\Gamma \vdash v_i : t'_i[\overline{t/a}][\overline{v/x}]}{\Gamma \vdash D\ \bar{t}\ \bar{v} : t''[\overline{t/a}][\overline{v/x}]} \qquad \frac{\Gamma, a{::}\kappa \vdash v : t}{\Gamma \vdash \Lambda a{::}\kappa.v : \forall \alpha{::}\kappa.t} \qquad \frac{\Gamma \vdash v : \forall a{::}\kappa.t' \quad \Gamma \vdash t :: \kappa}{\Gamma \vdash v\ t : t'[t/a]}$$

$$\frac{\Gamma, x{:}t \vdash e : \mathsf{M}\ t'\ \phi}{\Gamma \vdash \lambda x{:}t.e : x{:}t \to \mathsf{M}\ t'\ \phi} \qquad \frac{\Gamma \vdash v : t' \quad \Gamma \vdash t' <: t}{\Gamma \vdash (v : t) : t} \qquad \frac{\Gamma \vdash v : t}{\Gamma \vdash v : \mathsf{M}\ t\ (\Sigma.\mathsf{ret}\ t\ v)} \qquad \frac{\Gamma \vdash e_1 : \mathsf{M}\ t_1\ \phi_1 \quad \Gamma, x{:}t_1 \vdash e_2 : \mathsf{M}\ t_2\ \phi_2 \quad x \notin FV(t_2)}{\Gamma \vdash \textbf{let}\ x = e_1\ \textbf{in}\ e_2 : \mathsf{M}\ t_2\ (\Sigma.\mathsf{bind}\ t_1\ t_2\ \phi_1\ (\lambda x{:}t_1.\phi_2))}$$

$$\frac{\Gamma \vdash v_1 : x{:}t \to \mathsf{M}\ t'\ \phi \quad \Gamma \vdash v_2 : t}{\Gamma \vdash v_1\ v_2 : \mathsf{M}\ t'\ \phi[v_2/x]} \qquad \frac{\Gamma \vdash v : t_0 \quad \Gamma' = \overline{a{::}\kappa}, \overline{x{:}t'} \quad \Gamma,\Gamma' \vdash D\ \bar{a}\ \bar{x} : t_0 \quad \Gamma,\Gamma' \vdash e_1 : \mathsf{M}\ t\ \phi_1 \quad \Gamma \vdash e_2 : \mathsf{M}\ t\ \phi_2}{\Gamma \vdash \textbf{match}\ v\ \textbf{with}\ D\ \bar{a}\ \bar{x} \to e_1\ \textbf{else}\ e_2 : \mathsf{M}\ t\ (\Lambda p.\lambda h.(\forall \bar{a}\bar{x}.v = D\ \bar{a}\ \bar{x} \Longrightarrow \phi_1\ p\ h) \wedge (v \neq D_{\_} \Longrightarrow \phi_2\ p\ h))}$$

Figure 2. Verification condition generation for monadic F*

as equi-satisfiability.

(1) $\Sigma.\mathsf{bind}\ t\ t\ (\Sigma.\mathsf{ret}\ \mathsf{v})\ \mathsf{wp} = \mathsf{wp}\ \mathsf{v}$ *(left identity)*
(2) $\Sigma.\mathsf{bind}\ t\ t\ \mathsf{wp}\ \Sigma.\mathsf{ret} = \mathsf{wp}$ *(right identity)*
(3) $\Sigma.\mathsf{bind}\ t_2\ t_3 (\Sigma.\mathsf{bind}\ t_1\ t_2\ \mathsf{wp1}\ \mathsf{wp2})\ \mathsf{wp3} =$ *(associativity)*
$\Sigma.\mathsf{bind}\ t_1\ t_3\ \mathsf{wp1}\ (\lambda \mathsf{x}.\Sigma.\mathsf{bind}\ t_2\ t_3\ (\mathsf{wp2}\ \mathsf{x})\ \mathsf{wp3})$

It is easy to check that the laws are satisfied for the DST and eDST monads (where $\Sigma.\mathsf{ret}{=}\lambda \mathsf{x}.\Lambda \mathsf{p}.\mathsf{p}\ (\mathsf{V}\ \mathsf{x})$ and $\Sigma.\mathsf{bind} = \mathsf{wpBindE}$), and when the δ function is reflexive, for the iDST monad as well.

Kinding and well-formedness of environments. We write Γ ok for an environment that binds unique names at well-formed kinds and well-kinded types. We omit the judgments for well-formedness of kinds and the kinding judgment—these are inherited from F* without any change and we refer the reader to Swamy et al. (2011a) for details. Additionally, we require each inductive definition in the signature Σ to be well-formed (again, this is inherited from F*).

Value typing. The first six rules in Figure 2 compute non-monadic types for values and type applications. The first four rules are straightforward. In the fifth rule, notice how we compute specifications for functions independently of any particular post-condition. The sixth rule is a subsumption rule triggered by a programmer-supplied ascription. The subtyping relation $\Gamma \vdash t' <: t$ is inherited from F*, and is implemented by a call to an SMT solver (Swamy et al. 2011a). The main interesting case is in proving a subtyping relation between two monadic types. We have $\Gamma \vdash \mathsf{M}\ t_1\ \mathsf{wp}_1 <: \mathsf{M}\ t_2\ \mathsf{wp}_2$ when $\Gamma \vdash t_1 <: t_2$ and when $\Gamma, \mathsf{p{::}KPost(t)}, \mathsf{h{:}heap} \models \mathsf{wp}_2\ \mathsf{p}\ \mathsf{h} \Longrightarrow \mathsf{wp}_1\ \mathsf{p}\ \mathsf{h}$.

Expression typing. The first expression typing rule corresponds to a monadic unit—it allows a value v to be injected into the monad using $\Sigma.\mathsf{ret}$. We interpret **let**-bindings as a monadic bind—we compute the type of each component, insist that the let-bound variable does not escape in the result type (although it may appear in ϕ_2), and compose the results using $\Sigma.\mathsf{bind}$. The rule for function application is standard for a dependently typed language. To type a **match**, we type each branch and compute a predicate transformer by guarding the pre-conditions of each branch by the branch condition and closing over the pattern-bound variables. We do not show specific typing rules for operations on references; these are typed according to the signatures of **ref**, (!) and (:=) shown previously.

Soundness. We prove the soundness of the type system against the operational semantics for F*—a standard small-step, call-by-value reduction relation $(H,e) \to_\Sigma (H',e')$, which relates a pair of runtime configurations consisting of a store H (mapping locations to values) and an expression e. We prove the soundness for specific instantiations of KPost(a)—here, for $\mathsf{KPost(a)} = \mathsf{result\ a} \Rightarrow \mathsf{heap} \Rightarrow E$, i.e., for a language whose primitive effects include state and exceptions. Layering other monadic effects (e.g., probabilities, or reactivity, etc.) over the the primitive ones is also possible, and the same metatheory should carry over. In the theorem below, we write $\Sigma;\Gamma \vdash (H,e) : \mathsf{M}\ t\ \phi$ to type a runtime configuration—this extends expression typing with a typing for the store H in a standard way. We also write *asResult* v for V v and *asResult* (raise e) for E e.

THEOREM 1 (Soundness). *Given Σ ok, and Γ, H, e, t, and wp such that $\Sigma;\Gamma \vdash (H,e) : M\ t$ wp; and an interpretation function asHeap from runtime stores H to the type heap; and a post-condition p such that $\Sigma;\Gamma \models$ wp p (asHeap H) is derivable; either: (1) e is a result r and $\Sigma;\Gamma \models$ p (asResult r) (asHeap H); or, (2) there exist H', e', wp', such that $(H,e) \to_\Sigma (H',e')$, $\Sigma;\Gamma \vdash (H',e') : M\ t\ wp'$ and $\Sigma;\Gamma \models wp'$ p (asHeap H').*

First-order VCs. We also prove that the VC generation does not introduce higher-kinded quantification where none exists. To state this theorem, we introduce a judgment $\vdash (\Sigma;\Gamma)$ ord1, which is true of first-order contexts, i.e., those that do not use higher-order formulas in the refinement logic like $\forall \alpha{::}\kappa.\phi$ where $\kappa \neq \star$. The theorem states that when computing a wp for a term in such a first-order context, and when that wp is applied to a first-order post-condition and a heap, the resulting VC can be reduced to a first-order normal form, e.g., no Λs remain—this is the essence of the judgment $\Sigma;\Gamma \vdash \phi$ ord1, below. This result is important since we aim to translate VCs to SMT solvers which do not support quantification over predicates.

THEOREM 2 (First-order VCs). *If $\Sigma;\Gamma \vdash e : M\ t$ wp; and $\vdash (\Sigma;\Gamma)$ ord1; and $\Sigma;\Gamma \vdash$ p ord1; then $\Sigma;\Gamma, h : \mathsf{heap} \vdash (\mathsf{wp\ p\ h})$ ord1.*

3. Abstract predicates and local state

While Theorem 2 (First-order VCs) ensures that programs without higher-order assertions yield VCs that are first-order, this does not rule out the use of higher-order specifications. Indeed, careful use of higher-order logic in monadic F* makes it possible to reason modularly about features like local state, while still allowing automated verification via an SMT solver. We briefly present an example for illustration.

Consider the two functions below, evens and evens'.

```
let evens () = let x, y = ref 0, ref 0 in λ(). let r = !x + !y in incr x; incr y; r
let evens' () = let x = ref 0 in λ(). let r = 2*!x in incr x; r
```

Both these functions return closures which yield the same sequence of even numbers when they are called. To see why, we can reason informally that the closure returned by evens captures two references x and y that remain local to the closure, both references always contain the same value at the entry and exit of the closure, so !x + !y is always even. A similar line of reasoning applies to evens', although it uses only one reference.

We would like to be able to give specifications to both evens and evens' that state that the references they allocate are owned by their respective closures; that their invariants are maintained irrespective of the actions of their clients; and, finally, for the clients' view of the specifications of evens and evens' to be identical, hiding the differences in the representation of their internal data structures, e.g., the number of references they use.

This is a classic problem of information hiding and modular verification considered in many lines of work (Barnett et al. 2004; Nanevski et al. 2007; O'Hearn et al. 2004; Parkinson and Bierman 2005). Monadic F* can capture the specification style of several of these approaches naturally, e.g., the higher-order style of existentially quantified predicates of Nanevski et al. (2007), while still retaining the ability to automatically discharge proof obligations. Our solution, sketched in the remainder of this section, also illustrates common idioms we employ to control and simplify the use of the DST monad.

Note, from here on, we use the concrete syntax of F* in our examples. This is based closely on the syntax of the previous section and notations from F# and OCaml. We also use several conveniences such as curried function types and dependent pairs that are supported by our implementation.

3.1 Notation to structure the use of the DST monad

For many kinds of programs, exposing the full generality of the Dijkstra monad in specifications can be overwhelming. For example, it would be preferable to not have to think about state, exceptions, and other unrelated concerns when using the DST monad to write specifications for a pure function. To facilitate this, we define abbreviations for several common special cases of the DST monad, each a monad in its own right.

```
type Pure t requires ensures =
     DST t (Λpost h. requires ∧ ∀x. ensures x ⟹ post x h)
type Reader t requires ensures =
     DST t (Λpost h. requires h ∧ ∀x. ensures x h ⟹ post x h)
type Writer t requires ensures m =
     DST t (Λpost h. requires h ∧
          (∀ x h'. ensures h x h' ∧ Mods m h h' ⟹ post x h'))
and Mods m h h' = ∀x. x ∈ dom h ∧ x∉ m
          ⟹ x ∈ dom h' ∧ select h x = select h' x
```

For example, we use Writer t requires ensures m to type t-computations that read the heap, whose writes are confined to the set of references m, and which may also allocate new references. Notice the definition of Mods m h h'—it states that h and h' agree on all references that exist in h, except for the ones in the set m.

To make it easy to remember the interpretation of the last three indexes of Writer, we tag them with the following identifiers, each an identity function.

```
type Requires r = r      type Ensures r = r      let Modifies m = m
```

Using these tags, a function that increments an integer reference can be given the type below, hiding the complexity of predicate transformers under a notation evocative of that used by other Hoare-style verifiers.

```
x:ref int → Writer unit (Requires λh.True)
                        (Ensures λh () h'. select h' x = select h x + 1)
                        (Modifies {x})
```

3.2 Heap permissions and fragments

Monadic F* provides the flexibility to work with many different styles of specifications. For example, we can introduce a permission model (shown below) to control the use of references. We use an abstract predicate Perm r h to indicate that the program has permission to use the reference r in heap h. The pre-condition to read, write or free a reference r requires the caller to hold the permission to r. The specification of write r v ensures that the caller retains permission on r after the heap is updated. The alloc function returns a new reference r and ensures the caller has permission to use it, while free consumes the permission of the deallocated reference.

We also use features inherited from F* to axiomatize and internalize spatial connectives (like the separating conjunction from separation logic) into monadic F*. The listing below introduces a logical value Frag whose semantics is axiomatized (using the three **assume** expressions) so that Frag h fp is a heap whose domain is precisely the set of references fp and whose values on that domain agree with h. We call Frag h fp the fp-fragment of h.

```
(* Permissions on heap references*)
type Perm :: ref a ⇒ heap ⇒ E
val read: r:ref a → Reader a (Requires (Perm r))
                             (Ensures λh v. v=select h r)
val write: r:ref a → v:a → Writer unit (Requires (Perm r))
                                       (Ensures λh () h'. Perm r h'
                                                     ∧ select h' r=v)
                                       (Modifies {r})
type Fresh s h = ∀r. r ∈ s ⟹ r ∉ dom h
val alloc: v:a → Writer (ref a) (Requires λh.True)
                         (Ensures λh r h'. Fresh{r}h ∧ r∈dom h'
                                   ∧ select h r = v ∧ Perm r h')
                         (Modifies {})
val free: r:ref a → Writer unit (Requires (Perm r))
                         (Ensures λh r h'. r∉dom h')
                         (Modifies {r})

(* Fragments of heaps *)
logic val Frag : heap → refset → heap
assume ∀fp h x. x ∈ fp ⟹ select (Frag h r) x = select h x
assume ∀fp h x. if x ∈ fp then x ∈ dom (Frag h fp) ⟺ x ∈ dom h
           else x ∉ dom (Frag h fp)
assume ∀h1 h2 fp. (∀ x. x ∈ fp ⟹ select h1 x = select h2 x)
           ⟹ Frag h1 fp = Frag h2 fp
type Star P Q h = ∃f1 f2. f1 ∩ f2 = ∅ ∧ P (Frag h f1) ∧ Q (Frag h fp2)
type On fp P h = P (Frag h fp)
```

Using Frag, we define the heap-predicate Star P Q to be valid on a heap h if h contains disjoint fragments fp1 and fp2 such that P and Q are valid on each of those fragments. We also define On fp P, a heap predicate valid if P holds on the fp-fragment of a heap.

3.3 Specifying and verifying evens and evens'

With the heap permission model in place, we show how to program and verify our examples, evens and evens'. The main idea structuring our solution is to package a closure with an existentially quantified invariant on its local state, where the invariant encapsulates the permissions required to use the references private to the closure (thereby ensuring that a client cannot access these references). The type t below defines this existential package:

```
type t = MkT: Inv::heap ⇒ E → fp:refset → (unit → evens_t Inv fp) → t
and evens_t Inv fp =
    Writer int (Requires (On fp Inv))
               (Ensures λh x h'. x mod 2 = 0 ∧ On fp Inv h')
               (Modifies fp)
```

A t-value MkT Inv fp f is a triple consisting of a heap-predicate Inv, a set fp of references (representing the footprint of the invariant), and a closure f:unit → evens_t Inv fp, a function in the Writer monad whose pre-condition requires that Inv be valid on the fp-fragment of the input heap, and which ensures that it returns an even integer; that Inv remains valid on the same fragment of the output heap; and that only references in fp may be modified. Observe that this type reveals no information about the structure of the local state of f, although it guarantees that f always returns an even integer. (Note, if we wanted to prove that each call to f returned the next even integer, we would have to augment MkT with additional (ghost) state. This is relatively straightforward to do, although we omit it here for simplicity.)

Next, we show the type of evens and evens' (the same for both).

```
val evens,evens': unit → Writer t
  (Requires λ h. True)
  (Ensures λ h v h'. Fresh (fp v) h ∧ On (fp v) (Inv v) h')
  (Modifies {})
```

This is the type of a function in the Writer monad with a trivial pre-condition returning a t-value. To state the post-condition, we project the footprint and the invariant component of the v:t result using the logical projectors fp:t → refset and Inv::t ⇒ heap ⇒ E that are provided in F*'s logic for the data type t. We assert, first, that the references in the footprint (fp v) are freshly allocated, and second, that the existentially bound invariant (Inv v) is valid on the fragment of the output heap h' corresponding to the footprint. Additionally, both functions do not modify any existing reference.

The listing below shows the implementation of evens and evens', each returning the closures we showed earlier packaged as a t-value with a suitable invariant. The invariant for evens is Inv1 x y, which states that the closure holds the permission to x and y, and that the values of these references are always the same in the heap. The invariant for evens' is just Perm x, just stating that its closure holds permission to x.

```
type Inv1 x y h = Perm x h ∧ Perm y h ∧ select h x=select h y
let evens () = let x,y = alloc 0, alloc 0 in
               let f () : evens_t (Inv1 x y) {x,y} =
                 let r = read x + read y in incr x; incr y; r in
                 MkT (Inv1 x y) {x,y} f

let evens' () = let x = alloc 0 in
                let f () : evens_t (Perm x) {x} =
                  let r = read x in incr x; 2*r in
                  MkT (Perm x) {x} f
```

These examples, while particularly simple, illustrate a general pattern in monadic F* for writing specifications over local state. We make use of this pattern in programming other, more complex examples, e.g., a verified ring buffer programmed using arrays, local state, and a record of closures to mimic an object-oriented programming style. We discuss this briefly in §5.

4. Dynamic typing in monadic F*

We turn now to our main case study, JavaScript verification. While JavaScript is increasingly used for both web and server-side programming, it is a challenging language for verification and analysis, in part due to its highly dynamic nature. We implement a translation, JS2JS*, from JavaScript to F*, based closely on λJS (Guha et al. 2010). The image of this translation is JS*, an idiomatic subset of monadic F*.

A first difficulty in translating JavaScript to F* is to represent JavaScript's dynamic typing. In principle, to handle dynamic typing in an ML-like language, one simply provides a variant type dyn, with cases for each primitive type constructor in the language, e.g., Int : int → dyn, Fun: (dyn → dyn) → dyn, while systematically inserting injections and projections to and from type dyn. So, intuitively, we compose the λJS translation with a translation that adds type dyn systematically to produce a JS* program. JS* programs are linked against a library called JSPrims, which includes type dyn, as well as functions providing runtime support for coercions, object manipulation, prototype traversal, etc. The formalization of JS2JS* and the full JSPrims library are available online.

4.1 A refined type dynamic

The basic approach of inserting the standard type dyn systematically throughout the program is conceptually simple, but also not very useful—nearly every term is typed at dyn. Our first step towards verifying JavaScript programs, then, is a new *refined* type dyn that recovers the precision of static typing.

The listing below shows the (partial) definition of our type dyn, suitable for use with JavaScript programs translated to JS*. For example, we have the constructor Num, which allows a number n:float to be injected into the dyn type. However, the type of Num n is d:dyn{TypeOf d = float}, where TypeOf: a::⋆ ⇒ a ⇒ E is an uninterpreted function from values to types in the refinement logic. In effect, the refinement formula recovers the static type information. The case of strings and objects is similar—note, an object is represented as a mutable map from strings to dyn values.

```
type dyn =
  | Num : float → d:dyn{TypeOf d = float}
  | Str : string → d:dyn{TypeOf d = string}
  | Obj : ref (map string dyn) → d:dyn{TypeOf d = object}
  | Fun : ∀wp::dyn ⇒ dyn ⇒ (dyn ⇒ heap ⇒ E) ⇒ heap ⇒ E.
        (this:dyn → args:dyn → DST dyn (wp args this))
      → d:dyn{TypeOf d = AsE wp}
  | Undef : d:dyn{TypeOf d = undef} ...
```

The type of Fun merits closer attention. JavaScript functions always take two arguments—the first is for the implicit `this` parameter; the second is an object containing a variable number of fields, one for each of the variable number of actual parameters. So, to a first approximation, the type of Fun is (dyn → dyn → dyn) → dyn, but this is, of course, too imprecise. To recover precision, we type each function in the DST monad and refine the type of Fun to record the predicate transformer of the function in the refinement logic. From the type d:dyn{TypeOf d = AsE wp}, we can conclude that the underlying value is a function of type this:dyn → args:dyn → DST dyn (wp args this). (Note, AsE is just a type constructor that coerces the kind of wp to E-kind.)

Our full library includes other JavaScript primitive types; a more complicated type for Fun, which allows functions to also be treated as objects (as required by JavaScript); and types/functions to model exceptions and JavaScript's control operators. We leave them out of this paper due to space constraints.

4.2 An API for JS*

Next we discuss some key fragments of JSPrims, simplified substantially for the purposes of the paper. JSPrims defines the set of JavaScript runtime errors we capture.

Safe field selection. To select a field f:string from an object o:dyn, JS* programs call selField o f (corresponding to the JavaScript source operation `o.f` or `o["f"]`). The implementation of selField (line 8 below) elides several details of prototype chain traversal, functions as objects, etc. In its most basic form, selecting a field requires o to be an object. We dereference the map location, lookup the key f and return the value, if it exists.

```
1  define SelField h (Obj l) f = Map.select (select h l) f
2  define HasField h (Obj l) f = In f (Map.domain (select h l))
3  val unreachable: unit → DST a (Λp.λh. false)
4  val lookup: m:map a b → x:a → option (y:b{y=Map.select m x})
5  val selField: o:dyn → f:string → Reader dyn
6     (Requires λh.TypeOf o=object∧HasField h o f)
7     (Ensures λh v. v=SelField h o f)
8  let selField o f = match o with
9  | Undef | Str _ | Int _ | Fun _ → unreachable ()
10 | Obj l → match lookup !l f with Some v → v
11 | None → unreachable()
```

We aim to give a specification to selField that ensures that well-typed JS* clients avoid various JavaScript errors. Projecting a field from a non-object is prevented by the clause in the precondition (line 6) which requires TypeOf o = object. We also ensure that the field f be among the defined fields of the objects (HasField h o f).

If the field does not exist, JavaScript semantics permits returning the `undefined` value, which is, strictly speaking, not an error condition. However, checking for the absence of unexpected `undefined` values in a JavaScript program is generally considered a good idea (Crockford 2008), so we check for it here. At line 7, the specification ensures that selField returns the contents of the f field of o, and that the heap is unchanged.

Note, the definitions at lines 1-2 provide two functions in the logic, corresponding to projecting a field from an object and to testing whether a key exists among the fields of an object. We interpret the map type as a functional array, and use functions Map.select/Map.update/Map.domain, with the usual interpretation.

Safe field update. To update a field f:string from an object o:dyn with a value v:dyn, JS* programs call updField o f v (corresponding to the JavaScript source operation `o.f = v` or `o["f"] = v`).

The specification of updField has a similar form to that of selField. The caller is required, first, to prove that o is an object (trying to update a non-object is a JavaScript error). Note, the field f need not exist in o—JavaScript permits adding fields to an object "on the fly". The specification also states that updField returns Undef and updates just the heap accordingly. The modifies clause uses a projector provided in F*'s logic Obj_proj_0 to state that only the reference held in o is modified.

```
define UpdField h (Obj l) f v =
  update h l (Map.update (select h l) f v)
val insert: m:map a b →x:a →y:b
                →m':map a b{m'=Map.update m x y}
val updField: o:dyn →f:string →v:dyn →Writer dyn
    (Requires λh. TypeOf o=object)
    (Ensures λh u h'.u=Undef ∧ h'=UpdField h o f v)
    (Modifies {Obj_proj_0 o})
let updField o f v 'Post h = match o with
 ... | Undef | Str _ | Int _ | Fun _ →unreachable ()
 | Obj l →l := insert !l f v; Undef
```

Safe function application. Informally, for f:dyn, this:dyn, args:dyn, the term apply f this args corresponds (roughly) to the JavaScript construct `this.f(a1,...,an)`, where args is an object containing the n actual parameters. As in the other cases, our goal is to ensure that function applications in JS* (and hence in JavaScript) do not cause errors. There are two things that could potentially go wrong. First, f may not be a function—it is an error in JavaScript to apply, say, an integer. Second, f's pre-condition may not be satisfied.

Addressing both these concerns, we show the type and implementation of apply below.

```
val apply: f:dyn →this:dyn →args:dyn →DST dyn (Λp.λh.
    ∃ wp. TypeOf f = AsE wp ∧ wp args this p h)
let apply f this args = match f with Fun _ fn →fn this args
 ... | Undef | Str _ | Int _ | Obj _ →unreachable ()
```

The implementation of apply is straightforward—it checks that f is a function and applies it. The specification of apply requires the client to prove that f is indeed a function with some wp, and then to prove the pre-condition computed by that wp for the particular arguments and post-condition needed at the call site.

4.3 Computing VCs for JS*

We prove that VC generation always succeeds for any loop-free JS* program. Programs with loops must be annotated with invariants. We write $[\![e]\!]$ for the translation of a λJS program to JS*.

THEOREM 3 (VC generation is complete on JS*). *Given a loop-free λJS term e. Then, for the signature $\Sigma_{JSPrims}$, there exists wp such that $\cdot \vdash [\![e]\!] : M\ dyn\ wp$.*

By default, the VC for a JS* program is not first-order. Notably, each call to apply introduces an existentially bound predicate transformer. Our full paper shows how such existentially bound transformer variables can be eliminated using the model-finding features of an SMT solver. However, this procedure can be quite expensive (cf. the verification time of Facepalm in the next section).

We describe here a more efficient approach that we also implement. Specifically, instead of apply we use apply_hint shown below, where, instead of existentially quantifying over the wp, we require the caller to instantiate the wp explicitly.

```
val apply_hint: wp::dyn⇒ dyn⇒ (dyn⇒ heap⇒ E)⇒ heap⇒ E
→f:dyn →this:dyn →args:dyn
→DST dyn (fun post h ⇒ TypeOf f=AsE wp ∧ wp args this post h)
```

Unlike apply, the type of apply_hint satisfies our ord1-restriction, and the VCs produced when calling apply_hint can be handled within a first-order solver like Z3.

Of course, one still needs a way to compute the type argument of apply_hint. We use Gatekeeper, a pointer analysis for JavaScript, to produce a set of possible function call targets. We carry this information in the JS2JS* translation and use it to compute the type arguments of apply_hint. The example below illustrates this procedure, where the JavaScript program on the left is translated to the JS* program on the right.

```
function foo(x) {...}
foo({f:0});
foo = 17;
```

```
let foo this args = ... in
update global "foo" (Fun 'U0 foo);
apply_hint 'U0 (select global "foo")
       global (...);
update global "foo" (Int 17)
```

Each lambda-term in the translated program produces an application of the Fun constructor. For each such function, JS2JS* inserts a *new unification variable*, 'U0 in our example, as the first argument to Fun. When the type inference algorithm computes a predicate transformer for foo, say FooTX, 'U0 is unified with FooTX. Next, at each call site where Gatekeeper is able to definitively resolve a function call to a particular closure (say, foo), JS* inserts a call to apply_hint, passing as a first parameter the same unification variable ('U0) that was used when translating foo. As type inference proceeds and 'U0 is unified with FooTX, the witness argument to apply_hint is suitably unified too. We also support variants of apply_hint in case Gatekeeper cannot resolve a call target to a singleton. Note, we do not rely on the soundness of Gatekeeper (in fact, it is occasionally unsound)—an incorrect instantiation will be trapped by the theorem prover.

5. Experimental evaluation

To date, we have verified nearly 3,000 lines of F* code using the Dijkstra monad, summarized in Figure 3. The verification time (column **TC**) was collected on a 3.2GHz Windows 7 machine. The first class of examples is a set of 26 programs, listed in a single line in the table as ex0–ex25, and totaling 400 lines of code. These examples include the code discussed in §2.1, and others of a similar flavor. We have also ported three programs implemented by Chen et al. (2010) in Fine to monadic F*. The first, ac, is a simple access control scheme. Next, automaton is a program that implements a type-state protocol on files—coded in monadic F*, we no longer need to thread affine tokens and a store. Finally, iflow is a monadic encoding of information flow control. Ported to monadic F*, it highlights monadic layering—we can easily combine the Dijkstra state monad with a programmer-defined information flow monad. The programs auth and auth2 implement variations of a protocol that used digital signatures for authentication. They use the iDST monad to maintain an invariant on mutable memory that is used to track a collection of protocol events. The examples evens is the local state example of §3. The programs ringbuf1 and ringbuf2 program and verify a ring buffer based on a problem specification provided by the 2012 VSTTE verification competition. JSPrims is our most complex example: it provides a precise type interface suitable for verifying functional correctness of JS* programs, while implementing runtime support including coercions, prototype traversal, and the JavaScript calling convention. It uses the eDST and iDST monads to include reasoning about exceptions and a two-state invariant that controls how the JavaScript heap evolves.

The remaining programs are JavaScript web-browser extensions translated to JS* for verification. These extensions are based on those studied by Guha et al. (2011). We prove each extension free of runtime errors, assuming a sequential model for the DOM. Our

Name	LOC(JS)	TC (sec)	Description
ex0–ex25	406	9.1	Classic combinators and data struct.
ac	38	6.5	Access control (PLDI '10)
automaton	53	7.5	Typestate on files (PLDI '10)
iflow	115	10.1	Information flow monad (PLDI '10)
auth	52	6.2	Digital sig. with monotonic state
auth2	53	6.8	Variation of authentication above
evens	59	2.9	Local state for even streams
ringbuf-1	192	22.0	Ring buffer with global invariants
ringbuf-2	154	21.8	Ring buffer with local state
JSPrims	1,131	63.5	Runtime support for JavaScript
Untiny	59 (9)	11.0	Send selected URL
Delicious	65 (13)	11.3	Bookmark selected text
Passward	111 (29)	42.7	Store and retrieve passwords
HoverMagn	60 (23)	38.1	Magnify text under the cursor
Typograf	106 (28)	65.5	Format text a user inputs
Facepalm	270 (82)	718.0	Find contacts from Facebook
Total	**2,924 (184)**	**17m 23s**	

Figure 3. Summary of experiments

verification methodology is designed for proving the functional correctness of programs, although, in the absence of specifications for JavaScript programs in the wild, our tool checks for safety.

To simplify verification, in some cases, we model collections of objects by iterators, whereas the standard DOM API provides collections of objects as arrays encoded using dictionaries. We expect to support the array idioms in the near future, although precisely modeling asynchrony in the DOM is substantial future work. The remainder of this section discusses three extensions in detail.

5.1 HoverMagnifier

Our first extension is HoverMagnifier, an accessibility extension. It magnifies the text under the cursor. A key part of its code is shown below—it involves the manipulation of a collection of DOM elements.

```
1 function magnify(evt) { ... }
2 var elts = document.getElementsByTagName("body");
3 var body = elts.Next();
4 if (body !== undefined) {
5   body.onmousemove = function (evt){magnify(evt);};
6   body.onmousemove(dummyEv);} //for verif. harness
```

At line 2 it calls the DOM function `getElementsByTagName` to get all the `<body>` elements in a web page. Line 3 gets the first element in the result set. Then, it checks if the body is `undefined` and line 5 sets an event handler, `magnify`, to be called whenever the user's mouse moves—we elide the definition of `magnify`.

Setting up a verification harness for such a program involves two main elements. First, we need some "driver" code to ensure that all the relevant parts of the program are exercised. For example, we add the code at line 6 to mock the firing of a mouse-move event, so that the code in `magnify` becomes reachable. Without this, our verification tool would still infer a weakest pre-condition for `magnify`, but since no call to it appears in the program, the pre-condition would be trivially satisfied. (In §5.3, we show how one can avoid writing such driver code by instead writing better specifications for library functions.)

We also have to provide specifications for all the APIs used by the program. For our extensions, this API is the DOM. For each kind of DOM concept (`document`, `element`, `style`, etc.), we define a corresponding F* type—a predicate stating that an object is an instance of the concept. For `element`, a predicate EltTyping h elt means that elt is an element in heap h.

```
1 type EltTyping h elt =
2  TypeOf elt = object ∧ ... ∧ HasField h elt "text"
3  ∧ TypeOf (SelField h elt "text")=string
4  ∧ HasField h elt "getFirstChild"
5  ∧ TypeOf (SelField h elt "getFirstChild") =
6     AsE (λargs this post h'. IsElt h this ∧
7        ∀child. (child=Undef ∨ IsElt h' child) ⟹ post child h')
8 and IsElt :: heap ⇒ dyn ⇒ E
9 assume IsElt_trans:∀ h1 h2 x.
10   (IsElt h1 x ∧
11   (SelField h1 x "text")=(SelField h2 x "text") ∧ ...
12   (SelField h1 x "getFirstChild")=
13      (SelField h2 x "getFirstChild"))
14   ⟹ IsElt h2 x
15 assume IsElt_typ:∀ h x. IsElt h x ⟹ EltTyping h x
```

The predicate EltTyping (line 1) states that elt is an object, it has (among others) a field `"getFirstChild"`, and that this field is a function whose specification is given by the predicate transformer at lines 6–7. Informally, `"getFirstChild"` expects its first argument (the implicit this pointer) to be a DOM element e, and, if e is not a leaf node, it returns another DOM element (otherwise returning Undef). Capturing this specification involves the use of an abstract inductive predicate IsElt, and then providing two assumptions (at the bottom of the display) giving it an interpretation. The assumption IsElt_trans states that IsElt is transitive in its heap argument (if the relevant fields of the element elt have not changed), and IsElt_typ expands IsElt back into EltTyping.

The next listing shows the predicate DocTyping, a partial specification for the `document` object (line 1). It states that the object doc contains a field `"getElementsByTagName"` that stores a function-typed value. The pre-condition for this function requires that it be called with its this argument set to the doc object itself. Statically predicting the `this` pointer of a function is non-trivial. For example, in the following program, the final function call receives the object o as the `this` parameter: `o.f = document.getElementsByTagName ; o.f()`. This can be problematic, and, in the case of the DOM, leads to a runtime error. We rule out this kind of error by requiring that every call to getElementsByTagName must pass a this parameter equal to the document object doc.

```
1 type DocTyping h doc = HasField h doc "getElementsByTagName"
2  ∧ ... ∧ TypeOf (SelField h doc "getElementsByTagName") =
3  AsE (λargs this post h1.
4   (this = doc ∧ SingletonString h1 args ∧
5   (∀ x. Enum IsElt h1 x ⟹ post x h1)))
6 and Enum p h d = TypeOf d=object ∧ d ∈ dom h ∧
7   HasField h d "Next" ∧ TypeOf (SelField h d "Next") =
8   AsE (λargs this post h'. this = d ∧
9     ∀x. (x=Undef ∨ p h' x) ⟹ post x h')
```

The pre-condition of getElementsByTagName also requires that its arguments object args contain a single string field (the predicate SingletonString, elided here for brevity). The post-condition of getElementsByTagName is captured by line 5. It states that the function does not change the heap, and that the object x returned satisfies the predicate Enum IsElt h1 x.

The predicate Enum is shown at line 6. It is parameterized by a predicate p that applies to each of the elements in the collection. Enumerable collections are objects that have a function-typed `"Next"` field which does not mutate the heap. The function either returns Undef (if the collection is exhausted), or returns a value satisfying the predicate p h' x. As with other functions, `"Next"` expects its this pointer to be the enclosing collection.

Finally, to connect these specifications of the DOM to the program itself, we type the program in an initial heap h0 satisfying the InitialHeap h0 predicate overleaf, which states that a document object is reachable from the global object.

```
val global : dyn
type InitialHeap h0 = TypeOf global = object ∧ ...
 ∧ HasField h0 global "document"
 ∧ TypeOf (SelField h0 global "document")=object
 ∧ DocTyping h0 (SelField h0 global "document")
```

5.2 Facepalm

Our next example is Facepalm, an extension that helps build a user's address book by automatically recording the contact information of a user's friends as they browse Facebook. The verification time of Facepalm was dominated by the time spent in Z3. Our query compiler asked about 1,300 Z3 queries, and required producing models to resolve 27 function calls. Gatekeeper was able to successfully provide us with a hint 11 times, but the remaining 16 times we fell back on Z3's model finding feature, which dominated the Z3 time—so, a reduction in the number of queries that require producing models (via better hints) is likely to reduce the verification time substantially. We expect better stubs for the DOM when configuring Gatekeeper to help.

```
1 function getPath(root, p) {
2     var cur=root; var path=p;
3     while(path !== undefined ∧ //needs loop invariant
4           cur !== undefined) {
5        cur = cur.getChild(path.hd); //needs a hint
6        path = path.tl; }
7     return cur; }
8 function start() {
9     var friendName, href;
10    if (document.domain === 'facebook.com') {
11        friendName = findName();
12        href = findWebsite();
13        if (href) {
14            console.log("Website on " + href);
15            console.log("Name is " + friendName);
16            saveWebsite(friendName, href); }}}
```

The main function of Facepalm is shown above (start at line 8). At a high level, this extension checks to see if the page currently being viewed is a Facebook page (line 10). If the check succeeds, it traverses the DOM structure of the page looking for a specific fragment that mentions the name of the user's friend (line 11).

A second traversal finds the friend's contact and website information (line 12). If this information is successfully found, the extension logs it and saves it to the user's address book maintained on a third-party bookmarking service (line 16).

The main interest in verifying Facepalm is in verifying the two DOM traversals, findName and findWebsite. Both of these involve while-loops to iterate over the structure of the DOM. They do this by eventually calling the function getPath, shown at line 1. The loop in getPath iterates simultaneously over a list (path) of integers as well as the DOM tree rooted at cur, where the integer in the list indicates which sub-tree of cur to visit. Function getChild(n) returns the *n*th child of an element.

To verify this code, the programmer needs to supply a loop invariant. The next listing shows the translation (slightly cleaned up) of getPath to JS* for verification, starting with the signature of a function get which returns the current heap (useful for stating invariants).

At lines 3–5, we initialize the two local variables corresponding to cur and path in the source program. The while-loop is translated to a call to the while-combinator from §2.1. The first three arguments to while (at line 8) are the predicate arguments—the first argument Inv locals h0 is provided by the programmer; the next two are wild cards (_) whose instantiation is inferred by F*. The fourth argument is the thunk representing the loop guard, and the last argument is a thunk for the loop body.

```
1 val get: unit →DST heap (λp h. p h h)
2 let getPath this args =
3  let locals = allocObject () in
4  updField locals "cur" (selField args "0");
5  updField locals "path" (selField args "1");
6
7  let h0 = get () in
8  let _ = while (Inv locals h0) _ _
9   (λ_. (not ((selField locals "path") = Undef)) ∧
10             (not ((selField locals "cur") = Undef)))
11  (λ_.
12    let ps = allocObject () in
13    let getChild = selField (selField locals "cur") "getChild" in
14    let hd = selField (selField locals "path") "hd" in
15    updField ps "0" hd;
16    updField locals "cur" (apply getChild (selField locals "cur") ps);
17    updField locals "path" (selField (selField locals "path") "tl");
18    ( ))
19  in selField locals "cur"
```

The code of the loop guard is straightforward. The body allocates an object ps to pass arguments to the function getChild. The parameters at the call on line 16 is a singleton integer containing the head of the list "path". We then update the locals "cur" and "path" and iterate.

Intuitively, verifying this code for the absence of runtime errors requires two properties: at each iteration, the "path" local must either be Undef or contain an integer hd field and also a tl field, while the "cur" local must contain a DOM element (or be Undef). We state just this using the loop invariant shown below.

```
1 (* Typing polymorphic lists *)
2 type IsObject h o = TypeOf o=object ∧ InDom h o
3 type IsList :: E ⇒ heap ⇒ dyn ⇒ E
4 type ListTyping a h l =
5     (l=Undef ∨
6     (IsObject h l ∧
7       HasField h l "hd" ∧ TypeOf (SelField h l "hd")=a ∧
8       HasField h l "tl" ∧ IsList a h (SelField h l "tl")))
9 assume typing1:∀ a h d.
10          IsList a h d ⟺ ListTyping a h d
11 assume trans:∀ a h1 h2 d.
12          (IsList a h1 d ∧
13          (SelField h1 d "hd")=(SelField h2 d "hd") ∧
14          (SelField h1 d "tl")=(SelField h2 d "tl")) ⟹ IsList a h2 d
15 (* The loop invariant *)
16 type CutIsElt h d = IsObject h d ∧ (IsObject h d ⟹ IsElt h d)
17 type Inv locs h0 h1 =
18   (GetFields h0 global)=(GetFields h1 global) ∧
19   IsObject h1 locs ∧
20   HasField h1 locs "path" ∧
21   HasField h1 locs "cur" ∧
22   IsList int h1 (SelField h1 locs "path") ∧
23   ((SelField h1 locs "cur")=Undef ∨
24     CutIsElt h1 (SelField h1 locs "cur"))
```

The invariant comes in two parts. First, at lines 2–14 we define an inductive predicate IsList a h l, which states that in the heap h, the value l is either Undef or a list of a-typed values. The style of this inductive specification is similar to the specification of IsElt. The invariant Inv itself is defined at line 17. The invariant is a ternary predicate relating an object holding the local variables locs, the heap h0 at the start of the loop, to a heap h1, which represents the heap at the beginning of each loop iteration.

The invariant states that: (1) the loop does not mutate the global object (necessary to verify the code after the loop); (2) the locs object has fields "path" and "cur"; (3) "path" is a list of integers; and (4) "cur" is either Undef or a DOM element. Stating and proving (4) required an additional hint (CutIsElt) for Z3 to first prove that "cur" is an object and then that it is a DOM element.

Writing such an invariant took considerable manual effort. This is unsurprising—verifying loops in a more well-behaved language, say, C#, also requires writing invariants, although, of course, many simple invariants in C# can be stated using just its type system.

With more experience, we hope to discover JavaScript idioms that make writing loop invariants easier, and further, to apply ideas ranging from abstract interpretation to interpolants to automatically infer these invariants.

5.3 Typograf

Our final example is Typograf, an extension that formats text a user enters in a form. When Typograf receives a request to capture the text, it calls `captureText`, which calls the `callback` function in the request (line 3). At line 9, Typograf registers `listener`, which calls `captureText`, as an event handler with the Chrome extension framework, by calling the function `addListener`. We verified Typograf for the absence of runtime errors. We show a simplified fragment of its code below.

```
1 function captureText(elt, callback) {
2  if(elt.tagName==='INPUT')
3  { callback({text:elt.value}); }
4 }
5 function listener(request, callback) {
6  if (request.command === 'captureText') {
7   captureText(document.activeElement, callback);
8 }}
9 chromeExtensionOnRequest.addListener(listener);
```

Verifying this extension requires providing a specification for `addListener`, a third-order function—it receives a second-order function (`listener`) as an argument. As the example below shows, our verification methodology works naturally at higher order, and the same methodology can be used to write specifications for functions of an arbitrary order.

```
1  type ChromeTyping h chrome =
2   IsObject h chrome ∧
3   HasField h chrome "addListener" ∧
4   TypeOf (SelField h chrome "addListener")) =
5   AsE (λargs this post h'.
6     (∃ wp. TypeOf (SelField h' args "0") = AsE wp ∧
7     (∀ args' h''.
8       (not (InDom h' (Loc args)) ∧
9        h'' = Alloc h' args' ∧
10       IsObject h'' args' ∧ HasField h'' args' "0" ∧
11       HasField h'' args' "1" ∧
12       IsObject h'' (SelField h'' args' "0") ∧
13       HasField h'' (SelField h'' args' "0") "command" ∧
14       TypeOf (SelField h'' args' "1") =
15        AsE (λ_ _ postcb hcb. postcb Undef hcb))
16     ⟹ wp args' Undef post h'')))
```

Since we do not yet model asynchrony, we require a sequential verification harness. However, (in contrast with HoverMagnifier), we show how instead of writing driver code to include a call to `listener`, we give a specification to `addListener` that, in effect, treats it as a function that immediately calls the function it receives as an argument. Using more realistic drivers is future work.

The listing above shows our (partial) specification of the Chrome API. It states that Chrome contains an `"addListener"` function, which (at line 6) expects a function as its first argument, i.e., `listener`, in our example). The specification states that it calls `listener` immediately in a heap h'' that differs from the input heap in that it contains a new object args' (line 9). This arguments object args' itself, in its zeroth field, contains an object with a `"command"` field; and in its first field, contains another function, the callback passed to `listener`. The callback in this case is very simple—it is the constant Undef function—but clearly, it could be given a more elaborate specification.

6. Related work

Our verification methodology is connected to a long line of literature of Hoare logic and dependently typed programming languages. In addition to the connections already discussed, our methodology is related to the characteristic formulae of Charguéraud (2011). These formulae represent programs in higher-order logic, such that two programs are equivalent if and only if their characteristic formulae are logically equivalent. Chargueraud shows how to compute a characteristic formula and manipulate it interactively in a theorem prover. In contrast, our predicate transformers are designed to be provable using an automated first-order theorem prover.

Also related is work on $F^\star$ and related languages. Borgström et al. (2009) present an application of the Hoare monad within F7, a language subsumed by $F^\star$. Borgstrom et al. (2011) use substructural state on top of a Hoare-like monad to model local state. Bhargavan et al. (2010) adopt syntactic conventions to verify higher-order programs in a language with only first-order refinement types. However, none attempts the combination of type inference, higher-orderness, and state.

Fournet et al. (2013) use our JSPrims library to prove a compiler from F* to JavaScript fully abstract. A key part of their proof methodology involves the use of the Dijkstra monad to state and prove invariants of the translation. As such, their work constitutes separate validation of the expressiveness of the Dijkstra monad and the effectiveness of our verification methodology.

Another line of work on verifying higher-order programs is via higher-order model checking (Kobayashi et al. 2011) or via liquid types (Rondon et al. 2008). These approaches aim to be automated by discovering invariants. However, these systems generally do not handle state. Combining model checking or abstract interpretation based approaches with our work is likely to pay dividends, particularly in the inference of invariants.

Our case study of JavaScript verification is related to work that equips dynamic languages with static typing, starting perhaps with Cartwright (1976). More recently, Henglein and Rehof (1995) defined a translation from Scheme to ML by encoding Scheme terms using the algebraic ML type dynamic. They were able to statically discover certain kinds of runtime errors in Scheme programs via their translation to ML. Our JS2JS* translation makes use of a similar translation (combined with λJS). Because of the richness of our target language, we are able to verify programs in a much more precise (and only semi-automated) manner. Besides, we need not stop at simply proving runtime safety—our methodology enables proofs of functional correctness.

There are several recent systems for dynamic typing based on dependent typing. Dminor (Bierman et al. 2010) provides semantic subtyping for a first-order dynamically typed language. Tobin-Hochstadt and Felleisen (2010) provide refinement types for a pure subset of Scheme. System D (Chugh et al. 2012b) is a refinement type system for a pure higher-order language with dictionary-based objects. Our type dyn bears some resemblance to these in that the refinement formulas speak about a typing property. However, none of these prior systems gives stateful refinements to functions, which prevents them from handling both higher-order functions and mutable state, as we do. Chugh et al. (2012a) extends System D to provide a type system for JavaScript. They rely on explicit type annotations, and do not provide type inference or soundness of the type system.

Gardner et al. (2012) provide an axiomatic semantics for JavaScript based on separation logic. Their semantics enables precise reasoning about first-order, `eval`-free JavaScript programs, including those that explicitly manipulate scope objects and prototype chains. Technically, supporting this idiom is possible in our system with a richer heap model. However, automated proving for such complex idioms is still hard. Indeed, at present, Gardner et al. provide only pencil and paper proofs about small, first-order JavaScript programs. Nevertheless, a potential direction for future work is to embed a subset of Gardner et al's separation logic style within F* for JavaScript verification. Gardner et al. (2008) show how to write specifications and reason about the DOM using context logic. Our specification of the DOM, in contrast, uses classical logic, and is not nearly as amenable to modular reasoning about the DOM, which has many complex aliasing patterns layered on top of a basic n-ary tree data structure. Understanding how to better structure our specifications of the DOM, perhaps based on the insights of Gardner et al., is another line of future work.

Many tools for automated analyses of various JavaScript subsets have also been constructed. We have already mentioned Gatekeeper, a pointer analysis for JavaScript used by JS2JS*. The CFA2 analysis (Vardoulakis and Shivers 2011) has been implemented in the Doctor JS tool to recover information about the call structure of a JavaScript program. Our method of reasoning about JavaScript programs by extracting heap models in Z3 can also be seen as a precise control flow analysis. As discussed previously, there is ample opportunity to improve our tool to consume the results of a source-level control-flow analysis as hints to our solver.

Jensen et al. (2009) build a whole-program abstract interpretation to recover more precise type information of JavaScript programs in order to statically find program errors. The goals are similar to our JavaScript verification, but our modular approach does not rely on complete program analysis. They assume relatively small, complete programs while our approach allows for modular verification of portions of a program.

7. Conclusions

Structuring specifications for higher order, stateful programs in the style of the Dijkstra monad has a number of benefits. As we have argued, it lends itself naturally to type inference, the VCs it computes can be handled by an SMT solver, and it is flexible enough to accommodate various language disciplines (ranging from dynamic typing, local state, and higher order stores, to exceptions and monotonic state). Indeed, the basic methodology makes very few assumptions about the underlying monad, allowing our tools to be repurposed for other verification tasks—our initial experience combining the Dijkstra monad with an information flow monad is illustrative. Going further in this direction, we conjecture that adapting existing monads for functional reactivity to the Dijkstra-style is a natural way for handling asynchrony within our framework.

Using our JavaScript verification tool chain we have shown that with the right abstractions for reasoning about higher-order, dynamically typed stores, automated program verification tools are within reach for JavaScript. Despite some limitations, ours is the first tool to enable sound, precise, semi-automated, modular verification for a sizeable subset of JavaScript, including its higher-order and stateful features.

References

M. Barnett, R. DeLine, M. Fahndrich, K. R. M. Leino, and W. Schulte. Verification of object-oriented programs with invariants. *JOT*, 3, 2004.

K. Bhargavan, C. Fournet, and N. Guts. Typechecking higher-order security libraries. In *APLAS*, pages 47–62, 2010.

G. M. Bierman, A. D. Gordon, C. Hriţcu, and D. Langworthy. Semantic subtyping with an SMT solver. In *ICFP*, 2010.

J. Borgström, A. Gordon, and R. Pucella. Roles, stacks, histories: A triple for Hoare. Technical Report TR-2009-97, Microsoft Research, 2009.

J. Borgstrom, J. Chen, and N. Swamy. Verifying stateful programs with substructural state and hoare types. In *PLPV*, Jan. 2011.

R. Cartwright. *A Practical Formal Semantic Definition and Verification System for TYPED LISP*. Garland Publishing, New York, 1976.

R. Cartwright and M. Fagan. Soft typing. In *PLDI*, 1991.

A. Charguéraud. Characteristic formulae for the verification of imperative programs. In *ICFP*, 2011.

J. Chen, R. Chugh, and N. Swamy. Type-preserving compilation of end-to-end verification of security enforcement. In *PLDI*, 2010.

R. Chugh, D. Herman, and R. Jhala. Dependent types for JavaScript. In *OOPSLA*, 2012a.

R. Chugh, P. M. Rondon, and R. Jhala. Nested refinements: a logic for duck typing. In *POPL*, 2012b.

D. Crockford. *JavaScript: The Good Parts*. O'Reilly Media Inc., 2008.

L. de Moura and N. Bjørner. Z3: An efficient SMT solver. In *TACAS*, 2008.

E. W. Dijkstra. Guarded commands, nondeterminacy and formal derivation of programs. *Commun. ACM*, 18:453–457, August 1975.

J.-C. Filliâtre and C. Marché. The why/krakatoa/caduceus platform for deductive program verification. In *CAV*, pages 173–177, 2007.

C. Fournet, N. Swamy, J. Chen, P. Evariste-Dagand, P.-Y. Strub, and B. Livshits. Fully abstract compilation to JavaScript. In *POPL*, 2013.

P. A. Gardner, G. D. Smith, M. J. Wheelhouse, and U. D. Zarfaty. Local Hoare reasoning about DOM. In *PODS*, 2008.

P. A. Gardner, S. Maffeis, and G. D. Smith. Towards a program logic for Javascript. In *POPL*, 2012.

S. Guarnieri and B. Livshits. Gatekeeper: Mostly static enforcement of security and reliability policies for JavaScript code. In *USENIX Security*, 2009.

A. Guha, C. Saftoiu, and S. Krishnamurthi. The essence of JavaScript. In *ECOOP*, 2010.

A. Guha, M. Fredrikson, B. Livshits, and N. Swamy. Verified security for browser extensions. In *IEEE Symposium on Security and Privacy*, 2011.

F. Henglein. Dynamic typing: syntax and proof theory. *Science of Computer Programming*, 22:197–230, 1994.

F. Henglein and J. Rehof. Safe polymorphic type inference for Scheme: Translating Scheme to ML. In *FPCA*, pages 192–203, 1995.

S. H. Jensen, A. Møller, and P. Thiemann. Type analysis for JavaScript. In *SAS*, pages 238–255, 2009.

N. Kobayashi, R. Sato, and H. Unno. Predicate abstraction and CEGAR for higher-order model checking. In *PLDI*, pages 222–233, 2011.

K. R. M. Leino. Dafny: An automatic program verifier for functional correctness. In *LPAR (Dakar)*, pages 348–370, 2010.

K. R. M. Leino and P. Rümmer. A polymorphic intermediate verification language: Design and logical encoding. In *TACAS*, 2010.

J. McCarthy. Towards a mathematical science of computation. In *IFIP Congress*, pages 21–28, 1962.

A. Nanevski, A. Ahmed, G. Morrisett, and L. Birkedal. Abstract predicates and mutable adts in hoare type theory. In *ESOP*, pages 189–204, 2007.

A. Nanevski, G. Morrisett, A. Shinnar, P. Govereau, and L. Birkedal. Ynot: dependent types for imperative programs. In *ICFP*, 2008a.

A. Nanevski, J. G. Morrisett, and L. Birkedal. Hoare type theory, polymorphism and separation. *J. Funct. Program.*, 18(5-6):865–911, 2008b.

P. W. O'Hearn, H. Yang, and J. C. Reynolds. Separation and information hiding. In *POPL*, 2004.

M. Parkinson and G. Bierman. Separation logic and abstraction. In *POPL*, 2005.

P. M. Rondon, M. Kawaguchi, and R. Jhala. Liquid types. In *PLDI*, 2008.

N. Swamy, J. Chen, C. Fournet, P.-Y. Strub, K. Bhargavan, and J. Yang. Secure distributed programming with value-dependent types. In *ICFP*, 2011a.

N. Swamy, N. Guts, D. Leijen, and M. Hicks. Lightweight monadic programming in ML. In *ICFP*, 2011b.

S. Tobin-Hochstadt and M. Felleisen. Logical types for untyped languages. In *ICFP*, 2010.

D. Vardoulakis and O. Shivers. CFA2: a Context-Free Approach to Control-Flow Analysis. *Logical Methods in Computer Science*, 7(2:3), 2011.

Monadic Abstract Interpreters

Ilya Sergey
IMDEA Software Institute, Spain
ilya.sergey@imdea.org

Dominique Devriese
iMinds – DistriNet, KU Leuven, Belgium
dominique.devriese@cs.kuleuven.be

Matthew Might
University of Utah, USA
might@cs.utah.edu

Jan Midtgaard
Aarhus University, Denmark
jmi@cs.au.dk

David Darais
Harvard University, USA
darais@seas.harvard.edu

Dave Clarke Frank Piessens
iMinds – DistriNet, KU Leuven, Belgium
{firstname.lastname}@cs.kuleuven.be

Abstract

Recent developments in the systematic construction of abstract interpreters hinted at the possibility of a broad unification of concepts in static analysis. We deliver that unification by showing context-sensitivity, polyvariance, flow-sensitivity, reachability-pruning, heap-cloning and cardinality-bounding to be independent of any particular semantics. Monads become the unifying agent between these concepts and between semantics. For instance, by plugging the same "context-insensitivity monad" into a monadically-parameterized semantics for Java or for the lambda calculus, it yields the expected context-insensitive analysis.

To achieve this unification, we develop a systematic method for transforming a concrete semantics into a monadically-parameterized abstract machine. Changing the monad changes the behavior of the machine. By changing the monad, we recover a spectrum of machines—from the original concrete semantics to a monovariant, flow- and context-insensitive static analysis with a singly-threaded heap and weak updates.

The monadic parameterization also suggests an abstraction over the ubiquitous monotone fixed-point computation found in static analysis. This abstraction makes it straightforward to instrument an analysis with high-level strategies for improving precision and performance, such as abstract garbage collection and widening.

While the paper itself runs the development for continuation-passing style, our generic implementation replays it for direct-style lambda-calculus and Featherweight Java to support generality.

Categories and Subject Descriptors F.3.2 [*Logics and Meanings of Programs*]: Semantics of Programming Languages—Program analysis, Operational semantics

General Terms Languages, Theory

Keywords abstract machines, abstract interpretation, monads, operational semantics, collecting semantics, abstract garbage collection, interpreters

1. Introduction

Recent work on systematizing the construction of abstract interpreters [15, 23, 24] hints at the possibility of broad theoretical unification within static analysis. Van Horn and Might [23] sketch a method for abstracting abstract machines into static analyzers by bounding the store of the abstract machine: once the store is bounded, the abstraction and then the analysis follows.

But, bounding the store is an act of design—of human intervention. How a designer bounds the store immediately determines classical properties of the analysis such as its context-sensitivity and its polyvariance. While not directly expressed in terms of a bound on the store, other classical properties are also related to the abstraction and handling of the store, including heap-cloning, reachability-pruning and cardinality-bounding. But, other properties, such as flow-sensitivity, path-sensitvity and some kinds of widening, have little to do with the store, and more to with the (re-)interpretation of the abstract semantics during analysis.

Fortunately, there is a construct that encompasses all of these concerns: the monad. Monads were originally adapted to programming languages to provide a durable abstraction for mutation in a purely functional language. As such, expressing a semantics monadically allows the monad to fully veil the details of interacting with a store. Yet monads have always provided more than just a means for hiding effects in a purely functional manner: they also allow a near-complete reinterpretation of computations expressed monadically, *e.g.*, the instant and powerful non-determinism of the list monad. This semantic reflection in precisely the right dimensions allows monads to encapsulate a variety of concepts in static analysis.

The payoff of this realization is immediate: we can monadically refactor semantics for languages as diverse as the lambda calculus and Java, yet define notions like context-sensitivity for both at the same time, with the same monad.

Our presentation details every step of the monadic refactoring for continuation-passing style lambda calculus, and then develops the monadic parameters that induce static analyzers. The implementation of the approach in the accompanying code repository replays the same monadic refactoring for a direct-style lambda calculus and for Featherweight Java. *The monads remain the same.*

We have chosen Haskell in lieu of formal mathematics for the presentation for two reasons: (1) Haskell is directly executable, and (2) Haskell has concise, convenient and readable syntax for expressing monads—the central actor in our work. Our fundamental results are no more restricted to Haskell than monads are restricted to Haskell.

1.1 Overview

Van Horn and Might's systematic abstraction relies on breaking down recursive structure in the concrete state-space and threading that structure through a store. This refactoring of the state-space imposes a corresponding store-passing-style transformation on the semantics.

Were we writing an *interpreter in Haskell* rather than a *formal semantics*, we would recognize store-passing style as an anti-pattern: in Haskell, monads are the right generalization for capturing artifacts like a store in a purely functional manner. When we apply a monadic transformation in lieu of a store-passing transformation to a concrete semantics, the resulting monad erupts as the catalyst for unifying what appeared as *ad hoc* choices in the design of classical static analyses. Even the nondeterminism that arises during abstraction of an operational semantics can be captured, explained and throttled entirely monadically.

By delegating interaction with the store into a monad, the monad determines not only the polyvariance and context-sensitivity of the analysis, but also the degree to which the analysis prunes the abstract heap based on reachability (abstract garbage collection) and bounds the cardinality of abstract addresses for shape analysis. In fact, it suggests a refactoring of the traditional fixed-point iteration such that path-sensitivity and flow-sensitivity also fall out as natural parameters.

Our monadic abstraction of the semantics orthogonalizes the classic dimensions of static analysis, independent of the specific semantics in use.

We illustrate a systematic method for transforming a concrete semantics into a monadically-parameterized machine, comprising both *concrete* and *abstract* interpretation, such that the monad determines the classical properties of an analysis. As in recent work on abstracting abstract machines [23], our semantic transformation implicitly utilizes the techniques of Danvy *et al.* [1, 2, 7] in order to calculate an abstract[1] machine equivalent to the concrete semantics. It diverges with this line of work by applying a monadic-normal-form transformation [6] (instead of a store-passing-style transformation) to the rules for the machine.

1.2 Contributions

- The central theoretical contribution of the paper is identifying and employing monads as a mechanism to abstract over the fundamental characteristics of the analysis.
- The central practical contribution is an executable proof-of-concept implementation of the described decomposition for a series of calculi.[2]
- We decouple the interpretation of the semantics from a monotonic fixed-point computation, which makes it possible to define analysis widening strategies independently of the semantics and of the analysis' other parameters.
- We illustrate degrees of freedom when constructing the analysis using our framework and show that components implementing non-deterministic transitions, polyvariance and abstract counting are semantics-independent and can be reused for different calculi (*e.g.*, Java and the lambda calculus) and analysis families.

[1] *Abstract* in the sense that it models the salient intensional behavior of a program.

[2] The implementation is available for the lambda-calculus (both in the form of CPS [15] and CESK-machine [23]) and Featherweight Java [19]:

`http://github.com/ilyasergey/monadic-cfa`

$$v \in \mathsf{Var} \text{ is a set of identifiers}$$
$$lam \in \mathsf{Lam} ::= (\lambda\ (v_1 \ldots v_n)\ call)$$
$$f, æ \in \mathsf{AExp} = \mathsf{Var} + \mathsf{Lam}$$
$$call \in \mathsf{Call} ::= (f\ æ_1 \ldots æ_n) + \mathsf{Exit}$$

$$\varsigma \in \Sigma = \mathsf{Call} \times Env \qquad \rho \in Env = \mathsf{Var} \rightharpoonup D$$
$$d \in D = Clo \qquad clo \in Clo = \mathsf{Lam} \times Env$$

Figure 1: A grammar for CPS and a concrete state-space.

2. Setting the Scene: Analyzing Continuation-Passing Style

We start our discovery of the monadic refactoring process with a minimalist higher-order language: continuation-passing style λ-calculus (CPS). We will apply the systematic abstraction process as described by Van Horn and Might [23] in full to CPS. Afterward, we'll modify the process by transforming the semantics into monadic normal form after the store-passing transformation. Thus, all interaction with the store will pass through a monad. Because interaction with the store is central to describing facets of modern flow analysis, such as context-sensitivity and heap-cloning, we will be able to describe these facets independently of a particular semantics.

In CPS (Figure 1), the lambda calculus is partitioned into two worlds: call sites and atomic expressions. Atomic expressions are lambda terms and variable references. Call sites encode the application of a function to arguments. A classical abstract machine for CPS [9] needs only two components in its state-space Σ—see Figure 1—a control component (Call) and an environment (Env). The domain D contains denotable values. CPS is so simple that there is only one kind of denotable value—closures.

The injector $\mathcal{I} : \mathsf{Call} \to \Sigma$ maps a program into this state-space:

$$\mathcal{I}(call) = (call, []),$$

In CPS, there is only one rule to describe the transition relation, $(\Rightarrow) \subseteq \Sigma \times \Sigma$. We don't write index ranges explicitly for series of meta-expressions, assuming $i = 1..n$ is obvious form the context.

$$([\![(f\ æ_1 \ldots æ_n)]\!], \rho) \Rightarrow (call, \rho''), \text{ where}$$
$$([\![(\lambda\ (v_1 \ldots v_n)\ call)]\!], \rho') = \mathcal{A}(f, \rho)$$
$$d_i = \mathcal{A}(æ_i, \rho) \qquad \rho'' = \rho'[v_i \mapsto d_i],$$

where the evaluator $\mathcal{A} : \mathsf{AExp} \times Env \rightharpoonup Clo$ evaluates an atomic expression:

$$\mathcal{A}(v, \rho) = \rho(v) \qquad \mathcal{A}(lam, \rho) = (lam, \rho).$$

2.1 Attempting structural abstraction

A structural abstraction carries abstraction component-wise across the state-space and then lifts naturally over internal domains. However, a structural abstraction of the state-space for CPS yields:

$$\hat{\Sigma} = \mathsf{Call} \times \widehat{Env} \qquad \widehat{Env} = \mathsf{Var} \rightharpoonup \hat{D}$$
$$\hat{D} = \mathcal{P}(\widehat{Clo}) \qquad \widehat{Clo} = \mathsf{Lam} \times \widehat{Env}.$$

A structural abstraction preserves mutual recursion between closures and environments, and with it, the unboundedness of the abstract state-space. Since our goal with this abstraction was a finite abstract state-space (hence a trivially computable abstract semantics), structural abstraction alone is insufficient.

2.2 Cutting recursion with a store

To arrive at a finite state-space, the systematic method detailed in "Abstracting Abstract Machines" [23] calls for transforming the abstract machine into store-passing style, which cuts the recursive knot between environments and closures by introducing addresses. With the introduction of a store, $\sigma \in Store = Addr \rightharpoonup D$, the store-passing transform produces the following state-space:

$$\varsigma \in \Sigma = \mathsf{Call} \times Env \times Store$$
$$\rho \in Env = \mathsf{Var} \rightharpoonup Addr$$
$$d \in D = Clo$$
$$clo \in Clo = \mathsf{Lam} \times Env$$
$$a \in Addr \text{ is an infinite set of addresses.}$$

The modification of the transition relation is straightforward:

$$\overbrace{(\llbracket (f\ æ_1 \ldots æ_n) \rrbracket, \rho, \sigma)}^{\varsigma} \Rightarrow (call, \rho'', \sigma'), \text{ where}$$
$$(\llbracket (\lambda\ (v_1 \ldots v_n)\ call) \rrbracket, \rho') = \mathcal{A}(f, \rho, \sigma)$$
$$d_i = \mathcal{A}(æ_i, \rho, \sigma) \qquad a_i = alloc(v_i, \varsigma)$$
$$\rho'' = \rho'[v_i \mapsto a_i] \qquad \sigma' = \sigma[a_i \mapsto d_i].$$

The evaluator $\mathcal{A} : \mathsf{AExp} \times Env \times Store \rightharpoonup D$ is modified to take the store as an additional argument:

$$\mathcal{A}(v, \rho, \sigma) = \sigma(\rho(v)) \qquad \mathcal{A}(lam, \rho, \sigma) = (lam, \rho).$$

And, the (presently opaque) address-allocator $alloc : \mathsf{Var} \times \Sigma \to Addr$ yields a fresh address for each variable.

2.3 A second attempt at abstraction

With the recursion sliced from the state-space by the store-passing transformation, a structural abstraction succeeds in producing a finite abstract state-space:

$$\hat{\varsigma} \in \hat{\Sigma} = \mathsf{Call} \times \widehat{Env} \times \widehat{Store}$$
$$\hat{\rho} \in \widehat{Env} = \mathsf{Var} \rightharpoonup \widehat{Addr}$$
$$\hat{\sigma} \in \widehat{Store} = \widehat{Addr} \to \mathcal{P}(\hat{D})$$
$$\hat{d} \in \hat{D} = \widehat{Clo}$$
$$\widehat{clo} \in \widehat{Clo} = \mathsf{Lam} \times \widehat{Env}$$
$$\hat{a} \in \widehat{Addr} \text{ is a finite set of abstract addresses,}$$

and it induces a straightforward abstract transition relation:

$$\overbrace{(\llbracket (f\ æ_1 \ldots æ_n) \rrbracket, \hat{\rho}, \hat{\sigma})}^{\hat{\varsigma}} \rightsquigarrow (call, \hat{\rho}'', \hat{\sigma}'), \text{ if}$$
$$(\llbracket (\lambda\ (v_1 \ldots v_n)\ call) \rrbracket, \hat{\rho}') \in \hat{\mathcal{A}}(f, \hat{\rho}, \hat{\sigma})$$
$$\hat{d}_i \in \hat{\mathcal{A}}(æ_i, \hat{\rho}, \hat{\sigma}) \qquad \hat{a}_i = \widehat{alloc}(v_i, \hat{\varsigma})$$
$$\hat{\rho}'' = \hat{\rho}'[v_i \mapsto \hat{a}_i] \qquad \hat{\sigma}' = \hat{\sigma} \sqcup [\hat{a}_i \mapsto \{\hat{d}_i\}].$$

Branching to every possible abstract closure introduces a subtle nondeterminism.

Naturally, the abstract argument evaluator wraps closures as singletons, but looks up variables as in the concrete version:

$$\hat{\mathcal{A}}(v, \hat{\rho}, \hat{\sigma}) = \hat{\sigma}(\hat{\rho}(v)) \qquad \hat{\mathcal{A}}(lam, \hat{\rho}, \hat{\sigma}) = \{(lam, \hat{\rho})\}.$$

The join on the abstract store allows each address in the finite set of abstract addresses to soundly represent multiple concrete addresses:

$$\hat{\sigma} \sqcup \hat{\sigma}' = \lambda \hat{a}.\hat{\sigma}(\hat{a}) \cup \hat{\sigma}'(\hat{a}).$$

And, it should now be clear that the abstract allocator $\widehat{alloc} : \mathsf{Var} \times \hat{\Sigma} \to \widehat{Addr}$ determines the polyvariance of the analysis (*i.e.*, distinguishing between bindings of the same variable in different evaluation contexts [22, 19]) because $\widehat{alloc}$ determines how many abstract variants are associated with each variable. For instance, allocating each time a new address corresponds to associating just *one* value with a variable at each moment of the program execution.

2.3.1 Example: Monovariant analysis (0CFA)

For example, a classical monovariant analysis (0CFA) comes from defining the set of abstract addresses to be the set of variables ($\widehat{Addr}_{\text{0CFA}} = \mathsf{Var}$), and then using variables as their own abstract addresses:

$$\widehat{alloc}_{\text{0CFA}}(v, \hat{\varsigma}) = v.$$

2.4 Introducing context with time-stamps

Van Horn and Might [23] realize that the abstract state-space as it stands lacks sufficient information to instantiate classical strategies for polyvariance (like k-CFA). To fix this, they introduce time-stamps (to the concrete and abstract semantics) as a new component of the state.

Time-stamps are used to remember execution context, and are directly responsible for the context-sensitivity of the analysis:

$$\hat{\varsigma} \in \hat{\Sigma} = Call \times \widehat{Env} \times \widehat{Store} \times \widehat{Time}$$
$$\hat{t} \in \widehat{Time} \text{ is a finite set of abstract times.}$$

Each transition augments the time through an opaque function, $\widehat{tick} : \widehat{Clo} \times \hat{\Sigma} \to \widehat{Time}$ and by giving the allocator $\widehat{alloc} : \mathsf{Var} \times \widehat{Time} \to \widehat{Addr}$ access to this context instead of the whole state:

$$\overbrace{(\llbracket (f\ æ_1 \ldots æ_n) \rrbracket, \hat{\rho}, \hat{\sigma}, \hat{t})}^{\hat{\varsigma}} \rightsquigarrow (call, \hat{\rho}'', \hat{\sigma}', \hat{t}'), \text{ if}$$
$$\underbrace{(\llbracket (\lambda\ (v_1 \ldots v_n)\ call) \rrbracket, \hat{\rho}')}_{\widehat{clo}} \in \hat{\mathcal{A}}(f, \hat{\rho}, \hat{\sigma})$$
$$\hat{d}_i \in \hat{\mathcal{A}}(æ_i, \hat{\rho}, \hat{\sigma}) \qquad \hat{t}' = \widehat{tick}(\widehat{clo}, \hat{\varsigma})$$
$$\hat{a}_i = \widehat{alloc}(v_i, \hat{t}') \qquad \hat{\rho}'' = \hat{\rho}'[v_i \mapsto \hat{a}_i]$$
$$\hat{\sigma}' = \hat{\sigma} \sqcup [\hat{a}_i \mapsto \{\hat{d}_i\}].$$

2.4.1 Example: k-CFA-style context-sensitivity

The introduction of this component makes it possible to model k-CFA [22] by defining times to be sequences of up to k call sites and addresses to be pairs of variables and call sites:

$$\widehat{Time}_{k\text{-CFA}} = \mathsf{Call}^{\leqslant k}$$
$$\widehat{Addr}_{k\text{-CFA}} = \mathsf{Var} \times \widehat{Time}_{k\text{-CFA}},$$

and using corresponding definitions

$$\widehat{tick}_{k\text{-CFA}}(\widehat{clo}, (call, \ldots, \hat{t})) = \lfloor call : \hat{t} \rfloor_k$$
$$\widehat{alloc}_{k\text{-CFA}}(v, (\ldots, \hat{t}')) = (v, \hat{t}')$$

where $\lfloor \cdot \rfloor_k$ limits its argument to at most length k.

3. Abstracting through a Monad

In flow analysis, interaction with the store determines essential properties of the analysis. Thus, by abstracting away interaction with the store through a monad, we introduce an abstraction layer for these essential properties.

In pure functional programming, the introduction of store-passing style to mimic side effects is an anti-pattern. The established remedy for this anti-pattern is the use of monadic form in conjunction with a state-transformer monad. We can apply this remedy to our semantics as well.

To make the presentation unambiguous (and executable), we first transliterate the abstract semantics (for k-CFA at the moment) into Haskell, starting with the syntax for CPS:

$$\begin{array}{lll}
\mathbf{type}\ Var & = String & \\
\mathbf{data}\ Lambda & = [\,Var\,] \Rightarrow CExp\ \mathbf{deriving}\ (Eq, Ord) & \\
\mathbf{data}\ AExp & = Ref\ Var & \\
 & \mid\ Lam\ Lambda & \mathbf{deriving}\ (Eq, Ord) \\
\mathbf{data}\ CExp & = Call\ AExp\ [\,AExp\,] & \\
 & \mid\ Exit & \mathbf{deriving}\ (Eq, Ord)
\end{array}$$

The set Call from the definition of the state-space corresponds to the type $CExp$ in the implementation. The type for the state-space is a 4-tuple:

$$\begin{array}{ll}
\mathbf{type}\ \Sigma & = (CExp, Env, Store, Time) \\
\mathbf{type}\ k \rightharpoonup v & = Map\ k\ v \\
\mathbf{type}\ Env & = Var \rightharpoonup Addr \\
\mathbf{type}\ Store & = Addr \rightharpoonup \mathcal{P}\ Val \\
\mathbf{data}\ Val & = Clo\ (Lambda, Env) \\
 & \quad\ \mathbf{deriving}\ (Eq, Ord) \\
\mathbf{type}\ Addr & = (Var, Time) \\
\mathbf{type}\ Time & = [\,CExp\,]
\end{array}$$

where we utilize Haskell's unicode support to keep the implementation and the math as close as possible (*e.g.*, writing $\mathcal{P}\ Val$ instead of $Set\ Val$). The transition relation becomes a function $next$ on states into lists of states:

$$\begin{array}{l}
next :: \Sigma \to [\Sigma] \\
next\ \varsigma@(Call\ f\ aes, \rho, \sigma, t) = [(call, \rho'', \sigma', t') \mid \\
\quad proc@(Clo\ (vs \Rightarrow call, \rho')) \leftarrow Set.toList\ (arg\ (f, \rho, \sigma)), \\
\quad \mathbf{let}\ t' = tick\ (proc, \varsigma) \\
\qquad as = [alloc\ (v, t', proc, \varsigma) \mid v \leftarrow vs] \\
\qquad ds = [arg\ (æ, \rho, \sigma) \mid æ \leftarrow aes] \\
\qquad \rho'' = \rho' /\!\!/ [v \Longrightarrow a \mid v \leftarrow vs \mid a \leftarrow as] \\
\qquad \sigma' = \sigma \sqcup [a \Longrightarrow d \mid a \leftarrow as \mid d \leftarrow ds]] \\
next\ \varsigma = [\varsigma]
\end{array}$$

The function arg is the transliteration of the argument evaluator, $\hat{\mathcal{A}}$. The function $tick$ is the transliteration of the $\widehat{tick}$ function. And, the function $alloc$ is the transliteration of the $\widehat{alloc}$ function. Finally, the utility infix operator $(/\!\!/) :: Ord\ k \Rightarrow (k \rightharpoonup v) \to [(k, v)] \to (k \rightharpoonup v)$ is used to update a map with a list of key-value pairs, and $(\Longrightarrow)$ is just a synonym for pair constructor.

3.1 Capturing nondeterminism in the monad

The function $next$ uses the list comprehension notation to more closely mimic the formalism. The list comprehension notation is syntactic sugar for the list comprehension monad.

We can tiptoe into monadic normal form by expanding the list comprehension $[(call, \rho'', \sigma', t') \mid ...]$ into its monadic form:

$$\begin{array}{l}
mnext :: \Sigma \to [\Sigma] \\
mnext\ \varsigma@(Call\ f\ aes, \rho, \sigma, t) = \mathbf{do} \\
\quad proc@(Clo\ (vs \Rightarrow call, \rho')) \leftarrow Set.toList\ (arg\ (f, \rho, \sigma)) \\
\quad \mathbf{let}\ t' = tick\ (proc, \varsigma) \\
\qquad as = [alloc\ (v, t', proc, \varsigma) \mid v \leftarrow vs] \\
\qquad ds = [arg\ (æ, \rho, \sigma) \mid æ \leftarrow aes] \\
\qquad \rho'' = \rho' /\!\!/ [v \Longrightarrow a \mid v \leftarrow vs \mid a \leftarrow as] \\
\qquad \sigma' = \sigma \sqcup [a \Longrightarrow d \mid a \leftarrow as \mid d \leftarrow ds] \\
\quad return\ (call, \rho'', \sigma', t') \\
mnext\ \varsigma = return\ \varsigma
\end{array}$$

Since function evaluation is the only source of nondeterminism, we can clean up these semantics by creating a new function fun as a special version of arg for evaluating functions:

$$\begin{array}{l}
fun :: (AExp, Env, Store) \to [\,Val\,] \\
fun = Set.toList \circ arg
\end{array}$$

Thus, we can rewrite $mnext$:

$$\begin{array}{l}
mnext :: \Sigma \to [\Sigma] \\
mnext\ \varsigma@(Call\ f\ aes, \rho, \sigma, t) = \mathbf{do} \\
\quad proc@(Clo\ (vs \Rightarrow call, \rho')) \leftarrow fun\ (f, \rho, \sigma) \\
\quad \cdots\ \text{-- the rest is unchanged}
\end{array}$$

To reformulate this function fully into monadic normal form, we must refactor and recurry fun, arg, $tick$, $alloc$ to return singleton lists as well (hence fun and arg now have the same type):

$$\begin{array}{ll}
fun & :: (Env, Store) \to AExp \to [\,Val\,] \\
arg & :: (Env, Store) \to AExp \to [\,Val\,] \\
tick & :: Val \to State \to [\,Time\,] \\
alloc & :: (Time, Val, State) \to Var \to [\,Addr\,]
\end{array}$$

which allows us to rewrite $mnext$ in monadic normal form, replacing list comprehensions with a standard function $mapM :: Monad\ m \Rightarrow (a \to m\ b) \to [a] \to m\ [b]$ from a monadic toolset.

$$\begin{array}{l}
mnext :: \Sigma \to [\Sigma] \\
mnext\ \varsigma@(Call\ f\ aes, \rho, \sigma, t) = \mathbf{do} \\
\quad proc@(Clo\ (vs \Rightarrow call, \rho')) \leftarrow fun\ (\rho, \sigma)\ f \\
\quad t' \leftarrow tick\ proc\ \varsigma \\
\quad \mathbf{let}\ as = mapM\ (alloc\ (t', proc, \varsigma))\ vs \\
\qquad\ \ ds = mapM\ (arg\ (\rho, \sigma))\ aes \\
\quad \cdots\ \text{-- the rest is unchanged}
\end{array}$$

3.2 Pulling the store into the monad

In the previous section, we refactored the abstract semantics so that nondeterminism is explicitly threaded through the list monad. In this section, we subtly reformulate the semantics in terms of a *CPSInterface* type class that hides interaction with the store, abstracting over five functions that form a *semantic interface* of the CPS calculus:

$$\begin{array}{l}
\mathbf{class}\ Monad\ m \Rightarrow CPSInterface\ m\ \mathbf{where} \\
\quad fun\ \ :: Env \to AExp \to m\ Val \\
\quad arg\ \ :: Env \to AExp \to m\ Val \\
\quad (\mapsto)\ :: Addr \to Val \to m\ () \\
\quad alloc :: Time \to Var \to m\ Addr \\
\quad tick\ \ :: Val \to P\Sigma \to m\ Time
\end{array}$$

where the type $P\Sigma$ encodes a partial state (with no store):

$$P\Sigma = (CExp, Env, Time)$$

Under this interface, we can separate the specification of the abstract semantics from the specific details of how it interacts with the store:

$$\begin{array}{l}
mnext :: (CPSInterface\ m) \Rightarrow P\Sigma \to m\ P\Sigma \\
mnext\ ps@(Call\ f\ aes, \rho, t) = \mathbf{do} \\
\quad proc@(Clo\ (vs \Rightarrow call, \rho')) \leftarrow fun\ \rho\ f \\
\quad t' \leftarrow tick\ proc\ ps \\
\quad as \leftarrow mapM\ (alloc\ t')\ vs \\
\quad ds \leftarrow mapM\ (arg\ \rho)\ aes \\
\quad \mathbf{let}\ \rho'' = \rho' /\!\!/ [v \Longrightarrow a \mid v \leftarrow vs \mid a \leftarrow as] \\
\quad sequence\ [a \mapsto d \mid a \leftarrow as \mid d \leftarrow ds] \\
\quad return\ (call, \rho'', t') \\
mnext\ \varsigma = return\ \varsigma
\end{array}$$

3.3 Pulling time into the monad

Like the store, time-stamps were another *ad hoc* addition to the original semantics to engineer them into a form favorable for static analysis. We can lift time-stamps out of partial states and into monads as well, so that $P\Sigma = (CExp, Env)$.

The analysis monad can now assume internal access to the current time, which simplifies the interface:

$$
\begin{array}{l}
\textbf{class } Monad\ m \Rightarrow CPSInterface\ m \textbf{ where}\\
\quad fun\ \ :: Env \rightarrow AExp \rightarrow m\ Val\\
\quad arg\ \ :: Env \rightarrow AExp \rightarrow m\ Val\\
\quad (\mapsto) :: Addr \rightarrow Val \rightarrow m\ ()\\
\quad alloc :: Var \rightarrow m\ Addr\\
\quad tick\ \ :: Val \rightarrow P\Sigma \rightarrow m\ ()
\end{array}
$$

Because the allocator $alloc$ can assume access to time (and the store) inside the monad, it no longer needs to take it as a parameter, leaving the variable to be bound as its *only remaining parameter*. The simplification in the analysis monad is reflected in a simplification of the definition for transition function $mnext$ as well, as time is no longer a component of the abstract states datatype $P\Sigma$:

$$
\begin{array}{l}
mnext :: (CPSInterface\ m) \Rightarrow P\Sigma \rightarrow m\ P\Sigma\\
mnext\ ps@(Call\ f\ aes, \rho) = \textbf{do}\\
\quad proc@(Clo\ (vs \Rightarrow call, \rho')) \leftarrow fun\ \rho\ f\\
\quad tick\ proc\ ps\\
\quad as \leftarrow mapM\ alloc\ vs\\
\quad \cdots\ \ \text{-- the rest is unchanged}
\end{array}
$$

3.4 Abstracting over addresses

At this point, we have a monadically abstracted abstracted[3] abstract machine. Plugging in a monad controls nondeterminism, context and access to the store. However, we still have one component left to be abstracted.

Until now, we have assumed that abstract addresses are represented by a fixed datatype. In practice, the nature of the addresses determines the polyvariance and context-sensitivity of the analysis, since they usually divide bindings according to different contexts (also known as *contours* [22]). For example, Shivers' 1CFA allocates distinct contexts for each call site. Lakhotia *et al.* [12] introduce ℓ-contexts to build a static analysis for obfuscated x86 binaries, employing finite sequences of unique enclosed function calls. Finally, one can take a bounded set of naturals $\{n \in \mathbb{N} \mid n \leq N\}$ for some N as contexts, which will give a good precision for sufficiently big N.

Thus, we must abstract over the structure of addresses in order to cover at least all the options from above. Unfortunately, addresses form a part of the state-space as a codomain of Env; thus, we need to parameterize our semantic domains by the type of addresses—a:

$$
\begin{array}{lll}
\textbf{type } P\Sigma\ a & = & (CExp, Env\ a)\\
\textbf{type } Env\ a & = & Var \rightharpoonup a\\
\textbf{data } Val\ a & = & Clo\ (Lambda, Env\ a)\\
 & & \quad \textbf{deriving } (Eq, Ord)\\
\textbf{type } Store\ a & = & a \rightharpoonup \mathcal{P}\ (Val\ a)
\end{array}
$$

With this shift, we are no longer attached to the k-CFA-like representation of addresses, as both $Addr$ and $Time$ are gone.

Of course, the signature of the $CPSInterface$ monad and $mnext$ change accordingly, although the body of $mnext$ remains unchanged. The final definition of the $CPSInterface$ class and the function $mnext$ are represented in Figure 2 and are not going to change in the remainder of our story. What *is* going to change is the implementation of the semantic interface $CPSInterface$ as well as the choice of the underlying monad for the analysis logic.

[3] This is not a typo.

$$
\begin{array}{l}
\textbf{class } Monad\ m \Rightarrow CPSInterface\ m\ a \textbf{ where}\\
\quad fun\ \ :: Env\ a \rightarrow AExp \rightarrow m\ (Val\ a)\\
\quad arg\ \ :: Env\ a \rightarrow AExp \rightarrow m\ (Val\ a)\\
\quad (\mapsto)\ :: a \rightarrow Val\ a \rightarrow m\ ()\\
\quad alloc :: Var \rightarrow m\ a\\
\quad tick\ \ :: Val\ a \rightarrow P\Sigma\ a \rightarrow m\ ()\\
mnext :: CPSInterface\ m\ a \Rightarrow P\Sigma\ a \rightarrow m\ (P\Sigma\ a)\\
mnext\ ps@(Call\ f\ aes, \rho) = \textbf{do}\\
\quad proc@(Clo\ (vs \Rightarrow call', \rho')) \leftarrow fun\ \rho\ f\\
\quad tick\ proc\ ps\\
\quad as \leftarrow mapM\ alloc\ vs\\
\quad ds \leftarrow mapM\ (arg\ \rho)\ aes\\
\quad \textbf{let } \rho'' = \rho'\ /\!/\ [v \Longrightarrow a \mid v \leftarrow vs \mid a \leftarrow as]\\
\quad sequence\ [a \mapsto d \mid a \leftarrow as \mid d \leftarrow ds]\\
\quad return\ (call', \rho'')\\
mnext\ \varsigma = return\ \varsigma
\end{array}
$$

Figure 2: Semantic interface and a small-step semantics of CPS in a monadic form.

4. Recovering a Concrete Interpreter

With non-determinism, interaction with the store and time pulled into an analysis monad, and addresses abstracted, our semantics has become highly parameterized. As a result, we can easily recover a concrete interpreter as a "sanity" check for adequacy. With the standard IO monad as an underlying analysis monad, we can use the "real" heap as the store and implement mutable references as a datatype $IOAddr$ containing essentially a pointer:

$$\textbf{data } IOAddr = IOAddr\ \{lookup :: IORef\ (Val\ IOAddr)\}$$

We will also need two simple administrative functions in order to write to and read from $IOAddr$s:

$$
\begin{array}{l}
readIOAddr :: IOAddr \rightarrow IO\ (Val\ IOAddr)\\
readIOAddr = readIORef \circ lookup\\
writeIOAddr :: IOAddr \rightarrow Val\ IOAddr \rightarrow IO\ ()\\
writeIOAddr = writeIORef \circ lookup
\end{array}
$$

The implementation of the $CPSInterface$ type class directly mimics the concrete semantics defined in Section 2.2:

$$
\begin{array}{lll}
\multicolumn{3}{l}{\textbf{instance } CPSInterface\ IO\ IOAddr \textbf{ where}}\\
\quad fun\ \rho\ (Lam\ l) & = & return\ \$\ Clo\ (l, \rho)\\
\quad fun\ \rho\ (Ref\ v) & = & readIOAddr\ (\rho\ !\ v)\\
\quad arg\ \rho\ (Lam\ l) & = & return\ \$\ Clo\ (l, \rho)\\
\quad arg\ \rho\ (Ref\ v) & = & readIOAddr\ (\rho\ !\ v)\\
\quad addr \mapsto v & = & writeIOAddr\ addr\ v\\
\quad alloc\ v & = & liftM\ IOAddr\ \$\ newIORef\ \bot\\
\quad tick\ \_\ \_ & = & return\ ()
\end{array}
$$

When a new address is allocated, we pass the function $newIORef$ $\bot$ as the initial value of the new reference, since the actual value to be bound at this address is not yet defined at the moment of allocation. The function $tick$ is a no-op: in the real world, time advances without our help.

With this interpretation of the semantic interface, the concrete interpreter is simply a recursively defined driver loop that iterates the semantic transition function $mnext$ until an $Exit$ state is reached.

```
interpret :: CExp → IO (PΣ IOAddr)
interpret e = go (e, Map.empty)
  where go :: (PΣ IOAddr) → IO (PΣ IOAddr)
        go s = do s′ ← mnext s
                  case s′ of x@(Exit, _) → return x
                             y           → go y
```

5. Recovering a Collecting Semantics

In this section, we recall key notions from lattice theory and abstract interpretation, crucial for constructing an interpreter for concrete or abstract small-step collecting semantics of a program. We proceed by translating the theory into programs in Haskell and demonstrate an implementation of a simple collecting semantics.

5.1 Basics of lattice theory and abstract interpretation

A *complete lattice* $\langle C; \sqsubseteq, \bot, \top, \sqcup, \sqcap \rangle$ is a partial order $\langle C; \sqsubseteq \rangle$ such that there exists a least upper bound (or join) $\sqcup S$ and a greatest lower bound (or meet) $\sqcap S$ of all subsets $S \subseteq C$. In particular $\sqcup C = \top$ and $\sqcap C = \bot$.

A point x is a fixed point of a function f if $f(x) = x$. Given two partial orders, $\langle C, \sqsubseteq \rangle$ and $\langle A, \leq \rangle$, a function f of type $C \to A$ is monotone if $\forall x, y : x \sqsubseteq y \implies f(x) \leq f(y)$. By the Knaster-Tarski fixed-point theorem a monotone functional f over a complete lattice has a *least fixed point* $\mathrm{lfp}_{\sqsubseteq} f = \sqcap \{x \mid f(x) \sqsubseteq x\}$. Algorithmically the least fixed point of a monotone function f over a complete lattice of finite height can be computed by Kleene iteration: $\bot \sqsubseteq f(\bot) \sqsubseteq f^2(\bot) \sqsubseteq f^3(\bot) \sqsubseteq \ldots$ since

$$\mathrm{lfp}_{\sqsubseteq} f = \bigsqcup_{i \geq 0} f^i(\bot). \tag{1}$$

A *Galois connection* is a pair of functions α, γ connecting two partial orders $\langle C, \sqsubseteq \rangle$ and $\langle A, \leq \rangle$, such that $\forall a, c : \alpha(c) \leq a \iff c \sqsubseteq \gamma(a)$. We typeset Galois connections as: $\langle C, \sqsubseteq \rangle \underset{\alpha}{\overset{\gamma}{\longleftrightarrow}} \langle A, \leq \rangle$.

Given a Galois connection $\langle C, \sqsubseteq \rangle \underset{\alpha}{\overset{\gamma}{\longleftrightarrow}} \langle A, \leq \rangle$ and a monotone function $F_c : C \to C$, an *abstract* function F_a can be constructed as $\alpha \circ F_c \circ \gamma \stackrel{.}{\leq} F_a$. Therefore, by the *fixed-point transfer theorem* [5], we have $\alpha(\mathrm{lfp}\ F_c) \leq \mathrm{lfp}\ F_a$ when F_a is monotone.

The reachable states collecting semantics for a set of program states Σ, a transition function $(\leadsto) \subseteq \Sigma \times \Sigma$, and a set of initial states $\Sigma_0 \subseteq \Sigma$ is defined on a complete lattice $\langle \mathcal{P}(\Sigma), \subseteq, \emptyset, \Sigma, \cup, \cap \rangle$ as a least fixed point of a monotone functional $\mathcal{F}$, where

$$\mathcal{F}(\mathcal{X}) = \Sigma_0 \cup \{s' \mid s \in \mathcal{X} \wedge s \leadsto s'\}. \tag{2}$$

$\mathcal{F}$ is uncomputable in general, which makes it a usual starting point for construction of an abstract, monotone transition function $\widehat{\mathcal{F}}$, such that $\alpha \circ \mathcal{F} \circ \gamma \stackrel{.}{\leq} \widehat{\mathcal{F}}$ and computing an approximate fixed point as $\mathrm{lfp}\, \widehat{\mathcal{F}}$.

In the remainder of the section we will systematically abstract over computation of a small-step collecting semantics for CPS.

5.2 Implementing lattices and fixed point computations

We define a type class for a lattice following its algebraic definition:

```
class Lattice a where
  ⊥   :: a
  ⊤   :: a
  (⊑) :: a → a → Bool
  (⊔) :: a → a → a
  (⊓) :: a → a → a
```

We provide the following instances of *Lattice* for the standard container types that we use heavily for systematic abstraction of abstract machines [15]: unit, pairs, powersets and maps:

```
instance Lattice ()
instance (Lattice a, Lattice b) ⇒ Lattice (a, b)
instance (Ord s, Eq s) ⇒ Lattice (P s)
instance (Ord k, Lattice v) ⇒ Lattice (k ⇀ v)
```

The monadic interpreter from Figure 2, which we presented at the end of Section 3, is reminiscent of the definition (2) of the collecting semantics. However, the fact it uses a monad and is not an endo-function, prevents us from using it directly as a relation $(\leadsto)$ in a functional $\mathcal{F}$. What we can do is to explicitly make a separation of concerns between *mnext* as an implementation of an abstract transition function and a computation of a least fixed point. We define the type class *Collecting* to let the implementor of the analysis define the logic of initiating the semantics (*i.e.*, providing an initial set Σ_0 from (2)) and "making a step":

```
class Collecting m a fp | fp → a, fp → m where
  applyStep :: (a → m a) → fp → fp
  inject :: a → fp
```

The functional dependencies $fp \to a$ and $fp \to m$ state that the choice of a domain *fp* determines in which monad m the step function should be interpreted [11], as well as what the transition's domain and co-domain a should be.[4] The computation of the collecting semantics as a least fixed point can be then defined directly from the Kleene iteration (1):

```
kleeneIt :: (Lattice a) ⇒ (a → a) → a
kleeneIt f = loop ⊥
  where loop c = let c′ = f c in
                 if c′ ⊑ c then c else loop c′
```

Finally, the collecting semantics (2) translates gracefully to the following function, mapping a transition function *step* and an initial state c to a result of the analysis.

```
exploreFP :: (Lattice fp, Collecting m a fp) ⇒
             (a → m a) → a → fp
exploreFP step c = kleeneIt F
  where F s = inject c ⊔ applyStep step s
```

It is now straightforward to implement a function that, given an expression, runs the analysis:

```
runAnalysis :: (CPSInterface m a, Lattice fp,
                Collecting m (PΣ a) fp) ⇒
                CExp → fp
runAnalysis e = exploreFP mnext (e, Map.empty)
```

The signature of *runAnalysis* outlines precisely the three degrees of freedom that can be changed in order to obtain different collecting semantics:

1. A monad, accounting for nondeterminism and passing analysis-specific state components (*i.e.*, time and store),
2. An implementation of the semantic interface of a language (*e.g.*, the one in Figure 2), and
3. The analysis lattice and an implementation of a fixed point computation that extracts the result of a single step from the analysis monad and augments the lattice argument appropriately.

5.3 *StorePassing*—a simple implementation of a collecting semantics for CPS

At this point we are ready to reconstruct a simple abstract interpreter computing a collecting, store-passing semantics of CPS by

[4] Alternatively, we could use associated types to express the same sort of dependencies [3].

gradually instantiating three main aspects of the analysis, outlined at the end of the previous section.

5.3.1 A two-level analysis monad

We start from constructing a monad for a simple collecting, store-passing semantics by employing standard monad transformers $StateT$ and the list monad:

$$\mathbf{type}\ StorePassing\ s\ g = StateT\ g\ (StateT\ s\ [\,])$$

The analysis parameters of type s and g carry state components. They carry the store and the analysis' *guts* respectively, where the latter can contain for example a "time" value.

In a desugared form, the type $StorePassing$ is equivalent to the functional type $g \to s \to [((a, g), s)]$ for some a, g and s, so the stack representation of a monad should be read "inside-out". That is, a value of type $StorePassing$ produces a set (represented by a list) of results of type a, coupled with components of type g and s.

5.3.2 A simple implementation of a CPS semantic interface

To turn the $StorePassing$ monad into an interpretation of the semantics, we have to implement the $CPSInterface$ type class. So far, we choose to implement addresses as Haskell $Integer$s for simplicity. The store is represented as a map from integer addresses to sets of values. The implementation of the semantic interface is provided below.

```
instance CPSInterface
  (StorePassing (Store Integer) Integer) Integer
  where
    fun ρ (Lam l) = return $ Clo (l, ρ)
    fun ρ (Ref v) = lift $ getsNDSet $ λσ → σ ! (ρ ! v)
    arg ρ (Lam l) = return $ Clo (l, ρ)
    arg ρ (Ref v) = lift $ getsNDSet $ λσ → σ ! (ρ ! v)
    a ↦ d         = lift $ modify $
                      Map.insert a (singleton d)
    alloc v       = gets id
    tick proc ps  = modify $ λt → t + 1
```

The function $getsNDSet$ is a crux of handling non-determinism in a monadic implementation of the analysis as a stateful monad. It allows one to examine the state, get multiple results and non-deterministically choose one. Its signature needs explanation:

```
getsNDSet :: (MonadPlus m, MonadState s m) ⇒
               (s → Set a) → m a
```

However, the type class constraints before $\Rightarrow$ provide a clue. One can see that m is required to be a state monad, *i.e.*, carry an implicit state component of type s, which can be accessed and modified. The argument type $s \to Set\ a$ accounts for the non-deterministic result of type a that might come out of examining the state s. Finally, $MonadPlus\ m$ is a constraint that ensures that m has a notion of non-deterministic choice, so the obtained results can be combined in a wrapped result $m\ a$. What comes as a nice surprise is that $StorePassing$ is an instance of both $MonadPlus$ and $MonadState$.

lift is a standard Haskell function for explicit management of the monadic stack, which is used explicitly to disambiguate the targets of accesses to the monad stack [13, 21]. In our implementation of $CPSInterface$ the outermost state is reserved to carry "guts" (*i.e.*, the time component), so we need to employ *lift* to access the store σ, located on a "second level" of the monad stack. Finally, *gets* and *modify* are standard higher-order functions that allow one to examine and modify internal state of the monad.

```
gets   :: MonadState s m ⇒ (s → a) → m a
modify :: MonadState s m ⇒ (s → s) → m ()
```

For instance, the implementation of *tick* modifies the time component on the first level of the monadic stack (therefore, no explicit lifting is required).[5]

5.3.3 Computing a collecting semantics of CPS

The last missing ingredient we need to compute the collecting semantics of CPS is the definition of a fixed point computation that uses the $StorePassing$ monad. We can reach a fix-point of type $\mathcal{P}\ ((P\Sigma\ a, g), s)$ step by step with the following definitions of $applyStep$ and $inject$.

```
instance (Ord s, Ord a, Ord g, HasInitial g, Lattice s) ⇒
         Collecting (StorePassing s g)
                    (PΣ a)
                    (𝒫 ((PΣ a, g), s)) where
  inject p = singleton $ ((p, initial), ⊥)
  applyStep step fp = joinWith runStep fp where
    runStep ((ς, t), s) =
      Set.fromList $ runStateT (runStateT (step ς) t) s
```

The implementation of $inject$ instruments a provided state with initial "guts", defined by the value $initial$ of the class $HasInitial$ for g and the lattice minimum $\bot$ for s, and wraps it into a singleton set. The class $HasInitial$ is defined as

```
class HasInitial g where initial :: g
```

and its implementation for $Integer$s is trivial (*e.g.*, $initial = 0$).

The most interesting element of the implementation is the utility function $joinWith$, defined as follows:

```
joinWith :: (Lattice a) ⇒
              (b → a) → Set b → a
joinWith f = Set.foldr ((⊔) ∘ f) ⊥
```

That is, given a set of values of type b and a function f of type $b \to a$ for a lattice a, $joinWith$ traverses the structure, applying f to each of its leaf elements and combines the results using the lattice join $(\sqcup)$.

In the definition of $applyStep$, $joinWith$ takes a function that simply passes the state ς and the components t and s to the provided function $step$, runs a monad and collects the result into a set. This function is applied to *all* states in *fp* and the results are joined.

All ingredients to run the analysis are now in place, and all we need to do is to use the function $runAnalysis$ from Section 5.2 to compute the result:

```
exp :: CExp = ...
runAnalysis exp :: 𝒫 ((PΣ Integer, Integer), Store Integer)
```

6. Monadic Parameters for Abstract Abstract Machines

In Section 5 we have demonstrated how to restore a simple collecting semantics from the monadically-parametrized semantic interface, presenting a $StorePassing$ monad and an analysis with domain $\mathcal{P}\ ((P\Sigma\ Integer, Integer), Store\ Integer)$. More complex analyses differ from this simple analysis in a number of aspects. In this section, we will discuss how our $StorePassing$ monad and $CPSInterface$ and $Collecting$ instances can be abstracted further to accomodate this. Specifically, we show how to control polyvariance, store representation, abstract counting, abstract garbage collection and store cloning.

[5] In the present implementation, we allow the time component to grow infinitely for simplicity, so in principle some implementation of the analysis may not terminate, which can be restricted by modifying the function *tick*.

6.1 Controlling polyvariance

So far, we have used Haskell's *Integers* as abstract addresses in the collecting semantics. To allow experimentation with different addresses, we introduce the following class that provides a uniform view on addresses which may (optionally) incorporate context:

```
class (Ord a, Eq a) ⇒ Addressable a c | c → a where
  τ0      :: c
  valloc  :: Var → c → a
  advance :: Val a → PΣ a → c → c
```

The type class *Addressable* has two type parameters: a for actual addresses and c for the type of the context. Contexts unambiguously define the nature of addresses. The type class contains three functions. τ_0 generates an initial context, used to instantiate the *HasInitial* class from Section 5.3.3. The function *valloc*, given a variable name and a context, allocates a new address. Finally, the function *advance* has the opportunity to internalize components of the partial state within the monad, based on the function called, the current state processed, and a given context.

A meaningful instance of the *Addressable* type class uses a combination of time-stamps, represented by lists of calls of length bounded by some k, and addresses that simply pair the time-stamps with variable names. This defines an analysis' *polyvariance*:

```
data KTime = KCalls [CExp]       deriving (Eq, Ord)
data KAddr = KBind Var KTime deriving (Eq, Ord)
```

Here is the instance of *Addressable* for this pair, relying on the auxiliary class *KCFA* for generic controlling of polyvariance:

```
class KCFA a where
  getK :: a → Int
instance Addressable KAddr KTime where
  τ0          = KCalls []
  valloc v t  = KBind v t
  advance proc (call, ρ) t@(KCalls calls)
              = KCalls $ (getK t) (call : calls)
```

The *CPSInterface* instance for *StorePassing* requires a small change in order to accomodate polyvariance:

```
instance (Addressable a t) ⇒
    CPSInterface (StorePassing (Store a) t) a
  where
    alloc v        = gets (valloc v)
    tick proc ps   = modify $ λt → advance proc ps t
    ···              -- the rest is unchanged
```

Accroding to the *A Posteriori* soundness theorem of Might and Manolios [17], *any* allocation policy for a non-deterministic abstract interpreter (which our analysis is a particular case of) leads to a *sound* abstraction of a concrete store-based collecting semantics that uses uniques addresses for each allocation (*e.g.*, integers, as in the example in Section 5.3.2). Thus, abstracting over addresses yields a family of sound abstract interpreters and requires *no* change in the semantics interface (Figure 2).

6.2 Abstracting over the store component

The store component is essential for efficient implementation of the analysis but can also itself be a source of valuable measurements (*e.g.*, computing the *flows-to* information), so our next step is to make an analysis store-generic. We do so by defining a *StoreLike* class enabling creation of initial store, binding, update, and lookup as well as providing a mechanism to clean the store up:

```
class (Eq a, Lattice s, Lattice d) ⇒
      StoreLike a s d | s → a, s → d where
  σ0          :: s
  bind        :: s → a → d → s
  replace     :: s → a → d → s
  fetch       :: s → a → d
  filterStore :: s → (a → Bool) → s
```

The *StoreLike* class binds together three components: addresses (a), the store implementation itself (s) and the store codomain (d). To save space, we refer the reader to our public implementation for implementations of *StoreLike* instances for *Store a*.

Again, we need small changes in the *CPSInterface* instance for *StorePassing* in order to abstract over stores:

```
instance (Addressable a t, StoreLike a s (P (Val a))) ⇒
    CPSInterface (StorePassing s t) a
  where
    fun ρ (Ref v) = lift $ getsNDSet $ flip fetch (ρ ! v)
    arg ρ (Ref v) = lift $ getsNDSet $ flip fetch (ρ ! v)
    a ↦ d = lift $ modify $ λσ → bind σ a (singleton d)
    ···   -- the rest is unchanged
```

6.3 Controlling abstract counting

Abstract counting is a technique to track how many times an abstract resource has been allocated [18]. It provides a simple but powerful way of bounding cardinalities over abstractions. Specifically, it bounds them in a way that it enables *must*-alias analysis in imperative languages or environment analysis in higher-order languages. Counting enables additional shape analyses or predicate abstractions to be layered on top of an existing analysis [16]. This, in turn, enables an analysis' client to perform environmental analysis to perform advanced optimization, such as super β-inlining [14].

To introduce an abstract counter for CPS, we need to make a small addition to the state-space:

$$\begin{aligned} \hat{\varsigma} \in \hat{\Sigma} &= \mathit{Call} \times \widehat{\mathit{Env}} \times \widehat{\mathit{Store}} \times \widehat{\mathit{Count}} \times \widehat{\mathit{Time}} \\ \hat{\mu} \in \widehat{\mathit{Count}} &= \widehat{\mathit{Addr}} \to \widehat{\mathbb{N}} \\ \hat{n} \in \widehat{\mathbb{N}} &= \{0, 1, \infty\}\,. \end{aligned}$$

The abstract transition relation changes correspondingly to take possible changes of $\hat{\mu}$ into account:

$$\overbrace{([\![(f\ \mathit{æ}_1 \ldots \mathit{æ}_n)]\!], \hat{\rho}, \hat{\sigma}, \hat{\mu}, \hat{t})}^{\hat{\varsigma}} \leadsto (\mathit{call}, \hat{\rho}'', \hat{\sigma}', \hat{\mu}', \hat{t}'), \text{ where } \underbrace{([\![(\lambda\ (v_1 \ldots v_n)\ \mathit{call})]\!], \hat{\rho}')}_{\widehat{clo}} \in \hat{\mathcal{A}}(f, \hat{\rho}, \hat{\sigma})$$

$$\begin{aligned} \hat{d}_i &\in \hat{\mathcal{A}}(\mathit{æ}_i, \hat{\rho}, \hat{\sigma}) & \hat{\rho}'' &= \hat{\rho}'[v_i \mapsto \hat{a}_i] \\ \hat{t}' &= \widehat{\mathit{tick}}(\widehat{clo}, \hat{\varsigma}) & \hat{\sigma}' &= \hat{\sigma} \sqcup [\hat{a}_i \mapsto \{\hat{d}_i\}] \\ \hat{a}_i &= \widehat{\mathit{alloc}}(v_i, \hat{t}') & \hat{\mu}' &= \hat{\mu} \oplus [\hat{a}_i \mapsto 1] \end{aligned}$$

The operator $\oplus$ is the point-wise lifted natural abstraction of addition over $\widehat{\mathbb{N}}$. In fact, the structure of the set $\widehat{\mathbb{N}}$ can vary depending on the requirements for the analysis' results. The only requirement is that $\widehat{\mathbb{N}}$ should be a lattice. For instance, in a degenerate case, one can turn abstract counting off by setting $\widehat{\mathbb{N}} = \{\infty\}$.

Since abstract counts are modified in tandem with the abstract store, counting and dependent enhancements like strong update can be hidden entirely within and tuned from the monad. We need no refactoring of the state-space or the semantics needed to introduce abstract counting, thanks to the introduction of the class *StoreLike* in Section 6.2. All we need to do is supply a different instance of store, namely, a "counting" one. First, we define a datatype for $\widehat{\mathbb{N}}$, make it a lattice and define abstract addition:

```
data AbsNat = AZero | AOne | AMany
  deriving (Ord, Eq, Show)
(⊕) :: AbsNat → AbsNat → AbsNat
AZero ⊕ n     = n
n     ⊕ AZero = n
n     ⊕ m     = AMany
instance Lattice AbsNat where ···
```

Second, we define a type class for abstract counter, a counting store and make the latter an instance of the former:

```
class StoreLike a s d ⇒ ACounter a s d where
  count :: s → a → AbsNat
type CountingStore a d = a ⇀ (d, AbsNat)
instance (Ord a, Lattice d) ⇒
        ACounter a (CountingStore a d) d where
  count σ a = snd $ σ ! a
```

Because the counter is parameterized over addresses, it too is independent of specific semantics, and in fact can be used with any other semantics.

For a full implementation of *StoreLike a (CountingStore a d) d*, we invite the reader to puzzle through it or reference our public implementation. Once the instance is provided, a *CountingStore* can be directly plugged into the *StorePassing*, so the abstract counting does not require any changes in the analysis logic, implicitly adding the component $\widehat{Count}$ to $\hat{\Sigma}$.

6.4 Controlling abstract garbage collection

Abstract garbage collection [18] is a store-sensitive analysis technique that prunes unreachable structure (exactly as ordinary garbage collection does). The net effect is an often dramatic increase in precision as well as a corresponding drop in analysis time. The technique is defined in terms of touchability of a value by a binding, the adjacency of bindings and reachability of bindings from some entity. In essence, abstract *garbage collection* stands for finding the set of reachable bindings for a particular state and restricting the domain of the store σ to solely these bindings.

The abstract bindings $\hat{\mathcal{T}}(æ, \hat{\rho})$, touched by some abstract closure pair $(æ, \hat{\rho})$ are defined as follows:

$$\begin{aligned}\hat{\mathcal{T}}(æ, \hat{\rho}) &= \{\hat{\rho}(v) : v \in \mathit{free}(æ)\}\\ \hat{\mathcal{T}}\,\{(æ_1, \hat{\rho}_1), \ldots, (æ_n, \hat{\rho}_n)\} &= \hat{\mathcal{T}}(æ_1, \hat{\rho}_1) \cup \ldots \cup \hat{\mathcal{T}}(æ_n, \hat{\rho}_n)\end{aligned}$$

We extend the notion of touching to call sites and abstract states:

$$\begin{aligned}\hat{\mathcal{T}}((f\ æ_1 \ldots æ_n), \hat{\rho}) &= \hat{\mathcal{T}}(f, \hat{\rho}) \cup \hat{\mathcal{T}}(æ_1, \hat{\rho}) \cup \ldots \hat{\mathcal{T}}(æ_n, \hat{\rho})\\ \hat{\mathcal{T}}(call, \hat{\rho}, \hat{\sigma}, \hat{t}) &= \hat{\mathcal{T}}(call, \hat{\rho})\end{aligned}$$

and define the abstract adjacency relation for bindings:

$$\hat{a} \hat{\leadsto}_{\hat{\sigma}} \hat{a}' \iff \hat{a}' \in \hat{\mathcal{T}}(\hat{\sigma}(\hat{a}))$$

Next, the abstract reachable-bindings function

$$\hat{\mathcal{R}} : \hat{\Sigma} \to \mathcal{P}\left(\widehat{Addr}\right)$$

for a given abstract state $\hat{\varsigma}$ computes the set of *reachable* bindings as all bindings we can reach from $\hat{\varsigma}$ with chains of $\hat{\leadsto}_{\hat{\sigma}}$ links:

$$\hat{\mathcal{R}}(\hat{\varsigma}) = \left\{\hat{a}' : \hat{a} \in \hat{\mathcal{T}}(\hat{\varsigma}) \text{ and } \hat{a} \hat{\leadsto}^*_{\hat{\sigma}_{\hat{\varsigma}}} \hat{a}'\right\}.$$

We define the abstract Garbage Collection function, $\hat{\Gamma} : \hat{\Sigma} \to \hat{\Sigma}$ that removes unreachable bindings from the domain of $\hat{\sigma}$:

$$\hat{\Gamma}(call, \hat{\rho}, \hat{\sigma}, \hat{t}) = \quad (call, \hat{\rho}, \hat{\sigma}|\hat{\mathcal{R}}(\hat{\varsigma}), \hat{t}),$$

where the vertical bar '|' operator denotes map restriction, *i.e.*, $f|X$ is the function f defined at most over elements in the set X.

Finally, using the function $\hat{\Gamma}$, we can define the alternate, GC abstract transition rule, $\leadsto_{\hat{\Gamma}}$, so the abstract transition becomes:

$$\frac{\hat{\Gamma}(\hat{\varsigma}) \leadsto \hat{\varsigma}'}{\hat{\varsigma} \leadsto_{\hat{\Gamma}} \hat{\varsigma}'} \qquad (\text{STEP-GC})$$

From the implementor's point of view, an abstract garbage collector modifies the *internal* part of the state, *i.e.*, an abstract store, by removing unreachable addresses. Therefore, it is natural to define abstract garbage collection abstractly as an operation in the analysis monad:

```
class Monad m ⇒ GarbageCollector m a where
  gc :: a → m ()
  gc _ = return ()   -- default implementation
```

The function *gc* takes a partial state as a parameter and returns a monad operation. We also supply a *default* implementation of the function *gc* as a no-op.

The structure of the class *StoreLike* makes it easy to implement a garbage collector thanks to the function *filterStore* (Section 6.2). Weaving the GC into the semantics requires only little change in the fixed point computation for *StorePassing*:

```
applyStep step =
  joinWith (λ((ς, t), s) →
   ... runStateT (do {ς' ← step ς; gc ς'; return ς'}) t...)
```

6.5 Controlling store-cloning

By default, the abstracted abstract machine approach to static analysis yields a heap-(/store-)cloning analysis: every state contains a store. Ordinarily, store-cloning should be reserved for situations in which the extra precision benefit the target applications.

However, for an analysis implemented this way it can take time exponential in the size of the input program when computing the reachable states of the abstracted machine [19]. The standard technique to reduce the complexity is to employ widening in the form of Shivers' single-threaded store [22]. To use a single-threaded store, we have to reconsider the abstract evaluation function itself. Instead of seeing it as a function that returns the set of reachable states, it is a function that returns a pair, consisting of a set of partial states and a single globally approximating store.

Although this change requires a significant reworking in the definition of the semantics, it is quite easy to implement in our framework, since the store is *not* a component of the program states, but rather an element supplied by an analysis monad. One can also notice that the new semantics can be captured by establishing the following Galois connection:

$$\langle \mathcal{P}(\widehat{\Sigma_t} \times \widehat{Store}), \subseteq\rangle \underset{\alpha}{\overset{\gamma}{\leftrightarrows}} \langle \mathcal{P}(\widehat{\Sigma_t}) \times \widehat{Store}, \sqsubseteq\rangle, \qquad (3)$$

where $\widehat{\Sigma_t} = \mathsf{Call} \times \widehat{Env} \times \widehat{Time}$. Bounding the space of addresses (Section 6.1) implies finiteness of both lattices involved in the Galois connection (3), which means that both α and γ are computable. It is straightforward to express them in Haskell:

```
alpha :: (Lattice s, Ord a, Ord g) ⇒
         P ((PΣ a, g), s) → (P (PΣ a, g), s)
alpha = joinWith (λ((p, g), σ) → (singleton (p, g), σ))
gamma :: (Ord a, Ord g, Ord s) ⇒
         (P (PΣ a, g), s) → P ((PΣ a, g), s)
gamma (states, σ) = Set.map (λ(p, g) → ((p, g), σ)) states
```

In words, *alpha* combines together all per-state store components (given the stores form a lattice, hence *Lattice s*). Conversely, *gamma* spreads the store σ among all provided states.

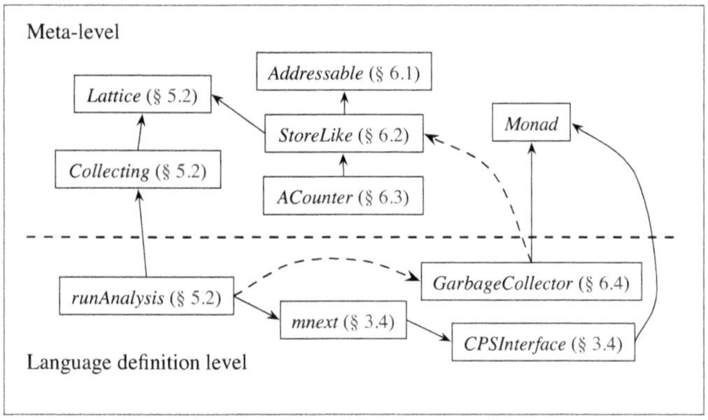

Figure 3: Overview of the framework concepts

The easiest way to construct a single-store analysis is to redefine the instance of *Collecting*, taking $F_c = applyStep'\ step$:[6]

$$\begin{array}{l}\textbf{instance}\ (Ord\ g, Ord\ a, Ord\ s, Lattice\ s, HasInitial\ g) \Rightarrow \\ \quad Collecting\ (StorePassing\ s\ g) \\ \qquad\qquad (P\Sigma\ a) \\ \qquad\qquad (\mathcal{P}\ (P\Sigma\ a, g), s)\ \textbf{where} \\ \quad inject\ a \qquad\quad = (singleton\ (a, initial), \bot) \\ \quad applyStep\ step = alpha \circ (applyStep'\ step) \circ gamma\end{array}$$

7. Pulling It All Together

A high-level overview of the described framework is given in Figure 3. The *concepts* in the upper half are defined on the *meta-level*, *i.e.*, *can be* implemented in a way so they might be reused by different languages and analyses. The lower half describes language-dependent concepts, which rely, in particular, on the fixed syntax, semantics and the structure of values. Solid arrows denote type dependencies between *instances* of the components, and dashed arrows are for the optional logical dependencies, which are, however, not strictly enforced by types. Curiously, the diagram confirms our point that store logic and abstract counting strategy are orthogonal to the analysis implementation (Sections 6.2 and 6.3).

As opposite to the abstract *concepts*, it is much harder to provide a straightforward hierarchy of actual concept *implementations* with strict "level" distinctions. For instance, one can encode the store and monad logic directly into the semantic interface definition, moving it, therefore to the bottom part of the diagram. Alternatively, one can implement the store and the monad independently from the encoding of the semantic interface, just as we did in Section 3, getting as close as possible to the conceptual decomposition. This approach pays off when composing the resulting analysis, as we demonstrate in the following section.

8. Further Examples: k-CFA Family

In this section, we expand our original examples from Section 3 to a family of k-CFA-based abstract interpreters, following the recipe described in Sections 5 and 6. We omit a few tedious implementation details for the sake of brevity; the full development and test programs can be found in the accompanying code repository:

`http://github.com/ilyasergey/monadic-cfa`

[6] We use $applyStep'$ to refer to the definition of $applyStep$ for a domain with per-state store. It is slightly different from the actual implementation in Haskell, as one is required to wrap the "per-state store"-version of $StorePassing$ into a separate datatype in order to make it possible for a type checker to distinguish between two versions of $applyStep$. We elaborate more on this in Section 8.

8.1 A simple abstract interpreter for k-CFA

First, we fix the k-degree of the analysis by instantiating the class $KCFA$ from Section 6.1 for $k = 1$:

$$\begin{array}{l}\textbf{instance}\ KCFA\ KTime\ \textbf{where} \\ \quad getK = const\ 1\end{array}$$

Second, we define the analysis function $analyseKCFA$ by employing the $runAnalysis$ function from Section 5.2:

$$\begin{array}{l}analyseKCFA :: CExp \rightarrow \\ \quad \mathcal{P}\ ((P\Sigma\ KAddr, KTime), Store\ KAddr) \\ analyseKCFA = runAnalysis\end{array}$$

The refined type of $analyseKCFA$ is of particular interest. After flattening the tuples, one can see that it reflects the abstract domain of the analysis: abstract states coupled with timestamps and abstract stores.

8.2 An abstract interpreter with a shared store

As a next step, we apply the widening strategy via a shared store, as described in Section 6.5. We directly use the definitions of $alpha$ and $gamma$ and redefine the instance of $Collecting$ by providing a new implementation of the $applyStep$ function (Section 5.2). In order to overcome Haskell's conventions for type resolution in the case of the function $applyStep$, we might need to define a *wrapper* record type for the analysis result.

$$\begin{array}{l}\textbf{newtype}\ Wrap\ a\ g\ s = \\ \quad Wrap\ \{unWrap :: \mathcal{P}\ ((P\Sigma\ a, g), s)\}\ \textbf{deriving}\ Lattice\end{array}$$

The definition of $applyStep$ for store-sharing widening looks as follows:

$$\begin{array}{l}applyStep\ step = \\ \quad alpha \circ unWrap \circ applyStep\ step \circ Wrap \circ gamma\end{array}$$

Note, the implementation is *not* recursive, but the inner call to $applyStep$ operates with a different domain. The definition of the analysis function has the same implementation, thanks to the type class-based polymorphism [25], however, its return type is conceptually different, as it accounts for a set of states, coupled with a *single* store:

$$\begin{array}{l}analyseShared :: CExp \rightarrow \\ \quad (\mathcal{P}\ (P\Sigma\ KAddr, KTime), Store\ KAddr) \\ analyseShared = runAnalysis\end{array}$$

8.3 An abstract interpreter with a counting store

As the analysis is parametrized with the store explicitly, its instrumentation with a counting machinery is trivial: we just replace the second component of the result of the single-store-passing analysis with a specialized counting store (Section 6.3).

$$\begin{array}{l}\textbf{type}\ KCFACountingStore = \\ \quad CountingStore\ KAddr\ (\mathcal{P}\ (Val\ KAddr)) \\ analyseWithCount :: CExp \rightarrow \\ \quad (\mathcal{P}\ (P\Sigma\ KAddr, KTime), KCFACountingStore) \\ analyseWithCount = runAnalysis\end{array}$$

9. Related Work and Conclusion

We have illustrated a systematic method for transforming a *concrete* semantics into a monadically-parameterized machine, such that the monad determines the classical properties of an *abstract* analysis. Our work is situated firmly in the abstract interpretation tradition established by Cousot and Cousot [4, 5].

Following a series of complex power-domain constructions, Hudak and Young [10] devised simpler set-based collecting interpretations for both first-order and higher-order functional languages. They furthermore outline how to modify their approach to express *relational* properties. This requires generalizing their collecting interpretation to sets of value-environment pairs, remniscent of our sets-of-states starting point. Like Hudak and Young, our framework can thereby describe relational properties.

The way we factor the concrete semantics is very much in the spirit of Nielson's two-level meta-language [20]. Nielson proposes an abstract interpretation framework based on the idea of decomposing a *denotational* language definition into two parts: a *core semantics*, containing semantic rules and their types, but leaving some function symbols and domain names uninterpreted, and an *interpretation* that fills out the missing definition of function symbol and domain names. thereby allowing alternate non-standard interpretations in addition to the "standard" semantics defining the meaning of programs.

Such a decomposition is formulated in terms of a *two-level* metalanguage, where some types are considered to be 'dynamically'-interpreted,[7] and 'dynamic' functions symbols are represented by combinators, closed over variables of dynamically-interpreted types. This makes it possible to define the "meaning" of dynamic types and combinators in different ways to express a lazy standard semantics, detection of signs, strictness, and liveness on top of the same semantics interface. Also, Nielson further illustrates that both forward and backward analyses, independent-attribute and relational methods can be formulated in terms of the same *core* semantics given different *interpretations*. In contrast, our work focuses on abstractions of the *operational* small-step collecting semantics, since it delivers data for most of the interesting analyses in the setting of a higher-order language. In a sense, the functions from the class *CPSInterface*, such as *fun*, *arg* and others, play an analogous role to Nielson's dynamic function symbols, and type parameters such as a, s or g are the dynamic types.

Our framework gains from giving function symbols monadic types: unlike Nielson's framework, where all information about properties of interest is captured by the treatment of values of specific types, our implementation also allows us to track *temporal* properties of execution and tweak interpretation properties depending on the context of execution. Moreover, the sharing of stores as a widening strategy, is trivial to implement in our decomposition. The *well-formedness* of an interpretation in our framework is ensured by the type system of the host language (Haskell, in our case).

The core semantics we present using monads is of a more denotational flavour, as it is expressed by the *CPSInterface* type class. Recent work by Filinski, however, demonstrates that a complementary, operational representation, is possible using *reflection* and *reification* [8]. This correspondence could be used to translate the monad-based definitions of the semantics functions into specialized operational rules, which were usually hand-crafted [23].

Our publicly available implementation indicates the robustness of the approach, allowing re-use of multiple semantic aspects between different analyses and semantic formalisms.

Acknowledgements We wish to thank Olivier Danvy for discussions on Nielson's work as well as for his hospitality during Sergey and Might's visit to Aarhus University in December 2011, where the idea of the work was discussed for the first time. We are grateful to the PLDI 2013 reviewers for their excellent feedback. The work of Ilya Sergey has been partially supported by EU Marie Curie CO-FUND Action 291803 "Amarout-II Europe". This research is partially funded by the Research Foundation - Flanders (FWO), and by the Research Fund KU Leuven. Dominique Devriese holds a Ph.D. fellowship of the Research Foundation - Flanders (FWO). Different parts of Might's effort on this work were partially supported by the DARPA programs APAC and CRASH.

[7] *I.e.*, those, which can be given a specific interpretation as a domain or a lattice.

References

[1] M. S. Ager, O. Danvy, and J. Midtgaard. A functional correspondence between monadic evaluators and abstract machines for languages with computational effects. *Theor. Comput. Sci.*, 342(1):149–172, 2005.

[2] M. Biernacka and O. Danvy. A syntactic correspondence between context-sensitive calculi and abstract machines. *Theor. Comput. Sci.*, 375(1-3):76–108, 2007.

[3] M. M. T. Chakravarty, G. Keller, S. L. P. Jones, and S. Marlow. Associated types with class. In *POPL*, 2005.

[4] P. Cousot and R. Cousot. Abstract interpretation: a unified lattice model for static analysis of programs by construction or approximation of fixpoints. In *POPL*, 1977.

[5] P. Cousot and R. Cousot. Systematic design of program analysis frameworks. In *POPL*, 1979.

[6] O. Danvy. A new one-pass transformation into monadic normal form. In *CC*, volume 2622 of *LNCS*, 2003.

[7] O. Danvy. Defunctionalized interpreters for programming languages. In *ICFP*, 2008.

[8] A. Filinski. Monads in action. In *POPL*, 2010.

[9] C. Flanagan, A. Sabry, B. F. Duba, and M. Felleisen. The essence of compiling with continuations. In *PLDI*, 1993.

[10] P. Hudak and J. Young. Collecting interpretations of expressions. *ACM Trans. Prog. Lang. Syst.*, 13(2):269–290, 1991.

[11] M. P. Jones. Type Classes with Functional Dependencies. In *ESOP*, volume 1782 of *LNCS*, 2000.

[12] A. Lakhotia, D. R. Boccardo, A. Singh, and A. Manacero, Jr. Context-sensitive analysis of obfuscated x86 executables. In *PEPM*, 2010.

[13] S. Liang, P. Hudak, and M. Jones. Monad transformers and modular interpreters. In *POPL*, 1995.

[14] M. Might. *Environment analysis of higher-order languages*. PhD thesis, Georgia Institute of Technology, 2007.

[15] M. Might. Abstract interpreters for free. In *SAS*, volume 6337 of *LNCS*, 2010.

[16] M. Might. Shape analysis in the absence of pointers and structure. In *VMCAI*, volume 5944 of *LNCS*, 2010.

[17] M. Might and P. Manolios. A posteriori soundness for non-deterministic abstract interpretations. In *VMCAI*, volume 5944 of *LNCS*, 2009.

[18] M. Might and O. Shivers. Improving flow analyses via ΓCFA: abstract garbage collection and counting. In *ICFP*, 2006.

[19] M. Might, Y. Smaragdakis, and D. Van Horn. Resolving and exploiting the k-CFA paradox: illuminating functional vs. object-oriented program analysis. In *PLDI*, 2010.

[20] F. Nielson. Two-level semantics and abstract interpretation. *Theor. Comput. Sci.*, 69(2):117–242, 1989.

[21] T. Schrijvers and B. C. Oliveira. Monads, zippers and views: virtualizing the monad stack. In *ICFP*, 2011.

[22] O. G. Shivers. *Control-flow analysis of higher-order languages or taming lambda*. PhD thesis, Carnegie Mellon University, 1991.

[23] D. Van Horn and M. Might. Abstracting abstract machines. In *ICFP*, 2010.

[24] D. Van Horn and M. Might. Abstracting abstract machines: a systematic approach to higher-order program analysis. *Commun. ACM*, 54(9):101–109, 2011.

[25] P. Wadler and S. Blott. How to make ad-hoc polymorphism less ad-hoc. In *POPL*, 1989.

Asynchronous Functional Reactive Programming for GUIs

Evan Czaplicki
Harvard University
evan.czaplicki@post.harvard.edu

Stephen Chong
Harvard University
chong@seas.harvard.edu

Abstract

Graphical user interfaces (GUIs) mediate many of our interactions with computers. Functional Reactive Programming (FRP) is a promising approach to GUI design, providing high-level, declarative, compositional abstractions to describe user interactions and time-dependent computations. We present Elm, a practical FRP language focused on easy creation of responsive GUIs. Elm has two major features: simple declarative support for *Asynchronous FRP*; and purely functional graphical layout.

Asynchronous FRP allows the programmer to specify when the global ordering of event processing can be violated, and thus enables efficient concurrent execution of FRP programs; long-running computation can be executed asynchronously and not adversely affect the responsiveness of the user interface.

Layout in Elm is achieved using a purely functional declarative framework that makes it simple to create and combine text, images, and video into rich multimedia displays.

Together, Elm's two major features simplify the complicated task of creating responsive and usable GUIs.

Categories and Subject Descriptors D.3.2 [*Language Classifications*]: Data-flow languages; Applicative (functional) languages

General Terms Languages, Design

Keywords Functional Reactive Programming, Graphical User Interfaces

1. Introduction

Elm is a functional reactive programming language that aims to simplify the creation of responsive graphical user interfaces (GUIs), and specifically targets GUIs for web applications. Functional reactive programming (FRP) applies pure functional programming paradigms to time-varying values, known as *signals*. FRP is a highly promising approach for implementing GUIs, where time-varying values can represent input and output (including user interaction, server requests and responses), and other information about the execution environment. By enforcing a purely functional programming style, programmers can explicitly model complex time-dependent relationships in a high-level declarative way.

However, previous FRP languages and implementations have suffered from at least two kinds of inefficiencies: *unnecessary recomputation* and *global delays*.

PLDI'13, June 16–19, 2013, Seattle, WA, USA.

Semantics of most FRP languages assume that signals change continuously. Thus, their implementations sample input signals as quickly as possible, and continually recompute the program with the latest values for the signals. In practice, however, many signals change discretely and infrequently, and so constant sampling leads to unnecessary recomputation. By contrast, Elm assumes that all signals are discrete, and uses this assumption to detect when a signal is unchanged, and in that case, avoid unnecessary recomputation.

In Elm, signals change only when a discrete *event* occurs. An event occurs when a program input (such as the mouse position) changes. Events require recomputation of the program, as the result of the program may have changed. Previous FRP systems require that events are processed synchronously: one at a time in the exact order of occurrence. In general, synchronization is required to allow the programmer to reason about the behavior of the FRP system, and ensure correct functionality.

However, processing an event may take significant time, resulting in delays to the entire FRP system. Pipelining event processing can help to reduce latency, but because the global order of events must be respected, an event cannot finish processing until all previous events have finished. In GUIs, this is unacceptable behavior: the user interface should remain responsive, even if a previous user action triggered a long-running computation.

Elm provides programmers with a simple abstraction to specify when computation can occur asynchronously. Combined with pipelined execution of event processing, this allows long-running computation to execute concurrently with other event processing, avoids global delays, and allows GUIs to remain responsive.

The ability to specify asynchronous computation within an FRP paradigm is the key novelty of Elm. We formalize this language feature by presenting the semantics of a core Asynchronous FRP calculus. However, Elm is also a practical and expressive programming language, which we demonstrate through the implementation of an Elm compiler, and the use of the resulting compiler to develop rich, responsive GUIs that perform non-trivial computation. The Elm compiler produces JavaScript code that can be immediately and easily deployed in web applications. Elm is publicly available.[1]

Like previous work on efficient FRP (e.g., [25, 30, 31]), Elm restricts use of signals to enable efficient implementation. Elm is strictly more expressive than these previous approaches, since (1) discrete signals generalize continuous signals [31], (2) we embed a discrete version of Arrowized FRP [25] in Elm, and (3) we additionally allow the programmer to specify when signal updates should be computed asynchronously.

The rest of the paper is structured as follows. In Section 2 we describe key features of Elm through several simple Elm programs. In Section 3 we present a formalization of the core language of Elm, including semantics and a type system. The full Elm language

[1] Available at http://elm-lang.org/.

Figure 1. Purely functional graphics: basic layout

extends the core language with libraries and syntactic sugar to simplify the creation of expressive GUIs. In Section 4 we describe some of these libraries (including the embedding of discrete Arrowized FRP [25]). Elm has a fully functional compiler that compiles Elm programs to JavaScript and HTML, suitable for immediate inclusion in web applications. We describe the compiler in Section 5. We discuss related work in Section 6 and conclude in Section 7.

2. Elm through Examples

We present key features of Elm through several simple Elm programs. The first example highlights Elm's purely functional graphical layout. The second example demonstrates how Elm's graphics primitives use FRP to easily produce rich interactive GUIs. The third example shows Elm's `async` construct, which allows programmers to specify that potentially long-running computation should execute asynchronously, and thus ensures that the user interface remains responsive.

Example 1 The following Elm program lays out three graphical elements vertically, as shown in Figure 1.

```
content = flow down [ plainText "Welcome to Elm!"
                    , image 150 50 "flower.jpg"
                    , asText (reverse [1..9]) ]

main = container 180 100 middle content
```

Variable `main` is distinguished in Elm: the value of this variable will be displayed on the screen when the program is executed. In the program above, `main` is defined to be a 180 by 100 container with content defined by variable `content`. The content is placed in the middle of the container. (Positioning elements is notoriously difficult in HTML; Elm provides a simple abstraction, allowing the position of content within a container to be specified as `topLeft`, `midTop`, `topRight`, `midLeft`, `middle`, and so on.)

Variable `content` has type `Element`, indicating that it is a graphical element that can be displayed, and/or composed with other graphical elements. The value of `content` at runtime is a composite element, comprising three elements stacked vertically. The three elements are the text `"Welcome to Elm!"`, a 150 by 50 image, and the text representation of a list containing numbers from 9 down to 1, which are combined together using function `flow : Direction -> [Element] -> Element` (i.e., `flow` is a function that takes a value of type `Direction`, a list of `Elements`, and produces an `Element`).

Values of type `Element` occupy a rectangular area of the screen when displayed, making `Elements` easy to compose. Elm provides primitives and library functions to create more complex `Element` values, and non-rectangular graphical elements. Elm and its libraries provide a simple declarative syntax and semantics, making layout easy to reason about.

Example 2 This example displays the position of the mouse pointer, as seen in Figure 2. Although extremely simple to describe, this is often head-scratchingly difficult to implement in today's GUI frameworks, since the content is dynamically updated. In Elm, however, it is a one liner:

Figure 2. A basic FRP program: tracking mouse movement

```
main = lift asText Mouse.position
```

This code relies on *signals*, which are the key abstraction of FRP. A signal is a value that changes over time. In Elm, a signal that represents a value of type τ changing over time has type `Signal` τ. For example, a graphical element that changes over time, such as an animation, is a `Signal Element`. Indeed, variable `main` typically has type `Signal Element`, since what to display on the screen changes over time.[2]

In the code above, the position of the mouse is represented as a signal of a pair of integers, indicating the coordinates of the mouse.

```
Mouse.position : Signal (Int,Int)
```

Function `lift : (a -> b) -> Signal a -> Signal b` takes a function from values of type `a` to values of type `b`, and a signal of values of type `a`, and applies the function to each value, resulting in a signal of type `b`. In the example above, function `asText : a -> Element` (which converts Elm values into a textual representation) is applied to every value of the signal `Mouse.position`, thus converting a signal of coordinates into a signal of `Elements`. As the position of the mouse changes, so does the `Element` that is being displayed. This is shown in Figure 2.

In Elm, all signals are discrete. That means that instead of the system needing to frequently sample a continuously changing value (i.e., the system *pulls* values from the external environment), the system waits to be notified when the value has changed (i.e., values are *pushed* to the system only when they change). Elm is a push-based system [12], meaning that computation is performed only when values change. This reduces needless recomputation. In the example above, function `asText` is only applied to a mouse coordinate when the mouse position changes.

Example 3 This example highlights Elm's ability to perform asynchronous computation over signals. It uses words entered by the user to find and fetch an image from a web service (such as Flickr), which may take significant time. The program simultaneously displays the current position of the mouse, with the position being updated in a timely manner, regardless of how long image fetching takes.

```
(inputField, tags) = Input.text "Enter a tag"

getImage tags =
  lift (fittedImage 300 200)
       (syncGet (lift requestTag tags))

scene input pos img =
  flow down [ input, asText pos, img ]

main = lift3 scene inputField
                   Mouse.position
                   (async (getImage tags))
```

[2] Variable `main` is also allowed to have type `Element`, as in Example 1.

Code `Input.text "Enter a tag"` creates a text input field, and returns a pair `(inputField, tags)`, where `inputField` is a signal of graphical elements for the input field, and `tags` is a signal of strings. Each time the text in the input field changes (due to the user typing), both signals produces a new value: the updated element and the current text in the input field.

Function `getImage` takes a signal of strings, and returns a signal of images. For each string that the user enters, this function requests from the server a URL of an image with tags (i.e., keywords) that match the string. Function `requestTag` takes a string, and constructs an appropriate HTTP request to the server. (We elide the definition of `requestTag`, which simply performs string concatenation.) Expression `lift requestTag tags` is thus a signal of HTTP requests. Built-in function `syncGet` issues the requests, and evaluates to a signal of image URLs (actually, a signal of JSON objects returned by the server requests; the JSON objects contain image URLs). Function `fittedImage` (definition elided) takes dimensions and an image URL and constructs an image `Element`.

Function `scene` takes as its arguments `input` (an `Element`), `pos` (an arbitrary value) and `img` (an `Element`), and composes them vertically.

Value `main` puts the pieces together, applying function `scene` to three signals: the signal of elements representing the text field in which the user types, the mouse position (`Mouse.position`), and the signal of images derived from the user's input (`getImage tags`). Primitive function `lift3` is similar to function `lift` described above, but takes a function `a -> b -> c -> d`, a signal of values of type `a`, a signal of values of type `b`, and a signal of values of type `c`, and applies the function to the current values of the three signals, each time any of the three signals produces a new value.

Keyword `async` indicates that the `getImage` computation should run asynchronously. Without the `async` keyword, the program must respect the global ordering of events: when the `tags` signal produces a new string, processing of new `Mouse.position` values must wait until an image is fetched from the server. The result would be an unresponsive GUI that hangs (i.e., does not display the current mouse position) from when the user types in the input field until an image is fetched. By contrast, with the `async` keyword, the program does not have to respect the order of values generated by `getImage tags` with respect to values generated by `Mouse.position`. The GUI remains responsive, regardless of how long it takes to fetch an image from the web service.

The `async` construct can be applied to any signal, and provides a simple, composable way for the programmer to specify when computation over a signal may occur asynchronously, and thus to ensure that long-running computation does not cause the GUI to become unresponsive.

The behavior of this example Elm program is difficult to implement in most practical programming frameworks. For example, implementation with JavaScript+AJAX requires nested call-backs. Also, such an example is impossible to implement in current FRP languages as no previous work permits explicit asynchrony and concurrent execution.

3. Core Language

The full Elm language contains libraries and syntactic sugar that simplify the creation of rich and responsive GUIs. In this section, we present a simple core language—FElm, for "Featherweight Elm"—that presents the semantics of Elm's key abstractions.

FElm combines a simply-typed functional language with a small set of reactive primitives. Programmers have direct access to signals, which can be transformed and combined with the full power of a functional language. A type system restricts the use of reactive primitives to ensure that the program can be executed efficiently. FElm uses a two-stage semantics. In the first stage, functional constructs are evaluated, and signals are left uninterpreted. In the second stage, signals are evaluated: as the external environment generates new values for input signals, the new values are processed as appropriate.

Numbers	$n \in \mathbb{Z}$
Variables	$x \in \mathsf{Var}$
Input signals	$i \in \mathsf{Input}$
Expressions	$e ::= () \mid n \mid x \mid \lambda x\!:\!\eta.\ e \mid e_1\ e_2 \mid e_1 \oplus e_2$
	$\mid \mathtt{if}\ e_1\ e_2\ e_3 \mid \mathtt{let}\ x = e_1\ \mathtt{in}\ e_2 \mid i$
	$\mid \mathtt{lift}_n\ e\ e_1\ ...\ e_n \mid \mathtt{foldp}\ e_1\ e_2\ e_3$
	$\mid \mathtt{async}\ e$
Simple types	$\tau ::= \mathsf{unit} \mid \mathsf{int} \mid \tau \to \tau'$
Signal types	$\sigma ::= \mathsf{signal}\ \tau \mid \tau \to \sigma \mid \sigma \to \sigma'$
Types	$\eta ::= \tau \mid \sigma$

Figure 3. Syntax of FElm

3.1 Syntax

The syntax of FElm is presented in Figure 3. Expressions include the unit value (), integers n, variables x, functions $\lambda x : \eta.\ e$, applications $e_1\ e_2$, let expressions $\mathtt{let}\ x = e_1\ \mathtt{in}\ e_2$, and conditional expressions $\mathtt{if}\ e_1\ e_2\ e_3$ which are all standard constructs for functional languages. (Conditional expression $\mathtt{if}\ e_1\ e_2\ e_3$ evaluates to e_2 if e_1 evaluates to a non-zero value, e_3 otherwise.) Metavariable $\oplus$ ranges over total binary operations on integers.

We assume a set of identifiers Input that denote input signals from the external environment, and use i to range over these identifiers. Signals can be thought of as streams of values. For example, an input signal representing the width of a window can be thought of as a stream of integer values such that every time the window width changes, a new value for the signal is generated. An input signal representing whether the left mouse button is currently pressed down may be represented as a stream of boolean values. Input signals may also include special signals, for example, to generate a new unit value at fixed time intervals, creating a timer.

An *event* occurs when an input signal generates a new value. Events may trigger computation. In FElm, every signal always has a "current" value: it is the most recent value generated by the signal, or, for an input signal that has not yet generated a new value, it is an appropriate default value associated with that input signal. Thus, every input signal is required to have a default value, which then induces default values for other signals.

The remaining expressions ($\mathtt{lift}_n\ e\ e_1\ ...\ e_n$, $\mathtt{foldp}\ e_1\ e_2\ e_3$, and $\mathtt{async}\ e$) are primitives for manipulating signals, and are described in more detail below.

Transforming and combining signals For each natural number $n \geq 0$, we have primitive $\mathtt{lift}_n\ e\ e_1\ ...\ e_n$ which allows a function e to transform and combine signals $e_1 \ldots e_n$.

Intuitively, if e is a function of type $\tau_1 \to \tau_2 \to \cdots \to \tau_n \to \tau$, and expressions e_i are of type $\mathsf{signal}\ \tau_i$ respectively, then $\mathtt{lift}_n\ e\ e_1\ ...\ e_n$ applies function e to the values from signals $e_1 \ldots e_n$, and has type $\mathsf{signal}\ \tau$ (i.e., it is a signal that produces values of type τ). For example,

$$\mathtt{lift}_1\ (\lambda \mathtt{x}\!:\!\mathsf{int}.\ \mathtt{x}\!+\!\mathtt{x})\ \mathtt{Window.width}$$

is a signal of integers obtained by doubling the values from input signal `Window.width`.

Signals can also be combined. For example, expression

```
lift₂ (λy:int. λz:int. y ÷ z) Mouse.x Window.width
```

takes two input signals of integers (`Mouse.x` and `Window.width`), and produces a signal of integers by combining values from the two input signals. It computes the relative position of the mouse's x-coordinate with respect to the window width. Note that the relative position is computed each time an event occurs for *either* input signal. Moreover, events are globally ordered, and signal computation is synchronous in that it respects the global order of events: the sequence of relative positions will reflect the order of events on `Mouse.x` and `Window.width`.

Past-dependent transformation The $\texttt{lift}_n$ primitives operate only on the current values of signals. By contrast, the `foldp` primitive can compute on both the current and previous values of a signal. Primitive `foldp` performs a fold on a signal from the past, similar to the way in which the standard function `foldl` performs a fold on lists from the left of the list. The type of `foldp` is

$$(\tau \to \tau' \to \tau') \to \tau' \to \mathsf{signal}\ \tau \to \mathsf{signal}\ \tau'$$

for any τ and τ'. Consider $\texttt{foldp}\ e_1\ e_2\ e_3$. Here, e_1 is a function of type $\tau \to \tau' \to \tau'$, e_2 is a value of type τ' and e_3 is a signal that produces values of type τ. Type τ' is the type of the accumulator, and e_2 is the initial value of the accumulator. As values are produced by signal e_3, function e_1 is applied to the new value and the current accumulator, to produce a new accumulator value. Expression $\texttt{foldp}\ e_1\ e_2\ e_3$ evaluates to the signal of accumulator values.

For example, suppose that `Keyboard.lastPressed` is an input signal that indicates the latest key that has been pressed. Then the following signal counts the number of key presses. (We assume that which key is pressed is encoded as an integer.)

```
foldp (λk:int. λc:int. c+1) 0 Keyboard.lastPressed
```

Asynchronous composition The `async` primitive allows a programmer to specify when certain computations on signals can be computed asynchronously with respect to the rest of the program. This annotation allows the programmer to specify when it is permissible to ignore the global ordering of events. The use and benefit of this construct is described in more detail, including a thorough example, in Section 3.3.2.

3.2 Type System

FElm's type system ensures that FElm programs cannot produce signals of signals. There are two kinds of types: *simple types* τ and *signal types* σ. Type syntax is presented in Figure 3. Simple types include base types (unit for the unit value and int for integers) and functions from simple types to simple types ($\tau \to \tau'$). Signal types σ include type $\mathsf{signal}\ \tau$ (for signals that produce values of type τ), and functions that produce signal types ($\tau \to \sigma$ and $\sigma \to \sigma'$).

The type system rules out programs that use signals of signals, for the following reason. Intuitively, if we have signals of signals, then after a program has executed for, say 10 minutes, we might create a signal that (through the use of `foldp`) depends on the history of an input signal, say `Window.width`. To compute the current value of this signal, should we use the entire history of `Window.width`? But that would require saving all history of `Window.width` from the beginning of execution, even though we do not know whether the history will be needed later. Alternatively, we could compute the current value of the signal just using the current and new values of `Window.width` (i.e., ignoring the history). But this would allow the possibility of having two identically defined signals that have different values, based on when they were created. We avoid these issues by ruling out signals of signals. This

$$\textsc{T-Unit}\ \frac{}{\Gamma \vdash () : \mathsf{unit}} \qquad \textsc{T-Number}\ \frac{}{\Gamma \vdash n : \mathsf{int}} \qquad \textsc{T-Var}\ \frac{\Gamma(x) = \eta}{\Gamma \vdash x : \eta} \qquad \textsc{T-Input}\ \frac{\Gamma(i) = \mathsf{signal}\ \tau}{\Gamma \vdash i : \mathsf{signal}\ \tau}$$

$$\textsc{T-Lam}\ \frac{\Gamma, x{:}\eta \vdash e : \eta'}{\Gamma \vdash \lambda x{:}\eta.\ e : \eta \to \eta'} \qquad \textsc{T-Async}\ \frac{\Gamma \vdash e : \mathsf{signal}\ \tau}{\Gamma \vdash \texttt{async}\ e : \mathsf{signal}\ \tau}$$

$$\textsc{T-Op}\ \frac{\Gamma \vdash e_1 : \mathsf{int} \quad \Gamma \vdash e_2 : \mathsf{int}}{\Gamma \vdash e_1 \oplus e_2 : \mathsf{int}} \qquad \textsc{T-App}\ \frac{\Gamma \vdash e_1 : \eta \to \eta' \quad \Gamma \vdash e_2 : \eta}{\Gamma \vdash e_1\ e_2 : \eta'}$$

$$\textsc{T-Cond}\ \frac{\Gamma \vdash e_1 : \mathsf{int} \quad \Gamma \vdash e_2 : \eta \quad \Gamma \vdash e_3 : \eta}{\Gamma \vdash \texttt{if}\ e_1\ e_2\ e_3 : \eta} \qquad \textsc{T-Let}\ \frac{\Gamma \vdash e_1 : \eta \quad \Gamma, x : \eta \vdash e_2 : \eta'}{\Gamma \vdash \texttt{let}\ x = e_1\ \texttt{in}\ e_2 : \eta'}$$

$$\textsc{T-Lift}\ \frac{\Gamma \vdash e : \tau_1 \to \cdots \to \tau_n \to \tau \quad \Gamma \vdash e_i : \mathsf{signal}\ \tau_i\ \ \forall i \in 1..n}{\Gamma \vdash \texttt{lift}_n\ e\ e_1\ \ldots\ e_n : \mathsf{signal}\ \tau}$$

$$\textsc{T-Fold}\ \frac{\Gamma \vdash e_f : \tau \to \tau' \to \tau' \quad \Gamma \vdash e_b : \tau' \quad \Gamma \vdash e_s : \mathsf{signal}\ \tau}{\Gamma \vdash \texttt{foldp}\ e_f\ e_b\ e_s : \mathsf{signal}\ \tau'}$$

Figure 4. Inference rules for typing judgment $\Gamma \vdash e : \eta$

does not overly restrict the expressiveness of the language, which we discuss further in Section 4.

The typing judgment for FElm has the form $\Gamma \vdash e : \eta$, indicating that expression e has type η under type context Γ, which maps variables and input signal identifiers to types. Figure 4 presents inference rules for this judgment. The rules for the primitive operators that manipulate signals are as described above, and the remaining inference rules are mostly standard. Note that the typing rule for conditional expressions $\texttt{if}\ e_1\ e_2\ e_3$ requires that the test expression e_1 has type int, and in particular, cannot be a signal. A program e is *well typed* if $\Gamma_{input} \vdash e : \eta$ holds for a type environment Γ_{input} that maps every input $i \in \mathsf{Input}$ to a signal type.

3.3 Semantics

FElm programs are evaluated in two stages. In the first stage, all and only functional constructs are evaluated, resulting in a term in an intermediate language that clearly shows how signals are connected together. The intermediate language is similar to the source language of Real-Time FRP [30] and Event-Driven FRP [31]. In the second stage, signals are evaluated: new values arriving on input signals trigger computation in a push-based manner.

3.3.1 Functional Evaluation

We define an intermediate language according to the grammar in Figure 5. The intermediate language separates values of simple types (unit, numbers, and functions over simple types), and signal terms (which will be the basis for the evaluation of signals).

A small step operational semantics for evaluation of FElm programs to the intermediate language is given in Figure 6. A FElm program e will evaluate to a final term, which is either a simple value v, or a signal term s. The inference rules use evaluation contexts E to implement a left-to-right call-by-value semantics. Rule Application converts function applications to let expres-

$$\begin{array}{rl} \text{Values} & v ::= () \mid n \mid \lambda x\!:\!\tau.\ e \\ \text{Signal terms} & s ::= x \mid \texttt{let}\ x = s\ \texttt{in}\ u \mid i \mid \texttt{lift}_n\ v\ s_1\ \dots\ s_n \\ & \quad \mid \texttt{foldp}\ v_1\ v_2\ s \mid \texttt{async}\ s \\ \text{Final terms} & u ::= v \mid s \end{array}$$

Figure 5. Syntax of intermediate language

$$\begin{array}{l} E ::= [\cdot] \mid E\ e \mid E \oplus e \mid v \oplus E \mid \\ \quad \texttt{if}\ E\ e_2\ e_3 \mid \texttt{let}\ x = E\ \texttt{in}\ e \mid \texttt{let}\ x = s\ \texttt{in}\ E \mid \\ \quad \texttt{lift}_n\ E\ e_1\ \dots\ e_n \mid \texttt{lift}_n\ v\ s_1\ \dots\ E\ \dots\ e_n \mid \\ \quad \texttt{foldp}\ E\ e_2\ e_3 \mid \texttt{foldp}\ v_1\ E\ e_3 \mid \texttt{foldp}\ v_1\ v_2\ E \mid \\ \quad \texttt{async}\ E \\ F ::= [\cdot]\ e \mid [\cdot] \oplus e \mid v \oplus [\cdot] \mid \texttt{if}\ F\ e_2\ e_3 \mid \\ \quad \texttt{lift}_n\ [\cdot]\ e_1\ \dots\ e_n \mid \texttt{foldp}\ [\cdot]\ e_2\ e_3 \mid \texttt{foldp}\ v_1\ [\cdot]\ e_3 \end{array}$$

CONTEXT
$$\frac{e \longrightarrow e'}{E[e] \longrightarrow E[e']}$$

OP
$$\frac{v = v_1 \oplus v_2}{v_1 \oplus v_2 \longrightarrow v}$$

COND-TRUE
$$\frac{v \neq 0}{\texttt{if}\ v\ e_2\ e_3 \longrightarrow e_2}$$

COND-FALSE
$$\frac{}{\texttt{if}\ 0\ e_2\ e_3 \longrightarrow e_3}$$

APPLICATION
$$\frac{}{(\lambda x\!:\!\eta.\ e_1)\ e_2 \longrightarrow \texttt{let}\ x = e_2\ \texttt{in}\ e_1}$$

REDUCE
$$\frac{}{\texttt{let}\ x = v\ \texttt{in}\ e \longrightarrow e[v/x]}$$

EXPAND
$$\frac{x \notin fv(F[\cdot])}{F[\texttt{let}\ x = s\ \texttt{in}\ u] \longrightarrow \texttt{let}\ x = s\ \texttt{in}\ F[u]}$$

Figure 6. Semantics for functional evaluation

sions. Rule REDUCE performs beta-reduction for let expressions $\texttt{let}\ x = v\ \texttt{in}\ e$, but only when x is bound to a simple value. If x is bound to a signal term, then (as shown by context $\texttt{let}\ x = s\ \texttt{in}\ E$) subexpression e is evaluated without substitution of x. This ensures that signal expressions are not duplicated, and reduces unnecessary computation in the second stage of evaluation, which is described in Section 3.3.2. (This is similar to a call-by-need calculus [5, 22], which avoids duplication of unevaluated expressions.)

Rule EXPAND expands the scope of a let expression to allow evaluation to continue. Contexts F describe where Rule EXPAND can be applied, and includes all contexts where a simple value v is required. For a context F, we write $fv(F[\cdot])$ for the set of free variables in F. We assume that expressions are equivalent up to renaming of bound variables, and an appropriate variable x can always be chosen such that $x \notin fv(F[\cdot])$.

If a FElm program is well typed, then the first stage of evaluation does not get stuck, and always evaluates to a final term. (We write $\longrightarrow^*$ for the reflexive transitive closure of the relation $\longrightarrow$.)

Theorem 1 (Type Soundness and Normalization). Let type environment Γ_{input} map every input $i \in \mathsf{Input}$ to a signal type. If $\Gamma_{input} \vdash e : \eta$ then $e \longrightarrow^* u$ and $\Gamma_{input} \vdash u : \eta$ for some final term u.

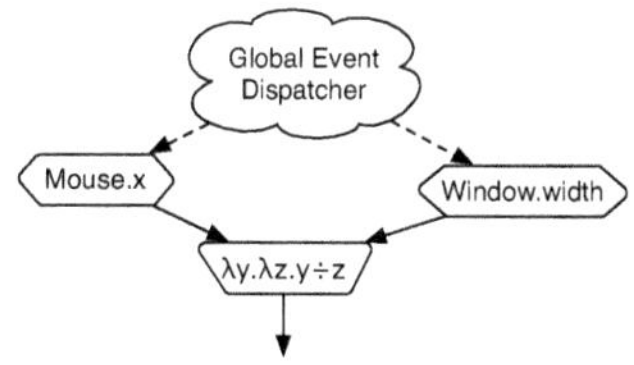

$\texttt{lift}_2\ (\lambda\texttt{y:int}.\ \lambda\texttt{z:int}.\ \texttt{y} \div \texttt{z})\ \texttt{Mouse.x Window.width}$

Figure 7. Signal graph for relative x-position of mouse

3.3.2 Signal Evaluation

If a FElm program evaluates to a simple value v, then the program does not use signals, and is not a reactive program. If, however, it evaluates to a signal term s then we perform the second stage of evaluation, performing computation as input signals produce new values. We first present the intuition behind signal evaluation, then present a working example to solidify the intuition. We then provide a semantics for signal terms by translation to Concurrent ML (CML) [27].

Intuition A signal term can be visualized as a directed acyclic graph, where nodes are input signals ($i \in \mathsf{Input}$), $\texttt{lift}_n$ terms, and `foldp` terms. The definition and use of variables define edges between the nodes. (Asynchronous terms $\texttt{async}\ s$ are described below.) We refer to these visualizations as *signal graphs*.

Nodes representing input signals have no incoming edges from other signal nodes, a node representing term $\texttt{lift}_n\ v\ s_1\ \dots\ s_n$ has n incoming edges, and a node representing term $\texttt{foldp}\ v_1\ v_2\ s$ has a single incoming edge. Signal graphs are acyclic since FElm has no way to construct recursive signal terms. Figure 7 shows an example of a signal graph for a simple FElm program.

We refer to nodes with no incoming edges as *source nodes*. Source nodes include input signals, and, as we will see below, $\texttt{async}\ s$ nodes. Source nodes are the source of new values. An *event* occurs when the signal represented by a source node produces a new value. Input signal events are triggered by the external environment, for example, mouse clicks or key presses. A *global event dispatcher* is responsible for notifying source nodes when events occur. The global event dispatcher ensures that events are totally ordered and no two events occur at exactly the same time. In signal graphs, we draw dashed lines from the global event dispatcher to all source nodes.

Nodes for $\texttt{lift}_n$ and `foldp` terms perform computation on values produced by signals. Lift terms perform (pure) computation on the current values of signals: term $\texttt{lift}_n\ v\ s_1\ \dots\ s_n$ applies function v to the current values of the n signals to produce a new value. A node for term $\texttt{foldp}\ v_1\ v_2\ s$ maintains the current value of the accumulator (initially v_2), and when a new value is received from signal s, applies function v_1 to the new value and the current value of accumulator, to produce the new value of the accumulator, which is also the new value for the signal $\texttt{foldp}\ v_1\ v_2\ s$.

Conceptually, signal computation is *synchronous*: when an event occurs (i.e., a source node produces a new value), then it is as if the new value propagates completely through the signal graph before the next event is processed. However, if the actual semantics used this approach, then global delays would occur, as processing of a new event would be blocked until processing of all previous events has finished.

We maintain the simple synchronous semantics, but allow more efficient implementations, by pipelining the execution of the signal graph: conceptually, each node in a signal graph has its own thread of control to perform computation, and each edge in a signal graph holds an unbounded FIFO queue of values. Whenever an event occurs, *all* source nodes are notified by the global event dispatcher:

the one source node to which the event is relevant produces the new value, and all other source nodes generate a special value noChange v, where v is the current (unchanged) value of the signal. Thus, every source node produces one value for each event. When a node in the signal graph performs computation, it must take a value from the front of each incoming edge's queue: computation at the node is blocked until values are available on all incoming edges. If all incoming values indicate no change, then the node does not perform any new computation, but instead propagates the value noChange v', where v' is the latest value of the signal represented by the node. If any value on the incoming edge is a new value (i.e., is not a noChange v value), then the node performs computation (which, in the case of a `foldp` node, updates the state) and propagates the newly computed value. This preserves the simple synchronous semantics, but allows computation at each node to occur in parallel.

The noChange v' values are a form of memoization—allowing nodes to avoid needless recomputation—but in the case of `foldp` nodes, are also critical to ensure correct execution. For example, a `foldp` term that counts the number of key presses (as in Section 3.1) should increment the counter only when a key is actually pressed, not every time any event occurs.

The synchrony of execution can be bypassed with the `async` construct. The node for a term `async` s is a source node: it has no incoming edges from other signal nodes, and whenever an event at another source node occurs, a noChange v value is propagated from the node. When signal s produces a new value, then a new event for term `async` s is generated. That is, when s produces a value, it is treated like an event from the external environment, and will be processed in a pipelined manner by the signal graph. The `async` construct, combined with pipelined execution of the signal graph, allows the programmer to easily separate long-running computations, while maintaining a relatively straightforward semantics for the FRP program. This allows a programmer to ensure that a GUI remains responsive even in the presence of significant computation trigged by user actions.

Example Consider the following program which takes in a signal of English words, pairing both the original word and the French translation of the word in a 2-tuple:

```
wordPairs = lift2 (,) words (lift toFrench words)
```

For simplicity, we assume that `words` is an input signal (i.e., words are given by the external environment), and function `toFrench` takes an English word and produces a French word, and may take significant time to perform the translation. Function `(,)` takes two arguments and constructs a pair from them. The signal graph for `wordPairs` is shown in Figure 8(a). Although function `toFrench` may take significant time, it is important that the propagation of values from signal `words` is synchronous, as each English word must be matched up with its translation. This example motivates the need for FRPs to be synchronous: the programmer must be able to ensure that values from signals are matched up appropriately.

However, there is a tension between synchronization and fast updates. Consider an expression that combines our `wordPairs` signal with the mouse position.

```
lift2 (,) wordPairs Mouse.position
```

The intent of this program is to display the current position of the mouse, in addition to translating English words to French. Figure 8(b) shows the signal graph for this program. However, synchronous update means that while translation is occurring, the mouse position will not be updated. In this case, it is not important to maintain the synchronization between updates of the mouse position and updates of the `wordPairs` signal: it is perfectly fine

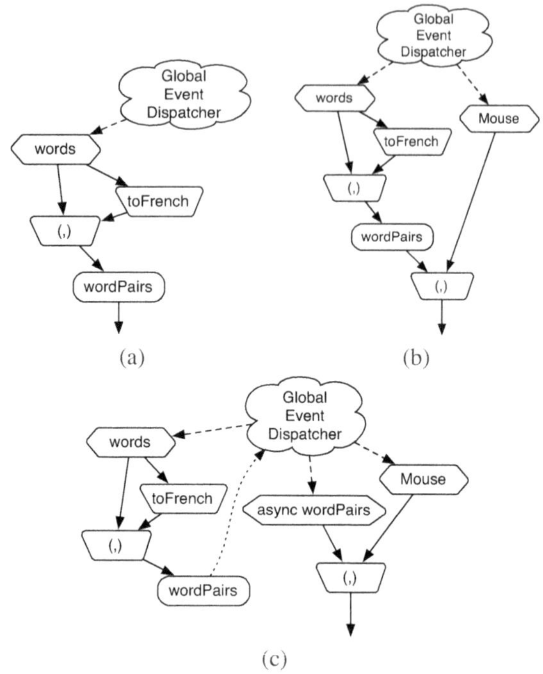

Figure 8. Example signal graphs

(and, in this case, preferable) to allow the mouse events to "jump ahead" of the translation computation.

The `async` primitive allows the programmer to break this synchronization in a controlled way. Informally, the annotation says "this subgraph does not need to respect the global order of events".

The following code uses `async` to indicate that the `wordPairs` subgraph should not block mouse updates.

```
lift2 (,) (async wordPairs) Mouse.position
```

The signal graph for this program, shown in Figure 8(c), has two distinct sections: the "primary subgraph" that combines translation pairs with the mouse position and the "secondary subgraph" that produces translation pairs. Effectively, the `async` primitive breaks a fully synchronous graph into one primary subgraph and an arbitrary number of secondary subgraphs. Event order is maintained *within* each subgraph, but not *between* them. The resulting graph is more responsive, but it does not respect global event ordering. In the example above, this is a desirable improvement.

Translation to Concurrent ML We define the semantics of FElm by translation to Concurrent ML (CML) [27]. We target CML because it has simple support for concurrency, it is type safe, and its theory is well understood.

The translation to CML is a direct instantiation of the intuition given above: each node in the signal graph has a thread that performs computation for the node, there is a channel for each edge in the signal graph (representing the FIFO queue for the edge), and the global event dispatcher is explicitly represented. Figure 9 defines a datatype and several CML helper functions that assist with the translation. The `event` data type wraps a value to indicate whether the value of the signal has changed. Function `change` takes an event value, and indicates whether it represents a changed value or not, and function `bodyOf` unwraps an `event` value to return the actual value. Function `guid` is used to obtain unique identifiers for source nodes.

Figure 10 presents the translation of signal terms to CML. Translation of signal s, denoted $[\![s]\!]$, produces a pair `(v,c)`, where

```
datatype 'a event = NoChange 'a | Change 'a
change e = case e of | NoChange _ => False
                     | Change _   => True
bodyOf e = case e of | NoChange v => v
                     | Change v   => v

counter = ref 0
guid () = counter := !counter + 1; !counter
```

Figure 9. Translation helper functions

```
[[i]] = [[ ⟨i, mc_i, v_i⟩ ]]

[[ ⟨id, mc, v⟩ ]] = spawn (fn _ => loop v) ; (v, c_out)
  where c_out = mailbox ()
        loop prev =
          let msg = if (recv (port eventNotify)) == id
                    then Change (recv (port mc))
                    else NoChange prev
          in  send c_out msg ; loop (bodyOf msg)

[[lift_n f s_1 ... s_n]] = spawn (fn _ => loop v) ; (v, c_out)
  where (v_1, c_1), ... , (v_n, c_n) = [[s_1]], ... , [[s_n]]
      v, c_out = [[f]]_V v_1 ... v_n, mailbox ()
      loop prev =
        let (m_1, ... , m_n) = (recv c_1, ... , recv c_n)
          msg = if exists change [m_1, ... , m_n] then
                  Change ([[f]]_V (bodyOf x_1) ... (bodyOf x_n))
                else NoChange prev
        in  send c_out msg ; loop (bodyOf msg)

[[foldp f v s]] = spawn (fn _ => loop [[v]]_V) ; ([[v]]_V, c_out)
  where (_, c_in), c_out = [[s]], mailbox ()
        loop acc =
          let msg = case recv c_in of
                      | NoChange _ -> NoChange acc
                      |   Change v -> Change ([[f]]_V v acc)
              in  send c_out msg ; loop (bodyOf msg)

[[let x = s_in in s_out]] = spawn loop ;
                            (let x_v,x_ch = v,mc_out in [[s_out]])
  where (v, c_in), mc_out = [[s_in]], mChannel ()
        loop () = send mc_out (recv c_in) ; loop ()

[[x]] = (x_v, port x_ch)

[[v]] = [[v]]_V

[[async s]] = spawn loop ; [[ ⟨id, c_out, d⟩ ]]
  where (d, c_in), c_out, id = [[s]], mChannel (), guid ()
      loop () = case recv c_in of
                | NoChange _ -> loop ()
                |   Change v -> send c_out v ;
                                send newEvent id ; loop ()
```

Figure 10. Translation from signal terms to CML

v is the default and initial value of the signal, and c is a *mailbox*, a buffered non-blocking channel to which new values of the signal are sent. Recall that we assume that every input signal has an appropriate default value, which then induces default values for all other signals. We assume a translation function $[\![\cdot]\!]_{\mathcal{V}}$ that translates values (i.e., unit (), integers n, and functions $\lambda x:\tau.\ e$) to CML.

The translation of each signal term creates a new thread that performs computation to produce values for the signal. For source nodes, this involves listening on a multicast channel for messages sent from the global dispatcher. For other nodes, the thread waits for input on all incoming edges, then either performs the appropriate computation for the node (if at least one of the incoming values is an `event` of the form `Change v`), or propagates an `event` value `NoChange v` where `v` is the latest computed value for the signal. We now describe the translation of each signal term in more detail.

The translation for input signal i assumes that i is a CML integer value, that there is a suitable default value $\mathtt{v}_i$ for the signal, and that there is a multicast channel $\mathtt{mc}_i$ on which new values for the input signal will be sent. We abstract translation of this triple $\langle i, \mathtt{mc}_i, \mathtt{v}_i\rangle$, since it is re-used by the translation for `async`. Translation of the triple creates a mailbox $\mathtt{c}_{out}$ to publish values for the input signal. It creates a thread that receives messages from the global event dispatcher on the `eventNotify` multicast channel ("`recv (port eventNotify)`"). For each event, the global event dispatcher sends a message on the `eventNotify` channel that contains the unique integer identifier of the source node for which the event is relevant. If this is the `id` of the input signal, then the thread takes a value v from the input signal channel ("`recv (port mc)`") and sends `Change` v on $\mathtt{c}_{out}$. Otherwise, the thread sends value `NoChange` v', where v' is the last value of the input signal.

Translation of $\mathtt{lift}_n\ f\ s_1\ ...\ s_n$ creates a mailbox $\mathtt{c}_{out}$ on which to send new values for the signal. It spawns a thread that waits to receive an `event` value from each of n signals. If any of the values indicate a change has occurred, then function f is applied to the current value of the signals to produce a value v and `Change` v is sent on the signal's channel. Otherwise, `NoChange` v' is sent on the channel, where v' is the last value of the input signal.

Translation of `foldp` $f\ v\ s$ is similar to a lift term, except that the fold has a single input signal, the initial value for the signal is the explicitly specified value v, and function f is given the previous value of the `fold` signal in addition to values received on signal s.

Translation of let expressions and variables work together to ensure that FElm's runtime system does not have duplicate nodes. A let expression node serves as a multicast station, forwarding messages to possibly many different nodes. Translation of `let` $x = s_{in}$ `in` s_{out} translates s_{in}, and binds variables x_v and x_{ch} in the translation of s_{out} to be, respectively, the initial value of signal s_{in} and a multicast channel on which values produced by s_{in} are multicast. Thus, variables are translated to the pair (x_v, `port` x_{ch}), where `port` x_{ch} returns a port that allows receipt of messages sent on the multicast channel.

Translation of `async` s returns the translation of the triple $\langle$`id`$, \mathtt{c}_{out}, \mathtt{v}\rangle$, where `id` is a newly generated unique identifier for the source node representing the term, $\mathtt{c}_{out}$ is a newly created multicast channel, and `d` is the default value for signal s. The translation spawns a thread that listens for `Change` v events to be produced by signal s, upon receiving a new value, sends that value on multicast channel $\mathtt{c}_{out}$, and notifies the global event dispatcher that source node `id` has a new event ("`send newEvent id`").

The translation of program s is executed within the context of the FElm CML runtime system, presented in Figure 11. There are two important loops: the global event dispatcher `eventDispatch` receives events from the `newEvent` mailbox, and notifies all source nodes of the new event, using the `eventNotify` multicast channel; the display loop `displayLoop` updates the user's view as new display values are produced by the translation of the program s. Together, these loops are the input and output for a FElm program, with `eventDispatch` feeding values in and `displayLoop` outputting values to the screen. Note that the `newEvent` mailbox is a FIFO queue, preserving the order of events sent to the mailbox.

The `displayLoop` depends on the translation of a signal term s. The translation produces both the `initialDisplay` which is the first screen to be displayed and the `nextDisplay` channel upon which display updates are sent. The display loop just funnels values from the `nextDisplay` channel to the screen.

```
newEvent = mailbox ()
eventNotify = mChannel ()
eventDispatch () =
    let id = recv newEvent in
           send eventNotify id ; eventDispatch ()

(initialDisplay, nextDisplay) = [[s]]
send display initialDisplay
displayLoop () = let v = recv nextDisplay in
                 send display v ; displayLoop ()

spawn eventDispatch ; spawn displayLoop
```

Figure 11. FElm CML runtime system

4. Building GUIs with Elm

Elm extends the FElm core calculus to a full language for building rich interactive GUIs, including libraries for constructing and composing GUI components. Elm can represent quite complex interactions with a small amount of code. The signal abstraction encourages a separation between reactive code and code focused on the layout of GUI components. This separation is due in part to Elm's purely functional and declarative approach to graphical layout, which allows a programmer to say *what* they want to display, without specifying *how* this should be done.

Elm has additional base values, including strings, floating point numbers, time, tuples, and graphical values such as `Elements` and `Forms`. Elm libraries provide data structures such as options, lists, sets, and dictionaries. Elm provides support for receiving input from mouse, keyboard, and touch devices, for accessing window attributes, and for network communication via HTTP. Elm supports JSON data structures and Markdown (making text creation easier). Elm's type system allows let-polymorphism and recursive simple types (but not recursive signal types). Elm supports type inference, has extensible records, and has a module system.

In this section we describe some key concepts and libraries for building GUIs with Elm, focusing on features unique to Elm.

4.1 Elements and Forms

Elm has two major categories of graphical primitives: elements and forms. An *element* (a value of type `Element`) is a rectangle with a known width and height. Elements can contain text, images, or video. They can be easily created and composed, making it simple to quickly lay out a multimedia display. Elements can be resized using functions `width` and `height`, both of which have type `Int -> Element -> Element`. Examples in the Introduction demonstrated the composition of elements.

A *form* (a value of type `Form`) allows non-rectangular shapes and text to be defined and composed. A form is an arbitrary 2D shape (including lines, shapes, text, and images) and a form can be enhanced by specifying texture and color. Forms can be moved, rotated, and scaled.

There are several subtypes of `Form`, including `Line` and `Shape`. Primitive functions can be used to construct forms, including `line` (which takes a list of points, and returns a line that goes through each point), `polygon` (which takes a list of points and returns an irregular polygon that goes through each of the points), and library functions such as `rect` to create rectangles, `oval` to construct ovals, and `ngon` to construct regular polygons.

Several functions allow lines and shapes to be given different colors, fills, and rendering. Forms can be moved, scaled, and rotated using primitive functions `move`, `scale`, and `rotate`.

Function `collage` provides the ability to combine forms in an unstructured way to produce an element. It takes as arguments width, height, and list of forms.

```
collage : Int -> Int -> [Form] -> Element
```

Figure 12 shows an example of creating several forms, changing their attributes, transforming them, and using `collage` to combine them into an element.

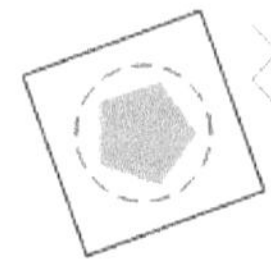

```
square   = rect 70 70
pentagon = ngon  5 20
circle   = oval 50 50
zigzag   = path [ (0,0), (10,10), (0,30), (10,40) ]

main = collage 140 140
      [ filled green pentagon,
        outlined (dashed blue) circle,
        rotate (degrees 70)
               (outlined (solid black) square),
        move 40 40 (trace (solid red) zigzag) ]
```

Figure 12. Creating and combining shapes

Signal	Type and Description
`Mouse.position`	`Signal (Int, Int)` Current coordinates of the mouse.
`Mouse.clicks`	`Signal ()` Triggers on mouse clicks.
`Window.dimensions`	`Signal (Int, Int)` Current dimensions of window.
`Time.every`	`Time -> Signal Time` Update every *t* milliseconds.
`Time.fps`	`Float -> Signal Time` Time deltas, updating at the given FPS.
`Touch.touches`	`Signal [Touch]` List of ongoing touches. Useful for defining gestures.
`Touch.taps`	`Signal { x:Int, y:Int }` Position of the latest tap.
`Keyboard.keysDown`	`Signal [KeyCode]` List of keys that are currently pressed.
`Keyboard.arrows`	`Signal { x:Int, y:Int }` Arrow keys pressed. e.g., up+right is `{x=1,y=1}`
`Keyboard.shift`	`Signal Bool` Is the shift key down?
`Input.text`	`String -> (Signal Element, Signal String)` Create a text input field.

Figure 13. Some Elm input signals and signal constructors

4.2 Reactive GUIs

To allow programmers to write GUIs that interact with the user, and react to user input and events in the external environment, Elm provides several primitive signals that can be used in Elm programs. These are the identifiers Input used in FElm to denote input signals from the external environment. Figure 13 describes some of Elm's signals and signal constructors. Signal constructor

```
pics = [ "shells.jpg", "car.jpg", "book.jpg" ]
display i =
    image 475 315 (ith (i 'mod' length pics) pics)

count s = foldp (\_ c -> c + 1) 0 s
index1 = count Mouse.clicks
index2 = count (Time.every (3 * second))
index3 = count Keyboard.lastPressed

main = lift display index1
```

Figure 14. A simple slide-show: reacting to user input

`Time.every` takes a floating point number t. The resulting signal is the current time, updated every t milliseconds. This signal enables time-indexed animations and allows update rates to be tuned by the programmer. Signal constructor `Time.fps` allows a programmer to specify a desired frame rate. The resulting signal is a sequence of time deltas (i.e., the time elapsed since the last event), making it easy to do time-stepped animations. The frame rate is managed by the Elm runtime system, accommodating performance constraints.

Input components such as text boxes, buttons, and sliders are represented as a pair of signals: an element (for the graphical component) and a value (for the value input). For example, the library function

```
Input.text :
     String -> (Signal Element, Signal String)
```

allows a programmer to construct a text input component. The code

```
(Input.text "Name")
```

returns a pair of a signal of `Elements` (for the graphical input field) and a signal of `Strings` representing the current user input. The graphical element uses the string `"Name"` as the greyed-out default text, indicating the desired user input. The element can be displayed on the screen, and the signals will be updated every time the text in the field changes.

Figure 14 shows how different user inputs can be used to implement a slide show. The code displays a single image from a list of images, `pics`. The user can cycle through the images by clicking the mouse. (In the accompanying diagram, the arrows indicate possible transitions between pictures, not actual graphical elements.) The program could easily be modified to change images using a timer as seen in `index2` which increments every three seconds. It could also change images when a key is pressed as in `index3`. The `Keyboard.lastPressed` signal updates to the latest character pressed.

4.3 Signal Functions

Elm embeds an implementation of discrete Arrowized FRP (AFRP), based on the naive continuation-based implementation described in the first AFRP paper [25]. To better capture the fact that our implementation is discrete (stepping forward only when provided with an input) this is called the `Automaton` library in Elm.

Arrowized FRP is a purely functional way to structure stateful programs. It introduced *signal functions* [25] which can encapsulate state and safely be switched in and out of a program. A signal function is conceptually equivalent to Elm's signal nodes: a set of external inputs, internal state, and an output. Although signal functions and signal nodes are equivalent, Elm's core language does not allow one to work with signal nodes directly. Arrowized FRP allows this, making it possible to dynamically reconfigure a single node. This direct embedding of AFRP gives Elm the flexibility of signal functions without resorting to the use of signals-of-signals.

An `Automaton` is defined as a continuation that when given an input `a`, produces the next continuation and an output `b`.

```
data Automaton a b = Step (a -> (Automaton a b, b))
```

This allows state to be kept around by continually placing it in the next continuation (the next step). Dynamic collections and dynamic switching are possible because an automaton is a pure data structure with no innate dependencies on inputs (whereas signals depend on an input by definition). Elm provides the following functions to make it easier to create pure and stateful automata:

```
pure : (a -> b) -> Automaton a b
init : (a -> b -> b) -> b -> Automaton a b
```

This lets a programmer create stateful components that can be switched in and out of a program. Notice the similarity between the types of `init` and `foldp`.

To use an `Automaton`, Elm provides the `step` function which steps an automaton forward once, and the `run` function which feeds a signal into an automaton, stepping it forward on each change.

```
step : a -> Automaton a b -> (Automaton a b, b)
step input (Step f) = f input

run : Automaton a b -> b -> Signal a -> Signal b
run automaton base inputs =
  let step' input (Step f, _) = f input
  in  lift snd (foldp step' (automaton,base) inputs)
```

Functions `run` and `foldp` are equivalent in expressive power. We defined `run` using `foldp`, but we could have taken `Automatons` as primitives and defined `foldp` using `run`, as follows.

```
foldp : (a -> b -> b) -> b -> Signal a -> Signal b
foldp f base inputs = run (init f base) base inputs
```

We chose `foldp` as our underlying abstraction partly because it makes Elm more accessible to users unfamiliar with arrows, arrow notation, type classes, and category theory. It also allows us to improve on our naive embedding of discrete AFRP, or add alternate embeddings, without changing the core language.

5. Implementation

We have implemented an Elm-to-JavaScript compiler, and have a prototype implementation of Elm as an embedded domain-specific language (DSL) in Haskell.

The use of Asynchronous FRP has the potential to ensure that GUIs remain responsive despite long-running computation. We do not provide direct performance evaluations of Elm, although in our experience GUIs implemented with Elm have not required any performance tuning other than identifying signals to mark as asynchronous. We note that it is easy to write programs such that Elm provides arbitrarily better responsiveness over synchronous FRP. For example, in the following code, function `f` can be made arbitrarily long-running. While the asynchronous code (signal `asyncEg`) will remain responsive (continuing to display `Mouse.x`), the synchronous case (signal `syncEg`) will be unresponsive until evaluation of `f` completes.

```
syncEg  = lift2 (,) Mouse.x (lift f Mouse.y)
asyncEg =
       lift2 (,) Mouse.x (async (lift f Mouse.y))
```

Similarly, it is possible to write programs such that the pipelined evaluation of signals has arbitrarily better performance than non-pipelined execution by ensuring that the signal graph of the program is sufficiently deep.

Elm-to-JavaScript compiler The Elm-to-JavaScript compiler is implemented in about 2,700 lines of Haskell code. The output of compiling an Elm program is an HTML file. The compiler can also output a JavaScript file for embedding an Elm program into an existing project. The compiler output works on any modern browser. We provide a Foreign Function Interface to JavaScript to allow Elm to integrate with existing JavaScript libraries.

We have targeted JavaScript as it is extremely expressive for graphics and has unmatched cross-platform support. It is perhaps the most widely used and supported GUI platform, albeit notoriously difficult to reason about its graphical layout model and to create readable asynchronous code.

JavaScript has poor support for concurrency, and as such the Elm-to-JavaScript compiler supports concurrent execution only for asynchronous requests, such as HTTP requests and non-blocking file I/O. JavaScript does provide heavy-weight threads, called Web Workers, but communication and interaction between threads is limited. We investigated using Web Workers to implement `async`, but found their overhead to be too high compared with simpler approaches. We anticipate that if and when JavaScript supports light-weight threads, we will be able to more fully support asynchrony and concurrency in the Elm-to-JavaScript compiler.

Elm programs typically take longer to execute than an equivalent hand-written JavaScript program, in a similar way that hand-tuned assembly code is often more efficient than compiled high-level language code. Indeed, a key benefit of Elm is providing better abstractions to programmers for building GUIs. However, the current prototype Elm-to-JavaScript compiler is efficient enough to execute all existing Elm programs while providing a responsive user experience on commodity web browsers on standard laptop and desktop machines.

The Elm-to-JavaScript compiler has been used to build the Elm website (http://elm-lang.org/) along with nearly 200 examples, including a nine-line analog clock, forms with client-side error checking, a graphing library that handles cartesian and radial coordinates, a slide-show API, and a Flickr image search interface. Elm has also been used to make Pong and other games, which require highly interactive GUIs.

Elm-in-Haskell library We also have a prototype Elm-in-Haskell library (144 lines of Haskell code) that supports the key features of Elm. While it does not have as extensive a suite of libraries and syntactic sugar, it does fully support the `async` construct and implement concurrent (pipelined) evaluation of signals. We use the `Control.Concurrent.Chan.Strict` module and Generalized Abstract Data Types to provide a type-safe implementation of Elm. By using strict channels we ensure that unevaluated expressions do not escape and cause unintended sequentialization.

6. Related Work

Elm is an asynchronous FRP programming language for creating rich and interactive GUIs. We focus on work related to the efficient FRP implementation, and to FRP frameworks for creating GUIs.

6.1 Efficient FRP Implementation

"Traditional" Functional Reactive Programming (FRP) was introduced in the Fran system [13] which suffered severe efficiency problems as a result of its expressive semantics. It permitted signals that depended on any past, present, or future value. As a result, its implementation had to save all past values of a signal just in case, growing memory linearly with time.

Real-time FRP (RT-FRP) [30, 32] ensures that signals cannot be used in ways that do not have an efficient implementation. Like Elm, RT-FRP uses a two-tiered language: an unrestricted base language (λ-calculus with recursion) and a limited reactive language for manipulating signals, which supports recursion but not higher-order functions (making it less expressive than traditional FRP). RT-FRP ensures that reactive updates will terminate as long as the base language terms terminate, and memory will not grow unless it grows in the base language. Although not strong guarantees, they are a significant improvement over traditional FRP, which might (needlessly) use space linear in a program's running time.

Event-Driven FRP (E-FRP) [31] builds on the efficiency gains of RT-FRP by introducing *discrete* signals. E-FRP programs are *event-driven* in that no changes need to be propagated unless an event has occurred (i.e., the value of a signal has changed) which improves efficiency of the computation.

Xu and Khoo [32] suggest a concurrent runtime for RT-FRP as future work but to the best of our knowledge, this has not been pursued. Like RT-FRP, Elm uses a two-tiered language to restrict the inefficient use of signals. However, whereas RT-FRP uses different syntactic constructs to separate functional and signal terms, Elm has a unified syntax but a stratified type system. This allows Elm to avoid non-standard syntactic constructs and accept more expressions, while restricting inefficient use of signals. Like E-FRP, Elm uses discrete signals to ensure efficiency and does not support recursively defined signals. The original paper on E-FRP suggests that discrete signals may be compatible with RT-FRP style recursion [31], but we have found that such an extension is not particularly important for creating GUIs. Improving upon these systems, we provide a concurrent runtime, and introduce a simple mechanism—the `async` annotation—to allow programmers to easily take advantage of concurrency.

Arrowized FRP (AFRP) [20, 21, 24, 25, 29] aims to regain much of the expressiveness of traditional FRP and keep the efficiency gains of RT-FRP. This is achieved by requiring programmers to use *signal functions* instead of having direct access to signals. Signal functions are conceptually equivalent to functions that take a signal of type `a` as an input, and return a signal of type `b`.

Signal functions solve the semantic problems associated with dynamically-created stateful signals by keeping state in signal functions instead of in signals. Unlike traditional FRP, a signal function cannot depend on arbitrary past values. Thus, AFRP allows programs to dynamically change how signals are processed without space leaks. Although there is no direct access to signals, AFRP achieves the expressiveness of traditional FRP via continuation-based switching and dynamic collections of signal functions.

Signal functions can be embedded in Elm (see Section 4.3), which brings the benefits of discrete AFRP to Elm programmers, allowing programs to dynamically create graphical components, without requiring signals of signals. Elm's discrete semantics make it clear how to allow asynchrony and concurrency, which appears to be semantically problematic in a continuous AFRP.

Parallel FRP [26], like Elm, enables concurrent signal processing. Parallel FRP relaxes the order of events *within* a single signal, allowing events to be processed out of order. In a server setting, this means that requests do not need to be processed in the order received, so responses can be computed in parallel and returned immediately. In a GUI setting, such intra-signal asynchrony is typically inappropriate, as it would allow, for example, key presses to be processed out of order. Instead, Elm permits *inter*-signal asynchrony: relaxing the order of events *between* multiple signals. We believe that intra- and inter-signal asynchrony are compatible, but inter-signal asynchrony is more useful in GUI programming.

Self-adjusting computation (e.g., [1, 2, 11]) is motivated by the desire to reduce redundant re-computation. As seen in FElm's pipelined signal evaluation (Section 3.3.2), avoiding needless recomputation helps performance and is required for correctness (due to the stateful nature of the `foldp` construct). Although FElm avoids some needless recomputation, it currently propagates many noChange v messages through the signal graph. Insights from self-adjusting computation could be used to reduce these messages and improve performance. Indeed, it appears likely that modifiable references [1] (used in self-adjusting computation to represent values that may change and thus trigger recomputation) can be used to encode signals, and can also express asynchronous signals [3].

6.2 FRP GUI Frameworks

Both traditional FRP and Arrowized FRP have been used as the basis of several Haskell-embedded GUI frameworks, including: FranTk [28] (the original GUI framework for Fran [13]); Fruit [9] and Yampa/Animas [10, 16] (based on Arrowized FRP); and Reactive Banana [4] (based on traditional FRP but avoids time leaks with carefully restricted APIs, disallowing signals-of-signals). Each of these Haskell-embedded libraries suffer from two problems. First, due to its lazy semantics, embedding the language in Haskell can lead to unexpectedly slow updates and unnecessary memory usage, which can be an issue for GUIs. Second, these Haskell-embedded libraries are a wrapper around a Haskell wrapper around an imperative GUI framework. This complicates both the design and the installation of the frameworks. Indeed, FranTk [28] includes event listeners—an imperative abstraction—because they map more naturally onto the Tcl/Tk backend.

Several frameworks embed FRP in imperative languages. Flapjax [23] extends JavaScript with traditional FRP. Flapjax interoperates easily with existing JavaScript code, as it is simply a JavaScript library. Frappé [8] adds FRP functionality to Java. Ignatoff et al. [18] adapt an object-oriented GUI library for use with the FRP language FrTime [7]. By necessity, these projects—including Elm—all rely on imperative GUI frameworks. This creates incentive to "work well" with existing code using these frameworks, or to be "close to the metal" of the framework. However, these incentives can be destructive, with imperative constructs muddying the clarity and simplicity of FRP. To maintain the declarative nature of FRP, Elm introduces a purely functional graphics library on a platform that is widely supported and easy to install. Interaction between Elm and JavaScript is handled by a simple foreign function interface (FFI) that maintains a clean separation between functional and imperative code.

Elm provides a functional abstraction for graphical layout. Elm's `collage` API is similar to previous work on free-form functional graphics [6, 14, 15, 17, 19]. Unlike this previous work, Elm supports user interaction and designs for animation, enabling creation of GUIs as opposed to purely static pictures and graphics.

7. Conclusion

We have developed the Elm programming language, a practical asynchronous FRP language focused on easy creation of responsive GUIs. We introduced *Asynchronous FRP* to allow programmers to easily specify when a potentially long-running signal computation should be computed asynchronously, and thus enable efficient concurrent execution of FRP programs. We captured the key concepts of asynchronous FRP in a core calculus.

By combining asynchronous FRP with purely functional layout of graphical elements, Elm simplifies the complicated task of creating responsive and usable graphical user interfaces.

Acknowledgments

We thank Greg Morrisett, Stuart Shieber, the anonymous reviewers, Umut Acar, Stefan Muller, David Darais, Jan Midtgaard, and the Aarhus Programming Languages group for their helpful comments and feedback. We thank the Elm user community. This research is supported in part by the National Science Foundation under Grant No. 1054172.

References

[1] U. A. Acar, G. E. Blelloch, and R. Harper. Adaptive functional programming. In *Proceedings of the 29th ACM SIGPLAN-SIGACT Symposium on Principles of Programming Languages*, pages 247–259, New York, NY, USA, 2002. ACM.

[2] U. A. Acar, A. Ahmed, and M. Blume. Imperative self-adjusting computation. In *Proceedings of the 35th Annual ACM SIGPLAN-SIGACT Symposium on Principles of Programming Languages*, pages 309–322, New York, NY, USA, 2008. ACM.

[3] U. A. Acar, G. E. Blelloch, K. Tangwongsan, and D. Türkoğlu. Robust kinetic convex hulls in 3D. In *Proceedings of the 16th Annual European Symposium on Algorithms*, pages 29–40, Berlin, Heidelberg, 2008. Springer-Verlag.

[4] H. Apfelmus. Reactive-banana. Haskell library available at `http://www.haskell.org/haskellwiki/Reactive-banana`, 2012.

[5] Z. M. Ariola and M. Felleisen. The call-by-need lambda calculus. *Journal of Functional Programming*, 7(3):265–301, May 1997.

[6] E. Chailloux, G. Cousineau, and A. Suàrez. MLgraph. `http://www.pps.univ-paris-diderot.fr/~cousinea/MLgraph/mlgraph.html`, 1992.

[7] G. H. Cooper. *Integrating Dataflow Evaluation into a Practical Higher-Order Call-by-Value Language*. PhD thesis, Brown University, May 2008.

[8] A. Courtney. Frappé: Functional reactive programming in Java. In *Proceedings of the Third International Symposium on Practical Aspects of Declarative Languages*, pages 29–44, London, UK, 2001. Springer-Verlag.

[9] A. Courtney and C. Elliott. Genuinely functional user interfaces. In *Proceedings of the 2001 ACM SIGPLAN Workshop on Haskell*, pages 41–69, 2001.

[10] A. Courtney, H. Nilsson, and J. Peterson. The Yampa arcade. In *Proceedings of the 2003 ACM SIGPLAN Workshop on Haskell*, pages 7–18, New York, NY, 2003. ACM.

[11] A. Demers, T. Reps, and T. Teitelbaum. Incremental evaluation for attribute grammars with application to syntax-directed editors. In *Proceedings of the 8th ACM SIGPLAN-SIGACT Symposium on Principles of Programming Languages*, pages 105–116, New York, NY, USA, 1981. ACM.

[12] C. Elliott. Push-pull functional reactive programming. In *Proceedings of the 2nd ACM SIGPLAN Symposium on Haskell*, pages 25–36, New York, NY, 2009. ACM.

[13] C. Elliott and P. Hudak. Functional reactive animation. In *Proceedings of the 2nd ACM SIGPLAN International Conference on Functional Programming*, pages 263–273, New York, NY, 1997. ACM.

[14] R. B. Findler and M. Flatt. Slideshow: functional presentations. In *Proceedings of the Ninth ACM SIGPLAN International Conference on Functional Programming*, pages 224–235, New York, NY, USA, 2004. ACM.

[15] S. Finne and S. Peyton Jones. Pictures: A simple structured graphics model. In *Proceedings of the Glasgow Functional Programming Workshop*, 1995.

[16] G. Giorgidze and H. Nilsson. Switched-on Yampa: declarative programming of modular synthesizers. In *Proceedings of the 10th International Conference on Practical Aspects of Declarative Languages*, pages 282–298, Berlin, Heidelberg, 2008. Springer-Verlag.

[17] P. Henderson. Functional geometry. In *Proceedings of the 1982 ACM Symposium on LISP and Functional Programming*, pages 179–187, New York, NY, USA, 1982. ACM.

[18] D. Ignatoff, G. H. Cooper, and S. Krishnamurthi. Crossing state lines: Adapting object-oriented frameworks to functional reactive languages. In *Proceedings of the International Symposium on Functional and Logic Programming*, 2006.

[19] S. N. Kamin and D. Hyatt. A special-purpose language for picture-drawing. In *Proceedings of the Conference on Domain-Specific Languages on Conference on Domain-Specific Languages (DSL), 1997*, pages 23–23, Berkeley, CA, USA, 1997. USENIX Association.

[20] H. Liu and P. Hudak. Plugging a space leak with an arrow. *Electron. Notes Theor. Comput. Sci.*, 193:29–45, Nov. 2007.

[21] H. Liu, E. Cheng, and P. Hudak. Causal commutative arrows and their optimization. In *Proceedings of the 14th ACM SIGPLAN International Conference on Functional Programming*, pages 35–46, New York, NY, 2009. ACM.

[22] J. Maraist, M. Odersky, and P. Wadler. The call-by-need lambda calculus. *Journal of Functional Programming*, 8(3):275–317, May 1998.

[23] L. A. Meyerovich, A. Guha, J. Baskin, G. H. Cooper, M. Greenberg, A. Bromfield, and S. Krishnamurthi. Flapjax: a programming language for Ajax applications. In *Proceedings of the 24th ACM SIGPLAN Conference on Object Oriented Programming Systems Languages and Applications*, pages 1–20, New York, NY, 2009. ACM.

[24] H. Nilsson. Dynamic optimization for functional reactive programming using generalized algebraic data types. In *Proceedings of the 10th ACM SIGPLAN International Conference on Functional Programming*, pages 54–65, New York, NY, 2005. ACM.

[25] H. Nilsson, A. Courtney, and J. Peterson. Functional reactive programming, continued. In *Proceedings of the 2002 ACM SIGPLAN Workshop on Haskell*, pages 51–64, New York, NY, 2002. ACM.

[26] J. Peterson, V. Trifonov, and A. Serjantov. Parallel functional reactive programming. In *Proceedings of the Second International Workshop on Practical Aspects of Declarative Languages*, pages 16–31, London, UK, 2000. Springer-Verlag.

[27] J. H. Reppy. *Concurrent programming in ML*. Cambridge University Press, 1999. ISBN 9780521480895.

[28] M. Sage. FranTk - a declarative GUI language for Haskell. In *Proceedings of the 5th ACM SIGPLAN International Conference on Functional Programming*, pages 106–117, New York, NY, 2000.

[29] N. Sculthorpe and H. Nilsson. Safe functional reactive programming through dependent types. In *Proceedings of the 14th ACM SIGPLAN International Conference on Functional Programming*, pages 23–34, New York, NY, 2009. ACM.

[30] Z. Wan, W. Taha, and P. Hudak. Real-time FRP. In *Proceedings of the 6th ACM SIGPLAN International Conference on Functional Programming*, pages 146–156, New York, NY, 2001. ACM.

[31] Z. Wan, W. Taha, and P. Hudak. Event-driven FRP. In *Proceedings of the 4th International Symposium on Practical Aspects of Declarative Languages*, pages 155–172, London, UK, UK, 2002. Springer-Verlag.

[32] D. N. Xu and S.-C. Khoo. Compiling real time functional reactive programming. In *Proceedings of the ASIAN Symposium on Partial Evaluation and Semantics-Based Program Manipulation*, pages 83–93, New York, NY, 2002. ACM.

Hybrid Context-Sensitivity for Points-To Analysis

George Kastrinis   Yannis Smaragdakis

Department of Informatics
University of Athens
{gkastrinis,smaragd}@di.uoa.gr

Abstract

Context-sensitive points-to analysis is valuable for achieving high precision with good performance. The standard flavors of context-sensitivity are call-site-sensitivity (kCFA) and object-sensitivity. Combining both flavors of context-sensitivity increases precision but at an infeasibly high cost. We show that a selective combination of call-site- and object-sensitivity for Java points-to analysis is highly profitable. Namely, by keeping a combined context only when analyzing selected language features, we can closely approximate the precision of an analysis that keeps both contexts at all times. In terms of speed, the selective combination of both kinds of context not only vastly outperforms non-selective combinations but is also faster than a mere object-sensitive analysis. This result holds for a large array of analyses (e.g., 1-object-sensitive, 2-object-sensitive with a context-sensitive heap, type-sensitive) establishing a new set of performance/precision sweet spots.

Categories and Subject Descriptors F.3.2 [*Logics and Meanings of Programs*]: Semantics of Programming Languages—Program Analysis; D.3.4 [*Programming Languages*]: Processors—Compilers

General Terms Algorithms, Languages, Performance

Keywords points-to analysis; context-sensitivity; object-sensitivity; type-sensitivity

1. Introduction

Points-to analysis is a static program analysis that consists of computing all objects (typically identified by allocation site) that a program variable may point to. The area of points-to analysis (and its close relative, *alias analysis*) has been the focus of intense research and is among the most standardized and well-understood of inter-procedural analyses. The emphasis of points-to analysis algorithms is on combining fairly precise modeling of pointer behavior with scalability. The challenge is to pick judicious approximations that will allow satisfactory precision at a reasonable cost. Furthermore, although increasing precision often leads to higher asymptotic complexity, this worst-case behavior is rarely encountered in actual practice. Instead, techniques that are effective at maintaining good precision often also exhibit better average-case performance, since smaller points-to sets lead to less work.

PLDI'13, June 16–19, 2013, Seattle, WA, USA.

One of the major tools for exploiting sweet spots in the precision/performance tradeoff has been *context-sensitivity*. Context-sensitivity consists of qualifying local variables and objects with context information: the analysis unifies executions that map to the same context value, while separating executions that map to different contexts. This approach tries to counter the loss of precision that naturally results in any static analysis from conflating information from different dynamic program paths. Two main kinds of context-sensitivity have been explored in the literature: *call-site-sensitivity* [22, 23] and *object-sensitivity* [18, 19, 24].

A call-site-sensitive/kCFA analysis uses method call-sites (i.e., labels of instructions that may call the method) as context elements. That is, the analysis separates information on local variables (e.g., method arguments) per call-stack (i.e., sequence of k call-sites) of method invocations that led to the current method call. Similarly, the analysis separates information on heap objects per call-stack of method invocations that led to the object's allocation. For instance, in the code example below, a 1-call-site-sensitive analysis (unlike a *context-insensitive* analysis) will distinguish the two call-sites of method `foo` on lines 7 and 9. This means that the analysis will treat `foo` separately for two cases: that of its formal argument, `o`, pointing to anything `obj1` may point to, and that of `o` pointing to anything `obj2` may point to.

```
1  class C {
2   void foo(Object o) { ... }
3  }
4
5  class Client {
6   void bar(C c1, C c2) { ...
7     c1.foo(obj1);
8     ...
9     c2.foo(obj2);
10  }
11 }
```

In contrast, object-sensitivity uses object allocation sites (i.e., labels of instructions containing a `new` statement) as context elements. (Hence, a better name for "object-sensitivity" might have been "allocation-site sensitivity".) That is, when a method is called on an object, the analysis separates the inferred facts depending on the allocation site of the receiver object (i.e., the object on which the method is called), as well as other allocation sites used as context. Thus, in the above example, a 1-object-sensitive analysis will analyze `foo` separately depending on the allocation sites of the objects that `c1` and `c2` may point to. It is not apparent from this code fragment neither whether `c1` and `c2` may point to different objects, nor to how many objects: the allocation site of the receiver object may be remote and unrelated to the method call itself. Similarly, it is not possible to compare the precision of an object-sensitive and a call-site-sensitive analysis in principle. In this example, it is not even clear whether the object sensitive analysis will examine all calls to `foo` as one case, as two, or as many more, since this depends on the allocation sites of all objects *that the analysis itself computes to flow into* `c1` *and* `c2`.

The question behind our work is whether the two kinds of contexts can be fruitfully combined, since they are quite dissimilar. In order to address this question, we map the design space of *hybrid call-site- and object-sensitive* analyses and describe the combinations that arise. Naive hybrids, such as always maintaining as context *both* a call-site and an allocation site, do not pay off, due to extremely high cost. For instance, keeping one call-site and one allocation site as context yields a very expensive analysis, on average 3.9x slower than a simple 1-object-sensitive analysis.

However, we find that more sophisticated hybrids are highly beneficial. Specifically, we show that we can switch per-language-feature between a combined context and an object-only context. For instance, contexts for static method calls are computed differently from contexts for dynamic method calls. This approach yields analyses with both low cost and high precision. Furthermore, adapting contexts per program feature defines a complex design space and allows even further optimization. Design choices arise, such as, how should the context adapt when a dynamic method call, or an object allocation are made inside a static method?

The end result is analyses that closely track the precision of combined call-site-and-object-sensitivity while incurring none of the cost. In fact, the cost of the resulting analysis is usually less (and occasionally much less) than that of just an object-sensitive analysis, due to increased precision. This effect is shown to apply widely, to several variants of analyses. Accordingly, this outcome establishes new sweet spots for the analyses most relevant for practical applications: 1-object-sensitive, 2-object-sensitive with a 1-context-sensitive heap, and analogous type-sensitive [24] analyses. For all of them, a selective hybrid context is typically both more precise and faster than the original analysis.

In all, our paper makes the following contributions:

- We model the parameter space of context-sensitive points-to analysis in a way that allows both call-site- and object-sensitivity, as well as combinations and switching of context at key points (virtual calls vs. static calls). In this space, we map out choices that produce entirely different flavors of algorithms.
- We introduce the idea of hybrid call-site- and object-sensitivity where the two kinds of context are freely mixed and the mix is adjusted in response to analyzing different program features. The goal is to achieve the precision of keeping *both* kinds of context together, but at the same cost as keeping only one.
- We implement our approach in the DOOP framework by Bravenboer et al. [4] and apply it to a large variety of algorithms with varying context depth.
- We show experimentally, over large Java benchmarks and the Java JDK, that hybrid context-sensitivity works remarkably well. The selective application of a combined context achieves the same effective precision as keeping both contexts at all times, at a fraction of the cost, and is typically faster even than keeping only an object context. For instance, in the practically important case of a 2-object-sensitive analysis with a context-sensitive heap, we get an average speedup of 1.53x *and* a more precise analysis. Similarly, for the simple and popular 1-object-sensitive analysis, we get an average speedup of 1.12x combined with significant increase in precision.

The rest of the paper introduces a model for points-to analysis (Section 2) and shows how instantiating the model yields several well-known analyses. In Section 3 we discuss the many choices for combining object- and call-site-sensitivity, as well as the most promising points in this design space. Our evaluation results follow in Section 4, before describing related work (Section 5).

2. Modeling of Points-To Analysis

We begin with a concise modeling of the relevant points-to analyses and their context choices.

2.1 Background: Parameterizable Model

We model a spectrum of flow-insensitive points-to analyses and joint (online) call-graph construction as a parametric Datalog program. Datalog rules are monotonic logical inferences that repeatedly apply to infer more facts until fixpoint. Our rules do not use negation in a recursive cycle, or other non-monotonic logic constructs, resulting in a declarative specification: the order of evaluation of rules or examination of clauses cannot affect the final result. The same abstract model applies to a wealth of analyses. We use it to model a context-insensitive Andersen-style [2] analysis, as well as several context-sensitive analyses, both call-site-sensitive and object-sensitive.

The input language is a representative simplified intermediate language with a) a "new" instruction for allocating an object; b) a "move" instruction for copying between local variables; c) "store" and "load" instructions for writing to the heap (i.e., to object fields); d) a "virtual method call" instruction that calls the method of the appropriate signature that is defined in the dynamic class of the receiver object; e) a "static method call" instruction that calls a statically known target method. This language models well the Java bytecode representation, but also other high-level intermediate languages. (It does not, however, model languages such as C or C++ that can create pointers through an address-of operator. The techniques used in that space are fairly different—e.g., [8, 9]—although our main hybrid approach is likely to be applicable. Also, even though we model regular object fields and static methods, we omit static fields. Their treatment is a mere engineering complexity, as it does not interact with context choice.) The specification of our points-to analysis as well as the input language are in line with those in past literature [6, 16], although we also integrate elements such as on-the-fly call-graph construction, static calls, and field-sensitivity.

Specifying the analysis logically as Datalog rules has the advantage that the specification is close to the actual implementation. Datalog has been the basis of several implementations of program analyses, both low-level [4, 11, 20, 30, 31] and high-level [5, 7]. Indeed, the analysis we show is a faithful model of the implementation in the DOOP framework [4], upon which our work builds. Our specification of the analysis (Figures 1-2) is an abstraction of the actual implementation in the following ways:

- The implementation has many more rules. It covers the full complexity of Java, including rules for handling reflection, native methods, static fields, string constants, implicit initialization, threads, and a lot more. The DOOP implementation[1] currently contains over 600 rules in the common core of all analyses, and several more rules specific to each analysis, as opposed to the 9 rules we examine here. (Note, however, that these few rules are the most crucial for points-to analysis. They also correspond fairly closely to the algorithms specified in other formalizations of points-to analyses in the literature [17, 24].)
- The implementation also reflects considerations for efficient execution. The most important is that of defining indexes for the key relations of the evaluation. Furthermore, it designates some relations as functions, defines storage models for relations (e.g., how many bits each variable uses), designates intermediate relations as "materialized views" or not, etc. No such considerations are reflected in our model.

[1] Available at http://doop.program-analysis.org/

V is a set of program variables
H is a set of heap abstractions (i.e., allocation sites)
M is a set of method identifiers
S is a set of method signatures (including name, type signature)
F is a set of fields
I is a set of instructions (mainly used for invocation sites)
T is a set of class types
$\mathbb{N}$ is the set of natural numbers
C is a set of contexts
HC is a set of heap contexts

ALLOC (*var : V, heap : H, inMeth : M*)	*# var = new ...*
MOVE (*to : V, from : V*)	*# to = from*
LOAD (*to : V, base : V, fld : F*)	*# to = base.fld*
STORE (*base : V, fld : F, from : V*)	*# base.fld = from*
VCALL (*base : V, sig : S, invo : I, inMeth : M*)	*# base.sig(..)*
SCALL (*meth : M, invo : I, inMeth : M*)	*# Class.meth(..)*

FORMALARG (*meth : M, i : ℕ, arg : V*)
ACTUALARG (*invo : I, i : ℕ, arg : V*)
FORMALRETURN (*meth : M, ret : V*)
ACTUALRETURN (*invo : I, var : V*)
THISVAR (*meth : M, this : V*)
HEAPTYPE (*heap : H, type : T*)
LOOKUP (*type : T, sig : S, meth : M*)

VARPOINTSTO (*var : V, ctx : C, heap : H, hctx : HC*)
CALLGRAPH (*invo : I, callerCtx : C, meth : M, calleeCtx : C*)
FLDPOINTSTO (*baseH: H, baseHCtx: HC, fld: F, heap: H, hctx: HC*)
INTERPROCASSIGN (*to : V, toCtx : C, from : V, fromCtx : C*)
REACHABLE (*meth : M, ctx : C*)

RECORD (*heap : H, ctx : C*) = ***newHCtx : HC***
MERGE (*heap : H, hctx : HC, invo : I, ctx : C*) = ***newCtx : C***
MERGESTATIC (*invo : I, ctx : C*) = ***newCtx : C***

Figure 1: Our domain, input relations (representing program instructions—with the matching program pattern shown in a comment—and type information), output relations, and constructors of contexts.

Figure 1 shows the domain of our analysis (i.e., the different value sets that constitute the space of our computation), its input relations, the intermediate and output relations, as well as three constructor functions, responsible for producing new contexts. Figure 2 shows the points-to analysis and call-graph computation. The rule syntax is simple: the left arrow symbol (←) separates the inferred facts (i.e., the *head* of the rule) from the previously established facts (i.e., the *body* of the rule). For instance, the first rule states that, if we have computed a call-graph edge between invocation site *invo* and method *meth* (under some contexts—see later), then we infer an inter-procedural assignment to the i-th formal argument of *meth* from the i-th actual argument at *invo*, for every i.

We explain the contents of both figures in more detail below:

- The input relations correspond to the intermediate language for our analysis. They are logically grouped into relations that represent instructions and relations that represent name-and-type information. For instance, the ALLOC relation represents every instruction that allocates a new heap object, *heap*, and assigns it to local variable *var* inside method *inMeth*. (Note that every local variable is defined in a unique method, hence the *inMeth* argument is also implied by *var* but is included to simplify later rules.) There are similar input relations for all other instruction types (MOVE, LOAD, STORE, VCALL, and SCALL). Similarly, there are relations that encode pertinent symbol table information. Most of these are self-explanatory but some deserve explanation. LOOKUP matches a method signature to the actual method definition inside a type. HEAPTYPE matches an object to its type, i.e., is a function on its first argument. (Note that we are shortening the term "heap object" to just "heap" and represent heap objects as allocation sites throughout.) ACTUALRETURN is also a function on its first argument (a method invocation site) and returns the local variable at the call-site that receives the method call's return value.

INTERPROCASSIGN (*to, calleeCtx, from, callerCtx*) ←
  CALLGRAPH (*invo, callerCtx, meth, calleeCtx*),
  FORMALARG (*meth, i, to*), ACTUALARG (*invo, i, from*).

INTERPROCASSIGN (*to, callerCtx, from, calleeCtx*) ←
  CALLGRAPH (*invo, callerCtx, meth, calleeCtx*),
  FORMALRETURN (*meth, from*), ACTUALRETURN (*invo, to*).

RECORD (*heap, ctx*) = ***hctx***,
VARPOINTSTO (*var, ctx, heap, hctx*) ←
  REACHABLE (*meth, ctx*), ALLOC (*var, heap, meth*).

VARPOINTSTO (*to, ctx, heap, hctx*) ←
  MOVE (*to, from*), VARPOINTSTO (*from, ctx, heap, hctx*).

VARPOINTSTO (*to, toCtx, heap, hctx*) ←
  INTERPROCASSIGN (*to, toCtx, from, fromCtx*),
  VARPOINTSTO (*from, fromCtx, heap, hctx*).

VARPOINTSTO (*to, ctx, heap, hctx*) ←
  LOAD (*to, base, fld*), VARPOINTSTO (*base, ctx, baseH, baseHCtx*),
  FLDPOINTSTO (*baseH, baseHCtx, fld, heap, hctx*).

FLDPOINTSTO (*baseH, baseHCtx, fld, heap, hctx*) ←
  STORE (*base, fld, from*), VARPOINTSTO (*from, ctx, heap, hctx*),
  VARPOINTSTO (*base, ctx, baseH, baseHCtx*).

MERGE (*heap, hctx, invo, callerCtx*) = ***calleeCtx***,
REACHABLE (*toMeth, calleeCtx*),
VARPOINTSTO (*this, calleeCtx, heap, hctx*),
CALLGRAPH (*invo, callerCtx, toMeth, calleeCtx*) ←
  VCALL (*base, sig, invo, inMeth*), REACHABLE (*inMeth, callerCtx*),
  VARPOINTSTO (*base, callerCtx, heap, hctx*),
  HEAPTYPE (*heap, heapT*), LOOKUP (*heapT, sig, toMeth*),
  THISVAR (*toMeth, this*).

MERGESTATIC (*invo, callerCtx*) = ***calleeCtx***,
REACHABLE (*toMeth, calleeCtx*),
CALLGRAPH (*invo, callerCtx, toMeth, calleeCtx*) ←
  SCALL (*toMeth, invo, inMeth*), REACHABLE (*inMeth, callerCtx*).

Figure 2: Datalog rules for the points-to analysis and call-graph construction.

- There are five output or intermediate computed relations (VARPOINTSTO, ..., REACHABLE). Every occurrence of a method or local variable in computed relations is qualified with a context (i.e., an element of set *C*), while every occurrence of a heap object is qualified with a heap context (i.e., an element of *HC*). The main output relations are VARPOINTSTO and CALLGRAPH, encoding our points-to and call-graph results. The VARPOINTSTO relation links a variable (*var*) to a heap object (*heap*). Other intermediate relations (FLDPOINTSTO, INTERPROCASSIGN, REACHABLE) correspond to standard concepts and are introduced for conciseness. For instance, INTERPROCASSIGN (which encodes all parameter and return value passing) unifies much of the treatment of static and virtual method calls.

- The base rules are not concerned with what kind of context-sensitivity is used. The same rules can be used for a context-insensitive analysis (by only ever creating a single context object and a single heap context object), for a call-site-sensitive analysis, or for an object-sensitive analysis, for any context depth. These aspects are completely hidden behind constructor functions **RECORD**, **MERGE**, and **MERGESTATIC**. The first two follow the usage and naming convention of Smaragdakis et al. [24], while **MERGESTATIC** is new and used to differentiate the treatment of static calls—this is a crucial element of our approach.

  RECORD is the function that creates a new heap context. It is invoked whenever an object allocation site (input relation ALLOC) is analyzed. Thus, **RECORD** is only used in the rule treating allocation instructions (3rd rule in Figure 2). **RECORD** takes all available information at the allocation site of an object and combines it to produce a new heap context. The rule merely says that an allocation instruction in a reachable method leads us to infer a points-to fact between the allocated object and the variable it is directly assigned to.

  MERGE and **MERGESTATIC** are used to create new calling contexts (or just "contexts"). These contexts are used to qualify method calls, i.e., they are applied to all local variables in a program. The **MERGE** and **MERGESTATIC** functions take all available information at the call-site of a method (virtual or static) and combine it to create a new context (if one for the same combination of parameters does not already exist). These functions are sufficient for modeling a very large variety of context-sensitive analyses, as we show in Sections 2.2 and 3.

  Note that the use of constructors, such as **RECORD**, **MERGE**, and **MERGESTATIC**, is not part of regular Datalog and can result in infinite structures (e.g., one can express unbounded call-site sensitivity) if care is not taken. All our later definitions statically guarantee to create contexts of a pre-set depth.
- The rules of Figure 2 show how each input instruction leads to the inference of facts for the five output or intermediate relations. The most complex rule is the second-to-last, which handles virtual method calls (input relation VCALL). The rule says that if a reachable method of the program has an instruction making a virtual method call over local variable *base* (this is an input fact), and the analysis so far has established that *base* can point to heap object *heap*, then the called method is looked up inside the type of *heap* and several further facts are inferred: that the looked up method is reachable, that it has an edge in the call-graph from the current invocation site, and that its *this* variable can point to *heap*. Additionally, the **MERGE** function is used to possibly create (or look up) the right context for the current invocation.

2.2 Instantiating the Model: Standard Analyses

By modifying the definitions of the **RECORD**, **MERGE** and **MERGESTATIC** functions as well as domains *HC* and *C*, one can create endless variations of points-to analyses. We next discuss the most interesting combinations from past literature, before we introduce our own (in Section 3). For every analysis name we also list a common abbreviation, which we often use later.

Context-insensitive (insens). As already mentioned, our context-sensitive analysis framework can yield a context-insensitive analysis by merely picking singleton *C* and *HC* sets (i.e., $C = HC = \{\star\}$, where $\star$ is merely a name for a distinguished element) and constructor functions that return the single element of the set:

RECORD (*heap,ctx*) = $\star$
MERGE (*heap, hctx, invo, ctx*) = $\star$
MERGESTATIC (*invo, ctx*) = $\star$

Note that the absence of contexts does not mean that the identity of input elements is forgotten. Objects are still represented by their allocation site (i.e., the exact program instruction that allocated the object) and local variables are still distinguished (e.g., by their declaration location in the input program). The absence of context just means that there is no *extra* distinguishing information. This can also be seen in the rules of Figure 2, where the *var* and *heap* predicate arguments are present, separately from the context arguments.

1-call-site-sensitive (1call). A 1-call-site-sensitive analysis has no heap context to qualify heap abstractions ($HC = \{\star\}$) and uses the current invocation site as a context ($C = I$). The following definitions describe such an analysis.

RECORD (*heap, ctx*) = $\star$
MERGE (*heap, hctx, invo, ctx*) = ***invo***
MERGESTATIC (*invo, ctx*) = ***invo***

In words: the analysis stores no context when an object is created (**RECORD**) and keeps the invocation site as context in both virtual and static calls.

1-call-site-sensitive with a context-sensitive heap (1call+H). The analysis is defined similarly to 1call.[2] The heap context as well as the main context consist of an invocation site ($HC = C = I$).

RECORD (*heap, ctx*) = ***ctx***
MERGE (*heap, hctx, invo, ctx*) = ***invo***
MERGESTATIC (*invo, ctx*) = ***invo***

In words: the analysis uses the current method's context as a heap context for objects allocated inside the method. The invocation site of a method call is the context of the method for both virtual and static calls.

1-object-sensitive (1obj). Object sensitivity uses allocation sites as context components. A 1-object-sensitive analysis has no heap context ($HC = \{\star\}$) and uses the allocation site of the receiver object as context ($C = H$). The following definitions complete the description.

RECORD (*heap, ctx*) = $\star$
MERGE (*heap, hctx, invo, ctx*) = ***heap***
MERGESTATIC (*invo, ctx*) = ***ctx***

In words: the analysis stores no context for allocated objects. For virtual method calls, the context is the allocation site of the receiver object. For static method calls, the context for the called method is that of the calling method.

The above definition offers a first glimpse of the possibilities that we explore in this paper, and can serve as motivation. In static calls, the context of the caller method is copied, i.e., the receiver object of the caller method is used as the new context. Why not try **MERGESTATIC** (*invo, ctx*) = ***invo***, instead of the current **MERGESTATIC** (*invo, ctx*) = ***ctx***? Isn't it perhaps better to use call-sites to differentiate static invocations, instead of blindly copying the context of the last non-static method called? A simple answer is that *invo* is an entity of the wrong type, since $C = H$. The only entity of type *H* we have available at a static call-site is the current context, *ctx*. But if we let $C = H \cup I$, we have a context type that is a hybrid of both an allocation site and an invocation site, and which allows the above alternative definition of **MERGESTATIC**. We explore this and other such directions in depth in Section 3.

2-object-sensitive with a 1-context-sensitive heap (2obj+H). In this case, the heap context consists of one allocation site ($HC = H$)

[2] The standard convention in the points-to analysis literature is to name an analysis first according to the context of methods, and, if a heap context exists, designate it in a suffix such as *context-sensitive heap* or *heap cloning*.

and the context consists of two allocation sites ($C = H \times H$). The definitions of constructor functions are:[3]

RECORD (*heap, ctx*) = ***first(ctx)***
MERGE (*heap, hctx, invo, ctx*) = ***pair(heap, hctx)***
MERGESTATIC (*invo, ctx*) = ***ctx***

In words: the context of a virtual method (see **MERGE**) is a 2-element list consisting of the receiver object and its (heap) context. The heap context of an object (fixed at allocation, via **RECORD**) is the first context element of the allocating method, i.e., the receiver object on which it was invoked. Therefore, the context of a virtual method is the receiver object together with the "parent" receiver object (the receiver object of the method that allocated the receiver object of the virtual call). Again, static calls just copy the context of the caller method.

Although there can be other definitions of the **MERGE** function, yielding alternative 2-obj+H analyses, it has been shown [24] that the above is the most precise and scalable. In intuitive terms, we use as method context the most precise abstraction of the receiver object available to the analysis.

2-type-sensitive with a 1-context-sensitive heap (2type+H). A type-sensitive analysis is step-by-step analogous to an object-sensitive one, but instead of using allocation sites (i.e., instructions) a type-sensitive analysis uses the name of the class containing the allocation site. In this way, all allocation sites in methods declared in the same class (though not inherited methods) are merged. This approximation was introduced by Smaragdakis et al. [24] and yields much more scalable analyses at the expense of moderate precision loss (as we also determine in our experiments).

In order to define type-sensitive analyses we need an auxiliary function which maps each heap abstraction to the class containing the allocation.

$\mathcal{C}_{\mathcal{A}} : H \to T$

Now we can define a 2type+H analysis by mapping $\mathcal{C}_{\mathcal{A}}$ over the context of a 2obj+H analysis. The heap context uses a type instead of an allocation site ($HC = T$) and the calling context uses two types ($C = T \times T$).

RECORD (*heap, ctx*) = ***first(ctx)***
MERGE (*heap, hctx, invo, ctx*) = ***pair($\mathcal{C}_{\mathcal{A}}$(heap), hctx)***
MERGESTATIC (*invo, ctx*) = ***ctx***

Other Analyses. The above discussion omits several analyses in the literature, in order to focus on a manageable set with practical relevance. We do not discuss a 1-object-sensitive analysis with a context-sensitive heap (1obj+H) because it is a strictly inferior choice to other analyses (especially 2type+H) in practice: it is both much less precise and much slower. We do not present other varieties of type-sensitivity for a similar reason. Deeper contexts or heap contexts (e.g., 2call+H, 2obj+2H, 3obj, etc.) quickly make an analysis intractable for a substantial portion of realistic programs and modern JDKs. In short, we focus on the specific analyses (1call, 1call+H, 1obj, 2obj+H, 2type+H) that are of most practical interest: they are quite scalable over a variety of medium-to-large programs, and no other analysis supplants them by being uniformly better in both precision and performance.

[3] We use auxiliary constructor functions *pair*, *triple* and accessors *first*, *second*, and *third*, with the expected meaning, in order to construct and deconstruct contexts with 2 or 3 elements. This has the added advantage that our context-depth is statically bounded—we never create lists of unknown length. Since our most complex constructor is *triple*, the possible number of distinct contexts is cubic in the size of the input program.

3. Hybrid Context-Sensitive Analyses

We can now explore interesting combinations of call-site- and object-sensitivity. The design space is large and we will be selective in our presentation and later experiments. Our choice of analyses in this space leverages insights from past studies on what kinds of context are beneficial.[4] Such insights include:

- A call-site-sensitive heap is far less attractive than an object-sensitive heap. Generally, adding a heap context to a call-site-sensitive analysis increases precision very slightly, compared to the overwhelming cost.
- When there is a choice between keeping an object-context or a call-site-context, the former is typically more profitable. This is well validated in extensive past measurements by Lhoták and Hendren [14], comparing call-site-sensitive and object-sensitive analyses of various depths. In other words, call-site-sensitivity is best added as *extra* context over an object-sensitive analysis and will almost never pay off as a replacement context, for an object-oriented language.

3.1 Uniform Hybrid Analyses

The first kind of context combination is a straightforward one: both kinds of context are kept. We term such combinations *uniform hybrid analyses*. In the variants we describe, a uniform hybrid analysis is guaranteed to be more precise[5] than the base analysis being enhanced. The question is whether such precision will justify the added cost.

Uniform 1-object-sensitive hybrid (U-1obj). Enhancing a 1-object-sensitive analysis with call-site sensitivity results in an analysis with an empty heap context ($HC = \{\star\}$) but with a context that consists of both the allocation site of the receiver object and the invocation site of the method ($C = H \times I$). The following definitions describe the analysis:

RECORD (*heap, ctx*) = $\star$
MERGE (*heap, hctx, invo, ctx*) = ***pair(heap, invo)***
MERGESTATIC (*invo, ctx*) = ***pair(first(ctx), invo)***

In words: a virtual method has as context the abstraction of its receiver object, extended with the method's invocation site. A static method keeps a context consisting of the most significant part of the caller's context and the method's invocation site.

Note that under the above definitions, the context of a U-1obj analysis is always a superset of that of 1obj, hence the analysis is strictly more precise.

Uniform 2-object-sensitive with 1-context-sensitive heap hybrid (U-2obj+H). A 2-object-sensitive analysis with a context-sensitive heap can be enhanced in the same way. A heap context consists of an allocation site ($HC = H$) and a method context consists of two allocation sites and one invocation site ($C = H \times H \times I$). The constructor definitions for the analysis are:

RECORD (*heap, ctx*) = ***first(ctx)***
MERGE (*heap, hctx, invo, ctx*) = ***triple(heap, hctx, invo)***
MERGESTATIC (*invo, ctx*) = ***triple(first(ctx), second(ctx), invo)***

In words: an object's heap context is the receiver object of the method doing the allocation. A virtual method's context is its receiver object's allocation site and context (the latter being the allocation site of the object that allocated the receiver), followed by the

[4] We have validated these insights with extensive measurements on our experimental setup, and have generally explored a much larger portion of the design space than is possible to present in our evaluation section.

[5] We use the term "more precise" colloquially. Strictly speaking, the analysis is guaranteed to be "at least as precise".

invocation site of the method. On a static call, the heap part (i.e., first two elements) of the method context is kept unchanged, and extended with the invocation site of the call.

This analysis is also strictly more precise than the "plain" analysis it is based on, 2obj+H. Note that this is achieved partly by placing the receiver object's allocation site in the most significant position of the context triple. In this way, the **RECORD** function produces the same heap context as 2obj+H on an object's allocation. Alternative definitions are possible for the same sets of contexts, C and HC. For instance, one could choose to place *hctx* in the most significant position. Similarly, one could produce a hybrid analysis based on 2obj+H but with a different kind of heap context, e.g., $HC = I$, therefore using the invocation site in a method's context as an allocation context. These definitions make decisively less sense, however, per the insights mentioned earlier: invocation sites are rarely advantageous as heap contexts, and, similarly, it is not reasonable to invert the natural significance order of *heap* vs. *hctx*. (We have also verified experimentally that such combinations yield bad analyses.)

Uniform 2-type-sensitive with 1-context-sensitive heap hybrid (U-2type+H). Isomorphically to object-sensitivity, we can enhance type-sensitive analyses with call-site information in the same way. When applied to a 2-type-sensitive analysis with a context-sensitive heap, this results in an analysis with a heap context of one type ($HC = T$) and a context of two types and an invocation site ($C = T \times T \times I$)—mirroring the 2-object-sensitive analysis with a context sensitive heap. The definitions are almost identical:

RECORD (*heap, ctx*) = ***first(ctx)***
MERGE (*heap, hctx, invo, ctx*) = ***triple($\mathcal{C}_A$(heap), hctx, invo)***
MERGESTATIC (*invo, ctx*) = ***triple(first(ctx), second(ctx), invo)***

3.2 Selective Hybrid Analyses

Another approach to hybrid call-site- and object-sensitive analyses is to maintain a context that varies inside the same analysis. We call such analyses *selective hybrid analyses*, as opposed to the earlier "uniform hybrid" ones. In a selective hybrid analysis, the sets of contexts, C and HC, will be formed as the cartesian product of unions of sets. Depending on the information available at different analysis points where new contexts are formed, we shall create contexts of a different kind, instead of always keeping a combination of rigid form. We have already hinted at such opportunities in Section 2.2: at a static method call, an object-sensitive analysis does not have a heap object available to create a new context, hence it can at best propagate the context of the caller. Yet, an invocation site is available and can be used to distinguish different static calls, as long as we are allowed to use it as context. This observation generalizes: static invocations are a language feature that benefits highly from the presence of call-site-sensitive elements in the context. This is not hard to explain: For object-sensitive analyses, when analyzing a static invocation, we do not have much information to use in creating a new context, in contrast to a "normal" virtual invocation. Consequently, it is beneficial to be able to use the invocation site as a differentiator of static calls.

Selective hybrid analyses are among the most interesting parts of our work and, to our knowledge, have never before arisen in the literature, far less specified, implemented, and evaluated.

Selective 1-object-sensitive hybrid A (S_A-1obj). Trying to selectively enhance a 1-object-sensitive analysis ($HC = \{\star\}$) with call-site sensitive elements, we are presented with two options, relative to how contexts are created in static invocations. The first option is quite simple: we can keep only a single context element in both virtual and static invocations. Consequently, in virtual invocations the context will be an allocation site, but in static invocations it will be an invocation site ($C = H \cup I$). The definitions needed are the following:

RECORD (*heap, ctx*) = $\star$
MERGE (*heap, hctx, invo, ctx*) = ***heap***
MERGESTATIC (*invo, ctx*) = ***invo***

Note that this analysis is *not* guaranteed to be more precise than the 1obj analysis it is based on. Nevertheless, it should be an excellent reference point for comparison and insights: it will suggest how much precision can be gained or lost by call-site-sensitivity as a replacement of object-sensitivity in static method calls.

Selective 1-object-sensitive hybrid B (S_B-1obj). The second option for a selective hybrid enhancement of a 1-object-sensitive analysis is to add *extra* information to the context of static calls. This means that context in virtual invocations is still an allocation site, but context in static invocations now consists of both the allocation site copied from the caller *and* the invocation site. In this way, $C = H \times (I \cup \{\star\})$. That is, the context can be either just an allocation site or an allocation site and an invocation site. (This could also be written equivalently as $C = H \cup (H \times I)$, but the earlier form streamlines the definitions of constructors, as it makes all contexts be pairs, thus avoiding case-based definitions.) In this way the constructor definitions become:

RECORD (*heap, ctx*) = $\star$
MERGE (*heap, hctx, invo, ctx*) = ***pair(heap, $\star$)***
MERGESTATIC (*invo, ctx*) = ***pair(first(ctx), invo)***

This analysis has a context that is always a superset of the 1obj context and, therefore, is guaranteed to be more precise.

Selective 2-object-sensitive with 1-context-sensitive heap hybrid (S-2obj+H). When dealing with deeper analyses, the possible design decisions start to vary. For example, for a 2-object-sensitive analysis with a context-sensitive heap, an interesting choice is to have allocation sites as heap contexts ($HC = H$), and for method contexts to keep standard object-sensitive information for virtual calls but favor call-site-sensitivity for static calls. The constructor definitions for the above analysis are:

RECORD (*heap, ctx*) = ***first(ctx)***
MERGE (*heap, hctx, invo, ctx*) = ***triple(heap, hctx, $\star$)***
MERGESTATIC (*invo, ctx*) = ***triple(first(ctx), invo, second(ctx))***

(In this way, we have $C = H \times (H \cup I) \times (H \cup I \cup \{\star\})$.) Note the interesting behavior of such an analysis: for virtual calls, the context is equivalent to that of 2obj+H. For the first static call (i.e., from inside a virtually called method), the context is a superset of 2obj+H, augmented by an invocation site. For further static calls (i.e., static calls inside statically called methods), however, the analysis favors call-site sensitivity (both the last two elements of context are invocation sites) and otherwise only remembers the most-significant element of the object-sensitive context. (The latter is important for creating high-quality heap contexts, when allocating objects.) It is interesting to see how this analysis fares relative to 2obj+H, since the analyses are in principle incomparable in precision.

Selective 2-type-sensitive with 1-context-sensitive heap hybrid (S-2type+H). Finally, type-sensitive analyses can be enhanced with call-site sensitive information in much the same way. Mirroring our choices in S-2obj+H, the S-2type+H analysis has heap context $HC = T$ and method context $C = T \times (T \cup I) \times (T \cup I \cup \{\star\})$. The constructor definitions are isomorphic to the S-2obj+H analysis:

RECORD (*heap, ctx*) = ***first(ctx)***
MERGE (*heap, hctx, invo, ctx*) = ***triple($\mathcal{C}_A$(heap), hctx, $\star$)***
MERGESTATIC (*invo, ctx*) = ***triple(first(ctx), invo, second(ctx))***

Other analyses. The above discussion does not nearly exhaust the space of hybrid combinations. Consider selective hybrids for a 2obj+H analysis: Many more design choices are possible than the one shown. One could change the heap context into an invocation site, or into a union of invocation and call-site ($HC = H \cup I$). This combination is a bad choice, due to the poor payoff of call-site heap contexts. One could create context structures that let call-site- and object-sensitive context elements freely merge, e.g., $C = (H \cup I) \times (H \cup I) \times (H \cup I \cup \{\star\})$. This allows several different definitions of context constructors, but has the drawback of diverging significantly from object-sensitivity (i.e., allowing to skip even the most-significant object-sensitive context element), which misses the well documented precision and performance advantages of object-sensitivity, especially as a heap context.

4. Evaluation

We implemented and evaluated all aforementioned analyses using the DOOP framework [4]. There are interesting and subtle aspects in our measurements, but the executive summary is clear: uniform hybrid analyses are typically not good choices in practice: their precision is offset by a very high performance cost. (A relative exception is the uniform type-sensitive hybrid analysis, U-2type+H, which, although higher-cost, is not prohibitively expensive and offers a reasonable precision/performance tradeoff.) Selective hybrid analyses, on the other hand, are not just interesting tradeoffs but clear winners: they match or (usually) outperform the object-sensitive analyses they are based on, while offering better precision, closely approaching the precision of the much more costly uniform hybrids. Overall, the best analyses in our evaluation set, both for highest-precision and for high performance with good precision, are selective hybrids.

Our evaluation setting uses the LogicBlox Datalog engine, v.3.9.0, on a Xeon X5650 2.67GHz machine with only one thread running at a time and 24GB of RAM (i.e., ample for the analyses studied). We analyze the DaCapo benchmark programs (v.2006-10-MR2) under JDK 1.6.0_37. (This is a much larger set of libraries than earlier work [4, 24], which also results in differences in measurements, since the numbers shown integrate application- and library-level metrics.) (All numbers shown are medians of three runs.) All runtime numbers are medians of three runs. As in other published work [1, 24], jython and hsqldb are analyzed with reflection disabled and hsqldb has its entry point set manually in a special harness.

4.1 Illustration

For an illustration of the precision and performance spectrum, consider Figure 3, which plots analyses on precision/performance axes. The figure plots execution time against precision in the "may-fail casts" metric, i.e., the number of casts that the analysis cannot statically prove safe. Lower numbers are better on both axes, thus an analysis that is to the left and below another is better in both precision and performance. Values that are disproportionately high on the Y axis (i.e., large execution times) are clipped and plotted at the top of the figure, with the actual number included in parentheses. (Note that the Y axis starts at zero, while the X axis starts at an arbitrary point—we cannot know what is the "ideal" reference value for this metric.)

In terms of pre-existing analyses, Figure 3 illustrates what has been past experience: 2obj+H is the most precise analysis, but often heavy. 1obj and 2type+H are both quite fast, with 2type+H also showing very good precision, often approaching 2obj+H. The two call-site-sensitive analyses (1call, 1call+H) are mostly shown for reference and to demonstrate the insights discussed in Section 3. 1call is a fast analysis but vastly imprecise, while 1call+H is a bad tradeoff: its cost grows quite significantly relative to 1call without much precision added—call-site sensitivity is a bad choice for heap contexts.

As can be seen, the selective hybrid analyses (S_A-1obj, S_A-1obj, S-2obj+H, S-2type+H) usually offer an advantage over the corresponding base analysis (1obj, 2type+H, 2obj+H) in both precision and performance. In fact, selective hybrids are typically imperceptibly less precise than the corresponding uniform hybrid, yet much more precise than the base analysis. For instance, the plot points for S-2obj+H are always barely to the right of those for the theoretically more precise U-2obj+H (but significantly lower—uniform hybrids are very expensive), while they are clearly to the left of 2obj+H.

4.2 Detailed Results

Detailed results of our experiments are presented in Table 1. The table shows precision and performance metrics for all analyses. The precision metrics are the average points-to set size (i.e., average over all variables of their points-to sets sizes), the number of edges in the computed call-graph (which is typically a good proxy for the overall precision of the analysis, in broad strokes), and the results of two client analyses: the number of virtual calls that could not be de-virtualized, and the number of casts that could not be statically proven safe. A combination of these four metrics gives a reliable picture of the precision of an analysis. (Note that the average points-to set size alone is not necessarily reliable, because it is influenced by a small number of library variables with enormous points-to sets. For comparison, the *median* points-to set size is 1, for all analyses and benchmarks.)

Performance is shown with two metrics: time and total size of all *context-sensitive* points-to sets. Although time is the ultimate performance metric, it is brittle: one can argue that our time measurements are influenced by a multitude of implementation or environment factors, among which are the choice of underlying data structures, indexing, and the overall implementation of the points-to analysis, especially since it is running on a Datalog engine, with its own complex implementation choices hidden. The context-sensitive points-to set size metric does not suffer from any such measurement or implementation bias. It is the foremost internal complexity metric of a points-to analysis, and typically correlates well with time, for analyses of the same flavor. Note that analysis implementations that fundamentally differ from ours also try hard to minimize this metric in order to achieve peak performance: Lhoták's PADDLE framework [12] is using binary decision diagrams (BDDs) for representing relations. The best BDD variable ordering (yielding "impressive results" [3]) is one that minimizes the total size of context-sensitive points-to sets. In short, it is reasonable to expect that improvements in this internal metric reinforce the verdict of which analysis yields better performance, not just in our setting but generally. Furthermore, the size of context-sensitive points-to sets serves as a valuable indicator of the internally different computation performed by various analyses: Analyses with almost identical precision metrics (e.g., context-insensitive points-to set sizes, call-graph edges) have vastly different context-sensitive points-to set sizes.

Since Table 1 has a high information density, we guide the reader through some of the most important findings below (see also a partial illustration in Figure 3, later).

- ***General observations.*** The analyses shown are in 4 groups of closely related analyses: call-site sensitive, 1-object-sensitive, 2-object-sensitive with a 1-context-sensitive heap, and 2-type-sensitive with a 1-context-sensitive heap. These analyses span a large performance and precision spectrum. For instance, for the chart benchmark, the least precise analysis, 1call, runs for under 5mins and computes an average points-to size of over 45, while the most precise, U-2obj+H, runs for over 53mins and computes

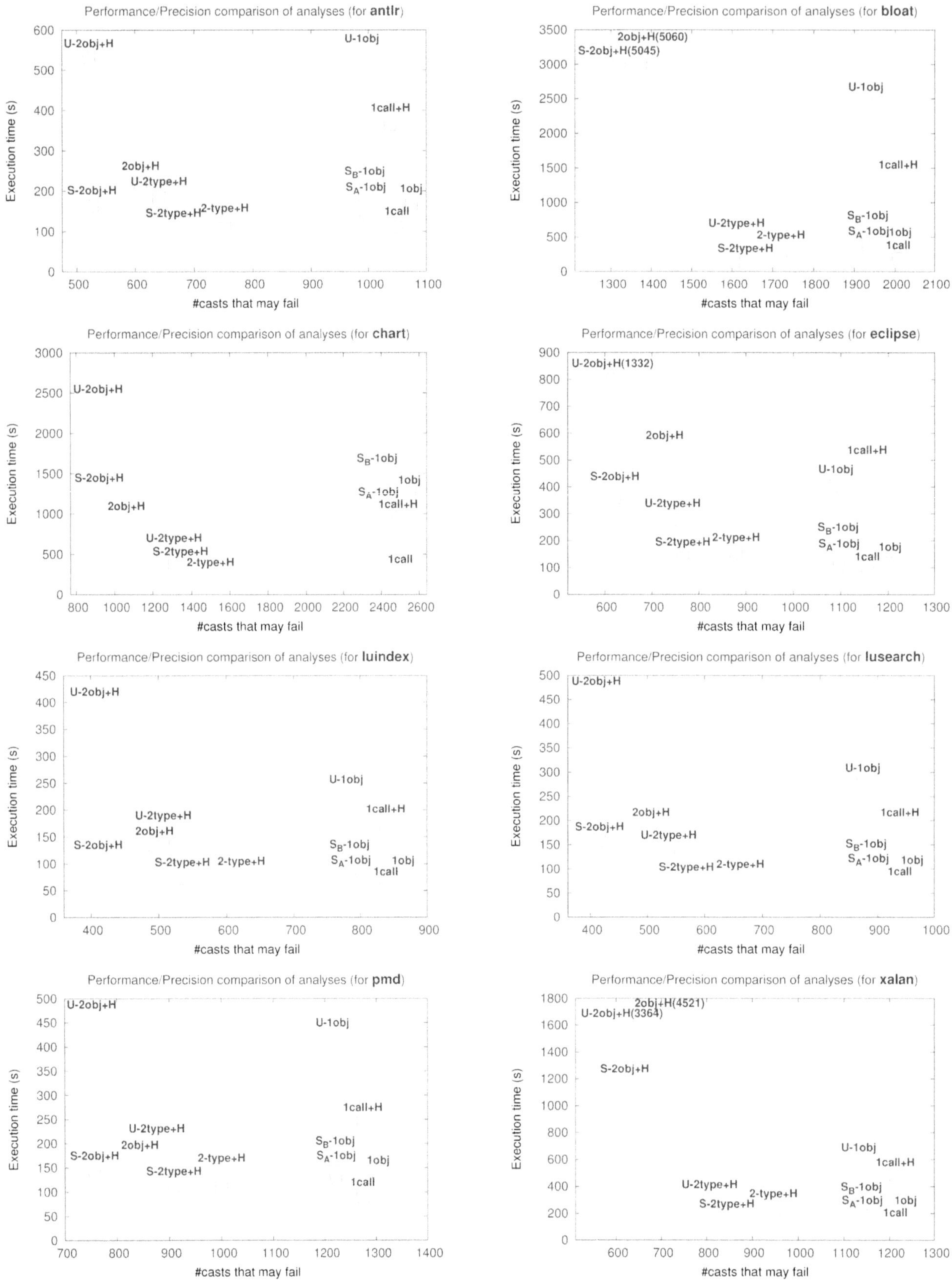

Figure 3: Graphical depiction of performance vs. precision metrics for eight of our benchmarks over all analyses. Lower is better on both axes. The Y axis is truncated for readability. Out-of-bounds points are included at lower Y values, with their real running time in parentheses.

		1call	*1call+H*	*1obj*	*U-1obj*	S_A*-1obj*	S_B*-1obj*	*2obj+H*	*U-2obj+H*	*S-2obj+H*	*2type+H*	*U-2type+H*	*S-2type+H*
antlr	avg. objs per var	29.79	29.58	24.86	24.55	24.90	24.61	6.42	6.26	6.27	17.60	7.14	17.39
	edges (over ~8.8K meths)	60999	60999	60194	60194	60202	60194	55548	55548	55548	55850	55765	55850
	poly v-calls (of ~33K)	1994	1994	1933	1933	1936	1933	1707	1707	1707	1759	1746	1759
	may-fail casts (of ~1.7K)	1049	1038	1074	989	996	994	609	521	526	752	640	665
	elapsed time (s)	110	366	166	544	**142**	182	217	532	**162**	108	184	**106**
	sensitive var-points-to (M)	16	54.8	14.3	65	**10.5**	17.3	19.9	39.5	**13.9**	5.3	8.9	**4.8**
bloat	avg. objs per var	43.96	43.94	41.26	41.16	41.32	41.18	13.25	-	13.10	16.28	14.71	16.10
	edges (over ~10.2K meths)	70506	70506	69501	69501	69511	69501	60726	-	60726	62115	61753	62115
	poly v-calls (of ~31K)	2138	2138	2076	2076	2080	2076	1640	-	1640	1888	1827	1888
	may-fail casts (of ~2.8K)	2008	2008	2013	1928	1935	1933	1403	-	1320	1720	1611	1633
	elapsed time (s)	186	1351	374	2473	**353**	391	5060	-	**5045**	142	353	**140**
	sensitive var-points-to (M)	32.9	150.5	21.9	287.1	**20.1**	24	153.5	-	**149.8**	11.4	30.3	**11**
chart	avg. objs per var	45.12	45.11	40.80	-	40.72	40.11	5.30	4.99	5.00	7.02	5.89	6.57
	edges (over ~15K meths)	82156	82078	81423	-	81075	81012	59162	59142	59152	62290	62172	62280
	poly v-calls (of ~35K)	2900	2897	2821	-	2815	2808	1610	1603	1610	1775	1756	1775
	may-fail casts (of ~3.5K)	2500	2488	2548	-	2385	2378	1062	915	920	1498	1309	1343
	elapsed time (s)	288	957	1240	-	**1059**	1477	**896**	2363	1199	**211**	362	276
	sensitive var-points-to (M)	49.6	120.9	62.5	-	**39.7**	89.7	67.6	115.7	**53**	**13.3**	21.3	16.5
eclipse	avg. objs per var	21.84	21.65	18.65	18.41	18.59	18.43	5.75	5.60	5.61	7.93	6.41	7.61
	edges (over ~9.3K meths)	53006	53001	52114	51935	51958	51936	44900	44899	44900	45318	45123	45235
	poly v-calls (of ~23K)	1515	1514	1429	1404	1412	1404	1163	1163	1163	1233	1202	1229
	may-fail casts (of ~2K)	1156	1155	1204	1089	1096	1094	727	616	621	879	744	766
	elapsed time (s)	81	478	117	406	**105**	126	532	1332	**359**	152	278	**135**
	sensitive var-points-to (M)	12.3	61.5	9.4	42.3	**7.6**	10.8	44.6	89.8	**32.3**	13.6	24.4	**11.5**
hsqldb	avg. objs per var	18.56	18.53	15.41	15.30	15.58	15.32	-	-	-	7.92	6.71	7.74
	edges (over ~10K meths)	54619	54619	53726	53724	53730	53724	-	-	-	49421	49319	49421
	poly v-calls (of ~26K)	1552	1552	1480	1479	1482	1479	-	-	-	1276	1263	1276
	may-fail casts (of ~2K)	1360	1360	1385	1302	1320	1308	-	-	-	1031	923	948
	elapsed time (s)	90	332	218	1351	**183**	329	-	-	-	**195**	583	238
	sensitive var-points-to (M)	9.6	39.8	13.9	74.3	**9.6**	29.5	-	-	-	**13.7**	42.9	20.5
jython	avg. objs per var	20.64	20.57	18.21	18.01	18.19	18.09	-	-	-	8.55	7.18	8.30
	edges (over ~8.5K meths)	50494	50480	49622	49614	49622	49614	-	-	-	43269	43138	43269
	poly v-calls (of ~21K)	1525	1524	1448	1448	1453	1448	-	-	-	1268	1236	1268
	may-fail casts (of ~1.9K)	1140	1140	1157	1087	1094	1092	-	-	-	909	822	840
	elapsed time (s)	88	401	119	375	**102**	138	-	-	-	731	1363	**676**
	sensitive var-points-to (M)	10.4	50.6	8.7	43.2	**6.7**	10.8	-	-	-	**52**	118.4	56.5
luindex	avg. objs per var	17.65	17.58	14.94	14.81	14.97	14.83	4.77	4.55	4.55	6.20	5.15	5.92
	edges (over ~7.9K meths)	41992	41992	41103	41103	41111	41103	36580	36580	36580	36889	36796	36889
	poly v-calls (of ~18K)	1180	1180	1119	1119	1122	1119	894	894	894	949	932	949
	may-fail casts (of ~1.4K)	838	838	864	779	786	784	494	406	411	622	507	535
	elapsed time (s)	59	172	76	227	**70**	81	131	377	**105**	75	132	**73**
	sensitive var-points-to (M)	7.8	26.1	5.4	26.3	**4.1**	6.4	11.1	22.4	**7.2**	4.5	7.6	**3.5**
lusearch	avg. objs per var	18.64	18.47	15.71	15.57	15.79	15.60	4.71	4.49	4.50	6.13	5.10	5.86
	edges (over ~8.4K meths)	45270	45270	44371	44365	44379	44371	39452	39446	39452	39763	39662	39763
	poly v-calls (of ~19K)	1360	1360	1299	1299	1302	1299	1065	1065	1065	1122	1103	1122
	may-fail casts (of ~1.5K)	939	939	961	874	884	880	506	410	416	662	537	568
	elapsed time (s)	63	187	89	279	**84**	95	183	464	**158**	76	137	**74**
	sensitive var-points-to (M)	8.7	28.5	6.2	30.3	**5.3**	7.2	13.2	26.3	**10**	4.2	7.8	**3.6**
pmd	avg. objs per var	19.94	19.82	17.36	17.22	17.37	17.24	4.87	4.68	4.68	6.35	5.28	6.10
	edges (over ~9.2K meths)	49097	49097	48250	48250	48258	48250	43068	43067	43067	43401	43315	43400
	poly v-calls (of ~21K)	1249	1249	1187	1187	1190	1187	937	937	937	988	976	988
	may-fail casts (of ~2K)	1274	1274	1304	1215	1222	1220	844	752	757	1000	876	909
	elapsed time (s)	90	245	135	420	**128**	142	167	465	**145**	114	201	**113**
	sensitive var-points-to (M)	11.4	35.9	7.9	42.6	**6.9**	9.2	13.2	30.5	**10**	4.5	9.7	**3.9**
xalan	avg. objs per var	25.50	25.38	21.86	21.59	21.84	21.69	5.48	5.22	5.23	7.52	6.19	7.16
	edges (over ~10.5K meths)	57168	57168	56412	56158	56404	56395	50148	50054	50054	50539	50432	50526
	poly v-calls (of ~26K)	1976	1976	1920	1905	1921	1918	1619	1615	1615	1677	1660	1677
	may-fail casts (of ~2K)	1213	1213	1236	1132	1140	1138	718	613	619	946	806	844
	elapsed time (s)	108	470	189	591	**161**	205	4521	3364	**1105**	168	299	**161**
	sensitive var-points-to (M)	14.5	59.8	15.5	67.5	**10.9**	18.2	166.6	171.7	**63.3**	10.2	17.4	**9**

Table 1: Precision and performance metrics for all benchmarks and analyses, grouped by relevance. In all cases *lower is better*. Dash (-) entries are for analyses that did not terminate in 90mins. The 4 precision metrics shown are the average size of points-to sets (how many heap objects are computed to be pointed-to per-var), the number of edges in the computed call-graph, the number of virtual calls whose target cannot be disambiguated by the analysis, and the number of casts that cannot be statically shown safe by the analysis. Reference numbers (e.g., total reachable casts in the program) are shown in parentheses in the metric's heading. These numbers change little per-analysis. Performance is shown as running time and size of context-sensitive var-points-to data (the main platform-independent internal complexity metric). Best performance numbers per-analysis-group are **in bold**.

an average points-to size of under 5. The difference in precision is also vividly shown in the "may-fail casts" metric: the 1call analysis cannot prove 2500 casts safe, while the U-2obj+H fails to prove safe just 915 casts (both numbers from a total of about 3.5K reachable casts—the exact number varies slightly due to method reachability variation per analysis).

- ***Uniform hybrid analyses.*** Recall that uniform hybrid analyses (U-1obj, U-2obj+H, U-2type+H) were defined to always keep a combination of object-sensitive and call-site-sensitive context. As a result, the analyses are more precise than their respective base analyses (1obj, 2obj+H, 2type+H), especially in the "may-fail casts" metric. However, this precision comes at great cost: uniform hybrid analyses are often 3x or more slower than their base analyses with twice as large, or more, context-sensitive points-to sets. U-1obj and U-2obj+H are plainly bad tradeoffs in the design space: for a slight increase in precision, the performance cost is heavy. U-2type+H is a bit more reasonable: it achieves more significant precision gains and its performance toll is often under 2x while still terminating comfortably for all our benchmarks. In fact, a surprising finding was that U-2type+H is a tempting alternative to 2obj+H for applications that need very high precision, given its good scalability.
- ***1obj hybrids.*** We presented two selective hybrids of a 1-object-sensitive analysis: S_A-1obj (which keeps either an allocation site or a call-site as context, but not both) and S_B-1obj (which always keeps an allocation site as context and occasionally adds a call-site to it). They both turn out to be interesting analyses from a practical standpoint. The former is consistently faster than the base 1obj analysis, with roughly similar precision and occasionally (for the "may-fail casts" metric) higher precision. The size of context-sensitive points-to sets also confirms that this is a "lighter" analysis that is likely to cost less in any context. The S_B-1obj analysis is always more precise than 1obj (as is statically guaranteed) for a slight extra cost. Indeed, S_B-1obj is a good approximation of the uniform hybrid analysis, U-1obj, in terms of precision, for a fraction (typically less than a third) of the cost.
- ***2obj+H hybrids.*** The selective hybrid idea yields even more dividends when applied to the very precise 2obj+H analysis. S-2obj+H is more precise than 2obj+H and only very slightly less precise than the uniform hybrid, U-2obj+H. In terms of performance, however, the analysis is typically well over 3 times faster than U-2obj+H, and significantly faster (an average of 53% speedup) than 2obj+H. This is interesting, given the practical value of 2obj+H, since it establishes a new sweet spot in the space of relatively scalable but highly precise analyses: S-2obj+H is both more precise than 2obj+H (especially for "may-fail casts") and substantially faster.
- ***2type+H hybrids.*** The 2type+H analysis variations are also highly interesting in practice. This is an analysis space that yields excellent precision relative to its low cost. There are few cases in which one might prefer some other inexpensive analysis over 2type+H given the combination of precision and competitive performance of the latter. As we saw, the uniform hybrid, U-2type+H, is an interesting tradeoff in this space. The selective hybrid, S-2type+H, also performs quite well. It is just as fast or slightly faster than the base analysis 2type+H, while also being more precise.

5. Related Work

We have discussed directly related work throughout the paper. Here we selectively mention a few techniques that, although not directly related to ours, offer alternative approaches to sweet spots in the precision/performance tradeoff.

Special-purpose combinations of context-sensitivity have been used in the past, but have required manual identification of classes to be treated separately (e.g., Java collection classes, or library factory methods). An excellent representative is the TAJ work for taint analysis of Java web applications [27]. In contrast, we have sought to map the space and identify interesting hybrids for general application of context-sensitivity, over the entire program.

The analyses we examined are context-sensitive but flow-insensitive. We can achieve several of the benefits of flow-sensitivity by applying the analysis on the static single assignment (SSA) intermediate form of the program. This is easy to do with a mere flag setting on the DOOP framework. However, the impact of the SSA transformation on the input is minimal. The default intermediate language used as input in DOOP (the Jimple representation of the Soot framework [28, 29]) is already close to SSA form, although it does not guarantee that every variable is strictly single-assignment without requesting it explicitly. Recent work by Lhoták and Chung [13] has shown that much of the benefit of flow-sensitivity derives from the ability to do strong updates of the points-to information. Lhoták and Chung then exploited this insight to derive analyses with similar benefit to a full flow-sensitive analysis at lower cost.

A demand-driven evaluation strategy reduces the cost of an analysis by computing only those results that are necessary for a client program analysis [10, 25, 26, 32]. This is a useful approach for client analyses that focus on specific locations in a program, but if the client needs results from the entire program, then demand-driven analysis is typically slower than an exhaustive analysis.

Reps [21] showed how to use the standard magic-sets optimization to automatically derive a demand-driven analysis from an exhaustive analysis (like ours). This optimization combines the benefits of top-down and bottom-up evaluation of logic programs by adding side-conditions to rules that limit the computation to just the required data.

An interesting recent approach to demand-driven analyses was introduced by Liang and Naik [15]. Their "pruning" approach consists of first computing a coarse over-approximation of the points-to information, while keeping the provenance of this derivation, i.e., recording which input facts have affected each part of the output. The input program is then pruned so that parts that did not affect the interesting points of the output are eliminated. Then a precise analysis is run, in order to establish the desired property.

6. Conclusions and Future Work

We presented a comprehensive map for the exploration of context combinations in points-to analysis, and used it to discover several interesting design points. Object-sensitivity and call-site-sensitivity had never been fruitfully combined in the past, although the idea is clearly tempting. We speculate that the reasons for the paucity of hybrid context-sensitivity results have been a) the difficulty of having a good enough model for the space of combinations and a convenient implementation to explore it; b) a belief that nothing fruitful will come out of such a combination, because call-site sensitivity incurs a high performance cost, which is more profitably spent on an extra level of object-sensitivity. The latter insight is mostly true, but only if one considers uniform hybrid analyses. As we saw, much of the benefit of call-site and object-sensitive hybrids comes from allowing the context to vary between pure object-sensitive and extended. The result of our work has been new sweet spots, in both precision and performance, for some of the most practically relevant analysis variations.

There are several interesting directions for further work that open up. First, our model gives the ability for further experimentation, e.g., with deeper-context analyses. Furthermore, it is interesting to examine if a hybrid context should perhaps change form more aggressively. The **Merge** and **MergeStatic** functions could examine the context passed to them as argument and create different kinds of contexts in return. For instance, the context of a statically called method could have a different form (e.g., more elements) for a call made inside another statically called method vs. a call made in a virtual method. Similarly, objects could have different context, via the **Record** function, depending on the context form of their allocating method. To explore this space without blind guessing, one needs to understand what programming patterns are best handled by hybrid contexts and how. For deep contexts this remains a challenge, as it is hard to reason about how context elements affect precision. (E.g., past work had to offer involved arguments for why the allocator object of the receiver object of a method is a better context element than the caller object [24].) This challenge is, however, worth addressing for the next level of benefit in context-sensitive points-to analysis.

Acknowledgments

We gratefully acknowledge funding by the European Union under a Marie Curie International Reintegration Grant and a European Research Council Starting/Consolidator grant; and by the Greek Secretariat for Research and Technology under an Excellence (Aristeia) award. We thank the anonymous reviewers, who offered several valuable suggestions, and LogicBlox Inc. for providing our Datalog engine, as well as technical and material support.

References

[1] K. Ali and O. Lhoták. Application-only call graph construction. In *European Conf. on Object-Oriented Programming (ECOOP)*, 2012.

[2] L. O. Andersen. *Program Analysis and Specialization for the C Programming Language*. PhD thesis, DIKU, University of Copenhagen, 1994.

[3] M. Berndl, O. Lhoták, F. Qian, L. J. Hendren, and N. Umanee. Points-to analysis using BDDs. In *Conf. on Programming Language Design and Implementation (PLDI)*, 2003.

[4] M. Bravenboer and Y. Smaragdakis. Strictly declarative specification of sophisticated points-to analyses. In *Conf. on Object Oriented Programming, Systems, Languages, and Applications (OOPSLA)*, 2009.

[5] M. Eichberg, S. Kloppenburg, K. Klose, and M. Mezini. Defining and continuous checking of structural program dependencies. In *Int. Conf. on Software engineering (ICSE)*, 2008.

[6] S. Guarnieri and B. Livshits. GateKeeper: mostly static enforcement of security and reliability policies for Javascript code. In *Proceedings of the 18th USENIX Security Symposium*, 2009.

[7] E. Hajiyev, M. Verbaere, and O. de Moor. Codequest: Scalable source code queries with Datalog. In *European Conf. on Object-Oriented Programming (ECOOP)*, 2006.

[8] B. Hardekopf and C. Lin. The ant and the grasshopper: fast and accurate pointer analysis for millions of lines of code. In *Conf. on Programming Language Design and Implementation (PLDI)*, 2007.

[9] B. Hardekopf and C. Lin. Semi-sparse flow-sensitive pointer analysis. In *Symposium on Principles of Programming Languages (POPL)*, 2009.

[10] N. Heintze and O. Tardieu. Demand-driven pointer analysis. In *Conf. on Programming Language Design and Implementation (PLDI)*, 2001.

[11] M. S. Lam, J. Whaley, V. B. Livshits, M. C. Martin, D. Avots, M. Carbin, and C. Unkel. Context-sensitive program analysis as database queries. In *Symposium on Principles of Database Systems (PODS)*, 2005.

[12] O. Lhoták. *Program Analysis using Binary Decision Diagrams*. PhD thesis, McGill University, 2006.

[13] O. Lhoták and K.-C. A. Chung. Points-to analysis with efficient strong updates. In *Symposium on Principles of Programming Languages (POPL)*, 2011.

[14] O. Lhoták and L. Hendren. Evaluating the benefits of context-sensitive points-to analysis using a BDD-based implementation. *ACM Trans. Softw. Eng. Methodol.*, 18(1):1–53, 2008.

[15] P. Liang and M. Naik. Scaling abstraction refinement via pruning. In *Conf. on Programming Language Design and Implementation (PLDI)*, 2011.

[16] M. Madsen, B. Livshits, and M. Fanning. Practical static analysis of Javascript applications in the presence of frameworks and libraries. Technical Report MSR-TR-2012-66, Microsoft Research, 2012.

[17] M. Might, Y. Smaragdakis, and D. Van Horn. Resolving and exploiting the k-CFA paradox: Illuminating functional vs. object-oriented program analysis. In *Conf. on Programming Language Design and Implementation (PLDI)*, 2010.

[18] A. Milanova, A. Rountev, and B. G. Ryder. Parameterized object sensitivity for points-to and side-effect analyses for Java. In *International Symposium on Software Testing and Analysis (ISSTA)*, 2002.

[19] A. Milanova, A. Rountev, and B. G. Ryder. Parameterized object sensitivity for points-to analysis for Java. *ACM Trans. Softw. Eng. Methodol.*, 14(1):1–41, 2005.

[20] T. Reps. Demand interprocedural program analysis using logic databases. In *Applications of Logic Databases*, 1994.

[21] T. W. Reps. Solving demand versions of interprocedural analysis problems. In *Int. Conf. on Compiler Construction (CC)*, 1994.

[22] M. Sharir and A. Pnueli. Two approaches to interprocedural data flow analysis. In *Program Flow Analysis*, 1981.

[23] O. Shivers. *Control-Flow Analysis of Higher-Order Languages*. PhD thesis, Carnegie Mellon University, 1991.

[24] Y. Smaragdakis, M. Bravenboer, and O. Lhoták. Pick your contexts well: Understanding object-sensitivity (the making of a precise and scalable pointer analysis). In *Symposium on Principles of Programming Languages (POPL)*, 2011.

[25] M. Sridharan and R. Bodík. Refinement-based context-sensitive points-to analysis for Java. In *Conf. on Programming Language Design and Implementation (PLDI)*, 2006.

[26] M. Sridharan, D. Gopan, L. Shan, and R. Bodík. Demand-driven points-to analysis for Java. In *Conf. on Object Oriented Programming, Systems, Languages, and Applications (OOPSLA)*, 2005.

[27] O. Tripp, M. Pistoia, S. J. Fink, M. Sridharan, and O. Weisman. Taj: effective taint analysis of web applications. In *Conf. on Programming Language Design and Implementation (PLDI)*, 2009.

[28] R. Vallée-Rai, E. Gagnon, L. J. Hendren, P. Lam, P. Pominville, and V. Sundaresan. Optimizing Java bytecode using the Soot framework: Is it feasible? In *Int. Conf. on Compiler Construction (CC)*, 2000.

[29] R. Vallée-Rai, L. Hendren, V. Sundaresan, P. Lam, E. Gagnon, and P. Co. Soot - a Java optimization framework. In *Proceedings of CASCON 1999*, 1999.

[30] J. Whaley, D. Avots, M. Carbin, and M. S. Lam. Using Datalog with binary decision diagrams for program analysis. In *APLAS*, 2005.

[31] J. Whaley and M. S. Lam. Cloning-based context-sensitive pointer alias analysis using binary decision diagrams. In *Conf. on Programming Language Design and Implementation (PLDI)*, 2004.

[32] X. Zheng and R. Rugina. Demand-driven alias analysis for c. In *Symposium on Principles of Programming Languages (POPL)*, 2008.

Fast Algorithms for Dyck-CFL-Reachability with Applications to Alias Analysis

Qirun Zhang Michael R. Lyu
The Chinese University of Hong Kong
{qrzhang, lyu}@cse.cuhk.edu.hk

Hao Yuan *
BOPU Technologies
hao@bopufund.com

Zhendong Su
University of California, Davis
su@cs.ucdavis.edu

Abstract

The context-free language (CFL) reachability problem is a well-known fundamental formulation in program analysis. In practice, many program analyses, especially pointer analyses, adopt a restricted version of CFL-reachability, Dyck-CFL-reachability, and compute on edge-labeled bidirected graphs. Solving the all-pairs Dyck-CFL-reachability on such bidirected graphs is expensive. For a bidirected graph with n nodes and m edges, the traditional dynamic programming style algorithm exhibits a subcubic time complexity for the Dyck language with k kinds of parentheses. When the underlying graphs are restricted to bidirected trees, an algorithm with $O(n \log n \log k)$ time complexity was proposed recently. This paper studies the Dyck-CFL-reachability problems on bidirected trees and graphs. In particular, it presents two fast algorithms with $O(n)$ and $O(n + m \log m)$ time complexities on trees and graphs respectively. We have implemented and evaluated our algorithms on a state-of-the-art alias analysis for Java. Results on standard benchmarks show that our algorithms achieve orders of magnitude speedup and consume less memory.

Categories and Subject Descriptors F.2.2 [*Nonnumerical Algorithms and Problems*]: Computations on discrete structures; D.3.4 [*Processors*]: Compilers; F.3.2 [*Semantics of Programming Languages*]: Program analysis

General Terms Algorithms, Design, Experimentation, Languages

Keywords Dyck-CFL-reachability; alias analysis

1. Introduction

The context-free language (CFL) reachability problem is a generalization of the traditional graph reachability problem [27]. Many program analyses have been formulated as CFL-reachability problems, such as interprocedural data flow analysis [29], program slicing [28], shape analysis [26], type-based flow analysis [22, 25], and pointer analysis [31–33, 36, 37, 40]. When the underlying CFL is restricted to a Dyck language which generates matched parentheses, the CFL-reachability problem is referred to as Dyck-CFL-reachability. Although a restricted version of CFL-reachability, Dyck-CFL-reachability can express "almost all of the applications of CFL-reachability" in program analysis [19].

Solving Dyck-CFL-reachability of size k (*i.e.*, k kinds of parentheses) is expensive in practice. The traditional dynamic programming style CFL-reachability algorithm [29, 38] runs in $O(k^3 n^3)$ time. Only recently, the first subcubic algorithm was proposed, reducing the cubic time complexity by a factor of $\log n$ [7]. Scaling Dyck-CFL-reachability-based analyses on real-world applications is challenging. Various enhancements have been proposed, such as leveraging demand-driven properties in specific analyses [33, 37, 40], making use of a specialized reduction to set constraints [19], and approximating the client problems [32, 33]. However, all existing Dyck-CFL-reachability algorithms relying on the dynamic programming scheme exhibit a subcubic time complexity. When the underlying graphs are restricted to bidirected trees, Yuan and Eugster proposed an algorithm with $O(n \log n \log k)$ time complexity [39].

In this paper, we focus on the bidirected version of Dyck-CFL-reachability, as detailed in Section 2.2. The bidirected Dyck-CFL-reachability is particularly suitable for pointer analysis. All state-of-the-art demand-driven pointer analyses [31–33, 37, 40] are formulated by extending Dyck-CFL-reachability and compute on edge-labeled bidirected graphs. Specifically, matched parentheses derived from Dyck-CFL-reachability can be used to capture field accesses (*i.e.*, `load`/`store`) in Java [32, 33, 36, 37] and indirections (*i.e.*, references/dereferences) in C [40]. The bidirectness of graphs is also a prerequisite for CFL-reachability formulations of pointer analyses as discussed by Reps [27]. Namely, edges in the original graph need to be augmented with reverse edges (*a.k.a.* barred edges). Otherwise, two nodes may not be reachable even via standard graph reachability.

This paper proposes two fast algorithms for solving the bidirected Dyck-CFL-reachability on trees and graphs respectively. The key insight behind our algorithms is the observation of an equivalence property on bidirected structures that has not been fully utilized in previous work. We exploit this property to obtain asymptotically much faster algorithms by safely collapsing nodes that belong to the same equivalence class. Table 1 compares our new algorithms and some of the existing algorithms for bidirected Dyck-CFL-reachability, where n and m denote the numbers of nodes and edges in the graph respectively. We also present the design and implementation of our algorithms, and apply them to a state-of-the-art alias analysis [37]. Empirical results on the standard benchmarks show that our proposed algorithms achieve orders of magnitude speedup and consume less memory compared to the traditional CFL-reachability algorithm.

The principal contributions of our work are as follows:

- For the case of bidirected trees, we give an algorithm that runs in $O(n)$ time and $O(n)$ space, which answers the Dyck-CFL-

* Part of this work was done while the author was working at City University of Hong Kong.

PLDI'13, June 16–19, 2013, Seattle, WA, USA.

Type	Time	Space	Reference
Tree	$O(n \log n \log k)$	$O(n \log n)$	[39]
Graph	$O(k^3 n^3)$	$O(kn^2)$	[29, 38]
Graph	$O(kn^3)$	$O(kn^2)$	[19]
Graph	$O(kn^3/\log n)$	$O(kn^2)$	[7]
Tree	$O(n)$	$O(n)$	Algorithm 4
Graph	$O(n + m \log m)$	$O(n + m)$	Algorithm 5

Table 1. Bidirected Dyck-CFL-reachability algorithms.

reachability queries for any node pair in $O(1)$ time. This result improves the $O(n \log n \log k)$ time and $O(n \log n)$ space algorithm proposed by Yuan and Eugster [39].

- For the case of bidirected graphs, we give an algorithm that runs in $O(n + m \log m)$ time and $O(n + m)$ space, which answers the Dyck-CFL-reachability queries for any node pair in $O(1)$ time. This result improves the traditional subcubic time result in the literature [7].
- We apply our algorithms to a state-of-the-art context-insensitive alias analysis for Java [37]. Our fast algorithms can be directly used in the analysis. Experimental results show that our algorithm achieves orders of magnitude speedup on real-world benchmarks.

The rest of the paper is structured as follows. Section 2 reviews the background material on Dyck-CFL-reachability. Section 3 discusses the equivalence property and a naïve all-pairs Dyck-CFL-reachability algorithm. Sections 4 and 5 present our fast algorithms on bidirected trees and graphs respectively. Section 6 describes an existing state-of-the-art alias analysis for Java as the client application for our algorithms. Section 7 describes our empirical comparison of the performance of our algorithm versus the performance of the CFL-reachability algorithm using the client alias analysis. Section 8 surveys related work, and Section 9 concludes.

2. Preliminaries

This section reviews basic background on Dyck-CFL-reachability and defines its bidirected variants. We also include the traditional subcubic solution for reference and completeness.

2.1 Dyck-CFL-Reachability

Let $CFG = (\Sigma, N, P, S)$ be a context-free grammar with alphabet Σ, nonterminal symbols N, production rules P and start symbol S. Given a context-free grammar $CFG = (\Sigma, N, P, S)$ and a directed graph $G = (V, E)$ with each edge $(u, v) \in E$ labeled by a terminal $\mathcal{L}(u, v)$ from the alphabet Σ or ε, each path $p = v_0, v_1, v_2, \ldots, v_m$ in G *realizes* a string $R(p)$ over the alphabet Σ by concatenating the edge labels in the path in order, *i.e.*, $R(p) = \mathcal{L}(v_0, v_1)\mathcal{L}(v_1, v_2)\mathcal{L}(v_2, v_3) \ldots \mathcal{L}(v_{m-1}, v_m)$. A path in G is an S-path if the *realized* string can be derived from the start symbol S. Node v is S-reachable from node u iff there exists an S-path from u to v.

The CFL-reachability problem has four variants:

(1) *The all-pairs S-path problem:* For every pair of nodes u and v, is there an S-path in the graph from u to v?

(2) *The single-source S-path problem:* Given a source node u, for all nodes v, is there an S-path in the graph from u to v?

(3) *The single-target S-path problem:* Given a target node v, for all nodes u, is there an S-path in the graph from u to v?

(4) *The single-source-single-target problem:* Given two nodes u and v, is there an S-path in the graph from u to v?

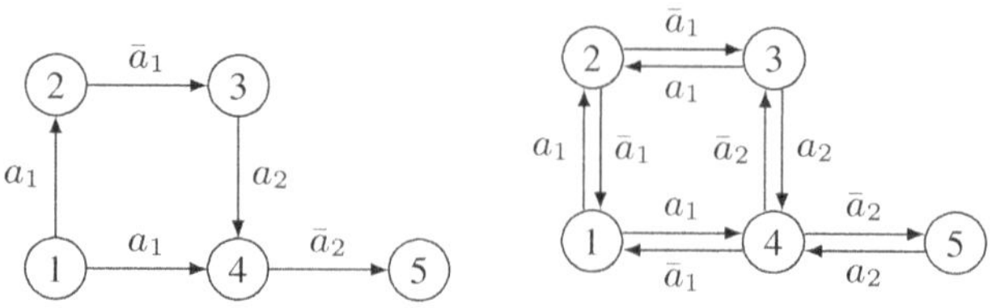

(a) The directed graph case. (b) The bidirected graph case.

Figure 1. Example graphs illustrating a directed graph and its corresponding bidirected graph.

The Dyck-CFL-reachability is defined similarly by restricting the underlying CFL to a Dyck language, which generates strings of properly balanced parentheses. Consider an alphabet Σ over the set of opening parentheses $A = \{a_1, a_2, \ldots, a_k\}$ and the set of their matching closing parentheses $\bar{A} = \{\bar{a}_1, \bar{a}_2, \ldots, \bar{a}_k\}$. The Dyck language of size k (*i.e.*, k kinds of parentheses) is defined by the following context-free grammar:

$$S \to SS \mid a_1 S \bar{a}_1 \mid \ldots \mid a_k S \bar{a}_k \mid \varepsilon$$

where S is the start symbol and ε is the empty string. Specially, we say node v is *Dyck-reachable* from node u iff there exists an S-path from u to v, where S is the start symbol in the Dyck grammar above. We call such a path joining nodes u and v a *Dyck-path*.

2.2 Bidirected Dyck-CFL-Reachability

In this paper, we focus on the bidirected Dyck-CFL-reachability problems, which require the underlying graph to be bidirected and edge-labeled. For any directed edge (u, v) in the graph that is not labeled by ε, if it is labeled by an opening parenthesis $a_i \in A$, there must be a reverse edge (v, u) which is labeled by a matching closing parenthesis $\bar{a}_i \in \bar{A}$, and vice versa. Formally, we have the following definition.

DEFINITION 1 (Bidirected Dyck-CFL-Reachability). *Given a bidirected graph $G = (V, E)$ and a Dyck language of size k, the labels of directed edges in the graph must satisfy the following constraints:*

- $\forall u, v \in V$, *if* $\mathcal{L}(u, v) = \varepsilon$, $\mathcal{L}(v, u)$ *must be* ε;
- $\forall u, v \in V$, *if* $\mathcal{L}(u, v) = a_i$, $\mathcal{L}(v, u)$ *must be* $\bar{a}_i$;
- $\forall u, v \in V$, *if* $\mathcal{L}(u, v) = \bar{a}_i$, $\mathcal{L}(v, u)$ *must be* a_i.

The bidirected Dyck-CFL-Reachability and its four variants are defined similarly as Dyck-CFL-Reachability.

The Dyck-CFL-reachable node pairs (u, v) can be defined as a binary relation $\mathbb{D}$.

DEFINITION 2 (Dyck-CFL-Relation). *Given a bidirected graph $G = (V, E)$, we call a binary relation $\mathbb{D}$ on $V \times V$ a Dyck-CFL-relation iff for all $(u, v) \in \mathbb{D}$, v is* Dyck-reachable *from u in G.*

We give an example to illustrate the Dyck-CFL-reachability and the bidirected Dyck-CFL-reachability problems.

EXAMPLE 1. *Consider the two graphs in Figure 1. The graph to the left shows a directed graph for Dyck-CFL-reachability, and the one to the right is its bidirected counterpart. In both graphs, the* realized *string $R(p)$ of the path $p = 1, 2, 3, 4, 5$ is "$a_1 \bar{a}_1 a_2 \bar{a}_2$", with properly matched parentheses. Therefore, node 5 is* Dyck-reachable *from node 1. However, the path $1, 4, 5$ is not a valid* Dyck-path.

The bidirected Dyck-CFL-reachability formulation has wide applications in pointer analysis. For pointer analysis problems, the

Algorithm 1: The standard CFL-reachability algorithm.

Input : Edge-labeled directed graph $G = (V, E)$, normalized $CFG = (\Sigma, N, P, S)$

Output: the set $\{(i, j) \mid S\langle i, j\rangle \in G\}$

1 add E to W
2 **foreach** *production* $X \to \epsilon \in P$ **do**
3   **foreach** *node* $v \in V$ **do**
4   **if** $X\langle v, v\rangle \notin E$ **then**
5   add $X\langle v, v\rangle$ to E and to W
6 **while** $W \neq \emptyset$ **do**
7   select and remove an edge $Y\langle i, j\rangle$ from W
8   **foreach** *production* $X \to Y \in P$ **do**
9   **if** $X\langle i, j\rangle \notin E$ **then**
10   add $X\langle i, j\rangle$ to E and to W
11   **foreach** *production* $X \to YZ \in P$ **do**
12   **foreach** *outgoing edge* $Z\langle j, k\rangle$ *from node* j **do**
13   **if** $X\langle i, k\rangle \notin E$ **then**
14   add $X\langle i, k\rangle$ to E and to W
15   **foreach** *production* $X \to ZY \in P$ **do**
16   **foreach** *incoming edge* $Z\langle k, i\rangle$ *to node* i **do**
17   **if** $X\langle k, j\rangle \notin E$ **then**
18   add$X\langle k, j\rangle$ to E and to W

directed edges in the underlying graph must be augmented with reverse edges (*a.k.a.* barred edges) [27], otherwise, two nodes may not be reachable from each other even by standard graph reachability. All existing CFL-reachability formulations for pointer analysis require the underlying graph to be bidirected. In addition, many pointer analyses employ Dyck-CFL-reachability to match certain properties, such as field accesses (*i.e.*, `load/store`) in Java [32, 33, 36, 37] and indirections (*i.e.*, references/dereferences) in C [40], which naturally satisfy the requirements of bidirected Dyck-CFL-reachability.

2.3 CFL-Reachability Algorithm

In the literature, there is a popular dynamic programming style algorithm [29, 38] for solving the CFL and Dyck-CFL-reachability problems. The algorithm is in Algorithm 1, where W denotes a worklist, and $X\langle u, v\rangle$ denotes the directed edge (u, v) with label $\mathcal{L}(u, v) = X$. The main algorithm has two steps: (1) *CFG Normalization* — The underlying CFG must be converted to a normal form, similar to the Chomsky Normal Form. When the grammar is in the normal form, all production rules are of the form $X \to YZ$, $X \to Y$ or $X \to \varepsilon$, where X is nonterminal, Y and Z are terminals or nonterminals, and ε denotes the empty string; and (2) *"Filling in" New Edges* — In order to compute the S-paths, new edges are added to the graph. For example, lines 11-14 describe that for the production rule $X \to YZ$ and edge $Y\langle i, j\rangle$,all outgoing edges of node j are considered. If there is an outgoing edge $Z\langle j, k\rangle$, a new edge $X\langle i, k\rangle$ is added to E if it is not already in E. The algorithm terminates if there are no more new edges to be inserted.

The complexity of Algorithm 1 is cubic in terms of the number of nodes in the input graph [21]. Chaudhuri [7] shows that the well-known Four Russians' Trick [5] can be employed on lines 12-13 and 16-17 in the CFL-reachability algorithm to immediately yield a subcubic algorithm with $O(n^3/\log n)$ time complexity.

3. Dyck-CFL-Relation

3.1 An Equivalence Property

We first study an equivalence property of Dyck-CFL-relations $\mathbb{D}$ on bidirected trees and graphs, which has not been fully utilized in previous work. Since trees are simply graphs without cycles, we use the more general term "graph" to illustrate the equivalence property. A binary relation $\sim \subseteq B \times B$ on a set B is an equivalence relation iff it is reflexive, symmetric and transitive. Specifically,

- $\sim$ is reflexive if $\forall a \in B,\ a \sim a$;
- $\sim$ is symmetric if $\forall a, b \in B,\ a \sim b \implies b \sim a$; and
- $\sim$ is transitive if $\forall a, b, c \in B,\ a \sim b \wedge b \sim c \implies a \sim c$.

For a given bidirected graph $G = (V, E)$, we consider the Dyck-CFL-relation $\mathbb{D}$ over $V \times V$. Based on the definition of relation $\mathbb{D}$, node $v \in V$ is *Dyck-reachable* from node $u \in V$ iff $(u, v) \in \mathbb{D}$. We list below the properties of relation $\mathbb{D}$ on bidirected graphs:

- *Relation* $\mathbb{D}$ *is reflexive:* This is because the start symbol S in the Dyck grammar is nullable (*i.e.*, it generates the empty string ε). Therefore, $(u, u) \in \mathbb{D}$ for all $u \in V$.
- *Relation* $\mathbb{D}$ *is symmetric:* One can identify a symmetric relation by showing it is equal to its inverse. For the bidirected graphs, the *realized* string $R(p)$ on a path p from node u to v is the reverse of $R(p')$ on the reverse path p' from v to u. It is easy to show $R(p)$ is generated by the Dyck grammar iff $R(p')$ is generated by the Dyck grammar with a simple induction on the path length. As a result, if v is *Dyck-reachable* from u (*i.e.*, $(u, v) \in \mathbb{D}$), u is also *Dyck-reachable* from v (*i.e.*, $(v, u) \in \mathbb{D}$).
- *Relation* $\mathbb{D}$ *is transitive:* That is, for any three nodes $u, v, w \in V$ in graph $G = (V, E)$, if v is *Dyck-reachable* from u (*i.e.*, $(u, v) \in \mathbb{D}$) and w is *Dyck-reachable* from v (*i.e.*, $(v, w) \in \mathbb{D}$), w is *Dyck-reachable* from u (*i.e.*, $(u, w) \in \mathbb{D}$). It is immediate that the *realized* string $R(p_1)$ for any path p_1 connecting node u and v can be derived from the start symbol S in the Dyck grammar. Similarly, the *realized* string $R(p_2)$ for any path p_2 connecting nodes v and w is also generated from the Dyck grammar. Consequently, the concatenated string $R(p_1)R(p_2)$ is generated by the Dyck grammar because of the rule $S \to SS$. Hence, the path p_1p_2 from node u to w is also a *Dyck-path*.

The discussions above lead to the following lemma.

LEMMA 1. *The Dyck-CFL-relation* $\mathbb{D}$ *on a bidirected graph is an equivalence relation.*

The key insight in our algorithms is that the equivalence property can be exploited to obtain asymptotically much faster algorithms. All nodes in the Dyck-CFL-relation $\mathbb{D}$ are equal to the other nodes in the graph, and thus nodes that belong to the same equivalence class can be safely collapsed to a single representative node. For example, in Figure 1(b), node 3 is *Dyck-reachable* from 1, thus, they can be collapsed into a single representative node $\{1, 3\}$ indicating that they are in the same equivalence class. Similarly, node 5 can be collapsed to the representative node $\{1, 3\}$ as well. Finally, we have a representative node $\{1, 3, 5\}$ reflecting the fact that the three nodes are *Dyck-reachable* from each other in the graph.

3.2 A Naïve Approach

We proceed to give a naïve all-pairs Dyck-CFL-reachability algorithm by collapsing the nodes in the graph that are in the Dyck-CFL-relation $\mathbb{D}$. Let $a_i\langle u, v\rangle$ denote the directed edge (u, v) labeled by $a_i \in A$. We note that while collapsing two *Dyck-reachable* nodes x and y in the graph, there always exists a node

z such that $a_i\langle x, z\rangle = a_i\langle y, z\rangle$. For example, in Figure 1(b), we have $a_1\langle 1, 2\rangle = a_1\langle 3, 2\rangle$. Without loss of generality, given a bidirected graph $G(V, E)$, the naïve algorithm can work on a directed graph $G'(V', E')$ by removing all edges labeled by closing parentheses from the original graph, *i.e.*, $V' = V$ and $a_i\langle u, v\rangle \in E'$ iff $a_i\langle u, v\rangle \in E$ for all labeled edges in E'. The basic idea of the naïve approach is to explicitly maintain a list W of nodes. For every item z popped from W, we pick two incoming neighbors x and y whose edges are labeled by the same opening parenthesis *i.e.*, $\exists a_i\langle x, z\rangle = a_i\langle y, z\rangle$, and then collapse x and y since they are *Dyck-reachable* via z. Due to the collapsing between nodes, E' may possibly contain *multiple edges*. The whole algorithm terminates if W is empty.

The naïve algorithm is given in Algorithm 2, where `Eq_nodes`$[v]$ denotes the equivalence set of node v and `Set`$[v]$ denotes the equivalence set number that node v belongs to. The procedure HAS-SAME-IN(v) traverses all incoming neighbors of node v, and returns true if there exist two neighbors u_1 and u_2 such that $a_i\langle u_1, v\rangle = a_i\langle u_2, v\rangle$. In Algorithm 2, line 1 transforms the given graph G to G', and lines 2-5 initialize W and `Eq_nodes[`v`]`. Lines 10-26 collapse node y to x *w.r.t.* node z, and remove y. The detailed procedure on collapsing y to x is given in Section 5.1.1. Finally, lines 29-31 assign the equivalence set number to each node v, such that any query can be answered in $O(1)$ time.

Complexity Analysis. The time complexity of the naïve algorithm is $O(kn^2)$. We begin by analyzing the maximum number of steps that the "while" loop on line 6 can be executed. We note that Algorithm 2 adds items to W only through lines 5 and 25. On line 25, item x can be added to W for at most $n - 1$ times, since line 26 can be executed for at most $n - 1$ times. On line 5, W is initialized with n items. Therefore, the worklist W can be filled with at most $2n - 1$ items by Algorithm 2. In the "while" loop, only line 28 removes an item from W, thus, the "else" part of the "if" statement can be executed for at most $2n - 1$ times. Since the "then" part of the same "if" statement can be executed for at most $n - 1$ times, the "while" loop can be executed for at most $(n - 1) + (2n - 1) = 3n - 2 = O(n)$ times. For each item z popped from W in the "while" loop, lines 8-28 take $O(kn)$ time to process. Specifically, the procedure HAS-SAME-IN(v) on lines 8 and 25 takes $O(kn)$ time to traverse all neighbors of node v, and the two "foreach" loops on lines 15 and 16 are bounded by $|A| = k$ and $|V'| = n$ respectively. Therefore, Algorithm 2 takes $O(kn^2)$ time. The space complexity is $O(n + m)$, since the input graph can be stored using FDLL to be introduced in Section 5.1.2 with $O(m)$ space and the worklist W takes $O(n)$ space. Putting everything together, we have the following theorem:

THEOREM 1. *Algorithm 2 pre-processes the input graph in $O(kn^2)$ time and $O(n + m)$ space to answer any online bidirected Dyck-CFL-reachability query in $O(1)$ time.*

In the following two sections, we describe two improved algorithms. They share the same insight with the the naïve approach, which have better time complexities on bidirected trees and graphs respectively. Specifically, our tree algorithm in Section 4 uses a single tree walk to find all equivalence sets because trees do not contain cycles. Our graph algorithm in Section 5 employs improved data structures to track nodes in W and to merge edges on x and y.

Algorithm 2: A naïve Dyck-CFL-reachability algorithm.

Input : Edge-labeled directed graph $G = (V, E)$
Output: `Set`$[v]$ for all $v \in V$

1 transform the input graph G to $G' = (V', E')$
2 initialize W to be empty
3 **foreach** $v \in V'$ **do**
4   `Eq_nodes`$[v] = \{v\}$
5   **if** HAS-SAME-IN(v) **then** add v to W
6 **while** $W \neq \emptyset$ *and* $|V'| > 1$ **do**
7   let z be the front node from W
8   **if** $z \in V'$ *and* HAS-SAME-IN(z) **then**
9   let x, y be two nodes such that $\exists a_i\langle x, z\rangle = a_i\langle y, z\rangle$
10   `Eq_nodes`$[x]$ = `Eq_nodes`$[y] \cup$ `Eq_nodes`$[x]$
11   **foreach** $a_i \in A$ **do**
12   **if** $a_i\langle y, y\rangle \in E'$ **then**
13   **if** $a_i\langle x, x\rangle \notin E'$ **then** add $a_i\langle x, x\rangle$ to E'
14   remove $a_i\langle y, y\rangle$ from E'
15   **foreach** $a_i \in A$ **do**
16   **foreach** $w \in V'$ **do**
17   **if** $a_i\langle w, y\rangle \in E'$ **then**
18   **if** $a_i\langle w, x\rangle \notin E'$ **then**
19   add $a_i\langle w, x\rangle$ to E'
20   remove $a_i\langle w, y\rangle$ from E'
21   **if** $a_i\langle y, w\rangle \in E'$ **then**
22   **if** $a_i\langle x, w\rangle \notin E'$ **then**
23   add $a_i\langle x, w\rangle$ to E'
24   remove $a_i\langle y, w\rangle$ from E'
25   add x to W if $x \notin W$ and HAS-SAME-IN(x)
26   remove y from V'
27   **else**
28   remove z from W
29 **foreach** $v \in V'$ **do**
30   **foreach** $u \in$ `Eq_nodes`$[v]$ **do**
31   `Set`$[u] = v$

4. Dyck-CFL-Reachability Algorithm on Bidirected Trees

This section presents our algorithm for solving the all-pairs Dyck-CFL-reachability problem on bidirected trees. Its time and space complexities are $O(n)$ and $O(n)$ respectively, and it answers any reachability query in $O(1)$ time. We remind the reader that the previous best result on bidirected trees [39] has $O(n \log n \log k)$ time and $O(n \log n)$ space complexities. First, we describe a linear-sized data structure to store the all-pairs reachability information. We then show how to utilize the equivalence property to solve the all-pairs Dyck-CFL-reachability problem using a single walk on trees.

4.1 The STRATIFIED-SETS Representation

In our algorithm, the all-pairs Dyck-CFL-reachability information is stored in disjoint sets. Two nodes u and v are *Dyck-reachable* from each other in the tree iff they belong to the same set. In other words, each disjoint set C corresponds to an equivalence class described by relation $\mathbb{D}$, *i.e.*, $u, v \in C$ iff $(u, v) \in \mathbb{D}$. We name the disjoint set representation in our main algorithm as STRATIFIED-SETS.

The STRATIFIED-SETS consist of several disjoint sets spanning over different layers. Each disjoint set stores the nodes that are *Dyck-reachable* from each other in the bidirected tree. The layers are indexed by an integer i. Note that the layer information is only used for providing a better explanation. The layer index i grows downward, *i.e.*, layer i is the upper layer in any two adjacent layers

i and $i+1$. The disjoint sets on the same layer i have no edges directly connecting each other. For any two adjacent layers i and $i+1$, there exists at least one edge connecting two disjoint sets C from layer i and C' from layer $i+1$. Specially, the connecting edge is labeled by $\mathcal{L}(u,v) \in A$, respecting the fact that there exist $u \in C$ and $v \in C'$ such that (u,v) is a directed edge in the tree with the same label $\mathcal{L}(u,v) \in A$. Note that there can be at most k edges connecting the set C' with the distinct sets from the upper layer i. However, more than k edges are possible for connecting the set C with the distinct sets from the lower layer $i+1$. Figure 2(b) shows an example STRATIFIED-SETS representation, where there are seven sets spanning four layers.

The STRATIFIED-SETS representation is implemented using three ingredients: one integer variable `curset`, two integer arrays `Set`$[v]$ and `Up`$[$`Set`$[v]][a_i]$. `Set`$[v]$ records the equivalence set number that node v belongs to, and `Up`$[$`Set`$[v]][a_i]$ stores the equivalence set number of the set from the upper layer that is connected to `Set`$[v]$ *w.r.t.* the edge labeled by the opening parenthesis $a_i \in A$. The STRATIFIED-SETS uses the integer variable `curset` to keep track of the *current* total number of disjoint sets. Due to the `Up` array, the tree algorithm does not need the layer information explicitly. The STRATIFIED-SETS implementation also permits three operations: `Init`(v), `Find`(v) and `Add`(v,e) described in Procedure 3. The functioning of procedures `Init`(v) and `Find`(v) is fairly straightforward. The procedure `Init`(v) takes a node v as input, assigns it to a new set indexed by `curset` in STRATIFIED-SETS, and increases the `curset` count. `Find`(v) returns the equivalence set number that node v belongs to.

We detail the description of procedure `Add`(v,e) to illustrate the idea of collapsing nodes in relation $\mathbb{D}$. We use `Add`(v,e) to insert the node v to the STRATIFIED-SETS with regard to the edge $e=(u,v)$ and the edge label $\mathcal{L}(u,v)$ in the tree. Node v is added to STRATIFIED-SETS by either assigning it to an new set (lines 3 and 9) or collapsing it to an existing set (line 13). Consider the example input tree in Figure 2(a), node 3 and edge $(2,3)$ are processed by `Add`(v,e). The resulting STRATIFIED-SETS is in Figure 2(b). Node 3 is assigned to a new set on layer 3. The new set is then linked with the set containing node 2 on layer 2 respecting the fact that $\mathcal{L}(2,3)=a_1$. Then, node 4 and edge $(3,4)$ are processed. Node 4 is collapsed to the set on layer 2 that contains node 2 respecting the facts that $\mathcal{L}(3,4)=\bar{a}_1$ and node 4 is *Dyck-reachable* from node 2 (*i.e.*, $(2,4)\in\mathbb{D}$). Formally, if the edge label $\mathcal{L}(u,v)$ in the tree is an opening parenthesis $a_i \in A$, v is assigned to a new set indexed by `curset` in STRATIFIED-SETS. This new set is then linked with the set returned by `Find`(u) on the upper layer as described by lines 2-5 . If the edge label is a closing parenthesis $\bar{a}_i \in \bar{A}$, we simply collapse node v to the equivalence set that is connected via a matched opening parenthesis $a_i \in A$ from u's upper layer. The equivalence set is indexed by `Up`$[$`Find`$(u)][a_i]$ as described by line 13. Lines 9-11 indicate that, for node u whose link node does not exist, we assign node v to a new set indexed by `curset` and link the set returned by `Find`(u) to the new set from the upper layer.

Note that the `Up` array used in Procedure 3 is indeed a map: $(Num \to A) \to Num$, where Num denotes the domain of the set numbers. For each set in STRATIFIED-SETS, line 8 in Procedure 3 needs to find a particular edge a_i from $O(k)$ link edges in `Up`$[s]$, where $s \in Num$. The time taken to search such $O(k)$ edges depends on the actual implementation of the `Up` array. For example, if the `Up` array stores such $O(k)$ edges for each set s using a binary search tree, the lookup for an a_i edge in `Up`$[s]$ takes $O(\log k)$ time as mentioned in Yuan and Eugster's work [39]. In our algorithm, we implement the `Up` array using the FDLL data structure illustrated as Example 3 in Section 5.1.2, thus a lookup takes *expected* $O(1)$ time. The space required is $O(m)$ since there are m edges in a tree,

Procedure 3: Add(v,e) to add a node v to STRATIFIED-SETS according to the directed edge $e=(u,v)$.

1 **if** $\mathcal{L}(u,v) \in A$ **then**
2   let $a_i = \mathcal{L}(u,v)$
3   `Set`$[v]$ = `curset`
4   `Up`$[$`curset`$][a_i]$ = `Find` (u)
5   `curset ++`
6 **if** $\mathcal{L}(u,v) \in \bar{A}$ **then**
7   let $\bar{a}_i = \mathcal{L}(u,v)$
8   **if** `Up`$[$`Find`$(u)][a_i]$ *does not exist* **then**
9   `Set`$[v]$ = `curset`
10   `Up`$[$`Find`$(u)][a_i]$ = `curset`
11   `curset ++`
12   **else**
13   `Set`$[v]$ = `Up`$[$`Find`$(u)][a_i]$

where $m=n-1$. Therefore, the time complexity of Procedure 3 is $O(1)$, and the space complexity of the `Up` array is $O(n)$.

4.2 Main Algorithm

This section presents the main algorithm. The key idea is to operate on the linear-sized STRATIFIED-SETS data structure to build the all-pairs Dyck-CFL-reachability information during a single tree walk.

The goal of our algorithm is to assign nodes u and v to the same set in STRATIFIED-SETS, for all $(u,v)\in\mathbb{D}$. The overall algorithm takes two steps:

(1) *Initializing a leaf node:* In this step, we pick an arbitrary leaf node v from the tree and invoke the `Init`(v) procedure to initialize the given node v.

(2) *Processing each encountered edge:* For each edge (u,v) with label $\mathcal{L}(u,v)$ encountered during the tree walk, we process the edge *w.r.t.* the edge label and insert the node v to STRATIFIED-SETS according to the `Add`(v,e) procedure.

The complete algorithm is shown as Algorithm 4. In the main algorithm, lines 1-6 initialize the relevant data structures, and lines 7-14 describe a standard depth-first search (DFS) starting at node v. For a given bidirected tree $T=(V,E)$ with n nodes, DFS takes $O(n)$ time. For every node v, the `Add`(v,e) procedure takes $O(1)$ time. The space required by Algorithm 4 depends on the STRATIFIED-SETS representation, which is essentially implemented using the `Up` array. Therefore, the space complexity is $O(n)$.

EXAMPLE 2. *We consider the bidirected tree in Figure 2(a), where reverse edges are omitted for brevity. Algorithm 4 outputs the* STRATIFIED-SETS *in Figure 2(b). The* STRATIFIED-SETS *representation contains seven disjoint sets:* $\{1,5,7,8,11,12\}$, $\{2,4\}$, $\{6\}$, $\{9\}$, $\{10\}$, $\{3\}$ *and* $\{13\}$. *The nodes in the same set are* Dyck-reachable *from each other in the tree. Note that the layer information is only used for providing a better explanation. Algorithm 4 uses the* `Up` *array for finding a set from the upper layer in* STRATIFIED-SETS.

After constructing the STRATIFIED-SETS, any Dyck-CFL-reachability query (u,v) can be answered in $O(1)$ time by simply checking whether the indices returned by `Find`(u) and `Find`(v) are the same. Putting everything together, we have the following theorem.

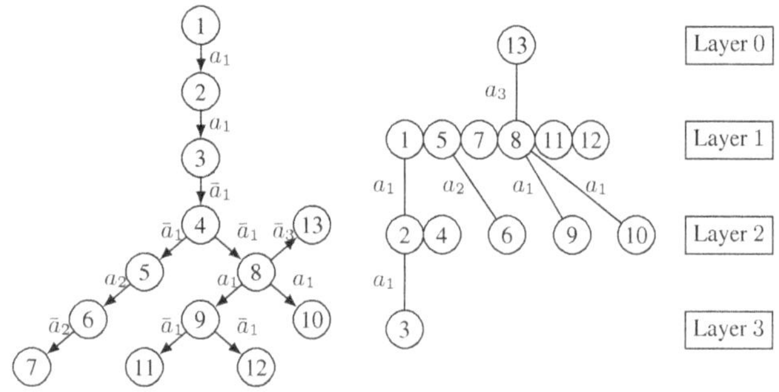

(a) Input tree. (b) STRATIFIED-SETS representation.

Figure 2. A running example for Dyck-CFL-reachability on trees.

Algorithm 4: Dyck-CFL-reachability algorithm on trees.

```
Input  : Edge-labeled bidirected tree T = (V, E)
Output: the STRATIFIED-SETS
initialize the Up array to be empty
foreach v ∈ V do
    visited[v] = false
    Set[v] = 0
stack.push(a leaf node v)
curset = 0
Init (v)
while stack is not empty do
    v = stack.pop
    if not visited[v] then
        visited[v] = true
        foreach unvisited neighbor u of v do
            stack.push(u)
            Add (u, e(v, u))
```

THEOREM 2. *The bidirected Dyck-CFL-reachability problem on trees can be pre-processed in $O(n)$ time and $O(n)$ space to answer any online query in $O(1)$ time.*

5. Dyck-CFL-Reachability Algorithm on Bidirected Graphs

In this section, we study the Dyck-CFL-reachability problems on bidirected graphs. Computing Dyck-CFL-reachability on graphs is harder than that on trees because graphs may contain cycles. Consequently, the algorithm introduced in Section 4 based on the STRATIFIED-SETS representation cannot be directly applied to graphs.

Although Dyck-CFL-reachability on bidirected graphs is more complicated, the Dyck-CFL-relation $\mathbb{D}$ shares the same equivalence properties as for trees. For bidirected graphs, we utilize the idea of edge merging to collapse the node pairs $(u, v) \in \mathbb{D}$. For a bidirected graph with n nodes and $2m$ edges, our algorithm processes the given graph in $O(n + m \log m)$ time with $O(n + m)$ space, and can answer any Dyck-CFL-reachability query over any pair of nodes (u, v) in $O(1)$ time.

5.1 Basic Idea

As the naïve approach, given a bidirected graph $G(V, E)$, our algorithm works on the same directed graph $G'(V', E')$ by removing all edges labeled by closing parentheses from the original graph, *i.e.*, $V' = V$ and $a_i\langle u, v\rangle \in E'$ iff $a_i\langle u, v\rangle \in E$ for all labeled edges in E'. Therefore, G' has n nodes and m edges. The key idea behind our algorithm is to collapse any node pair (u, v) connected by a *Dyck-path* in the graph because such pairs (u, v) are in the Dyck-CFL-relation $\mathbb{D}$. As in the naïve approach, E' may possibly contain *multiple edges* due to the collapsing between nodes.

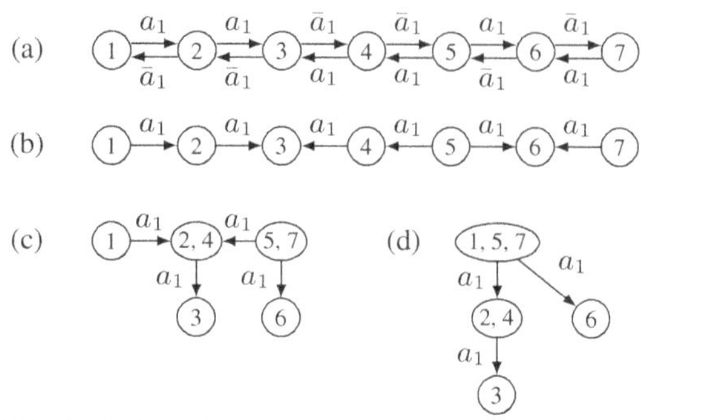

Figure 3. A Dyck-path example.

To make the above idea more concrete, we consider the example in Figure 3. Figure 3(a) shows the original path in G which contains two non-trivial sets of nodes that are *Dyck-reachable* from each other: $\{1, 5, 7\}$ and $\{2, 4\}$. Figure 3(b) shows the corresponding reduced path in G'. In such directed cases, node 5 is "connected" to node 7 via node 6, and $a_1\langle 5, 6\rangle = a_1\langle 7, 6\rangle$. Since nodes 5 and 7 are *Dyck-reachable* from each other, the two edges $a_1\langle 5, 6\rangle$ and $a_1\langle 7, 6\rangle$ should be merged to collapse nodes 5 and 7 into a single representative node $\{5, 7\}$ in Figure 3(c). We define a node like node 6 to be the *merging node*. Formally, we have the following definition.

DEFINITION 3 (Merging Node). *If a node $v \in V$ has at least two incoming edges labeled by $a_i \in A$, we say node v merges a_i edges. We define a node as a* merging node *iff it merges some $a_i \in A$ edges.*

Like the naïve algorithm in Algorithm 2, our main algorithm fulfills the following two tasks:

(1) *Merge edges for each merging node:* For any merging node in the graph G', the algorithm finds the incoming nodes with the same labeled edges, and merges the two edges to collapse the nodes. In the path in Figure 3(b), nodes 3 and 6 are two merging nodes. The relevant incoming edges should be merged.

(2) *Track the new merging nodes:* During edge merging, new merging nodes can be introduced into the graph G'. The algorithm tracks all new merging nodes in order to perform another edge merging. For the same example in Figure 3(c), collapsing nodes 2 and 4 generates a new representative node $\{2, 4\}$, which is also a merging node. Its corresponding edges should also be merged. The final output is shown in Figure 3(d).

In the naïve approach, nodes x and y are arbitrarily picked on line 9. Merging edges from y to x by enumerating all neighbors of y exhaustively takes $O(kn)$ time. Moreover, node tracking is achieved by simply traversing all neighbors of node z on line 8, which takes $O(kn)$ time as well. When the given graph is sparse, we can use additional data structures to improve the two tasks of merging edges and tracking nodes. Next, we describe them in detail.

5.1.1 Merging Edges

For the directed graph G', edge merging in G' picks a merging node z that has two incoming edges (x, z) and (y, z) with $a_i\langle x, z\rangle =$

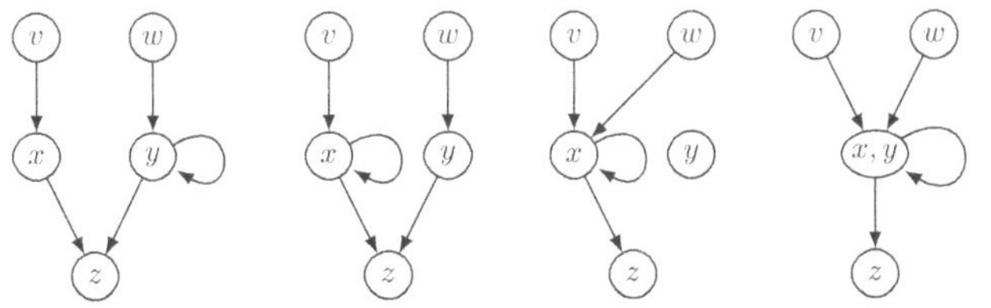

(a) Before edge merging. (b) Collapsing self loops. (c) Collapsing all neighbors. (d) After edge merging.

Figure 4. Steps in edge merging.

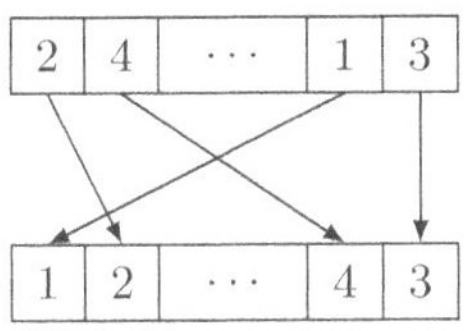

Figure 5. The illustration of the FDLL data structure.

$a_i\langle y, z\rangle$, and collapses nodes x and y. Specifically, if we choose to merge edge (y, z) to edge (x, z), all edges connecting y and its neighbor w should be deleted from G'. Node w is made a neighbor of x by inserting the relevant edges to G'. Finally, node y is removed from G', because it has been collapsed to x.

The order of edge merging is important. The naïve method in Algorithm 2 performs edge merging by collapsing nodes x and y arbitrarily with regard to the merging node z. If one adopts this approach, the time complexity can be $O(kn^2)$. When the graphs are sparse, it is possible to do edge merging faster. To this end, we employ a technique that is similar to the weighted-union heuristic (also known as the "union-by-size" heuristic) used in the disjoint sets data structures [9]. Namely, for each edge merging operation, we always collapse the node with a smaller degree to the node with a larger degree. Our new method bounds the total numbers of edge merging for *each edge* to $O(\log m)$. We provide a detailed complexity analysis in Section 5.3.

Taking the naïve approach in Algorithm 2 as an example, we discuss the process of edge merging. Specifically, our handling of edge merging from node y to node x has three phases, as illustrated in Figure 4. We assume that the degree of node x is larger than that of y, and all irrelevant edges are omitted in Figure 4. Figure 4(a) shows the original graph before edge merging. Figure 4(b) illustrates the handling in the first phase. If y has a self loop, the self loop is removed and added to x if x does not already have one (lines 11-14 in Algorithm 2). Second, we consider all neighbors of node y. As in Figure 4(c), for all shared neighbors z of x and y, those edges between z and y are removed; for those neighbors w that only belong to y, new edges between w and x are inserted (lines 15-24 in Algorithm 2). Finally, Figure 4(d) shows that node y is removed from the graph and degrees for relevant nodes in edge merging are updated.

5.1.2 Tracking Nodes

During edge merging, the in-degrees of merging nodes may change. We need to explicitly maintain a list of merging nodes whose in-degrees *w.r.t.* an opening parenthesis are at least 2. This section describes the design of our data structure to effectively maintain this information.

In the naïve algorithm, tracking nodes is achieved using a worklist W, which is typically implemented using a list. In our improved algorithm, we uses a doubly-linked list (DLL) and a hash map. We name the data structure FAST-DOUBLY-LINKED-LIST (FDLL). It is important to note that traditional list W used by the naïve approach on line 25 takes $O(n)$ time to find an element while FDLL takes *expected* $O(1)$ time. Figure 5 depicts an example FDLL. All elements in the FDLL are stored using a DLL and a hash map. The hash map associates each element with its position in the DLL, represented by arrows in Figure 5, to help quickly locate every element in the DLL. The *insertion* and *pop* operations on FDLL are nearly identical to DLL (or list), both of which take $O(1)$ time. Moreover, the FDLL supports two additional operations in *expected* $O(1)$ time:

- *Query:* Querying the membership of a particular element in FDLL is the same as querying the relevant membership in the hash map, which can be done in *expected* $O(1)$ time.
- *Deletion:* According to the hash map, the position of the element to be deleted can be found in *expected* $O(1)$ time. Thus removing the element at the specified position in the DLL can also be done in $O(1)$ time. Finally, the hash map entry associated with that element is erased in $O(1)$ time.

EXAMPLE 3. *In the tree algorithm, the* `Up` *array can be implemented using FDLL to support the* expected $O(1)$ *time lookup. Recall that the* `Up` *array is indeed a map:* $(Num \rightarrow A) \rightarrow Num$. *For each set* $s \in Num$, *we use an FDLL* $A[s]$ *to store the set of opening parentheses* a_i, *such that there exists an* a_i *labeled edge connecting set* s *and the set from the upper layer. For each* $a_i \in A[s]$, *we use another FDLL* $U[s\_i]$ *to store the corresponding set from the upper layer. For example, to look up an edge* a_3 *of set* 2, *we query whether* $a_3 \in A[2]$. *If such an* a_3 *exists,* $U[2\_3]$ *keeps the corresponding set number. The two lookups both take* expected $O(1)$ *time.*

5.2 Main Algorithm

We now present our algorithm solving bidirected Dyck-CFL-reachability on graphs in Algorithm 5, combining the ideas of merging edges and tracking nodes.

Before delving into the main algorithm, we first illustrate the use of FDLL in our main algorithm. For each node v in the input graph $G' = (V', E')$, the set of opening parentheses of v's incoming edges is represented using an FDLL, denoted as $A_{\text{in}}[v]$. For each $a_i \in A_{\text{in}}[v]$, we use the FDLL `In[v_i]` to store all v's incoming neighbors. We denote the size of `In[v_i]` as `In[v_i].size()`. Node v merges edge a_i iff `In[v_i].size()` > 1. We represent `Out[v_i]` and $A_{\text{out}}[v]$ similarly. Finally, the worklist FDLL$_w$ is also represented using an FDLL.

Algorithm 5 uses the array $\hat{D}[v]$ to represent the *total degree* of node v, which is initialized to v's degree in the original graph. Notations `eq_nodes[v]` and `Set[v]` are defined in the same way as the naïve approach. The functioning of the algorithm proceeds as follows. On line 1, the original bidirected graph G is pre-processed to obtain the directed graph $G' = (V', E')$. From lines 2-5, the equivalence set `Eq_nodes[v]` is initialized with node v and the FDLL$_w$ is initialized with v_i indicating node v merges a_i. The FDLL$_w$ in the main algorithm is used to implement the idea of node tracking. The main algorithm then proceeds to handle edge merging as follows:

- Lines 7-11: The algorithm pops one z_i from the FDLL$_w$, then chooses its two neighbors x and y for edge merging. Specifically, node y with a smaller *total degree* is collapsed to node x with a larger *total degree*.
- Lines 12-18: The self loop on node y is handled as described in Figure 4(b). During edge merging, if a node v becomes a non-merging node for a_i (*i.e.*, `In[v_i].size()` < 2), v_i is removed from the FDLL$_w$. Similarly, when node v becomes a merging node that merges a_i edges, v_i is inserted to the FDLL$_w$. Note

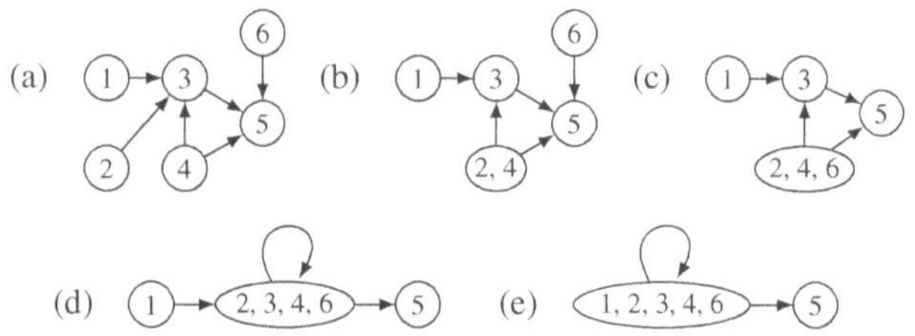

Figure 6. A running example for bidirected Dyck-CFL-reachability on graphs.

that when an edge is inserted/removed from E', all of $\texttt{In}[v\_i]$, $A_{\text{in}}[v]$, $\texttt{Out}[v\_i]$ and $A_{\text{out}}[v]$ need to be updated accordingly.

- Lines 19-31: All incoming and outgoing neighbors of y are handled as described in Figure 4(c). The update on FDLL_w for merging nodes is similar to the handling of self loop.
- Line 32: Node y is removed from V'. Note that we do not need to remove z_i because it was once w_i.

The edge merging ends when the FDLL_w is empty, *i.e.*, there are no merging nodes in the final graph. Lines 33-35 indicate that all nodes u in the equivalence set $\texttt{Eq\_nodes}[v]$ are enumerated to associate $\texttt{Set}[u]$ with v.

After the main algorithm terminates, $\texttt{Set}[v]$ stores the equivalence set number that node v belongs to. Similar to the tree case, any Dyck-CFL-reachability query (u, v) can be answered in $O(1)$ time by simply checking the equivalence set numbers of nodes u and v.

EXAMPLE 4. *Figure 6 shows an example. All edges are labeled by $a_1 \in A$. The original edges labeled by $\bar{a}_1 \in \bar{A}$ are removed first. Nodes 3 and 5 are two merging nodes. In the first iteration, nodes 2 and 4 are collapsed by edge merging. Then node 6 is collapsed as well. Finally, node 1 is collapsed due to its self loop in the graph. In the final graph, all of the nodes in the original graph are distributed into two disjoint sets.*

5.3 Algorithm Correctness and Complexity Analysis

This section discusses the correctness and complexity of our proposed algorithm. First, we establish its correctness.

THEOREM 3 (Correctness). *Algorithm 5 correctly finds all* Dyck-paths *in the input graph.*

Proof. It is clear that any *Dyck-path* reported by Algorithm 5 is indeed a *Dyck-path* due to the observed equivalence property (Lemma 1). Thus, our proof focuses on the other direction, that is Algorithm 5 finds all *Dyck-paths* in the input graph.

Any trivial *Dyck-path* generated by rule $S \to \varepsilon$ is handled correctly, because every node v in the graph is marked as *Dyck-reachable* from itself due to line 3 in Algorithm 5. Dyck grammar essentially generates the properly matched parentheses. Therefore, the length of any non-trivial *Dyck-path* in the graph is even. We prove by induction on the length $|p|$ of any non-trivial *Dyck-path*.

Base case. $|p| = 2$. Let the *Dyck-path* be $p = v_1v_2v_3$, with the *realized* string $R(p) = \mathcal{L}(v_1, v_2)\mathcal{L}(v_2, v_3) = a_i\bar{a}_i$. Because the graph is bidirected, we have $\mathcal{L}(v_3, v_2) = \mathcal{L}(v_1, v_2) = a_i$. Nodes v_1 and v_3 are collapsed due to the merging node v_2.

Inductive step. Suppose Algorithm 5 correctly finds all non-trivial *Dyck-paths* of length $|p|$ in the graph. According to the Dyck grammar, any non-trivial *Dyck-path* of length $|p| + 2$ is generated by the following two rules:

- $S \to a_iS\bar{a}_i$ indicates that the new S-path is generated by prepending an open parenthesis and appending by a matching closing parenthesis. Let the path be $p = v_1v_2 \ldots v_3v_4$, where $\mathcal{L}(v_1, v_2) = a_i$ and $\mathcal{L}(v_3, v_4) = \bar{a}_i$. The *realized* string $R(v_2 \ldots v_3) = S$ indicates that nodes v_2 and v_3 are *Dyck-reachable*, where the *Dyck-path* joining v_2 and v_3 is of length $|p|$. According to the induction hypothesis, they have been collapsed into a single representative node. Such a node is the merging node for v_1 and v_4. Thus, v_1 and v_4 are collapsed according to Algorithm 5.
- $S \to SS$ indicates that the new S-path is composed of two S-paths. Let the path be $p = v_1 \ldots v_2 \ldots v_3$, where $R(v_1 \ldots v_2) = R(v_2 \ldots v_3) = S$. Note that the length of

Algorithm 5: Dyck-CFL-reachability algorithm on graphs.

Input : Edge-labeled bidirected graph $G = (V, E)$
Output: $\texttt{Set}[v]$ for all $v \in V$

1 transform the input graph G to $G' = (V', E')$
2 **foreach** $v \in V'$ **do**
3    $\texttt{Eq\_nodes}[v] = \{v\}$
4   **foreach** $a_i \in A_{in}[v]$ **do**
5   add v_i to FDLL_w if $\texttt{In}[v\_i]\texttt{.size()} > 1$
6 **while** $FDLL_w \neq \emptyset$ **do**
7   let z_i be the front item from FDLL_w
8   let x and y be two front nodes from $\texttt{In}[z\_i]$
9   let x denote the node such that $\hat{D}[x] \geqslant \hat{D}[y]$
10    $\hat{D}[x] = \hat{D}[x] + \hat{D}[y]$
11    $\texttt{Eq\_nodes}[x] = \texttt{Eq\_nodes}[y] \cup \texttt{Eq\_nodes}[x]$
12   **foreach** $a_i \in A_{in}[y]$ **do**
13   **if** $a_i\langle y, y\rangle \in E'$ **then**
14   **if** $a_i\langle x, x\rangle \notin E'$ **then**
15   add $a_i\langle x, x\rangle$ to E'
16   add x_i to FDLL_w if $x\_i \notin \text{FDLL}_w$ and $\texttt{In}[x\_i]\texttt{.size()} > 1$
17   remove $a_i\langle y, y\rangle$ from E'
18   remove y_i from FDLL_w if $y\_i \in \text{FDLL}_w$ and $\texttt{In}[y\_i]\texttt{.size()} < 2$
19   **foreach** $a_i \in A_{in}[y]$ **do**
20   **foreach** $w \in \texttt{In}[y\_i]$ **do**
21   **if** $a_i\langle w, x\rangle \notin E'$ **then**
22   add $a_i\langle w, x\rangle$ to E'
23   add x_i to FDLL_w if $x\_i \notin \text{FDLL}_w$ and $\texttt{In}[x\_i]\texttt{.size()} > 1$
24   remove $a_i\langle w, y\rangle$ from E'
25   remove y_i from FDLL_w if $y\_i \in \text{FDLL}_w$ and $\texttt{In}[y\_i]\texttt{.size()} < 2$
26   **foreach** $a_i \in A_{out}[y]$ **do**
27   **foreach** $w \in \texttt{Out}[y\_i]$ **do**
28   **if** $a_i\langle x, w\rangle \notin E'$ **then**
29   add $a_i\langle x, w\rangle$ to E'
30   remove $a_i\langle y, w\rangle$ from E'
31   remove w_i from FDLL_w if $w\_i \in \text{FDLL}_w$ and $\texttt{In}[w\_i]\texttt{.size()} < 2$
32   remove y from V'
33 **foreach** $v \in V'$ **do**
34   **foreach** $u \in \texttt{Eq\_nodes}[v]$ **do**
35      $\texttt{Set}[u] = v$

any non-trivial *Dyck-path* is at least 2. Since the new S-path is of length $|p|+2$, the lengths of both path $v_1, \ldots, v_2$ and path $v_2, \ldots, v_3$ are less than or equal to $|p|$. According to the induction hypothesis, both v_1, v_2 and v_2, v_3 are collapsed into a single representative node. As a result, v_1 and v_3 are collapsed into the same representation node as well. □

Next we analyze the complexity of Algorithm 5. Note that the *total degree* $\hat{D}[v]$ used in our algorithm is different from the degree $D[v]$ of node v respecting the fact that the *total degree* $\hat{D}[v]$ admits duplicated edges. For example, in Figure 4(c), $\hat{D}[x] = 4 + 2 = 6$, but $D[x] = 5$, because edge (y, z) is duplicated with (x, z) according to the final representative node $\{x, y\}$ in Figure 4(d). Therefore, the *total degree* $\hat{D}[v]$ never decreases during edge merging. Our algorithm processes the merging node z and collapses its neighbor y with a smaller $\hat{D}[y]$ to node x with a larger $\hat{D}[x]$. Nodes y and x are collapsed into a single representative node $\{x, y\}$. As a result, the *total degree* of y after merging is the same as the *total degree* of x according to line 10, namely, $\hat{D}[x] = \hat{D}[x] + \hat{D}[y]$. On line 9, we have $\hat{D}[x] \geqslant \hat{D}[y]$. Combining the analysis of the two lines, the following lemma is immediate:

LEMMA 2. *For each edge merging in Algorithm 5, $\hat{D}[y]$ is doubled.*

Let m denote the number of edges in graph G', *i.e.*, $2m = \sum_{v \in V} D[v]$. Due to the duplicated edges, $D[v]$ may decrease during edge merging. Similarly, $\hat{m}$ denotes the *total number* of edges in graph G' *w.r.t.* $\hat{D}[v]$ that admits duplicated edges, *i.e.*, $\hat{m} = \sum_{v \in V} \hat{D}[v]$. For each edge (x, z) in graph G', we say it is "moved" if either the *total degree* $\hat{D}[x]$ or $\hat{D}[z]$ is doubled according to Lemma 2. For all $v \in V$, we have $\hat{D}[v] \leqslant \hat{m} \leqslant 2m$, because in the worst case, all nodes are collapsed into a single representative node (with m duplicated edges) in the final graph. Combined with Lemma 2, an edge is "moved" at most $(\log \hat{D}[x] + \log \hat{D}[z] \leqslant 2 \log 2m)$ times. The "while" loop on line 6 in Algorithm 5 takes time proportional to the number of times that an edge is "moved". Therefore, the total running time for the "while" loop is $O(m \log m)$. For lines 33-35, it takes $O(n)$ time to enumerate all nodes u in the equivalence set `Eq_nodes`$[v]$ and to associate `Set`$[u]$ with v. Therefore, the time complexity of our algorithm is $O(n + m \log m)$. At the beginning, each node is associated with two FDLLs `In[v_i]` and `Out[v_i]`. In each iteration of edge merging, there is one node removed from G', decreasing the number of edges m in G'. As a result, $O(n + m)$ space is required for processing the graph. Putting all these together, we have the following theorem:

THEOREM 4. *Algorithm 5 pre-processes the input graph in $O(n + m \log m)$ time and $O(n + m)$ space to answer any online bidirected Dyck-CFL-reachability query in $O(1)$ time.*

In practice, since the graphs in client analyses are typically sparse, Algorithm 5 performs in $O(n \log n)$ time. When the graphs are dense, we can use the naïve approach in Algorithm 2 for preprocessing. As a result, we have the following theorem:

THEOREM 5. *The bidirected Dyck-CFL-reachability problem on graphs can be pre-processed in $O(min\{kn^2, n + m \log m\})$ time and $O(n + m)$ space to answer any online query in $O(1)$ time.*

6. Application: Scaling an Alias Analysis for Java

This section describes a practical application of our results in speeding up an alias analysis for Java [37]. The goal of alias analysis is to determine if two pointer variables can point to the same memory location during program execution. The aliasing information obtained by an alias analysis is a prerequisite for many compiler optimizations and static analysis tools (*e.g.*, software verifiers [10], data race detectors [23], and static slicers [18]).

Many state-of-the-art alias analyses [31, 36, 37, 40] are formulated using CFL-reachability. Dyck-CFL-reachability plays an important role in these analyses. For instance, it has been used to model the matched references and dereferences in C [40], and has also been employed to describe the field loads and stores in Java [36, 37] to capture the "balanced-parentheses property" observed by Sridharan *et al.* [33]. Yuan and Eugster's recent work [39] further shows that Dyck-CFL-reachability on bidirected trees can be used to solve a simplified *context-insensitive pointers-to analysis* problem.

To demonstrate the practical applicability of our results, we leverage a recent demand-driven *context-sensitive* alias analysis for Java [37] formulated using CFL-reachability. Dyck-CFL-reachability is used to formulate its *context-insensitive* variant. The analysis is demand-driven in the sense that it solves the *single-source-single-target* Dyck-CFL-reachability problem. We show that our fast algorithms for *all-pairs* Dyck-CFL-reachability applies directly to this *context-insensitive* alias analysis.

6.1 Symbolic Points-to Graph

The underlying graph representation of the alias analysis is called the Symbolic Points-to Graph (SPG) [36, 37]. It extends the locally-resolved points-to graph representation [33] by introducing additional symbolic nodes as placeholders for abstract heap objects. The SPG contains three kinds of nodes: *variable nodes* $v \in \mathcal{V}$ representing variables, *allocation nodes* $o \in \mathcal{O}$ representing allocations for `new` expressions, and *symbolic nodes* $s \in \mathcal{S}$ representing abstract heap objects. It also consists of the following three types of edges:

- edges $v \rightarrow o_i \in \mathcal{V} \times \mathcal{O}$ to represent that variable v points to object o_i;
- edges $v \rightarrow s_i \in \mathcal{V} \times \mathcal{S}$ to represent that variable v points to an abstract heap object.
- edges $o_i \xrightarrow{f} o_j \in (\mathcal{O} \cup \mathcal{S}) \times \text{Fields} \times (\mathcal{O} \cup \mathcal{S})$ to represent that field f of o_i points to o_j.

A Java program's SPG is constructed in three steps. First, symbolic nodes are introduced for each procedure parameter, method invocation and field access. Second, the set of abstract heap locations $\mathcal{O} \cup \mathcal{S}$ that a variable may point to[1] is computed. The relevant points-to edges are inserted to the SPG. Third, the field access edges $o_i \xrightarrow{f} o_j$ are added with regard to field loads and stores. The SPG also includes the barred edges (*i.e.* $o_j \xrightarrow{\bar{f}} o_i$ edges) implicitly.

6.2 Context-Insensitive Alias Analysis

The context-insensitive alias analysis computes the aliasing relation over variables within a method. In the analysis, the method invocation edges (*i.e.*, entry and exit edges) are of no interest. Specifically, the *memory aliasing* between the allocation or symbolic nodes that variable nodes x and y may points-to indicates the aliasing relation between x and y. The memory alias relation defined in [37] over $(\mathcal{O} \cup \mathcal{S}) \times (\mathcal{O} \cup \mathcal{S})$ is described by the following context-free

[1] In the original work that using SPG [36, 37], the *flowsTo* edges are used. A *flowsTo* edge is obtained on the flow graph by computing a regular language reachability. An abstract heap object *flowsTo* a variable if it is in the points-to set of that variable.

```
x = w.f;
w.f = y;
u = x.g;
v = y.g;
v = w.g;
```

(a) A code snippet.

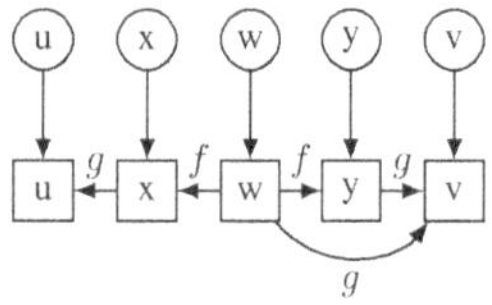

(b) Its SPG.

Figure 7. An example of alias analysis with the SPG.

grammar:

$$memAlias \rightarrow \bar{f}_1\ memAlias\ f_1 \mid \ldots \mid \bar{f}_k\ memAlias\ f_k \mid memAlias\ memAlias \mid \varepsilon$$

Note that the alias analysis based on $memAlias$ reachability is a simplification of the $alias$ reachability presented by Sridharan *et al.* [32, 33]. The field edges between abstract symbolic nodes in an SPG approximate the field loads and stores in the flow graph [32, 33]. The approximation may lead spurious aliasing as detailed by Xu *et al.* [36, Section 4]. However, the experimental results show that the overall performance is better than that proposed by Sridharan *et al.* [32, 33] in practice. The precision loss is insignificant enough compared to the performance gains.

EXAMPLE 5. *Consider the example in Figure 7. The Java code snippet (left) and its SPG (right) are shown. In the SPG, the boxes denote symbolic nodes, and the circles denote variable nodes. The reverse edges* (a.k.a. *barred edges) are omitted for brevity. Note that the Dyck-CFL-reachability formulation used in the client alias analysis represents the barred edges as the opening parentheses. There are two pairs of memAlias nodes: (x, y) and (u, v), because the realized strings of the two joining paths are "$\bar{f}f$" and "$\bar{g}\bar{f}fg$" respectively, which can be generated from the $memAlias$ grammar. However, the node pair (x, v) is not memAlias because the realized strings of two possible joining paths are "$\bar{f}g$" and "$\bar{f}fg$", such that the parentheses along the paths are not properly matched.*

6.3 Applying Our Fast Algorithms

Since the CFL used to describe the context-insensitive memory aliasing is a Dyck-CFL with k kinds of parentheses, the two Dyck-CFL-reachability algorithms presented in this paper can be directly applied. Note also that this alias analysis is demand-driven in the sense that the original algorithm solves the "single-source-single-target" Dyck-CFL-reachability problem, because solving "all-pairs" reachability is considered computationally much more expensive in these analyses. Both our algorithms are intended to solve the "all-pairs" Dyck-CFL-reachability problem. Next, we show how our "all-pairs" algorithm performs in practice.

7. Empirical Evaluation

In this section, we compare the traditional CFL-reachability algorithm with our proposed algorithm for solving the *all-pairs* Dyck-CFL-reachability problem on graphs for standard, real-world Java benchmarks. The input graphs are generated from the *context-insensitive* alias analysis for Java described in Section 6. The results show that our algorithm outperforms the traditional CFL-reachability algorithm by several orders of magnitude.

7.1 Experimental Setup

Benchmark Selection. The benchmark suite used in our evaluation is the DaCapo suite [1]. We include the entire DaCapo-2006-10-MR2 suite which consists of 11 benchmarks with five additional large benchmarks form the DaCapo-9.12bach suite. Table 2 describes the benchmarks. For each benchmark, columns 2 and 3 list the numbers of methods and statements in intermediate representations of the underlying analysis infrastructure, respectively.

Graph Collection. We have used the same code as Xu *et al.* [36] and Yan *et al.* [37] to generate the Symbolic Points-to Graphs (SPGs). The analysis is built on top of the Soot program analysis framework for Java [34].

All benchmarks are processed with the nightly-build version[2] of Soot. To measure scalability, we use the latest release of JDK 1.6 (version 1.6u37) as the base analysis library for Soot. The five large benchmarks from DaCapo-9.12bach are processed with the help of Tamiflex [6] for reflection resolution.

Implementation. We implemented the proposed graph algorithm to compare with the traditional CFL-reachability algorithm. Both algorithms are implemented in C++ with extensive use of the Standard Template Library (STL). The FDLL data structure described in Section 5 is implemented using STL `unordered_map` and `list`. The underlying graphs are represented using adjacency lists implemented with FDLL.

Our code is compiled using gcc-4.6.3 with the "-O2" optimization flag. Both algorithms take the same SPG as input. Their outputs are verified to ensure the consistency and correctness . All experiments are conducted on a Dell Optiplex 780 machine with Intel Core2 Quad Q9650 CPU and 8 GB RAM, running Ubuntu-12.04.

7.2 Time and Memory Consumption

Table 2 shows the performance comparison of the two algorithms over our benchmark set. Column 4 and 5 list the numbers of nodes and edges in each SPG respectively. Column 6 lists the aliasing pair counts. Column 7 shows the number of different kinds of parentheses (*i.e.*, the size of each Dyck grammar) in each SPG. The remaining columns list the time and memory consumption of the traditional CFL-reachability algorithm versus that of our algorithm. We denote our algorithm as FAST-DYCK.

The results indicate that our algorithm significantly improves over the traditional CFL-reachability algorithm. We observe that the running time of our algorithm grows very slowly *w.r.t.* the growth of the number of nodes. For example, the running time of the CFL-reachability algorithm on "jython09" is 30 times over that on "xalan06". While, it is only 4 times for our algorithm on the same benchmarks. We also note that our algorithm consumes less memory than the traditional CFL-reachability algorithm.

7.3 Discussion

Understanding the Asymptotic Behavior. The SPGs generated from the benchmarks are very sparse — there are fewer edges than nodes across all SPGs. This is expected for the client alias analysis and is consistent with the information in the original papers [36, 37]. For sparse graphs with $m = O(n)$, the asymptotic complexity of our algorithm is $O(n \log n)$.

Moreover, in the traditional CFL-reachability algorithm, the grammar rules should be scanned for each iteration for inserting new summary edges. Specifically, for the Dyck language of size k, each edge popped from the worklist (line 7) in Algorithm 1 needs to be compared with the $O(k)$ rules in the given grammar. However, in our algorithms, the above is unnecessary. It takes *expected* $O(1)$ time to find a relevant edge labeled by a matched parenthesis in both our tree algorithm and graph algorithm due to the use of the FDLL.

Understanding the Memory Consumption. Both our algorithm and the traditional CFL-reachability algorithm demand moderate amount of memory for the client alias analysis. The memory cost for representing the input graphs in both algorithm is similar. The

[2] As of 2012-10-23.

Benchmark	#Methods	#Statements	SPG				Time		Memory	
			#Nodes	#Edges	#S-pair	#para	CFL	FAST-DYCK	CFL	FAST-DYCK
antlr	9904	170402	16735	13878	19385	1087	37.42	0.041	29.68	20.21
bloat	11818	206857	20320	16224	23080	1197	43.09	0.048	35.09	23.89
chart	25184	448984	44584	36329	50670	2948	253.06	0.119	76.75	52.02
eclipse	10447	181101	17527	14411	20335	1182	42.26	0.042	30.97	21.19
fop	23643	431569	39977	31515	45837	2724	219.53	0.101	67.99	46.08
hsqldb	9177	156265	15015	12693	17615	998	33.39	0.038	27.10	18.22
jython	12802	216068	21615	17381	24487	1240	49.57	0.052	37.20	25.32
luindex	9668	164598	16098	13336	18716	1071	35.15	0.040	28.64	19.45
lusearch	10196	175354	17003	14195	19911	1117	40.22	0.043	30.34	20.73
pmd	11167	193375	18167	14958	20843	1168	40.28	0.046	32.00	21.90
xalan	9181	155180	15030	12645	17608	996	32.93	0.038	26.93	18.21
batik	22938	404097	40273	32052	46225	2565	206.50	0.100	68.77	46.60
eclipse	18741	354818	37531	31889	54471	2221	366.39	0.103	70.82	44.54
jython	41518	642242	63516	49005	85552	2855	947.49	0.163	112.14	72.18
sunflow	22346	385873	39321	31339	45161	2484	196.23	0.096	67.22	45.57
tomcat	25123	441606	45966	37338	63414	3013	622.36	0.124	83.98	53.56

Table 2. Benchmarks and performance comparison: time in seconds and memory in MB.

traditional CFL-reachability algorithm needs more iterations to compute the graph closure than those in our algorithm, therefore, it requires more space as well.

Note that we only used the cubic CFL-reachability algorithm (without applying the Four Russians' Trick) in our comparison. The subcubic CFL-reachability algorithm demands non-trivial memory for storing the input graphs in our client application. For instance, given a medium-sized graph from our client analysis with 15000 nodes and 1000 parentheses, the subcubic algorithm needs about 26.2 GB memory to store the graph. It is an interesting topic to scale the subcubic CFL-reachability algorithm on real-world analysis.

Interpreting the Alias Analysis. In the *field-sensitive, context-insensitive alias analysis* for Java, the aliasing pairs are typically sparse. All benchmarks in our evaluation have $O(n)$ aliasing pairs (the #S-pair column in Table 2). This indicates that for real-world applications, most of the variables are not aliases. We have also observed from the experiments that the length of an aliasing path is small; almost all of the aliasing paths are simple paths without cycles. This observation is consistent with the state-of-the-art demand-driven analyses [33, 37, 40].

Demand-Driven vs. Exhausted. We now discuss perhaps one of the most interesting implications from our study. We have noticed that the performance of our all-pairs algorithm for *field-sensitive, context-insensitive* alias analysis is extremely fast. Such an exhaustive analysis with small time and memory cost is particularly suitable for application scenarios that need client analyses to be able to respond instantly, such as just-in-time (JIT) optimizations and interactive development environments (IDEs). Compared to demand-driven analyses, our exhaustive alias analysis can answer any query in $O(1)$ time.

In practice, the two algorithms introduced in this paper can be combined to achieve better performance. For a connected component of the SPG encountered during analysis, it is straightforward to check whether the component is a graph or a tree by counting the number of nodes and edges. Furthermore, one can design an effective analysis switching between our tree and graph algorithms to achieve even better performance.

8. Related Work

There are two strands of closely related work: CFL-reachability and alias analysis.

8.1 CFL-Reachability

The CFL-reachability framework was initially proposed by Yannakakis [38] for Datalog chain query evaluation. Later, it has been used to formulate interprocedural dataflow analysis [29] and many other program analysis problems [11, 19, 22, 25, 27, 31–33, 36, 40]. The central theme in the CFL formulations is that many program analyses have the balanced-parentheses property that can be captured by Dyck-CFL-reachability. The CFL and Dyck-CFL-reachability problems are also studied in the context of recursive state machines [4], visibly pushdown languages [3] and streaming XML [2]. Specially, when the recursive state machines are restricted to allow a constant number of entry/exit nodes per module, reachability is solvable in linear-time. CFL-reachability-based algorithms have cubic worst-case complexity, commonly known as "the cubic bottleneck in flow analysis" [14]. Finding more efficient algorithms for CFL-reachability is a difficult problem as any breakthrough in CFL-reachability may lead to faster algorithms for CFL parsing [27]. Chaudhuri showed that the well-known Four Russians' Trick [5] could be employed to speed up in the original CFL-reachability algorithm to immediately yield a subcubic algorithm [7]. Similar techniques were used in Rytter's work [30] for CFL parsing. Besides the subcubic result, Kodumal and Aiken [19] described a specialized set constraint reduction for Dyck-CFL-reachability on graphs and Yuan and Eugster [39] proposed an efficient Dyck-CFL-reachability algorithm on bidirected trees. Our paper introduces asymptotically faster algorithms for Dyck-CFL-reachability on both bidirected trees and graphs.

8.2 Alias Analysis

Alias analysis has been extensively studied in the literature. Its goal is to decide if two pointer variables may point to the same memory location during program execution. The problem is first formulated by Choi *et al.* [8] and Landi and Ryder [20]. Points-to analysis is recognized as a natural approach to alias analysis because aliasing relation can be decided by consulting the points-to sets of the two variables. We refer the reader to Hind's survey paper [16] on a large body of points-to analysis work.

Deciding aliasing is a computationally hard problem [17, 24]. Approximations must be made for any practical alias analysis. Various techniques have been proposed to scale alias analyses, such as improving the underlying points-to analysis [12, 13], making the analysis demand-driven [15, 37], and using novel data structures [35]. Specifically, Zheng and Rugina [40] proposed an approach based on CFL-reachability such that the aliasing information can be directed computed without first obtaining the points-to information. The client alias analysis [36, 37] in our evaluation is built on the same insight. We show in this paper that our fast algorithms help dramatically speed up the *context-insensitive* alias analysis.

9. Conclusion

In this paper, we have proposed two fast algorithms for solving Dyck-CFL-reachability on bidirected trees and graphs respectively. We have also applied our graph algorithm to a state-of-the-art alias analysis. The experimental results show that our graph algorithm help bring orders of magnitude speedup on real-world benchmarks. The key insight behind both our algorithms is that the reachability relation is an equivalence relation. However, this property does not hold over general trees or graphs. Some existing analyses (*e.g.*, dataflow analysis) do not seem to be good applications for the bidirected restriction. As a result, fast results for solving Dyck-CFL-reachability on general trees and graphs are still of both theoretical and practical interests.

Acknowledgments

We would like to thank Vu Le, Earl Barr, and the anonymous reviewers for helpful comments on earlier drafts of this paper. Special thanks to Dacong Yan and Guoqing Xu for providing us with their alias analysis implementation. The work described in this paper was significantly supported by the Research Grants Council of the Hong Kong Special Administrative Region, China (Project No. CUHK 415311 of General Research Fund and Project No. N_CUHK405/11 of the NSFC/RGC Joint Research Scheme), and partially supported by United States NSF grants 0917392 and 1117603.

References

[1] DaCapo benchmark suite. `http://dacapobench.org/`.

[2] R. Alur. Marrying words and trees. In *PODS*, pages 233–242, 2007.

[3] R. Alur and P. Madhusudan. Visibly pushdown languages. In *STOC*, pages 202–211, 2004.

[4] R. Alur, M. Benedikt, K. Etessami, P. Godefroid, T. W. Reps, and M. Yannakakis. Analysis of recursive state machines. *ACM Trans. Program. Lang. Syst.*, 27(4):786–818, 2005.

[5] V. Arlazarov, E. Dinic, M. Kronrod, and I. Faradzev. On economic construction of the transitive closure of a directed graph. *Soviet Mathematics Doklady*, 11:1209–1210, 1970.

[6] E. Bodden, A. Sewe, J. Sinschek, H. Oueslati, and M. Mezini. Taming reflection: Aiding static analysis in the presence of reflection and custom class loaders. In *ICSE*, pages 241–250, 2011.

[7] S. Chaudhuri. Subcubic algorithms for recursive state machines. In *POPL*, pages 159–169, 2008.

[8] J.-D. Choi, M. G. Burke, and P. R. Carini. Efficient flow-sensitive interprocedural computation of pointer-induced aliases and side effects. In *POPL*, pages 232–245, 1993.

[9] T. H. Cormen, C. E. Leiserson, R. L. Rivest, and C. Stein. *Introduction to Algorithms (3rd ed.)*. MIT Press, 2009.

[10] M. Das, S. Lerner, and M. Seigle. ESP: Path-sensitive program verification in polynomial time. In *PLDI*, pages 57–68, 2002.

[11] C. Earl, I. Sergey, M. Might, and D. V. Horn. Introspective pushdown analysis of higher-order programs. In *ICFP*, pages 177–188, 2012.

[12] M. Fähndrich, J. S. Foster, Z. Su, and A. Aiken. Partial online cycle elimination in inclusion constraint graphs. In *PLDI*, pages 85–96, 1998.

[13] B. Hardekopf and C. Lin. The ant and the grasshopper: Fast and accurate pointer analysis for millions of lines of code. In *PLDI*, pages 290–299, 2007.

[14] N. Heintze and D. A. McAllester. On the cubic bottleneck in subtyping and flow analysis. In *LICS*, pages 342–351, 1997.

[15] N. Heintze and O. Tardieu. Ultra-fast aliasing analysis using CLA: A million lines of C code in a second. In *PLDI*, pages 254–263, 2001.

[16] M. Hind. Pointer analysis: Haven't we solved this problem yet? In *PASTE*, pages 54–61, 2001.

[17] S. Horwitz. Precise flow-insensitive may-alias analysis is NP-Hard. *ACM Trans. Program. Lang. Syst.*, 19(1):1–6, 1997.

[18] S. Horwitz, T. W. Reps, and D. Binkley. Interprocedural slicing using dependence graphs. *ACM Trans. Program. Lang. Syst.*, 12(1):26–60, 1990.

[19] J. Kodumal and A. Aiken. The set constraint/CFL reachability connection in practice. In *PLDI*, pages 207–218, 2004.

[20] W. Landi and B. G. Ryder. A safe approximate algorithm for interprocedural pointer aliasing. In *PLDI*, pages 235–248, 1992.

[21] D. Melski and T. W. Reps. Interconvertibility of a class of set constraints and context-free-language reachability. *Theor. Comput. Sci.*, 248(1-2):29–98, 2000.

[22] P. Pratikakis, J. S. Foster, and M. Hicks. Existential label flow inference via CFL reachability. In *SAS*, pages 88–106, 2006.

[23] P. Pratikakis, J. S. Foster, and M. Hicks. Locksmith: Practical static race detection for C. *ACM Trans. Program. Lang. Syst.*, 33(1):3, 2011.

[24] G. Ramalingam. The undecidability of aliasing. *ACM Trans. Program. Lang. Syst.*, 16(5):1467–1471, 1994.

[25] J. Rehof and M. Fähndrich. Type-base flow analysis: from polymorphic subtyping to CFL-reachability. In *POPL*, pages 54–66, 2001.

[26] T. W. Reps. Shape analysis as a generalized path problem. In *PEPM*, pages 1–11, 1995.

[27] T. W. Reps. Program analysis via graph reachability. *Information & Software Technology*, 40(11-12):701–726, 1998.

[28] T. W. Reps, S. Horwitz, S. Sagiv, and G. Rosay. Speeding up slicing. In *SIGSOFT FSE*, pages 11–20, 1994.

[29] T. W. Reps, S. Horwitz, and S. Sagiv. Precise interprocedural dataflow analysis via graph reachability. In *POPL*, pages 49–61, 1995.

[30] W. Rytter. Fast recognition of pushdown automaton and context-free languages. *Information and Control*, 67(1-3):12–22, 1985.

[31] L. Shang, X. Xie, and J. Xue. On-demand dynamic summary-based points-to analysis. In *CGO*, pages 264–274, 2012.

[32] M. Sridharan and R. Bodík. Refinement-based context-sensitive points-to analysis for Java. In *PLDI*, pages 387–400, 2006.

[33] M. Sridharan, D. Gopan, L. Shan, and R. Bodík. Demand-driven points-to analysis for Java. In *OOPSLA*, pages 59–76, 2005.

[34] R. Vallée-Rai, E. Gagnon, L. J. Hendren, P. Lam, P. Pominville, and V. Sundaresan. Optimizing java bytecode using the Soot framework: Is it feasible? In *CC*, pages 18–34, 2000.

[35] J. Whaley and M. S. Lam. Cloning-based context-sensitive pointer alias analysis using binary decision diagrams. In *PLDI*, pages 131–144, 2004.

[36] G. Xu, A. Rountev, and M. Sridharan. Scaling CFL-reachability-based points-to analysis using context-sensitive must-not-alias analysis. In *ECOOP*, pages 98–122, 2009.

[37] D. Yan, G. H. Xu, and A. Rountev. Demand-driven context-sensitive alias analysis for Java. In *ISSTA*, pages 155–165, 2011.

[38] M. Yannakakis. Graph-theoretic methods in database theory. In *PODS*, pages 230–242, 1990.

[39] H. Yuan and P. T. Eugster. An efficient algorithm for solving the Dyck-CFL reachability problem on trees. In *ESOP*, pages 175–189, 2009.

[40] X. Zheng and R. Rugina. Demand-driven alias analysis for C. In *POPL*, pages 197–208, 2008.

Static Analysis for Probabilistic Programs: Inferring Whole Program Properties from Finitely Many Paths

Sriram Sankaranarayanan
University of Colorado, Boulder
srirams@colorado.edu

Aleksandar Chakarov
University of Colorado, Boulder
aleksandar.chakarov@colorado.edu

Sumit Gulwani
Microsoft Research, Redmond
sumitg@microsoft.com

Abstract

We propose an approach for the static analysis of probabilistic programs that sense, manipulate, and control based on uncertain data. Examples include programs used in risk analysis, medical decision making and cyber-physical systems. Correctness properties of such programs take the form of *queries* that seek the probabilities of assertions over program variables. We present a static analysis approach that provides guaranteed interval bounds on the values (assertion probabilities) of such queries. First, we observe that for probabilistic programs, it is possible to conclude facts about the behavior of the entire program by choosing a finite, *adequate set* of its paths. We provide strategies for choosing such a set of paths and verifying its adequacy. The queries are evaluated over each path by a combination of symbolic execution and probabilistic volume-bound computations. Each path yields interval bounds that can be summed up with a "coverage" bound to yield an interval that encloses the probability of assertion for the program as a whole. We demonstrate promising results on a suite of benchmarks from many different sources including robotic manipulators and medical decision making programs.

Categories and Subject Descriptors D.2.4 [**Software Engineering**] Software/Program Verification.

Keywords: Probabilistic Programming, Program Verification, Volume Bounding, Symbolic Execution, Monte-Carlo Sampling.

1. Introduction

The goal of this paper is to study static analysis techniques for proving properties of probabilistic programs that manipulate *uncertain* quantities defined by probability distributions. Uncertainty is a common aspect of many software systems, especially systems that manipulate error-prone data to make medical decisions (eg., should the doctor recommend drugs or dialysis to a patient based on the calculated eGFR score?); systems that predict long term risks of catastrophic events such as floods and earthquakes (eg., should a nuclear power plant be built at a certain location?); and control systems that operate in the presence of sensor errors and external environmental disturbances (eg., robotic manipulators and air traffic control systems). It is essential to learn how the presence of uncertainty in the inputs can affect the program's behavior.

PLDI'13, June 16–19, 2013, Seattle, WA, USA.

In general, the problem of reasoning about uncertain systems is quite challenging due to (a) real-valued variables that are used to model physical quantities such as space, time and temperature; (b) imprecision in the input, modeled by different distributions such as uniform, Poisson and Gaussian; and (c) control flow that is mediated by conditions over the program variables and random variables. These aspects make the resulting programs infinite state, requiring techniques that go beyond the exhaustive exploration of concrete sets of states.

In this paper, we study infinite state programs that manipulate real-valued variables and uncertain quantities belonging to a wide variety of distributions. Our modeling approach is simple: we use standard imperative programs augmented with probabilistic constructs to model uncertainties. The overall goal of our approach is to answer questions about the probability of assertions at the exit of the program.

Monte-Carlo simulation [34] can be used to answer this question upto some desired level of precision. However, these techniques do not provide formal guarantees on the accuracy of the answers. In this work, we provide a static analysis approach that can place guaranteed interval bounds on the possible values of the assertion probabilities. As a side effect, our approach can perform a *stratified sampling* to provide more accurate answers than standard rejection sampling. Our static analysis approach has two main components: (A) choosing an adequate set of paths and (B) path probability bound computation.

Adequate Set of Paths: Unlike static analysis in the non-probabilistic case, it suffices to consider a carefully chosen finite set of *adequate program paths* for estimating probability bounds. Let us assume that a set of syntactic program paths S is provided with a lower bound c on their combined path probabilities. We can proceed to estimate the probability of any assertion φ over the finitely many paths in the set S and know that the contribution from the unexplored paths is at most $1 - c$.

Therefore, given some target "coverage" probability c (eg., $c = 0.95$), we wish to find a set S of syntactic program paths (if such a set exists) such that an execution of the program yields a path in the set S with probability at least c. We achieve this in two steps: (a) we use a statistical procedure to find a set S that achieves the coverage bound with high confidence, and (b) we then compute a formal lower bound on the actual coverage of S. Using a two-step approach guarantees that the symbolic execution is always performed over feasible program paths. Secondly, executing probabilistic programs is a natural way of sampling the paths of the program according to their path probabilities.

Path Probability Computation: We use symbolic execution along the chosen paths to compute bounds on the path probability: i.e, the probability that an execution of the program follows the chosen path. In turn, this reduces to finding the probability of satisfaction for a system of constraints, given probability distributions on the individual variables. This is a hard problem both in theory and in practice [2]. Therefore, rather than compute the precise answer, we seek to bound the probability of satisfaction. We present a scheme that can estimate probability bounds for linear assertions over integers and reals. Furthermore, given more time our technique can generate bounds that are tighter.

Our overall framework weaves the two ideas together to yield upper and lower bounds for the probability of the assertion for the program as a whole. The paper makes the following contributions:

1. We present an approach to infer bounds on assertion probability for the whole program by considering a suitably chosen finite set of program paths.
2. We present branch-and-bound techniques over polyhedra to derive tight bounds on path and assertion probabilities.
3. We present an experimental evaluation of our approach over a set of small but compelling benchmarks. We showcase some of the successes of our approach and identify limitations to motivate future work.

However, we have by no means solved every aspect of the complex problem of probabilistic program analysis.

1. Our approach is restricted to programs with linear assignments and conditionals (see Figure 3 in Section 3). As such, the high level ideas presented here directly extend to programs with non-linearities that arise from multiplications, exponentiations and bitwise operations. The current limitation lies in the volume computation technique (Section 4.2) that handles convex polyhedra over reals and integers.
2. We support the generation of random variables with known distributions and known correlations specified, for instance, by a given covariance matrix. However, our framework does not handle non-deterministic uncertainties or distributions with unknown (arbitrary) correlations.
3. Our focus is on estimating probability bounds for safety properties. We do not consider liveness properties (termination) or expectation queries in this paper.

2. Approach At A Glance

In this section, we first motivate the main contributions of this paper using an example from medical decision making. The probabilistic programming language and its semantics are described in the subsequent section.

Estimating Kidney Disease Risk in Adults Chronic kidney disease in adults is characterized by the gradual loss of kidney function. A common measure of chronic kidney disease is a quantity called the *Estimated Glomerular Filtration Rate* (eGFR), which is computed based on the age, gender, ethnicity and the measured serum Creatinine levels of the patient [1]. There are many formulae that are used for computing eGFR, which is typically a log-linear function of its inputs. Figure 1 shows the function that computes the value of eGFR according to the widely used CKD-EPI formula [2]. Kidney disease risk in adults is typically diagnosed if $\log(eGFR) < 4.5$, or equivalently $eGFR < 90$. However, the values of age and measured serum Creatinine levels can be erroneous. Age is typically rounded up or down causing a ± 1 variation, while the lab values of serum Creatinine levels are assumed to have a 10% variation. While gender and ethnicity are often mistake-free, it is sometimes possible to record a wrong gender or ethnicity due to transcription mistakes in the (electronic) medical record. Figure 2 shows a model that adds the appropriate amount of noise to the inputs of the eGFR calculation. Given these input uncertainties, one naturally worries about the problem of patients being mis-classified purely due to the noise in the recorded patient data. Therefore, we ask the question: what is the probability that the presence of noise causes 10% or larger variation in the EGFR values (≥ 0.1 absolute variation in the logarithmic scale)? Such a query is expressed at the end of the function `compareWithNoise` in Figure 2.

```
real estimateLogEGFR( real logScr, int age,
                      bool isFemale, bool isAA){
   var k,alpha: real;
   var f: real;
   f= 4.94;
   if (isFemale) {
      k = -0.357;
      alpha = -0.329;
   } else {
      k = -0.105;
      alpha = -0.411;
   }

   if ( logScr < k ) {
      f = alpha * (logScr - k);
   } else {
      f = -1.209 * (logScr - k);
   }
   f = f - 0.007 *  age;

   if (isFemale)  f = f + 0.017;
   if (isAA) f = f + 0.148;
   return f;
}
```

Figure 1. A program that computes the logarithm of the eGFR given the logarithm of the measured serum Creatinine value (logScr), the patient's age, whether the patient is female (isFemale) and whether the patient is African American (isAA). We assume that the inputs to the function are noisy and wish to know how the noise affects the output value f.

```
void compareWithNoise(real logScr, real age,
                      bool isFemale, bool isAA) {
  f1 = estimateLogEGFR(logScr, age, isFemale,isAA);
  logScr = logScr + uniformRandom(-0.1, 0.1);
  age = age + uniformRandomInt(-1,1);
  if (flip(0.01))
    isFemale = not( isFemale );
  if (flip(0.01))
    isAA = not( isAA );
  f2 = estimateLogEGFR(logScr, age, isFemale,isAA);
  estimateProbability (f1 - f2 >= 0.1);
  estimateProbability (f2 - f1 >= 0.1);
}
```

Figure 2. A probabilistic program that simulates noise in patient data, comparing the error between original and noisy outputs.

Modeling Input Distributions: The distributions of serum Creatinine values are highly correlated with age, gender and race. A detailed population survey is provided by Jones et al. [19]. For illustration, we assume a 50% chance of the person being female and 10% chance of being African American. Based on these outcomes, different distributions are chosen for the patients based on their gender. We model input serum Creatinine levels as drawn from a normal distribution around the mean with a fixed standard devi-

[1] Cf. http://www.kidney.org/kidneydisease/aboutckd.cfm

[2] Cf. http://nephron.com/epi_equation.

ation of 0.1 around a mean that varies based on gender: 1.0 for women and 1.2 for men. A full model based on population data can be constructed and used in our static analysis. Table 3 summarizes the two basic primitives that we expect from any distribution supported by our analysis.

Estimating Probability of Assertions: For the example at hand, our approach proceeds in three steps:

1. We first generate a finite, adequate set of paths S such that the probability that a random execution yields a path in S is at least c for some fixed c. Fixing $c = 0.95$, we use the procedure in Algorithm 2 to yield 49 distinct paths.
2. Next, we analyze each of these paths and estimate intervals for the path probability and the probability for each of the assertions. For the example at hand, this requires less than 5 seconds of computational time for all paths and assertions.
3. We add up the path probability intervals for individual paths in the set S to infer a bound of $[0.98117, 0.98119]$ on the total probability of paths in S. This means that the paths in S are guaranteed to be encountered with probability at least 0.98117. Therefore, the probability of drawing a path not in S is at most 0.01883. We will make use of this fact in the next step.
4. We add up path probability intervals for the assertion `f1-f2 >= 0.1` to obtain a bound $[0.12630, 0.126306]$. However, since we did not cover all paths in the program, this bound is not valid for the whole program. To address this, we add 0.01883, an upper bound on the probability of encountering a path outside S. This yields a guaranteed bound of $[0.126306, 0.145136]$ for the probability that a given execution satisfies the assertion. Likewise, the probability of the assertion `f2-f1 >= 0.1` is estimated at $[0.08503, 0.10386]$.
5. We simulated the program for $1,000,000$ iterations in Matlab and estimated the probability of the assertions, taking nearly as much time as our static analysis. The bounds obtained by our analysis are confirmed.

Thus, our analysis provides bounds on the probability of obtaining a 10% or larger deviation in the computed risk score due to errors in the input data.

The rest of the paper is organized as follows: Section 3 presents the syntax and semantics of probabilistic programs, the process of bounding probabilities is explained in Section 4, Section 5 discusses our implementation and some experimental results on an interesting set of benchmarks. Related work is discussed in Section 6. We conclude by discussing future directions. Supplementary materials, including our prototype implementation and the benchmarks used in this paper are available on-line from our project page [3].

3. Probabilistic Programs

We now consider imperative programs with constructs that can generate random values according to a fixed set of distributions. We then describe queries over probabilistic programs that seek (conditional) probabilities of assertions.

Fig. 3 presents the key parts of the syntax for a probabilistic programming language for specifying programs. Let $X = \{x_1, \ldots, x_k\}$ be a set of program variables partitioned into subsets Q and I of real and integer typed variables, respectively. The language consists of assignments, conditional statements and loops. The expressions in the language are restricted in two ways: (1) The language is *strongly typed*: integer values cannot be converted to reals, or vice-versa. (2) The expressions involving integer and real variables are affine.

```
program      →  declarations init {initSpec*}stmt*queries
stmt         →  assign | condStmt | while
initSpec     →  intVariable := intConst | realVariable := realConst
             |  intVariable ~ intRandom
             |  realVariable ~ realRandom
assign       →  intAssign | realAssign
condStmt     →  if boolExpr stmt+ else stmt+
while        →  while boolExpr stmt+
intAssign    →  intVariable := intExpr
realAssign   →  realVariable := realExpr
intExpr      →  intConst | intExpr ± intExpr
             |  intConst * intExpr | intRandom
realExpr     →  realConst | realExpr ± realExpr
             |  realConst * realExpr | realRandom
intRandom    →  uniformInt (intConst, intConst)
             |  Bernoulli (intConst, realConst)
             |  ...
realRandom   →  uniformReal (realConst, realConst)
             |  Gaussian (realConst, realConst)
             |  ...
boolExpr     →  boolExpr ∧ boolExpr
             |  intExpr relop intExpr | realExpr relop realExpr
             |  true | false
relop        →  < | > | ≥ | ≤ | =
intVariable  →  I
realVariable →  Q
queries      →  estimateProbability boolExpr( given boolExpr)?
```

Figure 3. Partial syntax specification for imperative language for modeling programs.

Inbuilt Random Value Generators: The programs in our language can call a set of inbuilt random number generators to produce values according to known distributions, as summarized in Table 2.

Some distributions can be automatically implemented based on other available ones. For instance, a coin flip with success probability $p \in [0, 1]$ can be simulated by a uniform random variable $r \sim \mathsf{uniformReal}(0, 1)$ and the conditional statement involving the condition $r \leq p$.

Initializer: The program has an initialization section that is assumed to initialize every variable $x_i \in X$. The initialization for a variable x_i can assign it to a concrete value c_i, or to a randomly distributed value by calling an in-built random number generator.

Queries: Queries in our language involve probabilities of Boolean expressions over program variables, possibly conditioned on other Boolean expressions. Table 1 summarizes the intended meaning of each of the two types of queries. For simplicity of presentation, we restrict queries to conjunctions of linear inequalities. However, queries involving disjunctions $\varphi_1 \vee \varphi_2$ can be expressed by using a special indicator variable x, which can be set to 1 iff either disjunct is true. The transformed query evaluates the probability of $x = 1$.

3.1 Semantics of Probabilistic Programs

The operational semantics of the execution of assignments, if-then-else, and while statements are quite standard. We focus on defining the semantics of the initialization, the random number generators, and the queries.

Let P be a probabilistic program written using the syntax in Fig. 3. We associate a set of *control locations*, $Loc = \{\ell_0, \ldots, \ell_k\}$,

[3] Cf. `http://systems.cs.colorado.edu/research/cyberphysical/probabilistic-program-analysis/`

Query	Remark
`estimateProbability(`φ`)`	The execution terminates AND variables at exit satisfy φ.
`estimateProbability(`φ `given` ψ`)`	The execution terminates AND variables satisfy φ under the condition that they satisfy ψ.

Table 1. Queries on the final state of the program and their informal meaning.

Name	Support	Density Function
`uniformReal(a,b)`	$[a,b] \subseteq \mathbb{R}$	$\frac{1}{b-a}\mathbb{1}_{[a,b]}, a < b.$
`uniformInt(a,b)`	$[a,b] \subseteq \mathbb{Z}$	$\begin{cases} \frac{1}{b-a}\mathbb{1}_{[a,b]} & b > a \\ 1 & a = b \end{cases}.$
`Binomial(n,p)`	$[0,n] \subseteq \mathbb{Z}$	$\binom{n}{x}p^x(1-p)^{n-x}$, $n \geq 1,\ p \in [0,1].$
`Gaussian(m,s)`	$\mathbb{R}$	$\frac{1}{\sqrt{2\pi s}}e^{-\frac{1}{2}\frac{(x-m)}{s}^2}, s > 0$

Table 2. Specification of the inbuilt random value generators. Note that the function $\mathbb{1}_X(x)$ is the indicator function for the set X.

```
state x: real;
state c: int;
init {  x := uniformReal(-1,3);
        c := 0;  }
-- ℓ0: while (x <= 4) {
-- ℓ1:    x := x + uniformReal(-1,3);
            c := c + uniformInt(0,2);
          }
-- ℓF: estimateProbability(c <= 4);
```

Figure 4. A simple probabilistic program with a probability estimation query. We consider the assignments to variables x,c as a simultaneous assignment.

such that each statement in P is associated with a unique control location. The set of labels define a control flow graph with nodes corresponding to statement labels and edges corresponding to conditional tests and assignments between program variables. Let ℓ_0 be the location after the initializer and ℓ_F be the end of the program, where queries may be posed. A state of the program is a tuple $\langle \ell_j, \vec{x}_j \rangle$ given by its current control location $\ell_j \in Loc$ and valuations to the program variables $\vec{x}_j \in \mathbb{R}^{|Q|} \times \mathbb{Z}^{|I|}$.

The initializer assigns each variable to a fixed constant value or a random value sampled according to a known probability distribution. All random variables are assumed to be mutually independent.

Since our main goal is to define and evaluate queries, we define the semantics operationally. Let $\Pi = \{\pi_1, \ldots, \pi_N, \ldots\}$ be a set of syntactic program paths that start from location ℓ_0 and lead to the final location ℓ_F. Each path π_j is a finite sequence $\pi_j : \ell_0 \rightarrow \ell_1 \rightarrow \cdots \rightarrow \ell_l \rightarrow \ell_F$, where each (ℓ_i, ℓ_{i+1}) is an edge in the program's CFG. Note that locations may repeat in π_j.

Symbolic Execution: First, we define symbolic execution of paths in the presence of random variables.

Definition 3.1 (Symbolic State). *The symbolic state of a program P is a tuple $s : \langle \ell, R, \psi, T \rangle$ wherein*

1. *ℓ denotes the current location.*
2. *$R = \{r_1, \ldots, r_k\}$ represents a set of random variables. This includes random variables for the initial condition, and the RHS of assignments involving calls to the random value generators (RVG). Fresh variables will be added to the set R, as RVGs are encountered along a path.*
3. *ψ is an assertion involving the variables in R representing the path condition. The syntax of the program ensures that ψ does not involve any program variables and is a conjunction of linear inequalities over R.*
4. *T is an affine transformation that maps each program variable $x_i \in X$ to an affine expression involving variables in R.*

Initial Symbolic State: The initial symbolic state s_0 is given by $\langle \ell_0, R_0, true, T_0 \rangle$ wherein R_0 is an initial set of random variables corresponding to each initialization of a program variable x_j by a call to an inbuilt random value generator. The transformation T_0 associates each program variable x_j with a constant c or a random variable $r_j \in R$ depending on how x_j is initialized.

Symbolic Step: We may now define the single-step execution of the program along a path $\pi : \ell_0 \rightsquigarrow \ell_F$ by means of symbolic states $s_0 \rightarrow s_1 \ldots \rightarrow s_F$. To do so, we specify the update of a symbolic state across an edge (ℓ, m) in the control-flow graph.

First, we handle any calls to random value generators on the edge (ℓ, m). Each such call results in the addition of a fresh random variable to the set R with appropriate type, set of support, and probability density function. Table 2 lists the formal specification of the random variable generated by various inbuilt random value generators. Next, depending on the type of the edge being traversed, we define the subsequent symbolic state:

1. The edge is labeled by a condition $\gamma[X, R]$, wherein calls to random value generators have been substituted by fresh random variables introduced in R. In this case, we update the path condition ψ to $\psi' : \psi \wedge \gamma[x_1 \mapsto T(x_1), \ldots, x_n \mapsto T(x_n)]$, wherein each occurrence of the program variable x_i in γ is substituted by $T(x_i)$.
2. The edge is labeled by an assignment $x_i := e[X, R]$ involving variables $x_j \in X$ and calls to random value generators replaced by fresh random variables. In this case, we update the transformation T to yield a new transformation T' defined as

$$T'(x_j) = \begin{cases} T(x_j) & x_j \neq x_i \\ e[x_1 \mapsto T(x_1), \ldots, x_n \mapsto T(x_n)] & \text{otherwise} \end{cases}$$

As a result, we have defined the transformation of the symbolic state $s : (\ell, R, \psi, T)$ to a new state $s' : (m, R', \psi', T')$ involving the addition of fresh random variables, updates to the path condition ψ or the transformation T.

Example 3.1. *Fig. 4 shows a simple program P that updates a real variable x and an integer c. Each step updates the value of x and c by drawing a uniform random variable of appropriate type from fixed ranges. Consider the path that iterates through the while loop twice: $\pi : \ell_0 \rightarrow \ell_1 \rightarrow \ell_0 \rightarrow \ell_1 \rightarrow \ell_0 \rightarrow \ell_F$. The initial state $s_0 : \langle \ell_0, R_0, \psi_0, T_0 \rangle$ is given by*

$$R_0 : \{r_1 : \mathsf{uniformReal}[-1,3]\}, \psi_0 : true,\ T_0 : (x \mapsto r_1, c \mapsto 0)$$

We may verify that the state at the end of the path is given by

$$\left\langle \ell_F, \left\{ \begin{array}{c} r_1, r_2, r_3, \\ z_1, z_2 \end{array} \right\}, \begin{array}{c} r_1 \leq 4 \wedge r_1 + r_2 \leq 4 \\ \wedge r_1 + r_2 + r_3 > 4 \end{array}, \left(\begin{array}{c} x : r_1 + r_2 + r_3, \\ c : z_1 + z_2 \end{array} \right) \right\rangle$$

The real-valued variables r_1, r_2, r_3 are distributed as $\mathsf{uniformReal}(-1,3)$*, while z_1, z_2 are distributed as* $\mathsf{uniformInt}(0,2)$.

Let $\pi : \ell_0 \rightsquigarrow \ell_F$ be a finite path from initial to exit node and $s(\pi) : \langle \ell_F, R_\pi, \psi_\pi, T_\pi \rangle$ be the final symbolic state obtained by propagating the initial symbolic state s_0 along the edges in π. A program path π is *feasible* iff the path condition ψ_π is satisfiable.

Lemma 3.1. *For any feasible state $s : (\ell, R, \psi, T)$ encountered during symbolic execution, the following properties hold:*

1. *ψ is a linear arithmetic assertion that can be decomposed into $\psi : \psi_Q \wedge \psi_I$ where ψ_Q involves real-valued random variables from R while ψ_I involves integer-valued random variables.*
2. *$T(x_j)$ is an affine expression for each x_j involving integer random variables/constants if x_j is integer typed and involving real-valued random variables/constants if x_j is real typed.*

3.2 Semantics of Queries

We may use the notion of a symbolic state propagated across program paths to define the semantics of queries. We first start with *unconditional queries* that estimate the probability of an assertion $\varphi[X]$ over the program variables. We then extend our definition to define the semantics of conditional probability queries.

To answer the queries, we start with the set of all feasible program paths $\Pi = \{\pi_j : \ell_0 \rightsquigarrow \ell_F \mid \pi_j \text{ is feasible}\}$, where $|\Pi|$ may be finite or countably infinite.

Probability of an Assertion: Consider a query that seeks the probability of an assertion φ over the program variables. We denote the outcome of the query as $\mathbb{P}(\varphi)$.

$$\mathbb{P}(\varphi) = \sum_{\pi_j \in \Pi} \mathbb{P}_{\pi_j}(\varphi),$$

wherein $\mathbb{P}_{\pi_j}(\varphi)$ denotes the probability of the event that the execution proceeds along the path π_j, reaching the location ℓ_F *and* φ is true in the resulting state at location ℓ_F.

We now formally define $\mathbb{P}_{\pi_j}(\varphi)$ for $\pi_j \in \Pi$. First, let $s_j : \langle \ell_F, R_j, \psi_j, T_j \rangle$ denote the symbolic state obtained by executing along the path π_j. The transformation T_j maps the program variables at ℓ_F to affine expressions over R_j, the random variables encountered along π_j. Let $\varphi' : \varphi[X \mapsto T_j(X)]$ denote the transformation of the program variables in φ using T_j.

We partition R_j into integer valued variables Z_j and real valued variables Q_j. Next, we split ψ_j into an integer part ψ_j^I conjoined with a real part ψ_j^Q. Similarly, we split the condition φ' into φ^I and φ^Q. The value $\mathbb{P}_{\pi_j}(\varphi)$ can be defined in two parts:

1. For the real part, we define the integral over the sets of support for the variables in $Q_j = \{y_1, \ldots, y_k\}$
$$p_r : \int_{\mathcal{Q}} \mathbb{1}(\psi_j^Q \wedge \varphi^Q)\, p_1(y_1) p_2(y_2) \cdots p_k(y_k) dy_1 \cdots dy_k,$$
wherein each y_j has a density function $p_i(y_i)$ and $\mathcal{Q}$ is the joint region of support for the variables $y_1, \ldots, y_k$ taken as the Cartesian product of their individual intervals of support. The notation $\mathbb{1}(\varphi)$ for an assertion φ stands for the *indicator function* that maps to 1 wherever φ is satisfied and 0 elsewhere.
2. For the integer part, we define a summation over the sets of support for variables in $Z_j = \{z_1, \ldots, z_l\}$
$$p_z : \sum_{z_1 \in I_1} \cdots \sum_{z_l \in I_l} \mathbb{1}(\psi_j^I \wedge \varphi^I) i_1(z_1) i_2(z_2) \cdots i_l(z_l),$$
wherein I_j is the set of support for z_j and $i_j(z_j)$ is the mass function for the distribution defining z_j.

The overall value $\mathbb{P}_{\pi_j}(\varphi)$ is the product $p_r \times p_z$. Note that the restrictions to the structure of the conditional statements and queries guarantee that ψ_j and φ' are defined by conjunctions of linear inequalities. Therefore, the sets defined by them are a union of polyhedra over the reals and Z-polyhedra over the integers. They are measurable under the Lebesgue and discrete measures, so that integrals and summations over them are well defined.

Example 3.2. *Consider again the symbolic execution from Ex. 3.1. The set of random variables is $R_F : \{r_1, r_2, r_3, z_1, z_2\}$ with the real-valued variables r_1, r_2, r_3 which are all of the type* uniformReal$(-1, 3)$. *The integer variables z_1, z_2 are of the type* uniformInt$(0, 2)$. *We wish to find the probability $\mathbb{P}_\pi(c \le 4)$ corresponding to the query* estimateProbability$(c \le 4)$. *First, we transform $c \le 4$ according to the transformation $c \mapsto z_1 + z_2$ to obtain $z_1 + z_2 \le 4$.*

The overall probability reduces to finding the probability that the following assertion holds

$$\psi^Q : r_1 + r_2 \le 4 \wedge r_1 + r_2 + r_3 > 4 \wedge \varphi^I : z_1 + z_2 \le 4$$

given the distributions of r_1, r_2, r_3, z_1, z_2. The constraint $r_1 \le 4$ is seen to be redundant given $r_1 \in [-1, 3]$ and therefore is dropped.

We split the computation into an integral over the real part

$$\int_{[-1,3]^3} \mathbb{1}(r_1 + r_2 \le 4 \wedge r_1 + r_2 + r_3 > 4) \left(\frac{1}{4}\right)^3 dr_1 dr_2 dr_3 .$$

and an integer part $\sum_{z_1=0}^{2} \sum_{z_2=0}^{2} \mathbb{1}(z_1 + z_2 \le 4) \left(\frac{1}{3}\right)^2$.

The second half of this paper describes how to restrict the probability computation to a suitably chosen finite set of paths, while bounding the influence of the unexplored paths and for each path, place tight bounds on the summation and the integral above. We also use Monte-Carlo simulations to estimate the actual values to some degree of confidence.

Conditional Assertions: We now consider queries of the form estimateProbability(φ_1 given φ_2) that seeks to estimate the probability of assertion φ_1 under the condition that the state at the exit satisfies φ_2. However, unlike the previous case, it is possible that the conditional probability may be ill defined. This is especially the case when no execution reaches the end of the program or all executions reaching the exit do not satisfy φ_2.

It is well-known that

$$\mathbb{P}(\varphi_1 | \varphi_2) = \frac{\mathbb{P}(\varphi_1 \wedge \varphi_2)}{\mathbb{P}\varphi_2} = \frac{\sum_{\pi \in \Pi} \mathbb{P}_\pi(\varphi_1 \wedge \varphi_2)}{\sum_{\pi \in \Pi} \mathbb{P}_\pi(\varphi_2)} .$$

As a result, we can use the definitions established for computing the probabilities of assertions unconditionally, and derive conditional probabilities. In general, however, it is incorrect to split the conditional probabilities as a whole as a summation of the conditional probabilities measured along paths.

4. Computing Probabilities

In this section, we present techniques to estimate the probabilities of assertions by sampling program paths. The probability of the assertion (overall probability) is simply the summation of the probabilities computed over individual paths. We consider three types of estimation: (a) computing guaranteed lower and upper bounds on the individual path probabilities and the overall probability of the assertion and (b) approximation (Monte-Carlo simulation) of path probabilities.

The overall path probability estimation proceeds in two steps: (a) choose a finite set of paths in the program using a heuristic strategy, so that with high confidence, the sum of the path probabilities of the chosen paths exceeds a *coverage bound c*; and (b) for each path chosen, estimate probability efficiently from the path condition. Finally, we show how both parts can be tied together to yield guaranteed whole program bounds and approximations.

Let us fix a program P and let φ be an assertion whose probability we wish to estimate. We assume a path coverage target

```
Data: Program P, assertion φ and coverage c ∈ (0, 1).
Result: Probability estimate p̂ and bounds [p̲, p̄].
/* 1. Heuristically elect a set of paths.               */
C := PathSelect(P, c) ;
q̲ := 0 ;            /* lower bound on path probability */
(p̲, p̄) := (0, 0) ;        /* path + assertion bounds */
p̂ := 0 ;                     /* Monte-Carlo Estimate */
/* 2. Iterate through paths in C                        */
for (π ∈ C) do
    /* 2.1 Compute path condition and transformation
       */
    (R, ψ, T) := SymbolicExecute(P, π);
    /* 2.2 Transform condition φ                        */
    φ' := φ[X ↦ T(X)];
    /* 2.3 Lower bound on path probability              */
    q̲ := q̲ + PolyhedronLowerBound(R, ψ) ;
    /* 2.4 Bounds on path and assertion probability
       */
    p̲ := p̲ + PolyhedronLowerBound(R, ψ ∧ φ') ;
    p̄ := p̄ + PolyhedronUpperBound(R, ψ ∧ φ') ;
    /* 2.5 Monte-Carlo estimation                       */
    p̂ := p̂ + MonteCarloSample(R, ψ ∧ φ') ;
end
/* 3. Adjust upper bound estimate to account for
   uncovered paths.                                     */
p̄ := p̄ + (1 − q̲) ;
```

Algorithm 1: Algorithm for estimating the probability of an assertion.

$0 < c < 1$ wherein c is assumed to be very close to 1 (say $c = 0.99$). Let Π denote the set of all terminating, feasible program paths that lead from the initial location ℓ_0 to the final location ℓ_F. Algorithm 1 shows the overall algorithm for providing bounds and estimates of probabilities for an assertion. The idea is to compute a finite set of paths C according to the coverage criterion and compute the probabilities for the assertion φ to hold at the end of each path. Next, an actual lower bound on the total probability of all paths in C is also estimated and used to yield an upper bound on the overall assertion probability.

4.1 Heuristic Path Selection Strategy

The first step is to select finitely many feasible, terminating program paths $C = \{\pi_1, \ldots, \pi_k\}$. The path probability of a path π_j is defined as $\mathbb{P}_{\pi_j}(\mathit{true})$. This denotes the probability that a randomly chosen initial condition results in taking the path π_j in the first place. We write $\mathbb{P}(\pi_j)$ to denote the path probability.

A subset $C \subseteq \Pi$ satisfies a coverage goal c iff $\sum_{\pi \in C} \mathbb{P}(\pi) \geq c$.

Satisfying any given coverage goal c is not guaranteed since it is not known a priori if a finite subset C satisfies the coverage goal. For instance, the program may fail to terminate with probability $p_{\text{non-terminating}} \geq 1 - c$. However, most programs of interest do terminate *almost surely* with probability 1.

Lemma 4.1. *Let P be an almost surely terminating program. For any coverage goal $c \in (0,1)$, there is a finite set of paths C such that $\sum_{\pi \in C} \mathbb{P}(\pi) \geq c$.*

Therefore, assuming that we are able to find enough paths C whose cumulative path probability is known to be at least c, we may proceed to estimate the probability of φ along paths $\pi \in C$. We use the notation $\mathbb{P}_C(\varphi)$ to denote the sum of path probabilities for φ along all paths belonging to the set C: $\mathbb{P}_C(\varphi) = \sum_{\pi \in C} \mathbb{P}_\pi(\varphi)$.

Theorem 4.1. *For any assertion φ and set of paths C that satisfy the coverage criterion c, $\mathbb{P}_C(\varphi) \leq \mathbb{P}(\varphi) \leq \mathbb{P}_C(\varphi) + (1 - c)$.*

```
Data: Program P, assertion φ, run length K > 0.
Result: Set of paths C such that a run of K continuously drawn
        program paths belong to C .
count := 0 ;
C = { } ;
while count < K do
    π := simulatePath(P) ;
    if π ∉ C then
        count := 0 ;
        C := C ∪ {π};
    else
        count := count + 1 ;
    end
end
```

Algorithm 2: Algorithm for collecting a set of paths C through random simulation until a run of $K > 0$ continuous paths already belonging to C is obtained.

Proof. Since we have $C \subseteq \Pi$, the lower bound is immediate. For the upper bound, we note that

$$\begin{array}{rcl} \mathbb{P}(\varphi) & = & \sum_{\pi \in \Pi} \mathbb{P}_\pi(\varphi) = \sum_{\pi \in C} \mathbb{P}_\pi(\varphi) + \sum_{\pi \notin C} \mathbb{P}_\pi(\varphi) \\ & \leq & \sum_{\pi \in C} \mathbb{P}_\pi(\varphi) + \sum_{\pi \notin C} \mathbb{P}_\pi(\mathit{true}) \\ & \leq & \sum_{\pi \in C} \mathbb{P}_\pi(\varphi) + (1 - c) \end{array}$$

□

Our approach uses a statistical approach based on simulation to select an initial set C of paths such that the sum of path probabilities of individual paths in C exceeds the coverage bound c with high confidence. Our overall strategy proceeds in two steps:

1. Fix integer parameter $K > 0$. The criterion for choosing K is described below.
2. The simple procedure shown in Algorithm 2 repeatedly runs the program and records the syntactic path taken by each run. If the current path was previously unseen, then it is added to the set C. If K consecutive paths belong to C, the algorithm terminates.

The strategy outlined above obtains a set of program paths C that is *likely*, but not guaranteed to satisfy the coverage criterion c desired by the user. As such, this strategy is unsuitable for static analysis. We employ it simply as a convenient heuristic to choose an initial set of paths. Our algorithm then proceeds to use probability bounding to find guaranteed bounds on the actual coverage. These bounds are then used to actually estimate coverage.

Selecting the Run Length: We now outline our heuristic strategy for selecting a suitable run length K. Suppose C be a current set of paths that is claimed to satisfy a coverage bound c. We wish to test this claim quickly. This can be viewed as a statistical hypothesis testing problem of choosing between two hypotheses:

$$\mathcal{H}_0 : \mathbb{P}(C) \geq c \text{ vs. } \mathcal{H}_1 : \mathbb{P}(C) < c .$$

In statistical testing terms, $\mathcal{H}_0$ is called the null hypothesis and $\mathcal{H}_1$, the alternative. Our goal is to witness $K > 0$ successive samples that belong to C, where K is set sufficiently large to convince us of $\mathcal{H}_0$ as opposed to $\mathcal{H}_1$. This can be attempted using the sequential probability ratio test (with a slight modification of $\mathcal{H}_0$ and $\mathcal{H}_1$ to introduce an indifference region, see Younes and Simmons [37] and references therein), or using a Bayesian factor test following Jeffreys (see Jha et al. [17], and references therein). Either approach gives rise to a formula that fixes K as a function of c. For illustration, Jeffreys test with uniform prior yields a simple formula

$$K \geq \left\lceil \frac{-\log B}{\log c} \right\rceil .$$

The factor B in the numerator is called the Bayes factor and can be set to 100 to yield a answer with high confidence. For instance, setting $c = 0.95$, we require $K \geq 90$ to satisfy the Bayes factor test at a confidence level given by $B = 100$.

However, this does not imply that we can be *absolutely certain* (rather than just *highly confident*!) that the set of paths satisfy the coverage guarantee. Therefore, we derive guaranteed lower bounds on the coverage of the set of paths C collected. This lower bound forms the basis of our bound estimations.

In our approach, the purpose of hypothesis testing is two-fold: (a) It guarantees that all chosen paths in the set C are feasible. As a result, our approach does not waste time exploring infeasible paths. (b) Sampling the program guarantees that paths with high probability are explored first before lower probability (tail) paths. This can potentially result in fewer paths explored by our analysis.

Path Slicing: The use of dynamic path slicing techniques can further enhance the efficiency of the procedure in Algorithm 2. The paths in the set C are sliced with respect to the variables involved in the query assertion φ being evaluated. The use of path slicing ensures that fewer path fragments in C are generated and each path fragment yields a simpler system of constraints over a smaller set of random variables. Our approach uses the path slicing approach originally proposed by Jhala et al. for predicate abstraction [18].

4.2 Computing Path Probabilities

We now describe techniques for computing the probability of an assertion φ at the exit of a given path π. As described previously, we perform a symbolic execution along π to obtain a symbolic state at the and of the program $\langle \ell_F, R, \psi, T\rangle$. We then consider the assertion $\psi \wedge \varphi[X \mapsto T(X)]$, involving random variables in R.

As a result, the computation of path probabilities reduces to the problem of estimating the probability that a sample point from R drawn according to the distribution of the individual variables also satisfies φ. We present algorithms for (a) computing lower and upper bounds; and (b) estimating the probability.

First, we observe that given the structure of the program, the path condition is a conjunction of linear inequalities and is therefore a convex polyhedron over R. How do we then compute the probability of drawing a sample point inside a given polyhedron? First, we note that computing the exact probability is closely related to the problem of computing the volume of a n-dimensional convex polyhedron. This is known to be $\sharp P$-hard and therefore computationally hard to solve precisely once the number of dimensions is large [2]. We proceed by using bounding boxes that bounds the region of interest from inside as well as outside.

Let $R = Q \cup Z$, where $Q = \{r_1, \ldots, r_k\}$ are the real-valued random variables and $Z = \{z_1, \ldots, z_l\}$ are the integer valued random variables. Let $\psi : \psi^Q \wedge \psi^Z$ be a conjunction of linear inequalities wherein ψ^Q involves the real-valued variables and ψ^Z involves the integer valued variables. Each random variable r_j (or z_k) is distributed according to a known probability distribution function $p_j(r_j)$ (or $p_k(z_k)$) over some set of support.

Our goal is to compute the probability that a randomly drawn sample $\hat{r} : (\hat{r_1}, \ldots, \hat{r_k}, \hat{z_1}, \ldots, \hat{z_l})$ satisfies the assertion ψ. We split this problem into two parts one for the integer part and one for the real part.

Random Variable Primitives: We ignore the details of the distributions, assuming instead that some primitive functions can be computed: (a) given a range $[a, b]$, we can compute its probability $\mathbb{P}_{r_i}([a, b]) = \int_a^b p_i(r_i)dr_i$; and (b) we can obtain samples $\widehat{r_{i,j}}$ for $j = 1, \ldots, N$ that are distributed according to p_i. The same assumptions are held for the integer-valued random variables as well. Table 3 summarizes the primitives.

sample ()	generate a (pseudo) random sample standard Monte-Carlo methods [34].
probability (a,b)	estimate probability mass of interval $[a, b]$ using cumulative distribution function (CDF).

Table 3. Primitives needed for each distribution type to support probability and expectation estimation.

Input: Polyhedron $\varphi[r_1, \ldots, r_n]$, each $r_i \sim \mathcal{D}_i$.
Output: Interval bounds $[\underline{p}, \overline{p}]$ and stratified MC sample estimate $\hat{p}$

```
queue := {φ} ;
(p̲, p̄, p̂) := (0, 0, 0);
while |queue| > 0 do
    ξ := deque(queue) ;
    if stopping criterion then
        H := boxOverApproximation(ξ);
        B := boxUnderApproximation(ξ);
        ( p̄ )    ( p̄ + boxProbability(H) )
        ( p̲ ) := ( p̲ + boxProbability(B) ) ;
        p̂ := p̂ + p̄ * stratifiedSample(ξ, H);
    else
        (d, l) = selectDimension(R) ;
        /* Perform Branch and Bound                */
        (ξ1, ξ2) := (ξ ∧ r_d ≥ l), (ξ ∧ r_d < l);
        queue := enqueue(queue, {ξ1, ξ2}) ;
    end
end
```

Algorithm 3: Basic algorithm to compute bounds on the probability of a polyhedron represented by a linear assertion φ.

Computing Probability of Hypercubes: A hypercube over $\mathbb{R}^k$ can be written as the Cartesian product of intervals:

$$\mathcal{H} : [a_1, b_1] \times [a_2, b_2] \times \cdots \times [a_k, b_k] .$$

To compute the probability of $\mathcal{H}$, we use the available primitives directly. $\mathbb{P}_Q(\mathcal{H}) = \mathbb{P}_{r_1}([a_1, b_1])\mathbb{P}_{r_2}([a_2, b_2]) \cdots \mathbb{P}_{r_k}([a_k, b_k])$. The same calculation holds over the integers as well with minor modifications to ensure that a_j, b_j values are rounded to the nearest integer above/below, respectively. For a disjoint union of $N \geq 0$ hypercubes, we have $\mathbb{P}_Q(\mathcal{H}_1 \uplus \cdots \uplus \mathcal{H}_N) = \sum_{k=1}^N \mathbb{P}_Q(\mathcal{H}_k)$.

4.3 Computing Bounds on Polyhedral Probabilities

We now address the issue of computing bounds on the probability of a given polyhedral set specified by assertion φ over a set of real-valued variables $Q = \{r_1, \ldots, r_k\}$ (or integer valued variables $Z = \{z_1, \ldots, z_k\}$), where each r_i is drawn from a known distribution.

The basis of our approach is to over approximate $[\![\varphi]\!]$ by a union of hypercubes $\overline{H_1} \cup \overline{H_2} \cup \cdots \cup \overline{H_p}$ and under approximate by a union $\underline{H_1} \cup \cdots \cup \underline{H_s}$. The number of hypercubes p, s can be varied to control the quality of the approximation. The overall idea is to bound the probability of φ by computing the probability of the over approximation and the under approximation.

Lemma 4.2. *Let $\underline{H} \subseteq [\![\varphi]\!] \subseteq \overline{H}$. It follows that $\mathbb{P}_Q(\underline{H}) \leq \mathbb{P}_Q(\varphi) \leq \mathbb{P}_Q(\overline{H})$.*

We now consider how to obtain over approximations and under approximations of polyhedral sets.

Figure 5. A worst-case scenario for over- and under approximation by a single hypercube (left) and a less pessimistic over- and under approximation using many hypercubes.

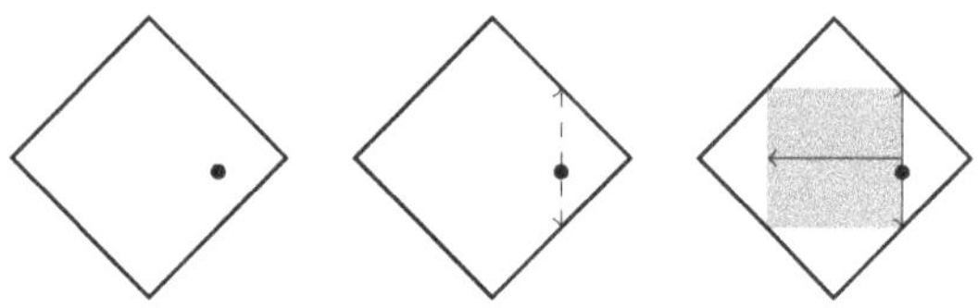

Figure 6. Underapproximation by interior ray shooting.

Over approximation: Linear programming (LP) solvers can be used to directly over approximate a given polyhedron by a single hypercube. To obtain upper (lower) bounds for r_j we solve the LP: $\max(\min)\ r_j$ s.t. φ. The resulting hypercube given by the product of intervals obtained for each r_j over approximates the region defined by φ. However, the hypercube may be a gross over approximation of the original set, yielding quite pessimistic upper bounds. Fig. 5 shows a polyhedron whose over approximation by a single hypercube is quite pessimistic. However, if multiple hypercubes were used, then the accuracy improves. As explained in Algorithm 3, this is achieved by repeated splitting along a chosen dimension and finding bounding boxes using LP solvers.

Under approximation: The goal is to find an under approximation of a polyhedron φ by a hypercube. As depicted in Fig. 5, there is no best under approximation for a given polyhedron. This is unlike the case for an over approximation, where LP solvers can yield a single best bounding box.

Our approach is to find a sample point $\hat{r}$ in the interior of the polyhedron, treating it as a hypercube of volume zero where the upper and lower bounds along each dimension are specified by $[\hat{r}_j, \hat{r}_j]$. Next, we use a simple "*ray-shooting*" approach (Cf. Fig. 6) to expand the current box along each dimension while satisfying the constraints. This is carried out by iterating over the dimensions in a fixed order. Upon termination, this process is guaranteed to yield an under approximation. The size of the hypercube depends on the sample point chosen. In practice, we choose multiple sample points and choose the hypercube with the largest probability mass.

Z-polyhedra: As such, the approach presented so far extends to Z-polyhedra with minor modifications. One modification is to ensure that the bounds of each interval are rounded up/down to account for the integer variables. Additionally, the use of an ILP solver to derive the over approximation can yield tighter bounds. On the other hand, since ILP is a harder problem than LP, using LP solvers to over approximate the polyhedron yields safe upper bounds. The computation of an inner approximation can also be performed using ray shooting.

Monte-Carlo Estimation We have discussed techniques for bounding the probability using boxes. We can extend this to find unbiased estimators of the probability by sampling. This is performed by drawing numerous samples $\widehat{s_1}, \ldots, \widehat{s_N}$ according to the underlying distributions for each variable in R for a large number N and count the number N_φ that satisfies φ. We simply compute the ratio $\hat{p} = \frac{N_\varphi}{N}$.

In some cases, it may take a prohibitively large number N of samples to approximate $\hat{p}$ to some given confidence. To circumvent this, it is possible to fold the computation of $\hat{p}$ with the branch-and-bound decomposition in Algorithm 3. Here, we over approximate the polyhedron φ as the union of K disjoint hypercubes $[\![\varphi]\!] \subseteq \mathcal{H}_1 \uplus \cdots \uplus \mathcal{H}_K$. Next, we draw N_j samples from inside each $\mathcal{H}_j$ and estimate the number of samples $N_{\varphi,j}$ inside $\mathcal{H}_j$ that satisfy φ. This yields an estimate $\widehat{p_j}$ for $\mathcal{H}_j$. The overall probability is given by $\widehat{p} = \sum_{j=1}^{K} \widehat{p_j}\mathbb{P}(\mathcal{H}_j)$. Note that $\mathbb{P}(\mathcal{H}_j)$ is computed exactly and efficiently. This scheme integrates the ideas of *stratified sampling* and *importance sampling*, both of which are well-known variance reduction techniques for Monte-Carlo sampling [34].

ID	#var	Description
EGFR-EPI	11	log egfr calc. using the ckd-epi formula.
ARTRIAL	15	Framingham artrial fibrillation risk calculation.
CORONARY	16	Framingham coronary risk calculation.
INVPEND	7+	Inverted pendulum controller with noise.
PACK	10+	Packing objects with varying weights.
VOL	8+	Filling a tank with fluid at uncertain rates.
ALIGN-1,2	6+	Pointing to a target with error feedback.
CART	7+	Steering a cart against disturbances.

Table 4. Benchmarks used in our evaluation with descriptions. The benchmarks are available on-line at our project page, or upon request. #var: number of input variables to the program. + indicates random value generation inside loops.

5. Implementation and Experiments

We now describe the implementation and evaluation of the ideas presented thus far.

Implementation: Our prototype implementation accepts programs whose syntax is along the lines of Figure 3 in Section 3. Our front-end simulates the program and collects the unique paths observed until no new paths are seen for K consecutive iterations (Algorithm 2). The value of K was chosen for $c = 0.95$ using a Bayes factor test with $B = 100$. This yields $K = 90$ for achieving a coverage of at least 0.95 with a 99% confidence (under a uniform prior). Symbolic execution is performed along the collected paths, yielding the path conditions and transforming the probabilistic queries into assertions involving the random variables produced along the path. Finally, we implement the technique for bounds estimation described in Algorithms 1 and 3. Rather than use an expensive linear programming instance at each step of our branch and bound algorithm, we use a cheaper interval constraint propagation (ICP) to find bounding boxes efficiently [15]. Other optimizations used in our implementation include the use of on-the-fly Cartesian product decomposition of polyhedra and repeated simplification with redundancy elimination.

Benchmark Programs: We evaluate our program over a set of benchmarks described in Table 4. A detailed description of the benchmarks used along with our latest implementation are available on-line from our project page [4].

The first class of benchmarks consists of medical decision making formulae including the eGFR calculation described in Section 2 (EGFR-EPI). We also include a common heart risk calculator and a hypertension risk calculator that uses the results of the Framingham heart study (ARTRIAL, CORONARY) [5]. The results of this calculation are often taken into account if a patient is a candidate for drugs such as Statins to prevent long term heart attack risk.

[4] Cf. `http://systems.cs.colorado.edu/research/cyberphysical/probabilistic-program-analysis/`

[5] Cf. `http://www.framinghamheartstudy.org/`

ID	N_s	N_u	T_s, T_{vc}	p_{mc}	$[lb, ub]$
EGFR EPI	563	45	0.1, 1.1	0.97803	[0.97803,0.97803]
ARTIRAL	19547	2520	15.6, 1095	0.94094	[0.82809,1.0]
CORONARY	7181	1239	3.9, 998.5	0.91992	[0.87239,1.0]
INVPEND	90	1	18.5, 0.1	1	[1,1]
PACK	8043	1010	4.6, 24.1	0.95052	[0.95051,0.95052]
ALIGN-1	4464	529	3.9, 25.7	0.90834	[0.90769,0.90846]
ALIGN-2	17892	1606	8.9 , 75.1	0.93110	[0.9304,0.9384]
VOL	121	9	3.6 , 1766	0.835	**[0,1]**
CART	5799	774	4.2 , 1612	0.94898	**[0.0176,1]**

Table 5. Experimental evaluation of initial adequate path exploration strategy. Our coverage goal was $c = 0.95$ at a 95% confidence level. N_s, N_u: number of simulated paths and unique paths, respectively, T_s: simulation time in seconds, T_{vc}: total volume computation time (branch-and-bound depth is set to 15), p_{mc}: monte-carlo probability estimate, $[lb, ub]$: coverage bounds.

The second class of benchmarks consist of programs that carry out control tasks over physical artifacts. This includes models of linear feedback control systems with noise such as the inverted pendulum controller (INVPEND), a model of a robot that packs objects of uncertain weights in a carton with the goal that the overall weight of carton has to be within some tolerance (PACK), a model of an actuator that fills a tank with fluid where the rate at which the fluid flows can vary with the goal that the fluid waste has to be minimized (VOL) and models of a manipulator that attempts to point a laser at a desired stationary target, wherein alignments can fail due to actuator uncertainties. Each failed attempt results in a feedback that reveals the amount and direction of error that can be used to design the displacement for the next attempt. We propose two versions that differ in terms of the error distributions and the feedback correction mechanisms (ALIGN-1, ALIGN-2).

Experimental Evaluation: Table 5 shows the performance of the path selection and coverage estimation strategies. We note that for most of our benchmarks, the selection of adequate paths required less than 10^4 simulations and resulted in a smaller set of unique paths that are potentially adequate. The time for symbolic execution is a small fraction of the total time taken (T_s). The probability bounds computation (T_{vc}) time dominates the overall analysis time.

The probability bounds computation performs well on many of the examples, solving large problems with as many as 50 integer and real variables. In many cases, the probability bounds obtained are quite tight, indicating that the volume computation converged to fairly precise bounds rapidly. There are two notable exceptions that include the VOL and CART examples. The path conditions in these examples produce highly skewed polyhedra that are the worst-cases for a branch and bound approach. As a result, the bounds produced are quite pessimistic. We are investigating the use of zonotope and ellipsoidal based approximations that can handle such instances effectively. Next, we observe that while 0.95 is the target coverage, the coverage goal is not confirmed by the probability bounds in two instances (ALIGN-1,2). However, the actual reported coverages in these examples are fairly close to the target. Note that a failure to achieve coverage goal is not a failure of the technique. Our ability to deduce rigorous bounds on the path probability helps ensure that the overall result can be made sound regardless of what coverage we aim for. Furthermore, we may remedy the situation by iteratively searching for more paths until the goals are satisfied.

Table 6 shows the results on many probabilistic queries over the benchmarks. Once again, we report on the time taken for the volume computation and the bounds on the queries. We note that whenever path coverage returns a tight bound on the path probabilities, the estimation of assertion probabilities also yields similar tight bounds. The bounds provide non-trivial information about the behavior of these programs and are quite hard to estimate by hand even if the programs in question are small.

Query	T_{vc}	p_{mc}	$[lb, ub]$
ARTRIAL (2520 paths, $c \geq 0.82809$)			
score $>= 10$	252	0.13455	[0.12379,0.31685]
err $>= 5$	48	0.0003637	[0.000257,0.17754]
err $<= 5$	1076	0.94057	[0.82783,1]
CORONARY (1239 paths, $c \geq 0.87239$)			
err $>= 5.0$	22	0.000154	[0,0.12778]
err $>= 7.0$	17	0	[0,0.12778]
err $>= 10.0$	17	0	[0,0.12778]
err $<= -5.0$	16	0.0001	[0,0.12778]
err $<= -7.0$	17	0	[0,0.12778]
err $<= -10.0$	17	0	[0,0.12778]
ALIGN-1 (529 paths, $c \geq .90834$)			
attempts $>= 10$	17.0	0.00726	[.00722,0.09889]
attempts $>= 6$	24.7	0.11796	[0.11773,0.20997]
attempts $>= 2$	25.6	0.630489	[0.62991,0.72234]
err $>= 12$	11.1	0.001580	[0.001570,.093245]
err $<= -12$	10.5	0.001841	[0.001834,0.0935130]
err $>= 5$	21.7	0.084092	[0.084035,.175794]
err $<= -5$	21.8	0.084455	[0.084396,.176163]
PACK (1010 paths, $c \geq 0.95051$)			
count ≥ 5	24.3	0.95051	[0.95051 , 1.0]
count ≥ 6	24.3	0.40364	[0.40364 , 0.45312]
count ≥ 7	22.7	0.14192	[0.14192 , 0.19140]
count ≥ 10	21.0	0.000467	[0.000467 , 0.04995]
totalWeight ≥ 6	43.7	0.27269	[0.25223 , 0.3420]
totalWeight ≥ 5	34.9	0.67754	[0.61734 , 0.78481]
totalWeight ≥ 4	24.0	0.95051	[0.95051 , 1.0]
INVPEND (1 path, $c = 1$)			
pAng $<= 1$	4.1	0.05138	[0,0.13653]
pAng $>= -1$	0.1	1	[1,1]
pAng $<= 0.1$	0.1	0	[0,0]
pAng $>= -0.1$	0.1	1	[1,1]

Table 6. Query processing results on the benchmark examples. Table 5 explains the abbreviations used. Bounds in the table include the over-estimation from uncovered paths inferred from the lower bound on c reported in Table 5.

6. Discussion and Related Work

Reasoning about infinite-state probabilistic programs is considered to be a hard problem. The execution of small and seemingly simple programs that use standard uniform random number generators can yield complex probability distributions over the program variables. Arithmetic operations often give rise to highly correlated program variables whose joint distributions cannot be factored as a product of marginals. Conditional branches and loops can lead to discontinuous distributions that cannot be described by simple probability density functions, in general.

Therefore, analysis algorithms for probabilistic programs must provide solutions to three basic questions: (a) *Representing* the possible intermediate distributions of variables, (b) *Propagating* the chosen representation according to the program semantics, and (c) *Reasoning* about the probabilities of assertions using the given intermediate distribution representation. Any viable solution for infinite state probabilistic programs must restrict the set of programs analyzed through some syntactic or semantic criteria, or deal with *information loss* due to the abstraction of intermediate probability distributions. We now compare our work against other approaches for probabilistic program analysis using these criteria.

Probabilistic Abstract Interpretation Monniaux's work constructs probabilistic analyses by annotating abstract domains such as intervals, octagons and polyhedra with *upper bounds* on the probability measure associated with the abstract objects [28]. However, the abstraction used by Monniaux associates a measure bound for the entire object, *without tracking how the overall measure is distributed amongst the individual states present in the concretization*. This restriction makes the resulting analysis quite conservative. The bounds associated with abstract objects become coarser during the course of analysis due to repeated meet and join operations. The domain of Mardziel et al [25] addresses this limitation for the case of integer-valued program variables. Their approach tracks upper and lower bounds for the object as a whole, as well as bounds on the measure associated with each lattice point. This allows the measure associated with an abstract object to be updated due to meet, join and projection operations.

Our "*domain*" can be seen as a disjunction of symbolic states (see Def. 3.1), and furthermore our analysis does not require meet or join operations over distributions. Similarly, no *upfront* explicit probabilistic bounds are attached to symbolic states during our analysis, unlike the work of Monniaux or Mardziel et al [25, 28]. On the other hand, the probabilistic bounds on symbolic states are computed "after the fact" (using probability bounds computation) when the entire path has been analyzed. The sources of loss in our approach include the probability bounds computation and the unexplored program paths.

The approaches mentioned thus far, including ours, do not handle non-linear operations. Furthermore, the high complexity of domain operations on convex polyhedra and approximate volume bound computations can limit the size of programs that can be analyzed. The work of Bouissou et al tackles these problems through the domain of *probabilistic affine forms* [3] by combining techniques from the AI community such as p-Boxes and Dempster-Shafer structures [9, 35] with affine forms [7]. Their approach represents variables as affine expressions involving two types of random variables (noise symbols): noise symbols that are correlated with the other symbols in an arbitrary, unspecified manner, and independent noise symbols. The concept of arbitrarily correlated noise symbols is a key contribution that supports transfer functions for nonlinear operations. However, at the time of writing, Bouissou et al do not provide meet, join and widening operations. Therefore, their technique is currently restricted to straight line probabilistic programs without conditional tests. Our approach uses symbolic states (see Def. 3.1) that are a special case of "constrained" probabilistic affine forms with linear inequality constraints over the random variables. However, our approach does not currently handle random variables with arbitrary, unspecified correlations. Extending our approach to treat correlated noise symbols will form an important part of our future work in this space.

Whereas the techniques described so far perform a forward propagation of the distribution information, it is possible to use backward abstract interpretation starting from an assertion whose probability is to be established, and exploring its preconditions backwards along the program paths. McIver and Morgan proposed a backward abstract interpretation for probabilistic programs with discrete Bernoulli random variables and demonic non-determinism. Their approach uses "expectations" that are real-valued functions of the program state [26] rather than assertions over the program variable. Expectations can be seen as abstractions of distributions. A notable aspect of their work lies in the use of *quantitative loop invariants* that are invariant expectations of loops in the program. The automatic inference of such invariants was addressed by the recent work of Katoen et al [20]. It is notable that very few approaches, including ours, have sought to provide a complete treatment of loops. It is common to assume that the loops terminate in all cases after a fixed number of iterations. The combination of quantitative loop invariants and the idea of using pre-/post-condition annotations are notable in the work of McIver and Morgan (ibid). A combined approach will form an interesting topic for future work.

DiPierro et al proposed an entirely different approach to probabilistic abstract interpretation that views concrete and abstract domains as Hilbert spaces, with the abstraction operator as a non-invertible linear operator [32]. Rather than defining the inverse in terms of a set of concrete states, as is traditionally done in abstract interpretation, the authors propose to use a Moore-Penrose pseudo-inverse, which corresponds to a least squares approximation in finite dimensional vector spaces. This approach exposes an interesting alternative to the traditional abstract interpretation approach to program analysis. However, a key problem lies in relating the results of the analysis proposed by DiPierro et al that provide a "close approximation" to the probability of a query assertion with the "classical" approach that provides a guaranteed interval bound enclosing the actual probability, such as the approach presented in this paper.

The recent work of Cousot and Monerau provides a general framework that encompasses a variety of probabilistic abstract interpretation schemes [6]. Various techniques mentioned thus far, including ours, can be seen as instances of this general framework [3, 6, 25, 28].

The program analysis techniques mentioned thus far focus on providing bounds on the probabilities of assertions for the program as a whole. In many cases, the same questions may be asked of a single path or a finite set of paths in the program. Recently, Geldenhuys et al proposed the integration of symbolic execution with exact model counting techniques to estimate the probabilities of violating assertions along individual paths of the program [13]. The tool LattE was used to count lattice points, and thus estimate polyhedral volumes for the constraints obtained along each path [8]. Like Geldenhuys et al, the approach here also performs a symbolic execution along a chosen set of program. However, our work goes further to infer *whole program bounds*. Our work computes probability bounds using a branch-and-bound technique, whereas Geldenhuys et al use the solver LattE off the shelf for computing precise probabilities. Finally, the approach of Geldenhuys et al is restricted to discrete, uniform random variables that take on a finite set of values.

An extension by Filieri et al., that is contemporaneous to our work, performs probabilistic symbolic execution with a user-specified cutoff on the path length [11]. Their approach uses the concept of "confidence" to estimate the probability of the paths that are cutoff prematurely. This is remarkably similar to the concept "coverage bounds" used in our work. On one hand, the work of Filieri et al. goes beyond ours to consider the effect of non-deterministic schedulers on multi-threaded programs. On the other, their work continues to use LattE as a lattice counting tool to estimate probabilities. Therefore, it is restricted to uniform distributions or discretized distributions over finite data domains. Integrating the contributions of Filieri et al. with our volume bounding approach can help us move towards a technique that can support integers along with reals and a wide variety of distributions without requiring discretization.

Visser et al presented a set of optimizations that can be used to reduce and simplify the constraints occurring in a program in a canonical form, so that the answer from one volume computation can be cached and reused [36]. Currently, we observe that different program paths explored in our framework necessarily yield different constraints. However, the idea of caching and reusing can be useful for intermediate polyhedra that are obtained during the branch and bound volume computation process. We plan to explore this idea as part of our future work.

A large volume of work has focused purely on verifying properties of finite state discrete and continuous time Markov chains and Markov decision processes [23]. The tool PRISM integrates many of these techniques, and has been used successfully in many scientific and engineering applications as showcased on-line [24]. A key aspect of PRISM is the integration of symbolic techniques for representing discrete distributions over a large but finite set of states using extensions to decision diagrams called MTBDDs [25]. Recently, infinite state systems such as probabilistic timed and hybrid automata have been considered (Cf. [16, 22], for instance) in the context of the model-checking approach embodied by PRISM. However, these extensions remain inside the decidable sub-classes. Our approach, on the other hand, considers Turing complete, infinite state programs, incorporating a rich set of probability distributions. Therefore, we do not compute probabilities precisely, settling for intervals that can be useful in many cases. Whereas work on PRISM uses a very rich temporal specification language, our work is currently restricted to (conditional) probabilities of assertions.

Sources of Probabilistic Programs: Probabilistic programs arise in many forms of computation involving erroneous or noisy inputs. These include risk analysis, medical decision making, data analysis [1], randomized algorithms [30], differential privacy mechanisms [10], simulations of fundamental physical processes (Monte-Carlo simulations) [12]. Certain loop optimizations such as *loop perforation* depend on the use of randomization to trade off performance against the precision of the computed results [27]. Program smoothing is an approach to program synthesis proposed by Chaudhuri et al [4]. It creates a probabilistic program that is a "smoothed version" of the original program obtained by adding noise to the inputs of the program.

Many programming language formalisms have been considered for expressing probabilistic programs including IBAL, a declarative language for specifying probabilistic models [31] probabilistic scheme [33] and Church, an extension of probabilistic scheme [14]. These languages support a variety of functions such as simulations, computing expectations, parameter estimations and computing marginal distributions based on Monte-Carlo simulations.

Probabilistic Program Semantics: The semantics of imperative probabilistic programs was first studied in detail by Kozen. [21]. Significantly, Kozen provides two types of semantics that are mathematically equivalent but represent different views of the probabilistic program. The first semantics is operational, wherein the program's execution is seen as essentially deterministic but governed by a countable set of random numbers generated up front. The second semantics considered by Kozen uses measure theoretic concepts to describe the program as a transformer of probability measure starting from the initial measure which is transformed by the execution of the program. This semantics has been the basis for further work, notably by Monniaux [29] and recently by Cousot and Monerau [6] on defining the semantics of programs that combine probabilistic and non-deterministic behaviors. Our work here uses a simple operational definition for the meaning of probabilistic programs. As a result, we lose the generality that can be achieved by a fundamental measure theoretic treatment espoused by the separate works of Kozen, Monniaux and Cousot. On the other hand, the simplicity of our semantics ensures that we can make inferences on individual program paths and combine them to reason about the program as a whole. Doing so also avoids a loss in precision for many of our benchmarks.

Abstract Monte-Carlo The *abstract Monte-Carlo* (AMC) approach of Monniaux reasons about programs that combine probabilistic and non-deterministic choices [28]. Therein, calls to random variables are dealt with using numerical sampling while the non-deterministic choices are explored using abstract interpretation. The AMC approach cannot, in general, be used to guarantee rigorous bounds on path probabilities, unlike our approach which can derive such bounds. However, our approach does not incorporate non-determinism.

Statistical Model Checking Statistical Model Checking (SMC) is yet another recent approach to verify probabilistic properties of systems with high confidence by using techniques from the field of statistical hypothesis testing [5, 37]. Using finitely many samples from the program, their approach can provide high confidence answers to questions about the probabilities of assertions. Whereas the SMC approach seeks to estimate whether a given lower or upper bound holds on the actual probability with high confidence, we attempt to estimate guaranteed bounds.

Volume Computation Our technique integrates the path constraints with the problem of finding the probability of satisfaction of constraints. This is known to be a $\sharp P$-complete problem and hence computationally hard (almost as hard as PSPACE-complete problems) [2]. The tool LattE Machiato integrates many state of the art techniques for counting lattice points in integer polyhedra and volume computation for convex polyhedra over the reals [8]. As mentioned earlier, the probabilistic symbolic execution approach of Geldenhuys et al [13] and the probabilistic abstract interpretation proposed by Mardziel et al [25] use the tool LattE to count the number of lattice points exactly. While LattE computes exact counts/volumes, our approach focuses on finding interval bounds for the probabilities. We observed two limitations of LattE that make it less ideal for probabilistic program analysis tasks: (a) the existing implementation does not handle non-uniform distributions (over the reals or integers), and (b) exact volume determination for real polyhedra is quite expensive, and often runs out of time/memory on the constraints that are obtained from our benchmarks. *We attempted to complete at least one of the benchmark examples in our approach using LattE, but were unsuccessful due to timeouts or more often out-of-memory errors.* Our approach, which focuses on finding interval bounds rather than exact computation, can handle programs over reals as well as integers, and a wide variety of distributions in addition to the uniform distribution.

7. Conclusion and Future Work

We have developed an analysis framework for probabilistic programs based on considering finitely many paths and estimating the probability of the remainder. Our initial experimental results are promising. However, we have also identified some challenges for motivating further work. Our future work will focus on more efficient polyhedral probability estimators using ellipsoidal and zonotope approximations, and the problem of synthesizing sketches, complementing recent approaches to this problem [4].

Acknowledgments

We thank Prof. Michael Hicks and the anonymous reviewers for their detailed comments. Sankaranarayanan and Chakarov acknowledge support from the US National Science Foundation (NSF) under award numbers CNS-0953941, CNS-1016994 and CPS-1035845. All opinions expressed are those of the authors and not necessarily of the NSF.

References

[1] C. C. Aggarwal and P. S. Yu. A survey of uncertain data algorithms and applications. *IEEE Transactions on Knowledge and Data Engineering (TKDE)*, 21(5), May 2009.

[2] S. Arora and B. Barak. *Computational Complexity: A Modern Approach.* Cambridge University Press, 2009.

[3] O. Bouissou, E. Goubault, J. Goubault-Larrecq, and S. Putot. A generalization of p-boxes to affine arithmetic. *Computing*, 2012.

[4] S. Chaudhuri and A. Solar-Lezama. Smoothing a program soundly and robustly. In *CAV*, volume 6806 of *LNCS*, pages 277–292. Springer, 2011.

[5] E. Clarke, A. Donze, and A. Legay. Statistical model checking of analog mixed-signal circuits with an application to a third order $\delta - \sigma$ modulator. In *Hardware and Software: Verification and Testing*, volume 5394/2009 of *LNCS*, pages 149–163, 2009.

[6] P. Cousot and M. Monerau. Probabilistic abstract interpretation. In *ESOP*, volume 7211 of *LNCS*, pages 169–193. Springer, 2012.

[7] L. H. de Figueiredo and J. Stolfi. Self-validated numerical methods and applications. In *Brazilian Mathematics Colloquium monograph*. IMPA, Rio de Janeiro, Brazil, 1997. Cf. `http://www.ic.unicamp.br/~stolfi/EXPORT/papers/by-tag/fig-sto-97-iaaa.ps.gz`.

[8] J. De Loera, B. Dutra, M. Koeppe, S. Moreinis, G. Pinto, and J. Wu. Software for Exact Integration of Polynomials over Polyhedra. *ArXiv e-prints*, July 2011.

[9] A. Dempster. A generalization of bayesian inference. *Journal of the Royal Statistical Society*, 30:205–247, 1968.

[10] C. Dwork. Differential privacy: A survey of results. In *TAMC*, volume 4978 of *LNCS*, pages 1–19. Springer, 2008.

[11] A. Filieri, C. S. Păsăreanu, and W. Visser. Reliability analysis in symbolic pathfinder. In *Intl. Conference on Software Engg. (ICSE)*, 2013. (To Appear, May 2013).

[12] D. Frenkel and B. Smit. *Understanding Molecular Simulation: From Algorithms to Applications*. Academic Press, 2002.

[13] J. Geldenhuys, M. B. Dwyer, and W. Visser. Probabilistic symbolic execution. In *ISSTA*, pages 166–176. ACM, 2012.

[14] N. D. Goodman, V. K. Mansinghka, D. M. Roy, K. Bonawitz, and J. B. Tenenbaum. Church: a language for generative models. In *Uncertainty in Artificial Intelligence*, pages 220–229, 2008.

[15] L. Granvilliers and F. Benhamou. Algorithm 852: Realpaver: an interval solver using constraint satisfaction techniques. *ACM Trans. On Mathematical Software*, 32(1):138–156, 2006.

[16] H. Hermanns, B. Wachter, and L. Zhang. Probabilistic CEGAR. In *CAV*, volume 5123 of *LNCS*, pages 162–175. Springer, 2008.

[17] S. K. Jha, E. M. Clarke, C. J. Langmead, A. Legay, A. Platzer, and P. Zuliani. A bayesian approach to model checking biological systems. In *CMSB*, volume 5688 of *Lecture Notes in Computer Science*, pages 218–234. Springer, 2009.

[18] R. Jhala and R. Majumdar. Path slicing. In *PLDI '05*, pages 38–47. ACM, 2005.

[19] C. Jones, G. McQuillan, and *et al.* Serum creatinine levels in the US population: Third national health and nutrition examination survey. *Am. J. Kidney Disease*, 32(6):992–999, 1998.

[20] J.-P. Katoen, A. McIver, L. Meinicke, and C. Morgan. Linear-invariant generation for probabilistic programs. In *Static Analysis Symposium (SAS)*, volume 6337 of *LNCS*, page 390406. Springer, 2010.

[21] D. Kozen. Semantics of probabilistic programs. *J. Computer and System Sciences*, 22:328–350, 1981.

[22] M. Kwiatkowska, G. Norman, and D. Parker. A framework for verification of software with time and probabilities. In *FORMATS*, volume 6246 of *LNCS*, pages 25–45. Springer, 2010.

[23] M. Kwiatkowska, G. Norman, and D. Parker. PRISM 4.0: Verification of probabilistic real-time systems. In *CAV*, volume 6806 of *LNCS*, pages 585–591. Springer, 2011.

[24] Kwiatkowska et al. The PRISM model checker. `http://www.prismmodelchecker.org`.

[25] P. Mardziel, S. Magill, M. Hicks, and M. Srivatsa. Dynamic enforcement of knowledge-based security policies. In *Computer Security Foundations Symposium (CSF)*, pages 114–128, JUN 2011.

[26] A. McIver and C. Morgan. *Abstraction, Refinement and Proof for Probabilistic Systems*. Monographs in Computer Science. Springer, 2004.

[27] S. Misailovic, D. M. Roy, and M. C. Rinard. Probabilistically accurate program transformations. In *Static Analysis Symposium*, volume 6887 of *LNCS*, pages 316–333. Springer, 2011.

[28] D. Monniaux. An abstract monte-carlo method for the analysis of probabilistic programs. In *POPL*, pages 93–101. ACM, 2001.

[29] D. Monniaux. Abstract interpretation of programs as markov decision processes. *Sci. Comput. Program.*, 58(1-2):179–205, 2005.

[30] R. Motwani and P. Raghavan. *Randomized Algorithms*. Cambridge University Press, 1995.

[31] A. Pfeffer. IBAL: a probabilistic rational programming language. In *In Proc. 17th IJCAI*, pages 733–740. Morgan Kaufmann Publishers, 2001.

[32] A. D. Pierro, C. Hankin, and H. Wiklicky. Probabilistic λ-calculus and quantitative program analysis. *J. Logic and Computation*, 15(2): 159–179, 2005.

[33] A. Radul. Report on the probabilistic language scheme. In *DLS*, pages 2–10. ACM, 2007.

[34] R. Y. Rubinstein and D. P. Kroese. *Simulation and the Monte Carlo Method*. Wiley Series in Probability and Mathematical Statistics, 2008.

[35] G. Shafer. *A Mathematical Theory of Evidence*. Princeton University Press, 1976.

[36] W. Visser, J. Geldenhuys, and M. B. Dwyer. Green: reducing, reusing and recycling constraints in program analysis. In *SIGSOFT FSE*, page 58. ACM, 2012.

[37] H. L. S. Younes and R. G. Simmons. Statistical probabilitistic model checking with a focus on time-bounded properties. *Information & Computation*, 204(9):1368–1409, 2006.

Modular Verification of Linearizability with Non-Fixed Linearization Points

Hongjin Liang Xinyu Feng

University of Science and Technology of China

lhj1018@mail.ustc.edu.cn xyfeng@ustc.edu.cn

Abstract

Locating linearization points (LPs) is an intuitive approach for proving linearizability, but it is difficult to apply the idea in Hoare-style logic for formal program verification, especially for verifying algorithms whose LPs cannot be statically located in the code. In this paper, we propose a program logic with a lightweight instrumentation mechanism which can verify algorithms with non-fixed LPs, including the most challenging ones that use the helping mechanism to achieve lock-freedom (as in HSY elimination-based stack), or have LPs depending on unpredictable future executions (as in the lazy set algorithm), or involve both features. We also develop a thread-local simulation as the meta-theory of our logic, and show it implies contextual refinement, which is equivalent to linearizability. Using our logic we have successfully verified various classic algorithms, some of which are used in the `java.util.concurrent` package.

Categories and Subject Descriptors D.2.4 [*Software Engineering*]: Software/Program Verification – Correctness proofs, Formal methods; F.3.1 [*Logics and Meanings of Programs*]: Specifying and Verifying and Reasoning about Programs

General Terms Theory, Verification

Keywords Concurrency; Rely-Guarantee Reasoning; Linearizability; Refinement; Simulation

1. Introduction

Linearizability is a standard correctness criterion for concurrent object implementations [16]. It requires the fine-grained implementation of an object operation to have the same effect with an instantaneous atomic operation. To prove linearizability, the most intuitive approach is to find a linearization point (LP) in the code of the implementation, and show that it is the single point where the effect of the operation takes place.

However, it is difficult to apply this idea when the LPs are not fixed in the code of object methods. For a large class of lock-free algorithms with *helping* mechanism (*e.g.*, HSY elimination-based stack [14]), the LP of one method might be in the code of some other method. In these algorithms, each thread maintains a descriptor recording all the information required to fulfill its intended operation. When a thread A detects conflicts with another thread B, A may access B's descriptor and help B finish its intended operation first before finishing its own. In this case, B's operation takes effect at a step from A. Thus its LP should *not* be in its own code, but in the code of thread A.

Besides, in optimistic algorithms and lazy algorithms (*e.g.*, Heller *et al.*'s lazy set [13]), the LPs might depend on unpredictable future interleavings. In those algorithms, a thread may access the shared states as if no interference would occur, and validate the accesses later. If the validation succeeds, it finishes the operation; otherwise it rolls back and retries. Its LP is usually at a prior state access, but only if the later validation succeeds.

Reasoning about algorithms with non-fixed LPs has been a long-standing problem. Most existing work either supports only simple objects with static LPs in the implementation code (*e.g.*, [2, 5, 19, 30]), or lacks formal soundness arguments (*e.g.*, [32]). In this paper, we propose a program logic for verification of linearizability with non-fixed LPs. For a concrete implementation of an object method, we treat the corresponding abstract atomic operation and the abstract state as auxiliary states, and insert auxiliary commands at the LP to execute the abstract operation simultaneously with the concrete step. We verify the instrumented implementation in an existing concurrent program logic (we will use LRG [8] in this paper), but extend it with new logic rules for the auxiliary commands. We also give a new relational interpretation to the logic assertions, and show that at the LP, the step of the original concrete implementation has the same effect as the abstract operation. We handle non-fixed LPs in the following way:

- To support the helping mechanism, we collect a pending thread pool as auxiliary state, which is a set of threads and their abstract operations that might be helped. We allow the thread that is currently being verified to use auxiliary commands to help execute the abstract operations in the pending thread pool.
- For future-dependent LPs, we introduce a try-commit mechanism to reason with uncertainty. The **try** clause guesses whether the corresponding abstract operation should be executed and keeps all possibilities, while **commit** chooses a specific possible case when we know which guess is correct later.

Although our program logic looks intuitive, it is challenging to prove that the logic is sound *w.r.t.* linearizability. Recent work has shown the equivalence between linearizability and contextual refinement [5, 9, 10]. The latter is often verified by proving simulations between the concrete implementation and the atomic operation [5]. The simulation establishes some correspondence between the executions of the two sides, showing there exists one step in the concrete execution that fulfills the abstract operation. Given the equivalence between linearizability and refinement, we would expect the simulations to justify the soundness of the LP method and to serve as the meta-theory of our logic. However, existing thread-

PLDI'13, June 16–19, 2013, Seattle, WA, USA.

local simulations do not support non-fixed LPs (except the recent work [31], which we will discuss in Sec. 7). We will explain the challenges in detail in Sec. 2.

Our work is inspired by the earlier work on linearizability verification, in particular the use of auxiliary code and states by Vafeiadis [32] and our previous work on thread-local simulation RGSim [19], but makes the following new contributions:

- We propose the first program logic that has a formal soundness proof for linearizability with non-fixed LPs. Our logic is built upon the unary program logic LRG [8], but we give a relational interpretation of assertions and rely/guarantee conditions. We also introduce new logic rules for auxiliary commands used specifically for linearizability proofs.
- We give a light instrumentation mechanism to relate concrete implementations with abstract operations. The systematic use of auxiliary states and commands makes it possible to execute the abstract operations synchronously with the concrete code. The try-commit clauses allow us to reason about future-dependent uncertainty without resorting to prophecy variables [1, 32], whose existing semantics (*e.g.*, [1]) is unsuitable for Hoare-style verification.
- We design a novel thread-local simulation as the meta-theory for our logic. It generalizes RGSim [19] and other compositional reasoning of refinement (*e.g.*, [5, 30]) with the support for non-fixed LPs.
- Instead of ensuring linearizability directly, the program logic and the simulation both establish contextual refinement, which we prove is equivalent to linearizability. A program logic for contextual refinement is interesting in its own right, since contextual refinement is also a widely accepted (and probably more natural) correctness criterion for library code.
- We successfully apply our logic to verify 12 well-known algorithms. Some of them are used in the `java.util.concurrent` package, such as MS non-blocking queue [23] and Harris-Michael lock-free list [11, 22].

In the rest of this paper, we first analyze the challenges in the logic design and explain our approach informally in Sec. 2. Then we give the basic technical setting in Sec. 3, including a formal operational definition of linearizability. We present our program logic in Sec. 4, and the new simulation relation as the meta-theory in Sec. 5. In Sec. 6 we summarize all the algorithms we have verified and sketch the proofs of three representative algorithms. We discuss related work and conclude in Sec. 7.

2. Challenges and Our Approach

Below we start from a simple program logic for linearizability with fixed LPs, and extend it to support algorithms with non-fixed LPs. We also discuss the problems with the underlying meta-theory, which establishes the soundness of the logic *w.r.t.* linearizability.

2.1 Basic Logic for Fixed LPs

We first show a simple and intuitive logic which follows the LP approach. As a working example, Fig. 1(a) shows the implementation of push in Treiber stack [29] (let's first ignore the blue code at line `7'`). The stack object is implemented as a linked list pointed to by `S`, and `push(v)` repeatedly tries to update `S` to point to the new node using compare-and-swap (`cas`) until it succeeds.

To verify linearizability, we first locate the LP in the code. The LP of `push(v)` is at the `cas` statement when it succeeds (line 7). That is, the successful `cas` can correspond to the abstract atomic `PUSH(v)` operation: `Stk := v::Stk`; and all the other concrete steps cannot. Here we simply represent the abstract stack `Stk` as

```
1 push(int v) {
2   local x, t, b;
3   x := new node(v);
4   do {
5     t := S;
6     x.next := t;
7     <b := cas(&S,t,x);
7'     if(b) linself;>
8   } while(!b);
9 }
```

(a) Treiber Stack

```
1 readPair(int i, j) {
2   local a, b, v, w;
3   while(true) {
4     <a := m[i].d; v := m[i].v;>
5     <b := m[j].d; w := m[j].v;
5'     trylinself;>
6     if(v = m[i].v) {
6'       commit(cid ↣ (end, (a, b)));
7       return (a, b); }
8   } }
9 write(int i, d) {
10  <m[i].d := d; m[i].v++;> }
```

(c) Pair Snapshot

```
1  push(int v) {
2    local p, him, q;
3    p := new thrdDescriptor(cid, PUSH, v);
4    while(true) {
5      if (tryPush(v)) return;
6      loc[cid] := p;
7      him := rand(); q := loc[him];
8      if (q != null && q.id = him && q.op = POP)
9        if (cas(&loc[cid], p, null)) {
10         <b := cas(&loc[him], q, p);
10'         if(b) {lin(cid); lin(him);}>
11         if (b) return; }
12     ...
13 } }
```

(b) HSY Elimination-Based Stack

Figure 1. LPs and Instrumented Auxiliary Commands

a sequence of values with "`::`" for concatenation. Then `push(v)` can be linearized at the successful `cas` since it is the single point where the operation takes effect.

We can encode the above reasoning in an existing (unary) concurrent program logic, such as Rely-Guarantee reasoning [17] and CSL [24]. Inspired by Vafeiadis [32], we embed the abstract operation γ and the abstract state θ as auxiliary states on the concrete side, so the program state now becomes $(\sigma, (\gamma, \theta))$, where σ is the original concrete state. Then we instrument the concrete implementation with an auxiliary command **linself** (shorthand for "linearize self") at the LP to update the auxiliary state. Intuitively, **linself** will execute the abstract operation γ over the abstract state θ, as described in the following operational semantics rule:

$$\frac{(\gamma, \theta) \leadsto (\mathbf{end}, \theta')}{(\mathbf{linself}, (\sigma, (\gamma, \theta))) \longrightarrow (\mathbf{skip}, (\sigma, (\mathbf{end}, \theta')))}$$

Here $\leadsto$ encodes the transition of γ at the abstract level, and **end** is a termination marker. We insert **linself** into the same atomic block with the concrete statement at the LP, such as line `7'` in Fig. 1(a), so that the concrete and abstract sides are executed simultaneously. Here the atomic block $\langle C \rangle$ means C is executed atomically. Then we reason about the instrumented code using a traditional concurrent logic extended with a new inference rule for **linself**.

The idea is intuitive, but it cannot handle more advanced algorithms with non-fixed LPs, including the algorithms with the helping mechanism and those whose locations of LPs depend on the future interleavings. Below we analyze the two challenges in detail and explain our solutions using two representative algorithms, the HSY stack and the pair snapshot.

2.2 Support Helping Mechanism with Pending Thread Pool

HSY elimination-based stack [14] is a typical example using the helping mechanism. Figure 1(b) shows part of its push method implementation. The basic idea behind the algorithm is to let a push and a pop cancel out each other.

At the beginning of the method in Fig. 1(b), the thread allocates its *thread descriptor* (line 3), which contains the thread id, the name of the operation to be performed, and the argument. The current thread `cid` first tries to perform Treiber stack's push (line `5`). It returns if succeeds. Otherwise, it writes its descriptor in the global `loc` array (line `6`) to allow other threads to eliminate its push. The elimination array `loc`$[1..n]$ has one slot for each thread, which holds the pointer to a thread descriptor. The thread randomly reads a slot `him` in `loc` (line `7`). If the descriptor `q` says `him` is doing pop, `cid` tries to eliminate itself with `him` by two `cas` instructions. The first clears `cid`'s entry in `loc` so that no other thread could eliminate with `cid` (line `9`). The second attempts to mark the entry of `him` in `loc` as "eliminated with `cid`" (line `10`). If successful, it should be the LPs of *both* the push of `cid` and the pop of `him`, with the push happening immediately before the pop.

The helping mechanism allows the current thread to linearize the operations of other threads, which cannot be expressed in the basic logic. It also breaks modularity and makes thread-local verification difficult. For the thread `cid`, its concrete step could correspond to the steps of both `cid` and `him` at the abstract level. For `him`, a step from its environment could fulfill its abstract operation. We must ensure in the thread-local verification that the two threads `cid` and `him` always take consistent views on whether and how the abstract operation of `him` is done. For example, if we let a concrete step in `cid` fulfill the abstract pop of `him`, we must know `him` is indeed doing pop and its pop has not been done before. Otherwise, we will not be able to compose `cid` and `him` in parallel.

We extend the basic logic to express the helping mechanism. First we introduce a new auxiliary command **lin**(`t`) to linearize a specific thread `t`. For instance, in Fig. 1(b) we insert line `10'` at the LP to execute both the push of `cid` and the pop of `him` at the abstract level. We also extend the auxiliary state to record both abstract operations of `cid` and `him`. More generally, we embed a pending thread pool U, which maps threads to their abstract operations. It specifies a set of threads whose operations might be helped by others. Then under the new state $(\sigma, (U, \theta))$, the semantics of **lin**(`t`) just executes the thread `t`'s abstract operation in U, similarly to the semantics of **linself** discussed before.

The shared pending thread pool U allows us to recover the thread modularity when verifying the helping mechanism. A concrete step of `cid` could fulfill the operation of `him` in U as well as its own abstract operation; and conversely, the thread `him` running in parallel could check U to know if its operation has been finished by others (such as `cid`) or not. We gain consistent abstract information of other threads in the thread-local verification. Note that the need of U itself does not break modularity because the required information of other threads' abstract operations can be inferred from the concrete state. In the HSY stack example, we know `him` is doing pop by looking at its thread descriptor in the elimination array. In this case U can be viewed as an abstract representation of the elimination array.

2.3 Try-Commit Commands for Future-Dependent LPs

Another challenge is to reason about optimistic algorithms whose LPs depend on the future interleavings.

We give a toy example, pair snapshot [27], in Fig. 1(c). The object is an array `m`, each slot of which contains two fields: `d` for the data and `v` for the version number. The `write(i,d)` method (lines `9`) updates the data stored at address `i` and increments the version number instantaneously. The `readPair(i,j)` method intends to perform an atomic read of two slots `i` and `j` in the presence of concurrent writes. It reads the data at slots `i` and `j` separately at lines `4` and `5`, and validate the first read at line `6`. If `i`'s version number has not been increased, the thread knows that when it read `j`'s data at line `5`, `i`'s data had not been updated. This means the two reads were at a consistent state, thus the thread can return. We can see that the LP of `readPair` should be at line `5` when the thread

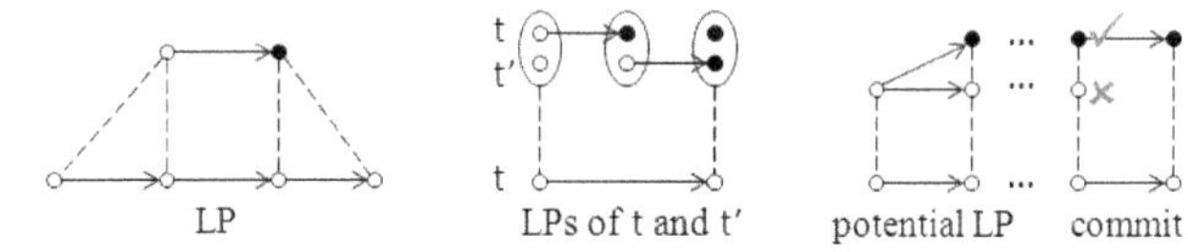

(a) Simple Simulation (b) Pending Thread Pool (c) Speculation

Figure 2. Simulation Diagrams

reads `j`'s data, but only if the validation at line `6` succeeds. That is, whether we should linearize the operation at line `5` depends on the future unpredictable behavior of line `6`.

As discussed a lot in previous work (*e.g.*, [1, 32]), the future-dependent LPs cannot be handled by introducing history variables, which are auxiliary variables storing values or events in the past executions. We have to refer to events coming from the unpredictable future. Thus people propose prophecy variables [1, 32] as the dual of history variables to store future behaviors. But as far as we know, there is no semantics of prophecy variables suitable for Hoare-style local and compositional reasoning.

Instead of resorting to prophecy variables, we follow the speculation idea [31]. For the concrete step at a potential LP (*e.g.*, line `5` of `readPair`), we execute the abstract operation speculatively and keep both the result and the original abstract configuration. Later based on the result of the validation (*e.g.*, line `6` in `readPair`), we keep the appropriate branch and discard the other.

For the logic, we introduce two new auxiliary commands: **trylinself** is to do speculation, and **commit**(p) will commit to the appropriate branch satisfying the assertion p. In Fig. 1(c), we insert lines `5'` and `6'`, where `cid` $\rightarrowtail$ (**end**, (`a`, `b`)) means that the current thread `cid` should have done its abstract operation and would return (`a`, `b`). We also extend the auxiliary state to record the multiple possibilities of abstract operations and abstract states after speculation.

Furthermore, we can combine the speculation idea with the pending thread pool. We allow the abstract operations in the pending thread pool as well as the current thread to speculate. Then we could handle some trickier algorithms such as RDCSS [12], in which the location of LP for thread `t` may be in the code of some other thread and also depend on the future behaviors of that thread. Please see Sec. 6 for one such example.

2.4 Simulation as Meta-Theory

The LP proof method can be understood as building simulations between the concrete implementations and the abstract atomic operations, such as the simple weak simulation in Fig. 2(a). The lower-level and higher-level arrows are the steps of the implementation and of the abstract operation respectively, and the dashed lines denote the simulation relation. We use dark nodes and white nodes at the abstract level to distinguish whether the operation has been finished or not. The only step at the concrete side corresponding to the single abstract step should be the LP of the implementation (labeled "LP" in the diagram). Since our program logic is based on the LP method, we can expect simulations to justify its soundness. In particular, we want a *thread-local* simulation which can handle both the helping mechanism and future-dependent LPs and can ensure linearizability.

To support helping in the simulation, we should allow the LP step at the concrete level to correspond to an abstract step made by a thread other than the one being verified. This requires information from other threads at the abstract side, thus makes it difficult to build a thread-local simulation. To address the problem, we introduce the pending thread pool at the abstract level of the simulation, just as in the development of our logic in Sec. 2.2. The new simula-

$$
\begin{array}{rrcl}
(\mathit{MName}) & f & \in & \mathit{String} \\
(\mathit{Expr}) & E & ::= & x \mid n \mid E+E \mid \ldots \\
(\mathit{BExp}) & B & ::= & \mathbf{true} \mid \mathbf{false} \mid E=E \mid !B \mid \ldots \\
(\mathit{Instr}) & c & ::= & x := E \mid x := [E] \mid [E] := E \mid \mathbf{print}(E) \\
 & & & \mid x := \mathbf{cons}(E,\ldots,E) \mid \mathbf{dispose}(E) \mid \ldots \\
(\mathit{Stmt}) & C & ::= & \mathbf{skip} \mid c \mid x := f(E) \mid \mathbf{return}\ E \mid \mathbf{noret} \\
 & & & \mid \langle C \rangle \mid C;C \mid \mathbf{if}\ (B)\ C\ \mathbf{else}\ C \mid \mathbf{while}\ (B)\{C\} \\
(\mathit{Prog}) & W & ::= & \mathbf{skip} \mid \mathbf{let}\ \Pi\ \mathbf{in}\ C \,\|\ldots\|\, C \\
(\mathit{ODecl}) & \Pi & ::= & \{f_1 \leadsto (x_1, C_1), \ldots, f_n \leadsto (x_n, C_n)\}
\end{array}
$$

Figure 3. Syntax of the Programming Language

$$
\begin{array}{rrcl}
(\mathit{ThrdID}) & \mathtt{t} & \in & \mathit{Nat} \\
(\mathit{Mem}) & \sigma & \in & (\mathit{PVar} \cup \mathit{Nat}) \rightharpoonup \mathit{Int} \\
(\mathit{CallStk}) & \kappa & ::= & (\sigma_l, x, C) \mid \circ \\
(\mathit{ThrdPool}) & \mathcal{K} & ::= & \{\mathtt{t}_1 \leadsto \kappa_1, \ldots, \mathtt{t}_n \leadsto \kappa_n\} \\
(\mathit{PState}) & \mathcal{S} & ::= & (\sigma_c, \sigma_o, \mathcal{K}) \\
(\mathit{LState}) & s & ::= & (\sigma_c, \sigma_o, \kappa) \\
(\mathit{Evt}) & e & ::= & (\mathtt{t}, f, n) \mid (\mathtt{t}, \mathbf{ok}, n) \mid (\mathtt{t}, \mathbf{obj}, \mathbf{abort}) \\
 & & & \mid (\mathtt{t}, \mathbf{out}, n) \mid (\mathtt{t}, \mathbf{clt}, \mathbf{abort}) \\
(\mathit{ETrace}) & H & ::= & \epsilon \mid e :: H
\end{array}
$$

Figure 4. States and Event Traces

tion is shown in Fig. 2(b). We can see that a concrete step of thread t could help linearize the operation of t′ in the pending thread pool as well as its own operation. Thus the new simulation intuitively supports the helping mechanism.

As forward simulations, neither of the simulations in Fig. 2(a) and (b) supports future-dependent LPs. For each step along the concrete execution in those simulations, we need to decide immediately whether the step is at the LP, and cannot postpone the decision to the future. As discussed a lot in previous work (*e.g.*, [1, 3, 6, 21]), we have to introduce backward simulations or hybrid simulations to support future-dependent LPs. Here we exploit the speculation idea and develop a forward-backward simulation [21]. As shown in Fig. 2(c), we keep both speculations after the potential LP, where the higher black nodes result from executing the abstract operation and the lower white nodes record the original abstract configuration. Then at the validation step we commit to the correct branch.

Finally, to ensure linearizability, the thread-local simulation has to be *compositional*. As a counterexample, we can construct a simple simulation (like the one in Fig. 2(a)) between the following implementation C and the abstract atomic increment operation γ, but C is not linearizable *w.r.t.* γ.

```
C : local t; t := x; x := t + 1;          γ : x++
```

The reason is that the simple simulation is not compositional *w.r.t.* parallel compositions. To address this problem, we proposed a compositional simulation RGSim [19] in previous work. The idea is to parameterize the simple simulation with the interference with the environment, in the form of rely/guarantee conditions (R and G) [17]. RGSim says, the concrete executions are simulated by the abstract executions under interference from the environment R, and all the related state transitions of the thread being verified should satisfy G. For parallel composition, we check that the guarantee G of each thread is permitted in the rely R of the other. Then the simulation becomes compositional and can ensure linearizability.

We combine the above ideas and develop a new compositional simulation with the support of non-fixed LPs as the meta-theory of our logic. We will discuss our simulation formally in Sec. 5.

3. Basic Technical Settings and Linearizability

In this section, we formalize linearizability of an object implementation *w.r.t.* its specification, and show that linearizability is equivalent to contextual refinement.

3.1 Language and Semantics

As shown in Fig. 3, a program W contains several client threads in parallel, each of which could call the methods declared in the object Π. A method is defined as a pair (x, C), where x is the formal argument and C is the method body. For simplicity, we assume there is only one object in W and each method takes one argument only, but it is easy to extend our work with multiple objects and arguments.

We use a runtime command **noret** to abort methods that terminate but do not execute **return** E. It is automatically appended to the method code and is not supposed to be used by programmers. Other commands are mostly standard. Clients can use $\mathbf{print}(E)$ to produce observable external events. We do not allow the object's methods to produce external events. To simplify the semantics, we also assume there are no nested method calls.

Figure 4 gives the model of program states. Here we partition a global state $\mathcal{S}$ into the client memory σ_c, the object σ_o and a thread pool $\mathcal{K}$. A client can only access the client memory σ_c, unless it calls object methods. The thread pool maps each thread id t to its local call stack frame. A call stack κ could be either empty ($\circ$) when the thread is not executing a method, or a triple (σ_l, x, C), where σ_l maps the method's formal argument and local variables (if any) to their values, x is the caller's variable to receive the return value, and C is the caller's remaining code to be executed after the method returns. To give a thread-local semantics, we also define the thread local view s of the state.

Figure 5 gives selected rules of the operational semantics. We show three kinds of transitions: $\longmapsto$ for the top-level program transitions, $\longrightarrow_{\mathtt{t},\Pi}$ for the transitions of thread t with the methods' declaration Π, and $\longrightarrow\!\!\!\!\triangleright_{\mathtt{t}}$ for the steps inside method calls of thread t. To describe the operational semantics for threads, we use an execution context $\mathbf{E}$:

$$(\mathit{ExecContext})\ \mathbf{E} ::= [\,] \mid \mathbf{E}; C$$

The hole $[\,]$ shows the place where the execution of code occurs. $\mathbf{E}[\,C\,]$ represents the code resulting from placing C into the hole.

We label transitions with events e defined in Fig. 4. An event could be a method invocation $(\mathtt{t}, f, n)$ or return $(\mathtt{t}, \mathbf{ok}, n)$, a fault $(\mathtt{t}, \mathbf{obj}, \mathbf{abort})$ produced by the object method code, an output $(\mathtt{t}, \mathbf{out}, n)$ generated by $\mathbf{print}(E)$, or a fault $(\mathtt{t}, \mathbf{clt}, \mathbf{abort})$ from the client code. The first two events are called object events, and the last two are observable external events. The third one $(\mathtt{t}, \mathbf{obj}, \mathbf{abort})$ belongs to both classes. An event trace H is then defined as a finite sequence of events.

3.2 Object Specification and Linearizability

Next we formalize the object specification Γ, which maps method names to their abstract operations γ, as shown in Fig. 6. γ transforms an argument value and an initial abstract object to a return value with a resulting abstract object in a single step. It specifies the intended sequential behaviors of the method. The abstract object representation θ is defined as a mapping from program variables to abstract values. We leave the abstract values unspecified here, which can be instantiated by programmers.

Then we give an abstract version of programs $\mathbb{W}$, where clients interact with the abstract object specification Γ instead of its implementation Π. The semantics is almost the same as the concrete language shown in Sec. 3.1, except that the abstract atomic operation γ is executed when the method is called, which now operates over the abstract object θ instead of over the concrete one σ_o. The

$$\frac{(C_i, (\sigma_c, \sigma_o, \mathcal{K}(i))) \xrightarrow{e}_{i,\Pi} (C'_i, (\sigma'_c, \sigma'_o, \kappa'))}{(\textbf{let } \Pi \textbf{ in } C_1 \| \ldots C_i \ldots \| C_n, (\sigma_c, \sigma_o, \mathcal{K})) \overset{e}{\longmapsto} (\textbf{let } \Pi \textbf{ in } C_1 \| \ldots C'_i \ldots \| C_n, (\sigma'_c, \sigma'_o, \mathcal{K}\{i \leadsto \kappa'\}))}$$

(a) Program Transitions

$$\frac{\Pi(f) = (y, C) \quad \llbracket E \rrbracket_{\sigma_c} = n \quad x \in \mathit{dom}(\sigma_c) \quad \kappa = (\{y \leadsto n\}, x, \mathbf{E}[\,\textbf{skip}\,])}{(\mathbf{E}[\,x := f(E)\,], (\sigma_c, \sigma_o, \circ)) \xrightarrow{(\mathsf{t}, f, n)}_{\mathsf{t},\Pi} (C; \textbf{noret}, (\sigma_c, \sigma_o, \kappa))}
\qquad
\frac{f \notin \mathit{dom}(\Pi) \text{ or } \llbracket E \rrbracket_{\sigma_c} \textit{ undefined} \text{ or } x \notin \mathit{dom}(\sigma_c)}{(\mathbf{E}[\,x := f(E)\,], (\sigma_c, \sigma_o, \circ)) \xrightarrow{(\mathsf{t}, \textbf{clt}, \textbf{abort})}_{\mathsf{t},\Pi} \textbf{abort}}$$

$$\frac{\kappa = (\sigma_l, x, C) \quad \llbracket E \rrbracket_{\sigma_o \uplus \sigma_l} = n \quad \sigma'_c = \sigma_c\{x \leadsto n\}}{(\mathbf{E}[\,\textbf{return } E\,], (\sigma_c, \sigma_o, \kappa)) \xrightarrow{(\mathsf{t}, \textbf{ok}, n)}_{\mathsf{t},\Pi} (C, (\sigma'_c, \sigma_o, \circ))}
\qquad
\frac{\llbracket E \rrbracket_{\sigma_c} = n}{(\mathbf{E}[\,\textbf{print}(E)\,], (\sigma_c, \sigma_o, \circ)) \xrightarrow{(\mathsf{t}, \textbf{out}, n)}_{\mathsf{t},\Pi} (\mathbf{E}[\,\textbf{skip}\,], (\sigma_c, \sigma_o, \circ))}$$

$$\frac{}{(\textbf{noret}, s) \xrightarrow{(\mathsf{t}, \textbf{obj}, \textbf{abort})}_{\mathsf{t},\Pi} \textbf{abort}}
\qquad
\frac{(C, \sigma_o \uplus \sigma_l) \longrightarrow_{\mathsf{t}} (C', \sigma'_o \uplus \sigma'_l) \quad \mathit{dom}(\sigma_l) = \mathit{dom}(\sigma'_l)}{(C, (\sigma_c, \sigma_o, (\sigma_l, x, C_c))) \longrightarrow_{\mathsf{t},\Pi} (C', (\sigma_c, \sigma'_o, (\sigma'_l, x, C_c)))}$$

(b) Thread Transitions

$$\frac{\llbracket E_j \rrbracket_{\sigma} \textit{ undefined} \ (1 \le j \le i) \text{ or } x \notin \mathit{dom}(\sigma)}{(\mathbf{E}[\,x := \textbf{cons}(E_1, \ldots, E_i)\,], \sigma) \longrightarrow_{\mathsf{t}} \textbf{abort}}
\qquad
\frac{(C, \sigma) \longrightarrow^*_{\mathsf{t}} (\textbf{skip}, \sigma')}{(\mathbf{E}[\,\langle C \rangle\,], \sigma) \longrightarrow_{\mathsf{t}} (\mathbf{E}[\,\textbf{skip}\,], \sigma')}
\qquad
\frac{(C, \sigma) \longrightarrow^*_{\mathsf{t}} \textbf{abort}}{(\mathbf{E}[\,\langle C \rangle\,], \sigma) \longrightarrow_{\mathsf{t}} \textbf{abort}}$$

(c) Thread Transitions Inside Method Calls

Figure 5. Selected Rules of Concrete Operational Semantics

$$\begin{array}{rlcl}
(\mathit{AbsObj}) & \theta & \in & \mathit{PVar} \rightharpoonup \mathit{AbsVal} \\
(\mathit{MSpec}) & \gamma & \in & \mathit{Int} \to \mathit{AbsObj} \rightharpoonup \mathit{Int} \times \mathit{AbsObj} \\
(\mathit{OSpec}) & \Gamma & ::= & \{f_1 \leadsto \gamma_1, \ldots, f_n \leadsto \gamma_n\} \\
(\mathit{AbsProg}) & \mathbb{W} & ::= & \textbf{skip} \mid \textbf{with } \Gamma \textbf{ do } C \| \ldots \| C
\end{array}$$

Figure 6. Object Specification and Abstract Program

abstract operation generates a pair of invocation and return events atomically. Due to space limit, we give the semantics in TR [18].

Linearizability. Linearizability [16] is defined using the notion of histories, which are special event traces H consisting of only object events (*i.e.*, invocations, returns and object faults).

Below we use $H(i)$ for the i-th event of H, and $|H|$ for the length of H. $H|_{\mathsf{t}}$ represents the sub-history consisting of all the events whose thread id is t. The predicates $\mathsf{is\_inv}(e)$ and $\mathsf{is\_res}(e)$ mean that the event e is a method invocation and a response (*i.e.*, a return or an object fault) respectively. We say a response e_2 *matches* an invocation e_1 iff they have the same thread id.

A history H is *sequential* iff the first event of H is an invocation, and each invocation, except possibly the last, is immediately followed by a matching response. Then H is *well-formed* iff, for all t, $H|_{\mathsf{t}}$ is sequential. H is *complete* iff it is well-formed and every invocation has a matching response. An invocation is *pending* if no matching response follows it. We handle pending invocations in an incomplete history H following the standard linearizability definition [16]: we append zero or more response events to H, and drop the remaining pending invocations. Then we get a set of complete histories, which is denoted by $\mathsf{completions}(H)$. We give formal definitions of the above concepts in TR [18].

Definition 1 (Linearizable Histories). $H \preceq_{\mathsf{lin}} H'$ iff

1. $\forall \mathsf{t}.\ H|_{\mathsf{t}} = H'|_{\mathsf{t}}$;
2. there exists a bijection $\pi : \{1, \ldots, |H|\} \to \{1, \ldots, |H'|\}$ such that $\forall i.\ H(i) = H'(\pi(i))$ and
$$\forall i, j.\ i < j \wedge \mathsf{is\_res}(H(i)) \wedge \mathsf{is\_inv}(H(j)) \implies \pi(i) < \pi(j).$$

That is, H is linearizable *w.r.t.* H' if the latter is a permutation of the former, preserving the order of events in the same threads and the order of the non-overlapping method calls.

We use $\mathcal{H}\llbracket W, (\sigma_c, \sigma_o) \rrbracket$ to represent the set of histories produced by the executions of W with the initial client memory σ_c, the object σ_o, and empty call stacks for all threads, and use $\mathcal{H}\llbracket \mathbb{W}, (\sigma_c, \theta) \rrbracket$ to generate histories from the abstract program $\mathbb{W}$ with the initial client memory σ_c and the abstract object θ.

A *legal* sequential history H is a history generated by any client using the specification Γ and an initial abstract object θ.

$$\Gamma \rhd (\theta, H) \stackrel{\text{def}}{=} \exists n, C_1, \ldots, C_n, \sigma_c.\ H \in \mathcal{H}\llbracket (\textbf{with } \Gamma \textbf{ do } C_1 \| \ldots \| C_n), (\sigma_c, \theta) \rrbracket$$

Then an *object* is linearizable iff all its completed concurrent histories are linearizable *w.r.t.* some legal sequential histories.

Definition 2 (Linearizability of Objects). The object's implementation Π is linearizable *w.r.t.* its specification Γ under a refinement mapping φ, denoted by $\Pi \preceq_{\varphi} \Gamma$, iff

$$\begin{array}{l}
\forall n, C_1, \ldots, C_n, \sigma_c, \sigma_o, \theta, H. \\
H \in \mathcal{H}\llbracket (\textbf{let } \Pi \textbf{ in } C_1 \| \ldots \| C_n), (\sigma_c, \sigma_o) \rrbracket \wedge (\varphi(\sigma_o) = \theta) \\
\implies \exists H_c, H'.\ H_c \in \mathsf{completions}(H) \wedge \Gamma \rhd (\theta, H') \wedge H_c \preceq_{\mathsf{lin}} H'
\end{array}$$

Here the mapping φ relates concrete objects to abstract ones:

$$(\mathit{RefMap}) \quad \varphi \in \mathit{Mem} \rightharpoonup \mathit{AbsObj}$$

The side condition $\varphi(\sigma_o) = \theta$ in the above definition requires the initial concrete object σ_o to be a well-formed data structure representing a valid object θ.

3.3 Contextual Refinement and Linearizability

Next we define contextual refinement between the concrete object and its specification, and prove its equivalence to linearizability. This equivalence will serve as the basis of our logic soundness *w.r.t.* linearizability.

Informally, the contextual refinement says, for any set of client threads, the program W has no more observable behaviors than the corresponding abstract program $\mathbb{W}$. Below we use $\mathcal{O}\llbracket W, (\sigma_c, \sigma_o) \rrbracket$ to represent the set of observable event traces generated during the executions of W with the initial state (σ_c, σ_o) (and empty stacks). It is defined similarly as $\mathcal{H}\llbracket W, (\sigma_c, \sigma_o) \rrbracket$, but now the traces consist of observable events only (output events, client faults or object faults). The observable event traces $\mathcal{O}\llbracket \mathbb{W}, (\sigma_c, \theta) \rrbracket$ generated by the abstract program is defined similarly.

$$
\begin{array}{llll}
(\mathit{InsStmt}) & \widetilde{C} & ::= & \mathbf{skip} \mid c \mid \mathbf{return}\ E \mid \mathbf{noret} \\
& & \mid & \mathbf{linself} \mid \mathbf{lin}(E) \mid \mathbf{trylinself} \\
& & \mid & \mathbf{trylin}(E) \mid \mathbf{commit}(p) \mid \langle \widetilde{C} \rangle \mid \widetilde{C};\widetilde{C} \\
& & \mid & \mathbf{if}\ (B)\ \widetilde{C}\ \mathbf{else}\ \widetilde{C} \mid \mathbf{while}\ (B)\{\widetilde{C}\} \\
(\mathit{RelState}) & \Sigma & ::= & (\sigma, \Delta) \\
(\mathit{SpecSet}) & \Delta & ::= & \{(U_1, \theta_1), \ldots, (U_n, \theta_n)\} \\
(\mathit{PendThrds}) & U & ::= & \{\mathsf{t}_1 \leadsto \Upsilon_1, \ldots, \mathsf{t}_n \leadsto \Upsilon_n\} \\
(\mathit{AbsOp}) & \Upsilon & ::= & (\gamma, n) \mid (\mathbf{end}, n) \\
(\mathit{RelAss}) & p, q, I & ::= & \mathsf{true} \mid \mathsf{false} \mid E = E \mid \mathsf{emp} \mid E \mapsto E \\
& & \mid & x \Mapsto E \mid E \rightarrowtail (\gamma, E) \mid E \rightarrowtail (\mathbf{end}, E) \\
& & \mid & p * q \mid p \oplus q \mid p \vee q \mid \ldots \\
(\mathit{RelAct}) & R, G & ::= & p \ltimes q \mid [p] \mid R * R \mid R \oplus R \mid \ldots
\end{array}
$$

Figure 7. Instrumented Code and Relational State Model

$$\bullet \stackrel{\text{def}}{=} \{(\emptyset, \emptyset)\} \qquad \text{where } \bullet \in \mathit{SpecSet}$$

$$f \bot g \stackrel{\text{def}}{=} \mathit{dom}(f) \cap \mathit{dom}(g) = \emptyset$$

$$\Delta_1 \sharp \Delta_2 \stackrel{\text{def}}{=} U_1 \bot U_2 \wedge \theta_1 \bot \theta_2\,, \text{ where } (U_1,\theta_1) \in \Delta_1 \wedge (U_2,\theta_2) \in \Delta_2$$

$$\Delta_1 * \Delta_2 \stackrel{\text{def}}{=} \{(U_1 \uplus U_2, \theta_1 \uplus \theta_2) \mid (U_1,\theta_1) \in \Delta_1 \wedge (U_2,\theta_2) \in \Delta_2\}$$

$$\Sigma_1 * \Sigma_2 \stackrel{\text{def}}{=} (\sigma_1 \uplus \sigma_2, \Delta_1 * \Delta_2) \quad \text{where } \Sigma_1 = (\sigma_1, \Delta_1), \Sigma_2 = (\sigma_2, \Delta_2), \sigma_1 \bot \sigma_2 \text{ and } \Delta_1 \sharp \Delta_2$$

$$\Sigma_1 \oplus \Sigma_2 \stackrel{\text{def}}{=} \begin{cases} (\sigma, \Delta_1 \cup \Delta_2) & \text{if } \Sigma_1 = (\sigma,\Delta_1) \text{ and } \Sigma_2 = (\sigma,\Delta_2) \\ \mathit{undefined} & \text{otherwise} \end{cases}$$

$$\{\!\!\{E\}\!\!\}_\sigma \stackrel{\text{def}}{=} \begin{cases} [\![E]\!]_\sigma & \text{if } \mathit{dom}(\sigma) = \mathit{fv}(E) \\ \mathit{undefined} & \text{otherwise} \end{cases}$$

$$
\begin{array}{l}
(\sigma, \Delta) \models E_1 = E_2 \ \text{ iff } \{\!\!\{(E_1 = E_2)\}\!\!\}_\sigma = \mathbf{true} \wedge \Delta = \bullet \\
(\sigma, \Delta) \models \mathsf{emp} \quad \text{iff } \sigma = \emptyset \wedge \Delta = \bullet \\
(\sigma, \Delta) \models E_1 \mapsto E_2 \ \text{ iff } \exists l, n, \sigma'.\ \{\!\!\{(E_1, E_2)\}\!\!\}_{\sigma'} = (l, n) \\
\qquad\qquad \wedge\, \sigma = \sigma' \uplus \{l \leadsto n\} \wedge \Delta = \bullet \\
(\sigma, \Delta) \models x \Mapsto E \quad \text{iff } \exists n, \theta.\ \{\!\!\{E\}\!\!\}_\sigma = n \wedge \theta = \{x \leadsto n\} \\
\qquad\qquad \wedge\, \Delta = \{(\emptyset, \theta)\} \\
(\sigma, \Delta) \models E_1 \rightarrowtail (\gamma, E_2) \quad \text{iff } \exists \sigma_1, \sigma_2, \mathsf{t}, n.\ \sigma = \sigma_1 \uplus \sigma_2 \\
\qquad\qquad \wedge \{\!\!\{E_1\}\!\!\}_{\sigma_1} = \mathsf{t} \wedge \{\!\!\{E_2\}\!\!\}_{\sigma_2} = n \\
\qquad\qquad \wedge\, \Delta = \{(\{\mathsf{t} \leadsto (\gamma, n)\}, \emptyset)\} \\
(\sigma, \Delta) \models E_1 \rightarrowtail (\mathbf{end}, E_2) \ \text{ iff } \exists \sigma_1, \sigma_2, \mathsf{t}, n.\ \sigma = \sigma_1 \uplus \sigma_2 \\
\qquad\qquad \wedge \{\!\!\{E_1\}\!\!\}_{\sigma_1} = \mathsf{t} \wedge \{\!\!\{E_2\}\!\!\}_{\sigma_2} = n \\
\qquad\qquad \wedge\, \Delta = \{(\{\mathsf{t} \leadsto (\mathbf{end}, n)\}, \emptyset)\} \\
\Sigma \models p * q \ \text{ iff } \exists \Sigma_1, \Sigma_2.\ \Sigma = \Sigma_1 * \Sigma_2 \wedge \Sigma_1 \models p \wedge \Sigma_2 \models q \\
\Sigma \models p \oplus q \ \text{ iff } \exists \Sigma_1, \Sigma_2.\ \Sigma = \Sigma_1 \oplus \Sigma_2 \wedge \Sigma_1 \models p \wedge \Sigma_2 \models q \\
\mathsf{SpecExact}(p) \ \text{ iff } \forall \Delta, \Delta'.\ ((\_,\Delta) \models p) \wedge ((\_,\Delta') \models p) \Longrightarrow (\Delta = \Delta')
\end{array}
$$

Figure 8. Semantics of State Assertions

Definition 3 (Contextual Refinement). $\Pi \sqsubseteq_\varphi \Gamma$ iff

$$
\begin{array}{l}
\forall n, C_1, \ldots, C_n, \sigma_c, \sigma_o, \theta.\ \varphi(\sigma_o) = \theta \\
\quad \Longrightarrow \mathcal{O}[\![(\mathbf{let}\ \Pi\ \mathbf{in}\ C_1 \parallel \ldots \parallel C_n), (\sigma_c, \sigma_o)]\!] \\
\qquad \subseteq \mathcal{O}[\![(\mathbf{with}\ \Gamma\ \mathbf{do}\ C_1 \parallel \ldots \parallel C_n), (\sigma_c, \theta)]\!].
\end{array}
$$

Following Filipović *et al.* [9], we can prove that linearizability is equivalent to contextual refinement. We give the proofs in TR [18].

Theorem 4 (Equivalence). $\Pi \preceq_\varphi \Gamma \iff \Pi \sqsubseteq_\varphi \Gamma$.

4. A Relational Rely-Guarantee Style Logic

To prove object linearizability, we first instrument the object implementation by introducing auxiliary states and auxiliary commands, which relate the concrete code with the abstract object and operations. Our program logic extends LRG [8] with a relational interpretation of assertions and new rules for auxiliary commands.

$$
\begin{array}{l}
(\Sigma, \Sigma') \models p \ltimes q \ \text{ iff } \Sigma \models p \wedge \Sigma' \models q \\
(\Sigma, \Sigma') \models [p] \ \text{ iff } \Sigma \models p \wedge \Sigma = \Sigma' \\
(\Sigma, \Sigma') \models R_1 * R_2 \ \text{ iff} \\
\qquad \exists \Sigma_1, \Sigma_2, \Sigma_1', \Sigma_2'.\ (\Sigma = \Sigma_1 * \Sigma_2) \wedge (\Sigma' = \Sigma_1' * \Sigma_2') \\
\qquad \wedge (\Sigma_1, \Sigma_1') \models R_1 \wedge (\Sigma_2, \Sigma_2') \models R_2 \\
(\Sigma, \Sigma') \models R_1 \oplus R_2 \ \text{ iff} \\
\qquad \exists \Sigma_1, \Sigma_2, \Sigma_1', \Sigma_2'.\ (\Sigma = \Sigma_1 \oplus \Sigma_2) \wedge (\Sigma' = \Sigma_1' \oplus \Sigma_2') \\
\qquad \wedge (\Sigma_1, \Sigma_1') \models R_1 \wedge (\Sigma_2, \Sigma_2') \models R_2
\end{array}
$$

$$\mathsf{Id} \stackrel{\text{def}}{=} [\mathsf{true}] \qquad \mathsf{True} \stackrel{\text{def}}{=} \mathsf{true} \ltimes \mathsf{true}$$

$$\frac{}{(\emptyset, n) \xrightarrow{\gamma} (\emptyset, n')} \qquad \frac{\gamma(n)(\theta) = (n', \theta') \quad (\Delta, n) \xrightarrow{\gamma} (\Delta', n')}{(\{(U, \theta)\} \uplus \Delta, n) \xrightarrow{\gamma} (\{(U, \theta')\} \uplus \Delta', n')}$$

$$
\begin{array}{l}
[E, p]\gamma[E', q] \ \text{ iff} \\
\quad \forall \sigma, \Delta, n.\ (\sigma, \Delta) \models (E = n) * p \\
\quad \Longrightarrow \exists \Delta', n'.\ (\Delta, n) \xrightarrow{\gamma} (\Delta', n') \wedge ((\sigma, \Delta') \models (E' = n') * q) \\
I \rhd R \ \text{ iff } ([I] \Rightarrow R) \wedge (R \Rightarrow I \ltimes I) \wedge \mathsf{Precise}(I)
\end{array}
$$

Figure 9. Semantics of Actions

Although our logic is based on LRG [8], this approach is mostly independent with the base logic. Similar extensions can also be made over other logics, such as RGSep [32].

Our logic is proposed to verify object methods only. Verified object methods are guaranteed to be a contextual refinement of their abstract atomic operations, which ensures linearizability of the object. We discuss verification of whole programs consisting of both client code and object code at the end of Sec. 4.3.

4.1 Instrumented Code and States

In Fig. 7 we show the syntax of the instrumented code and its state model. As explained in Sec. 2, program states Σ for the object method executions now consist of two parts, the physical object states σ and the auxiliary data Δ. Δ is a *nonempty* set of (U, θ) pairs, each pair representing a speculation of the situation at the abstract level. Here θ is the current abstract object, and U is a pending thread pool recording the remaining operation to be fulfilled by each thread. It maps a thread id to its remaining abstract operation, which is either (γ, n) (the operation γ needs to be executed with argument n) or $(\mathbf{end}, n)$ (the operation has been finished with the return value n). We assume Δ is always *domain-exact*, defined as follows:

$$
\begin{array}{l}
\mathsf{DomExact}(\Delta) \stackrel{\text{def}}{=} \forall U, \theta, U', \theta'.\ (U, \theta) \in \Delta \wedge (U', \theta') \in \Delta \\
\qquad \Longrightarrow \mathit{dom}(U) = \mathit{dom}(U') \wedge \mathit{dom}(\theta) = \mathit{dom}(\theta').
\end{array}
$$

It says, all the speculations in Δ should describe the same set of threads and the same domain of abstract objects. Any Δ containing a single speculation is domain-exact. Also domain-exactness can be preserved under the step of any command in our instrumented language, thus it is reasonable to assume it always holds.

Below we informally explain the effects over Δ of the newly introduced commands. We leave their formal semantics to Sec. 4.4. The auxiliary command **linself** executes the unfinished abstract operation of the current thread in every U in Δ, and changes the abstract object θ correspondingly. **lin**(E) executes the abstract operation of the thread with id E. **linself** or **lin**(E) is executed when we know for sure that a step is the linearization point. The **trylinself** command introduces uncertainty. Since we do not know if the abstract operation of the current thread is fulfilled or not at the current point, we consider both possibilities. For each (U, θ) pair in Δ that contains unfinished abstract operation of the current thread, we add in Δ a new speculation (U', θ') where the abstract operation is done and θ' is the resulting abstract object. Since the original (U, θ) is also kept, we have both speculations in Δ. Similarly, the

$$\frac{[E_1,p]\gamma[E_2,q]}{\vdash_{\mathsf{t}} \{\mathsf{t} \rightarrowtail (\gamma, E_1) * p\}\textbf{linself}\{\mathsf{t} \rightarrowtail (\textbf{end}, E_2) * q\}}\ (\text{LINSELF}) \qquad \frac{}{\vdash_{\mathsf{t}} \{\mathsf{t} \rightarrowtail (\textbf{end}, E)\}\textbf{linself}\{\mathsf{t} \rightarrowtail (\textbf{end}, E)\}}\ (\text{LINSELF-END})$$

$$\frac{[E_1,p]\gamma[E_2,q]}{\vdash_{\mathsf{t}} \{E \rightarrowtail (\gamma, E_1) * p\}\textbf{trylin}(E)\{(E \rightarrowtail (\gamma, E_1) * p) \oplus (E \rightarrowtail (\textbf{end}, E_2) * q)\}}\ (\text{TRY})$$

$$\frac{}{\vdash_{\mathsf{t}} \{E \rightarrowtail (\textbf{end}, E')\}\textbf{trylin}(E)\{E \rightarrowtail (\textbf{end}, E')\}}\ (\text{TRY-END}) \qquad \frac{\mathsf{SpecExact}(p) \quad p' \Rightarrow p}{\vdash_{\mathsf{t}} \{p' \oplus \mathsf{true}\}\textbf{commit}(p)\{p'\}}\ (\text{COMMIT})$$

$$\frac{}{\vdash_{\mathsf{t}} \{\mathsf{t} \rightarrowtail (\textbf{end}, E)\}\mathbf{E}[\,\textbf{return}\ E\,]\{\mathsf{t} \rightarrowtail (\textbf{end}, E)\}}\ (\text{RET}) \qquad \frac{\vdash_{\mathsf{t}} \{p\}\widetilde{C}\{q\}}{\vdash_{\mathsf{t}} \{p * r\}\widetilde{C}\{q * r\}}\ (\text{FRAME}) \qquad \frac{\vdash_{\mathsf{t}} \{p\}\widetilde{C}\{q\} \quad \vdash_{\mathsf{t}} \{p'\}\widetilde{C}\{q'\}}{\vdash_{\mathsf{t}} \{p \oplus p'\}\widetilde{C}\{q \oplus q'\}}\ (\text{SPEC-CONJ})$$

$$\frac{\vdash_{\mathsf{t}} \{p\}\widetilde{C}\{q\} \quad (p \ltimes q) \Rightarrow G * \mathsf{True} \quad I \rhd G \quad p \vee q \Rightarrow I * \mathsf{true}}{[I], G, I \vdash_{\mathsf{t}} \{p\}\langle\widetilde{C}\rangle\{q\}}\ (\text{ATOM}) \qquad \frac{[I], G, I \vdash_{\mathsf{t}} \{p\}\langle\widetilde{C}\rangle\{q\} \quad \mathsf{Sta}(\{p,q\}, R * \mathsf{Id}) \quad I \rhd R}{R, G, I \vdash_{\mathsf{t}} \{p\}\langle\widetilde{C}\rangle\{q\}}\ (\text{ATOM-R})$$

Figure 10. Selected Inference Rules

trylin(E) command introduces speculations about the thread E. When we have enough knowledge p about the situation of the abstract objects and operations, the **commit**(p) step keeps only the subset of speculations consistent with p and drops the rest. Here p is a logical assertion about the state Σ, which is explained below.

4.2 Assertions

Syntax of assertions is shown in Fig. 7. Following rely-guarantee style reasoning, assertions are either single state assertions p and q or binary rely/guarantee conditions R and G. Note here states refer to the relational states Σ.

We use standard separation logic assertions such as true, $E_1 = E_2$, emp and $E_1 \mapsto E_2$ to specify the memory σ. As shown in Fig. 8, their semantics is almost standard, but for $E_1 = E_2$ to hold over σ we require the domain of σ contains only the free variables in E_1 and E_2. Here we use $\{\!|E|\!\}_\sigma$ to evaluate E with the extra requirement that σ contains the exact resource to do the evaluation.

New assertions are introduced to specify Δ. $x \Mapsto E$ specifies the abstract object θ in Δ, with no speculations of U (abstract operations), while $E_1 \rightarrowtail (\gamma, E_2)$ (and $E_1 \rightarrowtail (\textbf{end}, E_2)$) specifies the singleton speculation of U. Semantics of separating conjunction $p * q$ is similar as in separation logic, except that it is now lifted to assertions over the relational states Σ. Note that the underlying "disjoint union" over Δ for separating conjunction should not be confused with the normal disjoint union operator over sets. The former (denoted as $\Delta_1 * \Delta_2$ in Fig. 8) describes the split of pending thread pools and/or abstract objects. For example, the left side Δ in the following equation specifies two speculations of threads t_1 and t_2 (we assume the abstract object part is empty and omitted here), and it can be split into two sets Δ_1 and Δ_2 on the right side, each of which describes the speculations of a single thread.

$$\left\{ \begin{matrix} \mathsf{t}_1 \boxed{\Upsilon_1} \\ \mathsf{t}_2 \boxed{\Upsilon_2} \end{matrix}, \begin{matrix} \mathsf{t}_1 \boxed{\Upsilon_1} \\ \mathsf{t}_2 \boxed{\Upsilon_2'} \end{matrix} \right\} = \begin{matrix} \{\mathsf{t}_1 \boxed{\Upsilon_1}\} \\ * \\ \{\mathsf{t}_2 \boxed{\Upsilon_2},\ \mathsf{t}_2 \boxed{\Upsilon_2'}\} \end{matrix}$$

The most interesting new assertion is $p \oplus q$, where p and q specify two different speculations. It is this assertion that reflects uncertainty about the abstract level. However, the readers should not confuse $\oplus$ with disjunction. It is more like conjunction since it says Δ contains both speculations satisfying p *and* those satisfying q. As an example, the above equation could be formulated at the assertion level using $*$ and $\oplus$:

$$\begin{array}{rl} & (\mathsf{t}_1 \rightarrowtail \Upsilon_1 * \mathsf{t}_2 \rightarrowtail \Upsilon_2) \oplus (\mathsf{t}_1 \rightarrowtail \Upsilon_1 * \mathsf{t}_2 \rightarrowtail \Upsilon_2') \\ \Leftrightarrow & \mathsf{t}_1 \rightarrowtail \Upsilon_1 * (\mathsf{t}_2 \rightarrowtail \Upsilon_2 \oplus \mathsf{t}_2 \rightarrowtail \Upsilon_2') \end{array}$$

Rely and guarantee assertions specify transitions over Σ. Here we follow the syntax of LRG [8], with a new assertion $R_1 \oplus R_2$ specifying speculative behaviors of the environment. The semantics is given in Fig. 9. We will show the use of the assertions in the examples of Sec. 6.

4.3 Inference Rules

The rules of our logic are shown in Fig. 10. Rules on the top half are for sequential Hoare-style reasoning. They are proposed to verify code $\widetilde{C}$ in the atomic block $\langle\widetilde{C}\rangle$. The judgment is parameterized with the id t of the current thread.

For the **linself** command, if the abstract operation γ of the current thread has not been done, this command will finish it. Here $[E_1, p]\gamma[E_2, q]$ in the LINSELF rule describes the behavior of γ, which transforms abstract objects satisfying p to new ones satisfying q. E_1 and E_2 are the argument and return value respectively. The definition is given in Fig. 9. The LINSELF-END rule says **linself** has no effects if we know the abstract operation has been finished. The LIN rule and LIN-END rule are similar and omitted here.

The TRY rule says that if the thread E has not finished the abstract operation γ, it can do speculation using **trylin**(E). The resulting state contains both cases, one says γ does not progress at this point and the other says it does. If the current thread has already finished the abstract operation, **trylin**(E) would have no effects, as shown in the TRY-END rule. We omit the TRYSELF rule and TRYSELF-END rule for the current thread, which are similar.

The above two pairs of rules require us to know for sure either the abstract operation has been finished or not. If we want to support uncertainty in the pre-condition, we could first consider different cases and then apply the SPEC-CONJ rule, which is like the conjunction rule in traditional Hoare logic.

The COMMIT rule allows us to commit to a specific speculation and drop the rest. **commit**(p) keeps only the speculations satisfying p. We require p to describe an exact set of speculations, as defined by $\mathsf{SpecExact}(p)$ in Fig. 8. For example, the following p_1 is speculation-exact, while p_2 is not:

$$\begin{array}{rcl} p_1 & \stackrel{\text{def}}{=} & \mathsf{t} \rightarrowtail (\gamma, n) \oplus \mathsf{t} \rightarrowtail (\textbf{end}, n') \\ p_2 & \stackrel{\text{def}}{=} & \mathsf{t} \rightarrowtail (\gamma, n) \vee \mathsf{t} \rightarrowtail (\textbf{end}, n') \end{array}$$

In all of our examples in Sec. 6, the assertion p in **commit**(p) describes a singleton speculation, so $\mathsf{SpecExact}(p)$ trivially holds.

Before the current thread returns, it must know its abstract operation has been done, as required in the RET rule. We also have a standard FRAME rule as in separation logic for local reasoning.

Rules in the bottom half show how to do rely-guarantee style concurrency reasoning, which are very similar to those in LRG [8]. As in LRG, we use a precise invariant I to specify the boundary of the well-formed shared resource. The ATOM rule says we could reason sequentially about code in the atomic block. Then we can lift it to the concurrent setting as long as its effects over the shared resource satisfy the guarantee G, which is fenced by the invariant I. In this step we assume the environment does not update shared resource, thus using Id as the rely condition (see Fig. 9). To allow general environment behaviors, we should apply the ATOM-R rule later, which requires that R be fenced by I and the pre- and post-conditions be stable with respect to R. Here $\mathsf{Sta}(\{p,q\},R)$ requires that p and q be stable with respect to R, a standard requirement in rely-guarantee reasoning. More rules are shown in TR [18].

Linking with client program verification. Our relational logic is introduced for object verification, but it can also be used to verify client code, since it is just an extension over the general-purpose concurrent logic LRG (which includes the rule for parallel composition). Moreover, as we will see in Sec. 5, our logic ensures contextual refinement. Therefore, to verify a program W, we could replace the object implementation with the abstract operations and verify the corresponding abstract program $\mathbb{W}$ instead. Since $\mathbb{W}$ abstracts away concrete object representation and method implementation details, this approach provides us with "separation and information hiding" [26] over the object, but still keeps enough information (*i.e.*, the abstract operations) about the method calls in concurrent client verification.

4.4 Semantics and Partial Correctness

We first show some key operational semantics rules for the instrumented code in Fig. 11.

A single step execution of the instrumented code by thread t is represented as $(\widetilde{C},\Sigma) \hookrightarrow_{\mathsf{t}} (\widetilde{C}',\Sigma')$. When we reach the **return** E command (the second rule), we require that there be no uncertainty about thread t at the abstract level in Δ. That is, in every speculation in Δ, we always know t's operation has been finished with the same return value E. Meanings of the auxiliary commands have been explained before. Here we use the auxiliary definition $\Delta \rightarrow_{\mathsf{t}} \Delta'$ to formally define their transitions over Δ. The semantics of $\mathbf{commit}(p)$ requires p to be speculation-exact (see Fig. 8). Also it uses $(\sigma,\Delta)|_p = (\sigma',\Delta')$ to filter out the wrong speculations. To ensure locality, this filter allows Δ to contain some extra resource such as the threads and their abstract operations other than those described in p. For example, the following Δ describes two threads t_1 and t_2, but we could mention only t_1 in $\mathbf{commit}(p)$.

$$\Delta : \left\{ \begin{array}{ll} \mathsf{t}_1 & \boxed{(\gamma_1, n_1)} \\ \mathsf{t}_2 & \boxed{(\gamma_2, n_2)} \end{array}, \quad \begin{array}{ll} \mathsf{t}_1 & \boxed{(\mathbf{end}, n_1')} \\ \mathsf{t}_2 & \boxed{(\mathbf{end}, n_2')} \end{array} \right\}$$

If p is $\mathsf{t}_1 \rightarrowtail (\gamma_1, n_1)$, then $\mathbf{commit}(p)$ will keep only the left speculation and discard the other. p can also be $\mathsf{t}_1 \rightarrowtail (\gamma_1, n_1) \oplus \mathsf{t}_1 \rightarrowtail (\mathbf{end}, n_1')$, then $\mathbf{commit}(p)$ will keep both speculations.

Given the thread-local semantics, we could next define the transition $(\widetilde{C},\Sigma) \overset{R}{\hookrightarrow}_{\mathsf{t}} (\widetilde{C},\Sigma)$, which describes the behavior of thread t with interference R from the environment.

Semantics preservation by the instrumentation. It is easy to see that the newly introduced auxiliary commands do not change the physical state σ, nor do they affect the program control flow. Thus the instrumentation does not change program behaviors, unless the auxiliary commands are inserted into the wrong places and they get stuck, but this can be prevented by our program logic.

Soundness w.r.t. partial correctness. Following LRG [8], we could give semantics of the logic judgment as $R, G, I \models_{\mathsf{t}} \{p\}\widetilde{C}\{q\}$, which encodes partial correctness of $\widetilde{C}$ *w.r.t.* the pre- and post-conditions. We could prove the logic ensures partial correctness by showing $R, G, I \vdash_{\mathsf{t}} \{p\}\widetilde{C}\{q\}$ implies $R, G, I \models_{\mathsf{t}} \{p\}\widetilde{C}\{q\}$. The details are shown in TR [18]. In the next section, we give a stronger soundness of the logic, *i.e.* soundness *w.r.t.* linearizability.

$$\frac{(C,\sigma) \longrightarrow_{\mathsf{t}} (C',\sigma') \qquad C \neq \mathbf{E}[\,\mathbf{return}\ \_\,]}{(C,(\sigma,\Delta)) \hookrightarrow_{\mathsf{t}} (C',(\sigma',\Delta))}$$

$$\frac{\forall U.\ (U,\_) \in \Delta \implies U(\mathsf{t}) = (\mathbf{end}, [\![E]\!]_\sigma)}{(\mathbf{E}[\,\mathbf{return}\ E\,],(\sigma,\Delta)) \hookrightarrow_{\mathsf{t}} (\mathbf{skip},(\sigma,\Delta))}$$

$$\frac{\Delta \rightarrow_{\mathsf{t}} \Delta'}{(\mathbf{E}[\,\mathbf{linself}\,],(\sigma,\Delta)) \hookrightarrow_{\mathsf{t}} (\mathbf{E}[\,\mathbf{skip}\,],(\sigma,\Delta'))}$$

$$\frac{[\![E]\!]_\sigma = \mathsf{t}' \qquad \Delta \rightarrow_{\mathsf{t}'} \Delta'}{(\mathbf{E}[\,\mathbf{trylin}(E)\,],(\sigma,\Delta)) \hookrightarrow_{\mathsf{t}} (\mathbf{E}[\,\mathbf{skip}\,],(\sigma,\Delta \cup \Delta'))}$$

$$\frac{\mathsf{SpecExact}(p) \qquad (\sigma,\Delta)|_p = (\_,\Delta')}{(\mathbf{E}[\,\mathbf{commit}(p)\,],(\sigma,\Delta)) \hookrightarrow_{\mathsf{t}} (\mathbf{E}[\,\mathbf{skip}\,],(\sigma,\Delta'))}$$

$$\frac{(\widetilde{C},\Sigma) \hookrightarrow_{\mathsf{t}} (\widetilde{C}',\Sigma')}{(\widetilde{C},\Sigma) \overset{R}{\hookrightarrow}_{\mathsf{t}} (\widetilde{C}',\Sigma')} \qquad \frac{(\Sigma,\Sigma') \models R}{(\widetilde{C},\Sigma) \overset{R}{\hookrightarrow}_{\mathsf{t}} (\widetilde{C},\Sigma')}$$

Auxiliary Definitions:

$$\frac{U(\mathsf{t}) = (\gamma, n) \qquad \gamma(n)(\theta) = (n', \theta')}{(U,\theta) \dashrightarrow_{\mathsf{t}} (U\{\mathsf{t} \rightsquigarrow (\mathbf{end}, n')\}, \theta')} \qquad \frac{U(\mathsf{t}) = (\mathbf{end}, n)}{(U,\theta) \dashrightarrow_{\mathsf{t}} (U,\theta)}$$

$$\frac{}{\emptyset \rightarrow_{\mathsf{t}} \emptyset} \qquad \frac{(U,\theta) \dashrightarrow_{\mathsf{t}} (U',\theta') \qquad \Delta \rightarrow_{\mathsf{t}} \Delta'}{\{(U,\theta)\} \uplus \Delta \ \rightarrow_{\mathsf{t}}\ \{(U',\theta')\} \cup \Delta'}$$

$$\begin{array}{l} (\sigma,\Delta)|_p = (\sigma',\Delta') \ \text{ iff} \\ \quad \exists \sigma'',\Delta'',\Delta_p.\ (\sigma = \sigma' \uplus \sigma'') \wedge (\Delta = \Delta' \uplus \Delta'') \wedge ((\sigma',\Delta_p) \models p) \\ \qquad\qquad \wedge (\Delta'|_{dom(\Delta_p)} = \Delta_p) \wedge (\Delta''|_{dom(\Delta_p)} \cap \Delta_p = \emptyset) \end{array}$$

$$\Delta|_D \stackrel{\text{def}}{=} \{(U,\theta) \mid dom(\{(U,\theta)\}) = D \wedge \exists U',\theta'.\ (U \uplus U', \theta \uplus \theta') \in \Delta\}$$

$$dom(\Delta) \stackrel{\text{def}}{=} (dom(U), dom(\theta)) \qquad \text{where } (U,\theta) \in \Delta$$

Figure 11. Operational Semantics in the Relational State Model

5. Soundness via Simulation

Our logic intuitively relates the concrete object code with its abstract level specification. In this section we formalize the intuition and prove that the logic indeed ensures object linearizability. The proof is constructed in the following steps. We propose a new rely-guarantee-based forward-backward simulation between the concrete code and the abstract operation. We prove the simulation is compositional and implies contextual refinement between the two sides, and our logic indeed establishes such a simulation. Thus the logic establishes contextual refinement. Finally we get linearizability following Theorem 4.

Below we first define a rely-guarantee-based forward-backward simulation. It extends RGSim [19] with the support of the helping mechanism and speculations.

Definition 5 (Simulation for Method). $(x, C) \preceq^{\mathsf{t}}_{R;G;p} \gamma$ iff

$$\begin{array}{l} \forall n, \sigma, \Delta.\ (\sigma,\Delta) \models (\mathsf{t} \rightarrowtail (\gamma, n) * (x = n) * p) \\ \qquad \implies (C; \mathbf{noret}, \sigma) \preceq^{\mathsf{t}}_{R;G;p} \Delta\,. \end{array}$$

Whenever $(C,\sigma) \preceq^{\mathsf{t}}_{R;G;p} \Delta$, we have the following:

1. if $C \neq \mathbf{E}[\,\mathbf{return}\ \_\,]$, then
   (a) for any C' and σ', if $(C,\sigma) \longrightarrow_{\mathsf{t}} (C',\sigma')$, then there exists Δ' such that $\Delta \rightrightarrows \Delta'$, $((\sigma,\Delta),(\sigma',\Delta')) \models (G * \mathsf{True})$ and $(C',\sigma') \preceq^{\mathsf{t}}_{R;G;p} \Delta'$;

(b) $(C, \sigma) \not\longrightarrow_{\mathsf{t}}$ **abort**;

2. for any σ' and Δ', if $((\sigma, \Delta), (\sigma', \Delta')) \models (R * \mathsf{Id})$, then $(C, \sigma') \preceq^{\mathsf{t}}_{R;G;p} \Delta'$;
3. if $C = \mathbf{E}[\,\textbf{return}\ E\,]$, then there exists n' such that $[\![E]\!]_\sigma = n'$ and $(\sigma, \Delta) \models (\mathsf{t} \rightarrowtail (\textbf{end}, n')) * (x = \_) * p)$.

As in RGSim, $(x, C) \preceq^{\mathsf{t}}_{R;G;p} \gamma$ says, the implementation C is simulated by the abstract operation γ under the interference with the environment, which is specified by R and G. The new simulation holds if the executions of the concrete code C are related to the *speculative* executions of some Δ. The Δ could specify abstract operations of other threads that might be helped, as well as the current thread t. Initially, the abstract operation of t is γ, with the same argument n as the concrete side (*i.e.*, $x = n$). The abstract operations of other threads can be known from the precondition p.

For each step of the concrete code C, we require it to be safe, and correspond to some steps of Δ, as shown in the first condition in Definition 5. We define the transition $\Delta \rightrightarrows \Delta'$ as follows.

$$\Delta \rightrightarrows \Delta' \text{ iff } \forall U', \theta'.\, (U', \theta') \in \Delta' \Longrightarrow \exists U, \theta.\, (U, \theta) \in \Delta \wedge (U, \theta) \dashrightarrow^{*} (U', \theta'),$$

where $(U, \theta) \dashrightarrow (U', \theta') \stackrel{\text{def}}{=} \exists \mathsf{t}.\, (U, \theta) \dashrightarrow_{\mathsf{t}} (U', \theta')$
and $(U, \theta) \dashrightarrow_{\mathsf{t}} (U', \theta')$ has been defined in Fig. 11.

It says, any (U', θ') pair in Δ' should be "reachable" from Δ. Specifically, we could execute the abstract operation of some thread t' (which could be the current thread t or some others), or drop some (U, θ) pair in Δ. The former is like a step of **trylin**(t') or **lin**(t'), depending on whether or not we keep the original abstract operation of t'. The latter can be viewed as a **commit** step, in which we discard the wrong speculations.

We also require the related steps at the two levels to satisfy the guarantee $G * \mathsf{True}$, G for the shared part and True (arbitrary transitions) for the local part. Symmetrically, the second condition in Definition 5 says, the simulation should be preserved under the environment interference $R * \mathsf{Id}$, R for the shared part and Id (identity transitions) for the local part.

Finally, when the method returns (the last condition in Definition 5), we require the current thread t has finished its abstract operation, and the return values match at the two levels.

Like RGSim, our new simulation is *compositional*, thus can ensure contextual refinement between the implementation and the abstract operation, as shown in the following lemma.

Lemma 6 (Simulation Implies Contextual Refinement).
For any Π, Γ and φ, if there exist R, G, p and I such that the following hold for all t,

1. for any f such that $\Pi(f) = (x, C)$, we have $\Pi(f) \preceq^{\mathsf{t}}_{R_{\mathsf{t}};G_{\mathsf{t}};p_{\mathsf{t}}} \Gamma(f)$, and $x \notin dom(I)$;
2. $R_{\mathsf{t}} = \bigvee_{\mathsf{t}' \neq \mathsf{t}} G_{\mathsf{t}'}$, $\;I \triangleright \{R_{\mathsf{t}}, G_{\mathsf{t}}\}$, $\;p_{\mathsf{t}} \Rightarrow I$, and $\mathsf{Sta}(p_{\mathsf{t}}, R_{\mathsf{t}})$;
3. $\lfloor \varphi \rfloor \Rightarrow \bigwedge_{\mathsf{t}} p_{\mathsf{t}}$;

then $\Pi \sqsubseteq_\varphi \Gamma$.

Here $x \notin dom(I)$ means the formal argument x is always in the local state, and $\lfloor \varphi \rfloor$ lifts φ to a state assertion:

$$\lfloor \varphi \rfloor \stackrel{\text{def}}{=} \{(\sigma, \{(\emptyset, \theta)\}) \mid \varphi(\sigma) = \theta\}.$$

Lemma 6 allows us to prove contextual refinement $\Pi \sqsubseteq_\varphi \Gamma$ by showing the simulation $\Pi(f) \preceq^{\mathsf{t}}_{R_{\mathsf{t}};G_{\mathsf{t}};p_{\mathsf{t}}} \Gamma(f)$ for each method f, where R, G and p are defined over the shared states fenced by the invariant I, and the interference constraint $R_{\mathsf{t}} = \bigvee_{\mathsf{t}' \neq \mathsf{t}} G_{\mathsf{t}'}$ holds following Rely-Guarantee reasoning [17]. Its proof is similar to the compositionality proofs of RGSim [19], but now we need to be careful with the helping between threads and the speculations. We give the proofs in TR [18].

Objects	Helping	Fut. LP	Java Pkg	HS Book
Treiber stack [29]				√
HSY stack [14]	√			√
MS two-lock queue [23]				√
MS lock-free queue [23]		√	√	√
DGLM queue [6]		√		
Lock-coupling list				√
Optimistic list [15]				√
Heller *et al.* lazy list [13]	√	√		√
Harris-Michael lock-free list	√	√	√	√
Pair snapshot [27]		√		
CCAS [31]	√	√		
RDCSS [12]	√	√		

Table 1. Verified Algorithms Using Our Logic

Lemma 7 (Logic Ensures Simulation for Method).
For any t, x, C, γ, R, G and p, if there exist I and $\widetilde{C}$ such that

$$R, G, I \vdash_{\mathsf{t}} \{\mathsf{t} \rightarrowtail (\gamma, x) * p\}\ \widetilde{C}\ \{\mathsf{t} \rightarrowtail (\textbf{end}, \_) * (x = \_) * p\},$$

and $\mathsf{Er}(\widetilde{C}) = (C; \textbf{noret})$, then $(x, C) \preceq^{\mathsf{t}}_{R;G;p} \gamma$.

Here we use $\mathsf{Er}(\widetilde{C})$ to erase the instrumented commands in $\widetilde{C}$. The lemma shows that, verifying $\widetilde{C}$ in our logic establishes simulation between the original code and the abstract operation. It is proved by first showing that our logic ensures the standard rely-guarantee-style partial correctness (see Sec. 4.4). Then we build the simulation by projecting the instrumented semantics (Fig. 11) to the concrete semantics of C (Fig. 5) and the speculative steps $\rightrightarrows$ of Δ.

Finally, from Lemmas 6 and 7, we get the soundness theorem of our logic, which says our logic can verify linearizability.

Theorem 8 (Logic Soundness). For any Π, Γ and φ, if there exist R, G, p and I such that the following hold for all t,

1. for any f, if $\Pi(f) = (x, C)$, there exists $\widetilde{C}$ such that
$$R_{\mathsf{t}}, G_{\mathsf{t}}, I \vdash_{\mathsf{t}} \{\mathsf{t} \rightarrowtail (\Gamma(f), x) * p_{\mathsf{t}}\}\ \widetilde{C}\ \{\mathsf{t} \rightarrowtail (\textbf{end}, \_) * (x = \_) * p_{\mathsf{t}}\},$$
$\mathsf{Er}(\widetilde{C}) = (C; \textbf{noret})$, and $x \notin dom(I)$;
2. $R_{\mathsf{t}} = \bigvee_{\mathsf{t}' \neq \mathsf{t}} G_{\mathsf{t}'}$, $\;p_{\mathsf{t}} \Rightarrow I$, and $\mathsf{Sta}(p_{\mathsf{t}}, R_{\mathsf{t}})$;
3. $\lfloor \varphi \rfloor \Rightarrow \bigwedge_{\mathsf{t}} p_{\mathsf{t}}$;

then $\Pi \sqsubseteq_\varphi \Gamma$, and thus $\Pi \preceq_\varphi \Gamma$.

6. Examples

Our logic gives us an effective approach to verify linearizability. As shown in Table 1, we have verified 12 algorithms, including two stacks, three queues, four lists and three algorithms on atomic memory reads or writes. Table 1 summarizes their features, including the helping mechanism (**Helping**) and future-dependent LPs (**Fut. LP**). Some of them are used in the `java.util.concurrent` package (**Java Pkg**). The last column (**HS Book**) shows whether it occurs in Herlihy and Shavit's classic textbook on concurrent algorithms [15]. We have almost covered all the fine-grained stacks, queues and lists in the book. We can see that our logic supports various objects ranging from simple ones with static LPs to sophisticated ones with non-fixed LPs. Although many of the examples can be verified using other approaches, we provide the first program logic which is proved sound and useful enough to verify all of these algorithms. Their complete proofs are given in TR [18].

In general we verify linearizability in the following steps. First we instrument the code with the auxiliary commands such as **linself**, **trylin**(E) and **commit**(p) at proper program points. The instrumentation should not be difficult based on the intuition of the algorithm. Then, we specify the assertions (as in Theorem 8)

```
readPair(int i, j) {  local a, b, v, w;
  {I ∗ (cid ↣ (γ, (i, j)))}
1 while(true) {
    {I ∗ (cid ↣ (γ, (i, j)) ⊕ true)}
2   < a := m[i].d; v := m[i].v; >
    {∃v'. (I ∧ readCell(i, a, v; v')) ∗ (cid ↣ (γ, (i, j)) ⊕ true)}
3   < b := m[j].d; w := m[j].v; trylinself; >
    {∃v'. (I ∧ readCell(i, a, v; v') ∧ readCell(j, b, w; _)) ∗ afterTry}
4   if (v = m[i].v) {
      {I ∗ (cid ↣ (end, (a, b)) ⊕ true)}
5     commit(cid ↣ (end, (a, b)));
      {I ∗ (cid ↣ (end, (a, b)))}
6     return (a, b);
      {I ∗ (cid ↣ (end, (a, b)))}
7 } } }
```

Auxiliary definitions:

$$\mathsf{readCell}(i, d, v; v') \stackrel{\text{def}}{=} (\mathsf{cell}(i, d, v) \vee (\mathsf{cell}(i, \_, v') \wedge v \neq v')) * \mathsf{true}$$

$$\mathsf{absRes} \stackrel{\text{def}}{=} (\mathtt{cid} \rightarrowtail (\mathbf{end}, (\mathtt{a}, \mathtt{b})) \wedge v' = \mathtt{v}) \vee (\mathtt{cid} \rightarrowtail (\mathbf{end}, (\_, \mathtt{b})) \wedge v' \neq \mathtt{v})$$

$$\mathsf{afterTry} \stackrel{\text{def}}{=} \mathtt{cid} \rightarrowtail (\gamma, (\mathtt{i}, \mathtt{j})) \oplus \mathsf{absRes} \oplus \mathsf{true}$$

Figure 12. Proof Outline of `readPair` in Pair Snapshot

and reason about the instrumented code by applying our inference rules, just like the usual partial correctness verification in LRG. In our experience, handling the auxiliary commands usually would not introduce much difficulty over the plain verification with LRG. Below we sketch the proofs of three representative examples: the pair snapshot, MS lock-free queue and the CCAS algorithm.

6.1 Pair Snapshot

As discussed in Sec. 2.3, the pair snapshot algorithm has a future-dependent LP. In Fig. 12, we show the proof of `readPair` for the current thread `cid`. We will use γ for its abstract operation, which atomically reads the cells `i` and `j` at the abstract level.

First, we insert **trylinself** and **commit** as highlighted in Fig. 12. The **commit** command says, when the validation at line 4 succeeds, we must have $\mathtt{cid} \rightarrowtail (\mathbf{end}, (\mathtt{a}, \mathtt{b}))$ as a possible speculation. This actually requires a correct instrumentation of **trylinself**. In Fig. 12, we insert it at line 3. It cannot be moved to other program points since line 3 is the only place where we could get the abstract return value $(\mathtt{a}, \mathtt{b})$ when executing γ. Besides, we cannot replace it by a **linself**, because if line 4 fails later, we have to restart to do the original abstract operation.

After the instrumentation, we can define the precise invariant I, the rely R and the guarantee G. The invariant I simply maps every memory cell (d, v) at the concrete level to a cell with data d at the abstract level, as shown below:

$$I \stackrel{\text{def}}{=} \circledast_{i \in [1..\mathtt{size}]} . (\exists d, v.\ \mathsf{cell}(i, d, v))$$
$$\text{where } \mathsf{cell}(i, d, v) \stackrel{\text{def}}{=} (\mathtt{m}[i] \mapsto (d, v)) * (\mathtt{m}[i] \Rrightarrow d))$$

Every thread guarantees that when writing a cell, it increases the version number. Here we use $[G]_I$ short for $(G \vee \mathsf{Id}) * \mathsf{Id} \wedge (I \ltimes I)$.

$$G \stackrel{\text{def}}{=} [\mathsf{Write}]_I \qquad \mathsf{Write} \stackrel{\text{def}}{=} \exists i, v.\ \mathsf{cell}(i, \_, v) \ltimes \mathsf{cell}(i, \_, v+1)$$

The rely R is the same as the guarantee G.

Then we specify the pre- and post-conditions, and reason about the instrumented code using our inference rules. The proof follows the intuition of the algorithm. Note that we relax $\mathtt{cid} \rightarrowtail (\gamma, (\mathtt{i}, \mathtt{j}))$ in the precondition of the method to $\mathtt{cid} \rightarrowtail (\gamma, (\mathtt{i}, \mathtt{j})) \oplus \mathsf{true}$ to ensure the loop invariant. The latter says, `cid` *may* just start (or restart) its operation and have not done yet.

The `readPair` method in the pair snapshot algorithm is "read-only" in the sense that the abstract operation does not update the abstract object. This perhaps means that it does not matter to linearize the method multiple times. In Sec. 6.3 we will verify an algorithm with future-dependent LPs, CCAS, which is not "read-only". We *can* still "linearize" a method with side effects multiple times.

```
 1 enq(v) {                          16 deq() {
 2  local x, t, s, b;                17  local h, t, s, v, b;
 3  x := cons(v, null);              18  while (true) {
 4  while (true) {                   19   h := Head; t := Tail;
 5   t := Tail; s := t.next;         20   s := h.next;
 6   if (t = Tail) {                 21   if (h = Head)
 7    if (s = null) {                22    if (h = t) {
 8     b:=cas(&(t.next),s,x);        23     if (s = null)
 9     if (b) {                      24      return EMPTY;
10      cas(&Tail, t, x);            25     cas(&Tail, t, s);
11      return; }                    26    }else {
12    }else cas(&Tail, t, s);        27     v := s.val;
13   }                               28     b:=cas(&Head,h,s);
14  }                                29     if(b) return v; }
15 }                                 30  } }
```

Figure 13. MS Lock-Free Queue Code

6.2 MS Lock-Free Queue

The widely-used MS lock-free queue [23] also has future-dependent LPs. We show its code in Fig. 13.

The queue is implemented as a linked list with `Head` and `Tail` pointers. `Head` always points to the first node (a sentinel) in the list, and `Tail` points to either the last or second to last node. The `enq` method appends a new node at the tail of the list and advances `Tail`, and `deq` replaces the sentinel node by its next node and returns the value in the new sentinel. If the list contains only the sentinel node, meaning the queue is empty, then `deq` returns `EMPTY`.

The algorithm employs the helping mechanism for the `enq` method to swing the `Tail` pointer when it lags behind the end of the list. A thread should first try to help the half-finished `enq` by advancing `Tail` (lines 12 and 25 in Fig. 13) before doing its own operation. But this helping mechanism would not affect the LP of `enq` which is statically located at line 8 when the `cas` succeeds, since the new node already becomes visible in the queue after being appended to the list, and updating `Tail` will not affect the abstract queue. We simply instrument line 8 as follows to verify `enq`:

```
< b := cas(&(t.next), s, x); if (b) linself; >
```

On the other hand, the original queue algorithm [23] checks `Head` or `Tail` (line 6 or 21 in Fig. 13) to make sure that its value has not been changed since its local copy was read (at line 5 or 19), and if it fails, the operation will restart. This check can improve efficiency of the algorithm, but it makes the LP of the `deq` method for the empty queue case depend on future executions. That LP should be at line 20, if the method returns `EMPTY` at the end of the same iteration. The intuition is, when we read `null` from `h.next` at line 20 (indicating the abstract queue must be empty there), we do not know how the iteration would terminate at that time. If the later check over `Head` at line 21 fails, the operation would restart and line 20 may not be the LP. We can use our try-commit instrumentation to handle this future-dependent LP. We insert **trylinself** at line 20, as follows:

```
< s := h.next; if (h = t && s = null) trylinself; >
```

Before the method returns `EMPTY`, we commit to the finished abstract operation, *i.e.*, we insert $\mathtt{commit(cid} \rightarrowtail \mathtt{(end, EMPTY))}$ just before line 24. Also, when we know we have to do another iteration, we can commit to the original DEQ operation, *i.e.*, we insert $\mathtt{commit(cid} \rightarrowtail \mathtt{DEQ)}$ at the end of the loop body.

For the case of nonempty queues, the LP of the `deq` method is statically at line 28 when the `cas` succeeds. Thus we can instrument **linself** there, as shown below.

```
< b := cas(&Head, h, s); if (b) linself; >
```

After the instrumentation, we can define I, R and G and verify the code using our logic rules. The invariant I relates all the nodes

```
1 CCAS(o, n) {
2  local r, d;
3  d := cons(cid, o, n);
4  r := cas(&a, o, d);
5  while(IsDesc(r)) {
6    Complete(r);
7    r := cas(&a, o, d);
8  }
9  if(r = o) Complete(d);
10 return r; }
11 Complete(d) {
12  local b;
13  b := flag;
14  if (b)
15    cas(&a, d, d.n);
16  else
17    cas(&a, d, d.o);
18 }
19 SetFlag(b){ flag := b;}
```

Figure 14. CCAS Code

in the concrete linked list to the abstract queue. R and G specify the related transitions at both levels, which simply include all the actions over the shared states in the algorithm. The proof is similar to the partial correctness proof using LRG, except that we have to specify the abstract objects and operations in assertions and reason about the instrumented code. We show the full proof in TR [18].

6.3 Conditional CAS

Conditional compare-and-swap (CCAS) [31] is a simplified version of the RDCSS algorithm [12]. It involves both the helping mechanism and future-dependent LPs. We show its code in Fig. 14.

The object contains an integer variable `a`, and a boolean bit `flag`. The method `SetFlag` (line 19) sets the bit directly. The method `CCAS` takes two arguments: an expected current value `o` of the variable `a` and a new value `n`. It atomically updates `a` with the new value if `flag` is true and `a` indeed has the value `o`; and does nothing otherwise. `CCAS` always returns the old value of `a`.

The implementation in Fig. 14 uses a variant of `cas`: instead of a boolean value indicating whether it succeeds, `cas(&a,o,n)` returns the old value stored in `a`. When starting a `CCAS`, a thread first allocates its descriptor (line 3), which contains the thread id and the arguments for CCAS. It then tries to put its descriptor in `a` (line 4). If successful (line 9), it calls the auxiliary `Complete` function, which restores `a` to the new value `n` (line 15) or to the original value `o` (line 17), depending on whether `flag` is true. If it finds `a` contains a descriptor (*i.e.*, `IsDesc` holds), it will try to help complete the operation in the descriptor (line 6) before doing its own. Since we disallow nested function calls to simplify the language, the auxiliary `Complete` function should be viewed as a macro.

The LPs of the algorithm are at lines 4, 7 and 13. If `a` contains a different value from `o` at lines 4 and 7, then CCAS fails and they are LPs of the current thread. We can instrument these lines as follows:

```
<r := cas(&a, o, d); if(r!=o && !IsDesc(r)) linself;>
```

If the descriptor `d` gets placed in `a`, then the LP should be in the `Complete` function. Since any thread can call `Complete` to help the operation, the LP should be at line 13 of the thread which will succeed at line 15 or 17. It is a future-dependent LP which may be in other threads' code. We instrument line 13 using **trylin**(`d.id`) to speculatively execute the abstract operation for the thread in `d`, which may not be the current thread. That is, line 13 becomes:

```
< b := flag; if (a = d) trylin(d.id); >
```

The condition `a=d` requires that the abstract operation in the descriptor has not been finished. Then at lines 15 and 17, we commit the correct guess. We show the instrumentation at line 15 below (where `s` is a local variable), and line 17 is instrumented similarly.

```
< s := cas(&a, d, d.n);
  if(s = d) commit(d.id ↣(end, d.o) * a⇛d.n); >
```

That is, it should be possible that the thread in `d` has finished the operation, and the current abstract `a` is the new value `n`.

Then we can define I, R and G, and verify the code by applying the inference rules. The invariant I says, the shared state includes `flag` and `a` at the abstract and the concrete levels; and when `a` is a descriptor `d`, the descriptor and the abstract operation of the thread `d.id` are also shared.

The rely R and the guarantee G should include the action over the shared states at each line. The action at line 4 (or 7) is interesting. If it succeeds, *both* the descriptor `d` and the abstract operation will be transferred from the local state to the shared part. This puts the abstract operation in the pending thread pool and enables other threads to help execute it.

The action at line 13 guarantees $\mathsf{TrylinSucc} \vee \mathsf{TrylinFail}$, which demonstrates the use of our logic for both helping and speculation.

$$\begin{aligned}\mathsf{TrylinSucc} &\stackrel{\text{def}}{=} (\exists t, o, n.\ (\mathtt{flag} \Mapsto \mathbf{true} * \mathsf{notDone}(t, o, n)) \\ &\qquad \ltimes (\mathtt{flag} \Mapsto \mathbf{true} * \mathsf{endSucc}(t, o, n))) \oplus \mathsf{Id}\\ \text{where } \mathsf{notDone}(t, o, n) &\stackrel{\text{def}}{=} t \rightarrowtail (\mathsf{CCAS}, o, n) * \mathtt{a} \Mapsto o\\ \mathsf{endSucc}(t, o, n) &\stackrel{\text{def}}{=} t \rightarrowtail (\mathbf{end}, o) * \mathtt{a} \Mapsto n\end{aligned}$$

$\mathsf{TrylinFail}$ is symmetric for the case when $\mathtt{flag} \Mapsto \mathbf{false}$. Here we use $R \oplus \mathsf{Id}$ (defined in Fig. 8) to describe the action of **trylin**. It means, after the action we will keep the original state as well as the new state resulting from R as possible speculations. Also, in $\mathsf{TrylinSucc}$ and $\mathsf{TrylinFail}$, the current thread is allowed to help execute the abstract CCAS of some thread t.

The subtle part in the proof is to ensure that, no thread could cheat by imagining another thread's help. In any program point of CCAS, the environment may have done **trylin** and helped the operation. But whether the environment has helped it or not, the **commit** at line 15 or 17 cannot fail. This means, we should not confuse the two kinds of nondeterminism caused by speculation and by environment interference. The former allows us to discard wrong guesses, while for the latter, we should consider *all* possible environments (including none).

7. Related Work and Conclusion

In addition to the work mentioned in Sec. 1 and 2, there is a large body of work on linearizability verification. Here we only discuss the most closely related work that can handle non-fixed LPs.

Our logic is similar to Vafeiadis' extension of RGSep to prove linearizability [32]. He also uses abstract objects and abstract atomic operations as auxiliary variables and code. There are two key differences between the logics. First he uses prophecy variables to handle future-dependent LPs, but there has been no satisfactory semantics given for prophecy variables so far. We use the simple try-commit mechanism, whose semantics is straightforward. Second the soundness of his logic *w.r.t.* linearizability is not specified and proved. We address this problem by defining a new thread-local simulation as the meta-theory of our logic. As we explained in Sec. 2, defining such a simulation to support non-fixed LPs is one of the most challenging issues we have to solve. Although recently Vafeiadis develops an automatic verification tool [33] with formal soundness for linearizability, his new work can handle non-fixed LPs for *read-only* methods only, and cannot verify algorithms like HSY stack, CCAS and RDCSS in our paper.

Recently, Turon *et al.* [31] propose logical relations to verify fine-grained concurrency, which establish contextual refinement between the library and the specification. Underlying the model a similar simulation is defined. Our pending thread pool is proposed concurrently with their "spec thread pool", while the speculation idea in our simulation is borrowed from their work, which traces back to forward-backward simulation [21]. What is new here is a new program logic and the way we instrument code to do relational reasoning. The set of syntactic rules, including the try-commit mechanism to handle uncertainty, is much easier to use than the semantic logical relations to construct proofs. On the other hand, they support higher-order features, recursive types and polymorphism, while we focus on concurrency reasoning and use only a simple first-order language.

O'Hearn *et al.* [25] prove linearizability of an optimistic variant of the lazy set algorithm by identifying the "Hindsight" property of the algorithm. Their Hindsight Lemma provides a *non-constructive* evidence for linearizability. Although Hindsight can capture the insights of the set algorithm, it remains an open problem whether the Hindsight-like lemmas exist for other concurrent algorithms.

Colvin *et al.* [3] formally verify the lazy set algorithm using a combination of forward and backward simulations between automata. Their simulations are not thread-local, where they need to know the program counters of all threads. Besides, their simulations are specifically constructed for the lazy set only, while ours is more general in that it can be satisfied by various algorithms.

The simulations defined by Derrick *et al.* [4] are thread-local and general, but they require the operations with non-fixed LPs to be read-only, thus cannot handle the CCAS example. They also propose a backward simulation to verify linearizability [28]. Although the method is proved to be complete, it does not support thread-local verification and there is no program logic given.

Elmas *et al.* [7] prove linearizability by incrementally *rewriting* the fine-grained code to the atomic operation. They do not need to locate LPs. Their rules are based on left/right movers and program refinements, but not for Hoare-style reasoning as in our work.

There are also lots of model-checking based tools (*e.g.*, [20, 34]) for *checking* linearizability. For example, Vechev *et al.* [34] check linearizability with user-specified non-fixed LPs. Their method is not thread modular. To handle non-fixed LPs, they need users to instrument the code with enough information about the actions of other threads, which usually demands a priori knowledge about the number of threads running in parallel, as shown in their example. Besides, although their checker can detect un-linearizable code, it will not terminate for linearizable methods in general.

Conclusion. We propose a new program logic to verify linearizability of algorithms with non-fixed LPs. The logic extends LRG [8] with new rules for the auxiliary commands introduced specifically for linearizability proof. We also give a relational interpretation of asssertions and rely/guarantee conditions to relate concrete implementations with the corresponding abstract operations. Underlying the logic is a new thread-local simulation, which gives us contextual refinement. Linearizability is derived based on its equivalence to refinement. Both the logic and the simulation support reasoning about the helping mechanism and future-dependent LPs. As shown in Table 1, we have applied the logic to verify various classic algorithms.

Acknowledgments

We would like to thank Matthew Parkinson, Zhong Shao, Jan Hoffmann and anonymous referees for their suggestions and comments on earlier versions of this paper. This work is supported in part by grants from National Natural Science Foundation of China (NSFC) under Grant No. 61073040 and 61229201, the National Hi-Tech Research and Development Program of China (Grant No. 2012AA010901), and Program for New Century Excellent Talents in Universities (Grant No. NCET-2010-0984). Part of the work is done during Hongjin Liang's visit to Yale University in 2012-2013, which is supported by China Scholarship Council.

References

[1] M. Abadi and L. Lamport. The existence of refinement mappings. *Theor. Comput. Sci.*, 82(2):253–284, 1991.

[2] D. Amit, N. Rinetzky, T. Reps, M. Sagiv, and E. Yahav. Comparison under abstraction for verifying linearizability. In *CAV'07*.

[3] R. Colvin, L. Groves, V. Luchangco, and M. Moir. Formal verification of a lazy concurrent list-based set algorithm. In *CAV'06*.

[4] J. Derrick, G. Schellhorn, and H. Wehrheim. Verifying linearisability with potential linearisation points. In *FM'11*.

[5] J. Derrick, G. Schellhorn, and H. Wehrheim. Mechanically verified proof obligations for linearizability. *ACM TOPLAS*, 33(1):4, 2011.

[6] S. Doherty, L. Groves, V. Luchangco, and M. Moir. Formal verification of a practical lock-free queue algorithm. In *FORTE'04*.

[7] T. Elmas, S. Qadeer, A. Sezgin, O. Subasi, and S. Tasiran. Simplifying linearizability proofs with reduction and abstraction. In *TACAS'10*.

[8] X. Feng. Local rely-guarantee reasoning. In *POPL'09*.

[9] I. Filipović, P. O'Hearn, N. Rinetzky, and H. Yang. Abstraction for concurrent objects. *Theor. Comput. Sci.*, 2010.

[10] A. Gotsman and H. Yang. Linearizability with ownership transfer. In *CONCUR'12*.

[11] T. L. Harris. A pragmatic implementation of non-blocking linked-lists. In *DISC'01*.

[12] T. L. Harris, K. Fraser, and I. A. Pratt. A practical multi-word compare-and-swap operation. In *DISC'02*.

[13] S. Heller, M. Herlihy, V. Luchangco, M. Moir, W. N. S. III, and N. Shavit. A lazy concurrent list-based set algorithm. In *OPODIS'05*.

[14] D. Hendler, N. Shavit, and L. Yerushalmi. A scalable lock-free stack algorithm. In *SPAA'04*.

[15] M. Herlihy and N. Shavit. *The Art of Multiprocessor Programming*. Morgan Kaufmann, Apr. 2008.

[16] M. Herlihy and J. Wing. Linearizability: a correctness condition for concurrent objects. *ACM TOPLAS*, 12(3):463–492, 1990.

[17] C. B. Jones. Tentative steps toward a development method for interfering programs. *ACM TOPLAS*, 5(4):596–619, 1983.

[18] H. Liang and X. Feng. Modular verification of linearizability with non-fixed linearization points. Technical report, USTC, March 2013. `http://kyhcs.ustcsz.edu.cn/relconcur/lin`.

[19] H. Liang, X. Feng, and M. Fu. A rely-guarantee-based simulation for verifying concurrent program transformations. In *POPL'12*.

[20] Y. Liu, W. Chen, Y. A. Liu, and J. Sun. Model checking linearizability via refinement. In *FM'09*.

[21] N. A. Lynch and F. W. Vaandrager. Forward and backward simulations: I. untimed systems. *Inf. Comput.*, 121(2):214–233, 1995.

[22] M. M. Michael. High performance dynamic lock-free hash tables and list-based sets. In *SPAA'02*.

[23] M. M. Michael and M. L. Scott. Simple, fast, and practical non-blocking and blocking concurrent queue algorithms. In *PODC'96*.

[24] P. W. O'Hearn. Resources, concurrency, and local reasoning. *Theor. Comput. Sci.*, 375(1-3):271–307, 2007.

[25] P. W. O'Hearn, N. Rinetzky, M. T. Vechev, E. Yahav, and G. Yorsh. Verifying linearizability with hindsight. In *PODC'10*, .

[26] P. W. O'Hearn, H. Yang, and J. C. Reynolds. Separation and information hiding. In *POPL'04*, .

[27] S. Qadeer, A. Sezgin, and S. Tasiran. Back and forth: Prophecy variables for static verification of concurrent programs. Tech Report.

[28] G. Schellhorn, H. Wehrheim, and J. Derrick. How to prove algorithms linearisable. In *CAV'12*.

[29] R. K. Treiber. System programming: coping with parallelism. Technical Report RJ 5118, IBM Almaden Research Center, 1986.

[30] A. Turon and M. Wand. A separation logic for refining concurrent objects. In *POPL'11*.

[31] A. Turon, J. Thamsborg, A. Ahmed, L. Birkedal, and D. Dreyer. Logical relations for fine-grained concurrency. In *POPL'13*.

[32] V. Vafeiadis. Modular fine-grained concurrency verification. Thesis.

[33] V. Vafeiadis. Automatically proving linearizability. In *CAV*, 2010.

[34] M. T. Vechev, E. Yahav, and G. Yorsh. Experience with model checking linearizability. In *SPIN'09*.

Translation Validation for a Verified OS Kernel

Thomas Sewell
NICTA & UNSW, Sydney, Australia
thomas.sewell@nicta.com.au

Magnus Myreen
Cambridge University, UK
magnus.myreen@cl.cam.ac.uk

Gerwin Klein
NICTA & UNSW, Sydney, Australia
gerwin.klein@nicta.com.au

Abstract

We extend the existing formal verification of the seL4 operating system microkernel from 9 500 lines of C source code to the binary level. We handle all functions that were part of the previous verification. Like the original verification, we currently omit the assembly routines and volatile accesses used to control system hardware.

More generally, we present an approach for proving refinement between the formal semantics of a program on the C source level and its formal semantics on the binary level, thus checking the validity of compilation, including some optimisations, and linking, and extending static properties proved of the source code to the executable. We make use of recent improvements in SMT solvers to almost fully automate this process.

We handle binaries generated by unmodified gcc 4.5.1 at optimisation level 1, and can handle most of seL4 even at optimisation level 2.

Categories and Subject Descriptors D.4.5 [*Operating Systems*]: Reliability—Verification; D.2.4 [*Software Engineering*]: Software/Program Verification

General Terms Verification, Languages

Keywords Binary Verification, seL4, Microkernel

1. Introduction

Our aim is to extend one of the largest formal verifications, that of the seL4 microkernel by Klein et al [11], from around 9 500 lines of C source code down to 11 736 instructions on the binary level.

Recent successes in the formal verification of sizeable programs at the implementation level, such as the CompCert C compiler [14], the Verisoft project [1], or the above mentioned seL4 microkernel [11], suggest that formal verification of small, high-importance software systems is feasible and may become more common in the future. Unfortunately such software systems tend to be written in old, low-level, but high-performance languages like C whose standards are difficult to formalise, are by necessity purposely violated by systems programmers, and are rarely implemented precisely by their toolchains. This leaves the prospective verifier with a difficult choice. Clean-room designs of modern low-level systems languages are an attractive research topic, but tend to come with pragmatic limitations, such as requiring garbage collection for type safety. The alternative is to proceed with the best available semantic model of the implementation language and program and hope that any compiler defect or difference between the compiler's and the verifier's interpretation can be found by testing or other means.

In their study on compiler testing, Yang et al reported 325 previously unknown defects in 11 different C compilers [34]. Even the formally verified CompCert was found to exhibit 5 defects, albeit in its unverified front-end only—it was the only compiler Yang et al did not manage to break in its code generation phase, despite devoting significant resources to the task. We have used this verified compiler on the verified C source of the seL4 microkernel, but in this case found the result unsatisfactory: There is a remaining chance of a mismatch between CompCert's interpretation of the C standard in the theorem prover Coq and the interpretation of the C standard the seL4 verification uses [32] in the theorem prover Isabelle/HOL [21], esp. in cases where the standard is purposely violated to implement machine-dependent, low-level operating system (OS) functionality. Reconciling these two semantics is non-trivial. Firstly the logics of Coq and Isabelle/HOL are not directly compatible. Secondly, since the seL4 semantics is largely shallowly embedded, an equivalence proof would have to be performed for each program, similar to our more direct method below.

In this paper we present a hybrid approach, in which we take precisely the semantics for that specific program (seL4) produced by Norrish's C parser [32] for Isabelle/HOL as used in the seL4 verification. We then produce a model of the compiled binary of this program, extending the approach of Myreen [17, 18] in the HOL4 theorem prover [29], and we check the soundness of this extracted model against the strongly validated Cambridge semantics for the ARM architecture [8]. Finally we use an SMT-based proof process to establish that the compiled binary matches the expected semantics of the C source. Formally, we prove that the binary is a refinement of the stated C source semantics. This property composes with the existing functional correctness proof of seL4.

Our method eliminates one of the Achilles' heels of the verified compiler approach: the parser and lexer for concrete C syntax. Since the high-level functional verification and the binary verification connect to precisely the same formal artefact, the output of the now untrusted C parser, the method by which we arrive at this artefact is irrelevant. Instead, this trust is replaced by trust in the binary verification tool and into the import of an executable file into hexadecimal numbers into the theorem prover HOL4.

In fact, it is not even important any more that the compiler conforms to the C standard, or that the C semantics in the theorem prover agrees with the C standard. All that matters is that compiler and prover semantics match and thereby transport high-level properties that have been proved on the C code down to the binary level. For seL4, this includes functional correctness, integrity, authority confinement, and non-interference [11, 15, 28].

We provide a full proof of correctness of the compilation by standard gcc 4.5.1 of all previously formally verified functions [11] in seL4 at optimisation level 1. We additionally produce proofs for all of seL4's unverified initialisation functions except for 3 nested loops. At optimisation level 2, which is the standard high-performance setting for seL4, we are able to automatically extract a model for all but four assembly routines (i.e. coverage of 98 %) and produce proofs of correctness for the vast majority of loop-free functions. Using optimisation level 1 rather than 2 incurs a performance cost of 15-20% depending on the system call.

Like the original seL4 verification, we do not handle the assembly routines and volatile accesses used to directly control the system hardware.

The verification strategy is to first build a representation of both the C program and the binary within a single restricted intermediate language. This language consists of simple control flow mechanisms and standard arithmetic operations which are common to the C language, CPU instruction sets and the SMT bit-vector theory. It is thus highly amenable to analysis by SMT solvers. To prove our refinement statement, we extract SMT formulas with consideration towards program loops as well as proof obligations and assumptions arising from the decompilation process and C semantics.

While our main target was extending the seL4 verification to the binary level, we believe that this approach generalises to other C verifications and to other compilers. We have for instance started experimenting with extending the decompilation phase to the output of CompCert. While there are still a number of limitations to overcome that we discuss in Section 4, we believe this work represents evidence for a general, flexible method of extending formal reasoning about C programs to the binary level using standard off-the-shelf compilers.

In the remainder of this paper, we first summarise the pieces of previous work we build on in Section 2, before describing the conversions and proof process in Section 3. Section 4 evaluates the performance and limitations of our verification method in more detail. We discuss related binary verification approaches in Section 5.

2. Background

In this section, we describe previous background work our binary verification of seL4 builds on. In particular, these are existing proofs on seL4 [11] together with its C semantics [32], and existing work on decompilation [17] and its validated ARM semantics [8].

2.1 The seL4 microkernel verification

The seL4 kernel is a general-purpose OS microkernel measuring about 9 500 source lines of C code[1] and 600 lines of assembly code. As usual for microkernels, it provides a minimal set of mechanisms, including threads, interrupts, virtual memory, and inter-process communication. Less usual is its capability-based mandatory access control model and explicitly user-controlled, but kernel-enforced memory allocation mechanism. It can be configured as a classical microkernel, as a hypervisor running Linux instances, or as a high-assurance pure separation kernel.

What makes this kernel special is that its functional correctness has been verified over multiple levels by formal refinement from an abstract specification down to the C source code level [11], and that further properties have been established over that specification [28]. It represents a large body of existing work, with over 200 000 lines of Isabelle/HOL proof, that our approach has to interface to if it is to extend this verification to the binary level.

Figure 1 illustrates the existing verification stack on top and our new work interfacing with it on the bottom. The existing work starts with high-level properties on top, abstract functional specification next, design-level specification further down, and the semantic C source code level at the bottom. Our work extends this stack by the semantic description of the binary, thereby removing compiler

[1] Klein et al report 8 700 lines [11]. We are basing our work on a newer version of seL4 that supports further API features.

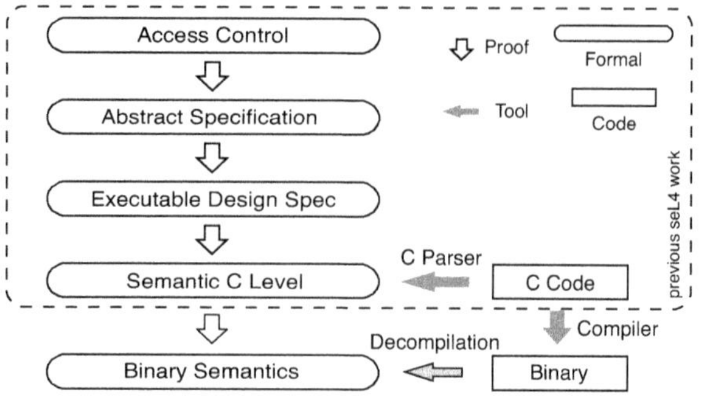

Figure 1. Existing seL4 verification stack.

and Isabelle/HOL C parser from the trust chain of the proof and replacing it with the ARM semantics and our tool set.

The kernel exists for multiple architectures, among them Intel x86 (unverified) and ARMv6/ARMv7 (verified). It is available as a commercial product under the name OKL4:verified and for free download for academic use [22].

Apart from its manageable size, key seL4 features for verifiability were that, as usual for microkernels, almost all device drivers and therefore most hardware interaction is outside the kernel in user-space, and the fact that seL4 is an event-based kernel for a uni-processor setting. This means, interrupts are switched off for most kernel operations. For long-running operations, seL4 contains specific preemption points where it explicitly checks for interrupts. This allows the verification to proceed on a sequential language model where the explicit coarse-grained preemption points are normal kernel exits. This is important, both for the C semantics used in the original verification as well as for the ARM semantics used in the binary decompilation work we build on.

As illustrated in Figure 1, the bottom level of the existing verification work is a semantic Isabelle/HOL model of the C source code of seL4, generated automatically by Norrish's C parser [32]. This parser instantiates a generic language framework for imperative languages by Schirmer [27], consisting of a generic operational semantics framework with a Hoare-logic and verification condition generator on top, which are proved sound and relatively complete in Isabelle/HOL. This instantiation covers a large subset of standard C99 [10] extended with architecture and compiler-specific assumptions, for instance about endianness and data layout, that systems programmers have to make. Its largest limitation is that it does not permit taking the address of local variables. This enables the C model to treat parameters and local variables on the stack separately from the pointer-addressable heap, thereby simplifying verification. This limitation could be lifted in future work at the expense of having to invest more explicit reasoning about this separation in C source-level verifications.

The memory model this parser uses in its semantic C embedding is due to Tuch [31, 32]. Its main feature is that it provides abstract C types and comparatively convenient type-based reasoning on top of a precise, byte-wise memory model that formalises the C heap merely as a function from 32-bit words to 8-bit words. Type information is kept as a so-called *heap type description* in ghost state for verification convenience, and Isabelle/HOL type classes establish abstractions on top. At the rare occasions where kernel code breaks type safety, such as memory allocation, reasoning can fall back to the explicit byte level. This model enables high-level reasoning in the existing verification, and is also compatible with the binary level in this work.

2.2 Decompilation from ARM into Higher-Order Logic

In this paper, we present how we proved seL4 correct down to the concrete ARM machine code that gcc produces. In order to reason formally about ARM machine code we require a semantics for this machine code, i.e. a formal specification of the ARM instruction set architecture (ISA). For this purpose, we build on the Cambridge ARM ISA specification [8] and proof tools, namely a proof-producing decompiler, which makes reasoning about such complex ISA specifications tractable.

The Cambridge ARM specification has evolved from a string of ARM related projects that started in 2000 with a hardware verification project where Fox formally specified the ARM ISA version 3 and proved, using the HOL4 theorem prover [29], that a hardware implementation (the ARM6) implements its ISA correctly. Later, the project's focus shifted to software verification: the ARM model was updated and extended to cover all modern versions of the ARM ISA, namely versions 4–7 including all operation modes and every instruction. Since the latest model is no longer directly connected via proof to modern hardware implementations, Fox and Myreen have extensively validated the latest specification against different real hardware implementations [8]. This latest ARM specification is the most comprehensive formal specification of a commercial ISA that is publicly available.

Due to its history, the Cambridge ARM specification is highly trustworthy, lengthy and very detailed. Reasoning manually in a theorem prover about such models is hopelessly tedious. For this reason, Myreen et al. developed automation that makes machine-code verification tractable even for very complex ISA specifications. The main tool is called a *decompiler*. This tool aids program verification by extracting a piece of the lengthy model, given a program to interpret the model on. More specifically, given a snippet of machine code, this decompiler extract a function describing the effect of running the code on the ISA specification. Loops in the machine code turn into recursion in the extracted functions. The decompiler is automatic and proof producing: for each run, the decompiler proves that the extracted function is indeed accurate w.r.t. the given code and the ISA specification. Myreen [16] has shown that decompilation can be used for verification of sizeable case studies, e.g. garbage collectors and Lisp implementations. This paper builds on decompilation, extends it and shows that it can be used in the verification of the seL4 microkernel.

3. Correctness Proof

This section describes our refinement approach between C source semantics and binary code.

The verification process involves a collection of representations of the input program which are outlined in Figure 2. The two inputs into the process are the C program and binary ELF file on the top of Figure 2. The three dotted boxes in the diagram represent the three main proof systems used in the binary verification: the interactive LCF-style provers Isabelle/HOL and HOL4, and our SMT-based proof tool that is centred around a common intermediate language describing control-flow graphs. On the left of the diagram, the C program is parsed into the theorem prover Isabelle/HOL using existing tools [32], and then transformed into a form closer to binary code. The first such transformation step is within Isabelle/HOL, the second in our external tool. On the right of Figure 2, the binary program is decompiled into HOL4, using the existing validated Cambridge ARM semantics [8]. Since the logics of the two theorem provers are almost identical, these can be translated into Isabelle/HOL in a straightforward way to be exported to the intermediate graph language. Once the C program and binary have both been represented in the common graph language, on the bottom of the diagram, refinement between them can be proven with the assistance of the two SMT solvers Z3 [7] and SONOLAR [23].

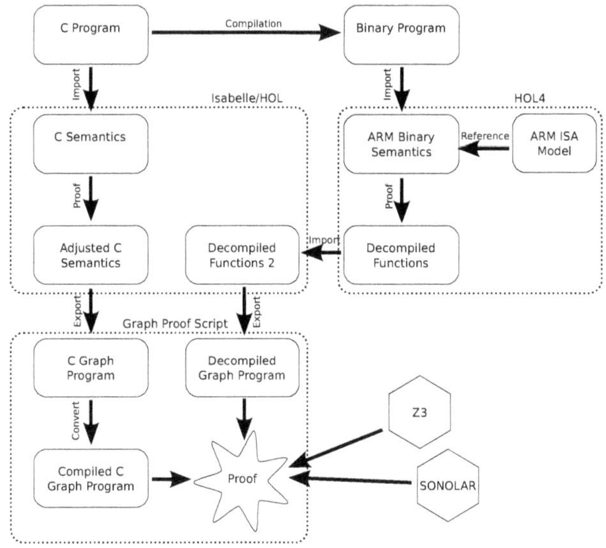

Figure 2. Artefacts in the correctness proof

The following subsections present each of these steps in more detail.

The SMT-based proof tool and some of the relevant Isabelle theories are available from `http://www.ssrg.nicta.com.au/software/TS/graph-refine/`.

3.1 Conversion from C Semantics to the Graph Language

This subsection describes the pseudo-compilation process which converts functions in the C model into the intermediate graph language. This also serves as an introduction to the graph language.

The idea of the graph conversion is to replace the language based control flow rules with a simpler control flow graph. An example conversion is given in Figure 3. All statements are numbered, and the steps between them become graph edges, giving us a labelled, directed graph. The point of doing this is that the context-dependent effects of `break`, `continue` and others are replaced by graph edges which simply specify the number of the next statement. The special label `Ret` represents return from the function.

The graph consists of three types of nodes. Conditional nodes are used to pick between execution paths, and correspond closely to decisions made by `if` and `while` statements in C. Basic nodes represent normal statements, and update the value of some variable with the result of some calculation (memory is represented as a variable). Call nodes are used to represent function calls, which are distinguished from other statements. A number of restrictions enforced by the C parser are relevant here: function calls may be embedded in other expressions and statements only in very limited ways, statements with multiple effects are forbidden, and switch statements must always be convertible into a chain of if-else statements.

The conversion also pseudo-compiles all C expressions. An example is on the right hand side of Figure 3. Insofar as C can be seen as a portable assembler, the conversion makes this explicit. Pointers become 32-bit words, with address operations of various kinds becoming explicit arithmetic. Local variables of structure and array type are replaced by collections of local variables representing their fields. Assignments of structure type are expanded into a sequence of assignments for each field. Reads and writes of global variables become reads and writes of memory, at symbolic addresses which

```
  struct node *
  find (struct tree *t, int k) {
1   struct node *p = t->trunk;
2   while (p) {
3     if (p->key == k)
4       return p;
5     else if (p->key < k)
6       p = p->right;
      else
7       p = p->left;
    }
8   return NULL;
  }
```

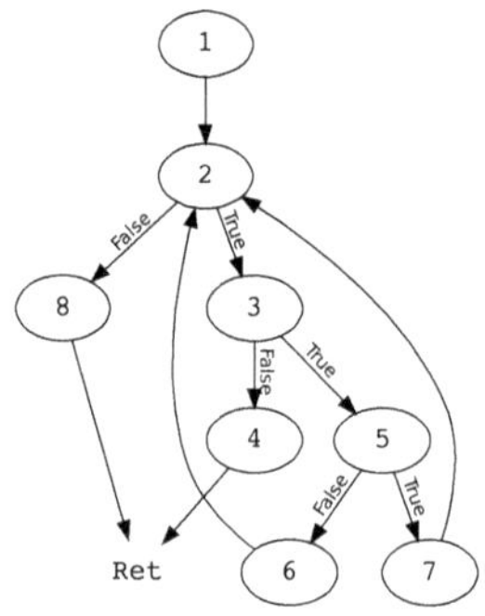


```
1: p := Mem[t + 4];

2: p == 0 ?

8: ret := 0
3: Mem[p] == k ?

4: ret := p;
5: Mem[p] < k ?

6: p := Mem[p + 4];
7: p := Mem[p + 8];
```

Figure 3. Example Conversion of Structure and Statements to Graph Language

are later instantiated by reading the ELF symbol table. The expressions that remain are entirely machine compatible: operations such as 32-bit addition and multiplication, left and right shifts, signed and unsigned less-than, and finally memory access and update of 32-bit and 8-bit values.

It is a theorem of the Tuch memory semantics [31] that memory writes of aggregate types are equivalent to sequences of writes of their fields, assuming the aggregate type contains no padding. Padding creates a number of headaches for us, and so for the purposes of this work we have adjusted the seL4 source to ensure that all structures of interest are packed (see Section 4.3).

The complication is that C is not merely a portable assembler. The C standard mandates a number of restrictions on the way various operations may be used, and some of these restrictions go beyond the scope of machine operations. One simple restriction is that arithmetic on signed operands may not overflow, and another is that dereferenced pointers must be aligned and nonzero. To ensure the standard is followed, the parser inserts a number of `Guard` statements into its output, which allow execution to continue only if some condition is met. The conditions become verification obligations in the existing verification work.

These guard statements are translated into condition nodes with one of the outbound edges pointing to the special label `Err`. Given that the guard conditions have all been established from the invariants in previous work, it will become an input assumption to the current work that these paths to `Err` are never taken. These guards were omitted from Figure 3 — there ought to be condition nodes immediately before all memory-using nodes which check pointer validity.

The key restriction from the C standard that cannot be realised in machine operations is the strict-aliasing rule. This allows the compiler to assume that a given memory address is not in use with two different incompatible types. In systems code, programmers occasionally break this assumption (see also Section 4.4), but most code conforms to it. Since optimisations frequently make use of the rule, we need to make the information it conveys available at the points where it does hold. To do this, we strengthened the checks made in the C parser output against the heap type description, a global variable which tracks the expected type of memory. The graph conversion then includes the heap type description and checks in its output. The stronger checks are of the form pvalid $htd\ \tau\ p$ for some heap type description htd, C type τ and pointer value p. The expected non-aliasing conditions are theorems of the Tuch memory model [31], for instance this rule about ints and floats:

$$\frac{\text{pvalid } htd \text{ int } p \quad \text{pvalid } htd' \text{ float } p}{\{x \mid p \le x < p+4\} \cap \{x \mid p' \le x < p'+4\} = \{\}}$$

The semantics of the graph language are straightforward to formalise in Isabelle/HOL or HOL4. The node types are introduced as datatype constructors `Basic`, `Cond` and `Call`. A single step starting from a `Basic` node updates local variables, and starting from a `Cond` node decides between two possible successor labels. The `Call` nodes create a new stack frame, with a new graph and new local variables, and steps from the `Ret` and `Err` labels fold the current stack frame into the previous one. The semantics of execution are given by the transitive closure of this single-step relation. Given this formal semantics, we have proven, in Isabelle/HOL, that the converted functions in the graph language refine the original C semantics. The details of this formalisation and proof are elided here, and are largely technical.

3.2 Decompiling Compiler Output into Logic

The next piece of the puzzle is the right-hand side of Figure 2, i.e. how we take binaries the compilers (recent versions of standard unmodified gcc) produce, decompile these binaries into functions, which we, in turn, translate into the graph language described above. By *decompilation* we mean proof-producing extraction of functional programs from concrete binaries. Here we build on previous work on such decompilation [17, 18], but in this text we do not assume any prior knowledge of the previous work. Instead, we use a few examples below to demonstrate what decompilation provides and what we had to alter in Myreen's original decompilation approach to make the decompiler's output better compatible with the C semantics to which the left-hand side of the Figure 2 connects the decompiler's output.

3.2.1 Simple Decompilation Example

To get a flavour of what decompilation provides, consider the following simple C function for taking the average of two integers.

```
uint avg (uint i, uint j) {
  return (i + j) / 2;
}
```

When compiled with gcc, this C code is translated into an ARM binary (an ELF file). Applying relevant `objdump` tools to the binary, one can produce a text file showing the generated ARM machine code (on the left below) and ARM assembly code (in the centre).

```
<avg>:
e0810000     add r0, r1, r0     // add r1 to r0
e1a000a0     lsr r0, r0, #1     // shift r0 right
e12fff1e     bx  lr             // return
```

To decompile the generated machine code, one simply provides the hex codes on the left to the decompiler together with the signature of the C function. The decompiler extracts from the machine code a function in logic that describes the state update the machine code performs. The machine code above is converted into the following logic function. Note that here, r_0 and r_1 are 32-bit integers and arithmetic + is over 32-bit integers (overflow wraps around).

$$\begin{array}{lcl}\mathsf{avg}\ (r_0, r_1) & = & \mathsf{let}\ r_0 = r_1 + r_0\ \mathsf{in} \\ & & \mathsf{let}\ r_0 = r_0 \ggg 1\ \mathsf{in} \\ & & \ r_0\end{array}$$

The decompiler also automatically proves a *certificate* theorem: a theorem relating the extracted function avg with the original machine code. These certificate theorems are stated in terms of a total-correctness Hoare logic with triples $\{pre\}code\{post\}$ for machine code. They are defined and proved in terms of the underlying specification of the ARM instruction set architecture [8]. Precise details on their definition be found elsewhere [16]. Informally, the following Hoare triple can be read to say: if the program counter p points to the start of the machine code and r_0, r_1 and lr hold initial values of registers 0, 1 and 14 respectively, then execution will reach a state where the postcondition is true, i.e. a state where the value of register 0 is described by avg (r_0, r_1) and the program counter is set to the return address lr. Informally, read $*$ below as 'and', formally this is a separating conjunction from separation logic [25] but here used to separate between any machine code resources [16].

$$\{\,\mathsf{R0}\ r_0 * \mathsf{R1}\ r_1 * \mathsf{R14}\ lr * \mathsf{PC}\ p\,\}$$
$$p : \mathtt{e0810000\ e1a000a0\ e12fff1e}$$
$$\{\,\mathsf{R0}\ (\mathsf{avg}\ (r_0, r_1)) * \mathsf{R1}\ \_ * \mathsf{R14}\ \_ * \mathsf{PC}\ lr\,\}$$

The benefit of decompilation is that the extracted functions provide a convenient abstraction of the machine code from which it is much more tractable to perform further proofs. Further proofs need only deal with the extracted function because the certificate theorem states that the behaviour of the extracted functions and the original machine code agree according to the specification of the instruction set architecture.

How is this form of proof-producing decompilation implemented in a theorem prover? The original approach does not use any heuristics and blindly follows the following steps:

1. For each instruction in the machine code, evaluate the specification of the instruction set architecture and prove a machine-code Hoare triple describing the effect of each instruction.
2. Construct a control-flow graph (CFG) based on these Hoare triples. Split the code into separate decompilation rounds, e.g. one round for each (nested) loop.
3. For each decompilation round:
   (a) Compose the Hoare triples for each path through the code segment, merge these Hoare triples to produce a single Hoare triple describing this code segment.
   (b) If there is a jump to one of the entry points, then apply a special loop rule which introduces a tail-recursive function,
   (c) The result is a theorem stated as a Hoare triple. Its postcondition mentions the effect of executing the code segment, expressed as a function applied to the initial values. We read off this function from the postcondition and return both the (certificate) theorem and the extracted function.

This form of decompilation is described in detail elsewhere [16] and has recently been extended [18] to also allow arbitrary use of code pointers, which the original approach struggled to handle.

3.2.2 C-Compatible (Stack Aware) Decompilation

Decompilation as outlined above can effectively extract functions from machine code. However, the functions the decompilation produces are not immediately compatible with the C semantics which we target. An extension of the avg example from above illustrates what goes wrong. Consider the following C function which takes eight integers as input and calculates their average.

```
uint avg8 (uint i1, i2, i3, i4, i5, i6, i7, i8) {
  return (i1+i2+i3+i4+i5+i6+i7+i8) / 2;
}
```

When this is compiled, gcc produces the following ARM assembly. Note that arguments i5-i8 are passed on the stack. Hence the memory load instructions ldr and ldm.

```
<avg8>:
e0811000    add r1, r1, r0
e0811002    add r1, r1, r2
e59d2000    ldr r2, [sp]         // load
e0811003    add r1, r1, r3
e0810002    add r0, r1, r2
e99d000c    ldmib sp, {r2, r3}  // load
e0800002    add r0, r0, r2
e0800003    add r0, r0, r3
e59d300c    ldr r3, [sp, #12]   // load
e0800003    add r0, r0, r3
e1a001a0    lsr r0, r0, #3
e12fff1e    bx   lr
```

The original decompiler knew nothing about how C uses the stack and thus treats the stack accesses as ordinary memory accesses. This results in extracted functions where stack accesses touch memory explicitly, e.g. the last load from above turns into a line:

$$\ldots\ \mathsf{let}\ r_3 = m(r_{13} + 12)\ \mathsf{in}\ \ldots$$

This fits very badly with the C semantics for which this spilling into the stack is completely hidden. The C semantics we use treats all local variables as simple 'register' variables, i.e. according to the C semantics avg8 does not make any memory accesses.

To remedy this mismatch, we made the decompiler aware of the stack and the C calling convention for ARM. We made the decompiler treat the stack as a separate datastructure. We formalised a new separation-logic inspired stack assertion

$$\mathsf{stack}\ sp\ n\ stack$$

which is true if the stack pointer (register 13) holds a value sp such that the list of elements $stack$ are on the stack and there is space for n elements above the stack pointer, i.e. n elements can safely be pushed onto the stack. We can keep this datastructure separate from the rest of memory by proving pre/postconditions where the 'heap' memory is separate from the stack using the separating conjunction $*$ from separation logic [16, 25].

$$\mathsf{stack}\ sp\ n\ stack * \mathsf{memory}\ m$$

The altered decompiler now has a new *stack simulation* phase which attempts to discover where and how the stack pointer can travel through the code, i.e. it attempts to identify which instructions access the stack and what offsets are used, i.e. which stack elements are accessed. This phase comes immediately after CFG exploration (i.e. step 2 of the original algorithm).

When run on the simple avg8 example, this stack heuristic finds that all the load instructions are stack accesses. For each of the stack accesses, it derives a new Hoare triple stated in terms of the stack assertion. For example, the last load in the example above is described by the following Hoare triple. Here :: is list cons.

$$\{\,\mathsf{R3}\ r_3 * \mathsf{stack}\ sp\ n\ (s_0{::}s_1{::}s_2{::}s_3{::}ss) * \mathsf{PC}\ p\,\}$$
$$p : \mathtt{e59d300c}$$
$$\{\,\mathsf{R3}\ s_3 * \mathsf{stack}\ sp\ n\ (s_0{::}s_1{::}s_2{::}s_3{::}ss) * \mathsf{PC}\ (p{+}4)\,\}$$

Given these Hoare triples stated in terms of stack, the rest of the decompiler runs just as before. The Hoare triple above turns into a let-expression of the following form:

$$\ldots\ \mathsf{let}\ r_3 = s_2\ \mathsf{in}\ \ldots$$

With the stack-aware decompiling, the entire code for avg8 turns into the following function which does not mention memory. We have expanded the let-expressions for brevity below.

$$\mathsf{avg8}\ (r_0, r_1, r_2, r_3, s_0, s_1, s_2, s_3) = \\ (r_1 + r_0 + r_2 + r_3 + s_0 + s_1 + s_2 + s_3) >>> 3$$

The generated certificate theorem is stated in terms of the stack assertion. For avg8, this theorem is:

$$\{\mathsf{R0}\ r_0 * \mathsf{R1}\ r_1 * \ldots * \mathsf{stack}\ sp\ n\ (s_0{::}s_1{::}s_2{::}s_3{::}ss) * \mathsf{PC}\ p\}$$
$$p : \texttt{e0811000 e0811002 ... e12fff1e}$$
$$\{\mathsf{let}\ r_0 = \mathsf{avg8}\ (r_0, r_1, r_2, r_3, s_0, s_1, s_2, s_3)\ \mathsf{in}$$
$$\mathsf{R0}\ r_0 * \mathsf{R1}\ \_ * \ldots * \mathsf{stack}\ sp\ n\ (s_0{::}s_1{::}s_2{::}s_3{::}ss) * \mathsf{PC}\ lr\}$$

Care is taken to make these Hoare triples adhere exactly to the calling convention so that they can be used in future decompilations of code that call this function. Using this certificate theorem, we can decompile a call to avg8 into a let-expression of the following form in the decompilation of a caller.

$$\ldots\ \mathsf{let}\ r_0 = \mathsf{avg8}\ (r_0, r_1, r_2, r_3, s_0, s_1, s_2, s_3)\ \mathsf{in}\ \ldots$$

Given that we do not allow C code to take the address of a local variable, this stack simulation is relatively straightforward to implement in practice, i.e. it is reasonably easy to automatically find which locations access the stack and which do not (even without use of any debug information). If we were to allow taking the address of a local variable, then this approach would fall apart very quickly as the distinction between memory and stack locations becomes blurred.

Having said that, there is one situation where the C compiler will produce code that passes an address of a stack location around, even if the C code does not seem to do so. This happens in cases where a function is to return a struct that does not fit into a single machine word, i.e. does not fit into a single register. When a function is to return a struct, it expects to get an address into the caller's stack space. This address points to a segment in the caller's part of the stack into which the callee is to write its result.

Our approach to dealing with the stack can manage this form of passing around of pointers into the stack. The solution is to initialise the stack heuristic appropriately. Instead of starting the stack heuristic off from a state where the caller's stack is an opaque untouchable part of state, we start it off with a slot for the return struct. If the result is n-words long, then we start the stack simulation from a stack which consists of an initial segment ss, the result slots $[t_1, t_2, \ldots, t_n]$ and finally the rest of the stack $stack$:

$$\mathsf{stack}\ sp\ n\ (ss +\!\!+ [t_1, t_2, \ldots, t_n] +\!\!+ stack)$$

We also assume (according to the calling convention) that register 0 holds, on entry to the function, the address of the first result slot in the stack, i.e. $sp + 4 \times \mathsf{length}\ ss$. With such an initialisation, we can deal with the case of returning a struct directly into the stack. The rest of the decompiler runs exactly as before.

The new stack heuristic brings with it a number of new limitations, since the decompiler now tries to discover what the compiler did with the stack and prove that the stack is kept separate from the heap. Limitations are discussed in Section 4.2.

3.2.3 Converting Extracted Functions into Graph Format

The pure functions extracted here can be easily converted into the graph representation. An example is shown in Figure 4. We invent a collection of unique variable names for the input values (x and y in the example), the (anonymous) output values (we pick $r0$ and $r1$ in the example), and each variable fixed in a let expression (a, b and c). If-then-else expressions become condition nodes. Values, such as $(3, x)$, become updates to variables, in this case to a and b as set by the let expression they appear in. Let expressions control order of

```
f x y =
  let (a, b) = if x < y
    then (1, 2)
    else (3, x)
  in let c = a + b - y
  in (c, 0)
```

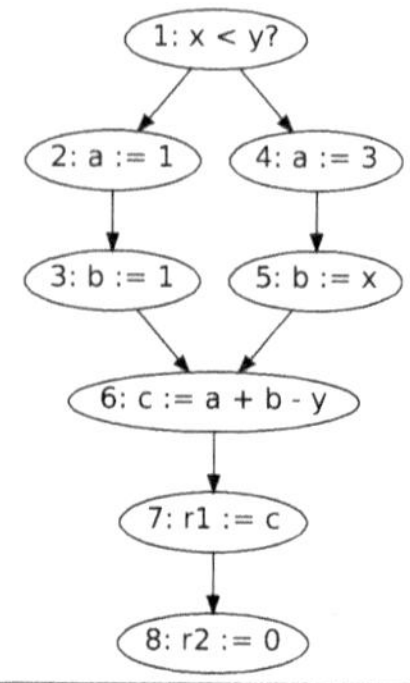

Figure 4. Example conversion of let-expression to graph

operations but create no nodes. Function calls become function call nodes. Tail recursion becomes a graph arc back to the beginning of the function.

This conversion is currently done automatically, but without proof of correctness. If more assurance is desired, the transformation could in future work be included on the Isabelle/HOL side of the tool and produce a corresponding certificate theorem.

3.3 Proof of Refinement

The final step in our process is the refinement proof, which we decompose function by function. We assume that we can treat other called functions as black boxes fully specified by their corresponding refinement theorem, with the calling convention giving us enough information to relate the C and binary behaviour. If the compiler makes use of inter-procedural analysis this may invalidate our assumption; we currently do not support this case. This compositional approach reduces our large code base to a series of manageable problems.

As recommended in Pnueli et al's original definition of translation validation [24], we divide the validation process into a search process and a checker, with the search process discovering a proof script which the checker then validates. This separation is partial, with the two processes sharing some code and the proof steps checked being far from minimal. The proof script consists of a problem space description together with a tree of proof rules `Restrict`, `Split` and `Leaf`. The rules give structure to the proof, but all the heavy lifting is done by converting proof goals on the problem space into SMT problems. We will describe these proof components as the proof checker sees them.

3.3.1 Inlining and The Problem Space

The first step in building a proof script is to establish a problem space, a shared graph namespace into which the binary and C bodies of the function of interest are copied. The problem space is free to be modified, in particular by inlining function calls. The search process attempts to inline sufficiently that the two function graphs in the problem space can be proven equivalent.

Inlining is done on the binary side of the problem whenever the called function does not match any C function, which may be because the compiler invented the function or modified its signature.

Inlining is done on the C side of the problem at any call site which is reachable and which calls a function name that does not appear on the binary side. This simple heuristic may fail in the presence of selective inlining. It could also potentially inline far too much source code in the case where a function designated pure or const was dropped because its result was ignored. This heuristic has, however, worked well at the optimisation levels we currently address.

This heuristic considers the C and binary functions completely separately, ignoring the relationship between them for now. This is a deliberate design decision allowing us to perform all inlining before any other analyses.

The problem space produced after inlining is included in the proof script, and the checker trusts that this problem space is derivable from the functions of interest. Checking that inlining was performed correctly did not seem worthwhile.

3.3.2 Conversion to SMT

The search and checker processes both use SMT solvers extensively to make judgements about the C and binary execution. These executions will form a sequence of visits to nodes in the problem space graph. The items of interest for a given node n will be the values of variables, should n be visited, at the point in execution that n is reached, and also the conditions under which n is reached. The final objective of the proof process is to reason about the values of returned variables should `Ret` be reached, and the conditions under which `Err` is reached.

These valuations and conditions can be represented in the SMT logic. Figure 5 shows nearly all of the steps of interest. The boxes show the path condition and variable values immediately before execution of each node. The function input variables are simply named, for instance x_i, and are unknowns in SMT. The path condition at the starting node, 1, is simply true. Basic nodes, such as 1 and 3, update the variable state with values taken from the existing variable state substituted into their expression, for instance, at node 1, $x+1$ is evaluated as x_i+1, and this is used to update the value of y. Condition nodes, such as 2, substitute their expression and add it to the path condition, such as the path condition at 3. When paths converge, such as at 4, the path condition to the node is the union of the conditions on each path, and the variable values are constructed using if-then-else expressions — if the path via 3 was taken, x has the value from 3, otherwise from 2.

Conveniently omitted from Figure 5 was the variable state after calling function f at 4. The return value is named, for instance z_after_4, and becomes another SMT unknown. The SMT conversion process notes the input and output values, and if any other call to f is made, adds SMT assertions that f will return the same values given the same inputs. If the two calls are on the C and binary side, the argument types may differ slightly, in which case the assertion takes into account the calling convention.

Figure 5 is inaccurate in that it is fully expanded. The expressions computed at nodes 1 and 2 would have been given names using SMTLIB2's definition feature, for instance $y\_after\_1 = x_i+1$, $cond\_at\_2 = y\_after\_1 < 3$. This reduces the syntactic expansion that already is seen at node 4.

This process does not handle loops, and the generalisation will be discussed in Section 3.3.4.

The values here are all encoded in the SMTLIB2 QF_ABV logic (quantifier-free formulae over arrays and bit-vectors). The variables and registers are all represented by 8-bit and 32-bit vectors. Memory is represented as an SMTLIB array, mapping 30-bit to 32-bit words. We find that this representation results in better SMT solver performance than the obvious 32-bit to 8-bit array, since it makes the most common operations—aligned 32-bit reads and writes—simple array operations, while the rarer 8-bit reads and writes become more complex.

Some values cannot be simply encoded, for instance the heap type description and pointer validity assertions described earlier. Workarounds for this are discussed in Section 3.3.6.

3.3.3 Simple Cases and the Leaf Rule

With the problem space established, and a process available for converting variable values and path conditions to SMT expressions, the proof checker explores the proof tree. The starting assumptions are that the input variables equate as specified by the calling convention, for example $x = r_0, y = r_1$ etc.

The main objective is to show that the output variables, those taken on the arcs to the `Ret` label, are equal as specified by the calling convention. It may be assumed in proving this that the path to the `Err` label is never taken on the C side. It must also be shown that the path to `Err` is never taken on the binary side.

The `Leaf` rule instructs the proof checker to attempt to prove these final goals immediately, by converting the values of variables at `Ret` and the path conditions to `Err` into SMT values and checking that the negation of the required propositions is unsatisfiable.

3.3.4 Path Restrictions and the Restrict Rule

The conversion of variables and path conditions to SMT depends on the node of interest being reachable via some finite collection of paths. This is problematic for points which are reachable via a loop, which may be reachable after any number of loop iterations.

Consider a C function containing a single loop of this form:

```
for (i = 0; i < 4; i ++) { ...}
```

The compiler may well fully unroll this loop in the binary, since only 4 copies are needed, making the binary loop-free. The proof script must replicate this logic.

The SMT conversion process cannot describe in general the state at a node in a loop, but it can describe the 1st, 2nd or n-th visit to that node, for small values of n. The path condition for the 5th visit to the head of the loop described here can be converted to SMT, and the key observation is that this condition is always false.

The `Restrict` rule names a node and a bound n, and instructs the proof checker to check that the path condition to the nth visit to that node is unsatisfiable by SMT. The proof checker then introduces a restriction, which asserts that this node is reached less than n times. This promotes the semantic limit on the loop iterations into a syntactic limit used by the SMT conversion process, which can now handle nodes in and beyond the loop.

`Restrict` proof script nodes have a single child, which continues the proof with the new restriction in force. In the case described, the subproof may be the `Leaf` rule, which, with the restriction available, can reason about `Ret` and `Err` and finish the proof.

3.3.5 Split Induction

The `Split` rule is used to handle cases that cannot be finitely enumerated. The rule names a C split point c_sp, a binary split point b_sp, an equality predicate P and a bound n. Roughly speaking, the checker will prove by induction that for each visit to b_sp along the binary execution path, c_sp is also visited with the variable state related by P. Formally, we define c_pc_i to be the condition that c_sp is visited at least i times, b_pc_i similarly, and $|P|_i$ to be condition that the P holds on the values of the variables at the i-th visit to c_sp and b_sp respectively. Define I_i to be the property that b_pc_i implies both c_pc_i and $|P|_i$. The checker shows $\forall i > 0.\ I_i$ by n-ary induction, that is, by proving $I_1, I_2, \ldots I_n$ directly and also that the induction hypotheses $I_i, I_{i+1}, \ldots I_{i+n-1}$ and $i > 0$ imply I_{i+n}.

Having established that the sequence of visits to b_sp is matched at c_sp, we consider three cases on the length of the sequence. If the sequence is infinite, then the binary execution and C execution are both non-terminating, and this is a valid refinement. The sequence may also contain n elements, in which case it ends with the elements $i, i+1 \ldots i+n-1$. Thirdly, the sequence may contain less than n elements. The proof script considers the latter two cases via two subproofs, which are children of the `Split` node in the proof tree. In the loop proof, new hypotheses are introduced: b_pc_{i+n-1}, $\neg b\_pc_{i+n}$, $I_i, I_{i+1}, \ldots I_{i+n-1}$. In the non-

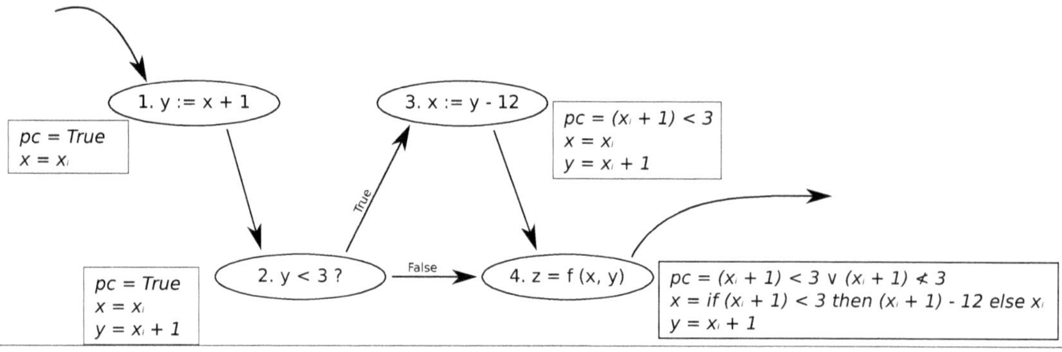

Figure 5. Example Conversion to SMT

looping case, the new hypothesis is $\neg b\_pc_n$. In each case it is expected that the subproof will begin with two `Restrict` rules which use these hypotheses to restrict the number of visits into some finite set. In the looping case, the set of possible visit counts will be of the form $\{x \mid i \leq x < i + k\}$ rather than $\{x \mid x < k\}$. This is an alternative form of the `Restrict` rule.

Some slight generalisations to this induction are needed. Firstly, the `Split` rule may define a sequence offset on either side. A C sequence offset of 2 means that we ignore the first two visits to b_sp, so b_pc_i is the condition that b_sp is visited at least $i + 2$ times, and $|P|_i$ is computed on the variable state at the second visit after the i-th visit. This may be needed to handle various optimisations which affect the initial few iterations of a loop, including a case where the binary sequence is shorter than the C sequence because some iterations have been unpacked entirely. Secondly, the predicate P may be a function not only of the variable states at the respective i-th visits, but also of the value i and the variable states at the first visit. If a C variable is incremented by 1 each iteration, it is simplest to record that it is $i - 1$ more than its first valuation.

The search process discovers the `Split` rules essentially by an exhaustive search with some minor optimisations. In practice this seems to be sufficient, although loop problems are by far the slowest problems for us to solve. In 33 of our 43 loops, the induction proof succeeds for the first candidate P for which $I_0, I_1, \ldots I_{n-1}$ hold, whereas in the remaining 10 cases the early check was mostly irrelevant and an average of 15 attempts were required to find a successful condition. The variation in these numbers is large, with the worst offending loop contributing 84 attempts, nearly half the total.

3.3.6 Assertions

Assertions are checks introduced by the C parser to ensure the standard is respected. These checks have all been handled as proof obligations in the seL4 verification, and may now be used as assumptions in this proof.

One assertion of the C standard is that no NULL pointer ever be dereferenced. The C parser produces a guard at every statement that uses a pointer which checks that the pointer is non-NULL and appropriately aligned. These guards are converted into inequalities and bit checks for the SMT solver, as are similar guards for arithmetic overflow, division by zero, etc.

Note that, for clarity, we omit these guards in our examples. There should, for instance, be a guard before the $x + 1$ calculation in Figure 5 to check that $x + 1$ does not overflow to negative.

The most involved guards relate to the strict-aliasing rule in C. The compiler is entitled to assume that no address is simultaneously in use with two different types. We adjusted the C parser to generate strong pointer validity assumptions pvalid $htd\ \tau\ p$ for every pointer p that is used with type τ when the global heap type description is htd. These assertions cannot be translated accurately into any

	gcc -O1	gcc -O2
Instructions in Binary	11 736	12 299
Decompiled Functions	260	259
- Placeholders		3
Function Pairings	260	225
Successes	234	145
Failures	0	18
Aborted	26	62
- Machine Operations	21	13
- Nested Loops	3	2
- Machine Operations Inlined	2	47
Time Taken in Proof	59m	4h 23m

Table 1. Decompilation and Proof Results

SMT theory. Instead, each time we encounter and expression of this form, we introduce new booleans $pvalid_1$, $pvalid_2$, etc to represent them. We then translate the following key theorem:

$$\frac{\text{pvalid } htd\ \tau\ p \quad \text{pvalid } htd'\ \tau'\ p \quad \text{distinct\_types } \tau\ \tau'}{\{x \mid p \leq x < p + \text{size}(\tau)\} \cap \{x \mid p' \leq x < p' + \text{size}(\tau')\} = \{\}}$$

The SMT form of this fact is $pvalid_1 \wedge pvalid_2 \longrightarrow p + \text{size}(\tau) - 1 < p' \vee p' + \text{size}(\tau') - 1 < p$. We produce all such theorems, a possibly quadratic expansion, though the largest group of pvalid assertions on the same heap type description which we have seen in successful runs is 20.

These assertions appear in path conditions in the C function graph. The proof checker always assumes the negation of the path condition to `Err` in all its SMT checks, thus this information is always available.

4. Evaluation and Discussion

4.1 Results

We report on two runs of the decompilation and proof, both for gcc builds of seL4 at optimisation level 1 and 2 respectively. Table 1 shows the results. Proof timings are taken on a single core of an Intel Core 2 Duo E8400. The majority of the time taken is spent in the SMT solvers. A full decompilation run with proof certificates takes an additional 6–8 hours on modern hardware. Our implementation is based on the original decompiler implementation by Myreen et al. [17], which was not optimised for speed. Recent advances [18] may significantly improve this speed.

There are 540 functions in seL4, but far less symbols in the binary after inlining. Our proof-producing decompiler is able to process the whole binary for gcc -O1 and, at the time of writing, all but 3 routines[2] (i.e. 98 % of the binary) at -O2. Some functions at -O2 have optimised function signatures, and thus cannot be paired via the calling convention with their C counterparts (we address this problem at the refinement stage by inlining these functions everywhere).

We produce proofs for all -O1 functions except for the 21 machine interface functions left abstract in the seL4 verification, 3 system initialisation functions involving nested loops, and 2 functions from the optional fastpath optimisation which inline machine interface operations. In the -O2 binary far more functions inline machine interface operations. There are also a number of explicit proof failures, most of which are failures to find split points, usually because of loop unrolling, loop invariant code motion and other loop structure optimisations.

We use the SMT solvers SONOLAR [23] and Z3 [7]. SONOLAR solves all of the problems we pose to it whereas Z3 times out on many of the larger problems. We suspect this is because of our heavy use of the theory of arrays (to represent memory) which SONOLAR is specifically designed to support. However Z3 supports all of the SMTLIB2 input standard, including retraction of assertions, whereas SONOLAR must be restarted for each new problem, thus we get best performance by invoking Z3 with a timeout of 2 seconds and SONOLAR if Z3 fails.

4.2 Constraints of the Approach

We aim to be general in supporting various flavours of C source, compiler and optimisation level. In practice we are limited by the restrictions of Norrish's C parser [32] we build on, our stack heuristic and the loop heuristics.

The largest single restriction imposed by the existing C parser is that it forbids taking the addresses of stack variables. The parser also forbids many uses of function pointers and all uses of variable-length argument lists [32]. In the seL4 verification this restriction simplified reasoning. As discussed in Section 3.2, it also enforces a static separation of stack accesses and heap accesses here which is needed for the decompilation process stack heuristic.

The C parser also mandates a level of conformity to the C standard which turns out to be rare in practice. For instance, duplicating a `typedef` statement, usually because of duplication of header files, is illegal in the C standard and rejected by the parser. Global variables with names beginning with underscores are also rejected. Compilers such as gcc are flexible in this regard, and various open source projects we had hoped to use as additional case studies tend to abuse this flexibility w.r.t. the standard. Both restrictions could be lifted easily in future work, since adherence to the standard becomes less important when binary verification is available.

The existing C semantics [32] as well as our graph language design fail to handle the case where the compiler has a genuine choice in data layout, such as when writing to a structure containing padding. In principle the parser and graph language could include some kind of unspecified decision node here, which would then become an existentially quantified value in the SMT problem. In practice we choose not to handle this situation, because embedded systems code often intentionally avoids padding anyway and the elimination of padding is easy to achieve on the source level.

The stack heuristic tries to discover how the binary handles the stack and tries to prove that the stack is kept separate from the heap. The exact use of the stack depends on the compiler, which means that our heuristics are fragile and at present only target recent versions of gcc. During the project, we switched gcc versions a few times. Each time the stack heuristic required some fine-tuning.

[2] These break the calling convention, i.e. gcc -O2 has performed aggressive interprocedural optimisations.

The new decompiler uses the ARM/C calling convention to make sure that the functions it extracts take input and produce output that match the input and output signatures of the corresponding C functions. This correspondence between signatures is important because it allows us to modularise the verification problem. However, when compiling with gcc -O2 we noticed that this correspondence breaks down in certain places. Sometimes gcc optimises function signatures, e.g. removing unused arguments where it can. This required special care. In the verification, we avoid these 'broken' function boundaries by inlining (in the logic) these problematic functions, i.e. such function boundaries disappear.

The loop heuristic presented in Section 3.3 depends on the existence of a split point pair, a point in the loop in the compiled binary code at which execution synchronises with a point in the C loop. There is no logical reason such a point need exist. In the case where a memory write is moved before or after an entire loop, no such point exists, and a more general formulation of problem splitting is required. This heuristic has proved sufficient at low optimisation levels, however such generalisations will be needed at higher levels of optimisation.

The loop heuristic presented here also does not handle nested loops, which do not occur in the previously verified part of seL4. To deal with nested loops, or with the compilation of loops with very complex control structure, it may be necessary to search for multiple split point pairs. This could be attempted in roughly the same manner as searching for a single split point pair, although the computational cost is likely to be high. Again, embedded systems code usually does not exhibit such complex control flow within loops, even though simple nested loops may occur. We aim to handle these in future work.

4.3 Workarounds

While we aim to support all situations as automatically as possible, we had to make a small number of changes to seL4 for the proof to work. As mentioned above, we choose not to handle the situation where the compiler is given a genuine choice in data layout. The most common cause of this in seL4 was C enumeration constants, which the C standard defines as being of a type of the compiler's choice, which must accommodate all the enumerated values. It happens that gcc on ARM picks the shortest type available, leading to padding in many structures. Furthermore the C parser guessed incorrectly that these types would be 32-bit. In principle the parser could make this flexible, but in practice in Isabelle/HOL it is more difficult to have unknown types than it is to have unknown terms.

We worked around this issue by changing the `typedef` statements used to define the types actually used in seL4 to `uint_32t` rather than any `enum` types or `uint_8t`. This eliminates all padding. There is a slight memory cost in a small number of structure types, but most structure types remain the same size.

We also adjusted a single function which loops over a short array stored in a struct in a stack variable, it being difficult for the stack heuristic to compute the bounds on the offset used in the array. Finally, we optimised a function which called a number of generic seL4 capability queries on capabilities of known type within a loop. The switch statement on the capability type appeared in every unrolling of the loop and led to an explosion in the number of possible paths causing the SMT solvers to diverge. Calling the query function specific to the capability type solved the problem.

4.4 Issues Found

We did not find any genuine compiler flaws during this analysis. The seL4 team has reported experience with compiler defects in the past and fixed all known issues by rearranging code, selecting appropriate compiler versions and disabling some compiler flags, such as -fwhole-program.

We did, however, find a number of small mismatches between C semantics and compiler. None of them were serious, but some effort was expended in removing them. These include the treatment of the strict-aliasing rule and the handling of reserved sections.

The existing proof for seL4 did not specifically address the strict-aliasing condition. It is one of the standard violations that systems code must make at some point. The C parser generated guards asserting that pointers dereferenced were aligned and not NULL, but no more. We strengthened these guards to assert that the pointers were to objects given the correct type in the heap type description to make use of that information in our SMT refinement proofs. The verification proof can be replayed essentially unchanged, since this fact was nearly always used as a step in proving the alignment conditions where they occurred anyway. Two problems remain where this strict-aliasing condition is broken.

Firstly, as a microkernel, seL4 does not use malloc and free, instead implementing its own retype mechanism. The heap type description changes during retypes, potentially invalidating the strict-aliasing condition, and there is no way to inform the compiler of this. Fortunately this will never create a problem since objects are never both accessed and retyped in the one system call.

Secondly, like standard C libraries, the kernel contains an optimised word-at-a-time memset function which is used during this retype operation. This word-wise access in memset is not compatible with the later type of these allocated objects. We had to tweak our C parser guard strengthening to explicitly omit these writes. In principle the compiler might produce unwanted code if it sufficiently inlined and reordered these functions. The fact that we prove refinement in these functions is evidence this has not happened.

Reserved sections are regions of memory which should not be adjusted by normal operations. These include the code, constant global objects and certain lookup tables generated by the compiler. With the strict stack/heap separation mandated by the C parser, this also includes the stack. The existing verification did not provide sufficient mechanisms for proving such regions were not adjusted. To include them, we once again strengthened C parser guards for the heap type description, making it clear at all locations in the C code that a given set of addresses is not covered by any type and thus unused. This set of addresses models the reserved regions.

We then produce assumptions within the SMT proof that the code and data sections created by the compiler live within this set of reserved addresses, as does the stack. While we can prove this condition is maintained, we have to assume it for the initial state. It would be desirable to make this assumption into a proof in future work, which would essentially extend the verification to the binary image as loaded in memory, as opposed to the binary image in the ELF file, i.e. it would further remove loading and in-memory relocation from the trusted computing base.

5. Related Work

Pnueli et al [24] proposed translation validation as a pragmatic alternative to compiler verification. Over a decade of competition between these two approaches has yielded a collection of translation validation experiments [4, 9, 12, 19, 26, 30, 35, 36] as well as a few verified compilers [5, 13]. This distinction is frequently blurred: some phases of the CompCert C compiler use translation validation whereas others are directly verified.

Our approach is yet another variation within the space of possible translation validations. Like Tristan et al [30], we do not make use of any hints from the compiler. Like Ryabtsev [26], we target the end-to-end transformation rather than any internal compiler step. Furthermore we do not accept any failures or false positives in the process. However, unlike other authors, we are prepared to make small adjustments to our source code if necessary.

What differentiates this approach is that it is strongly grounded in existing semantics at both ends, rather than the compiler's view of its input and output. At the binary level we connect to the extensively validated Cambridge ARM semantics, and at the source level we connect to the verifier's view of the C language which has been validated as useful through the existing seL4 proofs.

The Verisoft project [1] also uses a verified source to binary conversion to produce a verified binary. The project developed a verified compiler for a Pascal-like language with C-like syntax which shared its semantic framework with the verification environment. While the project clearly showed that end-to-end theorems to the binary level are feasible, practical considerations such as performance were not goals of the project.

The CompCert [13] verified C compiler could also be used to transport source-level proofs to the binary, by building a program logic on the semantics associated with the compiler's specification [2]. In our case those semantics are presented differently to those assumed in seL4's verification, and in an incompatible logic.

An alternative approach to binary verification is to prove results directly on the binary semantics with interactive tools. For instance, Bevier's KIT [3] was the first operating system to be completely verified at the assembly level. However, it measured only a few hundred lines of assembly in total. More recently, Ni et al [20] verified modern context switching code using the XCAP x86 model. Chlipala [6] presents a more sophisticated suite of tools for automating most of such reasoning.

Yang and Hawblitzel [33] used binary verification on a minimal type safe language runtime, including garbage collection, to implement an OS kernel. The verification establishes type safety for user-level programs, but forces all applications into the same language framework. Our verification achieves full functional correctness of the kernel instead, and seL4 uses hardware mechanisms to enforce isolation for arbitrary application programs.

6. Conclusion

We have extended the existing formal functional correctness proof of the seL4 microkernel from the C source code down to the binary level. This means, the seL4 binary conforms to its high level correctness properties stated in Isabelle/HOL. The C source, its semantics, and the compiler need no longer be trusted.

Our approach validates the output of compiler and linker by proving refinement between the formal semantics of a program on the C source level and its formal semantics on the binary level. Our refinement theorem composes with further refinement stacks on top of the source code such as in seL4, and transports Hoare-logic properties proved on the source code down to the binary.

We achieved this by building on an existing well-established C semantics and strongly validated ARM semantics and decompilation framework, extending both frameworks and translating them to a common intermediate format particularly amenable to modern high-performance SMT solvers.

While our main target was the seL4 microkernel, we believe that this approach in principle generalises to other C verifications, to other compilers, and even to other similar programming languages. We think that the limitations of the C parser front-end and the prover back-end, such as nested loops, can be overcome in future work to result in a tool chain for fully automatically extending formal C verification down to the binary level. This removes compilers from the trusted computing base of high-assurance systems, while still enabling the use of off-the-shelf compilation tool chains.

Acknowledgements

NICTA is funded by the Australian Government as represented by the Department of Broadband, Communications and the Digital Economy and the Australian Research Council through the ICT Centre of Excellence program. The second author is funded by the Royal Society, UK. This work was partially supported by EPSRC Research Grant EP/G007411/1.

References

[1] E. Alkassar, W. Paul, A. Starostin, and A. Tsyban. Pervasive verification of an OS microkernel: Inline assembly, memory consumption, concurrent devices. In P. O'Hearn, G. T. Leavens, and S. Rajamani, editors, *VSTTE 2010*, volume 6217 of *LNCS*, pages 71–85, Edinburgh, UK, Aug 2010. Springer.

[2] A. W. Appel. Verified software toolchain—(invited talk). In G. Barthe, editor, *Proc. 20th ESOP*, volume 6602 of *LNCS*, pages 1–17, Saarbrücken, Germany, Mar. 2011. Springer.

[3] W. R. Bevier. Kit: A study in operating system verification. *IEEE Trans. Softw. Engin.*, 15(11):1382–1396, 1989.

[4] J. O. Blech, I. Schaefer, and A. Poetzsch-Heffter. Translation validation of system abstractions. In *Proc. 7th Int. Conf. on Runtime verification*, RV'07, pages 139–150, Vancover, Canada, 2007. Springer.

[5] A. Chlipala. A certified type-preserving compiler from lambda calculus to assembly language. In J. Ferrante and K. S. McKinley, editors, *Proc. PLDI'07*, pages 54–65. ACM, 2007.

[6] A. Chlipala. Mostly-automated verification of low-level programs in computational separation logic. In *Proc. 32nd PLDI*, pages 234–245, San Jose, California, USA, 2011. ACM.

[7] L. M. de Moura and N. Bjørner. Z3: An efficient SMT solver. In C. R. Ramakrishnan and J. Rehof, editors, *14th TACAS*, volume 4963 of *LNCS*, pages 337–340, Budapest, Hungary, Mar. 2008. Springer.

[8] A. Fox and M. Myreen. A trustworthy monadic formalization of the ARMv7 instruction set architecture. In M. Kaufmann and L. C. Paulson, editors, *1st Int. Conf. Interactive Theorem Proving*, volume 6172 of *LNCS*, pages 243–258, Edinburgh, UK, July 2010. Springer.

[9] B. Goldberg, L. D. Zuck, and C. W. Barrett. Into the loops: Practical issues in translation validation for optimizing compilers. Proc 3rd Int. Workshop on Compiler Optimization Meets Compiler Verification (COCV '04). *Electr. Notes Theor. Comput. Sci.*, 132(1):53–71, 2005.

[10] ISO/IEC. Programming languages — C. Technical Report 9899:TC2, ISO/IEC JTC1/SC22/WG14, May 2005.

[11] G. Klein, K. Elphinstone, G. Heiser, J. Andronick, D. Cock, P. Derrin, D. Elkaduwe, K. Engelhardt, R. Kolanski, M. Norrish, T. Sewell, H. Tuch, and S. Winwood. seL4: Formal verification of an OS kernel. In *Proc. 22nd SOSP*, pages 207–220, Big Sky, MT, USA, 2009. ACM.

[12] S. Kundu, S. Lerner, and R. K. Gupta. Translation validation of high-level synthesis. *Trans. Comp.-Aided Des. Integ. Cir. Sys.*, 29(4):566–579, Apr. 2010.

[13] X. Leroy. Formal certification of a compiler back-end or: programming a compiler with a proof assistant. In J. G. Morrisett and S. L. P. Jones, editors, *Proc. 33rd POPL*, pages 42–54. ACM, 2006.

[14] X. Leroy. A formally verified compiler back-end. *J. Automated Reasoning*, 43(4):363–446, 2009.

[15] T. Murray, D. Matichuk, M. Brassil, P. Gammie, T. Bourke, S. Seefried, C. Lewis, X. Gao, and G. Klein. seL4: from general purpose to a proof of information flow enforcement. In *IEEE Symp. Security & Privacy*, Oakland, CA, May 2013.

[16] M. O. Myreen. *Formal verification of machine-code programs*. PhD thesis, University of Cambridge, 2009.

[17] M. O. Myreen, M. J. C. Gordon, and K. Slind. Machine-code verification for multiple architectures - an application of decompilation into logic. In A. Cimatti and R. B. Jones, editors, *Formal Methods in Computer-Aided Design (FMCAD)*, pages 1–8. IEEE, 2008.

[18] M. O. Myreen, M. J. C. Gordon, and K. Slind. Decompilation into logic — improved. In G. Cabodi and S. Singh, editors, *Formal Methods in Computer-Aided Design (FMCAD)*, pages 78–81. IEEE, 2012.

[19] G. C. Necula. Translation validation for an optimizing compiler. In *Proc. PLDI'00*, pages 83–94, Vancouver, BC, Canada, 2000. ACM.

[20] Z. Ni, D. Yu, and Z. Shao. Using XCAP to certify realistic systems code: machine context management. In *Proc. 20th TPHOLs*, volume 4732 of *LNCS*, pages 189–206. Springer, 2007.

[21] T. Nipkow, L. Paulson, and M. Wenzel. *Isabelle/HOL — A Proof Assistant for Higher-Order Logic*, volume 2283 of *LNCS*. Springer, 2002.

[22] Open Kernel Labs. seL4 research and evaluation download. `http://ertos.nicta.com.au/software/seL4/`, 2011.

[23] J. Peleska, E. Vorobev, and F. Lapschies. Automated test case generation with SMT-solving and abstract interpretation. In *Proc 3rd Int. Conf. NASA Formal methods*, NFM'11, pages 298–312, Pasadena, CA, 2011. Springer.

[24] A. Pnueli, M. Siegel, and E. Singerman. Translation validation. In B. Steffen, editor, *Proc. 4th TACAS*, volume 1384 of *LNCS*, pages 151–166. Springer, 1998.

[25] J. C. Reynolds. Separation logic: A logic for shared mutable data structures. In *Logic in Computer Science (LICS)*, pages 55–74. IEEE Computer Society, 2002.

[26] M. Ryabtsev and O. Strichman. Translation validation: From Simulink to C. In *Proc. 21st Int. Conf. on Computer Aided Verification*, CAV '09, pages 696–701, Grenoble, France, 2009. Springer.

[27] N. Schirmer. *Verification of Sequential Imperative Programs in Isabelle/HOL*. PhD thesis, Technische Universität München, 2006.

[28] T. Sewell, S. Winwood, P. Gammie, T. Murray, J. Andronick, and G. Klein. seL4 enforces integrity. In M. C. J. D. van Eekelen, H. Geuvers, J. Schmaltz, and F. Wiedijk, editors, *2nd Int. Conf. on Interactive Theorem Proving*, volume 6898 of *LNCS*, pages 325–340, Nijmegen, The Netherlands, Aug. 2011. Springer.

[29] K. Slind and M. Norrish. A brief overview of HOL4. In *20th Int. Conf. on Theorem Proving in Higher Order Logics*, pages 28–32, Montreal, Canada, Aug. 2008.

[30] J.-B. Tristan, P. Govereau, and G. Morrisett. Evaluating value-graph translation validation for llvm. In *Proc. 32nd PLDI*, pages 295–305, San Jose, CA, USA, 2011. ACM.

[31] H. Tuch. Formal verification of C systems code: Structured types, separation logic and theorem proving. *J. Automated Reasoning: Special Issue on OS Verification*, 42(2–4):125–187, Apr. 2009.

[32] H. Tuch, G. Klein, and M. Norrish. Types, bytes, and separation logic. In M. Hofmann and M. Felleisen, editors, *Proc. 34th POPL*, pages 97–108, Nice, France, Jan. 2007. ACM.

[33] J. Yang and C. Hawblitzel. Safe to the last instruction: automated verification of a type-safe operating system. In *Proc. PLDI'10*, pages 99–110, Toronto, Canada, 2010. ACM.

[34] X. Yang, Y. Chen, E. Eide, and J. Regehr. Finding and understanding bugs in C compilers. In M. W. Hall and D. A. Padua, editors, *Proc. 32nd PLDI*, pages 283–294, San Jose, CA, USA, June 2011. ACM.

[35] L. D. Zuck, A. Pnueli, Y. Fang, B. Goldberg, and Y. Hu. Translation and run-time validation of optimized code. Runtime Verification 2002 (RV'02). *Electr. Notes Theor. Comput. Sci.*, 70(4):179–200, 2002.

[36] L. D. Zuck, A. Pnueli, and B. Goldberg. VOC: A methodology for the translation validation of optimizing compilers. *J. UCS*, 9(3):223–247, 2003.

Machine-Verified Network Controllers

Arjun Guha
Cornell University
arjun@cs.cornell.edu

Mark Reitblatt
Cornell University
reitblatt@cs.cornell.edu

Nate Foster
Cornell University
jnfoster@cs.cornell.edu

Abstract

In many areas of computing, techniques ranging from testing to formal modeling to full-blown verification have been successfully used to help programmers build reliable systems. But although networks are critical infrastructure, they have largely resisted analysis using formal techniques. Software-defined networking (SDN) is a new network architecture that has the potential to provide a foundation for network reasoning, by standardizing the interfaces used to express network programs and giving them a precise semantics.

This paper describes the design and implementation of the first machine-verified SDN controller. Starting from the foundations, we develop a detailed operational model for OpenFlow (the most popular SDN platform) and formalize it in the Coq proof assistant. We then use this model to develop a verified compiler and run-time system for a high-level network programming language. We identify bugs in existing languages and tools built without formal foundations, and prove that these bugs are absent from our system. Finally, we describe our prototype implementation and our experiences using it to build practical applications.

Categories and Subject Descriptors F.3.1 [*Specifying and Verifying and Reasoning about Programs*]: Mechanical verification

Keywords Software-defined networking, OpenFlow, formal verification, Coq, domain-specific languages, NetCore, Frenetic.

1. Introduction

Networks are some of the most critical infrastructure in modern society and also some of the most fragile! Networks fail with alarming frequency, often due to simple misconfigurations or software bugs [8, 19, 30]. The recent news headlines contain numerous examples of network failures leading to disruptions: a configuration error during routine maintenance at Amazon triggered a sequence of cascading failures that brought down a datacenter and the customer machines hosted there; a corrupted routing table at GoDaddy disconnected their domain name servers for a day and caused a widespread outage; and a network connectivity issue at United Airlines took down their reservation system, leading to thousands of flight cancellations and a "ground stop" at their San Francisco hub.

One way to make networks more reliable would be to develop tools for checking important network invariants automatically. These tools would allow administrators to answer questions such as: "does this configuration provide connectivity to every host in the network?" or "does this configuration correctly enforce the access control policy?" or "does this configuration have a forwarding loop?" or "does this configuration properly isolate trusted and untrusted traffic?" Unfortunately, until recently, building such tools has been effectively impossible due to the complexity of today's networks. A typical enterprise or datacenter network contains thousands of heterogeneous devices, from routers and switches, to web caches and load balancers, to monitoring middleboxes and firewalls. Moreover, each device executes a stack of complex protocols and is configured through a proprietary and idiosyncratic interface. To reason formally about such a network, an administrator (or tool) must reason about the proprietary programs running on each distributed device, as well as the asynchronous interactions between them. Although formal models of traditional networks exist, they have either been too complex to allow effective reasoning, or too abstract to be useful. Overall, the incidental complexity of networks has made reasoning about their behavior practically infeasible.

Fortunately, recent years have seen growing interest in a new kind of network architecture that could provide a foundation for network reasoning. In a *software-defined network* (SDN), a program on a logically-centralized *controller machine* defines the overall policy for the network, and a collection of *programmable switches* implement the policy using efficient packet-processing hardware. The controller and switches communicate via an open and standard interface. By carefully installing packet-processing rules in the hardware tables provided on switches, the controller can effectively manage the behavior of the entire network.

Compared to traditional networks, SDNs have two important simplifications that make them amenable to formal reasoning. First, they relocate control from distributed algorithms running on individual devices to a single program running on the controller. Second, they eliminate the heterogeneous devices used in traditional networks—switches, routers, load balancers, firewalls, etc.—and replace them with stock programmable switches that provide a standard set of features. Together, this means that the behavior of the network is determined solely by the sequence of configuration instructions issued by the controller. To verify that the network has some property, an administrator (or tool) simply has to reason about the states of the switches as they process instructions.

In the networking community, there is burgeoning interest in tools for checking network-wide properties automatically. Systems such as FlowChecker [1], Header Space Analysis [12], Anteater [17], VeriFlow [13], and others, work by generating a logical representation of switch configurations and using an automatic solver to check properties of those configurations. The configurations are obtained by "scraping" state off of the switches or inspecting the instructions issued by an SDN controller at run-time.

These tools represent a good first step toward making networks more reliable, but they have two important limitations. First, they are based on ad hoc foundations. Although SDN platforms such as OpenFlow [21] have precise (if informal) specifications, the tools make simplifying assumptions that are routinely violated by real

PLDI'13, June 16–19, 2013, Seattle, WA, USA.

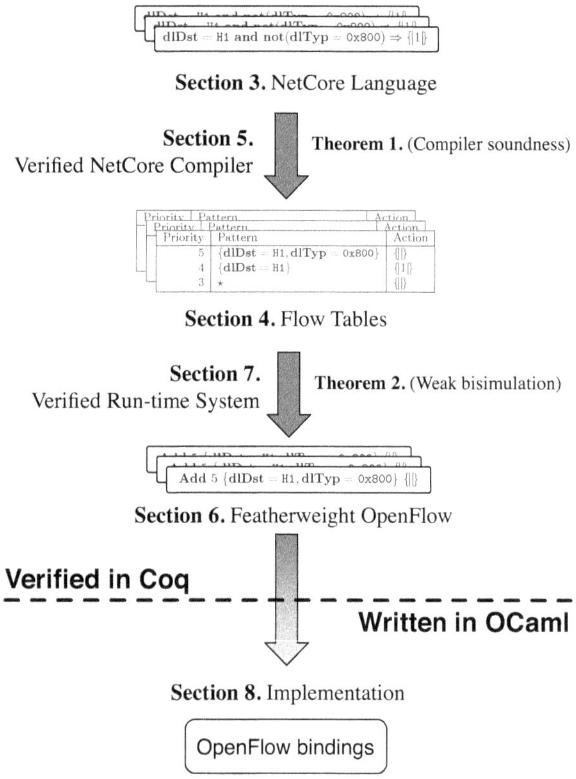

Figure 1: System architecture.

hardware switches. For example, some tools assume that switches will process instructions emitted by the controller in sequence, even though actual switches often reorder messages. This means that properties they consider verified do not always actually hold. Second, the tools are expensive to run and do not scale well. For example, most tools take several minutes to run, even in small to medium-sized networks (VeriFlow [13] is a notable exception). This is too slow to be used in large dynamic networks where configurations change on the order of seconds. Overall, although these tools are useful for finding bugs, they cannot provide the rigorous guarantees that networks, as critical infrastructure, require.

Our approach. This paper presents a different approach. Rather than building tools to find bugs in SDN controllers at run-time, we develop a verified SDN controller in the Coq proof assistant and prove it correct against a formal specification and a detailed operational model of SDN. With our controller, programmers specify the behavior of the network using the NetCore programming language [22], which abstracts away from the details of the underlying switch hardware and distributed system, and allows programmers to reason in terms of simple hop-by-hop packet-processing steps. The NetCore compiler and run-time system translates programs written in this language down to low-level packet-processing rules. Because its behavior is verified in Coq, we establish the correctness of our controller once and for all, obviating the need for run-time or post hoc verification as in most current tools.

Architecturally, our system is organized as a verified software stack that translates through the following levels of abstraction:

- **NetCore.** The highest level of abstraction is the NetCore language, proposed in prior work by Monsanto *et al.* [22]. NetCore is a declarative language that allows programmers to describe *what* network behavior they want, without specifying *how* it should be implemented. It offers a collection of intuitive constructs for matching, filtering, and transforming packets, as well as natural logical operators for combining smaller programs into bigger ones such as union and domain restriction. Although NetCore programs are ultimately executed in a distributed system—the network—they have a simple semantics that models their behavior as functions from packets to packets.
- **Flow tables.** The intermediate level of abstraction is *flow tables*, a representation that sits between NetCore programs and switch-level configurations. There are two main differences between NetCore programs and flow tables. First, NetCore programs describe the forwarding behavior of a whole network, while flow tables describe the behavior of a single switch. Second, flow tables process packets using a linear scan through a list of prioritized rules. Hence, to translate operators such as union and negation, the NetCore compiler must generate a sequence of rules that encodes the same semantics. However, because flow table matching uses a lower-level packet representation (as nested frames of Ethernet, IP, TCP, etc. packets), flow tables must satisfy a well-formedness condition to rule out invalid patterns that are inconsistent with this representation.
- **Featherweight OpenFlow.** The lowest level of abstraction is *Featherweight OpenFlow*, a new foundational model we have designed that captures the essential features of SDNs. Featherweight OpenFlow models switches, the controller, the network topology, as well as their internal transitions and interactions in a small-step operational semantics. This semantics is nondeterministic, modeling the asynchrony inherent in networks. To implement a flow table in a Featherweight OpenFlow network, the controller instructs switches to install or uninstall rules as appropriate while dealing with two important issues: First, switches process instructions concurrently with packets flowing through the network, so it must ensure that at all times the rules installed on switches are consistent with the flow table. Second, switches are allowed to buffer instructions and apply them in any order, so it must ensure that the behavior is correct no matter how instructions are reordered through careful use of synchronization primitives.

Figure 1 depicts the architecture of our system, and provides an outline for this paper. Overall, our main contributions are as follows:

- We present the first machine-verified SDN controller, which gives network programmers robust static guarantees backed by machine-checked proofs against a foundational model.
- We develop Featherweight OpenFlow, the first formal model of OpenFlow. It includes all sources of asynchrony and nondeterminism mentioned in the informal OpenFlow specification, as well as a precise model of switch flow table semantics.
- We formalize NetCore, flow tables, and Featherweight OpenFlow in Coq, and develop machine-checked proofs of correctness for the translations between them.
- We present our prototype implementation, obtained by extracting our Coq development to OCaml, and present experimental results comparing the performance of our system against unverified controllers on simple benchmarks.

Besides their use in our system, we hope that the abstractions and theorems presented in this paper will be useful to others. Flow tables are a canonical representation of switch state that appear in many other systems. Likewise, Featherweight OpenFlow is a comprehensive model that captures the essential forwarding behavior of SDNs in a minimal core calculus. Our design and Coq formalization of flow tables and Featherweight OpenFlow provide

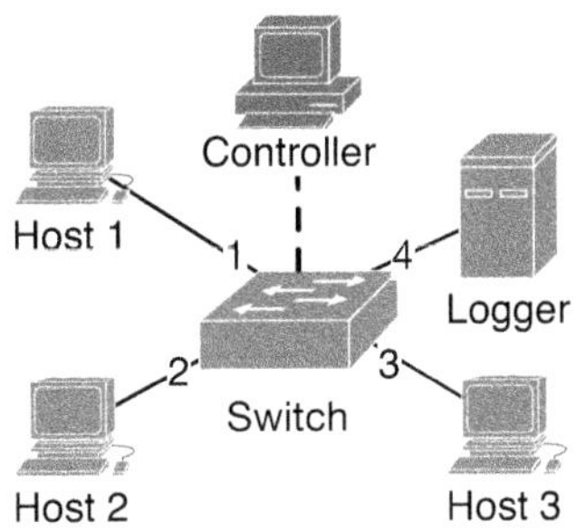

Figure 2: Example network topology.

a starting point for developing extensions that model additional SDN features and a foundation for other verified systems.

2. Overview

To motivate the need for verified SDN controllers, consider the simple network depicted in Fig. 2. It consists of a single switch connected to four hosts: three clients and a middlebox that monitors HTTP requests. The ports on the switch are numbered 1 to 4; the clients are connected to ports 1 to 3 and the middlebox to port 4. In addition, the switch has a dedicated link to the controller that is not considered part of the data network.

Now imagine we want to build an SDN controller that implements the following high-level network policy: block SSH traffic, log HTTP requests, and allow clients to send non-SSH traffic to each other. It is straightforward to formalize this policy as a packet-processing function that maps input packets to (possibly several) output packets: the function drops SSH packets, forwards HTTP packets both to their destination and to the middlebox, and forwards all other packets to their destination alone.

To implement this function in an SDN, however, we would need to specify several additional low-level details, since switches cannot implement general packet-processing functions directly. First, the controller would need to encode the function as a *flow table*—a set of prioritized forwarding rules. Second, it would need to send the switch a series of control messages to add individual entries from the flow table, incrementally building up the complete table.

More concretely, the controller could first send a message instructing the switch to add a flow table entry that blocks SSH traffic:

$$\textbf{Add}\ 10\ \{\textbf{tpDst} = 22\}\ \{\!|\,|\!\}$$

Here 10 is a priority number, $\{\textbf{tpDst} = 22\}$ is a pattern that matches SSH traffic (TCP port 22), and $\{\!|\,|\!\}$ is an empty multiset of ports, which drops packets, as intended. Next, the controller could add an entry to process HTTP requests:

$$\textbf{Add}\ 9\ \{\textbf{dlDst} = \mathit{H1}, \textbf{tpDst} = 80\}\ \{\!|1, 4|\!\}$$

Note that this rule duplicates HTTP (TCP port 80) packets, sending them to the monitor and to their destination.[1] Finally, the controller could add an entry to forward other packets to their destination:

$$\textbf{Add}\ 1\ \{\textbf{dlDst} = \mathit{H1}\}\ \{\!|1|\!\}$$

Note that this rule does not apply to SSH and HTTP traffic, since those packets are handled by the higher-priority rules.

After these control messages have been sent, it would be natural to expect that the network correctly implements the packet-processing function described above. But the situation is actually more complicated: switches have substantial latitude in how they process messages from the controller, and packets may arrive at any time during processing. Establishing that the network correctly implements this function—in particular, that it blocks SSH traffic and logs HTTP traffic—requires additional reasoning.

[1] The controller would actually need to create rules for each client. To save space, we have only given the rules for *H1* here.

Packet	pk	::= **Eth** *dlSrc dlDst dlTyp nwPk*
Network layer	$nwPk$	::= **IP** *nwSrc nwDst nwProto tpPk*
		| **Unknown** *payload*
Transport layer	$tpPk$	::= **TCP** *tpSrc tpDst payload*
		| **Unknown** *payload*

Figure 3: Logical packet structure.

Controller-switch consistency. Switches process packets and control messages concurrently. In our example, the switch may receive an HTTP request before the flow table entry that handles HTTP packets arrives. In this case, the switch will send the packet to the controller for further processing. Since the controller is a general-purpose machine, it can implement the packet-processing function directly, apply it to the incoming packet, and send the results back to the switch. However, this means that SDN controllers typically have two *different* implementations of the function: one residing at the controller and another on the switches. A key property we verify is that these two implementations are consistent.

Message reordering. SDN switches may process control messages in any order, and many switches do, to maximize performance. But unrestricted reordering can cause implementations to violate their intended specifications. For example, if the rule to drop SSH traffic is installed after the final, low-priority rule that forwards all traffic, then SSH traffic will temporarily be forwarded by the low-priority rule, breaking the intended security policy. To ensure that such reorderings do not occur, a controller must carefully insert *barrier messages*, which force the switch to process all outstanding messages. A key property we verify is that controllers use barriers correctly (several unverified controllers ignore this issue).

Natural patterns. Another complication is that the patterns presented earlier in this section, such as $\{\textbf{tpDst} = 22\}$, are actually invalid. To match SSH traffic, it is not enough to simply state that the destination port must be 22. The pattern must also specify that the Ethernet frame type must be IP, and the transport protocol must be TCP. Without these additional constraints, switches will interpret the pattern as a wildcard that matches all packets. Several earlier controller platforms did not properly account for this behavior, and had bugs as a result. We develop a semantics for patterns and identify a class of *natural patterns* that are closed under the algebraic operations used by our compiler and flow table optimizer.

Roadmap. The rest of this paper develops techniques for establishing that a given packet-processing function is implemented correctly by an OpenFlow network. More specifically, we tackle the problem of verifying high-level programming abstractions, using NetCore [22] as a concrete instance of a high-level network language. The next section presents NetCore in detail. The following sections describe general and reusable techniques for establishing the correctness of SDN controllers, including NetCore.

3. NetCore

This section presents the highest layer of our verified stack: the NetCore language. A NetCore program specifies how the switches process packets at each hop through the network. More formally, a program denotes a total function from port-packet pairs to multisets of port-packet pairs. The syntax and semantics of a core NetCore

Switch ID	sw	$\in \mathbb{N}$	
Port ID	pt	$\in \mathbb{N}$	
Headers	h	$::=$ **dlSrc** | **dlDst**	*MAC address*
		| **dlTyp**	*Ethernet frame type*
		| **nwSrc** | **nwDst**	*IP address*
		| **nwProto**	*IP protocol code*
		| **tpSrc** | **tpDst**	*transport port*
Predicate	pr	$::= \star$	*wildcard*
		| $h = n$	*match header*
		| **at** sw	*match switch*
		| **not** pr	*predicate negation*
		| pr_1 **and** pr_2	*predicate conjunction*
Program	pg	$::= pr \Rightarrow \{\!\mid pt_1 \cdots pt_n \mid\!\}$	*basic program*
		| $pg_1 \uplus pg_2$	*program union*
		| **restrict** pg **by** pr	*program restriction*

$\boxed{[\![pr]\!]\ sw\ pt\ pk}$

$$
\begin{aligned}
&[\![\star]\!]\ sw\ pt\ pk = \textbf{true}\\
&[\![\textbf{dlSrc}{=}n]\!]\ sw\ pt\ (\textbf{Eth}\ dlSrc\ \_\ \_\ \_) = dlSrc{=}n\\
&[\![\textbf{nwSrc}{=}n]\!]\ sw\ pt\ (\textbf{Eth}\ \_\ \_\ \_\ (\textbf{IP}\ nwSrc\ \_\ \_\ \_)) = nwSrc{=}n\\
&[\![\textbf{nwSrc}{=}n]\!]\ sw\ pt\ (\textbf{Eth}\ \_\ \_\ \_\ (\textbf{Unknown}\ \_)) = \textbf{false}\\
&\qquad\cdots\\
&[\![\textbf{at}\ sw']\!]\ sw\ pt\ pk = sw{=}sw'\\
&[\![\textbf{not}\ pr]\!]\ sw\ pt\ pk = \neg([\![pr]\!]\ sw\ pt\ pk)\\
&[\![pr_1\ \textbf{and}\ pr_2]\!]\ sw\ pt\ pk = [\![pr_1]\!]\ sw\ pt\ pk \wedge [\![pr_2]\!]\ sw\ pt\ pk
\end{aligned}
$$

$\boxed{[\![pg]\!]\ sw\ pt\ pk = \{\!\mid (pt_1, pk_1) \cdots (pt_n, pk_n) \mid\!\}}$

$$
\begin{aligned}
&[\![pr \Rightarrow \{\!\mid pt_1 \cdots pt_n \mid\!\}]\!]\ sw\ pt\ pk =\\
&\quad \textbf{if}\ [\![pr]\!]\ sw\ pt\ pk\ \textbf{then}\ \{\!\mid (pt_1, pk) \cdots (pt_n, pk) \mid\!\}\ \textbf{else}\ \{\!\mid\mid\!\}\\
&[\![pg_1 \uplus pg_2]\!]\ sw\ pt\ pk =\\
&\quad [\![pg_1]\!]\ sw\ pt\ pk \uplus [\![pg_2]\!]\ sw\ pt\ pk\\
&[\![\textbf{restrict}\ pg\ \textbf{by}\ pr]\!]\ sw\ pt\ pk =\\
&\quad \{\!\mid (pt', pk') \mid (pt', pk') \in [\![pg]\!]\ sw\ pt\ pk \wedge [\![pr]\!]\ sw\ pt\ pk \mid\!\}
\end{aligned}
$$

Figure 4: NetCore syntax and semantics (extracts).

fragment are shown in Fig. 4. To save space, we have elided several header fields and operators not used in this paper.

We can build a NetCore program that implements the example from the previous section by composing several smaller NetCore program fragments. The first fragment forwards traffic to *H1*:

$$pg_1 \triangleq \textbf{dlDst}{=}H1 \Rightarrow \{\!\mid 1 \mid\!\}$$

This basic program consists of a predicate pr and a multiset of actions $\{\!\mid pt_1 \cdots pt_n \mid\!\}$. The predicate denotes a set of port-packet pairs, and the actions denote the ports (if any) where those packets should be forwarded on the next hop. In this instance, the predicate denotes the set of all packets whose Ethernet destination (**dlDst**) address has the specified value, and the actions denote a transformation that forwards matching packets to port 1. Note that we represent packets as nested sequences of frames (Ethernet, IP, TCP, etc.) as shown in Fig. 3. NetCore provides predicates for matching on well-known header fields as well as logical operators such as **and** and **or**, unlike hardware switches, which only provide prioritized sets of rules.

The next two fragments are similar to pg_1, but forward traffic to *H2* and *H3* instead of *H1*:

$$pg_2 \triangleq \textbf{dlDst}{=}H2 \Rightarrow \{\!\mid 2 \mid\!\}$$
$$pg_3 \triangleq \textbf{dlDst}{=}H3 \Rightarrow \{\!\mid 3 \mid\!\}$$

Using the union operator, we can combine these programs into a single program that implements forwarding between all clients:

$$pg_{fwd} \triangleq pg_1 \uplus pg_2 \uplus pg_3$$

Semantically, the $\uplus$ operator produces the (multiset) union of the results produced by each sub-program. Using the union operator again, we can extend this program to one that also forwards HTTP requests to the middlebox:

$$pg_{fwd} \uplus \textbf{tpDst}{=}80 \Rightarrow \{\!\mid 4 \mid\!\}$$

Note that this program duplicates packets sent to port 80, forwarding to their destination and also to the logging machine. Finally, we can add the security policy using the **restrict by** operator, which restricts a program by a predicate:

$$\textbf{restrict}\ (pg_{fwd} \uplus \textbf{tpDst}{=}80 \Rightarrow \{\!\mid 4 \mid\!\})\ \textbf{by}\ (\textbf{not tpDst}{=}22)$$

This program is similar the previous one, but drops SSH traffic.

The advantages of using a declarative language such as NetCore should be clear: it provides abstractions that make it easy to establish network-wide properties through compositional reasoning. For example, simply by inspecting the final program and using the denotational semantics (Fig. 4), we can easily verify that the network blocks SSH traffic, forwards HTTP traffic to the middlebox, and provides pair-wise connectivity between the clients. In particular, even though a controller, switches, flow tables, forwarding rules, are all involved in implementing this program, we do not have to reason about them! This is in contrast to lower-level controller platforms, which require programmers to explicitly construct switch-level forwarding rules, issue messages to install those rules on switches, and reason about the asynchronous interactions between switches and controller. Of course, the complexity of the underlying system is not eliminated, but relocated from the programmer to the language implementers. This is an efficient tradeoff: functionality common to many programs can be implemented just once, proved correct, and reused broadly.

4. Flow Tables

The first step toward executing a NetCore program in an SDN involves compiling it to a prioritized set of forwarding rules—a *flow table*. Flow tables are an intermediate representation that play a similar role in NetCore to register transfer language (RTL) in traditional compilers. Flow tables are more primitive than NetCore programs because they lack the logical structure induced by NetCore operators such as union, intersection, negation, and restriction. Also, the patterns used to match packets in flow tables are more restrictive than NetCore predicates. And unlike NetCore programs, which denote total functions, flow tables are partial: switches redirect unmatched packets to the controller.

As defined in Fig. 5, a *flow table* consists of a multiset of rules (n, pat, pts) where n is an integer priority, pat is a pattern, and pts is a multiset of ports. A *pattern* is a record that associates each header field to either an integer constant n or the special *wildcard* value $\star$. When writing flow tables, we often elide headers set to $\star$ in patterns as well as priorities when they are clear from context.

Pattern semantics. The semantics of patterns is given by the function $pk\#pat$, as defined in Fig. 5. This turns out to be subtly complicated, due to the representation of packets as sequences of nested frames—a pattern contains a (possibly wildcarded) field for every header field, but not all packets contain every header field. Some fields only exist in specific frame types (**dlTyp**) or protocols (**nwProto**). For example, only IP packets (**dlTyp** $=$ 0x800) have IP source and destination addresses. Likewise, TCP (**nwProto** $=$ 6) and UDP (**nwProto** $=$ 17) packets have source and destination ports, but ICMP (**nwProto** $=$ 1) packets do not.

$$\begin{array}{lll}
\text{Wildcard} & w & ::= n \mid \star \\
\text{Pattern} & pat & ::= \{\mathbf{dlSrc} = w, \mathbf{dlDst} = w, \mathbf{dlTyp} = w, \\
& & \quad \mathbf{nwSrc} = w, \mathbf{nwDst} = w, \mathbf{nwProto} = w, \\
& & \quad \mathbf{tpSrc} = w, \mathbf{tpDst} = w\} \\
\text{Flow table} & FT & \in \{\!|n \times pat \times \{\!|pt|\!\}|\!\}
\end{array}$$

$$\boxed{[\![FT]\!]\ pt\ pk \rightsquigarrow \{\!|pt_1 \cdots pt_n|\!\} \times \{\!|pk_1 \cdots pk_m|\!\}}$$

$$\frac{\begin{array}{l}\exists (n, pat, \{\!|pt_1 \cdots pt_n|\!\}) \in FT. \\ \quad pk\#pat = \mathbf{true} \\ \quad \forall (n', pat', pts') \in FT.\ n' > n \Rightarrow \\ \quad\quad pk\#pat' = \mathbf{false}\end{array}}{[\![FT]\!]\ pt\ pk \rightsquigarrow (\{\!|(pt_1) \cdots (pt_n)|\!\}, \{\!||\!\})}\ (\text{MATCHED})$$

$$\frac{\forall (n, pat, pts) \in FT \qquad pk\#pat = \mathbf{false}}{[\![FT]\!]\ pt\ pk \rightsquigarrow (\{\!||\!\}, \{\!|(pt, pk)|\!\})}\ (\text{UNMATCHED})$$

$$\boxed{pk\#pat}$$

$$\begin{array}{l}
(\mathbf{Eth}\ dlSrc\ dlDst\ dlTyp\ nwPk)\#pat = \\
\quad dlSrc \sqsubseteq pat.\mathbf{dlSrc} \wedge dlDst \sqsubseteq pat.\mathbf{dlDst} \wedge \\
\quad dlTyp \sqsubseteq pat.\mathbf{dlTyp} \wedge \\
\quad (pat.\mathbf{dlTyp} = \texttt{0x800} \Rightarrow nwPk\#_{nw}pat)
\end{array}$$

$$\boxed{nwPk\#_{nw}pat}$$

$$\begin{array}{l}
(\mathbf{IP}\ nwSrc\ nwDst\ nwProto\ tpPk)\#_{nw}pat = \\
\quad nwSrc \sqsubseteq pat.\mathbf{nwSrc} \wedge nwDst \sqsubseteq pat.\mathbf{nwDst} \wedge \\
\quad nwProto \sqsubseteq pat.\mathbf{nwProto} \wedge \\
\quad (pat.\mathbf{nwProto} = 6 \Rightarrow tpPk\#_{tp}pat) \\
(\mathbf{Unknown}\ payload)\#_{nw}pat = \mathbf{true}
\end{array}$$

$$\boxed{tpPk\#_{tp}pat}$$

$$\begin{array}{l}
(\mathbf{TCP}\ tpSrc\ tpDst\ payload)\#_{tp}pat = \\
\quad tpSrc \sqsubseteq pat.\mathbf{tpSrc} \wedge tpDst \sqsubseteq pat.\mathbf{tpDst} \\
\mathbf{Unknown}\ payload\#_{tp}pat = \mathbf{true}
\end{array}$$

$$\boxed{n \sqsubseteq w}$$

$$m \sqsubseteq n = m{=}n \qquad n \sqsubseteq \star = \mathbf{true}$$

Figure 5: Flow table syntax and semantics.

To match on a given field, a pattern must specify values for all other fields it depends on. For example, to match on IP addresses, the pattern must also specify that the Ethernet frame type is IP:

$$\{\mathbf{dlTyp} = \texttt{0x800}, \mathbf{nwSrc} = \texttt{10.0.0.1}\}$$

If the frame type is elided, the value of the dependent header is silently ignored and the pattern is equivalent to a wildcard:

$$\{\mathbf{nwSrc} = \texttt{10.0.0.1}\} \equiv \{\}$$

In effect, patterns not only match packets, but also determine how they are parsed. This behavior, which was ambiguous in early versions of the OpenFlow specification (and later fixed) has lead to real bugs in existing controllers (Section 5). Although unintuitive for programmers, this behavior is completely consistent with how packet processing is implemented in modern switch hardware.

Flow table semantics. The semantics of flow tables is given by the relation $[\![\cdot]\!]$. The relation has two cases: one for matched packets and another for unmatched packets. Each flow table entry is a tuple containing a priority n, pattern pat, and a multiset of ports $\{\!|pt_1 \cdots pt_n|\!\}$. Given a packet and its input port, the semantics forwards the packet to all ports in the multiset associated with the highest-priority matching rule in the table. Otherwise, if no matching rule exists, it diverts the packet to the controller. In the formal semantics, the first component of the result pair represents forwarded packets while the second component represents diverted packets. Note that flow table matching is non-deterministic if there are multiple matching entries with the same priority. This has serious implications for a compiler—*e.g.*, naively combining flow tables with overlapping priorities could produce incorrect results. In the NetCore compiler, we avoid this issue by always working with unambiguous and total flow tables.

$$\boxed{\mathcal{P} : sw \times pr \to [(pat, \mathbf{bool})]}$$

$$\begin{array}{lll}
\mathcal{P}(sw, \mathbf{dlSrc} = n) & = & [(\{\mathbf{dlSrc} = n\}, \mathbf{true})] \\
\mathcal{P}(sw, \mathbf{nwSrc} = n) & = & [(\{\mathbf{dlTyp} = \texttt{0x800}, \mathbf{nwSrc} = n\}, \mathbf{true})] \\
& \cdots & \\
\mathcal{P}(sw, \mathbf{at}\ sw) & = & [(\star, \mathbf{true})] \\
\mathcal{P}(sw, \mathbf{at}\ sw') & = & [(\star, \mathbf{false})] \quad \text{where } sw \neq sw' \\
\mathcal{P}(sw, \mathbf{not}\ pr) & = & [(pat_1, \neg b_1) \cdots (pat_n, \neg b_n), (\star, \mathbf{false})] \\
\multicolumn{3}{l}{\quad \text{where } [(pat_1, b_1) \cdots (pat_n, b_n)] = \mathcal{P}(sw, pr)} \\
\mathcal{P}(sw, pr\ \mathbf{and}\ pr') & = & \\
\multicolumn{3}{l}{\quad [(pat_1 \cap pat'_1, b_1 \wedge b'_1) \cdots (pat_m \cap pat'_n, b_m \wedge b'_n)]} \\
\multicolumn{3}{l}{\quad\quad \text{where } [(pat_1, b_1) \cdots (pat_m, b_m)] = \mathcal{P}(sw, pr)} \\
\multicolumn{3}{l}{\quad\quad \text{where } [(pat'_1, b'_1) \cdots (pat'_n, b'_n)] = \mathcal{P}(sw, pr')}
\end{array}$$

$$\boxed{\mathcal{C} : sw \times pg \to [(pat, pt)]}$$

$$\begin{array}{l}
\mathcal{C}(sw, pr \Rightarrow pt) = [(pat_1, pt_1) \cdots (pat_n, pt_n), (\star, \{\!||\!\})] \\
\quad \text{where } [(pat_1, b_1), \cdots, (pat_n, b_n)] = \mathcal{P}(sw, pr) \\
\quad \text{where } pt_i = pt \text{ if } b_i = \mathbf{true} \\
\quad \text{where } pt_i = \{\!||\!\} \text{ if } b_i = \mathbf{false} \\
\mathcal{C}(sw, pg \uplus pg') = \\
\quad [(pat_1 \cap pat'_1, pt_1 \uplus pt'_1), \cdots, (pat_m \cap pat'_n, pt_m \uplus pt'_n)] +\!\!+ \\
\quad [(pat_1, pt_1) \cdots (pat_m, pt_m)] +\!\!+ \\
\quad [(pat'_1, pt'_1) \cdots (pat'_n, pt'_n)] \\
\quad\quad \text{where } [(pat_1, pt_1) \cdots (pat_m, pt_m)] = \mathcal{P}(sw, pg) \\
\quad\quad \text{where } [(pat'_1, pt'_1) \cdots (pat'_n, pt'_n)] = \mathcal{P}(sw, pg')
\end{array}$$

Figure 6: NetCore compilation.

5. Verified NetCore Compiler

With the syntax and semantics of NetCore and flow tables in place, we now present a verified compiler for NetCore. The compiler takes programs as input and generates a set of flow tables as output, one for every switch. The compilation algorithm is based on previous work [22], but we have verified its implementation in Coq. While building the compiler, we found two serious bugs in the original algorithm related to the handling of (unnatural) patterns in the compiler and flow table optimizer.

The compilation function $\mathcal{C}$, defined in Fig. 6, generates a flow table for a given switch sw. It uses the auxiliary function $\mathcal{P}$ to compile predicates. The compiler produces a list of pattern-action pairs, but priority numbers are implicit: the pair at the head has highest priority and each successive pair has lower priority.

Because NetCore programs denote total functions, packets not explicitly matched by any predicate are dropped. In contrast, flow tables divert unmatched packets to the controller. The compiler resolves this discrepancy by adding a catch-all rule that drops unmatched packets. For instance:

$$\mathcal{C}(sw, \mathbf{dlSrc} = H1 \Rightarrow \{\!|5|\!\}) = \{\!|(2, \{\mathbf{dlSrc} = H1\}, \{\!|5|\!\}), (1, \star, \{\!||\!\})|\!\}$$

The key operator used by the compiler constructs the cross-product of the flow tables provided as input. This operator can be used to compute intersections and unions of flow tables. Note that implementing union in the "obvious" way—by concatenating flow tables—would be wrong. The cross-product operator performs an element-wise intersection of the input flow tables and then merges their actions. To compile a union, we first use cross-product to build a flow table that represents the intersection, and then concatenate the flow tables for the sub-policies at lower priority. For example, the following NetCore program,

$$\mathbf{dlSrc} = \mathit{H1} \Rightarrow \{\!|5|\!\} \uplus \mathbf{dlDst} = \mathit{H2} \Rightarrow \{\!|10|\!\}$$

compiles to a flow table:

Priority	Pattern	Action
4	$\{\mathbf{dlSrc} = \mathit{H1}, \mathbf{dlDst} = \mathit{H2}\}$	$\{\!|5, 10|\!\}$
3	$\{\mathbf{dlSrc} = \mathit{H1}\}$	$\{\!|5|\!\}$
2	$\{\mathbf{dlDst} = \mathit{H2}\}$	$\{\!|10|\!\}$
1	$\star$	$\{\!||\!\}$

The first rule matches all packets that match both sub-programs, while the second and third rules match packets only matched by the left and the right programs respectively. The final rule drops all other packets. The compilation of other predicates uses similar manipulations on flow tables.

We have built a large library of flow table manipulation operators in Coq, along with several lemmas that state useful algebraic properties about these operators. With this library, proving the correctness theorem for the NetCore compiler is simple—only about 200 lines of code in Coq.

Theorem 1 (NetCore Compiler Soundness). *For all NetCore programs pg, switches sw, ports pt, and packets pk we have* $[\![\mathcal{C}(sw, pg)]\!]\ pt\ pk = [\![pg]\!]\ sw\ pt\ pk$.

Intuitively, this theorem states that a flow table compiled from a NetCore program for a switch sw, has the same behavior as the NetCore program evaluated on packets at sw.

Compiler bugs. In the course of our work, we discovered that several unverified compilers from high-level network programming languages to flow tables suffer from bugs due to subtle pattern semantics. Section 4 described inter-field dependencies in patterns. For example, to match packets from IP address `10.0.0.1`, we write

$$\{\mathbf{nwSrc} = \texttt{10.0.0.1}, \mathbf{dlTyp} = \texttt{0x800}\}$$

and if we omit the **dlTyp** field, the IP address is silently ignored. This unintuitive behavior has led to bugs in PANE [6] and Nettle [27] as well as an unverified version of NetCore [22]. To illustrate, consider the following program:

$$\mathbf{nwSrc} = \texttt{10.0.0.1} \Rightarrow \{\!|5|\!\}$$

In NetCore, this program matches all IP packets from `10.0.0.1` and forwards them out port 5. But the original NetCore compiler produced the following flow table for this program:

Priority	Pattern	Action
2	$\{\mathbf{nwSrc} = \texttt{10.0.0.1}\}$	$\{\!|5|\!\}$
1	$\star$	$\{\!||\!\}$

Because the first pattern is equivalent to the all-wildcard pattern, this flow table sends *all* traffic out port 5. Both PANE and Nettle have similar bugs. Nettle has a special case to handle patterns with IP addresses that do not specify **dlTyp** = `0x800`, but it does not correctly handle patterns that specify a transport port number but not the **nwProto** field. PANE suffers from the same bug. Even worse, these invalid patterns lead to further bugs when flow tables are combined and optimized by the compiler.

Natural patterns. The verified NetCore compiler does not suffer from the bug above. In our formal development, we require that all patterns manipulated by the compiler be what we call *natural patterns*. A natural pattern has the property that if the pattern specifies the value of a field, then all of that field's dependencies are also met. This rules out patterns such as $\{\mathbf{nwSrc} = \texttt{10.0.0.1}\}$, which omits the Ethernet frame type necessary to parse the IP address. Natural patterns are easy to define using dependent types in Coq. Moreover, we can calculate the cross-product of two natural patterns by intersecting fields point-wise. Hence, it is easy to prove that natural patterns are closed under intersection.

Lemma 1. *If* pat_1 *and* pat_2 *are natural patterns, then* $pat_1 \cap pat_2$ *is also a natural pattern.*

Another important property is that all patterns can be expressed as some equivalent natural pattern (where patterns are equivalent if they denote the same set of packets). This property tells us that we do not lose expressiveness by restricting to natural patterns.

Lemma 2. *If* pat *is an arbitrary pattern, then there exists a natural pattern* pat'*, such that* $pat \equiv pat'$.

These lemmas are used extensively in the proofs of correctness for our compiler and flow table optimizer.

Flow table optimizer. The basic NetCore compilation algorithm described so far generates flow tables that correctly implement the semantics of the input program. But many flow tables have redundant entries that could be safely removed. For example, a naive compiler might translate the program $(\star \Rightarrow \{\!|5|\!\})$ to the flow table $\{\!|(2, \star, \{\!|5|\!\}), (1, \star, \{\!||\!\})|\!\}$, which is equivalent to $\{\!|(2, \star, \{\!|5|\!\})|\!\}$. Worse, because the compilation rule for union uses a cross-product operator to combine the flow tables computed for sub-programs, the output can be exponentially larger than the input. Without an optimizer, such a naive compiler is essentially useless—*e.g.*, we built an unoptimized implementation of the algorithm in Fig. 6 and found that it ran out of memory when compiling a program consisting of just 9 operators!

Our compiler is parameterized on a function $\mathcal{O} : FT \rightarrow FT$, that it invokes at each recursive call. Because even simple policies can see a combinatorial explosion during compilation, this inline reduction is necessary. We stipulate that $\mathcal{O}$ must produce equivalent flow tables: $[\![\mathcal{O}(FT)]\!] = [\![FT]\!]$.

We have built an optimizer that eliminates low-priority entries whose patterns are fully subsumed by higher-priority rules and proved that it satisfies the above condition in Coq. Although this optimization is quite simple, it is effective in practice. In addition, earlier attempts to implement this optimization in NetCore had a bug that incorrectly identified certain rules as overlapping which we did not discover until developing this proof. The PANE optimizer also had a bug—it assumed that combining identical actions is always idempotent. Both of these bugs led to incorrect behavior.

6. Featherweight OpenFlow

The next step towards executing NetCore programs is a controller that configures the switches in the network. To prove that such a controller is correct, we need a model of the network. Unfortunately, the OpenFlow 1.0 specification, consisting of 42 pages of informal prose and C definitions, is not amenable to rigorous proof.

This section presents Featherweight OpenFlow, a detailed operational model that captures the essential features of OpenFlow networks, and yet still fits on a single page. The model elides a number of details such as error codes, counters, packet modification, and advanced configuration options such as the ability to enable and disable ports. But it does include all of the features related to how packets are forwarded and how flow tables are modified. Many existing SDN bug-finding and property-checking tools are based on

Switch	S	$::= \mathbb{S}(sw, pts, FT, in_p, out_p, in_m, out_m)$
Controller	C	$::= \mathbb{C}(\sigma, f_{in}, f_{out})$
Link	L	$::= \mathbb{L}((sw_{src}, pt_{src}), pks, (sw_{dst}, pt_{dst}))$
Link to Controller	M	$::= \mathbb{M}(sw, SMS, CMS)$

Devices

Ports on switch	pts	$\in \{pt\}$
Input/output buffers	in_p, out_p	$\in \{\!\lvert (pt, pk) \rvert\!\}$
Messages from controller	in_m	$\in \{\!\lvert SM \rvert\!\}$
Messages to controller	out_m	$\in \{\!\lvert CM \rvert\!\}$

Switch Components

Controller state	σ
Controller input relation	$f_{in} \in sw \times CM \times \sigma \rightsquigarrow \sigma$
Controller output relation	$f_{out} \in \sigma \rightsquigarrow sw \times SM \times \sigma$

Controller Components

Message queue from controller	$SMS \in [SM_1 \cdots SM_n]$
Message queue to controller	$CMS \in [CM_1 \cdots CM_n]$

Controller Link

From controller	SM	$::= \textbf{FlowMod}\ \delta \mid \textbf{PktOut}\ pt\ pk \mid \textbf{BarrierRequest}\ n$
To controller	CM	$::= \textbf{PktIn}\ pt\ pk \mid \textbf{BarrierReply}\ n$
Table update	δ	$::= \textbf{Add}\ n\ pat\ act \mid \textbf{Del}\ pat$

Abstract OpenFlow Protocol

$$\frac{[\![FT]\!](pt, pk) \rightsquigarrow (\{\!\lvert pt'_1 \cdots pt'_n \rvert\!\}, \{\!\lvert pk'_1 \cdots pk'_m \rvert\!\})}{\begin{array}{l}\mathbb{S}(sw, pts, FT, \{\!\lvert (pt, pk) \rvert\!\} \uplus in_p, out_p, in_m, out_m) \\ \xrightarrow{(sw,pt,pk)} \mathbb{S}(sw, pts, FT, in_p, \{\!\lvert (pt'_1, pk) \cdots (pt'_n, pk) \rvert\!\} \uplus out_p, in_m, \{\!\lvert \textbf{PktIn}\ pt\ pk'_1 \cdots \textbf{PktIn}\ pt\ pk'_m \rvert\!\} \uplus out_m)\end{array}} \quad (\textsc{Fwd})$$

$$\frac{}{\begin{array}{l}\mathbb{S}(sw, pts, FT, in_p, \{\!\lvert (pt, pk) \rvert\!\} \uplus out_p, in_m, out_m) \mid \mathbb{L}((sw, pt), pks, (sw', pt')) \\ \longrightarrow \mathbb{S}(sw, pts, FT, in_p, out_p, in_m, out_m) \mid \mathbb{L}((sw, pt), [pk] +\!\!+ pks, (sw', pt'))\end{array}} \quad (\textsc{Wire-Send})$$

$$\frac{}{\begin{array}{l}\mathbb{L}((sw', pt'), pks +\!\!+ [pk], (sw, pt)) \mid \mathbb{S}(sw, pts, FT, in_p, out_p, in_m, out_m) \\ \longrightarrow \mathbb{L}((sw', pt'), pks, (sw, pt)) \mid \mathbb{S}(sw, pts, FT, \{\!\lvert (pt, pk) \rvert\!\} \uplus in_p, out_p, in_m, out_m)\end{array}} \quad (\textsc{Wire-Recv})$$

$$\frac{}{\mathbb{S}(sw, pts, FT, in_p, out_p, \{\!\lvert \textbf{FlowMod Add}\ m\ pat\ act \rvert\!\} \uplus in_m, out_m) \longrightarrow \mathbb{S}(sw, pts, FT \uplus \{\!\lvert (m, pat, act) \rvert\!\}, in_p, out_p, in_m, out_m)} \quad (\textsc{Add})$$

$$\frac{FT_{rem} = \{\!\lvert (n', pat', act') \mid (n', pat', act') \in FT \text{ and } pat \neq pat' \rvert\!\}}{\mathbb{S}(sw, pts, FT, in_p, out_p, \{\!\lvert \textbf{FlowMod Del}\ pat \rvert\!\} \uplus in_m, out_m) \longrightarrow \mathbb{S}(sw, pts, FT_{rem}, in_p, out_p, in_m, out_m)} \quad (\textsc{Del})$$

$$\frac{pt \in pts}{\mathbb{S}(sw, pts, FT, in_p, out_p, \{\!\lvert \textbf{PktOut}\ pt\ pk \rvert\!\} \uplus in_m, out_m) \longrightarrow \mathbb{S}(sw, pts, FT, in_p, \{\!\lvert (pt, pk) \rvert\!\} \uplus out_p, in_m, out_m)} \quad (\textsc{PktOut})$$

$$\frac{f_{out}(\sigma) \rightsquigarrow (sw, SM, \sigma')}{\mathbb{C}(\sigma, f_{in}, f_{out}) \mid \mathbb{M}(sw, SMS, CMS) \longrightarrow \mathbb{C}(\sigma', f_{in}, f_{out}) \mid \mathbb{M}(sw, [SM] +\!\!+ SMS, CMS)} \quad (\textsc{Ctrl-Send})$$

$$\frac{f_{in}(sw, \sigma, CM) \rightsquigarrow \sigma'}{\mathbb{C}(\sigma, f_{in}, f_{out}) \mid \mathbb{M}(sw, SMS, CMS +\!\!+ [CM]) \longrightarrow \mathbb{C}(\sigma', f_{in}, f_{out}) \mid \mathbb{M}(sw, SMS, CMS)} \quad (\textsc{Ctrl-Recv})$$

$$\frac{SM \neq \textbf{BarrierRequest}\ n}{\begin{array}{l}\mathbb{M}(sw, SMS +\!\!+ [SM], CMS) \mid \mathbb{S}(sw, pts, FT, in_p, out_p, in_m, out_m) \\ \longrightarrow \mathbb{M}(sw, SMS, CMS) \mid \mathbb{S}(sw, pts, FT, in_p, out_p, \{\!\lvert SM \rvert\!\} \uplus in_m, out_m)\end{array}} \quad (\textsc{Switch-Recv-Ctrl})$$

$$\frac{}{\begin{array}{l}\mathbb{M}(sw, SMS +\!\!+ [\textbf{BarrierRequest}\ n], CMS) \mid \mathbb{S}(sw, pts, FT, in_p, out_p, \{\!\lvert \rvert\!\}, out_m) \\ \longrightarrow \mathbb{M}(sw, SMS, CMS) \mid \mathbb{S}(sw, pts, FT, in_p, out_p, \{\!\lvert \rvert\!\}, \{\!\lvert \textbf{BarrierReply}\ n \rvert\!\} \uplus out_m)\end{array}} \quad (\textsc{Switch-Recv-Barrier})$$

$$\frac{}{\begin{array}{l}\mathbb{S}(sw, pts, FT, in_p, out_p, in_m, \{\!\lvert CM \rvert\!\} \uplus out_m) \mid \mathbb{M}(sw, SMS, CMS) \\ \longrightarrow \mathbb{S}(sw, pts, FT, in_p, out_p, in_m, out_m) \mid \mathbb{M}(sw, SMS, [CM] +\!\!+ CMS)\end{array}} \quad (\textsc{Switch-Send-Ctrl})$$

$$\frac{Sys_1 \longrightarrow Sys'_1}{Sys_1 \mid Sys_2 \longrightarrow Sys'_1 \mid Sys_2} \quad (\textsc{Congruence})$$

Figure 7: Featherweight OpenFlow syntax and semantics.

similar (informal) models [3, 12, 13]. We believe Featherweight OpenFlow could also serve as a foundation for these tools.

6.1 OpenFlow Semantics

Initially, every switch has an empty flow table that diverts all packets to the controller. Using **FlowMod** messages, the controller can insert new table entries to have the switch process packets itself. A non-trivial program may compile to several thousand flow table entries, but **FlowMod** messages only add a single entry at a time. In general, many **FlowMod** messages will be needed to fully configure a switch. However, OpenFlow is designed to give switches a lot of latitude to enable efficient processing, often at the expense of programmability and understandability:

- **Pattern semantics.** As discussed in preceding sections, the semantics of flow tables is non-trivial: patterns have implicit dependencies and flow tables can have multiple, overlapping entries. (The OpenFlow specification itself notes that scanning the table to find overlaps is expensive.) Therefore, it is up to the controller to avoid overlaps that introduce non-determinism.
- **Packet reordering.** Switches may reorder packets arbitrarily. For example, switches often have both a "fast path" that uses custom packet-processing hardware and a "slow path" that processes packets using a slower general-purpose CPU.
- **No acknowledgments.** Switches do not acknowledge when **FlowMod** messages are processed, except when errors occur. The controller can explicitly request acknowledgements by sending a *barrier request* after a **FlowMod**. When the switch has processed the **FlowMod** (and all other messages received before the *barrier request*), it responds with a *barrier reply*.
- **Control message reordering.** Switches may process control messages, including **FlowMod** messages, in any order. This is based on the architecture of switches, where the logical flow table is implemented by multiple physical tables working in parallel—each physical table typically only matches headers for one protocol. To process a rule with a pattern such as $\{\textbf{nwSrc} = \texttt{10.0.0.1}, \textbf{dlTyp} = \texttt{0x800}\}$, which matches headers across several protocols, several physical tables may need to be reconfigured, which takes longer to process than a simple pattern such as $\{\textbf{dlDst} = \texttt{H2}\}$.

Figure 7 defines the syntax and semantics of Featherweight OpenFlow, which faithfully models all of these behaviors. The rest of this section discusses the key elements of the model in detail.

6.2 Network Elements

Featherweight OpenFlow has four kinds of elements: switches, controllers, links between switches (carrying data packets), and links between switches and the controller (carrying OpenFlow messages). The semantics is specified using a small-step relation, with elements interacting by passing messages and updating their state non-deterministically.

Switches. A switch $\mathbb{S}$ comprises a unique identifier sw, a set of ports pts, and input and output packet buffers in_p and out_p. The buffers are multisets of packets tagged with ports, (pt, pk). In the input buffer, packets are tagged with the port on which they were received. In the output buffer, packets are tagged with the port on which they will be sent out. Since buffers are unordered, switches can process packets in any order. Switches also have a flow table, FT, which determines how the switch processes packets. As detailed in Section 4, the table is a collection of flow table entries, where each entry has a priority, pattern and, a multiset of output ports. Each switch also has a multiset of messages to and from the controller, out_m and in_m. There are three kinds of messages from the controller:

- **PktOut** $pt\ pk$ instructs the switch to emit packet pk on port pt.
- **FlowMod** δ instructs the switch to add or delete entries from its flow table. When δ is **Add** $n\ pat\ act$, a new entry is created, whereas **Del** pat deletes all entries that match pat exactly. In our model, we assume that flow tables on switches can be arbitrarily large. This is not the case for hardware switches, where the size of flow tables is often constrained by the amount of silicon used, and varies from switch-to-switch. It would be straightforward to modify our model to bound the size of the table on each switch.
- **BarrierRequest** n forces the switch to process all outstanding messages before replying with a **BarrierReply** n message.

Controllers. A controller $\mathbb{C}$ is defined by its local state σ, an input relation f_{in}, and an output relation f_{out}. The local state and these relations are application-specific, so Featherweight OpenFlow can be instantiated with any controller whose behavior can be modeled in this way. The f_{out} relation sends a message to a switch while f_{in} receives a message from a switch. Both relations update the state σ. There are two kinds of messages a switch can send to the controller:

- **PktIn** $pt\ pk$ indicates that packet pk was received on pt and did not match any entry in the flow table.
- **BarrierReply** n indicates that sw has processed all messages up to and including a **BarrierRequest** n sent earlier.

Data links. A data link $\mathbb{L}$ is a unidirectional queue of packets between two switch ports. To model bidirectional links we use symmetric unidirectional links. Featherweight OpenFlow does not model packet-loss in links and packet-buffers. It would be easy to extend our model so that packets are lost, for example, with some probability. Without packet loss, a packet traces paths from its source to its destinations (or loops forever). With packet loss, a packet traces a prefix of the complete path given by our model under ideal conditions.

Control links. A control link $\mathbb{M}$ is a bidirectional link between the switch and the controller that contains a queue of controller messages for the switch and a queue of switch messages headed to the controller. Messages between the controller and the switch are sent and delivered in order, but may be processed in any order.

7. Verified Run-Time System

So far, we have developed a semantics for NetCore (Section 3), a compiler from NetCore to flow tables (Section 4), and a low-level semantics for OpenFlow (Section 6). To actually execute NetCore programs, we also need to develop a run-time system that installs rules on switches and prove it correct.

7.1 NetCore Run-Time System

There are many ways to build a controller that implements a NetCore run-time system. A trivial solution is to simply process all packets on the controller. The controller receives input packets as **PktIn** messages, evaluates them using the NetCore semantics, and emits the outputs using **PktOut** messages.

Of course, we can do much better by using the NetCore compiler to actually generate flow tables and install those rules on switches using **FlowMod** messages. For example, given the following program,

$$\textbf{dlDst} = \texttt{H1}\ \textbf{and}\ \textbf{not}(\textbf{dlTyp} = \texttt{0x800}) \Rightarrow \{\!|1|\!\}$$

Location	$loc ::= sw \times pt$	
Located packet	$lp ::= loc \times pk$	
Topology	$T \in loc \rightharpoonup loc$	

$$\boxed{pg, T \vdash \{\!|lp|\!\} \xRightarrow{lp} \{\!|lp|\!\}}$$

$$\frac{lps' = \{\!|(T(sw, pt_{out}), pk) \mid (pt_{out}, pk) \in [\![pg]\!]\ sw\ pt\ pk|\!\}}{pg, T \vdash \{\!|((sw, pt), pk)|\!\} \uplus \{\!|lp_1 \cdots lp_n|\!\} \xRightarrow{(sw,pt,pk)} lps' \uplus \{\!|lp_1 \cdots lp_n|\!\}}$$

Figure 8: Network semantics.

the compiler might generate the following flow table,

Priority	Pattern	Action
5	$\{$**dlDst** $=$ `H1`, **dlTyp** $=$ `0x800`$\}$	$\{\!\|\|\!\}$
4	$\{$**dlDst** $=$ `H1`$\}$	$\{\!\|1\|\!\}$
3	$\star$	$\{\!\|\|\!\}$

and the controller would emit three **FlowMod** messages:

Add 5 $\{$**dlDst** $=$ `H1`, **dlTyp** $=$ `0x800`$\}$ $\{\!|\,|\!\}$
Add 4 $\{$**dlDst** $=$ `H1`$\}$ $\{\!|1|\!\}$
Add 3 $\star$ $\{\!|\,|\!\}$

However, it would be unsafe to emit just these messages. As discussed in Section 6, switches can reorder messages to maximize throughput. This can lead to transient bugs by creating intermediate flow tables that are inconsistent with the intended policy. For example, if the **Add** 3 $\star$ $\{\!|\,|\!\}$ message is processed first, all packets will be dropped. Alternatively, if **Add** 4 $\{$**dlDst** $=$ `H1`$\}$ $\{\!|1|\!\}$ is processed first, traffic that should be dropped will be incorrectly forwarded. Of the six possible permutations, only one has the property that all intermediate states either (i) process packets according to the program, or (ii) send packets to the controller (which can evaluate them using the program). Therefore, to ensure the switch processes the messages in order, the run-time system must intersperse **BarrierRequest** messages between **FlowMod** messages.

Network semantics. The semantics of NetCore presented in Section 3 defines how a program processes a single packet at a single switch at a time. But Featherweight OpenFlow models the behavior of an entire network of inter-connected switches with multiple packets in-flight. To reconcile the difference between these two, we need a *network semantics* that models the processing of all packets in the network. In this semantics (Fig. 8), the system state is a bag of in-flight located packets $\{\!|lp|\!\}$. At each step, the system:

1. Removes a located packet $((sw, pt), pk)$, from its state,
2. Processes the packet according to the program to produce a new multiset of located packets,
$$\{\!|lp_1 \cdots lp_n|\!\} = [\![pg]\!]\ sw\ pt\ pk,$$
3. Transfers these packets to input ports, using the topology, $T(lp_1) \cdots T(lp_n)$, and
4. Adds the transferred packets to the system state.

Note that this approach to constructing a network semantics is not specific to NetCore: any hop-by-hop packet processing function could be used. Below, we refer to any semantics constructed in this way as a *network semantics*.

7.2 Run-Time System Correctness

Now we are ready to prove the correctness of the NetCore run-time system. However, rather than proving this directly, we instead develop a general framework for establishing controller correctness, and obtain the result for NetCore as a special case.

Bisimulation equivalence. The inputs to our framework are: (i) the high-level, hop-by-hop function the network is intended to implement, and (ii) the controller implementation, which is required to satisfy natural safety and liveness conditions. Given these parameters, we construct a *weak bisimulation* between the network semantics of the high-level function and an OpenFlow network instantiated with the controller implementation. This construction handles a number of low-level details once and for all, freeing developers to focus on essential controller correctness properties.

We prove a weak (rather than strong) bisimulation because Featherweight OpenFlow models the mechanics of packet processing in much greater detail than in the network semantics. For example, consider a NetCore program that forwards a packet pk from one switch to another, say *S1* to *S2*, in a single step. An equivalent Featherweight OpenFlow implementation would require at least three steps: (i) process pk at *S1*, move pk from the input buffer to the output buffer, (ii) move pk from *S1*'s output buffer to the link to *S2*, and (iii) move pk from the link to *S2*'s input buffer. If there were other packets on the link (which is likely!), additional steps would be needed. Moreover, pk could take an even more circuitous route if it is redirected to the controller.

The weak bisimulation states that the NetCore and FeatherWeight OpenFlow are indistinguishable modulo "internal" steps. Hence, any reasoning about the trajectory of a packet at the NetCore level will be preserved in FeatherWeight OpenFlow.

Observations. To define a weak bisimulation, we need a notion of observation (called an action in the π-calculus). We say that the NetCore network semantics observes a packet (sw, pt, pk) when it removes the packet from its state—i.e., just before evaluating it. Likewise, a Featherweight OpenFlow program observes a packet (sw, pt, pk) when it removes (pt, pk) from the input buffer on sw to process it using the FWD rule.

Bisimulation relation. Establishing a weak bisimulation requires exhibiting a relation $\approx_{OF}$ between the concrete and abstract states with certain properties. We relate packets located in links and buffers in Featherweight OpenFlow to packets in the abstract network semantics. We elide the full definition of the relation, but describe some of its key characteristics:

- Packets (pt, pk) in input buffers in_p on sw are related to packets $((sw, pt), pk)$ in the abstract state.
- Packets (pt, pk) in output buffers out_p on sw are related to packets located at the other side of the link connected to pt.
- Likewise, packets on a data link (or contained in **PktOut** messages) are related to packets located at the other side of the data link (or the link connected to the port in the message).

Intuitively, packets in output buffers have already been processed and observed. The network semantics moves packets to new locations in one step whereas OpenFlow requires several more steps, but we must not be able to observe these intermediate steps. Therefore, after Featherweight OpenFlow observes a concrete packet pk (in the FWD rule), subsequent copies of pk must be related to packets at the ultimate destination.

The structure of the relation is largely straightforward and dictated by the nature of Featherweight OpenFlow. However, a few parts are application specific. In particular, packets at the controller and packets sent to the controller in **PktIn** messages may relate to the state in the network semantics in application-specific ways.

Abstract semantics. So far, we have focused on NetCore to build intuitions. But our bisimulation can be obtained for any controller that implements a high-level packet-processing function. We now make this precise with a few additional definitions.

Definition 1 (Abstract Semantics). *An abstract semantics is defined by the following components:*

1. *An abstract packet-processing function on located packets:*
$$f(lp) = \{\!|lp_1 \cdots lp_n|\!\}$$
2. *An abstraction function,* $c : \sigma \rightarrow \{\!|lp|\!\}$*, that identifies the packets the controller has received but not yet processed.*

Note that the type of the NetCore semantics (Fig. 8) matches the type of the function above. In addition, because the NetCore controller simply holds the multiset of **PktIn** messages, the abstraction function is trivial. Given such an abstract semantics, we can lift it to a network semantics $\stackrel{lp}{\Longrightarrow}$ as we did for NetCore.

We say that an abstract semantics is *compatible* with a concrete controller implementation, consisting of a type of controller state σ, and input and output relations f_{in} and f_{out}, if the two satisfy the following conditions relating their behavior:

Definition 2 (Compatibility). *An abstract semantics and controller implementation are* compatible *if:*

1. *The controller ensures that all times packets are either (i) processed by switches in accordance with the packet-processing function or (ii) sent to the controller for processing;*
2. *Whenever the controller receives a packet,*
$$(sw, \textbf{\textit{PktIn}}\ pt\ pk, \sigma) \leadsto \sigma'$$
it applies the packet-processing function f to pk to get a multiset of located packets and adds them to its state
$$c(\sigma') = c(\sigma) \uplus f(pk)$$
3. *Whenever the controller emits a packet,*
$$\sigma \leadsto (sw, \textbf{\textit{PktOut}}\ pt\ pk, \sigma')$$
it removes the packet from its state:
$$c(\sigma') = c(\sigma) \setminus \{\!|(sw, pt, pk)|\!\}$$
4. *The controller eventually processes all packets (sw, pt, pk) in its state $c(\sigma)$ according to the packet-processing function, and*
5. *The controller eventually processes all OpenFlow messages.*

The first property is essential. If it did not hold, switches could process packets contrary to the intended packet-processing relation. Proving it requires reasoning about the messages sent to the switches by the controller. In particular, because switches may reorder messages, barriers must be interspersed appropriately. The second and third properties relate the abstraction function c and the controller implementation. The fourth property requires the controller to correctly process every packet it receives. The fifth property is a liveness condition requiring the controller to eventually process every OpenFlow message. This holds in the absence of failures on the control link and the controller itself.

Given such a semantics, we show that our relation between abstract and Featherweight OpenFlow states and its inverse are weak simulations. This implies that the relation is a weak bisimulation, and thus that the two systems are weakly bisimilar.

Theorem 2 (Weak Bisimulation). *For all compatible abstract semantics and controller implementations, all Featherweight OpenFlow states s and s', and all abstract states t and t':*

- *If $s \approx_{OF} t$ and $s \xrightarrow{(sw,pt,pk)} s'$, then there exists an abstract network state t'' such that $t \stackrel{(sw,pt,pk)}{\Longrightarrow} t''$ and $s' \approx_{OF} t''$, and*
- *If $s \approx_{OF} t$ and $t \stackrel{(sw,pt,pk)}{\Longrightarrow} t'$, then there exists a Featherweight OpenFlow state s'', and abstract network states s_i, s_i' such that*
$$s \longrightarrow^* s_i \xrightarrow{(sw,pt,pk)} s_i' \longrightarrow^* s''$$
and $s'' \approx_{OF} t'$.

In this theorem, portions of the $\approx_{OF}$ relation are defined in terms of the controller abstraction function, c supplied as a parameter. In addition, the proofs themselves rely on compatibility (Definition 2).

Finally, we instantiate this theorem for the NetCore controller:

Corollary 1 (NetCore Run-Time Correctness). *The network semantics of NetCore is weakly bisimilar to the concrete semantics of the NetCore controller in Featherweight OpenFlow.*

8. Implementation and Evaluation

We have built a complete working implementation of the system described in this paper, including machine-checked proofs of each of the lemmas and theorems. Our implementation is available under an open-source license at the following URL:

`http://frenetic-lang.org`

Our system consists of 12 KLOC of Coq, which we extract to OCaml and link against two unverified components:

- A library to serialize OpenFlow data types to the OpenFlow wire format. This code is a lightly modified version of the Mirage OpenFlow library [16] (1.4K LOC).
- A module to translate between the full OpenFlow protocol and the fragment used in Featherweight OpenFlow (200 LOC).

We have deployed our NetCore controllers on real hardware and used them to build a number of useful network applications including host discovery, shortest-path routing, spanning tree, access control, and traffic monitoring. Using the union operator, it is easy to compose these modules with others to form larger applications.

NetCore at home. For the past month, we have used a NetCore controller to manage the home network of one of the authors. Home networks are small, but they are dynamic as devices regularly connect and disconnect. Our controller monitors the state of the network and dynamically reconfigures an OpenFlow-enabled wireless router to support the current devices. Because Featherweight OpenFlow does not model dynamic configurations, this controller's run-time system is necessarily unverified. However, it uses the NetCore compiler as a verified sub-system. In the future, we plan to enrich our OpenFlow model with additional features, including support for dynamic configurations.

Controller throughput. Controller throughput is important for the performance of SDNs. The CBench [26] tool quantifies controller throughput by flooding the controller with **PktIn** messages and measuring the time taken to receive **PktOut** messages in response. This is a somewhat crude metric, but it is still effective, since any controller must respond to **PktIn** messages. We used CBench to compare the throughput of our verified controller with our previous unverified NetCore controller, written in Haskell, and with the popular POX and NOX controllers, written in Python and C++ respectively. To ensure that the experiment tested throughput and not the application running on it, we had each controller execute a trivial program that floods all packets. We ran the experiment on a dual-core 3.3 GHz Intel i3 with 8GB RAM with Ubuntu 12.04 and obtained the results shown in Fig. 9 (a).

Our unverified NetCore controller is significantly faster than our verified controller. We attribute this to (i) a more mature backend that uses an optimized library from Nettle [27] to serialize

Controller	Messages/sec
Unverified NetCore (Haskell)	26,022
NOX (Python and C++)	16,997
Verified NetCore (OCaml)	**9,437**
POX (Python)	6,150

(a)

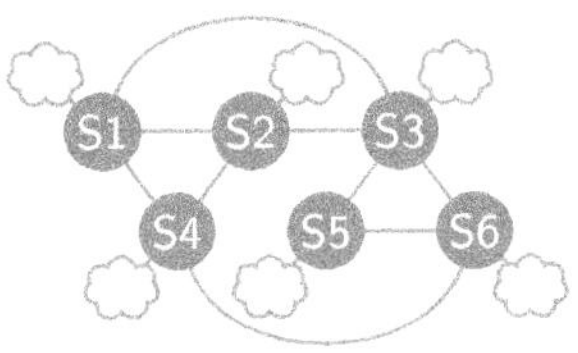

(b)

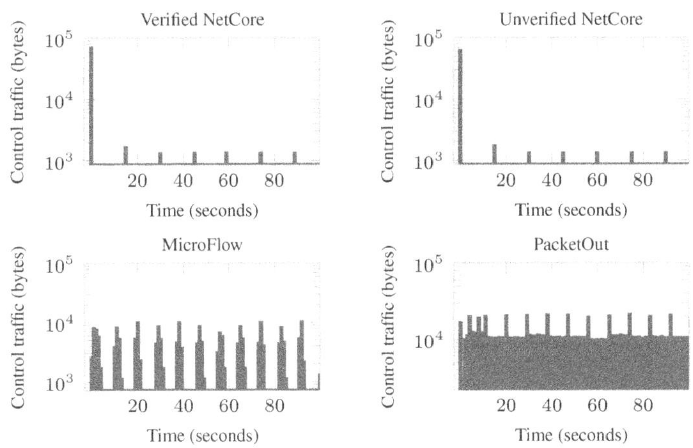

(c)

Figure 9: Experiments: (a) controller throughput results; (b) control traffic topology; (c) control traffic results.

messages, and (ii) Haskell's superior multicore support, which the controller exploits heavily. However, despite being slower than the original NetCore, the new controller is still fast enough to be useful—indeed, it is faster than the popular POX controller (although POX is not tuned for performance). We plan to optimize our controller to improve its performance in the future.

Control traffic. Another key factor that affects SDN performance is the amount of traffic that the controller must handle. This metric measures the effectiveness of the controller at compiling, optimizing, and installing forwarding rules rather than processing packets itself. To properly assess a controller on these points, we need a more substantial application than "flood all packets." Using NetCore, we built an application that computes shortest path forwarding rules as well as a spanning tree for broadcast. We ran this program on the six-switch Waxman topology shown in Fig. 9 (b), with two hosts connected to each switch.

In the experiment, every host sent 10 ICMP (ping) broadcast packets along the spanning tree, and received the replies from other hosts along shortest path routes. We used Mininet [9] to simulate the network and collected traffic traces using `tcpdump`. The total amount of network traffic during the experiment was 372 Kb.

We compared our Verified NetCore controller to several others: a (verified) "PacketOut" controller that never installs forwarding rules and processes all packets itself; our previous "Unverified NetCore" controller, written in Haskell; and a reactive "MicroFlow" controller [7] written in Haskell. The results of the experiment are shown in Fig. 9 (c). The graphs plot time-series data for every controller, showing the amount of control traffic in each one-second interval. Note that the y axis is on a logarithmic scale.

In the plot for our Verified NetCore controller, there is a large spike in control traffic at the start of the experiment, where the controller sends messages to install the forwarding rules generated from the program. Additional control traffic appears every 15 seconds; these messages implement a simple keep-alive protocol between the controller and switches. The Unverified NetCore controller uses the same compilation and run-time system algorithms as our verified controller, so its plot is nearly identical. The MicroFlow controller installs individual fine-grained rules in response to individual traffic flows rather than proactively compiling complete flow tables. Accordingly, its plot shows that there is much more control traffic than for the two NetCore controllers. The graph shows how traffic spikes when multiple hosts respond simultaneously to an ICMP broadcast. The fourth plot shows the behavior of the PacketOut controller. Because this controller does not install any forwarding rules on the switches, all data traffic flows to the controller and then back into the network.

Although these results are preliminary, we believe they demonstrate that the performance of our verified NetCore controller can be competitive with other controllers. In particular, our verified controller generates the same flow tables and handles a similar amount of traffic as the earlier unverified NetCore controller, which was written in Haskell. Moreover, our system is not tuned for performance. As we optimize and extend our system, we expect that its performance will only improve.

9. Related Work

Verification technology has progressed dramatically in the past decades, making it feasible to prove useful theorems about real systems including databases [18], compilers [15], and even whole operating systems [14]. Compilers have been particularly fruitful targets for verification efforts [11]. Most prominently, the CompCert compiler translates programs in a large subset of C to PowerPC, ARM, and x86 executables [15]. The Verified Software Toolchain project provides machine-checked infrastructure for connecting properties obtained by program analysis to guarantees at the machine level [2]. Rocksalt verifies a tool for analyzing machine code against a detailed model of x86 [23]. Another system, Bedrock provides rich Coq libraries for verifying low-level programs [5]. Much earlier, a compiler for a Pascal-like language was formalized and verified as a part of the CLInc stack [31]. Significant portions of many other compilers have been formalized and verified, including the LLVM intermediate representation [33], the F* typechecker [25], and an extension of CompCert with garbage collection [20]. Our work is inspired by all of these efforts, but is the first to tackle the challenge of building a verified SDN controller.

Over the past few years, a number of researchers have proposed high-level programming languages for controlling networks, including COOLAID [4], FML [10], Frenetic [7], NetCore [22], and PANE [6]. This work uses NetCore [22] as a high-level network programming language. NetCore's original semantics was defined in terms of handwritten proofs and a complex abstract machine while we use machine-checked proofs and Featherweight OpenFlow. In proving our compiler and run-time system correct, we discovered several bugs in the unverified NetCore compiler and runtime. A portion of the PANE compiler was formalized in Coq, but since the proof did not model several subtleties of flow tables, the compiler still had bugs. Unlike our system, PANE does not model or verify any portion of its run-time system. We used some of the PANE proofs during early development of our system. Lastly, Mirage [16], a language for writing cloud applications, includes an SDN interface. Our OpenFlow serializers are based on Mirage's.

Formally Verifiable Networking (FVN) [28] is a platform for synthesizing protocol implementations from formal specifications (though the synthesizer is unverified). Our work attacks the problem of generating and deploying correct network-wide configurations, rather than building distributed routing protocols. We use formal methods to build compilers, shifting the need for expertise with formal methods away from programmers.

Xie et al. introduced techniques for statically analyzing the reachability properties of networks [29]. A number of tools for verifying network configurations have been built using these techniques, including Header Space Analysis [12], Anteater [17], and VeriFlow[13]. These tools check whether the installed network rules have properties specified by the programmer. Our system guarantees that the generated network rules preserve the properties of the input program, enabling higher-level verification.

NICE [3] uses model-checking and symbolic execution to find bugs in OpenFlow controllers written in Python. Portions of our Featherweight OpenFlow model are inspired by the bugs discovered in NICE. Automatic Test Packet Generation [32] analyzes network configurations and constructs packets to achieve complete configuration testing coverage. Retrospective Causal Inference [24] detects minimal input sequences to induce bugs in SDN systems.

10. Conclusions

This paper presents a new foundation for network reasoning: a detailed model of OpenFlow, formalized in the Coq proof assistant, and a machine-verified compiler and run-time system for the NetCore programming language. Our main result is a general framework for establishing controller correctness that reduces the proof obligation to a small number of safety and liveness properties. In the future, we plan to develop program logics for network programs, extend Featherweight OpenFlow with additional features not included in our current core calculus, and improve the engineering aspects of our system.

Acknowledgements. The authors wish to thank Andrew Ferguson and the PLDI reviewers for many helpful comments, and members of the Mirage project, especially Anil Madhavapeddy, for developing the OCaml CStruct and OpenFlow libraries. This work is supported in part by the NSF under grant CNS-1111698, the ONR under award N00014-12-1-0757, and by a Google Research Award.

References

[1] E. Al-Shaer and S. Al-Haj. FlowChecker: Configuration analysis and verification of federated OpenFlow infrastructures. In *SafeConfig*, 2010.

[2] A. W. Appel. Verified software toolchain. In *ESOP*, 2011.

[3] M. Canini, D. Venzano, P. Perešíni, D. Kostić, and J. Rexford. A NICE way to test OpenFlow applications. In *NSDI*, 2012.

[4] X. Chen, Y. Mao, Z. M. Mao, and J. van der Merwe. Declarative configuration managaement for complex and dynamic networks. In *CoNEXT*, 2010.

[5] A. Chlipala. Mostly-automated verification of low-level programs in computational separation logic. In *PLDI*, 2011.

[6] A. D. Ferguson, A. Guha, C. Liang, R. Fonseca, and S. Krishnamurthi. Hierarchical policies for software defined networks. In *HotSDN*, 2012.

[7] N. Foster, R. Harrison, M. J. Freedman, C. Monsanto, J. Rexford, A. Story, and D. Walker. Frenetic: A network programming language. In *ICFP*, 2011.

[8] P. Gill, N. Jain, and N. Nagappan. Understanding network failures in data centers: measurement, analysis, and implications. In *SIGCOMM*, 2011.

[9] N. Handigol, B. Heller, V. Jeyakumar, B. Lantz, and N. McKeown. Reproducible network experiments using container-based emulation. In *CoNEXT*, 2012.

[10] T. L. Hinrichs, N. S. Gude, M. Casado, J. C. Mitchell, and S. Shenker. Practical declarative network management. In *WREN*, 2009.

[11] T. Hoare. The verifying compiler: A grand challenge for computing research. *JACM*, 50(1):63–69, Jan 2003.

[12] P. Kazemian, G. Varghese, and N. McKeown. Header space analysis: Static checking for networks. In *NSDI*, 2012.

[13] A. Khurshid, X. Zou, W. Zhou, M. Caesar, and P. B. Godfrey. Veriflow: Verifying network-wide invariants in real time. In *NSDI*, 2013.

[14] G. Klein, K. Elphinstone, G. Heiser, J. Andronick, D. Cock, P. Derrin, D. Elkaduwe, K. Engelhardt, R. Kolanski, M. Norrish, T. Sewell, H. Tuch, and S. Winwood. sel4: Formal verification of an OS kernel. In *SOSP*, 2009.

[15] X. Leroy. Formal verification of a realistic compiler. *CACM*, 52(7): 107–115, Jul 2009.

[16] A. Madhavapeddy, R. Mortier, C. Rotsos, D. Scott, B. Singh, T. Gazagnaire, S. Smith, S. Hand, and J. Crowcroft. Unikernels: Library operating systems for the cloud. In *ASPLOS*, 2013.

[17] H. Mai, A. Khurshid, R. Agarwal, M. Caesar, P. B. Godfrey, and S. T. King. Debugging the data plane with Anteater. In *SIGCOMM*, 2011.

[18] G. Malecha, G. Morrisett, A. Shinnar, and R. Wisnesky. Towards a verified relational database management system. In *POPL*, 2010.

[19] A. Markopoulou, G. Iannaccone, S. Bhattacharyya, C.-N. Chuah, Y. Ganjali, and C. Diot. Characterization of failures in an operational IP backbone network. *IEEE/ACM Transactions on Networking*, 16(4): 749–762, Aug 2008.

[20] A. McCreight, T. Chevalier, and A. Tolmach. A certified framework for compiling and executing garbage-collected languages. In *ICFP*, 2010.

[21] N. McKeown, T. Anderson, H. Balakrishnan, G. Parulkar, L. Peterson, J. Rexford, S. Shenker, and J. Turner. Openflow: Enabling innovation in campus networks. *SIGCOMM CCR*, 38(2):69–74, 2008.

[22] C. Monsanto, N. Foster, R. Harrison, and D. Walker. A compiler and run-time system for network programming languages. In *POPL*, 2012.

[23] G. Morrisett, G. Tan, J. Tassarotti, J.-B. Tristan, and E. Gan. RockSalt: Better, faster, stronger SFI for the x86. In *PLDI*, 2012.

[24] R. C. Scott, A. Wundsam, K. Zarifis, and S. Shenker. What, Where, and When: Software Fault Localization for SDN. Technical Report UCB/EECS-2012-178, EECS Department, University of California, Berkeley, 2012.

[25] P.-Y. Strub, N. Swamy, C. Fournet, and J. Chen. Self-certification: Bootstrapping certified typecheckers in F* with Coq. In *POPL*, 2012.

[26] A. Tootoonchian, S. Gorbunov, Y. Ganjali, M. Casado, and R. Sherwood. On controller performance in software-defined networks. In *HotICE*, 2012.

[27] A. Voellmy and P. Hudak. Nettle: Functional reactive programming of OpenFlow networks. In *PADL*, 2011.

[28] A. Wang, L. Jia, C. Lio, B. T. Loo, O. Sokolsky, and P. Basu. Formally verifiable networking. In *HotNets*, 2009.

[29] G. G. Xie, J. Zhan, D. A. Maltz, H. Zhang, A. G. Greenberg, G. Hjálmtýsson, and J. Rexford. On static reachability analysis of IP networks. In *INFOCOM*, 2005.

[30] Z. Yin, M. Caesar, and Y. Zhou. Towards understanding bugs in open source router software. In *SIGCOMM CCR*, 2010.

[31] W. Young. Verified compilation in micro-Gypsy. In *TAV*, 1989.

[32] H. Zeng, P. Kazemian, G. Varghese, and N. McKeown. Automatic test packet generation. In *CoNEXT*, 2012.

[33] J. Zhao, S. Nagarakatte, M. M. Martin, and S. Zdancewic. Formalizing the LLVM intermediate representation for verified program transformations. In *POPL*, 2012.

A General Constraint-centric Scheduling Framework for Spatial Architectures

Tony Nowatzki† Michael Sartin-Tarm† Lorenzo De Carli† Karthikeyan Sankaralingam†
Cristian Estan* Behnam Robatmili‡[1]

†University of Wisconsin-Madison *Broadcom ‡ Qualcomm Research Silicon Valley
(tjn@cs.wisc.edu, msartintarm@wisc.edu, lorenzo@cs.wisc.edu, karu@cs.wisc.edu, cristian@estan.org, behnamr@qti.qualcomm.com)

Abstract

Specialized execution using spatial architectures provides energy efficient computation, but requires effective algorithms for spatially scheduling the computation. Generally, this has been solved with architecture-specific heuristics, an approach which suffers from poor compiler/architect productivity, lack of insight on optimality, and inhibits migration of techniques between architectures.

Our goal is to develop a scheduling framework usable for all spatial architectures. To this end, we expresses spatial scheduling as a constraint satisfaction problem using Integer Linear Programming (ILP). We observe that architecture primitives and scheduler responsibilities can be related through five abstractions: placement of computation, routing of data, managing event timing, managing resource utilization, and forming the optimization objectives. We encode these responsibilities as 20 general ILP constraints, which are used to create schedulers for the disparate TRIPS, DySER, and PLUG architectures. Our results show that a general declarative approach using ILP is implementable, practical, and typically matches or outperforms specialized schedulers.

Categories and Subject Descriptors D.3.4 [*Processors*]: optimization, retargetable compilers; G.1.6 [*Optimization*]: Integer programming, Linear programming

Keywords Spatial Architectures; Spatial Architecture Scheduling; Integer Linear Programming

1. Introduction

Hardware specialization has emerged as an important way to sustain microprocessor performance improvements to address transistor energy efficiency challenges and general purpose processing's inefficiencies [6, 8, 19, 28]. The fundamental insight of many specialization techniques is to "map" large regions of computation to the hardware, breaking away from instruction-by-instruction pipelined execution and instead adopting a *spatial architecture* paradigm. Pioneering examples include RAW [50], Wavescalar [46] and TRIPS [9], motivated primarily by performance, and recent energy-focused proposals include Tartan [39], CCA [10], PLUG [13, 35], FlexCore [47], SoftHV [15], MESCAL [31], SPL [51], C-Cores [48], DySER [25, 26], BERET [27], and NPU [20]. A fundamental problem in all spatial architectures is the scheduling of computation to the hardware resources. Specifically, five intuitive abstractions in terms of graph-matching describe the scheduling problem: i) *placement of computation* on the hardware substrate, ii) *routing of data* on the substrate to reflect and carry out the computation semantics - including interconnection network assignment, network contention, and network path assignment, iii) *managing the timing of events* in the hardware, iv) *managing utilization* to orchestrate concurrent usage of hardware resources, and v) forming the *optimization objectives* to meet the architectural performance goals.

Thus far, these abstractions have not been modeled directly, and the typically NP-complete (depending on the hardware architecture) spatial architecture scheduling problem is side-stepped. Instead, the focus of architecture-specific schedulers has typically been on developing polynomial-time algorithms that approximate the optimal solution using knowledge about the architecture. Chronologically, this body of work includes the BUG scheduler for VLIW proposed in 1985 [17], UAS scheduler for clustered VLIW [41], synchronous data-flow graph scheduling [7], RAW scheduler [36], CARS VLIW code-generation and scheduler [33], TRIPS scheduler [12, 40], Wavescalar scheduler [37], and CCA scheduler proposed in 2008 [43]. While heuristic-based approaches are popular and effective, they have three problems: i) *poor compiler developer/architect productivity* since new algorithms, heuristics, and implementations are required for each architecture, ii) *lack of insight* on optimality of solution, and iii) *sandboxing of heuristics* to specific architectures — understanding and using techniques developed for one spatial architecture in another is very hard.

Considering these problems, others have looked at exact mathematical and constraint-theory based formulations of the scheduling problem. Table 1 classifies these prior efforts, which are based on integer linear programming (ILP) or Satisfiability Modulo Theory (SMT). They lack in some prominent ways - which perhaps explains why the heuristic-based approaches continue to be preferred. In particular, Feautrier [22] is the most related - but it lacks three of five abstractions required, and the static-placement/static-issue of VLIW restrict its applicability to the general problem. These techniques and their associated problems serve as the goal and inspiration for our work, which is to develop a declarative, constraint-theory based universal spatial architecture scheduler.

By unifying multiple facets of the related work above, specifically the past experience of architecture-specific spatial schedulers, the principal of attaining architectural generality, and the mathematical power of integer linear programming, we seek to create a solution which allows high developer productivity, provides provable properties on results, and enables true architectural generality. Achieving architectural generality through the five scheduling abstractions mentioned above is the key novelty of our work.

Implementation: In this paper, we use Integer Linear Programming (ILP) because it allows a high degree of constraint expressability, can provide strong bounds on the solution's optimality, and has fast commercial solvers like CPLEX, GUROBI, and XPRESS.

[1] Majority of work completed while author was a PhD student at UT-Austin

PLDI'13, June 16–19, 2013, Seattle, WA, USA.

Year	Technique	Comments or differences to our approach
1950	ILP machine sched. [49]	M-Job-DAG to N-resource scheduling. No job communication modeling, or network contention modeling. (missing ii,iv)
1992	ILP for VLIW[22]	Modulo scheduling. Cannot model an interconnection network, spatial resources, or network contention. (missing i,ii,iv)
1997	Inst scheduling [16]	Single-Processor Modulo Scheduling. (missing i,ii,iv)
2001	Process scheduling [18]	M-Job-DAG to N-resource scheduling using dynamic programming. Has no network routing or contention modeling, fixed job delays, and no flexible objective. (missing ii,iv,v)
2002	ILP for RAW [3]	M-Job-DAG to N-resource scheduling. Not generalizable as it does not model network routing or contention, just fixed network delays. (missing ii,iv)
2007	Multiproc Sched. [34,45]	M-Job-DAG to N-resource scheduling - No path assignment or contention modeling, just fixed delays. (missing ii,iv)
2008	SMT for PLA [21]	Strict communication and computation requirements: no network contention or path assignment modeling (missing ii,iv).

Table 1. Related work – Legend: i) computation placement ii) data routing iii) event timing iv) utilization v) optimization objective

Specifically, we use the GAMS modeling language. We show that a total of 20 constraints specify the problem. We implement these constraints and report on results for three architectures picked to stress our ILP scheduler in various ways. To stress the performance deliverable by our general ILP approach, we consider TRIPS because it is a mature architecture with sophisticated specialized schedulers resulting from multi-year efforts [1, 9, 12, 40]. To represent the emerging class of energy-centric specialized spatial architectures, we consider DySER [26]. Finally, to demonstrate the generality of our technique, we consider PLUG [13, 35], which uses a radically different organization. Respectively, only 3, 1, and 10 additional (and quite straightforward) constraints are required to handle architecture-specific details. We show that standard ILP solvers allows succinct implementation (our code is less than 50 lines in GAMS), provide solutions in tractable run-times, and the mappings produced are either competitive with or significantly better than those of specialized schedulers. The general and declarative approach allows schedulers to be *specified, implemented, evaluated* rapidly. Our implementation is provided as an open-source download, allowing the community to build upon our work.

Paper Organization: The next section presents background on the three architectures and an ILP primer. Section 3 presents an overview of our approach, Section 4 presents the detailed ILP formulation, Section 5 discusses architecture-specific modeling constraints. Section 6 presents evaluation and Section 7 concludes. Related work was covered in the introduction.

2. Spatial Architectures and ILP Primer

2.1 Spatial Architectures

We use the term *spatial architecture* to refer to an architecture in which some subset of the hardware resources, namely functional units, interconnection network, or storage, are exposed to the compiler, whose job, as part of the scheduling phase, is to map computation and communication primitives in the instruction set architecture to these hardware resources. VLIW architectures, dataflow machines likes TRIPS and Wavescalar, tiled architectures like RAW and PLUG, and accelerators like CCA, SoftHV, and DySER all fit this definition. We now briefly describe the three spatial architectures we consider in detail, and a short primer on ILP. A detailed diagram of all three architectures is in Figure 8 (page 7).

The **TRIPS architecture** is organized into 16 tiles, with each tile containing 64 slots, with these slots grouped into sets of eight. The slots from one group are available for mapping one block of code, with different groups used for concurrently executing blocks. The tiles are interconnected using a 2-D mesh network, which implements dimension-ordered routing and provides support for flow-control and network contention. The scheduler must perform computation mapping: it takes a block of instructions (which can be no more than 128 instructions long) and assigns each instruction to one of the 16 tiles and within them, to one of the 8 slots.

The **DySER architecture** consists of *functional units* (FUs) and *switches*, and is integrated into the execution stage of a conventional processor. Each FU is connected to four neighboring switches from where it gets input values and injects outputs. The switches allow datapaths to be dynamically specialized. Using a compiler, applications are profiled to extract the most commonly executed regions, called path-trees, which are then mapped to the DySER array. The role of the scheduler is to map nodes in the path-trees to tiles in the DySER array and to determine switch configurations to assign a path for the data-flow graph edges. There is no hardware support for contention, and some mappings may result in unroutable paths. Hence, the scheduler must ensure the mappings are correct, have low latencies and have high throughput.

The **PLUG architecture** is designed to work as an accelerator for data-structure lookups in network processing. Each PLUG tile consists of a set of SRAM banks, a set of no-buffering routers, and an array of statically scheduled in-order cores. The only memory access allowed by a core is to its local SRAM, which makes all delays statically determinable. Applications are expressed as dataflow graphs with code-snippets (the PLUG literature refers to them as code-blocks) and memory associated with each node of the graph. Execution of programs is data-flow driven by messages sent from tile to tile - the ISA provides a *send* instruction. The scheduler must perform computation mapping and network mapping (dataflow edges $\rightarrow$ networks). It must ensure there is no contention for any network link, which it can do by scheduling when *send* instructions execute in a code-snippet or adjusting the mapping of graph nodes to tiles. It must also handle flow-control.

In all three architectures, multiple instances of a block, region, or dataflow graph are executing concurrently on the same hardware, resulting in additional contention and flow-control.

2.2 ILP Primer

Integer Linear Programs (ILP) are algebraic models of systems used for optimization [52]. They are composed of three parts: 1) decision variables describing the possible outcomes, 2) linear equations on these variables describing the set of valid solutions, 3) an objective function which orders solutions by desirability. A short tutorial on ILP modeling and solving techniques is here: `http://wpweb2.tepper.cmu.edu/fmargot/introILP.html`.

2.3 Non goals

Graph abstractions and ILP (Integer Linear Programming) techniques are common in architecture and programming languages, and are used for a variety of applications unrelated to spatial scheduling. *Our goal is not to unify this wide and diverse domain.* In the following we discuss a few examples of "non-related work" and "non-goals", highlighting the difference from our techniques.

Notably, uses of ILP in register allocation, code-generation, and optimization ordering for conventional architectures [32, 42] are unrelated to the primitives of spatial architecture scheduling. Affine loop analysis and resulting instruction scheduling/code-generation for superscalar processors is a popular use of mathematical models [2, 5, 44], and since it falls within the data-dependence analysis role of the compiler, not its scheduler, is a non-goal for us. In general, modeling loops or any form of back-edges is meaningless for

#	Architecture feature	Scheduler responsibility	TRIPS	DySER	PLUG
1	Compute HW organization	Placement of computation	Homogeneous compute units	Heterogeneous compute units	Homogeneous compute units
2	Network HW organization	Routing of data	2-D grid, dimension-order routing	2-D grid, unconstrained routing	2-D multi-network grid, dimension-order routing
3	HW timing and synchronization	Manage timing of events	Data-flow execution and dynamic network arbitration	Data-flow execution and conflict-free network assignment + flow control	Hybrid data-flow and in-order execution with static compute and network timing
4	Concurrent HW usage **within a block**	Manage utilization	8-slots per compute-unit, reg-tile, data-tile	No concurrent usage; dedicated compute units, switches, links	32 slots per compute-unit; bundled links and multicast communication
	Concurrent HW usage **across blocks**		Concurrent execution of different blocks	Concurrent usage across blocks with pipelined execution	Pipelined execution across different tiles
5	Performance Goal **architecturally mandated**	Naturally enforced by ILP constraints	Any assignment legal	Throughput	Throughput
	Performance Goal **high efficiency**	ILP objective formulation	Throughput and Latency	Latency & Latency Mismatch	Latency

Table 2. Relationship between architectural primitives and scheduler responsibilities.

our work because of the nature of our scheduler's role (scheduling happens at a finer granularity than loops, so we always deal with Directed Acyclic Graphs by design).

On the architecture side, ILP and similar optimization theories have been used for hardware synthesis and VLSI CAD problems [4, 11, 31]. These techniques focus on taking a fixed computational kernel and generating a specialized hardware implementation. This is generally accomplished by extending/customizing a well-defined hardware pipeline structure. Therefore, even if in principle they share some responsibilities with our scheduler, the concrete approach they take differs significantly and cannot be applied to our case. For example, in [4] contention and timing issues are avoided by design, by provisioning enough functional units to meet the target latency, and by statically adjusting the system to timing constraints. In [31], ILP is used as a sub-step to synthesize pipelined hardware implementations of loops. Their formulation is specific to the problem and system, and does not apply to the more general scheduling problem. Finally, performance modeling frameworks, such as [38], are also orthogonal to our work. We emphasize that we have cited only a small subset of representative literature in the interest of space.

3. Overview

We present below the main insights of our approach in using constraint-solving for specifying the scheduling problem for spatial architectures. We distill the formulation into five responsibilities, each corresponding to one architectural primitive of the hardware. For a more general discussion of limitations and concerns related to our approach, see the comments in section 7 (Conclusions).

The scheduler for a spatial architecture works at the granularity of "blocks" of code, which could be basic-blocks, hyper-blocks, code-regions, or other more sophisticated partitions of program code. These blocks, which we represent as directed acyclic graphs (DAGs) consist of computation instructions, control-flow instructions, and memory access instructions that must be mapped to the hardware. We formulate the scheduling problem as spatially mapping a typed computation DAG G to a hardware graph H under certain constraints as shown by Figure 1 on page 4. For ease of explanation, we describe G as comprised of vertices and edges, while H is comprised of nodes, routers and links(formal definitions and details follow in Section 4).

To design and implement a general scheduler applicable to many spatial architectures, we observe that five fundamental architectural primitives, each with a corresponding scheduler responsibility, capture the problem as outlined in Table 2 (columns 2 and 3). Implementing these responsibilities mathematically is a matter of constraint and objective formulas involving integer variables, which form an ILP model, covered in depth in Section 4. Below we describe the insight connecting the primitives and responsibilities and highlight the mathematical approach. Table 2 summarizes this correspondence (in columns 2 and 3), and describes these primitives for three different architectures.

Computation HW organization → Placement of computation: The spatial organization of the computational resources, which could have a homogeneous or heterogeneous mix of computational units, requires the scheduler to provide an assignment of individual operations to hardware locations. As part of this responsibility, vertices in G are mapped to nodes in the H graph.

Network HW organization → Routing of data: The capabilities and organization of the network dictate how the scheduler must handle the mapping of communication between operations to the hardware substrate, i.e. the scheduler must create a mapping from edges in G to the links represented in H. As shown in the 2nd row of Table 2, the network organization consists of the spatial layout of the network, the number of networks, and the network routing algorithm. The flow of data required by the computation block and the placement of operations defines the required communication. Depending on the architecture, the scheduler may have to select a network for each message, or even select the exact path it takes.

Hardware timing/synchronization → Manage timing of events: The scheduler must take into consideration the timing properties of computation and network together with architectural restrictions, as shown in the 3rd row of table 2. In some architectures, the scheduler cannot determine the exact timing of events because it is affected by dynamic factors (e.g. memory latency through the caching hierarchy). For all architectures, the scheduler must have at least a partial view of timing of individual operations and individual messages to be able to minimize the latency of the computation block. In some architectures, the scheduler must exert extensive fine-grained control over timing to achieve static synchronization of certain events.

Concurrent hardware resource usage → Managing Utilization: Central to the difficulties of the scheduling problem is the concurrent usage of hardware resources by multiple vertices/edges in G of one node/link in H. We formalize this concurrent usage with a notion of *utilization*, which represents the amount of work a single hardware resource performs. Such concurrent usage (and hence > 1 *utilization*) can occur *within* a DAG and across concurrently executing DAGs. Overall, the scheduler must be aware of resource

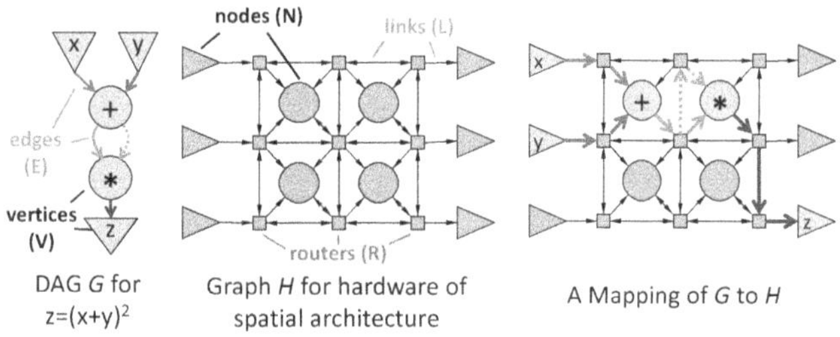

Figure 1. Example of computation G mapped to hardware H.

limits in H and which resources can be shared as shown in Table 2 row 4. For example, in TRIPS, within a single DAG, 8 instruction-slots share a single ALU (node in H), and across concurrent DAGs, 64 slots share a single ALU in TRIPS. In both cases, this node-sharing leads to contention on the links as well.

Performance goal → Formulate ILP objective: The performance goals of an architecture generally fall into two categories: those which are enforced by certain architectural limitations or abilities, and those which can be influenced by the schedule. For instance, both PLUG and DySER are throughput engines that try to perform one computation per cycle, and *any legal* schedule will naturally enforce this behavior. For this type of performance goal, the scheduler relies on the ILP constraints already present in the model. On the other hand, the scheduler generally has control over multiple quantities which can improve the performance. This often means deciding between the conflicting goals of minimizing the latency of individual blocks and managing the utilization among the available hardware resources to avoid creating bottlenecks, which it manages by prioritizing optimization quantities.

4. General ILP framework

This section presents our general ILP formulation in detail. Our formal notation closely follows our ILP formulation in GAMS instead of the more conventional notation often used for graphs in literature. We represent the computation graph as a set of vertices V, and a set of edges E. The computation DAG, represented by the adjacency matrix $G(V \cup E, V \cup E)$, explicitly represents edges as the connections between vertices. For example, for some $v \in V$ and $e \in E$, $G(v,e) = 1$ means that edge e is an output edge from vertex v. Likewise, $G(e,v) = 1$ signifies that e is an input to vertex v. For convenience, lowercase letters represents elements of the corresponding uppercase letters' set.

We similarly represent the hardware graph as a set of hardware computational resource nodes N, a set of routers R which serve as intermediate points in the routing network, and a set of L unidirectional links which connect the routers and resource nodes. The graph which describes the network organization is given by the adjacency matrix $H(N \cup R \cup L, N \cup R \cup L)$. To clarify, for some $l \in L$ and $n \in N$, if the parameter $H(l,n)$ was 0, link l would not be an input of node n. Hardware graphs are allowed to take any shape, and typically do contain cycles. Terms vertex/edge refer to members in G, and node/link to members in H.

Some of the vertices and nodes represent not only computation, but also inputs and outputs. To accommodate this, vertices and nodes are "typed" by the operations they can perform, which also enables the support of general heterogeneity in the architecture. For the treatment here, we abstract the details of the "types" into a compatibility matrix $C(V,N)$, indicating whether a particular vertex is compatible with a particular node. When equations depend on specific types of vertices, we will refer this set as V_{type}.

Figure 1 shows an example G graph, representing the computation $z = (x+y)^2$, and an H graph corresponding to a simplified version of the DySER architecture. Here, triangles represent input/output nodes and vertices, and circles represent computation nodes and vertices. Squares represent elements of R, which are routers composing the communication network. Elements of E are shown as unidirectional arrows in the computation DAG, and elements of L as bidirectional arrows in H representing two unidirectional links in either direction.

Inputs: Computation DAG Description (G)	
V	Set of computation vertices.
E	Set of Edges representing data flow of vertices
$G(V \cup E, V \cup E)$	The computation DAG
$\Delta(E)$	Delay between vertex activation and edge activation.
$\Delta(V)$	Duration of vertex.
$\Gamma(E)$ (PLUG)	Delay between vertex activation and edge reception.
B_e	Set of bundles which can be overlapped in network.
B_v (PLUG only)	Set of mutually exclusive vertex bundles.
$B(E \cup V, B_e \cup B_v)$	Parameter for edge/vertex bundle membership.
P (TRIPS only)	Set of control flow paths the computation can take
$A_v(P,V)$, $A_e(P,E)$ (TRIPS)	Activation matrices defining which vertices and edges get activated by given path
Inputs: Hardware Graph Description (H)	
N	Set of hardware resource Nodes.
R	Routers which form the network
L	Set of unidirectional point-to-point hardware Links
$H(N \cup R \cup L, N \cup R \cup L)$	Directed graph describing the Hardware
$I(L,L)$	Link pairs incompatible with Dim. Order Routing.
Inputs: Relationship between G/H	
$C(V,N)$	Vertex-Node Compatibility Matrix
MAX_N, MAX_L	Maximum degree of mapping for nodes and links.
Variables: Final Outputs	
$M_{vn}(V,N)$	Mapping of computation vertices to hardware nodes.
$M_{el}(E,L)$	Mapping of edges to paths of hardware links
$M_{bl}(B_e,L)$	Mapping of edge bundles to links
$M_{bn}(B_v,N)$ (PLUG only)	Mapping of vertex bundles to nodes
$\delta(E)$ (PLUG)	Padding cycles before message sent.
$\gamma(E)$ (PLUG)	Padding cycles before message received.
Variables: Intermediates	
$O(L)$	The order a link is traversed in.
$U(L \cup N)$	Utilization of links and nodes.
$U_p(P)$ (TRIPS)	Max Utilization for each path P.
$T(V)$	Time when a vertex is activated
$X(E)$	Extra cycles message is buffered.
$\lambda(b,e)$ (PLUG)	Cycle when e is activated for bundle b
LAT	Total latency for scheduled computation
SVC	Service interval for computation.
MIS	Largest Latency Mismatch.

Table 3. Summary of formal notation used.

The scheduler's job is to use the description of the typed computation DAG and hardware graph to find a mapping from computation vertices to computation resource nodes and determine the hardware paths along which individual edges flow. Figure 1 also shows a correct mapping of the computation graph to the hardware graph. This mapping is defined by a series of constraints and variables described in the remainder of this Section, and these variables and scheduler inputs are summarized in Table 3.

We now describe the ILP constraints which pertain to each scheduler responsibility, then show a diagram capturing this responsibility pictorially for our running example in Figure 1.

Responsibility 1: Placement of computation.

The first responsibility of the scheduler is to map vertices from the computation DAG to nodes from the hardware graph. Formally, the scheduler must compute a mapping from V to N, which we represent with the matrix of binary variables $M_{vn}(V,N)$. If $M_{vn}(v,n) = 1$, then vertex v is mapped to node n, while

$M_{vn}(v,n) = 0$ means that v is not mapped to n. Each vertex $v \in V$ must be mapped to exactly one compatible hardware node $n \in N$ in accordance with $C(v,n)$. The mapping for incompatible nodes must also be disallowed. This gives us:

$$\forall v \;\; \Sigma_{n|C(v,n)=1} M_{vn}(v,n) = 1 \qquad (1)$$

$$\forall v, n | C(v,n) = 0, \;\; M_{vn}(v,n) = 0 \qquad (2)$$

An example mapping with corresponding assignments to M_{vn} is shown in Figure 2.

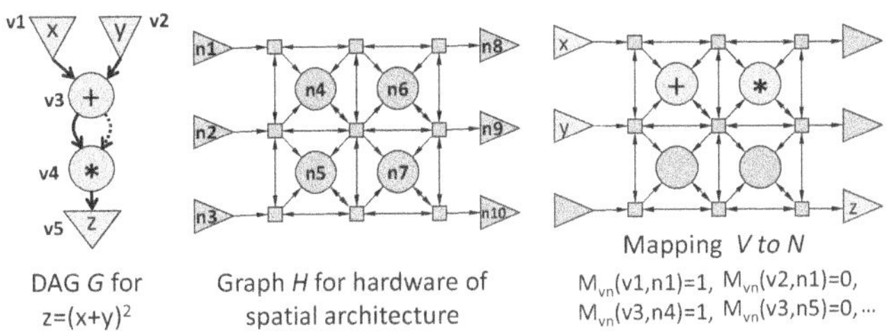

Figure 2. Placement of computation

Responsibility 2: Routing of data

The second responsibility of the scheduler is to map the required flow of data to the communication paths in the hardware. We use a matrix of binary variables $M_{el}(E, L)$ to encode the mapping of edges to links. Each edge e must be mapped to a sequence of one or more links l. This sequence must start from and end at the correct hardware nodes. We constrain the mappings such that if a vertex v is mapped to a node n, every edge e leaving from v must be mapped to one link leaving from n. Similarly, every edge arriving to v must be mapped to a link arriving to n.

$$\forall v, e, n | G(v,e), \Sigma_{l|H(n,l)}, M_{el}(e,l) = M_{vn}(v,n) \qquad (3)$$

$$\forall v, e, n | G(e,v), \Sigma_{l|H(l,n)}, M_{el}(e,l) = M_{vn}(v,n) \qquad (4)$$

In addition, the scheduler must ensure that each edge is mapped to a *contiguous* path of links. We achieve this by enforcing that for each router, either we have no incoming or outgoing links mapped to a given edge, or we have exactly one incoming and exactly one outgoing link mapped to the edge.

$$\forall e \in E, r \in R \quad \Sigma_{l|H(l,r)}, M_{el}(e,l) = \Sigma_{l|H(r,l)} M_{el}(e,l) \quad (5)$$

$$\forall e \in E, r \in R \qquad \Sigma_{l|H(l,r)}, M_{el}(e,l) \leq 1 \qquad (6)$$

Figure 3 shows these constraints applied to the example.

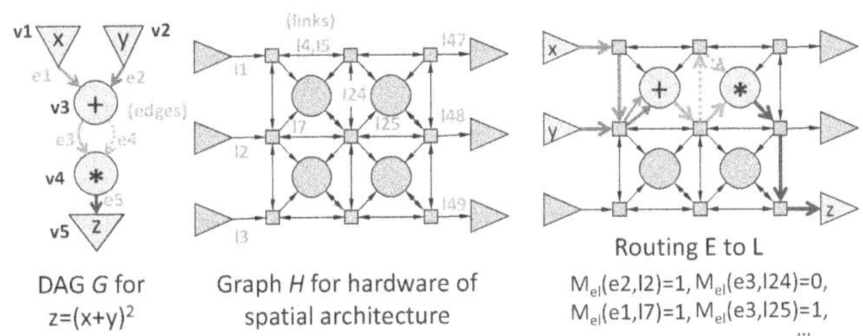

Figure 3. Routing of data.

Some architectures require dimension order routing: a message propagating along the X direction may continue on a link along the Y direction, but a message propagating along the Y direction cannot continue on a link along the X direction. To enforce this restriction, we expand the description of the hardware with $I(L,L)$, the set of link pairs that cannot be mapped to the same edge (i.e. an edge cannot be assigned to a path containing any link pair in this set).

$$\forall l, l' | I(l,l'), e \in E, \; M_{el}(e,l) + M_{el}(e,l') \leq 1 \qquad (7)$$

Responsibility 3: Manage timing of events

We capture the timing through a set of variables $T(V)$ which represents the time at which a vertex $v \in V$ starts executing. For each edge connecting the vertices v_{src} and v_{dst}, we compute the $T(v_{dst})$ based on $T(v_{src})$. This time is affected by three components. First, we must take into account the $\Delta(E)$, which is the number of clock cycles between the start time of the vertex and when the data is ready. Next is the total routing delay, which is the sum of the number of mapped links between v_{src} and v_{dest}. Since the data carried by all input edges for a vertex might not all arrive at the same time, the variable $X(E)$ describes this mismatch.

$$\forall v_{src}, e, v_{dest} | G(v_{src}, e) \& G(e, v_{dest}),$$
$$T(v_{src}) + \Delta(e) + \Sigma_{l \in L} M_{el}(e,l) + X(e) = T(v_{dest}) \qquad (8)$$

The equation above cannot fully capture dynamic events like cache misses. Rather than consider all possibilities, the scheduler simply assumes best-case values for unknown latencies (alternatively, these could be attained through profiling or similar means). Note that this is an issue for specialized schedulers as well.

With the constraints thus far, it is possible for the scheduler to overestimate edge latency because the link mapping allows fictitious cycles. As shown by the cycle in the bottom-left quadrant of Figure 4, the links in this cycle falsely contribute to the time between input "x" and vertex "+". This does not violate constraint 5 because each router involved contains the correct number of incoming / outgoing links.

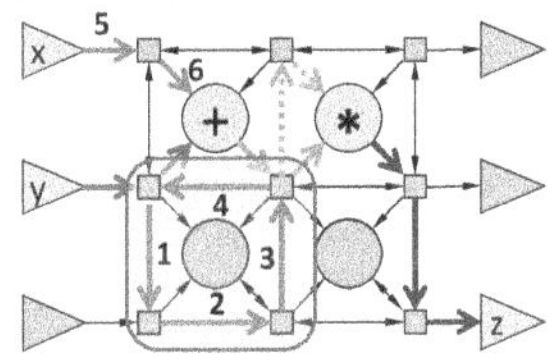

Figure 4. Fictitious cycles.

In many architectures, routing constraints (see constraint 7) make such loops impossible, but when this is not the case we eliminate cycles through a new constraint. We add a new set of variables $O(L)$, indicating the partial order in which links activated. If an edge is mapped to two connected links, this constraint enforces that the second link must be of later order.

$$\forall l, l', e \in E | H(l,l'), \; O(l) + M_{el}(e,l) + M_{el}(e,l') - 1 \leq O(l') \qquad (9)$$

Figure 5 shows the intermediate variable assignments that the constraints for timing provide.

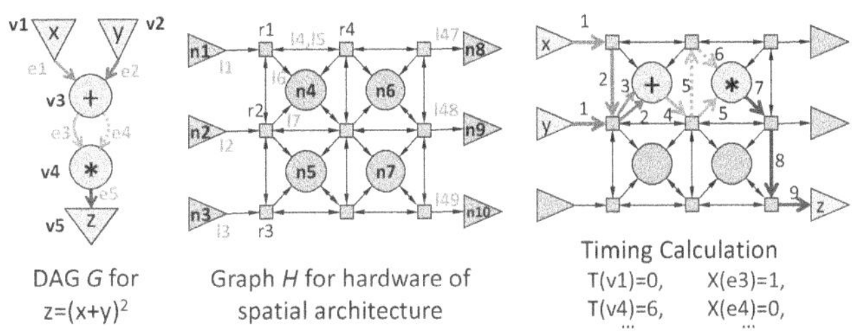

Figure 5. Timing of computation and communication.

Responsibility 4: Managing Utilization

The utilization of a hardware resource is simply the number of cycles for which it can not accept a new unit of work (computation or communication) because it is handling work corresponding to another computation. We first discuss the modeling of link utilization $U(L)$, then discuss node utilization $U(N)$.

$$\forall l \in L, \quad U(l) = \Sigma_{e \in E} M_{el}(e,l) \qquad (10)$$

The equation above models a link's utilization as the sum of its mapped edges and is effective when each edge takes up a resource. On the other hand, some architectures allow for edges to be overlapped, as in the case of multicast, or if it is known that sets of messages are mutually exclusive (will never activate at the same time). This requires us to extend our notion of utilization with the concept of *edge-bundles*, which represent edges that can be mapped to the same link at no cost. The set B_e denotes edge-bundles, and $B(E, B_e)$ defines its relationship to edges. The following three constraints ensure the correct correspondence between the mapping of edges to links and bundles to links, and compute the link's utilization based on the edge-bundles.

$$\forall e, b_e | B(e, b_e), l \in L, \qquad M_{bl}(b_e, l) \geq M_{el}(e, l) \quad (11)$$

$$\forall b_e \in B_e, l \in L, \quad \Sigma_{e \in B(e,b_e)} M_{el}(e, l) \geq M_{bl}(b_e, l) \quad (12)$$

$$\forall l \in L, \qquad U(l) = \Sigma_{b_e \in B} M_{bl}(b, l) \quad (13)$$

To compute the vertices' utilization, we must additionally consider the amount of time that a vertex fully occupies a node. This time, $\Delta(V)$, is always 1 when the architecture is fully pipelined, but increases when the lack of pipelining limits the use of a node n in subsequent cycles. To compute utilization, we simply sum $\Delta(V)$ over vertices mapped to a node:

$$\forall n \in N \;\; U(n) = \Sigma_{v \in V} \Delta(v) M_{vn}(v, l) \quad (14)$$

For many spatial architectures we use utilization-limiting constraints such as those below. One application of these constraints are hardware limitations in the number of registers available, instruction slots, etc. Also, they ensure lack of contention with operations or messages from within the same block or other blocks executing concurrently.

$$\forall l \in L, \quad U(l) \leq MAX_L \quad (15)$$

$$\forall n \in N, \quad U(n) \leq MAX_N \quad (16)$$

As shown in the running DySER example below in Figure 6, we limit the utilization of each link $U(l)$ to $MAX_L = 1$. This ensures that only a single message per block traverses the link, allowing the DySER's arbitration-free routers to operate correctly.

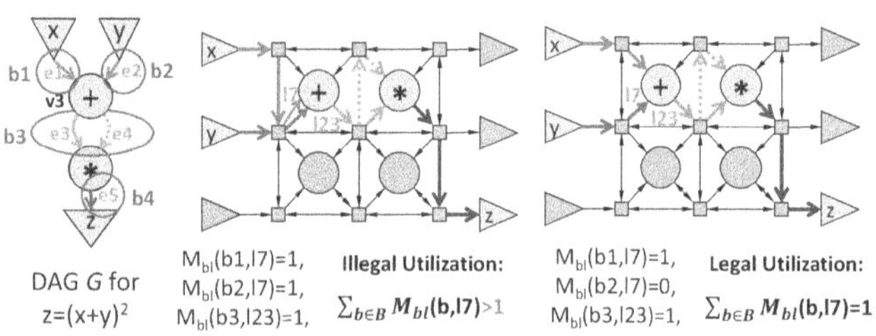

Figure 6. Utilization Management.

Responsibility 5: Optimizing performance

The constraints governing the previous sections model the quantities which capture only *individual* components for correctness and performance. However, the final responsibility of the scheduler is to manage the overall correctness while providing performance in the context of the overall system. In practice, this means that the scheduler must balance notions of latency and throughput. Having multiple conflicting targets requires strategic resolution, since there is not necessarily a single solution which optimizes both. The strategy we take is to supply to the scheduler a set of variables to optimize for with their associated priority.

To calculate the critical path latency, we first initialize the input vertices to zero (or some known value) then find the maximum latency of an output vertex LAT. This represents the scheduler's estimate of how long the block would take to complete.

$$\forall v \in V_{in}, \qquad T(v) = 0 \quad (17)$$

$$\forall v \in V_{out}, \quad T(v) \leq LAT \quad (18)$$

To model the throughput aspects, we utilize the concept of the service interval SVC, which is defined as the minimum number of cycles between successive invocations when no data dependencies between invocations exists. We compute SVC by finding the maximum utilization on any resource.

$$\forall n \in N, \quad U(n) \leq SVC \quad (19)$$

$$\forall l \in L, \quad U(l) \leq SVC \quad (20)$$

For fully pipelined architectures, SVC is naturally forced to 1, so it is not an optimization target. Other notions of throughput are possible, as in the case of DySER, where minimizing the latency mismatch MIS is the throughput objective (see Section 5.2).

For our running example, the final solution is shown in Figure 7, where the critical path latency LAT and the latency mismatch MIS (mentioned above), are both optimized by the scheduler.

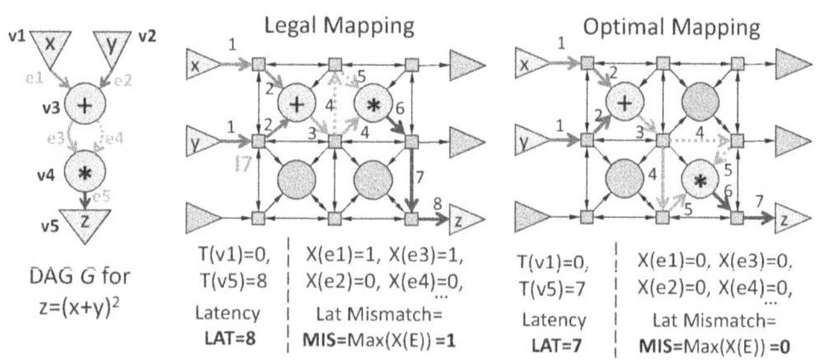

Figure 7. Optimizing performance.

5. Architecture-specific modeling

In this section, we describe how the general formulation presented above is used by three diverse architectures. Figure 8 shows schematics and H graphs for the three architectures.

5.1 Architecture-specific details for TRIPS

Computation organization → Placement of computation: Figure 8 depicts the graph H we use to describe a 4-tile TRIPS architecture. A tile in TRIPS is comprised of nodes $n \in N$ denoting a functional unit in the tile and $r \in R$ representing its router - the two are connected with one link in either direction. The router also connects to the routers in the neighboring tiles. The functional unit has a self-loop that denotes the bypass of the tile's router to move results into input slots for operations scheduled on the same tile.

Network organization → Routing data: Since messages are dedicated and point-to-point (as opposed to multicast), we use constraints modeling each edge as consuming a resource and contributing to the total utilization. The TRIPS routers implement dimension-order routing, i.e. messages first travel along the X axis, then along the Y axis. TRIPS uses the $I(L, L)$ parameter, which disallows the mapping of certain link pairs, to invalidate any paths which are not compatible with dimension-order.

HW timing → Managing timing of events: We can calculate network timing without any additions to the general formulation.

Concurrent HW usage → Utilization: TRIPS allows significant level of concurrent hardware usage which affects both the latency and throughput of blocks. Specifically, the maximum number of vertices per node is $MAX_N = 8$. The utilization on links is used to finally formulate the objective function.

Extensions: For TRIPS, the scheduler must also account for control flow when computing the utilization and ultimately the service interval for throughput. Simple extensions, as explained below, can in general handle control flow for any architecture and could

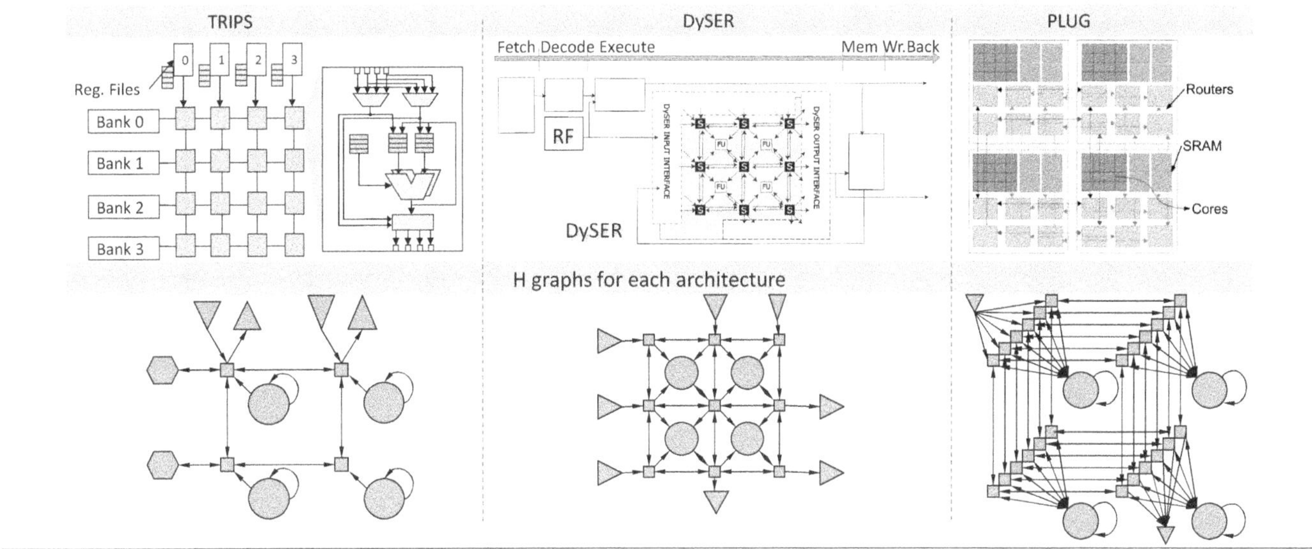

Figure 8. Three candidate architectures and corresponding H graphs, considering 4 tiles for each architecture.

Architecture	Description	ILP Modeling and scheduler responsibility	ILP Constraints
Compute HW organization	16 titles, 6 routers per tile	Each tile is 7 nodes in *H*, one in *N*, and six in *R*.	Gen. ILP framework
	4 mem-banks per tile	Handled with utilization	Gen. ILP framework
	32 cores per tile	Handled with utilization	Gen. ILP framework
Network HW organization	2D nearest neighbor mesh	Node *n* connected to *r*; *r* connected to 4 neighbors	Gen. ILP framework
	Dimension order routing	*I(L,L)* configure for dimension-order routing	Gen. ILP framework
	Multicast messages deliver values at every intermediate node on path	Enforce mapping of multicast messages to link to computation node	Eq. 25
HW timing and synchronization	Code-scheduling of network send instructions	Variables for send timing and receive time	$\Delta(E)$; $\Gamma(E)$
	Send instructions scheduled to avoid n/w conflicts	Variables for delaying send/receive timing by padding with no-ops	Eq. 26, 27a-c, 28
Concurrent HW usage	4 mem-banks per tile	Manage utilization ($MAX_N = 4$)	Gen. ILP framework
	Dedicated network per message	Manage utilization (MAX_L=1)	Gen. ILP framework
	Mutually exclusive activation of nodes in G	Concept of vertex bundles and utilization refined	Eq. 29, 30, 31
	Code-length limitations (maximum is 32) handled for all code on tile	Manage utilization and combine with vertex bundles	Eq. 32, 33, 34

Table 4. Description of ILP model implementation for PLUG

belong in the general ILP formulation as well. Let P be the set of control flow paths that the computation can take through G. Note that $p \in P$ is not actually a path through G, but the subset of its vertices and edges activated in a given execution. Let $A_v(P, V)$ and $A_e(P, E)$ be the activation matrices defining, for each vertex and edge of the computation, whether they are activated when a given path is taken or not. For each path we define the maximum utilization on this path $W_p(P)$. These constraints are similar to the original utilization constraints (10, 14), but also take control flow activation matrices into account.

$$\forall l \in L, p \in P, \quad \Sigma_{e \in E} M_{el}(e,l) A_e(p,e) \leq W_p(p) \qquad (21)$$

$$\forall n \in N, p \in P, \quad \Sigma_{v \in V} M_{vn}(v,n) \Delta(v) A_v(p,v) \leq W_p(p) \qquad (22)$$

And an additional constraint for calculating overall service interval:

$$SVC = \Sigma_{p \in P} W_p(p) \qquad (23)$$

Note that this heuristic provides the same importance to all control-flow paths. With profiling or other analysis, differential weighting can be implemented.

Objective formulation: For the TRIPS architecture, we empirically found that optimizing for throughput is of higher importance, in most cases, then for latency. Therefore, our strategy is to first minimize the SVC, add the lowest value as a constraint, and then optimize for LAT. The following is our solution procedure, where numbers refer to constraints from the formulation:

$$min\ SVC\ s.t.\ [\,1,2,3,4,5,6,7,8,10,14,15,16,17,18,21,22,23]$$

$$min\ LAT\ s.t.\ [\,1,2,3,4,5,6,7,8,10,14,15,16,17,18,21,22,23]$$

$$and\ SVC \ = \ SVC_{optimal}$$

5.2 Architecture-specific details for DySER

Computation organization → Placement of computation: We model DySER with the hardware graph H shown in Figure 8; heterogeneity is captured with the $C(V, N)$ compatibility matrix.

Network organization → Routing data: We use bundle-link mapping constraints to model multicast, and constraint 9 to prevent fictitious cycles. Since the network has the ability to perform multicast messages and can route multiple edges on the same link, we use the bundle-link mapping constraints. Since there is no ordering constraint on the network, we need to prevent fictitious cycles.

HW timing → Managing timing of events: No additions to the general formulation are required.

Concurrent HW usage → Utilization: Since DySER can only route one message per link, and max one vertex to a node, both MAX_L and MAX_N are set to 1.

Objective Formulation: DySER throughput can be as much as one computation G per cycle, since the functional units themselves are pipelined. However, throughput degradation can occur because of the limited buffering available for messages. The utilization defined in the general framework does not capture this problem because it only measures the usage of functional units and links, not of buffers. Unlike TRIPS, where all operands are buffered as long as needed in named registers, DySER buffers messages at routers and at most one message per edge is buffered at each router. Thus, two paths that diverge and then converge, but have different lengths, will also have different amounts of buffering. Combined with backpressure, this can reduce throughput.

Computing the exact throughput achievable by a DySER schedule is difficult, as multiple such pairs of converging paths may exist - even paths that converge after passing through functional units affect throughput. Instead we note that latency mismatches always manifest themselves as extra buffering delays $X(e)$ for some edges, so we model latency mismatch as MIS:

$$\forall e \in E, X(e) \leq MIS \tag{24}$$

Empirically, we found that external limitations on the throughput of inputs is greater than that of computation. For this reason, the DySER scheduler first optimizes for latency, adds the latency of the solution as a constraint, then optimizes for throughput by minimizing latency mismatch MIS, as below:

$$min\ LAT\ s.t.\ [1,2,3,4,5,6,8,9,11,12,13,14,15,16,17,18,24]$$
$$min\ MIS\ s.t.\ [1,2,3,4,5,6,8,9,11,12,13,14,15,16,17,18,24]$$
$$and\ LAT = LAT_{optimal}$$

5.3 Architecture-specific details for PLUG

The PLUG architecture is radically different from the previous two architectures since all decisions are static. Our formulation is general enough that it works for PLUG with only 10 predominantly simple additional constraints. In the interest of clarity, we summarize the key concepts of the PLUG architecture, corresponding ILP model, and additional equations in Table 4. The grayed rows summarize the extensions, and this section's text describes them.

Computation organization → Placement of computation: See Table 4, row 1. No additional constraints required.

Network organization → Routing data: See Table 4, row 2. *Additional constraints:* Multicast handled with edge-bundles: Let $B_{multi} \subset B_e$ be the subset of edge-bundles that involve multicast edges. The following constraint, which considers links through a router to a node, then enforces that the bundle mapped to the router link must also be mapped to the node's incoming link.

$$\forall b \in B_{multi}, l, r, l', n | H(l,r) \& H(r,l') \& H(l',n),$$
$$M_{bl}(b,l) \leq M_{bl}(b,l') \tag{25}$$

HW timing → Managing timing of events: See Table 4, row 3. *Additional constraints:* We need to handle the timing of send instructions. We use $\Delta(E)$ and the newly-introduced $\Gamma(E)$ to respectively indicate the relative cycle number of the corresponding send instruction and use instruction.

Network contention is avoided by code-scheduling the send instructions with NOP padding to create appropriate delays and equalize all delay mismatch. $\delta(E)$ denotes sending delay added, and $\gamma(E)$ denotes receiving delay added. To model the timing for PLUG, we augment equation 8 as follows:

$$\forall v_{src}, e, v_{dst} | G(v_{src}, e) \& G(e, v_{dst}),$$
$$T(v_{src}) + \Sigma_{l \in L} M_{el}(e,l) + \Delta(e) + \delta(e) = T(v_{dst}) + \Gamma(e) + \gamma(e) \tag{26}$$

Because the insertion of no-ops can only change timing in specific ways, we use two constraints to further link $\delta(E)$ and $\gamma(E)$ to $\Delta(E)$ and $\Gamma(E)$. The first ensures that the scheduler never attempts to pad a negative number of NOPs. The second ensures that sending delay $\delta(E)$ is the same for all multicast edges carrying the same message.

To implement these constraints we use the following 4 sets concerning distinct edges e, e': $SI(e,e')$ has the set of pairs of edges arriving to the same vertex such that $\Gamma(e) < \Gamma(e')$, $LIFO(e,e')$ has, for each vertex with both input and output edges, the last input edge e and the first output edge e', $SO(e,e')$ has the pairs of output edges with the same source vertex such that $\Delta(e) < \Delta(e')$, and $EQO(e,e')$ has the pairs of output edges leaving the same node concurrently.

$$\forall e, e' | SI(e,e'), \gamma(e) \leq \gamma(e') \tag{27a}$$
$$\forall e, e' | LIFO(e,e'), \gamma(e) \leq \delta(e') \tag{27b}$$
$$\forall e, e' | SO(e,e'), \delta(e) \leq \delta(e') \tag{27c}$$
$$\forall e, e' | EQO(e,e'), \delta(e) = \delta(e') \tag{28}$$

Concurrent HW usage → Utilization: See Table 4, row 4. *Additional constraints:* PLUG groups nodes in G into "super-nodes" (logical-page), and programmatically only a single node executes in every super-node. This mutual exclusion behavior is modeled by partitioning V into a set of vertex bundles B_v with $B(V, B_v)$ indicating to which bundle a vertex $v \in V$ belongs. We introduce $M_{bn}(b,n)$ to model the mapping of bundles to nodes, enforced by the following constraints:

$$\forall v, b_v | B(v, b_v), n \in N, \quad M_{bn}(b_v, n) \geq M_{vn}(v, n) \tag{29}$$
$$\forall b_v \in B_v, n \in N, \quad \Sigma_{v \in B(v,b_v)} M_{vn}(v,n) \geq M_{bn}(b_v, n) \tag{30}$$

We then define the utilization based on the number of vertex bundles mapped to a node. We also instantiate edge bundles b_e for all the set of edges coming from the same vertex bundle and going to the same destination. Since all the edges in such a bundle are *logically* a single message source, the schedule must equalize the receiving times of the message they send. Let $B_{mutex} \subseteq B_e$ be the set of edge-bundles described above. Then we add the following timing constraint:

$$\forall e, e', b_x \in B_{mutex} | B(e, b_x) \& B(e', b_x), \quad \gamma(e) = \gamma(e') \tag{31}$$

Additionally, architectural constraints require the total length in instructions of the vertex bundles mapped to the same node to be ≤ 32. This requires defining, for each bundle, the maximum bundle length $\lambda(b_v)$ as a function of the last send message of the vertex. This length can then be constrained to be ≤ 32.

To achieve this, we first define the set $LAST(B_v, B_e)$, which pairs each vertex bundle with its last edge bundle, corresponding to the last send message of the vertex. This enables to define the maximum bundle length $\lambda(b_v)$ as:

$$\forall e, b_e, b_v | LAST(b_v, b_e) \& B(e, b_e),$$
$$\Delta(e) + \delta(e) \leq \lambda(b_v) \tag{32}$$

We finally define $Q(B_v, N)$ as the required number of instructions on node n from vertex bundle b_v and limit it to 32 (the code-snippet length).

$$\forall b_v, n \in N, \quad Q(b_v, n) - 32 * M_{bn}(b_v, n) \geq \lambda(b_v) - 32 \tag{33}$$
$$\forall n, \quad \Sigma_{b_v \in B_v} Q(b_v, n) \leq 32 \tag{34}$$

Objective Formulation: For PLUG, the smallest service interval is achieved and enforced for any legal schedule, and we optimize solely for latency LAT.

$$min\ LAT\ s.t.\ [1,2,3,4,5,6,7,11,12,13,14,$$
$$15,16,17,18,25,26,27,28,29,30,31,32,33,34]$$

6. Implementation and Evaluation

In this section, we describe our implementation of the constraints in an off-the-shelf ILP solver and evaluate its performance compared to native specialized schedulers for the three architectures.

6.1 Implementation

We use the GAMS modeling language to specify our constraints as mixed integer linear programs, and we use the commercial CPLEX solver to obtain the schedules. Our implementation strategy for

	TRIPS	DySER	PLUG
Benchmarks	• Same as prior TRIPS scheduler papers [9]: SPEC microbenchmarks and EEMBC • Full SPEC benchmarks can't run to completion on simulator and don't stress scheduler (since blocks are small)	• DySER data-parallel workloads since they produce large blocks and complete code from compiler [25]. • Additional throughput microbenchmark (details below)[1] • SPEC2006 and PARSEC in [25] are not usable because they don't produce high quality code on compiler. [25] used a trace-simulation based approach (not compiler-based code-generation).	• PLUG benchmarks from [13]
Native scheduler	• Optimized SPS scheduler [9]	• Specialized greedy algorithm in toolchain & hand scheduled [26]	• Hand scheduled [13]
Metric	• Total execution cycles for program	• Total execution cycles for program	• Total execution cycles for lookups

1. DySER "throughput" microbenchmark: This performs the calculation $y = x - x^{2i}$ in the code-region. Paths diverge at the input node x, into one long path which computes the x^{2i} with a series of i multiplies, and along a short path which routes x to the subtraction. This pattern tends to cause latency mismatch because one of these converging paths naturally takes less resources.

Table 5. Tools and methodology for quantitative evaluation

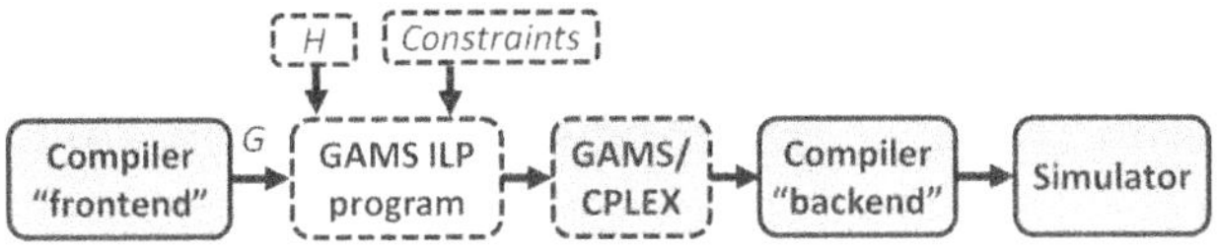

"frontend": passes in the compiler that produce pre-scheduled code; "backend": passes that convert scheduled code into binary.

Figure 9. Implementation of our ILP scheduler. Dotted boxes indicate the new components added.

prioritizing multiple variables follows a standard approach: we define an allowable percentage optimization gap (of between 2% to 10%, depending on the architecture), and optimize for each variable in prioritized succession, finishing the solver when the percent gap is within the specified bounds. After finding the optimal value for each variable, we add a constraint which restricts that variable to be no worse in future iterations.

Figure 9 shows our implementation and how we integrated with the compiler/simulator toolchains [1, 13, 25]. For all three architectures, we use their intermediate output converted into our standard directed acyclic graph (DAG) for G and fed to our GAMS ILP program. We specified H for each architecture. To evaluate our approach, we compare the performance of the final binaries on the architectures varying only the scheduler. Table 5 summarizes the methodology and infrastructure used.

6.2 Results

Is this ILP-based approach implementable? Yes, it is possible to express the scheduling problem as an ILP problem and implement it for real architectures. Considering the ILP constraint formulation for the general framework, our GAMS implementation is around 50 lines of code.

Result-1: A declarative and general approach to expressing and implementing spatial-architecture schedulers is possible.

Is the execution time of standard ILP-solvers fast enough to be practical? Table 6 (page 10) summarizes the mathematical characteristics of the workloads and corresponding scheduling behavior. The three right-hand columns respectively show the number of software nodes to schedule, the amount of single ILP equations created, and the solver time.[2] There is a rough correlation between the workload "size" and scheduling time, but it is still highly variable.

The solver time of the specialized schedulers in comparison is typically on the order of seconds or less. Although some blocks may take minutes to solve, these times are still tractable, demonstrating the practicality of ILP as a scheduling technique.

Result-2: Our general ILP scheduler runs in tractable time.

[2] For TRIPS, the per-benchmark number of DAGs can range from 50 to 5000, and the metrics provided are average per DAG. For DySER, #DAGs is 1 to 4 per benchmark, and PLUG is always 1.

Are the output solutions produced good? How do they compare against the output of specialized schedulers? Figure 10 (page 10) shows the performance of our ILP scheduler. It shows the cycle-count reduction for the executed programs as a normalized percentage of the program produced by the specialized compiler (higher is better, negative numbers mean execution time was increased). We discuss these results in terms of each architecture.

Compared to the TRIPS SPS specialized scheduler (a cumulated multi-year effort spanning several publications [9, 12, 40]), our ILP scheduler performs competitively as summarized below.[3]

Compared to SPS		
(a)Better on 22 of 43 benchmarks	up to 21%	GM +2.9%
(b)Worse on 18 of 43 benchmarks	within 4.9% **(typically 2%)**	GM -1.9%
(c)5.4%, 6.04%, and 13.2% worse on ONLY 3 benchmarks		
Compared to GRST		
Consistently better, up to 59% better; GM +30%		

Groups (a) and (b) show the ILP scheduler is capturing the architecture/scheduler interactions well. The small slowdowns/speedups compared to SPS are due to dynamic events which disrupt the scheduler's view of event timing, making its node/link assignments sub-optimal, typically by only 2%. After detailed analysis, we discovered the reason for the performance gap of group (c) is the lack of information that could be easily integrated in our model. First, the SPS scheduler took advantage of information regarding the specific cache banks of loads and stores, which is not available in the modular scheduling interface exposed by the TRIPS compiler. This knowledge would improve the ILP scheduler's performance and would only require changes to the compatibility matrix $C(V, N)$. Second, knowledge of limited resources was available to SPS, allowing it to defer decisions and interact with code-generation to map movement-related instructions. What these results show overall is that our first-principles based approach is capturing all the architecture behavior in a general fashion and arguably aesthetically cleaner fashion than SPS's indirect heuristics. Our ILP scheduler consistently exceeds by appreciable amounts a previous generation TRIPS scheduler, GRST, that did not model contention [40], as shown by the hatched bars in the figure.

On DySER, the ILP scheduler outperforms the specialized scheduler on all benchmarks, as shown in Figure 10, for a 64-unit DySER. Across the benchmarks, the ILP scheduler reduces *individual* block latencies by 38% on average. When the latency of DySER execution is the bottleneck, especially when there are dependencies between instances of the computation (like the needle benchmark), this leads to significant speedup of up to 15%. We

[3] We did not run on SPEC benchmarks for three reasons: prior TRIPS scheduler work uses this set; TRIPS simulator does not have sim-point etc. to meaningfully simulate TRIPS benchmarks; TRIPS compiler does not produce good enough code on SPEC (10-15 inst blocks only) to make scheduler a factor [12, 23]. Using TRIPS hardware was impractical for us.

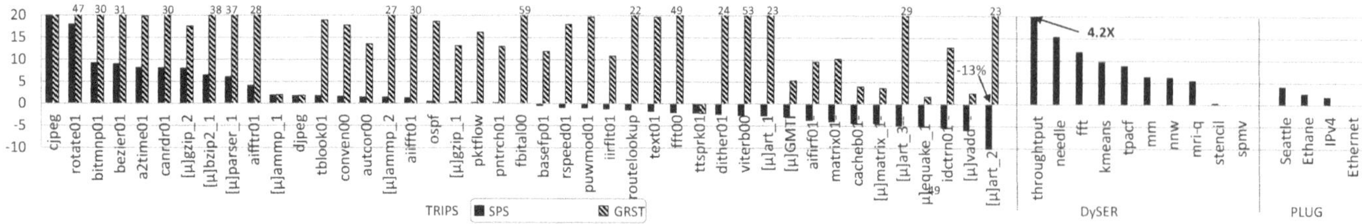

Figure 10. Normalized percentage improvement in execution cycles of ILP scheduler compared to specialized scheduler.

(a) TRIPS

Suite	Applications	#nodes	#eqns	Solver time (sec)	Applications	#nodes	#eqns	Solver time (sec)
Microbenchmarks [9]	ammp_1	17	3744	76	gzip_1	23	4480	1
	ammp_2	8	1593	<1	gzip_2	22	4506	111
	art_1	22	4547	74	matrix_1	19	3797	18
	art_2	27	5506	76	parser_1	33	7248	174
	art_3	33	7042	20	transp_GMTI	20	4159	115
	bzip_1	13	2655	10	vadd	30	7313	315
	equake_1	24	4455	3				
EEMBC [9]	a2time01	11	1914	5	ttsprk01	11	1993	8
	aifftr01	12	2173	25	cjpeg	12	2280	3
	aifirf01	11	1933	7	djpeg	12	2277	1
	aiifft01	11	2025	1	ospf	10	1778	3
	basefp01	10	1863	6	pktflow	10	1774	3
	bitmnp01	9	1535	3	routelookup	10	1747	3
	cacheb01	27	2745	76	bezier01	10	1788	2
	canrdr01	10	1871	8	dither01	10	3579	4
	idctrn01	11	1947	3	rotate01	10	1910	5
	iirflt01	11	2080	2	text01	10	1781	3
	matrix01	11	1426	2	autcor00	10	1746	2
	pntrch01	10	1819	5	conven00	10	1758	4
	puwmod01	10	1779	3	fbital00	9	1699	3
	rspeed01	10	1816	7	fft00	10	1808	5
	tblook01	10	1818	4	viterb00	10	1870	5
					TRIPS Avg.	14	2832	31

(b) DySER

Data-Parallel Benchmarks [26]

Applications	#nodes	#eqns	Solver time (sec)
fft	20	120250	365
mm	32	159231	77
mri-q	19	98615	66
spmv	32	155068	72
stencil	30	153428	74
tpacf	40	211584	368
nnw	25	169197	102
kmeans	40	232399	218
Needle	34	181686	183
Throughput	9	45138	62
DySER Avg.	**28**	**152660**	**159**

(c) PLUG

PLUG benchmarks [13]

Applications	#nodes	#eqns	Solver time (sec)
Ethernet	18	25603	57
Ethane	11	13905	14
IPv4	12	38741	384
Seattle	16	14531	26
PLUG Avg.	14	23195	120

Table 6. Benchmark characteristics and ILP scheduler behavior.

also implemented an extra DySER benchmark, which elucidates the importance of latency mismatch and is described in Table 5. The specialized scheduler tries to minimize the extra path length at each step, exacerbating the latency mismatch of the short and long paths in the program. The ILP scheduler, on the other hand, pads the length of the shorter path to reduce latency mismatch, increasing the potential throughput and achieving a 4.2× improvement over the specialized scheduler. Finally, we also compared to manually scheduled code on an *16-unit* DySER (since hand-scheduling for 64unit DySER is exceedingly tedious). The ILP scheduler always matched or out-performed it by a small ($< 2\%$) percentage.

The ILP scheduler matches or out-performs the PLUG hand-mapped schedules. It is able to both find schedules that force $SVC = 1$ and provide latency improvements of a few percent. Of particular note is solver time, because PLUG's DFGs are more complex. In fact, each DFG represents an *entire* application. The most complex benchmark, IPV4, contains 74 edges (24 more than any others) split between 30 mutually exclusive or multicast groups. Despite these difficulties, it completes in tractable time.

Result-3: Our ILP scheduler outperforms or matches the performance of specialized schedulers.

Modeling Concerns	Approach
Can constraints be modeled precisely?	• Most constraints are directly expressible • Nonlinear constraints do not arise • Logical operations can be modeled using known techniques [24, 29, 30]
Can other constraint theories be used?	• Constraints can be specified in SMT theory • Our Z3[14] implementation shows that SMT solving takes significantly longer than ILP
Implementation Concerns	
Can dynamic effects (cache misses, network contention) be taken into account?	• We optimize for best-case scenario (same approach as existing specialized schedulers) • Stochastic techniques can optimize concurrently for multiple scenarios (future work)
How does implementing objective functions compare to implementing scheduling heuristics?	• Declarative formulation is more intuitive & simplifies implementation. • Example: the TRIPS SPS scheduler uses several indirect heuristics to model utilization, whereas utilization directly captures it
Productivity Concerns	
Is a deep understanding of architecture required?	• Full understanding of the target architecture is required regardless of the approach • We streamline process by defining sets of responsibilities & direct modeling of behavior

Table 7. Feasibility concerns

7. Discussion and Conclusions

Scheduling is a fundamental problem for spatial architectures, which are increasingly used to address energy efficiency. Compared to the architecture-specific schedulers, which are the current state-of-the-art, this paper provides a general formulation of spatial scheduling as a constraint-solving problem. We applied this formulation to three diverse architectures, ran them on a standard ILP solver, and demonstrated such a general scheduler outperforms or matches the respective specialized schedulers. Some potential limitations and concerns about our work are outlined in Table 7, but do not detract from its central contributions.

We conclude with a discussion of some broader extensions and implications of our work. Specifically, we discuss the possibility of improving the scheduling time through algorithmic specialization, and how our scheduler delivers on its promises of compiler-developer productivity/extensibility, cross-architecture applicability, and insights on optimality.

Specializing ILP Solvers: While the benefits of using Integer Linear Programming come at the cost of additional scheduler execution time, we suspect that there may be further opportunities for improvement. One strategy is to specialize the solver's algorithms to the problem domain. The Network Simplex algorithm for the minimum cost flow problem is a widely known example. To create a specialized algorithm for our problem, a detailed investigation of the constraints from a solver design perspective would be required, as well as the modification of existing ILP solvers. This is one critical direction for future work.

Responsibility	RAW	WaveScalar	Neural Processing Unit
Placement	Homogeneous Cores (Tiles)	Homogeneous Processing Elements	8 Processing Elements, 1 Shared Bus
Routing	2-D grid, unconstrained routing	Hierarchical Network. First two levels are fully connected, last level grid uses dynamic routing	Responsibility Not Applicable -- Broadcast bus used for communication.
Timing	In-order execution inside tile, dataflow between tiles (Secondary list scheduler orders inter-stream events)	Data-flow execution, and dynamic network arbitration; network latency varies by hierarchy level	Fully Static execution. "No-ops" between bus events maintain synchronization.
Utilization	Many instructions per tile. Shared network links	64-Instuctions/PE; Shared Network Links	Shared Processing Elements
Objective	Latency & Throughput	Contention & Latency	Latency

Table 8. Applicability to other Spatial Architectures

Formulation Extensibility: In our experience, our model formulation was easily adaptable and extensible for modeling various problem variations or optimizations. For example, we improved upon our TRIPS scheduler's performance by identifying blocks with carried-loop cache dependencies (commonly the most frequently executed), and extended our formulation to only optimize for relevant paths.

Application to Example Architectures: Table 8 shows how our framework could be applied to three other systems. For both WaveScalar and RAW, we can attain optimal solutions by refraining from making early decisions, essentially avoiding the drawbacks of multi-stage solutions. For WaveScalar, our scheduler would consider all levels of the network hierarchy at once, using different latencies for links in different networks. For RAW, our scheduler would consider both the partitioning of instructions into streams, and the spatial placement of these instructions simultaneously.

As a more recent example, NPU [20] is a statically-scheduled architecture like PLUG, but uses a broadcast network instead of a point-to-point, tiled network. Instead of using the routing equations for communication, the NPU bus is more aptly modeled as a computation type. Timing would be modeled similarly to PLUG, where "no-ops" prevent bus contention, allowing a fully static schedule.

Insights on Optimality: Since our approach provides insights on optimality, it has potentially broader uses as well. For instance, in the context of a dynamic compilation framework, even though the compilation time of seconds is impractical, the ILP scheduler still has significant practical value – it enables developers to easily formulate and evaluate objectives that can guide the implementation of specialized heuristic schedulers.

Revisiting NPU scheduling, we can observe another potential use of ILP models, specifically in designing the hardware itself. For the NPU, the fifo depth of each processing element is expensive in terms of hardware, so we could easily extend the model to calculate the fifo depth as a function of the schedule. One strategy would be to first optimize for performance, then fix the performance and optimize for lowest maximum fifo depth. Doing this across a set of benchmarks would give the best lower-bound fifo depth which does not sacrifice performance.

Finally, while our approach is general, in that we have demonstrated implementations across three disparate architectures and shown extensions to others, a somewhat open question remains on "universality": what spatial architecture organization could render our framework ineffective? This is subject to debate and is future work. Overall, our general scheduler can form an important component for future spatial architectures.

Acknowledgments

We thank the anonymous reviewers for comments. Thanks to Mark Hill and Daniel Luchaup for their valuable insights and comments on the paper. Support for this research was provided by NSF under the following grants: CCF-0845751, CNS-0917213, and CNS-0917238.

References

[1] Trips toolchain, http://www.cs.utexas.edu/ trips/dist/.

[2] A. V. Aho, M. S. Lam, R. Sethi, and J. D. Ullman. *Compilers: Principles, Techniques, and Tools*.

[3] S. Amarasinghe, D. R. Karger, W. Lee, and V. S. Mirrokni. A theoretical and practical approach to instruction scheduling on spatial architectures. Technical report, MIT, 2002.

[4] S. Amellal and B. Kaminska. Functional synthesis of digital systems with tass. *Computer-Aided Design of Integrated Circuits and Systems, IEEE Transactions on*, 13(5):537 –552, 1994.

[5] C. Ancourt and F. Irigoin. Scanning polyhedra with do loops. In *PPOPP 1991*.

[6] O. Azizi, A. Mahesri, B. C. Lee, S. J. Patel, and M. Horowitz. Energy-performance tradeoffs in processor architecture and circuit design: a marginal cost analysis. In *ISCA 2010*.

[7] S. S. Battacharyya, E. A. Lee, and P. K. Murthy. *Software Synthesis from Dataflow Graphs*. Kluwer Academic Publishers, 1996.

[8] S. Borkar and A. A. Chien. The future of microprocessors. *Commun. ACM*, 54(5):67–77, 2011.

[9] D. Burger, S. W. Keckler, K. S. McKinley, M. Dahlin, L. K. John, C. Lin, C. R. Moore, J. Burrill, R. G. McDonald, W. Yoder, and the TRIPS Team. Scaling to the end of silicon with EDGE architectures. *IEEE Computer*, 37(7):44–55, 2004.

[10] N. Clark, M. Kudlur, H. Park, S. Mahlke, and K. Flautner. Application-specific processing on a general-purpose core via transparent instruction set customization. In *MICRO 2004*.

[11] J. Cong, K. Gururaj, G. Han, and W. Jiang. Synthesis algorithm for application-specific homogeneous processor networks. *IEEE Trans. Very Large Scale Integr. Syst.*, 17(9), Sept. 2009.

[12] K. Coons, X. Chen, S. Kushwaha, K. S. McKinley, and D. Burger. A Spatial Path Scheduling Algorithm for EDGE Architectures. In *ASPLOS 2006*.

[13] L. De Carli, Y. Pan, A. Kumar, C. Estan, and K. Sankaralingam. Plug: Flexible lookup modules for rapid deployment of new protocols in high-speed routers. In *SIGCOMM 2009*.

[14] L. de Moura and N. Bjørner. Z3: An efficient SMT solver. In *TACAS*, 2008.

[15] A. Deb, J. M. Codina, and A. Gonzales. Softhv: A hw/sw co-designed processor with horizontal and vertical fusion. In *International Conference on Computing Frontiers 2011*.

[16] A. E. Eichenberger and E. S. Davidson. Efficient formulation for optimal modulo schedulers. In *PLDI 1997*.

[17] J. R. Ellis. *Bulldog: a compiler for vliw architectures*. PhD thesis, 1985.

[18] D. W. Engels, J. Feldman, D. R. Karger, and M. Ruhl. Parallel processor scheduling with delay constraints. In *SODA 2001*.

[19] H. Esmaeilzadeh, E. Blem, R. S. Amant, K. Sankaralingam, and D. Burger. Dark Silicon and the End of Multicore Scaling. In *ISCA 2011*.

[20] H. Esmaeilzadeh, A. Sampson, L. Ceze, and D. Burger. Neural acceleration for general-purpose approximate programs. In *MICRO 2012*.

[21] K. Fan, H. h. Park, M. Kudlur, and S. o. Mahlke. Modulo scheduling for highly customized datapaths to increase hardware reusability. In *CGO 2008*.

[22] P. Feautrier. Some efficient solutions to the affine scheduling problem. *International Journal of Parallel Programming*, 21:313–347, 1992.

[23] M. Gebhart, B. A. Maher, K. E. Coons, J. Diamond, P. Gratz, M. Marino, N. Ranganathan, B. Robatmili, A. Smith, J. Burrill, S. W. Keckler, D. Burger, and K. S. McKinley. An evaluation of the trips computer system. In *ASPLOS 2009*.

[24] G. J. Gordon, S. A. Hong, and M. Dudík. First-order mixed integer linear programming. In *UAI 2009*.

[25] V. Govindaraju, C.-H. Ho, T. Nowatzki, J. Chhugani, N. Satish, K. Sankaralingam, and C. Kim. Dyser: Unifying functionality and parallelism specialization for energy efficient computing. *IEEE Micro*, 33(5), 2012.

[26] V. Govindaraju, C.-H. Ho, and K. Sankaralingam. Dynamically specialized datapaths for energy efficient computing. In *HPCA 2011*.

[27] S. Gupta, S. Feng, A. Ansari, S. Mahlke, and D. August. Bundled execution of recurring traces for energy-efficient general purpose processing. In *MICRO 2011*.

[28] N. Hardavellas, M. Ferdman, B. Falsafi, and A. Ailamaki. Toward dark silicon in servers. *IEEE Micro*, 31(4):6–15, 2011.

[29] J. N. Hooker. Logic, optimization and constraint programming. *INFORMS Journal on Computing*, 14:295–321, 2002.

[30] J. N. Hooker and M. A. Osorio. Mixed logical-linear programming. *Discrete Appl. Math.*, 96-97(1), Oct. 1999.

[31] Z. Huang, S. Malik, N. Moreano, and G. Araujo. The design of dynamically reconfigurable datapath coprocessors. *ACM Trans. Embed. Comput. Syst.*, 3(2):361–384, May 2004.

[32] R. Joshi, G. Nelson, and K. Randall. Denali: a goal-directed superoptimizer. In *PLDI 2002*.

[33] K. Kailas and A. Agrawala. Cars: A new code generation framework for clustered ilp processors. In *HPCA 2001*.

[34] M. Kudlur and S. Mahlke. Orchestrating the execution of stream programs on multicore platforms. In *PLDI 2008*.

[35] A. Kumar, L. De Carli, S. J. Kim, M. de Kruijf, K. Sankaralingam, C. Estan, and S. Jha. Design and implementation of the plug architecture for programmable and efficient network lookups. In *PACT 2010*.

[36] W. Lee, R. Barua, M. Frank, D. Srikrishna, J. Babb, V. Sarkar, and S. Amarasinghe. Space-time scheduling of instruction-level parallelism on a raw machine. In *ASPLOS 1998*.

[37] M. Mercaldi, S. Swanson, A. Petersen, A. Putnam, A. Schwerin, M. Oskin, and S. J. Eggers. Instruction scheduling for a tiled dataflow architecture. In *ASPLOS 2006*.

[38] M. Mercaldi, S. Swanson, A. Petersen, A. Putnam, A. Schwerin, M. Oskin, and S. J. Eggers. Modeling instruction placement on a spatial architecture. In *SPAA 2006*.

[39] M. Mishra, T. J. Callahan, T. Chelcea, G. Venkataramani, M. Budiu, and S. C. Goldstein. Tartan: Evaluating spatial computation for whole program execution. In *ASPLOS 2006*.

[40] R. Nagarajan, S. K. Kushwaha, D. Burger, K. S. McKinley, C. Lin, and S. W. Keckler. Static placement, dynamic issue (spdi) scheduling for edge architectures. In *PACT 2004*.

[41] E. Özer, S. Banerjia, and T. M. Conte. Unified assign and schedule: a new approach to scheduling for clustered register file microarchitectures. In *MICRO 31*.

[42] J. Palsberg and M. Naik. Ilp-based resource-aware compilation, 2004.

[43] H. Park, K. Fan, S. A. Mahlke, T. Oh, H. Kim, and H.-s. Kim. Edge-centric modulo scheduling for coarse-grained reconfigurable architectures. In *PACT 2008*.

[44] W. Pugh. The omega test: a fast and practical integer programming algorithm for dependence analysis. In *Supercomputing 1991*.

[45] N. Satish, K. Ravindran, and K. Keutzer. A decomposition-based constraint optimization approach for statically scheduling task graphs with communication delays to multiprocessors. In *DATE 2007*.

[46] S. Swanson, K. Michelson, A. Schwerin, and M. Oskin. Wavescalar. In *MICRO 2003*.

[47] M. Thuresson, M. Sjalander, M. Bjork, L. Svensson, P. Larsson-Edefors, and P. Stenstrom. Flexcore: Utilizing exposed datapath control for efficient computing. In *IC-SAMOS 2007*.

[48] G. Venkatesh, J. Sampson, N. Goulding, S. Garcia, V. Bryksin, J. Lugo-Martinez, S. Swanson, and M. B. Taylor. Conservation cores: reducing the energy of mature computations. In *ASPLOS 2010*.

[49] H. M. Wagner. An integer linear-programming model for machine scheduling. *Naval Research Logistics Quarterly*, 6(2):131–140, 1959.

[50] E. Waingold, M. Taylor, D. Srikrishna, V. Sarkar, W. Lee, V. Lee, J. Kim, M. Frank, P. Finch, R. Barua, J. Babb, S. Amarasinghe, and A. Agarwal. Baring It All to Software: RAW Machines. *Computer*, 30(9):86–93, 1997.

[51] M. Watkins, M. Cianchetti, and D. Albonesi. Shared reconfigurable architectures for cmps. In *FPGA 2008*.

[52] L. A. Wolsey and G. L. Nemhauser. *Integer and Combinatorial Optimization*.

Steal Tree: Low-Overhead Tracing of Work Stealing Schedulers

Jonathan Lifflander
Dept. of Computer Science
University of Illinois Urbana-Champaign
jliffl2@illinois.edu

Sriram Krishnamoorthy
Comp. Sci. & Math. Division
Pacific Northwest National Lab
sriram@pnnl.gov

Laxmikant V. Kale
Dept. of Computer Science
University of Illinois Urbana-Champaign
kale@illinois.edu

Abstract

Work stealing is a popular approach to scheduling task-parallel programs. The flexibility inherent in work stealing when dealing with load imbalance results in seemingly irregular computation structures, complicating the study of its runtime behavior. In this paper, we present an approach to efficiently trace async-finish parallel programs scheduled using work stealing. We identify key properties that allow us to trace the execution of tasks with low time and space overheads. We also study the usefulness of the proposed schemes in supporting algorithms for data-race detection and retentive stealing presented in the literature. We demonstrate that the perturbation due to tracing is within the variation in the execution time with 99% confidence and the traces are concise, amounting to a few tens of kilobytes per thread in most cases. We also demonstrate that the traces enable significant reductions in the cost of detecting data races and result in low, stable space overheads in supporting retentive stealing for async-finish programs.

Categories and Subject Descriptors D.2.5 [*Software*]: Software Engineering—Testing and Debugging; D.3.3 [*Software*]: Programming Languages—Language Constructs and Features

Keywords work-stealing schedulers; tracing; async-finish parallelism

1. Introduction

The increase in number of processor cores anticipated in both commodity and high-end systems has motivated the study of dynamic task parallelism. The structured parallel programming idioms simplify performance-portable programming and tackle problems related to frequent synchronization on large-scale systems.

Work stealing is a well-studied dynamic load balancing strategy with several useful characteristics—composability, understandable space and time bounds, provably efficient scheduling, etc. [5]. Several programming models support dynamic task parallelism using work stealing, including OpenMP 3.0 [3], Java Concurrency Utilities [11], Intel Thread Building Blocks [14], Cilk [5, 6], and X10 [15]. While several properties have been proven about work stealing schedulers, their dynamic behavior remains hard to analyze. In particular, the flexibility exhibited by work stealing in responding to load imbalances leads to less structured mapping of work to threads, complicating subsequent analysis.

PLDI'13, June 16–19, 2013, Seattle, WA, USA.

In this paper, we focus on studying work stealing schedulers that operate on programs using `async` and `finish` statements—the fundamental concurrency constructs in modern parallel languages such as X10 [15]. In particular, we derive algorithms to trace work stealing schedulers operating on async-finish programs.

Tracing captures the order of events of interest and is an effective approach to studying runtime behavior, enabling both online characterization and offline analysis. While useful, the size of a trace imposes a limit on what can be feasibly analyzed, and perturbation of the application's execution can make it impractical at scale. Tracing individual tasks in an async-finish program is a prohibitive challenge due to the fine granularity and sheer number of individual tasks. Such programs often expose far more concurrency than the number of computing threads to maximize scheduling flexibility.

In this paper, we derive algorithms to efficiently trace the execution of async-finish programs. Rather than trace individual tasks, we exploit the structure of work stealing schedulers to coarsen the events traced. In particular, we construct a steal tree: a tree of steal operations that partitions the program execution into groups of tasks. We identify the key properties of two scheduling policies—help-first and work-first [9]—that enables the steal tree to be compactly represented.

In addition to presenting algorithms to trace and replay async-finish programs scheduled using work stealing, we demonstrate the usefulness of the proposed algorithms in two distinct contexts—optimizing data race detection for structured parallel programs [13] and supporting retentive stealing without requiring explicit enumeration of tasks [12].

The following are the primary contributions of this paper:

- identification of key properties of work-first and help-first schedulers operating on async-finish programs to compactly represent the stealing relationships;
- algorithms that exploit these properties to trace and replay async-finish programs by efficiently constructing the *steal tree*;
- demonstration of low space overheads and within-variance perturbation of execution in tracing work stealing schedulers;
- reduction in the cost of data race detection using an algorithm that maintains and traverses the dynamic program structure tree [13]; and
- retentive stealing algorithms for recursive parallel programs, while prior work required explicitly enumerated task collections [12].

2. Background and Related Work

2.1 Async-Finish Parallelism

An `async` statement identifies the associated statement as a task, the basis unit of concurrent execution. A task identified by the async statement can be executed in parallel with the enclosing task, referred to as the parent task. A finish statement identifies the bounds of concurrency. All computation enclosed by a finish statement, including nested concurrent tasks, are required to complete before any statement subsequent to the finish can be executed.

This async-finish parallelism model, supported in X10, enables both fully strict and terminally strict computations. In fully strict computations, exemplified by Cilk, a finish statement implicitly encloses all execution in a task, requiring all tasks transitively nested within a task to complete before it returns. The async-finish model extends the fully strict model by supporting *escaping asyncs*, allowing a task to return before its nested concurrent tasks need to complete.

2.2 Work Stealing Schedulers

We shall assume that the computation begins with a single task and terminates when the task and its descendents complete execution. Concurrent tasks can be executed in parallel by distinct threads or processes. Each thread maintains a local deque of tasks and alternates between two phases until termination. In the *working phase*, each thread executes tasks from its local deque. When no more local work is available, a thread enters the *stealing phase* to steal from a victim's deque. A stealing thread (a *thief*) attempts to steal a task until work is found or termination is detected. The thief pushes the stolen task onto its local deque and enters a new working phase. Each thread pushes and pops tasks from the *local end* of its deque, while the thief steals from the other end (*steal end*) of the victim's deque.

We consider two scheduling policies (outlined in Figure 1) for async-finish programs identified by Guo et al. [9]. In the *work-first* policy, a thread, upon encountering an async or a finish statement, pushes the currently executing task onto the deque and begins to execute the nested task identified. A thief can steal the partially-executed task (a *continuation*) once it is pushed onto the deque. In the absence of steal operations, this policy mirrors the sequential execution order and has been shown to exhibit efficient space and time bounds.

In the *help-first* policy, the working thread continues to execute the current task, pushing any encountered concurrent tasks onto the deque. Encountering a finish statement, the current task's continuation is pushed onto the deque to complete processing of the tasks nested within the finish scope. Finish scopes constrain the help-first scheduler, requiring the tasks in the finish scope to be processed before tasks sequentially following the finish scope can be spawned. This scheduling policy was shown to speedup work propagation by Guo et al. [9].

2.3 Tracing and Performance Analysis

Several papers have noted for work-first schedulers that steals can be recorded for the purposes of maintaining series-parallel relationships using the SP-hybrid algorithm—for data-race detection [4, 10] and for optimizing transactional memory conflict detection [2]. However, these do not provide a general tracing algorithm and require a global lock to store "threads" of work. We provide a general tracing algorithm that does not require global synchronization or locking. We are not aware of any prior work on tracing the more complex help-first scheduling policy. The limitations of the prior work in tracing work stealing schedulers is evidenced by the fact that some of the most recent work on data-race detection for async-finish programs [13] does not exploit the steal relationship—a beneficial approach that we demonstrate later in this paper.

Work stealing has typically been studied empirically (e.g., [1, 12]). Tallent and Mellor-Crummey [16] presented blame shifting to relate lack of parallel slack in work stealing to code segments.

```
@async(Task t, Cont this):
  deque.push(t);

@finish(Task t, Cont this):
  deque.push(this);
  process(t);

@taskCompletion:
  t = deque.pop();
  if(t) process(t);
  //else this phase ends

@steal(Cont c, int victim):
  c=attemptSteal(victim);
```

(b) Help-first scheduler

```
@async(Task t, Cont this):
  deque.push(this);
  process(t);

@finish(Task t, Cont this):
  deque.push(this);
  process(t);

@taskCompletion:
  //same as help first minus
  //some finish scope mgmt

@steal(int victim):
  //same as help-first
```

(a) Work-first scheduler

Figure 1. Basic actions in the two scheduling policies

They assume global information about the number of active and idle workers.

3. Notation

We define a *continuation step* (or simply *step*) to be the dynamic sequence of instructions with no interleaving async, finish, at, or when statements. Each continuation step will be executed by exactly one thread and cannot be migrated between threads during execution.

A continuation is the portion of execution, in terms of continuation steps, reachable from a given continuation step. In other words, a continuation represents the remainder of the execution that begins with the given continuation step. A task is a continuation marked by an async or finish statement, representing all steps executed in the task. In shared-memory environments, all continuations of a task occupy the same storage and transform the state from one step to the next. The term continuation is used in places where a task is used, except when we intend to specifically distinguish a task from a continuation. A partial continuation is a continuation that represents a proper subset of the computation represented by a task.

A task is said to spawn another task when the task's execution encounters an async statement. Without changing program semantics, we treat a finish statement synonymously with a finish async. Thus a finish statement leads to the spawning of a task as well. All child tasks spawned from a given task are referred to as siblings and are ordered from left to right. We also refer to a task's left and right siblings, if they exist.

Each task is associated with a level. The initial task in a working phase is at level 0. A level of a spawned task is one greater than that of the spawning task.

4. Problem Statement

An example async-finish program is shown in Figure 2a. In the figure, s1, s2, etc. are continuation steps. Tasks spawned using async statements need to be processed before the execution can proceed past the immediately enclosing finish statement. async statements that are not ordered by a finish statement (e.g., the async statements enclosing s5 and s9) can be executed in any order. The objective is to compactly track the execution of each continuation step.

The execution in each worker is grouped into phases with each phase executing continuation steps in a well-defined order, starting from a single continuation. In each working phase, the computation begins with a single continuation step and involves the execution of all steps reached from the initial step minus the continuations that were stolen. The tracing overheads (space and time) can be

```
fn() {
 s1;
 async { s5; async x; s6; }
 s2;
 async {
  s7;
  async { s9; async x; s10;
          async x; s11; .. }
  s8;..
 }
 s3;
 async { s12; finish {s13;..}..}
 s4;
}
```

(a) async-finish program

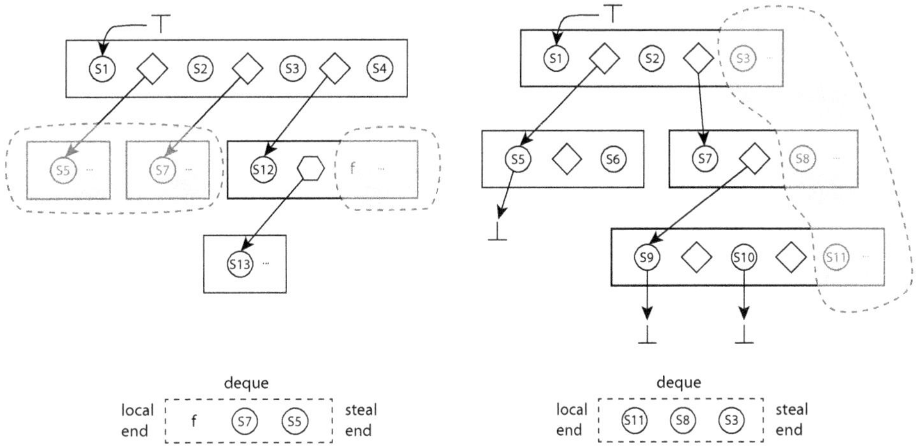

(b) Help-first (c) Work-first

Figure 2. An example async-finish parallel program and a snapshot of its execution. Legend: ⊤ represents the root task; ⊥ represents a sequential task; a circle represents a step; a diamond represents an `async` statement; a hexagon represents a `finish` statement; '..' represents a continuation; an arrow represents a spawn relationship; a rectangular box represents a task; and the shaded region represents the region that is stolen. The deque depicted at the bottom has a *steal end* that is accessed by thieves and a *local end* that is accessed by the worker thread.

significantly reduced if the steps executed in each working phase can be compactly represented.

Note the difference in the stealing structure between the work-first and help-first schedulers in Figure 2. While continuations stolen in the work-first schedule seem to follow the same structure across all the levels shown, the help-first schedule can produce more complicated steal relationships. This distinction is the result of the difference in the scheduling actions of the two policies—especially when an `async` statement encountered, as shown in Figure 1. The challenge is to identify the key properties of help-first and work-first scheduling policies to compactly identify the the leafs of the tree of steps rooted at the initial step in each working phase.

5. Tracing Help-First Schedulers

Under help-first scheduling, spawned tasks are pushed onto the deque, while the current task is executed until the end or a finish scope is reached. Children of task spawned by `async` statements are in the same finish scope as the parent. Encountering a `finish` statement, the current task's continuation is enqueued onto the deque and the spawned task in the new finish scope is immediately executed. When all the tasks nested within the `finish` statement have been processed, the finish scope is exited and the execution of the parent task is continued, possibly spawning additional tasks. We refer the reader to Guo et al. [9] for the detailed algorithm.

Figure 2b shows a snapshot of the help-first scheduling of the program in Figure 2a. The steps in the outermost task, represented by `fn()`—s1, s2, s3, and s4—are processed before any other steps.

OBSERVATION 5.1. *Two tasks are in the same immediately enclosing finish scope if the closest finish scope that encloses each of them also encloses their common ancestor.*

LEMMA 5.2. *A task at a level is processed only after all its younger siblings in the same immediately enclosing finish scope are processed.*

Proof. A work-first scheduler enqueues the spawned tasks from the start of the task's lexical scope. The spawned tasks are enqueued onto the deque with the newer child tasks enqueued closer to the local-end than the older ones. The child tasks are enqueued until the executing task completes or a `finish` statement is encountered. Tasks under the encountered `finish` statement are immediately processed and the execution continues with enqueuing tasks spawned using the `async` statement. This property, combined with the fact that tasks popped from the local end are immediately processed, requires all younger siblings of a task to be processed before it can be processed. □

LEMMA 5.3. *A task is stolen at a level only after all its older siblings in the same immediately enclosing finish scope are stolen.*

Proof. Recall that all `async` statements in a task are in the same immediately enclosing finish scope, and `finish` statements introduce new finish scopes.

1. Consider the case when two `async` statements in a task have no intervening `finish` statement. In this case, the corresponding tasks are pushed onto the deque with the older sibling first. Thus the older sibling is stolen before the younger sibling.
2. Now consider the case where siblings in the same immediate finish scope are separated by one of more intervening `finish` statements. In particular, consider the execution of the following sequence of statements in a task: *async n; ... finish p; ... async m*. Tasks n and m are in the same immediately enclosing finish scope, while task p is not. Task n is first enqueued onto the deque. When the `finish` statement is processed, the current task's continuation c is then pushed onto the deque with the worker immediately processing statement p. At this point, if a steal occurs, n and c are at the steal end of the deque followed by tasks spawned from p. Hence, all older siblings (n and c) in the same immediately enclosing finish scope will be stolen before tasks generated from p. The execution proceeds past the `finish` statement only after all the tasks nested by p are complete. Once they are executed, the continuation of the current task c is dequeued (unless it was stolen) and task m is enqueued on top of n in the deque. The execution now devolves onto case 1 and the older sibling is stolen before the younger.

□

LEMMA 5.4. *At most one partial continuation is stolen at any level and it belongs to the last executed task at that level.*

Proof. A task's partial continuation is enqueued only when it encounters a `finish` statement. Consider such a task. When the task is being processed, its parent's continuation is in the deque, or it has completed processing. Based on lemma 5.2, all the parent's younger siblings have been processed. Hence, the queue has the parent's older siblings followed by a possible partial continuation of the parent followed by this task's older siblings, then this task. By lemma 5.3, this task's partial continuation will not be stolen until all the parent's older siblings are stolen. By lemma 5.2 all younger siblings of this task, if any, have been processed at this point. Thus the deque only has the partial continuation's children, all of which are at levels higher than this task. After this task's partial continuation is stolen, all subsequent tasks will be at higher levels, making this task the last one at this level. □

LEMMA 5.5. *All tasks and continuations stolen at a level l are immediate children of the last task processed at level $l-1$.*

Proof. We first prove by contradiction that the all tasks stolen at a given level are children of the same parent task. Let two stolen tasks at a given level be children of distinct parent tasks. Let t_a be the lowest common ancestor of of these tasks, and t_1 and t_2 be the immediate children of t_a that are ancestors of the two tasks of interest. t_1 and t_2 are thus sibling tasks. Without loss of generality, let t_1 be the older sibling. By lemma 5.2, t_2 is processed before t_1. By lemma 5.3, t_1 is stolen before any descendent of t_2 can be stolen. Thus no descendent of t_1 can be enqueued if a descendent of t_2 is stolen, resulting in a contradiction: either the steals will be at different levels because descendents of t_1 cannot be enqueued, or they will be children of the same parent task.

We now prove that the parent task q of all tasks stolen at level l is the last task processed at level $l-1$. Let t be any task at level $l-1$ that is not q. By lemma 5.2, task t must be an older sibling of the parent task q. From lemma 5.3, any task t must be stolen before q. By the above proof, any task with a higher level y must be a child of the same parent task. We now show by contradiction that y must be a child of q, the last task processed at level $l-1$. If y is a child of some task t, then t is currently being processed. By lemma 5.2, q is processed before t. q has not been processed, hence we have a contradiction. □

LEMMA 5.6. *The parent q of the tasks stolen at level $l+1$ is a sibling of the tasks stolen at level l.*

Proof. We prove this by contradiction. By lemma 5.5, q is last task processed on level l. By lemma 5.2, all younger tasks on level l have been processed. If q is not a sibling of the tasks stolen at level l, q could not have been processed. Thus the stolen tasks at level $l+1$ could not have been created, resulting in a contradiction. □

LEMMA 5.7. *The parent of the tasks stolen at level $l+1$ is either the immediate younger sibling of the last stolen task at level l, or the immediate younger sibling of the last stolen task at level l in the same immediately enclosing finish scope.*

Proof. From lemmas 5.4, 5.5, and 5.6, the last task in the same immediately enclosing finish scope that is executed is the closest younger sibling of stolen task that is in the same enclosing finish scope. Thus the last task executed at that level is either the immediate right sibling of the last stolen task, say t_1, or the closest right sibling in the immediate enclosing finish scope, say t_2. When both are identical, the outcome is clear. When they are distinct, the immediate younger sibling of the last stolen task is in a distinct finish scope. If the `finish` statement is stolen, no further tasks can be processed that are not descendents of this statement, making t_1 the last executed task. If the `finish` statement is not stolen, no descendent tasks of this statement can be stolen, making t_2 the last executed task. □

THEOREM 5.8. *The tasks executed and steal operations encountered in each working phase can be fully described by (a) the level of the root in the total ordering of the steal operations on the victim's working phase, and (b) the number of tasks and step of the continuation stolen at each level.*

Proof. The tasks stolen at a level can be determined from the number of tasks stolen at that level and the identification of these tasks' parent (by lemma 5.7) (transitively until level 0 which has just one task). The position of the partial continuation stolen at a level can be determined from the fact it is the last processed task at a given level (lemma 5.4) and from the number of tasks stolen at that level in the same finish scope as the parent. Together with the step information tracking, this uniquely identifies all stolen continuations. □

Illustration. A snapshot of execution under the help-first work stealing policy is shown in Figure 2b. Steps `s1`, `s2`, `s3`, `s4`, and `s11` have been executed. Because `s13` is encountered in a finish scope, `s12` spawns the task starting with step `s13` and continues recursive execution before continuing the execution past the finish scope. Meanwhile, the deque consists of tasks `s5`, `s7`, and the continuation past the finish scope, represented by `f`, and were stolen. Note that the help-first scheduler steals from left-to-right when stealing full tasks, and right-to-left (similar to a work-first scheduler) when stealing a partial continuation.

The subtrees executed in each working phase form a steal tree. The root of the tree is the subtree that includes the main continuation that began the program. Each child is a subtree stolen from the victim's subtree. Each node in the steal tree contains information about the continuations stolen from it, bounding the actual steps executed in that subtree. Each edge in the steal tree contains information about the position of the steal from the parent subtree.

6. Tracing Work-First Schedulers

Under work-first scheduling, spawning a task involves pushing the currently executing step's successor onto the deque, with the execution continuing with the first step in the spawned task.

The continuation that starts the working phase is at level 0, referred to as the root continuation. Tasks spawned by continuations at level l are at level $l+1$. The work-first scheduling policy results in exactly one continuation at levels $0, \ldots, l-1$, where l is the number of continuations in the deque. We observe the tasks spawned during a working phase and prove that there is at most one steal per level, and a steal at all levels $0, \ldots, l-1$ before a task can be stolen at level l. This allows us to represent all the steals for a given working phase as a contiguous vector of integers that identify the continuation step stolen at each level, starting at level 0.

OBSERVATION 6.1. *The deque, with l tasks in it, consists of one continuation at levels 0 through $l-1$ with 0 at the steal-end and the continuation at level i spawned by the step that precedes the continuation at level $i-1$.*

The execution of the work-first scheduler mirrors the sequential execution. The task executing at level l is pushed onto the deque before spawning a task at level $l+1$. Thus the deque corresponds to one path from the initial step to the currently executing task in terms of the spawner-spawnee relationship.

LEMMA 6.2. *When a continuation is stolen at level l (a) at least one task has been stolen at each level 0 through $l-1$, (b) no additional tasks are created at level l.*

Proof. The first part follows from observation 6.1 and the structure of the deque—because stealing starts from the steal-end tasks at levels 0 through $l-1$ must stolen before level l.

We prove the second part by induction. Consider the base case when the root of the subtree is the only continuation at level 0 in the deque. After the root of the subtree is stolen, no continuation exists at level 0 to create another task at level 1. Let the lemma be true for all levels $0, \ldots, l$. When a continuation at level l is stolen, no further tasks can be created at level l. Now consider the lemma for level $l+1$. After a steal at level l, no further tasks can be created at level $l+1$. Once the current continuation at level $l+1$ is stolen, no subsequent tasks are created at level $l+1$. □

THEOREM 6.3. *The tasks executed and steal operations encountered in each working phase can be fully described by (a) the level of the root in the total ordering of the steal operations on the victim's working phase, and (b) the step of the continuation stolen at each level.*

Proof. By lemma 6.2, steal operations on a victim are totally ordered, implying that each task stolen from a victim during distinct working phase is at a unique level. Because no additional tasks can be created at that level (again by lemma 6.2), the step of the continuation stolen at that level is sufficient to uniquely identify it. □

These observations allow the steal points to be maintained in a contiguous array. The size of the array corresponds to the number of steals in this working phase, and the value at position l in the array corresponds to the index of the continuation stolen at level l. The stolen continuations can be identified to absolute or relative indices. Absolute indices—counting the number of steps executed in this phase at each level—does not effectively support retentive stealing, as explained later. We employ relative indices, with the value at index l corresponding to the number of steps executed in the last task executed at this level. Note that the last task executed at level l is a child of a predecessor step of the continuation stolen at level $l-1$. Given there is only one task at level 0, we store the number of steps by this worker for this initial step.

Illustration. A snapshot of execution under the work stealing scheduler is shown in Figure 2c. The thread began execution from step `s1` and has completed execution of s1, s2, s5, s6, s7, s9, and s10. It is currently executing the task spawned by s10 with the the deque consisting of steps s3, s8, and s11—bottom to top. These steps have been created but not yet processed. During some point in the execution, these tasks have been stolen by thieves. The steal order is s3, s8, followed by s11. Note that the execution in the work-first scheduling policy is *left-to-right*, while the steals are *right-to-left*.

7. Tracing and Replay Algorithms

We now present the algorithms for tracing and replay based on the properties identified for help-first and work-first schedulers. in Sections 5 and 6. These properties simplify the state to be managed to trace and replay both schedulers. The algorithms rely on some state in addition to the basic scheduler actions. This shared state is shown as C++-style pseudo-code in Figure 3.

Every continuation and task has an associated ContinuationHdr that stores the level and step. When a new working phase is started or an `async` or `finish` is encountered, the bookkeeping keeps track of the current level for each continuation. Each working phase that is executed by a worker maintains the state shown in WorkingPhaseInfo as part of the trace. A worker's trace is an ordered list of working phases it has executed so far, retained as one WorkerStateHdr object per worker. The root task of the entire computation is not stolen and its victim is set to -1. Each continuation's step is tracked as an integer and is updated on each `async` or `finish` statement.

7.1 Tracing

The tracing algorithms augment the steal operation to track the steal relationship and construct the steal tree. From the earlier discussion, we know that, unlike work-first schedulers, help-first schedulers allow multiple tasks to be stolen at each level. Thus for tracing a help-first scheduler, we store the number of tasks stolen at each level:

```
struct HelpFirstInfo : WorkingPhaseInfo {
  vector<int> nTasksStolen; //num. tasks stolen at each
        level, init to 0
};
```

When a continuation is stolen under help-first scheduling, the thief marks the steal in the victim's HelpFirstInfo. The HelpFirstInfo for the current working phase on the victim can only be accessed by a single thief, and hence requires no synchronization. myrank is the thief thread's rank. Note that just the number of stolen tasks at each level and the partial continuation's step is sufficient to reconstruct all information about the tasks executed in a given working phase.

```
@steal(Cont c, int victim, int myrank):
  // c is the continuation stolen by the thief
  if c.step == 0: // this is a full task
    wsh[victim].wpi.back().nTasksStolen[c.level] += 1;
  else: //this is a partial continuation
    wsh[victim].wpi.back().stepStolen[c.level] = c.step;
  wsh[victim].wpi.back().thieves.push_back(myrank);
  WorkingPhaseInfo phase;
  phase.victim = victim;
  wsh[myrank].wpi.push_back(phase);
```

When a continuation is stolen under work-first scheduling, the following marks the steal in the victim's WorkingPhaseInfo. For the work-first policy, the actions required are less complex because at most one task can be stolen per level.

```
@steal(Cont c, int victim, int myrank):
  wsh[victim].wpi.back().stepStolen[c.level] = c.step;
  wsh[victim].wpi.back().thieves.push_back(myrank);
  WorkingPhaseInfo phase;
  phase.victim = victim;
  wsh[myrank].wpi.push_back(phase);
```

Note that none of these actions require additional synchronizations, and all the tracing overhead incurred is on the steal path.

7.2 Replay

The collected traces include timing information, which allows the traces to be replayed. During replay, each thread executes the working phases assigned to it in order. Whenever a stolen task is spawned, rather than adding it to the deque, the corresponding thief is informed of its creation. Each thread executes its set of subtrees at the same time point as in the original run, after ensuring that the given subtree's root task has been spawned by the corresponding victim. The creation of the initial task in working phase indicates that all dependences before a task in that working phase have been satisfied.

During replay, each task tracks whether its children could have been stolen in the trace, i.e., the task is at the *frontier*, using the following additional field in the ContinuationHdr:

```
struct ContinuationHdr {
  int level; //this task's async level
  int step; //this continuation's step
};
struct Task : ContinuationHdr { ... };
struct Cont : ContinuationHdr { ... };
struct WorkingPhaseInfo {
  int victim; // victim stolen from
  vector<int> stepStolen; //step stolen at
        each level, init to -1
  vector<int> thieves; // list of thieves
};
```

```
struct WorkerStateHdr {
  //state for each working phase
  vector<WorkingPhaseInfo> wpi;
};

WorkerStateHdr wsh[NWORKERS]; //one
      per worker

//initializing computation's first task
@init(Task initialTask):
  initialTask.victim=-1;//victim set to -1
```

```
//start of working phase with continuation c
@startWorkingPhase(Cont c):
  c.level = 0; // level of starting frame

//spawning task t when executing task 'this'
@async(Task t, Cont this):
  t.level=this.level+1;
  t.step=0; this.step+=1;

//spawning task t in new finish scope when
      executing task 'this'
@finish(Task t, Cont this):
  t.level = this.level + 1; this.step += 1;
```

Figure 3. Common data structures and level management for all algorithms

```
struct ReplayContinuationHeader : ContinuationHdr {
  bool atFrontier; // could any of its children have been
        stolen, initially false
};
```

When a worker encounters a task that was stolen, it marks it as stolen and notifies (in shared-memory) or sends (in distributed memory) the task to the thief. When a thread starts the execution of a working phase, it waits for the initial task to be created by the victim. The worker with the initial task for the entire computation begins execution, identifying the initial task as being at the frontier.

```
markStolen(Task t):
  // enqueue 't' for sending or directly send to the next thief
        in current working phase info's thieves
  // drop 't' from execution on this worker

@startWorkingPhase(WorkingPhaseInfo wpi):
  // get initial task from wpi.victim, if wpi.victim>=0

@init(Task initialTask, int myrank):
  if(wsh[myrank].wpi[0].victim == -1):
    initialTask.atFrontier = true;
```

The above actions are used to replay traces from both help-first and work-first schedulers.

When help-first traces are replayed, the number of child tasks spawned by each task in the same finish scope is tracked by augmenting the following to the HelpFirstInfo structure.

```
struct HelpFirstReplayInfo : HelpFirstInfo {
  vector<int> childCount; //num children for current
        executing task
};

// at the beginning of execution of a task
@taskEntry(Task this, int myrank):
  wsh[myrank].childCount[this.level + 1] = 0;
```

A task spawned by an `async` statement is marked as being at the frontier if it is the immediate younger sibling of the last child task stolen from this task. When the executing task is at the frontier and the child count is less than the number of tasks stolen at the next level, the spawned task is marked as stolen. A task spawned by a `finish` statement can mark the executing task as stolen as well. If the partial continuation of the `finish` statement is not stolen, none of its descendents is stolen either.

```
@async(Task t, Continuation this, int myrank,
      WorkingPhaseInfo current_wpi):
  t.level = this.level + 1; t.step=0; this.step+=1;
  if this.atFrontier:
    if wsh[myrank].childCount[t.level] < current_wpi.
          stealCount[t.level]:
      markStolen(t);
    else if wsh[myrank].childCount[t.level] == current_wpi.
          stealCount[t.level]:
      t.atFrontier = true;
  wsh[myrank].childCount[t.level] += 1;

@finish(Continuation t, Continuation this, int myrank,
      WorkingPhaseInfo current_wpi):
  // t does not contribute to calculation of childCount
  t.level = this.level+1;
  if this.atFrontier:
    if this.step == wsh[myrank].stepStolen[this.level]:
      markStolen(this); // continuation of this after spawning
            the finish
      t.atFrontier = true; // only child of stolen parent is
            -- also at frontier
      if wsh[myrank].childCount[t.level] < current_wpi.
            stealCount[t.level]:
        assert(wsh[myrank].childCount[t.level] ==
              current_wpi.stealCount[t.level]-1);
        markStolen(t);
```

When replaying work-first traces, the primary action is determining whether a task is at a frontier. When an `async` or `finish` statement is encountered, the following actions are executed:

```
@async(Task t, Cont this, int myrank):
  t.level = this.level+1; t.step=0; this.step += 1;
  if this.atFrontier:
    if this.step == wsh[myrank].stepStolen[this.level]:
      markStolen(this);
      t.atFrontier = true;

@finish(Task t, Cont this, int myrank):
  //same action as for async(t, this, myrank)
```

7.3 Space Utilization

The space overhead can be quickly computed from the data structures employed in the algorithms. In the following formulæ, b_h and b_w describe the total number of bytes required to trace help-first and work-first schedulers, respectively:

$$b_h = \sum_{i=0}^{n} v(1+s_i) + s_i(m+k) \qquad \text{(Total bytes for help-first)}$$

$$b_w = \sum_{i=0}^{n} v(1+s_i) + s_i m \qquad \text{(Total bytes for work-first)}$$

where n is the total number of working phases, v is the number of bytes required for a thread identifier, s_i is the number of steals in a working phase, m is the number of bytes required for a step identifier, and k is number of bytes required to store the maximum number of tasks at a given level.

For Figures 5 and 7 that graph the storage required, we use integers to store the thread and step identifiers, and assume that the maximum number of tasks spawned at a given level does not exceed the size of an integer: $k = m = v = \text{sizeof(int)} - 4$ bytes.

8. Applications

8.1 Data-race Detection for Async-Finish Programs

Raman et al. [13] perform data race detection by building a dynamic program structure tree (DPST) at runtime that captures the relationships between `async` and `finish` instances. The `async` and `finish` nodes in the tree are internal and the leaves are `step` nodes that represent a step (same as the continuation step in this paper) in the program execution where data accesses may occur. The DPST is built dynamically at runtime by inserting nodes into the tree in parallel. Raman et al. present a DPST implementation that exploits the tree structure to insert nodes into the DPST in parallel without synchronization in $O(1)$ time. Here, we summarize the key cost factors in that implementation and refer readers to Raman et al. [13] for the full description.

To detect races, if an application performs a data access during a step, a reference to the step is stored in shadow memory so other steps that read/write this same address can reference it. If two steps access the same memory address, the structure of the tree is used to determine if these steps can possibly execute in parallel for any possible schedule. Conflicting access to the same memory location by concurrent steps is detected as a data race.

Two steps can execute concurrently, identified as satisfying the dynamically-may-happen-in-parallel relationship, if their lowest common ancestor (LCA) in the DPST tree is an `async` node. Each memory location is associated with two steps that read the location and one that last wrote that location. The two read operations form the extremal bounds of a DPST sub-tree that contains all concurrent reads to the memory location since the last synchronization point. Rather than comparing with every step performing a read, a step performing a write-operation might be flagged as causing a data race if it can execute concurrent with the three steps whose reads and writes are being tracked. Data-race detection for read operations is similar but also involves operations to track the extremal bounds of the sub-tree of concurrent reads.

It can be seen that computing the lowest common ancestor (LCA) of two steps in computing the dynamically-may-happen-in-parallel relation is a performance critical operation, invoked several times for each read and write operation. In particular, finding the LCA is among the most expensive parts of the data-race detection. The DPST creation takes constant time and requires no synchronization and updating the memory address locations atomically only happens when a memory address is written or read and the step is higher in the tree than the previous steps that read. On the other hand, computing the LCA between two steps involves walking the DPST from the two steps to their parent, with the cost proportional to the number of edges walked. Because the DPST contains the entire async-finish tree, it may be very deep if the application is fine-grained, leading to very expensive LCA calculations.

We observe that the steal tree can be used to partition the DPST based on the steal relationships. In particular, it can be seen that the LCA of two steps in distinct working phases is the LCA of the initial steps of the two working phases. Exploiting this additional structural information allows us to bypass potentially large portions of the tree when traversing upward to locate the LCA. We relate a step/async/finish in the DPST with the steal tree as we create the DPST. For each node (`step`, `async`, or `finish`) in the DPST a pointer is added to store the working phase it belongs to. If a step accesses data, a reference to that step may be stored in the shadow memory. We compute and track the absolute level of the initial task executed in each working phase, referred to as the depth of the subtree executed in that working phase. The algorithm below shows how we traverse the tree when two steps accessing the same memory address are executed in different working phases. If the depths of the subtrees are different, we traverse up the deeper one. If they are equal we traverse up both until the depths are different or the ancestors of both steps are in the same working phase subtrees. Once we are in the same subtree, we invoke the LCA method in [13] on the initial tasks of the two subtrees.

```
subtreeLCA(Cont s1, Cont s2):
  while(s1 and s2 are in different subtrees):
    while(s1 subtree depth != s2 subtree depth):
      if (s1 subtree depth < s2 subtree depth):
        s1 = initial task in s1's working phase
      else:
        s2 = initial task in s2's working phase
    if((s1 subtree depth == s2 subtree depth) &&
       (s1 and s2 in different subtrees)):
      s1 = initial task in s1's working phase
      s2 = initial task in s2's working phase
  return LCA(s1,s2) //Raman et al.'s algorithm
```

8.2 Retentive Stealing for Async-Finish Programs

Iterative applications that have identical or slowly evolving characteristics are said to exhibit the principle of persistence [18]. Such applications can be incrementally rebalanced based on performance profiles gathered from prior iterations. Lifflander et al. [12] exploited the property of persistence to improve the scalability of work stealing in iterative applications. In their approach to load balancing, each worker begins an iteration with the a collection of tasks executed by it in the previous iteration. This was shown to significantly improve parallel efficiency as the iterations progressed, in some cases from about 10% to about 90%.

Async-finish programs that exclusively exploit recursive parallelism have similar performance challenges. First, the slow propagation of work from the single initial task available at the beginning of the computation incurs significant ramp-up time. While help-first scheduling ameliorates some of the performance challenges, the challenges remains. Second, expanding from a single initial task for every iteration discards the application information on persistence.

While retentive stealing presented by Lifflander et al. [12] can address these issues, their approach was presented in the context of explicit enumeration of tasks to enable retentive stealing. This not only increases the storage overhead, but is also infeasible when intervening `finish` statements are involved. The key insight in enabling retentive stealing is to allow the execution in each worker to begin with the working phases in the previous iteration, while also allowing work stealing to improve load balance. We observe that retentive stealing can be applied to recursive parallel programs by building on the replay algorithms presented earlier. In particular, we explain the extensions to the replay algorithms to allow stealing of tasks from a working phase being replayed.

During normal execution, a worker can execute a stolen task to completion barring synchronization constraints imposed by the `finish` statement. However, a working phase being replayed completes execution when all the tasks in that phase are complete. In particular, the tasks at the frontier of a working phase need to be distinguished from other tasks. When stealing from a working phase, we therefore check whether the stolen task is at the frontier. In addition to the replay actions, a steal operation correctly identifies the steps represented by the stolen continuation, which can be extracted from the WorkingPhaseInfo structure. A task can be at the frontier,

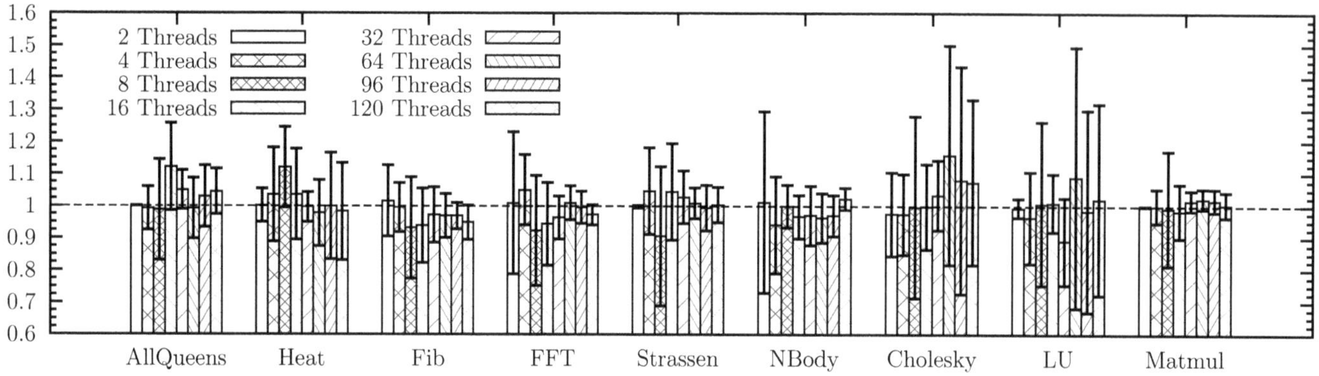

Figure 4. The ratio of mean execution time with tracing versus without tracing with a sample size of 15 on the POWER 7 architecture using the shared-memory Cilk runtime. The error bars represent the error in the difference of means at 99% confidence, using a Student's t-test.

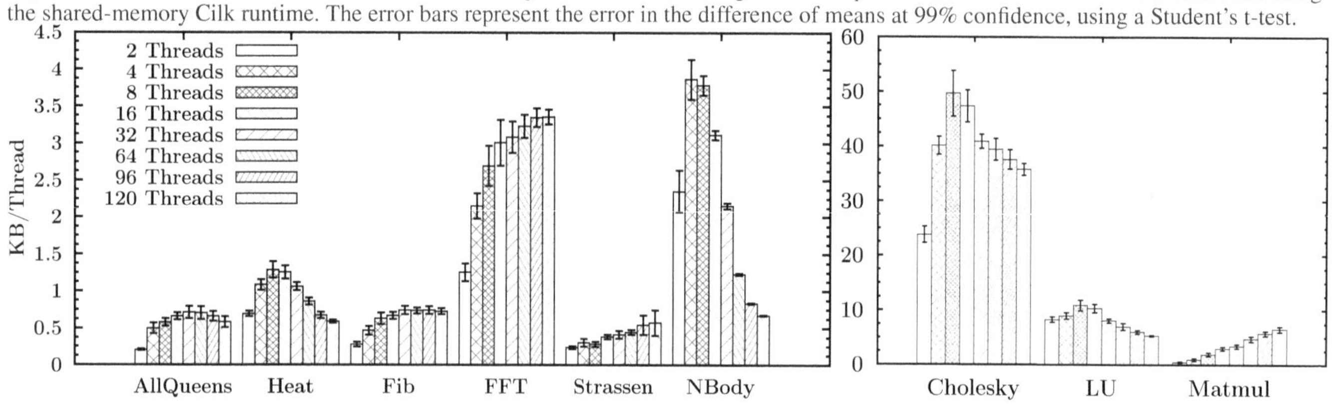

Figure 5. The storage overhead in KB/thread with our tracing scheme using the shared-memory Cilk runtime on the POWER 7 architecture. The error bars represent the standard deviation of storage size with a sample size of 15.

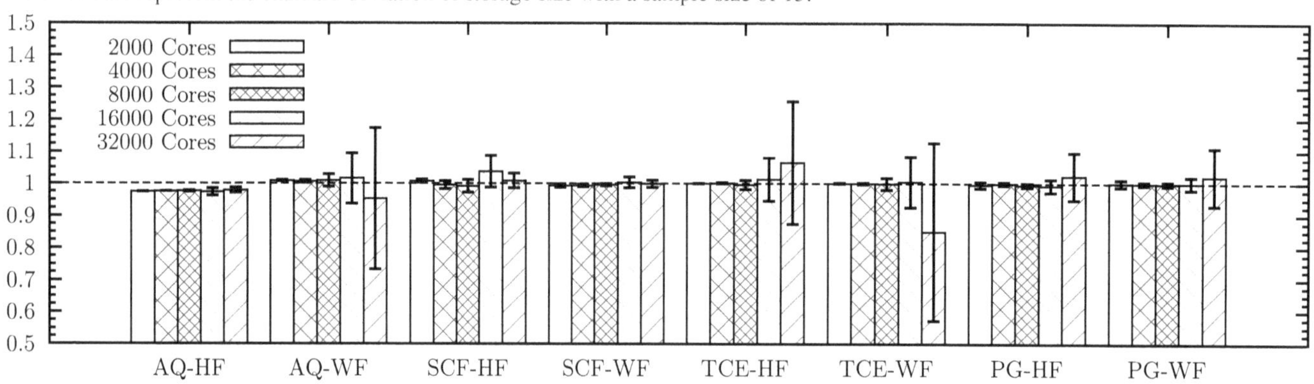

Figure 6. The ratio of mean execution time with tracing versus without tracing with a sample size of 15 on Cray XK6 Titan in distributed-memory. The error bars represent the error in the difference of means at 99% confidence, using a Student's t-test.

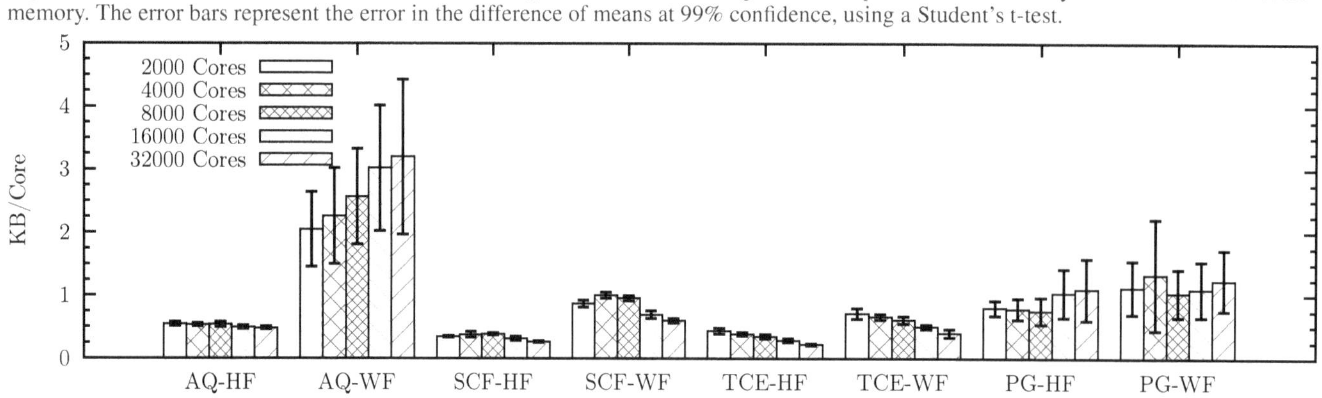

Figure 7. The storage overhead in KB/core with our tracing scheme for distributed-memory on Cray XK6 Titan. The error bars represent the standard deviation of storage size with a sample size of 15.

Shared-memory	
Benchmark	Configuration
AllQueens	nq = 14, sequential cutoff 8
Heat	nt = 5, nx = 4096, ny = 4096
Fib	n = 43
FFT	n = 67108864
Strassen	n = 4096
NBody	iterations = 15, nbodies = 8192
Cholesky	n = 2048, z = 20000
LU	n = 1024
Matmul	n = 3000
Distributed-memory	
AQ	nq = 19, sequential cutoff 10
SCF	128 beryllium atoms, chunk size 40
TCE	$C[i, j, k, l] += A[i, j, a, b] * B[a, b, k, l]$
	O-blocks 20 14 20 26, V-blocks 120 140 180 100
PG	13K sequences

Table 1. Benchmark configurations.

i.e., its descendents stolen in the current working phase, only if its parent is at the frontier. Thus a thief stealing a step not at the frontier can execute all tasks reachable from that step. When a stolen task is at the frontier, the WorkingPhaseInfo structure associated with victim's current working phase is also copied. This allows the thief to ensure that it does not execute steps reachable from the stolen continuation past the work represented by the victim's working phase. The calculations that use the task's level to determine the frontier during replay are adapted to take into account the level of the stolen task in the victim's working phase.

In this approach, steals of tasks not at frontier just steal the step information and incur the same cost as a steal during normal execution. Steals at the frontier, also need to copy the frontier information from the victim's working phase, and thus incur greater data movement overhead on distributed-memory systems. Stealing from working phases to enable retentive stealing can also lead to working phase "fragmentation", potentially increasing the number of working phases and hence the storage overhead as the iterations progress. In section 9, we show that these overheads do not adversely impact performance and the storage required stays well below the amount required to explicitly enumerate all tasks.

9. Experimental Evaluation

The shared-memory experiments were performed on a POWER 7 system composed of 128 GB of memory and a quad-chip module with eight cores per chip running at 3.8 GHz and supporting four-way simultaneous multi-threading. The distributed-memory experiments were performed on the OLCF Cray XK6 'Titan', an 18688-node system with one AMD sixteen-core 2.2GHz 'Bulldozer' processor and 32GB DDR3 memory per node.

The implementations were compiled with GCC 4.4.6 on the POWER 7 and PGI 12.5.0 on Titan. The distributed-memory benchmarks used MPI (MPICH2 5.5.0) for communication. We implemented the tracing algorithms for shared-memory systems in Cilk 5.4.6, and distributed-memory versions using the implementation in [12]. We tried to reproduce the configurations used by Lifflander et al. [12] in their distributed-memory experiments.

9.1 Tracing on Shared-Memory Systems

We evaluated seven of the example benchmarks in the Cilk suite and have added two more—NBody and AllQueens; the configurations are shown in Table 1. AllQueens is a variant of the NQueens Cilk benchmark that searches for all valid board configurations rather than just one. The NBody benchmark is from the "Computer Language Benchmarks Game" suite [8]; we have parallelized the benchmark by spawning a task per nbody calculation and using synchronization between iterations for the n-body updates.

For these nine benchmarks, we graph the ratio of execution time with our tracing versus the execution time without tracing in Figure 4. Each bar is the ratio of the mean of 15 runs with and without tracing for each benchmark and the error bars are the standard error in the difference of means at 99% confidence, using a Student's t-test [7]. This figure shows that our tracing overhead is low and within the run-to-run variability on the machine. We performed these same comparisons on another shared-memory architecture (an AMD x86-64 system) and observed the same trend: low overhead but high variability between runs.

Figure 5 shows the storage overhead in KB/thread that was incurred with tracing as we strong-scale the nine Cilk benchmarks. The error bars represent the standard deviation from a sample of 15 runs. For all the runs the standard deviation is low, demonstrating that different random stealing schedules do not significantly impact storage overhead. To make the trends more visible, we graph six of the benchmarks that have less overhead on the left and three on the right that have more overhead with different y-axis. For the first few scaling points all the benchmarks increase in storage per thread, but this increase scales sub-linearly (note that the threads are doubled each time, except for the 96-thread point) with thread count. This graph demonstrates that our storage requirements are small, grow slowly with thread count, and have low variation even with differing schedules. The total storage overhead continues to increase with thread count, reflecting the fact that increasing thread counts increases the number of steals. Despite this increase, we observe that the total trace size, even on 120 threads, is small enough to be analyzed on a commodity desktop system.

The traces were replayed to determine the utilization across time. Some of the results are shown in Figure 8. These plots, quickly computed from the traces, show the variation in executing identical iterations of Heat on 120 threads and the significant under-utilization when running LU even at moderate thread counts.

9.2 Tracing on Distributed-Memory Systems

For distributed-memory, we evaluate four benchmarks with two different scheduling strategies to measure the execution time and storage overhead that our tracing incurs (the configurations are shown in Table 1). The AllQueens (AQ) benchmark is a distributed-memory variant of the AllQueens benchmark. When the depth of recursion exceeds a threshold the benchmark executes an optimized sequential kernel. SCF and TCE are computational chemistry benchmarks designed by Lifflander et al. [12]. PG is a work stealing implementation of the pair-wise sequence alignment application designed by Wu et al. [17]. We refer the readers to the corresponding papers for details.

We execute the four benchmarks under both work-first and help-first scheduling policies. Figure 6 shows the ratio of execution time with tracing versus the execution time without tracing. For all the configurations, the overhead is low and mostly within the error bars, which represent the standard error in the difference of means at 99% confidence, using a Student's t-test. Some of the variation is due to obtaining a different job partition on the machine between runs (most likely the reason a couple points execute faster with tracing).

Figure 7 shows the storage overhead in KB/core that we incur with our tracing schemes. Note that for all the configurations except for AQ-WF, the overhead is less than 75 KB/core and is constant or decreases with core count. At 32,000 cores the total storage for the traces, assuming 75 KB/core, is 2.3 GB, which would

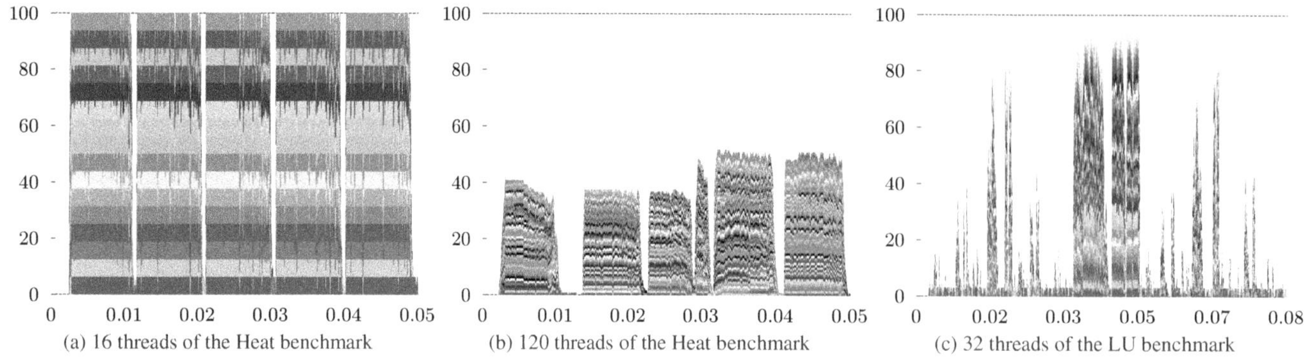

Figure 8. Percent utilization (y-axis) over time in seconds (x-axis) using the steal tree traces, colored by a random color for each thread.

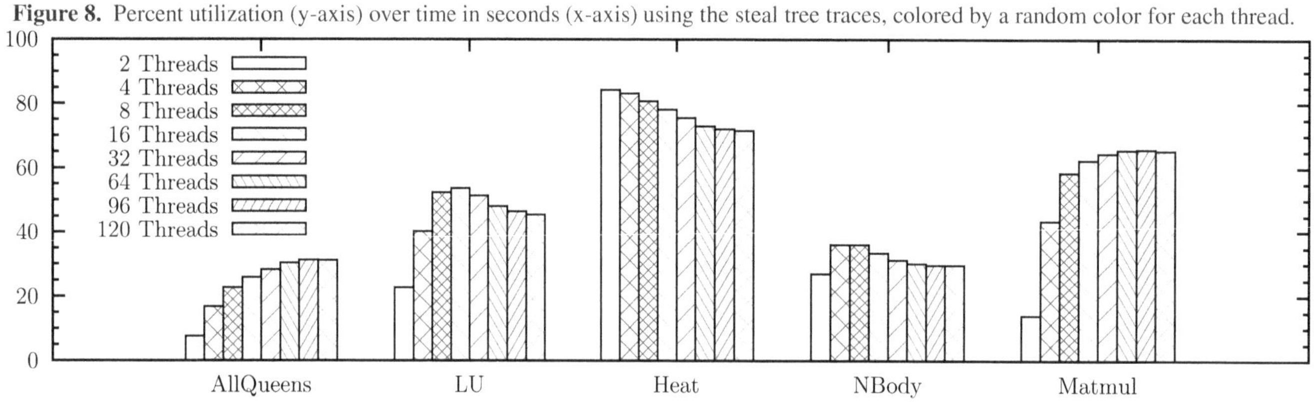

Figure 9. The percent reduction attained by exploiting our traces to reduce the tree traversals of the DPST (dynamic program structure tree) to detect races in a shared-memory application [13].

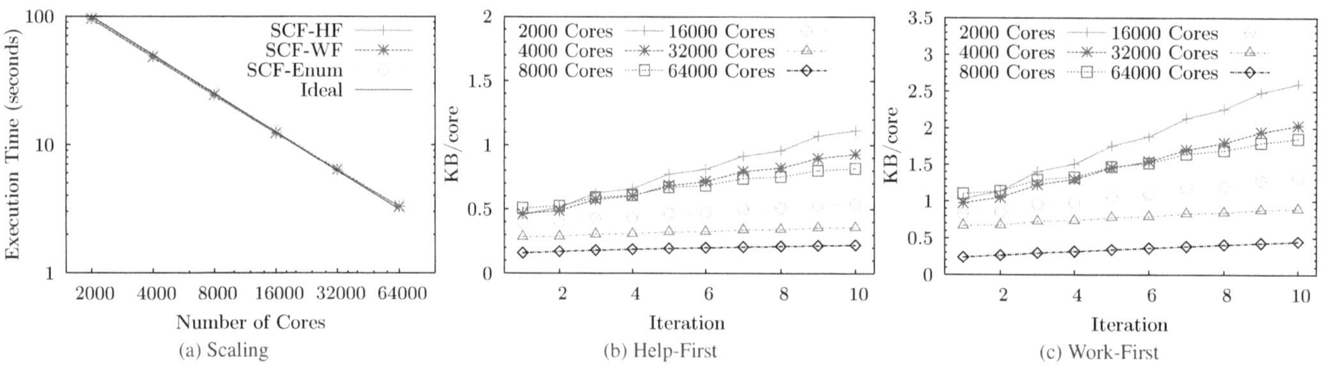

Figure 10. Retentive stealing using our tracing algorithms on recursive specification of the SCF benchmark on Cray XK6 Titan.

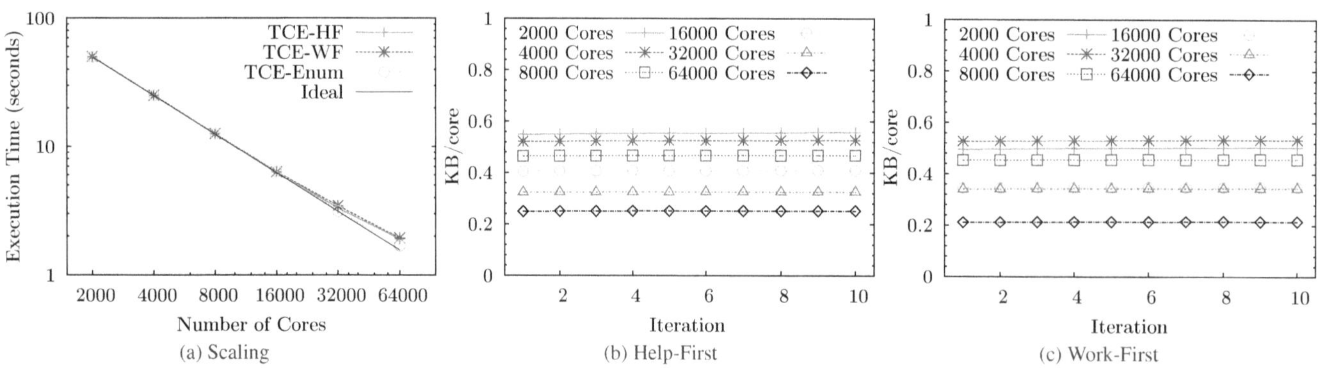

Figure 11. Retentive stealing using our tracing algorithms on recursive specification of the TCE benchmark on Cray XK6 Titan.

allow performance analysis to be performed easily on a shared-memory machine or a medium-scale work station. The AQ-WF configuration shows a somewhat different trend because the grain size for AQ is very fine and the WF scheme reduces parallel slack compared to the HF scheme.

9.3 Optimizing Data-Race Detection

For several benchmarks in Cilk, we show in Figure 9 the percent reduction of tree traversals achieved by exploiting the subtree information to bypass traversing regions of the tree. For the Heat benchmark we observe over a 70% reduction in tree traversals; for Matmul around 50–60% reduction; for NBody over 30% reduction; for LU around a 40–50% reduction; and for AllQueens around a 20–30% reduction. The general trend is that increasing the thread count partitions the tree more, causing a further reduction in the number of tree traversals required. Depending on the structure, further segmentation beyond some point may not be beneficial if the LCA is high up in the tree. Heat has this behavior where the best partitions are few and high up in the tree, with further segmentation causing an increase in tree traversals.

9.4 Retentive Stealing

We evaluated retentive stealing for the two iterative distributed-memory benchmarks: Self-Consistent Field (SCF) and Tensor Contraction Engine (TCE) (retentive stealing is not applicable for the others). In Figures 10a and 11a we show the scaling behavior of both benchmarks after several warm-up iterations and then running them 10 iterations to convergence with retentive stealing. The help-first and work-first schemes scale almost perfectly and the scaling results are comparable to the result in [12]. We graph the full task enumeration scheme used in that paper as TCE-Enum and SCF-Enum. We are able to reproduce this result without incurring the overhead of enumerating every task and storing them. For SCF, fully enumerating the tasks requires 20.7 KB/core on 2K cores; for TCE, full enumerating the tasks requires 8.3 KB/core on 2K cores. For both benchmarks, the steal tree uses significantly less storage per core compared to enumerating all the tasks. For instance, on 2K cores of SCF with help-first scheduling we only require 0.34 KB/core to store the traces; this decreases to 0.26 KB/core on 32K cores.

Also, our queue size is bounded by d (where d is the depth of the computational tree) for the work-first scheme or bd (where b is the branching factor) for the help-first scheme. With explicit enumeration the queue size is bounded by the number of tasks, which may require signification memory overhead.

In Figures 10b, 10c, 11b and 11c we graph the amount of storage per core required over time for retentive stealing because steals in subsequent iterations cause more partitioning of the work. We observe that the convergence rate is application- and scale-dependent. For the SCF benchmark, the convergence rate increases with scale under strong scaling as the benchmark approaches the limits of its concurrency. We thus anticipate the storage overhead to remain constant or increase very slowly for such an iterative application at large scales. TCE appears to be very well-behaved, with subsequent iterations causing almost no increase in storage overhead.

10. Conclusions

The widespread use of work stealing necessitates the development of mechanisms to study the behavior of individual executions. The algorithms presented in this paper to efficiently construct steal trees enable low overhead tracing and replay of async-finish programs scheduled using work-first or help-first work stealing schedulers.

We demonstrated the broader applicability of this work, beyond replay-based performance analysis, by demonstrating its usefulness in optimizing data race detection and extending the class of programs that can employ retentive stealing. As future work, we are considering the use of these tracing algorithms to construct skeletons for dynamic task-parallel programs that help study the stealing and execution structure of complex applications without requiring an understanding of the detailed domain-specific operations.

Acknowledgments

This work was supported in part by the U.S. Department of Energy's (DOE) Office of Science, Office of Advanced Scientific Computing Research, under award number 59193, and by Pacific Northwest National Laboratory under the Extreme Scale Computing Initiative. This research used resources of the Oak Ridge Leadership Computing Facility at the Oak Ridge National Laboratory, which is supported by the Office of Science under Contract No. DE-AC05-00OR22725. We thank Vivek Sarkar and Raghavan Raman for discussions on their data-race detection algorithm [13].

References

[1] U. A. Acar, G. E. Blelloch, and R. D. Blumofe. The data locality of work stealing. *Theory of Computing Systems*, 35(3):321–347, 2002. ISSN 1432-4350.

[2] K. Agrawal, J. T. Fineman, and J. Sukha. Nested parallelism in transactional memory. In *Proceedings of the 13th ACM SIGPLAN Symposium on Principles and practice of parallel programming*, PPoPP '08, pages 163–174, 2008.

[3] E. Ayguadé, N. Copty, A. Duran, J. Hoeflinger, Y. Lin, F. Massaioli, X. Teruel, P. Unnikrishnan, and G. Zhang. The design of OpenMP tasks. *Parallel and Distributed Systems, IEEE Transactions on*, 20(3): 404–418, 2009.

[4] M. A. Bender, J. T. Fineman, S. Gilbert, and C. E. Leiserson. On-the-fly maintenance of series-parallel relationships in fork-join multithreaded programs. In *Proceedings of the sixteenth annual ACM symposium on Parallelism in algorithms and architectures*, SPAA '04, pages 133–144, 2004.

[5] R. D. Blumofe. *Executing multithreaded programs efficiently*. PhD thesis, Massachusetts Institute of Technology, 1995.

[6] R. D. Blumofe, C. F. Joerg, B. C. Kuszmaul, C. E. Leiserson, K. H. Randall, and Y. Zhou. Cilk: an efficient multithreaded runtime system. In *Proceedings of the fifth ACM SIGPLAN symposium on Principles and practice of parallel programming*, PPOPP '95, pages 207–216, 1995.

[7] J. F. Box. Guinness, Gosset, Fisher, and Small Samples. *Statistical Science*, 2(1):45–52, Feb. 1987. ISSN 0883-4237. doi: 10.1214/ss/1177013437.

[8] B. Fulgham. Computer language benchmarks game, August 2012. URL `http://shootout.alioth.debian.org/`.

[9] Y. Guo, R. Barik, R. Raman, and V. Sarkar. Work-first and help-first scheduling policies for async-finish task parallelism. In *IEEE International Symposium on Parallel & Distributed Processing*, IPDPS '09, pages 1–12. IEEE, 2009.

[10] T. Karunaratna. *Nondeterminator-3: a provably good data-race detector that runs in parallel*. PhD thesis, Massachusetts Institute of Technology, 2005.

[11] D. Lea et al. Java specification request 166: Concurrency utilities, 2004.

[12] J. Lifflander, S. Krishnamoorthy, and L. V. Kale. Work stealing and persistence-based load balancers for iterative overdecomposed applications. In *Proceedings of the 21st international symposium on High-Performance Parallel and Distributed Computing*, HPDC '12, pages 137–148, 2012.

[13] R. Raman, J. Zhao, V. Sarkar, M. Vechev, and E. Yahav. Scalable and precise dynamic datarace detection for structured parallelism. In *Proceedings of the 33rd ACM SIGPLAN conference on Programming Language Design and Implementation*, PLDI '12, pages 531–542, 2012.

[14] J. Reinders. *Intel Threading Building Blocks: Outfitting C++ for Multi-Core Processor Parallelism*. O'Reilly Media, 2007.

[15] V. A. Saraswat, V. Sarkar, and C. von Praun. X10: concurrent programming for modern architectures. In *Proceedings of the 12th ACM SIGPLAN symposium on Principles and practice of parallel programming*, PPoPP '07, pages 271–271, 2007.

[16] N. R. Tallent and J. M. Mellor-Crummey. Identifying performance bottlenecks in work-stealing computations. *IEEE Computer*, 42(12): 44–50, 2009.

[17] C. Wu, A. Kalyanaraman, and W. R. Cannon. PGraph: efficient parallel construction of large-scale protein sequence homology graphs. *IEEE Transactions on Parallel and Distributed Systems*, 23(10):1923–1933, 2012.

[18] G. Zheng. *Achieving high performance on extremely large parallel machines: performance prediction and load balancing*. PhD thesis, Department of Computer Science, University of Illinois at Urbana-Champaign, 2005.

Halide: A Language and Compiler for Optimizing Parallelism, Locality, and Recomputation in Image Processing Pipelines

Jonathan Ragan-Kelley
MIT CSAIL

Connelly Barnes
Adobe

Andrew Adams
MIT CSAIL

Sylvain Paris
Adobe

Frédo Durand
MIT CSAIL

Saman Amarasinghe
MIT CSAIL

Abstract

Image processing pipelines combine the challenges of stencil computations and stream programs. They are composed of large graphs of different stencil stages, as well as complex reductions, and stages with global or data-dependent access patterns. Because of their complex structure, the performance difference between a naive implementation of a pipeline and an optimized one is often an order of magnitude. Efficient implementations require optimization of both parallelism and locality, but due to the nature of stencils, there is a fundamental tension between parallelism, locality, and introducing redundant recomputation of shared values.

We present a systematic model of the tradeoff space fundamental to stencil pipelines, a *schedule* representation which describes concrete points in this space for each stage in an image processing pipeline, and an optimizing compiler for the Halide image processing language that synthesizes high performance implementations from a Halide *algorithm* and a *schedule*. Combining this compiler with stochastic search over the space of schedules enables terse, composable programs to achieve state-of-the-art performance on a wide range of real image processing pipelines, and across different hardware architectures, including multicores with SIMD, and heterogeneous CPU+GPU execution. From simple Halide programs written in a few hours, we demonstrate performance up to 5× faster than hand-tuned C, intrinsics, and CUDA implementations optimized by experts over weeks or months, for image processing applications beyond the reach of past automatic compilers.

Categories and Subject Descriptors D.3.4 [*Programming Languages*]: Processors – compilers, optimization, code generation

Keywords domain specific language; compiler; image processing; locality; parallelism; redundant computation; optimization; GPU; vectorization

1. Introduction

Image processing pipelines are everywhere, and are essential to capturing, analyzing, mining, and rendering the rivers of visual information gathered by our countless cameras and imaging-based sensors. Applications from raw processing, to object detection and recognition, to Microsoft's Kinect, to Instagram and Photoshop, to medical imaging and neural scanning all demand extremely high performance to cope with the rapidly rising resolution and frame rate of image sensors and the increasing complexity of algorithms. At the same time, the shrinking cameras and mobile devices on which they run require extremely high efficiency to last more than a few minutes on battery power. While power-hungry radios and video CODECs can implement slow-changing standards in custom hardware, image processing pipelines are rapidly evolving and diverse, requiring high performance software implementations.

Image processing pipelines combine the challenges of stencil computation and stream programs. They are composed of large graphs of many different operations, most of which are stencil computations. These pipelines are simultaneously wide and deep: each stage exhibits data parallelism across the many pixels which it must process, and whole pipelines consist of long sequences of different operations, which individually have low arithmetic intensity (the ratio of computation performed to data read from prior stages and written to later stages). For example, an implementation of one recent algorithm, local Laplacian filters [3, 22], is a graph of 99 different stages (Fig. 1), including many different stencils and a large data-dependent resampling.

As a result of this structure, the performance difference between a naive implementation of a given pipeline and a highly optimized one is frequently an order of magnitude or more. With current tools, often the only way to approach peak performance is by hand-writing parallel, vectorized, tiled, and globally fused code in low-level C, CUDA, intrinsics, and assembly. Simple pipelines become hundreds of lines of intricately interleaved code; complex pipelines, like Adobe's Camera Raw engine, become hundreds of thousands. Tuning them requires immense effort by expert programmers, and the end result is not portable to different architectures, nor composable with other algorithms, without sacrificing much of this painstakingly earned performance. Libraries of optimized subroutines do not solve the problem, either, since many critical optimizations involve fusion for producer-consumer locality across stages.

We address this challenge by raising the level of abstraction, and decoupling the algorithm definition from its execution strategy, to improve portability and composability, while automating the search for optimized mappings of the resulting pipelines to parallel machines and complex memory hierarchies. Effective abstraction and automatic optimization enable radically simpler programs to achieve higher performance than hand-tuned expert implementations, while running across a wide range of architectures.

1.1 Image Processing Pipelines

Stencils have been well studied in scientific applications in the form of iterated stencil computations, where one or a few small stencils are applied to the same grid over many iterations [10, 16, 19]. In contrast, we are interested in other applications, in image processing

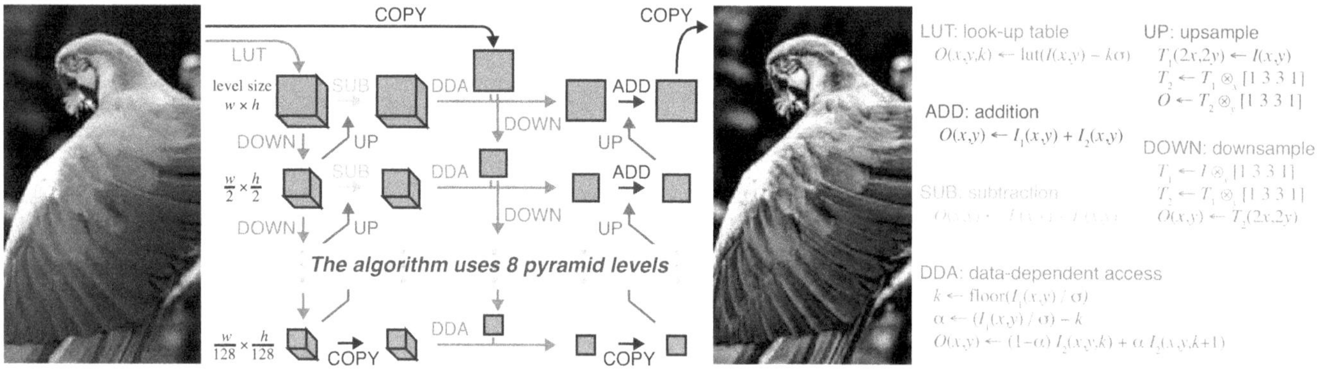

Figure 1. Imaging pipelines employ large numbers of interconnected, heterogeneous stages. Here we show the structure of the local Laplacian filter [3, 22], which is used for a variety of tasks in photographic post-production. Each box represents intermediate data, and each arrow represents one or more functions that define that data. The pipeline includes horizontal and vertical stencils, resampling, data-dependent gathers, and simple pointwise functions.

and computer graphics, where stencils are common, but often in a very different form: stencil pipelines. Stencil pipelines are graphs of different stencil computations. Iteration of the same stencil occurs, but it is the exception, not the rule; most stages apply their stencil only once before passing data to the next stage, which performs different data parallel computation over a different stencil.

Graph-structured programs have been studied in the context of streaming languages [4, 11, 29]. Static communication analysis allows stream compilers to simultaneously optimize for data parallelism and producer-consumer locality by interleaving computation and communication between kernels. However, most stream compilation research has focussed on 1D streams, where sliding window communication allows 1D stencil patterns. Image processing pipelines can be thought of as programs on 2D and 3D streams and stencils. The model of computation required by image processing is also more general than stencils, alone. While most stages are point or stencil operations over the results of prior stages, some stages gather from arbitrary data-dependent addresses, while others scatter to arbitrary addresses to compute operations like histograms.

Pipelines of simple map operations can be optimized by traditional loop fusion: merging multiple successive operations on each point into a single compound operation improves arithmetic intensity by maximizing producer-consumer locality, keeping intermediate data values in fast local memory (caches or registers) as it flows through the pipeline. But traditional loop fusion does not apply to stencil operations, where neighboring points in a consumer stage depend on overlapping regions of a producer stage. Instead, stencils require a complex tradeoff between producer-consumer locality, synchronization, and redundant computation. Because this tradeoff is made by interleaving the order of allocation, execution, and communication of each stage, we call it the pipeline's *schedule*. These tradeoffs exist in scheduling individual iterated stencil computations in scientific applications, and the complexity of the choice space is reflected by the many different tiling and scheduling strategies introduced in past work [10, 16, 19]. In image processing pipelines, this tradeoff must be made for each producer-consumer relationship between stages in the graph—often dozens or hundreds—and the ideal schedule depends on the global interaction among every stage, often requiring the composition of many different strategies.

1.2 Contributions

Halide is an open-source domain-specific language for the complex image processing pipelines found in modern computational photography and vision applications [26]. In this paper, we present the optimizing compiler for this language. We introduce:

- a systematic model of the tradeoffs between locality, parallelism, and redundant recomputation in stencil pipelines;
- a scheduling representation that spans this space of choices;
- a DSL compiler based on this representation that combines Halide programs and schedule descriptions to synthesize points anywhere in this space, using a design where the choices for *how* to execute a program are separated not just from the definition of *what* to compute, but are pulled all the way outside the black box of the compiler;
- a loop synthesizer for data parallel pipelines based on simple interval analysis, which is simpler and less expressive than polyhedral model, but more general in the class of expressions it can analyze;
- a code generator that produces high quality vector code for image processing pipelines, using machinery much simpler than the polyhedral model;
- and an autotuner that can infer high performance schedules—up to 5× faster than hand-optimized programs written by experts—for complex image processing pipelines using stochastic search.

Our scheduling representation composably models a range of tradeoffs between locality, parallelism, and avoiding redundant work. It can naturally express most prior stencil optimizations, as well as hierarchical combinations of them. Unlike prior stencil code generation systems, it does not describe just a single stencil scheduling strategy, but separately treats every producer-consumer edge in a graph of stencil and other image processing computations.

Our split representation, which separates schedules from the underlying algorithm, combined with the inside-out design of our compiler, allows our compiler to automatically search for the best schedule. The space of possible schedules is enormous, with hundreds of inter-dependent dimensions. It is too high dimensional for the polyhedral optimization or exhaustive parameter search employed by existing stencil compilers and autotuners. However, we show that it is possible to discover high quality schedules using stochastic search.

Given a schedule, our compiler automatically synthesizes high quality parallel vector code for x86 and ARM CPUs with SSE/AVX and NEON, and graphs of CUDA kernels interwoven with host management code for hybrid GPU execution. It automatically infers all internal allocations and a complete loop nest using simple but general interval analysis [18]. Directly mapping data parallel dimensions to SIMD execution, including careful treatment of strided access patterns, enables high quality vector code generation, without requiring any general-purpose loop auto-vectorization.

The end result is a system which enables terse, composable programs to achieve state-of-the-art performance on a wide range of real image processing pipelines, and across different hardware architectures, including multicores with SIMD, and heterogeneous CPU+GPU execution. From simple Halide programs written in a few hours, we demonstrate performance up to 5× faster than hand-tuned C, intrinsics, and CUDA implementations written by experts over weeks or months, for image processing applications beyond the reach of past automatic compilers.

2. The Halide DSL

We use the Halide DSL to describe image processing pipelines in a simple functional style [26]. A simple C++ implementation of local Laplacian filters (Fig. 1) is described by dozens of loop nests and hundreds of lines of code. This is not practical to globally optimize with traditional loop optimization systems. The Halide version distills this into 62 lines describing just the essential dataflow and computation in the 99 stage pipeline, and all choices for how the program should be synthesized are described separately (Sec. 3).

In Halide, values that would be mutable arrays in an imperative language are instead functions from coordinates to values. It represents images as pure functions defined over an infinite integer domain, where the value of a function at a point represents the color of the corresponding pixel. Pipelines are specified as chains of functions. Functions may either be simple expressions in their arguments, or reductions over a bounded domain. The expressions that define functions are side-effect free, and are much like those in any simple functional language, including:

- Arithmetic and logical operations;
- Loads from external images;
- If-then-else expressions;
- References to named values (which may be function arguments, or expressions defined by a functional *let* construct);
- Calls to other functions, including external C ABI functions.

For example, a separable 3×3 unnormalized box filter is expressed as a chain of two functions in x, y:

```
UniformImage in(UInt(8), 2)
Var x, y
Func blurx(x,y) =  in(x-1,y) +    in(x,y) +    in(x+1,y)
Func out(x,y) = blurx(x,y-1) + blurx(x,y) + blurx(x,y+1)
```

This representation is simpler than most functional languages. It does not include higher-order functions, dynamic recursion, or additional data structures like lists. Functions simply map from integer coordinates to a scalar result. Constrained versions of more advanced features such as higher-order functions are added as syntactic sugar, but do not change the underlying representation.

This representation is sufficient to describe a wide range of image processing algorithms, and these constraints enable flexible analysis and transformation of algorithms during compilation. Critically, this representation is naturally data parallel within the domain of each function. Also, since functions are defined over an infinite domain, boundary conditions can be handled safely and efficiently by computing arbitrary *guard bands* of extra values as needed. Guard bands are a common pattern in image processing code, both for performance concerns like alignment, and for safety. Wherever specific boundary conditions matter to the meaning of an algorithm, the function may define its own.

Reduction functions. In order to express operations like histograms and general convolutions, Halide also needs a way to express iterative or recursive computations, like summation, histogram, and scan. Reductions are defined in two parts:

- An *initial value function*, which specifies a value at each point in the *output domain*.
- A recursive *reduction function*, which redefines the value at points given by an *output coordinate expression* in terms of prior values of the function.

Unlike a pure function, the meaning of a reduction depends on the order in which the reduction function is applied. The programmer specifies the order by defining a *reduction domain*, bounded by minimum and maximum expressions for each dimension. The value at each point in the output domain is defined by the final value of the reduction function at that point, after recursing in lexicographic order across the reduction domain.

This pattern can describe a range of algorithms outside the scope of traditional stencil computation, but essential to image processig pipelines, in a way that bounds side effects. For example, histogram equalization combines multiple reductions and a data-dependent gather. A scattering reduction computes a histogram, a recursive scan integrates it into a CDF, and a point-wise operation remaps the input using the CDF:

```
UniformImage in(UInt(8), 2)
RDom r(0..in.width(), 0..in.height()), ri(0..255)
Var x, y, i
Func histogram(i) = 0; histogram(in(r.x, r.y))++
Func cdf(i) = 0; cdf(ri) = cdf(ri-1) + histogram(ri)
Func out(x, y) = cdf(in(x, y))
```

The iteration bounds for the reduction and scan are expressed by the programmer using explicit *reduction domains* (**RDoms**).

3. Scheduling Image Processing Pipelines

Halide's representation of image processing algorithms avoids imposing constraints on the order of execution and placement of data. Values need to be computed before they can be used, to respect the fundamental dependencies in the algorithm, but many choices remain unspecified:

- When and where should the value at each coordinate in each function be computed?
- Where should they be stored?
- How long are values cached and communicated across multiple consumers, and when are they independently recomputed by each?

These choices can not change the meaning or results of the algorithm, but they *are* essential to the performance of the resulting implementation. We call a specific set of choices for when and where values are computed the pipeline's *schedule*.

In the presence of stencil access patterns, these choices are bound by a fundamental tension between producer-consumer locality, parallelism, and redundant recomputation of shared values. To understand this tradeoff space, it is useful to look at an example.

3.1 Motivation: Scheduling a Two-Stage Pipeline

Consider the simple two-stage blur algorithm, which computes a 3×3 box filter as two 3×1 passes. The first stage, **blurx**, computes a horizontal blur of the input by averaging over a 3×1 window:

```
blurx(x,y) = in(x-1,y) + in(x,y) + in(x+1,y)
```

The second stage, **out**, computes the final isotropic blur by averaging a 1×3 window of the output from the first stage:

```
out(x,y) = blurx(x,y-1) + blurx(x,y) + blurx(x,y+1)
```

A natural way to think about scheduling the pipeline is from the perspective of the output stage: how should it compute its input? There are three obvious choices for this pipeline.

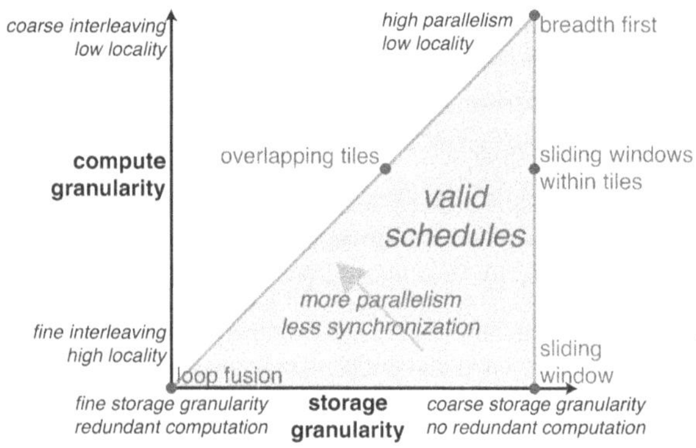

Figure 2. A natural way to visualize the space of scheduling choices is by granularity of storage (x-axis), and granularity of computation (y-axis). Breadth-first execution does coarse-grain computation into coarse-grain storage. Total fusion performs fine-grain computation into fine-grain storage (small temporary buffers). Sliding window strategies allocate enough space for the entire intermediate stage, but compute it in in fine-grain chunks as late as possible. These extremes each have their pitfalls. Breadth-first execution has poor locality, total fusion often does redundant work, and using sliding windows to avoid redundant recomputation constrains parallelism by introducing dependencies across loop iterations. The best strategies tend to be mixed, and lie somewhere in the middle of the space.

First, it could compute and store every required point in **blurx** before evaluating any points in **out**. Applied to a 6 megapixel ($3k \times 2k$) image, this is equivalent to the loop nest:

```
alloc blurx[2048][3072]
for each y in 0..2048:
  for each x in 0..3072:
    blurx[y][x] = in[y][x-1] + in[y][x] + in[y][x+1]
alloc out[2046][3072]
for each y in 1..2047:
  for each x in 0..3072:
    out[y][x]=blurx[y-1][x] + blurx[y][x] + blurx[y+1][x]
```

This is the most common strategy in hand-written pipelines, and what results from composing library routines together: each stage executes breadth-first across its input before passing its entire output to the next stage. There is abundant parallelism, since all the required points in each stage can be computed and stored independently, but there is little producer-consumer locality, since all the values of **blurx** must be computed and stored before the first one is used by **out**.

At the other extreme, the **out** stage could compute each point in **blurx** immediately before the point which uses it. This opens up a further choice: should points in **blurx** which are used by multiple points in **out** be stored and reused, or recomputed independently by each consumer?

Interleaving the two stages, without storing the intermediate results across uses, is equivalent to the loop nest:

```
alloc out[2046][3072]
for each y in 1..2047:
  for each x in 0..3072:
    alloc blurx[-1..1]
    for each i in -1..1:
      blurx[i]= in[y-1+i][x-1]+in[y-1+i][x]+in[y-1+i][x+1]
    out[y][x] = blurx[0] + blurx[1] + blurx[2]
```

Each pixel can be computed independently, providing the same abundant data parallelism from the breadth-first strategy. The distance from producer to consumer is small, maximizing locality. But because shared values in **blurx** are not reused across iterations, this strategy performs redundant work. This can be seen as the result of applying classical loop fusion through a stencil dependence pattern: the body of the first loop is moved into the second loop, but its work is amplified by the size of the stencil.

Strategy	Span (iterations)	Max. reuse dist. (ops)	Work ampl.
Breadth-first	$\geq 3072 \times 2046$	$3072 \times 2048 \times 3$	$1.0\times$
Full fusion	$\geq 3072 \times 2046$	3×3	$2.0\times$
Sliding window	3072	$3072 \times (3+3)$	$1.0\times$
Tiled	$\geq 3072 \times 2046$	$34 \times 32 \times 3$	$1.0625\times$
Sliding in tiles	$\geq 3072 \times 2048/8$	$3072 \times (3+3)$	$1.25\times$

Figure 3. Different points in the choice space in Figure 2 each make different trade-offs between locality, redundant recomputation, and parallelism. Here we quantify these effects for our two-stage blur pipeline. The *span* measures the degree of parallelism available, by counting how many threads or simd lanes could be kept busy doing useful work. The *Max. reuse distance* measures locality, by counting the maximum number of operations that can occur between computing a value and reading it back. *Work amplification* measures redundant work, by comparing the number of arithmetic operations done to the breadth-first case. Each of the first three strategies represent an extreme point of the choice space, and is weak in one regard. The fastest schedules are mixed strategies, such as the tiled ones in the last two rows.

The two stages can also be interleaved while storing the values of **blurx** across uses:

```
alloc out[2046][3072]
alloc blurx[3][3072]
for each y in -1..2047:
  for each x in 0..3072:
    blurx[(y+1)%3][x]=in[y+1][x-1]+in[y+1][x]+in[y+1][x+1]
    if y < 1: continue
    out[y][x] = blurx[(y-1)%3][x]
              + blurx[ y % 3 ][x]
              + blurx[(y+1)%3][x]
```

This interleaves the computation over a sliding window, with **out** trailing **blurx** by the stencil radius (one scanline). It wastes no work, computing each point in **blurx** exactly once, and the maximum distance between a value being produced in **blurx** and consumed in **out** is proportional to the stencil height (three scanlines), not the entire image. But to achieve this, it has introduced a dependence between the loop iterations: a given iteration of **out** depends on the last three outer loop iterations of **blurx**. This only works if these loops are evaluated sequentially. Interleaving the stages while producing each value only once requires tightly synchronizing the order of computation, sacrificing parallelism.

Each of these strategies has a major pitfall: lost locality, redundant work, or limited parallelism (Fig. 3). In practice, the right choice for a given pipeline is almost always somewhere in between these extremes. For our two-stage example, a better balance can be struck by interleaving the computation of **blurx** and **out** at the level of *tiles*:

```
alloc out[2046][3072]
for each ty in 0..2048/32:
  for each tx in 0..3072/32:
    alloc blurx[-1..33][32]
    for y in -1..33:
      for x in 0..32:
        blurx[y][x] = in[ty*32+y][tx*32+x-1]
                    + in[ty*32+y][tx*32+x]
                    + in[ty*32+y][tx*32+x+1]
    for y in 0..32:
      for x in 0..32:
        out[ty*32+y][tx*32+x] = blurx[y-1][x]
                              + blurx[y  ][x]
                              + blurx[y+1][x]
```

This trades off a small amount of redundant computation on tile boundaries for much greater producer-consumer locality, while still

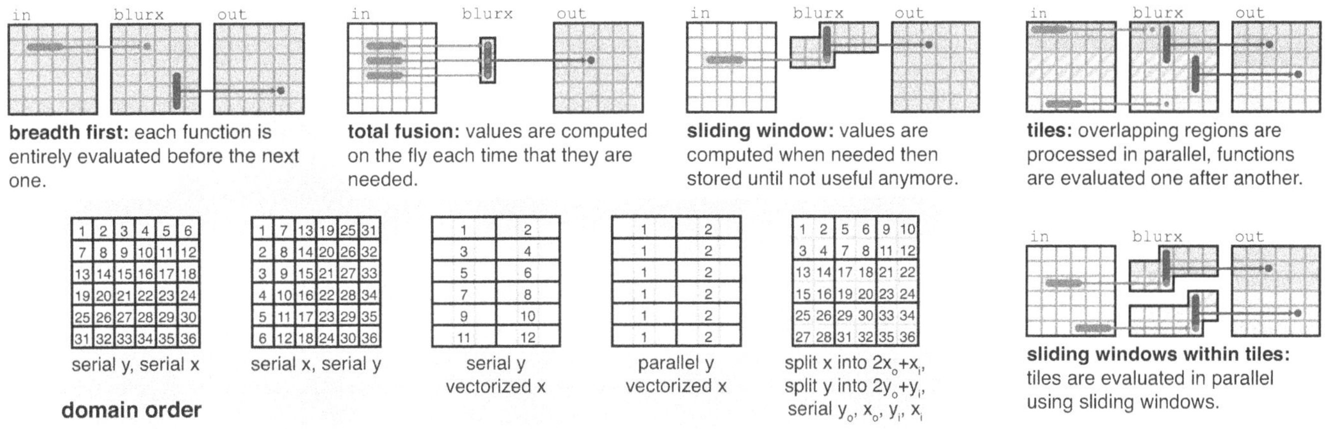

Figure 4. Even simple pipelines exhibit a rich space of scheduling choices, each expressing its own trade-off between parallelism, locality, and redundant recompute. The choice made for each stage is two-fold. The simpler choice is the *domain order*, which can express thread parallelism, vectorization, and traversal order (row-major vs column-major). Dimensions can be split into inner and outer components, which recursively expands the choice space, and can express tiling strategies. The more complex question each stage must answer is when its inputs should be computed. Choices include computing all dependencies ahead of time (breadth-first), computing values as late as possible and then discarding them (total fusion), and computing values as late as possible, but reusing previous computations (sliding window). The two categories of choice interact. For example, the fastest schedules often split the domain into tiles processed in parallel, and then compute either breadth-first or with sliding windows within each tile.

leaving parallelism unconstrained both within and across tiles. (In the iterated stencil computation literature, the redundant regions are often called "ghost zones," and this strategy is sometimes called "overlapped tiling" [17, 31].) On a modern x86, this strategy is $10\times$ faster than the breadth-first strategy using the same amount of multithreaded and vector parallelism. This is because the lack of producer-consumer locality leaves the breadth-first version limited by bandwidth. This difference grows as the pipeline gets longer, increasing the ratio of intermediate data to inputs and outputs, and it will only grow further as the computational resources scale exponentially faster than external memory bandwidth under Moore's Law.

The very fastest strategy we found on this architecture interleaves the computation of the two stages using a sliding window over scanlines, while splitting the image into strips of independent scanlines which are treated separately:

```
alloc out[2046][3072]
for each ty in 0..2048/8:
  alloc blurx[-1..1][3072]
  for y in -2..8:
    for x in 0..3072:
        blurx[(y+1)%3][x] = in[ty*8+y+1][tx*32+x-1]
                          + in[ty*8+y+1][tx*32+x]
                          + in[ty*8+y+1][tx*32+x+1]
    if y < 0: continue
    for x in 0..3072:
      out[ty*8+y][x] = blurx[(y-1)%3][x]
                     + blurx[ y % 3][x]
                     + blurx[(y+1)%3][x]
```

Relative to the original sliding window strategy, this sacrifices two scanlines of redundant work on the overlapping tops and bottoms of independently-processed strips of **blurx** to instead reclaim fine-grained parallelism within each scanline and coarse-grained parallelism across scanline strips. The end result is 10% faster still than the tiled strategy on one benchmark machine, but 10% slower on another. The best choice between these and many other strategies varies across different target architectures. There are also global consequences to the decision made for each stage in a larger pipeline, so the ideal choice depends on the composition of stages, not just each individual stages in isolation. Real image processing pipelines often have tens to hundreds of stages, making the choice space enormous.

3.2 A Model for the Scheduling Choice Space

We introduce a model for the space of important choices in scheduling stencil pipelines, based on each stage choosing at what granularity to *compute* each of its inputs, at what granularity to *store* each for reuse, and within those grains, in what *order* its domain should be traversed (Fig. 4).

The Domain Order Our model first defines the order in which the required region of each function's domain should be traversed, which we call the *domain order*, using a traditional set of loop transformation concepts:

- Each dimension can be traversed *sequentially* or in *parallel*.
- Constant-size dimensions can be *unrolled* or *vectorized*.
- Dimensions can be *reordered* (e.g. from column- to row-major).
- Finally, dimensions can be *split* by a factor, creating two new dimensions: an outer dimension, over the old range divided by the factor, and an inner dimension, which iterates within the factor. After splitting, references to the original index become $outer \times factor + inner$.

Splitting recursively opens up further choices, and enables many common patterns like tiling when combined with other transformations. Vectorization and unrolling are modeled by first splitting a dimension by the vector width or unrolling factor, and then scheduling the new inner dimension as *vectorized* or *unrolled*. Because Halide's model of functions is data parallel by construction, dimensions can be interleaved in any order, and any dimension may be scheduled serial, parallel, or vectorized.

For reduction functions, the dimensions of the reduction domain may only be reordered or parallelized if the reduction update is associative. Free variable dimensions may be scheduled in any order, just as with pure functions.

Our model considers only axis-aligned bounding regions, not general polytopes—a practical simplification for image processing and many other applications. But this also allows the regions to be defined and analyzed using simple interval analysis. Since our model of scheduling relies on later compiler inference to determine the bounds of evaluation and storage for each function and loop, it is essential that bounds analysis be capable of analyzing *every* expression and construct in the Halide language. Interval analysis is simpler than modern tools like polyhedral analysis, but it can effectively analyze through a wider range of expressions, which is essential for this design.

The Call Schedule In addition to the order of evaluation *within* the domain of each function, the schedule also specifies the granularity of interleaving the computation of a function with the storage and computation of each function on which it depends. We call these choices the *call schedule*. We specify a unique call schedule for each function in the entire call graph of a Halide pipeline. Each function's call schedule is defined as the points in the loop nest of its callers where it is stored and computed (Fig. 4, top). For example, the three extremes from the previous section can be viewed along these axes:

- The *breadth-first* schedule both *stores* and *computes* **blurx** at the coarsest granularity (which we call the *root* level—outside any other loops).
- The *fused* schedule both *stores* and *computes* **blurx** at the finest granularity, inside the innermost (**x**) loop of **out**. At this granularity, values are produced and consumed in the same iteration, but must be reallocated and recomputed on each iteration, independently.
- The *sliding window* schedule *stores* at the *root* granularity, while *computing* at the finest granularity. With this interleaving, values of **blurx** are computed in the same iteration as their first use, but persist across iterations. To exploit this by reusing shared values in subsequent iterations, the loops between the *storage* and *computation* levels must be strictly ordered, so that a single unique first iteration exists for each point, which can compute it for later consumers.

Together, the call schedule and domain order define an algebra for scheduling stencil pipelines on rectangular grids. Composing these choices can define an infinite range of schedules, including the vast majority of common patterns exploited by practitioners in hand-optimized image processing pipelines.

The loop transformations defined by the domain order interact with the inter-stage interleaving granularity chosen by the call schedule because the call schedule is defined by specifying the loop level at which to store or compute. A function call site may be stored or computed at any loop from the innermost dimensions of the directly calling function, to the surrounding dimensions at which it is itself scheduled to be computed, and so on through its chain of consumers. Splitting dimensions allows the call schedule to be specified at finer granularity than the intrinsic dimensionality of the calling functions, for example interleaving by blocks of scanlines instead of individual scanlines, or tiles of pixels instead of individual pixels. Since every value computed needs a logical location into which its result can be stored, *the storage granularity must be equal to, or coarser than, the computation granularity*.

Schedule Examples Revisiting the optimized examples from Sec. 3.1, the tiled schedule can be modeled as follows:

- The domain order of **out** is $split(\mathtt{y}, 32) \rightarrow \mathtt{ty}, \mathtt{y}$; $split(\mathtt{x}, 32) \rightarrow \mathtt{tx}, \mathtt{x}$; $order(\mathtt{ty}, \mathtt{tx}, \mathtt{y}, \mathtt{x})$. (This is similar to the tiled domain order shown rightmost in Fig. 4.) All dimensions may be *parallel*. **x** is *vectorized* for performance.
- The call schedule of **blurx** is set to both *store* and *compute* for each iteration of **tx** in **out**.
- The domain of **blurx** under **tx** is scheduled $order(\mathtt{y}, \mathtt{x})$, and **x** is *vectorized* for performance.

The parallel tiled sliding window schedule is modeled by making the call schedule of **blurx** *store* at **ty** in **out**, but *compute* at finer granularity, at **out**'s **y** dimension. Then:

- The domain order of **out** is $split(\mathtt{y}, 8) \rightarrow \mathtt{ty}, \mathtt{y}$; $order(\mathtt{ty}, \mathtt{y}, \mathtt{x})$. **ty** may be *parallel*, **x** is *vectorized* for performance. **y** must be *sequential*, to enable reuse.
- The domain of **blurx** under **y** only has dimension **x**, which is *vectorized* for performance.

4. Compiling Scheduled Pipelines

Our compiler combines the functions describing a Halide pipeline, with a fully-specified schedule for each function, to synthesize the machine code for a single procedure which implements the entire pipeline. The generated pipeline is exposed as a C ABI callable function which takes buffer pointers for input and output data, as well as scalar parameters. The implementation is multithreaded and vectorized according to the schedule, internally manages the allocation of all intermediate storage, and optionally includes synthesized GPU kernels which it also manages automatically.

The compiler makes no heuristic decisions about which loop transformations to apply or what will generate fast code. For all such questions we defer to the schedule. At the same time, the generated code is safe by construction. The bounds of all loops and allocations are inferred. Bounds inference generates loop bounds that ultimately depend only on the size of the output image. Bounded loops are our only means of control flow, so we can guarantee termination. All allocations are large enough to cover the regions used by the program.

Given the functions defining a Halide pipeline and a fully specified schedule as input (Fig. 5, left), our compiler proceeds through the major steps below.

4.1 Lowering and Loop Synthesis

The first step of our compiler is a lowering process that synthesizes a single, complete set of loop nests and allocations, given a Halide pipeline and a fully-specified schedule (Fig. 5, middle).

Lowering begins from the function defining the output (in this case, **out**). Given the function's domain order from the schedule, it generates a loop nest covering the required region of the output, whose body evaluates the function at a single point in that domain (Fig. 5, middle-top). The order of loops is given by the schedule, and includes additional loops for split dimensions. Loops are defined by their minimum value and their extent, and all loops implicitly stride by 1. This process rounds up the total traversed domain of dimensions which have been split to the nearest multiple of the split factor, since all loops have a single base and extent expression.

At this stage, loop bounds are left as simple symbolic expressions of the *required region* of the output function, which is resolved later. The bounds cannot have inter-dependent dimensions between the loops for a single function, so they represent a dense iteration over an axis-aligned bounding box. Each loop is labeled as being serial, parallel, unrolled, or vectorized, according to the schedule.

Lowering then proceeds recursively up the pipeline, from callers to callees (here, from **out** to **blurx**). Callees (apart from those scheduled *inline*) are scheduled to be computed at the granularity of some dimension of some caller function. This corresponds to an existing loop in the code generated so far. This site is located, and code evaluating the callee is injected at the beginning of that loop body. This code takes the form of a loop nest constructed using the domain order of the callee. The allocation for the callee is similarly injected at some containing loop level specified by the schedule. In Fig. 5, middle, **blurx** is allocated at the level of tiles ($\mathtt{out.x}_0$), while it is computed as required for each scanline within the tile

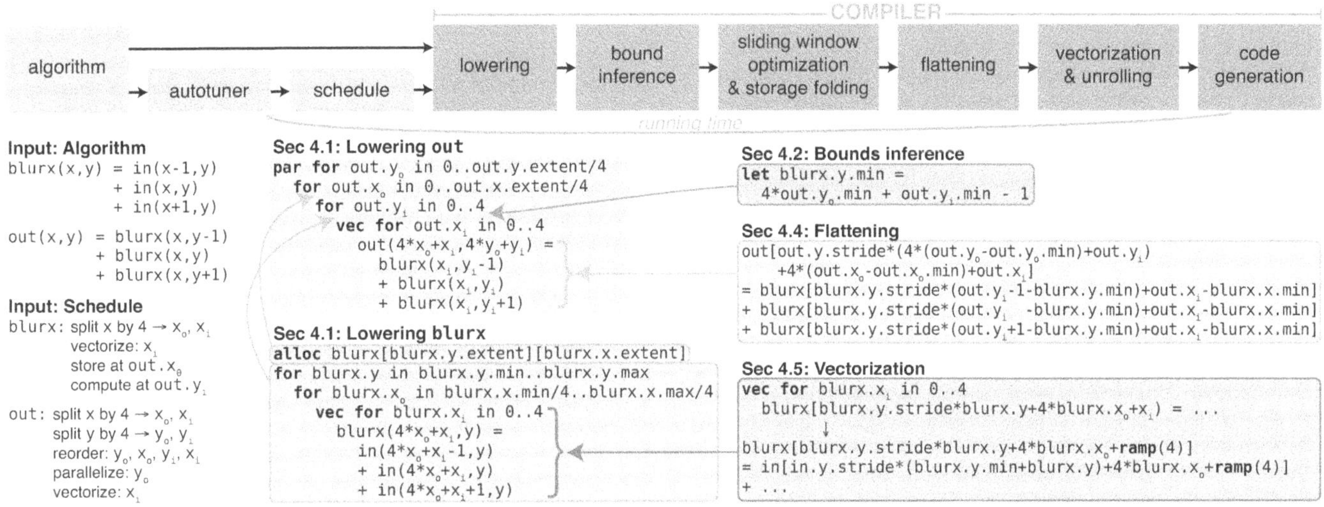

Figure 5. Our compiler is driven by an autotuner, which stochastically searches the space of valid schedules to find a high performance implementation of the given Halide program. The core of the compiler lowers a functional representation of an imaging pipeline to imperative code using a *schedule*. It does this by first constructing a loop nest producing the final stage of the pipeline (in this case **out**), and then recursively injecting the storage and computation of earlier stages of the pipeline at the loop levels specified by the schedule. The locations and sizes of regions computed are symbolic at this point. They are resolved by the subsequent bound inference pass, which injects interval arithmetic computations in a preamble at each loop level that set the region produced of each stage to be at least as large as the region consumed by subsequent stages. Next, sliding window optimization and storage folding remove redundant computation and excess storage where the storage granularity is above the compute granularity. A simple flattening transform converts multidimensional coordinates in the infinite domain of each function into simple one-dimensional indices relative to the base of the corresponding buffer. Vectorization and unrolling passes replace loops of constant with k scheduled as *vectorized* or *unrolled* with the corresponding k-wide vector code or k copies of the loop body. Finally, backend code generation emits machine code for the scheduled pipeline via LLVM.

(**out.y**$_i$). The allocation and computation for **blurx** are inserted at the corresponding points in the loop nest.

Reductions are lowered to a pair of loop nests: the first initializes the domain, and the second applies the reduction rule. Both allocation and loop extents are tracked as symbols of the required region of the function used by its callers. Once lowering has recursed to the end of the pipeline, all functions have been synthesized into a single set of loops.

4.2 Bounds Inference

At this stage, for allocation sizes and loop bounds the pipeline relies on symbolic bounds variables for each dimension of each function. The next stage of lowering generates and injects appropriate definitions for these variables. Like function lowering, bounds inference proceeds recursively back from the output. For each function, it symbolically evaluates the bounds of each dimension based on the bounds required of its caller and the symbolic indices at which the caller invokes it. At each step, the required bounds of each dimension are computed by interval analysis of the expressions in the caller which index that dimension, given the previously computed bounds of all downstream functions.

After bounds inference has recursed to the top of the pipeline, it walks back down to the output, injecting definitions for the bounds variables used as stand-ins during lowering. They are defined by expressions which compute concrete bounds as a preamble at each loop level (e.g., in Fig. 5, right, the minimum bound of **blurx.y** is computed from interval analysis of the index expressions at which it is accessed combined with the bounds of the calling function, **out**). In practice, hoisting dynamic bounds evaluation expressions to the outermost loop level possible makes the runtime overhead of more complex bounds expressions negligible.

Interval analysis is an unusual choice in a modern loop synthesis and code generation system. The resulting min/max bounds for each dimension are less expressive than the polyhedral model. They can only describe iteration over axis-aligned boxes, rather than arbitrary polytopes. However, it is trivial to synthesize efficient loops for any set of intervals, in contrast to the problem of scanning general polyhedra. For many domains, including image processing, this is an acceptable simplification: most functions *are* applied over rectilinear regions.

Most critically, interval analysis can analyze a more general class of expressions: it is straightforward to compute intervals through nearly any computation, from basic arithmetic, to conditional expressions, to transcendentals, and even loads from memory. As a result, this analysis can be used pervasively to infer the complete bounds of every loop and allocation in any pipeline represented in Halide. It also generalizes through constructs like symbolic tile sizes, which are beyond the scope of polyhedral analysis. For cases where interval analysis is over-conservative (e.g., when computing the bounds of a floating point number loaded from memory which the programmer knows will be between 0 and 1), Halide includes a simple *clamp* operator, which simultaneously declares and enforces a bound on an expression.

4.3 Sliding Window Optimization and Storage Folding

After bounds inference, the compiler traverses the loop nests seeking opportunities for sliding window optimizations. If a realization of a function is stored at higher loop level than its computation, with an intervening serial loop, then iterations of that loop can reuse values generated by previous iterations. Using the same interval analysis machinery as in bounds inference, we shrink the interval to be computed at each iteration by excluding the region computed by all previous iterations. It is this transformation that lets us trade off parallelism (because the intervening loop must be serial) for reuse (because we avoid recomputing values already computed by previous iterations.)

For example, in Fig. 5, `blurx` is stored for reuse within each tile of `out`, but computed as needed, for each scanline within the tile. Because scanlines ($\texttt{out.y}_i$) are traversed sequentially, intermediate values of `blurx` are computed immediately before the first scanline of `out` which needs them, but may be reused my later scanlines within the tile. For each iteration of $\texttt{out.y}_i$, the range of `blurx.y` is computed to exclude the interval covered by all prior iterations computed within the tile.

Storage folding is a second similar optimization employed at this stage of lowering. If a region is allocated outside of a serial loop but only used within it, and the subregion used by each loop iteration marches monotonically across the region allocated, we can "fold" the storage, by rewriting indices used when accessing the region by reducing them modulo the maximum extent of the region used in any given iteration. For example, in Fig. 5, each iteration of $\texttt{out.y}_i$ only needs access to the last 3 scanlines of `blurx`, so the storage of `blurx` can be reduced to just 3 scanlines, and the value `blurx(x,y+3)` will reuse the same memory address as `blurx(x,y)`, `blurx(x,y-3)`, and so on. This reduces peak memory use and working set size.

4.4 Flattening

Next, the compiler flattens multi-dimensional loads, stores, and allocations into their single-dimensional equivalent. This happens in the conventional way: a stride and a minimum offset are computed for each dimension, and the buffer index corresponding to a multidimensional site is the dot product of the site coordinates and the strides, minus the minimum. (Cf. Fig. 5, right.) By convention, we always set the stride of the innermost dimension to 1, to ensure we can perform dense vector loads and stores in that dimension. For images, this lays them out in memory in scanline order. While our model of scheduling allows extreme flexibility in the order of execution, we do not support more unusual layouts memory, such as tiled or sparse storage. (We have found that modern caching memory hierarchies largely obviate the need for tiled storage layouts, in practice.)

4.5 Vectorization and Unrolling

After flattening, vectorization and unrolling passes replace loops of constant size scheduled as vectorized or unrolled with transformed versions of their loop bodies. Unrolling replaces a loop of size n with n sequential statements performing each loop iteration in turn. That is, it completely unrolls the loop. Unrolling by lesser amounts is expressed by first splitting a dimension into two, and then unrolling the inner dimension.

Vectorization completely replaces a loop of size n with a single statement. For example, in Fig. 5 (lower right), the vector loop over $\texttt{blurx.x}_i$ is replaced by a single 4-wide vector expression. Any occurrences of the loop index ($\texttt{blurx.x}_i$) are replaced with a special value $\texttt{ramp}(n)$ representing the vector $[0\ 1 \ldots n-1]$. A type coercion pass is then run over this to promote any scalars combined with this special value to n-wide broadcasts of the scalar expression. All of our IR nodes are meaningful for vector types: loads become gathers, stores become scatters, arithmetic becomes vector arithmetic, ternary expressions become vector selects, and so on. Later, during code generation, loads and stores of a linear expression of $k*\texttt{ramp}(n)+o$ will become dense vector loads and stores if the coefficient $k = 1$, or strided loads and stores with stride k otherwise. In contrast to many languages, Halide has no divergent control flow, so this transformation is always well-defined and straight-forward to apply. In our representation, we never split a vector into a bundle of scalars. It is always a single expression containing `ramp`s and broadcast nodes. We have found that this yields extremely efficient code *without* any sort of generalized loop auto-vectorization.

4.6 Back-end Code Generation

Finally, we perform low-level optimizations and emit machine code for the resulting pipeline. Our primary backends use LLVM for low-level code generation. We first run a standard constant-folding and dead-code elimination pass on our IR, which also performs symbolic simplification of common patterns produced by bounds inference. At this point, the representation is ready to be lowered to LLVM IR. There is mostly a one-to-one mapping between our representation and LLVM's, but two specific patterns warrant mention.

First, parallel for loops are lowered to LLVM code that first builds a closure containing state referred to in the body of a for loop. The loop body is lowered to a separate function that accepts the closure as an argument and performs one iteration of the loop. We finally generate code that enqueues the iterations of the loop onto a task queue, which a thread pool consumes at runtime.

Second, many vector patterns are difficult to express or generate poor code if passed directly to LLVM. We use peephole optimization to reroute these to architecture-specific intrinsics. For example, we perform our own analysis pass to determine alignment of vector loads and stores, and we catch common patterns such as interleaving stores, strided loads, vector averages, clamped arithmetic, fixed-point arithmetic, widening or narrowing arithmetic, etc. By mapping specific expression IR patterns to specific SIMD opcodes on each architecture, we provide a means for the programmer to make use of all relevant SIMD operations on ARM (using NEON) and x86 (using SSE and AVX).

GPU Code Generation The data parallel grids defining a Halide pipeline are a natural fit for GPU programming models. Our compiler uses the same scheduling primitives, along with a few simple conventions, to model GPU execution choices. GPU kernel launches are modeled as dimensions (loops) scheduled to be *parallel* and annotated with the GPU *block* and *thread* dimensions to which they correspond.

The limitations of GPU execution place a few constraints on how these dimensions can be scheduled. In particular, a sequence of block and thread loops must be contiguous, with no other intervening loops between the block and thread levels, since a kernel launch corresponds to a single multidimensional, tiled, parallel loop nest. Sets of kernel loops may not be nested within each other on current GPUs which do not directly implement nested data parallelism. Additionally, the extent of the thread loops must fit within the corresponding limits of the target device. Other than that, all the standard looping constructs may still be scheduled outside or within the block and grid dimensions. This corresponds to loops which internally launch GPU kernels, and loops within each thread of a GPU kernel, respectively.

Given a schedule annotated with GPU block and thread dimensions, our compiler proceeds exactly as before, synthesizing a single set of loop nests for the entire pipeline. No stage before the backend is aware of GPU execution; block and thread dimensions are treated like any other loops. The GPU backend extends the x86 backend, including its full feature set. Outside the loops over block and thread dimensions, the compiler generates the same optimized SSE code as it would in the pure CPU target. At the start of each GPU block loop nest, we carve off the sub-nest much like a parallel for loop in the CPU backend, only it is spawned on the GPU. We first build a closure over all state which flows into the GPU loops. We then generate a GPU kernel from the body of those loops. And finally, we generate the host API calls to launch that kernel at the corresponding point in the host code, passing the closure as an argument. We also generate dynamic code before and after launches to track which buffers need to be copied to or from the device. Every allocated buffer which is used on the GPU has a corresponding device memory allocation, and their contents are lazily copied only when needed.

The end result is not individual GPU kernels, but large graphs of hybrid CPU/GPU execution, described by the same scheduling model which drives the CPU backends. A small change in the schedule can transform a graph of dozens of GPU kernels and vectorized CPU loop nests, tied together by complex memory management and synchronization, into an *entirely different* graph of kernels and loops which produce the same result, expressively modeling an enormous space of possible fusion and other choices in mapping a given pipeline to a heterogeneous machine.

5. Autotuning Pipeline Schedules

We apply stochastic search to automatically find good schedules for Halide pipelines. The automatic optimizer takes a fixed algorithm and attempts to optimize the running time by searching for the most efficient schedule. The schedule search space is enormous—far too large to search exhaustively. For example in the local Laplacian filters pipeline, we estimate a lower bound of 10^{720} schedules. This is derived by labeling functions with three tilings per function and all possible store and compute granularities. The actual dimensionality of the space is likely much higher. The optimal schedule dependends on machine architecture, image dimensions, and code generation in complex ways, and exhibits global dependencies between choices due to loop fusion and caching behavior.

In this section, we describe our autotuner. Because the search problem has many local minima, we use a genetic algorithm to seek out a plausible approximate solution, inspired by the search procedure in PetaBricks [2]. We first describe the schedule search space. We show how domain-specific knowledge can be used to select reasonable starting points. Then we explain the general operations of the genetic algorithm. Finally, we show how further knowledge can be incorporated as search priors for more effective mutation rules.

Schedule Search Space Our full model of scheduling is per call but to simplify autotuning we schedule each function identically across all call sites. The domain transformations include splitting and reordering dimensions, and marking them parallel, vectorized, or unrolled, or mapping a pair of dimensions to a GPU grid launch. Variable and block size arguments are randomized and chosen from small powers of two.

Because schedules have complex global dependencies, not all schedules are valid: for example, a schedule could be computed or stored inside a dimension that does not exist in the caller's loop order. Genetic operations such as mutate and crossover may invalidate correct parent schedules. In general therefore we reject any partially completed schedules that are invalid, and continue sampling until we obtain valid schedules. We also verify the program output against a correct reference schedule, over several input images. This is just a sanity check: all valid schedules should generate correct code. Finally to prevent explosion of generated code due to complex pipelines, we limit the number of domain scheduling operations for each function.

Search Starting Point One valid starting schedule is to label all functions as computed and stored breadth first (at the outermost, *root* granularity). The tuner converges from this starting point, albeit slowly. We can often do better by seeding the initial population with reasonable schedules. For each function we find its rectangular footprint relative to the caller (via bounds inference) and inline functions with footprint one. Remaining functions are stochastically scheduled as either (1) *fully parallelized and tiled* or (2) simply parallelized over y. We define *fully parallelized and tiled* as tiled over x and y, vectorized within the tile's inner x coordinate, and parallelized over the y outer tile dimension. These choices are selected by a weighted coin that has fixed weight from zero to one depending on the individual. This allows us to often discover good starting points for functions that vectorize well, or fall back to naive parallelism when that is not the case. The dimensions x and y are chosen from adjacent dimensions at random, except when there are optional bounds annotations provided by the Halide programmer (such as the number of color channels): dimensions with small bound are not tiled.

Genetic Algorithm Search We use a fixed population size (128 individuals per generation, for all examples in this paper) and construct each new generation with population frequencies of elitism, crossover, mutated individuals, and random individuals. Elitism copies the top individuals from the previous generation. Crossover selects parents by tournament selection, followed by two-point crossover, with crossover points selected at random between functions. Random individuals are generated either by the reasonable schedules described previously, or with equal probability, by scheduling each function independently with random schedule choices. This is directly derived from the PetaBricks autotuner [2].

Schedule Mutation Rules We incorporate further prior knowledge about schedules into our mutation rules. Mutation selects a function at random and modifies its schedule with one of eight operations selected at random. Six are fairly generic: randomize constants, replace a function's schedule with one randomly generated, copy from a randomly selected function's schedule, and for the function's list of domain transformations, either add, remove, or replace with a randomly selected transformation.

Our remaining two mutations incorporate specific knowledge about imaging. These are chosen with higher probability. First, a pointwise mutation of compute or storage granularity is generally ineffective at fusing loops. Thus we have a loop fusion rule which schedules the chosen function as *fully parallelized and tiled*, followed by scheduling callees as vectorized by x, and computed and stored under the tile's inner x dimension. The callee scheduling is repeated recursively until a coin flip fails. Finally, we incorporate prior knowledge by applying a template: we replace a function's schedule with one of three common schedule patterns sampled from a text file. These are: (1) compute and store under x, and vectorize by x, (2) *fully parallelized and tiled*, and (3) parallelized over y and vectorized over x. If generating a CUDA schedule we inject a fourth pattern which simply tiles on the GPU. The x and y dimensions are determined as in the starting point.

6. Results

To evaluate our representation and compiler, we applied them to a range of image processing applications, and compared the best autotuned result found by our compiler to the best previously published expert implementation we could find. We selected this set of examples to cover a diversity of algorithms and communication patterns. It includes pipelines ranging from two to 99 stages, and including many different stencils, data-dependent access patterns, and histogram reductions. We describe each application below. Fig. 6 summarizes their properties, and Fig. 7 summarizes their performance. All evaluation was performed on a quad core Xeon W3520 x86 CPU, an NVIDIA Tesla C2070 GPU.

Blur is the simple example used in Sec. 3.1, which convolves the image with two 3×1 box kernels in two steps, a horizontal 3×1 kernel then a vertical 1×3 kernel. This is a simple example of two consecutive stencils. Our reference comparison is a hand-optimized, manually fused and multithreaded loop nest defined entirely in SSE intrinsics [26]. This version is $12\times$ faster than a simple pair of loops in C compiled by GCC 4.7. The version found by our autotuner is 10% faster, still, while being generated from a two line Halide algorithm rather than 35 lines of intrinsics.

	# functions	# stencils	graph structure
Blur	2	2	simple
Bilateral grid	7	3	moderate
Camera pipeline	32	22	complex
Local Laplacian filters	99	85	very complex
Multi-scale interpolation	49	47	complex

Figure 6. Properties of the example applications. In some cases, the number of functions exceeds the number of program lines in Fig. 7, because Halide functions are meta-programmed using higher-order functions.

Camera pipeline transforms the raw data recorded by the camera sensor into a usable image. Its demosaicking, alone, is a complex combination of 21 interleaved and inter-dependent stencils.

The reference comparison is a single carefully tiled and fused loop nest from the Frankencamera, expressed in 306 lines of C++ [1]. All producer-consumer communication is staged through scratch buffers, tiles are distributed over parallel threads using OpenMP, and the tight loops are autovectorized by GCC. The Halide algorithm is 145 lines describing 32 functions and 22 different stencils, literally translated from the pseudocode in the comments explaining the original source. It compiles to an implementation 3.4× faster than the hand-tuned original. The autotuned schedule fuses long chains of stages through complex, interleaved stencils on overlapping tiles, fully fuses other stages, vectorizes every stage, and distributes blocks of scanlines across threads.

Multi-scale interpolation uses an image pyramid to interpolate pixel data for seamless compositing. This requires dealing with data at many different resolutions. The resulting pyramids are chains of stages which locally resample over small stencils, but through which dependence propagates globally across the entire image.

The reference implementation is a carefully-structured set of loop nests which were hand-tuned by an Adobe engineer to generate a fully vectorized implementation in GCC. The Halide algorithm is substantially simpler, but compiles to an implementation 1.7× faster than the original parallel vector code. The same Halide algorithm also automatically compiles to a graph of CUDA kernels and x86 code which is 5.9× faster.

Bilateral grid is an efficient implementation of the bilateral filter, which smoothes an image while preserving its main edges [5, 21]. It first scatters the image data into a 3D grid, effectively building a windowed histogram in each column of the grid, then blurs the grid along each of is axes with three 5-point stencils. Finally, the output image is constructed by trilinear interpolation within the grid at locations determined by the input image.

The CPU reference code is a tuned but clean implementation from the original authors in 122 lines of C++. It is partially autovectorized by GCC, but is nontrivial to multithread (a naive OpenMP parallelization of major stages results in a slowdown on our benchmark CPU), so the reference is single-threaded. The Halide algorithm is 34 lines, and compiles to an implementation 4.2× faster than the original. The speedup comes from a combination of parallelism, tile-level fusion of some stages, and careful reordering of dimensions to control parallel grain size in the grid.

We also compared our implementation to a hand-tuned GPU implementation from the original authors, written in 370 lines of CUDA code. The same Halide algorithm—less than 1/10th the code—found a different schedule which was 2.3× faster than the hand-written CUDA. The Halide compiler generates similar CUDA code to the reference, but the autotuner found an unintuitive point in the schedule space which sacrificed some parallelism in the grid construction step to reduce synchronization overhead in the scattering reduction. It also uses a tiled fusion strategy which passes intermediate results through GPU scratchpad memory to improve locality through the blur steps at the expense of redundant computation. These tradeoffs were counter-intuitive to the original author, and also much harder to express in CUDA, but are easily described by our schedule representation and found by our autotuner.

x86

	Halide tuned (ms)	Expert tuned (ms)	Speedup	Lines Halide	Lines expert	Factor shorter
Blur	11	13	1.2×	2	35	18×
Bilateral grid	36	158	4.4×	34	122	4×
Camera pipe	14	49	3.4×	123	306	2×
Interpolate	32	54	1.7×	21	152	7×
Local Laplacian	113	189	1.7×	52	262	5×

CUDA

	Halide tuned (ms)	Expert tuned (ms)	Speedup	Lines Halide	Lines expert	Factor shorter
Bilateral grid	8.1	18	2.3×	34	370	11×
Interpolate	9.1	*54**	*5.9×*	21	*152**	7×
Local Laplacian	21	*189**	*9×*	52	*262**	5×

Figure 7. Comparison of autotuned Halide program running times to hand-optimized programs created by domain experts in C, intrinsics, and CUDA. Halide programs are both faster and require fewer code lines. *(*No GPU reference available, compared to CPU reference.)*

Local Laplacian filters uses a multi-scale approach to tone map images and enhance local contrast in an edge-respecting fashion [3, 22]. It is used in the clarity, tone mapping, and other filters in Adobe Photoshop and Lightroom. The algorithm builds and manipulates several image pyramids with complex dependencies between them. The filter output is produced by a data-dependent resampling from several pyramids. With the parameters we used, the pipeline contains 99 different stages, operating at many scales, and with different computational patterns.

The reference implementation is 262 lines of C++, developed at Adobe, and carefully parallelized with OpenMP, and offloading most intensive kernels to tuned assembly routines from Intel Performance Primitives [14, 20]. It has very similar performance to a version deployed in their products, which took several months to develop, including 2-3 weeks dedicated to optimization. It is 10× faster than an algorithmically identical reference version written by the authors in pure C++, without IPP or OpenMP. The Halide version was written in one day, in 52 lines of code. It compiles to an implementation which is 1.7× faster than the highly optimized expert implementation (roughly 20× faster than the clean C++ without IPP and OpenMP). The resulting schedule is enormously complex, mixing different fusion, tiling, vectorization, and multithreading strategies throughout the expansive 99 stage graph. In C, it would correspond to hundreds of loops over more than 10,000 lines of code.

The same program compiles with a different automatically generated schedule to a hybrid CPU/GPU program with 58 unique GPU kernels, each representing a differently tiled and partially fused subset of the overall graph, and with the lookup table and several smaller levels of the pyramids scheduled as vector code on the CPU. *The generated program has more distinct CUDA kernels than the Halide algorithm describing it has lines of code.* It runs 7.5× faster than the hand-tuned Adobe implementation, and is more than 4× faster than the best parallel vector implementation on the CPU. This

	Source size (MP)	Target size (MP)	Cross-tested time (ms)	Autotuned on target (ms)	Slowdown (vs target autotuned)
Blur	0.3	30	13	11	1.2×
Bilateral grid	0.3	2	35	36	0.97×
Interpolate	0.3	2	31	32	0.97×
Blur	30	0.3	1.1	0.07	16×
Bilateral grid	2	0.3	9.6	6.7	1.4×
Interpolate	2	0.3	9.7	5.2	1.9×

Figure 8. Cross-testing of autotuned schedules across resolutions. Each program is autotuned on a source image size. The resulting schedule is tested on a target image size giving a "cross-tested time." This is compared to the result of running the autotuner directly on the target resolution. We report the ratio of the cross-tested time to the autotuned-on-target time as the "slowdown." Note that schedules generalize better from low resolutions to high resolutions. In theory the slow-down should always be at least one, but due to the stochastic nature of the search some schedules were slower when autotuned on the target.

is by far the fastest implementation of local Laplacian filters we know of.

6.1 Autotuning Performance

These examples took between 2 hours and 2 days to tune (from 10s to 100s of generations). In all cases, the tuner converged to within 15% of the final performance after less than one day tuning on a single machine. Improvements to the compiling and tuning infrastructure (for example, distributing tests across a cluster) could reduce these times significantly.

We generally found the tuned schedules to be insensitive to moderate changes in resolution or architecture, but extreme changes can cause the best schedule to change dramatically. Table 8 shows experiments in cross-testing schedules tuned at different resolutions. We observe that schedules generalize better from low resolutions to high resolutions. We also mapped the best GPU schedule for local Laplacian filter to the CPU, and found that this is 7× slower than the best CPU schedule.

6.2 Discussion

Across a range of image processing applications and target architectures, our scheduling representation is able to model, our compiler is able to generate, and our autotuner is able to discover implementation strategies which deliver state-of-the-art performance. This performance comes from careful navigation of the extremely high dimensional space of tradeoffs between locality, parallelism, and redundant recomputation in image processing pipelines. Making these tradeoffs by hand is challenging enough, as shown by the much greater complexity of hand-written implementations, but finding the ideal points is daunting when each change a programmer might want to test can require completely rewriting a complex loop nest hundreds of lines long. The performance advantage of the Halide implementations is a direct result of simply *testing many more points in the space* than a human programmer ever could manually describe at the level of explicit loops.

Nonetheless, based on our experience, brute force autotuning still poses significant challenges of robustness and usability in a real system. The tuning process is an entire extra stage added to a programmer's normal development process. Straightforward implementations are sensitive to noise in testing environment and many other factors. In Halide, while simple pipelines (like blur) can tune effectively with only trivial mutation rules, we found heuristic mutation rules are essential to converge in a reasonable amount of time when tuning more complex imaging pipelines. However these rules may be specific to the algorithm structure. For example, different template mutation rules may be necessary for 3D voxel data or unconventional color layouts. We also found that it is necessary to maintain diversity to avoid becoming trapped in local minima, which we did by using a large population (128 individuals per generation). Even so, the tuner can occasionally become trapped, requiring restarting with a new random initialization, and taking the best of several runs. In general, we feel that high dimensional stochastic autotuning has not yet developed the robust methodology or infrastructure for real-world use found elsewhere in the compiler community.

7. Prior Work

Image processing pipelines include similar structure to several problems well studied in compilers.

Split Compilers Sequoia's "mappings" and SPIRAL's loop synthesis algebra echo our separation of the model of *scheduling* from the description of the algorithm, and its lifting outside our compiler [9, 25].

Stream Programs Compiler optimization of stream programs was studied extensively in the StreamIt and Brook projects [4, 11, 29]. In this framework, sliding window communication implements stencils on 1D streams [12, 24, 30]. Stream compilers generally did not consider the introduction of redundant work as a major optimization choice, and nearly all work in stream compilation has focussed on these 1D streams. Image processing pipelines, in contrast, are effectively stream programs over 2D-4D streams.

Stencil Optimization Iterated stencil computations are important to many scientific applications, and have been studied for decades. Frigo and Strumpen proposed a cache oblivious traversal for efficient stencil computation [10]. This view of locality optimization by interleaving stencil applications in space and time inspired our model of scheduling. The Pochoir compiler automatically transforms stencil codes from serial form into a parallel cache oblivious form using similar algorithms [28].

Overlapping tiling is a strategy which divides a stencil computation into tiles, and trades off redundant computation along tile boundaries to improve locality and parallelism [16], modeled in our schedule representation as interleaving both storage and computation inside the tile loops. Other tiling strategies represent different points in the tradeoff space modeled by our representation [19]. Past compilers have automatically synthesized parallel loop nests with overlapped tiling on CPUs and GPUs using the polyhedral model [13, 16]. These compilers focussed on synthesizing high quality code given a single, user-defined set of overlapped tiling parameters. Autotuning has also been applied to iterated stencil computations, but past tuning work has focussed on exhaustive search of small parameter spaces for one or a few strategies [15].

Image Processing Languages Critically, many optimizations for iterated stencil computations are based on the assumption that the time dimension of iteration is large relative to the spatial dimension of the grid. In image processing pipelines, most individual stencils are applied only once, while images are millions of pixels in size. Image processing pipelines also include more types of computation than stencils alone, and scheduling them requires choices not only of different parameters, but of entirely different strategies, for each of many heterogeneous stages, which is infeasible with either exhaustive search or polyhedral optimization. Most prior image processing languages and systems have focused on efficient expression of individual kernels, as well as simple fusion in the absence of stencils [6, 8, 23, 27]. Recently, Cornwall et al. demonstrated fast

GPU code generation for image processing code using polyhedral optimization [7].

Earlier work on the Halide language included a weaker model of schedules, and required programmers to explicitly specify schedules by hand [26]. This is the first automatic optimizer, and therefore the first fully automatic compiler, for Halide programs. We show how they can be automatically inferred, starting from just the algorithm defining the pipeline stages, and using relatively little domain-specific knowledge beyond the ability to enumerate points in the space of schedules. Our state-of-the-art performance shows the effectiveness of our scheduling model for representing the underlying choice space. The scheduling model presented here is also richer than in past work. In particular, it separates computation frequency from storage frequency in the call schedule, enabling sliding window schedules and similar strategies which trade off parallelism for redundant work while maintaining locality.

In all, this gives a dramatic new result: automatic optimization of stencil computations, including full consideration of the parallelism, locality, and redundancy tradeoffs. Past automatic stencil optimizations have targeted individual points in the space, but have not automatically chosen *among* different strategies spanning these multi-dimensional tradeoffs, and none have automatically optimized large heterogeneous pipelines, only individual or small multi-stencils.

Acknowledgments

Eric Chan provided feedback and inspiration throughout the design of Halide, and helped compare our local Laplacian filters implementation to his in Camera Raw. Jason Ansel helped inform the design of our autotuner. This work was supported by DOE Award DE-SC0005288, NSF grant 0964004, grants from Intel and Quanta, and gifts from Cognex and Adobe.

References

[1] A. Adams, E. Talvala, S. H. Park, D. E. Jacobs, B. Ajdin, N. Gelfand, J. Dolson, D. Vaquero, J. Baek, M. Tico, H. P. A. Lensch, W. Matusik, K. Pulli, M. Horowitz, and M. Levoy. The Frankencamera: An experimental platform for computational photography. *ACM Trans. Graph.*, 29(4), 2010.

[2] J. Ansel, C. Chan, Y. L. Wong, M. Olszewski, Q. Zhao, A. Edelman, and S. Amarasinghe. PetaBricks: A language and compiler for algorithmic choice. In *ACM Programming Language Design and Implementation*, 2009.

[3] M. Aubry, S. Paris, S. W. Hasinoff, J. Kautz, and F. Durand. Fast and robust pyramid-based image processing. Technical Report MIT-CSAIL-TR-2011-049, Massachusetts Institute of Technology, 2011.

[4] I. Buck, T. Foley, D. Horn, J. Sugerman, K. Fatahalian, M. Houston, and P. Hanrahan. Brook for GPUs: Stream computing on graphics hardware. In *SIGGRAPH*, 2004.

[5] J. Chen, S. Paris, and F. Durand. Real-time edge-aware image processing with the bilateral grid. *ACM Trans. Graph.*, 26(3), 2007.

[6] CoreImage. Apple CoreImage programming guide, 2006.

[7] J. L. T. Cornwall, L. Howes, P. H. J. Kelly, P. Parsonage, and B. Nicoletti. High-performance SIMT code generation in an active visual effects library. In *Conf. on Computing Frontiers*, 2009.

[8] C. Elliott. Functional image synthesis. In *Proceedings of Bridges*, 2001.

[9] K. Fatahalian, D. R. Horn, T. J. Knight, L. Leem, M. Houston, J. Y. Park, M. Erez, M. Ren, A. Aiken, W. J. Dally, and P. Hanrahan. Sequoia: programming the memory hierarchy. In *ACM/IEEE conference on Supercomputing*, 2006.

[10] M. Frigo and V. Strumpen. Cache oblivious stencil computations. In *ICS*, 2005.

[11] M. I. Gordon, W. Thies, M. Karczmarek, J. Lin, A. S. Meli, C. Leger, A. A. Lamb, J. Wong, H. Hoffman, D. Z. Maze, and S. Amarasinghe. A stream compiler for communication-exposed architectures. In *International Conf. on Architectural Support for Programming Languages and Operating Systems*, 2002.

[12] P. L. Guernic, A. Benveniste, P. Bournai, and T. Gautier. Signal – A data flow-oriented language for signal processing. *IEEE Transactions on Acoustics, Speech and Signal Processing*, 34(2):362–374, 1986.

[13] J. Holewinski, L. Pouchet, and P. Sadayappan. High-performance code generation for stencil computations on gpu architectures. In *ICS*, 2012.

[14] IPP. Intel Integrated Performance Primitives. `http://software.intel.com/en-us/articles/intel-ipp/`.

[15] S. Kamil, C. Chan, L. Oliker, J. Shalf, , and S. Williams. An auto-tuning framework for parallel multicore stencil computations. In *IPDPS*, 2010.

[16] S. Krishnamoorthy, M. Baskaran, U. Bondhugula, J. Ramanujam, A. Rountev, and P. Sadayappan. Effective automatic parallelization of stencil computations. In *PLDI*, 2007.

[17] J. Meng and K. Skadron. A performance study for iterative stencil loops on gpus with ghost zone optimizations. In *IJPP*, 2011.

[18] R. Moore. *Interval Analysis*. 1966.

[19] A. Nguyen, N. Satish, J. Chhugani, C. Kim, and P. Dubey. 3.5-d blocking optimization for stencil computations on modern cpus and gpus. In *Supercomputing*, 2010.

[20] OpenMP. OpenMP. `http://openmp.org/`.

[21] S. Paris, P. Kornprobst, J. Tumblin, and F. Durand. Bilateral filtering: Theory and applications. Foundations and Trends in Computer Graphics and Vision, 2009.

[22] S. Paris, S. W. Hasinoff, and J. Kautz. Local Laplacian filters: Edge-aware image processing with a Laplacian pyramid. *ACM Trans. Graph.*, 30(4), 2011.

[23] PixelBender. Adobe PixelBender reference, 2010.

[24] H. Printz. *Automatic Mapping of Large Signal Processing Systems to a Parallel Machine*. Ph.D. Thesis, Carnegie Mellon University, 1991.

[25] M. Puschel, J. M. F. Moura, J. R. Johnson, D. Padua, M. M. Veloso, B. W. Singer, J. Xiong, F. Franchetti, A. Gacic, Y. Voronenko, K. Chen, R. W. Johnson, and N. Rizzolo. SPIRAL: Code generation for DSP transforms. In *Proceedings of the IEEE*, volume 93, 2005.

[26] J. Ragan-Kelley, A. Adams, S. Paris, M. Levoy, S. Amarasinghe, and F. Durand. Decoupling algorithms from schedules for easy optimization of image processing pipelines. *ACM Trans. Graph.*, 31(4), 2012.

[27] M. A. Shantzis. A model for efficient and flexible image computing. In *ACM SIGGRAPH*, 1994.

[28] Y. Tang, R. Chowdhury, B. Kuszmaul, C.-K. Luk, and C. Leiserson. The Pochoir stencil compiler. In *SPAA*, 2011.

[29] W. Thies, M. Karczmarek, and S. Amarasinghe. StreamIt: A language for streaming applications. In *International Conference on Compiler Construction*, 2002.

[30] P.-S. Tseng. *A Parallelizing Compiler for Disributed Memory Parallel Computers*. PhD thesis, Carnegie Mellon University, 1989.

[31] X. Zhou, J.-P. Giacalone, M. J. Garzarán, R. H. Kuhn, Y. Ni, and D. Padua. Hierarchical overlapped tiling.

Author Index

Adams, Andrew 519
Aiken, Alex 105
Alur, Rajeev 287
Amarasinghe, Saman 519
Anand, Kapil 51
Apinis, Kalmer 377
August, David I. 39
Barnes, Connelly 519
Barua, Rajeev 51
Blackburn, Stephen M. 297
Blackshear, Sam 209, 275
Bodden, Eric 355
Borba, Paulo 355
Brabrand, Claus 355
Burckhardt, Sebastian 95
Burger, Doug 297
Burnim, Jacob 153
Chakarov, Aleksandar 447
Chang, Bor-Yuh Evan 275
Chen, Juan 387
Chen, Mingyu 117
Chen, Yang 197
Cheung, Alvin 3
Chong, Stephen 411
Clarke, Dave 399
Cohen, Nachshon 309
Cook, Byron 219
Czaplicki, Evan 411
Darais, David 399
De Carli, Lorenzo 495
de Halleux, Peli 95
Desai, Ankush 321
Deshmukh, Jyotirmoy V. 287
DeVito, Zachary 105
Devriese, Dominique 399
Dolby, Julian 141, 165
Durand, Frédo 519
Eide, Eric 197
Elmas, Tayfun 153
Elver, Marco 61
ElWazeer, Khaled 51
Ernst, Michael D. 73
Estan, Cristian 495
Fähndrich, Manuel 95
Feng, Xinyu 459
Fern, Xiaoli 197
Foster, Nate 483
Franchetti, Franz 127
Gao, Tiejun 297
Garg, Pranav 231
Garg, Vijay K. 253
Golan-Gueta, Guy 263
Gordon, Colin S. 73
Green, Alexander S. 333
Groce, Alex 197
Grossman, Dan 73
Guha, Arjun 483
Gulwani, Sumit 15, 447
Gupta, Vivek 321
Gvero, Tihomir 27
Hanrahan, Pat 105
Hegarty, James 105
Huang, Jeff 141
Hung, Wei-Lun 253
Isradisaikul, Chinawat 343
Jackson, Ethan 321
Johnson, Nick P. 39
Kale, Laxmikant V. 507
Kastrinis, George 423
Kato, Jun 95
Klein, Gerwin 471
Ko, Hou-Jen 243
Kong, Martin 127
Koskinen, Eric 219
Kotha, Aparna 51
Krishnamoorthy, Sriram 507
Kuncak, Viktor 27
Kuraj, Ivan 27
Lahiri, Shuvendu K. 209
Larus, James R. 1, 297
Li, Jiajia 117
Li, Zhiyuan 243
Liang, Hongjin 459
Lifflander, Jonathan 507
Livshits, Benjamin 387
Lumsdaine, Peter LeFanu 333
Lyu, Michael R. 435
Madden, Samuel 3
Madhusudan, Parthasarathy 231
Mador-Haim, Sela 287
Martin, Milo M. K. 175, 287
McDirmid, Sean 95
McKinley, Kathryn S. 297
Mezini, Mira 355
Midtgaard, Jan 399
Might, Matthew 399
Morisset, Robin 187
Moskal, Michal 95
Myers, Andrew C. 343
Myreen, Magnus 471
Nagarajan, Vijay 61
Nagarakatte, Santosh 175
Naik, Mayur 365
Nardelli, Francesco Zappa 187
Necula, George 153
Nowatzki, Tony 495
Oh, Taewook 39
Paris, Sylvain 519
Pawan, Pankaj 187
Petrank, Erez 309
Piessens, Frank 399
Piskac, Ruzica 27
Pouchet, Louis-Noël 127
Qadeer, Shaz 321
Qiu, Xiaokang 231
Ragan-Kelley, Jonathan 519
Raghavan, Arun 287
Rajamani, Sriram 321
Rajaram, Bharghava 61
Ramalingam, G. 263

Regehr, John 197
Reitblatt, Mark 483
Ribeiro, Márcio 355
Robatmili, Behnam 495
Ross, Neil J. 333
Sadayappan, P. 127
Sagiv, Mooly 263
Sankaralingam, Karthikeyan 495
Sankaranarayanan, Sriram 447
Sarkar, Susmit 61
Sartin-Tarm, Michael 495
Schäfer, Max 165
Schlesinger, Cole 387
Schneider, Fred B. 139
Seidl, Helmut 377
Selinger, Peter 333
Sen, Koushik 153
Sergey, Ilya 399
Sewell, Thomas 471
Singh, Rishabh 15
Smaragdakis, Yannis 423
Smithson, Matthew 51
Solar-Lezama, Armando 3, 15
Sridharan, Manu 165, 275
Ştefănescu, Andrei 231
Stock, Kevin 127
Strauss, Karin 297
Su, Zhendong 435
Sun, Ninghui 117
Swamy, Nikhil 387
Tan, Guangming 117
Tillmann, Nikolai 95
Tip, Frank 165
Titzer, Ben L. 85
Tolêdo, Társis 355
Udupa, Abhishek 287
Valiron, Benoît 333
Veras, Richard 127
Vitek, Jan 105
Vojdani, Vesal 377
Weinberger, Joel 387
Wong, Weng-Keen 197
Yahav, Eran 263
Yang, Hongseok 365
Yu, Hongtao 243
Yuan, Hao 435
Zaks, Ayal 39
Zdancewic, Steve 175
Zhang, Chaoqiang 197
Zhang, Charles 141
Zhang, Qirun 435
Zhang, Xin 365
Zhao, Jianzhou 175
Zufferey, Damien 321

www.ingramcontent.com/pod-product-compliance
Ingram Content Group UK Ltd.
Pitfield, Milton Keynes, MK11 3LW, UK
UKHW051416290926
15471UKWH00009B/1625